Minnesota Rules of Court

Volume I – State

2014

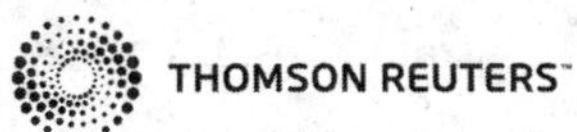

Mat #41418959

ISBN: 978–0–314–66355–9

PREFACE

This edition of *Minnesota Rules of Court, Volume I – State, 2014*, replaces the 2013 edition and 2013 supplement. This volume provides in convenient form the court rules governing state practice in Minnesota and is current with amendments received through January 1, 2014.

For additional information or research assistance call the West reference attorneys at 1-800-REF-ATTY (1-800-733-2889). Contact West's editorial department directly with your questions and suggestions by e-mail at west.editor@thomson.com.

Visit West's home page at legalsolutions.thomsonreuters.com.

THE PUBLISHER

February, 2014

TABLE OF CONTENTS

TRIAL AND APPELLATE RULES

TABLE OF CONTENTS

PROFESSIONAL RULES

RULES OF CIVIL PROCEDURE

Effective January 1, 1989

Including Amendments Received Through January 1, 2014

Research Note

See Minnesota Statutes Annotated, *Volume 48, for case annotations, historical notes, and library references. The Rules of Civil Procedure are discussed in Herr and Haydock, 1, 1A, 2, and 2A* Minnesota Practice–Civil Rules Annotated (4th Edition), *and related practice forms are provided in Haydock, Herr and Peterson, 15 and 16* Minnesota Practice–Civil Practice Forms (2nd Edition).

Superseded Statutes

Various statutes were superseded by the Rules of Civil Procedure for the District Courts. See Rule 81.01(c) and Appendix B(2) set forth following the Rules for a listing of specific statutes.

Comments

The orders of the Minnesota Supreme Court dated November 10, 1967, November 14, 1974, and March 21, 1985, provided in part that the Advisory Committee Notes included within the order were made for convenience and did not necessarily reflect court approval of the comments made therein. The order of the Minnesota Supreme Court dated October 18, 1988, provided in part that "(t)he inclusion of Advisory Committee notes, if any, is made for convenience and does not reflect court approval of the comments made therein." The order of the Minnesota Supreme Court dated September 5, 1991, in part amending the Rules of Civil Procedure, provided in part that "the inclusion of Task Force notes, if any, is made for convenience and does not reflect court approval of the comments." The order of the Minnesota Supreme Court [C6–84–2134] dated December 20, 1993, provides in part that "(t)he comments of the Advisory Committee are those of the committee and their inclusion with the amendments does not imply either agreement or adoption by this Court of the statements contained therein."

I. SCOPE OF RULES—ONE FORM OF ACTION

RULE 1. SCOPE OF RULES

These rules govern the procedure in the district courts of the State of Minnesota in all suits of a civil nature, with the exceptions stated in Rule 81. They shall be construed and administered to secure the just, speedy, and inexpensive determination of every action.

It is the responsibility of the court and the parties to examine each civil action to assure that the process and the costs are proportionate to the amount in controversy and the complexity and importance of the issues. The factors to be considered by the court in making a proportionality assessment include, without limitation: needs of the case, amount in controversy, parties' resources, and complexity and importance of the issues at stake in the litigation.

Adopted June 25, 1951, eff. Jan. 1, 1952. Revised Oct. 18, 1988, eff. Jan. 1, 1989. Amended Nov. 22, 1996, eff. Jan. 1, 1997; May 7, 2013, eff. July 1, 2013.

Advisory Committee Comments—1996 Amendments

This change conforms the rule to its federal counterpart. The amendment is intended to make clear that the goals of just, speedy, and inexpensive resolution of litigation are just as important—if not more important—in questions that do not involve interpretation of the rules. These goals should guide all aspects of judicial administration, and this amendment expressly so states.

Historical Notes

The order of the Minnesota Supreme Court [C6-84-2134] dated November 22, 1996, provides in part that the "(a)mendments shall apply to all actions pending on the effective date [January 1, 1997] and to those filed thereafter" and that "(t)he inclusion of Advisory Committee comments is made for convenience and does not reflect court approval of the comments made therein".

The order of the Minnesota Supreme Court [ADM04–8001, ADM09–8009, ADM10–8051] dated May 7, 2013, provided in part that the amendments be effective July 1, 2013, and further provided in part that "[t]hese amendments apply to all actions or proceedings pending on or commenced after the effective date", and also provided that the "February 4, 2013 and February 12, 2013 orders of the court are hereby rescinded to the extent inconsistent with this order."

RULE 2. ONE FORM OF ACTION

There shall be one form of action to be known as "civil action."

Adopted June 25, 1951, eff. Jan. 1, 1952. Revised Oct. 18, 1988, eff. Jan. 1, 1989.

II. COMMENCEMENT OF THE ACTION; SERVICE OF PROCESS, PLEADINGS, MOTIONS AND ORDERS

RULE 3. COMMENCEMENT OF THE ACTION; SERVICE OF THE COMPLAINT; FILING OF THE ACTION

Rule 3.01. Commencement of the Action

A civil action is commenced against each defendant:

(a) when the summons is served upon that defendant, or

(b) at the date of acknowledgement of service if service is made by mail, or

(c) when the summons is delivered to the sheriff in the county where the defendant resides for service; but such delivery shall be ineffectual unless within 60 days thereafter the summons is actually served on that defendant or the first publication thereof is made.

Filing requirements are set forth in Rule 5.04, which requires filing with the court within one year after commencement for non-family cases.

Adopted June 25, 1951, eff. Jan. 1, 1952. Amended March 21, 1985, eff. July 1, 1985. Revised Oct. 18, 1988, eff. Jan. 1, 1989. Amended May 7, 2013, eff. July 1, 2013.

Advisory Committee Note—1985

The Rules have permitted service by any non-minor, non-party for a substantial period of time. The changes recommended to Minn.R.Civ.P. 4.02 underscore and clarify the availability of service by any individual.

The most common method for commencing an action is by service of the summons and complaint upon a defendant. A different commencement time may apply to individual defendants based upon the times upon which the summons and complaint are actually served. An alternative method for commencing an action contained in the rule provides that an action may be commenced upon delivery of the summons and complaint to a sheriff in the county where the defendant resides for service. One change to Rule 3.a [1] is intended to clarify who is a "proper officer" for service. The Committee felt this language should be clarified to remove ambiguity or uncertainty. Commencement by delivery to the sheriff is effective only, however, if service is actually made within 60 days thereafter. The amendment to the rule is intended to make it clear that delivery to a private process server is not effective to commence an action on the date of delivery even though service is actually made within 60 days thereafter. In such a case, service will be effective, but the action will be deemed commenced as of the date service is actually made. Similarly, delivery of the summons to the Postal Service for service by mail does not commence an action. The action is commenced by mail when the defendant acknowledges service. If no acknowledgement is signed and returned, the action is not commenced until service is effected by some other authorized means.

[1] Probably was intended to be Rule 3.01(c).

Historical and Statutory Notes

The order of the Minnesota Supreme Court [ADM04–8001, ADM09–8009, ADM–10-8051] dated May 7, 2013, provided in part that the amendments be effective July 1, 2013, and further provided in part that "[t]hese amendments apply to all actions or proceedings pending on or commenced after the effective date", and further provided that the "February 4, 2013 and February 12, 2013 orders of the court are hereby rescinded to the extent inconsistent with this order."

Rule 3.02. Service of Complaint

A copy of the complaint shall be served with the summons, except when the service is by publication as provided in Rule 4.04.

Adopted June 25, 1951, eff. Jan. 1, 1952. Revised Oct. 18, 1988, eff. Jan. 1, 1989.

RULE 4. SERVICE

Rule 4.01. Summons; Form

The summons shall state the name of the court and the names of the parties, be subscribed by the plaintiff or by the plaintiff's attorney, give an address within the state where the subscriber may be served in person and by mail, state the time within which these rules require the defendant to serve an answer, and notify the defendant that if the defendant fails to do so judgment by default will be rendered against the defendant for the relief demanded in the complaint.

Adopted June 25, 1951, eff. Jan. 1, 1952. Amended March 3, 1959, eff. July 1, 1959. Revised Oct. 18, 1988, eff. Jan. 1, 1989.

Rule 4.02. By Whom Served

Unless otherwise ordered by the court, the sheriff or any other person not less than 18 years of age and not a party to the action, may make service of a summons or other process.

Adopted June 25, 1951, eff. Jan. 1, 1952. Amended March 21, 1985, eff. July 1, 1985. Revised Oct. 18, 1988, eff. Jan. 1, 1989.

Advisory Committee Note—1985

The language of the first paragraph of the existing rule 4.02 was deleted because it is no longer necessary. Under current Minnesota law, a prevailing party may recover the cost of service of process, whether by sheriff or private process server as costs and disbursements. *See* Minn.Stat. § 549.04 (Supp.1983).

The changes to the second paragraph are intended to clarify the language of the rule and incorporate provisions for service of process other than summonses and subpoenas presently contained in Rule 4.05. Under the rule any person who is not a party to the action and is 18 years of age or over may serve a summons or other process. Service of subpoenas is governed by Rule 45.03, and the changes in Rule 4.02 are intended to be make the two rules consistent. The rule provides that the court may direct service of any process by any means it deems appropriate. As a practical matter, courts will rarely have occasion to direct a specific means of service of process.

Rule 4.03. Personal Service

Service of summons within the state shall be as follows:

(a) Upon an Individual. Upon an individual by delivering a copy to the individual personally or by leaving a copy at the individual's usual place of abode with some person of suitable age and discretion then residing therein.

If the individual has, pursuant to statute, consented to any other method of service or appointed an agent to receive service of summons, or if a statute designates a state official to receive service of summons, service may be made in the manner provided by such statute.

If the individual is confined to a state institution, by serving also the chief executive officer at the institution.

If the individual is an infant under the age of 14 years, by serving also the individual's father or mother, and if neither is within the state, then a resident guardian if the infant has one known to the plaintiff, and if the infant has none, then the person having control of such defendant, or with whom the infant resides, or by whom the infant is employed.

(b) Upon Partnerships and Associations. Upon a partnership or association which is subject to suit under a common name, by delivering a copy to a member or the managing agent of the partnership or association. If the partnership or association has, pursuant to statute, consented to any other method of service or appointed an agent to receive service of summons, or if a statute designates a state official to receive service of summons, service may be made in the manner provided by such statute.

(c) Upon a Corporation. Upon a domestic or foreign corporation, by delivering a copy to an officer or managing agent, or to any other agent authorized expressly or impliedly or designated by statute to receive service of summons, and if the agent is one authorized or designated under statute to receive service any statutory provision for the manner of such service shall be complied with. In the case of a transportation or express corporation, the summons may be served by delivering a copy to any ticket, freight, or soliciting agent found in the county in which the action is brought, and if such corporation is a foreign corporation and has no such agent in the county in which the plaintiff elects to bring the action, then upon any such agent of the corporation within the state.

(d) Upon the State. Upon the state by delivering a copy to the attorney general, a deputy attorney general or an assistant attorney general.

(e) Upon Public Corporations. Upon a municipal or other public corporation by delivering a copy

(1) To the chair of the county board or to the county auditor of a defendant county;

(2) To the chief executive officer or to the clerk of a defendant city, village or borough;

(3) To the chair of the town board or to the clerk of a defendant town;

(4) To any member of the board or other governing body of a defendant school district; or

(5) To any member of the board or other governing body of a defendant public board or public body not hereinabove enumerated.

If service cannot be made as provided in this Rule 4.03(e), the court may direct the manner of such service.

Adopted June 25, 1951, eff. Jan. 1, 1952. Revised Oct. 18, 1988, eff. Jan. 1, 1989.

Rule 4.04. Service By Publications; Personal Service out of State

(a) Service by Publications. Service by publication shall be sufficient to confer jurisdiction:

(1) When the defendant is a resident individual domiciliary having departed from the state with intent to defraud creditors, or to avoid service, or remains concealed therein with the like intent;

(2) When the plaintiff has acquired a lien upon property or credits within the state by attachment or garnishment, and

(A) The defendant is a resident individual who has departed from the state, or cannot be found therein, or

(B) The defendant is a nonresident individual or a foreign corporation, partnership or association;

When quasi in rem jurisdiction has been obtained, a party defending the action thereby submits personally to the jurisdiction of the court. An appearance solely to contest the validity of quasi in rem jurisdiction is not such a submission.

(3) When the action is for marriage dissolution or separate maintenance and the court has ordered service by published notice;

(4) When the subject of the action is real or personal property within the state in or upon which the defendant has or claims a lien or interest, or the relief demanded consists wholly or partly in excluding the defendant from any such interest or lien;

(5) When the action is to foreclose a mortgage or to enforce a lien on real estate within the state.

The summons may be served by three weeks' published notice in any of the cases enumerated herein when the complaint and an affidavit of the plaintiff or the plaintiff's attorney have been filed with the court. The affidavit shall state the existence of one of the enumerated cases, and that affiant believes the defendant is not a resident of the state or cannot be found therein, and either that the affiant has mailed a copy of the summons to the defendant at the defendant's place of residence or that such residence is not known to the affiant. The service of the summons shall be deemed complete 21 days after the first publication.

(b) Personal Service Outside State. Personal service of such summons outside the state, proved by the affidavit of the person making the same sworn to before a person authorized to administer an oath, shall have the same effect as the published notice provided for herein.

(c) Service Outside United States. Unless otherwise provided by law, service upon an individual, other than an infant or an incompetent person, may be effected in a place not within the state:

(1) by any internationally agreed means reasonably calculated to give notice, such as those means authorized by the Hague Convention on the Service Abroad of Judicial and Extrajudicial Documents; or

(2) if there is no internationally agreed means of service or the applicable international agreement allows other means of service, provided that service is reasonably calculated to give notice:

(A) in the manner prescribed by the law of the foreign country for service in that country in an action in any of its courts of general jurisdiction; or

(B) as directed by the foreign authority in response to a letter rogatory or letter of request; or

(C) unless prohibited by the law of the foreign country, by

(i) delivery to the individual personally of a copy of the summons and the complaint; or

(ii) any form of mail requiring a signed receipt, to be addressed and dispatched by the court administrator to the party to be served; or

(3) by other means not prohibited by international agreement as may be directed by the court.

Adopted June 25, 1951, eff. Jan. 1, 1952. Amended March 3, 1959, eff. July 1, 1959; Nov. 10, 1967, eff. Feb. 1, 1968; March 21, 1985, eff. July 1, 1985. Revised Oct. 18, 1988, eff. Jan. 1, 1989. Amended Nov. 22, 1996, eff. Jan. 1, 1997.

Advisory Committee Note—1968

The amendment to Rule 4.04 prohibits limited appearances in Minnesota in quasi in rem actions. Prior to the amendment it was an open question in Minnesota whether or not a defendant in a quasi in rem action could defend on the merits without submitting generally to the jurisdiction of the court. A limited appearance must be distinguished from a special appearance and a motion to dismiss for lack of jurisdiction over the person. Special appearances were abolished by the rules in 1952. Under existing rule practice the defense of lack of jurisdiction over the person is properly raised by motion or pleading under Rule 12.02. A limited appearance is an appearance in which the defendant in a quasi in rem action is permitted to defend on the merits and submit to the court's jurisdiction only to the extent of the property seized. In the opinion of the Committee, limited appearances are inconsistent with the general philosophy of rule procedure requiring that all litigation be handled with dispatch. Limited appearances merely permit the defendant to litigate the same question more than once. 38 Minn.L.Rev. 676, 679; 51 Columbia L.Rev. 242. A majority of the state and federal courts considering the question have rejected the limited appearance. Brignall v. Merkle, 28 N.E.2d 311 (Ill.1940); Cunningham v. Kansas City Ry., 56 P. 502 (Kan.1899); State ex rel. Methodist Old Peoples' Home v. Crawford, 80 P.2d 873 (Ore.1938); Sands v. Lefcourt Realty Corp., 117 A.2d 365 (Del.1955); Burg v. Winquist, 124 N.Y.S.2d 133 (N.Y.Sup.Ct.1953); U.S. v. Balanovski, 131 F.Supp. 898 (S.D.N.Y.1955); Anderson v. Benson, 117 F.Supp. 765 (D.Neb.1753); Grant v. Kellogg, 3 F.R.D. 229 (1943); Contra, Cheshire Nat'l v. Jaynes, 112 N.E. 500 (Mass.1916); McInnes v. McKay, 141 A. 699 (Me.1928); Miller Bros. Co. v. State, 95 A.2d 286 (Md.1953); Osborn v. White Eagle Oil Co., 355 P.2d 1041 (Okla.1960); Salmon Falls Mfg. Co. v. Midland Tire and Rubber Co., 285 F. 214 (6th Cir.1922); McQuillan v. Nat'l Cash Register Co., 112 F.2d 877 (4th Cir.1940).

The only strong arguments that can be made in favor of limited appearances are: (1) an undue extension of state jurisdiction in personal claims through the fiction of asserting jurisdiction against property located within the state (2) the question of local prejudice or inconvenient forum for defendant. The matter of fictitious exercise of jurisdiction was resolved long ago when the United States Supreme Court approved of quasi in rem jurisdiction in Pennoyer v. Neff, 95 U.S. 714, 24 L.Ed. 565 (U.S.1877). With regard to local prejudice or an inconvenient forum the defendant may have the possibility of removal to a federal court on diversity jurisdiction in spite of his submission to the personal jurisdiction of the state court. Similarly, the defendant may move to dismiss on the basis of forum non conveniens after submitting to the personal jurisdiction of the court. The court in resolving the forum non conveniens question should decide the issue after personal jurisdiction has attached on the same grounds as would have been applicable were the action commenced by personal service within the state rather than by quasi in rem jurisdiction. The only factor that would distinguish the case from a typical forum non conveniens case is the security the plaintiff acquired to insure partial satisfaction of any resultant judgment, which security would be lost if the action were dismissed. The existence of security is merely a factor to be considered with all the other factors in determining whether or not to dismiss the action.

Under the last sentence of the amendment to Rule 4.04, a motion to dismiss which contests plaintiff's compliance with the statutory and rule requirements for quasi in rem jurisdiction may still be made without submitting to the personal jurisdiction of the court. Such a jurisdictional attack is not a defense going to the merits.

Advisory Committee Comments—1996 Amendments

Rule 4.04 is amended to conform the rule to its federal counterpart, in part. The new provision adopts verbatim the provisions for service of process outside the United States contained in the federal rules. This modification is appropriate because this subject is handled well by the federal rule and because it is advantageous to have the two rules similar. This is particularly valuable given the dearth of state-court authority on foreign service of process. Existing portions of the rule are renumbered for clarity.

Historical Notes

The order of the Minnesota Supreme Court [C6-84-2134] dated November 22, 1996, provides in part that the "(a)mendments shall apply to all actions pending on the effective date [January 1, 1997] and to those filed thereafter" and that "(t)he inclusion of Advisory Committee comments is made for convenience and does not reflect court approval of the comments made therein".

Rule 4.041. Additional Information to be Published

In all cases where publication of summons is made in an action in which the title to, or any interest in or lien upon, real property is involved or affected or is brought in question, the publication shall also contain a description of the real property involved, affected or brought in question thereby, and a statement of the object of the action. No other notice of the pendency of the action need be published.

Adopted June 25, 1951, eff. Jan. 1, 1952. Amended March 3, 1959, eff. July 1, 1959. Revised Oct. 18, 1988, eff. Jan. 1, 1989.

Advisory Committee Note—1959

The additional information required by the rule is substantially identical with the notice of lis pendens published with the summons in actions for partition and to determine adverse claims (M.S.A. §§ 558.02 and 559.02, both preserved by Appendix A). The publication of either would probably be sufficient, but the existing confusion warrants the amendment and corresponding changes in the Appendices and the Forms. The form of summons prescribed by M.S.A. § 284.16 for actions involving tax titles is not changed.

Rule 4.042. Service of the Complaint

If the defendant shall appear within 10 days after the completion of service by publication, the plaintiff, within 5 days after such appearance, shall serve the complaint, by copy, on the defendant or the defendant's attorney. The defendant shall then have at least 10 days in which to answer the same.

Adopted June 25, 1951, eff. Jan. 1, 1952. Revised Oct. 18, 1988, eff. Jan. 1, 1989.

Rule 4.043. Service by Publication; Defendant May Defend; Restitution

If the summons is served by publication, and the defendant receives no actual notification of the action, the defendant shall be permitted to defend upon application to the court before judgment and for sufficient cause; and, except in an action for marriage dissolution, the defendant, in like manner, may be permitted to defend at any time within one year after judgment, on such terms as may be just. If the defense is sustained, and any part of the judgment has been enforced, such restitution shall be made as the court may direct.

Adopted June 25, 1951, eff. Jan. 1, 1952. Amended March 21, 1985, eff. July 1, 1985. Revised Oct. 18, 1988, eff. Jan. 1, 1989.

Advisory Committee Note—1985

The only change in [Rules 4.043 and 4.044] is to substitute "marriage dissolution" for "divorce" in order to conform the language of the rule to that of the statute governing such actions. *See* Minn.Stat. § 518.002 (1982).

Rule 4.044. Nonresident Owner of Land Appointing an Agent

If a nonresident person or corporation owning or claiming any interest or lien in or upon lands in the state appoints an agent pursuant to Minn.Stat. § 557.01, service of summons in an action involving such real estate shall be made upon the agent or the principal in accordance with Rule 4.03, and service by publication shall not be made upon the principal.

Adopted June 25, 1951, eff. Jan. 1, 1952. Revised Oct. 18, 1988, eff. Jan. 1, 1989.

Rule 4.05. Service by Mail

In any action service may be made by mailing a copy of the summons and of the complaint (by first-class mail, postage prepaid) to the person to be served, together with two copies of a notice and acknowledgment conforming substantially to Form 22 and a return envelope, postage prepaid, addressed to the sender. If acknowledgment of service under this rule is not received by the sender within the time defendant is required by these rules to serve an answer, service shall be ineffectual.

Unless good cause is shown for not doing so, the court shall order the payment of the costs of personal service by the person served if such person does not complete and return the notice and acknowledgment of receipt of summons within the time allowed by these rules.

Adopted March 21, 1985, eff. July 1, 1985. Revised Oct. 18, 1988, eff. Jan. 1, 1989.

Advisory Committee Note—1985

Existing Rule 4.05 is deleted in its entirety because it is now covered by Rule 4.02. The Committee also determined it is unnecessary to place an apparent burden on the Court to direct service of all process other than summonses and subpoenas. *See* Minn.R.Civ.P. 4.02, Notes of Advisory Committee—1984 amendment.

The Committee considered various alternatives permitting service by mail, including two amendments to the Federal Rules of Civil Procedure which were adopted in 1983. The United States Supreme Court first amended Fed.R.Civ.P. 4 to authorize service by mail. *See* Fed.R.Civ.P. 4(c)(2)(C)(ii). Congress then adopted a further amendment which superseded the Supreme Court's action. *See* P.L. # 97462 [H.R. 7154] [96 Stat. 2527]. Under the present federal rule, service may be effected by mail. The Minnesota Supreme Court has also recognized the effectiveness of service by mail under the Minnesota Long-Arm Statute, Minn. Stat. § 543.19 (1980). The Minnesota Supreme Court in *Stonewall Insurance Co. v. Horak,* 325 N.W.2d 134 (Minn.1982), recognized that actual receipt of the summons and complaint by mail, evidenced by a certified mail receipt signed by the individual defendant, constituted delivery under Minn.R.Civ.P. 4.03(a) and the statute. This rule does not modify the holding in *Stonewall.*

The change in Minn.R.Civ.P. 4.05 permitting service by mail adopts the essential provisions of Fed. R.Civ.P. 4. The rule authorizes use of the mails to deliver the summons and complaint to a defendant within or without the state, and makes service effective if the defendant acknowledges receipt of the summons and complaint. The Committee recommends that a new form (Form 22) be adopted to provide notice of the effect of the service by mail upon the defendants served. The form advises the defendant that by signing the acknowledgment of receipt the defendant admits only actual receipt of the summons and complaint and that signing does not constitute an appearance or a submission to the jurisdiction of the court and does not waive any other defenses. If an acknowledgement is not signed and returned, the plaintiff may then serve the summons and complaint by any other means authorized by the rules or by statute. There is no restriction on the means of service that may be used following unsuccessful service by mail. The Minnesota rule differs from the federal rule. *See Federal Deposit Insurance Co. v. Sims,* 100 F.R.D. 792 (N.D.Ala.1984) (attempted mail service prevents service by publication under federal rule).

The rule retains the provision of its federal counterpart shifting the cost of personal service to a defendant who declines to acknowledge receipt of the summons and complaint by mail. The Committee believes this provision is an essential part of the system for service by mail, and is necessary to discourage defendants from unjustifiedly refusing to acknowledge receipt. *Eden Foods, Inc. v. Eden's Own Products, Inc.,* 101 F.R.D. 96 (E.D.Mich.1984).

Historical Notes

Former Rule: A former Rule 4.05, adopted June 25, 1951, and revised March 3, 1959, and November 10, 1967, related to the service of process other than summons and subpoena. The subject matter of former Rule 4.05 was incorporated into Rule 4.02 by court order dated March 21, 1985.

Rule 4.06. Return

Service of summons and other process shall be proved by the certificate of the sheriff or other peace officer making it, by the affidavit of any other person making it, by the written admission or acknowledgement of the party served, or if served by publication, by the affidavit of the printer or the printer's designee. The proof of service in all cases other than by published notice shall state the time, place, and manner of service. Failure to make proof of service shall not affect the validity of the service.

Adopted June 25, 1951, eff. Jan. 1, 1952. Amended March 21, 1985, eff. July 1, 1985. Revised Oct. 18, 1988, eff. Jan. 1, 1989. Amended June 20, 2000, eff. Aug. 1, 2000.

Advisory Committee Note—1985

The change in this rule is intended to reflect that an acknowledgment of receipt, as permitted by Rule 4.05 and as contained in Form 22, constitutes adequate proof of service.

Rule 4.07. Amendments

The court in its discretion and on such terms as it deems just may at any time allow any summons or other process or proof of service thereof to be amended, unless it clearly appears that substantial rights of the person against whom the process issued would be prejudiced thereby.

Adopted June 25, 1951, eff. Jan. 1, 1952. Revised Oct. 18, 1988, eff. Jan. 1, 1989.

RULE 5. SERVICE AND FILING OF PLEADINGS AND OTHER PAPERS

Rule 5.01. Service; When Required; Appearance

Except as otherwise provided in these rules, every order required by its terms to be served, every pleading subsequent to the original complaint unless the court otherwise orders because of numerous defendants, every written motion other than one that may be heard ex parte, and every written notice, appearance, demand, offer of judgment, designation of record on appeal, and similar document shall be served upon each of the parties. No service need be made on parties in default for failure to appear except that pleadings asserting new or additional claims for relief against them shall be served upon them in the manner provided for service of summons in Rule 4. A party appears when that party serves or files any document in the proceeding.

Adopted June 25, 1951, eff. Jan. 1, 1952. Amended Nov. 10, 1967, eff. Feb. 1, 1968. Revised Oct. 18, 1988, eff. Jan. 1, 1989. Amended May 24, 2012, eff. Sept. 1, 2012.

Advisory Committee Note—1968

This rule is changed to clarify the rule and to conform the rule to the companion federal rule as amended in 1963. The words "affected thereby" are stricken and the rule now provides for a full exchange of documents between the parties by service of all documents on all of the other parties. Pursuant to this rule, all parties will receive copies of all documents that are to be served unless the specific rule that relates to that document provides to the contrary. For an example of a rule providing to the contrary, see Rule 14.

Historical and Statutory Notes

The order of the Minnesota Supreme Court [ADM 10–8011] dated May 24, 2012, provided in part that "These amendments shall apply to all actions or proceedings commenced on or after the effective date."

Rule 5.02. Service; How Made

(a) Methods of Service. Whenever under these rules service is required or permitted to be made upon a party represented by an attorney, the service shall be made upon the attorney unless service upon the party is ordered by the court. Written admission of service by the party or the party's attorney shall be sufficient proof of service. Service upon the attorney or upon a party shall be made by delivering a copy to the attorney or party; transmitting a copy by facsimile machine to the attorney's or party's office; or by mailing a copy to the attorney or party at the attorney's or party's last known address or, if no address is known, by leaving it with the court administrator. Delivery of a copy within this rule means: Handing it to the attorney or to the party; or leaving it at the attorney's or party's office with a clerk or other person in charge thereof; or, if there is no one in charge, leaving it in a conspicuous place therein; or, if the office is closed or the person to be served has no office, leaving it at the attorney's or party's dwelling house or usual place of abode with some person of suitable age and discretion then residing therein. If service is either authorized or required to be made by electronic means by these rules, delivery shall be accomplished by compliance with subdivision (b) of this rule.

(b) E–Service. Service of all documents after the original complaint may, and where required by these rules shall, be made by electronic means other than facsimile transmission if authorized by Rule 14 of the Minnesota General Rules of Practice and if service is made in accordance with that rule.

(c) Effective Date of Service. Service by mail is complete upon mailing. Service by facsimile is complete upon completion of the facsimile transmission. Service by authorized electronic means using the court's E–Filing System as defined by Rule 14 of the Minnesota General Rules of Practice is complete:

(1) upon completion of the electronic transmission of the document(s) to the E–Filing System if the E–Filing System service command is used; and

(2) upon acceptance of the electronic filing by the court, as provided in Rule 14, if the E–Filing System joint service and filing command is used.

(d) Technical Errors; Relief. Upon satisfactory proof that electronic filing or electronic service of a document was not completed, any party may obtain relief in accordance with Rule 14.01(f) of the General Rules of Practice. That relief may be available because of:

(1) an error in the transmission of the document to the authorized electronic filing and service system that was unknown to the sending party;

(2) a failure of the system to process the document when received, or

(3) other technical problems experienced by any party or system.

The court may enter an order permitting the document to be deemed filed or served as of the date it was first attempted to be transmitted electronically. If appropriate, the court may adjust the schedule for responding to these documents or the court's hearing, or provide other relief.

Adopted June 25, 1951, eff. Jan. 1, 1952. Revised Oct. 18, 1988, eff. Jan. 1, 1989. Amended Nov. 22, 1996, eff. Jan. 1, 1997; Oct. 21, 2010, eff. Oct. 21, 2010; May 24, 2012, eff. Sept. 1, 2012.

Advisory Committee Comments—1996 Amendments

Most of Rule 5.02 is new and for the first time provides for service by facsimile. Service by this method has become widespread, generally handled either by express agreement of counsel or acquiescence in a service method not explicitly authorized by rule.

The committee considered a suggestion that the provision for leaving a document with the court administrator be changed, deleted, or clarified. Although it is not clear from the rule what the administrator should do in the rare event that a document is filed with the administrator rather than delivered or mailed to the attorney, the committee believes the rule should be retained as it provides notice to the court that although service may comply with the rule, effective notice has not been received by the party entitled to notice. This will facilitate the court's consideration of the sufficiency of service under all of the circumstances.

The amendment to Rule 5.02 provides an express mechanism for service by facsimile. Service by facsimile has become widely accepted and is used in Minnesota either by agreement or presumption that it is acceptable under the rules or at least has not been objected to by the parties. The committee believes an express authorization for service by facsimile is appropriate and preferable to the existing silence on the subject. The committee's recommendation is modeled on similar provisions in the Wisconsin and Florida rules. *See* Wis.Stat. §§ 801.14(2) & .15(5)(b); Fla.R.Civ.P. 1.080(b)(5). Service by facsimile is allowed in other jurisdictions as well. *See, e.g.,* Ill.S.Ct.R. 11(b)(4); S.Dak.R. 15–6–5(b); Cal.R.Civ.P. 2008.

In addition providing for service by facsimile, Rule 6.05 is amended to create a specific deadline for timely service. This rule adds an additional day for response to any paper served by any means other than mail (where 3 extra days are allowed under existing Rule 6.05, which is retained) and where service is not effected until after 5:00 p.m. local time. This rule is intended to discourage, or at least make unrewarding, the inappropriate practice of serving papers after the close of a normal business day. Service after 5:00 p.m. is still *timely* as of the day of service if the deadline for service is that day, but if a response is permitted, the party served has an additional day to respond. This structure parallels directly the mechanism for dealing with service by mail under the existing rule.

Rule 5.05 is amended to add a provision relating to filing that was adopted as part of Fed.R.Civ.P. 5(e) in 1991. It is important that Rule 5 specifically provide that the court administrator must accept for filing documents tendered for that purpose regardless of any technical deficiencies they may contain. The court may, of course, direct that those deficiencies be remedied or give substantive importance to the deficiencies of the documents. The sanction of closing the courthouse to the filing should not be imposed or if imposed, should be imposed by a judge only after reviewing the document and the circumstances surrounding its filing. The rejection of documents for filing may have dire consequences for litigants and is not authorized by statute or rule.

Advisory Committee Comment—2010 Amendment

Rule 5.02 is amended to provide for service by electronic means, other than by facsimile as allowed by the existing rule, if authorized by an order of the Minnesota Supreme Court. This amendment is intended to facilitate a pilot project on electronic service and filing in one or two districts, but is designed to be a model for the implementation of electronic filing and service if the pilot project is made permanent and statewide. The rule makes service by electronic means effective when transmission is complete, just as the existing rules provide for filing and service by mail and facsimile transmission.

Service by electronic means is allowed for documents served after the original summons. Service under Rule 4 is required for summonses, and electronic service is not one of the means of service under that rule.

This amendment is modeled on rules 5(b)(2)(D) & (3) of the Federal Rules of Civil Procedure, as amended to implement electronic filing and service in the federal courts.

Advisory Committee Comment—2012 Amendment

Rule 5.02 is amended to authorize service by use of an authorized e-filing and e-service system where allowed or required by court rule or supreme court order. This amendment takes effect in conjunction with the adoption of Rule 14 of the General Rules of Practice; that rule defines the cases in which electronic filing and service are either required or permitted, as well as what constitutes proof of service. Rule 5.02(c) addresses the fact of service. Just as service by postal mail is complete upon dropping the properly addressed and postage paid document into the mailbox, service using the court's E–Filing System is complete upon transmitting the electronic document to the E–Filing system using the appropriate service command. Rule 5.02(d) provides specific guidance for courts dealing with the rare, but probably inevitable, circumstance of the e-filing system either not being available or not functioning as intended. If applicable, the rule authorizes the court to deem pleadings served or filed (or both) when attempted and to adjust the time to respond as appropriate.

Historical Notes

The order of the Minnesota Supreme Court [C6-84-2134] dated November 22, 1996, provides in part that the "(a)mendments shall apply to all actions pending on the effective date [January 1, 1997] and to those filed thereafter" and that "(t)he inclusion of Advisory Committee comments is made for convenience and does not reflect court approval of the comments made therein".

The order of the Minnesota Supreme Court [ADM 10–8011] dated May 24, 2012, provided in part that "These amendments shall apply to all actions or proceedings commenced on or after the effective date."

Rule 5.03. Service; Numerous Defendants

If the defendants are numerous, the court, upon motion or upon its own initiative, may order that service of the pleadings of the defendants and replies thereto need not be made as between the defendants and that any cross-claim, counterclaim, or matter constituting an avoidance or affirmative defense contained therein shall be deemed to be denied or avoided by all other parties and that the filing of any such pleading with the court and service thereof upon the plaintiff constitutes due notice of it to the parties. A copy of every such order shall be served upon the parties in such manner and form as the court directs.

Adopted June 25, 1951, eff. Jan. 1, 1952. Revised Oct. 18, 1988, eff. Jan. 1, 1989.

Rule 5.04. Filing; Certificate of Service

Any action that is not filed with the court within one year of commencement against any party is deemed dismissed with prejudice against all parties unless the parties within that year sign a stipulation to extend the filing period. This paragraph does not apply to family cases governed by rules 301 to 378 of the General Rules of Practice for the District Courts.

All documents after the complaint required to be served upon a party, together with a certificate of service, shall be filed with the court within a reasonable time after service, except disclosures under Rule 26, expert disclosures and reports, depositions upon oral examination and interrogatories, requests for documents, requests for admission, and answers and responses thereto shall not be filed unless upon order of the court or for use in the proceeding.

The administrator shall not refuse to accept for filing any document presented for that purpose solely because it is not presented in proper form as required by these rules or any local rules or practices. Documents may be rejected for filing if tendered without a required filing fee or a correct assigned file number, or are tendered to an administrator other than for the court where the action is pending.

Adopted June 25, 1951, eff. Jan. 1, 1952. Amended March 21, 1985, eff. July 1, 1985. Revised Oct. 18, 1988, eff. Jan. 1, 1989. Amended Dec. 20, 1993, eff. March 1, 1994; Nov. 22, 1996, eff. Jan. 1, 1997; Dec. 6, 1996, eff. Jan. 1, 1997; Dec. 19, 2000, eff. March 1, 2001; May 24, 2012, eff. Sept. 1, 2012; May 7, 2013, eff. July 1, 2013.

Advisory Committee Note—1985

Rule 5.04 is revised in its entirety to create a uniform requirement for the filing of documents. Essentially, the rule requires all papers which were served upon other parties to be filed with the Court. The Committee rejected any fixed deadlines for the filing of such papers, and rather, determined simply that the papers should be filed within a reasonable period of time. The rule creates a single exception for discovery requests and responses. Filing of depositions, interrogatories, requests for admissions, and requests for production of documents, and any answers or responses to those requests, is not required and is specifically proscribed unless ordered by the Court. The purpose of this change is to reduce the burden of processing and storing documents which are rarely required by the court. The change also protects the important privacy interests of litigants. *See Tavoulareas v. Washington Post Co.,* 724 F.2d 1010 (D.C.Cir.1984) (en banc).

If it is necessary to bring the court's attention to materials contained in such documents a party may incorporate relevant portions of any discovery requests or responses in a brief, affidavit, or motion, or attach copies thereof, or may request an order permitting the filing of a selected document, or directing the filing of all discovery documents.

Advisory Committee Comment—1993 Amendments

The amendment to Rule 5.04 makes it unnecessary to file notice of taking depositions in the vast majority of cases. Filing may be required as a condition precedent to issuance of a deposition subpoena pursuant to Minn.R.Civ.P. 45.04(a), though that rule only requires proof of service to be shown, not filed, and does not require filing of the notice itself in either event. The notice need not be filed because court administrators should issue subpoenas without the filing of the notice. In practice, courts have little use for deposition notices in court files, and in those rare circumstances where reference to them is necessary, they can be attached as exhibits to an affidavit, filed by leave of court, or offered in evidence just as any other discovery request or response.

Advisory Committee Comment—2000 Amendments

The last sentence of Rule 5.04 is changed to broaden the direction to court administrators not to reject documents for filing for noncompliance with the form requirements of the rules. The rule as amended makes it clear that those form requirements, regardless of which set of rules contains them, should not be the basis for a refusal to file the document. Any deficiency as to form should be dealt with by appropriate court order, including in most cases an opportunity to cure the defect.

Advisory Committee Comment—2012 Amendment

Rule 5.04 is amended to specify the limited situations where courts are not required to accept documents tendered for filing. These situations apply equally to documents tendered for filing electronically, by mail, or by hand-delivery to the court. Rejection for filing is not required in each of these situations, and it may be possible that certain format defects might be "fixed" at the time of filing. For example, if an incorrect file number is used on a document and it is detected at the time of attempted filing, it might be corrected; the administrator is still authorized to reject it for filing. An attempt to file a case using a new case number when the case has previously been filed may also be treated as not having the correct file number.

Historical Notes

The order of the Minnesota Supreme Court [C6-84-2134] dated November 22, 1996, provides in part that the "(a)mendments shall apply to all actions pending on the effective date [January 1, 1997] and to those filed thereafter" and that "(t)he inclusion of Advisory Committee comments is made for convenience and does not reflect court approval of the comments made therein".

The order of the Minnesota Supreme Court [CX-84-2134] dated December 19, 2000, provides in part that these amendments are effective March 1, 2001, and shall apply to all actions or proceedings pending on or commenced on or after the effective date, with the exception of the amendments to Rule 59, which shall apply to all actions or proceedings commenced on or after the effective date and all actions or proceedings pending on or decided before the effective date in which the time periods stated in the former Rule 59 have not expired.

The order of the Minnesota Supreme Court [CX-84-2134] dated December 19, 2000, provides in part that "(t)he inclusion of Advisory Committee comments is made for convenience and does not reflect court approval of the statements made therein".

The order of the Minnesota Supreme Court [ADM 10–8011] dated May 24, 2012, provided in part that "These amendments shall apply to all actions or proceedings commenced on or after the effective date."

The order of the Minnesota Supreme Court [ADM04–8001, ADM09–8009, ADM–10-8051] dated May 7, 2013, provided in part that the amendments be effective July 1, 2013, and further provided in part that "[t]hese amendments apply to all actions or proceedings pending on or commenced after the effective date provided that: (a) no action shall be involuntarily dismissed pursuant to Minn. R. Civ. P. 5.04 until one year after the effective date", and further provided that the "February 4, 2013 and February 12, 2013 orders of the court are hereby rescinded to the extent inconsistent with this order."

Rule 5.05. Filing; Facsimile Transmission

Except where filing is required by electronic means by rule of court, any document may be filed with the court by facsimile transmission. Filing shall be deemed complete at the time that the facsimile transmission is received by the court and the filed facsimile shall have the same force and effect as the original. Only facsimile transmission equipment that satisfies the published criteria of the Supreme Court shall be used for filing in accordance with this rule.

Within five days after the court has received the transmission, the party filing the document shall forward the following to the court:

(a) a $25 transmission fee for each 50 pages, or part thereof, of the filing;

(b) any bulky exhibits or attachments; and

(c) the applicable filing fee or fees, if any.

If a document is filed by facsimile, the sender's original must not be filed but must be maintained in the files of the party transmitting it for filing and made available to the court or any party to the action upon request.

Upon failure to comply with the requirements of this rule, the court in which the action is pending may make such orders as are just, including but not limited to, an order striking pleadings or parts thereof, staying further proceedings until compliance is complete, or dismissing the action, proceeding, or any part thereof.

Adopted Oct. 18, 1988, eff. Jan. 1, 1989. Amended Nov. 22, 1996, eff. Jan. 1, 1997; Dec. 6, 1996, eff. Jan. 1, 1997; Nov. 30, 2005, eff. Jan. 1, 2006; May 24, 2012, eff. Sept. 1, 2012.

Advisory Committee Comments—1996 Amendments

Most of Rule 5.02 is new and for the first time provides for service by facsimile. Service by this method has become widespread, generally handled either by express agreement of counsel or acquiescence in a service method not explicitly authorized by rule.

The committee considered a suggestion that the provision for leaving a document with the court administrator be changed, deleted, or clarified. Although it is not clear from the rule what the administrator should do in the rare event that a document is filed with the administrator rather than delivered or mailed to the attorney, the committee believes the rule should be retained as it provides notice to the court that although service may comply with the rule, effective notice has not been received by the party entitled to notice. This will facilitate the court's consideration of the sufficiency of service under all of the circumstances.

The amendment to Rule 5.02 provides an express mechanism for service by facsimile. Service by facsimile has become widely accepted and is used in Minnesota either by agreement or presumption that it is acceptable under the rules or at least has not been objected to by the parties. The committee believes an express authorization for service by facsimile is appropriate and preferable to the existing silence on the subject. The committee's recommendation is modeled on similar provisions in the Wisconsin and Florida rules. *See* Wis.Stat. §§ 801.14(2) & .15(5)(b); Fla.R.Civ.P. 1.080(b)(5). Service by facsimile is allowed in other jurisdictions as well. *See, e.g.,* Ill.S.Ct.R. 11(b)(4); S.Dak.R. 15–6–5(b); Cal.R.Civ.P. 2008.

In addition providing for service by facsimile, Rule 6.05 is amended to create a specific deadline for timely service. This rule adds an additional day for response to any paper served by any means other than mail (where 3 extra days are allowed under existing Rule 6.05, which is retained) and where service is not effected until after 5:00 p.m. local time. This rule is intended to discourage, or at least make unrewarding, the inappropriate practice of serving papers after the close of a normal business day. Service after 5:00 p.m. is still *timely* as of the day of service if the deadline for service is that day, but if a response is permitted, the party served has an additional day to respond. This structure parallels directly the mechanism for dealing with service by mail under the existing rule.

Rule 5.05 is amended to add a provision relating to filing that was adopted as part of Fed.R.Civ.P. 5(e) in 1991. It is important that Rule 5 specifically provide that the court administrator must accept for filing documents tendered for that purpose regardless of any technical deficiencies they may contain. The court may, of course, direct that those deficiencies be remedied or give substantive importance to the deficiencies of the documents. The sanction of closing the courthouse to the filing should not be imposed or if imposed, should be imposed by a judge only after reviewing the document and the circumstances surrounding its filing. The rejection of documents for filing may have dire consequences for litigants and is not authorized by statute or rule.

Advisory Committee Comment—2006 Amendment

Rule 5.05 is amended to delete the requirement that an "original" document follow the filing by facsimile. The requirement of a double filing causes confusion and unnecessary burdens for court administrators, and with the dramatic improvement in quality of received faxes since this rule was adopted in 1988, it no longer serves a useful purpose. Under the amended rule, the document filed by facsimile is the original for all purposes unless an issue arises as to its authenticity, in which case the version transmitted electronically and retained by the sender can be reviewed.

The filing fee for fax filings in Rule 5.05 is changed from $5.00 to $25.00 because fax filings, even under the streamlined procedures of the amended rule, still impose significant administrative burdens on court staff, and it is therefore appropriate that this fee, unchanged since the rule's adoption in 1988, be increased. A number of committee members expressed the view that facsimile filing was, and still is, intended to be a process used on a limited basis in exigent or at least unusual circumstances. It is not intended to be a routine filing method.

The rule does not provide a specific mechanism for collecting the transmission fee required under the rule. Because prejudice may occur to a party if a filing is deemed ineffective, the court should determine the appropriate consequences of failure to pay the necessary fee.

Advisory Committee Comment—2012 Amendment

Rule 5.05 is amended to dovetail the facsimile filing and service provisions to mandatory use of e-filing and e-service in certain cases. Where the court rules require e-filing and e-service, filing and service by facsimile are not authorized. When e-filing and e-service are in use throughout the state and in all categories of cases, facsimile filing and service is likely to become unavailable.

Historical Notes

The order of the Minnesota Supreme Court [C6-84-2134] dated November 22, 1996, provides in part that the "(a)mendments shall apply to all actions pending on the effective date [January 1, 1997] and to those filed thereafter" and that "(t)he inclusion of Advisory Committee comments is made for convenience and does not reflect court approval of the comments made therein".

The order of the Minnesota Supreme Court [ADM 10–8011] dated May 24, 2012, provided in part that "These amendments shall apply to all actions or proceedings commenced on or after the effective date."

Rule 5.06. Filing Electronically

Where authorized or required by rule promulgated by the Minnesota Supreme Court, documents may be filed electronically by following the procedures of such rules and will be deemed filed in accordance with the provisions of this rule.

A document that is electronically filed is deemed to have been filed by the court administrator on the date and time of its transmittal to the court through the E-Filing System as defined by Rule 14 of the Minnesota General Rules of Practice, and the filing shall be stamped with this date and time subject to acceptance by the court administrator. If the filing is not subsequently accepted by the court administrator for reasons authorized by Rule 5.04, the date stamp shall be removed and the document electronically returned to the person who filed it.

Adopted Oct. 21, 2010, eff. Oct. 21, 2010. Amended May 24, 2012, eff. Sept. 1, 2012.

Advisory Committee Comment—2010 Amendment

Rule 5.06 is a new rule to provide for filing by electronic means, if authorized by an order of the Minnesota Supreme Court. This amendment is intended to facilitate a pilot project on electronic service and filing in one or two districts, but is designed to be a model for the implementation of electronic filing if the pilot project is made permanent and statewide. The rule makes filing by electronic means effective in accordance with the rule for the pilot project.

Advisory Committee Comment—2012 Amendment

Rule 5.06 is amended to clarify when electronic filing through the court's e-filing system is effective. E-filings are subject to acceptance by the court administrator and acceptance may or may not occur on the same day as the transmittal of the filing. If accepted by the court administrator, however, the e-filing party will get the benefit of the date and time of their transmittal as the effective date of their filing.

Historical and Statutory Notes

The order of the Minnesota Supreme Court [ADM 10–8011] dated May 24, 2012, provided in part that "These amendments shall apply to all actions or proceedings commenced on or after the effective date."

RULE 5A. NOTICE OF CONSTITUTIONAL CHALLENGE TO A STATUTE

A party that files a pleading, written motion, or other paper drawing into question the constitutionality of a federal or state statute must promptly:

(1) file a notice of constitutional question stating the question and identifying the paper that raises it, if:

(A) a federal statute is questioned and neither the United States nor any of its agencies, officers, or employees is a party in an official capacity, or

(B) a state statute is questioned and neither the state nor any of its agencies, officers, or employees is a party in an official capacity; and

(2) serve the notice and paper on the Attorney General of the United States if a federal statute is challenged, or on the Minnesota Attorney General if a state statute is challenged, by United States Mail to afford the Attorney General an opportunity to intervene.

Adopted May 21, 2007, eff. July 1, 2007.

Advisory Committee Comment—2007 Amendment

Rule 5A is a new rule, though it addresses subject matter covered by Minn. R. Civ. P. 24.04 prior to the adoption of this rule. The rule imposes an express requirement for notice to the appropriate Attorney General—the Minnesota Attorney General for challenges to Minnesota statutes and the Attorney General of the United States for challenges to federal statutes. The rule requires the giving of notice, and the purpose of the notice is to permit the Attorney General receiving it to decide whether to intervene in the action. The rule does not require any action by the Attorney General and in many instances intervention will not be sought until the litigation reaches the appellate courts. The federal rule requires service on the appropriate attorney general by certified or registered mail. The committee believes that service of this notice by U.S. Mail is sufficient for this purpose.

As part of this change, Minn. R. Civ. P. 24.04 is abrogated as it duplicates this rule's mechanism.

RULE 6. TIME

Rule 6.01. Computation

(a) Computation of Time Periods. In computing any period of time prescribed or allowed by these rules, by the local rules of any district court, by order of court, or by any applicable statute, the day of the act, event, or default from which the designated period of time begins to run shall not be included. The last day of the period so computed shall be included, unless it is a

- Saturday,
- Sunday,
- legal holiday, or,
- when the act to be done is the filing of a document in court, a day on which weather or other conditions result in the closing of the office of the court administrator of the court where the action is pending, or
- where filing or service is either permitted or required to be made electronically, a day on which unavailability of the computer system used by the court for electronic filing and service makes it impossible to accomplish service or filing,

in which event the period runs until the end of the next day that is not one of the aforementioned days.

(b) Periods Shorter than 7 Days. When the period of time prescribed or allowed is less than seven days, intermediate Saturdays, Sundays, and legal holidays shall be excluded in the computation.

(c) Definition of Legal Holiday. As used in this rule and in Rule 77(c), "legal holiday" includes any holiday designated in Minn. Stat. § 645.44, subd. 5, as a holiday for the state or any state-wide branch of government and any day that the United States Mail does not operate.

Adopted June 25, 1951, eff. Jan. 1, 1952. Amended Nov. 10, 1967, eff. Feb. 1, 1968. Revised Oct. 18, 1988, eff. Jan. 1, 1989. Amended Nov. 22, 1996, eff. Jan. 1, 1997; May 21, 2007, eff. July 1, 2007; May 24, 2012, eff. Sept. 1, 2012.

Advisory Committee Comments—1996 Amendments

The amendment to Rule 6.01 conforms the rule to its federal counterpart. The committee believes it is desirable to define explicitly what constitutes a "legal holiday." Given the nature of Minnesota's weather, the committee believes specific provision for dealing with inclement weather should be made in the rules. The federal rule enumerates specific holidays. That drafting approach is not feasible in Minnesota because Minn.Stat. § 645.44, subd. 5, defines legal holidays, but allows the judiciary to pick either Columbus Day or the Friday after Thanksgiving as a holiday. Whichever is selected is defined to be a holiday under the rule.

The amendment to Rule 6.05 conforms the rule to the federal rule except for the last sentence which is new and has no federal counterpart. This provision is intended to discourage the unseemly practices of sliding a "service" under the door of opposing counsel or sending a facsimile transmission after the close of business and asserting timely service. Such service will be timely under the rules, but will add a day to the time to respond. If the paper is due to be served a fixed number of days before an event, that number should be increased by one as well, making it necessary to serve late in the day before the deadline.

Advisory Committee Comment—2012 Amendment

Rule 6.01 is amended to add unavailability of the court-authorized e-filing and e-service system as a circumstance that would result in the extension of the time period. This extension applies only where the system problem occurs on the last day of the period and should only apply where the problem is not momentary. The rule requires that unavailability of the e-filing system actually prevent compliance with the service or filing requirements. This certainly eliminates use of a short-lived shutdown from extending the deadline except, possibly, where it occurs right at the end of the day. Where the shutdown occurs for a substantial part of the day and where it continues through the close of business, then the additional day would be automatically applied.

Historical Notes

The order of the Minnesota Supreme Court [C6-84-2134] dated November 22, 1996, provides in part that the "(a)mendments shall apply to all actions pending on the effective date [January 1, 1997] and to those filed thereafter" and that "(t)he inclusion of Advisory Committee comments is made for convenience and does not reflect court approval of the comments made therein".

The order of the Minnesota Supreme Court [ADM 10-8011] dated May 24, 2012, provided in part that "These amendments shall apply to all actions or proceedings commenced on or after the effective date."

Rule 6.02. Enlargement

When by statute, by these rules, by a notice given thereunder, or by order of court an act is required or allowed to be done at or within a specified time, the court for cause shown may, at any time in its discretion, (1) with or without motion or notice order the period enlarged if request therefor is made before the expiration of the period originally prescribed or as extended by a previous order, or (2) upon motion made after the expiration of the specified period permit the act to be done where the failure to act was the result of excusable neglect; but it may not extend the time for taking any action under Rules 4.043, 59.03, 59.05, and 60.02 except to the extent and under the conditions stated in them.

Adopted June 25, 1951, eff. Jan. 1, 1952. Amended Dec. 6, 1951. Revised Oct. 18, 1988, eff. Jan. 1, 1989.

Rule 6.03. Unaffected by Expiration of Term

The continued existence or the expiration of a term of court does not affect or limit the period of time provided for the taking of any action or proceeding, or affect the power of the court to act or take any proceeding in any action which has been pending before it.

Adopted June 25, 1951, eff. Jan. 1, 1952. Revised Oct. 18, 1988, eff. Jan. 1, 1989.

Rule 6.04. For Motions; Affidavits

A written motion, other than one which may be heard ex parte, and notice of the hearing thereof shall be served no later than 5 days before the time specified for the hearing, unless a different period is fixed by these rules or by order of the court. Such an order may for cause shown be made on ex parte application. When a motion is supported by affidavit, the affidavit shall be served with the motion; and, except as otherwise provided in Rule 59.04, opposing affidavits may be served not later than one day before the hearing, unless the court permits them to be served at some other time.

Adopted June 25, 1951, eff. Jan. 1, 1952. Revised Oct. 18, 1988, eff. Jan. 1, 1989. Amended Nov. 22, 1996, eff. Jan. 1, 1997.

Historical Notes

The order of the Minnesota Supreme Court [C6-84-2134] dated November 22, 1996, provides in part that the "(a)mendments shall apply to all actions pending on the effective date [January 1, 1997] and to those filed thereafter" and that "(t)he inclusion of Advisory Committee comments is made for convenience and does not reflect court approval of the comments made therein".

Rule 6.05. Additional Time After Service by Mail or Service Late in Day

Whenever a party has the right or is required to do some act or take some proceedings within a prescribed period after the service of a notice or other document upon the party, and the notice or document is served upon the party by United States Mail, three days shall be added to the prescribed period. If service is made by any means other than United States Mail and accomplished after 5:00 p.m. local time on the day of service, one additional day shall be added to the prescribed period.

Adopted June 25, 1951, eff. Jan. 1, 1952. Amended March 3, 1959, eff. July 1, 1959. Revised Oct. 18, 1988, eff. Jan. 1, 1989. Amended Nov. 22, 1996, eff. Jan. 1, 1997; May 21, 2007, eff. July 1, 2007; May 24, 2012, eff. Sept. 1, 2012.

Advisory Committee Comments—1996 Amendments

The amendment to Rule 6.01 conforms the rule to its federal counterpart. The committee believes it is desirable to define explicitly what constitutes a "legal holiday." Given the nature of Minnesota's weather, the committee believes specific provision for dealing with inclement weather should be made in the rules. The federal rule enumerates specific holidays. That drafting approach is not feasible in Minnesota because Minn.Stat. § 645.44, subd. 5, defines legal holidays, but allows the judiciary to pick either Columbus Day or the Friday after Thanksgiving as a holiday. Whichever is selected is defined to be a holiday under the rule.

The amendment to Rule 6.05 conforms the rule to the federal rule except for the last sentence which is new and has no federal counterpart. This provision is intended to discourage the unseemly practices of sliding a "service" under the door of opposing counsel or sending a facsimile transmission after the close of business and asserting timely service. Such service will be timely under the rules, but will add a day to the time to respond. If the paper is due to be served a fixed number of days before an event, that number should be increased by one as well, making it necessary to serve late in the day before the deadline.

Advisory Committee Comment—2007 Amendment

Rule 6.01 is amended to remove potential ambiguity in the existing rule. The rule is ambiguous because of the odd definition of "holiday" in MINN. STAT. § 645.44, subd. 5, and its ambiguity over how Columbus Day is treated, Additionally, because the rules explicitly provide for service by mail, the court recognized that a "mail holiday" should be a "legal holiday" for the purpose of this rule.

The rule excuses filing on the last day of a time period if the court administrator's office is inaccessible. The amended rule replaces an indefinite concept of the court administrator's office being "inaccessible" with a more definite formulation: the office of the administrator of the court where the action is pending must actually be closed.

Rule 6.05 is amended to make the rule definite as to what forms of service qualify as "service by mail." The rule as amended explicitly allows three additional days only for service by United States Mail; the use of any other delivery or courier service does not constitute "United States Mail," and therefore does not qualify for additional time. This rule is now consistent with Minn. R. Civ. P. 4.05, which specifies "first-class mail" as the means for service by mail.

Historical Notes

The order of the Minnesota Supreme Court [C6-84-2134] dated November 22, 1996, provides in part that the "(a)mendments shall apply to all actions pending on the effective date [January 1, 1997] and to those filed thereafter" and that "(t)he inclusion of Advisory Committee comments is made for convenience and does not reflect court approval of the comments made therein".

The order of the Minnesota Supreme Court [ADM 10–8011] dated May 24, 2012, provided in part that "These amendments shall apply to all actions or proceedings commenced on or after the effective date."

III. PLEADINGS AND MOTIONS

RULE 7. PLEADINGS ALLOWED; FORM OF MOTIONS

Rule 7.01. Pleadings

There shall be a complaint and an answer (including such pleadings in a third-party proceeding when a third-party claim is asserted); a reply to a counterclaim denominated as such; and an answer to a cross-claim if the answer contains a cross-claim. No other pleading shall be allowed except that the court may order a reply to an answer. Demurrers, pleas and exceptions for insufficiency of a pleading shall not be used.

Adopted June 25, 1951, eff. Jan. 1, 1952. Amended March 3, 1959, eff. July 1, 1959. Revised Oct. 18, 1988, eff. Jan. 1, 1989.

Advisory Committee Note—1959

Reference to leave of court is deleted as unnecessary and as inconsistent with Rule 14.01 as now amended.

Rule 7.02. Motions and Other Papers

(a) An application to the court for an order shall be by motion which, unless made during a hearing or trial, shall be in writing, shall state with particularity the grounds therefor, and shall set forth the relief or order sought. The requirement of writing is fulfilled if the motion is stated in a written notice of the hearing of the motion. Motions provided in these rules are motions requiring a written notice to the party and a hearing before the order can be issued unless the particular rule under which the motion is made specifically provides that the motion may be made ex parte. The parties may agree to written submission to the court for decision without oral argument unless the court directs otherwise. Upon the request of a party or upon its own initiative, the court may hear any motion by telephone conference.

(b) The rules applicable for captions, signing, and other matters of form of pleadings apply to all motions and other papers provided for by these rules.

(c) All motions will be signed in accordance with Rule 11.

Adopted June 25, 1951, eff. Jan. 1, 1952. Amended Nov. 14, 1974, eff. Jan. 1, 1975; Nov. 30, 1981; March 21, 1985, eff. July 1, 1985. Revised Oct. 18, 1988, eff. Jan. 1, 1989.

Advisory Committee Note—1975

This amendment is purely a clarifying amendment. No substantive change in the rule is made but an ambiguity evidenced in application of some of the rules is clarified where the rule reference to a motion did not indicate whether it was ex parte motion or a motion upon notice and hearing. This change has no counterpart in the corresponding Federal rule.

Advisory Committee Note—1985

Rule 7.02(1) is amended to make it clear that the court can properly conduct motion hearings by telephone conference call. The use of telephone conference calls for hearings, in appropriate cases, is intended to facilitate prompt and inexpensive hearings on motions submitted to the courts.

This rule is also changed by the addition of a third subdivision reflecting the change in Rule 11 which requires motions to be signed after reasonable inquiry. This change reflects an identical change made in Fed.R.Civ.P. 7 by the 1983 amendment.

RULE 8. GENERAL RULES OF PLEADING

Rule 8.01. Claims for Relief

A pleading which sets forth a claim for relief, whether an original claim, counterclaim, cross-claim, or third-party claim, shall contain a short and plain statement of the claim showing that the pleader is entitled to relief and a demand for judgment for the relief sought; if a recovery of money is demanded, the amount shall be stated. Relief in the alternative or of several different types may be demanded. If a recovery of money for unliquidated damages is demanded in an amount less than $50,000, the amount shall be stated. If a recovery of money for unliquidated damages in an amount greater than $50,000 is demanded, the pleading shall state merely that recovery of reasonable damages in an amount greater than $50,000 is sought.

Adopted June 25, 1951, eff. Jan. 1, 1952. Amended March 21, 1985, eff. July 1, 1985. Revised Oct. 18, 1988, eff. Jan. 1, 1989.

Advisory Committee Note—1985

This change is made to conform the language of the rule to the limitations of Minn.Stat. § 544.36 (1982) which was adopted in 1978.

Rule 8.02. Defenses; Form of Denials

A party shall state in short and plain terms any defenses to each claim asserted and shall admit or deny the averments upon which the adverse party relies. If a party is without knowledge or information sufficient to form a belief as to the truth of an averment, the party shall so state and this has the effect of a denial. Denials shall fairly meet the substance of the averments denied. A pleader who intends in good faith to deny only a part or to qualify an averment shall specify so much of it as is true and material and shall deny only the remainder. Unless the pleader intends in good faith to controvert all the averments of the preceding pleading, the pleader may make denials as specific denials of designated averments or paragraphs, or may generally deny all the averments except such designated averments or paragraphs as the pleader expressly admits. However, a pleader who intends to controvert all its averments may do so by general denial subject to the obligations set forth in Rule 11.

Adopted June 25, 1951, eff. Jan. 1, 1952. Revised Oct. 18, 1988, eff. Jan. 1, 1989.

Rule 8.03. Affirmative Defenses

In pleading to a preceding pleading, a party shall set forth affirmatively accord and satisfaction, arbitration and award, assumption of risk, contributory negligence, discharge in bankruptcy, duress, estoppel, failure of consideration, fraud, illegality, injury by fellow servant, laches, license, payment, release, res judicata, statute of frauds, statute of limitations, waiver, and any other matter constituting an avoidance or affirmative defense. When a party has mistakenly designated a defense as a counterclaim or a counterclaim as a defense, the court, on such terms as justice may require, shall treat the pleading as if there had been a proper designation.

Adopted June 25, 1951, eff. Jan. 1, 1952. Revised Oct. 18, 1988, eff. Jan. 1, 1989.

Rule 8.04. Effect of Failure to Deny

Averments in a pleading to which a responsive pleading is required, other than those as to amount of damage, are admitted when not denied in the responsive pleading. Averments in a pleading to which no responsive pleading is required or permitted shall be taken as denied or avoided.

Adopted June 25, 1951, eff. Jan. 1, 1952. Revised Oct. 18, 1988, eff. Jan. 1, 1989.

Rule 8.05. Pleading to be Concise and Direct; Consistency

(a) Each averment of a pleading shall be simple, concise, and direct. No technical forms of pleading or motions are required.

(b) A party may set forth two or more statements of a claim or defense alternatively or hypothetically, either in one count or defense or in separate counts or defenses. When two or more statements are made in the alternative and one of them if made independently would be sufficient, the pleading is not made insufficient by the insufficiency of one or more of the alternative statements. A party may also state as many separate claims or defenses as the party has regardless of consistency and whether based on legal or equitable grounds or both. All statements shall be made subject to the obligations set forth in Rule 11.

Adopted June 25, 1951, eff. Jan. 1, 1952. Revised Oct. 18, 1988, eff. Jan. 1, 1989.

Rule 8.06. Construction of Pleadings

All pleadings shall be so construed as to do substantial justice.

Adopted June 25, 1951, eff. Jan. 1, 1952. Revised Oct. 18, 1988, eff. Jan. 1, 1989.

RULE 9. PLEADING SPECIAL MATTERS

Rule 9.01. Capacity

It is not necessary to aver the capacity of a party to sue or be sued, the authority of a party to sue or be sued in a representative capacity, or the legal existence of a partnership or an organized association of persons that is made a party. A party who desires to raise an issue as to the legal existence of any party, the capacity of any party to sue or be sued, or the authority of a party to sue or be sued in a representative capacity shall do so by specific negative averment, which shall include such supporting particulars as are peculiarly within the pleader's knowledge.

Adopted June 25, 1951, eff. Jan. 1, 1952. Revised Oct. 18, 1988, eff. Jan. 1, 1989.

Rule 9.02. Fraud, Mistake, Condition of Mind

In all averments of fraud or mistake, the circumstances constituting fraud or mistake shall be stated with particularity. Malice, intent, knowledge, and other condition of mind of a person may be averred generally.

Adopted June 25, 1951, eff. Jan. 1, 1952. Revised Oct. 18, 1988, eff. Jan. 1, 1989.

Rule 9.03. Conditions Precedent

In pleading the performance or occurrence of conditions precedent, it is sufficient to aver generally that all conditions precedent have been performed or have occurred. A denial of performance or occurrence shall be made specifically and with particularity.

Adopted June 25, 1951, eff. Jan. 1, 1952. Revised Oct. 18, 1988, eff. Jan. 1, 1989.

Rule 9.04. Official Document or Act

In pleading an official document or official act, it is sufficient to aver that the document was issued or the act was done in compliance with law; and in pleading any ordinance of a city, village, or borough or any special or local statute or any right derived from either, it is sufficient to refer to the ordinance or statute by its title and the date of its approval.

Adopted June 25, 1951, eff. Jan. 1, 1952. Revised Oct. 18, 1988, eff. Jan. 1, 1989.

Rule 9.05. Judgment

In pleading a judgment or decision of a domestic or foreign court, judicial or quasi-judicial tribunal, or of a board or officer, it is sufficient to aver the judgment or decision without setting forth matter showing jurisdiction to render it.

Adopted June 25, 1951, eff. Jan. 1, 1952. Revised Oct. 18, 1988, eff. Jan. 1, 1989.

Rule 9.06. Time and Place

For the purpose of testing the sufficiency of a pleading, averments of time and place are material and shall be considered like all other averments of material matter.

Adopted June 25, 1951, eff. Jan. 1, 1952. Revised Oct. 18, 1988, eff. Jan. 1, 1989.

Rule 9.07. Special Damages

When items of special damage are claimed, they shall be specifically stated.

Adopted June 25, 1951, eff. Jan. 1, 1952. Revised Oct. 18, 1988, eff. Jan. 1, 1989.

Rule 9.08. Unknown Party; How Designated

When a party is ignorant of the name of an opposing party and so alleges in the party's pleading, the opposing party may be designated by any name and when that opposing party's true name is discovered the process and all pleadings and proceedings in the action may be amended by substituting the true name.

Adopted June 25, 1951, eff. Jan. 1, 1952. Revised Oct. 18, 1988, eff. Jan. 1, 1989.

RULE 10. FORM OF PLEADINGS

Rule 10.01. Caption; Names of Parties

Every pleading shall have a caption setting forth the name of the court and the county in which the action is brought, the title of the action, the court file number if one has been assigned, and a designation as in Rule 7, and, in the upper right hand corner, the appropriate case type indicator as set forth in the subject matter index included in the appendix as Form 23. If a case is assigned to a particular judge for all subsequent proceedings, the name of that judge shall be included in the caption and adjacent to the file number. In the complaint, the title of the action shall include the names of all the parties, but in other pleadings it is sufficient to state the first party on each side with an appropriate indication of other parties.

Adopted June 25, 1951, eff. Jan. 1, 1952. Amended June 12, 1986, eff. July 1, 1986. Revised Oct. 18, 1988, eff. Jan. 1, 1989. Amended Dec. 20, 1993, eff. March 1, 1994; Dec. 19, 2000, eff. March 1, 2001.

Advisory Committee Comment—1993 Amendments

The only change made to this rule is to correct a typographical or grammatical error in the existing rule. No change in meaning or interpretation is intended.

Advisory Committee Comments—2000 Amendments

Rule 10.01 is amended to facilitate case management and document management in cases where a judge has been assigned to the case. By placing the judge's name on the caption, it is often possible to expedite the delivery of filed documents to that judge. This provision is commonly required in federal court cases where all matters are assigned to a judge, including in the United States District Court for the District of Minnesota. See LR 5.1 (D. Minn.). The rule is also amended to require the inclusion of a court file number if one has been assigned.

Historical Notes

The order of the Minnesota Supreme Court [CX-84-2134] dated December 19, 2000, provides in part that these amendments are effective March 1, 2001, and shall apply to all actions or proceedings pending on or commenced on or after the effective date, with the exception of the amendments to Rule 59, which shall apply to all actions or proceedings commenced on or after the effective date and all actions or proceedings pending on or decided before the effective date in which the time periods stated in the former Rule 59 have not expired.

The order of the Minnesota Supreme Court [CX-84-2134] dated December 19, 2000, provides in part that "(t)he inclusion of Advisory Committee comments is made for convenience and does not reflect court approval of the statements made therein".

Rule 10.02. Paragraph; Separate Statements

All averments of claim or defense shall be made in numbered paragraphs, the contents of each of which shall be limited as far as practicable to a statement of a single set of circumstances; and a paragraph may be referred to by number in all succeeding pleadings. Each claim founded upon a separate transaction or occurrence and each defense other than denials shall be stated in a separate count or defense whenever a separation facilitates the clear presentation of the matters set forth.

Adopted June 25, 1951, eff. Jan. 1, 1952. Revised Oct. 18, 1988, eff. Jan. 1, 1989.

Rule 10.03. Adoption by Reference; Exhibits

Statements in a pleading may be adopted by reference in a different part of the same pleading or in another pleading or in any motion. A copy of any written instrument which is an exhibit to a pleading is a part of the statement of claim or defense set forth in the pleading.

Adopted June 25, 1951, eff. Jan. 1, 1952. Revised Oct. 18, 1988, eff. Jan. 1, 1989.

Rule 10.04. Failure to Comply

If a pleading, motion or other paper fails to indicate the case type as required by Rule 10.01, it may be stricken by the court unless the appropriate case type indicator is communicated to the court administrator promptly after the omission is called to the attention of the pleader or movant.

Adopted June 12, 1986, eff. July 1, 1986. Revised Oct. 18, 1988, eff. Jan. 1, 1989.

RULE 11. SIGNING OF PLEADINGS, MOTIONS, AND OTHER PAPERS; REPRESENTATIONS TO COURT; SANCTIONS

Rule 11.01. Signature

Every pleading, written motion, and other similar document shall be signed by at least one attorney of record in the attorney's individual name, or, if the party is not represented by an attorney, shall be signed by the party. Each document shall state the signer's address and telephone number, if any, and attorney registration number if signed by an attorney. Except when otherwise specifically provided by rule or statute, pleadings need not be verified or accompanied by affidavit. An unsigned document shall be stricken unless omission of the signature is corrected promptly after being called to the attention of the attorney or party. If authorized by order of the Minnesota Supreme Court, a document filed, signed, or verified by electronic means in accordance with that order constitutes a signed document for the purposes of applying these rules.

The filing or submitting of a document using an E–Filing System established by rule of court constitutes certification of compliance with the signature requirements of applicable court rules.

Adopted June 25, 1951, eff. Jan. 1, 1952. Amended March 21, 1985, eff. July 1, 1985. Revised Oct. 18, 1988, eff. Jan. 1, 1989. Amended Sept. 5, 1991, eff. Jan. 1, 1992; April 13, 2000, eff. July 1, 2000; June 20, 2000, eff. Aug. 1, 2000; Oct. 21, 2010, eff. Oct. 21, 2010; May 24, 2012, eff. Sept. 1, 2012.

Advisory Committee Comment—2010 Amendment

Rule 11.01 is amended to add the last sentence. This amendment makes it clear that "signing" in accordance with a rule allowing for filing and service by electronic means where authorized by an order of the Minnesota Supreme Court is treated as a signature for the purpose of Rule 11 or other provision in the rules. This amendment is intended to facilitate a pilot project on electronic filing in one or two districts, but is designed to be a model for the implementation of electronic filing and service if the pilot project is made permanent and statewide.

Advisory Committee Comment—2012 Amendment

Rule 11.01 is amended to add the second paragraph. The sole purpose of the amendment is to make explicit the status of "signatures" affixed to pleadings and other documents that are electronically served. Whatever means is used to sign these documents, whether quill pen and ink, facsimile of a signature, or an indication that the document is signed (such as a "/s/ Pat Smith" notation), each will be treated the same way and deemed to be signatures for all purposes under the rule.

Historical and Statutory Notes

The order of the Minnesota Supreme Court [ADM 10–8011] dated May 24, 2012, provided in part that "These amendments shall apply to all actions or proceedings commenced on or after the effective date."

Rule 11.02. Representations to Court

By presenting to the court (whether by signing, filing, submitting, or later advocating) a pleading, written motion, or other paper, an attorney or unrepresented party is certifying that to the best of the person's knowledge, information, and belief, formed after an inquiry reasonable under the circumstances,

(a) it is not being presented for any improper purpose, such as to harass or to cause unnecessary delay or needless increase in the cost of litigation;

(b) the claims, defenses, and other legal contentions therein are warranted by existing law or by a nonfrivolous argument for the extension, modification, or reversal of existing law or the establishment of new law;

(c) the allegations and other factual contentions have evidentiary support or, if specifically so identified, are likely to have evidentiary support after a reasonable opportunity for further investigation or discovery; and

(d) the denials of factual contentions are warranted on the evidence or, if specifically so identified, are reasonably based on a lack of information or belief.

Adopted June 25, 1951, eff. Jan. 1, 1952. Amended March 21, 1985, eff. July 1, 1985. Revised Oct. 18, 1988, eff. Jan. 1, 1989. Amended Sept. 5, 1991, eff. Jan. 1, 1992; April 13, 2000, eff. July 1, 2000; June 20, 2000, eff. Aug. 1, 2000.

Rule 11.03. Sanctions

If, after notice and a reasonable opportunity to respond, the court determines that Rule 11.02 has been violated, the court may, subject to the conditions stated below, impose an appropriate sanction upon the attorneys, law firms, or parties that have violated Rule 11.02 or are responsible for the violation.

(a) How Initiated.

(1) *By Motion.* A motion for sanctions under this rule shall be made separately from other motions or requests and shall describe the specific conduct alleged to violate Rule 11.02. It shall be served as provided in Rule 5, but shall not be filed with or presented to the court unless, within 21 days after service of the motion (or such other period as the court may prescribe), the challenged paper, claim, defense, contention, allegation, or denial is not withdrawn or appropriately corrected. If warranted, the court may award to the party prevailing on the motion the reasonable expenses and attorney fees incurred in presenting or opposing the motion. Absent exceptional circumstances, a law firm shall be held jointly responsible for violations committed by its partners, associates, and employees.

(2) *On Court's Initiative.* On its own initiative, the court may enter an order describing the specific conduct that appears to violate Rule 11.02 and directing an attorney, law firm, or party to show cause why it has not violated Rule 11.02 with respect thereto.

(b) Nature of Sanction; Limitations. A sanction imposed for violation of this rule shall be limited to what is sufficient to deter repetition of such conduct or comparable conduct by others similarly situated. Subject to the limitations in Rules 11.03(a)(1) and (2), the sanction may consist of, or include, directives of a nonmonetary nature, an order to pay a penalty into court, or, if imposed on motion and warranted for effective deterrence, an order directing payment to the movant of some or all of the reasonable attorney fees and other expenses incurred as a direct result of the violation.

(1) Monetary sanctions may not be awarded against a represented party for a violation of Rule 11.02(b).

(2) Monetary sanctions may not be awarded on the court's initiative unless the court issues its order to show cause before a voluntary dismissal or settlement of the claims made by or against the party which is, or whose attorneys are, to be sanctioned.

(c) Order. When imposing sanctions, the court shall describe the conduct determined to constitute a violation of this rule and explain the basis for the sanction imposed.

Adopted June 25, 1951, eff. Jan. 1, 1952. Amended March 21, 1985, eff. July 1, 1985. Revised Oct. 18, 1988, eff. Jan. 1, 1989. Amended Sept. 5, 1991, eff. Jan. 1, 1992; April 13, 2000, eff. July 1, 2000; June 20, 2000, eff. Aug. 1, 2000.

Rule 11.04. Inapplicability to Discovery

Rules 11.01–.03 do not apply to discovery requests, responses, objections, and motions that are subject to the provisions of Rules 26 through 37.

Adopted June 25, 1951, eff. Jan. 1, 1952. Amended March 21, 1985, eff. July 1, 1985. Revised Oct. 18, 1988, eff. Jan. 1, 1989. Amended Sept. 5, 1991, eff. Jan. 1, 1992; April 13, 2000, eff. July 1, 2000; June 20, 2000, eff. Aug. 1, 2000.

Advisory Committee Note—1985

The changes in this rule follow the changes made in Fed.R.Civ.P. 11 by the 1983 amendments. First, it is now clear that the certification requirements of the rule apply to motions and other papers in addition to pleadings. This change is also found in the language of new Rule 26.07 relating to the signing of discovery requests, responses, and objections. Second, an attorney or party is required to make reasonable inquiry in order to determine the soundness of the position being advanced. Third, sanctions may be imposed for improper certification of a pleading or motion. The rule in the past permitted the offending document to be stricken under Minn.R.Civ.P. 12.06, and subjected the attorney to disciplinary action. The proposed rule permits a pleading or motion to be stricken, but affords the pleader or movant the opportunity to sign the pleading if it has not been signed. If the pleading or motion is signed in violation of the rule, the Court is authorized and encouraged to impose sanctions against the party or attorney. Rule 11 was seldom used as a basis for a discipline. The rule provides clear authority to impose sanctions for misconduct. The new rule focuses on the Court's interest in preserving the integrity of the litigation process and preventing abuse. The rule permits sanctions to be imposed against either a party or the attorney, or both, and awards damages that are essentially compensatory in nature.

Although compensatory in purpose, the imposition of costs should also deter violations of the rule. Sanctions under Rule 11 may be substantial, even though limited to compensation for unnecessary expenses incurred by opponents. *See, e.g., Nemeroff v. Abelson,* 620 F.2d 339 (2d Cir.1983); *Van Berkel v. Fox Farm & Road Mach.,* 581 F.Supp. 1248 (D.Minn.1984). The court may order that a penalty imposed against an attorney is actually borne by the attorney, and not shifted to the client.

Task Force Comment—1991

This rule amendment is patterned after 4th Dist.R. 1.01(c) & (e).

The Task Force believes that the simple additional requirement for signing pleadings, widely followed in practice, should best be made part of this rule governing signing of pleadings, motions and other papers.

Advisory Committee Comments—2000 Amendments

Rule 11 is amended to conform completely to the federal rule. While Rule 11 has worked fairly well in its current form under the Supreme Court's guidance in *Uselman v. Uselman,* 464 N.W.2d 130 (Minn. 1990), the federal rules have been amended and create both procedural and substantive differences between state and federal court practices. Additionally, the Minnesota Legislature has created a statutory mechanism that follows the federal procedure, resulting in a confusing array of practice requirements and remedies. *See* MINN. STAT. § 549.211. On balance, the Committee believes that the amendment of the Rule to conform to its federal counterpart makes the most sense, given this Committee's long-standing preference for minimizing the differences between state and federal practice unless compelling local interests or long-entrenched reliance on the state procedure makes changing a rule inappropriate.

It is the intention of the Committee that the revised Rule would modify the procedure for seeking sanctions, but would not significantly change the availability of sanctions or the conduct justifying the imposition of sanctions. Courts and practitioners should be guided by the *Uselman* decision, cited above, and should continue to reserve the seeking of sanctions and their imposition for substantial departures from acceptable litigation conduct.

RULE 12. DEFENSES AND OBJECTIONS; WHEN AND HOW PRESENTED; BY PLEADING OR MOTION; MOTION FOR JUDGMENT ON PLEADINGS

Rule 12.01. When Presented

Defendant shall serve an answer within 20 days after service of the summons upon that defendant unless the court directs otherwise pursuant to Rule 4.043. A party served with a pleading stating a cross-claim against that party shall serve an answer thereto within 20 days after the service upon that party. The plaintiff shall serve a reply to a counterclaim in the answer within 20 days after service of the answer or, if a reply is ordered by the court, within 20 days after service of the order, unless the order otherwise directs. The service of a motion permitted under this rule alters these periods of time as follows unless a different time is fixed by order of the court: (1) If the court denies the motion or postpones its disposition until the trial on the merits, the responsive pleading shall be served within 10 days after service of notice of the court's action; (2) if the court grants a motion for a more definite statement, the responsive pleading shall be served within 10 days after the service of the more definite statement.

Adopted June 25, 1951, eff. Jan. 1, 1952. Revised Oct. 18, 1988, eff. Jan. 1, 1989.

Rule 12.02. How Presented

Every defense, in law or fact, to a claim for relief in any pleading, whether a claim, counterclaim, cross-claim, or third-party claim, shall be asserted in the responsive pleading thereto if one is required, except that the following defenses may at the option of the pleader be made by motion:

(a) lack of jurisdiction over the subject matter;

(b) lack of jurisdiction over the person;

(c) insufficiency of process;

(d) insufficiency of service of process;

(e) failure to state a claim upon which relief can be granted; and

(f) failure to join a party pursuant to Rule 19.

A motion making any of these defenses shall be made before pleading if a further pleading is permitted. No defense or objection is waived by being joined with one or more defenses or objections in a responsive pleading or motion. If a pleading sets forth a claim for relief to which the adverse party is not required to serve a responsive pleading, the adverse party may assert at the trial any defense in law or fact to that claim for relief. If, on a motion asserting the defense that the pleading fails to state a claim upon which relief can be granted, matters outside the pleading are presented to and not excluded by the court, the motion shall be treated as one for summary judgment and disposed of as provided in Rule 56, and all parties shall be given reasonable opportunity to present all material made pertinent to such a motion by Rule 56.

Adopted June 25, 1951, eff. Jan. 1, 1952. Amended Nov. 10, 1967, eff. Feb. 1, 1968. Revised Oct. 18, 1988, eff. Jan. 1, 1989.

Rule 12.03. Motion for Judgment on the Pleadings

After the pleadings are closed but within such time as not to delay the trial, any party may move for judgment on the pleadings. If, on such motion, matters outside the pleadings are presented to and not excluded by the court, the motion shall be treated as one for summary judgment and disposed of as provided for in Rule 56, and all parties shall be given reasonable opportunity to present all material made pertinent to such a motion by Rule 56.

Adopted June 25, 1951, eff. Jan. 1, 1952. Revised Oct. 18, 1988, eff. Jan. 1, 1989. Amended Dec. 20, 1993, eff. March 1, 1994.

Advisory Committee Comment—1993 Amendments

The only change made to this rule is to correct a typographical or grammatical error in the existing rule. No change in meaning or interpretation is intended.

Rule 12.04. Preliminary Hearing

The defenses and relief enumerated in Rules 12.02 and 12.03, whether made in a pleading or by motion, shall be heard and determined before trial on application of any party unless the court orders that the hearing and determination thereof be deferred until the trial.

Adopted June 25, 1951, eff. Jan. 1, 1952. Revised Oct. 18, 1988, eff. Jan. 1, 1989.

Rule 12.05. Motion for More Definite Statement, for Paragraphing and for Separate Statement

If a pleading to which a responsive pleading is permitted violates the provisions of Rule 10.02, or is so vague and ambiguous that a party cannot reasonably be required to frame a responsive pleading, the party may move for a compliance with Rule 10.02 or for a more definite statement before interposing a responsive pleading. The motion shall point out the defects complained of and the details desired. If the motion is granted and the order of the court is not obeyed within 10 days after service of notice of the order or within such other time as the court may fix, the court may strike the pleading to which the motion was directed or make such order as it deems just.

Adopted June 25, 1951, eff. Jan. 1, 1952. Revised Oct. 18, 1988, eff. Jan. 1, 1989.

Rule 12.06. Motion to Strike

Upon motion made by a party before responding to a pleading or, if no responsive pleading is permitted by these rules, upon motion made by a party within 20 days after the service of the pleading upon the party, or upon its own initiative at any time, the court may order any pleading not in compliance with Rule 11 stricken as sham and false, or may order stricken from any pleading any insufficient defense or any redundant, immaterial, impertinent or scandalous matter.

Adopted June 25, 1951, eff. Jan. 1, 1952. Revised Oct. 18, 1988, eff. Jan. 1, 1989.

Rule 12.07. Consolidation of Defenses in Motion

A party who makes a motion pursuant to this rule may join with it other motions then available to the party. If a party makes a motion under this rule but omits therefrom any then available defense or objection which this rule permits to be raised by motion, that party shall not thereafter make a motion based on the defense or objection so omitted, except a motion as provided in Rule 12.08(b) hereof on any of the grounds there stated.

Adopted June 25, 1951, eff. Jan. 1, 1952. Amended Nov. 10, 1967, eff. Feb. 1, 1968. Revised Oct. 18, 1988, eff. Jan. 1, 1989.

Advisory Committee Note—1968

Minnesota Rule 12.07 and Federal Rule 12(g) have been identical. The purpose of Rule 12.07 is to forbid a defendant who has made a motion asserting Rule 12 defenses, with the exceptions noted in Rule 12.08, from asserting other Rule 12 defenses not included in the original motion either in his answer or in a subsequent motion. The language of the existing Rule 12.07 is ambiguous. It is clear that Rule 12.07 intended to require consolidation of Rule 12 defenses if raised by motion and to prevent piecemeal assertion of technical defenses. However, the language of Rule 12.07 when considered with Rule 12.08 did not clearly spell out this effect of Rules 12.07 and 12.08. A few courts have permitted omitted defenses to be asserted by an answer or by an amended motion. The amendment to Rule 12.07 and the subsequent amendment to Rule 12.08 are for purposes of clarification. No change in existing practice is involved.

Rule 12.08. Waiver or Preservation of Certain Defenses

(a) A defense of lack of jurisdiction over the person, insufficiency of process, or insufficiency of service of process is waived (1) if omitted from a motion in the circumstances described in Rule 12.07, or (2) if it is neither made by motion pursuant to this rule nor included in a responsive pleading or an amendment thereof permitted by Rule 15.01 to be made as a matter of course.

(b) A defense of failure to state a claim upon which relief can be granted, a defense of failure to join a party indispensable under Rule 19, and an objection of failure to state a legal defense to a claim may be made in any pleading permitted or ordered pursuant to Rule 7.01, or by motion for judgment on the pleadings, or at the trial on the merits.

(c) Whenever it appears by suggestion of the parties or otherwise that the court lacks jurisdiction of the subject matter, the court shall dismiss the action.

Adopted June 25, 1951, eff. Jan. 1, 1952. Amended Nov. 10, 1967, eff. Feb. 1, 1968. Revised Oct. 18, 1988, eff. Jan. 1, 1989.

Advisory Committee Note—1968

The existing Minnesota Rule 12.08 and the former Federal Rule 12(h) were identical. As stated in the Note to Rule 12.07, clarification of Rules 12.07 and 12.08 is desired. Subdivision (1)(A) eliminates the existing ambiguity and specifies the defenses that are waived by the party when a motion is made prior to answer and the motion did not include the specified defenses. The Minnesota rule and federal rule are not identical in that the Minnesota rule does not include the defense of lack of proper venue as a nonwaivable Rule 12 defense.

Subdivision (1)(B) eliminates the possibility of using a discretionary amendment of a pleading under Rule 15.01 to raise waivable Rule 12 defenses. Subdivision (1)(B) now refers only to that part of Rule 15.01 where an amendment to a pleading could be made as a matter of right. The new subdivisions (2) and (3) are identical in effect with the existing rule.

RULE 13. COUNTERCLAIM AND CROSS-CLAIM

Rule 13.01. Compulsory Counterclaims

A pleading shall state as a counterclaim any claim which at the time of serving the pleading the pleader has against any opposing party, if it arises out of the transaction that is the subject matter of the opposing party's claim and does not require for its adjudication the presence of third parties over whom the court cannot acquire jurisdiction, except that such a claim need not be so stated if, at the time the action was commenced, the claim was the subject of another pending action.

Adopted June 25, 1951, eff. Jan. 1, 1952. Amended Dec. 6, 1951. Revised Oct. 18, 1988, eff. Jan. 1, 1989.

Rule 13.02. Permissive Counterclaims

A pleading may state as a counterclaim any claim against an opposing party not arising out of the transaction that is the subject matter of the opposing party's claim.

Adopted June 25, 1951, eff. Jan. 1, 1952. Amended Dec. 6, 1951. Revised Oct. 18, 1988, eff. Jan. 1, 1989.

Rule 13.03. Counterclaim Exceeding Opposing Claim

A counterclaim may or may not diminish or defeat the recovery sought by the opposing party. It may claim relief exceeding in amount or different in kind from that sought in the pleading of the opposing party.

Adopted June 25, 1951, eff. Jan. 1, 1952. Revised Oct. 18, 1988, eff. Jan. 1, 1989.

Rule 13.04. Counterclaim Against the State of Minnesota

These rules shall not be construed to enlarge beyond the limits now fixed by law the right to assert counterclaims or to claim credits against the State of Minnesota or an officer or agency thereof.

Adopted June 25, 1951, eff. Jan. 1, 1952. Revised Oct. 18, 1988, eff. Jan. 1, 1989.

Rule 13.05. Counterclaim Maturing or Acquired After Pleading

A claim which either matured or was acquired by the pleader after serving a pleading may, by leave of court, be presented as a counterclaim by supplemental pleading.

Adopted June 25, 1951, eff. Jan. 1, 1952. Revised Oct. 18, 1988, eff. Jan. 1, 1989.

Rule 13.06. Omitted Counterclaim

When a pleader fails to set up a counterclaim through oversight, inadvertence, or excusable neglect, or when justice requires, the pleader may, by leave of court, set up the counterclaim by amendment.

Adopted June 25, 1951, eff. Jan. 1, 1952. Revised Oct. 18, 1988, eff. Jan. 1, 1989.

Rule 13.07. Cross–Claim Against Co–Party

A pleading may state as a cross-claim any claim by one party against a co-party arising out of the transaction or occurrence that is the subject matter either of the original action or of a counterclaim therein or relating to any property that is the subject matter of the original action. Such cross-claim may include a claim that the party against whom it is asserted is or may be liable to the cross-claimant for all or part of a claim asserted in the action against the cross-claimant.

Adopted June 25, 1951, eff. Jan. 1, 1952. Revised Oct. 18, 1988, eff. Jan. 1, 1989.

Rule 13.08. Joinder of Additional Parties

Persons other than those made parties to the original action may be made parties to a counterclaim or cross-claim in accordance with the provisions of Rules 19 and 20.

Adopted June 25, 1951, eff. Jan. 1, 1952. Amended Nov. 10, 1967, eff. Feb. 1, 1968. Revised Oct. 18, 1988, eff. Jan. 1, 1989.

Advisory Committee Note—1968

The amendment is a clarifying amendment and conforms the Minnesota rule to a similar amendment to Federal Rule 13(h). The reference in the former rule to those persons whose presence is "required" for the granting of complete relief has been considered by some courts to refer only to Rule 19 parties. In fact, Rule 13.08 should properly refer to both Rule 19 and Rule 20 parties. The amendment makes this provision clear.

Rule 13.09. Separate Trials; Separate Judgment

If the court orders separate trials as provided in Rule 42.02, judgment on a counterclaim or cross-claim may be rendered in accordance with the terms of Rule 54.02 even if the claims of the opposing party have been dismissed or disposed of otherwise.

Adopted June 25, 1951, eff. Jan. 1, 1952. Revised Oct. 18, 1988, eff. Jan. 1, 1989.

RULE 14. THIRD–PARTY PRACTICE

Rule 14.01. When Defendant May Bring in Third Party

Within 90 days after service of the summons upon a defendant, and thereafter either by written consent of all parties to the action or by leave of court granted on motion upon notice to all parties to the action, a defendant as a third-party plaintiff may serve a summons and complaint, together with a copy of plaintiff's complaint upon a person, whether or not the person is a party to the action, who is or may be liable to the third-party plaintiff for all or part of the plaintiff's claim against the third-party plaintiff and after such service shall forthwith serve notice thereof upon all other parties to the action. Copies of third-party pleadings shall be furnished by the pleader to any other party to the action within 5 days after request therefor. The person so served, hereinafter called the third-party defendant, shall make any defenses to the third-party plaintiff's claim as provided in Rule 12 and any counterclaims against the third-party plaintiff and cross-claims against other third-party defendants as provided in Rule 13. The third-party defendant may assert against the plaintiff any defenses which the third-party plaintiff has to the plaintiff's claim. The third-party defendant may also assert any claim against the plaintiff arising out of the transaction or occurrence that is the subject matter of the plaintiff's claim against the third-party plaintiff. The plaintiff may assert any claim against the third-party defendant arising out of the transaction or occurrence that is the subject matter of the plaintiff's claim against the third-party plaintiff, and the third-party defendant thereupon shall assert any defenses as provided in Rule 12 and any counterclaims and cross-claims as provided in Rule 13. A third-party defendant may proceed in accordance with this rule against any person who is or may be liable to the third-party defendant for all or part of the claim made in the action against the third-party defendant.

Adopted June 25, 1951, eff. Jan. 1, 1952. Amended March 3, 1959, eff. July 1, 1959; Nov. 30, 1981. Revised Oct. 18, 1988, eff. Jan. 1, 1989.

Advisory Committee Note—1959

Under the amendment a defendant may assert a third-party claim without leave of court at any time within 45 days after service of summons upon him, and thereafter by leave of court upon notice to all other parties. Notice of service of the third-party summons must be given to all parties to the action and copies of third-party pleadings furnished to other parties when requested.

The 45-day free period will afford time to develop the facts, by discovery procedures or otherwise, and thus avoid the assertion of third-party claims for which there is no sound basis, as now sometimes occurs. On the other hand, it will encourage the assertion of such claims before the free period expires, for it is to be anticipated that, with notice to all of the parties and sharper scrutiny by the court, an application made after the free period will be granted only under exceptional circumstances. The present state of the jury calendars in the metropolitan areas is such that the free period proposed will not give rise to delay. The new Rule 14.03, which applies to third-party claims whenever asserted, should enable judges of all districts to prevent the tardy injection of such claims. See 43 Minn.L.R., p. 115.

The inclusion by the amendment as a third-party defendant of one who is already a party to the action is intended to cover situations not provided for by cross-claims under Rule 13.07 and does not limit or impair procedures under that rule.

Rule 14.02. When Plaintiff May Bring in Third Party

When a counterclaim is asserted against a plaintiff, the plaintiff may cause a third party to be brought in under circumstances which, pursuant to Rule 14.01, would entitle defendant to do so.

Adopted June 25, 1951, eff. Jan. 1, 1952. Revised Oct. 18, 1988, eff. Jan. 1, 1989.

Rule 14.03. Orders for Protection of Parties and Prevention of Delay

The court may make such orders to prevent a party from being embarrassed or put to undue expense, or to prevent delay of the trial or other proceeding by the assertion of a third-party claim, and may dismiss the third-party claim, order separate trials, or make other orders to prevent delay or prejudice. Unless otherwise specified in the order, a dismissal pursuant to this rule is without prejudice.

Adopted March 3, 1959, eff. July 1, 1959. Amended Nov. 10, 1967, eff. Feb. 1, 1968. Revised Oct. 18, 1988, eff. Jan. 1, 1989.

Advisory Committee Note—1959

Under the amendment a defendant may assert a third-party claim without leave of court at any time within 45 days after service of summons upon him, and thereafter by leave of court upon notice to all other parties. Notice of service of the third-party summons must be given to all parties to the action and copies of third-party pleadings furnished to other parties when requested.

The 45-day free period will afford time to develop the facts, by discovery procedures or otherwise, and thus avoid the assertion of third-party claims for which there is no sound basis, as now sometimes occurs. On the other hand, it will encourage the assertion of such claims before the free period expires, for it is to be anticipated that, with notice to all of the parties and sharper scrutiny by the court, an application made after the free period will be granted only under exceptional circumstances. The present state of the jury calendars in the metropolitan areas is such that the free period proposed will not give rise to delay. The new Rule 14.03, which applies to third-party claims whenever asserted, should enable judges of all districts to prevent the tardy injection of such claims. See 43 Minn.L.R., p. 115.

The inclusion by the amendment as a third-party defendant of one who is already a party to the action is intended to cover situations not provided for by cross-claims under Rule 13.07 and does not limit or impair procedures under that rule.

RULE 15. AMENDED AND SUPPLEMENTAL PLEADINGS

Rule 15.01. Amendments

A party may amend a pleading once as a matter of course at any time before a responsive pleading is served or, if the pleading is one to which no responsive pleading is permitted and the action has not been placed upon the trial calendar, the party may so amend it at any time within 20 days after it is served. Otherwise a party may amend a pleading only by leave of court or by written consent of the adverse party; and leave shall be freely given when justice so requires. A party shall plead in response to an amended pleading within the time remaining for response to the original pleading or within 10 days after service of the amended pleading, whichever period may be longer, unless the court otherwise orders.

Adopted June 25, 1951, eff. Jan. 1, 1952. Revised Oct. 18, 1988, eff. Jan. 1, 1989.

Rule 15.02. Amendments to Conform to the Evidence

When issues not raised by the pleadings are tried by express or implied consent of the parties, they shall be treated in all respects as if they had been raised in the pleadings. Such amendment of the pleadings as may be necessary to cause them to conform to the evidence and to raise these issues may be made upon motion of any party at any time, even after judgment; but failure so to amend does not affect the result of a trial of these issues. If evidence is objected to at the trial on the ground that it is not within the issues raised by the pleadings, the court may allow the pleadings to be amended and shall do so freely when the presentation of the merits of the action will be subserved thereby and the objecting party fails to satisfy the court that admission of such evidence would prejudice maintenance of the action or defense upon the merits. The court may grant a continuance to enable the objecting party to meet such evidence.

Adopted June 25, 1951, eff. Jan. 1, 1952. Revised Oct. 18, 1988, eff. Jan. 1, 1989.

Rule 15.03. Relation Back of Amendments

Whenever the claim or defense asserted in the amended pleading arose out of the conduct, transaction, or occurrence set forth or attempted to be set forth in the original pleading, the amendment relates back to the date of the original pleading. An amendment changing the party against whom a claim is asserted relates back if the foregoing provision is satisfied and, within the period provided by law for commencing the action against the party, the party to be brought in by amendment (1) has received such notice of the institution of the action that the party will not be prejudiced in maintaining a defense on the merits, and (2) knew or should have known that, but for a mistake concerning the identity of the proper party, the action would have been brought against that party.

Adopted June 25, 1951, eff. Jan. 1, 1952. Amended Nov. 10, 1967, eff. Feb. 1, 1968. Revised Oct. 18, 1988, eff. Jan. 1, 1989.

Advisory Committee Note—1968

The amendment conforms Minnesota Rule 15.03 to Federal Rule 15(c). The amendment permits substitution of parties and relation back of the claim, where the intended party knows that the lawsuit has been commenced and should know that a mistake in naming the party has been made. See Nelson v. Glenwood Hills Hospital, 240 Minn. 505, 62 N.W.2d 73 (1953); Halloran v. Blue and White Liberty Cab Co., Inc., 253 Minn. 436, 92 N.W.2d 794 (1958). The relation back of amendments changing plaintiff is not expressly provided for in Rule 15.03. This problem generally is one of a real party in interest under Rule 17.

Rule 15.04. Supplemental Pleadings

Upon motion of a party the court may, upon reasonable notice and upon such terms as are just, permit the party to serve a supplemental pleading setting forth transactions, occurrences, or events which have happened since the date of the pleading sought to be supplemented, whether or not the original pleading is defective in its statement of a claim for relief or of a defense. If the court deems it advisable that the adverse party plead thereto, it shall so order, specifying the time therefor.

Adopted June 25, 1951, eff. Jan. 1, 1952. Amended March 3, 1959, eff. July 1, 1959. Revised Oct. 18, 1988, eff. Jan. 1, 1989.

RULE 16. PRETRIAL CONFERENCES; SCHEDULING; MANAGEMENT

Rule 16.01. Pretrial Conferences; Objectives

In any action, the court may in its discretion direct the attorneys for the parties and any unrepresented parties to appear before it for a conference or conferences before trial for such purposes as

(a) expediting the disposition of the action;

(b) establishing early and continuing control so that the case will not be protracted because of lack of management;

(c) discouraging wasteful pretrial activities;

(d) improving the quality of the trial through more thorough preparation; and

(e) facilitating the settlement of the case.

Adopted March 21, 1985, eff. July 1, 1985. Revised Oct. 18, 1988, eff. Jan. 1, 1989.

Advisory Committee Note—1985

Rule 16

The Committee has recommended a complete revision of Rule 16. The changes adopt the important features of the 1983 amendments to Fed.R.Civ.P. 16, with certain modifications reflecting unique features of Minnesota practice. The most important difference between State and Federal Rules is the retention of the voluntary nature of pre-trial conferences under the Minnesota Rule. The Committee considered, and rejected, the notion that the rule should require pre-trial and scheduling conferences in every case. Although the Committee believes pre-trial conferences and scheduling conferences will be of great value in many cases, it is not satisfied that their use should be compelled in every case.

Rule 16.01

Subdivision 5 of this rule reflects one of the important purposes of pre-trial conference, providing a constructive vehicle for exploring settlement of the case.

Historical Notes

Former Rule: A former Rule 16, adopted June 25, 1951, related to pre-trial procedure. The order of the Minnesota Supreme Court dated September, 14, 1984, rewrote former Rule 16 as Rule 16.01 and added Rules 16.02 to 16.06.

Rule 16.02. Scheduling and Planning

The court may, and upon written request of any party with notice to all parties, shall, after consulting with the attorneys for the parties and any unrepresented parties, by a scheduling conference, telephone, mail, or other suitable means, enter a scheduling order that limits the time

(a) to join other parties and to amend the pleadings;

(b) to file and hear motions; and

(c) to complete discovery.

The scheduling order also may include

(d) provisions for disclosure or discovery of electronically stored information;

(e) any agreements the parties reach for asserting claims of privilege or of protection as trial-preparation materials after production;

(f) the date or dates for conferences before trial, a final pretrial conference, and trial; and

(g) any other matters appropriate in the circumstances of the case.

A schedule shall not be modified except by leave of court upon a showing of good cause.

Adopted March 21, 1985, eff. July 1, 1985. Revised Oct. 18, 1988, eff. Jan. 1, 1989. Amended May 21, 2007, eff. July 1, 2007.

Advisory Committee Note—1985

The Committee determined that scheduling conferences should be made optional, although it concluded they would be of value in many cases.

Rule 16.03. Subjects for Consideration

At any conference under this rule consideration may be given, and the court may take appropriate action, with respect to:

(a) the formulation and simplification of the issues, including the elimination of frivolous claims or defenses;

(b) the necessity or desirability of amendments to the pleadings;

(c) the possibility of obtaining admissions of fact and of documents which will avoid unnecessary proof, stipulations regarding the authenticity of documents, and advance rulings from the court on the admissibility of evidence;

(d) the avoidance of unnecessary proof and of cumulative evidence, and limitations or restrictions on the use of testimony under Rule 702 of the Minnesota Rules of Evidence;

(e) the appropriateness and timing of summary adjudication under Rule 56;

(f) the control and scheduling of discovery, including orders affecting discovery pursuant to Rule 26 and Rules 29 through 37;

(g) the identification of witnesses and documents, the need and schedule for filing and exchanging pretrial briefs, and the date or dates for further conferences and for trial;

(h) the advisability of referring matters pursuant to Rule 53;

(i) settlement and the use of special procedures to assist in resolving the dispute when authorized by statute or rule;

(j) the form and substance of the pretrial order;

(k) the disposition of pending motions;

(*l*) the need for adopting special procedures for managing potentially difficult or protracted actions that may involve complex issues, multiple parties, difficult legal questions, or unusual proof problems;

(m) an order for a separate trial pursuant to Rule 42.02 with respect to a claim, counterclaim, cross-claim, or third-party claim, or with respect to any particular issue in the case;

(n) an order directing a party or parties to present evidence early in the trial with respect to a manageable issue that could, on the evidence, be the basis for a judgment as a matter of law under Rule 50.01 or an involuntary dismissal under Rule 41.02(b);

(*o*) an order establishing a reasonable limit on the time allowed for presenting evidence; and

(p) such other matters as may facilitate the just, speedy, and inexpensive disposition of the action.

At least one of the attorneys for each party participating in any conference before trial shall have authority to enter into stipulations and to make admissions regarding all matters that the participants may reasonably anticipate may be discussed. If appropriate, the court may require that a party or its representative be present or reasonably available by telephone in order to consider possible settlement of the dispute.

Adopted March 21, 1985, eff. July 1, 1985. Revised Oct. 18, 1988, eff. Jan. 1, 1989. Amended Nov. 22, 1996, eff. Jan. 1, 1997; Nov. 30, 2005, eff. Jan. 1, 2006.

Advisory Committee Comments—1996 Amendments

This change conforms Rule 16.03 to its federal counterpart. The rule is expanded to enumerate many of the functions with which pretrial conferences must deal. Although the courts have inherent power to deal with these matters even in the absence of a rule, it is desirable to have the appropriate subjects for consideration at pretrial conferences expressly provided for by rule. The federal changes expressly provide for discussion of settlement, in part, to remove any confusion over the power of the court to order participation in court-related settlement efforts. *See, e.g., G. Heileman Brewing Co. v. Joseph Oat Corp.*, 871 F.2d 648 (7th Cir.1989); *Strandell v. Jackson County, Ill. (In re Tobin)*, 838 F.2d 884 (7th Cir.1988); *Klothe v. Smith*, 771 F.2d 667 (2d Cir.1985); *Buss v. Western Airlines, Inc.*, 738 F.2d 1053 (9th Cir.1984).

Advisory Committee Comment—2006 Amendment

Rule 16.03(n) is amended to reflect the new name for motions under Rule 50.01 as amended effective January 1, 2006.

Advisory Committee Comment—2007 Amendment

Rule 16 is amended to allow the court to include provision for discovery of electronically stored information. Although this discovery may not require special attention in a pretrial order, in many cases it may be helpful to address this subject separately. The rule also permits the pretrial order to memorialize the court's approval of agreements relating to claims of privilege. The rule specifically contemplates that parties may desire to permit documents to be reviewed or sampled, in order to permit the requesting parties to assess the reasonable need for further production without prejudice to any privilege claims.

Historical Notes

The order of the Minnesota Supreme Court [C6-84-2134] dated November 22, 1996, provides in part that the "(a)mendments shall apply to all actions pending on the effective date [January 1, 1997] and to those filed thereafter" and that "(t)he inclusion of Advisory Committee comments is made for convenience and does not reflect court approval of the comments made therein".

Rule 16.04. Final Pretrial Conference

Any final pretrial conference may be held as close to the time of trial as reasonable under the circumstances. The participants at any such conference shall formulate a plan for trial, including a program for facilitating the admission of evidence. The conference shall be attended by at least one of the attorneys who will conduct the trial for each of the parties and by any unrepresented parties.

Adopted March 21, 1985, eff. July 1, 1985. Revised Oct. 18, 1988, eff. Jan. 1, 1989.

Rule 16.05. Pretrial Orders

After any conference held pursuant to this rule, an order shall be entered reciting the action taken. This order shall control the subsequent course of the action and shall be modified only to prevent manifest injustice.

Adopted March 21, 1985, eff. July 1, 1985. Revised Oct. 18, 1988, eff. Jan. 1, 1989.

Rule 16.06. Sanctions

If a party or party's attorney fails to obey a scheduling or pretrial order, or if no appearance is made on behalf of a party at a scheduling or pretrial conference, or if a party or party's attorney is substantially unprepared to participate in the conference, or if a party or party's attorney fails to participate in good faith, the court, upon motion or upon its own initiative, may make such orders with regard thereto as are just, including any of the orders provided in Rule 37.02(b)(2), (3), (4). In lieu of or in addition to any other sanction, the court shall require the party or the attorney representing the party or both to pay the reasonable expenses incurred because of any noncompliance with this rule, including attorney fees, unless the court finds that the noncompliance was substantially justified or that other circumstances make an award of expenses unjust.

Adopted March 21, 1985, eff. July 1, 1985. Revised Oct. 18, 1988, eff. Jan. 1, 1989.

IV. PARTIES

RULE 17. PARTIES PLAINTIFF AND DEFENDANT; CAPACITY

Rule 17.01. Real Party in Interest

Every action shall be prosecuted in the name of the real party in interest. An executor, administrator, guardian, bailee, trustee of an express trust, a party with whom or in whose name a contract has been made for the benefit of another, or a party authorized by statute may sue in that person's own name without joining the party for whose benefit the action is brought. No action shall be dismissed on the ground that it is not prosecuted in the name of the real party in interest until a reasonable time has been allowed after objection for ratification of commencement of the action by, or joinder or substitution of, the real party in interest; and such ratification, joinder, or substitution shall have the same effect as if the action had been commenced in the name of the real party in interest.

Adopted June 25, 1951, eff. Jan. 1, 1952. Amended Nov. 10, 1967, eff. Feb. 1, 1968. Revised Oct. 18, 1988, eff. Jan. 1, 1989.

Advisory Committee Note—1968

The amended Federal Rule 17(a) and amended Minnesota Rule 17.01 are identical to the point where the Minnesota rule terminates. The federal rule also contains a provision for actions brought for the use and benefit of another in the name of the United States pursuant to a United States Statute. Such a provision is not needed in Minnesota. The new portion of Rule 17.01 will permit the substitution of plaintiffs when objection has been made on the ground of lack of a real party in interest. Bailees have been added as parties who may due in a representative capacity.

Rule 17.02. Infants or Incompetent Persons

Whenever a party to an action is an infant or is incompetent and has a representative duly appointed under the laws of this state or the laws of a foreign state or country, the representative may sue or defend on behalf of such party. A party who is an infant or is incompetent and is not so represented shall be represented by a guardian ad litem appointed by the court in which the action is pending or is to be brought. The guardian ad litem shall be a resident of this state, shall file a consent and oath with the court administrator, and shall give such bond as the court may require. A guardian ad litem appointed under this Rule is not a guardian ad litem within the meaning of the Rules of Guardian Ad Litem Procedure in Juvenile and Family Court and is not governed by those Rules.

Any person, including an infant party over the age of fourteen (14) years and under no other legal disability, may apply under oath for the appointment of a guardian ad litem. The application of the party or the party's spouse or parents or testamentary or other guardian shall have priority over other applications. If no such appointment is made on behalf of a defendant party before answer or default, the adverse party or a party's attorney may apply for such appointment, and in such case the court shall allow the guardian ad litem a reasonable time to respond to the complaint.

The application for appointment shall show (1) the name, age and address of the party, (2) if the party is a minor, the names and addresses of the parents, and, in the event of their death or the abandonment of the minor, the name and address of the party's custodian or testamentary or other guardian, if any, (3) the name and address of the party's spouse, if any, and (4) the name, age, address, and occupation of the person whose appointment is sought.

If the appointment is applied for by the party or by a spouse, parent, custodian or testamentary or other guardian of the party, the court may hear the application with or without notice. In all other cases written notice of the hearing on the application shall be given at such time as the court shall prescribe, and shall be served upon the party, the party's spouse, parent, custodian and testamentary or other guardian, if any, and if the party is an inmate of a public institution, the chief executive officer thereof. If the party is a nonresident or, after diligent search, cannot be found within the state, notice shall be given to such persons and in such manner as the court may direct.

Adopted June 25, 1951, eff. Jan. 1, 1952. Amended March 3, 1959, eff. July 1, 1959. Revised Oct. 18, 1988, eff. Jan. 1, 1989; Sept. 30, 2004, eff. Jan. 1, 2005; Dec. 1, 2006, eff. Jan. 1, 2007.

Advisory Committee Note—1959

There has been some apprehension that the rules abolished the action by a trustee for death by wrongful act in behalf of decedent's next of kin (including minors) under M.S.A. § 573.02 and the action by a parent under M.S.A. § 540.08 for injury to a minor child. The doubt will be resolved by listing both sections in Appendix A.

Although the present Rule 17.02, except for its first sentence, follows the former statute (M.S.A. § 540.06) providing for the appointment of a guardian ad litem, it has been the subject of some criticism. The amendment expands the present rule and conforms it more nearly to probate court procedure for the appointment of a general guardian.

RULE 18. JOINDER OF CLAIMS AND REMEDIES

Rule 18.01. Joinder of Claims

A party asserting a claim to relief as an original claim, counterclaim, cross-claim, or third-party claim, may join, either as independent or as alternate claims, as many claims, legal, or equitable, as the party has against an opposing party.

Adopted June 25, 1951, eff. Jan. 1, 1952. Amended Nov. 10, 1967, eff. Feb. 1, 1968. Revised Oct. 18, 1988, eff. Jan. 1, 1989.

Advisory Committee Note—1968

The amendment removes an ambiguity in Rule 18 where the action involves multiple parties and the claimant wishes to assert more than one claim against some but not all of the parties. A possible interpretation of the prior Rule 18 has led some courts to hold that the rules regulating joinder of parties (Rules 19, 20 and 22) carry back to Rule 18 and impose some limits on joinder of claims in multi-party cases. In particular, Rule 20.01 has been read to prohibit joinder of claims unless all parties are interested in all claims. See Federal Housing Administrator v. Christianson, 26 F.Supp. 419 (D.Conn.1939).

Rule 18.01 is amended to clarify the rule and to override the Christianson decision by clearly stating that a party may assert a claim as an original claim, a counterclaim, a cross-claim, or a third-party claim and join with it as many claims as he has against an opposing party. No distinction is made between single party and multiple party actions. The joinder of parties is governed by different rules operating independently from Rule 18. In the opinion of the Committee, it is more compatible with the purpose of the rules to permit free joinder of claims in all cases and leave to the trial court's discretion separation of trials of the various claims if fairness or convenience dictate separate trials. The present amendment makes the Minnesota rule identical with Federal Rule 18(a).

Rule 18.02. Joinder of Remedies; Fraudulent Conveyances

Whenever a claim is one heretofore cognizable only after another claim has been prosecuted to a conclusion, the two claims may be joined in a single action; but the court shall grant relief in that action only in accordance with the relative substantive rights of the parties. In particular, a plaintiff may state a claim for money and a claim to have set aside a conveyance fraudulent as to that plaintiff, without first having obtained a judgment establishing the claim for money.

Adopted June 25, 1951, eff. Jan. 1, 1952. Revised Oct. 18, 1988, eff. Jan. 1, 1989.

RULE 19. JOINDER OF PERSONS NEEDED FOR JUST ADJUDICATION

Rule 19.01. Persons to be Joined if Feasible

A person who is subject to service of process shall be joined as a party in the action if (a) in the person's absence complete relief cannot be accorded among those already parties, or (b) the person claims an interest relating to the subject of the action and is so situated that the disposition of the action in the person's absence may (1) as a practical matter impair or impede the person's ability to protect that interest or (2) leave any one already a party subject to a substantial risk or incurring double, multiple, or otherwise inconsistent obligations by reason of the person's claimed interest. If the person has not been so joined, the court shall order that the person be made a party. If the person should join as a plaintiff but refuses to do so, the person may be made a defendant, or, in a proper case, an involuntary plaintiff.

Adopted June 25, 1951, eff. Jan. 1, 1952. Amended Nov. 10, 1967, eff. Feb. 1, 1968. Revised Oct. 18, 1988, eff. Jan. 1, 1989.

Comment—Rule 19

See comment following Rule 19.04.

Rule 19.02. Determination by Court Whenever Joinder Not Feasible

If a person as described in Rule 19.01 cannot be made a party, the court shall determine whether in equity and good conscience the action should proceed among the parties before it, or should be dismissed, the absent person being thus regarded as indispensable. The factors to be considered by the court include:

(a) to what extent a judgment rendered in the person's absence might be prejudicial to the person or those already parties;

(b) the extent to which, by protective provisions in the judgment, by the shaping of relief, or other measures, the prejudice can be lessened or avoided;

(c) whether a judgment rendered in the person's absence will be adequate; and

(d) whether the plaintiff will have an adequate remedy if the action is dismissed for nonjoinder.

Adopted June 25, 1951, eff. Jan. 1, 1952. Amended Nov. 10, 1967, eff. Feb. 1, 1968. Revised Oct. 18, 1988, eff. Jan. 1, 1989.

Comment—Rule 19

See comment following Rule 19.04.

Rule 19.03. Pleading Reasons for Nonjoinder

A pleading asserting a claim for relief shall state the names, if known to the pleader, of any persons as described in Rule 19.01 who are not joined, and the reasons why they are not joined.

Adopted June 25, 1951, eff. Jan. 1, 1952. Amended Nov. 10, 1967, eff. Feb. 1, 1968. Revised Oct. 18, 1988, eff. Jan. 1, 1989.

Comment—Rule 19

See comment following Rule 19.04.

Rule 19.04. Exception of Class Actions

This rule is subject to the provisions of Rule 23.

Adopted Nov. 10, 1967, eff. Feb. 1, 1968. Revised Oct. 18, 1988, eff. Jan. 1, 1989.

Advisory Committee Note—1968

The amendment conforms Minnesota Rule 19 to the amended Federal Rule 19. Since 1952, Minnesota Rule 19 has been substantially identical to Federal Rule 19. In 1966, Federal Rule 19 was amended to remove ambiguities in the rule and to overcome certain decisions interpreting Rule 19 in a manner not deemed desirable by the Federal Advisory Committee. The purpose of Rule 19 is to compel joinder of parties whenever feasible so that a complete disposition of a claim can be made in the pending case. Decisional law interpreting the word "indispensable" under the original subdivision (b) of the federal rule equated indispensable party with persons having a joint interest in subdivision (a). The Federal Advisory Committee indicated that such restrictive definition of indispensable was not the original intent of the rule. The expression "indispensable" was intended to be an all inclusive reference to those persons in whose absence it would be advisable, all factors considered, to dismiss the action. In addition, several federal decisions equated lack of an indispensable party with lack of jurisdiction over the cause of action. Such an interpretation again was not intended in the original rule. For a discussion of the defects in the original rule, see Notes of Federal Advisory Committee, Rule 19 and Reed, Compulsory Joinder of Parties in Civil Actions, 55 Mich.L.Rev. 327.

Most courts, including Minnesota, have used the basic test of Shields v. Barrow, 58 U.S. (17 How.) 130 (U.S.1854), to classify parties as necessary or indispensable. Minnesota by decisional law has adopted the Shields test but recognized that that test was not an absolute one and that determination of an indispensable party involves balancing many considerations and rests ultimately on the facts of each particular case. McAndrew v. Krause, 245 Minn. 85, 71 N.W.2d 153 (1955). Thus Minnesota of decisional law has avoided many of the difficulties experienced by the federal courts in interpreting Rule 19. As such, the existing law in Minnesota is compatible with the amended provisions of Rule 19.

As set forth in the Federal Advisory Committee's notes, the intent of each of the new subdivisions is as follows: (Minnesota rule numbering is adopted as are the interpretations in the Federal Advisory Committee Notes) Rule 19.01 defines persons whose joinder in the action is desirable. Clause (1) of Rule 19.01 stresses the desirability of joining all persons in whose absence the court would be obligated to grant less than complete relief to the parties before the court. This reflects the public's interest in having a single lawsuit rather than repeated lawsuits on essentially the same subject matter. Clause (2)(i) of Rule 19.01 recognizes the importance of protecting a person whose joinder is in question against the practical prejudice to him which may arise through a disposition of the case in his absence. Clause (2)(ii) recognizes the importance of considering whether or not a party may be left in the situation where he will be subject to a double or otherwise inconsistent liability by later claims of non joined parties. Rule 19.01 defines persons who should be joined but eliminates the abstract terms of the former rule regarding the nature of their interest, i.e. joint, united, separable, etc. The new description of parties does not effect the existing decisional law holding that a tortfeasor with the normal joint and several liability is merely a permissive party and not a Rule 19 party.

In adopting Minnesota Rule 19.01 the Minnesota Committee eliminated reference to joinder of a party whose joinder would deprive the court of jurisdiction, as that provision involves matters particularly related to diversity jurisdiction in the federal court and does not have a similar counterpart in state practice. In like measure, Minnesota Rule 19.01 has eliminated the last sentence of Federal Rule 19(a) since dismissal for improper venue is not compatible with existing state practice.

Rule 19.02 sets forth factors to be considered by the court in determining whether in equity and good conscience the lawsuit should continue in the absence of a person described in 19.01 or if the action should be dismissed. This decision ultimately is to be made in light of pragmatic considerations. The factors set forth in 19.02 are acknowledged to be overlapped to some extent and are not intended to exclude other considerations which may be particularly applicable in certain cases. The first factor set forth in Rule 19.02 is consideration of what impact, if any, a judgment in the pending action would have on the absentee. Would the absentee be adversely affected in a practical sense and, if so, would the prejudice be immediate and serious or remote and minor? The second factor requires consideration of methods whereby the prejudice to absent parties may be averted or lessened by shaping relief. The court is also to consider the extent to which a party may avoid prejudice by other means such as intervention. A third factor is whether or not an adequate judgment can be rendered in the absence of a given person. This focuses attention on the extent and nature of the relief that can be accorded among the parties actually joined. The fourth factor looks to the practical effect of a dismissal and indicates that the court should consider among other things, whether the action could be more effectively sued out in another jurisdiction. The word "indispensable" is used only as a short hand expression to designate a person who must be joined upon consideration of all the factors and if not joined his absence would require dismissal of the action.

Rule 19.03 is identical in effect with the former provisions of Rule 19.03.

Rule 19.04 repeats an exception contained in the prior Rule 19.01.

RULE 20. PERMISSIVE JOINDER OF PARTIES

Rule 20.01. Permissive Joinder

All persons may join in one action as plaintiffs if they assert any right to relief, jointly, severally, or in the alternative with respect to or arising out of the same transaction, occurrence, or series of transactions or occurrences and if any question of fact or law common to all these persons will arise in the action. All persons may be joined in one action as defendants if there is asserted against them jointly, severally, or in the alternative, any right to relief with respect to or arising out of the same transaction, occurrence, or series of transactions or occurrences and if any question of law or fact common to all defendants will arise in the action. A plaintiff or defendant need not be interested in obtaining or defending against all the relief demanded. Judgment may be given for one or more of the plaintiffs according to their respective rights to relief, and against one or more defendants according to their respective liabilities.

Adopted June 25, 1951, eff. Jan. 1, 1952. Amended Nov. 10, 1967, eff. Feb. 1, 1968. Revised Oct. 18, 1988, eff. Jan. 1, 1989.

Advisory Committee Note—1968

The Minnesota amendment adopts the federal amendment to Rule 20. The change in Rule 20 is purely a clarification change necessitated by the amendment to Rule 18. The word "them" is now changed to "defendants" to eliminate the interpretation given to Rule 18 and Rule 20 in Federal Housing Administrator v. Christianson, 26 F.Supp. 419 (D.Conn.1939).

Rule 20.02. Separate Trials

The court may make such order as will prevent a party from being embarrassed, delayed, or put to expense by the inclusion of a party against whom the party asserts no claim and who asserts no claim against the party, and may order separate trials or make other orders to prevent delay or prejudice.

Adopted June 25, 1951, eff. Jan. 1, 1952. Revised Oct. 18, 1988, eff. Jan. 1, 1989.

RULE 21. MISJOINDER AND NONJOINDER OF PARTIES

Misjoinder of parties is not ground for dismissal of an action. Parties may be dropped or added by order of the court on motion of any party or upon the court's own initiative at any stage of the action and on such terms as are just. Any claim against a party may be severed and proceeded with separately.

Adopted June 25, 1951, eff. Jan. 1, 1952. Revised Oct. 18, 1988, eff. Jan. 1, 1989.

RULE 22. INTERPLEADER

Persons having claims against the plaintiff may be joined as defendants and required to interplead, in an action brought for that purpose, when their claims are such that the plaintiff is or may be exposed to multiple liability. A defendant exposed to similar liability may obtain such interpleader by way of cross-claim or counterclaim. If such a defendant admits being subject to liability, that defendant may, upon paying the amount claimed or delivering the property claimed or its value into court or to such person as the court may direct, move for an order to substitute the claimants other than the plaintiff as defendants in the movant's stead. On compliance with the terms of such order, the defendant shall be discharged and the action shall proceed against the substituted defendants. It is not ground for objection to such joinder or to such motion that the claims of the several claimants or the titles on which their claims depend do not have a common origin or are not identical with but are adverse to and independent of one another, or that the plaintiff denies liability in whole or in part to any or all of the claimants. The provisions of this rule do not restrict the joinder of parties permitted in Rule 20.

Adopted June 25, 1951, eff. Jan. 1, 1952. Amended Dec. 6, 1951. Revised Oct. 18, 1988, eff. Jan. 1, 1989.

RULE 23. CLASS ACTIONS

Rule 23.01. Prerequisites to a Class Action

One or more members of a class may sue or be sued as representative parties on behalf of all only if

(a) the class is so numerous that joinder of all members is impracticable;

(b) there are questions of law or fact common to the class;

(c) the claims or defenses of the representative parties are typical of the claims or defenses of the class; and

(d) the representative parties will fairly and adequately protect the interests of the class.

Adopted June 25, 1951, eff. Jan. 1, 1952. Amended Nov. 10, 1967, eff. Feb. 1, 1968. Revised Oct. 18, 1988, eff. Jan. 1, 1989.

Comment—Rule 23

See comment following Rule 23.10.

Rule 23.02. Class Actions Maintainable

An action may be maintained as a class action if the prerequisites of Rule 23.01 are satisfied, and in addition:

(a) the prosecution of separate actions by or against individual members of the class would create a risk of

(1) inconsistent or varying adjudications with respect to individual members of the class which would establish incompatible standards of conduct for the party opposing the class, or

(2) adjudications with respect to individual members of the class which would as a practical matter be dispositive of the interests of the other members not parties to the adjudications or substantially impair or impede their ability to protect their interests; or

(b) the party opposing the class has acted or refused to act on grounds generally applicable to the class, thereby making appropriate final injunctive relief or corresponding declaratory relief with respect to the class as a whole; or

(c) the court finds that the questions of law or fact common to the members of the class predominate over any questions affecting only individual members, and that a class action is superior to other available methods for the fair and efficient adjudication of the controversy. The matters pertinent to the findings include: (1) the interest of members of the class in individually controlling the prosecution or defense of separate actions; (2) the extent and nature of any litigation concerning the controversy already commenced by or against members of the class; (3) the desirability or undesirability of concentrating the litigation of the claims in the particular forum; and (4) the difficulties likely to be encountered in the management of a class action.

Adopted Nov. 10, 1967, eff. Feb. 1, 1968. Revised Oct. 18, 1988, eff. Jan. 1, 1989.

Comment—Rule 23

See comment following Rule 23.10.

Historical Notes

Former Rule: A former Rule 23.02 adopted June 25, 1951, and revised March 3, 1959, related to secondary actions by shareholders. The subject matter of former Rule 23.02 was incorporated into Rule 23.06 by court order dated November 10, 1967.

Rule 23.03. Determining by Order Whether to Certify a Class Action; Appointing Class Counsel; Notice and Membership in Class; Judgment; Multiple Classes and Subclasses

(a) Certification Order.

(1) When a person sues or is sued as a representative of a class, the court must—at an early practicable time—determine by order whether to certify the action as a class action.

(2) An order certifying a class action must define the class and the class claims, issues, or defenses, and must appoint class counsel under Rule 23.07.

(3) An order under Rule 23.03(a)(1) may be altered or amended before final judgment.

(b) Notice.

(1) For any class certified under Rule 23.02(a) or (b), the court may direct appropriate notice to the class.

(2) For any class certified under Rule 23.02(c), the court must direct to class members the best notice practicable under the circumstances, including individual notice to all members who can be identified through reasonable effort. The notice must concisely and clearly state in plain, easily understood language:

(A) the nature of the action,

(B) the definition of the class certified,

(C) the class claims, issues, or defenses,

(D) that a class member may enter an appearance through counsel if the member so desires,

(E) that the court will exclude from the class any member who requests exclusion, stating when and how members may elect to be excluded, and

(F) the binding effect of a class judgment on class members under Rule 23.03(c).

(c) Identification of Class Members. The judgment in an action maintained as a class action under Rule 23.02(a) or (b), whether or not favorable to the class, shall include and describe those whom the court finds to be members of the class. The judgment in an action maintained as a class action under Rule 23.02(c), whether or not favorable to the class, shall include and specify or describe those to whom the notice provided in Rule 23.03(b) was directed, and who have not requested exclusion, and whom the court finds to be members of the class.

(d) Issue Classes and Subclasses. When appropriate (1) an action may be brought or maintained as a class action with respect to particular issues, or (2) a class may be divided into subclasses and each subclass treated as a class; and the provisions of this rule shall then be construed and applied accordingly.

Adopted Nov. 10, 1967, eff. Feb. 1, 1968. Revised Oct. 18, 1988, eff. Jan. 1, 1989. Amended Nov. 30, 2005, eff. Jan. 1, 2006.

Comment—Rule 23

See comment following Rule 23.10.

Historical Notes

Former Rule: A former Rule 23.03 adopted June 25, 1951, and revised March 3, 1959, related to the dismissal or compromise of an action. The subject matter of former Rule 23.03 was incorporated into Rule 23.05 by court order November 10, 1967.

Rule 23.04. Orders in Conduct of Action

In the conduct of actions to which this rule applies, the court may make appropriate orders:

(a) determining the course of proceedings or prescribing measures to prevent undue repetition or complication in the presentation of evidence or argument;

(b) requiring, for the protection of the members of the class or otherwise for the fair conduct of the action, that notice be given in such manner as the court may direct to some or all members of any step in the action, or of the proposed extent of the judgment, or of the opportunity of members to signify whether they consider the representation fair and adequate, to intervene and present claims or defenses, or otherwise to enter the action;

(c) imposing conditions on the representative parties or intervenors;

(d) requiring that the pleadings be amended to eliminate therefrom allegations as to representation of absent persons, and that the action proceed accordingly; or

(e) dealing with similar procedural matters.

The orders may be combined with an order pursuant to Rule 16, and may be altered or amended whenever necessary.

Adopted March 3, 1959, eff. July 1, 1959. Amended Nov. 10, 1967, eff. Feb. 1, 1968. Revised Oct. 18, 1988, eff. Jan. 1, 1989.

Comment—Rule 23

See comment following Rule 23.10.

Rule 23.05. Settlement, Voluntary Dismissal, or Compromise

(a) Court Approval.

(1) A settlement, voluntary dismissal, or compromise of the claims, issues, or defenses of a certified class is effective only if approved by the court.

(2) The court must direct notice in a reasonable manner to all class members who would be bound by a proposed settlement, voluntary dismissal, or compromise.

(3) The court may approve a settlement, voluntary dismissal, or compromise that would bind class members only after a hearing and on finding that the settlement, voluntary dismissal, or compromise is fair, reasonable, and adequate.

(b) Disclosure Required. The parties seeking approval of a settlement, voluntary dismissal, or compromise under Rule 23.05(a) must file a statement identifying any agreement made in connection with the proposed settlement, voluntary dismissal, or compromise.

(c) Additional Opt–Out Period. In an action previously certified as a class action under Rule 23.02(c), the court may refuse to approve a settlement unless it affords a new opportunity to request exclusion to individual class members who had an earlier opportunity to request exclusion but did not do so.

(d) Objection to Settlement.

(1) Any class member may object to a proposed settlement, voluntary dismissal, or compromise that requires court approval under Rule 23.05(a)(1).

(2) An objection made under Rule 23.05(d)(1) may be withdrawn only with the court's approval.

Adopted Nov. 10, 1967, eff. Feb. 1, 1968. Revised Oct. 18, 1988, eff. Jan. 1, 1989. Amended Nov. 30, 2005, eff. Jan. 1, 2006.

Comment—Rule 23

See comment following Rule 23.10.

Rule 23.06. Appeals

The court of appeals may in its discretion permit an appeal from an order of a district court granting or denying class action certification under this rule. An application to appeal must be sought within the time provided in Rule 105 of the Minnesota Rules of Civil

Appellate Procedure, and shall be subject to the other provisions of that rule. An appeal does not stay proceedings in the district court unless the district judge or the court of appeals so orders.

Adopted Nov. 30, 2005, eff. Jan. 1, 2006.

Comment—Rule 23

See comment following Rule 23.10.

Historical Notes

Former Rule: Former Rule 23.06, which related to derivative actions by shareholders and members was renumbered as Rule 23.09 by court order dated November 30, 2005.

Rule 23.07. Class Counsel

(a) Appointing Class Counsel.

(1) Unless a statute provides otherwise, a court that certifies a class must appoint class counsel.

(2) An attorney appointed to serve as class counsel must fairly and adequately represent the interests of the class.

(3) In appointing class counsel, the court

(A) must consider:

(i) the work counsel has done in identifying or investigating potential claims in the action,

(ii) counsel's experience in handling class actions, other complex litigation, and claims of the type asserted in the action,

(iii) counsel's knowledge of the applicable law, and

(iv) the resources counsel will commit to representing the class;

(B) may consider any other matter pertinent to counsel's ability to fairly and adequately represent the interests of the class;

(C) may direct potential class counsel to provide information on any subject pertinent to the appointment and to propose terms for attorney fees and nontaxable costs; and

(D) may make further orders in connection with the appointment.

(b) Appointment Procedure.

(1) The court may designate interim counsel to act on behalf of the putative class before determining whether to certify the action as a class action.

(2) When there is one applicant for appointment as class counsel, the court may appoint that applicant only if the applicant is adequate under Rule 23.07(a)(2) and (3). If more than one adequate applicant seeks appointment as class counsel, the court must appoint the applicant best able to represent the interests of the class.

(3) The order appointing class counsel may include provisions about the award of attorney fees or nontaxable costs under Rule 23.08.

Adopted Nov. 30, 2005, eff. Jan. 1, 2006.

Comment—Rule 23

See comment following Rule 23.10.

Historical Notes

Former Rule: Former Rule 23.07, which related to actions relating to unincorporated associations, was renumbered as Rule 23.10 by court order dated November 30, 2005.

Rule 23.08. Attorney Fees Award

In an action certified as a class action, the court may award reasonable attorney fees and nontaxable costs authorized by law or by agreement of the parties as follows:

(a) Motion for Award of Attorney Fees. A claim for an award of attorney fees and nontaxable costs must be made by motion, subject to the provisions of this subdivision, at a time set by the court. Notice of the motion must be served on all parties and, for motions by class counsel, directed to class members in a reasonable manner.

(b) Right to Object. A class member, or a party from whom payment is sought, may object to the motion.

(c) Hearing and Findings. The court may hold a hearing and must find the facts and state its conclusions of law on the motion under Rule 52.01.

(d) Reference to Special Master. The court may refer issues related to the amount of the award to a special master as provided in Rule 53.01(a).

Adopted Nov. 30, 2005, eff. Jan. 1, 2006.

Comment—Rule 23

See comment following Rule 23.10.

Rule 23.09. Derivative Actions by Shareholders or Members

In a derivative action brought by one or more shareholders or members to enforce a right of a corporation or of an unincorporated association, the corporation or association having failed to enforce a right which may properly be asserted by it, the complaint shall allege that the plaintiff was a shareholder or member at the time of the transaction of which the plaintiff complains or that the plaintiff's share or membership thereafter devolved on the plaintiff by operation of law. The complaint shall also allege with particularity the efforts, if any, made by the plaintiff to obtain the desired action from the directors or comparable authority and, if necessary, from the shareholders or members, and the reasons for the plaintiff's failure to obtain the action or for not making the effort. The derivative action may not be maintained if it appears that the plaintiff does not fairly and adequately represent the interest of the shareholders or members similarly situated in enforcing the right of the corporation or association. The action shall not be dismissed or compromised without the approval of the court, and notice of the proposed dismissal or compromise shall be given to shareholders or members in such manner as the court directs.

Former Rule 23.06, adopted Nov. 10, 1967, eff. Feb. 1, 1968. Revised Oct. 18, 1988, eff. Jan. 1, 1989. Renumbered Rule 23.09, Nov. 30, 2005, eff. Jan. 1, 2006.

Comment—Rule 23

See comment following Rule 23.10.

Rule 23.10. Actions Relating to Unincorporated Associations

An action brought by or against the members of an unincorporated association as a class by naming certain members as representative parties may be maintained only if it appears that the representative parties will fairly and adequately protect the interests of the association and its members. In the conduct of the action the court may make appropriate orders corresponding with those described in Rule 23.04 and the procedure for dismissal or compromise of the action shall correspond with that provided in Rule 23.05.

Former Rule 23.07, adopted Nov. 10, 1967, eff. Feb. 1, 1968. Revised Oct. 18, 1988, eff. Jan. 1, 1989. Renumbered Rule 23.10, Nov. 30, 2005, eff. Jan. 1, 2006.

Advisory Committee Note—1968

Prior to 1966, Minnesota Rule 23.01 and Federal Rule 23(a) were identical in their respective provisions. The Minnesota rule adopted the interpretation of the federal rule establishing three separate classifications for class actions, namely true, hybrid, and spurious. Minnesota also adopted the federal case interpretation regarding the effect of the class action in each of the three classifications, namely true class action—binding upon all members of the class; hybrid class action—binding upon all persons joined in the action or who received notice and an invitation to participate in the action; spurious class action—binding only upon those actually named or joined as parties to the lawsuit. Minnesota also followed the general federal format requiring that the class be so numerous as to make it impracticable to try the lawsuits individually and requiring that the representation be adequate to insure fairness to all represented.

As the commerce to the amended federal rules indicates, substantial difficulty has been encountered in applying the three classifications to the various fact situations arising in class actions. The words "joint," "common," etc., also have proven to be obscure and uncertain. In many respects, the federal cases classified the class action in accordance with the opinion of the trial court regarding the best res judicata application for that particular action. The pre 1966 federal rule did not give the trial court discretion to adjust the class actions to conform to the most desirable procedural implications and res judicata implications as the case developed through the course of discovery, etc. Further, the original federal rule did not specifically set forth measures that might be taken during the pendency of the action to assure procedural fairness to members of the class. Minnesota corrected many of the difficulties in the federal rule by adoption of Rule 23.04 in March of 1959. Federal Rule 23 had no counterpart to the former Minnesota Rule 23.04. The amended federal rule in many respects gives the trial court the same powers as set forth in the former Minnesota Rule 23.04. In view of the close legal effect of the former Minnesota provision and the new federal provision, it is desirable to adopt the new federal provisions so that consistency between federal decisions and the Minnesota decisions will be more likely.

The amended rule describes in practical terms the occasions when a class action can be maintained. The familiar concept of a large number of persons composing the class and adequate representation for the interests of all members of the class is retained in the new Rule 23.01. The new Rule 23.01 abolishes the arbitrary classifications of the classes. The court is given the power throughout the course of the lawsuit to determine what the res judicata effect of the actions will be. Guidelines are set forth in the rule to guide the exercise of discretion by the judges. Specifically, subdivision (.01) states the prerequisites for maintaining a class action in terms of numbers and qualifications of representatives. Subdivision (.02) sets forth the elements to be considered in determining if a class action can be maintained. The considerations stated in clauses 23.02(1)(A) and (B) are somewhat comparable to the elements used in determining whether or not a person is a Rule 19 party. Clause (A) relates to claims by an individual or against an individual where conflicting standards or decisions would be incompatible with proper judicial results; *e.g.* separate actions by individuals against a municipality to declare a bond issue invalid or to condition or limit it, would be incompatible with the need of the municipality to finance government services because of multiplicity and the desirability for a single result.

Clause (B) of Rule 23.02(1) concerns itself with cases where as a practical matter persons not included in the lawsuit might be bound, i.e. policyholders in a fraternal benefit association where the issue is the propriety of a reorganization of the association. The primary consideration under this clause is the adverse practical effect upon the interest of the other members of the class who are similarly situated but not joined as technical parties to the lawsuit and thus not bound by the result unless considered a member of a class.

Subdivision (2) of Rule 23.02 involves situations where injunctive relief or declaratory action is taken and it effects the interest of a large number of persons. Illustrative of this type of case is the civil rights litigation. No case involving money damages falls under this subdivision.

Subdivision (3) of Rule 23.02 involves cases that have not traditionally fallen within the class action concept but might well be tried better as a class action to achieve economies of time and expense and to promote uniformity of decision without sacrificing procedural fairness to the individuals who might be involved. A prerequisite to defining a class action under this subdivision is that the common questions predominate over the individual questions. Generally the mass accident cases would not fall within the subdivision because of the individual liability and damage issues, but a group fraud case might well be a class action on liability even though separate damage issues are involved.

Rule 23.03(1) requires the court to determine as early in a proceeding as practicable whether or not the class action may be maintained as a class action. Under Rule 23.03(1) the court can make a conditional determination that a class action will or will not be maintained. Such a determination can be altered or amended before final disposition of the case. The court has the power to condition its order that the action will be a class action, e.g. additional or different representatives, notice to the members of the class, etc.

Rule 23.03(2) protects the interests of individuals who may be the subject of a class action under Rule 23.02(3) by requiring that notice be given to each member of the class of that member's right to be excluded from the lawsuit in the event that he requests such exclusion. A person receiving such notice may, if he wishes, enter an appearance through his own counsel, may permit the action to continue as a class action, or, upon his request, may be excluded.

Rule 23.03(3) makes specific provision for the various types of class actions set forth in Rule 23.02(1)(2)(3). It provides generally that class actions maintained under Rule 23.02(1) or (2), whether or not favorable to the class, shall include and describe those whom the court finds to be members of the class. If the judgment is maintained as an action under Rule 23.02(3) the court shall specify by name or describe those to whom the notice was sent and who have not requested exclusion and whom the court finds to have been included as members of the class in the lawsuit. Rule 23.02(3) excludes a procedural device known as a one way intervention. Under existing federal practice many federal courts have permitted parties to intervene in spurious class actions after decision or judgment for purposes of being included in the class when the judgment was favorable to the class. Rule 23.03(3) will bar this procedure and will require that the class be determined prior to judgment.

Rule 23.03(4) permits class actions with respect to particular issues and permits classes to be divided into subclasses and each subclass treated as a class.

Rule 23.04 is concerned with the fair and efficient conduct of the trial. It makes provisions for discretionary power in the court to determine the best method of conducting the class action, including handling of evidence, amendment of pleadings, etc. In many respects the power set forth under Rule 23.04 is similar to the power of the court under Rule 16 and contains some of the features formerly set forth in the Minnesota Rule 23.04.

Rule 23.05 preserves the present requirement of court approval for dismissal or compromise of class actions.

A new Rule 23.06 is added to the rules. It is similar to the former Minnesota Rule 23.02. The new rule relates to derivative action by shareholders. Shareholders as a class may bring class actions to enforce shareholder rights under the other subsections of Rule 23, e.g. action to compel declaration of a dividend. A derivative lawsuit by a shareholder or a member of an unincorporated association has distinctive aspects which require special treatment. The rule recognizes that the class may be composed of one or more than one shareholder. The rule requires that the plaintiff be a shareholder at the time of the transaction of which he complains or that his share was obtained by him by operation of law. The purpose is to prevent persons from purchasing stock solely for purposes of maintaining shareholders' derivative actions. Derivative actions require approval of the court if the action is to be dismissed or compromised. The rule also recognizes the power of the court to question the adequacy of the representation by the plaintiff shareholders. Minnesota Rule 23.06 eliminates the federal requirement of verification of the complaint and the federal provision prohibiting a collusive action to confer diversity jurisdiction upon a United States court. The latter provision has no state jurisdiction counterpart. Verification under this rule as an exception to the complaint form generally seems undesirable and could constitute an unnecessary technical trap for counsel.

A new Rule 23.07 is added relating to actions against unincorporated associations. Actions against unincorporated associations have traditionally been treated as class actions. Rule 23.07 will permit this type of class action subject to the general rules regarding class actions or derivative actions when for some reason the association cannot be sued as an entity under local procedure.

Advisory Committee Comment—2006 Amendment

Rule 23 is extensively revamped by these amendments. The recommended changes primarily adopt the amendments made to federal rule 23 in 2003. The reasons for these amendments are set forth in the advisory committee notes that accompanied the federal rule amendments. *See* Fed. R. Civ. P. 23, Advis. Comm. Notes—2003 Amends., *reprinted in* FED. CIV. JUD. PROC. & RULES 132–37 (West 2005 ed.). Those notes provide useful information on the purposes for these amendments and may be consulted for interpretation of these rules.

Rule 23.03(a)(1) requires class certification to be taken up "at an early practicable time" rather than "as soon as practicable." Although these standards are substantially similar, the former rule's phrasing occasionally prompted courts to feel they did not have the leeway to defer ruling on certification until a later, more logical time. In many cases, certification cannot be decided without consideration of the practicalities of trying the case, making early certification impractical. *See generally* MANUAL FOR COMPLEX LITIGATION (FOURTH) § 21.133 (Fed. Jud. Ctr. 2004). Rule 23.03(a)(2) places in the rule an express requirement that the class be defined at the time of certification and that class counsel be appointed. Precise definition of the class is necessary to identify the persons entitled to relief, bound by a judgment in the case, and entitled to notice. *Id.* § 21.222. The procedures for appointment of class counsel are set forth in Rule 23.07. The rule omits reference to a "conditional" certification, reflecting the disfavor this device has earned, but preserves the ability of courts to amend a certification order any time before final judgment is entered.

Rule 23.03(b) establishes the power of the court to direct notice to the class in actions certified under Rule 23.02(a) or (b) (where notice is not generally required) and also states the requirement that notice be given to members of classes certified under Rule 23.02(c). Rule 23.03(b)(2) provides guidance on the content and form of these required notices, and requires the use of plain language. Sample plain-language class notice documents are available on the Federal Judicial Center's website, http://www.fic.gov. These requirements are intended to improve the amount of useful information available to potential class members and to inform their decision on class participation.

Rule 23.05 is expanded to define the procedures for review and approval of class settlements. The rule adopts the changes in Fed. R. Civ. P. 23(e) with one stylistic modification. The federal rule, read literally, might appear to suggest that a trial court must approve every settlement submitted for approval; the language is reworked in the proposed rule to make it clear that although court approval is required for a settlement to be effective, the court's options are not constrained. Indeed, many proposed settlements are properly rejected for not being in the interest of class members. Rule 23.05(a)(3) requires that a hearing be held, and Rule 23.05(b) creates an express requirement that any "side" agreements relating to the settlement must be identified in a statement filed with the court. Rule 23.05(a)(1) removes an ambiguity that existed under the old rule, and now expressly requires court approval only of claims of a certified class.

Rule 23.05(c) authorizes the court to allow a "second opt-out" right in actions certified under Rule 23.02(c). In these actions an opt-out deadline is typically established early in the period following certification. This provision allows the court to permit class members who have not opted out to do so with knowledge of the actual settlement terms.

Rule 23.06 makes it clear that decisions relating to class certification are subject to appellate review on a discretionary basis. This rule is slightly different from its federal counterpart because Minnesota has an established process for discretionary appeals of interlocutory orders, Minn. R. Civ. App. P. 105, that is not present in the federal system. This new provision does not substantially change existing Minnesota practice, as the Minnesota appellate courts have allowed discretionary appeals under Rule 105. *See, e.g., Gordon v. Microsoft Corp.*, 645 N.W.2d 393 (Minn. 2002). The federal rule adopts a shorter 10-day deadline for seeking appellate review of decisions relating to class certification decisions. The committee believes that consistency with the requirements for other discretionary appeals in Minnesota is more important than consistency with the federal rule on this point. The other provisions of Rule 105 and the appellate rules generally apply to appeals under Rule 23.06.

RULE 24. INTERVENTION

Rule 24.01. Intervention of Right

Upon timely application anyone shall be permitted to intervene in an action when the applicant claims an interest relating to the property or transaction which is the subject of the action and the applicant is so situated that the disposition of the action may as a practical matter impair or impede the applicant's ability to protect that interest, unless the applicant's interest is adequately represented by existing parties.

Adopted June 25, 1951, eff. Jan. 1, 1952. Amended Nov. 10, 1967, eff. Feb. 1, 1968. Revised Oct. 18, 1988, eff. Jan. 1, 1989.

Advisory Committee Note—1968

The Minnesota amendment adopts the amended Federal Rule 24(a)(2) as Minnesota Rule 24.01. The prior Minnesota Rule 24.01 and Federal Rule 24(a) were not identical. The prior Minnesota Rule 24.01(1) had been interpreted as a rule codification of the Minnesota Supreme Court's decision in Faricy v. St. Paul Investment and Society, 110 Minn. 311, 125 N.W. 676 (1910). See In Re Application of Sister Kenny Foundation, Inc., 267 Minn. 352, 126 N.W.2d 640 (1964); Wright, Joinder of Claims and Parties, 36 Minn.L.Rev. 580, 628. In the Sister Kenny case the court stressed that the language did not contemplate a "possible" gain or loss as opposed to a "necessary" gain or loss. Subdivision (2) and subdivision (3) of prior Minnesota Rule 24.01 were identical to the former federal provisions (2) and (3). It is fair to say that the prior subdivisions (2) and (3) are meaningless in the former Minnesota rule since all cases encompassed within those two clauses would also be encompassed within the Minnesota version of subdivision (1).

The amendment to the federal rule eliminates federal subdivisions (2) and (3) and substitutes as subdivision (2) provisions permitting intervention as a matter of right if the party is so situated that as a practical matter decision in the pending action would impair or impede his ability to protect his interest. Federal rule provision (1) is not included in the present Minnesota rule and is not adopted in the amended Minnesota Rule 24.01. Federal subdivision (1) relates to intervention in an action when a statute of the United States confers an unconditional right to intervene. This subdivision merely states the necessary result if there is a statutory right to intervene.

The amended Rule 24.01 represents a change in Minnesota law. Minnesota has been much more stringent in determining necessity of gain or loss by direct legal effect of the judgment than have the federal courts. The proposed federal provision, while closer to the former Minnesota subdivision (1) than the prior federal rules, still permits the court to permit intervention as of right if a practical result of the decision rather than a necessary result of the decision will injure the plaintiff. The amendment is desirable purely for clarification and for the sake of consistency with the federal rule. The former provision in the Minnesota rule is an ambiguous provision in the sense that the court is to speculate whether or not the person would lose or gain if he became a party. It is difficult to see how a person would not gain or lose if he became a party.

Rule 24.02. Permissive Intervention

Upon timely application anyone may be permitted to intervene in an action when an applicant's claim or defense and the main action have a common question of law or fact. When a party to an action relies for ground of claim or defense upon any statute or executive order administered by a federal or state governmental officer or agency or upon any regulation, order, requirement, or agreement issued or made pursuant to the statute or executive order, the officer or agency upon timely application may be permitted to intervene in the action. In exercising its discretion, the court shall consider whether the intervention will unduly delay or prejudice the adjudication of the rights of the original parties.

Adopted June 25, 1951, eff. Jan. 1, 1952. Revised Oct. 18, 1988, eff. Jan. 1, 1989.

Rule 24.03. Procedure

A person desiring to intervene shall serve on all parties to the action and file a notice of intervention which shall state that in the absence of objections by an existing party to the action within 30 days after service thereof upon the party, such intervention shall be deemed to have been accomplished. The notice of intervention shall be accompanied by a pleading setting forth the nature and extent of every claim or defense as to which intervention is sought and the reasons for the claim of entitlement to intervention. Within 30 days after service upon the party seeking to intervene of a notice of objection to intervention, the party shall serve a motion to intervene upon all parties as provided in Rule 5.

Upon written consent of all parties to the action, anyone interested may intervene under this rule without notice.

Adopted June 25, 1951, eff. Jan. 1, 1952. Amended Nov. 30, 1981. Revised Oct. 18, 1988, eff. Jan. 1, 1989. Amended Dec. 20, 1993, eff. March 1, 1994.

Advisory Committee Note—1968

This amendment conforms Rule 24.03 to the requirements in the amended Rule 5.01.

Advisory Committee Comment—1993 Amendments

The only change made to this rule is to correct a typographical or grammatical error in the existing rule. No change in meaning or interpretation is intended.

Rule 24.04. Notice to Attorney General [Deleted May 21, 2007, eff. July 1, 2007]

Advisory Committee Comment—2007 Amendment

Rule 24.04 is deleted because the subject matter is now addressed by new Rule 5A.

RULE 25. SUBSTITUTION OF PARTIES

Rule 25.01. Death

(a) If a party dies and the claim is not extinguished or barred, the court may order substitution of the proper parties. The motion for substitution may be made by the successors or representatives of the deceased party or by any party and, together with the notice of hearing, shall be served on the parties as provided in Rule 5 and upon persons not parties in the manner provided in Rule 4 for the service of process.

(b) In the event of the death of one or more of the plaintiffs or of one or more of the defendants in an action in which the right sought to be enforced survives only to the surviving plaintiffs or only against the surviving defendants, the action does not abate. The death shall be indicated upon the record and the action shall proceed in favor of or against the surviving parties.

Adopted June 25, 1951, eff. Jan. 1, 1952. Revised Oct. 18, 1988, eff. Jan. 1, 1989.

Rule 25.02. Incompetency

If a party becomes incompetent, the action shall not abate because of the disability, and the court upon motion served as provided in Rule 25.01 may allow it to be continued by or against the party's representative.

Adopted June 25, 1951, eff. Jan. 1, 1952. Revised Oct. 18, 1988, eff. Jan. 1, 1989.

Rule 25.03. Transfer of Interest

In case of any transfer of interest, the action may be continued by or against the original party, unless the court upon motion directs the person to whom the interest is transferred to be substituted in the action or joined with the original party. Service of this motion shall be made as provided in Rule 25.01.

Adopted June 25, 1951, eff. Jan. 1, 1952. Revised Oct. 18, 1988, eff. Jan. 1, 1989.

Rule 25.04. Public Officers; Death or Separation from Office

When any public officer is a party to an action and during its pendency dies, resigns, or otherwise ceases to hold office, the action may be continued and maintained by or against the officer's successor if it is satisfactorily shown to the court that there is a substantial need for so continuing and maintaining it. Substitution pursuant to this rule may be made when it is shown by supplemental pleading that the successor of any officer adopts or continues or threatens to adopt or continue the action of the officer's predecessor. Before a substitution is made, the party or officer to be affected, unless expressly assenting thereto, shall be given reasonable notice of the application therefor and accorded an opportunity to object.

Adopted June 25, 1951, eff. Jan. 1, 1952. Amended March 3, 1959, eff. July 1, 1959. Revised Oct. 18, 1988, eff. Jan. 1, 1989.

Advisory Committee Note—1959

The limitation of six months for substitution is dropped as unnecessary and to conform to Rule 25.01.

V. DEPOSITIONS AND DISCOVERY

RULE 26. DUTY TO DISCLOSE; GENERAL PROVISIONS GOVERNING DISCOVERY

Rule 26.01. Required Disclosures

(a) Initial Disclosure.

(1) *In General.* Except as exempted by Rule 26.01(a)(2) or as otherwise stipulated or ordered by the court, a party must, without awaiting a discovery request, provide to the other parties:

(A) the name and, if known, the address and telephone number of each individual likely to have discoverable information—along with the subjects of that information—that the disclosing party may use to support its claims or defenses, unless the use would be solely for impeachment;

(B) a copy—or a description by category and location—of all documents, electronically stored information, and tangible things that the disclosing party has in its possession, custody, or control and may use to support its claims or defenses, unless the use would be solely for impeachment;

(C) a computation of each category of damages claimed by the disclosing party—who must also make available for inspection and copying as under Rule 34 the documents or other evidentiary material, unless privileged or protected from disclosure, on which each computation is based, including materials bearing on the nature and extent of injuries suffered; and

(D) for inspection and copying as under Rule 34, any insurance agreement under which an insurance business may be liable to satisfy all or part of a possible judgment in the action or to indemnify or reimburse for payments made to satisfy the judgment.

(2) *Proceedings Exempt from Disclosure.* Unless otherwise ordered by the court in an action, the following proceedings are exempt from disclosures under Rule 26.01(a), (b), and (c):

(A) an action for review on an administrative record;

(B) a forfeiture action in rem arising from a state statute;

(C) a petition for habeas corpus or any other proceeding to challenge a criminal conviction or sentence;

(D) an action brought without an attorney by a person in the custody of the United States, a state, or a state subdivision;

(E) an action to enforce or quash an administrative summons or subpoena;

(F) a proceeding ancillary to a proceeding in another court;

(G) an action to enforce an arbitration award;

(H) family court actions under Gen. R. Prac. 301—378;

(I) Torrens actions;

(J) conciliation court appeals;

(K) forfeitures;

(L) removals from housing court to district court;

(M) harassment proceedings;

(N) name change proceedings;

(O) default judgments;

(P) actions to either docket a foreign judgment or re-docket a judgment within the district;

(Q) appointment of trustee;

(R) condemnation appeal;

(S) confession of judgment;

(T) implied consent;

(U) restitution judgment; and

(V) tax court filings.

(3) *Time for Initial Disclosures—In General.* A party must make the initial disclosures at or within 60 days after the original due date when an answer is required, unless a different time is set by stipulation or court order, or unless an objection is made in a proposed discovery plan submitted as part of a civil cover sheet required under Rule 104 of the General Rules of Practice for the District Courts. In ruling on the objection, the court must determine what disclosures, if any, are to be made and must set the time for disclosure.

(4) *Time for Initial Disclosures—For Parties Served or Joined Later.* A party that is first served or otherwise joined after the initial disclosures are due under Rule 26.01(a)(3) must make the initial disclosures within 30 days after being served or joined, unless a different time is set by stipulation or court order.

(5) *Basis for Initial Disclosure; Unacceptable Excuses.* A party must make its initial disclosures based on the information then reasonably available

to it. A party is not excused from making its disclosures because it has not fully investigated the case or because it challenges the sufficiency of another party's disclosures or because another party has not made its disclosures.

(b) Disclosure of Expert Testimony.

(1) *In General.* In addition to the disclosures required by Rule 26.01(a), a party must disclose to the other parties the identity of any witness it may use at trial to present evidence under Minnesota Rule of Evidence 702, 703, or 705.

(2) *Witnesses Who Must Provide a Written Report.* Unless otherwise stipulated or ordered by the court, this disclosure must be accompanied by a written report—prepared and signed by the witness—if the witness is one retained or specially employed to provide expert testimony in the case or one whose duties as the party's employee regularly involve giving expert testimony. The report must contain:

(A) a complete statement of all opinions the witness will express and the basis and reasons for them;

(B) the facts or data considered by the witness in forming them;

(C) any exhibits that will be used to summarize or support them;

(D) the witness's qualifications, including a list of all publications authored in the previous 10 years;

(E) a list of all other cases in which, during the previous 4 years, the witness testified as an expert at trial or by deposition; and

(F) a statement of the compensation to be paid for the study and testimony in the case.

(3) *Witnesses Who Do Not Provide a Written Report.* Unless otherwise stipulated or ordered by the court, if the witness is not required to provide a written report, this disclosure must state:

(A) the subject matter on which the witness is expected to present evidence under Minnesota Rule of Evidence 702, 703, or 705; and

(B) a summary of the facts and opinions to which the witness is expected to testify.

(4) *Time to Disclose Expert Testimony.* A party must make these disclosures at the times and in the sequence that the court orders. Absent a stipulation or a court order, the disclosures must be made:

(A) at least 90 days before the date set for trial or for the case to be ready for trial; or

(B) if the evidence is intended solely to contradict or rebut evidence on the same subject matter identified by another party under Rule 26.01(b)(2) or (3), within 30 days after the other party's disclosure.

(5) *Supplementing the Disclosure.* The parties must supplement these disclosures when required under Rule 26.05.

(c) Pretrial Disclosures.

(1) *In General.* In addition to the disclosures required by Rule 26.01(a) and (b), a party must provide to the other parties the following information about the evidence that it may present at trial other than solely for impeachment:

(A) the name and, if not previously provided, the address and telephone number of each witness—separately identifying those the party expects to present and those it may call if the need arises;

(B) the designation of those witnesses whose testimony the party expects to present by deposition and, if not taken stenographically, a transcript of the pertinent parts of the deposition; and

(C) an identification of each document or other exhibit, including summaries of other evidence—separately identifying those items the party expects to offer and those it may offer if the need arises.

(2) *Time for Pretrial Disclosures; Objections.* Unless the court orders otherwise, these disclosures must be made at least 30 days before trial. Within 14 days after they are made, unless the court sets a different time, a party may serve and promptly file a list of the following objections: any objections to the use under Rule 32.01 of a deposition designated by another party under Rule 26.01(c)(1)(B); and any objection, together with the grounds for it, that may be made to the admissibility of materials identified under Rule 26.01(c)(1)(C). An objection not so made—except for one under Minnesota Rule of Evidence 402 or 403—is waived unless excused by the court for good cause.

(d) Form of Disclosures. Unless the court orders otherwise, all disclosures under Rule 26.01 must be in writing, signed, and served.

Adopted Nov. 14, 1974, eff. Jan. 1, 1975. Amended March 21, 1985, eff. July 1, 1985. Revised Oct. 18, 1988, eff. Jan. 1, 1989. Amended May 7, 2013, eff. July 1, 2013.

Advisory Committee Note—1975

Existing Rule 26.01 is transferred to Rules 30.01 and 31.01. As now recommended, Rule 26.01 lists all discovery devices provided by the discovery rules and establishes the relationship between the general provisions of Rule 26 and the specific rules for the various discovery devices. Rule 26.01 now specifically provides that the use of the various discovery devices is not limited unless a protective order is obtained from the court under Rule 26.03. Rule 33.01 contains its own specific limitations regarding the use and frequency of use of that discovery device.

Advisory Committee Note—1985

Most of the changes made in Rule 26 were made to adopt changes which were made in the Federal Rules of Civil Procedure in 1982 and 1983, with appropriate adaptation to Minnesota practice.

Rule 26.01

The last sentence of the existing rule is deleted to remove any impression of approval of unlimited use of discovery. The recommended addition to Rule 26.02(1) specifically permits the court to limit either frequency or extent of use of any discovery procedure, and the language of existing Rule 26.01 is inconsistent with the new language. The change does not specifically limit the use of discovery, but makes it clear that the court is empowered—and encouraged—to limit discovery when appropriate.

Historical Notes

Former Rule: A former Rule 26.01 adopted June 25, 1951, and revised March 3, 1959, and November 10, 1967, related to when depositions may be taken. The subject matter of former Rule 26.01 was incorporated into Rules 30.01 and 31.01 by court order dated November 14, 1974.

The order of the Minnesota Supreme Court [ADM04–8001, ADM09–8009, ADM–10-8051] dated May 7, 2013, provided in part that the amendments be effective July 1, 2013, further provided in part that "[t]hese amendments apply to all actions or proceedings pending on or commenced after the effective date provided that ... amendments to Minn. R. Civ. P. 26 apply only to actions commenced on or after the effective date provided that the court may in any case direct the parties to comply with all or part of the rule as part of a pretrial order.", and further provided that the "February 4, 2013 and February 12, 2013 orders of the court are hereby rescinded to the extent inconsistent with this order."

Rule 26.02. Discovery Methods, Scope and Limits

Unless otherwise limited by order of the court in accordance with these rules, the methods and scope of discovery are as follows:

(a) Methods. Parties may obtain discovery by one or more of the following methods: depositions by oral examination or written questions; written interrogatories; production of documents or things or permission to enter upon land or other property; for inspection and other purposes; physical (including blood) and mental examinations; and requests for admission.

(b) Scope and Limits. Discovery must be limited to matters that would enable a party to prove or disprove a claim or defense or to impeach a witness and must comport with the factors of proportionality, including without limitation, the burden or expense of the proposed discovery weighed against its likely benefit, considering the needs of the case, the amount in controversy, the parties' resources, the importance of the issues at stake in the action, and the importance of the discovery in resolving the issues. Subject to these limitations, parties may obtain discovery regarding any matter, not privileged, that is relevant to a claim or defense of any party, including the existence, description, nature, custody, condition and location of any books, documents, or other tangible things and the identity and location of persons having knowledge of any discoverable matter. Upon a showing of good cause and proportionality, the court may order discovery of any matter relevant to the subject matter involved in the action. Relevant information sought need not be admissible at the trial if the discovery appears reasonably calculated to lead to the discovery of admissible evidence.

(1) *Authority to Limit Frequency and Extent.* The court may establish or alter the limits on the number of depositions and interrogatories and may also limit the length of depositions under Rule 30 and the number of requests under Rule 36. The court may act upon its own initiative after reasonable notice or pursuant to a motion under Rule 26.03.

(2) *Limits on Electronically Stored Evidence for Undue Burden or Cost.* A party need not provide discovery of electronically stored information from sources that the party identifies as not reasonably accessible because of undue burden or cost. On motion to compel discovery or for a protective order, the party from whom discovery is sought must show that the information is not reasonably accessible because of undue burden or cost. If that showing is made, the court may nonetheless order discovery from such sources if the requesting party shows good cause and proportionality, considering the limitations of Rule 26.02(b)(3). The court may specify conditions for the discovery.

(3) *Limits Required When Cumulative; Duplicative; More Convenient Alternative; and Ample Prior Opportunity.* The frequency or extent of use of the discovery methods otherwise permitted under these rules shall be limited by the court if it determines that: (i) the discovery sought is unreasonably cumulative or duplicative, or is obtainable from some other source that is more convenient, less burdensome, or less expensive; or (ii) the party seeking discovery has had ample opportunity by discovery in the action to obtain the information sought. The court may act upon its own initiative after reasonable notice or pursuant to a motion under Rule 26.03.

(c) Insurance Agreements. In any action in which there is an insurance policy that may afford coverage, any party may require any other party to disclose the coverage and limits of such insurance and the amounts paid and payable thereunder and, pursuant to Rule 34, may obtain production of the insurance policy; provided, however, that this provision will not permit such disclosed information to be introduced into evidence unless admissible on other grounds.

(d) Trial Preparation: Materials. Subject to the provisions of Rule 26.02(e) a party may obtain discovery of documents and tangible things otherwise discoverable pursuant to Rule 26.02(b) and prepared in anticipation of litigation or for trial by or for another party or by or for that other party's representative (including the other party's attorney, consultant, surety, indemnitor, insurer, or agent) only upon a showing that the party seeking discovery has substantial need of the materials in the preparation of the party's case and that the party is unable without undue hardship to obtain the substantial equivalent of the materials by other means. In ordering discovery of such materials when the required showing has been made, the court shall protect against disclosure of the mental impressions, conclusions, opinions, or legal theories of an attorney or other representative of a party concerning the litigation.

A party may obtain without the required showing a statement concerning the action or its subject matter previously made by that party. Upon request, a party or other person may obtain without the required showing a statement concerning the action or its subject matter previously made by that person who is not a party. If the request is refused, the person may move for a court order. The provisions of Rule 37.01(d) apply to the award of expenses incurred in relation to the motion. For purposes of this paragraph, a statement previously made is (1) a written statement signed or otherwise adopted or approved by the person making it, or (2) a stenographic, mechanical, electrical, or other recording, or a transcription thereof, that is a substantially verbatim recital of an oral statement by the person making it and contemporaneously recorded.

(e) Trial Preparation: Experts. Discovery of facts known and opinions held by experts, otherwise discoverable pursuant to Rule 26.02(b) and acquired or developed in anticipation of litigation or for trial, may be obtained only as follows:

(1)(A) A party may through interrogatories require any other party to identify each person whom the other party expects to call as an expert witness at trial, to state the subject matter on which the expert is expected to testify, and to state the substance of the facts and opinions to which the expert is expected to testify and a summary of the grounds for each opinion. (B) Upon motion, the court may order further discovery by other means, subject to such restrictions as to scope and such provisions, pursuant to Rule 26.02 (e)(3), concerning fees and expenses, as the court may deem appropriate.

(2) A party may discover facts known or opinions held by an expert who has been retained or specially employed by another party in anticipation of litigation or preparation for trial and who is not expected to be called as a witness at trial, only as provided in Rule 35.02 or upon a showing of exceptional circumstances under which it is impracticable for the party seeking discovery to obtain facts or opinions on the same subject by other means.

(3) Unless manifest injustice would result, (A) the court shall require the party seeking discovery to pay the expert a reasonable fee for time spent in responding to discovery pursuant to Rules 26.02(e)(1)(B) and 26.02(e)(2); and (B) with respect to discovery obtained pursuant to Rule 26.02(e)(1)(B), the court may require, and with respect to discovery obtained pursuant to Rule 26.02(e)(2) the court shall require, the party seeking discovery to pay the other party a fair portion of the fees and expenses reasonably incurred by the latter party in obtaining facts and opinions from the expert.

(f) Claims of Privilege or Protection of Trial Preparation Materials.

(1) When a party withholds information otherwise discoverable under these rules by claiming that it is privileged or subject to protection as trial preparation material, the party shall make the claim expressly and shall describe the nature of the documents, communications, or things not produced or disclosed in a manner that, without revealing information itself privileged or protected, will enable other parties to assess the applicability of the privilege or protection.

(2) If information is produced in discovery that is subject to a claim of privilege or of protection as trial-preparation material, the party making the claim may notify any party that received the information of the claim and the basis for it. After being notified, a party must promptly return, sequester, or destroy the specified information and any copies it has and may not use or disclose the information until the claim is resolved. A receiving party may promptly present the information to the court under seal for a determination of the claim. If the receiving party disclosed the information before being notified, it must take reasonable steps to retrieve it. The producing party must preserve the information until the claim is resolved.

Adopted June 25, 1951, eff. Jan. 1, 1952. Amended Nov. 10, 1967, eff. Feb. 1, 1968; Nov. 14, 1974, eff. Jan. 1, 1975; March 21, 1985, eff. July 1, 1985. Revised Oct. 18, 1988, eff. Jan. 1, 1989. Amended April 13, 2000, eff. July 1, 2000; Nov. 30, 2005, eff. Jan. 1, 2006; May 21, 2007, eff. July 1, 2007; May 28, 2008, eff. May 28, 2008; May 7, 2013, eff. July 1, 2013.

Advisory Committee Note—1975

Subd. (1).

Subdivision (1), of proposed amended Rule 26.02, is applicable to all discovery rules. It regulates the discovery obtainable through any of the various discovery procedures. This general provision regarding the scope of discovery is subject to protective orders as may be issued by the court under proposed amended Rule 26.03. Rule 26.03 gives the court broad powers to regulate or prevent discovery even though the information or material sought are within the general scope of discovery under this rule. The proposed amended Rule 26.02 does not change the existing law regarding the scope of discovery or the court's power to regulate the scope of discovery by appropriate order.

The four general limitations on the scope of discovery are:

(1) Privileged matter (evidence and constitutional privileges).

(2) Material prepared in anticipation of litigation.

(3) Physical and mental examinations under Rule 35.

(4) Protective orders under Rule 26.03.

Subd. (2).

Federal Rule 26(b)(2) contains provisions permitting discovery of liability insurance coverage in a manner substantially similar to that provided in the existing Minnesota Rule 26.02. While the language difference is not substantial, the Committee believed the existing Minnesota rule was more liberal than the Federal rule and the differences were substantial enough to recommend retention of the language of the existing Minnesota rule rather than conform the rule to the Federal rule language. The Advisory Committee's recommendation restates the insurance discovery rule as provided in Rule 26.02. The primary difference between the Federal rule and the Minnesota rule is the application of the insurance discovery clause to all relevant insurance policies, including liability insurance, in the Minnesota rule while the Federal rule is limited to insurance obligating the company to satisfy all or part of the judgment or to indemnify or reimburse for payments made to satisfy a judgment. The proposed Minnesota rule does not contain a provision similar to Federal Rule 26.02 regarding applications for insurance to be treated as an insurance agreement even though there is no specific provision regarding this matter.

Subd. (3).

A party may obtain discovery of documents and tangible things within the scope of discovery under Rule 26.02(1) which were prepared in anticipation of litigation or for trial by or for another party or by or for that other party's representative (including his attorney, surety, indemnitor, insurer, or agent) only upon a showing that the party seeking the discovery has a substantial need of the materials in the preparation of his case and he is unable without undue hardship to obtain the substantial equivalent of the materials by other means. This work product limitation on the scope of discovery is also subject to Rule 26.02(4). In ordering discovery of such work product materials when the required showing has been made, the court must still protect against disclosure of the mental impressions, conclusions, opinions, or legal theories of the attorney or other representative of a party.

A party may obtain without the required showing of need and hardship any statement concerning the action or its subject matter previously made by that party. Upon request, a person not a party may obtain without the required showing a statement concerning the action or its subject matter previously made by that person. If the request for the statement is refused, the party or person seeking discovery may move for a court order. The provisions of Rule 37.01(4) apply to the award of expenses incurred in relation to the motion. For purposes of this paragraph a statement previously made is (a) a written statement signed or otherwise adopted or approved by the person making it, or (b) a stenographic, mechanical, electrical, or other recording, or a transcription thereof, which is a substantially verbatim recital of an oral statement by the person making it and contemporaneously recorded.

This rule is the "work product" rule. It resolves many of the questions raised by the present rule and by the application of the work product doctrine in Taylor v. Hickman, 67 S.Ct. 385, 329 U.S. 495, 91 L.Ed. 451 (1947). The rule is applicable to documents or things prepared in anticipation of litigation or prepared for trial. Prior to these proposed amendments of the discovery rules, the requirement in Rule 34 for a showing of "good cause" for the production of documents imposed a substantial limitation on the discovery on work product material. A large body of law was developed in the Federal court regarding the relationship of Rule 26(b)(26.02) and Rule 34. The amended Rule 26.02(3) resolves these questions. Rule 34 has been amended to eliminate the required showing of good cause. For documents and other tangible things, prepared in anticipation of litigation or for trial, a showing of "substantial need" is required plus an inability to obtain substantially equivalent materials by other means without "undue hardship". Rule 26.02(3) imposes a less burdensome "good cause" type requirement upon the discovery of these documents and tangible things. The rule is not expressed in "good cause" terms since that phrase had created a substantial body of case law interpretation under the old Rule 34 that should not be applicable under the amended rule. For that reason, Rule 26.02(3) contains its own factual statement of cause. This rule reflects existing case law protection for the work efforts of counsel and persons related to the attorney or the party in trial preparation. The rule also recognizes the fairness of requiring production in those situations where substantially equivalent materials cannot be obtained by other means without undue hardship.

The amended rule also prevents a fishing expedition by requiring a showing that the party has substantial need for the materials in preparation of his case. The last sentence of the first paragraph in Rule 26.02(3) contains absolute protection against disclosure of documents or tangible things containing the mental impressions, conclusions, opinions, or legal theories of the attorney or other representative of the party concerning the litigation. As proposed the rule is consistent with Leininger v. Swadner, 279 Minn. 251, 156 N.W.2d 254 (1968). If the document contains both factual and conclusionary material, it would be appropriate under this rule for the court to compel disclosure of those things not involving mental impressions, conclusions, etc. of the attorney.

The second paragraph of the rule is merely a restatement of the existing practice permitting a party or non-party to obtain a copy of his own statement. If a party or a non-party desires to obtain his own statement, no showing of special circumstances are set forth in the first paragraph is required. A request should be made directly to the party having custody of the statements. Recourse to the court for a court order is provided only if the request is refused.

The Committee has eliminated the word "consultant" from the first paragraph of the Federal rule primarily because that word contained such a breadth of possible application that its use without further definition or limitation seemed undesirable. The Committee believes that all proper representatives are included even though they may not be specifically mentioned in the parenthetical provision in the first sentence of Rule 26.02(3).

The rule as recommended contains the language "or a party" in the second sentence of the second paragraph of the rule. This language was recommended by the Minnesota State Bar Committee on Rules and differs in that respect from the corresponding Federal rule. The purpose of the addition of the language "or a party" is to make it clear that a party without a necessity of seeking a routine motion has the right to obtain statements made by non-party witnesses.

Subd. (4).

This rule relating to discovery of information from experts is a new provision and contains substantially new concepts. The subdivision distinguishes those experts whom a party expects to call as a trial witness from those experts who have been retained or consulted but who will not be called by the party. An expert who was consulted prior to the time the party could anticipate litigation or before preparation for trial is not subject to the provisions of this rule, but rather is covered by the discovery rules relating to non-expert witnesses. In view of the frequency with which expert testimony is now required for trial purposes, this rule must represent a substantial change in existing practice.

With regard to experts whom a party expects to call as a witness at trial, discovery takes the form of disclosure by the lawyer pursuant to interrogatories. The rule proceeds on the basis that a primary difficulty in cross-examining opposing experts at trial is lack of general information regarding the expert and the nature and content of his opinion. Trial preparation is substantially hampered by an inability to anticipate fully the expected testimony of opposing experts. Thus Rule 26.02(a)(A)(i) requires a party to respond to interrogatories requiring him to identify each person whom the party expects to call as an expert at trial, to state the subject matter on which the expert will testify, and to state the substance of the facts and opinions of the expert. If the interrogatory is fully answered the court normally should not order further discovery of the expert's opinion. If further discovery of the expert's findings and conclusions is to be had, it must be by a court order and subject to the restrictions set forth in Rule 26.02(4)(C). See Rule 26.02(4)(A)(ii). If the details required in the interrogatories relating to the expert's opinion become oppressive or unnecessarily expensive or time consuming to a party, a protective order can be obtained which could include a requirement that the expert's opinion be obtained through the use of other discovery devices.

With regard to experts who have been retained or specially consulted, but whose presence is not anticipated at trial, there is a general prohibition against discovery of the opinions held by such an expert. Rule 26.02(4)(B) permits discovery of opinions and facts known to such an expert only as provided in Rule 35.02 or upon a showing of exceptional circumstances under which it is impracticable to obtain the same facts or opinions by other means. Thus there is not a total prohibition against discovery of opinions from experts who are not anticipated to be called at trial, but the availability of such opinions will be quite limited. Obviously, the rule encourages parties to consult many experts in an effort to fully prepare their case without incurring the risk that such an expert's opinion may be used against the party at trial unless the party undertakes to call that expert as his witness. Under this portion of the rule, experts who are employed by attorneys in anticipation of trial or in preparation of trial cannot be considered as agents of the lawyer and therefore protected by the attorney-client privilege.

Rule 26.02(4)(C)(i) provides for the party seeking discovery to pay the expert a reasonable fee for time spent in responding to discovery under Rule 26.02(4)(A)(ii) and Rule 26.02(4)(B). Paragraph (ii), of Rule 26.02(4)(C), provides for payment of a part of the fees and expenses incurred by the other party in obtaining the expert's opinions and facts if the court orders further discovery under 26.02(4)(A)(ii) and requires the sharing of these and expenses which have reasonably been incurred if discovery is permitted under Rule 26.02(4)(B). There is no provision for payment of expert fees to those experts whose opinions are disclosed pursuant to interrogatories or those experts who are considered ordinary witnesses because their relationship to the case occurred prior to the time that counsel commenced preparation for trial.

Advisory Committee Note—1985

The recommended change to Rule 26.02 mirrors a change to Federal Rule 26(d). That change is intended to provide the court specific authority to manage discovery in order to prevent abusive discovery practices. This approach was considered, both by the federal committee and this Committee, to be superior to arbitrary limitations on the scope of discovery. The Committee determined that limitations on the amount or extent of discovery will be useful in certain cases, and should not be imposed in other cases. The courts are given specific guidelines relating to the exercise of their discretion. Courts are encouraged to require the parties to use discovery devices well-suited to their legitimate needs and consistent with Rule 1. The use of mandatory language is intended. The committee intends that the rule be a useful tool to curtail discovery abuse, and cannot foresee a circumstance in which a court should decline to limit discovery if it makes the determination that subdivisions (a), (b), or (c) would exist. The rule grants additional authority for entry of an order preventing duplicative discovery. The rule permits the entry of an order prospectively limiting the amount and type of discovery which may be used. Such a prospective order may be entered even before discovery is sought. The Committee anticipates that Rule 26.02(1), as amended, will be of value in controlling "runaway" discovery in smaller cases. The Committee believes that the over-discovery in small cases is a significant problem, and encourages the use of this rule by attorneys and judges to provide reasonable limitations on discovery. Other jurisdictions have considered specific, pre-determined limits on the availability of discovery in "small" cases. *See generally* R. Haydock & D. Herr, Discovery Practice § 12.6.1, at 521–22 (1982). The Committee has recommended rules which will give the trial courts power to control discovery abuse. It is important for trial judges to be aggressive in curtailing unnecessary discovery. *See* Renfrew, *Discovery Sanctions: A Judicial Perspective,* 2 Rev. Litigation 71 (1981); Schwarzer, *Managing Litigation: The Trial Judge's Role,* 61 Judicature 400 (1978).

Advisory Committee Comment—2006 Amendment

The amendment to Rule 26.02 is simple but potentially quite important. The rule is amended to conform to Fed. R. Civ. P. 26(b) as amended in 2000. Although the proposed changes were expected to create as many problems as they solved, *see, e.g.*, John S. Beckerman, *Confronting Civil Discovery's Fatal Flaws,* 84 MINN. L. REV. 505, 537–43 (2000); Jeffrey W. Stempel & David F. Herr, *Applying Amended Rule* 26(b)(1) *in Litigation: The New Scope of Discovery, in* 199 F.R.D. 396 (2001), the change in the scope of discovery, to limit it to the actual claims and defenses raised in the pleadings, has worked well in federal court, and most feared problems have not materialized. *See generally* Thomas D. Rowe, Jr., *A Square Peg in a Round Hole? The 2000 Limitation on the Scope of Federal Civil Discovery,* 69 TENN. L. REV. 13, 25–27 (2001); Note, *The Sound and the Fury or the Sound of Silence?: Evaluating the Pre-Amendment Predictions and Post-Amendment Effects of the Discovery Scope-Narrowing Language in the 2000 Amendments to Federal Rule of Civil Procedure 26(b)(1),* 37 GA. L. REV. 1039 (2003). Courts have simply not found the change dramatic nor given it a draconian interpretation. *See, e.g., Sanyo Laser Prod., Inc. v. Arista Records, Inc.*, 214 F.R.D. 496 (S.D. Ind. 2003).

The narrowing of the scope of discovery as a matter of right does not vitiate in any way the traditional rule that discovery should be liberally allowed. It should be limited to the claims and defenses raised by the pleadings, but the requests should still be liberally construed. *See, e.g., Graham v. Casey's General Stores,* 206 F.R.D. 251, 253 (S.D. Ind. 2002) ("Even after the recent amendments to Federal Rule of Civil Procedure 26, courts employ a liberal discovery standard.").

Advisory Committee Comment—2007 Amendment

Rule 26.02(b)(2) is a new provision that establishes a two-tier standard for discovery of electronically stored information. The rule makes information that is not "reasonably accessible because of undue burden or cost" not normally discoverable. This rule is identical to its federal counterpart, adopted in 2006. The rule requires that it be identified in response to an appropriate request, but if it is identified as "not reasonably accessible," it need not be produced in the absence of further order. It is not strictly exempt from discovery, as the court may, upon motion that "shows good cause," order disclosure of the information. The rule explicitly authorizes the court to impose conditions on any order for disclosure of this information, and conditions that either ease the undue burden or minimize the total cost or cost borne by the producing party would be appropriate.

Rule 26.02(f)(2) is a new provision that creates a uniform procedure for dealing with assertions of privilege that are made following production of information in discovery. The rule creates a mandatory obligation to return, sequester, or destroy information that is produced in discovery if the producing party asserts that it is subject to a privilege or work-product protection. The information cannot be used for any purpose until the privilege claim is resolved. The rule provides a mechanism for the receiving party to have the validity of the privilege claim resolved by the court. The rule does not create any presumption or have any impact on the validity of the claim of privilege, nor does it excuse the inadvertent or regretted production. If the court determines that that production waived an otherwise valid privilege, then the information should be ordered for production or release from sequestration of the information.

Historical and Statutory Notes

The order of the Minnesota Supreme Court [ADM04-8001, ADM09-8009, ADM-10-8051] dated May 7, 2013, provided in part that the amendments be effective July 1, 2013, further provided in part that "[t]hese amendments apply to all actions or proceedings pending on or commenced after the effective date provided that ... amendments to Minn. R. Civ. P. 26 apply only to actions commenced on or after the effective date provided that the court may in any case direct the parties to comply with all or part of the rule as part of a pretrial order.", and further provided that the "February 4, 2013 and February 12, 2013 orders of the court are hereby rescinded to the extent inconsistent with this order."

Rule 26.03. Protective Orders

Upon motion by a party or by the person from whom discovery is sought, and for good cause shown, the court in which the action is pending or alternatively, on matters relating to a deposition, the court in the district where the deposition is to be taken may make any order which justice requires to protect a party or person from annoyance, embarrassment, oppression, or undue burden or expense, including one or more of the following:

(a) that the discovery not be had;

(b) that the discovery may be had only on specified terms and conditions, including a designation of the time or place;

(c) that the discovery may be had only by a method of discovery other than that selected by the party seeking discovery;

(d) that certain matters not be inquired into, or that the scope of the discovery be limited to certain matters;

(e) that discovery be conducted with no one present except persons designated by the court;

(f) that a deposition, after being sealed, be opened only by order of the court;

(g) that a trade secret or other confidential research, development, or commercial information not be disclosed or be disclosed only in a designated way; or

(h) that the parties simultaneously file specified documents or information enclosed in sealed envelopes to be opened as directed by the court.

If the motion for a protective order is denied in whole or in part, the court may, on such terms and conditions as are just, order that any party or person provide or permit discovery. Rule 37.01(d) applies to the award of expenses incurred in connection with the motion.

Adopted Nov. 14, 1974, eff. Jan. 1, 1975. Revised Oct. 18, 1988, eff. Jan. 1, 1989.

Advisory Committee Note—1975

Protective orders formally contained in Rule 30.02 have been transferred to Rule 26.03. The protective orders now are specifically applicable to all forms of discovery. Sanctions under Rule 37.01(4) are applicable for enforcement of the discovery rules. The proposed amended rule provides that the court in which the action is pending may respond to a motion by a party or by the deponent for a protective order and in addition a protective order may be sought on matters relating to depositions by a party or a deponent in the district in which the deposition is to be taken. Expanding the authority of the district in which the deposition is to be taken to cover all depositions reflects a desire to permit quick and ready access to a court for protective orders. The scope of the protective orders is substantially the same as provided in the former Rule 30.02. As drafted, the rule will now clearly permit protective orders related to extension of time as well as to a change of the place for discovery. Protective orders may be obtained on the ground that the discover sought would place an undue burden or expense upon the party or deponent. Trade secrets and other confidential research development or commercial information can be protected under subdivision (7).

Historical Notes

Former Rule: A former Rule 26.03 adopted June 25, 1951, and revised March 3, 1959, and November 10, 1967, related to the examination and cross-examination of witnesses. The subject matter of former Rule 26.03 was incorporated into Rule 30.03 by court order dated November 14, 1974.

Rule 26.04. Timing and Sequence of Discovery

(a) Timing. Notwithstanding the provisions of Rules 26.02, 30.01, 31.01(a), 33.01(a), 34.02, 36.01, and 45, parties may not seek discovery from any source before the parties have conferred and prepared a discovery plan as required by Rule 26.06(c) except in a proceeding exempt from initial disclosure under Rule 26.01(a)(2), or when allowed by stipulation or court order.

(b) Sequence. Unless the court upon motion, for the convenience of parties and witnesses and in the interests of justice, orders otherwise, methods of discovery may be used in any sequence and the fact that a party is conducting discovery, whether by deposition or otherwise, shall not operate to delay any other party's discovery.

(c) Expedited Litigation Track. Expedited timing and modified content of certain disclosure and discovery obligations may be required by order of the supreme court adopting special rules for the pilot expedited civil litigation track.

Adopted Nov. 14, 1974, eff. Jan. 1, 1975. Revised Oct. 18, 1988, eff. Jan. 1, 1989. Amended May 7, 2013, eff. July 1, 2013.

Advisory Committee Note—1975

The proposed amended rule eliminates the former provision in Rule 30 establishing a priority for discovery to the party first giving notice of discovery. Under the amended rule the court may establish priority between parties by order, otherwise discovery will take place as properly noted in the notice of discovery without regard as to who gave notice first. The pendency of one form of discovery will not operate to delay or otherwise extend the use of other forms of discovery or similar forms of discovery if the timing is not inherently inconsistent.

Historical Notes

Former Rule: A former Rule 26.04 adopted June 25, 1951, and revised March 3, 1959, and November 10, 1967, related to the use of depositions. The subject matter of former Rule 26.04 was incorporated into Rule 32.01 by court order dated November 14, 1974.

The order of the Minnesota Supreme Court [ADM04–8001, ADM09–8009, ADM-10-8051] dated May 7, 2013, provided in part that the amendments be effective July 1, 2013, and further provided in part that "[t]hese amendments apply to all actions or proceedings pending on or commenced after the effective date provided that ... amendments to Minn. R. Civ. P. 26 apply only to actions commenced on or after the effective date provided that the court may in any case direct the parties to comply with all or part of the rule as part of a pretrial order."

Rule 26.05. Supplementation of Responses

A party who has responded to a request for discovery is under a duty to supplement or correct the response to include information thereafter acquired if ordered by the court or in the following circumstances:

A party is under a duty seasonably to amend a prior response to an interrogatory, request for production, or request for admission if the party learns that the response is in some material respect incomplete or incorrect and if the additional or corrective information has not otherwise been made known to the other parties during the discovery process or in writing. With respect to testimony of an expert, the duty extends to information contained in interrogatory responses, in any report of the expert, and to information provided through a deposition of the expert.

Adopted Nov. 14, 1974, eff. Jan. 1, 1975. Revised Oct. 18, 1988, eff. Jan. 1, 1989. Amended April 13, 2000, eff. July 1, 2000.

Advisory Committee Note—1975

The obligation of a party to supplement his responses to interrogatories or depositions is not provided by the existing discovery rules. Gebhard v. Niedzwiecki, 265 Minn. 471, 122 N.W.2d 110 (1963), and case law in other jurisdictions, impose a continuing obligation to respond upon a party under Rule 33. The proposed new Rule 26.05 clarifies the practice and makes explicit the obligation to provide new information in the specified situations. There is no duty to supplement the responses except as provided in the rule. Of particular significance is the requirement that a party when he has new information and knows that that information makes his previous response incorrect, even though it was correct when made, must correct his error by providing the new information. The court may specifically impose an obligation to supplement responses upon the party with or without a motion or order and the agreement of the parties made at the time of the deposition or interrogatories may impose such an obligation to respond. Since there is no limitation on the frequency of the use of the discovery procedures, new discovery procedures obviously may also produce supplemental material.

Advisory Committee Comments—2000 Amendments

The changes made to Rule 26 include some of the recent amendments to the federal rule made in 1993. The changes made to the Minnesota rule have been modified to reflect the fact that Minnesota practice does not include the automatic disclosure mechanisms that have been adopted in some federal courts; the resulting differences in the rules are minor, and the authorities construing the federal rule should be given full weight to the extent applicable.

The changes in Rule 26.02(a) adopt similar amendments made to Fed. R. Civ. P. 26(b) in 1993. The new rule is intended to facilitate greater judicial control over the extent of discovery. The rule does not limit or curtail any form of discovery or establish numeric limits on its use, but does clarify the broad discretion courts have to limit discovery.

Rule 26.02(e) is a new rule adopted directly from its federal counterpart. The requirement of a privilege log is necessary to permit consideration, by opposing counsel and ultimately by the courts, of the validity of privilege claims. Privilege logs have been in use for years and are routinely required when a dispute arises. *See generally Nevada Power Co. v. Monsanto Co.*, 151 F.R.D. 118, 122 & n.6 (D. Nev. 1993) (enumerating deficiencies in log); *Allendale Mutual Ins. Co. v. Bull Data Sys., Inc.*, 145 F.R.D. 84 (N.D. Ill. 1992) (ordering privilege log and specifying requirements); *Grossman v. Schwarz*, 125 F.R.D. 376, 386–87 (S.D.N.Y. 1989)(holding failure to provide privilege log deemed "presumptive evidence" claim of privilege not meritorious). The requirement of the log should not, however, be an invitation to require detailed identification of every privileged document within an obviously privileged category. Courts should not require a log in all circumstances, especially where a request seeks broad categories of non-discoverable information. *See, e.g., Durkin v. Shields (In re Imperial Corp. of Am.)*, 174 F.R.D. 475 (S.D. Cal. 1997)(recognizing document-by-document log would be unduly burdensome). It is the intention of the rule, however, to require the production of logs routinely to encourage the earlier resolution of privilege disputes and to discourage baseless assertions of privilege.

Fed. R. Civ. P. 45(d)(2) expressly requires production of a privilege log by a non-party seeking to assert a privilege in response to a subpoena. Although the Committee does not recommend adoption of the extensive changes that have been made in federal Rule 45, this recommendation is made to minimize disruption in existing Minnesota subpoena practice. The difference in rules should not prevent a court from ordering production of a privilege log by a non-party in appropriate cases. The cost of producing a privilege log may be properly shifted to the party serving the subpoena under Rule 45.06.

Rule 26.05 is amended to adopt in Minnesota the same supplementation requirement as exists in federal court. It is a more stringent and more explicit standard, and reflects a sounder analysis of when supplementation is necessary. It states affirmatively the duty to disclose. The Committee believes it is particularly desirable to have state supplementation practice conform to federal practice in order that compliance with the requirements is more common and sanctions can more readily be imposed for failure to supplement. The rule relaxes the supplementation requirement to obviate supplementation where the information has been disclosed either in discovery (i.e., in other discovery responses or by deposition testimony) or in writing. The writing need not be a discovery response, and could be a letter to all counsel identifying a witness or correcting a prior response.

Historical Notes

Former Rule: A former Rule 26.05 adopted June 25, 1951, and revised November 10, 1967, related to objections to the admissibility of a deposition. The subject matter of former Rule 26.05 was incorporated into Rule 32.02 by court order dated November 14, 1974.

Rule 26.06. Discovery Conference

(a) Conference Timing. Except in a proceeding exempted from initial disclosure under Rule 26.01(a)(2) or when the court orders otherwise, the parties must confer as soon as practicable—and in any event within 30 days from the initial due date for an answer.

(b) Conference Content; Parties' Responsibilities. In conferring, the parties must consider the nature and basis of their claims and defenses and the possibilities for promptly settling or resolving the case; make or arrange for the disclosures required by Rule 26.01(a), (b); discuss any issues about preserving discoverable information; and develop a proposed discovery plan. The attorneys of record and all unrepresented parties that have appeared in the case are jointly responsible for arranging the conference, and for attempting in good faith to agree on the proposed discovery plan. A written report outlining the discovery plan must be filed with the court within 14 days after the conference or at the time the action is filed, whichever is later. The court may order the parties or attorneys to attend the conference in person.

(c) Discovery Plan. A discovery plan must state the parties' views and proposals on:

(1) what changes should be made in the timing, form, or requirement for disclosures under Rule 26.01, including a statement of when initial disclosures were made or will be made;

(2) the subjects on which discovery may be needed, when discovery should be completed, and whether discovery should be conducted in phases or be limited to or focused on particular issues;

(3) any issues about disclosure or discovery of electronically stored information, including the form or forms in which it should be produced;

(4) any issues about claims of privilege or of protection as trial-preparation materials, including—if the parties agree on a procedure to assert these claims after production—whether to ask the court to include their agreement in an order;

(5) what changes should be made in the limitations on discovery imposed under these rules or by local rule, and what other limitations should be imposed; and

(6) any other orders that the court should issue under Rule 26.03 or under Rule 16.02 and .03.

(d) Conference with the Court. At any time after service of the summons, the court may direct the attorneys for the parties to appear before it for a conference on the subject of discovery. The court shall do so upon motion by the attorney for any party if the motion includes:

(1) A statement of the issues as they then appear;

(2) A proposed plan and schedule of discovery;

(3) Any issues relating to disclosure or discovery of electronically stored information, including the form or forms in which it should be produced;

(4) Any issues relating to claims of privilege or of protection as trial-preparation material, including—if the parties agree on a procedure to assert such claims after production—whether to ask the court to include their agreement in an order;

(5) Any limitations proposed to be placed on discovery;

(6) Any other proposed orders with respect to discovery; and

(7) A statement showing that the attorney making the motion has made a reasonable effort to reach agreement with opposing attorneys on the matter set forth in the motion. All parties and attorneys are under a duty to participate in good faith in the framing of any proposed discovery plan.

Notice of the motion shall be served on all parties. Objections or additions to matters set forth in the motion shall be served not later than 10 days after the service of the motion.

Following the discovery conference, the court shall enter an order tentatively identifying the issues for discovery purposes, establishing a plan and schedule for discovery, setting limitations on discovery, if any, and determining such other matters, including the allocation of expenses, as are necessary for the proper management of discovery in the action. An order may be altered or amended whenever justice so requires.

Subject to the right of a party who properly moves for a discovery conference to prompt convening of the conference, the court may combine the discovery conference with a pretrial conference authorized by Rule 16.

Adopted March 21, 1985, eff. July 1, 1985. Revised Oct. 18, 1988, eff. Jan. 1, 1989. Amended May 21, 2007, eff. July 1, 2007; May 7, 2013, eff. July 1, 2013.

Advisory Committee Note—1985

Rule 26.06 adopts in Minnesota the discovery conference as a tool to manage discovery. This procedure was established in the Federal Rules of Civil Procedure by the 1983 amendment. *See* Fed. R.Civ.P. 26(f). The discovery conference is optional. The court may, however, require the parties to attend one upon its own motion. Additionally, any party may request a discovery conference under this rule, and, if one is properly requested, the court is required to hold a conference. The Committee anticipates that discovery conferences will be the exception, rather than the rule, in Minnesota practice. A discovery conference may also be held as part of a pretrial conference under Minn.Rule 16.01, or a scheduling conference held under Minn.Rule 16.02. In cases involving complex issues, multiple parties, or other factors which make the litigation complex or complicated, discovery conferences should be used in order to ease the burdens of litigation upon the parties, their attorneys, and the judicial system.

Advisory Committee Comment—2007 Amendment

Rule 26.06 is amended to add to the required provisions in a motion for a discovery conference.

These changes require the party seeking a discovery conference to address electronic discovery issues, but do not dictate any particular resolution or conference agenda for them. Many cases will not involve electronic discovery issues, and there is no need to give substantial attention to them in a request for a conference under this rule.

Historical Notes

Former Rule: A former Rule 26.06, adopted June 25, 1951, and revised March 3, 1959, and November 10, 1967, related to the effect of taking or using depositions. The subject matter of former Rule 26.06 was incorporated into Rule 32.03 by court order dated November 14, 1974.

The order of the Minnesota Supreme Court [ADM04–8001, ADM09–8009, ADM–10-8051] dated May 7, 2013, provided in part that the amendments be effective July 1, 2013, further provided in part that "[t]hese amendments apply to all actions or proceedings pending on or commenced after the effective date provided that ... amendments to Minn. R. Civ. P. 26 apply only to actions commenced on or after the effective date provided that the court may in any case direct the parties to comply with all or part of the rule as part of a pretrial order.", and further provided that the "February 4, 2013 and February 12, 2013 orders of the court are hereby rescinded to the extent inconsistent with this order."

Rule 26.07. Signing of Discovery Requests, Responses and Objections

In addition to the requirements of Rule 33.01(d), every request for discovery or response or objection thereto made by a party represented by an attorney shall be signed by at least one attorney of record in the attorney's individual name, whose address shall be stated. A party who is not represented by an attorney shall sign the request, response, or objection and state the party's address. The signature constitutes a certification that the attorney or party has read the request, response, or objection, and that to the best of the signer's knowledge, information, and belief formed after a reasonable inquiry it is: (1) consistent with these rules and warranted by existing law or a good faith argument for the extension, modification, or reversal of existing law; (2) not interposed for any improper purpose, such as to harass or to cause unnecessary delay or needless increase in the cost of litigation; and (3) not unreasonable or unduly burdensome or expensive, given the needs of the case, the discovery had in the case, the amount in controversy, and the importance of the issues at stake in the litigation. If a request, response, or objection is not signed, it shall be stricken unless it is signed promptly after the omission is called to the attention of the party making the request, response or objection and a party shall not be obligated to take any action with respect to it until it is signed.

If a certification is made in violation of this rule, the court, upon motion or upon its own initiative, shall impose upon the person who made the certification, the party on whose behalf the request, response, or objection is made, or both, an appropriate sanction, which may include an order to pay the amount of the reasonable expenses incurred because of the violation, including reasonable attorney fees.

Adopted March 21, 1985, eff. July 1, 1985. Revised Oct. 18, 1988, eff. Jan. 1, 1989.

Advisory Committee Note—1985

Rule 26.07 is entirely new. The rule adopts the 1982 amendment to the Federal Rules, particularly Rule 26(g), verbatim. Discovery requests and responses are subject to the certification requirements of Rule 11. All discovery requests and responses must be signed by an attorney if a party is represented by an attorney. This requirement is in addition to Rule 33.01(4)'s requirement that interrogatory answers be signed under oath by the party. The purpose of the rule is to discourage parties from engaging in unjustifiable discovery conduct, including making frivolous or unnecessary discovery requests, making deceptive or non-responsive answers to discovery requests, and interposing ill-founded and groundless objections to discovery.

The Committee believes the discovery practices of most Minnesota attorneys presently comply with the spirit and purpose of the rule. The Committee considers the change appropriate, however, to discourage those attorneys who abuse discovery, thereby increasing the cost of litigation and imposing an unnecessary burden on the court system.

Historical Notes

Former Rule: A former Rule 26.07, adopted June 25, 1951, and revised March 3, 1959, and November 10, 1967, related to depositions in arbitration.

RULE 27. DEPOSITIONS BEFORE ACTION OR PENDING APPEAL

Rule 27.01. Before Action

(a) Petition. A person who desires to perpetuate testimony regarding any matter may file a verified petition in the district court of the county of the residence of an expected adverse party. The petition shall be entitled in the name of the petitioner and shall show

(1) that the petitioner expects to be a party to an action but is presently unable to bring it or cause it to be brought;

(2) the subject matter of the expected action and the petitioner's interest therein;

(3) the facts which the petitioner desires to establish by the proposed testimony and the reasons for desiring to perpetuate it;

(4) the names or a description of the persons the petitioner expects will be adverse parties and their addresses so far as known; and

(5) the names and addresses of the persons to be examined and the substance of the testimony which the petitioner expects to elicit from each.

The petition shall ask for an order authorizing the petitioner to take the deposition of those persons to be examined as named in the petition, for the purpose of perpetuating their testimony.

(b) Notice and Service. The petitioner shall thereafter serve a notice upon each person named in the petition as an expected adverse party, together with a copy of the petition, stating that the petitioner will apply to the court, at a time and place named therein, for the order described in the petition. At least 20 days before the date of hearing, the notice shall be served either within or outside the state in the manner provided in Rule 4.03 for service of summons; but if such service cannot with due diligence be made upon any expected adverse party named in the petition, the court may make such order as is just for service by publication or otherwise, and shall appoint, for persons not served in the manner provided in Rule 4.03, an attorney who shall represent them, and, in case they are not otherwise represented, shall cross-examine the deponent. If any expected adverse party is a minor or incompetent, the provisions of Rule 17.02 apply.

(c) Order and Examination. If the court is satisfied that the perpetuation of testimony may prevent a failure or delay of justice, it shall make an order designating and describing the persons whose depositions may be taken and specifying the subject matter of the examination and whether the depositions shall be taken upon oral examination or written interrogatories. The deposition may then be taken in accordance with these rules and the court may make orders authorized by Rules 34 and 35. For the purpose of applying these rules to depositions for perpetuating testimony, each reference therein to the court in which the action is pending shall be deemed to refer to the court in which the petition for such deposition was filed.

(d) Use of Deposition. If a deposition to perpetuate testimony is taken pursuant to these rules or if, although not so taken, it would be admissible in evidence in the courts of the state in which it is taken, it may be used in any action involving the same subject matter subsequently brought in this state, in accordance with the provisions of Rule 32.01.

Adopted June 25, 1951, eff. Jan. 1, 1952. Amended Dec. 6, 1951. Revised Oct. 18, 1988, eff. Jan. 1, 1989.

Rule 27.02. Pending Appeal

If an appeal has been taken from a judgment or order, or before the taking of an appeal if the time therefor has not expired, the district court in which the judgment or order was rendered may allow the taking of the deposition of witnesses to perpetuate their testimony for use in the event of further proceedings in the district court. In such case, the party who desires to perpetuate the testimony may make a motion in the district court for leave to take the depositions, upon the same notice and service thereof as if the action was pending in the district court. The motion shall show the names, addresses, the substance of the testimony expected to be elicited from each person to be examined, and the reasons for perpetuating their testimony. If the court finds that the perpetuation of the testimony is proper to avoid a failure or delay of justice, it may make an order allowing the depositions to be taken and may make orders authorized by Rules 34 and 35, and thereupon the depositions may be taken and used in the same manner and under the same conditions as are prescribed in these rules for depositions taken in actions pending in the district court.

Adopted June 25, 1951, eff. Jan. 1, 1952. Amended Nov. 26, 1969. Revised Oct. 18, 1988, eff. Jan. 1, 1989.

Rule 27.03. Perpetuation by Action

This rule does not limit the power of the court to entertain an action to perpetuate testimony.

Adopted June 25, 1951, eff. Jan. 1, 1952. Revised Oct. 18, 1988, eff. Jan. 1, 1989.

RULE 28. PERSONS BEFORE WHOM DEPOSITIONS MAY BE TAKEN

Rule 28.01. Within the United States

Within the United States or within a territory or insular possession subject to the jurisdiction of the United States, depositions shall be taken before an officer authorized to administer oaths by the laws of the United States or of the place where the examination is held, or before a person appointed by the court in which the action is pending. The term "officer" as used in Rules 28, 30, 31 and 32 includes a person appointed by the court or designated by the parties pursuant to Rule 29. A person so appointed has power to administer oaths and take testimony.

Adopted June 25, 1951, eff. Jan. 1, 1952. Amended Nov. 30, 1981. Revised Oct. 18, 1988, eff. Jan. 1, 1989.

Rule 28.02. In Foreign Countries

Depositions may be taken in a foreign country (1) pursuant to any applicable treaty or convention, or (2) pursuant to a letter of request (whether or not captioned a letter rogatory), or (3) on notice before a person authorized to administer oaths in the place where the examination is held, either by the law thereof or by the law of the United States, or (4) before a person commissioned by the court, and a person so commissioned shall have the power by virtue of the commission to administer any necessary oath and take testimony. A commission or a letter of request shall be issued on application and notice and on terms that are just and appropriate. It is not requisite to the issuance of a commission or a letter of request that the taking of the deposition in any other manner is impracticable or inconvenient; and both a commission and a letter of request may be issued in proper cases. A notice or commission may designate the person before whom the deposition is to be taken either by name or descriptive title. A letter of request may be addressed "To the Appropriate Authority in [here name the country]." When a letter of request or any other device is used pursuant to any applicable treaty or convention, it shall be captioned in the form prescribed by that treaty or convention. Evidence obtained in response to a letter of request need not be excluded merely because it is not a verbatim transcript, because the testimony was not taken under oath, or because of any similar departure from the requirements for depositions taken within the United States under these rules.

Adopted June 25, 1951, eff. Jan. 1, 1952. Amended Nov. 10, 1967, eff. Feb. 1, 1968. Revised Oct. 18, 1988, eff. Jan. 1, 1989. Amended Nov. 22, 1996, eff. Jan. 1, 1997.

Advisory Committee Comments—1996 Amendments

This change conforms the rule to its federal counterpart. The committee believes it is especially desirable to have this rule identical to the federal rule because of its subject matter. In addition to the usual factors favoring uniformity, this is a provision governed largely by federal law and which may need to be understood and applied by court reporters, consular or embassy officials, and other nonlawyers. Conformity to the federal rule increases the prospects that the rule will be followed and will not impose significant additional burdens on the litigants.

Historical Notes

The order of the Minnesota Supreme Court [C6-84-2134] dated November 22, 1996, provides in part that the "(a)mendments shall apply to all actions pending on the effective date [January 1, 1997] and to those filed thereafter" and that "(t)he inclusion of Advisory Committee comments is made for convenience and does not reflect court approval of the comments made therein".

Rule 28.03. Disqualification for Interest

No deposition shall be taken before or reported by any person who is a relative or employee or attorney or counsel of any of the parties, or is a relative or employee of such attorney or counsel, or is financially interested in the action, or who has a contract with the party, attorney, or person with an interest in the action that affects or has a substantial tendency to affect impartiality.

Adopted June 25, 1951, eff. Jan. 1, 1952. Revised Oct. 18, 1988, eff. Jan. 1, 1989.

RULE 29. STIPULATIONS REGARDING DISCOVERY PROCEDURE

Unless otherwise directed by the court the parties may by stipulation (1) provide that depositions may be taken before any person, at any time or place, upon any notice, and in any manner, and when so taken may be used like other depositions, and (2) modify other procedures governing or limitations placed upon discovery, except that stipulations extending the time provided in Rules 33, 34, and 36 for responses to discovery may, if they would interfere with any time set for completion of discovery, for hearing of a motion, or for trial, be made only with the approval of the court.

Adopted June 25, 1951, eff. Jan. 1, 1952. Amended Nov. 14, 1974, eff. Jan. 1, 1975. Revised Oct. 18, 1988, eff. Jan. 1, 1989. Amended Nov. 22, 1996, eff. Jan. 1, 1997.

Advisory Committee Comments—1996 Amendments

This change conforms the rule to its federal counterpart. The committee believes it is desirable to permit stipulations regarding discovery whenever those stipulations do not impact the court's handling of the action. Particularly in state court practice, it is often necessary to extend discovery deadlines—without affecting other case management deadlines—and the parties should be encouraged to do so. Counsel agreeing to discovery after a deadline should not expect court assistance in enforcing discovery obligations nor should non-completion affect any other motions, hearings, or other case management procedures.

Historical Notes

The order of the Minnesota Supreme Court [C6-84-2134] dated November 22, 1996, provides in part that the "(a)mendments shall apply to all actions pending on the effective date [January 1, 1997] and to those filed thereafter" and that "(t)he inclusion of Advisory Committee comments is made for convenience and does not reflect court approval of the comments made therein".

RULE 30. DEPOSITIONS UPON ORAL EXAMINATION

Rule 30.01. When Depositions May Be Taken

After service of the summons, any party may take the testimony of any person, including a party, by deposition upon oral examination. Leave of court, granted with or without notice, must be obtained only if the plaintiff seeks to take a deposition prior to the expiration of 30 days after service of the summons and complaint upon any defendant or service made pursuant to Rule 4.04, except that leave is not required if a defendant has served a notice of taking deposition or otherwise sought discovery. The attendance of witnesses may be compelled by subpoena as provided in Rule 45.

Adopted Nov. 14, 1974, eff. Jan. 1, 1975. Revised Oct. 18, 1988, eff. Jan. 1, 1989. Amended May 21, 2007, eff. July 1, 2007.

Advisory Committee Note—1975

Rule 30 contains the provisions in the former Rule 26.01 which under the amendments becomes Rule 30.01, and former Rule 26.03 which under the amendments becomes Rule 30.03. Protective orders formerly contained in Rule 30.02 have been transferred to Rule 26.03.

The proposed amended Rule 30.01 liberalizes the procedure for serving notice of taking of deposition. Changes made in the proposed Rule 30.01 from the former provision in Rule 26.01 are as follows:

1. The prohibition against a plaintiff taking a deposition is extended to 30 days from 20 days.

2. The 30 day prohibition period is measured from the service of the summons and complaint rather than from the technical commencement of the action.

3. The rule no longer provides that discovery may be used for discovery or for evidence or for both purposes although this multiple and alternative use is still applicable.

4. Leave of court is not required for plaintiff to take a deposition if defendant has served notice of taking of deposition or has otherwise sought discovery.

5. Reference to taking the deposition of a person confined in prison has been eliminated from this rule.

6. Leave of court is not required if a special situation exists as provided in Rule 30.02(2).

In particular, it must be noted that the critical time under the amended Rule 30.01 is the time of the taking of the discovery deposition, not the time of giving the notice. The notice of taking a deposition can be served immediately by the plaintiff if the deposition is not to be taken until more than 30 days after service of the summons and complaint. Service of notice no longer gives that party priority for the taking of depositions under Rule 26.04.

Advisory Committee Comment—2007 Amendment

Rule 30.01 is amended only to delete a reference to a notice procedure in former Rule 30.02(b), which was abrogated in 1996. The amendment merely conforms the rule to the current procedure.

Historical Notes

Former Rule: A former Rule 30.01 adopted June 25, 1951, and revised March 3, 1959, and November 10, 1967, related to notice of a deposition upon oral examination. The subject matter of former Rule 30.01 was incorporated into Rule 30.02 by court order dated November 14, 1974.

Rule 30.02. Notice of Examination; General Requirements; Special Notice; Non–Stenographic Method of Recording; Production of Documents and Things; Deposition of Organization; Depositions by Telephone

(a) Notice. A party desiring to take the deposition of any person upon oral examination shall give reasonable notice in writing to every other party to the action. The notice shall state the name and place for taking the deposition and the name and address of each person to be examined, if known, and, if the name is not known, a general description sufficient to identify the person or the particular class or group to which the person belongs. If a subpoena duces tecum is to be served on the person to be examined, the designation of the materials to be produced as set forth in the subpoena shall be attached to or included in the notice.

(b) Notice of Method of Recording. The party taking the deposition shall state in the notice the method by which the testimony shall be recorded. Unless the court orders otherwise, it may be recorded by sound, sound-and-visual, or stenographic means, and the party taking the deposition shall bear the cost of the recording. Any party may arrange for a transcription to be made from the recording of a deposition taken by non-stenographic means.

(c) Additional Recording Method. With prior notice to the deponent and other parties, any party may designate another method to record the deponent's testimony in addition to the method specified by the person taking the deposition. The additional record or transcript shall be made at that party's expense unless the court otherwise orders.

Any deposition pursuant to these rules may be taken by means of simultaneous audio and visual electronic recording without leave of court or stipulation of the parties if the deposition is taken in accordance with the provisions of this rule.

In addition to the specific provisions of this rule, the taking of video depositions is governed by all other rules governing the taking of depositions unless the nature of the video deposition makes compliance impossible or unnecessary.

(d) Role of Officer. Unless otherwise agreed by the parties, a deposition shall be conducted before an officer appointed or designated under Rule 28 and shall begin with a statement on the record by the officer that includes (A) the officer's name and business address; (B) the date, time, and place of the deposition; (C) the name of the deponent; (D) the administration of the oath or affirmation to the deponent; and (E) an identification of all persons present. If the deposition is recorded other than stenographically, the officer shall repeat items (A) through (C) at the beginning of each unit of recorded tape or other recording medium. The appearance or demeanor of deponents or attorneys shall not be distorted through camera or sound-recording techniques. At the end of the deposition, the officer shall state on the record that the deposition is complete and shall set forth any stipulations made by counsel concerning the custody of the transcript or recording and the exhibits, or concerning other pertinent matters.

(e) Production of Documents. The notice to a party deponent may be accompanied by a request made in compliance with Rule 34 for the production of documents and tangible things at the taking of the deposition. The procedure of Rule 34 shall apply to the request.

(f) Deposition of Organization. A party may in the party's notice and in a subpoena name as the deponent a public or private corporation or a partnership, association, or governmental agency and describe with reasonable particularity the matters on which examination is requested. In that event, the organization so named shall designate one or more officers, directors, or managing agents, or other persons who consent to testify on its behalf, and may set forth, for each person designated, the matters on which the person will testify. A subpoena shall advise a non-party organization of its duty to make such a designation. The persons so designated shall testify as to matters known or reasonably available to the organization. This provision does not preclude taking a deposition by any other procedure authorized in these rules.

(g) Telephonic Depositions. The parties may stipulate in writing or the court may upon motion order that a deposition be taken by telephone or other remote electronic means. For the purposes of this rule and Rules 28.01, 37.01(a), 37.02(a) and 45.03, a deposition taken by such means is taken in the district and at the place where the deponent is to answer questions.

Adopted Nov. 14, 1974, eff. Jan. 1, 1975. Revised Oct. 18, 1988, eff. Jan. 1, 1989. Amended Dec. 20, 1993, eff. March 1, 1994; Nov. 22, 1996, eff. Jan. 1, 1997; Nov. 30, 2005, eff. Jan. 1, 2006.

Advisory Committee Note—1975

Subd. (1).

The provisions in existing Rule 30.02 providing protective orders have been transferred to Rule 26.03. The provisions in Rule 30.01 relating to notice of the taking of depositions have been transferred to proposed amended Rule 30.02(1). A subpoena duces tecum can be used in conjunction with the taking of the deposition notice under Rule 30.02(1). If a party desires to obtain production of documents from another party, Rule 34 should be used rather than the subpoena duces tecum. Rule 30.02(5) requires a party to use the liberalized Rule 34 for the production of documents.

Subd. (2).

This rule is not applicable if a party has obtained an ex parte court order for an early deposition under Rule 30.01. The unnumbered second paragraph of this rule is not applicable to an early deposition obtained pursuant to court order under Rule 30.01. The amended Federal Rule 30(b)(2) followed a procedure in maritime law in which an early deposition was authorized when there was difficulty or impossibility in taking a deposition because the witness was about to part from the court's jurisdiction. The purpose for the amendment is to expedite the taking of depositions in those circumstances where leave of court may be difficult or too time consuming. It also reflects the general policy of the rules to encourage deposition practice without unnecessary court intervention. In applying the Federal provision to state practice the Advisory Committee and the State Bar Committee agreed that the Federal Court's 100 mile limitation and reference to court districts were not applicable to state practice. Subpoenas in Minnesota district courts are state-wide.

"Unavailability" should mean to all forms of unavailability for the taking of the deposition including absence from the state or a witness being beyond the jurisdiction of the subpoena power of the state. The fact that a deposition may be taken in a foreign jurisdiction at an increased expense or a later time is not deemed to be a sufficient alternative option to the taking of the deposition within the state within the 30 day prohibited period. The second paragraph protects a party if through the exercise of due diligence he is unable to obtain an attorney to represent him at the taking of the deposition. The Advisory Committee clarified the language proposed by the State Bar Committee to make clear that the unavailability for examination relates to unavailability to be examined within the state. In like measure, the second paragraph was clarified to provide that the rule applies to the deposition of both party and non-party deponents.

Subd. (3).

The rule conforms to the recommendations of the Minnesota State Bar Association Committee and the corresponding Federal rule. The rule anticipates a motion upon notice and hearing rather than an ex parte motion. The primary reason for requiring notice and a showing of cause is to permit the party noting the taking of the deposition to have an equal opportunity to explain to the court why the deposition was set at a particular time. Both parties will now have an opportunity to explain their position to the court before a change is made in the time set.

Subd. (4).

The rule follows the corresponding Federal rule and does not require that every electronic recording of the deposition have a backup stenographic recording of the deposition also. However, the rule recognizes that the court in its order should consider the nature of the electronic means being employed, the importance of the testimony and the need to assure accuracy and the preservation of the testimony.

Subd. (5).

The rule is as provided by the Minnesota State Bar Association Committee and conforms to the corresponding Federal rule. A subpoena duces tecum is not available to a party deponent when the person noting the taking of the deposition desires production of documents to be used at the time of the deposition and therefore the party must use the procedure of Rule 34.

Subd. (6).

As proposed by the Advisory Committee, this rule should be considered as a new discovery procedure. The rule permits a public or private corporation, partnership, association or governmental agency to designate one or more of its officers, directors, managing agents or other persons to testify on its behalf. This procedure eliminates problems formerly associated with taking the deposition of legal entities when the party desiring to take the deposition did not know either the name or status of proper entity officers or managing agents. This rule also is intended to eliminate the situation where depositions of numerous officers, agents or representatives would be noticed by a party and each of the deponents would indicate that he did not have the particularized knowledge of the matter under examination, but that some other representative had the desired information. Under the rule as proposed, the party in his notice can name the entity as the deponent and describe with reasonable particularity the matters on which he desires examination. Such a notice then imposes a responsibility upon the organization to designate one or more persons to testify on its behalf. The organization may by its response limit the areas in which each person designated will testify. Persons so designated must testify as to all matters known or reasonably available to the organization.

The last sentence of the proposed rule removes any uncertainty regarding the availability of depositions specifically naming designated corporate officers or others when the party believes that the deposition of such designated corporate officer, managing agent, etc. must be taken. A further clear effect of the proposed amended rule is to permit a corporation to protect itself by designating those who can make evidentiary admissions on behalf of the corporation through the deposition procedure.

The rule as proposed is substantially identical with the corresponding Federal rule. The only changes made are to clarify a possible ambiguity regarding the nature of the notice by adding in the first sentence the words "and in a subpoena" following the word "notice," and to change the word "designate" to the word "describe" in the first sentence of the rule. A new sentence has been added to clarify any possible ambiguity regarding the application of this procedure to a non-party organization whose deposition is to be taken and who will be asked to produce documents under Rule 45. The sentence provides that the subpoena shall advise a non-party organization of its duty to make such a designation.

Advisory Committee Comment—1993 Amendments

Rule 30.02(d)(1) is amended to change slightly the arrangements for handling the videotape record of a deposition taken by that means. At the present time the rule requires the videotape operator to retain possession of the videotape, a circumstance which sometimes makes it difficult to procure the videotape for use at a trial which takes place long after the deposition was taken. The amendment directs the lawyer for the party taking the deposition to retain custody of the video recording after it has been sealed and marked for identification purposes. This procedure is consistent with the procedure for handling original typewritten deposition transcripts pursuant to Minn.R.Civ.P. 30.06(a).

When the Advisory Committee recommended the addition of Rule 30.02(h) in 1988, the members of the committee hoped that it would be a useful device for curbing discovery abuses, but it appears that the rule is almost never used. The deletion of this portion of the rule should not be taken as any support for expanded discovery. The authority to control discovery is amply set forth in other rules, see, e.g., Minn.Gen.R.Prac. 111 & 112, and the committee encourages the continued vigorous exercise of this authority for the protection of all litigants and to carry out the mandate of Minn. R.Civ.P. 1, which provides that the Rules of Civil Procedure "shall be construed to secure the just, speedy, and inexpensive determination of every action."

Advisory Committee Comment—2006 Amendment

Rule 30.02 is amended only to add subsection titles. This change is made for convenience and consistency with the style of other rules, and is not intended to affect the rule's interpretation. Rule 30.02(g) is amended to renumber one of the rule cross-references to reflect the amendment and renumbering of Rule 45 as part of the amendments effective January 1, 2006.

Historical Notes

The order of the Minnesota Supreme Court [C6-84-2134] dated November 22, 1996, provides in part that the "(a)mendments shall apply to all actions pending on the effective date [January 1, 1997] and to those filed thereafter" and that "(t)he inclusion of Advisory Committee comments is made for convenience and does not reflect court approval of the comments made therein".

Former Rule: A former Rule 30.02 adopted June 25, 1951, and amended March 3, 1959, related to orders for the protection of parties and witnesses. The subject matter of former Rule 30.01 was incorporated into Rule 26.03 by court order dated November 14, 1974.

Rule 30.03. Examination and Cross-Examination; Record of Examination; Oath; Objections

Examination and cross-examination of witnesses may proceed as permitted at the trial under the provisions of the Minnesota Rules of Evidence except Rules 103 and 615. The officer before whom the deposition is to be taken shall put the witness on oath or affirmation and shall personally, or by someone acting under the officer's direction and in the officer's presence, record the testimony of the witness. The testimony shall be taken stenographically or recorded by any other means ordered in accordance with Rule 30.02(d). If requested by one of the parties, the testimony shall be transcribed.

All objections made at the time of the examination to the qualifications of the officer taking the deposition, to the manner of taking it, to the evidence presented, to the conduct of any party, or to any other aspect of the proceedings shall be noted by the officer upon the deposition; but the examination shall proceed, with the testimony being taken subject to the objections. In lieu of participating in the oral examination, a party may serve written questions in a sealed envelope on the party taking the deposition and the party taking the deposition shall transmit them to the officer, who shall propound them to the witness and record the answers verbatim.

Adopted June 25, 1951, eff. Jan. 1, 1952. Amended Nov. 14, 1974, eff. Jan. 1, 1975. Revised Oct. 18, 1988, eff. Jan. 1, 1989. Amended Nov. 22, 1996, eff. Jan. 1, 1997.

Advisory Committee Note—1975

The rule is identical to the corresponding Federal rule. In the first paragraph the rule has been changed from the former Minnesota rule by requiring that a party request the stenographic transcription if the testimony is to be transcribed. The former rule required the transcription unless all parties agreed that it need not be transcribed.

Historical Notes

The order of the Minnesota Supreme Court [C6-84-2134] dated November 22, 1996, provides in part that the "(a)mendments shall apply to all actions pending on the effective date [January 1, 1997] and to those filed thereafter" and that "(t)he inclusion of Advisory Committee comments is made for convenience and does not reflect court approval of the comments made therein".

Rule 30.04. Schedule and Duration; Motion to Terminate or Limit Examination

(a) Objections. Any objection to evidence during a deposition shall be stated concisely and in a non-argumentative and non-suggestive manner. A person may instruct a deponent not to answer only when necessary to preserve a privilege, to enforce a limitation on evidence directed by the court, or to present a motion under paragraph (d).

(b) Duration. Unless otherwise authorized by the court or stipulated by the parties, a deposition is limited to one day of seven hours. The court must allow additional time consistent with Rule 26.02(a) if needed for a fair examination of the deponent or if the deponent or another person, or other circumstance, impedes or delays the examination.

(c) Sanctions. If the court finds such an impediment, delay, or other conduct that has frustrated the fair examination of the deponent, it may impose upon the persons responsible an appropriate sanction, including the reasonable costs and attorney's fees incurred by any parties as a result thereof.

(d) Suspension of Examination. At any time during a deposition, on motion of a party or of the deponent and upon a showing that the examination is being conducted in bad faith or in such manner as unreasonably to annoy, embarrass, or oppress the deponent or party, the court in which the action is pending or the court in the district where the deposition is being taken may order the officer conducting the examination to cease forthwith from taking the deposition, or may limit the scope and manner of the taking of the deposition as provided in Rule 26.03. If the order made terminates the examination, it shall be resumed thereafter only upon the order of the court in which the action is pending. Upon demand of the objecting party or deponent, the taking of the deposition shall be suspended for the time necessary to make a motion for an order. The provisions of Rule 37.01(d) apply to the award of expenses incurred in relation to the motion.

Adopted June 25, 1951, eff. Jan. 1, 1952. Amended Dec. 6, 1951; Nov. 14, 1974, eff. Jan. 1, 1975. Revised Oct. 18, 1988, eff. Jan. 1, 1989. Amended Nov. 22, 1996, eff. Jan. 1, 1997; Nov. 30, 2005, eff. Jan. 1, 2006; Feb. 29, 2008, eff. Feb. 29, 2008.

Advisory Committee Note—1975

The proposed amendment to Rule 30.04 makes minor modifications in the existing Rule 30.04. A primary difference is found in the last sentence of the proposed rule where the court in granting or refusing the motion may impose expenses and costs upon the attorney as well as upon the party or witness.

Advisory Committee Comments—1996 Amendments

These amendments substantially conforms the rule to its federal counterpart. The committee believes it is particularly desirable to have the rules governing the mechanics of taking depositions conform to the federal rules because many depositions are taken for use in parallel state and federal proceedings or in distant locations before reporters who can be expected to know the federal procedures but may not know idiosyncratic Minnesota rules.

Rule 30.04 is largely new and includes important provisions governing the conduct of depositions. Most important is Rule 30.04(a), which is intended to constrain the conduct of attorneys at depositions. The rule limits deposition objections to concise statements that are directed to the record and not so suggesting a possible answer to the deponent. This rule is intended to set a high standard for conduct of depositions. The problem of deposition misconduct, though probably not as severe as has been noted in some reported cases, is still a frequent and unfortunate part of Minnesota practice. *See, e.g., Hall v. Clifton Precision*, 150 F.R.D. 525 (E.D.Pa.1993); *Paramount Communications, Inc. v. QVC Network, Inc.*, 637 A.2d 34, 51–57 (Del.1994); *Kelvey v. Coughlin*, 625 A.2d 775 (R.I.1993).

Rule 30.06 is amended to follow its federal counterpart, retaining the existing mechanism for delivering transcripts of depositions to the lawyer or party noticing the deposition rather than filing them with the court. This difference is necessary because Minn.R.Civ.P. 5.04 does not permit filing discovery in the absence of an order.

Advisory Committee Comment—2006 Amendment

Rule 30.04(a) is amended to remove an ambiguity in the current rule. As amended, the rule expressly extends the prohibition against improper instruction of a deponent not to answer to all persons (including counsel for a non-party witness), instead of just "parties."

Rule 30.04(b) is amended to adopt a specific time limit on depositions. Although parties may agree to a longer deposition and the court can determine that longer examination is appropriate, a deposition is made subject to a limit of one day lasting seven hours. This amendment is identical to the change in Fed. R. Civ. P. 30(d)(2) made in 2000. The purpose of this amendment is to decrease the burden of discovery on witnesses and to encourage focused examination of all deponents. Where the examining party engages in proper and focused examination and encounters unhelpful responses or inappropriate objections, or where the issues in the case dictate that additional time is necessary to permit a fair examination, the court is required to provide it. The rule establishes a presumptive limit on the length of depositions, not the presumptive length. Most depositions will continue to be much shorter than seven hours, and the rule does not limit courts from establishing shorter time limits in particular cases.

Historical Notes

The order of the Minnesota Supreme Court [C6-84-2134] dated November 22, 1996, provides in part that the "(a)mendments shall apply to all actions pending on the effective date [January 1, 1997] and to those filed thereafter" and that "(t)he inclusion of Advisory Committee comments is made for convenience and does not reflect court approval of the comments made therein".

Rule 30.05. Review by Witness; Changes; Signing

If requested by the deponent or a party before completion of the deposition, the deponent shall have 30 days after being notified by the officer that the transcript or recording is available in which to review the transcript or recording and, if there are changes in form or substance, to sign a statement reciting such changes and the reasons given by the deponent for making them. The officer shall indicate in the certificate prescribed by Rule 30.06(1) whether any review was requested and, if so, shall append any changes made by the deponent during the period allowed.

Adopted June 25, 1951, eff. Jan. 1, 1952. Amended Nov. 14, 1974, eff. Jan. 1, 1975. Revised Oct. 18, 1988, eff. Jan. 1, 1989. Amended Nov. 22, 1996, eff. Jan. 1, 1997.

Advisory Committee Note—1975

A primary change in the proposed rule is the provision permitting the officer to sign the deposition if the witness does not do so in 30 days of the time it is submitted to him. If the deposition is signed by the officer it may be used as though it was signed by the party unless a motion to suppress it has been made under Rule 32.04(4).

In the first sentence the Advisory Committee has changed the word "fully" to the word "stenographically" to conform more clearly to the recommended procedure of Rule 30.02(4). In the second sentence the word "desired" has been changed to "desires" to conform more clearly to the present tense of the rules.

Historical Notes

The order of the Minnesota Supreme Court [C6-84-2134] dated November 22, 1996, provides in part that the "(a)mendments shall apply to all actions pending on the effective date [January 1, 1997] and to those filed thereafter" and that "(t)he inclusion of Advisory Committee comments is made for convenience and does not reflect court approval of the comments made therein".

Rule 30.06. Certification and Filing by Officer; Exhibits; Copies; Notices of Filing

(a) Certification by Officer; Exhibits. The officer shall certify that the witness was duly sworn by the officer and that the deposition is a true record of the testimony given by the witness, and shall certify that the deposition has been transcribed, that the cost of the original has been charged to the party who noticed the deposition, and that all parties who ordered copies have been charged at the same rate for such copies. This certificate shall be in writing and accompany the record of the deposition. Unless otherwise ordered by the court or agreed to by the parties the officer shall securely seal the deposition in an envelope or package endorsed with the title of the action and marked "Deposition of (herein insert the name of witness)," and shall promptly send it to the attorney or party who arranged for the transcript or recording, who shall store it under conditions that will protect it against loss, destruction, tampering, or deterioration.

Documents and things produced for inspection during the examination of the witness shall, upon the request of a party, be marked for identification and annexed to the deposition and may be inspected and copied by any party, except that if the person producing the materials desires to retain them, the person may (1) offer copies to be marked for identification and annexed to the deposition and to serve thereafter as originals if the person affords to all parties fair opportunity to verify the copies by comparison with the originals, or (2) offer the originals to be marked for identification, after giving each party an opportunity to inspect and copy them, in which event the materials may then be used in the same manner as if annexed to the deposition. Any party may move for an order that the original be annexed to and returned with the deposition pending final disposition of the case.

(b) Duties of Officer. Unless otherwise ordered by the court or agreed by the parties, the officer shall retain stenographic notes of any deposition taken stenographically or a copy of the recording of any deposition taken by another method. Upon payment of reasonable charges therefor, the officer shall furnish a copy of the transcript or other recording of the deposition to any party or to the deponent.

(c) Notice of Receipt of Transcript. The party taking the deposition shall give prompt notice of its receipt from the officer to all other parties.

Adopted June 25, 1951, eff. Jan. 1, 1952. Amended March 3, 1959, eff. July 1, 1959; Nov. 14, 1974, eff. Jan. 1, 1975; Nov. 30, 1981; March 21, 1985, eff. July 1, 1985. Revised Oct. 18, 1988, eff. Jan. 1, 1989. Amended Nov. 22, 1996, eff. Jan. 1, 1997; Nov. 30, 2005, eff. Jan. 1, 2006.

Advisory Committee Note—1975

Subd. (1).

The Advisory Committee recommended modification in the first paragraph by striking the last clause "or, if the deposition was taken under Rule 26.07 (32.04) to an arbitrator". The Advisory Committee determined that the use of depositions in the arbitration proceeding as provided in Rule 32.04, as recommended by the State Bar Committee, was a reference to a procedure no longer applicable under existing state law. M.S.A. § 572.30, subd. 3, provides that the Rules of Civil Procedure shall not apply to arbitration insofar as they may be inconsistent with the statute. Under the existing statute the Committee believed that a special rule relative to arbitrations is no longer desirable.

The second paragraph provides a more flexible procedure for the handling of exhibits produced for inspection during the examination of a witness. Upon the request of a party such documents may be marked for identification and annexed to and returned with the deposition. It may be inspected and copied thereafter by any party. A party producing the original may substitute copies to be marked for identification if he affords all parties a full opportunity to verify the accuracy of the copies by comparison with the original. Originals may be returned to party producing them under the provision of Rule 30.06(1)(B). If the originals are to be annexed and retained with the deposition, a court order is appropriate for such purpose.

Subd. (2).

The rule as proposed is identical to the existing Rule 30.06(2) except the word "witness" has been changed to "deponent".

Subd. (3).

The rule as proposed is identical to the existing Rule 30.06(3).

Advisory Committee Note—1985

The change to Rule 30.06 is made in conjunction with the recommended changes to Rule 5. Because Rule 5 does not require deposition transcripts routinely to be filed, Rule 30 should be amended to remove the requirement that the court reporter file the transcripts.

The Committee also considered the question of whether the court reporter or the attorneys for the parties are more suitable custodians of the deposition transcripts. The Committee determined that it is more efficient and convenient for the attorney or party taking the deposition to have custody of the original transcripts. The rule continues to require that the court reporter seal the deposition in an envelope with the title of the action on the outside. This requirement will become especially important as attorneys retain custody of the original transcripts. In order to avoid any uncertainty about the retention of the original transcript, the rule requires that the person to whom the deposition is sent should be identified on the record.

Because the rule is changed to delete the requirement for filing, the requirement of Rule 30.06(3) is changed to make it unnecessary for notice of filing to be given. Notice of receipt of the transcripts by the party taking the deposition is required, although that notice may be waived by stipulation.

Advisory Committee Comments—1996 Amendments

These amendments substantially conforms the rule to its federal counterpart. The committee believes it is particularly desirable to have the rules governing the mechanics of taking depositions conform to the federal rules because many depositions are taken for use in parallel state and federal proceedings or in distant locations before reporters who can be expected to know the federal procedures but may not know idiosyncratic Minnesota rules.

Rule 30.04 is largely new and includes important provisions governing the conduct of depositions. Most important is Rule 30.04(a), which is intended to constrain the conduct of attorneys at depositions. The rule limits deposition objections to concise statements that are directed to the record and not so suggesting a possible answer to the deponent. This rule is intended to set a high standard for conduct of depositions. The problem of deposition misconduct, though probably not as severe as has been noted in some reported cases, is still a frequent and unfortunate part of Minnesota practice. *See, e.g., Hall v. Clifton Precision*, 150 F.R.D. 525 (E.D.Pa.1993); *Paramount Communications, Inc. v. QVC Network, Inc.*, 637 A.2d 34, 51–57 (Del.1994); *Kelvey v. Coughlin*, 625 A.2d 775 (R.I.1993).

Rule 30.06 is amended to follow its federal counterpart, retaining the existing mechanism for delivering transcripts of depositions to the lawyer or party noticing the deposition rather than filing them with the court. This difference is necessary because Minn.R.Civ.P. 5.04 does not permit filing discovery in the absence of an order.

Advisory Committee Comment—2006 Amendment

Rule 30.06 is amended only to add subsection titles. This change is made for convenience and consistency with the style of other rules, and is not intended to affect the rule's interpretation

Historical Notes

The order of the Minnesota Supreme Court [C6-84-2134] dated November 22, 1996, provides in part that the "(a)mendments shall apply to all actions pending on the effective date [January 1, 1997] and to those filed thereafter" and that "(t)he inclusion of Advisory Committee comments is made for convenience and does not reflect court approval of the comments made therein".

Rule 30.07. Failure to Attend or to Serve Subpoena; Expenses

(a) Failure of Party Noticing Deposition to Attend. If the party giving the notice of the taking of a deposition fails to attend and proceed therewith and another party attends in person or by attorney pursuant to the notice, the court may order the party giving the notice to pay to such other party the amount of the reasonable expenses incurred by the other party and the other party's attorney in so attending, including reasonable attorney fees.

(b) Failure to Serve Subpoena on Non–Party Witness. If the party giving the notice of the taking of a deposition of a witness fails to serve a subpoena upon that witness, and the witness because of such failure does not attend, and if another party attends in person or by attorney on the expectation that the deposition of that witness is to be taken, the court may order the party giving notice to pay to such other party the amount of the reasonable expenses incurred by those individuals in so attending, including reasonable attorney fees.

Adopted June 25, 1951, eff. Jan. 1, 1952. Amended Nov. 14, 1974, eff. Jan. 1, 1975. Revised Oct. 18, 1988, eff. Jan. 1, 1989. Amended Nov. 30, 2005, eff. Jan. 1, 2006.

Advisory Committee Note—1975

The rule as proposed is identical to the existing Rule 30.07.

Advisory Committee Comment—2006 Amendment

Rule 30.07 is amended only to add subsection titles. This change is made for convenience and consistency with the style of other rules, and is not intended to affect the rule's interpretation

RULE 31. DEPOSITIONS OF WITNESSES UPON WRITTEN QUESTIONS

RULE 31.01. Serving Questions; Notice

(a) A party may take the testimony of any person, including a party, by deposition upon written questions without leave of court except as provided in paragraph (2). The attendance of witnesses may be compelled by the use of subpoena as provided in Rule 45.

(b) A party must obtain leave of court, which shall be granted to the extent consistent with the principles stated in Rule 26.02(a), if the person to be examined is confined in prison or if, without the written stipulation of the parties, the person to be examined has already been deposed in the case.

(c) A party desiring to take a deposition upon written questions shall serve them upon every other party with a notice stating (1) the name and address of the person who is to answer them, if known, and if the name is not known, a general description sufficient to identify the person or the particular class or group to which the person belongs, and (2) the name or descriptive title and address of the officer before whom the deposition is to be taken. A deposition upon written questions may be taken of a public or private corporation or a partnership or association or governmental agency in accordance with the provisions of Rule 30.02(f).

(d) Within 14 days after the notice and written questions are served, a party may serve cross questions upon all other parties. Within 7 days after being served with cross questions, a party may serve redirect questions upon all other parties. Within 7 days after being served with redirect questions, a party may serve recross questions upon all other parties. The court may for cause shown enlarge or shorten the time.

Adopted June 25, 1951, eff. Jan. 1, 1952. Amended Nov. 14, 1974, eff. Jan. 1, 1975. Revised Oct. 18, 1988, eff. Jan. 1, 1989. Amended Nov. 22, 1996, eff. Jan. 1, 1997.

Advisory Committee Comments—1996 Amendments

This change conforms the rule to its federal counterpart. The federal rule was amended in 1993 to create a more usable mechanism for exchanging questions and submitting them to the witness. One goal of this change is to make depositions on written questions a more useful discovery device, recognizing that if it can be used effectively it has good potential for reducing the cost of litigation.

The amendment of this rule also serves the goal of facilitating the handling of these depositions by court reporters and others not regularly exposed to Minnesota practice.

Historical Notes

The order of the Minnesota Supreme Court [C6-84-2134] dated November 22, 1996, provides in part that the "(a)mendments shall apply to all actions pending on the effective date [January 1, 1997] and to those filed thereafter" and that "(t)he inclusion of Advisory Committee comments is made for convenience and does not reflect court approval of the comments made therein".

Rule 31.02. Officer to Take Responses and Prepare Record

A copy of the notice and copies of all questions served shall be delivered by the party taking the deposition to the officer designated in the notice, who shall proceed promptly, in the manner provided by Rules 30.03, 30.05, and 30.06, to take the testimony of the witness in response to the questions and to prepare, certify, and file or mail the deposition, attaching thereto the copy of the notice and the questions received by the officer.

Adopted June 25, 1951, eff. Jan. 1, 1952. Amended Nov. 14, 1974, eff. Jan. 1, 1975; March 21, 1985, eff. July 1, 1985. Revised Oct. 18, 1988, eff. Jan. 1, 1989. Amended Nov. 22, 1996, eff. Jan. 1, 1997.

Advisory Committee Comments—1996 Amendments

This change conforms the rule to its federal counterpart. The federal rule was amended in 1993 to create a more usable mechanism for exchanging questions and submitting them to the witness. One goal of this change is to make depositions on written questions a more useful discovery device, recognizing that if it can be used effectively it has good potential for reducing the cost of litigation.

The amendment of this rule also serves the goal of facilitating the handling of these depositions by court reporters and others not regularly exposed to Minnesota practice.

Historical Notes

The order of the Minnesota Supreme Court [C6-84-2134] dated November 22, 1996, provides in part that the "(a)mendments shall apply to all actions pending on the effective date [January 1, 1997] and to those filed thereafter" and that "(t)he inclusion of Advisory Committee comments is made for convenience and does not reflect court approval of the comments made therein".

Rule 31.03. Notice of Filing

When the deposition is received from the officer, the party taking it shall promptly give notice thereof to all other parties.

Adopted June 25, 1951, eff. Jan. 1, 1952. Amended Nov. 14, 1974, eff. Jan. 1, 1975; March 21, 1985, eff. July 1, 1985. Revised Oct. 18, 1988, eff. Jan. 1, 1989.

Advisory Committee Note—1975

The rule as proposed is identical to the former Rule 31.03.

Rule 31.04. Deleted Nov. 14, 1974, eff. Jan. 1, 1975

Advisory Committee Note—1975

Protective orders have been moved to Rule 26.03 in the renumbering and rearrangement of the rules. Former Rule 31.04 has been eliminated as surplusage.

Historical Notes

Former Rule 31.04, adopted June 25, 1951, related to orders for the protection of parties and witnesses. The subject matter of former Rule 31.04 was incorporated into Rule 26.03 by court order dated November 14, 1974.

RULE 32. USE OF DEPOSITIONS IN COURT PROCEEDINGS

Rule 32.01. Use of Depositions

At the trial or upon the hearing of a motion or an interlocutory proceeding, any part or all of a deposition, so far as admissible under the Minnesota Rules of Evidence applied as though the witness were then present and testifying, and subject to the provisions of Rule 32.02, may be used against any party who was present or represented at the taking of the deposition or who had reasonable notice thereof in accordance with any one of the following provisions:

(a) Any deposition may be used by any party for the purpose of contradicting or impeaching the testimony of deponent as a witness or for any purpose permitted by the Minnesota Rules of Evidence.

(b) The deposition of a party or of any one who at the time of taking the deposition was an officer, director, employee or managing agent or a person designated pursuant to Rules 30.02(f) or 31.01 to testify on behalf of a public or private corporation, partnership, association, or governmental agency which is a party may be used by an adverse party for any purpose.

(c) The deposition of a witness, whether or not a party, may be used by any party for any purpose if the court finds:

(1) that the witness is dead; or

(2) that the witness is at a greater distance than 100 miles from the place of trial or hearing, or is out of the state, unless it appears that the absence of the witness was procured by the party offering the deposition; or

(3) that the witness is unable to attend or testify because of age, sickness, infirmity, or imprisonment; or

(4) that the party offering the deposition has been unable to procure the attendance of the witness by subpoena; or

(5) upon application and notice, that such exceptional circumstances exist as to make it desirable, in the interest of justice and with due regard to the importance of presenting the testimony of witness orally in open court, to allow the deposition to be used.

(d) If only part of a deposition is offered in evidence by a party, an adverse party may require the offering party to introduce any other part which ought in fairness to be considered with the part introduced and any party may introduce any other parts.

Substitution of parties pursuant to Rule 25 does not affect the right to use depositions previously taken; and, when an action has been brought in any court of the United States or any state and another action involving the same subject matter is afterward brought between the same parties or their representatives or successors in interest, all depositions lawfully taken and duly filed in the former action may be used in the latter as if originally taken therefor. A deposition previously taken may also be used as permitted by the Minnesota Rules of Evidence.

Adopted Nov. 14, 1974, eff. Jan. 1, 1975. Amended Nov. 30, 1981. Revised Oct. 18, 1988, eff. Jan. 1, 1989.

Advisory Committee Note—1975

Rule 32 has been substantially changed in the rearrangement of the discovery rules. Rules 32.01, 32.02 and 32.03 represent the transfer of former Rules 26.04, 26.05 and 26.06. The provisions of the rule are generally the same although modifications have been made to conform with other amendments made in the discovery rules.

The Advisory Committee determined that M.S.A. § 572.14 eliminates the need for a special rule relative to depositions in arbitrations and therefore has recommended that the former Rule 26.07 not be readopted as Rule 32.04.

The first paragraph of Rule 32.01 has been modified to clearly provide that a deposition may be used at the hearing on a motion or at a trial insofar as it is admissible under the rules of evidence applied as though the witness was then present and testifying. The first paragraph was further amended by the Advisory Committee to provide that use of the deposition against a party who was present or represented at the taking is also subject to the provisions of Rule 32.02.

Amended Rule 32.01(1) has been modified by striking the final four words from the former rule. Impeachment or contradicting on material matters will occur as a matter of course and the limitation in the rule is confusing.

Rule 32.01(2) differs from the corresponding Federal rule by the addition of the word "employee" after the word "director." This variance from the Federal rule is in accordance with the recommendation of the Minnesota State Bar Association Committee. Inclusion of "employee" follows traditional practice in Minnesota to treat an employee the same as an officer, director or managing agent for discovery purposes. Even though the provisions of Rule 32.01(2) permit the use of the deposition of a party or a designated representative of the organization which is a party by an adverse party, the Committee stresses the importance for trial purposes of calling a witness to give his testimony on the witness stand rather than using the deposition as permitted under Rule 32.01(2). It is generally desirable for trial purposes to have a witness testify directly in the presence of the jury and thus enable the jury to determine credibility of the witness by personal observation. See Clark v. Wolkoff, 250 Minn. 504, 85 N.W.2d 401 (1957).

No change has been made in the proposed amendment to Rule 32.01(3) from the former Rule 26.04(3).

Rule 32.01(4) is modified by eliminating reference to parts of a deposition relevant to parts which the adverse party introduced and substituting a provision indicating that a part may be compelled which in fairness ought to be considered with the part introduced.

Historical Notes

Former Rule: A former Rule 32.01, adopted June 25, 1951, related to errors and irregularities in the notice for taking a deposition. The subject matter of former Rule 32.01 was incorporated into Rule 32.04 by court order dated November 14, 1974.

Rule 32.02. Objections to Admissibility

Subject to the provisions of Rules 28.02 and 32.04(c), objection may be made at the trial or hearing to receiving in evidence any deposition or part thereof for any reason which would require the exclusion of evidence if the witness were then present and testifying.

Adopted Nov. 14, 1974, eff. Jan. 1, 1975. Revised Oct. 18, 1988, eff. Jan. 1, 1989.

Advisory Committee Note—1975

With the exception of change in reference to the rule numbers, the proposed Rule 32.02 is identical to the former Rule 26.05.

Historical Notes

Former Rule: A former Rule 32.02 adopted June 25, 1951, related to disqualification of the officer before whom the deposition is taken. The subject matter of former Rule 32.02 was incorporated into Rule 32.04 by court order dated November 14, 1974.

Rule 32.03. Form of Presentation

Except as otherwise directed by the court, a party offering deposition testimony pursuant to this rule may offer it in stenographic or nonstenographic form, but, if in nonstenographic form, the party shall also provide the court with a transcript of the portions so offered. On request of any party in a case tried before a jury, deposition testimony offered other than for impeachment purposes shall be presented in nonstenographic form, if available, unless the court for good cause orders otherwise.

Adopted Nov. 14, 1974, eff. Jan. 1, 1975. Revised Oct. 18, 1988, eff. Jan. 1, 1989. Amended Nov. 22, 1996, eff. Jan. 1, 1997.

Advisory Committee Note—1975

The rule as recommended is substantially identical with the former Rule 26.06. A clarifying change of language has been made in the first sentence and reference to Rule 32.01(2) has been substituted for reference to Rule 26.04(2).

Advisory Committee Comments—1996 Amendments

This change conforms the rule to its federal counterpart. As is true for the amendments to Rules 30 and 31, the committee believes it is advantageous to have great uniformity in practice in the area of deposition practice because of the likelihood that some of the players in many depositions are totally unfamiliar with Minnesota Procedure.

Historical Notes

The order of the Minnesota Supreme Court [C6-84-2134] dated November 22, 1996, provides in part that the "(a)mendments shall apply to all actions pending on the effective date [January 1, 1997] and to those filed thereafter" and that "(t)he inclusion of Advisory Committee comments is made for convenience and does not reflect court approval of the comments made therein".

Former Rule: A former Rule 32.03 adopted June 25, 1951, related to the effect of taking or using depositions. The subject matter of former Rule 32.03 was incorporated into Rule 32.04 by court order dated November 14, 1974.

Rule 32.04. Effect of Errors and Irregularities in Depositions

(a) As to Notice. All errors and irregularities in the notice for taking a deposition are waived unless written objection is promptly served upon the party giving the notice.

(b) As to Disqualification of Officer. Objection to taking a deposition because of disqualification of the officer before whom it is to be taken is waived unless made before the taking of the deposition begins or as soon thereafter as the disqualification becomes known or could be discovered with reasonable diligence.

(c) As to Taking of Deposition.

(1) Objections to the competency of a witness or to the competency, relevancy, or materiality of testimony are not waived by failure to make them before or during the taking of the deposition, unless the ground of the objection is one which might have been obviated or removed if presented at that time.

(2) Errors and irregularities occurring at the oral examination in the manner of taking the deposition,

in the form of the questions or answers, in the oath or affirmation, or in the conduct of parties, and errors of any kind which might be obviated, removed, or cured if promptly presented, are waived unless seasonable objection thereto is made at the taking of the deposition.

(3) Objections to the form of written questions submitted pursuant to Rule 31 are waived unless served in writing upon the party propounding them within the time allowed for serving the succeeding cross or other questions and within 5 days after service of the last questions authorized.

(d) As to Completion and Return of Deposition. Errors and irregularities in the manner in which the testimony is transcribed, preserved or the deposition is prepared, signed, certified, sealed, endorsed, transmitted, filed, or otherwise dealt with by the officer pursuant to Rules 30 and 31 are waived unless a motion to suppress the deposition or some part thereof is made with reasonable promptness after such defect is, or with due diligence might have been, ascertained.

Adopted June 25, 1951, eff. Jan. 1, 1952. Amended Nov. 14, 1974, eff. Jan. 1, 1975. Revised Oct. 18, 1988, eff. Jan. 1, 1989.

Advisory Committee Note—1975

The provisions in Rule 32.04(1), (2), (3), (4) are substantially identical to the provisions in former Rules 32.01, 32.02, 32.03 and 32.04, and are substantially identical to the corresponding Federal rule. The only change of substance recommended by the Advisory Committee is in Rule 32.04(4), the word "preserved" was added in recognition of the use of recording methods other than the stenographic transcription as provided under the proposed amended rules.

Time for objection to the form of written interrogatories has been extended from three to five days under the proposed Rule 32.04(3)(c).

Rule 32.05. Use of Videotape Depositions

Video depositions may be used in court proceedings to the same extent as stenographically recorded depositions.

Adopted Oct. 18, 1988, eff. Jan. 1, 1989.

RULE 33. INTERROGATORIES TO PARTIES

Rule 33.01. Availability

(a) Any party may serve written interrogatories upon any other party. Interrogatories may, without leave of court, be served upon any party after service of the summons and complaint. No party may serve more than a total of 50 interrogatories upon any other party unless permitted to do so by the court upon motion, notice and a showing of good cause. In computing the total number of interrogatories each subdivision of separate questions shall be counted as an interrogatory.

(b) The party upon whom the interrogatories have been served shall serve separate written answers or objections to each interrogatory within 30 days after service of the interrogatories, except that a defendant may serve answers or objections within 45 days after service of summons and complaint upon that defendant. The court, on motion and notice and for good cause shown, may enlarge or shorten the time.

(c) Objections shall state with particularity the grounds for the objection and may be served either as a part of the document containing the answers or separately. The party submitting the interrogatories may move for an order under Rule 37.01 with respect to any objection to or other failure to answer an interrogatory. Answers to interrogatories to which objection has been made shall be deferred until the objections are determined.

(d) Answers to interrogatories shall be stated fully in writing and shall be signed under oath by the party served or, if the party served is the state, a corporation, a partnership, or an association, by any officer or managing agent, who shall furnish such information as is available. A party shall restate the interrogatory being answered immediately preceding the answer to that interrogatory.

Without leave of court or written stipulation, any party may serve upon any other party written interrogatories, not exceeding 50 in number including all discrete subparts, to be answered by the party served or, if the party served is a public or private corporation or a partnership or association or governmental agency, by any officer or agent, who shall furnish such information as is available to the party. Leave to serve additional interrogatories shall be granted to the extent consistent with the principles of Rule 26.02(a).

Adopted Nov. 14, 1974, eff. Jan. 1, 1975. Revised Oct. 18, 1988, eff. Jan. 1, 1989. Amended Nov. 22, 1996, eff. Jan. 1, 1997.

Advisory Committee Note—1968

Rule 33 has been rearranged and subdivided for purposes of clarity. The word "adverse" in Rule 33 has been eliminated. The Committee believes that any party should have the right to direct interrogatories to any other party without regard to the assertion or non assertion of a claim between the parties. Amended Rule 33 requires objection by the responding party to each interrogatory served and permits the objection to be stated separately or within the same document containing the answers to the other interrogatories. If objection is made to an interrogatory, the grounds for the objection must be stated with particularity. The amended Rule 33 casts upon the inquiring party the obligation of bringing the objection on for hearing. If notice for hearing is not served within 15 days from the service of the objection, the right to require a response to the interrogatory is waived. This amendment is designed to permit greater flexibility in the use of Rule 33 and to relieve the trial court from the automatic hearing now required under Rule 33 if objections are made to interrogatories. Often an inquiring party, obtaining the information from some other source or not deeming it that important, does not desire or does not feel the need to compel a response to the particular interrogatory to which objection has been made. This amendment overrules in part State v. Boening, 276 Minn. 151, 149 N.W.2d 87 (1967).

The rule has been clarified to clearly impose upon the answering party the obligation of signing the responses to the interrogatory. All responses to interrogatories are to be signed under oath.

Rule 33 has been amended to limit the number of interrogatories that may be served by any party upon any other party, without prior approval by the court, to 50 separate questions. All 50 questions may be contained in one set of interrogatories or may be divided between two or more sets of interrogatories. The amended rule states that each separate question shall be counted as a separate interrogatory even though it is related to a prior question or is a subdivision of a question.

Advisory Committee Note—1975

Rule 33 has been substantially rewritten by the Advisory Committee to retain in general the provisions in the existing Minnesota Rule 33. Amendments to the Minnesota rule have been proposed which adopt desirable recommendations made by the State Bar Committee and as exist in the interrogatory practice in the amended Federal Rule 33. Rather than using the Federal rule as a base for proposing an amended Minnesota Rule 33, the Advisory Committee used the existing Minnesota rule. In this instance the Committee believed that the variance between desirable Minnesota practice under Rule 33, which should be continued, and the proposed Federal Rule 33 was sufficient to warrant an exception to the general policy of adopting the Federal language wherever possible.

Major changes in Rule 33 relate to the time elements applicable to the interrogatory procedure. Under Rule 33.01(1) interrogatories may be served without leave of court after service of the summons and complaint upon the defending party or at any time upon the plaintiff. Sufficient time for defendants to secure the services of counsel and to respond are provided in Rule 33.01(2) by extending the answer or objection time to 30 days with a specific provision for defendants to answer or object within 45 days after service of the summons and complaint upon that defendant. Under the proposed amended rule, the plaintiff may serve interrogatories upon the defendant with the service of the summons and complaint.

Proposed Rule 33.01(3) preserve the existing practice of requiring the objections state with particularity the ground for the objection. The procedural burden is cast upon the inquiring party to serve notice of hearing within 15 days after service of objections to the interrogatories or the inquiring party waives his right to require answers to each interrogatory that has been objected to.

A new provision has been added to Rule 33.01(4). The proposed rule requires that the party answering the interrogatories to restate the interrogatory immediately prior to his answer. The purpose of this change is to permit more convenient use of the interrogatories at the time of trial or upon hearings by eliminating the necessity of referring back and forth between the questions and the answers. The duty to supplement answers is now contained in the proposed Rule 26.05.

Rule 33.01(1) preserves the 50 interrogatories limitation contained in the existing Minnesota rule. The procedure for signing and submitting answers and objections differ from the corresponding provisions in the Federal rule. The rule as proposed continues existing Minnesota practice which permits the service of interrogatories upon all parties, not merely adverse parties.

Advisory Committee Comments—1996 Amendments

This change retains the existing rule on interrogatories, and does not adopt the 1993 amendment to its federal counterpart. The federal courts adopted in 1993 an express numerical limitation on the number of interrogatories, limiting them to 25. Minnesota took this action to limit discovery in the 1975 amendments to the rules, limiting interrogatories to 50, and this limit has worked well in practice. The committee believes that the other changes in the federal rules are not significant enough in substance to warrant adoption in Minnesota.

The rule, however, is amended in one important way. The existing provision requiring a party receiving objections to interrogatories to move within 15 days to have the objections determined by the court and the waiver of a right to answers if such a motion is not made within the required time has not worked well. There is no reason to require such prompt action, and much to commend more orderly consideration of the objections. The absolute waiver of the old rule gives way to an explicit right to have the matter resolved by the court, and permits that to be done at any time. This permits the party receiving objections to determine their validity, attempt to resolve any dispute, consider the eventual importance of the information, and possibly to take the matter up with the court in conjunction with other matters. All of these reasons favor a more flexible rule.

Historical Notes

The order of the Minnesota Supreme Court [C6-84-2134] dated November 22, 1996, provides in part that the "(a)mendments shall apply to all actions pending on the effective date [January 1, 1997] and to those filed thereafter" and that "(t)he inclusion of Advisory Committee comments is made for convenience and does not reflect court approval of the comments made therein".

Former Rule: A former Rule 33 adopted June 25, 1951, and amended November 10, 1967, related to interrogatories to parties. The order of the Minnesota Supreme Court dated November 14, 1974, rewrote former Rule 33 as Rules 33.01 to 33.03.

Rule 33.02. Scope; Use at Trial

Interrogatories may relate to any matters which can be inquired into pursuant to Rule 26.02, and the answers may be used to the extent permitted by the Minnesota Rules of Evidence.

An interrogatory otherwise proper is not necessarily objectionable merely because its answer involves an opinion or contention that relates to fact or the application of law to fact, but the court may order that such an interrogatory need not be answered until after designated discovery has been completed, a pretrial conference has been held, or at another later time.

Adopted Nov. 14, 1974, eff. Jan. 1, 1975. Revised Oct. 18, 1988, eff. Jan. 1, 1989.

Advisory Committee Note—1975

The first paragraph is identical to the first sentence of the existing Rule 33(5) except the language has been changed in the final clause to provide that the answers will be used to the extent permitted under the rules of evidence rather than making specific reference to Rule 26.04 (now Rule 32.01). The second paragraph resolves a question which has involved substantial division and debate in the federal and state courts. Interrogatories relating to opinions and conclusions of the party are permitted under the proposed Rule 33.02. Pure questions of law are not proper under the proposed rule. Mixed questions of law and fact can be the proper subject for a Rule 33 interrogatory. The rule specifically provides that the court may by order delay the answer to the interrogatory until other discovery has been completed or until the pre-trial conference or such other time. This rule implements the proposed change in Rule 26.02(4) interrogatories to parties relating to experts expected to testify at trial.

Rule 33.03. Option to Produce Business Records

Where the answer to an interrogatory may be derived or ascertained from the business records, including electronically stored information, of the party upon whom the interrogatory has been served or from an examination, audit, or inspection of such business records, including a compilation, abstract, or summary thereof, and the burden of deriving or ascertaining the answer is substantially the same for the party serving the interrogatory as for the party served, it is a sufficient answer to such interrogatory to specify the records from which the answer may be derived or ascertained and to afford to the party serving the interrogatory reasonable opportunity to examine, audit, or inspect such records and to make copies, compilations, abstracts, or summaries. A specification shall be in sufficient detail as to permit the interrogating party to locate and to identify, as readily as can the party served, the records from which the answer may be ascertained.

Adopted Nov. 14, 1974, eff. Jan. 1, 1975. Amended Nov. 30, 1981. Revised Oct. 18, 1988, eff. Jan. 1, 1989. Amended May 21, 2007, eff. July 1, 2007.

Advisory Committee Note—1975

The proposed rule is a new provision designed to simplify the answering process when business records or documents provide the answer. If the burden of ascertaining the answer from existing records is substantially the same for the party inquiring as for the party answering, it is sufficient for the answering party to specify the records and to afford the acquiring party reasonable opportunity to examine or inspect the record.

Advisory Committee Comment—2007 Amendment

The amendment to Rule 33.03 in 2007 is simple but important. The existing rule allows a party to respond to an interrogatory by directing the requesting party to discover the information from designated documents. The amended rule does not change this procedure, but simply allows the responding party to designate electronic records from which the requested information can be obtained.

RULE 34. PRODUCTION OF DOCUMENTS, ELECTRONICALLY STORED INFORMATION, AND THINGS AND ENTRY UPON LAND FOR INSPECTION AND OTHER PURPOSES

Rule 34.01. Scope

Any party may serve on any other party a request (1) to produce and permit the party making the request, or someone acting on the requesting party's behalf, to inspect and copy, test, or sample any designated documents or electronically stored information—(including writings, drawings, graphs, charts, photographs, sound recordings, images, phono records, and other data or data compilations stored in any medium from which information can be obtained—, translated, if necessary, by the respondent through detection devices into reasonably usable form), or to inspect and copy, test, or sample any designated tangible things that constitute or contain matters within the scope of Rule 26.02 and that are in the possession, custody or control of the party upon whom the request is served, or (2) to permit entry upon designated land or other property in the possession or control of the party upon whom the request is served for the purpose of inspection and measuring, surveying, photographing, testing, or sampling the property or any designated object or operation thereon, within the scope of Rule 26.02.

Adopted Nov. 14, 1974, eff. Jan. 1, 1975. Revised Oct. 18, 1988, eff. Jan. 1, 1989. Amended May 21, 2007, eff. July 1, 2007.

Advisory Committee Note—1975

The proposed rule simplifies the practice under Rule 34 and conforms to the informal procedure presently adopted by many lawyers in requesting production of documents. In particular, the amendments (a) eliminate the requirement of showing "good cause;" (b) eliminate the requirement of a court order for production; and (c) specifically includes the testing and sampling of tangible property as a permissible inspection form. Documents as now defined include all forms used to preserve information including electronic forms.

Advisory Committee Comment—2007 Amendment

Rule 34.01 is amended to make two changes. First, the rule explicitly applies to "electronically stored information" ("ESI") as well as other forms. A more important change is to add provisions allowing the discovering party to require production of information for the purposes of testing or sampling. Testing and sampling are important tools in managing discovery, particularly discovery of ESI. Testing and sampling allow a party to inspect a small subset of requested information to determine whether it is worth conducting additional or broader discovery. These tools may be useful to the court in determining whether to allow additional discovery or discovery of information that is not reasonably accessible, as defined in Rule 26.02(b)(2).

Historical Notes

Former Rule: A former Rule 34, adopted June 25, 1951, related to discovery and production of documents and things for inspection, copying, and photographing. The order of the Minnesota Supreme Court dated November 14, 1974, rewrote former Rule 34 as Rules 34.01 to 34.03.

Rule 34.02. Procedure

The request may, without leave of court, be served upon any party with or after service of the summons and complaint. The request shall set forth the items to be inspected either by individual item or by category, and describe each item and category with reasonable particularity. The request shall specify a reasonable time, place, and manner of making the inspection and performing the related acts. The request may specify the form or forms in which electronically stored information is to be produced.

The party upon whom the request is served shall serve a written response within 30 days after the service of the request, except that a defendant may serve a response within 45 days after service of the summons and complaint upon that defendant. The court may allow a shorter or longer time. The response shall state, with respect to each item or category, that inspection and related activities will be permitted as requested, unless the request is objected to, including an objection to the requested form or forms for producing electronically stored information, stating the reasons for objection. If objection is made to part of an item or category, that part shall be specified and inspection permitted of the remaining parts. If objection is made to the requested form or forms for producing electronically stored information—or if no form was specified in the request—the responding party must state the form or forms it intends to use. The party submitting the request may move for an order pursuant to Rule 37 with respect to any objection to or other failure to respond to the request or any part thereof, or any failure to permit inspection as requested.

Unless the parties otherwise agree, or the court otherwise orders:

(a) A party who produces documents for inspection shall produce them as they are kept in the usual course of business at the time of the request or, at the option of the producing party, shall organize them to correspond with the categories in the request;

(b) If a request does not specify the form or forms for producing electronically stored information, a responding party must produce the information in a form or forms in which it is ordinarily maintained or in a form or forms that are reasonably usable; and

(c) A party need not produce the same electronically stored information in more than one form.

Adopted Nov. 14, 1974, eff. Jan. 1, 1975. Amended Nov. 30, 1981. Revised Oct. 18, 1988, eff. Jan. 1, 1989; May 21, 2007, eff. July 1, 2007.

Advisory Committee Note—1975

The procedure for production has been substantially changed. No longer need a party establish good cause or secure a court order prior to production. A simple request specifying the items to be inspected and describing each item with reasonable particularity is all that is required. The request must specify a reasonable time, place and manner of making the inspection, testing, etc. The party responding to the request must respond within 30 days after service of the request upon him except a defendant may respond within 45 days after service of summons and complaint upon him. Time may be extended or shortened by court order. If objection is made to all or a part of the request, production is not required and the parties seeking production must move for an order under Rule 37.

Advisory Committee Comment—2007 Amendment

Rule 34.02 is amended to establish presumptive rules for the procedural aspects of discovery of electrically stored information. These include allowing the party seeking discovery to specify the form or medium for response, providing a default rule that applies if the request does not specify a form, and making it clear that a party does not need to produce information in more than one form.

Rule 34.03. Persons Not Parties

This rule does not preclude an independent action against a person not a party for production of documents and things and permission to enter upon land.

Adopted Nov. 14, 1974, eff. Jan. 1, 1975. Revised Oct. 18, 1988, eff. Jan. 1, 1989.

Advisory Committee Note—1975

The proposed rule resolves the former uncertainty in the federal courts regarding the preempting nature of Rule 34. Rule 34 applies only to parties. Often it is necessary to enter land or inspect tangible property in the possession of a person not a party. In such a situation an independent action in the nature of an equity bill will lie. The proposed rule merely permits continuance of such independent procedure by providing that Rule 34 is not the exclusive remedy.

RULE 35. PHYSICAL, MENTAL, AND BLOOD EXAMINATION OF PERSONS

Rule 35.01. Order of Examinations

In an action in which the physical or mental condition or the blood relationship of a party, or of an agent of a party, or of a person under control of a party, is in controversy, the court in which the action is pending may order the party to submit to, or produce such agent or person for a physical, mental or blood examination by a suitably licensed or certified examiner. The order may be made only on motion for good cause shown and upon notice to the party or person to be examined and to all other parties and shall specify the time, place, manner, conditions, and scope of the examination and the person or persons by whom it is made.

Adopted June 25, 1951, eff. Jan. 1, 1952. Amended March 3, 1959, eff. July 1, 1959. Revised Oct. 18, 1988, eff. Jan. 1, 1989. Amended Dec. 20, 1993, eff. March 1, 1994.

Advisory Committee Note—1959

The amendments follow those proposed for the federal rules and provide for the examination of the agent of a party and of a person under his control, broaden its provisions for exchange of reports of examination, delete surplusage from Rule 37.02(2), and add sanctions against a party for failure to produce for examination his agent or a person under his control.

Advisory Committee Comment—1993 Amendments

The amendments to Rule 35 are intended to expand the power of the courts to order examinations by professionals other than physicians. This amendment is generally consistent with amendments made to Fed.R.Civ.P. 35 in 1991, though the state and federal rules have always been somewhat different.

This amendment recognizes that examination may be appropriate by, for example, a licensed psychologist, dentist, audiologist, or physical or occupational therapist. These licensed professionals are not physicians but may, and often do, provide valuable information or testimony. See Fed.R.Civ.P. 35, Notes of Advisory Committee—1991 Amendment, reprinted in Federal Civil Judicial Procedure & Rules 126 (West pamph. 1993).

Rule 35.02. Report of Findings

(a) If requested by the party against whom an order is made pursuant to Rule 35.01 or by the person examined, the party causing the examination to be made shall deliver to the requesting party a copy of a detailed written report of the examination setting out the examiner's findings and conclusions, together with like reports of all earlier examinations of the same condition. After such request and delivery, the party causing the examination to be made shall be entitled, upon request, to receive from the party or person examined a like report of any examination, previously or thereafter made, of the same physical, mental, or blood condition. If the party or person examined refuses to deliver such report, the court, on motion and notice, may make an order requiring delivery on such terms as are just, and, if an examiner fails or refuses to make such a report, the court may exclude the examiner's testimony if offered at the trial.

(b) By requesting and obtaining a report of the examination so ordered or by taking the deposition of the examiner, the adverse party waives any privilege the party may have in that action or any other involving the same controversy, regarding the testimony of every other person who has examined or may thereafter examine the party or the person under the party's control with respect to the same physical, mental, or blood condition.

Adopted June 25, 1951, eff. Jan. 1, 1952. Amended March 3, 1959, eff. July 1, 1959. Revised Oct. 18, 1988, eff. Jan. 1, 1989. Amended Dec. 20, 1993, eff. March 1, 1994.

Advisory Committee Note—1959

The amendments follow those proposed for the federal rules and provide for the examination of the agent of a party and of a person under his control, broaden its provisions for exchange of reports of examination, delete surplusage from Rule 37.02(2), and add sanctions against a party for failure to produce for examination his agent or a person under his control.

Advisory Committee Comment—1993 Amendments

The amendments to Rule 35 are intended to expand the power of the courts to order examinations by professionals other than physicians. This amendment is generally consistent with amendments made to Fed.R.Civ.P. 35 in 1991, though the state and federal rules have always been somewhat different.

This amendment recognizes that examination may be appropriate by, for example, a licensed psychologist, dentist, audiologist, or physical or occupational therapist. These licensed professionals are not physicians but may, and often do, provide valuable information or testimony. See Fed.R.Civ.P. 35, Notes of Advisory Committee—1991 Amendment, reprinted in Federal Civil Judicial Procedure & Rules 126 (West pamph. 1993).

Rule 35.03. Waiver of Medical Privilege

If at any stage of an action a party voluntarily places in controversy the physical, mental, or blood condition of that party, a decedent, or a person under that party's control, such party thereby waives any privilege that party may have in that action regarding the testimony of every person who has examined or may thereafter examine that party or the person under that party's control with respect to the same physical, mental, or blood condition.

Adopted Nov. 10, 1967, eff. Feb. 1, 1968. Revised Oct. 18, 1988, eff. Jan. 1, 1989.

Advisory Committee Note—1968

Waiver of medical privilege by the person affirmatively putting his physical, mental or blood condition in issue in a lawsuit is in accordance with the general purpose and philosophy of rule procedure. Mutual fact knowledge regarding all facts in issue by all parties is a foundation stone of rule procedure. Fifteen states do not recognize medical privilege. Five other states provide for compulsory waiver by a claimant seeking damages for personal injury, or by a party who puts his physical condition in issue. The amendment is consistent with the concept that medical privilege should exist as a shield, not a sword. See Nelson v. Ackerman, 249 Minn. 582, 83 N.W.2d 500 (1957); Snyker v. Snyker, 245 Minn. 405, 72 N.W.2d 357 (1955).

The amendment requires that the person who has the medical privilege or who has control over the person with the privilege affirmatively place the physical, mental or blood condition in issue. A denial of an affirmative allegation by an opposing party is not an affirmative placing of the condition in issue and is not a "voluntary" act by the person with the privilege. In such a situation, there would be no waiver. As an example, a plaintiff seeking damages for personal injury has voluntarily and affirmatively put his physical condition in issue by his complaint and has waived medical privilege regarding that condition. If, however, plaintiff in his complaint should allege or should otherwise assert that defendant was negligent in driving an automobile without eye glasses because defendant had extremely poor vision, defendant by denying the allegation or by taking issue with the quality of his vision, has not voluntarily or affirmatively raised an issue regarding his physical condition. In such a case, there would be no waiver of the medical privilege.

Rule 35.04. Medical Disclosures and Depositions of Medical Experts

When a party has waived medical privilege pursuant to Rule 35.03, such party within 10 days of a written request by any other party,

(a) shall furnish to the requesting party copies of all medical reports previously or thereafter made by any treating or examining medical expert, and

(b) shall provide written authority signed by the party of whom request is made to permit the inspection of all hospital and other medical records, concerning the physical, mental, or blood condition of such party as to which privilege has been waived.

Disclosures pursuant to this rule shall include the conclusions of such treating or examining medical expert.

Depositions of treating or examining medical experts shall not be taken except upon order of the court for good cause shown upon motion and notice to the parties and upon such terms as the court may provide.

Adopted Nov. 10, 1967, eff. Feb. 1, 1968. Revised Oct. 18, 1988, eff. Jan. 1, 1989.

Advisory Committee Note—1968

Medical records as used in this Rule include the office records of any medical expert, and x-rays, E.E.G.'s and all similar items. The limitation on depositions of medical experts is applicable to both treating and examining medical experts. The purpose for the limitation is to insure that depositions of medical experts will be taken only upon court order. In making its order the court can and should consider the extent of medical disclosure through medical reports and inspection of hospital and medical records. Protective orders under Rule 30.02 are available to the parties to further limit or prevent involuntary medical examination or disclosure of medical information in those cases where the protection provided in Rule 35.04 is not sufficient. Rule 37 will provide the means for obtaining a court order requiring a party to comply with the disclosure requirements of Rule 35.04. At such Rule 37 hearing, the court may properly determine whether or not the medical information sought is the same physical, mental or blood condition as to which privilege has been waived.

The limitation on depositions is not applicable to the taking of the testimonial deposition of a party's own medical expert.

RULE 36. REQUESTS FOR ADMISSION

Rule 36.01. Request for Admission

A party may serve upon any other party a written request for the admission, for purposes of the pending action only, of the truth of any matters within the scope of Rule 26.02 set forth in the request that relate to statements, opinions of fact, or the application of law to fact, including the genuineness of any documents described in the request. Copies of documents shall be served with the request, unless they have been or are otherwise furnished or made available for inspection and copying. The request may, without leave of court, be served after service of the summons and complaint.

Each matter of which an admission is requested shall be separately set forth. The matter is admitted unless within 30 days after service of the request, or within such shorter or longer time as the court may allow, the party to whom the request is directed serves upon the party requesting the admission a written answer or objection addressed to the matter, signed by the party or by the party's attorney; but, unless the court shortens the time, a defendant shall not be required to serve answers or objections before the expiration of 45 days after service of the summons and complaint upon that defendant. If objection is made, the reasons therefor shall be stated. The answer shall specifically deny the matter or set forth in detail the reasons why the answering party cannot truthfully admit or deny the matter. A denial shall fairly meet the substance of the requested admission, and, when good faith requires that a party qualify an answer or deny only a part of the matter of which an admission is requested, the party shall specify so much of it as is true and qualify or deny the remainder. An answering party may not give lack of information or knowledge as a reason for failure to admit or deny unless the party states that a reasonable inquiry has been made and that the information known or readily obtainable by the party is insufficient to enable the party to admit or deny. A party who considers that a matter of which an admission has been requested presents a genuine issue for trial may not, on that ground alone, object to the request; the party may, subject to the provisions of Rule 37.03, deny the matter or set forth reasons why the party cannot admit or deny it.

The party who has requested the admissions may move to determine the sufficiency of the answers or objections. Unless the court determines that an objection is justified, it shall order that an answer be served. If the court determines that an answer does not comply with the requirements of this rule, it may order either that the matter is admitted or that an amended answer be served. The court may, in lieu of these orders, determine that final disposition of the request is to be made at a pretrial conference or at a designated time prior to trial. The provisions of Rule 37.01(d) apply to the award of expenses incurred in connection with the motion.

Adopted June 25, 1951, eff. Jan. 1, 1952. Amended Nov. 10, 1967, eff. Feb. 1, 1968; Nov. 14, 1974, eff. Jan. 1, 1975. Revised Oct. 18, 1988, eff. Jan. 1, 1989.

Advisory Committee Note—1975

As proposed, the rule eliminates the existing provision in Rule 36 that the request for admission be limited to matters of "fact." The rule now permits inquiry into mixed questions of law and fact and matters of opinion and conclusion. As proposed, Rule 36.01 equates to the provisions of proposed amended Rule 33.02. The rule as proposed continues to impose a reasonable burden of searching out available facts upon the answering party. The rule requires the answering party to make a reasonable inquiry and to state that the information is not known or readily available to him in order to deny on the basis of lack of information or knowledge. Time for response has been extended to 30 days except defendants may answer or object within 45 days after service of the summons and complaint upon that defendant. The inquiring party has the obligation of moving the court for an order determining the sufficiency of the answers or objections. A failure to respond by answer or objection within 30 days after service of the request constitutes an admission.

Rule 36.02. Effect of Admission

Any matter admitted pursuant to this rule is conclusively established unless the court on motion permits withdrawal or amendment of the admission. Subject to Rule 16 governing amendment of a pre-trial order, the court may permit withdrawal or amendment when the presentation of the merits of the action will be subserved thereby and the party who obtained the admission fails to satisfy the court that withdrawal or amendment will prejudice that party in maintaining the action or defense on the merits. Any admission made by a party hereunder is for the purpose of the pending action only and is not an admission by that party for any other purpose nor may it be used against that party in any other proceeding.

Adopted June 25, 1951, eff. Jan. 1, 1952. Amended Nov. 14, 1974, eff. Jan. 1, 1975. Revised Oct. 18, 1988, eff. Jan. 1, 1989.

Advisory Committee Note—1975

The effect of an admission is clarified under this rule. In addition, provision is made for withdrawing or amending an admission. The rule now provides that an admission is a judicial admission unless the court on motion permits its withdrawal or amendment. The provisions related to amendment or withdrawal of admissions indicates the desirability to having the matter presented on the merits and not to be determined by factual or procedural errors of the party.

RULE 37. FAILURE TO MAKE DISCLOSURES OR TO COOPERATE IN DISCOVERY: SANCTIONS

Rule 37.01. Motion for Order Compelling Disclosure or Discovery

(a) Appropriate Court. An application for an order to a party shall be made to the court in which the action is pending. An application for an order to a person who is not a party shall be made to the court in the county where the discovery is being, or is to be, taken.

(b) Specific Motions.

(1) *To Compel Disclosure.* If a party fails to make a disclosure required by Rule 26.01, any other party may move to compel disclosure and for appropriate sanctions.

(2) *To Compel a Discovery Response.* A party seeking discovery may move for an order compelling an answer, designation, production, or inspection. This motion may be made if:

(A) a deponent fails to answer a question propounded or submitted under Rules 30 or 31;

(B) a corporation or other entity fails to make a designation under Rule 30.02(f) or 31.01(c);

(C) a party fails to answer an interrogatory submitted under Rule 33; or

(D) if a party, in response to a request for inspection submitted under Rule 34, fails to respond that inspection will be permitted as requested or fails to permit inspection as requested.

The motion must include a certification that the movant has in good faith conferred or attempted to confer with the person or party failing to make the discovery in an effort to secure the information or material without court action. When taking a deposition on oral examination, the proponent of the question may complete or adjourn the examination before applying for an order.

(c) Evasive or Incomplete Answer, or Response. For purposes of this subdivision an evasive or incomplete disclosure, answer, or response is to be treated as a failure to disclose, answer, or respond.

(d) Expenses and Sanctions.

(1) If the motion is granted, or if the requested discovery is provided after the motion was filed, the court shall, after affording an opportunity to be heard, require the party or deponent whose conduct necessitated the motion or the party or attorney advising such conduct or both of them to pay to the moving party the reasonable expenses incurred in making the motion, including attorney fees, unless the court finds that the motion was filed without the movant's first making a good faith effort to obtain the discovery without court action, or that the opposing party's nondisclosure, response, or objection was substantially justified or that other circumstances make an award of expenses unjust.

(2) If the motion is denied, the court may enter any protective order authorized under Rule 26.03 and shall, after affording an opportunity to be heard, require the moving party or the attorney filing the motion or both of them to pay to the party or deponent who opposed the motion the reasonable expenses incurred in opposing the motion, including attorney fees, unless the court finds that the making of the motion was substantially justified or that other circumstances make an award of expenses unjust.

(3) If the motion is granted in part and denied in part, the court may enter any protective order authorized under Rule 26.03 and may, after affording an opportunity to be heard, apportion the reasonable expenses incurred in relation to the motion among the parties and persons in a just manner.

Adopted June 25, 1951, eff. Jan. 1, 1952. Amended Nov. 14, 1974, eff. Jan. 1, 1975. Revised Oct. 18, 1988, eff. Jan. 1, 1989. Amended Nov. 22, 1996, eff. Jan. 1, 1997; May 7, 2013, eff. July 1, 2013.

Advisory Committee Comments—1996 Amendments

This change conforms the rule to its federal counterpart, consistent with the ongoing differences between the two rules.

Historical Notes

The order of the Minnesota Supreme Court [C6-84-2134] dated November 22, 1996, provides in part that the "(a)mendments shall apply to all actions pending on the effective date [January 1, 1997] and to those filed thereafter" and that "(t)he inclusion of Advisory Committee comments is made for convenience and does not reflect court approval of the comments made therein".

The order of the Minnesota Supreme Court [ADM04–8001, ADM09–8009, ADM–10-8051] dated May 7, 2013, provided in part that the amendments be effective July 1, 2013, and further provided in part that "[t]hese amendments apply to all actions or proceedings pending on or commenced after the effective date", and further provided that the "February 4, 2013 and February 12, 2013 orders of the court are hereby rescinded to the extent inconsistent with this order.".

Rule 37.02. Failure to Comply with Order

(a) Sanctions by Court in County Where Deposition Is Taken. If a deponent fails to be sworn or to answer a question after being directed to do so by the court in the county in which the deposition is being taken, the failure may be considered a contempt of that court.

(b) Sanctions by Court in Which Action Is Pending. If a party or an officer, director, employee, or managing agent of a party or a person designated in Rules 30.02(f) or 31.01 to testify on behalf of a party fails to obey an order to provide or permit discovery, including an order made pursuant to Rules 35 or 37.01, the court in which the action is pending may make such orders in regard to the failure as are just, and among others the following:

(1) An order that the matters regarding which the order was made or any other designated facts shall be taken to be established for the purposes of the action in accordance with the claim of the party obtaining the order;

(2) An order refusing to allow the disobedient party to support or oppose designated claims or defenses, or prohibiting that party from introducing designated matters in evidence;

(3) An order striking pleadings or parts thereof, staying further proceedings until the order is obeyed, dismissing the action or proceeding or any part thereof, or rendering a judgment by default against the disobedient party;

(4) In lieu of any of the foregoing orders or in addition thereto, an order treating as a contempt of court the failure to obey any orders except an order to submit to a physical or mental examination;

(5) Where a party has failed to comply with an order pursuant to Rule 35.01 requiring that party to produce another for examination, such orders as are listed herein in paragraphs (1), (2), and (3), unless the party failing to comply shows that that party is unable to produce such person for examination.

In lieu of any of the foregoing orders or in addition thereto, the court shall require the party failing to obey the order or the attorney advising that party or both to pay the reasonable expenses, including attorney fees, caused by the failure, unless the court finds that the failure was substantially justified or that other circumstances make an award of expenses unjust.

Adopted June 25, 1951, eff. Jan. 1, 1952. Amended Dec. 6, 1951; March 3, 1959, eff. July 1, 1959; Nov. 14, 1974, eff. Jan. 1, 1975. Revised Oct. 18, 1988, eff. Jan. 1, 1989.

Advisory Committee Note—1959

The amendments follow those proposed for the federal rules and provide for the examination of the agent of a party and of a person under his control, broaden its provisions for exchange of reports of examination, delete surplusage from Rule 37.02(2), and add sanctions against a party for failure to produce for examination his agent or a person under his control.

Advisory Committee Note—1975

Subd. (1).

The rule is substantially identical to the former Rule 37.02(1) except the word "refuse" has been changed to "fail" to remove the concept of wilfulness as a consideration in imposing the sanctions.

Subd. (2).

The proposed amendment is substantially identical to the previous Rule 37.02(2). The rule has been modified to provide a "failure" to make discovery rather than a "refusal" to make discovery.

Sub-paragraph (e) now permits the imposition of sanctions upon a party when a party has failed to comply with an order to produce a third person for examination under Rule 35.

Rule 37.03. Failure to Disclose, to Supplement an Earlier Response, or to Admit

(a) Failure to Disclose or Supplement. If a party fails to provide information or identify a witness as required by Rule 26.01 or .05, the party is not allowed to use that information or witness to supply evidence on a motion, at a hearing, or at a trial, unless the failure was substantially justified or is harmless. In addition to or instead of this sanction, the court, on motion and after giving an opportunity to be heard:

(1) may order payment of the reasonable expenses, including attorney's fees, caused by the failure;

(2) may inform the jury of the party's failure; and

(3) may impose other appropriate sanctions, including any of the orders listed in Rule 37.02.

(b) Failure to Admit. If a party fails to admit the genuineness of any documents or the truth of any matter as requested pursuant to Rule 36, and if the party requesting the admissions thereafter proves the genuineness of the document or the truth of any such matter, the requesting party may apply to the court for an order requiring the other party to pay the reasonable expenses incurred in making that proof, including reasonable attorney fees. The court shall make the order unless it finds that (1) the request was held objectionable pursuant to Rule 36.01, or (2) the admission sought was of no substantial importance, or (3) the party failing to admit had reasonable ground to believe that the party might prevail on the matter, or (4) there was other good reason for the failure to admit.

Adopted June 25, 1951, eff. Jan. 1, 1952. Amended Nov. 14, 1974, eff. Jan. 1, 1975. Revised Oct. 18, 1988, eff. Jan. 1, 1989; May 7, 2013, eff. July 1, 2013.

Advisory Committee Note—1975

The proposed amended Rule 37.03 is substantially identical to the existing Minnesota Rule 37.03. The rule as proposed clarifies an ambiguity existing in the present rule which does not specifically provide sanctions where a party fails to admit as requested under Rule 36 on the basis of an inability to admit or deny due to lack of knowledge or information. As amended, the rule imposes the same obligation upon the party in the latter situation as in the sworn denial situation.

Historical and Statutory Notes

The order of the Minnesota Supreme Court [ADM04–8001, ADM09–8009, ADM–10–8051] dated May 7, 2013, provided in part that the amendments be effective July 1, 2013, and further provided in part that "[t]hese amendments apply to all actions or proceedings pending on or commenced after the effective date", and further provided that the "February 4, 2013 and February 12, 2013 orders of the court are hereby rescinded to the extent inconsistent with this order."

Rule 37.04. Failure of a Party to Attend at Own Deposition or Serve Answers

If a party or an officer, director, employee, or managing agent of a party or a person designated in Rules 30.02(f) or 31.01 to testify on behalf of a party fails (1) to appear before the officer who is to take the deposition, after being served with a proper notice, or (2) to serve answers or objections to interrogatories submitted pursuant to Rule 33, after proper service of the interrogatories, or (3) to serve a written response to a request for inspection submitted pursuant to Rule 34, after proper service of the request, the court in which the action is pending on motion may make such orders in regard to the failure as are just, including any action authorized in Rule 37.02(b)(1), (2), and (3). In lieu of any order or in addition thereto, the court shall require the party failing to act or the attorney advising that party or both to pay the reasonable expenses, including attorney fees, caused by the failure, unless the court finds that the failure was substantially justified or that other circumstances make an award of expenses unjust.

The failure to act described herein may not be excused on the ground that the discovery sought is objectionable unless the party failing to act has applied for a protective order as provided by Rule 26.03.

Adopted June 25, 1951, eff. Jan. 1, 1952. Amended Nov. 14, 1974, eff. Jan. 1, 1975. Revised Oct. 18, 1988, eff. Jan. 1, 1989.

Advisory Committee Note—1975

The rule as amended eliminates the requirement of wilfulness found in the former Rule 37.04. The rule has also been expanded to encompass orders under Rule 34. The court is specifically given authority to make such orders as may be "just" in addition to the specified sanctions. The last paragraph is added to impose upon the answering party an obligation to seek a protective order in the event that he believes the discovery sought is objectionable or otherwise invalid. No longer can a party remain silent and take no affirmative action when properly served with a notice of discovery.

Rule 37.05. Electronically Stored Information

Absent exceptional circumstances, a court may not impose sanctions under these rules on a party for failing to provide electronically stored information lost as a result of the routine, good-faith operation of an electronic information system.

Adopted May 21, 2007, eff. July 1, 2007.

Advisory Committee Comment—2007 Amendment

Rule 37.05 is a new rule; it is identical to Fed. R. Civ. P. 37(f), adopted in 2006. It provides some protection against the automatic imposition of sanctions that might otherwise be required under the rules. This rule applies only to discovery of electronically stored information, and prevents the imposition of sanctions for spoliation of evidence where the loss of information arises from the routine operation of a computer system. The good-faith part of this test is important and is not met if a party fails to take appropriate steps to preserve data once a duty to preserve arises.

Rule 37.06. Failure to Participate in Framing a Discovery Plan

If a party or its attorney fails to participate in good faith in developing and submitting a proposed discovery plan as required by Rule 26.06, the court may, after giving an opportunity to be heard, require that party or attorney to pay to any other party the reasonable expenses, including attorney's fees, caused by the failure.

Adopted May 7, 2013, eff. July 1, 2013.

Historical and Statutory Notes

The order of the Minnesota Supreme Court [ADM04-8001, ADM09-8009, ADM-10-8051] dated May 7, 2013, provided in part that the amendments be effective July 1, 2013, and further provided in part that "[t]hese amendments apply to all actions or proceedings pending on or commenced after the effective date", and further provided that the "February 4, 2013 and February 12, 2013 orders of the court are hereby rescinded to the extent inconsistent with this order."

VI. TRIALS

RULE 38. JURY TRIAL OF RIGHT

Rule 38.01. Right Preserved

In actions for the recovery of money only, or of specific real or personal property, the issues of fact shall be tried by a jury, unless a jury trial is waived or a reference is ordered.

Adopted June 25, 1951, eff. Jan. 1, 1952. Amended March 21, 1985, eff. July 1, 1985. Revised Oct. 18, 1988, eff. Jan. 1, 1989.

Advisory Committee Note—1985

This change is made to conform the language of the rule to the statute governing marriage dissolution actions and establishing the grounds for marriage dissolution. *See* Minn.Stat. § 518.002 *et seq.* (1982).

Rule 38.02. Waiver

In actions arising on contract, and by permission of the court in other actions, any party thereto may waive a jury trial by:

(a) failing to appear at the trial;

(b) written consent, by the party or the party's attorney, filed with the court administrator; or

(c) oral consent in open court, entered in the minutes.

Neither the failure to file any document requesting a jury trial nor the failure to pay a jury fee shall be deemed a waiver of the right to a jury trial.

Adopted June 25, 1951, eff. Jan. 1, 1952. Revised Oct. 18, 1988, eff. Jan. 1, 1989. Amended Dec. 20, 1993, eff. March 1, 1994.

Advisory Committee Comment—1993 Amendments

The committee is of the opinion that waiver of the right to a jury trial should not be found from inaction or failure to pay a jury fee. The amendment, coupled with the abolition of the note of issue, should obviate any confusion or inadvertent waiver of the constitutionally protected right to a jury trial. *See Schweich v. Ziegler, Inc.,* 463 N.W.2d 722 (Minn.1991).

Rule 38.03. Repealed Sept. 5, 1991, eff. Jan. 1, 1992

Task Force Comment—1991 Adoption

This amendment to repeal this rule is appropriate because the use of notes of issue filed by the parties will be replaced by the court-initiated scheduling. See proposed Minn.Gen.R.Prac. 111.

Historical Notes

Repealed Rule 38.03, adopted June 25, 1951, and amended March 3, 1959, and November 10, 1967, related to notes of issue.

See, now, generally, Minn. R. Gen. Prac., Rule 111.01 et seq.

RULE 39. TRIAL BY JURY OR BY THE COURT

Rule 39.01. By Court

Issues of fact not submitted to a jury as provided in Rule 38 shall be tried by the court.

Adopted June 25, 1951, eff. Jan. 1, 1952. Revised Oct. 18, 1988, eff. Jan. 1, 1989.

Rule 39.02. Advisory Jury and Trial by Consent

In all actions not triable of right by a jury, the court, upon motion or upon its own initiative, may try an issue with an advisory jury, or the court, with the consent of both parties, may order a trial with a jury whose verdict has the same effect as if trial by jury had been a matter of right.

Adopted June 25, 1951, eff. Jan. 1, 1952. Revised Oct. 18, 1988, eff. Jan. 1, 1989.

Rule 39.03. Preliminary Instructions in Jury Trials

After the jury has been impaneled and sworn, and before opening statements of counsel, the court may instruct the jury as to the respective claims of the parties and as to such other matters as will aid the jury in comprehending the trial procedure and sequence to be followed. Preliminary instructions may also embrace such matters as burden of proof and preponderance of evidence, the elements which the jury may consider in weighing testimony or determining credibility of witnesses, rules applicable to opinion evidence, and such other rules of law as the court may deem essential to the proper understanding of the evidence.

Adopted Nov. 10, 1967, eff. Feb. 1, 1968. Revised Oct. 18, 1988, eff. Jan. 1, 1989.

Advisory Committee Note—1968

This rule is permissive, not mandatory. In some cases preliminary instructions may not be desirable. In other cases substantive rules of law may not be desirable for preliminary instructions, but "boiler plate" instructions would be helpful. Preliminary instructions on such matters as are commonly encompassed in the "boiler plate" instructions will generally aid the jury in their decisional process. Such procedure will also protect trial counsel better than the present procedure of preinstructing juries only at the time of welcoming or orienting the new jury panel. Group instructions given at the time jurors are called for jury service without regard to a particular case prevent trial counsel from knowing the instructions and other material given to the jury and does not give him an opportunity to correct any errors. Rule 39.03 will correct this difficulty.

Rule 39.04. Opening Statements by Counsel

Before any evidence is introduced, plaintiff may make an opening statement, whereupon any other party may make an opening statement or may reserve the same until that party's case in chief is opened. Opening statements may be waived by any party to the action without affecting the right of any other party to make such an opening statement.

Adopted Nov. 10, 1967, eff. Feb. 1, 1968. Revised Oct. 18, 1988, eff. Jan. 1, 1989.

Advisory Committee Note—1968

The amendment adding Rule 39.04 restates the existing law of Minnesota. However, to clarify the law and to conform generally to the procedure set forth in the local rules of procedure for the Federal District Courts for the District of Minnesota, Rule 39.04 is added.

RULE 40. ASSIGNMENT OF CASES FOR TRIAL

The judges of the court may, by order or by rule of court, provide for the setting of cases for trial upon the calendar, the order in which they shall be heard, and the resetting thereof.

Adopted June 25, 1951, eff. Jan. 1, 1952. Revised Oct. 18, 1988, eff. Jan. 1, 1989.

RULE 41. DISMISSAL OF ACTIONS

Rule 41.01. Voluntary Dismissal; Effect Thereof

(a) By Plaintiff by Stipulation. Subject to the provisions of Rules 23.05, 23.09 and 66, an action may be dismissed by the plaintiff without order of court (1) by filing a notice of dismissal at any time before service by the adverse party of an answer or of a motion for summary judgment, whichever first occurs, or (2) by filing a stipulation of dismissal signed by all parties who have appeared in the action. Unless otherwise stated in the notice of dismissal or stipulation the dismissal is without prejudice, except that a notice of dismissal operates as an adjudication upon the merits when filed by a plaintiff who has once dismissed in any court of the United States or of any state an action based on or including the same claim.

(b) By Order of Court. Except as provided in clause (a) of this rule, an action shall not be dismissed at the plaintiff's instance except upon order of the court and upon such terms and conditions as the court deems proper. If a counterclaim has been pleaded by a defendant prior to the service upon the defendant of the plaintiff's motion to dismiss, the action shall not be dismissed against the defendant's objection unless the counterclaim may remain pending for independent adjudication by the court. Unless otherwise specified in the order, a dismissal herein is without prejudice.

Adopted June 25, 1951, eff. Jan. 1, 1952. Revised Oct. 18, 1988, eff. Jan. 1, 1989. Amended Dec. 20, 1993, eff. March 1, 1994; Nov. 30, 2005, eff. Jan. 1, 2006.

Advisory Committee Comment—1993 Amendments

The amendment to this rule is made to conform the rule to its counterpart in the Federal Rules of Civil Procedure, Fed.R.Civ.P. 41(a)(1). The existing rule in Minnesota seems to the committee archaic, establishing time requirements on the commencement of terms of court. Since 1977, Minnesota trial courts have had continuous terms. Minn.Stat. § 484.08 (1992).

The former rule has permitted parties to dismiss claims without prejudice even after extensive discovery or other pretrial proceedings have taken place. Dismissal without prejudice has also been possible after the trial court has issued orders on preliminary matters. The right to dismiss on the eve of trial has prejudiced defendants or has required courts to consider motions to deny a plaintiff the right to dismiss without prejudice. The committee is of the opinion that the right to dismiss without prejudice ought to be limited to a fairly short period after commencement of the action when prejudice to opponents is likely to be minimal.

Advisory Committee Comment—2006 Amendment

Rule 41.01(a) is amended to renumber one of the rule cross-references to reflect the amendment and renumbering of Rule 23 as part of the amendments effective January 1, 2006.

Rule 41.02. Involuntary Dismissal; Effect Thereof

(a) The court may upon its own initiative, or upon motion of a party, and upon such notice as it may prescribe, dismiss an action or claim for failure to prosecute or to comply with these rules or any order of the court.

(b) After the plaintiff has completed the presentation of evidence, the defendant, without waiving the right to offer evidence in the event the motion is not granted, may move for a dismissal on the ground that upon the facts and the law, the plaintiff has shown no right to relief. In an action tried by the court without a jury, the court as trier of the fact may then determine the facts and render judgment against the plaintiff or may decline to render any judgment until the close of all the evidence. If the court renders judgment on the merits against the plaintiff, the court shall make findings as provided in Rule 52.01.

(c) Unless the court specifies otherwise in its order, a dismissal pursuant to this rule and any dismissal not provided for in this rule or in Rule 41.01, other than a dismissal for lack of jurisdiction, for forum non conveniens, or for failure to join a party indispensable pursuant to Rule 19, operates as an adjudication upon the merits.

Adopted June 25, 1951, eff. Jan. 1, 1952. Amended Dec. 6, 1951; March 3, 1959, eff. July 1, 1959; Nov. 10, 1967, eff. Feb. 1, 1968. Revised Oct. 18, 1988, eff. Jan. 1, 1989.

Advisory Committee Note—1959

There is added a provision for dismissal by the court on its own motion and a provision that dismissal for lack of an indispensable party be without prejudice. The rule has been divided into three paragraphs.

Advisory Committee Note—1968

Minnesota Rule 41.02 and Federal Rule 41(b) are not identical at the present time. The Minnesota rule is more liberal than the federal rule regarding the court's power to dismiss matters upon the court's own motion. No change is made in that portion of Rule 41.02. The amended Rule 41.02(3) reflects the change in Rule 19 to modify the indispensable party concept and adds dismissals now permitted under forum non conveniens as a dismissal not considered to be on the merits.

Rule 41.03. Dismissal of Counterclaim, Cross-Claim, or Third-Party Claim

The provisions of Rules 41.01 and 41.02 apply to the dismissal of any counterclaim, cross-claim, or third-party claim.

Adopted June 25, 1951, eff. Jan. 1, 1952. Revised Oct. 18, 1988, eff. Jan. 1, 1989.

Rule 41.04. Costs of Previously Dismissed Action

If a plaintiff who has once dismissed an action in any court commences an action based upon or including the same claim against the same defendant, the court may make such order for the payment of costs of the action previously dismissed as it may deem proper and may stay the proceedings in the action until the plaintiff has complied with the order.

Adopted June 25, 1951, eff. Jan. 1, 1952. Revised Oct. 18, 1988, eff. Jan. 1, 1989.

RULE 42. SEPARATE TRIALS

Rule 42.01. Consolidation

When actions involving a common question of law or fact are pending before the court, it may order a joint hearing or trial of any or all the matters in issue in the actions; it may order all the actions consolidated; and it may make such orders concerning proceedings therein as may tend to avoid unnecessary costs or delay.

Adopted June 25, 1951, eff. Jan. 1, 1952. Revised Oct. 18, 1988, eff. Jan. 1, 1989.

Rule 42.02. Separate Trials

The court, in furtherance of convenience or to avoid prejudice, or when separate trials will be conducive to expedition and economy, may order a separate trial of one or any number of claims, cross-claims, counterclaims, or third-party claims, or of any separate issues.

Adopted June 25, 1951, eff. Jan. 1, 1952. Amended Nov. 10, 1967, eff. Feb. 1, 1968. Revised Oct. 18, 1988, eff. Jan. 1, 1989.

Advisory Committee Note—1968

The amendment conforms generally to the federal amendment. Separation of liability and damage issues are permitted under the existing Rules of Civil Procedure. The amendment merely reflects that one of the grounds for separation will be expedition and economy.

RULE 43. TAKING OF TESTIMONY

Rule 43.01. Form

In all trials the testimony of witnesses shall be taken orally in open court, unless otherwise provided by statute or by these rules, the Minnesota Rules of Evidence, or other rules adopted by the Supreme Court.

Adopted June 25, 1951, eff. Jan. 1, 1952. Amended March 21, 1985, eff. July 1, 1985. Revised Oct. 18, 1988, eff. Jan. 1, 1989. Amended Nov. 22, 1996, eff. Jan. 1, 1997.

Advisory Committee Note—1985

This rule is changed to conform the Rules of Civil Procedure to practice under the Minnesota Rules of Evidence, adopted in 1977 and which govern proceedings in the courts of the State. *See* Minn. R.Evid. 101 & 1101(a).

Advisory Committee Comments—1996 Amendments

The changes to this rule conforms it to its federal counterpart. The existing rule predates the adoption of the Minnesota Rules of Evidence, and creates conflicts with those rules in practice. It is appropriate to have all provisions relating to evidence contained in a single location, and to have the rules of civil procedure only refer to those rules where necessary.

Historical Notes

The order of the Minnesota Supreme Court [C6-84-2134] dated November 22, 1996, provides in part that the "(a)mendments shall apply to all actions pending on the effective date [January 1, 1997] and to those filed thereafter" and that "(t)he inclusion of Advisory Committee comments is made for convenience and does not reflect court approval of the comments made therein".

Rules 43.02, 43.03. Abrogated Nov. 22, 1996, eff. Jan. 1, 1997

Advisory Committee Comments—1996 Amendments

The changes to this rule conforms it to its federal counterpart. The existing rule predates the adoption of the Minnesota Rules of Evidence, and creates conflicts with those rules in practice. It is appropriate to have all provisions relating to evidence contained in a single location, and to have the rules of civil procedure only refer to those rules where necessary.

Historical Notes

The abrogated rules related to the examination of hostile witnesses and adverse parties and a record of excluded evidence, respectively.

The order of the Minnesota Supreme Court [C6-84-2134] dated November 22, 1996, provides in part that the "(a)mendments shall apply to all actions pending on the effective date [January 1, 1997] and to those filed thereafter" and that "(t)he inclusion of Advisory Committee comments is made for convenience and does not reflect court approval of the comments made therein".

Rule 43.04. Affirmation in Lieu of Oath

Whenever under these rules an oath is required to be taken, a solemn affirmation may be accepted in lieu thereof.

Adopted June 25, 1951, eff. Jan. 1, 1952. Revised Oct. 18, 1988, eff. Jan. 1, 1989.

Rule 43.05. Evidence and Motions

Whenever a motion is based on facts not appearing of record, the court may hear the matter on affidavits presented by the respective parties, but the court may direct that the matter be heard wholly or partly on oral testimony or depositions.

Adopted June 25, 1951, eff. Jan. 1, 1952. Revised Oct. 18, 1988, eff. Jan. 1, 1989.

Rule 43.06. Abrogated Nov. 22, 1996, eff. Jan. 1, 1997

Advisory Committee Comments—1996 Amendments

The changes to this rule conforms it to its federal counterpart. The existing rule predates the adoption of the Minnesota Rules of Evidence, and creates conflicts with those rules in practice. It is appropriate to have all provisions relating to evidence contained in a single location, and to have the rules of civil procedure only refer to those rules where necessary.

Historical Notes

The abrogated rule related to res ipsa loquitur.

The order of the Minnesota Supreme Court [C6-84-2134] dated November 22, 1996, provides in part that the "(a)mendments shall apply to all actions pending on the effective date [January 1, 1997] and to those filed thereafter" and that "(t)he inclusion of Advisory Committee comments is made for convenience and does not reflect court approval of the comments made therein".

Rule 43.07. Interpreters

The court may appoint an interpreter of its own selection and may fix reasonable compensation. The compensation shall be paid out of funds provided by law.

Adopted Nov. 10, 1967, eff. Feb. 1, 1968. Revised Oct. 18, 1988, eff. Jan. 1, 1989. Amended Nov. 30, 2005, eff. Jan. 1, 2006.

Advisory Committee Note—1968

Minnesota previously had no rule relating to interpreters. The rule follows the federal rule. Presently no state funds are available to compensate interpreters except under M.S.A. 253.053. This rule would permit interpreters for deaf or dumb persons.

Advisory Committee Comment—2006 Amendment

Rule 43.07 is amended to conform the rule to the statutory requirement that the "fees and expenses of a qualified per diem interpreter for a court must be paid by the state courts." Minn. Stat. § 546.44, subd. 3 (2004). Language is stricken from the second sentence to eliminate the conflict between the rule and statute regarding payment of court-appointed interpreters.

This amendment is drawn from the language of Minn. R. Crim. P. 26.03, subd. 16.

RULE 44. PROOF OF OFFICIAL RECORD

Rule 44.01. Authentication

(a) Domestic. An official record kept within the United States, or any state, district, commonwealth, or within a territory subject to the administrative or judicial jurisdiction of the United States, or an entry therein, when admissible for any purpose, may be evidenced by an official publication thereof or by a copy attested by the officer having the legal custody of the record, or by the officer's deputy, and accompanied by a certificate that such officer has the custody. The certificate may be made by a judge of a court of record of the district or political subdivision in which the record is kept, authenticated by the seal of the court, or may be made by any public officer having a seal of office and having official duties in the district or political subdivision in which the record is kept, authenticated by the seal of the officer's office.

(b) Foreign. A foreign official record, or an entry therein, when admissible for any purpose, may be evidenced by an official publication thereof; or a copy thereof, attested by a person authorized to make the attestation, and accompanied by a final certification as to the genuineness of the signature and official position (i) of the attesting person, or (ii) of any foreign official whose certificate of genuineness of signature and official position relates to the attestation or is in a chain of certificates of genuineness of signature and official position relating to the attestation. A final certification may be made by a secretary of embassy or legation, consul general, vice consul, or consular agent of the United States, or a diplomatic or consular official of the foreign country assigned or accredited to the United States. If reasonable opportunity has been given to all parties to investigate the authenticity and accuracy of the documents, the court may, for good cause shown, (i) admit an attested copy without final certification or (ii) permit the foreign official record to be evidenced by an attested summary with or without a final certification. The final certification is unnecessary if the record and the attestation are certified as provided in a treaty or convention to which the United States and the foreign country in which the official record is located are parties.

Adopted June 25, 1951, eff. Jan. 1, 1952. Amended Nov. 10, 1967, eff. Feb. 1, 1968. Revised Oct. 18, 1988, eff. Jan. 1, 1989. Amended Nov. 22, 1996, eff. Jan. 1, 1997.

Comment—Rule 44

See comment following Rule 44.04.

Historical Notes

The order of the Minnesota Supreme Court [C6-84-2134] dated November 22, 1996, provides in part that the "(a)mendments shall apply to all actions pending on the effective date [January 1, 1997] and to those filed thereafter" and that "(t)he inclusion of Advisory Committee comments is made for convenience and does not reflect court approval of the comments made therein".

Rule 44.02. Lack of Record

A written statement that after diligent search no record or entry of a specified tenor is found to exist in the records designated by the statement, authenticated as provided in Rule 44.01(a) in the case of a domestic record, or complying with the requirements of Rule 44.01(b) for a summary in the case of a foreign record, is admissible as evidence that the records contain no such record or entry.

Adopted June 25, 1951, eff. Jan. 1, 1952. Amended Nov. 10, 1967, eff. Feb. 1, 1968. Revised Oct. 18, 1988, eff. Jan. 1, 1989.

Comment—Rule 44

See comment following Rule 44.04.

Rule 44.03. Other Proof

This rule does not prevent the proof of official records or of entry or lack of entry therein by any other method authorized by law.

Adopted June 25, 1951, eff. Jan. 1, 1952. Amended Nov. 10, 1967, eff. Feb. 1, 1968. Revised Oct. 18, 1988, eff. Jan. 1, 1989.

Comment—Rule 44

See comment following Rule 44.04.

Rule 44.04. Abrogated Nov. 22, 1996, eff. Jan. 1, 1997

Advisory Committee Comments—1996 Amendments

These changes conform the rule to its federal counterpart. These amendments reflect the view that questions of evidence should be determined under the Minnesota Rules of Evidence and the decisional law arising under those rules. The existing rule is not helpful to courts or litigants.

Historical Notes

The abrogated rule related to the determination of foreign law.

The order of the Minnesota Supreme Court [C6-84-2134] dated November 22, 1996, provides in part that the "(a)mendments shall apply to all actions pending on the effective date [January 1, 1997] and to those filed thereafter" and that "(t)he inclusion of Advisory Committee comments is made for convenience and does not reflect court approval of the comments made therein".

RULE 45. SUBPOENA

Rule 45.01. Form; Issuance

(a) Form. Every subpoena shall

(1) state the name of the court from which it is issued; and

(2) state the title of the action, the name of the court in which it is pending, and its court file number, if one has been assigned; and

(3) command each person to whom it is directed to attend and give testimony or to produce and permit inspection, copying, testing, or sampling of designated books, documents, electronically stored information, or tangible things in the possession, custody or control of that person, or to permit inspection of premises, at a time and place therein specified; and

(4) contain a notice to the person to whom it is directed advising that person of the right to reimbursement for certain expenses pursuant to Rule 45.03(d), and the right to have the amount of those expenses determined prior to compliance with the subpoena.

A command to produce evidence or to permit inspection, copying, testing, or sampling may be joined with a command to appear at trial or hearing or at deposition, or may be issued separately. A subpoena may specify the form or forms in which electronically stored information is to be produced.

(b) Subpoenas Issued in Name of Court. A subpoena commanding attendance at a trial or hearing, for attendance at a deposition, or for production, or inspection, copying, testing, or sampling shall be issued in the name of the court where the action is pending.

(c) Issuance by Court or by Attorney. The court administrator shall issue a subpoena, signed but otherwise in blank, to a party requesting it, who shall complete it before service. An attorney as officer of the court may also issue and sign a subpoena on behalf of the court where the action is pending.

(d) Subpoena for Taking Deposition, Action Pending in Foreign Jurisdiction. A subpoena for attendance at a deposition to be taken in Minnesota for an action pending in a foreign jurisdiction may be issued by the court administrator or by an attorney admitted to practice in Minnesota in the name of the court for the county in which the deposition will be taken, provided that the deposition is allowed and has been properly noticed under the law of the jurisdiction in which the action is pending. The subpoena may command the person to whom it is directed to produce and permit inspection and copying of designated books, papers, documents, electronically stored information, or tangible things that constitute or contain matters within the scope of the examination permitted by the law of the jurisdiction in which the action is pending, but in that event, the subpoena will be subject to the provisions of Rules 26.03 and 45.03(b)(2).

(e) Notice to Parties. Any use of a subpoena, other than to compel attendance at a trial, without prior notice to all parties to the action, is improper and may subject the party or attorney issuing it, or on whose behalf it was issued, to sanctions.

Adopted Nov. 30, 2005, eff. Jan. 1, 2006. Amended May 21, 2007, eff. July 1, 2007.

Comment—Rule 45

See comment following Rule 45.05.

Rule 45.02. Service

(a) Who May Serve and Method of Service; Timing of Notice. A subpoena may be served by any person who is not a party and is not less than 18 years of age. Service of a subpoena upon a person named therein shall be made by delivering a copy thereof to such person or by leaving a copy at the person's usual place of abode with some person of suitable age and discretion then residing therein and, if the person's attendance is commanded, by tendering to that person the fees for one day's attendance and the mileage allowed by law. When the subpoena is issued on behalf of the state of Minnesota or an officer or agency thereof, fees and mileage need not be tendered. A subpoena commanding production for inspection, copying, testing, or sampling of designated books, papers, documents, or electronically stored information, tangible things, or inspection of premises, must be served on the subject of the subpoena, and notice of the required production must be served in the manner prescribed by Rule 5.02 on each party to the action, at least 7 days before the required production.

(b) Statewide Service. Subject to Rule 45.03(c)(1)(B), a subpoena may be served at any place within the state of Minnesota.

(c) Proof of Service. Proof of service when necessary shall be made by filing with the court administrator of the court on behalf of which the subpoena is issued a statement of the date and manner of service and of the names of the persons served, certified by the person who made the service.

(d) Compensation of Subpoenaed Person. The party serving the subpoena shall make arrangements for reasonable compensation as required under Rule 45.03(d) prior to the time of commanded production or the taking of such testimony. If such reasonable arrangements are not made, the person subpoenaed may proceed under Rule 45.03(c) or 45.03(b)(2). The party serving the subpoena may, if objection has been made, move upon notice to the deponent and all parties for an order directing the amount of such compensation at any time before the taking of the deposition. Any amounts paid shall be subject to the provisions of Rule 54.04.

Adopted Nov. 30, 2005, eff. Jan. 1, 2006. Amended May 21, 2007, eff. July 1, 2007; May 3, 2010, eff. July 1, 2010.

Comment—Rule 45

See comment following Rule 45.05.

Rule 45.03. Protection of Persons Subject to Subpoenas

(a) Requirement to Avoid Undue Burden. A party or an attorney responsible for the issuance and service of a subpoena shall take reasonable steps to avoid imposing undue burden or expense on a person subject to that subpoena. The court on behalf of which the subpoena was issued shall enforce this duty and impose upon the party or attorney in breach of this duty an appropriate sanction, which may include, but is not limited to, lost earnings and a reasonable attorney's fee.

(b) Subpoena for Document Production Without Deposition.

(1) A person commanded to produce and permit inspection, copying, testing, or sampling of designated electronically stored information, books, papers, documents, or tangible things, or inspection of premises need not appear in person at the place of production or inspection unless commanded to appear for deposition, hearing, or trial.

(2) Subject to Rule 45.04(b), a person commanded to produce and permit inspection, copying, testing, or sampling may, within 14 days after service of the subpoena or before the time specified for compliance if such time is less than 14 days after service, serve upon the party or attorney designated in the subpoena written objection to producing any or all of the designated materials or inspection of the premises—or to producing electronically stored information in the form or forms requested. If objection is made, the party serving the subpoena shall not be entitled to inspect, copy, test, or sample the materials or inspect the premises except pursuant to an order of the court by which the subpoena was issued. If objection has been made, the party serving the subpoena may, upon notice to the person commanded to produce, move at any time for an order to compel the production, inspection, copying, testing, or sampling. Such an order to compel production shall protect any person who is not a party or an officer of a party from significant expense resulting from the inspection, copying, testing, or sampling commanded.

(c) Motion to Quash or Modify Subpoena.

(1) On timely motion, the court on behalf of which a subpoena was issued shall quash or modify the subpoena if it

(A) fails to allow reasonable time for compliance;

(B) requires a person who is not a party or an officer of a party to travel to a place outside the county where that person resides, is employed or regularly transacts business in person, except that, subject to the provisions of Rule 45.03(c)(2)(C), such a person may in order to attend trial be commanded to travel from any such place within the state of Minnesota, or

(C) requires disclosure of privileged or other protected matter and no exception or waiver applies, or

(D) subjects a person to undue burden.

(2) If a subpoena

(A) requires disclosure of a trade secret or other confidential research, development, or commercial information, or

(B) requires disclosure of an unretained expert's opinion or information not describing specific events or occurrences in dispute and resulting from the expert's study made not at the request of any party, or

(C) requires a person who is not a party or an officer of a party to incur substantial expense to travel outside the county where that person resides, is employed or regularly transacts business in person to attend trial, the court may, to protect a person subject to or affected by the subpoena, quash or modify the subpoena or, if the party in whose behalf the subpoena is issued shows a substantial need for the testimony or material that cannot be otherwise met without undue hardship and assures that the person to whom the subpoena is addressed will be reasonably compensated, the court may order appearance or production only upon specified conditions.

(d) Compensation of Certain Non–Party Witnesses. Subject to the provisions of Rules 26.02 and 26.03, a witness who is not a party to the action or an employee of a party [except a person appointed pursuant to Rule 30.02(f)] and who is required to give testimony or produce documents relating to a profession, business, or trade, or relating to knowledge, information, or facts obtained as a result of activities in such profession, business, or trade, is entitled to reasonable compensation for the time and expense involved in preparing for and giving such testimony or producing such documents.

Adopted Nov. 30, 2005, eff. Jan. 1, 2006. Amended May 21, 2007, eff. July 1, 2007.

Comment—Rule 45

See comment following Rule 45.05.

Rule 45.04. Duties in Responding to Subpoena

(a) Form of Production; Participation of Other Parties; Rescheduling.

(1) A person responding to a subpoena to produce documents shall produce them as they are kept in the usual course of business or shall organize and label them to correspond with the categories in the demand.

(2) If a subpoena does not specify the form or forms for producing electronically stored information, a person responding to a subpoena must produce the information in a form or forms in which the person ordinarily maintains it or in a form or forms that are reasonably usable.

(3) A person responding to a subpoena need not produce the same electronically stored information in more than one form.

(4) A person responding to a subpoena need not provide discovery of electronically stored information from sources that the person identifies as not reasonably accessible because of undue burden or cost. On motion to compel discovery or to quash, the person from whom discovery is sought must show that the information sought is not reasonably accessible because of undue burden or cost. If that showing is made, the court may nonetheless order discovery from such sources if the requesting party shows good cause, considering the limitations of Rule 26.02(b)(3). The court may specify conditions for the discovery.

(5) The party issuing a subpoena for production or inspection shall make available to all parties any books, papers, documents or electronically stored information obtained from any person following issuance of a subpoena to that person. If production or inspection is made at a time or place, in a manner, or to an extent and scope, different from that commanded in the subpoena, the party issuing the subpoena must give notice to all parties to the action at least 7 days in advance of the rescheduled production. Any party may attend and participate in any noticed or rescheduled production or inspection and may also require production or inspection within the scope of the subpoena for inspection or copying.

(b) Claims of Privilege.

(1) When information subject to a subpoena is withheld on a claim that it is privileged or subject to protection as trial-preparation materials, the claim shall be made expressly and shall be supported by a description of the nature of the documents, communications, or things not produced that is sufficient to enable the demanding party to contest the claim.

(2) If information is produced in response to a subpoena that is subject to a claim of privilege or of protection as trial-preparation material, the person making the claim may notify any party that received the information of the claim and the basis for it. After being notified, a party must promptly return, sequester, or destroy the specified information and any copies it has and may not use or disclose the information until the claim is resolved. A receiving party may promptly present the information to the court under seal for a determination of the claim. If the receiving party disclosed the information before being notified, it must take reasonable steps to retrieve it. The person who produced the information must preserve the information until the claim is resolved.

Adopted Nov. 30, 2005, eff. Jan. 1, 2006. Amended May 21, 2007, eff. July 1, 2007; May 3, 2010, eff. July 1, 2010.

Comment—Rule 45

See comment following Rule 45.05.

Rule 45.05. Contempt

Failure by any person without adequate excuse to obey a subpoena served upon that person may be deemed a contempt of the court on behalf of which the subpoena was issued. An adequate cause for failure to obey exists when a subpoena purports to require a non-party to attend or produce at a place not within the limits provided by Rule 45.03(c)(1)(B).

Adopted Nov. 30, 2005, eff. Jan. 1, 2006.

Advisory Committee Comment—2006 Amendment

Rule 45 is replaced, virtually in its entirety, by its federal counterpart. Provisions of the federal rule that do not apply in state court practice are deleted or replaced by comparable provisions consistent with current Minnesota practice. The new rule recognizes the scope of the subpoena power in the existing rule and does not significantly change it. Portions of the federal rule not relevant to state practice have been deleted. The rule adopts the language of the federal rules referring to the court where an action is pending. Because Minnesota allows actions to be commenced by service, the action is "pending" before the court named in the caption after service even though it is not on file with the court. *See* Minn. R. Civ. P. 3.01. The rule is not intended to change the existing practice that permitted subpoenas to be issued even though an action had not been filed.

The most significant "new" provisions of the rule are the authorization of issuance of subpoenas by attorneys as officers of the court (Rule 45.01(c)) and the adoption of a mechanism for requiring production of documents without requiring a deposition to be conducted (Rule 45.01(a)(3)). The rule retains the provisions of former Rule 45.06, which provide for expenses of non-parties put to particular expense of complying with a subpoena. Those provisions are now bifurcated, with portions relating to notice of the right to costs in Rule 45.01, dealing with the form of subpoenas, and the provision requiring payment in Rule 45.03(d). Additionally, Rule 45.03(a) places an affirmative duty on the attorney issuing or serving a subpoena to avoid imposing undue burden or expense on the person receiving it.

Advisory Committee Comment—2007 Amendment

Rule 45.01 is amended to add a process, in Rule 45.01(d), for issuance of a subpoena to compel attendance in Minnesota at a deposition in an action pending in another jurisdiction. The procedure in this section essentially follows that contained in former Rule 45.04(a), which was abrogated in 2005.

Rule 45.01(e) is a new rule intended to clarify the existing rule because of continuing confusion over the need to provide notice to all parties before issuance of a subpoena for pretrial discovery. Existing Rule 45.02(a) explicitly requires notice, but that provision has been overlooked in a number of instances reported to the advisory committee. Accordingly, Rule 45.01(e) is included to make the requirement of notice more prominent and to make it clearly apply to every use of a subpoena prior to trial. The rule does not specify the form of notice required, but it would normally be accomplished by providing either a copy of the subpoena at the time it is served on the non-party or by unambiguous notice in some other way that a non-party is being subpoenaed.

Rule 45.02(d) is amended to establish an explicit deadline for making arrangements for compensation by a party receiving a subpoena that requires only the production of documents without a deposition. By adding the words "commanded production or" to the first sentence, the rule applies explicitly to this situation, and establishes the same deadline as for a deposition.

Rule 45 is also amended to include provisions for use of subpoenas to obtain discovery of electronically stored information. These amendments relate to the discovery of electronically stored information, and generally just incorporate into Rule 45 for subpoena practice the procedures of Rules 26, 30, 33, 34, and 37 for discovery from parties.

Advisory Committee Comment—2010 Amendment

Rule 45 is amended in several ways to prevent misuse of subpoenas. These amendments are consistent with the purpose of two provisions of the existing rule. Under Rule 45.01(e), notice of issuance of a subpoena is required in order that all parties have an opportunity to participate in the production and to curtail use of a subpoena for ex parte investigation. Rule 45.03(a) explicitly recognizes that the costs of discovery from non-parties should be borne, to the extent feasible, by the parties to the action and the burden on subpoenaed parties should be minimized. The amendment in 2010 adds language to Rule 45.02(a) that is intended to make even more explicit the proper notice for use of a subpoena for production of documents, etc.

Rule 45.04(a) is amended by the addition of paragraph (5) that is intended to reinforce that the proper use of a subpoena for production is to obtain information for use by all parties to the litigation, and not for ex parte use by a single party. Once a subpoena is issued to a non-party, information produced or testimony by that non-party must be made available to all parties. The new language also facilitates the orderly production of information. Rule 45 was amended in 2006 to permit use of subpoenas to require production of documents and other information from non-parties without requiring a deposition to be scheduled and, indeed, without even requiring a personal appearance. *See* Rule 45.03(b). Where the non-party and the party that issued a subpoena make alternative arrangements for production in response to the subpoena—which may be entirely proper—the potential exists that the production would occur without the knowledge of the other parties to the action. That production, without notice to the parties, is improper and essentially prevents participation by the parties who had received notice of another time of production. The amended rule places a duty on the party issuing the subpoena either to arrange production at a time agreeable to all parties and the non-party or to give notice to the other parties.

The amended rule is intended to create a streamlined process that minimizes the burdens of discovery on non-parties and reinforces the rights of all parties to participate in court-sanctioned discovery on an equal footing. There may still be circumstances where other parties will want to serve separate subpoenas to the same non-party, either to request additional documents or inspection or copying, or to obtain documents in a different format. Ideally, the parties will coordinate their efforts to minimize the costs and other burdens of production on the person receiving a subpoena.

Notice of the intention to comply with a subpoena in some manner other than that noticed in the subpoena is important because one of the parties may have valid objections to the production taking place at all. Under the revised rule, no production can properly occur without all parties having at least seven days notice, providing any party the opportunity either to participate in the production or to seek a protective order to prevent the production from taking place. Because of the expedited hearing requirement for commitment proceedings under Minn. Stat. ch. 253B, subpoenas for production in those proceedings are subject to a 24–hour notice requirement as provided in a new Rule 25 added to the Special Rules of Procedure Governing Proceedings Under the Minnesota Commitment and Treatment Act.

RULE 46. EXCEPTIONS UNNECESSARY

Formal exceptions to rulings or orders of the court are unnecessary; but for all purposes for which an exception has heretofore been taken it is sufficient that a party, at the time the ruling or order of the court is made or sought, makes known to the court the action which the party desires the court to take or any objection to the action of the court and the grounds therefor; and, if a party has no opportunity to object to a ruling or order at the time it is made, the absence of an objection does not thereafter prejudice the party. A minute of the objection to the ruling or order shall be made by the judge or reporter.

Adopted June 25, 1951, eff. Jan. 1, 1952. Amended Nov. 26, 1969. Revised Oct. 18, 1988, eff. Jan. 1, 1989.

RULE 47. JURORS

Rule 47.01. Examination of Jurors

The court may permit the parties or their attorneys to conduct the examination of prospective jurors or may itself conduct the examination. In the latter event, the court shall permit the parties or their attorneys to supplement the examination by such further inquiry as it deems proper. Supplemental juror questionnaires completed by jurors shall not be accessible to the public unless formally admitted into evidence in a publicly accessible hearing or trial.

Adopted June 25, 1951, eff. Jan. 1, 1952. Revised Oct. 18, 1988, eff. Jan. 1, 1989; May 6, 2005, eff. July 1, 2005.

Comment—Rule 47

See Comment following Rule 47.04

Rule 47.02. Abrogated Aug. 27, 1998, eff. Jan. 1, 1999

Comment—Rule 47

See Comment following Rule 47.04

Historical Notes

The abrogated rule related to alternate jurors.

Rule 47.03. Separation of Jury

After the jury has retired for its deliberations, the court, in its discretion, may permit the jury to separate overnight and return to its deliberations the following morning.

Adopted Nov. 10, 1967, eff. Feb. 1, 1968. Revised Oct. 18, 1988, eff. Jan. 1, 1989.

Advisory Committee Note—1968

The practice of requiring the jury to remain together from the time the case is submitted to the jury until the final verdict of the jury creates hardships and undue expense in many cases. In many counties suitable accommodations for sleeping are not in existence. In other counties the cost of providing such sleeping accommodations is becoming prohibitive. Few, if any, civil cases require that the jury be locked up during the course of its deliberations. An adequate warning to the jury by the trial judge prior to the jury's separation should be sufficient in most cases to prevent any outside influence on the verdict. The proposed rule permits the trial judge in his sole discretion to allow the jury to separate during the deliberations. In some cases, such as protracted trials or cases involving substantial public interest, the trial judge may feel that separation is not desirable. In many other cases the trial judge may believe that separation will not effect the integrity of the jury verdict. In the opinion of the Committee, it is better practice to permit separation of the jury during its deliberations than to compel the jury to remain at the deliberations throughout the night and, perhaps, coercing a verdict through physical exhaustion.

The purpose of the amendment is related to solving the problem of overnight sleeping accommodations and is not intended to permit separation of the jury over weekends or holidays, or to permit the jury to avoid early evening deliberations. The trial judge is not to instruct the jury that they may adjourn at a given time in the evening, but rather should permit the separation at a time when it is clear that deliberations should not continue further into the night.

The proposed rule is consistent with the Minnesota practice in the use of sealed verdicts. See Colstad v. Levine, 243 Minn. 279, 64 N.W.2d 648 (1954). The same considerations set forth in the Colstad case should be considered by the trial judge in determining whether or not a separation should be permitted.

Rule 47.04. Excuse

The court may for good cause excuse a juror from service during trial or deliberation.

Adopted Aug. 27, 1998, eff. Jan. 1, 1999.

Advisory Committee Comment—1998 Amendments

Rule 47.02 is abrogated. Under this amendment, alternate jurors are no longer part of the jury trial process. Rather than seat "alternate" jurors who will, or may, then participate in the deliberations, the rule simply does not provide for two classes of jurors. Jurors who begin the case by being sworn in as jurors continue to the discharge of the jury, unless they are excused for cause as provided for by Rule 47.04. This amendment parallels the abandonment of using alternates in federal court in 1991, and is intended to resolve an ongoing source of dissatisfaction with jury service by jurors. *See* Fed. R. Civ. P. 47(b), Notes of Advisory Comm.—1991 Amends., *reprinted in* FEDERAL CIVIL JUDICIAL PROCEDURE AND RULES 205 (West 1998).

Rule 47.04 is new and is identical to Fed. R. Civ. P. 47(c). Although courts presently have the inherent power to excuse jurors even in the absence of a rule, there is no reason to have the federal rule be different from the state rule on this issue. Other than obviating confusion over whether there might be some substantive difference in intent, this amendment is not intended to change the existing practice. *See* Minn. Stat. § 546.13 (1996) (codifying authority to excuse juror).

Advisory Committee Comment—2005 Amendments

The addition of the last sentence in Rule 47.01 precluding public access to completed supplemental juror questionnaires recognizes both the legitimate privacy interests of jurors and the interests of the public in otherwise publicly accessible court proceedings. This rule does not apply to juror qualification questionnaires submitted by jurors in accordance with Minn. Gen. R. Prac. 807; public access to completed qualification questionnaires is governed by Minn. Gen. R. Prac. 814.

RULE 48. NUMBER OF JURORS; PARTICIPATION IN VERDICT

The court shall seat a jury of not fewer than six and not more than twelve members and all jurors shall participate in the verdict unless excused from service by the court pursuant to Rule 47.04. Unless otherwise provided by law or the parties otherwise stipulate, (1) the verdict shall be unanimous and (2) no verdict shall be taken from a jury reduced in size to fewer than six members.

Adopted June 25, 1951, eff. Jan. 1, 1952. Revised Oct. 18, 1988, eff. Jan. 1, 1989. Amended August 27, 1998, eff. Jan. 1, 1999; Sept. 1, 1998, eff. Jan. 1, 1999.

Advisory Committee Comment—1998 Amendments

This rule requires the court to permit all jurors to participate in deliberations. Rule 47.02 is abrogated to abolish alternate jurors, and Rule 48 expressly provides that all jurors participate in the deliberations. The rule prohibits a verdict from a jury of fewer than six jurors, unless the parties agree to a lesser number.

The rule does not provide any constraints on what size jury is appropriate in any particular case. Practical considerations of cost, courtroom design, and imposition on potential jurors as well as those seated may militate toward a jury of six. Where the trial is likely to be long, or where other considerations make it likely that jurors will need to be excused from service, more than six jurors should be seated. The rule also permits a twelve-person jury as was historically used in civil trials. Juries of twelve significantly reduce the likelihood of unusual or aberrant jury verdicts, and should be considered where the issues are unusually complex or important, or present difficult fact-finding challenges to the jury. *See generally Developments in the Law—The Civil Jury*, 110 Harv. L. Rev. 1408, 1468–80 (1997).

This rule expressly mandates seating a jury of from six to twelve jurors. Seating a larger jury is not provided for, and should be considered only in very unusual circumstances where more than six jurors are likely to be excused, making it inevitable that fewer than six will remain. Rather than risk a mistrial in that situation, the court should seek a stipulation of the parties that a verdict may be taken from a jury smaller than six. *See generally* Manual For Complex Litigation § 22.41 & n.408 (3rd ed. 1995). It may be permissible to seat a jury of larger than twelve, so long as twelve or fewer remain for deliberations, but there is no clear authority or precedent for this. If the parties stipulate to a larger jury, it should certainly not be error to seat one.

The last sentence of the rule requires a verdict to be unanimous unless there is an agreement to a less-than-unanimous verdict or it is otherwise provided by law. Both the Minnesota Constitution and statutory law allow verdicts in civil cases, even without stipulation of the parties, to be returned by 5/6ths of the jurors after six hours of deliberations. *See* Minn. Const. art. 1. § 4 and Minn. Stat. § 546.17 (1996). Where jury of more than six, but fewer than twelve, jurors deliberates, a 6/7ths, 7/8ths, 8/9ths, 9/10ths or 10/11ths verdict is permitted. For a twelve-person jury, ten of the twelve jurors (the equivalent of 5/6ths) can return a verdict.

RULE 49. SPECIAL VERDICTS AND INTERROGATORIES

Rule 49.01. Special Verdicts

(a) The court may require a jury to return only a special verdict in the form of a special written finding upon each issue of fact. In that event the court may submit to the jury written questions susceptible of categorical or other brief answer or may submit written forms of the several special findings which might properly be made under the pleadings and evidence; or it may use such other method of submitting the issues and require written findings thereon as it deems most appropriate. The court shall give to the jury such explanations and instructions concerning the matter thus submitted as may be necessary to enable the jury to make its findings upon each issue. If in so doing the court omits any issue of fact raised by the pleadings or by the evidence, each party waives the right to a trial by jury of the issue so omitted unless before the jury retires the party demands its submission to the jury. As to an issue omitted without such demand, the court may make a finding; or, if it fails to do so, it shall be deemed to have made a finding in accord with the judgment on the special verdict. Except as provided in Rule 49.01(b), neither the court nor counsel shall inform the jury of the effect of its answers on the outcome of the case.

(b) In actions involving Minn.Stat. c. 604 the court shall inform the jury of the effect of its answers to the comparative fault question and shall permit counsel to comment thereon, unless the court is of the opinion that doubtful or unresolved questions of law or complex issues of law or fact are involved which may render such instruction or comment erroneous, misleading, or confusing to the jury.

Adopted June 25, 1951, eff. Jan. 1, 1952. Amended Jan. 5, 1973. Revised Oct. 18, 1988, eff. Jan. 1, 1989.

Rule 49.02. General Verdict Accompanied by Answer to Interrogatories

The court may submit to the jury, together with appropriate forms for a general verdict, written interrogatories upon one or more issues of fact the decision of which is necessary to a verdict. The court shall give such explanation or instruction as may be necessary to enable the jury both to make answers to the interrogatories and to render a general verdict, and the court shall direct the jury both to make written answers and to render a general verdict. When the general verdict and the answers are harmonious, the court shall direct the entry of the appropriate judgment upon the verdict and answers. When the answers are consistent with each other, but one or more is inconsistent with the general verdict, the court may direct the entry of judgment in accordance with the answers, notwithstanding the general verdict, or may return the jury for further consideration of its answers and verdict, or may order a new trial. When the answers are inconsistent with each other and one or more is likewise inconsistent with the general verdict, the court shall not direct the entry of judgment, but may return the jury for further consideration of its answers and verdict, or may order a new trial.

Adopted June 25, 1951, eff. Jan. 1, 1952. Revised Oct. 18, 1988, eff. Jan. 1, 1989.

RULE 50. JUDGMENT AS A MATTER OF LAW IN JURY TRIALS; ALTERNATIVE MOTION FOR NEW TRIAL; CONDITIONAL RULINGS

Rule 50.01. Judgment as a Matter of Law During Trial

(a) Standard. If during a trial by jury a party has been fully heard on an issue and there is no legally sufficient evidentiary basis for a reasonable jury to find for that party on that issue, the court may decide the issue against that party and may grant a motion for judgment as a matter of law against that party with respect to a claim or defense that cannot under the controlling law be maintained or defeated without a favorable finding on that issue.

(b) Timing and Content. Motions for judgment as a matter of law during trial may be made at any time before submission of the case to the jury. Such a motion shall specify the judgment sought and the law and the facts on which the moving party is entitled to the judgment.

Adopted Nov. 30, 2005, eff. Jan. 1, 2006. Amended Jan. 9, 2006.

Comment—Rule 50

See comment following Rule 50.04.

Historical Notes

The order of the Minnesota Supreme Court dated January 9, 2006, provides in part:

"1. The attached amendments to Rule 50 of the Rules of Civil Procedure be, and the same are, prescribed and promulgated to be effective retroactive to January 2, 2006.

"2. These amendments shall apply to all actions or proceedings pending on or commenced on or after the effective date, provided that in cases in which a timely and otherwise proper motion is made under Rule 50.02 of the Rules of Civil Procedure; the time for appeal will be governed by Rule 104.01, subdivision 2, of the Rules of Civil Appellate Procedure, regardless of the nomenclature used for the Rule 50.02 motion.

"3. The inclusion of advisory committee comments is made for convenience and does not reflect court approval of the statements made therein."

Rule 50.02. Making or Renewing Motion for Judgment After Trial; Alternative Motion for New Trial

If, for any reason, the court does not grant a motion for judgment as a matter of law made during trial, the court is considered to have submitted the action to the jury subject to the court's later deciding the legal questions raised by the motion. Whether or not the party has moved for judgment as a matter of law before submission of the case to the jury, a party may make or renew a request for judgment as a matter of law by serving a motion within the time specified in Rule 59 for the service of a motion for a new trial—and may alternatively request a new trial or join a motion for a new trial under Rule 59. In ruling on such a motion, the court may:

(a) if a verdict was returned:

(1) allow the judgment to stand,

(2) order a new trial, or

(3) direct entry of judgment as a matter of law; or

(b) if no verdict was returned:

(1) order a new trial, or

(2) direct entry of judgment as a matter of law.

Adopted Nov. 30, 2005, eff. Jan. 1, 2006. Amended Jan. 9, 2006.

Comment—Rule 50

See comment following Rule 50.04.

Historical Notes

The order of the Minnesota Supreme Court dated November 30, 2005, provides in part:

"1. The attached amendments to the Rules of Civil Procedure, the General Rules of Practice, and the Rules of Civil Appellate Procedure be, and the same are, prescribed and promulgated to be effective on January 1, 2006.

"2. These amendments shall apply to all actions or proceedings pending on or commenced on or after the effective date, provided that in cases in which a timely and otherwise proper motion is brought under either the old or the new version of Rule 50.02 of the Rules of Civil Procedure, the time for appeal will be governed by Rule 104.01, subd. 2, of the Rules of Civil Appellate Procedure, even if the wrong version of Rule 50.02 is used."

The order of the Minnesota Supreme Court dated January 9, 2006, provides in part:

"1. The attached amendments to Rule 50 of the Rules of Civil Procedure be, and the same are, prescribed and promulgated to be effective retroactive to January 2, 2006.

"2. These amendments shall apply to all actions or proceedings pending on or commenced on or after the effective date, provided that in cases in which a timely and otherwise proper motion is made under Rule 50.02 of the Rules of Civil Procedure; the time for appeal will be governed by Rule 104.01, subdivision 2, of the Rules of Civil Appellate Procedure, regardless of the nomenclature used for the Rule 50.02 motion.

"3. The inclusion of advisory committee comments is made for convenience and does not reflect court approval of the statements made therein."

Rule 50.03. Granting Motion for Judgment as a Matter of Law; Conditional Rulings; New Trial Motion

(a) Conditional Rulings. If the motion for judgment as a matter of law is granted, the court shall also rule on the motion for a new trial, if any, by determining whether it should be granted if the judgment is thereafter vacated or reversed, and shall specify the grounds for granting or denying the motion for the new trial. If the motion for a new trial is thus conditionally granted, the order thereon does not affect the finality of the judgment. In case the motion for a new trial has been conditionally granted and the judgment is reversed on appeal, the new trial shall proceed unless the appellate court has otherwise ordered. In case the motion for a new trial has been conditionally denied, the respondent on appeal may assert error in that denial; and if the judgment is reversed on appeal, subsequent proceedings shall be in accordance with the order of the appellate court.

(b) Timing. Any motion for a new trial under Rule 59 by a party against whom judgment as a matter of law is rendered shall be served and heard within the times specified in Rule 59 for the service and hearing of a motion for a new trial.

Adopted Nov. 30, 2005, eff. Jan. 1, 2006. Amended Jan. 9, 2006.

Comment—Rule 50

See comment following Rule 50.04.

The order of the Minnesota Supreme Court dated January 9, 2006, provides in part:

"1. The attached amendments to Rule 50 of the Rules of Civil Procedure be, and the same are, prescribed and promulgated to be effective retroactive to January 2, 2006.

"2. These amendments shall apply to all actions or proceedings pending on or commenced on or after the effective date, provided that in cases in which a timely and otherwise proper motion is made under Rule 50.02 of the Rules of Civil Procedure; the time for appeal will be governed by Rule 104.01, subdivision 2, of the Rules of Civil Appellate Procedure, regardless of the nomenclature used for the Rule 50.02 motion.

"3. The inclusion of advisory committee comments is made for convenience and does not reflect court approval of the statements made therein."

Rule 50.04. Denial of Motion for Judgment as a Matter of Law

If the motion for judgment as a matter of law is denied, the party who prevailed on that motion may, as respondent on appeal, assert grounds entitling the party to a new trial in the event the appellate court concludes that the trial court erred in denying the motion for judgment. If the appellate court reverses the judgment, nothing in this rule precludes it from determining that the respondent is entitled to a new trial, or from directing the trial court to determine whether a new trial shall be granted.

Adopted Nov. 30, 2005, eff. Jan. 1, 2006.

Advisory Committee Comment—2006 Amendment

Rule 50 is amended in toto to adopt various changes made in 1991 to Fed. R. Civ. P. 50. The 1991 amendment of the federal rule was made to remove the archaic language and procedures of directing verdicts and granting j.n.o.v. The amended rule states a standard that the former rule already recognized: a uniform standard for motions made after trial begins of a "motion for judgment as a matter of law." The purpose of the change is two-fold: to adopt names that better describe the role of the motions and, because the motions essentially apply the same standard, to give them a common name.

This change is not intended to change substantive practice relating to these motions. The federal rule amendment in 1991 was not intended to change the actual practice under that rule. See Fed. R. Civ. P. 50(a), Advisory Comm. Notes—1991 Amend. The federal courts have recognized the non-substantive nature of the amendment. See 9A Charles Alan Wright & Arthur R. Miller, Federal Practice & Procedure § 2521, at 243 n.15 and accompanying text (2d ed. 1995) (collecting cases).

Minnesota practice differs from federal practice in one important respect—former Fed. R. Civ. P. 50 did not have the express provision of Minn. R. Civ. P. 50.02(a) allowing a motion for judgment n.o.v. to be brought "whether or not the party has moved for a directed verdict," and the current version of Fed. R. Civ. P. 50 lacks equivalent language with regard to motions for judgment as a matter of law. Because the amended Minnesota Rule 50.02 is not intended to change Minnesota practice in this respect, the amended rule retains the concept that a motion for judgment as a matter of law may be brought after submission of the case to the jury, whether or not such a motion was brought before submission to the jury.

The timing provisions of the federal rule have been changed slightly to accommodate Minnesota procedure including that relating to the service and filing of post-decision motions. Like the current rule, motions under Rule 50 must be served and filed in accordance with the timing mechanism and deadlines of Minn. R. Civ. P. 59.

RULE 51. INSTRUCTIONS TO THE JURY; OBJECTIONS; PRESERVING A CLAIM OF ERROR

Rule 51.01. Requests

(a) At or Before the Close of Evidence. A party may, at the close of the evidence or at an earlier reasonable time that the court directs, file and furnish to every other party written requests that the court instruct the jury on the law as set forth in the requests.

(b) After the Close of Evidence. After the close of the evidence, a party may:

(1) file requests for instructions on issues that could not reasonably have been anticipated at an earlier time for requests set under Rule 51.01(a), and

(2) with the court's permission file untimely requests for instructions on any issue.

Adopted Nov. 30, 2005, eff. Jan. 1, 2006.

Comment—Rule 51

See comment following Rule 51.04.

Rule 51.02. Instructions

The court:

(a) must inform the parties of its proposed instructions and proposed action on the requests before instructing the jury and before final jury arguments;

(b) must give the parties an opportunity to object on the record and out of the jury's hearing to the proposed instructions and actions on requests before the instructions and arguments are delivered; and

(c) may instruct the jury at any time after trial begins and before the jury is discharged.

Adopted Nov. 30, 2005, eff. Jan. 1, 2006.

Comment—Rule 51

See comment following Rule 51.04.

Rule 51.03. Objections

(a) Form. A party who objects to an instruction or the failure to give an instruction must do so on the record, stating distinctly the matter objected to and the grounds of the objection.

(b) Timeliness. An objection is timely if:

(1) a party that has been informed of an instruction or action on a request before the jury is instructed and before final jury arguments, as provided by Rule 51.02(a), objects at the opportunity for objection required by Rule 51.02(b); or

(2) a party that has not been informed of an instruction or action on a request before the time for objection provided under Rule 51.02(b) objects promptly after learning that the instruction or request will be, or has been, given or refused.

Adopted Nov. 30, 2005, eff. Jan. 1, 2006.

Comment—Rule 51

See comment following Rule 51.04.

Rule 51.04. Assigning Error; Plain Error

(a) Assigned Error. A party may assign as error:

(1) an error in an instruction actually given if that party made a proper objection under Rule 51.03, or

(2) a failure to give an instruction if that party made a proper request under Rule 51.01, and—unless the court made a definitive ruling on the record rejecting the request—also made a proper objection under Rule 51.03.

(b) Plain Error. A court may consider a plain error in the instructions affecting substantial rights that has not been preserved as required by Rule 51.04(a)(1) or (2).

Adopted Nov. 30, 2005, eff. Jan. 1, 2006.

Advisory Committee Comment—2006 Amendment

Rule 51 is entirely new with this amendment. The new rule is modeled on its federal counterpart, Fed. R. Civ. P. 51, as it was amended in 2003. The changes are intended primarily to provide detailed procedural guidance where the existing rule is either silent or vague. *See generally* Fed. R. Civ. P. 51, Advis. Comm. Notes—2003 Amend., *reprinted in* FED. CIV. JUD. PROC. & RULES 227 (West 2005 ed.).

Rule 51.02(c) continues to recognize that the court may give instructions to the jury at any time after trial begins, including preliminary instructions before opening statements or the taking of evidence, during the trial, and at the end of trial either before or after the arguments of counsel.

RULE 52. FINDINGS BY THE COURT

Rule 52.01. Effect

In all actions tried upon the facts without a jury or with an advisory jury, the court shall find the facts specially and state separately its conclusions of law thereon and direct the entry of the appropriate judgment; and in granting or refusing interlocutory injunctions the court shall similarly set forth the findings of fact and conclusions of law which constitute the grounds for its action. Requests for finding are not necessary for purposes of review. Findings of fact, whether based on oral or documentary evidence, shall not be set aside unless clearly erroneous, and due regard shall be given to the opportunity of the trial court to judge the credibility of the witnesses. The findings of a referee, to the extent adopted by the court, shall be considered as the findings of the court. It will be sufficient if the findings of fact and conclusions of law are stated orally and recorded in open court following the close of the evidence or appear in an opinion or memorandum of decision filed by the court or in an accompanying memorandum. Findings of fact and conclusions of law are unnecessary on decisions on motions pursuant to Rules 12 or 56 or any other motion except as provided in Rules 23.08(c) and 41.02.

Adopted June 25, 1951, eff. Jan. 1, 1952. Amended March 21, 1985, eff. July 1, 1985. Revised Oct. 18, 1988, eff. Jan. 1, 1989. Amended Nov. 30, 2005, eff. Jan. 1, 2006.

Advisory Committee Note—1985

The changes to Rule 52.01 are intended to permit trial courts to make findings of fact and conclusions of law orally or in a written memorandum. This change follows the change to Federal Rule 52(a) made by the 1983 amendments, and is intended to provide trial courts with greater latitude in the means of delivering decisions. The prior rule did not prohibit oral findings, and the amendment specifically allows them. The change is not intended to relax in any way the requirement that some specific statement be made of the facts found and the legal conclusions drawn from those facts. The purpose of requiring findings is to permit meaningful review upon appeal and it is therefore necessary that trial courts find facts and state conclusions clearly and specifically. For this reason, the oral findings and conclusions must be stated on the record, in the presence of the parties, in order that they are adequately preserved.

The Committee also determined that the rule should be changed to permit a written opinion or memorandum of decision to stand as findings of fact and conclusions of law in certain cases. The changes are intended to permit the trial court to issue a decision in a form suited to the case. The written opinion or memorandum must include a separate statement of the facts, and explain the legal conclusions drawn therefrom. It is not necessary that the findings of fact be identified in separately numbered paragraphs or that the conclusions of law be similarly stated.

Advisory Committee Comment—2006 Amendment

Rule 52.01 is amended to renumber one of the rule cross-references to reflect the amendment and renumbering of Rule 23 as part of the amendments effective January 1, 2006.

Rule 52.02. Amendment

Upon motion of a party served and heard not later than the times allowed for a motion for new trial pursuant to Rule 59.03, the court may amend its findings or make additional findings, and may amend the judgment accordingly if judgment has been entered. The motion may be made with a motion for a new trial and may be made on the files, exhibits, and minutes of the court. When findings of fact are made in actions tried by the court without a jury, the question of the sufficiency of the evidence to support the findings may thereafter be raised whether or not the party raising the question has made in the district court an objection to such findings or has made a motion to amend them or a motion for judgment.

Adopted June 25, 1951, eff. Jan. 1, 1952. Amended March 3, 1959, eff. July 1, 1959; Nov. 10, 1967, eff. Feb. 1, 1968. Revised Oct. 18, 1988, eff. Jan. 1, 1989. Amended Dec. 19, 2000, eff. March 1, 2001.

Advisory Committee Note—1968

This amendment is a clarifying amendment and conforms to the provisions of Rule 59.02.

Advisory Committee Comment—2000 Amendments

Although the text of this Rule 52.02 is not changed substantively by these amendments, it is worth noting that Rule 59.03, governing the time for filing a motion for a new trial is changed to expand the time from 15 days to 30 days for filing the motion and from 30 days to 60 days for having the motion heard. This amendment has the practical effect of extending the time for filing a motion for amended findings under Rule 52 because Rule 52.02 incorporates the filing and hearing time limits of Rule 59.

Historical Notes

The order of the Minnesota Supreme Court [CX-84-2134] dated December 19, 2000, provides in part that these amendments are effective March 1, 2001, and shall apply to all actions or proceedings pending on or commenced on or after the effective date, with the exception of the amendments to Rule 59, which shall apply to all actions or proceedings commenced on or after the effective date and all actions or proceedings pending on or decided before the effective date in which the time periods stated in the former Rule 59 have not expired.

The order of the Minnesota Supreme Court [CX-84-2134] dated December 19, 2000, provides in part that "(t)he inclusion of Advisory Committee comments is made for convenience and does not reflect court approval of the statements made therein".

RULE 53. MASTERS

Rule 53.01. Appointment

(a) Authority for Appointment. Unless a statute provides otherwise, a court may appoint a master only to:

(1) perform duties consented to by the parties;

(2) hold trial proceedings and make or recommend findings of fact on issues to be decided by the court without a jury if appointment is warranted by

(A) some exceptional condition, or

(B) the need to perform an accounting or resolve a difficult computation of damages; or

(3) address pretrial and post-trial matters that cannot be addressed effectively and timely by an available district judge.

(b) Disqualification. A master must not have a relationship to the parties, counsel, action, or court that would require disqualification of a judge, unless the parties consent with the court's approval to appointment of a particular person after disclosure of any potential grounds for disqualification.

(c) Expense. In appointing a master, the court must consider the fairness of imposing the likely expenses on the parties and must protect against unreasonable expense or delay.

Adopted Nov. 30, 2005, eff. Jan. 1, 2006.

Comment—Rule 53

See comment following Rule 53.09.

Rule 53.02. Order Appointing Master

(a) Notice. The court must give the parties notice and an opportunity to be heard before appointing a master. A party may suggest candidates for appointment.

(b) Contents. The order appointing a master must direct the master to proceed with all reasonable diligence and must state:

(1) the master's duties, including any investigation or enforcement duties, and any limits on the master's authority under Rule 53.03;

(2) the circumstances—if any—in which the master may communicate ex parte with the court or a party;

(3) the nature of the materials to be preserved and filed as the record of the master's activities;

(4) the time limits, method of filing the record, other procedures, and standards for reviewing the master's orders, findings, and recommendations; and

(5) the basis, terms, and procedure for fixing the master's compensation under Rule 53.08.

(c) Entry of Order. The court may enter the order appointing a master only after the master has filed an affidavit disclosing whether there is any ground for disqualification and, if a ground for disqualification is disclosed, after the parties have consented with the court's approval to waive the disqualification.

(d) Amendment. The order appointing a master may be amended at any time after notice to the parties and an opportunity to be heard.

Adopted Nov. 30, 2005, eff. Jan. 1, 2006.

Comment—Rule 53

See comment following Rule 53.09.

Rule 53.03. Master's Authority

Unless the appointing order expressly directs otherwise, a master has authority to regulate all proceedings and take all appropriate measures to perform fairly and efficiently the assigned duties. The master may by order impose upon a party any noncontempt sanction provided by Rule 37 or 45, and may recommend a contempt sanction against a party and sanctions against a nonparty.

Adopted Nov. 30, 2005, eff. Jan. 1, 2006.

Comment—Rule 53

See comment following Rule 53.09.

Rule 53.04. Evidentiary Hearings

Unless the appointing order expressly directs otherwise, a master conducting an evidentiary hearing may exercise the power of the appointing court to compel, take, and record evidence.

Adopted Nov. 30, 2005, eff. Jan. 1, 2006.

Comment—Rule 53

See comment following Rule 53.09.

Rule 53.05. Master's Orders

A master who makes an order must file the order and promptly serve a copy on each party. The court administrator must enter the order on the docket.

Adopted Nov. 30, 2005, eff. Jan. 1, 2006.

Comment—Rule 53

See comment following Rule 53.09.

Rule 53.06. Master's Reports

A master must report to the court as required by the order of appointment. The master must file the report and promptly serve a copy of the report on each party unless the court directs otherwise.

Adopted Nov. 30, 2005, eff. Jan. 1, 2006.

Comment—Rule 53

See comment following Rule 53.09.

Rule 53.07. Action on Master's Order, Report, or Recommendations

(a) Action. In acting on a master's order, report, or recommendations, the court must afford an opportunity to be heard and may receive evidence, and may: adopt or affirm; modify; wholly or partly reject or reverse; or resubmit to the master with instructions.

(b) Time To Object or Move. A party may file objections to—or a motion to adopt or modify—the master's order, report, or recommendations no later than 20 days from the time the master's order, report, or recommendations are served, unless the court sets a different time.

(c) Fact Findings. The court must decide de novo all objections to findings of fact made or recommended by a master unless the parties stipulate with the court's consent that:

(1) the master's findings will be reviewed for clear error, or

(2) the findings of a master appointed under Rule 53.01(a)(1) or (3) will be final.

(d) Legal Conclusions. The court must decide de novo all objections to conclusions of law made or recommended by a master.

(e) Procedural Matters. Unless the order of appointment establishes a different standard of review, the court may set aside a master's ruling on a procedural matter only for an abuse of discretion.

Adopted Nov. 30, 2005, eff. Jan. 1, 2006.

Comment—Rule 53

See comment following Rule 53.09.

Rule 53.08. Compensation

(a) Fixing Compensation. The court must fix the master's compensation before or after judgment on the basis and terms stated in the order of appointment, but the court may set a new basis and terms after notice and an opportunity to be heard.

(b) Payment. The compensation fixed under Rule 53.08(a) must be paid either:

(1) by a party or parties; or

(2) from a fund or subject matter of the action within the court's control.

(c) Allocation. The court must allocate payment of the master's compensation among the parties after considering the nature and amount of the controversy, the means of the parties, and the extent to which any party is more responsible than other parties for the reference to a master. An interim allocation may be amended to reflect a decision on the merits.

Adopted Nov. 30, 2005, eff. Jan. 1, 2006.

Comment—Rule 53

See comment following Rule 53.09.

Rule 53.09. Appointment of Statutory Referee

A statutory referee employed in the judicial branch is subject to this rule only when the order referring a matter to the statutory referee expressly provides that the reference is made under this rule.

Adopted Nov. 30, 2005, eff. Jan. 1, 2006.

Advisory Committee Comment—2006 Amendment

Rule 53 is replaced by a new rule derived nearly verbatim from its federal counterpart, Fed. R. Civ. P. 53. The federal rule was extensively revised by amendment in 2003. That amendment was taken up by the federal advisory committee after it had received empirical research on the use of masters in federal court. *See* THOMAS E. WILLGING *ET AL.*, SPECIAL MASTERS' INCIDENCE AND ACTIVITY (Fed. Jud. Ctr. 2000).

The federal rule provides significantly more detailed guidance to courts and litigants on the proper use of masters than either its predecessor or the current Minnesota rule. The committee believes that the changes to the federal rule are thoughtful and are valuable to litigants, and therefore appropriate for adoption in Minnesota.

The rule is not intended to expand the use of masters, but is designed to make the use of masters more readily accomplished in the minority of cases where their use is warranted.

Rule 53.01 includes specific guidance on the circumstances justifying or permitting the appointment of a master. Most significantly, the rule clarifies that in the absence of consent a master cannot be assigned to try issues on which the parties are entitled to a jury trial; mere press of other business would not trump the jury trial right. Although the court has greater latitude under the rule for issues triable to the court, either consent or some truly exceptional circumstances must be present. Short of trying issues, however, there are many roles that masters may play in civil cases, particularly in complex cases where the parties consent to the appointment. *See generally* Lynn Jokela & David F. Herr, *Special Masters in State Court Complex Litigation: An Available and Underused Case Management Tool*, 31 WM. MITCHELL L. REV. 1299 (2005).

Rule 53.02 establishes specific requirements for the order appointing a master. These subjects reflect a form of "best practices" for the use of masters, and they define procedures to be followed upon referral to a master. The rule intentionally makes these provisions mandatory because they are matters prone to dispute if not resolved at the time of appointment.

Rule 53.03 clarifies the extent of a master's authority and defines those powers expansively within the confines of the duties assigned to the master. The rule explicitly authorizes the imposition of discovery sanctions other than contempt by a master, and allows a master to recommend imposition of contempt sanctions.

The procedures established under Rule 53.07 are intended to clarify the role of master and ensure that all parties, including the appointing judge and appointed master, understand the master's role. The standards of review of a master's decisions are particularly important to the parties and the court, and are set forth with special detail.

Compensation of masters under this rule should be established in the order of appointment. *See* Rule 53.02(b)(5). In the majority of cases, compensation will be ordered to be paid by the parties pursuant to Rule 53.08(b)(1). The provision of Rule 53.08(b)(2) provides for payment from a fund created by the litigation, as where fees are awarded under the "common fund" doctrine, or by a fund that is the subject matter of the litigation. The federal rule advisory committee has recognized that it may be appropriate to revise the allocation ordered on an interim basis once the action is concluded. *See* Fed. R. Civ. P. 53(h), Advis. Comm. Notes—2003 Amend., *reprinted in* FED. CIV. JUD. PROC. & RULES 237 (West 2005 ed.).

Rule 53.09 distinguishes between masters under this rule, and regular court employees authorized as "referees" by statute. "Statutory referees" as used in the rule refers to court employees, whether full- or part-time, who serve regularly in multiple cases or calendars. *See, e.g.*, Minn. Stat. §§ 260.031 (juvenile court referees authorized); 484.013, subd. 3 (referees authorized for housing calendar consolidation program); 484.70 (referees generally in district court); 491A.03, subd. 1 (2004) (referees in conciliation court in second and fourth districts). In certain situations, a "referee" appointed pursuant to statute for a single case should be viewed as a master under Rule 53. *See, e.g.*, Minn. Stat. §§ 116B.05 (referee in particular environmental action); 558.04 (2004) (referees for partition of real estate). The procedures governing statutory referees are generally found in the statutes authorizing their use.

RULE 54. JUDGMENTS; COSTS

Rule 54.01. Definition; Form

Judgment as used in these rules includes a decree and means the final determination of the rights of the parties in an action or proceeding. A judgment shall not contain a recital of pleadings, the report of a referee, or the record of prior proceedings.

Adopted June 25, 1951, eff. Jan. 1, 1952. Revised Oct. 18, 1988, eff. Jan. 1, 1989.

Rule 54.02. Judgment upon Multiple Claims

When multiple claims for relief or multiple parties are involved in an action, the court may direct the entry of a final judgment as to one or more but fewer than all of the claims or parties only upon an express determination that there is no just reason for delay and upon an express direction for the entry of judgment. In the absence of such determination and direction, any order or other form of decision, however designated, which adjudicates fewer than all the claims or the rights and liabilities of fewer than all the parties shall not terminate the action as to any of the claims or parties, and the order or other form of decision is subject to revision at any time before the entry of judgment adjudicating all the claims and the rights and liabilities of all the parties.

Adopted June 25, 1951, eff. Jan. 1, 1952. Amended March 3, 1959, eff. July 1, 1959. Revised Oct. 18, 1988, eff. Jan. 1, 1989.

Advisory Committee Note—1959

Some federal courts have held that final judgment may be entered only on fewer than all of the claims, and not as to fewer than all of the parties. The amendment follows the majority rule and clarifies the language.

Rule 54.03. Demand for Judgment

A judgment by default shall not be different in kind from or exceed in amount that prayed for in the demand for judgment. Except as to a party against whom a judgment is entered by default, every other judgment shall grant the relief to which the party in whose favor it is rendered is entitled.

Adopted June 25, 1951, eff. Jan. 1, 1952. Revised Oct. 18, 1988, eff. Jan. 1, 1989.

Rule 54.04. Costs

(a) Costs and disbursements allowed. Costs and disbursements shall be allowed as provided by law.

(b) Application for costs and disbursements. A party seeking to recover costs and disbursements must serve and file a detailed sworn application for taxation of costs and disbursements with the court administrator, substantially in the form as published by the State Court Administrator. The application must be served and filed not later than 45 days after entry of a final judgment as to the party seeking costs and disbursements. A party may, but is not required to, serve and file a memorandum of law with an application for taxation of costs and disbursements.

(c) Objections. Not later than 7 days after service of the application by any party, any other party may file a separate sworn application as in section (b), above, or may file written objections to the award of any costs or disbursements sought by any other party, specifying the grounds for each objection.

(d) Decision. Costs and disbursements may be taxed by the court administrator or a district court judge at any time after all parties have been allowed an opportunity to file applications and to object to the application of any other party as provided in this rule. The judge or court administrator may tax any costs and disbursements allowed by law.

(e) Review by Judge. If costs and disbursements are taxed by the court administrator, any party aggrieved by the action of the court administrator may serve and file a notice of appeal not later than 7 days after the court administrator serves notice of taxation on all parties. Any other party may file a response to the appeal not later than 7 days after the appeal is served. The appeal shall thereupon be decided by a district court judge and determined upon the record before the court administrator.

(f) Judgment for Costs. When costs and disbursements have been determined, whether by a district court judge or by the court administrator with no appeal taken to a district court judge, they shall promptly be inserted in the judgment.

Adopted June 25, 1951, eff. Jan. 1, 1952. Revised Oct. 18, 1988, eff. Jan. 1, 1989. Amended May 3, 2010, eff. July 1, 2010.

Advisory Committee Comment—2010 Amendment

Rule 54.04 is amended both to clarify its operation and to improve the procedure for taxing costs by the court administrator and the review of those decisions by the district court judge. The amended process is commenced by filing an application on a form established by the State Court Administrator and made available on the Judicial Branch website (or in substantially the same form).

Historical Notes

INTEREST RATES ON STATE COURT JUDGMENTS AND ARBITRATION AWARDS

The state court administrator has issued the following notice relating to the 2014 interest rates on state court judgments and arbitration awards:

"**2014 INTEREST RATES ON STATE COURT JUDGMENTS AND ARBITRATION AWARDS.** M.S. 549.09 directs the State Court Administrator to determine the annual interest rate applicable to certain state court judgments, verdicts, and arbitration awards. For judgments and awards governed by section 549.091 the annual interest rate for calendar year 2014 shall be 4%, provided that for judgments exceeding $50,000 that are finally entered on or after August 1, 2009, except a judgment or award for or against the state or a political subdivision of the state entered on or after April 16, 2010, the interest rate shall be 10% per year until paid.[2] M.S. 548.091, subd. 1a, provides that the interest rate applicable to child support judgments shall be the rate provided in M.S. 549.09, subject to a 18% maximum rate.

"The following lists the judgment rates in effect for state courts for the periods noted:

YEAR	M.S. 549.09 Annual Rate	M.S. 549.09 Rate for Judgment exceeding $50,000 Finally entered on or after 8/1/09 But not judgments for or against The state or a political subdivision	M.S. 548.091 Rate for Child Support Judgments

		Finally entered on or after 4/16/2010	
2001	6%		8%
2002	2%		4%
2003	4%		6%
2004	4%		6%
2005	4%		6%
2006	4%		6%
2007	5%		7%
2008	4%		4%
2009	4%	10%	Follow 549.09 rate (but not more than 18%)
2010	4%	10%	Follow 549.09 rate (but not more than 18%)
2011	4%	10%	Follow 549.09 rate (but not more than 18%)
2012	4%	10%	Follow 549.09 rate (but not more than 18%)
2013	4%	10%	Follow 549.09 rate (but not more than 18%)
2014	4%	10%	Follow 549.09 rate (but not more than 18%)

"1 The interest rate determined pursuant to section 549.09 does not apply to judgments for the recovery of taxes and employment arbitrations pursuant to M.S. Chapters 179 or 179A, and may not apply to judgments in condemnation cases. In condemnation cases governed by M.S. 117.195, the interest rate determined pursuant to section 549.09 is presumed to satisfy the constitutional requirement of just compensation unless the landowner shows that this rate does not provide what a reasonable and prudent investor would have earned while investing so as to maximize the rate of return, yet guarantee safety of principle. *State by Humphrey v. Jim Lupient Oldsmobile Co.*, 509 N.W. 2d 361, 364 (Minn. 1993).

"The interest rate on judgments for the recovery of taxes owed to the Commissioner of the Department of Revenue, such as income, excise, and sales taxes, is established by the Commissioner pursuant to M.S. 270C.40, subd. 5. The interest rate for state tax judgments also applies to judgments for the recovery of real or personal property taxes, subject to a ten percent minimum and fourteen percent maximum, and double that in certain cases, pursuant to M.S. 279.03, subd. 1a. These rates may be obtained from the Department of Revenue.

"M.S. 549.09, subd. 1(d) provides that section 549.09 does not apply to arbitrations between employers and employees under Chapter 179 or 179A, and that an arbitrator is neither required to nor prohibited from awarding interest under Chapter 179 or M.S. 179A.16 for essential employees.

"2 As amended by 2002 Minn. Laws Chap. 247, Sec. 1, 2009 Minn. Laws Chap. 83, Art. 2, Sec. 35, and 2010 Minn. Laws Chap 249, Section 549.09 directs that the annual rate is to be determined by using the monthly one-year constant maturity treasury yield reported in the latest statistical release of the federal reserve board of governors rounded to the nearest one per cent, subject to a four percent minimum; provided that for certain judgments exceeding $50,000 entered on or after August 1, 2009, the interest rate shall be 10% per year until paid."

RULE 55. DEFAULT

Rule 55.01. Judgment

When a party against whom a judgment for affirmative relief is sought has failed to plead or otherwise defend within the time allowed therefor by these rules or by statute, and that fact is made to appear by affidavit, judgment by default shall be entered against that party as follows:

(a) When the plaintiff's claim against a defendant is upon a contract for the payment of money only, or for the payment of taxes and penalties and interest thereon owing to the state, the court administrator, upon request of the plaintiff and upon affidavit of the amount due, which may not exceed the amount demanded in the complaint or in a written notice served on the defendant in accordance with Rule 4 if the complaint seeks an unspecified amount pursuant to Rule 8.01, shall enter judgment for the amount due and costs against the defendant.

(b) In all other cases, the party entitled to a judgment by default shall apply to the court therefor. If a party against whom judgment is sought has appeared in the action, that party shall be served with written notice of the application for judgment at least 3 days prior to the hearing on such application. If the action is one for the recovery of money only, the court shall ascertain, by a reference or otherwise, the amount to which the plaintiff is entitled, and order judgment therefor.

(c) If relief other than the recovery of money is demanded and the taking of an account, or the proof of any fact, is necessary to enable the court to give judgment, it may take or hear the same or order a reference for that purpose, and order judgment accordingly.

(d) When service of the summons has been made by published notice, or by delivery of a copy outside the state, no judgment shall be entered on default until the plaintiff shall have filed a bond, approved by the court, conditioned to abide such order as the court may make concerning restitution of any property collected or obtained by virtue of the judgment in case a defense is thereafter permitted and sustained; provided, that in actions involving the title to real estate or to foreclose mortgages thereon such bond shall not be required.

(e) When judgment is entered in an action upon a promissory note, draft or bill of exchange under the provisions of this rule, such promissory note, draft or bill of exchange shall be filed with the court administrator and made a part of the files of the action.

Adopted June 25, 1951, eff. Jan. 1, 1952. Amended March 3, 1959, eff. July 1, 1959. Revised Oct. 18, 1988, eff. Jan. 1, 1989. Amended Sept. 5, 1991, eff. Jan. 1, 1992.

Advisory Committee Note—1959

The addition of provision relating to taxes in para. (1) was made at the suggestion of the Attorney General to obviate the need of applying to the court for an order for default judgment in the numerous actions for collection of income and certain other taxes.

Task Force Comment—1991 Adoption

Rule 55.01(e) is derived from Rule 12(c) of the Code of Rules for the District Courts.

The change in subsection (a) is intended to deal with the situation of notice of the amount of judgment sought in those cases where the complaint seeks only an unspecified amount in excess of

$50,000 pursuant to Minn.R.Civ.P. 8.01 (rule limits ad damnum clauses for unliquidated damages) and Minn.Stat. § 544.36 (1990) (statute providing same limitation).

Rule 55.02. Plaintiffs; Counterclaimants; Cross-Claimants

This rule is applicable whether the party entitled to judgment by default is a plaintiff, a third-party plaintiff, or a party who has pleaded a cross-claim or counterclaim. In all cases, a judgment by default is subject to the limitations of Rule 54.03.

Adopted June 25, 1951, eff. Jan. 1, 1952. Revised Oct. 18, 1988, eff. Jan. 1, 1989.

RULE 56. SUMMARY JUDGMENT

Rule 56.01. For Claimant

A party seeking to recover upon a claim, counterclaim, or cross-claim or to obtain a declaratory judgment may, at any time after the expiration of 20 days from the service of the summons, or after service of a motion for summary judgment by the adverse party, move with or without supporting affidavits for a summary judgment in the party's favor upon all or any part thereof.

Adopted June 25, 1951, eff. Jan. 1, 1952. Revised Oct. 18, 1988, eff. Jan. 1, 1989. Amended Dec. 20, 1993, eff. March 1, 1994.

Advisory Committee Comment—1993 Amendments

The amendment to Rule 56.01 is intended to correct a typographical or grammatical error in the existing rule. No change in meaning or interpretation is intended.

Rule 56.02. For Defending Party

A party against whom a claim, counterclaim, or cross-claim is asserted or a declaratory judgment is sought may, at any time, move with or without supporting affidavits for a summary judgment in the party's favor as to all or any part thereof.

Adopted June 25, 1951, eff. Jan. 1, 1952. Revised Oct. 18, 1988, eff. Jan. 1, 1989.

Rule 56.03. Motion and Proceedings Thereon

Service and filing of the motion shall comply with the requirements of Rule 115.03 of the General Rules of Practice for the District Courts, provided that in no event shall the motion be served less than 10 days before the time fixed for the hearing. Judgment shall be rendered forthwith if the pleadings, depositions, answers to interrogatories, and admissions on file, together with the affidavits, if any, show that there is no genuine issue as to any material fact and that either party is entitled to a judgment as a matter of law. A summary judgment, interlocutory in character, may be rendered on the issue of liability alone although there is a genuine issue as to the amount of damages.

Adopted June 25, 1951, eff. Jan. 1, 1952. Amended March 3, 1959, eff. July 1, 1959. Revised Oct. 18, 1988, eff. Jan. 1, 1989. Amended Dec. 20, 1993, eff. March 1, 1994.

Advisory Committee Note—1959

Answers to interrogatories under Rule 33 are added to the matters that may be considered. Provision is made for entry of summary judgment against as well as for the moving party, in conformity with decisions of several federal courts.

Advisory Committee Comment—1993 Amendments

The amendment to Rule 56.03 is intended to make clear the relationship between this rule and Minn.Gen.R.Prac. 115. Rule 56.03 includes a strict ten-day notice requirement before a summary judgment motion may be heard. This minimum notice period is mandatory unless waived by the parties. *See McAllister v. Independent School District No. 306*, 276 Minn. 549, 149 N.W.2d 81 (1967). The rule is intended to provide protection before claims or defenses are summarily determined by requiring a minimum of ten days' notice.

Rule 56.04. Case not Fully Adjudicated on Motion

If, on motion pursuant to this rule, judgment is not rendered upon the whole case or for all the relief asked and a trial is necessary, the court at the hearing on the motion, by examining the pleadings and the evidence before it and by interrogating counsel, shall, if practicable, ascertain what material facts exist without substantial controversy and what material facts are actually and in good faith controverted. It shall thereupon make an order specifying the facts that appear without substantial controversy, including the extent to which the amount of damages or other relief is not in controversy, and directing such further proceedings in the action as are just. Upon the trial of the action the facts so specified shall be deemed established, and the trial shall be conducted accordingly.

Adopted June 25, 1951, eff. Jan. 1, 1952. Revised Oct. 18, 1988, eff. Jan. 1, 1989.

Rule 56.05. Form of Affidavits; Further Testimony; Defense Required

Supporting and opposing affidavits shall be made on personal knowledge, shall set forth such facts as would be admissible in evidence, and shall show affirmatively that the affiant is competent to testify to the matters stated therein. Sworn or certified copies of all papers or parts thereof referred to in an affidavit shall be attached thereto or served therewith. The court may permit affidavits to be supplemented or opposed by depositions or by further affidavits. When a motion for summary judgment is made and supported as provided in Rule 56, an adverse party may not rest upon the mere averments or denials of the adverse party's pleading but must present specific facts showing that there is a genuine issue for trial. If the adverse party does not so respond, summary judgment, if appropriate, shall be entered against the adverse party.

Adopted June 25, 1951, eff. Jan. 1, 1952. Amended March 3, 1959, eff. July 1, 1959. Revised Oct. 18, 1988, eff. Jan. 1, 1989.

Advisory Committee Note—1959

Some federal courts have held that a formal averment or a naked denial in a pleading suffices to create an issue of fact for summary judgment purposes. The amendment adopts the majority rule that since the movant must support his motion by specific facts the effective operation of the rule requires that the adverse party support his opposition to the motion in like manner.

Rule 56.06. When Affidavits are Unavailable

Should it appear from the affidavits of a party opposing the motion that the party cannot for reasons stated present, by affidavit, facts essential to justify the party's opposition, the court may refuse the application for judgment or may order a continuance to permit affidavits to be obtained or depositions to be taken or discovery to be had or may make such other order as is just.

Adopted June 25, 1951, eff. Jan. 1, 1952. Revised Oct. 18, 1988, eff. Jan. 1, 1989.

Rule 56.07. Affidavits Made in Bad Faith

Should it appear to the satisfaction of the court at any time that any of the affidavits presented pursuant to this rule are presented in bad faith or solely for the purpose of delay, the court shall forthwith order the party submitting them to pay to the other party the amount of the reasonable expenses which the filing of the affidavits causes the other party to incur, including reasonable attorney fees, and any offending party or attorney may be adjudged guilty of contempt.

Adopted June 25, 1951, eff. Jan. 1, 1952. Revised Oct. 18, 1988, eff. Jan. 1, 1989.

RULE 57. DECLARATORY JUDGMENTS

The procedure for obtaining a declaratory judgment pursuant to Minn.Stat. c. 555, shall be in accordance with these rules, and the right to trial by jury is retained under the circumstances and in the manner provided in Rules 38 and 39. The existence of another adequate remedy does not preclude a judgment for declaratory relief in cases where it is appropriate. The court may order a speedy hearing of an action for a declaratory judgment and may advance it on the calendar.

Adopted June 25, 1951, eff. Jan. 1, 1952. Revised Oct. 18, 1988, eff. Jan. 1, 1989.

RULE 58. ENTRY OF JUDGMENT; STAY

Rule 58.01. Entry

Unless the court otherwise directs, and subject to the provisions of Rule 54.02, judgment upon the verdict of a jury, or upon an order of the court for the recovery of money only or for costs or that all relief be denied, shall be entered forthwith by the court administrator; but the court shall direct the appropriate judgment to be entered upon a special verdict or upon a general verdict accompanied by answers to interrogatories returned by a jury pursuant to Rule 49 or upon an order of the court for relief other than money or costs. Entry of judgment shall not be delayed for the taxation of costs, and the omission of costs shall not affect the finality of the judgment. The judgment in all cases shall be entered and signed by the court administrator in the judgment roll; this entry constitutes the entry of the judgment; and the judgment is not effective before such entry.

Adopted June 25, 1951, eff. Jan. 1, 1952. Amended March 3, 1959, eff. July 1, 1959; July 16, 1981, eff. Aug. 1, 1981. Revised Oct. 18, 1988, eff. Jan. 1, 1989.

Advisory Committee Note—1959

The amendment puts orders for the recovery of money only or for costs or denying relief in the same category as a general verdict. The provision for entry of judgment without taxation of costs follows the federal Rule and supersedes the Minnesota decision law that a judgment is not final until costs are taxed or are waived. A party can protect himself against entry of judgment without notice by obtaining an anticipatory stay under the amended Rule 58.02.

Rule 58.02. Stay

The court may order a stay of entry of judgment upon a verdict or decision for a period not exceeding the time required for the hearing and determination of a motion for new trial or for judgment notwithstanding the verdict or to set the verdict aside or to dismiss the action or for amended findings, and after such determination may order a stay of entry of judgment for not more than 30 days. In granting a stay of entry of judgment pursuant to this rule for any period exceeding 30 days after verdict or decision, the court, in its discretion, may impose such conditions for the security of the adverse party as may be deemed proper.

Adopted June 25, 1951, eff. Jan. 1, 1952. Amended March 3, 1959, eff. July 1, 1959; Nov. 10, 1967, eff. Feb. 1, 1968. Revised Oct. 18, 1988, eff. Jan. 1, 1989.

Advisory Committee Note—1959

Under the terms of the present Rule a stay may be entered only after the return of the verdict or the filing of the decision. The amendment permits an anticipatory stay. Federal Courts of Appeals have upheld local court rules providing for an automatic stay for a limited period.

Advisory Committee Note—1968

Although Rule 62.01 provides security to the prevailing party as a condition for staying the execution of a judgment pending disposition of various motions made under the Rules and M.S.A. 550.36 provides for staying execution on a money judgment for six (6) months on posting bond, there has been no express provision providing for any security during a stay of the entry of judgment where delays may be encountered in disposing of various post-trial motions. The amendment to Rule 58.02 is designed to cover this need.

RULE 59. NEW TRIALS

Rule 59.01. Grounds

A new trial may be granted to all or any of the parties and on all or part of the issues for any of the following causes:

(a) Irregularity in the proceedings of the court, referee, jury, or prevailing party, or any order or abuse of discretion, whereby the moving party was deprived of a fair trial;

(b) Misconduct of the jury or prevailing party;

(c) Accident or surprise which could not have been prevented by ordinary prudence;

(d) Material evidence newly discovered, which with reasonable diligence could not have been found and produced at the trial;

(e) Excessive or insufficient damages, appearing to have been given under the influence of passion or prejudice;

(f) Errors of law occurring at the trial, and objected to at the time or, if no objection need have been made pursuant to Rules 46 and 51, plainly assigned in the notice of motion;

(g) The verdict, decision, or report is not justified by the evidence, or is contrary to law; but, unless it be so expressly stated in the order granting a new trial, it shall not be presumed, on appeal, to have been made on the ground that the verdict, decision, or report was not justified by the evidence.

On a motion for a new trial in an action tried without a jury, the court may open the judgment if one has been entered, take additional testimony, amend findings of fact and conclusions of law or make new findings and conclusions, and direct entry of a new judgment.

Adopted June 25, 1951, eff. Jan. 1, 1952. Amended March 3, 1959, eff. July 1, 1959; Nov. 10, 1967, eff. Feb. 1, 1968. Revised Oct. 18, 1988, eff. Jan. 1, 1989.

Advisory Committee Note—1968

There is no longer a need for Subdivision 5 [former] as a ground for a new trial since other amendments to Rule 59 eliminate the necessity for a transcript or a settled case as a basis for a motion for a new trial. Under the amended Rule 59 the inability to obtain a transcript relates solely to appellate practice. If a transcript cannot be obtained or a record cannot be established sufficient to present the questions properly on appeal, the appellate court should resolve the matter by dismissing the appeal or granting a new trial as that court deems best.

Rule 59.02. Basis of Motion

A motion made pursuant to Rule 59.01 shall be made and heard on the files, exhibits, and minutes of the court. Pertinent facts that would not be a part of the minutes may be shown by affidavit. A full or partial transcript of the court reporter's notes may be used on the hearing of the motion.

Adopted June 25, 1951, eff. Jan. 1, 1952. Amended March 3, 1959, eff. July 1, 1959; Nov. 10, 1967, eff. Feb. 1, 1968. Revised Oct. 18, 1988, eff. Jan. 1, 1989.

Advisory Committee Note—1968

The amendment to Rule 59 eliminates the prior practice of basing the motion either on a transcript or the minutes of the court plus affidavits for certain enumerated grounds. Under the amended Rule 59.02 the motion will be heard on the minutes of the court plus the exhibits introduced and other matter on file. Affidavits are permitted to supply facts not otherwise shown as a part of the minutes. Minutes include the unofficial and untranscribed notes of the court reporter, notes of the deputy clerk of court indicating which exhibits have been received, and the notes made by the trial judge during the course of the trial. The file includes the pleadings, depositions on file, etc. Exhibits relate to exhibits introduced into evidence.

Rule 63.01 adequately covers the problem of presenting new trial motions in the event of the death or incapacity of the trial judge following the trial and before determination of the motion for a new trial.

Rule 59.03. Time for Motion

A notice of motion for a new trial shall be served within 30 days after a general verdict or service of notice by a party of the filing of the decision or order; and the motion shall be heard within 60 days after such general verdict or notice of filing, unless the time for hearing be extended by the court within the 60–day period for good cause shown.

Adopted June 25, 1951, eff. Jan. 1, 1952. Amended Nov. 10, 1967, eff. Feb. 1, 1968. Revised Oct. 18, 1988, eff. Jan. 1, 1989. Amended Dec. 19, 2000, eff. March 1, 2001.

Advisory Committee Note—1968

The rule preserves the existing practice of requiring notice from the adverse party in all cases, except those involving a general jury verdict, in order to start the time running for the motion for a new trial. The clerk's notice of the decision or order is not a notice which will commence time running under Rule 59.03. Either party may serve a notice of the filing of the decision or order for purposes of commencing the running of time. Time for the new trial motion is limited to and is identical with the time requirement under the former Rule 59.03(3). Former Rules 59.03(1) and 59.03(2) are eliminated. The 15 day provision in Rule 59.03 is subject to the three day extension of time when notice is given by mail as provided in Rule 6.05.

Special verdicts under Rule 49.01 and general verdict with interrogatories under Rule 49.02 are not "verdicts" within Rule 59.03, but are verdict forms looking toward a decision or order by the trial judge prior to the time that it is an effective conclusion to the litigation. Rule 58.01 clearly imposes upon the trial judge the obligation of directing the appropriate judgment upon a special verdict or upon a general verdict accompanied by interrogatories. Time will not commence running on either a Rule 49.01 verdict or a Rule 49.02 verdict until notice has been given by a party of the filing of the decision or order following such verdicts. In like respect, the report of a referee is subject to the time limitation for decisions or order of the court.

Advisory Committee Comment—2000 Amendments

The single purpose of the amendment of this Rule 59.03 in 2000 is to create a longer and more reasonable period in which to hear post-trial motions. At the time this rule was adopted, post-trial motions were often heard in a somewhat perfunctory manner and court assignment practices permitted the scheduling of cases in this manner.

This amendment will also reduce, although not eliminate, the potential consequences of failing to have a post-trial motion heard in a timely manner.

The change in Rule 59 will serve to extend the deadline for other post-trial motions as well, because the current rules specifically tie the deadlines for those motions to Rule 59. *See* MINN. R. CIV. P. 50.02(c) (judgment notwithstanding the verdict); 52.02 (motion for amended findings). It will also have an indirect impact on Rule 60.02(b), which allows for relief from an order or judgment on the grounds of newly discovered evidence which could not have been discovered in time to move for a new trial. This latter impact will be negligible.

Historical Notes

The order of the Minnesota Supreme Court [CX-84-2134] dated December 19, 2000, provides in part that these amendments are effective March 1, 2001, and shall apply to all actions or proceedings pending on or commenced on or after the effective date, with the exception of the amendments to Rule 59, which shall apply to all actions or proceedings commenced on or after the effective date and all actions or proceedings pending on or decided before the effective date in which the time periods stated in the former Rule 59 have not expired.

The order of the Minnesota Supreme Court [CX-84-2134] dated December 19, 2000, provides in part that "(t)he inclusion of Advisory Committee comments is made for convenience and does not reflect court approval of the statements made therein".

Rule 59.04. Time for Serving Affidavits

When a motion for a new trial is based upon affidavits, they shall be served with the notice of motion. The opposing party shall have 10 days after such service in which to serve opposing affidavits, which period may be extended by the court pursuant to Rule 59.03. The court may permit reply affidavits.

Adopted June 25, 1951, eff. Jan. 1, 1952. Amended Nov. 10, 1967, eff. Feb. 1, 1968. Revised Oct. 18, 1988, eff. Jan. 1, 1989.

Advisory Committee Note—1968

The amendment eliminates the provision of former Rule 59.04 permitting the parties by written stipulation or the court by order to extend the time for serving opposing affidavits for an additional period not exceeding 20 days. Rule 59.04 now permits such extension only upon court order made upon a motion also seeking to extend the time for the hearing under Rule 59.03. The former provision in Rule 59.04 permitted the parties to extend the time for hearing by written stipulation without the concurrence of the trial judge. In view of the change in Rule 59.02 requiring the hearing to be on the minutes of the court, the trial judge should have the discretion to decide whether or not the hearing time will be extended.

Rule 59.05. On Initiative of Court

Not later than 15 days after a general verdict or the filing of the decision or order, the court upon its own initiative may order a new trial for any reason for which it might have granted a new trial on motion of a party. After giving the parties notice and an opportunity to be heard on the matter, the court may grant a motion for a new trial, timely served, for a reason not stated in the motion. In either case, the court shall specify in the order the grounds therefor.

Adopted June 25, 1951, eff. Jan. 1, 1952. Amended Nov. 10, 1967, eff. Feb. 1, 1968. Revised Oct. 18, 1988, eff. Jan. 1, 1989.

Advisory Committee Note—1968

Judges in some judicial districts in Minnesota stay the entry of judgment automatically following a jury verdict. In other districts the clerks of court do not comply with Rule 58 requiring entry of judgment forthwith but rather delay the entry of judgment until time for motions has elapsed or until costs and disbursements have been filed. Further, Minnesota practice permits appeals from intermediate orders rather than limiting appeals as the federal courts generally do to final judgments. For these reasons it is desirable to change Rule 59.05 by eliminating the word "judgment" and substituting therefor the words "after a general verdict or the filing of the decision or order." In federal practice, judgment is generally entered immediately following the verdict or order and is generally entered before appeal. Equating 15 days from the general verdict or filing of order for judgment under Minnesota practice to the 15 days following judgment in federal practice gives the Minnesota trial judges in practical terms the same power to grant new trials immediately after termination of the case as the federal judges have. The former Rule 59.05 permitted a trial judge to grant a new trial on his own initiative long after the case had been completed and even after the case had been appealed and decided on appeal by the Supreme Court of Minnesota. Rule 60.02 is amended to provide that the trial judge has the power to grant a new trial if the judge finds grounds to vacate the judgment.

A narrow interpretation of former Rules 59.03 and 59.05 would seem to limit the trial court's power to grant a motion for a new trial, timely made by a party, to the grounds stated by the party in his motion. The amendment clearly specifies that the court may grant a motion for a new trial made by a party for reasons not specified by the party in his motion if the court gives the parties notice and an opportunity to be heard upon the matter. Whether the new trial is granted upon the court's own motion or upon grounds not stated in the party's motion, the court is required to specify in its order the grounds for the order. This portion of the amendment conforms Minnesota practice to Federal Rule 59(d).

Rule 59.06. Stay of Entry of Judgment

A stay of entry of judgment pursuant to Rule 58 shall not be construed to extend the time within which a party may serve a motion hereunder.

Adopted June 25, 1951, eff. Jan. 1, 1952. Amended Nov. 10, 1967, eff. Feb. 1, 1968. Revised Oct. 18, 1988, eff. Jan. 1, 1989.

Advisory Committee Note—1968

Amendment to Rule 59.02 renders the last four words of Rule 59.06 unnecessary.

[Last four words were "or settle a case"].

Rule 59.07. Deleted Nov. 10, 1967, eff. Feb. 1, 1968

Advisory Committee Note—1968

The procedure set forth in Rule 59.02 eliminates the need for a settled case. A transcript of all or part of the proceeding can be ordered and used in support of the new trial motion under Rule 59.02, but the transcript is not official and has no greater standing than other items constituting the minutes of the court. Inability to obtain the unofficial transcript in time for the hearing is not grounds for automatic delay of the hearing on the new trial motion.

Historical Notes

Deleted Rule 59.07, adopted June 25, 1951, and amended March 3, 1959, related to how and when a case is settled.

Rule 59.08. Deleted Nov. 10, 1967, eff. Feb. 1, 1968

Advisory Committee Note—1968

Since there is no longer a settled case, no provision is needed to handle the problem arising upon the incapacity of the judge. Rule 63.01 adequately covers the situations that may arise under Rule 59.

Historical Notes

Deleted Rule 59.08, adopted June 25, 1951, related to settling the case when the judge who tried the case is incapacitated.

RULE 60. RELIEF FROM JUDGMENT OR ORDER

Rule 60.01. Clerical Mistakes

Clerical mistakes in judgments, orders, or other parts of the record and errors therein arising from oversight or omission may be corrected by the court at any time upon its own initiative or on the motion of any party and after such notice, if any, as the court orders. During the pendency of an appeal, such mistakes may be so corrected with leave of the appellate court.

Adopted June 25, 1951, eff. Jan. 1, 1952. Amended Nov. 26, 1969. Revised Oct. 18, 1988, eff. Jan. 1, 1989.

Rule 60.02. Mistakes; Inadvertence; Excusable Neglect; Newly Discovered Evidence; Fraud; etc.

On motion and upon such terms as are just, the court may relieve a party or the party's legal representatives from a final judgment (other than a marriage dissolution decree), order, or proceeding and may order a new trial or grant such other relief as may be just for the following reasons:

(a) Mistake, inadvertence, surprise, or excusable neglect;

(b) Newly discovered evidence which by due diligence could not have been discovered in time to move for a new trial pursuant to Rule 59.03;

(c) Fraud (whether heretofore denominated intrinsic or extrinsic), misrepresentation, or other misconduct of an adverse party;

(d) The judgment is void;

(e) The judgment has been satisfied, released, or discharged or a prior judgment upon which it is based has been reversed or otherwise vacated, or it is no longer equitable that the judgment should have prospective application; or

(f) Any other reason justifying relief from the operation of the judgment.

The motion shall be made within a reasonable time, and for reasons (a), (b), and (c) not more than 1 year after the judgment, order, or proceeding was entered or taken. A Rule 60.02 motion does not affect the finality of a judgment or suspend its operation. This rule does not limit the power of a court to entertain an independent action to relieve a party from a judgment, order, or proceeding, or to grant relief to a defendant not actually personally notified as provided in Rule 4.043, or to set aside a judgment for fraud upon the court. Writs of coram nobis, coram vobis, audita querela, and bills of review and bills in the nature of a bill of review are abolished, and the procedure for obtaining any relief from a judgment shall be by motion as prescribed in these rules or by an independent action.

Adopted June 25, 1951, eff. Jan. 1, 1952. Amended Nov. 10, 1967, eff. Feb. 1, 1968. Revised Oct. 18, 1988, eff. Jan. 1, 1989. Amended Dec. 20, 1993, eff. March 1, 1994.

Advisory Committee Note—1968

The amendment to Rule 59.05 makes the amendment to Rule 60.02 desirable for purposes of clarification. By amendment to Rule 59.05, the trial court is deprived of its existing power to grant a new trial upon its own motion for a period of time limited by the entry of judgment. Under existing practice if a trial judge grants a motion to vacate a judgment, then obviously under Rule 59.05, no judgment now being in existence, the court also has the power to grant a new trial. By limiting the power to grant a new trial to a time period following a general verdict or notice of decision or order, the addition of new trial power under Rule 60.02 in the event that the judgment is vacated is necessary.

Advisory Committee Comment—1993 Amendments

The only change made to this rule is to correct the reference to marriage dissolution as that is the current name for the proceeding. This amendment is intended to be consistent with similar amendments to the rules made in 1988.

RULE 61. HARMLESS ERROR

No error in either the admission or the exclusion of evidence and no error or defect in any ruling or order or in anything done or omitted by the court or by any of the parties is ground for granting a new trial or for setting aside a verdict or for vacating, modifying, or otherwise disturbing a judgment or order, unless refusal to take such action appears to the court inconsistent with substantial justice. The court at every stage of the proceeding must disregard any error or defect in the proceeding which does not affect the substantial rights of the parties.

Adopted June 25, 1951, eff. Jan. 1, 1952. Revised Oct. 18, 1988, eff. Jan. 1, 1989.

RULE 62. STAY OF PROCEEDINGS TO ENFORCE A JUDGMENT

Rule 62.01. Stay on Motions

In its discretion and on such conditions for the security of the adverse party as are proper, the court may stay the execution of or any proceedings to enforce a judgment pending the disposition of a motion for a new trial made pursuant to Rule 59, or of a motion for relief from a judgment or order made pursuant to Rule 60, or of a motion for judgment as a matter of law made pursuant to Rule 50.02, or of a motion for amendment to the findings or for additional findings made pursuant to Rule 52.02.

Adopted June 25, 1951, eff. Jan. 1, 1952. Amended March 3, 1959, eff. July 1, 1959. Revised Oct. 18, 1988, eff. Jan. 1, 1989. Amended Nov. 30, 2005, eff. Jan. 1, 2006.

Advisory Committee Comment—2006 Amendment

Rule 62.01 is amended to reflect the new name for motions under Rule 50.01 as amended effective January 1, 2006.

Rule 62.02. Injunction Pending Appeal

When an appeal is taken from an interlocutory or final judgment granting, dissolving, or denying an injunction, the court in its discretion may suspend, modify, restore, or grant an injunction during the pendency of the appeal upon such terms as to bond or otherwise as it considers proper for the security of the rights of the adverse party.

Adopted June 25, 1951, eff. Jan. 1, 1952. Revised Oct. 18, 1988, eff. Jan. 1, 1989.

Rule 62.03. Stay Upon Appeal

When an appeal is taken, the appellant may obtain a stay only when authorized and in the manner provided in Rules 107 and 108, Rules of Civil Appellate Procedure.

Adopted June 25, 1951, eff. Jan. 1, 1952. Amended Nov. 26, 1969. Revised Oct. 18, 1988, eff. Jan. 1, 1989.

Rule 62.04. Stay in Favor of the State or Agency Thereof

When an appeal is taken by the state or an officer, agency, or governmental subdivision thereof, and the operation or enforcement of the judgment is stayed, no bond, obligation, or other security shall be required from the appellant.

Adopted June 25, 1951, eff. Jan. 1, 1952. Revised Oct. 18, 1988, eff. Jan. 1, 1989.

Rule 62.05. Power of Appellate Court Not Limited

The provisions of Rule 62 do not limit any power of an appellate court or of a judge or justice thereof to stay proceedings during the pendency of an appeal or to suspend, modify, restore, or grant an injunction during the pendency of an appeal or to make any order appropriate to preserve the status quo or the effectiveness of the judgment subsequently to be entered.

Adopted June 25, 1951, eff. Jan. 1, 1952. Revised Oct. 18, 1988, eff. Jan. 1, 1989.

Rule 62.06. Stay of Judgment Upon Multiple Claims

When a court has ordered a final judgment on some but not all of the claims presented in the action under the conditions stated in Rule 54.02, the court may stay enforcement of that judgment until the entering of a subsequent judgment or judgments and may prescribe such conditions as are necessary to secure the benefits thereof to the party in whose favor the judgment is entered.

Adopted June 25, 1951, eff. Jan. 1, 1952. Revised Oct. 18, 1988, eff. Jan. 1, 1989.

RULE 63. DISABILITY OR DISQUALIFICATION OF JUDGE; NOTICE TO REMOVE; ASSIGNMENT OF A JUDGE

Rule 63.01. Disability of Judge

If by reason of death, sickness, or other disability a judge before whom an action has been tried is unable to perform judicial duties after a verdict is returned or findings of fact and conclusions of law are filed, any other judge regularly sitting in or assigned to the court in which the action was tried may perform those duties; but if such other judge is satisfied that the duties cannot be performed because that judge did not preside at the trial or for any other reason, that judge may exercise discretion to grant a new trial.

Adopted June 25, 1951, eff. Jan. 1, 1952. Revised Oct. 18, 1988, eff. Jan. 1, 1989.

Rule 63.02. Interest or Bias

No judge shall sit in any case if that judge is interested in its determination or if that judge might be excluded for bias from acting therein as a juror. If there is no other judge of the district who is qualified, or if there is only one judge of the district, such judge shall forthwith notify the chief justice of the supreme court of that judge's disqualification.

Adopted June 25, 1951, eff. Jan. 1, 1952. Revised Oct. 18, 1988, eff. Jan. 1, 1989.

Rule 63.03. Notice to Remove

Any party or attorney may make and serve on the opposing party and file with the administrator a notice to remove. The notice shall be served and filed within ten days after the party receives notice of which judge or judicial officer is to preside at the trial or hearing, but not later than the commencement of the trial or hearing.

No such notice may be filed by a party or party's attorney against a judge or judicial officer who has presided at a motion or any other proceeding of which the party had notice, or who is assigned by the Chief Justice of the Minnesota Supreme Court. A judge or judicial officer who has presided at a motion or other proceeding or who is assigned by the Chief Justice of the Minnesota Supreme Court may not be removed except upon an affirmative showing of prejudice on the part of the judge or judicial officer.

After a party has once disqualified a presiding judge or judicial officer as a matter of right that party may disqualify the substitute judge or judicial officer, but only by making an affirmative showing of prejudice. A showing that the judge or judicial officer might be excluded for bias from acting as a juror in the matter constitutes an affirmative showing of prejudice.

Upon the filing of a notice to remove or if a litigant makes an affirmative showing of prejudice against a substitute judge or judicial officer, the chief judge of the judicial district shall assign any other judge of any court within the district, or a judicial officer in the case of a substitute judicial officer, to hear the cause.

Adopted June 25, 1951, eff. Jan. 1, 1952. Amended March 21, 1985, eff. July 1, 1985. Revised Oct. 18, 1988, eff. Jan. 1, 1989. Amended Sept. 5, 1991, eff. Jan. 1, 1992; Dec. 19, 2000, eff. March 1, 2001.

Advisory Committee Note—1985

Rule 63.03 has been substantially rewritten in order to adapt the rule to statutory changes made by the Minnesota Legislature. The rule revisions are intended to follow in large part the notice of removal procedure established by Minn.Stat. § 542.16 (1982). The Committee has attempted to make it clear that a party must file a notice to remove with respect to any individual judge the first time that judge presides in an action. The rule is intended to prevent counsel from using the notice to remove procedures to remove an assigned judge after that judge has presided at one or more pretrial hearings.

The Committee also considered various time limits in which a notice of removal should be filed, and determined that a party should be allowed ten days in which to file a notice to remove if the identity of the presiding judge is known that far in advance. The Committee determined this time period was appropriate in part because it recognized that the decision to remove an individual judge is frequently made by the party rather than the attorney, and a ten-day period was deemed appropriate to permit consultation with the client and to permit a decision to be made. The Committee also determined that a decision to remove a judge should be made before any proceedings before that judge take place, and the period in which the judge may be removed therefore ends absolutely at the time the trial or hearing commences. This final limitation applies regardless of the length of time during which the parties have known the identity of the judge to preside at the hearing or trial.

Task Force Comment—1991 Adoption

This amendment to Minn.R.Civ.P. 63.03 is intended to provide a uniform mechanism for removing any judicial officer, whether a judge or referee. This rule would replace various inconsistent provisions of the existing rules. 4th Dist.R. 16.01 requires objections to any referee to be filed one court day before the hearing. 2d Dist.R. 23 requires objection within 10 days after notice of assignment and not later than commencement, consistent with the statute and rule governing judges.

Advisory Committee Comments—2000 Amendments

Rule 63.03 is amended to make clear the fact that a judge specially assigned by the Chief Justice to hear cases originally pending in more than one district cannot be removed by mere filing of a notice to remove. This amendment is a companion to the amendment of Rule 113.03 of the Minnesota General Rules of Practice in 2000, effective March 1, 2001, to provide a formal mechanism for requesting the Chief Justice to make such an assignment. This rule codifies the existing practice in special cases such as special assignment of a judge by the Chief Justice. The rule makes it clear that even a judge assigned by the Chief Justice may be removed for cause.

Historical Notes

The order of the Minnesota Supreme Court [CX-84-2134] dated December 19, 2000, provides in part that these amendments are effective March 1, 2001, and shall apply to all actions or proceedings pending on or commenced on or after the effective date, with the exception of the amendments to Rule 59, which shall apply to all actions or proceedings commenced on or after the effective date and all actions or proceedings pending on or decided before the effective date in which the time periods stated in the former Rule 59 have not expired.

The order of the Minnesota Supreme Court [CX-84-2134] dated December 19, 2000, provides in part that "(t)he inclusion of Advisory Committee comments is made for convenience and does not reflect court approval of the statements made therein".

Rule 63.04. Assignment of Judge

Upon receiving notice as provided in Rules 63.02 and 63.03, the chief justice shall assign a judge of another district, accepting such assignment, to preside at the trial or hearing, and the trial or hearing shall be postponed until the judge so assigned can be present.

Adopted June 25, 1951, eff. Jan. 1, 1952. Revised Oct. 18, 1988, eff. Jan. 1, 1989.

VII. PROVISIONAL AND FINAL REMEDIES AND SPECIAL PROCEEDINGS

RULE 64. SEIZURE OF PERSON OR PROPERTY

At the commencement of and during the course of an action, all remedies providing for seizure of person or property for the purpose of securing satisfaction of the judgment ultimately to be entered in the action are available under the circumstances and in the manner provided by the law of the state.

Adopted June 25, 1951, eff. Jan. 1, 1952. Revised Oct. 18, 1988, eff. Jan. 1, 1989.

RULE 65. INJUNCTIONS

Advisory Committee Note—1968

The amended rule is based upon Federal Rule 65, modified to reflect state practice under M.S.A. 585.03 and 585.04. Rule 65.01 contemplates an informal conference prior to the issue of the restraining order if time and circumstances permit such a preliminary conference. The notice of conference can be oral or written. In the event notice cannot be given or if circumstances will not permit a conference, the facts evidencing the reasons must be contained in the attorney's statement. An ex parte restraining order (without notice) can be dissolved or modified upon oral or written notice to the party obtaining the order. Rule 65.02 generally follows existing practice regarding the hearing on the temporary injunction. Rule 65.02(3) permits the court by order to consolidate the temporary injunction hearing with the trial on the merits.

Rule 65.01. Temporary Restraining Order; Notice; Hearing; Duration

A temporary restraining order may be granted without written or oral notice to the adverse party or that party's attorney only if (1) it clearly appears from specific facts shown by affidavit or by the verified complaint that immediate and irreparable injury, loss, or damage will result to the applicant before the adverse party or that party's attorney can be heard in opposition, and (2) the applicant's attorney states to the court in writing the efforts, if any, which have been made to give notice or the reasons supporting the claim that notice should not be required. In the event that a temporary restraining order is based upon any affidavit, a copy of such affidavit must be served with the temporary restraining order. In case a temporary restraining order is granted without notice, the motion for a temporary injunction shall be set down for hearing at the earliest practicable time and shall take precedence over all matters except older matters of the same character; and when the motion comes on for hearing, the party who obtained the temporary restraining order shall proceed with the application for a temporary injunction, and, if the party does not do so, the court shall dissolve the temporary restraining order. On written or oral notice to the party who obtained the ex parte temporary restraining order, the adverse party may appear and move its dissolution or modification, and in that event the court shall proceed to hear and determine such motion as expeditiously as the ends of justice require.

Adopted Nov. 10, 1967, eff. Feb. 1, 1968. Revised Oct. 18, 1988, eff. Jan. 1, 1989.

Historical Notes

Former Rule: A former Rule 65 adopted June 25, 1951, related to injunctions. The order of the Minnesota Supreme Court dated November 10, 1967, rewrote former Rule 65 as Rules 65.01 to 65.03.

Rule 65.02. Temporary Injunction

(a) No temporary injunction shall be granted without notice of motion or an order to show cause to the adverse party.

(b) A temporary injunction may be granted if by affidavit, deposition testimony, or oral testimony in court, it appears that sufficient grounds exist therefor.

(c) Before or after the commencement of the hearing on a motion for a temporary injunction, the court may order the trial of the action on the merits to be advanced and consolidated with the hearing on the motion. Even when this consolidation is not ordered, any evidence received upon a motion for a temporary injunction which would be admissible at the trial on the merits becomes part of the trial record and need not be repeated at trial. This provision shall be so construed and applied as to preserve any rights the parties may have to trial by jury.

Adopted Nov. 10, 1967, eff. Feb. 1, 1968. Revised Oct. 18, 1988, eff. Jan. 1, 1989.

Rule 65.03. Security

(a) No temporary restraining order or temporary injunction shall be granted except upon the giving of security by the applicant, in such sum as the court deems proper, for the payment of such costs and damages as may be incurred or suffered by any party who is found to have been wrongfully enjoined or restrained.

(b) Whenever security is given in the form of a bond or other undertaking with one or more sureties, each surety submits to the jurisdiction of the court and irrevocably appoints the court administrator as the surety's agent upon whom any papers affecting liability on the bond or undertaking may be served. The surety's liability may be enforced on motion without the necessity of an independent action. The motion and such notice of the motion as the court prescribes may be served on the court administrator, who shall forthwith mail copies to the sureties if their addresses are known.

Adopted Nov. 10, 1967, eff. Feb. 1, 1968. Revised Oct. 18, 1988, eff. Jan. 1, 1989.

Rule 65.04. Form and Scope of Injunction or Restraining Order

Every order granting an injunction and every restraining order shall set forth the reasons for its issuance; shall be specific in terms; shall describe in reasonable detail, and not by reference to the complaint or other document, the act or acts sought to be restrained; and is binding only upon the parties to the action, their officers, agents, servants, employees, and attorneys, and upon those persons in active concert or participation with them who receive actual notice of the order by personal service or otherwise.

Adopted Dec. 19, 2000, eff. March 1, 2001.

Advisory Committee Comments—2000 Amendments

This rule is entirely new in the Minnesota rules; it is drawn directly from Fed. R. Civ. P. 65(d). There is no comparable provision currently in the Minnesota rules and questions do arise about what is necessary to make sure that a party is subject to a court's injunctive order. The amended rule is intended to resolve those questions.

Historical Notes

The order of the Minnesota Supreme Court [CX-84-2134] dated December 19, 2000, provides in part that these amendments are effective March 1, 2001, and shall apply to all actions or proceedings pending on or commenced on or after the effective date, with the exception of the amendments to Rule 59, which shall apply to all actions or proceedings commenced on or after the effective date and all actions or proceedings pending on or decided before the effective date in which the time periods stated in the former Rule 59 have not expired.

The order of the Minnesota Supreme Court [CX-84-2134] dated December 19, 2000, provides in part that "(t)he inclusion of Advisory Committee comments is made for convenience and does not reflect court approval of the statements made therein".

RULE 66. RECEIVERS

An action wherein a receiver has been appointed shall not be dismissed except by order of the court. A foreign receiver shall have capacity to sue in any district court, but the receiver's rights are subordinate to those of local creditors. The practice in the administration of estates by the court shall be in accordance with Minn.Stat. c. 576 and with the practice heretofore followed in the courts of this state or as provided in rules promulgated by the district courts. In all other respects, the action in which the appointment of a receiver is sought or which is brought by or against a receiver is governed by these rules.

Adopted June 25, 1951, eff. Jan. 1, 1952. Revised Oct. 18, 1988, eff. Jan. 1, 1989.

RULE 67. DEPOSIT IN COURT

Rule 67.01. In an Action

In an action in which any part of the relief sought is a judgment for a sum of money or the disposition of a sum of money or the disposition of any other thing capable of delivery, a party, upon notice to every other party, and by leave of court, may deposit with the court all or any part of such money or thing.

Adopted June 25, 1951, eff. Jan. 1, 1952. Revised Oct. 18, 1988, eff. Jan. 1, 1989.

Rule 67.02. When No Action is Brought

When money or other personal property in the possession of any person, as bailee or otherwise, is claimed adversely by two or more other persons, and the right thereto as between such claimants is in doubt, the person in possession, though no action is commenced against that person by any of the claimants, may place the property in the custody of the court. The person in possession shall apply to the court of the county in which the property is situated, setting forth by petition the facts which bring the case within the provisions of this rule, and the names and places of residence of all known claimants of such property. If satisfied of the truth of such showing, the court, by order, shall accept custody of the money or other property, and direct that, upon delivery and upon giving notice thereof to all persons interested, personally or by registered mail as prescribed in such order, the petitioner is relieved from further liability on account thereof. This rule shall apply to cases where property held under like conditions is garnished in the hands of the possessor; but in such cases the application shall be made to the court in which the garnishment proceedings are pending.

Adopted June 25, 1951, eff. Jan. 1, 1952. Revised Oct. 18, 1988, eff. Jan. 1, 1989.

Rule 67.03. Court May Order Deposit or Seizure of Property

When it is admitted by the pleading or examination of a party that the party has possession or control of any money or other thing capable of delivery which, being the subject of the litigation, is held by that party as trustee for another party, or which belongs or is due to another party, the court may order the same to be deposited in court or delivered to such other party, with or without security, subject to further direction. If such order is disobeyed, the court may punish the disobedience as a contempt, and may also require the sheriff or other proper officer to take the money or property and deposit or deliver it in accordance with the direction given.

Adopted June 25, 1951, eff. Jan. 1, 1952. Revised Oct. 18, 1988, eff. Jan. 1, 1989.

Rule 67.04. Money Paid into Court

Where money is paid into the court pending the result of any legal proceedings, the judge may order it deposited in a designated state or national bank or savings bank. In the absence of such order, the court administrator is the official custodian of all moneys, and the judge, on application of any person paying such money into court, may require the court administrator to give an additional bond, conditioned as the bond authorized in Minn.Stat. § 485.01 in such amount as the judge shall order.

Adopted June 25, 1951, eff. Jan. 1, 1952. Revised Oct. 18, 1988, eff. Jan. 1, 1989.

RULE 68. OFFER OF JUDGMENT OR SETTLEMENT

Comment—Rule 68

See comment following Rule 68.04.

Rule 68.01. Offer

(a) Time of Offer. At any time more than 10 days before the trial begins, any party may serve upon an adverse party a written damages-only or total-obligation offer to allow judgment to be entered to the effect specified in the offer, or to settle the case on the terms specified in the offer.

(b) Applicability of Rule. An offer does not have the consequences provided in Rules 68.02 and 68.03 unless it expressly refers to Rule 68.

(c) Damages-only Offers. An offer made under this rule is a "damages-only" offer unless the offer expressly states that it is a "total-obligation" offer. A damages-only offer does not include then-accrued applicable prejudgment interest, costs and disbursements, or applicable attorney fees, all of which shall be added to the amount stated as provided in Rules 68.02(b)(2) and (c).

(d) Total-obligation Offers. The amount stated in an offer that is expressly identified as a "total-obligation" offer includes then-accrued applicable prejudgment interest, costs and disbursements, and applicable attorney fees.

(e) Offer Following Determination of Liability. When the liability of one party to another has been determined by verdict, order, or judgment, but the amount or extent of the liability remains to be determined by further proceedings, the party adjudged liable may make an offer of judgment, which shall have the same effect as an offer made before trial if it is served within a reasonable time not less than 10 days before the commencement of a hearing or trial to determine the amount or extent of liability.

(f) Filing. Notwithstanding the provisions of Rule 5.04, no offer under this rule need be filed with the court unless the offer is accepted.

Amended Feb. 29, 2008, eff. July 1, 2008.

Comment—Rule 68

See comment following Rule 68.04.

Historical Notes

Former Rule: A former Rule 68.01 adopted June 25, 1951, related to an offer of judgment. The subject matter of former Rule 68.01 was incorporated into Rule 68 by court order dated March 21, 1985.

Former Rule: A former Rule 68 adopted March 21, 1985, and amended October 18, 1988, related to an offer of judgment or settlement. The subject matter of former Rule 68 was incorporated into Rules 68.01 to 68.04 by court order dated February 29, 2008.

Rule 68.02. Acceptance or Rejection of Offer

(a) Time for Acceptance. Acceptance of the offer shall be made by service of written notice of acceptance within 10 days after service of the offer. During the 10–day period the offer is irrevocable.

(b) Effect of Acceptance of Offer of Judgment. If the offer accepted is an offer of judgment, either party may file the offer and the notice of acceptance, together with the proof of service thereof, and the court shall order entry of judgment as follows:

(1) If the offer is a total-obligation offer as provided in Rule 68.01(d), judgment shall be for the amount of the offer.

(2) If the offer is a damages-only offer, applicable prejudgment interest, the plaintiff-offeree's costs and disbursements, and applicable attorney fees, all as accrued to the date of the offer, shall be determined by the court and included in the judgment.

(c) Effect of Acceptance of Offer of Settlement. If the offer accepted is an offer of settlement, the settled claim(s) shall be dismissed upon

(1) the filing of a stipulation of dismissal stating that the terms of the offer, including payment of applicable prejudgment interest, costs and disbursements, and applicable attorney fees, all accrued to the date of the offer, have been satisfied or

(2) order of the court implementing the terms of the agreement.

(d) Offer Deemed Withdrawn. If the offer is not accepted within the 10–day period, it shall be deemed withdrawn.

(e) Subsequent Offers. The fact that an offer is made but not accepted does not preclude a subsequent offer. Any subsequent offer by the same party under this rule supersedes all prior offers by that party.

Amended Feb. 29, 2008, eff. July 1, 2008.

Comment—Rule 68

See comment following Rule 68.04.

Historical Notes

Former Rule: A former Rule 68.02 adopted June 25, 1951, related to tender of money in lieu of judgment.

Rule 68.03. Effect of Unaccepted Offer

(a) Unaccepted Offer Not Admissible. Evidence of an unaccepted offer is not admissible, except in a proceeding to determine costs and disbursements.

(b) Effect of Offer on Recovery of Costs. An unaccepted offer affects the parties' obligations and entitlements regarding costs and disbursements as follows:

(1) If the offeror is a defendant, and the defendant-offeror prevails or the relief awarded to the plaintiff-offeree is less favorable than the offer, the plaintiff-offeree must pay the defendant-offeror's costs and disbursements incurred in the defense of the action after service of the offer, and the plaintiff-offeree shall not recover its costs and disbursements incurred after service of the offer, provided that applicable attorney fees available to the plaintiff-offeree shall not be affected by this provision.

(2) If the offeror is a plaintiff, and the relief awarded is less favorable to the defendant-offeree than the offer, the defendant-offeree must pay, in addition to the costs and disbursements to which the plaintiff-offeror is entitled under Rule 54.04, an amount equal to the plaintiff-offeror's costs and disbursements incurred after service of the offer. Applicable attorney fees available to the plaintiff-offeror shall not be affected by this provision.

(3) If the court determines that the obligations imposed under this rule as a result of a party's failure to accept an offer would impose undue hardship or otherwise be inequitable, the court may reduce the amount of the obligations to eliminate the undue hardship or inequity.

(c) Measuring Result Compared to Offer. To determine for purposes of this rule if the relief awarded is less favorable to the offeree than the offer:

(1) a damages-only offer is compared with the amount of damages awarded to the plaintiff; and

(2) a total-obligation offer is compared with the amount of damages awarded to the plaintiff, plus applicable prejudgment interest, the plaintiff's taxable costs and disbursements, and applicable attorney fees, all as accrued to the date of the offer.

Adopted Feb. 29, 2008, eff. July 1, 2008. Amended May 28, 2008, eff. July 1, 2008.

Comment—Rule 68

See comment following Rule 68.04.

Rule 68.04. Applicable Attorney Fees and Prejudgment Interest

(a) "Applicable Attorney Fees" Defined. "Applicable attorney fees" for purposes of Rule 68 means any attorney fees to which a party is entitled by statute, common law, or contract for one or more of the claims resolved by an offer made under the rule. Nothing in this rule shall be construed to create a right to attorney fees not provided for under the applicable substantive law.

(b) "Applicable Prejudgment Interest" Defined. "Applicable prejudgment interest" for purposes of Rule 68 means any prejudgment interest to which a party is entitled by statute, rule, common law, or contract for one or more of the claims resolved by an offer made under the rule. Nothing in this rule shall be construed to create a right to prejudgment interest not provided for under the applicable substantive law.

Adopted Feb. 29, 2008, eff. July 1, 2008.

Advisory Committee Comment—2008 Amendment

Rule 68 is extensively revamped both to clarify its operation and to make it more effective in its purpose of encouraging the settlement of litigation. The overarching goal of this set of amendments is to add certainty to the operation of the rule and to remove surprises both to parties making offers and those receiving and deciding whether to accept them. Additionally, Rule 68.03 is revised to make the mechanism of Rule 68 better address the goal of providing incentives for both claimants and parties opposing claims. This rule is not as closely modeled on its federal counterpart, Fed. R. Civ. P. 68, as is the existing rule, so that rule and decisions construing it may not be persuasive guidance in construing this rule.

Rule 68 uses the term "offer" to include offers to settle made by any party. Thus, both an offer by a defendant to pay a sum in return for a dismissal of a claim and an offer by a claimant to accept a sum in return for dismissal—often termed a "demand" and not an "offer"—are offers for the purposes of the rule.

Rule 68.01(b) is a new provision that requires that in order to be given the cost-shifting effect of the rule an offer must include express reference to the rule. *See Matheiu v. Freeman*, 472 N.W.2d 187 (Minn. App. 1991). This provision is intended to make it unlikely that an offer would come within the scope of the rule without the offeror intending that and the offeree having notice that it is an offer with particular consequences as defined in the rule.

The revised rule carries forward the former rule's application both to offers of judgment and to offers of settlement. The effects of these two types of offer are different, and are clarified in Rule 68.02. Rules 68.01(c) and (d) create an additional dichotomy in the rule, creating new categories of "damages-only" and "total-obligation" offers. This dichotomy is important to the operation of the rule, and is intended to remove a significant "trap for the unwary" where an accepted offer may be given two substantially different interpretations by offeror and offeree. Under the former rule, if a statute allowed the recovery of attorney fees as costs and a Rule 68 offer were made and did not expressly include reference to attorney fees, fees could be recovered in addition to the amount offered. *See, e.g., Collins v. Minn. Sch. of Business, Inc.*, 655 N.W.2d 320 (Minn. 2003). Fees recoverable by contract, rather than statute, would be subsumed within the offer, and not be recoverable in addition to the amount of the accepted offer. *See, e.g., Schwickert, Inc. v. Winnebago Seniors, Ltd.*, 680 N.W.2d 79 (Minn. 2004). Similar uncertainty may exist as to whether prejudgment interest is included in or to be added to the amount of an offer. *See, e.g., Collins; Stinson v. Clark Equip. Co.*, 743 N.W.2d 333 (Minn. App. 1991). Discussion of other ambiguities under the federal counterpart to Rule 68, Fed. R. Civ. P. 68, is included in Danielle M. Shelton, *Rewriting Rule 68: Realizing the Benefits of the Federal Settlement Rule by Injecting Certainty into Offers of Judgment*, 91 MINN. L. REV. 865 (2007).

The "damages-only" or "total obligation" offer choice allows the party making the offer to control and understand the effect of the offer, if accepted; similarly, a party deciding how to respond to an offer should be able to determine the total cost of accepting an offer. Rule 68.01(c) creates a presumption that an offer made under Rule 68 is a "damages-only" offer unless it expressly meets the criteria of Rule 68.01(d) by stating that it is a "total-obligation" offer. The added precision allowed by distinguishing the types of offers permits the new rule to provide greater clarity and certainty as to the effect both of accepted offers and unaccepted offers.

Rule 68.03(b)(1) changes the effect of Rule 68 on costs and disbursements when a defendant's offer is rejected and the judgment is less favorable to the plaintiff offeree. Under the former rule, the offeree would nevertheless recover its costs and disbursements from the offeror. *Borchert v. Maloney*, 581 N.W.2d 838 (Minn. 1998). The revised rule provides that the offeree does not recover its costs and disbursements incurred after service of the offer. But this change does not affect a prevailing plaintiff's right to attorney fees to which it is entitled under law or contract. In this respect the revised rule, like the former rule, does not incorporate the cut-off of attorney fees that occurs under the federal Rule 68 as interpreted in *Marek v. Chesney*, 473 U.S. 1 (1986). Additionally, under the former rule, the offeror was entitled to its costs and disbursements incurred from the beginning of the case. *Vandenheuvel v. Wagner*, 690 N.W.2d 757 (Minn. 2005). As to this issue, the revised rule now has the same effect as the federal rule (although with language that is not identical), requiring the offeree to pay the offeror's costs and disbursements incurred after service of the offer.

Rule 68.03(b)(2) introduces a consequence for a defendant's rejection of a plaintiff's Rule 68 offer if the judgment is less favorable to the defendant offeree. In that circumstance, this new provision requires the defendant to pay double the offeror's costs and disbursements incurred after service of the offer. If the defendant is merely required to pay the offeror's costs, as under the current rule, there is no adverse consequence for a defendant who rejects a Rule 68 offer. In contrast, under the revised rule, a plaintiff who rejects a Rule 68 offer suffers dual adverse consequences: loss of the right to recover his costs and required payment of the defendant's costs.

Rule 68.04(a) expressly provides that the rule does not create a right to recover attorney fees. This provision is intended only to avoid confusion. The rule might affect the extent of fees recoverable by statute, common law, or by contract, but it does not create any right to recover fees that does not exist outside of Rule 68.

Similarly, Rule 68.04(b) provides that the rule does not create a right to prejudgment interest, which right must rather be drawn from an applicable statute, rule, contract, or common law. It is noteworthy that MINN. STAT. § 549.09, subd. 1(b), which governs prejudgment interest in most cases, contains a mechanism analogous to this rule that adjusts calculation of prejudgment interest based on the relationship between the parties' offers of settlement and the ultimate judgment or award in the case.

RULE 69. EXECUTION

Process to enforce a judgment for the payment of money shall be a writ of execution, unless the court directs otherwise. The procedure on execution, in proceedings supplementary to and in aid of a judgment, and in proceedings on and in aid of execution shall be in accordance with Minn.Stat. c. 550. In aid of the judgment or execution, the judgment creditor, or successor in interest when that interest appears of record, may obtain discovery from any person, including the judgment debtor, in the manner provided by these rules.

Adopted June 25, 1951, eff. Jan. 1, 1952. Amended Nov. 14, 1974, eff. Jan. 1, 1975. Revised Oct. 18, 1988, eff. Jan. 1, 1989.

Advisory Committee Note—1975

The change provided in this rule is to make available to the judgment creditor all of the discovery procedures, not merely the procedure of depositions. In particular the rule will now permit application of the amended Rule 34.

RULE 70. JUDGMENT FOR SPECIFIC ACTS; VESTING TITLE

If a judgment directs a party to execute a conveyance of land or to deliver deeds or other documents or to perform any other specific act and the party fails to comply within the time specified, the court may direct the act to be done at the cost of the disobedient party by some other person appointed by the court, and the act when so done has like effect as if done by the party. On application of the party entitled to performance, the court administrator shall issue a writ of attachment against the property of the disobedient party to compel obedience to the judgment. The court may also in proper cases adjudge the party in contempt. If real or personal property is within the state, the court, in lieu of directing a conveyance thereof, may enter a judgment divesting the title of any party and vesting it in others; and such judgment has the effect of a conveyance executed in due form of law. When any order or judgment is for the delivery of possession, the party in whose favor it is entered is entitled to a writ of execution upon application to the court administrator.

Adopted June 25, 1951, eff. Jan. 1, 1952. Revised Oct. 18, 1988, eff. Jan. 1, 1989.

RULE 71. PROCESS IN BEHALF OF AND AGAINST PERSONS NOT PARTIES

When an order is made in favor of a person who is not a party to the action, that person may enforce obedience to the order by the same process as if a party; and, when obedience to an order may be lawfully enforced against a person who is not a party, that person is liable to the same process for enforcing obedience to the order as if that person were a party.

Adopted June 25, 1951, eff. Jan. 1, 1952. Revised Oct. 18, 1988, eff. Jan. 1, 1989.

RULES 72 to 76. [RESERVED FOR FUTURE USE]

VIII. DISTRICT COURTS AND COURT ADMINISTRATORS

RULE 77. DISTRICT COURTS AND COURT ADMINISTRATORS

Rule 77.01. District Courts Always Open

The district courts shall be deemed always open for the purpose of filing any pleading or other proper paper, of issuing and returning mesne and final process, and of making and directing all interlocutory motions, orders, and rules.

Adopted June 25, 1951, eff. Jan. 1, 1952. Revised Oct. 18, 1988, eff. Jan. 1, 1989.

Rule 77.02. Trials and Hearings; Orders in Chambers

All trials upon the merits shall be conducted in open court and so far as convenient in a regular courtroom. All other acts or proceedings may be done or conducted by a judge in chambers, without the attendance of the court administrator or other court officials and at any place either within or outside the district; but no hearing, other than one ex parte, shall be conducted outside the district without the consent of all parties affected thereby.

Adopted June 25, 1951, eff. Jan. 1, 1952. Revised Oct. 18, 1988, eff. Jan. 1, 1989.

Rule 77.03. Court Administrator's Office and Orders by Court Administrator

All motions and applications in the court administrator's office for issuing mesne process, for issuing final process to enforce and execute judgments, for entering judgments by default, and for other proceedings which do not require allowance or order of the court are grantable of course by the court administrator; but the court administrator's action may be suspended, altered, or rescinded by the court upon cause shown.

Adopted June 25, 1951, eff. Jan. 1, 1952. Revised Oct. 18, 1988, eff. Jan. 1, 1989.

Rule 77.04. Notice of Orders or Judgments

Immediately upon the filing of an order or decision or entry of a judgment, the court administrator shall transmit a notice of the filing or entry by mail, e-mail, or by use of an e-filing and e-service system, to every party affected thereby or upon such party's attorney of record, whether or not such party has appeared in the action, at the party or attorney's last known mail or e-mail address, and shall note the transmission in the court records. Notice under this rule shall not limit the time for taking an appeal or other proceeding on such order, decision, or judgment.

Adopted June 25, 1951, eff. Jan. 1, 1952. Revised Oct. 18, 1988, eff. Jan. 1, 1989. Amended May 24, 2012, eff. Sept. 1, 2012.

Advisory Committee Comment—2012 Amendment

Rule 77.04 is amended to permit any notice required by the rule to be sent by electronic means in all cases. Although this will necessarily occur in cases using mandatory e-filing and e-service, the rule permits court administrators to use e-mail or electronic noticing in any other case where it is feasible.

Notice is required to be provided to the last known address of the party or attorney. The burden is squarely on the party or attorney to advise the court of any change in address. This rule should be read in conjunction with Rule 13.02 of the General Rules of Practice which permits the court administrator to discontinue providing postal notice where that last known address is known to be obsolete, typically by the return of prior mailings by the postal service.

Historical and Statutory Notes

The order of the Minnesota Supreme Court [ADM 10–8011] dated May 24, 2012, provided in part that "These amendments shall apply to all actions or proceedings commenced on or after the effective date."

RULES 78, 79. [RESERVED FOR FUTURE USE]

RULE 80. STENOGRAPHIC REPORT OR TRANSCRIPT AS EVIDENCE

Whenever the testimony of a witness at a trial or hearing which was stenographically reported is admissible in evidence at a later trial, it may be proved by a reading of the transcript thereof duly certified by the person who reported the testimony. Such evidence is rebuttable and not conclusive.

Adopted June 25, 1951, eff. Jan. 1, 1952. Revised Oct. 18, 1988, eff. Jan. 1, 1989.

RULE 81. APPLICABILITY; IN GENERAL

Rule 81.01. Statutory and Other Procedures

(a) Procedures Preserved. These rules do not govern pleadings, practice and procedure in the statutory and other proceedings listed in Appendix A insofar as they are inconsistent or in conflict with the rules.

(b) Procedures Abolished. [Abrogated].

(c) Statutes Superseded. Subject to provision (a) of this rule, the statutes listed in Appendix B and all other statutes inconsistent or in conflict with these rules are superseded insofar as they apply to pleading, practice, and procedure in the district court.

Adopted June 25, 1951, eff. Jan. 1, 1952. Amended March 3, 1959, eff. July 1, 1959; Nov. 10, 1967, eff. Feb. 1, 1968. Revised Oct. 18, 1988, eff. Jan. 1, 1989. Amended Nov. 22, 1996, eff. Jan. 1, 1997.

Advisory Committee Note—1968

Difficulty has been experienced by the bench and bar regarding the proper form of civil action to accomplish the purposes of the former writ of mandamus. By statute M.S.A. 586.03, the writ of mandamus was either alternative or peremptory. M.S.A. 586.04 permitted the court to enter a peremptory writ in those cases where no valid excuse for non performance could be given. Under the existing provision of Rule 81.01(2) elimination of the writ of mandamus also had the practical effect of eliminating the peremptory writ. This result was not intended by the Rules Committee. Members of the bench expressed great reluctance to sign a mandatory order when an action had not previously been commenced by a summons and complaint. If the action had been commenced by a summons and complaint the bench was reluctant to summarily decide the matter on ex parte application before answer time had expired.

Further confusion has arisen regarding the proper form of civil action to secure the mandatory relief. Declaratory judgment and the injunction form have been used. See William v. Rolfe, 257 Minn. 237, 101 N.W.2d 923 (1960); Maine v. Whipple, 259 Minn. 18, 104 N.W.2d 657 (1960). Under either of these forms, 20 days must be allowed for answer in the main action. Such time lag may well be detrimental in the ordinary mandamus type action. In addition, bond requirements for mandatory injunctions created some difficulty in applying this rule. In view of the uncertainty existing in the minds of the bench and bar regarding proper procedures, the Committee felt it appropriate to resolve the questions by restoring the writ as a statutory writ not affected by the Rules of Civil Procedure in its initial stages.

Advisory Committee Comments—1996 Amendments

Rule 81.01(b) should be abrogated to reflect the decision of the Minnesota Supreme Court in *Rice v. Connolly,* 488 N.W.2d 241, 244 (Minn.1992), in which the court held: "[W]e have determined that quo warranto jurisdiction as it once existed in the district court must be reinstated and that petitions for the writ of quo warranto and information in the nature of quo warranto shall be filed in the first instance in the district court. The court recognized its retention of original jurisdiction under Minn. Stat. § 480.04 (1990), and also indicated its "future intention to exercise that discretion in only the most exigent of circumstances. We comment further that the reinstatement of quo warranto jurisdiction in the district court is intended to exist side by side with the appropriate alternative forms of remedy heretofore available. . . ." 488 N.W.2d at 244. The continued existence of a rule purporting to recognize a procedural remedy now expressly held to exist can only prove misleading or confusing in future litigation. Abrogation of the rule is appropriate to obviate any lack of clarity.

Although Rule 81.01(a) is not amended, the committee recommends that the list of special proceedings exempted from the rules by this rule be updated. An updated Appendix A is included in these proposed amendments.

Historical Notes

The order of the Minnesota Supreme Court [C6-84-2134] dated November 22, 1996, provides in part that the "(a)mendments shall apply to all actions pending on the effective date [January 1, 1997] and to those filed thereafter" and that "(t)he inclusion of Advisory

Committee comments is made for convenience and does not reflect court approval of the comments made therein".

Rule 81.02. Appeals to District Courts

These rules do not supersede the provisions of statutes relating to appeals to the district courts.

Adopted June 25, 1951, eff. Jan. 1, 1952. Revised Oct. 18, 1988, eff. Jan. 1, 1989.

Rule 81.03. Rules Incorporated into Statutes

Where any statute heretofore or hereafter enacted, whether or not listed in Appendix A, provides that any act in a civil proceeding shall be done in the manner provided by law, such act shall be done in accordance with these rules.

Adopted June 25, 1951, eff. Jan. 1, 1952. Revised Oct. 18, 1988, eff. Jan. 1, 1989.

RULE 82. JURISDICTION AND VENUE

These rules shall not be construed to extend or limit the jurisdiction of the district courts of Minnesota or the venue of actions therein.

Adopted June 25, 1951, eff. Jan. 1, 1952. Revised Oct. 18, 1988, eff. Jan. 1, 1989.

RULE 83. RULES BY DISTRICT COURTS

Any court may recommend rules governing its practice not in conflict with these rules or with the General Rules of Practice for the District Courts, and those rules shall become effective as ordered by the Supreme Court.

Adopted June 25, 1951, eff. Jan. 1, 1952. Amended Dec. 6, 1951. Revised Oct. 18, 1988, eff. Jan. 1, 1989. Amended Sept. 5, 1991, eff. Jan. 1, 1992.

Task Force Comment—1991 Adoption

This rule replaces existing Minn.R.Civ.P. 83.

The purpose of this rule is to insure a mechanism to maintain uniformity in the local rules. The Task Force believes it is imperative that some method be enforced to provide for uniformity of rules that may be adopted in the future. This rule will allow either local rules, or statewide rules based on proposed local rules, and will permit the Supreme Court to review and coordinate the adoption of those rules. In the absence of this provision, uniformity would be achieved on the day these rules are adopted, but would disappear as soon as one court adopted a rule to supplement or vary the new Code of Rules.

The American Bar Association Standards Relating to Court Administration also favor the promulgation of uniform rules of practice issued by a central court. Standard 1.11(c) provides:

> (c) Uniform standards of justice. The procedures by which the court system administers justice should be based on principles applicable throughout the system, and, so far as practicable, should be uniform in their particulars. The court system should have:
>
> (i) Uniform rules of procedure, promulgated by a common authority;
>
> (ii) Rules of court administration that are uniform so far as possible and have local variations only as approved by an appropriate central authority in the court system;

ABA Standards Relating to Court Administration, Standard 1.11(c)(i) & (ii) (1990).

RULE 84. APPENDIX OF FORMS

The forms contained in the Appendix of Forms sufficiently reflect the rules and are intended to indicate the simplicity and brevity of statement which the rules contemplate.

Adopted June 25, 1951, eff. Jan. 1, 1952. Revised Oct. 18, 1988, eff. Jan. 1, 1989.

RULE 85. TITLE

These rules are known and cited as Rules of Civil Procedure.

Adopted June 25, 1951, eff. Jan. 1, 1952. Revised Oct. 18, 1988, eff. Jan. 1, 1989.

RULE 86. EFFECTIVE DATE

Rule 86.01. Effective Date and Application to Pending Proceedings

(a) These rules as originally adopted took effect on January 1, 1952. They govern all proceedings and actions brought after that effective date, and also all further proceedings in actions then pending, except to the extent that in the opinion of the court their application in a particular action pending when the rules take effect would not be feasible, or would work injustice, in which event the procedure existing at the time the action was brought applies.

(b) Unless otherwise specified by the court, all amendments will take effect on either January 1 or July 1 in the year of or the year following their adoption. They govern all proceedings in actions brought after they take effect, and also all further proceedings in actions then pending, except as to the extent that in the opinion of the court their application in a particular action pending when the amendments take effect would not be feasible, or would work injustice, in which event the former procedure applies.

Adopted June 25, 1951, eff. Jan. 1, 1952. Revised Oct. 18, 1988, eff. Jan. 1, 1989.

Rule 86.02. Deleted Oct. 18, 1988, eff. Jan. 1, 1989

Historical Notes

Deleted Rule 86.02 adopted March 3, 1959, and revised November 10, 1967, related to the effective date of amendments. The subject matter of former Rule 86.02 was incorporated into Rule 86.01 by court order dated October 18, 1988.

Former Rule: A former Rule 86.02, adopted June 25, 1951, provided that the statutes in Appendices B(1) and B(2) are superseded in respect to practice and procedure in the district courts. The subject matter of former Rule 86.02 was incorporated into Rule 81.01 by court order dated March 3, 1959.

APPENDICES

APPENDIX A. Special Proceedings Under Rule 81.01

Following is a list of statutes and special proceedings which will be excepted from these rules insofar as they are inconsistent or in conflict with the procedure and practice provided by these rules:

Minn.Stat. (1996)	
64B.30	Quo warranto against fraternal benefit association
67A.241	Quo warranto against town mutual fire insurance company
Chapters 103A–110A	Drainage
Chapter 117	Eminent domain proceedings (see also Gen. R.Prac. 141)
Chapter 209	Election contests
Chapter 253B	Civil commitment
Chapter 259	Adoption; change of name
Chapter 271.06(7)	Proceedings in tax court
Chapter 277	Delinquent personal property taxes
Chapter 278	Objections and defenses to taxes on real estate
Chapter 279	Delinquent real estate taxes
284.07 to 284.26	Actions involving tax titles
Chapter 299F.10–.17	Actions on orders of state fire marshal
501.33 to 501.38	Proceedings relating to trusts
Chapter 503	Townsite lands
Chapter 508	Registration of title to lands (see also Gen.R.Prac. 201–216)
514.01 to 514.17	Mechanics liens
Chapter 518	Dissolution of marriage
540.08	Insofar as it provides for action by parent for injury to minor child (see also Gen.R.Prac. 145)
Chapter 556	Action by attorney general for usurpation of office, etc.
Chapter 558	Partition of real estate (except that part of second sentence of 558.02 beginning 'a copy of which')
Chapter 559	Actions to determine adverse claims (except that part of third sentence of 559.02 beginning 'a copy of which')
561.11 to 561.15	Petition by mortgagor to cultivate lands
573.02	Action for death by wrongful act (see also Gen. R.Prac. 142–144)
Chapter 579	Actions against boats and vessels

Writ of certiorari
Writ of habeas corpus
Writ of ne exeat
Writ of mandamus

Advisory Committee Note—1968

Amendment to Rule 81.01(2) by deleting the writ of mandamus as one of the writs subject to the rules, necessitates that the writ of mandamus be restored in Appendix A as one of the writs excepted from the rules. Chapter 586 of the Minnesota Statutes will control procedure for the issuance of the writ.

Historical Notes

The order of the Minnesota Supreme Court [C6-84-2134] dated November 22, 1996, provides in part that the "(a)mendments shall apply to all actions pending on the effective date [January 1, 1997] and to those filed thereafter" and that "(t)he inclusion of Advisory Committee comments is made for convenience and does not reflect court approval of the comments made therein".

APPENDIX B(1). List of Rules Superseding Statutes

Certain statutes and rules included within Appendix B(1) have been repealed. The user should check individual sections and rules for the current status of the law.

Rule	Statute Superseded M.S.A.1949	
2.01	540.01	
3.01	541.12	
	543.01	
3.02	543.04	1st sentence
4.01	543.02	
4.02	543.03	
4.03		
(a)	543.05	
(b)	540.15	the clause "and the summons may be served on one or more of them"
	540.151	the clause "and the summons may be served on one or more of them"
(c) 1st sentence:	543.08	1st paragraph, 1st sentence of 3d paragraph, and 4th paragraph
(c) 2d sentence:	543.08	2d clause of 1st sentence of 3d paragraph
	543.09	
	543.10	
(d)	543.07	
(e)	543.06	
	365.40)	
	373.07)	superseded to extent inconsistent
	411.07)	
4.04	543.11	
	543.12	
	543.15	last clause of 1st sentence
4.042	543.04	2d and 3d sentences
4.043	543.13	
4.044	557.01	3d sentence through "but" following semicolon
4.05	None	484.03, 586.05 and 587.02 contain same provision
4.06	543.14	
4.07	544.30)	
	544.32)	superseded in part
	544.34)	
5.01	543.16	
5.02	543.09	last sentence
	543.10	last sentence
	543.17	
	543.18	
	557.01	clause following semicolon in 3d sentence
	Dist.Ct. Rule 25	
5.04	544.35	
6.02	544.32)	
	544.34)	superseded in part
6.03	544.32	superseded in part
6.04	545.01	
6.05	543.18	
7.01	544.01	
	544.03	
	544.06	3d sentence
	544.08	
	544.09	
	546.02	1st sentence
	Dist.Ct. Rule 7 and Rule 22(c)	
7.02	545.01	1st sentence
	Dist.Ct. Rule 20	
8.01	544.02	(2) and (3)

Rule	Statute Superseded M.S.A.1949	
	544.04	(2)
8.02	544.04	(1), (2), and (3)
8.04	544.18	
8.05	544.05	
	544.06	1st sentence
	544.27	
8.06	544.16	
9 Generally	544.24	
	544.25	
	544.26	
9.03	544.23	
9.04	544.20	
9.05	544.19	
9.08	544.28	
10.01	544.02	(1)
10.02	544.06	2d sentence
	544.27	
	Dist.Ct. Rule 22(d) to extent inconsistent	
11	544.15	last paragraph and that part of 1st sentence as follows: "in a court of record shall be subscribed by the party or his attorney, and"
12.01	543.02	1st sentence
	544.29	2d sentence
	546.29	
12.02	544.03	
	Dist.Ct. Rule 7 and Rule 22(c)	
	543.15	2d sentence
	544.04	
	544.06	
	544.08	
	544.18	
12.05	544.10	
12.06	544.17	
12.08	544.03	subd. 3
13.01	544.05	
13.02	544.05	
13.05	544.05	
13.08	540.16	
14.01	540.16	
14.02	540.16	
15.01	544.29	1st sentence
	544.30	
15.02	544.30	
	544.31	
15.04	544.11	
17.01	540.02	
	540.04	
17.02	540.06	
18.01	544.27	
19.02	540.16	
20.01	540.10	
	544.05	
	544.27	
	548.02	(548.20 covers 2d sentence of 548.02)
22	50.12	to extent inconsistent
	227.17	
	228.20	
	544.12	
23.01	540.02	

Rule	Statute Superseded M.S.A.1949	
24.01	50.12	to extent inconsistent
	544.13	
24.03	544.13	
25.01	540.12	to extent inconsistent
25.03	540.12	to extent inconsistent
26.01	597.01	
	597.04	
	597.05	
26.04	597.12	
	597.15	
	597.16	
26.05	597.12	
26.07	597.01	
27.01	598.01	
	598.02	
	598.03	
	598.05	to 598.11, inclusive
28.01	597.01	
	597.04	
28.02	597.01	
	597.04	
29	597.06	
30.01	597.01	
	597.02	
30.03	597.07	
	597.10	
30.05	597.07	
	597.08	
30.06	597.08	
	597.09	
30.07	597.14	
31.01	597.04	
	597.05	
31.02	597.07	
	597.08	
	597.09	
	597.10	
32.01	597.13	
32.02	597.13	
32.03	597.12	
	597.13	
32.04	597.13	
34	603.01	
37.02	597.11	
	603.01	
38.01	546.03	2d sentence
38.02	546.26	
38.03	546.05	1st four sentences
39.01	546.03	1st clause of 3d sentence
39.02	546.03	last clause of 3d sentence
40	546.05	5th sentence
41.01	546.39	
41.02	546.38	
	546.39	
42.01	546.04	1st sentence
42.02	546.04	2d sentence
43.02	595.03	
43.04	595.05	
45.04	597.11	

Rule	Statute Superseded M.S.A.1949	
46	547.03	
	Dist.Ct. Rule 27(a)	
47.02	546.095	
49.01	546.14	(Laws 1971, Ch. 715)
	546.20	
49.02	546.20	
50.02	605.06	1st and 2d sentences
51	546.14	(Laws 1971, Ch. 715)
	547.03	
52.01	546.27	1st sentence
53.01	546.33	1st paragraph
	546.34	
53.03	546.36	
53.04	546.36	
53.05	546.36	
54.03	548.01	
54.04	549.10	
55.01	544.07	
58.01	548.03	
58.02	546.25	2d sentence
	547.023	
	Dist.Ct. Rule 26	
59.01	547.01	
59.02	547.02	
59.03	547.02	
59.07	547.04	
	547.05	
59.08	547.06	
60.01	544.32	
	544.34	
60.02	544.32	
	544.34	
61	544.33	
63.02	542.13	
63.03	542.16	
63.04	542.13	
	542.16	
65	585.01–585.04 to extent inconsistent	
67.02	544.14	
67.03	576.02	
67.04	485.02	1st sentence
68.01	546.40	
68.02	546.41	
70	557.04	
77.01	546.30	1st sentence
77.04	546.30	3d sentence

Adopted June 25, 1951, eff. Jan. 1, 1952. Amended Dec. 6, 1951; March 3, 1959, eff. July 1, 1959; Nov. 10, 1967, eff. Feb. 1, 1968; Jan. 5, 1973.

APPENDIX B(2). List of Statutes Superseded by Rules

Certain statutes and rules included within Appendix B(2) have been repealed. The user should check individual sections and rules for the current status of the law.

Statute Superseded M.S.A.1949	By Rule
50.12 to extent inconsistent	22; 24.01

Statute Superseded M.S.A.1949	By Rule
227.17 to extent inconsistent	22
228.20 to extent inconsistent	22
365.40 to extent inconsistent	4.03(e)
373.07 to extent inconsistent	4.03(e)
411.07 to extent inconsistent	4.03(e)
485.02 1st sentence	67.04
540.01	2.01
540.02	17.01; 23.01
540.04	17.01
540.06	17.02
540.10	20.01
540.12 to extent inconsistent	25.01; 25.03
540.15 the clause "and the summons may be served on one or more of them"	4.03(b)
540.151 the clause "and the summons may be served on one or more of them"	4.03(b)
540.16	13.08; 14.01; 14.02; 19.02
541.12	3.01
542.13	63.02; 63.04
542.16	63.03; 63.04
543.01	3.01
543.02	4.01; 12.01
543.03	4.02
543.04	3.02; 4.042
543.05	4.03(a)
543.06	4.03(e)
543.07	4.03(d)
543.08 all except 2d paragraph and 2d sentence of 3d paragraph	4.03(c)
543.09	4.03(c); 5.02
543.10	4.03(c); 5.02
543.11	4.04
543.12	4.04
543.13	4.043
543.14	4.06
543.15	4.04; 12.01; & generally
543.16	5.01
543.17	5.02
543.18	5.02; 6.05
544.01	7.01
544.02	8.01; 10.01
544.03	7.01; 12.02; 12.08
544.04	8.01; 8.02; 12.02
544.05	8.05; 13.01; 13.02; 13.05; 20.01
544.06	8.05; 7.01; 10.02; 12.02
544.07	55.01
544.08	7.01; 12.02
544.09	7.01
544.10	12.06
544.11	15.04
544.12	22
544.13	24.01; 24.03
544.14	67.02
544.15 last paragraph and part of 1st sentence reading "in a court of record shall be subscribed by the party or his attorney, and"	11
544.16	8.06

Statute Superseded M.S.A.1949		By Rule
544.17		12.05; 12.06
544.18		8.04; 12.02
544.19		9.05
544.20		9.04
544.23		9.03
544.24		Generally
544.25		Generally
544.26		Generally
544.27		8.05; 10.02; 18.01; 20.01
544.28		9.08
544.29		12.01; 15.01
544.30		4.07; 6.02; 15.01; 15.02
544.31		15.02
544.32		4.07; 6.02; 6.03; 60.01; 60.02; 61
544.33		61
544.34		4.07; 6.02; 60.01; 60.02
544.35		5.04
545.01		6.04; 7.02
546.02	1st sentence	7.01
546.03	2d and 3d sentences	38.01; 39.01; 39.02
546.04		42.01; 42.02
546.05	all except last 3 sentences	38.03; 40
546.095		47.02
546.14	(Laws 1971, Ch. 715)	49.01; 51
546.20		49.01; 49.02
546.25	beginning with "or, in its discretion * * * "	58.02
546.26		38.02
546.27	1st sentence	52.01
546.29		12.01
546.30	1st and 3d sentences	77.01; 77.04
546.33	1st paragraph	53.01
546.34		53.01
546.36		53.03; 53.04; 53.05
546.38		41.02
546.39		41.01; 41.02
546.40		68.01
546.41		68.02
547.01		59.01
547.02		59.02; 59.03
547.023		58.02
547.03		46; 51
547.04		59.07
547.05		59.07
547.06		59.08
548.01		54.03
548.02		20.01
548.03		58.01
549.10		54.04
557.01	3d sentence	4.044; 5.02
557.04		70
576.02		67.03
585.01–585.04	to extent inconsistent	65
595.03		43.02
595.05		43.04

Statute Superseded M.S.A.1949	By Rule
597.01	26.01; 26.07; 28.01; 28.02; 30.01
597.02	30.01
597.04	26.01; 28.01; 28.02; 31.01
597.05	26.01; 31.01
597.06	29
597.07	30.03; 30.05; 31.02
597.08	30.05; 30.06; 31.02
597.09	30.06; 31.02
597.10	30.03; 31.02
597.11	37.02; 45.04
597.12	26.04; 26.05; 32.03
597.13	32.01; 32.02; 32.03; 32.04
597.14	30.07
597.15	26.04
597.16	26.04
598.01	27.01
598.02	27.01
598.03	27.01
598.05	27.01
598.06	27.01
598.07	27.01
598.08	27.01
598.09	27.01
598.10	27.01
598.11	27.01
603.01	34; 37.02
605.06 1st and 2d sentences	50.02

District Court Rules Superseded

Dist. Rule	By Rule
7	7.01; 12.02
20 to extent inconsistent	7.02
22(c) & (d) to extent inconsistent	7.01; 10.02; 12.02
25	5.02
26	58.02

Adopted June 25, 1951, eff. Jan. 1, 1952. Amended Dec. 6, 1951; March 3, 1959, eff. July 1, 1959; Nov. 10, 1967, eff. Feb. 1, 1968; Jan. 5, 1973.

APPENDIX OF FORMS

[See Rule 84]

INTRODUCTORY STATEMENT

1. The following forms are intended for illustration only. They are limited in number. No attempt is made to furnish a manual of forms.

2. Except where otherwise indicated, each pleading, motion, and other paper should have a caption similar to that of the summons, with the designation of the particular paper substituted for the word "SUMMONS." In the caption of the summons and in the caption of the complaint all parties must be named, but in other pleadings and papers it is sufficient to state the name of the first party on either side, with an appropriate indication of other parties. See Rules 4.01, 7.02(2), 10.01.

3. Each pleading, motion, and other paper is to be signed in his individual name by at least one attorney of record (Rule 11). The attorney's name is to be followed by his address as indicated in Form 2. In forms following Form 2 the signature and address are not indicated.

4. If a party is not represented by an attorney, the signature and address of the party are required in place of those of the attorney.

State of Minnesota **District Court**

County of_____________ **____Judicial District**

____________________, Court File Number: ______

Case Type: __________

Plaintiff,

vs. **Summons**

____________________,

Defendant.

THIS SUMMONS IS DIRECTED TO _________

1. **YOU ARE BEING SUED.** The Plaintiff has started a lawsuit against you. The Plaintiff's Complaint against you [is attached to this summons] [is on file in the office of the court administrator of the above-named court].* Do not throw these papers away. They are official papers that affect your rights. You must respond to this lawsuit even though it may not yet be filed with the Court and there may be no court file number on this summons.

2. **YOU MUST REPLY WITHIN 20**DAYS TO PROTECT YOUR RIGHTS.** You must give or mail to the person who signed this summons **a written response** called an Answer within 20** days of the date on which you received this Summons. You must send a copy of your Answer to the person who signed this summons located at:

__________.

3. **YOU MUST RESPOND TO EACH CLAIM.** The Answer is your written response to the Plaintiff's Complaint. In your Answer you must state whether you agree or disagree with each paragraph of the Complaint. If you believe the Plaintiff should not be given everything asked for in the Complaint, you must say so in your Answer.

4. **YOU WILL LOSE YOUR CASE IF YOU DO NOT SEND A WRITTEN RESPONSE TO THE COMPLAINT TO THE PERSON WHO SIGNED THIS SUMMONS.** If you do not Answer within 20** days, you will lose this case. You will not get to tell your side of the story, and the Court may decide against you and award the Plaintiff everything asked for in the complaint. If you do not want to contest the claims stated in the complaint, you do not need to respond. A default judgment can then be entered against you for the relief requested in the complaint.

5. **LEGAL ASSISTANCE.** You may wish to get legal help from a lawyer. If you do not have a lawyer, the Court Administrator may have information about places where you can get legal assistance. **Even if you cannot get legal help, you must still provide a written Answer to protect your rights or you may lose the case.**

6. **ALTERNATIVE DISPUTE RESOLUTION.** The parties may agree to or be ordered to participate in an alternative dispute resolution process under Rule 114 of the Minnesota General Rules of Practice. You must still send your written response to the Complaint even if you expect to use alternative means of resolving this dispute.

[7. To be included only if this lawsuit affects title to real property:

THIS LAWSUIT MAY AFFECT OR BRING INTO QUESTION TITLE TO REAL PROPERTY located in _________ County, State of Minnesota, legally described as follows:

[Insert legal description of property]

The object of this action is __________.]

______________________________ __________

Plaintiff's attorney's signature Dated

____

Print or type plaintiff's attorney's name

Adopted June 25, 1951, eff. Jan. 1, 1952. Amended March 3, 1959, eff. July 1, 1959; May 3, 2010, eff. July 1, 2010.

* Use language in the first bracket when the complaint is served with the summons, language in the second bracket when the complaint is filed and the summons is served by publication.

** Use 20 days, except that in the exceptional situations where a different time is allowed by the court in which to answer, the different time should be inserted.

FORM 2. COMPLAINT ON A PROMISSORY NOTE

1. Defendant on or about June 1, 1948, executed and delivered to the plaintiff a promissory note [*in the following words and figures: (here set out the note verbatim)*]; [*a copy of which is hereto annexed as Exhibit A*]; [*whereby defendant promised to pay to plaintiff or order on June 1, 1949 the sum of one thousand dollars with interest thereon at the rate of six percent per annum*].

2. Defendant owes to plaintiff the amount of said note and interest.

Wherefore plaintiff demands judgment against defendant for the sum of one thousand dollars, interest, costs, and disbursements.

Signed: ______________________,
Attorney for Plaintiff.
Address: ______________________.

Adopted June 25, 1951, eff. Jan. 1, 1952.

FORM 3. COMPLAINT ON AN ACCOUNT

1. Defendant owes plaintiff one thousand dollars according to the account hereto annexed as Exhibit A.

Wherefore [*etc., as in Form 2*].

Adopted June 25, 1951, eff. Jan. 1, 1952.

FORM 4. COMPLAINT FOR GOODS SOLD AND DELIVERED

1. Defendant owes plaintiff one thousand dollars for goods sold and delivered by plaintiff to defendant between June 1, 1948 and December 1, 1948.

Wherefore [*etc., as in Form 2*].

Adopted June 25, 1951, eff. Jan. 1, 1952.

FORM 5. COMPLAINT FOR MONEY LENT

1. Defendant owes plaintiff one thousand dollars for money lent by plaintiff to defendant on June 1, 1948.

Wherefore [*etc., as in Form 2*].

Adopted June 25, 1951, eff. Jan. 1, 1952.

FORM 6. COMPLAINT FOR MONEY PAID BY MISTAKE

1. Defendant owes plaintiff one thousand dollars for money paid by plaintiff to defendant by mistake on June 1, 1948, under the following circumstances: [*here state the circumstances with particularity—see Rule 9.02*].

Wherefore [*etc., as in Form 2*].

Adopted June 25, 1951, eff. Jan. 1, 1952.

FORM 7. COMPLAINT FOR MONEY HAD AND RECEIVED

1. Defendant owes plaintiff one thousand dollars for money had and received from one G.H. on June 1, 1948, to be paid by defendant to plaintiff.

Wherefore [*etc., as in Form 2*].

Adopted June 25, 1951, eff. Jan. 1, 1952.

FORM 8. COMPLAINT FOR NEGLIGENCE

1. On June 1, 1948, in a public highway called University Avenue, in St. Paul, Minnesota, defendant negligently drove a motor vehicle against plaintiff who was then crossing said highway.

2. As a result plaintiff was thrown down and had his leg broken and was otherwise injured, was prevented from transacting his business, suffered great pain of body and mind, and incurred expenses for medical attention and hospitalization in the sum of one thousand dollars.

Wherefore plaintiff demands judgment against defendant in the sum of ten thousand dollars and costs.

Adopted June 25, 1951, eff. Jan. 1, 1952.

FORM 9. COMPLAINT FOR NEGLIGENCE WHERE PLAINTIFF IS UNABLE TO DETERMINE DEFINITELY WHETHER THE PERSON RESPONSIBLE IS C.D. OR E.F. OR WHETHER BOTH ARE RESPONSIBLE AND WHERE HIS EVIDENCE MAY JUSTIFY A FINDING OF WILFULNESS OR OF RECKLESSNESS OR OF NEGLIGENCE

A.B.,)
Plaintiff)
vs.) COMPLAINT
C.D. and E.F.,)
Defendants)

1. On June 1, 1948, in a public highway called University Avenue in St. Paul, Minnesota, defendant C.D. or defendant E.F., or both defendants C.D. and E.F. wilfully or recklessly or negligently drove or caused to be driven a motor vehicle against plaintiff who was then crossing said highway.

2. As a result plaintiff was thrown down and had his leg broken and was otherwise injured, was prevented from transacting his business, suffered great pain of body and mind, and incurred expenses for

medical attention and hospitalization in the sum of one thousand dollars.

Wherefore plaintiff demands judgment against C.D. or against E.F. or against both in the sum of ten thousand dollars and costs and disbursements.

Adopted June 25, 1951, eff. Jan. 1, 1952.

FORM 10. COMPLAINT FOR CONVERSION

1. On or about December 1, 1948, defendant converted to his own use ten bonds of the ________ Company [*here insert brief identification as by number and issue*] of the value of one thousand dollars, the property of plaintiff.

Wherefore plaintiff demands judgment against defendant in the sum of one thousand dollars, interest, costs, and disbursements.

Adopted June 25, 1951, eff. Jan. 1, 1952.

FORM 11. COMPLAINT FOR SPECIFIC PERFORMANCE OF CONTRACT TO CONVEY LAND

1. On or about December 1, 1948, plaintiff and defendant entered into an agreement in writing, a copy of which is hereto annexed as Exhibit A.

2. In accordance with the provisions of said agreement plaintiff tendered to defendant the purchase price and requested a conveyance of the land, but defendant refused to accept the tender and refused to make the conveyance.

3. Plaintiff now offers to pay the purchase price.

Wherefore plaintiff demands (1) that defendant be required specifically to perform said agreement, (2) damages in the sum of one thousand dollars, and (3) that if specific performance is not granted plaintiff have judgment against defendant in the sum of ten thousand dollars.

Adopted June 25, 1951, eff. Jan. 1, 1952.

FORM 12. COMPLAINT ON CLAIM FOR DEBT AND TO SET ASIDE FRAUDULENT CONVEYANCE UNDER RULE 18.02

A.B.,)
Plaintiff)
vs.) COMPLAINT
C.D. and E.F.,)
Defendants)

1. Defendant C.D. on or about ______ executed and delivered to plaintiff a promissory note [*in the following words and figures: (here set out the note verbatim)*]: [*a copy of which is hereto annexed as Exhibit A*]; [*whereby defendant C.D. promised to pay to plaintiff or order on ______ the sum of five thousand dollars with interest thereon at the rate of ______ percent per annum*].

2. Defendant C.D. owes to plaintiff the amount of said note and interest.

3. Defendant C.D. on or about ______ conveyed all his property, real and personal [or specify and describe] to defendant E.F. for the purpose of defrauding plaintiff and hindering and delaying the collection of the indebtedness evidenced by the note above referred to.

Wherefore plaintiff demands:

(1) That plaintiff have judgment against defendant C.D. for five thousand dollars and interest; (2) that the aforesaid conveyance to defendant E.F. be declared void and the judgment herein be declared a lien on said property; (3) that plaintiff have judgment against the defendants for costs and disbursements.

Adopted June 25, 1951, eff. Jan. 1, 1952.

FORM 13. COMPLAINT FOR INTERPLEADER AND DECLARATORY RELIEF

1. On or about June 1, 1948, plaintiff issued to G.H. a policy of life insurance whereby plaintiff promised to pay to K.L. as beneficiary the sum of ten thousand dollars upon the death of G.H. The policy required the payment by G.H. of a stipulated premium on June 1, 1948, and annually thereafter as a condition precedent to its continuance in force.

2. No part of the premium due June 1, 1948 was ever paid and the policy ceased to have any force or effect on July 1, 1948.

3. Thereafter, on September 1, 1948, G.H. and K.L. died as the result of a collision between a locomotive and the automobile in which G.H. and K.L. were riding.

4. Defendant C.D. is the duly appointed and acting executor of the will of G.H.; defendant E.F. is the duly appointed and acting executor of the will of K.L.; defendant X.Y. claims to have been duly designated as beneficiary of said policy in place of K.L.

5. Each of defendants, C.D., E.F., and X.Y., is claiming that the above-mentioned policy was in full force and effect at the time of the death of G.H.; each of them is claiming to be the only person entitled to receive payment of the amount of the policy and has made demand for payment thereof.

6. By reason of these conflicting claims of the defendants, plaintiff is in great doubt as to which defendant is entitled to be paid the amount of the policy, if it was in force at the death of G.H.

Wherefore plaintiff demands that the court adjudge:

(1) That none of the defendants is entitled to recover from plaintiff the amount of said policy or any part thereof.

(2) That each of the defendants be restrained from instituting any action against plaintiff for the recovery of the amount of said policy or any part thereof.

(3) That, if the court shall determine that said policy was in force at the death of G.H., the defendants be required to interplead and settle between themselves their rights to the money due under said

policy, and that plaintiff be discharged from all liability in the premises except to the person whom the court shall adjudge entitled to the amount of said policy.

(4) That plaintiff recover its costs and disbursements.

Adopted June 25, 1951, eff. Jan. 1, 1952.

FORM 14. MOTION TO DISMISS, PRESENTING DEFENSES OF FAILURE TO STATE A CLAIM, OF LACK OF SERVICE OF PROCESS, AND OF LACK OF JURISDICTION UNDER RULE 12.02

The defendant moves the court as follows:

1. To dismiss the action because the complaint fails to state a claim against defendant upon which relief can be granted.

2. To dismiss the action or in lieu thereof to quash the return of service of summons on the grounds: [Here state reasons, such as, (a) that the defendant is a corporation organized under the laws of Delaware and was not and is not subject to service of process within the State of Minnesota; (b) that the defendant has not been properly served with process in this action, all of which more clearly appears in the affidavits of M.N. and X.Y. hereto annexed as Exhibit A and Exhibit B respectively].

3. To dismiss the action on the ground that the court lacks jurisdiction because [no justiciable controversy is presented, or as the case may be].

Signed: ______________________,
Attorney for Defendant.
Address: ______________________.

Notice of Motion

To: ______________________
Attorney for Plaintiff.

* * * * * * * * * *

Please take notice, that the undersigned will bring the above motion on for hearing before the court at a special term thereof, to be held at the court house in the City of ______ on the ______ day of ______, 19__, at ______ o'clock in the [*forenoon*] [*afternoon*] or as soon thereafter as counsel can be heard.

Signed: ______________________,
Attorney for Defendant.
Address: ______________________.

Adopted June 25, 1951, eff. Jan. 1, 1952.

FORM 15. ANSWER PRESENTING DEFENSES UNDER RULE 12.02

First Defense

The complaint fails to state a claim against defendant upon which relief can be granted.

Second Defense

If defendant is indebted to plaintiffs for the goods mentioned in the complaint, he is indebted to them jointly with G.H. G.H. is alive; is a citizen and resident of this state; is subject to the jurisdiction of this court, as to both service of process and venue; can be made a party, but has not been made one.

Third Defense

Defendant admits the allegation contained in paragraphs 1 and 4 of the complaint; alleges that he is without knowledge or information sufficient to form a belief as to the truth of the allegation contained in paragraph 2 of the complaint; and denies each and every other allegation contained in the complaint.

Fourth Defense

The right of action set forth in the complaint did not accrue within six years next before the commencement of this action.

Counterclaim

[*Here set forth any claim as a counterclaim in the manner in which a claim is pleaded in a complaint.*]

Cross–Claim Against Defendant M.N.

[*Here set forth the claim constituting a cross-claim against defendant M.N. in the manner in which a claim is pleaded in a complaint.*]

Adopted June 25, 1951, eff. Jan. 1, 1952.

FORM 16. ANSWER TO COMPLAINT SET FORTH IN FORM 7, WITH COUNTERCLAIM FOR INTERPLEADER

Defense

Defendant denies the allegations stated to the extent set forth in the counterclaim herein.

Counterclaim for Interpleader

1. Defendant received the sum of one thousand dollars as a deposit from E.F.

2. Plaintiff has demanded the payment of such deposit to him by virtue of an assignment of it which he claims to have received from E.F.

3. E.F. has notified the defendant that he claims such deposit, that the purported assignment is not valid, and that he holds the defendant responsible for the deposit.

Wherefore defendant demands:

(1) That the court order E.F. to be made a party defendant to respond to the complaint and to this counterclaim.[1]

(2) That the court order the plaintiff and E.F. to interplead their respective claims.

(3) That the court adjudge whether the plaintiff or E.F. be entitled to the sum of money.

(4) That the court discharge defendant from all liability in the premises except to the person it shall adjudge entitled to the sum of money.

(5) That the court award to the defendant its costs and attorney's fees.

Adopted June 25, 1951, eff. Jan. 1, 1952.

[1] Rule 13.08 provides for the court ordering parties to a counterclaim, but who are not parties to the original action, to be brought in as defendants.

FORM 17. SUMMONS AND COMPLAINT AGAINST THIRD–PARTY DEFENDANT

STATE OF MINNESOTA, District Court
COUNTY OF ______ ______ Judicial District

A.B.,)
Plaintiff)
vs.)
C.D.,)
Defendant and) SUMMONS
Third–Party Plaintiff)
vs.)
E.F.,)
Third–Party Defendant)

State of Minnesota to the Above–Named Third–Party Defendant:

You are hereby summoned and required to serve upon ______, plaintiff's attorney whose address is ______, and upon ______, who is attorney for C.D., defendant and third-party plaintiff, and whose address is ______, an answer to the third-party complaint which is herewith served upon you within 20 days after the service of this summons upon you exclusive of the day of service. If you fail to do so, judgment by default will be taken against you for the relief demanded in the third-party complaint.

There is also served upon you herewith a copy of the complaint of the plaintiff which you may answer.

Signed: ______,
Attorney for Defendant and
Third–Party Plaintiff.
Address: ______.

A.B.,)
Plaintiff)
vs.)
C.D.,) THIRD–PARTY
Defendant and) COMPLAINT
Third–Party Plaintiff)
vs.)
E.F.,)
Third–Party Defendant)

1. Plaintiff A.B. has served upon C.D. a complaint, a copy of which is hereto attached as Exhibit ______.

2. [*Here state the grounds upon which C.D. is entitled to recover from E.F. all or part of what A.B. may recover from C.D. The statement should be framed as in an original complaint.*]

Wherefore C.D. demands judgment against third-party defendant E.F. for all sums that may be adjudged against defendant C.D. in favor of plaintiff A.B.

Signed: ______,
Attorney for C.D.,
Third–Party Plaintiff.
Address: ______.

Adopted June 25, 1951, eff. Jan. 1, 1952. Amended March 3, 1959, eff. July 1, 1959.

FORM 18. MOTION TO INTERVENE AS A DEFENDANT UNDER RULE 24

STATE OF MINNESOTA, District Court
COUNTY OF ______. ______ Judicial District

A.B.,)
Plaintiff)
vs.) MOTION TO
) INTERVENE AS
C.D.,) A DEFENDANT
Defendant)
E.F.,)
Applicant for Intervention)

E.F. moves for leave to intervene as a defendant in this action, in order to assert the defenses set forth in his proposed answer, of which a copy is hereto attached, on the grounds [*here state them*] and as such has a defense to plaintiff's claim presenting [*both questions of law and of fact*] which are common to the main action.

Signed: ______,
Attorney for E.F.,
Applicant for Intervention.
Address: ______.

Notice of Motion

[*Contents the same as in Form 14*]

STATE OF MINNESOTA, District Court
COUNTY OF ______. ______ Judicial District

A.B.,)
Plaintiff)
vs.)
C.D.,) INTERVENER'S
) ANSWER
Defendant)
E.F.,)
Intervener)

First Defense

Intervener admits the allegations stated in paragraphs ___ and ___ of the complaint; denies the allegations in paragraphs ___ and ___.

Second Defense

[*Set forth any defenses.*]

Signed: ______________________,
Attorney for E.F., Intervener.
Address: ______________________.

Adopted June 25, 1951, eff. Jan. 1, 1952.

FORM 19. REQUEST FOR PRODUCTION OF DOCUMENTS, ETC., UNDER RULE 34

Plaintiff A.B. requests defendant C.D. to respond within ___ days to the following requests:

(1) That defendant produce and permit plaintiff to inspect and to copy each of the following documents:

[*Here list the documents either individually or by category and describe each of them.*]

[*Here state the time, place, and manner of making the inspection and performance of any related acts.*]

(2) That defendant produce and permit plaintiff to inspect and to copy, test, or sample each of the following objects:

[*Here list the objects either individually or by category and describe each of them.*]

[*Here state the time, place, and manner of making the inspection and performance of any related acts.*]

(3) That defendant permit plaintiff to enter [*here describe property to be entered*] and to inspect and to photograph, test or sample [*here describe the portion of the real property and the objects to be inspected*].

[*Here state the time, place, and manner of making the inspection and performance of any related acts.*]

Signed: ______________________,
Attorney for Plaintiff.
Address: ______________________

Adopted June 25, 1951, eff. Jan. 1, 1952. Amended Nov. 14, 1974, eff. Jan. 1, 1975.

Advisory Committee Note—1975

The amendments conform Form 19 to changes made in Rule 34. This form may also be used under Rule 30.02(5).

FORM 20. REQUEST FOR ADMISSION UNDER RULE 36

Plaintiff A.B. requests defendant C.D. within ___ days after service of this request to make the following admissions for the purpose of this action only and subject to all pertinent objections to admissibility which may be interposed at the trial:

1. That each of the following documents, exhibited with this request, is genuine.

[*Here list the documents and describe each document.*]

2. That each of the following statements is true.

[*Here list the statements.*]

Signed: ______________________,
Attorney for Plaintiff.
Address: ______________________

Adopted June 25, 1951, eff. Jan. 1, 1952.

FORM 21. ALLEGATION OF REASON FOR OMITTING PARTY

When it is necessary, under Rule 19.03, for the pleader to set forth in his pleading the names of persons who ought to be made parties, but who are not so made, there should be an allegation such as the one set out below:

John Doe named in this complaint is not made a party to this action [*because he is not subject to the jurisdiction of this court*] or [*for reasons stated*].

Adopted June 25, 1951, eff. Jan. 1, 1952.

FORM 22. NOTICE AND ACKNOWLEDGEMENT OF SERVICE BY MAIL

NOTICE

TO: (insert the name and address of the person to be served.)

The enclosed summons and complaint are served pursuant to Rule 4.05 of the Minnesota Rules of Civil Procedure.

You must complete the acknowledgment part of this form and return one copy of the completed form to the sender within 20 days.

Signing this Acknowledgment of Receipt is only an admission that you have received the summons and complaint, and does not waive any other defenses.

You must sign and date the acknowledgment. If you are served on behalf of a corporation, unincorporated association (including a partnership), or other entity, you must indicate under your signature your relationship to that entity. If you are served on behalf of another person and you are authorized to receive process, you must indicate under your signature your authority.

If you do not complete and return the form to the sender within 20 days, you (or the party on whose behalf you are being served) may be required to pay any expenses incurred in serving a summons and complaint in any other manner permitted by law.

If you do complete and return this form, you (or the party on whose behalf you are being served) must answer the complaint within 20 days. If you fail to do so, judgment by default will be taken against you for the relief demanded in the complaint.

I declare, under penalty of perjury, that this Notice and Acknowledgment of Receipt of Summons and Complaint was mailed on (insert date).

____
Signature

____
Date of Signature

ACKNOWLEDGMENT OF RECEIPT OF SUMMONS AND COMPLAINT

I declare, under penalty of perjury, that I received a copy of the summons and of the complaint in the above-captioned matter at (insert address).

____
Signature

____
Relationship to Entity/Authority to
Receive Service of Process

____
Date of Signature

Adopted March 21, 1985, eff. July 1, 1985.

FORM 23. SUBJECT MATTER INDEX FOR CIVIL CASES

1. Appeal from Conciliation Court

[All cases in which there has been an appeal from conciliation court decision]

2. Condemnation

3A. Consumer Credit Contract

[Plaintiff is a corporation or organization, not an individual; defendant is an individual; and contract amount does not exceed $20,000]

3B. Other Contracts

[all other contracts not included in 3A, above]

4. Dissolution With Children
5. Dissolution Without Children
6. Drivers License Revocation [Implied Consent]
7. Employment
8. Harassment [except for Employment related cases]
9. Medical Malpractice
10. Property Damage
11. Personal Injury
12. Unlawful Detainer
13. Wrongful Death
14. Other Civil

[All other civil cases not covered by items 1 through 13 above, including but not limited to the following:

Appeals From Administrative Agencies
Attorney Malpractice
Change of Name
Corporate Dissolution
Declaratory Judgment
Discrimination
Minor Settlement
Mortgage Foreclosure
Quiet Title
Real Estate Tax Petitions
Receivership
Torrens
Writs of Attachment, Certiorari, Habeas Corpus, Mandamus and Prohibition]

Adopted June 12, 1986, eff. July 1, 1986. Amended July 17, 1992, eff. Aug. 1, 1992; Dec. 10, 2008, eff. Jan. 1, 2009.

INDEX TO RULES OF CIVIL PROCEDURE

RULES OF CRIMINAL PROCEDURE

Effective January 1, 1990

Including Amendments Received Through January 1, 2014

Research Note

See Minnesota Statutes Annotated, *Volume 49, for case annotations, historical notes, and library references. The Rules of Criminal Procedure are discussed in McCarr and Nordby, 7, 8, 9, and 9A* Minnesota Practice–Criminal Law and Procedure (3d Edition).

RULE 10. PLEADINGS AND MOTIONS BEFORE TRIAL; DEFENSES AND OBJECTIONS

RULE 11. THE OMNIBUS HEARING

RULE 12. PRETRIAL CONFERENCE AND EVIDENTIARY HEARING IN MISDEMEANOR CASES

RULE 13. ARRAIGNMENT IN FELONY AND GROSS MISDEMEANOR CASES [DELETED OCT. 27, 2009, EFF. JAN. 1, 2010]

RULE 14. PLEAS

RULE 15. GUILTY PLEA PROCEDURES

RULE 16. MISDEMEANOR PROSECUTION BY INDICTMENT

RULE 17. INDICTMENT, COMPLAINT AND TAB CHARGE

RULE 18. GRAND JURY

RULE 19. WARRANT OR SUMMONS UPON INDICTMENT; APPEARANCE BEFORE DISTRICT COURT

RULE 20. MENTALLY ILL OR MENTALLY DEFICIENT DEFENDANTS

RULE 21. DEPOSITIONS

Superceded Statutes

Various statutes were modified or superceded by the Rules of Criminal Procedure. See M.S.A. § 480.059, subd. 7, relating to the effect of the Rules upon statutes.

Application

The General Rules of Practice for the District Courts, enacted by Order of the Minnesota Supreme Court dated September 5, 1991, effective January 1, 1992, contain Title VIII, entitled Rules Relating to Criminal Matters, consisting of Rules 701 to 706. Rule 701 provides that these rules apply in all criminal actions, and supplement the Minnesota Rules of Criminal Procedure. See M.S.A. General Rules of Practice for the District Courts.

RULE 1. SCOPE AND PURPOSE OF THE RULES

Rule 1.01. Scope and Application

These rules govern the procedure in prosecutions for felonies, gross misdemeanors, misdemeanors, and petty misdemeanors in the district courts in the State of Minnesota.

Adopted Feb. 26, 1975, eff. July 1, 1975. Revised Dec. 13, 1989. Amended Oct. 27, 2009, eff. Jan. 1, 2010.

Comment—Rule 1

See comment following Rule 1.06.

Historical Notes

The order of the Minnesota Supreme Court [C1–84–2137] dated December 13, 1989, provides in part that "(t)hese amended Rules of Criminal Procedure shall govern all criminal actions commenced or arrests made after 12 o'clock midnight January 1, 1990, except amendments to 8.04, 11.07, and 19.04, subd. 5, shall govern all criminal actions commenced or arrests made after 12 o'clock midnight January 1, 1991."

Rule 1.02. Purpose and Construction

These rules are intended to provide a just determination of criminal proceedings, and ensure a simple and fair procedure that eliminates unjustified expense and delay. The rules must be applied without discrimination based upon race, color, creed, religion, national origin, sex, marital status, public-assistance status, disability, including disability in communication, sexual orientation, or age.

Adopted Feb. 26, 1975, eff. July 1, 1975. Revised Dec. 13, 1989. Amended May 9, 1994; Oct. 27, 2009, eff. Jan. 1, 2010.

Comment—Rule 1

See comment following Rule 1.06.

Historical Notes

The order of the Minnesota Supreme Court [C1–84–2137] dated December 13, 1989, provides in part that "(t)hese amended Rules of Criminal Procedure shall govern all criminal actions commenced or arrests made after 12 o'clock midnight January 1, 1990, except amendments to 8.04, 11.07, and 19.04, subd. 5, shall govern all criminal actions commenced or arrests made after 12 o'clock midnight January 1, 1991."

The order of the Minnesota Supreme Court [C1–84–2137] dated May 9, 1994, provides in part that "(t)hese amendments to the Rules of Criminal Procedure shall govern all criminal actions commenced or arrests made after 12 o'clock midnight July 1, 1994, except that the amendments in the first sentence of the third paragraph in Rule 2.01 shall govern all criminal actions commenced or arrests made after 12 o'clock midnight January 1, 1995."

Rule 1.03. Local Rules by District Court

A court may recommend local rules governing its practice if they do not conflict with these rules or with the General Rules of Practice for the District Courts. Local rules become effective only if ordered by the Supreme Court.

Adopted May 9, 1994. Amended Oct. 27, 2009, eff. Jan. 1, 2010.

Comment—Rule 1

See comment following Rule 1.06.

Historical Notes

The order of the Minnesota Supreme Court [C1–84–2137] dated May 9, 1994, provides in part that "(t)hese amendments to the Rules of Criminal Procedure shall govern all criminal actions commenced or arrests made after 12 o'clock midnight July 1, 1994, except that the amendments in the first sentence of the third paragraph in Rule 2.01 shall govern all criminal actions commenced or arrests made after 12 o'clock midnight January 1, 1995."

Rule 1.04. Definitions

As used in these rules, the following terms have the meanings given.

(a) Misdemeanor. Unless these rules direct otherwise, "misdemeanor" includes state statutes, local ordinances, charter provisions, or rules or regulations punishable—either alone or alternatively—by a fine or imprisonment of not more than 90 days.

(b) Designated Gross Misdemeanor. A "designated gross misdemeanor" is a gross misdemeanor charged or punishable under Minnesota Statutes, sections 169A.20, 169A.25, 169A.26, or 171.24.

(c) Tab Charge. A "tab charge" is a brief statement of the charge entered in the record by the court administrator that includes a reference to the statute, rule, regulation, ordinance, or other provision of law the defendant is alleged to have violated. A tab charge is not synonymous with "citation" as defined in paragraph (e).

(d) Aggravated Sentence. An "aggravated sentence" is a sentence that is an upward durational or dispositional departure from the presumptive sentence provided for in the Minnesota Sentencing Guidelines based on aggravating circumstances or a statutory sentencing enhancement.

(e) Citation. A "citation" is a charging document issued under Rule 6. The citation may be filed in paper form or by electronic means.

(f) Electronic Citation. An "electronic citation" is a citation transmitted to the court by electronic means.

(g) Violations Bureau. "Violations bureau" refers to court staff who process citations. A violations bureau may consist of one or more employees within a single court location, a dedicated court division, or the Minnesota Court Payment Center implemented and operated by the State Court Administrator.

Adopted Aug. 21, 1998, eff. Jan. 1, 1999. Amended Dec. 23, 2002, eff. Feb. 1, 2003; Aug. 17, 2006, eff. Oct. 1, 2006; Oct. 27, 2009, eff. Jan. 1, 2010; Jan. 13, 2011, eff. Jan. 1, 2012.

Comment—Rule 1

See comment following Rule 1.06.

Rule 1.05. Use of Interactive Video Teleconference in Criminal Proceedings

Subd. 1. Definitions.

(1) *ITV.* "ITV" refers to interactive video teleconference.

(2) *Terminal Site.* A "terminal site" is any location where ITV is used for any part of a court proceeding.

(3) *Venue County.* The "venue county" is the county where pleadings are filed and hearings are held under current court procedures.

(4) *District.* The "district" is the judicial district in which the venue county is located.

Subd. 2. Appearance; How Made. Appearances in proceedings governed by the Minnesota Rules of Criminal Procedure must be made in person except as authorized to be made by ITV in this rule, by written petition in Rules 14.02, subd. 2 and 15.03, subd. 2, and by phone in Rule 26.03, subd. 1(3)5.

Subd. 3. Permissible Use of ITV. ITV may be used to conduct the proceedings specified in subdivisions 4 and 5:

(1) When no judge is available in the venue county;

(2) When the defendant is in custody and is being held in a location other than the venue county; or

(3) In the interests of justice.

Subd. 4. Felony, Gross Misdemeanor, or Misdemeanor Proceedings.

(1) Subject to the requirements in subdivisions 6 and 7, ITV may be used to conduct the following felony, gross misdemeanor, or misdemeanor proceedings:

(a) Rule 5 or Rule 6 hearings;

(b) Rule 8 hearings;

(c) Rule 11 hearings for the purpose of waiving an omnibus hearing;

(d) Plea;

(e) Sentencing;

(f) Probation revocation hearings;

(g) Any hearing for which the defendant's personal presence is not required under Rules 14.02, subd. 2 and 26.03, subd. 1(3).

(2) ITV cannot be used to conduct a trial, contested omnibus hearing, contested pretrial hearing, or any other evidentiary matter except as provided in this rule.

Subd. 5. Petty Misdemeanor and Regulatory or Administrative Criminal Offenses. A defendant may appear by ITV for all hearings, including trials, related to petty misdemeanors and regulatory or administrative criminal offenses not punishable by imprisonment.

Subd. 6. Request for In-Person Hearing; Consent Requirements.

(1) *Rule 5 or Rule 6 Hearings.* When a defendant appears before the court by ITV for a Rule 5 or Rule 6 hearing, the defendant may request to appear in person before a judge. If the request is made, the hearing will be held within 3 business days of the ITV hearing and is deemed a continuance of the ITV hearing.

(2) *Other Hearings; Consent.* In all proceedings other than a Rule 5 or Rule 6 hearing, prior to the commencement of the hearing, the defendant, defense attorney, prosecutor, and judge must consent to holding the hearing by ITV. Otherwise, an in-person court appearance for that hearing must be scheduled to be held within the time limits as otherwise provided by these rules or other law.

Subd. 7. Location of Participants.

(1) *Defendant's Attorney.* The defendant and the defendant's attorney must be present at the same terminal site except in unusual or emergency circumstances specifically related to the defendant's case, and then only if all parties agree on the record. This exception for unusual or emergency circumstances does not apply to:

(a) felony or gross misdemeanor plea proceedings when the defendant is entering a guilty plea or

(b) felony or gross misdemeanor sentencing proceedings.

(2) *Prosecutor.* Subject to paragraph (4), the prosecutor may appear from any terminal site.

(3) *Judge.* Subject to paragraph (4), the judge may appear from any terminal site.

(4) *Defendant's Attorney or Prosecutor at Same Terminal Site as Judge.* When the right to counsel applies, ITV cannot be used in a situation in which only the defense attorney or prosecutor is physically present before the judge unless all parties agree on the record.

(5) *Witnesses, Victims, Other Persons.* Witnesses, victims, and other persons may be located at any terminal site.

Subd. 8. Consolidated Proceeding for Charges Pending in Multiple Counties.

(1) *Consolidated Proceeding.* When a defendant has pending charges in more than one county,the charges may be heard in a consolidated proceeding conducted by ITV.

(2) *Judge.* The proceedings shall be heard by a judge in the county in which the most serious offense is pending, unless the parties agree otherwise.

(3) *Prosecutor.* Each prosecutor having authority to charge the offenses included in the proceeding may attend the hearing in person or by ITV or waive appearance. Any prosecutor authorized to appear on behalf of another prosecutor in the ITV proceeding must make an oral record of the authorization.

(4) *Defense Attorney.* If the defendant is represented by multiple defense attorneys, each attorney may choose to attend the hearing in person or by ITV or assign responsibility as the attorney of record to one attorney. Any defense attorney appearing in the ITV proceeding must make an oral record of representation.

Subd. 9. Witness Testimony. Witnesses may testify by ITV if the court and all parties agree.

Subd. 10. Proceedings; Record; Decorum.

(1) *Where Conducted.* When an ITV proceeding is conducted, the terminal site(s) for the defendant, defense attorney, prosecutor, and judge must be located in a courtroom. The terminal site(s) for witnesses, victims, or other persons may be located in a courtroom or another suitable room reasonably accessible to the public as approved by the judge conducting the proceeding.

(2) *Effect of ITV Hearing.* Regardless of the physical location of any party to the ITV hearing, any waiver, stipulation, motion, objection, order, or any other action taken by the court or a party at an ITV hearing has the same effect as if done in person.

(3) *Defendant Right to Counsel.* The court must ensure that the defendant has adequate opportunity to confidentially communicate with counsel, including, where appropriate, suspension of the audio transmission and recording or allowing counsel to leave the conference table to communicate with the defendant in private.

(4) *Record.* The court administrator of the venue county must maintain court records as if the proceeding were heard in person. If the hearing requires a written record, a court reporter must be in simultaneous voice communication with all ITV terminal sites, and must make the appropriate verbatim record of the proceeding as if heard in person. No recording of the ITV proceeding other than the recording made as the official court record is permitted.

(5) *Decorum.* Courtroom decorum during ITV hearings must conform to the extent possible to that required during traditional court proceedings. This may include the presence of one or more sheriff's personnel at any ITV site.

Subd. 11. Administrative Procedures. Administrative procedures for conducting ITV hearings are governed by the General Rules of Practice.

Adopted Nov. 19, 2007, eff. Jan. 1, 2008. Amended Oct. 27, 2009, eff. Jan. 1, 2010; June 9, 2010, eff. July 1, 2010; June 5, 2012, eff. Aug. 1, 2012.

Comment—Rule 1

See comment following Rule 1.06.

Historical Notes

The order of the Minnesota Supreme Court [ADM 10–8049] dated June 5, 2012, provided in part that the amendments "be effective August 1, 2012, and shall apply to all actions or proceedings pending on or commenced on or after the effective date."

Rule 1.06. Use of Electronic Filing for Charging Documents

Subd. 1. Definitions.

(1) *Charging Document.* A "charging document" is a complaint, indictment, citation, or tab charge.

(2) *E-filing.* "E-filing" is the electronic transmission of the charging document to the court administrator.

Subd. 2. Authorization. E-filing may be used to file with the court administrator in a criminal case any charging document except an indictment.

Subd. 3. Signatures.

(1) *How Made.* If the charging document is e-filed, all signatures required under these rules must be affixed electronically. Any individual required to sign the charging document under these rules can choose to print the charging document and sign it manually. Once any individual prints the charging document and affixes a manual signature, all subsequent signatures must be affixed manually, and the printed copy is the original and must be filed with the court.

(2) *Signature Standard.* Each signature affixed electronically must comply with the electronic signa-

ture standard approved by the State Court Administrator, except that electronic signatures affixed by law enforcement officers serving as the complainant must be authenticated using biometric identification.

(3) *Effect of Electronic Signature.* A printed copy of a charging document showing that an electronic signature was properly affixed under paragraph (2) prior to the printout is prima facie evidence of the authenticity of the electronic signature.

Subd. 4. Electronic Notarization. If the probable cause statement in an e-filed complaint is made under oath before a notary public, it must be electronically notarized in accordance with state law.

Subd. 5. Paper Submission. E-filed documents are in lieu of paper submissions. An e-filed document should not be transmitted to the court administrator by any other means unless the court requests a printed copy.

Adopted Nov. 17, 2008, eff. Dec. 1, 2008. Amended Oct. 27, 2009, eff. Jan. 1, 2010; Dec. 18, 2009, eff. Jan. 1, 2010; June 30, 2010, eff. July 15, 2010.

Comment—Rule 1

Beyond the procedures required by these rules, prosecutors, courts, and law enforcement agencies should also be aware of the rights of crime victims as provided in chapter 611A of the Minnesota Statutes.

Rule 1.04 (d) defines "aggravated sentence" for the purpose of the provisions in these rules governing the procedure that a sentencing court must follow to impose an upward sentencing departure in compliance with Blakely v. Washington, 542 U.S. 296, 301–305 (2004). On June 24, 2004, the United States Supreme Court decided in Blakely that an upward departure in sentencing under the State of Washington's determinate sentencing system violated the defendant's Sixth Amendment rights where the additional findings required to justify the departure were not made beyond a reasonable doubt by a jury. The definition is in accord with existing Minnesota case law holding that Blakely applies to upward departures under the Minnesota Sentencing Guidelines and under various sentencing enhancement statutes requiring additional factual findings. See, e.g., State v. Shattuck, 704 N.W.2d 131, 140–142 (Minn. 2005) (durational departures); State v. Allen, 706 N.W.2d 40, 44–47 (Minn. 2005) (dispositional departures); State v. Leake, 699 N.W.2d 312, 321–324 (Minn. 2005) (life sentence without release under Minnesota Statutes, section 609.106); State v. Barker, 705 N.W.2d 768, 771–773 (Minn. 2005) (firearm sentence enhancements under Minnesota Statutes, section 609.11); and State v. Henderson, 706 N.W.2d 758, 761–762 (Minn. 2005) (career offender sentence enhancements under Minnesota Statutes section 609.1095, subd. 4).

These Blakely-related protections and procedures do not apply retroactively to sentences that were imposed and were no longer subject to direct appeal by the time that Blakely was decided on June 24, 2004. State v. Houston, 702 N.W.2d 268, 773 (Minn. 2005). Also, the protections and procedures do not apply to sentencing departures and enhancements that are based solely on a defendant's criminal conviction history such as the assessment of a custody status point under the Minnesota Sentencing Guidelines. State v. Allen, 706 N.W.2d 40, 47–48 (Minn. 2005).

For aggravated sentence procedures related to Blakely, see Rule 7.03 (notice of prosecutor's intent to seek an aggravated sentence in proceedings prosecuted by complaint); Rule 9.01, subd. 1(7) (discovery of evidence relating to an aggravated sentence); Rule 11.04, subd. 2 (Omnibus Hearing decisions on aggravated sentence issues); Rule 15.01, subd. 2 and Appendices E and F (required questioning and written petition provisions concerning defendant's admission of facts supporting an aggravated sentence and accompanying waiver of rights); Rule 19.04, subd. 6 (notice of prosecutor's intent to seek an aggravated sentence in proceedings prosecuted by indictment); Rule 26.01, subd. 1(2)(b) (waiver of right to a jury trial determination of facts supporting an aggravated sentence); Rule 26.01, subd. 3 (stipulation of facts to support an aggravated sentence and accompanying waiver of rights); Rules 26.03, subd. 18(1) and (3) (motion that evidence submitted to jury was insufficient to support an aggravated sentence); Rule 26.03, subd. 19(7) (verdict forms); Rule 26.03, subd. 20(5) (polling the jury); and Rule 26.04, subd. 1 (new trial on aggravated sentence issue). The procedures provided in these rules for the determination of aggravated sentence issues supersede the procedures concerning those issues in Minnesota Statutes, section 244.10 (see 2005 Minnesota Laws, chapter 136, article 16, sections 3–6) or other statutes.

Rule 1.05, subd. 8(3) and (4) clarify that when charges from multiple counties are consolidated into single ITV proceeding, each prosecutor having authority to charge the offenses and each defense attorney representing the defendant for any of those offenses may choose to attend the hearing in person or by ITV or to waive appearance. But the provision in paragraph (4) permitting one defense attorney to represent the defendant on all pending charges is not intended to be invoked by the court when a defense attorney is simply delayed by a proceeding occurring in another courtroom. Rather, the decision to attend the hearing is individual to the attorney.

The signatures of the following persons must be affixed electronically when a complaint is e-filed pursuant to Rule 1.06:

- the complainant, as required under Rule 2.01, subd. 1;
- the judge, court administrator, or notary public before whom a complaint is made upon oath, as required under Rule 2.01, subd. 2;
- the prosecutor, as required under Rule 2.02; and
- the judge, indicating a written finding of probable cause, as required under Rule 4.03, subd. 4.

There are currently no signature requirements in the rules for citations or tab charges.

It is anticipated that if a complaint is commenced electronically, any actor in the chain (e.g., prosecutor or judge) could choose to print the complaint and proceed by filing a hard copy. If paper filing occurs, Rule 1. 06, subd. 3, clarifies that any signatures affixed electronically and shown on the hard copy complaint are valid so long as the signatures were affixed in compliance with the electronic signature standard under paragraph (2).

Electronic Notarization, as required under Rule 1.06, subd. 4, is governed by Minnesota Statutes, chapters 358 and 359.

Historical Notes

The order of the Minnesota Supreme Court [C1–84–2137] dated November 17, 2008, provides in part that this rule "is effective December 1, 2008, and shall be in effect for two years thereafter, unless abrogated earlier by this court."

The order of the Minnesota Supreme Court [C1–84–2137] dated December 18, 2009, provided:

"1. The attached amendments to temporary Minnesota Rule of Criminal Procedure 1.06 are prescribed and promulgated effective January 1, 2010.

"2. The temporary rule shall be effective in the following counties for participants in the echarging/e-filing pilot project: Carver, Freeborn, Goodhue, Isanti, Kandiyohi, Lyon, Olmsted, Otter Tail, Rice, and St. Louis.

"3. The temporary rule shall remain in effect as amended until November 30, 2010, unless earlier abrogated by this court."

The order of the Minnesota Supreme Court [C1–84–2137] dated June 30, 2010, provided:

"Minn.R.Crim.P. 1.06 is amended and promulgated as a permanent Rule of Criminal Procedure effective statewide as of July 15, 2010."

RULE 2. COMPLAINT

Rule 2.01. Contents; Before Whom Made

Subd. 1. Contents. The complaint is a written signed statement of the facts establishing probable cause to believe that the charged offense has been committed and that the defendant committed it, except as modified by Rules 6.01, subd. 4, 11.08, and 15.08. The probable cause statement can be supplemented by supporting affidavits or by sworn witness testimony taken by the issuing judge. The complaint must specify the offense charged, the statute allegedly violated, and the maximum penalty. The complaint must also conform to the requirements in Rule 17.02.

Subd. 2. Before Whom Made. The probable cause statement must be made under oath before a judge, court administrator, or notary public, except as otherwise provided in Rules 11.08 and 15.08. If sworn witness testimony is taken under subdivision 3, the oath must be administered by a judge, but the oath may be administered by telephone, ITV, or similar device.

Subd. 3. Witness Testimony; How Made. If the court takes sworn witness testimony, the court must note that fact on the complaint. The testimony must be recorded by a reporter or recording instrument and must be transcribed and filed.

Subd. 4. Probable Cause Determination. The judge must determine whether probable cause exists to believe an offense has been committed and the defendant committed it. When the alleged offense is punishable by a fine only, the probable cause determination can be made by the court administrator if authorized by court order.

Adopted Feb. 26, 1975, eff. July 1, 1975. Revised Dec. 13, 1989. Amended May 9, 1994; May 19, 2008, eff. July 1, 2008; Oct. 27, 2009, eff. Jan. 1, 2010.

Comment—Rule 2

See comment following Rule 2.02.

Historical Notes

The order of the Minnesota Supreme Court [C1–84–2137] dated December 13, 1989, provides in part that "(t)hese amended Rules of Criminal Procedure shall govern all criminal actions commenced or arrests made after 12 o'clock midnight January 1, 1990, except amendments to 8.04, 11.07, and 19.04, subd. 5, shall govern all criminal actions commenced or arrests made after 12 o'clock midnight January 1, 1991."

The order of the Minnesota Supreme Court [C1–84–2137] dated May 9, 1994, provides in part that "(t)hese amendments to the Rules of Criminal Procedure shall govern all criminal actions commenced or arrests made after 12 o'clock midnight July 1, 1994, except that the amendments in the first sentence of the third paragraph in Rule 2.01 shall govern all criminal actions commenced or arrests made after 12 o'clock midnight January 1, 1995."

Rule 2.02. Approval of Prosecutor

A complaint must not be issued without the prosecutor's signature, unless a judge certifies on the complaint that the prosecutor is unavailable and that issuance of the complaint should not be delayed.

Adopted Feb. 26, 1975, eff. July 1, 1975. Revised Dec. 13, 1989. Amended Oct. 27. 2009, eff. Jan. 1, 2010.

Comment—Rule 2

Rule 2.01 notes exceptions to the probable cause requirement in the complaint. Rule 6.01, subd. 4 permits probable cause to be contained in a separate attachment to the citation. Rules 11.08 and 15.08, which authorize the substitution of a new complaint to permit a plea to a misdemeanor or different offense, do not require a showing of probable cause.

Even if affidavits, testimony, or other reports supplement the complaint, the complaint must still include a statement of the facts establishing probable cause. Under this rule, the complaint and any supporting affidavits can be sworn to before a court administrator or notary public. The documents can then be submitted to the judge or judicial officer by any method permitted under the rule and the law enforcement officer or other complainant need not personally appear before the judge. However, if sworn oral testimony is taken to supplement the complaint, it must be taken before the judge and cannot be taken before a court administrator or notary public.

The prosecutors referred to in Rule 2.02 are those authorized by law to prosecute the offense charged. See Minn. Stat. § 484.87 (allocating prosecutorial responsibilities amongst city, township, and county prosecutors); Minn. Stat. §§ 8.01and

8.03 (Attorney General); Minn. Stat. § 388.051 (County Attorney).

Rule 2.02 does not define the remedy available when a local prosecutor refuses to approve a complaint.

Because the complaint is accessible to the public, and documents supporting the statement of probable cause can contain irrelevant material that is injurious to innocent third persons, as well as material prejudicial to the defendant's right to a fair trial, it is recommended that a statement be drafted containing the facts establishing probable cause, in or with the complaint, and that irrelevant material be omitted.

Historical Notes

The order of the Minnesota Supreme Court [C1–84–2137] dated December 13, 1989, provides in part that "(t)hese amended Rules of Criminal Procedure shall govern all criminal actions commenced or arrests made after 12 o'clock midnight January 1, 1990, except amendments to 8.04, 11.07, and 19.04, subd. 5, shall govern all criminal actions commenced or arrests made after 12 o'clock midnight January 1, 1991."

Rule 2.03. Repealed May 19, 2008, eff. July 1, 2008

Historical Notes

Repealed Rule 2.03, adopted April 14, 1980, and amended December 13, 1989, related to felony or gross misdemeanor complaint forms.

RULE 3. WARRANT OR SUMMONS UPON COMPLAINT

Rule 3.01. Issuance

If the facts in the complaint and any supporting affidavits or supplemental sworn testimony establish probable cause to believe an offense has been committed and the defendant committed it, a summons or warrant must issue. A summons rather than a warrant must issue unless a substantial likelihood exists that the defendant will fail to respond to a summons, the defendant's location is not reasonably discoverable, or the defendant's arrest is necessary to prevent imminent harm to anyone. A warrant for the defendant's arrest must be issued to any person authorized by law to execute it.

The warrant or summons must be issued by a judge of the district court. If the offense is punishable by fine only, a court administrator may issue the summons when authorized by court order.

A summons must issue in lieu of a warrant if the offense is punishable by fine only in misdemeanor cases.

A judge must issue a summons whenever requested to do so by the prosecutor.

If a defendant fails to appear in response to a summons, a warrant must issue.

Adopted Feb. 26, 1975, eff. July 1, 1975. Revised Dec. 13, 1989. Amended May 9, 1994; Oct. 27, 2009, eff. Jan. 1, 2010.

Comment—Rule 3

See comment following Rule 3.04.

Historical Notes

The order of the Minnesota Supreme Court [C1–84–2137] dated December 13, 1989, provides in part that "(t)hese amended Rules of Criminal Procedure shall govern all criminal actions commenced or arrests made after 12 o'clock midnight January 1, 1990, except amendments to 8.04, 11.07, and 19.04, subd. 5, shall govern all criminal actions commenced or arrests made after 12 o'clock midnight January 1, 1991."

The order of the Minnesota Supreme Court [C1–84–2137] dated May 9, 1994, provides in part that "(t)hese amendments to the Rules of Criminal Procedure shall govern all criminal actions commenced or arrests made after 12 o'clock midnight July 1, 1994, except that the amendments in the first sentence of the third paragraph in Rule 2.01 shall govern all criminal actions commenced or arrests made after 12 o'clock midnight January 1, 1995."

Rule 3.02. Contents of Warrant or Summons

Subd. 1. Warrant. The warrant must be signed by a judge and must contain the name of the defendant, or, if unknown, any name or description by which the defendant can be identified with reasonable certainty. It must describe the offense charged in the complaint. The warrant and complaint may be combined in one form. For all offenses, the amount of bail must be set, and other conditions of release may be set, by a judge and endorsed on the warrant.

Subd. 2. Directions of Warrant. The warrant must direct that the defendant be brought promptly before the court that issued the warrant if the court is in session.

If the court specified is not in session, the warrant must direct that the defendant be brought before the court without unnecessary delay, and not later than 36 hours after the arrest, exclusive of the day of arrest, or as soon as a judge is available.

Subd. 3. Summons. The summons must summon the defendant to appear at a stated time and place to answer the complaint before the court issuing it, and must be accompanied by a copy of the complaint.

Adopted Feb. 26, 1975, eff. July 1, 1975. Revised Dec. 13, 1989. Amended May 9, 1994; Oct. 27, 2009, eff. Jan. 1, 2010.

Comment—Rule 3

See comment following Rule 3.04.

Historical Notes

The order of the Minnesota Supreme Court [C1–84–2137] dated December 13, 1989, provides in part that "(t)hese amended Rules of Criminal Procedure shall govern all criminal actions commenced or arrests made after 12 o'clock midnight January 1, 1990, except amendments to 8.04, 11.07, and 19.04, subd. 5, shall govern all criminal actions commenced or arrests made after 12 o'clock midnight January 1, 1991."

The order of the Minnesota Supreme Court [C1–84–2137] dated May 9, 1994, provides in part that "(t)hese amendments to the Rules of Criminal Procedure shall govern all criminal actions commenced or arrests made after 12 o'clock midnight July 1, 1994, except that the amendments in the first sentence of the third paragraph in Rule 2.01 shall govern all criminal actions commenced or arrests made after 12 o'clock midnight January 1, 1995."

Rule 3.03. Execution or Service of Warrant or Summons; Certification

Subd. 1. By Whom. The warrant must be executed by an officer authorized by law. The summons may be served by any officer authorized to serve a warrant, and if served by mail, it may also be served by the court administrator.

Subd. 2. Territorial Limits. The warrant may be executed or the summons may be served at any place within the State, except where prohibited by law.

Subd. 3. Manner. A warrant is executed by the defendant's arrest. If the offense charged is a misdemeanor, the defendant must not be arrested on Sunday or, on any other day of the week, between the hours of 10:00 p.m. and 8:00 a.m. except, when exigent circumstances exist, by direction of the judge, stated on the warrant. A misdemeanor warrant may also be executed at any time if the person is found on a public highway or street. The officer need not have the warrant in possession when the arrest occurs, but must inform the defendant of the warrant's existence and of the charge.

The summons must be served on an individual defendant by delivering a copy to the defendant personally, or by leaving it at the defendant's usual place of abode with a person of suitable age and discretion residing there, or by mailing it to the defendant's last known address. A summons directed to a corporate defendant must be issued and served in the manner prescribed by law for service of summons on corporations in civil actions, or by mail addressed to the corporation at its principal place of business, or to an agent designated by the corporation to receive service of process.

Subd. 4. Certification; Unexecuted Warrant or Summons. The officer executing the warrant must certify the execution to the court before which the defendant is brought.

On or before the date set for appearance, the officer or clerk of court to whom a summons was delivered for service must certify its service to the court before which the defendant was summoned to appear.

At the prosecutor's request, an unexecuted warrant, an unserved summons, or a duplicate may be delivered by a judge to any authorized officer or person for execution or service.

Adopted Feb. 26, 1975, eff. July 1, 1975. Revised Dec. 13, 1989. Amended Oct. 27, 2009, eff. Jan. 1, 2010.

Comment—Rule 3

See comment following Rule 3.04.

Historical Notes

The order of the Minnesota Supreme Court [C1–84–2137] dated December 13, 1989, provides in part that "(t)hese amended Rules of Criminal Procedure shall govern all criminal actions commenced or arrests made after 12 o'clock midnight January 1, 1990, except amendments to 8.04, 11.07, and 19.04, subd. 5, shall govern all criminal actions commenced or arrests made after 12 o'clock midnight January 1, 1991."

Rule 3.04. Defective Warrant, Summons or Complaint

Subd. 1. Amendment. A person arrested under a warrant or appearing in response to a summons must not be discharged from custody or dismissed because of any defect in form in the warrant or summons if the warrant or summons is amended to remedy the defect.

Subd. 2. Issuance of New Complaint, Warrant or Summons. Pre-trial proceedings may be continued to permit a new complaint to be filed and a new warrant or summons issued if the prosecutor promptly moves for a continuance on the ground that:

(a) the initial complaint does not properly name or describe the defendant or the offense charged; or

(b) the evidence presented establishes probable cause to believe that the defendant has committed a different offense from that charged in the complaint, and the prosecutor intends to charge the defendant with that offense.

If the proceedings are continued, the new complaint must be filed and process promptly issued. In misdemeanor cases, if the defendant during the continuance is unable to post bail that might be required under Rule 6.02, subd. 1, then the defendant must be released subject to such non-monetary conditions as the court deems necessary under that Rule.

Adopted Feb. 26, 1975, eff. July 1, 1975. Revised Dec. 13, 1989. Amended Oct. 27, 2009, eff. Jan. 1, 2010.

Comment—Rule 3

Rule 3.01 does not define probable cause for the purpose of obtaining a warrant of arrest or to prescribe the evidence that may be considered on that issue. These issues are determined by federal Fourth Amendment constitutional law. See e.g., State ex rel. Duhn v. Tahash, 275 Minn. 377, 147 N.W.2d 382 (1966); State v. Burch, 284 Minn. 300, 170 N.W.2d 543 (1969).

See Rule 4.02, subd. 5(3) for restrictions on the issuance of a warrant for an offense for which the prosecution has obtained a valid complaint after the time in which the court had ordered the complaint to be prepared.

Issuance of a warrant instead of a summons should not be grounds for objection to the arrest, to the jurisdiction of the court, or to any subsequent proceedings. In overcoming the presumption for issuing a summons rather than a warrant, the prosecutor may, among other factors, cite to the nature and circumstances of the particular case, the past history of response to legal process and the defendant's criminal record. The remedy of a defendant who has been arrested by warrant is to request the imposition of conditions of release under Rule 6.02, subd. 1 upon the initial court appearance.

Minnesota law requires that the defendant be taken before the court "without unreasonable delay." See, e.g., Stromberg v. Hansen, 177 Minn. 307, 225 N.W. 148 (1929). See also Minn. Stat. § 629.401. Rule 3.02, subd. 2 imposes more definite time limitations while permitting a degree of flexibility. The first limitation (Rule 3.02, subd. 2) is that the defendant must be brought directly before the court if it is in session. The second limitation (Rule 3.02, subd. 2) is that if the court is not in session, the defendant must be taken before the nearest available judge of the issuing court without unnecessary delay, but not more than 36 hours after the arrest or as soon after the 36–hour period as a judge of the issuing court is available.

In computing the 36–hour time limit in Rule 3.02, subd. 2, the day of arrest is not counted. The 36 hours begin to run at midnight following the arrest. Also, Rule 34.01 expressly does not apply to Rule 3.02, subd. 2. Saturdays are to be counted in computing the 36–hour time limit under this rule. See also Rule 4.02, subd. 5.

The provisions of Rule 3.03, subd. 2 that a warrant may be executed or a summons served at any place within the State is in accord with existing law governing service of criminal process. The phrase "except where prohibited by law" was added to exclude those places, such as federal reservations, where state service of process may be prohibited by law.

For service of summons on corporations, Rule 3.03, subd. 3 adopts the method prescribed by law for service of process in civil actions. See Minn. R.Civ.P. 4.03(c).

Historical Notes

The order of the Minnesota Supreme Court [C1–84–2137] dated December 13, 1989, provides in part that "(t)hese amended Rules of Criminal Procedure shall govern all criminal actions commenced or arrests made after 12 o'clock midnight January 1, 1990, except amendments to 8.04, 11.07, and 19.04, subd. 5, shall govern all criminal actions commenced or arrests made after 12 o'clock midnight January 1, 1991."

RULE 4. PROCEDURE UPON ARREST WITH A WARRANT FOLLOWING A COMPLAINT OR WITHOUT A WARRANT

Rule 4.01. Arrest With a Warrant

A defendant arrested with a warrant must be taken before a judge as directed in the warrant.

Adopted Feb. 26, 1975, eff. July 1, 1975. Revised Dec. 13, 1989. Amended Oct. 27, 2009, eff. Jan. 1, 2010.

Comment—Rule 4

See comment following Rule 4.03.

Historical Notes

The order of the Minnesota Supreme Court [C1–84–2137] dated December 13, 1989, provides in part that "(t)hese amended Rules of Criminal Procedure shall govern all criminal actions commenced or arrests made after 12 o'clock midnight January 1, 1990, except amendments to 8.04, 11.07, and 19.04, subd. 5, shall govern all criminal actions commenced or arrests made after 12 o'clock midnight January 1, 1991."

Rule 4.02. Arrest Without a Warrant

Following an arrest without a warrant:

Subd. 1. Release by Arresting Officer. If the arresting officer or the officer's superior determines that further detention is not justified, the arrested person must be immediately released.

Subd. 2. Citation. The arresting officer or the officer's superior may issue a citation and release the arrested person, and must do so if ordered by the prosecutor or by a judge of the district court where the alleged offense occurred.

Subd. 3. Notice to Prosecutor. The arresting officer or the officer's superior must notify the prosecutor of the arrest as soon as practicable.

Subd. 4. Release by Prosecutor. The prosecutor may order the arrested person released from custody.

Subd. 5. Appearance Before Judge.

(1) *Before Whom and When.* An arrested person who is not released under this rule or Rule 6, must be brought before the nearest available judge of the county where the alleged offense occurred. The defendant must be brought before a judge without unnecessary delay, and not more than 36 hours after the arrest, exclusive of the day of arrest, Sundays, and legal holidays, or as soon as a judge is available. In misdemeanor cases, a defendant who is not brought before a judge within the 36–hour limit must be released upon citation, as provided in Rule 6.01, subd. 1.

(2) *Complaint Filed; Order of Detention; Felonies and Gross Misdemeanors Not Charged as Designated Gross Misdemeanors Under Rule 1.04(b).* A complaint must be presented to the judge before the appearance under Rule 4.02, subd. 5(1). The complaint must be filed promptly, except as provided by Rule 33.04, and an order for detention of the defendant may be issued, provided: (1) the complaint contains the written approval of the prosecutor or the certificate of the judge as provided by Rule 2.02; and (2) the judge determines from the facts presented in writing in or with the complaint, and any supporting affidavits or supplemental sworn testimony, that probable cause exists to believe that an offense has been committed and that defendant committed it. Otherwise, the defendant must be released, the complaint and any supporting papers must not be filed, and no record made of the proceedings.

(3) *Complaint or Tab Charge; Misdemeanors; Designated Gross Misdemeanors.* If no complaint is filed by the time of the defendant's first appearance in court as required by this rule for a misdemeanor charge or a gross misdemeanor charge for offenses designated under Rule 1.04(b), the court administrator must enter upon the records a tab charge, as defined in Rule 1.04(c) of these rules. However, in a misdemeanor case, if the judge or-

ders, or if requested by the person charged or defense counsel, a complaint must be filed.

In a designated gross misdemeanor case commenced by a tab charge, the complaint must be served and filed within 48 hours of the defendant's appearance on the tab charge if the defendant is in custody, or within 10 days of the appearance if the defendant is not in custody, provided that the complaint must be served and filed before the court accepts a guilty plea to any designated gross misdemeanor. Service of a gross misdemeanor complaint must be as provided by Rule 33.02 and may include service by U.S. mail.

In a misdemeanor case, the complaint must be filed within 48 hours after demand if the defendant is in custody, or within 30 days of the demand if the defendant is not in custody.

If no complaint is filed within the time required by this rule, the defendant must be discharged, the complaint and any supporting papers must not be filed, and no record will be made of the proceedings.

A complaint is valid when it: (1) complies with the requirements of Rule 2; and (2) the judge has determined from the complaint and any supporting affidavits or supplemental sworn testimony that probable cause exists to believe that an offense has been committed and that the defendant committed it.

Upon the filing of a valid complaint in a misdemeanor case, the defendant must be arraigned. When a charge has been dismissed for failure to file a valid complaint, and the prosecutor later files a valid complaint, a warrant must not be issued on that complaint unless a summons has been issued first and either could not be served, or, if served, the defendant failed to appear in response.

Adopted Feb. 26, 1975, eff. July 1, 1975. Revised Dec. 13, 1989. Amended May 9, 1994; Aug. 21, 1998, eff. Jan. 1, 1999; Oct. 27, 2009, eff. Jan. 1, 2010.

Comment—Rule 4

See comment following Rule 4.03.

Historical Notes

The order of the Minnesota Supreme Court [C1–84–2137] dated December 13, 1989, provides in part that "(t)hese amended Rules of Criminal Procedure shall govern all criminal actions commenced or arrests made after 12 o'clock midnight January 1, 1990, except amendments to 8.04, 11.07, and 19.04, subd. 5, shall govern all criminal actions commenced or arrests made after 12 o'clock midnight January 1, 1991."

The order of the Minnesota Supreme Court [C1–84–2137] dated May 9, 1994, provides in part that "(t)hese amendments to the Rules of Criminal Procedure shall govern all criminal actions commenced or arrests made after 12 o'clock midnight July 1, 1994, except that the amendments in the first sentence of the third paragraph in Rule 2.01 shall govern all criminal actions commenced or arrests made after 12 o'clock midnight January 1, 1995."

Rule 4.03. Probable Cause Determination

Subd. 1. Time Limit. When a person arrested without a warrant is not released under this rule or Rule 6, a judge must make a probable cause determination without unnecessary delay, and in any event within 48 hours from the time of the arrest, including the day of arrest, Saturdays, Sundays, and legal holidays. If the Court determines that probable cause does not exist or does not make a determination as to probable cause within the time provided by this rule, the person must be released immediately.

Subd. 2. Application and Record. The facts establishing probable cause to believe that an offense has been committed, and that the person arrested committed it, must be submitted under oath, either orally or in writing. The oath may be administered by the court administrator or notary public for any facts submitted in writing. If oral testimony is taken, the oath must be administered by a judge, but it may be administered by telephone, ITV, or similar device. Any oral testimony must be recorded by reporter or recording instrument and must be retained by the court or by the judge's designee.

The person requesting a probable cause determination must advise the reviewing judge of any prior request for a probable cause determination on this same incident, or of any prior release of the arrested person on this same incident, for failure to obtain a probable cause determination within the time limit as provided by this rule.

Subd. 3. Prosecutor. No request for determination of probable cause may proceed without the approval of the prosecutor authorized to prosecute the matter, or by affirmation of the applicant that the applicant contacted the prosecutor and the prosecutor approved the request, or unless the judge reviewing probable cause certifies in writing that the prosecutor is unavailable and the determination of probable cause should not be delayed. A complaint complying with Rule 2, approved by the court, satisfies the probable cause requirement of this rule.

Subd. 4. Determination. If the information presented satisfies the court that probable cause exists to believe that an offense has been committed and the person arrested committed it, the court may set bail or other conditions of release, or release the arrested person without bail, under Rule 6. If probable cause is not found, the arrested person must be released immediately. The court's finding of probable cause must be in writing, and must indicate the offense, whether oral testimony was received, and the amount of any bail or other conditions of release the court may set. A written notice of the court's determination must be provided promptly to the arrested person.

Adopted Oct. 23, 1992. Amended Oct. 27, 2009, eff. Jan. 1, 2010.

Comment—Rule 4

It is anticipated that complaints will be requested by defendants in only a small percentage of misdemeanor cases because discovery is permitted under

Rule 9.04, and most defendants will not wish to make an additional appearance to receive the complaint.

Where a charge has been dismissed by the court for failure of the prosecutor to file a valid, timely complaint (Rule 4.02, subd. 5(3)) as required, and the prosecutor subsequently files a valid complaint, a summons must issue instead of a warrant. If it is impossible to locate the defendant to serve the summons or if the defendant fails to respond to the summons, a warrant may be issued. See also Rule 3.01. This restriction is necessary because it is unfair to subject a defendant to a possibly unnecessary arrest when the defendant has appeared in court once to answer the minor charge, and, through no fault of the defendant, a complaint was not issued.

Rule 4.03 is based upon the constitutional requirement as set forth in County of Riverside v. McLaughlin, 500 U.S. 44 (1991) for a prompt judicial determination of probable cause following a warrantless arrest. Pursuant to that case and Rule 4.03, subd. 1, the determination must occur without unreasonable delay and in no event later than 48 hours after the arrest. There are no exclusions in computing the 48–hour time limit. Rule 6.01 provides for the mandatory and permissive issuance of citations and an arrested person released on citation prior to the 48–hour time limit need not receive a probable cause determination pursuant to Rule 4.03.

Under Rule 4.03, subd. 2 the facts submitted to the court to establish probable cause may be either by written affidavit or sworn oral testimony. See Form 44, Application for Judicial Determination of Probable Cause to Detain, following these rules.

Rule 4.03, subd. 4, sets out the elements to be included in the court's written determination of probable cause. See Form 45, Judicial Determination of Probable Cause to Detain, following these rules.

Historical Notes

The order of the Minnesota Supreme Court [C1–84–2137] dated October 23, 1992, provides in part that "(t)hese amendments to the Rules of Criminal Procedure shall govern all criminal actions commenced or arrests made after 12 o'clock midnight January 1, 1993."

RULE 5. PROCEDURE ON FIRST APPEARANCE

Rule 5.01. Purpose of First Appearance

(a) The purpose of the first appearance is for the court to inform the defendant of the:

(1) charge(s);

(2) defendant's rights, including the right to have counsel appointed if eligible; and

(3) opportunity to enter a plea as permitted by Rules 5.06, 5.07, and 5.08.

(b) The court must first determine whether a defendant is disabled in communication as defined in Rule 5.02.

(c) The court must ensure the defendant has a copy of the complaint, citation, or written tab charge.

(d) The court must set bail and other conditions of release under Rule 6.02.

(e) On the prosecutor's motion, the court must require that the defendant be booked, photographed, and fingerprinted.

Adopted Oct. 27, 2009, eff. Jan. 1, 2010.

Comment—Rule 5

See comment following Rule 5.09.

Historical Notes

Former Rule: Former Rule 5.01 related to the court's statement to the defendant at the defendant's first appearance. See, now, Rules Crim.Proc., Rules 5.02 and 5.03.

Rule 5.02. Requirement for Interpreter

A defendant is disabled in communication if, due to a hearing, speech or other communications disorder or difficulty in speaking or comprehending the English language, the defendant cannot fully understand the proceedings or any charges made, or is incapable of presenting or assisting in the presentation of a defense.

If a defendant is disabled in communication, the judge must appoint a qualified interpreter under Rule 8 of the Minnesota Rules of General Practice for the District Courts to assist the defendant throughout the proceedings. The proceedings that require a qualified interpreter include any proceeding attended by the defendant.

Former Rule 5.01 adopted Feb. 26, 1975, eff. July 1, 1975. Revised Dec. 13, 1989. Amended May 9, 1994; Aug. 21, 1998, eff. Jan. 1, 1999; Dec. 29, 2006, eff. April 1, 2007. Renumbered Rule 5.02 and amended Oct. 27, 2009, eff. Jan. 1, 2010.

Comment—Rule 5

See comment following Rule 5.09.

Historical Notes

Former Rule: Former Rule 5.02 related to the appointment of the public defender. See, now, Rules Crim.Proc., Rule 5.04.

Rule 5.03. Statement of Rights

The court must advise the defendant of the following:

(a) The right to remain silent and not submit to interrogation;

(b) Anything the defendant says may be used against the defendant in this or any subsequent proceeding;

(c) The right to counsel in all proceedings, including police line-ups and interrogations;

(d) If the defendant appears without counsel and is financially unable to obtain counsel, counsel will be appointed if the defendant has been charged with an offense punishable by incarceration;

(e) The right to communicate with defense counsel, and that a continuance will be granted if necessary to permit this;

(f) The right to a jury trial or a trial to the court;

(g) If the offense is a misdemeanor, the defendant may plead guilty or not guilty, or demand a complaint before entering a plea;

(h) If the offense is a designated gross misdemeanor as defined in Rule 1.04(b) and a complaint has not yet been filed, a complaint must be issued within 10 days if the defendant is not in custody or within 48 hours if the defendant is in custody;

(i) If the offense is a gross misdemeanor and the defendant has had an opportunity to consult with an attorney, the defendant may plead guilty in accordance with Rule 15.02.

Former Rule 5.01 adopted Feb. 26, 1975, eff. July 1, 1975. Revised Dec. 13, 1989. Amended May 9, 1994; Aug. 21, 1998, eff. Jan. 1, 1999; Dec. 29, 2006, eff. April 1, 2007. Renumbered Rule 5.03 and amended Oct. 27, 2009, eff. Jan. 1, 2010. Amended June 5, 2012, eff. Aug. 1, 2012.

Comment—Rule 5

See comment following Rule 5.09.

Historical Notes

The order of the Minnesota Supreme Court [ADM 10-8049] dated June 5, 2012, provided in part that the amendments "be effective August 1, 2012, and shall apply to all actions or proceedings pending on or commenced on or after the effective date."

Former Rule: Former Rule 5.03 related to the date of a Rule 8 appearance and to the consolidation of appearances under Rule 5 and Rule 8. See, now, Rules Crim.Proc., Rule 5.05.

Rule 5.04. Appointment of Counsel

Subd. 1. Notice of Right to Counsel; Appointment of the District Public Defender; Waiver of Counsel.

(1) *Notice of Right to Counsel.* If a defendant charged with a felony, gross misdemeanor, or misdemeanor punishable by incarceration appears without counsel, the court must advise the defendant of the right to counsel, and that the court will appoint the district public defender if the defendant has been determined to be financially unable to obtain counsel.

The court must also advise the defendant that the defendant has the right to request counsel at any stage of the proceedings.

(2) *Appointment of the Public Defender.* The court must appoint the district public defender on request of a defendant who is:

(a) charged with a felony, gross misdemeanor, or misdemeanor punishable by incarceration, or subject to an extradition proceeding or probation revocation proceeding;

(b) not represented by counsel; and

(c) financially unable to obtain counsel.

The court must not appoint a district public defender if the defendant is financially able to retain private counsel but refuses to do so.

(3) *Waiver of Counsel, Misdemeanor or Gross Misdemeanor.* Defendants charged with a misdemeanor or gross misdemeanor punishable by incarceration who appear without counsel, do not request counsel, and wish to represent themselves, must waive counsel in writing or on the record. The court must not accept the waiver unless the court is satisfied that it is voluntary and has been made by the defendant with full knowledge and understanding of the defendant's rights. The court may appoint the district public defender for the limited purpose of advising and consulting with the defendant about the waiver.

(4) *Waiver of Counsel, Felony.* The court must ensure that defendants charged with a felony who appear without counsel, do not request counsel, and wish to represent themselves, enter on the record a voluntary and intelligent written waiver of the right to counsel. If the defendant refuses to sign the written waiver form, the waiver must be made on the record. Before accepting the waiver, the court must advise the defendant of the following:

(a) nature of the charges;

(b) all offenses included within the charges;

(c) range of allowable punishments;

(d) there may be defenses;

(e) mitigating circumstances may exist; and

(f) all other facts essential to a broad understanding of the consequences of the waiver of the right to counsel, including the advantages and disadvantages of the decision to waive counsel.

The court may appoint the district public defender for the limited purpose of advising and consulting with the defendant as to the waiver.

Subd. 2. Appointment of Advisory Counsel. The court may appoint advisory counsel to assist a defendant who voluntarily and intelligently waives the right to counsel.

(1) If the court appoints advisory counsel because of concerns about fairness of the process, the court must state that on the record. The court must advise the defendant and advisory counsel on the record that the defendant retains the right to decide when and how to use advisory counsel, and that decisions about the use of advisory counsel may affect a later request by the defendant to allow advisory counsel to assume full representation.

(2) If the court appoints advisory counsel because of concerns about delays in completing the trial, the potential disruption by the defendant, or the complexity or length of the trial, the court must state that on the record.

The court must then advise the defendant and advisory counsel on the record that advisory counsel will assume full representation of the defendant if the defendant:

(a) becomes so disruptive during the proceedings that the defendant's conduct is determined to constitute a waiver of the right of self representation; or

(b) requests advisory counsel to take over representation during the proceeding.

(3) Advisory counsel must be present in the courtroom during all proceedings and must be served with all documents that would otherwise be served upon an attorney of record.

Subd. 3. Standards for District Public Defender Eligibility. A defendant is financially unable to obtain counsel if the defendant meets the standards for eligibility defined in Minn. Stat. § 611.17.

Subd. 4. Financial Inquiry. The court has a duty to conduct a financial inquiry to determine the financial eligibility of a defendant for the appointment of a district public defender as required under Minn. Stat. § 611.17.

Subd. 5. Partial Eligibility and Reimbursement. The ability to pay part of the cost of adequate representation at any time while the charges are pending against a defendant must not preclude the appointment of the district public defender for the defendant. If the court, after finding the defendant eligible for district public defender services, determines that the defendant now has the ability to pay part of the costs, it may require a defendant to make partial payment as provided in Minn. Stat. § 611.20.

Former Rule 5.02 adopted Feb. 26, 1975, eff. July 1, 1975. Revised Dec. 13, 1989. Amended Aug. 21, 1998, eff. Jan. 1, 1999; Dec. 10, 2003, eff. Feb. 1, 2004. Renumbered Rule 5.04 and amended Oct. 27, 2009, eff. Jan. 1, 2010. Amended June 5, 2012, eff. Aug. 1, 2012.

Comment—Rule 5

See comment following Rule 5.09.

Historical Notes

The order of the Minnesota Supreme Court [ADM 10–8049] dated June 5, 2012, provided in part that the amendments "be effective August 1, 2012, and shall apply to all actions or proceedings pending on or commenced on or after the effective date."

Former Rule: Former Rule 5.04 related to pleas in misdemeanor cases. See, now, Rules Crim.Proc., Rule 5.06.

Rule 5.05. Date of Rule 8 Appearance; Consolidation of Appearances Under Rule 5 and Rule 8

If the defendant is charged with a felony or gross misdemeanor, the court must set a date for a Rule 8 appearance before the court having jurisdiction to try the charged offense no later than 14 days after the defendant's initial appearance under Rule 5, unless the defendant waives the right to a separate Rule 8 appearance.

The defendant must be informed of the time and place of the Rule 8 appearance and ordered to appear as scheduled. The time for appearance may be extended by the court for good cause.

In felony and gross misdemeanor cases, the defendant may waive the separate appearances otherwise required by this rule and Rule 8. The waiver must be made either in writing or on the record in open court. If the defendant waives a separate appearance under Rule 8, all of the functions and procedures provided for by Rules 5 and 8 must take place at the Rule 5 hearing.

Former Rule 5.03 adopted Feb. 26, 1975, eff. July 1, 1975. Revised Dec. 13, 1989. Renumbered Rule 5.05 and amended Oct. 27, 2009, eff. Jan. 1, 2010.

Comment—Rule 5

See comment following Rule 5.09.

Historical Notes

Former Rule: Former Rule 5.05 related to bail and conditions for release.

Rule 5.06. Plea and Post–Plea Procedure in Misdemeanor Cases

Subd. 1. Entry of Plea in Misdemeanor Cases. In misdemeanor cases, the arraignment must be conducted in open court. The court must ask the defendant to enter a plea, or set a date for entry of the plea. A defendant may appear by counsel and a corporation must appear by counsel or by an authorized officer.

Subd. 2. Guilty Plea; Offenses From Other Jurisdictions. If the defendant enters a plea of guilty, the presentencing and sentencing procedures provided by these rules must be followed. The defendant may also request permission under Rule 15.10 to plead guilty to other misdemeanor offenses committed within the jurisdiction of other courts in the state.

Subd. 3. Not Guilty Plea and Jury Trial. If the defendant enters a plea of not guilty to a charge for which the defendant would be entitled to a jury trial, the defendant must exercise or waive that right. The defendant may waive the right to a jury trial either on the record or in writing. If the defendant fails to waive or demand a jury trial, a jury trial demand must be entered in the record.

Subd. 4. Demand or Waiver of Evidentiary Hearing. If the defendant pleads not guilty and a notice of evidence and identification procedures has been given by the prosecutor as required by Rule 7.01, the defendant and prosecutor must each either waive or demand an evidentiary hearing under Rule 12.04. The demand or waiver may be made either on the record or in writing and must be made at the first court appearance after the notice has been given by the prosecutor.

Former Rule 5.04 adopted Feb. 26, 1975, eff. July 1, 1975. Revised Dec. 13, 1989. Renumbered Rule 5.06 and amended Oct. 27, 2009, eff. Jan. 1, 2010.

Comment—Rule 5

See comment following Rule 5.09.

Historical Notes

Former Rule: Former Rule 5.06 related to a record of the proceedings. See, now, Rules Crim.Proc., Rule 5.09.

Rule 5.07. Plea and Post–Plea Procedure in Gross Misdemeanor Cases

Subd. 1. Entry of Guilty Plea in Gross Misdemeanor Cases.

The defendant may plead guilty to a gross misdemeanor charge in accordance with Rule 15.02 if the defendant has counsel, or has had the opportunity to consult with counsel before pleading guilty. If the defendant does not plead guilty, entry of a plea must await the Rule 8 or Omnibus Hearing. A corporation must appear by counsel or by an authorized officer.

Subd. 2. Guilty Plea; Offenses From Other Jurisdictions.

The procedure in Rule 5.06, subd. 2 applies to gross misdemeanor cases.

Adopted Oct. 27, 2009, eff. Jan. 1, 2010. Amended June 5, 2012, eff. Aug. 1, 2012.

Comment—Rule 5

See comment following Rule 5.09.

Historical Notes

The order of the Minnesota Supreme Court [ADM 10–8049] dated June 5, 2012, provided in part that the amendments "be effective August 1, 2012, and shall apply to all actions or proceedings pending on or commenced on or after the effective date."

Former Rule: Former Rule 5.07 related to the handling of court papers and was deleted August 1, 1987.

Rule 5.08. Plea in Felony Cases

In felony cases, a defendant may plead guilty as early as the Rule 8 hearing. The defendant cannot enter any other plea until the Omnibus hearing under Rule 11.

Adopted Oct. 27, 2009, eff. Jan. 1, 2010.

Comment—Rule 5

See comment following Rule 5.09.

Historical Notes

Former Rule: Former Rule 5.08 related to the initial appearance of a defendant among county, municipal, and district courts and was deleted August. 1, 1987.

Rule 5.09. Record

Minutes of the proceedings must be kept unless the court directs that a verbatim record be made. Any plea of guilty to an offense punishable by incarceration must comply with the requirements of Rule 15.09.

Former Rule 5.06 adopted Feb. 26, 1975, eff. July 1, 1975. Revised Dec. 13, 1989. Renumbered Rule 5.09 and amended Oct. 27, 2009, eff. Jan. 1, 2010.

Comment—Rule 5

Rule 5 prescribes the procedure at the defendant's initial appearance. In most misdemeanor cases, the initial appearance will also be the time of arraignment and disposition.

Rule 5.02 requires the appointment of a qualified interpreter for a defendant disabled in communication. Minn. Stat. § 611.32, subd. 1 mandates the appointment. The definition for "disabled in communication" contained in Rule 5.02 is the same as that contained in Minn. Stat. § 611.31. Minn. Stat. § 611.33 and Rule 8 of the Minnesota Rules of General Practice for the District Courts should be referred to for the definition of qualified interpreter.

The warning under Rule 5.03 as to the defendant's right to counsel continues the requirement of Minn. Stat. § 611.15. See St. Paul v. Whidby, 295 Minn. 129, 203 N.W.2d 823 (1972), recognizing that misdemeanors authorizing a sentence of incarceration are criminal offenses and criminal procedures must be followed.

Under Rules 5.03(i) and 5.07, a defendant may plead guilty to a gross misdemeanor at the first appearance under Rule 5 in accordance with the guilty plea provisions of Rule 15.02. If that is done, the defendant must first have the opportunity to consult with an attorney. If the guilty plea is to a designated gross misdemeanor prosecuted by tab charge, a complaint must be filed before the court accepts the guilty plea. See Rule 4.02, subd. 5(3), and the comments to that rule. See also Rule 5.04, subd. 1(3), concerning waiver of the right to counsel. Rule 5.03(i) does not permit a defendant to enter a plea of not guilty to a gross misdemeanor at the first appearance under Rule 5. Rather, in accordance with Rules 8.01 and 11.08, a not-guilty plea in felony and gross misdemeanor cases is not entered until the Omnibus Hearing or later.

Minnesota law requires that a waiver of counsel be in writing unless the defendant refuses to sign the written waiver form. In that case, a record of the waiver is permitted. Minn. Stat. § 611.19. In practice, a Petition to Proceed As Pro Se Counsel may fulfill the dual requirements of providing the defendant with the information necessary to make a voluntary and intelligent waiver of the right to counsel as well as providing a written waiver. See Form 11. Also see Appendix C to Rule 15 for the Petition to Enter Plea of Guilty by Pro Se Defendant.

The decision in Faretta v. California, 422 U.S. 806 (1975), held that counsel may be appointed over the defendant's objection, to assist and consult if requested to do so by the defendant. Rule 5.04

establishes standards for appointing advisory counsel in cases where the defendant waives counsel and the court believes it is appropriate to appoint advisory counsel.

In most cases, the primary role of counsel appointed over the defendant's objection will be advisory. In fewer cases, the role of appointed counsel may be to take over representation of the defendant during trial. The term "standby counsel" is too broad a term to cover the role of appointed counsel in every case or even most cases where counsel is appointed over the objection of the defendant. Because the primary purpose of counsel appointed over the objection of the defendant is to help the accused understand and negotiate through the basic procedures of the trial and "to relieve the trial judge of the need to explain and enforce basic rules of [the] courtroom," counsel appointed over the objection of the accused may be more properly called "advisory counsel."

Two main reasons exist for appointing advisory counsel for defendants who wish to represent themselves: (1) the fairness of a criminal process where lay people choose to represent themselves—to aid the court in fulfilling its responsibility for insuring a fair trial, to further the public interest in an orderly, rational trial, or if the court appoints advisory counsel to assist the pro se defendant—and (2) the disruption of the criminal process before its completion caused by the removal of an unruly defendant or a request for counsel during a long or complicated trial.

These general reasons for the appointment of counsel to the pro se defendant suggest a natural expectation of the level of readiness of advisory counsel. If the court appoints advisory counsel as a safeguard to the fairness of the proceeding, it would not be expected that counsel would be asked to take over the representation of the defendant during the trial and counsel should not be expected and need not be prepared to take over representation should this be requested or become necessary. If this unexpected event occurred and a short recess of the proceeding would be sufficient to allow counsel to take over representation, the court could enter that order. If the circumstances constituted a manifest injustice to continue with the trial, a mistrial could be granted and a date for a new trial, allowing counsel time to prepare, could be set. The court could also deny the request to allow counsel to take over representation if the circumstances would not make this feasible or practical.

If the court appoints advisory counsel because of the complexity of the case or the length of the trial or the possibility that the defendant may be removed from the trial because of disruptive behavior, advisory counsel must be expected to be prepared to take over as counsel in the middle of the trial so long as the interests of justice are served.

Whenever counsel is appointed over the defendant's objection, counsel's participation must not be allowed to destroy the jury's perception that the accused is representing himself or herself. In all proceedings, especially those before the jury, advisory counsel must respect the defendant's right to control the case and not interfere with it. The accused must authorize appointed counsel before the counsel can be involved, render impromptu advice, or ever appear before the court. If the accused does not wish appointed counsel to participate, counsel must simply attend the trial.

Even where appointed counsel is not expected to be ready to take over representation in the middle of the proceedings, it is appropriate and necessary that all advisory counsel be served with the same disclosure and discovery items as counsel of record so that counsel can at least be familiar with this information in acting in an advisory role. All counsel appointed for the pro se defendant must be served with the pleadings, motions, and discovery.

It is essential that at the outset the trial court explain to the accused and counsel appointed in these situations what choices the accused has and what the consequences of those choices may be later in the proceedings. In State v. Richards, 552 N.W.2d 197, 206 (Minn. 1996), the Supreme Court repeated the rule it set in State v. Richards, 463 N.W.2d 499 (Minn. 1990): the defendant's request for the "substitution of standby counsel [shall not be granted] unless, in the trial court's discretion, his request is timely and reasonable and reflects extraordinary circumstances." Trial courts should consider the progress of the trial, the readiness of standby counsel, and the possible disruption of the proceedings. Statement of the expectations of advisory counsel at the outset should make it clear to all concerned about what will happen should there be a change in the representation of the defendant during the proceeding.

A defendant appearing pro se with advisory counsel should be informed that the duties and costs of investigation, legal research, and other matters associated with litigating a criminal matter are the responsibility of the defendant and not advisory counsel. It should be made clear to the pro se defendant that advisory counsel is not a functionary of the defendant who can be directed to perform tasks by the defendant. A motion under Minn. Stat. § 611.21 is available to seek funds for hiring investigators and expert witnesses.

In certain circumstances, a separate appearance to fulfill the requirements of Rule 8 may serve very little purpose. Originally these rules required the appearance under Rule 5 to be in the county court and the appearance under Rule 8 to be in the district court. Now, both appearances are held in the district court. The additional time and judicial resources invested in a separate appearance under Rule 8 may yield little or no benefit. Therefore, Rule 5.05 permits the appearances required by Rule 5 and Rule 8 to be consolidated upon request of the defendant.

When the appearances are consolidated under Rule 5.05, all of the provisions in Rule 8 are applied to the consolidated hearing. This means that under Rule 8.04 the Omnibus Hearing provided for by Rule 11 must be scheduled for a date no later than 28 days after the consolidated hearing. This requirement is subject, however, to the power of the court under Rule 8.04(c) to extend the time for good cause related to the particular case upon motion of the defendant or the prosecution or upon the court's initiative. Also, the notice of evidence and identification procedures required by Rule 7.01 must be given at or before the consolidated hearing.

Under Rule 5.06, subd. 4 if the defendant pleads not guilty in a misdemeanor case and the prosecution has given the notice of evidence and identification prescribed by Rule 7.01, then both the defendant and the prosecution shall either waive or demand a Rasmussen (State ex rel. Rasmussen v. Tahash, 272 Minn. 539, 141 N.W.2d 3 (1965)) hearing. The waiver or demand is necessary only in cases where a jury trial is to be held since the notice is not required under Rule 7.01 if no jury trial is to be held in a misdemeanor case.

RULE 6. PRETRIAL RELEASE

Rule 6.01. Release on Citation

Subd. 1. Mandatory Citation Issuance in Misdemeanor Cases.

(a) *By Arresting Officer.* In misdemeanor cases, peace officers who decide to proceed with prosecution and who act without a warrant must issue a citation and release the defendant unless it reasonably appears:

(1) the person must be detained to prevent bodily injury to that person or another;

(2) further criminal conduct will occur; or

(3) a substantial likelihood exists that the person will not respond to a citation.

If the officer has already arrested the person, a citation must issue in lieu of continued detention, and the person must be released, unless any of the circumstances in subd. 1(a)(1)–(3) above exist.

(b) *At Place of Detention.* When an officer brings a person arrested without a warrant for a misdemeanor to a police station or county jail, the officer in charge of the police station, sheriff in charge of the jail, or officer designated by the sheriff must issue a citation in lieu of continued detention unless it reasonably appears to the officer that any of the circumstances in subd. 1(a)(1)–(3) exist.

(c) *Offenses Not Punishable by Incarceration.* A citation must be issued for petty misdemeanors and misdemeanors not punishable by incarceration. If an arrest has been made, a citation must be issued in lieu of continued detention.

(d) *Reporting Requirements.* If the defendant is not released at the scene or place of detention, the officer in charge of the place of detention must report to the court the reasons why.

Subd. 2. Permissive Authority to Issue Citations in Gross Misdemeanor and Felony Cases at Place of Detention.

When an officer brings a person arrested without a warrant for a felony or gross misdemeanor to a police station or county jail, the officer in charge of the police station, sheriff in charge of the jail, or officer designated by the sheriff may issue a citation and release the defendant unless it reasonably appears to the officer that any of the circumstances in subd. 1(a)(1)–(3) exist.

Subd. 3. Mandatory Release on Citation When Ordered by Prosecutor or Court.

In felony, gross misdemeanor, and misdemeanor cases, a person arrested without a warrant must be issued a citation and released if so ordered by the prosecutor or by the district court, or by any person designated by the court to perform that function.

Subd. 4. Form of Citation.

(a) *General Form.* Any citation, including an electronic citation, filed or e-filed with the court must be in a form prescribed by this rule and approved by the State Court Administrator and the Commissioner of Public Safety, who shall, to the extent practicable, include in the citation the information required by Minnesota Statutes, section 169.99, subds. 1, 1a, 1b, and 1c, and Minnesota Statutes, section 97A.211, subd. 1. The citation must contain the summons and complaint, and must direct the defendant to appear at a designated time and place or to contact the court or violations bureau to schedule an appearance.

(b) *Notices Regarding Failure to Appear.* The citation must state that failure to appear or contact the court or violations bureau as directed may result in the issuance of a warrant. A summons or warrant issued after failure to respond to a citation may be based on sworn facts establishing probable cause contained in or with the citation and attached to the complaint.

The citation must contain notice regarding failure to appear when the offense is a petty misdemeanor as required in Minnesota Statutes, sections 169.99, subd. 1(b), and 609.491, subd. 1.

(c) *Notice Regarding Fine Payment.* The citation must contain the notice regarding fine payment and waiver of rights in Rule 23.03, subd. 3.

(d) *Electronic Citation.* If the defendant is charged by electronic citation, the defendant must be issued a copy of the citation. This copy must include:

(1) the directive to appear or contact the court or violations bureau in paragraph (a); and

(2) the notices in paragraphs (b) and (c).

Subd. 5. Lawful Searches. The issuance of a citation does not affect an officer's authority to conduct an otherwise lawful search.

Subd. 6. Persons in Need of Care. Even if a citation has been issued, an officer can take the person cited to an appropriate medical or mental health facility if that person appears mentally or physically incapable of self care.

Adopted Feb. 26, 1975, eff. July 1, 1975. Revised Dec. 13, 1989. Amended May 9, 1994; Oct. 27, 2009, eff. Jan. 1, 2010; Jan. 13, 2011, eff. Jan. 1, 2012.

Comment—Rule 6

See comment following Rule 6.06.

Historical Notes

The order of the Minnesota Supreme Court [C1–84–2137] dated December 13, 1989, provides in part that "(t)hese amended Rules of Criminal Procedure shall govern all criminal actions commenced or arrests made after 12 o'clock midnight January 1, 1990, except amendments to 8.04, 11.07, and 19.04, subd. 5, shall govern all criminal actions commenced or arrests made after 12 o'clock midnight January 1, 1991."

The order of the Minnesota Supreme Court [C1–84–2137] dated May 9, 1994, provides in part that "(t)hese amendments to the Rules of Criminal Procedure shall govern all criminal actions commenced or arrests made after 12 o'clock midnight July 1, 1994, except that the amendments in the first sentence of the third paragraph in Rule 2.01 shall govern all criminal actions commenced or arrests made after 12 o'clock midnight January 1, 1995."

Rule 6.02. Release by Court or Prosecutor

Subd. 1. Conditions of Release. A person charged with an offense must be released without bail when ordered by the prosecutor, court, or any person designated by the court to perform that function. On appearance before the court, a person must be released on personal recognizance or an unsecured appearance bond unless a court determines that release will endanger the public safety or will not reasonably assure the defendant's appearance. When this determination is made, the court must, either in lieu of or in addition to the above methods of release, impose the first of the following conditions of release that will reasonably assure the person's appearance as ordered, or, if no single condition gives that assurance, any combination of the following conditions:

(a) Place the defendant under the supervision of a person who, or organization that, agrees to supervise;

(b) Place restrictions on travel, association, or residence during release;

(c) Require an appearance bond, cash deposit, or other security; or

(d) Impose other conditions necessary to assure appearance as ordered.

If the court sets conditions of release, it must issue a written order containing them. A copy of the order must be provided to the defendant and to the law enforcement agency that has or had custody. The law enforcement agency must also be provided with the victim's name and location.

The court must set money bail without other conditions on which the defendant may be released by posting cash or sureties.

The defendant's release must be conditioned on appearance at all future court proceedings.

Subd. 2. Release Conditions. In determining conditions of release the court must consider:

(a) the nature and circumstances of the offense charged;

(b) the weight of the evidence;

(c) family ties;

(d) employment;

(e) financial resources;

(f) character and mental condition;

(g) length of residence in the community;

(h) criminal convictions;

(i) prior history of appearing in court;

(j) prior flight to avoid prosecution;

(k) the victim's safety;

(*l*) any other person's safety;

(m) the community's safety.

Subd. 3. Pre-Release Investigation. To determine conditions of release, the court may investigate the defendant's background before or at the defendant's court appearance. The investigation may be conducted by probation services or by any other qualified agency as directed by the court.

Information obtained in the pre-release investigation from the defendant in response to an inquiry during the investigation and any derivative evidence must not be used against the defendant at trial. Evidence obtained by independent investigation may be used.

Subd. 4. Review of Release Conditions. The court must review conditions of release on request of any party.

Adopted Feb. 26, 1975, eff. July 1, 1975. Revised Dec. 13, 1989. Amended Aug. 21, 1998, eff. Jan. 1, 1999; Dec. 23, 2002, eff. Feb. 1, 2003; Oct. 27, 2009, eff. Jan. 1, 2010.

Comment—Rule 6

See comment following Rule 6.06.

Historical Notes

The order of the Minnesota Supreme Court [C1–84–2137] dated December 13, 1989, provides in part that "(t)hese amended Rules of Criminal Procedure shall govern all criminal actions commenced or arrests made after 12 o'clock midnight January 1, 1990, except amendments to 8.04, 11.07, and 19.04, subd. 5, shall govern all criminal actions commenced or arrests made after 12 o'clock midnight January 1, 1991."

Rule 6.03. Violation of Release Conditions

Subd. 1. Authority to Apply for a Summons or Warrant. On application by the prosecutor, court services, or probation officer alleging probable cause that defendant violated a release condition, the court may issue a summons or warrant, using the procedure in paragraphs (a) and (b).

(a) *Summons.* A summons must be issued instead of a warrant unless a warrant is authorized under paragraph (b). The summons must direct the defendant to appear in court and include a date and time for a hearing.

(b) *Warrant.* The court may issue a warrant instead of a summons if a substantial likelihood exists that the defendant will fail to respond to a summons, that continued release of the defendant will endanger any person, or the defendant's location is not known. The warrant must direct the defendant's arrest and prompt appearance in court.

Subd. 2. Arrest Without Warrant. A peace officer may arrest a released defendant if the officer has probable cause to believe a release condition has been violated and it reasonably appears continued release will endanger the safety of any person. The officer must promptly take the defendant before a judge. When possible, a warrant should be obtained before making an arrest under this rule.

Subd. 3. Hearing. The defendant is entitled to a hearing on alleged violations of release conditions. If the court finds a violation, the court may revise the conditions of release as provided in Rule 6.02, subd. 1.

Subd. 4. Commission of Crime. When a complaint is filed or indictment returned charging a defendant with committing a crime while released pending adjudication of a prior charge, the court with jurisdiction over the prior charge may, after notice and hearing, review and revise the conditions of release as provided for in Rule 6.02, subd. 1.

Adopted Feb. 26, 1975, eff. July 1, 1975. Revised Dec. 13, 1989. Amended Dec. 28, 2005, eff. March 1, 2006; Oct. 27, 2009, eff. Jan. 1, 2010.

Comment—Rule 6

See comment following Rule 6.06.

Historical Notes

The order of the Minnesota Supreme Court [C1–84–2137] dated December 13, 1989, provides in part that "(t)hese amended Rules of Criminal Procedure shall govern all criminal actions commenced or arrests made after 12 o'clock midnight January 1, 1990, except amendments to 8.04, 11.07, and 19.04, subd. 5, shall govern all criminal actions commenced or arrests made after 12 o'clock midnight January 1, 1991."

The order of the Minnesota Supreme Court [C1–84–2137] dated December 28, 2005, provides in part that "(t)he attached amendments shall govern all criminal actions commenced or arrests made after 12 o'clock midnight March 1, 2006."

Rule 6.04. Forfeiture

Forfeiture of an appearance bond must be as provided by law.

Adopted Feb. 26, 1975, eff. July 1, 1975. Revised Dec. 13, 1989. Amended Oct. 27, 2009, eff. Jan. 1, 2010.

Comment—Rule 6

See comment following Rule 6.06.

Historical Notes

The order of the Minnesota Supreme Court [C1–84–2137] dated December 13, 1989, provides in part that "(t)hese amended Rules of Criminal Procedure shall govern all criminal actions commenced or arrests made after 12 o'clock midnight January 1, 1990, except amendments to 8.04, 11.07, and 19.04, subd. 5, shall govern all criminal actions commenced or arrests made after 12 o'clock midnight January 1, 1991."

Rule 6.05. Detention Supervision

The court must supervise a defendant's detention to eliminate all unnecessary detention. A detention facility must make at least bi-weekly reports to the prosecutor and the court listing prisoners in custody for more than 10 days in felony and gross misdemeanor cases, and prisoners in custody more than 2 days in misdemeanor cases.

Adopted Feb. 26, 1975, eff. July 1, 1975. Revised Dec. 13, 1989. Amended Oct. 27, 2009, eff. Jan. 1, 2010.

Comment—Rule 6

See comment following Rule 6.06.

Historical Notes

The order of the Minnesota Supreme Court [C1–84–2137] dated December 13, 1989, provides in part that "(t)hese amended Rules of Criminal Procedure shall govern all criminal actions commenced or arrests made after 12 o'clock midnight January 1, 1990, except amendments to 8.04, 11.07, and 19.04, subd. 5, shall govern all criminal actions commenced or arrests made after 12 o'clock midnight January 1, 1991."

Rule 6.06. Misdemeanor Trial Dates

A defendant must be tried promptly after entering a not guilty plea. If a defendant or the prosecutor demands a speedy trial in writing or on the record, the trial must begin within 60 days.

The 60–day period begins to run on the day of the not guilty plea, and may be extended for good cause shown on motion of the prosecutor or the defendant, or on the court's initiative. If an in-custody defendant's trial does not begin in 10 days, the defendant must be released subject to nonmonetary release conditions as set by the court under Rule 6.02, subd. 1.

Adopted Feb. 26, 1975, eff. July 1, 1975. Revised Dec. 13, 1989. Amended Oct. 27, 2009, eff. Jan. 1, 2010.

Comment—Rule 6

In misdemeanor cases a citation must be issued if the misdemeanor charged is not punishable by incarceration. A person should not be taken into custody for an offense that cannot be punished by incarceration. Rule 1.04(a) defines misdemeanors.

The "uniform traffic ticket" as defined in Minn. Stat. § 169.99 is used to issue a citation under Rule 6. The citation is used to charge not only traffic offenses under Minnesota Statutes Chapter 169, but also criminal or Department of Natural Resources

(DNR) offenses defined in other chapters. The State Court Administrator and the Commissioner of Public Safety determine the required content of the citation in consultation with the courts, law enforcement, and other affected agencies, including the DNR.

Rule 6.01, subd. 4(b) reiterates that the citation must contain the statutorily required notice that failure to appear for a petty misdemeanor offense results in a conviction. As stated in the rule, the citation must direct the defendant to either appear or contact the court by a particular date. This means a conviction will be entered: (1) if the defendant fails to appear on the scheduled court date; (2) if the defendant fails to pay the fine or otherwise contact the court by the scheduled deadline; or (3) if the defendant requests an initial hearing on the citation but then fails to appear for it.

Rule 6.01, subd. 4(d) sets forth the content that must be included on the defendant's copy of an electronic citation. The defendant's copy of a paper citation typically contains additional information such as court contact information, payment methods, and collateral consequences. Since the Rules do not specifically require this information to be on the citation, when the defendant is issued an electronic citation, the additional information could be given to the defendant by other means such as directing the defendant to a website or providing a separate information sheet.

The arresting officer is to decide whether to issue a citation using the information available at the time. If that officer decides not to issue a citation, the officer-in-charge of the stationhouse will then make a determination from all the information then available, including any additional information disclosed by further interrogation and investigation.

Rule 6.01, subd. 6 is intended merely to stress that issuing a citation in lieu of a custodial arrest or continued detention does not affect a law enforcement officer's statutory right to transport a person in need of care to an appropriate medical facility. A law enforcement officer's power to transport a person for such purposes is still governed by statute and is neither expanded nor contracted by Rule 6.01, subd. 6. See, e. g., Minn. Stat. § 609.06, subd. 1(9) about the right to use reasonable force, in certain situations, toward mentally ill or mentally defective persons and Minn. Stat. § 253B.05, subd. 2 governing the right of a health or peace officer to transport mentally ill or intoxicated persons to various places for care.

These rules do not prescribe the consequences of failing to obey a citation. The remedy available is the issuance of a warrant or summons upon a complaint.

Rule 6.02, subd. 1 specifies the conditions of release that can be imposed on a defendant at the first appearance. If conditions of release are endorsed on the warrant (Rule 3.02, subd. 1), the defendant must be released on meeting those conditions.

Release on "personal recognizance" is a release without bail on defendant's promise to appear at appropriate times. An "Order to Appear" is an order issued by the court releasing the defendant from custody or continuing the defendant at large pending disposition of the case, but requiring the defendant to appear in court or in some other place at all appropriate times.

The conditions of release must proceed from the least restrictive to the ultimate imposition of cash bail depending on the circumstances in each case. Release on monetary conditions should only be required when no other conditions will reasonably ensure the defendant's appearance. When monetary conditions are imposed, bail should be set at the lowest level necessary to ensure the defendant's reappearance.

Rule 341(g)(2) of the Uniform Rules of Criminal Procedure (1987) and Standard 10–5.3(d) of the American Bar Association Standards for Criminal Justice (1985) provide for release upon posting of 10 percent of the face value of an unsecured bond and upon posting of a secured bond by an uncompensated surety. Although Rule 6.02 does not expressly authorize these options, the rule is broad enough to permit the court to set such conditions of release in an unusual case. If the 10 percent cash option is authorized by the district court, it should be in lieu of, not in addition to, an unsecured bond, because there is generally no reasonable expectation of collecting on the unsecured bond and the public should not be deluded into thinking it will be collected. The court should consider the availability of a reliable person to help assure the defendant's appearance. If cash bail is deposited with the court it is deemed the property of the defendant under Minn. Stat. § 629.53 and according to that statute the court can apply the deposit to any fine or restitution imposed.

For certain driving while intoxicated prosecutions under Minn. Stat. § 169A.20, if the defendant has prior convictions under that or related statutes, the court may impose the conditions of release set forth in Minn. Stat. § 169A.44. Conditions may include alcohol testing and license plate impoundment. However, Rule 6.02, subd. 1 requires that the court must set the amount of money bail without any other conditions on which the defendant can obtain release. The Advisory Committee was of the opinion that this is required by the defendant's constitutional right to bail. Minn. Const. Art. 1, § 7 makes all persons bailable by sufficient sureties for all offenses. It would violate this constitutional provision for the court to require that the monetary bail could be satisfied only by a cash deposit. The defendant must also be given the option of satisfying the monetary bail by sufficient sureties. State v. Brooks, 604 N.W.2d 345 (Minn. 2000).

If the court sets conditions of release, aside from an appearance bond, then the court must issue a written order stating those conditions. Any written order must be issued promptly and the defendant's release must not be delayed. In addition to providing a copy of the order to the defendant, the court must immediately provide it to the law enforcement agency that has or had custody of the defendant along with information about the named victim's whereabouts. This provision for a written order is in accord with Minn. Stat. § 629.715 which concerns conditions of release for defendants charged with crimes against persons. Written orders are required because it is important that the defendant, concerned persons, and law enforcement officers know precisely the conditions that govern the defendant's release.

When setting bail or other conditions of release, see Minn. Stat. § 629.72, subd. 7 and Minn. Stat. § 629.725 as to the court's duty to provide notice of a hearing on the defendant's release from pretrial detention in domestic abuse, harassment or crimes of violence cases. Also see Minn. Stat. § 629.72, subd. 6 and Minn. Stat. § 629.73 as to the duty of the law enforcement agency having custody of the defendant in such cases to provide notice of the defendant's impending release.

When imposing release conditions under Rule 6.02, subd. 2, Recommendation 5, concerning sexual assault, in the Final Report of the Minnesota Supreme Court Task Force on Gender Fairness in the Courts, 15 Wm.Mitchell L.Rev. 827 (1989), states that "Minnesota judges should not distinguish in setting bail, conditions of release, or sentencing in non-familial criminal sexual conduct cases on the basis of whether the victim and defendant were acquainted." This prohibition should be applied in setting bail in other cases as well.

NOTE: Rule 6 does not cover appeal of the release decision nor does it include release after a conviction. Appeal of the release decision is permitted under Rules 28 and 29. These rules also set standards and procedures for releasing a defendant after conviction.

Rule 6.03 prescribes the procedures followed when conditions of release are violated. The Rule requires issuing a summons rather than a warrant under circumstances similar to those required under Rule 3.01. Rule 6.03, subd. 3, requires only an informal hearing and does not require a showing of willful default, but leaves it to the court's discretion to determine under all of the circumstances whether to continue or revise the possible release conditions. On finding a violation, the court is not authorized to revoke the defendant's release without setting bail because such action is not permitted under Minn. Const. art. 1, § 5. The court must continue or revise the release conditions, governed by the considerations set forth in Rule 6.02, subds. 1 and 2. Under those rules, the court may increase the defendant's bail. If the defendant is unable to post the increased bail or to meet alternative conditions of release, the defendant may be kept in custody.

There are no provisions similar to Rule 6.03 in existing Minnesota statutory law except Minn. Stat. § 629.58, which provides that if a defendant fails to perform the conditions of a recognizance, process must be issued against the persons so bound. Rule 6.03, subds. 1 and 2 take the place of that statute.

Minn. Stat. § 629.63 providing for surrender of the defendant by the surety on the defendant's bond is not affected by Rule 6.03. To the extent that it is inconsistent with Rule 6.03 and Rule 6.02, subds. 1 and 2, however, Minn. Stat. § 629.64, requiring that in the event a defendant is surrendered by such surety money bail must be set, is superseded.

As to sanctions for violating Rule 6.06 speedy trial provisions, see State v. Kasper, 411 N.W.2d 182 (Minn.1987) and State v. Friberg, 435 N.W.2d 509 (Minn.1989). As to the right to a speedy trial generally, see the comments to Rule 11.09.

Historical Notes

The order of the Minnesota Supreme Court [C1–84–2137] dated December 13, 1989, provides in part that "(t)hese amended Rules of Criminal Procedure shall govern all criminal actions commenced or arrests made after 12 o'clock midnight January 1, 1990, except amendments to 8.04, 11.07, and 19.04, subd. 5, shall govern all criminal actions commenced or arrests made after 12 o'clock midnight January 1, 1991."

RULE 7. NOTICE BY PROSECUTOR OF OMNIBUS ISSUES, OTHER OFFENSES EVIDENCE, AND INTENT TO SEEK AGGRAVATED SENTENCE

Rule 7.01. Notice of Omnibus Issues

(a) In any case where a right to a jury trial exists, the prosecutor must notify the defendant or defense counsel of:

(1) any evidence against the defendant obtained as a result of a search, search and seizure, wiretapping, or any form of electronic or mechanical eavesdropping;

(2) any confessions, admissions, or statements in the nature of confessions made by the defendant;

(3) any evidence against the defendant discovered as a result of confessions, admissions, or statements in the nature of confessions made by the defendant; or

(4) any evidence of lineups, show-ups, or other procedures used to identify the defendant or any other person.

(b) In felony and gross misdemeanor cases, notice must be given in writing on or before the date set for the defendant's initial appearance in the district court under Rule 5.05.

(c) In misdemeanor cases, notice must be given either in writing or orally on the record in court on or before the date set for the defendant's pretrial conference, if one is scheduled, or 7 days before trial if no pretrial conference is held.

(d) Written notice may be served:

(1) personally on the defendant or defense counsel;

(2) by ordinary mail sent to the defendant's last known mailing address or left at this address with a person of suitable age and discretion residing there;

(3) by ordinary mail sent to defense counsel's business address or left at this address with a person of suitable age and discretion working there; or

(4) by electronic means if authorized by Minnesota Supreme Court Order and if service is made in accordance with that order.

Adopted Feb. 26, 1975, eff. July 1, 1975. Revised Dec. 13, 1989. Amended Oct. 27, 2009, eff. Jan. 1, 2010; July 26, 2012, eff. Sept. 1, 2012.

Comment—Rule 7

See comment following Rule 7.04.

Historical Notes

The order of the Minnesota Supreme Court [C1–84–2137] dated December 13, 1989, provides in part that "(t)hese amended Rules of Criminal Procedure shall govern all criminal actions commenced or arrests made after 12 o'clock midnight January 1, 1990, except amendments to 8.04, 11.07, and 19.04, subd. 5, shall govern all criminal actions commenced or arrests made after 12 o'clock midnight January 1, 1991."

The order of the Minnesota Supreme Court [ADM10–8049] dated July 26, 2012, provides in part that "(t)he attached amendments to the Rules of Criminal Procedure be, and the same are, prescribed and promulgated to be effective September 1, 2012," and further provides "(t)hese amendments shall apply to all actions or proceedings pending or commenced on or after the effective date."

Rule 7.02. Notice of Other Offenses

Subd. 1. Notice of Other Crime, Wrong, or Act. The prosecutor must notify the defendant or defense counsel in writing of any crime, wrong, or act that may be offered at the trial under Minnesota Rule of Evidence 404(b). No notice is required for any crime, wrong, or act:

(a) previously prosecuted,

(b) offered to rebut the defendant's character evidence, or

(c) arising out of the same occurrence or episode as the charged offense.

Subd. 2. Notice of a Specific Instance of Conduct. The prosecutor must notify the defendant or defense counsel in writing of the intent to cross-examine the defendant or a defense witness under Minnesota Rule of Evidence 608(b) about a specific instance of conduct.

Subd. 3. Contents of Notice. The notice required by subdivisions 1 and 2 must contain a description of each crime, wrong, act, or specific instance of conduct with sufficient particularity to enable the defendant to prepare for trial.

Subd. 4. Timing.

(a) In felony and gross misdemeanor cases, the notice must be given at or before the Omnibus Hearing under Rule 11, or as soon after that hearing as the other crime, wrong, act, or specific instance of conduct becomes known to the prosecutor.

(b) In misdemeanor cases, the notice must be given at or before a pretrial conference under Rule 12, if held, or as soon after the hearing as the other crime, wrong, act, or specific instance of conduct becomes known to the prosecutor. If no pretrial conference occurs, the notice must be given at least 7 days before trial or as soon as the prosecutor learns of the other crime, wrong, act, or specific instance of conduct.

Adopted Feb. 26, 1975, eff. July 1, 1975. Revised Dec. 13, 1989. Amended May 9, 1994; Oct. 27, 2009, eff. Jan. 1, 2010; June 22, 2011, eff. Sept. 1, 2011.

Comment—Rule 7

See comment following Rule 7.04.

Historical Notes

The order of the Minnesota Supreme Court [C1–84–2137] dated December 13, 1989, provides in part that "(t)hese amended Rules of Criminal Procedure shall govern all criminal actions commenced or arrests made after 12 o'clock midnight January 1, 1990, except amendments to 8.04, 11.07, and 19.04, subd. 5, shall govern all criminal actions commenced or arrests made after 12 o'clock midnight January 1, 1991."

The order of the Minnesota Supreme Court [C1–84–2137] dated May 9, 1994, provides in part that "(t)hese amendments to the Rules of Criminal Procedure shall govern all criminal actions commenced or arrests made after 12 o'clock midnight July 1, 1994, except that the amendments in the first sentence of the third paragraph in Rule 2.01 shall govern all criminal actions commenced or arrests made after 12 o'clock midnight January 1, 1995."

The order of the Minnesota Supreme Court [ADM10–8049] dated June 22, 2011, provides in part that "the amendment to Rule 7.02 shall govern all criminal actions commenced on or after the effective date."

Rule 7.03. Notice of Intent to Seek an Aggravated Sentence

The prosecutor must give written notice at least 7 days before the Omnibus Hearing of intent to seek an aggravated sentence. Notice may be given later if permitted by the court on good cause and on conditions that will not unfairly prejudice the defendant. The notice must include the grounds or statutes relied upon and a summary statement of the factual basis supporting the aggravated sentence.

Adopted Aug. 17, 2006, eff. Oct. 1, 2006. Amended Oct. 27, 2009, eff. Jan. 1, 2010.

Comment—Rule 7

See comment following Rule 7.04.

Rule 7.04. Completion of Discovery

Before the date set for the Omnibus Hearing, in felonies and gross misdemeanor cases, the prosecutor and defendant must complete the discovery that is required by Rules 9.01 and 9.02 to be made without the necessity of an order of the court. Rule 9.04 governs completion of discovery for misdemeanor cases.

Former Rule 7.03 adopted Feb. 26, 1975, eff. July 1, 1975. Revised Dec. 13, 1989. Amended Dec. 23, 2002, eff. Feb. 1, 2003. Renumbered Rule 7.04 and amended Aug. 17, 2006, eff. Oct. 1, 2006; May 19, 2008, eff. July 1, 2008; Oct. 27, 2009, eff. Jan. 1, 2010.

Comment—Rule 7

Under Rule 7.01 the Rasmussen notice (State ex rel. Rasmussen v. Tahash, 272 Minn. 539, 553–54, 141 N.W.2d 3, 13 (1965)) of evidence obtained from the defendant and of identification procedures must be given on or before the defendant's appearance in the district court under Rule 8 (within 14 days after the first appearance in the court under Rule 5) so that the defendant may determine at the time of the Rule 8 appearance whether to waive or demand a Rasmussen hearing (Rule 8.03). If the defendant then demands a Rasmussen hearing, it will be included in the Omnibus Hearing (Rule 11) no more than 28 days later. It is permissible for the prosecutor to attach to a complaint for service a notice under Rule 7.01 or a discovery request under Rule 9.02.

In misdemeanor cases under Rule 7.01, the Rasmussen notice of evidence obtained from the defendant and of identification procedures may be given at arraignment, and in such a case the waiver or demand of a hearing takes place at that time (Rule 5.06, subd. 4). However, since misdemeanor arraignments are often within one day or even a few hours of an arrest, a prosecutor may not have sufficient knowledge of the case to issue a Rasmussen notice at that time. Rather than discourage such prompt arraignments, this rule provides that the Rasmussen notice may be served as late as the pretrial conference, if held, or at least seven days before trial if no pretrial conference is held. The Rasmussen notice procedure is required only where a jury trial is to be held. Even where no notice is required, the discovery permitted by Rule 9.04 will give the defendant and defense counsel notice of any evidentiary or identification issues that would have been the subject of a formal Rasmussen notice.

If the notice required by Rule 7.01 is not actually received, the court may grant a continuance to prevent any prejudice due to surprise.

Rule 7.02 requires that the Spreigl notice be given on or before the date of the Omnibus Hearing (Rule 11) in order that any issues that may arise as to the admissibility of the evidence of these offenses at trial may be ascertained and determined at the Omnibus Hearing. If the prosecutor learns of any such offenses after the Omnibus Hearing, the prosecutor must immediately give notice to the defendant.

Rule 7.03 establishes the notice requirements for a prosecutor to initiate proceedings seeking an aggravated sentence in compliance with Blakely v. Washington, 542 U.S. 296, 301–305 (2004). See Rule 1.04(d) as to the definition of "aggravated sentence." See also the comments to that rule. The written notice required by Rule 7.03 must include not only the grounds or statute relied upon, but also a summary statement of the supporting factual basis. However, there is no requirement that the factual basis be given under oath. This rule balances the competing interests of the parties: the prosecution may not have sufficient evidence at charging to make the Blakely decision and the defense requires notice as early as possible to prepare an adequate defense. The rule recognizes that it may not always be possible to give notice by 7 days before the Omnibus Hearing and the court may permit a later notice for good cause so long as the later notice will not unfairly prejudice the defendant. In making that decision the court can consider whether a continuance of the proceedings or other conditions would cure any unfair prejudice to the defendant. Pretrial issues concerning a requested aggravated sentence will be considered and decided under the Omnibus Hearing provisions of Rule 11.

Rule 7.04 provides that discovery required under Rule 9 in felony and gross misdemeanor cases must be completed by the prosecution and defense before the Omnibus Hearing (Rule 11). This will permit the court to resolve any issues that may have arisen between the parties with respect to discovery (Rules 9.03, subd. 8) at the Omnibus Hearing. It may also result in a plea of guilty at the Omnibus Hearing (Rule 11.08). All notices under Rule 7 must also be filed with the court (Rule 33.04). The discovery requirements for misdemeanor cases are set forth in Rule 9.04.

Rule 7.01(d)(4) is a new rule to provide for service by electronic means, if authorized by an order of the Minnesota Supreme Court. This amendment is intended to facilitate a pilot project on electronic service and filing in certain pilot districts, but is designed to be a model for the implementation of electronic filing if the pilot project is made permanent and statewide. The rule makes service by electronic means effective in accordance with the rule for the pilot project.

Historical Notes

The order of the Minnesota Supreme Court [C1–84–2137] dated December 13, 1989, provides in part that "(t)hese amended Rules of Criminal Procedure shall govern all criminal actions commenced or arrests made after 12 o'clock midnight January 1, 1990, except amendments to 8.04, 11.07, and 19.04, subd. 5, shall govern all criminal actions commenced or arrests made after 12 o'clock midnight January 1, 1991."

RULE 8. PROCEDURE ON SECOND APPEARANCE IN FELONY AND GROSS MISDEMEANOR CASES

Rule 8.01. Purpose of Second Appearance

(a) The purpose of this hearing is to again advise defendants of their rights, to allow defendants to plead guilty, or if the defendant does not plead guilty, to request or waive an Omnibus Hearing under Rule 11.

(b) At this hearing, the court must again inform the defendant of the:

(1) charge(s);

(2) defendant's rights, including the right to counsel, and to have counsel appointed under Rule 5.04 if eligible, and;

(3) opportunity to enter a guilty plea as permitted by Rule 8.02.

(c) The court must ensure the defendant has a copy of the complaint or indictment.

(d) The court may continue or modify the defendant's bail or other conditions of release previously ordered.

Adopted Oct. 27, 2009, eff. Jan. 1, 2010.

Comment—Rule 8

See comment following Rule 8.06.

Historical Notes

Former Rule: Former Rule 8.01 related to a defendant's place of initial appearance and arraignment. See, now, Rules Crim.Proc. Rule 8.02.

Rule 8.02. Arraignment

Subd. 1. Entry of Plea. The arraignment must be conducted in open court. Except as provided in subdivision 2, the court must ask the defendant to enter a plea. The only plea a defendant may enter at the Rule 8 hearing is a guilty plea.

If the defendant pleads guilty, the pre-sentencing and sentencing procedures in these rules must be followed.

If the defendant does not wish to plead guilty, the arraignment must be continued until the Omnibus Hearing.

Subd. 2. Homicide or Offenses Punishable by Life Imprisonment. If the complaint charges a homicide, and the prosecuting attorney notifies the court that the case will be presented to the grand jury, or if the offense is punishable by life imprisonment, the defendant cannot enter a plea at the Rule 8 hearing.

Presentation of the case to the grand jury must commence within 14 days from the date of defendant's appearance in the court under this rule, and an indictment or report of no indictment must be returned within a reasonable time. If an indictment is returned, the Omnibus Hearing under Rule 11 must be held as provided by Rule 19.04, subd. 5.

Rule 8.02, former Rules 8.01 and 13.01 adopted Feb. 26, 1975, eff. July 1, 1975. Revised Dec. 13, 1989. Former Rule 8.01 amended May 9, 1994; Aug. 21, 1998, eff. Jan. 1, 1999. Rule 8.02 amended and former Rules 8.01 and 13.01 renumbered Rule 8.02 and amended Oct. 27, 2009, eff. Jan. 1, 2010.

Comment—Rule 8

See comment following Rule 8.06.

Historical Notes

This rule, as amended Oct. 27, 2009, eff. Jan. 1, 2010, also incorporates former Rules 8.01 and 13.01.

Rule 8.03. Demand or Waiver of Hearing

If the defendant does not plead guilty, the defendant and the prosecutor must each either waive or demand a hearing as provided in Rule 11.02 on the admissibility at trial of evidence specified in the prosecutor's Rule 7.01 notice, or on the admissibility of any evidence obtained as a result of the specified evidence.

Adopted Feb. 26, 1975, eff. July 1, 1975. Revised Dec. 13, 1989. Amended Oct. 27, 2009, eff. Jan. 1, 2010.

Comment—Rule 8

See comment following Rule 8.06.

Rule 8.04. Plea and Time of Omnibus Hearing

(a) If the defendant does not plead guilty, the Omnibus Hearing on the issues as provided for in Rules 11.03 and 11.04 must be held within the time specified in this rule.

(b) If a hearing on either of the issues set forth in Rule 8.03 is demanded, the Omnibus Hearing must also include the issues provided for in Rule 11.02.

(c) The Omnibus Hearing provided for in Rule 11 must be scheduled for a date not later than 28 days after the defendant's appearance before the court under this rule. The court may extend the time for good cause related to the particular case on motion of the prosecutor or defendant or on the court's initiative.

Adopted Feb. 26, 1975, eff. July 1, 1975. Revised Dec. 13, 1989. Amended Nov. 29, 1990; Oct. 27, 2009, eff. Jan. 1, 2010.

Comment—Rule 8

See comment following Rule 8.06.

Rule 8.05. Record

A verbatim record must be made of the proceedings under this rule.

Rule 8.05 and former Rule 13.05 adopted Feb. 26, 1975, eff. July 1, 1975. Revised Dec. 13, 1989. Rule 8.05 amended and former Rule 13.05 renumbered Rule 8.05 and amended Oct. 27, 2009, eff. Jan. 1, 2010.

Comment—Rule 8

See comment following Rule 8.06.

Rule 8.06. Deleted Oct. 27, 2009, eff. Jan. 1, 2010

Comment—Rule 8

If the Rasmussen hearing is waived under Rule 8.03 by both the prosecution and the defense, the Omnibus Hearing provided by Rule 11 must be held without a Rasmussen hearing.

If the Rasmussen hearing is demanded, the hearing must be held as part of the Omnibus Hearing as provided by Rule 11.02.

The Omnibus Hearing must be commenced not later than 28 days after the defendant's initial appearance in court under Rule 8 unless the time is extended for good cause related to the particular case. See Minn. Stat. § 611A.033 regarding the prosecutor's duties under the Victim's Rights Act to make reasonable efforts to provide advance notice of any change in the schedule of court proceedings. This would include the Omnibus Hearing as well as trial or any other hearing.

Historical Notes

Deleted Rule 8.06 related to the conditions of a defendant's release. See, now, Rules Crim.Proc., Rule 8.01(d).

RULE 9. DISCOVERY IN FELONY, GROSS MISDEMEANOR, AND MISDEMEANOR CASES

Rule 9.01. Prosecution Disclosure in Felony and Gross Misdemeanor Cases

Subd. 1. Prosecution Disclosure Without Court Order. The prosecutor must, at the defense's request and before the Rule 11 Omnibus Hearing, allow access at any reasonable time to all matters within the prosecutor's possession or control that relate to the case, except as provided in Rule 9.01, subd. 3, and make the following disclosures:

(1) Trial Witnesses; Other Persons; Grand Jury Witnesses.

(a) Trial Witnesses. The names and addresses of witnesses who may be called at trial, along with their record of convictions, if any, within the prosecutor's actual knowledge. The defense must not make any comment in the jury's presence that a name is on a witness list furnished by the prosecutor.

(b) Other Persons. The names and addresses of anyone else with information relating to the case.

(c) Grand Jury Witnesses. If the defendant has been charged by indictment, the names and addresses of the grand jury witnesses.

(2) Statements. Any of the following known to the prosecutor that relate to the case:

(a) written or recorded statements;

(b) written summaries of oral statements;

(c) the substance of oral statements.

The obligation to disclose the preceding types of statements applies whether or not the person who made the statement is listed as a witness.

(3) Documents and Tangible Objects. Any of the following that relate to the case:

(a) books, papers, documents;

(b) photographs;

(c) law enforcement officer reports;

(d) tangible objects;

(e) the location of buildings and places;

(f) grand jury transcripts;

(g) reports on prospective jurors.

(4) Reports of Examinations and Tests.

(a) The results or reports of physical or mental examinations, scientific tests, experiments, or comparisons made that relate to the case.

(b) In addition, the prosecutor must allow the defendant to conduct reasonable tests. If a test or experiment, other than those conducted under Minn. Stat. ch. 169A, might preclude any further tests or experiments, the prosecutor must give reasonable notice and opportunity to the defense so that a qualified expert may observe the test or experiment.

(c) A person who will testify as an expert but who created no results or reports in connection with the case must provide to the prosecutor for disclosure to the defense a written summary of the subject matter of the expert's testimony, along with any findings, opinions, or conclusions the expert will give, the basis for them, and the expert's qualifications.

(5) Criminal Records of Defendant and Defense Witnesses. The conviction records of the defendant and of any defense witnesses disclosed under Rule 9. 02, subd. 1(3) and (8) that are known to the prosecutor, provided the defense informs the prosecutor of any of these records known to the defendant.

(6) Exculpatory Information. Material or information in the prosecutor's possession and control that tends to negate or reduce the defendant's guilt.

(7) Evidence Relating to Aggravated Sentence. Evidence the prosecutor may rely on in seeking an aggravated sentence.

Subd. 1a. Scope of Prosecutor's Obligations; Inspection, Reproduction, and Documentation.

(1) Scope of Prosecutor's Obligations. The prosecutor's obligations under this rule extend to material and information in the possession or control of members of the prosecution staff and of any others who have participated in the investigation or evaluation of the case and who either regularly report, or with reference to the particular case have reported, to the prosecutor's office.

(2) Inspection, Reproduction, and Documentation. The prosecutor must allow the defendant to inspect and reproduce any information required to be disclosed under this rule, as well as to inspect and photograph any object, place, or building required to be disclosed under this rule.

Subd. 2. Discretionary Disclosure By Court Order.

(1) Matters Possessed by Other Governmental Agencies. On the defendant's motion, the court for good cause must require the prosecutor, except as provided by Rule 9.01, subd. 3, to assist the defendant in seeking access to specified matters relating to the case that are within the possession or control of an official or employee of any governmental agency, but not within the prosecutor's control.

The prosecutor must use diligent good faith efforts to cause the official or employee to allow the defense reasonable access to inspect, photograph, copy, or have reasonable tests made.

(2) Nontestimonial Evidence from Defendant on Defendant's Motion. On the defendant's motion, the court for good cause may require the prosecutor to permit the defendant to participate in a lineup, to speak for identification by witnesses, or to participate in other procedures.

(3) Other Relevant Material. On the defendant's motion, the trial court at any time before trial may, in its discretion, require the prosecutor to disclose to defense counsel and to permit the inspection, reproduction, or testing of any relevant material and information not subject to disclosure without order of court under Rule 9.01, subd. 1, provided, however, a showing is made that the information may relate to the guilt or innocence of the defendant or negate guilt or reduce the culpability of the defendant as to the offense charged. If the motion is denied, the court upon application of the defendant must inspect and preserve any relevant material and information.

Subd. 3. Non-Discoverable Information. The following information is not discoverable by the defendant:

(1) Work Product.

(a) Opinions, Theories, or Conclusions. Unless otherwise provided by these rules, legal research, records, correspondence, reports, or memoranda to the extent they contain the opinions, theories, or conclusions of the prosecutor, the prosecutor's staff or officials, or official agencies participating in the prosecution.

(b) Reports. Except as provided in Rule 9.01, subd. 1(1) to (7), reports, memoranda, or internal documents made by the prosecutor or members of the prosecutor's staff, or by prosecution agents in connection with the investigation or prosecution of the case against the defendant.

(2) Prosecution Witnesses Under Prosecutor's Certificate. The information concerning the witnesses and other persons described in Rule 9.01, subd. 1(1) and (2) is not subject to disclosure if the prosecutor files a written certificate with the trial court that to do so may endanger the integrity of a continuing investigation or subject witnesses or other persons to physical harm or coercion. Non-disclosure under this rule must not extend beyond the time the witnesses or persons are sworn to testify at the trial.

Adopted Feb. 26, 1975, eff. July 1, 1975. Revised Dec. 13, 1989. Amended Aug. 17, 2006, eff. Oct. 1, 2006; May 19, 2008, eff. July 1, 2008; Oct. 27, 2009, eff. Jan. 1, 2010.

Comment—Rule 9

See comment following Rule 9.05.

Rule 9.02. Defendant's Disclosure in Felony and Gross Misdemeanor Cases

Subd. 1. Information Subject to Discovery Without Court Order. The defendant must, at the prosecutor's request and before the Rule 11 Omnibus Hearing, make the following disclosures and permit the prosecutor to inspect and reproduce them:

(1) Documents and Tangible Objects. Any of the following the defense intends to introduce at trial:

(a) books, papers, documents;

(b) photographs;

(c) tangible objects;

(d) the locations of buildings and places concerning which the defendant intends to offer evidence. As to this disclosure, the defense must also permit photographing;

(e) without regard to use at trial, any reports on prospective jurors.

(2) Reports of Examinations and Tests.

(a) Any of the following results or reports the defense intends to introduce at trial that were made in connection with the case and are within the defense's possession or control, or were prepared by a witness the defense intends to call at trial, when the results and reports are of:

(i) physical or mental examinations;

(ii) scientific tests, experiments, or comparisons.

(b) In addition, a person who will testify as an expert but who created no results or reports in connection with the case must provide to the defense for disclosure to the prosecutor a written summary of the subject matter of the expert's testimony, along with any findings, opinions, or conclusions the expert will give, the basis for them, and the expert's qualifications.

(3) Notice of Defense Witnesses. The defendant must disclose the names and addresses of witnesses who may be called at trial, along with their record of convictions, if any, within the defendant's actual knowledge.

The prosecutor must not make any comment in the jury's presence that a name is on a witness list furnished by the defendant.

(4) Statements of Defense and Prosecution Witnesses. The defendant must disclose:

(a) Relevant written or recorded statements of the persons the defendant intends to call at trial;

(b) Statements of prosecution witnesses obtained by the defendant, defense counsel, or persons participating in the defense within the defendant's possession or control;

(c) Written summaries known to the defense of the substance of any oral statements made by prosecution witnesses to defense counsel or persons participating in the defense, or obtained by the defendant at the defense counsel's direction.

(d) The substance of any oral statements that relate to the case made by persons the defendant intends to call as witnesses at trial, and that were made to defense counsel or persons participating in the defense.

(e) The defendant is not required to disclose statements made by the defendant to defense counsel or agents of defense counsel that are protected by the attorney-client privilege or by state or federal constitutional guarantees.

(5) Notice of defense.

The defense must inform the prosecutor in writing of any defense, other than not guilty, that the defendant intends to assert, including but not limited to:

(a) self-defense;

(b) entrapment;

(c) mental illness or deficiency;

(d) duress;

(e) alibi;

(f) double jeopardy;

(g) statute of limitations;

(h) collateral estoppel;

(i) defense under Minn. Stat. § 609.035;

(j) intoxication.

A defendant who gives notice of intent to assert the defense of mental illness or mental deficiency must also notify the prosecutor of any intent to also assert the defense of not guilty.

(6) Entrapment.

(a) If the defendant intends to offer evidence of entrapment, the defendant must inform the prosecutor of the facts supporting the defense, and elect to submit the defense to the court or jury.

(b) The entrapment defense may be submitted to the court only if the defendant waives a jury trial on that issue as provided in Rule 26.01, subd. 1(2).

(c) If the defendant submits entrapment to the court, the hearing on entrapment must be included in the Omnibus Hearing under Rule 11 or in the evidentiary hearing under Rule 12. The court must make findings of fact and conclusions of law on the record supporting its decision.

(7) Alibi. If the defendant intends to offer evidence of an alibi, the defendant must inform the prosecutor of:

(a) the specific place or places where the defendant was when the alleged offense occurred;

(b) the names and addresses of the witnesses the defendant intends to call at the trial in support of the alibi.

As soon as practicable, the prosecutor must then inform the defendant of the names and addresses of the witnesses the prosecutor intends to call at trial to rebut the testimony of any of the defendant's alibi witnesses.

(8) Criminal Record. The defendant must inform the prosecutor of any convictions the defendant has, provided the prosecutor informs the defense of the defendant's record of convictions known to the prosecutor.

Subd. 2. Discovery by Court Order.

(1) Disclosures Permitted. On the prosecutor's motion, with notice to the defense and a showing that one or more of the discovery procedures described below will materially aid in determining whether the defendant committed the offense charged, the court before trial may, subject to constitutional limitations, order a defendant to:

(a) Appear in a lineup;

(b) Speak for the purpose of voice identification or for taking voice prints;

(c) Permit finger, palm, or foot-printing;

(d) Permit body measurements;

(e) Pose for photographs not involving re-enactment of a scene;

(f) Permit the taking of blood, hair, saliva, urine, or samples of other bodily materials that do not involve unreasonable intrusion, but the court must not permit a blood sample to be taken except on a showing of probable cause to believe that the test will aid in establishing the defendant's guilt;

(g) Provide specimens of the defendant's handwriting; and

(h) Submit to reasonable physical or medical inspection.

(2) Notice of Time and Place of Disclosures. The prosecutor must give the defense reasonable notice of the time and place the defendant must appear for any discovery purpose listed above.

(3) Medical Supervision. Blood tests must be conducted under medical supervision. The court may require medical supervision for any other test ordered under this rule. On the defendant's motion, the court may delay the defendant's appearance for a reasonable time, or may order that it take place at the defendant's residence, or some other convenient place.

(4) Notice of Results of Disclosure. The prosecutor must tell the defense the results of the procedures within 5 days of learning the result, unless the court orders otherwise.

(5) Other Methods Not Excluded. The discovery procedures provided in this rule do not exclude other lawful methods available for obtaining the evidence discoverable under this rule.

Subd. 3. Information Not Subject to Disclosure by Defendant; Work Product. Unless these rules direct otherwise, legal research, records, correspondence, reports, or memoranda, to the extent they contain the opinions, theories, or conclusions of the defendant or defense counsel or persons participating in the defense, are not subject to disclosure.

Adopted Feb. 26, 1975, eff. July 1, 1975. Revised Dec. 13, 1989. Amended Dec. 23, 2002, eff. Feb. 1, 2003; Oct. 27, 2009, eff. Jan. 1, 2010.

Comment—Rule 9

See comment following Rule 9.05.

Rule 9.03. Regulation of Discovery

Subd. 1. Investigations Not to be Impeded. Counsel for the parties and other prosecution or defense personnel must not tell anyone with relevant information (except the accused) not to discuss the case with opposing counsel, or not to show opposing counsel relevant material, or otherwise impede opposing counsel's investigation of the case.

This rule does not apply to matters not subject to discovery under this rule or that are covered by a protective order.

Subd. 2. Timely Disclosure and Continuing Duty to Disclose.

(a) All material and information to which a party is entitled must be disclosed in time to afford counsel the opportunity to make beneficial use of it.

(b) If, after compliance with any discovery rules or orders, a party discovers additional material, information, or witnesses subject to disclosure, that party must promptly notify the other party of what it has discovered and disclose it.

(c) Each party has a continuing duty of disclosure before and during trial.

Subd. 3. Time, Place, and Manner of Discovery and Inspection. A court granting discovery must specify the time, place, and manner of discovery, and may impose reasonable terms and conditions.

Subd. 4. Custody of Materials. Materials furnished to a party under discovery rules or orders must remain in the party's custody and be used by the party only to conduct that attorney's side of the case, and may be subject to other conditions the court orders.

Subd. 5. Protective Orders. The court may order disclosures restricted, deferred, or made subject to other conditions.

Subd. 6. In Camera Proceedings. On any party's motion, with notice to the other parties, the court for good cause may order a discovery motion to be made in camera. A record must be made. If the court orders an in camera hearing, the entire record of the motion must be sealed and preserved in the court's records, and be available to reviewing courts.

Subd. 7. Excision. When parts of materials are discoverable under these rules and other parts are not, the discoverable portions must be disclosed. Material excised under judicial order must be sealed and be made available to reviewing courts.

Subd. 8. Sanctions. If a party fails to comply with a discovery rule or order, the court may, on notice and motion, order the party to permit the discovery, grant a continuance, or enter any order it deems just in the circumstances. Any person who willfully disobeys a court's discovery order may be held in contempt.

Subd. 9. Filing. Unless the court directs otherwise, discovery disclosures made under Rule 9 are not subject to the filing requirements in Rule 33.04. The party making disclosures must prepare an itemized descriptive list identifying the disclosures but without disclosing their contents, and must file the list as provided by Rule 33.04.

Subd. 10. Reproduction. When an obligation exists to permit reproduction of a report, statement, document, or other tangible thing discoverable under this rule, it may be satisfied by any method that provides an exact reproduction, including e-mail, facsimile, or similar method if available to both parties.

Adopted Feb. 26, 1975, eff. July 1, 1975. Revised Dec. 13, 1989. Amended Dec. 23, 2002, eff. Feb. 1, 2003; Oct. 27, 2009, eff. Jan. 1, 2010.

Comment—Rule 9

See comments following Rule 9.05.

Rule 9.04. Discovery in Misdemeanor Cases

In misdemeanor cases, before arraignment or at any time before trial the prosecutor must, on request and without a court order, permit the defendant or defense counsel to inspect the police investigatory reports.

Upon request, the prosecutor must also disclose any material or information within the prosecutor's possession and control that tends to negate or reduce the guilt of the accused as to the offense charged.

After arraignment and on request, the defendant or defense counsel must be provided a copy of the police investigatory reports.

Any other discovery must be by consent of the parties or by motion to the court.

The obligation to provide discovery after arraignment may be satisfied by any method that provides the defendant or defense counsel a copy of the reports, including e-mail, facsimile, or similar method if available to both parties.

Former Rule 7.03 adopted Feb. 26, 1975, eff. July 1, 1975. Revised Dec. 13, 1989. Amended Dec. 23, 2002, eff. Feb. 1, 2003. Renumbered Rule 7.04 and amended Aug. 17, 2006, eff. Oct. 1, 2006; May 19, 2008, eff. July 1, 2008. Renumbered Rule 9.04 and amended Oct. 27, 2009, eff. Jan. 1, 2010. Amended Feb. 11, 2010, eff. Feb. 11, 2010.

Comment—Rule 9

See comment following Rule 9.05.

Rule 9.05. Charges and Exemptions for Reproduction of Discovery in All Cases

A reasonable charge may be made to cover the actual costs of reproduction, but no charges may be assessed to a defendant who is:

(1) represented by the public defender or by an attorney working for a public defense corporation under Minn. Stat. § 611.216; or

(2) determined by the court under Rule 5.04 to be financially unable to obtain counsel.

Former Rules 7.03, 9.03 adopted Feb. 26, 1975, eff. July 1, 1975. Revised Dec. 13, 1989. Amended Dec. 23, 2002, eff. Feb. 1, 2003. Former Rule 7.03 renumbered Rule 7.04 and amended Aug. 17, 2006, eff. Oct. 1, 2006; May 19, 2008, eff. July 1, 2008. Former Rules 7.04 and 9.03 renumbered Rule 9.05 and amended Oct. 27, 2009, eff. Jan. 1, 2010.

Comment—Rule 9

Rule 9, with Rules 7.01, 19.04, subd. 6, and 18.04, subds. 1 and 2 (recorded testimony of grand jury witnesses), provide a comprehensive method of discovery of the prosecution (Rule 9.01) and defense (Rule 9.02) cases. The rules are intended to give the parties complete discovery subject to constitutional limitations.

The object of the rules is to complete discovery procedures so far as possible by the Omnibus Hearing under Rule 11, which will be held within 42 days after the defendant's first appearance in court following a complaint under Rule 5, where the Rule 5 and Rule 8 appearances are not consolidated, or within 7 days after the first appearance in district court following an indictment (Rule 19.04), and that all issues arising from the discovery process, including the need for additional discovery, will be resolved at the Omnibus Hearing (Rules 11.04; 9.01, subd. 2; 9.03, subd. 8).

Rule 9.01, subd. 1 provides generally for access by defense counsel to unprotected materials in the prosecution file, and also for numerous specific disclosures that must be made by the prosecutor on defense request. The general "open file" policy established by the rule is based on Unif.R. Crim.P. 421(a) (1987). Of course, this "open file" policy does not require the prosecuting attorney to give defense counsel access to any information that would be deemed non-discoverable under Rule 9.01, subd. 3.

Rule 9.01 does not require any specific form of request. It is anticipated that the discovery provided for by Rule 9.01, subd. 1, as well as the disclosures required of the defense by Rule 9.02 without order of court, will be accomplished informally between the prosecutor and defense counsel.

Rule 9.01, subd. 1(1)(a), forbidding comment to the jury on the fact that a person was named on the list of prosecution witnesses, is not intended to affect any right defense counsel may have under existing law to comment concerning the prosecution's failure to call a particular witness, but prevents defense counsel from commenting that the witness was on the prosecution's list.

Rule 9.01, subd. 1(3)(f) permits the defendant to obtain grand jury transcripts possessed by the prosecutor. If the defendant wants portions of the grand jury record not yet transcribed or possessed by the prosecutor, a request must be made under Rule 18.04.

Rule 9.01, subd. 1(4) permits discovery of reports of examinations and tests. If a test or experiment done by the prosecution does not destroy the evidence and preclude further tests or experiments, it is not necessary under this rule to notify the defendant or to allow a defense expert to observe the test or experiment.

Rule 9.01, subd. 1(5) provides for the reciprocal discovery of the criminal records of any defense witness disclosed to the prosecution under Rule 9.02, subd. 1(3). Under Rule 9.03, subd. 2, a continuing duty exists to disclose this information through trial. If the prosecutor intends to impeach the defendant or any defense witnesses with evidence of prior convictions the prosecutor is required by State v. Wenberg, 289 N.W.2d 503, 504–05 (Minn.1980) to request a pretrial hearing on the admissibility of this evidence under the Rules of Evidence. The pretrial hearing may be made a part of the Omnibus Hearing under Rule 11 or the pretrial conference under Rule 12.

Rule 9.01, subd. 1(7) requires the prosecutor to disclose to the defendant or defense counsel all evidence not otherwise disclosed on which the prosecutor intends to rely in seeking an aggravated sentence under Blakely v. Washington, 542 U.S. 296 (2004).

The requirement under Rule 9.02, subd. 1(1)(e) to disclose reports on prospective jurors does not require disclosure of opinions or conclusions concerning jurors given by persons assisting counsel on the case. Such material would be protected as work product under Rule 9.02, subd. 3.

The provision in Rule 9.02 subd. 1(4)(d) that defense counsel and the defendant disclose the substance of any oral statements obtained from persons whom the defendant intends to call at the trial is not intended to support a claim that if counsel or the defendant interviewed the witness without a third party present that defense counsel can be disqualified in order to permit counsel to testify to any discrepancy between the oral statement disclosed and the witness's trial testimony, or that if the defendant declines to testify to the discrepancy that the witness's testimony should be stricken. Other solutions should be sought, such as stipulating that in the interview that counsel or the defendant conducted, the witness made the statement the prosecutor now seeks to impeach.

Rule 9.02, subd. 1(5) requires written notice of any defense—other than not guilty—on which the defendant intends to rely at the trial, along with the names and addresses of the witnesses the defendant intends to call at the trial. The defendant is not required to indicate the witnesses intended to be used for each defense except for the defense of alibi (Rule 9. 02, subd. 1(7)).

Rule 9.02, subd. 2 regulates orders for nontestimonial identification or other procedures. This rule applies after a defendant has been charged. Precharging nontestimonial procedures are usually accomplished by search warrant.

Following the charging of a felony or gross misdemeanor, the order may be obtained at the first appearance of the defendant under Rule 4.02, subd. 5(1), and Rule 5, or at or before the Omnibus Hearing under Rule 11. The order may be obtained from the district court at any time before trial, but preferably at or before the Omnibus Hearing.

In making protective orders under Rule 9.03, subd. 5 or in ruling on motions to compel discovery under Rules 9.01, subd. 2, and 9.03, subd. 8, the court may avail itself of Rule 9.03, subds. 6 and 7 authorizing in camera proceedings and excision.

Under Rule 9.04 the prosecutor should reveal not only the reports physically in the prosecutor's possession, but also those concerning the case that are in the possession of the police.

In those rare cases where additional discovery is considered necessary by either party, it shall be by consent of the parties or by motion to the court. In such cases it is expected that the parties and the court will be guided by the extensive discovery provisions of these rules. Rule 9 provides guidelines for deciding any such motions, but they are not mandatory and the decision is within the discretion of the district court judge. State v. Davis, 592 N.W.2d 457, 459 (Minn. 1999).

Under Rule 9.05, the provision of the rule permitting free copies to public defenders and attorneys working for a public defense corporation under Minn. Stat. § 611.216 is in accord with Minn. Stat. § 611.271.

RULE 10. PLEADINGS AND MOTIONS BEFORE TRIAL; DEFENSES AND OBJECTIONS

Rule 10.01. Pleadings and Motions

Subd. 1. Pleadings. The pleadings consist of the indictment, complaint, or tab charge and any plea permitted by Rule 14.

Subd. 2. Motions; Waiver. Defenses, objections, issues, or requests that can be determined without trial on the merits must be made before trial by a motion to dismiss or to grant appropriate relief. The motion must include all defenses, objections, issues, and requests then available. Failure to include any of them in the motion constitutes waiver, but lack of jurisdiction over the offense or failure of the indictment or complaint to charge an offense can be noticed by the court at any time during the proceeding.

The court can grant relief from the waiver for good cause. The defendant does not waive any defenses or objections by including them in a motion with other defenses, objections, or issues.

Rule 10.01 and former Rule 10.03 adopted Feb. 26, 1975, eff. July 1, 1975. Revised Dec. 13, 1989. Former rule 10.03 renumbered Rule 10.01, subd. 2, and amended Oct. 27, 2009, eff. Jan. 1, 2010.

Comment—Rule 10

See comment following Rule 10.04.

Historical Notes

The order of the Minnesota Supreme Court [C1–84–2137] dated December 13, 1989, provides in part that "(t)hese amended Rules of Criminal Procedure shall govern all criminal actions commenced or arrests made after 12 o'clock midnight January 1, 1990, except amendments to 8.04, 11.07, and 19.04, subd. 5, shall govern all criminal actions commenced or arrests made after 12 o'clock midnight January 1, 1991."

Rule 10.02. Motions Attacking Court Jurisdiction in Misdemeanor Cases

A motion to dismiss for lack of personal jurisdiction in a misdemeanor case cannot be made until after the prosecutor files a complaint and the defendant pleads not guilty, unless the court hears and determines the motion summarily. Notice of the motion must be given orally on the record in court or in writing to the prosecutor. The notice must be given no later than 7 days after entry of the not guilty plea, or else the jurisdictional challenge is waived. The court for good cause can grant relief from the waiver.

Adopted Feb. 26, 1975, eff. July 1, 1975. Revised Dec. 13, 1989. Amended Oct. 27, 2009, eff. Jan. 1, 2010.

Comment—Rule 10

See comment following Rule 10.04.

Rule 10.03. Service of Motions; Hearing Date

Subd. 1. Service. In felony and gross misdemeanor cases, motions must be made in writing and served upon opposing counsel no later than 3 days before the Omnibus Hearing unless the court for good cause permits the motion to be made and served later.

In misdemeanor cases, except as permitted in subdivision 2, motions must be made in writing and served—along with any supporting affidavits—on opposing counsel at least 3 days before the hearing and no more than 30 days after the arraignment unless the court for good cause permits the motion to be made and served later.

Subd. 2. Hearing Date. In felony and gross misdemeanor cases, unless the motion is served after the Omnibus Hearing, it must be heard at that hearing and determined as provided in Rule 11.07.

In misdemeanor cases, if a pretrial conference is held, the motion must be heard then unless the court directs otherwise for the purpose of hearing witnesses, or for other good cause. If the motion is not heard at a pretrial conference, it must be heard before trial, unless the court—upon agreement by the prosecutor and defense attorney—hears and determines the motion at arraignment. If the court hears the motion at the arraignment, it need not be in writing, but a record must be made of the proceedings, and witnesses can be called in the court's discretion. The motion must be determined before trial as provided in Rule 12.07.

Subd. 3. Discovery. A party intending to call witnesses at a motion hearing must disclose them at least 3 days before the hearing and must comply with Rule 9 as if the witnesses were to be called at the trial.

Former Rule 10.04 adopted Feb. 26, 1975, eff. July 1, 1975. Revised Dec. 13, 1989. Amended May 19, 2008, eff. July 1, 2008. Renumbered Rule 10.03 and amended Oct. 27, 2009, eff. Jan. 1, 2010.

Comment—Rule 10

See comment following Rule 10.04.

Historical Notes

Former Rule: Former Rule 10.03 related to waivers. See, now, Rules Crim.Proc., Rule 10.01, subd. 2.

Rule 10.04. Deleted Oct. 27, 2009, eff. Jan. 1, 2010

Comment—Rule 10

Rule 10 does not require pre-trial motions to be made before a plea is entered.

As a general rule, under Rule 10.02 no challenge to the court's personal jurisdiction can be made in a misdemeanor case until after a complaint has been filed. Therefore, a defendant who has been tab charged must first demand a complaint under Rule 4.02, subd. 5(3) before raising the jurisdictional challenge. If no complaint is issued, the charge must be dismissed under Rule 4.02, subd. 5(3). If a complaint is issued, it will often make any possible challenge moot, since a valid complaint would give the court jurisdiction even if the arrest was illegal. See City of St. Paul v. Webb, 256 Minn. 210, 97 N.W.2d 638 (1959). Once the complaint is issued, the jurisdictional challenge becomes a sufficiency of the complaint question.

If the defendant's motion to dismiss is denied, Rule 17.06, subd. 4(1) provides that the defendant can continue to raise the jurisdictional issue on direct appeal if convicted after a trial. This procedure avoids the necessity of seeking review by an extraordinary writ that oftentimes would delay a trial otherwise ready to proceed.

Rule 17.06, subd. 4 describes the effect of determining a motion to dismiss under this rule.

In misdemeanor cases, Rule 10.03, subd. 2 provides an alternative method to dispose of a motion to dismiss—including a motion to dismiss for want of personal jurisdiction—at the time of arraignment. When there is no dispute over the facts, and the law can be quickly and adequately argued, this alternative procedure can provide an immediate disposition and avoid the delay and expense of further court appearances.

Historical Notes

Deleted Rule 10.04 related to service of motions and hearing dates. See, now, Rules Crim.Proc., Rules 10.03.

RULE 11. THE OMNIBUS HEARING

If the defendant does not plead guilty in a felony case at the initial appearance under Rule 8 or, in a gross misdemeanor case at the first appearance under Rule 5 or at the initial appearance under Rule 8, a hearing shall be held as follows:

Amended Aug. 21, 1998, eff. Jan. 1, 1999; Dec. 29, 2006, eff. April 1, 2007.

Comment—Rule 11

See comments following Rule 11.11.

Rule 11.01. Time and Place of Hearing

In felony and gross misdemeanor cases, if the defendant has not pled guilty, an Omnibus Hearing must be held.

(a) The Omnibus Hearing must start within 42 days of the Rule 5 appearance if it was not combined with the Rule 8 hearing, or within 28 days of the Rule 5 appearance if it was combined with the Rule 8 hearing.

(b) The Omnibus Hearing must be held in the district where the alleged offense occurred.

Adopted Feb. 26, 1975, eff. July 1, 1975. Revised Dec. 13, 1989. Amended Oct. 27, 2009, eff. Jan. 1, 2010.

Comment—Rule 11

See comment following Rule 11.11.

Historical Notes

The order of the Minnesota Supreme Court [C1–84–2137] dated December 13, 1989, provides in part that "(t)hese amended Rules of Criminal Procedure shall govern all criminal actions commenced or arrests made after 12 o'clock midnight January 1, 1990, except amendments to 8.04, 11.07, and 19.04, subd. 5, shall govern all criminal actions commenced or arrests made after 12 o'clock midnight January 1, 1991."

Rule 11.02. Scope of the Hearing

If the prosecutor or defendant demands a hearing under Rule 8.03, the court must conduct an Omnibus Hearing and hear all motions relating to:

(a) Probable cause;

(b) Evidentiary issues;

(c) Discovery;

(d) Admissibility of other crimes, wrongs or bad acts under Minnesota Rule of Evidence 404(b);

(e) Admissibility of relationship evidence under Minn. Stat. § 634.20;

(f) Admissibility of prior sexual conduct under Minnesota Rule of Evidence 412;

(g) Constitutional issues;

(h) Procedural issues;

(i) Aggravated sentence;

(j) Any other issues relating to a fair and expeditious trial.

Adopted Feb. 26, 1975, eff. July 1, 1975. Revised Dec. 13, 1989. Amended Aug. 21, 1998, eff. Jan. 1, 1999; Oct. 27, 2009, eff. Jan. 1, 2010.

Comment—Rule 11

See comment following Rule 11.11.

Rule 11.03. General Procedures

(a) The court may receive evidence offered by the prosecutor or defendant on any omnibus issue. A party may cross-examine any witness called by any other party.

(b) Before or during the Omnibus Hearing or any other pretrial hearing, witnesses may be sequestered or excluded from the courtroom.

Rule 11.03, former Rule 11.11 adopted Feb. 26, 1975, eff. July 1, 1975. Revised Dec. 13, 1989. Amended Oct. 27, 2009, eff. Jan. 1, 2010. Former Rule 11.11 renumbered Rule 11.03(b) and amended Oct. 27, 2009, eff. Jan. 1, 2010.

Comment—Rule 11

See comment following Rule 11.11.

Historical Notes

The order of the Minnesota Supreme Court [C1–84–2137] dated December 13, 1989, provides in part that "(t)hese amended Rules of Criminal Procedure shall govern all criminal actions commenced or arrests made after 12 o'clock midnight January 1, 1990, except amendments to 8.04, 11.07, and 19.04, subd. 5, shall govern all criminal actions commenced or arrests made after 12 o'clock midnight January 1, 1991."

Rule 11.04. Omnibus Motions

Subd. 1. Probable Cause Motions.

(a) The court must determine whether probable cause exists to believe that an offense has been committed and that the defendant committed it.

(b) The prosecutor and defendant may offer evidence at the probable cause hearing.

(c) The court may find probable cause on the face of the complaint or the entire record, including reliable hearsay. Evidence considered on the issue of probable cause is subject to the requirements of Rule 18.05, subd. 1.

Subd. 2. Aggravated Sentence Motion.

(a) If the prosecutor gave notice under Rule 7.03 or 19.04, subd. 6 of intent to seek an aggravated sentence, the court must determine whether the law and proffered evidence support an aggravated sentence. The court must also determine whether to conduct a unitary or bifurcated trial.

(b) In deciding whether to bifurcate, the court must determine whether the evidence supporting an aggravated sentence is otherwise admissible in the guilt phase of trial and whether a unitary trial would unfairly prejudice the defendant. The court must order a bifurcated trial if the evidence supporting an aggravated sentence includes evidence otherwise inadmissible at the guilt phase of the trial or if that evidence would unfairly prejudice the defendant in the guilt phase.

(c) If the court orders a unitary trial, the court may order separate final arguments on the issues of guilt and the aggravated sentence.

Adopted Feb. 26, 1975, eff. July 1, 1975. Revised Dec. 13, 1989. Amended Dec. 11, 1990; May 9, 1994; Aug. 17, 2006, eff. Oct. 1, 2006; Oct. 27, 2009, eff. Jan. 1, 2010.

Comment—Rule 11

See comment following Rule 11.11.

Historical Notes

The order of the Minnesota Supreme Court [C1–84–2137] dated December 13, 1989, provides in part that "(t)hese amended Rules of Criminal Procedure shall govern all criminal actions commenced or arrests made after 12 o'clock midnight January 1, 1990, except amendments to 8.04, 11.07, and 19.04, subd. 5, shall govern all criminal actions commenced or arrests made after 12 o'clock midnight January 1, 1991."

The order of the Minnesota Supreme Court [C1–84–2137] dated December 11, 1990, provides in part that "(t)his amendment to the Rules of Criminal Procedure shall govern all criminal actions commenced or arrests made after 12 o'clock midnight January 1, 1991."

The order of the Minnesota Supreme Court [C1–84–2137] dated May 9, 1994, provides in part that "(t)hese amendments to the Rules of Criminal Procedure shall govern all criminal actions commenced or arrests made after 12 o'clock midnight July 1, 1994, except that the amendments in the first sentence of the third paragraph in Rule 2.01 shall govern all criminal actions commenced or arrests made after 12 o'clock midnight January 1, 1995."

Rule 11.05. Pretrial Conference

The Omnibus Hearing may also include a pretrial conference to determine whether the case can be resolved before trial.

Adopted Oct. 27, 2009, eff. Jan. 1, 2010.

Comment—Rule 11

See comment following Rule 11.11.

Historical Notes

Former Rule: Former Rule 11.05 related to the amendment of a complaint.

Rule 11.06. Continuances

The court may continue the hearing or any part of the hearing for good cause related to the case.

Former Rule 11.07 adopted Feb. 26, 1975, eff. July 1, 1975. Revised Dec. 13, 1989. Amended Nov. 29, 1990. Renumbered Rule 11.06 and amended Oct. 27, 2009, eff. Jan. 1, 2010.

Comment—Rule 11

See comment following Rule 11.11.

Historical Notes

Former Rule: Former Rule 11.06 related to pleas. See, now, Rules Crim.Proc., Rule 11.08.

Rule 11.07. Determination of Issues

The court must make findings and determinations on the omnibus issues in writing or on the record within 7 business days of the Omnibus Hearing.

Adopted Oct. 27, 2009, eff. Jan. 1, 2010.

Comment—Rule 11

See comment following Rule 11.11.

Historical Notes

Former Rule: Former Rule 11.07 related to continuances. See, now, generally, Rules Crim.Proc., Rule 11.06.

Rule 11.08. Pleas

(a) The defendant may enter a plea to the charged offense or to a lesser included offense as permitted in Rule 15 anytime after the commencement of the Omnibus Hearing.

(b) Entry of a plea other than guilty does not waive any jurisdictional or other issue raised for determination in the Omnibus Hearing.

Former Rules 11.06, 11.10 adopted Feb. 26, 1975, eff. July 1, 1975. Revised Dec. 13, 1989. Amended May 9, 1994; Aug. 21, 1998, eff. Jan. 1, 1999. Renumbered Rule 11.08 and amended Oct. 27, 2009, eff. Jan. 1, 2010.

Comment—Rule 11

See comment following Rule 11.11.

Historical Notes

Former Rule: Former Rule 11.08 related to the record of the proceedings. See, now, Rules Crim.Proc., Rule 11.10.

Rule 11.09. Trial Date

(a) If the defendant enters a plea other than guilty, a trial date must be set.

(b) A defendant must be tried as soon as possible after entry of a plea other than guilty. On demand of any party the trial must start within 60 days of the demand unless the court finds good cause for a later trial date. The time period begins on the date of the plea other than guilty.

Unless exigent circumstances exist, if trial does not start within 120 days from the date the plea other than guilty is entered and the demand is made, the defendant must be released under any nonmonetary conditions the court orders under Rule 6.01, subd. 1.

Former Rule 11.10 adopted Feb. 26, 1975, eff. July 1, 1975. Revised Dec. 13, 1989. Amended May 9, 1994; Aug. 21, 1998, eff. Jan. 1, 1999. Renumbered Rule 11.09 and amended Oct. 27, 2009, eff. Jan. 1, 2010.

Comment—Rule 11

See comment following Rule 11.11.

Historical Notes

Former Rule: Former Rule 11.09, which related to district court review of omnibus hearings in felony and gross misdemeanor cases, was deleted effective August 1, 1987.

Rule 11.10. Record

Subd. 1. Record. A verbatim record must be made.

Subd. 2. Transcript. When a party has timely requested a transcript of the proceedings from the court reporter, it must be provided on the following conditions:

(a) If the defendant has ordered the transcript, the cost must be prepaid unless the public defender or assigned counsel represents the defendant, or the defendant makes a sufficient affidavit of inability to pay or secure the costs and the court orders that the defendant be supplied with the transcript at the expense of the appropriate governmental unit.

(b) The transcript must be provided to the prosecutor without prepayment.

(c) Transcripts provided to counsel must be filed with the court.

(d) A party offering video or audio evidence may also provide a transcript of the exhibit, which becomes part of the record.

Subd. 3. Papers and Exhibits. All papers and exhibits must be filed with the court administrator. On motion, any exhibit may be returned to the offering party.

Former Rule 11.08 adopted Feb. 26, 1975, eff. July 1, 1975. Revised Dec. 13, 1989. Amended May 9, 1994; Aug. 21, 1998, eff. Jan. 1, 1999. Renumbered Rule 11.10 and amended Oct. 27, 2009, eff. Jan. 1, 2010.

Comment—Rule 11

See comment following Rule 11.11.

Historical Notes

Former Rule: Former Rule 11.10 related to pleas and trial dates. See, now, Rules Crim.Proc., Rules 11.08 and 11.09.

Rule 11.11. Deleted Oct. 27, 2009, eff. Jan. 1, 2010

Comment—Rule 11

If a probable cause motion is made, the court must base its probable cause determination upon the evidence set forth in Rule 18.05, subd. 1. In State v. Florence, 306 Minn. 442, 446, 239 N.W.2d 892, 896 (1976), the Supreme Court discussed the type of evidence that may be presented and considered on a motion to dismiss the complaint for lack of probable cause. Nothing in that case or in the rule prohibits a defendant from calling any witness to testify for the purpose of showing an absence of probable cause. In determining whether to dismiss a complaint under Rule 11.04 for lack of probable cause, the trial court is not simply reassessing whether or not probable cause existed to warrant the arrest. Rather, under Florence, the trial court must determine based upon the facts disclosed by the record whether it is fair and reasonable to require the defendant to stand trial.

By the Omnibus Hearing, the prosecution will have given the Rasmussen and Spreigl notices; the Rasmussen hearing will have been either waived or demanded; the discovery required without order of court will have been completed; and pretrial motions will have been served. (In the case of an indictment the pre-trial motions should include any motion to suppress based on the disclosures contained in the Rasmussen notice under Rule 19.04, subd. 6).

The purpose of the Omnibus Hearing is to avoid a multiplicity of court appearances on these issues with a duplication of evidence and to combine all of the issues that can be disposed of without trial into one appearance. Early resolution of motions provides for more efficient handling of criminal cases at subsequent stages. This includes suppression motions, evidentiary motions, and nonevidentiary motions such as motions to disclose the identity of an informant or to consolidate or sever trials or codefendants. Early resolution of these motions also helps to focus the lawyers' attention on a smaller number of witnesses, including law enforcement officers and victims of crimes. When such motions are resolved early, uncertainty with respect to many significant issues in a case are removed. This early resolution of motions also permits timely and meaningful pretrial dispositional conferences at which time the parties can engage in significant plea agreement discussions. Setting a firm trial date and commencing a trial on that date are also important factors in minimizing delays.

By Rule 11.02 the court must also hear all motions made by the parties under Rule 10. A failure to raise known issues at the Omnibus Hearing waives that issue except lack of jurisdiction or failure of the complaint or indictment to state an offense, unless the court grants an exception to the waiver (Rule 10.03).

Rule 11.02 specifically permits a motion to dismiss a complaint for lack of probable cause, but does not permit a motion to dismiss an indictment upon this ground.

The court must also on its initiative under Rule 11.02 ascertain and hear any other issues that can be heard and disposed of before trial and any other matters that would promote a fair and expeditious trial. This would include requests or issues arising respecting discovery (Rule 9), evidentiary issues arising from the Spreigl notice (Rules 7.02, 19.04, subd. 6), or other evidentiary issues, and expressly permits a pretrial dispositional conference if the court considers it necessary. See Fed. R. Crim. P. 17.1. If such resolution is not possible, the conference may be used to determine the nature of the case so that further hearings or trial may be scheduled as appropriate. The use of such dispositional conferences is commendable and highly recommended by the Advisory Committee. To assure that the pretrial dispositional conference portion of the Omnibus Hearing is meaningful, trial courts should insist on timely discovery by the parties before the date of the Omnibus Hearing as required by Rule 9.01, subd. 1.

If the prosecutor has given notice under Rules 7.03 or 19.04, subd. 6(3) of intent to seek an aggravated sentence, Rule 11.04 requires the court to have a hearing to determine any pretrial issues that need to be resolved in connection with that request. This could include issues as to the timeliness of the notice under Rules 7.03 or 19.04, subd. 6. The court must determine whether the proposed grounds legally support an aggravated sentence and whether or not the proffered evidence is sufficient to proceed to trial. The rule does not provide a standard for determining insufficiency of the evidence claims and that is left to case law development. If the aggravated sentence claim will be presented to a jury, the court must also decide whether the evidence will be presented in a unitary or a bifurcated trial and the rule provides the standards for making that determination. Even if a unitary trial is ordered for the presentation of evidence, the rule recognizes that presentation of argument on an aggravated sentence during the guilt phase of the proceedings may unduly prejudice a defendant. The rule therefore allows the court to order separate final arguments on the aggravated sentence issue, if necessary, after the jury renders its verdict on the issue of guilt.

Under State v. Wenberg, 289 N.W.2d 503, 504–05 (Minn. 1980), if the prosecutor intends to impeach the defendant or any defense witness with evidence of prior convictions, the prosecutor must request a pretrial hearing on the admissibility of such evidence. If possible this issue should be heard at the Omnibus Hearing. See Rules 9.01, subd. 1(5) and 9.02, subd. 1(8) as to the reciprocal duties of the prosecutor and defense counsel to disclose the criminal records of the defendant and any defense witnesses. As to the standards for determining the admissibility of the impeachment evidence, see Rule 609 of the Minnesota Rules of Evidence, State v. Jones, 271 N.W.2d 534 (Minn. 1978) and State v. Brouillette, 286 N.W.2d 702 (Minn. 1979).

By Rule 11.06 the Omnibus Hearing or any part may be continued if necessary to dispose of the issues presented. At any conference portion of an Omnibus Hearing it is permissible under Rule 11.06 to continue the evidence suppression portion of the Omnibus Hearing until the day of trial if the court determines that resolution of the evidentiary issues would not dispose of the case. Such a continuance would be "for good cause related to the case" under Rule 11.06, and under that rule the court could enter an order continuing both the Omnibus Hearing and the court's decision on the evidentiary issues until the day of trial. Other grounds may also support a continuance as long as the court finds that the continuance is justified under the rule. However, the court should not as a general rule or practice bifurcate the Omnibus Hearing or delay the hearing or any part of it until the day of trial when that is not justified by the circumstances of the case. To do so violates the purpose of these rules. See Minn. Stat. § 611A.033 regarding the prosecutor's duties under the Victim's Rights Act to make reasonable efforts to provide advance notice of any change in the schedule of court proceedings. This would include the Omnibus Hearing as well as trial or any other hearing.

Rule 11.07 requires appropriate findings for the determinations made on the Omnibus Hearing issues.

The intent of the Omnibus Hearing rule is that all issues that can be determined before trial must be heard at the Omnibus Hearing and decided before trial. Consequently, when the Omnibus Hearing is held before a judge other than the trial judge, the trial judge, except in extraordinary circumstances will adhere to the findings and determinations of the Omnibus Hearing judge. See State v. Coe, 298 N.W.2d 770, 771–72 (Minn. 1980) and State v. Hamling, 314 N.W.2d 224, 225 (Minn. 1982) (where this issue was discussed, but not decided).

Rule 11.08 further provides that the defendant may enter a plea including a not guilty plea at the first Omnibus Hearing appearance. This assures that if a defendant wishes to demand a speedy trial under Rule 11.09, the running of the time limit for that will not be delayed by continuing the plea until the continued Omnibus Hearing. If the trial date is continued, see Minn. Stat. § 611A.033 regarding the prosecutor's duties under the Victim's Rights Act to make reasonable efforts to provide advance notice of the continuance.

For good cause the trial may be postponed beyond the 60–day time limit upon request of the prosecutor or the defendant or upon the court's initiative. Good cause for the delay does not include court calendar congestion unless exceptional circumstances exist. See McIntosh v. Davis, 441 N.W.2d 115, 120 (Minn. 1989). Even if good cause exists for postponing the trial beyond the 60–day time limit, the defendant, except in exigent circumstances, must be released, subject to such nonmonetary release conditions as may be required by the court under Rule 6.02, subd. 1, if trial has not yet commenced within 120 days after the demand is made and the not guilty plea entered. Other sanctions for violation of these speedy trial provisions are left to case law. See State v. Kasper, 411 N.W.2d 182 (Minn. 1987) and State v. Friberg, 435 N.W.2d 509 (Minn. 1989).

Rule 11.09 does not attempt to set arbitrary time limits (other than those resulting from the demand), because they would have to be circumscribed by numerous specific exclusions (See ABA Standards, Speedy Trial, 2.3 (Approved Draft, 1968)) which are covered in any event by the more general terms of the rule. See ABA Standards, Speedy Trial, 4.1, Pre–Trial Release, 5.10 (Approved Drafts, 1968) in which the consequences are set forth.

The consequences and the time limits beyond which a defendant is considered to have been denied the constitutional right to a speedy trial are left to judicial decision. See Barker v. Wingo, 407 U.S. 514, 519–36 (1972). The constitutional right to a speedy trial is triggered not when the plea is entered but when a charge is issued or an arrest is made. State v. Jones, 392 N.W.2d 224, 235 (Minn. 1986). The existence or absence of the demand under Rule 11.09 provides a factor that may be taken into account in determining whether the defendant has been unconstitutionally denied a speedy trial. See Barker v. Wingo, supra.

Historical Notes

Former Rule: Former Rule 11.11 related to the exclusion of witnesses. See, now, Rules Crim.Proc., Rule 11.03(b).

RULE 12. PRETRIAL CONFERENCE AND EVIDENTIARY HEARING IN MISDEMEANOR CASES

Rule 12.01. Pretrial Conference

In misdemeanor cases, the court may schedule a pretrial conference. If the court does not hold a pretrial conference, pretrial motions and other issues must be heard immediately before trial.

Adopted Feb. 26, 1975, eff. July 1, 1975. Revised Dec. 13, 1989. Amended Oct. 27, 2009, eff. Jan. 1, 2010.

Comment—Rule 12

See comment following Rule 12.08.

Rule 12.02. Motions

The court must hear and determine all motions made by the parties and receive evidence offered in support of or opposition to the motion. A party may cross-examine any witness called by any other party.

Adopted Feb. 26, 1975, eff. July 1, 1975. Revised Dec. 13, 1989. Amended Oct. 27, 2009, eff. Jan. 1, 2010.

Comment—Rule 12

See comment following Rule 12.08.

Rule 12.03. Other Issues

The court must hear and determine any constitutional, evidentiary, procedural and other issues that may be resolved before trial and resolve other matters that promote a fair and expeditious trial. The court may continue the hearing for that purpose.

Adopted Feb. 26, 1975, eff. July 1, 1975. Revised Dec. 13, 1989. Amended Oct. 27, 2009, eff. Jan. 1, 2010.

Comment—Rule 12

See comment following Rule 12.08.

Rule 12.04. Hearing on Evidentiary Issues

Subd. 1. Evidence and Identification Procedures. The court must hear and determine any issues specified in Rule 7.01 if the defendant or prosecutor demands a hearing.

Subd. 2. Additional Offenses. If the prosecutor gives notice under Rule 7.02 of additional offenses and the defendant moves for a hearing, the court must determine the admissibility of that evidence under Rule 404(b) of the Minnesota Rules of Evidence, and also determine whether clear and convincing evidence exists that the defendant committed the additional offenses.

Subd. 3. Time. When a trial is to be heard by a jury, the evidentiary hearing must be held separately from the jury trial. When a trial is to be heard by the court, the evidentiary hearing may be held separately or as part of the court trial. A separate evidentiary hearing must be held immediately before trial unless the court finds good cause to otherwise order.

Adopted Feb. 26, 1975, eff. July 1, 1975. Revised Dec. 13, 1989. Amended Aug. 21, 1998, eff. Jan. 1, 1999; Oct. 27, 2009, eff. Jan. 1, 2010.

Comment—Rule 12

See comment following Rule 12.08.

Rule 12.05. Amended Complaint

The complaint, if any, may be amended at the pretrial conference as prescribed by these rules.

Adopted Feb. 26, 1975, eff. July 1, 1975. Revised Dec. 13, 1989. Amended Oct. 27, 2009, eff. Jan. 1, 2010.

Comment—Rule 12

See comment following Rule 12.08.

Rule 12.06. Pleas

The defendant may enter a guilty plea to the charged offense or a different offense, as permitted in Rule 15.08.

Adopted Feb. 26, 1975, eff. July 1, 1975. Revised Dec. 13, 1989. Amended Oct. 27, 2009, eff. Jan. 1, 2010.

Comment—Rule 12

See comment following Rule 12.08.

Rule 12.07. Continuances and Determination of Issues

The pretrial conference may be continued to take testimony or for other good cause, and may be continued to the day of trial to determine issues and motions.

All motions and issues, including evidentiary issues, must be decided before trial unless otherwise agreed to by the parties. Decisions must be in writing or on the record.

Adopted Feb. 26, 1975, eff. July 1, 1975. Revised Dec. 13, 1989. Amended Oct. 27, 2009, eff. Jan. 1, 2010.

Comment—Rule 12

See comment following Rule 12.08.

Rule 12.08. Record

Subd. 1. Record. A verbatim record of the proceedings must be made unless waived by the parties.

Subd. 2. Audio and Video Evidence. If any party offers video or audio evidence, that party may provide a transcript of the evidence, which will be made a part of the record.

Subd. 3. Transcript and Filing. Rule 11.10, subds. 2 and 3 govern filings and obtaining a transcript.

Adopted Feb. 26, 1975, eff. July 1, 1975. Revised Dec. 13, 1989. Amended Oct. 27, 2009, eff. Jan. 1, 2010.

Comment—Rule 12

This rule permits the court to order a pre-trial conference. Any Rasmussen issues will ordinarily be heard immediately before trial. At the pretrial conference the court will consider the same matters for which an Omnibus Hearing must be held in felony and gross misdemeanor cases (see Rule 11).

Rule 12.08, subd. 2, permits any party offering video or audio evidence to also provide to the court a transcript of the evidence. This rule does not govern whether any such transcript is admissible as evidence in the case. That issue is governed by Article 10 of the Minnesota Rules of Evidence. However, upon an appeal of the proceedings, the transcript of the exhibit will be part of the record if the other party stipulated to the accuracy of the tape transcript as provided in Rule 28.02, subd. 9.

Rule 12.07 provides for the continuation of the pretrial conference if necessary to dispose of the issues presented. For the purpose of taking testimony or other good cause the court may continue the determination of issues or motions until the day of trial. Such a continuance, where testimony is required, will save witnesses an additional court appearance where those witnesses would be testifying at trial.

RULE 13. ARRAIGNMENT IN FELONY AND GROSS MISDEMEANOR CASES [Deleted Oct. 27, 2009, eff. Jan. 1, 2010]

Rules 13.01 to 13.05. Deleted Oct. 27, 2009, eff. Jan. 1, 2010

Historical Notes

Deleted Rules 13.01 to 13.05 related to arraignments in felony and gross misdemeanor cases. For the subject matter of deleted Rule 13.01, which required the arraignment to be conducted in open court, and deleted Rule 13.05, which related to the record of the proceedings, see Rules Crim.Proc., Rules 8.02 and 8.05, respectively.

RULE 14. PLEAS

Rule 14.01. Pleas Permitted

A defendant may plead:

(a) Guilty.

(b) Not guilty.

(c) Not guilty by reason of mental illness or mental deficiency.

(d) Double jeopardy or prosecution barred by Minn. Stat. § 609.035. Either may be plead with or without the plea of not guilty.

Adopted Feb. 26, 1975, eff. July 1, 1975. Revised Dec. 13, 1989. Amended Oct. 27, 2009, eff. Jan. 1, 2010.

Comments—Rule 14

See comment following Rule 14.03.

Rule 14.02. Who May Plead

Subd. 1. Felony Charges. A plea in cases involving felony charges must be made by an individual defendant in person on the record.

Subd. 2. Gross Misdemeanor and Misdemeanor Charges. A plea in cases involving misdemeanor or gross misdemeanor charges may be made by an individual defendant either in person on the record, by ITV, or by petition to plead guilty under Rule 15.03, subd. 2. The plea may be entered by counsel or by ITV if the court is satisfied that the defendant has knowingly and voluntarily waived the right to be present.

Subd. 3. Corporate Defendant. A plea by a corporate defendant must be made by counsel or an authorized corporate officer. The plea may be made on the record or in writing.

Subd. 4. Defendant's Refusal to Plead. If the defendant refuses to plead, or if the court refuses to accept a plea of guilty, the court must proceed as if the defendant had entered a plea of not guilty.

Subd. 5. Defendant Corporation's Failure to Appear. If a defendant corporation fails to appear, the court may enter judgment of conviction and impose sentence as may be appropriate on proof of commission of the charged offense.

Adopted Feb. 26, 1975, eff. July 1, 1975. Revised Dec. 13, 1989. Amended Aug. 21, 1998, eff. Jan. 1, 1999; Nov. 19, 2007, eff. Jan. 1, 2008; Oct. 27, 2009, eff. Jan. 1, 2010; June 5, 2012, eff. Aug. 1, 2012.

Comments—Rule 14

See comment following Rule 14.03.

Historical Notes

The order of the Minnesota Supreme Court [ADM 10-8049] dated June 5, 2012, provided in part that the amendments "be effective August 1, 2012, and shall apply to all actions or proceedings pending on or commenced on or after the effective date."

Rule 14.03. Timing of Pleas

(a) In misdemeanor cases, the defendant may enter any plea, including a guilty plea, as early as the Rule 5 hearing.

(b) In gross misdemeanor cases, the defendant may plead guilty at the Rule 5 hearing if the defendant has had an opportunity to consult with counsel; otherwise entry of a guilty plea must await the Rule 8 or Omnibus Hearing. The defendant cannot enter any other plea until the Omnibus Hearing.

(c) In felony cases, a defendant may plead guilty as early as the Rule 8 hearing. The defendant cannot enter any other plea until the Omnibus Hearing.

(d) A defendant may also appear in court at proceedings after those listed above to plead guilty to the charged offense. To schedule an appearance, the defendant must file a written request with the court indicating the offense to which the defendant wishes to plead guilty. The court must schedule a hearing within 14 days after the request is filed. The court must then notify the defendant and the prosecutor of the time and place of the hearing.

Adopted March 31, 1977. Revised Dec. 13, 1989. Amended Oct. 27, 2009, eff. Jan. 1, 2010.

Comment—Rule 14

Notice of a defense or defenses under Rule 9.02, subd. 1(5) does not obviate the necessity for a plea under Rule 14.

Rule 20.02, subds. 6(2) and 7, governing the procedure upon the defense of mental illness or mental deficiency, contemplate that a defendant shall plead both not guilty and not guilty by reason of mental illness or deficiency when intending to put in issue both guilt on the elements of the offense charged and mental responsibility by reason of mental illness or deficiency.

A conditional plea of guilty may not be entered when the defendant reserves the right to appeal the denial of a motion to suppress evidence or any other pretrial order. State v. Lothenbach, 296 N.W.2d 854 (Minn. 1980). One option, as authorized by Rule 26.01 subd. 3, is to plead not guilty, stipulate the facts, waive the jury trial, and, if there is a finding of guilty, appeal the judgment of conviction. Id. A guilty plea also waives any appellate challenge to an order certifying the defendant as an adult. Waynewood v. State, 552 N.W.2d 718 (Minn. 1996).

In misdemeanor and gross misdemeanor cases, by Rule 14.02, subd. 2, before accepting such a plea through counsel, the court should determine whether counsel has advised the defendant of the rights and information contained in Rule 15.02. See also Rule 26.03, subd. 1(3) (defendant's presence at trial and sentencing) and Rule 27.03, subd. 2 (defendant's presence at sentencing).

RULE 15. GUILTY PLEA PROCEDURES

Rule 15.01. Felony Cases

Subdivision 1. Guilty Plea. Before the judge accepts a guilty plea, the defendant must be sworn and questioned by the judge with the assistance of counsel as to the following:

1. Name, age, date and place of birth, and whether the defendant is disabled in communication and, if so, whether a qualified interpreter has been provided for the defendant under Rule 8 of the General Rules of Practice for the District Courts.

2. Whether the defendant understands that the crime charged is (name of offense) committed on or about (month) (day) (year) in ________ County, Minnesota.

3. Whether the defendant understands the defendant is pleading guilty to the offense of (name of offense) committed on or about (month) (day) (year) in ________ County, Minnesota, and understands the terms of the plea agreement, if any (state the terms with specificity).

4. The judge must ensure:

a. The defendant had sufficient time to discuss the case with defense counsel.

b. The defendant is satisfied that defense counsel is fully informed as to the facts of the case, and defense counsel represented the defendant's interests and fully advised the defendant.

c. Neither the defendant nor any other person has been given any promises other than those in the plea agreement, or been threatened by anyone, to get the defendant to plead guilty.

d. The defendant had an opportunity to ask questions of the court or make a statement before stating the facts of the crime.

5. The judge must determine whether the defendant:

a. is under the influence of drugs or intoxicating liquor;

b. has a mental disability; or

c. is undergoing medical or psychiatric treatment.

6. The judge must also ensure defense counsel has told the defendant and the defendant understands:

a. Upon a plea of not guilty, there is a right to a trial by jury and a finding of guilty is not possible unless all jurors agree.

b. There will not be a trial by either a jury or a judge without a jury if the defendant pleads guilty.

c. By pleading guilty the defendant waives the right to a trial by a jury or a judge on the issue of guilt.

d. If the defendant pleads not guilty and has a trial by jury or judge, the defendant will be presumed to be innocent until proven guilty beyond a reasonable doubt.

e. If the defendant pleads not guilty and has a trial, the prosecutor will be required to have the witnesses testify in open court in the defendant's presence, and the defendant will have the right, through defense counsel, to question these witnesses.

f. The defendant waives the right to have witnesses testify in the defendant's presence in court and be questioned by defense counsel.

g. If the defendant pleads not guilty and has a trial, the defendant will be entitled to require any defense witnesses to appear and testify.

h. The defendant waives the right to subpoena witnesses.

i. The maximum penalty the judge could impose for the crime charged (taking into consideration any prior convictions) is imprisonment for ___ months or ___ years.

j. If a minimum sentence is required by statute, the judge may impose a sentence of imprisonment of not less than ___ months for the crime charged.

k. For felony driving while impaired offenses and most sex offenses, a mandatory period of conditional release will be imposed to follow any executed prison sentence, and violating the terms of that conditional release may increase the time the defendant serves in prison.

l. If the defendant is not a citizen of the United States, a guilty plea may result in deportation, exclusion from admission to the United States, or denial of naturalization as a United States citizen.

m. The prosecutor is seeking an aggravated sentence (if applicable).

n. If the court does not approve the plea agreement, the defendant has an absolute right to withdraw the guilty plea and have a trial.

o. If the plea of guilty is not accepted by the court, or is withdrawn by the defendant, or is vacated on appeal or other review, the defendant will stand trial on the original charge(s), including any charges dismissed under the plea agreement, and the prosecutor may proceed just as if there had never been an agreement.

p. If the defendant pleads not guilty and has a jury trial, the defendant can decide to testify at trial, but if the defendant decided not to testify, neither the prosecutor nor the judge could comment to the jury about the failure to testify.

q. The defendant waives the right to testify, and agrees to tell the court about the facts of the crime.

r. The defendant with knowledge and understanding of all these rights still wishes to enter a plea of guilty or instead wishes to plead not guilty.

7. The judge must inquire whether the defendant makes any claim of innocence.

8. The defendant must state the factual basis for the plea.

Subd. 2. Aggravated Sentence. Before the judge accepts an admission of facts in support of an aggravated sentence, the defendant must be sworn and questioned by the judge with the assistance of defense counsel. This must be done separately from the inquiry that is required by subdivision 1. The inquiry must include whether the defendant:

1. Understands that the prosecutor is seeking a sentence greater than the presumptive guideline sentence or an aggravated sentence.

2. Understands that the presumptive guideline sentence for the crime to which the defendant has pled guilty or otherwise has been found guilty is _________, and that the defendant could not be given an aggravated sentence greater than the presumptive guideline sentence unless the prosecutor proves facts in support of an aggravated sentence beyond a reasonable doubt.

3. Understands that the sentence in this case will be an aggravated sentence of _________, or will be left to the judge to decide.

4. Has had sufficient time to discuss this aggravated sentence with defense counsel.

5. Is satisfied that defense counsel is fully informed as to the facts supporting an aggravated sentence and has represented defendant's interests and fully advised the defendant.

6. The judge must also ensure defense counsel has told the defendant and defendant understands that:

a. Even though the defendant has pled guilty to or has otherwise been found guilty of the crime of _________, defendant may contest the facts alleged by the prosecutor that would support an aggravated sentence.

b. If defendant contests the facts alleged in support of an aggravated sentence, the defendant has a right to a trial by a jury or a judge to determine whether the facts have been proven, and a finding that the facts are proven is not possible unless all jurors agree.

c. The defendant waives the right to a trial by a jury or a judge of the facts in support of an aggravated sentence.

d. At trial before a jury or a judge, the defendant would be presumed not to be subject to an aggravated sentence, and the court could not impose an aggravated sentence unless the facts in support of the aggravated sentence are proven beyond a reasonable doubt.

e. If the defendant contests the facts alleged in support of an aggravated sentence and has a trial by a jury or a judge, the prosecutor will be required to have the prosecution witnesses testify in open court in the defendant's presence, and the defendant will have the right, through defense counsel, to question these witnesses.

f. The defendant waives the right to have witnesses testify in the defendant's presence and be questioned by defense counsel.

g. If the defendant contests the facts alleged in support of an aggravated sentence and has a trial by a jury or a judge, the defendant will be entitled to require any defense witnesses to appear and testify.

h. The defendant waives the right to subpoena witnesses.

i. If the defendant contests the facts in support of an aggravated sentence and has a trial by a jury or a judge, the defendant can decide to testify if the defendant wishes, but if the defendant decides not to testify, neither the prosecutor nor the judge could comment to the jury about the failure to testify.

j. The defendant waives the right to remain silent and agrees to tell the court about the facts supporting an aggravated sentence.

k. With knowledge and understanding of these rights, the defendant still wants to admit the facts in support of an aggravated sentence or instead wants to contest these facts and have a trial by a jury or a judge.

7. The defendant must state the factual basis for an aggravated sentence.

Adopted Feb. 26, 1975, eff. July 1, 1975. Revised Dec. 13, 1989. Amended May 9, 1994; Aug. 21, 1998, eff. Jan. 1, 1999; Dec. 23, 2002, eff. Feb. 1, 2003; Aug. 17, 2006, eff. Oct. 1, 2006; Oct. 27, 2009, eff. Jan. 1, 2010; June 5, 2012, eff. Aug. 1, 2012.

Comments—Rule 15

See comment after appendices following Rule 15.11.

Historical Notes

The order of the Minnesota Supreme Court [ADM 10–8049] dated June 5, 2012, provided in part that the amendments "be effective August 1, 2012, and shall apply to all actions or proceedings pending on or commenced on or after the effective date."

Rule 15.02. Gross Misdemeanor and Misdemeanor Cases

Subd. 1. Guilty Plea. Before the court accepts a plea of guilty to any misdemeanor or gross misdemeanor offense punishable upon conviction by incarceration, the plea agreement must be explained in open court. The defendant must then be questioned by the court or counsel as to whether the defendant:

1. Understands that the crime charged is (name the offense) committed on or about (Month) (Day) (Year) _________ in County, Minnesota, and that the defendant is pleading guilty to the crime of (name of offense) committed on or about (Month) (Day) (Year) in _________ County, Minnesota.

2. Understands that the maximum possible sentence is 90 days imprisonment for a misdemeanor and 1 year imprisonment for a gross misdemeanor, and a fine in the amount allowed by applicable law. (Under

the applicable law, if the maximum sentence is less, it should be so stated.)

3. Understands that, if the defendant is not a citizen of the United States, a guilty plea may result in deportation, exclusion from admission to the United States, or denial of naturalization as a United States citizen.

4. Understands there is a right to the assistance of counsel at every stage of the proceedings and that defense counsel will be appointed for a defendant unable to afford counsel.

5. Understands and waives the right to:

(a) trial by the court or a jury and that a finding of guilty is not possible in a jury trial unless all jurors agree;

(b) confront and cross-examine all prosecution witnesses;

(c) subpoena and present defense witnesses;

(d) testify or remain silent at trial or at any other time;

(e) be presumed innocent and that the prosecutor must prove the case beyond a reasonable doubt; and

(f) a pretrial hearing to contest the admissibility at trial of any confessions or admissions or of any evidence obtained from a search and seizure.

6. Understands the nature of the offense or offenses charged.

7. Believes that what the defendant did constitutes the offense to which the defendant is pleading guilty.

Subd. 2. Factual Basis. After explaining the defendant's rights, the judge, with the assistance of counsel, must question the defendant to determine a factual basis for all elements of the offense to which the defendant is pleading guilty.

Subd. 3. Guilty Plea at First Appearance. If the guilty plea is entered at the defendant's first appearance in court, the statement as to the defendant's rights required by Rule 5.01 may be combined with the questioning required above prior to entry of a guilty plea.

Adopted Feb. 26, 1975, eff. July 1, 1975. Revised Dec. 13, 1989. Amended Aug. 21, 1998, eff. Jan. 1, 1999; Oct. 27, 2009, eff. Jan. 1, 2010; June 5, 2012, eff. Aug. 1, 2012.

Comments—Rule 15

See comment after appendices following Rule 15.11.

Historical Notes

The order of the Minnesota Supreme Court [ADM 10–8049] dated June 5, 2012, provided in part that the amendments "be effective August 1, 2012, and shall apply to all actions or proceedings pending on or commenced on or after the effective date."

Rule 15.03. Alternative Methods in Misdemeanor and Gross Misdemeanor Cases

Subd. 1. Group Warnings. The judge may advise a number of defendants at once as to their constitutional rights as specified in Rule 15.02, subd. 1, questions 2 through 5 above, and as to the consequences of a plea.

The court must first determine whether any defendant is disabled in communication. If so, the court must provide the services of a qualified interpreter to that defendant and should provide the warnings contemplated by this rule to that defendant individually. The judge's statement in a group warning must be recorded and each defendant when called before the court must be asked whether the defendant heard and understood the statement. The defendant must then be questioned on the record as to the remaining matters specified in Rule 15.02.

Subd. 2. Petition to Plead Guilty. As an alternative to the defendant personally appearing in court, the defendant or defense counsel may file with the court a petition to plead guilty. The petition must be signed by the defendant indicating that the defendant is pleading guilty to the specified misdemeanor or gross misdemeanor offense with the understanding and knowledge required of defendants personally entering a guilty plea under Rule 15.02.

Adopted Feb. 26, 1975, eff. July 1, 1975. Revised Dec. 13, 1989. Amended May 9, 1994; Oct. 27, 2009, eff. Jan. 1, 2010; June 5, 2012, eff. Aug. 1, 2012.

Comments—Rule 15

See comment after appendices following Rule 15.11.

Historical Notes

The order of the Minnesota Supreme Court [ADM 10–8049] dated June 5, 2012, provided in part that the amendments "be effective August 1, 2012, and shall apply to all actions or proceedings pending on or commenced on or after the effective date."

Rule 15.04. Plea Discussions and Agreements

Subd. 1. Propriety of Plea Discussions and Agreements. The prosecutor must engage in plea discussions and reach a plea agreement with the defendant only through defense counsel unless the defendant is pro se.

Subd. 2. Relationship Between Defense Counsel and Defendant. Defense counsel must enter into a plea agreement only with the consent of the defendant and must ensure that the decision to enter a plea of guilty is made by the defendant.

Subd. 3. Responsibilities of the Trial Court Judge.

(1) When a plea is entered and the defendant questioned, the trial court judge must reject or accept the plea of guilty on the terms of the plea agreement. The court may postpone its acceptance or rejection until it has received the results of a pre-sentence

investigation. If the court rejects the plea agreement, it must advise the parties in open court and then call upon the defendant to either affirm or withdraw the plea.

(2) The judge may accept a plea agreement of the parties when the interest of justice would be served. Among the considerations appropriate in determining whether acceptance should be given are that:

(a) defendant by pleading guilty has aided in ensuring the prompt and certain application of correctional measures;

(b) defendant has acknowledged guilt and shown a willingness to assume responsibility for the criminal conduct;

(c) concessions will make possible the application of alternative correctional measures, which are better adapted to achieving rehabilitative, protective, deterrent or other purposes of correctional treatment, or will prevent undue harm to the defendant;

(d) defendant has made trial unnecessary when good reasons exist for not having a trial;

(e) defendant has given or offered cooperation, which has resulted or may result in the successful prosecution of other offenders engaged in serious criminal conduct;

(f) defendant by pleading has aided in avoiding delay in the disposition of other cases and has contributed to the efficient administration of criminal justice.

Adopted Feb. 26, 1975, eff. July 1, 1975. Revised Dec. 13, 1989. Amended Oct. 27, 2009, eff. Jan. 1, 2010.

Comments—Rule 15

See comment after appendices following Rule 15.11.

Rule 15.05. Plea Withdrawal

Subd. 1. To Correct Manifest Injustice. At any time the court must allow a defendant to withdraw a guilty plea upon a timely motion and proof to the satisfaction of the court that withdrawal is necessary to correct a manifest injustice. Such a motion is not barred solely because it is made after sentencing. If a defendant is allowed to withdraw a plea after sentencing, the court must set aside the judgment and the plea.

Subd. 2. Before Sentence. In its discretion the court may allow the defendant to withdraw a plea at any time before sentence if it is fair and just to do so. The court must give due consideration to the reasons advanced by the defendant in support of the motion and any prejudice the granting of the motion would cause the prosecution by reason of actions taken in reliance upon the defendant's plea.

Subd. 3. Withdrawal of Guilty Plea Without Asserting Innocence. The defendant may move to withdraw a plea of guilty without an assertion of not guilty of the charge to which the plea was entered.

Adopted Feb. 26, 1975, eff. July 1, 1975. Revised Dec. 13, 1989. Amended Oct. 27, 2009, eff. Jan. 1, 2010.

Comments—Rule 15

See comment after appendices following Rule 15.11.

Rule 15.06. Plea Discussions and Agreements Not Admissible

If the defendant enters a plea of guilty that is not accepted or is withdrawn, any plea discussions, plea agreements, and the plea are not admissible as evidence against or in favor of the defendant in any criminal, civil, or administrative proceeding.

Adopted Feb. 26, 1975, eff. July 1, 1975. Revised Dec. 13, 1989. Amended Oct. 27, 2009, eff. Jan. 1, 2010.

Comments—Rule 15

See comment after appendices following Rule 15.11.

Rule 15.07. Plea to Lesser Offenses

With the prosecutor's consent and the court's approval, the defendant may plead guilty to a lesser included offense or to an offense of lesser degree. On the defendant's motion and after hearing, the court, without the prosecutor's consent, may accept a guilty plea to a lesser included offense or to an offense of lesser degree, provided the court is satisfied that the prosecutor cannot introduce sufficient evidence to justify the submission of the offense charged to the jury or that it would be a manifest injustice not to accept the plea. In either event, the plea may be entered without amendment of the indictment, complaint or tab charge. However, in felony cases, if the indictment or complaint is not amended, the reduction of the charge to an included offense or an offense of lesser degree must be done in writing or on the record. If done only on the record, the proceedings must be transcribed and filed.

Adopted Feb. 26, 1975, eff. July 1, 1975. Revised Dec. 13, 1989. Amended Oct. 27, 2009, eff. Jan. 1, 2010.

Comments—Rule 15

See comment after appendices following Rule 15.11.

Rule 15.08. Plea to Different Offense

With the consent of the prosecutor and the defendant, the defendant may enter a guilty plea to a different offense than that charged in the original tab charge, indictment, or complaint. If the different offense is a felony or gross misdemeanor, a new complaint must be signed by the prosecutor and filed in the district court. The complaint must be in the form prescribed by Rule 2.01 except that it need not be made upon oath, and the facts establishing probable cause to believe the defendant committed the offense charged need not be provided. If the different offense is a misdemeanor, the defendant may be charged with the new offense by complaint or tab charge, as provided in Rule 4.02, subd. 5(3), and the original charge must be dismissed.

Adopted Feb. 26, 1975, eff. July 1, 1975. Revised Dec. 13, 1989. Amended Aug. 21, 1998, eff. Jan. 1, 1999; Oct. 27, 2009, eff. Jan. 1, 2010.

Comments—Rule 15

See comment after appendices following Rule 15.11.

Rule 15.09. Record of Proceedings

Whenever a guilty plea to an offense punishable by incarceration is entered and accepted by the court, a verbatim record of the proceedings must be made, or in the case of misdemeanors or gross misdemeanors, a petition to enter a plea of guilty must be filed with the court. If a written petition to enter a guilty plea is submitted to the court, it must be in the form as set forth in the Appendices to this rule. Any person may, at their expense, order a transcript of the verbatim record made in accordance with this rule. When requested, the transcript must be completed within 30 days of the date the transcript was requested in writing and satisfactory financial arrangements were made for the transcription.

Adopted Feb. 26, 1975, eff. July 1, 1975. Revised Dec. 13, 1989. Amended May 9, 1994; Oct. 31, 2003, eff. Nov. 5, 2003; Dec. 28, 2005, eff. March 1, 2006; Oct. 27, 2009, eff. Jan. 1, 2010; June 5, 2012, eff. Aug. 1, 2012.

Comments—Rule 15

See comment after appendices following Rule 15.11.

Historical Notes

The order of the Minnesota Supreme Court [ADM 10-8049] dated June 5, 2012, provided in part that the amendments "be effective August 1, 2012, and shall apply to all actions or proceedings pending on or commenced on or after the effective date."

Rule 15.10. Guilty Plea to Offenses From Other Jurisdictions

Following a guilty plea or a verdict or finding of guilty, the defendant may request permission to plead guilty to any other offense committed by the defendant within the jurisdiction of other courts in the state. The offense must be charged, and the plea must be approved, by the prosecutor having authority to charge the offenses. The prosecutor having authority to charge the offenses may participate in the plea and sentencing hearings by ITV under Rule 1.05.

Adopted Dec. 13, 1989. Amended Oct. 27, 2009, eff. Jan. 1, 2010; June 9, 2010, eff. July 1, 2010.

Comments—Rule 15

See comment after appendices following Rule 15.11.

Rule 15.11. Use of Guilty Plea Petitions When Defendant is Disabled in Communication

Whenever a defendant is disabled in communication, the court must not accept a guilty plea petition unless the defendant is first able to review it with the assistance of a qualified interpreter and the court establishes on the record that this has occurred. Whenever practicable, the court should use multilingual guilty plea petitions approved by the State Court Administrator to insure that the defendant understands all rights being waived, the nature of the proceedings, and the petition.

Adopted May 9, 1994. Amended Oct. 27, 2009, eff. Jan. 1, 2010.

Comments—Rule 15

See comment after appendices following this rule.

APPENDIX A TO RULE 15

STATE OF MINNESOTA	IN DISTRICT COURT
COUNTY OF __________	_____ JUDICIAL DISTRICT

____

State of Minnesota,	PETITION TO ENTER PLEA OF GUILTY
vs.	

____

____

TO: THE ABOVE NAMED COURT

I, ______________, defendant in the above entitled action do respectfully represent and state as follows:

1. My full name is ______________. I am ___ years old, my date of birth is ______________. The last grade that I went through in school is ______________.

2. If filed in my case, I have received, read and discussed a copy of the (Indictment) (Complaint).

3. I understand the charge made against me in this case.

4. Specifically, I understand that I have been charged with the crime of ______________ committed on or about (month) (day) (year) in ________ County, Minnesota.

5. I am represented by an attorney whose name is ______________ and:

   a. I feel that I have had sufficient time to discuss my case with my attorney.

   b. I am satisfied that my attorney is fully informed as to facts of this case.

   c. My attorney has discussed possible defenses to the crime that I might have.

d. I am satisfied that my attorney has represented my interests and has fully advised me.

6. I (have) (have never) been a patient in a mental hospital.

7. I (have) (have not) talked with or been treated by a psychiatrist or other person for a nervous or mental condition.

8. I (have) (have not) been ill recently.

9. I (have) (have not) recently been taking pills or other medicines.

10. I (do) (do not) make the claim that I was so drunk or so under the influence of drugs or medicine that I did not know what I was doing at the time of the crime.

11. I (do) (do not) make the claim that I was acting in self-defense or merely protecting myself or others at the time of the crime.

12. I (do) (do not) make the claim that the fact that I have been held in jail since my arrest and could not post bail caused me to decide to plead guilty in order to get the thing over with rather than waiting for my turn at trial.

13. I (was) (was not) represented by an attorney when I (had a probable cause hearing). (If I have not had a probable cause hearing)

a. I know that I could now move that the complaint against me be dismissed for lack of probable cause and I know that if I do not make such a motion and go ahead with entering my plea of guilty, I waive all right to successfully object to the absence of a probable cause hearing.

b. I also know that I waive all right to successfully object to any errors in the probable cause hearing when I enter my plea of guilty.

14. My attorney has told me and I understand:

a. That the prosecutor for the case against me, has:

i. physical evidence obtained as a result of searching for and seizing the evidence;

ii. evidence in the form of statements, oral or written that I made to police or others regarding this crime;

iii. evidence discovered as a result of my statements or as a result of the evidence seized in a search;

iv. identification evidence from a lineup or photographic identification;

v. evidence the prosecution believes indicates that I committed one or more other crimes.

b. That I have a right to a pre-trial hearing before a judge to determine whether or not the evidence the prosecution has could be used against me if I went to trial in this case.

c. That if I requested such a pre-trial hearing I could testify at the hearing if I wanted to, but my testimony could not be used as substantive evidence against me if I went to trial and could only be used against me if I was charged with the crime of perjury. (Perjury means testifying falsely).

d. That I (do) (do not) now request such a pre-trial hearing and I specifically (do) (do not) now waive my right to have such a pre-trial hearing.

e. That whether or not I have had such a hearing I will not be able to object tomorrow or any other time to the evidence that the prosecutor has.

15. I have been told by my attorney and I understand:

a. That if I wish to plead not guilty I am entitled to a trial by a jury on the issue of guilt, and all jurors would have to agree I was guilty before the jury could find me guilty.

b. That if I plead guilty I will not have a trial by either a jury or by a judge without a jury.

c. That with knowledge of my right to a trial on the issue of guilt, I now waive my right to a trial.

16. I have been told by my attorney and I understand that if I wish to plead not guilty and have a trial by jury or trial by a judge I would be presumed innocent until my guilt is proved beyond a reasonable doubt.

17. I have been told by my attorney and I understand:

a. That if I wish to plead not guilty and have a trial the prosecutor would be required to have the witnesses testify against me in open court in my presence and that I would have the right, through my attorney, to question these witnesses.

b. That with knowledge of my right to have the prosecution's witnesses testify in open court in my presence and questioned by my attorney, I now waive this right.

18. I have been told by my attorney and I understand:

a. That if I wish to plead not guilty and have a trial I would be entitled to require any witnesses that I think are favorable to me to appear and testify at trial.

b. That with knowledge of my right to require favorable witnesses to appear and testify at trial I now waive this right.

19. I have been told by my attorney and I understand:

a. That a person who has prior convictions or a prior conviction can be given a longer prison term because of this.

b. That the maximum penalty that the court could impose for this crime (taking into consideration any prior conviction or convictions) is imprisonment for ___ years. That if a minimum sentence is required by statute the court may impose a sentence of imprisonment of not less than ___ months for this crime.

c. That for felony driving while impaired offenses and most sex offenses, a mandatory period of conditional release will follow any executed prison sentence that is imposed. Violating the terms of this conditional release may increase the time I serve in prison. In this case, the period of conditional release is ___ years.

d. That a person who participates in a crime by intentionally aiding, advising, counseling and conspiring with another person or persons to commit a crime is just as guilty of that crime as the person or persons who are present and participating in the crime when it is actually committed.

e. That my present probation or parole could be revoked because of the plea of guilty to this crime.

f. That the prosecutor is seeking an aggravated sentence of __________.

20. I have been told by my attorney and I understand:

a. That my attorney discussed this case with one of the prosecuting attorneys and that my attorney and the prosecuting attorney agreed that if I entered a plea of guilty, the prosecutor will do the following:

(Give the substance of the agreement)

b. That if the court does not approve this agreement:

i. I have an absolute right to then withdraw my plea of guilty and have a trial.

ii. Any testimony that I have given concerning the guilty plea could not be used against me unless I am charged with the crime of perjury based on this testimony.

21. That except for the agreement between my attorney and the prosecuting attorney:

a. No one—including my attorney, any police officer, prosecutor, judge, or any other person—has made any promises to me, to any member of my family, to any of my friends or other persons, in order to obtain a plea of guilty from me.

b. No one—including my attorney, any police officer, prosecutor or judge, or any other person—has threatened me or any member of my family or my friends or other persons, in order to obtain a plea of guilty from me.

22. My attorney has told me and I understand that if my plea of guilty is for any reason not accepted by the court, or if I withdraw the plea, with the court's approval, or if the plea is withdrawn by court order on appeal or other review:

a. I would then stand trial on the original charge (charges).

b. The prosecution could proceed against me just as if there had been no plea of guilty and no plea agreement.

23. My attorney has told me and I understand that if my plea of guilty is accepted by the judge I have the right to appeal, but that any appeal or other court action I may take claiming error in the proceedings probably would be useless and a waste of my time and the court's.

24. My attorney has told me and I understand that a judge will not accept a plea of guilty for anyone who claims to be innocent.

25. I now make no claim that I am innocent.

26. I have been told by my attorney and I understand that if I wish to plead not guilty and have a jury trial:

a. That I could testify at trial if I wanted to but I could not be forced to testify.

b. That if I decided not to testify neither the prosecutor nor the judge could comment on my failure to testify.

c. That with knowledge of my right not to testify and that neither the judge nor the prosecutor could comment on my failure to testify at trial I now waive this right and I will tell the judge about the facts of the crime.

27. My attorney has told me and I understand that if I am not a citizen of the United States this plea of guilty may result in deportation, exclusion from admission to the United States of America or denial of citizenship.

28. That in view of all above facts and considerations I wish to enter a plea of guilty.

Dated this ______ day of ______, 19___

____
DEFENDANT

Adopted Feb. 26, 1975, eff. July 1, 1975. Revised Dec. 13, 1989. Amended Aug. 21, 1998, eff. Jan. 1, 1999; Dec. 23, 2002, eff. Feb. 1, 2003; Aug. 17, 2006, eff. Oct. 1, 2006.

Historical Notes

The order of the Minnesota Supreme Court [C1-84-2137] dated December 13, 1989, provides in part that "(t)hese amended Rules of Criminal Procedure shall govern all criminal actions commenced or arrests made after 12 o'clock midnight January 1, 1990, except amendments to 8.04, 11.07, and 19.04, subd. 5, shall govern all criminal actions commenced or arrests made after 12 o'clock midnight January 1, 1991."

APPENDIX B TO RULE 15

STATE OF MINNESOTA IN DISTRICT COURT
COUNTY OF ________ ____ JUDICIAL DISTRICT

____

________________,
Plaintiff, MISDEMEANOR

vs. /GROSS MISDEMEANOR PETITION TO ENTER PLEA OF GUILTY
District Court File No.

____________________,
Defendant.

TO: THE ABOVE-NAMED COURT:

I wish to enter a plea of guilty in the above-entitled case and I hereby state to the Court the following:

1. I am the Defendant in this case, my full name is _________ and my date of birth is _________.

2. I am charged with (name of offense) in violation of (statute or ordinance).

3. I hereby plead guilty to the offense of (name of offense) in violation of (statute or ordinance).

4. I am pleading guilty because on (date) in the City of _________, County of _________, and State of Minnesota I committed the following acts: (state sufficient facts to establish a factual basis for all elements of the offense to which the defendant is pleading guilty).

5. I understand that the maximum possible sentence for any misdemeanor offense to which I am pleading guilty is 90 days imprisonment or a fine of (amount) or both, and that the maximum possible sentence for any gross misdemeanor offense to which I am pleading guilty is 1 year imprisonment or a fine of (amount) or both. Further, I understand that if I am not a citizen of the United States, my plea of guilty to this crime may result in deportation, exclusion from admission to the United States or denial of naturalization as a United States citizen.

6. RIGHT TO AN ATTORNEY. I understand that I have the right to be represented by an attorney and that an attorney will be appointed to represent me without cost to me if I cannot afford to pay for an attorney.

7. I have fully discussed the charge(s), my constitutional rights, and this petition with my attorney, (name of attorney).

[or]

7a. WAIVER OF ATTORNEY. I give up my right to be represented by an attorney and any right I might have to request that an attorney be appointed to represent me.

8. I understand that I also have the following constitutional rights which I knowingly and voluntarily give up:

a. The right to a trial to the court or to a jury in which I am presumed innocent until proven guilty beyond a reasonable doubt and in which all jurors in a jury trial must agree I am guilty before the jury could find me guilty.

b. The right to confront and cross-examine all witnesses against me.

c. The right to remain silent or to testify for myself.

d. The right to subpoena and present witnesses to testify for me in my defense.

e. The right to a pretrial hearing to contest the admissibility at trial of any confessions or admissions or of any evidence obtained from a search and seizure.

9. I am entering my plea of guilty freely and voluntarily and without any promises except as indicated in number 10 below.

10. I am entering my plea of guilty based on the following plea agreement with the prosecutor: (if none so state).

11. I understand that if the Court does not approve this agreement I have the right to withdraw my plea of guilty and have a trial.

12. I understand that if this plea of guilty is accepted I have the right to be present at the time of sentencing and to speak and to present evidence on my behalf.

13. I hereby request to be present at the time of sentencing.

[or]

13a. I hereby knowingly and voluntarily give up my right to be present upon (entry of my plea and) sentencing and request that the court sentence me in my absence, but according to any plea agreement that might be contained in this petition.

Dated this ___ day of _________, ___.

____
Signature of Defendant

____
Printed Name of Defendant

I, (name of attorney) state that I am the attorney for the defendant in the above-entitled criminal action; that I personally explained the contents of the above petition to the defendant; and that I personally observed the defendant date and sign the above petition.

Dated this ___ day of _________, ___.

____
Attorney for Defendant

PETITION AND PLEA OF GUILTY ACCEPTED BY

________________ ________________
Judge of District Court Date

Adopted Feb. 26, 1975, eff. July 1, 1975. Revised Dec. 13, 1989. Amended Aug. 21, 1998, eff. Jan. 1, 1999; June 5, 2012, eff. Aug. 1, 2012.

Historical Notes

The order of the Minnesota Supreme Court [C1–84–2137] dated December 13, 1989, provides in part that "(t)hese amended Rules of Criminal Procedure shall govern all criminal actions commenced or arrests made after 12 o'clock midnight January 1, 1990, except amendments to 8.04, 11.07, and 19.04, subd. 5, shall govern all criminal actions commenced or arrests made after 12 o'clock midnight January 1, 1991."

The order of the Minnesota Supreme Court [ADM 10–8049] dated June 5, 2012, provided in part that the amendments "be effective August 1, 2012, and shall apply to all actions or proceedings pending on or commenced on or after the effective date."

APPENDIX C TO RULE 15

STATE OF MINNESOTA IN DISTRICT COURT

COUNTY OF __________ ____ JUDICIAL DISTRICT

____

State of Minnesota,
Plaintiff,
vs.

____________________,
Defendant.

____

PETITION TO ENTER PLEA OF GUILTY BY PRO SE DEFENDANT

TO: THE ABOVE NAMED COURT

I, ____________, defendant in the above-entitled action do respectfully represent and state as follows:

1. My full name is __________. I am __________ years old. My date of birth is __________. The last grade that I went through in school is __________.

2. If filed in my case, I have received and read a copy of the (Indictment) (Complaint).

3. I understand the charge made against me in this case.

4. Specifically, I understand that I have been charged with the crime of __________ committed on or about _____ (month) _____ (day) _____ (year) in __________ County, Minnesota, (and that the crime I am talking about is __________ which is a lesser degree or lesser included offense of the crime charged).

5. a. I understand that I have an absolute right to have an attorney represent me at any stage of these proceedings, including a guilty plea.

b. I have read over and completed a Petition to Proceed as Pro Se Counsel (Form 11) and provided that Petition to the Court on __________.

c. I have been advised of the nature of the charges and statutory offenses included in the charges against me, the maximum sentence permitted, the possible defenses, mitigating circumstances, and other relevant facts so that I understand the advantages and disadvantages of waiving my right to an attorney.

d. Knowing the consequences of giving up my right to counsel, I waive my right to be represented by an attorney during the entry of my guilty plea.

6. I (have) (have not) been a patient in a mental hospital.

7. I (have) (have not) talked with or been treated by a psychiatrist or other person for a nervous or mental condition.

8. I (have) (have not) been ill recently.

9. I (have) (have not) recently been taking pills or other medicines.

10. I (do) (do not) make the claim that I was so drunk or so under the influence of drugs or medicine that I did not know what I was doing at the time of the crime.

11. I (do) (do not) make the claim that I was acting in self-defense or merely protecting myself or others at the time of the crime.

12. I (do) (do not) make the claim that the fact that I have been held in jail since my arrest and could not post bail caused me to decide to plead guilty in order to get the thing over with rather than waiting for my turn at trial.

13. I (was) (was not) represented by an attorney when I (had a probable cause hearing). (If I have not had a probable cause hearing.)

a. I know that I could now move that the complaint against me be dismissed for lack of probable cause and I know that if I do not make such a motion and go ahead with entering my plea of guilty, I waive all right to successfully object to the absence of a probable cause hearing.

b. I also know that I waive all right to successfully object to any errors in the probable cause hearing when I enter my plea of guilty.

14. I understand:

a. That the prosecutor for the case against me, has:

i. physical evidence obtained as a result of searching for and seizing the evidence;

ii. evidence in the form of statements, oral or written that I made to police or others regarding this crime;

iii. evidence discovered as a result of my statements or as a result of the evidence seized in a search;

iv. identification evidence from a lineup or photographic identification;

v. evidence the prosecution believes indicates that I committed one or more other crimes.

b. That I have a right to a pre-trial hearing before a judge to determine whether or not the evidence the prosecution has could be used against me if I went to trial in this case.

c. That if I requested such a pre-trial hearing I could testify at the hearing if I wanted to, but my testimony could not be used as substantive evidence against me if I went to trial and could only be used against me if I was charged with the crime of perjury. (Perjury means testifying falsely.)

d. That I (do) (do not) now request such a pre-trial hearing and I specifically (do) (do not) now waive my right to have such a pre-trial hearing.

e. That whether or not I have had such a hearing I will not be able to object tomorrow or any other time to the evidence that the prosecutor has.

15. I understand:

a. That if I wish to plead not guilty I am entitled to a trial by a jury on the issue of guilt, and all jurors would have to agree I was guilty before the jury could find me guilty.

b. That if I plead guilty I will not have a trial by either a jury or by a judge without a jury.

c. That with knowledge of my right to a trial on the issue of guilt, I now waive my right to a trial.

16. I understand that if I wish to plead not guilty and have a trial by jury or trial by a judge I would be presumed innocent until my guilt is proved beyond a reasonable doubt.

17. I understand:

a. That if I wish to plead not guilty and have a trial the prosecutor would be required to have the witnesses testify against me in open court in my presence and that I would have the right to question these witnesses.

b. That with knowledge of my right to have the prosecution's witnesses testify in open court in my presence and questioned by me, I now waive this right.

18. I understand:

a. That if I wish to plead not guilty and have a trial I would be entitled to require any witnesses that I think are favorable to me to appear and testify at trial.

b. That with the knowledge of my right to require favorable witnesses to appear and testify at trial I now waive this right.

19. I understand:

a. That a person who has prior convictions or a prior conviction can be given a longer prison term because of this.

b. That the maximum penalty that the court could impose for this crime (taking into consideration any prior conviction or convictions) is imprisonment for ___ years. That if a minimum sentence is required by statute the court may impose a sentence of imprisonment of not less than ___ months for this crime.

c. That a person who participates in a crime by intentionally aiding, advising, counseling and conspiring with another person or persons to commit a crime is just as guilty of that crime as the person or persons who are present and participating in the crime when it is actually committed.

d. That my present probation or parole could be revoked because of the plea of guilty to this crime.

e. That if I am not a citizen of the United States, my plea of guilty to this crime may result in deportation, exclusion from admission to the United States or denial of naturalization as a United States citizen.

f. That the prosecutor is seeking an aggravated sentence of ________.

20. I understand:

a. That I have discussed this case with one of the prosecuting attorneys and that the prosecuting attorney and I agreed that if I entered a plea of guilty, the prosecutor will do the following:

(Give the substance of the agreement)

b. That if the court does not approve this agreement:

i. I have an absolute right to then withdraw my plea of guilty and have a trial.

ii. Any testimony that I have given concerning the guilty plea could not be used against me unless I am charged with the crime of perjury based on this testimony.

21. That except for the agreement between the prosecuting attorney and me:

a. No one— including any police officer, prosecutor, judge, or any other person— has made any promises to me, to any member of my family, to any of my friends or other persons, in order to obtain a plea of guilty from me.

b. No one— including any police officer, prosecutor or judge, or any other person— has threatened me or any member of my family or my friends or other persons, in order to obtain a plea of guilty from me.

22. I understand that if my plea of guilty is for any reason not accepted by the court, or if I withdraw the plea, with the court's approval, or if the plea is withdrawn by court order on appeal or other review:

a. I would then stand trial on the original charge (charges) against me, namely ____________ (which would include any charges that were dismissed as a result of the plea agreement entered into by the prosecuting attorney and me.)

b. The prosecution could proceed against me just as if there had been no plea of guilty and no plea agreement.

23. I understand that if my plea of guilty is accepted by the judge I have the right to appeal, but that any appeal or other court action I may take claiming error in the proceedings probably would be useless and a waste of my time and the court's time.

24. I understand that a judge will not accept a plea of guilty for anyone who claims to be innocent.

25. I now make no claim that I am innocent.

26. I understand that if I wish to plead not guilty and have a jury trial:

a. That I could testify at trial if I wanted to, but I could not be forced to testify.

b. That if I decided not to testify neither the prosecutor not the judge could comment on my failure to testify.

c. That with knowledge of my right not to testify and that neither the judge nor the prosecutor could comment on my failure to testify at trial I now waive this right and I will tell the judge about the facts of the crime.

27. That in view of all the above facts and considerations I wish to enter a plea of guilty.

Dated this ___ day of ____________, ___.

____
DEFENDANT

Adopted Aug. 21, 1998, eff. Jan. 1, 1999. Amended Aug. 17, 2006, eff. Oct. 1, 2006.

APPENDIX D TO RULE 15

PLEA AGREEMENT

STATE OF MINNESOTA DISTRICT COURT
COUNTY OF ________ ___ JUDICIAL DISTRICT

____

State of Minnesota,
Plaintiff,
vs.
______________________,
Defendant.

PLEA AGREEMENT

District Court File No. ___

____

1. Negotiation Status

___ The terms and conditions outlined in this agreement are a joint recommendation to the Court, but the Court is not bound to those terms and may impose different terms than those outlined in this agreement.

___ The terms and conditions outlined in this negotiation are required by the agreement. If the Court will not sentence the defendant to the terms outlined in this agreement, either party may withdraw from the agreement.

2. Charges/Dismissals/Deferrals

___ The defendant will enter a plea of guilty to the following counts from the following files: ______________________
____
____
____

___ This case will be deferred pursuant to a pretrial diversion program. If the defendant successfully completes this program, the case will be dismissed.

___ This case will be deferred pursuant to Minn. Stat. § 152.18 with conditions outlined in Section 4. If the defendant successfully completes those conditions, the case will be dismissed.

___ This matter will be continued for dismissal for a period of ________ on condition that the defendant abide by the following conditions: ______________________
____
____

___ Successful completion of probation will result in vacation of plea and dismissal of charge.

___ The following counts in this case or other criminal complaints will be dismissed: ______________________
____
____

___ This complaint will be amended to the lesser included offense(s) (or amended to the separate offense) of: ________
____

___ The State will not seek criminal charges arising out of the following conduct: ______________________
____

3. Level of Conviction

___ The parties agree to a misdemeanor or gross misdemeanor sentence of ______________________
____

___ The parties agree to a stay of imposition of sentence for ___ years.

___ The parties agree to a stay of execution of sentence with a stayed sentence of ___ months and a stay for ___ years.

___ The parties agree to an executed sentence of ___ months.

___ The parties agree to a waiver of the mandatory minimums found in Minn. Stat. § 609.11.

___ **(If sentenced on multiple counts/files)** The prison term in this case is arrived at by the following sentences from the following counts/files to be served consecutively/concurrently (circle one): ______________________
____
____

___ The parties agree to whatever sentence is presumed by the Minnesota Sentencing Guidelines.

___ The parties agree this is a departure from the Minnesota Sentencing Guidelines (or other sentencing enhancement) based on the following factors: ______________________
____
____

___ The parties agree to a sentencing range of ___ months to ___ months.

___ **(DWI and Criminal Sexual Conduct cases)** If this is an executed sentence or if this sentence is ever executed, the parties understand that the defendant is subject to an extended term of conditional release for five or ten years after any term of imprisonment.

___ The parties also understand the defendant will be required to provide a biological sample for the state DNA database.

4. If this is a probationary sentence the parties agree to the following terms and conditions:

___ All terms of probation left to discretion of the Court.

___ A probationary term of ______________________

___ A workhouse or jail term of ______________________

___ A workhouse or jail term not to exceed ('a cap' of) ________

___ This term may be served intermittently on the following dates: ______________________

___ The defendant will be eligible for Huber release for the following purposes: ______________________
____

___ Community service for ___ hours.

___ Sentence to Serve for ___ days.

___ Electronic home monitoring for ___ days.

___ Undergo any treatment-related evaluation recommended by Probation or the Department of Court Services.

___ Enter and successfully complete the following programs: ___
____

___ Enter and successfully complete any program recommended by Probation or the Department of Court Services.

___ No contact in person, by mail, by phone, by third party, or electronically with: ______________________

___ A fine of ________ and applicable surcharges.
___ Other: ____________________

5. Restitution

___ Defendant agrees to make restitution in the amount of ________.

___ Restitution to be determined by the Court.

6. Miscellaneous Provisions

____

Dated: __________ __________
Defendant

__________ __________
Prosecuting Attorney Defense Attorney

Adopted Oct. 31, 2003, 2005, eff. Nov. 5, 2003. Amended Dec. 28, 2005, eff. March 1, 2006.

Historical Notes

The order of the Minnesota Supreme Court [C1–84–2137] dated December 28, 2005, provides in part that "(t)he attached amendments shall govern all criminal actions commenced or arrests made after 12 o'clock midnight March 1, 2006."

APPENDIX E TO RULE 15

STATE OF MINNESOTA IN DISTRICT COURT
COUNTY OF ________ ___ JUDICIAL DISTRICT

State of Minnesota,
Plaintiff,

vs.

____
Defendant.

PETITION REGARDING AGGRAVATED SENTENCE

TO: THE ABOVE NAMED COURT

I, ________, defendant in the above entitled action do respectfully represent and state as follows:

1. I have pled guilty to or have otherwise been found guilty of the crime of ________.

2. I understand the presumptive guideline sentence for this offense is ________, and I could not be given an aggravated sentence greater than the presumptive sentence unless the prosecution proves facts in support of such an aggravated sentence.

3. I understand the prosecution is seeking a sentence greater than that called for in the sentencing guidelines. Specifically, I understand the sentence in this case will be ________ or will be left to the judge to decide.

4. I am represented by attorney ________ and:

a) I feel I have had sufficient time to discuss the issue of an aggravated sentence with my attorney.

b) I am satisfied my attorney is fully informed as to the facts related to an aggravated sentence and that my attorney has discussed possible defenses I have to an aggravated sentence.

c) I am satisfied that my attorney has represented my interests and has fully advised me about an aggravated sentence.

5. My attorney has told me and I understand that even though I have pled guilty to or been otherwise found guilty of the crime of ________, I have the right to deny the facts alleged by the prosecution in support of an aggravated sentence.

6. My attorney has told me and I understand that I am entitled to a trial by either a jury or a judge to determine whether an aggravated sentence may be imposed upon me.

7. My attorney has told me and I understand that at such trial I have the following rights:

a) I am presumed not to be subject to an aggravated sentence.

b) The prosecution must prove facts supporting an aggravated sentence to either a jury or a judge beyond a reasonable doubt.

c) That before a jury could find facts supporting an aggravated sentence, all jurors would have to agree. That means the jury's decision must be unanimous.

d) That at a trial before either a jury or a judge, the prosecution will be required to call witnesses in open court and in my presence, and I, through my attorney, will have the right to question the witnesses.

e) That I may require any witnesses I think are favorable to me to appear and testify on my behalf.

f) That I may testify at such a trial if I wish to, but that if I choose not to testify, neither the prosecution nor the judge could comment to the jury about the failure to testify.

g) That if I admit the facts in support of an aggravated sentence, I will not have a trial by either a jury or a judge.

8. That with knowledge of my right to a trial on the facts in support of an aggravated sentence, I now waive my right to a trial.

9. I now waive my right not to testify and I will tell the judge about the facts which support an aggravated sentence.

Dated: ________ __________
Signature of Defendant

Adopted Aug. 17, 2006, eff. Oct. 1, 2006.

APPENDIX F TO RULE 15

STATE OF MINNESOTA IN DISTRICT COURT
COUNTY OF ________ ___ JUDICIAL DISTRICT

State of Minnesota,
Plaintiff,

vs.

____
Defendant.

PETITION REGARDING AGGRAVATED SENTENCE BY PRO SE DEFENDANT

TO: THE ABOVE NAMED COURT

I, __________, defendant in the above entitled action do respectfully represent and state as follows:

1. I have pled guilty to or have otherwise been found guilty of the crime of __________.

2. I understand the presumptive guideline sentence for this offense is __________, and I could not be given an aggravated sentence greater than the presumptive sentence unless the prosecution proves facts in support of such an aggravated sentence.

3. I understand the prosecution is seeking a sentence greater than that called for in the sentencing guidelines. Specifically, I understand the sentence in this case will be __________ or will be left to the judge to decide.

4. I understand that although I have pled guilty to or have otherwise been found guilty of the crime of __________, I have the right to deny the facts alleged by the prosecution in support of an aggravated sentence.

5. I understand that I am entitled to a trial by either a jury or a judge to determine whether an aggravated sentence may be imposed upon me.

6. I understand that I have an absolute right to have an attorney represent me at such trial and knowing the consequences of giving up my right to counsel, I waive my right to be represented by an attorney.

7. I understand that at a trial by a jury or a judge to determine if an aggravated sentence may be imposed upon me, I have the following rights:

a) I am presumed not to be subject to an aggravated sentence.

b) The prosecution must prove facts supporting an aggravated sentence to either a jury or a judge beyond a reasonable doubt.

c) That before a jury could find facts supporting an aggravated sentence, all jurors would have to agree. That means the jury's decision would have to be unanimous.

d) That at a trial before either a jury or a judge, the prosecution will be required to call witnesses in open court and in my presence, and that I would have the right to question the witnesses.

e) That I may require any witnesses I think are favorable to me to appear and testify on my behalf.

f) That I may testify at such a trial if I wish to, but that if I choose not to testify, neither the prosecution nor the judge could comment to the jury about the failure to testify.

g) That if I admit the facts in support of an aggravated sentence, I will not have a trial by either a jury or a judge.

8. That with knowledge of my right to a trial on the facts in support of an aggravated sentence, I now waive my right to a trial.

9. I now waive my right not to testify and I will tell the judge about the facts which support an aggravated sentence.

Dated: __________ ____________________
Signature of Defendant

Adopted Aug. 17, 2006, eff. Oct. 1, 2006.

Comment—Rule 15

Although a failure to include all of the interrogation set forth in Rule 15.01 will not in and of itself invalidate a plea of guilty, a complete inquiry as provided for by the rule will in most cases assure and provide a record for a valid plea. The requirement that the court make certain that a defendant disabled in communication has a qualified interpreter comports with Rule 8 of the Minnesota General Rules of Practice and the general requirement for interpreter services established in Rule 5.01 and Minn. Stat. §§ 611.31–611.34, and emphasizes the critical importance of this service in the guilty plea process.

The inquiry required by paragraph 6.l. of Rule 15.01, subd. 1 and by paragraph 3 of Rule 15.02, subd. 1 (concerning deportation and related consequences), is similar to that required in a number of other states. See, e.g., California, Cal. Penal Code § 1016.5; Connecticut, Conn. Gen. Stat. Ann. § 54–1 j; Massachusetts, Mass. Gen. Laws Ann. ch. 278, § 29D; New York, N.Y. Crim. Proc. Law § 220.50 (7); Ohio, Ohio Rev. Code Ann. § 2943.031; Oregon, Or. Rev. Stat. § 135.385(2)(d); Texas, Tex. Code Crim. Proc. Ann. art. 26.13(a)(4); and Washington, Wash. Rev. Code Ann. § 10.40.200(2). In the Antiterrorism and Effective Death Penalty Act of 1996, Pub. L. No. 104–132, 110 Stat. 1214 (1996) and the Illegal Immigration Reform and Immigrant Responsibility Act of 1996, Pub. L. No. 104–208, 110 Stat. 3009 (1996), Congress extensively amended the Immigration and Nationality Act and greatly expanded the grounds for deportation of non-citizens convicted of crimes. Consequently, non-citizens pleading guilty will subject themselves to deportation proceedings. The consequences of such proceedings will often be more severe and more important to the non-citizen defendant than the consequences of the criminal proceedings. It is therefore appropriate that defense counsel advise non-citizen defendants of those consequences and that the court inquire to be sure that has been done. As to the obligation of defense counsel in such situations, see ABA Standards for Criminal Justice, Pleas of Guilty, 14–3.2 (3d ed. 1999). The requirement of inquiring into deportation and immigration consequences does not mean that other unanticipated non-criminal consequences of a guilty plea will justify later withdrawal of that plea. See Kim v. State, 434 N.W.2d 263 (Minn. 1989) (unanticipated employment consequences).

Before entry of a guilty plea, defense counsel should review with the defendant the effect of the Minnesota Sentencing Guidelines on the case. Further, it may be desirable for the court to order a pre-plea sentencing guidelines worksheet to be prepared so that the court, the defendant, and both counsel will be aware of the effect of the guidelines at the time the guilty plea is entered.

It is suggested by the Advisory Committee that the defendant sign a Petition to Plead Guilty in the form appearing in the Appendices to these rules (which contain in even more detailed form the information showing the defendant's understanding of defense rights and the consequences of pleading), and that the defendant be asked upon the inquiry under Rule 15.01 to acknowledge signing the petition, that the defendant has read the questions set forth in the petition or that they have been read to the defendant, and that the defendant understands them, that the defendant gave the answers in the petition, and that they are true.

The court in State v. Casarez, 295 Minn. 534, 203 N.W.2d 406 (1973), applied the Boykin standard to misdemeanors, holding that a misdemeanor guilty plea must be vacated where the record does not show a knowing and voluntary waiver of the defendant's constitutional rights. It is clear then that at least some limited inquiry is necessary on the record before a misdemeanor guilty plea is accepted, and Rule 15.02 prescribes the minimal standards for this questioning.

A prior guilty plea without the assistance of defense counsel cannot be used to aggravate a later charge absent a valid waiver of counsel on the record for the earlier plea. State v. Nordstrom, 331 N.W.2d 901 (Minn. 1983). Also, a prior guilty plea which lacks a factual basis on the record cannot be used to aggravate a later charge. State v. Stewart, 360 N.W.2d 463 (Minn. Ct. App. 1985).

Under Rule 15.03, subd. 2, a "Misdemeanor/Gross Misdemeanor Petition to Enter Plea of Guilty" as provided for in the Appendix B to Rule 15, may be completed and filed with the court. This petition in written form contains in substance the information and questions required by Rule 15. 02, subd. 1, questions 2–5. When properly completed, the petition may be filed by either the defendant or defense counsel. It is not necessary for the defendant to personally appear in court when the petition is presented to the court. If the court is satisfied that the plea is being knowingly and voluntarily entered according to the standards of Rule 15.02, subd. 1 it will dispose of the plea in the same manner as if the defendant entered the plea in person.

See Minn. Stat. § 611A.03 regarding the prosecutor's duties under the Victim's Rights Act to make a reasonable and good faith effort to inform victims of proposed plea agreements and to notify of the right to be present at sentencing to make an objection to the plea agreement or to the proposed disposition.

When the defendant is questioned as to the plea agreement under Rule 15.01, the court must inform the defendant if the plea agreement is rejected, unless the court decides to postpone a decision on acceptance or rejection until the pre-sentence report is received. Whenever a plea agreement has been rejected, the defendant must be afforded the opportunity to withdraw a plea of guilty, if entered. Rules 15.04, subd. 3(1); 15.01. If the defendant has made factual disclosures tending to disclose guilt of the offense charged, the judge should disqualify himself or herself from the trial of the case.

Rule 15.04, subd. 3(2)(d) includes situations in which certain witnesses, such as young children involved in sexual offenses, may be protected from unnecessary publicity.

Rule 15.05, subd. 1 authorizing the withdrawal of a guilty plea to correct manifest injustice does not provide guidelines for determining whether a motion for withdrawal of the plea is timely or whether withdrawal is necessary to correct manifest injustice. This is left by the rule to judicial decision. See, e.g., Chapman v. State, 282 Minn. 13, 162 N.W.2d 698 (1968).

Rule 15.06 is consistent with Rule 410 of the Minnesota Rules of Evidence, which also governs the admissibility of evidence of a withdrawn plea of guilty. Rule 410 is broader in that it makes inadmissible evidence relating to withdrawn pleas from other jurisdictions, including withdrawn pleas of nolo contendere from those jurisdictions that allow such a plea.

Before proceeding under Rule 15.10, the prosecutor in the jurisdiction having venue must charge the defendant. This may be done by complaint or indictment or, for misdemeanors, by tab charge. The charging document may be transmitted to the jurisdiction where the plea is to be entered by facsimile transmission under Rule 33.05.

It is strongly recommended that when the defendant is disabled in communication due to difficulty in speaking or comprehending English, a multilingual guilty plea petition be used that is in English as well as the language in which the defendant is able to communicate. The use of a multilingual petition would help assure that the translation is accurate and is preferable to the use of a petition that contains only the language other than English.

RULE 16. MISDEMEANOR PROSECUTION BY INDICTMENT

In misdemeanor cases prosecuted by indictment, Rule 19 (Warrant or Summons Upon Indictment) governs to the extent that it conflicts with those rules that would otherwise govern the misdemeanor prosecution.

Adopted Feb. 26, 1975, eff. July 1, 1975. Revised Dec. 13, 1989. Amended Oct. 27, 2009, eff. Jan. 1, 2010.

Comment—Rule 16

The grand jury, with its power under Minn.Stat. § 628.02 to inquire into all "public offenses", could indict a defendant on misdemeanor charges. In those rare cases, Rule 16 provides that the prosecution shall be governed by Rule 19 in those instances where Rule 19 conflicts with those rules that would otherwise govern the misdemeanor prosecution.

RULE 17. INDICTMENT, COMPLAINT AND TAB CHARGE

Rule 17.01. Prosecution by Indictment, Complaint or Tab Charge

Subd. 1. Offenses Punishable by Life Imprisonment. An offense punishable by life imprisonment must be prosecuted by indictment. The prosecutor may initially proceed by a complaint after an arrest without a warrant or as the basis to issue an arrest warrant. Subsequent procedure must be in accordance with Rules 8 and 19. Any other offense defined by state law may be prosecuted by indictment or by a complaint as provided by Rule 2.

Subd. 2. Misdemeanor and Gross Misdemeanor Offenses. Misdemeanors and designated gross misdemeanors as defined by Rule 1.04(a)–(b) may be prosecuted by tab charge. A complaint must be subsequently served and filed for designated gross misdemeanors as required by Rule 4.02, subd. 5(3).

Subd. 3. Indictment Following Arrest or Complaint. The arrest of a person by arrest warrant issued in a complaint under Rule 3 or the filing of a complaint under Rule 4.02, subd. 5(2) against a person arrested without a warrant will not preclude an indictment for the offense charged or for an offense arising out of the same conduct.

Adopted Feb. 26, 1975, eff. July 1, 1975. Revised Dec. 13, 1989. Amended May 9, 1994; Aug. 21, 1998, eff. Jan. 1, 1999; Oct. 27, 2009, eff. Jan. 1, 2010.

Comment—Rule 17

See comment following Rule 17.06.

Historical Notes

The order of the Minnesota Supreme Court [C1–84–2137] dated December 13, 1989, provides in part that "(t)hese amended Rules of Criminal Procedure shall govern all criminal actions commenced or arrests made after 12 o'clock midnight January 1, 1990, except amendments to 8.04, 11.07, and 19.04, subd. 5, shall govern all criminal actions commenced or arrests made after 12 o'clock midnight January 1, 1991."

The order of the Minnesota Supreme Court [C1–84–2137] dated May 9, 1994, provides in part that "(t)hese amendments to the Rules of Criminal Procedure shall govern all criminal actions commenced or arrests made after 12 o'clock midnight July 1, 1994, except that the amendments in the first sentence of the third paragraph in Rule 2.01 shall govern all criminal actions commenced or arrests made after 12 o'clock midnight January 1, 1995."

Rule 17.02. Nature and Contents

Subd. 1. Complaint. A complaint must be substantially in the form required by Rule 2.

Subd. 2. Indictment. An indictment must contain a written statement of the essential facts constituting the offense charged and be signed by the grand jury foreperson.

Subd. 3. Indictment and Complaint. For each count, the indictment or complaint must cite the statute, rule, regulation, or other provision of law the defendant allegedly violated. Error in the citation or its omission is not a ground to dismiss or reverse a conviction if the error or omission did not prejudice the defendant. Each count can charge only one offense. Allegations made in one count may be incorporated by reference in another count. An indictment or complaint may contain counts for the different degrees of the same offense, or counts for lesser or other included offenses. The same indictment or complaint may contain counts for murder and manslaughter. The indictment or complaint may allege in one count alternative theories of committing the offense or that the means by which the defendant committed the offense are unknown.

Subd. 4. Administrative Information. The indictment or complaint must contain other administrative information as authorized and published by the State Court Administrator.

Adopted Feb. 26, 1975, eff. July 1, 1975. Revised Dec. 13, 1989. Amended May 9, 1994; May 19, 2008, eff. July 1, 2008; Oct. 27, 2009, eff. Jan. 1, 2010.

Comment—Rule 17

See comment following Rule 17.06.

Historical Notes

The order of the Minnesota Supreme Court [C1–84–2137] dated December 13, 1989, provides in part that "(t)hese amended Rules of Criminal Procedure shall govern all criminal actions commenced or arrests made after 12 o'clock midnight January 1, 1990, except amendments to 8.04, 11.07, and 19.04, subd. 5, shall govern all criminal actions commenced or arrests made after 12 o'clock midnight January 1, 1991."

The order of the Minnesota Supreme Court [C1–84–2137] dated May 9, 1994, provides in part that "(t)hese amendments to the Rules of Criminal Procedure shall govern all criminal actions commenced or arrests made after 12 o'clock midnight July 1, 1994, except that the amendments in the first sentence of the third paragraph in Rule 2.01 shall govern all criminal actions commenced or arrests made after 12 o'clock midnight January 1, 1995."

Rule 17.03. Joinder of Offenses and of Defendants

Subd. 1. Joinder of Offenses. When the defendant's conduct constitutes more than one offense, each offense may be charged in the same indictment or complaint in a separate count.

Subd. 2. Joinder of Defendants. When two or more defendants are charged with the same offense, they may be tried separately or jointly at the court's discretion. To determine whether to order joinder or separate trials, the court must consider:

(1) the nature of the offense charged;

(2) the impact on the victim;

(3) the potential prejudice to the defendant; and

(4) the interests of justice.

In all cases any one or more of the defendants may be convicted or acquitted.

Subd. 3. Severance of Offenses or Defendants.

(1) *Severance of Offenses.* On motion of the prosecutor or the defendant, the court must sever offenses or charges if:

(a) the offenses or charges are not related;

(b) before trial, the court determines severance is appropriate to promote a fair determination of the defendant's guilt or innocence of each offense or charge; or

(c) during trial, with the defendant's consent or on a finding of manifest necessity, the court determines severance is necessary to fairly determine the defendant's guilt or innocence of each offense or charge.

(2) *Severance from Codefendant because of Codefendant's Out-of-Court Statement.* On a defendant's motion for severance from a codefendant because a codefendant's out-of-court statement refers to but is not admissible against the defendant, the court must determine whether the prosecutor intends to offer the statement as evidence during its case in chief. If so, the court must require the prosecutor to elect one of the following options:

(a) a joint trial at which the statement is not received in evidence;

(b) a joint trial at which the statement is only received in evidence after all references to the defendant have been deleted, if the statement's admission with the deletions will not prejudice the defendant; or

(c) the defendant's severance.

(3) *Severance of Defendants During Trial.* The court must sever defendants during trial, with the defendant's consent or on a finding of manifest necessity, if the court determines severance is necessary to fairly determine the guilt or innocence of one or more of the defendants.

Subd. 4. Consolidation of Indictments, Complaints or Tab Charges for Trial.

(a) The court, on the prosecutor's motion, or on its initiative, may order two or more indictments, complaints, tab charges, or any combination thereof to be tried together if the offenses and the defendants could have been joined in a single indictment, complaint, or tab charge.

(b) On a defendant's motion, the court may order two or more indictments, complaints, tab charges, or any combination of them to be tried together even if the offenses and the defendants could not have been joined in a single indictment, complaint, or tab charge.

(c) In all cases, the procedure will be the same as if the prosecution were under a single indictment, complaint, or tab charge.

Subd. 5. Dual Representation. When 2 or more defendants are jointly charged or will be tried jointly under subdivisions 2 or 4 of this rule, and 2 or more of them are represented by the same attorney, the following procedure must be followed before plea and trial.

(1) The court must:

(a) address each defendant personally on the record;

(b) advise each defendant of the potential danger of dual representation; and

(c) give each defendant an opportunity to question the court on the complexities and possible consequences of dual representation.

(2) The court must elicit from each defendant in a narrative statement that the defendant:

(a) has been advised of the right to effective representation;

(b) understands the details of defense counsel's possible conflict of interest and the potential perils of such a conflict;

(c) has discussed the matter with defense counsel, or if the defendant wishes, with outside counsel; and

(d) voluntarily waives the constitutional right to separate counsel.

Adopted Feb. 26, 1975, eff. July 1, 1975. Revised Dec. 13, 1989. Amended Oct. 27, 2009, eff. Jan. 1, 2010.

Comment—Rule 17

See comment following Rule 17.06.

Historical Notes

The order of the Minnesota Supreme Court [C1–84–2137] dated December 13, 1989, provides in part that "(t)hese amended Rules of Criminal Procedure shall govern all criminal actions commenced or arrests made after 12 o'clock midnight January 1, 1990, except amendments to 8.04, 11.07, and 19.04, subd. 5, shall govern all criminal actions commenced or arrests made after 12 o'clock midnight January 1, 1991."

Rule 17.04. Surplusage

The court on motion may strike surplusage from the indictment, complaint, or tab charge.

Adopted Feb. 26, 1975, eff. July 1, 1975. Revised Dec. 13, 1989. Amended Oct. 27, 2009, eff. Jan. 1, 2010.

Comment—Rule 17

See comment following Rule 17.06.

Historical Notes

The order of the Minnesota Supreme Court [C1–84–2137] dated December 13, 1989, provides in part that "(t)hese amended Rules of Criminal Procedure shall govern all criminal actions commenced or arrests made after 12 o'clock midnight January 1, 1990, except amendments to 8.04, 11.07, and 19.04, subd. 5, shall govern all criminal actions commenced or arrests made after 12 o'clock midnight January 1, 1991."

Rule 17.05. Amendment of Indictment or Complaint

The court may permit an indictment or complaint to be amended at any time before verdict or finding if no additional or different offense is charged and if the defendant's substantial rights are not prejudiced.

Adopted Feb. 26, 1975, eff. July 1, 1975. Revised Dec. 13, 1989. Amended Oct. 27, 2009, eff. Jan. 1, 2010.

Comment—Rule 17

See comment following Rule 17.06.

Historical Notes

The order of the Minnesota Supreme Court [C1–84–2137] dated December 13, 1989, provides in part that "(t)hese amended Rules of Criminal Procedure shall govern all criminal actions commenced or arrests made after 12 o'clock midnight January 1, 1990, except amendments to 8.04, 11.07, and 19.04, subd. 5, shall govern all criminal actions commenced or arrests made after 12 o'clock midnight January 1, 1991."

Rule 17.06. Motions Attacking Indictment, Complaint or Tab Charge

Subd. 1. Defects in Form. No indictment, complaint, or tab charge will be dismissed nor will the trial, judgment, or other proceedings be affected by reason of a defect or imperfection in matters of form that does not prejudice the defendant's substantial rights.

Subd. 2. Motion to Dismiss or for Appropriate Relief. All objections to an indictment, complaint, or tab charge must be made by motion under Rule 10.01, subd. 2 and may be based on the following grounds without limit:

(1) With regard to an indictment:

(a) The evidence admissible before the grand jury was not sufficient to establish an offense charged or any lesser or other included offense;

(b) The grand jury was illegally constituted;

(c) The grand jury proceeding was conducted before fewer than 16 grand jurors;

(d) Fewer than 12 grand jurors concurred in the finding of the indictment;

(e) The indictment was not found or returned as required by law; or

(f) An unauthorized person was in the grand jury room during the presentation of evidence on the charge contained in the indictment, or during the grand jury's deliberations or voting.

(2) With regard to an indictment, complaint, or tab charge:

(a) The indictment, complaint or tab charge does not substantially comply with the requirements prescribed by law to the prejudice of the defendant's substantial rights;

(b) The court lacks jurisdiction over the offense charged;

(c) The law defining the offense charged is unconstitutional or otherwise invalid;

(d) In the case of an indictment or complaint, the facts stated do not constitute an offense;

(e) The prosecution is barred by the statute of limitations;

(f) The defendant has been denied a speedy trial;

(g) There exists some other jurisdictional or legal impediment to the defendant's prosecution or conviction for the offense charged, unless provided by Rule 10.02; or

(h) Double jeopardy, collateral estoppel, or that prosecution is barred by Minn. Stat. § 609.035.

Subd. 3. Time for Motion. A motion to dismiss the indictment, complaint, or tab charge must be made within the time prescribed by Rule 10.03, subd. 1. At any time during the pendency of a proceeding an objection may be made to the court's jurisdiction over the offense or that the indictment, complaint or tab charge fails to charge an offense.

Subd. 4. Effect of Determining Motion to Dismiss.

(1) *Motion Denied.* If the court denies a motion to dismiss the indictment, complaint, or tab charge, the defendant must be permitted to plead if the defendant has not previously entered a plea. A plea previously entered will stand. In all cases, the defendant may continue to raise the issues on appeal if convicted after a trial.

(2) *Grounds for Dismissal.* When the court grants a motion to dismiss an indictment, complaint or tab charge for a defect in the institution of prosecution or in the indictment, complaint, or tab charge, the court must specify the grounds on which the motion is granted.

(3) *Dismissal for Curable Defect.* If the dismissal is for failure to file a timely complaint as required by Rule 4.02, subd. 5(3), or for a defect that could be cured or avoided by an amended or new indictment or complaint, further prosecution for the same offense will not be barred. On the prosecutor's motion made within 7 days after notice of the order granting the motion to dismiss, the court must order that defendant's bail or the other conditions of his release be continued or modified for a specified reasonable time pending an amended or new indictment or complaint.

In misdemeanor cases, if the defendant is unable to post any bail that may be required under Rule 6.02, subd. 1, the defendant must be released subject to such non-monetary conditions as the court deems appropriate. The specified time for such amended or new indictment or complaint must not exceed 60 days for filing a new indictment or 7 days for amending an indictment or complaint or for filing a new complaint. During the 7–day period for making the motion and during the time specified by the order, if such motion is made, the indictment or complaint's dismissal must be stayed. If the prosecutor does not make the motion within the 7–day period or if the indictment or complaint is not amended or if a new indictment or complaint is not filed within the time specified, the defendant must be discharged and further prosecution for the same offense is barred unless the prosecutor has appealed as provided by law, or the defendant is charged with murder and the court has granted a motion to dismiss on the ground of the insufficiency of the evidence before the grand jury. In misdemeanor and designated gross misdemeanor cases (as defined in Rule 1.04(a)–(b)) dismissed for failure to file a timely complaint within the time limits as provided by Rule 4.02 subd. 5(3), further prosecution will not be barred unless the court has so ordered.

Adopted Feb. 26, 1975, eff. July 1, 1975. Revised Dec. 13, 1989. Amended May 9, 1994; Aug. 21, 1998, eff. Jan. 1, 1999; Oct. 27, 2009, eff. Jan. 1, 2010.

Comment—Rule 17

The complaint under Rule 2.01 and the indictment under Rule 17.02, subd. 2 must contain a written statement of the essential facts constituting the offense charged. The statement of the evidence, supporting affidavits, or sworn testimony, showing probable cause required by Rule 2.01 are not a part of the indictment.

The required legal content of the complaint and indictment is set forth in Rules. 2.01 and 17.02, and serves the function of informing the court of the offense(s) charged and the facts establishing probable cause. In addition to this legal information, the court requires administrative information to identify the defendant and the case, as well as additional factual information about the defendant or the status of the defendant's case to fulfill the court's statutory obligations to provide such information to other agencies. There is no requirement that the complaint or indictment be submitted to the court in any particular form or format. Rule 17.02, subd. 4 requires the State Court Administrator to identify and publish the administrative content of the complaint or indictment required by the courts. A sample complaint/indictment and a listing of the administrative content approved by the State Court Administrator will be published on the Minnesota Judicial Branch website. This flexibility will allow for e-filing of the complaint or indictment.

Except to the extent that existing statutes (Minn. Stat. §§ 628.10, 628.12–628.13, 628.15–628.18, 628.20–628.24, 628.27) that govern the contents of an indictment or information are inconsistent with Rule 17.02, they are not abrogated by these rules. So, to the extent they are consistent with the provisions of Rule 17.02, they may be followed in drawing complaints and indictments under these rules.

Rule 17.02, subd. 3 permits counts to be used but prohibits duplication by charging more than one offense in a single count.

Rule 17.03, subd. 5 sets forth procedures for representing two or more defendants who are jointly charged or tried, as set forth in State v. Olsen, 258 N.W.2d 898 (Minn. 1977). That case requires defendants to clearly and unequivocally waive their constitutional right to separate counsel. If a record is not made as required or if the record fails to show that the procedures were followed in every important respect, State v. Olsen, supra, places the burden on the prosecutor to establish beyond a reasonable doubt that a prejudicial conflict of interest did not exist.

Rule 17.05 leaves district courts to determine whether the defendant will be substantially prejudiced by an amendment and what steps, if any, including a continuance, may be taken to remove any prejudice that might otherwise result from an amendment. Rule 17.05 does not govern a complaint's amendment after a mistrial and before the start of the second trial. Rather, Rule 3.04, subd. 2, which provides for the free amendment of the complaint, controls. State v. Alexander, 290 N.W.2d 745 (Minn. 1980).

Grounds for a motion for dismissal of an indictment only and for a motion for dismissal of an indictment or complaint are set forth in Rule 17.06, subd. 2(1) and (2). These grounds are not intended to be exclusive.

Rule 17.06, subd. 2(1)(a) is available because Rule 18.04, subd. 1 requires a record to be made of the evidence taken before the grand jury. (See also the provisions of 18.04, subd. 1 for the conditions in which the record may be disclosed to the defendant. And see also Rule 18.05, subd. 2.) Upon such a motion, the admissibility and sufficiency of evidence pertaining to indictments is governed by Rules 18.05, subd. 1, and 18.05, subd. 2.

Rule 17.06, subd. 2(2)(f) leaves to judicial decision the constitutional or other requirements of a speedy trial as well as the effect of denying a defendant's demand for trial under Rule 11.08–.09 and Rule 6.06.

By Rule 10.03, subd. 1, a motion to dismiss an indictment or complaint must be served no later than 3 days before the Omnibus Hearing under Rule 11 unless the time is extended for good cause. In misdemeanor cases, by Rule 17.06, subd. 3, a motion to dismiss a complaint or tab charge must be served at least 3 days before the pretrial conference or, at least 3 days before the trial if no pretrial conference is held, unless this time is extended for good cause.

The first sentence of Rule 17.06, subd. 4 contemplates that a defendant may plead not guilty and also make a motion to dismiss if the defendant wishes.

To make the basis for dismissal based on a defect in the institution of the prosecution or in the indictment or complaint apparent, Rule 17.06, subd. 4 requires the court to specify the grounds for granting the motion. Under Rule 17.06, subd. 4(3), if the dismissal is for failure to file a timely complaint as required by Rule 4.02, subd. 5(3) for misdemeanor cases, or for designated gross misdemeanor cases as defined in Rule 1.04(b), or for a defect which could be cured by a new complaint, the prosecutor may within 7 days after notice of entry of the order dismissing the case move to continue the case for the purpose of filing a new complaint. On such a motion, the court must continue the case for no more than 7 days pending the filing of a new complaint, or amending of the complaint or indictment, or for 60 days pending the filing of a new indictment. This filing requirement for a new or amended complaint is not satisfied until the complaint is signed by the judge or other appropriate issuing officer and then filed with the court administrator.

During the time for such a motion and during any continuance, dismissal of the charge is stayed. In a misdemeanor case, the defendant must not be kept in custody. Rule 17.06, subd. 4(3), does not govern dismissals for defects that could not be cured at the time of dismissal by a new or amended complaint or indictment. Therefore, when a complaint or indictment has been dismissed because of insufficient evidence to establish probable cause, the prosecutor may re-prosecute if further evidence is later discovered to establish probable cause. Also under Rule 4.02, subd. 5(3), even if prosecution is reinstituted within the specified period after having been dismissed for failure to file a timely complaint, a summons rather than a warrant must be issued to secure the defendant's appearance in court.

Historical Notes

The order of the Minnesota Supreme Court [C1–84–2137] dated December 13, 1989, provides in part that "(t)hese amended Rules of Criminal Procedure shall govern all criminal actions commenced or arrests made after 12 o'clock midnight January 1, 1990, except amendments to 8.04, 11.07, and 19.04, subd. 5, shall govern all criminal actions commenced or arrests made after 12 o'clock midnight January 1, 1991."

The order of the Minnesota Supreme Court [C1–84–2137] dated May 9, 1994, provides in part that "(t)hese amendments to the Rules of Criminal Procedure shall govern all criminal actions commenced or arrests made after 12 o'clock midnight July 1, 1994, except that the amendments in the first sentence of the third paragraph in Rule 2.01 shall govern all criminal actions commenced or arrests made after 12 o'clock midnight January 1, 1995."

RULE 18. GRAND JURY

Rule 18.01. Summoning Grand Juries

Subd. 1. When Summoned. The court must order that one or more grand juries be drawn at least annually. The grand jury must be summoned and convened whenever required by the public interest, or whenever requested by the county attorney.

On being drawn, each juror must be notified of selection. The court must prescribe by order or rule the time and manner of summoning grand jurors. Vacancies in the grand jury panel must be filled in the same manner as this rule provides.

Subd. 2. How Selected and Drawn. Except as provided for St. Louis County, the grand jury must be drawn from a list composed of the names of persons selected at random from a fair cross-section of the statutorily qualified residents of the county.

In St. Louis County, a grand jury list must be selected from residents of each of the 3 districts of St. Louis County. When the offense is committed nearer to Virginia or Hibbing than to the county seat, the case must be submitted to the grand jury in Virginia or Hibbing.

Adopted Feb. 26, 1975, eff. July 1, 1975. Revised Dec. 13, 1989. Amended Oct. 27, 2009, eff. Jan. 1, 2010.

Comment—Rule 18

See comment following Rule 18.09.

Historical Notes

The order of the Minnesota Supreme Court [C1–84–2137] dated December 13, 1989, provides in part that "(t)hese amended Rules of Criminal Procedure shall govern all criminal actions commenced or arrests made after 12 o'clock midnight January 1, 1990, except amendments to 8.04, 11.07, and 19.04, subd. 5, shall govern all criminal actions commenced or arrests made after 12 o'clock midnight January 1, 1991."

Rule 18.02. Organization of Grand Jury

Subd. 1. Members; Quorum. A grand jury consists of not more than 23 nor fewer than 16 persons, and must not proceed unless at least 16 members are present.

Subd. 2. Organization and Proceedings. The grand jury must be organized and its proceedings conducted as provided by statute, unless these rules direct otherwise.

Subd. 3. Charge. After swearing the grand jury, the court must instruct it on its duties.

Former Rule 18.03 adopted Feb. 26, 1975, eff. July 1, 1975. Revised Dec. 13, 1989. Renumbered Rule 18.02 and amended Oct. 27, 2009, eff. Jan. 1, 2010.

Comment—Rule 18

See comment following Rule 18.09.

Historical Notes

The order of the Minnesota Supreme Court [C1–84–2137] dated December 13, 1989, provides in part that "(t)hese amended Rules of Criminal Procedure shall govern all criminal actions commenced or arrests made after 12 o'clock midnight January 1, 1990, except amendments to 8.04, 11.07, and 19.04, subd. 5, shall govern all criminal actions commenced or arrests made after 12 o'clock midnight January 1, 1991."

Former Rule. Former Rule 18.02 related to objections to the grand jury and grand jurors. See, now, Rules Crim.Proc., Rule 18.09.

Rule 18.03. Who May Be Present

Prosecutors, the witness under examination, qualified interpreters for witnesses disabled in communication, or for jurors with a sensory disability, and for the purpose of recording the evidence, a reporter or operator of a recording instrument may be present while the grand jury is in session. No person other than the jurors and any qualified interpreters for any jurors with a sensory disability may be present while the grand jury is deliberating or voting.

On the court's order and a showing of necessity, for security purposes, a designated peace officer may be present while a specified witness testifies.

If a witness at the grand jury requests, and has effectively waived the privilege against self-incrimination, or has been granted use immunity, the attorney for the witness may be present while the witness testifies, provided the attorney is present for that purpose, or the attorney's presence can be secured without unreasonably delaying the grand jury proceedings. The attorney cannot participate in the grand jury proceedings except to advise and consult with the witness while the witness testifies.

By order of the court based on a particularized showing of need, a witness under the age of 18 may be accompanied by a parent, guardian or other supportive person while that child witness testifies at the grand jury. The parent, guardian or other supportive person must not participate in the grand jury proceedings, and must not be permitted to influence the content of the witness's testimony.

In choosing the parent, guardian or other supportive person, the court must determine whether the person is appropriate, including whether the person may become a witness in the case, or may exert undue influence over the child witness. The court must instruct the person on the proper role for that person in the grand jury proceedings.

Former Rule 18.04 adopted Feb. 26, 1975, eff. July 1, 1975. Revised Dec. 13, 1989. Renumbered Rule 18.03 and amended Oct. 27, 2009, eff. Jan. 1, 2010.

Comment—Rule 18

See comment following Rule 18.09.

Historical Notes

The order of the Minnesota Supreme Court [C1–84–2137] dated December 13, 1989, provides in part that "(t)hese amended Rules of Criminal Procedure shall govern all criminal actions commenced or arrests made after 12 o'clock midnight January 1, 1990, except amendments to 8.04, 11.07, and 19.04, subd. 5, shall govern all criminal actions commenced or arrests made after 12 o'clock midnight January 1, 1991."

Former Rule: Former Rule 18.03 related to the organization of the grand jury. See, now, Rules Crim.Proc., Rule 18.02.

Rule 18.04. Record of Proceedings

Subd. 1. Verbatim Record. A verbatim record must be made of all statements made, evidence taken, and events occurring before the grand jury except deliberations and voting.

The record must not include any grand juror's name. The record may be disclosed only to the court or prosecutor unless the court, on the defendant's motion for good cause, or on a showing that grounds may exist for a motion to dismiss the indictment because of matters occurring before the grand jury, orders disclosure of the record or designated portions of it to the defendant or defense counsel.

Subd. 2. Transcript. On the defendant's motion, and with notice to the prosecutor, the court at any time before trial must, subject to a protective order as may be granted under Rule 9.03, subd. 5, order that defense counsel may obtain a transcript or copy of:

(1) defendant's grand jury testimony;

(2) the grand jury testimony of witnesses the prosecutor intends to call at the defendant's trial; or

(3) the grand jury testimony of any witness, if defense counsel makes an offer of proof that a witness the defendant expects to call at trial will give relevant and favorable testimony for the defendant.

Former Rule 18.05 adopted Feb. 26, 1975, eff. July 1, 1975. Revised Dec. 13, 1989. Amended May 9, 1994; Aug. 21, 1998, eff. Jan. 1, 1999; Dec. 23, 2002, eff. Feb. 1, 2003. Renumbered Rule 18.04 and amended Oct. 27, 2009, eff. Jan. 1, 2010.

Comment—Rule 18

See comment following Rule 18.09.

Historical Notes

The order of the Minnesota Supreme Court [C1–84–2137] dated December 13, 1989, provides in part that "(t)hese amended Rules of Criminal Procedure shall govern all criminal actions commenced or arrests made after 12 o'clock midnight January 1, 1990, except amendments to 8.04, 11.07, and 19.04, subd. 5, shall govern all criminal actions commenced or arrests made after 12 o'clock midnight January 1, 1991."

The order of the Minnesota Supreme Court [C1–84–2137] dated May 9, 1994, provides in part that "(t)hese amendments to the Rules of Criminal Procedure shall govern all criminal actions commenced or arrests made after 12 o'clock midnight July 1, 1994, except that the amendments in the first sentence of the third paragraph in Rule 2.01 shall govern all criminal actions commenced or arrests made after 12 o'clock midnight January 1, 1995."

Former Rule: Former Rule 18.04 related to who may be present during grand jury proceedings. See, now, Rules Crim.Proc., Rule 18.03.

Rule 18.05. Kind and Character of Evidence

Subd. 1. Admissibility of Evidence. An indictment must be based on evidence that would be admissible at trial, with these exceptions:

(1) Hearsay evidence offered only to lay the foundation for the admissibility of otherwise admissible evidence if admissible foundation evidence is available and will be offered at the trial.

(2) A report by a physician, chemist, firearms identification expert, examiner of questioned documents, fingerprint technician, or an expert or technician in some comparable scientific or professional field, concerning the results of an examination, comparison, or test performed by the person in connection with the investigation of the case against the defendant, when certified by the person as the person's report.

(3) Unauthenticated copies of official records if authenticated copies will be available at trial.

(4) Written sworn statements of the persons who claim to have title or an interest in property to prove ownership or that the property was obtained without the owner's consent, and written sworn statements of these persons or of experts to prove the value of the property, if admissible evidence to

prove ownership, value, or nonconsent is available and will be presented at the trial.

(5) Written sworn statements of witnesses who for reasons of ill health, or for other valid reasons, are unable to testify in person if the witnesses, or otherwise admissible evidence, will be available at the trial to prove the facts contained in the statements.

(6) Oral or written summaries made by investigating officers or other persons, who are called as witnesses, of the contents of books, records, papers and other documents that they have examined but that are not produced at the hearing or were not previously submitted to defense counsel for examination, if the documents and summaries would otherwise be admissible. A police officer in charge of the investigation may give an oral summary.

Subd. 2. Evidence Warranting Finding of Indictment. The grand jury may find an indictment if the evidence establishes probable cause to believe an offense has been committed and the defendant committed it. Reception of inadmissible evidence does not provide grounds for dismissing the indictment if sufficient admissible evidence exists to support the indictment.

Subd. 3. Presentments Abolished. The grand jury may not find or return a presentment.

Former Rule 18.06 adopted Feb. 26, 1975, eff. July 1, 1975. Revised Dec. 13, 1989. Renumbered Rule 18.05 and amended Oct. 27, 2009, eff. Jan. 1, 2010.

Comment—Rule 18

See comment following Rule 18.09.

Historical Notes

The order of the Minnesota Supreme Court [C1–84–2137] dated December 13, 1989, provides in part that "(t)hese amended Rules of Criminal Procedure shall govern all criminal actions commenced or arrests made after 12 o'clock midnight January 1, 1990, except amendments to 8.04, 11.07, and 19.04, subd. 5, shall govern all criminal actions commenced or arrests made after 12 o'clock midnight January 1, 1991."

Former Rule: Former Rule 18.05 related to a record of the proceedings. See, now, Rules Crim.Proc., Rule 18.04.

Rule 18.06. Finding and Return of Indictment

An indictment may only issue if at least 12 jurors concur. The indictment must be signed by the foreperson, whether the foreperson was one of the 12 who concurred or not, and delivered to a judge in open court. If 12 jurors do not concur in issuing an indictment, the foreperson must promptly inform the court in writing. Charges filed against the defendant for offenses on which no indictment was issued must be dismissed. The failure to issue an indictment or the dismissal of the charge does not prevent the case from again being submitted to a grand jury as often as the court directs.

Former Rule 18.07 adopted Feb. 26, 1975, eff. July 1, 1975. Revised Dec. 13, 1989. Renumbered Rule 18.06 and amended Oct. 27, 2009, eff. Jan. 1, 2010.

Comment—Rule 18

See comment following Rule 18.09.

Historical Notes

The order of the Minnesota Supreme Court [C1–84–2137] dated December 13, 1989, provides in part that "(t)hese amended Rules of Criminal Procedure shall govern all criminal actions commenced or arrests made after 12 o'clock midnight January 1, 1990, except amendments to 8.04, 11.07, and 19.04, subd. 5, shall govern all criminal actions commenced or arrests made after 12 o'clock midnight January 1, 1991."

Former Rule: Former Rule 18.06 related to the kind and character of evidence. See, now, Rules Crim.Proc., Rule 18.05.

Rule 18.07. Secrecy of Proceedings

Every grand juror and every qualified interpreter for a grand juror with a sensory disability present during deliberations or voting must keep secret whatever that juror or any other juror has said during deliberations and how that juror or any other juror voted.

Disclosure of matters occurring before the grand jury, other than its deliberations and the vote of any juror, may be made to the prosecutor for use in the performance of the prosecutor's duties, and to the defendant or defense counsel under Rule 18.04 governing the record of the grand jury proceedings. Otherwise, no one may disclose matters occurring before the grand jury unless directed to do so by the court in connection with a judicial proceeding.

Unless the court otherwise directs, no person may disclose the finding of an indictment until the defendant is in custody or appears before the court, unless necessary for the issuance and execution of a summons or warrant. However, disclosure may be made by the prosecutor by notice to the defendant or defense counsel of the indictment and the time of defendant's appearance in the district court, if in the prosecutor's discretion the notice suffices to insure defendant's appearance.

Former Rule 18.08 adopted Feb. 26, 1975, eff. July 1, 1975. Revised Dec. 13, 1989. Renumbered Rule 18.07 and amended Oct. 27, 2009, eff. Jan. 1, 2010.

Comment—Rule 18

See comment following Rule 18.09.

Historical Notes

The order of the Minnesota Supreme Court [C1–84–2137] dated December 13, 1989, provides in part that "(t)hese amended Rules of Criminal Procedure shall govern all criminal actions commenced or arrests made after 12 o'clock midnight January 1, 1990, except amendments to 8.04, 11.07, and 19.04, subd. 5, shall govern all criminal actions commenced or arrests made after 12 o'clock midnight January 1, 1991."

Former Rule: Former Rule 18.07 related to the finding and return of indictment. See, now, Rules Crim.Proc., Rule 18.06.

Rule 18.08. Tenure and Excusal

Subd. 1. Tenure. A grand jury must be drawn for a specified period of service, not to exceed 12 months, as designated by court order. The grand jury must not be discharged, and its powers must continue until the latest of the following:

(a) the period of service is completed;

(b) its successor is drawn; or

(c) it has completed an investigation, already begun, of a particular offense.

Subd. 2. Excusal. For cause shown, the court may excuse a juror temporarily or permanently. The court may impanel another person in place of the excused juror.

Former Rule 18.09 adopted Feb. 26, 1975, eff. July 1, 1975. Revised Dec. 13, 1989. Amended Aug. 21, 1998, eff. Jan. 1, 1999; Dec. 23, 2002, eff. Feb. 1, 2003. Renumbered Rule 18.08 and amended Oct. 27, 2009, eff. Jan. 1, 2010.

Comment—Rule 18

See comment following Rule 18.09.

Historical Notes

The order of the Minnesota Supreme Court [C1–84–2137] dated December 13, 1989, provides in part that "(t)hese amended Rules of Criminal Procedure shall govern all criminal actions commenced or arrests made after 12 o'clock midnight January 1, 1990, except amendments to 8.04, 11.07, and 19.04, subd. 5, shall govern all criminal actions commenced or arrests made after 12 o'clock midnight January 1, 1991."

Former Rule: Former Rule 18.08 related to the secrecy of grand jury proceedings. See, now, Rules Crim.Proc., Rule 18.07.

Rule 18.09. Objections to Grand Jury and Grand Jurors

Subd. 1. Motion to Dismiss Indictment. Objections to the grand jury panel and to individual grand jurors must be made by motion to dismiss the indictment as this rule provides.

Subd. 2. Grounds for Dismissal. A motion to dismiss an indictment may be based on any of the following:

(a) the grand jury was not selected, drawn or summoned in accordance with law;

(b) an individual juror was not legally qualified; or

(c) the juror's state of mind prevented the juror from acting impartially.

An indictment must not be dismissed on the ground that one or more of the grand jurors was not statutorily qualified if it appears from the records that 12 or more qualified jurors concurred in finding the indictment.

Former Rule 18.02 adopted Feb. 26, 1975, eff. July 1, 1975. Revised Dec. 13, 1989. Renumbered Rule 18.09 and amended Oct. 27, 2009, eff. Jan. 1, 2010.

Comment—Rule 18

Rule 18.01, subd. 2 complies with the constitutional requirement that the persons on the grand jury list must be selected at random from a fair cross section of the qualified residents of the county. The method by which this must be done is left to the determination of the jury commission or judges making the selection of persons for the list.

Rule 18.01, subd. 2 includes special provisions governing St. Louis County based on Minn. Stat. §§ 484.46 and 484.48.

Rule 18.03 allows qualified interpreters for jurors with sensory disabilities to be present during grand jury proceedings including deliberations or voting. This is in accord with Minn. Stat. § 593.32 and Rule 809 of the Jury Management Rules in the General Rules of Practice for District Courts, which prohibit exclusion from jury service for certain reasons including sensory disability. Further, this provision allows the court to make reasonable accommodation for such jurors under the Americans with Disabilities Act. 42 U.S.C. § 12101 et seq.

Under Rule 18.04, subd. 1, the record may be disclosed to the court or to the prosecutor, and to the defendant for good cause, which would include a "particularized need," Dennis v. United States, 384 U.S. 855, 869–70 (1966), or on a showing that grounds exist for a motion to dismiss the indictment because of occurrences before the grand jury. In addition, the defendant, under Rule 9.01, subd. 1, may obtain from the prosecutor any portions of the grand jury proceedings already transcribed and possessed by the prosecutor.

Rule 18.04, subd. 2, supplementing the discovery rules (Rule 9.01, subd. 1), permits the defendant to obtain a transcript of the testimony of grand jury witnesses, subject to protective orders under Rule 9.03, subd. 5. See ABA Standards, Discovery and Procedure Before Trial, 2.1(a)(iii) (Approved Draft, 1970). This rule does not preclude the court from ordering that the defendant be supplied with the transcript during the trial, on a showing of good cause.

Canon 5 of the Code of Professional Responsibility for Interpreters in the Minnesota State Court System bolsters the confidentiality requirement of interpreters under Rule 18.07.

Rule 18.07 leaves it to the discretion of the prosecutor to determine whether to notify the defendant or defense counsel of the indictment without the issuance of a warrant or summons. But see Minn. Stat. § 628.68 (leaving it to the court's, not prosecutor's, discretion).

The effect of a dismissal of an indictment under Rule 18.09 is covered by Rule 17.06, subd. 4.

Historical Notes

The order of the Minnesota Supreme Court [C1–84–2137] dated December 13, 1989, provides in part that "(t)hese amended Rules of Criminal Procedure shall govern all criminal actions commenced or arrests made after 12 o'clock midnight January 1, 1990, except amendments to 8.04, 11.07, and 19.04, subd. 5, shall govern all criminal actions commenced or arrests made after 12 o'clock midnight January 1, 1991."

Former Rule: Former Rule 18.09 related to the tenure of a grand jury and the excusal of grand jurors. See, now, Rules Crim.Proc., Rule 18.08.

RULE 19. WARRANT OR SUMMONS UPON INDICTMENT; APPEARANCE BEFORE DISTRICT COURT

Rule 19.01. Issuance

On the filing of an indictment, the court must issue a warrant for the arrest of each defendant named in the indictment, except that the court may issue a summons instead of a warrant when the prosecutor requests or the court directs, or if the defendant is a corporation.

The court may order an indicted defendant already in custody to be brought before the court at a specified date and time.

More than one warrant or summons may be issued for the same defendant. If a defendant, other than a corporation, fails to appear in response to a summons, a warrant must issue.

Adopted Feb. 26, 1975, eff. July 1, 1975. Revised Dec. 13, 1989. Amended Oct. 27, 2009, eff. Jan. 1, 2010.

Comment—Rule 19

See comment following Rule 19.06.

Historical Notes

The order of the Minnesota Supreme Court [C1–84–2137] dated December 13, 1989, provides in part that "(t)hese amended Rules of Criminal Procedure shall govern all criminal actions commenced or arrests made after 12 o'clock midnight January 1, 1990, except amendments to 8.04, 11.07, and 19.04, subd. 5, shall govern all criminal actions commenced or arrests made after 12 o'clock midnight January 1, 1991."

Rule 19.02. Form

Subd. 1. Warrant. The warrant must:

(a) be signed by a judge;

(b) contain the defendant's name or, if unknown, any name or description by which the defendant can be identified with reasonable certainty;

(c) describe the offense charged; and

(d) command the defendant's arrest and appearance in court.

The amount of bail and other conditions of release may be set by the court and stated in the warrant.

Subd. 2. Summons. The summons must be signed by the court and must summon the defendant to appear before the court at a specified time and place to answer to the indictment. A copy of the indictment must be attached to the summons.

Adopted Feb. 26, 1975, eff. July 1, 1975. Revised Dec. 13, 1989. Amended Oct. 27, 2009, eff. Jan. 1, 2010.

Comment—Rule 19

See comment following Rule 19.06.

Historical Notes

The order of the Minnesota Supreme Court [C1–84–2137] dated December 13, 1989, provides in part that "(t)hese amended Rules of Criminal Procedure shall govern all criminal actions commenced or arrests made after 12 o'clock midnight January 1, 1990, except amendments to 8.04, 11.07, and 19.04, subd. 5, shall govern all criminal actions commenced or arrests made after 12 o'clock midnight January 1, 1991."

Rule 19.03. Service of the Indictment

Subd. 1. By Whom. Any officer authorized by law may execute the warrant, and if authorized may also serve the summons. The court administrator may serve the summons by mail.

Subd. 2. Territorial Limits. The warrant may be executed or the summons served any place in the state, except where prohibited by law.

Subd. 3. Manner. The warrant must be executed or the summons served as specified in Rule 3.03, subd. 3.

Subd. 4. Certification. The execution of a warrant or the service of a summons must be certified as specified in Rule 3.03, subd. 4.

Subd. 5. Unexecuted Warrants. At the prosecutor's request made during the pendency of the indictment, a warrant returned unexecuted or a summons returned unserved, or a duplicate of either, may be delivered to any authorized officer or person for execution or service.

Adopted Feb. 26, 1975, eff. July 1, 1975. Revised Dec. 13, 1989. Amended Oct. 27, 2009, eff. Jan. 1, 2010.

Comment—Rule 19

See comment following Rule 19.06.

Historical Notes

The order of the Minnesota Supreme Court [C1–84–2137] dated December 13, 1989, provides in part that "(t)hese amended Rules of Criminal Procedure shall govern all criminal actions commenced or arrests made after 12 o'clock midnight January 1, 1990, except amendments to 8.04, 11.07, and 19.04, subd. 5, shall govern all criminal actions commenced or arrests made after 12 o'clock midnight January 1, 1991."

Rule 19.04. Defendant's Appearance in Court

Subd. 1. Appearance. The defendant must be taken promptly before the district court that issued the warrant.

Subd. 2. Statement to Defendant. A defendant appearing initially in the district court under an arrest warrant, or in response to a summons, must be advised of the charges. If the defendant has not received a copy of the indictment, the defendant must be provided with one.

The court must also advise the defendant in accordance with Rule 5.03 (Statement of Rights).

Subd. 3. Appointment of Counsel. If the defendant is not represented by counsel and cannot financially afford counsel, the court must appoint counsel as set out in Rule 5.04.

Subd. 4. Date for Arraignment. The court may arraign the defendant at the defendant's initial appearance on the indictment, if the defendant so requests and the court consents.

If the court does not arraign the defendant at the initial appearance, it must set a date for the arraignment not more than 7 days from the initial appearance. The court may extend this date for good cause.

At the arraignment, whether at the initial appearance or at some later appearance before the Omnibus Hearing, the defendant may only enter a plea of guilty. A defendant who does not wish to plead guilty must not be asked to enter any other plea, and the arraignment must be continued until the Omnibus Hearing, where, under Rule 11.08 (Pleas), the defendant must plead to the indictment, or be given additional time to plead.

Subd. 5. Omnibus Hearing Date and Procedure. If at arraignment the defendant does not plead guilty, the court must schedule an Omnibus Hearing under Rule 11 not more than seven 7 days from the arraignment, unless the court extends the time for good cause.

Subd. 6. Notice by Prosecutor. The procedures set out in Rules 7.01 (Notice of Omnibus Issues), 7.02 (Notice of Other Offenses), and 7.03 (Notice of Intent to Seek Aggravated Sentence) apply to cases prosecuted by indictment.

Subd. 7. Completion of Discovery. The procedure set out in Rule 7.04 for completion of discovery in felony, gross misdemeanor, and misdemeanor cases applies to cases prosecuted by indictment.

Adopted Feb. 26, 1975, eff. July 1, 1975. Revised Dec. 13, 1989. Amended Aug. 17, 2006, eff. Oct. 1, 2006; Oct. 27, 2009, eff. Jan. 1, 2010.

Comment—Rule 19

See comment following Rule 19.06.

Historical Notes

The order of the Minnesota Supreme Court [C1–84–2137] dated December 13, 1989, provides in part that "(t)hese amended Rules of Criminal Procedure shall govern all criminal actions commenced or arrests made after 12 o'clock midnight January 1, 1990, except amendments to 8.04, 11.07, and 19.04, subd. 5, shall govern all criminal actions commenced or arrests made after 12 o'clock midnight January 1, 1991."

Rule 19.05. Bail or Conditions of Release

At the defendant's initial appearance in the district court following indictment, the court may, in accordance with Rule 6 (Pretrial Release), set bail or other conditions of release, or may continue or modify bail or conditions of release previously ordered.

Adopted Feb. 26, 1975, eff. July 1, 1975. Revised Dec. 13, 1989. Amended Oct. 27, 2009, eff. Jan. 1, 2010.

Comment—Rule 19

See comment following Rule 19.06.

Historical Notes

The order of the Minnesota Supreme Court [C1–84–2137] dated December 13, 1989, provides in part that "(t)hese amended Rules of Criminal Procedure shall govern all criminal actions commenced or arrests made after 12 o'clock midnight January 1, 1990, except amendments to 8.04, 11.07, and 19.04, subd. 5, shall govern all criminal actions commenced or arrests made after 12 o'clock midnight January 1, 1991."

Rule 19.06. Record

A verbatim record must be made at the defendant's initial appearance, arraignment, and Omnibus Hearing.

Adopted Feb. 26, 1975, eff. July 1, 1975. Revised Dec. 13, 1989. Amended Oct. 27, eff. Jan. 1, 2010.

Comment—Rule 19

Rule 19 relating to the warrant or summons on an indictment and the subsequent procedures parallels for the most part Rules 3, 4, 5, 8, and 11 governing the warrant or summons on a complaint and the procedures subsequently followed, all of which lead up to the Omnibus Hearing under Rule 11. Rule 19 reflects the necessary differences between the procedures under an indictment and under a complaint.

If a corporation does not respond to a summons issued under Rule 19.01 the court may proceed as provided in Rule 14.02, subd. 5.

The parties must serve their motions under Rule 10 at least 3 days before the Omnibus Hearing (Rule 10.03) (including motions to suppress based on the Rasmussen notice given under Rule 19.04, subd. 6). See also comments to Rules 11.02 and 11.04.

The Omnibus Hearing must be held in the district court in accordance with the provisions of Rule 11. See comments to Rule 11. If at the Omnibus Hearing the defendant wishes to challenge the sufficiency of the evidence heard by the grand jury to support the indictment, Rules 17.06, subd. 2(1)(a) and 18.05, subds. 1 and 2 govern that challenge. The provision in Rule 11.03 concerning a motion that an insufficient showing of probable cause has been made applies only to complaints and not to indictments.

Historical Notes

The order of the Minnesota Supreme Court [C1–84–2137] dated December 13, 1989, provides in part that "(t)hese amended Rules of Criminal Procedure shall govern all criminal actions commenced or arrests made after 12 o'clock midnight January 1, 1990, except amendments to 8.04, 11.07, and 19.04, subd. 5, shall govern all criminal actions commenced or arrests made after 12 o'clock midnight January 1, 1991."

RULE 20. MENTALLY ILL OR MENTALLY DEFICIENT DEFENDANTS

Rule 20.01. Competency Proceedings

Subd. 1. Waiver of Counsel in Competency Proceedings. A defendant must not be allowed to waive counsel if the defendant lacks ability to:

(a) knowingly, voluntarily, and intelligently waive the right to counsel;

(b) appreciate the consequences of proceeding without counsel;

(c) comprehend the nature of the charge;

(d) comprehend the nature of the proceedings;

(e) comprehend the possible punishment; or

(f) comprehend any other matters essential to understanding the case.

The court must not proceed under this rule before a lawyer consults with the defendant and has an opportunity to be heard.

Subd. 2. Competency to Participate in the Proceedings. A defendant is incompetent and must not plead, be tried, or be sentenced if the defendant lacks ability to:

(a) rationally consult with counsel; or

(b) understand the proceedings or participate in the defense due to mental illness or deficiency.

Subd. 3. Competency Motion. If the prosecutor, defense counsel, or the court, at any time, doubts the defendant's competency, the prosecutor or defense counsel must make a motion challenging competency, or the court on its initiative must raise the issue. The defendant's consent is not required. The motion must provide supporting facts, but must not include communications between the defendant and defense counsel if disclosure would violate the attorney-client privilege. By bringing the motion, defense counsel does not waive the attorney-client privilege. If the court determines that reason exists to doubt the defendant's competency, the court must suspend the criminal proceedings and proceed as follows.

(a) In misdemeanor cases, the court must:

(1) proceed under this rule as in felony or gross misdemeanor cases;

(2) begin civil commitment proceedings; or

(3) dismiss the case, unless dismissal would be contrary to the public interest.

(b) In felony or gross misdemeanor cases, the court must, on motion, determine probable cause. If probable cause exists, the court must order an examination of the defendant's mental condition. If no probable cause exists, the charges must be dismissed.

Subd. 4. Examination and Report.

(a) Medical Examination. The court must appoint at least one examiner as defined in Minn. Stat. ch. 253B, or successor statute, to examine the defendant and report to the court on the defendant's mental condition.

If the defendant is entitled to release, and the examination can be done on an outpatient basis, the court cannot order the defendant to be confined for the examination. The court may make appearance for the examination a condition of release. If the defendant is not entitled to release or the examination cannot be done on an outpatient basis, the court may order the defendant confined in a state hospital or other suitable facility for up to 60 days to complete the examination.

If the prosecutor or defense counsel has a qualified examiner, the court, on request, must allow the examiner to observe the examination and examine the defendant. Any examiner may obtain and review the report of any prior examination under this rule.

The court must order that if any examiner appointed to examine the defendant concludes that the defendant presents an imminent risk of serious danger to another, is imminently suicidal, or otherwise needs emergency intervention, the examiner must promptly notify the prosecutor, defense counsel, and the court.

(b) Report of Examination. The court-appointed examiner must forward a written report to the judge who ordered the examination. The court must promptly provide a copy of the report to the prosecutor and defense counsel. The report must not be otherwise disclosed until the competency hearing. The report must include:

(1) A diagnosis of the defendant's mental condition.

(2) If the defendant is mentally ill or deficient, an opinion as to:

(a) the defendant's capacity to understand the proceedings or participate in the defense;

(b) whether the defendant presents an imminent risk of serious danger to another, is imminently suicidal, or otherwise needs emergency intervention;

(c) any treatment required for the defendant to attain or maintain competence and an explanation of appropriate treatment alternatives by order of preference, including the extent to which the defendant can be treated without commitment to an institution and the reasons for rejecting such treatment if institutionalization is recommended;

(d) whether a substantial probability exists that the defendant will ever attain competency to proceed;

(e) the estimated time required to attain competency to proceed; and

(f) the availability of acceptable treatment programs in the geographic area including the provider and type of treatment.

(3) The factual basis for the diagnosis and opinions.

(4) If the examination could not be conducted because of the defendant's unwillingness to participate, an opinion, if possible, as to whether the unwillingness resulted from mental illness or deficiency.

Subd. 5. Competency Determination.

(a) Request for Hearing. The court must hold a hearing if a party files written objections to the competency report within ten (10) days after receipt.

(b) Hearing Process. The party that requested the competency hearing must present evidence first. If the court requested the competency report, the prosecutor must present evidence first unless the court otherwise orders.

(c) Evidence. Evidence of the defendant's mental condition may be admitted, including the court-appointed examiner's report. The court-appointed examiner or any person designated by the examiner as a source of information for preparation of the report other than the defendant or defense counsel, is considered the court's witness and may be called and cross-examined by any party.

(d) Defense Counsel as Witness. Defense counsel may testify, subject to the prosecutor's cross-examination, but must not violate the attorney-client privilege. Testifying does not automatically disqualify defense counsel from continuing to represent the defendant. The court may inquire of defense counsel regarding the attorney-client relationship and the defendant's ability to communicate with counsel. The court must not require counsel to divulge communications protected by the attorney-client privilege, and the prosecutor cannot cross-examine defense counsel concerning responses to the court's inquiry.

(e) Determination Without Hearing. If no party timely filed objections and the court did not hold a competency hearing, the court may determine the defendant's competency on the examiner's report.

(f) Burden of Proof and Decision. If the court finds by the greater weight of the evidence that the defendant is competent, it must enter an order finding the defendant competent. Otherwise, the court must enter an order finding the defendant incompetent.

Subd. 6. Procedure After Competency Proceedings.

(a) Finding of Competency. If the court finds the defendant competent, the criminal proceedings must resume.

(b) Finding of Incompetency. If the court finds the defendant incompetent, and the charge is a misdemeanor, the charge must be dismissed. If the court finds the defendant incompetent, and the charge is a felony or gross misdemeanor, the proceedings must be suspended except as provided in Rule 20.01, subd. 8.

(1) Finding of Mental Illness. If the court finds the defendant mentally ill so as to be incapable of understanding the criminal proceedings or participating in the defense, and the defendant is under civil commitment as mentally ill, the court must order the commitment to continue. If the defendant is not under commitment, the court must commence a civil commitment proceeding. The court must supervise the commitment as provided in Rule 20.01, subd. 7.

(2) Finding of Mental Deficiency. If the court finds the defendant mentally deficient so as to be incapable of understanding the criminal proceedings or participating in the defense, and the defendant is under commitment as mentally deficient to the guardianship of the commissioner of public welfare, the court must order the defendant remanded to the care and custody of the commissioner. If the defendant is not under commitment, the court must cause civil commitment proceedings to be instituted against the defendant. The court must supervise the commitment as provided in Rule 20.01, subd. 7.

(3) Appeal. Any party may appeal a civil commitment determination to the Court of Appeals. The appeal must be under Rule 28 and on the record made in the court. A verbatim record must be made in all civil commitment proceedings instituted under this rule.

Subd. 7. Continuing Supervision. The head of the institution to which the defendant is committed, or if the defendant is not committed to an institution, the person charged with the defendant's supervision, must report to the court periodically, not less than once every six months, on the defendant's mental condition with an opinion as to competency to proceed. The court may order a different period. Reports must be furnished to the prosecutor and defense counsel.

The prosecutor, defense counsel, the defendant, or the person charged with the defendant's supervision may apply to the court for a hearing to review the defendant's competency. All parties are entitled to notice before the hearing. If the court finds the defendant competent to proceed, the criminal proceedings must resume. The court and the prosecutor must be notified of any proposed institutional transfer, partial institutionalization status, and any proposed termination, discharge, or provisional discharge of the civil commitment. The prosecutor has the right to participate as a party in any proceedings concerning proposed changes in the defendant's civil commitment or status.

Subd. 8. Dismissal of Criminal Charge.

(1) Felonies. Except when the defendant is charged with murder, the criminal charges must be dismissed three years after the date of finding the defendant incompetent to proceed unless the prosecutor, before the expiration of the three-year period, files a written notice of intent to prosecute when the defendant regains competency.

(2) Gross Misdemeanors. The criminal charges must be dismissed 30 days after the date of finding the defendant incompetent to proceed unless before that date the prosecutor files a written notice of intent to prosecute when the defendant regains competency. If a notice has been filed, the charges must be dismissed when the defendant would be entitled under these rules to custody credit of at least one year if convicted.

Subd. 9. Issues Not Requiring Defendant's Participation. The defendant's incompetence does not preclude defense counsel from making an objection or defense before trial that can be fairly determined without the defendant's participation.

Subd. 10. Admissibility of Defendant's Statements. When a defendant is examined under this rule, any statement made by the defendant for the purpose of the examination and any evidence derived from the examination is admissible at the competency proceeding.

Subd. 11. Credit for Confinement. If the defendant is convicted, any time spent confined to a hospital or other facility for a mental examination under this rule must be credited as time served.

Adopted Feb. 26, 1975, eff. July 1, 1975. Revised Dec. 13, 1989. Amended Dec. 28, 2005, eff. March 1, 2006; Dec. 29, 2006, eff. April 1, 2007; Oct. 27, 2009, eff. Jan. 1, 2010.

Comments—Rule 20

See comment following Rule 20.04.

Historical Notes

The order of the Minnesota Supreme Court [C1–84–2137] dated December 13, 1989, provides in part that "(t)hese amended Rules of Criminal Procedure shall govern all criminal actions commenced or arrests made after 12 o'clock midnight January 1, 1990, except amendments to 8.04, 11.07, and 19.04, subd. 5, shall govern all criminal actions commenced or arrests made after 12 o'clock midnight January 1, 1991."

The order of the Minnesota Supreme Court [C1–84–2137] dated December 28, 2005, provides in part that "(t)he attached amendments shall govern all criminal actions commenced or arrests made after 12 o'clock midnight March 1, 2006."

Rule 20.02. Defense of Mental Illness or Deficiency—Mental Examination

Subd. 1. Authority to Order Examination. The trial court may order the defendant's mental examination if:

(a) the defense notifies the prosecutor of its intent to assert a mental illness or deficiency defense pursuant to Rule 9.02, subd. 1(5);

(b) the defendant in a misdemeanor case pleads not guilty by reason of mental illness or deficiency; or

(c) the defendant offers evidence of mental illness or deficiency at trial.

Subd. 2. Defendant's Examination. If the court orders a mental examination of the defendant, it must appoint at least one examiner as defined in Minn. Stat. ch. 253B, or successor statute, to examine the defendant and report to the court on the defendant's mental condition. The court may order the defendant to be confined to a hospital or other facility for up to 60 days to complete the examination if special need is shown. If any party has retained an examiner, the examiner must be permitted to observe the mental examination and examine the defendant.

Subd. 3. Defendant's Refusal to be Examined. If the defendant does not participate in the examination and thereby prevents the examiner from making an adequate report to the court, the court may:

(a) prohibit the defendant from introducing evidence of the defendant's mental condition;

(b) strike any previously introduced evidence of the defendant's mental condition;

(c) permit any party to introduce evidence of the defendant's refusal to cooperate and to comment on it to the trier of fact;

(d) make any other ruling as it deems just.

Subd. 4. Report of Examination. The examiner must forward a written examination report to the court. The court must provide copies of the report to the prosecutor and defense. The contents of the report must not otherwise be disclosed except as provided in this rule. The report must contain:

(a) A diagnosis of the defendant's mental condition as requested by the court;

(b) If directed by the court, an opinion as to whether, because of mental illness or deficiency, the defendant, at the time of committing the alleged criminal act, was laboring under such a defect of reason as not to know the nature of the act or that it was wrong;

(c) Any opinion requested by the court that is based on the examiner's diagnosis;

(d) A statement of the factual basis on which the diagnosis and any opinion are based; and

(e) If the examination could not be conducted because of the defendant's unwillingness to participate, an opinion, if possible, as to whether the defendant's unwillingness resulted from mental illness or deficiency.

Subd. 5. Admissibility of Examination. Evidence derived from the examination is not admissible against the defendant unless the defendant has previously made his or her mental condition an issue in the case. If the defendant's mental condition is an issue, any party may call the court-appointed examiner to testify as a witness at trial, and the examiner is subject to cross-examination by any other party. The report or portions of it may be received in evidence to impeach the examiner.

Subd. 6. Admissibility of Defendant's Statements. When a defendant is examined under Rule 20.01, Rule 20.02, or both, the admissibility at trial of any statements the defendant made for the purpose of the examination and any evidence derived from the statements must be determined by the following rules.

(1) *Sole Defense of Mental Condition.* If a defendant notifies the prosecutor under Rule 9.02, subd. 1(5), of intent to rely solely on the defense of mental illness or deficiency, or if the defendant in a misdemeanor case relies solely on the plea of not guilty by reason of mental illness or deficiency under Rule 14.01(c), statements the defendant made for the purpose of the mental examination and evidence derived from the statements are admissible at the trial on the issue of the defendant's mental condition.

(2) *Multiple Defenses.* If a defendant relies on the defense of mental illness or deficiency together with a defense of not guilty, or if the defendant in a misdemeanor case pleads both not guilty and not guilty by reason of mental illness or deficiency, the statements the defendant made for the purpose of the mental examination and any evidence derived from the statements are admissible against the defendant only at the mental illness or deficiency stage of the trial.

Subd. 7. Trial Procedure for Multiple Defenses.

(a) Order of Proof. If a defendant notifies the prosecutor under Rule 9.02, subd. 1(5), of intent to rely on the defense of mental illness or deficiency together with a defense of not guilty, or if the defendant in a misdemeanor case pleads both not guilty and not guilty by reason of mental illness or deficiency, the court must separate the two defenses. The defense of not guilty must be heard and determined first. The defense of mental illness or deficiency must be heard and determined second.

(b) Jury Instructions. The jury must be informed at the start of the trial that:

(1) the defendant has offered two defenses;

(2) the defense of not guilty will be tried first and the defense of mental illness or deficiency will be tried second;

(3) if the jury finds that the elements of the offense have not been proved, the defendant will be acquitted;

(4) if the jury finds the elements of the offense have been proved then the defense of mental illness or deficiency will be tried and determined by the jury.

(c) Proof of Elements—Effect. The court or jury must determine whether the elements of the offense have been proved beyond a reasonable doubt. If the elements of the offense have not been proved, a judgment of acquittal must be entered.

If the defendant has been convicted in the guilt phase, then the defense of mental illness or deficiency must be tried. The jury must render a verdict or the court make a finding of:

(1) not guilty by reason of mental illness;

(2) not guilty by reason of mental deficiency; or

(3) guilty.

The defendant bears the burden of proving mental illness or deficiency by a preponderance of the evidence.

Subd. 8. Effect of Not Guilty by Reason of Mental Illness or Deficiency.

(1) *Mental Illness.* When a defendant is found not guilty by reason of mental illness, and the defendant is under civil commitment as mentally ill, the court must order the commitment to continue. If the defendant is not under commitment, the court must commence a civil commitment proceeding and order the defendant to be detained in a state hospital or other facility pending completion of the proceedings. In felony and gross misdemeanor cases, the court must supervise the commitment as provided in Rule 20.02, subd. 8(4).

(2) *Mental Deficiency.* When a defendant is found not guilty by reason of mental deficiency and the defendant is under commitment to the guardianship of the commissioner of public welfare, the court must order the defendant remanded to the care and custody of the commissioner. If the defendant is not under such commitment, the court must commence a civil commitment proceeding. In felony and gross misdemeanor cases, the court must supervise the commitment as provided in Rule 20.02, subd. 8(4).

(3) *Appeal.* Any party may appeal a civil commitment determination to the Court of Appeals. The appeal must be under Rule 28 and on the record made in court. In all civil commitment proceedings instituted under this rule, a verbatim record of the proceedings must be made.

(4) *Continuing Supervision.* In felony and gross misdemeanor cases, the court and the prosecutor must be notified of any proposed institutional transfer, partial hospitalization status, and any proposed termination, discharge, or provisional discharge of the civil commitment. The prosecutor has the right to participate as a party in any proceedings concerning proposed changes in the defendant's civil commitment or status.

Adopted Feb. 26, 1975, eff. July 1, 1975. Revised Dec. 13, 1989. Amended Oct. 27, 2009, eff. Jan. 1, 2010.

Comments—Rule 20

See comment following Rule 20.04.

Historical Notes

The order of the Minnesota Supreme Court [C1–84–2137] dated December 13, 1989, provides in part that "(t)hese amended Rules of Criminal Procedure shall govern all criminal actions commenced or arrests made after 12 o'clock midnight January 1, 1990, except amendments to 8.04, 11.07, and 19.04, subd. 5, shall govern all criminal actions commenced or arrests made after 12 o'clock midnight January 1, 1991."

Rule 20.03. Disclosure of Reports and Records of Defendant's Mental Examinations

Subd. 1. Disclosure Order. If a defendant notifies the prosecutor under Rule 9.02, subd. 1(5), of an intent to rely on the defense of mental illness or deficiency, the court, on the prosecutor's motion with notice to defense counsel, may order the defendant to furnish to the court or to the prosecutor copies of all medical reports and records previously or subsequently made concerning the defendant's mental condition that are relevant to the mental illness or deficiency defense. The court must inspect any reports and records furnished to it, and if the court finds them relevant, order them disclosed to the prosecutor. Otherwise, they must be returned to the defendant.

A subpoena duces tecum may be issued under Rule 22 if the defendant cannot comply with the court's disclosure order.

Subd. 2. Use of Reports and Records. Reports and records furnished to the prosecutor under Rule 20.03, subd. 1, and any evidence obtained from them, may be admitted in evidence only on the defense of mental illness or deficiency when it is the sole defense, or during the mental illness or deficiency phase when there are multiple defenses, as specified by Rule 20.02, subd. 7.

Adopted Feb. 26, 1975, eff. July 1, 1975. Revised Dec. 13, 1989. Amended Oct. 27, 2009, eff. Jan. 1, 2010.

Comments—Rule 20

See comment following Rule 20.04.

Historical Notes

The order of the Minnesota Supreme Court [C1–84–2137] dated December 13, 1989, provides in part that "(t)hese amended Rules of Criminal Procedure shall govern all criminal actions commenced or arrests made after 12 o'clock midnight January 1, 1990, except amendments to 8.04, 11.07, and 19.04, subd. 5, shall govern all criminal actions commenced or arrests made after 12 o'clock midnight January 1, 1991."

Rule 20.04. Simultaneous Examinations.

The court may order a civil commitment examination under Minn. Stat. ch. 253B, or successor statute, a competency examination under Rule 20.01, and an examination under Rule 20.02 to all be conducted simultaneously.

Former Rule 20.02, subd. 7, adopted Feb. 26, 1975, eff. July 1, 1975. Revised Dec. 13, 1989. Renumbered Rule 20.04 and amended Oct. 27, 2009, eff. Jan. 1, 2010.

Comment—Rule 20

Rule 20.01, subd. 4(a), provides that the examiners may obtain and review any reports of prior examinations conducted under the rule. This includes prior reports conducted under both Rules 20.01 and 20.02. This express authorization, which was adopted in 2005, is intended merely to clarify the rule and not to change it.

No limitation exists for the time or number of hearings that may be held under Rule 20.01 to determine the defendant's competency.

The definitions of mental illness and mental deficiency contained in Minn. Stat. § 611.026 and its judicial interpretations are not affected by these rules.

Rule 20.02, subd. 2, providing for the examination on a defense of mental illness or deficiency, is the same as Rule 20.01, subd. 4(a), governing the examination for competency to proceed.

Rule 20.02, subd. 8, addresses the constitutional requirements of equal protection and due process. No continuing supervision by the trial court exists in misdemeanor cases.

The prosecutor has the right to participate as a party in any civil proceedings being conducted under Minn. Stat. ch. 253B. The prosecutor could question and present witnesses and argue for the continued commitment of the defendant in the civil proceedings.

If the court orders simultaneous examinations under Rule 20.04, the examiner appointed must be qualified to provide a report for all necessary purposes.

RULE 21. DEPOSITIONS

Rule 21.01. When Taken

The court may order that the testimony of a witness be taken by oral deposition before any person authorized to administer oaths, and that any designated book, paper, document, record, recording or other material, not privileged, be produced at the same time and place if all of the following circumstances exist:

(a) there is a reasonable probability that the testimony of the prospective witness will be used at hearing or at trial under any of the conditions specified in Rule 21.06, subd. 1;

(b) the prosecutor has filed a complaint or indictment, or a tab charge has been entered; and

(c) the requesting party has filed a motion and provided notice of the motion to the parties.

The order must also direct the defendant's presence at the deposition, and if the defendant is disabled in communication, direct the presence of a qualified interpreter.

Adopted Feb. 26, 1975, eff. July 1, 1975. Revised Dec. 13, 1989. Amended May 9, 1994; Oct. 27, 2009, eff. Jan. 1, 2010.

Comment—Rule 21

See comment following Rule 21.08.

Historical Notes

The order of the Minnesota Supreme Court [C1–84–2137] dated December 13, 1989, provides in part that "(t)hese amended Rules of Criminal Procedure shall govern all criminal actions commenced or arrests made after 12 o'clock midnight January 1, 1990, except amendments to 8.04, 11.07, and 19.04, subd. 5, shall govern all criminal actions commenced or arrests made after 12 o'clock midnight January 1, 1991."

The order of the Minnesota Supreme Court [C1–84–2137] dated May 9, 1994, provides in part that "(t)hese amendments to the Rules of Criminal Procedure shall govern all criminal actions commenced or arrests made after 12 o'clock midnight July 1, 1994, except that the amendments in the first sentence of the third paragraph in Rule 2.01 shall govern all criminal actions commenced or arrests made after 12 o'clock midnight January 1, 1995."

Rule 21.02. Notice of Taking

The party or person at whose request the court ordered the deposition must give to every other party reasonable notice of the time and place for taking the deposition.

The notice must state the name and address of each person to be examined. Unless the court directs otherwise, the notice must be served personally on the defendants. The notice must inform the defendant of the requirement to personally attend the deposition. A copy of the court order must be attached to the notice.

An officer having custody of any of the defendants must be notified of the time and place set for the deposition, produce the defendant at the examination, and keep the defendant in the presence of the witness during the examination.

On motion of a party served with notice of the deposition, the court for cause shown may extend or shorten the time or change the place for taking the deposition.

Adopted Feb. 26, 1975, eff. July 1, 1975. Revised Dec. 13, 1989. Amended Oct. 27, 2009, eff. Jan. 1, 2010.

Comment—Rule 21

See comment following Rule 21.08.

Historical Notes

The order of the Minnesota Supreme Court [C1–84–2137] dated December 13, 1989, provides in part that "(t)hese amended Rules of Criminal Procedure shall govern all criminal actions commenced or arrests made after 12 o'clock midnight January 1, 1990, except amendments to 8.04, 11.07, and 19.04, subd. 5, shall govern all criminal actions commenced or arrests made after 12 o'clock midnight January 1, 1991."

Rule 21.03. Expenses of Defendant and Counsel; Failure to Appear

Subd. 1. Expenses. If a defendant cannot afford travel, meals, and lodging expenses for the defendant and defense counsel's attendance at the examination, the court must direct payment of their expenses at public expense.

Subd. 2. Failure to Appear. If, after having received notice, a defendant who is not confined fails to appear at the examination without reasonable excuse, the deposition may be taken and used as though the defendant had been present.

Adopted Feb. 26, 1975, eff. July 1, 1975. Revised Dec. 13, 1989. Amended Oct. 27, 2009, eff. Jan. 1, 2010.

Comment—Rule 21

See comment following Rule 21.08.

Historical Notes

The order of the Minnesota Supreme Court [C1–84–2137] dated December 13, 1989, provides in part that "(t)hese amended Rules of Criminal Procedure shall govern all criminal actions commenced or arrests made after 12 o'clock midnight January 1, 1990, except amendments to 8.04, 11.07, and 19.04, subd. 5, shall govern all criminal actions commenced or arrests made after 12 o'clock midnight January 1, 1991."

Rule 21.04. How Taken

Subd. 1. Oral Deposition. Depositions must be taken upon oral examination, with accommodation for those who are disabled in communication.

Subd. 2. Oath and Record of Examination. The witness must be sworn, and a verbatim record of the testimony of the witness must be taken.

The testimony must be taken stenographically and transcribed unless the court directs otherwise.

If the court orders recording of the deposition testimony by other than stenographic means, the order must designate the manner of recording, preserving, and filing the deposition, and may include other provisions to assure that the recorded testimony will be accurate and trustworthy. A party may arrange to have a stenographic transcription made at that party's own expense.

Subd. 3. Scope and Manner of Examination—Objections—Motion to Terminate.

(a) The defendant's deposition cannot be taken without that defendant's consent.

(b) The scope and manner of examination and cross-examination must be the same as that allowed at trial. Each party possessing a statement of the witness being deposed must make it available to the other party for examination and use at the deposition if the other party would be entitled to it at trial.

(c) The person taking the deposition must record all objections made during the examination to the qualifications of the person taking the deposition, the manner of taking it, the evidence presented, the conduct of any party, or any other objection to the proceedings. Objected-to evidence is taken subject to the objections.

(d) On motion of a party or of the deponent during the deposition, and on a showing that the examination is being conducted in bad faith, or in a manner that annoys, embarrasses, or oppresses the deponent or party or elicits privileged testimony, the court that ordered the deposition may order the person conducting the examination to stop taking the deposition. The court may also limit the deposition by one or both of the following:

(1) restricting its subject matter;

(2) requiring that the examination be conducted with no one present except persons designated by the court.

On demand of the objecting party or deponent, the taking of the deposition must be suspended for the time necessary to move for the order.

Adopted Feb. 26, 1975, eff. July 1, 1975. Revised Dec. 13, 1989. Amended Oct. 27, 2009, eff. Jan. 1, 2010.

Comment—Rule 21

See comment following Rule 21.08.

Historical Notes

The order of the Minnesota Supreme Court [C1-84-2137] dated December 13, 1989, provides in part that "(t)hese amended Rules of Criminal Procedure shall govern all criminal actions commenced or arrests made after 12 o'clock midnight January 1, 1990, except amendments to 8.04, 11.07, and 19.04, subd. 5, shall govern all criminal actions commenced or arrests made after 12 o'clock midnight January 1, 1991."

Rule 21.05. Transcription, Certification and Filing

When the testimony is transcribed, the person who took the deposition must certify that the witness was duly sworn and that the deposition is a verbatim record of the witness's testimony. The person must then securely seal the deposition in an envelope endorsed with the title of the case and marked "Deposition of (here insert name of witness)." The person must promptly file it with the court, or send it by registered or certified mail to the court administrator for filing.

On a party's request, documents and other things produced during the examination of a witness, or copies of them, must be marked for identification and annexed as exhibits to the deposition, and may be inspected and copied by any party.

If the person producing the exhibits requests their return, the person taking the deposition must mark them, and, after giving each party an opportunity to inspect and copy them, return the exhibits to the parties producing them. The exhibits may then be used as if annexed to the deposition.

Adopted Feb. 26, 1975, eff. July 1, 1975. Revised Dec. 13, 1989. Amended Oct. 27, 2009, eff. Jan. 1, 2010.

Comment—Rule 21

See comment following Rule 21.08.

Historical Notes

The order of the Minnesota Supreme Court [C1-84-2137] dated December 13, 1989, provides in part that "(t)hese amended Rules of Criminal Procedure shall govern all criminal actions commenced or arrests made after 12 o'clock midnight January 1, 1990, except amendments to 8.04, 11.07, and 19.04, subd. 5, shall govern all criminal actions commenced or arrests made after 12 o'clock midnight January 1, 1991."

Rule 21.06. Use of Deposition

Subd. 1. Unavailability of Witness. A part or all of a deposition may be used as substantive evidence at the trial or hearing to the extent it would be otherwise admissible under the rules of evidence if:

(a) the witness is dead or unable to be present or to testify at the trial or hearing because of a physical or mental illness or infirmity; or

(b) the party offering the deposition has been unable to obtain the attendance of the witness by subpoena, order of court, or other reasonable means.

Subd. 2. Inconsistent Testimony. A deposition may be used as substantive evidence at the trial or hearing to the extent it would be otherwise admissible under the rules of evidence if the witness:

(a) testifies inconsistently with the deposition; or

(b) persists in refusing to testify despite a court order to do so.

Subd. 3. Impeachment. Any deposition may also be used by any party to contradict or impeach the deponent's testimony as a witness.

A deposition may not be used if it appears that the party offering the deposition caused the deposed witness's absence, unless part of the deposition has previously been offered by another party.

Adopted Feb. 26, 1975, eff. July 1, 1975. Revised Dec. 13, 1989. Amended Oct. 27, 2009, eff. Jan. 1, 2010.

Comment—Rule 21

See comment following Rule 21.08.

Historical Notes

The order of the Minnesota Supreme Court [C1-84-2137] dated December 13, 1989, provides in part that "(t)hese amended Rules of Criminal Procedure shall govern all criminal actions commenced or arrests made after 12 o'clock midnight January 1, 1990, except amendments to 8.04, 11.07, and 19.04, subd. 5, shall govern all criminal actions commenced or arrests made after 12 o'clock midnight January 1, 1991."

Rule 21.07. Effect of Errors and Irregularities in Depositions

Subd. 1. As to Order or Notice. All errors and irregularities in the order or notice for taking a deposition are waived unless the objecting party promptly serves a written objection on the party giving the notice.

Subd. 2. As to Disqualification of Officer. Objection to taking a deposition because of a disqualification of the person taking it is waived unless made before the taking of the deposition begins, or as soon as the grounds for disqualification become known or could be discovered with reasonable diligence.

Subd. 3. As to Taking of Deposition. Objections to the competency, relevancy, or materiality of testimony are not waived by failure to make them before or during the taking of the deposition unless the ground of the objection is one that might have been obviated or removed if presented at that time.

Errors and irregularities occurring at the deposition that might be remedied if promptly presented are waived unless timely objected to at the deposition.

Subd. 4. As to Completion and Return of Deposition. Errors and irregularities in the transcription of the testimony, or in the way the deposition is prepared, recorded, certified, sealed, endorsed, transmitted, filed, or otherwise dealt with by the person taking the deposition under these rules, are waived unless a motion to suppress the deposition or some part of it occurs with reasonable promptness after a party discovers the defect, or with due diligence might have done so.

Adopted Feb. 26, 1975, eff. July 1, 1975. Revised Dec. 13, 1989. Amended Oct. 27, 2009, eff. Jan. 1, 2010.

Comment—Rule 21

See comment following Rule 21.08.

Historical Notes

The order of the Minnesota Supreme Court [C1–84–2137] dated December 13, 1989, provides in part that "(t)hese amended Rules of Criminal Procedure shall govern all criminal actions commenced or arrests made after 12 o'clock midnight January 1, 1990, except amendments to 8.04, 11.07, and 19.04, subd. 5, shall govern all criminal actions commenced or arrests made after 12 o'clock midnight January 1, 1991."

Rule 21.08. Deposition by Stipulation

The parties may by written stipulation provide that a deposition may be taken before any person, at any time or place, upon any notice, and in any manner, and that it may be used like other depositions. These rules, unless inconsistent with the stipulation, govern the taking of the deposition.

Adopted Feb. 26, 1975, eff. July 1, 1975. Revised Dec. 13, 1989. Amended Oct. 27, 2009, eff. Jan. 1, 2010.

Comment—Rule 21

The requirement that a qualified interpreter be present for defendants disabled in communication is based upon Rule 8 of the General Rules of Practice for the District Courts and Minn. Stat. §§ 611.31—611.34.

The deposition may be taken before any person authorized to administer oaths designated by the order. If the deposition is taken outside the State of Minnesota, this would include any person authorized to administer oaths by the laws of Minnesota or of the state where the deposition is taken. See Moore v. Keesey, 26 Wash.2d 31, 173 P.2d 130 (1946).

Notice must normally be personally served on the defendant. But, in cases where the defendant is unavailable and time is of the essence, the court may order that notice be served on the defendant's attorney instead of the defendant. These rules do not deal with the constitutionality of the use of a deposition at trial when the defendant has not been personally notified.

Rule 21.05 does not require that the deposition be submitted to and signed by the witness. It requires only that the person before whom the deposition is taken certify that the deposition is a true record of the testimony given by the witness. Any dispute over the accuracy of the record must be dealt with under Rule 21.07, subd. 4 (completion and return of deposition).

Historical Notes

The order of the Minnesota Supreme Court [C1–84–2137] dated December 13, 1989, provides in part that "(t)hese amended Rules of Criminal Procedure shall govern all criminal actions commenced or arrests made after 12 o'clock midnight January 1, 1990, except amendments to 8.04, 11.07, and 19.04, subd. 5, shall govern all criminal actions commenced or arrests made after 12 o'clock midnight January 1, 1991."

RULE 22. SUBPOENA

Rule 22.01. For Attendance of Witnesses; For Documents

Subd. 1. Witnesses. A subpoena may be issued for attendance of a witness:

(a) before a grand jury;

(b) at a hearing before the court;

(c) at a trial before the court; or

(d) for the taking of a deposition.

The subpoena must command attendance and testimony at the time and place specified.

Subd. 2. Documents.

(a) A subpoena may command a person to produce books, papers, documents, or other designated objects.

(b) The court may direct production in court of the books, papers, documents, or objects designated in the subpoena, including medical reports and records ordered disclosed under Rule 20.03, subd. 1, before the trial or before being offered in evidence, and may permit the parties or their attorneys to inspect them.

Subd. 3. Unrepresented Defendant. A defendant not represented by an attorney may obtain a subpoena only by court order. The request and order may be written or oral. An oral order must be noted in the court's record.

Subd. 4. Grand Jury Subpoena. A grand jury subpoena must be captioned "In the matter of the investigation by the grand jury of __________. " (Insert here the name of the county or counties conducting the investigation.)

Subd. 5. Motion to Quash. The court on motion promptly made may quash or modify a subpoena if compliance would be unreasonable.

Adopted Feb. 26, 1975, eff. July 1, 1975. Revised Dec. 13, 1989. Amended Oct. 27, 2009, eff. Jan. 1, 2010; June 22, 2011, eff. Sept. 1, 2011.

Comment—Rule 22

See comment following Rule 22.06.

Historical Notes

The order of the Minnesota Supreme Court [C1–84–2137] dated December 13, 1989, provides in part that "(t)hese amended Rules of Criminal Procedure shall govern all criminal actions commenced or arrests made after 12 o'clock midnight January 1, 1990, except amendments to 8.04, 11.07, and 19.04, subd. 5, shall govern all criminal actions commenced or arrests made after 12 o'clock midnight January 1, 1991."

The order of the Minnesota Supreme Court [ADM10–8049] dated June 22, 2011, provided in part that "The amendments shall govern all criminal actions currently pending on or commenced on or after the effective date."

Rule 22.02. By Whom Issued

Subd. 1. By the Court. The court administrator issues a subpoena under the court's seal, signed but otherwise blank, to the attorney for the party requesting it, who must fill in the blanks before service. The subpoena must state the name of the court and the title of the proceeding if the subpoena is for a hearing, trial, or deposition.

Subd. 2. By an Attorney. Alternatively, an attorney, as an officer of the court, may issue a subpoena in a case in which the attorney represents a party. The attorney must personally sign the completed subpoena on behalf of the court, using the attorney's name. A subpoena issued by an attorney need not bear a seal, but must otherwise comply with the format requirements in subdivision 1. The completed subpoena must include:

(a) the attorney's printed name;

(b) attorney-registration number;

(c) office address and phone number; and

(d) the party the attorney represents.

Subd. 3. Deposition and Grand Jury Subpoenas. Subpoenas for a deposition may be issued only if the court under Rule 21.01 has ordered a deposition, or the parties under Rule 21.08 have stipulated to one. When so ordered or stipulated, deposition subpoenas may be issued only as provided in subdivisions 1 or 2 above, or in the case of unrepresented defendants, only by court order under Rule 22.01, subd. 3. Grand jury subpoenas may be issued only by the court administrator.

Adopted Feb. 26, 1975, eff. July 1, 1975. Revised Dec. 13, 1989. Amended May 9, 1994; Oct. 27, 2009, eff. Jan. 1, 2010; June 22, 2011, eff. Sept. 1, 2011.

Comment—Rule 22

See comment following Rule 22.06.

Historical Notes

The order of the Minnesota Supreme Court [C1–84–2137] dated December 13, 1989, provides in part that "(t)hese amended Rules of Criminal Procedure shall govern all criminal actions commenced or arrests made after 12 o'clock midnight January 1, 1990, except amendments to 8.04, 11.07, and 19.04, subd. 5, shall govern all criminal actions commenced or arrests made after 12 o'clock midnight January 1, 1991."

The order of the Minnesota Supreme Court [ADM10–8049] dated June 22, 2011, provided in part that "The amendments shall govern all criminal actions currently pending on or commenced on or after the effective date."

Rule 22.03. Service

A subpoena may be served by the sheriff, a deputy sheriff, or any person at least 18 years of age who is not a party.

Service of a subpoena on a person must be made by delivering a copy to the person or by leaving a copy at the person's usual place of abode with a person of suitable age and discretion who resides there.

A subpoena may also be served by U.S. mail, but service is effective only if the person named returns a signed admission acknowledging personal receipt of the subpoena. Fees and mileage need not be paid in advance.

Adopted Feb. 26, 1975, eff. July 1, 1975. Revised Dec. 13, 1989. Amended May 9, 1994; Oct. 27, 2009, eff. Jan. 1, 2010.

Comment—Rule 22

See comment following Rule 22.06.

Historical Notes

The order of the Minnesota Supreme Court [C1–84–2137] dated December 13, 1989, provides in part that "(t)hese amended Rules of Criminal Procedure shall govern all criminal actions commenced or arrests made after 12 o'clock midnight January 1, 1990, except amendments to 8.04, 11.07, and 19.04, subd. 5, shall govern all criminal actions commenced or arrests made after 12 o'clock midnight January 1, 1991."

The order of the Minnesota Supreme Court [C1–84–2137] dated May 9, 1994, provides in part that "(t)hese amendments to the Rules of Criminal Procedure shall govern all criminal actions commenced or arrests made after 12 o'clock midnight July 1, 1994, except that the amendments in the first sentence of the third paragraph in Rule 2.01 shall govern all criminal actions commenced or arrests made after 12 o'clock midnight January 1, 1995."

Rule 22.04. Place of Service

A subpoena may be served anywhere in the state.

Adopted Feb. 26, 1975, eff. July 1, 1975. Revised Dec. 13, 1989. Amended Oct. 27, 2009, eff. Jan. 1, 2010; June 22, 2011, eff. Sept. 1, 2011.

Comment—Rule 22

See comment following Rule 22.06.

Historical Notes

The order of the Minnesota Supreme Court [C1–84–2137] dated December 13, 1989, provides in part that "(t)hese amended Rules of Criminal Procedure shall govern all criminal actions commenced or arrests made after 12 o'clock midnight January 1, 1990, except amendments to 8.04, 11.07, and 19.04, subd. 5, shall govern all criminal actions commenced or arrests made after 12 o'clock midnight January 1, 1991."

The order of the Minnesota Supreme Court [ADM10–8049] dated June 22, 2011, provided in part that "The amendments shall govern all criminal actions currently pending on or commenced on or after the effective date."

Rule 22.05. Contempt

Failure to obey a subpoena without adequate excuse is a contempt of court.

Adopted Feb. 26, 1975, eff. July 1, 1975. Revised Dec. 13, 1989. Amended Oct. 27, 2009, eff. Jan. 1, 2010.

Comment—Rule 22

See comment following Rule 22.06.

Historical Notes

The order of the Minnesota Supreme Court [C1–84–2137] dated December 13, 1989, provides in part that "(t)hese amended Rules of Criminal Procedure shall govern all criminal actions commenced or arrests made after 12 o'clock midnight January 1, 1990, except amendments to 8.04, 11.07, and 19.04, subd. 5, shall govern all criminal actions commenced or arrests made after 12 o'clock midnight January 1, 1991."

Rule 22.06. Witness Outside the State

The attendance of a witness who is outside the state may be secured as provided by Minn. Stat. § 634.07 (Nonresidents Required to Testify in State).

Adopted Feb. 26, 1975, eff. July 1, 1975. Revised Dec. 13, 1989. Amended Oct. 27, 2009, eff. Jan. 1, 2010; June 22, 2011, eff. Sept. 1, 2011.

Comment—Rule 22

In addition to Rule 22.01, subd. 3, Minn. Stat. § 611.06 also addresses the issuance of subpoenas to unrepresented defendants and states that Rule 22.01, subd. 3 applies. The statute also requires that the issuance of subpoenas to self-represented defendants is without cost to the defendant.

Rule 22 applies only to criminal proceedings in Minnesota. It does not affect Minn. Stat. § 634.06, which provides a method for compelling Minnesota residents to testify in criminal cases in other states.

Historical Notes

The order of the Minnesota Supreme Court [C1–84–2137] dated December 13, 1989, provides in part that "(t)hese amended Rules of Criminal Procedure shall govern all criminal actions commenced or arrests made after 12 o'clock midnight January 1, 1990, except amendments to 8.04, 11.07, and 19.04, subd. 5, shall govern all criminal actions commenced or arrests made after 12 o'clock midnight January 1, 1991."

The order of the Minnesota Supreme Court [ADM10–8049] dated June 22, 2011, provided in part that "The amendments shall govern all criminal actions currently pending on or commenced on or after the effective date."

RULE 23. PETTY MISDEMEANORS AND VIOLATIONS BUREAUS

Rule 23.01. Definition of Petty Misdemeanor

"Petty misdemeanor" means an offense punishable by a fine of not more than $300 or other amount established by statute as the maximum fine for a petty misdemeanor.

Adopted Feb. 26, 1975, eff. July 1, 1975. Revised Dec. 13, 1989. Amended Oct. 27, 2009, eff. Jan. 1, 2010.

Comment—Rule 23

See comment following Rule 23.06.

Historical Notes

The order of the Minnesota Supreme Court [C1–84–2137] dated December 13, 1989, provides in part that "(t)hese amended Rules of Criminal Procedure shall govern all criminal actions commenced or arrests made after 12 o'clock midnight January 1, 1990, except amendments to 8.04, 11.07, and 19.04, subd. 5, shall govern all criminal actions commenced or arrests made after 12 o'clock midnight January 1, 1991."

Rule 23.02. Certification as Petty Misdemeanor by Sentence Imposed

A conviction is deemed a petty misdemeanor if the sentence imposed is within petty misdemeanor limits.

Adopted Feb. 26, 1975, eff. July 1, 1975. Revised Dec. 13, 1989. Amended Oct. 27, 2009, eff. Jan. 1, 2010.

Comment—Rule 23

See comment following Rule 23.06.

Historical Notes

The order of the Minnesota Supreme Court [C1–84–2137] dated December 13, 1989, provides in part that "(t)hese amended Rules of Criminal Procedure shall govern all criminal actions commenced or arrests made after 12 o'clock midnight January 1, 1990, except amendments to 8.04, 11.07, and 19.04, subd. 5, shall govern all criminal actions commenced or arrests made after 12 o'clock midnight January 1, 1991."

Rule 23.03. Violations Bureaus

Subd. 1. Establishment. The district court may implement and operate violations bureaus. The State Court Administrator may implement and operate the Minnesota Court Payment Center.

Subd. 2. Fine Schedules.

(1) Uniform Fine Schedule. The Judicial Council must adopt and, as necessary, revise a uniform fine schedule setting fines for statutory petty misdemeanors and for statutory misdemeanors as it selects. The uniform schedule is applicable statewide, and is known as the Statewide Payables List.

(2) County Fine Schedules. Each district court may establish by court rule for each county a fine for any ordinance that may be paid to the violations bureau in lieu of a court appearance by the defendant. When an ordinance offense is substantially the same as an offense included on the uniform fine schedule, the fine established must be the same.

Subd. 3. Fine Payment. A defendant must be advised in writing before paying a fine to a violations bureau that payment constitutes a plea of guilty to the charge and an admission that the defendant understands and waives the right to:

a. a court or jury trial;

b. counsel;

c. be presumed innocent until proven guilty beyond a reasonable doubt;

d. confront and cross-examine all witnesses; and

e. to remain silent or to testify for the defense.

Adopted Feb. 26, 1975, eff. July 1, 1975. Revised Dec. 13, 1989. Amended Oct. 27, 2009, eff. Jan. 1, 2010; Jan. 13, 2011, eff. Jan. 1, 2012; June 5, 2012, eff. Aug. 1, 2012.

Comment—Rule 23

See comment following Rule 23.06.

Historical Notes

The order of the Minnesota Supreme Court [C1–84–2137] dated December 13, 1989, provides in part that "(t)hese amended Rules of Criminal Procedure shall govern all criminal actions commenced or arrests made after 12 o'clock midnight January 1, 1990, except amendments to 8.04, 11.07, and 19.04, subd. 5, shall govern all criminal actions commenced or arrests made after 12 o'clock midnight January 1, 1991."

The order of the Minnesota Supreme Court [ADM 10–8049] dated June 5, 2012, provided in part that the amendments "be effective August 1, 2012, and shall apply to all actions or proceedings pending on or commenced on or after the effective date."

Rule 23.04. Certification as a Petty Misdemeanor in a Particular Case

Before trial, the prosecutor may certify a misdemeanor offense as a petty misdemeanor if the prosecutor does not seek incarceration, and seeks a fine at or below the statutory maximum for a petty misdemeanor. Subject to the following exception, certification takes effect only on approval of the court and consent of the defendant. Certification does not require the defendant's consent if the offense is included on the Statewide Payables List on the date of the alleged offense.

Adopted Feb. 26, 1975, eff. July 1, 1975. Revised Dec. 13, 1989. Amended Oct. 27, 2009, eff. Jan. 1, 2010; June 5, 2012, eff. Aug. 1, 2012.

Comment—Rule 23

See comment following Rule 23.06.

Historical Notes

The order of the Minnesota Supreme Court [C1–84–2137] dated December 13, 1989, provides in part that "(t)hese amended Rules of Criminal Procedure shall govern all criminal actions commenced or arrests made after 12 o'clock midnight January 1, 1990, except amendments to 8.04, 11.07, and 19.04, subd. 5, shall govern all criminal actions commenced or arrests made after 12 o'clock midnight January 1, 1991."

The order of the Minnesota Supreme Court [ADM 10–8049] dated June 5, 2012, provided in part that the amendments "be effective August 1, 2012, and shall apply to all actions or proceedings pending on or commenced on or after the effective date."

Rule 23.05. Procedure in Petty Misdemeanor Cases

Subd. 1. No Right to Jury Trial. No right to a jury trial exists in a misdemeanor charge certified as a petty misdemeanor under Rule 23.04.

Subd. 2. Right to Public Defender Representation. Upon certification of a misdemeanor as a petty misdemeanor, the defendant is not entitled to representation by the public defender. In cases that require the defendant's consent to certification, and the prosecutor moves for certification, the judge must advise an unrepresented defendant of the right to apply for a public defender.

Subd. 3. General Procedure. A defendant charged with a petty misdemeanor violation is presumed innocent until proven guilty beyond a reasonable doubt. Except as otherwise provided in Rule 23, the procedure in petty misdemeanor cases must be the same as for misdemeanors punishable by incarceration.

Subd. 4. Failure to Appear. If a defendant charged with a petty misdemeanor, or a misdemeanor on the Statewide Payables List that is certified as a petty misdemeanor, fails to appear or respond as directed on the citation or complaint, a guilty plea and conviction may be entered, the payable fine amount no greater than the maximum fine for a petty misdemeanor, and any applicable fees and surcharges may be imposed, and the matter referred to collections. Conviction must not be entered until 10 days after the failure to appear.

Subd. 5. Withdrawal of Plea. A defendant convicted under subdivision 4 may move under Rule 15.05 to withdraw the guilty plea and vacate the conviction.

Adopted Feb. 26, 1975, eff. July 1, 1975. Revised Dec. 13, 1989. Amended Oct. 27, 2009, eff. Jan. 1, 2010; June 5, 2012, eff. Aug. 1, 2012; Jan. 17, 2013, eff. Feb. 1, 2013.

Comment—Rule 23

See comment following Rule 23.06.

Historical Notes

The order of the Minnesota Supreme Court [C1–84–2137] dated December 13, 1989, provides in part that "(t)hese amended Rules of Criminal Procedure shall govern all criminal actions commenced or arrests made after 12 o'clock midnight January 1, 1990, except amendments to 8.04, 11.07, and 19.04, subd. 5, shall govern all criminal actions commenced or arrests made after 12 o'clock midnight January 1, 1991."

The order of the Minnesota Supreme Court [ADM 10–8049] dated June 5, 2012, provided in part that the amendments "be effective August 1, 2012, and shall apply to all actions or proceedings pending on or commenced on or after the effective date."

The order of the Minnesota Supreme Court [ADM 10–8049] dated January 17, 2013, provided in part that the amendments "be effective February 1, 2013", and further provided that the amendments "shall apply to all actions or proceedings pending or commenced on or after the effective date."

Rule 23.06. Effect of Conviction

A petty misdemeanor is not considered a crime.

Adopted Feb. 26, 1975, eff. July 1, 1975. Revised Dec. 13, 1989. Amended Oct. 27, 2009, eff. Jan. 1, 2010.

Comment—Rule 23

The definition of petty misdemeanor as used in Rule 23 is broader than the definition provided by Minn. Stat. § 609.02, subd. 4a, which refers to a statutory violation punishable only by a fine of not more than the specified amount. Under Rule 23.01, read in conjunction with the definition of "misdemeanor" in Rule 1.04(a), the term "petty misdemeanor" refers also to violations of local ordinances, charter provisions, rules, or regulations.

These rules do not specify any procedures or sanctions for enforcing payment of fines in petty misdemeanor cases. Existing law permits some enforcement methods. The court may delay acceptance of a plea until the defendant has the money to pay the fine. If a defendant is unable to pay a fine when imposed, the court may set a date by which the defendant must either pay the fine or reappear in court. If the fine is not paid by the date set and the defendant does not reappear as ordered to explain why it has not been paid, the court may issue a bench warrant for the defendant's arrest and set bail in the amount of the fine. Any bail collected could then be used under Minn. Stat. § 629.53 to pay the fine. Contempt procedures under Minn. Stat. ch. 588 can also be used to enforce payment of a fine when the defendant has willfully refused payment. An administrative sanction may exist if the defendant has failed to pay a fine imposed upon conviction of violating a law regulating the operation or parking of motor vehicles. In such cases, the commissioner of public safety is required under Minn. Stat. § 171.16, subd. 3, to suspend the defendant's license for 30 days or until the fine is paid if the court determines that the defendant has the ability to pay the unpaid fine. Similar sanctions for non-traffic offenses might prove effective, but would require legislative action.

Rule 23.02, which deems a conviction a petty misdemeanor if the sentence imposed is within petty misdemeanor limits, is similar to Minn. Stat. § 609.13, which provides for the reduction of a felony to a gross misdemeanor or misdemeanor and for the reduction of a gross misdemeanor to a misdemeanor.

For uniformity in fines imposed for certain misdemeanors throughout the state, see Minn. Stat. § 609.101, subd. 4.

The written advice required by Rule 23.03, subd. 3 may be included upon the citation issued for the offense. This citation may be set forth in the form of an envelope for mailing the fine to the bureau. This rule does not require a defendant to sign a written plea of guilty.

See also Rule 5.04 as to appointment of counsel upon request of the defendant or interested counsel when the prosecution is for a misdemeanor not punishable by incarceration.

Contrary to what Rule 23.04 provides, Minn. Stat. § 609.131, enacted by the legislature in 1987 (Chapter 329, Section 6), purports to allow the reduction of any misdemeanor to a petty misdemeanor without the defendant's consent. The Advisory Committee is aware of this statute, but after consideration rejected fully conforming the Rule to the statute. On these matters of procedure, the Rules of Criminal Procedure take precedence over statutes to the extent any inconsistency exists. State v. Keith, 325 N.W.2d 641 (Minn. 1982).

Historical Notes

The order of the Minnesota Supreme Court [C1–84–2137] dated December 13, 1989, provides in part that "(t)hese amended Rules of Criminal Procedure shall govern all criminal actions commenced or arrests made after 12 o'clock midnight January 1, 1990, except amendments to 8.04, 11.07, and 19.04, subd. 5, shall govern all criminal actions commenced or arrests made after 12 o'clock midnight January 1, 1991."

Rule 23.07. Deleted

Historical Notes

The deleted rule related to trials de novo in the district court.

The order of the Minnesota Supreme Court dated June 9, 1983 [which in part deleted this rule], provides in part that "(t)hese amendments to the Rules of Criminal Procedure shall govern all criminal actions commenced or arrests made after 12 o'clock midnight July 31, 1983."

RULE 24. VENUE

Rule 24.01. Place of Trial

The case must be tried in the county where the offense was committed unless these rules direct otherwise.

Adopted Feb. 26, 1975, eff. July 1, 1975. Revised Dec. 13, 1989. Amended Oct. 27, 2009, eff. Jan. 1, 2010.

Comment—Rule 24

See comment following Rule 24.03.

Historical Notes

The order of the Minnesota Supreme Court [C1–84–2137] dated December 13, 1989, provides in part that "(t)hese amended Rules of Criminal Procedure shall govern all criminal actions commenced or arrests made after 12 o'clock midnight January 1, 1990, except amendments to 8.04, 11.07, and 19.04, subd. 5, shall govern all criminal actions commenced or arrests made after 12 o'clock midnight January 1, 1991."

Rule 24.02. Venue in Special Cases

Subd. 1. Offense Committed on a Conveyance. When an offense occurs within the state on a conveyance, and doubt exists as to where the offense occurred, the case may be prosecuted in any county through which the conveyance traveled in the course of the trip during which the offense was committed.

Subd. 2. Offenses Committed on County Lines. Offenses committed on or within 1,500 feet (457.2M) of the boundary line between two counties may be alleged in the complaint or indictment to have been committed in either of them, and may be prosecuted in either county.

Subd. 3. Injury or Death in One County from an Act Committed in Another County. If a person commits an act in one county causing injury or death in another county, the offense may be prosecuted in either county. If doubt exists as to where the act, injury, or death occurred, the offense may be prosecuted in any of the counties.

Subd. 4. Prosecution in County Where Injury or Death Occurs. If a person commits an act either within or outside the limits of the state and injury or death results, the offense may be prosecuted in the county of this state where the injury or death occurs, or where the body of the deceased is found.

Subd. 5. Prosecution When Death Occurs Outside State. If a person commits an assault in this state resulting in death outside the state, the homicide may be prosecuted in the county where the assault occurred.

Subd. 6. Kidnapping. Kidnapping may be prosecuted in any county through which the person kidnapped was taken or kept while under confinement or restraint.

Subd. 7. Libel. Publication of a libel contained in a newspaper published in the state may be prosecuted in any county where the paper was published or circulated. A person cannot be prosecuted for publication of the same libel against the same person in more than one county.

Subd. 8. Bringing Stolen Goods Into State. Whoever brings stolen property into the state in violation of Minn. Stat. § 609.525 may be prosecuted in any county into or through which the property was brought.

Subd. 9. Obscene or Harassing Telephone Calls; Wireless or Electronic Communication. Violations of Minn. Stat. § 609.79 may be prosecuted at the place where the call is made or where it is received or, in the case of wireless or electronic communication, where the sender or receiver resides.

Subd. 10. Fair Campaign Practices. Violations of Minn. Stat. § 211B.15 prohibiting corporate contributions to political campaigns may be prosecuted in the county where the payment or contribution was made, where services were rendered, or where money was paid or distributed.

Subd. 11. Series of Offenses Aggregated. When a series of offenses is aggregated under Minn. Stat. § 609.52, subd. 3(5), and the offenses have been committed in more than one county, the case may be prosecuted in any county in which one or more of the offenses occurred.

Subd. 12. Non-Support of Spouse or Child. Violations of Minn. Stat. § 609.375 for non-support of spouse or child may be prosecuted in the county in which the person obligated to pay or entitled to receive support resides, or where the child resides.

Subd. 13. Refusal to Submit to Chemical Test Crime. Violations of Minn. Stat. § 169A.20, subd. 2 for refusal to submit to a chemical test may be prosecuted in the jurisdiction where the arresting officer observed the defendant driving, operating, or in the control of the motor vehicle, or in the jurisdiction where the refusal occurred.

Subd. 14. Contributing to Need for Protection or Services for a Child. Violations of Minn. Stat. § 260C.425 for contributing to need for protection or services for a child, may be prosecuted in the county where the child is found, resides, or where the alleged act occurred.

Subd. 15. Criminal Tax Penalties. If a person commits violations of Minn. Stat. § 289A.63 in more than one county, the person may be prosecuted for all of the violations in any county in which one of the violations occurred.

Subd. 16. Municipalities in More than One County. Offenses occurring within a municipality located in more than one county or district must be prosecuted in the county where the municipality's city hall is located, unless the municipality designates by ordinance some other county or district in which part of the municipality is located.

Subd. 17. Depriving Another of Custodial or Parental Rights. Violations of Minn. Stat. § 609.26 for depriving another of custodial or parental rights may be prosecuted in the county in which the child was taken, concealed, or detained, or the county of lawful residence of the child.

Subd. 18. Child Abuse. A criminal action arising out of an incident of alleged child abuse may be prosecuted in the county where the alleged abuse occurred or the county where the child is found.

Adopted Feb. 26, 1975, eff. July 1, 1975. Revised Dec. 13, 1989. Amended Dec. 23, 2002, eff. Feb. 1, 2003; Oct. 27, 2009, eff. Jan. 1, 2010.

Comment—Rule 24

See comment following Rule 24.03.

Historical Notes

The order of the Minnesota Supreme Court [C1–84–2137] dated December 13, 1989, provides in part that "(t)hese amended Rules of Criminal Procedure shall govern all criminal actions commenced or arrests made after 12 o'clock midnight January 1, 1990, except amendments to 8.04, 11.07, and 19.04, subd. 5, shall govern all criminal actions commenced or arrests made after 12 o'clock midnight January 1, 1991."

Rule 24.03. Change of Venue

Subd. 1. Grounds. The case may be transferred to another county:.

a. If the court is satisfied that a fair and impartial trial cannot be had in the county in which the case is pending;

b. For the convenience of parties and witnesses;

c. In the interests of justice;

d. As provided by Rule 25.02 governing prejudicial publicity.

Subd. 2. County to Which Transferred. For the purposes of change of venue under this rule the district referred to in Minn. Const. Art. I, § 6 is the area within the geographical boundaries of the State of Minnesota.

Subd. 3. Time for Motion for Change of Venue. Except as permitted by Rule 25.02, a motion for change of venue must be made at the time prescribed in Rule 10 for making pretrial motions.

Subd. 4. Proceedings on Transfer. If the case is transferred under these rules, all records in the case, or certified copies of them, must be transmitted to the court to which the case is transferred. If the defendant is in custody, the court may order that the defendant be transported to the sheriff of the county to which the case is transferred. Unless the Supreme Court orders otherwise, the case must be tried before the judge who ordered the change of venue. If the defendant has been released upon conditions of release, those conditions must be continued on the further condition that the defendant must appear as ordered by the court for trial and other proceedings in the county to which the case has been transferred.

Adopted Feb. 26, 1975, eff. July 1, 1975. Revised Dec. 13, 1989. Amended Oct. 27, 2009, eff. Jan. 1, 2010.

Comment—Rule 24

By Rule 11.01, Omnibus Hearings may be held in any county in the district court's judicial district in which the offense was committed. Objections to the place of trial are waived unless asserted before commencement of the trial.

Rule 24.02, subd. 16 (Municipalities in More Than One County) is derived from Minn. Stat. § 484.80.

Rule 24.02, subd. 18 (Child Abuse) is derived from Minn. Stat. § 627.15.

Rule 24.03, subd. 1 (Grounds for Change of Venue) permits a change of venue upon motion of the defendant or prosecution, or on the court's initiative upon any of the grounds specified in the rule.

Minn. Const. Art. I, § 6 provides that the accused shall enjoy the right to a speedy and public trial by an impartial jury of the county or district wherein the crime shall have been committed, which county or district shall have been previously ascertained by law. Under Rule 24.03, subd. 2 (County to Which Transferred), change of venue may be ordered upon any of the specified grounds to any county of the state.

Historical Notes

The order of the Minnesota Supreme Court [C1-84-2137] dated December 13, 1989, provides in part that "(t)hese amended Rules of Criminal Procedure shall govern all criminal actions commenced or arrests made after 12 o'clock midnight January 1, 1990, except amendments to 8.04, 11.07, and 19.04, subd. 5, shall govern all criminal actions commenced or arrests made after 12 o'clock midnight January 1, 1991."

RULE 25. SPECIAL RULES GOVERNING PREJUDICIAL PUBLICITY

Rule 25.01. Pretrial Hearings—Motion to Exclude Public

The following rules govern orders excluding the public from any pretrial hearing and restricting access to the orders or to transcripts of the closed proceeding.

Subd. 1. Grounds for Exclusion of Public. Any part of a pretrial hearing may be closed to the public on motion of any party or the court's initiative on the ground that dissemination of evidence or argument presented at the hearing may interfere with an overriding interest, including disclosure of inadmissible evidence and the right to a fair trial.

Subd. 2. Notice to Adverse Counsel. If any party has evidence that may be subject to a closure order, the party must advise opposing counsel and request a closed meeting with counsel and the court.

Subd. 3. Meeting in Closed Court and Notice of Hearing. In closed court, the court must review the evidence that could be the subject of a restrictive order. If the court determines restriction may be appropriate, the court must schedule a hearing on the potential restrictive order. A hearing notice must be issued publicly at least 24 hours before the hearing and must afford the public and the news media an opportunity to be heard on whether the claimed overriding interest justifies closure.

Subd. 4. Hearing. At the hearing, the court must advise all present that evidence exists that may be the subject of a closure order. The court must allow the public, including reporters, to suggest alternatives to a restrictive order.

The court must consider alternatives to closure. The court may order closure of the pretrial hearing only if it finds a substantial likelihood exists that conducting the hearing in open court would interfere with an overriding interest. Any closure must be no broader than necessary to protect the overriding interest.

Subd. 5. Findings. Any order excluding the public from a pretrial hearing must be issued in writing and state the reasons for closure. The order must address any possible alternatives to closure and explain why the alternatives are inadequate. Any matter relevant to the court's decision that does not present the risk of revealing inadmissible, prejudicial information must be decided on the record in open court.

Subd. 6. Records. If the court closes all or part of a pretrial hearing, a complete record of the nonpublic proceedings must be made. On request, the record must be transcribed and filed at public expense. The record must be publicly available after trial or disposition of the case. The court may redact or substitute names in the record to protect innocent persons.

Subd. 7. Appellate Review. Anyone represented at the hearing or aggrieved by an order granting or denying public access may petition the Court of Appeals for review. This is the exclusive method for obtaining review.

The Court of Appeals must determine whether the party who moved for public exclusion met the burden of justifying exclusion under this rule. The Court of Appeals may reverse, affirm, or modify the district court's order.

Adopted Feb. 26, 1975, eff. July 1, 1975. Revised Dec. 13, 1989. Amended Oct. 27, 2009, eff. Jan. 1, 2010.

Comment—Rule 25

See comment following Rule 25.03.

Historical Notes

The order of the Minnesota Supreme Court [C1–84–2137] dated December 13, 1989, provides in part that "(t)hese amended Rules of Criminal Procedure shall govern all criminal actions commenced or arrests made after 12 o'clock midnight January 1, 1990, except amendments to 8.04, 11.07, and 19.04, subd. 5, shall govern all criminal actions commenced or arrests made after 12 o'clock midnight January 1, 1991."

Rule 25.02. Continuance or Change of Venue

This rule governs a motion for continuance or change of venue because of prejudicial publicity.

Subd. 1. How Obtained. A continuance or change of venue may be granted on motion of any party or on the court's initiative.

Subd. 2. Methods of Proof. The following are permissible methods of proof of grounds for a motion for change of venue due to pretrial publicity:

(a) Testimony or affidavits from individuals in the community;

(b) Qualified public opinion surveys; or

(c) Other material having probative value.

Testimony or affidavits from individuals in the community must not be required as a condition for granting the motion.

Subd. 3. Standards for Granting the Motion. A motion for continuance or change of venue must be granted whenever potentially prejudicial material creates a reasonable likelihood that a fair trial cannot be had. Actual prejudice need not be shown.

Subd. 4. Time of Disposition. If a motion for continuance or change of venue is made before the jury is sworn, the motion must be determined before the jury is sworn. A motion or reconsideration of a prior denial may be granted even after a jury has been sworn.

Subd. 5. Limitations; Waiver. The court may grant more than one change of venue. The waiver of a jury or the failure to exercise all available peremptory challenges does not constitute a waiver of the right to a continuance or change of venue if a motion has been timely made.

Adopted Feb. 26, 1975, eff. July 1, 1975. Revised Dec. 13, 1989. Amended Oct. 27, 2009, eff. Jan. 1, 2010.

Comment—Rule 25

See comment following Rule 25.03.

Historical Notes

The order of the Minnesota Supreme Court [C1–84–2137] dated December 13, 1989, provides in part that "(t)hese amended Rules of Criminal Procedure shall govern all criminal actions commenced or arrests made after 12 o'clock midnight January 1, 1990, except amendments to 8.04, 11.07, and 19.04, subd. 5, shall govern all criminal actions commenced or arrests made after 12 o'clock midnight January 1, 1991."

Rule 25.03. Restrictive Orders

Subd. 1. Scope. Except as provided in Rules 25.01, 26.03, subd. 6, and 33.04, this rule governs the issuance of any court order restricting public access to public records relating to a criminal proceeding.

Subd. 2. Motion and Notice.

(a) A restrictive order may be issued only on motion and after notice and hearing.

(b) Notice of the hearing must be given in the time and manner and to interested persons, including the news media, as the court may direct. The notice must be issued publicly at least 24 hours before the hearing and must afford the public and the news media an opportunity to be heard.

Subd. 3. Hearing.

(a) At the hearing, the moving party has the burden of establishing a factual basis for the issuance of the order under the conditions specified in subd. 4.

(b) The public and news media have a right to be represented and to present evidence and arguments in support of or in opposition to the motion, and to suggest any alternatives to the restrictive order.

(c) A verbatim record of the hearing must be made.

Subd. 4. Grounds for Restrictive Order. The court may issue a restrictive order under this rule only if the court concludes that:

(a) Access to public records will present a substantial likelihood of interfering with the fair and impartial administration of justice.

(b) All reasonable alternatives to a restrictive order are inadequate.

A restrictive order must be no broader than necessary to protect against the potential interference with the fair and impartial administration of justice.

Subd. 5. Findings of Fact. The Court must make written findings of the facts and reasons supporting the conclusions on which an order granting or denying the motion is based. If a restrictive order is granted, the order must address possible alternatives to the restrictive order and explain why the alternatives are inadequate.

Subd. 6. Appellate Review.

(a) Anyone aggrieved by an order granting or denying a restrictive order may petition the Court of Appeals for review. This is the exclusive method for obtaining review.

(b) The Court of Appeals must determine whether the moving party met the burden of justifying the restrictive order under the conditions specified in subd. 3. The Court of Appeals may reverse, affirm, or modify the district court's order.

Adopted Feb. 26, 1975, eff. July 1, 1975. Revised Dec. 13, 1989. Amended Oct. 27, 2009, eff. Jan. 1, 2010.

Comment—Rule 25

The Rules of Public Access to Records of the Judicial Branch generally govern access to case records of all judicial courts. However, Rule 4, subd. 1(d) and Rule 4, subd. 2 of those rules provide that the Rules of Criminal Procedure govern what criminal case records are inaccessible to the public and the procedure for restraining access to those records.

Rule 25.01 (Motion to Exclude Public) setting forth the procedure and standard for excluding the public from pretrial hearings is based on Minneapolis Star and Tribune Co. v. Kammeyer, 341 N.W.2d 550 (Minn. 1983). For a defendant an overriding interest includes interference with the defendant's right to a fair trial by reason of the dissemination of evidence or argument presented at the hearing. As to the sufficiency of the alleged overriding interest to justify closure of the hearing see Waller v. Georgia, 467 U.S. 39 (1984) (Closure of suppression hearing over the defendant's objection), Press–Enterprise Co. v. Superior Court, 464 U.S. 501 (1984) (Closure of voir dire proceedings), and Globe Newspaper Co. v. Superior Court, 457 U.S. 596 (1982) (Closure of courtroom when the minor victim of a sex offense testifies). This determination would include the situation in which the news media agreed not to disseminate these matters until completion of the trial. The provision for appellate review is intended to give the defendant, as well as any person aggrieved, standing to seek immediate review of the court's ruling on exclusion.

This rule does not interfere with the power of the court in any pretrial hearing to caution those present that dissemination of certain information by means of public communication may jeopardize the right to a fair trial by an impartial jury.

The procedure in Rule 25.03 is based upon Minneapolis Star and Tribune Co. v. Kammeyer, 341 N.W.2d 550 (Minn. 1983) and Northwest Publications, Inc. v. Anderson, 259 N.W.2d 254 (Minn. 1977). Rule 25.03 governs only the restriction of access to public records concerning a criminal case. It does not authorize the court under any circumstances to prohibit the news media from broadcasting or publishing any information in their possession relating to a criminal case.

Possible alternatives to a restrictive order indicated in Rule 25.03, subd. 3(b) are the following:

- a continuance or change of venue under Rule 25.02;
- sequestration of jurors on voir dire under Rule 26.02, subd. 4(2)(b);
- regulation of use of the courtroom under Rule 26.03, subd. 3;
- sequestration of jury under Rule 26.03, subd. 5(1);
- exclusion of the public from hearings or arguments outside of the presence of the jury under Rule 26.03, subd. 6;
- cautioning or ordering parties, witnesses, jurors, and judicial employees and sequestration of witnesses under Rule 26.03, subds. 7 and 8;
- admonitions to jurors about exposure to prejudicial material under Rule 26.03, subd. 9.

Historical Notes

The order of the Minnesota Supreme Court [C1–84–2137] dated December 13, 1989, provides in part that "(t)hese amended Rules of Criminal Procedure shall govern all criminal actions commenced or arrests made after 12 o'clock midnight January 1, 1990, except amendments to 8.04, 11.07, and 19.04, subd. 5, shall govern all criminal actions commenced or arrests made after 12 o'clock midnight January 1, 1991."

RULE 26. TRIAL

Rule 26.01. Trial by Jury or by the Court

Subd. 1. Trial by Jury.

(1) *Right to Jury Trial.*

(a) Offenses Punishable by Incarceration. A defendant has a right to a jury trial for any offense punishable by incarceration. All trials must be in the district court.

(b) Misdemeanors Not Punishable by Incarceration. In any prosecution for the violation of a misdemeanor not punishable by incarceration, trial must be to the court.

(2) *Waiver of Trial by Jury.*

(a) Waiver on the Issue of Guilt. The defendant, with the approval of the court, may waive a jury trial on the issue of guilt provided the defendant does so personally, in writing or on the record in open court, after being advised by the court of the right to trial by jury, and after having had an opportunity to consult with counsel.

(b) Waiver on the Issue of an Aggravated Sentence. Where the prosecutor seeks an aggravated sentence, the defendant, with the approval of the court, may waive a jury trial on the facts in support of an aggravated sentence provided the defendant does so personally, in writing or on the record in open court, after being advised by the court of the right to a trial by jury, and after having had an opportunity to consult with counsel.

(c) Waiver Necessitated by Prejudicial Publicity. The defendant must be permitted to waive a jury trial whenever the court determines:

(i) the defendant knowingly and voluntarily waived that right; and

(ii) reason exists to believe that, because of the dissemination of potentially prejudicial material, the waiver must be granted to assure a fair trial.

(3) *Withdrawal of Jury-Trial Waiver.* The defendant may withdraw the waiver of a jury trial any time before trial begins.

(4) *Waiver of Number of Jurors Required by Law.* Any time before verdict, the parties, with the approval of the court, may stipulate that the jury consist of a number of jurors fewer than that provided by law. The court must not approve this stipulation unless the defendant, personally in writing or on the record in open court, agrees to trial by a reduced jury after being advised by the court of the right to trial by a jury consisting of the number of jurors provided by law.

(5) *Number Required for Verdict.* The jury's verdict must be unanimous in all cases.

(6) *Waiver of Unanimous Verdict.* Any time before verdict, the parties, with the approval of the court, may stipulate that the jury may render a verdict on the concurrence of a specified number of jurors fewer than that required by law or these rules. The court must not approve this stipulation unless the defendant waives this right personally in writing or on the record, after being advised by the court of the right to a verdict on the concurrence of the number of jurors specified by law.

Subd. 2. Trial Without a Jury.

(a) In a case tried without a jury, the court, within 7 days after the completion of the trial, must make a general finding of guilty; not guilty; or if the applicable pleas have been made, a general finding of not guilty by reason of mental illness or deficiency, double jeopardy, or that Minn. Stat. § 609.035 bars the prosecution.

(b) The court, within 7 days after making its general finding in felony and gross misdemeanor cases, must in addition make findings in writing of the essential facts.

(c) In misdemeanor and petty misdemeanor cases, findings must be made within 7 days after the defendant has filed a notice of appeal.

(d) An opinion or memorandum of decision filed by the court satisfies the requirement to find the essential facts if they appear in the opinion or memorandum.

(e) If the court omits a finding on any issue of fact essential to sustain the general finding, it must be deemed to have made a finding consistent with the general finding.

Subd. 3. Trial on Stipulated Facts.

(a) The defendant and the prosecutor may agree that a determination of defendant's guilt, or the existence of facts to support an aggravated sentence, or both, may be submitted to and tried by the court based on stipulated facts. Before proceeding, the defendant must acknowledge and personally waive the rights to:

(1) testify at trial;

(2) have the prosecution witnesses testify in open court in the defendant's presence;

(3) question those prosecution witnesses; and

(4) require any favorable witnesses to testify for the defense in court.

(b) The agreement and the waiver must be in writing or be placed on the record.

(c) If the parties use this procedure to determine the issues of the defendant's guilt, and the existence of facts to support an aggravated sentence, the defendant must make a separate waiver of the above-listed rights as to each issue.

(d) On submission of the case on stipulated facts, the court must proceed under subdivision 2 of this rule as in any other trial to the court.

(e) If the court finds the defendant guilty based on the stipulated facts, the defendant may appeal from the judgment of conviction and raise issues on appeal as from any trial to the court.

Subd. 4. Stipulation to Prosecution's Case to Obtain Review of a Pretrial Ruling.

(a) When the parties agree that the court's ruling on a specified pretrial issue is dispositive of the case, or that the ruling makes a contested trial unnecessary, the following procedure must be used to preserve the issue for appellate review.

(b) The defendant must maintain the plea of not guilty.

(c) The defendant and the prosecutor must acknowledge that the pretrial issue is dispositive, or that a trial will be unnecessary if the defendant prevails on appeal.

(d) The defendant, after an opportunity to consult with counsel, must waive the right to a jury trial under Rule 26.01, subdivision 1(2)(a), and must also waive the rights specified in Rule 26.01, subdivision 3(a).

(e) The defendant must stipulate to the prosecution's evidence in a trial to the court, and acknowledge that the court will consider the prosecution's evidence, and that the court may enter a finding of guilt based on that evidence.

(f) The defendant must also acknowledge that appellate review will be of the pretrial issue, but not of the defendant's guilt, or of other issues that could arise at a contested trial.

(g) The defendant and the prosecutor must make the preceding acknowledgments personally, in writing or on the record.

(h) After consideration of the stipulated evidence, the court must make an appropriate finding, and if that finding is guilty, the court must also make findings of fact on the record or in writing as to each element of the offense(s).

Adopted Feb. 26, 1975, eff. July 1, 1975. Revised Dec. 13, 1989. Amended Aug. 21, 1998, eff. Jan. 1, 1999; Aug. 17, 2006, eff. Oct. 1, 2006; Dec. 29, 2006, eff. April 1, 2007; Oct. 27, 2009, eff. Jan. 1, 2010.

Comment—Rule 26

See comment following Rule 26.04.

Historical Notes

The order of the Minnesota Supreme Court [C1–84–2137] dated December 13, 1989, provides in part that "(t)hese amended Rules of Criminal Procedure shall govern all criminal actions commenced or arrests made after 12 o'clock midnight January 1, 1990, except amendments to 8.04, 11.07, and 19.04, subd. 5, shall govern all criminal actions commenced or arrests made after 12 o'clock midnight January 1, 1991."

Rule 26.02. Jury Selection

Subd. 1. Jury List. The jury list must be composed of persons randomly selected from a fair cross-section of qualified county residents. The jury must be drawn from the jury list.

Subd. 2. Juror Information.

(1) *Jury Panel List.* Unless the court orders otherwise after a hearing, the court administrator must furnish to any party, upon request, a list of persons on the jury panel, including name, city as reported on the juror questionnaire, occupation, education, children's ages, spouse's occupation, birth date, reported race and whether or not of Hispanic origin, gender, and marital status.

(2) *Anonymous Jurors.* On any party's motion, the court may restrict access to prospective and selected jurors' names, addresses, and other identifying information if a strong reason exists to believe that the jury needs protection from external threats to its members' safety or impartiality.

The court must hold a hearing on the motion and make detailed findings of fact supporting its decision to restrict access to juror information.

The findings of fact must be made in writing or on the record in open court. If ordered, jurors may be identified by number or other means to protect their identity. The court may restrict access to juror identity as long as necessary to protect the jurors. The court must minimize any prejudice the restriction has on the parties.

(3) *Jury Questionnaire.* On the request of a party or on its own initiative, the court may order use of a jury questionnaire as a supplement to voir dire. The questionnaire must be approved by the court. The court must tell prospective jurors that if sensitive or embarrassing questions are included on the questionnaire, instead of answering any particular questions in writing they may request an opportunity to address the court in camera, with counsel and the defendant present, concerning their desire that the answers not be public. When a prospective juror asks to address the court in camera, the court must proceed under Rule 26.02, subd. 4(4) and decide whether the particular questions may be answered during oral voir dire with the public excluded. The court must make the completed questionnaires available to counsel.

Subd. 3. Challenge to Panel. Any party may challenge the jury panel if a material departure from law has occurred in drawing or summoning jurors. The challenge must be made in writing and before the court swears in the jury. The challenge must specify grounds. The court must conduct a hearing to determine the sufficiency of the challenge.

Subd. 4. Voir Dire Examination.

(1) *Purpose—How Made.* The court must allow the parties to conduct voir dire examination to discover grounds for challenges for cause and to assist in the exercise of peremptory challenges. The examination must be open to the public unless otherwise ordered under Rule 26.02, subd. 4(4). The court must begin by identifying the parties and their respective counsel and by outlining the nature of the case. The court must question jurors about their qualifications to serve and may give the preliminary instructions in Rule 26.03, subd. 4. A verbatim record of the voir dire examination must be made at any party's request.

(2) *Sequestration of Jurors.*

(a) Court's Discretion. The court may order that the examination of each juror take place outside of the presence of other chosen and prospective jurors.

(b) Prejudicial Publicity. Whenever a significant possibility exists of exposure to prejudicial material, the examination of each juror with respect to the juror's exposure must take place outside the presence of other prospective and selected jurors.

(3) *Order of Drawing, Examination, and Challenge.*

(a) Jury Selection Methods. Three methods exist for selecting a jury:

(i) the preferred method found in paragraph (b), in which the parties make peremptory challenges at the end of voir dire;

(ii) the alternate method found in paragraph (c), in which a party exercises any peremptory challenge after questioning the prospective juror;

(iii) the preferred method for first-degree murder cases found in paragraph (d), in which each party questions the prospective juror out of the hearing of the other prospective and selected jurors.

(b) Preferred Method; Cases Other Than First–Degree Murder.

(i) The court must draw prospective jurors comprising the number of jurors required, the number of peremptory challenges, and the number of alternates.

(ii) The prospective jurors must take their place in the jury box and be sworn in.

(iii) The prospective jurors must be examined, first by the court, then by the parties, commencing with the defendant.

(iv) A challenge for cause may be made at any time during voir dire by any party. At the close of voir dire any additional challenges for cause must be made, first by the defense and then by the prosecutor.

(v) When the court excuses a prospective juror for cause, another must be drawn so that the number in the jury box remains the same as the number initially called.

(vi) After all challenges for cause have been made, the parties may alternately exercise peremptory challenges, starting with the defendant.

(vii) The jury consists of the remaining panel members in the order they were called.

(c) Alternate Method; Cases Other Than First–Degree Murder.

(i) The court must draw prospective jurors comprising the total of the number of jurors required and the number of alternates.

(ii) The prospective jurors must take their place in the jury box and be sworn in.

(iii) The prospective jurors must be examined, first by the court, then by the parties, commencing with the defendant.

(iv) On completion of the defendant's examination of a prospective juror, the defendant must be permitted to exercise a challenge for cause or a peremptory challenge.

(v) On completion of the defendant's examination and any challenge of a prospective juror, the prosecutor may examine the prospective juror and may exercise a challenge for cause or a peremptory challenge.

(vi) An excused prospective juror must be replaced by another. The replacement must be examined and challenged after all previously drawn jurors have been examined and challenged.

(viii) This process continues until the number of persons who will constitute the jury, including the alternates, have been selected.

(d) Preferred Method; First–Degree Murder Cases.

(i) The court must direct that one prospective juror at a time be drawn from the jury panel for examination.

(ii) The prospective juror must be sworn in.

(iii) The prospective juror must be examined, first by the court, then by the parties, commencing with the defendant.

(iv) On completion of defendant's examination, the defendant may exercise a challenge for cause or peremptory challenge.

(v) A prospective juror who is not excused after examination by the defendant may be examined by the state. The state may exercise a challenge for cause or peremptory challenge.

(vi) This process must continue until the number of jurors equals the number required plus alternates.

(4) *Exclusion of the Public From Voir Dire.* In those rare cases where it is necessary, the following rules govern orders excluding the public from any part of voir dire or restricting access to the orders or to transcripts of the closed proceeding.

(a) Advisory. When it appears prospective jurors may be asked sensitive or embarrassing questions during voir dire, the court may on its own initiative or on request of either party, advise the prospective jurors that they may request an opportunity to address the court in camera, with counsel and defendant present, concerning their desire to exclude the public from voir dire when the sensitive or embarrassing questions are asked.

(b) In Camera Hearing. If a prospective juror requests an opportunity to address the court in camera during sensitive or embarrassing questioning, the request must be granted. The hearing must be on the record with counsel and the defendant present.

(c) Standards. In considering the request to exclude the public during voir dire, the court must balance the juror's privacy interests, the defendant's right to a fair and public trial, and the public's interest in access to the courts. The court may order voir dire closed only if it finds a substantial likelihood that conducting voir dire in open court would interfere with an overriding interest, including the defendant's right to a fair trial and the juror's legitimate privacy interests in not disclosing deeply personal matters to the public. The court must consider alternatives to closure. Any closure must be no broader than necessary to protect the overriding interest.

(d) Refusal to Close Voir Dire. If the court determines no overriding interest exists to justify excluding the public from voir dire, the voir dire must continue in open court on the record.

(e) Closure of Voir Dire. If the court determines that an overriding interest justifies closure of any part of voir dire, that part of voir dire must be conducted in camera on the record with counsel and the defendant present.

(f) Findings of Fact. Any order excluding the public from a part of voir dire must be issued in writing or on the record. The court must set forth the reasons for the order, including findings as to why the defendant's right to a fair trial and the jurors' interests in privacy would be threatened by an open voir dire. The order must address any possible alternatives to closure and explain why the alternatives are inadequate.

(g) Record. A complete record of the in camera proceedings must be made. On request, the record must be transcribed within a reasonable time and filed with the court administrator. The transcript must be publicly available, but only if disclosure can be accomplished while safeguarding the overriding interests involved. The court may order the transcript or any part of it sealed, the name of a juror withheld, or parts of the transcript excised if the court finds these actions necessary to protect the overriding interest that justified closure.

Subd. 5. Challenge for Cause.

(1) *Grounds.* A juror may be challenged for cause on these grounds:

1. The juror's state of mind—in reference to the case or to either party—satisfies the court that the juror cannot try the case impartially and without prejudice to the substantial rights of the challenging party.

2. A felony conviction unless the juror's civil rights have been restored.

3. The lack of any qualification prescribed by law.

4. A physical or mental disability that renders the juror incapable of performing the duties of a juror.

5. The consanguinity or affinity, within the ninth degree, to the person alleged to be injured by the offense charged, or to the person on whose complaint the prosecution was instituted, or to the defendant, or to any of the attorneys in the case.

6. Standing as a guardian, ward, attorney, client, employer, employee, landlord, tenant, family member of the defendant, or person alleged to have been injured by the offense, or whose complaint instituted the prosecution.

7. Being a party adverse to the defendant in a civil action, or a party who complained against the defendant, or whom the defendant accused, in a criminal prosecution.

8. Service on the grand jury that found the indictment or an indictment on a related offense.

9. Service on a trial jury that tried another person for the same or a related offense as the pending charge.

10. Service on any jury previously sworn to try the pending charge.

11. Service as a juror in any case involving the defendant.

(2) *How and When Exercised.* A challenge for cause may be oral and must state grounds. The challenge must be made before the juror is sworn to try the case, but the court for good cause may permit it to be made after the juror is sworn but before all the jurors constituting the jury are sworn. If the court sustains a challenge for cause, the juror must be excused.

(3) *By Whom Tried.* If a party objects to the challenge for cause, the court must determine the challenge.

Subd. 6. Peremptory Challenges. In cases punishable by life imprisonment the defendant has 15 peremptory challenges and the prosecutor has 9. For any other offense, the defendant has 5 peremptory challenges and the prosecutor has 3. In cases with more than one defendant, the court may allow the defendants additional peremptory challenges and permit them to be exercised separately or jointly. The prosecutor's peremptory challenges must be correspondingly increased. All peremptory challenges must be exercised out of the hearing of the jury panel.

Subd. 7. Objections to Peremptory Challenges.

(1) *Rule.* No party may purposefully discriminate on the basis of race or gender in the exercise of peremptory challenges.

(2) *Procedure.* Any party, or the court, at any time before the jury is sworn, may object to a peremptory challenge on the ground of purposeful racial or gender discrimination. The objection and all arguments must be made out of the hearing of all prospective or selected jurors. All proceedings on the objection must be on the record. The objection must be determined by the court as promptly as possible, and must be decided before the jury is sworn.

(3) *Determination.* The trial court must use a three-step process for determining whether a party purposefully discriminated on the basis of race or gender:

(a) First, the party making the objection must make a prima facie showing that the responding party exercised its peremptory challenges on the basis of race or gender. If the court raised the objection, the court must determine, after any hearing it deems appropriate, whether a prima facie showing exists. If no prima facie showing is found, the objection must be overruled.

(b) Second, if the prima facie showing has been made, the responding party must articulate a race- or gender-neutral explanation for exercising the peremptory challenge(s). If the responding party fails to articulate a race- or gender-neutral explanation, the objection must be sustained.

(c) Third, if the court determines that a race- or gender-neutral explanation has been articulated, the objecting party must prove that the explanation is pretextual. If the court initially raised the objection, it must determine, after any hearing it deems appropriate, whether the party exercised the peremptory challenge in a purposefully discriminatory manner on the basis of race or gender. If purposeful discrimination is proved, the objection must be sustained; otherwise the objection must be overruled.

(4) *Remedies.* If the court overrules the objection, the prospective juror must be excused. If the court sustains the objection, the court must—based upon its determination of what the interests of justice and a fair trial to all parties in the case require—either:

(a) Disallow the discriminatory peremptory challenge and resume jury selection with the challenged prospective juror reinstated on the panel; or

(b) Discharge the entire jury panel and select a new jury from a jury panel not previously associated with the case.

Subd. 8. Order of Challenges. Challenges must be made in the following order:

a. To the panel.

b. To an individual prospective juror for cause, except that under subd. 5(2) a challenge for cause may be made at any time before a jury is sworn.

c. Peremptory challenge to an individual prospective juror.

Subd. 9. Alternate Jurors. The court may impanel alternate jurors. An alternate juror who does not replace a principal juror must be discharged when the jury retires to consider its verdict. If a juror becomes unable to serve, an alternate juror must replace that juror. Alternate jurors replace jurors in the order the alternates were drawn. No additional peremptory challenges are allowed for alternate jurors. If a juror becomes unable or disqualified to perform a juror's duties after the jury has retired to consider its verdict, a mistrial must be declared unless the parties agree under Rule 26.01, subd. 1(4) that the jury consist of a lesser number than that selected for the trial.

Adopted Feb. 26, 1975, eff. July 1, 1975. Revised Dec. 13, 1989. Amended May 9, 1994; Aug. 21, 1998, eff. Jan. 1, 1999; Dec. 10, 2003, eff. Feb. 1, 2004; Oct. 27, 2009, eff. Jan. 1, 2010; June 22, 2011, eff. Sept. 1, 2011.

Comment—Rule 26

See comment following Rule 26.04.

Historical Notes

The order of the Minnesota Supreme Court [C1–84–2137] dated December 13, 1989, provides in part that "(t)hese amended Rules of Criminal Procedure shall govern all criminal actions commenced or arrests made after 12 o'clock midnight January 1, 1990, except amendments to 8.04, 11.07, and 19.04, subd. 5 shall govern all criminal actions commenced or arrests made after 12 o'clock midnight January 1, 1991."

The order of the Minnesota Supreme Court [C1–84–2137] dated May 9, 1994, provides in part that "(t)hese amendments to the Rules of Criminal Procedure shall govern all criminal actions commenced or arrests made after 12 o'clock midnight July 1, 1994, except that the amendments in the first sentence of the third paragraph in Rule 2.01 shall govern all criminal actions commenced or arrests made after 12 o'clock midnight January 1, 1995."

The order of the Minnesota Supreme Court [ADM10–8049] dated June 22, 2011, provided in part that "The amendments shall govern all criminal actions currently pending on or commenced on or after the effective date."

Rule 26.03. Procedures During Trial

Subd. 1. Defendant's Presence.

(1) *Presence Required.* The defendant must be present at arraignment, plea, and for every stage of the trial including:

(a) jury selection;

(b) opening statements;

(c) presentation of evidence;

(d) closing argument;

(e) jury instructions;

(f) any jury questions dealing with evidence or law;

(g) the verdict;

(h) sentencing.

If the defendant is disabled in communication, a qualified interpreter must also be present at each proceeding.

(2) *Presence Waived.* The trial may proceed to verdict without the defendant's presence if:

1. The defendant is absent without justification after the trial starts; or

2. The defendant, after warning, engages in conduct that justifies expulsion from the courtroom because it disrupts the trial or hearing. But, as an alternative to expulsion, the court may use restraints if necessary to ensure order in the courtroom.

(3) *Presence Not Required.*

1. Corporations. A corporation may appear by counsel.

2. Felony. In felony cases, the court may, on the defendant's motion, excuse the defendant's presence except at arraignment, plea, trial, and sentencing.

3. Gross Misdemeanors. In gross misdemeanor cases, the court may, on the defendant's motion, excuse the defendant's presence except at trial.

4. Misdemeanors. In misdemeanor cases, if the defendant consents either in writing or on the rec-

ord, the court must excuse the defendant from appearing for arraignment or plea, and the court may excuse the defendant from appearing at trial or sentencing.

5. ITV or Telephone. If a defendant consents, the court may allow the parties, lawyers, or the court to appear using ITV or telephone in any proceeding where the defendant could waive appearance under these rules.

Subd. 2. Custody and Restraint of Defendants and Witnesses.

a. During trial, the defendant must be seated to permit effective consultation with defense counsel and to see and hear the proceedings.

b. During trial, an incarcerated defendant or witness must not appear in court in the distinctive attire of a prisoner.

c. Defendants and witnesses must not be subjected to physical restraint while in court unless the court:

1. Finds the restraint necessary to maintain order or security; and

2. States the reasons for the restraints on the record outside the hearing of the jury.

d. If the restraint is apparent to the jury, and the defendant requests, the judge must instruct the jury that the restraint must not be considered in reaching the verdict.

Subd. 3. Media Access and Courtroom Decorum.

(a) The court must ensure the preservation of decorum in the courtroom.

(b) The court may reserve seats in the courtroom for reporters.

(c) The court may advise reporters about the proper use of the courtroom and other court facilities, or about courtroom decorum.

Subd. 4. Preliminary Instructions. After the jury has been impaneled and sworn, and before the opening statements, the court may instruct the jury on the parties' respective claims and on other matters that will aid the jury in comprehending the order of trial and trial procedures. Preliminary instructions may include the:

(a) burden of proof;

(b) presumption of innocence;

(c) necessity of proof of guilt beyond a reasonable doubt;

(d) factors the jury may consider in weighing testimony or determining credibility of witnesses;

(e) rules applicable to opinion evidence;

(f) elements of the offense;

(g) other rules of law essential to the proper understanding of the evidence.

The preliminary instructions must be disclosed to the parties before they are given, and any party may object to specific instructions or propose other instructions.

Subd. 5. Jury Sequestration.

(1) *Discretion of the Court.* From the time the jurors are sworn until they retire for deliberations, the court may permit them and any alternate jurors to separate during recesses and adjournments, or direct that they remain together continuously under the supervision of designated officers.

(2) *On Motion.* Any party may move for sequestration of the jury at the beginning of trial or at any time during trial. Sequestration must be ordered if the case is of such notoriety or the issues are of such a nature that, in the absence of sequestration, highly prejudicial matters are likely to come to the jurors' attention. Whenever sequestration is ordered, the court in advising the jury of the decision must not disclose which party requested sequestration.

(3) *During Deliberations.* Unless the court has ordered sequestration under paragraph (2), the court may allow the jurors to separate over night during deliberations.

(4) *No Outside Contact.* The supervising officers must not communicate with any juror concerning any subject connected with the trial, nor permit any other person to do so, and must return the jury to the courtroom as ordered by the court.

Subd. 6. Exclusion of the Public From Hearings or Arguments Outside the Presence of the Jury. The following rules govern orders restricting public access to portions of the trial conducted outside the presence of the jury or restricting access to trial transcripts, or an order arising from a closed portion of the trial.

(1) *Grounds for Exclusion of Public.*

(a) If the jury is not sequestered, on motion of a party or the court's own motion, the court may order that the public be excluded from portions of the trial held outside the jury's presence if the court finds that public dissemination of evidence or argument at the hearing would likely interfere with an overriding interest, including the right to a fair trial.

(b) *Alternative Measures.* Before restricting public access, the court must consider reasonable alternatives to restricting public access. The restriction must be no broader than necessary to protect the overriding interest involved, including the right to a fair trial.

(2) *Notice.* If any party wishes to bring a motion excluding the public, the party must request a closed meeting with counsel and the court.

(3) *Closed Hearing and Public Notice.* At the closed hearing, the court must review the evidence sought to be excluded from public access. If the court

finds restriction appropriate, the court must schedule a hearing on the potential restrictive order. A hearing notice must be issued publicly at least 24 hours before the hearing. The notice must allow the public, including reporters, an opportunity to be heard on whether any overriding interests exist, including the right to a fair trial, that would justify closing the hearing to the public.

(4) *Hearing.* At the hearing the court must disclose that evidence exists that may justify restricting access. The court must allow the public, including reporters, to suggest alternatives to a restrictive order.

(5) *Findings.* An order and supporting findings of fact restricting public access must be in writing. The order must address alternatives to closure and explain why the alternatives are inadequate. Any matter relevant to the court's decision that does not endanger the overriding interests involved, including the right to a fair trial, must be decided on the record in open court.

(6) *Records.* If the court closes a portion of the trial, a record of the non-public proceedings must be made. If anyone makes a request, the record must be transcribed at public expense. The record must be publicly available after the trial. The court may redact names from the record to protect the innocent.

(7) *Appellate Review.* Anyone represented at the hearing or aggrieved by an order granting or denying public access may petition the Court of Appeals for review. This is the exclusive method for obtaining review.

The Court of Appeals must determine whether the party who moved for public exclusion met the burden justifying the exclusion under this rule. The Court of Appeals may reverse, affirm, or modify the district court's order.

Subd. 7. Cautioning Parties, Witnesses, Jurors and Judicial Employees. The court may order attorneys, parties, witnesses, jurors, and employees and officers of the court not to make extra-judicial statements relating to the case or the issues in the case for public dissemination during the trial.

Subd. 8. Sequestration. The court may sequester witnesses from the courtroom before their appearance.

Subd. 9. Admonitions to Jurors. The court may advise the jurors not to read, listen to, or watch news reports about the case.

Subd. 10. Questioning Jurors About Exposure to Potentially Prejudicial Material in the Course of a Trial. If the court determines that material disseminated outside the trial proceedings raises questions of possible prejudice, the court may on its initiative, and must on motion of either party, question each juror, out of the presence of the others, about the juror's exposure to that material. The examination must take place in the presence of counsel, and a record of the examination must be made.

Subd. 11. View by Jury.

a. The court may allow the jury to view a place relevant to a case at any time before closing arguments if doing so would be helpful to the jury in deciding a material factual issue.

b. At the viewing:

(1) The jury must be kept together under the supervision of an officer appointed by the court;

(2) The judge and the court reporter must be present;

(3) The prosecutor, defendant and defense attorney have the right to be present; and

(4) Others may be present if authorized by the court.

c. The purpose of the viewing is limited to visual observation of the place in question, and neither the parties, nor counsel or the jurors while viewing the place may discuss the significance or implications of anything under observation or any issue in the case.

Subd. 12. Order of Jury Trial.

a. The jury is selected and sworn.

b. The court may deliver preliminary jury instructions.

c. The prosecutor may make an opening statement limited to the facts the prosecutor expects to prove.

d. The defendant may make an opening statement after the prosecutor's opening statement, or make an opening statement at the beginning of the defendant's case. The defendant's statement must be limited to the defense and the facts the defendant expects to offer supporting that defense.

e. The prosecutor presents evidence in support of the state's case.

f. The defendant may offer evidence in defense.

g. The prosecutor may rebut the defense evidence, and, the defense may rebut the prosecutor's evidence. In the interests of justice, the court may allow any party to reopen that party's case to offer additional evidence.

h. The prosecutor may make a closing argument.

i. The defendant may make a closing argument.

j. The prosecutor may make a rebuttal argument limited to a direct response to the defendant's closing argument.

k. On motion, the court may allow a defense rebuttal if the court finds the prosecution has made a misstatement of law or fact or an inflammatory or prejudicial statement in rebuttal. Rebuttal must be limited to a direct response to the misstatement of law or fact or the inflammatory or prejudicial statement.

l. Outside the jury's presence, the court must allow the parties to object to the other party's argument and request curative instructions. The parties may also object and seek curative instructions before or during argument.

m. The court instructs the jury.

n. The jury deliberates and, if possible, renders a verdict.

Subd. 13. Note Taking. Jurors may take notes during the presentation of evidence and use them during deliberation.

Subd. 14. Substitution of Judge.

(1) *Before or During Trial.* If a judge is unable to preside over pretrial or trial proceedings due to death, illness, or other disability, any other judge in the district, once familiar with the record, may finish the proceedings or trial.

(2) *After Verdict or Finding of Guilt.* If a judge is unable to preside due to death, illness or other disability after verdict or finding of guilt, any other judge in the district may finish the proceedings. If the subsequent judge determines the proceedings cannot be finished because the judge did not preside at the trial, the judge may order a new trial.

(3) *Interest or Bias of Judge.* A judge must not preside at a trial or other proceeding if disqualified under the Code of Judicial Conduct. A request to disqualify a judge for cause must be heard and determined by the chief judge of the district or by the assistant chief judge if the chief judge is the subject of the request.

(4) *Notice to Remove.* A party may remove a judge assigned to preside at a trial or hearing as follows:

(a) A notice to remove must be served on the opposing counsel and filed with district court within 7 days after the party receives notice of the name of the presiding judge at the trial or hearing;

(b) The notice must be filed before the start of the trial or hearing; and

(c) The notice is not effective against a judge who already presided at the trial, Omnibus Hearing, or evidentiary hearing if the removing party had notice the judge would preside at the hearing.

(5) After a party removes a judge under subdivision 14(4) that party may remove a subsequent judge only for cause.

(6) *Recusal.* The court may recuse itself from presiding over a case without a motion.

(7) *Assignment of New Judge.* If a judge is unavailable for any reason under this rule, the chief judge of the judicial district must assign another judge within the district to hear the matter. If no other judge in the district is available, the chief judge must notify the chief justice. The chief justice must assign a judge of another district to preside over the matter.

Subd. 15. Objections. An objection to a court order or ruling is preserved for appeal if the party indicates on the record its objection or position. If no opportunity existed to object or indicate a position, the absence of an objection or stated position does not prejudice the party.

Subd. 16. Evidence. At trial, witness testimony must be taken in open court, unless these rules provide otherwise.

Jurors may not submit questions to a witness directly or through the judge or attorneys.

If either party offers an audio or video recording, that party may offer a transcript of the recording, which will be part of the record.

Subd. 17. Interpreters. The court must appoint and compensate interpreters as provided under Rule 8 of the General Rules of Practice for District Courts. Interpreters may be appointed and be present during deliberations for a juror with a sensory disability.

Subd. 18. Motion for Judgment of Acquittal or Insufficient Evidence for an Aggravated Sentence.

(1) *Before Deliberations.*

(a) Charged Offense. At the close of evidence for either party, the defendant may move for, or the court on its own may order, a judgment of acquittal on one or more of the charges if the evidence is insufficient to sustain a conviction.

(b) Aggravated Sentence. The defendant may move for, or the court on its own may order, that any aggravating factors be withdrawn from consideration by the jury if the evidence is insufficient to prove them.

(2) *Reservation of Decision.* If the defendant's motion is made at the close of the prosecution's case, the court must rule on the motion. If the defendant's motion is made at the close of the defendant's case, the court may reserve ruling on the motion, submit the case to the jury, and rule before or after verdict. If the court grants the defendant's motion after a verdict of guilty, the court must make a written finding stating the reason for the order.

(3) *After Verdict or Discharge.*

(a) If the jury returns a verdict of guilty or is discharged without verdict, a motion for a judgment of acquittal may be brought within 15 days after the jury is discharged or within any further time as the court may fix during the 15–day period.

(b) If the jury finds aggravating factors, the defendant may move the court to determine that the evidence is insufficient to sustain them.

(c) If the court grants the defendant's motion for a judgment of acquittal or determines that the evidence is insufficient to sustain the aggravating factors, the court must make written findings stating the reasons for the order.

(d) If no verdict is returned, the court may enter judgment of acquittal. If no finding of an aggravating factor is made, the court may enter a finding of insufficient evidence to support an aggravated sentence.

(e) A motion for a judgment of acquittal or that the evidence is insufficient to sustain an aggravated sentence is not barred by a failure to move before deliberations.

Subd. 19. Instructions.

(1) *Requests for Instructions.* Any party may request specific jury instructions at or before the close of evidence. The request must be provided to all parties.

(2) *Proposed Instructions.* The court may, and on request must, tell the parties on the record before the arguments to the jury what instructions will be given to the jury including a ruling on the requests made by any party.

(3) *In Argument.* Any party may refer to the instructions during final argument.

(4) *Objections.*

(a) No party may claim error for any instruction not objected to before deliberation.

(b) The party's objection must state specific grounds.

(c) The court must give the parties the opportunity to object outside the jury's presence.

(d) The objection must be made on the record.

(e) All instructions, given or refused, must be made a part of the record.

(f) Objections to instructions claiming error in fundamental law or controlling principle may be included in a motion for a new trial even if not raised before deliberations.

(5) *Giving of Instructions.* The court may instruct the jury before or after argument. Preliminary instructions need not be repeated. The instructions may be in writing and may be taken into the jury room during deliberations.

(6) *Contents of Instructions.* The court must instruct the jury on all matters of law necessary to render a verdict and must instruct the jury that they are the exclusive judges of the facts. The court must not comment on evidence or witness credibility, but may state the respective claims of the parties.

(7) *Verdict Forms.* The court must submit appropriate verdict forms to the jury. An aggravated sentence form must be in the form of a special interrogatory.

Subd. 20. Jury Deliberations and Verdict.

(1) *Materials Allowed in Jury Room.* The court must permit received exhibits or copies, except depositions and audio or video material, into the jury room. The court may permit a copy of jury instructions into the jury room.

(2) *Requests to Review Evidence.* The court may allow the jury to review specific evidence.

(a) If the jury requests review of specific evidence during deliberations, the court may permit review of that evidence after notice to the parties and an opportunity to be heard.

(b) Any jury review of depositions, or audio or video material must occur in open court. The court must instruct the jury to suspend deliberations during the review.

(c) The prosecutor, defense counsel, and the defendant must be present for the proceedings described in paragraphs (a) and (b), but the defendant may personally waive the right to be present.

(d) The court need not submit evidence beyond what the jury requested but may submit additional evidence on the same issue to avoid giving undue prominence to the requested evidence.

(3) *Additional Instructions.* If the jury asks for additional instruction on the law during deliberation, the court must give notice to the parties. The court's response must be given in the courtroom.

(a) The court may give additional instructions.

(b) The court may reread portions of the original instructions.

(c) The court may tell the jury that the request deals with matters not in evidence or not related to the law of the case.

(d) The court may tell the jury that the request is a factual matter that the jury, not the judge, must determine.

(e) The court need not give instructions beyond the jury's request, but may do so to avoid giving undue prominence to the requested instructions.

(f) The court may give additional instructions without a jury request during deliberations. The court must give notice to the parties of its intent to give additional instructions.

(4) *Deadlocked Jury.* The jury may be discharged without a verdict if the court finds there is no reasonable probability of agreement.

(5) *Polling the Jury.*

(a) When a verdict is returned, or the jury answered special interrogatories related to an aggravated sentence, and before the jury is discharged, either party may request that the jury be polled. The court must poll the jury on request. The court may poll the jury on its own initiative.

(b) The poll must be done by the court or the court's clerk. Each juror must be asked individually whether the announced verdict or finding is that juror's verdict or finding.

(c) If a juror indicates the announced verdict or finding is not that juror's verdict or finding, the court may return the jury to deliberations or discharge the jury.

(6) *Verdict Impeachment.* A defendant may move the court for a hearing to impeach the verdict. Juror affidavits are not admissible to impeach a verdict. At an impeachment hearing, jurors must be examined under oath and their testimony recorded. Minnesota Rule of Evidence 606(b) governs the admissibility of evidence at an impeachment hearing.

(7) *Partial Verdicts.* The court may accept a partial verdict if the jury has reached a verdict on fewer than all of the charges and is unable to reach a verdict on the rest.

Adopted Feb. 26, 1975, eff. July 1, 1975. Revised Dec. 13, 1989. Amended May 9, 1994; Aug. 21, 1998, eff. Jan. 1, 1999; Feb. 11, 2000, eff. March 14, 2000; Dec. 23, 2002, eff. Feb. 1, 2003; Dec. 10, 2003, eff. Feb. 1, 2004; Aug. 17, 2006, eff. Oct. 1, 2006; Nov. 19, 2007, eff. Jan. 1, 2008; Oct. 27, 2009, eff. Jan. 1, 2010; June 22, 2011, eff. Sept. 1, 2011; June 5, 2012, eff. Aug. 1, 2012.

Comment—Rule 26

See comment following Rule 26.04.

Supersedure

Laws 1999, c. 72, § 2, provides that subd. 11 [now subd. 12] is superseded to the extent that it conflicts with Laws 1999, c. 72, § 1 (amending § 631.07).

Historical Notes

The order of the Minnesota Supreme Court [C1–84–2137] dated December 13, 1989, provides in part that "(t)hese amended Rules of Criminal Procedure shall govern all criminal actions commenced or arrests made after 12 o'clock midnight January 1, 1990, except amendments to 8.04, 11.07, and 19.04, subd. 5, shall govern all criminal actions commenced or arrests made after 12 o'clock midnight January 1, 1991."

The order of the Minnesota Supreme Court [C1–84–2137] dated May 9, 1994, provides in part that "(t)hese amendments to the Rules of Criminal Procedure shall govern all criminal actions commenced or arrests made after 12 o'clock midnight July 1, 1994, except that the amendments in the first sentence of the third paragraph in Rule 2.01 shall govern all criminal actions commenced or arrests made after 12 o'clock midnight January 1, 1995."

Laws 1999, c. 72, § 2, provides that subd. 11 is superseded to the extent it conflicts with Laws 1999, c. 72, § 1 (amending § 631.07).

Laws 1999, c. 72, § 3, provides in part that § 2, superseding subd. 11 to the extent it conflicts with Laws 1999, c. 72, § 1 (amending § 631.07), is effective August 1, 1999, and applies to crimes committed on or after that date.

The order of the Minnesota Supreme Court [ADM10–8049] dated June 22, 2011, provided in part that "The amendments shall govern all criminal actions currently pending on or commenced on or after the effective date."

The order of the Minnesota Supreme Court [ADM 10–8049] dated June 5, 2012, provided in part that the amendments "be effective August 1, 2012, and shall apply to all actions or proceedings pending on or commenced on or after the effective date."

Rule 26.04. Post–Verdict Motions

Subd. 1. New Trial On Defendant's Motion.

(1) *Grounds.* The court may—on written motion of a defendant—grant a new trial on the issue of guilt or the existence of facts to support an aggravated sentence, or both, on any of the following grounds:

1. The interests of justice;
2. Irregularity in the proceedings, or any order or abuse of discretion that deprived the defendant of a fair trial;
3. Prosecutorial or jury misconduct;
4. Accident or surprise that could not have been prevented by ordinary prudence;
5. Newly discovered material evidence, which with reasonable diligence could not have been found and produced at the trial;
6. Errors of law at trial, and objected to at the time unless no objection is required by these rules;
7. A verdict or finding of guilty that is not justified by the evidence, or is contrary to law.

(2) *Basis of Motion.* A motion for new trial must be based on the record. Pertinent facts that are not in the record may be submitted by affidavit, except as otherwise provided by these rules. A full or partial transcript or other verbatim recording of the testimony taken at trial may be used during the motion hearing.

(3) *Time for Motion.* Notice of a motion for a new trial must be served within 15 days after a verdict or finding of guilty. The motion must be heard within 30 days after the verdict or finding of guilty, unless the time for hearing is extended by the court for good cause within the 30–day period.

(4) *Time for Serving Affidavits.* If a motion for a new trial is based on affidavits, the affidavits must be served with the notice of motion. The opposing party will then have 10 days to serve affidavits. The 10–day period may be extended by the court for good cause. The court may permit reply affidavits.

Subd. 2. New Trial on Court's Initiative. The court may—on its own initiative and with the consent of the defendant—order a new trial on any of the grounds specified in subdivision 1(1) within 15 days after a verdict or finding of guilty.

Subd. 3. Motion to Vacate Judgment. The court must—on motion of a defendant—vacate judgment, if entered, and dismiss the case if the indictment, complaint, or tab charge does not charge an offense, or if the court did not have jurisdiction over the offense charged. The motion must be made within 15 days after a verdict or finding of guilty, after a plea of guilty, or within a time set by the court during the 15–day period. If the motion is granted, the court must make written findings specifying its reasons for vacating the judgment and dismissing the case.

Adopted Feb. 26, 1975, eff. July 1, 1975. Revised Dec. 13, 1989. Amended May 9, 1994; Aug. 17, 2006, eff. Oct. 1, 2006; Oct. 27, 2009, eff. Jan. 1, 2010.

Comments—Rule 26

Rule 26.01, subd. 1(1) (Right to Jury Trial). In cases of felonies and gross misdemeanors, the defendant has the right to a jury trial under Minn. Const. Art. 1, § 6, which guarantees the right to jury trial in "all criminal prosecutions." The term "criminal prosecution" includes prosecutions for all crimes defined by Minn. Stat. § 609.02. See Peterson v. Peterson, 278 Minn. 275, 281, 153 N.W.2d 825, 830 (1967); State v. Ketterer, 248 Minn. 173, 176, 79 N.W.2d 136, 139 (1956). The defendant's right to jury trial for offenses punishable by more than six months imprisonment is also guaranteed by the Fourteenth and Sixth Amendments to the United States Constitution. Duncan v. Louisiana, 391 U.S. 145, 159 (1968); Baldwin v. New York, 399 U.S. 66, 69 (1970).

Since misdemeanors in Minnesota are punishable by no more than 90 days of incarceration or a fine or both, Minn. Stat. § 609.03, subd. 3, no federal constitutional right exists to a jury trial on a misdemeanor. However, a state constitutional right to a jury trial exists in any prosecution for the violation of a misdemeanor statute punishable by incarceration. See Minn. Const. Art. 1, § 6 as interpreted in State v. Hoben, 256 Minn. 436, 444, 98 N.W.2d 813, 819 (1959).

Rule 26.01, subd. 1(2)(b) establishes the procedure for waiver of a jury on the issue of an aggravated sentence. See generally Blakely v. Washington, 542 U.S. 296 (2004) and State v. Shattuck, 704 N.W.2d 131 (Minn. 2005) as to the constitutional limitations on imposing aggravated sentences based on findings of fact beyond the elements of the offense and the conviction history. Also, see Rules 1.04 (d), 7.03, and 11.04, subd. 2 and the comments to those rules. Whether a defendant has waived or demanded a jury trial on the issue of guilt, that defendant may still have a jury trial on the issue of an aggravated sentence, and a valid waiver under Rule 26.01, subd. 1(2)(b) must be made before an aggravated sentence may be imposed based on findings not made by jury trial.

Rule 26.01, subd. 1(3) (Withdrawal of Jury-Trial Waiver) provides that waiver of jury trial may be withdrawn before commencement of trial. Trial begins when jeopardy attaches.

The rules do not permit conditional pleas of guilty by which the defendant reserves the right to appeal the denial of a motion to suppress evidence or other pretrial order. Rule 26.01, subd. 4 implements the procedure authorized by State v. Lothenbach, 296 N.W.2d 854 (Minn. 1980). This rule supersedes Lothenbach as to the procedure for stipulating to the prosecution's case to obtain review of a pretrial ruling.

This rule also distinguishes the Lothenbach-type procedure it implements from Rule 26.01, subd. 3 (Trial on Stipulated Facts). Rule 26.01, subd. 3 should be used if there is no pretrial ruling dispositive of the case, and if the defendant wishes to have the full scope of appellate review, including a challenge to the sufficiency of the evidence. See State v. Busse, 644 N.W.2d 79, 89 (Minn. 2002).

The phrase in the first sentence of Rule 26.01, subd. 4(a)—"or that the ruling makes a contested trial unnecessary"—recognizes that a pretrial ruling will not always be dispositive of the entire case, but that a successful appeal of the pretrial issue could nonetheless make a trial unnecessary, such as in a DWI case where the only issue is the validity of one or more qualified prior impaired driving incidents as a charge enhancement. See, e.g., State v. Sandmoen, 390 N.W.2d 419, 423 (Minn. App. 1986). The parties could agree that if the defendant prevailed on appeal, the defendant would still have a conviction for an unenhanced DWI offense. Where a conviction for some offense is supportable regardless of the outcome of the appeal, but a contested trial would serve no purpose, Rule 26. 01, subd. 4 could be used.

On a finding under Rule 26.02, subd. 2(2) that there is strong reason to believe dissemination of juror information poses a threat to juror safety or impartiality, the court may enter an order that information regarding identity, including names, telephone numbers, and addresses of prospective jurors be withheld from the public, parties, and counsel. See State v. Bowles, 530 N.W.2d 521, 530–31 (Minn. 1995); State v. McKenzie, 532 N.W.2d 210, 219 (Minn. 1995). The restrictions ordered by the court may extend through trial and beyond as necessary to protect the safety and impartiality interests involved. To protect the identity of jurors and prospective jurors, the court may order that they be identified by number or other method and may prohibit pictures or sketches in the courtroom. The court's decision will be reviewed under an abuse of discretion standard.

The court must recognize that not every trial where there is a threat to jurors' impartiality will require restriction on access to information about jurors. The decision to restrict access to information on jurors must be made in the light of reason, principle, and common sense.

In ensuring that restriction on the parties' access to information about the jurors does not have a prejudicial effect on the defendant, the court must take reasonable precautions to minimize the potential for prejudice. The court must allow voir dire on the effect that restricting access to juror identification may have on the impartiality of the jurors. The court should also instruct the jurors that the jury selection procedures do not in any way suggest the defendant's guilt.

The use of a written jury questionnaire (Rule 26.02, subd. 2(3)) has proved to be a useful tool in obtaining information from prospective jurors in criminal cases. The written questionnaire provided in the Criminal Forms following these rules includes generally non-sensitive questions relevant to jury selection in any criminal case. See Form 50 for the Jury Questionnaire. Additionally the court on its own initiative or on request of counsel may submit to the prospective jurors as part of the questionnaire other questions that might be helpful based on the particular case to be tried.

Once the panel of prospective jurors for a particular case has been determined, the judge or court personnel will instruct the panel on the use of the questionnaire. The preamble at the beginning of the Jury Questionnaire (Form 50) provides the basic information to the prospective jurors including their right to ask the court to permit them to answer any sensitive question orally or privately. On completion of the questionnaire, the court must make the questionnaire available to counsel for use in the jury selection process. The questionnaire may be sworn to either when signed or when the prospective juror appears in court at the time of the voir dire examination. Because of the information contained in the questionnaire, counsel will not need to expend court time on this information, but can move directly to follow-up questions on particular information already available in the questionnaire. However, the written questionnaire is intended only to supplement and not to substitute for the oral voir dire examination provided for by Rule 26.02, subd. 4.

The use and retention of jury questionnaires have been subject to a variety of practices. This rule provides that the questionnaire is a part of the jury selection process and part of the record for appeal and reflects current law. As such, the questionnaires should be preserved as part of the court record of the case. See Rule 814 of the General Rules of Practice for the District Courts as to the length of time such records must be retained. Additionally, see Rule 26.02, subd. 2(2) as to restricting public access to the names, addresses, telephone numbers, and other identifying information concerning jurors and prospective jurors when the court determines that an anonymous jury is necessary.

It is recognized that the idea of the privacy of the questionnaire adds to the candor and honesty of the responses of the prospective jurors. However, in light of other applicable laws and the fact that the questionnaire is part of the record in the case, prospective jurors cannot be told that the questionnaire is confidential or will be destroyed at the conclusion of the case. Rather, the jurors can be told, as reflected in the preamble to the Jury Questionnaire (Form 50), that they can ask the court to permit them to answer sensitive questions orally and privately under Rule 26. 02, subd. 4(4). This procedure should minimize the sensitive or embarrassing information in the written questionnaires and consequently the need for sealing or destroying them.

Jury selection is a part of the criminal trial record, which is presumed to be open to the public. Press–Enterprise Co. v. Superior Court of California (Press–Enterprise I), 464 U.S. 501, 505 (1984). The use of a jury questionnaire as part of jury selection is also a part of the open proceeding and therefore the public and the media have a right of access to that information in the usual case. See, e.g., Lesher Commc'ns, Inc. v. Superior Court of Contra Costa County, 224 Cal. App. 3d 774, 779 (1990).

The provision of Rule 26.02, subd. 4(1) governing the purpose for which voir dire examination must be conducted and the provision for initiation of the examination by the judge is taken from ABA Standards, Trial by Jury, 2.4. The court has the right and the duty to assure that the inquiries by the parties during the voir dire examination are "reasonable". The court may therefore restrict or prohibit questions that are repetitious, irrelevant, or otherwise improper. See State v. Greer, 635 N.W. 2d 82, 87 (Minn. 2001) (holding no error in district court's restrictions on voir dire); State v. Bauer, 189 Minn. 280, 282, 249 N.W. 40, 41 (1933). However, the Minnesota Supreme Court's Task Force on Racial Bias in the Judicial System recommends in its Final Report, dated May 1993, that during voir dire lawyers should be given ample opportunity to inquire of jurors as to racial bias.

The purpose of Rule 26.02, subd. 4(3) is to achieve uniformity in the order of drawing, examination, and challenge of jurors, and also to provide a limited number of alternatives that may be followed, in the court's discretion. Hence, a uniform rule (26.02, subd. 4(3)(b)) is prescribed, which is to be followed unless the court orders the alternative. Rule 26.02, subd. 4(3)(c). An exception is that in cases of first degree murder, Rule 26.02, subd. 4(3)(d) is to be preferred unless otherwise ordered by the court.

Rule 26.02, subd. 4(3)(b) is the rule to be followed unless the court orders otherwise and substantially adopts the method used in civil cases, so that in a criminal case 20 members of the jury panel are first drawn for a 12–person jury. See Minn. Stat. § 546.10; Minn. R. Civ. P. 48. After each party has exercised challenges for cause, commencing with the defendant, they exercise their peremptory challenges alternately, commencing with the defendant. If all peremptory challenges are not exercised, the jury must be selected from the remaining prospective jurors in the order in which they were called.

For the definition of a felony conviction that would disqualify a person from service on the jury under Rule 26.02, subd. 5(1), see Minn. Stat. § 609.13. The term "related offense" in the rule is intended to be more comprehensive than the conduct or behavioral incident covered by Minn. Stat. § 609.035.

Rule 26.02, subd. 7 (Objections to Peremptory Challenges) adopts and implements the equal protection prohibition against purposeful racial and gender discrimination in the exercise of peremptory challenges established in Batson v. Kentucky, 476 U.S. 79 (1986) and subsequent cases, including J.E.B. v. Alabama ex rel. T.B., 511 U.S. 127 (1994) (extending the rule to gender-based discrimination). In applying this rule, the bench and bar should thoroughly familiarize themselves with the case law that has developed, particularly with respect to meanings of the terms "prima facie showing," "race-neutral explanation," "pretextual reasons," and "purposeful discrimination" used in the rule. See also State v. Davis, 504 N.W.2d 767 (Minn. 1993) (declining to extend the rule to religion), cert. denied sub. nom Davis v. Minnesota, 511 U.S. 1115 (1994).

The interpreter requirement in Rule 26.03, subd. 1(1) derives from Rule 8 of the General Rules of Practice for the District Courts and Minn. Stat. §§ 611.30–611.34.

A defendant's refusal to wear non-jail attire waives the provision in Rule 26.03, subd. 2 (Custody and Restraint of Defendants and Witnesses) and is not grounds for delaying the trial. A list of factors relevant to the decision to employ restraints is found in State v. Shoen, 578 N.W.2d 708, 713 (Minn. 1998).

Rule 26.03, subd. 5(3) requires the consent of the defendant and prosecutor when ordering jurors to separate overnight during deliberation. In State v. Green, 719 N.W.2d 664, 672–73 (Minn. 2006), the Minnesota Supreme Court concluded that a district court did not commit error in releasing jurors for the night when no hotel accommodations could be found within a reasonable distance of the courthouse despite an exhaustive effort, neither party could propose a means of accomplishing sequestration, and the trial court instructed jurors to have no discussions about the case and to not read newspapers, watch television, or listen to the radio.

Rule 26.03, subd. 6 (Exclusion of Public From Hearings or Arguments Outside the Presence of the Jury) reflects Minneapolis Star and Tribune Company v. Kammeyer, 341 N.W.2d 550, 559–60 (Minn. 1983), which established similar procedures for excluding the public from pretrial hearings. See the comment to Rule 25.01 concerning those procedures.

Rule 26.03, subd. 12 (Order of Jury Trial) substantially continues the order of trial under existing practice. See Minn. Stat. § 546.11. The order of closing argument, under sections "h," "i," "j," and "k" of this rule reflects a change. The prosecution argues first, then the defense. The prosecution is then automatically entitled to rebuttal argument. However, this argument must be true rebuttal and is limited to directly responding to matters raised in the defendant's closing argument. Allowance of the rebuttal argument to the prosecution should result in a more efficient and less confusing presentation to the jury. The prosecution will need to address only those defenses actually raised by the defendant rather than guessing, perhaps wrongly, about those defenses. In the event that the prosecution engages in improper rebuttal, paragraph "k" of the rule provides, upon motion, for a limited right of rebuttal to the defendant to address misstatements of law or fact and any inflammatory or prejudicial statements. The court has the inherent power and duty to assure that any rebuttal or surrebuttal arguments stay within the limits of the rule and do not simply repeat matters from the earlier arguments or address matters not raised in earlier arguments. It is the responsibility of the court to ensure that final argument to the jury is kept within proper bounds. ABA Standards for Criminal Justice: Prosecution Function and Defense Function, standards 3–5.8 & 4–7.7 (3d ed. 1993). If the argument is sufficiently improper, the trial judge should intervene, even without objection from opposing counsel. See State v. Salitros, 499 N.W.2d 815, 817 (Minn. 1993); State v. White, 295 Minn. 217, 223, 203 N.W.2d 852, 857 (1973).

Under Rule 26.03, subd. 14, a party is not foreclosed from later serving and filing a notice to remove a judge who simply presided at an appearance under Rule 5 or Rule 8 in the case. Also under that rule, a judge should disqualify himself or herself "whenever the judge has any doubt as to his or her ability to preside impartially or whenever his or her impartiality reasonably might be questioned." ABA Standards for Criminal Justice: Special Functions of the Trial Judge, standard 6–1.9 (3d ed. 2000).

Rule 26.03, subd. 16 (Evidence) leaves to the Minnesota Rules of Evidence the issues of the admissibility of evidence and the competency of witnesses except as otherwise provided in these rules. As to the use of a deposition at a criminal trial, Rule 21.06 controls rather than the Minnesota Rules of Evidence if there is any conflict between them. See Rule 802 and the comments to Rule 804 in the Minnesota Rules of Evidence. The prohibition in Rule 26.03, subd. 16 against jurors submitting questions to witnesses is taken from State v. Costello, 646 N.W.2d 204, 214 (Minn. 2002).

Rule 26.03, subd. 16 provides that any party offering a videotape or audiotape exhibit may also provide to the court a transcript of the tape. This rule does not govern whether any such transcript is admissible as evidence. That issue is governed by Article 10 of the Minnesota Rules of Evidence. However, upon an appeal of the proceedings, the transcript of the exhibit will be part of the record if the other party stipulates to the accuracy of the tape transcript as provided in Rule 28.02, subd. 9.

The provision in Rule 26.03, subd. 17 (Interpreters) allowing qualified interpreters for any juror with a sensory disability to be present in the jury room during deliberations and voting was added to the rule to conform with Minn. Stat. § 593.32 and Rule 809 of the Jury Management Rules in the General Rules of Practice for District Courts, which prohibit exclusion from jury service for certain reasons including sensory disability. Further, this provision allows the court to make reasonable accommodation for such jurors under the Americans with Disabilities Act. 42 U.S.C. § 12101 et seq. Caselaw holding that the presence of an alternate juror during deliberations is considered to be presumptively prejudicial—e.g., State v. Crandall, 452 N.W.2d 708, 711 (Minn. App. 1990)—would not apply to such qualified interpreters present during deliberations. As to an interpreter's duties of confidentiality and to refrain from public comment, see respectively Canons 5 and 6 of the Code of Professional Responsibility for Interpreters in the Minnesota State Court System.

A defendant is entitled to a jury determination of any facts beyond the elements of the offense or conviction history that might be used to aggravate the sentence. Blakely v. Washington, 542 U.S. 296, 301 (2004); State v. Shattuck, 704 N.W.2d 131, 135 (Minn. 2005). If such a trial is held, Rule 26.03, subd. 18 provides that the defendant may challenge the sufficiency of the evidence presented.

Rule 26.03, subd. 19(7) (Verdict Forms) requires that where aggravated sentence issues are presented to a jury, the court shall submit the issues to the jury by special interrogatory. For a sample form for that purpose see CRIMJIG 8.01 of the Minnesota Criminal Jury Instruction Guide. When that is done, Rule 26.03, subd. 20(5) permits any of the parties to request that the jury be polled as to their answers.

Under Rule 26.03, subd. 20(4) (Deadlocked Jury), the kind of instruction that may be given to a deadlocked jury is left to judicial decision. In State v Buggs, 581 N.W.2d 329, 338 (Minn. 1998), the Supreme Court suggested the risk of error in jury instructions can be significantly reduced if the trial court uses CRIMJIG 3.04 when the jury asks for further instruction.

Rule 26.03, subd. 20(6) (Verdict Impeachment) adopts the procedure outlined in Schwartz v. Minneapolis Suburban Bus Company, 258 Minn. 325, 328, 104 N.W.2d 301, 303 (1960).

Acceptance of a partial verdict under Rule 26.03, subd. 20(7) (Partial Verdicts) may bar further prosecution of any counts over which the jury has deadlocked. See Minn. Stat. § 609.035, subd. 1.

Historical Notes

The order of the Minnesota Supreme Court [C1–84–2137] dated December 13, 1989, provides in part that "(t)hese amended Rules of Criminal Procedure shall govern all criminal actions commenced or arrests made after 12 o'clock midnight January 1, 1990, except amendments to 8.04, 11.07, and 19.04, subd. 5, shall govern all criminal actions commenced or arrests made after 12 o'clock midnight January 1, 1991."

The order of the Minnesota Supreme Court [C1–84–2137] dated May 9, 1994, provides in part that "(t)hese amendments to the Rules of Criminal Procedure shall govern all criminal actions commenced or arrests made after 12 o'clock midnight July 1, 1994, except that the amendments in the first sentence of the third paragraph in Rule 2.01 shall govern all criminal actions commenced or arrests made after 12 o'clock midnight January 1, 1995."

RULE 27. SENTENCE AND JUDGMENT

Rule 27.01. Conditions of Release

After conviction but before sentencing, the court may continue or alter the terms of release, or the court may confine the defendant. The factors in Rule 6.02, subds. 1 and 2 apply, but the defendant bears the burden of showing the defendant will not flee and is not a danger to others.

Adopted Feb. 26, 1975, eff. July 1, 1975. Revised Dec. 13, 1989. Amended Oct. 27, 2009, eff. Jan. 1, 2010.

Supersedure

Laws 1997, c. 96, § 10, provides in part that this rule is superseded to the extent it conflicts with §§ 244.09, subd. 5, or 244.11.

Comment—Rule 27

See comment following Rule 27.05.

Historical Notes

The order of the Minnesota Supreme Court [C1–84–2137] dated December 13, 1989, provides in part that "(t)hese amended Rules of Criminal Procedure shall govern all criminal actions commenced or arrests made after 12 o'clock midnight January 1, 1990, except amendments to 8.04, 11.07, and 19.04, subd. 5, shall govern all criminal actions commenced or arrests made after 12 o'clock midnight January 1, 1991."

Laws 1997, c. 96, § 10, provides in part that this rule is superseded to the extent it conflicts with §§ 244.09, subd. 5, or 244.11.

Laws 1997, c. 96, § 12, provides in part that § 10 is effective August 1, 1997, and applies to crimes committed on or after that date.

Rule 27.02. Presentence Investigation in Misdemeanor and Gross Misdemeanor Cases

The court may permit that an oral presentence report be given in misdemeanor and gross misdemeanor cases. If an oral report is given, the parties must be permitted to hear it.

Adopted Feb. 26, 1975, eff. July 1, 1975. Revised Dec. 13, 1989. Amended Oct. 27, 2009, eff. Jan. 1, 2010; June 5, 2012, eff. Aug. 1, 2012.

Supersedure

Laws 1997, c. 96, § 10, provides in part that this rule is superseded to the extent it conflicts with §§ 244.09, subd. 5, or 244.11.

Comment—Rule 27

See comment following Rule 27.05.

Historical Notes

The order of the Minnesota Supreme Court [C1–84–2137] dated December 13, 1989, provides in part that "(t)hese amended Rules of Criminal Procedure shall govern all criminal actions commenced or arrests made after 12 o'clock midnight January 1, 1990, except amendments to 8.04, 11.07, and 19.04, subd. 5, shall govern all criminal actions commenced or arrests made after 12 o'clock midnight January 1, 1991."

Laws 1997, c. 96, § 10, provides in part that this rule is superseded to the extent it conflicts with §§ 244.09, subd. 5, or 244.11.

Laws 1997, c. 96, § 12, provides in part that § 10 is effective August 1, 1997, and applies to crimes committed on or after that date.

The order of the Minnesota Supreme Court [ADM 10–8049] dated June 5, 2012, provided in part that the amendments "be effective August 1, 2012, and shall apply to all actions or proceedings pending on or commenced on or after the effective date."

Rule 27.03. Sentencing Proceedings

Subd. 1. Hearings. Sentencing hearings must be held as provided by law:

(A) Misdemeanor and Gross Misdemeanor Hearings. Before the sentencing proceeding in a misdemeanor or gross misdemeanor case:

(1) Either party is permitted to contest any part of an oral presentence investigation. The court may continue the hearing to give the parties this opportunity.

(2) A party must notify the opposing party and the court if the party intends to present evidence to contest any part of the presentence investigation.

(B) Felony Sentencings

(1) Within 3 days of a plea or finding or verdict of guilty in a felony case, the court may:

(a) order a presentence investigation and set a date for its return;

(b) order a mental or physical examination of the defendant;

(2) Within the same 3 days, the court must:

(a) order completion of a sentencing guidelines worksheet;

(b) set a date for sentencing;

(c) order the defendant to appear on the sentencing date.

(3) If the court intends to consider a mitigated departure from the sentencing guidelines, the court must advise the parties. This notice may be given when the presentence investigation is completed or when the presentence investigation is forwarded to the parties.

(4) The presentence investigation report, if ordered, must conform to Minn. Stat. § 609.115, subd. 1, and include a sentencing guidelines worksheet and any other information the court ordered included. The report must be submitted in triplicate.

(5) The court must forward the guidelines worksheet and the nonconfidential portion of the presentence investigation to the parties except as limited by Minn. Stat. § 609.115, subd. 4. The confidential information section of the presentence investigation need not be forwarded, but counsel for the parties must be told it is available for inspection.

(6) Any party may move for a sentencing hearing after receipt of the presentence investigation and guidelines worksheet.

(a) The motion must be served on the opposing party and filed with the court.

(b) The motion must be served and filed no later than 8 days before the hearing, but if the presentence investigation is received less than 8 days before the sentencing date, then the motion must be served and filed within a reasonable time.

(c) The court may continue a sentencing hearing to accommodate a sentencing motion.

(d) The motion must state the reasons for the hearing, including the portion of the presentence investigation or worksheet being challenged, and include any affidavits or other documents supporting the motion.

(e) Opposing counsel must serve and file a reply no later than 3 days before the sentencing hearing.

(7) At the sentencing hearing:

(a) The contested sentencing motions must be heard.

(b) The parties may raise other sentencing issues.

(c) The court must allow the record to be supplemented with relevant testimony.

(d) The court may make findings of fact and conclusions of law on the record or, if in writing, within 20 days of the hearing.

(e) If the court determines the guidelines worksheet or supplement is wrong, the court may order a corrected worksheet submitted to the sentencing guidelines commission.

(8) The court may impose sentence immediately following the conclusion of the sentencing hearing.

Subd. 2. Defendant's Presence.

(A) The defendant must be present at the sentencing hearing and sentencing, unless excused under Rule 26.03, subd. 1(3).

(B) If the defendant is disabled in communication, a qualified interpreter must be present.

(C) A corporation may be sentenced in the absence of counsel if counsel fails to appear, after notice, at sentencing.

Subd. 3. Statements at Time of Sentencing. Before pronouncing sentence, the court must allow statements from:

(A) the prosecutor, victim, and defense counsel concerning any sentencing issues and a recommended sentence;

(B) persons on behalf of the defendant;

(C) the defendant, personally.

The court must not accept any off-the-record communications relating to sentencing unless the contents are disclosed to the parties.

Subd. 4. Sentencing. When pronouncing sentence the court must:

(A) State precisely the terms of the sentence.

(B) State the number of days spent in custody in connection with the offense or behavioral incident being sentenced. That credit must be deducted from the sentence and term of imprisonment and must include time spent in custody from a prior stay of imposition or execution of sentence.

(C) If the court imposes a departure from the sentencing guidelines, the court must make findings of fact supporting the departure. The grounds for departure must be: (a) stated in the sentencing order; or (b) recorded in the departure report as provided by the sentencing guidelines commission and attached to the sentencing order required under subdivision 7. The sentencing order and any attached departure report must be filed with the commission within 15 days after sentencing.

(D) If the court is considering a departure from the sentencing guidelines, and no contested sentencing hearing was held, and no notice was given to the parties that the court was considering a departure, the court must allow either party to request a sentencing hearing.

(E) If the court stays imposition or execution of sentence:

(1) The court must state the length of the stay.

(2) In felony cases, the court must tell the defendant that noncustodial probation time will not be

credited against a future prison term if the stay is revoked.

(3) If lawful conduct could violate the defendant's terms of probation, the court must tell the defendant what that conduct is.

(4) A written copy of the terms of probation must be given to the defendant at sentencing or as soon as possible afterwards.

(5) The court must inform the defendant that if the defendant disagrees with the probation agent concerning the terms and conditions of probation, the defendant may return to court for clarification.

Subd. 5. Right of Appeal. After sentencing, the court must tell the defendant of the right to appeal both the conviction and sentence, and, if eligible, of the right to appeal at state expense by contacting the state public defender.

Subd. 6. Record. A verbatim record must be made of the sentencing proceedings. If either party requests a transcript, it must be prepared within 30 days of a written request. The party requesting the transcript must pay for it and must make satisfactory arrangements for payment.

Subd. 7. Sentencing Order. When the court pronounces sentence for any counts for which the offense level before sentencing was a felony or gross misdemeanor, the court must record the sentence using an order generated from the court's case management system. This order must at a minimum contain:

(1) the defendant's name;

(2) the case number;

(3) for each count:

(a) if the defendant pled guilty or was found guilty:

i. the offense date;

ii. the statute violated;

iii. the pronouncements made under subdivision 4 (precise terms of sentence including any fine, time spent in custody, whether the sentence is a departure and if so, the departure reasons, whether the defendant is placed on probation and if so, the terms and conditions of probation);

iv. the level of sentence;

v. any restitution ordered, and whether it is joint and several with others;

(b) if the defendant did not plead guilty or was not found guilty, whether the defendant was acquitted or the count was dismissed;

(4) any court costs, library fee, treatment evaluation cost or other financial charge;

(5) other administrative information determined by the State Court Administrator to be necessary to facilitate transmission of the sentence to the Bureau of Criminal Apprehension, the Commissioner of Corrections, county jails, or probation services;

(6) the judge's signature.

The sentencing order must be provided in place of the transcript required by Minn. Stat. §§ 243.49 and 631.41.

Subd. 8. Judgment. The record of a judgment of conviction must contain the plea, verdict, adjudication of guilt, and sentence. If a defendant is found not guilty or is otherwise discharged, judgment must be entered accordingly. A sentence or stay of imposition of sentence is an adjudication of guilt.

Subd. 9. Correction or Reduction of Sentence. The court may at any time correct a sentence not authorized by law. The court may modify a sentence during a stay of execution or imposition of sentence if the court does not increase the period of confinement.

Subd. 10. Clerical Mistakes. Clerical mistakes in a judgment, order, or in the record arising from oversight or omission may be corrected by the court at any time, or after notice if ordered by the court.

Adopted Feb. 26, 1975, eff. July 1, 1975. Revised Dec. 13, 1989. Amended May 9, 1994; Aug. 21, 1998, eff. Jan. 1, 1999; Oct. 31, 2003, eff. Nov. 5, 2003; June 9, 2005, eff. Aug. 1, 2005; Dec. 28, 2005, eff. March 1, 2006; Aug. 17, 2006, eff. Oct. 1, 2006; Oct. 27, 2009, eff. Jan. 1, 2010; Jan. 21, 2010, eff. July 1, 2010.

Supersedure

Laws 1997, c. 96, § 10, provides in part that this rule is superseded to the extent it conflicts with §§ 244.09, subd. 5, or 244.11.

Comment—Rule 27

See comment following Rule 27.05.

Historical Notes

The order of the Minnesota Supreme Court [C1–84–2137] dated December 13, 1989, provides in part that "(t)hese amended Rules of Criminal Procedure shall govern all criminal actions commenced or arrests made after 12 o'clock midnight January 1, 1990, except amendments to 8.04, 11.07, and 19.04, subd. 5, shall govern all criminal actions commenced or arrests made after 12 o'clock midnight January 1, 1991."

The order of the Minnesota Supreme Court [C1–84–2137] dated May 9, 1994, provides in part that "(t)hese amendments to the Rules of Criminal Procedure shall govern all criminal actions commenced or arrests made after 12 o'clock midnight July 1, 1994, except that the amendments in the first sentence of the third paragraph in Rule 2.01 shall govern all criminal actions commenced or arrests made after 12 o'clock midnight January 1, 1995."

Laws 1997, c. 96, § 10, provides in part that this rule is superseded to the extent it conflicts with §§ 244.09, subd. 5, or 244.11.

Laws 1997, c. 96, § 12, provides in part that § 10 is effective August 1, 1997, and applies to crimes committed on or after that date.

The order of the Minnesota Supreme Court [C1-84-2137] dated October 31, 2003, provides in part:

"1. The attached amendments to the Minnesota Rules of Criminal Procedure are prescribed and promulgated for the regulation of practice and procedure in criminal matters in the courts of the State of Minnesota to be effective November 5, 2003. Minn. Stat. §§ 243.49 and 631.41 (2002) are superceded to the extent that they conflict with these amendments. The Advisory Committee on Rules of Criminal Procedure is requested to amend the comments to the rules to reflect these amendments.

"2. Transcripts for guilty plea and sentencing hearings held prior to November 5, 2003 shall be paid in accordance with Minn. R. Crim. P. 15.09 and 27.03, subd. 6 as they existed prior to the amendments provided for in this order if the transcripts for those hearings are filed within thirty days of the guilty plea and/or sentencing hearing.

"3. Forms 49A and 49B are models of the sentencing form provided for in Minn. R. Crim. P. 27.03, subd. 6, as amended by this order. These forms will be made available in electronic format in the Court Rules section of the Supreme Court public website: http://www.courts.state.mn.us. The Supreme Court Technology Planning Committee is directed to develop, through the MNCIS project and in consultation with appropriate criminal justice partners, a standardized, uniform state-wide sentencing form or order that captures for immediate transmission essential sentencing information consistent with Minn. R. Crim. P. 27.03, subd. 6 as amended herein. The form shall be completed and implemented in conjunction with the MNCIS rollout.

"4. Court reporters and operators of electronic recording equipment shall file the stenographic notes or tape recordings of guilty plea or sentencing hearings with the court administrator within 90 days of sentencing. The reporter or operator may retrieve the notes or recordings if necessary. Minnesota Statutes § 486.03 (2002) is superceded to the extent that it conflicts with this procedure.

"5. No charge may be assessed for preparation of a transcript for the district court's own use; any other person may order a transcript at their own expense.

"6. The maximum rate charged for the transcription of any proceeding shall be established by the Conference of Chief Judges. Minnesota Statutes § 486.06 (2002) is superceded to the extent that it conflicts with this procedure.

"7. The Supreme Court Advisory Committee on General Rules of Practice shall draft rules in accordance with paragraphs 4, 5 and 6 of this order, and may recommend additional procedures for ensuring the availability and transcribability of the record, such as requiring that the court reporter file or make available his or her personal stenographic dictionary."

The order of the Minnesota Supreme Court [C1–84–2137] dated December 28, 2005, provides in part that "(t)he attached amendments shall govern all criminal actions commenced or arrests made after 12 o'clock midnight March 1, 2006."

The order of the Minnesota Supreme Court [C1–84–2137] dated January 21, 2010, provides in part that "on or after July 1, 2010, any district court issuing a sentencing order under Minn. R. Crim. P. 27.03, subd. 7, as amended herein must generate that order using the judicial branch's case management system."

Rule 27.04. Probation Revocation

Subd. 1. Initiation of Proceedings.

(1) *Warrant or Summons.*

(a) Probation revocation proceedings must be initiated by a summons or warrant based on a written report showing probable cause to believe a probationer violated probation.

(b) The court must issue a summons unless the court believes a warrant is necessary to secure the probationer's appearance or prevent harm to the probationer or another. If the probationer fails to appear on the summons, the court may issue a warrant.

(2) *Contents.* The warrant or summons must include:

(a) the name of the probationer;

(b) a description of the sentence and the probationary terms allegedly violated;

(c) the judge's signature;

(d) a factual statement supporting probable cause to believe the probationer violated the terms of probation;

(e) the amount of bail or other conditions of release the court may set on the warrant;

(f) for a warrant, an order directing that the probationer be brought before the court promptly, and in any event not later than 36 hours after arrest, not including the day of arrest.

(g) for a summons, an order directing the probationer to appear at a specific date, time, and place.

(3) *Execution, Service, Certification of Warrant or Summons.* Execution, service, and certification of the warrant or summons are as provided in Rule 3.03.

Subd. 2. First Appearance.

(1) When the probationer initially appears on the warrant or summons the court must:

(a) Appoint an interpreter if the probationer is disabled in communication.

(b) Give the probationer a copy of the violation report, if not already provided.

(c) Tell the probationer of the right to:

a. a lawyer, including an appointed lawyer if the probationer cannot afford a lawyer;

b. a revocation hearing to determine whether clear and convincing evidence of a probation violation exists and whether probation should be revoked;

c. disclosure of all evidence used to support revocation and of official records relevant to revocation;

d. present evidence, subpoena witnesses, and call and cross-examine witnesses, except the court may prohibit the probationer from confrontation if the court believes a substantial likelihood of serious harm to others exists;

e. present mitigating evidence or other reasons why the violation, if proved, should not result in revocation;

f. appeal any decision to revoke probation.

(2) *Appointment of Counsel.* Rule 5.04 governs the appointment of counsel for a probationer unable to afford counsel.

(3) *Conditions of Release.*

(a) A probationer may be released pending the revocation hearing.

(b) The conditions of release must consider the factors found in Rule 6.02 and the risk the probationer will flee or pose a danger to any person or the community.

(c) The probationer bears the burden of establishing no risk of flight or danger to any person or the community.

(4) *Time of Revocation.*

(a) The revocation hearing must be held within a reasonable time.

(b) If the probationer is in custody because of the violation report, the hearing must be within 7 days.

(c) If the violation report alleges a new crime, the revocation hearing may be postponed pending disposition of the criminal case.

(5) *Record.* A verbatim record must be made of the probationer's initial appearance.

Subd. 3. Revocation Hearing.

(1) *Procedure.* The revocation hearing must be conducted consistent with the rights outlined in subd. 2(1)(c)a–e above.

(2) *Findings.*

(a) No Violation. If the court finds no violation of the conditions of probation, the proceedings must be dismissed and the probationer continued on probation under the terms previously ordered.

(b) Violation Found. If the court finds or the probationer admits a probation violation, the court may:

(i) continue an existing stay of imposition and order probation as provided in Minn. Stat. § 609.135;

(ii) impose sentence but stay execution and order probation as provided in Minn. Stat. § 609.135;

(iii) impose and execute a sentence;

(iv) continue an existing stay of execution and order probation as provided in Minn. Stat. § 609.135;

(v) execute a sentence.

(3) *Record.* A verbatim record must be made of the probation revocation hearing. If a contested revocation hearing is held, the court must make written findings of fact, including a summary of the evidence relied on in reaching a revocation decision and the basis for the court's decision.

(4) *Appeal.*

(a) The defendant or the prosecutor may appeal the revocation decision.

(b) Rule 28.05 governs the appeal, except that if an appellant files a notice of appeal within 90 days of the revocation hearing, the appellant's brief must be identified as a probation revocation brief and must be filed within 30 days after delivery of the transcript.

(c) The Minnesota Rules of Civil Appellate Procedure govern preparation of the transcript.

Adopted June 9, 1983. Revised Dec. 13, 1989. Amended May 9, 1994; Aug. 21, 1998, eff. Jan. 1, 1999; Dec. 23, 2002, eff. Feb. 1, 2003; Dec. 28, 2005, eff. March 1, 2006; Oct. 27, 2009, eff. Jan. 1, 2010.

Supersedure

Laws 1997, c. 96, § 10, provides in part that this rule is superseded to the extent it conflicts with §§ 244.09, subd. 5, or 244.11.

Comment—Rule 27

See comment following Rule 27.05.

Historical Notes

The order of the Minnesota Supreme Court dated June 9, 1983, provides in part that "(t)hese amendments to the Rules of Criminal Procedure shall govern all criminal actions commenced or arrests made after 12 o'clock midnight July 31, 1983."

The order of the Minnesota Supreme Court [C1–84–2137] dated December 13, 1989, provides in part that "(t)hese amended Rules of Criminal Procedure shall govern all criminal actions commenced or arrests made after 12 o'clock midnight January 1, 1990, except amendments to 8.04, 11.07, and 19.04, subd. 5, shall govern all criminal actions commenced or arrests made after 12 o'clock midnight January 1, 1991."

The order of the Minnesota Supreme Court [C1–84–2137] dated May 9, 1994, provides in part that "(t)hese amendments to the Rules of Criminal Procedure shall govern all criminal actions commenced or arrests made after 12 o'clock midnight July 1, 1994, except that the amendments in the first sentence of the third paragraph in Rule 2.01 shall govern all criminal actions commenced or arrests made after 12 o'clock midnight January 1, 1995."

Laws 1997, c. 96, § 10, provides in part that this rule is superseded to the extent it conflicts with §§ 244.09, subd. 5, or 244.11.

Laws 1997, c. 96, § 12, provides in part that § 10 is effective August 1, 1997, and applies to crimes committed on or after that date.

The order of the Minnesota Supreme Court [C1–84–2137] dated December 28, 2005, provides in part that "(t)he attached amendments shall govern all criminal actions commenced or arrests made after 12 o'clock midnight March 1, 2006."

Rule 27.05. Pretrial Diversion

Subd. 1. Agreements.

(1) A prosecution may be suspended for a specified time and then dismissed under subdivision 6 if:

(a) the agreement is in writing and signed by the parties;

(b) the victim's views are considered;

(c) the court consents;

(d) the court finds a substantial likelihood of conviction and that the benefits of rehabilitation outweigh the harm to society from suspending prosecution.

(2) The agreement must provide that the defendant not commit a new crime or petty misdemeanor and that the defendant waive the right to a speedy trial. In addition, the agreement may:

(a) include stipulations of fact or of the admissibility of specified testimony, other evidence, and depositions if the diversion agreement is terminated and the case is tried;

(b) provide for any term a court could impose as a condition of probation except the defendant may not be incarcerated as a condition of diversion.

(3) *Limitations.* The agreement cannot suspend prosecution longer than the period of probation the court could impose if the defendant were convicted. The agreement cannot include a condition the court could not impose as a condition of probation.

Subd. 2. Filing of Agreement; Release. If a diversion agreement is reached, the prosecutor must file the agreement along with a statement suspending the prosecution for a specified time with the court. The defendant must be released when the agreement is filed.

Subd. 3. Modification. The parties, with the court's approval, may agree to modify the terms of the diversion.

Subd. 4. Termination of Agreement and Resumption of Prosecution.

(1) *Defendant's Notice.* The defendant may terminate the agreement by filing a termination notice with the court. The prosecution will then proceed.

(2) *Prosecutor's Motion.* The court may terminate the agreement on the prosecutor's motion if the court finds:

a. the defendant or defense counsel misrepresented material facts affecting the agreement and the prosecutor moves to terminate the agreement within 6 months after it commences; or

b. the defendant has committed a material violation of the agreement, and the prosecutor makes the motion no later than 1 month after the suspension period specified in the agreement expires.

(3) *Issuance of Warrant or Summons.* The court may order the defendant's arrest and prompt appearance for the hearing on the prosecutor's motion if the court, based on affidavit or testimony, finds:

(a) probable cause exists to believe the defendant committed a material violation of the agreement; and

(b) a substantial likelihood exists that the defendant will not appear at a termination hearing.

In lieu of a warrant, the court may issue a summons ordering the defendant to appear.

Subd. 5. Release Status upon Resumption of Prosecution. If the agreement is terminated, the defendant must return to the release status in effect before the agreement, unless the court alters those terms under Rule 6.

Subd. 6. Termination of Agreement and Dismissal of Charges.

(A) Automatic Dismissal. The charges must be dismissed 1 month after the suspension period specified in the agreement expires unless the prosecutor earlier moved to terminate the agreement.

(B) Dismissal of Motion. If the court denies the motion to resume prosecution, and the specified suspension time has elapsed, the charges must be dismissed.

(C) Effect of Dismissal. If the court dismisses the charge under this rule, the defendant cannot be prosecuted for it.

Subd. 7. Termination and Dismissal on a Showing of Rehabilitation. The court may terminate the agreement, dismiss the charges, and prohibit further prosecution if:

(1) a party moves for termination and provides facts supporting it;

(2) the court gives the parties an opportunity to be heard;

(3) the court finds the defendant has not committed any additional offenses; and

(4) the court finds the defendant appears to be rehabilitated.

Subd. 8. Modification or Termination. If the court finds the prosecutor obtained the defendant's agreement to diversion because of a material misrepresentation by the prosecutor or a person covered by Rule 9.01, subd. 1a(1), the court may:

(1) modify the parts of the agreement related to the misrepresentation; or

(2) if justice requires, terminate the agreement and prohibit further prosecution of the charge.

Adopted Dec. 13, 1989. Amended May 9, 1994; Oct. 27, 2009, eff. Jan. 1, 2010.

Supersedure

Laws 1997, c. 96, § 10, provides in part that this rule is superseded to the extent it conflicts with §§ 244.09, subd. 5, or 244.11.

Comment—Rule 27

Minn. Const. Art. I, § 7, provides that all persons before conviction must be bailable by sufficient sureties. The defendant is not entitled to bail as a matter of right after conviction.

If pursuant to Rule 27.02 a presentence report is prepared, the officer conducting the investigation is required by Minn. Stat. § 609.115, subd. 1 and Minn. Stat. § 611A.037 to advise the victim of the crime concerning the victim's rights under those statutes and under Minn. Stat. § 611A.038. Those rights include the rights to request restitution and to submit an impact statement to the court at sentencing.

The sentencing hearings "as provided by law" under Rule 27.03, subd. 1 would include restitution proceedings under Minn. Stat. §§ 611A.04 and 611A.045.

The Sentencing Guidelines Commission recommends that when the felony being sentenced involves a sexual offense, the trial court should order a physical or mental examination of the offender as a supplement to the presentence investigation permitted by Minn. Stat. § 609.115. Minnesota Sentencing Guidelines and Commentary, Training Material, III. E. Rule 27.03, subd. 1(B) permits the court to order these examinations. This rule does not preclude a post-sentence investigation whenever required by statute (Minn. Stat. § 609.115, subd. 2 (sentence of life imprisonment)) or whenever the court considers one necessary. The presentence investigation may include the information obtained on the pretrial release investigation under Rule 6.02, subd. 3. If a defendant is convicted of a domestic abuse offense as defined by Minn. Stat. § 609.2244, subd. 1, a presentence domestic abuse investigation must be conducted. A report must then be submitted to the court that meets the requirements in Minn. Stat. § 609.2244, subd. 2.

The Advisory Committee strongly commends the practice, now in effect in some counties, of preparing the Sentencing Guidelines Worksheet before the Omnibus Hearing. This may be done in connection with a pre-release investigation under Rule 6.02, subd. 3 and may later be included with any presentence investigation report required under Rule 27.03, subd. 1.

The date for the return of the presentence investigation report should be set sufficiently in advance of sentencing to allow counsel sufficient time to make any motion under Rule 27.03, subd. 1(B)(6). The officer conducting the presentence investigation is required by Minn. Stat. § 609.115 and Minn. Stat. § 611A.037 to advise any victim of the crime concerning the victim's rights under those statutes and under Minn. Stat. § 611A.038. Those rights include the rights to request restitution and to submit an impact statement to the court at sentencing.

Rule 27.03, subd. 1(B)(7) is in accord with Minn. Stat. § 244.10, subd. 1, which requires that the court issue written findings of fact, conclusions of law and appropriate order on the issues raised at the sentencing hearing at the conclusion of the hearing or within twenty days afterwards.

In Rule 27.03, subd. 1(B)(8) the term "sentencing hearing" refers to the hearing required by Minn. Stat. § 244.10, subd. 1 on issues of sentencing. In the usual case, actual sentencing should immediately follow.

Minn. Stat. § 611A.06 requires the Commissioner of Corrections or other custodial authority to notify the victim of the crime when an offender is to be released from imprisonment. Minn. Stat. § 611A.0385 further requires that the court or its designee shall at the time of the sentencing make reasonable good faith efforts to inform any identifiable victims of their right to such notice under Minn. Stat. § 611A.06.

Minn. Stat. § 244.10, subd. 2 requires written findings of fact as to the reasons for departure from the sentencing guidelines. The court's statement into the record under Rule 27.03, subd. 4(C), should satisfy this requirement, but the rule further requires that the reasons for departure must be stated in a sentencing order or in a departure report attached to the sentencing order. Whichever document is used, it must be filed with the sentencing guidelines commission within 15 days of the date of the sentencing.

Rule 27.03, subd. 4(D) is designed to eliminate any possible due process notice problems where a defendant does not request a sentencing hearing because of an expectation of receiving a sentence in conformance with the sentencing guidelines. It is also anticipated that fewer sentencing hearings will be requested by the prosecution and defense so long as an opportunity exists to request such a hearing after notice that the court might depart from the guidelines.

Rule 27.03, subd. 4(E) avoids any due process notice problems if the court revokes probation and executes the sentence. Except as provided in Minn. Stat. § 609.135, subd.7, a defendant has a right to refuse probation when the conditions of the probation are more onerous than a prison sentence, State v. Randolph, 316 N.W.2d 508 (Minn.1982).

Rule 27.04 does not require an initial probable cause hearing on the probation violation report. The hearing is not constitutionally required if the defendant is not in custody or if the final revocation hearing is held within the time that the preliminary hearing would otherwise be required. Pearson v. State, 308 Minn. 287, 241 N.W.2d 490 (1976). It is, however, necessary under Rule 27.04, subd. 1(2) that the defendant be brought before the court after arrest within the same time limits as set forth under Rule 3. 02, subd. 2 for arrests upon warrant.

Rule 27.05 (Pretrial Diversion) does not preclude the prosecutor and defendant from agreeing to diversion of a case without court approval if charges are not pending before the court. The requirement in subd. 1(1) that the prosecutor give "due consideration of the victim's views" is in accord with the requirement in Minn. Stat. § 611A.031 that the prosecuting attorney "make every reasonable effort to notify and seek input from the victim" before employing pretrial diversion for certain specified offenses.

With the approval of the court, the pretrial diversion agreement may provide for any term a court could impose as a condition of probation, including restitution. See Minn. Stat. §§ 611A.04 and 611A.045 as to requiring restitution as part of a sentence.

Under Rule 27.05, subd. 1(3), no condition may be included in the pretrial diversion agreement that could not be imposed upon probation after conviction of the crime charged. See Minn. Stat. § 609.135 as to the permissible conditions of probation. See Minn. Stat. § 611A.031 regarding the prosecutor's duties under the Victim's Rights Act, for certain designated offenses, to make every reasonable effort to notify and seek input before placing a person into a pretrial diversion program.

Historical Notes

The order of the Minnesota Supreme Court [C1–84–2137] dated December 13, 1989, provides in part that "(t)hese amended Rules of Criminal Procedure shall govern all criminal actions commenced or arrests made after 12 o'clock midnight January 1, 1990, except amendments to 8.04, 11.07, and 19.04, subd. 5, shall govern all criminal actions commenced or arrests made after 12 o'clock midnight January 1, 1991."

The order of the Minnesota Supreme Court [C1–84–2137] dated May 9, 1994, provides in part that "(t)hese amendments to the Rules of Criminal Procedure shall govern all criminal actions commenced or arrests made after 12 o'clock midnight July 1, 1994, except that the amendments in the first sentence of the third paragraph in Rule 2.01 shall govern all criminal actions commenced or arrests made after 12 o'clock midnight January 1, 1995."

Laws 1997, c. 96, § 10, provides in part that this rule is superseded to the extent it conflicts with §§ 244.09, subd. 5, or 244.11.

Laws 1997, c. 96, § 12, provides in part that § 10 is effective August 1, 1997, and applies to crimes committed on or after that date.

RULE 28. APPEALS TO COURT OF APPEALS

Rule 28.01. Scope of Rule

Subd. 1. Appeals from District Court. In misdemeanor, gross misdemeanor, and felony cases, Rule 28 governs the procedure for appeals from the district courts to the Court of Appeals unless the defendant has been convicted of first-degree murder.

Subd. 2. Applicability of Rules of Civil Appellate Procedure. To the extent applicable, the Minnesota Rules of Civil Appellate Procedure govern appellate procedure unless these rules direct otherwise.

Subd. 3. Suspension of Rules. For good cause, the Court of Appeals may suspend application of any of these rules on its own initiative or on a party's motion, and may order proceedings as it directs, but it may not alter the time for filing the notice of appeal unless permitted by Rule 28.02, subd. 4(3)(g).

Adopted Feb. 26, 1975, eff. July 1, 1975. Revised Dec. 13, 1989. Amended Oct. 27, 2009, eff. Jan. 1, 2010.

Supersedure

Laws 1997, c. 96, § 10, provides in part that this rule is superseded to the extent it conflicts with §§ 244.09, subd. 5, or 244.11.

Comment—Rule 28

See comment following Rule 28.06.

Historical Notes

The order of the Minnesota Supreme Court [C1–84–2137] dated December 13, 1989, provides in part that "(t)hese amended Rules of Criminal Procedure shall govern all criminal actions commenced or arrests made after 12 o'clock midnight January 1, 1990, except amendments to 8.04, 11.07, and 19.04, subd. 5, shall govern all criminal actions commenced or arrests made after 12 o'clock midnight January 1, 1991."

Laws 1997, c. 96, § 10, provides in part that this rule is superseded to the extent it conflicts with §§ 244.09, subd. 5, or 244.11.

Laws 1997, c. 96, § 12, provides in part that § 10 is effective August 1, 1997, and applies to crimes committed on or after that date.

Former rule: Former rule 28.01 related to trials de novo and appeals to the district court.

Rule 28.02. Appeal by Defendant

Subd. 1. Review by Appeal. A defendant may obtain Court of Appeals review of district court orders and rulings only as these rules permit, or as permitted by the law for the issuance of the extraordinary writs and for the Post–Conviction Remedy. Writs of error are abolished.

Subd. 2. Appeal as of Right.

(1) *Final Judgment and Postconviction Appeal.* A defendant may appeal as of right from any adverse final judgment, or from an order denying in whole or in part a petition for postconviction relief under Minn. Stat. ch. 590. A final judgment within the meaning of these rules occurs when the district court enters a judgment of conviction and imposes or stays a sentence.

(2) *Orders.* A defendant cannot appeal until the district court enters an adverse final judgment, but may appeal:

(a) from an order refusing or imposing conditions of release; or

(b) in felony and gross misdemeanor cases from an order:

1. granting a new trial, and the defendant claims that the district court should have entered a final judgment in the defendant's favor;

2. not on the defendant's motion, finding the defendant incompetent to stand trial; or

3. denying a motion to dismiss a complaint following a mistrial, and the defendant claims retrial would violate double jeopardy.

(3) *Sentences.* A defendant may appeal as of right from any sentence imposed or stayed in a felony case. Rule 28.02, subd. 3 governs sentencing appeals in nonfelony cases.

Subd. 3. Discretionary Review. In the interests of justice and on petition of the defendant, the Court of Appeals may allow an appeal from an order not otherwise appealable, but not from an order made during trial. The petition must be served and filed within 30 days after entry of the order appealed. Minnesota Rule of Civil Appellate Procedure 105 governs the procedure for the appeal.

Subd. 4. Procedure for Appeals Other than Sentencing Appeals.

(1) *Service and Filing.* A defendant appeals by filing a notice of appeal with the clerk of the appellate courts with proof of service on the prosecutor, the Minnesota Attorney General, and the court administrator for the county in which the judgment or order appealed from is entered. The defendant need not file a certified copy of the judgment or order appealed from, or the statement of the case provided for in Minnesota Rule of Civil Appellate Procedure 133.03 unless the appellate court directs otherwise. The defendant does not have to post bond to appeal. The defendant's failure to take any step other than timely filing the notice of appeal does not affect the validity of the appeal, but permits action the Court of Appeals deems appropriate, including dismissal.

(2) *Contents of Notice of Appeal.* The notice of appeal must specify:

(a) the party or parties taking the appeal;

(b) the names, addresses, and telephone numbers of all counsel and whom they represent;

(c) the judgment or order from which appeal is taken; and

(d) that the appeal is to the Court of Appeals.

(3) *Time for Taking an Appeal.*

(a) In felony and gross misdemeanor cases, an appeal by the defendant must be filed within 90 days after final judgment or entry of the order being appealed. Other charges that were joined for prosecution with the felony or gross misdemeanor may be included in the appeal.

(b) In misdemeanor cases, an appeal by the defendant must be filed within 30 days after final judgment or entry of the order being appealed.

(c) In postconviction relief cases, an appeal by the defendant from an order denying a petition for postconviction relief must be filed within 60 days after entry of the order.

(d) A notice of appeal filed after the announcement of a decision or order—but before sentencing or entry of judgment or order—must be treated as filed after, but on the same day as sentencing or entry of judgment.

(e) A timely motion to vacate the judgment, for judgment of acquittal, or for a new trial tolls the time for an appeal from a final judgment until the entry of an order denying the motion, and the order denying the motion may be reviewed in the appeal from the judgment.

(f) A judgment or order is entered under these appellate rules when the court administrator enters it in the record.

(g) For good cause, the district court or a judge of the Court of Appeals may, before or after the time for appeal has expired, with or without motion and notice, extend the time for filing a notice of appeal up to 30 days from the expiration of the time prescribed by these rules.

(4) *Stay of Appeal for Postconviction Proceedings.* If, after filing a notice of appeal, a defendant determines that a petition for postconviction relief is appropriate, the defendant may file a motion to stay the appeal for postconviction proceedings.

Subd. 5. Proceeding in Forma Pauperis. A defendant who wishes to proceed in forma pauperis under this rule must follow this process:

(1) An indigent defendant wanting to appeal or to obtain postconviction relief must apply to the State Public Defender's office.

(2) The State Public Defender's office must promptly send the applicant a financial inquiry form, preliminary questionnaire form, and other forms as deemed appropriate.

(3) The applicant must completely fill out these forms, sign them, and have his or her signature notarized if indicated.

(4) The applicant must then return these completed documents to the State Public Defender's office for further processing.

(5) The State Public Defender's office must determine if the applicant is financially and otherwise eligible for representation. If the applicant qualifies, then the State Public Defender's office must provide representation in felony cases regarding a judicial review or an evaluation of the merits of a judicial review of the case, and may so represent the applicant in misdemeanor or gross misdemeanor cases.

Upon the administrative determination by the State Public Defender's office that it will represent an applicant for a judicial review or an evaluation of the merits of a judicial review of the case, the office is automatically appointed without order of the court. The State Public Defender's office must notify the applicant of its decision on representation and advise the applicant of any problem relative to the applicant's qualifications to obtain its services. Any applicant who contests a decision of the State Public Defender's office that the applicant does not qualify for representation may apply to the Minnesota Supreme Court for relief.

(6) If the court receives a request for transcripts necessary for judicial review or other efforts to have cases reviewed from a defendant who does not have counsel, the court must refer the request to the State Public Defender's office for processing as in paragraphs (2) through (5) above.

(7) The State Public Defender's office's obligation to order and pay for transcripts for indigent defendants represented by private counsel on appeal is limited to the types of appeals or proceedings for which the State Public Defender's office is required to provide representation. If the court receives a request for transcripts made by an indigent defendant represented by private counsel, the court must submit the request to the State Public Defender's office for processing as follows:

a. The State Public Defender's office must determine eligibility of the applicant as in paragraphs (2) through (5) above.

b. If the defendant qualifies, he or she may request the State Public Defender to order all parts of the trial transcript necessary for effective appellate review. The State Public Defender's office must order and pay for these transcripts.

c. If a dispute arises about the parts of the trial transcript necessary for effective appellate review, the defendant or the State Public Defender's office may make a motion for resolution of the matter to the appropriate court.

d. The State Public Defender's office must provide the transcript to the indigent defendant's attorney for use in the direct appeal. The attorney must sign a receipt for the transcript agreeing to return it to the State Public Defender's office after the appeal process.

(8) All court administrators must furnish the State Public Defender's office without charge copies of any documents relevant to the case.

(9) All fees—including appeal fees, hearing fees, or filing fees—ordinarily charged by the clerk of the appellate courts or court administrators are waived when the State Public Defender's office, or other public defender's office, represents the defendant. The court must also waive these fees on a sufficient showing by any other attorney that the defendant cannot pay them.

(10) The State Public Defender's office must be appointed to represent all eligible indigent defendants in all appeal or postconviction cases as provided above, regardless of the county where the prosecution occurred, unless the Supreme Court directs otherwise.

(11) In appeal cases and postconviction cases, the State of Minnesota must bear the cost of transcripts and other necessary expenses from funds available to the State Public Defender's office, if approved by that office, regardless of where the prosecution occurred.

(12) For defendants represented on appeal by the State Public Defender's office, Minnesota Rule of Civil Appellate Procedure 110.02, subd. 2, concerning the certificate as to transcript, does not apply. In these cases, the State Public Defender's office on ordering the transcript must mail a copy of the written request for transcript to the court administrator, the clerk of the appellate courts, and the prosecutor.

The court reporter must promptly acknowledge its receipt and indicate acceptance in writing, with copies to the court administrator, the clerk of the appellate courts, the State Public Defender's office, and the prosecutor. In so doing, the court reporter must state the estimated number of pages of the transcript and the estimated completion date. That date cannot exceed 60 days, but for guilty plea and sentencing transcripts, it cannot exceed 30 days. Upon delivery of the transcript, the reporter must file with the clerk of the appellate courts a certificate evidencing the date and manner of delivery.

(13) A defendant may proceed pro se on appeal only after the State Public Defender's office has first had the opportunity to file a brief on the defendant's behalf. When that office files and serves the brief, it must also provide a copy of the brief to the defendant. If the defendant then chooses to proceed pro se on appeal or to file a supplemental brief, the defendant must so notify the State Public Defender's office.

(14) Upon receiving notice under paragraph (13) that the defendant has chosen to proceed pro se on appeal or to file a supplemental brief, the State Public Defender's office must confer with the defendant about the reasons for choosing to do so and advise the defendant concerning the consequences of that choice.

(15) To proceed pro se on appeal following consultation, the defendant must sign and return to the State Public Defender's office a detailed waiver of counsel as provided by that office for the particular case.

(16) If the State Public Defender's office believes, after consultation, that the defendant may not be competent to waive counsel it must assist the defendant in seeking an order from the district court determining the defendant's competency or incompetency.

(17) The court must consider the brief filed by the State Public Defender's office on the defendant's behalf. A defendant, whether or not choosing to proceed pro se, may also file with the court a supplemental brief. The supplemental brief must be filed within 30 days after the State Public Defender's office files its initial brief.

(18) If a defendant requests a copy of the transcript, the State Public Defender's office must confer with the defendant concerning the need for the transcript. If the defendant still requests a copy of it, one must be provided to the defendant temporarily.

(19) Upon receiving the transcript, the defendant must sign a receipt for it including an agreement not to make it available to other persons and to return the transcript to the State Public Defender's office when the time to file any supplemental brief expires.

(20) The transcript remains the property of the State Public Defender's office and must be returned upon expiration of the time to file any supplemental brief. Upon return of the transcript, the State Public Defender's office must provide the defendant with a copy of a signed receipt for it. The State Public Defender's office must promptly file the original of the receipt with the clerk of the appellate courts, and until that occurs, the clerk will not accept the supplemental brief for filing.

Subd. 6. Stay. When a defendant files an appeal, this does not stay execution of the judgment or sentence unless a district court judge or a judge of the appellate court grants a stay.

Subd. 7. Release of Defendant.

(1) *Conditions of Release.* If a defendant appeals, and a court grants a stay, Rule 6.02, subds. 1 and 2, govern the conditions for defendant's release and the factors determining the conditions of release, except as provided by this rule. The court must also take into consideration that the defendant may be compelled to serve the sentence imposed before the appellate court decides the case.

(2) *Burden of Proof.* If a defendant was sentenced to incarceration, a court must not grant release pending appeal from a judgment of conviction unless the defendant establishes to the court's satisfaction that:

(a) the appeal is not frivolous or taken for delay; and

(b) no substantial risk exists that the defendant:

(i) will fail to appear to answer the judgment following the conclusion of the appellate proceedings;

(ii) is likely commit a serious crime, intimidate witnesses, or otherwise interfere with the administration of justice.

(3) *Application for Release Pending Appeal.* A defendant must first apply to the district court for release pending appeal. If the district court denies release pending appeal or imposes conditions of release, the court must state on the record the reasons for the action taken.

If the defendant appeals and has previously applied to the district court for release pending appeal, the defendant may file a motion for release, or for modification of the conditions of release, to the applicable appellate court or to a judge or justice of that court. The motion must be determined promptly upon such papers, affidavits, and portions of the record as the parties may present, and after reasonable notice to the prosecutor. The appellate court or one of its judges or justices may order the defendant's release pending the motion's disposition.

(4) *Credit for Time Spent in Custody.* All time the defendant spends in custody pending an appeal must be deducted from the sentence the district court imposed.

(5) When a defendant obtains release pending appeal under this rule, the prosecution must make reasonable good faith efforts as soon as possible to advise the victim of the defendant's release.

Subd. 8. Record on Appeal. The record on appeal consists of the papers filed in the district court, the offered exhibits, and the transcript of the proceedings, if any.

In lieu of the record as defined by this rule, the parties may—within 60 days after filing of the notice of appeal—prepare, sign, and file with the court administrator a statement of the case showing how the issues presented by the appeal arose and how the district court decided them, stating only the claims and facts essential to a decision. The district court, after making any additions it considers necessary to present the issues raised by the appeal, may approve the statement, which will then be the record on appeal. Any recitation of the essential facts of the case, conclusions of law, and any relevant district court memorandum of law must be included with the record.

An appellant who intends to proceed on appeal with a statement of the case under this rule rather than by obtaining a transcript, or without either a statement of the case or transcript, must serve notice of intent to do so on respondent and the court administrator and also file the notice with the clerk of the appellate courts, all within the time provided for ordering a transcript.

Subd. 9. Transcript of Proceedings and Transmission of the Transcript and Record. To the extent applicable, the Minnesota Rules of Civil Appellate Procedure govern preparation of the transcript of the proceedings and the transmission of the transcript and record to the Court of Appeals, except that the transcript must be ordered within 30 days after filing of the notice of appeal and may be extended by the appellate court for good cause, and that the appellant must order an original and two copies of any transcript. The original transcript must be filed with the court administrator and a copy transmitted promptly to the attorney for each party. Upon the termination of the appeal, the clerk of the appellate courts must transmit the original transcript along with the remainder of the record to the court administrator.

If the parties have stipulated to the accuracy of a transcript of videotape or audiotape exhibits and made it part of the district court record, it becomes part of the record on appeal and it is not necessary for the court reporter to transcribe the exhibits. If no such transcript exists, a transcript need not be prepared unless expressly requested by the appellant or the respondent. If the exhibit must be transcribed, the court reporter need not certify the correctness of this transcript.

If the appellant does not order the entire transcript, then within the 30 days permitted to order it, the appellant must file with the clerk of the appellate courts and serve on the court administrator and respondent a description of the parts of the transcript the appellant intends to include in the record, and a statement of the issues the appellant intends to present on appeal. If the respondent deems a transcript of other parts of the proceedings necessary, the respondent must order from the reporter, within 10 days of service of the description or notification of no transcript, those other parts deemed necessary, or serve and file a motion in the district court for an order requiring the appellant to do so.

Subd. 10. Briefs. The appellant must serve and file the appellant's brief within 60 days after the court reporter delivers the transcript, or after the filing of the district court's approval of the statement under subd. 8 of this rule or under Minnesota Rule of Civil Appellate Procedure 110.03. In all other cases, if the parties obtain the transcript before the appeal, or if the record on appeal does not include a transcript, the appellant must serve and file the appellant's brief within 60 days after the appellant filed the notice of appeal. The respondent must serve and file the respondent's brief within 45 days after service of the appellant's brief. The appellant may serve and file a reply brief within 15 days after service of the respondent's brief. In all other respects, the Minnesota Rules of Civil Appellate Procedure govern, to the extent applicable, the form and filing of briefs, but the appellant's brief must contain a procedural history.

Subd. 11. Scope of Review. On appeal from a judgment, the court may review any order or ruling of the district court or any other matter, as the interests of justice may require.

Subd. 12. Action on Appeal. If the appellate court affirms the judgment, it must direct execution of the sentence as pronounced by the district court or as modified by the appellate court under Rule 28.05, subd. 2. If it reverses the judgment, it must:

(a) direct a new trial;

(b) vacate the conviction and enter a judgment of acquittal; or

(c) reduce the conviction to a lesser included offense or to an offense of lesser degree, as the case may require. If the court reduces the conviction, it must remand for resentencing.

Subd. 13. Oral Argument.

(1) Oral argument must be held in every case if either party serves on adverse counsel and files with the clerk of the appellate courts a request for it when the party serves and files its initial brief, unless:

1. the respondent forfeits oral argument under Minnesota Rule of Civil Appellate Procedure 134.01(b) for failure to timely file a brief, and appellant has either waived oral argument or not requested it;

2. the parties waive oral argument by joint agreement under Minnesota Rule of Civil Appellate Procedure 134.06; or

3. the appellate court determines that oral argument is unnecessary because:

a. the dispositive issue or set of issues has been authoritatively settled; or

b. the briefs and record adequately present the facts and legal arguments, and the decisional process would not be significantly aided by oral argument.

The clerk of the appellate court must notify the parties when oral argument will not be allowed under this provision. Any party so notified may request the court to reconsider its decision by serving on all other parties and filing with the clerk of the appellate courts a written request for reconsideration within 5 days of receipt of the notification that no oral argument will be allowed. If, under this provision, the court does not allow oral argument, the case must be considered as submitted to the court when the clerk of the appellate courts notifies the parties that oral argument has been denied.

The Court of Appeals may direct presentation of oral argument in any case.

(2) Except in exigent circumstances, the oral argument must be heard by the full panel assigned to decide the case, and in any event must be considered and decided by the full panel. The procedure on oral argument, including waiver and forfeiture of oral argument, must be as prescribed by the Minnesota Rules of Civil Appellate Procedure, unless this rule directs otherwise.

Adopted Feb. 26, 1975, eff. July 1, 1975. Revised Dec. 13, 1989. Amended Aug. 21, 1998, eff. Jan. 1, 1999; Dec. 23, 2002, eff. Feb. 1, 2003; Feb. 28, 2003, eff. March 17, 2003; Dec. 28, 2005, eff. March 1, 2006; Oct. 27, 2009, eff. Jan. 1, 2010; June 22, 2011, eff. Sept. 1, 2011; June 5, 2012, eff. Aug. 1, 2012; July 25, 2012, eff. Aug. 1, 2012.

Supersedure

Laws 1997, c. 96, § 10, provides in part that this rule is superseded to the extent it conflicts with §§ 244.09, subd. 5, or 244.11.

Comment—Rule 28

See comment following Rule 28.06.

Historical Notes

The order of the Minnesota Supreme Court [C1–84–2137] dated December 13, 1989, provides in part that "(t)hese amended Rules of Criminal Procedure shall govern all criminal actions commenced or arrests made after 12 o'clock midnight January 1, 1990, except amendments to 8.04, 11.07, and 19.04, subd. 5, shall govern all criminal actions commenced or arrests made after 12 o'clock midnight January 1, 1991."

Laws 1997, c. 96, § 10, provides in part that this rule is superseded to the extent it conflicts with §§ 244.09, subd. 5, or 244.11.

Laws 1997, c. 96, § 12, provides in part that § 10 is effective August 1, 1997, and applies to crimes committed on or after that date.

The order of the Minnesota Supreme Court [C1–84–2137] dated December 28, 2005, provides in part that "(t)he attached amendments shall govern all criminal actions commenced or arrests made after 12 o'clock midnight March 1, 2006."

The order of the Minnesota Supreme Court [ADM10–8049] dated June 22, 2011, provided in part that "The amendments shall govern all criminal actions currently pending on or commenced on or after the effective date."

Former rule: Former rule 28.02 related to de novo review of conditions of release.

The order of the Minnesota Supreme Court [ADM 10–8049] dated June 5, 2012, provided in part that the amendments "be effective August 1, 2012, and shall apply to all actions or proceedings pending on or commenced on or after the effective date."

The order of the Minnesota Supreme Court [ADM10–8049] dated July 25, 2012, provides in part that "(t)he attached amendment to the Minnesota Rules of Criminal Procedure be, and the same is, prescribed and promulgated for the regulation of practice and procedure in criminal matters in the courts of the State of Minnesota to be effective August 1, 2012", and further provides that "(t)he amendment shall apply to all actions or proceedings pending on, or commenced on or after, the effective date."

Rule 28.03. Certification of Proceedings

In the following circumstances, when any question of law arises that in the district court's opinion is so important or doubtful that the Court of Appeals should decide it, and the defendant requests or consents, the judge must report the case to present the question of law, and certify the report to the Court of Appeals:

(1) at the trial of any person convicted in any court;

(2) upon any motion to dismiss a tab charge, complaint, or indictment; or

(3) upon any motion relating to the tab charge, complaint, or indictment.

Certification stays all proceedings in the district court until the Court of Appeals decides the question presented. The prosecutor must, upon certification of the report, promptly furnish a copy to the Minnesota Attorney General at the expense of the governmental unit responsible for the prosecution.

The court may stay other criminal cases it has pending that involve or depend on the same question, if the defendant so requests or consents to the stay, until the appellate court decides the certified question. Briefs must be filed and served as provided in Rule 28.04, subd. 2(3), unless the appellate court directs otherwise.

Adopted Feb. 26, 1975, eff. July 1, 1975. Revised Dec. 13, 1989. Amended Oct. 27, 2009, eff. Jan. 1, 2010.

Supersedure

Laws 1997, c. 96, § 10, provides in part that this rule is superseded to the extent it conflicts with §§ 244.09, subd. 5, or 244.11.

Comment—Rule 28

See comment following Rule 28.06.

Historical Notes

The order of the Minnesota Supreme Court [C1–84–2137] dated December 13, 1989, provides in part that "(t)hese amended Rules of Criminal Procedure shall govern all criminal actions commenced or arrests made after 12 o'clock midnight January 1, 1990, except amendments to 8.04, 11.07, and 19.04, subd. 5, shall govern all criminal actions commenced or arrests made after 12 o'clock midnight January 1, 1991."

Laws 1997, c. 96, § 10, provides in part that this rule is superseded to the extent it conflicts with §§ 244.09, subd. 5, or 244.11.

Laws 1997, c. 96, § 12, provides in part that § 10 is effective August 1, 1997, and applies to crimes committed on or after that date.

Rule 28.04. Appeal by Prosecutor

Subd. 1. Right of Appeal. The prosecutor may appeal as of right to the Court of Appeals:

(1) in any case, from any pretrial order, including probable cause dismissal orders based on questions of law. But a pretrial order cannot be appealed if the court dismissed a complaint for lack of probable cause premised solely on a factual determination, or if the court dismissed a complaint under Minn. Stat. § 631.21;

(2) in felony cases, from any sentence imposed or stayed by the district court;

(3) in any case, from an order granting postconviction relief under Minn. Stat. ch. 590;

(4) in any case, from an order staying adjudication of an offense for which the defendant pleaded guilty or was found guilty at a trial. An order for a stay of adjudication to which the prosecutor did not object is not appealable;

(5) in any case, from a judgment of acquittal by the district court entered after the jury returns a verdict of guilty under Rule 26.03, subd. 18(2) or (3);

(6) in any case, from an order of the district court vacating judgment and dismissing the case made after the jury returns a verdict of guilty under Rule 26.04, subd. 3;

(7) in any case, from an order for a new trial granted under Rule 26.04, subd. 1, after a verdict or judgment of guilty, if the district court expressly stated in its order or in an accompanying memorandum that it based its order exclusively on a question of law that, in the opinion of the district court, is so important or doubtful that the appellate courts should decide it. However, an order for a new trial cannot be appealed if based on the interests of justice.

Subd. 2. Procedure Upon Appeal of Pretrial Order. The procedure upon appeal of a pretrial order by the prosecutor is as follows:

(1) *Stay.* Upon oral notice that the prosecutor intends to appeal a pretrial order, the district court must stay the proceedings for 5 days to allow time to perfect the appeal.

The oral notice must include a statement for the record explaining how the district court's alleged error, unless reversed, will have a critical impact on the outcome of the trial.

(2) *Notice of Appeal.* The prosecutor must file with the clerk of the appellate courts:

(a) a notice of appeal;

(b) the statement of the case provided for by Minnesota Rule of Civil Appellate Procedure 133.03, which must also include a summary statement by the prosecutor explaining how the district court's alleged error, unless reversed, will have a critical impact on the outcome of the trial; and

(c) a copy of the written request to the court reporter for a transcript of the proceedings as appellant deems necessary.

The prosecutor must submit with the notice of appeal, the statement of the case, and request for transcript at the time of filing, proof of service of these documents on the defendant or defense counsel, the State Public Defender's office, the Minnesota Attorney General, and the court administrator.

Failure to serve or file the statement of the case, to request the transcript, to file a copy of such request, or to file proof of service, does not deprive the Court of Appeals of jurisdiction over the prosecutor's appeal, but permits action the Court of Appeals deems appropriate, including dismissal of the appeal. The contents of the notice of appeal must be as set out in Rule 28.02, subd. 4(2).

(3) *Briefs.* The prosecutor must file the appellant's brief with the clerk of appellate courts, with proof of service on the respondent, within 15 days of delivery of the transcript.

If the court reporter delivered the transcript before the prosecutor filed the notice of appeal, or if the prosecutor did not request any transcript under Rule 28.04, subd. 2(2), appellant must file the appellant's brief with the clerk of the appellate courts together with proof of service upon the respondent within 15 days after the prosecutor filed the notice of appeal.

Within 8 days of service of appellant's brief upon respondent, the respondent must file the respondent's brief together with proof of service on the appellant. In all other respects, and to the extent applicable, the Minnesota Rules of Civil Appellate Procedure govern the form and filing of briefs and appendices, but the appellant's brief must contain a procedural history.

(4) *Dismissal by the Minnesota Attorney General.* In appeals by the prosecutor, the attorney general may, within 20 days after entry of the order staying proceedings, dismiss the appeal, and must within 3 days after the dismissal give notice of it to the court administrator and file it with the clerk of the appellate courts. The district court must then proceed as if no appeal had been taken.

(5) *Oral Argument and Consideration.* Rule 28.02, subd. 13 concerning oral argument applies to appeals by the prosecutor, but the date of oral argument or submission of the case to the court without oral argument cannot be later than 3 months after all briefs have been filed. The Court of Appeals must not hear or accept as submitted any appeals not argued or submitted before this period elapsed. If the case has not been argued or submitted within 3 months, the district court must proceed as if no appeal had been taken.

(6) *Attorney Fees.* Reasonable attorney fees and costs incurred must be allowed to the defendant on such appeal, and they must be paid by the governmental unit responsible for the prosecution.

(7) *Joinder.* The prosecutor may appeal several of the orders under this rule joined in a single appeal.

(8) *Time for Appeal.* The prosecutor may not appeal under this rule until after the Omnibus Hearing has been held under Rule 11, or the evidentiary hearing and pretrial conference, if any, have been held under Rule 12, and the district court has decided all issues raised.

The appeal then must be taken within 5 days after the defense, or the court administrator under Rule 33.03, serves notice of entry of the order to be appealed from on the prosecutor, or within 5 days after the district court notifies the prosecutor in court on the record of the order, whichever occurs first.

All pretrial orders entered and noticed to the prosecutor before the district court's final determination of all issues raised in the Omnibus Hearing under Rule 11, or in the evidentiary hearing and pretrial conference under Rule 12, may be included in this appeal.

An appeal by the prosecutor under this rule bars any further appeal by the prosecutor from any existing orders not included in the appeal. No appeal of a pretrial order by the prosecutor can be taken after jeopardy has attached.

An appeal under this rule does not deprive the district court of jurisdiction over pending matters not included in the appeal.

Subd. 3. Cross–Appeal by Defendant. When the prosecutor appeals, the defendant may obtain review of any adverse pretrial or postconviction order by filing a notice of cross-appeal with the clerk of the appellate courts, with proof of service on the prosecutor, within 10 days after the prosecutor serves notice of the appeal. In postconviction cases, the notice of cross-appeal may be filed within 60 days after the entry of the order granting or denying postconviction relief, if that is later.

Failure to serve the notice does not deprive the Court of Appeals of jurisdiction over defendant's cross-appeal, but permits action the Court of Appeals deems appropriate, including dismissal of the cross-appeal.

Subd. 4. Conditions of Release. Upon appeal by the prosecutor of a pretrial order, Rule 6.02, subds. 1 and 2 govern the conditions for defendant's release. The court must also consider that the defendant, if not released, may be confined for a longer time pending the appeal than would be possible under the potential sentence for the offense charged.

Subd. 5. Proceedings in Forma Pauperis. An indigent defendant who wants the services of an attorney in an appeal by the prosecutor under this rule must proceed under Rule 28.02, subd. 5.

Subd. 6. Procedure Upon Appeal of Postconviction Order.

(1) *Service and Filing.* The prosecutor may appeal an order granting postconviction relief by filing a notice of appeal with the clerk of the appellate courts, with proof of service on the opposing counsel, the court administrator, and the Minnesota Attorney General. No fees or bond for costs are required for the appeal.

A certified copy of the order appealed and the statement of the case in Minnesota Rule of Civil Appellate Procedure 133.03 need not be filed, unless the appellate court directs otherwise.

Failure of the prosecutor to take any step other than timely filing the notice of appeal does not affect the validity of the appeal, but permits action the Court of Appeals deems appropriate, including dismissal of the appeal.

(2) *Time for Taking an Appeal.* An appeal by the prosecutor of an order granting postconviction relief must be taken within 60 days after entry of the order.

(3) *Other Procedures.* The following rules govern the below-listed aspects of prosecution appeals from an order granting postconviction relief under this rule:

(a) Rule 28.02, subd. 4(2): the contents of the notice of appeal;

(b) Rule 28.02, subd. 8: the record on appeal;

(c) Rule 28.02, subd. 9: transcript of the proceedings and transmission of the transcript on record;

(d) Rule 28.02, subd. 10: briefs;

(e) Rule 28.02, subd. 13: oral argument;

(f) Rule 28.04, subd. 2(4): dismissal by the Minnesota Attorney General;

(g) Rule 28.04, subd. 2(6): attorney fees; and

(h) Rule 28.06; voluntary dismissal.

Subd. 7. Procedure Upon Appeal From Order Staying Adjudication.

(1) *Service and Filing.* The prosecutor may appeal an order staying adjudication by filing a notice of appeal with the clerk of the appellate courts, with proof of service on opposing counsel, the court administrator, the State Public Defender's office, and the Minnesota Attorney General.

The notice must be accompanied by a copy of a written request to the court reporter for a transcript of the proceedings, as appellant deems necessary. No fees or bond for costs are required for the appeal.

A certified copy of the order to be appealed or the statement of the case in Minnesota Rule of Civil Appellate Procedure 133.03 need not be filed, unless the appellate court directs otherwise.

Failure of the prosecutor to take any step other than timely filing the notice of appeal does not affect the validity of the appeal, but permits action the Court of Appeals deems appropriate, including dismissal of the appeal.

(2) *Time for Taking an Appeal.* An appeal by the prosecutor from an order staying adjudication must be taken within 10 days after entry of the order.

(3) *Briefs.* The prosecutor must file and serve the appellant's brief and proof of service on the respondent with the clerk of the appellate courts within 15 days after delivery of the transcript.

If the court reporter delivered the transcript before the prosecutor filed the notice of appeal, or if the prosecutor did not request a transcript, the appellant must file the appellant's brief and proof of service on the respondent with the clerk of the appellate courts together within 15 days after the prosecutor filed the notice of appeal. The brief must identify itself as a stay of adjudication brief.

Within 8 days after service of the appellant's brief, the respondent must file the respondent's brief and proof of service on the appellant. In all other respects, and to the extent applicable, the Minnesota Rules of Civil Appellate Procedure govern the form and filing of briefs and appendices, but the appellant's brief must contain a procedural history.

(4) *Other Procedures.* The following rules govern the below-listed aspects of prosecution appeals from an order staying adjudication:

(a) Rule 28.02, subd. 4(2): the contents of the notice of appeal;

(b) Rule 28.02, subd. 5: proceedings in forma pauperis;

(c) Rule 28.02, subd. 7: release of the defendant pending appeal;

(d) Rule 28.02, subd. 8: the record on appeal; and

(e) Rule 28.02, subd. 13: oral argument.

Subd. 8. Procedure Upon Appeal From Judgment of Acquittal or Vacation of Judgment After a Jury Verdict of Guilty, or From an Order Granting a New Trial.

(1) *Service and Filing.* The prosecutor may appeal these judgments or orders by filing with the clerk of the appellate courts a notice of appeal and proof of service on the opposing counsel, the court administrator, and the Minnesota Attorney General. No fees or bond for costs are required for the appeal.

A certified copy of the judgment or order appealed and the statement of the case in Minnesota Rule of Civil Appellate Procedure 133.03 need not be filed, unless the appellate court directs otherwise.

Failure of the prosecutor to take any step other than timely filing the notice of appeal does not affect the validity of the appeal, but permits action the Court of Appeals deems appropriate, including dismissal of the appeal.

(2) *Time for Appeal.* An appeal by the prosecutor under this subdivision must be made within 10 days after entry of the judgment or order.

(3) *Stay and Conditions of Release.* Upon oral notice that the prosecutor intends to appeal under this subdivision, the district court must order execution of the judgment or order stayed for 10 days to allow time to perfect the appeal. The district court must also determine the conditions for defendant's release pending the appeal, which are governed by Rule 6.02, subds. 1 and 2.

(4) *Other Procedures.* The following rules govern the below-listed aspects of appeals by the prosecutor under this subdivision:

(a) Rule 28.02, subd. 4(2): the contents of the notice of appeal;

(b) Rule 28.02, subd. 8: the record on appeal;

(c) Rule 28.02, subd. 9: transcript of the proceedings and transmission of the transcript and record;

(d) Rule 28.02, subd. 10: briefs;

(e) Rule 28.02, subd. 13: oral argument;

(f) Rule 28.04, subd. 2(4): dismissal by the Minnesota Attorney General; and

(g) Rule 28.04, subd. 2(6): attorney fees.

(5) *Cross–Appeals.* When the prosecutor appeals under this subdivision, the defendant may obtain review of any adverse pretrial and trial orders and issues by filing a notice of cross-appeal with the clerk of the appellate courts, with proof of service on the prosecutor, within 30 days of the prosecutor filing notice of appeal, or within 10 days after delivery of the transcript by the reporter, whichever is later.

If the defendant makes this election, and the jury's verdict is ultimately reinstated, the defendant may not file a second appeal from the entry of judgment of conviction unless it is limited to issues, such as sentencing, that could not have been raised in the cross-appeal.

The defendant may also elect to respond to the issues raised in the prosecutor's appeal and reserve appeal of any other issues until such time as the jury's verdict of guilty is reinstated. If reinstatement occurs, the defendant may appeal from the judgment using the procedures in Rule 28.02, subd. 2.

Adopted Feb. 26, 1975, eff. July 1, 1975. Revised Dec. 13, 1989. Amended Nov. 29, 1990; May 9, 1994; Aug. 21, 1998, eff. Jan. 1, 1999; Dec. 23, 2002, eff. Feb. 1, 2003; Dec. 29, 2006, eff. April 1, 2007; Oct. 27, 2009, eff. Jan. 1, 2010; June 22, 2011, eff. Sept. 1, 2011.

Supersedure

Laws 1997, c. 96, § 10, provides in part that this rule is superseded to the extent it conflicts with §§ 244.09, subd. 5, or 244.11.

Comment—Rule 28

See comment following Rule 28.06.

Historical Notes

The order of the Minnesota Supreme Court [C1–84–2137] dated December 13, 1989, provides in part that "(t)hese amended Rules of Criminal Procedure shall govern all criminal actions commenced or arrests made after 12 o'clock midnight January 1, 1990, except amendments to 8.04, 11.07, and 19.04, subd. 5, shall govern all criminal actions commenced or arrests made after 12 o'clock midnight January 1, 1991."

The order of the Minnesota Supreme Court [C1–84–2137] dated November 29, 1990, provides in part that "(t)hese amendments to the Rules of Criminal Procedure shall govern all criminal actions commenced or arrests made after 12 o'clock midnight January 1, 1991."

The order of the Minnesota Supreme Court [C1–84–2137] dated May 9, 1994, provides in part that "(t)hese amendments to the Rules of Criminal Procedure shall govern all criminal actions commenced or arrests made after 12 o'clock midnight July 1, 1994, except that the amendments in the first sentence of the third paragraph in Rule 2.01 shall govern all criminal actions commenced or arrests made after 12 o'clock midnight January 1, 1995."

Laws 1997, c. 96, § 10, provides in part that this rule is superseded to the extent it conflicts with §§ 244.09, subd. 5, or 244.11.

Laws 1997, c. 96, § 12, provides in part that § 10 is effective August 1, 1997, and applies to crimes committed on or after that date.

The order of the Minnesota Supreme Court [ADM10–8049] dated June 22, 2011, provided in part that "The amendments shall govern all criminal actions currently pending on or commenced on or after the effective date."

Former rule: Former rule 28.04 related to the certification of proceedings in order to present a question of law. See, now, Rules Crim.Proc., Rule 28.03.

Rule 28.05. Appeal from Sentence Imposed or Stayed

Subd. 1. Procedure. The following procedures apply to the appeal of a sentence imposed or stayed under these rules:

(1) *Notice of Appeal and Briefs.* Any party appealing a sentence must file with the clerk of the appellate courts, within 90 days after judgment and sentencing:

(a) a notice of appeal; and

(b) an affidavit of service of the notice on opposing counsel, the Minnesota Attorney General, the court administrator, and in the case of prosecution appeals the State Public Defender's office.

If all transcripts necessary for the appeal have already been transcribed when the appellant files the notice of appeal, the party appealing the sentence must file with the notice of appeal 9 copies of an informal letter brief, which must identify itself as a sentencing appeal brief, with an affidavit of service on opposing counsel, the Minnesota Attorney General, and in the case of prosecution appeals the State Public Defender's office. The brief must set out the arguments concerning the illegality or inappropriateness of the sentence.

When the transcripts necessary for the appeal have not been transcribed, the appellant must file with the notice of appeal a request for transcripts, and an affidavit of service of the request on opposing counsel, the Minnesota Attorney General, the court administrator, and in the case of prosecution appeals, the State Public Defender's office.

Appellant's brief must be identified as a sentencing appeal brief and must be served and filed within 30 days after delivery of the transcript. The clerk of the appellate courts must not accept a notice of appeal from sentence unless accompanied by the requisite briefs or transcript request and affidavit of service.

A defendant appealing the sentence and the judgment of conviction may combine the two into a single appeal; when this option is selected, the procedures in Rule 28.02 continue to apply.

(2) *Transmission of Record.* Upon receiving a copy of the notice of appeal, the court administrator must immediately forward to the clerk of the appellate courts:

(a) a transcript of the sentencing hearing, if any;

(b) the sentencing order required in Rule 27.03, subd. 7, with the departure report, if any, attached;

(c) the sentencing guidelines worksheet; and

(d) any presentence investigation report.

(3) *Respondent's Brief.* Within 10 days of service on respondent of appellant's brief, a respondent choosing to respond must serve an informal letter brief on appellant and file with the clerk of the appellate courts 9 copies of the brief.

(4) *Reply Brief.* Appellant may serve and file a reply brief within 5 days after service of the respondent's brief.

(5) *Other procedures.* The following rules govern the below-listed aspects of sentencing appeals:

(a) Rule 28.02, subd. 4(2): the contents of the notice of appeal;

(b) Rule 28.02, subd. 5: proceedings in forma pauperis;

(c) Rule 28.02, subd. 6: stays;

(d) Rule 28.02, subd. 7: release of the defendant on appeal; and

(e) Rule 28.02, subd. 13: oral argument.

Subd. 2. Action on Appeal. The appellate court may review the sentence imposed or stayed to determine whether the sentence is inconsistent with statutory requirements, unreasonable, inappropriate, excessive, unjustifiably disparate, or not warranted by the sentencing court's findings of fact. This review exists in addition to all other powers of review.

The court may:

(a) dismiss or affirm the appeal;

(b) vacate or set aside the sentence imposed or stayed and direct entry of an appropriate sentence; or

(c) order further proceedings as it may direct.

Adopted Feb. 26, 1975, eff. July 1, 1975. Revised Dec. 13, 1989. Amended Dec. 23, 2002, eff. Feb. 1, 2003; Oct. 31, 2003, eff. Nov. 5, 2003; Dec. 28, 2005, eff. March 1, 2006; Oct. 27, 2009, eff. Jan. 1, 2010; Jan. 21, 2010, eff. July 1, 2010.

Supersedure

Laws 1997, c. 96, § 10, provides in part that this rule is superseded to the extent it conflicts with §§ 244.09, subd. 5, or 244.11.

Comment—Rule 28

See comment following Rule 28.06.

Historical Notes

The order of the Minnesota Supreme Court [C1–84–2137] dated December 13, 1989, provides in part that "(t)hese amended Rules of Criminal Procedure shall govern all criminal actions commenced or arrests made after 12 o'clock midnight January 1, 1990, except amendments to 8.04, 11.07, and 19.04, subd. 5, shall govern all criminal actions commenced or arrests made after 12 o'clock midnight January 1, 1991."

Laws 1997, c. 96, § 10, provides in part that this rule is superseded to the extent it conflicts with §§ 244.09, subd. 5, or 244.11.

Laws 1997, c. 96, § 12, provides in part that § 10 is effective August 1, 1997, and applies to crimes committed on or after that date.

The order of the Minnesota Supreme Court [C1-84-2137] dated October 31, 2003, provides in part:

"1. The attached amendments to the Minnesota Rules of Criminal Procedure are prescribed and promulgated for the regulation of practice and procedure in criminal matters in the courts of the State of Minnesota to be effective November 5, 2003. Minn. Stat. §§ 243.49 and 631.41 (2002) are superceded to the extent that they conflict with these amendments. The Advisory Committee on Rules of Criminal Procedure is requested to amend the comments to the rules to reflect these amendments.

"2. Transcripts for guilty plea and sentencing hearings held prior to November 5, 2003 shall be paid in accordance with Minn. R. Crim. P. 15.09 and 27.03, subd. 6 as they existed prior to the amendments provided for in this order if the transcripts for those hearings are filed within thirty days of the guilty plea and/or sentencing hearing.

"3. Forms 49A and 49B are models of the sentencing form provided for in Minn. R. Crim. P. 27.03, subd. 6, as amended by this order. These forms will be made available in electronic format in the Court Rules section of the Supreme Court public website: http://www.courts.state.mn.us. The Supreme Court Technology Planning Committee is directed to develop, through the MNCIS project and in consultation with appropriate criminal justice partners, a standardized, uniform state-wide sentencing form or order that captures for immediate transmission essential sentencing information consistent with Minn. R. Crim. P. 27.03, subd. 6 as amended herein. The form shall be completed and implemented in conjunction with the MNCIS rollout.

"4. Court reporters and operators of electronic recording equipment shall file the stenographic notes or tape recordings of guilty plea or sentencing hearings with the court administrator within 90 days of sentencing. The reporter or operator may retrieve the notes or recordings if necessary. Minnesota Statutes § 486.03 (2002) is superceded to the extent that it conflicts with this procedure.

"5. No charge may be assessed for preparation of a transcript for the district court's own use; any other person may order a transcript at their own expense.

"6. The maximum rate charged for the transcription of any proceeding shall be established by the Conference of Chief Judges. Minnesota Statutes § 486.06 (2002) is superceded to the extent that it conflicts with this procedure.

"7. The Supreme Court Advisory Committee on General Rules of Practice shall draft rules in accordance with paragraphs 4, 5 and 6 of this order, and may recommend additional procedures for ensuring the availability and transcribability of the record, such as requiring that the court reporter file or make available his or her personal stenographic dictionary."

The order of the Minnesota Supreme Court [C1–84–2137] dated December 28, 2005, provides in part that "(t)he attached amendments shall govern all criminal actions commenced or arrests made after 12 o'clock midnight March 1, 2006."

Former rule: Former rule 28.05 related to appeals to the district court and to trials de novo.

Rule 28.06. Voluntary Dismissal

If the appellant files with the clerk of the appellate courts a notice of voluntary dismissal, with proof of service upon counsel for respondent, the appellate court may dismiss the appeal. If the appellant was the defendant in the district court, the notice must be signed by the appellant, as well as appellant's legal counsel, if the appellant is represented.

Adopted June 22, 2011, eff. Sept. 1, 2011.

Comment—Rule 28

Under Rule 28.02, subd. 1 the defendant may obtain review of lower court orders and rulings only by appeal except as may be provided in the case of the extraordinary writ authorized by Minn. Const. Art. VI, § 2, and the postconviction remedy, Minn. Stat. ch. 590. The statutory authorization for the extraordinary writs is contained in Minn. Stat.

§ 480A.06, subd. 5 and chs. 586 (Mandamus), 589 (Habeas Corpus), and 606 (Certiorari). The procedure for obtaining writs of mandamus or prohibition appears in Minn. R. Civ. App. P. 120 and 121.

A defendant cannot as a matter of right appeal from a stay of adjudication entered under Minn. Stat. § 152.18, subd. 1, which requires the consent of the defendant. However, a defendant may seek discretionary review of such a stay under Rule 28.02, subd. 3. State v. Verschelde, 595 N. W.2d 192 (Minn. 1999).

Rule 28.02, subd. 3 (Discretionary Review) is taken from Minn. R. Civ. App. P. 105, which sets forth the procedure to be followed by a defendant in seeking permission to proceed with an appeal from an order not otherwise appealable. A defendant seeking to appeal from a sentence imposed or stayed in a misdemeanor or gross misdemeanor case would have to proceed under this rule.

Rule 28.02, subd. 4(4) establishes a procedure by which a defendant who has initiated a direct appeal may nonetheless pursue postconviction relief. Certain types of claims are better suited to the taking of testimony and fact-finding possible in the district court, and defendants are encouraged to bring such claims, such as ineffective assistance of counsel where explanation of the attorney's decision is necessary, through postconviction proceedings rather than through direct appeal. See Black v. State, 560 N.W.2d 83, 85 n.1 (Minn. 1997). The order staying the appeal may provide for a time limit within which to file the postconviction proceeding.

Under Rule 28.02, subd. 9 (Transcript of Proceedings and Transmission of the Transcript and Record), the transcript must be ordered within 30 days after filing of the notice of appeal rather than within 10 days as otherwise provided by Minn. R. Civ. App. P. 110.02, subd. 1. The provisions of Minn. R. Civ. App. P. 110 and 111 concerning the content and transmission of the record and transcripts apply to criminal appeals under Rule 28. Therefore, it is necessary in a criminal appeal on ordering the transcript to serve and file a Certificate as to Transcript as required by Minn. R. Civ. App. P. 110. 02, subd. 2. If either of the parties questions the accuracy of the court reporter's transcript of a videotape or audiotape exhibit, that party may seek to correct the transcript either by stipulation with the other party or by motion to the district court under Minn. R. Civ. App. P. 110.05.

To the extent that an order granting a defendant a new trial also suppresses evidence, it will be viewed as a pretrial order concerning the retrial and the prosecutor may appeal the suppression part of the order under Rule 28.04, subd. 1(1). State v. Brown, 317 N.W.2d 714 (Minn. 1982). In response to State v. Lee, 706 N.W.2d 491 (Minn. 2005), Rule 28.04, subd. 1(4), was revised to expressly permit a prosecutor to appeal a stay of adjudication ordered by the district court over the objection of the prosecutor.

A timely, good-faith motion by the prosecutor for clarification or rehearing of an appealable order extends the time to appeal from that order. State v. Wollan, 303 N.W.2d 253 (Minn. 1981). Originally under Rules 28.04, subd. 2(2) and (8) the prosecutor had five days from entry of an appealable pretrial order to perfect the appeal. It was possible for this short time limit to expire before the prosecutor received actual notice of the order sought to be appealed. These rules as revised eliminate this unfairness and assure that notice of the pretrial order will be served on or given to the prosecutor before the five-day time limit begins to run. In State v. Hugger, 640 N.W.2d 619 (Minn. 2002), the court held that in computing the five-day time period within which an appeal must be taken under Rule 28.04, subd. 2(8), intermediate Saturdays, Sundays, and legal holidays are excluded under Rule 34.01 before the additional 3 days for service by mail are added under Rule 34.04.

Under Rule 28.04, subd. 2(2), failure to timely serve the notice of appeal on the State Public Defender is a jurisdictional defect requiring dismissal of the appeal. State v. Barrett, 694 N.W.2d 783 (Minn. 2005).

Absent special circumstances, failure of the prosecutor to file the appellant's brief within the 15 days as provided by Rule 28.04, subd. 2(3) will result in dismissal of the appeal. State v. Schroeder, 292 N.W.2d 758 (Minn. 1980).

Rule 28.05, subd. 2 (Action on Appeal) is taken from Minn. Stat. § 244.11.

Historical Notes

The order of the Minnesota Supreme Court [ADM10-8049] dated June 22, 2011, provided in part that "The amendments shall govern all criminal actions currently pending on or commenced on or after the effective date."

Former rule: Former rule 28.06 related to the procedure for trials de novo.

Rules 28.07, 28.08. Deleted

Historical Notes

Rules 28.07 and 28.08 related to the procedure for appeals on the record to the district court and to appeals by the prosecuting authority to the district court, respectively.

RULE 29. APPEALS TO SUPREME COURT

Rule 29.01. Scope of Rule

Subd. 1. Appeals from Court of Appeals and in First–Degree Murder Cases. Rule 29 governs the procedure in misdemeanor, gross misdemeanor, and felony cases for appeals from the Court of Appeals to the Supreme Court and from the district court to the Supreme Court if the defendant has been convicted of first-degree murder.

Subd. 2. Applicability of Rules of Civil Appellate Procedure. To the extent applicable, the Minnesota Rules of Civil Appellate Procedure govern appellate procedure unless these rules direct otherwise.

Subd. 3. Suspension of Rules. For good cause, the Supreme Court may suspend application of any of these rules on a party's motion or on its own initiative, and may order proceedings as it directs, but cannot alter the time for filing a notice of appeal or a petition for review, unless permitted by Rules 29.03, subd. 3(f) or 29.04, subd. 2.

Adopted Feb. 26, 1975, eff. July 1, 1975. Revised Dec. 13, 1989. Amended Oct. 27, 2009, eff. Jan. 1, 2010.

Comment—Rule 29

See comment following Rule 29.06.

Historical Notes

The order of the Minnesota Supreme Court [C1–84–2137] dated December 13, 1989, provides in part that "(t)hese amended Rules of Criminal Procedure shall govern all criminal actions commenced or arrests made after 12 o'clock midnight January 1, 1990, except amendments to 8.04, 11.07, and 19.04, subd. 5, shall govern all criminal actions commenced or arrests made after 12 o'clock midnight January 1, 1991."

Former rule: A former rule 29.01 predating the creation of the Court of Appeals also related to the scope of the rules governing appeals.

Rule 29.02. Right of Appeal

Subd. 1. Appeals in First–Degree Murder Cases.

(a) A defendant may appeal as of right from the district court to the Supreme Court from a final judgment of conviction of first-degree murder.

(b) Either the defendant or the prosecutor may appeal as of right from the district court to the Supreme Court, in a first-degree murder case, from an adverse final order deciding a petition for postconviction relief under Minn. Stat. ch. 590.

(c) The prosecutor may appeal as of right from the district court to the Supreme Court, in a first-degree murder case, from:

(i) a judgment of acquittal after a jury verdict of guilty of first-degree murder;

(ii) an order vacating judgment and dismissing the case after a jury verdict of guilty of first-degree murder; or

(iii) an order granting a new trial under Rule 26.04, subd. 1, after a verdict or judgment of guilty of first-degree murder, if the district court expressly states in the order, or in an accompanying memorandum, that the order is based exclusively on a question of law that the district court concludes is so important or doubtful that it requires a decision by the appellate courts. An order for a new trial is not appealable if based on the interests of justice.

(d) Other charges that were joined for prosecution with the first-degree murder charge may be included in the appeal. No other direct appeals can be taken from the district court to the Supreme Court except as provided in Minnesota Rule of Civil Appellate Procedure 118 (accelerated review by the Supreme Court of cases pending in the Court of Appeals).

Subd. 2. Appeals from Court of Appeals. A party may appeal from a final decision of the Court of Appeals to the Supreme Court only with leave of the Supreme Court.

Adopted Feb. 26, 1975, eff. July 1, 1975. Revised Dec. 13, 1989. Amended May 9, 1994; Dec. 23, 2002, eff. Feb. 1, 2003; Oct. 27, 2009, eff. Jan. 1, 2010.

Comment—Rule 29

See comment following Rule 29.06.

Historical Notes

The order of the Minnesota Supreme Court [C1–84–2137] dated December 13, 1989, provides in part that "(t)hese amended Rules of Criminal Procedure shall govern all criminal actions commenced or arrests made after 12 o'clock midnight January 1, 1990, except amendments to 8.04, 11.07, and 19.04, subd. 5, shall govern all criminal actions commenced or arrests made after 12 o'clock midnight January 1, 1991."

The order of the Minnesota Supreme Court [C1–84–2137] dated May 9, 1994, provides in part that "(t)hese amendments to the Rules of Criminal Procedure shall govern all criminal actions commenced or arrests made after 12 o'clock midnight July 1, 1994, except that the amendments in the first sentence of the third paragraph in Rule 2.01 shall govern all criminal actions commenced or arrests made after 12 o'clock midnight January 1, 1995."

Former rule: A former rule 29.02 predating the creation of the Court of Appeals related to appeals by defendants.

Rule 29.03. Procedure for Appeals by Defendant in First–Degree Murder Cases

Subd. 1. Service and Filing. A defendant appeals by filing a notice of appeal to the Supreme Court with the clerk of the appellate courts, with proof of service on the prosecutor, the Minnesota Attorney General, and the court administrator for the county in which the judgment appealed from is entered. The defendant does not have to post a bond to appeal. The defendant need not file a certified copy of the judgment or order appealed from, or the statement of the case in Minnesota Rule of Civil Appellate Procedure 133.03. The defendant's failure to take any step other than timely filing the notice of appeal does not affect the validity of the appeal, but permits action the Supreme Court deems appropriate, including dismissal of the appeal.

Subd. 2. Contents of Notice of Appeal. The notice of appeal must specify:

(a) the party or parties filing the appeal;

(b) the names, addresses, and telephone numbers of all counsel and whom they represent;

(c) the judgment or order from which appeal is taken; and

(d) that the appeal is to the Supreme Court.

Subd. 3. Time for Taking an Appeal.

(a) An appeal by a defendant from a final judgment of conviction of first-degree murder must be filed within 90 days after the final judgment. A judgment is final within the meaning of these rules when there is a judgment of conviction upon the verdict of a jury, or the finding of the court, and sentence is imposed.

(b) A notice of appeal filed after the announcement of a decision or order—but before sentencing or entry of judgment or order—must be treated as occurring after these events, but on the same day.

(c) A timely motion to vacate the judgment, for a judgment of acquittal, or for a new trial tolls the time for an appeal from a final judgment until the entry of an order denying the motion, and the order denying the motion may be reviewed in an appeal from the final judgment.

(d) An appeal by a defendant from an adverse final order in a postconviction proceeding in a first-degree murder case must be filed within 60 days after its entry.

(e) A judgment or order is entered under these appellate rules when the court administrator enters it in the record.

(f) For good cause, the district court or a justice of the Supreme Court may, before or after the time for appeal has expired, with or without motion or notice, extend the time for filing a notice of appeal up to 30 days from the expiration of the time prescribed by these rules.

Subd. 4. Other Procedures. The following rules govern the below-listed aspects of an appeal in a first-degree murder case:

(a) Rule 28.02, subd. 4(4): stay of appeal for post-conviction proceedings;

(b) Rule 28.02, subd. 5: proceeding in forma pauperis;

(c) Rule 28.02, subd. 6: stay;

(d) Rule 28.02, subd. 7: release of defendant;

(e) Rule 28.02, subd. 9: transcript of proceedings and transmission of the transcript and record;

(f) Rule 28.02, subd. 10: briefs;

(g) Rule 28.02, subd. 11: scope of review;

(h) Rule 28.02, subd. 12: action on appeal;

(i) Rule 28.06; voluntary dismissal; and

(j) Rule 29.04, subd. 9: oral argument.

Adopted Feb. 26, 1975, eff. July 1, 1975. Revised Dec. 13, 1989. Amended Dec. 23, 2002, eff. Feb. 1, 2003; Feb. 28, 2003, eff. March 17, 2003; Oct. 27, 2009, eff. Jan. 1, 2010; June 22, 2011, eff. Sept. 1, 2011.

Comment—Rule 29

See comment following Rule 29.06.

Historical Notes

The order of the Minnesota Supreme Court [C1–84–2137] dated December 13, 1989, provides in part that "(t)hese amended Rules of Criminal Procedure shall govern all criminal actions commenced or arrests made after 12 o'clock midnight January 1, 1990, except amendments to 8.04, 11.07, and 19.04, subd. 5, shall govern all criminal actions commenced or arrests made after 12 o'clock midnight January 1, 1991."

The order of the Minnesota Supreme Court [ADM10–8049] dated June 22, 2011, provided in part that "The amendments shall govern all criminal actions currently pending on or commenced on or after the effective date."

Former rule: A former rule 29.03 predating the creation of the Court of Appeals related to appeals by prosecutors. See, now, Rules Crim.Proc., Rule 29.06.

Rule 29.04. Procedure for Appeals from Court of Appeals

Subd. 1. Service and Filing. A party petitioning for review to the Supreme Court from the Court of Appeals must file 4 copies of a petition for review with the clerk of the appellate courts, with proof of service on opposing counsel and the Minnesota Attorney General. A defendant does not have to file a bond to petition for review.

A party's failure to take any step other than timely filing the petition for review does not affect the validity of the appeal, but permits action the Supreme Court deems appropriate, including dismissal of the appeal.

Subd. 2. Time for Petitioning. A party petitioning for review to the Supreme Court from the Court of Appeals must serve and file the petition for review within 30 days after the Court of Appeals files its decision.

For good cause, a judge of the Court of Appeals or a justice of the Supreme Court may, before or after the time to serve and file a petition for review has expired, with or without motion or notice, extend the time to do so up to 30 days from the expiration of the time prescribed by these rules.

Subd. 3. Contents of Petition for Review. The petition for review must not exceed 10 pages, exclusive of the appendix, and must identify the petitioner, state that petitioner is seeking permission to appeal to the Supreme Court from the Court of Appeals, and contain in order the following information:

(1) the names, addresses, and telephone numbers of the attorneys for all parties;

(2) the date the Court of Appeals filed its decision, and a designation of the judgment or order from which petitioner had appealed to the Court of Appeals;

(3) a concise statement of the legal issue or issues presented for review, indicating how the district court and the Court of Appeals decided each issue;

(4) a procedural history of the case from commencement of prosecution through filing of the decision in the Court of Appeals, including a designation of the district court and district court judge, and the disposition of the case in the district court and in the Court of Appeals;

(5) a concise statement of facts indicating briefly the nature of the case, and including only the facts relevant to the issue(s) sought to be reviewed;

(6) a concise statement of the reasons why the Supreme Court should exercise its discretion to review the case; and

(7) an appendix containing a copy of the written decision of the Court of Appeals, and a copy of any district court recitation of the essential facts of the case, conclusions of law, and memoranda.

Subd. 4. Discretionary Review. The Supreme Court may exercise discretionary review of any Court of Appeals' decision. The following criteria may be considered:

(1) the decision presents an important question on which the Supreme Court should rule;

(2) the Court of Appeals has ruled on the constitutionality of a statute;

(3) the Court of Appeals has decided a question in direct conflict with an applicable precedent of a Minnesota appellate court;

(4) the lower courts have so far departed from the accepted and usual course of justice that the Supreme Court should exercise its supervisory powers; or

(5) a Supreme Court decision will help develop, clarify, or harmonize the law; and

1. the case calls for the application of a new principle or policy;

2. the resolution of the question presented has possible statewide impact; or

3. the question will likely recur unless resolved by the Supreme Court.

Subd. 5. Response to Petition. When a petition for review has been filed, the respondent must file with the clerk of the appellate courts within 20 days after service of the petition on respondent 4 copies of any response, not to exceed 10 pages exclusive of the appendix, and proof of service on appellant. Failing to respond to the petition will not be considered agreement with it.

Subd. 6. Cross–Petition. A party cross-petitioning for review to the Supreme Court must file with the clerk of the appellate courts within 20 days after service of the petition for review, or within 30 days after filing of the decision of the Court of Appeals, whichever is later, 4 copies of a cross-petition for review, not to exceed 10 pages exclusive of the appendix, and proof of service on the petitioner. The cross-petition must conform to Rule 29.04, subd. 3, but the procedural history, statement of facts, and appendix need not be included unless the cross-petitioner disagrees with them as they appear in the petition for review.

The court may permit a party, without filing a cross-petition, to defend a decision or judgment on any ground that the law and record permit that would not expand the relief that has been granted to the party.

Subd. 7. Action on Petition or Cross–Petition. The Supreme Court must file its order granting or denying review or cross-review within 60 days from the date the petition was filed. Upon the filing of the order, the clerk of the appellate courts must mail a copy of it to the attorneys for the parties.

Subd. 8. Briefs.

(1) Except as subdivision 10 (pretrial appeals) of this rule directs:

(a) appellant must serve and file the appellant's brief and appendix within 30 days after entry of the order granting permission to appeal;

(b) respondent must serve and file the respondent's brief and appendix, if any, within 30 days after service of appellant's brief; and

(c) appellant may serve and file a reply brief within 10 days after service of the respondent's brief.

(2) In all other respects, the Minnesota Rules of Civil Appellate Procedure govern, to the extent applicable, the form and filing of briefs, but appellant's brief must also contain a procedural history.

Subd. 9. Oral Argument. Each party must serve and file with the party's initial brief a notice stating whether the party requests oral argument. Oral argument must be granted unless the court determines it is unnecessary because:

(1) neither party has requested oral argument in the notice served and filed with the initial briefs;

(2) a party forfeits oral argument under Minnesota Rule of Civil Appellate Procedure 134.01 for not timely filing its brief; or

(3) the parties waive oral argument by joint agreement under Minnesota Rule of Civil Appellate Procedure 134.06.

The Supreme Court may direct presentation of oral argument in any case.

Subd. 10. Appeals Involving Pretrial Orders.

(1) Briefs. In cases originally appealed to the Court of Appeals by the prosecutor under Rule 28.04, the appellant must, within 15 days from the date of entry of the order granting review, serve the appellant's brief on respondent and file 14 copies with the clerk of the appellate courts.

Within 8 days of service, respondent must serve the respondent's brief on appellant and file 14 copies with the clerk of appellate courts.

(2) Hearing. In pretrial appeals, the date of oral argument or submission of the case to the court without oral argument must not be later than 3 months after all briefs have been filed.

The Supreme Court must not hear or accept as submitted any pretrial appeal not argued or submitted within this 3–month period. If the case has not been argued or submitted within 3 months, the district court must proceed under the judgment of the Court of Appeals as if no appeal had been taken to the Supreme Court.

(3) Attorney Fees. Reasonable attorney fees and costs incurred must be allowed to the defendant on an appeal to the Supreme Court by the prosecutor in a case originally appealed by the prosecutor to the Court of Appeals under Rule 28.04. The fees and costs must be paid by the governmental unit responsible for the prosecution.

(4) Conditions of Release. Upon an appeal to the Supreme Court in a case originally appealed by the prosecutor under Rule 28.04, Rule 6.02, subds. 1 and 2, govern the conditions for defendant's release pending the appeal.

Subd. 11. Other Procedures. The following rules govern the below-listed aspects of an appeal to the Supreme Court from the Court of Appeals:

(1) Rule 28.02, subd. 4(4): stay of appeal for postconviction proceedings;

(2) Rule 28.02, subd. 5: proceeding in forma pauperis;

(3) Rule 28.02, subd. 6: stay;

(4) Rule 28.02, subd. 7: release of defendant;

(5) Rule 28.02, subd. 8: record on appeal;

(6) Rule 28.02, subd. 11: scope of review;

(7) Rules 28.02, subd. 12, and 28.05, subd. 2: action on appeal; and

(8) Rule 28.06; voluntary dismissal.

Adopted June 9, 1983. Revised Dec. 13, 1989. Amended Dec. 23, 2002, eff. Feb. 1, 2003; Feb. 28, 2003, eff. March 17, 2003; Nov. 24, 2003, eff. Dec. 1, 2003; Dec. 2, 2003, eff. Dec. 2, 2003; Oct. 27, 2009, eff. Jan. 1, 2010; June 22, 2011, eff. Sept. 1, 2011.

Comment—Rule 29

See comment following Rule 29.06.

Historical Notes

The order of the Minnesota Supreme Court dated June 9, 1983, provides in part that "(t)hese amendments to the Rules of Criminal Procedure shall govern all criminal actions commenced or arrests made after 12 o'clock midnight July 31, 1983."

The order of the Minnesota Supreme Court [C1–84–2137] dated December 13, 1989, provides in part that "(t)hese amended Rules of Criminal Procedure shall govern all criminal actions commenced or arrests made after 12 o'clock midnight January 1, 1990, except amendments to 8.04, 11.07, and 19.04, subd. 5, shall govern all criminal actions commenced or arrests made after 12 o'clock midnight January 1, 1991."

The order of the Minnesota Supreme Court [ADM10 8049] dated June 22, 2011, provided in part that "The amendments shall govern all criminal actions currently pending on or commenced on or after the effective date."

Rule 29.05. Procedure for Appeals by the Prosecutor in Postconviction Cases

Rule 28.04, subd. 6, applies to an appeal to the Supreme Court by the prosecutor from an adverse final order of the district court in postconviction proceedings in a first-degree murder case.

Adopted Dec. 13, 1989. Amended Oct. 27, 2009, eff. Jan. 1, 2010.

Comment—Rule 29

See comment following Rule 29.06.

Historical Notes

The order of the Minnesota Supreme Court [C1–84–2137] dated December 13, 1989, provides in part that "(t)hese amended Rules of Criminal Procedure shall govern all criminal actions commenced or arrests made after 12 o'clock midnight January 1, 1990, except amendments to 8.04, 11.07, and 19.04, subd. 5, shall govern all criminal actions commenced or arrests made after 12 o'clock midnight January 1, 1991."

Rule 29.06. Procedure for Prosecutor Appeals from a Judgment of Acquittal, Vacation of Judgment after a Jury Verdict of Guilty, or Order Granting a New Trial

In first-degree murder cases, Rule 28.04, subd. 8 governs appeals by the prosecutor to the Supreme Court from:

(1) a judgment of acquittal after a jury verdict of guilty;

(2) an order vacating judgment and dismissing the case after a jury verdict of guilty; or

(3) an order granting a new trial.

Adopted May 9, 1994. Amended Dec. 23, 2002, eff. Feb. 1, 2003; Feb. 8, 2007, eff. April 1, 2007; Oct. 27, 2009, eff. Jan. 1, 2010.

Comment—Rule 29

After a first-degree murder conviction, only the Supreme Court has appellate jurisdiction. See Minn. Stat. §§ 480A.06, subd. 1 and 632.14. This includes appeals from orders denying postconviction relief from convictions in first-degree murder cases. See Minn. Stat. § 590.06. However, appeals in first-degree murder cases before conviction are decided by the Court of Appeals under Rule 28, and may be reviewed by the Supreme Court via a petition for further review.

Under Minn. R. Civ. App. P. 136.02, the clerk of the appellate courts is to enter judgment under the decision of the Court of Appeals not less than 30 days after that decision is filed. The filing of a petition for review under Rule 29.04 stays entry of the judgment and transmission of the judgment back to the clerk of the district court according to Minn. R. Civ. App. P. 136.02 and 136.03. If the petition for review is denied, the judgment is to be entered and transmitted immediately.

Historical Notes

The order of the Minnesota Supreme Court [C1–84–2137] dated May 9, 1994, provides in part that "(t)hese amendments to the Rules of Criminal Procedure shall govern all criminal actions commenced or arrests made after 12 o'clock midnight July 1, 1994, except that the amendments in the first sentence of the third paragraph in Rule 2.01 shall govern all criminal actions commenced or arrests made after 12 o'clock midnight January 1, 1995."

RULE 30. DISMISSAL

Rule 30.01. By Prosecutor

The prosecutor may dismiss a complaint or tab charge without the court's approval, and may dismiss an indictment with the court's approval. The prosecutor must state the reasons for the dismissal in writing or on the record. In felony cases, if the dismissal is on the record, it must be transcribed and filed.

Adopted Feb. 26, 1975, eff. July 1, 1975. Revised Dec. 13, 1989. Amended Oct. 27, 2009, eff. Jan. 1, 2010; June 5, 2012, eff. Aug. 1, 2012.

Comment—Rule 30

See comment following Rule 30.02.

Historical Notes

The order of the Minnesota Supreme Court [C1–84–2137] dated December 13, 1989, provides in part that "(t)hese amended Rules of Criminal Procedure shall govern all criminal actions commenced or arrests made after 12 o'clock midnight January 1, 1990, except amendments to 8.04, 11.07, and 19.04, subd. 5, shall govern all criminal actions commenced or arrests made after 12 o'clock midnight January 1, 1991."

The order of the Minnesota Supreme Court [ADM 10–8049] dated June 5, 2012, provided in part that the amendments "be effective August 1, 2012, and shall apply to all actions or proceedings pending on or commenced on or after the effective date."

Rule 30.02. By Court

The court may dismiss the complaint, indictment, or tab charge if the prosecutor has unnecessarily delayed bringing the defendant to trial.

Adopted Feb. 26, 1975, eff. July 1, 1975. Revised Dec. 13, 1989. Amended Oct. 27, 2009, eff. Jan. 1, 2010.

Comment—Rule 30

Stated reasons for dismissal under Rule 30.01 may include satisfactory completion of a pretrial diversion program.

According to State v. Aubol, 309 Minn. 323, 244 N.W.2d 636 (1976), leave to dismiss an indictment must be granted if the prosecutor has provided a factual basis for the insufficiency of the evidence to support a conviction, and the court is satisfied that the prosecutor has not abused prosecutorial discretion.

Prosecutors and judges should be aware of their obligations under Minn. Stat. § 611A.0315 of the Minnesota Crime Victims Rights Act concerning notice to domestic abuse victims upon dismissal or refusal to prosecute the charge.

Historical Notes

The order of the Minnesota Supreme Court [C1–84–2137] dated December 13, 1989, provides in part that "(t)hese amended Rules of Criminal Procedure shall govern all criminal actions commenced or arrests made after 12 o'clock midnight January 1, 1990, except amendments to 8.04, 11.07, and 19.04, subd. 5, shall govern all criminal actions commenced or arrests made after 12 o'clock midnight January 1, 1991."

RULE 31. HARMLESS ERROR AND PLAIN ERROR

Rule 31.01. Harmless Error

Any error that does not affect substantial rights must be disregarded.

Adopted Feb. 26, 1975, eff. July 1, 1975. Revised Dec. 13, 1989. Amended Oct. 27, 2009, eff. Jan. 1, 2010.

Comment—Rule 31

See comment following Rule 31.02.

Historical Notes

The order of the Minnesota Supreme Court [C1–84–2137] dated December 13, 1989, provides in part that "(t)hese amended Rules of Criminal Procedure shall govern all criminal actions commenced or arrests made after 12 o'clock midnight January 1, 1990, except amendments to 8.04, 11.07, and 19.04, subd. 5, shall govern all criminal actions commenced or arrests made after 12 o'clock midnight January 1, 1991."

Rule 31.02. Plain Error

Plain error affecting a substantial right can be considered by the court on motion for new trial, posttrial motion, or on appeal even if it was not brought to the trial court's attention.

Adopted Feb. 26, 1975, eff. July 1, 1975. Revised Dec. 13, 1989. Amended Oct. 27, 2009, eff. Jan. 1, 2010.

Comment—Rule 31

On appeal, the plain error doctrine applies to unobjected-to prosecutorial misconduct. The defendant bears the burden of showing that error occurred and that it was plain. Once the defendant has made that showing, the burden rests with the prosecutor to show that the error did not affect the defendant's substantial rights. See State v. Ramey, 721 N.W.2d 294, 299–300 (Minn. 2006).

Historical Notes

The order of the Minnesota Supreme Court [C1–84–2137] dated December 13, 1989, provides in part that "(t)hese amended Rules of Criminal Procedure shall govern all criminal actions commenced or arrests made after 12 o'clock midnight January 1, 1990, except amendments to 8.04, 11.07, and 19.04, subd. 5, shall govern all criminal actions commenced or arrests made after 12 o'clock midnight January 1, 1991."

RULE 32. MOTIONS

Requests to the court for an order must be by motion. A motion other than one made during a trial or hearing must be in writing, unless the court or these rules permit it to be made orally. The motion must state the grounds on which it is made and must set forth the relief or order sought. A motion may be supported by affidavit.

Adopted Feb. 26, 1975, eff. July 1, 1975. Revised Dec. 13, 1989. Amended Oct. 27, 2009, eff. Jan. 1, 2010.

Historical Notes

The order of the Minnesota Supreme Court [C1–84–2137] dated December 13, 1989, provides in part that "(t)hese amended Rules of

Criminal Procedure shall govern all criminal actions commenced or arrests made after 12 o'clock midnight January 1, 1990, except amendments to 8.04, 11.07, and 19.04, subd. 5, shall govern all criminal actions commenced or arrests made after 12 o'clock midnight January 1, 1991."

RULE 33. SERVICE AND FILING OF PAPERS

Rule 33.01. Service; Where Required

Written motions—other than those heard ex parte—written notices, and other similar papers must be served on each party.

Adopted Feb. 26, 1975, eff. July 1, 1975. Revised Dec. 13, 1989. Amended Oct. 27, 2009, eff. Jan. 1, 2010.

Comment—Rule 33

See comment following Rule 33.05.

Historical Notes

The order of the Minnesota Supreme Court [C1–84–2137] dated December 13, 1989, provides in part that "(t)hese amended Rules of Criminal Procedure shall govern all criminal actions commenced or arrests made after 12 o'clock midnight January 1, 1990, except amendments to 8.04, 11.07, and 19.04, subd. 5, shall govern all criminal actions commenced or arrests made after 12 o'clock midnight January 1, 1991."

Rule 33.02. Service; On Whom Made

Service required or permitted to be made on a represented party must be made on the attorney unless the court orders personal service on the party. Service on the attorney or party must be made in the manner provided in civil actions, as ordered by the court, or as required by these rules. Service may be made by electronic means if authorized by an order of the Minnesota Supreme Court and if service is made in accordance with that order; service by electronic means is complete as provided in that order.

Adopted Feb. 26, 1975, eff. July 1, 1975. Revised Dec. 13, 1989. Amended Oct. 27, 2009, eff. Jan. 1, 2010; July 26, 2012, eff. Sept. 1, 2012.

Comment—Rule 33

See comment following Rule 33.05.

Historical Notes

The order of the Minnesota Supreme Court [C1–84–2137] dated December 13, 1989, provides in part that "(t)hese amended Rules of Criminal Procedure shall govern all criminal actions commenced or arrests made after 12 o'clock midnight January 1, 1990, except amendments to 8.04, 11.07, and 19.04, subd. 5, shall govern all criminal actions commenced or arrests made after 12 o'clock midnight January 1, 1991."

The order of the Minnesota Supreme Court [ADM10–8049] dated July 26, 2012, provides in part that "(t)he attached amendments to the Rules of Criminal Procedure be, and the same are, prescribed and promulgated to be effective September 1, 2012," and further provides "(t)hese amendments shall apply to all actions or proceedings pending or commenced on or after the effective date."

Rule 33.03. Notice of Orders

Upon entry of an order made on a written motion subsequent to arraignment, the court administrator must promptly mail a copy to each party and must make a record of the mailing. The court administrator may provide a copy by electronic means if authorized by an order of the Minnesota Supreme Court and if provided in accordance with that order. Lack of notice of entry by the court administrator does not affect the time to appeal or relieve or authorize the court to relieve a party for failure to appeal within the time allowed, unless these rules direct otherwise.

Adopted Feb. 26, 1975, eff. July 1, 1975. Revised Dec. 13, 1989. Amended Oct. 27, 2009, eff. Jan. 1, 2010; July 26, 2012, eff. Sept. 1, 2012.

Comment—Rule 33

See comment following Rule 33.05.

Historical Notes

The order of the Minnesota Supreme Court [C1–84–2137] dated December 13, 1989, provides in part that "(t)hese amended Rules of Criminal Procedure shall govern all criminal actions commenced or arrests made after 12 o'clock midnight January 1, 1990, except amendments to 8.04, 11.07, and 19.04, subd. 5, shall govern all criminal actions commenced or arrests made after 12 o'clock midnight January 1, 1991."

The order of the Minnesota Supreme Court [ADM10–8049] dated July 26, 2012, provides in part that "(t)he attached amendments to the Rules of Criminal Procedure be, and the same are, prescribed and promulgated to be effective September 1, 2012," and further provides "(t)hese amendments shall apply to all actions or proceedings pending or commenced on or after the effective date."

Rule 33.04. Filing

(a) Search warrants and search warrant applications, affidavits, and inventories—including statements of unsuccessful execution—and papers required to be served must be filed with the court administrator. Papers must be filed as in civil actions, except that when papers are filed by facsimile transmission, a facsimile filing fee is not required and the originals of the papers described in Rule 33.05 must be filed as Rule 33.05 provides. Where authorized by order of the Minnesota Supreme Court, documents may be filed electronically by following the procedures of such order and will be deemed filed in accordance with the provisions of that order.

(b) Search warrants and related documents need not be filed until after execution of the search or the expiration of 10 days, unless this rule directs otherwise. If the search warrant is filed with the court when signed by the judge, the warrant must remain sealed until the expiration of 10 days or a longer period of time if so ordered by the court.

(c) The prosecutor may request that a complaint, indictment, application, arrest warrant, search warrant, supporting affidavits, and any order granting the request not be filed.

(d) An order must be issued granting the request in whole or in part if, from affidavits, sworn testimony, or other evidence, the court finds reasonable grounds exist to believe that: (1) in the case of complaint, indictment, or arrest documents, filing may cause a potential arrestee to flee, hide, or otherwise prevent the execution of the warrant; or, (2) in the case of a search warrant application or affidavit, filing may cause the search or a related search to be unsuccessful, create a substantial risk of injury to an innocent person, or severely hamper an ongoing investigation.

(e) The order must further direct that on execution and return of an arrest warrant, the filing required by paragraph (a) must be complied with immediately. For a search warrant, following the commencement of any criminal proceeding utilizing evidence obtained in or as a result of the search, the supporting application or affidavit must be filed either immediately or at any other time as the court directs. Until such filing, the documents and materials ordered withheld from filing must be retained by the judge or the judge's designee.

Adopted Feb. 26, 1975, eff. July 1, 1975. Revised Dec. 13, 1989. Amended Oct. 27, 2009, eff. Jan. 1, 2010; June 22, 2011, eff. Sept. 1, 2011; July 26, 2012, eff. Sept. 1, 2012.

Comment—Rule 33

See comment following Rule 33.05.

Historical Notes

The order of the Minnesota Supreme Court [C1–84–2137] dated December 13, 1989, provides in part that "(t)hese amended Rules of Criminal Procedure shall govern all criminal actions commenced or arrests made after 12 o'clock midnight January 1, 1990, except amendments to 8.04, 11.07, and 19.04, subd. 5, shall govern all criminal actions commenced or arrests made after 12 o'clock midnight January 1, 1991."

The order of the Minnesota Supreme Court [ADM10–8049] dated June 22, 2011, provided in part that "The amendments shall govern all criminal actions currently pending on or commenced on or after the effective date."

The order of the Minnesota Supreme Court [ADM10–8049] dated July 26, 2012, provides in part that "(t)he attached amendments to the Rules of Criminal Procedure be, and the same are, prescribed and promulgated to be effective September 1, 2012," and further provides "(t)hese amendments shall apply to all actions or proceedings pending or commenced on or after the effective date."

Rule 33.05. Facsimile and Electronic Transmission

Complaints, orders, summons, warrants, and supporting documents—including orders and warrants authorizing the interception of communications under Minnesota Statutes, Chapter 626A—may be sent via facsimile transmission. The transmission may be by other electronic means if authorized by order of the Minnesota Supreme Court and if provided in accordance with that order. Procedural and statutory requirements for the issuance of a warrant or order must be met, including the making of a record of the proceedings. A facsimile order or warrant issued by the court has the same force and effect as the original for procedural and statutory purposes. The original order or warrant, along with any supporting documents and affidavits, must be delivered to the court administrator of the county in which the request or application was made. The original of any facsimile transmissions received by the court under this rule must be promptly filed.

Adopted Dec. 13, 1989. Amended May 9, 1994; May 19, 2008, eff. July 1, 2008; Oct. 27, 2009, eff. Jan. 1, 2010; June 22, 2011, eff. Sept. 1, 2011; July 26, 2012, eff. Sept. 1, 2012.

Comment—Rule 33

Minn.R.Civ.P.5.02 provides the method for service in civil actions.

The amendments to Rule 33 provide for service and filing by electronic means, other than by facsimile as allowed by the existing rule, if authorized by an order of the Minnesota Supreme Court. This amendment is intended to facilitate a pilot project on electronic service and filing in certain pilot districts, but is designed to be a model for the implementation of electronic filing and service if the pilot project is made permanent and statewide.

Service by electronic means is allowed for documents served under Rule 33. Personal service or service by mail of documents such as summonses, subpoenas, and warrants is still required under the rules that govern those documents, and electronic service is therefore not an authorized means of service.

Historical Notes

The order of the Minnesota Supreme Court [C1–84–2137] dated December 13, 1989, provides in part that "(t)hese amended Rules of Criminal Procedure shall govern all criminal actions commenced or arrests made after 12 o'clock midnight January 1, 1990, except amendments to 8.04, 11.07, and 19.04, subd. 5, shall govern all criminal actions commenced or arrests made after 12 o'clock midnight January 1, 1991."

The order of the Minnesota Supreme Court [C1–84–2137] dated May 9, 1994, provides in part that "(t)hese amendments to the Rules of Criminal Procedure shall govern all criminal actions commenced or arrests made after 12 o'clock midnight July 1, 1994, except that the amendments in the first sentence of the third paragraph in Rule 2.01 shall govern all criminal actions commenced or arrests made after 12 o'clock midnight January 1, 1995."

The order of the Minnesota Supreme Court [ADM10–8049] dated June 22, 2011, provided in part that "The amendments shall govern all criminal actions currently pending on or commenced on or after the effective date."

The order of the Minnesota Supreme Court [ADM10–8049] dated July 26, 2012, provides in part that "(t)he attached amendments to the Rules of Criminal Procedure be, and the same are, prescribed and promulgated to be effective September 1, 2012," and further provides "(t)hese amendments shall apply to all actions or proceedings pending or commenced on or after the effective date."

RULE 34. TIME

Rule 34.01. Computation

Time must be computed as follows except as provided by Rules 3.02, subd. 2; 4.02, subd. 5(1); 4.02, subd. 5(3); and 4.03.

The day of the act or event from which the designated period of time begins to run must not be included. The last day of the period must be included, unless it is a Saturday, a Sunday, or a legal holiday, in which event the period runs until the end of the next day that is not a Saturday, a Sunday, or a legal holiday. When a period of time prescribed or allowed is 7 or fewer days, intermediate Saturdays, Sundays, and legal holidays must be excluded in the computation. As used in these rules, "legal holiday" includes any holiday defined or designated by statute, and any other day appointed as a holiday by the President or the Congress of the United States or by the State.

Adopted Feb. 26, 1975, eff. July 1, 1975. Revised Dec. 13, 1989. Amended Oct. 23, 1992; Dec. 23, 2002, eff. Feb. 1, 2003; Oct. 27, 2009, eff. Jan. 1, 2010.

Comment—Rule 34

See comment following Rule 34.05.

Historical Notes

The order of the Minnesota Supreme Court [C1–84–2137] dated December 13, 1989, provides in part that "(t)hese amended Rules of Criminal Procedure shall govern all criminal actions commenced or arrests made after 12 o'clock midnight January 1, 1990, except amendments to 8.04, 11.07, and 19.04, subd. 5, shall govern all criminal actions commenced or arrests made after 12 o'clock midnight January 1, 1991."

The order of the Minnesota Supreme Court [C1–84–2137] dated October 23, 1992, provides in part that "(t)here amendments to the Rules of Criminal Procedure shall govern all criminal actions commenced or arrests made after 12 o'clock midnight January 1, 1993."

Rule 34.02. Extension

When an act is required or allowed to be done within a specified time, the court may for cause:

(a) within the time allowed, extend the time, with or without motion or notice, if a party requests the extension before the original time, or the previously-extended time, expires;

(b) after the time allowed has expired, permit the act to be done, upon motion, if failure to act was the result of excusable neglect.

The court may not extend the time for taking any action under Rules 26.03, subd. 18(3); 26.04, subd. 1(3); or 26.04, subd. 3, or extend the time to appeal except as provided by Rules 28.02, subd. 4(3)(g); 29.03, subd. 3(f); and 29.04, subd. 2.

Adopted Feb. 26, 1975, eff. July 1, 1975. Revised Dec. 13, 1989. Amended Oct. 27, 2009, eff. Jan. 1, 2010.

Comment—Rule 34

See comment following Rule 34.05.

Historical Notes

The order of the Minnesota Supreme Court [C1–84–2137] dated December 13, 1989, provides in part that "(t)hese amended Rules of Criminal Procedure shall govern all criminal actions commenced or arrests made after 12 o'clock midnight January 1, 1990, except amendments to 8.04, 11.07, and 19.04, subd. 5, shall govern all criminal actions commenced or arrests made after 12 o'clock midnight January 1, 1991."

Rule 34.03. For Motions; Affidavits

A written notice of motion and motion, other than one that may be heard ex parte, must be served at least five days before the time specified for the hearing, unless a rule or court order fixes a different time. For cause, an order fixing a different time may be granted on ex parte application.

When a party supports a motion by affidavit, the affidavit must be served at least one day before the hearing, unless the court permits it to be served later.

Adopted Feb. 26, 1975, eff. July 1, 1975. Revised Dec. 13, 1989. Amended Oct. 27, 2009, eff. Jan. 1, 2010.

Comment—Rule 34

See comment following Rule 34.05.

Historical Notes

The order of the Minnesota Supreme Court [C1–84–2137] dated December 13, 1989, provides in part that "(t)hese amended Rules of Criminal Procedure shall govern all criminal actions commenced or arrests made after 12 o'clock midnight January 1, 1990, except amendments to 8.04, 11.07, and 19.04, subd. 5, shall govern all criminal actions commenced or arrests made after 12 o'clock midnight January 1, 1991."

Rule 34.04. Additional Time After Service by Mail

When a party is served with a notice or other paper by mail, three days must be added to the time the party has the right, or is required, to act.

Adopted Feb. 26, 1975, eff. July 1, 1975. Revised Dec. 13, 1989. Amended Oct. 27, 2009, eff. Jan. 1, 2010.

Comment—Rule 34

See comment following Rule 34.05.

Historical Notes

The order of the Minnesota Supreme Court [C1–84–2137] dated December 13, 1989, provides in part that "(t)hese amended Rules of Criminal Procedure shall govern all criminal actions commenced or arrests made after 12 o'clock midnight January 1, 1990, except amendments to 8.04, 11.07, and 19.04, subd. 5, shall govern all criminal actions commenced or arrests made after 12 o'clock midnight January 1, 1991."

Rule 34.05. Unaffected by Expiration

The expiration of a term of court does not affect the time-period for doing any act or taking any proceeding, or affect the court's power to do any act or take any proceeding in any pending action.

Adopted Feb. 26, 1975, eff. July 1, 1975. Revised Dec. 13, 1989. Amended Oct. 27, 2009, eff. Jan. 1, 2010.

Comment—Rule 34

Rule 34.01 (Computation) adopts Minn.R.Civ.P. 6.01 except that it excludes Saturdays, Sundays, and legal holidays from computation when the period of time allowed is "7 days or less" rather than "less than 7 days." Minnesota Statutes § 645.44, subd. 5, sets forth the legal holidays for the State of Minnesota.

In State v. Hugger, 640 N.W.2d 619 (Minn. 2002), the Supreme Court held that when calculating the five-day period within which an appeal must be taken under Rule 28.04, subd. 2(8), intermediate Saturdays, Sundays, and legal holidays must be excluded from the computation of the period allowed under Rule 34.01 before the additional three days by mail are added under Rule 34.04.

Historical Notes

The order of the Minnesota Supreme Court [C1–84–2137] dated December 13, 1989, provides in part that "(t)hese amended Rules of Criminal Procedure shall govern all criminal actions commenced or arrests made after 12 o'clock midnight January 1, 1990, except amendments to 8.04, 11.07, and 19.04, subd. 5, shall govern all criminal actions commenced or arrests made after 12 o'clock midnight January 1, 1991."

RULE 35. COURTS AND CLERKS

The district courts are deemed open at all times for the purpose of filing any proper paper, issuing and returning or certifying process, and making motions and orders. Unless otherwise ordered, the courts are deemed open at all times, except legal holidays, for the transaction of any other business that may be presented. The court administrator's office, with the court administrator or a deputy in attendance, must be open during business hours on all days except Saturdays, Sundays, or legal holidays.

Adopted Feb. 26, 1975, eff. July 1, 1975. Revised Dec. 13, 1989. Amended Oct. 27, 2009, eff. Jan. 1, 2010.

Comment—Rule 35

Legal holidays are defined by Minn. Stat. § 645.44, subd. 5. The rule supersedes Minn. Stat. §§ 484.07 and 484.08 to the extent inconsistent.

Historical Notes

The order of the Minnesota Supreme Court [C1–84–2137] dated December 13, 1989, provides in part that "(t)hese amended Rules of Criminal Procedure shall govern all criminal actions commenced or arrests made after 12 o'clock midnight January 1, 1990, except amendments to 8.04, 11.07, and 19.04, subd. 5, shall govern all criminal actions commenced or arrests made after 12 o'clock midnight January 1, 1991."

RULE 36. SEARCH WARRANTS ON ORAL TESTIMONY

Rule 36.01. General Rule

A request for a search warrant may be made, in whole or in part, on sworn oral testimony, to a judge, subject to the limitations in this rule. Oral testimony may be presented via telephone, radio, or other similar means of communication. Written submissions may be presented by facsimile transmission, or by other appropriate means.

Adopted May 9, 1994. Amended Oct. 27, 2009, eff. Jan. 1, 2010.

Comment—Rule 36

See comment following Rule 36.08.

Historical Notes

The order of the Minnesota Supreme Court [C1–84–2137] dated May 9, 1994, provides in part that "(t)hese amendments to the Rules of Criminal Procedure shall govern all criminal actions commenced or arrests made after 12 o'clock midnight July 1, 1994, except that the amendments in the first sentence of the third paragraph in Rule 2.01 shall govern all criminal actions commenced or arrests made after 12 o'clock midnight January 1, 1995."

Rule 36.02. When Request by Oral Testimony Appropriate

An oral request for a search warrant may only be made in circumstances that make it reasonable to dispense with a written affidavit. The judge must make this determination the initial focus of the oral warrant request.

Adopted May 9, 1994. Amended Oct. 27, 2009, eff. Jan. 1, 2010.

Comment—Rule 36

See comment following Rule 36.08.

Historical Notes

The order of the Minnesota Supreme Court [C1–84–2137] dated May 9, 1994, provides in part that "(t)hese amendments to the Rules of Criminal Procedure shall govern all criminal actions commenced or arrests made after 12 o'clock midnight July 1, 1994, except that the amendments in the first sentence of the third paragraph in Rule 2.01 shall govern all criminal actions commenced or arrests made after 12 o'clock midnight January 1, 1995."

Rule 36.03. Application

The person requesting the warrant must prepare a duplicate original warrant and must read the duplicate original warrant, verbatim, to the judge. The judge must prepare an original warrant by recording, verbatim, what has been read by the applicant. The judge may direct modifications, which must be included on the original and the duplicate original warrant.

Adopted May 9, 1994. Amended Oct. 27, 2009, eff. Jan. 1, 2010.

Comment—Rule 36

See comment following Rule 36.08.

Historical Notes

The order of the Minnesota Supreme Court [C1–84–2137] dated May 9, 1994, provides in part that "(t)hese amendments to the Rules of Criminal Procedure shall govern all criminal actions commenced or arrests made after 12 o'clock midnight July 1, 1994, except that the amendments in the first sentence of the third paragraph in Rule 2.01 shall govern all criminal actions commenced or arrests made after 12 o'clock midnight January 1, 1995."

Rule 36.04. Testimony Requirements

When the officer informs the judge that the purpose of the communication is to request a search warrant, the judge must:

(1) Immediately begin recording, electronically, stenographically, or longhand verbatim the testimony of all persons involved in making the warrant application. Alternatively, with the permission of the judge, the recording may be done by the applicant for the search warrant, but the tape or other medium used to make the record must be submitted to the issuing

judge as soon as practical, and no later than the time for filing in Rule 33. 04.

(2) Identify and place under oath each person whose testimony forms a basis of the application, and each person applying for the warrant.

(3) As soon as is practical after receiving the testimony, the judge must direct that the record of the oral warrant request be transcribed. The judge must certify the accuracy of the transcription. If a longhand verbatim record is made, the judge must sign it.

Adopted May 9, 1994. Amended Oct. 27, 2009, eff. Jan. 1, 2010.

Comment—Rule 36

See comment following Rule 36.08.

Historical Notes

The order of the Minnesota Supreme Court [C1–84–2137] dated May 9, 1994, provides in part that "(t)hese amendments to the Rules of Criminal Procedure shall govern all criminal actions commenced or arrests made after 12 o'clock midnight July 1, 1994, except that the amendments in the first sentence of the third paragraph in Rule 2.01 shall govern all criminal actions commenced or arrests made after 12 o'clock midnight January 1, 1995."

Rule 36.05. Issuance of Warrant

The judge must order issuance of a warrant if:

(a) the circumstances make it reasonable to dispense with a written affidavit;

(b) the warrant request conforms with the law; and

(c) probable cause exists for issuance of the warrant.

The judge must order the issuance of a warrant by directing the applicant to sign the judge's name on the duplicate original warrant. The judge must immediately sign the original warrant and enter on the face of the original warrant the exact time the judge signed the warrant. The finding of probable cause may be based on the same kind of evidence as is sufficient for a warrant upon affidavit.

Adopted May 9, 1994. Amended Oct. 27, 2009, eff. Jan. 1, 2010.

Comment—Rule 36

See comment following Rule 36.08.

Historical Notes

The order of the Minnesota Supreme Court [C1–84–2137] dated May 9, 1994, provides in part that "(t)hese amendments to the Rules of Criminal Procedure shall govern all criminal actions commenced or arrests made after 12 o'clock midnight July 1, 1994, except that the amendments in the first sentence of the third paragraph in Rule 2.01 shall govern all criminal actions commenced or arrests made after 12 o'clock midnight January 1, 1995."

Rule 36.06. Filing

The original warrant, the duplicate original warrant, the certified transcript of the oral application for the warrant, any longhand verbatim record, and any related documents must be filed as Rule 33.04 requires. If the oral warrant request is recorded on tape or other electronic recording device, the original tape or other medium must also be filed with the court.

Adopted May 9, 1994. Amended Oct. 27, 2009, eff. Jan. 1, 2010.

Comment—Rule 36

See comment following Rule 36.08.

Historical Notes

The order of the Minnesota Supreme Court [C1–84–2137] dated May 9, 1994, provides in part that "(t)hese amendments to the Rules of Criminal Procedure shall govern all criminal actions commenced or arrests made after 12 o'clock midnight July 1, 1994, except that the amendments in the first sentence of the third paragraph in Rule 2.01 shall govern all criminal actions commenced or arrests made after 12 o'clock midnight January 1, 1995."

Rule 36.07. Contents of Warrant

The contents of a warrant issued on oral testimony must be the same as the contents of a warrant on affidavit.

Adopted May 9, 1994. Amended Oct. 27, 2009, eff. Jan. 1, 2010.

Comment—Rule 36

See comment following Rule 36.08.

Historical Notes

The order of the Minnesota Supreme Court [C1–84–2137] dated May 9, 1994, provides in part that "(t)hese amendments to the Rules of Criminal Procedure shall govern all criminal actions commenced or arrests made after 12 o'clock midnight July 1, 1994, except that the amendments in the first sentence of the third paragraph in Rule 2.01 shall govern all criminal actions commenced or arrests made after 12 o'clock midnight January 1, 1995."

Rule 36.08. Execution

The execution of a warrant obtained through oral testimony is subject to the same laws and principles that govern execution of any other search warrant. In addition, the person who executes the warrant must enter the exact time of execution on the face of the duplicate original warrant.

Adopted May 9, 1994. Amended Oct. 27, 2009, eff. Jan. 1, 2010.

Comment—Rule 36

The procedure found in Rule 36 is derived from State v. Lindsey, 473 N.W.2d 857 (Minn. 1993).

Minn. Stat. § 626.16, which requires that a written document be prepared for presentation to the person whose premises or property is searched, or that can be left on the premises if no persons are present, mandates the preparation of the duplicate warrant in Rule 36.03. Judges and judicial officers who may receive oral warrant requests at home are advised to have appropriate forms available for preparation of the original warrant.

Judges are cautioned to avoid engaging in any preliminary unrecorded and unsworn conversation with the officer or prosecutor. See ABA Guidelines for the Issuance of Search Warrants, Guideline 11(3) (1990).

The officer and the judge must keep in mind that in addition to the special requirements for issuance of an oral warrant, all other requirements for the issuance of a warrant must also be met, including the basis for a no-knock and nighttime warrant. See Minn. Stat. §§ 626.01–.18; 629.30.

Rules 36.07 and 36.08 emphasize that the use of the oral warrant process does not justify any other departures from traditional warrant law and practice.

Historical Notes

The order of the Minnesota Supreme Court [C1–84–2137] dated May 9, 1994, provides in part that "(t)hese amendments to the Rules of Criminal Procedure shall govern all criminal actions commenced or arrests made after 12 o'clock midnight July 1, 1994, except that the amendments in the first sentence of the third paragraph in Rule 2.01 shall govern all criminal actions commenced or arrests made after 12 o'clock midnight January 1, 1995."

CRIMINAL FORMS

INTRODUCTORY STATEMENT

The following forms are limited in number. No attempt is made to furnish a complete manual of forms. For all complaints charging a misdemeanor offense the prosecuting attorney, judge, judicial officer or clerk of court authorized to issue process shall use the appropriate form as set forth in the following criminal forms or a form substantially in compliance with these forms. The other forms provided herein are not mandatory, but shall be accepted by the court if offered by any party or counsel for their designated purpose.

Comment

The Final Report of the Minnesota Supreme Court Task Force on Racial Bias in the Judicial System (1993) recommends that all judicial forms and documents be drafted in easily translatable English, and be translated by approved legal translators into such additional languages as the State Court Administrator approves. It is recommended that any criminal forms that are translated consist of both English and the additional language.

FORM 1. COMPLAINT—SUMMONS FOR MISDEMEANOR OR PETTY MISDEMEANOR [Deleted May 19, 2008, eff. July 1, 2008]

FORM 2. COMPLAINT—WARRANT FOR MISDEMEANOR [Deleted May 19, 2008, eff. July 1, 2008]

FORM 3. COMPLAINT—ORDER OF DETENTION FOR MISDEMEANOR [Deleted May 19, 2008, eff. July 1, 2008]

FORM 4. CITATION FOR MISDEMEANOR OR PETTY MISDEMEANOR [Deleted June 5, 2012, eff. August 1, 2012]

FORM 4A. GROSS MISDEMEANOR CHARGING BY TAB CHARGE

STATE OF MINNESOTA — DISTRICT COURT
COUNTY OF ______ — ______ JUDICIAL DISTRICT

State of Minnesota,

______
Plaintiff,

vs.

TAB CHARGE PURSUANT TO MINN. R. CRIM. P. 4.02, SUBD. 5(3)

______
Defendant.

To: ______ County District Court and ______ County Jail
From: Arresting Officer: (Please Print) ______ Badge Number: ______

Pursuant to Minnesota Rules of Criminal Procedure 4.02, subd. 5(3), the above-named officer hereby requests that the named defendant be processed for the designated Gross Misdemeanor (GM) indicated below and as defined by Minnesota Rules of Criminal Procedure 1.04 (b).

Defendant Name: ______ **DOB:** __/__/__
Driver's License No. ______ **State:** ______ **Date of Offense:** __/__/__
City of Occurrence: ______ **Controlling Agency:** MN-______
Control Number/ICR: ______ **Court File No. (Provided by Court/Jail):** ______

(Check Boxes)

Designated GM Offense	**Charge**	**Penalty (must check one)** 2nd Degree (E)	3rd Degree (F)	**MOC** Circle E or F
☐ UI Alcohol	169A.20, 1(1)	☐ 169A.25	☐ 169A.26	J__501 E F
☐ UI Controlled Substance	169A.20, 1(2)	☐ 169A.25	☐ 169A.26	J__601 E F
☐ UI Hazardous Substance	169A.20, 1(3)	☐ 169A.25	☐ 169A.26	J__H01 E F
☐ UI Combination	169A.20, 1(4)	☐ 169A.25	☐ 169A.26	J__G01 E F
☐ Alcohol .08 or More Within 2 Hours of Driving	169A.20, 1(5)	☐ 169A.25	☐ 169A.26	J__W01 E F
☐ Alcohol .04 or More Within 2 Hours of Driving – Commercial Vehicle	169A.20, 1(6)	☐ 169A.25	☐ 169A.26	J__K01 E F
☐ Schedule I or II Controlled Substance	169A.20, 1(7)	☐ 169A.25	☐ 169A.26	J__S01 E F
☐ Refusal to Submit To Test	169A.20, 2	☐ 169A.25	☐ 169A.26	J__R01 E F

☐ Other (specify): ______

Court Status: (Check One)
☐ Defendant incarcerated in ______ County Jail to be held in custody pending court appearance.
☐ Defendant released on his/her own recognizance and assigned the following court date.
Date: __/__/__ Time: ______
Location: ______ County Courthouse
Address: ______

Bail/Bond Status: (Check One) Date: __/__/__
☐ Maximum $12,000 bail under Minn. Stat. § 629.471 or conditional release under Minn. Stat. § 169A.44.
☐ Bail was posted in the amount of $______
☐ Bond was posted in the amount of $______
☐ No bail/bond was required.

Dated: __/__/__

______
Officer's signature

______
Officer's Name and Badge Number (if different from arresting officer)

Adopted Sept. 29, 2000. Amended Dec. 28, 2005, eff. March 1, 2006.

Historical Notes

The order of the Minnesota Supreme Court [C1–84–2137] dated December 28, 2005, provides in part that "(t)he attached amendments shall govern all criminal actions commenced or arrests made after 12 o'clock midnight March 1, 2006."

FORM 5. CITATION FOR FELONY OR GROSS MISDEMEANOR

[Deleted June 5, 2012, eff. August 1, 2012]

FORM 6. COMPLAINT—FOR MISDEMEANOR OR PETTY MISDEMEANOR

[Deleted May 19, 2008, eff. July 1, 2008]

FORM 7. APPLICATION AND SUMMONS FOR OBTAINING DEFENDANT'S APPEARANCE IN COURT FOR FAILURE TO APPEAR IN RESPONSE TO SUMMONS OR CITATION

STATE OF MINNESOTA DISTRICT COURT
COUNTY OF ____ ____ JUDICIAL DISTRICT

_______________,) APPLICATION AND
Plaintiff,) SUMMONS FOR OBTAIN-
) ING DEFENDANT'S
) APPEARANCE IN COURT
vs.) FOR FAILURE TO
) APPEAR IN RESPONSE
) TO SUMMONS OR
_______________,) CITATION
Defendant.) District Court File No. _____

APPLICATION FOR OBTAINING DEFENDANT'S APPEARANCE IN COURT

As the above-named Defendant has failed to appear in Court as instructed by the Complaint—Summons served upon the Defendant or Citation issued to the Defendant by __________ on the ____ day of ____________________, 19___, I therefore request that Defendant be summoned to appear in Court and otherwise be dealt with according to law.

Dated: ______ ____________________
(Prosecuting Attorney)
Name:
Attorney License No.:
Title:
Address:
Telephone No.:

SUMMONS

TO: The above-named Defendant.

AS PROBABLE CAUSE has previously been established by the Complaint—Summons or Complaint Following Citation dated and filed on the ____ day of ________, 19___, charging the Defendant with the offense of ______ and as you failed to appear in Court as instructed in the Complaint—Summons or Citation.

YOU ARE HEREBY SUMMONED to appear on the ___ day of _______, 19___, at ___ o'clock ___.m., before the above-named Court at ____________, (Room No.)
____________, ____________, for failing to appear
(Place) (Address)
in Court as instructed in the Complaint—Summons or Citation previously issued to you.

IF YOU FAIL TO APPEAR in response to this Summons, a warrant for your arrest may be issued.

____
Issuing Officer*

* The name and title of the Issuing Officer should be printed or stamped following the Issuing Officer's signature.

Adopted Dec. 13, 1989.

Historical Note

The order of the Minnesota Supreme Court [C1–84–2137] dated December 13, 1989, provides in part that "(t)hese amended Rules of Criminal Procedure shall govern all criminal actions commenced or arrests made after 12 o'clock midnight January 1, 1990, except amendments to 8.04, 11.07, and 19.04, subd. 5, shall govern all criminal actions commenced or arrests made after 12 o'clock midnight January 1, 1991."

FORM 8. APPLICATION AND WARRANT FOR OBTAINING DEFENDANT'S APPEARANCE IN COURT FOR FAILURE TO APPEAR IN RESPONSE TO SUMMONS OR CITATION

STATE OF MINNESOTA DISTRICT COURT
COUNTY OF ____ ____ JUDICIAL DISTRICT

_______________,) APPLICATION AND
Plaintiff,) SUMMONS FOR OBTAIN-
) ING DEFENDANT'S
) APPEARANCE IN COURT
vs.) FOR FAILURE TO
) APPEAR IN RESPONSE
) TO SUMMONS OR
_______________,) CITATION
Defendant.) District Court File No. _____

APPLICATION FOR WARRANT

The above-named Defendant has failed to appear in Court as instructed in the Complaint—Summons served upon the Defendant or the Citation issued to the Defendant by __________ on the ____ day of __________, 19___; I therefore request that a Warrant of Arrest issue for the Defendant, so that the Defendant may be arrested to obtain the Defendant's appearance in Court and that the Defendant otherwise be dealt with according to law.

Dated: ______ ____________________
(Prosecuting Attorney)
Name:
Attorney License No.:
Title:
Address:
Telephone No.:

WARRANT

TO: The Sheriff of the above-named County or any other person authorized by law to execute this Warrant.

AS PROBABLE CAUSE has previously been established by the Complaint—Summons or Complaint following Citation dated and filed on the ____________ day of ________, 19___, charging the

Defendant with the offense of __________, and as the Defendant has failed to appear in Court as instructed in the Complaint—Summons or Citation; in the name of the State of Minnesota, I hereby order that the above-named Defendant be arrested and brought promptly before the above-named Court (if in session, and if not before a Judge or Judicial Officer of such Court without unnecessary delay, and in any event, not later than 36 hours after the arrest or as soon thereafter as such Judge or Judicial Officer is available) to be dealt with according to law.

Conditions of Release:

Amount of Bail: __________

Dated: ______ ____________________
Issuing Officer *

* The name and title of the Issuing Officer should be printed or stamped following the Issuing Officer's signature.

Adopted Dec. 13, 1989.

Historical Note

The order of the Minnesota Supreme Court [C1–84–2137] dated December 13, 1989, provides in part that "(t)hese amended Rules of Criminal Procedure shall govern all criminal actions commenced or arrests made after 12 o'clock midnight January 1, 1990, except amendments to 8.04, 11.07, and 19.04, subd. 5, shall govern all criminal actions commenced or arrests made after 12 o'clock midnight January 1, 1991."

FORM 9. APPLICATION AND SUMMONS FOR OBTAINING DEFENDANT'S APPEARANCE FOR VIOLATION OF CONDITIONS OF RELEASE, PURSUANT TO RULE 6.03, SUBD. 1

STATE OF MINNESOTA DISTRICT COURT
COUNTY OF _____ _____ JUDICIAL DISTRICT

________________, Plaintiff,
vs.
________________, Defendant.

) APPLICATION AND SUMMONS FOR OBTAINING DEFENDANT'S APPEARANCE FOR VIOLATION OF CONDITIONS OF RELEASE, PURSUANT TO RULE 6.03, SUBD. 1
) District Court File No. _____

APPLICATION FOR OBTAINING DEFENDANT'S APPEARANCE

The following facts constitute PROBABLE CAUSE to believe that the above-named Defendant has violated conditions of release:

THEREFORE, I request, that pursuant to Rule 6.03, subd. 1, Minnesota Rules of Criminal Procedure, that Defendant be summoned to appear and be otherwise dealt with according to law.

Dated: ______ ____________________
(Prosecuting Attorney)
Name:
Attorney License No.:
Title:
Address:
Telephone No.:

SUMMONS

TO: The above-named Defendant.

YOU ARE HEREBY SUMMONED to appear on the ___ day of _____, 19___, at ___ o'clock ___.m., before the above-named Court at __________ (Room No.), __________ (Place), __________ (Address), pursuant to Rule 6.03, Subd. 1, Minnesota Rules of Criminal Procedure, to determine if you have violated your conditions of release.

IF YOU FAIL TO APPEAR in response to this Summons, a warrant for your arrest may be issued.

____
Issuing Officer *

* The name and title of the Issuing Officer should be printed or stamped following the Issuing Officer's signature.

Adopted Dec. 13, 1989.

Historical Note

The order of the Minnesota Supreme Court [C1–84–2137] dated December 13, 1989, provides in part that "(t)hese amended Rules of Criminal Procedure shall govern all criminal actions commenced or arrests made after 12 o'clock midnight January 1, 1990, except amendments to 8.04, 11.07, and 19.04, subd. 5, shall govern all criminal actions commenced or arrests made after 12 o'clock midnight January 1, 1991."

FORM 10. APPLICATION AND WARRANT FOR OBTAINING DEFENDANT'S APPEARANCE FOR VIOLATION OF CONDITIONS OF RELEASE, PURSUANT TO RULE 6.03, SUBD. 1

STATE OF MINNESOTA DISTRICT COURT
COUNTY OF _____ _____ JUDICIAL DISTRICT

________________, Plaintiff,
vs.
________________, Defendant.

) APPLICATION AND WARRANT FOR OBTAINING DEFENDANT'S APPEARANCE FOR VIOLATION OF CONDITIONS OF RELEASE, PURSUANT TO RULE 6.03, SUBD. 1
) District Court File No. _____

APPLICATION FOR WARRANT

The following facts constitute PROBABLE CAUSE to believe that the above-named Defendant has violated conditions of release:

THEREFORE, I request that pursuant to Rule 6.03, subd. 1, Minnesota Rules of Criminal Procedure, a Warrant of Arrest issue for the above-named Defendant so that the Defendant may be arrested to obtain the Defendant's appearance, and that the Defendant otherwise be dealt with according to law.

Dated: ______ ____________________
(Prosecuting Attorney)
Name:
Attorney License No.:
Address:
Telephone No.:

WARRANT

(To be issued only if it reasonably appears that there is a substantial likelihood that the Defendant will fail to respond to a Summons or when the whereabouts of the Defendant is unknown.)

TO: The Sheriff of the above-named County or any other person authorized by law to execute this Warrant.

Upon the above Application by the Prosecuting Attorney and pursuant to Rule 6.03, subd. 1, Minnesota Rules of Criminal Procedure, in the name of the State of Minnesota, I hereby order that the above-named Defendant, having previously been released, be arrested and taken immediately before the Judge, Judicial Officer or Court which released the Defendant.

TO BE COMPLETED AND SIGNED BY ISSUING OFFICER IF APPLICABLE.

As the offense stated is a misdemeanor and as the following exigent circumstances exist:

I hereby direct that this warrant may be executed at any time of the day or night and on Sundays.

Conditions of Release:

Amount of Bail: ______________

Dated: ______ ______________________
Issuing Officer *

* The name and title of the Issuing Officer should be printed or stamped following the Issuing Officer's signature.

Adopted Dec. 13, 1989.

Historical Note

The order of the Minnesota Supreme Court [C1–84–2137] dated December 13, 1989, provides in part that "(t)hese amended Rules of Criminal Procedure shall govern all criminal actions commenced or arrests made after 12 o'clock midnight January 1, 1990, except amendments to 8.04, 11.07, and 19.04, subd. 5, shall govern all criminal actions commenced or arrests made after 12 o'clock midnight January 1, 1991."

FORM 11. PETITION TO PROCEED AS PRO SE COUNSEL

STATE OF MINNESOTA DISTRICT COURT

COUNTY OF JUDICIAL DISTRICT

____

State of Minnesota,

Plaintiff, PETITION TO PROCEED AS PRO SE COUNSEL

vs.

District Court File No. ______

____

Defendant.

TO: THE ABOVE-NAMED COURT

I, ______________ defendant in the above-entitled action, request the Court to allow me to represent myself, and do respectfully represent and state as follows:

1. My full name is ______________ I am __________ years old. My date of birth is __________. The last grade that I went through in __________ school is __________.

2. I have received and read the (complaint)(indictment).

3. I understand the charge(s) made against me.

4. Specifically, I understand that I have been charged with the crime(s) of ______________ alleged to have occurred on or about ______________, ___, in ______________, County, Minnesota.

5. I have discussed my desire to represent myself with an attorney whose name is ______________

6. I (have)(have never) been a patient in a mental hospital.

7. I (have)(have not) talked with or been treated by a psychiatrist or other person for a nervous or mental condition.

8. I (have)(have not) been ill recently.

9. I (have)(have not) recently been taking pills or medicine.

10. I understand that I have an absolute right to have an attorney represent me in these proceedings. I understand that if the Court grants my petition to represent myself, I will be responsible for preparing my case for trial and trying my case. I understand that I will be bound by the same rules as an attorney. I understand that if I fail to do something in a timely manner, or make a mistake because of my unfamiliarity with the law, I will be bound by those decisions and must deal with them myself.

11. That in making any decisions regarding the conduct of this case, I have the right to consult with advisory counsel assigned to this case.

12. I understand the Court will schedule a probable cause hearing, if one has not already been held. At the probable cause hearing, I can make a motion that the complaint or indictment filed against me be dismissed for lack of probable cause. That the preparation for, conduct of, and decisions made relating to that hearing will be my sole responsibility.

13. I understand that:

a. the prosecution for their case against me has:

i. physical evidence obtained as a result of searching for and seizing evidence.

ii. evidence in the form of statements, oral or written, that I made to the police or others regarding the charges;

iii. evidence discovered as a result of my statements or as a result of the evidence seized in a search.

iv. identification evidence from a line-up or photographic identification.

v. evidence the prosecution believes indicates that I committed one or more other crimes.

b. That I have the right to a pretrial hearing before a judge to determine whether or not the evidence the prosecution has could be used against me at trial in this case.

c. That I can testify at the hearing if I want to, but my testimony could not be used as substantive evidence against me if I went to trial and could only be used against me if I was charged with the crime of perjury. (Perjury means testifying falsely.)

d. That the preparation for, conduct of, and decisions made relating to that hearing will be my sole responsibility.

14. I understand that I am entitled to a trial by jury of 12 persons in a felony case and a jury of 6 persons in other cases and all jurors must agree before they can find me guilty. Also, all jurors must agree before they can find me not guilty. I also understand that I may ask for a trial to the judge and not a jury. I further understand that I will conduct all phases of the trial including, but not limited to: writing and filing motions, making arguments to the Court, selection of the jury, cross-examination of the witnesses for the prosecution, direct examination of my witnesses, making all objections, opening statement and closing argument.

15. I understand that I am entitled to require any witnesses that I think are favorable to me to appear and testify at my trial by use of a subpoena.

16. I understand:

a. That a person who has prior convictions or a prior conviction can be given a longer prison term.

b. That the maximum statutory penalty that the Court could impose for this crime (taking into consideration any prior conviction or convictions) is imprisonment for __________ years, and/or a fine of $__________. That if a minimum sentence is required by statute the Court may impose a sentence of imprisonment of not less than ______ months for this crime.

17. I understand that if I am eligible for the services of the public defender, the Court will appoint the Office of the __________ Public Defender. However, I am under no obligation to seek advice from advisory counsel. I understand that the role of advisory counsel is limited. I understand that:

a. Advisory counsel will be physically present in the courtroom during all proceedings in my case.

b. Advisory counsel will respond to request for advice from me. Advisory counsel will not initiate such discussions.

c. The support staff of the public defender - investigators, secretaries, law clerks, and legal service advisors will not be available to me.

d. If need investigative services, expert services, waivers of fees, research, secretarial services, or any other assistance, I must petition the Court for whatever relief or assistance I deem appropriate. Such request is pursuant to Minnesota Statute § 611.21.

e. If I am out of custody and desire to conduct legal research, I will be expected to do it myself at the library.

f. Advisory counsel will not be prepared to try my case on the trial date unless ordered to be prepared to do so by the court.

g. Advisory counsel will be present for all Court appearances to consult with me if I request. Advisory counsel will be seated either at the back of the courtroom or at counsel table, based on my wishes and the Court's wishes. In an effort to vindicate my constitutional right to self-representation, advisory counsel will not initiate motions, objections, arguments to the Court, or any other aspect of representation unless I have given prior approval to the specific aspect of representation.

h. If I wish to give up my right to represent myself, I know that the Court will not automatically grant my request. The Court will consider the following in either granting or denying that request: the stage of the proceedings, whether advisory counsel is prepared to take over, the length of the continuance necessary for the advisory counsel to assume representation, the prejudice to either party, whether the jury has been sworn, and any other relevant considerations.

i. If the Court grants my request to give up the right to represent myself and substitute advisory counsel, the trial date may be continued if requested by the advisory counsel. The trial date will then be reset at a date mutually agreeable between counsel for the prosecution and counsel for the defendant.

j. In the unlikely event that the Court orders advisory counsel to represent me after the trial has started and jeopardy has attached, the Court may grant a mistrial if requested by my new attorney and reset the trial date at a date mutually agreeable between counsel.

18. That in view of the above, I wish to waive my right to be represented by an attorney and represent myself.

Dated this __________ day of __________, ____.

____
Petitioner

Adopted Dec. 13, 1989. Amended Aug. 21, 1998, eff. Jan. 1, 1999.

Historical Notes

The order of the Minnesota Supreme Court [C1–84–2137] dated December 13, 1989, provides in part that "(t)hese amended Rules of Criminal Procedure shall govern all criminal actions commenced or arrests made after 12 o'clock midnight January 1, 1990, except amendments to 8.04, 11.07, and 19.04, subd. 5, shall govern all criminal actions commenced or arrests made after 12 o'clock midnight January 1, 1991."

FORM 12. DEMAND FOR TRIAL PURSUANT TO RULE 6.06 OR RULE 11.10

STATE OF MINNESOTA DISTRICT COURT
COUNTY OF ____ ____ JUDICIAL DISTRICT

______________,)
Plaintiff,) DEMAND FOR TRIAL
) PURSUANT TO RULE 6.06
vs.) OR RULE 11.10
)
______________,) District Court File No. ____
Defendant.)

I hereby demand that trial in the above-named case be commenced within sixty (60) days from the date of this demand or the entry of a plea of not guilty, whichever is later.

Dated: _____ __________________
Name:
Attorney License No.:
Title:
Address:
Telephone No.:

Adopted Dec. 13, 1989.

Historical Note

The order of the Minnesota Supreme Court [C1–84–2137] dated December 13, 1989, provides in part that "(t)hese amended Rules of Criminal Procedure shall govern all criminal actions commenced or arrests made after 12 o'clock midnight January 1, 1990, except amendments to 8.04, 11.07, and 19.04, subd. 5, shall govern all criminal actions commenced or arrests made after 12 o'clock midnight January 1, 1991."

FORM 13. NOTICE BY PROSECUTING ATTORNEY OF EVIDENCE AND IDENTIFICATION PROCEDURES, PURSUANT TO RULE 7.01

STATE OF MINNESOTA DISTRICT COURT
COUNTY OF ____ ____ JUDICIAL DISTRICT

______________,) NOTICE BY PROSECUT-
Plaintiff,) ING ATTORNEY OF
) EVIDENCE AND IDENTI-
vs.) FICATION PROCEDURES,
) PURSUANT TO RULE 7.01
______________,)
Defendant.) District Court File No. ____

TO: The above-named Defendant.

Pursuant to Rule 7.01, Minnesota Rules of Criminal Procedure, I hereby advise you that in the above-named case, the prosecution has:

______ Evidence against the defendant obtained as a result of a search, search and seizure, wiretapping, or any form of electronic or mechanical eavesdropping.

______ Confessions, admissions, or statements in the nature of confessions made by the defendant.

______ Evidence against the defendant discovered as the result of confessions, admissions, or statements in the nature of confessions made by the defendant.

______ Employed the following identification procedures during its investigation:

____ Lineups.
____ Other observations of the defendant.
____ The exhibition of photographs of the defendant or any other person.
____ Others ______________

(More specific information may be obtained by contacting the Prosecuting Attorney.)

Dated: _____ __________________
(Prosecuting Attorney)
Name:
Attorney License No.:
Title:
Address:
Telephone No.:

Adopted Dec. 13, 1989.

Historical Note

The order of the Minnesota Supreme Court [C1–84–2137] dated December 13, 1989, provides in part that "(t)hese amended Rules of Criminal Procedure shall govern all criminal actions commenced or arrests made after 12 o'clock midnight January 1, 1990, except amendments to 8.04, 11.07, and 19.04, subd. 5, shall govern all criminal actions commenced or arrests made after 12 o'clock midnight January 1, 1991."

FORM 14. NOTICE BY PROSECUTING ATTORNEY OF EVIDENCE OF ADDITIONAL OFFENSE(S) TO BE OFFERED AT TRIAL PURSUANT TO RULE 7.02

STATE OF MINNESOTA DISTRICT COURT
COUNTY OF ____ ____ JUDICIAL DISTRICT

______________,) NOTICE BY PROSECUT-
Plaintiff,) ING ATTORNEY OF EVI-
) DENCE OF ADDITIONAL
) OFFENSE(S) TO BE
vs.) OFFERED AT TRIAL
) PURSUANT TO RULE 7.02
)
______________,)
Defendant.) District Court File No. ____

TO: The above-named Defendant.

Pursuant to Rule 7.02, Minnesota Rules of Criminal Procedure, I hereby advise you that in the above-named case, the Prosecution may offer at trial, under any exception to the general exclusionary rule, evidence of the following additional offense(s):

1. That the above-named Defendant on the ____ day of ______, 19__, at ______________ in the (location) County of ____________, committed the following described

OFFENSE

Charge: ____________________, in violation of Section: ____________________:

(description)

2. That the above-named Defendant on the ____ day of ______, 19__, at ______________ in the (location) County of ____________, committed the following described

OFFENSE

Charge: ____________________, in violation of Section: ____________________:

(description)

3. That the above-named Defendant on the ____ day of ______, 19__, at ______________ in the (location) County of ____________, committed the following described

OFFENSE

(Further offenses should be set forth below using the above structure.)

TAKE NOTE: 1. Rule 7.02 states, "Such additional offenses shall be described with sufficient particularity to enable the defendant to prepare for trial."

2. This notice need not include offenses
(a) for which the Defendant has been previously prosecuted,
(b) that may be offered in rebuttal of the Defendant's character witnesses, or
(c) which are a part of the occurrence or episode out of which the offense charged against Defendant arose.

Dated: ______ ____________________
(Prosecuting Attorney)
Name:
Attorney License No.:
Title:
Address:
Telephone No.:

Adopted Dec. 13, 1989.

Historical Note

The order of the Minnesota Supreme Court [C1–84–2137] dated December 13, 1989, provides in part that "(t)hese amended Rules of Criminal Procedure shall govern all criminal actions commenced or arrests made after 12 o'clock midnight January 1, 1990, except amendments to 8.04, 11.07, and 19.04, subd. 5, shall govern all criminal actions commenced or arrests made after 12 o'clock midnight January 1, 1991."

FORM 15. DEMAND OR WAIVER OF MISDEMEANOR EVIDENTIARY HEARING PURSUANT TO RULES 5.04, SUBD. 4 AND 12.04

STATE OF MINNESOTA DISTRICT COURT
COUNTY OF ____ ____ JUDICIAL DISTRICT

____________, Plaintiff,) DEMAND OR WAIVER OF MISDEMEANOR EVIDENTIARY HEARING PURSUANT TO RULES 5.04, SUBD. 4 AND 12.04
____________, Defendant.) District Court File No. ____

The (Prosecuting Attorney) (Defendant) hereby (demands) (waives) an evidentiary hearing to determine in the above case the admissibility of evidence contained in the Notice by Prosecuting Attorney given pursuant to Rule 7.01, Minnesota Rules of Criminal Procedure.

Dated: ______ ____________________
Name:
Attorney License No.:
Title:
Address:
Telephone No.:

Adopted Dec. 13, 1989.

Historical Note

The order of the Minnesota Supreme Court [C1–84–2137] dated December 13, 1989, provides in part that "(t)hese amended Rules of Criminal Procedure shall govern all criminal actions commenced or arrests made after 12 o'clock midnight January 1, 1990, except amendments to 8.04, 11.07, and 19.04, subd. 5, shall govern all criminal actions commenced or arrests made after 12 o'clock midnight January 1, 1991."

FORM 16. NOTICE OF PROSECUTING ATTORNEY IN FELONY CASE THAT MATTER WILL BE PRESENTED TO GRAND JURY

STATE OF MINNESOTA DISTRICT COURT
COUNTY OF ____ ____ JUDICIAL DISTRICT

____________, Plaintiff,) NOTICE OF PROSECUTING ATTORNEY IN FELONY CASE THAT MATTER WILL BE PRESENTED TO GRAND JURY
____________, Defendant.) District Court File No. ____

Pursuant to Rule 8.01, Minnesota Rules of Criminal Procedure, the State advises the Court that the charge in the above entitled matter:

________ 1. is a homicide
________ 2. carries a penalty of life imprisonment
________ 3. is a homicide and carries a penalty of life imprisonment and will be presented to the Grand Jury on ____________ .
(date)

Dated: ______ ________________________
(Prosecuting Attorney)
Name:
Attorney License No.:
Title:
Address:
Telephone No.:

Adopted Dec. 13, 1989.

Historical Note

The order of the Minnesota Supreme Court [C1–84–2137] dated December 13, 1989, provides in part that "(t)hese amended Rules of Criminal Procedure shall govern all criminal actions commenced or arrests made after 12 o'clock midnight January 1, 1990, except amendments to 8.04, 11.07, and 19.04, subd. 5, shall govern all criminal actions commenced or arrests made after 12 o'clock midnight January 1, 1991."

FORM 17. MOTION TO EXTEND TIME OF OMNIBUS HEARING IN FELONY OR GROSS MISDEMEANOR CASE PURSUANT TO RULE 8.04(c)

STATE OF MINNESOTA DISTRICT COURT
COUNTY OF _____ _____ JUDICIAL DISTRICT

State of Minnesota,) MOTION TO EXTEND
Plaintiff,) TIME OF OMNIBUS
) HEARING IN FELONY OR
vs.) GROSS MISDEMEANOR
) CASE PURSUANT TO
______________,) RULE 8.04(c)
Defendant.) District Court File No. _____

Pursuant to Rule 8.04(c), Minnesota Rules of Criminal Procedure, the undersigned moves the Court to extend the time of the Omnibus Hearing in the above entitled matter to ____________. Said motion is based upon the following reasons:

Dated: ______ ________________________
Name:
Attorney License No.:
Title:
Address:
Telephone No.:

Adopted Dec. 13, 1989.

Historical Note

The order of the Minnesota Supreme Court [C1–84–2137] dated December 13, 1989, provides in part that "(t)hese amended Rules of Criminal Procedure shall govern all criminal actions commenced or arrests made after 12 o'clock midnight January 1, 1990, except amendments to 8.04, 11.07, and 19.04, subd. 5, shall govern all criminal actions commenced or arrests made after 12 o'clock midnight January 1, 1991."

FORM 18. NOTICE OF DEFENSE(S) AND DEFENSE WITNESSES FOR FELONY OR GROSS MISDEMEANOR CASES PURSUANT TO RULE 9.02, SUBD. 1(3)(a)

STATE OF MINNESOTA DISTRICT COURT
COUNTY OF _____ _____ JUDICIAL DISTRICT

______________,) NOTICE OF DEFENSE(S)
Plaintiff,) AND DEFENSE WITNESSES FOR FELONY OR
vs.) GROSS MISDEMEANOR
) CASES PURSUANT TO
______________,) RULE 9.02, SUBD. 1(3)(a)
Defendant.) District Court File No. _____

TO: The Prosecuting Attorney in the above-named case:

I hereby inform you, pursuant to Rule 9.02, subd. 1(3)(a), Minnesota Rules of Criminal Procedure, that in the above-named case, the Defendant intends to rely upon the following defense(s) at trial:

_____ Self–Defense
_____ Mental Illness or Deficiency
_____ Duress
_____ Alibi; following is the specific place or places where the Defendant contends he was when the alleged offense occurred:
_____ Double Jeopardy
_____ Statute of Limitations
_____ Collateral Estoppel
_____ Defense under Minnesota Statutes Section 609.035
_____ Intoxication
_____ Entrapment
Defendant on this issue elects trial by
_____ jury
_____ the Court at the Omnibus Hearing.

(NOTE: If this issue is submitted to the Court, defendant must waive jury trial on the issue. See Form Number 34 for the waiver.)

The following facts form the basis for the defense:

_____ Others (specify):

The following are the names and addresses of persons whom the Defendant intends to call as Witnesses at trial (specify if an alibi witness):

Dated: ______ ________________________
(Attorney for Defendant)
Name:
Attorney License No.:
Title:
Address:
Telephone No.:

Adopted Dec. 13, 1989.

Historical Note

The order of the Minnesota Supreme Court [C1-84-2137] dated December 13, 1989, provides in part that "(t)hese amended Rules of Criminal Procedure shall govern all criminal actions commenced or arrests made after 12 o'clock midnight January 1, 1990, except amendments to 8.04, 11.07, and 19.04, subd. 5, shall govern all criminal actions commenced or arrests made after 12 o'clock midnight January 1, 1991."

FORM 19. MOTION BY PROSECUTING ATTORNEY FOR DISCOVERY BY ORDER OF THE COURT IN FELONY OR GROSS MISDEMEANOR CASE

STATE OF MINNESOTA DISTRICT COURT
COUNTY OF ____ ____ JUDICIAL DISTRICT

________________,) MOTION BY PROSECUT-
Plaintiff,) ING ATTORNEY FOR
) DISCOVERY BY ORDER
vs.) OF THE COURT IN
) FELONY OR GROSS
________________,) MISDEMEANOR CASE
Defendant.) District Court File No. ____

Pursuant to Rule 9.02, subd. 2(1), Minnesota Rules of Criminal Procedure, the State informs the Court that one or more of the discovery procedure(s) marked below will be of material aid in determining whether the Defendant in the above entitled matter committed the offense charged, and moves this Court to order the Defendant to:

____ (a) Appear in a lineup;
____ (b) Speak for identification by witnesses to the offense or for the purpose of taking voice prints;
____ (c) Be fingerprinted or permit palm prints or footprints to be taken;
____ (d) Permit measurements of the Defendant's body to be taken;
____ (e) Pose for photographs not involving reenactment of a scene;
____ (f) Permit the taking of samples of the Defendant's (blood) (hair) (saliva) (urine) (other) ____;
____ (g) Provide specimens of the Defendant's handwriting;
____ (h) Submit to reasonable physical or medical inspection.

The discovery procedure(s) marked above will be of material aid in this case for the following reasons:

The following facts constitute probable cause to believe that a blood test will aid in establishing the guilt of the Defendant:

The state further moves that the Defendant be ordered to appear on ________________ (time) at ________________ (place) and submit to the aforementioned discovery procedure(s).

Dated: ______ ________________
(Prosecuting Attorney)
Name:
Attorney License No.:
Title:
Address:
Telephone No.:

Adopted Dec. 13, 1989.

Historical Note

The order of the Minnesota Supreme Court [C1-84-2137] dated December 13, 1989, provides in part that "(t)hese amended Rules of Criminal Procedure shall govern all criminal actions commenced or arrests made after 12 o'clock midnight January 1, 1990, except amendments to 8.04, 11.07, and 19.04, subd. 5, shall govern all criminal actions commenced or arrests made after 12 o'clock midnight January 1, 1991."

FORM 20. FINDINGS AND ORDER FOR DISCOVERY IN FELONY OR GROSS MISDEMEANOR CASE

STATE OF MINNESOTA DISTRICT COURT
COUNTY OF ____ ____ JUDICIAL DISTRICT

________________,) FINDINGS AND ORDER
Plaintiff,) FOR DISCOVERY
) IN FELONY OR GROSS
vs.) MISDEMEANOR CASE
)
________________,) District Court File No. ____
Defendant.)

Pursuant to Rule 9.02, subd. 2(1), Minnesota Rules of Criminal Procedure, the Court finds that the discovery procedure(s) marked below will be of material aid in determining whether the defendant in the above entitled matter committed the offense charged, and hereby orders the defendant to:

____ (a) Appear in a lineup;
____ (b) Speak for identification by witnesses to the offense or for the purpose of taking voice prints;
____ (c) Be fingerprinted or permit palm prints or footprints to be taken;
____ (d) Permit measurements of the Defendant's body to be taken;
____ (e) Pose for photographs not involving reenactment of a scene;
____ (f) Permit the taking of samples of the Defendant's (blood) (hair) (saliva) (urine) (other)____;

(The Court finds that there is probable cause to believe that a blood test will aid in establishing the guilt of the defendant.)

_____ (g) Provide specimens of the Defendant's handwriting;

_____ (h) Submit to reasonable physical or medical inspection.

The defendant is therefore ordered to appear at the time and place indicated below and submit to the aforementioned discovery procedure(s):

Dated: _____ ______________________

Judge of District Court

Adopted Dec. 13, 1989.

Historical Note

The order of the Minnesota Supreme Court [C1–84–2137] dated December 13, 1989, provides in part that "(t)hese amended Rules of Criminal Procedure shall govern all criminal actions commenced or arrests made after 12 o'clock midnight January 1, 1990, except amendments to 8.04, 11.07, and 19.04, subd. 5, shall govern all criminal actions commenced or arrests made after 12 o'clock midnight January 1, 1991."

FORM 21. MOTION TO DISMISS OR GRANT APPROPRIATE RELIEF, PURSUANT TO RULES 10, 11.03, 12.02, 17.06, 32 OR 33

STATE OF MINNESOTA DISTRICT COURT
COUNTY OF _____ _____ JUDICIAL DISTRICT

_______________,) MOTION TO DISMISS OR
Plaintiff,) GRANT APPROPRIATE
) RELIEF, PURSUANT TO
vs.) RULES 10, 11.03, 12.02,
) 17.06, 32, OR 33
)
_______________,) District Court File No. _____
Defendant.)

The undersigned moves:

_____ 1. That this case be dismissed.

_____ 2. That the following relief be granted:

Said motion to be granted for the following reasons:

TAKE NOTE: The failure to include any defense, objection, issue, or request available to the moving party at this time, constitutes a waiver thereof. (Lack of jurisdiction over the offense, failure of the indictment or complaint to charge an offense, and any other defense, which may be so designated in the future by judicial decision, are excepted.)

Dated: _____ ______________________

Name:
Attorney License No.:
Title:
Address:
Telephone No.:

Adopted Dec. 13, 1989.

Historical Note

The order of the Minnesota Supreme Court [C1–84–2137] dated December 13, 1989, provides in part that "(t)hese amended Rules of Criminal Procedure shall govern all criminal actions commenced or arrests made after 12 o'clock midnight January 1, 1990, except amendments to 8.04, 11.07, and 19.04, subd. 5, shall govern all criminal actions commenced or arrests made after 12 o'clock midnight January 1, 1991."

FORM 22. NO INDICTMENT RETURNED PURSUANT TO RULE 18.07

STATE OF MINNESOTA DISTRICT COURT
COUNTY OF _____ _____ JUDICIAL DISTRICT

_______________,) NO INDICTMENT
Plaintiff,) RETURNED (NO BILL)
) PURSUANT TO RULE 18.07
vs.)
) District Court File No. _____
_______________,)
Defendant.)

The Grand Jury, after due consideration, reports that no indictment (a "no bill") has been returned against the above-named Defendant relative to the offense of:

Charge: ______________ in violation of
Section: ______________

Dated: _____ ______________________

(Foreperson of the Grand Jury)

Adopted Dec. 13, 1989.

Historical Note

The order of the Minnesota Supreme Court [C1–84–2137] dated December 13, 1989, provides in part that "(t)hese amended Rules of Criminal Procedure shall govern all criminal actions commenced or arrests made after 12 o'clock midnight January 1, 1990, except amendments to 8.04, 11.07, and 19.04, subd. 5, shall govern all criminal actions commenced or arrests made after 12 o'clock midnight January 1, 1991."

FORM 23. WARRANT UPON INDICTMENT PURSUANT TO RULE 19.02, SUBD. 1

STATE OF MINNESOTA DISTRICT COURT
COUNTY OF _____ _____ JUDICIAL DISTRICT

_______________,) WARRANT UPON INDICT-
Plaintiff,) MENT PURSUANT TO
) RULE 19.02, SUBD. 1
vs.)
) District Court File No. _____
_______________,)
Defendant.)

TO: The Sheriff of the above-named County or any other person authorized by law to execute this Warrant.

WHEREAS the above-named Defendant has been indicted on the _____ day of _________, 19___, by the Grand Jury of the above-named County, Minnesota, for the offense of:

Charge: __________ in violation of Section: ______; in the name of the State of Minnesota, I hereby order that the above-named Defendant be apprehended and arrested without delay and brought promptly before this Court.

Conditions of Release: ______________________

____

____

Amount of Bail: ______
Dated: ______

____
Judge of District Court

Adopted Dec. 13, 1989.

Historical Note

The order of the Minnesota Supreme Court [C1–84–2137] dated December 13, 1989, provides in part that "(t)hese amended Rules of Criminal Procedure shall govern all criminal actions commenced or arrests made after 12 o'clock midnight January 1, 1990, except amendments to 8.04, 11.07, and 19.04, subd. 5, shall govern all criminal actions commenced or arrests made after 12 o'clock midnight January 1, 1991."

FORM 24. SUMMONS UPON INDICTMENT PURSUANT TO RULE 19.02, SUBD. 2

STATE OF MINNESOTA DISTRICT COURT
COUNTY OF ______ ______ JUDICIAL DISTRICT

________________,) SUMMONS UPON INDICT-
Plaintiff,) MENT PURSUANT TO
) RULE 19.02, SUBD. 2
vs.)
) District Court File No. ______
________________,)
Defendant.)

TO: The above-named Defendant.

YOU ARE HEREBY SUMMONED to appear on the ______ day of ________, 19___, at ____ o'clock ___.m., before the above-named Court at ____________, (room number) ____________, ____________ (place) (address) to answer the indictment, a copy of which is attached.

IF YOU FAIL TO APPEAR in response to this Summons, a Warrant for your arrest shall be issued.

____
Judge of District Court

Adopted Dec. 13, 1989.

Historical Note

The order of the Minnesota Supreme Court [C1–84–2137] dated December 13, 1989, provides in part that "(t)hese amended Rules of Criminal Procedure shall govern all criminal actions commenced or arrests made after 12 o'clock midnight January 1, 1990, except amendments to 8.04, 11.07, and 19.04, subd. 5, shall govern all criminal actions commenced or arrests made after 12 o'clock midnight January 1, 1991."

FORM 25. GRAND JURY SUBPOENA—SUBPOENA DUCES TECUM

STATE OF MINNESOTA DISTRICT COURT
COUNTY OF ______ ______ JUDICIAL DISTRICT

IN THE MATTER OF) GRAND JURY
THE INVESTIGATION OF) SUBPOENA—SUB-
THE GRAND JURY OF) POENA DUCES
____________ COUNTY) TECUM
) File No. ________

THE STATE OF MINNESOTA

TO: ________

You are hereby ordered to appear as a witness before the Grand Jury of the above-named County at ____________ (location) on the ____ day of ______, 19___ at ___ o'clock ___.m. and to:

______ bring with you
______ produce, prior to the above-stated time, on the ______ day of ________, 19___, at ____________ (location) the following books, papers, documents, or other objects:

WARNING: Failure to obey a Subpoena without adequate excuse is a Contempt of Court.

Dated: ______ WITNESS THE HONORABLE [JUDGE'S NAME]
Judge of District Court

____
Clerk of District Court

Adopted Dec. 13, 1989.

Historical Note

The order of the Minnesota Supreme Court [C1–84–2137] dated December 13, 1989, provides in part that "(t)hese amended Rules of Criminal Procedure shall govern all criminal actions commenced or arrests made after 12 o'clock midnight January 1, 1990, except amendments to 8.04, 11.07, and 19.04, subd. 5, shall govern all criminal actions commenced or arrests made after 12 o'clock midnight January 1, 1991."

FORM 26. DISTRICT COURT SUBPOENA—SUBPOENA DUCES TECUM [Deleted June 5, 2012, eff. August 1, 2012]

FORM 27. FINDINGS OF FACT AND ORDER INCLUDING PETITION FOR JUDICIAL COMMITMENT, FOR MISDEMEANOR CASE, PURSUANT TO RULE 20.01

STATE OF MINNESOTA DISTRICT COURT
COUNTY OF ____ ____ JUDICIAL DISTRICT

______________,) FINDINGS OF FACT
Plaintiff,) AND ORDER INCLUDING
) PETITION FOR JUDICIAL
vs.) COMMITMENT, FOR
) MISDEMEANOR CASE,
______________,) PURSUANT TO RULE 20.01
Defendant.)
) District Court File No. ____

This matter came on for hearing before the Court, the Honorable ______________ ______________, ______________ Judge presiding. ______________, Prosecuting Attorney, appeared for the State. The defendant appeared in person and was represented by Attorney ______________.

This Court finds that based on all the files, records, and proceedings in this case, there is reason to believe that the Defendant may be mentally ill or deficient and that proceedings should be commenced under the Minnesota Hospitalization and Commitment Act.

Pursuant to the Minnesota Hospitalization and Commitment Act, this Court represents that:

1. Defendant was born ______, 19__, at ______.

2. Defendant resides at ______, Minnesota.

3. Defendant's spouse and nearest kindred are:

(Name) (Relationship) (Age) (Address)

____

____

____

4. Defendant (is) (is not) a Veteran.

5. Defendant is believed to be (mentally ill) (mentally deficient) because ______________

____

____

6. Defendant is further believed to be (mentally ill) (mentally deficient), as evidenced by the physician's statement furnished herewith.

7. The Court has been unable to procure a physician's statement because ______________

____

8. Defendant is presently at ______________

____

9. Defendant was last committed to the State Hospital at ______, Minnesota, by the ______ Probate Court on or about ______, 19__, and has received psychiatric treatment at the following hospitals:

____

____

____

10. Defendant has been under the care of Dr. ______ whose office address is: ______

____

____

This Court orders that:

a. The prosecuting attorney shall immediately:

1. Deliver a copy of these Findings of Fact, and Order Including Petition for Judicial Commitment to the county welfare department.

2. File these Findings of Fact and Order Including Petition for Judicial Commitment in the probate court.

3. Request the probate court to immediately issue such orders as may be necessary to provide for the examination of the proposed patient.

4. Cause to be delivered to the sheriff any order of the probate court directing the sheriff to transport the proposed patient to a designated hospital or other place for the purpose of an examination prior to the hearing on the petition for judicial commitment.

b. The sheriff shall immediately transport the proposed patient to a designated hospital or other place as directed by any order of the probate court.

c. The county attorney shall appear and represent the petitioner at the commitment hearing.

d. If the determination is commitment or other reasonable alternative disposition including, but not limited to, out-patient care, informal or voluntary hospitalization in a private or public facility, appointment of a guardian or release before commitment as provided for in Minn.Stat. § 253B.09, subd. 4, the charge of ______ is dismissed in accordance with Rule 20.01 of the Minnesota Rules of Criminal Procedure.

e. If the determination is dismissal of the petition, the sheriff shall immediately cause the defendant to be brought before this court.

f. The proceedings in this matter are suspended pending the commitment and other determinations. Bail or other conditions of release as to this matter are continued subject to the order of this court or until and unless this matter is dismissed.

Dated: ______ ______________
District Court Judge

Adopted Dec. 13, 1989.

Historical Note

The order of the Minnesota Supreme Court [C1–84–2137] dated December 13, 1989, provides in part that "(t)hese amended Rules of Criminal Procedure shall govern all criminal actions commenced or arrests made after 12 o'clock midnight January 1, 1990, except amendments to 8.04, 11.07, and 19.04, subd. 5, shall govern all criminal actions commenced or arrests made after 12 o'clock midnight January 1, 1991."

FORM 28. FELONY OR GROSS MISDEMEANOR FINDINGS OF FACT; ORDER INCLUDING PETITION FOR JUDICIAL COMMITMENT; ORDER FOR MENTAL EXAMINATION TO DETERMINE: (1) DEFENDANT'S COMPETENCY TO PROCEED WITH CRIMINAL CASE (2) MENTAL ILLNESS OR DEFICIENCY AT TIME OF COMMISSION OF THE OFFENSE

STATE OF MINNESOTA DISTRICT COURT
COUNTY OF ____ ____ JUDICIAL DISTRICT

______________,) FELONY OR GROSS MISDE-
Plaintiff,) MEANOR FINDINGS OF
) FACT; ORDER INCLUDING
) PETITION FOR JUDICIAL
) COMMITMENT; ORDER
) FOR MENTAL EXAMINA-
vs.) TION TO DETERMINE:
) (1) DEFENDANT'S COMPE-
) TENCY TO PROCEED WITH
) CRIMINAL CASE (2) MEN-
) TAL ILLNESS OR DEFI-
______________,) CIENCY AT TIME OF COM-
Defendant.) MISSION OF THE OFFENSE
)
) District Court File No. ____

This matter came on for hearing before the Court, the Honorable __________, District Judge presiding. ____________, Assistant County Attorney, appeared for the State. The Defendant appeared in person and was represented by Attorney ____________.

This Court finds that based on all the files, records, and proceedings in this case: There is reason to believe that the Defendant may be mentally ill or deficient and that proceedings should be commenced under the Minnesota Hospitalization and Commitment Act; there is reason to believe the Defendant is incompetent to proceed with the criminal case; the Defendant has notified the prosecuting attorney of an intention to assert a defense of mental illness or mental deficiency.

Pursuant to the Minnesota Hospitalization and Commitment Act, this Court represents that:

1. Defendant was born ____________, 19__, at ____________.

2. Defendant resides at ______, Minnesota.

3. Defendant's spouse and nearest kindred are:

(Name) (Relationship) (Age) (Address)

____
____
____

4. Defendant (is) (is not) a Veteran.

5. Defendant is believed to be (mentally ill) (mentally deficient) because ____________
____
____

6. Defendant is further believed to be (mentally ill) (mentally deficient), as evidenced by the physician's statement furnished herewith.

7. The Court has been unable to procure a physician's statement because ____________
____

8. Defendant is presently at ____________
____

9. Defendant was last committed to the State Hospital at ____________, Minnesota, by the ____________ Probate Court on or about ________, 19__, and has received psychiatric treatment at the following hospitals:

____
____
____

10. Defendant has been under the care of Dr. ____________ whose office address is: ____________
____
____

This Court orders that:

A. The prosecuting attorney shall immediately:

1. Deliver a copy of these Findings of Fact, and Order Including Petition for Judicial Commitment to the county welfare department.

2. File these Findings of Fact and Order Including Petition for Judicial Commitment in the probate court.

3. Request the probate court to immediately issue such orders as may be necessary to provide for the examination of the proposed patient.

4. Cause to be delivered to the sheriff any order of the probate court directing the sheriff to transport the proposed patient to a designated hospital or other place for the purpose of an examination prior to the hearing on the petition for judicial commitment.

B. The sheriff shall immediately transport the proposed patient to a designated hospital or other place as directed by any order of the probate court.

C. The prosecuting attorney shall appear and represent the petitioner at the commitment hearing.

D. The criminal proceedings are continued pending the commitment and other determinations.

E. The Probate Court shall transmit its findings to the District Court, including:

1. Its findings of fact and conclusions of law.

2. A copy of the examiner's report.

3. A determination as to whether defendant may be committed under the Minnesota Hospitalization and Commitment Act, and if so whether the Defendant is dangerous to the public.

4. As to competency to proceed with the criminal case:

(a) A diagnosis of the mental condition of the Defendant.

(b) If the Defendant is mentally ill or mentally deficient, an opinion as to: (i) the Defendant's capacity to understand the criminal proceedings and to participate in the defense; (ii) whether the Defendant presents an imminent risk of serious danger to another person is imminently suicidal or otherwise needs emergency intervention; (iii) the treatment required, if any, for the Defendant to attain or maintain competence with an explanation of the appropriate treatment alternatives by order of choice, including the extent to which the Defendant can be treated without being committed to an institution and the reasons for rejecting such treatment if institutionalization is recommended; and (iv) whether there is a substantial probability that with treatment, or otherwise, the Defendant will ever attain the competency to proceed and if so, in approximately what period of time, and the availability of the various types of acceptable treatment in the local geographical area, specifying the agencies or settings in which the treatment might be obtained and whether it would be available to an outpatient.

(c) A statement of the factual basis upon which the diagnosis and opinion are based.

(d) If the examination could not be conducted by reason of the Defendant's unwillingness to participate therein, a statement to that effect with an opinion, if possible, as to whether the Defendant's unwillingness was the result of mental illness or deficiency.

5. As to mental illness or deficiency at time of commission of offense:

(a) A diagnosis of the Defendant's medical condition at the time of the commission of the offense.

(b) An opinion as to whether, because of mental illness or deficiency, the Defendant at the time of the commission of the offense charged was laboring under such a defect of reason as not to know the nature of the act constituting the offense with which Defendant is charged or that it was wrong.

(c) A statement of the factual basis upon which the diagnosis and any opinion are based.

(d) If the examination could not be conducted by reason of the Defendant's unwillingness to participate therein, a statement to that effect with an opinion, if possible, as to whether the Defendant's unwillingness was the result of mental illness or deficiency.

F. Following the examination by the Probate Court, the entry of the appropriate judgment is to be suspended and the Defendant returned to this Court.

G. If any of the mental-health professionals appointed to examine the Defendant concludes that the Defendant presents an imminent risk of serious danger to another person, is imminently suicidal, or otherwise needs emergency intervention, the mental-health professional shall promptly notify the prosecuting attorney, defense counsel, and this Court.

Dated: ______ ____________________________

District Court Judge

Adopted Dec. 13, 1989.

Historical Note

The order of the Minnesota Supreme Court [C1–84–2137] dated December 13, 1989, provides in part that "(t)hese amended Rules of Criminal Procedure shall govern all criminal actions commenced or arrests made after 12 o'clock midnight January 1, 1990, except amendments to 8.04, 11.07, and 19.04, subd. 5, shall govern all criminal actions commenced or arrests made after 12 o'clock midnight January 1, 1991."

FORM 29. FELONY OR GROSS MISDEMEANOR FINDINGS OF FACT; ORDER INCLUDING PETITION FOR JUDICIAL COMMITMENT OF A DEFENDANT FOUND INCOMPETENT TO PROCEED TO TRIAL, PURSUANT TO RULE 20.01, SUBDS. 4 AND 5

STATE OF MINNESOTA DISTRICT COURT
COUNTY OF _____ _____ JUDICIAL DISTRICT

________________,) FELONY OR GROSS MISDE-
Plaintiff,) MEANOR FINDINGS OF
) FACT; ORDER INCLUDING
) PETITION FOR JUDICIAL
vs.) COMMITMENT OF A DE-
) FENDANT FOUND INCOM-
) PETENT TO PROCEED TO
) TRIAL, PURSUANT TO
) RULE 20.01, SUBDS.
________________,) 4 AND 5
Defendant.) District Court File No. _____

This matter came on for hearing before the Court, the Honorable ________, District Judge presiding. ___________, Assistant County Attorney, appeared for the State. The Defendant appeared in person and was represented by Attorney ________.

This Court finds that based on all the files, records, and proceedings in this case: The Defendant is mentally ill or mentally deficient so as to be incapable of understanding the criminal proceedings or participating in the defense; there is reason to believe the Defendant may be mentally ill or deficient and that proceedings should be commenced under the Minnesota Hospitalization and Commitment Act.

Pursuant to the Minnesota Hospitalization and Commitment Act, this Court represents that:

1. Defendant was born ______, 19__, at ______.

2. Defendant resides at __________, Minnesota.

3. Defendant's spouse and nearest kindred are:

(Name) (Relationship) (Age) (Address)

____

____

____

4. Defendant (is) (is not) a Veteran.

5. Defendant is believed to be (mentally ill) (mentally deficient) because __________

____

____

6. Defendant is further believed to be (mentally ill) (mentally deficient), as evidenced by the physician's statement furnished herewith.

7. The Court has been unable to procure a physician's statement because __________

____

8. Defendant is presently at __________

____

9. Defendant was last committed to the State Hospital at __________, Minnesota, by the ______ Probate Court on or about ______, 19__, and has received psychiatric treatment at the following hospitals:

____

____

____

10. Defendant has been under the care of Dr. ______ whose office address is:

____

____

____

This Court orders that:

a. The prosecuting attorney shall immediately:

1. Deliver a copy of these Findings of Fact, and Order Including Petition for Judicial Commitment to the county welfare department.

2. File these Findings of Fact and Order Including Petition for Judicial Commitment in the probate court.

3. Request the probate court to immediately issue such orders as may be necessary to provide for the examination of the proposed patient.

4. Cause to be delivered to the sheriff any order of the probate court directing the sheriff to transport the proposed patient to a designated hospital or other place for the purpose of an examination prior to the hearing on the petition for judicial commitment.

b. The sheriff shall immediately transport the proposed patient to a designated hospital or other place as directed by any order of the probate court.

c. The prosecuting attorney shall appear and represent the petitioner at the commitment hearing.

d. The criminal proceedings are continued pending the commitment and other determinations.

e. If Defendant is committed, the head of the institution or designated place to which the Defendant is committed shall review the mental condition of the Defendant within 60 days from the date of the commitment order and report in writing to this District Court on the Defendant's mental condition with an opinion as to the Defendant's competency to proceed with the criminal case, and as to the need of the Defendant for further institutional care and treatment. Thereafter, if the commitment is continued, the head of the institution or designated place shall report to this District Court at least once every six months.

f. If Defendant is committed, the criminal proceedings are continued in accordance with Rule 20.01, Subd. 4(2) of the Minnesota Rules of Criminal Procedure.

g. If Defendant is not committed, the sheriff shall immediately cause the Defendant to be brought before this court.

h. Bail or other conditions of release as to the criminal proceedings are continued.

Dated: ______________

____
District Court Judge

Adopted Dec. 13, 1989.

Historical Note

The order of the Minnesota Supreme Court [C1–84–2137] dated December 13, 1989, provides in part that "(t)hese amended Rules of Criminal Procedure shall govern all criminal actions commenced or arrests made after 12 o'clock midnight January 1, 1990, except amendments to 8.04, 11.07, and 19.04, subd. 5, shall govern all criminal actions commenced or arrests made after 12 o'clock midnight January 1, 1991."

FORM 30. FINDINGS OF FACT AND ORDER FOR JUDICIAL COMMITMENT OF DEFENDANT FOUND INCOMPETENT TO PROCEED WITH FELONY OR GROSS MISDEMEANOR CASE, PURSUANT TO RULE 20.01

STATE OF MINNESOTA DISTRICT COURT
COUNTY OF ______ ______ JUDICIAL DISTRICT

______________) FINDINGS OF FACT AND
Plaintiff,) ORDER FOR JUDICIAL
) COMMITMENT OF DEFEN-
) DANT FOUND INCOMPE-
vs.) TENT TO PROCEED WITH
) FELONY OR GROSS MISDE-
) MEANOR CASE PURSUANT
______________) TO RULE 20.01
Defendant.) District Court File No. ______

This matter came on for hearing before the Court, the Honorable ________, District Judge presiding.

___________, Assistant County Attorney, appeared for the State. The Defendant appeared in person and was represented by Attorney _____________.

This Court finds that, based on all the files, records and proceedings in this case, the Defendant is mentally ill or mentally deficient so as to be incapable of understanding the criminal proceedings or participating in the defense.

This Court orders that:

1. The judicial commitment proceedings in the Probate Court immediately be continued and completed by the Probate Court issuing such orders as may be necessary to commit the Defendant.

2. The head of the institution or designated place to which the Defendant is committed shall review the mental condition of the Defendant within 60 days from the date of the commitment order and report in writing to this District Court on the Defendant's mental condition with an opinion as to the Defendant's competency to proceed with the criminal case, and as to the need of the Defendant for further institutional care and treatment. Thereafter, if the commitment is continued, the head of the institution or designated place shall report to this District Court at least once every six months.

3. Bail or other conditions of release as to the criminal proceedings are continued.

4. The criminal proceedings are continued in accordance with Rule 20.01, Subd. 4(2) of the Minnesota Rules of Criminal Procedure.

5. The County Attorney shall immediately file a copy of these findings of fact and order in the Probate Court and request the Probate Court to immediately issue such orders as may be necessary to commit the Defendant.

Dated: _____________ ____________________
District Court Judge

Adopted Dec. 13, 1989.

Historical Note

The order of the Minnesota Supreme Court [C1–84–2137] dated December 13, 1989, provides in part that "(t)hese amended Rules of Criminal Procedure shall govern all criminal actions commenced or arrests made after 12 o'clock midnight January 1, 1990, except amendments to 8.04, 11.07, and 19.04, subd. 5, shall govern all criminal actions commenced or arrests made after 12 o'clock midnight January 1, 1991."

FORM 31. DESIGNATION AS A PETTY MISDEMEANOR IN A PARTICULAR CASE

STATE OF MINNESOTA DISTRICT COURT
COUNTY OF _____ _____ JUDICIAL DISTRICT

_______________,) DESIGNATION AS A PETTY
Plaintiff,) MISDEMEANOR IN A PAR-
vs.) TICULAR CASE
_______________,)
Defendant.) District Court File No. _____

I, the Prosecuting Attorney, hereby certify to the above-named Court that in my opinion it is in the interests of justice that the above-named Defendant not be incarcerated, and thereby designate, subject to the consent of the above-named Defendant, that this alleged misdemeanor violation be treated as a petty misdemeanor.

Dated: ______ ____________________
(Prosecuting Attorney)
Name:
Attorney License No.:
Title:
Address:
Telephone No.:

I hereby consent to the treatment of the offense involved in this particular case as a petty misdemeanor.

____
(Defendant)

I hereby approve the designation of the offense involved in this particular case as a petty misdemeanor.

____
Judge or Judicial Officer *

* The name and title of the Judge or Judicial Officer should be printed or stamped following the signature.

Adopted Dec. 13, 1989.

Historical Note

The order of the Minnesota Supreme Court [C1–84–2137] dated December 13, 1989, provides in part that "(t)hese amended Rules of Criminal Procedure shall govern all criminal actions commenced or arrests made after 12 o'clock midnight January 1, 1990, except amendments to 8.04, 11.07, and 19.04, subd. 5, shall govern all criminal actions commenced or arrests made after 12 o'clock midnight January 1, 1991."

FORM 32. WAIVER OF JURY TRIAL PURSUANT TO RULE 26.01, SUBD. 1(2)(a)

STATE OF MINNESOTA DISTRICT COURT
COUNTY OF _____ _____ JUDICIAL DISTRICT

_______________,) WAIVER OF JURY TRIAL
Plaintiff) PURSUANT TO RULE 26.01,
vs.) SUBD. 1(2)(a)
_______________,)
Defendant.) District Court File No. _____

Having been advised by the Court of my right to trial by jury and having had an opportunity to consult with counsel, I do hereby, with the approval of this Court, waive my right to trial by jury.

Dated: ______ ____________________
(Defendant)

APPROVED BY:

____
Judge of District Court

Adopted Dec. 13, 1989.

Historical Note

The order of the Minnesota Supreme Court [C1–84–2137] dated December 13, 1989, provides in part that "(t)hese amended Rules of Criminal Procedure shall govern all criminal actions commenced or arrests made after 12 o'clock midnight January 1, 1990, except amendments to 8.04, 11.07, and 19.04, subd. 5, shall govern all criminal actions commenced or arrests made after 12 o'clock midnight January 1, 1991."

FORM 33. NOTICE OF APPEAL BY DEFENDANT TO COURT OF APPEALS

STATE OF MINNESOTA DISTRICT COURT
COUNTY OF ____ ____ JUDICIAL DISTRICT

__________, Plaintiff,
vs.
__________, Defendant.

NOTICE OF APPEAL BY DEFENDANT TO COURT OF APPEALS
District Court File No. ____
Date Judgment, Sentence or Order Entered: ______

TO: Clerk of Appellate Court
Minnesota Judicial Center
St. Paul, MN 55155

State Attorney General
Address: ______
Telephone No.: ____

Clerk of District Court
Address: ______
Telephone No.: ____

Prosecuting Attorney
Address: ______
Telephone No.: ____

PLEASE TAKE NOTICE that the above-named Defendant hereby appeals to the Court of Appeals of the State of Minnesota from the following judgment or orders of the above-named District Court:

____ Final judgment entered on the ___ day of ______, 19__;

____ Order refusing or imposing conditions of release entered on the ___ day of ______, 19__;

____ Order finding Defendant incompetent to stand trial entered on the ___ day of ______, 19__ (felony and gross misdemeanor cases only);

____ Order granting a new trial instead of entering judgment in Defendant's favor, entered on the ___ day of ______, 19__. (felony and gross misdemeanor cases only);

____ Sentence imposed on the ___ day of ______, 19__. (felony cases only).

____ Order denying in whole or in part a petition for postconviction relief under Minn.Stat. Ch. 590 entered on the ___ day of ______, 19__.

Dated: ____ __________

(Attorney for Defendant)
Name:
Attorney License No.:
Title:
Address:
Telephone No.:

Adopted Dec. 13, 1989.

Historical Note

The order of the Minnesota Supreme Court [C1–84–2137] dated December 13, 1989, provides in part that "(t)hese amended Rules of Criminal Procedure shall govern all criminal actions commenced or arrests made after 12 o'clock midnight January 1, 1990, except amendments to 8.04, 11.07, and 19.04, subd. 5, shall govern all criminal actions commenced or arrests made after 12 o'clock midnight January 1, 1991."

FORM 34. NOTICE OF APPEAL BY PROSECUTING ATTORNEY TO THE COURT OF APPEALS FROM PRETRIAL ORDER(S) OF THE DISTRICT COURT

STATE OF MINNESOTA DISTRICT COURT
COUNTY OF ______ ____ JUDICIAL DISTRICT

__________, Plaintiff,
vs.
__________, Defendant.

NOTICE OF APPEAL BY PROSECUTING ATTORNEY TO THE COURT OF APPEALS FROM PRETRIAL ORDER(S) OF THE DISTRICT COURT
District Court File No.: ____

TO: Clerk of Appellate Court
Minnesota Judicial Center
St. Paul, MN 55155

State Attorney General
Address: ______
Telephone No.: ____

(Name of county) Court Administrator
Address: ______
Telephone No.: ____

Attorney for Defendant
Address: ______
Telephone No.: ____

State Public Defender
Address: ______
Telephone No. ______

PLEASE TAKE NOTICE that the prosecuting attorney in the above-entitled case hereby appeals to the Court of Appeals of the State of Minnesota from the following pretrial order(s) of the above-named District Court entered on the following dates:

__ day of ______, 20__. (Description of Order)
__ day of ______, 20__. (Description of Order)
__ day of ______, 20__. (Description of Order)

Dated: ______ __________

(Prosecuting Attorney)
Name:
Attorney License No.:
Title:
Address:
Telephone No.:

Adopted Dec. 13, 1989. Amended Dec. 28, 2005, eff. March 1, 2006.

Historical Note

The order of the Minnesota Supreme Court [C1–84–2137] dated December 13, 1989, provides in part that "(t)hese amended Rules of Criminal Procedure shall govern all criminal actions commenced or arrests made after 12 o'clock midnight January 1, 1990, except amendments to 8.04, 11.07, and 19.04, subd. 5, shall govern all criminal actions commenced or arrests made after 12 o'clock midnight January 1, 1991."

The order of the Minnesota Supreme Court [C1–84–2137] dated December 28, 2005, provides in part that "(t)he attached amendments shall govern all criminal actions commenced or arrests made after 12 o'clock midnight March 1, 2006.

FORM 35. NOTICE OF CROSS–APPEAL TO COURT OF APPEALS BY DEFENDANT UPON APPEAL BY THE STATE

STATE OF MINNESOTA
IN COURT OF APPEALS

____________,	)
Plaintiff– Appellant	) NOTICE OF CROSS–APPEAL) COURT OF APPEALS BY
vs.	) DEFENDANT UPON APPEAL) BY THE STATE)
____________,	) District Court File No.: _____
Defendant– Respondent	) Court of Appeals File No.: _____)

TO: Clerk of Appellate Courts Minnesota Judicial Center St. Paul, MN 55155	State Attorney General Address: ____________ Telephone No.: _____
Clerk of District Court Address: ____________ Telephone No.: _______	Prosecuting Attorney Address: ____________ Telephone No.: _____

PLEASE TAKE NOTICE that the above-named Defendant hereby cross-appeals to the Court of Appeals of the State of Minnesota, upon the appeal of the prosecuting attorney filed on the _____ day of ____________, 19___, from the following pretrial order(s) of the above-named District Court entered on the following date(s):

_____ Pretrial order entered on the _____ day of ________, 19__. (Description of Order)

_____ Pretrial order entered on the _____ day of ________, 19__. (Description of Order)

_____ Order granting the Defendant postconviction relief under Minn.Stat. Ch. 590 entered on the _____ day of _______, 19__. (Description of Order)

Dated: _____

____
(Attorney for Defendant)
Name:
Attorney License No.:
Title:
Address:
Telephone No.:

Adopted Dec. 13, 1989.

Historical Note

The order of the Minnesota Supreme Court [C1–84–2137] dated December 13, 1989, provides in part that "(t)hese amended Rules of Criminal Procedure shall govern all criminal actions commenced or arrests made after 12 o'clock midnight January 1, 1990, except amendments to 8.04, 11.07, and 19.04, subd. 5, shall govern all criminal actions commenced or arrests made after 12 o'clock midnight January 1, 1991."

FORM 36. PETITION FOR REVIEW OF DECISION OF THE COURT OF APPEALS

STATE OF MINNESOTA
IN SUPREME COURT

____________, Respondent,	) PETITION FOR REVIEW OF) DECISION OF THE COURT
vs.	) OF APPEALS)
	) Appellate Court Case No.: ____
____________, Petitioner.	) Date of Filing of Court of) Appeals Decision: ________

TO: The Supreme Court of the State of Minnesota:

The Petitioner, ____________, requests Supreme Court review of the above-entitled decision of the Court of Appeals and in support thereof states:

1. Petitioner is represented by ____________, with offices at ____________, telephone number ____________. Respondent is represented by ____________, State Attorney General with offices at ____________, telephone number _____ and by ____________, the County Attorney for ____________ County, with offices at ____________, telephone number _____.

2. The decision of the Court of Appeals of which Petitioner seeks review was filed on _____. The appeal to the Court of Appeals was from (describe matter initially appealed) of the ____________ County District Court involving the offense of ____________ in violation of Minn.Stat. § _______ entered on _____.

3. The legal issue presented for review and the decision on those issues in the Court of Appeals are as follows:

4. The procedural history of this case is as follows:

5. The facts which give rise to this request for discretionary review are as follows:

6. The reasons why the Supreme Court should exercise its discretion to review this case are as follows:

7. An appendix containing the written decision of the Court of Appeals and the trial court's Findings of Fact, Conclusions of Law, and Memorandum is attached.

Dated: ______ ______________________
(Attorney for Petitioner)
Name:
Attorney License No.:
Title:
Address:
Telephone No.:

Adopted Dec. 13, 1989.

Historical Note

The order of the Minnesota Supreme Court [C1–84–2137] dated December 13, 1989, provides in part that "(t)hese amended Rules of Criminal Procedure shall govern all criminal actions commenced or arrests made after 12 o'clock midnight January 1, 1990, except amendments to 8.04, 11.07, and 19.04, subd. 5, shall govern all criminal actions commenced or arrests made after 12 o'clock midnight January 1, 1991."

FORM 37. WAIVER OF COUNSEL ON DIRECT APPEAL

STATE OF MINNESOTA
IN COURT OF APPEALS (SUPREME COURT)

______________,)
Respondent,) WAIVER OF COUNSEL
) ON APPEAL
)
vs.) D.C. File No. ______
) Appellate Court
______________,) File No. ______
Appellant.)

TO THE ABOVE–NAMED COURT:

I, __________, appellant in the above-entitled case, represent and state as follows:

1. My full name is __________. I am ___ years old, my date of birth is __________. I certify I am able to read, write and understand the English language.

2. I have been convicted of __________ _______, a felony (gross misdemeanor), in _______ County District Court. I was sentenced to __________ on __________, 19___.

3. I understand that I have the right to appeal my conviction to the (Court of Appeals) (Supreme Court), and that because I am indigent I have the right to be represented by the State Public Defender.

4. Notwithstanding my right to be represented on appeal by the State Public Defender, I wish to waive that right and represent myself on appeal *pro se.* I understand that by this waiver I am permanently waiving my right to the assistance of the attorneys in the State Public Defender's Office or any other attorney retained at public expense. I understand that the Supreme Court has said that if I choose to act as my own attorney, I will not receive any legal advice, research, library materials, or other assistance from the State Public Defender in any state court proceeding to challenge the legality of my conviction and/or sentence. In other words, as to any challenge of this conviction and/or sentence, I am on my own.

I further understand that I will have to do the necessary legal work on this appeal by myself. This includes complying with the limited time schedules required for appeals, the legal requirements as to the substantive content of briefs and other documents, the size of briefs, the number of copies of briefs and other documents required to be filed, and proper service on the necessary parties. I understand that the State Public Defender will not be available to answer any questions I have in this regard, nor can I expect the Clerk of Appellate Courts to answer any such questions. I acknowledge that the Supreme Court has said that I will be held to the same standard of responsibility as a licensed attorney. I understand that I may not later claim that because I made mistakes while representing myself on appeal that I am entitled to a new appeal.

5. I certify that I do not have the funds to pay for the necessary transcripts and I acknowledge that the Court will have access to any information regarding my finances.

6. I understand that a copy of the transcript will be made available to me by the State Public Defender. In order for my brief to be accepted for filing by the Court of Appeals (Supreme Court) the Supreme Court has said that I will have to return the entire transcript in an undamaged condition to the State Public Defender before the time for preparing, filing and serving the brief has expired. Failure to do so could result in the dismissal of my appeal. Additionally, failure to return the transcript, which is state property, is a violation of Rule 19 of the Inmate Discipline Regulations and I could be prosecuted within the prison disciplinary system. Any destruction, damage or alteration of the transcript is a violation of Rule 27 of the Inmate Discipline Regulations and I could be prosecuted within the prison disciplinary system.

I further understand that I cannot make the transcript available to any other inmate or other person, but it must remain in my personal possession until returned to the State Public Defender.

7. I understand that the Supreme Court has said no library services are required to be made available to me other than those available to other inmates in the institution.

8. I understand that all existing legal issues with respect to my present conviction and/or sentence must be raised by me in this court proceeding or they will be waived for the purpose of any further state or federal court proceedings.

9. I understand that I will not be permitted to be personally present to argue my case to the appellate court, nor will any other person appear on my behalf.

10. I understand that Minn.Stat. § 481.02, subd. 1, makes it a crime for any person who is not a lawyer to give legal advice or assistance to another person. Additionally, Rule 4 of the Inmate Discipline Regula-

tions prohibits one inmate from performing unauthorized tasks for another inmate. I understand that I may be required to certify that the brief I file was prepared by me before my brief will be accepted for filing by the Clerk of Appellate Courts.

11. I understand that if an attorney, other than an attorney from the State Public Defender's Office or any other attorney retained at public expense, agrees to assist me that the attorney must first agree to represent me through exhaustion of all state court remedies. In that case I would return the transcript to the State Public Defender so arrangements could be made to get the transcript to the private attorney.

12. I understand that in waiving assistance of the State Public Defender on appeal, I am certifying that I am competent to make this decision, that I am not under the influence of any drug, that I am not suffering from any mental illness or defect that would prevent me from representing myself on appeal, and I understand that if I did not waive counsel, the State Public Defender would be appointed to represent me on appeal.

I hereby acknowledge that I have read or have had read to me the above-entitled waiver and that I have been advised by the State Public Defender as to the risks involved in proceeding *pro se* and that I understand those risks and am voluntarily waiving my right to be represented by the State Public Defender.

Dated: ______ ____________________
Appellant

Subscribed and sworn to before me
this ___ day of ______.

____
Notary Public

Adopted Dec. 13, 1989.

Historical Note

The order of the Minnesota Supreme Court [C1–84–2137] dated December 13, 1989, provides in part that "(t)hese amended Rules of Criminal Procedure shall govern all criminal actions commenced or arrests made after 12 o'clock midnight January 1, 1990, except amendments to 8.04, 11.07, and 19.04, subd. 5, shall govern all criminal actions commenced or arrests made after 12 o'clock midnight January 1, 1991."

FORM 38. WAIVER OF COUNSEL ON POST–CONVICTION PROCEEDINGS

STATE OF MINNESOTA IN DISTRICT COURT
COUNTY OF _____ _____ JUDICIAL DISTRICT

_____________,)
Respondent,) WAIVER OF COUNSEL
) ON POST–CONVICTION
) PROCEEDINGS
vs.)
) D.C. File No. _____
)
_____________,)
Petitioner.)

TO THE ABOVE–NAMED COURT:

I, ___________, petitioner in the above-entitled case, represent and state as follows:

1. My full name is ______________. I am ___ years old, my date of birth is ___________. I certify I am able to read, write and understand the English language.

2. I have been convicted of _____________, a felony (gross misdemeanor), in ______ County District Court. I was sentenced to _____________ on ___________, 19__.

3. I understand that I have the right to challenge my conviction by filing a post-conviction petition in the district court where I was convicted and sentenced and that because I am indigent I have the right to be represented by the State Public Defender.

4. Notwithstanding my right to be represented in a post-conviction proceeding by the State Public Defender, I wish to waive that right and represent myself *pro se.* I understand that by this waiver I am permanently waiving my right to the assistance of the attorneys in the State Public Defender's Office or any other attorney retained at public expense. I understand that the Supreme Court has said that if I choose to act as my own attorney, I will not receive any legal advice, research, library materials, or other assistance from the State Public Defender in any state court proceeding to challenge the legality of my conviction and/or sentence. In other words, as to any challenge of this conviction and/or sentence, I am on my own in filing my post-conviction petition and in filing any appeal from that petition, should it be denied.

I further understand that I will have to do the necessary legal work on my post-conviction by myself. This includes filing my post-conviction petition in the district court where I was convicted and sentenced within 60 days after I receive my trial transcript, complying with any district court requirements regarding the format of my petition, and properly serving my petition on the appropriate parties. I understand that the State Public Defender will not be available to answer any questions I have in this regard, nor can I expect the Clerk of District Court to answer any such questions. I acknowledge that the Supreme Court has said that I will be held to the same standard of responsibility as a licensed attorney. I understand that I may not later claim that because I made mistakes while representing myself in my post-conviction action that I am entitled to a new post-conviction action.

5. I certify that I do not have the funds to pay for the necessary transcripts and I acknowledge that the Court will have access to any information regarding my finances.

6. I understand that a copy of the transcript will be made available to me by the State Public Defender.

I agree to return the entire transcript in an undamaged condition to the State Public Defender within 60 days after receiving it. Failure to return the transcript, which is state property, is a violation of Rule 19 of the Inmate Discipline Regulations and I could be prosecuted within the prison disciplinary system. Any destruction, damage or alteration of the transcript is a violation of Rule 27 of the Inmate Discipline Regulations and I could be prosecuted within the prison disciplinary system.

I further understand that I cannot make the transcript available to any other inmate or other person, but it must remain in my personal possession until returned to the State Public Defender.

7. I understand that the Supreme Court has said no library services are required to be made available to me other than those available to other inmates in the institution.

8. I understand that all existing legal issues with respect to my present conviction and/or sentence must be raised by me in my post-conviction petition or they will be waived for the purpose of any further state or federal court proceedings.

9. I understand that I will not be permitted to be personally present to argue my case to the district court unless the court so orders, nor will any other person appear on my behalf.

10. I understand that Minn.Stat. § 481.02, subd. 1, makes it a crime for any person who is not a lawyer to give legal advice or assistance to another person. Additionally, Rule 4 of the Inmate Discipline Regulations prohibits one inmate from performing unauthorized tasks for another inmate. I understand that I may be required to certify that the petition I file was prepared by me before my petition will be accepted for filing by the Clerk of District Court.

11. I understand that if an attorney, other than an attorney from the State Public Defender's Office or any other attorney retained at public expense, agrees to assist me, that the attorney must first agree to represent me through exhaustion of all state court remedies. In that case I would return the transcript to the State Public Defender so arrangements could be made to get the transcript to the private attorney.

12. I understand that in waiving assistance of the State Public Defender in my post-conviction action or on any appeal I may choose to file should my petition be denied, I am certifying that I am competent to make this decision, that I am not under the influence of any drug, that I am not suffering from any mental illness or defect that would prevent me from representing myself, and I understand that if I did not waive counsel, the State Public Defender would be appointed to represent me in my post-conviction action.

13. I understand that by alleging ineffective assistance of trial counsel in my post-conviction petition, I waive the attorney/client privilege to the extent necessary to establish this claim. I understand that my trial attorney will be permitted to respond to my specific allegations of ineffective assistance either by testifying or by submitting an affidavit to the Court. I understand that in responding to my allegations, my trial attorney will be permitted to reveal confidential information I disclosed to my trial attorney during the course of our relationship, which relates to my claim of ineffective representation.

14. I hereby acknowledge that I have read or have had read to me the above-entitled waiver and that I have been advised by the State Public Defender as to the risks involved in proceeding *pro se* and that I understand those risks and am voluntarily waiving my right to be represented by the State Public Defender.

Dated: _____ ________________

Petitioner

Subscribed and sworn to before me this ___ day of _______.

____

Notary Public

Adopted Dec. 13, 1989.

Historical Note

The order of the Minnesota Supreme Court [C1–84–2137] dated December 13, 1989, provides in part that "(t)hese amended Rules of Criminal Procedure shall govern all criminal actions commenced or arrests made after 12 o'clock midnight January 1, 1990, except amendments to 8.04, 11.07, and 19.04, subd. 5, shall govern all criminal actions commenced or arrests made after 12 o'clock midnight January 1, 1991."

FORM 39. REQUEST FOR DETERMINATION OF COMPETENCY TO PROCEED PRO SE ON APPEAL

STATE OF MINNESOTA
IN COURT OF APPEALS (SUPREME COURT)

____________,	) REQUEST FOR DETERMI-
Respondent,	) NATION OF COMPETENCY
	) TO PROCEED PRO SE ON
vs.	) APPEAL
	) D.C. File No. _____
____________,	) Appellate Court
Appellant.	) File No. _____

TO THE ABOVE–NAMED COURT:

I, __________, appellant in the above-entitled case, represent and state as follows:

1. My full name is __________. I am ___ years old, my date of birth is __________.

2. I have been convicted of ______________, a felony (gross misdemeanor), in __________ County District Court. I was sentenced to __________ on __________, 19___.

3. I understand that I have the right to appeal my conviction to the (Court of Appeals) (Supreme Court), and that because I am indigent I have the right to be represented by the State Public Defender.

4. Notwithstanding my right to be represented on appeal by the State Public Defender, I wish to waive that right and represent myself on appeal *pro se.* I understand that by this waiver I am permanently waiving my right to the assistance of the attorneys in the State Public Defender's Office or any other attorney retained at public expense. I understand that the Supreme Court has said that if I choose to act as my own attorney, I will not receive any legal advice, research, library materials, or other assistance from the State Public Defender in any state court proceeding to challenge the legality of my conviction and/or sentence. In other words, as to any challenge of this conviction and/or sentence, I am on my own.

I further understand that I will have to do the necessary legal work on this appeal by myself. This includes complying with the limited time schedules required for appeals, the legal requirements as to the substantive content of briefs and other documents, the size of briefs, the number of copies of briefs and other documents required to be filed, and proper service on the necessary parties. I understand that the State Public Defender will not be available to answer any questions I have in this regard, nor can I expect the Clerk of Appellate Courts to answer any such questions. I acknowledge that the Supreme Court has said that I will be held to the same standard of responsibility as a licensed attorney. I understand that I may not later claim that because I made mistakes while representing myself on appeal that I am entitled to a new appeal.

5. I certify that I do not have the funds to pay for the necessary transcripts and I acknowledge that the Court will have access to any information regarding my finances.

6. I understand that a copy of the transcript will be made available to me by the State Public Defender. In order for my brief to be accepted for filing by the Court of Appeals (Supreme Court) the Supreme Court has said that I will have to return the entire transcript in an undamaged condition to the State Public Defender before the time for preparing, filing and serving the brief has expired. Failure to do so could result in the dismissal of my appeal. Additionally, failure to return the transcript, which is state property, is a violation of Rule 19 of the Inmate Discipline Regulations and I could be prosecuted within the prison disciplinary system. Any destruction, damage or alteration of the transcript is a violation of Rule 27 of the Inmate Discipline Regulations and I could be prosecuted within the prison disciplinary system.

I further understand that I cannot make the transcript available to any other inmate or other person, but it must remain in my personal possession until returned to the State Public Defender.

7. I understand that the Supreme Court has said no library services are required to be made available to me other than those available to other inmates in the institution.

8. I understand that all existing legal issues with respect to my present conviction and/or sentence must be raised by me in this court proceeding or they will be waived for the purpose of any further state or federal court proceedings.

9. I understand that I will not be permitted to be personally present to argue my case to the appellate court, nor will any other person appear on my behalf.

10. I understand that Minn.Stat. § 481.02, subd. 1, makes it a crime for any person who is not a lawyer to give legal advice or assistance to another person. Additionally, Rule 4 of the Inmate Discipline Regulations prohibits one inmate from performing unauthorized tasks for another inmate. I understand that I may be required to certify that the brief I file was prepared by me before my brief will be accepted for filing by the Clerk of Appellate Courts.

11. I understand that if an attorney, other than an attorney from the State Public Defender's Office or any other attorney retained at public expense, agrees to assist me that the attorney must first agree to represent me through exhaustion of all state court remedies. In that case I would return the transcript to the State Public Defender so arrangements could be made to get the transcript to the private attorney.

12. I understand that in waiving assistance of the State Public Defender on appeal, I am certifying that I am competent to make this decision, that I am not under the influence of any drug, that I am not suffering from any mental illness or defect that would prevent me from representing myself on appeal, and I understand that if I did not waive counsel, the State Public Defender would be appointed to represent me on appeal.

13. I understand that the Supreme Court has said that I will not be permitted to represent myself on appeal in this case if there is a question as to my competence to proceed *pro se.* I understand that the Supreme Court has also said that it is the district court that will decide if I am competent to make this decision. I HEREBY REQUEST THE DISTRICT COURT TO REVIEW MY CASE AND MAKE A DETERMINATION AS TO MY COMPETENCE.

I hereby acknowledge that I have read or have had read to me the above-entitled waiver and that I have been advised by the State Public Defender as to the risks involved in proceeding *pro se* and that I understand those risks and am voluntarily waiving my right to be represented by the State Public Defender.

Dated: ______ ____________________

Appellant

Subscribed and sworn to before me
this ___ day of ______.

____

Notary Public

Adopted Dec. 13, 1989.

Historical Note

The order of the Minnesota Supreme Court [C1–84–2137] dated December 13, 1989, provides in part that "(t)hese amended Rules of Criminal Procedure shall govern all criminal actions commenced or arrests made after 12 o'clock midnight January 1, 1990, except amendments to 8.04, 11.07, and 19.04, subd. 5, shall govern all criminal actions commenced or arrests made after 12 o'clock midnight January 1, 1991."

FORM 40. RECEIPT OF TRANSCRIPT BY APPELLANT

STATE OF MINNESOTA
IN COURT OF APPEALS (SUPREME COURT)

________________,)
Respondent,) RECEIPT OF TRANSCRIPT
) BY APPELLANT
vs.)
) D.C. File No. _______
________________,) Appellate Court File No. _______
Appellant.)

I, ________________, acknowledge that I have received from the State Public Defender the ______ page transcript of the trial of State of Minnesota v. ______________ and the transcripts of ______________ proceedings.

I understand that the Supreme Court has said that the transcripts are state property and that the Supreme Court has also said that I must return them to the State Public Defender in an undamaged and complete condition before the appellate brief I have prepared will be accepted for filing by the Court of Appeals (Supreme Court). I understand that when I return the transcript to the State Public Defender, I will be given a return receipt and that the State Public Defender will file a duplicate receipt with the Court of Appeals (Supreme Court). I acknowledge that the *pro se* brief I have prepared will not be accepted for filing unless and until the State Public Defender files such a receipt with the appellate court.

I further understand that the Supreme Court has said that I cannot make the transcript available to any other inmate or other person, but it must remain in my personal possession until returned to the State Public Defender.

I agree to the above conditions and agree to return the transcript in an undamaged and complete condition to the State Public Defender on or before ______________.

Dated: ________ ____________________
Appellant

Adopted Dec. 13, 1989.

Historical Note

The order of the Minnesota Supreme Court [C1–84–2137] dated December 13, 1989, provides in part that "(t)hese amended Rules of Criminal Procedure shall govern all criminal actions commenced or arrests made after 12 o'clock midnight January 1, 1990, except amendments to 8.04, 11.07, and 19.04, subd. 5, shall govern all criminal actions commenced or arrests made after 12 o'clock midnight January 1, 1991."

FORM 41. CERTIFICATE OF RECEIPT OF TRANSCRIPT FROM APPELLANT

STATE OF MINNESOTA
IN COURT OF APPEALS (SUPREME COURT)

________________,)
Respondent,) CERTIFICATE OF RECEIPT
) OF TRANSCRIPT FROM
vs.) APPELLANT
)
________________,) D.C. File No. _______
Appellant.) Appellate Court File No. _______

This is to certify that ______________, Assistant State Public Defender, has received the ________ page transcript of the trial of State of Minnesota v. ____________ and the transcript of the ____________ proceedings from ______________, the appellant in the above-entitled case.

This is to further certify that the transcripts were returned to the Office of the State Public Defender in a complete and undamaged condition.

A copy of this certificate of receipt was left with the appellant.

Dated: ________ ____________________
Assistant State Public Defender

____
Appellant

Subscribed and sworn to before me this ____ day of ________.

____
Notary Public

Adopted Dec. 13, 1989.

Historical Note

The order of the Minnesota Supreme Court [C1–84–2137] dated December 13, 1989, provides in part that "(t)hese amended Rules of Criminal Procedure shall govern all criminal actions commenced or arrests made after 12 o'clock midnight January 1, 1990, except amendments to 8.04, 11.07, and 19.04, subd. 5, shall govern all criminal actions commenced or arrests made after 12 o'clock midnight January 1, 1991."

FORM 42. DISMISSAL OF COMPLAINT BY PROSECUTING ATTORNEY, PURSUANT TO RULE 30.01

STATE OF MINNESOTA DISTRICT COURT
COUNTY OF ________ ________ JUDICIAL DISTRICT

________________,)
Plaintiff,) DISMISSAL OF COMPLAINT,
) BY PROSECUTING ATTOR-
vs.) NEY, PURSUANT TO RULE
) 30.01
________________,)
Defendant.) District Court File No. _______

The Prosecuting Attorney hereby dismisses the Complaint in the above-named case for the following reasons:

Dated: ______ ____________________________

(Prosecuting Attorney)
Name:
Attorney License No.:
Title:
Address:
Telephone No.:

Adopted Dec. 13, 1989.

Historical Note

The order of the Minnesota Supreme Court [C1–84–2137] dated December 13, 1989, provides in part that "(t)hese amended Rules of Criminal Procedure shall govern all criminal actions commenced or arrests made after 12 o'clock midnight January 1, 1990, except amendments to 8.04, 11.07, and 19.04, subd. 5, shall govern all criminal actions commenced or arrests made after 12 o'clock midnight January 1, 1991."

FORM 43. STATE DISMISSAL OF INDICTMENT PURSUANT TO RULE 30.01

STATE OF MINNESOTA DISTRICT COURT
COUNTY OF _____ _____ JUDICIAL DISTRICT

________________,)
Plaintiff,) STATE DISMISSAL OF
) INDICTMENT, PURSUANT
vs.) TO RULE 30.01
)
________________,) District Court File No. ______
Defendant.)

The State of Minnesota, with leave of this Court, hereby dismisses the Indictment in the above-named case for the following reasons:

Dated: ______ ____________________________

(Prosecuting Attorney)
Name:
Attorney License No.:
Title:
Address:
Telephone No.:

APPROVED BY:

____
Judge of District Court

Adopted Dec. 13, 1989.

Historical Note

The order of the Minnesota Supreme Court [C1–84–2137] dated December 13, 1989, provides in part that "(t)hese amended Rules of Criminal Procedure shall govern all criminal actions commenced or arrests made after 12 o'clock midnight January 1, 1990, except amendments to 8.04, 11.07, and 19.04, subd. 5, shall govern all criminal actions commenced or arrests made after 12 o'clock midnight January 1, 1991."

FORM 44. APPLICATION FOR JUDICIAL DETERMINATION OF PROBABLE CAUSE TO DETAIN

STATE OF MINNESOTA
COUNTY OF ______ DISTRICT COURT
Name of Arrestee: ____________________
Date of Birth: ________ Present Location: ________
Arresting Agency: ______________ CN#: ________
Date of Arrest: ________ Time of Arrest: ________
Offense(s): ______________________________
____

Facts constituting probable cause to believe a crime was committed and arrestee committed it: ________
____
____
____
____

___ Yes ___ No Was a prior application for probable cause to detain this person submitted to the court. If so, explain: ____________________
____

___ I have contacted the prosecuting attorney, ______________, who approved this Application for
(Name)
Judicial Determination of Probable Cause to Detain.

___ I have attempted to contact the prosecuting attorney to approve this application and have been unable to do so for the following reasons: ________
____
____

The Complainant, being duly sworn, swears the above facts are true and correct to the best of Complainant's knowledge and belief and constitute probable cause to believe that the above-named arrestee committed the offense(s) described herein.
Complainant's Signature: ________________
Agency: ______________ Time: ________
Subscribed and sworn to before me this ________ day of __________, 19__.

____
Judge, Judicial Officer, Clerk or Notary Public

APPROVAL OF PROSECUTING ATTORNEY

__________, being duly authorized to prosecute the offense(s) specified in the attached Application, hereby approves this Application for Judicial Determination of Probable Cause to Detain.
Date and time: ________ ______(signature)______
Name
Office

Adopted Oct. 23, 1992.

Historical Note

The order of the Minnesota Supreme Court [C1–84–2137] dated October 23, 1992, provides in part that "(t)hese amendments to the

Rules of Criminal Procedure shall govern all criminal actions commenced or arrests made after 12 o'clock midnight January 1, 1993."

FORM 45. JUDICIAL DETERMINATION OF PROBABLE CAUSE TO DETAIN

STATE OF MINNESOTA
COUNTY OF ______ DISTRICT COURT

JUDICIAL DETERMINATION OF PROBABLE CAUSE TO DETAIN

Name of Arrestee: ______
Date of Birth: ______ Present Location: ______
Arresting Agency: ______ CN#: ______
Date of Arrest: ______ Time of Arrest: ______
Facts submitted by written application and sworn affidavit?
___ Yes ___ No
Facts submitted orally upon oath?
___ Yes ___ No
Application approved by prosecuting attorney?
___ Yes ___ No
FROM THE SWORN FACTS SUBMITTED TO THE COURT

IT IS DETERMINED:
___ that the application to detain was timely presented to the court.
___ that the application to detain was not timely presented to the court and the above-described arrestee shall be released immediately.
___ that no probable cause exists to detain the above-described arrestee and said arrestee shall be released immediately.
___ that probable cause exists to detain the above-described arrestee for the offense(s) of ______
______

It is hereby ordered that said arrestee be detained subject to the requirements of the Minnesota Rules of Criminal Procedure and further order of this court.

___ that bail without other conditions of release is set in the amount of ______.
___ that other conditions of release, with or without bail, are established as follows: ______
______.
___ that the prosecuting attorney authorized to prosecute the offense(s) specified in the Application is unavailable to approve the application and the determination as to probable cause should not be delayed.

The proceeding was submitted: [ ] in writing
[ ] in person
[ ] telephonically
[ ] by FAX.

DATE: ______ TIME: ______

Judge or Judicial Officer

Adopted Oct. 23, 1992.

Historical Note

The order of the Minnesota Supreme Court [C1–84–2137] dated October 23, 1992, provides in part that "(t)hese amendments to the Rules of Criminal Procedure shall govern all criminal actions commenced or arrests made after 12 o'clock midnight January 1, 1993."

FORM 46. NOTICE OF JUDICIAL DETERMINATION OF PROBABLE CAUSE TO DETAIN

STATE OF MINNESOTA
COUNTY OF ______ DISTRICT COURT

Name of Arrestee: ______
Date of Birth: ______ Present Location: ______
Arresting Agency: ______ CN#: ______
Date of Arrest: ______ Time of Arrest: ______

You, (name of arrestee), are hereby notified that at (time) on (date), Judge/Judicial Officer (name) reviewed whether there was probable cause to detain you further pending your first court appearance and determined:

___ that the application to detain was timely presented to the court.
___ that the application to detain was not timely presented to the court and you shall be released immediately.
___ that no probable cause exists to detain you further and that you shall be released immediately.
___ that probable cause exists to detain you for the offense(s) of ______
______
pending your appearance in court or the posting of any bail that may have been set.
___ that bail without other conditions of release is set in the amount of ______.
___ that other conditions of release, with or without bail, are established as follows: ______
______.

The facts upon which this determination was made were submitted:

___ by written application and sworn affidavit.
___ orally upon oath.

Date and time notice given: ______

______
(name of person giving notice)

Adopted Oct. 23, 1992.

Historical Note

The order of the Minnesota Supreme Court [C1–84–2137] dated October 23, 1992, provides in part that "(t)hese amendments to the

Rules of Criminal Procedure shall govern all criminal actions commenced or arrests made after 12 o'clock midnight January 1, 1993."

FORM 47. APPLICATION FOR PUBLIC DEFENDER [Deleted January 17, 2013, eff. February 1, 2013]

FORM 48. ORDER ON APPLICATION FOR PUBLIC DEFENDER

State of Minnesota **District Court**
County of ____________ **_____ Judicial District**
File No.: ____________

STATE OF MINNESOTA
v.
____
Defendant

ORDER ON APPLICATION FOR PUBLIC DEFENDER

Upon review of the verified application for a public defender, the Court finds:

The Defendant is:

- ☐ Not financially eligible
- ☐ Financially eligible because:
  - ☐ The defendant, or a dependent of theirs who lives in their household, receives a means tested government benefit.
  - ☐ Due to insufficient funds or other assets, the defendant was refused representation by two lawyers on a referral list maintained by the Court.
  - ☐ The Court does not maintain a lawyer referral list, but two lawyers in this judicial district refused representation of the defendant due to insufficient funds or other assets.
  - ☐ The defendant does not have sufficient income or assets to pay the reasonable costs for defense of their case charged by lawyers in this judicial district.

Therefore, **IT IS ORDERED** that defendant's application for a public defender is:

- ☐ Approved
- ☐ Not approved

The Court finds that reimbursement is:

- ☐ Not required
- ☐ Required as follows: ______________________________
- ☐ To be determined at a later date

Date: __________

____
District Court Judge

Adopted April 11, 1996, eff. July 1, 1996.

FORM 49. CRIMINAL JUDGMENT AND WARRANT OF COMMITMENT

[Deleted Oct. 31, 2003, eff. Nov. 5, 2003.]

Historical Notes

See, now, MN R. Crim. P. 27.03, subd. 7.

FORM 49A. CRIMINAL JUDGMENT/WARRANT OF COMMITMENT

[Deleted Jan. 21, 2010, eff. July 1, 2010.]

FORM 49B. ORDER FOR CONDITIONS PRIOR TO CRIMINAL JUDGMENT

[Deleted Jan. 21, 2010, eff. July 1, 2010.]

FORM 50. JURY QUESTIONNAIRE

The use of this Questionnaire is to assist lawyers and the court in the selection of a fair, impartial and neutral jury.

Your answers to the questions contained in the Questionnaire, like your answers to questions in open court during jury selection proceedings, are part of the public record in this case.

DO NOT DISCUSS YOUR ANSWERS WITH ANY OF THE OTHER PROSPECTIVE JURORS.

(If additional questions are asked that may elicit sensitive information, the following language should be included: If you object to answering any particular questions in writing because the answers will be sensitive or embarrassing to you, you may request an opportunity to address the court to ask that such answers be given orally and not disclosed to the public.)

1. Name______________________________
2. Place of residence (City, Village, or Township): ________________
   __________ Zip Code __________
3. How long have you lived in this location?_______________
4. Where did you grow up? ____
   How long have you lived in this County? ______________________________
5. Your age __________
6. Are you currently (check one) single (never married)_______ separated _______ divorced _______ married _______ widowed _______?
7. How many years of school have you completed? __________
8. What high school(s) did you attend and the last calendar year you attended? _______
   ____
9. If you attended college or vocational school after high school, list: 1. the name of the school, 2. major type of training, 3. dates attended, 4. degrees or certificates.
   ____
   ____
   ____
10. Are you currently: (check one) employed full time_____employed at more than one job_____ employed part time _____ temporarily laid off_____unemployed_____ retired_____homemaker_____disabled _____ student_____
11. If employed or temporarily laid off, list occupation, name of employer and duties:
    ____
    ____
12. How long have you worked for this employer?__________________________________
    What previous jobs have you held?____
    ____
13. Please describe the occupation and education of: other adults in your household or, if divorced, your ex-spouse ____
    ____
    your mother ____
    your father ____
14. If you have any children, please list their age, sex, occupation if employed:
    ____
    ____
    ____
    ____
    ____
    ____
15. Have you ever served in the military? Yes _____ No _____
    If yes, list the branch, place and date of service, rank at discharge and the type of discharge: ____
    ____
    ____
    Are you now serving in a reserve unit? Yes _____ No _____
16. Please list the organizations to which you belong, in which you participate, or in which you have ever held any office. For example, service clubs, governmental bodies, unions

or professional organizations, volunteer activities, educational or political groups, etc.:
____
____
____
____

Answer this question for other adults in your household:
____
____
____
____

17. Have you ever served on a jury? Yes ____ No ____
If yes, please list the year or years in which you served and whether the case was civil or criminal:

year	civil or criminal
________	________________
________	________________
________	________________

If you served on a criminal jury was a verdict reached?
Yes ____ No ____ What was the charge? ________________
____
____
____

18. Have you ever served on a grand jury? Yes ____ No ____
If yes, how many cases were presented to the grand jury on which you served?
____
If yes, did the grand jury return an indictment(s)? Yes ____ No ____

19. Have you ever been called as a witness in court or given a statement in any legal proceeding? Yes ____ No ____
If yes, please describe the circumstances:
____
____
____

20. Do you have any close relatives or friends who are lawyers, judges, or are employed in any other job within the legal profession? Yes ____ No ____
If yes, list the name(s), relationship(s) and occupation(s):
____
____
____
____

21. Have you or any close relatives or friends ever been sued or sued someone else?
Yes ____ No ____
If yes, please explain: ________________
____
____
____

22. Have you ever had any legal or medical training?
Yes ____ No ____
If yes, please describe: ________________
____
____
____

23. Have you or any close relatives or friends ever been the victim of a crime?
Yes ____ No ____
If yes, please explain: ________________
____
____
____

24. Have you ever been a witness to a crime, or ever been questioned by a law enforcement officer about a crime? Yes ____ No ____
If yes, please explain: ________________

____

____

____

25. Have you ever filed a complaint against someone with law enforcement?
Yes _____ No _____
If yes, please explain: ____

____

____

26. Have you or any close relatives or friends ever been charged with or accused of a crime?
Yes _____ No _____
If yes, please explain the circumstances and the results:

____

____

____

____

27. Have you or any close relatives or friends ever worked in law enforcement, such as for a police department, highway patrol, state crime bureau or sheriff?
Yes _____ No _____
If yes, please list their name(s) occupation(s) and employer(s): _______________

____

____

____

28. Have you or any close relatives or friends ever worked for a fire department or rescue squad? Yes _____ No _____
29. Do you have any close relatives or friends who have ever worked as a probation officer or in the prison system?
Yes _____ No _____
30. Do you have any religious or philosophical beliefs that would make it difficult for you to be a juror? Yes _____ No _____
If yes, please explain: ____

____

____

____

____

31. Do you have any disabilities, physical, mental, or other problems which would make it difficult for you to sit as a juror? Yes _____ No _____
If yes, please explain: ____

____

Do you have any limitations on your vision or hearing?
Yes _____ No _____
If yes, would a special seating assignment help you follow the trial and enable you to serve on the jury? Yes _____ No _____
32. Have you or any close relatives or friends ever been addicted to anything, such as alcohol or drugs of any kind?
Yes _____ No _____
33. Are there any pressing matters that would distract you or prevent you from giving jury service your complete and undivided attention? Yes _____ No _____
If yes, please explain: ____

____

____

____

____

____

____

____

____

____

I have given complete and honest answers to all of the questions above.

Dated: ______________________________

____
Signature

Adopted Aug. 21, 1998, eff. Jan. 1, 1999. Amended Dec. 10, 2003, eff. Feb. 1, 2004.

FORM 51. CONSENT TO ITV APPEARANCE

STATE OF MINNESOTA
COUNTY OF ____________

DISTRICT COURT
____ JUDICIAL DISTRICT

________________________________,
Plaintiff,

vs.

CONSENT TO ITV APPEARANCE

________________________________,
Defendant.

District Court File No. ____________

I, _________, Defendant in the above-entitled action do respectfully represent and state as follows:

1. I understand that I have the right to be personally present before the presiding Judge at all stages of these proceedings.

2. I have been requested to consent to appear by ITV for the (hearing type) hearing scheduled for (date).

3. I understand that if I do not consent to appear by ITV, an in-person court appearance for that hearing will be scheduled within the time limits provided by the Minnesota Rules of Criminal Procedure or other law.

3. I hereby consent to appear by ITV for the hearing.

4. This consent may not be extended to a future hearing without my later consent.

Dated: __________

____
Signature of Defendant

Adopted Nov. 19, 2007, eff. Jan. 1, 2008.

MANDATORY FELONY AND GROSS MISDEMEANOR COMPLAINT AND INDICTMENT FORMS

[Deleted May 19, 2008, eff. July 1, 2008]

INDEX TO RULES OF CRIMINAL PROCEDURE

MINNESOTA SENTENCING GUIDELINES AND COMMENTARY

Revised Effective August 1, 2013

Research Note

See Minnesota Statutes Annotated, *Volume 16, Ch. 244 Appendix, for case annotations and other research aids.*

Historical and Statutory Notes

Revised August 1, 2013

TABLE OF CONTENTS

MEMBERS AND STAFF

MINNESOTA SENTENCING GUIDELINES COMMISSION
309 Administration Building
50 Sherburne Avenue
St. Paul, Minnesota 55155

Voice: (651) 296–0144
FAX: (651) 297–5757

Website: mn.gov/sentencing-guidelines
Email: sentencing.guidelines@state.mn.us

MN Relay TTY: 1–800–627–3529; ask for (651) 296–0144

Commission Members

Jeffrey Edblad, Chair and Isanti County Attorney
Jason Anderson, Probation Representative, Itasca County Probation
Christopher Dietzen, Justice, Minnesota Supreme Court
Paul Ford, Peace Officer Representative, Washington County
Connie Larson, Vice-Chair and Citizen Representative
Caroline Lennon, Judge, First Judicial District
Tom Roy, Commissioner of Corrections
Heidi Schellhas, Judge, Minnesota Court of Appeals
John Stuart, State Public Defender
Yamy Vang, Citizen Representative
Sarah Walker, Citizen Representative

Commission Staff

Kelly Lyn Mitchell, Executive Director
Jackie Braun, Research Analyst
Kathleen Madland, Research Analyst Intermediate
Linda McBrayer, Management Analyst 4
Jill Payne, Research Analysis Specialist, Senior
Anne Wall, Research Analysis Specialist, Senior

1. Purpose and Definitions

A. Statement of Purpose and Principles

The purpose of the Sentencing Guidelines is to establish rational and consistent sentencing standards that reduce sentencing disparity and ensure that the sanctions imposed for felony convictions are proportional to the severity of the conviction offense and the offender's criminal history. Equity in sentencing requires that: (a) convicted felons with similar relevant sentencing criteria should receive similar sanctions; and (b) convicted felons with relevant sentencing criteria substantially different from a typical case should receive different sanctions.

The Sentencing Guidelines embody the following principles:

1. Sentencing should be neutral with respect to the race, gender, social, or economic status of convicted felons.

2. The severity of the sanction should increase in direct proportion to an increase in offense severity or the convicted felon's criminal history, or both. This promotes a rational and consistent sentencing policy.

3. Commitment to the Commissioner of Corrections is the most severe sanction that can be imposed for a felony conviction, but it is not the only significant sanction available to the court.

4. Because state and local correctional facility capacity is finite, confinement should be imposed only for offenders who are convicted of more serious offenses or who have longer criminal histories. To ensure such usage of finite resources, sanctions used in sentencing convicted felons should be the least restrictive necessary to achieve the purposes of the sentence.

5. Although the Sentencing Guidelines are advisory to the court, the presumptive sentences are deemed appropriate for the felonies covered by them. Therefore, departures from the presumptive sentences established in the Sentencing Guidelines should be made only when substantial and compelling circumstances can be identified and articulated.

B. Definitions

As used in these Sentencing Guidelines (or "Guidelines"), the following terms have the meanings given.

1. Commitment. "Commitment" occurs when the offender is sentenced to the custody of the Commissioner of Corrections.

2. Concurrent Sentence. When the court orders sentences to be "concurrent," the court is ordering that multiple sentences be served at the same time.

3. Consecutive Sentence. When the court orders sentences to be "consecutive," the court is ordering that multiple sentences be served one after the other.

4. Departure. A "departure" is a pronounced sentence other than that recommended in the appropriate cell on the applicable Grid, including a stayed or imposed gross misdemeanor or misdemeanor sentence.

a. *Dispositional Departure.* A "dispositional departure" occurs when the court orders a disposition other than that recommended in the Guidelines.

(1) Aggravated Dispositional Departure. An "aggravated dispositional departure" occurs when the Guidelines recommend a stayed sentence but the court pronounces a prison sentence.

(2) Mitigated Dispositional Departure. A "mitigated dispositional departure" occurs when the Guidelines recommend a prison sentence but the court stays the sentence.

b. *Durational Departure.* A "durational departure" occurs when the court orders a sentence with a duration other than the presumptive fixed duration or range in the appropriate cell on the applicable Grid.

(1) Aggravated Durational Departure. An "aggravated durational departure" occurs when the court pronounces a duration that is more than 20 percent higher than the fixed duration displayed in the appropriate cell on the applicable Grid.

(2) Mitigated Durational Departure. A "mitigated durational departure" occurs when the court pronounces a sentence that is more than 15 percent lower than the fixed duration displayed in the appropriate cell on the applicable Grid.

5. Departure Report. A "departure report" is a form completed by the sentencing court when the court pronounces a sentence that is a departure from the presumptive sentence. Under Minn. R. Crim. P. 27.03, subd. 4(c), the form must be completed and submitted to the Sentencing Guidelines Commission within 15 days after sentencing.

6. Executed Sentence. An "executed sentence" is the total period of time for which an inmate is committed to the custody of the Commissioner of Corrections (sent to prison). Under Minn. Stat. § 244.101, the sentence consists of two parts: a minimum term of imprisonment and a maximum period of supervised release.

a. *Term of Imprisonment.* For offenders committed to the Commissioner of Corrections for crimes committed on or after August 1, 1993, the "term of imprisonment" (incarceration) is equal to two-thirds of the executed sentence.

b. *Supervised Release Term.* For offenders committed to the Commissioner of Corrections for crimes committed on or after August 1, 1993, the "supervised release term" is a period of mandatory community supervision, which is served following the end of the term of imprisonment, and is equal to one-third of the executed sentence less any applicable disciplinary confinement period.

7. **Extended Jurisdiction Juvenile (EJJ).** An "extended jurisdiction juvenile" is a child who, under the procedures in Minn. Stat. § 260B.130, has been given a stayed adult sentence and a juvenile disposition, and for whom jurisdiction of the juvenile court may continue until the child's twenty-first birthday.

8. **Factfinder.** The "factfinder" or finder of fact determines the facts in the case, and may be either the court or the jury.

9. **Hernandize.** "Hernandize" (or "Hernandizing") is the unofficial term for the process described in section 2.B.1.e of counting criminal history when multiple offenses are sentenced on the same day before the same court.

10. **Local Confinement.** "Local confinement" is a term of incarceration of up to one year served in a local facility, and may be pronounced by the court as a condition of probation.

11. **Mandatory Minimum.** The "mandatory minimum" is a minimum executed sentence duration specified in statute for offenders convicted of certain felony offenses.

12. **Presumptive Sentence.** "Presumptive sentences" are those sentences provided on the Sentencing Guidelines Grids. They are presumptive because they are presumed to be appropriate for all typical cases sharing criminal history and offense severity characteristics.

a. *Presumptive Disposition.* The "presumptive disposition" is the recommendation for either a commitment or a stayed sentence.

(1) Presumptive Commitment. A "presumptive commitment" is a recommended disposition of imprisonment for cases contained in cells outside of the shaded area on the Grids.

(2) Presumptive Stayed Sentence. A "presumptive stayed sentence" is a recommendation for a stayed sentence for cases contained in the cells within the shaded area on the Grids.

b. *Presumptive Duration.* The "presumptive duration" is the recommended fixed sentence length in months found in the appropriate cell on the applicable Grid.

c. *Presumptive Range.* The "presumptive range" is provided for a sentence that is a presumptive commitment. Pursuant to Minn. Stat. § 244.09, subd. 5(2), the range is 15 percent lower and 20 percent higher than the fixed duration displayed in each cell on the Grids.

13. **Sentence Modifier.** A "sentence modifier" is a statute that aids in defining the punishment for the underlying offense. A sentence modifier can affect either or both the duration and the disposition of the presumptive sentence. See section 2.G for policies relating to determining the presumptive sentence for offenses that include a sentence modifier.

14. **Sentencing Guidelines Grids.** The "Sentencing Guidelines Grids" (or "Grids") display presumptive sentences for felony offenses according to the severity level of the offense (vertical axis) and offender's criminal history score (horizontal axis).

a. *Sex Offender Grid.* The "Sex Offender Grid" displays the presumptive sentences for criminal sexual conduct, failure to register as a predatory offender, and related offenses as shown on the Sex Offender Grid.

b. *Standard Grid.* The "Standard Grid" displays the presumptive sentences for felony offenses not on the Sex Offender Grid.

15. **Sentencing Worksheet.** The "Sentencing Worksheet" (or "Worksheet') is a form completed by probation at the direction of the court under Minn. Stat. § 609.115, subd. 2a. The Worksheet reflects the severity of the current conviction offense, applicable history as calculated under Sentencing Guidelines policies, and the presumptive sentence as reflected in the appropriate cell of the applicable Grid. A separate Worksheet should be completed for all felony-level offenses receiving a stayed or imposed sentence, or a stay of imposition. This includes offenses that receive a life sentence and felony convictions for which the court imposes a gross misdemeanor or misdemeanor sentence.

16. **Statutory Maximum.** The "statutory maximum" is the maximum sentence duration provided for the offense in statute (e.g., "imprisonment for not more than 15 years").

17. **Stayed Sentenced.** A "stayed sentence" may be accomplished by either a stay of imposition or a stay of execution. There are two steps in sentencing: the imposition of a sentence and the execution of the sentence imposed. The imposition of sentence consists of pronouncing the sentence to be served in prison (for example, three years imprisonment). The execution of an imposed sentence consists of transferring the felon to the custody of the Commissioner of Corrections to serve the prison sentence.

a. *Stay of Imposition.* A "stay of imposition" occurs when the court accepts and records a finding or plea of guilty, but does not impose (or pronounce) a prison sentence. If the offender successfully completes the stay, the case is discharged, and the conviction is deemed a misdemeanor under Minn.

Stat. § 609.13, but is still included in criminal history under section 2.B.

b. *Stay of Execution.* A "stay of execution" occurs when the court accepts and records a finding or plea of guilty, and a prison sentence is pronounced, but is not executed. If the offender successfully completes the stay, the case is discharged, but the offender continues to have a record of a felony conviction, which is included in criminal history under section 2.B.

2. Determining Presumptive Sentences

The presumptive sentence for any offender convicted of a felony committed on or after May 1, 1980, is determined by the Sentencing Guidelines in effect on the date of the conviction offense, except that:

- If multiple offenses are an element of the conviction offense, the date of the conviction offense must be determined by the factfinder.
- If offenses have been aggregated under one of the following statutes, or as otherwise permitted by statute, the date of the earliest offense should be used as the date of the conviction offense:

Statute Number	Offense Title
349.2127, subds. 2 and 6	Gambling Regulations
609.322, subd. 1c	Solicitation, Promotion, and Inducement of Prostitution; Sex Trafficking
609.52, subd. 3(5)	Theft
609.527, subd. 7	Identity Theft
609.535, subd. 2a(b)	Issuance of Dishonored Checks
609.551, subd. 3	Rustling and Livestock Theft
609.595	Criminal Damage to Property
609.631, subd. 4	Check Forgery
609.632, subd. 5	Counterfeiting Currency
609.763, subd. 3	Lawful Gambling Fraud
609.821, subd. 3	Financial Transaction Card Fraud
609.86, subd. 3(2)	Commercial Bribery
609.893, subd. 3	Telecommunications Fraud
609.895, subd. 3	Counterfeited Intellectual Property

The presumptive sentence is found in the cell of the appropriate Grid located at the intersection of the criminal history score and the severity level. The Grids represent the two dimensions most important in sentencing decisions.

A. Offense Severity

1. General Rule. The offense severity level is determined by the conviction offense. When an offender is convicted of two or more felonies, the severity level is determined by the most severe conviction offense. Felony offenses, other than sex offenses, are arranged on the Standard Grid into eleven levels of severity, ranging from high (Severity Level 11) to low (Severity Level 1). Sex offenses are arranged on a separate Sex Offender Grid into eight severity levels, ranging from high (Severity Level A) to low (Severity Level H). Offenses listed within each severity level are deemed to be equally serious. The severity level for each felony offense is governed by section 5A, Offense Severity Reference Table.

2. Theft and Damage to Property; Foreseeable Risk of Bodily Harm. For an offender sentenced for theft under Minn. Stat. § 609.52, subd. 3a, the severity level ranking is elevated by one severity level from that listed on the Offense Severity Reference Table if the offense creates a foreseeable risk of bodily harm to another and:

a. the violation involves a monetary value over $1,000; or

b. the violation involves a monetary value between $500 and $1,000, and the offender has been convicted within the preceding five years for an offense under Minn. Stat. § 609.52, subd. 3.

3. First Degree Murder. A severity level has not been assigned to first-degree murder because by law the punishment is a mandatory life sentence.

4. Unranked Offenses. Some offenses are designated as unranked offenses. When the court sentences an unranked offense, the court must assign an appropriate severity level for the offense and specify on the record why that particular level was assigned. The court may consider, but is not limited to, the following factors:

a. the gravity of the specific conduct underlying the unranked offense;

b. the severity level assigned to any ranked offense with elements that are similar to the elements of the unranked offense;

c. the conduct of and severity level assigned to other offenders for the same unranked offense; and

d. the severity level assigned to other offenders engaged in similar conduct.

If an offense is omitted from the Offense Severity Reference Table, the offense is considered unranked.

5. Attempts, Conspiracies, and Other Sentence Modifiers. When the current offense includes a sentence modifier, such as attempt or conspiracy, the severity level is found by determining the severity level for the underlying offense. Determining the presumptive sentence for these offenses is described in section 2.G.

Comment

2.A.01. The date of the offense is important because the offender's age at the time of the offense will determine whether the juvenile record is considered, and the date of the offense might determine whether a custody status point should be given and the order of sentencing with multiple convictions.

2.A.02. If multiple offenses are an element of the offense and the determination of which presumptive sentence applies depends on the offense date, the date of the conviction offense must be determined by the factfinder. See State v. DeRosier, 719 N.W.2d 900 (Minn. 2006) (where defendant was charged with first-degree criminal sexual conduct occurring from June through August of 2000 and the presumptive sentence increased on August 1, 2000 from 86 to 144 months, the court erred when it made a finding without a jury that the offense occurred after the effective date of the increased presumptive sentence).

2.A.03. If the offense occurred on or before April 30, 1980, the Sentencing Guidelines should not be used to sentence the case.

2.A.04. An unranked offense typically has one or more of the following characteristics: (1) the offense is rarely prosecuted; (2) the offense covers a wide range of underlying conduct; or (3) the offense is new and the severity of a typical offense cannot yet be determined. If a significant number of future convictions are obtained under one or more of the unranked offenses, the Commission will reexamine the ranking of these offenses and assign an appropriate severity level for a typical offense. Practitioners can contact the Commission for information on severity levels assigned to unranked offenses.

2.A.05. For Theft of a Motor Vehicle to be ranked at Severity Level 4, the offender must be convicted under the general theft statute, Minn. Stat. § 609.52, subd. 2(a)(1), and the offense must involve theft of a motor vehicle. It is the Commission's intent that any conviction involving the permanent theft of a motor vehicle be ranked at Severity Level 4, regardless of the value of the motor vehicle.

2.A.06. When a sentencing worksheet is completed under Minn. Stat. § 609.115, subd. 2a for first-degree murder, Severity Level 12 should be used.

B. Criminal History

The horizontal axis on the Sentencing Guidelines Grids is the criminal history score. An offender's criminal history score is the sum of points from eligible:

- prior felonies;
- custody status at the time of the offense;
- prior misdemeanors and gross misdemeanors; and
- prior juvenile adjudications.

This section details the requirements for calculating the criminal history points in each of these areas. This section also details the requirements for calculating criminal history points for convictions from jurisdictions other than Minnesota and convictions for enhanced felonies.

Comment

2.B.01. The Guidelines reduce the emphasis given to criminal history in sentencing decisions. Under past judicial practice, criminal history was the primary factor in dispositional decisions. Under the Guidelines, the conviction offense is the primary factor, and criminal history is a secondary factor in dispositional decisions. Prior to enactment of the Guidelines, there were no uniform standards regarding what should be included in an offender's criminal history, no weighting format for different types of offenses, and no systematic process to check the accuracy of the information on criminal history.

2.B.02. The Guidelines provide uniform standards for the inclusion and weighting of criminal history information. The sentencing hearing provides a process to assure the accuracy of the information in individual cases.

2.B.03. Minn. Stat. § 609A.03, subd. 7(b) provides that:

> Notwithstanding the issuance of an expungement order:
>
> (1) an expunged record may be opened for purposes of a criminal investigation, prosecution, or sentencing, upon an ex parte court order;
>
> . . .
>
> Upon request by law enforcement, prosecution, or corrections authorities, an agency or jurisdiction subject to an expungement order shall inform the requester of the existence of a sealed record and of the right to obtain access to it as provided by this paragraph....

1. Prior Felonies. Assign a particular weight, as set forth in paragraphs a and b, to each extended jurisdiction juvenile (EJJ) conviction and each felony conviction, provided that a felony sentence was stayed or imposed before the current sentencing or a stay of imposition of sentence was given before the current sentencing.

The severity level ranking in effect at the time the current offense was committed determines the weight assigned to the prior offense.

a. *Current Offense on Standard Grid.* If the current offense is **not** on the Sex Offender Grid, determine the weight assigned to each prior felony sentence according to its severity level, as follows:

SEVERITY LEVEL	POINTS
1—2	½
3—5	1
6—8	1½
9—11	2
Murder 1st Degree	2
A	2
B—E	1½
F—G	1
H	½ (for first offense); 1 (for subsequent offenses)

b. *Current Offense on Sex Offender Grid.* If the current offense is on the Sex Offender Grid, determine the weight assigned to each prior felony sentence according to its severity level, as follows:

SEVERITY LEVEL	POINTS
1—2	½
3—5	1
6—8	1½
9—11	2
Murder 1st Degree	2
A	3
B—C	2
D—E	1½
F—G	1
H	½ (for first offense); 1 (for subsequent offenses)

c. *Felony Decay Factor.* A prior felony sentence or stay of imposition following a felony conviction must not be used in computing the criminal history score if a period of fifteen years has elapsed since the date of discharge from or expiration of the sentence to the date of the current offense.

d. *Assigning Felony Weights—Previous Court Appearances Resulting in Multiple Sentences.* Following are exceptions to including prior felonies in criminal history when multiple felony sentences were imposed in a previous court appearance:

(1) Single Course of Conduct / Multiple Sentences. When multiple sentences for a single course of conduct were imposed under Minn. Stats. §§ 152.137, 609.585 or 609.251, include in criminal history only the weight from the offense at the highest severity level.

(2) Single Course of Conduct / Multiple Victims. When multiple offenses arising from a single course of conduct involving multiple victims were sentenced, include in criminal history only the weights from the two offenses at the highest severity levels.

e. *Assigning Felony Weights—Current Multiple Sentences.* Multiple offenses sentenced at the same time before the same court must be sentenced in the order in which they occurred. As each offense is sentenced, include it in the criminal history on the next offense to be sentenced (also known as "*Hernandizing*") except as follows:

(1) Single Course of Conduct / Multiple Sentences. When multiple current convictions arise from a single course of conduct and multiple sentences are imposed on the same day under Minn. Stats. §§ 152.137, 609.585, or 609.251, the conviction and sentence for the "earlier" offense does not increase the criminal history score for the "later" offense.

(2) Single Course of Conduct / Multiple Victims. When multiple current convictions arise out of a single course of conduct in which there were multiple victims, weights are given only to the two offenses at the highest severity levels.

f. *Prior Offense with Attempt, Conspiracy, or Other Sentence Modifier.* When a prior offense included a sentence modifier, such as attempt, conspiracy, or other sentence modifier as described in section 2.G, the prior conviction must be given the same felony weight as a completed offense.

g. *Prior Offenses with No Conviction.* Assign no weight to an offense for which a judgment of guilty has not been entered before the current sentencing, such as a stay of adjudication or continuance for dismissal.

h. *Non-Felony Sentence.* Except when a monetary threshold determines the offense classification of the prior offense (see section 2.B.7), when a prior felony conviction resulted in a non-felony sentence (misdemeanor or gross misdemeanor), the conviction must be counted in the criminal history score as a misdemeanor or gross misdemeanor conviction as indicated in section 2.B.3.

i. *Total Felony Points.* The felony point total is the sum of the felony weights. If the sum of the weights results in a partial point, the point value must be rounded down to the nearest whole number.

Comment

2.B.101. The basic rule for computing the number of prior felony points in the criminal history score is that the offender is assigned a particular weight for every felony conviction for which a felony sentence was stayed or imposed before the current sentencing or for which a stay of imposition of sentence was given for a felony level offense, no matter what period of probation is pronounced, before the current sentencing.

2.B.102. No partial points are given—thus, an offender with less than a full point is not given that point. For example, an offender with a total weight of 2 ½ would have 2 felony points.

2.B.103. The Commission determined that it was important to establish a weighting scheme for prior felony sentences to assure a greater degree of proportionality in the current sentencing. Offenders who have a history of serious felonies are considered more culpable than those offenders whose prior felonies consist primarily of low severity, nonviolent offenses.

2.B.104. The Commission recognized that determining the severity level of the prior felonies may be difficult in some instances. For that reason, the severity level of the prior offense is based on the severity level in effect when the offender commits the current offense.

2.B.105. If an offense has been repealed, but the elements of that offense have been incorporated into another felony statute, determine the appropriate severity level based on the severity level ranking for the current felony offense containing those similar elements. For example, in 2010, the Legislature recodified violations of domestic abuse no contact orders from Minn. Stat. § 518B.01, subd. 22(d) into Minn. Stat. § 629.75, subd. 2(d). This policy also applies to offenses that are currently assigned a severity level ranking, but were previously unranked and excluded from the Offense Severity

Reference Table. For example, possession of pornographic work involving minors under Minn. Stat. § 617.247, subd. 3(a) was unranked until August 1, 2006. It is currently ranked at Severity Level E, and receives a weight of 1 ½ points.

2.B.106. If an offense has been redefined by the Legislature, base the appropriate severity level on how the prior felony offense would currently be ranked in consideration of any new or removed elements. It was contemplated that the sentencing court, in its discretion, should make the final determination as to the weight accorded prior felony sentences.

2.B.107. In cases of multiple offenses occurring in a single course of conduct in which state law prohibits the offender from being sentenced on more than one offense, only the offense at the highest severity level should be considered. The phrase "before the current sentencing" means that in order for prior convictions to be used in computing the criminal history score, the felony sentence for the prior offense must have been stayed or imposed before sentencing for the current offense. When multiple current offenses are sentenced on the same day before the same court, sentencing must occur in the order in which the offenses occurred. The dates of the offenses must be determined according to the procedures in section 2.A.

2.B.108. The Commission established policies to deal with several specific situations that arise under Minnesota law: a conviction under Minn. Stat. § 152.137, under which offenders convicted of methamphetamine-related crimes involving children and vulnerable adults are subject to conviction and sentence for other crimes resulting from the same criminal behavior; Minn. Stat. § 609.585, under which offenders committing another felony offense during the course of a burglary could be convicted of and sentenced for both the burglary and the other felony; and a conviction under Minn. Stat. § 609.251 under which offenders who commit another felony during the course of a kidnapping can be convicted of and sentenced for both offenses. For purposes of computing criminal history, the Commission decided that consideration should only be given to the most severe offense when there are prior multiple sentences under provisions of Minn. Stats. §§ 152.137, 609.585, or 609.251. This was done to prevent inequities due to past variability in prosecutorial and sentencing practices with respect to these statutes, to prevent systematic manipulation of these statutes in the future, and to provide a uniform and equitable method of computing criminal history scores for all cases of multiple convictions arising from a single course of conduct, when single victims are involved.

When multiple current convictions arise from a single course of conduct and multiple sentences are imposed on the same day under Minn. Stats. §§ 152.137, 609.585, or 609.251, the conviction and sentence for the "earlier" offense should not increase the criminal history score for the "later" offense.

2.B.109. The Commission has carefully considered the application of the Hernandez method to sentencing in provisions of Minnesota law other than Minn. Stats. §§ 152.137, 609.585, and 609.251. The Commission's decision not to amend the Sentencing Guidelines is deliberate. See, State v. Williams, 771 N.W.2d 514 (Minn. 2009).

2.B.110. To limit the impact of past variability in prosecutorial discretion, the Commission decided that for prior multiple felony sentences arising out of a single course of conduct in which there were multiple victims, consideration should be given only for the two most severe offenses. For example, if an offender had robbed a crowded liquor store, he could be convicted of and sentenced for the robbery, as well as one count of assault for every person in the store at the time of the offense. Past variability in prosecutorial charging and negotiating practices could create substantial variance in the number of felony sentences arising from comparable criminal behavior. To prevent this past disparity from entering into the computation of criminal histories, and to prevent manipulation of the system in the future, the Commission limited consideration to the two most severe offenses in such situations. This still allows differentiation between those getting multiple sentences in such situations from those getting single sentences, but it prevents the perpetuation of gross disparities from the past.

This limit in calculating criminal history when there are multiple felony sentences arising out of a single course of conduct with multiple victims also applies when such sentences are imposed on the same day.

2.B.111. When an offender was convicted of a felony but was given a misdemeanor or gross misdemeanor sentence, the offense will be counted as a misdemeanor or gross misdemeanor for purposes of computing the criminal history score. The Commission also recognized that where such sentences were given, it was the opinion of the court that the offending behavior did not merit felonious punishment, or other circumstances existed that justified a limit on the severity of the sanction.

2.B.112. The decision to stay execution of sentence rather than to stay imposition of sentence as a means to a probationary term following a felony conviction is discretionary with the court. Considerable disparity appears to exist in the use of these options. In the case of two similar offenders it is not uncommon for one to receive a stay of execution and another to receive the benefit of a stay of imposition. There may also be geographical disparities. As a result of the disparity that exists in the use of stays of imposition, the Commission determined to treat stays of execution and stays of imposition the same with respect to criminal history point accrual. Similar treatment has the additional advantage of a simplified procedure for computing criminal history scores.

2.B.113. The Commission established a "decay factor" for the consideration of prior felony offenses in computing criminal history scores. The Commission decided it was important to consider not just the total number of felony sentences and stays of imposition, but also the age of the sentences and stays of imposition. The Commission decided that the presence of old felony sentences and stays of imposition should not be considered in computing criminal history scores after a significant period of time has elapsed. A prior felony sentence or stay of imposition would not be counted in criminal history score computation if fifteen years had elapsed from the date of discharge or expiration of that sentence or stay of imposition to the date of the current offense. While this procedure does not include a measure of the offender's subsequent criminality it has the overriding advantage of accurate and simple application.

2.B.114. An offense upon which a judgment of guilty has not been entered before the current sentencing (e.g., under Minn. Stat. § 152.18, subd. 1), must not be assigned any weight in computing the criminal history score.

2.B.115. Under Minn. Stat. § 260B.130, a child alleged to have committed a felony offense under certain circumstances may be prosecuted as an extended jurisdiction juvenile (EJJ). If the prosecution results in a guilty plea or finding of guilt and the court imposes a disposition according to Minn. Stat. § 260B.130, subd. 4 (a), the extended jurisdiction juvenile conviction must be treated the same as an adult felony sentence for purposes of calculating the prior felony record component of the criminal history score. All of the policies under section 2.B.1, and corresponding commentary apply to EJJ convictions. If the EJJ conviction resulted in execution of the stayed adult prison sentence, the offense can only be counted once in the criminal history.

2.B.116. Legal authorities use the terms "single course of conduct" and "single behavioral incident" interchangeably. In the Guidelines, this is referred to as "single course of conduct."

2. Custody Status at the Time of the Offense.

a. *One Custody Status Point.* Assign **one** custody status point when the conditions in paragraphs (1) through (3) are met:

(1) The offender was under one of the following custody statuses:

(i) probation;

(ii) parole;

(iii) supervised release;

(iv) conditional release following release from an executed prison sentence (see conditional release terms listed in section 2.E.3);

(v) release pending sentencing;

(vi) confinement in a jail, workhouse, or prison pending or after sentencing; or

(vii) escape from confinement following an executed sentence.

(2) The offender was under one of the custody statuses in paragraph (1) after entry of a guilty plea, guilty verdict, or conviction. This includes a guilty plea for an offense under Minn. Stat. § 152.18, subd. 1.

(3) The offender was under one of the custody statuses in paragraph (1) for one of the following:

(i) a felony;

(ii) extended jurisdiction juvenile (EJJ) conviction;

(iii) non-traffic gross misdemeanor;

(iv) gross misdemeanor driving while impaired or refusal to submit to a chemical test; or

(v) targeted misdemeanor.

(4) Early Discharge from Probation. Assign a custody point if the offender is discharged from probation but commits an offense within the initial period of probation pronounced by the court. **Do not** assign a point if probation is revoked and the offender serves an executed sentence.

(5) Assigning Points to Offenses Committed Over Time. Assign a custody status point when the offender meets the conditions in paragraphs (1) through (3) and the offender was placed under one of the custody statuses in paragraph (1) at any point in time during which the offense occurred when:

(i) multiple offenses are an element of the conviction offense; or

(ii) the conviction offense is an aggregated offense.

b. *Two Custody Status Points.* Assign **two** custody status points if:

(1) the current conviction offense is an offense on the Sex Offender Grid other than Failure to Register as a Predatory Offender (243.166);

(2) the offender was under any of the custody statuses in paragraph a(1) for an offense currently found on the Sex Offender Grid other than Failure to Register as a Predatory Offender (Minn. Stat. § 243.166).

c. *Additional Duration.* An **additional three months** must be added to the duration of the appropriate cell time, which then becomes the presumptive duration, when:

(1) a custody status point is assigned; and

(2) the offender's total Criminal History Score exceeds the maximum score on the applicable Grid (i.e., 7 or more).

Three months must also be added to the lower and upper end of the range provided in the appropriate cell on the applicable Grid.

If the current conviction is an attempt, conspiracy, or other offense with a sentence modifier that reduces the presumptive sentence, the three months must be added to the cell duration before the duration is reduced as outlined in section 2.G. The presumptive duration, however, cannot be less than one year and one day.

d. *No Custody Status Points Assigned.* The offender must not be assigned custody status points when:

(1) The offender was committed for treatment or examination under Minn. R. Crim. P. 20.

(2) The offender was on juvenile custody status other than for an extended jurisdiction juvenile (EJJ) conviction, at the time the adult felony was committed.

(3) The offender was on custody status for a misdemeanor or gross misdemeanor DWI committed when the offender was 16 or 17 years old, and the DWI was processed in adult court under Minn. Stat. § 260B.225, subds. 3 and 8.

Comment

2.B.201. The basic rule assigns offenders one point if they were under some form of eligible criminal justice custody status when they committed the offense for which they are now being sentenced.

2.B.202. The Commission determined that the potential for a custody status point should remain for the entire period of the probationary sentence. If an offender receives an initial term of probation that is definite, is released from probation prior to the expiration of that term and commits a new crime within the initial term, it is clear that a custody point will be assigned. For example, if the offender is put on probation for five years, is released from probation in three years, and commits a new crime in year four, at least one custody status point will be added to the offender's criminal history. When the offender is given an indefinite initial term of probation and commits a new crime at any time prior to the end date of the pronounced range, the offender will be assigned a custody status point. Thus, an initial term of probation "not to exceed three years" is, for this purpose, three years; "three to five years" is five years; "up to the statutory maximum" is the statutory maximum. If probation is revoked and the offender serves an executed prison sentence for the prior offense, eligibility for the custody status point ends with discharge from the sentence.

2.B.203. Probation given for an offense under Minn. Stat. § 152.18, subd. 1, will result in the assignment of a custody status point because a guilty plea has previously been entered and the offender has been on a probationary status.

2.B.204. Commitments under Minn. R. Crim. P. 20, and juvenile custody status are not included because, in those situations, there has been no conviction. However, a custody point will be assigned if the offender committed the current offense while under some form of custody following an extended jurisdiction juvenile (EJJ) conviction.

2.B.205. The custodial statuses covered by this policy are those occurring after conviction of a felony, non-traffic gross misdemeanor, gross misdemeanor driving while impaired or refusal to submit to a chemical test or misdemeanor on the targeted misdemeanor list provided in Minn. Stat. § 299C.10, subd. 1(e). Thus, an offender who commits a new felony while on pre-trial diversion or pre-trial release on another charge does not get a custody status point. Likewise, offenders serving a misdemeanor sentence for an offense not on the targeted misdemeanor list provided in Minn. Stat. § 299C.10, subd. 1(e), do not receive a custody status point, even if the court imposed the misdemeanor sentence upon conviction of a gross misdemeanor or felony.

2.B.206. As a general rule, the Commission excludes traffic offenses from consideration in computing the criminal history score. Given the increased penalties associated with driving while impaired (DWI) offenses and the serious impact on public safety, the Commission determined that these offenses should be considered for custody status points in the same manner as non-traffic offenses.

2.B.207. The most problematic consequence of a Criminal History Score of 7 or more (in excess of the maximum points differentiated by the Sentencing Guidelines Grids) is that no additional penalty accrues for engaging in felonious behavior while under custody supervision. For example, if an offender has a Criminal History Score of 7 and is released pending sentencing for a Severity Level 3 offense, and he or she commits another Severity Level 3 offense while awaiting sentencing, the presumptive sentence for the most recent offense is the same as for the prior offense. A presumption exists against consecutive sentences for most property offenses, and therefore no additional penalty results when this situation occurs. The addition of three months to the cell duration provides a uniform presumptive standard for dealing with this situation.

2.B.208. While the Commission believes that the impact of the custody status provision should be maintained for all cases, incrementing the sanction for each criminal history point above seven is deemed inappropriate. The primary determinant of the sentence is the seriousness of the current conviction offense. Criminal history is of secondary importance, and the Commission believes that proportionality in sentencing is served sufficiently with the criminal history differentiations incorporated in the Sentencing Guidelines Grids and with the special provision for maintaining the impact of the custody status provision. The Commission deems further differentiation unnecessary to achieve proportionality in sentencing.

2.B.209. The Commission believes that when multiple offenses are an element of the conviction offense or the conviction offense is an aggregated offense, offenders should receive a custody status point if they become subject to one of the custody status types listed in 2.B.2.a(1) at any point during the time period in which the offenses occurred. While the Commission recognizes that its policy for determining the presumptive sentence states that for aggregated offenses, the earliest offense date determines the date of offense, it believes that eligibility for a custody status point should not be limited to the offender's status at the time of the earliest date of offense.

2.B.210. When offenders on any custody status condition listed in section 2.B.2.b for a sex offense commit another sex offense, they are assigned an additional custody status point. The Commission believes that offenders who commit a subsequent sex offense pose so significant a risk to public safety that their criminal history scores should be enhanced to reflect this risk. This policy does not apply to the offense of Failure to Register as a Predatory Offender (Minn. Stat. § 243.166).

2.B.211. Assign a custody status point to an offender on any custody status type who absconds and commits a new felony offense. The custody status type depends on the form of supervision that exists when the offender commits a new offense. For example, assign a custody status point to an offender who absconds from supervised release and commits a new felony offense. The custody status type would be "supervised release."

3. Prior Gross Misdemeanors and Misdemeanors. Prior gross misdemeanor and misdemeanor convictions count as units comprising criminal history points. Four units equal one criminal history point; give no partial point for fewer than four units. Determine units as specified in this section.

a. *General Assignment of Units.* If the current conviction is for an offense other than criminal vehicular homicide or operation or felony driving while impaired (DWI), assign the offender one unit for each prior conviction of the following offenses provided the offender received a stayed or imposed sentence or stay of imposition for the conviction before the current sentencing:

(1) targeted misdemeanor, as defined in Minn. Stat. § 299C.10, subd. 1(e);

(2) non-traffic gross misdemeanor;

(3) gross misdemeanor driving while impaired;

(4) gross misdemeanor refusal to submit to a chemical test;

(5) a felony conviction resulting in a misdemeanor or gross misdemeanor sentence.

b. *Gross Misdemeanors Sentenced as Misdemeanors.* A gross misdemeanor conviction resulting in a misdemeanor sentence for an offense not defined as a targeted misdemeanor under Minn. Stat § 299C.10, subd. 1(e) must **not** be used to compute units.

c. *Single Course of Conduct/Multiple Sentences.* When multiple sentences for a single course of conduct were imposed under Minn. Stat. §§ 152.137, 609.585, or 609.251, the offender must not be assigned more than one unit.

d. *Single Course of Conduct / Multiple Victims.* When multiple offenses arising from a single course of conduct involving multiple victims were sentenced, assign only the two most severe offenses units in criminal history.

e. *Decay Factor.* A prior misdemeanor or gross misdemeanor sentence or stay of imposition following a misdemeanor or gross misdemeanor conviction must **not** be used in computing the criminal history score if ten years has elapsed between the date of discharge from or expiration of the sentence and the date of the current offense. However, misdemeanor sentences that result from the successful completion of a stay of imposition for a felony conviction are subject to the felony decay factor in section 2.B.1.c.

f. *Maximum Assignment of Points.* Except as provided in paragraph g, an offender cannot receive more than one point for prior misdemeanor or gross misdemeanor convictions.

g. *Assignment of Units for Criminal Vehicular Homicide or Operation or Felony Driving While Impaired (DWI).* If the current conviction is for criminal vehicular homicide or operation or felony DWI, assign previous violations of Minn. Stat. §§ 169A.20, 169A.31, 169.121, 169.1211, 169.129, 360.0752, or 609.21 two units each. There is no limit to the total number of misdemeanor points that can be included in the offender's criminal history score due to criminal vehicular homicide or operation or DWI offenses. For DWI offenses, see section 2.B.6 for exceptions to this policy relating to predicate offenses used for enhancement purposes.

h. *Prior Misdemeanor or Gross Misdemeanor Driving While Impaired (DWI) Committed by Juvenile Offenders.* Assign no units under this section if the offender was 16 or 17 years old when the prior misdemeanor or gross misdemeanor DWI was committed, and the DWI was processed in adult court under Minn. Stat. § 260B.225, subds. 3 and 8.

Comment

2.B.301. The Commission established a measurement procedure based on units for misdemeanor and gross misdemeanor sentences, which are totaled and then converted to a point value. The purpose of this procedure is to provide different weightings for convictions of felonies, gross misdemeanors, and misdemeanors. Under this procedure, misdemeanors and gross misdemeanors are assigned one unit. An offender must have a total of four units to receive one point in the criminal history score, thus an offender with three units is assigned no point value.

2.B.302. The Commission decided to reduce the weight of prior gross misdemeanors (other than DWI-related offenses) to create a more proportional weighting scheme for prior felonies at Severity Level 1 and Severity Level 2 which receive a weight of ½ point each. The Commission believes that a weighting scheme that sets the same weight for both misdemeanors and gross misdemeanors is more consistent and equitable.

2.B.303. The Commission placed a limit of one point on the consideration of misdemeanors or gross misdemeanors in the criminal history score. This was done because, with no limit on point accrual, offenders with lengthy, but relatively minor, misdemeanor records could accrue high criminal history scores and thus be subject to inappropriately severe sentences upon their first felony conviction. The Commission limited consideration of misdemeanors to particularly relevant misdemeanors under existing state statute. Offenders whose criminal record includes at least four prior sentences for misdemeanors on the targeted misdemeanor list provided in Minn. Stat. § 299C.10, subd. 1(e), non-traffic gross misdemeanors and gross misdemeanor driving while impaired or refusal to submit to a chemical test are considered more culpable and are given an additional criminal history point.

2.B.304. The Commission believes that offenders whose current conviction is for criminal vehicular homicide or operation or first degree (felony) driving while impaired, and who have prior violations under Minn. Stats. §§ 169A.20, 169A.31, 169.121, 1691211, 169.129, 360.0752, or 609.21, are also more culpable, and for these offenders there is no limit to the total number of misdemeanor points included in the criminal history score due to DWI or criminal vehicular homicide or operation (CVO) violations. To determine the total number of misdemeanor points under these circumstances, first add together any non DWI/CVO misdemeanor units. If there are less than four units, add in any DWI/CVO units. Four or more units would equal one point. Only DWI/CVO units can be used in calculating additional points. Each set of four DWI/CVO units would equal an additional point. For example, if an offender had two theft units and six DWI/CVO units, the theft would be added to the two DWI/CVO units to equal one point. The remaining four DWI/CVO units would equal a second point. In a second example, if an offender had six theft units and six DWI/CVO units, the first four theft units would equal one point. Four of the DWI/CVO units would equal a second point. The remaining two theft units could not be added to the remaining two DWI/CVO units for a third point. The total misdemeanor score would be two.

2.B.305. For purposes of computing criminal history, the Commission decided that consideration should only be given to the most severe offense when there are prior multiple sentences under provisions of Minn. Stats. §§ 152.137, 609.585 or 609.251. This was done to prevent inequities due to past variability in prosecutorial and sentencing practices with respect to these statutes, to prevent systematic manipulation of these statutes in the future, and to provide a uniform and equitable method of computing criminal history scores for all cases of multiple convictions arising from a single course of conduct, when single victims are involved. References are made to felony convictions under Minn. Stats. §§ 152.137, 609.585, and 609.251, in the event that they result in a misdemeanor or gross misdemeanor sentence.

The Commission has carefully considered the application of the Hernandez method to sentencing in provisions of Minnesota law other than Minn. Stats. §§ 152.137, 609.585 and 609.251. The Commission made a deliberate decision not to amend the Sentencing Guidelines. See, State v. Williams, 771 N. W.2d 514 (Minn. 2009).

2.B.306. The Commission also adopted a "decay" factor for prior misdemeanor and gross misdemeanor offenses for the same reasons articulated for felony offenses; however, given that these offenses are less serious, the decay period is 10 years rather than 15.

2.B.307. Convictions that are petty misdemeanors by statutory definition, that have been certified as petty misdemeanors under Minn. R. Crim. P. 23.04, or that are deemed to be petty misdemeanors under Minn. R. Crim. P. 23.02 are not used to compute the criminal history score.

2.B.308. When multiple misdemeanor or gross misdemeanor sentences arose out of a single course of conduct in which there were multiple victims, consideration should be given only for the two most severe offenses for purposes of computing criminal history. These are the same policies that apply to felony convictions and juvenile adjudications.

4. Prior Juvenile Adjudications.

a. *Assignment of Points for Juvenile Adjudications.* Assign an offender one point for every two adjudications for felony offenses the offender committed, and for which the offender was prosecuted as a juvenile, provided that:

(1) each adjudication must have been for a separate offense or must have involved separate victims in a single course of conduct, except as provided in paragraphs c and d below; and

(2) the juvenile adjudications must have been for offenses committed after the offender's fourteenth birthday; and

(3) the offender was under the age of twenty-five when the offender committed the current felony.

b. *Maximum Points for Juvenile Adjudications.* An offender may receive only **one point** for juvenile adjudications as described in this section, except that the point limit does not apply to juvenile adjudications for offenses for which the Sentencing Guidelines would presume imprisonment if the offenses had been committed by an adult. Make this determination regardless of the criminal history score, and include offenses that carry a mandatory minimum prison sentence and other presumptive imprisonment offenses described in section 2.C.

c. *Single Course of Conduct / Multiple Sentences.* When multiple adjudications for a single course of conduct were imposed under Minn. Stat. §§ 152.137, 609.585, or 609.251, only one offense may be used in the criminal history calculation.

d. *Single Course of Conduct / Multiple Victims.* When the prior adjudications involve multiple offenses arising from a single course of conduct involving multiple victims, include only the two most severe offenses in criminal history.

Comment

2.B.401. Juvenile history is included in the criminal history score to identify those young adult felons whose criminal careers were preceded by repeated felony-type offenses committed as a juvenile. The Commission held several public hearings devoted to the issue of using juvenile records in the criminal history score. Those hearings pointed out differences in legal procedures and safeguards between adult and juvenile courts, differing availability of juvenile records, and differing procedures among juvenile courts. As a result of these issues, the Commission decided to establish rigorous standards regulating the consideration of juvenile records in computing the criminal history score.

2.B.402. Only juvenile adjudications for offenses that are felonies under Minnesota law will be considered in computing the criminal history score. Status offenses, dependency and neglect proceedings, and misdemeanor or gross misdemeanor-type offenses will be excluded from consideration.

2.B.403. Consistent with Minn. Stat. § 609.035, which provides for a single sentence for adult offenders when multiple convictions arise from a single course of conduct, only juvenile adjudications for offenses arising from separate courses of conduct contribute to the juvenile point(s), unless multiple victims were involved.

2.B.404. The juvenile adjudications must result from offenses committed after the offender's fourteenth birthday. The Commission chose the date of the offense rather than the date of adjudication to eliminate variability in application based on differing juvenile court practices.

2.B.405. Juvenile adjudications will be considered in computing the criminal history score only for adult offenders who had not attained the age of 25 when they committed the felony for which they are now being sentenced. Again, the Commission chose to examine the age of the offender at the time of the offense rather than at time of sentencing to prevent disparities resulting from system processing variations.

2.B.406. The Commission decided that it would take two juvenile adjudications to equal 1 point on the criminal history score, and generally, an offender may not receive more than 1 point on the basis of prior juvenile adjudications. This point limit does not apply to offenses committed and prosecuted as a juvenile for which the Guidelines would presume imprisonment, regardless of criminal history, if committed by an adult. This includes offenses in the non-shaded portions of the applicable Grids at a Criminal History Score of 0 (e.g., Severity Level 8 or H), offenses subject to mandatory minimum laws (e.g., Assault in the Second Degree), or any other applicable policies under section 2. C. The criminal history record is not used to determine whether the juvenile offense carries a presumptive imprisonment sentence because of the difficulty in applying criminal history score computations to prior juvenile offenses. Two juvenile adjudications are required for each additional point. Again, no partial points are allowed, so an offender with only one juvenile adjudication meeting the above criteria would receive no point on the criminal history score.

2.B.407. To provide a uniform and equitable method of computing criminal history scores for cases of multiple felony offenses with adjudications arising from a single course of conduct when single victims are involved, and when the adjudications involved provisions of Minn. Stats. §§ 152.137, 609.585 or 609.251, consideration should be given to only the most severe offense with an adjudication when computing criminal history.

When there are multiple felony offenses with adjudications arising out of a single course of conduct in which there were multiple victims, consideration should be given only to the two most severe felony offenses with adjudications when computing criminal history. These are the same policies that apply to felony, gross misdemeanor and misdemeanor convictions for adults.

The Commission has carefully considered the application of the Hernandez method to sentencing in provisions of Minnesota law other than Minn. Stats. §§ 152.137, 609.585 and 609.251. The Commission made a deliberate decision not to amend the Sentencing Guidelines. See, State v. Williams, 771 N.W.2d 514 (Minn. 2009).

5. Convictions from Jurisdictions other than Minnesota.

a. *In General.* The offense definitions in effect when the offense was committed govern the designation of convictions from jurisdictions other than Minnesota as felonies, gross misdemeanors, or misdemeanors. Sections 2. B.1 through 2.B.7 govern the use of these convictions.

b. *Offense Equivalent.* The court makes the final determination of the Minnesota offense that is equivalent to the non-Minnesota offense. Where to place the offense in criminal history depends on:

- whether the offense is defined as a felony, gross misdemeanor, or targeted misdemeanor in Minnesota; and
- the sentence imposed.

An offense may be counted as a felony only if it would **both** be defined as a felony in Minnesota, and the offender received a sentence that in Minnesota would be a felony-level sentence, which includes the equivalent of a stay of imposition.

c. *Assigning Felony Weights.* Section 2.B.1 governs the weight of a prior felony conviction from a jurisdiction other than Minnesota, and must be based on the severity level of the equivalent Minnesota felony offense.

d. *Federal Offenses; No Minnesota Equivalent.* Federal felony offenses that received a sentence that in Minnesota would be a felony-level sentence, but for which no comparable Minnesota offense exists, must receive a weight of one in computing the criminal history score.

e. *Juvenile Offenses from other Jurisdictions.* Minnesota law governs the inclusion of a prior felony offense from jurisdictions other than Minnesota committed by an offender who was under 18 years old in the juvenile section or adult section of the criminal history score. The offense should be included in the juvenile history section only if it meets the requirements in section 2.B.4. The prior can be included in the adult history section only if the factfinder determines that it is an offense for which the offender would have been certified to adult court if it had occurred in Minnesota.

Comment

2.B.501. Convictions from jurisdictions other than Minnesota include convictions under the laws of any other state, or the federal government, including convictions under the Uniform Code of Military Justice, or convictions under the law of other nations.

2.B.502. The Commission concluded that convictions from other jurisdictions must, in fairness, be considered in the computation of an offender's criminal history score. No uniform nationwide characterization of the terms "felony," "gross misdemeanor," and "misdemeanor" exists. Therefore, the Commission recognizes that criminal conduct may be characterized differently by the various state and federal criminal jurisdictions. Generally, the classification of prior offenses as petty misdemeanors, misdemeanors, gross misdemeanors, or felonies should be determined by current Minnesota offense definitions and sentencing policies, except as provided in section 2.B.7. For example, an assault with a dangerous weapon committed in Texas that received a 365–day sentence would be given one gross misdemeanor unit due to the sentence length despite being the equivalent by definition of a Minnesota felony second-degree assault.

2.B.503. For prior non-Minnesota controlled substance convictions, the amount and type of the controlled substance should be considered in the determination of the appropriate weight to be assigned to a prior felony sentence for a controlled substance offense.

2.B.504. A non-Minnesota conviction committed by a juvenile can only be included in the adult section of the criminal history score if the offender would have been certified as an adult under Minnesota law. See State v. Marquetti, 322 N. W.2d 316 (Minn. 1982).

6. Felony Enhancement Due to Prior Misdemeanor or Gross Misdemeanor Convictions.

a. *Enhanced Felonies.* When the current offense is a felony solely because the offender has previous convictions for misdemeanor and gross misdemeanor offenses, the prior misdemeanor conviction(s) on the targeted misdemeanor list provided in Minn. Stat. § 299C.10, subd. 1(e) or gross misdemeanor conviction(s) upon which the enhancement is based may be used in determining custody status, but cannot be used in calculating the remaining components of the offender's criminal history score.

b. *Counting Prior Misdemeanors and Gross Misdemeanors; Future Felony.* Except as provide in paragraph c, misdemeanor and gross misdemeanor offenses used to enhance the current offense must be used in calculating the offender's criminal history score on future offenses that are not enhanced felonies. Prior felony offenses used for enhancement must always be used in calculating the offender's criminal history score.

c. *Counting Prior Misdemeanors and Gross Misdemeanors; Felony Driving While Impaired (DWI).* If the current offense is a felony DWI offense and the offender has a prior felony DWI offense, the prior felony DWI must be used in computing the criminal history score. The prior misdemeanor and gross misdemeanor offenses used to enhance the first prior felony DWI cannot be used in the offender's criminal history. Any other misdemeanor or gross misdemeanor DWI offenses may be included as provided in section 2.B.3.g.

Comment

2.B.601. A number of instances exist in Minnesota law in which misdemeanor or gross misdemeanor behavior carries a felony penalty as a result of the offender's prior record. The Commission decided that in the interest of fairness, a prior misdemeanor or gross misdemeanor offense that elevated the misdemeanor or gross misdemeanor behavior to a felony should not also be used in criminal history points other than custody status. Only one prior offense should be excluded from the criminal history score calculation, unless more than one prior was required for the offense to be elevated to a felony. For example, Assault in the Fifth Degree is a felony if the offender has two or more convictions for assaultive behavior. In those cases, the two related priors at the lowest level should be excluded. Similarly, theft crimes of more than $500 but less than $1,000 are felonies if the offender has at least one previous conviction for an offense specified in that statute. In those cases, the prior related offense at the lowest level should be excluded.

2.B.602. A first-time first degree (felony) driving while impaired (DWI) offense involves a DWI violation within ten years of the first of three or more prior impaired driving incidents. Because the DWI priors elevated this offense to the felony level, they should be excluded from the criminal history score. Those predicate misdemeanor and gross misdemeanor offenses should also be excluded for a subsequent felony DWI, but any prior felony DWI would be counted as part of the felony criminal history score.

7. Determining Offense Levels for Prior Offenses.

a. *Classification of Prior Offense.* The classification of a prior offense as a petty misdemeanor, misdemeanor, gross misdemeanor, or felony is determined by current Minnesota offense definitions (see Minn. Stat. § 609.02, subds. 2–4a) and sentencing policies. Offenses that are petty misdemeanors by statute, or that are certified as or deemed to be petty misdemeanors under Minn. R. Crim. P. 23, must not be used to compute the criminal history score.

b. *Monetary Threshold.* When a monetary threshold determines the offense classification, the monetary threshold in effect when the prior offense was committed, not the current threshold, determines the offense classification in calculating the criminal history score.

Comment

2.B.701. The Commission recognized that the classification of criminal conduct as a felony, gross misdemeanor, misdemeanor, or petty misdemeanor is determined legally by the sentence given rather than the conviction offense.

2.B.702. A monetary threshold determines the offense classification when the value of property or services is an element of the offense. Punishment for the offense typically increases as the dollar amount increases.

2.B.703. When the offense severity level is determined by a monetary threshold, the threshold in effect when the prior offense was committed determines the offense classification in criminal history. For example, beginning August 1, 2007, the monetary threshold for a felony level Theft of Moveable Property offense under Minn. Stat. § 609.52.2(a)(1) was divided between Severity Level 2 and Severity Level 3 by the dollar amount of $5,000. Prior to that, this offense would have been assigned a severity level based on a dollar amount of $2,500. Because this was a change by the Legislature for inflation and no change was made by the Commission to the severity levels, a Theft of Moveable Property offense over $2,500 which previously received a Severity Level of 3 and a weight of 1 point in criminal history would continue to receive that same weight.

C. Presumptive Sentence

1. Finding the Presumptive Sentence. The presumptive sentence for a felony conviction is found in the appropriate cell on the applicable Grid located at the intersection of the criminal history score (horizontal axis) and the severity level (vertical axis). The conviction offense determines the severity level. The offender's criminal history score is computed according to section 2.B above. For cases contained in cells outside of the shaded areas, the sentence should be executed. For cases contained in cells within the shaded areas, the sentence should be stayed unless the conviction offense carries a mandatory minimum sentence.

Each cell on the Standard Grid and the Sex Offender Grid provides a fixed sentence duration. Minn. Stat. § 244.09 requires that the Guidelines provide a range for sentences that are presumptive commitments. For cells above the solid line, the Guidelines provide both a fixed presumptive duration and a range of time for that sentence. The shaded areas of the grids do not display ranges. If the duration for a sentence that is a presumptive commitment is found in a shaded area, the standard range—15 percent lower and 20 percent higher than the fixed duration displayed—is permissible without departure, provided that the minimum sentence is not less than one year and one day, and the maximum sentence is not more than the statutory maximum.

2. Presumptive Sentence Durations that Exceed the Statutory Maximum Sentence. If the presumptive sentence duration in the appropriate cell on the applicable Grid exceeds the statutory maximum sentence for the conviction offense, the statutory maximum is the presumptive sentence.

3. Finding the Presumptive Sentence for Certain Offenses.

a. *Sex Offenses.* Under Minn. Stat. § 609.3455, certain sex offenders are subject to mandatory life sentences and certain repeat sex offenders are subject to presumptive executed prison sentences of at least 36 months.

(1) Mandatory Life Sentences. The Sentencing Guidelines presumptive sentence does not apply to offenders subject to mandatory life without the possibility of release under subdivision 2 of that statute. For offenders subject to life with the possibility of release under subdivisions 3 and 4 of that statute, the court must specify a minimum term of imprisonment, based on the Sentencing Guidelines presumptive sentence as determined in section 2.C, or any applicable mandatory minimum sentence not contained in Minn. Stat. § 609.3455, that must be served before the offender may be considered for release.

(2) Presumptive Executed Prison Sentences of at least 36 Months. Except when a life sentence applies, if the current conviction offense is criminal sexual conduct in the first, second, third, or fourth degree (Minn. Stat. §§ 609.342 to 345) or criminal sexual predatory conduct (609.3453) within 15 years of a previous sex offense conviction, under Minn. Stat. § 609.3455, subd. 10, the presumptive disposition is commitment. The presumptive duration is at least 36 months, or the fixed duration indicated in the appropriate cell on the Grid, whichever is longer.

b. *Burglary.* If the current conviction offense is burglary of an occupied dwelling (Minn. Stat. § 609.582, subd. 1 (a)) and there was a previous conviction for a felony burglary before the current offense occurred, the presumptive disposition is commitment. Prior burglary convictions trigger the presumptive commitment even if they have decayed for criminal history purposes as set forth in section 2.B.1.c. The presumptive duration for a burglary conviction falling under this section is the fixed duration indicated in the appropriate cell on the Grid.

c. *Controlled Substance Offenses.* If the current conviction offense is for a controlled substance crime in the first, second, or third degree and is a "subsequent controlled substance conviction" as defined in Minn. Stat. § 152.01, subd. 16a, the presumptive disposition is commitment. A stay of adjudication under Minn. Stat. § 152.18 that occurred before August 1, 1999 is not a prior disposition under Minn. Stat. § 152.01, subd. 16a. The prior dispositions listed in Minn. Stat. § 152.01, subd. 16a trigger the presumptive commitment unless more than ten years have elapsed since discharge from sentence or stay of adjudication. The presumptive duration for a controlled substance conviction falling under this section is the fixed duration indicated in the appropriate cell on the Grid, or the mandatory minimum, whichever is longer.

d. *Driving While Impaired (DWI) Offenses.* If the current conviction is for felony DWI and if, prior to the commission of the current offense, the offender had a previous conviction (as conviction is defined in Minn. Stat. § 609.02 subd. 5) for a felony DWI or for a criminal vehicular homicide or operation as defined in Minn. Stat. § 169A.24, subd. 1(3), the presumptive disposition is commitment. Prior felony DWI or criminal vehicular homicide or operation convictions trigger the presumptive commitment even if they have decayed for criminal history purposes as set forth in section 2.B.1.c.

e. *Offenses Committed While Under State Authority.* The presumptive disposition for escape from an executed sentence, felony assault committed by an inmate serving an executed term of imprisonment, or assault on secure treatment facility personnel is commitment. It is presumptive for escape from an executed sentence and for felony assault committed by an inmate serving an executed term of imprisonment to be sentenced consecutively to the offense for which the inmate was confined. The presumptive duration is determined by the presumptive sentencing consecutive policy (see section 2.F. 1, Presumptive Consecutive Sentences).

Comment

2.C.01. The dispositional policy adopted by the Commission was designed so that scarce prison resources would primarily be used for serious person offenders and community resources would be used for most property offenders. The Commission believes that a rational sentencing policy requires such trade-offs to ensure the availability of correctional resources for the most serious offenders For the first year of Guidelines' operation, this policy was reflected in sentencing practices. However, by the third year of guideline operation, the percentage of offenders with criminal history scores of four or more had increased greatly, resulting in a significant increase in imprisonment for property offenses. Given finite resources, increased use of imprisonment for property offenses results in reduced prison resources for person offenses. The allocation of scarce resources has been monitored and evaluated on an ongoing basis by the Commission. The Commission has determined that assigning particular weights to prior felony sentences in computing the criminal history score will address this problem. The significance of low severity level prior felonies is reduced, which should result in a lower imprisonment rate for property offenders. The significance of more serious prior felonies is increased, which should result in increased prison sentences for repeat serious person offenders.

2.C.02. In the cells outside the shaded areas of the grids, the Guidelines provide a fixed presumptive sentence length, and a range of time around that length. Presumptive sentence lengths are shown in months, and it is the Commission's intent that months be computed by reference to calendar months. Any sentence length given that is within the range of sentence length shown in the appropriate cell on the applicable Grid is not a departure from the Guidelines, and any sentence length given that is outside the range is a departure from the Guidelines. In the cells in the shaded areas of the grids, the Guidelines provide a single fixed presumptive sentence length.

2.C.03. The presumptive duration listed on the grids, when executed, includes both the term of imprisonment and the period of supervised release. According to Minn. Stat. § 244.101, when the court sentences an offender to an executed sentence for an offense occurring on or after August 1, 1993, the sentence consists of two parts: a specified minimum term of imprisonment equal to two-thirds of the total executed sentence; and a specified maximum supervised release term equal to one-third of the total executed sentence. Separate tables following the Grids illustrate how executed sentences are broken down into their two components.

The Commissioner of Corrections may extend the amount of time an offender actually serves in prison if the offender violates disciplinary rules while in prison or violates conditions of supervised release. This extension period could result in the offender serving the entire executed sentence in prison.

2.C.04. When a stay of execution is given, the presumptive sentence length shown in the appropriate cell should be pronounced, but its execution stayed. If the sentence length pronounced, but stayed, differs from that shown in the appropriate cell, the sentence is a departure from the Guidelines.

2.C.05. When a stay of imposition is given, no sentence length is pronounced, and the imposition of the sentence is stayed to some future date. If that sentence is ever imposed, the presumptive sentence length shown in the appropriate cell should be pronounced, and a decision should be made whether to execute the presumptive sentence length given. If the sentence length pronounced at the imposition of the sentence differs from that shown in the appropriate cell on the applicable Grid, the sentence is a departure from the Guidelines.

2.C.06. There are rare instances where the presumptive sentence length exceeds the statutory maximum sentence. If this situation occurs, the statutory maximum sentence becomes the presumptive sentence. For example, Terroristic Threats under Minn. Stat. § 609.713, subd. 3(a)(1) or (2) carries a statutory maximum sentence of 12 months and 1 day. At a Severity Level 1, the statutory maximum will be exceeded when the offender reaches a Criminal History Score of 3. As another example, Soliciting Children for Sexual Conduct under Minn. Stat. § 609.352 carries a statutory maximum sentence of three years. At Severity Level G, the statutory maximum will be exceeded when the offender reaches a Criminal History Score of 4.

2.C.07. When an offender is convicted of two or more offenses, and the most severe offense is a conviction for attempt or conspiracy under Minn. Stat. §§ 609.17 or 609.175, the presumptive sentence duration must be the longer of: (1) the duration for the attempt or conspiracy conviction; or (2) the duration for the next most severe conviction offense.

2.C.08. The 2005 Legislature enacted statutory changes allowing life sentences with the possibility of release for certain sex offenders. The statute requires the sentencing court to pronounce a minimum term of imprisonment, based on the Guidelines or any applicable mandatory minimum not contained in Minn. Stat. § 609.3455, that the offender must serve before being considered for release. All applicable Guidelines provisions, including the procedures for departing from the presumptive sentence, are applicable to determining the minimum term of imprisonment. See State v. Hodges, 770 N.W.2d 515 (Minn. 2009).

2.C.09. Sections 2.C.3.b and 2.C.3.d clarify that the court may consider decayed convictions when determining whether to execute a presumptively stayed sentence. See State v. Jones, 587 N.W.2d 854 (Minn. Ct. App. 1999).

D. Departures from the Guidelines

1. Departures in General. The sentence ranges provided in the Grids are presumed to be appropriate for the crimes to which they apply. The court must pronounce a sentence within the applicable range unless there exist identifiable, substantial, and compelling circumstances to support a sentence outside the appropriate range on the applicable Grid.

The court may depart from the presumptive disposition or duration provided in the Guidelines, and stay or impose a sentence that is deemed to be more appropriate than the presumptive sentence. A pronounced sentence for a felony conviction that is outside the appropriate range on the applicable Grid, including a stayed or imposed gross misdemeanor or misdemeanor sentence, is a departure from the Guidelines. A departure is not controlled by the Guidelines, but rather, is an exercise of judicial discretion constrained by statute or case law.

a. *Disposition and Duration.* Departures with respect to disposition and duration are separate decisions. A court may depart from the presumptive disposition without departing from the presumptive duration, and vice-versa. A court departing from the presumptive disposition as well as the presumptive duration has made two separate departure decisions, each requiring written departure reasons.

b. *Aggravated Departure.* When imposing a sentence that is an aggravated departure, it is recommended that the court pronounce a sentence proportional to the severity of the crime for which the sentence is imposed and the offender's criminal history, and take into consideration the purposes and underlying principles of the Guidelines.

c. *Departure Report.* In exercising the discretion to depart from a presumptive sentence, the court must disclose in writing or on the record the particular substantial and compelling circumstances that make the departure more appropriate than the presumptive sentence. The reasons must be stated in the sentencing order or recorded in the departure report and filed with the Commission.

d. *Departure Reasons.* Because departures are by definition exceptions to the Guidelines, the departure factors in this section are advisory, except as otherwise established by case law.

Comment

2.D.101. The departure report must be filed with the Commission within 15 days after sentencing. Minn. R. Crim. P. 27.03, subd. 4(C).

2.D.102. A defendant has the right to a jury trial to determine whether aggravating factors are proved beyond a reasonable doubt. See, e.g., Blakely v. Washington, 542 U.S. 296 (2004); State v. Shattuck, 704 N.W.2d 131 (Minn. 2005); State v. Allen, 706 N.W.2d 40 (Minn. 2005). See also Minn. R. Crim. P. 7.03, 11.04, and 27 (detailing the procedures for seeking an aggravated sentence). If the departure facts are proved beyond a reasonable doubt, the court may exercise its discretion to depart from the presumptive sentence.

2.D.103. The aggravating or mitigating factors and the written reasons supporting the departure must be substantial and compelling to overcome the presumption in favor of the Guidelines sentence. The purposes of the Guidelines cannot be achieved unless the presumptive sentences are applied with a high degree of regularity. Sentencing disparity cannot be reduced if courts depart from the Guidelines frequently. Certainty in sentencing cannot be attained if departure rates are high. Prison populations will exceed capacity if departures increase imprisonment rates significantly above past practice.

2.D.104. Plea agreements are important to our criminal justice system because it is not possible to support a system where all cases go to trial. However, it is important to have balance in the criminal justice system where plea agreements are recognized as legitimate and necessary and the goals of the Guidelines are supported. If a plea agreement involves a sentence departure and no other reasons are provided, there is little information available to make informed policy decisions or to ensure consistency, proportionality, and rationality in sentencing.

Departures and their reasons highlight both the success and problems of the existing Guidelines. When a plea agreement involves a departure from the presumptive sentence, the court should cite the reasons that underlie the plea agreement or explain its reasons for accepting the negotiation.

2.D.105. Under Minn. Stat. § 609.13, if a court pronounces a misdemeanor or gross misdemeanor sentence for a felony conviction, that conviction is deemed a gross misdemeanor or misdemeanor. The sentence is a departure because it is outside the appropriate range on the applicable Grid. Because courts sometimes fail to issue departure reports in these cases, section 2.D was amended to clarify that if the court stays or imposes a gross misdemeanor or misdemeanor sentence for a felony conviction, the sentence is a departure.

In contrast, if the prosecutor amends the charge to a gross misdemeanor or misdemeanor offense prior to conviction, a gross misdemeanor or misdemeanor sentence will not be a departure because the sentence will be consistent with the level of the charge. When the prosecutor amends the charge, the prosecutor must amend it to an existing offense. For example, there is no gross misdemeanor version of terroristic threats (Minn. Stat. § 609.713) in statute, so a terroristic threats charge cannot be amended from a felony to a gross misdemeanor.

2. Factors that should not be used as Reasons for Departure. The following factors should not be used as reasons for departing from the presumptive sentences provided in the appropriate cell on the applicable Grid:

a. Race

b. Sex

c. Employment factors, including:

(1) occupation or impact of sentence on profession or occupation;

(2) employment history;

(3) employment at time of offense;

(4) employment at time of sentencing.

d. Social factors, including:

(1) educational attainment;

(2) living arrangements at time of offense or sentencing;

(3) length of residence;

(4) marital status.

e. The defendant's exercise of constitutional rights during the adjudication process.

Comment

2.D.201. The Commission believes that sentencing should be neutral with respect to an offender's race, sex, and income level. Accordingly, the Commission has listed employment and social factors that should not be used as reasons for departure from the presumptive sentence, because these factors are highly correlated with sex, race, or income level. Employment is excluded as a reason for departure not only because of its correlation with race and income levels, but also because this factor is manipulable—e.g., offenders could lessen the severity of the sentence by obtaining employment between arrest and sentencing. While it may be desirable for offenders to obtain employment between arrest and sentencing, some groups (those with low income levels, low education levels, and racial minorities generally) find it more difficult to obtain employment than others. It is impossible to reward those employed without, in fact, penalizing those not employed at time of sentencing. The use of the factors "amenable to probation (or treatment)" or "unamenable to probation" to justify a dispositional departure, could be closely related to social and economic factors. The use of these factors, alone, to explain the reason for departure is insufficient, and the trial court should demonstrate that the departure is not based on any of the excluded factors.

2.D.202. The Commission determined that the severity of an offender's sanctions should not vary depending on whether the offender exercised constitutional rights during the adjudication process.

2.D.203. It follows from the Commission's use of the conviction offense to determine offense severity that departures from the Guidelines should not be permitted for elements of alleged offender behavior not within the definition of the conviction offense. For example, if an offender is convicted of simple robbery, a departure from the Guidelines to increase the severity of the sentence should not be permitted because the offender possessed a firearm or used another dangerous weapon.

3. Factors that may be used as Reasons for Departure. The following is a nonexclusive list of factors that may be used as reasons for departure:

a. *Mitigating Factors.*

(1) The victim was an aggressor in the incident.

(2) The offender played a minor or passive role in the crime or participated under circumstances of coercion or duress.

(3) The offender, because of physical or mental impairment, lacked substantial capacity for judgment when the offense was committed. The voluntary use of intoxicants (drugs or alcohol) does not fall within the purview of this factor.

(4) The offender's presumptive sentence is a commitment but not a mandatory minimum sentence, and either of the following exist:

(a) The current conviction offense is at Severity Level 1 or Severity Level 2 and the offender received all of his or her prior felony sentences during fewer than three separate court appearances; or

(b) The current conviction offense is at Severity Level 3 or Severity Level 4 and the offender received all of his or her prior felony sentences during one court appearance.

(5) Other substantial grounds exist that tend to excuse or mitigate the offender's culpability, although not amounting to a defense.

(6) The court is ordering an alternative placement under Minn. Stat. § 609.1055 for an offender with a serious and persistent mental illness.

b. *Aggravating Factors.*

(1) The victim was particularly vulnerable due to age, infirmity, or reduced physical or mental capacity, and the offender knew or should have known of this vulnerability.

(2) The victim was treated with particular cruelty for which the individual offender should be held responsible.

(3) The current conviction is for a criminal sexual conduct offense, or an offense in which the victim was otherwise injured, and is the offender has a prior felony conviction for a criminal sexual conduct offense or an offense in which the victim was otherwise injured.

(4) The offense was a major economic offense, identified as an illegal act or series of illegal acts committed by other than physical means and by concealment or guile to obtain money or property, to avoid payment or loss of money or property, or to obtain business or professional advantage. The presence of two or more of the circumstances listed below are aggravating factors with respect to the offense:

(a) the offense involved multiple victims or multiple incidents per victim;

(b) the offense involved an attempted or actual monetary loss substantially greater than the usual offense or substantially greater than the minimum loss specified in the statutes;

(c) the offense involved a high degree of sophistication or planning or occurred over a lengthy period of time;

(d) the defendant used his or her position or status to facilitate the commission of the offense, including positions of trust, confidence, or fiduciary relationships; or

(e) the defendant has been involved in other conduct similar to the current offense as evidenced by the findings of civil or administrative law proceedings or the imposition of professional sanctions.

(5) The offense was a major controlled substance offense, identified as an offense or series of offenses related to trafficking in controlled substances under circumstances more onerous than the usual offense. The presence of two or more of the circumstances listed below are aggravating factors with respect to the offense:

(a) the offense involved at least three separate transactions wherein controlled substances were sold, transferred, or possessed with intent to do so;

(b) the offense involved an attempted or actual sale or transfer of controlled substances in quantities substantially larger than for personal use;

(c) the offense involved the manufacture of controlled substances for use by other parties;

(d) the offender knowingly possessed a firearm during the commission of the offense;

(e) the circumstances of the offense reveal the offender to have occupied a high position in the drug distribution hierarchy;

(f) the offense involved a high degree of sophistication or planning or occurred over a lengthy period of time or involved a broad geographic area of disbursement; or

(g) the offender used his or her position or status to facilitate the commission of the offense, including positions of trust, confidence or fiduciary relationships (e.g., pharmacist, physician or other medical professional).

(6) The offender committed, for hire, a crime against the person.

(7) The offender is being sentenced as an "engrained offender" under Minn. Stat. § 609.3455, subd. 3a.

(8) The offender is being sentenced as a "dangerous offender who commits a third violent crime" under Minn. Stat. § 609.1095, subd. 2.

(9) The offender is being sentenced as a "career offender" under Minn. Stat. § 609.1095, subd. 4.

(10) The offender committed the crime as part of a group of three or more offenders who all actively participated in the crime.

(11) The offender intentionally selected the victim or the property against which the offense was committed, in whole or in part, because of the victim's, the property owner's, or another's actual or perceived race, color, religion, sex, sexual orientation, disability, age, or national origin.

(12) The offender used another's identity without authorization to commit a crime. This aggravating factor may not be used when use of another's identity is an element of the offense.

(13) The offense was committed in the presence of a child.

(14) The offense was committed in a location in which the victim had an expectation of privacy.

Comment

2.D.301. The Commission provides a non-exclusive list of factors that may be used as departure reasons. The factors are intended to describe specific situations involving a small number of cases. The Commission rejects factors that are general in nature, and that could apply to large numbers of cases, such as intoxication at the time of the offense. The factors cited are illustrative and are not intended to be an exclusive or exhaustive list. Some of these factors may be considered in establishing conditions of stayed sentences, even though they may not be used as reasons for departure. For example, whether an offender is employed at time of sentencing may be an important factor in deciding whether restitution should be used as a condition of probation, or in deciding the terms of restitution payment.

2.D.302. The Commission recognizes that the criminal history score does not differentiate between the crime spree offender who has been convicted of several offenses but has not been previously sanctioned by the criminal justice system, and the repeat offender who continues to commit new crimes despite receiving previous consequences from the criminal justice system. The Commission believes the nonviolent crime spree offender should perhaps be sanctioned in the community at least once or twice before a prison sentence is appropriate. The Commission believes that the court is best able to distinguish these offenders, and can depart from the Guidelines accordingly.

2.D.303. In section 2.D.3.b(3), an aggravated durational departure is permitted when the current conviction is for a criminal sexual conduct offense or an offense in which the victim was otherwise injured and there is a prior felony conviction for a criminal sexual conduct offense or an offense in which victim injury was established as an element of the offense. The departure is appropriate even if the prior felony offense had decayed in accordance with section 2.B.1.c. An aggravated durational departure is possible without jury determination of additional facts if victim injury is established in proving the elements of the current offense.

2.D.304. Special sentencing provisions were established by the legislature under Minn. Stat. §§ 609.3455, subd. 3a, 609.1095, subd. 2 and 609.1095, subd. 4, that are available to the courts when sentencing certain sex offenders, "dangerous offenders," and "career offenders." The use of one of these sentencing provisions would constitute a departure under the Guidelines and the court must provide written reasons specifying that the requirements of the statute have been met.

2.D.305. The aggravating factor involving groups of three or more offenders under section 2.D.3.b(10) cannot be used when an offender has been convicted under Minn. Stat. § 609.229, Crime Committed for Benefit of a Gang. See section 2.G, Convictions for Attempts, Conspiracies, and Other Sentence Modifiers, for the presumptive sentence for offenders convicted of Crime Committed for Benefit of a Gang, Minn. Stat. § 609.229, subd. 3 (a).

2.D.306. The aggravating factor involving bias motivation under section 2.D.3.b(11) cannot be used when an offender has been convicted under a statute that elevated the crime to a felony offense because of bias motivation (e.g., Minn. Stat. §§ 609.2231, subd. 4 (fourth-degree assault); 609.595, subd. 1a(a) (criminal damage to property); 609.749, subd. 3(a)(1) (stalking)). The Commission intends that a penalty for a bias-motivated offense be subject to enhancement only once.

In determining when domestic violence, sexual assault and sexual abuse cases are motivated by a victim's sex and may be appropriately enhanced, proof must be shown of at least one factor, such as: offender makes abusive or derogatory references based on gender; offender states hatred for a gender as a class; crime involves excessive violence, including mutilation; or there are multiple victims of the same gender.

E. Mandatory Sentences

1. In General. When an offender is convicted of an offense with a statutory mandatory minimum sentence of one year and one day or more, the presumptive disposition is commitment even if the presumptive sentence would ordinarily fall within the shaded area on the applicable Grid. The presumptive duration of the prison sentence is the mandatory minimum sentence in statute or the duration provided in the appropriate cell on the applicable Grid, whichever is longer. When an offender is sentenced for an attempted offense under Minn. Stat. § 609.17 or conspiracy to commit an offense under Minn. Stat. § 609.175, and the underlying offense has a mandatory minimum sentence of a year and a day or more, the presumptive duration is the mandatory minimum sentence in statute or one-half the duration found in the appropriate cell on the applicable Grid, whichever is longer. See Mandatory and Presumptive Sentences Reference Table in Appendix 1.

2. Specific Statutory Provisions. The following mandatory minimum provisions should be imposed as indicated.

a. *Second– and Third–Degree Murder.* Minn. Stat. § 609.107, Mandatory Penalty for Certain Murderers, determines the presumptive sentence for an offender sentenced under that statute.

b. *Dangerous Weapon or Firearm.* Minn. Stat. § 609.11 establishes the mandatory sentence for offenses committed with a dangerous weapon or firearm, or for possession of a firearm by an ineligible felon.

(1) Finding the Mandatory Sentence. Regardless of whether an offender would otherwise receive a presumptive stayed sentence under the Guidelines, the presumptive disposition for an offense subject to a mandatory sentence under Minn. Stat. § 609.11 is always commitment. The mandatory duration is established in the statute. See Dangerous Weapons—Minn. Stat. § 609.11 Table in Appendix 2.

(2) Departure. Minn. Stat. § 609.11, subd. 8 provides that the court, on its own motion or on the prosecutor's motion, may sentence without regard to the mandatory minimum sentence if the court finds substantial and compelling reasons to do so. Sentencing under subdivision 8 is a departure as follows:

(i) Dispositional Departure. A stay of execution or stay of imposition is a dispositional departure.

(ii) Durational Departure. A sentence other than the mandatory minimum or the presumptive duration or applicable range in the appropriate cell on the applicable Grid, whichever is longer, is a durational departure.

c. *Subsequent Drug Offenses Involving a Dangerous Weapon.* If an offender is sentenced for a second or subsequent drug offense and is subject to Minn. Stat. § 609.11, subd. 5a, the presumptive duration is the longer of either:

(1) the mandatory minimum sentence for the subsequent drug offense added to the mandatory minimum sentence for the dangerous weapon involvement; or

(2) the presumptive duration for the subsequent drug offense provided in the appropriate cell on the Standard Grid.

d. *Dangerous and Repeat Felony Offenders.* When an offender is sentenced under Minn. Stat. § 609.1095, subd. 3, the presumptive disposition is commitment. The court must impose and execute the presumptive duration unless a longer mandatory minimum sentence is otherwise required by law or the court imposes a longer aggravated durational departure.

e. *Felony Driving While Impaired (DWI).* When the court sentences an offender for first-degree felony driving while impaired, under Minn. Stat. § 169A.276, it must impose a sentence of at least 36 months. The court cannot stay imposition or adjudication of the sentence, but may stay execution.

3. **Conditional Release.** Several Minnesota statutes provide for mandatory conditional release terms that must be served by certain offenders once they are released from prison. The court must pronounce the conditional release term when sentencing for the following offenses:

- First degree (felony) driving while impaired. Minn. Stat. § 169A.276, subd. 1(d).
- Predatory offense registration violation committed by certain offenders. Minn. Stat. § 243.166, subd. 5a.
- Assault in the fourth degree against secure treatment facility personnel. Minn. Stat. § 609.2231, subd. 3a(d).
- First through fourth degree criminal sexual conduct and criminal sexual predatory conduct. Minn. Stat. § 609.3455, subds. 6–8.
- Use of minors in a sexual performance. Minn. Stat. § 617.246, subd. 7.
- Possession of pornographic work involving minors. Minn. Stat. § 617.247, subd. 9.

4. **Mandatory Life Sentences.** Mandatory life imprisonment sentences for first-degree murder and for sex offenses subject to Minn. Stat. § 609.3455, subdivision 2, are not governed by the Guidelines.

Comment

2.E.01. The Commission attempted to draw the dispositional line so that the great majority of offenses that might involve a mandatory sentence would fall outside the shaded areas of the grids. However, some cases carry a mandatory prison sentence under state law but fall within the shaded areas of the grids; e.g., Assault in the Second Degree. When that occurs, imprisonment of the offender is the presumptive disposition. The presumptive duration is the mandatory minimum sentence or the duration provided in the appropriate cell on the applicable Grid, whichever is longer. These crimes are ranked below the dispositional line because the Commission believes the durations at these levels are more proportional to the crime than the durations found at the higher severity levels where prison is recommended regardless of the criminal history score of the offender. For example, according to Minn. Stat. § 609.11, the mandatory minimum prison sentence for Assault in the Second Degree involving a knife is one year and one day. However, according to the Guidelines, the presumptive duration is the mandatory minimum or the duration provided in the appropriate cell on the Standard Grid, whichever is longer. Therefore, for someone convicted of Assault in the Second Degree with a Criminal History Score of 0, the Guidelines presume a 21 month prison duration based on the appropriate cell on the Standard Grid found at Severity Level 6. The Commission believes this duration is more appropriate than the 48 month prison duration that would be recommended if this crime were ranked at Severity Level 8, which is the first severity level ranked completely above the dispositional line.

2.E.02. When the mandatory minimum sentence is for less than one year and one day, the Commission interprets the minimum to mean any incarceration including time spent in local confinement as a condition of a stayed sentence. The presumptive disposition is not commitment unless the case falls above the dispositional line on the applicable Grid. An example is a conviction for a Fifth Degree Controlled Substance Crime. If the offender has previously been convicted of a controlled substance crime, the mandatory minimum law requires at least six months incarceration, which can be served in a local jail or workhouse. .

2.E.03. Some offenses by statutory definition involve a dangerous weapon, and therefore the mandatory minimum provision dealing with dangerous weapons always applies: Assault in the Second Degree under Minn. Stat. § 609.222; Certain Persons Not to Have Firearms under Minn. Stat. §§ 624.713, subd. 2(b) and 609.165, subd. 1b; Drive–By Shootings under Minn. Stat. § 609.66; and Stalking (Aggravated Violations) and Possessing a Dangerous Weapon under Minn. Stat. § 609.749, subd. 3(a)(3). The presumptive disposition for these types of offenses is imprisonment and the presumptive duration is the mandatory minimum sentence prescribed for the conviction offense or the cell time, whichever is longer.

2.E.04. The mandatory minimum provision dealing with the use of dangerous weapons in the commission of certain felonies (Minn. Stat. § 609.11) provides that the finder of fact must determine the firearm or other dangerous weapon use or firearm possession based upon the record of the trial or plea of guilty and does not require the citing of this provision. If the court finds that a dangerous weapon was involved, the mandatory minimum applies under Minn. Stat. § 609.11. This provision also provides prosecutors with the authority to make a motion to sentence apart from the mandatory minimum sentence. In State v. Olson, 325 N.W.2d 13 (Minn. 1982), the Supreme Court extended that authority to courts as well. When the prosecutor or court makes a motion to sentence apart from the mandatory minimum, it becomes legal to stay imposition or execution of sentence or to impose a lesser sentence than the mandatory minimum. When this motion is made, the presumptive disposition for the case is still imprisonment, and the presumptive duration is the mandatory minimum sentence prescribed for the conviction offense or the cell time, whichever is longer. A stay of imposition or execution for the case constitutes a mitigated dispositional departure. The imposition of a duration less than the mandatory minimum or cell time, if the latter is longer, constitutes a mitigated durational departure. Written reasons specifying the substantial and compelling nature of the circumstances and demonstrating why the sentence selected is more appropriate, reasonable or equitable than the presumptive sentence are required.

2.E.05. Minn. Stat. § 609.11, subd. 5a, states that for a subsequent drug offense involving a weapon, the mandatory minimum duration for the drug offense and the mandatory minimum duration for the weapon offense are added together. The Guidelines presumptive duration is determined by comparing the total sum of the combined mandatory minimums and the duration found in the appropriate cell on the Standard Grid for the subsequent drug offense; the presumptive duration is the longer of the two. For example: A third-degree drug offender with a Criminal History Score of 3 is convicted of a subsequent controlled substance offense and was in possession of a firearm.

Mandatory Minimums:	24 months	Mand. Min. (Minn. Stat. § 152.023, subd. 3(b))
	+ 36 months	Mand. Min (Minn. Stat. § 609.11, subd. 5(a))
	= 60 months	
vs.		
Grid Cell:	= 39 months (Severity Level 6; Criminal History Score of 3)	

F. Concurrent/Consecutive Sentences

Generally, when an offender is convicted of multiple current offenses, or when there is a prior felony sentence that has not expired or been discharged, concurrent sentencing is presumptive.

This section sets forth the criteria for imposing consecutive sentences. Imposition of consecutive sentences in any situation not described in this section is a departure. When the court imposes consecutive sentences, the court must sentence the offenses in the order in which they occurred.

Comment

2.F.01. Consecutive sentences are a more severe sanction because the intent is to confine the offender for a longer period than under concurrent sentences. If the severity of the sanction is to be proportional to the severity of the offense, consecutive sentences should be limited to more severe offenses. The Commission recommends that the court consider carefully whether the purposes of the Guidelines (in terms of punishment proportional to the severity of the offense and the offender's criminal history) would be served best by concurrent rather than consecutive sentences.

2.F.02. The service of the consecutive sentence begins at the end of any incarceration arising from the first sentence. The Commissioner of Corrections aggregates the separate durations into a single fixed sentence. The terms of imprisonment and the periods of supervised release are aggregated as well. For example, if a court executes a 44–month fixed sentence, and a 24–month fixed sentence to be served consecutively to the first sentence, the Commissioner of Corrections aggregates the sentences into a single 68–month fixed sentence, with a specified minimum 45.3–month term of imprisonment and a specified maximum 22.7–month period of supervised release.

44 months (first sentence)
+24 months consecutive (second sentence)
=68 months (fixed sentence)
45.3 months (2/3—term of imprisonment)
22.7 months (1/3—supervised release)

1. Presumptive Consecutive Sentences.

a. *Criteria for Imposing a Presumptive Consecutive Sentence.* Consecutive sentences are presumptive (required under the Guidelines) when:

(1) the offender is:

(i) serving an executed prison sentence;

(ii) on escape status from an executed prison sentence;

(iii) on supervised release; or

(iv) on conditional release following release from an executed prison sentence (see conditional release terms in section 2.E.3); and

(2) the presumptive disposition for the current offense(s) is commitment. The presumptive disposition for an escape from an executed sentence or for a felony assault committed by an inmate serving an executed term of imprisonment is always commitment.

b. *Finding the Presumptive Duration.* For each offense sentenced consecutively to another offense(s) under this section, the presumptive duration is the duration in the appropriate cell on the applicable Grid at a Criminal History Score of 1, or the mandatory minimum for the offense, whichever is longer.

c. *Exception When Presumptive Concurrent Sentence is Longer.* If the criteria in paragraph 2.F.1.a have been met but the total time to serve in prison would be longer if a concurrent sentence were imposed, a concurrent sentence is presumptive. Otherwise, a concurrent sentence is a departure.

d. *Departure Factor.* If there is evidence that the defendant has provided substantial and material assistance in the detection or prosecution of crime, the court may depart from the presumptive consecutive sentence and impose a concurrent sentence.

e. *Felony Driving While Impaired (DWI).* Minn. Stat. § 169A.28 subd. 1 requires a consecutive sentence when the court sentences an offender for a felony DWI and:

(1) the offender has a prior unexpired misdemeanor, gross misdemeanor or felony DWI sentence; and

(2) the disposition for the current offense will be probation; **but not**

(3) when the disposition for the current offense will be commitment.

If the court pronounces a consecutive sentence, the presumptive duration is based on a Criminal History Score of 1. Any pronounced probationary jail time should be served consecutively to any remaining time to be served on the prior DWI offense.

Comment

2.F.101. This section establishes criteria requiring the use of consecutive sentences under the Guidelines. These are called "presumptive consecutive sentences." When consecutive sentencing is presumptive, it is a departure to give concurrent sentences.

2.F.102. When the court pronounces presumptive consecutive sentences for multiple offenses, each new offense will be sentenced at a Criminal History Score of 1. The new offenses will run concurrently to each other, but consecutive to the prior offense.

For example, an offender is convicted of Escape from Custody and First–Degree Burglary of an Occupied Dwelling following escape from an executed sentence. The term of imprisonment remaining on the original offense from which the offender escaped is 18 months. Each of the new offenses will have a presumptive consecutive sentence duration found at a Criminal History Score of 1: Escape from Custody (Severity Level 3), 13 months; Burglary (Severity Level 6), 27 months. The two sentences will run concurrently to each other, and the longer of the two durations will be added to the time remaining on the original term of imprisonment (here, 27 months will be added to the time remaining on the original 18–month sentence). Aggregated, the new presumptive consecutive sentence duration is 45 months.

2.F.103. A concurrent sentence is presumptive if the result is that an offender will serve longer in prison. For example, an offender with a Criminal History Score of 6 is on supervised release. The offender has one month remaining until the sentence expires when the offender commits a theft over $5,000 (Severity Level 3). The Guidelines would typically recommend that the theft run consecutively to the unexpired prior except that a concurrent sentence is longer; therefore, a concurrent sentence is presumptive.

	1 month	(before expiration of sentence)
+	13 months	(Severity Level 3; Criminal History Score of 1)
=	14 months	consecutive

vs.

23 months concurrent (Severity Level 3; Criminal History Score of 6)

2.F.104. If the offense is an attempt under Minn. Stat. § 609.17, or a conspiracy under Minn. Stat. § 609.175, and the court pronounces a presumptive consecutive sentence, the presumptive duration for each offense sentenced consecutively to another offense is determined by first locating the duration in the appropriate cell on the applicable Grid at a Criminal History Score of 1, then applying the rules for attempts and conspiracy set forth in section 2.G.2. For example, for an attempted aggravated robbery offense sentenced presumptive consecutive to another offense, the duration found at Severity Level 8 and Criminal History Score of 1 (58 months), is divided in half — making the presumptive duration 29 months.

2. Permissive Consecutive Sentences.

a. *Criteria for Imposing a Permissive Consecutive Sentence.* Consecutive sentences are permissive (may be given without departure) only in the situations specified in this section. For each felony offense sentenced consecutively to another felony offense(s), the court must use a Criminal History Score of 0, or the mandatory minimum for the offense, whichever is longer, to determine the presumptive duration. A consecutive sentence at any other duration is a departure.

(1) Specific Offenses; Presumptive Commitment. Consecutive sentences are permissive if the presumptive disposition for the current offense(s) is commitment and paragraph (i), (ii), or (iii) applies. If the court pronounces a consecutive stayed sentence under one of these paragraphs, the stayed sentence is a mitigated dispositional departure, but the consecutive nature of the sentence is not a departure. The consecutive stayed sentence begins when the offender completes the term of imprisonment and is placed on supervised release.

(i) Prior Felony Sentence. A current felony conviction for a crime on the list in section 6 of offenses eligible for permissive consecutive sentences may be sentenced consecutively to a prior felony sentence that has not expired or been discharged if the prior felony conviction:

(a) is for a crime on the list in section 6 of offenses eligible for permissive consecutive sentences; or

(b) is from a jurisdiction other than Minnesota and would be equivalent to a crime on the list in section 6.

The presumptive disposition for the prior offense(s) must also be commitment as outlined in section 2.C. A non-Minnesota conviction is equivalent to a crime on the list in section 6 if it would both be defined as a felony in Minnesota, and received a sentence that in Minnesota would be a felony-level sentence, including the equivalent of a stay of imposition.

(ii) Multiple Current Felony Convictions. If the offender is being sentenced for multiple current felony convictions for crimes on the list of offenses eligible for permissive consecutive sentences in section 6, the convictions may be sentenced consecutively to each other.

(iii) Felony Conviction After Escape (Non–Executed Sentence). If the offender commits and is convicted for a new felony crime while on felony escape from lawful custody—as defined in Minn. Stat. § 609.485—from a non-executed felony sentence, the new felony conviction may be sentenced consecutively to the sentence for the escape or the offense for which the offender was confined.

(2) Other Offenses. Consecutive sentences for the following offenses are always permissive and there is no dispositional departure if the sentences are executed.

(i) Felony Escape. If the offender is convicted of felony escape from lawful custody—as defined in Minn. Stat. § 609.485—and the offender did not escape from an executed prison sentence, the escape may be sentenced consecutively to the sentence for which the offender was confined.

(ii) Felony Conviction After Escape (Executed Sentence). If the offender committed and is convicted for a new felony crime committed while on felony escape from lawful custody—as defined in Minn. Stat. § 609.485—from an executed felony sentence, the new felony may be sentenced consecutively to the sentence for the escape.

(iii) Fleeing a Police Officer; Criminal Sexual Conduct. The court may impose consecutive sentences as permitted under Minn. Stat. § 609.035, subds. 5 and 6 if both of the following occur:

(a) the offender is convicted of either of the following offenses:

- Fleeing a Peace Officer in a Motor Vehicle, as defined in Minn. Stat. § 609.487; or
- Criminal Sexual Conduct in the First through Fourth Degrees with force or violence, as defined in Minn. Stat. §§ 609.342 through 609.345; and

(b) the court imposes punishment for any other crime committed by the defendant as part of the same conduct.

(iv) Felony Assault in a Local Jail or Workhouse. If the offender is convicted of felony assault committed while in a local jail or workhouse, the felony assault conviction may be sentenced consecutively to any other executed prison sentence if the presumptive disposition for the other offense was commitment as outlined in section 2.C.

Comment

2.F.201. The Commission establishes criteria that permits, but does not require, the use of consecutive sentences in instances listed in the Guidelines. This is called "permissive consecutive sentences."

2.F.202. If an offender is given permissive consecutive sentences, the presumptive duration for each offense sentenced consecutive to another offense(s) is determined by using the zero criminal history column, or the mandatory minimum, whichever is longer. The purpose of this procedure is to count an offender's criminal history score only one time in the computation of consecutive sentence durations.

2.F.203. If the offense is an attempt under Minn. Stat. § 609.17, or a conspiracy under Minn. Stat. § 609.175, and the court pronounces a permissive consecutive sentence, the presumptive duration for each offense sentenced consecutively to another offense is determined by first locating the duration in the appropriate cell on the applicable Grid at a Criminal History Score of 0, then applying the rules for attempts and conspiracy set forth in section 2.G.2. For example, for an attempted aggravated robbery offense sentenced permissive consecutive to another offense, the duration found at Severity Level 8 and Criminal History Score of 0 (48 months), is divided in half — making the presumptive sentence 24 months.

2.F.204. The Commission's policies on permissive consecutive sentences outline the criteria that are necessary to permit consecutive sentences without the requirement to cite reasons for departure. Courts may pronounce consecutive sentences in any other situation by citing reasons for departure. Courts may also pronounce durational and dispositional departures both upward and downward in cases involving consecutive sentencing if reasons for departure are cited. The reasons for each type of departure should be specifically cited. The procedures for departures are outlined in section 2.D.

2.F.205. Consecutive sentences are permissive for multiple current felony convictions even when the offenses involve one victim and a single course of conduct, but only when the presumptive disposition is commitment. However, consecutive sentencing is not permissive for multiple current felony convictions involving one victim and a single course of conduct if the court is giving an upward durational departure on any of the current conviction offenses. The Commission believes that to give both an upward durational departure and a consecutive sentence when the circumstances involve one victim and a single course of conduct can result in disproportional sentencing unless additional aggravating factors exist to justify the consecutive sentence.

2.F.206. An offender given a consecutive sentence for a crime committed while using or possessing metal-penetrating bullets under Minn. Stat. § 624.7191, subd. 3, can get up to the three-year statutory maximum without departing from the Guidelines. The length of the consecutive sentence is left to the discretion of the court. For example, an offender with a Criminal History Score of 0 is sentenced to a presumptive 48 months prison for aggravated robbery in the first degree, and next is sentenced to 36 months prison consecutively for possessing metal-penetrating bullets.

3. Crime Committed for the Benefit of a Gang. When the court imposes a presumptive or permissive consecutive sentence for a crime committed for the benefit of a gang under Minn. Stat. § 609.229, subd. 3, the presumptive duration includes additional months as outlined in section 2.G.

4. Pre–Guidelines Cases. If a sentence is imposed consecutively to an offense committed before May 1, 1980, the consecutive sentence begins after completion of any incarceration arising from the prior sentence.

Comment

2.F.401. The Commissioner of Corrections has the authority to establish policies regarding durations of confinement for offenders sentenced for crimes committed before May 1, 1980, and will continue to establish policies for the durations of confinement for offenders revoked and re-imprisoned while on parole or supervised release, who were imprisoned for crimes committed on or after May 1, 1980.

If an offender is under the custody of the Commissioner of Corrections pursuant to a sentence for an offense committed on or before April 30, 1980, and if the offender is convicted of a new felony committed on or after May 1, 1980, and is given a presumptive sentence to run consecutively to the previous indeterminate sentence, the phrase "completion of any incarceration arising from the prior sentence" means the target release date the Commissioner of Corrections assigned to the inmate for the offense committed on or before April 30, 1980, or the date on which the inmate completes any incarceration assigned as a result of a revocation of parole for the pre-Guidelines offense.

G. Convictions for Attempts, Conspiracies, and Other Sentence Modifiers

1. In General. Sentence modifiers are statutes that aid in defining the punishment for the underlying offense. Modifiers can affect either or both the duration and the disposition of the presumptive sentence. Any change to the presumptive fixed sentence under this section must also be applied to the upper and lower ends of the range found in the appropriate cell on the applicable Grid, except that the presumptive sentence cannot be less than one year and one day, nor can it be less than any applicable mandatory minimum.

2. Attempt or Conspiracy. When an offender is sentenced for an attempted offense under Minn. Stat. § 609.17 or for conspiracy to commit an offense under Minn. Stat. § 609.175, the presumptive duration is one-half of that found in the appropriate cell on the applicable Grid for the underlying offense. When the underlying offense has a mandatory minimum sentence of a year and a day or more, the presumptive duration is the mandatory minimum sentence in statute or one-half the duration found in the appropriate cell on the applicable Grid, whichever is longer.

3. Solicitation of Juveniles or Mentally Impaired Persons. When an offender is sentenced for soliciting a juvenile under Minn. Stat. § 609.494, subd. 2(b), or for soliciting a mentally impaired person under Minn. Stat. § 609.493 subd. 2(b), the presumptive duration is one-half of that found in the appropriate cell on the applicable Grid for the underlying offense.

4. Conspiracy to Commit a Controlled Substance Offense. The modifying statute for Conspiracy to Commit a Controlled Substance offense under Minn. Stat. § 152.096 does not affect the presumptive sentence for the underlying offense.

5. Attempt or Conspiracy to Commit Criminal Sexual Conduct in the First or Second Degree. The Commission regards the provisions in Minn. Stat. § 609.342, subd. 2(b) and 609.343, subd. 2(b) as statutorily created presumptive sentences, not mandatory minimums. When an offender is sentenced for an attempt or conspiracy to commit Criminal Sexual Conduct in the First Degree under Minn. Stat. § 609.342 or Criminal Sexual Conduct in the Second Degree under Minn. Stat. § 609.343, subd. 1(c), (d), (e), (f), and (h), the presumptive duration is one-half of that found in the appropriate cell on the Sex Offender Grid for the underlying offense or any mandatory minimum, whichever is longer.

6. Taking Responsibility for Criminal Acts. When an offender is sentenced for taking responsibility for criminal acts under Minn. Stat. § 609.495, subd. 4, the presumptive duration is one-half of that found in the appropriate cell on the applicable Grid for the underlying offense.

7. Offense Committed in Furtherance of Terrorism. When an offender is sentenced for an offense committed in the furtherance of terrorism under Minn. Stat. § 609.714, the presumptive duration found in the appropriate cell on the applicable Grid for the underlying offense must be increased by fifty percent.

8. Criminal Sexual Predatory Conduct. When an offender is sentenced for criminal sexual predatory conduct under Minn. Stat. § 609.3453, the presumptive duration found in the appropriate cell on the applicable Grid for the underlying offense must be increased by:

a. twenty-five percent; or

b. fifty percent, if the violation was committed by an offender with a "previous sex offense conviction" as defined in Minn. Stat. § 609.3455, subd. 1.

9. Solicitation or Promotion of Prostitution; Sex Trafficking. When an offender is sentenced for Solicitation or Promotion of Prostitution or Sex Trafficking under Minn. Stat. § 609.322, subd. 1(b), the presumptive sentence is determined by locating the duration in the appropriate cell on the applicable Grid defined by the offender's criminal history score and the underlying crime with the highest severity level, or the mandatory minimum for the underlying crime, whichever is longer, and adding:

a. 48 months, if the underlying crime was completed; or

b. 24 months, if the underlying crime was an attempt or conspiracy.

10. Offense Committed for the Benefit of a Gang. When an offender is sentenced for an offense committed for the benefit of a gang under Minn. Stat. § 609.229, subd. 3(a):

a. Pursuant to Minn. Stat. § 609.229, subd. 4, the presumptive disposition is always commitment; and

b. The presumptive duration is determined by locating the duration in the appropriate cell on the applicable Grid defined by the offender's criminal history score and the underlying crime with the highest severity level, or the mandatory minimum for the underlying crime, whichever is longer, and adding:

(1) If the victim of the crime was under the age of eighteen:

(i) 24 months, if the underlying offense was completed; or

(ii) 12 months, if the underlying offense was an attempt or conspiracy; or

(2) If the victim was eighteen or older:

(i) 12 months, if the underlying offense was completed; or

(ii) 6 months, if the underlying offense was an attempt or conspiracy.

11. Attempt or Conspiracy to Commit First–Degree Murder. When an offender is sentenced for attempt or conspiracy to commit murder in the first degree under Minn. Stat. § 609.185 or murder of an unborn child in the first degree under Minn. Stat. § 609.2661, the presumptive disposition is commitment. The presumptive durations are as follows:

SEVERITY LEVEL OF CONVICTION OFFENSE	CRIMINAL HISTORY SCORE						
	0	1	2	3	4	5	6 or More
Conspiracy/ Attempted Murder, 1st Degree	180 *153–216*	190 *161.5–228*	200 *170–240*	210 *178.5–240*[1]	220 *187–240*[1]	230 *195.5–240*[1]	240 *204–240*[1]

1 Minn. Stat. § 244.09 requires that the Guidelines provide a range for sentences that are presumptive commitment to state imprisonment of 15% lower and 20% higher than the fixed duration displayed, provided that the minimum sentence is not less than one year and one day and the maximum sentence is not more than the statutory maximum. Guidelines section 2.C.1–2. Presumptive Sentence.

Comment

2.G.01. If the presumptive sentence is an odd number, division by two produces a presumptive sentence involving a half month. For example, 41 months divided by two equals 20.5 months. In that case, 20.5 months is the presumptive sentence length.

2.G.02. A modifier that reduces the duration of the presumptive sentence does not alter a presumptive disposition of commitment. For example, the presumptive sentence for completed simple robbery at a Criminal History Score of 3 is commitment for 33 months; the presumptive sentence for attempt is commitment for 16.5 months. Although 16.5 months appears to be in the shaded area on the Standard Grid, the presumptive disposition is still commitment.

3. Related Policies

A. Establishing Conditions of Stayed Sentences:

1. Method of Granting Stayed Sentences. When the appropriate cell on the applicable Grid specifies a stayed sentence, the court may pronounce a stay of execution or a stay of imposition. The court must pronounce the length of the stay, which may exceed the duration of the presumptive prison sentence, and may establish appropriate conditions.

a. *Stay of Execution.* When ordering a stay of execution, the court must pronounce the prison sentence duration, but its execution is stayed. The presumptive duration is shown in the appropriate cell.

b. *Stay of Imposition.* When ordering a stay of imposition, the court must not pronounce a sentence duration, and the imposition of the sentence is stayed.

The Commission recommends that stays of imposition be used for offenders who are convicted of lower severity offenses and who have low criminal history scores. The Commission further recommends that convicted felons be given one stay of imposition, although for very low severity offenses, a second stay of imposition may be appropriate.

Comment

3.A.101. The use of either a stay of imposition or stay of execution is at the discretion of the court. The Commission has provided a non-presumptive recommendation regarding which categories of offenders should receive stays of imposition, and has recommended that convicted felons generally should receive only one stay of imposition. The Commission believes that stays of imposition are a less severe sanction, and should be used for those convicted of less serious offenses and those with short criminal histories. Under current sentencing practices, courts use stays of imposition most frequently for these types of offenders.

3.A.102. When a court grants a stayed sentence, the duration of the stayed sentence may exceed the presumptive sentence length indicated in the appropriate cell on the applicable Grid, and may be as long as the statutory maximum for the conviction offense. See Minn. Stat. § 609.135, subd. 2. Thus, for an offender convicted of Theft over $5,000 (Severity Level 3), with a Criminal History Score of 1, the duration of the stay could be up to ten years. The 13–month sentence shown in the Guidelines is the presumptive sentence length and, if imposed, would be executed if: (a) the court departs from the dispositional recommendation and decides to execute the sentence; or (b) the stay is later revoked and the court decides to imprison the offender.

2. **Conditions of Stayed Sentences.** While the Commission has chosen not to develop specific guidelines for the conditions of stayed sentences, it recognizes that there are several penal objectives to be considered in establishing conditions of stayed sentences, including:

- deterrence;
- public condemnation of criminal conduct;
- public safety;
- rehabilitation;
- restitution;
- retribution; and
- risk reduction.

The Commission also recognizes that the relative importance of these objectives may vary with both offense and offender characteristics and that multiple objectives may be present in any given sentence. The Commission urges courts to utilize the least restrictive conditions of stayed sentences that are consistent with the objectives of the sanction. The Commission further urges courts to consider the following principles in establishing the conditions of stayed sentences:

(1) *Retribution.* If retribution is an important objective of the stayed sentence, the severity of the retributive sanction should be proportional to the severity of the offense and the prior criminal record of the offender. A period of confinement in a local jail or correctional facility may be appropriate.

(2) *Rehabilitation.* If rehabilitation is an important objective of the stayed sentence, the court should make full use of available local programs and resources. The absence of a rehabilitative resource, in general, should not be a basis for enhancing the retributive objective in sentencing and, in particular, should not be the basis for more extensive use of incarceration than is justified on other grounds.

(3) *Restitution.* The Commission urges courts to make expanded use of restitution and community work orders as conditions of a stayed sentence, especially for offenders with short criminal histories who are convicted of property crimes, although the use of these conditions in other cases may be appropriate.

(4) *Supervision.* Supervised probation should be a primary condition of stayed sentences.

(5) *Fines.* If fines are imposed, the Commission urges the expanded use of day fines, which standardizes the financial impact of the sanction among offenders with different income levels.

Comment

3.A.201. The court may attach any conditions to a stayed sentence that are permitted by law and that the court deems appropriate. The Guidelines neither enlarge nor restrict the conditions that courts may attach to a stayed sentence. Minn. Stat. § 244.09, subd. 5 permits, but does not require, the Commission to establish guidelines covering conditions of stayed sentences. The Commission chose not to develop guidelines during its initial guideline development effort. The Commission has provided some language in the above section of the Guidelines that provides general direction in the use of conditions of stayed sentences.

3.A.202. While the Commission has resolved not to develop guidelines for nonimprisonment sanctions at this time, the Commission believes it is important for the sentencing courts to consider proportionality when pronouncing a period of local confinement as a condition of probation. This is particularly important given Minn. Stat. § 609.135, subd. 7, which states that an offender may not demand execution of sentence. The period of local confinement should be proportional to the severity of the conviction offense and the criminal history score of the offender. Therefore, the period of local confinement should not exceed the term of imprisonment that would be served if the offender were to have received an executed prison sentence according to the presumptive Guidelines duration.

B. Revocation of Stayed Sentences

The Commission views revocation of a stayed sentence and commitment to be justified when:

- The offender is convicted of a new felony for which the Guidelines recommend prison; or
- The offender continues to violate conditions of the stay despite the court's use of expanded and more onerous conditions.

The decision to revoke an offender's stayed sentence should not be undertaken lightly. Great restraint should be exercised in imprisoning offenders who were originally convicted of low severity level offenses or who have short prior criminal histories. For these offenders, the Commission urges continuance of the stay and use of more restrictive and onerous conditions, such as periods of local confinement. Less judicial tolerance is urged for offenders who were convicted of a more severe offense or who had a longer criminal history. For both groups of offenders, however, the court should not reflexively order imprisonment for non-criminal violations of probationary conditions.

Comment

3.B.01. The Guidelines are based on the concept that the severity of the sanction is proportional to the severity of the current offense and the criminal history of the offender. Therefore, great restraint should be used when considering increasing the severity of the sanction based upon non-criminal technical violations of probationary conditions.

C. Jail Credit

1. In General. In order to promote the goals of the Sentencing Guidelines, it is important to ensure that jail credit is consistently applied. The court must assure that the record accurately reflects all time spent in custody—including examinations under Minn. R. Crim. P. 20 or 27.03, subd. 1(B)—for the offense or behavioral incident for which the offender is sentenced. Minnesota statutes, Rules of Criminal Procedure, relevant court decisions, and these Guidelines determine how jail credit is applied.

2. Applying Jail Credit. To uphold the proportionality of sentencing, jail credit should be applied in the following manner:

a. The Commissioner of Corrections must deduct jail credit from the sentence imposed by subtracting the time from the specified minimum term of imprisonment. If there is any remaining time, it must be subtracted from the specified maximum period of supervised release.

b. To avoid double credit when applying jail credit to consecutive sentences, the court must apply the jail credit to the first sentence only.

c. To avoid creating a concurrent sentence when a current offense is sentenced consecutively to a prior offense for which the offender is already serving time in a prison or jail, the court must not apply jail credit from the prior offense to the current offense.

d. When a stayed sentence is revoked and the offender is committed, jail credit must reflect time spent in confinement as a condition of the stayed sentence.

e. Jail credit must be awarded at the rate of one day for each day served for time spent in confinement under Huber Law (Minn. Stat. § 631.425).

Comment

3.C.01. Jail credit is governed by statute and rule—see, e.g., Minn. Stat. § 609.145 and Minn. R. Crim. P. 27.03, subd. 4(b)—and a great deal of case law. Granting jail credit to the time served in custody in connection with an offense ensures that a defendant who cannot post bail because of indigency will serve the same amount of time that an offender in identical circumstances who is able to post bail would serve. Also, the total amount of time a defendant is incarcerated should not turn on irrelevant concerns such as whether the defendant pleads guilty or insists on his right to trial.

3.C.02. Determining the appropriate application of jail credit for an individual can be very complicated, particularly when multiple offenses are involved. While the Commission recognizes the difficulty in interpreting individual circumstances, it believes that the court should award jail credit so that it does not turn on matters that are subject to the manipulation by the prosecutor.

3.C.03. The Commission also believes that jail credit should be awarded for time spent in custody as a condition of a stay of imposition or stay of execution when the stay is revoked and the offender is committed. The primary purpose of imprisonment is punishment, and the punishment imposed should be proportional to the severity of the conviction offense and the criminal history of the offender. If, for example, the presumptive duration in a case is 18 months, and the sentence was initially executed, the specified minimum term of imprisonment would be 12 months. If the execution of the sentence had initially been stayed and the offender had served four months in jail as a condition of the stay, and later the stay was revoked and the sentence executed, the offender would be confined for 16 months rather than 12 without awarding jail credit. By awarding jail credit for time spent in custody as a condition of a stay of imposition or execution, proportionality is maintained.

3.C.04. Credit for time spent in custody as a condition of a stay of imposition or stay of execution is appropriate for time spent in jails, workhouses, and regional correctional facilities. The Commission takes no position on the applicability of jail credit for time spent in other residential facilities, electronic monitoring, etc., and leaves it to the sentencing authority to determine whether jail credit should be granted in these situations.

3.C.05. In computing jail time credit, each day or portion of a day in jail should be counted as one full day of credit. For example, a defendant who spends part of a day in confinement on the day of arrest and part of a day in confinement on the day of release should receive a full day of credit for each day.

3.C.06. The Commission's policy is that sentencing should be neutral with respect to the economic status of felons. In order to ensure that offenders are not penalized for inability to post bond, credit for time in custody must be computed by the Commissioner of Corrections and subtracted from the specified minimum term of imprisonment. If there is any remaining jail credit left over, it should be subtracted from the specified maximum period of supervised release. If credit for time spent in custody were immediately deducted from the sentence instead, the incongruous result is that individuals who cannot post bond are confined longer than those who post bond.

3.C.07. For offenders sentenced for offenses committed before August 1, 1993, credit for time in custody must be computed by the Commissioner of Corrections after projected good time is subtracted from the executed sentence.

D. Juveniles

The Guidelines apply when determining:

- the appropriate sentence for a juvenile certified as an adult under Minn. Stat. § 260B.125; or

- the stayed adult sentence pronounced as part of the disposition imposed for a juvenile convicted as an extended jurisdiction juvenile under Minn. Stat. § 260B.130.

E. Presentence Mental or Physical Examinations for Sex Offenders

The Commission recommends that, under Minn. R. Crim. P. 27.03, subd. 1(B)(1)(b), the court order a physical or mental examination of the offender as a supplement to the presentence investigation required by Minn. Stat. § 609.115 when:

- an offender has been convicted under Minn. Stat. §§ 609.342 (first–degree criminal sexual conduct), 609.343 (second–degree criminal sexual conduct), 609.344 (third–degree criminal sexual conduct), 609.345 (fourth–degree criminal sexual conduct), or 609.365 (incest); or
- an offender is convicted under Minn. Stat. § 609.17 of an attempt to commit an act proscribed by Minn. Stat. §§ 609.342 (first–degree criminal sexual conduct) or 609.344 (third–degree criminal sexual conduct).

F. Military Veterans

Under Minn. Stat. § 609.115, subd. 10, when a defendant is convicted of a crime, the court must inquire whether the defendant is currently serving in or is a veteran of the armed forces of the United States, and if so, may take further action as permitted by that provision.

G. Modifications

1. Policy Modifications. Modifications to the Minnesota Sentencing Guidelines and associated commentary apply to offenders whose date of offense is on or after the specified modification effective date.

2. Clarifications of Existing Policy. Modifications to Commentary relating to existing Guidelines policy apply to offenders sentenced on or after the specified effective date.

4.A. Sentencing Guidelines Grid

Presumptive sentence lengths are in months. Italicized numbers within the grid denote the discretionary range within which a court may sentence without the sentence being deemed a departure. Offenders with stayed felony sentences may be subject to local confinement.

SEVERITY LEVEL OF CONVICTION OFFENSE (Example offenses listed in italics)		CRIMINAL HISTORY SCORE 0	1	2	3	4	5	6 or more
Murder, 2nd Degree (intentional murder; drive-by-shootings)	11	306 *261-367*	326 *278-391*	346 *295-415*	366 *312-439*	386 *329-463*	406 *346-480*[2]	426 *363-480*[2]
Murder, 3rd Degree Murder, 2nd Degree (unintentional murder)	10	150 *128-180*	165 *141-198*	180 *153-216*	195 *166-234*	210 *179-252*	225 *192-270*	240 *204-288*
Assault, 1st Degree Controlled Substance Crime, 1st Degree	9	86 *74-103*	98 *84-117*	110 *94-132*	122 *104-146*	134 *114-160*	146 *125-175*	158 *135-189*
Aggravated Robbery, 1st Degree Controlled Substance Crime, 2nd Degree	8	48 *41-57*	58 *50-69*	68 *58-81*	78 *67-93*	88 *75-105*	98 *84-117*	108 *92-129*
Felony DWI	7	36	42	48	54 *46-64*	60 *51-72*	66 *57-79*	72 *62-84*[2]
Controlled Substance Crime, 3rd Degree	6	21	27	33	39 *34-46*	45 *39-54*	51 *44-61*	57 *49-68*
Residential Burglary Simple Robbery	5	18	23	28	33 *29-39*	38 *33-45*	43 *37-51*	48 *41-57*
Nonresidential Burglary	4	12[1]	15	18	21	24 *21-28*	27 *23-32*	30 *26-36*
Theft Crimes (Over $5,000)	3	12[1]	13	15	17	19 *17-22*	21 *18-25*	23 *20-27*
Theft Crimes ($5,000 or less) Check Forgery ($251-$2,500)	2	12[1]	12[1]	13	15	17	19	21 *18-25*
Sale of Simulated Controlled Substance	1	12[1]	12[1]	12[1]	13	15	17	19 *17-22*

☐ Presumptive commitment to state imprisonment. First-degree murder has a mandatory life sentence and is excluded from the Guidelines under Minn. Stat. § 609.185. See Guidelines section 2.E. Mandatory Sentences, for policies regarding those sentences controlled by law.

■ Presumptive stayed sentence; at the discretion of the court, up to one year of confinement and other non-jail sanctions can be imposed as conditions of probation. However, certain offenses in the shaded area of the Grid always carry a presumptive commitment to state prison. Guidelines sections 2.C. Presumptive Sentence and 2.E. Mandatory Sentences.

[1] 12[1] =One year and one day

[2] Minn. Stat. § 244.09 requires that the Guidelines provide a range for sentences that are presumptive commitment to state imprisonment of 15% lower and 20% higher than the fixed duration displayed, provided that the minimum sentence is not less than one year and one day and the maximum sentence is not more than the statutory maximum. Guidelines section 2.C.1-2. Presumptive Sentence.

Examples of Executed Sentences (Length in Months) Broken Down by:
Term of Imprisonment and Supervised Release Term

Under Minn. Stat. § 244.101, offenders committed to the Commissioner of Corrections for crimes committed on or after August 1, 1993 will receive an executed sentence pronounced by the court consisting of two parts: a specified minimum term of imprisonment equal to two-thirds of the total executed sentence and a supervised release term equal to the remaining one-third. The court is required to pronounce the total executed sentence and explain the amount of time the offender will serve in prison and the amount of time the offender will serve on supervised release, assuming the offender commits no disciplinary offense in prison that results in the imposition of a disciplinary confinement period. The court must also explain that the amount of time the offender actually serves in prison may be extended by the Commissioner if the offender violates disciplinary rules while in prison or violates conditions of supervised release. This extension period could result in the offender's serving the entire executed sentence in prison.

Executed Sentence	Term of Imprisonment	Supervised Release Term	Executed Sentence	Term of Imprisonment	Supervised Release Term
12 and 1 day	8 and 1 day	4	78	52	26
13	8 2/3	4 1/3	86	57 1/3	28 2/3
15	10	5	88	58 2/3	29 1/3
17	11 1/3	5 2/3	98	65 1/3	32 2/3
18	12	6	108	72	36
19	12 2/3	6 1/3	110	73 1/3	36 2/3
21	14	7	122	81 1/3	40 2/3
23	15 1/3	7 2/3	134	89 1/3	44 2/3
24	16	8	146	97 1/3	48 2/3
27	18	9	150	100	50
28	18 2/3	9 1/3	158	105 1/3	52 2/3
30	20	10	165	110	55
33	22	11	180	120	60
36	24	12	190	126 2/3	63 1/3
38	25 1/3	12 2/3	195	130	65
39	26	13	200	133 1/3	66 2/3
42	28	14	210	140	70
43	28 2/3	14 1/3	220	146 2/3	73 1/3
45	30	15	225	150	75
48	32	16	230	153 1/3	76 2/3
51	34	17	240	160	80
54	36	18	306	204	102
57	38	19	326	217 1/3	108 2/3
58	38 2/3	19 1/3	346	230 2/3	115 1/3
60	40	20	366	244	122
66	44	22	386	257 1/3	128 2/3
68	45 1/3	22 2/3	406	270 2/3	135 1/3
72	48	24	426	284	142

4.B. Sex Offender Grid

Presumptive sentence lengths are in months. Italicized numbers within the grid denote the discretionary range within which a court may sentence without the sentence being deemed a departure. Offenders with stayed felony sentences may be subject to local confinement.

CRIMINAL HISTORY SCORE

SEVERITY LEVEL OF CONVICTION OFFENSE		**0**	**1**	**2**	**3**	**4**	**5**	**6 or More**
CSC 1st Degree	**A**	144 *144-172*	156 *144-187*	168 *144-201*	180 *153-216*	234 *199-280*	306 *261-360*	360 *306-360*[2]
CSC 2nd Degree–(c)(d)(e)(f)(h) *Prostitution; Sex Trafficking*[3] *1st Degree–1(a)*	**B**	90 *90*[3]*-108*	110 *94-132*	130 *111-156*	150 *128-180*	195 *166-234*	255 *217-300*	300 *255-300*[2]
CSC 3rd Degree–(c)(d)(g)(h)(i)(j)(k)(l)(m)(n)(o) *Prostitution; Sex Trafficking 2nd Degree–1a*	**C**	48 *41-57*	62 *53-74*	76 *65-91*	90 *77-108*	117 *100-140*	153 *131-180*	180 *153-180*[2]
CSC 2nd Degree–(a)(b)(g) *CSC 3rd Degree–(a)(b)*[2] *(e)(f)* *Dissemination of Child Pornography (Subsequent or by Predatory Offender)*	**D**	36	48	60 *51-72*	70 *60-84*	91 *78-109*	119 *102-142*	140 *119-168*
CSC 4th Degree–(c)(d)(g)(h)(i)(j)(k)(l)(m)(n)(o) *Use Minors in Sexual Performance* *Dissemination of Child Pornography*[2]	**E**	24	36	48	60 51-72	78 *67-93*	102 *87-120*	120 *102-120*[2]
CSC 4th Degree–(a)(b)(e)(f) *Possession of Child Pornography (Subsequent or by Predatory Offender)*	**F**	18	27	36	45 *39-54*	59 *51-70*	77 *66-92*	84 *72-100*
CSC 5th Degree *Indecent Exposure* *Possession of Child Pornography* *Solicit Children for Sexual Conduct*[2]	**G**	15	20	25	30	39 *34-46*	51 *44-60*	60 *51-60*[2]
Registration Of Predatory Offenders	**H**	12[1] *12*[1]*-14*	14 *12*[1]*-16*	16 *14-19*	18 *16-21*	24 *21-28*	30 *26-36*	36 *31-43*

☐ Presumptive commitment to state imprisonment. Sex offenses under Minn. Stat. § 609.3455, subd. 2, have mandatory life sentences and are excluded from the Guidelines. See Guidelines section 2.E. Mandatory Sentences, for policies regarding those sentences controlled by law, including conditional release terms for sex offenders.

■ Presumptive stayed sentence; at the discretion of the court, up to one year of confinement and other non-jail sanctions can be imposed as conditions of probation. However, certain offenders in the shaded area of the Grid may qualify for a mandatory life sentence under Minn. Stat. § 609.3455, subd. 4. Guidelines sections 2.C. Presumptive Sentence and 2.E. Mandatory Sentences.

[1] 12[1]=One year and one day

[2] Minn. Stat. § 244.09 requires that the Guidelines provide a range for sentences that are presumptive commitment to state imprisonment of 15% lower and 20% higher than the fixed duration displayed, provided that the minimum sentence is not less than one year and one day and the maximum sentence is not more than the statutory maximum. Guidelines section 2.C.1-2. Presumptive Sentence.

[3] Prostitution; Sex Trafficking is not subject to a 90-month minimum statutory presumptive sentence so the standard range of 15% lower and 20% higher than the fixed duration applies. (The range is 77-108.)

Examples of Executed Sentences (Length in Months) Broken Down by: Term of Imprisonment and Supervised Release Term

Under Minn. Stat. § 244.101, offenders committed to the Commissioner of Corrections for crimes committed on or after August 1, 1993 will receive an executed sentence pronounced by the court consisting of two parts: a specified minimum term of imprisonment equal to two-thirds of the total executed sentence and a supervised release term equal to the remaining one-third. The court is required to pronounce the total executed sentence and explain the amount of time the offender will serve in prison and the amount of time the offender will serve on supervised release, assuming the offender commits no disciplinary offense in prison that results in the imposition of a disciplinary confinement period. The court must also explain that the amount of time the offender actually serves in prison may be extended by the Commissioner if the offender violates disciplinary rules while in prison or violates conditions of supervised release. This extension period could result in the offender's serving the entire executed sentence in prison.

Executed Sentence	Term of Imprisonment	Supervised Release Term	Executed Sentence	Term of Imprisonment	Supervised Release Term
12 and 1 day	8 and 1 day	4	84	56	28
14	9 1/3	4 2/3	90	60	30
15	10	5	91	60 2/3	30 1/3
16	10 2/3	5 1/3	102	68	34
18	12	6	110	73 1/3	36 2/3
20	13 1/3	6 2/3	117	78	39
24	16	8	119	79 1/3	39 2/3
25	16 2/3	8 1/3	120	80	40
27	18	9	130	86 2/3	43 1/3
30	20	10	140	93 1/3	46 2/3
36	24	12	144	96	48
39	26	13	150	100	50
40	26 2/3	13 1/3	153	102	51
45	30	15	156	104	52
48	32	16	168	112	56
51	34	17	180	120	60
59	39 1/3	19 2/3	195	130	65
60	40	20	234	156	78
62	41 1/3	20 2/3	255	170	85
70	46 2/3	23 1/3	300	200	100
76	50 2/3	25 1/3	306	204	102
77	51 1/3	25 2/3	360	240	120
78	52	26			

5. Offense Severity Reference Table

Offenses subject to a mandatory life sentence, including first-degree murder and certain sex offenses under Minn. Stat. § 609.3455, subdivision 2, are excluded from the Guidelines by law.

Severity Level	Offense Title	Statute Number
11	Adulteration	609.687, subd. 3(1)
	Murder 2nd Degree (Intentional Murder; Unintentional Drive–By Shootings)	609.19, subd. 1
	Murder of an Unborn Child 2nd Degree	609.2662(1)
10	Fleeing a Peace Officer (Death)	609.487, subd. 4(a)
	Murder 2nd Degree (Unintentional Murder)	609.19, subd. 2
	Murder of an Unborn Child 2nd Degree	609.2662(2)

Severity Level	Offense Title	Statute Number
	Murder 3rd Degree	609.195(a)
	Murder of an Unborn Child 3rd Degree	609.2663
9	Assault 1st Degree	609.221
	Assault of an Unborn Child 1st Degree	609.267
	Controlled Substance Crime 1st Degree	152.021
	Manufacture Any Amount of Methamphetamine	152.021, subd. 2a(a)
	Criminal Abuse of Vulnerable Adult (Death)	609.2325, subd. 3(a)(1)
	Death of an Unborn Child in the Commission of Crime	609.268, subd. 1
	Engage or Hire a Minor to Engage in Prostitution	609.324, subd. 1(a)
	Importing Controlled Substances Across State Borders	152.0261
	Kidnapping (Great Bodily Harm)	609.25, subd. 2(2)
	Manslaughter 1st Degree	609.20(1), (2) & (5)
	Manslaughter of an Unborn Child 1st Degree	609.2664(1) & (2)
	Murder 3rd Degree	609.195(b)
	Tampering with Witness, Aggravated 1st Degree	609.498, subd. 1b
8	Aggravated Robbery 1st Degree	609.245, subd. 1
	Arson 1st Degree	609.561
	Burglary 1st Degree (w/Weapon or Assault)	609.582, 1(b) & (c)
	Controlled Substance Crime 2nd Degree	152.022
	Criminal Abuse of Vulnerable Adult (Great Bodily Harm)	609.2325, subd. 3(a)(2)
	Criminal Vehicular Homicide or Operation (Death)	609.21, subd. 1a(a)
	Deprivation of Vulnerable Adult (Great Bodily Harm)	609.233, subd. 2a(1)
	Drive–By Shooting (Toward a Person or Occupied Motor Vehicle or Building)	609.66, subd. 1e(b)
	Emergency Telephone Calls and Communications (Reporting Fictitious Emergency Resulting in Serious Injury or Death)	609.78, subd. 2a
	Escape with Violence from Felony Offense	609.485, subd. 4(b)
	Great Bodily Harm Caused by Distribution of Drugs	609.228
	Identity Theft	609.527, subd. 3(5)
	Kidnapping (Not in Safe Place or Victim Under 16)	609.25, subd. 2(2)
	Malicious Punishment of Child (Great Bodily Harm)	609.377, subd. 6
	Manslaughter 1st Degree	609.20 (3) & (4)

Severity Level	Offense Title	Statute Number
	Manslaughter of an Unborn Child 1st Degree	609.2664(3)
	Manslaughter 2nd Degree—Culpable Negligence	609.205 (1) & (5)
	Manslaughter of an Unborn Child 2nd Degree	609.2665(1)
	Riot 1st Degree	609.71, subd. 1
	Wildfire Arson (Damage over 100 Dwellings, Burns 1,500 Acres or More, or Crops in Excess of $250,000)	609.5641 subd. 1a(c)
7	Financial Exploitation of a Vulnerable Adult (Over $35,000)	609.2335
	Felony Driving While Impaired 1st Degree	169A.24
	Wildfire Arson (Damage over Five Dwellings, Burns 500 Acres or More, or Crops in Excess of $100,000)	609.5641 subd. 1a(b)
6	Aggravated Robbery 2nd Degree	609.245, subd. 2
	Assault 2nd Degree	609.222
	Burglary 1st Degree (Occupied Dwelling)	609.582, subd. 1(a)
	Certain Persons Not to Have Firearms	624.713, subd. 2(b); 609.165, subd. 1b
	Controlled Substance Crime 3rd Degree	152.023
	Discharge of Firearm at Occupied Transit Vehicle/Facility	609.855, subd. 5
	Explosive Device or Incendiary Device	609.668, subd. 6
	Failure to Affix Stamp on Cocaine	297D.09, subd. 1
	Failure to Affix Stamp on Hallucinogens or PCP	297D.09, subd. 1
	Failure to Affix Stamp on Heroin	297D.09, subd. 1
	Failure to Affix Stamp on Remaining Schedule I & II Narcotics	297D.09, subd. 1
	Fleeing Peace Officer (Great Bodily Harm)	609.487, subd. 4(b)
	Kidnapping (Safe Release/No Great Bodily Harm)	609.25, subd. 2(1)
	Price Fixing/Collusive Bidding	325D.53, subd. 1(2)(a)
	Theft Over $35,000	609.52, subd. 2(3), (4), (15), & (16) with 609.52, subd. 3(1)
5	Arson 2nd Degree	609.562
	Burglary 2nd Degree	609.582, subd. 2(a)(1)&(2), 2(b)
	Check Forgery (Over $35,000)	609.631, subd. 4(1)
	Criminal Vehicular Homicide or Operation (Great Bodily Harm)	609.21, subd. 1a(b)
	Deprivation of Vulnerable Adult (Substantial Bodily Harm)	609.233, subd. 2a(2)
	Emergency Telephone Calls and Communications (Blocks, Interferes, Prevents Using Multiple Communication Devices or Electronic Means)	609.78, subd. 2b(2)

Severity Level	Offense Title	Statute Number
	Engage or Hire a Minor to Engage in Prostitution	609.324, subd. 1(b)
	Financial Exploitation of a Vulnerable Adult (Over $5,000)	609.2335
	Financial Transaction Card Fraud (Over $35,000)	609.821, subd. 3(1)(i)
	Interference with Emergency Communications	609.776
	Manslaughter 2nd Degree—Hunting Accident	609.205 (2), (3), & (4)
	Manslaughter of an Unborn Child 2nd Degree	609.2665 (2), (3), & (4)
	Negligent Discharge of Explosive	299F.83
	Perjury	609.48, subd. 4(1)
	Possession of Substances with Intent to Manufacture Methamphetamine	152.0262
	Possession or Use (Unauthorized) of Explosives	299F.79; 299F.80, subd. 1; 299F.82, subd. 1
	Price Fixing/Collusive Bidding	325D.53, subd. 1(1), and subd. 1(2)(b) & (c)
	Simple Robbery	609.24
	Stalking (3rd or Subsequent Violations)	609.749, subd. 4(b)
	Stalking (Pattern of Stalking Conduct)	609.749, subd. 5
	Tampering with Witness in the First Degree	609.498, subd. 1a
	Wildfire Arson (Demonstrable Bodily Harm)	609.5641 subd. 1a(d)
4	Adulteration	609.687, subd. 3(2)
	Assault of an Unborn Child 2nd Degree	609.2671
	Assault 3rd Degree	609.223, subd. 1,2, & 3
	Assault 5th Degree (3rd or Subsequent Violation)	609.224, subd. 4
	Bribery	609.42; 90.41; 609.86
	Bribery, Advancing Money, and Treating	211B.13
	Bring Contraband into State Prison	243.55
	Bring Dangerous Weapon into County Jail	641.165, subd. 2(b)
	Burglary 2nd Degree (Pharmacy/Tool)	609.582, subd. 2(a)(3) & (4)
	Burglary 3rd Degree (Non Residential)	609.582, subd. 3
	Controlled Substance Crime 4th Degree	152.024
	Criminal Abuse of Vulnerable Adult (Substantial Bodily Harm)	609.2325, subd. 3(a)(3)
	Dangerous Weapons on School Property	609.66, 1d(a)
	Domestic Assault	609.2242, subd. 4
	Domestic Assault by Strangulation	609.2247

Severity Level	Offense Title	Statute Number
	Emergency Telephone Calls and Communications (3rd or Subsequent, Making Calls When No Emergency Exists)	609.78, subd. 2b(1)
	False Imprisonment (Substantial Bodily Harm)	609.255, subd. 3(c)
	Financial Exploitation of a Vulnerable Adult ($5,000 or Less)	609.2335
	Fleeing a Peace Officer (Substantial Bodily Harm)	609.487, subd. 4(c)
	Injury of an Unborn Child in Commission of Crime	609.268, subd. 2
	Malicious Punishment of Child (2nd or Subsequent Violation)	609.377, subd. 3
	Malicious Punishment of Child (Bodily Harm)	609.377, subd. 4
	Malicious Punishment of Child (Substantial Bodily Harm)	609.377, subd. 5
	Negligent Fires (Great Bodily Harm)	609.576, subd. 1(1)
	Perjury	609.48, subd. 4(2)
	Precious Metal and Scrap Metal Dealers, Receiving Stolen Goods (2nd or Subsequent Violations)	609.526
	Receiving Stolen Property (Firearm)	609.53
	Security Violations (Over $2,500)	80A.68; 80B.10, subd. 1; 80C.16, subd. 3(a) & (b)
	Sports Bookmaking	609.76, subd. 2
	Stalking (Aggravated Violations)	609.749, subd. 3(a), (b)
	Stalking (2nd or Subsequent Violation)	609.749, subd. 4(a)
	Terroristic Threats	609.713, subd. 1
	Theft From Person	609.52
	Theft of Controlled Substances	609.52, subd. 3(2)
	Theft of Firearm	609.52, subd. 3(1)
	Theft of Incendiary Device	609.52, subd. 3(2)
	Theft of Motor Vehicle	609.52, subd. 2(1)
	Use of Drugs to Injure or Facilitate Crime	609.235
	Violation of a Domestic Abuse No Contact Order	629.75, subd. 2(d)
	Violation of an Order for Protection	518B.01, subd. 14(d)
	Violation of Harassment Restraining Order	609.748, subd. 6(d)
	Weapon in Courthouse or Certain State Buildings	609.66, subd. 1g
3	Anhydrous Ammonia (Tamper/Theft/Transport)	152.136
	Arson 3rd Degree	609.563
	Bringing Stolen Goods into State (Over $5,000)	609.525
	Check Forgery (Over $2,500)	609.631, subd. 4(2)
	Coercion (Threat Bodily Harm)	609.27, subd. 1(1)
	Coercion ($2,500 or More)	609.27, subd. 1(2), (3), (4), & (5)

Severity Level	Offense Title	Statute Number
	Computer Damage (Over $2,500)	609.88
	Computer Theft (Over $2,500)	609.89
	Criminal Vehicular Homicide or Operation (Substantial Bodily Harm)	609.21, subd. 1a(c)
	Damage or Theft to Energy Transmission, Telecommunications	609.593
	Damage to Property (Risk Bodily Harm)	609.595, subd. 1(1)
	Damages; Illegal Molestation of Human Remains; Burials; Cemeteries	307.08, subd. 2(a)
	Dangerous Smoking	609.576, subd. 2
	Dangerous Trespass, Railroad Tracks	609.85(1)
	Dangerous Weapons/Certain Persons Not to Have Firearms	609.67, subd. 2; 624.713, subd. 2(a)
	Depriving Another of Custodial or Parental Rights	609.26, subd. 6(a)(2)
	Disarming a Peace Officer	609.504
	Drive–By Shooting (Unoccupied Motor Vehicle or Building)	609.66, subd. 1e(a)
	Embezzlement of Public Funds (Over $2,500)	609.54
	Engage or Hire a Minor to Engage in Prostitution	609.324, subd. 1(c)
	Escape from Civil Commitment, Sexually Dangerous Persons	609.485, subd. 4(a)(5)
	Escape from Felony Offense	609.485, subd. 4(a)(1)
	False Imprisonment (Demonstrable Bodily Harm)	609.255 subd. 3(b)
	False Imprisonment (Restraint)	609.255, subd. 2
	False Traffic Signal	609.851, subd. 2
	Financial Transaction Card Fraud (Over $2,500)	609.821, subd. 2(1)(2)(5)(6) (7)(8)
	Firearm Silencer (Public Housing, School, or Park Zone)	609.66, subd. 1a (a)(1)
	Gambling Taxes	297E.13, subd. 1–4
	Hinder Logging (Great Bodily Harm)	609.591, subd. 3(1)
	Identity Theft	609.527, subd. 3(4)
	Insurance Tax	297I.90, subd. 1 & 2
	Intentional Release of Harmful Substance	624.732, subd. 2
	Methamphetamine Crimes Involving Children and Vulnerable Adults	152.137
	Motor Vehicle Use Without Consent	609.52, subd. 2(17)
	Obstructing Legal Process, Arrest, Firefighting, or Ambulance Service Personnel Crew	609.50, subd. 2
	Possession of Burglary Tools	609.59
	Possession of Code Grabbing Devices	609.586, subd. 2
	Possession of Shoplifting Gear	609.521
	Possession or Sale of Stolen or Counterfeit Check	609.528, subd. 3(4)

Severity Level	Offense Title	Statute Number
	Precious Metal and Scrap Metal Dealers, Receiving Stolen Goods ($1,000 or More)	609.526, subd. 2(1)
	Receiving Stolen Goods (Over $5,000)	609.53
	Rustling and Livestock Theft (Over $2,500)	609.551
	Security Violations ($2,500 or Less)	80A.68; 80B.10, subd. 1; 80C.16, subd. 3(a) & (b)
	Tampering with Fire Alarm System (Results in Bodily Harm)	609.686, subd. 2
	Tax Evasion Laws	289A.63
	Tear Gas & Tear Gas Compounds; Electronic Incapacitation Devices	624.731, subd. 8(a)
	Telecommunications and Information Services; Obtaining Services by Fraud (Over $2,500)	609.893, subd. 1
	Theft Crimes—Over $5,000	See section 7: Theft Offense List
	Theft of Controlled Substances	609.52, subd. 3(3)(b)
	Theft of Public Records	609.52
	Theft of Trade Secret	609.52, subd. 2(8)
	Unauthorized Presence at Camp Ripley	609.396, subd. 2
2	Accidents (Death)	169.09, subd. 14(a)(1)
	Aggravated Forgery (Misc. Non-Check)	609.625; 609.635; 609.64
	Bribery of Participant or Official in Contest	609.825, subd. 2
	Bringing Stolen Goods into State ($1,001–$5,000)	609.525
	Bringing Stolen Goods into State ($501–$1,000, w/Previous Conviction)	609.525
	Cellular Counterfeiting 1st Degree	609.894, subd. 4
	Check Forgery ($251—$2,500)	609.631, subd. 4(3)(a)
	Coercion ($301—$2,499)	609.27, subd. 1(2), (3), (4), & (5)
	Computer Damage ($2,500 or Less)	609.88
	Computer Theft ($2,500 or Less)	609.89
	Controlled Substance in the 5th Degree	152.025
	Counterfeited Intellectual Property	609.895, subd. 3(a)
	Damage to Property (Over $500/Service to Public)	609.595, subd. 1(2), (3), & (4)
	Discharge of Firearm (Intentional)	609.66, subd. 1a(a)(2)
	Discharge of Firearm (Public Housing, School, or Park Zone)	609.66, subd. 1a(a)(2) & (3)
	Dishonored Check (Over $500)	609.535, subd. 2a(a)(1)
	Duty to Render Aid (Death or Great Bodily Harm)	609.662, subd. 2(b)(1)
	Electronic Use of False Pretense to Obtain Identity	609.527, subd. 5a

Severity Level	Offense Title	Statute Number
	Embezzlement of Public Funds ($2,500 or Less)	609.54
	Failure to Affix Stamp on Remaining Schedule I, II, & III Non–Narcotics	297D.09, subd. 1
	Failure to Control a Regulated Animal, Resulting in Great Bodily Harm or Death	346.155, subd. 10(e)
	Financial Transaction Card Fraud ($2,500 or Less)	609.821, subd. 2(1)(2)(5)(6)(7)(8)
	Firearm Silencer	609.66, subd. 1a(a)(1)
	Furnishing a Dangerous Weapon	609.66, subd. 1c
	Furnishing Firearm to Minor	609.66, subd. 1b
	Gambling Regulations	349.2127, subd. 1–6; 349.22, subd. 4
	Identity Theft	609.527, subd. 3(3)
	Mail Theft	609.529
	Negligent Fires (Damage $2,500 or More)	609.576, subd. 1(3)(iii)
	Possession or Sale of Stolen or Counterfeit Check	609.528, subd. 3(3)
	Precious Metal and Scrap Metal Dealers, Receiving Stolen Goods (Less than $1,000)	609.526, subd. 2(2)
	Precious Metal Dealers, Regulatory Provisions	325F.743
	Receiving Stolen Goods ($5,000 or Less)	609.53
	Residential Mortgage Fraud	609.822
	Riot 2nd Degree	609.71, subd. 2
	Rustling and Livestock Theft ($2,500 or Less)	609.551
	Sale of Synthetic Cannabinoids	152.027, subd. 6(c)
	Telecommunications and Information Services; Obtaining Services by Fraud ($2,500 or Less)	609.893, subd. 1
	Telecommunications and Information Services; Facilitation of Telecommunications Fraud	609.893, subd. 2
	Terroristic Threats	609.713, subd. 2
	Theft Crimes—$5,000, or Less	See section 7: Theft Offense List
	Theft (Looting)	609.52
	Theft ($1,000 or Less; Risk of Bodily Harm)	609.52, subd. 3a(1)
	Transfer Pistol to Ineligible Person	624.7141, subd. 2
	Transfer Pistol to Minor	624.7132, subd. 15(b)
	Unlawful Possession or Use of Scanning Device or Reencoder	609.527, subd. 5b
	Wildfire Arson	609.5641, subd. 1a(a)
1	Accidents (Great Bodily Harm)	169.09, subd. 14(a)(2)
	Altering Livestock Certificate	35.824
	Assault 4th Degree	609.2231, subd. 1,2,3, & 3a

Severity Level	Offense Title	Statute Number
	Assault Weapon in Public if Under 21	624.7181, subd. 2
	Assaulting or Harming a Police Horse	609.597, subd. 3(3)
	Assaults Motivated by Bias	609.2231, subd. 4(b)
	Aiding Offender to Avoid Arrest	609.495, subd. 1
	Bullet–Resistant Vest During Commission of Crime	609.486
	Cable Communication Systems Interference	609.80, subd. 2
	Cellular Counterfeiting 2nd Degree	609.894, subd. 3
	Certification for Title on Watercraft	86B.865, subd. 1
	Check Forgery ($250 or Less)	609.631, subd. 4(3)(b)
	Child Neglect/Endangerment	609.378
	Counterfeited Intellectual Property	609.895, subd. 3(b)
	Crime Committed for Benefit of Gang	609.229, subd. 3(c)
	Criminal Damage to Property Motivated by Bias	609.595, subd. 1a, (a)
	Criminal Use of Real Property (Movie Pirating)	609.896
	Depriving Another of Custodial or Parental Rights	609.26, subd. 6(a)(1)
	Discharge of Firearm (Reckless)	609.66, subd. 1a(a)(3)
	Discharge of Firearm at Unoccupied Transit Vehicle/Facility	609.855, subd. 5
	Duty to Render Aid (Substantial Bodily Harm)	609.662, subd. 2(b)(2)
	Escape from Civil Commitment	609.485, subd. 4(a)(4)
	Escape, Mental Illness	609.485, subd, 4(a)(2)
	Failure to Affix Stamp on Marijuana/Hashish/Tetrahydrocannabinols	297D.09, subd. 1
	Failure to Affix Stamp on Schedule IV Substances	297D.09, subd. 1
	Failure to Appear in Court	609.49; 588.20, subd. 1
	False Bill of Lading	228.45, 47, 49, 50, 51
	False Certification by Notary Public	609.65 (1)
	False Declaration	256.984
	False Information—Certificate of Title Application	168A.30, subd. 1
	Financial Transaction Card Fraud	609.821, subd. 2(3) & (4)
	Fleeing A Peace Officer	609.487, subd. 3
	Forgery	609.63
	Fraudulent Drivers' Licenses and Identification Cards	609.652
	Fraudulent Statements	609.645
	Insurance Regulations	62A.41
	Interference with Privacy (Subsequent Violations & Minor Victim)	609.746, subd. 1(e)
	Interference with Transit Operator	609.855, subd. 2(c)(1)
	Leaving State to Evade Establishment of Paternity	609.31

Severity Level	Offense Title	Statute Number
	Liquor Taxation (Criminal Penalties)	297G.19, subd. 3,4(c), 5(c)
	Lottery Fraud	609.651, subd. 1 with subd. 4(a)
	Nonsupport of Spouse or Child	609.375, subd. 2a
	Pistol Without a Permit (Subsequent Violations)	624.714, subd. 1a
	Prize Notices and Solicitations	325F.755, subd. 7
	Prostitution Crimes (Gross Misdemeanor Level) Committed in School or Park Zones	609.3242, subd. 2(2)
	Remove or Alter Serial Number on Firearm	609.667
	Sale of Simulated Controlled Substance	152.097
	Tampering with a Fire Alarm (Potential for Bodily Harm)	609.686, subd. 2
	Tax on Petroleum and Other Fuels (Willful Evasion)	296A.23, subd. 2
	Terroristic Threats	609.713, subd. 3(a)
	Theft from Abandoned or Vacant Building ($1,000 or Less)	609.52, subd. 3(3)(d)(iii)
	Unlawful Acts Involving Liquor	340A.701
	Voting Violations	Chapter 201, 203B, & 204C
UNRANKED	Abortion	617.20; 617.22; 145.412
	Accomplice After the Fact	609.495, subd. 3
	Adulteration	609.687, subd. 3(3)
	Aiding Suicide	609.215
	Altering Engrossed Bill	3.191
	Animal Fighting	343.31 (a)(b)
	Assaulting or Harming a Police Horse	609.597, subd. 3 (1) & (2)
	Bigamy	609.355
	Cigarette Tax and Regulation Violations	297F.20
	Collusive Bidding/Price Fixing	325D.53, subds. 1(3), 2 & 3
	Computer Encryption	609.8912
	Concealing Criminal Proceeds; Engaging in Business	609.496; 609.497
	Corrupting Legislator	609.425
	Counterfeiting of Currency	609.632
	Damage to Property of Critical Public Service Facilities, Utilities, and Pipelines	609.594
	Escape with Violence from Gross Misdemeanor or Misdemeanor Offense	609.485, subd. 4(a)(3)
	Failure to Report	626.556, subd. 6
	Falsely Impersonating Another	609.83
	Female Genital Mutilation	609.2245
	Forced Execution of a Declaration	145B.105

Severity Level	Offense Title	Statute Number
	Fraudulent or Improper Financing Statements	609.7475
	Gambling Acts (Cheating, Certain Devices Prohibited; Counterfeit Chips; Manufacture, Sale, Modification of Devices; Instruction)	609.76, subd. 3,4,5,6, & 7
	Hazardous Wastes	609.671
	Horse Racing—Prohibited Act	240.25
	Incest	609.365
	Insurance Fraud—Employment of Runners	609.612
	Interstate Compact Violation	243.161
	Issuing a Receipt for Goods One Does Not Have	227.50
	Issuing a Second Receipt Without "Duplicate" on It	227.52
	Killing or Harming a Public Safety Dog	609.596, subd. 1
	Labor Trafficking	609.282
	Lawful Gambling Fraud	609.763
	Metal Penetrating Bullets	624.7191
	Midwest Interstate Low–Level Radioactive Waste Compact; Enforcement of Compact and Laws	116C.835
	Misprision of Treason	609.39
	Motor Vehicle Excise Tax	297B.10
	Obscene Materials; Distribution	617.241, subd. 4
	Obstructing Military Forces	609.395
	Pipeline Safety	299J.07, subd. 2
	Police Radios During Commission of Crime	609.856
	Racketeering, Criminal Penalties (RICO)	609.904
	Real and Simulated Weapons of Mass Destruction	609.712
	Refusal to Assist	6.53
	Sale of Membership Camping Contracts	82A.03; 82A.13; 82A.25
	Service Animal Providing Service	343.21, subd. 9(f)(h)
	State Lottery Fraud	609.651, subd. 1 with 4 (b) and subd. 2 & 3
	Subdivided Land Fraud	83.43
	Torture or Cruelty to Pet or Companion Animal	343.21, subd. 9(c)(d)(g)(i)
	Treason	609.385
	Unauthorized Computer Access	609.891
	Unlawful Conduct with Documents in Furtherance of Labor or Sex Trafficking	609.283
	Unlawful Transfer of Sounds; Sales	325E.201
	Warning Subject of Investigation	609.4971
	Warning Subject of Surveillance or Search	609.4975

Severity Level	Offense Title	Statute Number
	Wire Communications Violations	626A.02, subd. 4; 626A.03, subd. 1(b)(ii); 626A.26, subd. 2(1)(ii)
A	Criminal Sexual Conduct 1st Degree	609.342
B	Criminal Sexual Conduct 2nd Degree	609.343 subd. 1(c)(d)(e)(f)(h)
	Solicits, Promotes, or Receives Profit Derived from Prostitution; Sex Trafficking 1st Degree	609.322, subd. 1(a)
C	Criminal Sexual Conduct 3rd Degree	609.344 subd. 1(c)(d)(g)(h)(i)(j)(k) (*l*) (m)(n)(*o*)
	Solicits, Promotes, or Receives Profit Derived from Prostitution; Sex Trafficking 2nd Degree	609.322, subd. 1a
D	Criminal Sexual Conduct 2nd Degree	609.343 subd. 1(a)(b)(g)
	Criminal Sexual Conduct 3rd Degree	609.344 subd. 1(a)(b)(e)(f)
	Dissemination of Child Pornography (Subsequent or by Predatory Offender)	617.247 subd. 3
E	Criminal Sexual Conduct 4th Degree	609.345 subd. 1(c)(d)(g)(h)(i)(j)(k) (*l*) (m)(n)(*o*)
	Use Minors in Sexual Performance	617.246 subd. 2,3,4
	Dissemination of Child Pornography	617.247 subd. 3
F	Criminal Sexual Conduct 4th Degree	609.345 subd. 1(a)(b)(e)(f)
	Possession of Child Pornography (Subsequent or by Predatory Offender)	617.247 subd. 4
G	Criminal Sexual Conduct 5th Degree	609.3451, subd. 3
	Solicitation of Children to Engage in Sexual Conduct	609.352, subd. 2
	Solicitation of Children to Engage in Sexual Conduct (Electronic)	609.352, subd. 2a
	Indecent Exposure	617.23 subd. 3
	Possession of Child Pornography	617.247 subd. 4
H	Failure to Register as a Predatory Offender	243.166 subd. 5(b) (c)

Offenses subject to a mandatory life sentence, including first-degree murder and certain sex offenses under Minn. Stat. § 609.3455, subdivision 2, are excluded from the Guidelines by law.

Statute Number	Offense Title	Severity Level
3.191	Altering Engrossed Bill	Unranked
6.53	Refusal to Assist	Unranked
35.824	Altering Livestock Certificate	1
62A.41	Insurance Regulations	1
80A.68 or	Securities Violation (Over $2,500)	4

Statute Number	Offense Title	Severity Level
80B.10 subd. 1 or 80C.16 subd. 3(a)(b)		
80A.68 or 80B.10 subd. 1 or 80C.16 subd. 3(a)(b)	Securities Violation ($2,500 or Less)	3
82A.03; 82A.13 82A.25	Sale of Membership Camping Contracts	Unranked
83.43	Subdivided Land Fraud	Unranked
86B.865 subd. 1	Certification for Title on Watercraft	1
90.41 subd. 1	Bribery (State Appraiser and Scaler)	4
116C.835	Midwest Interstate Low–Level Radioactive Waste Compact; Enforcement of Compact and Laws	Unranked
145.412	Abortion	Unranked
145B.105	Forced Execution of a Declaration	Unranked
152.021	Controlled Substance Crime 1st Degree	9
152.021, subd. 2a(a)	Manufacture Any Amount of Methamphetamine	9
152.022	Controlled Substance Crime 2nd Degree	8
152.023	Controlled Substance Crime 3rd Degree	6 [1]
152.024	Controlled Substance Crime 4th Degree	4
152.025	Controlled Substance Crime 5th Degree	2
152.0261	Importing Controlled Substances Across State Borders	9
152.0262	Possession of Substances with Intent to Manufacture Methamphetamine	5
152.027, subd. 6(c)	Sale of Synthetic Cannabinoids	2
152.097	Sale of Simulated Controlled Substance	1
152.136	Anhydrous Ammonia (Tamper/Theft/Transport)	3
152.137	Methamphetamine Crimes Involving Children and Vulnerable Adults	3
168A.30, subd. 1	False Information—Certificate of Title Application	1
169.09 subd. 14(a)(1)	Accidents (Death)	2
169.09 subd. 14(a)(2)	Accidents (Great Bodily Harm)	1
169A.24	Felony Driving While Impaired 1st Degree	7 [1]
176.178	Workers Compensation Fraud (Over $5,000)	3
176.178	Workers Compensation Fraud ($5,000 or Less)	2
201, 203B, 204C (Chapters)	Voting Violations	1
211B.13	Bribery, Advancing Money, and Treating Prohibited	4
227.50	Issuing a Receipt for Goods One Does Not Have	Unranked

Statute Number	Offense Title	Severity Level
227.52	Issuing a 2nd Receipt without "Duplicate" on it	Unranked
228.45, 47, 49, 50, 51	False Bill of Lading	1
240.25	Horse Racing (Prohibited Act)	Unranked
243.161	Interstate Compact Violation	Unranked
243.166 subd. 5(b)	Registration of Predatory Offenders	H
243.166 subd. 5(c)	Registration of Predatory Offenders (2nd or Subsequent Violations)	H
243.55	Bringing Contraband into State Prison	4
256.98	Welfare Fraud (Over $5,000)	3
256.98	Welfare Fraud ($5,000 or Less)	2
256.984	False Declaration	1
268.182	False Representations (Over $5,000)	3
268.182	False Representations ($5,000 or Less)	2
289A.63	Tax Evasion Laws	3
296A.23 subd. 2	Tax on Petroleum and Other Fuels (Willful Evasion)	1
297B.10	Motor Vehicle Excise Tax	Unranked
297D.09 subd. 1	Failure to Affix Stamp on Cocaine	6
297D.09 subd. 1	Failure to Affix Stamp on Hallucinogens or PCP (Angel Dust), Incl. LSD	6
297D.09 subd. 1	Failure to Affix Stamp on Heroin	6
297D.09 subd. 1	Failure to Affix Stamp on Remaining Schedule I and II Narcotics	6
297D.09 subd. 1	Failure to Affix Stamp on Remaining Schedule I, II, & III Non Narcotics	2
297D.09 subd. 1	Failure to Affix Stamp on Marijuana/Hashish/Tetrahydrocannabinols	1
297D.09 subd. 1	Failure to Affix Stamp on Schedule IV Substance	1
297E.13 subd. 1–4	Gambling Taxes	3
297F.20	Cigarette Tax and Regulation Violations	Unranked
297G.19 subd. 3, 4(c), 5(c)	Liquor Taxation (Criminal Penalties)	1
297I.90 subd. 1 & 2	Insurance Tax	3
299F.79	Intent to Manufacture Explosives	5
299F.80 subd. 1	Possession of Explosives Without Permit	5
299F.82 subd. 1	Transfer of Explosives	5
299F.83	Negligent Discharge of Explosive	5
299J.07 subd. 2	Pipeline Safety	Unranked
307.08 subd. 2(a)	Damages; Illegal Molestation of Human Remains; Burials; Cemeteries	3
325D.53 subd. 1(2)(a)	Price Fixing/Collusive Bidding	6
325D.53 subd. 1(1) subd. 1(2)(b)(c)	Price Fixing/Collusive Bidding	5
325D.53 subd. 1(3) subd. 2 & 3	Price Fixing/Collusive Bidding	Unranked
325E.201	Unlawful Transfer of Sounds; Sales	Unranked
325F.743	Precious Metal Dealers, Regulatory Provisions	2
325F.755 subd. 7	Prize Notices and Solicitations	1
340A.701	Unlawful Acts Involving Liquor	1

Statute Number	Offense Title	Severity Level
343.21, subd. 9(c)(d)(g)(i)	Torture or Cruelty to Pet or Companion Animal	Unranked
343.21, subd. 9(f)(h)	Service Animal Providing Service	Unranked
343.31 (a)(b)	Animal Fighting	Unranked
346.155	Failure to Control a Regulated Animal (Great Bodily Harm or Death)	2
349.2127 subd. 1–6; 349.22 subd. 4	Gambling Regulations	2
393.07 subd.10	Federal Food Stamp Program (Over $5,000)	3
393.07 subd.10	Federal Food Stamp Program ($5,000 or Less)	2
471.392	False Declaration of Claim (Over $5,000)	3
471.392	False Declaration of Claim ($5,000 or Less)	2
514.02 subd. 1(b)	Non–payment for Improvement (Over $5,000; Proceeds of Payments; Acts Constituting Theft)	3
514.02 subd. 1(b)	Non–payment for Improvement ($5,000 or Less Proceeds of Payments; Acts Constituting Theft)	2
518B.01 subd. 14(d)	Violation of an Order for Protection	4
588.20 subd. 1	Failure to Appear in Court	1
609.165 subd. 1b	Certain Persons Not to Have Firearms	6
609.19 subd. 1	Murder 2nd Degree (Intentional Murder; Unintentional Drive–By–Shootings)	11
609.19 subd. 2	Murder 2nd Degree (Unintentional Murder)	10
609.195(a)	Murder 3rd Degree	10
609.195(b)	Murder 3rd Degree	9
609.20(1), (2) & (5)	Manslaughter 1st Degree	9
609.20(3) & (4)	Manslaughter 1st Degree	8
609.205(1) & (5)	Manslaughter 2nd Degree—Culpable Negligence	8
609.205(2), (3) & (4)	Manslaughter 2nd Degree—Hunting Accident	5
609.21 subd. 1a(a)	Criminal Vehicular Homicide or Operation (Death)	8
609.21 subd. 1a(b)	Criminal Vehicular Homicide or Operation (Great Bodily Harm)	5
609.21 subd. 1a(c)	Criminal Vehicular Homicide or Operation(Substantial Bodily Harm)	3
609.215	Aiding Suicide	Unranked
609.221	Assault 1st Degree (Great Bodily Harm)	9
609.222	Assault 2nd Degree (Dangerous Weapon)	6
609.223 subd. 1	Assault 3rd Degree (Substantial Bodily Harm)	4 [2]
609.223 subd. 2	Assault 3rd Degree (Bodily Harm, Pattern of Child Abuse)	4

Statute Number	Offense Title	Severity Level
609.223 subd. 3	Assault 3rd Degree (Bodily Harm, Victim under 4)	4
609.2231 subd. 1	Assault 4th Degree (Bodily Harm, Peace Officer)	1
609.2231 subd. 2	Assault 4th Degree (Bodily Harm, Firefighters and Emergency Medical Personnel)	1
609.2231 subd. 3	Assault 4th Degree (Bodily Harm, Corrections Employee)	1 [2]
609.2231 subd. 3a	Assault 4th Degree (Bodily Harm, Secure Treatment Facility Personnel)	1 [2]
609.2231 subd. 4 (b)	Assaults Motivated by Bias	1
609.224 subd. 4	Assault 5th Degree (3rd or Subsequent Violation)	4
609.2241	Knowing Transfer of Communicable Disease	See Note [3]
609.2242 subd. 4	Domestic Assault	4
609.2245	Female Genital Mutilation	Unranked
609.2247	Domestic Assault by Strangulation	4
609.228	Great Bodily Harm Caused by Distribution of Drugs	8
609.229 subd. 3 (a)	Crime Committed for Benefit of Gang	See Note [4]
609.229 subd. 3 (c)	Crime Committed for Benefit of Gang	1
609.2325 subd. 3(a)(1)	Criminal Abuse of Vulnerable Adult (Death)	9
609.2325 subd. 3(a)(2)	Criminal Abuse of Vulnerable Adult (Great Bodily Harm)	8
609.2325 subd. 3(a)(3)	Criminal Abuse of Vulnerable Adult (Substantial Bodily Harm)	4
609.233, subd. 2a(1)	Deprivation of Vulnerable Adult (Great Bodily Harm)	8
609.233, subd. 2a(2)	Deprivation of Vulnerable Adult (Substantial Bodily Harm)	5
609.2335	Financial Exploitation of Vulnerable Adult (Over $35,000)	7
609.2335	Financial Exploitation of Vulnerable Adult (Over $5,000)	5
609.2335	Financial Exploitation of Vulnerable Adult ($5,000 or Less)	4
609.235	Use of Drugs to Injure or Facilitate Crime	4
609.24	Simple Robbery	5
609.245 subd. 1	Aggravated Robbery 1st Degree	8
609.245 subd. 2	Aggravated Robbery 2nd Degree	6
609.25 subd. 2(1)	Kidnapping (Safe Release/No Great Bodily Harm)	6
609.25 subd. 2(2)	Kidnapping (Great Bodily Harm)	9
609.25 subd. 2(2)	Kidnapping (Unsafe Release)	8
609.25 subd. 2(2)	Kidnapping (Victim Under 16)	8
609.255 subd. 2	False Imprisonment (Restraint)	3
609.255 subd. 3(b)	False Imprisonment (Demonstrable Bodily Harm)	3

Statute Number	Offense Title	Severity Level
609.255 subd. 3(c)	False Imprisonment (Substantial Bodily Harm)	4
609.26 subd. 6(a) (1)	Depriving Another of Cust. or Parental Rights	1
609.26 subd. 6(a) (2)	Depriving Another of Cust. or Parental Rights	3
609.2662(1)	Murder of an Unborn Child 2nd Degree	11
609.2662(2)	Murder of an Unborn Child 2nd Degree	10
609.2663	Murder of an Unborn Child 3rd Degree	10
609.2664(1) & (2)	Manslaughter of an Unborn Child 1st Degree	9
609.2664 (3)	Manslaughter of an Unborn Child 1st Degree	8
609.2665 (1)	Manslaughter of an Unborn Child 2nd Degree	8
609.2665 (2), (3), & (4)	Manslaughter of an Unborn Child 2nd Degree	5
609.267	Assault of an Unborn Child 1st Degree	9
609.2671	Assault of an Unborn Child 2nd Degree	4
609.268 subd. 1	Death of an Unborn Child in Comm. of Crime	9
609.268 subd. 2	Injury of an Unborn Child in Comm. of Crime	4
609.27 subd. 1 (1)	Coercion (Threat Bodily Harm)	3
609.27 subd. 1(2)(3)(4)(5)	Coercion (Prop. Value over $2,500)	3
609.27 subd. 1(2)(3)(4)(5)	Coercion (Prop. Value $301–$2,500)	2
609.282	Labor Trafficking	Unranked
609.283	Unlawful Conduct with Documents in Furtherance of Labor or Sex Trafficking	Unranked
609.31	Leaving State to Evade Paternity	1
609.322 subd. 1(a)	Solicits, Promotes, or Receives Profit Derived from Prostitution; Sex Trafficking 1st Degree	B
609.322 subd. 1(b)	Aggravating Factors for Solicitation or Promotion of Prostitution; Sex Trafficking	See Note [5]
609.322 subd. 1a	Solicits, Promotes, or Receives Profit Derived from Prostitution; Sex Trafficking 2nd Degree	C
609.324 subd. 1(a)	Engage or Hire a Minor to Engage in Prostitution	9
609.324 subd. 1(b)	Engage or Hire a Minor to Engage in Prostitution	5
609.324 subd. 1(c)	Engage or Hire a Minor to Engage in Prostitution	3
609.3242 subd. 2(2)	Prostitution Crimes (Gross Misd. Level) Committed in School or Park Zones	1
609.342	Criminal Sexual Conduct 1st Degree	A
609.343 subd.1(a)(b)(g)	Criminal Sexual Conduct 2nd Degree	D
609.343 subd.1(c)(d)(e)(f)(h)	Criminal Sexual Conduct 2nd Degree	B

Statute Number	Offense Title	Severity Level
609.344 subd. 1(a)	Criminal Sexual Conduct 3rd Degree (By Definition Perpetrator Must be a Juvenile)	D
609.344 subd. 1(b)(e)(f)	Criminal Sexual Conduct 3rd Degree	D
609.344 subd. 1(c)(d)(g)(h)(i)(j)(k)(*l*)(m)(n)(*o*)	Criminal Sexual Conduct 3rd Degree	C
609.345 subd. 1(a)	Criminal Sexual Conduct 4th Degree (By Definition Perpetrator Must be a Juvenile)	F
609.345 subd. 1(b)(e)(f)	Criminal Sexual Conduct 4th Degree	F
609.345 subd. 1(c)(d)(g)(h)(i)(j)(k)(*l*)(m)(n)(*o*)	Criminal Sexual Conduct 4th Degree	E
609.3451 subd. 3	Criminal Sexual Conduct 5th Degree	G
609.3453	Criminal Sexual Predatory Conduct	See Note [6]
609.352 subd. 2	Solicitation of Children to Engage in Sexual Conduct	G
609.352 subd. 2a	Solicitation of Children to Engage in Sexual Conduct (Electronic)	G
609.355	Bigamy	Unranked
609.365	Incest	Unranked
609.375 subd. 2a	Nonsupport of Spouse or Child	1
609.377 subd. 3	Malicious Punishment of Child (2nd or Subsequent Violation)	4
609.377 subd. 4	Malicious Punishment of Child (Bodily Harm)	4
609.377 subd. 5	Malicious Punishment of Child (Substantial Bodily Harm)	4
609.377 subd. 6	Malicious Punishment of Child (Great Bodily Harm)	8
609.378	Child Neglect/Endangerment	1
609.385	Treason	Unranked
609.39	Misprision of Treason	Unranked
609.395	Obstructing Military Forces	Unranked
609.396 subd. 2	Unauthorized Presence at Camp Ripley	3
609.42 subd.1 all sections	Bribery	4
609.425	Corrupting Legislator	Unranked
609.445	Failure to Pay Over State Funds (Over $5,000)	3
609.445	Failure to Pay Over State Funds ($5,000 or Less)	2
609.455	Permitting False Claims against Government (Over $5,000)	3
609.455	Permitting False Claims against Government ($5,000 or Less)	2
609.465	Presenting False Claims to Public Officer(Over $5,000)	3
609.465	Presenting False Claims to Public Officer($5,000 or Less)	2
609.466	Medical Assistance Fraud (Over $5,000)	3
609.466	Medical Assistance Fraud ($5,000 or Less)	2

Statute Number	Offense Title	Severity Level
609.48 subd. 4(1)	Perjury (Felony Trial)	5
609.48 subd. 4(2)	Perjury (Other Trial)	4
609.485 subd. 4(a)(1)	Escape from Felony Offense	3 [7]
609.485 subd. 4(a)(2)	Escape, Mental Illness	1
609.485 subd. 4(a)(3)	Escape with Violence from Gross Misdemeanor or Misdemeanor Offense	Unranked
609.485 subd. 4(a)(4)	Escape from Civil Commitment	1
609.485 subd. 4(a)(5)	Escape from Civil Commitment, Sexually Dangerous Persons	3
609.485 subd. 4(b)	Escape with Violence from Felony Offense	8
609.486	Bullet–Resistant Vest During Crime	1
609.487 subd. 3	Fleeing Peace Officer	1
609.487 subd. 4(a)	Fleeing Peace Officer (Death)	10
609.487 subd. 4(b)	Fleeing Peace Officer (Great Bodily Harm)	6
609.487 subd. 4(c)	Fleeing Peace Officer (Substantial Bodily Harm)	4
609.49	Failure to Appear in Court	1
609.493	Solicitation of Mentally Impaired Persons	See Note [8]
609.494 subd. 2(b)	Solicitation of Juveniles	See Note [9]
609.495 subd. 1	Aiding an Offender to Avoid Arrest	1
609.495 subd. 3	Accomplice After the Fact	Unranked
609.495 subd. 4	Taking Responsibility for Criminal Acts	See Note [10]
609.496; 609.497	Concealing Criminal Proceeds; Engaging in Business	Unranked
609.4971	Warning Subject of Investigation	Unranked
609.4975	Warning Subject of Surveillance or Search	Unranked
609.498 subd. 1a	Tampering with a Witness 1st Degree	5
609.498 subd. 1b	Tampering with a Witness Aggravated 1st Degree	9
609.50 subd. 2	Obstructing Legal Process, Arrest, Firefighting, or Ambulance Service Personnel Crew	3
609.504	Disarming a Peace Officer	3
609.52 all sections [11]	Theft of Public Funds (Over $5,000)	3
609.52 all sections[11]	Theft of Public Funds ($5,000 or Less)	2
609.52 all sections[11]	Theft from Person	4
609.52 all sections[11]	Theft of Public Records	3
609.52 all sections[11]	Theft (Looting)	2
609.52 subd. 2(a)(1)	Theft (Over $5,000)	3
609.52 subd. 2(a)(1)	Theft ($5,000 or Less)	2
609.52 subd. 2(a)(1)	Theft of a Motor Vehicle	4 [12]
609.52 subd. 2(a)(2)	Taking Pledged Property (Over $5,000)	3
609.52 subd. 2(a)(2)	Taking Pledged Property ($5,000 or Less)	2
609.52 subd. 2(a)(3) with subd. 3(1)	Theft by Check/False Representation (Over $35,000)	6
609.52 subd. 2(a)(3)(i)	Theft by Check ($5,001—$35,000)	3
609.52 subd. 2(a)(3)(i)	Theft by Check ($5,000 or Less)	2

Statute Number	Offense Title	Severity Level
609.52 subd. 2(a)(3)(ii–v)	Theft by False Representation ($5,001–$35,000)	3
609.52 subd. 2(a)(3)(ii–v)	Theft by False Representation ($5,000 or Less)	2
609.52 subd. 2(a)(4) with subd. 3(1)	Theft by Trick (Over $35,000)	6
609.52 subd. 2(a)(4)	Theft by Trick ($5,001–$35,000)	3
609.52 subd. 2(a)(4)	Theft by Trick ($5,000 or Less)	2
609.52 subd. 2(a)(5)	Temporary Theft (Over $5,000)	3
609.52 subd. 2(a)(5)	Temporary Theft ($5,000 or Less)	2
609.52 subd. 2(a)(6)	Refusing to Return Lost Property (Over $5,000)	3
609.52 subd. 2(a)(6)	Refusing to Return Lost Property ($5,000 or Less)	2
609.52 subd. 2(a)(7)	Theft from Coin Operated Machine (Over $5,000)	3
609.52 subd. 2(a)(7)	Theft from Coin Operated Machine ($5,000 or Less)	2
609.52 subd. 2(a)(8)	Theft of Trade Secret	3
609.52 subd. 2(a)(9)	Theft of Leased Property (Over $5,000)	3
609.52 subd. 2(a)(9)	Theft of Leased Property ($5,000 or Less)	2
609.52 subd. 2(a)(10)&(11)	Altering Serial Number (Over $5,000)	3
609.52 subd. 2(a)(10)&(11)	Altering Serial Number ($5,000 or Less)	2
609.52 subd. 2(a)(12)	Theft of Cable TV Services (Over $5,000)	3
609.52 subd. 2(a)(12)	Theft of Cable TV Services ($5,000 or Less)	2
609.52 subd. 2(a)(12)	Theft of Services (Over $5,000)	3
609.52 subd. 2(a)(13)	Theft of Services ($5,000 or Less)	2
609.52 subd. 2(a)(14)	Theft of Telecommunication Services (Over $5,000)	3
609.52 subd. 2(a)(14)	Theft of Telecommunication Services ($5,000 or Less)	2
609.52 subd. 2(a)(15)(16) with subd. 3(1)	Diversion of Corporate Property (Over $35,000)	6
609.52 subd. 2(a)(15)(16)	Diversion of Corporate Property ($5,001—$35,000)	3
609.52 subd. 2(a)(15)(16)	Diversion of Corporate Property ($5,000, or Less)	2
609.52 subd. 2(a)(17) [13]	Motor Vehicle Use Without Consent	3 [14]
609.52 subd. 2(a)(18)	Theft of Motor Fuel from Retailer (Over $5,000)	3
609.52 subd. 2(a)(18)	Theft of Motor Fuel from Retailer ($5,000 or Less)	2
609.52 subd. 3a(1)	Theft ($1,000, or Less; Risk of Bodily Harm)	2
609.52 subd. 3a(2)	Theft (Over $1,000; Risk of Bodily Harm)	See Note [15]
609.52 subd. 3a(2)	Theft ($501–$1,000, and Prior Conviction; Risk of Bodily Harm)	See Note [16]

Statute Number	Offense Title	Severity Level
609.52 subd. 3(1)	Theft of Firearm	4
609.52 subd. 3(2)	Theft of Incendiary Device	4
609.52 subd. 3(2)	Theft of Controlled Substances	4
609.52 subd. 3(3)(b)	Theft of Controlled Substances	3
609.52 subd. 3(3)(d)(iii)	Theft from an Abandoned or Vacant Building ($1,000 or Less)	1
609.521	Possession of Shoplifting Gear	3
609.525 all sections	Bringing Stolen Goods into State (Over $5,000)	3
609.525 all sections	Bringing Stolen Goods into State ($1,001–$5,000)	2
609.525 all sections	Bringing Stolen Goods into State ($501–$1,000, w/Previous Conviction)	2
609.526	Precious Metal and Scrap Metal Dealers, Receiving Stolen Goods (2nd or Subsequent Violations)	4
609.526, subd. 2(1)	Precious Metal and Scrap Metal Dealers, Receiving Stolen Goods ($1,000 or More)	3
609.526, subd. 2(2)	Precious Metal and Scrap Metal Dealers, Receiving Stolen Goods (Less than $1,000)	2
609.527 subd. 3(3)	Identity Theft	2
609.527 subd. 3(4)	Identity Theft	3
609.527 subd. 3(5)	Identity Theft	8
609.527 subd. 5a	Electronic Use of False Pretense to Obtain Identity	2
609.527 subd. 5b	Unlawful Possession or Use of Scanning Device or Reencoder	2
609.528 subd. 3(3)	Possession or Sale of Stolen or Counterfeit Check	2
609.528 subd. 3(4)	Possession or Sale of Stolen or Counterfeit Check	3
609.529	Mail Theft	2
609.53	Receiving Stolen Goods (Over $5,000)	3
609.53	Receiving Stolen Goods ($5,000 or Less)	2
609.53	Receiving Stolen Property (Firearm)	4
609.535 subd. 2a(a)(1)	Dishonored Check (Over $500)	2
609.54 all sections	Embezzlement of Public Funds (Over $2,500)	3
609.54 all sections	Embezzlement of Public Funds ($2,500 or Less)	2
609.551 all sections	Rustling of Livestock (Over $2,500)	3
609.551 all sections	Rustling of Livestock ($2,500 or Less)	2
609.561 all sections	Arson 1st Degree	8
609.562	Arson 2nd Degree	5
609.563 all sections	Arson 3rd Degree	3
609.5641 subd. 1a(a)	Wildfire Arson	2
609.5641 subd. 1a(b)	Wildfire Arson (Damage over Five Dwellings, Burns 500 Acres or More, or Crops in Excess of $100,000)	7

Statute Number	Offense Title	Severity Level
609.5641 subd. 1a(c)	Wildfire Arson (Damage over 100 Dwellings, Burns 1,500 Acres or More, or Crops in Excess of $250,000)	8
609.5641 subd. 1a(d)	Wildfire Arson (Demonstrable Bodily Harm)	5
609.576 subd. 1(1)	Negligent Fires (Great Bodily Harm)	4
609.576 subd. 1(3)(iii)	Negligent Fires (Damage $2,500 or More)	2
609.576 subd. 2	Dangerous Smoking	3
609.582 subd. 1(a)	Burglary 1st Degree (Occupied Dwelling)	6 [17]
609.582 subd. 1(b)(c)	Burglary 1st Degree (w/Weapon or Assault)	8
609.582 subd. 2(a)(1)(2)	Burglary 2nd Degree (Dwelling/Bank)	5
609.582 subd. 2(a)(3)(4)	Burglary 2nd Degree (Pharmacy/Tool)	4
609.582 subd. 2(b)	Burglary 2nd Degree (Government Building, Religious Est., Historic Property, or School Building)	5
609.582 subd. 3	Burglary 3rd Degree (Non Residential)	4
609.586 subd. 2	Possession of Code Grabbing Devices	3
609.59	Possession of Burglary Tools	3
609.591 subd. 3(1)	Hinder Logging (Great Bodily Harm)	3
609.593	Damage or Theft (Energy Transmission or Telecommunications)	3
609.594	Damage to Property (Critical Service Facilities Utilities, and Pipelines)	Unranked
609.595 subd.1(1)	Damage to Property (Risk Bodily Harm)	3
609.595 subd. 1(2)(3)(4)	Damage to Property (Over $500/Service to Public)	2
609.595 subd. 1a (a)	Damage to Property (Motivated by Bias)	1
609.596 subd. 1	Killing or Harming a Public Safety Dog	Unranked
609.597 subd. 3(3)	Assaulting or Harming a Police Horse	1
609.597 subd. 3(1) & (2)	Assaulting or Harming a Police Horse	Unranked
609.611 all sections	Defrauding Insurer (Over $5,000)	3
609.611 all sections	Defrauding Insurer ($5,000 or Less)	2
609.612	Insurance Fraud (Employment of Runners)	Unranked
609.615 all sections	Defeating Security on Realty (Over $5,000)	3
609.615 all sections	Defeating Security on Realty ($5,000 or Less)	2
609.62 all sections	Defeating Security on Personalty (Over $5,000)	3
609.62 all sections	Defeating Security on Personalty ($5,000 or Less)	2
609.625 all sections	Aggravated Forgery (Non–Check)	2
609.63 all sections	Forgery	1
609.631 subd. 4(1)	Check Forgery (Over $35,000)	5
609.631 subd. 4(2)	Check Forgery (Over $2,500)	3
609.631 subd. 4(3)(a)	Check Forgery ($251–$2,500)	2

Statute Number	Offense Title	Severity Level
609.631 subd. 4(3)(b)	Check Forgery ($250 or Less)	1
609.632	Counterfeiting Currency	Unranked
609.635	Obtaining Signature by False Pretense	2
609.64	Recording, Filing of Forged Instrument	2
609.645	Fraudulent Statements	1
609.65 (1)	False Certification by Notary Public	1
609.651 subd. 1 with 4(a)	State Lottery Fraud	1
609.651 subd. 1 with 4(b) and subd. 2 & 3	State Lottery Fraud	Unranked
609.652	Fraudulent Drivers' Licenses and Identification Cards	1
609.66 subd. 1a(a)(1)	Firearm Silencer	2
609.66 subd. 1a(a)(1)	Firearm Silencer(Public Housing, School or Park Zone)	3
609.66 subd. 1a(a)(2)&(3)	Discharge of Firearm (Public Housing, School or Park Zone)	2
609.66 subd. 1a(a)(2)	Discharge of Firearm (Intentional)	2
609.66 subd. 1a(a)(3)	Discharge of Firearm (Reckless)	1
609.66 subd. 1b	Furnishing Firearm to a Minor	2
609.66 subd. 1c	Furnishing a Dangerous Weapon	2
609.66 subd. 1d(a)	Dangerous Weapons on School Property	4
609.66 subd. 1e(a)	Drive–By Shooting (Unoccupied Motor Vehicle or Building)	3
609.66 subd. 1e(b)	Drive–By Shooting (Toward a Person or Occupied Motor Vehicle or Building)	8
609.66 subd. 1g	Weapon in Courthouse/Certain State Buildings	4
609.662 subd. 2(b)(1)	Duty to Render Aid (Death or Great Bodily Harm)	2
609.662 subd. 2(b)(2)	Duty to Render Aid (Substantial Bodily Harm)	1
609.667	Remove or Alter Serial Number on Firearm	1
609.668 subd. 6	Explosive Devices/Incendiary Devices	6
609.67 subd. 2	Possession/Ownership of Machine and Shortbarreled Shotguns	3
609.671	Hazardous Wastes	Unranked
609.686 subd. 2	Tampering w/ Fire Alarm System (Results in Bodily Harm)	3
609.686 subd. 2	Tampering w/ Fire Alarm System(Potential for Bodily Harm)	1
609.687 subd. 3(1)	Adulteration Resulting in Death	11
609.687 subd. 3(2)	Adulteration Resulting in Bodily Harm	4
609.687 subd. 3(3)	Adulteration	Unranked
609.71 subd. 1	Riot 1st Degree	8
609.71 subd. 2	Riot 2nd Degree	2
609.712	Real/Simulated Weapons of Mass Destruction	Unranked
609.713 subd. 1	Terroristic Threats–Violence Threat/Evacuation	4
609.713 subd. 2	Terroristic Threats–Bomb Threat	2
609.713 subd. 3(a)	Terroristic Threats–Replica Firearm	1

Statute Number	Offense Title	Severity Level
609.714	Offense in Furtherance of Terrorism	See Note [18]
609.746 subd. 1(e)	Interference with Privacy (Subsequent Violations or Minor Victim)	1
609.7475	Fraudulent or Improper Financing Statements	Unranked
609.748 subd. 6(d)	Violation of Harassment Restraining Order	4
609.749 subd. 3(a)(b)	Stalking (Aggravated Violations)	4
609.749 subd. 4(a)	Stalking (2nd or Subsequent Violations)	4
609.749 subd. 4(b)	Stalking (3rd or Subsequent Violations)	5
609.749 subd. 5	Stalking (Pattern of Conduct)	5
609.76 subd. 2	Sports Bookmaking	4
609.76 subd. 3, 4, 5, 6 &7	Gambling Acts (Cheating, Certain Devices Prohibited; Counterfeit Chips; Manufacture, Sale, Modification of Devices; Instruction)	Unranked
609.763	Lawful Gambling Fraud	Unranked
609.776	Interference with Emergency Communications	5
609.78, subd. 2a	Emergency Telephone Calls and Communications (Reporting Fictitious Emergency Resulting in Serious Injury or Death)	8
609.78, subd. 2b(1)	Emergency Telephone Calls and Communications (3rd or Subsequent, Making Calls When No Emergency Exists)	4
609.78, subd. 2b(2)	Emergency Telephone Calls and Communications (Blocks, Interferes, Prevents Using Multiple Communication Devices or Electronic Means)	5
609.80 subd. 2	Cable Communication Systems Interference	1
609.82 all sections	Fraud in Obtaining Credit (Over $5,000)	3
609.82 all sections	Fraud in Obtaining Credit ($5,000 or Less)	2
609.821 subd. 2(1)(2)(5)(6)(7)(8)	Financial Transaction Card Fraud (Over $2,500)	3
609.821 subd. 2(1)(2)(5)(6)(7)(8)	Financial Transaction Card Fraud ($2,500 or Less)	2
609.821 subd. 2(3)(4)	Financial Transaction Card Fraud	1
609.821 subd. 3(1)(i)	Financial Transaction Card Fraud (Over $35,000)	5
609.822	Residential Mortgage Fraud	2
609.825 subd. 2	Bribery of Participant or Official in Contest	2
609.83	Falsely Impersonating Another	Unranked
609.85 (1)	Dangerous Trespass, Railroad Tracks	3
609.851 subd. 2	False Traffic Signal	3
609.855 subd. 2(c)(1)	Interference with Transit Operator	1
609.855 subd. 5	Discharge Firearm at Occupied Transit Vehicle/Facility	6
609.855 subd. 5	Discharge Firearm at Unoccupied Transit Vehicle/Facility	1

Statute Number	Offense Title	Severity Level
609.856	Police Radios During Commission of Crime	Unranked
609.86	Commercial Bribery	4
609.88	Computer Damage (Over $2,500)	3
609.88	Computer Damage ($2,500 or Less)	2
609.89	Computer Theft (Over $2,500)	3
609.89	Computer Theft ($2,500 or Less)	2
609.891	Unauthorized Computer Access	Unranked
609.8912	Computer Encryption	Unranked
609.893 subd. 1	Telecommunications and Information Services; Obtaining Services by Fraud (Over $2,500)	3
609.893 subd. 1	Telecommunications and Information Services; Obtaining Services by Fraud ($2,500 or Less)	2
609.893 subd. 2	Telecommunications and Information Services; Facilitation of Telecommunications Fraud	2
609.894 subd. 3	Cellular Counterfeiting 2nd Degree	1
609.894 subd. 4	Cellular Counterfeiting 1st Degree	2
609.895 subd. 3(a)	Counterfeited Intellectual Property	2
609.895 subd. 3(b)	Counterfeited Intellectual Property	1
609.896	Criminal Use of Real Property (Movie Pirating)	1
609.904	Racketeering (RICO)	Unranked
617.20	Abortion	Unranked
617.22	Abortion	Unranked
617.23 subd. 3	Indecent Exposure	G
617.241 subd. 4	Obscene Materials–Distribution	Unranked
617.246	Use of Minors in Sexual Performance Prohibited	E
617.247 subd.3	Dissemination of Pictorial Representation of Minors(Subsequent or by Predatory Offenders)	D
617.247 subd.3	Dissemination of Pictorial Representation of Minors	E
617.247 subd.4	Possession of Pictorial Representation of Minors(Subsequent or by Predatory Offenders)	F
617.247 subd.4	Possession of Pictorial Representation of Minors	G
624.713 subd. 2(a)	Certain Persons Not to Have Firearms	3
624.713 subd. 2(b)	Certain Persons Not to Have Firearms	6
624.7132 subd. 15(b)	Transfer Pistol to Minor	2
624.714 subd. 1a	Pistol Without Permit (Subsequent Violations)	1
624.7141 subd. 2	Transfer Pistol to Ineligible Person	2
624.7181 subd. 2	Assault Weapon in Public (Under 21)	1
624.731 subd. 8(a)	Tear Gas and Tear Gas Compounds; Electronic incapacitation devices	3
624.732 subd. 2	Intentional Release of Harmful Substance	3

Statute Number	Offense Title	Severity Level
624.7191	Metal Penetrating Bullets	Unranked
626A.02 subd. 4; 626A.03 subd.1(b)(ii); 626A.26 subd. 2(1)(ii)	Wire Communications Violations	Unranked
626.556 subd. 6	Failure to Report	Unranked
629.75 subd. 2(d)	Violation of a Domestic Abuse No Contact Order	4
641.165 subd. 2(b)	Bring Dangerous Weapon into County Jail	4

[1] See section 2.C and Appendix 1 to determine the presumptive disposition.

[1] See section 2.C and Appendix 1 to determine the presumptive disposition.

[2] See section 2.C and Appendix 1 to determine the presumptive disposition for a felony assault committed by an inmate serving an executed term of imprisonment or for assault on secure treatment facility personnel.

[2] See section 2.C and Appendix 1 to determine the presumptive disposition for a felony assault committed by an inmate serving an executed term of imprisonment or for assault on secure treatment facility personnel.

[2] See section 2.C and Appendix 1 to determine the presumptive disposition for a felony assault committed by an inmate serving an executed term of imprisonment or for assault on secure treatment facility personnel.

[3] See section 2.A.5 to determine the presumptive sentence.

[4] See section 2.G.10 to determine the presumptive sentence.

[5] See Guidelines section 2.G to determine the presumptive sentence.

[6] See section 2.G.8 to determine the presumptive sentence.

[7] See section 2.C and Appendix 1 to determine the presumptive disposition for an escape from an executed sentence.

[8] See section 2.G.3 to determine the presumptive sentence.

[9] See section 2.G.3 to determine the presumptive sentence.

[10] See section 2.G.6 to determine the presumptive sentence.

[11] Includes offenses sentenced according to Minn. Stat. § 609.52, subd. 3(3)(d).

[11] Includes offenses sentenced according to Minn. Stat. § 609.52, subd. 3(3)(d).

[11] Includes offenses sentenced according to Minn. Stat. § 609.52, subd. 3(3)(d).

[11] Includes offenses sentenced according to Minn. Stat. § 609.52, subd. 3(3)(d).

[11] Includes offenses sentenced according to Minn. Stat. § 609.52, subd. 3(3)(d).

[12] *See Comment 2.A.05* for commentary on motor vehicle offense severity levels.

[13] Includes offenses sentenced according to Minn. Stat. § 609.52, subd. 3(3)(d).

[14] *See Comment 2.A.05* for commentary on motor vehicle offense severity levels.

[15] See Guidelines section 2.A.2.a–b to determine the severity level.

[16] See Guidelines section 2.A.2.a–b to determine the severity level.

[17] See section 2.C.3.b and Appendix 1 to determine the presumptive disposition.

[18] See section 2.G.7 to determine the presumptive sentence.

6. Offenses Eligible for Permissive Consecutive Sentences

A. Convictions for attempted offenses or conspiracies to commit offenses listed below are eligible for permissive consecutive sentences as well as convictions for completed offenses.

B. Under section 2.F.2(a)(1)(i), it is permissive for a current felony conviction to run consecutively to a prior felony sentence from a jurisdiction other than Minnesota if the non-Minnesota conviction is for a crime that is equivalent to a crime listed below.

Statute Number	Offense Title
152.021, subd. 2a(a)	Manufacture any Amount of Methamphetamine
152.022, subd. 1(5)	Sells Cocaine/Narcotic to Minor/Employs Minor
152.023, subd. 1(3)	Sells Sch. I,II,III to Minor (not Narcotic)
152.023, subd. 1(4)	Sells Sch. I,II,III Employs Minor (not Narcotic)
152.024, subd. 1(2)	Schedule IV or V to Minor
152.024, subd. 1(3)	Employs Minor to Sell Schedule IV or V
152.0261, subd. 1a	Employing a Minor to Import Controlled Substances
152.137	Methamphetamine Crimes Involving Children or Vulnerable Adults
169.09, subd. 14(a)(1)	Accidents (Death)
169.09, subd. 14(a)(2)	Accidents (Great Bodily Harm)
169A.24	DWI 1st Degree
243.166, subd. 5(b)	Registration of Predatory Offenders
243.166, subd. 5(c)	Registration of Predatory Offenders (2nd or subsequent)
518B.01, subd. 14(d)	Violation of an Order for Protection
609.185	Murder 1st Degree
609.19	Murder 2nd Degree
609.195	Murder 3rd Degree
609.20	Manslaughter 1st Degree
609.205	Manslaughter 2nd Degree
609.21, subd. 1a(a)	Criminal Vehicular Homicide (Death)
609.21, subd. 1a(b)	Criminal Vehicular Operation (Great Bodily Harm)
609.21, subd. 1a(c)	Criminal Vehicular Operation (Substantial Bodily Harm)
609.215	Aiding Suicide
609.221	Assault 1st Degree
609.222	Assault 2nd Degree—Dangerous Weapon
609.223	Assault 3rd Degree
609.2231	Assault 4th Degree
609.224, subd. 4	Assault 5th Degree (3rd or Subsequent Violation)
609.2241	Knowing Transfer of Communicable Disease
609.2242, subd. 4	Domestic Assault
609.2245	Female Genital Mutilation
609.2247	Domestic Assault by Strangulation
609.228	Great Bodily Harm Caused by Distribution of Drugs
609.229, subd. 3	Crime Committed for Benefit of Gang
609.2325, subd. 3(1)	Criminal Abuse of Vulnerable Adult (Death)
609.2325, subd. 3(2)	Criminal Abuse of Vulnerable Adult (Great Bodily Harm)

Statute Number	Offense Title
609.2325, subd. 3(3)	Criminal Abuse of Vulnerable Adult (Substantial Bodily Harm)
609.233, subd. 2a	Deprivation of Vulnerable Adult
609.235	Use of Drugs to Injure or Facilitate Crime
609.24	Simple Robbery
609.245, subd. 1	Aggravated Robbery 1st Degree
609.245, subd. 2	Aggravated Robbery 2nd Degree
609.25	Kidnapping
609.255	False Imprisonment
609.2661	Consp./At. Murder of Unborn Child 1st Degree
609.2662	Murder of an Unborn Child 2nd Degree
609.2663	Murder of an Unborn Child 3rd Degree
609.2664	Manslaughter of an Unborn Child 1st Degree
609.2665	Manslaughter of an Unborn Child 2nd Degree
609.267	Assault of an Unborn Child 1st Degree
609.2671	Assault of an Unborn Child 2nd Degree
609.268	Death or Injury of an Unborn Child in Comm. of Crime
609.282	Labor Trafficking
609.322, subd. 1(a)	Solicit, Promote, or Profit from Prostitution; Sex Trafficking in the 1st Degree
609.322, subd. 1a	Solicit, Promote, or Profit from Prostitution; Sex Trafficking in the 2nd Degree
609.324, subd. 1(a)	Engage or Hire a Minor to Engage in Prostitution
609.324, subd. 1(b)	Engage or Hire a Minor to Engage in Prostitution
609.324, subd. 1(c)	Engage or Hire a Minor to Engage in Prostitution
609.342, subd. 1	Criminal Sexual Conduct 1st Degree
609.343, subd. 1	Criminal Sexual Conduct 2nd Degree
609.344, subd. 1	Criminal Sexual Conduct 3rd Degree
609.345, subd. 1	Criminal Sexual Conduct 4th Degree
609.3451, subd. 3	Criminal Sexual Conduct 5th Degree
609.3453	Criminal Sexual Predatory Conduct
609.352, subd. 2	Solicitation of Children to Engage in Sexual Conduct
609.352, subd. 2a	Solicitation of Children to Engage in Sexual Conduct (Internet or Computer)
609.365	Incest
609.377	Malicious Punishment of Child
609.378	Child Neglect/Endangerment
609.485, subd. 4(a)(3)	Escape with Violence from GM or Misd. Offense
609.485, subd. 4(b)	Escape with Violence from Felony Offense
609.487, subd. 3	Fleeing Peace Officer
609.487, subd. 4(a)	Fleeing Peace Officer (Resulting in Death)
609.487, subd. 4(b)	Fleeing Peace Officer (Great Bodily Harm)
609.487, subd. 4(c)	Fleeing Peace Officer (Substantial Bodily Harm)
609.498, subd. 1a	Tampering with a Witness in the 1st Degree
609.498, subd. 1b	Tampering with a Witness, Aggravated 1st Degree
609.527	Identity Theft
609.561	Arson in the 1st Degree
609.5641, subd. 1a(b)	Wildfire Arson (Damage over Five Dwellings, Burns 500 Acres or More, or Crops in Excess of $100,000)

Statute Number	Offense Title
609.5641, subd. 1a(c)	Wildfire Arson (Damage over 100 Dwellings, Burns 1,500 Acres or More, or Crops in Excess of $250,000)
609.5641, subd. 1a(d)	Wildfire Arson (Demonstrable Bodily Harm)
609.582, subd. 1(a)	Burglary 1st Degree—of Occupied Dwelling
609.582, subd. 1(b)	Burglary 1st Degree with Dangerous Weapon
609.582, subd. 1(c)	Burglary 1st Degree with Assault
609.582, subd. 2(a)(1)	Burglary 2nd Degree—Dwelling
609.582, subd. 2(a)(2)	Burglary 2nd Degree—Bank
609.591, subd. 3(1)	Hinder Logging (Great Bodily Harm)
609.594, subd.2	Damage to Property—Critical Public Service Facilities
609.66, subd. 1e	Drive–By Shooting
609.662, subd. 2(b)(1)	Duty to Render Aid (Death or Great Bodily Harm)
609.662, subd. 2(b)(2)	Duty to Render Aid (Substantial Bodily Harm)
609.671	Hazardous Wastes
609.687, subd. 3(1)	Adulteration Resulting in Death
609.687, subd. 3(2)	Adulteration Resulting in Bodily Harm
609.71, subd. 1	Riot 1st Degree
609.712	Real/Simulated Weapons of Mass Destruction
609.713, subd. 1	Terroristic Threats—Violence Threat/Evacuation
609.713, subd. 2	Terroristic Threats—Bomb Threat
609.713, subd. 3(a)	Terroristic Threats—Replica Firearm
609.714, subd. 2	Crimes Committed in Furtherance of Terrorism
609.748, subd. 6(d)	Violation of Harassment Restraining Order
609.749, subd. 3	Stalking (Aggravated Violations)
609.749, subd. 4	Stalking (Subsequent Violations)
609.749, subd. 5	Stalking (Pattern of Conduct)
609.78, subd. 2a	Emergency Telephone Calls and Communications (Reporting Fictitious Emergency Resulting in Serious Injury or Death)
609.78, subd. 2b(2)	Emergency Telephone Calls and Communications (Blocks, Interferes, Prevents Using Multiple Communication Devices or Electronic Means)
609.855, subd. 2(c)(1)	Interference with Transit Operator
609.855, subd. 5	Discharge Firearm at Occupied Transit Vehicle/Facility
617.23, subd. 3	Indecent Exposure
617.246, subd. 2	Use of Minors in Sexual Performance Prohibited
617.246, subd. 3	Operation/Owner–Use of Minors in Sexual Performance
617.246, subd. 4	Dissemination–Use of Minors in Sexual Performance
617.247, subd. 3(a)	Dissemination of Pictorial Representations of Minors
617.247, subd. 3(b)	Dissemination by Predatory Offender
617.247, subd. 4(a)	Possession of Pictorial Representations of Minors
617.247, subd. 4(b)	Possession by Predatory Offender
624.732, subd. 2	Intentional Release of Harmful Substance
624.7191	Metal Penetrating Bullets
629.75, subd. 2(d)	Violation of a Domestic Abuse No Contact Order

7. Theft Offense List

It is recommended that the following property crimes be treated similarly. Below is the Theft Offense List cited for the Theft Crimes ($5,000 or less and over $5,000) in section 5.A Offense Severity Reference Table. The severity level for these offenses is based on the monetary amount of the conviction offense. The monetary amount is contained in the penalty statute as cited below:

- Severity Level 2. When the monetary value of the Theft Crime is $5,000 or less, the penalty statute is Minn. Stat. § 609.52, subdivision 3(3)(a).
- Severity Level 3. When the monetary value of the Theft Crime is over $5,000, the penalty statute is Minn. Stat. § 609.52, subdivision 3(2).

Statute Number	Offense Title
176.178	Workers Compensation Fraud
256.98	Wrongfully Obtaining Assistance
268.182	False Representations
393.07 subd. 10	Federal Food Stamp Program
471.392	False Declaration of Claim
514.02 subd. 1(b)	Non-payment for Improvement (Proceeds of Payments; Acts Constituting Theft)
609.445	Failure to Pay Over State Funds
609.455	Permitting False Claims Against Government
609.465	Presenting False Claims to Public Officer or Body
609.466	Medical Assistance Fraud
609.52	Theft of Public Funds
609.52 subd. 2(a)(1)	Theft
609.52 subd. 2(a)(2)	Taking Pledged Property
609.52 subd. 2(a)(3)(i)	Theft By Check
609.52 subd. 2(a)(3) (ii), (iii), (iv), & (v)	Theft By False Representation
609.52 subd. 2(a)(4)	Theft by Trick
609.52 subd. 2(a)(5)	Temporary Theft
609.52 subd. 2(a)(6)	Refusing to Return Lost Property
609.52 subd. 2(a)(7)	Theft from Coin Operated Machines
609.52 subd. 2(a)(9)	Theft of Leased Property
609.52 subd. 2(a)(10) & (11)	Altering Serial Number
609.52 subd. 2(a)(12)	Theft of Cable TV Services
609.52 subd. 2(a)(13)	Theft of Services
609.52 subd. 2(a)(14)	Theft of Telecommunications Services
609.52 subd. 2(a)(15) & (16)	Diversion of Corporate Property
609.53	Receiving Stolen Property
609.611	Defrauding Insurer
609.615	Defeating Security on Realty
609.62	Defeating Security on Personalty
609.82	Fraud in Obtaining Credit

8. Targeted Misdemeanor List

(As provided for in Minn. Stat. § 299C.10, subd. 1(e))

Under Minn. Stat. § 299C.10, subd. 1(e), a targeted misdemeanor is a misdemeanor violation of:

Statute Number	Offense Title
169A.20	Driving While Impaired
518B.01; 629.75	Order for Protection Violation
609.224	Assault 5th Degree
609.2242	Domestic Assault
609.746	Interference with Privacy
609.748	Harassment or Restraining Order Violation
617.23	Indecent Exposure

Appendix 1. Mandatory and Presumptive Sentences Reference Table

This table is for convenience when applying mandatory sentences (section 2.E) and presumptive sentences (section 2.C). It is not exhaustive.

- Presumptive disposition. Commitment.
- Presumptive duration. Mandatory minimum or the duration in the appropriate cell on the applicable Grid, whichever is longer.
- Attempts and Conspiracies. Mandatory sentences generally apply to attempted offenses under Minn. Stat. § 609.17 and conspiracies under Minn. Stat. § 609.175. Mandatory minimums are not divided in half. The presumptive duration is the mandatory minimum duration found in statute or one-half of the duration in the appropriate cell on the applicable Grid, whichever is longer. (See section 2.G for more information on convictions for attempts, conspiracies and offenses with other sentence modifiers.)

Statute	Offense	Prerequisite or Conditions	Minimum Duration
169A.24, subd. 1(2)	Driving while Intoxicated	Prior Felony DWI	Grid Time
169A.24, subd. 1(3)	Driving while Intoxicated	Prior Criminal Vehicular Operation Minn. Stat. § 609.21.1(2) thru (6)	Grid Time
152.021	Controlled Substance Crime 1st Degree	Prior felony conviction per chapter Minn. Stat. § 152 or finding under Minn. Stat. § 152.18	48 Months
152.022	Controlled Substance Crime 2nd Degree	Prior felony conviction per chapter Minn. Stat. § 152 or finding under Minn. Stat. § 152.18	36 Months
152.023, subd. 3(a)	Controlled Substance Crime 3rd Degree	Prior felony conviction under Minn. Stat. § 152 or finding under Minn. Stat. § 152.18	Grid Time [1]
152.023, subd. 3(b)	Controlled Substance Crime 3rd Degree	Prior felony conviction under Minn. Stat. § 152 or finding under Minn. Stat. § 152.18	24 months
243.166, subd. 5(b)	Violation of Predatory Offender Registration		Grid Time
243.166, subd. 5(c)	Violation of Predatory Offender Registration—Subsequent offense	Prior felony Violation of Predatory Offender Registration	24 Months
609.1095, subd. 3	Dangerous Offender—3rd Violent Felony	Statute Cited	Grid Time
609.221, subd. 2(b)	Assault 1st Degree, Deadly Force—Peace Officer or Correctional Employee		120 Months
609.221—609.2231	Assault	Must commit during "Term of Imprisonment" portion of executed sentence	Grid Time
609.3455, subd. 3a	Dangerous (Engrained) Sex Offender	Statute Cited	At least double the Grid Time

Statute	Offense	Prerequisite or Conditions	Minimum Duration
609.485	Escape	Offense committed during "Term of Imprisonment" portion of executed sentence	Grid Time
609.582, subd. 1(a)	Burglary 1st Degree	Prior felony burglary	Grid Time [1]

[1] Presumptive commitment per Guidelines section 2.C.

Appendix 2. Dangerous Weapons Offense Reference Table

This table is for convenience when applying mandatory sentences (section 2.E) and presumptive sentences (section 2.C). It is not exhaustive.

- Presumptive disposition. Commitment.
- Presumptive duration. Mandatory minimum or the duration in the appropriate cell on the applicable Grid, whichever is longer.
- Attempts and Conspiracies. Mandatory sentences generally apply to attempted offenses under Minn. Stat. § 609.17 and conspiracies under Minn. Stat. § 609.175. Mandatory minimums are not divided in half. The presumptive duration is the mandatory minimum duration found in statute or one-half of the duration in the appropriate cell of the applicable Grid, whichever is longer. (See section 2.G for more information on convictions for attempts, conspiracies and offenses with other sentence modifiers.)

Dangerous Weapons—Minn. Stat. § 609.11

Statute	**Offense**	**Prerequisite or Conditions**	**Minimum Duration**
609.11, subd. 4	Dangerous Weapon (Other than Firearm)	Weapon is an element of crime	1 Year and 1 Day
609.11, subd. 4	Dangerous Weapon (Other than Firearm)—Subsequent offense	Current dangerous weapon offense (other than firearm) with prior dangerous weapon offense Weapon is an element of crime	36 Months
609.11, subd. 5(a)	Firearm	Weapon is an element of crime	36 Months
609.11, subd. 5(a)	Firearm—Subsequent Offense	Current firearm offense with prior firearm or dangerous weapon offense Weapon is an element of crime	60 Months
609.11, subd. 5(b)	Certain Persons not to have Firearms	Current conviction under Minn. Stat. § 609.165 or Minn. Stat. § 624.713 subd. 1(2)	60 Months

2012 Legislation

Laws 2012, c. 229, § 1, provided:

"Section 1. MODIFICATION TO SEX OFFENDER SENTENCING GRID.

"Notwithstanding the modification procedures described in Minnesota Statutes, section 244.09, subdivision 11, and Minnesota Rules, chapter 3000, the Sentencing Guidelines Commission, acting without a public hearing, shall modify the sex offender sentencing grid to ensure that it provides for an increase of not greater than 20 percent and a decrease of not greater than 15 percent in the presumptive fixed sentence. The modified grid shall be effective immediately upon issuance by the commission."

RULES OF EVIDENCE

Effective July 1, 1977

Including Amendments Received Through January 1, 2014

Research Note

See Minnesota Statutes Annotated, *Volume 50, for case annotations, historical notes, and library references. The Minnesota Rules of Evidence are discussed in Thompson, 11* Minnesota Practice–Evidence (3d Edition), *and Thompson and Herr, 11A Minnesota Practice–Courtroom Handbook of Minnesota Evidence* (2010 Ed.).

ARTICLE 1. GENERAL PROVISIONS

RULE 101. SCOPE

These rules govern proceedings in the courts of this state, to the extent and with the exceptions stated in Rule 1101.

Adopted April 1, 1977, eff. July 1, 1977.

Superseded Statutes:

To the extent that the rules conflict with existing statutes, the enabling legislation provides that the statutes will be superseded by the rules. There was an effort made in the comments to indicate when the rule of evidence directly contradicts a statute or an existing Minnesota precedent. Although the committee attempted to avoid a direct conflict with the federal and state constitutions, there was no effort made to codify constitutional provisions in these rules of evidence. If the facts in any given case give rise to a conflict between the constitution and the rule of evidence, obviously the rule of evidence will not be enforced.

Federal Rules of Evidence:

The committee reviewed each of the Federal Rules of Evidence and compared it to existing state practice. Unless there was a substantial state policy which required deviation from the federal rule, the committee recommended the federal rule of evidence exactly as enacted.

Obviously and difference in language could result in a change in the substance of the rule. However, in recommending rules of evidence certain deviations from the federal rules were required to make the rules suitable for use in the state system without intending any substantive change. These rules include: 301, 402, 802, 803(22), 901(b)(10), 902(4), 902(10), and 1002.

The following rules represent a change in language that could involve a substantive difference from the corresponding federal rule: 103(d), 410, 501, 601, 609(a)(1), 609(c), 609(d), 611(b), 612, 613(b), 615, 801(d)(1)(C), 803(6), 803(8)(B), 803(8)(C), 803(17), 803(24), 804(b)(1), 804(b)(5), and 1101.

The following recommended rules have no counterpart in the Federal Rules of Evidence: 404(c), 616, and 801(d)(1)(D).

The committee did not recommend rules 302 and 803(1) of the Federal Rules of Evidence.

RULE 102. PURPOSE AND CONSTRUCTION

These rules shall be construed to secure fairness in administration, elimination of unjustifiable expense and delay, and promotion of growth and development of the law of evidence to the end that the truth may be ascertained and proceedings justly determined.

Adopted April 1, 1977, eff. July 1, 1977.

Committee Comment—1977

Rule 102 sets the stage for the application of the evidentiary rules. In the interpretation of the rules, principles of fairness and convenience should be paramount. The rules should not be read narrowly but with a view for accomplishing essential fairness, with a minimum of formality and procedural obstacles in the search for the truth. The rules provide for a great deal of flexibility and discretion. This rule urges that such discretion and flexibility be exercised to accomplish the stated purpose.

RULE 103. RULINGS ON EVIDENCE

(a) Effect of erroneous ruling. Error may not be predicated upon a ruling which admits or excludes evidence unless a substantial right of the party is affected, and

(1) *Objection.* In case the ruling is one admitting evidence a timely objection or motion to strike appears of record, stating the specific ground of objection, if the specific ground was not apparent from the context; or

(2) *Offer of proof.* In case the ruling is one excluding evidence, the substance of the evidence was made known to the court by offer or was apparent from the context within which questions were asked.

Once the court makes a definitive ruling on the record admitting or excluding evidence, either at or before trial, a party need not renew an objection or offer of proof to preserve a claim of error.

(b) Record of offer and ruling. The court may add any other or further statement which shows the character of the evidence, the form in which it was offered, the objection made, and the ruling thereon. Upon request of any party, the court shall place its ruling on the record. The court may direct the making of an offer in question and answer form

(c) Hearing of jury. In jury cases, proceedings shall be conducted, to the extent practicable, so as to prevent inadmissible evidence from being suggested to the jury by any means, such as making statements or offers of proof or asking questions in the hearing of the jury.

(d) Error. Nothing in this rule precludes taking notice of errors in fundamental law or of plain errors affecting substantial rights although they were not brought to the attention of the court.

Adopted April 1, 1977, eff. July 1, 1977. Amended Dec. 28, 1989, eff. Jan. 1, 1990; July 18, 2006, eff. Sept. 1, 2006.

Committee Comment—1989

Rule 103(a)

Rule 103(a) codifies the existing practice in Minnesota. Only error affecting substantial rights is actionable. Minn.R.Civ.P. 61 and Minn.R.Crim.P. 31.01. The rule does not define what is meant by substantial rights but leaves this for case by case decision. Although there are many cases applying this standard no clear cut definition of substantial rights has emerged. The normal procedure in these cases appears to be an examination of the effect of the alleged error upon the trial as a whole for determination as to whether or not the error was prejudicial. See J. Hetland and O. Adamson, Minnesota Practice Rule 61 (1970) and cases cited therein. In criminal cases, certain constitutional errors require automatic reversal, see State v. Schmit, 273 Minn. 78, 88, 139 N.W.2d 800, 807 (1966), whereas others must be harmless beyond a reasonable doubt, Chapman v. California, 87 S.Ct. 824, 828, 386 U.S. 18, 24, 17 L.Ed.2d 705, 710, 711 (1967), and see State ex rel. Kopetka v. Tahash, 281 Minn. 52, 56, 160 N.W.2d 399, 402 (1968). See also C. Wright, Federal Practice and Procedure § 856, rule 52 (1969), and cases cited therein. In cases involving nonconstitutional errors, where the error has the effect of depriving the defendant of a fair trial, the court has applied the reasonable doubt standard, State v. White, 295 Minn. 217, 226, 203 N.W.2d 852, 859 (1973); and something akin to the automatic reversal standard, see, *e.g.*, State v. Flowers, 262 Minn. 164, 169, 114 N.W.2d 78, 81 (1962); State v. Reardon, 245 Minn. 509, 513, 514, 73 N.W.2d 192, 195 (1955). However, in cases involving error of a less grievous type, presumably error not affecting the fairness of the trial process, the Court has inquired into whether it is likely that the error played a substantial part in influencing the jury to convict. State v. Caron, 300 Minn. 123, 127, 128, 218 N.W.2d 197, 200 (1974). See State v. Van Alstine, Minn., 232 N.W.2d 899, 905 (1975); State v. Fields, Minn., 237 N.W.2d 634, 635 (1976); State v. Wilebski, Minn., 238 N.W.2d 213, 215 (1976).

The rule continues the existing practice of requiring not only a timely objection, but a specific objection unless the context of the question makes the grounds for objection obvious. See Kenney v. Chicago Great Western Ry., 245 Minn. 284, 289, 71 N.W.2d 669, 672, 673, certiorari denied 350 U.S. 903, 76 S.Ct. 182, 100 L.Ed. 793 (1955); Adelmann v. Elk River Lumber Co., 242 Minn. 388, 393, 394, 65 N.W.2d 661, 666 (1954). Under current practice, a motion in limine to strike or prohibit the introduction of evidence operates as a timely objection and obviates the requirement of any further objection with respect to such evidence. If the Court excludes evidence, an offer of proof must be made to preserve the issue for review unless the substance of the evidence is apparent from its context. See Auger v. Rofshus, 267 Minn. 87, 91, 125 N.W.2d 159, 162 (1963); Wozniak v. Luta, 258 Minn. 234, 241, 103 N.W.2d 870, 875 (1960); Minn.R.Civ.P. 43.03, see also Minn.R.Civ.P. 46, 59.01(6), and Minn. R.Crim.P. 26.03 subd. 14(1).

Rule 103(b)

This rule is adapted from Minn.R.Civ.P. 43.03. In order to determine on review whether or not a substantial right of a party was affected by the exclusion of evidence the reviewing court must have some information as to the nature of the excluded testimony. Parties are entitled to have the rulings of the court placed on the record if they so request. The rule gives the court authority to require that the offer of proof be in question and answer form to provide an accurate record for review. It would also be permissible to allow cross-examination of the witness making the offer of proof.

Rule 103(c)

The rule gives the court the discretion in the conduct of the trial to employ procedures that would minimize the possibility of inadmissible evidence being suggested to the jury. It puts to rest the issue that was unresolved in In re McConnell, 82 S.Ct. 1288, 370 U.S. 230, 8 L.Ed.2d 434 (1962) as to whether or not questions on which an offer of proof is based must be asked to a witness in the presence of the jury.

Rule 103(d)

This subdivision [(d)] makes it clear that the rule is not meant to affect the application of the "plain error" rule or the application of Minn.R.Civ.P. 51 with respect to error in fundamental law contained in instructions to the jury. Plain error is a federal term which has recently been adopted in Minn. R.Crim.P. 31.02. See State ex rel. Rasmussen v. Tahash, 272 Minn. 539, 550, 551, 141 N.W.2d 3, 11 (1965). The Minnesota Supreme Court has not formally recognized the plain error rule in civil cases although in several cases they have addressed issues on appeal that were not properly preserved by a timely specific objection. E.g., Rosenfeld v. Rosenfeld, Minn., 249 N.W.2d 168 (1976); Jones v. Peterson, 279 Minn. 241, 156 N.W.2d 733 (1968); Magistad v. Potter, 227 Minn. 570, 36 N.W.2d 400 (1949).

Advisory Committee Comment—2006 Amendments

Rule 103(a).

This amendment in rule 103(a) is taken from the corresponding Fed. R. Evid. 103 and would codify existing practice in Minnesota. *See* Minn. R. Evid. 103(a) comm. cmt.—1989 ("Under current practice, a motion in limine to strike or prohibit the introduction of evidence operates as a timely objection and obviates the requirement of any further objection with respect to such evidence."); *Myers v. Winslow R. Chamberlain Co.*, 443 N.W.2d 211, 216 (Minn. App. 1989) (ruling that objections on the record in chambers need not be repeated at trial to preserve the issue for review). *But see State v. Litzau*, 650 N.W.2d 177, 183 (Minn. 2002) ("Ordinarily, a party need not renew an objection to the admission of evidence to preserve a claim of error for appeal following a ruling on a motion in limine. If, however, excluded evidence is offered at trial because the court has changed its initial ruling, the objection should be renewed at trial.") (citation omitted).

The federal rule refers to preserving the claim of error "for appeal." In civil cases in Minnesota to preserve the evidentiary ruling for appeal, in addition to a timely and specific objection, the claim also must be included in a motion for new trial. *Sauter v. Wasemiller*, 389 N.W.2d 200, 201–02 (Minn. 1986).

The amendment does not prevent an attorney from making an offer of proof where appropriate, or from renewing an objection. Repetitive, cumulative objections should be avoided, but occasionally the context at trial is more developed and may be different from what was anticipated at the time of the former ruling, justifying a renewed objection and perhaps a different ruling.

RULE 104. PRELIMINARY QUESTIONS

(a) Questions of admissibility generally. Preliminary questions concerning the qualification of a person to be a witness, the existence of a privilege, or the admissibility of evidence shall be determined by the court, subject to the provisions of subdivision (b). In making its determination it is not bound by the rules of evidence except those with respect to privileges.

(b) Relevancy conditioned on fact. When the relevancy of evidence depends upon the fulfillment of a condition of fact, the court shall admit it upon, or in the court's discretion subject to, the introduction of evidence sufficient to support a finding of the fulfillment of the condition.

(c) Hearing of jury. Hearings on the admissibility of confessions shall in all cases be conducted out of the hearing of the jury. Hearings on other preliminary matters shall be so conducted when the interests of justice require or, when an accused is a witness, and so requests.

(d) Testimony by accused. The accused does not, by testifying upon a preliminary matter, become subject to cross-examination as to other issues in the case.

(e) Weight and credibility. This rule does not limit the right of a party to introduce before the jury evidence relevant to weight or credibility.

Adopted April 1, 1977, eff. July 1, 1977. Amended Dec. 28, 1989, eff. Jan. 1, 1990.

Committee Comment—1977

Rule 104(a)

Rule 104 sets out the relative function of the judge and jury in the trial process. It is clear that the application of the exclusionary rules of evidence rests in the hands of the court. To the extent that admissibility of evidence is conditioned on the resolution of a second question (unavailability of a witness, rule 804; qualification of expert witness, rule 702; existence of privilege, etc.) it is the function of the court to determine whether or not the condition has been fulfilled. Often the resolution of the second question will involve a factual determination, and to that extent the court acts as a trier of fact. In this capacity, the court is not bound by the exclusionary rules of evidence other than the rules dealing with privilege. The exclusionary rules of evidence reflect a concern over the capabilities of a lay jury to make technical legal and factual distinctions. The same considerations are not present when the decision as to such a preliminary question is to be made by the court. Furthermore, in the interest of judicial time and expense practicality dictates that the court be permitted to consider reliable hearsay, affidavit, or offers of proof on the preliminary questions as to the competence of an offer of evidence. See C. McCormick, Evidence § 53 (2d ed. 1972). Many existing rules of procedure permit the court to make important decisions based on affidavit. Minn.R.Civ.P. 43.05, 4.06, 56, 65.01, 65.02 and Minn.R.Crim.P. 28.05 subd. 5(2), 32. The policy behind preserving the confidentiality of certain communications would be destroyed by permitting the court to inquire into privilege.

The rule should continue existing practice in Minnesota. See State v. Martin, 293 Minn. 116, 125, 197 N.W.2d 219, 225 (1972) where the Court discusses this rule with apparent approval.

Rule 104(b)

Rule 104(a) must be read consistently with 104(b) and (c). Pursuant to rules 401–403 the court must make a determination as to the relevance and admissibility of an offer of evidence. If the relevance of the offer is dependent on the existence of a second fact the court's function is to determine whether there is sufficient evidence admitted for a jury decision as to the existence of the second fact. It is for the jury to determine whether or not the second fact is established and the weight to be given the original offer. Questions of fact are deemed to be appropriate for jury determination. To permit the court to determine preliminary questions of this nature would be to severely limit the fact finding function of the jury.

For specific application of this provision see rules 901 and 1008. The Committee recommends the rule as provided in the Uniform Rules of Evidence since it clearly preserves the court's control over the order of proof.

Rule 104(c)

Preliminary hearings on the admissibility of confessions must be heard outside of the presence of the jury. Jackson v. Denno, 84 S.Ct. 1774, 1790, 378 U.S. 368, 394, 12 L.Ed.2d 908, 925, 926, 1 A.L.R.3d 1205 (1964); State ex rel. Rasmussen v. Tahash, 272 Minn. 539, 554, 141 N.W.2d 3, 13 (1965), and Minn.R.Crim.P. 7.01, 8.03 and 11.02. The second sentence of the rule is applicable to both civil and criminal proceedings.

Hearings on preliminary questions should be heard outside of the presence of the jury when requested by the accused or where the interests of justice so require. This is consistent with rule 103(c). See Minn.R.Crim.P. 7.01, 8.03 and 11.02 for specific types of preliminary questions that are resolved at the omnibus hearing in a criminal case.

Rule 104(d)

This rule limits the court's discretion as to the scope of cross-examination pursuant to rule 611(b). The rule does not speak to the issue of the subsequent use of testimony on preliminary matters.

RULE 105. LIMITED ADMISSIBILITY

When evidence which is admissible as to one party or for one purpose but not admissible as to another party or for another purpose is admitted, the court, upon request, shall restrict the evidence to its proper scope and instruct the jury accordingly.

Adopted April 1, 1977, eff. July 1, 1977.

Committee Comment—1977

Consistent with rule 103 the rule places the burden on the opposing party to request a limiting instruction before a court is required to give such an instruction. This is generally consistent with existing practice. State v. DeZeler, 230 Minn. 39, 48, 41 N.W.2d 313, 319, 15 A.L.R.2d 1137 (1950); State v. Soltau, 212 Minn. 20, 25, 2 N.W.2d 155, 158 (1942). The rule should not be read to indicate that a limiting instruction in every case will cure any potential prejudice that might be encountered by the admission of the evidence. *E.g.,* Bruton v. United States, 88 S.Ct. 1620, 391 U.S. 123, 20 L.Ed.2d 476 (1968). Such a decision is for the court to make under rule 403 or applicable statutory or constitutional provisions.

RULE 106. REMAINDER OF OR RELATED WRITINGS OR RECORDED STATEMENTS

When a writing or recorded statement or part thereof is introduced by a party, an adverse party may require the introduction at that time of any other part or any other writing or recorded statement which ought in fairness to be considered contemporaneously with it.

Adopted April 1, 1977, eff. July 1, 1977. Amended Dec. 28, 1989, eff. Jan. 1, 1990.

Committee Comment—1977

The rule extends the present rule with regard to depositions to other writings and recordings. Minn. R.Civ.P. 32.01(4). The rule is not intended to apply to conversations.

ARTICLE 2. JUDICIAL NOTICE

RULE 201. JUDICIAL NOTICE OF ADJUDICATIVE FACTS

(a) Scope of rule. This rule governs only judicial notice of adjudicative facts in civil cases.

(b) Kinds of facts. A judicially noticed fact must be one not subject to reasonable dispute in that it is either (1) generally known within the territorial jurisdiction of the trial court or (2) capable of accurate and ready determination by resort to sources whose accuracy cannot reasonably be questioned.

(c) When discretionary. A court may take judicial notice, whether requested or not.

(d) When mandatory. A court shall take judicial notice if requested by a party and supplied with the necessary information.

(e) Opportunity to be heard. A party is entitled upon timely request to an opportunity to be heard as to the propriety of taking judicial notice and the tenor of the matter noticed. In the absence of prior notification, the request may be made after judicial notice has been taken.

(f) Time of taking notice. Judicial notice may be taken at any stage of the proceeding.

(g) Instructing jury. The court shall instruct the jury to accept as conclusive any fact judicially noticed.

Adopted April 1, 1977, eff. July 1, 1977. Amended Dec. 28, 1989, eff. Jan. 1, 1990.

Committee Comment—1989

Rule 201(a)

The rule governing judicial notice is applicable only to civil cases. The status of the law governing the use of judicial notice in criminal cases is unsettled and not appropriate for codification. While it is understood that a trial judge should not direct a verdict against an accused in a criminal case, it is less clear the extent to which the court can take judicial notice of uncontested and uncontradictable peripheral facts or facts establishing venue. See e.g. State v. White, 300 N.W.2d 176 (Minn.1980); State v. Trezona, 286 Minn. 531, 176 N.W.2d 95 (1970). Trial courts should rely on applicable case law to determine the appropriate use of judicial notice in criminal cases.

This rule is limited to judicial notice of "adjudicative" facts, and does not govern judicial notice of "legislative" facts. The distinction between adjudicative and legislative facts was developed by Professor Kenneth C. Davis. An Approach to Problems of Evidence in the Administrative Process, 55 Harv. L.Rev. 364, 404–407 (1942); Judicial Notice, 55 Colum.L.Rev. 945 (1955); Administrative Law Text, Ch. 15 (3d ed. 1972).

Adjudicative facts generally are the type of facts decided by juries. Facts about the parties, their activities, properties, motives, and intent, the facts that give rise to the controversy, are adjudicative facts.

Legislative facts involve questions of law and policy and normally are decided by the court. See Beaudette v. Frana, 285 Minn. 366, 372, 173 N.W.2d 416, 419, 420 (1969) where the Court notices the effect which various courses of conduct might have upon the integrity of the marriage relationship. See also McCormack v. Hankscraft Co., 278 Minn.

322, 338, 154 N.W.2d 488, 500 (1967) "[e]nlarging a manufacturer's liability to those injured by its products more adequately meets public policy demands to protect consumers from the inevitable risks of bodily harm created by mass production and complex marketing conditions." The Committee was in agreement with the promulgators of the federal rule of evidence in not limiting judicial notice of legislative facts. See United States Supreme Court Advisory Committee Note.

Rule 201(b)

Minnesota has traditionally limited judicial notice of adjudicative facts to situations incapable of serious dispute. See State ex rel. Remick v. Clousing, 205 Minn. 296, 301, 285 N.W. 711, 714, 123 A.L.R. 465 (1939). This includes matters capable of accurate and ready determination. See Bollenbach v. Bollenbach, 285 Minn. 418, 429, 175 N.W.2d 148, 156 (1970), as well as facts of common knowledge; In re Application of Baldwin, 218 Minn. 11, 16, 17, 15 N.W.2d 184, 187 (1944).

Rule 201(c), (d)

These issues have received little attention in Minnesota. See generally State, Department of Highways v. Halvorson, 288 Minn. 424, 429, 181 N.W.2d 473, 476 (1970). The net effect of the rule should be to encourage the taking of judicial notice in appropriate circumstances. The improper refusal to take judicial notice would not necessarily be reversible. See rule 103.

Rule 201(e)

The opportunity to be heard is a mainstay of procedural fairness. This right is protected by the rule. If the limits imposed upon the judicial notice by subdivision (b) of this rule are properly observed, there should be relatively little controversy concerning the right to be heard. The shape of the hearing on the issue of judicial notice rests in the discretion of the trial judge. However, in a jury trial such a hearing should always be outside of the presence of the jury. Rule 103(c). See also 104(c).

Rule 201(f)

This subdivision recognizes that the circumstances which make judicial notice of adjudicative facts appropriate are not limited to any particular stage of the judicial process.

Rule 201(g)

The conclusive nature of judicially noticed facts in civil cases is consistent with the restrictions which the rule places upon the kinds of facts which can be judicially noticed.

The rule does not affect judicial notice of foreign law. See Minn.R.Civ.P. 44.04. There are a number of existing statutes that deal with judicial notice of local laws, regulations, etc. See e.g., Minn.Stats. Ch. 599, and §§ 268.12(3), 410.11 (1974); Minn. Stats., (1975 Supp.) § 15.049.

ARTICLE 3. PRESUMPTIONS IN CIVIL ACTIONS AND PROCEEDINGS

RULE 301. PRESUMPTIONS IN GENERAL IN CIVIL ACTIONS AND PROCEEDINGS

In all civil actions and proceedings not otherwise provided for by statute or by these rules, a presumption imposes on the party against whom it is directed the burden of going forward with evidence to rebut or meet the presumption, but does not shift to such party the burden of proof in the sense of the risk of nonpersuasion, which remains throughout the trial upon the party on whom it was originally cast.

Adopted April 1, 1977, eff. July 1, 1977.

Committee Comment—1977

Only the burden of producing evidence is affected by a presumption. A presumption is a procedural device that satisfies the burden of producing evidence. Once the basic facts that give rise to the presumption are established the opponent must produce evidence to rebut the assumed fact or a verdict will be directed on the issue. If sufficient evidence is introduced that would justify a finding of fact contrary to the assumed fact the presumption is rebutted and has no further function at the trial.

The disappearance of the presumption does not deprive the offered evidence of whatever probative value and whatever effect to which it would otherwise be entitled. For example, it may be that the presumption is rebutted but the underlying facts that give rise to the presumption are sufficiently probative to justify an instruction as to a permissive inference. In approving the federal rule the United States Congress contemplated such instruction. 4 U.S.Code Cong. & Ad.News, 93d Cong., 2d Sess., House Conference Report No. 93–1597, Dec. 14, 1974, p. 7099. 4 U.S.Code Cong. & Ad.News, 93d Cong., 2d Sess., Senate Report No. 93–1277, Oct. 11, 1974, p. 7051. The Court's authority to give such an instruction does not flow from the presumption which has disappeared but from the Court's power and duty to sum up and instruct the jury. Under this rule a jury should never be instructed in terms of presumption. Furthermore, a presumption has no effect on the burden of persuasion.

The rule is largely consistent with the stated practice in Minnesota. Ryan v. Metropolitan Life Ins. Co., 206 Minn. 562, 289 N.W. 557 (1939); Te Poel v. Larson, 236 Minn. 482, 53 N.W.2d 468 (1952). However, the application of the rule has been inconsistent. See Jones v. Peterson, 279 Minn. 241, 246, 156 N.W.2d 733, 736 (1968); Krinke v. Faricy, 304 Minn. 450, 231 N.W.2d 491, 492 (1975); Thompson, Presumptions and the New Rules of Evidence in Minnesota, 2 Wm. Mitchell L.Rev. 167 (1976).

The rule does not define presumption, leaving this to court or statutory resolution. Because the term presumption has been used loosely in the past to refer to inferences, assumptions and matters of substantive law, the court must determine whether it is dealing with a true procedural presumption. For example, the statement that everyone is presumed to know the law is not based on presumption, but is a mere shorthand statement for the proposition that the substantive law does not recognize ignorance of the law as a permissible defense or excuse. J. Thayer, A Preliminary Treatise on Evidence at the Common Law, p. 335 (1898); Electric Short Line Term. Co. v. City of Minneapolis, 242 Minn. 1, 7, 64 N.W.2d 149, 153 (1954). Similarly, the so called presumption of legitimacy that attaches when a child is born during wedlock is not a true presumption but an operation of the substantive law that allocates the burden of persuasion in the litigation.

The rule applies to both common law presumptions and statutory presumptions with the exception of those statutory presumptions in which the legislature has specifically provided that the presumption shall have some other effect. See Minn.Stats. § 602.04 (1974). The rule applies only in civil actions and proceedings.

ARTICLE 4. RELEVANCY AND ITS LIMITS

RULE 401. DEFINITION OF "RELEVANT EVIDENCE"

"Relevant evidence" means evidence having any tendency to make the existence of any fact that is of consequence to the determination of the action more probable or less probable than it would be without the evidence.

Adopted April 1, 1977, eff. July 1, 1977.

Committee Comment—1977

The threshold test for the admissibility of evidence is the test of relevancy. Essentially, it is a test of logic, an assessment of probative value. Evidence must have some probative value or it should not be admitted. The rule adopts a liberal as opposed to restrictive approach to the question of relevancy. If the offer has any tendency to make the existence of a fact of consequence more or less probable than it would be without the evidence it is relevant. A slight probative tendency is sufficient under rule 401. Even where probative value is established and the evidence is relevant it still might be excluded under various other provisions in these rules, state and federal constitutions and other court rules. Rule 402.

The evidentiary offer must tend to prove or disprove a fact that is of consequence to the litigation. What is of consequence to the litigation depends upon the scope of the pleadings, the theory of recovery and the substantive law. The rule avoids reference to materiality, an overused term meaning different things in different situations. The fact to be established need not be an ultimate fact or a vital fact. It need only be a fact that is of some consequence to the disposition of the litigation.

The liberal approach to relevancy is consistent with Minnesota practice. In Boland v. Morrill, 270 Minn. 86, 98, 99, 132 N.W.2d 711, 719 (1965) the Court defined relevancy as a function of the effect the offered evidence might have upon the proof of a material fact in issue:

> If the offered evidence permits an inference to be drawn that will justify a desired finding of fact, it is relevant. Reduced to simple terms, any evidence is relevant which logically tends to prove or disprove a material fact in issue.

RULE 402. RELEVANT EVIDENCE GENERALLY ADMISSIBLE; IRRELEVANT EVIDENCE INADMISSIBLE

All relevant evidence is admissible, except as otherwise provided by the United States Constitution, the State Constitution, statute, by these rules, or by other rules applicable in the courts of this state. Evidence which is not relevant is not admissible.

Adopted April 1, 1977, eff. July 1, 1977.

RULE 403. EXCLUSION OF RELEVANT EVIDENCE ON GROUNDS OF PREJUDICE, CONFUSION, OR WASTE OF TIME

Although relevant, evidence may be excluded if its probative value is substantially outweighed by the danger of unfair prejudice, confusion of the issues, or misleading the jury, or by considerations of undue delay, waste of time, or needless presentation of cumulative evidence.

Adopted April 1, 1977, eff. July 1, 1977.

Committee Comment—1977

This rule along with rule 102 provides the guidance for the proper application of these rules. Rule 403 sets forth the appropriate considerations that must be addressed in resolving challenges to the admissibility of relevant evidence. The rule creates a balancing test. Probative value is balanced against other considerations of policy, fairness, and convenience. The rule favors the admission of relevant evidence by requiring a determination that its probative value be "substantially" outweighed by the dangers listed in the rule before relevant evidence will be excluded.

Conspicuously missing from the proposed rule is the exclusion of relevant evidence on the basis of surprise. Even with modern discovery methods the question of surprise may still come up in litigation but a continuance rather than the exclusion of the evidence is deemed to be the better method of handling such a case. Minnesota cases list surprise as a basis for excluding otherwise relevant evidence. However, few if any reported cases have excluded relevant evidence on this ground. Cf. State v. Spreigl, 272 Minn. 488, 139 N.W.2d 167 (1965), (new trial ordered essentially on a surprise analysis.) Otherwise the rule is consistent with existing Minnesota practice. State v. Gavle, 234 Minn. 186,

208, 48 N.W.2d 44, 56 (1951); State v. Haney, 219 Minn. 518, 520, 18 N.W.2d 315, 316 (1945).

RULE 404. CHARACTER EVIDENCE NOT ADMISSIBLE TO PROVE CONDUCT; EXCEPTIONS; OTHER CRIMES

(a) Character evidence generally. Evidence of a person's character or a trait of character is not admissible for the purpose of proving action in conformity therewith on a particular occasion, except:

(1) *Character of accused.* Evidence of a pertinent trait of character offered by an accused, or by the prosecution to rebut the same;

(2) *Character of victim.* Evidence of a pertinent trait of character of the victim of the crime offered by an accused, or by the prosecution to rebut the same, or evidence of a character trait of peacefulness of the victim offered by the prosecution in a homicide case to rebut evidence that the victim was the first aggressor.

(3) *Character of witness.* Evidence of the character of a witness, as provided in rules 607, 608, and 609.

(b) Other crimes, wrongs, or acts. Evidence of another crime, wrong, or act is not admissible to prove the character of a person in order to show action in conformity therewith. It may, however, be admissible for other purposes, such as proof of motive, opportunity, intent, preparation, plan, knowledge, identity, or absence of mistake or accident. In a criminal prosecution, such evidence shall not be admitted unless 1) the prosecutor gives notice of its intent to admit the evidence consistent with the rules of criminal procedure; 2) the prosecutor clearly indicates what the evidence will be offered to prove; 3) the other crime, wrong, or act and the participation in it by a relevant person are proven by clear and convincing evidence; 4) the evidence is relevant to the prosecutor's case; and 5) the probative value of the evidence is not outweighed by its potential for unfair prejudice to the defendant. Evidence of past sexual conduct of the victim in prosecutions involving criminal sexual conduct, including attempts or any act of criminal sexual predatory conduct is governed by rule 412.

(c) Renumbered Rule 412 effective Jan. 1, 1990.

Adopted April 1, 1977, eff. July 1, 1977. Amended Dec. 28, 1989, eff. Jan. 1, 1990; July 18, 2006, eff. Sept. 1, 2006.

Committee Comment—1989

Rules 404 to 411 give specific treatment to several areas where questions of relevancy commonly arise. To the extent that these rules call for the exclusion of certain offers of evidence, the court's discretion has been limited. All issues of admissibility are ultimately subject to the provisions of rules 401 and 403, which also serve to limit the court in its exercise of discretion.

Rule 404(a)

The use of character evidence to prove conduct is subject to the limitations of rule 404. The rule is generally consistent with the common law doctrine that character evidence is not admissible to prove that an individual acted in conformity with his character on a specific occasion. Certain exceptions to this general doctrine are contained in the rule.

The rule recognizes the traditional exception which permits the accused in a criminal case to introduce evidence of his good character as proof of the substantive issue of guilt or innocence. State v. Peery, 224 Minn. 346, 353, 28 N.W.2d 851, 855 (1947); State v. Dolliver, 150 Minn. 155, 184 N.W. 848 (1921). If the accused puts his character in issue the prosecutor may offer evidence in rebuttal. State v. Sharich, 297 Minn. 19, 23, 209 N.W.2d 907, 911 (1973).

The former Minnesota practice in civil actions which extended similar rights to a defendant where the cause of action was predicated upon defendant's "[d]epraved conduct or acts involving moral turpitude," State v. Oslund, 199 Minn. 604, 605, 273 N.W. 76 (1937), has been discontinued by this rule.

Rule 404(a)(2) continues the existing practice which permits the admission of a pertinent character trait of the victim to be offered by the accused in a criminal case. See State v. Keaton, 258 Minn. 359, 367, 104 N.W.2d 650, 656, 86 A.L.R.2d 649 (1960). Evidence of this type is most commonly offered in cases involving issues of self-defense. The rule also permits the prosecution in homicide cases to introduce evidence of the character trait of peacefulness of the victim to rebut any evidence that the victim was the first aggressor. Before an accused can introduce evidence of the victim's past sexual conduct in cases involving sexual offenses the provisions of rule 404(c) must be satisfied.

Rule 404(b)

The subdivision [(b)] suggests certain purposes for which evidence of other acts or crimes may be admitted subject to the provisions of Rule 403. The list of acceptable purposes is not meant to be exclusive. See Minn.R.Crim.P. 7.02 which provides that the prosecuting attorney must give notice of certain additional offenses that might be offered pursuant to this rule of evidence. See also State v. Billstrom, 276 Minn. 174, 149 N.W.2d 281 (1967); State v. Spreigl, 272 Minn. 488, 139 N.W.2d 167 (1965).

The Committee has revised Rule 404(b) by adding one sentence which codifies Minnesota case law. State v. Billstrom.

Rule 404(c)

The Committee renumbered the rules in Article 4, moving the rule addressing evidence of the victim's past sexual conduct to a new Rule 412 to conform to the numbering in the Federal Rules of Evidence and Uniform Rules of Evidence.

Advisory Committee Comment—2006 Amendments

Rule 404(b).

Rule 404(b) has been revised to reflect the five part test that trial courts must apply in determining whether to admit other act evidence under the rule. *See State v. Ness*, 707 N.W.2d 676, 685–86 (Minn.

2006); *State v. McLeod,* 705 N.W.2d 776, 787 (Minn. 2005); *Angus v. State,* 695 N.W.2d 109, 119 (Minn. 2005); *State v. Asfeld,* 662 N.W.2d 534, 542 (Minn. 2003). In applying the test, the court should first determine the precise purpose or fact for which the evidence was offered and the relevance of the proffered evidence to that particular purpose or fact. Only after finding that the proffered evidence is relevant to a pertinent purpose or fact should the trial court apply the fifth prong's balancing test. *See Ness,* 707 N.W.2d at 686. The *Ness* opinion further held that the "need" requirement first enunciated in *State v. Billstrom,* 276 Minn. 174, 178–79, 149 N.W.2d 281, 284 (1967), is not an "independent requirement of admissibility" but is to be addressed in the context of the fifth prong's balancing test. *Ness,* 707 N.W.2d at 690.

The intent of the revision is, in part, to provide a clear balancing test to be applied in determining the admissibility of other acts evidence. The Minnesota Supreme Court has used conflicting language when describing the trial court's task. *See generally* James A. Morrow, Peter N. Thompson & Alfred C. Holden, *Weighing* Spreigl *Evidence: In Search of a Standard,* 60 BENCH & B. OF MINN. 23 (November 2003). Consistent with the Court's longstanding view that because of the great potential for misuse of this evidence, the trial judge should exclude the evidence in the close case, the Court has instructed the trial judge to exclude the evidence if the probative value is outweighed by the potential for unfair prejudice. In some of the same opinions, however, the Court also referred to the rule 403 balancing test that requires the trial judge to admit the evidence in the close case. Rule 403 requires admission unless the probative value is "substantially" outweighed by the unfair prejudice. Even in *Ness,* an opinion designed to reconcile inconsistent decisions, the Court stated that other act evidence "may not be introduced if its probative value is substantially outweighed by its tendency to unfairly prejudice the factfinder." *Ness,* 707 N.W.2d at 685. However, the *Ness* Court, following *Angus,* 695 N.W.2d at 119, *Asfeld,* 662 N.W.2d at 542, and *State v. Kennedy,* 585 N.W.2d 385, 389 (Minn. 1998), held that the fifth prong as stated in rule 404(b)(5) is the appropriate balancing test for other acts evidence. *Ness,* 707 N.W.2d at 689–93. This test focuses on whether the probative value is outweighed by the potential for unfair prejudice. A slight balance in favor of unfair prejudice requires exclusion. Since this test is a more stringent test, evidence that satisfies this balancing test will certainly satisfy rule 403.

Rule 404(b) also changes the description of the cases where rule 412 is applicable. Consistent with rule 412, the description is no longer dependent on statute numbers thereby alleviating the need to revise the evidence rule whenever criminal statutes are renumbered, amended, or added.

Similar conduct by the accused against a victim of domestic abuse or against other family or household members is governed by Minn. Stat. § 634.20 (2004). In *State v. McCoy,* 682 N.W.2d 153, 159–61 (Minn. 2004), the supreme court held that the clear and convincing evidence standard of rule 404(b) does not apply when evidence is offered under the statute.

RULE 405. METHODS OF PROVING CHARACTER

(a) Reputation or opinion. In all cases in which evidence of character or a trait of character of a person is admissible, proof may be made by testimony as to reputation or by testimony in the form of an opinion. On cross-examination, inquiry is allowable into relevant specific instances of conduct.

(b) Specific instances of conduct. In cases in which character or trait of character of a person is an essential element of a charge, claim, or defense, proof may also be made of specific instances of that person's conduct.

Adopted April 1, 1977, eff. July 1, 1977. Amended Dec. 28, 1989, eff. Jan. 1, 1990.

Committee Comment—1977

While rule 404 determines when character evidence is admissible, rule 405 determines the proper methods of introducing character evidence. In the note to the federal rule the Supreme Court Advisory Committee explained the rationale for drawing distinctions as to the various methods of proving character:

> Of the three methods of proving character provided by the rule, evidence of specific instances of conduct is the most convincing. At the same time it possesses the greatest capacity to arouse prejudice, to confuse, to surprise, and to consume time. Consequently the rule confines the use of evidence of this kind to cases in which character is, in the strict sense, in issue and hence deserving of a searching inquiry. When character is used circumstantially and hence occupies a lesser status in the case, proof may be only by reputation and opinion. These latter methods are also available when character is in issue. This treatment is with respect to specific instances of conduct and reputation, conventional contemporary common law doctrine. Citing C. McCormick, Evidence § 153 (1954).

When character is not in issue the rule permits evidence by way of reputation or opinion. The rule is consistent with Minnesota law. Minnesota has long followed the minority rule and has permitted opinion evidence to establish good character. State v. Humphrey, 173 Minn. 410, 413, 217 N.W. 373, 374 (1928); State v. Lee, 22 Minn. 407, 409, 410 (1876). The foundation for the opinion and the competency of the witness to make the statement should be governed by the principles in Articles 6 and 7.

On cross-examination of a character witness the opposing party may inquire into specific instances in order to test the basis for the testimony on direct. The rule is not meant to provide an opportunity for attorneys to make points by innuendo by asking questions about unsubstantiated instances, and the Court should levy appropriate sanctions where such is the case. See gen. State v. Flowers, 262 Minn.

164, 114 N.W.2d 78 (1962); State v. Silvers, 230 Minn. 12, 40 N.W.2d 630 (1950).

RULE 406. HABIT; ROUTINE PRACTICE

Evidence of the habit of a person or of the routine practice of an organization, whether corroborated or not and regardless of the presence of eyewitnesses, is relevant to prove that the conduct of the person or organization on a particular occasion was in conformity with the habit or routine practice.

Adopted April 1, 1977, eff. July 1, 1977. Amended Dec. 28, 1989, eff. Jan. 1, 1990.

Committee Comment—1989

The change in the title of the rule conforms the title to the text of the rule and to the title of the corresponding Federal Rule and Uniform Rule 406. Habit is not defined in the rule, but the definition as set forth in McCormick is generally accepted and should be used in conjunction with this rule. Whereas character evidence is considered to be a "generalized description of one's disposition, or of one's disposition in respect to a generalized trait," habit describes "one's regular response to a repeated specific situation." C. McCormick, Evidence § 195 (2d ed. 1972). Whether the response is sufficiently regular and whether the specific situation has been repeated enough to constitute habit are questions for the trial court. See Lewan, Rationale of Habit Evidence, 16 Syracuse L.Rev. 39 (1964). The Court should make a searching inquiry to assure that a true habit exists. Once it is established that a habit does exist testimony as to that habit is highly probative. Such testimony has been received in Minnesota Courts. See Department of Employment Security v. Minnesota Drug Products, Inc., 258 Minn. 133, 138, 104 N.W.2d 540, 644 (1960); Evison v. Chicago, St. Paul, Minneapolis & Omaha Ry., 45 Minn. 370, 372, 373, 48 N.W. 6, 7, 11 (1891).

RULE 407. SUBSEQUENT REMEDIAL MEASURES

When, after an injury or harm allegedly caused by an event, measures are taken which, if taken previously, would have made the event less likely to occur, evidence of the subsequent measures is not admissible to prove negligence, culpable conduct, a defect in a product, a defect in a product's design, or a need for a warning or instruction. This rule does not require the exclusion of evidence of subsequent measures when offered for another purpose, such as proving ownership, control, or feasibility of precautionary measures, if controverted, or impeachment.

Adopted April 1, 1977, eff. July 1, 1977. Amended July 18, 2006, eff. Sept. 1, 2006.

Committee Comment—1989

The rule reflects the conventional approach to the admissibility of subsequent remedial measures. Based on policy considerations aimed at encouraging people to make needed repairs, along with the real possibility that subsequent repairs are frequently not indicative of past fault, such evidence is not admissible to establish negligence or culpable conduct. The evidence might be admissible to establish other controverted issues in the case or for impeachment purposes. The rule is consistent with existing Minnesota practice. See Faber v. Roelofs, 298 Minn. 16, 20–23, 212 N.W.2d 856, 859–860 (1973).

Under the rule subsequent remedial measures can be admissible to establish feasibility of precautionary measures in any case where such feasibility is in issue. Subsequent remedial measures are not admissible to prove defect in design defect cases. See Kallio v. Ford Motor Co., 407 N.W.2d 92 (Minn. 1987), rejecting Ault v. International Harvester Co., 13 Cal.3d 113, 117 Cal.Rptr. 812, 528 P.2d 1148 (1975). The Committee is of the view that such measures are also inadmissible in failure to warn cases in view of Bilotta v. Kelly Co. Inc., 346 N.W.2d 616 (Minn.1984), which held that design defect and failure to warn cases can be submitted to the jury on a single theory of products liability. See DeLuryea v. Winthrop Laboratories, 697 F.2d 222 (8th Cir.1983).

Advisory Committee Comment—2006 Amendments

The amendment comes from Fed. R. Evid. 407, which was added in 1997. The amending language makes it clear that to merit protection under the rule the remedial measure must come after the accident or injury. This approach is consistent with current practice in Minnesota. *See Myers v. Hearth Techs., Inc.*, 621 N.W.2d 787, 792 (Minn. App. 2001) (finding changes made before the accident do not qualify as subsequent remedial measures); *Beniek v. Textron, Inc.*, 479 N.W.2d 719, 723 (Minn. App. 1992) (finding that design changes after plaintiff purchased the product, but before the accident, are not excluded by this rule).

In addition, the language insures that the protection under the rule does not depend on the legal theory advanced at trial. The Minnesota Supreme Court has already ruled that subsequent remedial measures are not admissible to prove defect in design defect cases. *See Kallio v. Ford Motor Co.*, 407 N.W.2d 92, 97–98 (Minn. 1987). The 1989 Minnesota Supreme Court Advisory Committee Comment to rule 407 provided that subsequent remedial measures "are also inadmissible in failure to warn cases in view of *Bilotta v. Kelly Co. Inc.*, 346 N.W.2d 616 (Minn. 1984) which held that design defect and failure to warn cases can be submitted to the jury on a single theory of products liability." The amended language would also make subsequent remedial measures inadmissible to prove that a product was defective in a pure strict liability or a breach of warranty case.

RULE 408. COMPROMISE AND OFFERS TO COMPROMISE

Evidence of (1) furnishing or offering or promising to furnish, or (2) accepting or offering or promising to accept, a valuable consideration in compromising or attempting to compromise a claim which was disputed as to either validity or amount, is not admissible to prove liability for or invalidity of the claim or its amount. Evidence of conduct or statements made in compromise negotiations is likewise not admissible. This rule does not require the exclusion of any evidence otherwise discoverable merely because it is presented in the course of compromise negotiations. This rule also does not require exclusion when the evidence is offered for another purpose, such as proving bias or prejudice of a witness, negativing a contention of undue delay, or proving an effort to obstruct a criminal investigation or prosecution.

Adopted April 1, 1977, eff. July 1, 1977.

Committee Comment—1977

This rule will substantially alter present practice in Minnesota affording more protection to compromise discussions than presently exist. The increased protection is justified to the extent that it will encourage frank and free discussion to compromise negotiations and avoid the necessity for parties to speak in terms of hypotheticals. Not only are offers of compromise or the acceptance of compromise inadmissible but also all statements made in compromise negotiations. Contra, Esser v. Brophey, 212 Minn. 194, 196–99, 3 N.W.2d 3, 4, 5 (1942). Before the rule of exclusion is applicable there must be a genuine dispute as to either validity or amount. Absent such a dispute there is no real compromise. The rule does not immunize otherwise discoverable material merely because it was revealed within the context of an offer of compromise. Finally the rule only excludes evidence of compromise on the issue of liability, not for other possible purposes as suggested in the rule. See Esser, id. at 199, 200, 3 N.W.2d at 6.

RULE 409. PAYMENT OF MEDICAL AND SIMILAR EXPENSES

Evidence of furnishing or offering or promising to pay medical, hospital, or similar expenses occasioned by an injury is not admissible to prove liability for the injury.

Adopted April 1, 1977, eff. July 1, 1977.

Committee Comment—1977

The rule is based on many of the same considerations that give rise to rule 408. Unlike rule 408 there is no requirement that there be an actual dispute at the time the medical payments are made or offered. In addition, the rule does not preclude the admissibility of statements that accompany the payments or offers to pay. Consistent with rule 408 the rule only precludes such an offer of evidence when offered to prove liability for the injury. Subject to the provisions of rules 401–403 such evidence may be admissible to prove other issues of consequence to the litigation.

RULE 410. OFFER TO PLEAD GUILTY; NOLO CONTENDERE, WITHDRAWN PLEA OF GUILTY

Evidence of a plea of guilty, later withdrawn, or a plea of nolo contendere, or of an offer to plead guilty or nolo contendere to the crime charged or any other crime or of statements made in connection with any of the foregoing pleas or offers, is not admissible in any civil, criminal, or administrative action, case, or proceeding whether offered for or against the person who made the plea or offer.

Adopted April 1, 1977, eff. July 1, 1977.

Committee Comment—1977

At present the subsequent effect of a withdrawn plea of guilty or an offer to plead guilty is governed by Minn.R.Crim.P. 15.06 which provides:

> If the defendant enters a plea of guilty which is not accepted or which is withdrawn, neither the plea discussions, nor the plea agreement, nor the plea shall be received in evidence against or in favor of the defendant in any criminal, civil, or administrative proceeding.

The rule of evidence makes it clearer that not only the plea but also those statements that accompany the plea are inadmissible. See gen. Minn.R.Crim.P. 15.02.

Based on principles of comity as well as fairness to the person making the plea, the rule also precludes evidence of pleas or offers to plea nolo contendere in those jurisdictions that permit such a plea.

RULE 411. LIABILITY INSURANCE

Evidence that a person was or was not insured against liability is not admissible upon the issue whether the person acted negligently or otherwise wrongfully. This rule does not require the exclusion of evidence of insurance against liability when offered for another purpose, such as proof of agency, ownership, or control, or bias or prejudice of a witness.

Adopted April 1, 1977, eff. July 1, 1977. Amended Dec. 28, 1989, eff. Jan. 1, 1990.

Committee Comment—1977

The rule is in agreement with the approach currently followed in Minnesota that evidence as to whether a person is or is not insured against liability is inadmissible upon the issue of negligence or wrongful conduct. See Olson v. Prayfrock, 254 Minn. 42, 44, 94 N.W.2d 540, 542 (1958). Such evidence may be admissible to prove other issues, such as bias of a witness. See Scholte v. Brabec, 177 Minn. 13, 16, 224 N.W. 259, 260 (1929). The rule is obviously not intended to apply to those cases in which liability turns on whether or not a person was insured. See Minn.Stats. § 65B.67 (1974).

RULE 412. PAST CONDUCT OF VICTIM OF CERTAIN SEX OFFENSES

(1) In a prosecution for acts of criminal sexual conduct, including attempts or any act of criminal sexual predatory conduct, evidence of the victim's

previous sexual conduct shall not be admitted nor shall any reference to such conduct be made in the presence of the jury, except by court order under the procedure provided in rule 412. Such evidence can be admissible only if the probative value of the evidence is not substantially outweighed by its inflammatory or prejudicial nature and only in the following circumstances:

(A) When consent of the victim is a defense in the case,

(i) evidence of the victim's previous sexual conduct tending to establish a common scheme or plan of similar sexual conduct under circumstances similar to the case at issue, relevant and material to the issue of consent;

(ii) evidence of the victim's previous sexual conduct with the accused; or

(B) When the prosecution's case includes evidence of semen, pregnancy or disease at the time of the incident or, in the case of pregnancy, between the time of the incident and trial, evidence of specific instances of the victim's previous sexual conduct, to show the source of the semen, pregnancy or disease.

(2) The accused may not offer evidence described in rule 412(1) except pursuant to the following procedure:

(A) A motion shall be made by the accused prior to the trial, unless later for good cause shown, setting out with particularity the offer of proof of the evidence that the accused intends to offer, relative to the previous sexual conduct of the victim.

(B) If the court deems the offer of proof sufficient, the court shall order a hearing out of the presence of the jury, if any, and in such hearing shall allow the accused to make a full presentation of the offer of proof.

(C) At the conclusion of the hearing, if the court finds that the evidence proposed to be offered by the accused regarding the previous sexual conduct of the victim is admissible under the provisions of rule 412(1) and that its probative value is not substantially outweighed by its inflammatory or prejudicial nature, the court shall make an order stating the extent to which such evidence is admissible. The accused may then offer evidence pursuant to the order of the court.

(D) If new information is discovered after the date of the hearing or during the course of trial, which may make evidence described in rule 412(1) admissible, the accused may make an offer of proof pursuant to rule 412(2), and the court shall hold an in camera hearing to determine whether the proposed evidence is admissible by the standards herein.

Adopted April 1, 1977, eff. July 1, 1977. Amended Dec. 28, 1989, eff. Jan. 1, 1990; July 18, 2006, eff. Sept. 1, 2006.

Committee Comment—1989

The original draft of the rules contained a proposed rule which was intended to preserve the holdings of State v. Zaccardi, 280 Minn. 291, 159 N.W.2d 108 (1968) and State v. Warford, 293 Minn. 339, 200 N.W.2d 301 (1972), cert. denied 93 S.Ct. 1388, 410 U.S. 935, 35 L.Ed.2d 598 (1973). While the Committee was drafting the rules, the Legislature passed an extensive revision of the law relating to sex offenses. Criminal Code of 1963, ch. 374, 1975 Minn.Laws p. 1244, codified at Minn.Stat. § 609.341–.35 (Supp.1975). Included in the legislation was Minn.Stat. § 609.347 (Supp.1975), which contained provisions relating to evidence, procedure, substantive law and jury instructions. During the public hearings held on the rules, various persons appeared before the committee and a number of written comments were received, all in support of the provisions of Minn.Stat. § 609.347 (Supp.1975). As a result, the Committee decided to revise the original proposed evidentiary rule to incorporate the evidentiary and procedural provisions of the statute.

It is the intent of the Committee that subdivisions 1, 2, and 5 of the statute shall not be affected by the rule. Subdivision 1 relates to the weight of evidence; subdivision 2 relates to the substantive law defining the offenses; and subdivision 5 concerns jury instructions. It was the opinion of the Committee that none of these subjects should be incorporated into evidentiary rules. Accordingly, it is the Committee's intent that these subdivisions shall continue in effect after the rules take effect.

Subdivision 3 of the statute relates to admissibility, and subdivision 4 relates to the procedure for determining admissibility. Both of these subjects are properly within the scope of evidentiary rules, and the Committee incorporated their substance into the revised rule 412. The revised rule contains the substance of the statute's provision that evidence of the victim's previous sexual conduct can only be admitted in limited circumstances and the provision for mandatory notice and hearing before such evidence can be admitted.

The committee made various changes, some of style and some of substance. Among the changes of style are the substitution of the words "accused" for "defendant" and "victim" for "complainant" so as to be consistent with the balance of rule 404.

Although the Committee agreed in substance with the thrust of the statute, because of the many questions that were created by the language in the statute, the Committee could not recommend the entire statute as drafted. For example, although it appears that the purpose of the statute was to eliminate the unwarranted attack on the victim's character when such evidence does not relate to the issues at trial, the effect of the statute could be the opposite. Subdivision (3)(a) suggests that the victim's past sexual conduct would be admissible to prove "fabrication." This could have the effect of expanding the use of past sexual conduct to all contested trials, an unwise result that seems inconsistent with sound policy and the purposes of the legislation. The evidentiary rule does not make past conduct admissible to prove fabrication.

The statute did not make it clear that consent and identity of semen, disease, or pregnancy are the only two issues to which evidence of the victim's prior sexual conduct should be admitted. Furthermore, it is not clear from the statute the extent to which prior sexual conduct with the accused is admissible. The evidentiary rule makes it clear that this evidence is only admissible when consent or identity is in issue. Finally, portions of the statute could be subject to constitutional attack on due process or right of confrontation grounds. As a consequence, the Committee re-drafted these sections trying to remain true to the overall legislative intent which the Committee endorses.

The statute recognized three situations in which previous sexual conduct of the victim would be relevant and admissible. The first of these occurs when consent is in issue. Prior sexual conduct is offered in order to give rise to an inference that the victim acted in conformity with that past conduct on a particular occasion. In the case of a victim of a sex offense, this is only relevant to prove that the victim consented to the act. If consent is not a defense, as, for example, the accused denies he was involved in the incident, evidence of the victim's past conduct is not relevant. This type of evidence is treated in rule 412(1). The rule recognizes the same two categories of such evidence recognized by the statute: evidence tending to show a common scheme or plan [subsection (A)(i)]; and evidence of conduct involving both the accused and the victim [subsection (A)(ii)]. As in the statute, the rule allows only these two categories of past sexual conduct to be admitted to prove consent.

The second situation in which evidence of the victim's previous sexual conduct can be admitted under both the statute and the rule occurs when the prosecution has offered evidence concerning semen, pregnancy or disease, to show either that the offense occurred or that the accused committed it. In this case the accused may offer evidence of the victim's specific sexual activity to rebut the inferences raised by the prosecution's evidence. Rule 412(1)(B). In this situation consent is not material, and the rule admits such evidence without requiring consent to be a defense.

The third situation in which the statute admitted evidence of previous sexual conduct occurs when the victim testifies specifically concerning such sexual conduct—or more probably, lack of sexual conduct—on direct examination. The statute allowed evidence of previous sexual conduct to impeach the victim's testimony. Minn.Stat. § 609.347, Subd. 3(d) (Supp.1975). This provision was not incorporated in the rule because the Committee is of the opinion that the accused might not know whether the victim was going to testify about lack of sexual conduct until the victim had actually completed direct examination. To impose the notice and hearing requirement does not seem to be fair in such a case. Moreover, the prosecution and victim can obviate such impeaching testimony by avoiding general statements about the victim's sexual activity on direct examination. For these reasons subdivision 3(d) of the statute is not incorporated in the rule. The Committee has not attempted to codify rules about circumstances under which prosecution evidence of this nature opens the door to rebuttal evidence by the defense.

The Committee deleted the language, "Evidence of such conduct engaged in more than one year prior to the date of alleged offense is inadmissible," from subdivision 3(a) of the statute. Obviously, the longer time lapse between the past conduct and the date of the alleged consent, the less probative the evidence becomes. However, there might be situations in which the victim engaged in a common scheme or plan which began more than a year before the offense and which might be relevant. The year limitation is arbitrary and may be unconstitutional. A sufficient safeguard is contained in the requirement that the probative value must not be substantially outweighed by the inflammatory and prejudicial nature of the evidence. This standard of admissibility has been altered slightly from the statutory language to conform with the general standard of admissibility found in rule 403. The change was necessary so that it would not appear that the accused had to meet a more stringent test of admissibility when proving a defense, than did the prosecutor in proving the accused's guilt.

With the respect to the procedural portions of the rule, the Committee deleted the language "to the fact of consent" from subdivision 4(c) of the statute. The required finding is that the evidence be "admissible as prescribed by this rule." Under both the statute and the rule, certain evidence of previous sexual conduct—that concerning the source of semen, pregnancy or disease—is admissible whether or not consent is a defense.

The Committee deleted the language "and prescribing the nature of the questions to be permitted at trial," also from subdivision 4(c) of the statute. A court order stating the extent to which the evidence is admissible is a sufficient safeguard, especially when considered with the restrictive language, "nor shall any reference to such conduct be made in the presence of the jury," taken from the statute and incorporated in rule 412(1). Prescribing the nature of the questions to be asked by counsel is a marked and unnecessary departure from the adversary system and may be unconstitutional.

In rare cases, the due process clause, the right to confront accusers, or the right to present evidence will require admission of evidence not specifically described in Rule 412. See State v. Benedict, 397 N.W.2d 337, 341 (Minn.1986); State v. Caswell, 320 N.W.2d 417, 419 (Minn.1982).

Advisory Committee Comment—2006 Amendments

The amendment is intended to clarify the reach of the rape shield rule. The amendment provides a general description of the types of cases in which this rule is applicable. The rule is drafted broadly enough to incorporate offers of evidence against alleged victims in prosecutions brought under the new sexual predator laws. *See, e.g.*, Minn. Stat. § 609.3453 (Supp. 2005) (criminal sexual predatory conduct). The language in the amendment can accommodate future statutory changes without requiring that the rule be amended. Similar language is also included in the amendment to rule 404. The rape shield rule should be applicable in all cases where the accused is offering evidence of the past sexual conduct of the alleged victim.

ARTICLE 5. PRIVILEGES

RULE 501. GENERAL RULE

Nothing in these rules shall be deemed to modify, or supersede existing law relating to the privilege of a witness, person, government, state or political subdivision.

Adopted April 1, 1977, eff. July 1, 1977.

Committee Comment—1977

In the enabling legislation which created the committee, the legislature specifically attempted to limit the power of the Supreme Court to promulgate rules of evidence which conflicted, modified, or superseded "Statutes which relate to the competency of witnesses to testify, found in Minn.Stats. 595.02 to 595.025"; and "Statutes which relate to the privacy of communications." Minn.Stats. § 480.0591, subd. 6(a) and (d) (1974). Rule 501 reflects the committee's recognition of these limitations. The bulk of the existing law dealing with the traditional privileges is found in Minn.Stats. §§ 595.02 to 595.025 (1974).

ARTICLE 6. WITNESSES

RULE 601. COMPETENCY

Except as provided by these rules, the competency of a witness to give testimony shall be determined in accordance with law.

Adopted April 1, 1977, eff. July 1, 1977.

Committee Comment—1977

As with rule 501 this rule reflects the committee's adherence to the enabling legislation which attempts to limit the Court's authority to promulgate rules of evidence in this area. See Comment to rule 501. Although Minn.Stats. §§ 595.02 to 595.08 (1974) are referred to as competency statutes some in fact are statutes creating privilege. The general competency statutes are Minn.Stats. §§ 595.02(6) and 595.06 (1974).

RULE 602. LACK OF PERSONAL KNOWLEDGE

A witness may not testify to a matter unless evidence is introduced sufficient to support a finding that the witness has personal knowledge of the matter. Evidence to prove personal knowledge may, but need not, consist of the witness' own testimony. This rule is subject to the provisions of Rule 703, relating to opinion testimony by expert witnesses.

Adopted April 1, 1977, eff. July 1, 1977. Amended Dec. 28, 1989, eff. Jan. 1, 1990.

Committee Comment—1977

The rule states a fundamental principle of evidence law. Expert witnesses provide the only exception to the rule that witnesses must testify from firsthand knowledge. See rule 703. The rule, although phrased in terms of competency, is essentially a specific application of rule 104(b). Testimony simply is not relevant unless the witness testifies from firsthand knowledge.

The requirement of firsthand knowledge does not preclude a witness from testifying as to a hearsay statement which qualifies as an exception to the hearsay rule (see Article 8) and was heard by the witness. Whereas the witness in such circumstances could repeat the hearsay statements the witness could not testify as to the subject matter of the statements without firsthand knowledge. See United States Supreme Court Advisory Committee Note.

The rule requires that witnesses have firsthand knowledge. It does not specifically refer to the declarant of a hearsay statement that is admitted subject to an exception to the hearsay rule. With the exception of party admissions, which are admitted as a function of the adversary system (and are not hearsay under rule 801(d)(2)) the Courts have generally required that the declarant of a hearsay statement have firsthand knowledge, before the hearsay statement is admissible. The rule should be read to continue this practice. See C. McCormick, Evidence §§ 18, 264, 285, 300, 310 (2d ed. 1972).

RULE 603. OATH OR AFFIRMATION

Before testifying, every witness shall be required to declare that the witness will testify truthfully, by oath or affirmation administered in a form calculated to awaken the witness' conscience and impress the witness' mind with the duty to do so.

Adopted April 1, 1977, eff. July 1, 1977. Amended Dec. 28, 1989, eff. Jan. 1, 1990.

Committee Comment—1977

The Minnesota procedural rules permit an affirmation in lieu of oath. See Minn.R.Civ.P. 43.04. Cf. Minn.Stats. 595.01 (1974).

RULE 604. INTERPRETERS

An interpreter is subject to the provisions of these rules relating to qualification as an expert and the administration of an oath or affirmation to make a true translation.

Adopted April 1, 1977, eff. July 1, 1977. Amended Dec. 28, 1989, eff. Jan. 1, 1990.

Committee Comment—1977

This rule is intended to implement Minn.R.Civ.P. 43.07.

Advisory Committee Comment—2006 Amendments

Interpreters who have not been qualified as experts should not be allowed to provide their opinion about the content of questions and answers involving persons who do not speak English or are handicapped in communication. The specific rules governing the qualifications of interpreters are set forth in Minn. Gen. R. Prac. 8. This rule provides that an interpreter who is listed on the statewide roster as a certified court interpreter is presumed competent to interpret in all court proceedings. Minn. Gen. R. Prac. 8.02(a). Most court interpreters on the statewide roster, however, have not passed the stringent tests and are not certified. Interpreters on the statewide roster but not certified, or those interpreters not on the roster, must be qualified as expert witnesses before providing interpretation. Judges should use the screening standards developed by the State Court Administrator to determine whether the non-certified interpreter is qualified. *See* Minn. Gen. R. Prac. 8.02(c). The State Court Administrator standards are available at: http://www.courts.state.mn.us/documents/0/Public/Interpreter_Program/ voir_dire.doc

RULE 605. COMPETENCY OF JUDGE AS WITNESS

The judge presiding at the trial may not testify in that trial as a witness. No objection need be made in order to preserve the point.

Adopted April 1, 1977, eff. July 1, 1977.

Committee Comment—1977

The rule as provided states the general rule in Minnesota as well as the approach generally followed in the United States. State v. Sandquist, 146 Minn. 322, 178 N.W. 883 (1920). See also Annot., 157 A.L.R. 315 (1945).

RULE 606. COMPETENCY OF JUROR AS WITNESS

(a) At the trial. A member of the jury may not testify as a witness before that jury in the trial of the case in which the juror is sitting. If the juror is called to so testify, the opposing party shall be afforded an opportunity to object out of the presence of the jury.

(b) Inquiry into validity of verdict or indictment. Upon an inquiry into the validity of a verdict or indictment, a juror may not testify as to any matter or statement occurring during the course of the jury's deliberations or to the effect of anything upon that or any other juror's mind or emotions as influencing the juror to assent to or dissent from the verdict or indictment or concerning the juror's mental processes in connection therewith, except that a juror may testify on the question whether extraneous prejudicial information was improperly brought to the jury's attention, or whether any outside influence was improperly brought to bear upon any juror, or as to any threats of violence or violent acts brought to bear on jurors, from whatever source, to reach a verdict. Nor may a juror's affidavit or evidence of any statement by the juror concerning a matter about which the juror would be precluded from testifying be received for these purposes.

Adopted April 1, 1977, eff. July 1, 1977. Amended Dec. 28, 1989, eff. Jan. 1, 1990.

Committee Comment—1989

The rule is based on the same rationale that gives rise to rule 605. However, when a juror is called as a witness an objection is required by the party opposing this testimony. Opportunity should be provided for an objection out of the presence of the jury.

Rule 606(b) is a reasoned compromise between the view that jury verdicts should be totally immunized from review in order to encourage freedom of deliberation, stability, and finality of judgments; and the necessity for having some check on the jury's conduct. Under the rule, the juror's thought processes and mental operations are protected from later scrutiny. Only evidence of the use of extraneous prejudicial information or other outside influence that is improperly brought to bear upon a juror is admissible. In criminal cases such an intrusion on the jury's processes on behalf of the accused might be mandated by the Sixth Amendment. See Parker v. Gladden, 87 S.Ct. 468, 470, 385 U.S. 363, 364, 17 L.Ed.2d 420, 422 (1966).

The application of the rule may be simple in many cases, such as unauthorized views, experiments, investigations, etc., but in other cases the rule merely sets out guidelines for the court to apply in a case by case analysis. Compare Olberg v. Minneapolis Gas Co., 291 Minn. 334, 340, 191 N.W.2d 418, 422 (1971) in which the Court stated that evidence of a juror's general "bias, motives, or beliefs should not be considered" with State v. Hayden Miller Co., 263 Minn. 29, 35, 116 N.W.2d 535, 539 (1962) in which the Court holds that bias resulting from specialized or personal knowledge of the dispute and withheld on voir dire is subject to inquiry.

The rule makes the juror's statements by way of affidavit or testimony incompetent. The rule does not purport to set out standards for when a new trial should be granted on the grounds of juror misconduct. Nor does the rule set the proper procedure for procuring admissible information from jurors. In Minnesota it is generally considered improper to question jurors after a trial for the purpose of obtaining evidence for a motion for a new trial. If possible misconduct on behalf of a juror is suspected, it should be reported to the Court, and if necessary the jurors will be interrogated on the record and under oath in court. Schwartz v. Minneapolis Gas Co., 258 Minn. 325, 328, 104 N.W.2d 301, 303 (1960); Olberg v. Minneapolis Gas Co., 291 Minn. 334, 343, 191 N.W.2d 418, 424 (1971); Minn.R.Crim.P. 26.03, subd. 19(6). See also Rule 3.5 of the Rules of Professional Conduct in regard to communications with jurors. The amended rule allows jurors to testify about overt threats of violence or violent acts brought to bear on jurors by anyone, including by other jurors. Threats of violence and use of violence is clearly outside of the scope of the acceptable decisionmaking process of a jury. The pressures and dynamics of juror deliberations will frequently be stressful and jurors will, of course, become agitated from time to time. The trial court must distinguish between testimony about "psychological" intimidation, coercion, and persuasion, which would be inadmissible, as opposed to express acts or threats of violence. See State v. Scheerle, 285 N.W.2d 686 (Minn.1979); State v. Hoskins, 292 Minn. 111, 193 N.W.2d 802 (1972).

RULE 607. WHO MAY IMPEACH

The credibility of a witness may be attacked by any party, including the party calling the witness.

Adopted April 1, 1977, eff. July 1, 1977. Amended Dec. 28, 1989, eff. Jan. 1, 1990.

Committee Comment—1977

It has been settled for some time in Minnesota that absent surprise, a party cannot impeach his own witness. The Minnesota Court has recognized that attorneys must take their witnesses where they find them and cannot always vouch for their credibility, but has followed the rule in an effort to avoid subjecting the jury to hearsay statements, ostensibly admitted for impeachment purposes. State v. Saporen, 205 Minn. 358, 285 N.W. 898 (1939); Selover v. Bryant, 54 Minn. 434, 438, 439, 56 N.W. 58, 59 (1893). The Court has used the surprise doctrine as a means for screening those cases in which a prior inconsistent statement is improperly being offered to prejudice the jury with hearsay from the case where the introduction of the prior statement is essential to a fair presentation of the claims.

Not only has the application of the rule resulted in technical distinctions but occasionally operates to deprive the trier of fact of valuable, relevant evidence. A witness with firsthand knowledge might not be called by either party, or if a witness does testify the rule may preclude impeachment to place the testimony in proper perspective. Such results are inconsistent with the principles of these evidentiary rules as expressed in rule 102.

Some intrusions on the traditional rule have already been implemented in civil cases by Minn. R.Civ.P. 43.02 and by the operation of the Sixth Amendment Confrontation Clause in criminal cases. Chambers v. Mississippi, 93 S.Ct. 1038, 410 U.S. 284, 35 L.Ed.2d 297 (1973). It was the committee's belief that the "surprise doctrine" no longer was justified. Consequently, it is recommended that the proposed rule be adopted, bringing Minnesota into conformity with the modern trend.

RULE 608. EVIDENCE OF CHARACTER AND CONDUCT OF WITNESS

(a) Opinion and reputation evidence of character. The credibility of a witness may be attacked or supported by evidence in the form of opinion or reputation, but subject to these limitations: (1) the evidence may refer only to character for truthfulness or untruthfulness, and (2) evidence of truthful character is admissible only after the character of the witness for truthfulness has been attacked by opinion or reputation evidence or otherwise.

(b) Specific instances of conduct. Specific instances of the conduct of the witness, for the purpose of attacking or supporting the witness' character for truthfulness, other than conviction of crime as provided in rule 609, may not be proved by extrinsic evidence. They may, however, in the discretion of the court, if probative of truthfulness or untruthfulness, be inquired into on cross-examination of the witness (1) concerning the witness' character for truthfulness or untruthfulness, or (2) concerning the character for truthfulness or untruthfulness of another witness as to which character the witness being cross-examined has testified.

(c) Criminal cases. The prosecutor in a criminal case may not cross-examine the accused or defense witness under subdivision (b) unless (1) the prosecutor has given the defense notice of intent to cross-examine pursuant to the rule; (2) the prosecutor is able to provide the trial court with sufficient evidentiary support justifying the cross-examination; and (3) the prosecutor establishes that the probative value of the cross-examination outweighs its potential for creating unfair prejudice to the accused.

The giving of testimony, whether by an accused or by any other witness, does not operate as a waiver of the accused's or the witness' privilege against self-incrimination when examined with respect to matters which relate only to credibility.

Adopted April 1, 1977, eff. July 1, 1977. Amended Dec. 28, 1989, eff. Jan. 1, 1990; July 18, 2006, eff. Sept. 1, 2006.

Committee Comment—1977

Rule 608(a)

The rule permits impeachment by means of reputation or opinion evidence. Traditionally, Minnesota has distinguished between opinion and reputation when dealing with the issue of credibility. Reputation testimony has been permitted but personal opinion has been excluded. See Simon v. Carroll, 241 Minn. 211, 220, 221, 62 N.W.2d 822, 828, 829 (1954); State v. Kahner, 217 Minn. 574, 582, 15 N.W.2d 105, 109 (1944). However, since the Minnesota courts permit the witness to testify as to whether he would believe the testimony which the impeached witness would give under oath, Minnesota courts come very close to permitting opinion testimony as to credibility.

Evidence of truthful character is only admissible for rehabilitation purposes after the character of the witness is attacked. What is meant by "otherwise" in the rule is left for case by case analysis. The United States Supreme Court Advisory Committee Note indicates that impeachment of a witness by introducing evidence of bias is not an attack on the character of the witness sufficient to justify rehabilitation. It is further suggested that evidence of misconduct admitted under rules 608(b) or 609 is such an attack. Impeachment in the form of contradiction may justify rehabilitation, depending on the circumstances. See United States Supreme Court Advisory Committee Note.

Rule 608(b)

This subdivision [(b)] considers the use of specific conduct to attack or support the credibility of a witness. (See rule 609 for the admissibility of a criminal conviction.) The rule corresponds to existing practice in Minnesota. It is permissible to impeach a witness on cross-examination by prior misconduct if the prior misconduct is probative of untruthfulness. See State v. Gress, 250 Minn. 337, 343, 84 N.W.2d 616, 621 (1957); Note 36 Minn. L.Rev. 724, 733 (1952). However, because this is deemed an inquiry into a collateral matter the cross-examiner may not disprove an answer by extrinsic evidence. State v. Nelson, 148 Minn. 285, 296, 181 N.W. 850, 855 (1921). In criminal cases the courts have been somewhat reluctant to permit such evidence if it tends to involve matters that might prejudice the jury. See State v. Haney, 219 Minn. 518, 520, 18 N.W.2d 315, 316 (1945).

The last sentence in rule 608 preserves the rights of an accused or other witness to assert the Fifth Amendment privilege as to those questions which relate only to credibility. If the question relates to matters other than credibility this rule has no application.

Advisory Committee Comment—2006 Amendments

Rule 608 (b).

The amendment in rule 608(b) comes from the amendment to Fed. R. Evid. 608(b), which was added in 2003. The language clarifies that the restriction on extrinsic evidence applies only if the witness is being impeached on the issue of character for truthfulness. If the witness is impeached by evidence of bias the denial may be contradicted by extrinsic evidence. For example, if a witness denies the plaintiff is her son, the denial may be challenged by extrinsic evidence. If the witness denies that she lied on a job application, the denial may not be disproved by extrinsic evidence.

The limitation on extrinsic evidence applies only to evidence that requires testimony from another witness. Counsel may contradict the witness with evidence offered through the testimony of the witness being impeached. For example, if the witness denies lying on a job application, counsel may try to refresh the witness' recollection by showing the witness the application. Counsel may offer the job application if the foundation for admitting it can be established through the testimony of the witness being impeached. If the witness denies lying on a job application, and the lie cannot be established through cross-examination of that witness, counsel may not disprove the denial by calling another witness. Because this is an inquiry into a collateral matter counsel may not call a rebuttal witness to lay the foundation for admitting the job application and proving the lie. *Compare Carter v. Hewitt*, 617 F.2d 961, 969–70 (3d Cir. 1980) (admitting, as non-extrinsic evidence, a letter that defendant admitted authoring) *with United States v. Martz*, 964 F.2d 787, 788 (8th Cir. 1992) (precluding defendant from introducing witness' plea agreements after witness denied making any agreement stating that documents are not admissible under rule 608(b) "merely to show a witness' general character for truthfulness"). *See generally* Roger C. Park, David P. Leonard & Steven H. Goldberg, Evidence Law: A Student's Guide to the Law of Evidence as Applied in American Trials 485 (2d ed. 2004).

Rule 608 (c).

Rule 608(c) incorporates the holding in *State v. Fallin*, 540 N.W.2d 518, 522 (Minn. 1995) (placing burden on the prosecutor before allowing cross-examination of defendant or defense witnesses about acts of misconduct reflecting on truthfulness). The balancing test taken from *Fallin* is not the rule 403 test favoring admissibility unless probative value is "substantially outweighed" by unfair prejudice. Under this test the court should not allow the cross-examination if probative value and unfair prejudice are closely balanced. *Fallin*, 540 N.W.2d at 522. The evidence should not be allowed unless probative value on the issue of credibility outweighs the potential for unfair prejudice.

The rule follows the holding in *Fallin*. Neither the rule nor the Court's opinion addresses the issue of whether the accused or a party in a civil case must provide notice and satisfy the same evidentiary standard if counsel attempts to impeach a witness under this rule. Ethical requirements in Minn. R. Prof. Cond. 3.4(e) would be applicable in all cases to restrict lawyers from alluding "to any matter that the lawyer does not reasonably believe is relevant or that will not be supported by admissible evidence." Nothing in this rule would limit the rights and obligations in discovery. The Committee recognizes that in some circumstances Minn. R. Crim. P. 9 provides for differing obligations of discovery between the prosecutor and the defense. *See also State v. Patterson*, 587 N.W.2d 45, 50 (Minn. 1998) ("Discovery rules are 'based on the proposition that the ends of justice will best be served by a system of liberal discovery which gives both parties the maximum possible amount of information with which to prepare their cases and thereby reduces the possibility of surprise at trial' and are 'designed to enhance the search for truth'") (citations omitted).

RULE 609. IMPEACHMENT BY EVIDENCE OF CONVICTION OF CRIME

(a) General rule. For the purpose of attacking the credibility of a witness, evidence that the witness has been convicted of a crime shall be admitted only if the crime (1) was punishable by death or imprisonment in excess of one year under the law under which the witness was convicted, and the court determines that the probative value of admitting this evidence outweighs its prejudicial effect, or (2) involved dishonesty or false statement, regardless of the punishment.

(b) Time limit. Evidence of a conviction under this rule is not admissible if a period of more than ten years has elapsed since the date of the conviction or of the release of the witness from the confinement imposed for that conviction, whichever is the later date, unless the court determines, in the interests of justice, that the probative value of the conviction supported by specific facts and circumstances substantially outweighs its prejudicial effect. However, evidence of a conviction more than 10 years old as calculated herein, is not admissible unless the proponent gives to the adverse party sufficient advance written notice of intent to use such evidence to provide the adverse party with a fair opportunity to contest the use of such evidence.

(c) Effect of pardon, annulment, vacation or certificate of rehabilitation. Evidence of a conviction is not admissible under this rule if (1) the conviction has been the subject of a pardon, annulment, vacation or certificate of rehabilitation or other equivalent procedure based on a finding of the rehabilitation of the person convicted, and that person has not been convicted of a subsequent crime which was punishable by death or imprisonment in excess of one year, or (2) the conviction has been the subject of a pardon, annulment, vacation or other equivalent procedure based on a finding of innocence.

(d) Juvenile adjudications. Evidence of juvenile adjudications is not admissible under this rule unless permitted by statute or required by the state or federal constitution.

(e) Pendency of appeal. The pendency of an appeal therefrom does not render evidence of a conviction inadmissible. Evidence of the pendency of an appeal is admissible.

Adopted April 1, 1977, eff. July 1, 1977. Amended Dec. 28, 1989, eff. Jan. 1, 1990.

Committee Comment—1989

Rule 609(a)

The question of impeachment by past conviction has given rise to much controversy. Originally convicted felons were incompetent to give testimony in courts. It was later determined that they should be permitted to testify but that the prior conviction would be evidence which the jury could consider in assessing the credibility of the witness. However, not all convictions reflect on the individual's character for truthfulness. In cases where a conviction is not probative of truthfulness the admission of such evidence theoretically on the issue of credibility breeds prejudice. The potential for prejudice is greater when the accused in a criminal case is impeached by past crimes that only indirectly speak to character for truthfulness or untruthfulness. The rule represents a workable solution to the problem. Those crimes which involve dishonesty or false statement are admissible for impeachment purposes because they involve acts directly bearing on a person's character for truthfulness. Dishonesty in this rule refers only to those crimes involving untruthful conduct. When dealing with other serious crimes, which do not directly involve dishonesty or false statement the Court has some discretion to exclude the offer where the probative value is outweighed by prejudice. Convictions for lesser offenses not involving dishonesty or false statement are inadmissible.

The substantive amendment is designed to conform this rule to the accepted practice in Minnesota, which is to allow the accused to introduce evidence of past crimes in the direct examination of the accused.

Contrary to the practice in federal courts, the defendant can preserve the issue at a motion in limine and need not testify to litigate the issue in post trial motions and appeals. Compare State v. Jones, 271 N.W.2d 534 (Minn.1978) with Luce v. United States, 469 U.S. 38, 105 S.Ct. 460, 83 L.Ed.2d 443 (1984). The trial judge should make explicit findings on the record as to the factors considered and the reasons for admitting or excluding the evidence. If the conviction is admitted, the court should give a limiting instruction to the jury whether or not one is requested. State v. Bissell, 368 N.W.2d 281 (Minn.1985).

Rule 609(b)

The rule places a ten year limit on the admissibility of convictions. This limitation is based on the assumption that after such an extended period of time the conviction has lost its probative value on the issue of credibility. Provision is made for going beyond the ten year limitation in unusual cases where the general assumption does not apply.

The rule will supersede Minn.Stat. § 595.07 (1974).

Rule 609(c)

The rule is predicated on the assumption that if the conviction has been "set aside" for reasons that suggest rehabilitation, the probative value of the conviction on the issue of credibility is diminished. For example, pardons pursuant to Minn.Const. art. 5, § 7 (restructured 1974), or Minn.Stats. § 638.02 (1974) would operate to make a prior conviction inadmissible as would a vacation of the conviction or subsequent nullification pursuant to Minn.Stats. §§ 609.166–168 (1974), or Minn.Stats. § 242.01 et seq. (1974). A restoration of civil rights, which does not reflect findings of rehabilitation would not qualify under the rule. See Minn.Stats. § 609.165 (1974). If there is a later conviction, as defined in the rule, the assumption of rehabilitation is no longer valid. If otherwise relevant and competent both convictions may be used for impeachment purposes. Obviously, if the first conviction is "set aside" based on a finding of innocence, the conviction would have no more probative value under any circumstances. See rules 401–403.

Rule 609(d)

The amendment is a change in style not substance. Minn.Stats. § 260.211, subd. 2 (1988) does permit the disclosure of juvenile records in limited circumstances. Pursuant to Minn.Stats. § 260.211, subd. 1 (1988) a juvenile adjudication is not to be considered a conviction nor is it to impose civil liabilities that accompany the conviction of a crime. Rule 609(d) reflects this policy by precluding impeachment by evidence of a prior juvenile adjudication. It is conceivable that the state policy protecting juveniles as embodied in the statute and the evidentiary rule might conflict with certain constitutional provisions, e.g., the sixth amendment confrontation clause. Under these circumstances the evidentiary rule becomes inoperative. See Davis v. Alaska, 94 S.Ct. 1105, 415 U.S. 308, 39 L.Ed.2d 347 (1974), construed in State v. Schilling, 270 N.W.2d 769 (Minn.1978).

RULE 610. RELIGIOUS BELIEFS OR OPINIONS

Evidence of the beliefs or opinions of a witness on matters of religion is not admissible for the purpose of showing that by reason of their nature the witness' credibility is impaired or enhanced.

Adopted April 1, 1977, eff. July 1, 1977. Amended Dec. 28, 1989, eff. Jan. 1, 1990.

RULE 611. MODE AND ORDER OF INTERROGATION AND PRESENTATION

(a) Control by court. The court shall exercise reasonable control over the mode and order of interrogating witnesses and presenting evidence so as to (1) make the interrogation and presentation effective for the ascertainment of the truth, (2) avoid needless consumption of time, and (3) protect witnesses from harassment or undue embarrassment.

(b) Scope of cross-examination. Cross-examination should be limited to the subject matter of the direct examination and matters affecting the credibility of the witness. The court may, in the exercise of discretion, permit inquiry into additional matters as if on direct examination. An accused who testifies in a criminal case may be cross-examined on any matter relevant to any issue in the case, including credibility.

(c) Leading questions. Leading questions should not be used on the direct examination of a witness except as may be necessary to develop the witness testimony. Ordinarily leading questions should be permitted on cross-examination. When a party calls a hostile witness, an adverse party, or a witness identified with an adverse party, interrogation may be by leading questions.

Adopted April 1, 1977, eff. July 1, 1977. Amended Dec. 28, 1989, eff. Jan. 1, 1990.

Committee Comment—1977

Rule 611(a)

The mechanics of the trial process and the method and order of interrogating witnesses is left to the discretion of the trial court. The rule makes it clear that the court must bear the ultimate responsibility for the proper conduct of the trial. The rule presents three general principles which should guide the court in its exercise of "reasonable control." See also rule 102.

Rule 611(b)

The court is also given some discretion over the scope of cross-examination. Generally, the scope of cross-examination should be limited to the subject matter of the direct examination and matters affecting the credibility of the witness. Consistent with rule 611(a) and the court's power to control the order of proof, the court may permit a broader scope of cross-examination in the appropriate case. However, inquiries into matters which were not the subject of direct examination will be treated as if originating from direct examination. The rule makes it clear that the scope of cross-examination of an accused who takes the witness stand in a criminal trial is limited only by principles of relevancy and the Fifth Amendment. See, e.g., rules 104(d), 608(b).

Rule 611(c)

The use of leading questions is left to the discretion of the trial court. Generally, leading questions should not be permitted when the witness is sympathetic to the examiner. However, for preliminary matters and the occasional situation in which leading questions are necessary to develop testimony because of temporary lapse of memory, mental defect, immaturity of a witness, etc., the court may permit inquiry by leading questions on direct examination. When a party calls the opposing party, a witness identified with the opposing party, or a hostile witness leading questions should also be permitted.

Usually there is a right to ask leading questions on cross-examination. When the witness is clearly sympathetic to the examiner the court has discretion to prohibit the use of leading questions. For example, if a party defendant is called as a witness by the plaintiff for direct examination, leading questions should not be permitted on the cross-examination by the defendant's own attorney. This rule and rule 607 incorporate and expand Minn.R.Civ.P. 43.02. The committee urges that the procedural rule be repealed.

RULE 612. WRITING USED TO REFRESH MEMORY

Except as otherwise provided in criminal proceedings by the rules of criminal procedure, if a witness uses a writing to refresh memory for the purpose of testifying, either—

(1) while testifying, or

(2) before testifying, if the court in its discretion determines it is necessary in the interests of justice,—

an adverse party is entitled to have the writing produced at the hearing, to inspect it, to cross-examine the witness thereon, and if otherwise admissible to introduce in evidence those portions which relate to the testimony of the witness. If it is claimed that the writing contains matters not related to the subject matter of the testimony the court shall examine the writing in camera, excise any portions not so related, and order delivery of the remainder to the party entitled thereto. Any portion withheld over objections shall be preserved and made available to the appellate court in the event of an appeal. If a writing is not produced or delivered pursuant to order under this rule, the court shall make any order justice requires.

Adopted April 1, 1977, eff. July 1, 1977. Amended Dec. 28, 1989, eff. Jan. 1, 1990.

Committee Comment—1977

The rule continues existing practice, requiring disclosure of any statements that are used by a witness for the purpose of refreshing his recollection on the witness stand. Once the witness' recollection is refreshed the witness can testify from present recollection. Documents used for refreshing recollection need not satisfy any requirements of trustworthiness, authenticity, etc. This should be contrasted with the process involved when a witness has no present recollection and attempts to introduce a document into evidence pursuant to rule 803(5). The rule substantially expands the common law approach by requiring production, within the discretion of the Court, of writings that were reviewed by a witness in preparation for testifying. Most of the writings that would be used for these purposes would be discoverable prior to trial pursuant to Minn.R.Civ.P. 26–37 and Minn.R.Crim.P. 9. The rule is expressly made subject to the rules of criminal procedure. Specifically the operative provisions of the criminal rules would be rules 9.01 subd. 3 and 9.02 subd. 3 which preclude inquiry into legal theories, opinions, and conclusions as well as certain reports and internal documents. Additionally, rule 9.01 provides for the timing of the disclosure in certain cases.

Although it was the committee's view that in most cases the materials reviewed by a witness prior to testifying should be turned over upon request, it was thought that the trial court should have some discretion in the matter. *Cf.* State v. Grunau, 273 Minn. 315, 141 N.W.2d 815 (1966). Some flexibility might be necessary in the large case if the witness reviewed an extraordinary amount of documentary material and in the very small case where the attorney might not have access to all of the materials reviewed by a witness prior to trial.

If the statements are turned over, the opposing party may use the statements for cross-examination purposes. If admissible for impeachment purposes or otherwise the statements can be introduced into evidence. The rule should not be read to disregard applicable privileges that are validly asserted to protect the confidentiality of a communication. See rule 501. The rule does not speak to the issue that will be raised in civil cases if the document that is used to refresh a witness' recollection falls under the work product doctrine. See Minn.R.Civ.P. 26.02 subd. 3. The issue is left for development in the traditional common law fashion. See 3 J. Weinstein and M. Berger, Weinstein's Evidence ¶ 612(04) (1975).

RULE 613. PRIOR STATEMENTS OF WITNESSES

(a) Examining witness concerning prior statement. In examining a witness concerning a prior statement made by the witness, whether written or not, the statement need not be shown nor its contents disclosed to the witness at that time, but on request the same shall be shown or disclosed to opposing counsel.

(b) Extrinsic evidence of prior inconsistent statement. Extrinsic evidence of a prior inconsistent statement by a witness is not admissible unless the witness is afforded a prior opportunity to explain or deny the same and the opposite party is afforded an opportunity to interrogate the witness thereon, or the interests of justice otherwise require. This provision does not apply to admissions of a party-opponent as defined in Rule 801(d)(2).

Adopted April 1, 1977, eff. July 1, 1977. Amended Dec. 28, 1989, eff. Jan. 1, 1990.

Committee Comment—1977

Rule 613(a)

Prior statements of a witness may be used for cross-examination purposes without disclosing the statement to the witness. The rule deviates from the longstanding practice in most American jurisdictions which require disclosure to the witness before any such cross-examination. This practice has been soundly criticized as depriving the cross-examiner of a vital tool. See C. McCormick Evidence § 28 (2d ed. 1972); 4 Wigmore, Evidence § 1260 (Chadbourn ed. 1972). The rule is based on the belief that the truth finding function of cross-examination will be better served by permitting such examination without providing the witness with a warning as to where the examiner is going. The rule provides for disclosure to the opposing counsel to insure the integrity of the process.

Rule 613(b)

If a prior inconsistent statement is offered for impeachment purposes by means of extrinsic evidence this subdivision is applicable. The committee altered the federal rule in order to continue the existing practice of requiring prior disclosure to the witness and an opportunity to explain before offering a prior inconsistent statement into evidence. This procedure would obviate the necessity for proof by extrinsic evidence if the witness admits making the inconsistent statement. In the appropriate case the court has the discretion to waive this foundational requirement. See gen. Carroll v. Pratt, 247 Minn. 198, 203, 204, 76 N.W.2d 693, 697, 698 (1956).

The rule does not apply to party admissions that are admissible as substantive evidence. See rule 801(d)(2). See also Minn.R.Civ.P. 32.01 subd. 2.

RULE 614. CALLING AND INTERROGATING WITNESSES

(a) Calling by court. The court may, on its own motion or at the suggestion of a party, call witnesses, and all parties are entitled to cross-examine witnesses thus called.

(b) Interrogation by court. The court may interrogate witnesses, whether called by itself or by a party.

(c) Objections. Objections to the calling of witnesses by the court or to interrogation by it may be made at the time or at the next available opportunity when the jury is not present.

(d) Juror interrogation in criminal trials. Jurors may not suggest questions or interrogate witnesses in criminal trials.

Adopted April 1, 1977, eff. July 1, 1977. Amended July 18, 2006, eff. Sept. 1, 2006.

Committee Comment—1977

Trial courts have traditionally been vested with the power to call and interrogate witnesses. This right is consistent with the responsibility of the Court in insuring a speedy and just determination of the issues. See rules 102 and 611(a). The rule does not immunize the trial court's action from review. The right to call and question witnesses can be abused by the trial court which assumes an advocate's position, particularly in a jury trial. The precise manner and extent of questioning by the Court cannot be reduced to a simple rule of evidence and must be developed on a case by case basis. United States Supreme Court Advisory Committee Note. See also State v. Rasmussen, 268 Minn. 42, 44–46, 128 N.W.2d 289, 290, 291, certiorari denied 85 S.Ct. 267, 379 U.S. 916, 13 L.Ed.2d 187 (1964).

A specific objection is required to preserve the issue for appeal. See rule 103. However, the objection need not be made contemporaneously with the objectionable act if the jury is present. The objection can be made at the next available opportunity when the jury is absent.

Advisory Committee Comment—2006 Amendments

The amendment precluding juror questioning in criminal cases codifies the holding in *State v. Costello*, 646 N.W.2d 204, 214–15 (Minn. 2002). Consistent with the opinion in *Costello*, the rule does not address the issue of whether jurors may ask questions in civil cases.

RULE 615. EXCLUSION OF WITNESSES

At the request of a party the court may order witnesses excluded so that they cannot hear the testimony of other witnesses, and it may make the order of its own motion.

Adopted April 1, 1977, eff. July 1, 1977.

Committee Comment—1989

The rule conforms to existing law in Minnesota and is consistent with Minn.R.Crim.P. 26.03 subd. 7. The rule, unlike the federal rule, leaves the issue subject to the discretion of the trial court. A request for sequestration in criminal cases rarely should be denied. State v. Jones, 347 N.W.2d 796 (Minn.1984); State v. Garden, 267 Minn. 97, 125 N.W.2d 591 (1963). The committee agrees, however, with the Advisory Committee Note to Fed. R.Evid. 615 that investigating officers, agents who were involved in the transaction being litigated, or experts essential to advise counsel in the litigation can be essential to the trial process and should not be excluded.

RULE 616. BIAS OF WITNESS

For the purpose of attacking the credibility of a witness, evidence of bias, prejudice, or interest of the witness for or against any party to the case is admissible.

Adopted Dec. 28, 1989, eff. Jan. 1, 1990.

Committee Comment—1989

Rule 616 is adopted from the Uniform Rules of Evidence. Rule 616 codifies United States v. Abel, 469 U.S. 45, 105 S.Ct. 465, 83 L.Ed.2d 450 (1984) which in turn reaffirmed existing practice. Thus, the rule does not constitute a change in practice. The committee viewed the rule as useful, however, to reiterate that bias, prejudice, or interest of a witness is a fact of consequence under Rule 401. Further, the rule should make it clear that bias, prejudice, or interest is not a collateral matter, and can be established by extrinsic evidence. See State v. Underwood, 281 N.W.2d 337 (Minn.1979); State v. Waddell, 308 N.W.2d 303 (Minn.1981); State v. Garceau, 370 N.W.2d 34 (Minn.App.1985). Included in bias, prejudice, or interest is evidence that the witness is being paid by a party.

RULE 617. CONVERSATION WITH DECEASED OR INSANE PERSON

A witness is not precluded from giving evidence of or concerning any conversations with, or admissions of a deceased or insane party or person merely because the witness is a party to the action or a person interested in the event thereof.

Adopted April 1, 1977, eff. July 1, 1977. Amended Dec. 28, 1989, eff. Jan. 1, 1990.

Committee Comment—1989

This rule, former Minn.R.Evid. 616, was renumbered to permit the inclusion of Rule 616, Bias of Witness, in a manner consistent with the organization of the Uniform Rules of Evidence. This rule supersedes Minn.Stats. § 594.04 (1974), which is known to the bench and bar of Minnesota as the "Dead Man's Statute." The purpose of this statute was to reduce the possibility of perjury in cases of this type. However, the statute was subject to all the problems and potential for injustice which are inherent in a rule which excludes otherwise admissible evidence.

The evidentiary rule represents a considered opinion that the protection which the statute had offered to decedents' estates was not sufficient to justify the problems it created for honest litigants with legitimate claims. Much of the rationale for abolishing the "Dead Man's Statute" is set out in detail in In re Estate of Lea, 301 Minn. 253, 222 N.W.2d 92 (1974).

ARTICLE 7. OPINIONS AND EXPERT TESTIMONY

RULE 701. OPINION TESTIMONY BY LAY WITNESS

If the witness is not testifying as an expert, the witness' testimony in the form of opinion or inferences is limited to those opinions or inferences which are (a) rationally based on the perception of the witness and (b) helpful to a clear understanding of the witness' testimony or the determination of a fact in issue.

Adopted April 1, 1977, eff. July 1, 1977. Amended Dec. 28, 1989, eff. Jan. 1, 1990.

Committee Comment—1977

The rule is consistent with existing practice in Minnesota. The rule permits testimony by means of opinion and inference when it is based on first-hand knowledge and will be helpful to an effective presentation of the issues. Because the distinction between fact and opinion is frequently impossible to delineate, the rule is stated in the nature of a general principle, leaving specific application to the discretion of the trial court.

RULE 702. TESTIMONY BY EXPERTS

If scientific, technical, or other specialized knowledge will assist the trier of fact to understand the evidence or to determine a fact in issue, a witness qualified as an expert by knowledge, skill, experience, training, or education, may testify thereto in the form of an opinion or otherwise. The opinion must have foundational reliability. In addition, if the opinion or evidence involves novel scientific theory, the proponent must establish that the underlying scientific evidence is generally accepted in the relevant scientific community.

Adopted April 1, 1977, eff. July 1, 1977. Amended July 18, 2006, eff. Sept. 1, 2006.

Committee Comment—1977

The admissibility of expert opinion has traditionally rested in the discretion of the trial court. This discretion is primarily exercised in two areas:

1. determining if an opinion can assist the trier of fact in formulating a correct resolution of the questions raised; and

2. deciding if the witness is sufficiently qualified as an expert in a given subject area to justify testimony in the form of an opinion.

There will be no change in existing practice in this regard.

The rule is not limited to scientific, or technical areas, but is phrased broadly to include all areas of specialized knowledge. If an opinion could assist the trier of fact it should be admitted subject to proper qualification of the witness. The qualifications of the expert need not stem from formal training, and may include any knowledge, skill, or experience that would provide the background necessary for a meaningful opinion on the subject. The rule also contemplates expert testimony in the form of lecture or explanation. The expert may educate the jury so the jurors can draw their own inference or conclusion from the evidence presented.

Advisory Committee Comment—2006 Amendments

The amendment codifies existing Minnesota case law on the admissibility of expert testimony. The trial judge should require that all expert testimony under rule 702 be based on a reliable foundation. The proposed amendment does not purport to describe what that foundation must look like for all types of expert testimony. The required foundation will vary depending on the context of the opinion, but must lead to an opinion that will assist the trier of fact. If the opinion or evidence involves a scientific test, the case law requires that the judge assure that the proponent establish that "'the test itself is reliable and that its administration in the particular instance conformed to the procedure necessary to ensure reliability.'" *Goeb v. Tharaldson*, 615 N.W.2d 800, 814 (Minn. 2000) (quoting *State v. Moore*, 458 N.W.2d 90, 98 (Minn. 1990)).

In addition, if the opinion involves novel scientific theory, the Minnesota Supreme Court requires that the proponent also establish that the evidence is generally accepted in the relevant scientific community. The rule does not define what is novel, leaving this for resolution by the courts. *See, e.g., State v. Klawitter*, 518 N.W.2d 577, 578–86 (Minn. 1994) (addressing whether 12–step drug recognition protocol involves novel scientific theory); *State v. Hodgson*, 512 N.W.2d 95, 98 (Minn. 1994) (ruling that bite-mark analysis does not involve novel scientific theory).

The Minnesota Supreme Court provided the standard for admissibility of novel scientific testimony in *Goeb*. The court stated:

Therefore, when novel scientific evidence is offered, the district court must determine whether it is generally accepted in the relevant scientific community. *See Moore*, 458 N.W.2d at 97–98; *Schwartz*, 447 N.W.2d at 424–26. In addition, the particular scientific evidence in each case must be shown to have foundational reliability. *See Moore*, 458 N.W.2d at 98; *Schwartz*, 447 N.W.2d at 426–28. Foundational reliability "requires the 'proponent of a * * * test [to] establish that the test itself is reliable and that its administration in the particular instance conformed to the procedure necessary to ensure reliability.'" *Moore*, 458 N.W.2d at 98 (alteration in original) (quoting *State v. Dille*, 258 N.W.2d 565, 567 (Minn. 1977)). Finally, as with all testimony by experts, the evidence must satisfy the requirements of Minn. R. Evid. 402 and 702—be relevant, be given by a witness qualified as an expert, and be helpful to the trier of fact. *See State v. Nystrom*, 596 N.W.2d 256, 259 (Minn. 1999). *Goeb*, 615 N.W.2d at 814.

In *State v. Roman Nose*, 649 N.W.2d 815, 819 (Minn. 2002), the court described the standard in a different way:

Put another way, the *Frye–Mack* standard asks first whether experts in the field widely share the view that the results of scientific testing are scientifically reliable, and second whether the laboratory conducting the tests in the individual case complied with appropriate standards and controls.

Finally, in *State v. MacLennan*, 702 N.W.2d 219, 230 (Minn. 2005) the court explained the standard:

Under the *Frye–Mack* standard, a novel scientific theory may be admitted if two requirements are satisfied. The district court must first determine whether the novel scientific evidence offered is generally accepted in the relevant scientific community. Second, the court must determine whether the novel scientific evidence offered is shown to have foundational reliability. As with all expert testimony, the evidence must comply with Minn. R. Evid. Rules 402 and 702; that is, it must be relevant, helpful to the trier of fact, and given by a witness qualified as an expert. The proponent of the novel scientific evidence bears the burden of establishing the proper foundation for the admissibility of the evidence. (Citations omitted).

RULE 703. BASES OF OPINION TESTIMONY BY EXPERTS

(a) The facts or data in the particular case upon which an expert bases an opinion or inference may be those perceived by or made known to the expert at or before the hearing. If of a type reasonably relied upon by experts in the particular field in forming opinions or inferences upon the subject, the facts or data need not be admissible in evidence.

(b) Underlying expert data must be independently admissible in order to be received upon direct examination; provided that when good cause is shown in civil cases and the underlying data is particularly trustworthy, the court may admit the data under this rule for the limited purpose of showing the basis for the expert's opinion. Nothing in this rule restricts admissibility of underlying expert data when inquired into on cross-examination.

Adopted April 1, 1977, eff. July 1, 1977. Amended Dec. 28, 1989, eff. Jan. 1, 1990.

Committee Comment—1989

The rule represents a fresh approach to the question of expert testimony—one which more closely conforms to modern realities. Consistent with existing practice the expert can base an opinion on firsthand knowledge of the facts, facts revealed at trial by testimony of other witnesses, or by way of hypothetical questions. The rule also permits the opinion to be based on data or facts presented to the witness prior to trial. The sufficiency of facts or data in establishing an adequate foundation for receiving the opinion is subject to a two part test:

1. are these facts and data of a type relied upon by experts in this field when forming inferences or opinions on the subject;

2. is this reliance reasonable?

In explanation the United States Supreme Court Advisory Committee stated:

> [A] physician is his own practice bases his diagnosis on information from numerous sources and of considerable variety, including statements by patients and relatives, reports and opinions from nurses, technicians and other doctors, hospital records, and X-rays. Most of them are admissible in evidence, but only with the expenditure of substantial time in producing and examining various authenticating witnesses. The physician makes life and death decisions in reliance upon them. His validation, expertly performed and subject to cross-examination, ought to suffice for judicial purposes. (citations omitted)
>
> Supreme Court Advisory Committee Note

The requirement that the facts or data be of a type reasonably relied upon by experts in the field provides a check on the trustworthiness of the opinion and its foundation. In determining whether the reliance is reasonable, the judge must be satisfied that the facts and data relied on by the experts in the field are sufficiently trustworthy to insure the validity of the opinion. The sufficiency of the foundation for the opinion testimony could be treated as a preliminary question under rule 104.

The rule is aimed at permitting experts to base opinions on reliable hearsay and other facts that might not be admissible under these rules of evidence. Obviously, a prosecution witness could not base an opinion on evidence that had been seized from a defendant in violation of the Fourth or Fifth Amendments. The application of the "fruit of the poisonous tree doctrine" would mandate such a result. See Wong Sun v. United States, 83 S.Ct. 407, 371 U.S. 471, 9 L.Ed.2d 441 (1963). Similarly, where state policy considerations require that certain matters not be admitted at trial, the state policy should not be thwarted by allowing the same evidence to come in the "back door" in the form of an expert's opinion. See, *e.g.*, Minn.Stats. §§ 595.02 and 169.121 (1974).

This rule deals with the adequacy of the foundation for the opinion. Rule 705 determines the timing and necessity for establishing the foundation at trial. Great emphasis is placed on the use of cross-examination to provide the trier of fact with sufficient information to properly assess the weight to be given any opinion.

Although an expert may rely on inadmissible facts or data in forming an opinion, the inadmissible foundation should not be admitted into evidence simply because it forms the basis for an expert opinion.

In civil cases, upon a showing of good cause, the inadmissible foundation, if trustworthy, can be admitted on direct examination for the limited purpose of establishing the basis for the opinion. See generally Carlson, Policing the Bases of Modern Expert Testimony, 39 Vand.L.Rev. 577 (1986); Federal Rules of Evidence: A Fresh Review and Evaluation, ABA Criminal Justice Section, Rule 703 and accompanying comment, 120 F.R.D. 299, at 369 (1987).

In criminal cases, the inadmissible foundation should not be admitted. Admitting such evidence might violate the accused's right to confrontation. See State v. Towne, 142 Vt. 241, 453 A.2d 1133 (1982).

RULE 704. OPINION ON ULTIMATE ISSUE

Testimony in the form of an opinion or inference otherwise admissible is not objectionable because it embraces an ultimate issue to be decided by the trier of fact.

Adopted April 1, 1977, eff. July 1, 1977.

Committee Comment—1977

Expert and lay witnesses will not be precluded from giving an opinion merely because the opinion embraces an ultimate fact issue to be determined by the jury. If the witness is qualified and the opinion would be helpful to or assist the jury as provided in rules 701–703, the opinion testimony should be permitted. In determining whether or not an opinion would be helpful or of assistance under these rules a distinction should be made between opinions as to factual matters, and opinions involving a legal analysis or mixed questions of law and fact. Opinions of the latter nature are not deemed to be of any use to the trier of fact. The rule is consistent with existing practice in Minnesota as stated in In re Estate of Olson, 176 Minn. 360, 370, 223 N.W. 677, 681 (1929):

> ... Standing alone, the objection that the opinion of a qualified witness is asked upon the very issue and the ultimate one for decision is not sufficient. So long as the matter remains in the realm where opinion evidence is customarily resorted to, there is ordinarily no valid objection to permitting a person who has qualified himself to express an opinion upon the ultimate issue. That is a matter well left to the discretion of the trial judge. While in a will contest the opinion of a witness, lay or scientific, should not be asked as to the testator's capacity to make a valid will, there is certainly no objection to questions concerning his ability to comprehend his property and dispose of it understandingly.

See also In re Estate of Jenks, 291 Minn. 138, 144, 189 N.W.2d 695, 698 (1971).

RULE 705. DISCLOSURE OF FACTS OR DATA UNDERLYING EXPERT OPINION

The expert may testify in terms of opinion or inference and give reasons therefor without prior disclosure of the underlying facts or data, unless the court requires otherwise. The expert may in any event be required to disclose the underlying facts or data on cross-examination.

Adopted April 1, 1977, eff. July 1, 1977. Amended Dec. 28, 1989, eff. Jan. 1, 1990.

Committee Comment—1989

Rule 705 streamlines the presentation of expert testimony leaving it to cross examination to develop weaknesses in the expert's opinion. Obviously, if there is to be effective cross-examination the adverse party must have advance knowledge of the nature of the opinion and the basis for it. The procedural rules provide for much of this information by way of discovery. See Minn.R.Civ.P. 26 and Minn.R.Crim.P. 9.01, subd. 1(4). In the case where the adverse party has not been provided with the necessary information to conduct an effective cross-examination, the Court should, if requested by the adverse party, exercise its discretion under the rule and require that a full foundation be established on direct examination.

RULE 706. COURT APPOINTED EXPERTS

(a) Appointment. The court may on its own motion or on the motion of any party enter an order to show cause why expert witnesses should not be appointed, and may request the parties to submit nominations. The court may appoint any expert witnesses agreed upon by the parties, and may appoint expert witnesses of its own selection. An expert witness shall not be appointed by the court unless the witness consents to act. A witness so appointed shall be informed of the witness' duties by the court in writing, a copy of which shall be filed with the clerk, or at a conference in which the parties shall have opportunity to participate. A witness so appointed shall advise the parties of the witness' findings, if any; the witness' deposition may be taken by any party; and the witness may be called to testify by the court or any party. The witness shall be subject to cross-examination by each party, including a party calling the witness.

(b) Compensation. Expert witnesses so appointed are entitled to reasonable compensation in whatever sum the court may allow. The compensation thus fixed is payable from funds which may be provided by law in criminal cases and civil actions and proceedings involving just compensation under the fifth amendment. In other civil actions and proceedings the compensation shall be paid by the parties in such proportion and at such time as the court directs, and thereafter charged in like manner as other costs.

(c) Disclosure of appointment. In the exercise of its discretion, the court may authorize disclosure to the jury of the fact that the court appointed the expert witness.

(d) Parties' experts of own selection. Nothing in this rule limits the parties in calling expert witnesses of their own selection.

Adopted April 1, 1977, eff. July 1, 1977. Amended Dec. 28, 1989, eff. Jan. 1, 1990.

Committee Comment—1977

This rule implements rule 614 setting up the appropriate procedure to be used in calling an expert as a court witness. By recommending this rule the committee did not intend to encourage the use of court appointed expert witnesses. In the appropriate case, a trial judge might find that the use of a court expert would be necessary to a fair, expeditious, and inexpensive proceeding. See *e.g.*, Minn.Stats. § 176.391(2) (1974) which provides for the appointment of impartial experts in Workmen's Compensation proceedings.

However, court experts pose a potential danger. Particularly in a jury trial such an expert might unfairly tip the balance in the adversary process. The rule provides for ample opportunity for the parties to provide the court with the necessary information with which to make the decision whether to call an expert as a court witness.

ARTICLE 8. HEARSAY

RULE 801. DEFINITIONS

The following definitions apply under this article:

(a) Statement. A "statement" is (1) an oral or written assertion or (2) nonverbal conduct of a person, if it is intended by the person as an assertion.

(b) Declarant. A "declarant" is a person who makes a statement.

(c) Hearsay. "Hearsay" is a statement, other than one made by the declarant while testifying at the trial or hearing, offered in evidence to prove the truth of the matter asserted.

(d) Statements which are not hearsay. A statement is not hearsay if—

(1) *Prior statement by witness.* The declarant testifies at the trial or hearing and is subject to cross-examination concerning the statement, and the statement is (A) inconsistent with the declarant's testimony, and was given under oath subject to the penalty of perjury at a trial, hearing, or other proceeding, or in a deposition, or (B) consistent with the declarant's testimony and helpful to the trier of fact in evaluating the declarant's credibility as a witness, or (C) one of identification of a person made after perceiving the person, if the court is satisfied that the circumstances of the prior identification demonstrate the reliability of the prior identification, or (D) a statement describing or explaining an event or condition made while the declarant was perceiving the event or condition or immediately thereafter.

(2) *Statement by party-opponent.* The statement is offered against a party and is (A) the party's own statement, in either an individual or a representative capacity, or (B) a statement of which the party has manifested an adoption or belief in its truth, or (C) a statement by a person authorized by the party to make a statement concerning the subject, or (D) a statement by the party's agent or servant concerning a matter within the scope of the agency or employment, made during the existence of the relationship, or (E) a statement by a coconspirator of the party. In order to have a coconspirator's declaration admitted, there must be a showing, by a preponderance of the evidence, (i) that there was a conspiracy involving both the declarant and the party against whom the statement is offered, and (ii) that the statement was made in the course of and in furtherance of the conspiracy. In determining whether the required showing has been made, the Court may consider the declarant's statement; provided, however, the declarant's statement alone shall not be sufficient to establish the existence of a conspiracy for purposes of this rule. The statement may be admitted, in the discretion of the Court, before the required showing has been made. In the event the statement is admitted and the required showing is not made, however, the Court shall grant a mistrial, or give curative instructions, or grant the party such relief as is just in the circumstances.

Adopted April 1, 1977, eff. July 1, 1977. Amended Dec. 28, 1989, eff. Jan. 1, 1990; July 18, 2006, eff. Sept. 1, 2006.

Committee Comment—1989

Rule 801(a, b, c)

Rules 801(a), (b), and (c) provide the general definition of hearsay. The definition is largely consistent with the common law. Hearsay is an out of court statement that is used in court to prove the truth of the matter asserted in the statement. If the out of court statement is being offered for some other purpose, such as to prove knowledge, notice, or for impeachment purposes it is not hearsay. "Statement" is defined to include oral and written assertions as well as non-verbal conduct that is intended as an assertion, *e.g.*, nodding of the head up and down to signify assent to a proposition. Non-verbal conduct that is not intended as an assertion is not a statement and is not affected by the hearsay rule. Hence, the rule puts to rest whatever lingering authority Wright v. Tatham, 7 Ad. & Ell. 313 (Ex.Ch.1837), aff'd. 5 Cl. & Fin. 670, 7 Eng.Rep. 559 (H.L.1838) has in Minnesota. Wright involved a will contest in which it was claimed that the testator was not competent at the time he executed his will. To prove competence certain letters were introduced on the theory that the authors of the letters considered the testator to be fully alert or letters of this nature would not have been written.

As "implied assertions of the authors" the letters were excluded as hearsay. Under the rule the conduct of writing a letter would not be hearsay and the admissibility of such conduct would be determined under a relevancy analysis. See Article 4.

Rule 801(d)(1)

Adoption of this rule will change Minnesota law as stated in State v. Saporen, 205 Minn. 358, 285 N.W. 898 (1939). The Court in *Saporen* held that prior inconsistent statements of witnesses are admissible only for impeachment purposes. But see Gave v. Pyrofax Gas Corp., 274 Minn. 210, 214, 215, 143 N.W.2d 242, 246 (1966). However, the Court on two occasions has indicated its willingness to reconsider the *Saporen* rule in the appropriate circumstances. See State v. Slapnicher, 276 Minn. 237, 241, 149 N.W.2d 390, 393 (1967), State v. Marchand, 302 Minn. 510, 225 N.W.2d 537, 538 (1975).

Four reasons were cited to support the decision in *Saporen*:

1. Lack of oath;
2. Lack of cross-examination;
3. A different ruling might encourage the manufacture of evidence by third degree or entrapment methods;
4. If inconsistent statements were admitted, consistent statements should be admitted.

It was the Committee's belief that the rule eliminates all but the second concern of the Court in *Saporen*. The requirement that the statement must be given under oath subject to the penalty of perjury is retained. Secondly, the witness must be presently available for cross-examination or explanation of the prior statement.

As amended, Rule 801(d)(1)(B) permits prior consistent statements of a witness to be received as substantive evidence if they are helpful to the trier of fact in evaluating the credibility of the witness. Originally, Rule 801(d)(1)(B) applied only to statements that were offered to rebut a charge of recent fabrication or undue influence or motive. The language of the original rule, if read literally, was too restrictive. For example, evidence of a prior consistent statement should be received as substantive evidence to rebut an inference of unintentional inaccuracy, even in the absence of any charge of fabrication or impropriety. Also, evidence of prompt complaint in sexual assault cases should be received as substantive evidence in the prosecution's case in chief, without the need for any showing that the evidence is being used to rebut a charge of "recent fabrication or improper influence or motive."

The amended rule is consistent with the result in State v. Arndt, 285 N.W.2d 478 (Minn.1979). Because of the restrictive language of former Rule 801(d)(1)(B), however, the Arndt Court did not rely upon that rule. Instead, it relied upon the theory that the prior statement was not offered for the truth of the matter asserted, and hence was not hearsay under the definition set forth in Rule 801(c). As amended, Rule 801(d)(1)(B) eliminates the need for reliance upon this theory, and thereby eliminates the need for a limiting instruction informing the jury that the evidence cannot be used to prove the truth of the matter asserted.

Amended Rule 801(d)(1)(B) only applies to prior statements that are consistent with the declarant's trial testimony and that are helpful in evaluating the credibility of the declarant as a witness. Thus, when a witness' prior statement contains assertions about events that have not been described by the witness in trial testimony, those assertions are not helpful in supporting the credibility of the witness and are not admissible under this rule.

Even when a prior consistent statement deals with events described in the witness' trial testimony, amended Rule 801(d)(1)(B) does not make the prior statement automatically admissible. The trial judge has discretion under Rules 611 and 403 to control the mode and order of presenting evidence and to exclude cumulative evidence. Thus, the trial judge may prevent the witness from reading a prepared statement before giving oral testimony, or prevent the proponent from using direct examination of the witness merely as a vehicle for having the witness vouch for the accuracy of a written report prepared by the witness. The trial judge may also exclude prior consistent statements that are a waste of time because they do not substantially support the credibility of the witness. Mere proof that the witness repeated the same story in and out of court does not necessarily bolster credibility.

The rule continues the existing practice of permitting testimony about the witness' prior out of court identification. See *e.g.,* State v. Jones, 277 Minn. 174, 179, 152 N.W.2d 67, 72 (1967). The rationale for the rule stems from the belief that if the original identification procedures were conducted fairly, the prior identification would tend to be more probative than an identification at trial. Obviously, if the prior identification did not occur under circumstances insuring its trustworthiness, the identification should not be admissible. The Court must be satisfied as to the trustworthiness of the out of court identification before allowing it to be introduced as substantive evidence. See gen. Minn. R.Crim.P. 7.01 which requires that criminal defendants be given notice of certain identification procedures involved in their case.

Subdivision (d)(1)(D) represents a limited exception to the definition of hearsay. The subject matter of the statement must describe an event or condition at or near the time the declarant perceives the event or condition. The federal rules treat such a statement as hearsay but would include it as an exception to the hearsay rule without regard to the availability of the declarant at trial. Federal Rule 803(1). The committee was concerned with the trustworthiness of such statements when the declarant was not available to testify at trial. When the declarant does testify at trial the distinction between what he did or what he said contemporaneous with an event is frequently an artificial one. As a consequence the committee recommends treating such spontaneous statements as nonhearsay. Furthermore, the traditional concerns that gave rise to the hearsay rule of exclusion are satisfied by the requirement that the declarant be a witness and be subject to cross-examination.

Rule 801(d)(2)

The rule excludes party admissions from its definition of hearsay. The requirements of trustworthiness, firsthand knowledge, or rules against opinion which may be applicable in determining whether or not a hearsay statement should be admissible do not apply when dealing with party admissions. Because the rationale for their admissibility is based more on the nature of the adversary system than in principles of trustworthiness or necessity, it makes sense to treat party admissions as nonhearsay. In addition to a party's own statements and fully authorized statements made by agents of a party, the rule provides for the admissibility of adoptive admissions. For a discussion of the use of adoptive admissions in criminal cases see gen. Village of New Hope v. Duplessie, 304 Minn. 417, 231 N.W.2d 548, 551 (1975). These provisions should not change existing practice.

The admissibility of statements made by agents of a party has given rise to much litigation. The rule rejects the strict agency theory in determining whether or not the statement is admissible. Rather than focusing on the agent's authority to speak for the principal, the rule requires only that the statement be made concerning a matter within the scope of the agency. For example, the statement of a truck driver concerning an accident in which he was involved while driving the truck for his employer can be received as an admission of the employer. Statements made after the employment relationship terminates will not be admissions of the employer.

In Bourjaily v. United States, 483 U.S. 171, 107 S.Ct. 2775, 97 L.Ed.2d 144 (1987), the United States Supreme Court construed Fed.R.Evid. 801(d)(2)(E) so that the federal coconspirator rule differed from the Minnesota rule in two important particulars. First, Minnesota law required a prima facie showing of a conspiracy, and second, the showing had to be made without considering the coconspirator's statements. State v. Thompson, 273 Minn. 1, 139 N.W.2d 490 (1966). In Bourjaily the Court continued the prior federal rule that the showing had to be made by a preponderance of the evidence, which is a higher standard than the Minnesota standard of a prima facie showing. However, the Court held that the trial judge could consider the statements in determining whether a conspiracy had been shown, overruling a line of federal cases which held that the statements could not be considered. The amended rule adopts the Bourjaily holdings in the following respects: The quantum of proof required is a preponderance of the evidence, and under most circumstances the rule allows the judge to consider the statements in determining whether the showing has been made. The proviso in the amended rule precludes the declarant's statement by itself from establishing the conspiracy and is included to prevent the hearsay statement from becoming admissible solely on the basis of the content of the statement.

The amended rule continues prior Minnesota law that the order of proof rests in the discretion of the trial judge, who may admit the declaration before the required showing is made. Although there is a danger that the declarations will be admitted and the showing will not later be made, the Committee took the view that the danger is offset by the trial judge's authority to require the showing to be made outside the presence of the jury under Rule 104(c). Moreover, the amended rule expressly authorizes the judge to grant a mistrial or give such other relief as is just, in the event the statements are admitted and the foundation is not later shown.

The amended rule continues the prior limitation that the statement must be made in the course of and in furtherance of the conspiracy.

Advisory Committee Comment—2006 Amendments

Right to Confrontation.

In *Crawford v. Washington*, 541 U.S. 36 (2004), the United States Supreme Court adopted a new approach to Sixth Amendment confrontation analysis. The Court ruled that admitting against the accused "testimonial" hearsay from an unavailable declarant, violates the Sixth Amendment right to confrontation, absent a prior opportunity for cross-examination. The *Crawford* court stated,

Where nontestimonial hearsay is at issue, it is wholly consistent with the Framers' design to afford the States flexibility in the development of hearsay law—as does [*Ohio v.*] *Roberts*, and as would an approach that exempted such statement from Confrontation Clause scrutiny altogether. Where testimonial evidence is at issue, however, the Sixth Amendment demands what the common law required: unavailability and a prior opportunity for cross-examination.

Crawford, 541 U.S. at 68.

The *Crawford* court did not define what constitutes "testimonial" hearsay. *See id.* Some types of evidence appear to be testimonial no matter how the term is defined. For example, courtroom testimony, including testimony at a preliminary hearing, or affidavits are testimonial, as are guilty pleas, allocutions, and grand jury testimony. The *Crawford* court also stated, "Statements taken by police officers in the course of interrogations are also testimonial under even a narrow standard." *Id.* at 52.

The full implications of this new approach to Sixth Amendment interpretation is presently being worked out in the courts. *See, e.g., State v. Hannon*, 703 N.W.2d 498, 507 (Minn. 2005) (ruling that testimony from a witness at the defendant's prior trial did not violate the defendant's right of confrontation where the witness was unavailable, the defendant had an opportunity to cross-examine at the first trial, and the state's theory of the case had not substantially changed); *State v. Martin*, 695 N.W.2d 578, 584–86 (Minn. 2005) (holding that a dying declaration does not violate a defendant's Sixth Amendment right to confrontation because the Sixth Amendment did not repudiate dying declarations, which were readily admissible at early common law).

Rule 801(d)(2).

The change in the title to rule 801(d)(2) conforms the title of the rule to the text. The amended title clarifies that the statement by a party opponent need not be an "admission" of guilt or liability in order to be excluded from the definition of hearsay.

RULE 802. HEARSAY RULE

Hearsay is not admissible except as provided by these rules or by other rules prescribed by the Supreme Court or by the Legislature.

Adopted April 1, 1977, eff. July 1, 1977.

Committee Comment—1977

The general rule excluding hearsay is consistent with common law and existing Minnesota practice. Rules 803(24) and 804(5) control the common law development of additional hearsay exceptions. The authority of the legislature to create various exceptions to the hearsay rule is well established. See gen. Minn.Stats. Ch. 600 (1974) which contains several examples of legislative exceptions to the hearsay rule.

RULE 803. HEARSAY EXCEPTIONS; AVAILABILITY OF DECLARANT IMMATERIAL

The following are not excluded by the hearsay rule, even though the declarant is available as a witness:

(1) (Not Used).

(2) Excited utterance. A statement relating to a startling event or condition made while the declarant was under the stress of excitement caused by the event or condition.

(3) Then existing mental, emotional, or physical condition. A statement of the declarant's then existing state of mind, emotion, sensation, or physical condition (such as intent, plan, motive, design, mental feeling, pain, and bodily health), but not including a statement of memory or belief to prove the fact remembered or believed unless it relates to the execution, revocation, identification, or terms of declarant's will.

(4) Statements for purposes of medical diagnosis or treatment. Statements made for purposes of medical diagnosis or treatment and describing medical history, or past or present symptoms, pain, or sensations, or the inception or general character of the cause or external source thereof insofar as reasonably pertinent to diagnosis or treatment.

(5) Recorded recollection. A memorandum or record concerning a matter about which a witness once had knowledge but now has insufficient recollection to testify fully and accurately, shown to have been made or adopted by the witness when the matter was fresh in the witness' memory and to reflect that knowledge correctly. If admitted, the memorandum or record may be read into evidence but may not itself be received as an exhibit unless offered by an adverse party.

(6) Records of regularly conducted business activity. A memorandum, report, record, or data compilation, in any form, of acts, events, conditions, opinions, or diagnoses, made at or near the time by, or from information transmitted by, a person with knowledge, if kept in the course of a regularly conducted business activity, and if it was the regular practice of that business activity to make the memorandum, report, record, or data compilation, all as shown by the testimony of the custodian or other qualified witness, unless the source of information or the method or circumstances of preparation indicate lack of trustworthiness. The term "business" as used in this paragraph includes business, institution, association, profession, occupation, and calling of every kind, whether or not conducted for profit. A memorandum, report, record, or data compilation prepared for litigation is not admissible under this exception.

(7) Absence of entry in records kept in accordance with the provisions of paragraph (6). Evidence that a matter is not included in the memoranda reports, records, or data compilations, in any form, kept in accordance with the provisions of paragraph (6), to prove the nonoccurrence or nonexistence of the matter, if the matter was of a kind of which a memorandum, report, record, or data compilation was regularly made and preserved, unless the sources of information or other circumstances indicate lack of trustworthiness.

(8) Public records and reports. Unless the sources of information or other circumstances indicate lack of trustworthiness, records, reports, statements, or data compilations, in any form, of public offices or agencies, setting forth (A) the activities of the office or agency, or (B) matters observed pursuant to duty imposed by law as to which matters there was a duty to report, excluding, however, in criminal cases and petty misdemeanors matters observed by police officers and other law enforcement personnel, or (C) in civil actions and proceedings except petty misdemeanors and against the State in criminal cases and petty misdemeanors, factual findings resulting from an investigation made pursuant to authority granted by law.

(9) Records of vital statistics. Records or data compilations, in any form, of births, fetal deaths, deaths, or marriages, if the report thereof was made to a public office pursuant to requirements of law.

(10) Absence of public record or entry. To prove the absence of a record, report, statement, or data compilation, in any form, or the nonoccurrence or nonexistence of a matter of which a record, report, statement, or data compilation, in any form, was regularly made and preserved by a public office or agency, evidence in the form of a certification in accordance with rule 902, or testimony, that diligent search failed to disclose the record, report, statement, or data compilation, or entry.

(11) Records of religious organizations. Statements of births, marriages, divorces, deaths, legitimacy, ancestry, relationship by blood or marriage, or other similar facts of personal or family history, contained in a regularly kept record of a religious organization.

(12) Marriage, baptismal, and similar certificates. Statements of fact contained in a certificate that the maker performed a marriage or other ceremony or administered a sacrament, made by a clergyman, public official, or other person authorized by the rules or practices of a religious organization or by law to perform the act certified, and purporting to have been issued at the time of the act or within a reasonable time thereafter.

(13) Family records. Statements of fact concerning personal or family history contained in family Bibles, genealogies, charts, engravings on rings, inscriptions on family portraits, engravings on urns, crypts, or tombstones, or the like.

(14) Records of documents affecting an interest in property. The record of a document purporting to establish or affect an interest in property, as proof of the content of the original recorded document and its execution and delivery by each person by whom it purports to have been executed, if the record is a record of a public office and an applicable statute authorizes the recording of documents of that kind in that office.

(15) Statements in documents affecting an interest in property. A statement contained in a document purporting to establish or affect an interest in property if the matter stated was relevant to the purpose of the document, unless dealings with the property since the document was made have been inconsistent with the truth of the statement or the purport of the document.

(16) Statements in ancient documents. Statements in a document in existence twenty years or more the authenticity of which is established.

(17) Market reports, commercial publications. Market quotations, tabulations, lists, directories, or other published compilations, generally used and relied upon by the public or by persons in particular occupations unless the sources of information or other circumstances indicate lack of trustworthiness.

(18) Learned treatises. To the extent called to the attention of an expert witness upon cross-examination or relied upon by the expert witness in direct examination, statements contained in published treatises, periodicals, or pamphlets on a subject of history, medicine, or other science or art, established as a reliable authority by the testimony or admission of the witness or by other expert testimony or by judicial notice. If admitted, the statements may be read into evidence but may not be received as exhibits.

(19) Reputation concerning personal or family history. Reputation among members of a person's family by blood, adoption, or marriage, or among a person's associates, or in the community, concerning a person's birth, adoption, marriage, divorce, death, legitimacy, relationship by blood, adoption, or marriage, ancestry, or other similar fact of personal or family history.

(20) Reputation concerning boundaries or general history. Reputation in a community, arising before the controversy, as to boundaries of or customs affecting lands in the community, and reputation as to events of general history important to the community or State or nation in which located.

(21) Reputation as to character. Reputation of a person's character among associates or in the community.

(22) Judgment of previous conviction. Evidence of a final judgment, entered after a trial or upon a plea of guilty (but not upon a plea of nolo contendere), adjudging a person guilty of a crime punishable by death or imprisonment in excess of one year, to prove any fact essential to sustain the judgment, but not including, when offered by the state in a criminal prosecution for purposes other than impeachment, judgments against persons other than the accused. The pendency of an appeal may be shown but does not affect admissibility.

(23) Judgment as to personal, family or general history, or boundaries. Judgments as proof of matters of personal, family or general history, or boundaries, essential to the judgment, if the same would be provable by evidence of reputation.

Adopted April 1, 1977, eff. July 1, 1977. Amended Dec. 28, 1989, eff. Jan. 1, 1990; July 18, 2006, eff. Sept. 1, 2006.

Committee Comments—1989

The exceptions to the hearsay rule of exclusion (rule 802) are separated into two categories:

1. those exceptions which are not affected by the availability or unavailability of the declarant (rule 803), and

2. those exceptions which require that the declarant be unavailable before the hearsay statement might be admissible (rule 804).

The basis for the distinction is largely historical, and represents a judgment as to which hearsay statements are so trustworthy as to be admissible without requiring the production of the declarant when available.

Rules 803 and 804 provide certain exceptions to the general rule of exclusion for hearsay statements. A statement qualifying as an exception to the hearsay rule must satisfy other provisions in these rules before it is admissible. For example, a statement that qualifies as an exception to the hearsay rule must be relevant and admissible under Article 4 and be based on personal knowledge (rule 602) before it can be admitted into evidence.

Rule 803(1)

The committee did not recommend adoption of Fed.R.Evid. 803(1) "Present sense impressions." However, if the declarant testifies at trial and is subject to cross-examination, the declarant's present sense impressions are treated as non-hearsay under these rules. Rule 801(d)(1)(D).

Rule 803(2)

The excited utterance exception is one which traditionally has been treated in terms of "res gestae" in Minnesota. The rules avoid use of the term "res gestae" which is considered to be a general catchall phrase sanctioning the admission of several types of hearsay statements. See gen. Morgan, A Suggested Classification of Utterances Admissible as Res Gestae, 31 Yale L.J. 229 (1922). C. McCormick, Evidence § 288 (2d ed. 1972). The rules provide specific exceptions more clearly identifying the rationale and requirements of each. The major effect this rule will have on existing practice is a change in terminology which hopefully will result in better analysis and understanding.

In order to qualify as an excited utterance, the following three requirements must be met:

1. there must be a startling event or condition;
2. the statement must relate to the startling event or condition; and
3. the declarant must be under a sufficient aura of excitement caused by the event or condition to insure the trustworthiness of the statement.

The rationale stems from the belief that the excitement caused by the event eliminates the possibility of conscious fabrication, and insures the trustworthiness of the statement. As the time lapse between the startling event and subsequent statement increases so does the possibility for reflection and conscious fabrication. There can be no fixed guidelines. It is largely a matter for the trial judge to determine whether the statement was given at such a time when the aura of excitement was sufficient to insure a trustworthy statement. Rule 104(a). In reaching this decision the judge must consider all relevant factors including the length of time elapsed, the nature of the event, the physical condition of the declarant, any possible motive to falsify, etc.

Rule 803(3)

The rule [Exception (3)] combines two traditional exceptions to the hearsay rule; the state of mind exception and the statement of present bodily condition. Both are based on the belief that spontaneous statements of this nature are sufficiently trustworthy to justify their admission into evidence. State of mind or bodily condition are difficult matters to prove. When they are in issue or otherwise relevant, hearsay statements of this type may be the best proof available.

The rule makes it clear that hearsay statements probative of the declarant's state of mind or emotion are not made inadmissible by the hearsay rule. The more difficult evidentiary problems arise in the determination as to whether state of mind is relevant to the issues in the lawsuit. Clearly, when state of mind is in issue there is no problem. State of mind may also be admitted to prove that the declarant subsequently acted in conformity with his state of mind. See Scott v. Prudential Ins. Co., 203 Minn. 547, 552, 282 N.W. 467, 470 (1938); Mutual Life Ins. Co. v. Hillmon, 12 S.Ct. 909, 913, 145 U.S. 285, 296, 36 L.Ed. 706, 710, 711 (1892). The rule does not permit evidence of a declarant's present state of mind to be admitted to establish the declarant's previous actions, unless dealing with the execution, revocation, identification, or terms of declarant's will. Cf. Troseth v. Troseth, 224 Minn. 35, 28 N.W.2d 65 (1947). (Present state of mind used to prove previous intent in effectuating gift.)

In considering the admissibility of statements of present sensation, or bodily condition the Court should examine the circumstances surrounding the statements to determine if they were spontaneous statements or statements designed with a view to making evidence. Statements of the latter type should be excluded under rule 403. See C. McCormick, Evidence § 292 (2d ed. 1972).

Rule 803(4)

Statements to treating physicians traditionally have been admissible as an exception to the hearsay rule if reasonably pertinent to diagnosis and treatment. This includes statements as to present matters as well as past conditions. See Peterson v. Richfield Plaza, Inc., 252 Minn. 215, 228, 89 N.W.2d 712, 722 (1958). In Minnesota they have been admissible if the physician bases an opinion on the statement.

The rule extends this exception to cover statements made to a non-treating physician if made for the purpose of diagnosis. This rule is the logical outgrowth of rule 703 which permits a non-treating physician to base an opinion on such a statement if it is the type of statement upon which experts in the field reasonably rely.

Rule 803(5)

The introduction of hearsay documents under this exception [Rule 803(5)] must be distinguished from the use of documents to refresh the recollection of a witness. See rule 612. Only when a witness has insufficient present recollection of the event and attempts to read a hearsay document into the record are the requirements of this rule applicable.

The rule does not require a total lack of memory. If the present recollection of the witness is impaired to such an extent that he is unable to testify fully and accurately he may resort to a memorandum or record if it satisfies the other provisions of the rule. In these situations, the previously recorded statement will often be the best available evidence. See Walker v. Larson, 284 Minn. 99, 105, 169 N.W.2d 737, 741, 742 (1969). The provision that the hearsay document will not be received as an exhibit is intended to prevent the jury from placing undue emphasis on the statement.

Rule 803(6)

This provision [Exception (6)] will replace the existing statutory scheme dealing with the introduction of business records and shop records. See Minn.Stats. §§ 600.01–600.06 (1974). Minnesota had previously adopted the Uniform Business Records as Evidence Act to bring state law in this area into conformity with other states adopting the Uniform Act. In recommending the federal rule it was the committee's view that in the years to come it is of greater importance that the state rule corresponds to the rule in force in the federal courts.

The rule should be read broadly to accomplish the purposes set out in Rule 102 as well as to ensure that only trustworthy evidence is admitted. The application of the rule should not cause a substantive change in existing practice. Past decisions of the Minnesota Supreme Court should serve as guidelines for the proper interpretation of this rule. See gen. Brown v. St. Paul Ry., 241 Minn. 15, 62 N.W.2d 688, 44 A.L.R.2d 535 (1954); City of Fairmont v. Sjostrom, 280 Minn. 87, 157 N.W.2d 849 (1968).

Documents prepared solely for litigation purposes do not qualify under this exception. If the document is prepared in part for business purposes but with an eye toward litigation the court must decide if the interest in litigation sufficiently detracted from the trustworthiness of the report to preclude its admission. See Palmer v. Hoffman, 318 U.S. 109, 63 S.Ct. 477, 87 L.Ed. 645, 144 A.L.R. 719 (1943), cited with approval in Brown v. St. Paul Ry. Co., 241 Minn. 15, 36, 62 N.W.2d 688, 702 (dictum).

Rule 803(7)

Absence of an entry in a business record is not made inadmissible by the hearsay rule. The admissibility of such evidence is governed by rules of relevancy. See Article 4.

Rule 803(8)

The rationale for this exception rests in:

1. a belief in the trustworthiness of the work product of government agents operating pursuant to official duty;

2. the necessity for introducing the full reports as opposed to testimony of government agents whose memory may be faulty; and

3. a concern for the disruption that would result in government agencies if its employees were continually required to testify in trials. See United States Supreme Court advisory Committee Note. See also C. McCormick, Evidence § 315 (2d ed. 1972). Subdivisions (A) and (B) are consistent with existing practice.

The rule was amended to clarify that records and reports qualifying under each subdivision (A), (B) and (C) should be excluded if the report is not trustworthy. Among other matters, the court should consider the qualifications, bias, and motivation of the authors, the timeliness and methods of investigation or hearing procedures, and the reliability of the foundation upon which any factual finding, opinion, or conclusion is based.

Subdivision (C) permits introduction of factual findings resulting from investigations made pursuant to authority granted by law except when offered against the accused in criminal cases. Prior to the Minnesota Rules of Evidence, Minnesota courts did not admit reports which included discretionary conclusions and opinions Barnes v. Northwest Airlines, Inc., 233 Minn. 410, 433, 47 N.W.2d 180, 193 (1951); Clancy v. Daily News Corp., 202 Minn. 1, 7, 277 N.W. 264, 268 (1938). The rule makes no distinction among findings of historical fact, factual conclusions, or opinions. Beech Aircraft Corp. v. Rainey, 488 U.S., 109 S.Ct. 439, 102 L.Ed.2d 445 (1988) (investigator's report on cause of airplane crash was not excludable because it included investigator's opinion or conclusion). See also Pipestone v. Halbersma, 294 N.W.2d 271 (Minn.1980). The primary concern of the rule is a determination of whether the factual finding, conclusion, or opinion is trustworthy and helpful to the resolution of the issues. Considerations of whether the document contains historical facts as opposed to conclusions or discretionary factual findings is subordinate to this primary consideration.

At present public records are admitted pursuant to specific statutes. See, *e.g.*, Minn.Stats. § 600.13 (1974). This rule is not intended to supersede the many statutes that specifically provide for the admission or exclusion of certain public documents. *E.g.*, Minn.Stats. § 169.09 subd. 13 (1974).

Rule 803(9)

Minnesota has adopted the Uniform Vital Statistics Act, Minn.Stats. §§ 144.151–144.204, 144.49 (1974) which requires certain individuals to make reports to the State Board of Health concerning births, deaths, etc. Similarly Minn.Stats. § 517.10 (1974) requires the filing of marriage certificates. The documents, if properly admitted, will constitute prima facie evidence of certain facts included in the certificates. Minn.Stats. §§ 144.167 and 600.20 (1974). However, not all statements included in such certificates are admissible. See Backstrom v. New York Life Ins. Co., 183 Minn. 384, 236 N.W. 708 (1931). This rule should not change existing Minnesota practice.

Rule 803(10)

The absence of a public record or entry, like the absence of a business record is not made inadmissible by the hearsay rule. The admissibility would depend on principles of relevancy. See Article 4. The rule provides for proof by way of certification that a diligent search failed to disclose the record or entry. See Minn.R.Civ.P. 44.02.

Rule 803(11)

The rule [Exception (11)] is an extension of the business records exception. See rule 803(6). This exception is somewhat broader since there is no explicit directive that the court inquire into the trustworthiness of the statement. Unlike the business record exception the person furnishing the statement is not required to have a business or religious duty to report the information. Contra. Houlton v. Manteuffel, 51 Minn. 185, 187, 53 N.W. 541, 542 (1892).

Rule 803(12)

This provision [Exception (12)] excepts certain certificates from the hearsay rule. In cases where the certificate is filed or maintained in a church record this provision provides an alternative method of proof. See rules 803(8) and (10). See also Minn.Stats. § 600.20 (1974).

Rule 803(13)

The exception for family records is consistent with common law tradition, although at common law they were admissible only when the declarant was unavailable. See C. McCormick, Evidence § 322 (2d ed. 1972). See also Geisler v. Geisler, 160 Minn. 463, 467, 200 N.W. 742, 744 (1924). Cf. rule 804(b)(4).

Rule 803(14)

In many cases the proper recording of an interest in property requires or permits statements on the face of the record which assert proper execution and delivery of the document. See *e.g.,* Uniform Conveyancing Blanks prepared under authority granted by Minn.Stats.1975 Supp. § 507.09. The rule is intended to allow this record to be used as proof of proper execution and delivery of the document, as well as proving the contents of the record. This procedure is consistent with Minnesota practice. See Minn.Stats. § 600.13 (1974).

Rule 803(15)

The circumstances under which most dispositive documents are made will normally assure the reliability of statements relevant to the purpose of the document. Absent a showing that subsequent dealings with the property have been inconsistent with these statements, there is sufficient indicia of trustworthiness to warrant an exception to the general rule against hearsay.

Rule 803(16)

The admissibility of ancient documents will normally raise problems of authentication and hearsay. The requirements of proper authentication are set forth in rule 901(b)(8). If properly authenticated, these hearsay documents are deemed to be sufficiently trustworthy to warrant admission as evidence because:

1) they were compiled at a time prior to the litigation when there was no motive to falsify;

2) the documentary form of the evidence reduces the possibility of error in transmission;

3) it is unlikely that present testimony concerning these prior matters will be significantly more probative. Furthermore, in most instances witnesses with firsthand knowledge will not be available.

If the Court has reason to suspect the trustworthiness of the ancient document, it may exercise its discretion under rule 403 to exclude the evidence.

Rule 803(17)

Many commercial publications and market quotations are highly trustworthy and are relied upon by the general public as well as specialized groups.

The committee was concerned that this exception might permit certain credit reports, etc., reflecting unreliable hearsay to be received as substantive evidence. The distinction between the Minnesota rule and its federal counterpart is intended to emphasize that this exception will not be a universal sanction for the admission of market reports or commercial publications.

The rule makes it clear that the Court retains the power to exclude evidence offered pursuant to this exception if the evidence is not trustworthy. See gen. J. Weinstein & M. Berger, 4 Weinstein's Evidence § 803(17(01)) (1975). This provision is consistent with the authority given the Court under rule 403.

Rule 803(18)

The circumstances under which learned treatises will be admitted as substantive evidence are set forth by the rule. These limitations should serve to avoid dangers of misunderstanding or misapplication of this evidence.

The rule will expand the use of learned treatises in Minnesota courts. See gen. Briggs v. Chicago Great Western Ry., 238 Minn. 472, 57 N.W.2d 572 (1953); but see Ruud v. Hendrickson, 176 Minn. 138, 222 N.W. 904 (1929); see also Comment, 39 Minn.L.Rev. 905 (1955).

Rule 803(19, 20)

The rationale for the hearsay exception for reputation evidence is explained in the United States Supreme Court Advisory Committee Note:

> Trustworthiness in reputation evidence is found when the topic is such that the facts are likely to have been inquired about and that persons having personal knowledge have disclosed facts which have thus been discussed in the community; and thus the community conclusion, if any has been formed, is likely to be a trustworthy one. (citations omitted)

When dealing with reputation concerning personal or family history the community includes the family, associates, or general community. This may be somewhat broader than the traditional pedigree exception in Minnesota. See Houlton v. Manteuffel, 51 Minn. 185, 53 N.W. 541 (1892). See Minn.Stats. § 602.02 (1974) which permits reputation evidence to prove the fact of marriage.

Subdivision 20 codifies a common law exception to the hearsay rule. C. McCormick, Evidence § 324 (2d ed. 1972).

Rule 803(21)

Subdivision 21 provides that reputation as to character is not excluded by the hearsay rule. The admissibility of this type of evidence is governed by rules 404, 405, and 608.

Rule 803(22)

Prior to this rule [803(22)], convictions have not been admissible as substantive evidence. Guilty pleas could be received in a subsequent civil action as party admissions. Otherwise a conviction would be admissible in a subsequent civil case only for impeachment purposes. In addition, it is possible that a criminal conviction might serve as an estoppel in the civil action. See Travelers Ins. Co. v. Thompson, 281 Minn. 547, 163 N.W.2d 289 (1968). The rule gives evidentiary effect to criminal felony convictions, altering existing practice.

The rule is consistent with the modern trend in this area and has much to commend it. See Annot., 18 A.L.R.2d 1287 (1951). It represents a belief in the trustworthiness of verdicts based on the reasonable doubt standard. The rule is limited to convictions for serious crimes to insure that there was sufficient motivation to defend the criminal prosecution. To the extent that the defendant believes the criminal conviction was not accurate for any reason, *e.g.,* new evidence, lack of discovery at the criminal trial, restrictive evidentiary rulings, etc., these matters can be explained at the civil trial. The burden is placed on the party offering the prior conviction to establish what facts were essential to sustain the criminal conviction.

Rule 803(23)

This provision [Rule 803(23)] deals with the evidentiary effect to be given a judgment in a civil case concerning matters of personal, family, or general history and boundaries. At one time jury verdicts were essentially the equivalent of reputation. Although the historical rationale for this exception is no longer valid, judgments of this nature have continued to be admitted as an exception to the hearsay rule since such judgments are at least as trustworthy as reputation evidence. Rules 803(19) and (20). See United States Supreme Court Advisory Committee Note.

Rule 803(24)

This exception allows for the continued development of exceptions to the hearsay rule. It provides for sufficient flexibility to carry out the goals set out in Rule 102. The rule defines the common law power of the judge to fashion new exceptions to the hearsay doctrine. For hearsay to qualify under this provision it must be established that there is some need for the evidence and that the evidence has guarantees of trustworthiness equivalent to the specific exceptions set out in Rule 803.

Furthermore, there is a notice requirement to avoid the possibility of surprise and to lend more predictability to the litigation process. The Committee considered and rejected the federal cases that applied a less restrictive notice requirement. United States v. Bailey, 581 F.2d 341 (3d Cir.1978); United States v. Carlson, 547 F.2d 1346 (8th Cir. 1976) cert. denied 431 U.S. 914; United States v. Leslie, 542 F.2d 285 (5th Cir.1976).

Advisory Committee Comment—2006 Amendments

Rule 803(24).

The substance of this rule is combined with rule 804(b)(5) in new rule 807.

RULE 804. HEARSAY EXCEPTIONS; DECLARANT UNAVAILABLE

(a) Definitions of unavailability. "Unavailability as a witness" includes situations in which the declarant—

(1) is exempted by ruling of the court on the ground of privilege from testifying concerning the subject matter of the declarant's statement; or

(2) persists in refusing to testify concerning the subject matter of the declarant's statement despite an order of the court to do so; or

(3) testifies to a lack of memory of the subject matter of the declarant's statement; or

(4) is unable to be present or to testify at the hearing because of death or then existing physical or mental illness or infirmity; or

(5) is absent from the hearing and the proponent of a statement has been unable to procure the declarant's attendance (or in the case of a hearsay exception under subdivision (b)(2), (3), or (4), the declarant's attendance or testimony) by process or other reasonable means.

A declarant is not unavailable as a witness if the declarant's exemption, refusal, claim of lack of memory, inability, or absence is due to the procurement or wrongdoing of the proponent of the statement for the purpose of preventing the witness from attending or testifying.

(b) Hearsay exceptions. The following are not excluded by the hearsay rule if the declarant is unavailable as a witness:

(1) *Former testimony.* In a civil proceeding testimony given as a witness at another hearing of the same or a different proceeding, or in a deposition taken in compliance with law in the course of the same or another proceeding, if the party against whom the testimony is now offered or a party with substantially the same interest or motive with respect to the outcome of the litigation, had an opportunity and similar motive to develop the testimony by direct, cross, or redirect examination. In a criminal proceeding involving a retrial of the same defendant for the same or an included offense, testimony given as a witness at the prior trial or in a deposition taken in the course thereof.

(2) *Statement under belief of impending death.* In a prosecution for homicide or in a civil action or proceeding, a statement made by a declarant while believing that the declarant's death was imminent, concerning the cause or circumstances of what the declarant believed to be impending death.

(3) *Statement against interest.* A statement which was at the time of its making so far contrary to the declarant's pecuniary or proprietary interest, or so far tended to subject the declarant to civil or criminal liability, or to render invalid a claim by the declarant against another, that a reasonable person in the declarant's position would not have made the statement unless believing it to be true. A statement tending to expose the declarant to criminal liability and offered to exculpate the accused is not admissible unless corroborating circumstances clearly indicate the trustworthiness of the statement.

(4) *Statement of personal or family history.* (A) A statement concerning the declarant's own birth, adoption, marriage, divorce, legitimacy, relationship by blood, adoption, or marriage, ancestry, or other similar fact of personal or family history, even though declarant had no means of acquiring personal knowledge of the matter stated; or (B) a statement concerning the foregoing matters, and death also, of another person, if the declarant was related to the other by blood, adoption, or marriage or was so intimately associated with the other's family as to be likely to have accurate information concerning the matter declared.

Adopted April 1, 1977, eff. July 1, 1977. Amended Dec. 28, 1989, eff. Jan. 1, 1990; July 18, 2006, eff. Sept. 1, 2006.

Committee Comment—1989

Rule 804 includes those exceptions to the hearsay rule that are conditioned upon a showing that the declarant is unavailable. As with the exceptions in rule 803 the requirements of relevancy (Article 4) and firsthand knowledge (rule 602) must be satisfied. Of necessity the decision as to whether or not a hearsay declaration is based on first-hand knowledge must be made on circumstantial evidence, and this requirement should be sufficiently flexible to accomplish the purposes set out in rule 102.

Rule 804(a)

Traditionally the definition of unavailability varied among the several hearsay exceptions. The rule takes the general approach that the concept of unavailability should be applied consistently among each of the exceptions. Contra, rule 804(a)(5). The definition of unavailability indicates that the primary concern is the unavailability of the testimony and not necessarily the unavailability of the declarant. If the declarant is present at trial but will not or cannot testify as to an issue for any reason, whether justified or not, the declarant is deemed to be unavailable on that issue for the purposes of the rule. With the exception of rule 804(b)(1), a witness will not be deemed unavailable if his testimony can be procured by reasonable means, *e.g.,* by taking his deposition. This is a judgment that evidence by means of deposition would be preferable to the hearsay statement. In determining whether testimony could be procured by reasonable means the judge has some discretion. Appropriate considerations would include such things as the stakes involved, the nature of the testimony, and the expense that would be incurred by out of state depositions. See rule 102.

The application of the Sixth Amendment confrontation clause will dictate when the declarant must be produced in many criminal cases. See gen. Barber v. Page, 88 S.Ct. 1318, 390 U.S. 719, 20 L.Ed.2d 255 (1968); Mancusi v. Stubbs, 92 S.Ct. 2308, 408 U.S. 204, 33 L.Ed.2d 293 (1972); State v. Shotley, Minn., 233 N.W.2d 755, 757–758 (1975).

Rule 804(b)(1)

This exception [Rule 804(b)(1)] deals with the introduction of former testimony when the declarant is unavailable. Former testimony of a witness who testifies at trial might be admissible under rule 801(d)(1)(A) if inconsistent with the witness' present testimony. The rule distinguishes between civil and criminal cases.

In a civil case the former testimony in the same or different litigation is excepted from the hearsay rule if:

1. the declarant is unavailable; and

2. the party against whom the testimony is being offered or another party with substantially the same interest, had an opportunity and motive to develop the testimony. Briggs v. Chicago Great Western Ry., 248 Minn. 418, 426, 80 N.W.2d 625, 633 (1957).

In a criminal proceeding the rule is only applicable when there is a retrial of the same defendant for the same or an included offense. Even this limited application might raise issues under the confrontation clause. The rule is not intended to codify the scope of the Sixth Amendment.

To the extent that the admissibility of depositions is governed by rules of procedure, the procedural rules shall still be in effect pursuant to rule 802. See Minn.R.Civ.P. 32.01(3) and Minn.R.Crim.P. 21.06.

Rule 804(b)(2)

This provision [Rule 804(b)(2)] represents the traditional "dying declaration exception" to the hearsay rule. At common law the exception was limited to homicide prosecutions. The rule extends this to include civil actions. Otherwise the rule is consistent with the Minnesota approach as stated in State v. Eubanks, 277 Minn. 257, 262, 152 N.W.2d 453, 456, 457 (1967).

In prosecutions for homicide the dying declarations of the deceased as to the cause of his injury or as to the circumstances which resulted in the injury are admissible if it be shown, to the satisfaction of the trial court, that they were made when the deceased was in actual danger of death and had given up all hope of recovery. State v. Elias, 205 Minn. 156, 158, 285 N.W. 475, 476 (1939).

Rule 804(b)(3)

Declarations against interest have traditionally been excepted from the hearsay rule when the declarant is unavailable. Unlike the admission of a party (rule 801(d)(2)), the basis for this exception centers in notions of trustworthiness and necessity.

The statement must not only be contrary to the declarant's interest at the time made, but so far contrary to his interest that a reasonable person would not have made the statement unless he believed it to be true. Implicit in the rule is the requirement that the declarant have firsthand knowledge (rule 602), and that he understand or should understand that the statement is likely to be contrary to his interest at the time the statement is made.

The common law exception was originally limited to declarations against proprietary or pecuniary interests. Many jurisdictions, including Minnesota, have expanded this to include statements that might give rise to civil liability, Johnson v. Sleizer, 268 Minn. 421, 426, 129 N.W.2d 761, 764 (1964), and statements against penal interest, State v. Higginbotham, 298 Minn. 1, 212 N.W.2d 881 (1973). This rule was not intended to affect the application of Minn.Stat. § 169.94 (1974). See Warren v. Marsh, 215 Minn. 615, 11 N.W.2d 528 (1943).

The corroboration requirement in criminal cases for statements that exculpate the accused has been expressly approved by the Supreme Court. State v. Higginbotham, 298 Minn. 1, 212 N.W.2d 881 (1973).

Rule 804(b)(4)

Statements of personal or family history have traditionally been admissible as an exception to the hearsay rule. See gen. 5 Wigmore, Evidence § 1480 et seq. (Chadbourn ed. 1974). The rule does not require that the statement be made prior to the controversy, as was the case at common law. It is thought that the timing of the statement goes more to its evidentiary weight than admissibility. The relaxation of the requirement of first-hand knowledge will allow admission of the statement of an unavailable declarant relating to the date of his birth. See United States Supreme Court Advisory Committee Note.

Rule 804(b)(5)

Other than the requirement of unavailability, this exception is identical to Rule 803(24). Since the unavailability of the declarant will increase the necessity for resorting to hearsay statements, it is likely that this provision will be used more frequently than Rule 803(24) in fashioning new exceptions to the hearsay rule.

Advisory Committee Comment—2006 Amendments

Rule 804(b)(5).

The substance of this rule is combined with rule 803(24) in new rule 807.

RULE 805. HEARSAY WITHIN HEARSAY

Hearsay included within hearsay is not excluded under the hearsay rule if each part of the combined statements conforms with an exception to the hearsay rule provided in these rules.

Adopted April 1, 1977, eff. July 1, 1977.

Committee Comment—1977

Where double hearsay is involved the statement is admissible if each step in the transmission of the statement qualifies under an exception to the hearsay rule. Usually this question arises with respect to documentary evidence that includes a hearsay statement. For example, a hospital record that includes a spontaneous statement of a patient indicating present pain would not be excluded by the hearsay rule. See rules 803(6), (3) and (4).

RULE 806. ATTACKING AND SUPPORTING CREDIBILITY OF DECLARANT

When a hearsay statement, or a statement defined in Rule 801(d)(2)(C), (D), or (E), has been admitted in evidence, the credibility of the declarant may be attacked, and if attacked may be supported, by any evidence which would be admissible for those purposes if declarant had testified as a witness. Evidence of a statement or conduct by the declarant at any time, inconsistent with the declarant's hearsay statement, is not subject to any requirement that the declarant may have been afforded an opportunity to deny or explain. If the party against whom a hearsay statement has been admitted calls the declarant as a witness, the party is entitled to examine the declarant on the statement as if under cross-examination.

Adopted April 1, 1977, eff. July 1, 1977. Amended Dec. 28, 1989, eff. Jan. 1, 1990.

Committee Comment—1977

The evidentiary value of a hearsay statement is dependent upon the credibility of the declarant. The proper assessment of hearsay evidence requires an opportunity to impeach and if necessary rehabilitate the credibility of the declarant. The same rules governing impeachment and rehabilitation of witnesses at trial are applicable to a hearsay declarant. However, when impeaching a hearsay declarant with an inconsistent statement, the requirement set forth in rule 613(b) that a person be given an opportunity to explain the inconsistent statement is dispensed with. *Contra* Lerum v. Geving, 97 Minn. 269, 273, 105 N.W. 967, 969 (1906).

RULE 807. RESIDUAL EXCEPTION

A statement not specifically covered by rule 803 or 804 but having equivalent circumstantial guarantees of trustworthiness, is not excluded by the hearsay rule, if the court determines that (A) the statement is offered as evidence of a material fact; (B) the statement is more probative on the point for which it is offered than any other evidence which the proponent can procure through reasonable efforts; and (C) the general purposes of these rules and the interests of justice will best be served by admission of the statement into evidence. However, a statement may not be admitted under this exception unless the proponent of it makes known to the adverse party, sufficiently in advance of the trial or hearing, to provide the adverse party with a fair opportunity to prepare to meet it, the proponent's intention to offer the statement and the particulars of it, including the name, address and present whereabouts of the declarant.

Adopted July 18, 2006, eff. Sept. 1, 2006.

Advisory Committee Comment—2006 Amendments

The new rule 807 is taken from Fed. R. Evid. 807 and combines rules 803(24) and 804(b)(5). The rule requires the proponent to disclose, if known, the name, address and present whereabouts of the declarant. In criminal cases, offering hearsay statements against the accused from declarants who do not testify and are not subject to cross-examination, may implicate the constitutional right to confrontation.

ARTICLE 9. AUTHENTICATION AND IDENTIFICATION

RULE 901. REQUIREMENT OF AUTHENTICATION OR IDENTIFICATION

(a) General provision. The requirement of authentication or identification as a condition precedent to admissibility is satisfied by evidence sufficient to support a finding that the matter in question is what its proponent claims.

(b) Illustrations. By way of illustration only, and not by way of limitation, the following are examples of authentication or identification conforming with the requirements of this rule:

(1) *Testimony of witness with knowledge.* Testimony that a matter is what it is claimed to be.

(2) *Nonexpert opinion on handwriting.* Nonexpert opinion as to the genuineness of handwriting, based upon familiarity not acquired for purposes of the litigation.

(3) *Comparison by trier or expert witness.* Comparison by the trier of fact or by expert witnesses with specimens which have been authenticated.

(4) *Distinctive characteristics and the like.* Appearance, contents, substance, internal patterns, or other distinctive characteristics, taken in conjunction with circumstances.

(5) *Voice identification.* Identification of a voice, whether heard firsthand or through mechanical or electronic transmission or recording, by opinion based upon hearing the voice at any time under circumstances connecting it with the alleged speaker.

(6) *Telephone conversations.* Telephone conversations, by evidence that a call was made to the number assigned at the time by the telephone company to a particular person or business, if (A) in the case of a person, circumstances, including self-identification, show the person answering to be the one called, or (B) in the case of a business, the call was made to a place of business and the conversation related to business reasonably transacted over the telephone.

(7) *Public records or reports.* Evidence that a writing authorized by law to be recorded or filed and in fact recorded or filed in a public office, or a purported public record, report, statement, or data compilation, in any form, is from the public office where items of this nature are kept.

(8) *Ancient documents or data compilation.* Evidence that a document or data compilation, in any form, (A) is in such condition as to create no suspicion concerning its authenticity, (B) was in a place where it, if authentic, would likely be, and (C) has been in existence 20 years or more at the time it is offered.

(9) *Process or system.* Evidence describing a process or system used to produce a result and showing that the process or system produces an accurate result.

(10) *Methods provided by statute or rule.* Any method of authentication or identification provided by Legislative Act or by other rules prescribed by the Supreme Court pursuant to statutory authority.

Adopted April 1, 1977, eff. July 1, 1977.

Committee Comment—1977

Rule 901(a)

Authentication is simply a more specialized application of the principles of relevancy. Before probative value can be attached to an offer of evidence it must be established that the evidence, be it a chattel, a writing, or a conversation is precisely what the proponent claims it to be. The concept is frequently easy in application but most difficult to define. As a consequence the rule consists of a general statement followed by a number of illustrations setting forth possible applications of the general rule. The illustrations are not intended to limit the general rule in other areas, but are to serve only as examples of how the rule might be applied.

The general rule treats authentication in terms of a condition precedent to admissibility. To satisfy the condition precedent the proponent must present evidence "sufficient to support a finding" by the trier of fact that the offered evidence is what it is claimed to be. Authentication is governed by rule 104(b) which leaves the order of proof subject to the discretion of the court. Rule 901 does not distinguish between the authentication of writings and chattels, and applies equally to both.

Rule 901(b)

The illustrations are set out as guidelines to the application of the general rule. Rule 901(a) requires that the evidence be sufficient to support a finding that the matter in question is what it is purported to be. It is possible that a factual situation might fit within the letter of a particular illustration and yet, because of peculiar circumstances, lack the probative value required to satisfy the standard in subd. (a). Certainly there will be occasions when the authentication requirement is met by methods not suggested in subd. (b).

Rule 901(b)(1)

Perhaps the most common method of authentication is the use of testimony by a witness with knowledge that the offer of evidence is what it is represented to be. See rule 602.

Rule 901(b)(2)

This illustration makes it clear that a lay witness who is familiar with a person's handwriting should be able to give an opinion for authentication purposes. See rule 701. See also Johnson v. Burmeister, 182 Minn. 385, 386–387, 234 N.W. 590–591 (1931). However, the familiarity with the handwriting must not have been acquired for the purposes of the litigation.

Rule 901(b)(3)

In addition to the methods suggested in rules 901(b)(1) and (2), a letter could be authenticated by opinion testimony of a handwriting expert, or through comparison by the trier of fact with authenticated exemplars. The practice of allowing jurors to determine the authenticity of a writing has been approved in Minnesota. State v. Houston, 278 Minn. 41, 44, 153 N.W.2d 267, 269 (1967). The rule should not be read as a statement that jurors can authenticate other matters by comparison techniques without the benefit of expert testimony, *e.g.*, ballistics or fingerprints. These questions must be resolved on a case by case basis.

Rule 901(b)(4)

This illustration indicates that an offer of evidence can be authenticated by circumstantial evidence. Typically, letters and telephone conversations are authenticated by the well known "reply doctrine."

Rule 901(b)(5)

This provision is consistent with Minnesota law. A properly qualified witness may give his opinion as to the identity of a voice whether comparing voices heard firsthand or through a mechanical or electronic transmission or recording. State ex rel. Trimble v. Hedman, 291 Minn. 442, 450, 192 N.W.2d 432, 437 (1971). In addition, the Court in Trimble makes it clear that voiceprints are admissible at trial at least for the purposes of corroborating or impeaching other voice identifications. Id. at 457, 192 N.W.2d at 441. Although the illustration does not directly speak to voiceprints, their admission for identification purposes would not be inconsistent with the underlying rationale. See also rule 901(b)(9).

Rule 901(b)(6)

Telephone conversations can be authenticated by a number of methods, *e.g.*, the reply doctrine, rule 901(b)(4); or voice recognition, rule 901(b)(5). If the number was assigned to a person the conversation may be authenticated by introducing evidence that the call was made to the properly assigned number and the person answering the phone identified himself or his identity can be established by other circumstances. If the number was assigned to a business the conversation may be authenticated by introducing evidence that the call was made to the properly assigned number and the conversation related to the type of business reasonably transacted over the telephone.

Rule 901(b)(7)

To authenticate a public or official record, it need only be established that the document is from the custody of the appropriate office. See rules 902 and 1005 for the introduction of copies of public records. The hearsay aspects of certain public records are addressed in rules 803(8, 9, 10, 14, and 15). See generally, Minn.R.Civ.P. 44 and Minn.Stats. § 600.13 (1974).

Rule 901(b)(8)

The hearsay problems that are associated with the admissibility of ancient documents are covered in rule 803(16). The authenticity of a document or data compilation can be established by showing that it is at least 20 years old, found in a place where such documents or compilations are normally kept, and in such condition so as not to create suspicion as to its authenticity. The rule is drafted to reflect contemporary methods of data processing, retention, and storage.

Rule 901(b)(9)

The authentication of many different types of scientific testimony is addressed by this illustration. The admissibility of evidence based on X-rays, computer printouts, voice-prints, public opinion polls, etc., all depend upon a showing that the process or system used does produce an accurate result. The degree of accuracy required might vary with the purposes for which the evidence is being offered, the state of the art, and the type of method or process involved.

Rule 901(b)(10)

This illustration is intended to make it clear that rule 901 does not limit or supersede other forms of authentication. Existing statutes and court rules providing for authentication of certain evidence remain in effect. See *e.g.*, Minn.R.Civ.P. 44, 80 and 30.06. Minn.Stats. §§ 175.11 and 600.13 (1974).

RULE 902. SELF-AUTHENTICATION

Extrinsic evidence of authenticity as a condition precedent to admissibility is not required with respect to the following:

(1) Domestic public documents under seal. A document bearing a seal purporting to be that of the United States, or of any State, district, Commonwealth, territory, or insular possession thereof, or the Panama Canal Zone, or the Trust Territory of the Pacific Islands, or of a political subdivision, department, officer, or agency thereof, and a signature purporting to be an attestation or execution.

(2) Domestic public documents not under seal. A document purporting to bear the signature in the official capacity of an officer or employee of any entity included in paragraph (1) hereof, having no seal, if a public officer having a seal and having official duties in the district or political subdivision of the officer or employee certifies under seal that the signer has the official capacity and that the signature is genuine.

(3) Foreign public documents. A document purporting to be executed or attested in an official capacity by a person authorized by the laws of a foreign country to make the execution or attestation, and accompanied by a final certification as to the genuineness of the signature and official position (A) of the executing or attesting person, or (B) of any foreign official whose certificate of genuineness of signature and official position relates to the execution or attestation or is in a chain of certificates of genuineness of signature and official position relating to the execution or attestation. A final certification may be made by a secretary of embassy or legation, consul general, consul, vice consul, or consular agent of the United States, or a diplomatic or consular official of the foreign country assigned or accredited to the United States. If reasonable opportunity has been given to all parties to investigate the authenticity and accuracy of official documents, the court may, for good cause shown, order that they be treated as presumptively authentic without final certification or permit them to be evidenced by an attested summary with or without final certification.

(4) Certified copies of public records. A copy of an official record or report or entry therein, or of a document authorized by law to be recorded or filed and actually recorded or filed in a public office, including data compilations in any form, certified as correct by the custodian or other person authorized to make the certification, by certificate complying with paragraph (1), (2), or (3) of this rule or complying with any Legislative Act or rule prescribed by the Supreme Court pursuant to statutory authority.

(5) Official publications. Books, pamphlets, or other publications purporting to be issued by public authority.

(6) Newspapers and periodicals. Printed materials purporting to be newspapers or periodicals.

(7) Trade inscriptions and the like. Inscriptions, signs, tags, or labels purporting to have been affixed in the course of business and indicating ownership, control, or origin.

(8) Acknowledged documents. Documents accompanied by a certificate of acknowledgment executed in the manner provided by law by a notary public or other officer authorized by law to take acknowledgments.

(9) Commercial paper and related documents. Commercial paper, signatures thereon, and documents relating thereto to the extent provided by general commercial law.

(10) Presumptions under Legislative Acts. Any signature, document, or other matter declared by Legislative Act to be presumptively or prima facie genuine or authentic.

Adopted April 1, 1977, eff. July 1, 1977. Amended Dec. 28, 1989, eff. Jan. 1, 1990.

Committee Comment—1989

The rules retain the existing practice of dispensing with the authentication requirement for certain documentary evidence. Because of the difficulty and inconvenience that would result if formal authentication was required and the slight risk of fraud or forgery, certain documents are deemed to be self-authenticating. The fulfillment of the authentication requirement does not preclude the opposing party from attacking the genuineness of the evidence to detract from the weight to be given it by the trier of fact.

Rule 902(1)

Consistent with principles of common law, public documents under seal are self-authenticating. See gen. Minn.Stats. §§ 175.11 and 600.13 (1974). See also Minn.R.Civ.P. 44.01.

Rule 902(2)

The naked signature of a public employee or officer is not sufficient to authenticate the document. However, if accompanied by a certification under seal by a second public officer under the circumstances set out in the rule, the document becomes self-authenticating.

Rule 902(3)

Rule 902(3) was adapted from Fed.R.Civ.P. 44 (Minn.R.Civ.P. 44.01(2)).

Rule 902(4)

Consistent with the common law, certified copies of public records need no additional authentication. See Minn.Stats. § 600.13 (1974) and Minn.R.Civ.P. 44.01. The rule requires that the copy be of a public or official record, that the custodian or other authorized person certify the copy, and that the certificate comply with rule 902(1–3), a specific statute, or other court rule. The contents of the certificate should generally indicate the status of the signer in relation to the custody of the document, and the accuracy of the copy.

Rule 902(5)

This provision is generally consistent with existing practice. See *e.g.,* Minn.R.Civ.P. 44, Minn. Stats. §§ 599.02, 648.33 (1974).

Rule 902(6)

The provision alters the common law, by placing the burden to contest the genuineness of newspapers and other periodicals on the party opposing the offer. Cf. Minn.Stats. §§ 600.10–12 (1974). It is based on the theory that the likelihood of forgery in these matters is slight and the inconvenience and expense involved by requiring authentication is not justified. The rule speaks only to authentication. The admissibility of such evidence can be challenged pursuant to other rules of evidence.

Rule 902(7)

The rule is based on the unlikelihood of forgery of a trade inscription. In addition, the business community accepts and relies upon the trustworthiness of trade inscriptions. Although this rule is not unquestioned at common law, it represents a reasoned view that is supported in the case law. See United States Supreme Court Advisory Committee Note and cases cited therein.

Rule 902(8, 9)

These provisions are consistent with existing practice. Minn.Stats. § 600.14 (1974). See Minn. Stats. § 358.15 (1974) for the parties authorized to take acknowledgments and Minn.Stats. §§ 358.34–37 (1974) for the manner of taking acknowledgments. The evidentiary rule is not intended to affect the legal requirements for establishing a valid, executed will set forth by the Uniform Probate Code, Minn.Stats. § 524.1–101 et seq. (1974). See in particular, Minn.Stats.1975 Supp. § 524.2–501 et seq. The authentication of commercial paper is governed by statutory law. See *e.g.*, Minn.Stats. §§ 336.1–202, 336.3–307, 336.3–510 and 336.8–105 (1974).

Rule 902(10)

In addition to the provisions in these rules, evidence can be authenticated pursuant to specific statutes.

Rule 902(11)

Uniform Rule 902(11) adds business records to those writings that are self-authenticating. The committee considered Rule 902(11) and recommends against adopting it.

Under present Minnesota law, the authentication requirement for business records is found in Rule 803(6) (. . . "all as shown by the testimony of the custodian or other qualified witness, . . ."). The extensive discovery available in both civil and criminal procedures provides a vehicle for resolving authentication issues before trial. The authentication requirement is generally waived. With respect to the minority of cases in which the parties cannot resolve the issue prior to trial, the committee took the view that a party should have the right to insist upon the proof required by Rule 803(6). For these reasons the committee decided not to recommend that business records be added to the list of self-authenticating documents, and recommends that Uniform Rule 902(11) not be adopted.

RULE 903. SUBSCRIBING WITNESS' TESTIMONY UNNECESSARY

The testimony of a subscribing witness is not necessary to authenticate a writing unless required by the laws of the jurisdiction whose laws govern the validity of the writing.

Adopted April 1, 1977, eff. July 1, 1977.

Committee Comment—1977

To authenticate a writing there is no need to present subscribing witnesses unless otherwise required by the laws of the jurisdiction governing the validity of the writing. E.g., Minn.Stats.1975 Supp. § 524.3–406, which in certain circumstances requires the production of an attesting witness.

ARTICLE 10. CONTENTS OF WRITINGS, RECORDINGS, AND PHOTOGRAPHS

RULE 1001. DEFINITIONS

For purposes of this article the following definitions are applicable:

(1) Writings and recordings. "Writings" and "recordings" consist of letters, words, or numbers, or their equivalent, set down by handwriting, typewriting, printing, photostating, photographing, magnetic impulse, mechanical or electronic recording, or other form of data compilation.

(2) Photographs. "Photographs" include still photographs, X-ray films, video tapes, and motion pictures.

(3) Original. An "original" of a writing or recording is the writing or recording itself or any counterpart intended to have the same effect by a person executing or issuing it. An "original" of a photograph includes the negative or any print therefrom. If data are stored in a computer or similar device, any printout or other output readable by sight, shown to reflect the data accurately, is an "original".

(4) Duplicate. A "duplicate" is a counterpart produced by the same impression as the original, or from the same matrix, or by means of photography, including enlargements and miniatures, or by mechanical or electronic re-recording, or by chemical reproduction, or by other equivalent techniques which accurately reproduces the original.

Adopted April 1, 1977, eff. July 1, 1977.

Committee Comment—1977

Article 10 deals with the so called "best evidence rule." Rule 1001 is the definitional portion of the article. The rule is drafted sufficiently broad to encompass future scientific advances in the storage and retrieval of data and other information.

Consistent with existing practice, not only the writing itself is classified as an original, but also any counterpart intended to have the same effect by a person executing or issuing it. Thus executed carbon copies are treated as originals. The rule resolves two issues that have been raised in other jurisdictions.

1) Both the negative and the print of a photograph are treated as an original.

2) Data printouts, readable by sight, are treated as originals. Practicality and common usage justify this result. See United States Supreme Court Advisory Committee Note.

RULE 1002. REQUIREMENT OF ORIGINAL

To prove the content of a writing, recording, or photograph, the original writing, recording, or photograph is required, except as otherwise provided in these rules or by Legislative Act.

Adopted April 1, 1977, eff. July 1, 1977.

Committee Comment—1977

This provision is a straightforward statement of the general rule. Only when a party is attempting to prove the contents of a writing, recording, or photograph, must the original be produced. If a party is attempting to prove a different consequential fact there is no general requirement that he do so with the best available evidence. See generally C. McCormick, Evidence § 233 (2d ed. 1972). The rule does not address the question that arises when a party attempts to prove the contents of a writing inscribed on a chattel, e.g., a ring, a license plate, a billboard, etc. The question of whether the chattel must be produced in these cases is left to the discretion of the trial court. See, *e.g.*, Mattson v. Minnesota & North Wisconsin R.R., 98 Minn. 296, 298, 108 N.W. 517, 518 (1906).

RULE 1003. ADMISSIBILITY OF DUPLICATES

A duplicate is admissible to the same extent as an original unless (1) a genuine question is raised as to the authenticity of the original or (2) in the circumstances it would be unfair to admit the duplicate in lieu of the original.

Adopted April 1, 1977, eff. July 1, 1977.

Committee Comment—1977

With the development of accurate and convenient reproducing systems much of the concern about the admission of duplicates is eliminated. There remains the fear of possible fraud. However, in most instances where the accuracy of a duplicate is not contested it makes little sense to prohibit the introduction of a duplicate. It makes less sense in civil cases where the litigants by way of discovery usually can examine the original documents. The courts should not place a heavy burden on the party contesting the admission of the duplicates.

The rule will mark a change in Minnesota practice, but not a major change. At present copies made and kept in the ordinary course of business are treated as originals. Minn.Stats. § 600.135 (1974).

RULE 1004. ADMISSIBILITY OF OTHER EVIDENCE OF CONTENTS

The original is not required, and other evidence of the contents of a writing, recording, or photograph is admissible if—

(1) **Originals lost or destroyed.** All originals are lost or have been destroyed, unless the proponent lost or destroyed them in bad faith; or

(2) **Original not obtainable.** No original can be obtained by any available judicial process or procedure; or

(3) **Original in possession of opponent.** At a time when an original was under the control of the party against whom offered, that party was put on notice, by the pleadings or otherwise, that the contents would be a subject of proof at the hearing, and that party does not produce the original at the hearing; or

(4) **Collateral matters.** The writing, recording, or photograph is not closely related to a controlling issue.

Adopted April 1, 1977, eff. July 1, 1977. Amended Dec. 28, 1989, eff. Jan. 1, 1990.

Committee Comment—1977

This rule is a codification of the common law. In application the rule requiring the production of the original writing is a rule of preference. If the original is available it must be produced if the contents are at issue. However, where the original is not available courts have traditionally permitted the admission of secondary evidence in the circumstances set out in the rule.

RULE 1005. PUBLIC RECORDS

The contents of an official record, or of a document authorized to be recorded or filed and actually recorded or filed, including data compilations in any form, if otherwise admissible, may be proved by copy, certified as correct in accordance with rule 902 or testified to be correct by a witness who has compared it with the original. If a copy which complies with the foregoing cannot be obtained by the exercise of reasonable diligence, then other evidence of the contents may be given.

Adopted April 1, 1977, eff. July 1, 1977.

Committee Comment—1977

An official record or authorized document which has been filed or recorded may be proved by a certified copy. This is consistent with existing practice under Minn.Stat. § 600.13 (1974). If a certified copy is not obtainable, the record can be established by other types of evidence including oral testimony.

RULE 1006. SUMMARIES

The contents of voluminous writings, recordings, or photographs which cannot conveniently be examined in court may be presented in the form of a chart, summary, or calculation. The originals, or duplicates, shall be made available for examination or copying, or both, by other parties at a reasonable time and place. The court may order that they be produced in court.

Adopted April 1, 1977, eff. July 1, 1977. Amended Dec. 28, 1989, eff. Jan. 1, 1990.

Committee Comment—1977

In cases involving voluminous records, the only practical way to introduce the evidence in a meaningful fashion is by resorting to charts, summaries, or calculations. The rule does not require that the original documents be introduced into evidence. However, they must be made available for inspection or copying. The court has the power to require production of the original documents in court.

RULE 1007. TESTIMONY OR WRITTEN ADMISSION OF PARTY

Contents of writings, recordings, or photographs may be proved by the testimony or deposition of the party against whom offered or by that party's written admission, without accounting for the non-production of the original.

Adopted April 1, 1977, eff. July 1, 1977. Amended Dec. 28, 1989, eff. Jan. 1, 1990.

Committee Comment—1977

The original need not be produced if the contents of the writing can be established by the testimony, deposition or written admission of an opposing party. See Swing v. Cloquet Lumber Co., 121 Minn. 221, 225, 141 N.W. 117, 118 (1913). In each of these situations the policy rationale for requiring the original writing is satisfied, with the possible exception that the party opponent's admission might not be accurate. The nature of the adversary system justifies this result. In order to avoid the dangers of erroneous transmission, an oral out of court admission by an adversary is not sufficient to prove the contents of a writing.

RULE 1008. FUNCTIONS OF COURT AND JURY

When the admissibility of other evidence of contents of writings, recordings, or photographs under these rules depends upon the fulfillment of a condition of fact, the question whether the condition has been fulfilled is ordinarily for the court to determine in accordance with the provisions of rule 104. However, when an issue is raised (a) whether the asserted writing ever existed, or (b) whether another writing, recording, or photograph produced at the trial is the original, or (c) whether other evidence of contents correctly reflects the contents, the issue is for the trier of fact to determine as in the case of other issues of fact.

Adopted April 1, 1977, eff. July 1, 1977.

Committee Comment—1977

The rule is merely a specialized application of rule 104. Rule 104 sets out the respective functions of the judge and jury. The judge is to make all determinations as to the competency or admissibility of the evidence and the jury is to determine the relevance or probative worth of the evidence. The "best evidence rule" is essentially a rule of competency. Secondary evidence is not competent to prove the contents of an original writing unless the original is destroyed, not available, etc. It is a matter for the judge to decide pursuant to rules 1008 and 104(a) whether the condition precedent for admissibility has been established. Beyond the questions of admissibility certain factual disputes may arise. Three possible issues are listed in the rule:

1) whether the original ever existed;

2) which of two evidentiary items is the original; and

3) whether the secondary evidence correctly reflects the contents of the original.

As to these questions the judge's function is to determine whether there is sufficient evidence in the record to support a finding on the issue. If sufficient evidence is in the record the issues must be submitted to the trier of fact for resolution.

ARTICLE 11. MISCELLANEOUS RULES

RULE 1101. RULES APPLICABLE

(a) Except as otherwise provided in subdivision (b), these rules apply to all actions and proceedings in the courts of this state.

(b) Rules inapplicable. The rules other than those with respect to privileges do not apply in the following situations:

(1) *Preliminary questions of fact.* The determination of questions of fact preliminary to admissibility of evidence when the issue is to be determined by the court under Rule 104(a).

(2) *Grand jury.* Proceedings before grand juries.

(3) *Miscellaneous proceedings.* Proceedings for extradition or rendition; probable cause hearings; sentencing, or granting or revoking probation; issuance of warrants for arrest, criminal summonses, and search warrants; and proceedings with respect to release on bail or otherwise.

(4) Contempt proceedings in which the court may act summarily.

Adopted April 1, 1977, eff. July 1, 1977.

Committee Comment—1977

These rules of evidence are not applicable to certain procedures. However, these proceedings may be governed by evidentiary rules set forth in statutes, federal and state constitutions, and other court rules. See *e.g.,* Minn.R.Crim.P. 18.06.

INDEX TO RULES OF EVIDENCE

RULES OF CIVIL APPELLATE PROCEDURE

Effective August 1, 1983

Including Amendments Received Through January 1, 2014

Research Note

See Minnesota Statutes Annotated, *Volume 51, for case annotations, historical notes, and library references. The Rules of Civil Appellate Procedure are discussed in Magnuson, and Herr, 3* Minnesota Practice–Appellate Rules Annotated (2010 Ed.).

APPENDIX OF FORMS

1998 Order

The order of the Minnesota Supreme Court [C4-84-2133] dated July 7, 1998, provides in part:

"1. The attached amendments to the Rules of Civil Appellate procedure be, and the same hereby are, prescribed and promulgated to be effective on January 1, 1999.

"2. The Effective Date of these amendments is January 1, 1999. These amendments shall apply to all actions or proceedings pending on or commenced on or after the Effective Date. As to matters pending on the Effective Date of these rules, the following special rules apply:

"a. The time to appeal from appealable orders filed before the Effective Date shall be governed by Rule 104, as amended.

"b. As to appeals from judgments entered before the Effective Date of these rules, appeals may be taken within the time permitted by either the old or new version of Rule 104.

"c. For appeals of orders filed, or judgments entered, before the Effective Date of these rules and governed by former Rule 104.04 an appeal may be taken within the time permitted by either the old or new version of the rules, including consideration of any tolling effect of former Rule 104.04.

"d. As to all matters where post-trial motions as defined in new Rule 104.01, subd. 2, are served and filed but not decided as of the Effective Date, the time to appeal shall be governed by that rule.

"3. The inclusion of Advisory Committee comments is made for convenience and does not reflect court approval of the comments made therein."

TITLE I. APPLICABILITY OF RULES

RULE 101. SCOPE OF RULES; DEFINITIONS

Rule 101.01. Scope

These rules govern procedure in the Supreme Court and the Court of Appeals of Minnesota in civil appeals; in criminal appeals insofar as the rules are not inconsistent with the Rules of Criminal Procedure; in proceedings for review of orders of administrative agencies, boards or commissions; and on applications for writs or other relief in civil proceedings which the Supreme Court, the Court of Appeals or a justice or judge thereof is competent to give.

Amended June 17, 1983, eff. Aug. 1, 1983; Nov. 10, 1983, eff. Aug. 1, 1983.

Advisory Committee Note—1967

See note following Rule 101.02.

Rule 101.02. Definitions

Subdivision 1. When used in these rules, the words listed below have the meanings given them.

Subd. 2. "Appellate court" means the Supreme Court pursuant to Minnesota Statutes, Chapter 480, or the Court of Appeals pursuant to Minnesota Statutes, Chapter 480A.

Subd. 3. "Judge" means a justice of the Supreme Court or a judge of the Court of Appeals.

Subd. 4. "Trial court" means the court or agency whose decision is sought to be reviewed.

Subd. 5. "Clerk of the appellate courts" means the clerk of the Supreme Court and the Court of Appeals.

Subd. 6. "Appellant" means the party seeking review including relators and petitioners.

Amended June 17, 1983, eff. Aug. 1, 1983; Nov. 10, 1983, eff. Aug. 1, 1983; Dec. 6, 1991, eff. Jan. 1, 1992.

Advisory Committee Note—1967

This rule is substantially the same as P.Fed. R.App.P. 1(a), and is primarily introductory. There is no similar Minnesota Supreme Court Rule. All criminal proceedings are excluded from the scope of the rules. The term "trial court" is used to describe the district court, municipal court, or any other court or agency from which appeals to or review by the Supreme Court are or may be authorized.

While the rules do not directly apply to criminal proceedings, it is anticipated that the rules will be followed in respect to appeals of criminal matters insofar as the rules are not inconsistent with the several statutes (e.g., M.S.A. c. 632, c. 611) which govern criminal procedure.

RULE 102. SUSPENSION OF RULES

In the interest of expediting decision upon any matter before it, or for other good cause shown, the Supreme Court or the Court of Appeals, except as otherwise provided in Rule 126.02, may suspend the requirements or provisions of these rules on application of a party or on its own motion and may order proceedings in accordance with its direction.

Adopted Dec. 7, 1967, eff. Feb. 1, 1968. Amended June 17, 1983, eff. Aug. 1, 1983; Nov. 10, 1983, eff. Aug. 1, 1983.

Advisory Committee Note—1967

This rule is substantially the same as P.Fed. R.App.P. 2, and is similar to Minn.Sup.Ct.R. XXI. The primary purpose of this rule is to make clear the power of the Supreme Court to expedite the determination of cases of pressing concern to the public or to the litigants. Thus, it would permit the Supreme Court to decide an appeal where a party could have appealed from an appealable order but, through inadvertence, perfected a timely appeal from a non-appealable order. See Locke v. Henry, 273 Minn. 491, 141 N.W.2d 736 (1966). The rule also contains a procedure to relieve litigants of the consequences of default where manifest injustice would otherwise result. Rule 126.02 prohibits the Supreme Court from extending the time for taking appeal or seeking review.

TITLE II. APPEALS FROM JUDGMENTS AND ORDERS

RULE 103. APPEAL—HOW TAKEN

Rule 103.01. Manner of Making Appeal

Subdivision 1. Notice of Appeal and Filings. An appeal shall be made by filing a notice of appeal with the clerk of the appellate courts and serving the notice on the adverse party or parties within the appeal period. The notice shall contain:

(a) a statement specifying the judgment or order from which the appeal is taken; and

(b) the names, addresses, and telephone numbers of opposing counsel, indicating the parties they represent.

The notice shall be accompanied by:

(c) proof of service on the adverse party or parties; and

(d) proof of filing with the administrator of the trial court in which the judgment or order appealed from is entered or filed.

The appellant shall simultaneously file the following with the clerk of the appellate courts:

(1) two copies of the notice of appeal,

(2) a certified copy of the judgment or order from which the appeal is taken,

(3) two copies of the statement of the case required by Rule 133.03, and

(4) a filing fee of $550.

The appellant shall file the following simultaneously with the trial court administrator:

(1) a copy of the notice of appeal, and

(2) the cost bond required by Rule 107, or written waiver of it.

Subd. 2. Relief. When a party in good faith files and serves a notice of appeal from a judgment or an order, and omits, through inadvertence or mistake, to proceed further with the appeal, or to stay proceedings, the appellate court may grant relief on such terms as may be just.

Subd. 3. When Filing Fee Not Required. The filing fees set out in Rule 103.01, subdivision 1, shall not be required when:

(a) the appellant has been authorized to proceed without payment of the filing fee pursuant to Rule 109; or

(b) the appellant is represented by a public defender's office or a legal aid society; or

(c) the appellant is a party to a proceeding pursuant to Minnesota Statutes, chapter 253B; or

(d) the appellant is the state or a governmental subdivision of the state or an officer, employee or agency thereof; or

(e) the appeal has been remanded to the trial court or agency for further proceedings and, upon completion of those proceedings, the appeal is renewed; or

(f) the appellant is a party to a public assistance appeal pursuant to Minnesota Statutes, chapter 256; or

(g) the appeal is taken by a claimant for unemployment compensation benefits pursuant to Minnesota Statutes, chapter 268.

Adopted Dec. 7, 1967, eff. Feb. 1, 1968. Amended Oct. 23, 1969; Feb. 14, 1975; April 9, 1979; June 17, 1983, eff. Aug. 1, 1983; Nov. 10, 1983, eff. Aug. 1, 1983; June 28, 1989; May 10, 1990; Dec. 6, 1991, eff. Jan. 1, 1992; June 29, 1993, eff. July 1, 1993; July 7, 1998, eff. Jan. 1, 1999; Dec. 19, 2000, eff. March 1, 2001; June 13, 2003, eff. July 1, 2003; June 11, 2009, eff. July 1, 2009.

Comment—1983

Filing the notice of appeal with the clerk of the appellate courts, in addition to service on the adverse party, is required to initiate an appeal.

A substantial change has been made in Rule 103.01. Under the new rule service alone no longer initiates an appeal. The notice of appeal served on both the adverse party and the clerk of the trial court and filed with the clerk of the appellate courts is required in order to vest jurisdiction in the Court of Appeals.

Proof of service, a certified copy of the judgment or order from which the appeal is taken, and the statement of the case (described at Rule 133.03) must accompany the notice of appeal when it is filed. For purposes of these rules, filing is timely if the notice of appeal is deposited in the mail within the time fixed for filing. See Rule 125.01.

A change has been made in the amount of the filing fee and to which courts it is paid.

Since prehearing conferences will be held only if the court so directs, within 10 days after filing the notice of appeal the appellant must send to the clerk of the appellate courts a written order for the transcript or a notice of intent to proceed on a statement of the proceedings. See Rule 110.02.

See Appendix for form of notice of appeal (Forms 103A and 103B) and statement of the case (Form 133).

Advisory Committee Comment—1998 Amendments

The additional language in the first paragraph of the rule is intended to clarify the steps that must be taken to invoke appellate jurisdiction. Timely filing the notice of appeal with the clerk of the appellate courts and timely service on the adverse party are the jurisdictional steps required to initiate an appeal. Failure of an appellant to take any step other than the timely filing and service of the notice of appeal does not affect appellate jurisdiction, but is ground only for such action as the appellate court deems appropriate, which may include dismissal of the appeal. The reference to supersedeas bonds previously contained in the rule has been deleted, in light of the concurrent revisions made to Rule 108, which clarify the timing and procedure regarding filing supersedeas bonds.

Historical Notes

The order of the Minnesota Supreme Court [ADM–09–8006] dated June 11, 2009, amending the Rules of Civil Appellate Procedure by increasing filing fees, also provided that the amendments are effective July 1, 2009, and apply to all filings in the appellate courts on or after that date.

The order of the Minnesota Supreme Court [C4-84-2133] dated December 19, 2000, provides in part that these amendments are effective March 1, 2001, and shall apply to all actions or proceedings pending on or commenced on or after the effective date, with the exception of the amendments to Rule 132, which shall apply to all appeals or proceedings commenced in either the Court of Appeals or the Supreme Court on or after the effective date.

The order of the Minnesota Supreme Court [C4-84-2133] dated December 19, 2000, provides in part that "(t)he inclusion of Advisory Committee comments is made for convenience and does not reflect court approval of the statements made therein".

Rule 103.02. Joint Appeals; Related Appeals; Consolidated Appeals

Subdivision 1. Joint Appeals. If two or more parties are entitled to appeal from a judgment or order or to petition for certiorari in the same action and their interests are such as to make joinder practicable, they may file a joint notice of appeal or petition, or may join in the appeal after filing separate timely notices of appeal or petitions for certiorari, and they may then proceed on appeal as a single appellant.

Subd. 2. Related Appeals. After one party timely files a notice of appeal, any other party may seek review of a judgment or order in the same action by serving and filing a notice of related appeal. The notice of related appeal shall specify the judgment or order to be reviewed. The notice of related appeal shall be accompanied by:

(a) a filing fee of $100,

(b) a certified copy of the judgment or order from which the related appeal is taken if different than the judgment or order being challenged in the original appeal, and

(c) two copies of a statement of the case.

A separate cost bond is not required unless ordered by the court.

Subd. 3. Consolidated Appeals. Related appeals from a single trial court action or appeals in separate actions may be consolidated by order of the appellate court on its own motion or upon motion of a party.

Adopted Dec. 7, 1967, eff. Feb. 1, 1968. Amended June 17, 1983, eff. Aug. 1, 1983; Nov. 10, 1983, eff. Aug. 1, 1983; Oct. 16, 2009, eff. Jan. 1, 2010.

Advisory Committee Note—1967

Rule 103.02. This rule adopts P.Fed.R.App.P. 3(b) and Fed.R.Civ.P. 74 (as amended, July 1, 1966). It reflects the Minnesota Supreme Court's declaration that the common law rule against duplicity is not effective where there is no interference with orderly appellate procedure and the rights of the respondent are not prejudiced or adversely affected. See Common Sch. Dist. No. 1317 v. Board of County Com'rs, 267 Minn, 372, 127 N.W.2d 528, 533 (1964).

Advisory Committee Comment—2009 Amendments

Rule 103.02 is amended to add a new subdivision 2 to establish a new procedure for filing of a cross-appeal or another related appeal after any party has filed a notice of appeal. This rule applies in civil cases, as the Minnesota Rules of Criminal Procedure address the right to file a cross-appeal in criminal cases. *See* MINN. R. CRIM. P. 28.04, subd. 3. The new notice is denominated a "Notice of Related Appeal." *See* Appendix for form of Notice of Related Appeal (Form 103C). This procedure replaces the notice-of-review procedure formerly established by Rule 106. Existing subdivision 2 is renumbered as subdivision 3 and is amended to provide for consolidation of related appeals from a single trial court proceeding. This consolidation may be ordered by the court based on information in the statement of the case or may be ordered upon motion of any party to any related appeal.

Historical Notes

The order of the Supreme Court dated Oct. 16, 2009, provided:

"1. The attached amendments to the Rules of Civil Appellate Procedure be, and the same are, prescribed and promulgated to be effective on January 1, 2010.

"2. These amendments shall apply to all actions or proceedings pending on or commenced on or after the effective date.

"3. The inclusion of Advisory Committee comments is for convenience and does not reflect court approval of the statements made therein."

Rule 103.03. Appealable Judgments and Orders

An appeal may be taken to the Court of Appeals:

(a) from a final judgment, or from a partial judgment entered pursuant to Minn. R. Civ. P. 54.02;

(b) from an order which grants, refuses, dissolves or refuses to dissolve, an injunction;

(c) from an order vacating or sustaining an attachment;

(d) from an order denying a new trial, or from an order granting a new trial if the trial court expressly states therein, or in a memorandum attached thereto, that the order is based exclusively upon errors of law occurring at the trial, and upon no other ground; and the trial court shall specify such errors in its order or memorandum, but upon appeal, such order granting a new trial may be sustained for errors of law prejudicial to respondent other than those specified by the trial court;

(e) from an order which, in effect, determines the action and prevents a judgment from which an appeal might be taken;

(f) from a final order or judgment made or rendered in proceedings supplementary to execution;

(g) except as otherwise provided by statute, from a final order, decision or judgment affecting a substantial right made in an administrative or other special proceeding;

(h) from an order that grants or denies modification of custody, visitation, maintenance, or child support provisions in an existing judgment or decree;

(i) if the trial court certifies that the question presented is important and doubtful, from an order which denies a motion to dismiss for failure to state a claim upon which relief can be granted or from an order which denies a motion for summary judgment; and

(j) from such other orders or decisions as may be appealable by statute or under the decisions of the Minnesota appellate courts.

Adopted Dec. 7, 1967, eff. Feb. 1, 1968. Amended April 9, 1979; June 17, 1983, eff. Aug. 1, 1983; Nov. 10, 1983, eff. Aug. 1, 1983; July 7, 1998, eff. Jan. 1, 1999; Sept. 9, 1998, eff. Jan. 1, 1999; Dec. 19, 2000, eff. March 1, 2001.

Comment—1983

Two substantial changes have been made in Rule 103.03. The deletion from clause (a) of "order for judgment" marks a return to former practice: a judgment is appealable; an order for judgment is not appealable. Because of the uncertainties resulting from its broad, unspecific language, former clause (d) "From an order involving the merits of the action or some part thereof" has also been deleted. Review of any order not specifically enumerated in Rule 103.03 is discretionary only, and permission to appeal must be sought pursuant to Rule 105.

Advisory Committee Comment—1998 Amendments

While Rule 103.03 contains a nearly exhaustive list of appealable orders and judgments, it is not the exclusive basis for appellate jurisdiction. *See In re State & Regents Bldg. Asbestos Cases*, 435 N.W.2d 521 (Minn. 1989); *Anderson v. City of Hopkins*, 393 N.W.2d 363 (Minn. 1986). In these and other cases, the Minnesota Supreme Court has recognized that there are certain instances in which an appeal may be allowed as a matter of right even though the ground for that appeal is not found expressly in the provisions of Rule 103.03. Such instances include:

Orders granting or denying motions to dismiss or for summary judgment when the motions are based on the trial court's alleged lack of personal or subject matter jurisdiction, regardless of whether the motion seeks dismissal of the entire action. *See McGowan v. Our Savior's Lutheran Church*, 527 N.W.2d 830, 833 (Minn. 1995) (order denying summary judgment is appealable when motion is based on district court's lack of subject matter jurisdiction); *Hunt v. Nevada State Bank*, 285 Minn. 77, 88-89, 172 N.W.2d 292, 298 (1969) (order denying motion to dismiss for lack of personal jurisdiction immediately appealable of right).

Orders denying motions to dismiss or for summary judgment based on governmental immunity from suit, provided that the denial is not based on the existence of a question of fact. *See Anderson*, 393 N.W.2d at 364 (order denying defendant's motion for summary judgment is appealable when motion is based on governmental immunity from suit); *Carter v. Cole*, 526 N.W.2d 209 (Minn. App. 1995), *aff'd*, 539 N.W.2d 241 (Minn. 1995) (affirming dismissal of appeal from order denying government official's motion for summary judgment based solely on the finding that there is a genuine issue of material fact whether the official committed the acts alleged; reserving question of appealability of an order denying summary judgment where the genuine issues of material fact identified by the trial court are related to the issue of immunity, and not to the merits of the claim); *see also Johnson v. Jones*, 515 U.S. 304, 115 S.Ct. 2151, 132 L.Ed.2d 238 (1995) (order denying summary judgment on immunity grounds not appealable where motion is denied because of genuine issue of material fact).

Orders vacating final orders or judgments, when the orders are issued after the time to appeal the underlying orders or judgments has expired, or from orders refusing to vacate default judgments. *See State & Regents*, 435 N.W.2d at 522 (order vacating final judgment is appealable); *Spicer v. Carefree Vacations, Inc.*, 370 N.W.2d 424 (Minn. 1985) (denial of a Rule 60 motion is appealable if the judgment is rendered *ex parte* against a party who has made no appearance). *But see Carlson v. Panuska*, 555 N.W.2d 745 (Minn. 1996) (*Spicer* exception applies only to true default judgments and not to "default" judgments entered after contested hearings for failure to comply with discovery orders).

In addition, certain statutes provide for appeals as a matter of right, even though Rule 103.03 does not expressly so provide. *See, e.g.*, MINN. STAT. § 572.26, subd. I (listing appealable orders in arbitration proceedings, which are not "special" proceedings under Rule 103.03), *Pulju v. Metropolitan Property & Cas.*, 535 N.W.2d 608 (Minn. 1995).

These examples are not intended to be exhaustive, but rather to emphasize that there are limited grounds for appeal other than those set forth in Rule 103.03. *See generally* Scott W. Johnson, *Common Law Appellate Jurisdiction*, BENCH & BAR OF MINN., Sept. 1997, at 31.

Advisory Committee Comment—2000 Amendments

Rule 103.03 is amended to add a new subdivision (h) and renumber existing paragraphs (h) and (i) to become (i) and (j). The purpose of this amendment is to clarify that orders that grant or deny modification of custody, visitation, maintenance, and support provisions are appealable in accordance with *Angelos v. Angelos*, 367 N.W.2d 518 (Minn. 1985). These orders are appealable under paragraph (g) (final order in a special proceeding), but because of the volume of such orders, as well as the frequent involvement of *pro se* litigants, the Committee believes an explicit provision will minimize confusion. This change is not intended to expand appealability of otherwise unappealable orders, but rather, is meant to have the rule correctly identify these orders as appealable.

Historical Notes

The order of the Minnesota Supreme Court [C4-84-2133] dated December 19, 2000, provides in part that these amendments are effective March 1, 2001, and shall apply to all actions or proceedings pending on or commenced on or after the effective date, with the exception of the amendments to Rule 132, which shall apply to all appeals or proceedings commenced in either the Court of Appeals or the Supreme Court on or after the effective date.

The order of the Minnesota Supreme Court [C4-84-2133] dated December 19, 2000, provides in part that "(t)he inclusion of Advisory Committee comments is made for convenience and does not reflect court approval of the statements made therein".

Rule 103.04. Scope of Review

The appellate courts may reverse, affirm or modify the judgment or order appealed from or take any other action as the interest of justice may require.

On appeal from or review of an order the appellate courts may review any order affecting the order from which the appeal is taken and on appeal from a judgment may review any order involving the merits or affecting the judgment. They may review any other matter as the interest of justice may require. The scope of review afforded may be affected by whether proper steps have been taken to preserve issues for review on appeal, including the existence of timely and proper post-trial motions.

Adopted Dec. 7, 1967, eff. Feb. 1, 1968. Amended June 17, 1983, eff. Aug. 1, 1983; Nov. 10, 1983, eff. Aug. 1, 1983; July 7, 1998, eff. Jan. 1. 1999.

Advisory Committee Comment—1998 Amendments

The rule has been changed to make clear that the scope of review can and often does depend upon the scope of the trial proceedings. As a general proposition, appellate review is limited to review of the facts and legal arguments that are contained in the trial record. The conduct of the trial proceedings will affect the scope of review on appeal. *See Sauter v. Wasemiller*, 389 N.W.2d 200 (Minn. 1986); *Northwestern State Bank v. Foss*. 287 Minn. 508, 511, 177 N.W.2d 292, 294 (1970). This is true notwithstanding the broad statement of the appellate courts' scope of review contained in Rule 103.04. *See* MINN. CONST. art. 6, § 2.

Litigants often fail to recognize the importance of post-trial motions, and the sometimes dramatic consequences of the failure to bring them. Though commentators have alerted lawyers to this issue, *see* 3 ERIC J. MAGNUSON & DAVID F. HERR, MINNESOTA PRACTICE: APPELLATE RULES ANNOTATED § 103.17 (3d ed. 1996), problems associated with failure to file appropriate post-trial motions continues to be a significant, recurring problem. This rule amendment is intended to ameliorate the problem.

RULE 104. TIME FOR FILING AND SERVICE OF NOTICE OF APPEAL AND NOTICE OF RELATED APPEAL

Rule 104.01. Time for Filing and Service

Subdivision 1. Time for Appeal. Unless a different time is provided by statute, an appeal may be taken from a judgment within 60 days after its entry, and from an appealable order within 60 days after service by any party of written notice of its filing.

An appeal may be taken from a judgment entered pursuant to Rule 54.02, Minnesota Rules of Civil Procedure, within 60 days of the entry of the judgment only if the trial court makes an express determination that there is no just reason for delay and expressly directs the entry of a final judgment. The time to appeal from any other judgment entered pursuant to Rule 54.02 shall not begin to run until the entry of a judgment which adjudicates all the claims and rights and liabilities of the remaining parties.

Subd. 2. Effect of Post-Decision Motions. Unless otherwise provided by law, if any party serves and files a proper and timely motion of a type specified immediately below, the time for appeal of the order or judgment that is the subject of such motion runs for all parties from the service by any party of notice of filing of the order disposing of the last such motion outstanding. This provision applies to a proper and timely motion:

(a) for judgment as a matter of law under Minn. R. Civ. P. 50.02;

(b) to amend or make findings of fact under Minn.R.Civ.P. 52.02, whether or not granting the motion would alter the judgment;

(c) to alter or amend the judgment under Minn. R.Civ.P. 52.02;

(d) for a new trial under Minn.R.Civ.P. 59;

(e) for relief under Minn.R.Civ.P. 60 if the motion is filed within the time for a motion for new trial; or

(f) in proceedings not governed by the Rules of Civil Procedure, a proper and timely motion that seeks the same or equivalent relief as those motions listed in (a)-(e).

Subd. 3. Premature Appeal. A notice of appeal filed before the disposition of any of the above motions is premature and of no effect, and does not divest the trial court of jurisdiction to dispose of the motion. A new notice of appeal must be filed within the time prescribed to appeal the underlying order or judgment, measured from the service of notice of filing of the order disposing of the outstanding motion. If a party has already paid a filing fee in connection with a premature appeal, no additional fee shall be required from that party for the filing of a new notice of appeal or notice of related appeal pursuant to Rule 103.02, subdivision 2.

Subd. 4. Multiple Appeals. After one party timely files a notice of appeal, any other party may serve and file a notice of related appeal within 14 days after service of the first notice of appeal, or within the time otherwise prescribed by subdivisions 1 and 2 of this rule, whichever period ends later.

Adopted Dec. 7, 1967, eff. Feb. 1, 1968. Amended Dec. 4, 1980, eff. Jan. 1, 1981; June 17, 1983, eff. Aug. 1, 1983; Nov. 10, 1983, eff. Aug. 1, 1983; July 7, 1998, eff. Jan. 1, 1999; Nov. 30, 2005, eff. Jan. 1, 2006; Oct. 16, 2009, eff. Jan. 1, 2010.

Advisory Committee Note—1967

Rule 104.01. This rule is identical to M.S.A. § 605.08(1) (1963). P.Fed.R.App.P. 4 and Fed. R.Civ.P. 75(a) (as amended, July 1, 1966), contain a substantially dissimilar procedure. Neither the Supreme Court nor the trial court nor the parties may extend time to appeal. Tombs v. Ashworth, 255 Minn. 55, 95 N.W.2d 423 (1959); Eisenberg v. State Farm Mutual Automobile Ins. Co., 270 Minn. 487, 134 N.W.2d 144 (1965).

Comment—1983

The time for taking an appeal from a final judgment or an order remains unchanged.

The clerk of the appellate courts is authorized to reject the filing of a notice of appeal from a judgment after the expiration of the 90-day period.

The second paragraph follows federal practice with respect to judgments ordered pursuant to Rule 54.02, Minnesota Rules of Civil Procedure. An early right of appeal is provided as to those summary judgments that dispose of less than all claims against all parties if, but only if, the trial court expressly determines that there is no just reason for delay and expressly directs the entry of judgment. If an appeal is not taken within 90 days after entry of such a judgment, it becomes final and is not subject to later review. A judgment disposing of less than all claims against all parties entered pursuant to an order which does not contain the express determination and directions prescribed by Rule 54.02 is not appealable until entry of the final judgment disposing of all remaining claims of all parties.

This limited right of appeal recognizes that the trial court's use of the language prescribed by Rule 54.02 is likely to be confined to two situations: (1) where early review of the applicability of a rule of law may obviate a retrial, or (2) where the party obtaining judgment should not be required to await the conclusion of the case as to other parties and issues before the time for appeal begins to run.

Advisory Committee Comment—1998 Amendments

The 1998 amendments to this rule will significantly affect appellate practice. The rule is intended to simplify practice by establishing a 60-day period to effect appeals from both final judgments and appealable orders. This 60-day period will not necessarily result in an identical period to appeal from both an order and judgment, as the event that begins the running of the respective 60-day appeal periods usually will differ. However, the amendment will result in less confusion regarding the time period for appeal.

Subdivision 2 is new and enumerates the post-trial motions that will toll the running of the time to appeal. The rule serves two equally important purposes: to make it clear that an appeal is not necessary until the proper motion is decided, and to avoid a party's erroneous assumption that an improper or unauthorized motion would prevent the running of an appeal deadline. The list is intended to be exhaustive for civil actions in the district courts. Rule 104.01, subd. 2(f), provides that the procedural counterparts of these motions will also prevent the running of the time to appeal until the motion is decided. The motions enumerated in this subdivision exclude "motions for reconsideration" because these motions are never required by the rules and are considered only if the trial court permits the motion to be filed. *See* MINN. GEN. R. PRAC. 115.11, amended in 1997, effective Jan. 1, 1998.

Counsel must carefully determine whether post-trial motions are authorized in certain proceedings. *See Schiltz v. City of Duluth*, 449 N.W.2d 439 (Minn. 1990) (in special proceedings there must be statutory authority for new trial motions, and in the absence of such a provision, a "new trial" motion, even if considered by the trial court on the merits and denied, may not result in an appealable order) and *Steeves v. Campbell*, 508 N.W.2d 817 (Minn. App. 1993) (new trial motion in order for protection proceedings not authorized, and order denying such motion is not appealable). Subdivision 2 of Rule 104.01 replaces Rule 104.04 concerning post-trial and modification motions in marital dissolutions. Modification motions no longer extend the time in which to appeal. The affect of post-trial motions is clarified in subdivisions 2 and 3.

Advisory Committee Comment—2006 Amendment

Rule 104.01, subd. 2(a) is amended to reflect the new name for a motion challenging the legal sufficiency of a verdict under Minn. R. Civ. P. 50.02. As a result of the amendment to Minn. R. Civ. P. 50.02, the former "motion for directed verdict" and "motion for judgment notwithstanding the verdict" are both now referred to as motions for "judgment as a matter of law." Rule 104.01, subd. 2(a) is amended to reflect this nomenclature. During the short transition period during which timely appeals might be taken from cases where either motions for judgment notwithstanding the verdict or motions for judgment as a matter of law may have been filed after the trial court decision, the court should consider the two motions fungible in determining whether an appeal is timely.

Advisory Committee Comment—2008 Amendments

The absence of motions for reconsideration or rehearing in the list of motions given tolling effect in Rule 104.01, subd. 2, is intentional. Neither requesting leave to file such a motion (as contemplated by MINN. GEN. R. PRAC. 115.11), the granting of that request so the motion can be filed, nor the actual filing of the motion will toll or extend the time to appeal. A party seeking to proceed with a motion for reconsideration should pay attention to the appellate calendar and must perfect the appeal regardless of what progress has occurred with the reconsideration motion.

Failure to file a timely appeal may be fatal to later review. If a timely appeal is filed notwithstanding the pendency of a request for reconsideration in the trial court, the court of appeals can accept the appeal as timely, but stay it to permit consideration of the reconsideration motion. *See Marzitelli v. City of Little Canada*, 582 N.W.2d 904, 907 (Minn. 1998), where the court stated:

"We note that requiring parties to file a timely appeal while a post-trial motion is pending does not deny the parties the opportunity to have the district court decide their motions. Rather, the parties may apply to the appellate court for a stay on the appeal to give the district court time to decide the pending post-trial motion. This procedure not only preserves the time limitation on appeals, but also helps to ensure that the district court hears and rules on the motion in an expedient manner. This is particularly important when the case involves a special proceeding. In such cases, the time for appeal is abbreviated to ensure "speedy and summary determination of matters passed upon by the court[.]"

(Footnotes omitted.)

Advisory Committee Comment—2009 Amendments

Subdivision 4 of Rule 104.01 is a new provision. It is modeled on Fed. R. App. P. 4(a)(3) and, for respondents, replaces the notice of review under former Rule 106 of these rules. The amended rule explicitly recognizes that a party may elect to appeal an issue only after learning that another party has appealed. Where a prior appeal has been filed and remains pending, a subsequent notice of appeal should be denominated "Notice of Related Appeal" and will suffice to raise any issue arising from the same trial court action. *See* Appendix for form of Notice of Related Appeal (Form 103C). The rule permits a party to serve and file a subsequent notice of related appeal within 14 days of the service of the first notice of appeal by another party, even if that occurs on the last day to appeal; it does not shorten the normal appeal period even if a party serves and files an appeal on the first possible day.

Historical Notes

The order of the Supreme Court dated Oct. 16, 2009, provided:

"1. The attached amendments to the Rules of Civil Appellate Procedure be, and the same are, prescribed and promulgated to be effective on January 1, 2010.

"2. These amendments shall apply to all actions or proceedings pending on or commenced on or after the effective date.

"3. The inclusion of Advisory Committee comments is for convenience and does not reflect court approval of the statements made therein."

The order of the Minnesota Supreme Court dated November 30, 2005, provides in part:

"1. The attached amendments to the Rules of Civil Procedure, the General Rules of Practice, and the Rules of Civil Appellate Procedure be, and the same are, prescribed and promulgated to be effective on January 1, 2006.

"2. These amendments shall apply to all actions or proceedings pending on or commenced on or after the effective date, provided that in cases in which a timely and otherwise proper motion is brought under either the old or the new version of Rule 50.02 of the Rules of Civil Procedure, the time for appeal will be governed by Rule 104.01, subd. 2, of the Rules of Civil Appellate Procedure, even if the wrong version of Rule 50.02 is used."

Rule 104.02. Effect of Entry of Judgment and Insertion of Costs into the Judgment

No order made prior to the entry of judgment shall be appealable after the expiration of time to appeal from the judgment. Time to appeal from the judgment pursuant to this section shall not be extended by the subsequent insertion therein of costs and disbursements.

Adopted Dec. 7, 1967, eff. Feb. 1, 1968. Amended June 17, 1983, eff. Aug. 1, 1983; Nov. 10, 1983, eff. Aug. 1, 1983; July 7, 1998, eff. Jan. 1, 1999.

Rule 104.03. Special Proceedings [Deleted July 7, 1998, eff. Jan. 1, 1999]

Rule 104.04. Marital Dissolution [Deleted July 7, 1998, eff. Jan. 1, 1999]

RULE 105. DISCRETIONARY REVIEW

Rule 105.01. Petition for Permission to Appeal; Time

Upon the petition of a party, in the interests of justice the Court of Appeals may allow an appeal from an order not otherwise appealable pursuant to Rule 103.03 except an order made during trial, and the Supreme Court may allow an appeal from an order of the Tax Court or the Workers' Compensation Court of Appeals not otherwise appealable pursuant to Rule 116 or governing statute except an order made during trial. The petition shall be served on the adverse party and filed within 30 days of the filing of the order. The trial court should be notified that the petition has been filed and provided with a copy of the petition and any response. Four copies of the petition shall be filed with the clerk of the appellate courts, but the court may direct that additional copies be provided. A filing fee of $550 paid to the clerk of the appellate courts shall accompany the petition for permission to appeal.

Adopted Dec. 7, 1967, eff. Feb. 1, 1968. Amended April 9, 1979; Dec. 4, 1980, eff. Jan. 1, 1981; June 17, 1983, eff. Aug. 1, 1983; Nov. 10, 1983, eff. Aug. 1, 1983; June 28, 1989; May 10, 1990; June 29, 1993, eff. July 1, 1993; Dec. 19, 2000, eff. March 1, 2001; June 13, 2003, eff. July 1, 2003; June 11, 2009, eff. July 1, 2009.

Advisory Committee Note—1967

This rule is similar to P.Fed.R.App.P. 5. It follows the recommendation of the Judicial Council of Minnesota and permits the Supreme Court, in its discretion, to hear appeals from certain nonappealable orders and determinations. The writ procedure contained in Rule 120 provides an alternative method to obtain review of such orders.

Generally, either method may be used. However, the Supreme Court may permit a party to proceed pursuant to Rule 105 in cases where a writ may be inappropriate.

Comment—1983

A petition for discretionary review must be filed with the clerk of the appellate courts within 30 days after filing of the order.

Because a request for discretionary review of an interlocutory or other nonappealable order is usually prompted by some exigency and because it is not customary to give notice of making and filing of nonappealable orders, a petition for review must be served and filed with the clerk of the appellate courts within 30 days after the order was filed with the clerk of the trial court.

See Appendix for form of petition for discretionary review (Form 105).

Historical Notes

The order of the Minnesota Supreme Court [ADM–09–8006] dated June 11, 2009, amending the Rules of Civil Appellate Procedure by increasing filing fees, also provided that the amendments are effective July 1, 2009, and apply to all filings in the appellate courts on or after that date.

The order of the Minnesota Supreme Court [C4-84-2133] dated December 19, 2000, provides in part that these amendments are effective March 1, 2001, and shall apply to all actions or proceedings pending on or commenced on or after the effective date, with the exception of the amendments to Rule 132, which shall apply to all appeals or proceedings commenced in either the Court of Appeals or the Supreme Court on or after the effective date.

The order of the Minnesota Supreme Court [C4-84-2133] dated December 19, 2000, provides in part that "(t)he inclusion of Advisory Committee comments is made for convenience and does not reflect court approval of the statements made therein".

Rule 105.02. Content of Petition; Response

The petition shall be entitled as in the trial court, shall not exceed ten typewritten pages, and shall contain:

(a) a statement of facts necessary to an understanding of the questions of law or fact determined by the order of the trial court;

(b) a statement of the issues; and

(c) a statement why an immediate appeal is necessary and desirable.

A copy of the order from which the appeal is sought and any findings of fact, conclusions of law, or memorandum of law relating to it shall be attached to the petition. Any adverse party may, within five days after service of the petition, serve and file with the clerk of the appellate courts four copies of a response to the petition, which shall not exceed ten pages. Any reply shall be served within two days after service of the response and shall not exceed five pages. All papers may be typewritten in the form prescribed in Rule 132.02. No additional memoranda may be filed without leave of the appellate court.

The petition and any response shall be submitted without oral argument unless otherwise ordered.

Adopted Dec. 7, 1967, eff. Feb. 1, 1968. Amended April 9, 1979; June 17, 1983, eff. Aug. 1, 1983; Nov. 10, 1983, eff. Aug. 1, 1983; Dec. 6, 1991, eff. Jan. 1, 1992; July 7, 1998, eff. Jan. 1, 1999; Dec. 19, 2000, eff. March 1, 2001.

Advisory Committee Note—1967

This rule is similar to P.Fed.R.App.P. 5. It follows the recommendation of the Judicial Council of Minnesota and permits the Supreme Court, in its discretion, to hear appeals from certain nonappealable orders and determinations. The writ procedure contained in Rule 120 provides an alternative method to obtain review of such orders.

Generally, either method may be used. However, the Supreme Court may permit a party to proceed pursuant to Rule 105 in cases where a writ may be inappropriate.

Advisory Committee Comment—1998 Amendments

The rule has been amended to change the responsive time from seven to five days to be consistent with the time to file a response to a petition for an extraordinary writ and to a motion. *See* MINN. R. CIV. APP. P. 120.02, 127. The two-day period to file a reply is added to be consistent with the provision for a reply in the rule on motions. *See* MINN. R. CIV. APP. P. 127. Because intervening weekends and holidays are not counted when the time for response is less than 7 days, the change will not shorten the time for response, and may actually lengthen it in some cases. *See* MINN. R. CIV. APP. P. 126.01.

Advisory Committee Comment—2000 Amendments

Rule 105.01 is changed to authorize petitions to the Supreme Court seeking discretionary review of nonappealable orders of the Tax Court and the Workers' Compensation Court of Appeals. The Court has noted the advisability of such a provision. *See Tarutis v. Commissioner of Revenue*, 393 N.W.2d 667, 668–69 (Minn. 1986). The amendment to Rule 105.02 clarifies that the petition should not be accompanied by a separate memorandum of law, expands the page limit for the petition to ten pages and specifies page limits for the response and reply.

Historical Notes

The order of the Minnesota Supreme Court [C4-84-2133] dated December 19, 2000, provides in part that these amendments are effective March 1, 2001, and shall apply to all actions or proceedings pending on or commenced on or after the effective date, with the exception of the amendments to Rule 132, which shall apply to all appeals or proceedings commenced in either the Court of Appeals or the Supreme Court on or after the effective date.

The order of the Minnesota Supreme Court [C4-84-2133] dated December 19, 2000, provides in part that "(t)he inclusion of Advisory

Committee comments is made for convenience and does not reflect court approval of the statements made therein".

Rule 105.03. Grant of Permission—Procedure

If permission to appeal is granted, the clerk of the appellate courts shall notify the trial court administrator and the appellant shall file the bond as required by these rules, and then proceed as though the appeal had been noticed by filing an appeal. Two copies of a completed statement of the case shall be filed within 5 days of the order granting the petition. The time fixed by these rules for transmitting the record and for filing the briefs and appendix shall run from the date of the entry of the order granting permission to appeal.

Adopted Dec. 7, 1967, eff. Feb. 1, 1968. Amended April 9, 1979; June 17, 1983, eff. Aug. 1, 1983; Nov. 10, 1983, eff. Aug. 1, 1983; Dec. 6, 1991, eff. Jan. 1, 1992.

Advisory Committee Note—1967

This rule is similar to P.Fed.R.App.P. 5. It follows the recommendation of the Judicial Council of Minnesota and permits the Supreme Court, in its discretion, to hear appeals from certain nonappealable orders and determinations. The writ procedure contained in Rule 120 provides an alternative method to obtain review of such orders.

Generally, either method may be used. However, the Supreme Court may permit a party to proceed pursuant to Rule 105 in cases where a writ may be inappropriate.

Comment—1983

The filing of 2 copies of a completed statement of the case is required within 5 days from the date of the order granting the petition for discretionary review.

RULE 106. RESPONDENT'S RIGHT TO OBTAIN REVIEW

After an appeal has been filed, respondent may obtain review of a judgment or order entered in the same underlying action that may adversely affect respondent by filing a notice of related appeal in accordance with Rule 103.02, subdivision 2, and Rule 104.01, subdivision 4.

Adopted Dec. 7, 1967, eff. Feb. 1, 1968. Amended June 17, 1983, eff. Aug. 1, 1983; Nov. 10, 1983, eff. Aug. 1, 1983; June 28, 1989; May 10, 1990; Dec. 6, 1991, eff. Jan. 1, 1992; Sept. 15, 1994; July 7, 1998, eff. Jan. 1, 1999; Oct. 16, 2009, eff. Jan. 1, 2010.

Comment—1983

A respondent must file a notice of review with the clerk of the appellate courts within 15 days after service on the respondent of the notice of appeal.

See Appendix for form of notice of review (Form 106).

Advisory Committee Comment—1998 Amendments

This rule is amended to delete gender-specific language. This amendment is not intended to affect the interpretation and meaning of the rule.

Advisory Committee Comment—2009 Amendments

Rule 106 is amended to abolish the former notice of review, replacing it with the notice of related appeal for all situations where a respondent seeks appellate review of a trial court decision. The amendment avoids the limitations of the former notice of review that could be fatal to an attempt by a respondent to seek review. *See, e.g., Leaon v. Wash. County*, 397 N. W.2d 867, 872 (Minn. 1986) (holding that a respondent seeking appellate relief against parties other than the appellant may obtain review only by separate notice of appeal, but nonetheless considering issue raised improperly). As a practical matter, the amended rule serves only to give notice to a respondent that the proper procedure is no longer contained in this rule but is now found in Rule 103.02, subdivision 2, as to procedure, and Rule 104.01, subdivision 4, as to timing.

The amended rule is intended to create a single procedure that will allow a respondent seeking review to file a notice of related appeal. Under the amended rule a notice of related appeal should suffice to permit a respondent to obtain appellate review of any issues arising in the same trial court case but does not foreclose the right of any party to proceed by separate notice of appeal.

The new procedure is not intended to change the scope of appellate review. This notice of related appeal procedure is not meant to expand what can be reviewed on appeal or to limit that review. For example, the defendant's filing of an appeal under Minn. R. Crim. P. 28.02 does not currently create a right to file a cross-appeal or notice of review; and this amendment should not affect that result. *See State v. Schanus*, 431 N.W.2d 151, 152 (Minn. App. 1988). The court of appeals has recognized that the former notice of review could be used to seek review of an otherwise non-appealable order. *See Kostelnik v. Kostelnik*, 367 N.W.2d 665, 669 (Minn. App. 1985); *see also Arndt v. Am. Family Ins. Co.*, 394 N.W.2d 791, 793–94 (Minn. 1986) (citing *Kostelnik* with apparent approval). The committee intends that the notice of related appeal be treated similarly and that an independent basis for jurisdiction not be required.

Historical Notes

The order of the Supreme Court dated Oct. 16, 2009, provided:

"1. The attached amendments to the Rules of Civil Appellate Procedure be, and the same are, prescribed and promulgated to be effective on January 1, 2010.

"2. These amendments shall apply to all actions or proceedings pending on or commenced on or after the effective date.

"3. The inclusion of Advisory Committee comments is for convenience and does not reflect court approval of the statements made therein."

RULE 107. BOND OR DEPOSIT FOR COSTS

Rule 107.01. When Bond Required

Unless the appellant is exempt by law, a bond shall be executed by, or on behalf of, the appellant. The bond shall be conditioned upon the payment of all costs and disbursements awarded against the appellant on the appeal, not exceeding the penalty of the bond which shall be $500. In lieu of the bond, the appellant may deposit $500 with the trial court administrator as security for the payment.

Prior to filing the notice of appeal, the appellant may move the trial court for an order waiving the bond or setting a lesser amount or deposit. Upon the appellant's filing of the required cost bond or deposit, the respondent may move the trial court for an order requiring a supplemental bond or deposit.

The bond or deposit may be waived by written consent of the respondent, which consent shall be filed with the trial court administrator.

Adopted Dec. 7, 1967, eff. Feb. 1, 1968. Amended Jan. 5, 1976; June 17, 1983, eff. Aug. 1, 1983; Nov. 10, 1983, eff. Aug. 1, 1983; Dec. 6, 1991, eff. Jan. 1, 1992; July 7, 1998, eff. Jan. 1, 1999; Dec. 19, 2000, eff. March 1, 2001.

Advisory Committee Note—1967

See note following Rule 107.02.

Comment—1983

See note following Rule 107.02.

Advisory Committee Comment—1998 Amendment

See note following Rule 107.02.

Historical Notes

The order of the Minnesota Supreme Court [C4-84-2133] dated December 19, 2000, provides in part that these amendments are effective March 1, 2001, and shall apply to all actions or proceedings pending on or commenced on or after the effective date, with the exception of the amendments to Rule 132, which shall apply to all appeals or proceedings commenced in either the Court of Appeals or the Supreme Court on or after the effective date.

The order of the Minnesota Supreme Court [C4-84-2133] dated December 19, 2000, provides in part that "(t)he inclusion of Advisory Committee comments is made for convenience and does not reflect court approval of the statements made therein".

Rule 107.02. When Bond Not Required

No cost bond is required:

(a) in a criminal case; or

(b) in a case arising in juvenile court; or

(c) in a proceeding pursuant to Minnesota Statutes, chapter 253B; or

(d) when the appellant has been authorized to proceed without a cost bond pursuant to Rule 109; or

(e) when the appellant is the state or a governmental subdivision of the state or an officer, employee or agency thereof; or

(f) when the appellant is a party to a public assistance appeal pursuant to Minnesota Statutes, chapter 256; or

(g) when the appellant is a reemployment insurance benefits claimant pursuant to Minnesota Statutes, chapter 268.

Adopted Dec. 7, 1967, eff. Feb. 1, 1968. Amended Jan. 5, 1976; June 17, 1983, eff. Aug. 1, 1983; Nov. 10, 1983, eff. Aug. 1, 1983; Dec. 6, 1991, eff. Jan. 1, 1992; July 7, 1998, eff. Jan. 1, 1999; Dec. 19, 2000, eff. March 1, 2001.

Advisory Committee Note—1967

This rule is identical to M.S.A. § 605.10 (1963). P.Fed.R.App.P. 7 and Fed.R.Civ.P. 73(c) (as amended, July 1, 1966) contain a similar procedure. The bond may be waived by stipulation of the parties.

Comment—1983

A cost bond in the amount of $500 or a stipulation waiving the bond must be filed with the notice of appeal. See Rule 103.01, subdivision 1(d)(6). Rule 107 provides a mechanism for securing, prior to appeal, an order from the trial court waiving the bond or setting a bond in a lesser amount. It also affords the respondent a mechanism for securing a supplemental bond or deposit. Finally, it enumerates the categories of appeals in which a cost bond is not required.

Advisory Committee Comment—1998 Amendments

Under this rule as revised, the cost bond requirement is not automatically waived when an appeal is filed after a remand. Unless the cost bond from the first appeal remains on deposit, the respondent in the second appeal still needs the protection of a cost bond. Changes in (h) reflect the current terminology.

Historical Notes

The order of the Minnesota Supreme Court [C4-84-2133] dated December 19, 2000, provides in part that these amendments are effective March 1, 2001, and shall apply to all actions or proceedings pending on or commenced on or after the effective date, with the exception of the amendments to Rule 132, which shall apply to all appeals or proceedings commenced in either the Court of Appeals or the Supreme Court on or after the effective date.

The order of the Minnesota Supreme Court [C4-84-2133] dated December 19, 2000, provides in part that "(t)he inclusion of Advisory Committee comments is made for convenience and does not reflect court approval of the statements made therein".

RULE 108. STAYS PENDING APPEAL; SECURITY

Rule 108.01. Effect of Appeal on Proceedings in Trial Court

Subdivision 1. Generally No Stay of Enforcement of Judgment or Order on Appeal. Except as otherwise provided by rule or statute, an appeal from a judgment or order does not stay enforcement of the judgment or order in the trial court unless that court orders relief in accordance with Rule 108.02.

Subd. 2. Suspension of Trial Court's Authority to Make Orders Affecting Judgment or Order on Appeal. Except in appeals under Rule 103.03(b), the filing of a timely and proper appeal suspends the trial court's authority to make any order that affects the order or judgment appealed from, although the trial court retains jurisdiction as to matters independent of, supplemental to, or collateral to the order or judgment appealed from.

Adopted Dec. 7, 1967, eff. Feb. 1, 1968. Amended Oct. 29, 1968; Jan. 5, 1976; June 17, 1983, eff. Aug. 1, 1983; Nov. 10, 1983, eff. Aug. 1, 1983; Dec. 6, 1991, eff. Jan. 1, 1992; July 7, 1998, eff. Jan. 1, 1999; Oct. 16, 2009, eff. Jan. 1, 2010.

Advisory Committee Comment—1998 Amendments

The 1998 revisions to Rule 108 make explicit a number of principles regarding appellate jurisprudence previously found in case law. First, the mere filing of an appeal does not, except where provided by statute, rule, or case law, stay proceedings in the trial court to enforce the judgment or order which has been appealed. Second, while an appeal may (with some exceptions) suspend the authority of the trial court to modify the order or judgment appealed from, the suspension of the trial court's jurisdiction is not all-encompassing. Generally, the trial court retains authority to enforce the judgment, and to consider and rule on matters that are supplemental or collateral to the judgment. If there is uncertainty about the scope of the trial court's ongoing jurisdiction, a motion to resolve the question may be directed to the appellate court.

The posting of a supersedeas bond or a request for stay on other grounds is not required for an appeal to be perfected or proceed. However, because the order or judgment that is the subject of the appeal is not generally stayed automatically, a matter may, in some circumstances, become moot while the appeal is pending. Under prior practice, stays in appellate proceedings relating to administrative agency decisions were obtained under MINN. STAT. § 14.65 (1996).

The revisions also set out more clearly the procedure for obtaining a stay. Application for the stay is made in the first instance to the trial court, and not the appellate court. The bond, whether approved by the trial court, or upon review by the appellate court, is still filed in the trial court, and the rule now so specifies.

Advisory Committee Comment—2009 Amendments

Rule 108.01 is a new rule, but it is not intended to create new law. Its provisions are drawn from existing Rule 108.01, subdivision 1, and codify longstanding common law. Neither the filing of an appeal nor the posting of a cost bond required by Rule 107 stays the order or judgment appealed from. *See, e.g., Anderson v. Anderson*, 288 Minn. 514, 517, 179 N.W.2d 718, 721 (Minn. 1970) (stay available only upon filing of supersedeas bond, not cost bond). An appeal divests the trial court of jurisdiction over the matters appealed but only over matters necessarily involved in the order or judgment appealed from. *See Spaeth v. City of Plymouth*, 344 N.W.2d 815, 824 (Minn. 1984); *State v. Barnes*, 249 Minn. 301, 302–03, 81 N.W.2d 864, 866 (1957). The trial court retains jurisdiction over matters collateral to or supplemental to the order or judgment. *See, e.g., Kellar v. Von Holtum*, 605 N.W.2d 696, 700 (Minn. 2000) (trial court retained jurisdiction over motions for attorney fees and costs after appeal was perfected); *Phillips–Klein Cos. v. Tiffany P'ship*, 474 N.W.2d 370, 372 (Minn. App. 1991).

Historical Notes

The order of the Supreme Court dated Oct. 16, 2009, provided:

"1. The attached amendments to the Rules of Civil Appellate Procedure be, and the same are, prescribed and promulgated to be effective on January 1, 2010.

"2. These amendments shall apply to all actions or proceedings pending on or commenced on or after the effective date.

"3. The inclusion of Advisory Committee comments is for convenience and does not reflect court approval of the statements made therein."

Rule 108.02. Motion for Stay or Injunction in Trial Court; Security

Subdivision 1. Motion in Trial Court. A party seeking any of the following relief must move first in the trial court:

(a) a stay of enforcement of the judgment or order of a trial court pending appeal;

(b) approval of the form and amount of security, if any, to be provided in connection with such a stay; or

(c) an order suspending, modifying, restoring, or granting an injunction while an appeal is pending pursuant to Minn. R. Civ. P. 62.02.

Subd. 2. Security Required. Except as to cases in which a governmental body is the appellant or as otherwise provided by rule or statute, a trial court may grant the relief described in subdivision 1 of this rule if the appellant provides security in a form and amount that the trial court approves. The security provided for in this rule may be in one instrument or several. The appellant must serve proof of the security in accordance with Rule 125.02.

Subd. 3. Form of Security. The form of the security may be a supersedeas bond, a letter of credit, a deposit of cash or property with the trial court administrator, or any other form of security that the trial court approves as adequate under the circumstances. The appellant bears the burden of demonstrating the adequacy of any security to be given. Unless the trial court orders otherwise, a stay of an order or judgment does not take effect until any security ordered is filed and notice of filing is provided to all parties.

Subd. 4. Amount of Security.

(a) In all cases, the amount of the security, if any, must be fixed at such amount as the trial court determines will preserve the value of the judgment or order to the respondent during the pendency of appeal.

(b) When the judgment or order is for the payment of money not otherwise secured, the amount of the security normally must be fixed at such sum as will cover the unpaid amount of the judgment or order, costs on appeal (to the extent security for costs has not already been given under Rule 107), interest during the pendency of the appeal, and any other damages that may be caused by depriving the respondent of the right to enforce the judgment or order during the pendency of the appeal.

(c) When the judgment or order determines the possession, ownership, or use of real or personal property (such as in actions for replevin, foreclosure, or conveyance of real property), the amount of the security normally must be fixed at such sum as will compensate the respondent for the loss of use of the property during the pendency of the appeal, costs on appeal (to the extent security for costs has not already been given under Rule 107), interest during the pendency of the appeal, and any other damages (including waste) that may be caused by depriving the respondent of the right to enforcement of the judgment or order during the pendency of the appeal.

(d) If a party seeks to stay enforcement of only part of the judgment or order on appeal, the security must be fixed at such sum as the trial court determines is sufficient to secure that portion of the judgment or order on appeal.

Subd. 5. Providers Submit to Jurisdiction of District Court. If security is provided in the form of a bond, letter of credit, or undertaking with one or more sureties, each provider (whether surety, issuer, or other person liable for the security) submits to the jurisdiction of the district court. A provider's liability may be enforced on motion in the district court, served on the provider or providers in accordance with the Minnesota Rules of Civil Procedure as if the provider or providers were a party or parties to the action, without the necessity of an independent action.

Subd. 6. Review by Court of Appeals. On a motion under Rule 127, the Court of Appeals may review the trial court's determinations as to whether a stay is appropriate, the terms of any stay, and the form and amount of security pending appeal. The motion for review must:

(a) set forth the reasons for granting the relief requested and the facts relied on;

(b) include originals or copies of affidavits or other sworn statements supporting the facts that are subject to dispute; and

(c) include a copy of any submissions to the trial court, any order entered by the trial court relating to security pending appeal, and any other relevant parts of the record in the trial court.

If the Court of Appeals grants the motion, it may give relief on the same terms that a trial court may give relief under Rule 108.02, subds. 2, 3, and 4, and may require that any security that the appellant must provide be posted in the trial court.

Adopted Dec. 7, 1967, eff. Feb. 1, 1968. Amended June 17, 1983, eff. Aug. 1, 1983; Nov. 10, 1983, eff. Aug. 1, 1983; Dec. 6, 1991, eff. Jan. 1, 1992; Oct. 16, 2009, eff. Jan. 1, 2010.

Advisory Committee Comment—2009 Amendments

Rule 108.02, subdivision 1, requires that an application for stay of a judgment or order be brought in the trial court. Subdivision 6 of the rule provides for the trial court decision on the stay to be reviewed by the court of appeals and establishes the procedure for allowing the appellate court to conduct that review. Although the matter is raised by motion in the appellate court, the review is for abuse of fairly broad trial court discretion in these matters. *See Axford v. W. Syndicate Inv. Co.*, 141 Minn. 412, 414, 168 N.W. 97, 97 (1918).

Subdivision 3 recognizes that security may be provided in any of several forms. The former rule's apparent limitation to a surety bond as security is expressly removed in favor of a wider array of potential security arrangements. In many cases, a deposit into court or posting of a letter of credit may be preferable and less expensive. Deposit into court is also allowed by statute as a means not only to stay enforcement of a judgment but to remove a docketed judgment's lien against real property. *See* Minn. Stat. § 548.12 (2008).

Subdivision 4 is intended to provide guidance to litigants and judges on the appropriate standards for the setting of required security for a stay. The rule addresses the amount of security required and establishes a guiding principle in subdivision 4(a) of an amount sufficient to preserve the value of the judgment or order during the appeal. For money judgments, the unpaid amount of the judgment, costs on appeal (less $500 if secured by a cost bond), and interest during the appeal will be the usual amount. This calculation is consistent with the amount of security specified in statutes relating to supersedeas bonds. *See* Minn. Stat. § 550.36 (2008) (allowing stay upon posting of bond in the amount of judgment and interest or a lesser amount allowed by a court); Minn. Stat. § 548.12 (2008) (allowing a party to deposit money into court in amount of judgment, plus interest and costs). The determination of the amount of a bond ultimately lies in the discretion of the courts and can even be waived in its entirety, although the Minnesota Supreme Court has recognized that this discretion must be exercised sparingly. *See No Power Line, Inc. v. Minn. Envtl. Quality Council*, 262 N.W.2d 312, 330–31 (Minn. 1977).

Although not constrained by the rule, trial court discretion to determine the amount of required security may be limited by statute or common law. There are cases in which no stay may be available, regardless of the amount of security. Child custody orders take effect as directed by the trial court, notwithstanding an appealing party's willingness to post a bond for the purpose of obtaining a stay. *See Petersen v. Petersen*, 296 Minn. 147, 149, 206 N.W.2d 658, 659–60 (Minn. 1973) (stating, for the purpose of "future guidance of the bench and bar, . . . that orders changing the custody of children are not affected by supersedeas or cost bonds [,] but are to take effect at whatever date the trial court specifies"). For discussion of the factors to be weighed in deciding whether or not to change custody while an appeal is pending, see *Clark v. Clark*,

543 N.W.2d 685, 687 (Minn. App. 1996) (holding that trial court abused its discretion in denying a stay of custody modification order, in light of drastic changes to living arrangements that would result from modification and lack of endangerment or other exigency requiring immediate change). The court of appeals has addressed the criteria governing whether to grant a stay in the nature of an injunction pending a certiorari appeal in *DRJ, Inc. v. City of St. Paul*, 741 N.W.2d 141, 144 (Minn. App. 2007) (citing MINN. R. CIV. P. 62.02 as to injunctive relief pending appeal; two juvenile rules, one of which establishes a presumption that there will be no stay pending appeal and the other of which explicitly stays further proceedings; and a criminal rule that identifies criteria governing whether to grant release pending appeal). MINN. STAT. § 525.714 (2008) provides that the filing of an appeal stays a probate order, although an "additional bond" may be required to secure payment of any damages that may be awarded as a consequence of the appeal. *But see In re Estate of Goyette*, 376 N.W.2d 438, 441 (Minn. App. 1985) (holding that failure to post bond ordered by probate court precluded automatic stay of probate proceedings pending appeal).

Historical Notes

The order of the Supreme Court dated Oct. 16, 2009, provided:

"1. The attached amendments to the Rules of Civil Appellate Procedure be, and the same are, prescribed and promulgated to be effective on January 1, 2010.

"2. These amendments shall apply to all actions or proceedings pending on or commenced on or after the effective date.

"3. The inclusion of Advisory Committee comments is for convenience and does not reflect court approval of the statements made therein."

Former rule: Prior to its amendment by order of the Supreme Court dated October 16, 2009, rule 108.02 related to an appeal from a judgment directing the execution of a conveyance or other instrument.

Rule 108.03. Proceedings in Supreme Court

Where a petition to the Supreme Court for review of a decision of the Court of Appeals is filed, or a case is transferred to the Supreme Court in accordance with these rules, and security has previously been given to stay proceedings in the trial court, the security shall remain in full force and effect during the pendency of review in the Supreme Court unless otherwise ordered by the Supreme Court. The Supreme Court may make any order appropriate to preserve the status quo or require security or additional security to any person who may suffer damage due to the continued stay of proceedings in the trial court during the pendency of review in the Supreme Court.

Adopted Dec. 7, 1967, eff. Feb. 1, 1968. Amended June 17, 1983, eff. Aug. 1, 1983; Nov. 10, 1983, eff. Aug. 1, 1983; Oct. 16, 2009, eff. Jan. 1, 2010.

Advisory Committee Comment—2009 Amendments

Rule 108 is replaced by an entirely new rule. The changes are intended to provide greater guidance to parties, attorneys, and the courts on how stays of trial court orders and judgments can be obtained.

Historical Notes

The order of the Supreme Court dated Oct. 16, 2009, provided:

"1. The attached amendments to the Rules of Civil Appellate Procedure be, and the same are, prescribed and promulgated to be effective on January 1, 2010.

"2. These amendments shall apply to all actions or proceedings pending on or commenced on or after the effective date.

"3. The inclusion of Advisory Committee comments is for convenience and does not reflect court approval of the statements made therein."

Former rule: Prior to its amendment by order of the Supreme Court dated October 16, 2009, rule 108.03 related to the extent of a stay.

Rules 108.04 to 108.07. Deleted Oct. 16, 2009, eff. Jan. 1, 2010

Historical Notes

Deleted rule 108.04 related to a respondent's bond to enforce judgment.

Deleted rule 108.05 related to the joinder of bond provisions and to service on an adverse party.

Deleted rule 108.06 related to perishable property.

Deleted rule 108.07 related to the effect of proceedings in the Supreme Court.

The order of the Supreme Court dated October 16, 2009, provided:

"1. The attached amendments to the Rules of Civil Appellate Procedure be, and the same are, prescribed and promulgated to be effective on January 1, 2010.

"2. These amendments shall apply to all actions or proceedings pending on or commenced on or after the effective date.

"3. The inclusion of Advisory Committee comments is for convenience and does not reflect court approval of the statements made therein."

RULE 109. LEAVE TO PROCEED *IN FORMA PAUPERIS*

Rule 109.01. Authorized Relief

A party who is unable to pay the expenses of appeal may apply for leave to proceed *in forma pauperis*, which may include waiver of the filing fee and cost bond, and payment of costs for the transcript and reproducing briefs.

Adopted Dec. 19, 2000, eff. March 1, 2001.

Historical Notes

The order of the Minnesota Supreme Court [C4-84-2133] dated December 19, 2000, provides in part that these amendments are effective March 1, 2001, and shall apply to all actions or proceedings pending on or commenced on or after the effective date, with the exception of the amendments to Rule 132, which shall apply to all appeals or proceedings commenced in either the Court of Appeals or the Supreme Court on or after the effective date.

The order of the Minnesota Supreme Court [C4-84-2133] dated December 19, 2000, provides in part that "(t)he inclusion of Advisory Committee comments is made for convenience and does not reflect court approval of the statements made therein".

Rule 109.02. Motion for Leave to Proceed *In Forma Pauperis* in the Court of Appeals

A party who desires to proceed *in forma pauperis* in the Court of Appeals shall file in the trial court a motion for leave so to proceed, together with an affidavit showing the party's inability to pay fees and costs and a copy of the party's statement of the case as prescribed by Rule 133.03, showing the proposed issues on appeal. Any such motion by a party initiating an appeal shall be filed on or before the date the appeal is commenced. The trial court shall rule on the motion within 15 days after it is filed, unless the Court of Appeals grants additional time. The party shall file a copy of the motion with the clerk of the appellate courts simultaneously with the notice of appeal or the petition that initiates the appeal.

The trial court shall grant the motion if the court finds that the party is indigent and that the appeal is not frivolous. If the motion is denied, the trial court shall state in writing the reasons for the denial. The party shall promptly file a copy of the trial court's order on the motion with the clerk of the appellate courts.

If the trial court grants the motion, the party may proceed in forma pauperis without further application to the Court of Appeals. If a transcript is to be prepared for appeal, the party shall file the certificate as to transcript required by Rule 110.02, subdivision 2(a), within 10 days from the date of the trial court administrator's filing of the order granting leave to proceed *in forma pauperis* or within 10 days after filing the notice of appeal, whichever is later.

If the trial court denies the motion, the party shall, within 10 days from the date of the trial court administrator's filing of the order, either:

(a) pay the filing fee, post the cost bond, and file a completed transcript certificate, if a transcript is required; or

(b) serve and file a motion in the Court of Appeals for review of the trial court's order denying *in forma pauperis* status. The record on the motion shall be limited to the record presented to the trial court.

Adopted Dec. 19, 2000, eff. March 1, 2001.

Historical Notes

The order of the Minnesota Supreme Court [C4-84-2133] dated December 19, 2000, provides in part that these amendments are effective March 1, 2001, and shall apply to all actions or proceedings pending on or commenced on or after the effective date, with the exception of the amendments to Rule 132, which shall apply to all appeals or proceedings commenced in either the Court of Appeals or the Supreme Court on or after the effective date.

The order of the Minnesota Supreme Court [C4-84-2133] dated December 19, 2000, provides in part that "(t)he inclusion of Advisory Committee comments is made for convenience and does not reflect court approval of the statements made therein".

Rule 109.03. Civil Commitment and Juvenile Proceedings

A motion to proceed *in forma pauperis* on appeal from a civil commitment or juvenile proceeding may be granted based on the party's financial inability to pay appeal expenses alone. A finding that the appeal is not of a frivolous nature is not required.

Adopted Dec. 19, 2000, eff. March 1, 2001.

Historical Notes

The order of the Minnesota Supreme Court [C4-84-2133] dated December 19, 2000, provides in part that these amendments are effective March 1, 2001, and shall apply to all actions or proceedings pending on or commenced on or after the effective date, with the exception of the amendments to Rule 132, which shall apply to all appeals or proceedings commenced in either the Court of Appeals or the Supreme Court on or after the effective date.

The order of the Minnesota Supreme Court [C4-84-2133] dated December 19, 2000, provides in part that "(t)he inclusion of Advisory Committee comments is made for convenience and does not reflect court approval of the statements made therein".

Rule 109.04. Motion for Leave to Proceed *In Forma Pauperis* in the Supreme Court

A party who desires to proceed *in forma pauperis* in the Supreme Court shall file in that court a motion for leave so to proceed. Any such motion by a party initiating an appeal shall be filed on or before the date the Supreme Court proceeding is commenced. The motion shall specify the fees and costs for which *in forma pauperis* relief is sought. The motion shall be accompanied by:

(a) a copy of the order, if any, granting the party leave to proceed *in forma pauperis* in the court whose decision is to be reviewed by the Supreme Court and an affidavit stating that the party remains indigent; or

(b) an affidavit showing the party's inability to pay the fees and costs for which relief is sought.

Adopted Dec. 19, 2000, eff. March 1, 2001.

Historical Notes

The order of the Minnesota Supreme Court [C4-84-2133] dated December 19, 2000, provides in part that these amendments are effective March 1, 2001, and shall apply to all actions or proceedings pending on or commenced on or after the effective date, with the exception of the amendments to Rule 132, which shall apply to all appeals or proceedings commenced in either the Court of Appeals or the Supreme Court on or after the effective date.

The order of the Minnesota Supreme Court [C4-84-2133] dated December 19, 2000, provides in part that "(t)he inclusion of Advisory Committee comments is made for convenience and does not reflect court approval of the statements made therein".

Rule 109.05. Suspension of Time Periods

The time periods for a party to pay the filing fee, post a cost bond, and file a transcript certificate are suspended during the pendency of that party's timely motion to proceed *in forma pauperis*.

Adopted Dec. 19, 2000, eff. March 1, 2001.

Advisory Committee Comment—2000 Amendments

Rule 109 is a new rule, adopted in 2000. It is intended to collect and harmonize various provisions that apply to the procedure for *in forma pauperis* appeals. It is not intended to establish or modify any substantive rights to proceed *in forma pauperis*.

The rule requires that the application to proceed *in forma pauperis* in the Court of Appeals be submitted to the trial court for appropriate factual determinations. This requirement is consistent with the long-standing practice of the Court of Appeals. *See, e.g., Maddox v. Department of Human Servs.*, 400 N.W.2d 136, 139 n.1 (Minn. App. 1987). This requirement is consistent with the general preference of having trial courts, rather than appellate courts, make factual findings, and also obviates any appearance that the appellate court has prejudged the merits of the appeal before the transcript, record and briefs have been prepared. Even without a transcript or briefs, the trial court will be familiar with the issues raised by the parties and may be familiar with their financial resources, and is, therefore, better able to make the required findings early in the appellate process. MINN. STAT. § 563.01, subd. 3 defines "indigence" to include those receiving public assistance, being represented by a legal services attorney or volunteer attorney program on the basis of indigence, or having an annual income not greater than 125% of the poverty level. *See* 42 U.S.C. § 9902(2).

The requirement that a party seeking *in forma pauperis* relief establish that his or her appeal (or position on appeal, if such relief is being sought by a respondent) is "not frivolous" does not require a showing that the party is likely to prevail on appeal and does not require the trial court to evaluate the likelihood of success on appeal. *In forma pauperis* status in civil commitment and juvenile proceedings is based solely on indigency, and an indigent party is not required to establish that the position to be taken in the appellate court is not frivolous.

Rule 109.04 establishes procedures for seeking leave to proceed *in forma pauperis* in the Supreme Court. It permits a motion based on an order granting *in forma pauperis* status from the court whose decision is to be reviewed if accompanied by an affidavit that the party remains indigent.

Rule 109.05 provides for the suspension of the time periods to pay the filing fee, post a bond and file the transcript certificate while the trial court considers a motion to proceed *in forma pauperis*. A party who has made a timely motion to proceed *in forma pauperis* must file a copy of that motion with the appeal papers. The trial court must rule on the motion promptly and the party must inform the appellate court of the ruling, so that the appeal can proceed without delay.

Historical Notes

The order of the Minnesota Supreme Court [C4-84-2133] dated December 19, 2000, provides in part that these amendments are effective March 1, 2001, and shall apply to all actions or proceedings pending on or commenced on or after the effective date, with the exception of the amendments to Rule 132, which shall apply to all appeals or proceedings commenced in either the Court of Appeals or the Supreme Court on or after the effective date.

The order of the Minnesota Supreme Court [C4-84-2133] dated December 19, 2000, provides in part that "(t)he inclusion of Advisory Committee comments is made for convenience and does not reflect court approval of the statements made therein".

RULE 110. THE RECORD ON APPEAL

Rule 110.01. Composition of the Record on Appeal

The papers filed in the trial court, the exhibits, and the transcript of the proceedings, if any, shall constitute the record on appeal in all cases.

Adopted Dec. 7, 1967, eff. Feb. 1, 1968. Amended June 17, 1983, eff. Aug. 1, 1983; Nov. 10, 1983, eff. Aug. 1, 1983.

Advisory Committee Note—1967

Rule 110.01. This rule is substantially the same as P.Fed.R.App.P. 10(a) and is similar to Fed. R.Civ.P. 75(a) (as amended, July 1, 1966) and to Minn.Sup.Ct.R.V. The original trial court record is the official and only record on appeal. Wherever the unqualified word "record" is used in these rules, it refers to this record. The printed Record, which was required by the former Minnesota practice, is abolished by Rule 130.

Rule 110.02. The Transcript of Proceedings; Duty of Appellant to Order; Notice to Respondent if Partial Transcript is Ordered; Duty of Reporter; Form of Transcript

Subdivision 1. Duty to Order Transcript. Within 10 days after filing the notice of appeal, the appellant shall:

(a) pursuant to subdivision 2 of this rule, order from the reporter a transcript of those parts of the proceedings not already part of the record which are deemed necessary for inclusion in the record; or

(b) file a notice of intent to proceed pursuant to Rule 110.03 or Rule 110.04; or

(c) notify the respondent in writing that no transcript or statement will be ordered or prepared.

If the entire transcript is not to be included, the appellant, within the 10 days, shall file and serve on the respondent a description of the parts of the transcript which appellant intends to include in the record and a statement of the issues intended to be presented on appeal. If the respondent deems a transcript of other parts of the proceedings to be necessary, respondent shall order, within 10 days of service of the description or notification of no transcript, those other parts from the reporter, pursuant to subdivision 2 of this rule, or serve and file a motion in the trial court for an order requiring the appellant to do so. A copy of any order of the trial court affecting the transcript shall be filed by the appellant with the clerk of the appellate courts.

Subd. 2. Transcript Certificates. (a) If any part of the proceedings is to be transcribed by a court reporter, a certificate as to transcript signed by the designating counsel and by the court reporter shall be filed with the clerk of the appellate courts, with a copy to the trial court and all counsel of record within 10 days of the date the transcript was ordered. The certificate shall contain the date on which the transcript was requested; the estimated number of pages; the estimated completion date not to exceed 60 days; a statement that satisfactory financial arrangements have been made for the transcription; and the court reporter's address and telephone number.

(b) Upon filing of the transcript with the trial court administrator and delivery to counsel of record, the reporter shall file with the clerk of the appellate courts a certificate of filing and delivery. The certificate shall identify the transcript(s) delivered; specify the dates of filing of the transcript with the trial court administrator and delivery to counsel; and shall indicate the method of delivery. The certificate shall also contain the court reporter's address and telephone number.

Subd. 3. Overdue Transcripts. If any party deems the period of time set by the reporter to be excessive or insufficient, or if the reporter needs an extension of time for completion of the transcript, the party or reporter may request a different period of time within which the transcript must be delivered by written motion to the appellate court pursuant to Rule 127, showing good cause therefor. A justice, judge or a person designated by the appellate court shall act as a referee in hearing the motion and shall file with the appellate court appropriate findings and recommendations for a dispositional order. A failure to comply with the order of the appellate court fixing a time within which the transcript must be delivered may be punished as a contempt of court. The appellate court may declare a reporter ineligible to act as an official court reporter in any court proceeding and prohibit the reporter from performing any private reporting work until the overdue transcript is filed.

Subd. 4. Transcript Requirements. The transcript shall be typewritten or printed on 8½ by 11 inch or 8½ by 10½ inch unglazed opaque paper with double spacing between each line of text, shall be bound at the left-hand margin, and shall contain a table of contents. To the extent possible, the transcript of a trial or other single court proceeding shall be consecutively paginated, regardless of the number of volumes. The name of each witness shall appear at the top of each page containing that person's testimony. A question and its answer may be contained in a single paragraph. The original and first copy of the transcript shall be filed with the trial court administrator and a copy shall be transmitted promptly to the attorney for each party to the appeal separately represented. All copies must be legible. The reporter shall certify the correctness of the transcript.

The transcript should include transcription of any testimony given by audiotape, videotape, or other electronic means unless that testimony has previously been transcribed, in which case the transcript shall include the existing transcript of testimony, with appropriate annotations and verification of what portions were replayed at trial, as part of the official trial transcript.

In any matter, the parties may stipulate to file with the clerk of the appellate courts, in addition to the typewritten or printed transcripts, all transcripts prepared for an appeal in electronic form. The electronic form shall be on compact discs formatted for IBM-compatible computers and shall contain the transcript in ASCII or other self-contained format accessible by Windows-compatible operating systems with no additional software. The label on the disc must include the case name and the case file number. One copy of the disc must be served on each party separately represented by counsel. The filing party must certify that the disc has been scanned for viruses and that it is virus-free.

Adopted Dec. 7, 1967, eff. Feb. 1, 1968. Amended Aug. 8, 1973; Feb. 14, 1975; April 9, 1979; June 17, 1983, eff. Aug. 1, 1983; Nov. 10, 1983, eff. Aug. 1, 1983; Dec. 6, 1991, eff. Jan. 1, 1992; July 7, 1998, eff. Jan. 1, 1999; Dec. 19, 2000, eff. March 1, 2001; Dec. 11, 2008, eff. Jan. 1, 2009.

Advisory Committee Note—1967

Rule 110.02(1). This rule is substantially the same as P.Fed.R.App.P. 10(b) and Fed.R.Civ.P. 75(b). It abolishes the old settled case procedure formerly set forth in Minn.R.Civ.P. 59.07. No formal approval of the transcript by the trial court or the parties is necessary. Errors may be corrected by either party by motion under Rule 110.05.

In those cases where only part of the proceedings is transcribed, the requirement that appellant serve a statement of the issues he intends to present on appeal is made solely for the purpose of affording respondent an opportunity to determine whether the partial transcript will be adequate for the determination of the issues presented by the appeal. Such a statement is not equivalent to an assignment of errors, which is no longer required in these rules, and the statement does not limit the issues on appeal. The precise statement of the issues presented by the appeal is to be made in the brief. See Rule 128.01(2). A respondent, who can show that he was misled by the statement required by this rule and in consequence failed to designate for transcription material parts of the reported proceedings, may seek relief under Rule 110.05.

Rule 110.02(2) requires acknowledgment by the reporter of the order and acceptance of the order for a transcript. The reporter in his written acknowledgment must state the date when the transcript will be furnished which time shall not exceed 60 days. When the transcript is delivered, the reporter must file a certificate of such fact with the clerk of the Supreme Court. The date of delivery establishes the beginning of the 60 day period for the filing of appellant's brief and appendix. See Rule 131.01.

Rule 110.02(3) provides a procedure for the parties to extend or reduce the time of delivery of the transcript.

Rule 110.02(4) specifies the physical appearance and number of copies of the transcript and requires the reporter's certification of correctness.

Comment—1983

The transcript must be ordered within 10 days after the notice of appeal is filed.

Since a prehearing conference will be held only if the court so directs, within 10 days after filing the notice of appeal the appellant must order the transcript or file a notice of intent to proceed on a statement of the proceedings pursuant to Rule 110.03 or Rule 110.04 or notify the respondent that no transcript or statement will be ordered or prepared.

Rule 110.02, subdivision 2, introduces the certificate as to transcript, which includes a statement that financial arrangements satisfactory to the reporter and counsel have been made (see appendix for form). Rule 110.02, subdivision 3, provides sanctions in addition to contempt in the event of the reporter's failure to make timely delivery of the transcript. The certificate must be filed with the clerk of the appellate courts within 10 days after the date the transcript was ordered.

The typewritten transcript requirement of Rule 110.02, subdivision 4 is intended to authorize the use of legible computerized or mechanically produced transcripts.

See Appendix for form of certificate as to transcript (Form 110).

Advisory Committee Comment—1998 Amendments

Subdivision 2 is divided into two sections to emphasize that the court reporter has to file both a transcript certificate and a certificate of filing and delivery, each with different requirements. Court reporters sometimes do not include their telephone number on the certificates, which makes it difficult for the clerk's office to contact them if there is a problem with the certificate. The proposed amendment includes the reporter's telephone number as one of the pieces of information that must be included on the certificate.

Currently, the delivery certificates filed by most reporters only specify the date that the transcript was filed with the trial court administrator, together with a general statement that the transcript was "transmitted promptly" to counsel. The clerk's office uses the filing date as the delivery date for the purpose of calculating the briefing period, which may not be accurate if the reporter does not deliver the transcript on the same day filed. In addition, the certificates usually do not indicate the method of delivery. This makes a difference for calculation of the briefing period, because if the transcript is delivered by mail, three days are added to the briefing period. *See* MINN. R. CIV. APP. P. 125.03. The amended rule introduces the certificate of filing and delivery, which must specify the dates the transcript was filed with the court administrator and delivered to counsel. This certificate may show delivery by hand, by courier, or may show mailing. The court reporter and counsel should insure that the certificate accurately reflects the date and method of delivery of the transcript, because those factors determine the due date of appellant's brief. *See* MINN. R. CIV. APP. P. 125.03, 131.01.

Subdivision 4 includes a new requirement that the transcript be paginated consecutively, to the extent possible. This requirement is intended to reduce the number of transcripts requiring complicated citation forms. The goal is to have consecutive pagination of the entire trial, and any pretrial proceedings that immediately precede the trial as well as any other portions of the transcript that are ordered at the same time. If multiple court reporters were involved in transcribing the proceedings, various segments of the transcript can be assigned blocks of numbers so that pagination will be consecutive, albeit with potential for "missing" numbers. In that event, the transcript should clearly show that the missing numbers are intentionally omitted and identify the correct following transcript page number. There may be situations where it is impossible to paginate the transcript in this manner, and the rule recognizes such occasions may exist. The Committee believes that consecutive pagination should become the norm for transcripts, however, and this rule should make consecutive pagination the standard practice of court reporters.

The rule also includes the requirement that any testimony given by audio, video or other electronic means must be transcribed unless the court reporter provides an existing transcript of the videotape testimony, verifying its accuracy. The requirement for transcription applies only to testimony offered as such as trial, and not to non-testimonial evidence such as ordinary audio or video recordings, witness statements used for impeachment, or other recordings received as exhibits. If an existing transcript exists, it must be submitted with the electronic testimony and it is made part of the record on appeal. The reporter at trial certifies that what is included in the transcript is what transpired at the trial, but does not need to certify the accuracy or quality of the previously-prepared transcription. This rule change does not affect the procedure for criminal appeals, as they are governed by MINN. R. CRIM. P. 28.02, subd. 9.

See Appendix for form of certificate as to transcript and certificate of filing and delivery (Forms 110A and 110B).

Advisory Committee Comment—2000 Amendments

Rule 110.02, subd. 4 is amended to allow parties to file transcripts in electronic form. With increasing frequency, transcripts of trials and other proceedings are available to counsel and the courts in electronic format, in addition to the traditional typed or printed format. Electronic format offers some significant advantages in the areas of handling, storage, and use. There is no currently accepted standard for preparation of electronic transcripts, which are available in a variety of formats and software contexts. This amendment allows parties the opportunity to file an electronic version of transcripts in addition to the paper transcripts required under the rules; it does not permit this format to replace the traditional paper transcript.

As technology advances, additional forms of media may become acceptable.

Advisory Committee Comment—2008 Amendments

Rule 110.02, subd. 4, is amended to delete provision for filing a transcript in electronic form on 3½″ diskettes. That format is obsolescent, and CD-ROM is the format best suited to this use and most convenient for the courts and the parties.

Historical Notes

The order of the Minnesota Supreme Court [C4-84-2133] dated December 19, 2000, provides in part that these amendments are effective March 1, 2001, and shall apply to all actions or proceedings pending on or commenced on or after the effective date, with the exception of the amendments to Rule 132, which shall apply to all appeals or proceedings commenced in either the Court of Appeals or the Supreme Court on or after the effective date.

The order of the Minnesota Supreme Court [C4-84-2133] dated December 19, 2000, provides in part that "(t)he inclusion of Advisory Committee comments is made for convenience and does not reflect court approval of the statements made therein".

Rule 110.03. Statement of the Proceedings When No Report Was Made or When the Transcript is Unavailable

If no report of all or any part of the proceedings at a hearing or trial was made, or if a transcript is unavailable, the appellant may, prepare a statement of the proceedings from the best available means, including recollection. The statement is not intended to be a complete re-creation of testimony or arguments.

Appellant shall file the original proposed statement with the trial court administrator and the clerk of the appellate courts, and serve a copy on respondent, within 15 days after filing the notice of appeal. Within 15 days after service of appellant's statement, respondent may file with the trial court administrator and the clerk of the appellate courts objections or proposed amendments, and serve a copy on appellant.

The trial court may approve the statement submitted by appellant, or modify the statement based on respondent's submissions or the court's own recollection of the proceedings. The statement as approved by the trial court shall be included in the record. Within 60 days of the filing of the notice of appeal, the original trial court approval of the statement shall be filed with the trial court administrator and copies of the approval shall be served on counsel for the parties and filed with the clerk of the appellate court.

Adopted Dec. 7, 1967, eff. Feb. 1, 1968. Amended June 17, 1983, eff. Aug. 1, 1983; Nov. 10, 1983, eff. Aug. 1, 1983; Dec. 6, 1991, eff. Jan. 1, 1992; July 7, 1998, eff. Jan. 1, 1999.

Advisory Committee Note—1967

Rule 110.03. This rule is substantially the same as P.Fed.R.App.P. 10(c) and Fed.R.Civ.P. 75(c) (as amended, July 1, 1966), and permits the use of a court approved statement in cases where no report, in whole or in part, was made or where a report was made but cannot be transcribed.

Advisory Committee Comment—1998 Amendments

The statement of the proceedings under Rule 110.03 may not be used if a transcript is available. The use of an agreed statement as the record under Rule 110.04 is restricted to situations where the parties agree on the essential facts and the portions of the record necessary for appellate review.

It was not clear under the former rule who was responsible for submitting the proposed statement and any objections to the trial court, or what the time period for the submission was. Under the amended rule, each party is responsible for filing their documents with the trial court administrator at the same time that the documents are served.

The amendment requires service of the proposed statement and objections on the clerk of the appellate courts, to allow the clerk's office to monitor whether the statement is being processed in a timely fashion. In addition, the amendment clarifies that the original approval is to be filed with the trial court administrator, with copies to counsel and the clerk of the appellate courts. Under the rule, the original statement and approval were filed with the clerk of the appellate courts. The amendment requires that the original be filed with the trial court administrator, because it is part of the record of the proceedings.

The amendment is also intended to clarify that the trial court is not bound by the parties' submissions but may modify the statement based on the court's own recollection.

Rule 110.04. Agreed Statement as the Record

In lieu of the record as defined in Rule 110.01, the parties may prepare and sign a statement of the record showing how the issues presented by the appeal arose and were decided in the trial court and setting forth only the facts averred and proved or sought to be proved which are essential to a decision of the issues presented. The agreed statement shall be approved by the trial court with any additions the trial court may consider necessary to present the issues raised by the appeal and shall be the record on appeal. The trial court's approval of the statement shall be filed with the clerk of the appellate courts within 60 days of the filing of the notice of appeal.

Adopted Dec. 7, 1967, eff. Feb. 1, 1968. Amended June 17, 1983, eff. Aug. 1, 1983; Nov. 10, 1983, eff. Aug. 1, 1983.

Advisory Committee Note—1967

Rule 110.04. This rule is substantially the same as P.Fed.R.App.P. 10(d) and permits the parties to substitute a court approved statement of the case in lieu of a record. It is similar to the procedure authorized by M.S.A. § 548.24 which permits parties to submit cases to the trial court upon an agreed statement.

Comment—1983

Within 10 days after filing the notice of appeal the appellant must file notice of intent to proceed under either Rule 110.03 or Rule 110.04. The trial court's approval of the statement must be filed with the clerk of the appellate courts within 60 days after filing of the notice of appeal. The time for filing the appellant's brief and appendix begins to run with the filing of the trial court's approval. See Rule 131.01.

Rule 110.05. Correction or Modification of the Record

If any difference arises as to whether the record truly discloses what occurred in the trial court, the difference shall be submitted to and determined by the trial court and the record made to conform. If anything material to either party is omitted from the record by error or accident or is misstated in it, the parties by stipulation, or the trial court, either before or after the record is transmitted to the appellate court, or the appellate court, on motion by a party or on its own initiative, may direct that the omission or misstatement be corrected, and if necessary that a supplemental record be approved and transmitted. All other questions as to the form and content of the record shall be presented to the appellate court.

Adopted Dec. 7, 1967, eff. Feb. 1, 1968. Amended June 17, 1983, eff. Aug. 1, 1983; Nov. 10, 1983, eff. Aug. 1, 1983.

Advisory Committee Note—1967

Rule 110.05. This rule is substantially the same as P.Fed.R.App.P. 10(e) and Fed.R.Civ.P. 75(d), and replaces the cumbersome procedure formerly required by Minn.R.Civ.P. 59.07 to secure a settled case.

RULE 111. TRANSMISSION OF THE RECORD

Rule 111.01. Transmission of Record; Time

Within 10 days after the due date for the filing of the appellant's brief, the trial court administrator shall transmit the record to the clerk of the appellate courts, together with a numbered itemized list in quadruplicate of all documents and exhibits contained in the record, identifying each with reasonable definiteness; each document and exhibit shall be endorsed with the corresponding number from the itemized list. The trial court administrator shall send a copy of this list to all parties. A party having possession of exhibits shall transmit them with an itemized list in quadruplicate to the clerk of the appellate courts within 10 days after the due date for the filing of the respondent's brief. A party shall make advance arrangements with the clerk for the delivery of bulky or weighty exhibits and for the cost of transporting them to and from the appellate courts. Transmission of the record is effected when the trial court administrator mails or otherwise forwards the record to the appellate courts.

Amended Feb. 14, 1975; June 17, 1983, eff. Aug. 1, 1983; Nov. 10, 1983, eff. Aug. 1, 1983; Dec. 6, 1991, eff. Jan. 1, 1992; Nov. 16, 2009, eff. Jan. 1, 2010.

Advisory Committee Note—1967

Rules 111.01 and 111.02 [as promulgated in 1967. In 1975 Rule 111.01 was struck down and Rule 111.02 was renumbered as Rule 111.01]. These rules are similar to P.Fed.R.App.P. 11(a) and (b), and Fed.R.Civ.P. 75(e) (as amended, July 1, 1966). They modify substantially the procedure specified by Minn.Sup.Ct.R. V, 1st paragraph. The appellant has the duty of filing the transcript with his brief and appendix. The duty of transmission of the remainder of the original record to the Supreme Court is imposed on the clerk of the trial court. The clerk of the trial court also must prepare an adequate index of the record in the same manner as was specified in Minn.Sup.Ct.R. V, 6th paragraph. The appellant has the obligation of notifying the clerk of the trial court of the argument or submission date so that the clerk may transmit the record to the clerk of Supreme Court at the proper time. Normally, such notice should be given to the clerk of the trial court a week before the 30-day period.

If the record contains bulky or weighty exhibits, the party must make special arrangements for the transportation of such exhibits to the Supreme Court.

Rule 111.02. Exhibits and Models

The title of the case and the appellate court docket number shall be endorsed upon all exhibits sent to the clerk of the appellate courts. Exhibits and models will be returned to the trial court administrator with the remittitur when a new trial or further proceedings are ordered, but if the judgment of the appellate court is final and neither a new trial nor further proceedings are ordered, the clerk of the appellate courts may destroy all exhibits and models unless called for by the parties within 30 days after entry of the judgment of the appellate court.

Amended Feb. 14, 1975; June 17, 1983, eff. Aug. 1, 1983; Nov. 10, 1983, eff. Aug. 1, 1983; Dec. 6, 1991, eff. Jan. 1, 1992.

Rule 111.03. Record for Preliminary Hearing in the Appellate Courts

If prior to the time the record is transmitted, a party desires to make a motion for dismissal, for a stay pending appeal, for additional security on the bond on appeal or on a supersedeas bond, or for any intermediate order, the trial court administrator at the request of any party shall transmit to the appellate court those parts of the original record which the party designates.

Amended Feb. 14, 1975; June 17, 1983, eff. Aug. 1, 1983; Nov. 10, 1983, eff. Aug. 1, 1983; Dec. 6, 1991, eff. Jan. 1, 1992.

Rule 111.04. Disposition of Record after Appeal

Upon the termination of the appeal, the clerk of the appellate courts shall transmit the original transcript to the State Law Library and may transmit the remainder of the record to the trial court administrator.

Amended Feb. 14, 1975; June 17, 1983, eff. Aug. 1, 1983; Nov. 10, 1983, eff. Aug. 1, 1983; Dec. 6, 1991, eff. Jan. 1, 1992.

Rule 111.05. [Renumbered Rule 111.04 in 1975]

RULE 112. CONFIDENTIAL INFORMATION; SEALING OF PORTIONS OF RECORD

Rule 112.01. Status of Confidential Record Material on Appeal

Subdivision 1. Materials Not Available to the Public. Materials that are filed in the trial court under seal or in another manner that makes the materials unavailable to the public pursuant to statute, court rule, or trial court order, as well as any documents containing restricted identifiers as defined in Rule 11 of the General Rules of Practice, will remain under seal or not available to the public on appeal unless either the trial court or appellate court orders otherwise.

Subd. 2. Sealing of Materials on Appeal. In extraordinary situations where material in the record is confidential or trade-secret information that was not protected by a confidentiality order in the trial court, a party may move to have it filed under seal on appeal. The motion must demonstrate the need for sealing the information and must set forth the efforts made to maintain the confidentiality of the information before the motion was brought.

Adopted Oct. 16, 2009, eff. Jan. 1, 2010.

Advisory Committee Comment—2009 Amendments

Rule 112 is a new rule intended to codify existing practices relating to handling confidential information on appeal. The rule applies to information that is filed under seal pursuant to a court order for sealing, as well as to other information that is not available to the public by operation of law.

The general policy of the Minnesota courts is that court records are accessible to any member of the public. *See* Rule 2, Minnesota Rules of Public Access to Records of the Judicial Branch, *reprinted in* MINNESOTA RULES OF COURT: STATE 1083 (West 2009 ed.). This general policy is carried forward by Rule 4 governing accessibility of case records. Rule 4, subdivision 2, specifies that restricting access to case records is governed by court rules. Many statutes limit access to particular case types. *See* Rule 4, Minnesota Rules of Public Access to Records of the Judicial Branch, Advisory Committee Comment—2005, *reprinted in* MINNESOTA RULES OF COURT: STATE 1085–86 (West 2009 ed.) (collecting citations to statutes). In addition, Minn. Gen. R. Prac. 11 requires filing of personal identifying information in a separate document filed under seal.

The majority of orders restricting access to court records in civil cases are entered pursuant to Minn. R. Civ. P. 26.03(e) (limiting persons present during discovery), (f) (allowing court to order sealing of depositions), and (h) (allowing court to order parties to file other documents under seal). *See generally Minneapolis Star & Tribune v. Schumacher*, 392 N.W.2d 197 (Minn. 1986). Criminal case protective orders are governed by Minn. R. Crim. P. 25. *See generally Minneapolis Star & Tribune v. Kammeyer*, 341 N.W.2d 550 (Minn. 1983); *Nw. Publ'ns, Inc. v. Anderson*, 259 N.W.2d 254 (Minn. 1977).

The most common situation relating to sealed materials on appeal relates to the continued protection of materials filed under seal in the trial court. Subdivision 1 of Rule 112.01 restates the general rule that documents that are sealed in the trial court will remain sealed on appeal.

Historical Notes

The order of the Supreme Court dated Oct. 16, 2009, provided:

"1. The attached amendments to the Rules of Civil Appellate Procedure be, and the same are, prescribed and promulgated to be effective on January 1, 2010.

"2. These amendments shall apply to all actions or proceedings pending on or commenced on or after the effective date.

"3. The inclusion of Advisory Committee comments is for convenience and does not reflect court approval of the statements made therein."

Rule 112.02. Handling of Confidential Portions of the Appellate Record

Any materials that are filed under seal or in another manner that makes the materials unavailable to the public that need to be included in an addendum or appendix on appeal shall be prepared in a separately bound Confidential Addendum or Confidential Appendix and filed in a sealed envelope designated as "Filed under Seal pursuant to Order of the ________ Court dated ________" or in substantially similar form that describes the basis for the assertion of confidentiality.

Adopted Oct. 16, 2009, eff. Jan. 1, 2010.

Advisory Committee Comment—2009 Amendments

Rule 112.02 creates the required process for handling sealed records on appeal. The rule is intended to permit the ready handling of confidential documents by the court and to ensure that sealed information remains inaccessible to the public. Despite the additional expense that may be incurred, the duty to maintain confidentiality may require a more cumbersome process to permit the parties to advance their appellate arguments without compromising confidentiality rights that are recognized under law.

Historical Notes

The order of the Supreme Court dated Oct. 16, 2009, provided:

"1. The attached amendments to the Rules of Civil Appellate Procedure be, and the same are, prescribed and promulgated to be effective on January 1, 2010.

"2. These amendments shall apply to all actions or proceedings pending on or commenced on or after the effective date.

"3. The inclusion of Advisory Committee comments is for convenience and does not reflect court approval of the statements made therein."

Rule 112.03. Duty to Maintain Confidentiality

Every party to an appeal must take reasonable steps to prevent the disclosure of confidential information, both in oral argument and written submissions filed with the court, except in the manner prescribed in Rule 112.02.

Adopted Oct. 16, 2009, eff. Jan. 1, 2010.

Advisory Committee Comment—2009 Amendments

Rule 112.03 imposes an affirmative duty on all parties to maintain the confidentiality of information that is protected by statute, rule, or court order.

If the inability to discuss confidential information in motion papers or briefs would cause substantial hardship or prevent the fair presentation of a party's argument, a party may seek leave to file separate "public" and sealed versions of the motion or brief, with confidential information redacted in the public version and stated as necessary in the sealed version. Each separately represented party would have to be served with both the "public" and sealed versions of any documents filed with the court and served on all parties. Other means to minimize the disclosure of confidential information include referring to parties by their initials or description rather than by name, or by describing this information in terms of its specific location in the confidential part of the record without disclosing the information itself.

Historical Notes

The order of the Supreme Court dated Oct. 16, 2009, provided:

"1. The attached amendments to the Rules of Civil Appellate Procedure be, and the same are, prescribed and promulgated to be effective on January 1, 2010.

"2. These amendments shall apply to all actions or proceedings pending on or commenced on or after the effective date.

"3. The inclusion of Advisory Committee comments is for convenience and does not reflect court approval of the statements made therein."

Rule 112.04. Oral Argument

Appellate arguments are public hearings.

Adopted Oct. 16, 2009, eff. Jan. 1, 2010.

Advisory Committee Comment—2009 Amendments

Even in cases where portions of the record are confidential and filed under seal, the oral argument hearing will be in open court, open to the public, and possibly televised. The rule does not forbid closing a hearing to the public. Neither the Minnesota Supreme Court nor the Minnesota Court of Appeals has closed a hearing in the past.

Historical Notes

The order of the Supreme Court dated Oct. 16, 2009, provided:

"1. The attached amendments to the Rules of Civil Appellate Procedure be, and the same are, prescribed and promulgated to be effective on January 1, 2010.

"2. These amendments shall apply to all actions or proceedings pending on or commenced on or after the effective date.

"3. The inclusion of Advisory Committee comments is for convenience and does not reflect court approval of the statements made therein."

RULE 113. [RESERVED FOR FUTURE USE]

RULE 114. COURT OF APPEALS REVIEW OF ADMINISTRATIVE RULES

Rule 114.01. How Obtained

Review by the Court of Appeals of the validity of administrative rules pursuant to Minnesota Statutes, section 14.44 may be obtained by:

(a) filing a petition for declaratory judgment with the clerk of the appellate courts;

(b) paying the filing fee of $550 to the clerk of the appellate courts, unless no fee is required pursuant to Rule 103.01, subdivision 3;

(c) serving the petition upon the attorney general and the agency or body whose rule is to be reviewed;

(d) filing proof of service with the clerk of the appellate courts; and

(e) filing a cost bond or other security with the agency or body, unless no bond is required pursuant to Rule 107, subdivision 2, or the agency or board waives the bond.

Adopted July 7, 1998, eff. Jan. 1, 1999. Amended June 13, 2003, eff. July 1, 2003; June 11, 2009, eff. July 1, 2009.

Historical Notes

The order of the Minnesota Supreme Court [ADM–09–8006] dated June 11, 2009, amending the Rules of Civil Appellate Procedure by increasing filing fees, also provided that the amendments are effective July 1, 2009, and apply to all filings in the appellate courts on or after that date.

Rule 114.02. Contents of Petition for Declaratory Judgment

The petition shall briefly describe the specific rule to be reviewed and the errors claimed by petitioner. An original and one copy of the completed statement of the case pursuant to Rule 133.03 and a copy of the rule which is to be reviewed shall be attached to the petition. The title and form of the petition should conform to that shown in the appendix to these rules.

Adopted July 7, 1998, eff. Jan. 1, 1999.

Rule 114.03. Record on Review of Petition for Declaratory Judgment; Transmission of Record

Subdivision 1. Review of the Record. Review of the validity of administrative rules shall be on the record made in the agency rulemaking process. To the extent possible, the description of the record contained in Rule 110.01 and the provisions of Rules 110.02, 110.05, and 111 shall apply to declaratory-judgment actions.

Subd. 2. Transmission of Record. Unless the time is extended by order of the court on a showing of good cause, the record shall be forwarded by the agency or body to the clerk of the appellate courts with an itemized list as described in Rule 111.01 within 30 days after service of the petition. A copy of the itemized list shall be served on all parties.

Adopted July 7, 1998, eff. Jan. 1, 1999. Amended Oct. 16, 2009, eff. Jan. 1, 2010.

Historical Notes

The order of the Supreme Court dated Oct. 16, 2009, provided:

"1. The attached amendments to the Rules of Civil Appellate Procedure be, and the same are, prescribed and promulgated to be effective on January 1, 2010.

"2. These amendments shall apply to all actions or proceedings pending on or commenced on or after the effective date.

"3. The inclusion of Advisory Committee comments is for convenience and does not reflect court approval of the statements made therein."

Rule 114.04. Briefing

Petitioner shall serve and file a brief and appendix within 30 days after transmission of the record by the agency or body, and briefing shall proceed in accordance with Rule 131.01.

Adopted July 7, 1998, eff. Jan. 1, 1999. Amended Oct. 16, 2009, eff. Jan. 1, 2010.

Advisory Committee Comment—2009 Amendments

Rule 114 is amended to alter the timing rules for briefing. The change is made to delay the first deadline for filing a brief to 30 days after the record is transmitted to the appellate courts and the itemized list is provided to all parties.

Historical Notes

The order of the Supreme Court dated Oct. 16, 2009, provided:

"1. The attached amendments to the Rules of Civil Appellate Procedure be, and the same are, prescribed and promulgated to be effective on January 1, 2010.

"2. These amendments shall apply to all actions or proceedings pending on or commenced on or after the effective date.

"3. The inclusion of Advisory Committee comments is for convenience and does not reflect court approval of the statements made therein."

Rule 114.05. Participants

Persons other than the petitioner, agency, and attorney general, may participate in the declaratory judgment action only with leave of the Court of Appeals. Permission may be sought by filing a motion with the Court of Appeals pursuant to Rule 127 or Rule 129 and serving that motion upon all other parties. The motion shall describe the nature of the movant's participation below, the interest which would be represented in the declaratory judgment action, and the manner in which the rule affects the rights or privileges of the moving party.

Adopted July 7, 1998, eff. Jan. 1, 1999.

Advisory Committee Comment—1998 Amendments

By statute the Court of Appeals is granted original jurisdiction to review by declaratory judgment the validity of administrative rules promulgated by a state agency. MINN. STAT. § 14.44 (1996). The statute contains no provisions regarding the procedure by which this review is to be accomplished. The Court of Appeals promulgated MINN. APP. SPEC. R. PRACT. 10, effective October 25, 1991, to provide a procedural framework for such proceedings, but the Special Rules of Practice are not routinely referred to by the practicing bar when trying to determine matters of appellate procedure. To remedy this problem, a new rule, Rule 114, has been adopted.

A declaratory judgment action in the Court of Appeals is the proper method to challenge a rule prior to its application or enforcement. The grounds for challenging a rule, which must be described in the petition required by Rule 114.02, are prescribed by MINN. STAT. § 14.45 (1996). Only formally promulgated rules may be challenged in a pre-enforcement action under MINN. STAT. § 14.44. *Minnesota Educ. Ass'n v. Minnesota State Bd. of Educ.*, 499 N.W.2d 846, 849 (Minn. App. 1993). This pre-enforcement challenge must be distinguished from a contested case action in which a rule is applied to a particular party and the validity of the rule, as illustrated by the application in the individual case, may be considered. *See Mammenga v. State Dep't. of Human Servs.*, 442 N.W.2d 786 (Minn. 1989).

TITLE III. DECISIONS REVIEWABLE BY CERTIORARI TO THE COURT OF APPEALS OR THE SUPREME COURT

RULE 115. COURT OF APPEALS REVIEW OF DECISIONS OF THE DEPARTMENT OF EMPLOYMENT AND ECONOMIC DEVELOPMENT AND OTHER DECISIONS REVIEWABLE BY CERTIORARI AND REVIEW OF DECISIONS APPEALABLE PURSUANT TO THE ADMINISTRATIVE PROCEDURE ACT

Rule 115.01. How Obtained; Time for Securing Writ

Review by the Court of Appeals of decisions of the Department of Employment and Economic Development and other decisions reviewable by certiorari and review of decisions appealable pursuant to the Administrative Procedure Act may be had by securing issuance of a writ of certiorari. The appeal period and the acts required to invoke appellate jurisdiction are governed by the applicable statute.

Adopted Dec. 7, 1967, eff. Feb. 1, 1968. Amended Oct. 23, 1969; Feb. 14, 1975; Dec. 4, 1980, eff. Jan. 1, 1981; June 17, 1983, eff. Aug. 1, 1983; Nov. 10, 1983, eff. Aug. 1, 1983; Dec. 6, 1991, eff. Jan. 1, 1992; July 7, 1998, eff. Jan. 1, 1999; Oct. 16, 2009, eff. Jan. 1, 2010.

Comment—1983

See comment following Rule 115.06.

Advisory Committee Comment—2009 Amendments

Rule 115.01 is amended to change the reference, in both the title and body of the rule, to the Department of Employment and Economic Development, the current name of this agency. *See* MINN. STAT. § 15.01 (2008).

Historical Notes

The order of the Supreme Court dated Oct. 16, 2009, provided:

"1. The attached amendments to the Rules of Civil Appellate Procedure be, and the same are, prescribed and promulgated to be effective on January 1, 2010.

"2. These amendments shall apply to all actions or proceedings pending on or commenced on or after the effective date.

"3. The inclusion of Advisory Committee comments is for convenience and does not reflect court approval of the statements made therein."

Rule 115.02. Petition for Writ; How Secured

The petition and a proposed writ of certiorari shall be presented to the clerk of the appellate courts. The writ issued shall be in the name of the court.

Adopted Dec. 7, 1967, eff. Feb. 1, 1968. Amended June 17, 1983, eff. Aug. 1, 1983; Nov. 10, 1983, eff. Aug. 1, 1983.

Comment—1983

See comment following Rule 115.06.

Rule 115.03. Contents of the Petition and Writ; Filing and Service

Subdivision 1. Contents and Form of Petition, Writ and Response. The petition shall definitely and briefly state the decision, judgment, order or proceeding which is sought to be reviewed and the errors which the petitioner claims. A copy of the decision and an original and one copy of a completed statement of the case pursuant to Rule 133.03 shall be attached to the petition. The title and form of the petition and writ shall be as shown in the appendix to these rules. The respondent's statement of the case, if any, shall be filed and served not later than 14 days after service of the petitioner's statement.

Subd. 2. Bond or Security. (a) The petitioner shall file with the agency or body the cost bond pursuant to Rule 107, unless no bond is required under Rule 107, subd. 2, or by statute, or the bond is waived under Rule 107, subd. 1.

(b) The agency or body may stay enforcement of the decision in accordance with Rule 108, Application for a supersedeas bond or a stay on other terms must be made in the first instance to the agency or body. Upon motion, the Court of Appeals may review the agency's or body's decision on a stay and the terms of any stay.

Subd. 3. Filing; Fees. The clerk of the appellate courts shall file the original petition and issue the original writ. The petitioner shall pay $550 to the clerk of the appellate courts, unless no fee is required under Rule 103.01, subdivision 3, or by statute.

Subd. 4. Service. The petitioner shall serve copies of the petition and the writ, if issued, upon the agency or body to which it is directed and upon every party. Proof of service shall be filed with the clerk of the appellate courts within five days of service. A copy of the petition and writ shall be provided to the attorney general, unless the state is neither a party nor the body to which the writ is directed.

Adopted Dec. 7, 1967, eff. Feb. 1, 1968. Amended March 29, 1972; April 9, 1979; June 17, 1983, eff. Aug. 1, 1983; Nov. 10, 1983, eff. Aug. 1, 1983; June 28, 1989; May 10, 1990; Dec. 6, 1991, eff. Jan. 1, 1992; June 29, 1993, eff. July 1, 1993; July 7, 1998, eff. Jan. 1, 1999; June 13, 2003, eff. July 1, 2003; June 11, 2009, eff. July 1, 2009; Oct. 16, 2009, eff. Jan. 1, 2010.

Comment—1983

See comment following Rule 115.06.

Advisory Committee Comment—2009 Amendments

Rule 115.03, subdivision 1, is amended to change the timing for filing a statement of the case by a respondent to 14, rather than 10, days after service of the petitioner's statement of the case. This change makes the respondent's statement of the case due on the same day a notice of related appeal would be due. *See* Rule 104.01, subdivision 4, as amended.

Historical Notes

The order of the Minnesota Supreme Court [ADM-09-8006] dated June 11, 2009, amending the Rules of Civil Appellate Procedure by increasing filing fees, also provided that the amendments are effective July 1, 2009, and apply to all filings in the appellate courts on or after that date.

The order of the Supreme Court dated Oct. 16, 2009, provided:

"1. The attached amendments to the Rules of Civil Appellate Procedure be, and the same are, prescribed and promulgated to be effective on January 1, 2010.

"2. These amendments shall apply to all actions or proceedings pending on or commenced on or after the effective date.

"3. The inclusion of Advisory Committee comments is for convenience and does not reflect court approval of the statements made therein."

Rule 115.04. The Record on Review by Certiorari; Transmission of the Record; Timing of Briefing

Subdivision 1. General Application of Rules 110 and 111. To the extent possible, the provisions of Rules 110 and 111 respecting the record and manner of its transmission and filing or return in appeals shall govern upon the issuance of the writ; and the parties shall proceed as though the appeal had been commenced by the filing of a notice of appeal, unless otherwise provided by this rule, the court, or statute. Each reference in Rules 110 and 111 to the trial court, the trial court administrator, and the notice of appeal shall be read, where appropriate, as a reference to the body whose decision is to be reviewed, to the administrator, clerk or secretary thereof, and to the writ of certiorari respectively.

Subd. 2. Transcript of Audiotaped Proceedings. If a proceeding has been audiotaped and a record of the proceeding is necessary for the appeal, the relator shall order the transcript from the agency or body within ten days after the writ of certiorari is filed. The relator shall make appropriate financial arrangements with the agency or body for the transcription. The agency or body shall designate a court reporter or other qualified person to transcribe the audiotape. The agency or body shall serve and file a transcript certificate pursuant to Rule 110.02, subdivision 2(a) within ten days after the transcript is ordered. The reporter shall file the original and first copy of the transcript with the agency or body, deliver a copy to the attorney for each party to the appeal separately represented, and file a certificate of filing and delivery pursuant to Rule 110.02, subdivision 2(b).

Subd. 3. Notice of Contents of Record. Unless the time is extended by order of the court on a showing of good cause, the itemized list of the contents of the record as described in Rule 111.01 shall be served on all parties and filed with the clerk of the appellate courts by the agency or body within 30 days after service of the petition or 14 days after delivery of the transcript in accordance with subdivision 2 of this rule, whichever date is later. Service and filing shall be accomplished by notice of service and filing, as in Form 115C in the appendix to these rules, which shall constitute proof of service.

Subd. 4. Timing of Briefing. Relator shall serve and file a brief and appendix within 30 days after the service of the itemized list of contents of the record by the agency or body, and briefing shall proceed in accordance with Rule 131.01.

Subd. 5. Transmission of Record. The record shall be retained by the agency or body until the clerk of the appellate courts requests that it be transmitted to the court. The record shall thereupon be transmitted promptly to the clerk of the appellate courts with a copy of the itemized list of the contents, in quadruplicate.

Adopted Dec. 7, 1967, eff. Feb. 1, 1968. Amended June 17, 1983, eff. Aug. 1, 1983; Nov. 10, 1983, eff. Aug. 1, 1983; Dec. 6, 1991, eff. Jan. 1, 1992; July 7, 1998, eff. Jan. 1, 1999; Oct. 16, 2009, eff. Jan. 1, 2010.

Comment—1983

See comment following Rule 115.06.

Advisory Committee Comment—1998 Amendments

The amendments to this rule in 1998 update references to the Department of Economic Security, clarify that the time for appeal and jurisdictional acts are defined by statute, clarify the terms used to refer to the parties, and establish procedures for transcribing audiotapes of agency proceedings.

Because certiorari in Minnesota is a statutory remedy, the jurisdictional prerequisites for certiorari review are governed by the applicable statute, not by the appellate rules. Statutes governing various types of decisions reviewable by certiorari may establish different time limitations and contain different requirements for securing review by the Court of Appeals. Examples of different statutory requirements include: proceedings governed by the Administrative Procedure Act, MINN. STAT. §§ 14.63-.64(1996) (service and filing of petition for writ of certiorari not more than 30 days after party receives final decision and order of agency; timely motion for reconsideration extends time until service of order disposing of motion); reemployment benefits proceedings, MINN. STAT. § 268.105, subd. 7 (1996) (service and filing of petition for writ of certiorari within 30 days of mailing of Commissioner of Economic Security's decision); and proceedings under the general certiorari statute, MINN. STAT. §§ 606.01-.02 (1996) (issuance of writ and service of issued writ within 60 days after party applying for writ receives due notice of proceeding to be reviewed). The Rule has been modified to make clear that the applicable statutes will determine the time limitations and triggering events for review.

The rule has been modified to clarify the procedure for obtaining a stay of the order for which review is sought. As with other appellate proceedings, requests for stays should be addressed in the first instance to the agency or body which has issued the challenged decision.

A party seeking certiorari review is a petitioner unless and until the court issues a writ of certiorari. After a writ has been issued, the party seeking review is called the relator. The adverse party or parties and the agency or body whose decision is to be reviewed are the respondents.

Finally, the revisions clarify and make more specific the procedures for preparation and submission of the record for appellate review.

Advisory Committee Comment—2009 Amendments

Rule 115.04 is amended to change the timing rules for certiorari proceedings. Subdivision 3 establishes a new Form 115C to ensure that the itemized list is provided to all parties and to determine the date and means of service and filing. One of the purposes of this amendment is to defer briefing until the contents of the record are known to the parties. Subdivision 4 establishes the timing requirements for briefing.

Subdivision 5 clarifies that the record itself is then to be retained by the agency or body until needed by the appellate court. This provision does not directly affect the litigants—it is primarily a matter of administration of the appellate court clerk's office. The rule requires that the record be accompanied by the itemized list of the contents in quadruplicate because that form is used to document receipt by the appellate courts and again to document receipt when the record is returned to the agency or body.

Historical Notes

The order of the Supreme Court dated Oct. 16, 2009, provided:

"1. The attached amendments to the Rules of Civil Appellate Procedure be, and the same are, prescribed and promulgated to be effective on January 1, 2010.

"2. These amendments shall apply to all actions or proceedings pending on or commenced on or after the effective date.

"3. The inclusion of Advisory Committee comments is for convenience and does not reflect court approval of the statements made therein."

Rule 115.05. Costs and Disbursements

Costs and disbursements may be taxed by the prevailing party but not for or against the body to whom the writ is directed. If a writ appears to have been brought for the purpose of delay or vexation, the Court of Appeals may award double costs to the prevailing party.

Adopted Dec. 7, 1967, eff. Feb. 1, 1968. Amended June 17, 1983, eff. Aug. 1, 1983; Nov. 10, 1983, eff. Aug. 1, 1983.

Comment—1983

See comment following Rule 115.06.

Rule 115.06. Dismissal Costs

If any writ of certiorari is issued improperly or is not served as required by these rules, the party against whom it is issued may have it discharged on motion and affidavit showing the facts and shall be entitled to allowable costs.

Adopted Dec. 7, 1967, eff. Feb. 1, 1968. Amended June 17, 1983, eff. Aug. 1, 1983; Nov. 10, 1983, eff. Aug. 1, 1983.

Comment—1983

Rule 115 sets out the procedure for securing review by the Court of Appeals of decisions of the Commissioner of Jobs and Training, decisions appealable pursuant to the Administrative Procedure Act, and other decisions reviewable by certiorari to the Court of Appeals. The procedures are similar to those provided by former Rule 115 except that the time limitations set out in the rule have been shortened to conform with the time limitations presently provided in the statute governing review of unemployment compensation decisions. The rule cautions that statutes governing review of the various types of decisions reviewable by certiorari may establish different time limitations.

Proof of service of the petition and the writ must be filed with the clerk of the appellate courts within 5 days after service. A copy of the petition and the writ must be provided to the attorney general whenever the state or a department or agency of the state is a party or the body to whom the writ is directed.

A completed statement of the case shall be attached to the petition (Form 133).

See Appendix for form of the petition for a writ of certiorari (Form 115A) and of the writ of certiorari (Form 115B).

RULE 116. SUPREME COURT REVIEW OF DECISIONS OF THE WORKERS' COMPENSATION COURT OF APPEALS, DECISIONS OF THE TAX COURT, AND OTHER DECISIONS REVIEWABLE BY CERTIORARI

Rule 116.01. How Obtained; Time for Securing Writ

Supreme Court review of decisions of the Workers' Compensation Court of Appeals, decisions of the Tax Court, and of other decisions reviewable by certiorari may be had by securing issuance of a writ of certiorari within 30 days after the date the party applying for the writ was served with written notice of the decision sought to be reviewed, unless an applicable statute prescribes a different period of time.

Adopted June 17, 1983, eff. Aug. 1, 1983. Amended Nov. 10, 1983, eff. Aug. 1, 1983.

Comment—1983

See comment following Rule 116.06.

Rule 116.02. Petition for Writ; How Secured

The petition and a proposed writ of certiorari shall be presented to the clerk of the appellate courts. The writ issued shall be in the name of the court.

Adopted June 17, 1983, eff. Aug. 1, 1983. Amended Nov. 10, 1983, eff. Aug. 1, 1983.

Comment—1983

See comment following Rule 116.06.

Rule 116.03. Contents of the Petition and Writ; Filing and Service

Subdivision 1. Contents and Form of Petition, Writ and Response. The petition shall definitely and briefly state the decision, judgment, order or proceeding which is sought to be reviewed and the errors which the petitioner claims. A copy of the decision and two copies of a completed statement of the case pursuant to Rule 133.03 shall be attached to the petition. The title and form of the petition and writ should be as shown in the appendix to these rules. The respondent's statement of the case, if any, shall be filed and served within 14 days after service of the petitioner's statement.

Subd. 2. Bond or Security. The petitioner shall file the bond or other security required by statute or by the Supreme Court.

Subd. 3. Filing; Fees. The clerk of the appellate courts shall file the original petition and issue the original writ. The petitioner shall pay $550 to the clerk of the appellate courts, unless a different filing fee is required by statute.

Subd. 4. Service; Time. The petitioner shall serve copies of the petition and writ upon the court or body to whom it is directed and upon any party within 30 days after the petitioner was served with written notice of the decision to be reviewed, unless an applicable statute prescribes a different period of time. Proof of service shall be filed with the clerk of the appellate courts within 5 days of service. A copy of the petition and writ shall be provided to the Attorney General at the time of service.

Adopted June 17, 1983, eff. Aug. 1, 1983. Amended Nov. 10, 1983, eff. Aug. 1, 1983; June 28, 1989; May 10, 1990; Dec. 6, 1991, eff. Jan. 1, 1992; June 29, 1993, eff. July 1, 1993; June 13, 2003, eff. July 1, 2003; June 11, 2009, eff. July 1, 2009; Oct. 16, 2009, eff. Jan. 1, 2010.

Comment—1983

See comment following Rule 116.06.

Advisory Committee Comment—2009 Amendments

Rule 116.03, subdivision 1, is amended to change the timing for filing a statement of the case by a respondent to 14, rather than 10, days after service of the petitioner's statement of the case. This change makes the respondent's statement of the case due on the same day a notice of related appeal would be due. *See* Rule 104.01, subdivision 4, as amended.

Historical Notes

The order of the Minnesota Supreme Court [ADM-09-8006] dated June 11, 2009, amending the Rules of Civil Appellate Procedure by increasing filing fees, also provided that the amendments are effective July 1, 2009, and apply to all filings in the appellate courts on or after that date.

The order of the Supreme Court dated Oct. 16, 2009, provided:

"1. The attached amendments to the Rules of Civil Appellate Procedure be, and the same are, prescribed and promulgated to be effective on January 1, 2010.

"2. These amendments shall apply to all actions or proceedings pending on or commenced on or after the effective date.

"3. The inclusion of Advisory Committee comments is for convenience and does not reflect court approval of the statements made therein."

Rule 116.04. The Record on Review by Certiorari; Transmission of the Record

To the extent possible, the provisions of Rules 110 and 111 respecting the record and the time and manner of its transmission and filing or return in appeals shall govern upon the issuance of the writ, and the parties shall proceed as though the appeal had been commenced by the filing of a notice of appeal, unless otherwise provided by the court or by statute. Each reference in those rules to the trial court, the trial court administrator, and the notice of appeal shall be read, where appropriate, as a reference to the body whose decision is to be reviewed, to the administrator, clerk or secretary thereof, and to the writ of certiorari respectively.

Adopted June 17, 1983, eff. Aug. 1, 1983. Amended Nov. 10, 1983, eff. Aug. 1, 1983; Dec. 6, 1991, eff. Jan. 1, 1992.

Comment—1983

See comment following Rule 116.06.

Rule 116.05. Costs and Disbursements

Costs and disbursements may be taxed by the prevailing party but not for or against the body to whom the writ is directed. If a writ appears to have been brought for the purpose of delay or vexation, the Supreme Court may award double costs to the prevailing party.

Adopted June 17, 1983, eff. Aug. 1, 1983. Amended Nov. 10, 1983, eff. Aug. 1, 1983.

Comment—1983

See comment following Rule 116.06.

Rule 116.06. Dismissal Costs

If any writ of certiorari is issued improperly or is not served as required by these rules, the party against whom it is issued may have it discharged on motion and affidavit showing the facts and shall be entitled to allowable costs.

Adopted June 17, 1983, eff. Aug. 1, 1983. Amended Nov. 10, 1983, eff. Aug. 1, 1983.

Comment—1983

Rule 116 sets out the procedures for securing review by the Supreme Court of decisions of the Workers' Compensation Court of Appeals, decisions of the Tax Court, and other decisions reviewable by certiorari to the Supreme Court. The procedures are similar to those provided by former Rule 115 except that the time limitations set out in the rule have been shortened to conform with the time limitations presently provided in the statute governing review of workers' compensation decisions. The rule cautions that statutes governing review of the various types of decisions reviewable by certiorari may establish different time limitations.

Proof of service of the petition and writ must be filed with the clerk of the appellate courts within 5 days after service. A copy of the petition and the writ must also be provided to the attorney general.

See Appendix for form of the petition for a writ of certiorari (Form 116A) and of the writ of certiorari (Form 116B).

RULE 117. PETITION IN SUPREME COURT FOR REVIEW OF DECISIONS OF THE COURT OF APPEALS

Subdivision 1. Filing of Petition. Any party seeking review of a decision of the Court of Appeals shall separately petition the Supreme Court. The petition with proof of service shall be filed with the clerk of the appellate courts within 30 days of the filing of the Court of Appeals' decision. A filing fee of $550 shall be paid to the clerk of the appellate courts.

Subd. 2. Discretionary Review. Review of any decision of the Court of Appeals is discretionary with the Supreme Court. The following criteria may be considered:

(a) the question presented is an important one upon which the Supreme Court should rule; or

(b) the Court of Appeals has ruled on the constitutionality of a statute; or

(c) the lower courts have so far departed from the accepted and usual course of justice as to call for an exercise of the Supreme Court's supervisory powers; or

(d) a decision by the Supreme Court will help develop, clarify, or harmonize the law; and

(1) the case calls for the application of a new principle or policy; or

(2) the resolution of the question presented has possible statewide impact; or

(3) the question is likely to recur unless resolved by the Supreme Court.

Subd. 3. Petition Requirements. The petition for review shall not exceed five typewritten pages, exclusive of appendix, and shall contain:

(a) a statement of the legal issues sought to be reviewed, and the disposition of those issues by the Court of Appeals;

(b) a statement of the criteria relied upon to support the petition, or other substantial and compelling reasons for review;

(c) a statement of the case, including disposition in the trial court or administrative agency and the Court of Appeals, and of those facts not addressed by the Court of Appeals relevant to the issues presented for review, with appropriate references to the record; and

(d) a brief argument in support of the petition.

The appendix shall contain the decision and opinion of the Court of Appeals, the judgments, orders, findings of fact, conclusions of law, and memorandum decisions of the trial court or administrative agency, pertinent trial briefs, and any portion of the record necessary for an understanding of the petition.

Four copies of the petition and appendix shall be filed with the clerk of the appellate courts.

Subd. 4. Response and Request for Cross-Review. An opposing party may file with the clerk of the appellate courts a response to the petition within 20 days of service. The response shall comply with the requirements set forth for the petition and shall contain proof of service. Any responding party may, in its response, also conditionally seek review of additional designated issues not raised by the petition. In the event of such a conditional request, the party filing the initial petition for review shall not be entitled to file a response unless the court requests one on its own initiative.

Subd. 5. Amicus Curiae. A request for leave to participate in the appeal as amicus curiae is governed by Rule 129.

Adopted June 17, 1983, eff. Aug. 1, 1983. Amended Nov. 10, 1983, eff. Aug. 1, 1983; June 28, 1989; May 10, 1990; Dec. 6, 1991, eff. Jan. 1, 1992; June 29, 1993, eff. July 1, 1993; Feb. 5, 1998, eff. May 11, 1998; July 7, 1998, eff. Jan. 1, 1999; June 13, 2003, eff. July 1, 2003; Nov. 17, 2003, eff. Dec. 1, 2003; June 11, 2009, eff. July 1, 2009.

Comment—1983

This entirely new rule establishes the procedure for obtaining Supreme Court review of a decision of the Court of Appeals. Review is discretionary with the Supreme Court. While the rule enumerates criteria which may be considered by the court in exercising its discretion, they are intended to be instructive and are neither mandatory nor exclusive. The petition should be accompanied by any documents pertinent to the Supreme Court's review.

See Appendix for form of petition for review (Form 117).

Advisory Committee Comment—1998 Amendments

The 1998 revisions to Rule 117 eliminate the provision for "conditional" petitions for review. In its stead, the revised rule allows parties to include in their responses a conditional request to the court to review additional issues only if the petition is granted. This procedure mirrors the procedure used in criminal appeals. *See* MINN. R. CRIM. P. 29.04, subd. 6 (appeals to Court of Appeals). The revised rule does not provide for any expansion of the five-page limit for the response in order to accommodate the conditional request for review of additional issues. By the same token, the amended rule does not allow a reply by the party initially seeking review, since that party has already indicated to the court that the case satisfies some of the criteria of Rule 117.

A party who wishes to have issues reviewed by the Supreme Court regardless of the court's actions on a previously filed petition should file a petition within the 30-day time limit from decision, since the court is unlikely to deny an initial petition but grant review of issues raised only conditionally in a response. Likewise, a party who would feel constrained by the page limit of a response which includes a conditional request for review of additional issues should file a separate petition for review within the time provided by Rule 117 for an initial petition, thirty days from the date of filing the Court of Appeals' decision.

Historical Notes

The order of the Minnesota Supreme Court [ADM–09–8006] dated June 11, 2009, amending the Rules of Civil Appellate Procedure by increasing filing fees, also provided that the amendments are effective July 1, 2009, and apply to all filings in the appellate courts on or after that date.

RULE 118. ACCELERATED REVIEW BY THE SUPREME COURT PRIOR TO A DECISION BY THE COURT OF APPEALS

Subdivision 1. Filing Requirements. Any party may petition the Supreme Court for accelerated review of any case pending in the Court of Appeals upon a petition which shows, in addition to the criteria of Rule 117, subdivision 2, that the case is of such imperative public importance as to justify deviation from the normal appellate procedure and to require immediate determination in the Supreme Court. The petition for accelerated review with proof of service shall be filed with the clerk of the appellate courts together with a filing fee of $100. The filing of a petition for accelerated review shall not stay proceedings or extend the time requirements in the Court of Appeals.

Subd. 2. Petition Requirements. The petition for accelerated review shall not exceed ten typewritten pages, exclusive of appendix, and shall contain:

(a) a statement of the issues;

(b) a statement of the case, including all relevant facts, and disposition in the trial court or administrative agency; and

(c) a brief argument in support of the petition.

The appendix shall contain the judgments, orders, findings of fact, conclusions of law, and memorandum decisions of the trial court or administrative agency, pertinent trial briefs, and any portion of the record necessary for an understanding of the petition.

Four copies of the petition and appendix shall be filed with the clerk.

Subd. 3. Notice. If the Supreme Court orders accelerated review, whether on the petition of a party, on certification by the Court of Appeals pursuant to Minnesota Statutes, Section 480A.10, or on its own motion, notice of accelerated review shall be given by the clerk of the appellate courts to all parties.

Adopted June 17, 1983, eff. Aug. 1, 1983. Amended Nov. 10, 1983, eff. Aug. 1, 1983; June 28, 1989; May 10, 1990.

Comment—1983

This rule authorizes a party to request by-pass of the Court of Appeals in favor of immediate review by the Supreme Court. The decision to permit accelerated review is discretionary with the Supreme Court, and the rule contemplates that leave will be granted only in extraordinary cases.

There is statutory authority for certification of a case by the Court of Appeals and for transfer of a case by order of the Supreme Court.

See Appendix for form of petition for accelerated review (Form 118).

RULE 119. [RESERVED FOR FUTURE USE]

TITLE V. EXTRAORDINARY WRITS

RULE 120. WRITS OF MANDAMUS AND PROHIBITION DIRECTED TO A JUDGE OR JUDGES AND OTHER WRITS

Advisory Committee Note—1967

This rule governs the issuance of extraordinary writs by the Supreme Court to judges of lower courts. The issuance of writs of certiorari to administrative bodies is governed by Rule 115.

Today, writs of mandamus and prohibition are the only intercourt writs commonly used. The rule does not specify the grounds for the issuance of an extraordinary writ. The issuance of a writ lies within the sound discretion of the Supreme Court. No party is entitled to a writ as a matter of right. Generally, the Supreme Court will not issue a writ to review the broad discretionary powers vested in the lower courts, nor will a writ be issued where a right to appeal exists and may be properly exercised. Specifically, writs of mandamus are issued "to compel the performance of an act which the law specifically enjoins as a duty" or to compel a lower court "to exercise its judgment or proceed to the discharge of any of its functions." M.S.A. § 586.01. Writs of prohibition are issued to restrain action by the lower court "where it appears that the court is about to exceed its jurisdiction or where it appears the action of the court relates to a matter that is decisive of the case; where the court has ordered the production of information clearly not discoverable and there is no adequate remedy at law; or in rare instances where it will settle a rule of practice affecting all litigants." Thermorama, Inc. v. Shiller, 271 Minn. 79, 135 N.W.2d 43 (1965). E.g., Jallen v. Agre, 265 Minn. 578, 122 N.W.2d 207 (1963) (mandamus to compel trial court to comply with mandate of Supreme Court); State v. Moriarity, 203 Minn. 23, 279 N.W. 835 (1938) (mandamus to compel trial court to state grounds upon which new trial was granted); Planck v. Minneapolis, St. P. & S.S.M. Ry. Co., 143 N.W.2d 641 (Minn.1966) (mandamus to compel trial court to dismiss action on the ground of forum non conveniens); Jeppesen v. Swanson, 243 Minn. 547, 68 N.W.2d 649 (1955) (prohibition to prevent enforcement of discovery order); Bellows v. Erickson, 233 Minn. 320, 46 N.W.2d 654 (1951) (prohibition to prevent enforcement of order granting temporary injunction); Shacter v. Richter, 271 Minn. 87, 135 N.W.2d 66 (1965) (prohibition to prevent enforcement of order consolidating actions). In addition, it is customary to use mandamus to review orders refusing to change venue even though the order is discretionary. Castle v. Village of Baudette, 267 Minn. 140, 125 N.W.2d 416 (1963).

Rule 120.01. Petition for Writ

Application for a writ of mandamus or of prohibition or for any other extraordinary writ in the Supreme

Court directed to the Court of Appeals, the Tax Court, or the Workers' Compensation Court of Appeals, or in the Court of Appeals directed to a trial court shall be made by petition. The petition shall specify the lower court decision and the name of the judge and shall contain:

(a) a statement of the facts necessary to an understanding of the issues presented by the application;

(b) a statement of the issues presented and the relief sought; and

(c) a statement of the reasons why the extraordinary writ should issue.

Petitioner shall attach a copy of the trial court decision challenged in the petition, and if necessary to an understanding of the issues, additional pertinent lower court documents.

The petition shall be titled "In re [name of petitioner], Petitioner," followed by the trial court caption, and shall be captioned in the court in which the application is made, in the manner specified in Rule 120.04.

Adopted Dec. 7, 1967, eff. Feb. 1, 1968. Amended April 9, 1979; June 17, 1983, eff. Aug. 1, 1983; Nov. 10, 1983, eff. Aug. 1, 1983; July 7, 1998, eff. Jan. 1, 1999; Dec. 19, 2000, eff. March 1, 2001.

Advisory Committee Note—1967

Rule 120.01. This rule is similar to P.Fed. R.App.P. 20(a). The proceeding is initiated by a written petition requesting the issuance of the writ. The petition shall contain a brief statement of the pertinent facts, the legal issue, and the reasons why a writ should be issued. In addition, the petition should be accompanied by a copy of the trial court's order or other parts of the record (if readily available) which will be of aid to an understanding of the matters set forth in the petition, and may be accompanied by a brief résumé of the authorities upon which the petitioner relies.

[For general discussion of the provisions of Rules 120.01 to 120.04, see note preceding Rule 120.01.]

Comment—1983

See comment following Rule 121.03.

Advisory Committee Comment—1998 Amendments

See note following Rule 120.04.

Historical Notes

The order of the Minnesota Supreme Court [C4-84-2133] dated December 19, 2000, provides in part that these amendments are effective March 1, 2001, and shall apply to all actions or proceedings pending on or commenced on or after the effective date, with the exception of the amendments to Rule 132, which shall apply to all appeals or proceedings commenced in either the Court of Appeals or the Supreme Court on or after the effective date.

The order of the Minnesota Supreme Court [C4-84-2133] dated December 19, 2000, provides in part that "(t)he inclusion of Advisory Committee comments is made for convenience and does not reflect court approval of the statements made therein".

Rule 120.02. Submission of Petition; Response to the Petition

The petition shall be served on all parties and filed with the clerk of the appellate courts. In criminal cases, the State Public Defender and the Attorney General for the State of Minnesota shall also be served. If the lower court is a party, it shall be served; in all other cases, it should be notified of the filing of the petition and provided with a copy of the petition and any response. All parties other than the petitioner shall be deemed respondents and may answer jointly or separately within five days after the service of the petition. If a respondent does not desire to respond, the clerk of the appellate courts and all parties shall be advised by letter within the five-day period, but the petition shall not thereby be taken as admitted.

Adopted Dec. 7, 1967, eff. Feb. 1, 1968. Amended Feb. 14, 1975; April 9, 1979; Dec. 4, 1980, eff. Jan. 1, 1981; June 17, 1983, eff. Aug. 1, 1983; Nov. 10, 1983, eff. Aug. 1, 1983; Dec. 6, 1991, eff. Jan. 1, 1992; July 7, 1998, eff. Jan. 1, 1999; Dec. 11, 2008, eff. Jan. 1, 2009.

Advisory Committee Note—1967

Rule 120.02. This rule governs the manner of submission of the petition to the court and is flexible to suit the various situations with which the petitioner may be faced.

If an emergency situation exists, the attorney for the petitioner will submit the petition personally after notifying the attorneys of the other parties of his intention to do so. No formal notice is necessary nor is there any time limitation. All that is necessary is that the notice be reasonable under the circumstances. Thus, an informal, oral notice will usually be sufficient. If an extreme emergency exists and there is insufficient time to locate or notify the other attorneys, the court may waive the notice requirement.

Even though no emergency exists, if the petition involves a controversial or novel matter, the rule nevertheless contemplates the personal appearance of the attorneys of the parties at the time of the submission of the petition. In this situation, the notice may be either oral or written and shall give the other parties a reasonable opportunity to attend.

The personal appearance of the attorneys at the time of submission of the petition will permit the justice or justices present to engage in an informal discussion concerning the basis of the petition, the facts, and the problems facing the parties, and will enable the court to exercise its discretion with an understanding of both sides of the case. For this reason, the attendance of opposing counsel, while not compulsory, is desirable and expected.

If the petition involves a non-controversial routine matter concerning which the above described informal preliminary conference will be of no real value, personal appearance of counsel is not required and the petition may be submitted by mail. An example of this type of situation is a petition for mandamus to review a venue matter.

[For general discussion of the provisions of Rules 120.01 to 120.04, see note preceding Rule 120.01.]

Comment—1983

See comment following Rule 121.03.

Advisory Committee Comment—1998 Amendments

See note following Rule 120.04.

Advisory Committee Comment—2008 Amendments

Rule 120.02 is amended to add a single requirement for writ practice in criminal cases. The additional requirement of service on the public defender and attorney general is patterned on similar service requirements in the rules of criminal procedure. *See, e.g.*, MINN. R. CRIM. P. 28. 04, subd. 2(2)(appeal by prosecutor of pretrial order), subd. 6(1)(appeal of postconviction order), subd. 8(1)(appeal from judgment of acquittal, vacation of judgment after guilty verdict, or from order granting a new trial; MINN. R. CRIM. P. 28.02, subd. 4. The requirement for notice in petitions for extraordinary writs is especially appropriate given the short time periods for writ practice. *See generally State v. Barrett*, 694 N.W. 2d 783 (Minn. 2005)(discussing importance of service requirements).

Rule 120.03. Procedure Following Submission

If the reviewing court is of the opinion that the writ should not be granted, it shall deny the petition. Otherwise, it may:

(a) issue a peremptory writ, or

(b) grant temporary relief and direct the filing of briefs.

There shall be no oral argument unless the reviewing court otherwise directs.

Adopted Dec. 7, 1967, eff. Feb. 1, 1968. Amended April 9, 1979; June 17, 1983, eff. Aug. 1, 1983; Nov. 10, 1983, eff. Aug. 1, 1983.

Comment—1983

See comment following Rule 121.03.

Advisory Committee Note—1967

Rule 120.03. This rule is similar to P.Fed. R.App.P. 20(b).[1] Following submission of the petition, the court may do the following:

(1) If the court believes the petition to be without merit or if it decides not to exercise its discretionary powers, it may simply deny the petition.

(2) If the court is of the opinion that the petitioner is entitled to the requested relief, it may order the issuance of a peremptory writ without further proceedings.

(3) If the court believes that the petition may have merit and decides to exercise its discretion, it may order further proceedings to determine whether a peremptory writ should be issued.

In the last mentioned situation, the customary practice was the issuance of an order for an alternative writ. The order often granted temporary relief by restraining further proceedings below. Pursuant to the order, the clerk issued a formal alternative writ which was, in effect, an order directed to the lower court to show cause why the alternative writ should not be made absolute.

While the rule is broad enough to encompass the old alternative writ procedure, it is designed to permit the court to proceed without the issuance of an alternative writ. The court may simply issue an order directing the adverse parties to respond, and staying proceedings below until further order of the court. In addition, the order may direct the filing of formal briefs, or it may specify a simple answer to the petition. Further, the often fictional response of the trial court judge is no longer required although he may participate if he so desires. After the parties have complied with the order, the court will again consider the matter and either deny the petition or order the issuance of a peremptory writ granting, in whole or in part, the relief requested.

[For general discussion of the provisions of Rules 120.01 to 120.04, see note preceding Rule 120.01.]

[1] Proposed Fed.R.App.P. 20(b) was adopted as Rule 21(b) by the Supreme Court of the United States on December 4, 1967 with minor changes.

Rule 120.04. Filing; Form of Papers; Number of Copies

Upon receipt of a 550 filing fee, the clerk of the appellate courts shall file the petition. All papers and briefs may be typewritten and in the form specified in Rule 132.02. Four copies with proof of service shall be filed with the clerk of the appellate courts, but the reviewing court may direct that additional copies be provided. Service of all papers and briefs may be made by mail.

Adopted Dec. 7, 1967, eff. Feb. 1, 1968. Amended April 9, 1979; June 17, 1983, eff. Aug. 1, 1983; Nov. 10, 1983, eff. Aug. 1, 1983; June 28, 1989; May 10, 1990; June 29, 1993, eff. July 1, 1993; July 7, 1998, eff. Jan. 1, 1999; June 13, 2003, eff. July 1, 2003; June 11, 2009, eff. July 1, 2009.

Comment—1983

See comment following Rule 121.03.

Advisory Committee Comment—1998 Amendments

The primary purpose of these amendments is to modify extraordinary writ procedure to allow a party to seek relief without requiring that party to sue the trial court. This change follows in some respects the amendments made to the federal rules of appellate procedure in 1997. The rule, however, retains most of the remaining procedural requirements of the existing rule inasmuch as they work well in practice in Minnesota.

The rule eliminates any requirement that the trial court judge be named as a party. It is still possible to name the judge as a respondent in the writ proceeding, but this rule does not require it. This change is intended to make it less likely that the seeking of the writ will interfere with the orderly handling of ongoing proceedings in the trial court.

The rule also eliminates the requirement that a proposed writ be filed because that document is of little use to the courts.

The forms relating to this rule are also amended as part of these changes.

Historical Notes

The order of the Minnesota Supreme Court [ADM-09-8006] dated June 11, 2009, amending the Rules of Civil Appellate Procedure by increasing filing fees, also provided that the amendments are effective July 1, 2009, and apply to all filings in the appellate courts on or after that date.

Rule 120.05. Review in Supreme Court

Denial of a writ under this rule or Rule 121 by the Court of Appeals is subject to review by the Supreme Court through petition for review under Rule 117. Review of an order denying an extraordinary writ should not be sought by filing a petition for a writ under this rule with the Supreme Court unless the criteria for issuance of the writ are applicable to the Court of Appeals order for which review is sought.

Adopted Dec. 19, 2000, eff. March 1, 2001.

Advisory Committee Comment—2000 Amendments

Rule 120 is amended to make explicit two aspects of extraordinary writ practice that some practitioners have overlooked. First, an extraordinary writ directed to the Tax Court or the Workers' Compensation Court of Appeals may be sought in the Supreme Court. *See* MINN. STAT. § 480.04 (1998). Second, the normal method of seeking review in the Supreme Court of a denial of an extraordinary writ by the Court of Appeals is by petition for review under Rule 117, not by petition for a writ under this rule. The same is true for review of denial of an emergency writ under Rule 121.

Historical Notes

The order of the Minnesota Supreme Court [C4-84-2133] dated December 19, 2000, provides in part that these amendments are effective March 1, 2001, and shall apply to all actions or proceedings pending on or commenced on or after the effective date, with the exception of the amendments to Rule 132, which shall apply to all appeals or proceedings commenced in either the Court of Appeals or the Supreme Court on or after the effective date.

The order of the Minnesota Supreme Court [C4-84-2133] dated December 19, 2000, provides in part that "(t)he inclusion of Advisory Committee comments is made for convenience and does not reflect court approval of the statements made therein".

RULE 121. MANDAMUS AND PROHIBITION—EMERGENCY SITUATIONS

Rule 121.01. Communication to the Court

If an emergency situation exists and the provisions of Rule 120 are impractical, the attorney for a party seeking a writ of mandamus or of prohibition directed to a lower court may orally petition the reviewing court for such relief by telephoning or by personally contacting the Supreme Court Commissioner, if application is made in the Supreme Court, or the Chief Staff Attorney, if application is made in the Court of Appeals, who will communicate with the reviewing court relative to an early or immediate consideration of the petition. If the Commissioner or Chief Staff Attorney is unavailable, the oral petition may be made to a justice or judge of the reviewing court.

Adopted April 9, 1979. Amended June 17, 1983, eff. Aug. 1, 1983; Nov. 10, 1983, eff. Aug. 1, 1983.

Comment—1983

See comment following Rule 121.03.

Rule 121.02. Procedure

Except as provided in Rule 121.03, no written petition or other document need be filed unless the reviewing court so directs. If the reviewing court is of the opinion that either no emergency exists or no relief is available, it may either deny the oral petition or may direct the party to proceed under Rule 120. Otherwise, after affording all parties an opportunity to be heard, it may:

(a) issue a peremptory writ, or

(b) grant such other relief as the interest of justice requires.

Adopted April 9, 1979. Amended June 17, 1983, eff. Aug. 1, 1983; Nov. 10, 1983, eff. Aug. 1, 1983; Dec. 6, 1991, eff. Jan. 1, 1992.

Comment—1983

See comment following Rule 121.03.

Rule 121.03. Filing Fee

In the event the oral petition is granted, the attorney orally petitioning for a writ shall thereafter immediately transmit to the clerk of the appellate courts a $550 filing fee with a letter specifying:

(a) the name of the case,

(b) the lower court and the name of the judge,

(c) the type of writ sought, and

(d) the name, address, telephone number and attorney registration license number of each attorney.

No filing fee or transmission of documents shall be required in the event the oral petition is denied.

Adopted April 9, 1979. Amended June 17, 1983, eff. Aug. 1, 1983; Nov. 10, 1983, eff. Aug. 1, 1983; June 28, 1989; May 10, 1990; Dec. 6, 1991, eff. Jan. 1, 1992; June 29, 1993, eff. July 1, 1993; June 13, 2003, eff. July 1, 2003; June 11, 2009, eff. July 1, 2009.

Comment to Rules 120 and 121—1983

These two rules have been amended to reflect the judicial restructuring accomplished by the creation of the Court of Appeals. Jurisdiction to issue extraordinary writs directed to trial courts or other lower tribunals, previously existing in the Supreme Court, is vested by these rules in the Court of

Appeals. Once the Court of Appeals has acted on an application for an extraordinary writ, review by the Supreme Court is discretionary under Rule 117. Extraordinary relief in the Supreme Court pursuant to these rules relates solely to actions taken by the Court of Appeals in matters other than those arising under Rules 120 and 121.

The basic procedures and requirements remain the same in both courts as they were under the prior rules with the exception that the filing fee has been increased. The filing of a petition for extraordinary relief does not automatically stay the proceedings in the lower court.

See Appendix for form of petition for a writ of prohibition (Form 120A), the order for the writ (Form 120B), and the writ of prohibition (Form 120C).

Historical Notes

The order of the Minnesota Supreme Court [ADM–09–8006] dated June 11, 2009, amending the Rules of Civil Appellate Procedure by increasing filing fees, also provided that the amendments are effective July 1, 2009, and apply to all filings in the appellate courts on or after that date.

RULES 122 to 124. [RESERVED FOR FUTURE USE]

TITLE VII. GENERAL PROVISIONS

RULE 125. FILING AND SERVICE

Rule 125.01. Filing

Papers required or authorized by these rules shall be filed with the clerk of the appellate courts within the time limitations contained in the applicable rule. Filing may be accomplished by United States Mail addressed to the clerk of the appellate courts, but filing shall not be timely unless the papers are deposited in the mail within the time fixed for filing. Filing may be accomplished by use of a commercial courier service, and shall be effective upon receipt by the clerk of the appellate courts. Filing by facsimile or other electronic means is not allowed in the appellate courts, except with express leave of the court.

If a motion or petition requests relief that may be granted by a single judge, the judge may accept the document for filing, in which event the date of filing shall be noted on it and it shall be thereafter transmitted to the clerk. All papers filed shall include the attorney registration license number of counsel filing the paper and, if filed subsequent to the notice of appeal, shall specify the appellate court docket number.

Adopted Dec. 7, 1967, eff. Feb. 1, 1968. Amended June 17, 1983, eff. Aug. 1, 1983; Nov. 10, 1983, eff. Aug. 1, 1983; Dec. 6, 1991, eff. Jan. 1, 1992; Dec. 11, 2008, eff. Jan. 1, 2009.

Advisory Committee Note—1967

See note following Rule 125.04.

Comment—1983

See comment following Rule 125.04.

Rule 125.02. Service and Filing of All Papers Required

Copies of all papers filed by any party shall be served by that party, at or before the time of filing, on all other parties to the appeal or review. Papers shall be filed with the clerk of the appellate courts at the time of service or immediately thereafter. Service on a party represented by counsel shall be made on the attorney.

Adopted Dec. 7, 1967, eff. Feb. 1, 1968. Amended June 17, 1983, eff. Aug. 1, 1983; Nov. 10, 1983, eff. Aug. 1, 1983; Dec. 11, 2008, eff. Jan. 1, 2009.

Advisory Committee Note—1967

See note following Rule 125.04.

Comment—1983

See comment following Rule 125.04.

Rule 125.03. Manner of Service

Service may be personal or by United States Mail. Personal service includes delivery of a copy of the document to the attorney or other responsible person in the office of the attorney, or to the party, if not represented by counsel, in any manner provided by Rule 4, Minnesota Rules of Civil Procedure. Service by United States Mail is complete on mailing; however, whenever a party is required or permitted to do an act within a prescribed period after service and the paper is served by United States Mail, 3 days shall be added to the prescribed period. Personal service may be effected by use of a commercial courier service, and it shall be effective upon receipt. Service by facsimile or other electronic means is allowed only with the consent of the party to be served, and is effective upon receipt.

Adopted Dec. 7, 1967, eff. Feb. 1, 1968. Amended June 17, 1983, eff. Aug. 1, 1983; Nov. 10, 1983, eff. Aug. 1, 1983; Dec. 6, 1991, eff. Jan. 1, 1992; Dec. 11, 2008, eff. Jan. 1, 2009.

Advisory Committee Note—1967

See note following Rule 125.04.

Comment—1983

See comment following Rule 125.04.

Advisory Committee Comment—2008 Amendment

Rules 125.01 and .03 are amended to make clear the intent of the existing rule: that service and filing "by mail" under the rules requires use of the United States Mail. This clarification parallels a similar set of amendments to the Minnesota Rules of Civil Procedure. *Compare* Minn. R. Civ. P. 6.05 (amended in 2007 to specify U.S. Mail) *with* Minn. R. Civ. P. 4.05 (historically requiring use of first-class mail). The rule also makes it clear that it is permissible to use Federal Express, UPS, or other commercial courier for both filing and service, but delivery by that means is treated as any other hand delivery, and effective only upon receipt. Additional time for response to service by these services is thus neither required nor provided for, because the response period begins to run at the time of receipt.

These rules are also amended to make it clear that neither service nor filing by facsimile are ordinarily allowed in the appellate courts. In exigent circumstances the courts may request that courtesy copies of papers be provided by facsimile, but originals must be filed as provided in Rule 125.01. Service by facsimile is not generally permitted by rule, but if a party agrees to be served by facsimile it is permissible under the amended rule and is effective upon receipt. This provision recognizes that service by facsimile may be cost-effective and convenient for motions, notices, and other papers; it is unlikely to be used for briefs and appendices. The scope of any agreement to consent to service by facsimile should be carefully defined; it will be the unusual appeal where the parties really want their agreement to extend to the briefs and any appendices. The extension of this provision to service "by other electronic means" is intended to permit service by electronic mail, again only where the party to be served has agreed to it for the type of document involved.

Rule 125.04. Proof of Service

Papers presented for filing shall contain either a written admission of service or an affidavit of service. Proof of service may appear on or be affixed to the papers filed. The clerk of the appellate courts may permit papers to be filed without proof of service, but shall require proof of service to be filed promptly after filing the papers.

Adopted Dec. 7, 1967, eff. Feb. 1, 1968. Amended June 17, 1983, eff. Aug. 1, 1983; Nov. 10, 1983, eff. Aug. 1, 1983.

Advisory Committee Note—1967

This rule is substantially the same as P.Fed. R.App.P. 25. There is no similar Minnesota Supreme Court rule. Briefs and other papers must be received by the clerk of the Supreme Court on or before the due-date prescribed by these rules. Service on other parties must be accomplished before filing. The rules governing service are basically the same as those prescribed by Minn.R.Civ.P. 5.02.

Comment—1983

The filing of all papers must be made within the time designated in the applicable rule.

Filing by mail addressed to the clerk of the appellate courts is authorized but must be accomplished by deposit in the mail, first class postage prepaid, within the designated time period. To the extent practical, all papers shall include the appellate court docket number and attorney registration license numbers.

The clerk of the appellate courts is not authorized to file any papers unless and until the appropriate fee has been paid [Minn.Stat. § 357.08 (1983)] or the documents are accompanied by a written statement of the reason no fee is required.

Proof of service must be filed with the clerk of the appellate courts at the time the notice, petition or motion is filed or immediately thereafter.

RULE 126. COMPUTATION AND EXTENSION OR LIMITATION OF TIME

Rule 126.01. Computation

In computing any period of time prescribed or allowed by these rules, by order of court or by any applicable statute, the method of computation specified in Rules 6.01 and 6.05, Minnesota Rules of Civil Procedure, shall be used.

Adopted Dec. 7, 1967, eff. Feb. 1, 1968. Amended June 17, 1983, eff. Aug. 1, 1983; Nov. 10, 1983, eff. Aug. 1, 1983.

Rule 126.02. Extension or Limitation of Time

The appellate court for good cause shown may by order extend or limit the time prescribed by these rules or by its order for doing any act, and may permit an act to be done after the expiration of that time if the failure to act was excusable under the circumstances. The appellate court may not extend or limit the time for filing the notice of appeal or the time prescribed by law for securing review of a decision or an order of a court or an administrative agency, board, commission or officer, except as specifically authorized by law.

Adopted Dec. 7, 1967, eff. Feb. 1, 1968. Amended June 17, 1983, eff. Aug. 1, 1983; Nov. 10, 1983, eff. Aug. 1, 1983.

Advisory Committee Note—1967

Rule 126.02. This rule is similar to P.Fed. R.App.P. 26(b), and permits the Supreme Court to vary the time limitations contained in the rules other than the limitations prescribed by law for service of the notice of appeal or for initiating a review of an administrative ruling. See Rules 102 and 104.

Comment—1983

This rule specifically incorporates the method of computation specified in Rules 6.01 and 6.03, Minnesota Rules of Civil Procedure.

Rule 126.02 requires the showing of good cause for an extension or limitation of time prescribed by the rules. To obtain relief from a failure to act within the time prescribed, it is necessary to establish that the failure was excusable under the circumstances. The appellate court may not extend or limit the time for filing the notice of appeal or for petitioning for review.

RULE 127. MOTIONS

Unless another form is prescribed by these rules, an application for an order or other relief shall be made by serving and filing a written motion for the order or relief. The filing of a motion shall not stay any time period or action specified in these rules unless ordered by the appellate court. The motion shall state with particularity the grounds and set forth the order or relief sought. If the motion is supported by briefs, affidavits or other papers, they shall be served and filed with the motion. Any party may file a response within 5 days after service of the motion. Any reply shall be served within 2 days, at which time the motion shall be deemed submitted. The motion and all relative papers may be typewritten. Four copies of all papers shall be filed with proof of service. Oral argument will not be permitted except by order of the appellate court.

Adopted Dec. 7, 1967, eff. Feb. 1, 1968. Amended June 17, 1983, eff. Aug. 1, 1983; Nov. 10, 1983, eff. Aug. 1, 1983; Dec. 6, 1991, eff. Jan. 1, 1992.

Advisory Committee Note—1967

This rule is similar to P.Fed.R.App.P. 27 and varies considerably from the procedure formerly specified in Minn.Sup.Ct.R. IV. All supporting documents must be served and filed with the motion. No notice of motion is necessary. The written motion is deemed submitted on the date specified therein. There is no oral argument except by order of the Supreme Court. Orders to show cause are not permitted. However, a party may apply ex parte for an order pursuant to Rule 102 shortening the time periods specified for the submission of a motion if an emergency situation exists.

RULE 128. BRIEFS

Rule 128.01. Informal Briefs and Letter Briefs

Subdivision 1. Informal Briefs. Informal briefs may be authorized by the appellate court and shall contain a concise statement of the party's arguments on appeal, together with the appendix required by Rule 130.01. The informal brief shall have a cover and may be bound informally by stapling.

Subd. 2. Reliance Upon Trial Court Memoranda. If counsel elects, in the statement of the case, to rely upon memoranda submitted to the trial court supplemented by a short letter argument the submission shall be covered and may be informally bound by stapling. The trial court submissions and decision shall be attached as the appendix.

Adopted June 17, 1983, eff. Aug. 1, 1983. Amended Nov. 10, 1983, eff. Aug. 1, 1983; Dec. 6, 1991, eff. Jan. 1, 1992; July 7, 1998, eff. Jan. 1, 1999.

Historical Notes

Former Rule: Former Rule 128.01 specified the form of and items included in the brief of the appellant. See, now, Minn. R. Civ. App. P., Rule 128.02.

Rule 128.02. Formal Brief

Subdivision 1. Brief of Appellant. The formal brief of the appellant shall contain under appropriate headings and in the order here indicated:

(a) A table of contents, with page references, and an alphabetical table of cases, statutes, and other authorities cited, with references to the pages of the brief where they are cited.

(b) A concise statement of the legal issue or issues involved, omitting unnecessary detail. Each issue shall be stated as an appellate court would state the broad issue presented. Each issue shall be followed by:

(1) a description of how the issue was raised in the trial court, including citations to the record;

(2) a concise statement of the trial court's ruling;

(3) a description of how the issue was subsequently preserved for appeal, including citations to the record; and

(4) a list of the most apposite cases, not to exceed four, and the most apposite constitutional and statutory provisions.

(c) A statement of the case and the facts. A statement of the case shall first be presented identifying the trial court and the trial judge and briefly indicating the nature of the case and its disposition. There shall follow a statement of facts relevant to the grounds urged for reversal, modification or other relief. The facts must be stated fairly, with complete candor, and as concisely as possible. Where it is claimed that a verdict, finding of fact or other determination is not sustained by the evidence, the evidence, if any, tending directly or by reasonable inference to sustain the verdict, findings or determination shall be summarized. Each statement of a material fact shall be accompanied by a reference to the record, as provided in Rule 128.03.

(d) An argument. The argument may be preceded by a summary introduction, but it must include the contentions of the party with respect to the issues presented, the applicable standard of appellate review for each issue, the analyses, and the citations to the authorities. Each issue shall be separately presented. Needless repetition shall be avoided.

(e) A short conclusion stating the precise relief sought.

(f) The appendix required by Rule 130.01.

Subd. 2. Brief of Respondent. The formal brief of the respondent shall conform to the requirements of Rule 128.02, subdivision 1, except that a statement of the issues or of the case or facts need not be made unless the respondent is dissatisfied with the statement of the appellant. If a notice of related appeal is filed pursuant to Rule 103.02, subdivision 2, the respondent's brief shall present the issues specified in the notice of related appeal. A respondent who fails to file a brief either when originally due or upon expiration of an extension of time shall not be entitled to oral argument without leave of the appellate court.

Subd. 3. Addendum.

(a) Contents. Appellant must prepare an addendum and file it with the opening brief. The addendum must include:

(1) a copy of any order, judgment, findings, or trial court memorandum in the action directly relating to or affecting issues on appeal; and

(2) short excerpts from the record, other than from the transcript of testimony, that would be helpful in reading the brief without immediate reference to the appendix.

(b) Length. The addendum must not exceed 15 pages excluding the orders and judgments required by subdivision (1)(a) of this rule and any material reproduced in the addendum under Rule 128.04. The addendum must be incorporated into the back of the brief, unless it includes a long district court decision, in which event it may be bound separately. If bound separately, the appellant must file the same number of addenda as briefs.

(c) Respondent's Addendum. The respondent's brief may include an addendum not to exceed 15 pages, which must be incorporated into the back of the brief.

(d) Non-Duplication. A document or other material included in any party's addendum need not be included in any appendix.

Subd. 4. Reply Brief. The appellant may file a brief in reply to the brief of the respondent. The reply brief must be confined to new matter raised in the brief of the respondent.

Subd. 5. Additional Briefs. No further briefs may be filed except with leave of the appellate court.

Amended Dec. 7, 1967, eff. Feb. 1, 1968; Feb. 14, 1975; April 9, 1979; June 17, 1983, eff. Aug. 1, 1983; Nov. 10, 1983, eff. Aug. 1, 1983; July 7, 1998, eff. Jan. 1, 1999; Dec. 11, 2008, eff. Jan. 1, 2009; Oct. 16, 2009, eff. Jan. 1, 2010.

Advisory Committee Note—1967

Rule 128.01 [Now Rule 128.02]. This rule is substantially the same as P.Fed.R.App.P. 28(a) and is very similar in content to Minn.Sup.Ct.R. VIII (3) and (4) with two important exceptions. The formal procedural history and the assignment of errors required by Minn.Sup.Ct.R. VIII (3)(b) and (e) are abolished. The skeleton outline of a brief set forth in Form 8 in the Appendix will be of aid in following the rule.

Since assignments of errors are abolished, the correct statement of the legal issues is doubly important. Each legal issue should be stated as an abstract question of law with sufficient exactitude so that the court, after reading the legal issue, may understand the precise issue presented. The following are *not* proper statements of legal issues: "Is the verdict supported by the evidence?"; "Did the trial court correctly direct a verdict?"; "Did the trial court err in denying a new trial?" Examples of correct statements of legal issues may be found in Form 8 of the Appendix. Each legal issue must be separately briefed and argued.

This rule contains no limitation on the length of briefs as is found in P.Fed.R.App.P. 28(g). However, the court may deny costs and disbursements if unnecessarily long briefs are submitted. It may also deny costs and disbursements if the brief does not contain a fair and proper statement of the facts as required by Rule 128.01(3).

Rule 128.02. This rule is similar to P.Fed. R.App.P. 28(b) and Minn.Sup.Ct.R. VIII(4). The respondent's brief may contain a restatement of the legal issues or of the facts if the respondent so desires. In all other respects, the respondent's brief should comply with Rule 128.01. Respondents who have common interests may file a joint brief.

Rule 128.03 [Now Rule 128.02]. This rule is similar to P.Fed.R.App.P. 28(c). The reply brief should be confined to strict rebuttal and should not contain a re-argument of matters discussed in the appellant's brief.

Advisory Committee Comment—1998 Amendments

Rule 128.02 is amended in 1998 to add a requirement for listing the most apposite cases for each issue in the statement of issues. This rule is part of the briefing requirements for the United States Court of Appeals for the Eighth Circuit, and provides useful guidance on the issues. *See* 8th Cir. R. 28A(I)(4). MINN. R. CIV. APP. P. 128.02, subd. 2, does not expressly require a statement of issues in a responding brief, but if one is included, it should conform to this rule. In addition, the provisions concerning letter briefs formerly found in Rule 132.01, subd. 5, have been moved to Rule 128.01, subd. 2.

Advisory Committee Comment—2008 Amendments

Rule 128.02, subdivision 3, as amended, is a new rule, containing a new requirement for submission of an addendum. The rule requires the key trial court rulings, and permits up to 15 additional pages that would be helpful to reading the brief, to be bound with the brief. Presumably, the materials in the addendum would otherwise be contained in the appendix, so this rule really just reorganizes the location of the materials for the benefit of the parties and the appellate judges. The rule explicitly provides for inclusion of the relevant trial court orders or judgment in the addendum; it does not contemplate attachment of briefs of the parties. In the rare cases where memoranda of the parties are relevant to the appeal, they should be included in the appendix. The current subdivisions 3 and 4 of Rule 128.02 are re-numbered as subdivisions 4 and 5.

Advisory Committee Comment—2009 Amendments

Rule 128.02, subdivision 1(b), is amended to require specification of how each issue was raised in the record and preserved for appeal in the trial court, including citations to the record. These are matters that are important to many appeals and adding this requirement is intended to make it easier for the court to determine that each issue was properly raised, decided, and preserved for appeal. This requirement has been implemented by other courts, *see, e.g.*, Iowa R. App. P. 6.14, and the committee believes this requirement will improve the quality of briefing in Minnesota appeals. For example, subparagraph 1 requires specification of where an evidentiary objection or offer of evidence was made, including a transcript citation, and subparagraph 3 where it was raised in a motion for new trial to preserve it for appeal. The rule does not expand what is required to raise or preserve an issue for appeal; it only requires that specific information be provided in the statement of issues in the appellant's brief about how these steps were taken.

Rule 128.02, subdivision 1(d), is amended to require that a brief address the applicable standard of appellate review. The standard of review is crucial to the analysis of every issue by the appellate court. A useful compendium of the standards of review for particular issues is Minnesota Court of Appeals, Standards of Review (Aug. 2008), available for review or download at http://www.lawlibrary.state.mn.us/casofrev.html. The rule does not dictate how the standard of review be set forth—whether in a separate section or at the beginning of the argument for an issue—although in most cases it is best handled at the beginning of the argument for each issue. The applicable standard of review must be addressed for each issue in an argument.

Subdivision 2 is amended to reflect the amendment of Rule 106 to abolish the notice of review and adoption of Rule 103.02, subdivision 2, to adopt the notice of related appeal.

The order of the Supreme Court dated Oct. 16, 2009, provided:

"1. The attached amendments to the Rules of Civil Appellate Procedure be, and the same are, prescribed and promulgated to be effective on January 1, 2010.

"2. These amendments shall apply to all actions or proceedings pending on or commenced on or after the effective date.

"3. The inclusion of Advisory Committee comments is for convenience and does not reflect court approval of the statements made therein."

Rule 128.03. References in Briefs to Record

Whenever a reference is made in the briefs to any part of the record which is reproduced in the addendum or appendix or in a supplemental record, the reference shall be made to the specific pages of the addendum or appendix or the supplemental record where the particular part of the record is reproduced. Whenever a reference is made to a part of the record which is not reproduced in the addendum or appendix or in a supplemental record, the reference shall be made to the particular part of the record, suitably designated, and to the specific pages of it, e.g., Motion for Summary Judgment, p. 1; Transcript, p. 135; Plaintiff's Exhibit D, p. 3. Intelligible abbreviations may be used.

Amended June 17, 1983, eff. Aug. 1, 1983; Nov. 10, 1983, eff. Aug. 1, 1983; Dec. 11, 2008, eff. Jan. 1, 2009.

Advisory Committee Note—1967

Rule 128.04 [Now Rule 128.03]. Because of the abolition of the printed Record, references in the briefs to the records will ordinarily fall into these categories:

(a) If reference is made to a part of the record which is reproduced in the appendix required by Rule 130.01, a simple citation such as "A.3" or "A.11", indicating matters which appear at pages 3 or 11 of the appendix, will be sufficient. If the respondent files an appendix, (Rule 130.02), a citation such as "RA. 7" will be sufficient. Folio numbers are not required and are unnecessary.

(b) If reference is made to testimony or other matters contained in the transcript, a simple citation such as "T. 21" or "T. 104", indicating matters which appear at pages 21 or 104 of the transcript will be sufficient. It is not necessary to specify the line or lines of a page of the transcript.

(c) If reference is made to a pleading, exhibit or other document contained in the record, an intelligible abbreviation identifying such document and the page thereof is sufficient.

(d) If a party elects to print a supplemental record pursuant to Rule 130.04, the references to matters contained in the supplemental record should be "SR. 33" or "SR. 52", etc.

Rule 128.04. Reproduction of Statutes, Ordinances, Rules, Regulations, Etc.

If determination of the issues presented requires the study of statutes, ordinances, rules, regulations, etc., or relevant parts of them, they shall be reproduced in the brief or in an addendum, or they may be supplied to the court in pamphlet form.

Amended June 17, 1983, eff. Aug. 1, 1983; Nov. 10, 1983, eff. Aug. 1, 1983.

Advisory Committee Note—1967

Rule 128.05 [Now Rule 128.04]. This rule is substantially the same as P.Fed.R.App.P. 28(f). Statutes, ordinances, rules, etc. must be reproduced verbatim if they are material to a determination of the issues.

Comment—1983

See Appendix for form of formal brief (Form 128).

Rule 128.05. Citation of Supplemental Authorities

If pertinent and significant authorities come to a party's attention after the party's brief has been filed or after oral argument but before decision, a party may promptly advise the clerk of the appellate courts by letter, with a copy to all other parties, setting forth the citations. The letter must state without argument the reasons for the supplemental citations, referring either to the page of the brief or to the point argued orally. Any response must be made promptly and must be similarly limited.

Adopted Dec. 19, 2000, eff. March 1, 2001.

Advisory Committee Comment—2000 Amendments

Rule 128.05 is a new provision in the Minnesota Rules. It is patterned after FED. R. APP. P. 28(j), and is intended to allow a party to submit additional authorities to the court without requiring a motion and without providing an opportunity for argument. The rule contemplates a very short submission, simply providing the citation of the new authority and enough information so the court can determine what previously-made argument it relates to. The submission itself is not to contain argument, and a response, if any, is similarly constrained. Because a response is limited to the citation of authority and cannot provide argument, a response most frequently will not be necessary or proper. A submission or reply that does not conform to the rule is subject to being stricken. *See, e.g., Esicorp, Inc. v. Liberty Mut. Ins. Co.*, 193 F.3d 966, 972 (8th Cir. 1999) (granting motion to strike argumentative submission); *Anderson v. General Motors Corp.*, 176 F.3d 488 (10th Cir. 1999) (unpublished) (same).

Historical Notes

The order of the Minnesota Supreme Court [C4-84-2133] dated December 19, 2000, provides in part that these amendments are effective March 1, 2001, and shall apply to all actions or proceedings pending on or commenced on or after the effective date, with the exception of the amendments to Rule 132, which shall apply to all appeals or proceedings commenced in either the Court of Appeals or the Supreme Court on or after the effective date.

The order of the Minnesota Supreme Court [C4-84-2133] dated December 19, 2000, provides in part that "(t)he inclusion of Advisory Committee comments is made for convenience and does not reflect court approval of the statements made therein".

RULE 129. BRIEF OF AN AMICUS CURIAE

Rule 129.01. Request for Leave to Participate

Upon prior notice to the parties, a brief of an amicus curiae may be filed with leave of the appellate court. The applicant shall serve and file a request for leave no later than 15 days after the filing of the notice of appeal, the petition which initiates the appeal, the appellate petition for declaratory judgment, or the appellate court order granting review. A request for leave shall identify whether the applicant's interest is public or private in nature, identify the party supported or indicate whether the amicus brief will suggest affirmance or reversal, and shall state the reason why a brief of an amicus curiae is desirable.

Adopted Dec. 7, 1967, eff. Feb. 1, 1968. Amended April 9, 1979; June 17, 1983, eff. Aug. 1, 1983; Nov. 10, 1983, eff. Aug. 1, 1983; July 7, 1998, eff. Jan. 1, 1999; Dec. 19, 2000, eff. March 1, 2001.

Historical Notes

The order of the Minnesota Supreme Court [C4-84-2133] dated December 19, 2000, provides in part that these amendments are effective March 1, 2001, and shall apply to all actions or proceedings pending on or commenced on or after the effective date, with the exception of the amendments to Rule 132, which shall apply to all appeals or proceedings commenced in either the Court of Appeals or the Supreme Court on or after the effective date.

The order of the Minnesota Supreme Court [C4-84-2133] dated December 19, 2000, provides in part that "(t)he inclusion of Advisory Committee comments is made for convenience and does not reflect court approval of the statements made therein".

Rule 129.02. Time for Filing and Service

Copies of an amicus curiae brief shall be served on all parties and filed with the clerk of the appellate courts with proof of service no later than seven days after the time allowed for filing the brief of the party supported, or if in support of neither party, no later than the time allowed for filing the petitioner's or appellant's brief.

Adopted Dec. 7, 1967, eff. Feb. 1, 1968. Amended April 9, 1979; June 17, 1983, eff. Aug. 1, 1983; Nov. 10, 1983, eff. Aug. 1, 1983; July 7, 1998, eff. Jan. 1, 1999; Dec. 19, 2000, eff. March 1, 2001.

Historical Notes

The order of the Minnesota Supreme Court [C4-84-2133] dated December 19, 2000, provides in part that these amendments are effective March 1, 2001, and shall apply to all actions or proceedings pending on or commenced on or after the effective date, with the exception of the amendments to Rule 132, which shall apply to all appeals or proceedings commenced in either the Court of Appeals or the Supreme Court on or after the effective date.

The order of the Minnesota Supreme Court [C4-84-2133] dated December 19, 2000, provides in part that "(t)he inclusion of Advisory Committee comments is made for convenience and does not reflect court approval of the statements made therein".

Rule 129.03. Certification in Brief

A brief filed under this rule shall indicate whether counsel for a party authored the brief in whole or in part and shall identify every person or entity, other than the *amicus curiae*, its members, or its counsel, who made a monetary contribution to the preparation or submission of the brief. The disclosure shall be made in the first footnote on the first page of text.

Adopted Dec. 19, 2000, eff. March 1, 2001.

Historical Notes

The order of the Minnesota Supreme Court [C4-84-2133] dated December 19, 2000, provides in part that these amendments are effective March 1, 2001, and shall apply to all actions or proceedings pending on or commenced on or after the effective date, with the exception of the amendments to Rule 132, which shall apply to all appeals or proceedings commenced in either the Court of Appeals or the Supreme Court on or after the effective date.

The order of the Minnesota Supreme Court [C4-84-2133] dated December 19, 2000, provides in part that "(t)he inclusion of Advisory Committee comments is made for convenience and does not reflect court approval of the statements made therein".

Rule 129.04. Oral Argument

An amicus curiae shall not participate in oral argument except with leave of the appellate court.

Adopted Dec. 7, 1967, eff. Feb. 1, 1968. Amended April 9, 1979; June 17, 1983, eff. Aug. 1, 1983; Nov. 10, 1983, eff. Aug. 1, 1983; July 7, 1998, eff. Jan. 1, 1999; Dec. 19, 2000, eff. March 1, 2001.

Advisory Committee Comment—2000 Amendments

Rule 129.01 is amended to delete a provision that provided for an automatic stay of a briefing period until a request for leave to participate as *amicus curiae* was decided. Under the revised rule, the parties proceed with the normal briefing schedule without regard to whether *amici* will participate. A party or a potential *amicus curiae* who believes a delay in the briefing schedule is necessary may move for a stay. Rule 129.03 is a new provision requiring disclosure, in the brief, of whether any counsel for a party authored the brief in whole or in part and shall identify persons other than the *amicus curiae* who provided monetary contribution to its preparation or submission. This rule is patterned on Rule 37.6 of the Rules of the Supreme Court of the United States. This rule is intended to encourage participation of independent *amici*, and to prevent the courts from being misled about the independence of *amici* or being exposed to "a mirage of amicus support that really emanates from the petitioner's word processor." Stephen M. Shapiro, *Certiorari Practice: The Supreme Court's Shrinking Docket*, *reprinted at* 24 LITIGATION, Spring 1998, at 25, 74. The rule is not intended to discourage the normal cooperation between the parties to an action and the *amici*, including the providing of access to the record, the exchange of briefs in advance of submission, and other such activities that do not result in someone other than the *amicus* preparing the *amicus* brief.

The numbering of the rule is changed to conform it to the style predominantly used in the other rules. This change is not intended to modify the meaning or interpretation of the rule.

Historical Notes

The order of the Minnesota Supreme Court [C4-84-2133] dated December 19, 2000, provides in part that these amendments are effective March 1, 2001, and shall apply to all actions or proceedings pending on or commenced on or after the effective date, with the exception of the amendments to Rule 132, which shall apply to all appeals or proceedings commenced in either the Court of Appeals or the Supreme Court on or after the effective date.

The order of the Minnesota Supreme Court [C4-84-2133] dated December 19, 2000, provides in part that "(t)he inclusion of Advisory Committee comments is made for convenience and does not reflect court approval of the statements made therein".

RULE 130. THE APPENDIX TO THE BRIEFS; SUPPLEMENTAL RECORD

Rule 130.01. Record Not to be Printed; Appellant to File Appendix

Subdivision 1. Record; Portions. The record shall not be printed. The appellant shall prepare and file an appendix to its brief. The appendix shall be separately and consecutively numbered and shall contain the following portions of the record:

(a) the relevant pleadings;

(b) the relevant written motions and orders;

(c) the verdict or the findings of fact, conclusions of law and order for judgment;

(d) the relevant post trial motions and orders;

(e) any memorandum opinions;

(f) if the trial court's instructions are challenged on appeal, the instructions, any portion of the transcript containing a discussion of the instructions and any relevant requests for instructions;

(g) any judgments;

(h) the notice of appeal;

(i) if the constitutionality of a statute is challenged, proof of compliance with Rule 144; and

(j) the index to the documents contained in the appendix.

The parties shall have regard for the fact that the entire record is always available to the appellate court for reference or examination and shall not engage in unnecessary reproduction. Any documents included in an addendum to a party's brief need not be included in the appendix.

Subd. 2. Statement. If the record includes a statement of the proceedings made pursuant to Rule 110.03 or an agreed statement made pursuant to Rule 110.04, the statement shall be included in the appendix.

Adopted Dec. 7, 1967, eff. Feb. 1, 1968. Amended June 17, 1983, eff. Aug. 1, 1983; Nov. 10, 1983, eff. Aug. 1, 1983; Dec. 6, 1991, eff. Jan. 1, 1992; July 7, 1998, eff. Jan. 1, 1999; Nov. 9, 1998; Dec. 11, 2008, eff. Jan. 1, 2009.

Comment—1983

This rule no longer requires the inclusion of the trial court's instructions in the appendix unless they are challenged on appeal. In addition, it is now mandatory to provide an index to the documents contained in the appendix.

Advisory Committee Comment—1998 Amendments

Rule 144.04 requires notice to be provided to the Attorney General when the constitutionality of a statute is challenged. The amended rule requires the party challenging the constitutionality to include in the appendix proof of compliance with the rule.

Rule 130.02. Respondent May File Appendix

If the respondent determines that the appendix filed by the appellant omits any items specified in Rule 130.01, only those omitted items may be included in an appendix to the respondent's brief.

Adopted Dec. 7, 1967, eff. Feb. 1, 1968. Amended June 17, 1983, eff. Aug. 1, 1983; Nov. 10, 1983, eff. Aug. 1, 1983; Dec. 6, 1991, eff. Jan. 1, 1992.

Rule 130.03. Party May File Supplemental Record; Not Taxable Cost

A party may prepare and file a supplemental record, suitably indexed, containing any relevant portion of the record not contained in the appendix. The original pagination of each part of the transcript set out in the supplemental record shall be indicated by placing in brackets the number of the original page at the place where the page begins. If the transcript is abridged, the pages and parts of pages of the transcript omitted shall be clearly indicated following the index and at the place where the omission occurs. A question and its answer may be contained in a single paragraph. The cost of producing the supplemental records shall not be a taxable cost.

Adopted Dec. 7, 1967, eff. Feb. 1, 1968. Amended June 17, 1983, eff. Aug. 1, 1983; Nov. 10, 1983, eff. Aug. 1, 1983.

RULE 131. FILING AND SERVICE OF BRIEFS, THE APPENDIX, AND THE SUPPLEMENTAL RECORD

Rule 131.01. Time for Filing and Service

Subdivision 1. Appellant's Brief. The appellant shall serve and file a brief and appendix within 30 days after delivery of the transcript by the reporter or after the filing of the trial court's approval of the statement pursuant to Rules 110.03 and 110.04. If the transcript is delivered by United States Mail, three days are added to the briefing period, which is measured from the date the transcript was mailed. If the transcript is obtained prior to appeal or if the record on appeal does not include a transcript, then the appellant shall serve and file a brief and appendix with the clerk of the appellate courts within 30 days after the filing of the notice of appeal, the petition which initiates the appeal, the appellate petition for declaratory judgment, or the appellate court order granting review.

Subd. 2. Respondent's Brief. The respondent shall serve and file a brief and appendix, if any, within 30 days after service of the brief of the appellant or the last appellant's brief, if there are multiple appellants, or within 30 days after delivery of a transcript ordered by respondent pursuant to Rule 110.02, subdivision 1, whichever is later.

Subd. 3. Reply Brief. The appellant may serve and file a reply brief within ten days after the later of the following:

(a) service of the respondent's brief or the last respondent's brief if there are multiple respondents; or

(b) service of the brief of an amicus curiae granted leave to participate under Rule 129.

Subd. 4. Supplemental Record. If a party prepares a supplemental record, the supplemental records shall be served and filed with that party's first brief.

Subd. 5. Briefing Schedule for Cross–Appeals; Form of Briefs in Cross–Appeals.

(a) Cross–Appeal Defined. A cross-appeal, for the purpose of this rule, exists when a notice of appeal and at least one notice of related appeal or separate notice of appeal are filed by parties adverse to each other on appeal. Multiple notices of appeal or related appeal filed by parties who are not adverse to each other do not create cross-appeals.

(b) Designation of Appellant. The party who files a notice of appeal first is the appellant for the purposes of this rule. If notices are filed on the same day, the plaintiff in the proceeding below is the appellant. These designations may be modified by the parties' agreement or by court order.

(c) Schedule for Filing. In a case involving a cross-appeal, the appellant's principal brief shall be filed in accordance with Rule 131.01, subdivision 1, and the respondent/cross-appellant's principal brief shall be filed as one brief within 30 days after service of appellant's brief. Appellant/cross-respondent's response and reply brief shall be filed as one brief within 30 days after service of cross-appellant's brief. Respondent/cross-appellant's reply brief may be filed within 10 days after service of appellant/cross-respondent's response and reply brief.

(d) Form of Briefs in Cross–Appeals. In a case involving a cross-appeal:

(1) **Appellant's Principal Brief.** The appellant must file a principal brief in the appeal. That brief must comply with Rule 128.01 or Rule 128.02, subdivision 1.

(2) **Respondent/Cross–Appellant's Principal and Response Brief.** The respondent/cross-appellant must file a principal brief on the cross-appeal and may, in the same brief, respond to the appellant's principal brief. The respondent/cross-appellant's brief must comply with Rule 128.01 or 128.02, subdivision 1, as to the cross-appeal and Rule 128.02, subdivision 2, as to the appeal, except the brief need not include a statement of the case or a statement of the facts unless the respondent/cross-appellant is dissatisfied with the appellant's statement.

(3) **Appellant/Cross–Respondent's Response and Reply Brief.** The appellant/cross-respondent may file a brief that responds to the principal brief of the respondent/cross-appellant in the cross-appeal and may, in the same brief, reply to the response in the appeal. That brief must comply with Rule 128.02, subdivision 2, as to the response to the cross-appeal and Rule 128.02, subdivision 4, as to the reply on the original appeal.

(4) **Respondent/Cross–Appellant's Reply Brief.** The respondent/cross-appellant may file a brief in reply to the response in the cross-appeal. The brief must comply with Rule 128.02, subdivision 4, and must be limited to the issues presented by the cross-appeal.

(5) **No Further Briefs.** Unless the court permits, no further briefs may be filed in a case involving a cross-appeal.

(6) **Cover.** If briefs are formally bound, the cover of the appellant's principal brief must be blue;

the respondent/cross-appellant's principal and response brief, red; the appellant/cross-respondent's response and reply brief, yellow; the respondent/cross-appellant's reply brief, gray; and an intervenor's or amicus curiae's brief, green.

(7) Length limit.

(A) The appellant's principal brief is acceptable if it complies with the length limits of Rule 132.01, subdivision 3(a).

(B) The respondent/cross-appellant's principal and response brief is acceptable if:

(i) it contains no more than 16,500 words; or

(ii) it uses a monospaced font and contains no more than 1,500 lines of text.

(C) The appellant/cross-respondent's response and reply brief is acceptable if:

(i) it contains no more than 10,000 words; or

(ii) it uses a monospaced font and contains no more than 750 lines of text.

(D) The respondent/cross-appellant's reply brief is acceptable if it complies with the length limits of Rule 132.01, subdivision 3(b).

Adopted Dec. 7, 1967, eff. Feb. 1, 1968. Amended Oct. 29, 1968; June 6, 1972; June 17, 1983, eff. Aug. 1, 1983; Nov. 10, 1983, eff. Aug. 1, 1983; Dec. 6, 1991, eff. Jan. 1, 1992; July 7, 1998, eff. Jan. 1, 1999; Oct. 16, 2009, eff. Jan. 1, 2010.

Comment—October 1968

By order dated October 29, 1968, the Supreme Court amended Rule 131.01 of the Rules of Civil Appellate Procedure so as to require the appellant to file his brief and appendix within 60 days after service of the notice of the appeal, in those cases where a transcript of the testimony is not ordered. However, where a transcript is ordered, the time for filing briefs continues to run from the date of delivery of the transcript.

Comment—1983

Times for filing all briefs have been shortened.

This rule reduces the time for the filing of the appellant's brief from 60 to 30 days. The commencement of the briefing will depend upon a number of variables. If a transcript is ordered, the 30-day period begins with its delivery. If a transcript has been prepared prior to the appeal or the granting of a petition for review, or if no transcript is contemplated or necessary, the time runs from the date the notice of appeal was filed or the petition was granted. If a statement pursuant to either Rule 110.03 or 110.04 is submitted in lieu of a transcript, the time begins to run upon filing of the trial court's approval.

The time for filing the respondent's brief has been shortened from 45 to 30 days. All parties now have equal time for the preparation of their briefs.

Advisory Committee Comment—1998 Amendments

See note following Rule 131.03.

Advisory Committee Comment—2009 Amendments

Rule 131.01, subdivision 5, is a new rule to establish alternative rules for briefing in cases where a cross-appeal is filed. The provisions are drawn from Fed. R. App. P. 28.1. The amended Minnesota rule operates as a default timing and brief-length rule; in any case the parties may seek alternate limits by motion, and the court may impose them on its own initiative.

The briefing process for cross-appeals under the amended rule is summarized as follows:

	Brief (in order of filing)	Cover Color	Length limit (word count method)
1	Appellant's principal brief	Blue	14,000 words (unchanged)
2	Respondent/cross-appellant's principal and response brief	Red	16,500 words
3	Appellant/cross-respondent's response and reply brief	Yellow	10,000 word s
4	Respondent/cross-appellant's reply brief	Gray	7,000 words (unchanged)

Subdivision 5(a) makes it clear that only multiple appeals by adverse parties create cross-appeals. If several parties on the same side of a case file separate appeals that are not adverse to each other, the normal three-brief schedule of Rule 131.01 applies.

Historical Notes

The order of the Supreme Court dated Oct. 16, 2009, provided:

"1. The attached amendments to the Rules of Civil Appellate Procedure be, and the same are, prescribed and promulgated to be effective on January 1, 2010.

"2. These amendments shall apply to all actions or proceedings pending on or commenced on or after the effective date.

"3. The inclusion of Advisory Committee comments is for convenience and does not reflect court approval of the statements made therein."

Rule 131.011. [Deleted]

Historical Notes

The deleted rule related to applications for extension of time. See, now, Minn. R. Civ. App, P., Rule 131.02.

Rule 131.02. Application for Extension of Time

Subdivision 1. Motion for Extension. No extension of the time fixed for the filing of a brief will be granted except upon a motion pursuant to Rule 127 made within the time specified for the filing of the brief. The motion shall be considered by a justice, judge or a person designated by the appellate court, acting as a referee, and shall be granted only for good cause shown. Only an original of the motion shall be filed.

Subd. 2. Procedure. The date the brief is due shall be stated in the motion. The motion shall be supported by an affidavit which discloses facts showing that with due diligence, and giving reasonable priority to the preparation of the brief, it will not be possible to file the brief on time. All factual statements required by this rule shall be set forth with specificity.

Amended June 17, 1983, eff. Aug. 1, 1983; Nov. 10, 1983, eff. Aug. 1, 1983; July 7, 1998, eff. Jan. 1, 1999; Dec. 19, 2000, eff. March 1, 2001.

Comment—1983

This rule has been clarified to make explicit that a request for an extension of time to file a brief must be made within the time specified by rule or court order for the filing.

Advisory Committee Comment—1998 Amendments

See note following Rule 131.03.

Advisory Committee Comment—2000 Amendments

Subdivision 1 of Rule 131.02 is amended to delete the reference to periods of time fixed by Rule 131.01. The requirement for a motion to extend time applies to any time requirement, whether established by rule or scheduling order. The purpose of the amendment is to clarify the existing practice rather than to effect a significant change in practice.

Historical Notes

The order of the Minnesota Supreme Court [C4-84-2133] dated December 19, 2000, provides in part that these amendments are effective March 1, 2001, and shall apply to all actions or proceedings pending on or commenced on or after the effective date, with the exception of the amendments to Rule 132, which shall apply to all appeals or proceedings commenced in either the Court of Appeals or the Supreme Court on or after the effective date.

The order of the Minnesota Supreme Court [C4-84-2133] dated December 19, 2000, provides in part that "(t)he inclusion of Advisory Committee comments is made for convenience and does not reflect court approval of the statements made therein".

Rule 131.03. Number of Copies to be Filed and Served

Subdivision 1. Number of Copies. Unless otherwise specified by the appellate court, the following number of copies of each brief, appendix, and supplemental record, if any, shall be filed with the clerk of the appellate courts:

(a) In an appeal to the Supreme Court, 14 copies. Two copies of the 14 shall be unbound.

(b) In an appeal to the Court of Appeals, seven copies. One copy of the seven shall be unbound.

If counsel has elected, in the statement of the case form, to rely on memoranda submitted to the trial court, supplemented by a short letter argument, the number of copies required by this rule shall be filed with the clerk of the appellate courts.

Subd. 2. Service. Two copies of each brief, appendix, and supplemental record, if any, shall be served on the attorney for each party to the appeal separately represented and on each party appearing pro se. The clerk shall not accept a brief, appendix or supplemental record for filing unless it is accompanied by admission or proof of service as required by Rule 125.

Amended June 17, 1983, eff. Aug. 1, 1983; Nov. 10, 1983, eff. Aug. 1, 1983; Dec. 6, 1991, eff. Jan. 1, 1992; July 7, 1998, eff. Jan. 1, 1999.

Comment—1983

Fourteen copies of all briefs, appendices, and supplemental records must now be filed in the Supreme Court and nine copies in the Court of Appeals. Two unbound copies must be supplied to either court.

Advisory Committee Comment—1998 Amendments

This rule has been revised to make more clear the event from which the due date of the opening brief is calculated, the due date for responsive briefs, and the procedure for obtaining extensions of time to file briefs. The amended rule also reduces the number of copies of briefs that must be filed in the Court of Appeals.

In instances where it is not necessary to await the preparation of a transcript, the time for the opening brief begins to run when the appellate proceedings are formally commenced. When review is not as a matter of right, but depends on some grant of leave from the appellate court, the time for the opening brief does not begin to run until that permission is granted.

If either party has ordered a transcript, the time for the opening brief runs from the date the transcript is delivered. Consistent with Rule 125.03, three days are added to the briefing period if the transcript was delivered by United States Mail. The revised rule makes that calculation clear.

Generally, service of appellant's brief begins the 30-day period for the filing of respondent's brief. If respondent has ordered a transcript pursuant to Rule 110.02, subd. 1, respondent's briefing period does not begin until delivery of the transcript, if the transcript is delivered after appellant's brief is served.

Specific grounds for any extension of a brief due date must be shown in the affidavit accompanying the motion. Extensions of time to file briefs are not favored.

The rule has also been changed to reduce the number of briefs to be filed in the Court of Appeals from nine to seven. While the rule previously required two unbound copies for the Court of Appeals, it now only requires one such copy. The number of bound and unbound copies required by the Supreme Court is unchanged.

RULE 132. FORM OF BRIEFS, APPENDICES, SUPPLEMENTAL RECORDS, MOTIONS AND OTHER PAPERS

Rule 132.01. Form of Briefs, Appendices, and Supplemental Records

Subdivision 1. Form Requirements. Any process capable of producing a clear black image on white paper may be used. Briefs shall be printed or typed on unglazed opaque paper. If a monospaced font is used, printed or typed material (including headings and footnotes) must appear in a font that produces a maximum of 10½ characters per inch; if a proportional font is used, printed or typed material (including headings and footnotes) must appear in at least 13–point font. Formal briefs and accompanying appendices shall be bound together by a method that securely affixes the contents, and that is substantially equivalent to the list of approved binding methods maintained by the clerk of appellate courts. Methods of binding that are not approved include stapling, continuous coil spiral binding, spiral comb bindings and similar bindings. Pages shall be 8½ by 11 inches in size with written matter not exceeding 6½ by 9½ inches. Written matter in briefs and addenda shall appear on only one side of the paper; appendices and supplemental records may be produced in the same manner or using two-sided printing. The pages of the appendix shall be separately and consecutively numbered. Briefs shall be double-spaced, except for tables of contents, tables of authorities, statements of issues, headings and footnotes, which may be single-spaced. Carbon copies shall not be submitted.

Subd. 2. Front Cover. The front cover of the brief and appendix shall contain:

(a) the name of the court and the appellate court docket number, which number shall be printed or lettered in bold-face print or prominent lettering and shall be located one-half inch from the top center of the cover;

(b) the title of the case;

(c) the title of the document, e.g., Appellant's Brief and Appendix; and

(d) the names, addresses, and telephone numbers of the attorneys representing each party to the appeal, and attorney registration license numbers of the preparers of the brief.

The front cover shall not be protected by a clear plastic or mylar sheet.

If briefs are formally bound, the cover of the brief of the appellant should be blue; that of the respondent, red; that of an intervenor or amicus curiae, green; that of any reply brief, gray. The cover of the appendix, if separately printed, should be white. The cover of an amendment or supplement should be the same color as the document which it amends or supplements.

Subd. 3. Length Limit. Except for good cause shown and with permission of the appellate court, briefs, whether printed or typewritten, exclusive of pages containing the table of contents, tables of citations, any addendum containing statutes, rules, regulations, etc., and any appendix, shall not exceed 45 pages for principal briefs, 20 pages for reply briefs, and 20 pages for amicus briefs, unless the brief complies with one of these alternative measures:

(a) A principal brief is acceptable if:

(1) it contains no more than 14,000 words; or

(2) it uses a monospaced font and contains no more than 1,300 lines of text.

(b) A reply brief is acceptable if:

(1) it contains no more than 7,000 words; or

(2) it uses a monospaced font and contains no more than 650 lines of text.

(c) An amicus brief is acceptable if:

(1) it contains no more than 7,000 words; or

(2) it uses a monospaced font and contains no more than 650 lines of text.

A brief submitted under Rule 132.01, subd. 3(a), (b), or (c) must include a certificate that the brief complies with the word count or line count limitation. The person preparing the certificate may rely on the word or line count of the word-processing software used to prepare the brief. The certificate must state the name and version of the word processing software used to prepare the brief, state that the brief complies with the typeface requirements of this rule, and state either:

(1) the number of words in the brief; or

(2) the number of lines of monospaced font in the brief.

Application for filing an enlarged brief shall be filed at least 10 days prior to the date the brief is due.

Subd. 4. Supplemental Records. Supplemental records shall be bound in separate volumes and shall, in all other respects, comply with this rule.

Adopted Dec. 7, 1967, eff. Feb. 1, 1968. Amended April 3, 1980, eff. Jan. 1, 1981; Dec. 4, 1980, eff. Jan. 1, 1981; June 17, 1983, eff. Aug. 1, 1983; Nov. 10, 1983, eff. Aug. 1, 1983; Dec. 6, 1991; eff. Jan. 1, 1992; July 7, 1998, eff. Jan. 1, 1999; Dec. 19, 2000, eff. March 1, 2001; Dec. 11, 2008, eff. Jan. 1, 2009.

Comment—1983

There are page limitations on all briefs.

The form of briefs, appendices, and supplemental records to be submitted has been changed. Commercial typographical printing is no longer required; instead any process capable of producing a clear black image on white paper is acceptable.

The color coding system introduced is only applicable if commercially produced briefs are submitted.

The appellant and the respondent's briefs are limited to 50 pages exclusive of tables of contents and authorities, addenda, and appendices. Reply briefs shall not exceed 25 pages and briefs of amicus curiae are restricted to 20 pages. Any request to file an enlarged brief must be filed at least 10 days before the brief is due.

Advisory Committee Comment—1998 Amendments

Rule 132.01, subd. I has been modified to make clear the requirement that the written material in briefs should appear on only one side of the paper. The Clerk of Appellate Courts maintains a list of approved binding methods and this list is available upon request.

Rule 132.01, subd. 2 has been modified in two respects. First, the rule has been re-written to make clear that in all cases where formal bound briefs are submitted, the color coding requirements apply. The rule has also been changed to eliminate the provision regarding the color of brief covers in the Supreme Court. The rule previously provided that the parties would use the same color covers as they did in the Court of Appeals. This caused considerable confusion among the bar, and the requirement was dropped in favor of a rule that consistently requires the opening brief of the appellant to be blue, the opening brief of the party responding to that brief to be red, and reply briefs to be gray. Rule 101.02, subd. 6 defines "appellant" to mean the party seeking review, including relators and petitioners.

MINN. STAT. § 480.0515, subd. 2 (1996), requires documents submitted by an attorney to a court of this state, and all papers appended to the document be submitted on paper containing not less than ten percent postconsumer material, as defined in MINN. STAT. § 115A.03, subd. 24b. The statute also provides that a court may not refuse a document solely because the document was not submitted on recycled paper. Finally, subd. (3)(b) of the statute makes the entire section nonapplicable "if recycled paper is not readily available."

Subdivision 5 of this Rule regarding reliance upon trial court memoranda has been moved to Rule 128.01, subd. 2.

Advisory Committee Comment—2000 Amendments

The rule has been amended to provide for an alternative measure of length of appellate briefs, based on word volume and not page count. This alternative allows parties to choose type size that is more readable than they might choose if endeavoring to satisfy the page limit requirement. The word volume measure has been derived from the analogous provisions of the Federal Rules of Appellate Procedure, and in general will not significantly alter the amount of text that a party may submit, regardless of the method chosen to determine brief length. The amended rule provides for a certification of brief length that will enable the appellate courts to verify that the brief complies with the rule. The rule also increases the minimum permissible font size for briefs and shortens the maximum permissible length of principal briefs that are not measured on a word or line count basis. These amendments only apply to formal briefs, not to motions, petitions for further review, or other pleadings.

Advisory Committee Comment—2008 Amendments

Rule 132.01 is amended to permit, but not require, the preparation of appendices and supplemental records using two-sided copies. The rule's requirement for use of opaque paper is particularly important if a party elects to submit a two-sided appendix.

Historical Notes

The order of the Minnesota Supreme Court [C4-84-2133] dated December 19, 2000, provides in part that these amendments are effective March 1, 2001, and shall apply to all actions or proceedings pending on or commenced on or after the effective date, with the exception of the amendments to Rule 132, which shall apply to all appeals or proceedings commenced in either the Court of Appeals or the Supreme Court on or after the effective date.

The order of the Minnesota Supreme Court [C4-84-2133] dated December 19, 2000, provides in part that "(t)he inclusion of Advisory Committee comments is made for convenience and does not reflect court approval of the statements made therein".

Rule 132.02. Form of Motions and Other Papers

Subdivision 1. Form Requirements. Papers not required to be produced in the manner prescribed by Rule 132.01 shall be 8½ by 11 inches in size with typewritten matter not exceeding 6½ by 9½ inches. Any process capable of producing a clear black image on white paper may be used. All material must appear in at least 11 point type, or its equivalent of not more than 16 characters per inch, on unglazed opaque paper. Pages shall be bound or stapled at the top margin and numbered at the center of the bottom margin. Typewritten matters shall be double spaced. Carbon copies shall not be submitted.

Subd. 2. Caption. Each paper shall contain a caption setting forth the name of the court, the title of the case, the appellate court docket number, and a brief descriptive title of the paper; and shall be subscribed by the attorney preparing the paper together with the preparer's address, telephone number, and attorney registration license number.

Adopted Dec. 7, 1967, eff. Feb. 1, 1968. Amended April 3, 1980, eff. Jan. 1, 1981; Dec. 4, 1980, eff. Jan. 1, 1981; June 17, 1983, eff. Aug. 1, 1983; Nov. 10, 1983, eff. Aug. 1, 1983; Dec. 6, 1991, eff. Jan. 1, 1992.

RULE 133. PREHEARING CONFERENCE; CALENDAR; STATEMENT OF THE CASE

Rule 133.01. Prehearing Conference

The appellate courts may direct the parties, or their attorneys, to appear before a justice, judge or person designated by the appellate courts, either in person or by telephone, for a prehearing conference to consider settlement, simplification of the issues, and other matters which may aid in the disposition of the proceedings by the court. The justice, judge or person designated by the appellate courts shall make an order which recites the agreement made by the parties as to any of the matters considered and which limits the issues to those not disposed of by admission or agreement of counsel.

Unless exempted by the court for good cause shown, appeals in family law cases are subject to mandatory mediation. The court of appeals is authorized to issue special rules of practice governing the family law appellate mediation process. These special rules apply to appeals arising from marital dissolution actions; parentage actions; post-decree modification and enforcement proceedings, including civil contempt actions; child-support actions; and third-party custody and visitation actions.

Amended June 17, 1983, eff. Aug. 1, 1983; Nov. 10, 1983, eff. Aug. 1, 1983; Dec. 17, 2010, eff. Jan. 1, 2011.

Comment—1983

Prehearing conferences are still authorized by this rule, but it is anticipated that they will be held in very few cases and will be governed by internal operating procedures established by each of the appellate courts.

Advisory Committee Comment—2010 Amendment

This rule is amended to add a second paragraph to provide expressly for the family law mediation pilot program initiated by the court of appeals in September of 2008 and made permanent in 2010. The primary purpose of this rule is to provide notice to litigants that certain family law appeals are subject to mandatory mediation in the court of appeals.

Following a successful pilot project in which family law appeals were referred to mediation (over 50% of the appeals that were mediated in the pilot project were settled, resulting in substantial benefits to the litigants and the court), the court of appeals has recommended that the mediation requirement be made permanent. As part of the implementation of mediation as a standing requirement, the Special Rules of Practice for the Minnesota Court of Appeal Governing Family Law Appellate Mediation will include detailed guidance on the procedures involved in the mediation program. The program will be operated in accordance with the special rules of practice, which should be consulted by parties to family law appeals. The rules will be published as an adjunct to the Minnesota Rules of Civil Appellate Procedure and are accessible on the Minnesota Judicial Branch web site: www.mncourts.gov.

When those rules are adopted, this amendment to Rule 133.01 is appropriate to provide guidance to litigants of the existence of this program and the fact that it is generally mandatory. The rule includes reference to the possibility that good cause may exist for exemption from the mediation requirement. Exemption from mandatory mediation is governed by the Special Rules, and the Minnesota Court of Appeals Family Law Appellate Mediation Policies and Procedures provide explicitly for exemption in cases involving allegations of domestic violence. Other grounds for exemption from mandatory mediation may include making a convincing demonstration that post-trial ADR has been employed without success, geographical unavailability of a trained appellate mediator, persuasive arguments that appeal presents an unsettled legal issue upon which the court of appeals should rule, and other reasons.

Rule 133.02. Calendar

No case shall be placed on the calendar for argument, except by special order of the appellate court, until there has been filed in the appellate court the appellant's brief and appendix and the respondent's brief. If either the appellant or the respondent fails to file the required brief within the time provided, or an extension of that time, the case shall be disposed of in accordance with Rule 142.

No changes may be made on the calendar except by order of the court on its own motion or in response to a motion filed by counsel. No case scheduled for argument shall be withdrawn after being placed upon the calendar except upon a showing of extreme emergency.

Amended June 17, 1983, eff. Aug. 1, 1983; Nov. 10, 1983, eff. Aug. 1, 1983.

Comment—1983

This rule indicates that no case will be scheduled for argument until all briefing is completed. The significant amendment is that once placed on the calendar, a case may not be rescheduled except upon motion or by the court and only upon a showing of extreme emergency.

Rule 133.03. Statement of the Case

Two copies of a statement of the case in the form prescribed by the appellate court shall be filed with any of the following:

(a) a notice of appeal pursuant to Rule 103.01;

(b) a notice of related appeal pursuant to 103.02, subdivision 2;

(c) a petition for declaratory relief pursuant to Rule 114.02; or a petition for the writ of certiorari pursuant to Rule 115 or 116.

The appellant shall serve the attorney for each party separately represented and each party appearing pro se and shall file proof of service with the clerk of the appellate courts.

Within 14 days after service of the appellant's statement, the respondent may serve on all parties and file with proof of service two copies of its statement clarifying or supplementing the appellant's statement. If the respondent agrees with the particulars set forth in the appellant's statement, no additional statement need be filed. If a party desires oral argument, a request must be included in the statement of the case. If a party desires oral argument at a location other than that provided by Rule 134.09, subdivision 2(a) to (e), the location requested shall be included in the statement of the case.

Adopted June 17, 1983, eff. Aug. 1, 1983. Amended Nov. 10, 1983, eff. Aug. 1, 1983; Oct. 16, 2009, eff. Jan. 1, 2010.

Comment—1983

Any request for oral argument must be made in the statement of the case.

The former prehearing conference statement has now been replaced by a form entitled "Statement of the Case" as found in the appendix. The appellant must file 2 copies of it with the notice of appeal and 2 copies of the respondent's statement, if any, must be filed within 10 days of service. Any request for oral argument at a location other than that specified in Rule 134.09 must be included in the statement.

See Appendix for form of the statement of the case (Form 133).

Advisory Committee Comment—2009 Amendments

Rule 133.03 is amended to change the timing for filing a statement of the case by a respondent or cross-appellant to 14, rather than 10, days after service of the notice of appeal. This change is intended to create a single response date upon which any notice of related appeal and respondent's statement of the case are due. The rule is also amended to make it clear that the 14-day period is measured from the date of service, not the date of receipt of the notice of appeal.

The rule is also amended to include reference to declaratory relief proceedings, which also require a statement of the case. Because certiorari proceedings under Rules 115 and 116 are commenced by petition, a reference to notices of appeal under those rules is deleted.

Historical Notes

The order of the Supreme Court dated Oct. 16, 2009, provided:

"1. The attached amendments to the Rules of Civil Appellate Procedure be, and the same are, prescribed and promulgated to be effective on January 1, 2010.

"2. These amendments shall apply to all actions or proceedings pending on or commenced on or after the effective date.

"3. The inclusion of Advisory Committee comments is for convenience and does not reflect court approval of the statements made therein."

RULE 134. ORAL ARGUMENT

Rule 134.01. Allowance of Oral Argument

Oral argument will be allowed unless:

(a) no request for oral argument has been made by either party in the statement of the case required by Rule 133.03; or

(b) a party has failed to file a timely brief as required by Rule 128.02; or

(c) the parties have agreed to waive oral argument pursuant to Rule 134.06; or

(d) the appellate court, in the exercise of its discretion, determines that oral argument is unnecessary because:

(1) the dispositive issue or set of issues has been authoritatively settled; or

(2) the facts and legal arguments could be adequately presented by the briefs and record and the decisional process would not be significantly aided by oral argument.

The appellate court shall notify the parties when it has been determined that a request for oral argument has been denied. A party aggrieved by the decision may, within 5 days after the receipt of the notification and pursuant to Rule 127, request the court to reconsider its decision.

Amended June 17, 1983, eff. Aug. 1, 1983; Nov. 10, 1983, eff. Aug. 1, 1983; Dec. 6, 1991, eff. Jan. 1, 1992.

Rule 134.02. Notice of Hearing; Postponement

The clerk of the appellate courts shall notify all parties of the time and place of oral argument. A request for postponement of the hearing must be made by motion filed immediately upon receipt of the notice of the date of hearing.

Amended June 17, 1983, eff. Aug. 1, 1983; Nov. 10, 1983, eff. Aug. 1, 1983.

Rule 134.03. Time Allowed for Argument

Subdivision 1. Time Allowed. In the Court of Appeals, the appellant shall be granted time not to exceed 30 minutes and the respondent 20 minutes for oral argument. The appellant may reserve a portion of that time for rebuttal. In the Supreme Court, the appellant shall be granted time not to exceed 35 minutes and the respondent 25 minutes for oral argument. The appellant may reserve a portion of that time for rebuttal. If multiple parties to the appeal all wish to participate in oral argument, they shall mutually agree to divide the allotted time among themselves.

Subd. 2. Additional Time. If counsel is of the opinion that additional time is necessary for the adequate presentation of argument, additional time may be requested at the prehearing conference, if one is held, or by a motion filed in advance of the date fixed for hearing.

Subd. 3. Argument Limit. The appellate court may increase or reduce the time for argument on its own motion.

Amended June 17, 1983, eff. Aug. 1, 1983; Nov. 10, 1983, eff. Aug. 1, 1983.

Rule 134.04. Order and Content of Argument

The appellant is entitled to open and conclude the argument. It is the duty of counsel for the appellant to state the case and facts fairly, with complete candor, and as fully as necessary for consideration of the issues to be presented. The appellant shall precede the statement of facts with a summary of the questions to be raised. Counsel should not read at length from the record, briefs or authorities.

Amended June 17, 1983, eff. Aug. 1, 1983; Nov. 10, 1983, eff. Aug. 1, 1983.

Advisory Committee Note—1967

Rule 134.03 [Now Rule 134.04]. This rule is similar to P.Fed.R.App.P. 34(c) and Minn.Sup.Ct.R. VIII (4) and XIII. The appellant is required to state the issues and the facts prior to an argument of the issues. The closing argument of the appellant must be confined to rebuttal matters. If counsel intends to argue an authority not mentioned in the briefs, such as a case decided after the briefs are submitted, courtesy dictates that he give the other parties reasonable notice of his intent.

Rule 134.05. Non-Appearance of Counsel

If counsel for a party fails to appear to present argument, the court may hear argument on behalf of a party whose counsel is present, and the case will be decided on the briefs and the argument heard. If no counsel appears for any party, the case will be decided on the briefs unless the court shall otherwise order.

Amended June 17, 1983, eff. Aug. 1, 1983; Nov. 10, 1983, eff. Aug. 1, 1983.

Advisory Committee Note—1967

Rules 134.04 and 134.05 [Now Rules 134.05 and 134.06]. These rules are the same as P.Fed. R.App.P. 34(e) and (f) and similar to Minn.Sup.Ct.R. XIII. Failure to appear does not constitute a default. However, if counsel does not intend to appear, courtesy dictates that he should so inform the Court and the other parties. If the parties decide to waive oral argument, they should promptly inform the clerk.

Rule 134.06. Submission on Briefs

An appeal will be placed on a nonoral calendar and deemed submitted on the briefs on that calendar date in the following circumstances:

(a) When oral argument has not been requested;

(b) When oral argument once allowed has been waived by agreement of the parties and consent of the court; or

(c) If, pursuant to Rule 134.01(d), oral argument is not allowed.

Amended June 17, 1983, eff. Aug. 1, 1983; Nov. 10, 1983, eff. Aug. 1, 1983; Dec. 11, 2008, eff. Jan. 1, 2009.

Advisory Committee Comment—2008 Amendments

Rule 134.06 is amended to conform the rule to the uniform practice of the both the court of appeals and supreme court for cases to be submitted without argument. In all cases it is the practice of the courts to place these cases on an argument calendar for a specific date, noting that nonoral cases will be submitted without argument. The rule is simply amended to conform to this practice.

Rule 134.07. Trial Court Exhibits; Diagrams and Demonstrative Aids

Subdivision 1. Trial Court Exhibits. Counsel planning to use any trial court exhibits during oral argument must arrange before the day of argument with the clerk of the appellate courts to have them placed in the courtroom before the court convenes on the date of the hearing.

Subd. 2. Diagrams and Demonstrative Aids. In cases where a plat, diagram, or demonstrative aid will facilitate an understanding of the facts or of the issues involved, counsel shall either:

(a) Provide a copy in the addendum to the brief or in the appendix;

(b) Provide individual copies to opposing counsel and the court before the argument;

(c) If necessary, have in court a plat, diagram, or demonstrative aid of sufficient size and distinctness to be visible to the court and opposing counsel; or

(d) In advance of oral argument make arrangements with the court for the set-up and removal of any video projection or audio playback equipment needed for presentation of trial electronic exhibits or demonstrative aids.

Amended June 17, 1983, eff. Aug. 1, 1983; Nov. 10, 1983, eff. Aug. 1, 1983; Dec. 11, 2008, eff. Jan. 1, 2009.

Advisory Committee Note—1967

Rule 134.06(1) [Now Rule 134.07(1)]. This rule is similar to P.Fed.R.App.P. 34(g) and Minn.Sup. Ct.R. V. Oral argument is not to be interrupted or delayed to obtain exhibits from the clerk's office.

Rule 134.06(2) [Now Rule 134.07(2)]. This rule is similar to Minn.Sup.Ct.R. V. There is no comparable proposed federal rule. The rule is generally pertinent to land boundary disputes and intersectional automobile cases, but it may apply in a wide variety of situations. Failure to provide a necessary plat or diagram may result in a disallowance of costs and disbursements. The rule is applicable even though no such plat or diagram was used in the trial court. There is no prohibition in the rules against the use of any type of demonstrative aids (such as models, charts, enlarged photographs, etc.) provided that they correctly illustrate the facts and are legitimately helpful.

Advisory Committee Comment—2008 Amendments

Rule 134.07 is amended to broaden the rule and also to conform it to current court practices. Prior to amendment, Rule 134.07 spoke generally of "exhibits," referring either to trial court exhibits or possibly to demonstrative aids. As amended, subdivision 1 addresses trial court exhibits, and states the requirement that counsel seeking to use them in some way in argument must make arrangements for them to be in the courtroom. This is rarely necessary, as exhibits are available to the court and important exhibits are usually reproduced in a party's addendum or appendix. Subdivision 2 is revamped more extensively, to reflect the wider array of materials that might have a role at oral argument. Most importantly, the revised rule provides for what is probably the best way to provide demonstrative exhibits to the court: include them in the addendum or appendix, which makes them available to all judges both before and at argument or, if they are not included in the addendum or appendix, provide copies to the marshal for distribution to the judges or justices and to opposing counsel before the beginning of oral argument. "Blowups" of documents are notoriously ineffective at argument, as most typed documents—even if enlarged many times—are still difficult or impossible to read across a courtroom. The rule also makes it clear that in order to present video images or audio recordings at argument, whether for parts of the record or for demonstrative aids, counsel must arrange for the presence and operation of playback equipment. The inclusion of this provision is not to encourage the use of audio or video equipment at argument—it is often more distracting than useful—but there are circumstances where its use may be appropriate. The revised rule makes it clear how it may be used. The court will likely require that any equipment be set up before the first argument of the day or during a break, and removed at the end of the day or during a formal break.

Rule 134.08. Submission When Member of Appellate Court Not Present

Except in exigent circumstances, the oral argument shall be heard in the Court of Appeals before the full panel to which the case has been assigned or in the Supreme Court before the court sitting en banc. Whenever any member of the appellate court is not present at the oral argument of a case, the case shall be deemed submitted to that member of the court on the record and briefs. When, during the consideration of a case, there is a change in the personnel of the court, the case shall be deemed submitted to the new member or members on the record and briefs.

Amended June 17, 1983, eff. Aug. 1, 1983; Nov. 10, 1983, eff. Aug. 1, 1983.

Rule 134.09. Oral Argument—Place of Argument

Subdivision 1. Supreme Court. Argument to the Supreme Court shall take place at the State Capitol or Minnesota Judicial Center in St. Paul or at any other place designated by the Supreme Court.

Subd. 2. Court of Appeals. Argument to the Court of Appeals shall take place in the Minnesota Judicial Center in St. Paul or as specifically provided in this rule.

(a) Argument in appeals from trial courts shall be heard:

(1) in appeals from trial courts in Hennepin and Ramsey Counties, at a session of the Court of Appeals in Hennepin or Ramsey County;

(2) in appeals from trial courts in other counties, at a session of the Court of Appeals in the judicial district in which the county is located at a location convenient to the place of trial or counsel.

(b) Arguments on writs of certiorari to review decisions of the Commissioner of Economic Security shall be heard as follows:

(1) if the claimant for benefits is a real party in interest in the proceedings and resides in Hennepin or Ramsey County, in one of those counties;

(2) if the claimant for benefits is a real party in interest in the proceedings and resides elsewhere in the state, in the judicial district of the claimant's residence;

(3) otherwise, at a place designated by the court.

(c) Arguments on petitions to review the validity of administrative rules, pursuant to Minnesota Statutes, Section 14.44, shall be in Hennepin or Ramsey County.

(d) Arguments on petitions to review decisions of administrative agencies in contested cases, pursuant to Minnesota Statutes, Sections 14.63 to 14.68, shall be heard:

(1) if the petitioner resides outside of Hennepin and Ramsey Counties, but within Minnesota, either at the session of the Court of Appeals in Hennepin or Ramsey County or at a session of the Court of Appeals in the judicial district in which the petitioner resides, as designated by the petitioner in the petition for review;

(2) if the petitioner resides in Hennepin or Ramsey County, or outside of Minnesota, at a session of the Court of Appeals in Hennepin or Ramsey County.

(e) In all other cases, any oral argument shall be heard at a session of the court in Hennepin or Ramsey County.

(f) Upon the joint request of the parties and with the approval of the court, an argument may be heard at a location other than that provided in this rule. The request pursuant to this subsection shall be included in the statement of the case.

Adopted June 17, 1983, eff. Aug. 1, 1983. Amended Nov. 10, 1983, eff. Aug. 1, 1983; Dec. 6, 1991, eff. Jan. 1, 1992; July 7, 1998, eff. Jan. 1, 1999.

Comment—1983

This rule designates the place of oral argument in the Supreme Court and the Court of Appeals. In cases arising in counties other than Hennepin or Ramsey, the Court of Appeals will hear argument within the judicial district in which the county is located, to the extent practical, at a site convenient to either the place of trial or counsel.

Advisory Committee Comment—1998 Amendments

The rule has been amended to use the correct title of the Commissioner of Economic Security. The change is not intended to affect the meaning or interpretation of the rule.

Rule 134.10. Audio and Video Coverage of Appellate Court Proceedings

Subdivision 1. Unless notice is waived by the Chief Justice of the Supreme Court or the Chief Judge of the Court of Appeals, notice of intent to cover appellate court proceedings by either audio or video means shall be given by the media to the Clerk of the Appellate Courts at least 24 hours prior to the time of the intended coverage.

Subd. 2. Camera operators, technicians, and photographers covering a proceeding must:

(a) avoid activity which might distract participants or impair the dignity of the proceedings;

(b) remain seated within the restricted areas designated by the Court;

(c) observe the customs of the Court;

(d) conduct themselves in keeping with courtroom decorum; and

(e) not dress in a manner that sets them apart unduly from the participants in the proceeding.

Subd. 3. All broadcast and photographic coverage shall be on a pool basis, the arrangements for which must be made by the pooling parties in advance of the hearing. Not more than one (1) electronic news gathering camera producing the single video pool-feed shall be permitted in the courtroom. Not more than two (2) still-photographic cameras shall be permitted in the courtroom at any one time. Motor-driven still cameras may not be used.

Subd. 4. Exact locations for all camera and audio equipment within the courtroom shall be determined by the Court. All equipment must be in place and tested 15 minutes in advance of the time the Court is called to order and must be unobtrusive. All wiring, until made permanent, must be safely and securely taped to the floor along the walls.

Subd. 5. Only existing courtroom lighting may be used.

Adopted March 11, 2011, effective July 1, 2011.

Historical Notes

The order of the Minnesota Supreme Court [ADM09-8006] dated March 11, 2011, provides in part that these amendments be effective on July 1, 2011, and "shall apply to all appeals pending on the effective date and those filed thereafter."

RULE 135. EN BANC AND NONORAL CONSIDERATION BY THE SUPREME COURT

Cases scheduled for oral argument in the Supreme Court shall be heard and decided by the court en banc. Cases submitted on briefs may be considered by a nonoral panel of three or more members of the court assigned by the Chief Justice. The disposition proposed by the panel shall thereafter be circulated to the full court for review.

Adopted Dec. 7, 1967, eff. Feb. 1, 1968. Amended Oct. 24, 1969; Nov. 20, 1970; March 29, 1972; Dec. 4, 1980; June 17, 1983, eff. Aug. 1, 1983; Nov. 10, 1983, eff. Aug. 1, 1983.

RULE 136. NOTICE OF DECISION: JUDGMENT; REMITTITUR

Rule 136.01. Decision

Subdivision 1. Written Decision. (a) Each Court of Appeals disposition shall be written in the form of a published opinion, unpublished opinion, or an order opinion.

(b) Unpublished opinions and order opinions are not precedential except as law of the case, res judicata or collateral estoppel, and may be cited only as provided in Minn. Stat. § 480A.08, subd. 3 (1996).

Subd. 2. Notice of Decision. Upon the filing of a decision or order which determines the matter, the clerk of the appellate courts shall transmit a copy to the attorneys for the parties, to self-represented parties, and to the trial court. The transmittal shall constitute notice of filing.

Adopted Dec. 7, 1967, eff. Feb. 1, 1968. Amended Jan. 5, 1976; June 17, 1983, eff. Aug. 1, 1983; Nov. 10, 1983, eff. Aug. 1, 1983; July 7, 1998, eff. Jan. 1, 1999; June 20, 2011, eff. June 22, 2011.

Advisory Committee Comment—1998 Amendments

This rule is amended to remove any specific form requirements for Court of Appeals decisions. It embodies the different types of opinions issued by the court. The rule removes the prohibition against citation of order opinions in subd. (b) and treats both unpublished opinions and order opinions identically in the new subd. (b). It permits citation of these opinions in accordance with MINN. STAT. § 480A.08, subd. 3 (1996).

Rule 136.02. Entry of Judgment; Stay

Unless the parties stipulate to an immediate entry of judgment, the clerk of the appellate courts shall enter judgment pursuant to the decision or order not less than 30 days after the filing of the decision or order. The service and filing of a petition for review to, or rehearing in, the Supreme Court shall stay the entry of the judgment. Judgment shall be entered immediately upon the denial of a petition for review or rehearing.

Adopted Dec. 7, 1967, eff. Feb. 1, 1968. Amended June 17, 1983, eff. Aug. 1, 1983; Nov. 10, 1983, eff. Aug. 1, 1983.

Comment—1983

Judgment will not be entered for 30 days after the filing of a decision or order to allow the filing of a petition for review to, or rehearing in the Supreme Court. In the event either petition is made and denied, judgment will be entered immediately.

Rule 136.03. Remittitur

Subdivision 1. From the Court of Appeals. The clerk of the appellate courts shall transmit the judgment to the trial court administrator when judgment is entered. If the Supreme Court grants a petition for review, the clerk shall transmit the entire record on appeal, one copy of each brief on file, and the decision of the Court of Appeals to the Supreme Court unless the order granting review directs otherwise.

Subd. 2. From the Supreme Court. When judgment is entered, the clerk of the appellate courts shall either transmit the judgment to the trial court administrator or notify the Court of Appeals if the matter is remanded to the Court of Appeals with special instructions.

Adopted Dec. 7, 1967, eff. Feb. 1, 1968. Amended June 17, 1983, eff. Aug. 1, 1983; Nov. 10, 1983, eff. Aug. 1, 1983; Dec. 6, 1991, eff. Jan. 1, 1992.

Rule 136.04. [Deleted]

RULE 137. ENFORCEMENT OF MONEY JUDGMENTS

Subdivision 1. Cases Originating in the District Courts. Upon transmittal as provided by Rule 136.03, money judgments entered in the appellate courts are enforceable in the district court action as though originally entered in that court.

Subd. 2. Cases Not Originating in the District Courts. Appellate court judgments in cases not originating in the district courts are enforceable in the manner provided by the Uniform Enforcement of Foreign Judgments Act.

Amended June 17, 1983, eff. Aug. 1, 1983; Nov. 10, 1983, eff. Aug. 1, 1983; Dec. 6, 1991, eff. Jan. 1, 1992; July 7, 1998, eff. Jan. 1, 1999.

Advisory Committee Comment—1998 Amendments

This rule is amended to improve and clarify the procedures for enforcement of money judgments following appeal. Non-money judgments from the appellate courts are enforced by the district court on remand according to the direction of the appellate court, while money judgments are enforced by execution. The change essentially takes the appellate courts out of the business of issuing process for the enforcement of money judgments, and provides for the performance of those tasks by the district courts. A money judgment from the appellate courts, whether for costs, damages or any other form of relief, is treated like any other judgment in the district court and transmittal as provided for by Rule 136.03 acts as its entry. As with any other district court judgment, an affidavit of identification of judgment debtor and docketing are required prior to enforcement.

Subdivision 2 of the rule is intended to obviate any confusion over the status of appellate court judgments entered in original or other proceedings not originating in the district courts. Enforcement of those judgments is available in the manner provided by the Uniform Enforcement of Foreign Judgments Act, MINN. STAT. §§ 548.26-.33 (1996).

RULE 138. DAMAGES FOR DELAY

If an appeal delays proceedings on a judgment of the trial court and appears to have been taken merely for delay, the appellate court may award just damages and single or double costs to the respondent.

Adopted Dec. 7, 1967, eff. Feb. 1, 1968. Amended June 17, 1983, eff. Aug. 1, 1983; Nov. 10, 1983, eff. Aug. 1, 1983.

RULE 139. COSTS AND DISBURSEMENTS

Rule 139.01. Costs

Unless otherwise ordered by the appellate court, the prevailing party shall recover costs as follows:

(1) upon a judgment on the merits, costs in the amount of $300;

(2) upon a dismissal, $10.

Adopted Dec. 7, 1967, eff. Feb. 1, 1968. Amended June 17, 1983, eff. Aug. 1, 1983; Nov. 10, 1983, eff. Aug. 1, 1983; Sept. 15, 1994; Dec. 19, 2000, eff. March 1, 2001.

Historical Notes

The order of the Minnesota Supreme Court [C4-84-2133] dated December 19, 2000, provides in part that these amendments are effective March 1, 2001, and shall apply to all actions or proceedings pending on or commenced on or after the effective date, with the exception of the amendments to Rule 132, which shall apply to all appeals or proceedings commenced in either the Court of Appeals or the Supreme Court on or after the effective date.

The order of the Minnesota Supreme Court [C4-84-2133] dated December 19, 2000, provides in part that "(t)he inclusion of Advisory Committee comments is made for convenience and does not reflect court approval of the statements made therein".

Rule 139.02. Disbursements

Unless otherwise ordered by the appellate court, the prevailing party shall be allowed that party's disbursements necessarily paid or incurred. The prevailing party will not be allowed to tax as a disbursement the cost of preparing informal briefs or submissions designated in Rule 128.01, subd. 2.

Adopted Dec. 7, 1967, eff. Feb. 1, 1968. Amended Oct. 12, 1976, eff. Jan. 1, 1977; June 17, 1983, eff. Aug. 1, 1983; Nov. 10, 1983, eff. Aug. 1, 1983; Dec. 6, 1991, eff. Jan. 1, 1992; Dec. 19, 2000, eff. March 1, 2001.

Historical Notes

The order of the Minnesota Supreme Court [C4-84-2133] dated December 19, 2000, provides in part that these amendments are effective March 1, 2001, and shall apply to all actions or proceedings pending on or commenced on or after the effective date, with the exception of the amendments to Rule 132, which shall apply to all appeals or proceedings commenced in either the Court of Appeals or the Supreme Court on or after the effective date.

The order of the Minnesota Supreme Court [C4-84-2133] dated December 19, 2000, provides in part that "(t)he inclusion of Advisory Committee comments is made for convenience and does not reflect court approval of the statements made therein".

Rule 139.03. Taxation of Costs and Disbursements; Time

Costs and disbursements shall be taxed by the clerk of the appellate courts upon 5 days' written notice served and filed by the prevailing party. The costs and disbursements so taxed shall be inserted in the judgment. Failure to file and serve a notice of taxation of costs and disbursements within 15 days after the filing of the decision or order shall constitute a waiver of taxation, provided that upon reversal in the Supreme Court, a prevailing party in that Court who did not prevail in the Court of Appeals may file and serve a notice for costs and disbursements incurred in both appellate courts within 15 days after the filing of the decision of the Supreme Court, separately identifying costs and disbursements incurred in each court.

Adopted Dec. 7, 1967, eff. Feb. 1, 1968. Amended June 17, 1983, eff. Aug. 1, 1983; Nov. 10, 1983, eff. Aug. 1, 1983; Dec. 19, 2000, eff. March 1, 2001.

Historical Notes

The order of the Minnesota Supreme Court [C4-84-2133] dated December 19, 2000, provides in part that these amendments are effective March 1, 2001, and shall apply to all actions or proceedings pending on or commenced on or after the effective date, with the exception of the amendments to Rule 132, which shall apply to all appeals or proceedings commenced in either the Court of Appeals or the Supreme Court on or after the effective date.

The order of the Minnesota Supreme Court [C4-84-2133] dated December 19, 2000, provides in part that "(t)he inclusion of Advisory Committee comments is made for convenience and does not reflect court approval of the statements made therein".

Rule 139.04. Objections

Written objections to the taxation of costs and disbursements shall be served and filed with the clerk of the appellate courts within 5 days after service of the notice of taxation. Failure to serve and file timely written objections shall constitute a waiver. If no objections are filed, the clerk may tax costs and disbursements in accordance with these rules. If objections are filed, a person designated by the appellate courts, after conferring with the appropriate appellate court, shall determine the amount of costs and disbursements to be taxed. There shall be no appeal from the taxation of costs and disbursements.

Adopted Dec. 7, 1967, eff. Feb. 1, 1968. Amended Dec. 17, 1981, eff. Dec. 17, 1981; June 17, 1983, eff. Aug. 1, 1983; Nov. 10, 1983, eff. Aug. 1, 1983; Dec. 19, 2000, eff. March 1, 2001.

Comment—1983

No appeal may be taken from the taxation of costs.

Advisory Committee Comment—2000 Amendments

The amendment to Rule 139.01 clarifies the rule and, by deleting the statutory reference, makes an award of costs available in a greater variety of appellate proceedings. The amendment to Rule 139.03 allows a party who did not prevail in the Court of Appeals but obtains a reversal in the Supreme Court to seek costs and disbursements related to proceedings in both appellate courts. The notice must be served and filed within 15 days after the Supreme Court's decision. This allows the party who ultimately prevails in the Supreme Court to receive an award of costs and disbursements related to both appellate proceedings, whether or not the party initially prevailed in the Court of Appeals.

Historical Notes

The order of the Minnesota Supreme Court [C4-84-2133] dated December 19, 2000, provides in part that these amendments are effective March 1, 2001, and shall apply to all actions or proceedings pending on or commenced on or after the effective date, with the exception of the amendments to Rule 132, which shall apply to all appeals or proceedings commenced in either the Court of Appeals or the Supreme Court on or after the effective date.

The order of the Minnesota Supreme Court [C4-84-2133] dated December 19, 2000, provides in part that "(t)he inclusion of Advisory Committee comments is made for convenience and does not reflect court approval of the statements made therein".

Rule 139.05. Disallowance of Costs and Disbursements

The appellate court upon its own motion may disallow the prevailing party's costs or disbursements or both, in whole or in part, for a violation of these rules or for other good cause. The prevailing party will not be allowed to tax as a disbursement the cost of reproducing parts of the record in the appendix which are not relevant to the issues on appeal.

Adopted Dec. 7, 1967, eff. Feb. 1, 1968. Amended June 17, 1983, eff. Aug. 1, 1983; Nov. 10, 1983, eff. Aug. 1, 1983.

Rule 139.06. Attorneys' Fees on Appeal—Procedure

Subdivision 1. Request for Fees on Appeal. A party seeking attorneys' fees on appeal shall submit such a request by motion under Rule 127. The court may grant on its own motion an award of reasonable attorneys' fees to any party. All motions for fees must be submitted no later than within the time for taxation of costs, or such other period of time as the court directs. All motions for fees must include sufficient documentation to enable the appellate court to determine the appropriate amount of fees.

Subd. 2. Response. Any response to a motion for fees shall state the grounds for the objections with specificity and shall be filed within ten days of the date the motion is served, unless the appellate court allows a longer time. On the court's own motion or the request of a party, a request for attorneys' fees may be remanded to the district court for appropriate hearing and determination.

Subd. 3. Applications for Pre-Decision Awards of Fees. Where allowed by law, a pre-decision application for fees, and any response to such an application, may be made by motion as provided by Rule 127.

Adopted July 7, 1998, eff. Jan. 1, 1999.

Advisory Committee Comment—1998 Amendments

The rule has been amended to provide a procedure for seeking attorneys' fees in the appellate courts. The amendments are procedural only, and do not provide a substantive basis for claiming fees on appeal.

Attorneys' fees on appeal may be allowed as a matter of substantive law or as a sanction. If a party seeks an award of attorneys' fees for work done on the appeal, as opposed to seeking appellate court affirmance of an award made below, the party should seek the award in the appellate court. *Johnson v. City of Shorewood*, 531 N.W.2d 509, 511 (Minn. App. 1995). The appellate court may choose to remand the issue to the trial court for a determination of the fees, *see Richards v. Richards*, 472 N.W.2d 162, 166 (Minn. App. 1991); *Katz v. Katz*, 380 N.W.2d 527, 531 (Minn. App. 1986), *aff'd*, 408 N.W.2d 835, 840 (Minn. 1987); or may refuse such a suggestion, and make the determination itself. *See State Bank v. Ziehwein*, 510 N.W.2d 268, 270 (Minn. App. 1994); *Norwest Bank Midland v. Shinnick*, 402 N.W.2d 818 (Minn. App. 1987).

The request for fees must include sufficient information to enable the appellate court to determine the appropriate amount of fees. This generally will include specific descriptions of the work performed, the number of hours spent on each item of work, the hourly rate charged for that work, and evidence concerning the usual and customary charges for such work, or if the basis for the fees is other than hourly, information by which the court can judge the propriety of the request. Where appropriate, copies of bills submitted to the client, redacted if necessary to preserve privileged information and work-product, may be submitted with the motion.

RULE 140. PETITION FOR REHEARING IN SUPREME COURT

Rule 140.01. Petition for Rehearing

No petition for rehearing shall be allowed in the Court of Appeals.

A petition for rehearing in the Supreme Court may be filed within 10 days after the filing of the decision or order unless the time is enlarged by order of the Supreme Court within the 10–day period. The petition shall set forth with particularity:

(a) any controlling statute, decision or principle of law; or

(b) any material fact; or

(c) any material question in the case which, in the opinion of the petitioner, the Supreme Court has overlooked, failed to consider, misapplied or misconceived.

No petition for reconsideration or rehearing of a denial of a petition for review provided by Rule 117, or of a petition for accelerated review provided by Rule 118, shall be allowed in the Supreme Court.

Adopted June 17, 1983, eff. Aug. 1, 1983. Amended Nov. 10, 1983, eff. Aug. 1, 1983, Dec. 6, 1991, eff. Jan. 1, 1992.

Comment—1983

No petition for rehearing is allowed in the court of appeals.

Rule 140.02. Service; Filing

The petition shall be served upon the opposing party who may answer within 5 days after service. Oral argument in support of the petition will not be permitted. Fourteen copies of the petition, produced and sized as required by Rule 132.01, shall be filed with the clerk. A filing fee of $100 shall accompany the petition for rehearing.

Adopted June 17, 1983, eff. Aug. 1, 1983. Amended Nov. 10, 1983, eff. Aug. 1, 1983.

Rule 140.03. Stay of Judgment

The filing of a petition for rehearing shall stay the entry of judgment until disposition of the petition. It does not stay the taxation of costs. If the petition is denied, the party responding to the petition may be awarded attorney fees to be allowed by the court in the amount not to exceed $500.

Adopted June 17, 1983, eff. Aug. 1, 1983. Amended Nov. 10, 1983, eff. Aug. 1, 1983.

RULE 141. [RESERVED FOR FUTURE USE]

RULE 142. DISMISSAL; DEFAULT

Rule 142.01. Voluntary Dismissal

If the parties to an appeal or other proceeding execute and file with the clerk of the appellate courts a stipulation that the proceedings be dismissed, the matter may be dismissed upon the approval of the appellate court.

Adopted Dec. 7, 1967, eff. Feb. 1, 1968. Amended April 9, 1979; June 17, 1983, eff. Aug. 1, 1983; Nov. 10, 1983, eff. Aug. 1, 1983.

Rule 142.02. Default of Appellant

The respondent may serve and file a motion for judgment of affirmance or dismissal if the appellant fails or neglects to serve and file its brief and appendix as required by these rules. If the appellant is in default for 30 days and the respondent has not made a motion under this rule, the appellate court shall order the appeal dismissed without notice, subject to a motion to reinstate the appeal. In support of the motion, the appellant must show good cause for failure to comply with the rules governing the service and filing of briefs, that the appeal is meritorious and that reinstatement would not substantially prejudice the respondent's rights.

Adopted Dec. 7, 1967, eff. Feb. 1, 1968. Amended April 9, 1979; June 17, 1983, eff. Aug. 1, 1983; Nov. 10, 1983, eff. Aug. 1, 1983; Dec. 6, 1991, eff. Jan. 1, 1992.

Rule 142.03. Default of Respondent

If the respondent fails or neglects to serve and file its brief, the case shall be determined on the merits. If a defaulting respondent has filed a notice of related appeal pursuant to Rule 103.02, subdivision 2, the party opposing the related appeal may serve and file a motion for affirmance of the judgment or order specified in the notice of related appeal or for a dismissal of the respondent's related appeal proceedings, subject to a motion to reinstate the related appeal proceedings in accordance with the criteria specified in Rule 142.02.

If the appellant fails or neglects to serve and file its brief in response to a respondent/cross-appellant's brief in support of a cross-appeal, the case shall be determined on the merits as to those issues raised by the cross-appeal.

Adopted Dec. 7, 1967, eff. Feb. 1, 1968. Amended April 9, 1979; June 17, 1983, eff. Aug. 1, 1983; Nov. 10, 1983, eff. Aug. 1, 1983; Dec. 6, 1991, eff. Jan. 1, 1992; Oct. 16, 2009, eff. Jan. 1, 2010.

Historical Notes

The order of the Supreme Court dated Oct. 16, 2009, provided:

"1. The attached amendments to the Rules of Civil Appellate Procedure be, and the same are, prescribed and promulgated to be effective on January 1, 2010.

"2. These amendments shall apply to all actions or proceedings pending on or commenced on or after the effective date.

"3. The inclusion of Advisory Committee comments is for convenience and does not reflect court approval of the statements made therein."

RULE 143. PARTIES; SUBSTITUTION; ATTORNEYS

Rule 143.01. Parties

The party appealing shall be known as the appellant, relator or petitioner and the adverse party as the respondent. The title of the action shall not be changed in consequence of the appeal.

Adopted Dec. 7, 1967, eff. Feb. 1, 1968. Amended June 17, 1983, eff. Aug. 1, 1983; Nov. 10, 1983, eff. Aug. 1, 1983; Dec. 6, 1991, eff. Jan. 1, 1992.

Rule 143.02. Death of a Party

If any party dies while an appeal is pending in the appellate court, the surviving party or the legal representative or successor in interest of the deceased party, shall file with the clerk of the appellate courts an affidavit showing the death and the name and address of the legal representative or successor in interest by or against whom the appeal shall thereafter proceed. If the deceased party has no representative, any party may inform the clerk of the appellate courts of the death and proceedings shall then be had as the appellate court may direct. If a party against whom an appeal may be taken dies after the entry of a judgment or an order in the trial court but before a notice of appeal is filed, an appellant may proceed as if the death had not occurred. If a party entitled to appeal dies before filing a notice of appeal, the notice of appeal may be filed by the decedent's personal representative or, if there is no personal representative, by the attorney of record within the time prescribed by these rules. After the notice of appeal is filed, substitution shall be effected in the appellate court in accordance with this rule.

Adopted Dec. 7, 1967, eff. Feb. 1, 1968. Amended June 17, 1983, eff. Aug. 1, 1983; Nov. 10, 1983, eff. Aug. 1, 1983; Dec. 6, 1991, eff. Jan. 1, 1992.

Rule 143.03. Substitution for Other Causes

If substitution of a party in the appellate court is necessary for any reason other than death, substitution shall be effected in accordance with the procedure prescribed by Rule 143.02.

Adopted Dec. 7, 1967, eff. Feb. 1, 1968. Amended June 17, 1983, eff. Aug. 1, 1983; Nov. 10, 1983, eff. Aug. 1, 1983.

Rule 143.04. Public Officers

If a public officer dies, resigns or otherwise ceases to hold office during the pendency of an appeal or other appellate proceeding to which the officer is a party in an official capacity, the action does not abate and the successor in office is automatically substituted as a party. Proceedings following the substitution shall be in the name of the substituted party, but any misnomer not affecting the substantial rights of the parties shall be disregarded. An order of substitution may be entered at any time, but the omission to enter such an order shall not affect the substitution.

Adopted Dec. 7, 1967, eff. Feb. 1, 1968. Amended June 17, 1983, eff. Aug. 1, 1983; Nov. 10, 1983, eff. Aug. 1, 1983; Dec. 6, 1991, eff. Jan. 1, 1992.

Rule 143.05. Attorneys

Subdivision 1. Admission Required: Admission Pro Hac Vice. All pleadings filed with the appellate courts must be signed by an attorney licensed to practice in this State, or admitted pro hac vice to practice before the appellate courts. No attorney may present argument to the appellate courts unless licensed to practice in this State or admitted pro hac vice to appear before the appellate court as provided for by this rule.

An attorney licensed to practice law in Minnesota may move for the admission pro hac vice of an attorney admitted to practice law in another state or territory. The motion shall be accompanied by an affidavit of the attorney seeking pro hac vice admission attesting that he or she is a member in good standing of the bar of another state or territory.

Subd. 2. Withdrawal of Attorneys. (a) After a lawyer has appeared for a party in the appellate courts, withdrawal will be effective only if written notice of withdrawal is served on the client and all parties who have appeared, or their lawyers if represented by counsel, and is filed with the Clerk of Appellate Courts. The notice of withdrawal shall state the address at which the client can be served and the address and phone number at which the client can be notified of matters relating to the appeal and shall be accompanied by proof of service.

(b) Withdrawal of an attorney does not create any right to extend briefing deadlines or postpone argument.

Subd. 3. Certified Students. A law student who is certified pursuant to the Minnesota Student Practice

Rules may present oral argument only with leave of the appellate court. A motion for leave to present oral argument must be filed no later than 10 days before the date of the scheduled oral argument. The student may participate in oral argument only in the presence of the attorney of record.

Adopted July 7, 1998, eff. Jan. 1, 1999.

Advisory Committee Comment—1998 Amendments

This rule is amended to provide explicitly for admission of out-of-state attorneys, withdrawal of attorneys, and appearance by certified students. Out-of-state attorneys may be admitted *pro hac vice* upon motion by a Minnesota attorney. Courts have the inherent power to establish rules for admission and regulation of lawyers appearing before them. This rule is consistent with that power. The Minnesota Legislature has specifically recognized that formal admission *pro hac vice* exempts the lawyer from any concern about the unauthorized practice of law. *See* MINN. STAT. § 481.02, subd. 6 (1996). This rule is generally consistent with the rules used in the trial courts. *See* MINN. GEN. R. PRAC. 5, though that rule does not mandate a specific procedure.

The revised rule specifically prescribes when out-of-state lawyers must be admitted *pro hac vice*. Attorneys seeking to argue orally and those actually signing pleadings or briefs must be admitted; others appearing on the brief may wish to seek admission, but admission is not mandatory.

The rule does not require the motion for admission *pro hac vice* be brought at any particular time, but it should be brought sufficiently in advance of the time that a brief is to be submitted or argument is to be made so as to allow the appellate court to consider the motion and act upon it. Similarly, the rule does not provide for any responsive papers. In the unusual case that a motion for *pro hac vice* admission is opposed, the party opposing the motion should submit the opposition within the time for responding to any other motion.

Although the amended rule permits withdrawal upon notice to the court, counsel, and client, withdrawal should not impose any additional burdens on opposing parties or the court. It is imperative that the notice provide basic information to allow the court and opposing counsel to notify and serve the party whose counsel withdraws. This procedure is consistent with the procedure under MINN. GEN. R. PRAC. 108. Just as parties may elect to proceed *pro se* in the first instance, they may continue to represent themselves where their lawyers have withdrawn. This rule establishes the procedure for withdrawal of counsel; it does not itself authorize withdrawal nor does it change the rules governing a lawyer's right or obligation to withdraw in any way. The rule does not affect or lessen a lawyer's obligations to the client upon withdrawal. Those matters are governed by the Minnesota Rules of Professional Conduct. *See* MINN. R. PROF. COND. 1.16.

The rule makes it clear that the withdrawal of counsel does not, in itself, justify extension of the appellate deadlines or the postponement of argument. The existence of these impending deadlines should, however, be considered by counsel in determining if withdrawal can be effected without prejudicing the client. Withdrawal or substitution of counsel may be part of a set of circumstances justifying the exercise of the court's discretion to grant an extension or postponement.

The Minnesota Student Practice Rules allow certified law students to perform all functions that an attorney may perform in representing and appearing on behalf of a client. *See* MINN. R. STUDENT PRAC. 1.01 & 2.01. A motion is required to argue orally in the appellate courts.

RULE 144. CASES INVOLVING CONSTITUTIONAL QUESTIONS WHERE STATE IS NOT A PARTY

When the constitutionality of an act of the legislature is questioned in any appellate proceeding to which the state or an officer, agency or employee of the state is not a party, the party asserting the unconstitutionality of the act shall notify the attorney general within time to afford an opportunity to intervene.

Adopted Dec. 7, 1967, eff. Feb. 1, 1968. Amended June 17, 1983, eff. Aug. 1, 1983; Nov. 10, 1983, eff. Aug. 1, 1983; Dec. 6, 1991, eff. Jan. 1, 1992.

Advisory Committee Note—1967

This rule is similar to P.Fed.R.App.P. 44. The notice required by this rule must be given upon appeal even though the party has previously notified the attorney general pursuant to Minn.R.Civ.P. 24.04 while the matter was in the trial court. If the proper notice was not given to the attorney general pursuant to Rule 24.04, the Supreme Court will refuse to review the constitutional question on appeal unless the constitutional question pertains to the lack of jurisdiction of the court. Campbell v. Glenwood Hills Hospitals, 273 Minn. 525, 142 N.W.2d 255 (1966); Oak Center Creamery Co. v. Grobe, 264 Minn. 435, 119 N.W.2d 729 (1963). In original proceedings in the Supreme Court, notice pursuant to this rule is sufficient.

RULE 145. APPENDIX OF FORMS

The sample forms contained in the appendix to these rules satisfy the requirements of the rules.

Adopted Dec. 7, 1967, eff. Feb. 1, 1968. Amended June 17, 1983, eff. Aug. 1, 1983; Nov. 10, 1983, eff. Aug. 1, 1983.

Comment—1983

The appendix of forms is intended to guide counsel in the preparation of any application for relief in either of the appellate courts. For consistency of illustration the defending party has been designated as the appellant or petitioner in all forms. Accordingly, appropriate adjustment must be made when the plaintiff or claimant is the party seeking relief in an appellate court. The attorney registration license number of the attorney-preparer of each form is required to permit the computerized tracking of all cases in the appellate courts. While there is no other requirement for strict adherence to the forms, an inclusion of the information contained in them is viewed as a prerequisite to obtaining an informal decision from the appellate court.

RULE 146. TITLE

These rules may be known and cited as Rules of Civil Appellate Procedure.

Adopted Dec. 7, 1967, eff. Feb. 1, 1968. Amended June 17, 1983, eff. Aug. 1, 1983; Nov. 10, 1983, eff. Aug. 1, 1983.

RULE 147. EFFECTIVE DATE

These rules are effective on August 1, 1983 and govern all civil appeals and proceedings brought after that date.

Adopted June 17, 1983, eff. Aug. 1, 1983. Amended Nov. 10, 1983, eff. Aug. 1, 1983.

Comment—1983

The revised rules are effective on August 1, 1983, the effective date of Minnesota Statutes, Section 480A.06, which establishes the jurisdiction of the Court of Appeals, and will govern all civil appeals and proceedings initiated in either the Supreme Court or the Court of Appeals after that date. Appeals and other proceedings pending in the Supreme Court on July 31, 1983, will be governed by the former rules.

APPENDIX OF FORMS

FORM 103A. NOTICE OF APPEAL (COURT OF APPEALS)

STATE OF MINNESOTA ______ DISTRICT COURT
COUNTY OF ________ ______ COUNTY COURT
______ JUDICIAL DISTRICT

CASE TITLE:

Plaintiff, NOTICE OF APPEAL TO COURT OF APPEALS

vs.

TRIAL COURT CASE NUMBER:

Defendant. DATE OF ORDER:
OR
DATE JUDGMENT ENTERED:

TO: Clerk of the Appellate Courts
Minnesota Judicial Center
St. Paul, MN 55155

Please take notice that the above-named defendant appeals to the Court of Appeals of the State of Minnesota from an order (judgment) of the court filed (entered) on the date shown, denying defendant's motion for a new trial.

DATED:

NAME, ADDRESS, ZIP CODE, TELEPHONE NUMBER OF ATTORNEY(S) FOR PLAINTIFF

NAME, ADDRESS, ZIP CODE, TELEPHONE NUMBER, AND ATTORNEY REGISTRATION LICENSE NUMBER OF ATTORNEY(S) FOR DEFENDANT:

____
SIGNATURE

(The trial court caption is used on the notice of appeal. Subsequent documents shall bear the appropriate appellate court caption. RCAP 103.01, subd. 1 specifies the contents of the notice of appeal and filings required to perfect an appeal, including filing fees. RCAP 103.03 sets forth judgments and orders which are appealable to the Court of Appeals. RCAP 104.01 specifies time limits for filing and service of the notice of appeal. RCAP 107 provides for bond or deposit for costs. RCAP 108.01 provides for a supersedeas bond. This document must be accompanied by 2 copies of a completed statement of the case. RCAP 133.03.)

Adopted June 17, 1983, eff. Aug. 1, 1983. Amended Nov. 10, 1983, eff. Aug. 1, 1983; Dec. 6, 1991, eff. Jan. 1, 1992.

FORM 103B. NOTICE OF APPEAL (SUPREME COURT)

STATE OF MINNESOTA ______ DISTRICT COURT
COUNTY OF ________ ______ JUDICIAL DISTRICT

CASE TITLE:

Plaintiff, NOTICE OF APPEAL TO SUPREME COURT

vs.

TRIAL COURT CASE NUMBER:

Defendant. DATE OF FINAL JUDGMENT OF CONVICTION/ORDER:

TO: Clerk of the Appellate Courts
Minnesota Judicial Center
St. Paul, MN 55155

Please take notice that the above-named defendant appeals to the Supreme Court of the State of Minnesota from defendant's final judgment of conviction, date noted above, for the crime of murder in the first degree.

DATED:

NAME, ADDRESS, ZIP CODE, TELEPHONE NUMBER OF ATTORNEY(S) FOR PLAINTIFF

NAME, ADDRESS, ZIP CODE, TELEPHONE NUMBER, AND ATTORNEY REGISTRATION LICENSE NUMBER OF ATTORNEY(S) FOR DEFENDANT:

____
SIGNATURE

(The trial court caption is used on the notice of appeal. Subsequent documents shall bear the appropriate appellate court caption. Minnesota Statutes, Section 632.14 provides that appeals from a final judgment of conviction of the crime of murder in the first degree are taken directly to the Supreme Court. Rule 29, subdivision 1 of the Rules of Criminal Procedure specifies the procedure for service and filing of the notice of appeal; subdivision 2 itemizes the contents of the notice of appeal; subdivision 3 defines the time for taking an appeal; and subdivision 4 cites other relevant procedures in first-degree murder appeals.)

Adopted June 17, 1983, eff. Aug. 1, 1983. Amended Nov. 10, 1983, eff. Aug. 1, 1983; Dec. 6, 1991, eff. Jan. 1, 1992.

FORM 103C. NOTICE OF RELATED APPEAL (COURT OF APPEALS)

STATE OF MINNESOTA ______ DISTRICT COURT
COUNTY OF ________ ______ JUDICIAL DISTRICT

CASE TITLE:

Plaintiff, NOTICE OF RELATED APPEAL TO COURT OF APPEALS

vs.

TRIAL COURT CASE NUMBER:

Defendant. DATE OF ORDER OR JUDGMENT BEING CHALLENGED:

APPELLATE COURT FILE NUMBER: ________

TO: Clerk of the Appellate Courts
305 Minnesota Judicial Center
25 Rev. Dr. Martin Luther King Jr. Blvd.
St. Paul, MN 55155

Please take notice that the above-named [plaintiff/defendant] (state full name) appeals to the Minnesota Court of Appeals and seeks review of the (specify order or judgment by title) of the ________ court, which was [filed/entered] on the date noted above and [granting/denying (describe nature of ruling, such as plaintiffs motion for a new trial on liability)].

DATED:

NAME, ADDRESS, ZIP CODE, TELEPHONE NUMBER, AND ATTORNEY REGISTRATION LICENSE NUMBER OF ATTORNEY(S) FOR PLAINTIFF:

NAME, ADDRESS, ZIP CODE, TELEPHONE NUMBER, AND ATTORNEY REGISTRATION LICENSE NUMBER OF ATTORNEY(S) FOR DEFENDANT:

____

SIGNATURE

(The trial court caption is used on the notice of appeal and any notice of related appeal. Subsequent documents shall bear the appropriate appellate court caption. RCAP 103.02, subd. 1, specifies the contents of the notice of related appeal and filings required to perfect an appeal, including filing fees. RCAP 104.01, subd. 4, specifies time limits for filing and service of the notice of related appeal. This document must be accompanied by 2 copies of a completed statement of the case. RCAP 133.03.)

Advisory Committee Comment—2009 Amendments

This Form 103C is new as part of the amendments deleting Rule 106 and abolishing the notice of review and substituting the notice of related appeal. The caption provides information about the earlier appeal to which the later appeal related, including identification of the date of the order or judgment to be reviewed and the appellate court file number of that action, if known.

FORM 105. PETITION FOR DISCRETIONARY REVIEW

STATE OF MINNESOTA
IN COURT OF APPEALS

CASE TITLE:

Petitioner, PETITION FOR DISCRETIONARY REVIEW

vs. TRIAL COURT CASE NUMBER:

Respondent. DATE OF FILING ORDER:

TO: The Court of Appeals of the State of Minnesota:

The petitioner (name) requests discretionary review of the (date) order of the ________ Court.

1. Statement of facts necessary to an understanding of the issues presented.

2. Statement of the issues.

3. Statement why immediate review of interlocutory or otherwise nonappealable order necessary.

WHEREFORE, the petitioner requests an order of the court granting the petition for discretionary review.

DATED:

NAME, ADDRESS, ZIP CODE, TELEPHONE NUMBER, AND ATTORNEY REGISTRATION LICENSE NUMBER OF ATTORNEY(S) FOR PETITIONER

____

SIGNATURE

(The content requirements of the petition for discretionary review are found in RCAP 105. A memorandum of law and pertinent lower court documents should be attached to the petition. The submission and the requirements for filing, form and the number of copies are contained in RCAP 105.02.)

Adopted June 17, 1983, eff. Aug. 1, 1983. Amended Nov. 10, 1983, eff. Aug. 1, 1983; Dec. 6, 1991, eff. Jan. 1, 1992.

FORM 106. RESPONDENT'S NOTICE OF REVIEW

[Deleted Oct. 16, 2009, eff. Jan. 1, 2010]

FORM 110. CERTIFICATE AS TO TRANSCRIPT [Renumbered Form 110A July 7, 1998, eff. Jan. 1, 1999]

FORM 110A. CERTIFICATE AS TO TRANSCRIPT

(to be filed with the clerk of the appellate courts within 10 days from the date the transcript was ordered)

STATE OF MINNESOTA ______ DISTRICT COURT
COUNTY OF______
______ JUDICIAL DISTRICT

CASE TITLE:

Plaintiff, CERTIFICATE AS TO TRANSCRIPT

vs. ________ Supreme Court
________ Court of Appeals

Defendant. APPELLATE COURT CASE NUMBER:

TO: Clerk of the Appellate Courts
Minnesota Judicial Center
St. Paul, MN 55155

A transcript of the proceedings held on (specify dates) in the above-entitled action was requested by counsel for the (specify party) on (date) in accordance with Rule 110.02, subdivision 2 of the Rules of Civil Appellate Procedure. The estimated number of pages is (number) and the estimated date of completion is __________, a date not to exceed 60 days from the date of request.

Satisfactory financial arrangements have been made between counsel and the court reporter for the transcription.

DATED:

____
SIGNATURE OF ATTORNEY

____
ADDRESS AND TELEPHONE NUMBER

____
SIGNATURE OF COURT REPORTER
ADDRESS AND TELEPHONE NUMBER

cc: Trial Court Administrator of Record
All Counsel of Record

(Rule 110.02, subdivision 2, requires a certificate as to transcript if any part of the proceedings are to be transcribed by a court reporter. The original copy of the certificate shall be filed with the clerk of the appellate courts, with a copy to the trial court administrator and all counsel of record and shall be filed with the clerk of the appellate courts within 10 days from the date the transcript was ordered.)

Amended July 7, 1998, eff. Jan. 1, 1999.

Historical Notes

Form 110, adopted June 17, 1983, effective August 1, 1983, and amended November 10, 1983 and December 6, 1991 was renumbered Form 110A by court order dated July 7, 1998, effective January 1, 1999.

FORM 110B. CERTIFICATE OF FILING AND DELIVERY

(to be filed with the clerk of the appellate courts promptly after filing and delivery of the transcript)

STATE OF MINNESOTA __________DISTRICT COURT
COUNTY OF__________ ______JUDICIAL DISTRICT

CASE TITLE:

Plaintiff. CERTIFICATE OF FILING AND DELIVERY

vs. Supreme Court
Court of Appeals

Defendant. APPELLATE COURT CASE NUMBER:

TRIAL COURT CASE NUMBER:

TO: Clerk of the Appellate Courts
Minnesota Judicial Center
St. Paul, MN 55155

A transcript of the proceedings held on (specify dates) in the above-entitled action was filed with the trial court administrator on (date). The transcript was delivered to counsel of record on (date) by (specify method of delivery). The transcript was delivered to the following recipients:

____

DATED:

____
SIGNATURE OF COURT REPORTER
ADDRESS AND TELEPHONE NUMBER

cc: Trial Court Administrator of Record
All Counsel of Record

(Rule 110.02, subd. 2(b), requires the filing of a certificate to document the filing and delivery of the transcript. The certificate must specify the date the transcript was filed with the trial court administrator and the date and method of delivery of the transcript to counsel of record. The original copy of the certificate shall be filed with the clerk of the appellate courts, with a copy to the trial court administrator and all counsel of record and shall be filed with the clerk of the appellate courts immediately after filing and delivery of the transcript.)

Adopted July 7, 1998, eff. Jan. 1, 1999.

FORM 114. PETITION FOR DECLARATORY JUDGMENT

STATE OF MINNESOTA
IN COURT OF APPEALS

CASE TITLE:

Petitioner, PETITION FOR DECLARATORY JUDGMENT

vs. COURT OF APPEALS NUMBER:

Agency or Body,
Respondent. AGENCY OR BODY NUMBER:

TO: The Court of Appeals of the State of Minnesota

The above-named petitioner hereby petitions the Court of Appeals pursuant to Minn. Stat. § 14.44 for a declaratory judgment determining the validity of a rule adopted by (agency) on (date), upon the grounds that the rule (is unconstitutional/exceeds the statutory authority of the agency/was adopted without compliance with statutory rule-making procedures).

DATED:

NAME, ADDRESS, ZIP CODE AND
TELEPHONE NUMBER OF PETITIONER
(ATTORNEY REGISTRATION NUMBER
IF REPRESENTED BY COUNSEL)

SIGNATURE

(The procedure for obtaining a declaratory judgment on the validity of an administrative rule from the Court of Appeals is set forth in Rule 114, Rules of Civil Appellate Procedure. The rule prescribes the manner of obtaining review, contents of the petition, filing fees, and service requirements for obtaining review. An original and one copy of a completed statement of the case must accompany the petition.)

Adopted July 7, 1998, eff. Jan. 1, 1999.

FORM 115A. PETITION FOR WRIT OF CERTIORARI

STATE OF MINNESOTA
IN COURT OF APPEALS

CASE TITLE:

PETITION FOR WRIT OF CERTIORARI

Petitioner,

COURT OF APPEALS NUMBER:

vs.

Respondent,

(AGENCY OR BODY) NUMBER:

DATE OF DECISION:

(Agency or Body), Respondent.

DATE AND DESCRIPTION OF EVENT TRIGGERING APPEAL TIME (for example, mailing of decision, receipt of decision, or receipt of other notice):

TO: The Court of Appeals of the State of Minnesota:

The above-named petitioner hereby petitions the Court of Appeals for a Writ of Certiorari to review a decision of the (agency or body) issued on the date noted above, upon the grounds that (specify grounds and statute authorizing certiorari review).

DATED:

NAME, ADDRESS, ZIP CODE, TELEPHONE NUMBER, AND ATTORNEY REGISTRATION LICENSE NUMBER OF ATTORNEY(S) FOR PETITIONER:

SIGNATURE OF ATTORNEY

OR, IF NOT REPRESENTED BY COUNSEL:

NAME, ADDRESS, ZIP CODE, AND TELEPHONE NUMBER OF PETITIONER:

SIGNATURE OF PETITIONER

(The procedure for obtaining a writ of certiorari from the Court of Appeals is set forth in the applicable statutes and in Rule 115, Rules of Civil Appellate Procedure. The applicable statutes prescribes the subject matter of writs in the Court of Appeals,, time limitations, and requirements for service. The rule prescribes the manner of securing a writ, contents of the petition, bonds, filing and fees, and preparation of the record. An original and one copy of a completed statement of the case must accompany the petition.

The date of the event that triggered the appeal period must be indicated on the petition. The nature of this event varies, depending on the requirements of the statute authorizing certiorari review in the Court of Appeals. *See* MINN. R. CIV. APP. P. 115 comment.)

Adopted June 17, 1983, eff. Aug. 1, 1983. Amended Nov. 10, 1983, eff. Aug. 1, 1983; Dec. 6, 1991, eff. Jan. 1, 1992; July 7, 1998, eff. Jan. 1, 1999.

Historical Notes

This Form was subject to a correction provided by the Court on October 12, 1983. That correction was recognized by the order of November 10, 1983, as a minor amendment and was so incorporated.

FORM 115B. WRIT OF CERTIORARI

STATE OF MINNESOTA

IN COURT OF APPEALS

CASE TITLE:

WRIT OF CERTIORARI

Relator,

vs.

COURT OF APPEALS NUMBER:

Respondent,

AGENCY OR BODY) NUMBER:

(Agency or Body), Respondent.

DATE OF DECISION:

TO: (Agency or Body)

You are hereby ordered to return to the Court of Appeals and serve on all parties in accordance with Rule 115.04, subdivision 3, within 30 days after service of the petition or 14 days after delivery of a transcript, whichever is later, an itemized statement of the record, exhibits and proceedings in the above-entitled matter so that this court may review the decision of the (agency or body) issued on the date noted above.

You are further directed to retain the actual record, exhibits, and transcript of proceedings (if any) until requested by the clerk of the appellate courts to deliver them in accordance with Rule 115.04, subdivision 5.

Copies of this writ and accompanying petition shall be served forthwith either personally or by mail upon the respondent (agency or body) and upon the respondent or its attorney at:

____

____

(address)

Proof of service of the writ and of the itemized list shall be filed with the clerk of the appellate courts.

DATED:

Clerk of Appellate Courts

(Clerk's File Stamp)

By: ____________________

Assistant Clerk

Adopted June 17, 1983, eff. Aug. 1, 1983. Amended Nov. 10, 1983, eff. Aug. 1, 1983; Dec. 6, 1991, eff. Jan. 1, 1992; July 7, 1998, eff. Jan. 1, 1999; Oct. 16, 2009, eff. Jan. 1, 2010.

FORM 115C. CERTIFICATE OF SERVICE AND FILING OF ITEMIZED LIST

STATE OF MINNESOTA

IN COURT OF APPEALS

CASE TITLE:

Relator,	CERTIFICATE OF SERVICE AND FILING OF ITEMIZED LIST
vs.	Court of Appeals
Respondent,	APPELLATE COURT CASE NUMBER:
(Agency or Body), Respondent.	(AGENCY OR BODY) NUMBER:

TO: Clerk of the Appellate Courts
Minnesota Judicial Center
St. Paul, MN 55155

A copy of the itemized list of the contents of the record is attached to this certificate, was served on each separately-represented party to this proceeding, and is transmitted to the clerk of appellate courts in accordance with Rules 115.04, subdivision 3, and 111.01. Service was made as follows:

Party Name	Address	Date Served	Method of Service
Clerk of Appellate Courts	Minnesota Judicial Center St. Paul, MN 55155		

etc.

DATED:

____

SIGNATURE

ADDRESS AND TELEPHONE NUMBER

cc: All Counsel of Record

(Rule 115.04, subd. 3, requires the service and filing of the itemized list of the contents of the record as specified in Rule 111.01 to take place within 30 days after service of the petition for writ of certiorari or 14 days after delivery of a transcript, whichever is later. This notice requires service and filing of the itemized list of the record; the actual record is to be retained until the clerk of appellate courts requests that it be transmitted to the court. *See* Rule 115.04, subd. 5.)

FORM 116A. PETITION FOR WRIT OF CERTIORARI

STATE OF MINNESOTA
IN SUPREME COURT

CASE TITLE:

Employee–Realtor,	PETITION FOR WRIT OF CERTIORARI
vs.	SUPREME COURT NUMBER:
Employer–Respondent,	WORKERS' COMPENSATION COURT OF APPEALS NUMBER:
Insurer–Respondent.	DATE OF SERVICE OF WRITTEN NOTICE OF DECISION:

TO: The Supreme Court of the State of Minnesota:

The above-named relator hereby petitions the Supreme Court for a Writ of Certiorari to review a decision of the Workers' Compensation Court of Appeals, upon the grounds that it is not in conformity with the terms of the Workers' Compensation Act and is unwarranted by the evidence.

DATED:

NAME, ADDRESS, ZIP CODE, TELEPHONE NUMBER, AND ATTORNEY REGISTRATION LICENSE NUMBER OF ATTORNEY(S) FOR EMPLOYEE–RELATOR:

____

SIGNATURE

(The procedure for obtaining a writ of certiorari from the Supreme Court is set forth in RCAP 116. The rule prescribes the subject matter of writs in the Supreme Court, contents of the petition, bond or security, filing and fees, and requirements for service. Two copies of a completed statement of the case must accompany the petition.)

Adopted June 17, 1983, eff. Aug. 1, 1983. Amended Nov. 10, 1983, eff. Aug. 1, 1983; Dec. 6, 1991, eff. Jan. 1, 1992.

FORM 116B. WRIT OF CERTIORARI

STATE OF MINNESOTA
IN SUPREME COURT

CASE TITLE:

	WRIT OF CERTIORARI
Employee–Realtor,	
vs.	SUPREME COURT NUMBER: WORKERS' COMPENSATION COURT OF APPEALS NUMBER:
Employer–Respondent,	
Insurer–Respondent.	DATE OF SERVICE OF WRITTEN NOTICE OF DECISION:

TO: The Workers' Compensation Court of Appeals:

You are hereby ordered to return to the Supreme Court within 30 days from this date the record, exhibits and proceedings in the above-entitled matter so that this court may review the decision of the Workers' Compensation Court of Appeals.

Copies of this writ and accompanying petition shall be served forthwith either personally or by mail upon the Secretary of the Workers' Compensation Court of Appeals and upon the Employer–Respondent(s) above-named or their attorney(s) at:

____

____

(address)

Proof of service shall be filed with the clerk of the appellate courts.

DATED:

Clerk of Appellate Courts

(Clerk's File Stamp)

By: ____________________

Assistant Clerk

Adopted June 17, 1983, eff. Aug. 1, 1983. Amended Nov. 10, 1983, eff. Aug. 1, 1983; Dec. 6, 1991, eff. Jan. 1, 1992.

FORM 117. PETITION FOR REVIEW OF DECISION OF COURT OF APPEALS

STATE OF MINNESOTA
IN SUPREME COURT

CASE TITLE:

Petitioner,	PETITION FOR REVIEW OF DECISION OF COURT OF APPEALS
vs	APPELLATE COURT CASE NUMBER:
Respondent.	DATE OF FILING OF COURT OF APPEALS DECISION:

TO: The Supreme Court of the State of Minnesota:

The petitioner (name) requests Supreme Court review of the above-entitled decision of the Court of Appeals upon the following grounds:

1. Statement of legal issues and their resolution by the Court of Appeals.

2. Statement of the criteria of the rule relied upon to support the petition.

3. Statement of the case (facts and procedural history).

(The statement should be a concise summary because the decisions of the lower courts must be attached.)

4. A brief argument in support of petition.

(The petitioner shall identify and address the critical portion of the Court of Appeals decision and discuss the likelihood of success on the merits.)

For these reasons, the petitioner seeks an order granting review of the decision of the Court of Appeals.

DATED:

NAME, ADDRESS, ZIP CODE, TELEPHONE NUMBER, AND ATTORNEY REGISTRATION LICENSE NUMBER OF ATTORNEY(S) FOR PETITIONER

____

SIGNATURE

Appendix

(The content requirements of the petition are found in RCAP 117. The rule emphasizes that Supreme Court review is discretionary. The decisions of the Court of Appeals and trial court or agency must be attached as an appendix. The petition should not exceed 5 typewritten pages, exclusive of appendix.)

Adopted June 17, 1983, eff. Aug. 1, 1983. Amended Nov. 10, 1983, eff. Aug. 1, 1983; Dec. 6, 1991, eff. Jan. 1, 1992; Dec. 19, 2000, eff. March 1, 2001.

Historical Notes

The order of the Minnesota Supreme Court [C4-84-2133] dated December 19, 2000, provides in part that these amendments are effective March 1, 2001, and shall apply to all actions or proceedings pending on or commenced on or after the effective date, with the exception of the amendments to Rule 132, which shall apply to all appeals or proceedings commenced in either the Court of Appeals or the Supreme Court on or after the effective date.

The order of the Minnesota Supreme Court [C4-84-2133] dated December 19, 2000, provides in part that "(t)he inclusion of Advisory Committee comments is made for convenience and does not reflect court approval of the statements made therein".

FORM 118. PETITION FOR ACCELERATED REVIEW

STATE OF MINNESOTA
IN SUPREME COURT

CASE TITLE:

Petitioner,	PETITION FOR ACCELERATED REVIEW
vs.	APPELLATE COURT CASE NUMBER:
Respondent.	

TO: The Supreme Court of the State of Minnesota:

The petitioner (name) requests accelerated review by the Supreme Court of the above-entitled matter upon the following grounds:

1. Statement of legal issues.
2. Statement of the case.

(This should be a concise statement of the facts necessary to the Supreme Court's decision to accelerate the appeal; a summary of the trial court or agency's decision; and the status of the case—including the stage of the proceedings on the date of this petition—and the date of filing of the notice of appeal.)

3. A brief argument.

(The petitioner should discuss the applicable criteria of RCAP 117, subd. 2; and the question of why immediate review by the Supreme Court is necessary.)

For these reasons, the petitioner requests an order granting accelerated review of this appeal now pending in the Court of Appeals.

DATED:

NAME, ADDRESS, ZIP CODE, TELEPHONE NUMBER, AND ATTORNEY REGISTRATION LICENSE NUMBER OF ATTORNEY(S) FOR PETITIONER

____

SIGNATURE

Appendix

(This petition shall not exceed 10 typewritten pages, exclusive of appendix, and shall comply with the requirements of RCAP 118, subd. 2.)

Adopted June 17, 1983, eff. Aug. 1, 1983. Amended Nov. 10, 1983, eff. Aug. 1, 1983; Dec. 6, 1991, eff. Jan. 1, 1992.

FORM 120. PETITION FOR WRIT OF PROHIBITION

STATE OF MINNESOTA
IN COURT OF APPEALS

CASE TITLE:

	PETITION FOR WRIT OF PROHIBITION
Petitioner,	TRIAL COURT CASE NUMBER:
vs.	APPELLATE COURT CASE NUMBER:
Respondent.	

TO: The Court of Appeals of the State of Minnesota:

The petitioner (name) requests a writ of prohibition restraining the ________ County District Court from enforcing its order of (date).

1. Statement of facts necessary to an understanding of the issues presented.
2. Statement of the issues.
3. Argument and statement of the reasons extraordinary relief necessary.

WHEREFORE, the petitioner requests an order granting the petition for a writ of prohibition and the issuance of the writ.

DATED:

NAME, ADDRESS, ZIP CODE, TELEPHONE NUMBER, AND ATTORNEY REGISTRATION LICENSE NUMBER OF ATTORNEY(S) FOR PETITIONER

____

SIGNATURE

Appendix

(The content requirements of the petition for extraordinary relief are found in RCAP 120. A memorandum of law and pertinent lower court documents should be attached to the petition. The submission of the petition and time to respond are detailed in RCAP 120.02 and the requirements for filing, form and the number of copies are contained in RCAP 120.04.)

Amended July 7, 1998, eff. Jan. 1, 1999.

Historical Notes

Form 120A, adopted June 17, 1983, effective August 1, 1983, and amended November 10, 1983, and December 6, 1991, was renumbered Form 120 by court order dated July 7, 1998, effective January 1, 1999.

FORM 120A. PETITION FOR WRIT OF PROHIBITION

[Renumbered Form 120 July 7, 1998, eff. Jan. 1, 1999]

FORM 120B. ORDER FOR WRIT OF PROHIBITION
[Deleted July 7, 1998, eff. Jan. 1, 1999]

FORM 120C. WRIT OF PROHIBITION
[Deleted July 7, 1998, eff. Jan. 1, 1999]

FORM 128. APPELLANT'S FORMAL BRIEF AND APPENDIX

(Cover)

APPELLATE COURT CASE NUMBER
STATE OF MINNESOTA
IN COURT OF APPEALS

CASE TITLE:

Respondent,

vs.

Appellant.

APPELLANT'S BRIEF AND APPENDIX

JOHN BROWN Attorney for Respondent (address, zip code, and telephone number)	SMITH & JONES By John Jones Attorney for Appellant (address, zip code, telephone number, and attorney registration license number)

* * * * * *

TABLE OF CONTENTS

APPENDIX AND ITS INDEX

* * * * * *

TABLE OF AUTHORITIES

Statutes (list applicable statutes and page where argument found)

Minn.Stat. § 518.58 (1982)	8

Cases (list applicable authorities and page where argument found)

Jones v. Olson, ___ N.W.2d ___ (Minn.1982)	9
Smith v. Brown, ___ Minn. ___, ___ N.W.2d ___ (1965)	14

Secondary Authorities

McCormick, Damages § 83 (1935)	16

* * * * * *

LEGAL ISSUES

I. (Precise statement of each legal issue)
Trial court held: ___________

II.

* * * * * *

STATEMENT OF FACTS

(The facts should be stated in compliance with RCAP 128.02, subd. 1(c), accompanied by appropriate citations to the appendix and the transcript.)

* * * * * *

ARGUMENT

I. (Each legal issue should be argued separately. RCAP 128.02, subd. 1(d).)

* * * * * *

CONCLUSION

(The conclusion shall contain a statement of the precise relief sought.)

Respectfully submitted,
SMITH & JONES
By John Jones
Attorney for Appellant
(address, zip code, telephone number, and attorney registration license number)

* * * * * *

APPENDIX AND INDEX

(The index should precede the appendix and the pages of the appendix should be separately and consecutively numbered. RCAP 130.)

Adopted June 17, 1983, eff. Aug. 1, 1983. Amended Nov. 10, 1983, eff. Aug. 1, 1983; Dec. 6, 1991, eff. Jan. 1, 1992.

FORM 132. CERTIFICATION OF BRIEF LENGTH

STATE OF MINNESOTA
(IN SUPREME COURT
OR
IN COURT OF APPEALS)

CASE TITLE:

Appellant,	CERTIFICATION OF BRIEF LENGTH
vs.	
Respondent.	APPELLATE COURT CASE NUMBER:

I hereby certify that this brief conforms to the requirements of Minn. R. Civ. App. P. 132.01, subds. 1 and 3, for a brief produced with a [monospaced] [proportional] font. The length of this brief is.... [lines][words]. This brief was prepared using [name and version of word processing software].

DATED:

NAME, ADDRESS, ZIP CODE, TELEPHONE NUMBER, AND ATTORNEY REGISTRATION LICENSE NUMBER OF ATTORNEY(S) FOR PETITIONER

____

SIGNATURE

Adopted Dec. 19, 2000, eff. March 1, 2001.

Historical Notes

The order of the Minnesota Supreme Court [C4-84-2133] dated December 19, 2000, provides in part that these amendments are effective March 1, 2001, and shall apply to all actions or proceedings pending on or commenced on or after the effective date, with the exception of the amendments to Rule 132, which shall apply to all appeals or proceedings commenced in either the Court of Appeals or the Supreme Court on or after the effective date.

The order of the Minnesota Supreme Court [C4-84-2133] dated December 19, 2000, provides in part that "(t)he inclusion of Advisory Committee comments is made for convenience and does not reflect court approval of the statements made therein".

FORM 133. STATEMENT OF THE CASE

STATE OF MINNESOTA
IN (SUPREME COURT
OR
IN COURT OF APPEALS)

CASE TITLE:

STATEMENT OF THE CASE OF (APPELLANT) (RESPONDENT)

Appellant,

TRIAL COURT CASE NUMBER:

vs.

APPELLATE COURT CASE NUMBER:

Respondent.

1. Court or agency of case origination and name of presiding judge or hearing officer.

2. Jurisdictional statement

(A) Appeal from district court.

Statute, rule or other authority authorizing appeal:

Date of entry of judgment or date of service of notice of filing of order from which appeal is taken:

Authority fixing time limit for filing notice of appeal (specify applicable rule or statute):

Date of filing any motion that tolls appeal time:

Date of filing of order deciding tolling motion and date of service of notice of filing:

(B) Certiorari appeal.

Statute, rule or other authority authorizing certiorari appeal:

Authority fixing time limit for obtaining certiorari review (cite statutory section and date of event triggering appeal time, *e.g.*, mailing of decision, receipt of decision, or receipt of other notice):

(C) Other appellate proceedings.

Statute, rule or other authority authorizing appellate proceeding:

Authority fixing time limit for appellate review (cite statutory section and date of event triggering appeal time, *e.g.*, mailing of decision, receipt of decision, or receipt of other notice):

(D) Finality of order or judgment.

Does the judgment or order to be reviewed dispose of all claims by and against all parties, including attorney fees? Yes ( ) No ( )

If no:

Did the district court order entry of a final partial judgment for immediate appeal pursuant to MINN. R. CIV. APP. P. 104.01? Yes ( ) No ( ) or

If yes, provide date of order:

If no, is the order or judgment appealed from reviewable under any exception to the finality rule? Yes ( ) No ( )

If yes, cite rule, statute, or other authority authorizing appeal:

(E) Criminal only:

Has a sentence been imposed or imposition of sentence stayed? Yes ( ) No ( )

If no, cite statute or rule authorizing interlocutory appeal:

3. State type of litigation and designate any statutes at issue.

4. Brief description of claims, defenses, issues litigated and result below. For criminal cases, specify whether conviction was for a misdemeanor, gross misdemeanor, or felony offense.

5. List specific issues proposed to be raised on appeal.

6. Related appeals.

List all prior or pending appeals arising from the same action as this appeal. If none, so state.

List any known pending appeals in separate actions raising similar issues to this appeal. If none are known, so state.

7. Contents of record.

Is a transcript necessary to review the issues on appeal? Yes ( ) No ( )

If yes, full ( ) or partial ( ) transcript?

Has the transcript already been delivered to the parties and filed with the trial court administrator? Yes ( ) No ( )

If not, has it been ordered from the court reporter? Yes ( ) No ( )

If a transcript is unavailable, is a statement of the proceedings under Rule 110.03 necessary? Yes ( ) No ( )

In lieu of the record as defined in Rule 110.01, have the parties agreed to prepare a statement of the record pursuant to Rule 110.04? Yes ( ) No ( )

8. Is oral argument requested? Yes ( ) No ( )

If so, is argument requested at a location other than that provided in Rule 134.09, subd. 2? Yes ( ) No ( )

If yes, state where argument is requested:

9. Identify the type of brief to be filed.

Formal brief under Rule 128.02. ( )

Informal brief under Rule 128.01, subd. 1 (must be accompanied by motion to accept unless submitted by claimant for reemployment benefits). ( )

Trial memoranda, supplemented by a short letter argument, under Rule 128.01, subd. 2. ( )

10. Names, addresses, zip codes and telephone numbers of attorney for appellant and respondent.

NAME, ADDRESS, ZIP CODE, TELEPHONE NUMBER, AND ATTORNEY REGISTRATION LICENSE NUMBER OF ATTORNEY(S) FOR (APPELLANT) (RESPONDENT)

____

SIGNATURE

OR, IF NOT REPRESENTED BY COUNSEL:

NAME, ADDRESS, ZIP CODE AND TELEPHONE NUMBER OF (APPELLANT) (RESPONDENT)

____

SIGNATURE (OF APPELLANT) (OF RESPONDENT)

Dated:

(The Statement of Case is not a jurisdictional document, but it is important to the proper and efficient processing of the appeal by the appellate courts. The "jurisdictional statement" section is intended to provide sufficient information for the appellate court to easily determine whether the order or judgment is appealable and if the appeal is timely. The nature of the proceedings below and the notice of appeal determine the jurisdiction of the appellate court. The sections requesting information about the issues litigated in the lower court or tribunal, and the issues proposed to be raised on appeal are for the court's information, and do not expand or limit the issues that might be addressed on appeal. Likewise, the section asking counsel to identify and prior or pending appeals from the same case, and any separate appeals that raise similar issues is intended to provide more information about the procedural history of the case and to ensure that the court has early notice of other pending related matters in case consolidation is appropriate.)

Adopted June 17, 1983, eff. Aug. 1, 1983. Amended Nov. 10, 1983, eff. Aug. 1, 1983; Dec. 6, 1991, eff. Jan. 1, 1992; July 7, 1998, eff. Jan. 1, 1999.

FORM 133A. SUBJECT MATTER INDEX—COURT OF APPEALS

1. Administrative Law—
   Administrative Procedure Act
2. Agency
3. Appeal and Error
   a. Jurisdictional Question
   b. Standard of Review
   c. Scope of Review
4. Arbitration
5. Attorney Fees
6. Commercial Law
7. Constitutional Law (other than criminal)
8. Contracts
9. Corporations/Professional Associations/Partnerships
10. Criminal
    a. Police Practices
       —arrest
       —search and seizure
       —electronic surveillance
       —confessions
       —identification procedures
       —administration of exclusionary rules
    b. Pretrial Procedures
       —prosecutorial discretion in charging
       —indictment and complaint
       —bail
       —discovery
       —joinder
       —speedy trial
       —venue
       —competency of defendant
       —continuances
       —omnibus hearing
    c. Guilty Pleas
    d. Trial—Right to counsel
       —appointment of counsel
       —effective assistance of counsel
       —waiver of counsel
    e. Trial—Conduct of Prosecutor
       —improper argument
       —improper elicitation of evidence
    f. Evidentiary Rulings
    g. Trial Court's Instructions
    h. Defenses
    i. Sufficiency of Evidence
    j. Jury
    k. Sentencing
    l. Juveniles

m. Miscellaneous
11. Debtor–Creditor
12. Dissolution of Marriage
 a. Attorney Fees
 b. Child Custody, Support
 c. Spousal Maintenance
 d. Property Distribution
13. Dram Shop Act
14. Evidence
15. Governmental Immunity
16. Implied Consent Proceedings
17. Insurance
 a. No-fault Benefits
 b. Duty to Defend
 c. Coverage
18. Juveniles
 a. Dependency
 b. Neglect
 c. Termination of Parental Rights
19. Landlord-Tenant
20. Malpractice
 a. Legal
 b. Medical
21. Mental Health Commitment
22. Municipalities
23. Negligence
 a. Damages
 b. Liability
 c. Jury Instructions
 d. Sufficiency of Evidence
24. Negotiable Instruments
25. Probate–Trust Administration
26. Property
 a. Adverse Possession
 b. Conveyances
 c. Cancellation of Contracts
27. Public Officials—Duties
28. Schools
 a. Districts
 b. School Teacher—Employment
29. Statute at Issue (identify) ______
30. Torts
 a. Identify
31. Unemployment Compensation
 a. Voluntary termination
 b. Misconduct
 c. Other (identify) ______
32. Writs
33. Zoning
34. Miscellaneous (identify) ______

Adopted Oct. 12, 1983. Amended Nov. 10, 1983, eff. Aug. 1, 1983.

FORM 133B. SUBJECT MATTER INDEX—SUPREME COURT

1. Criminal—Murder in the First Degree
2. Mortgages
3. Tax Court
4. Workers' Compensation
 a. Apportionment
 b. Attorney Fees
 c. Computation of Award
 d. Coverage of the Act
 e. Procedure
 f. Settlement Agreements
5. Miscellaneous (identify) ______

Adopted Oct. 12, 1983. Amended Nov. 10, 1983, eff. Aug. 1, 1983.

FORM 139. TAXATION OF COSTS AND DISBURSEMENTS

STATE OF MINNESOTA

☐ Supreme Court
☐ Court of Appeals

Case Title

Appellate Court Case Number: ____________

NOTICE, STATEMENT AND CLAIM OF COSTS AND DISBURSEMENTS INCURRED BY PREVAILING PARTY

Prevailing Party: ____________

☐ Appellant ☐ Respondent ☐ Relator

COSTS AND DISBURSEMENTS

Statutory Costs $300.00

Clerk of The Appellate Courts Filing Fee .... $____

Transcript of case used for appeal to Appellate Courts only .... $____

Printing of Respondent's brief .... $____

Printing Appellant's brief and Appendix .... $____

Postage .... $____

Premium on appeal bond .... $____

Other .... $____

The above bill of Costs and Disbursements taxed and allowed ____________

Dated

Frederick K. Grittner
Clerk of the Appellate Courts

By ____________
Assistant Clerk

STATE OF MINNESOTA

County of ____________

Being duly sworn, I the attorney for the prevailing party in the above-entitled action, state that the above is a true and correct statement of costs incurred and disbursements made by the prevailing party in that action.

NOTARY STAMP, SIGNATURE AND DATE:

____
Dated

____
Signature

Respectfully,

____
Attorney's Name

____
Address

____
Signature

NOTICE TO ATTORNEY FOR ADVERSE PARTY(S):

Costs and disbursements will be taxed pursuant to Rule 139.03 (Rules of Civil Appellate Procedure), objections thereto may be filed pursuant to Rule 139.04.

ADVERSE PARTY(S) BEING TAXED:

____
ATTORNEY

For ____________
(Name of Party)

____
ATTORNEY

For ____________
(Name of Party)

____
ATTORNEY

For ____________

____
ATTORNEY

For ____________

(Name of Party) (Name of Party)

Adopted July 7, 1998, eff. Jan. 1, 1999.

INDEX TO RULES OF CIVIL APPELLATE PROCEDURE

CASE DISPOSITIONAL PROCEDURES OF THE MINNESOTA SUPREME COURT

Adopted October 19, 1988; revised January 2011

Including Amendments Received Through January 1, 2014

INTRODUCTION

This document has been prepared to assist the public and practicing bar in understanding the processes by which the Supreme Court performs its judicial business. The Court continually reviews and refines its internal operating procedures to accomplish its goal of effective and efficient processing of judicial and administrative responsibilities. As a result, this document is informational only and does not bind the Court; the processes described may be changed at any time without prior notice.

Adopted Oct. 19, 1988. Amended Jan. 1, 2011, eff. Jan. 1, 2011.

COURT SCHEDULE

The Court schedules its work based on an annual term that runs from September through August. The projected schedule of argument and special term dates for the full term is published on the judicial branch website, usually several months before the beginning of the term. While it generally adheres to the established schedule, the Court may supplement or otherwise modify the calendar as its workload requires.

The Court hears regularly-scheduled arguments each month, September through June. A typical monthly schedule for those months is as follows:

a. First week of the month: Oral arguments heard Monday through Thursday.

b. Second week: Oral arguments heard Monday through Wednesday; court meeting (administrative matters) on Thursday, unless conflict with Judicial Council meeting.

c. Third week: Special term conference on Tuesday; court meeting on Wednesday, if conflict with Judicial Council in the second week.

d. Fourth week: Special term conference on Wednesday.

Oral argument is typically not heard in July and August, with the exception of cases in which expedited consideration is warranted. One special term conference is scheduled on a Tuesday in mid-July and two special term conferences are scheduled in August. Court meetings are scheduled in July and August as needed.

Adopted Oct. 19, 1988. Amended Jan. 1, 2011, eff. Jan. 1, 2011.

JURISDICTION

The Minnesota Constitution, in Article VI, § 2, confers on the Supreme Court appellate jurisdiction in all cases, original jurisdiction in remedial cases as prescribed by law, and supervisory jurisdiction over all courts of the state. The Court's supervisory jurisdiction includes the authority to regulate procedural and evidentiary matters. The Court has authority to consider all petitions and motions relating to the exercise of its jurisdiction.

The Supreme Court has direct appellate jurisdiction over several categories of cases, as specified by law. Appeals may be taken directly to the Court from decisions of the Minnesota Tax Court and the Minnesota Workers' Compensation Court of Appeals. In addition, convictions of first-degree murder and decisions in postconviction proceedings involving convictions of first-degree murder are directly appealable to the Supreme Court, as are decisions in election contests involving a statewide or legislative office.

Most appeals, however, are taken initially to the Court of Appeals, and the Supreme Court has discretionary jurisdiction to review decisions of the Court of Appeals. That is, the Supreme Court may choose whether to grant review of a decision of the Court of Appeals. See "Obtaining Discretionary Review" below.

The Supreme Court has original jurisdiction in several categories of cases. These include petitions for writs of mandamus or prohibition, but only to the extent the relief sought is directed to the Court of Appeals, the Tax Court, or the Workers' Compensation Court of Appeals. The Supreme Court also has original jurisdiction over certain pre-election ballot challenges involving statewide or legislative office and over matters of attorney and judge discipline.

Adopted Oct. 19, 1988. Amended Jan. 1, 2011, eff. Jan. 1, 2011.

OBTAINING DISCRETIONARY REVIEW

A party may seek Supreme Court review of an adverse decision of the Court of Appeals by serving and filing a petition for review. The purpose of the petition is to persuade the Supreme Court that the case satisfies the criteria for review set out in the applicable appellate rule. (Minn. R. Civ. App. P. 117, subd. 2, for civil cases and Minn. R. Crim. P. 29.04, subd. 4, for criminal cases.) As the criteria for review reflect, the Supreme Court's primary role in reviewing Court of Appeals decisions is to set precedent that develops and clarifies the law on important issues of broad impact. The Supreme Court rarely grants review just to correct an erroneous decision that will affect only the parties to that case. As a result, the Court grants review in a small percentage of cases.

A petition for review must be served and filed within 30 days of the filing of the Court of Appeals' decision for which review is sought. Minn. R. Civ. App. P. 117, subd. 1; Minn. R. Crim. P. 29.04, subd. 2. The respondent has 20 days after service of the petition to file and serve a response.[1] Minn. R. Civ. App. P. 117, subd. 4; Minn. R. Crim. P. 29.04, subd. 5. A respondent may request conditional cross-review in its response (civil), Minn. R. Civ. App. P. 117, subd. 4, or file a cross-petition (criminal), Minn. R. Crim. P. 29.04, subd. 6, to raise additional issues not included in the petition for review.

The Clerk of Appellate Courts forwards all petitions for review and responses to the Supreme Court Commissioner's Office for analysis prior to the Court's consideration. The Commissioner's Office prepares a memorandum for the Court on every case in which a petition is filed. In the memorandum, the Commissioner's Office summarizes the facts and procedural history of the case, describes the legal issues on which the petitioner seeks review, discusses whether the case satisfies the criteria for review, and makes a recommendation whether review should be granted.

The Court considers petitions for review at its special term conferences. Petitions are generally considered within 60 days of filing, with only rare exceptions. The Commissioner's Office memorandum and the Court of Appeals' decision are distributed to the justices a week in advance of the special term conference at which the petition will be considered.

At the special term conference, the Court considers each case individually, discussing whether to grant or deny the petition and, if review is granted, whether to specify the issues on which review is granted, whether to allow oral argument, and whether to grant any related pending motions. A petition for review is granted if three or more justices vote for review.

After special term, the Commissioner's Office prepares an order for each case decided. If the petition is granted, the order specifies which party will proceed as the appellant (normally the petitioner), any limitation of issues on which review has been granted, and the briefing schedule, typically by reference to the applicable rule of appellate procedure. The orders are signed by a single member of the Court, usually the Chief Justice, on behalf of the Court and filed with the Clerk of Appellate Courts. The clerk sends copies of the orders to the parties. No petition for reconsideration or rehearing of a denial of a petition for review is allowed. Minn. R. Civ. App. P. 140.01.

An alternative procedure to request discretionary review by the Supreme Court is a petition for accelerated review. After an appeal has been filed in the Court of Appeals, a party may petition for "accelerated" review, which means Supreme Court review of the case before the Court of Appeals has ruled. A petition for accelerated review must demonstrate not only that the case satisfies the criteria for Supreme Court review stated in Minn. R. Civ. App. P. 117, subd. 2, but also that "the case is of such imperative public importance as to justify deviation from the normal appellate procedure and to require immediate determination in the Supreme Court." Minn. R. Civ. App. P. 118, subd. 1. The procedures described above for consideration of a petition for review are also used for consideration of a petition for accelerated review. Although Rule 118 does not expressly provide for a response to a petition for accelerated review, the Court will allow a response if it is served and filed within the time allowed for a response to a petition for review under Minn. R. Civ. App. P. 117, subd. 4.

Adopted Oct. 19, 1988. Amended Jan. 1, 2011, eff. Jan. 1, 2011.

DIRECT REVIEW

Decisions of the Tax Court and the Workers' Compensation Court of Appeals are subject to direct review by the Supreme Court. The proceeding is initiated by presenting a petition for writ of certiorari, with a statement of the case and two copies of the decision to be reviewed attached, and proposed writ to the Clerk of Appellate Courts. Minn. R. Civ. App. P. 116.02 and 116.03, subd. 1. The Clerk's Office issues the writ of certiorari, Minn. R. Civ. App. P. 116.03, subd. 3, which then must be served by the petitioner on opposing parties and the court whose decision is to be reviewed, *id.*, subd. 4.

The Commissioner's Office reviews the petition, the statement of the case, and the decision to be reviewed and recommends to the Supreme Court whether the matter should be considered on the en banc oral calendar. The criteria employed in that recommendation include whether the appeal is based on legal or factual issues and whether oral argument will significantly enhance the decisional process. The Commissioner's Office notifies the parties whether the Court will hear oral argument on the case or consider it without oral argument. Appeals from the Tax Court are scheduled on the Supreme Court's en banc monthly calendar, whether for oral or nonoral consideration. Appeals from the Workers' Compensation Court of Appeals that are considered without oral argument are conferenced and decided by the Supreme Court at special term, based on a bench memorandum and recommendation from the Commissioner's Office.

Adopted Oct. 19, 1988. Amended Jan. 1, 2011, eff. Jan. 1, 2011.

MOTIONS AND EXTRAORDINARY WRITS

A party may petition the Supreme Court for an extraordinary writ, that is, mandamus or prohibition, to review the action or decision of the Court of Appeals, the Tax Court, or the Workers' Compensation Court of Appeals. Minn. R. Civ. App. P. 120.01. Petitions for extraordinary writs are considered by the Supreme Court at special term.

Routine motions, such as motions for an extension of time or for leave to file an amicus curiae brief, are considered and decided on behalf of the Court by the Chief Justice, or the most senior associate justice available, based on the recommendation of the Commissioner's Office. Motions that are not routine are considered and decided by the entire Court at special term or based on circulated written materials. Decisions on some motions, such as motions to strike a portion of a brief or material in a party's appendix, may be deferred until the Court's consideration of the case on the merits.

In the event a motion or petition is filed with the Supreme Court seeking emergency relief, the Chief Justice calls a meeting of the available members of the Court for prompt consideration of the request. The Court will consider a request for emergency relief made orally only in the most extreme circumstances. The Court will require a written submission, by electronic means if necessary, and an opportunity for the opposing party to respond, unless the action complained of is imminent.

Adopted Oct. 19, 1988. Amended Jan. 1, 2011, eff. Jan. 1, 2011.

CALENDARING AND ASSIGNMENT OF CASES

Each month from August through May, the Commissioner's Office prepares the en banc calendar of cases to be considered by the Court the following month. A case is considered ready to be placed on the monthly calendar when the respondent's brief is filed. Cases are placed on the calendar roughly in the order of the filing of the respondents' briefs, although some categories of cases, such as juvenile protection and pretrial criminal appeals, are given priority. The calendar sets the date for oral argument or nonoral consideration. Generally, a case is designated for oral argument, rather than nonoral consideration, unless it appears from the briefs that argument would not sufficiently enhance the decisional process or a party is appearing pro se.

The Commissioner's Office tries to accommodate known scheduling conflicts of counsel, but it is difficult and disruptive for the Court to reschedule a case once it has been placed on the formal calendar. Counsel are therefore advised to anticipate that their case may be calendared starting with the first available calendar after the respondent's brief is filed and to notify the Commissioner's Office in advance, by letter filed with the Clerk of Appellate Courts, as soon as potential scheduling conflicts are known.

The monthly calendar is distributed to the Court at least 30 days before the first day set for argument on the calendar. At the same time, the Clerk of Appellate Courts sends a copy of the calendar to counsel for the parties in the scheduled cases, and the calendar is posted on the judicial branch website. Summaries of the issues presented by each case on the calendar are posted on the website approximately two weeks before the calendar begins.

The Commissioner's Office assigns the cases on the monthly calendar to members of the Court on a more-or-less rotational basis, modified based on an effort to equalize the workload and distribution of cases over the course of the annual term. After the calendar is distributed to the Court with these assignments, a law clerk prepares a bench memorandum on the assigned case that thoroughly analyzes the factual and legal issues in the case and recommends a disposition. The bench memo is distributed to all members of the Court a week before the case is scheduled for argument.

Adopted Oct. 19, 1988. Amended Jan. 1, 2011, eff. Jan. 1, 2011.

ORAL ARGUMENT

Generally speaking, oral arguments during the first week of the month's calendar are held in the State Capitol Courtroom, and arguments during the second week are held in Courtroom 300 in the Minnesota Judicial Center. As part of its outreach and public education efforts, the Court schedules two cases each term for oral argument at a high school in the metropolitan area or greater Minnesota. In addition, the Court hears arguments at the Minnesota law schools.

Usually two cases are heard each day of the calendar, with arguments beginning at 9:00 a.m. unless otherwise noted on the calendar. All counsel in all cases scheduled for the day must check in with the Court marshal in the courtroom by 8:40 a.m. and are to be present and prepared to argue at 9:00 a.m., in case the order in which the cases are argued must be changed. Counsel for the first case should be seated at the counsel tables before the Court enters the courtroom.

The appellant is allowed 35 minutes and the respondent 25 minutes, or such other time periods as the Court may specify. The appellant may reserve time for rebuttal, which should be communicated to the marshal when checking in. Counsel should be prepared to answer questions from the justices. Visual aids may be used at oral argument only with prior notice to the Court through the marshal. Use of such aids is not encouraged, however, because it is seldom effective and may be distracting in this setting.

Oral arguments are recorded and are available for viewing on the judicial branch website, usually by the next day. Other than the official video recording equipment, cameras and microphones are only permitted in the courtroom with prior Court approval, and use of such equipment is subject to the condition that it must not disrupt the proceedings or the formality of the courtroom.

Adopted Oct. 19, 1988. Amended Dec. 11, 1998, eff. Dec. 11, 1998; amended Jan. 1, 2011, eff. Jan. 1, 2011.

POST–ARGUMENT CONFERENCE

After each day's oral arguments, the Court meets in conference to discuss the cases just argued, as well as any case scheduled for nonoral consideration on that day. The Chief Justice presides at the conference and directs the Court's discussion. The justice to whom the case was assigned first reports the case, providing his or her analysis of the issues and recommendation for disposition. Discussion follows, with the comments and votes of the other members of the Court, in descending order of seniority, although the Chief Justice speaks last unless the Chief Justice reported on the case. Although the Court reaches a tentative decision in each case based on the conference discussion, the vote is preliminary and a final decision awaits the circulation and approval of a formal opinion or opinions. Any member of the Court may request an additional conference for further discussion of a case.

Adopted Oct. 19, 1988. Amended Jan. 1, 2011, eff. Jan. 1, 2011.

OPINION

If the justice to whom the case was assigned is in the majority at conference, he or she will prepare a draft opinion for the Court's consideration. Circulation of the draft majority opinion among the other members of the Court generally begins within 60 days after the case conference. If any member of the Court indicated at conference an intention to write a dissenting opinion, the draft of the majority opinion is circulated first to that justice, whose draft dissenting opinion is provided to the majority author for possible revision of the majority draft, which is then returned to the dissenting justice for potential revision of the dissent. A similar process occurs if any member of the Court is writing a concurring opinion. The majority draft and any dissenting or concurring drafts are then circulated together to each of the remaining justices. Each reviewing justice writes whatever comments or suggestions he or she has on the draft(s) and indicates on an accompanying cover sheet whether he or she will join the majority or some other opinion. After circulation is complete and the authoring justices have made any final revisions to their opinions based on the comments of their colleagues, the opinions are carefully cite-checked by a law clerk.

Adopted Oct. 19, 1988. Amended Jan. 1, 2011, eff. Jan. 1, 2011.

OPINION RELEASE

Opinions of the Supreme Court are formally filed with the Clerk of Appellate Courts and released to the parties and the public by posting on the judicial branch website on Wednesdays at 10 a.m. A notice is sent to the parties on Monday that the opinion in their case will be filed and posted the following Wednesday. Any concurring or dissenting opinions are filed and released with the majority opinion. The Clerk of Appellate Courts provides copies of the opinions to the parties and to publishers after the official release time.

Adopted Oct. 19, 1988. Amended Jan. 1, 2011, eff. Jan. 1, 2011.

REHEARING

A party may petition the Court for rehearing within 10 days of the filing of the Court's opinion. Minn. R. Civ. App. P. 140.01. An affirmative vote of a majority of the justices is necessary to grant rehearing. The grounds for rehearing are extremely narrow and, as a result, rehearing is seldom granted.

Adopted Oct. 19, 1988. Amended Jan. 1, 2011, eff. Jan. 1, 2011.

COSTS AND DISBURSEMENTS

The prevailing party may seek an award of costs and disbursements. *See* Minn. R. Civ. App. P. 139. The claim must be served and filed within 15 days of the filing of the Court's decision. Minn. R. Civ. App. P. 139.03. An adverse party may file objections to taxation of the requested costs and disbursements within 5 days. Minn. R. Civ. App. P. 139.04. If no objections are filed, the Clerk of Appellate Courts taxes costs and allowable disbursements. If objections are filed, the request for taxation and the objections are submitted to the chambers of the justice who authored the majority opinion, usually with a recommendation from the Commissioner's Office. The majority author will decide the issues, if routine, or circulate a proposed resolution to the Court, if not.

ENTRY OF JUDGMENT AND REMITTITUR

Unless the parties stipulate to immediate entry, the Clerk of Appellate Courts enters judgment not less than 30 days after filing of the Supreme Court's decision, except that judgment may be entered immediately on denial of a petition for review or rehearing. Minn. R. Civ. App. P. 136.02. When judgment has been entered, the Clerk of Appellate Courts transmits the judgment to the appropriate district court administrator or notifies the Court of Appeals if the case is remanded to that court. Minn. R. Civ. App. P. 136.03.

Adopted Oct. 19, 1988. Amended Jan. 1, 2011, eff. Jan. 1, 2011.

1 In juvenile protection matters, the deadline for serving and filing a petition for review is 15 days, and the deadline to respond is 10 days. Minn. R. Juv. Prot. P. 47.07.

RULES OF PRACTICE BEFORE THE MINNESOTA SUPREME COURT FOR FORMER JUSTICES AND EMPLOYEES OF THE COURT

Adopted March 11, 2011, effective April 1, 2011

Including Amendments Received Through January 1, 2014

Rule 1. Justices

A former member of the Minnesota Supreme Court shall not participate in any professional capacity in any case that was pending in the Supreme Court during the member's tenure on the court, or appear before the court as counsel for a client, in person or in writing, in any case or matter for a period of three years after leaving the court.

Adopted eff. April 1, 2011.

Rule 2. Employees

A former employee of the Minnesota Supreme Court shall not participate in any professional capacity in any case that was pending in the Supreme Court during the employee's tenure at the court, or appear before the court as counsel for a client, in person or in writing, in any case or matter for a period of one year after leaving employment with the court, except that a former employee of the court in the commissioner's office may not appear for a period of two years after leaving employment with the court.

Adopted eff. April 1, 2011.

SUPREME COURT RULES OF DECORUM

Adopted October 15, 1996

Including Amendments Received Through January 1, 2014

Rule 1. Display of Flags[1]

The flags of the United States and the State of Minnesota shall be displayed at all times while the court is in session.

Adopted Oct. 15, 1996.

1 Rule nameline editorially supplied.

Rule 2. Tobacco, Food, or Drink[1]

No tobacco in any form, food or drink shall be permitted in the courtroom.

Adopted Oct. 15, 1996.

1 Rule nameline editorially supplied.

Rule 3. Headgear and Overcoats[1]

No hats, caps or other headgear shall be worn in the courtroom. Overcoats and overshoes should be removed before entering the courtroom. No one may remain standing while court is in session.

Adopted Oct. 15, 1996.

1 Rule nameline editorially supplied.

Rule 4. Distracting or Disconcerting Behavior[1]

No signs or banners are allowed in the courtroom. There shall be no demonstrations of any kind in the courtroom while court is in session. There shall be no unnecessary conversation, loud whispering, newspaper or magazine reading in the courtroom while court is in session. In addition, pagers and cellular telephones must be turned off before entering the courtroom gallery. Any distracting or disconcerting activity will be grounds for removal from the courtroom.

Adopted Oct. 15, 1996.

1 Rule nameline editorially supplied.

Rule 5. Media Equipment[1]

Tape recorders, video cameras and still cameras are prohibited from the courtroom without the prior consent of the Court. All public media-related equipment to be utilized during court proceedings, may be set up 45 minutes before court begins. Any equipment not set up 15 minutes before court begins, will not be allowed into the courtroom. No microphone wire or camera cable shall obstruct access to or egress from the courtroom or the podium.

Adopted Oct. 15, 1996.

1 Rule nameline editorially supplied.

Rule 6. Children[1]

Children must be under the control and supervision of an adult at all times.

Adopted Oct. 15, 1996.

1 Rule nameline editorially supplied.

Rule 7. Spectators[1]

Spectators in the gallery must remain seated during arguments. Spectators may leave or enter the court during times when the attorneys are approaching or leaving the podium.

Adopted Oct. 15, 1996.

1 Rule nameline editorially supplied.

Rule 8. Opening of Court[1]

At the opening of each court day, the Court Marshal shall, by rap of the gavel, direct all present to stand, and shall clearly and distinctly say:

"All rise for the honorable justices of the Supreme Court of the state of Minnesota."

Adopted Oct. 15, 1996.

1 Rule nameline editorially supplied.

Rule 9. Duty of Court Marshal[1]

It shall be the duty of the Court Marshal to maintain order at all times as attorneys and the public assemble in the courtroom. This duty shall include removing persons for distracting or discordant behavior, admitting persons to the courtroom and directing them to seats, and refusing admittance to the courtroom when the courtroom is filled to its seating capacity.

Adopted Oct. 15, 1996.

1 Rule nameline editorially supplied.

Rule 10. Conduct of Lawyers[1]

Lawyers are officers of the court and shall at all times uphold the honor and maintain the dignity of the profession, maintaining at all times a respectful attitude toward the court and opposing counsel.

Adopted Oct. 15, 1996.

1 Rule nameline editorially supplied.

Rule 11. Oral Arguments[1]

Unless otherwise noted in a specific calendar, oral arguments on days assigned begin at 9:00 a.m. All attorneys in all cases are to be present and prepared to argue at 9:00 a.m. They must check in with the Court Marshal and be prepared to begin whenever they are called. (Case Dispositional Procedures—Oral Arguments, Minn.R.Civ.App.P.)

Adopted Oct. 15, 1996.

1 Rule nameline editorially supplied.

Rule 12. Attire of Lawyers and Court Personnel[1]

All lawyers and court personnel shall wear appropriate business attire to the courtroom.

Adopted Oct. 15, 1996.

1 Rule nameline editorially supplied.

Rule 13. Advising Clients of Rules[1]

All lawyers accompanied by clients shall advise their clients of all the formalities of the courtroom and courtroom appearances.

Adopted Oct. 15, 1996.

1 Rule nameline editorially supplied.

SPECIAL RULES OF PRACTICE FOR THE MINNESOTA COURT OF APPEALS

Effective October 25, 1991

Including Amendments Received Through January 1, 2014

INTRODUCTION

These rules are informational for the practitioner and directive for the court. They are complementary to the Rules of Civil Appellate Procedure. These rules are subject to change without prior notice.

The special rules enable lawyers to understand the mechanics of the Court's procedure, provide a basis for evaluation and improvement of the administration of the Court, and promote public understanding of the judicial deliberative process.

Adopted Oct. 25, 1991, eff. Oct. 25, 1991.

Rule 1. Scheduling Cases

Placement on the calendar is in order of filing, except that cases involving child custody or juvenile protection will be given priority. Other cases may be expedited by rule, by statute, or by motion, based on a showing of good cause. Cases may be scheduled as soon as one responsive brief is filed.

If a case pending in the Supreme Court will be dispositive of a case pending before the Court of Appeals, the Chief Judge may order that scheduling be deferred until the Supreme Court has acted. Counsel should inform the court if they believe a case may be controlled by a case pending in the Supreme Court.

Counsel must advise the clerk, in writing before the case is scheduled, of any conflicts which will limit their availability for argument, and counsel must continue to file updated notices until the case has been scheduled. The Clerk of the Appellate Courts will notify counsel approximately one month in advance of the conference or hearing date, specifying the location of oral argument, if any, and the identity of the panel members assigned to the case.

Adopted Oct. 25, 1991, eff. Oct. 25, 1991. Amended Oct. 7, 2010, eff. Oct. 7, 2010.

Rule 2. Oral Argument

Members of the Minnesota Bar and attorneys admitted pro hac vice by the Court of Appeals may argue before the court. If any litigant is without counsel, the case will be submitted on the briefs and record, without oral arguments by any party. Minn. R. Civ. App. P. 134.01 sets out circumstances in which oral argument will not be allowed. Waiver of argument is governed by Minn. R. Civ. App. P. 134.05 and 134.06.

Appellants are allowed 15 minutes to present their principal arguments, respondents are allowed 15 minutes (to be divided, in cases involving multiple respondents), and appellants are allowed 5 minutes for rebuttal. Arguments are held in the Judicial Center in St. Paul and at appropriate locations in other judicial districts, as provided in Minn. Stat. § 480A.09, subd. 1 and Minn. R. Civ. App. P. 134.09, subd. 2.

A motion to reset or postpone oral argument must be made in writing, with a copy to opposing counsel, in accordance with Minn. R. Civ. App. P. 134.02. Reasons for the request must be stated. The court will reset a case only upon a showing of extreme emergency and no more than once. However, the court may reschedule cases on its own motion.

Counsel may use exhibits and graphic aids during oral argument. Counsel must make arrangements prior to hearing with the court's receptionist or with the local court administrator for the use of easels or other equipment. It is the responsibility of counsel to ensure that any trial exhibit to be used is obtained prior to argument.

Arguments are recorded by the court for internal use only. Recordings are retained only until the opinion is released. Prior approval of the Chief Judge or presiding judge is required to take photographs or to record or videotape oral argument. The media may cover proceedings in accordance with rules adopted by the Supreme Court.

Adopted Oct. 25, 1991, eff. Oct. 25, 1991. Amended Oct. 7, 2010, eff. Oct. 7, 2010.

Rule 3. Panels

Oral and non-oral cases will be assigned to panels of at least three judges as set forth in Minn. Stat. § 480A.08. One of the judges will be named by the Chief Judge to preside. If a judge assigned to the panel does not participate, the Chief Judge will assign another judge to the panel. Panels decide cases immediately following oral arguments and hold scheduled conferences to decide non-oral cases. After a decision is made, the presiding judge assigns preparation of the opinion to a member of the panel.

Adopted Oct. 25, 1991, eff. Oct. 25, 1991.

Rule 4. Opinions

Opinions state the nature of the case and the reasons for the decision. The panel will decide at its conference whether to publish an opinion. The publication decision is guided by Minn. Stat. § 480A.08, subd. 3, which provides for publication of opinions which establish a new rule of law, overrule a previous Court of Appeals decision not reviewed by the Minnesota Supreme Court, provide important procedural guidelines in interpreting statutes or administrative rules, involve a significant legal issue, or significantly aid in the administration of justice. All other opinions are unpublished.

Unpublished opinions are not precedential and may not be cited unless copies are provided to other counsel at least 48 hours before their use at any pretrial conference, hearing, or trial. If an unpublished opinion is cited in a brief or memorandum, copies must be provided to all other counsel at the time the brief or memorandum is served.

Pursuant to Minn. R. Civ. App. P. 136.01, subd. 1(a), the panel may decide to issue an order opinion.

Adopted Oct. 25, 1991, eff. Oct. 25, 1991.

Rule 5. Circulation of Opinions

When a draft opinion has been prepared, the authoring judge will circulate it to other members of the court for their information and comments.

Adopted Oct. 25, 1991, eff. Oct. 25, 1991. Amended Oct. 7, 2010, eff. Oct. 7, 2010.

Rule 6. Opinion Issuance

Except in extraordinary circumstances, opinions will be filed on Tuesday of each week. Counsel of record and unrepresented parties will receive notice if an opinion is to be filed in their case on Tuesday, so they can check the appellate courts' website at the designated time.

The official publications of the Court of Appeals, for the purpose of notice to the public and the legal profession, are Finance and Commerce and the St. Paul Legal Ledger. Notices may be published elsewhere at the discretion of the Chief Judge.

After release, the panel may make clerical changes in an opinion at any time ex parte.

Adopted Oct. 25, 1991, eff. Oct. 25, 1991. Amended Oct. 7, 2010, eff. Oct. 7, 2010.

Rule 7. Procedures After Decision

The Clerk of the Appellate Courts taxes costs and disbursements pursuant to Minn. R. Civ. App. P. 139.03. After expiration of the 30–day period to petition for review, the Clerk of Appellate Courts will transmit the judgment to the trial court administrator and return the trial record.

Adopted Oct. 25, 1991, eff. Oct. 25, 1991.

Rule 8. Motion Procedure

The form, content, and time periods for motions are prescribed in Minn. R. Civ. App. P. 127.

Motions and requests for extraordinary remedies are disposed of by the Chief Judge or by a special term panel designated by the Chief Judge. Routine motions, including those seeking voluntary dismissal, postponements, or extensions of time to file briefs, are disposed of by the Chief Judge. Motions made after submission of a case will be referred to the panel to which the case is assigned.

Adopted Oct. 25, 1991, eff. Oct. 25, 1991. Amended Oct. 7, 2010, eff. Oct. 7, 2010.

Rule 9. Criminal Appeals

In all appeals taken under Minn. R. Crim. P. 28, a statement of the case shall be filed as prescribed by Minn. R. Civ. App. P. 133.03.

Adopted Oct. 25, 1991, eff. Oct. 25, 1991.

Rule 10. Recusal of Judges

Court of Appeals judges are subject to the Code of Judicial Conduct adopted by the Supreme Court. Counsel may request that a member of the panel assigned to the case recuse by writing to the particular judge, setting out the reasons for the request. Application of the principles governing recusal is ultimately the responsibility of the individual judge. If a judge recuses, the Chief Judge names a replacement to the panel.

Adopted Oct. 25, 1991, eff. Oct. 25, 1991; renumbered Oct. 1, 1999, eff. Oct. 1, 1999.

Historical Notes

Derivation:

Minn.R.Ct Appeals 11.

Oct. 23, 1996.

Oct. 25, 1991.

Former rule: Former rule 10, adopted by court order dated October 25, 1991, related to the review of administrative rules, and was deleted by court order dated October 1, 1999.

Rule 11. Amicus Briefs

Where the same attorney or law firm represents a party and a proposed amicus curiae, leave to file an additional brief as amicus curiae is not granted unless the amicus brief will represent a position not already before the court or unless the interests of justice require.

Adopted Oct. 25, 1991, eff. Oct. 25, 1991; renumbered Oct. 1, 1999, eff. Oct 1, 1999.

Historical Notes

Derivation:

Minn.R.Ct Appeals 12.

Oct. 25, 1991.

Former rule: Former rule 11, adopted by court order dated October 25, 1991, related to the recusal of judges, and was renumbered rule 10 by court order dated October 1, 1999.

Rule 12. Remand From the Supreme Court

When the Supreme Court remands a case to the Court of Appeals, the court may request additional briefing, direct that oral arguments be heard, or take other appropriate action.

Adopted Oct. 25, 1991, eff. Oct. 25, 1991; renumbered Oct. 1, 1999, eff. Oct. 1, 1999.

Historical Notes

Derivation:

Minn.R.Ct Appeals 11.

Oct. 25, 1991.

Former rule: Former rule 12, adopted by court order dated October 25, 1991, related to amicus briefs, and was renumbered rule 11 by court order dated October 1, 1999.

Rule 13. Full Court Conference

The Chief Judge, subject to the authority of the Chief Justice, exercises general administrative authority over the court. All matters passed on by the bench shall be considered policy matters to be carried out and implemented by the Chief Judge.

The judges of the Court of Appeals meet on the first Monday of each month. If a holiday or other conflict occurs on that day, the conference may be rescheduled. Conferences are also held at the call of the Chief Judge or a majority of the judges.

Adopted Oct. 25, 1991, eff. Oct. 25, 1991; renumbered Oct. 1, 1999, eff. Oct. 1, 1991; amended Oct. 7, 2010, eff. Oct. 7, 2010.

Historical Notes

Derivation:

Minn.R.Ct Appeals 14.

Oct. 25, 1991.

Former rule: Former rule 13, adopted by court order dated October 25, 1991, related to cases remanded from the Supreme Court, and was renumbered rule 12 by court order dated October 1, 1999.

Rule 14. [Renumbered Rule 13 Oct. 1, 1999, eff. Oct. 1, 1999]

APPENDIX

FORM
PETITION FOR DECLARATORY JUDGMENT

[Deleted Oct. 1, 1999, eff. Oct. 1, 1999.]

SPECIAL RULES OF PRACTICE FOR THE MINNESOTA COURT OF APPEALS GOVERNING FAMILY LAW APPELLATE MEDIATION

Adopted Effective January 1, 2011

Including Amendments Received Through January 1, 2014

Rule 1. General

(a) Authority. These special rules of practice are made in accordance with the appellate court's authority under Minn. R. Civ. App. P. 133.01 to direct the parties, or their attorneys, to appear before a judge or person delegated by the appellate courts, for a prehearing conference to consider settlement.

(b) Scope. These special rules apply to appeals arising from marital dissolution actions, parentage actions, post decree modification and enforcement proceedings, including civil contempt actions, child support actions, including IV–D cases, and third-party custody and visitation actions.

(c) Suspension of Processing Deadlines. In the interests of judicial economy and to facilitate the mediation process, there is good cause under Minn. R. Civ. App. P. 102 to suspend the requirements of certain appellate processing rules, as specified in these special rules.

(d) Applicability of the Rules of Civil Appellate Procedure. The Minnesota Rules of Civil Appellate Procedure apply unless these special rules direct otherwise.

(e) Time Periods to File a Direct Appeal or Notice of Related Appeal. These special rules do not extend or otherwise affect the time periods to file a direct appeal or notice of related appeal under Minn. R. Civ. App. P. 104.01.

Adopted eff. Jan. 1, 2011.

Rule 2. Transcripts

(a) The time periods to file a transcript certificate and for preparation of the transcript under Minn. R. Civ. App. P. 110.02 are stayed in appeals that are referred to appellate family law mediation.

(b) If a transcript has already been ordered before the appeal is referred to mediation, upon receipt of the order referring the case to mediation, the party, if unrepresented, or the attorney for the party ordering the transcript, shall immediately notify the court reporter that transcript preparation is stayed pending mediation.

(c) If a party chooses to have transcript preparation continue during mediation, the party, if unrepresented, or the attorney for the party, shall file with the Clerk of Appellate Courts a written notification to that effect, with proof of service on the court reporter and the other parties. A party who chooses to have transcript preparation continue during mediation is responsible for payment of transcript expenses, even if the case fully settles.

Adopted eff. Jan. 1, 2011.

Rule 3. Briefing

The time periods for filing briefs under Minn. R. Civ. App. P. 131.01 are stayed pending mediation.

Adopted eff. Jan. 1, 2011.

Rule 4. Other Processing Deadlines

In addition to the time periods for filing a direct appeal or notice of related appeal, the following processing requirements are not stayed in appeals subject to mediation: the filing of a certified copy of the order and judgment appealed from and proof of service for the appeal papers under Minn. R. Civ. App. P. 103.01, subd. 1, and the filing of a statement of the case under Minn. R. Civ. App. P. 133.03.

Adopted eff. Jan. 1, 2011.

Rule 5. Untimely Appeals

Untimely appeals are not subject to mediation. A party may file a motion to dismiss a direct appeal or notice of related appeal that is not filed and served within the time periods specified in Minn. R. Civ. App. P. 104.01.

Adopted eff. Jan. 1, 2011.

Rule 6. Screening Process

(a) The Family Law Appellate Mediation Office screens new family law appeals to determine their suitability for mediation.

(b) If the initial screening shows mediation suitability, the Court of Appeals shall issue an order staying processing of the appeal and directing the parties to file a confidential mediator selection form and confidential information form.

(c) A party may request an exemption from mediation by including in the confidential information form, the request and the reason(s) for the request. This request may be granted at the discretion of the Family Law Appellate Mediation Office. If the request is granted, the parties shall be notified in writing no later than ten (10) days after the Family Law Appellate Mediation Office receives the confidential information form from all parties. When the public agency responsible for child support enforcement is a party or is providing services to a party with respect to the action, the public agency may opt out of the mediation and will thereafter be bound by any mediated decision and order.

(d) When multiple appeals involving the same parties are filed, all pending issues on appeal shall be consolidated into a single mediation process.

Adopted eff. Jan. 1, 2011.

Rule 7. Confidentiality

(a) All information obtained for and through the mediation process shall remain confidential and shall not become part of the appellate record.

(b) To the extent applicable, Minn. R. Gen. Pract. 114.08, 114.10(c), and 114.10(d), which govern confidentiality in civil cases subject to Alternative Dispute Resolution processes, are incorporated into these special rules by reference.

Adopted eff. Jan. 1, 2011.

Rule 8. Appellate Mediator Roster

(a) Appointment to the Appellate Mediator Roster. The court shall maintain a roster of approved appellate mediators and shall recruit mediators as needed throughout the state.

(b) Removal from the Appellate Mediator Roster. An appellate mediator may be removed from the appellate mediator roster if the mediator violates the Rule 114 Code of Ethics, fails to maintain good standing with the licensing board for the profession in which the person practices, fails to comply with the rules and policies of this program, or for other good cause shown.

Adopted eff. Jan. 1, 2011.

Rule 9. Mediation Process–Timelines

(a) Within ten (10) days of the Court of Appeals order staying the process of the appeal and referring the case for family law appellate mediation, the parties shall file with the Family Law Appellate Mediation Office a confidential mediator selection form and confidential information form.

(b) After receiving from both parties the confidential mediator selection form and confidential information form, the Family Law Appellate Mediation Office shall issue a letter appointing the mediator and the Family Law Appellate Mediation Office shall contact attorneys and pro se parties to schedule a premediation conference call.

(c) Parties shall begin mediation as soon as practicable after the premediation conference call and shall complete mediation no later than seventy (70) days after the premediation conference call, unless the Family Law Appellate Mediation Office receives a request for and grants an extension.

Adopted eff. Jan. 1, 2011.

Rule 10. Assignment of Mediator

(a) The Family Law Appellate Mediation Office shall assign a mediator from the appellate mediator roster to each case to be mediated.

(b) Before the mediation process begins, the parties shall sign a written agreement to mediate.

Adopted eff. Jan. 1, 2011.

Rule 11. Appellate Mediation Fees

The Family Law Appellate Mediation Office shall establish a schedule of fees to be paid by the parties to the appellate mediator.

Adopted eff. Jan. 1, 2011.

Rule 12. Liability of Appellate Mediator

Mediators appointed by the court serve in a quasi-judicial role and in the absence of willful and wanton misconduct are immune to claims as provided by law.

Adopted eff. Jan. 1, 2011.

Rule 13. Finalization of Mediation Process

(a) Mediation Settlement Agreement. In the event that the parties reach an agreement resolving all or any issues involved in the appeal, the parties, and counsel, if any, shall sign a Mediated Settlement Agreement setting out the essential terms of all agreements reached in mediation and, if applicable, designating the individual responsible for drafting and filing any additional documents needed to implement the agreement in the district court and the time for completion of that drafting and filing in the district court. The purpose of the Mediated Settlement Agreement is to memorialize the essence of the agreement for the parties, counsel, and the mediator, each of whom shall be given a copy of the signed agreement. Because of the purpose of this agreement, it shall not be filed with the Court of Appeals or the Family Law Appellate Mediation Office.

(b) Mediator Case Closing Notice. When the parties reach agreement resolving all issues on appeal and have signed a Mediation Settlement Agreement, or when the mediator has declared mediation concluded without agreement resolving all issues, the mediator shall mail to the parties, or counsel if represented, and file with the Family Law Appellate Mediation Office a completed Mediator Case Closing Notice informing the parties that:

(1) In the event agreement is reached on all issues involved in the appeal, the appeal shall be dismissed when appellant (and respondent if a related appeal is involved) file a Voluntary Dismissal with the Court of Appeals. If appellant (and respondent if a related appeal is involved) fails to voluntarily dismiss the appeal (and any related appeal) within forty-five (45) days of the date of this notice, the Court of Appeals shall issue an order vacating the stay of the appeal, setting a deadline for a completed initial transcript certificate to be filed, and providing that briefing shall proceed under Rule 131.01.

(2) In the event mediation is concluded without a full resolution of all issues, the Court of Appeals shall immediately issue an order vacating the stay of the appeal, setting a deadline for a completed initial transcript certificate to be filed, and providing that briefing shall proceed under Rule 131.01.

Adopted eff. Jan. 1, 2011.

Rule 14. Reinstatement of the Appeal

In the event that the district court does not approve a Mediated Settlement Agreement of all issues on which an appeal was taken, the mediation shall be treated as a failure to reach a settlement, and the appeal shall be reinstated following motion to the Court of Appeals by the appellant. A reinstatement motion shall contain a certified copy of the district court's order and shall be filed within ten days of that order with no new filing fee.

Adopted eff. Jan. 1, 2011.

Rule 15. Sanctions

(a) The Court of Appeals may sanction a party for the failure to comply with the requirements of the appellate mediation program. Neither the Family Law Appellate Mediation Office nor the mediator is authorized to impose sanctions.

(b) The Family Law Appellate Mediation Office may file a deficiency notice with the Court of Appeals if a party fails to comply with the requirements of the program. The Court of Appeals may issue an order compelling the party to comply and may also impose sanctions.

(c) The Court of Appeals may impose sanctions against a party who refuses to attend a mediation session or sessions, unreasonably delays the scheduling of mediation, or otherwise unreasonably impedes the procedures required for the mediation program.

(d) The Court of Appeals may impose sanctions on its own motion or on the motion of a party made in compliance with Minn. R. Civ. App. P. 127. A party's motion for sanctions may not be filed until mediation has been closed. A motion for sanctions may be filed but no later than within the time for taxation of costs under Minn. R. Civ. App. P. 139.03.

(e) Sanctions may include, but are not limited to, assessment of reasonable expenses caused by the failure of mediation, including an amount equivalent to mediator and/or attorney fees, assessment of all or a portion of appellate costs, or dismissal of an appeal or a notice of related appeal.

Adopted eff. Jan. 1, 2011.

GENERAL RULES OF PRACTICE FOR THE DISTRICT COURTS

Effective January 1, 1992

Including Amendments Received Through January 1, 2014

Research Note

See Minnesota Statutes Annotated, *Volume 51, for historical notes, case annotations, and cross references. The General Rules of Practice for the District Courts are discussed in Herr, 3A* Minnesota Practice–General Rules of Practice Annotated (2008 Ed.).

TITLE I. RULES APPLICABLE TO ALL COURT PROCEEDINGS

RULE 1. SCOPE OF RULES; MODIFICATION; SERVICE ON PARTIES; APPLICABILITY TO PRO SE PARTIES

RULE 2. COURT DECORUM; CONDUCT OF JUDGES AND LAWYERS

RULE 3. EX PARTE ORDERS

RULE 4. PICTURES AND VOICE RECORDINGS

RULE 5. APPEARANCE BY OUT OF STATE LAWYERS

RULE 6. FORM OF PLEADINGS

RULE 7. PROOF OF SERVICE

RULE 8. INTERPRETERS

RULE 9. FRIVOLOUS LITIGATION

RULE 10. TRIBAL COURT ORDERS AND JUDGMENTS

Comments

The order of the Minnesota Supreme Court [CX–89–1863, C6–84–2134] dated September 15, 1991 adopting the General Rules of Practice for the District Courts provides in part that "(t)he inclusion of Task Force notes, if any, is made for convenience and does not reflect court approval of the comments made therein."

The order of the Minnesota Supreme Court [CX–89–1863, C6–84–2134] dated November 13, 1992 amending the General Rules of Practice for the District Courts provides in part that "(t)he inclusion of Advisory Committee comments is made for convenience and does not reflect court approval of the comments made therein."

The order of the Minnesota Supreme Court [CX–89–1863] dated December 2, 1993 amending the General Rules of Practice for the District Courts provides in part that "(t)he inclusion of Implementation Committee comments is made for convenience and does not reflect court approval of the comments made therein."

The order of the Minnesota Supreme Court [CX–89–1863] dated December 14, 1993 amending the General Rules of Practice for the District Courts provides in part that "(t)he inclusion of Advisory Committee comments is made for convenience and does not reflect court approval of the comments made therein."

The order of the Minnesota Supreme Court [CX–89–1863, C6–84–2134] dated December 14, 1995, amending the General Rules of Practice for the District Courts provides in part that "(t)he inclusion of Advisory Committee comments is made for convenience and does not reflect court approval of the comments made therein."

TITLE I. RULES APPLICABLE TO ALL COURT PROCEEDINGS

RULE 1. SCOPE OF RULES; MODIFICATION; SERVICE ON PARTIES; APPLICABILITY TO PRO SE PARTIES

Rule 1.01. Scope

These rules shall apply in all trial courts of the state. These rules may be cited as Minn. Gen. R. Prac. _____.

Adopted Sept. 5, 1991, eff. Jan. 1, 1992.

Rule 1.02. Modification

A judge may modify the application of these rules in any case to prevent manifest injustice.

Adopted Sept. 5, 1991, eff. Jan. 1, 1992.

Rule 1.03. Service on Parties

When a paper is to be served on a party under these rules, service shall be made on the party's lawyer if represented, otherwise on the nonrepresented party directly.

Adopted Sept. 5, 1991, eff. Jan. 1, 1992.

Rule 1.04. Responsibility of Parties Appearing Pro Se

Whenever these rules require that an act be done by a lawyer, the same duty is required of a party appearing pro se.

Adopted Sept. 5, 1991, eff. Jan. 1, 1992.

Task Force Comment—1991 Adoption

Cross Reference: Minn.R.Civ.P. 5.02, 83.

RULE 2. COURT DECORUM; CONDUCT OF JUDGES AND LAWYERS

Rule 2.01. Behavior and Ceremony in General

(a) Acceptable Behavior. Dignity and solemnity shall be maintained in the courtroom. There shall be no unnecessary conversation, loud whispering, newspaper or magazine reading or other distracting activity in the courtroom while court is in session.

(b) Flag. The flags of the United States and the State of Minnesota shall be displayed on or in close proximity to the bench when court is in session.

(c) Formalities in Opening Court. At the opening of each court day, the formalities to be observed shall consist of the following: court personnel shall direct all present to stand, and shall say clearly and distinctly:

Everyone please rise! The District Court of the ________ Judicial District, County of ________, State of Minnesota is now open. Judge ________ presiding. Please be seated.

(Rap gavel or give other signal immediately prior to directing audience to be seated.)

At any time thereafter during the day that court is reconvened court personnel shall give warning by gavel or otherwise, and as the judge enters, cause all to stand until the Judge is seated.

(The above rule (to) or (to not) apply to midmorning and midafternoon recesses of the court at the option of the judge.)

(d) The Jury. Jurors shall take their places in the jury box before the judge enters the courtroom. Court personnel shall assemble the jurors when court is reconvened.

When a jury has been selected and is to be sworn, the presiding judge or clerk shall request everyone in the courtroom to stand.

(e) Court Personnel. Court personnel shall maintain order as litigants, witnesses and the public assemble in the courtroom, during trial and during recesses. Court personnel shall direct them to seats and refuse admittance to the courtroom in such trials where the courtroom is occupied to its full seating capacity.

(f) Swearing of Witnesses. When the witness is sworn, court personnel shall request the witness's full name, and after being sworn, courteously invite the witness to be seated on the witness stand.

(g) Manner of Administration of Oath. Oaths and affirmations shall be administered to jurors and witnesses in a slow, clear, and dignified manner. Witnesses should stand near the bench, or witness stand as sworn. The swearing of witnesses should be an impressive ceremony and not a mere formality.

Adopted Sept. 5, 1991, eff. Jan. 1, 1992. Amended Dec. 8, 1997, eff. Jan. 1, 1998.

Historical Notes

The order of the Minnesota Supreme Court [CX–89–1863] dated December 8, 1997, provides in part that "(t)he attached amendments shall apply to all actions pending on the effective date and to those filed thereafter."

Rule 2.02. Role of Judges

(a) Dignity. The judge shall be dignified, courteous, respectful and considerate of the lawyers, the jury and witnesses. The judge shall wear a robe at all trials and courtroom appearances. The judge shall at all times treat all lawyers, jury members, and witnesses fairly and shall not discriminate on the basis of race, color, creed, religion, national origin, sex, marital status, sexual preference, status with regard to public assistance, disability, or age.

(b) Punctuality. The judge shall be punctual in convening court, and prompt in the performance of judicial duties, recognizing that the time of litigants, jurors and attorneys is of value and that habitual lack of punctuality on part of a judge justifies dissatisfaction with the administration of the business of the court.

(c) Impartiality. During the presentation of the case, the judge shall maintain absolute impartiality, and shall neither by word or sign indicate favor to any party to the litigation. The judge shall be impersonal in addressing the lawyers, litigants and other officers of the court.

(d) Intervention. The judge should generally refrain from intervening in the examination of witnesses or argument of counsel; however, the court shall intervene upon its own initiative to prevent a miscarriage of justice or obvious error of law.

(e) Decorum in Court. The judge shall be responsible for order and decorum in the court and shall see to it at all times that parties and witnesses in the case are treated with proper courtesy and respect.

(f) Accurate Record. The judge shall be in complete charge of the trial at all times and shall see to it that everything is done to obtain a clear and accurate record of the trial. It is a duty to see that the witnesses testify clearly so that the reporter may obtain a correct record of all proceedings in court.

(g) Comment Upon Verdict. The judge should not comment favorably or adversely upon the verdict of a jury when it may indirectly influence the action of the jury in causes remaining to be tried.

Adopted Dec. 8, 1997, eff. Jan. 1, 1998.

Historical Notes

The order of the Minnesota Supreme Court [CX–89–1863] dated December 8, 1997, provides in part that "(t)he attached amendments shall apply to all actions pending on the effective date and to those filed thereafter."

Rule 2.03. Role of Attorneys

(a) Officer of Court. The lawyer is an officer of the court and should at all times uphold the honor and maintain the dignity of the profession, maintaining at all times a respectful attitude toward the court.

(b) Addressing Court or Jury. Except when making objections, lawyers should rise and remain standing while addressing the court or the jury. In addressing the court, the lawyer should refer to the judge as "Your Honor" or "The Court." Counsel shall not address or refer to jurors individually or by name or occupation, except during voir dire, and shall never use the first name when addressing a juror in voir dire examination. During trial, counsel shall not exhibit familiarity with the judge, jurors, witnesses, parties or other counsel, nor address them by use of first names (except for children).

(c) Approaching Bench. The lawyers should address the court from a position at the counsel table. If a lawyer finds it necessary to discuss some question out of the hearing of the jury at the bench, the lawyer may so indicate to the court and, if invited, approach the bench for the purpose indicated. In such an instance, the lawyers should never lean upon the bench nor appear to engage the court in a familiar manner.

(d) Non–Discrimination. Lawyers shall treat all parties, participants, other lawyers, and court personnel fairly and shall not discriminate on the basis of race, color, creed, religion, national origin, sex, marital status, sexual preference, status with regard to public assistance, disability, or age.

(e) Attire. Lawyers shall appear in court in appropriate courtroom attire.

Adopted Dec. 8, 1997, eff. Jan. 1, 1998.

Advisory Committee Comment—1997 Amendment

The majority of this rule was initially derived from the former Rules of Uniform Decorum. The adoption of these rules in 1991 included these provisions in Part H, Minnesota Civil Trialbook. They are recodified here to make it clear that the standards for decorum, for lawyers and judges, apply in criminal as well as civil proceedings.

The Task Force on Uniform Local Rules considered the recommendations of the Minnesota Supreme Court Task Force on Gender Fairness, and recommended Rule 2.03(d) be adopted to implement, in part, the recommendations of that body. *See Minnesota Supreme Court Task Force for Gender Fairness in the Courts,* 15 Wm. Mitchell L.Rev. 825 (1989). The rule specifically incorporated the definition of discriminatory conduct in the Minnesota Human Rights Act, Minn.Stat. § 363.01, subd. 1(1) (1990). The Task Force added to the statutory definition of discrimination the category of sexual preference.

The inclusion of these provisions in the rules is intended to establish uniform standards to be followed in most cases. Nothing in this rule limits the power of the court to modify the rules or their application in a particular case. *See* Rule 1.02. It is not intended that the failure to follow these rules, in itself, would be the subject of claimed error in the conduct of the trial court proceedings in the absence of aggravating circumstances, such as repeated violations or persistent violation after objections by a party or direction from the court.

Historical Notes

The order of the Minnesota Supreme Court [CX–89–1863] dated December 8, 1997, provides in part that "(t)he attached amendments shall apply to all actions pending on the effective date and to those filed thereafter."

The order of the Minnesota Supreme Court [CX–89–1863] dated December 8, 1997, amending the General Rules of Practice for the District Courts provides in part that "(t)he inclusion of Advisory Committee comments is made for convenience and does not reflect court approval of the comments made therein."

RULE 3. EX PARTE ORDERS

Rule 3.01. Notice

In any application for ex parte relief, the court may require a demonstration or explanation of the efforts made to notify affected parties, or the reasons why such efforts were not made. The reasons supporting ex parte relief should be recited in the order.

Adopted Sept. 5, 1991, eff. Jan. 1, 1992.

Rule 3.02. Prior Application

Before an ex parte order is issued, an affidavit shall be submitted with the application showing:

(1) No prior applications for the relief requested or for a similar order have been made; or,

(2) The court and judge to whom the prior application was made; the result of the prior application; and what new facts are presented with the current application.

Failure to comply with this rule may result in vacation of any order entered.

Adopted Sept. 5, 1991, eff. Jan. 1, 1992.

Task Force Comment—1991 Adoption

Rule 3.01 is new, although it codifies the practice of the vast majority of judges.

Rule 3.02 is derived from Rule 10 of the Code of Rules for the District Courts. This rule applies in all trial court proceedings, including criminal actions. The Minnesota Supreme Court Advisory Committee on Criminal Procedure joins the Task Force in recommending that this rule apply in all trial court proceedings.

The review of the efforts made to provide notice is an integral part of permitting ex parte relief to be granted. The rule does not specify what showing must be made and does not state how it is to be made because the Task Force recognizes that a wide variety of circumstances apply to the seeking and obtaining of ex parte orders. In some circumstances, there may be proper reasons to justify ex parte relief even if notice could be given, and in those limited instances, a showing of those reasons should be made and reviewed by the court. The more common situation will involve description of the efforts made to give notice. The court may require the information in written or affidavit form, may take oral testimony, or may base the decision on the statements of counsel, either in person or by telephone. The Task Force also believes that if notice to affected parties is deemed unnecessary, the order should state the facts supporting ex parte relief without notice.

RULE 4. PICTURES AND VOICE RECORDINGS

Rule 4.01. General Rule

Except as set forth in this rule, no pictures or voice recordings, except the recording made as the official court record, shall be taken in any courtroom, area of a courthouse where courtrooms are located, or other area designated by order of the chief judge made available in the office of the court administrator in the county, during a trial or hearing of any case or special proceeding incident to a trial or hearing, or in connection with any grand jury proceedings.

This rule may be superseded by specific rules of the Minnesota Supreme Court relating to use of cameras in the courtroom for courtroom security purposes, for use of videotaped recording of proceedings to create the official recording of the case, or for interactive video hearings pursuant to rule or order of the supreme court. This Rule 4 does not supersede the provisions of the Minnesota Rules of Public Access to Records of the Judicial Branch.

Adopted Sept. 5, 1991, eff. Jan. 1, 1992. Amended Dec. 14, 1993, eff. Jan. 1, 1994; Feb. 11, 2009, eff. March 1, 2009.

Rule 4.02. Exception

(a) A judge may authorize the use of electronic or photographic means for the presentation of evidence, for the perpetuation of a record or for other purposes of judicial administration.

(b) A judge may authorize the broadcasting, televising, recording or photographing of investitive, ceremonial or naturalization proceedings.

(c) A judge may authorize, with the consent of all parties in writing or made on the record prior to the commencement of the trial in criminal proceedings, and without the consent of all parties in civil proceedings, the photographic or electronic recording and reproduction of appropriate court proceedings under the following conditions:

(i) There shall be no audio or video coverage of jurors at any time during the trial, including *voir dire*.

(ii) There shall be no audio or video coverage of any witness who objects thereto in writing or on the record before testifying.

(iii) Audio or video coverage of judicial proceedings shall be limited to proceedings conducted within the courtroom, and shall not extend to activities or events substantially related to judicial proceedings that occur in other areas of the court building.

(iv) There shall be no audio or video coverage within the courtroom during recesses or at any other time the judge is not present and presiding.

(v) During or preceding a jury trial, there shall be no audio or video coverage of hearings that take place outside the presence of the jury. Without limiting the generality of the foregoing sentence, such hearings in criminal proceedings would include those to determine the admissibility of evidence, and those to determine various motions, such as motions to suppress evidence, for judgment of acquittal, *in limine* and to dismiss. This provision does not prohibit audio or video coverage of appropriate pretrial hearings in civil proceedings, such as hearings on dispositive motions.

(vi) There shall be no audio or video coverage in cases involving child custody, marriage dissolution, juvenile proceedings, child protection proceedings, paternity proceedings, civil commitment proceedings, petitions for orders for protection, motions to suppress evidence, police informants, relocated witnesses, sex crimes, trade secrets, undercover agents, and proceedings that are not accessible to the public.

Adopted Feb. 11, 2009, eff. March 1, 2009. Amended March 12, 2009, eff. March 12, 2009; March 11, 2011, eff. July 1, 2011; April 21, 2011, eff. July 1, 2011.

Historical Notes

The order of the Minnesota Supreme Court dated March 11, 2011 provides in part that the amendments to 4.02, 4.03 and 4.04 are effective July 1, 2011, and that "except as otherwise provided, the attached amendments shall apply to all actions pending on the effective date of this order and those filed thereafter".

Rule 4.03. Procedures Relating to Requests for Audio or Video Coverage of Authorized District Court Civil Proceedings

The following procedures apply to audio and video coverage of civil proceedings where authorized under Rule 4.02(c):

(a) Notice. Unless notice is waived by the trial judge, the media shall provide written notice of their intent to cover authorized district court civil proceedings by either audio or video means to the trial judge, all counsel of record, and any parties appearing without counsel as far in advance as practicable, and at least 10 days before the commencement of the hearing or trial. A copy of the written notice shall also be provided to the State Court Administrator's Court Information Office. The media shall also notify their respective media coordinator, identified as provided under part (e) of this rule, of the request to cover proceedings in advance of submitting the request to the trial judge, if possible, or as soon thereafter as possible.

(b) Objections. If a party opposes audio or video coverage, the party shall provide written notice of the party's objections to the presiding judge, the other parties, and the media requesting coverage as soon as practicable, and at least 3 days before the commencement of the hearing or trial in cases where the media have given at least 10 days' notice of their intent to cover the proceedings. The judge shall rule on any objections and make a decision on audio or video coverage before the commencement of the hearing or trial. However, the judge has the discretion to limit, terminate, or temporarily suspend audio or video coverage of an entire case or portions of a case at any time.

(c) Witness Information and Objection to Coverage. At or before the commencement of the hearing or trial in cases with audio or video coverage, each party shall inform all witnesses the party plans to call that their testimony will be subject to audio or video recording unless the witness objects in writing or on the record before testifying.

(d) Appeals. No ruling of the trial judge relating to the implementation or management of audio or video coverage under this rule shall be appealable until the trial has been completed, and then only by a party.

(e) Media Coordinators. Media coordinators for various areas of the state shall be identified on the main state court web site. The media coordinators shall facilitate interaction between the courts and the electronic media regarding audio or video coverage of authorized district court civil proceedings. Responsibilities of the media coordinators include:

(i) Compiling basic information (e.g., case identifiers, judge, parties, attorneys, dates and coverage duration) on all requests for use of audio or video coverage of authorized civil trial court proceedings for their respective court location(s) as identified on the main state court web site, and making aggregate forms of the information publicly available;

(ii) Notifying the Minnesota Court Information Office of all requests for audio and video coverage of civil trial court proceedings for their respective court location(s) as identified on the main state court web site;

(iii) Explaining to persons requesting video or audio coverage of civil trial court proceedings for their respective court location(s) the local practices, procedures, and logistical details of the court related to audio and video coverage;

(iv) Resolving all issues related to pooling of cameras and microphones related to video or audio coverage of civil trial court proceedings for their respective court location(s).

Adopted March 11, 2011, eff. July 1, 2011. Amended Jan. 19, 2012, eff. May 1, 2012; Dec. 3, 2013, eff. Dec. 3, 2013.

Historical Notes

The order of the Minnesota Supreme Court dated March 11, 2011 provides in part that the amendments to 4.02, 4.03 and 4.03 are effective July 1, 2011, and that "except as otherwise provided, the attached amendments shall apply to all actions pending on the effective date of this order and those filed thereafter".

The order of the Minnesota Supreme Court [ADM09–8009] dated January 19, 2012, provides in part that the amendments to the General Rules of Practice for the District Courts are effective on May 1, 2012, and that the amendments "shall apply to all actions pending on the effective date and to those filed thereafter."

The order of the Minnesota Supreme Court [ADM09–8009] dated December 3, 2013, provided in part that the amendments were effective December 3, 2013, and "shall apply to all actions pending on the effective date and those filed thereafter."

Rule 4.04. Technical Standards for Photography, Electronic and Broadcast Coverage of Judicial Proceedings

The trial court may regulate any aspect of the proceedings to ensure that the means of recording will not distract participants or impair the dignity of the proceedings. In the absence of a specific order imposing additional or different conditions, the following provisions apply to all proceedings.

(a) Equipment and personnel.

(1) Not more than one portable television or movie camera, operated by not more than one person, shall be permitted in any district court proceeding.

(2) Not more than one still photographer, utilizing not more than two still cameras with not more than two lenses for each camera and related equipment for print purposes, shall be permitted in any proceeding in any district court.

(3) Not more than one audio system for radio broadcast purposes shall be permitted in any proceeding in any district court. Audio pickup for all media purposes shall be accomplished from existing audio systems present in the court. If no technically suitable audio system exists in the court, microphones and related wiring essential for media purposes shall be unobtrusive and shall be located in places designated in advance of any proceeding by the judge.

(4) Any "pooling" arrangements among the media required by these limitations on equipment and personnel shall be the sole responsibility of the media without calling upon the judge to mediate any dispute as to the appropriate media representative or equipment authorized to cover a particular proceeding. In the absence of advance media agreement on disputed equipment or personnel issues, the judge shall exclude from a proceeding all media personnel who have contested the pooling arrangement.

(b) Sound and light.

(1) Only television camera and audio equipment which does not produce distracting sound or light shall be employed to cover judicial proceedings. Excepting modifications and additions made pursuant to Paragraph (e) below, no artificial, mobile lighting device of any kind shall be employed with the television equipment.

(2) Only still camera equipment which does not produce distracting sound or light shall be employed to cover judicial proceedings.

(3) Media personnel must demonstrate to the trial judge adequately in advance of any proceeding that the equipment sought to be utilized meets the sound and light requirements of this rule. A failure to demonstrate that these criteria have been met for specific equipment shall preclude its use in any proceeding.

(c) Location of equipment and personnel.

(1) Television camera equipment shall be positioned in such location in the court as shall be designated by the judge. The area designated shall provide reasonable access to coverage. When areas that permit reasonable access to coverage are provided, all television camera and audio equipment must be located in an area remote from the court.

(2) A still camera photographer shall position himself or herself in such location in the court as shall be designated by the judge. The area designated shall provide reasonable access to coverage. Still camera photographers shall assume a fixed position within the designated area and, once a photographer has established himself or herself in a shooting position, he or she shall act so as not to attract attention by distracting movement. Still camera photographers shall not be permitted to move about in order to obtain photographs of court proceedings.

(3) Broadcast media representatives shall not move about the court facility while proceedings are in session.

(d) Movement of equipment during proceedings. News media photographic or audio equipment shall not be placed in, or removed from, the district court except before commencement or after adjournment of proceedings each day, or during a recess. Microphones or taping equipment, once positioned as required by Paragraph (a)(3) above, may not be moved from their position during the pendency of the proceeding. Neither television film magazines nor still camera film or lenses may be changed within a court except during a recess in the proceedings.

(e) Courtroom light sources. When necessary to allow news coverage to proceed, modifications and additions may be made in light sources existing in the facility, provided such modifications or additions do not produce distracting light and are installed and maintained without public expense. Such modifications or additions are to be presented to the judge for review before their implementation.

(f) Conferences of counsel. To protect the attorney-client privilege and the effective right to counsel, there shall be no video or audio pickup or broadcast of the conferences which occur in a court between attorneys and their client, co-counsel of a client, opposing counsel, or between counsel and the judge held at the bench. In addition, there shall be no video pickup or broadcast of work papers of such persons.

(g) Impermissible use of media material. None of the film, videotape, still photographs or audio reproductions developed during, or by virtue of, coverage of a judicial proceeding shall be admissible as evidence in the proceeding out of which it arose, any proceeding subsequent or collateral thereto, or upon any retrial or appeal of such proceedings.

Adopted Feb. 11, 2009, eff. March 1, 2009. Amended March 11, 2011, eff. July 1, 2011; Dec. 3, 2013, eff. Dec. 3, 2013.

Historical Notes

The order of the Minnesota Supreme Court dated March 11, 2011 provides in part that the amendments to 4.02, 4.03 and 4.04 are effective July 1, 2011, and that "except as otherwise provided, the attached amendments shall apply to all actions pending on the effective date of this order and those filed thereafter".

The order of the Minnesota Supreme Court [ADM09–8009] dated December 3, 2013, provided in part that these amendments were effective December 3, 2013, and "shall apply to all actions pending on the effective date and those filed thereafter."

RULE 5. APPEARANCE BY OUT OF STATE LAWYERS

Lawyers duly admitted to practice in the trial courts of any other jurisdiction may appear in any of the courts of this state provided (a) the pleadings are also signed by a lawyer duly admitted to practice in the State of Minnesota, and (b) such lawyer admitted in Minnesota is also present before the court, in chambers or in the courtroom or participates by telephone in any hearing conducted by telephone. In a subsequent appearance in the same action the out-of-state lawyer may, in the discretion of the court, conduct the proceedings without the presence of Minnesota counsel.

Any lawyer appearing pursuant to this rule shall be subject to the disciplinary rules and regulations governing Minnesota lawyers and by applying to appear or appearing in any action shall be subject to the jurisdiction of the Minnesota courts.

Adopted Sept. 5, 1991, eff. Jan. 1, 1992.

Task Force Comment—1991 Adoption

This rule is derived from 3rd Dist. R. 1.

This rule is intended to supplement Minn. Stat. § 481.02 (1990) and would supersede the statute to the extent the rule may be inconsistent with it. This rule recognizes and preserves the power and responsibility of the court to determine the proper role to be played by lawyers not admitted to practice in Minnesota.

RULE 6. FORM OF PLEADINGS

Rule 6.01. Format

All pleadings or other documents required to be filed shall be double spaced and legibly handwritten, typewritten, or printed on one side on plain unglazed paper of good texture. Every page shall have a top margin of not less than one inch, free from all typewritten, printed, or other written matter. Any pleading or document either permitted or required to be served or filed electronically must conform to the format requirements contained in the court rules or orders relating to electronic filing.

Amended Nov. 13, 1992, eff. Jan. 1, 1993; Nov. 30, 2005, eff. Jan. 1, 2006; May 24, 2012, eff. Sept. 1, 2012.

Advisory Committee Comment—2006 Amendment

Rule 6.01 is amended to delete a sentence dealing with filing by facsimile. The former provision is, in effect, superseded by Minn. R. Civ. P. 5.05, as amended effective January 1, 2006.

Advisory Committee Comment—2012 Amendment

Rule 6.01 is amended to dovetail the requirements for the form of paper pleadings, as set forth in the prior text of this rule, with the fundamentally different format required for documents electronically filed and served. Those format requirements are generally set forth in new Rule 14.05.

The order of the Minnesota Supreme Court [ADM 10–8011] dated May 24, 2012, provided in part that "These amendments shall apply to all actions or proceedings commenced on or after the effective date."

Rule 6.02. Paper Size

All papers served or filed by any party shall be on standard size 8½ X 11 inch paper.

Amended Nov. 13, 1992, eff. Jan. 1, 1993.

Rule 6.03. Backings Not Allowed

No pleading, motion, order, or other paper offered to the court administrator for filing shall be backed or otherwise enclosed in a covering. Any papers that cannot be attached by a single staple in the upper lefthand corner shall be clipped or tied by an alternate means at the upper lefthand corner.

Amended Nov. 13, 1992, eff. Jan. 1, 1993.

Advisory Committee Comment—1992 Amendments

This rule is based on 4th Dist. R. 1.01(a) & (b), with changes.

Although the rule permits the filing of handwritten documents, the clearly preferred practice in Minnesota is for typewritten documents. Similarly, commercially printed papers are rarely, if ever, used in Minnesota trial court practice, and the use of printed briefs in appellate practice is discouraged.

All courts in Minnesota converted to use of "letter size" paper in 1982. *See* Order Mandating 8½ x 11 Inch Size Paper For All Filings in All Courts in the State, Minn.Sup.Ct., Apr. 16, 1982 (no current file number assigned), *reprinted in* Minn.Rules of Ct. 665 (West pamph. ed. 1992). Papers filed in the appellate courts must also be on letter-sized paper. *See* Minn.R.Civ.App.P. 132.01, subd. 1. This rule simply reiterates the requirement for the trial courts.

Cross Reference: Minn.R.Civ.P. 5.05, 10.

RULE 7. PROOF OF SERVICE

When service has been made before filing, proofs of service shall be affixed to all documents so that the identity of the instrument is not obscured. If a document is filed before service, proof of service shall be filed within 10 days after service is made. When service is made electronically when authorized by and in accordance with Rule 14 of these rules, the record of service on the e-service system shall constitute proof of service.

Amended Nov. 13, 1992, eff. Jan. 1, 1993; Dec. 14, 1995, eff. Jan. 1, 1996; May 24, 2012, eff. Sept. 1, 2012.

Advisory Committee Comments—1995 Amendments

This rule derived from Rule 13 of the Code of Rules for the District Courts.

The second sentence is new, drafted to provide for filing of documents where service is to be made after filing.

The Committee recommends amendment of the rule to require a specific rather than subjective standard for the filing of proof of service. Although the Committee heard requests to change the rule to require that all documents be filed with proof of service attached, the Committee believes that such a rule is neither helpful nor necessary. Such a rule would make it difficult to serve and file documents at the same time, and would probably result in greater problems relating to untimely service and filing. Nonetheless, there appear to be a number of situations where proof of service is not filed for a substantial period of time, resulting in confusion in the courts. The rule is accordingly amended to change the requirement from filing "promptly" after service to "within ten days" after service. The Committee believes this period is more than sufficient for filing a proof of service. The Committee is also sensitive to a potential problem that would arise with a requirement that proof of service accompany documents at the time of filing. The Committee continues to believe that documents, in whatever form, should not be rejected for filing by the court administrators. Rather, documents should be filed as submitted and the court should deal with any deficiencies or irregularities in the documents in an orderly way, having in mind the mandate of Rule 1 of the Minnesota Rules of Civil Procedure that the rules be interpreted to advance the "just, speedy, and inexpensive" determination of every action.

Advisory Committee Comment—2012 Amendment

Rule 7 is amended to make it clear that a separate proof of service is not required for documents served using the court's e-service system in cases where that method is authorized by the rules. Proof of service exists in the system's records and that record of service suffices to prove service for all purposes.

The order of the Minnesota Supreme Court [ADM 10-8011] dated May 24, 2012, provided in part that "These amendments shall apply to all actions or proceedings commenced on or after the effective date."

RULE 8. INTERPRETERS

DEFINITIONS

1. "Review Panel" means the Minnesota Court Interpreter Review Panel, which is comprised of two district court judges and one court administrator appointed by the Chief Justice of the Minnesota Supreme Court.

2. "Coordinator" means the Court Interpreter Program Coordinator assigned to the State Court Administrator's Office.

3. "Good Character" means traits that are relevant to and have a rational connection with the present fitness or capacity of an applicant to provide interpretation services in court proceedings.

4. "Roster" means the Minnesota statewide roster of court interpreters.

Adopted Sept. 18, 1996, eff. Sept. 19, 1996. Amended October 13, 2005, eff. Jan. 1, 2006; Jan. 12, 2006.

Historical Notes

The order of the Minnesota Supreme Court dated January 12, 2006, provides in part that "the attached corrective amendments to Rule 8 of the General Rules of Practice for the District Courts are prescribed and promulgated to be effective retroactively to January 2, 2006".

Rule 8.01. Statewide Roster

The State Court Administrator shall maintain and publish annually a statewide roster of certified and non-certified interpreters which shall include:

(a) Certified Court Interpreters: To be included on the Statewide Roster, certified court interpreters must have satisfied all certification requirements pursuant to Rule 8.04.

(b) Non-certified Foreign Language Court Interpreters: To be included on the Statewide Roster, foreign language court interpreters must have: (1) completed the interpreter orientation program sponsored by the State Court Administrator; (2) filed with the State Court Administrator a written affidavit agreeing to be bound by the Code of Professional Responsibility for Interpreters in the Minnesota State Court System as the same may be amended from time to time; (3) received a passing score on a written ethics examination administered by the State Court Administrator; and (4) demonstrated minimal language proficiency in English and any foreign language(s) for which the interpreter will be listed, as established by protocols developed by the State Court Administrator.

(c) Non-certified Sign Language Court Interpreters: To be included on the Statewide Roster, non-certified sign language court interpreters must

(1) have satisfied the three requirements set forth above in Rule 8.01(b);

(2) be a member in good standing with the Registry of Interpreters for the Deaf (RID) or with the National Association of the Deaf (NAD); and,

(3) possess

(i) both a valid Certificate of Transliteration (CT) and a valid Certificate of Interpretation (CI) from RID; or

(ii) a valid Comprehensive Skills Certificate (CSC) from RID; or

(iii) a valid Level 5 certificate from NAD; or

(iv) a valid Certified Deaf Interpreter (CDI) or Certified Deaf Interpreter Provisional (CDIP) certificate from RID; or

(v) another equivalent valid certification approved by the State Court Administrator.

Adopted Nov. 9, 1995, eff. Jan. 1, 1996. Amended Aug. 5, 1997, eff. Jan. 1, 1998; March 14, 2002, eff. March 15, 2002; Oct. 13, 2005, eff. Jan. 1, 2006; Dec. 28, 2006, eff. Jan. 1, 2007.

Advisory Committee Comment 1997 Amendment

It is the policy of the state to provide interpreters to litigants and witnesses in civil and criminal proceedings who are handicapped in communication. Minn.Stat. §§ 611.30–.32 (1996); Minn.R.Crim.P. 5.01, 15. 03, 15.11, 21.01, 26.03, 27.04, subd. 2; Minn.Stat. § 546.44, subd. 3 (1996); *see also* 42 U.S.C. § 12101; 28 C.F.R. Part 35, § 130 (prohibiting discrimination in public services on basis of disability).

To effectuate that policy, the Minnesota Supreme Court has initiated a statewide orientation program of training for court interpreters and promulgated the Rules on Certification of Court Interpreters. Pursuant to Rule 8.01 of the General Rules of Practice for the District Courts, the State Court Administrator has established a statewide roster of court interpreters who have completed the orientation program on the Minnesota court system and court interpreting and who have filed an affidavit attesting that they understand and agree to comply with the Code of Professional Responsibility for Court Interpreters adopted by the Minnesota Supreme Court on September 18, 1995. The creation of the roster is the first step in a process that is being undertaken to ensure the competence of court interpreters. To be listed on the roster, a non-certified court interpreter must attend an orientation course provided or approved by the State Court Administrator. The purpose of the orientation is to provide interpreters with information regarding the Code of Professional Responsibility, the role of interpreters in our courts, skills required of court interpreters, the legal process, and legal terminology. Merely being listed on the roster does not certify or otherwise guarantee an interpreter's competence.

In 1997, two key changes were made to this rule. First, interpreters are now required to receive a passing score on the ethics examination before they are eligible to be listed on the Statewide Roster. This change was implemented to ensure that court interpreters on the Statewide Roster have a demonstrated knowledge of the Code of Professional Responsibility.

Second, to be eligible to be listed on the Statewide Roster, non-certified sign language court interpreters are required to possess certificates from the Registry of Interpreters for the Deaf (RID), which demonstrate that the interpreter has minimum competency skills in sign language. This change was recommended by the Advisory Committee because of reports to the Committee that courts were hiring sign language interpreters who completed the orientation training, but who were not certified by RID. This practice was troubling because prior to the promulgation of Rule 8, courts generally adopted the practice of using only RID certified sign language interpreters to ensure a minimum level of competency. Unlike most spoken language interpreting fields, the field of sign language interpreting is well established with nationally developed standards for evaluation and certification of sign language interpreters. Because of the long history of RID, its certification program, the availability of RID certified sign language interpreters in Minnesota and the recent incidents when courts have deviated from their general practice of appointing RID certified sign language interpreters, the Advisory Committee determined that it is appropriate and necessary to amend Rule 8 to maintain the current levels of professionalism and competency among non-certified sign language court interpreters.

Advisory Committee Comments—2007 Amendment

Rule 8.01(b) is amended to add a new subsection (4). This subsection imposes an additional requirement that court interpreters demonstrate proficiency in English as well as the foreign languages for which they will be listed. This provision is necessary because certification is currently offered only in 12 languages and many of the state's interpreters are not certified. This change is intended to minimize the current problems involving need to use non-certified interpreters who now often do not possess sufficient English language skills to be effective.

Historical Notes

The order of the Minnesota Supreme Court [C9-94-1898] dated August 5, 1997, amending the General Rules of Practice for the District Courts provides in part that "(t)he inclusion of Advisory Committee comments is made for convenience and does not reflect court approval of the comments made therein."

The order of the Minnesota Supreme Court [CX-89-1863] dated March 14, 2002, provides in part that the amendments to Rules 8.01 and 8.02 are effective March 15, 2002, that these amendments shall apply to all sign language interpreters used by the Minnesota Judiciary on or after the effective date, and that "(t)he inclusion of Advisory Committee comments is made for convenience and does not reflect court approval of the statements made therein."

Rule 8.02. Appointment

(a) Use of Certified Court Interpreter. Whenever an interpreter is required to be appointed by the court, the court shall appoint only a certified court interpreter who is listed on the statewide roster of interpreters established by the State Court Administrator under Rule 8.01, except as provided in Rule 8.02(b), (c) and (d). A certified court interpreter shall be presumed competent to interpret in all court proceedings. The court may, at any time, make further inquiry into the appointment of a particular certified court interpreter. Objections made by a party regarding special circumstances which render the certified court interpreter unqualified to interpret in the proceeding must be made in a timely manner.

(b) Use of Non-certified Court Interpreter On The Statewide Roster. If the court has made diligent efforts to obtain a certified court interpreter as required by Rule 8.02(a) and found none to be available, the court shall appoint a non-certified court interpreter who is otherwise competent and is listed on the Statewide Roster established by the State Court Administrator under Rule 8.01. In determining whether a non-certified court interpreter is competent, the court shall apply the screening standards developed by the State Court Administrator.

(c) Use of Non-certified Foreign Language Court Interpreter Not On The Statewide Roster. Only after the court has exhausted the requirements of Rule 8.02(a) and (b) may the court appoint a non-certified foreign language interpreter who is not listed on the Statewide Roster and who is otherwise competent. In determining whether a non-certified foreign language interpreter is competent, the court shall apply the screening standards developed by the State Court Administrator.

(d) Use of Non-certified Sign Language Court Interpreter Not On The Statewide Roster. Only after exhausting the requirements of Rule 8.02(a) and (b) may the court appoint a non-certified sign language interpreter(s) not on the Statewide Roster. The court must appoint an interpreter(s) who can establish effective communication and who is (are):

(1) an interpreter who is a member in good standing with RID or NAD who possesses both a valid CT and a valid CI; or a valid CSC from RID; or a valid Level 5 certificate from NAD; or a valid CDI or CDIP certificate; or another equivalent valid certification approved by the State Court Administrator. If no such interpreter is available.

(2) a team including an interpreter with a valid CDI or CDIP certificate and an interpreter who has a valid CI *or* a valid CT from RID. If no such interpreters are available, as a last resort.

(3) an interpreter with a valid CI from RID.

Adopted Nov. 9, 1995, eff. Jan. 1, 1996. Amended Aug. 5, 1997, eff. Jan. 1, 1998; March 14, 2002, eff. March 15, 2002.

Advisory Committee Comment 2002 Amendment

Rule 8.02(a) requires that courts use certified court interpreters. If certified court interpreters are not available or cannot be located, courts should next use only interpreters listed on the statewide roster maintained by the State Court Administrator. Rule 8.02 recognizes, however, that in rare circumstances it will not be possible to appoint an interpreter from the statewide roster. Non-roster interpreters and telephone interpreting services, such as AT & T's Language Lines Service, should be used only as a last resort because of the limitations of such services including the lack of a minimum orientation to the Minnesota Court System and to the requirements of court interpreting. For a detailed discussion of the issues, see Court Interpretation: Model Guides for Policy and Practice in the State Courts, chapter 8 (National Center for State Courts, 1995), a copy of which is available from the State Court Administrator's Office.

To avoid unreasonable objections to a certified court interpreter in a proceeding, the rule makes a presumption that the certified court interpreter is competent. However, the rule also recognizes that there are situations when an interpreter may be competent to interpret, but not qualified. Examples of such situations include when an interpreter has a conflict of interest or the user of the interpreter services has unique demands, such as services tailored to a person with minimal language skills, that the interpreter is not as qualified to meet.

Rule 8.02(b) requires that courts make "diligent" efforts to locate a certified court interpreter before appointing a non-certified court interpreter. Because the certification process is still in an early stage and because it is important to ensure that courts use competent interpreters, courts should seek the services of certified court interpreters who are located outside the court's judicial district if none can be found within its own district. In addition, courts should consider modifying the schedule for a matter if there is difficulty locating a certified interpreter for a particular time.

Because the certification program being implemented by the State Court Administrator is still new, interpreters are being certified in only certain languages at this time. The Advisory Committee recognizes that it may be some time before certification is provided for all languages used in our courts. However, the committee feels strongly that for those languages for which certification has been issued, the courts must utilize certified court interpreters to ensure that its interpreters are qualified. If a court uses non-certified court interpreters, court administrators should administer the screening standards prior to hiring an interpreter. However, the presiding judge is still primarily responsible for ensuring the competence and qualifications of the interpreter. A model voir dire to determine the competence and qualifications of an interpreter is set forth in the State Court Administrator's Best Practices Manual on Court Interpreters.

The Supreme Court has received reports that courts do not always comply with Rule 8.02(b)'s requirements that courts make "diligent" efforts to locate a certified court interpreter before appointing a non-certified court interpreter. Apparently there is some confusion about the meaning of "diligent" efforts. To clarify, to satisfy the diligent efforts requirement a court must demonstrate that, after receiving a request for an interpreter, the court made prompt attempts to hire a *certified* court interpreter. If the court could not find a certified court interpreter within its judicial district, it must show that it attempted to locate a certified interpreter in another judicial district. If no certified interpreter is available, the court must consider modifying the schedule for the matter before resorting to hiring a non-certified court interpreter.

Historical Notes

The order of the Minnesota Supreme Court [C9-94-1898] dated August 5, 1997, amending the General Rules of Practice for the District Courts provides in part that "(t)he inclusion of Advisory

Committee comments is made for convenience and does not reflect court approval of the comments made therein."

The order of the Minnesota Supreme Court [CX-89-1863] dated March 14, 2002, provides in part that the amendments to Rules 8.01 and 8.02 are effective March 15, 2002, that these amendments shall apply to all sign language interpreters used by the Minnesota Judiciary on or after the effective date, and that "(t)he inclusion of Advisory Committee comments is made for convenience and does not reflect court approval of the statements made therein."

Rule 8.03. Disqualification From Proceeding

A judge may disqualify a court interpreter from a proceeding for good cause. Good cause for disqualification includes, but is not limited to, an interpreter who engages in the following conduct:

(a) Knowingly and willfully making a false interpretation while serving in a proceeding;

(b) Knowingly and willfully disclosing confidential or privileged information obtained while serving in an official capacity;

(c) Failing to follow applicable laws, rules of court, or the Code of Professional Responsibility for Interpreters in the Minnesota State Court System.

Adopted Nov. 9, 1995, eff. Jan. 1, 1996. Amended Aug. 5, 1997, eff. Jan. 1, 1998.

Advisory Committee Comment 1995

Interpreters must take an oath or affirmation to make a true interpretation to the best of their ability, to the person handicapped in communication and to officials. Minn.Stat. §§ 546.44, subd. 2; 611.33, subd. 2 (1994). Interpreters cannot disclose privileged information without consent. Minn.Stat. §§ 546.44, subd. 4; 611.33, subd. 4 (1994). These and other requirements are also addressed in the Code of Professional Responsibility for Interpreters in the Minnesota State Court System.

Rule 8.04. General Requirement for Court Interpreter Certification

(a) Eligibility for Certification. An applicant is eligible for certification upon establishing to the satisfaction of the State Court Administrator:

1. age of at least 18 years;

2. good character and fitness;

3. inclusion on the Statewide Roster of court interpreters maintained by the State Court Administrator's office in accordance with Rule 8 of the General Rules of Practice for the District Courts;

4. passing score on legal interpreting competency examination administered or approved by the State Court Administrator's Office; and

5. passing score on a written ethics examination administered by the State Court Administrator's Office.

Adopted Sept. 18, 1996, eff. Sept. 19, 1996. Amended Oct. 13, 2005, eff. Jan. 1, 2006.

Rule 8.05. Examination for Legal Interpreting Competency

(a) Examination. Examinations for legal interpreting competency in specific languages shall be administered at such times and places as the Coordinator may designate.

1. **Scope of Examination.** Applicants for certification in interpreting in a spoken or sign language may be tested on any combination of the following:

   a. Sight Interpretation;

   b. Consecutive Interpretation;

   c. Simultaneous Interpretation; and

   d. Transliteration (when applicable).

2. **Denial of Opportunity to Test.** An applicant may be denied permission to take an examination if an application, together with the application fee, is not complete and filed in a timely manner.

3. **Results of Examination.** The results of the examination, which may include scores, shall be released to examinees by regular mail to the address listed in the Coordinator's files. Statistical information relating to the examinations, applicants, and the work of the State Court Administrator's Office may be released at the discretion of the State Court Administrator's Office. Pass/fail examination results may be released to (1) District Administrators by the State Court Administrator's Office for purposes of assuring that interpreters are appointed in accordance with Rule 8.02, and (2) any state court interpreter certification authority.

4. **Testing Accommodations.** A qualified applicant with a disability who requires reasonable accommodations must submit a written request to the Coordinator at the same time the application is filed. The Coordinator will consider timely requests and advise the applicant of what, if any, reasonable accommodations will be provided. The Coordinator may request additional information, including medical evidence, from the applicant prior to providing accommodations to the applicant.

5. **Confidentiality.** Except as otherwise provided in Rule 8.05(a)3, all information relating to the examinations is confidential unless the examinee waives confidentiality. The State Court Administrator's Office shall take steps to ensure the security and confidentiality of all examination information.

Adopted Sept. 18, 1996, eff. Sept. 19, 1996. Amended Oct. 13, 2005, eff. Jan. 1, 2006; Dec. 28, 2006, eff. Jan. 1, 2007.

Drafting Committee Comment—1996

The Minnesota Supreme Court is one of the founding states of the State Court Interpreter Certification Consortium. It is the function of the Consortium to develop tests for court interpretation in various languages and administration standards, and to provide testing materials to individual states and jurisdictions. The Minnesota State Court Administrator's Office will in most circumstances utilize tests and standards established by or in conjunction with the Consortium.

Advisory Committee Comments—2007 Amendment

Rule 8.05(a)(3) is amended to facilitate verification of interpreters' qualification by permitting the release of the interpreter test results to court administrators or interpreter program administrators.

Rule 8.05(a)(5) is amended to provide for the waiver of confidentiality by examinees for the purpose of permitting the release of examination information upon their request.

Rule 8.06. Application for Certification

(a) Complete Application. An applicant desiring legal interpreting certification in a particular language shall file with the Coordinator a complete and notarized application on a form prepared by the State Court Administrator's Office and pay the application fee established by the State Court Administrator's Office.

(b) Certification Standards.

1. Screening. The State Court Administrator's Office shall administer character, fitness and competency screening. It shall perform its duties in a manner that ensures the protection of the public by recommending for certification only those who qualify. A court interpreter should be one whose record of conduct justifies the trust of the courts, witnesses, jurors, attorneys, parties, and others with respect to the official duties owed to them. A record manifesting significant deficiency in the honesty, trustworthiness, diligence or reliability of an applicant may constitute a basis for denial of certification.

2. Relevant Conduct. The revelation or discovery of any of the following should be treated as cause for further inquiry before the State Court Administrator's Office decides whether the applicant possesses the character and fitness to qualify for certification to interpret in the courtroom:

a. conviction of a crime which resulted in a sentence or a suspended sentence;

b. misconduct involving dishonesty, fraud, deceit or misrepresentation;

c. revocation or suspension of certification as an interpreter, or for any other position or license for which a character check was performed in this state or in other jurisdictions; and

d. acts that indicate abuse of or disrespect for the judicial process.

3. Evaluation of Character and Fitness. The State Court Administrator's Office shall determine whether the present character and fitness of an applicant qualifies the applicant for certification. In making this determination, the following factors should be considered in assigning weight and significance to prior conduct:

a. the applicant's age at the time of the conduct;

b. the recency of the conduct;

c. the reliability of the information concerning the conduct;

d. the seriousness of the conduct;

e. the factors underlying the conduct;

f. the cumulative effect of the conduct;

g. the evidence of rehabilitation;

h. the applicant's positive social contributions since the conduct;

i. the applicant's candor in the certification process; and

j. the materiality of any admissions or misrepresentations.

(c) Notification of Application for Certification. The Coordinator shall notify applicants in writing and by regular mail of the decision on the applicant's request for certification.

(d) Information Disclosure.

1. Application File. An applicant may review the contents of his or her application file, except for the work product of the Coordinator and the State Court Administrator's Office, at such times and under such conditions as the State Court Administrator's Office may provide.

2. Investigation. Information may be released to appropriate agencies for the purpose of obtaining information related to the applicant's character and competency.

3. Confidentiality.

a. Investigative Data: Information obtained by the Coordinator and the State Court Administrator's Office during the course of their investigation is confidential and may not be released to anyone absent a court order. The court shall consider whether the benefit to the person requesting the release of the investigative data outweighs the harm to the public, the agency or any person identified in the data.

b. Applicant File Data: All information contained in the files of applicants for court interpreter certification in the State Court Administrator's Office except as otherwise provided in Rule 8.06(d)3 of these rules is confidential and will not be released to anyone except upon order of a court of competent jurisdiction or the consent of the applicant.

c. Examination Information: Examination Information shall be available as provided in Rule 8.05(a).

Adopted Sept. 18, 1996, eff. Sept. 19, 1996. Amended Oct. 13, 2005, eff. Jan. 1, 2006.

Drafting Committee Comment—1996

The primary purpose of character, fitness and competency screening is to ensure equal access to justice for people with limited English proficiency, or speech or hearing impairments. Such screening also ensures the efficient and effective operation of our judicial system. Our judicial system is adequately protected by a system that evaluates the character, fitness and competency of an interpreter as those elements relate to interpreting in the courtroom. The public interest requires that all participants in the courtroom be secure in their expectation that those who are certified interpreters are competent to render such services and are worthy of the trust that the courts, witnesses, jurors, attorneys and parties may reasonably place in the certified interpreter.

Rule 8.07. Appeal of Denial of Certification

(a) Appeal of Certification Denial. Any applicant who is denied certification by the State Court Administrator's Office may appeal to the Review Panel by filing a petition for review with the Review Panel within twenty (20) days of receipt by the applicant of a final decision by the State Court Administrator's Office.

The petition shall briefly state the facts that form the basis for the complaint and the applicant's reasons for believing that review is warranted. A copy of the petition must be provided to the State Court Administrator's Office.

(b) Response From State Court Administrator's Office. The State Court Administrator's Office shall submit to the Review Panel a response to the applicant's appeal of the denial of certification within a reasonable time after receipt of a copy of the applicant's petition for review. The response should set forth the reasons for the denial of certification.

(c) Decision by the Minnesota Court Interpreter Review Panel. The Review Panel shall give such directions, hold such hearings and make such order as it may deem appropriate.

Adopted Sept. 18, 1996, eff. Sept. 19, 1996. Amended Oct. 13, 2005, eff. Jan. 1, 2006.

Rule 8.08. Complaints and Investigation

(a) Procedure. Complaints of alleged unprofessional, illegal or unethical conduct by any certified or non-certified court interpreter on the Minnesota Court Interpreter Roster shall be governed by procedures established by the State Court Administrator's Office. These procedures shall include the following:

1. a description of the types of actions which may be grounds for discipline;

2. a description of the types of sanctions available;

3. a procedure by which a person can file a complaint against an interpreter;

4. a procedure for the investigation of complaints;

5. a procedure for the review of complaints;

6. a hearing procedure for cases involving more severe sanctions; and

7. an appeal process when applicable.

(b) Revocation or Suspension of Certification or Roster Status. The certification or roster status of a certified or non-certified interpreter on the Minnesota Court Interpreter Roster is subject to suspension or revocation by the State Court Administrator's Office in accordance with the procedures established by the State Court Administrator's Office.

Adopted Sept. 18, 1996, eff. Sept. 19, 1996. Amended Oct. 13, 2005, eff. Jan. 1, 2006.

Drafting Committee Comment—1996

The complaint procedure is not intended as a means for appealing claims of error by a court interpreter. The complaint procedure is available to address unprofessional or unethical conduct by certified and non-certified court interpreters. Consequently, in the absence of fraud, corrupt motive, bad faith, or pattern of established interpreter error, the Coordinator is not likely to initiate an investigation of a complaint of an error of a court interpreter.

It is contemplated that the power to revoke or suspend interpreter certification or roster status will be exercised sparingly and when exercised, consideration will be given to the appropriate procedure and the giving of notice and an opportunity to be heard if such process is due the interpreter.

Rule 8.09. Expenses and Fees

The expenses for administering the certification requirements, including the complaint procedures, may be paid from initial application, examination fees and renewal fees. The fees shall be set by the State Court Administrator's Office and may be revised as necessary with the approval of the Supreme Court.

Adopted Sept. 18, 1996, eff. Sept. 19, 1996. Amended Oct. 13, 2005, eff. Jan. 1, 2006; Jan. 12, 2006.

Historical Notes

The order of the Minnesota Supreme Court dated January 12, 2006, provides in part that "the attached corrective amendments to Rule 8 of the General Rules of Practice for the District Courts are prescribed and promulgated to be effective retroactively to January 2, 2006".

Rule 8.10. Continuing Education Requirements

The State Court Administrator's Office may establish continuing education requirements for certified and non-certified interpreters on the Minnesota Court Interpreter Roster with the approval of the Supreme Court.

Adopted Sept. 18, 1996, eff. Sept. 19, 1996. Amended Oct. 13, 2005, eff. Jan. 1, 2006; Jan. 12, 2006.

Historical Notes

The order of the Minnesota Supreme Court dated January 12, 2006, provides in part that "the attached corrective amendments to Rule 8 of the General Rules of Practice for the District Courts are prescribed and promulgated to be effective retroactively to January 2, 2006".

Rule 8.11. Confidentiality of Records

Subject to exceptions in rules 8.01, 8.04(a)(3), 8.05(a)(3), 8.05(a)(5), and 8.06(d) of these rules, and the Enforcement Procedures for the Code of Professional Responsibility for Court Interpreters, all information in the files of the Coordinator, the Review Panel, and the State Court Administrator relating to court interpreters shall be confidential and shall not be released to anyone other than the Supreme Court except upon order of the Supreme Court.

Adopted Sept. 18, 1996, eff. Sept. 19, 1996. Amended Oct. 13, 2005, eff. Jan. 1, 2006; Jan. 12, 2006.

Drafting Committee Comment—2000

This rule is being added in 2000 to provide a consistent and necessary level of confidentiality for information maintained in the court interpreter orientation and certification process, including for example testing materials, orientation and registration information, and non-roster contact information. Both certified and non-certified interpreters included on the statewide roster under rule 8.01 must attend orientation training and pass and ethics exam, but the confidentiality provisions in rules 8.05 and 8.06 are limited to those seeking formal certification. Rule 8.11 ensures consistent confidentiality for all testing, orientation, registration and non-roster contact information, and is consistent with the level of accessibility accorded similar information in the attorney licensing process.

Historical Notes

The order of the Minnesota Supreme Court dated January 12, 2006, provides in part that "the attached corrective amendments to Rule 8 of the General Rules of Practice for the District Courts are prescribed and promulgated to be effective retroactively to January 2, 2006".

Rule 8.12. Interpreters to Assist Jurors

Qualified interpreters appointed by the court for any juror with a sensory disability may be present in the jury room to interpret while the jury is deliberating and voting.

Adopted Nov. 30, 2005, eff. Jan. 1, 2006. Amended Jan. 12, 2006.

Advisory Committee Comment—2006 Amendment

Rule 8.12 is intended to provide guidance on the role of interpreters appointed for the benefit of jurors with a sensory disability. The requirement that such interpreters be allowed to join the juror in the jury room is logical and necessary to permit the juror to communicate in deliberations. In this situation the interpreter should be given an oath to follow other constraints placed on jurors (*e.g.*, not to discuss the case, not to read or listen to media accounts of the trial, etc.) and also that the interpreter will participate only in interpreting the statements of others, and will not become an additional juror. An interpreter in this situation should also not be allowed or required to testify as to any aspect of the jury's deliberations in any context a juror would not be allowed or required to testify.

This amendment is drawn from the language of Minn. R. Crim. P. 26.03, subd. 16.

The rule is limited by its terms to interpreters appointed for the benefit of jurors with a sensory disability only because that is the only condition generally resulting in the appointment for jurors. In other, unusual, situations where such an interpreter is appointed, these procedures would presumably apply as well.

Historical Notes

The order of the Minnesota Supreme Court dated January 12, 2006, provides in part that "the attached corrective amendments to Rule 8 of the General Rules of Practice for the District Courts are prescribed and promulgated to be effective retroactively to January 2, 2006".

Rule 8.13. Requirement for Notice of Anticipated Need for Interpreter

In order to permit the court to make arrangements for the availability of required interpreter services, parties shall, in the Civil Cover Sheet, Initial Case Management Statement or Joint Statement of the Case, and as may otherwise be required by court rule or order, advise the court of that need in advance of the hearing or trial where services are required.

When it becomes apparent that previously-requested interpreter services will not be required, the parties must advise the court.

Adopted Dec. 22, 2008, eff. March 1, 2009. Amended May 7, 2013, eff. July 1, 2013.

Advisory Committee Comment—2008 Amendment

Making a qualified interpreter available when needed in court often requires difficult prearrangement. Rule 8.13 is a simple rule drawing the attention of litigants to the likelihood they will encounter specific court rules or orders requiring identification of interpreter needs in advance of the need. *See* amendments to Rules 111.02, 111.03, 112.02, Forms 111.02 & 112.01, and Minnesota Civil Trialbook sections 5 & 11.

The second paragraph of the rule contains an obvious corollary: when it becomes clear that interpreter services will no longer be required, notice must be given to permit the court to avoid the expense that would otherwise be incurred. This notice would be required if a trial or hearing were obviated by settlement, and the requirement of notice is similar to that required by MINN. GEN. R. PRAC. 115.10 for the settlement of a motion, which would obviate a hearing and the court's preparation for the hearing.

Historical and Statutory Notes

The order of the Minnesota Supreme Court [ADM04-8001, ADM09-8009, ADM-10-8051] dated May 7, 2013, provided in part that the amendments be effective July 1, 2013, and further provided in part that "[t]hese amendments apply to all actions or proceedings pending on or commenced after the effective date", and further provided that the "February 4, 2013 and February 12, 2013 orders of the court are hereby rescinded to the extent inconsistent with this order.".

RULE 9. FRIVOLOUS LITIGATION

Rule 9.01. Motion for Order Requiring Security or Imposing Sanctions

Relief under this rule is available in any action or proceeding pending in any court of this state, at any time until final judgment is entered. Upon the motion of any party or on its own initiative and after notice and hearing, the court may, subject to the conditions stated in Rules 9.01 to 9.07, enter an order: (a) requiring the furnishing of security by a frivolous litigant who has requested relief in the form of a claim, or (b) imposing preconditions on a frivolous litigant's service or filing of any new claims, motions or requests. All motions under this rule shall be made separately from other motions or requests, and shall be served as provided in the Rules of Civil Procedure, but shall not be filed with or presented to the court unless, within 21 days after service of the motion (or such other period as the court may prescribe), the challenged claim, motion, or request is not withdrawn or appropriately corrected.

Adopted Sept. 1, 1999, eff. Sept. 1, 1999.

Rule 9.02. Hearing

(a) Evidence. At the hearing upon such motion the court shall consider such evidence, written or oral, by witnesses or affidavit, as may be material to the ground of the motion.

(b) Factors. In determining whether to require security or to impose sanctions, the court shall consider the following factors:

(1) the frequency and number of claims pursued by the frivolous litigant with an adverse result;

(2) whether there is a reasonable probability that the frivolous litigant will prevail on the claim, motion, or request;

(3) whether the claim, motion, or request was made for purposes of harassment, delay, or vexatiousness, or otherwise in bad faith;

(4) injury incurred by other litigants prevailing against the frivolous litigant and to the efficient administration of justice as a result of the claim, motion, or request in question;

(5) effectiveness of prior sanctions in deterring the frivolous litigant from pursuing frivolous claims;

(6) the likelihood that requiring security or imposing sanctions will ensure adequate safeguards and provide means to compensate the adverse party;

(7) whether less severe sanctions will sufficiently protect the rights of other litigants, the public, or the courts.

The court may consider any other factors relevant to the determination of whether to require security or impose sanctions.

(c) Findings. If the court determines that a party is a frivolous litigant and that security or sanctions are appropriate, it shall state on the record its reasons supporting that determination. An order requiring security shall only be entered with an express determination that there is no reasonable probability that the litigant will prevail on the claim. An order imposing preconditions on serving or filing new claims, motions, or requests shall only be entered with an express determination that no less severe sanction will sufficiently protect the rights of other litigants, the public, or the courts.

(d) Ruling Not Deemed Determination of Issues. No determination or ruling made by the court upon the motion shall be, or be deemed to be, a determination of any issue in the action or proceeding or of the merits thereof.

Adopted Sept. 1, 1999, eff. Sept. 1, 1999.

Rule 9.03. Failure to Furnish Security

If security is required and not furnished as ordered, the claim(s) subject to the security requirement may be dismissed with or without prejudice as to the offending party.

Adopted Sept. 1, 1999, eff. Sept. 1, 1999.

Rule 9.04. Stay of Proceedings

When a motion pursuant to Rule 9.01 is properly filed prior to trial, the action or proceeding is stayed and the moving party need not plead or respond to discovery or motions, until 10 days after the motion is denied, or if granted, until 10 days after the required security has been furnished and the moving party given written notice thereof. When a motion pursuant to Rule 9.01 is made at any time after commencement of trial, the action or proceeding may be stayed for such period after the denial of the motion or the furnishing of the required security as the court shall determine.

Adopted Sept. 1, 1999, eff. Sept. 1, 1999.

Rule 9.05. Appeal

An order requiring security or imposing sanctions under this rule shall be deemed a final, appealable order. Any appeal under this rule may be taken to the court of appeals as in other civil cases within 60 days after filing of the order to be reviewed.

Adopted Sept. 1, 1999, eff. Sept. 1, 1999.

Rule 9.06. Definitions

As used in this rule, the following terms have the following meanings:

(a) "Claim" means any relief requested in the form of a claim, counterclaim, cross claim, third party claim, or lien filed, served, commenced, maintained, or pending in any federal or state court, including conciliation court.

(b) "Frivolous litigant" means:

(1) A person who, after a claim has been finally determined against the person, repeatedly relitigates or attempts to relitigate either

(i) the validity of the determination against the same party or parties as to whom the claim was finally determined, or

(ii) the cause of action, claim, controversy, or any of the issues of fact or law determined or concluded by the final determination against the same party or parties as to whom the claim was finally determined; or

(2) A person who in any action or proceeding repeatedly serves or files frivolous motions, pleadings, letters, or other papers, conducts unnecessary discovery, or engages in oral or written tactics that are frivolous or intended to cause delay; or

(3) A person who institutes and maintains a claim that is not well grounded in fact and not warranted by existing law or a good faith argument for the extension, modification or reversal of existing law or that is interposed for any improper purpose, such as to harass or cause unnecessary delay or needless increase in the cost of litigating the claim.

(c) "Security" means either:

(1) an undertaking to assure payment, issued by a surety authorized to issue surety bonds in the State of Minnesota, to the party for whose benefit the undertaking is required to be furnished, of the party's reasonable expenses, including attorney's fees and not limited to taxable costs, incurred in or in connection with a claim instituted, caused to be instituted, or maintained or caused to be maintained by a frivolous litigant or;

(2) cash tendered to and accepted by the court administrator for that purpose.

Adopted Sept. 1, 1999, eff. Sept. 1, 1999.

Rule 9.07. Effect on Other Provisions

Sanctions available under this rule are in addition to sanctions expressly authorized by any other statute or rule, or in the inherent power of the court.

Adopted Sept. 1, 1999, eff. Sept. 1, 1999.

Advisory Committee Comment–1999 Amendment

This rule is intended to curb frivolous litigation that is seriously burdensome on the courts, parties, and litigants. This rule is intended to apply only in the most egregious circumstances of abuse of the litigation process, and the remedies allowed by the rule can be viewed as drastic. Because of the very serious nature of the sanctions under this rule, courts should be certain that all reasonable efforts have been taken to ensure that affected parties are given notice and an opportunity to be heard. Rule 9.01 also requires that the court enter findings of fact to support any relief ordered under the rule, and this requirement should be given careful attention in the rare case where relief under this rule is necessary.

It is appropriate for the court to tailor the sanction imposed under this rule to the conduct and to limit the sanction to what is necessary to curb the inappropriate conduct of the frivolous litigant. *See Cello–Whitney v. Hoover*, 769 F.Supp. 1155 (W.D. Wash. 1991).

This rule includes a specific provision relating to the possible appeal of an order for sanctions. The rule provides that an appeal may be taken within 60 days, the same period allowed for appeals from orders and judgment, but specifies that the 60–day period begins to run from entry of the date of filing of the order. This timing mechanism is preferable because the requirement of service of notice of entry may not be workable where only one party may be interested in the appeal or where the order is entered on the court's own initiative. The date of filing can be readily determined, and typically appears on the face of the order or is a matter of record, obviating confusion over the time to appeal.

RULE 10. TRIBAL COURT ORDERS AND JUDGMENTS

Rule 10.01. When Tribal Court Orders and Judgments Must Be Given Effect

(a) Recognition Mandated by Law. Where mandated by state or federal statute, orders, judgments, and other judicial acts of the tribal courts of any federally recognized Indian tribe shall be recognized and enforced.

(b) Procedure.

(1) *Generally.* Where an applicable state or federal statute establishes a procedure for enforcement of any tribal court order or judgment, that procedure must be followed.

(2) *Violence Against Women Act; Presumption.* An order that is subject to the Violence Against Women Act of 2000, 18 U.S.C. § 2265 (2003), that appears to be issued by a court with subject matter jurisdiction and jurisdiction over the parties, and that appears not to have expired by its own terms is presumptively enforceable, and shall be honored by Minnesota courts and law enforcement and other officials so long as it remains the judgment of the issuing court and the respondent has been given notice and an opportunity to be heard or, in the case of matters properly considered ex parte, the respondent will be given notice and an opportunity to be heard within a reasonable time. The presumptive enforceability of such a tribal court order shall continue until terminated by state court order but shall not affect the burdens of proof and persuasion in any proceeding.

Adopted Dec. 11, 2003, eff. Jan. 1, 2004.

Advisory Committee Comment—2007 Amendment

See comment following Rule 10.02.

Historical Notes

The order of the Minnesota Supreme Court [CX-89-1863] dated December 11, 2003, provides in part that these amendments are effective January 1, 2004, and shall apply to all actions or proceedings pending on or commenced on or after the effective date.

Rule 10.02. When Recognition of Tribal Court Orders and Judgments Is Discretionary.

(a) Factors. In cases other than those governed by Rule 10.01(a), enforcement of a tribal court order or judgment is discretionary with the court. In exercising this discretion, the court may consider the following factors:

(1) whether the party against whom the order or judgment will be used has been given notice and an opportunity to be heard or, in the case of matters properly considered ex parte, whether the respondent will be given notice and an opportunity to be heard within a reasonable time;

(2) whether the order or judgment appears valid on its face and, if possible to determine, whether it remains in effect;

(3) whether the tribal court possessed subject-matter jurisdiction and jurisdiction over the person of the parties;

(4) whether the issuing tribal court was a court of record;

(5) whether the order or judgment was obtained by fraud, duress, or coercion;

(6) whether the order or judgment was obtained through a process that afforded fair notice, the right to appear and compel attendance of witnesses, and a fair hearing before an independent magistrate;

(7) whether the order or judgment contravenes the public policy of this state;

(8) whether the order or judgment is final under the laws and procedures of the rendering court, unless the order is a non-criminal order for the protection or apprehension of an adult, juvenile or child, or another type of temporary, emergency order;

(9) whether the tribal court reciprocally provides for recognition and implementation of orders, judgments and decrees of the courts of this state; and

(10) any other factors the court deems appropriate in the interests of justice.

(b) Procedure. The court shall hold such hearing, if any, as it deems necessary under the circumstances.

Adopted Dec. 11, 2003, eff. Jan. 1, 2004.

Advisory Committee Comments—2007 Amendment

Introduction. Rule 10 is a new rule intended to provide a starting point for enforcing tribal court orders and judgments where recognition is mandated by state or federal law (Rule 10.01), and to establish factors for determining the effect of these adjudications where federal or state statutory law does not do so (Rule 10.02).

The rule applies to all tribal court orders and judgments and does not distinguish between tribal courts located in Minnesota and those sitting in other states. The only limitation on the universe of determinations is that they be from tribal courts of a federally-recognized Indian tribe. These courts are defined in 25 U.S.C. § 450b(e), and a list is published by the Department of the Interior, Bureau of Indian Affairs. *See, e.g.*, FED. REG. 1194 (Nov. 25, 2005).

Tribal court adjudications are not entitled to full faith and credit under the United States Constitution, which provides only for full faith and credit for "public acts, records, and judicial proceedings of every other state" U. S. CONST. Art IV, § 1. But state and federal statutes have conferred the equivalent of full faith and credit status on some tribal adjudications by mandating that they be enforced in state court. Where such full faith and credit is mandatory, a state does not exercise discretion in giving effect to the proper judgments of a sister state. *Baker v. Gen. Motors Corp.*, 522 U.S. 222, 233 (1998) ("A final judgment in one State, if rendered by a court with adjudicatory authority over the subject matter and persons governed by the judgment, qualifies for recognition throughout the land.") Through full faith and credit, a sister state's judgment is given res judicata effect in all other states. *See, e.g., id.; Hansberry v. Lee*, 311 U.S. 32, 42 (1940).

The enforcement in state court of tribal court adjudications that are not entitled to the equivalent of full faith and credit under a specific state or federal statute, is governed by the doctrine of comity. Comity is fundamentally a discretionary doctrine. It is rooted in the court's inherent powers, as was early recognized in United States jurisprudence in *Hilton v. Guyot*, 159 U.S. 113, 163–164 (1895), where the court said: "No law has any effect, of its own force, beyond the limits of the sovereignty from which its authority is derived. The extent to which the law of one nation, as put in force within its territory, whether by executive order, by legislative act, or by judicial decree, shall be allowed to operate within the dominion of another nation, depends upon what our greatest jurists have been content to call 'the comity of nations.'"

This inherent power was recognized in Minnesota in *Traders' Trust Co. v. Davidson*, 146 Minn. 224, 227, 178 N.W. 735, 736 (1920) (citing *Hilton*, 159 U.S. at 227) where the court said: "Effect is given to foreign judgments as a matter of comity and reciprocity, and it has become the rule to give no other or greater effect to the judgment of a foreign court than the country or state whose court rendered it gives to a like judgment of our courts." In *Nicol v. Tanner*, 310 Minn. 68, 75–79, 256 N. W.2d 796, 800–02 (1976) (citing the Restatement (Second) of Conflicts of Laws § 98 (1971)), the court further developed the doctrine of comity when it held that the statement in *Traders' Trust Co.* that enforcement required a showing of reciprocity was dictum; that 'reciprocity is not a prerequisite to enforcement of a foreign judgment in Minnesota;" and that the default status of a foreign judgment "should not affect the force of the judgment."

Statutory Mandates. Rule 10.01 reflects the normal presumption that courts will adhere to statutory mandates for enforcement of specific tribal court orders or judgments where such a statutory mandate applies. Federal statutes that do provide such mandates include:

1. Violence Against Women Act of 2000, 18 U.S.C. § 2265 (2003) (full faith and credit for certain protection orders).

2. Indian Child Welfare Act, 25 U.S.C. § 1911(d) (2003) ("full faith and credit" for certain custody determinations).

3. Full Faith and Credit for Child Support Orders Act, 28 U.S.C. § 1738B(a) (2003) ("shall enforce" certain child support orders and "shall not seek or make modifications ... except in accordance with [certain limitations]").

In addition to federal law, the Minnesota Legislature has addressed custody, support, child placement, and orders for protection. The Minnesota Legislature adopted the Uniform Child Custody Jurisdiction and Enforcement Act, MINN. STAT. §§ 518D.101–518D.317 (2002) which: (1) requires recognition and enforcement of certain child custody determinations made by a tribe "under factual circumstances in substantial conformity with the jurisdictional standards of" the Act; and (2) establishes a voluntary registration process for custody determinations with a 20–day period for contesting validity. MINN. STAT. §§ 518D.103; 104 (2002) (not applicable to adoption or emergency medical care of child; not applicable to extent ICWA controls). In addition, the Minnesota Legislature has adopted the Uniform Interstate Family Support Act, MINN. STAT. §§ 518C.101–518C.902 (2002), which provides the procedures for enforcement of support orders from another state ["state" is defined to include an Indian tribe, MINN. STAT. § 518C.101(s)(1) (2002)] with or without registration, and enforcement and modification after registration. The Minnesota Legislature has also adopted the Minnesota Indian Family Preservation Act, MINN. STAT. §§ 260.751—260.835 (2002), which provides, among other things, that tribal court orders concerning child placement (adoptive and pre-adoptive placement, involuntary foster care placement, termination of parental rights, and status offense placements) shall have the same force and effect as orders of a court of this state. MINN. STAT. § 260.771, subd. 4 (2002). In 2006 the Minnesota Legislature adopted MINN. STAT. § 518B.01, subd. 19a, which requires enforcement of certain foreign or tribal court orders for protection.

The facial validity provision in Rule 10.01(b)(2) fills in a gap in state law. MINN. STAT. § 518B.01, subd. 14(e) (2002), authorizes an arrest based on probable cause of violation of tribal court order for protection; although this law includes immunity from civil suit for a peace officer acting in good faith and exercising due care, it does not address facial validity of the order. Similar laws in other jurisdictions address this issue. *See, e.g.*, 720 ILL. COMP. STAT. 5/12–30(a)(2) (Supp. 2003); OKLA. STAT. tit. 22 § 60.9B(1) (2003); WISC. STAT. § 813.128(1) (2001–02).

The Minnesota Legislature has also addressed enforcement of foreign money judgments. The Minnesota Uniform Foreign Country Money–Judgments Recognition Act, MINN. STAT. § 548.35 (2002), creates a procedure for filing and enforcing judgments rendered by courts other than those of sister states. Tribal court money judgments fall within the literal scope of this statute and the statutory procedures therefore may guide Minnesota courts considering money judgments. *Cf. Anderson v. Engelke*, 954 P.2d 1106, 1110–11 (Mont. 1998) (dictum) (statute assumed to allow enforcement by state courts outside of tribal lands, but question not decided). In general, money judgments of tribal courts are not entitled to full faith and credit under the Constitution, and the court is allowed a more expansive and discretionary role in deciding what effect they have. Rule 10.02(a) is intended to facilitate that process.

Discretionary Enforcement: Comity. Where no statutory mandate expressly applies, tribal court orders and judgments are subject to the doctrine of comity. Rule 10.02(a) does not create any new or additional powers but only begins to describe in one convenient place the principles that apply to recognition of orders and judgments by comity.

Comity is also an inherently flexible doctrine. A court asked to decide whether to recognize a foreign order can consider whatever aspects of the foreign court proceedings it deems relevant. Thus Rule 10.02(a) does not dictate a single standard for determining the effect of these adjudications in state court. Instead, it identifies some of the factors a Minnesota judge may consider in determining what effect such a determination will be given. Rule 10.02(a) does not attempt to define all of the factors that may be appropriate for consideration by a court charged with determining whether a tribal court determination should be enforced. It does enumerate many of the appropriate factors. It is possible in any given case that one or more of these factors will not apply. For example, reciprocity is not a pre-condition to enforceability generally, *Nicol*, 310 Minn. at 75–79, 256 N.W.2d at 800–02, but may be relevant in some circumstances. Notice of the proceedings and an opportunity to be heard (or the prospect of notice and right to hearing in the case of ex parte matters) are fundamental parts of procedural fairness in state and federal courts and are considered basic elements of due process; it is appropriate at least to consider whether the tribal court proceedings extended these rights to the litigants. The issue of whether the tribal court is "of record" may be important to the determination of what the proceedings were in that court. A useful definition of "of record" is contained in the Wisconsin statutes. WIS. STAT. § 806.245(1)(c) (2001–02); *see also* WIS. STAT. § 806.245(3) (2001–02) (setting forth requirements for determining whether a court is "of record"). The rule permits the court to inquire into whether the tribal court proceedings offered similar protections to the parties, recognizing that tribal courts may not be required to adhere to the requirements of due process under the federal and state constitutions. Some of the considerations of the rule are drawn from the requirements of the Minnesota Uniform Enforcement of Foreign Judgments Act, MINN. STAT. §§ 548.26–.33 (2002). For example, contravention of the state's public policy is a specific factor for non-recognition of a foreign state's judgment under MINN. STAT. § 548.35, subd. 4(b)(3)(2002); it is carried forward into Rule 10.02(a)(7). Inconsistency with state public policy is a factor for non-recognition of tribal court orders under other states' rules. *See* MICH. R. CIV. P. 2.615(C)(2)(c); N.D. R. CT. 7.2(b)(4).

Hearing. Rule 10.02(b) does not require that a hearing be held on the issues relating to consideration of the effect to be given to a tribal court order or judgment. In some instances, a hearing would serve no useful purpose or would be unnecessary; in others, an evidentiary hearing might be required to resolve contested questions of fact where affidavit or documentary evidence is insufficient. The committee believes the discretion to decide when an evidentiary hearing is held should rest with the trial judge.

Historical Notes

The order of the Minnesota Supreme Court [CX-89-1863] dated December 11, 2003, provides in part that these amendments are effective January 1, 2004, and shall apply to all actions or proceedings pending on or commenced on or after the effective date.

The order of the Minnesota Supreme Court [CX-89-1863] dated December 11, 2003, provides in part that "(t)he inclusion of Advisory Committee comments is made for convenience and does not reflect court approval of the statements made therein".

RULE 11. SUBMISSION OF CONFIDENTIAL INFORMATION

Rule 11.01. Definitions

The following definitions apply for the purposes of this rule:

(a) "Restricted identifiers" shall mean the social security number, employer identification number, and financial account numbers of a party or other person.

(b) "Financial source documents" means income tax returns, W–2 forms and schedules, wage stubs, credit card statements, financial institution statements, check registers, and other financial information deemed financial source documents by court order.

Adopted May 6, 2005, eff. July 1, 2005. Amended April 27, 2007, eff. July 1, 2007.

Rule 11.02. Restricted Identifiers

(a) Pleadings and Other Documents Submitted by a Party. No party shall submit restricted identifiers on any pleading or other document that is to be filed with the court except:

(1) on a separate form entitled Confidential Information Form (see Form 11.1 as published by the state court administrator) filed with the pleading or other document; or

(2) on Sealed Financial Source Documents under Rule 11.03.

The parties are solely responsible for ensuring that restricted identifiers do not otherwise appear on the pleading or other document filed with the court. The court administrator will not review each pleading or document filed by a party for compliance with this rule. The Confidential Information Form shall not be accessible to the public.

(b) Records Generated by the Court. Restricted identifiers maintained by the court in its register of actions (i.e., activity summary or similar information that lists the title, origination, activities, proceedings, and filings in each case), calendars, indexes, and judgment docket shall not be accessible to the public. Courts shall not include restricted identifiers on judgments, orders, decisions, and notices except on the Confidential Information Form (Form 11.1), which shall not be accessible to the public.

Adopted May 6, 2005, eff. July 1, 2005. Amended Nov. 19, 2009, eff. Jan. 1, 2010; May 24, 2012, eff. Sept. 1, 2012.

Historical Notes

The order of the Supreme Court dated November 19, 2009, provided:

"1. The attached amendments to the General Rules of Practice for the District Courts and the Special Rules of Procedure Governing Proceedings under the Minnesota Commitment and Treatment Act be, and the same are, prescribed and promulgated to be effective on January 1, 2010.

"2. The attached amendments shall apply to all actions pending on the effective date and to those filed thereafter.

"3. The inclusion of Advisory Committee comments is made for convenience and does not reflect court approval of the comments made therein."

The order of the Minnesota Supreme Court [ADM 10–8011] dated May 24, 2012, provided in part that "These amendments shall apply to all actions or proceedings commenced on or after the effective date."

Rule 11.03. Sealing Financial Source Documents

Financial source documents shall be submitted to the court under a cover sheet designated "Sealed Financial Source Documents" and substantially in the form set forth as Form 11.2 as published by the state court administrator. Financial source documents submitted with the required cover sheet are not accessible to the public except to the extent that they are admitted into evidence in a testimonial hearing or trial or as provided in Rule 11.05 of these rules. The cover sheet or copy of it shall be accessible to the public. Financial source documents that are not submitted with the required cover sheet and that contain restricted identifiers are accessible to the public, but the court may, upon motion or on its own initiative, order that any such financial source document be sealed.

Adopted May 6, 2005, eff. July 1, 2005. Amended April 27, 2007, eff. July 1, 2007; Nov. 19, 2009, eff. Jan. 1, 2010.

Advisory Committee Comment—2009 Amendment

Rule 11 is amended to remove Forms 11.1 and 11.2 from the rules and to correct the reference to the forms in the rule. This amendment will allow for the maintenance and publication of the form by the state court administrator. The form, together with other court forms, can be found at http://www.mncourts.gov/.

Forms 11.1 and 11.2 should be deleted from the rules and maintained in the future on the court's website.

Historical Notes

The order of the Supreme Court dated November 19, 2009, provided:

"1. The attached amendments to the General Rules of Practice for the District Courts and the Special Rules of Procedure Governing Proceedings under the Minnesota Commitment and Treatment Act be, and the same are, prescribed and promulgated to be effective on January 1, 2010.

"2. The attached amendments shall apply to all actions pending on the effective date and to those filed thereafter.

"3. The inclusion of Advisory Committee comments is made for convenience and does not reflect court approval of the comments made therein."

Rule 11.04. Failure to Comply

If a party fails to comply with the requirements of this rule in regard to another individual's restricted identifiers or financial source documents, the court may upon motion or its own initiative impose appropriate sanctions, including costs necessary to prepare an appropriate document for filing.

Adopted May 6, 2005, eff. July 1, 2005.

Rule 11.05. Procedure for Requesting Access to Sealed Financial Source Documents

(a) Motion. Any person may file a motion, supported by affidavit showing good cause, for access to Sealed Financial Source Documents or portions of the documents. Written notice of the motion shall be required.

(b) Waiver of Notice. If the person seeking access cannot locate a party to provide the notice required under this rule, after making a good faith reasonable effort to provide such notice as required by applicable court rules, an affidavit may be filed with the court setting forth the efforts to locate the party and requesting waiver of the notice provisions of this rule. The court may waive the notice requirement of this rule if the court finds that further good faith efforts to locate the party are unlikely to be successful.

(c) Balancing Test. The court shall allow access to Sealed Financial Source Documents, or relevant portions of the documents, if the court finds that the public interest in granting access or the personal interest of the person seeking access outweighs the privacy interests of the parties or dependent children. In granting access the court may impose conditions necessary to balance the interests consistent with this rule.

Adopted May 6, 2005, eff. July 1, 2005.

Advisory Committee Comment—2005 Adoption

Rule 11 is a new rule, but is derived in part from former Rule 313. It is also based on WASH. GR 22 (2003). Under this rule, applicable in all court proceedings, parties are now responsible for protecting the privacy of restricted identifiers (social security numbers or employer identification numbers and financial account numbers) and financial source documents by submitting them with the proper forms. Failure to comply would result in the public having access to the restricted identifiers and financial source documents from the case file unless the party files a motion to seal them or the court acts on its own initiative under Rule 11.03. The Confidential Information Form from Rule 313 is retained, modified, and renumbered, and a new Sealed Financial Source Documents cover sheet has been added. The court retains authority to impose sanctions against parties who violate the rule in regard to another individual's restricted identifiers or financial source documents.

New in 2005 is the procedure for obtaining access to restricted identifiers and sealed financial source documents. This process requires the court to balance the competing interest involved. *See, e.g., Minneapolis Star & Tribune Co. v. Schumacher*, 392 N.W.2d 197 (Minn. 1986) (when party seeks to restrict access to settlement documents and transcripts of settlement hearings made part of civil court file by statute, court must balance interests favoring access, along with presumption in favor of access, against those asserted for restricting access).

Advisory Committee Comment—2007 Adoption

The 2007 amendment to Rule 11.01(a) expands the rule to protect the restricted identifiers of all persons, not just a party and a party's child. Records submitted to the court may include restricted identifiers of persons other than a party or the party's child, such as clients or other fiduciaries.

The 2007 amendment to Rule 11.03 recognizes that if a sealed financial source document is formally offered and admitted into evidence in a testimonial hearing or trial the document will be accessible to the public to the extent that it has been admitted. This is the result under WASH. GR 22 (2006) upon which this rule is based. In such situations, it is strongly recommended that restricted identifiers be redacted from the document before its admission into evidence.

Rule 11.06. When Documents May Be Filed as Confidential or under Seal

A party may submit a document for filing as "confidential" or "under seal" only if one of these circumstances exist:

(a) The court has entered an order permitting the filing of the particular document or class of documents under seal or as confidential.

(b) This rule or any applicable court rule, court order, or statute expressly authorizes or requires filing under seal or as confidential.

(c) The party files a motion for leave to file under seal or as confidential not later than at the time of submission of the document.

The court may require a filing party to specify the authority for asserting that a filing may be made as "confidential" or "under seal."

Adopted May 24, 2012, eff. Sept. 1, 2012.

Advisory Committee Comment—2012 Amendment

Rule 11.06 is a new rule intended to define the procedural prerequisites for filing of documents under seal. This rule is not intended to expand or limit the confidentiality concerns that might justify special treatment of any document. The rule is intended to make it clear that filing parties do not have a unilateral right to designate any filing as confidential, and that permission from the court is required. This permission may flow from a statute or rule explicitly requiring that a particular document or portion of a document be filed confidentially or from a court order that documents be filed under seal. Rule 112 of the Minnesota Rules of Civil Appellate Procedure contains useful guidance on how confidential information can be handled. Where documents contain both confidential and non-confidential information, it may be appropriate to file redacted "public" versions of documents filed under seal.

Historical Notes

The order of the Minnesota Supreme Court [ADM 10–8011] dated May 24, 2012, provided in part that "These amendments shall apply to all actions or proceedings commenced on or after the effective date."

RULE 12. REQUIREMENT FOR COMPARABLE MEANS OF SERVICE

In all cases, a party serving a paper on a party and filing the same paper with the court must select comparable means of service and filing so that the papers are delivered substantially contemporaneously. This rule does not apply to service of a summons or a subpoena. Pleadings and other papers need not be filed until required by Minn. R. Civ. P. 5.05 and motions for sanctions may not be filed before the time allowed by Minn. R. Civ. P. 11.03(a).

In emergency situations, where compliance with this rule is not possible, the facts of attempted compliance must be provided by affidavit.

Adopted Dec. 22, 2008, eff. March 1, 2009. Amended Nov. 19, 2009, eff. Jan. 1, 2010.

Advisory Committee Comment—2008 Amendment

Rule 12 is a new rule, recommended to codify a longstanding practice of professional courtesy: that papers served both to the court and to the other party be served and filed by comparable means. The rule does not require that the same means be used; but if hand delivery to the court is chosen for filing, then either hand delivery, overnight courier sent the day before, or facsimile transmission to other party must be used. The measure of compliance is approximate simultaneity; the purpose of the rule is to discourage gameplaying over service. Fairness requires that service and filing occur at about the same time; delivering papers immediately to the court and then serving them leisurely upon counsel is not justified and in some cases is not fair.

Advisory Committee Comment—2009 Amendment

Rule 12 is amended to add the last sentence of the first paragraph. The amendment is intended to clarify that the rule does not modify two facets of practice established before its adoption. It does not require that pleadings be filed before the time allowed under Rule 5.05, which generally makes it unnecessary to file pleadings until after a party files a pleading, thereby opening a court file. This rule is a part of Minnesota's "hip-pocket" service regime as established by Minn. R. Civ. P. 3. Rule 11 of the Minnesota Rules of Civil Procedure contains a 21–day "safe harbor" provision, requiring service of a motion for sanctions but prohibiting filing of the motion for 21 days. The amendment to Rule 12 of the general rules was not intended to modify that important provision.

Historical Notes

The order of the Supreme Court dated November 19, 2009, provided:

"1. The attached amendments to the General Rules of Practice for the District Courts and the Special Rules of Procedure Governing Proceedings under the Minnesota Commitment and Treatment Act be, and the same are, prescribed and promulgated to be effective on January 1, 2010.

"2. The attached amendments shall apply to all actions pending on the effective date and to those filed thereafter.

"3. The inclusion of Advisory Committee comments is made for convenience and does not reflect court approval of the comments made therein."

RULE 13. REQUIREMENT TO PROVIDE NOTICE OF CURRENT ADDRESS

Rule 13.01. Duty to Provide Notice

In all actions, it is the responsibility of the parties, or their counsel of record, to provide notice to all other parties and to the court administrator of their current address for delivery of notices, orders, and other documents in the case. Where a party or a party's attorney has provided an e-mail address for the purpose of allowing service or filing, this rule also requires that the party advise the court and all parties of any change in that e-mail address. Failure to provide this notice constitutes waiver of the right to notice until a current address is provided.

Adopted Nov. 19, 2009, eff. Jan. 1, 2009. Amended May 24, 2012, eff. Sept. 1, 2012.

Advisory Committee Comment—2012 Amendment

Rule 13.01 is amended to add the requirement that a party or attorney provide an updated e-mail address any time an attorney or party has submitted an e-mail address to the court. This change is intended to ensure that e-noticing under Minn. R. Civ. P. 77.04 and electronic filing and service under the rules will function and provide meaningful notice. Rule 13.02 is amended to make it clear that the giving of e-mail notice will not be ended upon two unsuccessful attempts to serve or notify by e-mail. The committee believes that there is no compelling reason to stop e-mailed notices given the minimal additional cost of continuing them.

Historical Notes

The order of the Supreme Court dated November 19, 2009, provided:

"1. The attached amendments to the General Rules of Practice for the District Courts and the Special Rules of Procedure Governing Proceedings under the Minnesota Commitment and Treatment Act be, and the same are, prescribed and promulgated to be effective on January 1, 2010.

"2. The attached amendments shall apply to all actions pending on the effective date and to those filed thereafter.

"3. The inclusion of Advisory Committee comments is made for convenience and does not reflect court approval of the comments made therein."

The order of the Minnesota Supreme Court [ADM 10–8011] dated May 24, 2012, provided in part that "These amendments shall apply to all actions or proceedings commenced on or after the effective date."

Rule 13.02. Elimination of Requirement to Provide Notice to Lapsed Address

In the event notices, pleadings, or other documents are returned by the postal service or noted as undelivered or unopened by the e-mail system after the court administrator's transmission by mailing (or e-mailing where authorized by rule) to a party or attorney's address of record on two separate occasions, the administrator should make reasonable efforts to obtain a valid, current address. If those efforts are not successful, the administrator may omit making further United States Mail transmissions to that party or attorney in that action, and shall place appropriate notice in the court file or docket indicating that notices are not being transmitted to all parties.

Adopted Nov. 19, 2009, eff. Jan. 1, 2009. Amended May 24, 2012, eff. Sept. 1, 2012.

Advisory Committee Comment—2009 Amendment

Rule 13 is a new rule intended to make explicit what has heretofore been expected of parties and their counsel: to keep the court apprised of a current address for mailing notices, orders, and other papers routinely mailed by the administrator to all parties. Where the court does not have a valid address, evidenced by two returned mailings, and cannot readily determine the correct address, the rule makes it unnecessary for the administrator to continue the futile mailing of additional papers until the party or attorney provides a current address.

The purpose of this rule is to require meaningful notice. If a party is a participant in the Secretary of State's address confidentiality program, there is no reason not to permit the use of that address to satisfy the requirement of this rule. *See* MINN. STAT. §§ 5B.01–.09 (2008).

Historical Notes

The order of the Supreme Court dated November 19, 2009, provided:

"1. The attached amendments to the General Rules of Practice for the District Courts and the Special Rules of Procedure Governing Proceedings under the Minnesota Commitment and Treatment Act be, and the same are, prescribed and promulgated to be effective on January 1, 2010.

"2. The attached amendments shall apply to all actions pending on the effective date and to those filed thereafter.

"3. The inclusion of Advisory Committee comments is made for convenience and does not reflect court approval of the comments made therein."

The order of the Minnesota Supreme Court [ADM 10–8011] dated May 24, 2012, provided in part that "These amendments shall apply to all actions or proceedings commenced on or after the effective date."

RULE 14. E-FILING AND E-SERVICE

Rule 14.01. Mandatory and Voluntary E-File and E-Service

(a) Definitions. The following terms have the following meanings:

(1) "Designated Provider" means the electronic filing service provider designated by the state court administrator.

(2) "E-Filing System" means the Designated Provider's Internet-accessible electronic filing and service system.

(3) "Pilot Project Case Types" means cases in the Fourth Judicial District and Second Judicial District, of the Selected Civil Case Types and Family Case Types as defined in this rule.

(4) "Selected Civil Case Types" means all general civil cases, including examiner of title cases (in the Fourth Judicial District, in addition to Torrens cases this includes 5–week redemptions) except Conciliation Court and Probate/Mental Health case types, and Family Case Types as defined in this rule.

(5) "Family Case Types" means Annulments, Custody, Dissolutions with Children, Dissolutions without Children, Domestic Abuse, Family Other, Legal Separation, Paternity, Separate Maintenance, Summary Dissolution, Support, and Transfers of Legal Custody.

(b) Cases Subject to Mandatory E-Filing and E-Service. Effective September 1, 2012, attorneys representing parties in any case of the Pilot Project Case Types in the Second and Fourth Judicial Districts, and effective September 1, 2013, or ninety (90) days after designation by the State Court Administrator, whichever is later, for attorneys representing parties in any case of the Pilot Project Case types in the districts or portions thereof designated by the State Court Administrator under Rule 14.01(e), and government agencies appearing in such cases, must register promptly upon filing of any document by any party with the Designated Provider and file documents electronically with the court in Pilot Project Case Types. Registered attorneys and government agencies must also electronically serve all documents required or permitted to be served on other registered attorneys and government agencies in that case, provided that the attorney to be served has designated an e-mail address for receiving electronic service in the E–Filing System after the District Court has accepted the initial filing in the case. Electronic filing and electronic service shall be accomplished through the E–Filing System.

(c) Prohibited E–Filing. The following case types may not be filed electronically in proceedings related to:

(1) Wills deposited for safekeeping under Minn. Stat. § 524.2–515; and

(2) Parental notification bypass proceedings under Minn. Stat. § 144.343.

(d) Request for Exception to Mandatory E–File and E–Service Requirement. An attorney or government agency required to file and serve electronically under this rule, may request to be excused from mandatory e-filing in a particular case by motion to the Chief Judge or his or her designee. An opt-out request may be granted for good cause shown. If an opt-out request is granted, the court shall scan all document filings into the court's computer system and may charge the filing party an appropriate fee.

(e) Voluntary E–File and E–Serve. During the pilot project, attorneys, and parties designated by the Fourth Judicial District and Second Judicial District may, upon registering with the Designated Provider, electronically file documents with the court in civil cases designated by the respective judicial district. For other districts, attorneys and parties designated by the State Court Administrator may, upon registering with the Designated Provider, electronically file documents with the court in the locations and civil cases designated by the State Court Administrator. In any designated case in which the designated and registered attorneys or parties have electronically filed a document with the District Court, any other attorney or law firm representing a party in the case and any party designated by the District Court (Second and Fourth Judicial Districts), or the State Court Administrator (all other districts), may also electronically file documents in the case after registering with the Designated Provider. Registered attorneys and parties may also electronically serve documents on other registered attorneys and parties in such cases provided that the attorney or party to be served has designated an e-mail address for receiving electronic service in the E–Filing System after the District Court has accepted the initial filing in the case.

(f) Relief from Operation of this Rule.

(1) Technical Errors; Relief for Sending Party. Upon motion and a showing that electronic filing or electronic service of a document was not completed because of: (1) an error in the transmission of the document to the E–File System that was unknown to the sending party; (2) a failure of the E–Filing System to process the document when received; or (3) other technical problems experienced by the sending party or E–Filing System, the court may enter an order permitting the document to be deemed filed or served on the date and time it was first attempted to be transmitted electronically. If appropriate, the court may adjust the schedule for responding to these documents or the court's hearing.

(2) Technical Errors; Relief for Other Parties. Upon motion and a showing that an electronically served document was unavailable to or not received by a party served, the court may enter an order extending the time for responding to that document.

Adopted May 24, 2012, eff. Sept. 1, 2012. Amended June 13, 2013, eff. Sept. 16, 2013.

Advisory Committee Comment—2012 Amendment

See note following Rule 14.07.

Historical and Statutory Notes

The order of the Minnesota Supreme Court [ADM09–8009] dated June 13, 2013, amended the effective date of an order dated June 7, 2013, from September 1, 2013, to September 16, 2013, and provided in part that "These amendments shall apply to all actions or proceedings commenced on or after the effective date [September 16, 2013.]."

Rule 14.02. Registration Process and Duty to Designate E–Mail Address for Service

An attorney or party registers with the Designated Provider for each case by entering into a subscriber agreement with the Designated Provider and obtaining a E–Filing System user identification and password provided by the Designated Provider. The registered attorney or party must also designate in the E–Filing System an e-mail address for receiving electronic service in the case. Once an initial filing has been accepted in a case, all other registered attorneys and parties shall, upon filing their initial document in a case, designate in the E–Filing System an e-mail address for receiving electronic service in the case. Registered attorneys and parties shall maintain a designated e-mail address for receiving electronic service until all applicable appeal periods have expired for the case.

Adopted May 24, 2012, eff. Sept. 1, 2012.

Advisory Committee Comment—2012 Amendment

See note following Rule 14.07.

Rule 14.03. Document Format

(a) Document Types. Documents filed electronically shall be submitted in searchable PDF format only.

(b) Format. Documents filed electronically shall comply with the following format requirements:

(1) 8½ × 11″ size with a portrait orientation.

(2) No Optical Character Recognition (OCR) data shall be contained in or associated with the document.

(3) At least 200 dot-per-inch ("DPI") resolution.

(4) No unintelligible images (e.g., no all-black images).

(5) Documents may not be secured, password-protected, or have other features limiting access.

(6) Black and white images (no color images will be retained). Color documents submitted via the E–Filing System are transformed into black and white images.

(7) No document shall contain any external references (e.g., hyperlinks, URLs, shortcuts).

(8) Only readable words, viewable pictures or images, and valid, non-corrupted tables shall be included.

(9) Documents shall not be corrupted (e.g., a corrupt file having 0 bytes of data).

(10) Documents may contain only standard fonts. No CID or Character Identifier fonts are permitted.

(11) Only standard CCIT image compression is permitted.

(12) Documents must comprise the complete image or file. A file that experiences an upload issue or time-out on file transfer from a submitting party usually appears as an incomplete image or file when opened.

(c) Document Size.

(1) No single electronic document should be greater than 5 MB; and

(2) No single envelope or filing should be greater than 25 MB.

Larger documents may be filed in several parts or in multiple envelopes.

(d) Non-conforming Documents. With leave of court, a color document or document containing color may be filed electronically with manual handling or in paper form to be retained by the court in a color format. A motion to file a color document or document containing color to be retained by the court in a color format must be filed and served electronically.

Adopted May 24, 2012, eff. Sept. 1, 2012. Amended June 13, 2013, eff. Sept. 16, 2013.

Advisory Committee Comment—2012 Amendment

See note following Rule 14.07.

Historical and Statutory Notes

The order of the Minnesota Supreme Court [ADM09–8009] dated June 13, 2013, amended the effective date of an order dated June 7, 2013, from September 1, 2013, to September 16, 2013, and provided in part that "These amendments shall apply to all actions or proceedings commenced on or after the effective date [September 16, 2013.]."

Rule 14.04. Signatures

(a) Judge and Administrator Signatures. All electronically filed and served documents that require a judge's, judicial officer's, or court administrator's signature shall either capture the signature electronically under a process approved by the state court administrator pursuant to judicial branch policy or begin with an actual signature on paper that is then scanned into an electronic document format such that the final electronic document has the judge's, judicial officer's, or court administrator's signature depicted thereon. The final electronic document shall constitute an original.

(b) Attorney or Declarant Signature. A document electronically filed or served using the E–Filing System shall be deemed to have been signed by the attorney or declarant and shall bear a facsimile or typographical signature of such person, along with the typed name, address, telephone number, and attorney registration number of a signing attorney. Typographical signatures of an attorney or declarant shall be treated as a personal signature and shall be in the form: */s/ Pat L. Smith.*

(c) Notary Signature, Stamp. A document electronically filed or served using the E–Filing System that requires a signature of a notary public shall be deemed signed by the notary public if, before filing or service, the notary public has signed a printed or electronic form of the document and the electronically filed or served document bears a facsimile or typographical notary signature and stamp.

(d) Perjury Penalty Acknowledgement. A document electronically filed or served using the E–Filing System that requires a signature under penalty of perjury is deemed signed by the declarant if, before filing or service, the declarant has signed a printed form of the document and the electronically filed or served document bears the declarant's facsimile or typographical signature.

(e) Certification; Retention. By electronically filing or submitting a document using the E–Filing System, the registered attorney or party filing or serving is certifying compliance with the signature requirements of these rules, and the signatures on the document shall have the same legal effect as the signatures on the original document.

Adopted May 24, 2012, eff. Sept. 1, 2012.

Advisory Committee Comment—2012 Amendment

See note following Rule 14.07.

Rule 14.05. Proof of Service

The records of the E–Filing System indicating transmittal to a registered recipient who has designated an e-mail address for service of process in the case shall be sufficient proof of service on the recipient for all purposes.

Adopted May 24, 2012, eff. Sept. 1, 2012.

Advisory Committee Comment—2012 Amendment

See note following Rule 14.07.

Rule 14.06. Sealed and Confidential Documents

A person electronically filing a document that is not accessible to the public in whole or in part under the Rules of Public Access to Records of the Judicial Branch or other applicable law, court rules or court order, is responsible for designating that document as confidential or sealed in the E–Filing System before transmitting it to the court.

A document marked as "confidential" (which may include "Confidential 1" and "Confidential 2", etc., as available and defined by the E–Filing System document security classifications) will not be accessible to the public, but will be accessible to court staff and, where applicable, to certain governmental entities as authorized by law, court rule, or court order. A document marked as "sealed" will not be accessible to the public but will be accessible to court staff with only the highest security level clearance.

Upon review, the court may modify the designation of any document incorrectly designated as sealed or confidential and shall provide prompt notice of any such change to the filing party. A filing party must seek advance approval from the court to submit a document designated as sealed or confidential if that document is not already inaccessible to the public under the Rules of Public Access to Records of the Judicial Branch or other applicable law, court rules, or court order.

A document to be filed under seal or as confidential may be filed in paper form if required or permitted by the court. A motion to file a document in paper form under seal or as confidential must be filed and served electronically.

Adopted May 24, 2012, eff. Sept. 1, 2012.

Advisory Committee Comment—2012 Amendment

See note following Rule 14.07.

Rule 14.07. Records: Official; Appeal; Certified Copies

Documents electronically filed are official court records for all purposes. Certified copies shall be issued in the conventional manner.

Adopted May 24, 2012, eff. Sept. 1, 2012.

Advisory Committee Comment—2012 Amendment

Rule 14 is a new rule, drafted to provide a uniform structure for implementation of e-filing and e-service in the district courts. The rule is derived in substantial part, with modification, from the Judicial District E–Filing Pilot Project Provisions, adopted by the Minnesota Supreme Court on October 21, 2010, and amended on March 10, 2011.

Rule 14.01 defines the cases that are subject to mandatory e-filing and e-service. This rule is intended to evolve by amendment by order of the supreme court as additional case categories or additional judicial districts are added to the pilot project. The other requirements for e-filing and e-service are not intended to see frequent amendment, and the committee believes the rules for e-filing and e-service, when authorized, should be maintained as uniform rules statewide.

Rule 14.01(d) provides for requests to be excused from required use of e-filing and e-service, and creates a "good cause" standard for granting that relief. There are few circumstances where the court should grant exemption from the requirements.

Because cases in Minnesota may be commenced by service rather than by filing with the court, the use of e-service under the court's system is possible only after the action has been commenced and is filed, and service may then be effected electronically only on an attorney or party who registers with the system and provides an e-mail address at which service from other parties and notices from the court can be delivered. Rule 14.02 sets forth this procedure. Rule 13.01 imposes an affirmative duty on parties and their attorneys to advise the court of any changes in their address, including their e-mail address.

The format requirements for documents are superficially the same as for other documents—they should be based on an 8½ by 11 inch format, with a caption at the top and signature block at the end. But they are in fact filed as electronic records on a computer service and served on other parties by e-mail. Rule 14.03 defines the available electronic format for these documents and other requirements applicable to e-filed and e-served documents.

Rule 14.04 establishes the means by which electronic documents are "signed." The rule explicitly states the standard that e-filed and e-served documents as they reside on the computer system used by the court constitute originals, and are not mere copies of documents. The rule does not require the signing or retention of a paper copy of any filed document. It may be prudent for a litigant to maintain copies of these documents as duplicate originals in some limited circumstances, such as where an affidavit is signed by a non-party who may not be available if a dispute were to arise over authenticity.

Rule 14.06 establishes a specific procedure for filing electronic documents that either contain confidential information or are filed under seal. This rule establishes the requirements for electronic documents that are consistent with the requirements in Rule 11.06. Neither rule is intended to expand or limit the confidentiality concerns that might justify special treatment of any document. Under Rule 11.06, filing parties do not have a unilateral right to designate any filing as confidential, and prior permission in some form is required. This permission may flow from a statute or rule explicitly requiring that a particular document or portion of a document be filed confidentially or from a court order that documents be filed under seal. Rule 112 of the Minnesota Rules of Civil Appellate Procedure contains useful guidance on how confidential information can be handled. Where documents contain both confidential and non-confidential information, it may be appropriate to file redacted "public" versions of confidential or sealed documents.

Rule 14.06 also permits a party to seek either permission or a requirement that certain sealed or confidential documents be filed in paper format. This provision recognizes that certain information may be so sensitive or valuable that placing it in a sealed envelope with a clear warning that it is not to be opened except by court order may be the appropriate means to assure confidentiality.

The security designations "confidential" and "sealed" reflect the security classifications available in the courts case management system. In addition to court staff access, some confidential documents (e.g., in Domestic Violence, Juvenile Delinquency, and Parent/Child relationship cases) may be accessible to certain government entities who have demonstrated a need for access and have signed appropriate nondisclosure agreements. See, e.g., Rule 8, subd. 4(b), of the Rules of Public Access to Records of the Judicial Branch (authorizing access by county attorneys and public defenders, among others).

Pursuant to Minn. R. Civ. P. 5.06, a document that is electronically filed is deemed to have been filed by the court administrator on the date and time of its transmittal to the District Court through the E-Filing System, and the filing shall be stamped with this date and time subject to acceptance by the court administrator. If the filing is not subsequently accepted by the court administrator for reasons authorized by Minn. R. Civ. P. 5.04, the date stamp shall be removed and the document electronically returned to the person who filed it.

APPENDIX OF FORMS FOR TITLE I. RULES APPLICABLE TO ALL COURT PROCEEDINGS

FORM 5. MOTION FOR ADMISSION PRO HAC VICE

State of Minnesota	**District Court**
______________________	______________________
County	Judicial District: __________
	Court File Number: __________
	Case Type:
______________________	______________________

STATE OF MINNESOTA)
) ss.
COUNTY OF __________)

______________________,
Plaintiff

vs.

Motion for Admission of
____
Pro Hac Vice

______________________,
Defendant.

________, being sworn/affirmed under oath, states:

I, ________, an active member in good standing of the bar of the State of Minnesota, move that this Court admit pro hac vice ________, an attorney admitted to practice in the trial courts of ________, but not admitted to the bar of this Court, who will be counsel for the ( ) Plaintiff ( ) Defendant in this case. I am aware that Rule 5 of the Minnesota General Rules of Practice requires me to (1) sign all pleadings in this case, (2) be present in person or by telephone at the proceeding at which this Motion is heard, and (3) be present in person or by telephone at all subsequent proceedings in this case unless the Court, in its discretion, conducts the proceedings without the presence of Minnesota counsel.

Dated: ________, 20 __.

Signature:

____
MN Attorney License Number:
Law Firm Name & Address:
Telephone: (   )

Affidavit of Proposed Admittee

STATE OF MINNESOTA)
) ss.
COUNTY OF __________)

________, being duly sworn, states the following under oath:

I am currently admitted to practice and in good standing in the trial courts of the following jurisdiction(s), but not admitted to the bar of this Court:

State	License #	Status	Admission Date

I understand that if this Court grants me admission pro hac vice, Rule 5 of the Minnesota General Rules of Practice requires the Minnesota lawyer bringing this Motion to (1) sign all pleadings in this case, (2) be present in person or by telephone at the proceeding at which this Motion is heard, and (3) be present in person or by telephone at all subsequent proceedings in this case unless the Court, in its discretion, conducts the proceedings without the presence of Minnesota counsel.

I also understand that Rule 5 of the Minnesota General Rules of Practice specifies that by appearing pursuant to that rule I am subject to the disciplinary rules and regulations governing Minnesota lawyers and that by applying to appear or appearing in any action I am subject to the jurisdiction of the Minnesota courts.

Dated: ________, 20 ___.

Signature:

____

Attorney License Number:
Law Firm Name & Address:
Telephone: ( )

Subscribed and sworn to before me this ___ day of ________, 20 __________.

____

ORDER

The foregoing Motion is hereby GRANTED.

Dated: ________, 20 ___.

____

Judge of District Court

Dated: ________, 20 ___.

For the Court:

______________________________,

Court Administrator

Note: The original of this form must be filed with Court Administrator before you will receive notices generated in this action.

Adopted Dec. 28, 2006, eff. Jan. 1, 2007.

Advisory Committee Comments—2007 Amendment

Form 5.1 is a new form recommended to facilitate compliance with Rule 5 on the admission of out-of-state lawyers *pro hac vice*. Neither the rule nor the adoption of this form limits the discretion of trial judges to determine whether to permit pro hac vice admission and to define the terms upon which a trial court may permit or refuse appearance by out-of-state lawyers. Courts may also require verification of a lawyers good standing in the bar of another court, either by verification on a public website or by requiring a certificate of good standing.

FORM 11.1. CONFIDENTIAL INFORMATION FORM

(Gen. R. Prac. 11.02)

State of Minnesota **District Court**

County of ________ ________ **Judicial District**

Case Type:

Case No. ___

____
Plaintiff/Petitioner

and

CONFIDENTIAL INFORMATION FORM
(Provided in Accordance With Rule 11 of the Minnesota General Rules of Practice)

____
Defendant/Respondent

The information on this form is confidential and shall not be placed in a publicly accessible portion of a file.

		NAME	SOCIAL SECURITY NUMBER EMPLOYER IDENTIFICATION NUMBER AND FINANCIAL ACCOUNT NUMBERS
Plaintiff/Petitioner	1.	______________	______________
	2.	______________	______________
	3.	______________	______________
Defendant/ Respondent	1.	______________	______________
	2.	______________	______________
	3.	______________	______________
Other Party (e.g., minor children)	1.	______________	______________
	2.	______________	______________

Information supplied by:

____
(print or type name of party submitting this form to the court)

Signed: _________________________
Attorney Reg. #: _________________________
Firm: _________________________
Address: _________________________
____
Date: _________________________

Adopted May 6, 2005, eff. July 1, 2005.

FORM 11.2. SEALED FINANCIAL SOURCE DOCUMENTS

(Gen. R. Prac. 11.02)

State of Minnesota **District Court**

County of ________ ________ **Judicial District**

Case Type: ________

Case No. ___

____
Plaintiff/Petitioner

and

____
Defendant/Respondent

SEALED FINANCIAL SOURCE DOCUMENTS
(Provided in Accordance With Rule 11.02 of the Minnesota General Rules of Practice)

THIS LISTING OF SEALED FINANCIAL SOURCE DOCUMENTS IS ACCESSIBLE TO THE PUBLIC BUT THE SOURCE DOCUMENTS SHALL NOT BE ACCESSIBLE TO THE PUBLIC EXCEPT AS AUTHORIZED BY COURT RULE OR ORDER

☐ Income tax records
Periods covered:

☐ Bank statements
Periods covered:

☐ Pay stubs
Periods covered:

☐ Credit card statement
Periods covered:

☐ Other:

Information supplied by:

____

(print or type name of party submitting this form to the court)

Signed: ______________________
Attorney Reg. #: ______________________
Firm: ______________________
Address: ______________________
____
Date: ______________________

Adopted May 6, 2005, eff. July 1, 2005.

TITLE II. RULES GOVERNING CIVIL ACTIONS

PART A. PLEADINGS, PARTIES, AND LAWYERS

RULE 101. SCOPE OF RULES

Rules 101 through 145 shall apply in all civil actions, except those governed by the Rules of Juvenile Procedure.

Adopted Sept. 5, 1991, eff. Jan. 1, 1992.

Rule 102. [RENUMBERED RULE 6 EFF. JAN. 1, 1993]

Historical Notes

Rule 102 relating to form of pleadings and other papers was renumbered to Rule 6 by a court order [CX–89–1863, C6–84–2134] dated November 13, 1992 effective on January 1, 1993.

RULE 103. [RENUMBERED RULE 7 EFF. JAN. 1, 1993]

Historical Notes

Rule 103 relating to proof of service was renumbered to Rule 7 by a court order [CX–89–1863, C6–84–2134] dated November 13, 1992 effective on January 1, 1993.

RULE 104. CIVIL COVER SHEET AND CERTIFICATE OF REPRESENTATION AND PARTIES

Except as otherwise provided in these rules for specific types of cases and in cases where the action is commenced by filing by operation of statute, a party filing a civil case shall, at the time of filing, notify the court administrator in writing of:

(a) If the case is a family case or a civil case listed in Rule 111.01 of this rule, the name, postal address, e-mail address, and telephone number of all counsel and unrepresented parties, if known, in a Certificate of Representation and Parties (see Form CIV102 promulgated by the state court administrator and published on the website www.mncourts.gov) or

(b) If the case is a non-family civil case other than those listed in Rule 111.01, basic information about the case in a Civil Cover Sheet (see Form CIV117 promulgated by the state court administrator and published on the website www.mncourts.gov) which shall also include the information required in part (a) of this rule. Any other party to the action may, within ten days of service of the filing party's civil cover sheet, file a supplemental civil cover sheet to provide additional information about the case.

If that information is not then known to the filing party, it shall be provided to the court administrator in writing by the filing party within seven days of learning it. Any party impleading additional parties shall provide the same information to the court administrator. The court administrator shall, upon receipt of the completed certificate, notify all parties or their lawyers, if represented by counsel, of the date of filing the action and the file number assigned.

Adopted Sept. 5, 1991, eff. Jan. 1, 1992. Amended Nov. 13, 1992, eff. Jan. 1, 1993; Dec. 14, 1995, eff. Jan. 1, 1996; May 7, 2013, eff. July 1, 2013.

Advisory Committee Comments—1995 Amendments

This rule is derived from 7th Dist.R. 7 (eff. Jan. 1, 1990).

The final sentence is derived from 2d Dist.R. 2(b).

This rule formalizes the requirement to provide information about all parties when an action is filed. Its need derives from the commencement of actions by service and the fact that many pleadings are routinely not filed. The certificate of representation and parties serves a purpose of allowing the court to give notice of assignment of a judge to the case (in those districts making that assignment prior to trial), thereby triggering for all parties the 10–day period to remove an assigned judge under Minn. R. Civ. P. 63.

This requirement now exists in the Fourth and Seventh districts, and seems to be the type of requirement the Task Force seeks to make uniform statewide. The required information may be submitted in typed form or on forms available from the court administrator. A sample form is included in the Appendix of Forms as Form 104.

The first clause of the rule is intended to make it clear that where other rules provide specific requirements relating to initiation of an action for scheduling purposes, those rules govern. For example, Minn. Gen. R. Prac. 144.01, as amended in 1992, states that the Certificate of Representation required under this rule is not required in wrongful death actions following the mere filing of a petition for appointment of the trustee, but is required after the action itself is commenced by service of the summons and papers are filed with the court. Rule 141.02, as amended in 1992, similarly provides that filing of a notice of appeal from a commissioner's award triggers the assignment process requirements in condemnation proceedings. In addition to cases exempted by rule, this rule was amended in 1995 to exempt its application to actions that are commenced by filing. In those cases, it is unfair and inappropriate to place additional burdens on the filing process that are not required by statute, and which might result in the rejection of a document for filing. The consequences of rejecting such a document can be dire, Minn.Stat. § 514.11, *Cf.AAA Electric & Neon Service, Inc. v. R. Design Co.,* 364 N.W.2d 869 (Minn.App.1985) (bar by not meeting filing requirement of action in a timely manner). The Advisory Committee believes it is not appropriate to reject such documents for filing in any event, but this rule now makes it clear that a certificate of representation and parties is not required in actions commenced by filing. For the convenience of the parties, frequently encountered examples of actions that are commenced by filing include mechanic's lien actions, quiet title actions, and actions to register title to real property (Torrens actions). This amendment is intended to remove the requirement that a certificate of representation and parties accompany the complaint for filing. It is not intended to prevent courts from obtaining this information, if still needed, after process has been served and the parties' representation known.

Cross Reference: Minn. R. Civ. P. 5.04.

Historical Notes

The order of the Minnesota Supreme Court [CX–89–1863, C6–84–2134] dated December 14, 1995, provides in part that "(t)he attached amendments shall apply to all actions pending on the effective date and to those filed thereafter."

The order of the Minnesota Supreme Court [ADM04–8001, ADM09–8009, ADM–10-8051] dated May 7, 2013, provided in part that the amendments be effective July 1, 2013, and further provided in part that "[t]hese amendments apply to all actions or proceedings pending on or commenced after the effective date", and further provided that the "February 4, 2013 and February 12, 2013 orders of the court are hereby rescinded to the extent inconsistent with this order."

RULE 105. WITHDRAWAL OF COUNSEL

After a lawyer has appeared for a party in any action, withdrawal will be effective only if written notice of withdrawal is served on all parties who have appeared, or their lawyers if represented by counsel, and is filed with the court administrator if any other paper in the action has been filed. The notice of withdrawal shall include the address and phone number where the party can be served or notified of matters relating to the action.

Withdrawal of counsel does not create any right to continuance of any scheduled trial or hearing.

Adopted Sept. 5, 1991, eff. Jan. 1, 1992. Amended Dec. 8, eff. Jan. 1, 1998.

Advisory Committee Comment—1997 Amendment

The Task Force believes that uniformity in withdrawal practice and procedure would be desirable. Existing practice varies, in part due to differing rules and in part due to differing practices in the absence of a rule of statewide application. The primary concern upon withdrawal is the continuity of the litigation. Withdrawal should not impose additional burdens on opposing parties. The Task Force considered various rules that would make it more onerous for lawyers to withdraw, but determined those rules are not necessary nor desirable. Consistent with the right of parties to proceed pro se, they may continue to represent themselves where their lawyers have withdrawn. This rule establishes the procedure for withdrawal of counsel; it does not itself authorize withdrawal nor does it change the rules governing a lawyer's right or obligation to withdraw in any way. *See* Minn. R.Prof.Cond. 1.16. The rule does not affect or lessen a lawyer's obligations to the client upon withdrawal. Those matters are governed by the Minnesota Rules of Professional Conduct. *See* Minn.R.Prof.Cond. 1.16. Enforcement of those rules is best left to the Lawyers Professional Responsibility Board.

The 1997 amendment removes any suggestion that the notice of withdrawal must be filed with the court if no other documents have been filed by any party. When other documents are filed by any party, however, it should be filed as required by Minn.R.Civ.P. 5.04.

The rule makes it clear that the withdrawal of counsel does not, in itself, justify continuance of any trial or hearing. Of course, withdrawal or substitution of counsel may be part of a set of circumstances justifying the exercise of the court's discretion to grant a continuance.

Historical Notes

The order of the Minnesota Supreme Court [CX–89–1863] dated December 8, 1997, provides in part that "(t)he attached amendments shall apply to all actions pending on the effective date and to those filed thereafter."

The order of the Minnesota Supreme Court [CX–89–1863] dated December 8, 1997, amending the General Rules of Practice for the District Courts provides in part that "(t)he inclusion of Advisory Committee comments is made for convenience and does not reflect court approval of the comments made therein."

RULE 106. HEARING ON MOTION TO REMOVE JUDGE FOR ACTUAL PREJUDICE OR BIAS

All motions for removal of a judge, referee, or judicial officer, on the basis of actual prejudice or bias shall be heard in the first instance by the judge sought to be removed. If that judge denies the motion, it may subsequently be heard and reconsidered by the Chief Judge of the district or another judge designated by the Chief Judge.

Adopted Sept. 5, 1991, eff. Jan. 1, 1992.

Task Force Comment—1991 Adoption

Minn. R. Civ. P. 63.02 does not currently specify the procedure to be followed when a motion is made to remove a judge from hearing a case on the grounds of actual bias or prejudice. This rule requires the motion to be heard initially by the judge sought to be removed, and allows the chief judge of the district to reconsider the motion if it is denied by the affected trial judge. The rule does not require the party seeking removal to bring the motion for reconsideration before the chief judge; it merely permits that reconsideration. Bringing the motion for reconsideration should not be construed as any condition precedent to appellate review, whether by appeal or extraordinary writ.

The rule intentionally allows a motion for reconsideration only if the trial court denies the motion for removal. If the motion is granted, it should only be addressed further on appeal.

The procedure for review by the chief judge of the district is not entirely satisfactory. Consideration should be given to facilitating appeal of these issues to the appellate courts, but the Task Force did not directly address this question because of the current limited jurisdiction of the appellate courts to hear appeals of decisions by judges declining to recuse themselves.

Cross Reference: Minn.R.Civ.P. 63.02.

RULE 107. PROCEDURE FOR CHALLENGE FOR HAVING A REFEREE HEAR A MATTER

Any party objecting to having any referee hear a contested trial, hearing, motion or petition shall serve and file the objection within ten days of notice of the assignment of a referee to hear any aspect of the case, but not later than the commencement of any hearing before a referee.

Adopted Sept. 5, 1991, eff. Jan. 1, 1992.

Task Force Comment—1991 Adoption

This rule serves to comply with the requirements of Minn. Stat. § 484.70, subd. 6 (1990), which provides:

> No referee may hear a contested trial, hearing, motion or petition if a party or lawyer for a party objects in writing to the assignment of the referee to hear the matter. The court shall, by rule, specify the time within which an objection must be filed.

This rule is intended to specify the procedure for filing this notice. The procedure and time limits are derived from the requirements of Minn. R. Civ. P. 63.03 for removing a judge by notice to remove. The Task Force believes it is desirable to use the same procedures, time limits, and time calculation rules for these different types of removal.

This rule should apply to all referee assignments with the exception of referees assigned in Housing Court in Ramsey and Hennepin Counties. These courts are governed by Rule 602 of these rules.

Cross Reference: Minn.R.Civ.P. 63.

RULE 108. GUARDIAN AD LITEM

Rule 108.01. Role of Guardian Ad Litem

Whenever the court appoints a guardian ad litem, the guardian ad litem shall be furnished copies of all pleadings, documents and reports by the party or agency which served or submitted them. A party or agency submitting, providing or serving reports and documents to or on a party or the court, shall provide copies promptly thereafter to the guardian ad litem.

Upon motion, the court may extend the guardian ad litem's powers as it deems necessary. Except upon a showing of exigent circumstance, the guardian ad litem shall submit any recommendations, in writing, to the parties and to the court at least 10 days prior to any hearing at which such recommendations shall be made. For purposes of all oral communications between a guardian ad litem and the court, the guardian ad litem shall be treated as a party.

Adopted Sept. 5, 1991, eff. Jan. 1, 1992. Amended Sept. 30, 2004, eff. Jan. 1, 2005.

Rule 108.02. Guardian Ad Litem Not Lawyer for Any Party

The guardian ad litem shall not be a lawyer for any party to the action.

Former Rule 108.03, adopted Sept. 5, 1991, eff. Jan. 1, 1992. Amended Sept. 30, 2004, eff. Jan. 1, 2005. Renumbered Rule 108.02 and amended Dec. 1, 2006, eff. Jan. 1, 2007.

Task Force Comment—1991 Adoption

This rule requires all discussions with a guardian ad litem regarding a case to be made as if the guardian ad litem were a party. It does not prohibit general discussions or briefing of guardians ad litem or potential guardians ad litem from taking place ex parte.

In personal injury actions, neither the lawyer nor any member of the lawyer's firm should be guardian. For the same reason, such a lawyer should not accept a referral fee with respect to the guardianship.

Rule 108.03. Guardian Ad Litem Not Lawyer for Any Party [Renumbered Rule 108.02, Dec. 1, 2006, eff. Jan. 1, 2007]

RULE 109. APPLICATION FOR LEAVE TO ANSWER OR REPLY

Rule 109.01. Requirement of Affidavit of Merits

Any application for leave to answer or reply after the time limited by statute or rule, or to open a judgment and for leave to answer and defend, shall be accompanied by a copy of the answer or reply, and an affidavit of merits and be served on the opposite party.

Adopted Sept. 5, 1991, eff. Jan. 1, 1992.

Rule 109.02. Contents of Required Affidavits

In an affidavit of merits made by the party, the affiant shall state with particularity the facts relied upon as a defense or claim for relief, that the affiant has fully and fairly stated the facts in the case to counsel, and that the affiant has a good and substantial defense or claim for relief on the merits, as the affiant is advised by counsel after such statement and believes true, and the affiant shall also give the name and address of such counsel.

An affidavit shall also be made by a lawyer who shall state that from the showing of the facts made by the party to the lawyer believes that such party has a good and substantial defense or claim for relief on the merits.

Adopted Sept. 5, 1991, eff. Jan. 1, 1992.

Task Force Comment—1991 Adoption

This rule is derived from Rule 22 of the Code of Rules for the District Courts.

Cross Reference: Minn.R.Civ.P. 4.043, 6.02, 59.03, 59.05, 60.02.

RULE 110. SELF–HELP PROGRAMS

Rule 110.01. Authority for Self–Help Programs

A District Court for any county may establish a Self–Help Program to facilitate access to the courts. The purpose of a Self–Help Program is to assist Self–Represented Litigants, within the bounds of this rule, to achieve fair and efficient resolution of their cases, and to minimize the delays and inefficient use of court resources that result from misuse of the court system by litigants who are not represented by lawyers. There is a compelling state interest in resolving cases efficiently and fairly, regardless of the financial resources of the parties.

Adopted Dec. 11, 2003, eff. Jan. 1, 2004.

Advisory Committee Comment—2003 Adoption

See comment following Rule 110.09.

Historical Notes

The order of the Minnesota Supreme Court [CX-89-1863] dated December 11, 2003, provides in part that these amendments are effective January 1, 2004, and shall apply to all actions or proceedings pending on or commenced on or after the effective date.

Rule 110.02. Staffing

The Self–Help Program may be staffed by lawyer and non-lawyer personnel, and volunteers under the supervision of regular personnel. Self–Help Personnel act at the direction of the district court judges to further the business of the court.

Adopted Dec. 11, 2003, eff. Jan. 1, 2004.

Advisory Committee Comment—2003 Adoption

See comment following Rule 110.09.

Historical Notes

The order of the Minnesota Supreme Court [CX-89-1863] dated December 11, 2003, provides in part that these amendments are effective January 1, 2004, and shall apply to all actions or proceedings pending on or commenced on or after the effective date.

Rule 110.03. Definitions

(a) "Self–Represented Litigant" means any individual who seeks information to file, pursue, or respond to a case without the assistance of a lawyer authorized to practice before the court.

(b) "Self–Help Personnel" means lawyer and non-lawyer personnel and volunteers under the direction of paid staff in a Self–Help Program who are performing the limited role under this rule. "Self–Help Personnel" does not include lawyers who are providing legal services to only one party as part of a legal services program that may operate along side or in conjunction with a Self–Help Program.

(c) "Self–Help Program" means a program of any name established and operating under the authority of this rule.

Adopted Dec. 11, 2003, eff. Jan. 1, 2004.

Advisory Committee Comment—2003 Adoption

See comment following Rule 110.09.

Historical Notes

The order of the Minnesota Supreme Court [CX-89-1863] dated December 11, 2003, provides in part that these amendments are effective January 1, 2004, and shall apply to all actions or proceedings pending on or commenced on or after the effective date.

Rule 110.04. Role of Self–Help Personnel

(a) Required Acts. Self–Help Personnel shall

(1) Educate Self–Represented Litigants about available pro bono legal services, low cost legal services, legal aid programs, lawyer referral services and legal resources provided by state and local law libraries;

(2) Encourage Self–Represented Litigants to obtain legal advice;

(3) Provide information about mediation services;

(4) Provide services on the assumption that the information provided by the litigant is true; and

(5) Provide the same services and information to all parties to an action, if requested.

(b) Permitted, but Not Required, Acts. Self–Help Personnel may, but are not required to:

(1) provide forms and instructions;

(2) assist in the completion of forms;

(3) provide information about court process, practice and procedure;

(4) offer educational sessions and materials on all case types, such as sessions and materials on marriage dissolution;

(5) answer general questions about family law and other issues and how to proceed with such matters;

(6) explain options within and outside of the court system;

(7) assist in calculating guidelines child support based on information provided by the Self–Represented Litigant;

(8) assist with preparation of court orders under the direction of the court; and

(9) provide other services consistent with the intent of this rule and the direction of the court, including programs in partnership with other agencies and organizations.

(c) Prohibited Acts. Self–Help Personnel may not:

(1) represent litigants in court;

(2) perform legal research for litigants;

(3) deny a litigant's access to the court;

(4) lead litigants to believe that they are representing them as lawyers in any capacity or induce the public to rely on them for personal legal advice;

(5) recommend one option over another option;

(6) offer legal strategy or personalized legal advice;

(7) tell a litigant anything she or he would not repeat in the presence of the opposing party;

(8) investigate facts pertaining to a litigants case, except to help the litigant obtain public records; or

(9) disclose information in violation of statute, rule, or case law.

Adopted Dec. 11, 2003, eff. Jan. 1, 2004.

Advisory Committee Comment—2003 Adoption

See comment following Rule 110.09.

Historical Notes

The order of the Minnesota Supreme Court [CX-89-1863] dated December 11, 2003, provides in part that these amendments are effective January 1, 2004, and shall apply to all actions or proceedings pending on or commenced on or after the effective date.

Rule 110.05. Disclosure

Self–Help Programs shall provide conspicuous notice that:

(a) no attorney-client relationship exists between Self–Help Personnel and Self–Represented Litigants;

(b) communications with Self–Help Personnel are neither privileged nor confidential;

(c) Self–Help Personnel must remain neutral and may provide services to the other party; and

(d) Self–Help personnel are not responsible for the outcome of the case.

Program materials should advise litigants to consult with their own attorney if they desire personalized advice or strategy, confidential conversations with an attorney, or if they wish to be represented by an attorney in court.

Adopted Dec. 11, 2003, eff. Jan. 1, 2004.

Advisory Committee Comment—2003 Adoption

See comment following Rule 110.09.

Historical Notes

The order of the Minnesota Supreme Court [CX-89-1863] dated December 11, 2003, provides in part that these amendments are effective January 1, 2004, and shall apply to all actions or proceedings pending on or commenced on or after the effective date.

Rule 110.06. Unauthorized Practice of Law

The performance of services by Self–Help Personnel in accordance with this rule shall not constitute the unauthorized practice of law.

Adopted Dec. 11, 2003, eff. Jan. 1, 2004.

Advisory Committee Comment—2003 Adoption

See comment following Rule 110.09.

Historical Notes

The order of the Minnesota Supreme Court [CX-89-1863] dated December 11, 2003, provides in part that these amendments are effective January 1, 2004, and shall apply to all actions or proceedings pending on or commenced on or after the effective date.

Rule 110.07. No Attorney–Client Privilege or Confidentiality

Except as provided in Rule 110.09, information given by a Self–Represented Litigant to court administration staff or Self–Help Personnel is neither confidential nor privileged. No attorney-client relationship exists between Self–Help Personnel and a Self–Represented Litigant. Notwithstanding the foregoing, Self–Help Personnel who are also lawyers and are permitted to practice law outside the role of Self–Help Personnel under this rule must abide by all applicable Rules of Professional Conduct regarding confidentiality and conflicts of interest.

Adopted Dec. 11, 2003, eff. Jan. 1, 2004.

Advisory Committee Comment—2003 Adoption

See comment following Rule 110.09.

Historical Notes

The order of the Minnesota Supreme Court [CX-89-1863] dated December 11, 2003, provides in part that these amendments are effective January 1, 2004, and shall apply to all actions or proceedings pending on or commenced on or after the effective date.

Rule 110.08. Conflict

Notwithstanding ethics rules that govern attorneys, certified legal interns, and other persons working under the supervision of an attorney, there shall be no conflict of interest when Self–Help Personnel provide services to both parties, provided, however, that Self–Help Personnel who are also lawyers and are permitted to practice law outside the role of Self–Help Personnel under this rule, must abide by all applicable Rules of Professional Conduct regarding conflicts of interest.

Adopted Dec. 11, 2003, eff. Jan. 1, 2004.

Advisory Committee Comment—2003 Adoption

See comment following Rule 110.09.

Historical Notes

The order of the Minnesota Supreme Court [CX-89-1863] dated December 11, 2003, provides in part that these amendments are effective January 1, 2004, and shall apply to all actions or proceedings pending on or commenced on or after the effective date.

Rule 110.09. Access to Records

All records made or received in connection with the official business of a Self-Help Program relating to the address, telephone number or residence of a Self-Represented Litigant are not accessible to the public or the other party.

Adopted Dec. 11, 2003, eff. Jan. 1, 2003.

Advisory Committee Comment—2003 Adoption

Rule 110 is a new rule adopted in 2003 on the recommendation of a pro se implementation committee to facilitate access to and use of the courts by pro se litigants. It is modeled after similar family law provisions in other jurisdictions. *See, e.g.,* CA. FAM. CODE §§ 10000 –100015 (West 2003); FLA. FAM. L. R. P. 12.750 (West 2003); OR.REV. STAT. § 3.428 (2003); WASH. REV. CODE § 26.12.240 (2003); WASH. R. GEN. GR 27 (West 2003).

The rule defines and communicates to interested parties the role of Self-Help Personnel. Definition of roles is important because of the potential for confusion. Rule 110.03(b) intentionally limits the definition of Self-Help Personnel to exclude lawyers who provide services to one party, as is commonly done by legal service program attorneys. Because of this definition, Rule 110.07 does not limit the creation of an attorney-client relationship in such attorney-client relationships. Rules 110.07–.08 recognize that Self-Help Personnel who are otherwise engaged in or authorized to engage in the practice of law may have obligations to clients outside the Self-Help Program that can affect their relationships to Self-Represented Litigants within the Self-Help Program.

Historical Notes

The order of the Minnesota Supreme Court [CX-89-1863] dated December 11, 2003, provides in part that these amendments are effective January 1, 2004, and shall apply to all actions or proceedings pending on or commenced on or after the effective date.

The order of the Minnesota Supreme Court [CX-89-1863] dated December 11, 2003, provides in part that "(t)he inclusion of Advisory Committee comments is made for convenience and does not reflect court approval of the statements made therein".

PART B. SCHEDULING

RULE 111. SCHEDULING OF CASES

Rule 111.01. Scope

The purpose of this rule is to provide a uniform system for scheduling matters for disposition and trial in civil cases, excluding only the following:

(a) Conciliation court actions and conciliation court appeals where no jury trial is demanded;

(b) Family court matters governed by Minn. Gen. R. Prac. 301 through 379;

(c) Public assistance appeals under Minnesota Statutes, section 256.045, subdivision 7;

(d) Unlawful detainer actions pursuant to Minnesota Statutes, sections 504B.281, et seq.;

(e) Implied consent proceedings pursuant to Minnesota Statutes, section 169.123;

(f) Juvenile court proceedings;

(g) Civil commitment proceedings subject to the Special Rules of Procedure Governing Proceedings Under the Minnesota Commitment Act of 1982;

(h) Probate court proceedings;

(i) Periodic trust accountings pursuant to Minn. Gen. R. Prac. 417;

(j) Proceedings under Minnesota Statutes, section 609.748 relating to harassment restraining orders;

(k) Proceedings for registration of land titles pursuant to Minnesota Statutes, chapter 508;

(*l*) Election contests pursuant to Minnesota Statutes, chapter 209; and

(m) Applications to compel or stay arbitration under Minnesota Statutes, chapter 572;

(n) consumer credit contract actions (see Case Type 3A, Minn. R. Civ. P. Form 23); and

(*o*) mechanics' lien actions.

The court may invoke the procedures of this rule in any action where not otherwise required.

Adopted Sept. 5, 1991, eff. Jan. 1, 1992. Amended Nov. 13, 1992, eff. Jan. 1, 1993; Dec. 14, 1993, eff. Jan. 1, 1994; Dec. 17, 1999, eff. Jan. 1, 2000; Sept. 5, 2001, eff. Sept. 5, 2001; Nov. 19, 2009, eff. Jan. 1, 2010; Dec. 1, 2009.

Advisory Committee Comment—1999 Amendments

Rule 111.01(d) is amended in 1999 to reflect the fact that Minn.Stat. § 566.01, et seq. were replaced by § 504B.281. This change is not intended to have any substantive effect other than to correct the statutory reference.

Advisory Committee Comment—2009 Amendment

Rule 111.01 is amended to exempt consumer credit contract actions and mechanics lien actions from the case scheduling regime generally followed in civil proceedings. These changes are made because these cases are required to be filed but are often either not ready for case scheduling or are unlikely ever to require it. "Consumer credit contract actions" refer to those cases properly carrying the case type identifier "3A. Consumer Credit Contracts," which as specified in Form 23 of the Minnesota Rules of Civil Procedure requires three things: (1) that the plaintiff is a corporation or other business organization, not an individual; (2) that the defendant is an individual; and (3) that the contract amount does not exceed $20,000.

Historical Notes

The order of the Supreme Court dated November 19, 2009, provided:

"1. The attached amendments to the General Rules of Practice for the District Courts and the Special Rules of Procedure Governing Proceedings under the Minnesota Commitment and Treatment Act be, and the same are, prescribed and promulgated to be effective on January 1, 2010.

"2. The attached amendments shall apply to all actions pending on the effective date and to those filed thereafter.

"3. The inclusion of Advisory Committee comments is made for convenience and does not reflect court approval of the comments made therein."

The order of the Minnesota Supreme Court [CX–89–1863, C6–84–2134] dated September 5, 1991 adopting the General Rules of Practice for the District Courts provided in part:

"In all pending actions in which any paper has been filed with the District Court prior to January 1, 1992, the filing date for purposes of Rules 111 and 304 of the attached General Rules of Practice for the District Courts shall be deemed to be January 1, 1992, unless otherwise ordered by the District Court."

Rule 111.02. The Party's Scheduling Input

The parties may submit scheduling information to the court as part of the civil cover sheet as provided in Rule 104 of these rules.

Adopted Sept. 5, 1991, eff. Jan. 1, 1992. Amended Dec. 2, eff. July 1, 1994; Dec. 22, 2008, eff. March 1, 2009; May 7, 2013, eff. July 1, 2013.

Historical and Statutory Notes

The order of the Minnesota Supreme Court [ADM04–8001, ADM09–8009, ADM–10-8051] dated May 7, 2013, provided in part that the amendments be effective July 1, 2013, and further provided in part that "[t]hese amendments apply to all actions or proceedings pending on or commenced after the effective date", and further provided that the "February 4, 2013 and February 12, 2013 orders of the court are hereby rescinded to the extent inconsistent with this order."

Rule 111.03. Scheduling Order

(a) When issued. No sooner than the due date of the last civil cover sheet under Rule 104, and no longer than 90 days after an action has been filed, the court shall enter its scheduling order. The court may issue the order after either a telephone or in-court conference, or without a conference or hearing if none is needed.

(b) Contents. The scheduling order shall provide for alternative dispute resolution as required by Rule 114.04(c) and shall establish a date for completion of discovery. The order may also establish any of the following:

(1) Deadlines for joining additional parties, whether by amendment or third-party practice;

(2) Deadlines for bringing non-dispositive or dispositive motions;

(3) Deadlines or specific dates for submitting particular issues to the court for consideration;

(4) A deadline for completing any independent physical, mental or blood examination pursuant to Minn. R. Civ. P. 35;

(5) A date for a formal discovery conference pursuant to Minn. R. Civ. P. 26.06, a pretrial conference or conferences pursuant to Minn. R. Civ. P. 16, or a further scheduling conference.

(6) Deadlines for filing any pre-trial submissions, including proposed instructions, verdicts, or findings of fact, witness lists, exhibits lists, statements of the case or any similar documents;

(7) Whether the case is a jury trial, or court trial if a jury has been waived by all parties;

(8) Identification of interpreter services (specifying language and, if known, particular dialect) any party anticipates will be required for any witness or party;

(9) A date for submission of a Joint Statement of the Case pursuant to Minn. Gen. R. Prac. 112; or

(10) A trial date.

Adopted Sept. 5, 1991, eff. Jan. 1, 1992. Amended Dec. 2, 1993, eff. July 1, 1994; Dec. 22, 2008, eff. March 1, 2009; May 7, 2013, eff. July 1, 2013.

Advisory Committee Comment—2008 Amendment

Rules 111.02(*l*) and 111.03(b)(8) are new provisions, adopted as part of amendments designed to foster earlier gathering of information about the potential need for interpreter services in a case, either for witnesses or for a party. *See* MINN. GEN. R. PRAC. 8.13.

Historical and Statutory Notes

The order of the Minnesota Supreme Court [ADM04–8001, ADM09–8009, ADM–10-8051] dated May 7, 2013, provided in part that the amendments be effective July 1, 2013, further provided in part that "[t]hese amendments apply to all actions or proceedings pending on or commenced after the effective date", and further provided that the "February 4, 2013 and February 12, 2013 orders of the court are hereby rescinded to the extent inconsistent with this order."

Rule 111.04. Amendment

A scheduling order pursuant to this rule may be amended at a pre-trial conference or upon motion for good cause shown. Except in unusual circumstances, a motion to extend deadlines under a scheduling order shall be made before the expiration of the deadline. The court may issue more than one scheduling order.

Adopted Sept. 5, 1991, eff. Jan. 1, 1992.

Advisory Committee Comment—1994 Amendments

This rule is new. This rule is intended to establish a uniform, mandatory practice of dealing with scheduling in every case by some court action. The rule does not establish, however, a single means of complying with the scheduling requirement nor does it set any rigid or uniform schedules. In certain instances, other rules establish the event giving rise to the requirement that the scheduling procedures be followed. *See, e.g.,* Rule 141 (condemnation scheduling triggered by appeal of commissioner's award); 144.01 (wrongful death scheduling triggered by filing paper in wrongful death action, not proceedings for appointment of trustee). Because applications to compel or stay arbitrations are, by statute, authorized to be handled by the

District Court in a summary matter and without the commencement of a separate action, it is appropriate that they be exempted from the formal case scheduling requirements of Rule 111.

Although the rule allows parties to submit scheduling information separately, this information may also be submitted jointly and required to be submitted jointly. In many cases, the efficient handling of the case may be fostered by the parties meeting to discuss scheduling issues and submitting a joint statement.

The rule contemplates establishment of a separate deadline for completion of an independent medical examination because the Task Force believes that it is frequently desirable to allow such an examination to take place after the conclusion of other discovery. The rule does not create any specific schedule for independent medical examinations, but allows, and encourages, the court to consider this question separately. The timing of these examinations is best not handled by rigid schedule, but rather, by the exercise of judgment on the part of the trial judge based upon the views of the lawyers, any medical information bearing on timing and the status of other discovery, as well as the specific factors set forth in Minn.R.Civ.P. 35. The Task Force considered a new rule expressly to exempt the use of requests for admissions pursuant to Minn.R.Civ.P. 36 from discovery completion deadlines in the ordinary case. The Task Force determined that a separate rule exempting requests for admissions from discovery deadlines in all cases was not necessary, but encourages use of extended deadlines for requests for admissions in most cases. The primary function served by these requests is not discovery, but the narrowing of issues, and their use is often most valuable at the close of discovery. *See* R. Haydock & D. Herr, *Discovery Practice* § 7.2 (2d ed. 1988). Because requests for admissions serve an important purpose of narrowing the issues for trial and resolving evidentiary issues relating to trial, it is often desirable to allow use of these requests after the close of other discovery.

Cross Reference: Minn.R.Civ.P. 16, 26.06, 35, 36, 38; Minn. Civ. Trialbook § 5.

Rule 111.05. Collaborative Law

(a) Collaborative Law Defined. Collaborative law is a process in which parties and their respective trained collaborative lawyers and other professionals contract in writing to resolve disputes without seeking court action other than approval of a stipulated settlement. The process may include the use of neutrals as defined in Rule 114.02(b), depending on the circumstances of the particular case. If the collaborative process ends without a stipulated agreement, the collaborative lawyers must withdraw from further representation.

(b) Deferral from Scheduling. Where the parties to an action request deferral in a form substantially similar to Form 111.03 and the court has agreed to attempt to resolve the action using a collaborative law process, the court shall defer setting any deadlines for the period specified in the order approving deferral.

(c) Additional ADR following Collaborative Law. When a case has been deferred pursuant to subdivision (b) of this rule and is reinstated on the calendar with new counsel or a collaborative law process has resulted in withdrawal of counsel prior to the filing of the case, the court should not ordinarily order the parties to engage in further ADR proceedings without the agreement of the parties.

Adopted Sept. 26, 2007, eff. Jan. 1, 2008.

Advisory Committee Comment—2007 Amendment

Rule 111.05 is a new rule to provide for the use of collaborative law processes in matters that would otherwise be in the court system. Collaborative law is a process that attempts to resolve disputes outside the court system. Where court approval or entry of a court document is necessary, such as for minor settlements or entry of a decree of marriage dissolution, the court's role may be limited to that essential task. Collaborative law is defined in Rule 111.05(a). The primary distinguishing characteristic of this process is the retention of lawyers for the parties, with the lawyers' and the parties' written agreement that if the collaborative law process is not successful and litigation ensues, each lawyer will withdraw from representing the client in the litigation.

Despite not being court-based, the committee believes the good faith use of collaborative law processes by the parties should be accommodated by the court in two ways. First, as provided in new Rule 111.05(b), the parties should be able to request deferral from scheduling for a duration to be determined appropriate by the parties. This can be accomplished through use of new Form 111.03 or similar submission providing substantially the same information. Second, if the parties have obtained deferral from scheduling for a collaborative law process that proves unsuccessful, the action should not normally or automatically ordered into another ADR process. The rule intentionally does not bar a second ADR process, as there may be cases where the court fairly views that such an effort may be worthwhile. These provisions for deferral and presumed exemption from a second ADR process are also made expressly applicable to family law matters by a new Rule 304.05.

RULE 112. JOINT STATEMENT OF THE CASE

Rule 112.01. When Required

As a case progresses, the court may find it advisable to implement the scheduling order and procedures of Minn.Gen.R.Prac. 111 by requiring the parties to report on the status of the case. This report shall be made in the form entitled Joint Statement of the Case (see Form 112.01 appended to these rules). The court may also choose to direct the filing of separate statements of the case. If the parties are directed to file a joint statement of the case, the plaintiff shall initiate and schedule the meeting and shall be responsible for filing the Joint Statement of the Case within these time limits. If the plaintiff is unable to obtain the cooperation, after genuine efforts, of the other parties in preparing a Joint Statement of the Case, the plaintiff may file a separate statement together with an affidavit setting forth the efforts made and reasons why a joint statement could not be filed.

Adopted Sept. 5, 1991, eff. Jan. 1, 1992. Amended Dec. 14, 1993, eff. Jan. 1, 1994.

Rule 112.02. Contents

The Joint Statement of the Case shall contain the following information to the extent applicable:

(a) a statement that all parties have been served, that the case is at issue, and that all parties have joined in the filing of the Statement of the Case.

(b) an estimated trial time.

(c) whether a jury trial has been requested, and if so, by which party.

(d) counsels' opinion whether the case should be handled as an expedited, standard, or complex case (determination to be made by the court).

(e) a concise statement of the case indicating the facts that Plaintiff(s) intend to prove and the legal basis for all claims.

(f) a concise statement of the case indicating the facts that Defendant(s) intend to prove and the legal basis for all defenses and counterclaims.

(g) names and addresses of all witnesses known to the lawyer or client who may be called at the trial by each party, including expert witnesses and the particular area of expertise each expert will be addressing. If any witness or party is likely to require interpreter services, that fact and the nature of the required services (specifying language and, if known, particular dialect) shall be provided.

Adopted Sept. 5, 1991, eff. Jan. 1, 1992. Amended Dec. 22, 2008, eff. March 1, 2009.

Advisory Committee Comment—2008 Amendment

Rule 112.02 is amended to include a provision designed to foster earlier gathering of information about the potential need for interpreter services in a case, either for witnesses or for a party. *See* MINN. GEN. R. PRAC. 8.13.

Rule 112.03. Contents—Personal Injury Actions

In cases involving personal injury, the Joint Statement of the Case shall also include a statement by each claimant, whether by complaint or counter-claim, setting forth the following:

(a) a detailed description of claimed injuries, including claims of permanent injury. If permanent injuries are claimed, the name of the doctor or doctors who will so testify;

(b) an itemized list of special damages to date including, but not limited to, auto vehicle damage and method of proof thereof; hospital bills, x-ray charges, and other doctor and medical bills to date; loss of earnings to date fully itemized; and

(c) whether parties will exchange medical reports (See Minn.R.Civ.P. 35.04).

Adopted Sept. 5, 1991, eff. Jan. 1, 1992.

Rule 112.04. Contents—Vehicle Accidents

In cases involving vehicle accidents, the Joint Statement shall also include the following:

(a) a description of vehicles and other instrumentalities involved with information as to ownership or other relevant facts; and

(b) name of insurance carriers involved, if any.

Adopted Sept. 5, 1991, eff. Jan. 1, 1992.

Rule 112.05. Hearing

If no Joint Statement has been timely filed, the court may set the matter for hearing.

Adopted Sept. 5, 1991, eff. Jan. 1, 1992.

Advisory Committee Comment—1994 Amendment

This rule is new. The procedures implemented by this rule supplement the procedures of Rule 111.

The rule does not require that a joint statement of the case be used. The court can direct the parties to file separate statements, although the same format should be followed for such separate statements of the case.

The requirement that the parties confer to prepare a statement does not require a face-to-face meeting; the conference can be by telephone if that is suited to the needs of the particular case.

The final sentence of Rule 112.01 is added to provide a mechanism for the plaintiff ordered to file a Joint Statement of the Case but unable to obtain cooperation of the opposing parties. Although the rule as originally drafted did not place an undue burden on the plaintiff, the trial courts have occasionally done so when the plaintiff's opposing parties have thwarted the preparation of the Statement of the Case and prevented its filing. The amendment allows the plaintiff to proceed individually in that circumstance.

Cross Reference: Minn.R.Civ.P. 16, 35.04; Minn. Civ. Trialbook § 5.

RULE 113. ASSIGNMENT OF CASE(S) TO A SINGLE JUDGE

Rule 113.01. Request for Assignment of a Single Case to a Single Judge

(a) In any case that the court or parties believe is likely to be complex, or where other reasons of efficiency or the interests of justice dictate, the chief judge of the district or the chief judge's designee may order that all pretrial and trial proceedings shall be heard before a single judge. The court may enter such an order at any time on its own initiative, in response to a suggestion in a party's civil cover sheet filed under Rule 104, or on the motion of any party, and shall enter such an order when the requirements of Rule 113.01(b) have been met. The motion shall comply with these rules and shall be supported by affidavit(s). In any case assigned to a single judge pursuant to this Rule that judge shall actively use enhanced judicial management techniques, including, but not limited to, the setting of a firm trial date, establishment of a discovery cut off date, and periodic case conferences.

(b) Grounds. Unless the court finds that court management of the claims and/or issues involved has become routine or that the interests of justice require otherwise, the court shall order that all pretrial and trial proceedings shall be heard before a single judge upon a showing that the action is likely to involve one or more of the following:

(1) numerous pretrial motions raising difficult or novel legal issues that will be time consuming to resolve;

(2) management of a large number of witnesses or substantial amount of documentary evidence;

(3) management of a large number of separately represented parties;

(4) the opportunity to coordinate with related actions pending in another court;

(5) substantial post-judgment judicial supervision.

Adopted Feb. 3, 1994, eff. July 1, 1994. Amended Dec. 19, 2000, eff. March 1, 2001; May 7, 2013, eff. July 1, 2013.

Historical Notes

The order of the Minnesota Supreme Court [CX-89-1863] dated December 19, 2000, provides in part that these amendments are effective March 1, 2001, and shall apply to all actions or proceedings pending on or commenced on or after the effective date, with the exception of the amendments to Rule 114.13, which shall become effective on further order of the court following the action of the Alternative Dispute Resolution (ADR) Review Board.

The order of the Minnesota Supreme Court [CX-89-1863] dated December 19, 2000, provides in part that "(t)he inclusion of Advisory Committee comments is made for convenience and does not reflect court approval of the statements made therein".

The order of the Minnesota Supreme Court [ADM04-8001, ADM09-8009, ADM-10-8051] dated May 7, 2013, provided in part that the amendments be effective July 1, 2013, and further provided in part that "[t]hese amendments apply to all actions or proceedings pending on or commenced after the effective date", and further provided that the "February 4, 2013 and February 12, 2013 orders of the court are hereby rescinded to the extent inconsistent with this order."

Rule 113.02. Consolidation of Cases Within a Judicial District

A motion for assignment of two or more cases pending within a single judicial district to a single judge shall be made to the chief judge of the district in which the cases are pending, or the chief judge's designee.

Adopted Feb. 3, 1994, eff. July 1, 1994. Amended Dec. 19, 2000, eff. March 1, 2001.

Historical Notes

The order of the Minnesota Supreme Court [CX-89-1863] dated December 19, 2000, provides in part that these amendments are effective March 1, 2001, and shall apply to all actions or proceedings pending on or commenced on or after the effective date, with the exception of the amendments to Rule 114.13, which shall become effective on further order of the court following the action of the Alternative Dispute Resolution (ADR) Review Board.

The order of the Minnesota Supreme Court [CX-89-1863] dated December 19, 2000, provides in part that "(t)he inclusion of Advisory Committee comments is made for convenience and does not reflect court approval of the statements made therein".

Rule 113.03. Assignment of Cases in More Than One District to a Single Judge

(a) Assignment by Chief Justice. When two or more cases pending in more than one judicial district involve one or more common questions of fact or are otherwise related cases in which there is a special need for or desirability of central or coordinated judicial management, a motion by a party or a court's request for assignment of the cases to a single judge may be made to the chief justice of the supreme court.

(b) Procedure. The motion shall identify by court, case title, case number, and judge assigned, if any, each case for which assignment to a single judge is requested. The motion shall also indicate the extent to which the movant anticipates that additional related cases may be filed. An original and two copies of the motion shall be filed with the clerk of appellate courts. A copy of the motion shall be served on other counsel and any unrepresented parties in all cases for which assignment is requested and the chief judge of each district in which such an action is pending. Any party may file and serve a response within 5 days after service of the motion. Any reply shall be filed and served within 2 days of service of the response. Except as otherwise provided in this rule, the motion and any response shall comply with the requirements of Minn. R. Civ. App. P. 127 and 132.02.

(c) Mechanics and Effect of Transfer. When such a motion is made, the chief justice may, after consultation with the chief judges of the affected districts and the state court administrator, assign the cases to a judge in one of the districts in which any of the cases is pending or in any other district. If the motion is to be granted, in selecting a judge the chief justice may consider, among other things, the scope of the cases and their possible impact on judicial resources, the availability of adequate judicial resources in the affected districts, and the ability, interests, training and experience of the available judges. As necessary, the chief justice may assign an alternate or back-up judge or judges to assist in the management and disposition of the cases. The assigned judge may refer any case to the chief judge of the district in which the case was pending for trial before a judge of that district selected by the chief judge.

Adopted Feb. 3, 1994, eff. July 1, 1994. Amended Dec. 19, 2000, eff. March 1, 2001; Nov. 30, 2005, eff. Jan. 1, 2006.

Advisory Committee Comment—2000 Amendments

Rule 113.01 applies to assignment of a single case within a judicial district or county that does not already use a so-called block assignment system whereby cases are routinely assigned to the same judge for all pretrial and trial proceedings. Although parties can request a single-judge assignment in the informational statement under Rule 111, this rule contemplates a formal motion with facts presented supporting the request in the form of sworn testimony. The grounds for the motion in Rule 113.01(b) were derived from rules 1800–1811 of the California Special Rules for Trial Courts, Div. V, Complex Cases. If the court finds that management of the claims or issues has become routine, the matter would not rise to the level of requiring assignment to a single judge. A motion to certify a class, for example, might be routine in terms of court management. Once a class has been certified and the matter becomes a class action, however, the complexity may rise to the level that requires a single judge assignment. Under Rule 113.01(a), the motion is to be made to the chief judge (or his or her designee) of the district in which the case is pending.

Rule 113.02 recognizes that motions for consolidation of cases within a single judicial district may be heard by the chief judge of the district or his or her designee.

Rule 113.03 is new, and is intended merely to establish a formal procedure for requesting the chief justice to exercise the power to assign multiple cases in different districts to a single judge when the interests of justice dictate. The power to assign cases has been recognized by the supreme court in a few decisions over the past decade or so. *See, e.g., In re Minnesota Vitamin Antitrust Litigation*, 606 N.W.2d 446 (Minn. 2000); *In re Minnesota Silicone Implant Litigation*, 503 N.W.2d 472 (Minn. 1993); *In re Minnesota L-tryptophan Litigation*, No. C0–91–706 (Minn. Sup. Ct., Apr. 24, 1991); *In re Minnesota Asbestos Litigation*, No. C4–87–2406 (Minn. Sup. Ct., Dec. 15, 1987). The power is derived from the inherent power of the court and specific statutory recognition of that power in MINN. STAT. §§ 480.16 & 2.724 (1998). The rule is intended to establish a procedure for seeking consideration of transfer by the chief justice. The procedure contemplates notice to interested parties and consultation with the affected judges so that the sound administration of the cases is not compromised. Transfer of cases for coordinated pretrial proceedings is an established practice in the federal court system under 28 U.S.C. § 1407. Although this rule is not as complex as its federal counterpart, its purpose is largely the same—to facilitate the efficient and fair handling of multiple cases. Practice under the federal statute has worked well, and is one of the most important tools of complex case management in the federal courts. *See generally* DAVID F. HERR, MULTIDISTRICT LITIGATION: HANDLING CASES BEFORE THE JUDICIAL PANEL ON MULTIDISTRICT LITIGATION (1986 & Supp. 1996). A companion change is made to MINN. R. CIV. P. 63.03, making it clear that when a judge is assigned by order of the chief justice pursuant to this rule that the judge so appointed may not be removed peremptorily under Rule 63 or the statutory restatement of the removal power contained in MINN. STAT. § 542.16 (1998).

Advisory Committee Comment — 2006 Amendment

The amendments to Rule 113.03 are intended to provide more detailed guidance about the procedures to be followed in seeking transfer of cases under the rule. The rule clarifies the existing practice and specifically incorporates the normal procedures for handling motions in the appellate courts. Because the motion is made to the chief justice rather than the entire court, fewer copies are necessary, but other procedures of Minn. R. Civ. App. P. 127 and 132.02 apply to these motions.

Historical Notes

The order of the Minnesota Supreme Court [CX-89-1863] dated December 19, 2000, provides in part that these amendments are effective March 1, 2001, and shall apply to all actions or proceedings pending on or commenced on or after the effective date, with the exception of the amendments to Rule 114.13, which shall become effective on further order of the court following the action of the Alternative Dispute Resolution (ADR) Review Board.

The order of the Minnesota Supreme Court [CX-89-1863] dated December 19, 2000, provides in part that "(t)he inclusion of Advisory Committee comments is made for convenience and does not reflect court approval of the statements made therein".

RULE 114. ALTERNATIVE DISPUTE RESOLUTION

Rule 114.01. Applicability

All civil cases are subject to Alternative Dispute Resolution (ADR) processes, except for those actions enumerated in Minn.Stat. § 484.76 and Rules 111.01 and 310.01 of these rules.

Adopted Dec. 2, 1993, eff. July 1, 1994. Amended Oct. 10, 1996.

Advisory Committee Comment—1996 Amendment

This change incorporates the limitations on use of ADR in family law matters contained in Minn.Gen. R.Prac. 310.01 as amended by these amendments. The committee believes it is desirable to have the limitations on use of ADR included within the series of rules dealing with family law, and it is necessary that it be included here as well.

Historical Notes

The order of the Minnesota Supreme Court [CX-89-1863] dated October 10, 1996, provides in part that these amendments are effective July 1, 1997, except that rules 119 and 418 are effective January 1, 1997, that these amendments shall apply to all actions pending on the effective dates and to those filed thereafter, and that "(t)he inclusion of Advisory Committee comments is made for convenience and does not reflect court approval of the comments made therein".

Rule 114.02. Definitions

The following terms shall have the meanings set forth in this rule in construing these rules and applying them to court-affiliated ADR programs.

(a) ADR Processes.

Adjudicative Processes

(1) *Arbitration.* A forum in which a neutral third party renders a specific award after presiding over an adversarial hearing at which each party and its counsel present its position. If the parties stipulate in writing that the arbitration will be binding, then the proceeding will be conducted pursuant to the Uniform Arbitration Act (Minn. Stat. §§ 572.08–.30.). If the parties do not stipulate that the arbitration will be binding, then the award is non-binding and will be conducted pursuant to Rule 114.09.

(2) *Consensual Special Magistrate.* A forum in which the parties present their positions to a neutral in the same manner as a civil lawsuit is presented to a judge. This process is binding and includes the right of appeal to the Minnesota Court of Appeals.

(3) *Summary Jury Trial.* A forum in which each party and their counsel present a summary of their position before a panel of jurors. The number of jurors on the panel is six unless the parties agree otherwise. The panel may issue a non-binding advisory opinion regarding liability, damages, or both.

Evaluative Processes

(4) *Early Neutral Evaluation (ENE).* A forum in which attorneys present the core of the dispute to a neutral evaluator in the presence of the parties. This occurs after the case is filed but before discovery is conducted. The neutral then gives an assessment of the strengths and weaknesses of the case. If settlement does not result, the neutral helps narrow the dispute and suggests guidelines for managing discovery.

(5) *Non–Binding Advisory Opinion.* A forum in which the parties and their counsel present their position before one or more neutral(s). The neutral(s) then issue(s) a non-binding advisory opinion regarding liability, damages or both.

Investigation and Report Process

(6) *Neutral Fact Finding.* A forum in which a neutral investigates and analyzes a factual dispute and issues findings. The findings are non-binding unless the parties agree to be bound by them.

Facilitative Processes

(7) *Mediation.* A forum in which a neutral third party facilitates communication between parties to promote settlement. A mediator may not impose his or her own judgment on the issues for that of the parties.

Hybrid Processes

(8) *Mini–Trial.* A forum in which each party and their counsel present its position before a selected representative for each party, a neutral third party, or both, to develop a basis for settlement negotiations. A neutral may issue an advisory opinion regarding the merits of the case. The advisory opinion is not binding unless the parties agree that it is binding and enter into a written settlement agreement.

(9) *Mediation–Arbitration (Med–Arb).* A hybrid of mediation and arbitration in which the parties initially mediate their disputes; but if they reach impasse, they arbitrate any deadlocked issues.

(10) *Other.* Parties may by agreement create an ADR process. They shall explain their process in the civil cover sheet.

(b) Neutral. A "neutral" is an individual or organization who provides an ADR process. A "qualified neutral" is an individual or organization included on the State Court Administrator's roster as provided in Rule 114.12. An individual neutral must have completed the training and continuing education requirements provided in Rule 114.13. An organization on the roster must certify that an individual neutral provided by the organization has met the training and continuing education requirements of Rule 114.13. Neutral fact-finders selected by the parties for their expertise need not undergo training nor be on the State Court Administrator's roster.

Adopted Dec. 2, 1993, eff. July 1, 1994. Amended Oct. 10, 1996; Aug. 31, 1998, eff. Aug. 31, 1998; Dec. 17, 2004, eff. Jan. 1, 2005; May 7, 2013, eff. July 1, 2013..

Implementation Committee Comments—1993

The definitions of ADR processes that were set forth in the 1990 report of the joint Task Force have been used. No special educational background or professional standing (e.g., licensed attorney) is required of neutrals.

Advisory Committee Comment—1996 Amendment

The amendments to this rule are limited, but important. In subdivision (a)(10) is new, and makes it explicit that parties may create an ADR process other than those enumerated in the rule. This can be either a "standard" process not defined in the rule, or a truly novel process not otherwise defined or used. This rule specifically is necessary where the parties may agree to a binding process that the courts could not otherwise impose on the parties. For example, the parties can agree to "baseball arbitration" where each party makes a best offer which is submitted to an arbitrator who has authority to select one of the offers as fairest, but can make no other decision. Another example is the Divorce with Dignity Program established in the Fourth Judicial District, in which the parties and the judge agree to attempt to resolve disputed issues through negotiation and use of impartial experts, and the judge determines unresolved preliminary matters by telephone conference call and unresolved dispositive matters by written submissions.

The individual ADR processes are grouped in the new definitions as "adjudicative," "evaluative," "facilitative," and "hybrid." These collective terms are important in the rule, as they are used in other parts of the rule. The group definitions are useful because many of the references elsewhere in the rules are intended to cover broad groups of ADR processes rather than a single process, and because the broader grouping avoids issues of precise definition. The distinction is particularly significant because of the different training requirements under Rule 114.13.

Historical Notes

The order of the Minnesota Supreme Court [CX-89-1863] dated October 10, 1996, provides in part that these amendments are effective July 1, 1997, except that rules 119 and 418 are effective January 1, 1997, that these amendments shall apply to all actions pending on the effective dates and to those filed thereafter, and that "(t)he inclusion of Advisory Committee comments is made for convenience and does not reflect court approval of the comments made therein".

The order of the Minnesota Supreme Court [CX–89–1863] dated December 17, 2004, provides in part that "(t)he attached amendments shall apply to all actions pending on the effective date and to those filed thereafter."

The order of the Minnesota Supreme Court [ADM04–8001, ADM09–8009, ADM–10–8051] dated May 7, 2013, provided in part that the amendments be effective July 1, 2013, and further provided in part that "[t]hese amendments apply to all actions or proceedings pending on or commenced after the effective date", and further provided that the "February 4, 2013 and February 12, 2013 orders of the court are hereby rescinded to the extent inconsistent with this order."

Rule 114.03. Notice of ADR Processes

(a) Notice. The court administrator shall provide, on request, information about ADR processes available to the county and the availability of a list of neutrals who provide ADR services in that county.

(b) Duty to Advise Clients of ADR Processes. Attorneys shall provide clients with the ADR information.

Adopted Dec. 2, 1993, eff.July 1, 1994. Amended Oct. 10, 1996; Dec. 17, 2004, eff. Jan. 1, 2005.

Implementation Committee Comments—1993

This rule is designed to provide attorneys and parties to a dispute with information on the efficacy and availability of ADR processes. Court personnel are in the best position to provide this information. A brochure has been developed which can be used by court administrators to give information about ADR processes to attorneys and parties. The State Court Administrator's Office will maintain a master list of all qualified neutrals and will update the list and distribute it annually to court administrators.

Advisory Committee Comment—1996 Amendment

This change is made only to remove an ambiguity in the phrasing of the rule and to add titles to the subdivisions. Neither change is intended to affect the meaning or interpretation of the rule.

Historical Notes

The order of the Minnesota Supreme Court [CX-89-1863] dated October 10, 1996, provides in part that these amendments are effective July 1, 1997, except that rules 119 and 418 are effective January 1, 1997, that these amendments shall apply to all actions pending on the effective dates and to those filed thereafter, and that "(t)he inclusion of Advisory Committee comments is made for convenience and does not reflect court approval of the comments made therein".

The order of the Minnesota Supreme Court [CX–89–1863] dated December 17, 2004, provides in part that "(t)he attached amendments shall apply to all actions pending on the effective date and to those filed thereafter."

Rule 114.04. Selection of ADR Process

(a) Conference. After the service of a complaint or petition, the parties shall promptly confer regarding case management issues, including the selection and timing of the ADR process. Following this conference ADR information shall be included in the civil cover sheet required by Rule 104 and in the initial case management statement required by Rule 304.02.

In family law matters, the parties need not meet and confer where one of the parties claims to be the victim of domestic abuse by the other party or where the court determines there is probable cause that one of the parties or a child of the parties has been physically abused or threatened with physical abuse by the other party. In such cases, both parties shall complete and submit form 9A or 9B, specifying the form(s) of ADR the parties individually prefer, not what is agreed upon.

(b) Court Involvement. If the parties cannot agree on the appropriate ADR process, the timing of the process, or the selection of a neutral, or if the court does not approve the parties' agreement, the court shall, in cases subject to Rule 111, schedule a telephone or in-court conference of the attorneys and any unrepresented parties within thirty days after the due date for filing initial case management statements pursuant to Rule 304.02 or the filing of a civil cover sheet pursuant to Rule 104 to discuss ADR and other scheduling and case management issues.

Except as otherwise provided in Minnesota Statutes, section 604.11 or Rule 310.01, the court, at its discretion, may order the parties to utilize one of the non-binding processes; provided that no ADR process shall be approved if the court finds that ADR is not appropriate or if it amounts to a sanction on a non-moving party. Where the parties have proceeded in good faith to attempt to resolve the matter using collaborative law, the court should not ordinarily order the parties to use further ADR processes.

(c) Scheduling Order. The court's Scheduling Order pursuant to Rule 111.03 or 304.03 shall designate the ADR process selected, the deadline for completing the procedure, and the name of the neutral selected or the deadline for the selection of the neutral. If ADR is determined to be inappropriate, the Scheduling Order pursuant to Rule 111.03 or 304.03 shall so indicate.

(d) Post–Decree Family Law Matters. Post–decree matters in family law are subject to ADR under this rule. ADR may be ordered following the conference required by Rule 303.03(c).

Adopted Dec. 2, 1993, eff. July 1, 1994. Amended Dec. 14, 1995, eff. Jan. 1, 1996; Oct. 10, 1996; Dec. 17, 2004, eff. Jan. 1, 2005; Oct. 29, 2007, eff. Jan. 1, 2008; May 7, 2013, eff. July 1, 2013.

Implementation Committee Comments–1993

Early case evaluation and referral to an appropriate ADR process has proven to facilitate speedy resolution of disputes, and should be encouraged whenever possible. Mandatory referral to a non-binding ADR process may result if the judge makes an informed decision despite the preference of one or more parties to avoid ADR. The judge shall not order the parties to use more than one non-binding ADR process. Seriatim use of ADR processes, unless desired by the parties, is inappropriate. The judge's authority to order mandatory ADR processes should be exercised only after careful consideration of the likelihood that mandatory ADR in specific cases will result in voluntary settlement.

Advisory Committee Comments—1995 Amendments

Rule 114.04 is amended to make explicit what was implicit before. The rule mandates a telephone or in-court conference if the parties cannot agree on an ADR process. The primary purpose of that conference is to resolve the disagreement on ADR, and the rule now expressly says that. The court can, and usually will, discuss other scheduling and case management issues at the same time. The court's action following the conference required by this rule may be embodied in a scheduling order entered pursuant to Rule 111.03 of these rules.

Advisory Committee Comment—1996 Amendment

The changes to this rule are made to incorporate Rule 114's expanded applicability to family law matters. The rule adopts the procedures heretofore followed for ADR in other civil cases. The beginning point of the process is the informational statement, used under either Rule 111.02 or 304.02. The rule encourages the parties to approach ADR in all matters by conferring and agreeing on an ADR method that best suits the need of the case. This procedure recognizes that ADR works best when the parties agree to its use and as many details about its use as possible.

Subdivision (a) requires a conference regarding ADR in civil actions and after commencement of family law proceedings. In family cases seeking post-decree relief, ADR must be considered in the meeting required by Rule 303.03(c). Cases involving domestic abuse are expressly exempted from the ADR meet-and-confer requirement and courts should accommodate implementing ADR in these cases without requiring a meeting nor compromising a party's right to choose an ADR process and neutral.

The rule is not intended to discourage settlement efforts in any action. In cases where any party has been, or claims to have been, a victim of domestic violence, however, courts need to be especially cautious. Facilitative processes, particularly mediation, are especially prone to abuse since they place the parties in direct contact and may encourage them to compromise their rights in situations where their independent decision-making capacity is limited. The rule accordingly prohibits their use where those concerns are present.

Advisory Committee Comment—2007 Amendment

Rule 114.04(b) is amended to provide a presumptive exemption from court-ordered ADR under Rule 114 where the parties have previously obtained a deferral on the court calendar of an action to permit use of a collaborative law process as defined in Rule 111.05(a).

Historical Notes

The order of the Minnesota Supreme Court [CX–89–1863, C6–84–2134] dated December 14, 1995, provides in part that "(t)he attached amendments shall apply to all actions pending on the effective date and to those filed thereafter."

The order of the Minnesota Supreme Court [CX-89-1863] dated October 10, 1996, provides in part that these amendments are effective July 1, 1997, except that rules 119 and 418 are effective January 1, 1997, that these amendments shall apply to all actions pending on the effective dates and to those filed thereafter, and that "(t)he inclusion of Advisory Committee comments is made for convenience and does not reflect court approval of the comments made therein".

The order of the Minnesota Supreme Court [CX–89–1863] dated December 17, 2004, provides in part that "(t)he attached amendments shall apply to all actions pending on the effective date and to those filed thereafter."

The order of the Minnesota Supreme Court [CX–89–1863] dated October 29, 2007, provides in part that "(t)he attached amendments shall apply to all actions pending on the effective date and to those filed thereafter" and "(t)his order shall supersede the September 26, 2007, order to the extent that it is inconsistent with this order".

The order of the Minnesota Supreme Court [ADM04–8001, ADM09–8009, ADM10–8051] dated February 4, 2013, provides in part that the "amendments apply to all actions or proceedings pending on or commenced on or after the effective date [July 1, 2013]".

The order of the Minnesota Supreme Court [ADM04–8001, ADM09–8009, ADM–10-8051] dated May 7, 2013, provided in part that the amendments be effective July 1, 2013, and further provided in part that "[t]hese amendments apply to all actions or proceedings pending on or commenced after the effective date", and further provided that the "February 4, 2013 and February 12, 2013 orders of the court are hereby rescinded to the extent inconsistent with this order."

Rule 114.05. Selection of Neutral

(a) Court Appointment. If the parties are unable to agree on either a neutral or the date upon which the neutral will be selected, the court shall, in those cases subject to Rule 111, appoint a qualified neutral at the time of the issuance of the scheduling order required by Rule 111.03 or 304.03. In cases not subject to Rule 111, the court may appoint a qualified neutral at its discretion, after obtaining the views of the parties. In all cases, the order may establish a deadline for the completion of the ADR process.

(b) Exception from Qualification. Except when mediation or med-arb is chosen as a dispute resolution process, the court, in its discretion, or upon recommendation of the parties, may appoint a neutral who does not qualify under Rule 114.12 of these rules, if the appointment is based on legal or other professional training or experience. A neutral so selected shall be deemed to consent to the jurisdiction of the ADR Review Board and compliance with the Code of Ethics set forth in the Appendix to Rule 114.

(c) Removal. Any party or the party's attorney may file with the court administrator within 10 days of notice of the appointment of the neutral and serve on the opposing party a notice to remove. Upon receipt of the notice to remove the court administrator shall immediately assign another neutral. After a party has once disqualified a neutral as a matter of right, a substitute neutral may be disqualified by the party only by making an affirmative showing of prejudice to the chief judge or his or her designee.

(d) Availability of Child Custody Investigator. A neutral serving in a family law matter may conduct a custody investigation, or evaluation only (1) where the parties agree in writing executed after the termination of mediation, that the neutral shall conduct the investigation or evaluation; or (2) where there is no other person reasonably available to conduct the investigation or evaluation. Where the neutral is also the sole investigator for a county agency charged with making recommendations to the court regarding child custody and visitation, the neutral may make such recommendations, but only after the court administrator has made all reasonable attempts to obtain reciprocal services from an adjacent county. Where such reciprocal services are obtainable, the custody evaluation must be conducted by a person from the adjacent county agency, and not by the neutral who served in the family law matter.

Adopted Dec. 2, 1993, eff. July 1, 1994. Amended Oct. 10, 1996; Dec. 17, 2004, eff. Jan. 1, 2005.

Implementation Committee Comments–1993

Parties should consult the statewide roster for information on the educational background and relevant training and experience of the proposed neutrals. It is important that the neutrals' qualifications can be provided to the parties so that the parties may make an informed choice. Unique aspects of a dispute and the preference of the parties may require special qualifications by the neutral.

Parties should have the ability, within reason, to choose a neutral with special expertise or experience in the subject matter of the dispute, even if they do not qualify under Rule 114.12, though it is anticipated that this will occur infrequently. Parties to mediation and med-arb processes must appoint an individual who qualifies under Rule 114.12.

Advisory Committee Comment—1996 Amendment

This rule is amended only to provide for the expanded applicability of Rule 114 to family law matters. The rule also now explicitly permits the court to establish a deadline for completion of a court-annexed ADR process. This change is intended only to make explicit a power courts have had and have frequently exercised without an explicit rule.

Rule 114.05(d) is derived from existing Rule 310.08. Although it is clearly not generally desirable to have a neutral subsequently serve as child custody investigator, in some instances it is necessary. The circumstances where this occurs are, and should be, limited, and are defined in the rule. Where other alternatives exist in a county and for an individual case, a neutral should not serve as child custody investigator.

Historical Notes

The order of the Minnesota Supreme Court [CX-89-1863] dated October 10, 1996, provides in part that these amendments are effective July 1, 1997, except that rules 119 and 418 are effective January 1, 1997, that these amendments shall apply to all actions pending on the effective dates and to those filed thereafter, and that "(t)he inclusion of Advisory Committee comments is made for convenience and does not reflect court approval of the comments made therein".

The order of the Minnesota Supreme Court [CX-89-1863] dated December 17, 2004, provides in part that "(t)he attached amendments shall apply to all actions pending on the effective date and to those filed thereafter."

Rule 114.06. Time and Place of Proceedings

(a) Notice. The court shall send to the neutral a copy of the Order of Appointment.

(b) Scheduling. Upon receipt of the court's order, the neutral shall promptly schedule the ADR process in accordance with the scheduling order and inform the parties of the date. ADR processes shall be held at a time and place set by the neutral, unless otherwise ordered by the court.

(c) Final Disposition. If the case is settled through an ADR process, the attorneys shall complete the appropriate court documents to bring the case to a final disposition.

Adopted Dec. 2, 1993, eff. July 1, 1994. Amended Oct. 10, 1996; Dec. 17, 2004, eff. Jan. 1, 2005.

Implementation Committee Comments–1993

The neutral will schedule the ADR process date unless, the parties agree on a date within the time frame contained in the scheduling order. If the neutral is selected at the time of scheduling order, such order can serve as the court order appointing the neutral. In scheduling the ADR process the neutral will attempt to accommodate the parties' schedules.

Advisory Committee Comment—1996 Amendment

The only changes to this rule are the inclusion of titles to the subparagraphs. This amendment is not intended to affect the meaning or interpretation of the rule, but is included to make the rule easier to use.

Historical Notes

The order of the Minnesota Supreme Court [CX-89-1863] dated October 10, 1996, provides in part that these amendments are effective July 1, 1997, except that rules 119 and 418 are effective January 1, 1997, that these amendments shall apply to all actions pending on the effective dates and to those filed thereafter, and that "(t)he inclusion of Advisory Committee comments is made for convenience and does not reflect court approval of the comments made therein".

The order of the Minnesota Supreme Court [CX-89-1863] dated December 17, 2004, provides in part that "(t)he attached amendments shall apply to all actions pending on the effective date and to those filed thereafter."

Rule 114.07. Attendance at ADR Proceedings

(a) Privacy. Non-binding ADR processes are not open to the public except with the consent of all parties.

(b) Attendance. The court may require that the attorneys who will try the case attend ADR proceedings.

(c) Attendance at Adjudicative Sessions. Individuals with the authority to settle the case need not attend adjudicative processes aimed at reaching a decision in the case, such as arbitration, as long as such individuals are reasonably accessible, unless otherwise directed by the court.

(d) Attendance at Non-Adjudicative Sessions. Individuals with the authority to settle the case shall attend non-adjudicative processes aimed at settlement of the case, such as mediation, mini-trial, or med-arb, unless otherwise directed by the court.

(e) Sanctions. The court may impose sanctions for failure to attend a scheduled ADR process only if this rule is violated.

Adopted Dec. 2, 1993, eff. July 1, 1994. Amended Oct. 10, 1996; Dec. 17, 2004, eff. Jan. 1, 2005.

Implementation Committee Comments–1993

Effective and efficient use of an ADR process depends upon the participation of appropriate individuals in the process. Attendance by attorneys facilitates discussions with clients about their case. Attendance of individuals with authority to settle the case is essential where a settlement may be reached during the process. In processes where a decision is made by the neutral, individuals with authority to settle need only be readily accessible for review of the decision.

Advisory Committee Comment—1996 Amendment

This rule is amended only to incorporate the collective definitions now incorporated in Rule 114.02. This change is not intended to create any significant difference in the requirements for attendance at ADR sessions.

Historical Notes

The order of the Minnesota Supreme Court [CX-89-1863] dated October 10, 1996, provides in part that these amendments are effective July 1, 1997, except that rules 119 and 418 are effective January 1, 1997, that these amendments shall apply to all actions pending on the effective dates and to those filed thereafter, and that "(t)he inclusion of Advisory Committee comments is made for convenience and does not reflect court approval of the comments made therein".

The order of the Minnesota Supreme Court [CX–89–1863] dated December 17, 2004, provides in part that "(t)he attached amendments shall apply to all actions pending on the effective date and to those filed thereafter."

Rule 114.08. Confidentiality

(a) Evidence. Without the consent of all parties and an order of the court, or except as provided in Rule 114.09(e)(4), no evidence that there has been an ADR proceeding or any fact concerning the proceeding may be admitted in a trial de novo or in any subsequent proceeding involving any of the issues or parties to the proceeding.

(b) Inadmissibility. Subject to Minn. Stat. § 595.02 and except as provided in paragraphs (a) and (d), no statements made nor documents produced in non-binding ADR processes which are not otherwise discoverable shall be subject to discovery or other disclosure. Such evidence is inadmissible for any purpose at the trial, including impeachment.

(c) Adjudicative Evidence. Evidence in consensual special master proceedings, binding arbitration, or in non-binding arbitration after the period for a demand for trial expires, may be used in subsequent proceedings for any purpose for which it is admissible under the rules of evidence.

(d) Sworn Testimony. Sworn testimony in a summary jury trial may be used in subsequent proceedings for any purpose for which it is admissible under the rules of evidence.

(e) Records of Neutral. Notes, records, and recollections of the neutral are confidential, which means that they shall not be disclosed to the parties, the public, or anyone other than the neutral, unless (1) all parties and the neutral agree to such disclosure or (2) required by law or other applicable professional codes. No record shall be made without the agreement of both parties, except for a memorandum of issues that are resolved.

Adopted Dec. 2, 1993, eff. July 1, 1994. Amended Oct. 10, 1996; Dec. 17, 2004, eff. Jan. 1, 2005.

Implementation Committee Comments–1993

If a candid discussion of the issues is to take place, parties need to be able to trust that discussions held and notes taken during an ADR proceeding will be held in confidence.

This proposed rule is important to establish the subsequent evidentiary use of statements made and documents produced during ADR proceedings. As a general rule, statements in ADR processes that are intended to result in the compromise and settlement of litigation would not be admissible under Minn. R. Evid. 408. This rule underscores and clarifies that the fact that ADR proceedings have occurred or what transpired in them.[1] Evidence and sworn testimony offered in summary jury trials and other similar related proceedings is not excluded from admissibility by this rule, but is explicitly treated as other evidence or as in the other sworn testimony or evidence under the rules of evidence. Former testimony is excepted from the hearsay rule if the witness is unavailable by Minn. R. Evid. 804(b)(1). Prior testimony may also be admissible under Minn. R. Evid. 613 as a prior statement.

[1] So in original.

Advisory Committee Comment—1996 Amendment

The amendment of this rule in 1996 is intended to underscore the general need for confidentiality of ADR proceedings. It is important to the functioning of the ADR process that the participants know that the ADR proceedings will not be part of subsequent (or underlying) litigation. Rule 114.08(a) carries forward the basic rule that evidence in ADR proceedings is not to be used in other actions or proceedings. Mediators and lawyers for the parties, to the extent of their participation in the mediation process, cannot be called as witnesses in other proceedings. Minn. Stat. § 595.02, subd. 1a. This confidentiality should be extended to any subsequent proceedings.

The last sentence of 114.08(e) is derived from existing Rule 310.05.

Historical Notes

The order of the Minnesota Supreme Court [CX-89-1863] dated October 10, 1996, provides in part that these amendments are effective July 1, 1997, except that rules 119 and 418 are effective January 1, 1997, that these amendments shall apply to all actions pending on the effective dates and to those filed thereafter, and that "(t)he inclusion of Advisory Committee comments is made for convenience and does not reflect court approval of the comments made therein".

The order of the Minnesota Supreme Court [CX–89–1863] dated December 17, 2004, provides in part that "(t)he attached amendments shall apply to all actions pending on the effective date and to those filed thereafter."

The order of the Minnesota Supreme Court [CX–89–1863] dated December 17, 2004, amending the General Rules of Practice for the District Courts provides in part that "(t)he inclusion of Advisory Committee comments is made for convenience and does not reflect court approval of the comments made therein."

Rule 114.09. Arbitration Proceedings

(a) General.

Parties are free to opt for binding or non-binding arbitration. Whether they elect binding or non-binding arbitration, the parties may construct or select a set of rules to govern the process. The agreement to arbitrate must state what rules govern. If the parties elect binding arbitration, and their agreement to arbitrate is otherwise silent, the arbitration will be deemed to be conducted pursuant to Minn. Stat. § 572.08 *et seq.* ("Uniform Arbitration Act"). If they elect non-binding arbitration, and their agreement is otherwise silent, they shall conduct the arbitration pursuant to Rule 114.09, subsections (b)–(f). Parties are free, however, to contract to use provisions from both processes or to modify the arbitration procedure as they deem appropriate to their case.

(b) Evidence.

(1) Except where a party has waived the right to be present or is absent after due notice of the hearing, the arbitrator and all parties shall be present at the taking of all evidence.

(2) The arbitrator shall receive evidence that the arbitrator deems necessary to understand and determine the dispute. Relevancy shall be liberally construed in favor of admission. The following principles apply:

(I) *Documents.* If copies have been delivered to all other parties at least 10 days prior to the hearing, the arbitrator may consider written medical and hospital reports, records, and bills; documentary evidence of loss of income, property damage, repair bills or estimates; and police reports concerning an accident which gave rise to the case. Any other party may subpoena as a witness the author of a report, bill, or estimate, and examine that person as if under cross-examination. Any repair estimate offered as an exhibit, as well as copies delivered to other parties, shall be accompanied by a statement indicating whether or not the property was repaired. If the property was repaired, the statement must indicate whether the estimated repairs were made in full or in part and must be accompanied by a copy of the receipted bill showing the items repaired and the amount paid. The arbitrator shall not consider any police report opinion as to ultimate fault. In family law matters, the arbitrator may consider property valuations, business valuations, custody reports and similar documents.

(II) *Other Reports.* The written statement of any other witness, including written reports of expert witnesses not enumerated above and statements of opinion which the witness would be qualified to express if testifying in person, shall be received in evidence if: (1) copies have been delivered to all other parties at least 10 days prior to the hearing; and (2) no other party has delivered to the proponent of the evidence a written demand at least 5 days before the hearing that the witness be produced in person to testify at the hearing. The arbitrator shall disregard any portion of a statement received pursuant to the rule that would be inadmissible if the witness were testifying in person, but the inclusion of inadmissible matter does not render the entire statement inadmissible.

(III) *Depositions.* Subject to objections, the deposition of any witness shall be received in evidence, even if the deponent is not unavailable as a witness and if no exceptional circumstances exist, if: (1) the deposition was taken in the manner provided for by law or by stipulation of the parties; and (2) not fewer than 10 days prior to the hearing, the proponent of the deposition serves on all other parties notice of the intention to offer the deposition in evidence.

(IV) *Affidavits.* The arbitrator may receive and consider witness affidavits, but shall give them only such weight to which they are entitled after consideration of any objections. A party offering opinion testimony in the form of an affidavit, statement, or deposition, shall have the right to withdraw such testimony, and attendance of the witness at the hearing shall not then be required.

(3) Attorneys must obtain subpoenas for attendance at hearings through the court administrator, pursuant to Minn. R. Civ. P. 45. The party requesting the subpoena shall modify the form of the

subpoena to show that the appearance is before the arbitrator and to give the time and place set for the arbitration hearing. At the discretion of the arbitrator, nonappearance of a properly subpoenaed witness may be grounds for an adjournment or continuance of the hearing. If any witness properly served with a subpoena fails to appear or refuses to be sworn or answer, the court may conduct proceedings to compel compliance.

(c) Powers of Arbitrator

The arbitrator has the following powers:

(1) to administer oaths or affirmations to witnesses;

(2) to take adjournments upon the request of a party or upon the arbitrator's initiative;

(3) to permit testimony to be offered by deposition;

(4) to permit evidence to be introduced as provided in these rules;

(5) to rule upon admissibility and relevance of evidence offered;

(6) To invite the parties, upon reasonable notice, to submit pre-hearing or post-hearing briefs or pre-hearing statements of evidence;

(7) to decide the law and facts of the case and make an award accordingly;

(8) to award costs, within statutory limits;

(9) to view any site or object relevant to the case; and

(10) any other powers agreed upon by the parties.

(d) Record

(1) No record of the proceedings shall be made unless permitted by the arbitrator and agreed to by the parties.

(2) The arbitrator's personal notes are not subject to discovery.

(e) The Award

(1) No later than 10 days from the date of the arbitration hearing or the arbitrator's receipt of the final post-hearing memorandum, whichever is later, the arbitrator shall file with the court the decision, together with proof of service by first class mail on all parties.

(2) If no party has filed a request for a trial within 20 days after the award is filed, the court administrator shall enter the decision as a judgment and shall promptly mail notice of entry of judgment to the parties. The judgment shall have the same force and effect as, and is subject to all provisions of law relating to, a judgment in a civil action or proceeding, except that it is not subject to appeal, and may not be attacked or set aside. The judgment may be enforced as if it had been rendered by the court in which it is entered.

(3) No findings of fact, conclusions of law, or opinions supporting an arbitrator's decision are required.

(4) Within 90 days after its entry, a party against whom a judgment is entered pursuant to an arbitration award may move to vacate the judgment on only those grounds set forth in Minnesota Statutes Chapter 572.

(f) Trial after Arbitration

(1) Within 20 days after the arbitrator files the decision with the court, any party may request a trial by filing a request for trial with the court, along with proof of service upon all other parties. This 20–day period shall not be extended.

(2) The court may set the matter for trial on the first available date, or shall restore the case to the civil calendar in the same position as it would have had if there had been no arbitration.

(3) Upon request for a trial, the decision of the arbitrator shall be sealed and placed in the court file.

(4) A trial de novo shall be conducted as if there had been no arbitration.

Adopted Dec. 2, 1993, eff. July 1, 1994. Amended Oct. 10, 1996; Dec. 17, 2004, eff. Jan. 1, 2005.

Implementation Committee Comments—1993

The Committee made a conscious decision not to formulate rules to govern other forms of ADR, such as mediation, early neutral evaluations, and summary jury trials. There is no consensus among those who conduct or participate in those forms of ADR as to whether any procedures or rules are necessary at all, let alone what those rules or procedures should be. The Committee urges parties, judges and neutrals to be open and flexible in their conduct of ADR proceedings (other than arbitration), and to experiment as necessary, at some time in the future, to revisit the issues of rules, procedures or other limitations applicable to the various forms of court-annexed ADR.

Hennepin County and Ramsey County both have had substantial experience with arbitrations, and have developed rules of procedure that have worked well. The Committee has considered those rules, and others, in developing its proposed rules.

Subd. (a) of this rule is modeled after rules presently in use by the Second and Fourth Judicial Districts and rules currently in use by the American Arbitration Association.

Subd. (b) of this Rule is modeled after rules presently in use in the Second and Fourth Judicial Districts. In non-binding arbitration, the arbitrator is limited to providing advisory awards, unless the parties do not request a trial.

Subd. (c) of this Rule is modeled after rules presently in use in the Second and Fourth Judicial Districts. Records of the proceeding include records made by a stenographer, court reporter, or recording device.

Subd. (d) of this Rule is modeled after Rule 25 VIII of the Special Rules of Practice for the Second Judicial District.

Advisory Committee Comment—1996 Amendment

The changes to this rule in 1996 incorporate the collective labels for ADR processes now recognized in Rule 114.02. These changes should clarify the operation of the rule, but should not otherwise affect its interpretation.

Historical Notes

The order of the Minnesota Supreme Court [CX-89-1863] dated October 10, 1996, provides in part that these amendments are effective July 1, 1997, except that rules 119 and 418 are effective January 1, 1997, that these amendments shall apply to all actions pending on the effective dates and to those filed thereafter, and that "(t)he inclusion of Advisory Committee comments is made for convenience and does not reflect court approval of the comments made therein".

The order of the Minnesota Supreme Court [CX-89-1863] dated December 17, 2004, provides in part that "(t)he attached amendments shall apply to all actions pending on the effective date and to those filed thereafter."

Rule 114.10. Communication with Neutral

(a) Adjudicative Processes. Neither the parties nor their representatives shall communicate ex parte with the neutral unless approved in advance by all parties and the neutral.

(b) Non-Adjudicative Processes. Parties and their counsel may communicate ex parte with the neutral in non-adjudicative ADR processes with the consent of the neutral, so long as the communication encourages or facilitates settlement.

(c) Communications to Court During ADR Process. During an ADR process the court may be informed only of the following:

(1) The failure of a party or an attorney to comply with the order to attend the process;

(2) Any request by the parties for additional time to complete the ADR process;

(3) With the written consent of the parties, any procedural action by the court that would facilitate the ADR process; and

(4) The neutral's assessment that the case is inappropriate for that ADR process.

(d) Communications to Court After ADR Process. When the ADR process has concluded, the court may only be informed of the following:

(1) If the parties do not reach an agreement on any matter, the neutral shall report the lack of an agreement to the court without comment or recommendations;

(2) If agreement is reached, any requirement that its terms be reported to the court should be consistent with the jurisdiction's policies governing settlements in general; and

(3) With the written consent of the parties, the neutral's report also may identify any pending motions or outstanding legal issues, discovery process, or other action by any party which, if resolved or completed, would facilitate the possibility of a settlement.

Adopted Dec. 2, 1993, eff. July 1, 1994. Amended Oct. 10, 1996; Dec. 17, 2004, eff. Jan. 1, 2005.

Implementation Committee Comments–1993

This Rule is modeled after Rule 25 VI of the special rules of Practice for the Second Judicial District.

Advisory Committee Comment—1996 Amendment

The changes to this rule in 1996 incorporate the collective labels for ADR processes now recognized in Rule 114.02. These changes should clarify the operation of the rule, but should not otherwise affect its interpretation.

Historical Notes

The order of the Minnesota Supreme Court [CX-89-1863] dated October 10, 1996, provides in part that these amendments are effective July 1, 1997, except that rules 119 and 418 are effective January 1, 1997, that these amendments shall apply to all actions pending on the effective dates and to those filed thereafter, and that "(t)he inclusion of Advisory Committee comments is made for convenience and does not reflect court approval of the comments made therein".

The order of the Minnesota Supreme Court [CX-89-1863] dated December 17, 2004, provides in part that "(t)he attached amendments shall apply to all actions pending on the effective date and to those filed thereafter."

Rule 114.11. Funding

(a) Setting of Fee. The neutral and the parties will determine the fee. All fees of neutral(s) for ADR services shall be fair and reasonable.

(b) Responsibility for Payment. The parties shall pay for the neutral. It is presumed that the parties shall split the costs of the ADR process on an equal basis. The parties may, however, agree on a different allocation. Where the parties cannot agree, the court retains the authority to determine a final and equitable allocation of the costs of the ADR process.

(c) Sanctions for Non-Payment. If a party fails to pay for the neutral, the court may, upon motion, issue an order for the payment of such costs and impose appropriate sanctions.

(d) Inability to Pay. If a party qualifies for waiver of filing fees under Minn. Stat. § 563.01 or if the court determines on other grounds that the party is unable to pay for ADR services, and free or low-cost ADR services are not available, the court shall not order that party to participate in ADR and shall proceed with the judicial handling of the case.

Adopted Dec. 2, 1993, eff. July 1, 1994. Amended Oct. 10, 1996; Dec. 17, 2004, eff. Jan. 1, 2005.

Implementation Committee Comments–1993

The marketplace in the parties' geographic area will determine the rates to be offered by neutrals for their services. The parties can then best determine the appropriate fee, after considering a number of factors, including availability, experience and expertise of the neutral and the financial abilities of the parties.

ADR providers shall be encouraged to provide pro bono and volunteer services to parties unable to pay for ADR processes. Parties with limited financial resources should not be denied access to an ADR process because of an inability to pay for a neutral. Judges and ADR providers should consider the financial abilities of all parties and accommodate those who are not able to share equally in costs of the ADR process. The State Court Administrator shall monitor access to ADR processes by individuals with limited financial resources.

Advisory Committee Comment—1996 Amendment

The payment of fees for neutrals is particularly troublesome in family law matters, where the expense may be particularly onerous. Subdivision (d) of this rule is intended to obviate some difficulties relating to inability to pay ADR fees. The advisory committee rejected any suggestion that these rules should create a separate duty on the part of neutrals to provide free neutral services. The committee hopes such services are available, and would encourage qualified neutrals who are attorneys to provide free services as a neutral as part of their obligation to provide pro bono services. See Minn. R. Prof. Cond. 6.1. If free or affordable ADR services are not available, however, the party should not be forced to participate in an ADR process and should suffer no ill-consequence of not being able to do so.

Historical Notes

The order of the Minnesota Supreme Court [CX-89-1863] dated October 10, 1996, provides in part that these amendments are effective July 1, 1997, except that rules 119 and 418 are effective January 1, 1997, that these amendments shall apply to all actions pending on the effective dates and to those filed thereafter, and that "(t)he inclusion of Advisory Committee comments is made for convenience and does not reflect court approval of the comments made therein".

The order of the Minnesota Supreme Court [CX–89–1863] dated December 17, 2004, provides in part that "(t)he attached amendments shall apply to all actions pending on the effective date and to those filed thereafter."

Rule 114.12. Rosters of Neutrals

(a) Roster. The State Court Administrator shall establish one roster of neutrals for civil matters and one roster of neutrals for family law. Each roster shall be updated and published on a regular basis. The State Court Administrator shall not place on, and shall delete from, the rosters the name of any applicant or neutral whose professional license has been revoked. A qualified neutral may not provide services during a period of suspension of a professional license. The State Court Administrator shall review applications from those who wish to be listed on the roster of qualified neutrals, which shall include those who meet the training requirements established in Rule 114.13, or who have received a waiver under Rule 114.14.

(b) Fees. The State Court Administrator shall establish reasonable fees for qualified individuals and organizations to be placed on either roster.

Adopted Oct. 10, 1996. Amended Dec. 17, 2004, eff. Jan. 1, 2005.

Advisory Committee Comment—1996 Amendment

This rule is primarily new, though it incorporates the procedure now in place administratively under Rule 114.12(b) for placement of neutrals on the roster and the establishment of fees.

This rule expands the State Court Administrator's neutral roster to create a new, separate roster for family law neutrals. It is intended that the new roster will function the same way the current roster for civil ADR under existing Rule 114 does. Subparagraph (b) is new, and provides greater detail of the specific sub-rosters for civil neutrals. It describes the roster as it is now created, and this new rule is not intended to change the existing practice for civil neutrals in any way. Subparagraph (c) creates a parallel definition for the new family law neutral roster, and it is intended that the new roster appear in form essentially the same as the existing roster for civil action neutrals.

Historical Notes

The order of the Minnesota Supreme Court [CX-89-1863] dated October 10, 1996, provides in part that these amendments are effective July 1, 1997, except that rules 119 and 418 are effective January 1, 1997, that these amendments shall apply to all actions pending on the effective dates and to those filed thereafter, and that "(t)he inclusion of Advisory Committee comments is made for convenience and does not reflect court approval of the comments made therein".

The order of the Minnesota Supreme Court [CX–89–1863] dated December 17, 2004, provides in part that "(t)he attached amendments shall apply to all actions pending on the effective date and to those filed thereafter."

Former rule: A former Rule 114.12, adopted Dec. 2, 1993, related to training neutrals. See, now, MN R. Civil App. Proc., Rule 114.13.

Rule 114.13. Training, Standards and Qualifications for Neutral Rosters

(a) Civil Facilitative/Hybrid Neutrals. All qualified neutrals providing facilitative or hybrid services in civil, non-family matters, must have received a minimum of 30 hours of classroom training, with an emphasis on experiential learning. The training must include the following topics:

(1) Conflict resolution and mediation theory, including causes of conflict and interest-based versus positional bargaining and models of conflict resolution;

(2) Mediation skills and techniques, including information gathering skills, communication skills, problem solving skills, interaction skills, conflict management skills, negotiation techniques, caucusing, cultural and gender issues and power balancing;

(3) Components in the mediation process, including an introduction to the mediation process, fact gathering, interest identification, option building, problem solving, agreement building, decision mak-

ing, closure, drafting agreements, and evaluation of the mediation process;

(4) Mediator conduct, including conflicts of interest, confidentiality, neutrality, ethics, standards of practice and mediator introduction pursuant to the Civil Mediation Act, Minn. Stat. § 572.31.

(5) Rules, statutes and practices governing mediation in the trial court system, including these rules, Special Rules of Court, and applicable statutes, including the Civil Mediation Act.

The training outlined in this subdivision shall include a maximum of 15 hours of lectures and a minimum of 15 hours of role-playing.

(b) Civil Adjudicative/Evaluative Neutrals. All qualified neutrals serving in arbitration, summary jury trial, early neutral evaluation and adjudicative or evaluative processes or serving as a consensual special magistrate must have received a minimum of 6 hours of classroom training on the following topics:

(1) Pre–hearing communications between parties and between parties and neutral; and

(2) Components of the hearing process including evidence; presentation of the case; witness, exhibits and objectives; awards; and dismissals; and

(3) Settlement techniques; and

(4) Rules, statutes, and practices covering arbitration in the trial court system, including Supreme Court ADR rules, special rules of court and applicable state and federal statutes; and

(5) Management of presentations made during early neutral evaluation procedures and moderated settlement conferences.

(c) Family Law Facilitative Neutrals.

All qualified neutrals serving in family law facilitative processes must have:

(1) Completed or taught a minimum of 40 hours of family mediation training which is certified by the Minnesota Supreme Court. The certified training shall include at least:

(a) 4 hours of conflict resolution theory;

(b) 4 hours of psychological issues related to separation and divorce, and family dynamics;

(c) 4 hours of the issues and needs of children in divorce;

(d) 6 hours of family law including custody and visitation, support, asset distribution and evaluation, and taxation as it relates to divorce;

(e) 5 hours of family economics; and,

(f) 2 hours of ethics, including: (I) the role of mediators and parties' attorneys in the facilitative process; (ii) the prohibition against mediators dispensing legal advice; and, (iii) a party's right of termination.

Certified training for mediation of custody issues only need not include 5 hours of family economics. The certified training shall consist of at least 40 percent role-playing and simulations.

(2) Completed or taught a minimum of 6 hours of certified training in domestic abuse issues, which may be a part of the 40–hour training above, to include at least:

(a) 2 hours about domestic abuse in general, including definition of battery and types of power imbalance;

(b) 3 hours of domestic abuse screening, including simulations or role-playing; and,

(c) 1 hour of legal issues relative to domestic abuse cases.

(d) Family Law Adjudicative Neutrals.

All qualified neutrals serving in a family law adjudicative capacity must have had at least 5 years of professional experience in the area of family law and be recognized as qualified practitioners in their field. Recognition may be demonstrated by submitting proof of professional licensure; professional certification; faculty membership of approved continuing education courses for family law; service as court-appointed adjudicative neutral, including consensual special magistrates; service as referees or guardians ad litem; or acceptance by peers as experts in their field. All qualified family law adjudicative neutrals shall have also completed or taught a minimum of 6 hours of certified training on the following topics:

(1) Pre–hearing communications among parties and between the parties and neutral(s);

(2) Components of the family court hearing process including evidence, presentation of the case, witnesses, exhibits, awards, dismissals, and vacation of awards;

(3) Settlement techniques; and,

(4) Rules, statutes, and practices pertaining to arbitration in the trial court system, including Minnesota Supreme Court ADR rules, special rules of court, and applicable state and federal statutes.

In addition to the 6–hour training required above, all qualified family law adjudicative neutrals must have completed or taught a minimum of 6 hours of certified training in domestic abuse issues, to include at least:

(1) 2 hours about domestic abuse in general, including definition of battery and types of power imbalance;

(2) 3 hours of domestic abuse screening, including simulations or role-playing; and,

(3) 1 hour of legal issues relative to domestic abuse cases.

(e) Family Law Evaluative Neutrals. All qualified neutrals offering early neutral evaluations or non-binding advisory opinions (1) shall have at least 5 years of experience as family law attorneys, as accountants dealing with divorce-related matters, as custody and visitation psychologists, or as other professionals working in the area of family law who are recognized as qualified practitioners in their field; and (2) shall have completed or taught a minimum of 2 hours of certified training on management of presentations made during evaluative processes. Evaluative neutrals shall have knowledge on all issues on which they render opinions.

In addition to the 2–hour training required above, all qualified family law evaluative neutrals must have completed or taught a minimum of 6 hours of certified training in domestic abuse issues, to include at least:

(1) 2 hours about domestic abuse in general, including definition of battery and types of power imbalance;

(2) 3 hours of domestic abuse screening, including simulations or role-playing; and,

(3) 1 hour of legal issues relative to domestic abuse cases.

(f) Exceptions to Roster Requirements. Neutral fact-finders selected by the parties for their expertise need not undergo training nor be included on the State Court Administrator's roster.

(g) Continuing Training. All qualified neutrals providing facilitative or hybrid services must attend 18 hours of continuing education about alternative dispute resolution subjects within the 3–year period in which the qualified neutral is required to complete the continuing education requirements. All other qualified neutrals must attend 9 hours of continuing education about alternative dispute resolution subjects during the 3–year period in which the qualified neutral is required to complete the continuing education requirements. These hours may be attained through course work and attendance at state and national ADR conferences. The qualified neutral is responsible for maintaining attendance records and shall disclose the information to program administrators and the parties to any dispute. The qualified neutral shall submit continuing education credit information to the State Court Administrator's office within sixty days after the close of the period during which his or her education requirements must be completed.

(h) Certification of Training Programs. The State Court Administrator shall certify training programs which meet the training criteria of this rule.

Adopted Dec. 2, 1993, eff. July 1, 1994. Amended Oct. 10, 1996; Dec. 19, 2000, eff. March 1, 2001; Dec. 17, 2004, eff. Jan. 1, 2005.

Implementation Committee Comments–1993

The training requirements are designed to emphasize the value of learning through experience. Training requirements can protect the parties and the integrity of the ADR processes from neutrals with little or no dispute resolution skills who offer services to the public and training to neutrals. These rules shall serve as minimum standards; individual jurisdictions may make requirements more stringent.

Advisory Committee Comment—1996 Amendment

The provisions for training and certification of training are expanded in these amendments to provide for the specialized training necessary for ADR neutrals. The committee recommends that six hours of domestic abuse training be required for all family law neutrals, other than those selected solely for technical expertise. The committee believes this is a reasonable requirement and one that should significantly facilitate the fair and appropriate consideration of the concerns of all parties in family law proceedings.

Advisory Committee Comment—2000 Amendments

Rule 114.13(g) is amended in 2000 to replace the current annual training requirement with a three-year reporting cycle. The existing requirements are simply tripled in size, but need only be accumulated over a three-year period. The rule is designed to require reporting of training for ADR on the same schedule required for CLE for neutrals who are lawyers. See generally Rule 3 of Rules of the Supreme Court for Continuing Legal Education of Members of the Bar and Rule 106 of Rules of the Board of Continuing Legal Education. Non–lawyer neutrals should be placed by the ADR Board on a similar three-year reporting schedule.

Historical Notes

The order of the Minnesota Supreme Court [CX-89-1863] dated October 10, 1996, provides in part that these amendments are effective July 1, 1997, except that rules 119 and 418 are effective January 1, 1997, that these amendments shall apply to all actions pending on the effective dates and to those filed thereafter, and that "(t)he inclusion of Advisory Committee comments is made for convenience and does not reflect court approval of the comments made therein".

The order of the Minnesota Supreme Court [CX–89–1863] dated December 17, 2004, provides in part that "(t)he attached amendments shall apply to all actions pending on the effective date and to those filed thereafter."

Former rule: A former Rule 114.13, adopted Dec. 2, 1993, related to the procedure to place applicants on the roster of qualified neutrals. See, now, MN R. Civil App. Proc., Rule 114.12.

Rule 114.14. Waiver of Training Requirement

A neutral seeking to be included on the roster of qualified neutrals without having to complete training requirements under Rule 114.13 shall apply for a waiver to the Minnesota Supreme Court ADR Review Board. Waivers may be granted when an individual's training and experience clearly demonstrate exceptional competence to serve as a neutral.

Adopted Dec. 2, 1993, eff. July 1, 1994. Amended Oct. 10, 1996; Dec. 17, 2004, eff. Jan. 1, 2005.

Implementation Committee Comment—1993

Some neutrals may be permitted to continue providing ADR services without completing the training requirements. A Board, made up of dispute resolution professionals, court officials, judges and attorneys, shall determine who qualifies.

Advisory Committee Comment—1996 Amendment

This rule is amended to allow "grandparenting" of family law neutrals. The rule is derived in form from the grandparenting provision included in initial adoption of this rule for civil neutrals.

Historical Notes

The order of the Minnesota Supreme Court [CX-89-1863] dated October 10, 1996, provides in part that these amendments are effective July 1, 1997, except that rules 119 and 418 are effective January 1, 1997, that these amendments shall apply to all actions pending on the effective dates and to those filed thereafter, and that "(t)he inclusion of Advisory Committee comments is made for convenience and does not reflect court approval of the comments made therein".

The order of the Minnesota Supreme Court [CX–89–1863] dated December 17, 2004, provides in part that "(t)he attached amendments shall apply to all actions pending on the effective date and to those filed thereafter."

RULE 114 APPENDIX. CODE OF ETHICS

INTRODUCTION

Rule 114 of the Minnesota General Rules of Practice provides that alternative dispute resolution (ADR) must be considered for nearly all civil cases filed in district court. The ADR Review Board, appointed by the Supreme Court, approves individuals and organizations who are qualified under Rule 114 to act as neutrals in court-referred cases.

Individuals and organizations approved by the ADR Review Board consent to the jurisdiction of the Board and to compliance with this Code of Ethics. The purpose of this code is to provide standards of ethical conduct to guide neutrals who provide ADR services, to inform and protect consumers of ADR services, and to ensure the integrity of the various ADR processes.

In order for ADR to be effective, there must be broad public confidence in the integrity and fairness of the process. Neutrals have a responsibility not only to the parties and to the court, but also to the continuing improvement of ADR processes. Neutrals must observe high standards of ethical conduct. The provisions of this Code should be construed to advance these objectives.

Neutrals should orient the parties to the process before beginning a proceeding. Neutrals should not practice, condone, facilitate, or promote any form of discrimination on the basis of race, color, creed, religion, national origin, sex, marital status, status with regard to public assistance, disability, sexual orientation, or age. Neutrals should be aware that cultural differences may affect a party's values and negotiating style.

This introduction provides general orientation to the Code of Ethics. Comments accompanying any rule explain and illustrate the meaning and purpose of the rule. The Comments are intended as guides to interpretation but the text of each rule is authoritative. Failure to comply with any provision in this Code of Ethics may be the basis for removal from the roster of neutrals maintained by the Office of the State Court Administrator and/or for such other action as may be taken by the Minnesota Supreme Court.

Violation of a provision of this Code shall not create a cause of action nor shall it create any presumption that a legal duty has been breached. Nothing in this Code should be deemed to establish or augment any substantive legal duty on the part of neutrals.

Adopted Aug. 27, 1997, eff. Aug. 27, 1997.

Rule I. Impartiality

A neutral shall conduct the dispute resolution process in an impartial manner and shall serve only in those matters in which she or he can remain impartial and evenhanded. If at any time the neutral is unable to conduct the process in an impartial manner, the neutral shall withdraw.

Adopted Aug. 27, 1997, eff. Aug. 27, 1997.

Advisory Task Force Comments—1997

1. The concept of impartiality of the neutral is central to all alternative dispute resolution processes. Impartiality means freedom from favoritism or bias either by word or action, and a commitment to serve all parties as opposed to a single party.

Historical Notes

The order of the Minnesota Supreme Court [C5-87-843] dated August 27, 1997, adopting the Code of Ethics for neutrals under Rule 114 of the Minnesota General Rules of Practice provides in part that "(t)he inclusion of Advisory Task Force Comments is made for convenience and does not reflect court approval of the comments made therein."

Rule II. Conflicts of Interest

A neutral shall disclose all actual and potential conflicts of interest reasonably known to the neutral. After disclosure, the neutral shall decline to participate unless all parties choose to retain the neutral. The need to protect against conflicts of interest shall govern conduct that occurs during and after the dispute resolution process. Without the consent of all parties, and for a reasonable time under the particular circumstances, a neutral who also practices in another profession shall not establish a professional relationship in that other profession with one of the parties, or any person or entity, in a substantially factually related matter.

Adopted Aug. 27, 1997, eff. Aug. 27, 1997.

Advisory Task Force Comments—1997

1. A conflict of interest is any direct or indirect financial or personal interest in the outcome of the proceeding or any existing or past financial, business, professional, family or social relationship which is likely to affect impartiality or which might reasonably create an appearance of partiality or bias. If all parties agree to proceed after being informed of conflicts, the neutral may proceed with the case. If, however, the neutral believes that the conflict of interest would inhibit the neutral's impartiality, the neutral should decline to proceed.

2. Guidance on these conflict of interests issues may be found in the cases under statutes regarding challenges to arbitration awards or mediated settlement agreements on the grounds of fraud for nondisclosure of a conflict of interest or material relationship or for partiality of an arbitrator or mediator. (Minnesota Civil Mediation Act, Uniform Arbitration Act, Federal Arbitration Act.)

3. In deciding whether to establish a relationship with one of the parties in an unrelated matter, the neutral should exercise caution in circumstances which would raise legitimate questions about the integrity of the ADR process.

4. A neutral should avoid conflicts of interest in recommending the services of other professionals.

5. The neutral's commitment must be to the parties and the process. Pressures from outside of the process should never influence the neutral's conduct.

6. There is no intent that the prohibition established in this rule which applies to an individual neutral shall be imputed to an organization, panel or firm of which the neutral is a part. However, the individual neutral should be mindful of the confidentiality requirements in Rule IV of this Code and the organization, panel, or firm should exercise caution.

Historical Notes

The order of the Minnesota Supreme Court [C5-87-843] dated August 27, 1997, adopting the Code of Ethics for neutrals under Rule 114 of the Minnesota General Rules of Practice provides in part that "(t)he inclusion of Advisory Task Force Comments is made for convenience and does not reflect court approval of the comments made therein."

Rule III. Competence

A neutral shall serve as a neutral only when she/he has the necessary qualifications to satisfy the reasonable expectations of the parties.

Adopted Aug. 27, 1997, eff. Aug. 27, 1997.

Advisory Task Force Comments—1997

1. Any person on the Minnesota Statewide ADR–Rule 114 Neutral Roster may be selected as a neutral, provided that the parties are satisfied with the neutral's qualifications. A person who offers neutral services gives parties and the public the expectations that she or he is competent to serve effectively as a neutral. A neutral should decline appointment, request technical assistance, or withdraw from a dispute which is beyond the neutral's competence.

2. Neutrals must provide information regarding their relevant training, education and experience to the parties (Minnesota Civil Mediation Act.)

Historical Notes

The order of the Minnesota Supreme Court [C5-87-843] dated August 27, 1997, adopting the Code of Ethics for neutrals under Rule 114 of the Minnesota General Rules of Practice provides in part that "(t)he inclusion of Advisory Task Force Comments is made for convenience and does not reflect court approval of the comments made therein."

Rule IV. Confidentiality

The neutral shall maintain confidentiality to the extent provided by Rule 114.08 and 114.10 and any additional agreements made with or between the parties.

Adopted Aug. 27, 1997, eff. Aug. 27, 1997.

Advisory Task Force Comments—1997

1. A neutral should discuss issues of confidentiality with the parties before beginning an ADR process including limitations on the scope of confidentiality and the extent of confidentiality provided in any private sessions that a neutral holds with a party.

2. Rule 114.08 reads: Confidentiality

(a) Evidence. Without the consent of all parties and an order of the court, or except as provided in Rule 114.09(e)(4), no evidence that there has been an ADR proceeding or any fact concerning the proceeding may be admitted in a trial de novo or in any subsequent proceeding involving any of the issues or parties to the proceeding.

(b) Inadmissibility. Statements made and documents produced in non-binding ADR processes which are not otherwise discoverable are not subject to discovery or other disclosure and are not admissible into evidence for any purpose at the trial, including impeachment, except as provided in paragraph (d).

(c) Adjudicative Evidence. Evidence in consensual special master proceedings, binding arbitration, or in non-binding arbitration after the period for a demand for trial expires, may be used in subsequent proceedings for any purpose for which it is admissible under the rules of evidence.

(d) Sworn Testimony. Sworn testimony in a summary jury trial may be used in subsequent proceedings for any purpose for which it is admissible under the rules of evidence.

(e) Records of Neutral. Notes, records, and recollections of the neutral are confidential, which means that they shall not be disclosed to the parties, the public, or anyone other than the neutral, unless (1) all parties and the neutral agree to such disclosure or (2) required by law or other applicable professional codes. No record shall be made without the agreement of both parties, except for a memorandum of issues that are resolved.

3. Rule 114.10 reads: Communication with Neutral

(a) Adjudicative Processes. The parties and their counsel shall not communicate ex parte with an arbitrator or a consensual special master or other adjudicative neutral.

(b) Non–Adjudicative Processes. Parties and their counsel may communicate ex parte with the neutral in non-adjudicative ADR processes with the consent of the neutral, so long as the communication encourages or facilitates settlement.

(c) Communications to Court During ADR Process. During an ADR process the court may be informed only of the following:

(1) The failure of a party or an attorney to comply with the order to attend the process;

(2) Any request by the parties for additional time to complete the ADR process;

(3) With the written consent of the parties, any procedural action by the court that would facilitate the ADR process; and

(4) The neutral's assessment that the case is inappropriate for that ADR process.

(d) Communications to Court After ADR Process. When the ADR process has been concluded, the court may only be informed of the following:

(1) If the parties do not reach an agreement on any matter, the neutral should report the lack of an agreement to the court without comment or recommendations;

(2) If agreement is reached, any requirement that its terms be reported to the court should be consistent with the jurisdiction's policies governing settlements in general; and

(3) With the written consent of the parties, the neutral's report also may identify any pending motions or outstanding legal issues, discovery process, or other action by any party which, if resolved or completed, would facilitate the possibility of a settlement.

Historical Notes

The order of the Minnesota Supreme Court [C5-87-843] dated August 27, 1997, adopting the Code of Ethics for neutrals under Rule 114 of the Minnesota General Rules of Practice provides in part that "(t)he inclusion of Advisory Task Force Comments is made for convenience and does not reflect court approval of the comments made therein."

Rule V. Quality of the Process

A neutral shall work to ensure a quality process. A quality process requires a commitment by the neutral to diligence and procedural fairness. A neutral shall not knowingly make false statements of fact or law. The neutral shall exert every reasonable effort to expedite the process including prompt issuance of written reports, awards, or agreements.

Adopted Aug. 27, 1997, eff. Aug. 27, 1997.

Advisory Task Force Comments—1997

1. A neutral should be prepared to commit the attention essential to the ADR process.

2. A neutral should satisfy the reasonable expectations of the parties concerning the timing of the process.

3. A neutral should not provide therapy to either party, nor should a neutral who is a lawyer represent either party in any matter during an ADR process.

4. A neutral should withdraw from an ADR process when incapable of serving or when unable to remain neutral.

5. A neutral should withdraw from an ADR process or postpone a session if the process is being used to further illegal conduct, or if a party is unable to participate due to drug or alcohol abuse, or other physical or mental incapacity.

Historical Notes

The order of the Minnesota Supreme Court [C5-87-843] dated August 27, 1997, adopting the Code of Ethics for neutrals under Rule 114 of the Minnesota General Rules of Practice provides in part that "(t)he inclusion of Advisory Task Force Comments is made for convenience and does not reflect court approval of the comments made therein."

Rule VI. Advertising and Solicitation

A neutral shall be truthful in advertising and solicitation for alternative dispute resolution. A neutral shall make only accurate and truthful statements about any alternative dispute resolution process, its costs and benefits, the neutral's role and her or his skills or qualifications. A neutral shall refrain from promising specific results.

In an advertisement or other communication to the public, a neutral who is on the Roster may use the phrase "qualified neutral under Rule 114 of the Minnesota General Rules of Practice." It is not appropriate to identify oneself as a "certified" neutral.

Adopted Aug. 27, 1997, eff. Aug. 27, 1997.

Rule VII. Fees

A neutral shall fully disclose and explain the basis of compensation, fees and charges to the parties. The parties shall be provided sufficient information about fees at the outset to determine if they wish to retain the services of a neutral. A neutral shall not enter into a fee agreement which is contingent upon the outcome of the alternative dispute resolution process. A neutral shall not give or receive any commission, rebate, or similar remuneration for referring a person for alternative dispute resolution services.

Adopted Aug. 27, 1997, eff. Aug. 27, 1997.

Advisory Task Force Comments—1997

1. The better practice in reaching an understanding about fees is to set down the arrangements in a written agreement.

2. A neutral who withdraws from a case should return any unearned fee to the parties.

Historical Notes

The order of the Minnesota Supreme Court [C5-87-843] dated August 27, 1997, adopting the Code of Ethics for neutrals under Rule 114 of the Minnesota General Rules of Practice provides in part that "(t)he inclusion of Advisory Task Force Comments is made for convenience and does not reflect court approval of the comments made therein."

MEDIATION

Rule I. Self-Determination:

A mediator shall recognize that mediation is based on the principle of self-determination by the parties. It requires that the mediation process rely upon the ability of the parties to reach a voluntary, uncoerced agreement. The primary responsibility for the resolution of a dispute and the shaping of a settlement agreement rests with the parties. A mediator shall not require a party to stay in the mediation against the party's will.

Adopted Aug. 27, 1997, eff. Aug. 27, 1997.

Advisory Task Force Comments—1997

1. The mediator may provide information about the process, raise issues, offer opinions about the strengths and weaknesses of a case, draft proposals, and help parties explore options. The primary role of the mediator is to facilitate a voluntary resolution of a dispute. Parties should be given the opportunity to consider all proposed options. It is acceptable for the mediator to suggest options in response to parties' requests, but not to coerce the parties to accept any particular option.

2. A mediator cannot personally ensure that each party has made a fully informed choice to reach a particular agreement, but it is a good practice for the mediator to make the parties aware of the importance of consulting other professionals, where appropriate, to help them make informed decisions.

Historical Notes

The order of the Minnesota Supreme Court [C5-87-843] dated August 27, 1997, adopting the Code of Ethics for neutrals under Rule 114 of the Minnesota General Rules of Practice provides in part that "(t)he inclusion of Advisory Task Force Comments is made for convenience and does not reflect court approval of the comments made therein."

RULE 114 APPENDIX. CODE OF ETHICS ENFORCEMENT PROCEDURE

INTRODUCTION

Inclusion on the list of qualified neutrals pursuant to Minnesota General Rules of Practice 114.12 is a conditional privilege, revocable for cause.

Adopted Aug. 31, 2000.

Rule I. Scope

This procedure applies to complaints against any individual or organization (neutral) placed on the roster of qualified neutrals pursuant to Rule 114.12 or serving as a court appointed neutral pursuant to 114.05(b) of the Minnesota General Rules of Practice. Collaborative attorneys or other professionals as defined in Rule 111.05(a) are not subject to the Rule 114 Code of Ethics and Enforcement Procedure while acting in a collaborative process under that rule.

Adopted Aug. 31, 2000; Sept. 26, 2007, eff. Jan. 1, 2008.

Advisory Committee Comment—2004 Amendment

A qualified neutral is subject to this complaint procedure when providing any ADR services. The complaint procedure applies whether the services are court ordered or not, and whether the services are or are not pursuant to Minnesota General Rules of Practice. The Board will consider the full context of the alleged misconduct, including whether the neutral was subject to other applicable codes of ethics, or representing a "qualified organization" at the time of the alleged misconduct

Minn. Gen. R. Prac. 114.02(b): "***Neutral.*** A 'neutral' is an individual or organization that provides an ADR process. A 'qualified neutral' is an individual or organization included on the State Court Administrator's roster as provided in Rule 114.12. An individual neutral must have completed the training and continuing education requirements provided in Rule 114.13. An individual neutral provided by an organization also must meet the training and continuing education requirements of Rule 114.13. Neutral fact-finders selected by the parties for their expertise need not undergo training nor be on the State Court Administrator's roster."

Attorneys functioning as collaborative attorneys are subject to the Minnesota Rules on Lawyers Professional Responsibility. Complaints against collaborative attorneys should be directed to the Lawyers Professional Responsibility Board.

Advisory Committee Comment—2007 Amendment

The committee believes it is worth reminding participants in collaborative law processes that the process is essentially adversary in nature, and collaborative attorneys owe the duty of loyalty to their clients. The Code of Ethics procedures apply to create standards of care for ADR neutrals, as defined in the rules; because collaborative lawyers, while acting in that capacity, are not neutrals, these enforcement procedures to not apply.

Historical Notes

The order of the Minnesota Supreme Court [CX–89–1863] dated December 17, 2004, amending the General Rules of Practice for the District Courts provides in part that "(t)he inclusion of Advisory Committee comments is made for convenience and does not reflect court approval of the comments made therein."

Rule II. Procedure

A. A complaint must be in writing, signed by the complainant, and mailed or delivered to the ADR Review Board at 25 Rev. Dr. Martin Luther King Jr. Blvd., Suite 120, Saint Paul, MN 55155–1500. The complaint shall identify the neutral and make a short and plain statement of the conduct forming the basis of the complaint.

B. The State Court Administrator's Office, in conjunction with one ADR Review Board member shall review the complaint and recommend whether the allegations(s), if true, constitute a violation of the Code of Ethics, and whether to refer the complaint to mediation. The State Court Administrator's Office and ADR Review Board member may also request additional information from the complainant if it is necessary prior to making a recommendation.

C. If the allegations(s) of the complaint do not constitute a violation of the Code of Ethics, the complaint shall be dismissed and the complainant and the neutral shall be notified in writing.

D. If the allegation(s) of the complaint, if true, constitute a violation of the Code of Ethics, the Board will undertake such review, investigation, and action it deems appropriate. In all such cases, the Board shall send to the neutral, by certified mail, a copy of the complaint, a list identifying the ethical rules which may have been violated, and a request for a written response to the allegations and to any specific questions posed by the Board. It shall not be considered a violation of Rule 114.08(e) of the Minnesota General Rules of Practice or of Rule IV of the Code of Ethics, Rule 114 Appendix, for the neutral to disclose notes, records, or recollections of the ADR process complained of as part of the complaint procedure. Except for good cause shown, if the neutral fails to respond to the complaint in writing within thirty (30) days, the allegations(s) shall be deemed admitted.

E. The complainant and neutral may agree to mediation or the State Court Administrator's Office or Board may refer them to mediation conducted by a qualified neutral to resolve the issues raised by the complainant. Mediation shall proceed only if both the complainant and neutral consent. If the complaint is resolved through mediation, the complaint shall be dismissed, unless the resolution includes sanctions to be imposed by the Board. If no agreement is reached in mediation, the Board shall determine whether to proceed further.

F. After review and investigation, the Board shall advise the complainant and neutral of the Board's action in writing by certified mail sent to their respective last known addresses. If the neutral does not file a request for an appeal hearing as prescribed in section G, the Board's decision becomes final.

G. The neutral shall be entitled to appeal the proposed sanctions and findings of the Board to the ADR Ethics Panel by written request within fourteen days from receipt of the Board's action on the complaint. The Panel shall be appointed by the Judicial Council and shall be composed of two sitting or retired district court judges and one qualified neutral in good standing on the Rule 114 roster. Members of the Panel shall serve for a period to be determined by the Judicial Council. One member of the Panel shall be designated as the presiding member.

(1) Discovery. Within 30 days after receipt of a request for an appeal hearing, counsel for the Board and the neutral shall exchange the names and addresses of all persons known to have knowledge of the relevant facts. The presiding member of the Panel shall set a date for the exchange of the names and addresses of all witnesses the parties intend to call at the hearing. The Panel may issue subpoenas for the attendance of witnesses and production of documents or other evidentiary material. Counsel for the Board and the neutral shall exchange nonprivileged evidence relevant to the alleged ethical violation(s), documents to be presented at the hearing, witness statements and summaries of interviews with witnesses who will be called at the hearing. Both the Board and the neutral have a continuing duty to supplement information required to be exchanged under this rule. All discovery must be completed within 10 days of the scheduled appeal hearing.

(2) Procedure. The neutral has the right to be represented by an attorney at all parts of the proceedings. In the hearing, all testimony shall be under oath. The Panel shall receive such evidence as the Panel deems necessary to understand and determine the issues. The Minnesota Rules of Evidence shall apply, however, relevancy shall be liberally construed in favor of admission. Counsel for the Board shall present the matter to the Panel. The Board has the burden of proving the facts justifying action by clear and convincing evidence. The neutral shall be permitted to adduce evidence and produce and cross-examine witnesses, subject to the Minnesota Rules of evidence. Every formal hearing conducted under this rule shall be recorded electronically by staff for the Panel. The Panel shall deliberate upon the close of evidence and shall present written Findings and Memorandum with regard to any ethical violations and sanction resulting there from. The panel shall serve and file the written decision on the Board, neutral and complainant within forty-five days of the hearing. The decision of the Panel is final.

Adopted Aug. 31, 2000. Amended Dec. 17, 2004, eff. Jan. 1, 2005; Dec. 28, 2006, eff. Jan. 1, 2007; Dec. 28, 2007, eff. Jan. 1, 2008.

Advisory Comment

A complaint form is available from the ADR Review Board by calling 651-297-7590 or emailing adr@courts.state.mn.us.

The Board, at its discretion, may establish a complaint review panel comprised of members of the Board. Staff under the Board's direction and control may also conduct investigations.

Advisory Committee Comments—2008 Amendments

Rule II. B. is amended in 2007 to implement a streamlined process so that one ADR Review Board member together with state court administration staff can make initial determinations. This will allow the process to proceed instead of waiting for monthly board meetings. Rule II.E. is amended to clarify that the parties may voluntarily elect mediation in addition to mediation being offered by the Board.

Historical Notes

The order of the Minnesota Supreme Court [CX-89-1863] dated December 17, 2004, provides in part that "(t)he attached amendments shall apply to all actions pending on the effective date and to those filed thereafter."

Rule III. Sanctions

A. The Board may impose sanctions, including but not limited to:

(1) Issue a private reprimand.

(2) Designate the corrective action necessary for the neutral to remain on the roster.

(3) Notify the appointing court and any professional licensing authority with which the neutral is affiliated of the complaint and its disposition.

(4) Publish the neutral's name, a summary of the violation, and any sanctions imposed.

(5) Remove the neutral from the roster of qualified neutrals, and set conditions for reinstatement if appropriate.

B. Sanctions shall only be imposed if supported by clear and convincing evidence. Conduct considered in previous or concurrent ethical complaints against the neutral is inadmissible, except to show a pattern of related conduct the cumulative effect of which constitutes an ethical violation.

C. Sanctions against an organization may be imposed for its ethical violation and its member's violation if the member is acting within the rules and directives of the organization.

Adopted Aug. 31, 2000. Amended Dec. 17, 2004, eff. Jan. 1, 2005; Dec. 28, 2006, eff. Jan. 1, 2007.

Historical Notes

The order of the Minnesota Supreme Court [CX–89–1863] dated December 17, 2004, provides in part that "(t)he attached amendments shall apply to all actions pending on the effective date and to those filed thereafter."

Rule IV. Confidentiality

A. Unless and until final sanctions are imposed, all files, records, and proceedings of the Board that relate to or arise out of any complaint shall be confidential, except:

(1) As between Board members and staff;

(2) Upon request of the neutral, the file maintained by the Board, excluding its work product, shall be provided to the neutral;

(3) As otherwise required or permitted by rule or statute; and

(4) To the extent that the neutral waives confidentiality.

B. If final sanctions are imposed against any neutral pursuant to Section III A (2)–(5), the sanction and the grounds for the sanction shall be of public record, and the Board file shall remain confidential.

C. Nothing in this rule shall be construed to require the disclosure of the mental processes or communications of the Board or staff.

D. Accessibility to records maintained by district court administrators relating to complaints or sanctions about neutrals shall be consistent with this rule.

Adopted Aug. 31, 2000. Amended Dec. 28, 2006, eff. Jan. 1, 2007; April 27, 2007, eff. July 1, 2007; Dec. 28, 2007, eff. Jan. 1, 2008.

Advisory Committee Comment–2007

The 2007 addition of Rule IV.D. is designed to make the treatment of complaint and sanction information consistent in the hands of both the statewide ADR Review Board, which has jurisdiction over any expeditor appointed by the court regardless of whether that expeditor is listed on the statewide ADR neutral rosters (Minn. Gen. R. Prac. 114.05(b)), and the local court administrator who is required by law to maintain a local roster of parenting time expeditors. Minn. Stat. § 518.1751, subds. 2b, 2c (2006). Although statutes address public access to records of the expeditors and their process, they do not address public access to complaints or sanctions about rostered expeditors.

Advisory Committee Comments–2008 Amendments

Rule IV. D. is amended in 2007 to clarify that accessibility to district court information about sanctions is consistent with Rule 114 for all neutrals. In addition to maintaining local rosters of parenting time expediters, district courts receive notice of sanctions imposed by the ADR Review Board.

Rule V. Privilege; immunity

A. Privilege. A statement made in these proceedings is absolutely privileged and may not serve as a basis for liability in any civil lawsuit brought against the person who made the statement.

B. Immunity. Board members and staff shall be immune from suit for any conduct in the course of their official duties.

Adopted Aug. 31, 2000.

PART C. MOTIONS

RULE 115. MOTION PRACTICE

Rule 115.01. Scope and Application

This rule shall govern all civil motions, except those in family court matters governed by Minn. Gen. R. Prac. 301 through 379 and in commitment proceedings subject to the Special Rules of Procedure Governing Proceedings Under the Minnesota Commitment and Treatment Act.

(a) Definitions. Motions are either dispositive or non-dispositive, and are defined as follows:

(1) Dispositive motions are motions which seek to dispose of all or part of the claims or parties, except motions for default judgment. They include motions to dismiss a party or claim, motions for summary judgment and motions under Minn.R.Civ.P. 12.02(a)–(f).

(2) Non-dispositive motions are all other motions, including but not limited to discovery, third party practice, temporary relief, intervention or amendment of pleadings.

(b) Time. The time limits in this rule are to provide the court adequate opportunity to prepare for and promptly rule on matters, and the court may modify the time limits, provided, however, that in no event shall the time limited be less than the time established by Minn.R.Civ.P. 56.03. Whenever this rule requires documents to be filed with the court administrator within a prescribed period of time before a specific event, filing may be accomplished by mail, subject to the following: (1) 3 days shall be added to the prescribed period; and (2) filing shall not be considered timely unless the documents are deposited in the mail within the prescribed period. Service of documents on parties by mail is subject to the provisions of Minn.R.Civ.P. 5.02 and 6.05.

(c) Post–Trial Motions. The timing provisions of sections 115.03 and 115.04 of this rule do not apply to post-trial motions.

Adopted Sept. 5, 1991, eff. Jan. 1, 1992. Amended Nov. 13, 1992, eff. Jan. 1, 1993; Sept. 5, 2001, eff. Sept. 5, 2001.

Advisory Committee Comments

See comments following Rule 115.11

Rule 115.02. Obtaining Hearing Date; Notice to Parties

A hearing date and time shall be obtained from the court administrator or a designated motion calendar deputy. A party obtaining a date and time for a hearing on a motion or for any other calendar setting, shall promptly give notice advising all other parties who have appeared in the action so that cross motions may, insofar as possible, be heard on a single hearing date.

Adopted Sept. 5, 1991, eff. Jan. 1, 1992. Amended Nov. 13, 1992, eff. Jan. 1, 1993.

Advisory Committee Comments

See comments following Rule 115.11

Rule 115.03. Dispositive Motions

(a) No motion shall be heard until the moving party pays any required motion filing fee, serves a copy of the following documents on opposing counsel, and files the original with the court administrator at least 28 days prior to the hearing:

(1) Notice of motion and motion;

(2) Proposed order;

(3) Any affidavits and exhibits to be submitted in conjunction with the motion; and

(4) Memorandum of law.

(b) The party responding to the motion shall pay any required motion filing fee, serve a copy of the following documents on opposing counsel, and file the originals with the Court Administrator at least 9 days prior to the hearing:

(1) Memorandum of law; and

(2) Supplementary affidavits and exhibits.

(c) Reply Memoranda. The moving party may submit a reply memorandum, limited to new legal or factual matters raised by an opposing party's response to a motion, by serving a copy on opposing counsel and filing the original with the court administrator at least 3 days before the hearing.

(d) Additional Requirement for Summary Judgment Motions. For summary judgment motions, the memorandum of law shall include:

(1) A statement by the moving party of the issues involved which are the grounds for the motion for summary judgment;

(2) A statement identifying all documents (such as depositions or excerpts thereof, pleadings, exhibits, admissions, interrogatory answers, and affidavits) which comprise the record on which the motion is made. Opposing parties shall identify in their responding Memorandum of Law any additional documents on which they rely;

(3) A recital by the moving party of the material facts as to which there is no genuine dispute, with a specific citation to that part of the record supporting each fact, such as deposition page and line or page and paragraph of an exhibit. A party opposing the motion shall, in like manner, make a recital of any material facts claimed to be in dispute; and

(4) The party's argument and authorities. These additional requirements apply also to a motion under Minn.R.Civ.P. 12 if factually based. Part (3) is excluded from the page limitations of this rule.

Adopted Sept. 5, 1991, eff. Jan. 1, 1992. Amended Nov. 13, 1992, eff. Jan. 1, 1993; Dec. 11, 2003, eff. Jan. 1, 2004.

Advisory Committee Comments

See comments following Rule 115.11

Historical Notes

The order of the Minnesota Supreme Court [CX-89-1863] dated December 11, 2003, provides in part that these amendments are effective January 1, 2004, and shall apply to all actions or proceedings pending on or commenced on or after the effective date.

Rule 115.04. Non–Dispositive Motions

(a) No motion shall be heard until the moving party pays any required motion filing fee, serves a copy of the following documents on the other party or parties and files the original with the court administrator at least 14 days prior to the hearing:

(1) Notice of motion and motion;

(2) Proposed order;

(3) Any affidavits and exhibits to be submitted in conjunction with the motion; and

(4) Any memorandum of law the party intends to submit.

(b) The party responding to the motion shall pay any required motion filing fee, serve a copy of the following documents on the moving party and other interested parties, and file the original with the court administrator at least 7 days prior to the hearing:

(1) Any memorandum of law the party intends to submit; and

(2) Any relevant affidavits and exhibits.

(c) Reply Memoranda. The moving party may submit a reply memorandum, limited to new legal or factual matters raised by an opposing party's response to a motion, by serving a copy on opposing counsel and filing the original with the court administrator at least 3 days before the hearing.

(d) Expedited, Informal Non–Dispositive Motion Process. The moving party is encouraged to consider whether the motion can be informally resolved through a telephone conference with the judge. The moving party may invoke this informal resolution process by written notice to the court and all parties. The moving party must also contact the appropriate court administrative or judicial staff to schedule a phone conference. The parties may (but are not required to) submit short letters, with or without a limited number of documents attached (no briefs, declarations or sworn affidavits are to be filed), prior to the conference to set forth their respective positions. The court will read the written submissions of the parties before the phone conference, hear arguments of counsel and unrepresented parties at the conference, and issue its decision at the conclusion of the phone conference or shortly after the conference. Depending on the nature of the dispute, the court may or may not issue a written order. The court may also determine that the dispute must be presented to the court via formal motion and hearing. Telephone conferences will not be recorded or transcribed.

Adopted Sept. 5, 1991, eff. Jan. 1, 1992. Amended Nov. 13, 1992, eff. Jan. 1, 1993; Dec. 11, 2003, eff. Jan. 1, 2004; May 7, 2013, eff. July 1, 2013.

Advisory Committee Comments

See comments following Rule 115.11

Historical Notes

The order of the Minnesota Supreme Court [CX-89-1863] dated December 11, 2003, provides in part that these amendments are effective January 1, 2004, and shall apply to all actions or proceedings pending on or commenced on or after the effective date.

The order of the Minnesota Supreme Court [ADM04–8001, ADM09–8009, ADM–10-8051] dated May 7, 2013, provided in part that the amendments be effective July 1, 2013, and further provided in part that "[t]hese amendments apply to all actions or proceedings pending on or commenced after the effective date", and further provided that the "February 4, 2013 and February 12, 2013 orders of the court are hereby rescinded to the extent inconsistent with this order."

Rule 115.05. Page Limits

No memorandum of law submitted in connection with either a dispositive or nondispositive motion shall exceed 35 pages, exclusive of the recital of facts required by Minn.Gen.R.Prac. 115.03(d)(3), except with permission of the court. For motions involving discovery requests, the moving party's memorandum shall set forth only the particular discovery requests and the response or objection thereto which are the subject of the motion, and a concise recitation of why the response or objection is improper. If a reply memorandum of law is filed, the cumulative total of the original memorandum and the reply memorandum shall not exceed 35 pages, except with permission of the court.

Adopted Sept. 5, 1991, eff. Jan. 1, 1992. Amended Nov. 13, 1992, eff. Jan. 1, 1993; Dec. 14, 1993, eff. Jan. 1, 1994.

Advisory Committee Comments

See comments following Rule 115.11

Rule 115.06. Failure to Comply

If the moving papers are not properly served and filed, the hearing may be cancelled by the court. If responsive papers are not properly served and filed in a non-dispositive motion, the court may deem the motion unopposed and may grant the relief requested without a hearing. For a dispositive motion, the court, in its discretion, may refuse to permit oral argument by the party not filing the required documents, may allow reasonable attorney's fees, or may take other appropriate action.

Adopted Sept. 5, 1991, eff. Jan. 1, 1992.

Advisory Committee Comments

See comments following Rule 115.11

Rule 115.07. Relaxation of Time Limits

If irreparable harm will result absent immediate action by the court, or if the interests of justice otherwise require, the court may waive or modify the time limits established by this rule.

Adopted Sept. 5, 1991, eff. Jan. 1, 1992.

Advisory Committee Comments

See comments following Rule 115.11

Rule 115.08. Witnesses

No testimony will be taken at motion hearings except under unusual circumstances. Any party seeking to present witnesses at a motion hearing shall obtain prior consent of the court and shall notify the adverse party in the motion papers of the names and addresses of the witnesses which that party intends to call at the motion.

Adopted Sept. 5, 1991, eff. Jan. 1, 1992.

Advisory Committee Comments

See comments following Rule 115.11

Rule 115.09. Telephone Hearings

When a motion is authorized by the court to be heard by telephone conference call, the moving party shall be responsible either to initiate the conference call or to comply with the court's instructions on initiation of the conference call. If necessary, adequate provision shall be made by the court for a record of the telephone hearing. No recording shall be made of any telephone hearing except the recording made as the official court record.

Adopted Sept. 5, 1991, eff. Jan. 1, 1992. Amended Dec. 14, 1995, eff. Jan. 1, 1996.

Advisory Committee Comments

See comments following Rule 115.11

Historical Notes

The order of the Minnesota Supreme Court [CX–89–1863, C6–84–2134] dated December 14, 1995, provides in part that "(t)he attached amendments shall apply to all actions pending on the effective date and to those filed thereafter."

Rule 115.10. Settlement Efforts

No motion will be heard unless the parties have conferred either in person, or by telephone, or in writing in an attempt to resolve their differences prior to the hearing. The moving party shall initiate the conference. The moving party shall certify to the court, before the time of the hearing, compliance with this rule or any reasons for not complying, including lack of availability or cooperation of opposing counsel. Whenever any pending motion is settled, the moving party shall promptly advise the court.

Adopted Sept. 5, 1991, eff. Jan. 1, 1992.

Advisory Committee Comments

See comments following Rule 115.11

Rule 115.11. Motions to Reconsider

Motions to reconsider are prohibited except by express permission of the court, which will be granted only upon a showing of compelling circumstances. Requests to make such a motion, and any responses to such requests, shall be made only by letter to the court of no more than two pages in length, a copy of which must be sent to opposing counsel.

Adopted Dec. 8, 1997, eff. Jan. 1, 1998.

Advisory Committee Comment—1997 Amendments

This rule is derived primarily from Rule 15 of the Local Rules of the Seventh District. Provisions are also included from Rule 8 of the Local Rules of the Second District (2d Dist. R. 8(h)(1) & 8(j)(1)).

This rule is intended to create uniform motion practice in all districts of the state. The existing practices diverge in many ways. The inconsistent requirements for having a motion heard impose significant burdens on litigants and their counsel. The Task Force is confident that this new rule will make civil practice more efficient and fairer, consistent with the goals of the rules of civil procedure set forth in Minn. R. Civ. P. 1.

The rule applies to all motions except the timing provisions do not apply to post-trial motions. These motions are excepted because they are governed by other, stringent timing requirements. *See* Minn. R.Civ.P. 59.03 (motions for a new trial), 52.02 (amendment of findings), 50.02(c) (time for j.n.o.v. motion same as for new trial motion). Other post-trial motions excluded from this rule include those relating to entry of judgment, stays, taxation of costs, and approval of supersedeas bonds. *See* Minn.R.Civ.App.P. 108.01, subd. 1. These matters are routinely and necessarily heard on shorter notice than that required by the rule.

The time limits set forth in this rule were arrived at after extensive discussion. The Task Force attempted to balance the needs of the courts to obtain information on motions sufficiently in advance of the hearing to permit judicial preparation and the needs of counsel and litigants to have prompt hearings after the submission of motions. The time limits for dispositive motions are admittedly longer than the 10–day requirement set forth in Minn.R.Civ.P. 56.03. The Task Force is of the view that these requirements are not necessarily inconsistent because the rules serve two different purposes. The civil procedure rule establishes a minimum notice period to the adversary, while this provision in the general rules of practice sets forth a standard to facilitate the court's consideration of the motions. The time requirements of this rule may be readily modified by the court, while the minimum notice requirements of Minn.R.Civ.P. 56.03 is mandatory unless waived by the parties themselves. *See McAllister v. Independent School District No. 306*, 276 Minn. 549, 149 N.W.2d 81 (1967). The time limits have been slightly modified from the Task Force's original report to reflect the motion practice deadlines now established and followed in the federal court by Minnesota. The local rules of the United States District Court for the District of Minnesota were recently amended, effective Feb. 1, 1991. *See* Rule LR7.1(b)(1) (D. Minn.) (moving papers for dispositive motions now due 28 days before hearing). The Task Force believes it is desirable to remove minor differences between state and federal court practice where no overriding purpose exists for the differences.

The amendment to this rule in 1992 added an express provision for reply briefs. Reply briefs are now allowed for all motions, with the total page limits remaining unchanged. This change is appropriate because of the number of situations where truly new factual or legal matters are raised in response to a motion. In many cases, however, a reply brief will be unnecessary or, where no new matters are raised, inappropriate. The requirement that reply briefs be served and filed three days before the hearing contemplates actual delivery three days before the hearing is scheduled. If service or filing will be accomplished by mail, the deadline is three days earlier by operation of Minn. R.Civ.P. 5.02 & 6.05 and Minn.Gen.R.Prac. 115.01(b).

The statements of facts required by this rule are made for the purpose of the then-pending motion only, and are not to be judicial admissions for other purposes. The Task Force modified the existing local rule in the seventh district to remove any provision that might suggest that summary judgment motions would be treated as defaults if the required statements of fact were not submitted or that might be interpreted to reduce the factual record for summary judgment motions from that specified in Minn.R.Civ.P. 56.05. This will avoid the conflict dealt with by the Minnesota Court of Appeals in *Bunkowske v. Briard,* 461 N.W.2d 392 (Minn. Ct. App. 1990). Counsel seeking to have the court consider matters located elsewhere in the court file will need to identify those materials in the statements of facts required by the rule, but will not have to refile the documents.

Rule 115.10 is a new requirement in the statewide rules, but is a familiar one to most lawyers. Many state and federal courts require parties to meet and confer in an attempt to resolve discovery disputes. *See* Second Dist. Rule 8(h); Fourth Dist. Rule 2.02; R. Haydock & D. Herr, *Discovery Practice* § 8.2 & n.3 (2d ed. 1988) (federal court local rules collected). The Task Force believes that it is reasonable and worthwhile to require informal efforts to attempt to resolve all motion disputes, not just discovery disputes. The Task Force also believes, however, that a rule requiring a face-to-face meeting in all situations would be unwise. This rule requires that some appropriate efforts be made to resolve motion disputes before hearing with the court, but does not specify a specific mechanism. In some instances, a face-to-face meeting will be productive; in other cases a short phone call will suffice to exhaust any possibility of resolution of the matter. The Task Force considered exempting dispositive motions from the requirements of the rule in view of the likely futility of conferring with adversaries over matters that would be dispositive, but determined that the effort expended in conferring in these matters is justified by the likely resolution or narrowing of some disputes or focusing of the dispute for judicial resolution.

Rule 115.02 is a new provision intended both [1] to give parties notice of hearings in advance of the minimum required by other rules. It is intended primarily to prevent a party from obtaining a hearing date and time weeks in advance of a hearing but then delaying giving notice until shortly before the hearing. This practice appears to give an unnecessary tactical advantage to one side. Additionally, by requiring that more than the minimum notice be given in many cases, it will be possible for the responding parties to set on for hearing any additional motions they may have. This may result in the more efficient hearing of multiple motions on a single hearing date.

The definitions of "dispositive" and "non-dispositive" motions should be fairly easy to follow in practice. The definitions are similar to those used in Minnesota federal court practice, *see* Local Rule 4 (D. Minn.), reprinted in Minn. Rules of Ct. 885–86 (West, 1990). Federal court practice treats motions for interlocutory injunctive relief as dispositive because these matters are heard with other dispositive motions before judges rather than magistrates, but there is no reason to treat these motions as dispositive in state-court practice. Indeed, most such motions in state court are heard on expedited schedules set at the time of initial appearance.

The language of Rule 115.06 permits the court, but does not require it, to strike a motion where the rule is not followed. The permissive language is included to make it clear the court retains the discretion to hear matters even if the rules have been ignored, but should not be viewed as suggesting that the court needs to provide a hearing on whether such a motion will be stricken. Courts may administratively provide that hearings on motions not served and filed in accordance with the rule will be automatically or routinely cancelled.

The Task Force considered the adoption of the Seventh District's rule that called for the trial judge to "make every effort" to rule on non-dispositive motions on the day of hearing and dispositive motions within 30 days of hearing. Seventh Dist. R. 15(8). That provision was adopted as part of the revision of motion practice in that district whereby earlier briefing was required with the expected result of earlier decision. Although the purpose of that rule is laudable, the Task Force decided it is not good practice to adopt rules that are purely hortatory in nature, and do not impose any specific requirements or standards. Nonetheless, the Task Force hopes that those benefits of early briefing will flow from the proposed changes on a statewide basis. The Task Force also noted that a statute governs the outer limits of the time for decision. *See* Minn. Stat. § 546.27, subd. 1 (1990) (establishing 90–day period for decision).

Rule 115.09 has been amended to make it clear that telephone hearings may not be recorded unofficially by one party. This rule is consistent with the broader mandate of Gen. R. Prac. 4 which prohibits pictures or voice recordings except if taken as the official record for matters that are heard in court rather than by phone.

Rule 115.11 is added to establish an explicit procedure for submitting motions for reconsideration. The rule permits such motions only with permission of the trial court. The request must be by letter, and should be directed to the judge who issued the decision for which reconsideration is sought. The rule is drawn from a similar provision in the Local Rules of the United States District Court for the District of Minnesota. The rule is intended to remove some of the uncertainty that surrounds use of these motions in Minnesota, especially after the Minnesota Court of Appeals decision in *Carter v. Anderson,* 554 N.W.2d 110 (Minn.Ct.App.1996). *See* Eric J. Magnuson, *Motions for Reconsideration,* 54 BENCH & BAR OF MINN., July 1997, at 36.

Motions for reconsideration play a very limited role in civil practice, and should be approached cautiously and used sparingly. It is not appropriate to prohibit them, however, as they occasionally serve a helpful purpose for the courts. Counsel should understand that although the courts may have the power to reconsider decisions, they rarely will exercise it. They are likely to do so only where intervening legal developments have occurred (*e.g.*, enactment of an applicable statute or issuance of a dispositive court decision) or where the earlier decision is palpably wrong in some respect. Motions for reconsideration are not opportunities for presentation of facts or arguments available when the prior motion was considered. Motions for reconsideration will not be allowed to "expand" or "supplement" the record on appeal. *See e.g., Sullivan v. Spot Weld, Inc.,* 560 N.W.2d 712 (Minn.App.1997); *Progressive Cas. Ins. Co. v. Fiedler,* 1997 WL 292332 (Minn.App.1997) (unpublished). Most importantly, counsel should remember that a motion for reconsideration does not toll any time periods or deadlines, including the time to appeal. See generally 3 ERIC J. MAGNUSON & DAVID F. HERR, MINNESOTA PRACTICE: APPELLATE RULES ANNOTATED § 103.17 (3rd ed. 1996, Supp.1997).

Advisory Committee Comment—2003 Amendments

The rule is amended in 2003 to include a reference to the requirement for paying a motion filing fee. A new statute in 2003 imposes a fee for "[f]iling a motion or response to a motion in civil, family, excluding child support, and guardianship case." *See* 2003 MINN. LAWS 1st Spec. Sess., ch. 2, art. 2, § 2, *to be codified at* MINN. STAT. § 357.021, subd. 2(4).

1 So in adopting court order.

Cross Reference: Minn.R.Civ.P. 7, 56.

Historical Notes

The order of the Minnesota Supreme Court [CX–89–1863] dated December 8, 1997, provides in part that "(t)he attached amendments shall apply to all actions pending on the effective date and to those filed thereafter."

The order of the Minnesota Supreme Court [CX–89–1863] dated December 8, 1997, amending the General Rules of Practice for the District Courts provides in part that "(t)he inclusion of Advisory Committee comments is made for convenience and does not reflect court approval of the comments made therein."

The order of the Minnesota Supreme Court [CX-89-1863] dated December 11, 2003, provides in part that these amendments are effective January 1, 2004, and shall apply to all actions or proceedings pending on or commenced on or after the effective date.

The order of the Minnesota Supreme Court [CX-89-1863] dated December 11, 2003, provides in part that "(t)he inclusion of Advisory Committee comments is made for convenience and does not reflect court approval of the statements made therein".

PART D. MISCELLANEOUS MOTION PRACTICE

RULE 116. ORDERS TO SHOW CAUSE

An order to show cause will be issued only in a case where a statute or rule of civil procedure provides that such an order may be issued or where the court deems it necessary to require the party to appear in person at the hearing.

Adopted Sept. 5, 1991, eff. Jan. 1, 1992.

Task Force Comment—1991 Adoption

This rule is derived from existing Rule 21 of the Code of Rules for the District Courts.

Cross Reference: Minn.R.Civ.P. 7.

RULE 117. DEFAULT HEARINGS

Rule 117.01. Scheduling Hearings

Default hearings are scheduled as motions, and a date and time for default hearings shall be obtained from the court administrator or a designated motion assignment deputy. None of the provisions of Rule 115 apply to default hearings.

Adopted Sept. 5, 1991, eff. Jan. 1, 1992. Amended Nov. 13, 1992, eff. Jan. 1, 1993.

Rule 117.02. Proof of Claim

A party entitled to judgment by default shall move the court for judgment in that party's favor, setting forth by affidavit the facts which entitle that party to relief. Either the party or the party's lawyer may make the affidavit, which may include reliable hearsay. This affidavit is not required in cases governed by Minn.R.Civ.P. 55.01(a).

Adopted Sept. 5, 1991, eff. Jan. 1, 1992. Amended Nov. 13, 1992, eff. Jan. 1, 1993.

Advisory Committee Comment—1992 Amendments

The procedure for scheduling a hearing on a default is the same as that under Rule 115.02 for scheduling motion hearings. This practice related only to the setting of a date for resolution. The other requirements of Rule 115.02 do not apply to default hearings and no additional service requirements are imposed beyond what is required by the Minnesota Rules of Civil Procedure. This rule has been amended explicitly to exempt defaults from all other requirements for motions contained in Rule 115.

Minn.R.Civ.P. 55.01(a) permits entry of judgment by the administrator in limited situations. In those cases, however, Rule 55.01 requires only an affidavit of the amount due, and not the more extensive affidavit required by Minn.Gen.R.Prac. 117.02.

Cross Reference: Minn.R.Civ.P. 54.03, 55.01.

RULE 118. INJUNCTIVE RELIEF AGAINST MUNICIPALITIES

No applications for temporary restraining orders against any city, county, state or governmental agency will be granted without prior oral or written notice to the adverse party. The applications shall be accompanied by a written statement describing the manner of notice.

Adopted Sept. 5, 1991, eff. Jan. 1, 1992.

Task Force Comment—1991 Adoption

This rule is derived from Second District Rule 8(j)(1).

Cross Reference: Minn.R.Civ.P. 65.

RULE 119. APPLICATIONS FOR ATTORNEY FEES

Rule 119.01. Requirement for Motion

In any action or proceeding in which an attorney seeks the award, or approval, of attorneys' fees in the amount of $1,000.00 for the action, or more, application for award or approval of fees shall be made by motion. As to probate and trust matters, application of the rule is limited to contested formal court proceedings. Unless otherwise ordered by the court in a particular proceeding, it does not apply to:

(a) informal probates,

(b) formal probates closed on consents,

(c) uncontested trust proceedings; and

(d) routine guardianship or conservatorship proceedings, except where the Court determines necessary to protect the interests of the ward.

Adopted Oct. 10, 1996. Amended Dec. 8, 1997, eff. Jan. 1, 1998.

Historical Notes

The order of the Minnesota Supreme Court [CX–89–1863] dated December 8, 1997, provides in part that "(t)he attached amendments shall apply to all actions pending on the effective date and to those filed thereafter."

Rule 119.02. Required Papers

The motion shall be accompanied by an affidavit of any attorney of record which establishes the following:

1. A description of each item of work performed, the date upon which it was performed, the amount of time spent on each item of work, the identity of the lawyer or legal assistant performing the work, and the hourly rate sought for the work performed;

2. The normal hourly rate for each person for whom compensation is sought, with an explanation of the basis for any difference between the amount sought and the normal hourly billing rate, if any;

3. A detailed itemization of all amounts sought for disbursements or expenses, including the rate for which any disbursements are charged and the verification that the amounts sought represent the actual cost to the lawyer or firm for the disbursements sought; and

4. That the affiant has reviewed the work in progress or original time records, the work was actually performed for the benefit of the client and was necessary for the proper representation of the client, and that charges for any unnecessary or duplicative work has been eliminated from the application or motion.

Adopted Oct. 10, 1996. Amended Dec. 8, 1997, eff. Jan. 1, 1998.

Historical Notes

The order of the Minnesota Supreme Court [CX–89–1863] dated December 8, 1997, provides in part that "(t)he attached amendments shall apply to all actions pending on the effective date and to those filed thereafter."

Rule 119.03. Additional Records; *In Camera* Review

The court may require production of copies of additional records, including any fee agreement relevant to the fee application, bills actually rendered to the client, work in progress reports, time sheets, invoices or statements for disbursements, or other relevant records. These documents may be ordered produced for review by all parties or for *in camera* review by the court.

Adopted Oct. 10, 1996. Amended Dec. 8, 1997, eff. Jan. 1, 1998.

Historical Notes

The order of the Minnesota Supreme Court [CX–89–1863] dated December 8, 1997, provides in part that "(t)he attached amendments shall apply to all actions pending on the effective date and to those filed thereafter."

Rule 119.04. Memorandum of Law

The motion should be accompanied by a memorandum of law that discusses the basis for recovery of attorneys' fees and explains the calculation of the award of fees sought and the appropriateness of that calculation under applicable law.

Adopted Oct. 10, 1996. Amended Dec. 8, 1997, eff. Jan. 1, 1998.

Advisory Committee Comment—1997 Amendment

This rule is intended to establish a standard procedure for supporting requests for attorneys' fees. The committee is aware that motions for attorneys' fees are either not supported by any factual information or are supported with conclusionary, non-specific information that is not sufficient to permit the court to make an appropriate determination of the appropriate amount of fees. This rule is intended to create a standard procedure only; it neither expands nor limits the entitlement to recovery of attorneys' fees in any case.

Where fees are to be determined under the "lodestar" method widely used in the federal courts and adopted in Minnesota in *Specialized Tours, Inc. v. Hagen*, 392 N.W.2d 520, 542–43 (Minn.1986), trial courts need to have information to support the reasonableness of the hours claimed to be expended as well as the reasonable hourly rate under the circumstances. This rule is intended to provide a standard set of documentation that allows the majority of fee applications to be considered by the court without requiring further information. The rule specifically acknowledges that cases involving complex issues or serious factual dispute over these issues may require additional documentation. The rule allows the court to require additional materials in any case where appropriate. This rule is not intended to limit the court's discretion, but is intended to encourage streamlined handling of fee applications and to facilitate filing of appropriate support to permit consideration of the issues.

This rule also authorizes the court to review the documentation required by the rule *in camera.* This is often necessary given the sensitive nature of the required fee information and the need to protect the party entitled to attorneys' fees from having to compromise its attorney's thoughts, mental impressions, or other work product in order to support its fee application. As an alternative to permitting in camera review by the trial judge, the court can permit submission of redacted copies, with privileged material removed from all copies.

The amendment in 1997, adding the exceptions to the requirements of the rule for certain probate and trust proceedings, is designed to obviate procedures that serve no purpose for the courts and unduly burden the parties. Probate and trust matters have separate statutes and case law relating to attorney fees. *See* Minn.Stat. §§ 524.3–721 and 525.515; *In re Great Northern Iron Ore Properties,* 311 N.W.2d 488 (Minn.1981) and *In re Living Trust Created by Atwood,* 227 Minn. 495, 35 N.W.2d 736 (1949). In probate and trust matters, if no interested party objects to the attorney fees, there is ordinarily no reason for the court to require the detail specified in Rule 119. In contested matters, however, such detail may be appropriate to enable the court to resolve the matter under the standards of applicable probate and trust law. The court may protect the sensitive and confidential information that may be contained in attorney time records by entering an appropriate order in a particular case. Similarly, the exemption of these cases from the requirements of the rule does not prevent the court from requiring any of the fee application documentation in a particular matter.

Historical Notes

The order of the Minnesota Supreme Court [CX–89–1863] dated December 8, 1997, provides in part that "(t)he attached amendments shall apply to all actions pending on the effective date and to those filed thereafter."

The order of the Minnesota Supreme Court [CX–89–1863] dated December 8, 1997, amending the General Rules of Practice for the District Courts provides in part that "(t)he inclusion of Advisory Committee comments is made for convenience and does not reflect court approval of the comments made therein."

Rule 119.05. Attorney Fees in Default Proceedings

(a) A party proceeding by default and seeking an award of attorney fees that has established a basis for the award under applicable law, including parties seeking to enforce a confession of judgment, may obtain approval of the fees administratively without a motion hearing, provided that:

(1) the fees requested do not exceed fifteen percent (15%) of the principal balance owing as requested in that party's pleadings, up to a maximum of $3,000.00. Such a party may seek a minimum of $250.00; and

(2) the requesting party's pleading includes a claim for attorney fees in an amount greater than or equal to the amount sought upon default; and

(3) the defaulting party, after default has occurred, has been provided notice of the right to request a hearing under section (c) of this rule, a form for making such a request substantially similar to Form 119.05 as published by the state court administrator, and the affidavit required under Rule 119.02.

(b) A party may request a formal hearing and seek fees in excess of the amount described herein if that party provides the court with evidence relevant to the amount of attorneys' fees requested as established by the factors a court considers when determining the reasonableness of the attorneys' fees.

(c) A defaulting party may request a hearing and further judicial review of the attorneys' fees requested by completing a "Request for Hearing" provided by the plaintiff substantially similar to Form 119.05 as published by the state court administrator. A party may serve the form, at any time after a default has occurred, provided that the defaulting party is given at least twenty (20) days notice before the request for judgment is made. A defaulting party must serve the Request for Hearing upon the requesting party or its counsel within twenty (20) days of its receipt. Upon timely receipt of a Request for Hearing the party seeking fees shall request a judicial assignment and have the hearing scheduled.

(d) Rule 119.05 does not apply to contested cases, ancillary proceedings (*e.g.,* motions to compel or show cause) or proceedings subsequent to the entry of judgment.

Adopted Dec. 11, 2003, eff. Jan. 1, 2004. Amended Dec. 17, 2004, eff. Jan. 1, 2005; Dec. 22, 2008, eff. March 1, 2009.

Advisory Committee Comment—1997 Amendment

This rule is intended to establish a standard procedure for supporting requests for attorney fees. The committee is aware that motions for attorney fees are either not supported by any factual information or are supported with conclusionary, non-specific information that is not sufficient to permit the court to make an appropriate determination of the appropriate amount of fees. This rule is intended to create a standard procedure only; it neither expands nor limits the entitlement to recovery of attorneys' fees in any case.

Where fees are to be determined under the "lodestar" method widely used in the federal courts and adopted in Minnesota in Specialized Tours, Inc. v. Hagen, 392 N.W.2d 520, 542–43 (Minn. 1986), trial courts need to have information to support the reasonableness of the hours claimed to be expended as well as the reasonable hourly rate under the circumstances. This rule is intended to provide a standard set of documentation that allows the majority of fee applications to be considered by the court without requiring further information. The rule specifically acknowledges that cases involving complex issues or serious factual dispute over these issues may require additional documentation. The rule allows the court to require additional materials in any case where appropriate. This rule is not intended to limit the court's discretion, but is intended to encourage streamlined handing of fee applications and to facilitate filing of appropriate support to permit consideration of the issues.

This rule also authorizes the court to review the documentation required by the rule in camera. This is often necessary given the sensitive nature of the required fee information and the need to protect the party entitled to attorney fees from having to compromise its attorney's thoughts, mental impressions, or other work product in order to support its fee application. As an alternative to permitting in camera review by the trial judge, the court can permit submission of redacted copies, with privileged material removed from all copies.

The amendment in 1997, adding the exceptions to the requirements of the rule for certain probate and trust proceedings, is designed to obviate procedures that serve no purpose for the courts and unduly burden the parties. Probate and trust matters have separate statutes and case law relating to attorney fees. See Minnesota Statutes, sections 524.3–721 and 525.515; In re Great Northern Iron Ore Properties, 311 N.W.2d 488 (Minn. 1981) and In re Living Trust Created by Atwood, 227 Minn. 495, 35 N.W.2d 736 (1949). In probate and trust matters, if no interested party objects to the attorney fees, there is ordinarily no reason for the court to require the detail specified in Rule 119. In contested matters, however, such detail may be appropriate to enable the court to resolve the matter under the standards of applicable probate and trust law. The court may protect the sensitive and confidential information that may be contained in attorney time records by entering an appropriate order in a particular case. Similarly, the exemption of these cases from the requirements of the rule does not prevent the court from requiring any of the fee application documentation in a particular matter.

Advisory Committee Comment—2003 Amendment

Rule 119.05 is a new rule to establish a streamlined procedure for considering attorney fees on matters that will be heard by default. The rule does not apply to situations other than default judgments, such as motions to compel discovery, motions to show cause, sanctions matters, or attorney fees in contested matters. This subsection is modeled on a rule adopted by the Fourth Judicial District and implemented as a local standing order. A simpler procedure for defaults is appropriate and will serve to conserve judicial resources, and it is appropriate to have a uniform rule throughout Minnesota.

New Form 119.05 is intended to provide useful information to the defaulting party and some care has gone into its drafting. Although use of the form is not required, the requirement that any notice conform "substantially" to the form should be heeded. The committee has attempted to use language that fairly advises the defaulting party of the procedure under Rule 119.05 without threatening consequences or confusing the defaulting party on the effect of either contesting or not contesting the fee award. The rule requires that notice be given after the defendant has defaulted. Notice given earlier is not effective to comply with the rule, as such notice is likely to confuse the recipient as to the differing procedures and timing for response to the Summons and responding to the request for fees. An affidavit detailing the basis for the award as required under Rule 119.02 must accompany the notice and the form.

The rule does not affect the amounts that may be recovered for attorney fees; it allows either side to obtain a hearing on the request for fees; the rule supplies an efficient mechanism for the numerous default matters where a full hearing is not required. Similarly, the rule does not remove the requirement that a party seeking fees file a motion; it simply provides a mechanism for resolution of some motions without formal hearings.

Advisory Committee Comment—2004 Adoption

Rule 119.05 was amended in 2004 in a single way: to make it clear that the mechanism for streamlined approval of attorney fees in default matters is also available for matters proceeding pursuant to confession of judgment, even if not technically a default. Confessions of judgment are authorized and limited by Minn. Stat. § 548.22 (2002), but that statute does not address how attorney fee requests that accompany confessions of judgment should be heard. Because the rule both allows streamlined entry of a judgment for attorney fees and provides procedural protection to the judgment debtor, the committee believes it is appropriate to apply this procedure to judgments pursuant to confession.

Advisory Committee Comment—2008 Amendment

Rule 119.05 is amended to remove Form 119.05 from the rules, and to permit the maintenance and publication of the form by the state court administrator. The form, together with other court forms, can be found at http://www.mncourts.gov/.

Historical Notes

The order of the Minnesota Supreme Court [CX-89-1863] dated December 11, 2003, provides in part that these amendments are effective January 1, 2004, and shall apply to all actions or proceedings pending on or commenced on or after the effective date.

The order of the Minnesota Supreme Court [CX-89-1863] dated December 11, 2003, provides in part that "(t)he inclusion of Advisory Committee comments is made for convenience and does not reflect court approval of the statements made therein".

The order of the Minnesota Supreme Court [CX–89–1863] dated December 17, 2004, provides in part that "(t)he attached amendments shall apply to all actions pending on the effective date and to those filed thereafter."

The order of the Minnesota Supreme Court [CX–89–1863] dated December 17, 2004, amending the General Rules of Practice for the

District Courts provides in part that "(t)he inclusion of Advisory Committee comments is made for convenience and does not reflect court approval of the comments made therein."

RULE 120. [RESERVED]

PART E. TRIAL MANAGEMENT

RULE 121. NOTICE OF SETTLEMENT

When any action in which any pleading or other paper has been filed is settled, counsel shall immediately advise the appropriate assignment office, and shall also advise the office of the judge assigned to the case or then assigned to hear any matter relating to the case.

Adopted Sept. 5, 1991, eff. Jan. 1, 1992.

Task Force Comment—1991 Adoption

This rule is based on 2d Dist. R. 9(a). Other districts have similar rules. This new rule, derived from current local rule provisions, makes explicit what courts now expect and which common courtesy requires.

Cross Reference: Minn.R.Civ.P. 40, 41.

RULE 122. CONTINUANCE

If a trial setting has been established by scheduling order after hearing the parties, the court shall decline to consider requests for continuance except those made by motion or when a judge determines that an emergency exists. A single request for a reasonable continuance of a trial setting set by notice without hearing should be granted by the court upon agreement of all parties, provided that the request is made within 20 days after notice of the setting to the parties. All other requests for continuance shall be made by motion with notice to all parties.

Adopted Sept. 5, 1991, eff. Jan. 1, 1992.

Task Force Comment—1991 Adoption

This rule reflects the result of extensive discussions by the Task Force. This rule is intended to create a uniform continuance practice statewide, consistent with the widely differing assignment practices. The rule creates a presumptive right to one continuance only in cases where a trial setting is made mechanically and without consultation of the parties and their lawyers and then only if all parties agree. If the setting has been made after hearing parties, there would be no presumed continuance. In any case, the court can deny requests for continuance.

Cross Reference: Minn.R.Civ.P. 40.

RULE 123. VOIR DIRE OF JURORS IN CASES IN WHICH INSURANCE COMPANY INTERESTED IN DEFENSE OR OUTCOME OF ACTION

In all civil jury cases, in which an insurance company or companies are not parties, but are interested in the defense or outcome of the action, the presiding judge shall, upon the request of any party, be advised of the name of such company or companies, out of the hearing of the jury, as well as the name of the local agent of such companies. When so disclosed, no inquiry shall be permitted by counsel as to such names in the hearing of the jury, nor shall disclosure be made to the jury that such insurance company is interested in the action.

During examination of the jurors by the court, the jurors shall, upon request of any party, be asked collectively whether any of them have any interest as policyholders, stockholders, officers, agents or otherwise in the insurance company or companies interested in the defense or outcome of the action, but such question shall not be repeated to each individual juror. If none of the jurors indicate any such interest in the company or companies involved, then no further inquiry shall be permitted with reference thereto.

If any of the jurors manifest an interest in any of the companies involved, then the court shall further inquire of such juror or jurors as to any interest in such company, including any relationship or connection with the local agent of such interested company, to determine whether such interests or relationship disqualifies such juror.

Adopted Sept. 5, 1991, eff. Jan. 1, 1992.

Task Force Comment—1991 Adoption

This rule is derived from Rule 31 of the Code of Rules for the District Courts. The rule is modified to specify that the court conducts the examination of potential jurors about their possible involvement with any interested insurers, thereby allowing the subject to be covered without the potential for introducing prejudice, rather than revealing it. The court should exercise its discretion to make certain that any affirmative answers to the court's questions be fully explored. *See Hunt v. Regents of Univ. of Minn.*, 460 N.W.2d 28, 33–34 (Minn. 1990).

Cross Reference: Minn.R.Civ.P. 47; Minn. Civ. Trialbook § 6.

RULE 124. REPORTING OF OPENING STATEMENT AND FINAL ARGUMENTS

Opening statements and final arguments shall be reported.

Adopted Sept. 5, 1991, eff. Jan. 1, 1992.

Task Force Comment—1991 Adoption

This rule is new. The practice of various courts in reporting opening statements and final arguments has not been uniform. The Task Force strongly recommends that the rules provide for reporting of all opening statements and final arguments so that these portions of the trial proceedings are available for transcription. Most judges now follow this practice. In some cases, parties exercising their right to make a record of these trial proceedings have been presented with bills from the official court reporter for this service. In the absence of an order for a transcript, the Task Force believes no extra charges should properly be made for the mere making of a record of what transpires in the trial court.

Cross Reference: Minn.R.Civ.P. 39.04; Minn. Civ. Trialbook § 8.

RULE 125. AUTOMATIC STAY

The court administrator shall stay entry of judgment for thirty days after the court orders judgment following a trial unless the court orders otherwise. Upon expiration of the stay, the court administrator shall promptly enter judgment.

Adopted Sept. 5, 1991, eff. Jan. 1, 1992. Amended Nov. 13, 1992, eff. Jan. 1, 1993.

Advisory Committee Comment—1992 Amendments

This rule is derived from 7th Dist. R. 11, and is similar to the local rules in other districts.

This rule reflects a common practice in the trial courts, even in those districts that do not have a specific rule requiring a stay. The Task Force believes it is desirable to make this practice both uniform and explicit. The stay allows parties to file post-trial motions and to perfect an appeal without entry of judgment or formal collection efforts. At the end of the 30–day period, stay is governed by Minn.R.Civ.P. 62.03 and the supersedeas bond requirements of the Minnesota Rules of Civil Appellate Procedure. The stay anticipated by this rule applies only following a trial. Where judgment is ordered pursuant to pretrial motion or by default (e.g., temporary hearings in family law), or in situations governed by other rules, including marriage dissolutions by stipulation (Rule 307(b)) and housing court matters (Rules 609 and 611(b)), the stay is not necessary and not intended by the rule.

The rule only creates a standard, uniform procedure for staying entry of judgment. The court can enter such a stay in any case and can order immediate entry of judgment in any case.

Cross Reference: Minn.R.Civ.P. 58.

RULE 126. JUDGMENT—ENTRY BY ADVERSE PARTY

When a party is entitled to have judgment entered in that party's favor upon the verdict of a jury, report of a referee, or decision or finding of the court, and neglects to enter the same for 10 days after the rendition of the verdict or notice of the filing of the report, decision or finding; or after the expiration of a stay, the opposite party may cause judgment to be entered on five days' notice to the party entitled thereto.

Adopted Sept. 5, 1991, eff. Jan. 1, 1992.

Task Force Comment—1991 Adoption

This rule is derived from existing Rule 17 of the Code of Rules for the District Courts.

Cross Reference: Minn.R.Civ.P. 58.

RULE 127. EXPERT WITNESS FEES

The amount allowed shall be in such amount as is deemed reasonable for such services in the community where the trial occurred and in the field of endeavor in which the witness has qualified as an expert. No allowance shall be made for preparation or in conducting of experiments outside the courtroom by an expert.

Adopted Sept. 5, 1991, eff. Jan. 1, 1992. Amended May 3, 2010, eff. July 1, 2010.

Advisory Committee Comment—2010 Amendment

This rule is amended to remove the $300 limit on expert fees contained in the former rule. This change is part of the new procedure established for taxation of expert costs established by amendment of Minn. R. Civ. P. 54. 04 in 2010. The rule allows taxation of costs by either the court administrator or district court judge, and there is no reason to continue a rule that limits the amount the court administrator can order, thereby making a two-step taxation process inevitable. The $300 limit in the former rule also had not been changed for several decades, so was unduly miserly in the 21st century.

Task Force Comment—1991 Adoption

This rule is derived from Rule 11 of the Code of Rules for the District Courts.

Cross Reference: Minn.R.Civ.P. 54.

Expert witnesses, court appointment, compensation, see Rules of Evid., Rule 706.

RULE 128. RETRIEVAL OR DESTRUCTION OF EXHIBITS

It shall be the duty of the lawyer or party offering exhibits in evidence to remove all exhibits from the custody of the court upon final disposition of a case. Failure to do so within 15 days of being notified to do so will be deemed authorization to destroy such exhibits.

Adopted Sept. 5, 1991, eff. Jan. 1, 1992.

Task Force Comment—1991 Adoption

This rule is derived from 2d Dist. R. 11, with changes.

Cross Reference: Minn.R.Civ.P. 43, 77; Minn. Civ. Trialbook §§ 13, 14.

RULE 129. USE OF ADMINISTRATOR'S FILES

No papers on file in a cause shall be taken from the custody of the court administrator except upon order of the court.

Adopted Sept. 5, 1991, eff. Jan. 1, 1992.

Task Force Comment—1991 Adoption

This rule is derived from Rule 12(b) of the Code of Rules for the District Courts, without substantial change.

Cross Reference: Minn.R.Civ.P. 77; Minn. Civ. Trialbook §§ 13, 14.

RULE 130. EXHIBIT NUMBERING

Exhibits proposed by any party shall be marked in a single series of arabic numbers, without designation of the party offering the exhibit. Exhibit numbers may be consecutive or may be preassigned in blocks to each party. If adhesive exhibit labels are used, they shall be white with black printing.

Adopted Dec. 14, 1993, eff. Jan. 1, 1994.

Advisory Committee Comment—1994 Amendments

This new rule requires a uniform method of marking exhibits, without the cumbersome prefixes that are frequently now encountered. The committee believes that a uniform numbering system will benefit the courts and litigants. The new system will permit exhibits to be used without labeling to show "ownership" or "lineage" of the exhibit. This system will also facilitate numbering of exhibits in multi-party cases, where the current practice creates complicated numbers at trial and burdensome citations on appeal. Attorneys and judges with experience in using this system believe it works fairly, predictably, and efficiently. The rule permits flexibility in assignment of exhibit numbers, allowing them to be issued seriatim at trial or in blocks of numbers assigned to each party prior to trial. The rule requires uniform exhibit labels to prevent any uncertainty or wasted effort by parties attempting to obtain a perceived advantage in identifying "ownership" of exhibits through the color of labels.

RULE 131. USE OF INTERACTIVE VIDEO TELECONFERENCE IN CIVIL CASES

Rule 131.01. Definitions.

(a) "ITV" refers to interactive video teleconference.

(b) A "terminal site" is any location where ITV is used for any portion of a court proceeding.

(c) The "venue county" is the county where pleadings are filed and hearings are held under current court procedures.

Adopted Dec. 22, 2008, eff. March 1, 2009.

Comment—Rule 131

See comment following Rule 131.07.

Rule 131.02. Permissible Uses; Initiation.

In all civil actions and proceedings including commitment proceedings subject to the Special Rules of Procedure Governing Proceedings Under the Minnesota Commitment and Treatment Act, the court may conduct hearings and admit oral testimony, subject to cross-examination, by live audio-visual means, where authorized by this rule.

(a) Scheduling Conflicts. All scheduling conflicts and priorities shall be determined by the judge(s).

(b) Use of ITV on Court's Initiative; Notice. If the court on its own initiative orders the use of live audio-visual means (ITV) to conduct hearings and proceedings, it shall give notice in accordance with the Rules of Civil Procedure and General Rules of Practice, which notice shall advise the parties of the duty to exchange information under Rule 131.04, and the prohibition on recording in Rule 131.06(i).

(c) Use of ITV Upon Stipulation. The parties may, subject to court approval and site availability, stipulate that a hearing or proceeding be conducted by ITV in accordance with the procedures established in this rule. The parties shall contact the court administrator as soon as possible to permit scheduling of ITV facilities. A written, signed stipulation requesting the use of ITV shall be filed with the court at least 24 hours prior to the date set for the ITV hearing or proceeding. The stipulation shall be substantially in the form set forth in the Stipulation and Approval form as published by the state court administrator. The parties are responsible for making arrangements to use any site that is outside the control of the court in the venue county, for providing the necessary contact information to the court administrator, and for ensuring the compatibility of the equipment.

(d) Use of ITV Upon Motion.

(1) **Request.** Any party may, by motion, request the use of ITV for a hearing or proceeding in accordance with this rule. No motion for use of ITV shall be heard until the moving party serves a copy of the motion on the opposing counsel and files the original with the court administrator at least seven (7) days prior to the scheduled hearing or proceeding for which ITV use is requested. The moving party may, ex parte, contact the court for an expedited hearing date on the motion for use of ITV and for waiver of the usual notice of hearing. The moving party is responsible under Rule 131.02(c) for making arrangements to use any site that is outside the control of the court in the venue county, for providing the necessary contact information to the court administrator, and for ensuring the compatibility of the equipment. The motion shall include, as an attachment, a notice advising the other parties of their right to object to use of ITV, the consequences of failing to timely file an objection, the duty to exchange information under Rule 131.04, and the prohibition on recording in Rule 131.06(i). A sample notice is published by the state court administrator.

(2) **Objection.** Any party objecting to a motion for use of ITV may file and serve a response to the motion 48 hours prior to the hearing on the motion for use of ITV.

(3) **Burden of Proof.** The moving party must establish good cause for use of ITV by a preponderance of the evidence.

(4) **Good Cause.** The Court shall consider the following factors to determine "good cause":

(i) Whether a timely objection has been made;

(ii) Whether any undue surprise or prejudice would result;

(iii) The convenience of the parties, counsel, and the court;

(iv) The cost and time savings;

(v) The importance and complexity of the proceeding;

(vi) Whether the proponent has been unable, after due diligence, to procure the physical presence of a witness;

(vii) The convenience to the parties and the proposed witness, and the cost of producing the witness in relation to the importance of the offered testimony;

(viii) Whether the procedure would allow effective cross-examination, especially where documents and exhibits available to the witness may not be available to counsel;

(ix) Whether the surroundings maintain the solemnity and integrity of the proceedings and thereby impress upon the witness the duty to testify truthfully;

(x) Whether the witness is presently in prison or incarcerated; and,

(xi) Such other factors as the court may, in each individual case, determine to be relevant.

(5) **Emergency Circumstances.** The court may shorten the time periods provided in this rule 131.02(d) upon a showing of good cause.

(6) **Determination.** If the use of ITV is thereafter allowed and ordered by the court, the hearing shall proceed, by ITV, in accordance with the provisions of this rule. If the court determines that good cause for the use of ITV has not been established, the hearing or proceeding shall be heard as provided by the Rules of Civil Procedure and General Rules of Practice.

Adopted Dec. 22, 2008, eff. March 1, 2009.

Comment—Rule 131

See comment following Rule 131.07.

Rule 131.03. Costs and Arrangements; Certification

(a) **Costs.** The party or parties, other than the court, requesting use of ITV for any hearing or proceeding shall be responsible for any additional use or other fees over and above those normally incurred by the venue county in connecting from one court site to another court site within the district or collaboration area.

(b) **Arrangements.** If the court on its own initiative orders ITV, the court shall, through the court administrator where the case is venued, establish and make arrangements to carry out the ITV procedures required in order for the court to hear the case as an ITV hearing or proceeding. In all other cases it will be the responsibility of the party requesting the use of ITV to contact the court administrator where the case is venued who shall, working with the judge assigned, establish a hearing date and time so that the case may be scheduled as an ITV hearing or proceeding. The court and counsel shall use reasonable efforts to confer with one another in scheduling ITV hearings or proceedings so as not to cause, delay or create scheduling conflicts.

(c) **Service.** The moving party shall have the responsibility of preparing, serving and filing the motion and notice of motion papers as required by this rule.

(d) **Certification.** By signing a stipulation or motion for use of ITV, a person certifies that the use of ITV will be in accordance with the provisions of this rule, including, without limitation, the requirement in Rule 131.06(i) that no recording shall be made of any ITV proceeding except the recording made as the official court record.

Adopted Dec. 22, 2008, eff. March 1, 2009.

Comment—Rule 131

See comment following Rule 131.07.

Rule 131.04. Exchange of information.

Whenever ITV is to be used to conduct a hearing or proceeding, evidentiary exhibits shall be exchanged with all other parties and submitted to the court, as appropriate, prior to the commencement of the hearing or proceeding.

Adopted Dec. 22, 2008, eff. March 1, 2009.

Comment—Rule 131

See comment following Rule 131.07.

Rule 131.05. Location of Participants.

During the ITV hearing:

(a) The judge may be at any terminal site.

(b) The court clerk shall be in the venue county unless otherwise authorized by the presiding judge.

(c) Except as otherwise provided in rule 131.05(d) regarding commitment proceedings, counsel for the parties shall be present at the site from which the party they represent will participate in the hearing, unless the court approves another location prior to the hearing, and witnesses and other interested parties may be located at any terminal site that will allow satisfactory video and audio reception at all other sites.

(d) In commitment proceedings, the respondent's attorney shall be present at the ITV site from which the respondent will participate in the proceedings.

Adopted Dec. 22, 2008, eff. March 1, 2009.

Comment—Rule 131

See comment following Rule 131.07.

Rule 131.06. Proceedings.

In any proceeding conducted by ITV under this rule:

(a) Parties entitled to be heard shall be given prior notice of the manner and time of the hearing or proceeding.

(b) Witnesses may testify by ITV at all hearings, including contested matters.

(c) Regardless of the physical location of any party to the ITV hearing or proceeding, any waiver, stipulation, motion, objection, decision, order or any other actions taken by the court or a party has the same effect as if done in person. Court orders that bear the presiding judge's signature may be transmitted electronically or via facsimile machine to the various ITV sites for the purpose of service.

(d) The court administrator of the venue county will keep court minutes and maintain court records as if the proceeding were heard in person.

(e) All proceedings held by ITV will be governed by the Minnesota Rules of Civil Procedure, the General Rules of Practice and state law, except as herein provided. Courtroom decorum during ITV hearings will conform to the extent possible to that required during traditional court proceedings.

(f) A sheriff, sheriff's deputy, bailiff or other licensed peace officer shall be present at each ITV site for the purpose of maintaining order, as the court deems necessary.

(g) The court shall ensure that each party has adequate opportunity to speak privately with counsel, including, where appropriate, suspension of the audio transmission and recording or allowing counsel to leave the conference table to communicate with the client in private.

(h) Judges may continue any hearing that cannot proceed due to ITV equipment problems or failure, unless other arrangements to proceed with the hearing are agreed upon by all parties.

(i) No recording shall be made of any ITV proceeding except the recording made as the official court record. This Rule 131 does not supersede the provisions of the Minnesota Rules of Public Access to Records of the Judicial Branch.

Adopted Dec. 22, 2008, eff. March 1, 2009.

Comment—Rule 131

See comment following Rule 131.07.

Rule 131.07. Administrative Procedures

The following administrative procedures are applicable to all ITV proceedings:

(a) Off–Camera Presence. During a hearing conducted by ITV, all off-camera persons at any participating ITV terminal site must be identified for the record. This shall not apply to members of the public located in general public seating areas of any courtroom.

(b) Court Administrator Duties. The Court Administrator for each county shall be responsible for the following:

(1) Ensure that the ITV equipment is ready and functioning properly in advance of any ITV hearing, so that there will be no interference with the punctual commencement of a hearing.

(2) Provide participants an opportunity to become familiar with use of the ITV equipment and courtroom procedure prior to commencement of the hearing.

(3) Set ITV system configuration as designated by the presiding judge. The presiding judge shall consider the objections or concerns of any party.

(4) Monitor audio and video quality, making adjustments and providing technical assistance throughout the hearing as necessary.

(5) Ensure that any court documents or exhibits that the judge will require prior to or during the course of the hearing are mailed or faxed to the judge prior to commencement of the hearing.

(6) Be familiar with problem management procedures, including steps to be taken in performing initial problem determination, identity and location of individual(s) who should be contacted if initial problem/resolution attempts fail, and service call placement procedures.

(c) Technical Standards. The following technical standards should be followed:

(1) To optimize picture clarity, the room should have diffused lighting and window shades to block external light.

(2) To optimize viewing, monitors should be placed in a darkened area of the room and be of sufficient size and number to allow convenient viewing by all participants.

(3) Cameras and microphones should be sufficient in number to allow video and audio coverage of all participants, prevent crowding of participants, facilitate security, and protect confidential communications.

(4) Audio and visual must be synchronized and undistorted.

(5) All hearing participants should speak directly into their microphones.

Adopted Dec. 22, 2008, eff. March 1, 2009.

Advisory Committee Comments—2008 Amendment

In October 1999 the Supreme Court informally approved the use of ITV in civil cases but did not adopt any specific rules. The addition of Rule 131 in 2008 is intended to provide a uniform procedure permitting the use of interactive video teleconferencing (ITV) to conduct hearings and admit oral testimony in civil cases. It is based on protocols developed and implemented for a pilot project in the Ninth Judicial District and later tweaked by a subcommittee of the Court's former Technology Planning Committee. The success of the pilot project is reported in NATIONAL CENTER FOR STATE COURTS, COURT SERVICES DIVISION, ASSESSMENT OF THE INTERACTIVE TELEVISION PROGRAM IN THE NINTH JUDICIAL DISTRICT OF MINNESOTA (Sept. 1999).

Rule 131.02 identifies the situations in which the district court may authorize the use of ITV by order: upon the court's own initiative, upon stipulation by the parties, or upon a showing of good cause. The court as part of its overall case management practice initiated the bulk of the orders in the Ninth Judicial District pilot project. It is anticipated that use of ITV will vary by district, depending on factors such as geographical size and the nature of the cases.

Rule 131.02(b) recognizes that when a court orders the use of ITV on its own initiative, the court must notify the parties of the use of ITV. Notices are to be in accordance with rules of civil procedure and the general rules of practice. Once an order is filed, MINN. R. CIV. P. 77.04 requires the court administrator to serve notice of the order immediately by mail, and MINN. GEN. R. PRAC. 1.03 requires that service be made on a party's attorney if represented, otherwise on the party directly. The notice of ITV use may also be incorporated into a scheduling order issued under MINN. GEN. R. PRAC. 111.03. Regardless of the precise mechanism, the notice of ITV use must include the information required in Rule 131.02(b). A sample notice is set forth for publication by the state court administrator.

Parties may, subject to court approval, stipulate to the use of ITV under rule 131.02(c). Upon reaching a stipulation, the parties must contact the court administrator as soon as possible to obtain a date and time for the ITV hearing. Failure to provide adequate lead time may result in rejection of the stipulation. The parties are responsible for making arrangements to use any site that is outside the control of the court in the venue county. Parties should be aware that use of court and other governmental terminal sites might be subject to collaboration agreements entered into between courts and other government agencies. This may limit the availability of, or control the costs of using or accessing certain terminal sites, particularly those outside the county or district where the action is venued or outside the state's dedicated MNET network. Under Rule 131.03 parties requesting use of ITV for any hearing or proceeding are responsible for any additional use or other fees over and above those normally incurred by the venue county in connecting from one collaboration site to another. Parties are also responsible for ensuring compatibility of equipment for sites outside the control of the venue county.

Finally, a written, signed stipulation in the format substantially similar to the form appended to the rule must be filed with the court no later than twenty-four (24) hours prior to the hearing. By signing the stipulation the parties certify that they will follow the protocol, including, without limitation, the requirement in Rule 131.06(i) that no recording shall be made of the ITV proceeding except a recording made as the official record of the proceeding. Access to recordings of proceedings is governed by Rule 4, subd. 3, of the RULES OF PUBLIC ACCESS TO RECORDS OF THE JUDICIAL BRANCH.

Rule 131.02(d) sets forth requirements for requesting ITV use when there is no stipulation by the parties. A formal motion is required, and it must be served and filed at least seven days prior to the scheduled hearing or proceeding for which ITV use is requested. The rule authorizes ex parte contact with the court for purposes of obtaining an expedited hearing date on the motion for use of ITV. *See* MINN. GEN. R. PRAC. 115.04 (non-dispositive motions normally must be served and filed at 14 days in advance of the hearing). The moving party is responsible under Rule 131.03 for making arrangements to use any site that is outside the control of the court in the venue county, for providing the necessary contact information to the court administrator, for ensuring the compatibility of the equipment, and paving any additional costs incurred by the court in facilitating the ITV session. The motion must also include or be accompanied by a notice informing opposing parties of their right to object, consequences of failure to object, requirements for exchange of information, and prohibitions on recording an ITV session (a sample notice is provided for publication by the state court administrator).

Objections to a motion for use of ITV must be made prior to the hearing on the motion. The failure of an opposing party to object may be considered along with other factors set forth in Rule 131.02(d)(4) that may determine good cause for use of ITV. The moving party has the burden of establishing good cause.

Rule 131.02(d)(5) permits the court to shorten the time periods provided for in Rule 131.02 in emergent circumstances upon a proper showing. As of the time of the drafting of this commentary, a different time period is established for requesting ITV use in commitment cases under Rule 14 of the SPECIAL RULES OF PROCEDURE UNDER THE MINNESOTA COMMITMENT AND TREATMENT ACT (requires notice to the other party at least 24 hours in advance of the hearing, and court approval). The drafting committee is of the opinion that following the protocol with the ability to shorten the time frames when necessary will be sufficient to address the needs of commitment and other matters covered by this rule.

Rule 131.03 places responsibility for costs and site arrangements with those seeking to use ITV. The court assumes this responsibility when ordering ITV on its own initiative, as is done for the bulk of the ITV proceedings in the Ninth Judicial District pilot project. When a party or parties initiate the request, however, Rules 131.02(c) and 131.02(d) shift some of the responsibility to the requesting party or parties. Parties also certify that they will comply with the protocol, including the prohibition in Rule 131.06(i) against recording ITV sessions.

Rule 131.04 attempts to highlight an important logistical requirement when ITV is used. Documents and other information need to be exchanged and submitted to the court, where appropriate, prior to the ITV session. This is particularly important when the parties are located at different sites.

Rule 131.07(b) recognizes that ITV use imposes new logistical duties on court administration staff. This section is intended to assist courts as they implement ITV use and to train new staff.

Rules 131.05–.07 set forth the ground rules for conducting ITV sessions. The prohibition on recording ITV sessions set forth in Rule 131.06(i) and echoed throughout the rule is identical to that applicable to telephone hearings under MINN. GEN. R. PRAC. 115.09. This requirement is consistent with the directives of the supreme court regarding use of cameras in the courtroom. *See In re Modification of Section 3A(10) of the Minnesota Code of Judicial Conduct*, No. C7–81–300 (Minn. S. Ct., filed Jan. 11, 1996) (order reinstating experimental program for audio and video coverage of trial court proceedings); *Order for Interactive Audio–Video Communications Experiment in First Judicial District–Mental Illness Commitment Proceedings*, No. C6–90–649 (Minn. S. Ct., filed April 5, 1995); *Order re Interactive Audio–Video communications Pilot Program in Third Judicial District Mental Illness Commitment Proceedings*, No. C6–90–649 (Minn. S. Ct., filed Jan. 29, 1999); *Order for Interactive Audio and Video Communications*, Fourth Judicial District, Mental Health Division, *Price and Jarvis Proceedings*, No. C6–90–649 (Minn. S. Ct., filed April 8, 1991).

Rule 131.05(c) requires that counsel and their party must be present at the same terminal site unless otherwise permitted by the court. In commitment cases, court rules do not permit counsel for the patient and the patient to be present at different sites. See rule 14 of the Special Rules of Procedure Under the Minnesota Commitment and Treatment Act. Witnesses and other participants may be located at any terminal site that allows satisfactory video and audio reception.

Rule 131.07(c) describes equipment and room standards in functional terms. A more detailed discussion of technical issues and terminology can be found in STATEWIDE VIDEOCONFERENCING COMMITTEE, BRIDGING THE DISTANCE: IMPLEMENTING VIDEOCONFERENCING IN WISCONSIN (10/30/2007) (a dynamic document that is continually updated and that is currently available for download from the Wisconsin Supreme Court website, located at http://www.wicourts.gov/about/committees/ppacvidconf.htm).

RULES 132 to 134. [RESERVED]

PART F. SPECIAL PROCEDURES

RULE 135. RESTRAINING ORDER—BOND

Before any restraining order shall be issued, except in aid of writs of execution or replevin, in harassment proceedings, in actions for dissolution of marriage or orders for protection in domestic abuse proceedings, or in any other case exempted by law, the applicant shall give a bond in the penal sum of at least $2,000, executed by the applicant or by some person for the applicant as a principal, approved by the court and conditioned for the payment to the party restrained of such damages as the restrained person shall sustain by reason of the order, if the court finally decides that the applicant was not entitled thereto.

Adopted Sept. 5, 1991, eff. Jan. 1, 1992.

Task Force Comment—1991 Adoption

This rule is derived from Rule 24 of the Code of Rules for the District Courts.

By statute, governmental entities are not required to post bonds for temporary restraining orders. Minn. Stat. § 574.18 (1990). In addition, the court may waive the bond requirement when granting an order temporarily restraining an action on a contract for the conveyance of real estate. Minn. Stat. § 559.211 (1990). Accordingly, a specific provision allowing waiver of the bond requirement is included in the rule for cases provided by law.

Cross Reference: Minn.R.Civ.P. 65.

RULE 136. GARNISHMENTS AND ATTACHMENTS—BONDS TO RELEASE—ENTRY OF JUDGMENT AGAINST GARNISHEE

Rule 136.01. Bond

Garnishments or attachments shall not be discharged through a personal bond under Minn. Stat. §§ 571.931 & .932 without one day's written notice of the application therefor to the adverse party; but if a surety company's bond is given, notice shall not be required.

Adopted Sept. 5, 1991, eff. Jan. 1, 1992. Amended Nov. 13, 1992, eff. Jan. 1, 1993.

Rule 136.02. Requirement of Notice

Judgment against a garnishee shall be entered only upon notice to the garnishee and the defendant, if known to be within the jurisdiction of the court, showing the date and amount of the judgment against the defendant, and the amount for which plaintiff proposes to enter judgment against the garnishee after deducting such fees and allowances as the garnishee is entitled to receive. If the garnishee appears and secures a reduction of the proposed judgment, the court may make an appropriate allowance for fees and expense incident to such appearance.

Adopted Sept. 5, 1991, eff. Jan. 1, 1992.

Advisory Committee Comment—1992 Amendments

This rule is derived from Rule 15 of the Code of Rules for the District Courts.

The statutes governing garnishment and attachment have been amended, and the statutory reference in the rule has been corrected to reflect this change.

Cross Reference: Minn.R.Civ.P. 64.

RULE 137. RECEIVERS

Rule 137.01. Venue

All actions or proceedings for the sequestration of the property of corporations or for the appointment of receivers thereof, except actions or proceedings instituted by the Attorney General in behalf of the state, shall be instituted in the county in which the principal place of business of said corporation is situated; provided, that for the convenience of witnesses and to promote the ends of justice the venue may be changed by order of court.

Adopted Sept. 5, 1991, eff. Jan. 1, 1992.

Rule 137.02. Appointment of Receivers

Receivers, trustees, guardians and others appointed by the court to aid in the administration of justice shall be wholly impartial and indifferent to all parties in interest, and selected with a view solely to their character and fitness. Except by consent of all parties interested, or where it clearly appears that prejudice will otherwise result, no person who is or has been during the preceding year a stockholder, director or officer of a corporation shall be appointed as receiver for such corporation. Receivers shall be appointed only upon notice to interested parties, such notice to be given in the manner ordered by the court; but if it shall be clearly shown that an emergency exists requiring the immediate appointment of a temporary receiver, such appointment may be made ex parte.

Adopted Sept. 5, 1991, eff. Jan. 1, 1992.

Rule 137.03. Bond

Every receiver after appointment shall give a bond to be approved by the court in such sum and conditioned as the court shall direct, and shall make and file with the court administrator an inventory and estimated valuation of the assets of the estate in the receiver's custody; and, unless otherwise ordered, appraisers shall then be appointed and their compensation fixed by order of the court.

Adopted Sept. 5, 1991, eff. Jan. 1, 1992.

Rule 137.04. Claims

Claims of creditors of corporations, the subject of sequestration or receivership proceedings, shall be duly verified and filed in the office of the court administrator. The court, by order, shall fix the time for presentation, examination and adjustment of claims and the time for objecting thereto, and notice of the order shall be given by such means, including publication if deemed desirable, as the court therein shall direct. Written objections to the allowance of any claim may be made by the party to the proceeding by serving a copy of such objection upon the claimant or the claimant's lawyer. Where no objection is made within the time fixed by said order, the claim may stand admitted and be allowed without proof. Issues of law and fact shall be tried as in other cases.

Adopted Sept. 5, 1991, eff. Jan. 1, 1992.

Rule 137.05. Annual Inventory and Report

Every receiver shall file an annual inventory and report showing the condition of the estate and a summary of the proceedings to date. The clerk shall keep a list of receiverships and notify each receiver and the court when such reports are due.

Adopted Sept. 5, 1991, eff. Jan. 1, 1992.

Rule 137.06. Lawyer as Receiver

When a lawyer has been appointed receiver, no lawyer for such receiver shall be employed except upon the order of the court, which shall be granted only upon the petition of the receiver, stating the name of counsel whom the receiver wishes to employ and showing the necessity for such employment.

Adopted Sept. 5, 1991, eff. Jan. 1, 1992.

Rule 137.07. Employment of Counsel

No receiver shall employ more than one counsel, except under special circumstances requiring the employment of additional counsel; and in such cases only after an order of the court made on a petition showing such circumstances, and on notice to the party or person on whose behalf or application the receiver was appointed. No allowance shall be made to any receiver for expenses paid or incurred in violation of this rule.

Adopted Sept. 5, 1991, eff. Jan. 1, 1992.

Rule 137.08. Use of Funds

No receiver or other trustee appointed by the court, nor any lawyer acting for such receiver or trustee, shall withdraw or use any trust funds to apply on the receiver's compensation for services except on written order of court, duly made after such notice as the court may direct, and filed in the proceeding.

Adopted Sept. 5, 1991, eff. Jan. 1, 1992.

Rule 137.09. Allowance of Fees

All applications for the allowance of fees to receivers and their lawyers shall be accompanied by an itemized statement of the services performed and the amount charged for each item shown.

Compensation of receivers and their lawyers shall be allowed only upon the order of the court after such notice to creditors and others interested as the court shall direct, of the amounts claimed, as compensation and of the time and place of hearing the application for their allowance.

Adopted Sept. 5, 1991, eff. Jan. 1, 1992.

Rule 137.10. Final Account

Every receiver shall take a receipt for all disbursements made by him in excess of one dollar, shall file the same with the final account, and shall recite such filing in a verified petition for the allowance of such account. Final accounts shall disclose the status of the property of the estate as to unpaid or delinquent taxes and the same shall be paid by the receiver to the extent that the funds in the receiver's custody permit, over and beyond costs and expenses of the receivership.

Adopted Sept. 5, 1991, eff. Jan. 1, 1992.

Task Force Comment—1991 Adoption

This rule is derived from Rule 23 of the Code of Rules for the District Courts.

Cross Reference: Minn.R.Civ.P. 66.

RULE 138. BANKS IN LIQUIDATION

Petitions for orders approving the sale or compounding of doubtful debts, or the sale of real or personal property, or authorizing a final dividend, of any bank, state or national, in liquidation, shall be heard after notice to all interested persons given as herein provided.

Upon the filing of the petition, the court shall enter an order reciting the substance of the petition and the time and place for hearing thereon, and advising all interested parties of their right to be heard.

A copy of the order shall be published once in a legal newspaper published near the location of the bank in liquidation, which publication shall be made at least ten days prior to the time fixed for the hearing; or the court may direct notice to be given by such other method as it shall deem proper. If it shall appear to the court that delay may prejudice the rights of those interested, the giving of notice may be dispensed with.

Adopted Sept. 5, 1991, eff. Jan. 1, 1992.

Task Force Comment—1991 Adoption

This rule is derived from Rule 5 of the Code of Rules for the District Court.

Cross Reference: Minn.R.Civ.P. 66.

RULE 139. LAWYERS AS SURETIES

No practicing lawyer shall be accepted as surety on a bond or undertaking required by law.

Adopted Sept. 5, 1991, eff. Jan. 1, 1992.

Task Force Comment—1991 Adoption

This rule is derived from Rule 4 of the Code of Rules for the District Courts.

Cross Reference: Minn.R.Civ.P. 67.

RULE 140. SUPPLEMENTAL PROCEEDINGS

Rule 140.01. Previous Applications

If an ex parte application is made, any previous applications for a supplemental proceeding order concerning the pending case shall be disclosed to the court in the form of an affidavit.

Adopted Sept. 5, 1991, eff. Jan. 1, 1992.

Rule 140.02. Referee

Referees in supplementary proceedings and in garnishment disclosures shall be notaries public or lawyers and shall not be the creditor's lawyer or an employee or partner of the creditor or of the creditor's lawyer and said referees must take and subscribe the appropriate oath.

Adopted Sept. 5, 1991, eff. Jan. 1, 1992.

Rule 140.03. Continuances

Orders in supplementary proceedings shall specify the name of the Referee and provide that in the examination of the judgment debtor the Referee shall not grant more than two continuances.

Adopted Sept. 5, 1991, eff. Jan. 1, 1992.

Task Force Comment—1991 Adoption

This rule is derived from 4th Dist. R. 12.

Cross Reference: Minn.R.Civ.P. 69.

RULE 141. CONDEMNATION

Rule 141.01. Objection to Commissioner

Within ten (10) days after the order appointing the commissioners has been filed, the petitioner or any respondent may serve on all other parties and file with the appointing judge an affidavit objecting to the appointment of any one or more of the commissioners and setting forth the reasons for the objection. Within five (5) days after receiving such an objection, the judge in the exercise of discretion may appoint a new commissioner to replace any commissioner concerning whom objection has been made. If the judge does not appoint a new commissioner within five (5) days, the objection shall be deemed overruled.

Adopted Sept. 5, 1991, eff. Jan. 1, 1992.

Rule 141.02. Notice of Appeal

In condemnation cases the notice of appeal from the award of the Commissioners shall be deemed the filing of the first paper in the case for the purposes of Minn. Gen. R. Prac. 104 and 111.

Adopted Sept. 5, 1991, eff. Jan. 1, 1992. Amended Nov. 13, 1992, eff. Jan. 1, 1993.

Advisory Committee Comment—1992 Amendments

This rule is derived from 4th Dist. R. 10 and is intended to supplement statutes providing for the appointment of commissioners and the filing of a notice of appeal. *See* Minn. Stat. §§ 117.075 & .145 (1990).

Rule 141.02 as amended in 1992 establishes that the appeal from the award of the commissioners, not any earlier proceedings relating to appointment of commissioners or a "quick take" of the property, triggers the scheduling requirements of Rules 104 and 111.

RULE 142. [RENUMBERED RULE 417 EFF. JAN. 1, 1993.]

Historical Notes

Rule 142 relating to trustees, accounting, and petition for appointment was renumbered to Rule 417 by a Court order [CX–89–1863, C6–84–2134] dated November 13, 1992 effective on January 1, 1993.

RULE 143. ACTIONS BY REPRESENTATIVES—ATTORNEYS' FEES

In actions for personal injury or death by wrongful act, brought by persons acting in a representative capacity, contracts for attorney's fees shall not be regarded as determinative of fees to be allowed by the court.

Adopted Sept. 5, 1991, eff. Jan. 1, 1992.

Task Force Comment—1991 Adoption

This rule is Rule 1 of the Code of Rules for the District Courts, without change.

Cross Reference: Minn.R.Civ.P. 17.

RULE 144. ACTIONS FOR DEATH BY WRONGFUL ACT

Rule 144.01. Application for Appointment of Trustee

Every application for the appointment of a trustee of a claim for death by wrongful act under Minnesota Statutes, section 573.02, shall be made by the verified petition of the surviving spouse or one of the next of kin of the decedent. The petition shall show the dates and places of the decedent's birth and death; the decedent's address at the time of death; the name, age and address of the decedent's surviving spouse, children, parents, grandparents, and siblings; and the name, age, occupation and address of the proposed trustee. The petition shall also show whether or not any previous application has been made, the facts with reference thereto and its disposition shall also be stated. The written consent of the proposed trustee to act as such shall be endorsed on or filed with such petition. The application for appointment shall not be considered filing of a document in the case for the purpose of any requirement for filing a certificate of representation or civil cover sheet.

Adopted Sept. 5, 1991, eff. Jan. 1, 1992. Amended Nov. 13, 1992, eff. Jan. 1, 1993; Dec. 17, 1999, eff. Jan. 1, 2000; May 7, 2013, eff. July 1, 2013.

Historical and Statutory Notes

The order of the Minnesota Supreme Court [ADM04–8001, ADM09–8009, ADM–10-8051] dated May 7, 2013, provided in part that the amendments be effective July 1, 2013, and further provided in part that "[t]hese amendments apply to all actions or proceedings pending on or commenced after the effective date", and further provided that the "February 4, 2013 and February 12, 2013 orders of the court are hereby rescinded to the extent inconsistent with this order."

Rule 144.02. Notice and Hearing

The petition for appointment of trustee will be heard upon such notice, given in such form and in such manner and upon such persons as may be determined by the court, unless waived by the next of kin listed in the petition or unless the court determines that such notice is not required.

Adopted Sept. 5, 1991, eff. Jan. 1, 1992. Amended Dec. 17, 1999, eff. Jan. 1, 2000.

Rule 144.03. Caption

The petition, any order entered thereon, and the trustee's oath, will be entitled: "In the matter of the appointment of a trustee for the next of kin of ________________, Decedent."

Adopted Sept. 5, 1991, eff. Jan. 1, 1992.

Rule 144.04. Transfer of Action

If the trustee, after appointment and qualification, commences an action for death by wrongful act in a county other than that in which the trustee was appointed, a certified copy of the petition, the order entered thereon and the oath shall be filed in the court where such action be commenced, at the time the summons and complaint are filed therein, and the court file and jurisdiction over the trust will thereupon be transferred to such court.

Adopted Sept. 5, 1991, eff. Jan. 1, 1992.

Rule 144.05. Distribution of Proceeds

Application for the distribution of money recovered under Minn. Stat. § 573.02 shall be by verified petition of the trustee. Such petition shall show the amount which has been received upon action or settlement; a detailed statement of disbursements paid or incurred, if any; the amount, if any, claimed for services of the trustee and of the trustee's lawyer; the amount of the funeral expenses and of demands for the support of the decedent; the name, age and address of the surviving spouse and each next of kin required to be listed in the petition for appointment of trustee and all other next of kin who have notified the trustee in writing of a claim for pecuniary loss, and the share to which each is entitled.

If an action was commenced, such petition shall be heard by the court in which the action was tried, or in the case of settlement, by the court in which the action was pending at the time of settlement. If an action was not commenced, the petition shall be heard by the court in which the trustee was appointed. The court hearing the petition shall approve, modify, or disapprove the proposed disposition and shall specify the persons to whom the proceeds are to be paid.

The petition for distribution will be heard upon notice, given in form and manner and upon such persons as may be determined by the court, unless waived by all next of kin listed in the petition for distribution or unless the court determines that such notice is not required. The court by order, or by decree of distribution, will direct distribution of the money to the persons entitled thereto by law. Upon the filing of a receipt from each distributee for the amount assigned to that distributee, the trustee shall be discharged.

The foregoing procedure will, so far as can be applicable, also govern the distribution of money recovered by personal representatives under the Federal Employers' Liability Act (45 U.S.C. § 51) and under Minn. Stat. § 219.77.

Adopted Sept. 5, 1991, eff. Jan. 1, 1992. Amended Dec. 17, 1999, eff. Jan. 1, 2000.

Rule 144.06. Validity and Timeliness of Action

The failure to name the next of kin in a petition required by Rule 144.01 or the failure to notify or obtain a waiver from the next of kin shall have no effect on the validity or timeliness of an action commenced by the trustee.

Adopted Dec. 17, 1999, eff. Jan. 1, 2000.

Advisory Committee Comment 2007 Amendment

This rule is derived from Rule 2 of the Code of Rules for the District Courts. The Task Force has amended the rule to refer to "next of kin" rather than "heirs." Minn. Stat. § 573.02 makes no requirements as to who must receive notification of petitions for appointment of trustees or for orders for distribution. Amendments to Rule 144.01, 144.02, and 144.05 codify the longstanding practice of requiring petitioners to name and notify only the decedent's surviving spouse and close relatives, not "all next of kin," which under *Wynkoop v. Carpenter*, 574 N.W.2d 422 (Minn. 1998), and recent changes to Minnesota's intestacy statute would include distant relatives such as nieces, nephews, aunts, uncles, and cousins. These amendments address only the matter of notification and are not intended to reduce substantive rights of any next of kin.

The Task Force considered the advisability of amending Rule 144.05 to require the court to consider and either approve, modify, or disapprove the settlement itself, in addition to the disposition of proceeds as required under the existing rule. Although it appears that good reasons exist to change the rule in this manner, the Minnesota Supreme Court has indicated that the trial court has no jurisdiction to approve or disapprove the settlement amounts agreed upon by the parties. The court can only approve the distribution of those funds among the heirs and next of kin. *See Minneapolis Star & Tribune Co. v. Schumacher*, 392 N.W.2d 197, 200 n.1 (Minn. 1986).

The final sentence of Rule 144.01 was added in 1992 to make it clear that it is the filing of papers in the actual wrongful death action, and not papers relating to appointment of a trustee to bring the action, that triggers the scheduling requirements of the rules, including the requirement to file a certificate of representation and parties (Rule 104) and an informational statement (Rule 111.02). Some have interpreted this comment to mean that the advisory committee intended there to be two separate actions for purposes of computing filing fees. Although a filing fee must be paid when the petition for appointment of a trustee is filed, a second filing fee should not be required in the wrongful death action, even when that wrongful death action is commenced in a different county or district.

Rule 144.06 codifies existing law holding that failure to notify some next of kin does not void an appointment. *See Stroud v. Hennepin County Medical Center*, 544 N.W.2d 42, 48–49 (Minn. App. 1996) (failure to list and obtain signatures of all next of kin did not invalidate trustee's appointment and commencement of a wrongful death action), *rev'd on other grounds*, 556 N.W.2d 552, 553–55, nn.3 & 5 (Minn. 1996) (trustee's original complaint effectively commenced wrongful death action despite her improper appointment).

RULE 145. ACTIONS ON BEHALF OF MINORS AND INCOMPETENT PERSONS

Rule 145.01. When Petition and Order are Required

No part of the proceeds of any action or claim for personal injuries on behalf of any minor or incompetent person shall be paid to any person except under written petition to the court and written order of the court as hereinafter provided. This rule governs a claim or action brought by a parent of a minor, by a guardian ad litem or general guardian of a minor or incompetent person, or by the guardian of a dependent, neglected or delinquent child, and applies whether the proceeds of the claim or action have become fixed in amount by a settlement agreement, jury verdict or court findings, and even though the proceeds have been reduced to judgment.

Adopted Sept. 5, 1991, eff. Jan. 1, 1992.

Rule 145.02. Contents and Filing of Petition

The petition shall be verified by the parent or guardian, shall be filed before the court makes its order, and shall include the following:

(a) The name and birth date of the minor or other incompetent person.

(b) A brief description of the nature of the claim if a complaint has not been filed.

(c) An attached affidavit, letter or records of a health care provider showing the nature of the injuries, the extent of recovery, and the prognosis if the court has not already heard testimony covering these matters.

(d) Whether the parent, or the minor or incompetent person, has collateral sources covering any part of the principal and derivative claims, including expenses and attorneys fees, and whether subrogation rights have been asserted by any collateral source.

(e) In cases involving proposed structured settlements, a statement from the parties disclosing the cost of the annuity or structured settlement to the tortfeasor.

Adopted Sept. 5, 1991, eff. Jan. 1, 1992. Amended Nov. 13, 1992, eff. Jan. 1, 1993; Dec. 14, 1993, eff. Jan. 1, 1994.

Rule 145.03. Representation

(a) If the lawyer who presents the petition has been retained by the tortfeasor or its insurer, the lawyer shall disclose to the court and to the petitioner the nature of the representation, how he or she is being paid, the frequency with which the lawyer has been retained by the tortfeasor or insurer, and whether the lawyer is giving legal advice to the petitioner. The petition shall not be denied by the court solely because of the petitioner's representation.

(b) The court may, at its discretion, refer the petitioner to a lawyer selected by the petitioner (or by the court if petitioner requests or declines to select a lawyer), to evaluate the proposed settlement and advise the court whether the settlement is reasonable considering all relevant facts. The opinion shall be in writing, and the court shall provide a copy to the petitioner and all tortfeasors or their representative, regardless of whether a filing fee has been paid by the tortfeasor. This appointment shall be made pursuant to Minn. R. Evid. 706.

(c) The lawyer accepting the referral must agree not to represent the petitioner or the minor or accept a referral fee in the event that the petition is denied by the court.

(d) For the legal opinion thus rendered to the court, the tortfeasor or the insurer shall pay a reasonable sum ordered by the court; however, the insurer or tortfeasor may be reimbursed from settlement proceeds up to one half of the sum so ordered, also upon order of the court. An order for attorney's fees payment in excess of $300.00 can issue only upon a court hearing with notice to the insurer or tortfeasor and the petitioner.

(e) The opinion of the referred-to lawyer shall not be binding upon the court.

Adopted Sept. 5, 1991, eff. Jan. 1, 1992.

Rule 145.04. Hearing on the Petition

The minor or incompetent person and the petitioner shall personally appear before the court at the hearing on the petition unless their appearance is specifically waived by the court because the action has been fully or partially tried or for other good cause. The reporter shall, when ordered by the court, keep a record of the hearing. The hearing shall be ex parte unless otherwise ordered.

Adopted Sept. 5, 1991, eff. Jan. 1, 1992.

Rule 145.05. Terms of the Order

The court's order shall:

(a) Approve, modify or disapprove the proposed settlement or disposition and specify the persons to whom the proceeds are to be paid.

(b) State the reason or reasons why the proposed disposition is approved if the court is approving a settlement for an amount which it feels is less than what the injuries and expenses, might seem to call for, e.g., limited insurance coverage, dubious liability, comparative fault or other similar considerations.

(c) Determine what expenses may be paid from the proceeds of any recovery by action or settlement, including the attorney's fee. Attorney's fees will not be allowed in any amount in excess of one-third of the recovery, except on a showing that: (1) an appeal to an appellate court has been perfected and a brief by the plaintiff's lawyer has been printed therein and (2) there has been an expenditure of time and effort throughout the proceeding which is substantially disproportionate to a one-third fee. No sum will be allowed, in addition to attorney fees, to reimburse any expense incurred in paying an investigator for services and mileage, except in those circumstances where the attorney's fee is not fully compensatory or where the investigation must be conducted in any area so distant from the principal offices of the lawyer so employed that expense of travel and related expense would be substantially equal to, or in excess of, usual investigating expenses.

(d) Specify what disposition shall be made of the balance of the proceeds of any recovery after payment of the expenses authorized by the court.

(1) The court may authorize investment of all or part of such balance of the proceeds in securities of the United States, or in an annuity or other form of structured settlement, including a medical assur-

ance agreement, but otherwise shall order the balance of the proceeds deposited in one or more banks, savings and loan associations or trust companies where the deposits will be fully covered by Federal deposit insurance.

(2) In lieu of such disposition of the proceeds, the order may provide for the filing by the petitioner of a surety bond approved by the court conditioned for payment to the ward in a manner therein to be specified of such moneys as the ward is entitled to receive, including interest which would be earned if the proceeds were invested.

(e) If part or all of the balance of the proceeds is ordered deposited in one or more financial institutions, the court's order shall direct:

(1) that the defendant pay the sum to be deposited directly to the financial institution;

(2) that the account be opened in the name of the minor or incompetent person and that any deposit document be issued in the name of the minor or incompetent person;

(3) that the petitioner shall, at the time of depositing, supply the financial institution with a tax identification number or a social security number for the minor and a copy of the order approving settlement; and

(4) that the financial institution forthwith acknowledge to the court receipt of the order approving settlement and the sum and that no disbursement of the funds will occur unless the court so orders, using the form substantially equivalent to Form 145.1;

(5) that the financial institution shall not make any disbursement from the deposit except upon order of the court; and

(6) that a copy of the court's order shall be delivered to said financial institution by the petitioner with the remittance for deposit. The financial institution(s) and the type of investment therein shall be as specified in MINN. STAT. § 540.08, as amended. Two or more institutions shall be used if necessary to have full Federal deposit insurance coverage of the proceeds plus future interest; and time deposits shall be established with a maturity date on or before the minor's age of majority. If automatically renewing instruments of deposit are used, the final renewal period shall be limited to the date of the age of majority.

(7) that the petitioner shall be ordered to file or cause to be filed timely state and federal income tax returns on behalf of the minor.

(f) Authorize or direct the investment of proceeds of the recovery in securities of the United States only if practicable means are devised comparable to the provisions of paragraphs (d) and (e) above, to insure that funds so invested will be preserved for the benefit of the minor or incompetent person, and the original security instrument be deposited with the court administrator consistent with paragraph (e) above.

(g) Provide that applications for release of funds, either before or upon the age of majority may be made using the form substantially similar to Form 145.2.

Adopted Sept. 5, 1991, eff. Jan. 1, 1992. Amended Nov. 13, 1992, eff. Jan. 1993; Dec. 17, 2002, eff. Jan. 1, 2003.

Rule 145.06. Structured Settlements

If the settlement involves the purchase of an annuity or other form of structured settlement, the court shall:

(a) Determine the cost of the annuity or structured settlement to the tortfeasor by examining the proposal of the annuity company or other generating entity;

(b) Require that the company issuing the annuity or structured settlement:

(1) Be licensed to do business in Minnesota;

(2) Have a financial rating equivalent to A.M. Best Co. A+, Class VIII or better;

(3) Has complied with the applicable provisions of MINN. STAT. § 549.30 to § 549.34;

or that a trust making periodic payments be funded by United States Government obligations; and

(4) If the company issuing the proposed annuity or structured settlement is related to either the settling party or its insurer, that the proposed annuity or structured settlement is at least as favorable to the minor or incompetent person as at least one other competitively-offered annuity obtained from an issuer qualified under this rule and not related to the party or its insurer. This additional proposal should be for an annuity with the same terms as to cost and due dates of payments.

(c) Order that the original annuity policy be deposited with the court administrator, without affecting ownership, and the policy be returned to the owner of the policy when:

(1) The minor reaches majority;

(2) The terms of the policy have been fully performed; or

(3) The minor dies, whichever occurs first.

(d) In its discretion, permit a "qualified assignment" within the meaning and subject to the conditions of Section 130(c) of the Internal Revenue Code;

(e) In its discretion, order the tortfeasor or its insurer, or both of them, to guarantee the payments contracted for in the annuity or other form of structured settlement; and

(f) Provide that:

(1) The person receiving periodic payments is entitled to each periodic payment only when the payment becomes due;

(2) That the person shall have no rights to the funding source; and

(3) That the person cannot designate the owner of the annuity nor have any right to control or designate the method of investment of the funding medium; and

(g) Direct that the appropriate party or parties will be entitled to receive appropriate receipts, releases or a satisfaction of judgment, pursuant to the agreement of the parties.

Adopted Sept. 5, 1991, eff. Jan. 1, 1992. Amended Nov. 14, 1991, eff. Jan. 1, 1992; Nov. 13, 1992, eff. Jan. 1, 1993; Dec. 14, 1995, eff. Jan. 1, 1996; Dec. 19, 2000, eff. March 1, 2001; Dec. 17, 2002, eff. Jan. 1, 2003.

Historical Notes

The order of the Minnesota Supreme Court [CX–89–1863, C6–84–2134] dated December 14, 1995, provides in part that "(t)he attached amendments shall apply to all actions pending on the effective date and to those filed thereafter."

The order of the Minnesota Supreme Court [CX-89-1863] dated December 19, 2000, provides in part that these amendments are effective March 1, 2001, and shall apply to all actions or proceedings pending on or commenced on or after the effective date, with the exception of the amendments to Rule 114.13, which shall become effective on further order of the court following the action of the Alternative Dispute Resolution (ADR) Review Board.

The order of the Minnesota Supreme Court [CX-89-1863] dated December 19, 2000, provides in part that "(t)he inclusion of Advisory Committee comments is made for convenience and does not reflect court approval of the statements made therein".

Rule 145.07. General Guardians

When an action is brought by a general guardian appointed and bonded by a court of competent jurisdiction, the requirements of this rule may be modified as deemed desirable by the court because of bonding or other action taken by the appointing court, except that there must be compliance with the settlement approval requirements of Section 540.08 of the Minnesota Statutes or amendments thereof.

Adopted Sept. 5, 1991, eff. Jan. 1, 1992.

Advisory Committee Comment—2000 Amendments

This rule is derived from Minn.Stat. § 540.08 (1990) and Rule 3 of the Code of Rules for the District Courts.

The Task Force considered it a thoughtful recommendation that a minor's social security number be required to be included on all minor settlement petitions. Such a requirement would make it easier to locate a minor at the time of reaching majority. The Task Force ultimately concluded, however, the privacy interests dictate that the inclusion of this number should not be mandatory. The information may nonetheless be required by the financial institution with which the funds are deposited, and many lawyers will routinely include it in petitions in order to facilitate locating the minor should the need arise.

The 1994 amendment of Rule 145.02(c) allows the filing of medical records in lieu of a full report of each health care provider where those records provide the information necessary to evaluate the settlement. This may be especially appropriate where the injuries are not severe, or where the cost of obtaining reports would represent a substantial portion of the settlement proceeds. The court can, in any case, require any further information or reports deemed necessary to permit the court to discharge its duty to evaluate the overall fairness of the settlement to the minor.

Rule 145.02(d) is new. It is designed to advise the court of factors to take into consideration when approving or disapproving a settlement on behalf of the minor or incompetent person. Rule 145.02(e) is added in 1992 to provide the court in the petition the information necessary for the court to make the determination required by Rule 145.06(a). Although the parties are the obvious source of the cost information necessary to make the cost determination, the rule explicitly requires the petition to include this information. This information must be disclosed by the parties, and not only the party filing the petition, as often the tortfeasor will have the only accurate information on this subject.

Rule 145.03 is new. It addresses a situation where a tortfeasor or insurer has negotiated a settlement with a minor's family or guardian, and court approval of that settlement is necessary. Oftentimes the plaintiff does not wish to incur attorney's fees to obtain that approval, so as a part of the settlement, the tortfeasor or the insurer makes the arrangements to draft and present the petition. The court needs to be satisfied that the settlement is fair. The Task Force discussed at length whether or not a lawyer hired and paid by an insurer or tortfeasor should be permitted to represent the minor or incompetent person to obtain the approval of the court. It was decided that the petitioner should not be compelled to obtain counsel, and that "arranged counsel" may appear, provided that there is full disclosure to the petitioner of the interests of the insurer or tortfeasor.

Rule 145.03(b) is new and is designed to provide a procedure for the court to obtain advice to evaluate the reasonableness of settlement. The court may appoint a lawyer selected by the petitioner or the court may designate a lawyer of its own choice. In either case, where a referral is made under this section, the lawyer accepting the referral may not represent the petitioner to pursue the claim, should the petition be denied by the court. Rule 145.03(d) provides that the cost of the consultation provided for in Rule 145.03(b) shall be borne equally by the petitioner and the tortfeasor or insurer.

Finally, Rule 145.03(d) provides that any opinions rendered by a selected lawyer on behalf of the minor or incompetent person are advisory only.

Rule 145.05(d) expands the types of investments that may be used in managing the settlement proceeds while retaining the requirements of security of investment. It incorporates Minn.Stat. § 540.08 (1990) regarding structured settlements, and it allows that settlements may include a medical assurance agreement. A medical assurance agreement is a contract whereby future medical expenses of an undetermined amount will be paid by a designated person or entity.

Rule 145.05(e)(5) requires that funds placed in certificates of deposit or other deposits with fixed maturities have those maturities adjusted so they do not mature after the age of majority. This rule places the burden on the financial institution by the notice to be included in the order for deposit.

Rule 145.06 is new. It establishes criteria for approval of structured settlements, and it requires the court to determine the cost of the annuity to insure that the periodic payments reflect a cost comparable to a reasonable settlement amount. Where a minor or incompetent receives a verdict representing future damages greater than $100,000.00 and the guardian determines that a structured settlement pursuant to Minn.Stat. § 549.25 (1990) would be in the best interests of the minor or incompetent person, this rule shall apply to the implementation of the election pursuant to the statute. The amendment of the rule in 1995 (effective January 1, 1996) is intended to make it clear that it is important that the original annuity policy be retained by the court administrator, and that this is for the purpose of security, not establishing any ownership interest which might affect the tax treatment of the settlement.

Rule 145.06 (b) is modified by amendment in 2000. The amendment is intended to require the court approving a minor settlement that includes a structured settlement provision to verify that the annuity issuer is licensed to do business and that MINN. STAT. § 549.30-.34 (1998) is followed. The amendment is not intended to impose any additional substantive requirements, as compliance with statutes is assumed under the current rule. The rule will require the trial court to verify the fact of compliance, however, and will probably require submitting this information to the court.

Advisory Committee Comment—2002 Amendment

Rule 145.05 is revamped to create a new procedure for handling the deposit of funds resulting from minor settlements. The new rule removes provisions calling for deposit of funds in "passbook" savings accounts, largely because this form of account is no longer widely available from financial institutions. The revised rule allows use of statement accounts, but requires that the financial institution acknowledge receipt of the funds at the inception of the account. A form for this purpose is included as Form 145.1. Additionally, the rule is redrafted to remove inconsistent provisions. Under the revised rule, release of funds is not automatic when the minor reaches majority; a separate order is required. A form to implement the final release of funds, as well as any permitted interim release of funds, is included as Form 145.2.

Rule 145.06(b)(4) is a new provision to require at least two competitive proposals for a structured settlement. This requirement applies only when one of the proposals is for an annuity issued by the settling party, its liability insurer, or by an insurer related to either of them. The rule requires that the competitive bids be issued by annuity companies that would be qualified to issue an annuity that complies with the requirements of Rule 145.06. In order to permit the trial court to determine that the proposed settlement adequately provides for the interests of the minor, the competitive bids must be for annuities with comparable terms. The rule requires only a second proposal, but permits the court to require additional proposals or analysis of available proposals in its discretion. The rule, as revised, does not direct how the trial court should exercise its discretion in approving or disapproving the proposed structure settlement. It is intended, however, to provide the court some information upon which it can base the decision.

Cross Reference: Minn. R. Civ. P. 17.

RULE 146. COMPLEX CASES

Rule 146.01. Purpose; Principles

The purposes of the Complex Case Program ("CCP") are to promote effective and efficient judicial management of complex cases in the district courts, avoid unnecessary burdens on the court, keep costs reasonable for the litigants and to promote effective decision making by the court, the parties and counsel.

The core principles that support the establishment of a mandatory CCP include:

(a) Early and consistent judicial management promotes efficiency.

(b) Mandatory disclosure of relevant information, rigorously enforced by the court, will result in disclosure of facts and information necessary to avoid unnecessary litigation procedures and discovery.

(c) Blocking complex cases to a single judge from the inception of the case results in the best case management.

(d) Firm trial dates result in better case management and more effective use of the parties' resources, with continuances granted only for good cause.

(e) Education and training for both judges and court staff will assist with the management of complex cases.

Adopted May 7, 2013, eff. July 1, 2013.

Historical and Statutory Notes

The order of the Minnesota Supreme Court [ADM04-8001, ADM09-8009, ADM-10-8051] dated May 7, 2013, provided in part that the "February 4, 2013 and February 12, 2013 orders of the court are hereby rescinded to the extent inconsistent with this order."

Rule 146.02. Definition of a Complex Case

(a) Definition. A "complex case" is an action that requires exceptional judicial management to avoid placing unnecessary burdens on the court or the litigants and to expedite the case, keep costs reasonable, and promote effective decision making by the court, the parties, and counsel.

(b) Factors. In deciding whether an action is a complex case under (a), the court must consider, among other things, whether the action is likely to involve:

(1) Numerous hearings, pretrial and dispositive motions raising difficult or novel legal issues that will be time-consuming to resolve;

(2) Management of a large number of witnesses or a substantial amount of documentary evidence;

(3) Management of a large number of separately represented parties;

(4) Multiple expert witnesses;

(5) Coordination with related actions pending in one or more courts in other counties, states, or countries, or in a federal court;

(6) Substantial post judgment judicial supervision; or

(7) Legal or technical issues of complexity.

(c) Provisional designation. An action is provisionally a complex case if it involves one or more of the following types of claims:

(1) Antitrust or trade regulation claims;

(2) Intellectual property matters, such as trade secrets, copyrights, patents, etc.;

(3) Construction defect claims involving many parties or structures;

(4) Securities claims or investment losses involving many parties;

(5) Environmental or toxic tort claims involving many parties;

(6) Product liability claims;

(7) Claims involving mass torts;

(8) Claims involving class actions;

(9) Ownership or control of business claims; or

(10) Insurance coverage claims arising out of any of the claims listed in (c)(1) through (c)(9).

(d) Parties' designation. In any action not enumerated above, the parties can agree to be governed by Rule 146 of these rules by filing a "CCP Election," in a form to be developed by the state court administrator and posted on the main state court website, to be filed along with the initial pleading.

(e) Motion to Exclude Complex Case Designation. A party objecting to the provisional assignment of a matter to the CCP must serve and file a motion setting forth the reasons that the matter should be removed from the CCP. The motion papers must be served and filed within 14 days of the date the moving party is served with the CCP Designation. The motion shall be heard during the Case Management Conference or at such other time as determined by the court. The factors that should be considered by the court in ruling on the motion include the factors set forth in Rule 146.02 (b) and (c) above.

Adopted May 7, 2013, eff. July 1, 2013.

Historical and Statutory Notes

The order of the Minnesota Supreme Court [ADM04–8001, ADM09–8009, ADM–10-8051] dated May 7, 2013, provided in part that the "February 4, 2013 and February 12, 2013 orders of the court are hereby rescinded to the extent inconsistent with this order."

Rule 146.03. Judge Assigned to Complex Cases

A single judge shall be assigned to all designated complex cases within 30 days of filing in accordance with Rule 113 of these rules. In making the assignment the assigning judge should consider, among other factors, the needs of the court, the judge's ability, interest, training, experience (including experience with complex cases), and willingness to participate in educational programs related to the management of complex cases.

Adopted Feb. 4, 2013, eff. July 1, 2013.

Historical and Statutory Notes

The order of the Minnesota Supreme Court [ADM04–8001, ADM09–8009, ADM–10-8051] dated May 7, 2013, provided in part that the "February 4, 2013 and February 12, 2013 orders of the court are hereby rescinded to the extent inconsistent with this order."

Rule 146.04. Mandatory Case Management Conferences

(a) Within 28 days of assignment, the judge assigned to a complex case shall hold a mandatory case management conference. Counsel for all parties and pro se parties shall attend the conference. At the conference, the court will discuss all aspects of the case as contemplated by Minn. R. Civ. P. 16.01.

(b) The court may hold such additional case management conferences, including a pretrial conference, as it deems appropriate.

Adopted May 7, 2013, eff. July 1, 2013.

Historical and Statutory Notes

The order of the Minnesota Supreme Court [ADM04–8001, ADM09–8009, ADM–10-8051] dated May 7, 2013, provided in part that the "February 4, 2013 and February 12, 2013 orders of the court are hereby rescinded to the extent inconsistent with this order."

Rule 146.05. Case Management Order and Scheduling Order

In all complex cases, the judge assigned to the case shall enter a Case Management Order and a Scheduling Order (together or separately) addressing the matters set forth in Minn. R. Civ. P. 16.02 and 16.03, and including without limitation the following:

(a) The dates for subsequent Case Management Conferences in the case;

(b) the deadline for the parties to meet and confer regarding discovery needs and the preservation and production of electronically stored information;

(c) the deadline for joining other parties;

(d) the deadline for amending the pleadings;

(e) the deadline by which fact discovery will close and provisions for disclosure or discovery of electronically stored information;

(f) the deadlines by which parties will make expert witness disclosures and deadlines for expert witness depositions;

(g) the deadlines for non-dispositive and dispositive motions;

(h) any modifications to the extent of required disclosures and discovery, such as, among other things, limits on:

(1) the number of fact depositions each party may take;

(2) the number of interrogatories each party may serve;

(3) the number of expert witnesses each party may call at trial;

(4) the number of expert witnesses each party may depose; and

(i) a date certain for trial subject to continuation for good cause only, and a statement of whether the case will be tried to a jury or the bench and an estimate of the trial's duration.

Adopted May 7, 2013, eff. July 1, 2013.

Historical and Statutory Notes

The order of the Minnesota Supreme Court [ADM04–8001, ADM09–8009, ADM–10-8051] dated May 7, 2013, provided in part that the "February 4, 2013 and February 12, 2013 orders of the court are hereby rescinded to the extent inconsistent with this order."

PART G. APPENDIX OF FORMS

FORM 104. CERTIFICATE OF REPRESENTATION AND PARTIES

State of Minnesota District Court

COUNTY JUDICIAL DISTRICT CASE NO.

CERTIFICATE OF REPRESENTATION AND PARTIES

(ONLY THE INITIAL FILING LAWYER/PARTY NEEDS TO COMPLETE THIS FORM)

Date Case Filed: ______________

______________________________ vs. ______________________________

This certificate must be filed pursuant to Rule 104 of the General Rules of Practice for the District Courts, which states: "A party filing a civil case shall, at the time of filing, notify the court administrator in writing of the name, address, and telephone number of all counsel and unrepresented parties, if known (see form 104 appended to these rules). If that information is not then known to the filing party, it shall be provided to the court administrator in writing by the filing party within seven days of learning it. Any party impleading additional parties shall provide the same information to the court administrator. The court administrator shall, upon receipt of the completed certificate, notify all parties or their lawyers, if represented by counsel, of the date of filing the action and the file number assigned."

LIST ALL LAWYERS/PRO SE PARTIES INVOLVED IN THIS CASE.

LAWYER FOR PLAINTIFF(S)	LAWYER FOR DEFENDANT(S) (If not known, name party and address)
Name of Party	Name of Party
Atty Name (Not firm name)	Atty Name (Not firm name)
Address	Address
Phone Number	Phone Number
MN Atty ID No.	MN Atty ID No.

(Please use other side for additional lawyers/parties.)

_______________	_______________
Date	Filing Lawyer/Party
Lawyer for:	Lawyer for:
_______________	_______________
Name of Party	Name of Party
_______________	_______________
Atty Name (Not firm name)	Atty Name (Not firm name)
_______________	_______________
Address	Address
_______________	_______________
_______________	_______________
_______________	_______________
Phone Number	Phone Number
_______________	_______________
MN Atty ID No.	MN Atty ID No.

Lawyer for:	Lawyer for:
_______________	_______________
Name of Party	Name of Party
_______________	_______________
Atty Name (Not firm name)	Atty Name (Not firm name)
_______________	_______________
Address	Address
_______________	_______________
_______________	_______________
_______________	_______________
Phone Number	Phone Number
_______________	_______________
MN Atty ID No.	MN Atty ID No.

Adopted Sept. 5, 1991, eff. Jan. 1, 1992.

FORM 111.02. INFORMATIONAL STATEMENT (Civil Matters—Non-Family)

State of Minnesota ______________ District Court

COUNTY ______________ JUDICIAL DISTRICT CASE NO. ______________

Case Type: __________

______________________________,
Plaintiff

and

INFORMATIONAL STATEMENT FORM

______________________________,
Defendant

1. All parties (have) (have not) been served with process.

2. All parties (have) (have not) joined in the filing of this form.

3. Brief description of the case: ____
____
____

4. It is estimated that the discovery specified below can be completed within ___ months from the date of this form. (Check all that apply, and supply estimates where indicated.)

   a. Factual Depositions No ___ Yes ___, estimated number: ________
   b. Medical Evaluations No ___ Yes ___, estimated number: ________
   c. Experts Subject to Discovery No ___ Yes ___, estimated number: ________

5. Assignment as an ___ expedited ___ standard ___ complex case is requested. (If not standard case assignment, include brief statement setting forth the reasons for the request.)

____
____

6. The dates and deadlines specified below are suggested.

   a. ____________ Deadline for joining additional parties, whether by amendment or third party practice.
   b. ____________ Deadline for bringing non-dispositive motions.
   c. ____________ Deadline for bringing dispositive motions.
   d. ____________ Deadline for submitting ________ to the court.
   (specify issue)
   e. ____________ Deadline for completing independent physical examination pursuant to Minn.R.Civ.P. 35.
   f. ____________ Date for formal discovery conference pursuant to Minn. R. Civ. P. 26.06.
   g. ____________ Date for pretrial conference pursuant to Minn. R. Civ. P. 16.
   h. ____________ Date for scheduling conference.
   i. ____________ Date for submission of a Joint Statement of the Case pursuant to Minn. Gen. R. Prac. 112.
   j. ____________ Trial Date.
   k. ____________ Deadline for filing (proposed instructions), (verdicts), (findings of fact), (witness list), (exhibit list).
   l. ____________ Deadline for ________________. (specify)

7. Estimated trial time: ___ days ___ hours (estimates less than a day must be stated in hours).

8. A jury trial is: ( ) waived by consent of ________ pursuant to R. Civ. P. 38.02.
   (specify party)
   ( ) requested by __________.(NOTE: Applicable fee must be
   (specify party)
   enclosed.)

9. a. Meeting: Counsel for the parties met on __________ (Date) to discuss case management issues.

b. ADR PROCESS (Check one):

[ ] Counsel agree that ADR is appropriate and choose the following:

  [ ] Mediation
  [ ] Arbitration (non-binding)
  [ ] Arbitration (binding)
  [ ] Med–Arb
  [ ] Early Neutral Evaluation
  [ ] Moderated Settlement Conference
  [ ] Mini–Trial
  [ ] Summary Jury Trial
  [ ] Consensual Special Magistrate
  [ ] Impartial Fact Finder
  [ ] Other (describe) ______________________________

____

[ ] Counsel agree that ADR is appropriate but request that the Court select the process.

[ ] Counsel agree that ADR is NOT appropriate because:

  [ ] the case implicates the federal or state constitution.
  [ ] other (explain with particularity) ______________________________

  ____

  [ ] domestic violence has occurred between the parties.

c. PROVIDER (Check one):

[ ] The parties have selected the following ADR neutral:

____

[ ] The parties cannot agree on an ADR neutral and request the Court to appoint one

[ ] The parties agreed to select an ADR neutral on or before

______________________________.

d. DEADLINE: The parties recommend that the ADR process be completed by ___. (Date)

10. Please identify any party or witness who will require interpreter services, and describe the services (specifying language and, if known, particular dialect) needed.

11. Please list any additional information which might be helpful to the court when scheduling this matter.

____

____

Signed: ______________________	Signed: ______________________
Lawyer for (Plaintiff) (Defendant)	Lawyer for (Plaintiff) (Defendant)
Attorney Reg. #: ______________	Attorney Reg. #: ______________
Firm: ______________________	Firm: ______________________
Address: ______________________	Address: ______________________
Telephone: ______________________	Telephone: ______________________
Date: ______________________	Date: ______________________

Adopted Sept. 5, 1991, eff. Jan. 1, 1992. Amended Nov. 13, 1992, eff. Jan. 1, 1993; Dec. 2, 1993, eff. July 1, 1994; Dec. 14, 1995, eff. Jan. 1, 1996; Dec. 22, 2008, eff. March 1, 2009.

Historical Notes

The order of the Minnesota Supreme Court [CX–89–1863, C6–84–2134] dated December 14, 1995, provides in part that "(t)he attached amendments shall apply to all actions pending on the effective date and to those filed thereafter."

FORM 111.03. REQUEST FOR DEFERRAL OF SCHEDULING DEADLINES

STATE OF MINNESOTA DISTRICT COURT
__________________ COUNTY ___________ JUDICIAL DISTRICT

CASE NO.:

Case Type: ________

____
Plaintiff

and REQUEST FOR DEFERRAL

____
Defendant

The undersigned parties request, pursuant to Minn. Gen. R. Prac. 111.05, that this action be deferred and excused from normal scheduling deadlines until _______ ___, ___, to permit the parties to engage in a formal collaborative law process. In support of this request, the parties represent to the Court as true:

1. All parties have contractually agreed to enter into a collaborative law process in an attempt to resolve their differences.

2. The undersigned attorneys are each trained as collaborative lawyers.

3. The undersigned attorneys each agree that if the collaborative law process is not concluded by the complete settlement of all issues between the parties, each attorney and his or her law firm will withdraw from further representation and will consent to the substitution of new counsel for the party.

4. The undersigned attorneys will diligently and in good faith pursue resolution of this action through the collaborative law process, and will promptly report to the Court when a settlement is reached or as soon as they determine that further collaborative law efforts will not be fruitful.

Signed: ________________________
Collaborative Lawyer for (Plaintiff)
(Defendant)

Attorney Reg. #: _______________
Firm: ________________________
Address: _______________________
Telephone: _____________________
Date: _________________________

Signed: ________________________
Collaborative Lawyer for (Plaintiff)
(Defendant)

Attorney Reg. #: _______________
Firm: ________________________
Address: _______________________
Telephone: _____________________
Date: _________________________

ORDER FOR DEFERRAL

The foregoing request is granted, and this action is deferred and placed on the inactive calendar until _________ ____, 20___, or until further order of this Court.

Dated: ______________, 20___.

____
Judge of District Court

Adopted Sept. 26, 2007, eff. Jan. 1, 2008.

Advisory Committee Comment—2007 Amendment

Form 111.03 is a new form, designed to facilitate the making of a request for deferral of a case from scheduling as permitted by Rule 111.05 when that case is going to be the subject to a collaborative law process as defined in that rule.

FORM 112.01. JOINT STATEMENT OF THE CASE

State of Minnesota	District Court
COUNTY	JUDICIAL DISTRICT CASE NO.
__________	__________

Case Type: __________

__________________________,
Plaintiff

and **JOINT STATEMENT OF THE CASE**

__________________________,
Defendant

1. All parties have been served with process. The case is at issue and all parties have joined in the filing of this Joint Statement of the Case.

2. Estimated trial time: ___ days ___ hours (estimates less than a day must be stated in hours).

3. Jury is requested by the ___ plaintiff ___ defendant. [If this is a change from a court to a jury request, then a $30 fee must be paid when filing this document.]

4. Concise statement of the case including facts plaintiff(s) intend to prove and legal basis for claims:
____
____
____

5. Concise statement of the case indicating facts defendant(s) intend to prove and legal basis for defenses and counterclaim:
____
____
____

6. List the names and addresses of witnesses known to either party that either party may call. Indicate the party who expects to call the witness and whether the party intends to qualify that witness as an expert. (Attach additional sheets if necessary.)

Party	Name/Addresses of Witnesses	Please Indicate if Expert Witness
__________	__________	__________ Yes
__________	__________	__________ Yes
__________	__________	__________ Yes

7. Identify any party or witness who will require interpreter services, and describe the services (specifying language, and, if known, particular dialect) needed.

   In claims involving personal injury, attach a statement by each claimant, whether by complaint or counterclaim, setting forth a detailed description of claimed injuries and an itemized list of special damages as required by the rule. Indicate whether parties will exchange medical reports.

9. In claims involving vehicle accidents, attach a statement describing the vehicles with information as to ownership and the name of insurance carriers, if any.

[Signature Blocks]

(If more space is needed to add additional information or parties, attach a separate sheet typed in the same format.)

The undersigned counsel have met and conferred this ___ day of __________ and certify the foregoing is true and correct.

____
Signature

____
Signature

____
Signature

____
Signature

Adopted Sept. 5, 1991, eff. Jan. 1, 1992. Amended Dec. 22, 2008, eff. March 1, 2009.

FORM 114.01. MN STATE COURT SYSTEM NEUTRAL ADR ORGANIZATION ROSTER REGISTRATION FORM [Deleted Dec. 8, 1997, eff. Jan. 1, 1998]

FORM 114.02. MN STATE COURT SYSTEM NEUTRAL ROSTER REGISTRATION FORM [Deleted Dec. 8, 1997, eff. Jan. 1, 1998]

FORM 119.05. NOTICE AND REQUEST FOR HEARING TO DETERMINE ATTORNEYS' FEES AWARD

STATE OF MINNESOTA DISTRICT COURT

COUNTY OF ________ ________ JUDICIAL DISTRICT

__________ (Plaintiff)

vs.

__________ (Defendant(s))

NOTICE AND REQUEST FOR HEARING TO DETERMINE ATTORNEYS' FEES AWARD

Court File No.: ______________

TO: ________________, JUDGMENT DEBTOR:
(Provide Name)

The above-named plaintiff has commenced an action against you and you are in default because you failed to timely serve an Answer. The plaintiff is now seeking an award of attorneys' fees in addition to the principal, interest and court costs in this action. If you do not contest the attorney fee award by completing this form and returning it to the (plaintiff)(plaintiff's attorney) identified below within twenty (20) days, the court may award fees up to the amount of $ ___, calculated as fifteen percent (15%) of the principal balance owing as requested in the Complaint up to a maximum of $3,000.00 but not less than $250.00. Attached to this notice is an affidavit from the plaintiff explaining its basis for an award of attorney fees. If you contest the reasonableness of the attorney fees, the plaintiff may seek an award of fees in excess of the amount indicated above, and the Court may award an amount larger or smaller than the amount indicated above.

You must return this form to the (plaintiff)(plaintiff's attorney) identified below within twenty (20) days of its receipt. Failure to timely return the form may result in judgment for the requested fees being granted.

NOTE: This form is not a substitute for an Answer to the action that has been commenced against you and will not preclude the entry of judgment for the principal claim. This form is limited solely to requesting a judicial review of the attorneys' fees requested by the plaintiff. Please contact legal counsel for advice related to serving an Answer or completing this form.

REQUEST FOR COURT HEARING

I request a hearing to determine the reasonableness of the attorneys' fees requested by the plaintiff.

____
(Defendant(s))

Return this form to:

____
(Plaintiff)(Plaintiff's Attorney)

____

____
(Address)

Adopted Dec. 11, 2003, eff. Jan. 1, 2004.

FORM 142.02. TRUSTEE'S ACCOUNTING [Renumbered Form 417.02 Nov. 13, 1992, eff. Jan. 1, 1993]

FORM 145.1. RECEIPT OF MINOR SETTLEMENT ORDER AND FUNDS

(Gen. R. Prac. 145.05)

State of Minnesota **District Court**

County of ______________ ________ **Judicial District**

Case Type: ________

____

Plaintiff/Petitioner **Case No.** ________

and

RECEIPT OF MINOR SETTLEMENT ORDER AND FUNDS
(Provided Pursuant to Rule 145 of the Minnesota General Rules of Practice)

____

Defendant/Respondent

1. ________ (**"Financial Institution"**) acknowledges receipt of the sum of $ ________ on behalf of ________ in this action.

2. **Financial Institution** acknowledges receipt of the Order Approving Settlement and For Deposit Into Restricted Account dated ________ in this action, and that the funds delivered remain subject to that order in the account specified below:

Name of Depository: ______________________
Branch Name: ______________________
Branch Address: ______________________
____
Account Number: (Place on separate form 11.1*)
Date Account Opened: ______________________
Current Balance: $ ______________________

3. This account is a federally insured, restricted account, and no withdrawal of either principal or interest shall be allowed by **Financial Institution** without a signed court order in this case.

Dated: ________ Type or Print Name ______________________
Signature: ______________________
Title: ______________________

Adopted Dec. 17, 2002, eff. Jan. 1, 2003. Amended July 24, 2013, eff. July 24, 2013.

* = As required by Rule 11.2 of the Minnesota General Rules of Practice

FORM 145.2. COMBINED MOTION AND ORDER FOR RELEASE OF MINOR SETTLEMENT FUNDS

(Gen. R. Prac. 145.05)

State of Minnesota **District Court**
County of ________ ________ **Judicial District**
Case Type: ________

____
Plaintiff/Petitioner **Case No.** ________

and

COMBINED MOTION AND ORDER FOR RELEASE OF MINOR SETTLEMENT FUNDS

____
Defendant/Respondent

(Pursuant to Rule 145 of the Minnesota General Rules of Practice)

1. ________ ("Movant") requests an order of permitting withdrawal of funds now held in a restricted account pursuant to a minor settlement approved in this action on ________. Movant brings this Motion as the

____ (Minor, now past the age of majority–Date of Birth ________)
or
____ ________________ to minor. (Specify whether trustee, custodian, parent, legal guardian, conservator, or other specified role).

2. Funds are now held on behalf of ________ in the following account:
Name of Depository: ________________
Branch Name: ________________
Branch Address: ________________
____
Account Number: (Place on separate form 11.1*)
Date Account Opened: ________________
Current Balance: $ ________________

* = As required by Rule 11.2 of the Minnesota General Rules of Practice

3. Previous withdrawals from the account, each of which was approved by the Court, are as follows:

____ None.
or
____ $ ________ on ________ for the purpose of ________________
$ ________ on ________ for the purpose of ________________
$ ________ on ________ for the purpose of ________________
☐ Check if additional space is necessary, and attach a separate sheet with that information.

4. Movant seeks the release of funds in the amount of $ ________ for the following reason:

____ Minor has reached the age of 18 and this is a final distribution
or
____ The funds will be used for the benefit of the minor in the following way:
____
____
____
☐ Check if additional space is necessary, and attach a separate sheet with that information.

5. Funds should be disbursed as follows:

$ ________ to ______________________________
$ ________ to ______________________________
$ ________ to ______________________________

☐ Check if additional space is necessary, and attach a separate sheet with that information.

I declare under oath and penalty of perjury under the laws of the State of Minnesota that the foregoing is true and correct and that any funds released pursuant to this request will be used for the benefit of the minor and in the way stated.

Dated: ____________. Type or Print Name

____

Signature: ______________________________

(sign only in front of notary public or court administrator)

Sworn/affirmed before me this

________ day of ________, ________
(DATE) (MONTH) (YEAR)

____

____

Notary Public/ Deputy Court Administrator

ORDER APPROVING RELEASE OF FUNDS

Pursuant to the foregoing Motion,

IT IS HEREBY ORDERED that

1. Movant is authorized to withdraw funds to be made payable as follows:
$ ________ to ______________________________
$ ________ to ______________________________

2. ____ This is a final distribution of funds from this account and the account may accordingly be closed following this final distribution

or

____ This is not a final distribution of funds and this account must be maintained as to the remaining funds and subject to all restrictions on distribution previous ordered.

3. Other provisions: ______________________________
____

Dated: ____________. ______________________________

Judge of District Court

Adopted Dec. 17, 2002, eff. Jan. 1, 2003. Amended Jan. 13, 2003, eff. Jan. 13, 2003; July 24, 2013, eff. July 24, 2013.

Historical Notes

The order of the Minnesota Supreme Court [CX–89–1863] dated January 13, 2003, provides in part that "(t)he attached amendments shall apply to all actions pending on the effective date and to those filed thereafter, except that any Form 145.2 filed prior to the effective date hereof that is otherwise in compliance with the rules at the time of filing shall be deemed also to comply with the attached amendments."

PART H. MINNESOTA CIVIL TRIALBOOK

Section 1. Scope; Policy

This trialbook is a declaration of practical policies and procedures to be followed in the civil trials in all the trial courts of Minnesota. It has been written to standardize practices and procedures throughout the state with the hope, and expectation, that trial time and expense will be reduced and that justice to the litigants and public acceptance of trial procedures will be increased.

It is recommended that the policies and procedures be generally and uniformly used. However, it is recognized that situations will arise where their use would violate the purpose for which they were drafted. In such circumstances, the policies and procedures should be disregarded so that justice, not form, may prevail. The provisions of this Trialbook may be cited as Minn. Civ. Trialbook § ___.

Adopted Sept. 5, 1991, eff. Jan. 1, 1992.

Sections 2 to 4. [Deleted Dec. 8, 1997, eff. Jan. 1, 1998]

Section 5. Pre–Trial Conferences

(a) Settlement Procedures. Settlement conferences are encouraged and recommended for case disposition. However, because of the diversity of approaches to be used, specific procedures are not set forth.

Lawyers will be notified by the court of the procedures to be followed in any action where settlement conferences are to be held.

(b) Procedures to be Followed. In those courts where a formal pre-trial conference is held prior to assignment for trial, a trial date shall be set and the conference shall cover those matters set forth in paragraphs (d) and (e) of this section.

(c) Settlement Discussions with Court. The court may request counsel to explore settlement between themselves further and may engage in settlement discussions.

(d) Pre-trial Chambers Conferences. At an informal chambers conference before trial the trial court shall:

(1) determine whether settlement possibilities have been exhausted;

(2) determine whether all pleadings have been filed;

(3) ascertain the relevance to each party of each cause of action; and,

(4) with a view to ascertaining and reducing the issues to be tried, shall inquire:

(i) whether the issues in the case may be narrowed or modified by stipulations or motions;

(ii) whether dismissal of any of the causes of actions or parties will be requested;

(iii) whether stipulations may be reached as to those facts about which there is no substantial controversy;

(iv) whether stipulations may be reached for waiver of foundation and other objections regarding exhibits, tests, or experiments;

(v) whether there are any requests for producing evidence out of order;

(vi) whether motions in limine to exclude or admit specified evidence or bar reference thereto will be requested; and

(vii) whether there are any unusual or critical legal or evidentiary issues anticipated;

(5) direct the parties to disclose the number and names of witnesses they anticipate calling, and to make good faith estimates as to the length of testimony and arguments;

(6) direct the parties to disclose whether any party or witness requires interpreter services and, if so, the nature of the interpreter services (specifying language and, if known, particular dialect) required;

(7) inquire whether the number of experts or other witnesses may be reduced;

(8) ascertain whether there may be time problems in presentation of the case, e.g., because of other commitments of counsel, witnesses, or the court and advise counsel of the hours and days for trial; and

(9) ascertain whether counsel have graphic devices they want to use during opening statements; and

(10) ascertain whether a jury, if previously demanded, will be waived. If a jury is requested, the judge shall make inquiries with a view to determining:

(i) the areas of proposed voir dire interrogation to be directed to prospective jurors, and whether there is any contention that the case is one of "unusual circumstances";

(ii) the substance of a brief statement to be made by the trial court to the prospective jurors outlining the case, the contentions of the parties, and the anticipated issues to be tried;

(iii) the number of alternate jurors (it is suggested that the identity of the alternates not be disclosed to the jury); and

(iv) in multiple party cases, whether there are issues as to the number of "sides" and allocation of peremptory challenges.

(e) Formal Conference. After conclusion of the informal chambers conference and any review of the court file and preliminary research the court finds advisable, a formal record shall be made of:

(1) arguments and rulings upon motions, bifurcation, and order of proof;

(2) statement of stipulations, including whether graphic devices can be used during opening statement; and

(3) in a jury trial, specification of:

(i) the brief statement the trial court proposes to make to prospective jurors outlining the case, contentions of the parties, and anticipated issues to be tried;

(ii) the areas of proposed voir dire interrogation to be directed to the prospective jurors;

(iii) whether any of the defendants have adverse interests to warrant individual peremptory challenges and number of them;

(iv) the number of alternate jurors, if any, and the method by which the alternates shall be determined;

(v) the need for any preliminary jury instructions.

Adopted Sept. 5, 1991, eff. Jan. 1, 1992. Amended Dec. 22, 2008, eff. March 1, 2009.

Task Force Comment—1991 Adoption

Subsection (a) is derived from existing Trialbook ¶ 6. The deleted language is unnecessary as it merely repeats other requirements.

Subsection (b) is derived from existing Trialbook ¶ 7.

Subsection (c) is derived from existing Trialbook ¶ 8.

Subsection (d) is derived from existing Trialbook ¶ 9.

Subsection (e) is derived from existing Trialbook ¶ 10.

This section sets forth many of the matters which can, and often should, be discussed in pretrial proceedings. The section does not enumerate all the subjects that can be discussed or resolved in pretrial conferences or other pretrial proceedings. The pretrial conference is intended to be a flexible device and the trial judge has considerable discretion to tailor the pretrial conference to suit the needs of an individual case. Many matters that may be useful in pretrial conferences are discussed in the Federal Judicial Center's *Manual for Complex Litigation* (2d ed. 1985).

The Task Force considered proposals and concerns expressed on the subject of the role of trial judges, both in jury trial matters and bench trial matters. The Task Force believes this is a difficult issue, and one on which trial judges and counsel should have guidance. The Task Force recommends that this problem area be given further study by the Minnesota Supreme Court and interested bar associations.

Cross Reference: Minn.R.Civ.P. 116; Minn.Gen.R.Prac. 111, 112.

Advisory Committee Comment—2008 Amendment

Section 5(d)(6) is new, added to reflect the amendments to Rules 111.02(*l*), 111.03(b)(8), and 112.02(g), requiring earlier disclosure of information about the potential need for interpreter services in a case, either for witnesses or for a party. *See* MINN. GEN. R. PRAC. 8.13.

Section 6. Voir Dire of Jurors

(a) Swearing Jurors to Answer. The entire panel shall be sworn by the clerk to truthfully answer the voir dire questions put to them. The clerk shall then draw the names of the necessary persons who shall take their appropriate seats in the jury box.

(b) Statement of the Case to and Examination of Prospective Jurors. The court shall make a brief statement to the prospective jurors introducing the counsel and parties and outlining the case, contentions of the parties, and anticipated issues to be tried and may then permit the parties or their lawyers to conduct voir dire or may itself do so. In the latter event, the court shall permit the parties or their lawyers to supplement the voir dire by such further nonrepetitive inquiry as it deems proper.

(c) Challenges for Cause. A challenge for cause may be made at any time during voir dire by any party or at the close of voir dire by all parties.

(d) Peremptory Challenges. Each adverse party shall be entitled to two peremptory challenges, which shall be made alternately beginning with the defendant. The parties to the action shall be deemed two, plaintiffs being one party, defendants the other. If the court finds that two or more defendants have adverse interests, the court shall allow each adverse defendant additional peremptory challenges. When there are multiple adverse parties, the court shall determine the order of exercising peremptory challenges.

(e) Voir Dire of Replacements. When a prospective juror is excused, the replacement shall be asked by the court:

(1) whether he or she heard and understood the brief statement of the case previously made by the judge;

(2) whether he or she heard and understood the questions;

(3) whether, other than to personal matters such as prior jury service, area of residence, employment, and family, the replacement's answers would be different from the previous answers in any substantial respect.

If the replacement answers in the affirmative to (3) above, the court shall inquire further as to those differing answers and counsel may make such supplemental examination as the court deems proper.

(f) Alternates. [Deleted Dec. 17, 1999, eff. Jan. 1, 2000].

Adopted Sept. 5, 1991, eff. Jan. 1, 1992. Amended Dec. 17, 1999, eff. Jan. 1, 2000.

Advisory Committee Comment—1999 Amendments

Subsections (a), (b), (d), and (f) are derived from existing Trialbook ¶ ¶ 11–15.

Subsection (c) is derived from the analogous provision of the rules of criminal procedure, Minn. R. Crim. P. 26.02(3)(a)(4). The present provisions relating to jury selection are spread among numerous different sets of rules. The civil rules have not heretofore specified a time for exercise of peremptory challenges. Some judges ask a party conducting voir dire examination before the conclusion of the jury selection process to "pass the jury for cause." This section will make it clear that challenges for cause can be made at any time, even after voir dire by other parties.

Although the section provides for administration of oaths to jurors, an affirmation should be used as to any juror or panel member preferring it.

Section 6(f) dealing with alternates is deleted in 1999 to conform this rule to the abolition of alternates under the Rules of Civil Procedure. Minn. R. Civ. P. 47.02 was abrogated by the 1998 amendments to the Rules of Civil Procedure, effective January 1, 1999.

Section 7. Preliminary Instructions

After the jury is sworn, but before opening statements, the judge shall instruct the jurors generally as follows:

(1) to refrain from communicating in writing or by other means about the case, to use the jury room rather than remaining in the courtroom or hallway, and to avoid approaching, or conversations with counsel, litigants, or witnesses, and that they must not discuss the case, or any aspect of it among themselves or with other persons;

(2) that if a juror has a question or communication for the court (e.g., as regards time scheduling), it should be taken up with, or transmitted through, the appropriate court personnel who is in charge of the jurors as to their physical facilities and supplies;

(3) that the jurors will be supplied with note pads and pencils, on request, and that they may only take notes on the subject of the case for their personal use, though they may bring such notes with them into the jury room once they commence deliberations in the case. The jury should receive a cautionary instruction that they are to rely primarily on their collective recollection of what they saw and heard in the courtroom and that extensive note taking may distract them from properly fulfilling this function;

(4) as to law which the judge determines to be appropriate; and

(5) that, as with other statements of counsel, the opening statement is not evidence but only an outline of what counsel expect to prove.

Upon submission of the case to the jury, the judge shall instruct the jury that they shall converse among themselves about the case only in the jury room and only after the entire jury has assembled.

Adopted Sept. 5, 1991, eff. Jan. 1, 1992.

Task Force Comment—1991 Adoption

This section was derived from existing Trialbook ¶ 16, without significant change.

Cross Reference: Minn.R.Civ.P. 39.03

Section 8. Opening Statement and Final Arguments

(a) Scope of Opening. Counsel on each side, in opening the case to the jury, shall only state the facts proposed to be proven. During opening statement counsel may use a blackboard or paper for illustration only. There shall be no display to the jury of, nor reference to, any chart, graph, map, picture, model or any other graphic device unless, outside the presence of the jurors:

(1) it has been admitted into evidence; or

(2) such display or reference has been stipulated to; or

(3) leave of court for such reference or display has been obtained.

(b) Final Arguments. Final arguments to the jury shall not misstate the evidence. During final argument counsel may use a blackboard or paper for illustration only. A graphic device, such as a chart, summary or model, which is to be used for illustration only in argument shall be prepared and shown to opposing counsel before commencement of the argument. Upon request by opposing counsel, it shall remain available for reference and be marked for identification.

(c) Objections. Objections to remarks by counsel either in the opening statement to the jury or in the closing argument shall be made while such statement or argument is in progress or at the close of the statement or argument. Any objection shall be argued outside the juror's hearing. If the court is uncertain whether there has been a misstatement of the evidence in final argument, the jurors shall be instructed to rely on their own recollections.

Adopted Sept. 5, 1991, eff. Jan. 1, 1992.

Task Force Comment—1991 Adoption

Subsection (a) is derived from Rule 27(a) of the Code of Rules for the District Court and existing Trialbook ¶ 17.

Subsection (b) is derived from existing Trialbook ¶¶ 30 and 44.

Subsection (c) is derived from Rule 27(f) of the Code of Rules and existing Trialbook ¶ 31.

Cross Reference: Minn.R.Civ.P. 39.04; Minn.Gen.R.Prac. 124.

Section 9. Availability of Witnesses

(a) Exchange of Information as to Future Scheduling. In order to facilitate efficient scheduling of future witnesses and court time, all parties shall communicate with one another and exchange good faith estimates as to the length of witness examinations together with any other information pertinent to trial scheduling.

(b) "On-Call" Witnesses. It is the responsibility of an "on-call" witness proponent to have the witness present in court when needed.

(c) Completion of Witness' Testimony. Except with the court's approval, a witness's testimony shall be pursued to its conclusion and not interrupted by the taking of other evidence.

Upon the conclusion of a witness's testimony the court should inquire of all counsel whether the witness may be excused from further attendance and if affirmative responses are given, the court may then excuse the witness.

(d) Excluding Witnesses. Exclusion of witnesses shall be in accordance with Minn.R.Evid. 615.

(e) Issuance of Warrants. A warrant for arrest or body attachment for failure of a witness to attend shall not be released for service unless it is shown by the applicant party, in a hearing outside the presence of jurors, that (1) service of the process compelling attendance was made at a time providing the witness with reasonable notice and opportunity to respond, and (2) no reasonable excuse exists for the failure to attend or, if the reason for the failure to attend is unknown to the applicant party, due diligence was used in attempting to communicate with such witness to ascertain the reason for the failure to attend.

Adopted Sept. 5, 1991, eff. Jan. 1, 1992.

Task Force Comment—1991 Adoption

Subsection (a) is derived from existing Trialbook ¶ 54.

Subsection (b) is derived from existing Trialbook ¶ 55.

Subsection (c) is derived from existing Trialbook ¶ 56.

Subsection (d) is derived from existing Trialbook ¶ 57, with significant change.

Subsection (e) is derived from existing Trialbook ¶ 61.

Subsection (d) now simply makes it clear that Minn. R. Evid. 615 governs the sequestration of witnesses. The existing provision of existing Trialbook ¶ 57 appears to be inconsistent with the Rules of Evidence, and should be superseded.

Cross Reference: Minn.R.Civ.P. 43.

Section 10. Examination of Witnesses

(a) Objections. Lawyers shall state objections succinctly, stating only the specific legal grounds for the objection without argument. Argument, if allowed by the court, and any offer of proof shall be made outside of the hearing of the jury and on the record.

(b) Caution to Witnesses. Before taking the stand and outside of the hearing of the jury, a witness called by counsel shall be cautioned by such counsel to be responsive to the questions and to wait in answering until a question is completed and a ruling made on any objection. Lawyers should advise their clients and witnesses of the formalities of court appearances.

Counsel may request the court to caution a witness while on the stand as to the manner of answering questions.

(c) Questions Not to be Interrupted. A question shall not be interrupted by objection unless then patently objectionable.

(d) Effect of Asking Another Question. An examiner shall not repeat the witness' answer to the prior question before asking another question.

An examiner shall wait until the witness has completed answering before asking another question. If a question is asked before the preceding question of the same examiner is answered or any objection is ruled upon, it shall be deemed a withdrawal of the earlier question.

(e) Number of Examinations. On the trial of actions only one counsel on each side shall examine or cross-examine a witness, and one counsel only on each side shall sum up the case to the jury, unless the judge otherwise orders.

(f) Counsel's Use of Graphic Devices. Counsel may use a graphic device to diagram, calculate, or outline chronology from witnesses' testimony.

(g) Familiarity with Witnesses, Jurors and Opposing Counsel. Lawyers and judges shall not exhibit undue familiarity with adult witnesses, parties, jurors or opposing counsel, or each other and the use of first names shall be avoided. In arguments to the jury, no juror shall be singled out and addressed individually. When addressing the jury, the lawyers shall first address the court, who shall recognize the lawyer.

(h) Matters to be Out of Jury's Hearing. The following matters shall be held outside the hearing of jurors. Counsel wishing to argue such matters shall request leave from the court. The first time this request is granted in a trial, the judge shall advise the jurors that matters of law are for the court rather than the jury and that discussions as to law outside the jurors' hearing are necessary and proper for counsel to request.

(1) Arguments: Evidentiary arguments and offers of proof as provided for in section 10(a) of this Trialbook;

(2) Offers to Stipulate: Counsel shall not confer about stipulations within possible jury hearing, nor

without leave of the court when such conference would impede trial progress;

(3) Requests for Objects: Other than requests to a witness during testimony, requests by a party to opposing counsel for objects or information purportedly in the possession of the opposing counsel or party shall be made outside the hearing of jurors;

(4) Motions: Motions for judgments on the pleadings, to exclude evidence, directed verdict, and mistrial shall be made and argued outside the hearing of the jurors. If the ruling affects the issues to be tried by the jury, the court, after consulting with counsel, shall advise the jurors. Immediately upon granting a motion to strike any evidence or arguments to the jury, the court shall instruct the jury to disregard the matter stricken; and

(5) Sensitive Areas of Inquiry: Areas of inquiry reasonably anticipated to be inflammatory, highly prejudicial, or inadmissible, shall be brought to the attention of opposing counsel and the court outside the hearing of jurors before inquiry. A question of a witness shall be framed to avoid the suggestion of any inadmissible matter.

(i) Questioning by Judge. The judge shall not examine a witness until the parties have completed their questions of such witness and then only for the purpose of clarifying the evidence. When the judge finishes questioning, all parties shall have the opportunity to examine the matters touched upon by the judge. If a lawyer wants to object to a question posed by the court, he or she shall make an objection on the record outside the presence of the jury. The lawyer shall make a "motion to strike" and ask for a curative instruction.

(j) Advice of Court as to Self-Incrimination. Whenever there is a likelihood of self-incrimination by a witness, the court shall advise the witness outside the hearing of the jurors of the privilege against self-incrimination.

(k) Policy Against Indication as to Testimony. Persons in the courtroom shall not indicate by facial expression, shaking of the head, gesturing, shouts or other conduct disagreement or approval of testimony or other evidence being given, and counsel shall so instruct parties they represent, witnesses they call, and persons accompanying them.

(*l*) Policy on Approaching the Bench. Except with approval of the court, persons in the courtroom shall not traverse the area between the bench and counsel table, and counsel shall so instruct parties they represent, witnesses they call, and persons accompanying them.

(m) Use of Depositions and Interrogatories. A party, before reading into evidence from depositions or interrogatories, shall cite page and line numbers to be read, and pause briefly for review by opposing counsel and the court and for any objections. The court may require designation of portions of depositions to be used at trial in a pretrial order.

Adopted Sept. 5, 1991, eff. Jan. 1, 1992.

Task Force Comment—1991 Adoption

Subsections (a)-(d) are derived from ¶¶ 48–53 of the existing Trialbook, in order.

Subsection (e) is derived from Rule 27(d) of the Code of Rules.

Subsection (f) is derived from ¶ 59 of the existing Trialbook.

Subsection (g) is derived from ¶ 58 of the existing Trialbook.

Subsection (h) is derived from ¶ 18 of the existing Trialbook

Subsections (i)-(*l*) are derived from ¶¶ 62–65 of the existing Trialbook, in order.

Subsection (m) is derived from existing Trialbook, ¶ 22.

Cross Reference: Minn.R.Civ.P. 43.

Section 11. Interpreters

The party calling a witness for whom an interpreter is required shall advise the court in the Civil Cover Sheet, Initial Case Management Statement, or Joint Statement of the Case of the need for an interpreter and interpreter services (specifying the language and, if known, particular dialect) expected to be required. Parties shall not use a relative or friend as an interpreter in a contested proceeding, except as approved by the court.

Adopted Sept. 5, 1991, eff. Jan. 1, 1992. Amended Dec. 22, 2008, eff. March 1, 2009; May 7, 2013, eff. July 1, 2013.

Task Force Comment—1991 Adoption

This section is derived from existing Trialbook ¶ 60.

Cross Reference: Minn.R.Civ.P. 43.

Advisory Committee Comment—2008 Amendment

This section is amended to incorporate the amendments to Rules 111.02(*l*), 111.03(b)(8), and 112.02(g), requiring earlier disclosure of information about the potential need for interpreter services in a case, either for witnesses or for a party. *See* MINN. GEN. R. PRAC. 8.13.

Historical and Statutory Notes

The order of the Minnesota Supreme Court [ADM04-8001, ADM09-8009, ADM-10-8051] dated May 7, 2013, provided in part that the amendments be effective July 1, 2013, and further provided in part that "[t]hese amendments apply to all actions or proceedings pending on or commenced after the effective date", and further provided that the "February 4, 2013 and February 12, 2013 orders of the court are hereby rescinded to the extent inconsistent with this order."

Section 12. Exhibits

(a) Pre-Trial Exchange of Lists of Exhibits. Each party shall prepare a list of exhibits to be offered in evidence, and exchange copies of such lists with other counsel prior to the pre-trial conference. Such lists shall briefly describe each exhibit anticipated to be offered in evidence. Prior to the commencement of trial, copies of all documents on the list of exhibits shall be made available by the proponent for examination and copying by any other party.

(b) Counsel to Organize Numerous Exhibits. If it can reasonably be anticipated that numerous exhibits will be offered in a trial, all counsel shall meet with designated court personnel shortly prior to or during a recess of the trial for the purpose of organizing and marking the exhibits.

All exhibits shall be marked for identification before any reference by counsel or by a witness.

(c) Marking of Exhibits First Disclosed During Trial. When an exhibit is first disclosed, the proponent shall have it marked for identification before referring to it.

(d) Collections of Similar and Related or Integrated Documents. Each collection of similar and related or integrated documents shall be marked with a single designation. If reference is made to a specific document or page in such collection, it shall be marked with a letter the arabic exhibit number assigned to the collection, e.g., "1–a," "21–b," "2–g," etc.

(e) Oral Identification of Exhibits at First Reference. Upon first reference to an exhibit the proponent shall briefly refer to its general nature, without describing the contents.

(f) When Exhibits to be Given to Jurors. Exhibits admitted into evidence, subject to cursory examination, such as photographs and some other demonstrative evidence, may be handed to jurors only after leave is obtained from the court.

Other exhibits admitted into evidence, not subject to cursory examination, such as writings, shall not be handed to jurors until they retire to the jury room upon the cause being submitted to them. If a party contends that an exhibit not subject to cursory examination is critical and should be handed to jurors in the jury box during the course of the trial, counsel shall request leave from the court. Such party shall be prepared to furnish sufficient copies of the exhibit, if reasonably practicable, for all jurors in the event such leave is granted; and upon concluding their examination, the jurors should return the copies to the bailiff. In lieu of copies, and if reasonably practicable, enlargements or projections of such exhibits may be utilized. The court may permit counsel to read short exhibits or portions of exhibits to the jury.

(g) Exhibits Admitted in Part. If an exhibit admitted into evidence contains some inadmissible matter, e.g., a reference to insurance, excluded hearsay, opinion or other evidence lacking foundation, the court, outside the hearing of the jury, shall specify the excluded matter and withhold delivery of such exhibit to the jurors unless and until the inadmissible matter is physically deleted.

Such redaction may be accomplished by photocopying or other copying which deletes the inadmissible portions, and in such event, the proponent of such exhibit shall prepare and furnish a copy.

If redaction by such copying is not accomplished, the parties shall seek to reach a stipulation as to other means; and failing so to do, the admissible matter may be read into evidence with leave of the court.

(h) Evidence Admitted for a Limited Purpose. When evidence is received for a limited purpose or against less than all other parties, the court shall so instruct the jury at the time of admission and, if requested by counsel, during final instructions.

Adopted Sept. 5, 1991, eff. Jan. 1, 1992. Amended Dec. 14, 1993, eff. Jan. 1, 1994.

Task Force Comment—1991 Adoption

Subsection (a) is derived from existing Trialbook ¶ 37.

Subsection (b) is derived from existing Trialbook ¶ 38.

Subsection (c) is derived from existing Trialbook ¶ 39.

Subsection (d) is derived, with change, from existing Trialbook ¶ 40.

Subsection (e) is derived from existing Trialbook ¶ 41.

Subsection (f) is derived from existing Trialbook ¶ 42.

Subsection (g) is derived from existing Trialbook ¶ 19.

Subsection (h) is derived from existing Trialbook ¶ 20.

Subsection (i) is derived from existing Trialbook ¶ 21.

The change made in subsection (d) expands on the uniformity attempted in the existing Trialbook. This new section requires a uniform method of marking exhibits, without the cumbersome prefixes that are frequently now encountered. The Task Force believes that a uniform numbering system will benefit the courts and litigants. The new system will permit exhibits to be used without labeling to show "ownership" or "lineage" of the exhibit. This system will also facilitate numbering of exhibits in multi-party cases, where the current practice creates complicated numbers at trial and burdensome citations on appeal. Lawyers and judges with experience in using this system believe it works fairly, predictably, and efficiently. The section permits flexibility in assignment of exhibit numbers, allowing them to be issued seriatim at trial or in blocks of numbers assigned to each party prior to trial.

The provisions of subsection (g) are not intended to limit in any way the discretion of the trial court as to what evidence is allowed to go to the jury room. Any evidence that is fragile, perishable, or hazardous may properly not be allowed into the jury deliberation room.

Advisory Committee Comment—1994 Amendment

Subsection (a) is derived from existing Trialbook ¶ 37.

Subsection (b) is derived from existing Trialbook ¶ 38.

Subsection (c) is derived from existing Trialbook ¶ 39.

Subsection (d) is derived from existing Trialbook ¶ 41.

Subsection (e) is derived from existing Trialbook ¶ 42.

Subsection (f) is derived from existing Trialbook ¶ 19.

Subsection (g) is derived from existing Trialbook ¶ 20.

Subsection (h) is derived from existing Trialbook ¶ 21.

Former subsection (d) is deleted because uniform exhibit marking is now covered by Minn.Gen. R.Prac. 130, a new rule effective on the same date. The remaining sections are renumbered for convenience.

The provisions of subsection (f) are not intended to limit in any way the discretion of the trial court as to what evidence is allowed to go to the jury room. Any evidence that is fragile, perishable, or hazardous may properly not be allowed into the jury deliberation room.

Cross Reference: Minn.R.Civ.P. 43.

Section 13. Custody of Exhibits

(a) Return of Exhibits to Court Personnel. Immediately after conclusion of the examination of a witness regarding an exhibit shown to a witness, counsel shall return it to the court personnel.

(b) Exhibits after Trial. Upon the completion of trial, the administrator shall index and retain all exhibits until the case is finally disposed of and all times for appeal have expired and they are either retrieved by the party offering them or destroyed pursuant to Minn. Gen.R. Prac. 128. In the event an appeal is taken, the court administrator shall deliver the exhibits to the Clerk of Appellate Courts in accordance with the procedures of the appellate courts.

(c) Bulky Exhibits. Any time after trial and upon the agreement of all parties, the court administrator may arrange the return of bulky exhibits to the party offering them at trial.

Adopted Sept. 5, 1991, eff. Jan. 1, 1992.

Task Force Comment—1991 Adoption

Subsection (a) is derived from existing Trialbook ¶ 43.

Subsection (b) is new, although the subject is covered in a number of current rules.

Cross Reference: Minn.R.Civ.P. 43, 77; Minn.Gen.R.Prac. 128, 129.

Section 14. Sealing and Handling of Confidential Exhibits

When briefs, depositions, and other documents or an exhibit such as a trade secret, formula or model are to be treated as confidential, if size permits, such an exhibit shall be placed in a sealed envelope clearly labeled as follows:

> "This envelope contains Exhibits ______ which are confidential and sealed by order of the court. This envelope shall not be opened, nor the contents hereof revealed, except by order of the court."

Such an envelope and other confidential exhibits shall be kept in a locked container such as a file cabinet or some other secure location under the supervision of the administration until released by order of the court.

If testimony is taken which would reveal the substance of confidential exhibits, the courtroom shall be cleared of all persons other than parties, their lawyers, and court personnel. Those present, including jurors, shall be directed by the court to refrain from disclosing the substance of the confidential exhibits.

The pertinent portions of the reporter's notes or transcript shall be kept in a locked container after being placed in a sealed envelope clearly labeled as follows:

> "This envelope contains confidential references sealed by order of the court. This envelope shall not be opened, nor the contents hereof revealed, except by order of the court."

Briefs and other papers submitted in or after trial ordinarily should not describe the substance of confidential exhibits but should refer to them only by number or letter designation pursuant to the uniform method of marking exhibits.

Adopted Sept. 5, 1991, eff. Jan. 1, 1992.

Task Force Comment—1991 Adoption

This section is derived from existing Trialbook ¶ 47. For a discussion of balancing tests applicable to requests to seal documents, see *Minneapolis Star & Tribune Co. v. Schumacher,* 392 N.W.2d 197, 202–206 (Minn. 1986).

Cross Reference: Minn.R.Civ.P. 26.03, 43, 77; Minn.Gen.R.Prac. 128, 129.

Section 15. Instructions

(a) When Jury Instructions to be Submitted. Jury instructions shall be submitted in accordance with Minn. R. Civ. P. 51. Written requests for instructions shall list authorities.

(b) Conference Regarding Instructions and Verdicts. Before final argument and after submission to the court of all proposed jury instructions and verdict forms, a conference shall be held outside the presence of jurors.

A reporter is not required at the beginning of the conference while the court reviews with counsel any proposed instructions or verdict forms and discusses:

(1) whether any proposed instructions or verdict forms are inappropriate and will be voluntarily withdrawn;

(2) whether there is any omission of instructions or verdict forms which are appropriate and shall be offered and given without objection; and

(3) whether there is any other modification of instructions or verdict forms to which the parties will stipulate.

Thereafter, the conference shall be reported and the court shall:

(1) specify those instructions and verdict forms the court proposes to give, refuse, or modify, whether at the request of a party or on its own initiative;

(2) hear formal argument, and rule upon any objections to, and offers of, the proposed instruction and verdict forms.

(c) Specifying Disposition of Instructions. Upon determining the instructions to be given, refused, or modified, the court shall indicate the disposition and sign or initial them.

(d) Stipulations Regarding Further Procedure. At a conference prior to the submission of the case to the jury, the court may request that the parties consider stipulating:

(1) that in the absence of any counsel the court may, upon request of the jury, read to the jury any and all instructions previously given;

(2) that in the absence of the court after the original submission of the case to the jury, any judge of the court may act in the court's place up to and including the time of dismissal of the jury;

(3) that a stay of entry of judgment for an agreed upon number of days shall be granted after a verdict;

(4) that a sealed verdict may be returned; and

(5) that the presence of the clerk and reporter, the right to poll the jury, and the right to have the verdict immediately recorded and filed in open court are waived.

(e) Changing Jury Instructions. If, after the chambers conference and at any time before giving the instructions and verdict form to the jurors, the court determines to make any substantive change the court shall so advise all parties outside the hearing of jurors. If the court determines to make a substantive change after final argument, the court shall permit additional final argument. The court shall also make a statement on the record regarding any changes.

(f) Use of Jury Instructions in Jury Room. Jury instructions may be sent to the jury room for use by the jurors if the court so directs. The number, title, citation of authority, and history shall be removed from each instruction. Stricken portions shall be totally obliterated and any additions shall be completely legible.

Adopted Sept. 5, 1991, eff. Jan. 1, 1992.

Task Force Comment—1991 Adoption

Subsection (a) is derived from existing Trialbook ¶ 24.

Subsection (b) is derived from existing Trialbook ¶ 25.

Subsection (c) is derived from existing Trialbook ¶ 26.

Subsection (d) is derived from existing Trialbook ¶ 27.

Subsection (e) is derived from existing Trialbook ¶ 28.

Subsection (f) is derived from existing Trialbook ¶ 32.

Cross Reference: Minn.R.Civ.P. 51.

Section 16. Questions by Jurors

If the jury has a question regarding the case during deliberations, the court shall instruct the foreperson to reduce it to writing and submit it through appropriate court personnel. Upon receipt of such a written question, the court shall review the propriety of an answer with counsel, unless counsel have waived the right to participate or cannot be found after reasonable and diligent search documented by the court. Such review may be in person or by telephone, and shall be on the record outside the hearing of the jury. The written question and answer shall be made a part of the record. The answer shall be given in open court, absent a stipulation to the contrary.

Adopted Sept. 5, 1991, eff. Jan. 1, 1992.

Task Force Comment—1991 Adoption

This section is derived from existing Trialbook ¶ 34.

Cross Reference: Minn.R.Civ.P. 47, 49.

Section 17. Special Verdicts

(a) Special Verdict Forms. A party requesting a special verdict form should prepare the proposed form and submit it to the court and serve it upon the other counsel prior to the chambers conference referred to in section 15 of this Trialbook.

(b) Filing. Proposed special verdict forms shall be filed and made part of the record in the case.

(c) Copies of Verdict. The court may provide copies of the verdict form to the jury or to each juror for use during arguments or instruction.

Adopted Sept. 5, 1991, eff. Jan. 1, 1992.

Task Force Comment—1991 Adoption

Subsection (a) is derived from existing Trialbook ¶ 33.

Subsection (b) is new.

Subsection (c) is new. The Task Force believes that it may be useful in some cases to allow the jury to have a copy or copies to be used during arguments of counsel or instructions by the court. It is not wise to permit multiple copies of the verdict form to be taken into the jury room, however.

Cross Reference: Minn.R.Civ.P. 49

Section 18. Polling and Discharge

(a) Polling the Jury. Upon the return of any verdict and at the request of a party the jury shall be polled. Polling shall be conducted by the trial court or by the clerk at the trial court's direction by asking each juror: "Is the verdict read your verdict?"

(b) Discharge of the Jury. In discharging the jury, the court shall:

(1) Thank the jury for its service;

(2) Not comment on the propriety of any verdict or failure to reach same;

(3) Advise the jurors that they may, but need not, speak with anyone about the case; and

(4) Specify where and when any jurors are to return for further service.

Adopted Sept. 5, 1991, eff. Jan. 1, 1992.

Task Force Comment—1991 Adoption

Subsection (a) is derived from existing Trialbook ¶ 35.

Subsection (b) is derived from existing Trialbook ¶ 36.

Cross Reference: Minn.R.Civ.P. 47–49.

TITLE III. REGISTRATION OF LAND TITLES

PART A. PROCEEDINGS FOR INITIAL REGISTRATION

RULE 201. APPLICABILITY OF RULES

Rules 201 through 222 of these rules apply to all actions and proceedings in the district court relating to registration of land titles, including proceedings subsequent to initial registration.

Adopted Sept. 5, 1991, eff. Jan. 1, 1992.

Task Force Comment—1991 Adoption

These rules include all of the provisions of the Code of Rules for the District Courts, Part II, and include additional rules derived from detailed local rules provisions dealing with subjects not addressed in the Code of Rules. No significant substantive changes have been made except to add these new provisions to the state-wide rules.

RULE 202. APPLICATIONS—INDORSEMENTS

Applications shall be approved as to form by the examiner, and there shall be indorsed thereon the name and address of the applicant's lawyer, or of the applicant if the applicant appears in person.

Adopted Sept. 5, 1991, eff. Jan. 1, 1992.

RULE 203. ABSTRACTS OF TITLE

The abstract when filed shall show the record of the patent or other conveyance from the United States, the record of the certified copy of the application, and shall include searches as to all state and federal judgments, federal and state tax liens, real estate taxes and tax and special assessment sales. The abstract also shall contain bankruptcy searches in the office of the County Recorder in the county in which the land is located. Additional bankruptcy searches in the office of the clerk of federal district court shall be required only in examination of title to lands in Hennepin, Ramsey and St. Louis counties.

Adopted Sept. 5, 1991, eff. Jan. 1, 1992.

RULE 204. TITLE BASED UPON AN ADJUDICATION NOT FINAL, OR UPON ESTOPPEL

When the title of the applicant or the release or discharge of any incumbrance thereon is based upon an adjudication not final, or upon estoppel, and there remains a right of appeal or contest, all parties having such right of appeal or contest shall be made parties defendant.

Adopted Sept. 5, 1991, eff. Jan. 1, 1992.

RULE 205. EXAMINER'S REPORT—PETITION AND ORDER FOR SUMMONS

The examiner's report shall specify the names of all parties deemed necessary parties defendant. Petitions for summons shall set forth those names and the names of such other parties as the applicant deems to be necessary, and the names, if known to the applicant, or ascertainable by reasonable inquiry of the successors in interest of such persons known to the applicant to be deceased. The petition shall recite that the petitioner has made a diligent effort by reasonable inquiry and search to ascertain the place of residence of all defendants named therein, and where the place of residence of a defendant is unknown to the petitioner, the petition shall so state such fact.

Adopted Sept. 5, 1991, eff. Jan. 1, 1992.

RULE 206. PAPERS TO BE FILED—EFFECT OF NOTICE AND APPEARANCE

A defendant who appears or files an answer, and who also serves a copy on the applicant or the applicant's lawyer, shall be entitled to notice of all subsequent proceedings in that action.

Adopted Sept. 5, 1991, eff. Jan. 1, 1992.

RULE 207. AFFIDAVIT OF NO ANSWER AND COURT ADMINISTRATOR'S CERTIFICATE OF DEFAULT

The default of defendants who fail to appear and answer shall be shown by the certificate of the court administrator of the district court in which the action is filed, and by the affidavit of the applicant's lawyer, if the applicant appears by lawyer; otherwise by the applicant's affidavit.

Adopted Sept. 5, 1991, eff. Jan. 1, 1992.

RULE 208. HEARINGS IN DEFAULT CASES—FILING PAPERS

Initial applications, where no issue has been joined, shall be heard by the court at any special term, or they may be heard by an examiner, to whom the matter has been specially referred. In counties where the examiner checks the proceedings in advance of the hearings, all papers necessary to complete the files shall be filed; and all documentary evidence proposed to be used by the applicant or petitioner shall be delivered to the examiner at least three days before the hearing, together with the proposed order for judgment and decree.

Adopted Sept. 5, 1991, eff. Jan. 1, 1992.

RULE 209. ISSUES RAISED BY ANSWER—REPLY

All facts alleged in an answer, which are not in accordance with the allegations of the application, shall be considered at issue without reply by the applicant. But if the answer sets up rights admitted in the application, or in a reply of the applicant, the hearing may proceed as in case of a default, and the registration shall be subject to such rights.

Adopted Sept. 5, 1991, eff. Jan. 1, 1992.

RULE 210. TRIAL OF CONTESTED ISSUES

In all cases where the answer raises an issue which is not disposed of by stipulation or otherwise, the matter shall be set for trial. The procedure and the method of determination shall be the same as in the trial of similar issues in civil actions or proceedings.

Adopted Sept. 5, 1991, eff. Jan. 1, 1992.

RULE 211. INTERLOCUTORY DECREE ESTABLISHING BOUNDARIES

When the applicant seeks to fix and establish all or some of the boundary lines of the land, the applicant shall have the premises surveyed by a registered land surveyor and shall cause to be filed in the proceeding a plat of the survey showing the correct boundaries of the premises. The applicant shall furnish the examiner with such abstracts of title of adjoining lands as the latter shall require in determining the necessary parties defendant in the fixing and establishing of such boundaries. The hearing upon such application may be separate from or in connection with the hearing upon the application to register, but before any final adjudication of registration, the court by order shall fix and establish such boundaries and direct the establishment of "judicial landmarks" in the manner provided by Minn. Stat. § 559.25. In the decree of registration thereafter entered, and in certificates of title thereafter issued, the description of the land shall contain appropriate reference to such "judicial landmarks."

Adopted Sept. 5, 1991, eff. Jan. 1, 1992.

RULE 212. PROTECTION OF INTERESTS ACQUIRED PENDENTE LITE—PROVISION FOR IMMEDIATE REGISTRATION AFTER HEARING

At the time of the hearing of the application for judgment, the applicant shall satisfy the court by continuation of abstract, if required by the examiner, and other proper proof, of any changes in the title, or in the incumbrances arising since the filing of the application. When the decree is signed, the applicant shall forthwith file it with the court administrator, together with a receipt of the registrar showing payment of all sums due for the registration of the decree, and the issuance of a certificate of title, and thereupon the court administrator shall certify a copy of the decree and file the same for registration with the registrar.

Adopted Sept. 5, 1991, eff. Jan. 1, 1992.

PART B. PROCEEDINGS SUBSEQUENT TO INITIAL REGISTRATION

RULE 213. TITLE OF PROCEEDINGS

Proceedings subsequent to the initial registration under Minn. Stat. §§ 508.44, 508.45, 508.58, 508.59, 508.61, 508.62, 508.67, 508.671, 508.70, 508.71, and 508.73, shall be commenced by filing with the court administrator a verified petition by a party in interest, which shall be entitled:

> In the Matter of the Petition of ____ in Relation to (description of property) registered in Certificate of Title No. ____ for (relief sought).

The petition shall allege the facts justifying the relief sought, the names of all interested parties as shown by the certificate of title, and their interests therein.

Adopted Sept. 5, 1991, eff. Jan. 1, 1992.

RULE 214. TRIAL AND HEARING

In proceedings where no notice is required and in proceedings where the required process or notice has been served and the time for appearance has expired without any issue having been raised, the proceedings shall be set for trial and heard the same as in proceedings upon default for initial registration. Issues raised in these proceedings shall be set for trial and disposed of the same as similar issues in other civil proceedings.

Adopted Sept. 5, 1991, eff. Jan. 1, 1992.

RULE 215. NEW CERTIFICATES, AMENDMENTS, ETC.

In proceedings under Minn. Stat. §§ 508.44, 508.45, 508.58, 508.59, 508.61, 508.62, 508.67, 508.671, 508.70, 508.71, and 508.73, the examiner shall make such examination as to the truth of the allegations contained in the petition as the examiner considers necessary, or as directed by the court. In all cases where notice is necessary and the manner of notice is not prescribed by statute, it shall be by an order to show cause, which shall designate the respondents, the manner of service, and the time within which service shall be made. Any final order or decree directed in such proceeding shall be approved as to form by the examiner before presentation to the court.

Adopted Sept. 5, 1991, eff. Jan. 1, 1992.

RULE 216. NEW DUPLICATE CERTIFICATE

Every petition for a new duplicate certificate shall be filed with the clerk and a certified copy thereof may be filed with the registrar for registration as a memorial on the certificate of title. Thereupon the court shall issue a citation addressed "To Whom It May Concern," fixing a time and place of hearing and prescribing the mode of service. No order shall be made for a new duplicate except upon hearing and due proof that the duplicate theretofore issued has been lost or destroyed, or cannot be produced. If it shall appear at the hearing that there are any known parties in interest to whom notice should be given, the hearing shall be continued and an order entered accordingly.

Adopted Sept. 5, 1991, eff. Jan. 1, 1992.

PART C. MISCELLANEOUS PROVISIONS

RULE 217. CASES NOT REQUIRING SPECIAL ORDER OF COURT

When the interest of a life tenant has been terminated by death, the Registrar may receive and enter a memorial of a duly certified copy of the official death certificate and an affidavit of identity of the decedent with the life tenant named in the certificate of title; and in such case the memorial of said certificate and affidavit shall be treated as evidence of the discharge of said life tenancy.

Adopted Sept. 5, 1991, eff. Jan. 1, 1992.

Task Force Comment—1991 Adoption

This rule is derived from 4th Dist. R. 11.02(d).

RULE 218. STATE TAX DEEDS

A deed from the State of Minnesota in favor of the registered owner shall be registered as a memorial on the certificate of title as a discharge of an Auditor's Certificate of forfeiture to the State.

In cases where the state deed of repurchase is dated subsequent to the date of any conveyance by the repurchasing registered owner to another, the County Auditor, a deputy Auditor, or the County Land Commissioner may endorse on the state deed a statement that the repurchase was made prior to or concurrent with the date of the conveyance by the registered owner.

Adopted Sept. 5, 1991, eff. Jan. 1, 1992.

Task Force Comment—1991 Adoption

This rule is derived from 4th Dist. R. 11.03.

RULE 219. DEEDS OF HOUSING AND URBAN DEVELOPMENT

In the registration of deeds or other instruments hereinafter listed for titles or interest registered in the name of an individual as Secretary of Housing and Urban Development, the Registrar of Titles shall be guided by 12 U.S.C. § 1710(g), which confers upon any designated officer, agent or employee the power to convey and to execute in the name of the Secretary deeds of conveyance, deeds of release, assignments of mortgages, satisfactions of mortgages, and any other written instrument relating to real property or any interest therein which has been acquired by the Secretary; and the Registrar of Titles shall accept the statement of the certificate of acknowledgement attached to any such instrument as evidence of the official character of the Secretary or the Secretary's designated officer, agent or employee executing the instrument.

Adopted Sept. 5, 1991, eff. Jan. 1, 1992.

Task Force Comment—1991 Adoption

This rule is derived from 4th Dist. R. 11.04.

RULE 220. BIRTH CERTIFICATES

The Registrar of Titles is authorized to receive for registration of memorials upon any outstanding certificate of title an official birth certificate pertaining to a registered owner named in said certificate of title showing the date of birth of said registered owner, providing there is attached to said birth certificate an affidavit of an affiant who states that he/she is familiar with the facts recited, stating that the party named in said birth certificate is the same party as one of the owners named in said certificate of title; and that thereafter the Registrar of Titles shall treat said registered owner as having attained the age of majority at a date 18 years after the date of birth shown by said certificate.

Adopted Sept. 5, 1991, eff. Jan. 1, 1992.

Task Force Comment—1991 Adoption

This rule is derived from 4th Dist. R. 11.05.

RULE 221. DEATH CERTIFICATES

The Registrar of Titles may receive official certificates of death issued by the United States Department of Defense or other military department in lieu of a certificate of death.

Adopted Sept. 5, 1991, eff. Jan. 1, 1992.

Task Force Comment—1991 Adoption

This rule is derived from 4th Dist. R. 11.06.

RULE 222. CONDOMINIUMS

The procedure for administration by the Registrar of the Uniform Condominium Act shall be as follows:

(a) The declaration, bylaws and any amendments thereto, to be filed in the office of the Registrar of Titles, must be executed and acknowledged and embrace land within the county.

(b) In order to have uniformity in the recording offices and to protect the interests of the public generally, the general requirements of Minn. Stat. § 505.08 as to the platting of land shall be followed, namely: as authorized by Minn. Stat. § 505.08, subd. 2a, only one set of transparencies shall be filed. The transparencies shall be of 4 mil. thickness, black on white on clear Mylar and be made by a fixed photo process. The transparencies shall be 20 by 30 inches in size. More detailed information on the drafting of the condominium plat may be obtained from the Registrar of Titles.

(c) The condominium plat is to be numbered serially beginning with the next number after the last apartment ownership number assigned pursuant to the Minnesota Condominium Act, Minn. Stat. ch. 515, and the numbers shall run consecutively within the offices of the County Recorder and the Registrar of Titles.

(d) Where registered land is to be submitted for administration under said act, the declarant, prior to filing the declaration and bylaws, shall obtain an Order of the Court in a Proceedings Subsequent to Initial Registration of land that the Declaration, including the condominium plat, and Bylaws, as submitted, comply with the various requirements of Minn. Stat. ch. 515A, and any amendments thereto. The Order shall direct the Registrar of Titles to accept such documents for registration and to enter them as separate memorials on the original Certificate of Title and on the Owner's Duplicate Certificate thereof. Reference to such documents, including the document numbers and dates of filing, shall be carried forward to each succeeding Certificate, including any Mortgagees' or Lessees' Duplicate Certificates.

(e) A condominium shall not include both registered land and unregistered land, but shall consist only of land that is all registered under Minnesota Statutes Chapter 508 or land of which no part is so registered.

Adopted Sept. 5, 1991, eff. Jan. 1, 1992.

Task Force Comment—1991 Adoption

This rule is derived from 4th Dist. R. 11.07.

TITLE IV. RULES OF FAMILY COURT PROCEDURE

PART A. PROCEEDINGS, MOTIONS, AND ORDERS

RULE 301. SCOPE; TIME

Rule 301.01. Applicability of Rules

(a) Applicable Rule or Statute. Rules 301 through 314 and, where applicable, the Minnesota Rules of Civil Procedure, shall apply to Family Law Actions except where they are in conflict with applicable statutes or the Expedited Child Support Process Rules, Minn. Gen. R. Prac. 351 through 379.

(b) Included Proceedings. The following types of proceedings are referred to in these rules as Family Court Actions:

1. Marriage dissolution, legal separation, annulment proceedings, and child custody actions (Minnesota Statutes, chapter 518, and section 260C.201, subd. 11(d)(1)(iii));
2. Child custody enforcement proceedings (Minnesota Statutes, chapter 518D);
3. Domestic abuse proceedings (Minnesota Statutes chapter 518B);
4. Proceedings to determine or enforce child support obligations (Minnesota Statutes, chapters 518A, 518C—U.I.F.S.A., sections 256.87; 289A.50, subd. 5; and 393.07, subd. 9);
5. Contempt proceedings in Family Court (Minnesota Statutes, chapter 588);
6. Parentage determination proceedings (Minnesota Statutes, sections 257.51–.74);
7. Proceedings for support, maintenance or county reimbursement judgments (Minnesota statutes, section 548.091);
8. Third-party custody proceedings (Minnesota Statutes, chapter 257C); and
9. Proceedings pursuant to the Hague Convention on Civil Aspects of International Child Abductions and the International Child Abduction Remedies Act.

Other matters may be treated as family court matters by order of the court.

(c) Excluded proceedings. Rules 301 through 314 do not apply to proceedings commenced in the Expedited Child Support Process, except for Rules 302.02, 303.05, 308.02, 309, 313, and 314.

(d) Applicability of Rules of Civil Procedure. The Minnesota Rules of Civil Procedure apply to Family Court Actions as to matters not addressed by these rules. To the extent there is any conflict in the rules, these rules govern.

Former Rule 301 adopted Sept. 5, 1991, eff. Jan. 1, 1992. Amended Dec. 19, 2000, eff. March 1, 2001; Sept. 5, 2001, eff. Sept. 5, 2001. Renumbered as Rule 301.01 and amended Jan. 19, 2012, eff. May 1, 2012.

Advisory Committee Comment—1992 Amendments

These rules are derived primarily from the Rules of Family Court Procedure. The advisory committee comments from the Rules of Family Court Procedure are included except where inconsistent with new provisions or where applicable rules are not retained.

These rules apply to the following specific types of proceedings that are generally treated as family court actions:

1. Marriage dissolution, legal separation, and annulment proceedings (Minn. Stat. ch. 518);
2. Child custody enforcement proceedings (Minn. Stat. ch. 518A);
3. Domestic abuse proceedings (Minn. Stat. ch. 518B);
4. Support enforcement proceedings (Minn. Stat. ch. 518C—R.U.R.E.S.A.);
5. Contempt actions in Family Court (Minn. Stat. ch. 588);
6. Parentage determination proceedings (Minn. Stat. §§ 257.51–.74);
7. Actions for reimbursement of public assistance (Minn. Stat. § 256.87);
8. Withholding of refunds from support debtors (Minn. Stat. § 289A.50, subd. 5);
9. Proceedings to compel payment of child support (Minn. Stat. § 393.07, subd. 9); and
10. Proceedings for support, maintenance or county reimbursement judgments (Minn. Stat. § 548.091).

Other matters may be heard and treated as family court matters.

Advisory Committee Comment—2001

Minn. Gen. R. Prac. 351.01 states that the Rules of Civil Procedure, Rules of Evidence, and General Rules of Practice shall apply to proceedings in the expedited process unless inconsistent with the Expedited Child Support Rules, Minn. Gen. R. Prac. 351 through 379. With the exception of Family Court Rules 302.04, 303.05, 303.06, 308.02, and 313, Minn. Gen. R. Prac. 301—313 are inconsistent with the Expedited Child Support Rules and therefore do not apply to the expedited process.

Advisory Committee Comment—2012 Amendments

Rules 301 through 314 were originally derived primarily from the Rules of Family Court Procedure as they existed in 1992. These rules have been revised in several important ways in the ensuing years, and were revised and completely restated in 2011. The prior Advisory Committee Comments have been incorporated into a single set of Advisory Committee Comments for the benefit of the Minnesota Supreme Court as well as for courts and litigants. As is consistently made clear by the orders that have amended the rules, the Advisory Committee Comments are not adopted by the Supreme Court and do not have any official status. They reflect the views of the Supreme Court's advisory committees that have recommended amendments of the rules from time to time.

Rules 301 through 314 apply in the enumerated proceedings, comprising the majority of types of cases involving family relations. Adoption proceedings are governed by separate Rules of Adoption Procedure, adopted effective January 1, 2005.

Minn. R. Gen. Prac. 351.01 states that the Rules of Civil Procedure, Rules of Evidence, and General Rules of Practice shall apply to proceedings in the expedited process unless inconsistent with the Expedited Child Support Rules, Minn. Gen. R. Prac. 351 through 379. With the exception of Family Court Rules 302.02, 303.05, 308.02, 309, 313 and 314, Rules 301–314 are inconsistent with the Expedited Child Support Rules and therefore do not apply to the expedited process.

Historical Notes

The order of the Minnesota Supreme Court [CX-89-1863] dated December 19, 2000, provides in part that these amendments are effective March 1, 2001, and shall apply to all actions or proceedings pending on or commenced on or after the effective date, with the exception of the amendments to Rule 114.13, which shall become effective on further order of the court following the action of the Alternative Dispute Resolution (ADR) Review Board.

The order of the Minnesota Supreme Court [CX-89-1863] dated December 19, 2000, provides in part that "(t)he inclusion of Advisory Committee comments is made for convenience and does not reflect court approval of the statements made therein".

The order of the Minnesota Supreme Court [ADM09–8009] dated January 19, 2012, provides in part that the amendments to the General Rules of Practice for the District Courts are effective on May 1, 2012, and that the amendments "shall apply to all actions pending on the effective date and to those filed thereafter."

Rule 301.02. Time

Computation of time under these rules is governed by Rule 6 of the Minnesota Rules of Civil Procedure.

Adopted Jan. 19, 2012, eff. May 1, 2012.

Advisory Committee Comment—2012 Amendments

The rules relating to computation of time are critical, and it is important that they be clear and predictable to all users of the court system. Rule 6 of the Minnesota Rules of Civil Procedure provides the appropriate clarity and makes it expressly applicable in family matters thereby eliminating any room for confusion. Rule 6 is consistent with the general day-counting rules set forth in Minn. Stat. § 645.15, and provides additional guidance for counting days where the periods of time are short and for responding to papers served by mail, or facsimile.

The time periods in the rules are intended to apply in most situations. Where unusual circumstances exist and justice so requires, the court may shorten the time limits. *See* Rule 1.02 of these rules.

Historical Notes

The order of the Minnesota Supreme Court [ADM09–8009] dated January 19, 2012, provides in part that the amendments to the General Rules of Practice for the District Courts are effective on May 1, 2012, and that the amendments "shall apply to all actions pending on the effective date and to those filed thereafter."

RULE 302. COMMENCEMENT; PARTIES

Rule 302.01. Commencement of Proceedings

(a) Methods of Commencement. Family Court Actions shall be commenced by service of a summons and petition or other means authorized by statute upon the person of the other party. Commencement can be accomplished by the following means:

(1) *Personal Service.* The summons and petition may be served upon the person of the party to be served.

(2) *Admission/Acknowledgment.* Service may be accomplished when the 211 party to be served signs an admission of service or acknowledges service as permitted in Minn. R. Civ. P. 4.05.

(3) *Alternate Means.* Service of the summons and petition may be made accomplished by alternate means as authorized by statute.

(4) *Publication.* Service of the summons and petition may be made by publication only upon an order of the court. If the respondent subsequently is located and has not been served personally or by alternate means, personal service shall be made before the final hearing.

(b) Service After Commencement. After a Family Law Action has been commenced, service may be accomplished in accordance with Minn. R. Civ. P. 5.

(c) Joint Petition in Marriage Dissolution Proceedings.

(1) No summons shall be required if a joint petition is filed to commence marriage dissolution proceedings. Proceedings shall be deemed commenced when both parties have signed the verified petition.

(2) Where the parties to a marriage dissolution proceeding agree on all issues, the parties may proceed using a joint petition, agreement, and judgment and decree for marriage dissolution.

(3) Upon filing of the "Joint Petition, Agreement and Judgment and Decree," and the Confidential Information Form (Form 11.1 as published by the state court administrator), and a Notice to the Public Authority if required by Minn. Stat. § 518A.44, the court administrator shall place the matter on the appropriate calendar pursuant to Minn. Stat. § 518.13, subd. 5. A Certificate of Representation and Parties and documents required

by Rules 306.01 shall not be required if the "Joint Petition, Agreement and Judgment and Decree" published by the state court administrator is used.

(4) The state court administrator shall develop forms that may be used by parties to file joint petitions to commence marriage dissolution proceedings.

Adopted Sept. 5, 1991, eff. Jan. 1, 1992. Amended Dec. 11, 2003, eff. Jan. 1, 2004; Nov. 30, 2005, eff. Jan. 1, 2006; Dec. 28, 2007, eff. Jan. 1, 2008; Jan. 19, 2012, eff. May 1, 2012.

Family Court Rules Advisory Committee Commentary

Original Advisory Committee Comment—Not kept current.

Proceedings for dissolution, legal separation and annulment are governed by Minn. Stat. Ch. 518. Minn. Stat. § 518.10 sets out the requisites for the petition. Minn. Stat. § 518.11 governs service by publication and precludes substitute service or service by mail under Minn. R. Civ. P. 4.05. The respondent's answer must be served within 30 days. Minn. Stat. § 518.12. The joint proceeding is commenced on the date when both parties have signed the petition; no summons is required. Minn. Stat. §§ 518.09 & .11. In cases involving foreign nationals, *see* Part I, Rule 30, Code of Rules for District Courts.

Custody proceedings under the Uniform Child Custody Jurisdiction Act are governed by Minn. Stat. Ch. 518A. Interstate service and notice must be accomplished at least 20 days prior to any hearing in Minnesota. Service within the state is set forth in Minn. R. Civ. P. 4.

Domestic abuse proceedings are governed by Minn. Stat. Ch. 518B. Ex parte orders for protection must include notice of a hearing within 14 days of the issuance of the order. Personal service upon the respondent must be effected not less than 5 days prior to the first hearing.

Support proceedings under the revised Uniform Reciprocal Enforcement of Support Act are governed by Minn. Stat. Ch. 518C. The time for answer is governed by the law of the responding jurisdiction.

Actions to establish parentage are governed by Minn. Stat. Ch. 257. Actions for reimbursement for public assistance are governed by Minn. Stat. § 256.87. Defendant has 20 days to answer the complaint in each action.

The Petitioner must notify the public agency responsible for support enforcement of all proceedings if either party is receiving or has applied for public assistance. Minn. Stat. § 518.551.

A party appearing pro se shall perform the acts required by rule or statute in the same manner as an attorney representing a party. An attorney dealing with a party pro se shall proceed in the same manner, including service of process, as in dealing with an attorney.

Task Force Comment—1991 Adoption

Subsection (a) is derived from Rule 1.01 of the Rules of Family Court Procedure.

Subsection (b) is derived from Second District Local Rule 1.011.

Subsection (c) is derived from Second District Local Rule 1.013. *See* Minn. Stat. § 518.11 (1990). This is to protect the children and help avoid secret proceedings if the respondent is able to be located.

Advisory Committee Comment—2003 Amendments

Subsections (2), (3), and (4), and Form 12, are new in 2003 and were recommended for adoption by the Minnesota State Bar Association's Pro Se Implementation Committee.

Subsections (2) and (3) of Rule 302.01(b) intended to provide a streamlined process for marriage dissolutions without children, where the parties agree on all property issues. These rule provisions essentially create a new process, commenced with a combined petition, stipulation and judgment and decree. Although intended to facilitate handling of cases by parties appearing without an attorney, it is available to represented parties as well. A new form is provided and should be made readily available to litigants. If either party to the proceedings is receiving public assistance, a Notice to Public Authority is also required. The Joint Petition, Agreement, and Judgment and Decree includes a statement regarding non-military status and a pro se waiver of right to be represented by a lawyer, thus satisfying the requirements of Rule 306.01(c). Court Administrators shall place the matter on the default calendar for final hearing without filing of Form 10 appended to the Rules. The Joint Petition, Agreement and Judgment and Decree may be used by parties represented by attorneys or parties representing themselves. The committee believes that the Joint Petition, Agreement, and Judgment and Decree procedure will reduce costs for litigants, reduce paper handling and storage expenses for the courts, and improve access to the courts.

Attorneys should approach the use of a Joint Petition with care. The amendment of this rule to allow use of a joint petition does not modify the professional liability constraints on joint representation of parties with divergent interests.

As part of this amendment, Rule 306.01 is also amended for internal consistency.

Advisory Committee Comment—2006 Amendment

Rule 302 is amended to incorporate procedures to deal with service "by alternate means" as authorized by statute. Minn. Stat. § 518.11 expressly provides authority for service by various other means. The rule retains provision for service by publication as well, because publication is authorized for a summons and petition that may affect title to real property. *See* Minn. Stat. § 518.11(c) (2004).

Advisory Committee Comments—2007 Amendment

Although Rule 302 is not amended, the amendment made to Rule 308.04 creates a procedure similar to that in Rule 302.01(b)(2). The Rule 302 procedure is available only in limited circumstances to allow for a completely streamlined procedure—use of a joint petition, agreement and judgment and decree of marriage dissolution without children. The Rule 308 procedure is a more limited streamlined procedure, although it is available in any case, but it does not obviate service of a petition (or use of a separate joint petition). That procedure simply allows the parties to combine the marital termination agreement and judgment and decree into a single document. The decision to use the procedure established in Rule 308.04 may be made at any time, while the procedure in Rule 302.01(b) is, by its nature, limited to a decision prior to commencement of the proceedings.

Advisory Committee Comments–2008 Amendments

Rule 302(b) is amended to expand the availability of the streamlined procedure allowing a marriage dissolution to proceed by use of a single pleading that combines a joint petition, marital termination agreement, and judgment and decree. The prior rule allowed this procedure only in marriages with no children; the amendment allows its use in marriage dissolution proceedings with children where the parties have agreed on all issues. The combined form permits the parties to proceed more expeditiously and make it easier for the parties and the court to verify that the judgment and decree to be entered by the court conforms to the parties' agreement.

The rule also deletes the reference to the former Rule 12 as part of a transition to maintain practice forms related to practice under the rules by court administration and available on the courts' website [www.mcourts.gov] rather than as part of the rule.

Advisory Committee Comment—2012 Amendments

Family court proceedings are generally governed by statute in Minnesota, and these rules implement the statutory procedures. Proceedings for dissolution, legal separation and annulment are governed in detail by Minnesota Statutes, chapter 518. *See generally* Minn. Stat. § 518.10 (requirements for petition); § 518.11 (service by publication and precluding substitute service or service by mail under Minn. R. Civ. P. 4.05); § 518.12 (requiring respondent's answer to be served within 30 days). Service "by alternate means" is authorized by statute. *See* Minn. Stat. § 518.11 (authorizing service by various other means). The rule retains provision for service by publication because publication is authorized for a summons and petition that may affect title to real property. *See* Minn. Stat. § 518.11(c) (2010).

A joint proceeding is commenced on the date when both parties have signed the petition, and no summons is required. Minn. Stat. §§ 518.09 & 518.11. Rule 308.04 creates a procedure similar to that in Rule 302.01(c)(2) & (3). The Rule 302 procedure is available only in limited circumstances to allow for a completely streamlined procedure—use of a joint petition, agreement and judgment and decree of marriage dissolution without children or with children where the parties have agreed on all issues. The Rule 308 procedure is a more limited streamlined procedure, although it is available in any case, but it does not obviate service of a petition (or use of a separate joint petition). That procedure simply allows the parties to combine the marital termination agreement and judgment and decree into a single document. The decision to use the procedure established in Rule 308.04 may be made at any time, while the procedure in Rule 302.01(c) is, by its nature, limited to a decision prior to commencement of the proceedings.

Custody proceedings under the Uniform Child Custody Jurisdiction and Enforcement Act are governed by Minnesota Statutes, chapter 518D. Interstate service and notice must be accomplished at least 20 days prior to any hearing in Minnesota. Service within the state is governed by Minn. R. Civ. P. 4.

Domestic abuse order for protection proceedings are governed by Minnesota Statutes, chapter 518B. Notice and the timing of personal service on the respondent varies according to the circumstances detailed in the statute. Support proceedings under the revised Uniform Interstate Family Support Act are governed by Minnesota Statutes, chapter 518C. The time for answer is governed by the law of the responding jurisdiction.

Statutes authorize commencement of certain Family Court Actions other than by summons and petition. Commencement of contempt proceedings under Minn. Stat. § 588.04 is addressed in Rule 309 of these rules. Court decisions set forth in *Rodewald v. Taylor*, 797 N.W.2d 729 (Minn. Ct. App. 2011), also permit commencement by motion following the signing of a Recognition of Parentage under Minn. Stat. § 257.75.

Actions to establish parentage are governed by Minnesota Statutes, chapter 257. Rule 314 of these rules addresses specific procedures applicable in these actions.

A child support proceeding that is not a IV–D case as defined in Rule 352.01(g)) must be commenced in district court and is subject to Rules 301–314. Actions for reimbursement for public assistance are governed by Minn. Stat. § 256.87 and are governed by the expedited process rules, Rules 351, et seq. The Petitioner must notify the public agency responsible for support enforcement of all proceedings if either party is receiving or has applied for public assistance. Minn. Stat. § 518A.44.

A party appearing pro se is required to perform the acts required by rule or statute in the same manner as an attorney representing a party. An attorney dealing with a party appearing pro se shall proceed in the same manner, including service of process, as in dealing with an attorney.

Historical Notes

The order of the Minnesota Supreme Court [ADM09–8009] dated January 19, 2012, provides in part that the amendments to the General Rules of Practice for the District Courts are effective on May 1, 2012, and that the amendments "shall apply to all actions pending on the effective date and to those filed thereafter."

Rule 302.02. Designation of Parties

(a) Petitioner and Respondent. Parties to Family Court Actions shall be designated as petitioner (joint petitioners or petitioner and co-petitioner) and respondent. After so designating the parties, it is permissible to refer to them as husband and wife, father and mother, or other designations if applicable by inserting the following in any petition, order, decree, etc.:

Petitioner is hereinafter referred to as (familial designation), and respondent as (familial designation).

(b) Guardians Ad Litem. Appointment of a guardian ad litem for minor children is governed by the Rules of Guardian Ad Litem Procedure in Juvenile and Family Court (Rules 901–907). The guardian ad litem shall carry out the responsibilities set forth in the Rules of Guardian Ad Litem Procedure in Juvenile and Family Court. The guardian ad litem shall have the rights set forth in the Rules of Guardian Ad Litem Procedure in Juvenile and Family Court.

A guardian ad litem for minor children may be designated a party to the proceedings in the order of appointment. If the child is made a party to the proceeding, then the child's guardian ad litem shall also be made a party.

Former Rule 302.04 adopted Sept. 5, 1991, eff. Jan. 1, 1992. Amended Sept. 30, 2004, eff. Jan. 1, 2005. Renumbered as Rule 302.02 and amended Jan. 19, 2012, eff. May 1, 2012.

Family Court Rules Advisory Committee Commentary*

A guardian appointed pursuant to Minnesota Statutes, section 257.60 becomes a party to the action if the child is made a party. The guardian then would be entitled to initiate and respond to motions, conduct discovery, call and cross-examine witnesses, make oral or written arguments or reports and appeal on behalf of a child without the necessity of applying to the court.

A guardian appointed under Minnesota Statutes, section 518.165 is not a party to the proceeding and may only initiate and respond to motions and make oral statements and written reports on behalf of the child.

A party has the right to cross-examine as an adverse witness the author of any report or recommendation on custody and visitation of a minor child. *Thompson v. Thompson*, 288 Minn. 41, 55 N.W. 329 (1952) and *Scheibe v. Scheibe*, 308 Minn. 449, 241 N.W.2d 100 (1976).

Practice among the courts may vary with respect to appointments. Some courts maintain panels of lay guardians while other courts maintain panels of attorney guardians. If a lay guardian is appointed, an attorney for the guardian may also be appointed. Guardians may volunteer or be paid for their services. An attorney requesting appointment of a guardian should inquire into local practice.

***Original Advisory Committee Comment—Not kept current.**

Task Force Comment—1991 Adoption

Subdivision (a) of this rule is derived from existing Second District R. 1.07. Subdivision (b) of this rule is derived from Rule 1.02 of the Uniform Rules of Family Court Procedure. The first sentence of the subdivision is new and is intended to make it clear that practice involving guardians ad litem is also governed by another rule provision.

Advisory Committee Comment—2012 Amendments

Rule 302.02(a) specifies that the proper designation of parties in family court proceedings is as petitioner and respondent. Where a proceeding is commenced jointly, both parties may be designated as co-petitioners. The rule permits the parties, once properly designated in the appropriate pleadings, to be designated by less formal terms that indicate their relationship. The rule is amended to recognize that those designations are not limited to husband and wife, and other forms of relationships are encountered in family court proceedings. The "petitioner" and "respondent" labels are to be used in parentage cases, despite the historic use of "plaintiff" and "defendant" in these cases. There is no statutory or other requirement for the use of those labels, although at least one statute uses the term "defendant" in specifying the proper venue for these actions. *See* Minn. Stat. § 257.59. It is particularly helpful to use common terminology given the fact parentage proceedings may be combined with or joined with an action for dissolution, annulment, legal separation, custody under Minn. Stat. ch. 518, or reciprocal enforcement of support pursuant to Minn. Stat. § 257.59, subd. 1.

Rule 302.02(b) deals with guardians ad litem. A guardian appointed pursuant to Minnesota Statutes, section 257.60 becomes a party to the action if the child is made a party. The guardian then would be entitled to initiate and respond to motions, conduct discovery, call and cross-examine witnesses, make oral or written arguments or reports and appeal on behalf of a child without the necessity of applying to the court. This rule applies to appointment of a guardian ad litem for minor children. Appointment of a guardian in other situations is governed by Rule 17.02 of the Minnesota Rules of Civil Procedure.

A guardian appointed under Minnesota Statutes, section 518.165 is not a party to the proceeding, but may initiate and respond to motions and make oral statements and written reports on behalf of the child. A party has the right to cross-examine as an adverse witness the author of any report or recommendation on custody and visitation of a minor child. *Scheibe v. Scheibe*, 308 Minn. 449, 241 N.W.2d 100 (1976); *Thompson v. Thompson*, 238 Minn. 41, 55 N.W.2d 329 (1952).

Historical Notes

The order of the Minnesota Supreme Court [ADM09–8009] dated January 19, 2012, provides in part that the amendments to the General Rules of Practice for the District Courts are effective on May 1, 2012, and that the amendments "shall apply to all actions pending on the effective date and to those filed thereafter."

RULE 303. MOTIONS; EMERGENCY RELIEF; ORDERS TO SHOW CAUSE

Rule 303.01. Scheduling of Motions

(a) Notice of Obtaining Hearing Date. Except in cases in which the parties reside in the same residence and there is a possibility of abuse, a party who obtains a date and time for hearing a motion shall promptly give written notice of the hearing date and time, name of the judicial officer, if known, and the primary issue(s) to be addressed at the hearing to all parties in the action. If the parties reside in the same residence and there is a possibility of abuse, notice shall be given in accordance with the Minnesota Rules of Civil Procedure.

(b) Notice of Motion. All motions shall be accompanied by either an order to show cause in accordance with Minn. R. Gen. Prac. 303.05 or by a notice of motion which shall state, with particularity, the date, time, and place of the hearing and the name of the judicial officer if known, as assigned by the local assignment clerk.

(c) Notice of Time to Respond. All motions and orders to show cause shall contain the following statement:

> The Rules establish deadlines for responding to motions. All responsive pleadings shall be served and mailed to or filed with the court administrator no later than five days prior to the scheduled hearing. The court may, in its discretion, disregard any responsive pleadings served or filed with the court administrator less than five days prior to such hearing in ruling on the motion or matter in question.

Adopted Sept. 5, 1991, eff. Jan. 1, 1992. Amended Jan. 19, 2012, eff. May 1, 2012.

Family Court Rules Advisory Committee Commentary

Original Advisory Committee Comment—Not kept current.

The scheduling of cases and the assignment of judges, judicial officers or referees is often a situation in which local calendaring practices prevail. Effective disposition of litigation requires immediate notice of the hearing officer's identity to preclude last minute filing of notices to remove or affidavits of prejudice.

Task Force Comment—1991 Adoption

Subdivision (a)(1) of this rule is derived from existing Rule 2.01 of the Rules of Family Court Procedure.

Subdivision (a)(2) is from the new Minn. Gen. R. Prac. 115.02. It is intended primarily to prevent a party from obtaining a hearing date and time weeks in advance of a hearing but then delaying giving notice until shortly before the hearing. This practice appears to give an unnecessary tactical advantage to one side. Additionally, by requiring that more than the minimum notice be given in many cases, it will be possible for the responding parties to set on for hearing any additional motions they may have. This may result in the more efficient hearing of multiple motions on a single hearing date.

Subdivision (b) of this rule is derived from Second Judicial District Rule 2.011.

Advisory Committee Comment—2012 Amendments

Rule 303.01 imposes a simple burden on any party, whether or not represented by counsel: to promptly advise the other parties when a hearing date is obtained from the court. The rule codifies common courtesy, but also serves specific purposes of reducing the need to reschedule motion hearings and permitting the other side to submit motions at the same hearing, if appropriate. "Promptly" is intentionally not rigidly defined, but notice should be sent the same day the hearing date is obtained. Notice of the assignment of a judicial officer also starts the time to remove an assigned judicial officer under Minn. R. Civ. P. 63.03 and Minn. Stat. § 542. 16.

The Rule exempts a party from giving prior notice if there is a "possibility of abuse" and where the two parties share the same residence. This admittedly subjective standard is retained in the rule for the protection of victims of domestic violence. The trial court retains the authority to impose sanctions for the improper use of this exception.

Historical Notes

The order of the Minnesota Supreme Court [ADM09–8009] dated January 19, 2012, provides in part that the amendments to the General Rules of Practice for the District Courts are effective on May 1, 2012, and that the amendments "shall apply to all actions pending on the effective date and to those filed thereafter."

Rule 303.02. Form of Motion

(a) Specificity and Supporting Documents. Motions shall set out with particularity the relief requested in individually numbered paragraphs. All motions must be supported by signed, sworn and notarized affidavits that contain facts relevant to the issues before the court.

(b) Temporary Relief. When temporary financial relief such as child support, maintenance, payment of debt and attorney's fees is requested, the Parenting/Financial Disclosure Statement form developed by the state court administrator shall be served and filed by the moving and responding parties, along with their motions and affidavits. Sanctions for failure to comply include, but are not limited to, the striking of pleadings or hearing.

Adopted Sept. 5, 1991, eff. Jan. 1, 1992. Amended Dec. 28, 2007, eff. Jan. 1, 2008; Jan. 19, 2012, eff. May 1, 2012.

Task Force Comment—1991 Adoption

Subdivision (a) of this rule is derived from existing Rule 2.02 of Rules of Family Court Procedure.

Subdivision (b) of this rule is derived from Second Judicial District Rule 2.021.

The local rule from which subdivision (b) is derived included a requirement that information be filed on forms, and that typewritten or word-processed documents would not be accepted for filing. The Task Force considered the desirability of requiring information to be submitted on pre-printed forms, and determined that such requirements should not be retained. Many modern law offices cannot readily prepare such documents as word processing machines have displaced the typewriters for which the forms are designed. The Task Force also believes that these requirements only increase the cost of litigation and limit access to the courts.

Historical Notes

The order of the Minnesota Supreme Court [ADM09-8009] dated January 19, 2012, provides in part that the amendments to the General Rules of Practice for the District Courts are effective on May 1, 2012, and that the amendments "shall apply to all actions pending on the effective date and to those filed thereafter."

Rule 303.03. Motion Practice

(a) Requirements for Motions.

(1) *Moving Party, Supporting Documents, Time Limits.* No motion shall be heard unless the moving party pays any required motion filing fee, properly serves a copy of the following documents on all parties and files them with the court administrator at least 14 days prior to the hearing:

(i) Notice of motion and motion in the form required by Minn. Gen. R. Prac. 303.01 and 303.02;

(ii) Relevant signed, sworn and notarized affidavits and exhibits; and

(iii) Any memorandum of law the party intends to submit.

(2) *Motion Raising New Issues.* A responding party raising new issues other than those raised in the initial motion shall pay any required motion filing fee, properly serve a copy of the following documents on all parties and file them with the court administrator at least 10 days prior to the hearing:

(i) Notice of motion and motion in the form required by Minn. Gen. R. Prac. 303.01and 303.02;

(ii) Relevant signed, sworn and notarized, affidavits and exhibits; and

(iii) Any memorandum of law the party intends to submit.

(3) *Responding Party, Supporting Documents, Time Limits.* The party responding to issues raised in the initial motion, or the party responding to a motion that raises new issues, shall pay any required motion filing fee, properly serve a copy of the following documents on all parties, and file them with the court administrator at least 5 days prior to the hearing, inclusive of Saturdays, Sundays, and holidays:

(i) Any memorandum of law the party intends to submit; and

(ii) Relevant signed, sworn and notarized affidavits and exhibits.

(4) *Computation of Time for Service.* Whenever this rule requires documents to be served and filed with the court administrator within a prescribed period of time before a specific event, service and filing must be accomplished as required by Minn. R. Civ. P. 5 and 6.

(5) *Post-Trial Motions.* The timing provisions of Rule 303.03(a) do not apply to post-trial motions.

(b) Failure to Comply. In the event a moving party fails to timely serve and file documents required in this rule, the hearing may be cancelled by the court. If responsive papers are not properly served and filed, the court may deem the initial motion unopposed and may issue an order without a hearing. The court, in its discretion, may refuse to permit oral argument by the party not filing the required documents, may consider the matter unopposed, may allow reasonable attorney's fees, or may take other appropriate action.

(c) Settlement Efforts. Except in parentage cases when there has been no court determination of the existence of the parent and child relationship, and except in situations where a court has ordered that no contact occur between the parties, the moving party shall, within 7 days of filing a motion, initiate a settlement conference either in person, or by telephone, or in writing in an attempt to resolve the issues raised. Unless ADR is not required under Rule 310, this conference shall include consideration of an appropriate ADR process under Rule 114. The moving party shall certify to the court compliance with this rule or any reasons for not complying. The moving party shall file a Certificate of Settlement Efforts in the form developed by the state court administrator not later than 24 hours before the hearing. Unless excused by the Court for good cause, no motion shall be heard unless the parties have complied with this rule. Whenever any pending motion is settled, the moving party shall promptly advise the court.

(d) Request for Oral Testimony.

(1) *General Rule.* Motions shall be submitted on affidavits, exhibits, documents subpoenaed to the hearing, memoranda, and arguments of counsel except for contempt proceedings or as otherwise provided for in these rules.

(2) *Request for Leave for Oral Testimony.* Requests for the taking of oral testimony must be made by motion served and filed not later than the filing of that party's initial motion papers. The motion shall include names of witnesses, nature and length of testimony, including cross-examination, and types of exhibits, if any.

(3) *Request for Hearing Longer Than One-Half Hour.* Requests for hearing time in excess of one-half hour must be submitted by separate written motion specifically setting forth the necessity and reason that evidence cannot be submitted by affidavit.

(4) *Conversion to Prehearing Conference.* If the matter cannot be heard adequately in the scheduled

time, the hearing shall be used as a prehearing conference.

(5) *Court Discretion to Solicit Oral Testimony.* If the request required by subdivision (2) of this rule has not been made, the court shall not take oral testimony at the scheduled hearing unless the court in its discretion solicits additional evidence from the parties by oral testimony.

(6) *Order.* In the event the court permits oral testimony, it may issue an order limiting the number of witnesses each party may call, the scope of their testimony, and the total time for each party to present evidence. Each party shall be afforded an opportunity to suggest appropriate limits.

(7) *Interviews of Minor Children.* Any motion relating to custody or visitation shall additionally state whether either party desires the court to interview minor children. No child under the age of fourteen years will be allowed to testify without prior written notice to the other party and court approval.

Adopted Sept. 5, 1991, eff. Jan. 1, 1992. Amended Dec. 14, 1993, eff. Jan. 1, 1994; Oct. 10, 1996; Dec. 11, 2003, eff. Jan. 1, 2004; Jan. 19, 2012, eff. May 1, 2012.

Family Court Rules Advisory Committee Commentary

Original Advisory Committee Comment— Not kept current.

Minn. Stat. § 518.131, subd. 8 grants a party the right to present oral testimony upon the filing of a demand either in the initial application for temporary relief or in the response thereto.

The party demanding oral testimony should provide a list of the proposed witnesses, the scope of their testimony and an estimate of the required time.

Advisory Committee Comment—1996 Amendment

Subdivisions (a)–(d) of this rule are new. They are derived from parallel provisions in new Minn. Gen.R.Prac. 115, and are intended to make motion practice in family court matters as similar to that in other civil actions as is possible and practical given the particular needs in family court matters.

Subdivision (d) of this rule is derived from Rule 2.04 of Rules of Family Court Procedure and from Second Judicial District Rules 2.041 and 2.042.

The requirement in subsection (c) of an attempt to resolve motion disputes requires that the efforts to resolve the matter be made before the hearing, not before bringing the motion. It is permissible under the rule to bring a motion and then attempt to resolve the motion. If the motion is resolved, subsection (c) requires the parties to advise the court immediately.

Rule 303.03(a)(5) is added by amendment to be effective January 1, 1994, in order to make it clear that the stringent timing requirements of the rule need not be followed on post-trial motions. This change is made to continue the uniformity in motion practice between family court matters and general civil cases, and is patterned on the change to Minn. Gen.R.Prac. 115.01(c) made effective January 1, 1993.

Subdivision (c) of this rule is amended in 1996 to require consideration of ADR in post-decree matters. The rule specifies how ADR proceedings are commenced in post-decree matters; the procedures for court-annexed ADR in these matters is generally the same under Rule 114 as for other cases.

Advisory Committee Comment—2003 Amendments

The rule is amended in 2003 to include a reference to the requirement for paying a motion filing fee. A new statute in 2003 imposes a fee for "filing a motion or response to a motion in civil, family, excluding child support, and guardianship case." *See* 2003 MINN. LAWS 1st Spec. Sess., ch. 2, art. 2, § 2, *to be codified at* MINN. STAT. § 357.021, subd. 2(4).

Advisory Committee Comment—2012 Amendments

Motion practice in family law matters is intended to mirror, where appropriate to the needs of family law issues, the procedures followed generally in civil cases in Minnesota courts. The prevailing practice in Minnesota courts is for the submission of evidence relating to motions by written submissions, with sworn testimony provided by affidavit, deposition, or other written submissions. Rule 303.03(d)(1) restates that rule. The balance of Rule 303.03(d) addresses the process to request leave to present oral testimony in the limited circumstances where it may be appropriate. Minn. Stat. § 518.131, subd. 8, provides for allowing oral testimony upon demand of a party in requests for a temporary order or restraining order.

Rule 303.03(a)(5) makes it clear that the stringent timing requirements of the rule need not be followed on post-trial motions, such as a motion for a new trial or for amended findings made shortly after the conclusion of trial. *See* Minn. R. Civ. P. 52 & 59. This change is made to continue the uniformity in motion practice between family court matters and general civil cases, and is patterned on Minn. Gen. R. Prac. 115.01(c). Support, spousal maintenance, and custody modification motions, often brought months or years later, are subject to the general timing rules for motions.

The requirement in subsection (c) of an attempt to resolve motion disputes requires that the efforts to resolve the matter be made before the hearing, not before bringing the motion. The rule requires the moving party to initiate settlement efforts. If the motion is resolved, subsection (c) requires the parties to advise the court immediately. Although mandated settlement efforts may create additional challenges for pro se parties, Rule 1.04 requires compliance with the rules by all parties, including pro se parties, subject to relief granted by the court to prevent a manifest injustice under rule 1.02.

The rule explicitly addresses the requirement for paying a motion filing fee. Since 2003, Minnesota law requires a fee for "filing a motion or response to a motion in civil, family, excluding child support, and guardianship cases." *See* Minn. Stat. § 357.021, subd. 2(4).

Historical Notes

The order of the Minnesota Supreme Court [CX-89-1863] dated October 10, 1996, provides in part that these amendments are effective July 1, 1997, except that rules 119 and 418 are effective January 1, 1997, that these amendments shall apply to all actions pending on the effective dates and to those filed thereafter, and that "(t)he inclusion of Advisory Committee comments is made for convenience and does not reflect court approval of the comments made therein".

The order of the Minnesota Supreme Court [CX-89-1863] dated December 11, 2003, provides in part that these amendments are effective January 1, 2004, and shall apply to all actions or proceedings pending on or commenced on or after the effective date.

The order of the Minnesota Supreme Court [CX-89-1863] dated December 11, 2003, provides in part that "(t)he inclusion of Advisory Committee comments is made for convenience and does not reflect court approval of the statements made therein".

The order of the Minnesota Supreme Court [ADM09-8009] dated January 19, 2012, provides in part that the amendments to the General Rules of Practice for the District Courts are effective on May 1, 2012, and that the amendments "shall apply to all actions pending on the effective date and to those filed thereafter."

Rule 303.04. Ex Parte and Emergency Relief

(a) Governing Rules. The court may grant emergency relief if the requirements in this Rule 303.04 are met. If emergency relief is sought ex parte, the party seeking the relief must demonstrate compliance with Rule 3 of these rules.

(b) Order to Show Cause. An order to show cause shall not be used except in those cases where permitted pursuant to Minn. Gen. R. Prac. 303.05.

(c) Requirement of Motion; Form. The party seeking emergency relief must state with specificity in a motion and affidavit:

(i) Why emergency relief is required;

(ii) The relief requested;

(iii) Disclosure of any other attempts to obtain the same or similar relief and the result;

(iv) If there was a prior attempt to obtain emergency relief, the name of the judicial officer to whom the request was made;

(v) If a prior request was denied for the same or similar relief, explain what new facts are presented to support the current motion.

(d) Proposed Order. The party seeking emergency relief must present a proposed order for the court's consideration.

(e) Notice. The party seeking emergency relief must serve the motion and affidavit, including notice of the time when and the place where the motion will be heard, on the other party or counsel, unless:

(i) the party seeking emergency relief provides a written statement that the party has made a good faith effort to contact the other party or counsel and has been unsuccessful; or

(ii) the supporting documents show good cause why notice to the other party should not be required and the court waives the notice requirement.

(f) Hearing. An order granting emergency relief without notice shall include a return hearing date before the judicial officer hearing the matter. If the relief obtained affects custody or parenting time, the court shall set the matter for hearing within 14 days of the date the emergency relief is granted.

Adopted Sept. 5, 1991, eff. Jan. 1, 1992. Amended Jan. 19, 2012, eff. May 1, 2012.

Family Court Rules Advisory Committee Commentary

Original Advisory Committee Comment— Not kept current.

Minn. R. Civ. P. 65.01 states the notice requirements for ex parte relief. Minn. Stat. § 518.131 controls ex parte temporary restraining orders.

Task Force Comment—1991 Adoption

Subdivisions (a), (b) and (c) of this rule are derived from existing Rule 2.05 of the Rules of Family Court Procedure.

Subdivision (d) of this rule is derived from Second District Local Rule 2.051.

Parties should be aware that Minn. Gen. R. Prac. 3 applies to all ex parte orders, including those relating to family court proceedings. Minn. R. Civ. P. 65.01 also applies in family court temporary restraining order practice.

Advisory Committee Comment—2012 Amendments

Rule 303.04 is amended to make clearer the circumstances that justify seeking either emergency or ex parte relief. "Emergency" and "ex parte" are not synonymous, though sometimes both might be justified in a particular situation. Emergency relief may be appropriate where there is urgency, not caused by lack of diligence on the part of the moving party, that makes the normal deadlines in the rules unworkable. Even where exigent circumstances justify shortening the deadlines, they do not generally excuse the giving of notice—or the attempt thereof—to the other side. Rare situations may, however, permit or even demand that notice not be given to the other side before seeking relief from the court. Where destruction of property or evidence is threatened, assets appear to be concealed or are threatened to be concealed, or the abduction of children has occurred or is threatened, or other situations exist where the giving of notice is likely to make any relief impossible to obtain, the court may consider the matter ex parte (without notice to the other side). Rule 3 of these rules provides clear guidelines on seeking ex parte relief. The standards of Rule 65.01 of the Minnesota Rules of Civil Procedure also provide guidance for relief in family law manners. *See* Minn. R. Civ. P. 65.01 (permitting relief without notice if "immediate and irreparable injury, loss, or damage will result.").

As is true for temporary restraining orders, any order granted without notice to all parties should be of extremely short duration and the court should hold a hearing upon notice to all parties before continuing or extending the relief. The availability of temporary relief, and the limits on that relief, are set forth in Minn. Stat. § 518.131.

Historical Notes

The order of the Minnesota Supreme Court [ADM09–8009] dated January 19, 2012, provides in part that the amendments to the General Rules of Practice for the District Courts are effective on May 1, 2012, and that the amendments "shall apply to all actions pending on the effective date and to those filed thereafter."

Rule 303.05. Orders to Show Cause

Orders to show cause shall be obtained in the same manner specified for ex parte relief in Rule 3 of these rules. Such orders may require production of limited financial information. An order to show cause shall be issued only where the motion seeks a finding of contempt under Rule 309 or the supporting affidavit makes an affirmative showing of:

(a) a need to require the party to appear in person at the hearing, or

(b) a need for interim support is warranted, or

(c) the production of limited financial information is deemed necessary by the court, or

(d) a need for the issuance of an order to show cause, subject to the discretion of the judge.

All orders to show cause must be appropriately signed out for service. A conformed file copy of such order shall be retained by the court administrator in the file.

Adopted Sept. 5, 1991, eff. Jan. 1, 1992. Amended Jan. 19, 2012, eff. May 1, 2012.

Family Court Rules Advisory Committee Commentary

Original Advisory Committee Comment—Not kept current.

The use of orders to show cause can be abused by requiring a personal appearance where none is necessary. A timely notice of motion informing a party of the time to appear, if he or she wishes, is adequate in most proceedings.

Task Force Comment—1991 Adoption

This rule is derived from existing Rule 2.06 of the Rules of Family Court Procedure. The Family Law Section of the Minnesota State Bar Association recommended additional specific language limiting use of orders to show cause and the Task Force agrees that this clarification should be useful. Orders to show cause are specifically authorized, in limited circumstances, by statute. *See, e.g.,* Minn. Stat. §§ 256.87, subd. 1a & 393.07, subd. 9 (1990).

Advisory Committee Comment—2012 Amendments

Orders to show cause should be issued only when it is necessary that a party appear at a hearing. In most situations, the provision of notice of a hearing, and allowing parties to appear if they choose to contest entry of the relief sought, is sufficient. Orders to show cause are specifically authorized, in limited circumstances, by statute. *See, e.g.,* Minn. Stat. §§ 256.87, subd. la; 393.07, subd. 9; 518A.73; and 543.20. It is often preferable to use a notice of motion, and if attendance is required, to issue a subpoena to a non-party. *See, e.g., Stevens County Social Service Dept. ex rel. Banken v. Banken,* 403 N.W.2d 693 (Minn. Ct. App. 1987). Orders to show cause are a recognized part of contempt proceedings. *See, e.g.,* Minn. Stat. § 588.04.

Parties should be aware that improper use of an order to show cause can result in the imposition of sanctions. *See, e.g., Nelson v. Quade,* 413 N.W.2d 824 (Minn. Ct. App. 1987).

Former Rule 303.06 setting forth notices to be included in a final decree have largely been obviated by statutorily required notices. Notices required under statute are discussed in Rule 308.02 and its accompanying advisory committee comment.

Historical Notes

The order of the Minnesota Supreme Court [ADM09–8009] dated January 19, 2012, provides in part that the amendments to the General Rules of Practice for the District Courts are effective on May 1, 2012, and that the amendments "shall apply to all actions pending on the effective date and to those filed thereafter."

RULE 304. SCHEDULING OF CASES

Rule 304.01. Scope

Rules 304.01 through 304.05 provide for scheduling matters for disposition and trial in all Family Court Actions, excluding only the following:

(a) Actions for reimbursement of public assistance (Minn. Stat. § 256.87);

(b) Contempt (Minn. Stat. ch. 588);

(c) Domestic abuse proceedings (Minn. Stat. ch. 518B);

(d) Child custody enforcement proceedings (Minn. Stat. ch. 518D);

(e) Support enforcement proceedings (Minn. Stat. ch. 518C—U.I.F.S.A.);

(f) Withholding of refunds from support debtors (Minn. Stat. § 289A.50, subd. 5);

(g) Proceedings to compel payment of child support (Minn. Stat. § 393.07, subd. 9);

(h) Proceedings for support, maintenance or county reimbursement judgments (Minn. Stat. § 548.091); and

(i) Expedited Child Support Proceedings (Minn. Gen. R. Prac. 351 through 379). Rule 304.06 applies to all Family Court Actions.

Adopted Sept. 5, 1991, eff. Jan. 1, 1992. Amended Jan. 19, 2012, eff. May 1, 2012.

Historical Notes

The order of the Minnesota Supreme Court [CX–89–1863, C6–84–2134] dated September 5, 1991 adopting the General Rules of Practice for the District Courts provided in part:

"In all pending actions in which any paper has been filed with the District Court prior to January 1, 1992, the filing date for purposes of Rules 111 and 304 of the attached General Rules of Practice for the District Courts shall be deemed to be January 1, 1992, unless otherwise ordered by the District Court."

The order of the Minnesota Supreme Court [ADM09–8009] dated January 19, 2012, provides in part that the amendments to the General Rules of Practice for the District Courts are effective on May 1, 2012, and that the amendments "shall apply to all actions pending on the effective date and to those filed thereafter."

Rule 304.02. Scheduling Statement

(a) Except where the court orders the parties to use an Initial Case Management Conference ("ICMC"), within 60 days after the initial filing in a case, or sooner if the court requires, the parties shall file a Scheduling Statement that substantially conforms to the form developed by the state court administrator.

(b) In cases where the court orders the parties to use an Initial Case Management Conference, the parties shall comply with the order issued by the court as to what form to submit, its due date, and whether it should be filed or submitted to the court without filing.

Adopted Sept. 5, 1991, eff. Jan. 1, 1992. Amended Nov. 13, 1992, eff. Jan. 1, 1993; Dec. 14, 1995, eff. Jan. 1, 1996; Oct. 10, 1996; Dec. 28, 2007, eff. Jan. 1, 2008; Nov. 19, 2009, eff. Jan. 1, 2010; Jan. 19, 2012, eff. May 1, 2012; Dec. 3, 2013, eff. Jan. 1, 2014.

Advisory Committee Comment—2009 Amendment

Rule 304.02 is amended to include section (b)(7) adopted to implement the gathering of information about the potential need for interpreter services in a case, either for witnesses or for a party. *See* Minn. Gen. R. Prac. 8.13.

Advisory Committee Comment—2012 Amendments

Rule 304.02 is amended to reflect the more varied approaches to case management being used in Minnesota courts. The Initial Case Management Statement replaces the former Party's Information Statement form and is intended to be a more flexible device for obtaining information to be used by the court in making case-management decisions. Supplemental information regarding local programs such as Early Case Management and/or Early Neutral Evaluation addressing may require submission of separate information on a separate time deadline.

Advisory Committee Comment—2014 Amendment

The amendments to Rules 304.02 and 304.03 recognize that different districts and counties use different processes for scheduling family law matters. Rule 304.02 is amended to rename the Initial Case Management Statement (formerly known as the Informational Statement) as the Scheduling Statement. This change is intended to make clear the distinction between it and the Initial Case Management Conference (ICMC) Data Sheet used in the many counties that hold Initial Case Management Conferences (ICMCs) and find them useful tools in managing their cases. Pursuant to Judicial Branch Policy 520.1 § IV, the ICMC Data Sheet is not to be filed with the court, but is provided to the court in advance of the ICMC to assist the court in preparing for and holding the ICMC. Further information on the ICMC process, if in use in a particular court, may be obtained on the individual court's websites, which may be accessed through the state court website, www. mncourts.gov.

The Scheduling Statement is formally filed with the court within 60 days of filing of the case. The court's management of the case from and after the ICMC ensures the case is concluded in a timely manner, alleviating the necessity of filing a Scheduling Statement. In counties that do not utilize ICMCs as part of case management, the filing of the Scheduling Statement will assist the court in scheduling appropriate court appearances to conclude the case in a timely manner.

Historical Notes

The order of the Minnesota Supreme Court [CX–89–1863, C6–84–2134] dated December 14, 1995, provides in part that "(t)he attached amendments shall apply to all actions pending on the effective date and to those filed thereafter."

The order of the Minnesota Supreme Court [CX-89-1863] dated October 10, 1996, provides in part that these amendments are effective July 1, 1997, except that rules 119 and 418 are effective January 1, 1997, that these amendments shall apply to all actions pending on the effective dates and to those filed thereafter, and that "(t)he inclusion of Advisory Committee comments is made for convenience and does not reflect court approval of the comments made therein".

The order of the Supreme Court dated November 19, 2009, provided:

"1. The attached amendments to the General Rules of Practice for the District Courts and the Special Rules of Procedure Governing Proceedings under the Minnesota Commitment and Treatment Act be, and the same are, prescribed and promulgated to be effective on January 1, 2010.

"2. The attached amendments shall apply to all actions pending on the effective date and to those filed thereafter.

"3. The inclusion of Advisory Committee comments is made for convenience and does not reflect court approval of the comments made therein."

The order of the Minnesota Supreme Court [ADM09–8009] dated January 19, 2012, provides in part that the amendments to the General Rules of Practice for the District Courts are effective on May 1, 2012, and that the amendments "shall apply to all actions pending on the effective date and to those filed thereafter."

The order of the Minnesota Supreme Court [ADM09–8009] dated December 3, 2013, provided in part that these amendments were effective January 1, 2014, and "shall apply to all actions pending on the effective date and those filed thereafter."

Rule 304.03. Scheduling Order

(a) When Issued. Within thirty days after the expiration of the time set forth in Rule 304.02 for filing a Scheduling Statement, the court shall enter its scheduling order. The court may issue the order after either a telephone or in court conference, or without a conference or hearing if none is needed.

(b) Contents of Order. The scheduling order shall provide for alternative dispute resolution as required by Rule 114.04(c) and may establish any of the following:

(1) Deadlines or specific dates for the completion of alternative dispute resolution including but not limited to mediation and early neutral evaluations;

(2) Deadlines or specific dates for the completion of discovery and other pretrial preparation;

(3) Deadlines or specific dates for serving, filing or hearing motions;

(4) A deadline or specific date for custody, parenting time or property evaluations;

(5) A deadline or specific date for the pretrial conference; and

(6) A deadline or specific date for the trial or final hearing.

Adopted Sept. 5, 1991, eff. Jan. 1, 1992. Amended Oct. 10, 1996; Jan. 19, 2012, eff. May 1, 2012; Dec. 3, 2013, eff. Jan. 1, 2014.

Advisory Committee Comment—2014 Amendment

The amendments to Rules 304.02 and 304.03 recognize that different districts and counties use different processes for scheduling family law matters. Rule 304.02 is amended to rename the Initial Case Management Statement (formerly known as the Informational Statement) as the Scheduling Statement. This change is intended to make clear the distinction between it and the Initial Case Management Conference (ICMC) Data Sheet used in the many counties that hold Initial Case Management Conferences (ICMCs) and find them useful tools in managing their cases. Pursuant to Judicial Branch Policy 520.1 § IV, the ICMC Data Sheet is not to be filed with the court, but is provided to the court in advance of the ICMC to assist the court in preparing for and holding the ICMC. Further information on the ICMC process, if in use in a particular court, may be obtained on the individual court's websites, which may be accessed through the state court website, www. mncourts.gov.

The Scheduling Statement is formally filed with the court within 60 days of filing of the case. The court's management of the case from and after the ICMC ensures the case is concluded in a timely manner, alleviating the necessity of filing a Scheduling Statement. In counties that do not utilize ICMCs as part of case management, the filing of the Scheduling Statement will assist the court in scheduling appropriate court appearances to conclude the case in a timely manner.

Historical Notes

The order of the Minnesota Supreme Court [CX-89-1863] dated October 10, 1996, provides in part that these amendments are effective July 1, 1997, except that rules 119 and 418 are effective January 1, 1997, that these amendments shall apply to all actions pending on the effective dates and to those filed thereafter, and that "(t)he inclusion of Advisory Committee comments is made for convenience and does not reflect court approval of the comments made therein".

The order of the Minnesota Supreme Court [ADM09–8009] dated January 19, 2012, provides in part that the amendments to the General Rules of Practice for the District Courts are effective on May 1, 2012, and that the amendments "shall apply to all actions pending on the effective date and to those filed thereafter."

The order of the Minnesota Supreme Court [ADM09–8009] dated December 3, 2013, provided in part that these amendments were effective January 1, 2014, and "shall apply to all actions pending on the effective date and those filed thereafter."

Rule 304.04. Amendment

A scheduling order pursuant to this rule may be amended at any pretrial or settlement conference, upon motion for good cause shown, or upon stipulation of the parties if approved by the court.

Adopted Sept. 5, 1991, eff. Jan. 1, 1992. Amended Jan. 19, 2012, eff. May 1, 2012.

Advisory Committee Comment—1996 Amendment

This rule is new. It is patterned after the similar new Minn.Gen.R.Prac. 111. The Task Force believes that the scheduling information and procedures in family court and other civil matters should be made as uniform as possible, consistent with the special needs in family court matters. It is amended in 1996 to include information needed for using alternative dispute resolution in family law matters as required by Minn.Gen.R.Prac. 301.01, also as amended in 1996. These amendments follow the form of similar provisions in Minn.Gen.R.Prac. 111, and should be interpreted in the same manner.

Matters not scheduled under the procedures of this rule are scheduled by motion practice under Minn.Gen.R.Prac. 303.

Rule 304.02 now provides a definite time by which informational statements are required, even if a temporary hearing is contemplated and postponed. Under the prior version of the rule, informational statements might never be due because a temporary hearing might be repeatedly postponed. If the parties seek to have a case excluded from the court scheduling process, they may do so by stipulation to have the case placed on "Inactive Status." This stipulation can be revoked by either party, but removes the case from active court calendar management for up to one year. *See* Minnesota Conference of Chief Judges (See Exhibit A), Resolution Relating to the Adoption of Uniform Local Rules, Jan. 25, 1991.

This rule provides for a separate Form 9B for use by unrepresented parties. This form contains additional information useful to the court in managing cases where one or both parties are not represented by a party. This form is updated in 1996 to request information about any history or claims of domestic abuse and the views of the parties on the use (or potential use) of alternative dispute resolution in the same manner as Form 9A for represented parties.

Historical Notes

The order of the Minnesota Supreme Court [ADM09–8009] dated January 19, 2012, provides in part that the amendments to the General Rules of Practice for the District Courts are effective on May 1, 2012, and that the amendments "shall apply to all actions pending on the effective date and to those filed thereafter."

Rule 304.05. Collaborative Law

A scheduling order under this rule may include provision for deferral on the calendar pursuant to Rule 111.05(b) of these rules and for exemption from additional ADR requirements pursuant to Rule 111.05(c).

Adopted Sept. 26, 2007, eff. Jan. 1, 2008.

Advisory Committee Comment—2007 Amendment

Rule 304.05 is a new provision, intended primarily to make it clear that the special scheduling procedures relating to collaborative law in Minn. Gen. R. Pract. 111.05 apply to scheduling of family law matters subject to Rule 304. The rule permits a scheduling order to include provision for collaborative law, but does not require it.

Rule 304.06. Continuances

(a) Trial. Minn. Gen. R. Prac. 122 governs continuances for trial settings unless the court directs otherwise.

(b) Motions and Pretrial. A request for a continuance of a motion or pretrial conference shall be in writing and set forth the basis for the request.

Adopted Jan. 19, 2012, eff. May 1, 2012.

Historical Notes

The order of the Minnesota Supreme Court [ADM09–8009] dated January 19, 2012, provides in part that the amendments to the General Rules of Practice for the District Courts are effective on May 1, 2012, and that the amendments "shall apply to all actions pending on the effective date and to those filed thereafter."

RULE 305. PRETRIAL CONFERENCES

Rule 305.01. Parenting/Financial Disclosure Statement

Each party shall complete a Parenting/Financial Disclosure statement in the form developed by the state court administrator which shall be served upon all parties and filed with the court at least 7 days prior to the date of the pretrial conference.

Adopted Sept. 5, 1991, eff. Jan. 1, 1992. Amended Dec. 28, 2007, eff. Jan. 1, 2008; Jan. 19, 2012, eff. May 1, 2012.

Task Force Comment—1991 Adoption

This rule is derived from existing Rule 4.02 of the Rules of Family Court Procedure. The existing family court rule includes a requirement that information be filed on forms, and that typewritten or word-processed documents would not be accepted for filing. The Task Force considered the desirability of requiring information to be submitted on preprinted forms, and determined that such requirements should not be retained. Many modern law offices cannot readily prepare such documents as word processing machines have displaced the typewriters for which the forms are designed. The Task Force also believes that these requirements only increase the cost of litigation and limit access to the courts.

Historical Notes

The order of the Minnesota Supreme Court [ADM09–8009] dated January 19, 2012, provides in part that the amendments to the General Rules of Practice for the District Courts are effective on May 1, 2012, and that the amendments "shall apply to all actions pending on the effective date and to those filed thereafter."

Rule 305.02. Pretrial Conference Attendance

(a) Parties and Counsel. Unless excused by the court for good cause, the parties and lawyers who will try the proceedings shall attend the pretrial conference, prepared to negotiate a final settlement. The lawyers attending the pretrial conference must have authority to settle the case. If a stipulation is reduced to writing prior to the pretrial conference, the case may be heard administratively or as a default at the time scheduled for the conference. In the event the matter will proceed as a default, then only the party obtaining the decree need appear.

(b) Failure to Appear—Sanctions. If a party fails to appear at a pretrial conference, the court may dispose of the proceedings without further notice to that party.

(c) Failure to Comply—Sanctions. Failure to comply with the rules relating to pretrial conferences may result in the case being stricken from the contested calendar, granting of partial relief to the appearing party, striking of the nonappearing party's pleadings and the hearing of the matter as a default, award of attorney fees and costs, and such other relief as the court finds appropriate, without further notice to the defaulting party.

Adopted Sept. 5, 1991, eff. Jan. 1, 1992. Amended Jan. 19, 2012, eff. May 1, 2012.

Family Court Rules Advisory Committee Commentary

Original Advisory Committee Comment— Not kept current.

In disposing of a proceeding, the Court may dismiss it entirely, grant relief to the party appearing, grant attorney fees, bifurcate the proceedings and grant partial relief, or grant any other relief which the court may deem appropriate. See Rule 306.2(c).

Task Force Comment—1991 Adoption

Subsection (a) of this rule is derived from existing Rule 4.03 of the Rules of Family Court Procedure.

Subsection (b) of this rule is derived from existing Rule 4.04 of the Rules of Family Court Procedure.

Subsection (c) of this rule is derived from existing Rule 4.05 of the Rules of Family Court Procedure.

A prehearing conference without both parties and lawyers familiar with the facts of the case and the parties is rarely a worthwhile exercise and usually is a waste of resources of the parties and the court. Nonetheless, the Task Force believes there may be situations, on rare occasion, where a party or lawyer should be excused from attendance or should be allowed to participate by conference phone call.

Historical Notes

The order of the Minnesota Supreme Court [ADM09–8009] dated January 19, 2012, provides in part that the amendments to the

General Rules of Practice for the District Courts are effective on May 1, 2012, and that the amendments "shall apply to all actions pending on the effective date and to those filed thereafter."

Rule 305.03. Order for Trial or Continued Pretrial Conference

If the parties are unable to resolve the case, in whole or in part, at the pretrial conference, the court shall issue an order that schedules any remaining discovery and any contemplated motions, identifies the contested issues for trial, and provides for the exchange of witness lists and exhibits to be offered at trial. The order shall identify and describe the resolution of uncontested issues that have been placed on the record.

Adopted Sept. 5, 1991, eff. Jan. 1, 1992. Amended Jan. 19, 2012, eff. May 1, 2012.

Task Force Comment—1991 Adoption

This rule is new. The Task Force believes it is useful to have an order entered to limit the issues and preserve any agreements reached at a pretrial conference. This rule is adapted from a recommendation of the Minnesota State Bar Association's Family Law Section.

Cross Reference: Minn. Civ. Trialbook § 5.

Historical Notes

The order of the Minnesota Supreme Court [ADM09-8009] dated January 19, 2012, provides in part that the amendments to the General Rules of Practice for the District Courts are effective on May 1, 2012, and that the amendments "shall apply to all actions pending on the effective date and to those filed thereafter."

RULE 306. DEFAULT

Rule 306.01. Scheduling of Final Hearing

Except when proceeding under Rule 302.01(b) by Joint Petition, Agreement and Judgment and Decree, to place a marriage dissolution matter on the default calendar for final hearing or for approval without hearing pursuant to Minnesota Statutes, section 518.13, subdivision 5, the moving party shall submit a Default Scheduling Request form developed by the state court administrator and shall comply with the following, as applicable:

(a) Without Stipulation—No Appearance. In all default proceedings where a stipulation has not been filed, an Affidavit of Default and of Nonmilitary Status of the defaulting party or a waiver by that party of any rights under the Servicemembers Civil Relief Act, as amended, shall be filed with the court.

(b) Without Stipulation—Appearance. Where the defaulting party has appeared by a pleading other than an answer, or personally without a pleading, and has not affirmatively waived notice of the other party's right to a default hearing, the moving party shall notify the defaulting party in writing at least 14 days before the final hearing of the intent to proceed to Judgment. The notice shall state:

> You are hereby notified that an application has been made for a final hearing to be held on _________, 20 ___, at ___: ___ ___.m. at _________ [a date not sooner than 14 days from the date of this notice]. You are further notified that the court will be requested to grant the relief requested in the petition at the hearing. You should contact the undersigned and the District Court Administrator immediately if you have any defense to assert to this default judgment and decree.

The default hearing will not be held until the notice has been mailed to the defaulting party at the last known address and an affidavit of service by mail has been filed.

If the case is to proceed administratively without a hearing under Minn. Stat. § 518.13, subdivision 5, then the notice shall be sent after the expiration of the 30-day answer period, but at least 14 days before submission of a default scheduling request as required by this rule, and shall state:

> You are hereby notified that an application will be made for a final judgment and decree to be entered not sooner than 14 days from the date of this notice. You are further notified that the court will be requested to grant the relief requested in the Petition. You should contact the undersigned and the District Court Administrator immediately if you have any defense to assert to this default judgment and decree.

(c) Default with Stipulation. Whenever a stipulation settling all issues has been executed by the parties, the stipulation shall be filed with an affidavit of nonmilitary status of the defaulting party or a waiver of that party's rights under the Servicemembers Civil Relief Act, as amended, if not included in the stipulation.

In a stipulation where a party appears pro se, the following waiver shall be executed by that party:

> I know I have the right to be represented by a lawyer of my choice. I hereby expressly waive that right and I freely and voluntarily sign the foregoing stipulation.

Adopted Sept. 5, 1991, eff. Jan. 1, 1992. Amended Nov. 13, 1992, eff. Jan. 1, 1993; Dec. 11, 2003, eff. Jan. 1, 2004; Nov. 30, 2005, eff. Jan. 1, 2006; Dec. 28, 2007, eff. Jan. 1, 2008; Jan. 19, 2012, eff. May 1, 2012.

Family Court Rules Advisory Committee Commentary

Original Advisory Committee Comment— Not kept current.

The stipulation should establish that one of the parties may proceed as if by default, without further notice to or appearance by the other party.

The waiver of counsel should be prepared as an addendum following the parties' signatures on the stipulation.

Advisory Committee Comment—1992 Amendments

Subsections (a) and (b) of this rule are derived from existing Rule 5.01 of the Rules of Family Court Procedure.

Subsection (c) of this rule is derived from existing Rule 5.02 of the Rules of Family Court Procedure.

The default scheduling request required by Rule 306.01, as amended in 1992, serves the purpose of permitting the court administrator's office to schedule the case for the right type of hearing. It is not otherwise involved in the merits. The affidavit of default is a substantive document establishing entitlement to relief by default.

Advisory Committee Comment—2003 Amendment

Rule 306.01 is amended in 2003 to add a new first clause. The purpose of this change is to include in the rules an express exemption of the proceedings from the requirements of the rule when the parties proceed by Joint Petition, Agreement and Judgment and Decree as allowed by new Rule 302.01(b).

Advisory Committee Comment—2006 Amendment

Rule 306 is amended to clarify the role of the notice required to be given to parties who are in default but who have "appeared" in some way. A party is not entitled to prevent entry of judgment if that party is in default by not serving and filing a timely written answer to the Petition. Nonetheless, the court may, in its discretion, consider some appropriate measures to prevent the case from being decided on a default basis and to obviate a motion for relief from the default judgment and decree. Accordingly, the rule is amended to afford more useful notice as to the request for a default.

The rule does not define how a party might appear either by "a pleading other than an answer," or "personally without a pleading." Both conditions should be limited to some actions that approach responding to the Petition despite the fact they may be insufficient as a matter of law to stand as a response. Sending a letter that responds to a Petition might suffice for the first condition, as might a letter to the court. Appearing at a court hearing despite having not answered would certainly meet the "appeared personally" condition. When in doubt as to other circumstances, the party seeking a default should, to comply with Rule 306.01(b), provide the required notice, with the expectation that many of these responses that fall short of an answer will not prevent entry of judgment.

The Soldiers' and Sailors' Civil Relief Act of 1940 was amended and renamed in 2003, and the rule is amended to use the new name as a matter of convenience. *See* Servicemembers Civil Relief Act, Pub. L. No. 108–189, § 1.117 Stat. 2835, 2840–42 (2003) (to be codified at 50 U.S.C. app. § 521). The former rule would still apply, however, because it included the "as amended" extension of the citation.

Advisory Committee Comment—2012 Amendments

Rule 306 attempts to make clear the role of notice required to be given to parties who are in default but who have "appeared" in some way in marriage dissolution proceedings. A party is not entitled to prevent entry of judgment if that party is in default by not serving and filing a timely written answer to the Petition. Nonetheless, the court may, in its discretion, consider some appropriate measures to prevent the case from being decided on a default basis and to obviate a motion for relief from the default judgment and decree. Accordingly, the rule is amended to afford more useful notice as to the request for a default. Defaults in other types of family proceedings are governed by Rule 55 of the Minnesota Rules of Civil Procedure.

The rule does not define how a party might appear either by "a pleading other than an answer," or "personally without a pleading." Both conditions should be limited to actions that approach responding to the Petition despite the fact they may be insufficient as a matter of law to stand as a response. Sending a letter that responds to a Petition might suffice for the first condition, as might a letter to the court. Appearing at a court hearing despite having not answered would certainly meet the "appeared personally" condition. When in doubt as to other circumstances, the party seeking a default should, to comply with Rule 306.01(b), provide the required notice, with the expectation that many of these responses that fall short of an answer will not prevent entry of judgment.

Historical Notes

The order of the Minnesota Supreme Court [CX-89-1863] dated December 11, 2003, provides in part that these amendments are effective January 1, 2004, and shall apply to all actions or proceedings pending on or commenced on or after the effective date.

The order of the Minnesota Supreme Court [CX-89-1863] dated December 11, 2003, provides in part that "(t)he inclusion of Advisory Committee comments is made for convenience and does not reflect court approval of the statements made therein".

The order of the Minnesota Supreme Court [ADM09-8009] dated January 19, 2012, provides in part that the amendments to the General Rules of Practice for the District Courts are effective on May 1, 2012, and that the amendments "shall apply to all actions pending on the effective date and to those filed thereafter."

Rule 306.02. Preparation of Decree [Abrogated]

Advisory Committee Comment—2012 Amendment

Rule 306.02 is abrogated because it sets forth procedures that do not need to be established by rule and in practice individual judges deal with the preparation of a decree in different ways. The court may still require the submission of proposed findings of fact, conclusions of law, order for judgment, and judgment and decree in advance of the hearing.

RULE 307. FINAL HEARINGS

RULE 307. FINAL HEARINGS

(a) Failure to Appear—Sanctions. Failure to appear at the scheduled final hearing may result in the case being stricken from the contested calendar, granting of partial relief to the appearing party, striking of the nonappearing party's pleadings and the hearing of the matter as a default, an award of attorney's fees and costs, and such other relief as the court finds appropriate, without further notice to the defaulting party.

(b) Stipulations Entered in Open Court—Preparation of Findings. Where a stipulation has been entered orally upon the record, the lawyer directed to prepare the decree shall submit it to the court with a copy to each party. Unless a written, fully executed stipulation is filed or unless the decree contains the written approval of the other party or their legal representative, a transcript of the oral stipulation shall be filed by the lawyer directed to prepare the decree. Responsibility for the cost of the transcript shall be determined by the court. Entry of the decree shall be deferred for fourteen (14) days to allow for objections unless the decree contains the written approval of the lawyer for each party, or the other party if not represented.

Adopted Sept. 5, 1991, eff. Jan. 1, 1992. Amended Jan. 19, 2012, eff. May 1, 2012.

Task Force Comment—1991 Adoption

Subsection (a) of this rule is derived from existing Rule 6.01 of the Rules of Family Court Procedure.

Subsection (b) of this rule is derived from existing Rule 6.02 of the Rules of Family Court Procedure.

Historical Notes

The order of the Minnesota Supreme Court [ADM09–8009] dated January 19, 2012, provides in part that the amendments to the General Rules of Practice for the District Courts are effective on May 1, 2012, and that the amendments "shall apply to all actions pending on the effective date and to those filed thereafter."

RULE 308. FINAL ORDER, JUDGMENT OR DECREE

Rule 308.01. Notices; Service

(a) Awards of Child Support and/or Maintenance. All orders, judgments, and decrees that include awards of child support or maintenance, unless otherwise directed by the court, shall include the provisions set forth in Minnesota Statutes section 518.68 (Appendix A).

(b) Public Assistance. When a party is receiving or has applied for public assistance, the party obtaining the judgment and decree shall serve a copy of the judgment and decree on the agency responsible for child support enforcement, and the decree shall direct that all payments of child support and spousal maintenance shall be made to the Minnesota Child Support Central Payment Center for as long as the custodial parent is receiving assistance.

(c) Child Support Enforcement. When a private party has applied for or is using the services of the local child support enforcement agency, a copy of the decree shall be served by mail by the party submitting the decree for execution upon the county agency involved.

(d) Supervised Parenting Time or Visitation. A copy of any judgment and decree or other order directing ongoing supervision of parenting time or visitation shall be provided to the appropriate agency by the party obtaining the decree or other order.

Adopted Sept. 5, 1991, eff. Jan. 1, 1992. Amended Jan. 19, 2012, eff. May 1, 2012.

Family Court Rules Advisory Committee Commentary

Original Advisory Committee Comment—Not kept current.

Minn. Stat. § 518.551 requires that maintenance or support must be ordered payable to the public agency so long as the obligee is receiving public assistance.

Agencies responsible for enforcement of child support in private cases also require a copy of the judgment and decree.

Task Force Comment—1991 Adoption

Subdivision (a) of this rule is derived from existing Rule 7.01 of the Rules of Family Court Procedure. The list of provisions is not set forth in this rule, as it was set forth in full in new Minn. Gen. R. Prac. 303.06.

Subdivision (b) is derived from Rule 7.02 of the Rules of Family Court Procedure, and also in part from Second District Local Rule 7.021.

Subdivision (c) is derived from Second District Local Rule 7.022.

Subdivision (d) of this rule, replacing existing Rule 7.03 of the Rules of Family Court Procedure, was recommended to the Task Force by the Minnesota State Bar Association Family Law Section.

Historical Notes

The order of the Minnesota Supreme Court [ADM09–8009] dated January 19, 2012, provides in part that the amendments to the General Rules of Practice for the District Courts are effective on May 1, 2012, and that the amendments "shall apply to all actions pending on the effective date and to those filed thereafter."

Rule 308.02. Statutorily Required Notices

Where statutes require that certain subjects be addressed by notices in an order or decree, the notices may be set forth in an attachment and incorporated by reference.

Adopted Sept. 5, 1991, eff. Jan. 1, 1992. Amended Jan. 19, 2012, eff. May 1, 2012.

Family Court Rules Advisory Committee Commentary

Original Advisory Committee Comment—Not kept current.

See Rule 10.01, Form 3, for the concept of the form of the attachment.

Task Force Comment—1991 Adoption

This rule is derived from existing Rule 7.04 of the Rules of Family Court Procedure.

Historical Notes

The order of the Minnesota Supreme Court [ADM09-8009] dated January 19, 2012, provides in part that the amendments to the General Rules of Practice for the District Courts are effective on May 1, 2012, and that the amendments "shall apply to all actions pending on the effective date and to those filed thereafter."

Rule 308.03. Sensitive Matters

Whenever the findings of fact include private or sensitive matters as determined by the court, a judgment and decree may be supported by separate documents comprising findings of fact, conclusions of law, and order for judgment.

Adopted Sept. 5, 1991, eff. Jan. 1, 1992. Amended Jan. 19, 2012, eff. May 1, 2012.

Task Force Comment—1991 Adoption

The Task Force recommends repeal of existing Rule 7.05 of the Rules of Family Court Procedure because the requirement for findings is well established by the common law, and a rule recodifying the settled law is surplusage.

The recommended rule is patterned after Second District Rule 7.051. Its purpose is to allow sensitive factual and legal matters to be preserved in separate documents so that the need for disseminating confidential and sensitive matters can be minimized. This rule does not create a right to maintain the privacy of any portion of the findings; it allows the court to create documents that may be useful for some public purposes without including all other parts of the findings.

Historical Notes

The order of the Minnesota Supreme Court [ADM09-8009] dated January 19, 2012, provides in part that the amendments to the General Rules of Practice for the District Courts are effective on May 1, 2012, and that the amendments "shall apply to all actions pending on the effective date and to those filed thereafter."

Rule 308.04. Joint Marital Agreement and Decree

The parties to any marital dissolution proceeding may use a combined agreement and judgment and decree. A judgment and decree that is subscribed to by each party before a notary public and contains a final conclusion of law with words to the effect that "the parties agree that the foregoing Findings of Fact and Conclusions of Law incorporate the complete and full agreement" shall, upon approval and entry by the court, constitute an agreement and judgment and decree for marriage dissolution for all purposes.

Adopted Dec. 28, 2006, eff. Jan. 1, 2007. Amended Jan. 19, 2012, eff. May 1, 2012.

Advisory Committee Comments—2007 Amendment

Rule 308.04 is new. The rule allows parties in any marriage dissolution proceeding, whether commenced by petition or joint petition, to use a combined marital termination agreement and judgment and decree. The primary benefit of this procedure is to reduce the risk of discrepancy between the terms of a marital termination agreement and the judgment and decree it purports to authorize. This procedure should benefit both the parties and the court in streamlining the court procedure where the parties are in agreement. The rule permits the parties to use this procedure by agreement, but does not require its use.

The procedure in Rule 308.04 is similar to the procedure for use of combined Joint Petition, Agreement and Judgment and Decree under Rule 302.01(b)(2), but it is available in all cases where the parties agree on all issues (the Rule 302 procedure may be used only in cases not involving children).

The use of this procedure will result in the marital termination agreement becoming an integral part of the judgment and decree, which will render it a public record. To the extent the parties' agreement contains confidential information, they should consider alternative methods of protecting that information, such as use of separate documents as provided for in Rule 308.03 so the agreement is not filed or the use of the confidentiality protection procedures contained in Minn. Gen. R. Prac. 11.

Advisory Committee Comment—2012 Amendment

Rule 308.02 refers to statutory notice. The legislature has established numerous forms of notice including those required by Minn. Stat. § 518.68. These requirements are met in a two-page notice form, which is known as Appendix A and labeled as FAM 301 on the state court website (www.mncourts.gov, under "Court Forms" click on "Other").

Rule 308.04 allows parties in any marriage dissolution proceeding, whether commenced by petition or joint petition, to use a combined agreement and judgment and decree. The agreement is often termed a "marital termination agreement," but that label is not required by the rule. The primary benefit of this procedure is to reduce the risk of discrepancy between the terms of a marital termination agreement and the judgment and decree it purports to authorize. This procedure should benefit both the parties and the court in streamlining the court procedure where the parties are in agreement. The rule permits the parties to use this procedure by agreement, but does not require its use.

The procedure in Rule 308.04 is similar to the procedure for use of a combined Joint Petition, Agreement and Judgment and Decree under Rule 302.01(b)(2), and is available in all cases where the parties agree on all issues.

The use of this procedure will result in the marital termination agreement becoming an integral part of the judgment and decree, which will render it a public record. To the extent the parties' agreement contains confidential information, they should consider alternative methods of protecting that information, such as use of separate documents as provided for in Rule 308.03 so the agreement is not filed or the use of the confidentiality protection procedures contained in Minn. Gen. R. Prac. 11.

Historical Notes

The order of the Minnesota Supreme Court [ADM09-8009] dated January 19, 2012, provides in part that the amendments to the

General Rules of Practice for the District Courts are effective on May 1, 2012, and that the amendments "shall apply to all actions pending on the effective date and to those filed thereafter."

RULE 309. CONTEMPT

Rule 309.01. Initiation

(a) Moving Papers—Service; Notice. Contempt proceedings may be initiated by notice of motion and motion or by an order to show cause served upon the person of the alleged contemnor together with motions accompanied by appropriate supporting affidavits. Pursuant to Rule 303.05 an order to show cause may be issued by the court without notice to the alleged contemnor provided the supporting affidavits credibly raise an issue of contempt.

(b) Content of Order to Show Cause or Notice of Motion and Motion. The order to show cause shall direct the alleged contemnor to appear and show cause why he or she should not be held in contempt of court and why the moving party should not be granted the relief requested by the motion. If proceeding by notice of motion and motion, the motion may seek that relief directly.

The notice of motion and motion or the order to show cause shall contain at least the following:

(1) a reference to the specific order or judgment of the court alleged to have been violated and the date of entry or filing of the order or judgment;

(2) a quotation of the specific applicable provisions ordered;

(3) the alleged failures to comply;

(4) notice to the alleged contemnor that his or her ability to pay is a crucial issue in the contempt proceeding and that a Parenting/Financial Disclosure Statement form for submitting ability to pay information is available from the state court website, and this form should be served and filed with the court at or before the contempt hearing; and

(5) a date to appear for a Rule 309.02 hearing no later than 60 days after the issuance of the notice of motion or order to show cause.

(c) Affidavits. The supportive affidavit of the moving party shall set forth each alleged violation of the order with particularity. Where the alleged violation is a failure to pay sums of money, the affidavit shall state the kind of payments in default and shall specifically set forth the payment dates and the amounts due, paid and unpaid for each failure.

Any responsive affidavit shall set forth with particularity any defenses the alleged contemnor will present to the court. Where the alleged violation is a failure to pay sums of money, the affidavit shall set forth the nature, dates and amount of payments, if any.

Adopted Sept. 5, 1991, eff. Jan. 1, 1992. Amended Nov. 19, 2009, eff. Jan. 1, 2010; Jan. 19, 2012, eff. May 1, 2012.

Family Court Rules Advisory Committee Commentary

Original Advisory Committee Comment— Not kept current.

Service of the order to show cause upon the person provides jurisdiction for the issuance of a writ of attachment or bench warrant, if necessary, and meets the requirement for an opportunity to be heard. See *Clausen v. Clausen,* 250 Minn. 293, 84 N.W.2d 675 (1976); *Hopp v. Hopp,* 279 Minn. 170, 156 N.W.2d 212 (1968).

Task Force Comment—1991 Adoption

Subdivision (a) of this rule is derived from existing Rule 8.01 of the Rules of Family Court Procedure.

Subdivision (b) of this rule is derived from existing Rule 8.01 of the Rules of Family Court Procedure. The new language is derived from Second District Local Rule 8.011.

Advisory Committee Comment—2009 Amendment

Rule 309.01 is amended in 2009 to remove an apparent requirement that any contempt proceeding be commenced by order to show cause. Although an order to show cause is an available mechanism for initiating contempt proceedings, the authorizing statute also recognizes that these proceedings may be commenced by motion accompanied by appropriate notice. *See* MINN. STAT. § 588.04. The amendment to Rule 309.01 is intended simply to recognize that both mechanisms are available. In many situations, proceeding by order to show cause is preferable. Use of an order to show cause, which is court process served with the same formality as a summons, permits the court to impose sanctions directly upon failure to comply. *See* MINN. STAT. § 588.04. It is the preferred means to commence a contempt proceeding if there is significant risk that the alleged contemnor is likely not to appear in response to a notice of motion.

Advisory Committee Comment—2012 Amendments

Rule 309.01 does not require that contempt proceeding be commenced by an order to show cause, even though that is the most common and most direct means of commencing the proceedings. Although an order to show cause is an available mechanism for initiating contempt proceedings, the authorizing statute also recognizes that these proceedings may be commenced by motion accompanied by appropriate notice. *See* Minn. Stat. § 588.04. The amendment to Rule 309.01 is intended simply to recognize that both mechanisms are available. In many situations, proceeding by order to show cause is preferable. Use of an order to show cause, which is court process served with the same formality as a summons, permits the court to impose sanctions directly upon failure to comply. *See* Minn. Stat. § 588.04. The order to show cause is still the preferred means to commence a contempt proceeding if there is meaningful risk that the alleged contemnor will not to appear in response to a notice of motion. Service of the order to show cause upon the person provides jurisdiction for the issuance of a writ of attachment or bench warrant, if necessary, and meets the requirement for notice of an opportunity to be heard. *See Clausen v. Clausen*, 250 Minn. 293, 84 N.W.2d 675 (1976); *Hopp v. Hopp*, 279 Minn. 170, 156 N.W.2d 212 (1968).

The requirement in Rule 309.01(b)(5) that a hearing be held within 60 days of issuance of an order or notice of motion is intended to create the standard rule and to underscore the importance of holding the hearing promptly so that the contempt issues may be resolved. Where exceptional circumstances are found to exist by the court, the hearing may be held later than 60 days from the order or notice, but it should still be heard by the court as promptly as possible.

Historical Notes

The order of the Supreme Court dated November 19, 2009, provided:

"1. The attached amendments to the General Rules of Practice for the District Courts and the Special Rules of Procedure Governing Proceedings under the Minnesota Commitment and Treatment Act be, and the same are, prescribed and promulgated to be effective on January 1, 2010.

"2. The attached amendments shall apply to all actions pending on the effective date and to those filed thereafter.

"3. The inclusion of Advisory Committee comments is made for convenience and does not reflect court approval of the comments made therein."

The order of the Minnesota Supreme Court [ADM09-8009] dated January 19, 2012, provides in part that the amendments to the General Rules of Practice for the District Courts are effective on May 1, 2012, and that the amendments "shall apply to all actions pending on the effective date and to those filed thereafter."

Rule 309.02. Hearing

The alleged contemnor must appear in person before the court to be afforded the opportunity to respond to the motion for contempt by sworn testimony. The court shall not act upon affidavit alone, absent express waiver by the alleged contemnor of the right to offer sworn testimony.

Adopted Sept. 5, 1991, eff. Jan. 1, 1992. Amended Jan. 19, 2012, eff. May 1, 2012.

Family Court Rules Advisory Committee Commentary

Original Advisory Committee Comment— Not kept current.

For the right to counsel in contempt proceedings, see *Cox v. Slama*, 355 N.W.2d 401 (Minn. 1984).

Task Force Comment—1991 Adoption

This rule is derived from existing Rule 8.02 of the Rules of Family Court Procedure.

Historical Notes

The order of the Minnesota Supreme Court [ADM09-8009] dated January 19, 2012, provides in part that the amendments to the General Rules of Practice for the District Courts are effective on May 1, 2012, and that the amendments "shall apply to all actions pending on the effective date and to those filed thereafter."

Rule 309.03. Sentencing

(a) Default of Conditions for Stay. Where the court has entered an order for contempt with a stay of sentence and there has been a default in the performance of the condition(s) for the stay, before a writ of attachment or a bench warrant will be issued, an affidavit of noncompliance and request for writ of attachment must be served upon the person of the defaulting party, unless the person is shown to be avoiding service.

(b) Writ of Attachment. The writ of attachment shall direct law enforcement officers to bring the defaulting party before the court for a hearing to show cause why the stay of sentence should not be revoked. A proposed order for writ of attachment shall be submitted to the court by the moving party.

Adopted Sept. 5, 1991, eff. Jan. 1, 1992.

Task Force Comment—1991 Adoption

Subdivision (a) of this rule is derived from existing Rule 8.03 of the Rules of Family Court Procedure.

Subdivision (b) of this rule is derived from existing Rule 8.03 of the Rules of Family Court Procedure, with the new language added from Second District Rule 8.031.

Rule 309.04. Findings

An order finding contempt must be accompanied by appropriate findings of fact.

Adopted Jan. 19, 2012, eff. May 1, 2012.

Advisory Committee Comment—2012 Amendments

Rule 309.04 requires findings. Findings are required to permit appellate review of a contempt order. In cases where incarceration is a consequence of a contempt finding, due process may require notice to the alleged contemnor of the right to show inability to pay and findings on that issue. *See Turner v. Rogers*, 564 U.S. ___, 131 S. Ct. 2507, 180 L. Ed. 2d 254 (2011).

Historical Notes

The order of the Minnesota Supreme Court [ADM09-8009] dated January 19, 2012, provides in part that the amendments to the General Rules of Practice for the District Courts are effective on May 1, 2012, and that the amendments "shall apply to all actions pending on the effective date and to those filed thereafter."

RULE 310. ALTERNATIVE DISPUTE RESOLUTION

Rule 310.01. Applicability

(a) When ADR Required. All family law matters in district court are subject to Alternative Dispute Resolution (ADR) processes as established in Rule 114, except for:

1. actions enumerated in Minn. Stat., ch. 518B (Domestic Abuse Act),
2. contempt actions, and

3. maintenance, support, and parentage actions when the public agency responsible for child support enforcement is a party or is providing services to a party with respect to the action.

(b) ADR When There Is Domestic Abuse. The court shall not require parties to participate in any facilitative process if one of the parties claims to be the victim of domestic abuse by the other party or if the court determines there is probable cause that one of the parties or a child of the parties has been physically abused or threatened with physical abuse by the other party. In circumstances when the court is satisfied that the parties have been advised by counsel and have agreed to an ADR process established in Rule 114 that will not require face-to-face meeting of the parties, the court may direct that the ADR process be used.

The court shall not require parties to attempt ADR if they have previously engaged in an ADR process under Rule 114 with a qualified neutral and reached an impasse.

Adopted Oct. 10, 1996. Amended Jan. 19, 2012, eff. May 1, 2012.

Advisory Committee Comment—1996 Amendment

This rule is changed from a limited rule dealing only with mediation to the main family law rule governing use of ADR. All of the provisions of the existing rule are deleted because their subject matter is now governed by either the amended rule or Minn.Gen.R.Prac. 114.

The committee believes that there are significant and compelling reasons to have all court-annexed ADR governed by a single rule. This will streamline the process and make it more cost-effective for litigants, and will also make the process easier to understand for ADR providers and neutrals, many of whom are not lawyers.

The rule is not intended to discourage settlement efforts in any action. In cases where any party has been, or claims to have been, a victim of domestic violence, however, courts need to be especially cautious. Facilitative processes, particularly mediation, are especially prone to abuse since they place the parties in direct contact and may encourage them to compromise their rights in situations where their independent decision-making capacity is limited. The rule accordingly prohibits their use where those concerns are present.

Historical Notes

The order of the Minnesota Supreme Court [CX-89-1863] dated October 10, 1996, provides in part that these amendments are effective July 1, 1997, except that rules 119 and 418 are effective January 1, 1997, that these amendments shall apply to all actions pending on the effective dates and to those filed thereafter, and that "(t)he inclusion of Advisory Committee comments is made for convenience and does not reflect court approval of the comments made therein".

The order of the Minnesota Supreme Court [ADM09–8009] dated January 19, 2012, provides in part that the amendments to the General Rules of Practice for the District Courts are effective on May 1, 2012, and that the amendments "shall apply to all actions pending on the effective date and to those filed thereafter."

Former Rule: A former Rule 310.01, adopted Sept. 5, 1991, related to an order for mediation.

Rule 310.02. Post–Decree Matters

The court may order ADR under Rule 114 in matters involving post-decree relief. The parties shall discuss the use of ADR as part of the settlement conference required by Rule 303.03(c).

Adopted Oct. 10, 1996.

Advisory Committee Comment—1996 Amendment

This rule expressly provides for use of ADR in post-decree matters. This is appropriate because such matters constitute a significant portion of the litigation in family law and because these matters are often quite susceptible to successful resolution in ADR.

The committee believes the existing mechanism requiring the parties to confer before filing any motion other than a motion for temporary relief provides a suitable mechanism for considering ADR and Rule 303.03(c) is amended to remind the parties of this obligation.

Historical Notes

The order of the Minnesota Supreme Court [CX-89-1863] dated October 10, 1996, provides in part that these amendments are effective July 1, 1997, except that rules 119 and 418 are effective January 1, 1997, that these amendments shall apply to all actions pending on the effective dates and to those filed thereafter, and that "(t)he inclusion of Advisory Committee comments is made for convenience and does not reflect court approval of the comments made therein".

Former Rule: A former Rule 310.02, adopted Sept. 5, 1991, related to the appointment of mediators.

Rule 310.03. Deleted Oct. 10. 1996

Historical Notes

The order of the Minnesota Supreme Court [CX-89-1863] dated October 10, 1996, provides in part that these amendments are effective July 1, 1997, except that rules 119 and 418 are effective January 1, 1997, that these amendments shall apply to all actions pending on the effective dates and to those filed thereafter, and that "(t)he inclusion of Advisory Committee comments is made for convenience and does not reflect court approval of the comments made therein".

Rule 310.04. Deleted Oct. 10, 1996

Historical Notes

The order of the Minnesota Supreme Court [CX-89-1863] dated October 10, 1996, provides in part that these amendments are effective July 1, 1997, except that rules 119 and 418 are effective January 1, 1997, that these amendments shall apply to all actions pending on the effective dates and to those filed thereafter, and that "(t)he inclusion of Advisory Committee comments is made for convenience and does not reflect court approval of the comments made therein".

Rule 310.05. Deleted Oct. 10, 1996

Historical Notes

The order of the Minnesota Supreme Court [CX-89-1863] dated October 10, 1996, provides in part that these amendments are effective July 1, 1997, except that rules 119 and 418 are effective January 1, 1997, that these amendments shall apply to all actions pending on the effective dates and to those filed thereafter, and that "(t)he inclusion of Advisory Committee comments is made for convenience and does not reflect court approval of the comments made therein".

Rule 310.06. Deleted Oct. 10, 1996

Historical Notes

The order of the Minnesota Supreme Court [CX-89-1863] dated October 10, 1996, provides in part that these amendments are effective July 1, 1997, except that rules 119 and 418 are effective January 1, 1997, that these amendments shall apply to all actions pending on the effective dates and to those filed thereafter, and that "(t)he inclusion of Advisory Committee comments is made for convenience and does not reflect court approval of the comments made therein".

Rule 310.07. Deleted Oct. 10, 1996

Historical Notes

The order of the Minnesota Supreme Court [CX-89-1863] dated October 10, 1996, provides in part that these amendments are effective July 1, 1997, except that rules 119 and 418 are effective January 1, 1997, that these amendments shall apply to all actions pending on the effective dates and to those filed thereafter, and that "(t)he inclusion of Advisory Committee comments is made for convenience and does not reflect court approval of the comments made therein".

Rule 310.08. Deleted Oct. 10, 1996

Historical Notes

The order of the Minnesota Supreme Court [CX-89-1863] dated October 10, 1996, provides in part that these amendments are effective July 1, 1997, except that rules 119 and 418 are effective January 1, 1997, that these amendments shall apply to all actions pending on the effective dates and to those filed thereafter, and that "(t)he inclusion of Advisory Committee comments is made for convenience and does not reflect court approval of the comments made therein".

Rule 310.09. Deleted Oct. 10, 1996

Historical Notes

The order of the Minnesota Supreme Court [CX-89-1863] dated October 10, 1996, provides in part that these amendments are effective July 1, 1997, except that rules 119 and 418 are effective January 1, 1997, that these amendments shall apply to all actions pending on the effective dates and to those filed thereafter, and that "(t)he inclusion of Advisory Committee comments is made for convenience and does not reflect court approval of the comments made therein".

RULE 311. FORMS

The forms developed by the state court administrator are sufficient under these rules. Forms are currently maintained on the state court website (www.mncourts.gov). Court Administrators in each Judicial District shall make the forms available to the public at a reasonable cost.

Adopted Sept. 5, 1991, eff. Jan. 1, 1992. Amended Dec. 28, 2007, eff. Jan. 1, 2008; Jan. 19, 2012, eff. May 1, 2012.

Task Force Comment—1991 Adoption

This rule is derived from existing Rule 10.01 of the Rules of Family Court Procedure.

Advisory Committee Comment

The responsibility for forms development and review is being handed off to the state court administrator to permit more effective forms management and review. This process is already followed for the expedited process. Gen. R. Prac. 379.02.

Advisory Committee Comment—2012 Amendments

Rule 311 establishes that court-established forms for family matters are deemed sufficient under the rules. These specific forms are not required to be used, but they contain what is required and are therefore appropriate for use.

These rules direct the state court administrator to develop various forms: See Rules 303.02(b) (Parenting/Financial Disclosure Statement); 303. 03(c) (Certificate of Settlement Efforts); 304.02(Initial Case Management Statement); 305.01(Parenting/Financial Disclosure Statement); and 306.01 (Default Scheduling Request). By maintaining the forms on the courts' website they can be readily updated and distributed to all potential users.

Historical Notes

The order of the Minnesota Supreme Court [ADM09–8009] dated January 19, 2012, provides in part that the amendments to the General Rules of Practice for the District Courts are effective on May 1, 2012, and that the amendments "shall apply to all actions pending on the effective date and to those filed thereafter."

RULE 312. REVIEW OF REFEREE'S FINDINGS OR RECOMMENDATIONS

Review of decisions of district court referees is controlled by applicable statutes and order of the supreme court.

Adopted Jan. 19, 2012, eff. May 1, 2012.

Advisory Committee Comment—2012 Amendments

Rule 312 is amended to replace the former rule, which established now-obsolete procedures for review of the findings or recommendations of a district court referee in family law matters. Family court referees are now used in limited circumstances in two districts, and the processes followed are established by statute and supreme court orders. Under Minn. Stat. § 484.65, subd. 9, recommended orders and findings of Fourth Judicial District referees are subject to confirmation by a district court judge, and once confirmed by the district court judge the orders and findings may be appealed directly to the court of appeals. Essentially the same is true in the Second Judicial District under a series of orders establishing a pilot project that is still operating. The history of the pilot project is set forth by the Minnesota Court of Appeals in its Special Term Opinion in *Culver v. Culver*, 771 N.W.2d 547 (Minn. Ct. App. 2009):

The pilot project came into existence in the Second Judicial District in 1996. *See* 1996 Minn. Laws ch. 365, § 2 (allowing Second Judicial District to implement pilot project assigning related family matters to single judge or referee); In re Second Judicial Dist. Combined Family, Civil Harassment, Juvenile Probate Jurisdiction Pilot Project, No. CX–89–1863 (Minn. Apr. 10, 1996) (suspending, in light of pilot project, Minn. R. Gen. Pract. 312.01, which recites procedure for district-court review upon filing of petition for review). The suspension is still in effect. *See* 1998 Minn. Laws ch. 367, art. 1142 11, § 26 (extending pilot-project legislation); 2000 Minn. Law ch. 452, § 1 (same); 2002 Minn.

Law ch. 242 (same); In re Second Judicial Dist. Combined Family, Civil Harassment, Juvenile Probate Jurisdiction Pilot Project, No. CX–89–1863 (Minn. June 17, 1998) (extending suspension); (Minn. May 23, 2000) (same); (Minn. June 3, 2002) (extending suspension until further order of supreme court).

Id., n.1.

RULE 313. CONFIDENTIAL NUMBERS AND TAX RETURNS

The requirements of Rule 11 of these rules regarding submission of restricted identifiers (e.g., social security numbers, employer identification numbers, financial account numbers) and financial source documents (e.g., tax returns, wage stubs, credit card statements) apply to all family court matters.

Amended May 6, 2005, eff. July 1, 2005.

RULE 314. PARENTAGE PROCEEDINGS

In proceedings to determine parentage, the following additional rules apply:

(a) Parentage proceedings are commenced by a Summons and Complaint.

(b) The parties in parentage proceedings are one or more Petitioners and one or more Respondents, and must be so named in the initial pleadings. After so designating the parties, it is permissible to use descriptive labels as allowed by Rule 302.02(a).

(c) Upon proper demand, the parties to parentage proceedings may obtain a jury trial.

Adopted Jan. 19, 2012, eff. May 1, 2012.

Advisory Committee Comment—2012 Amendments

Rule 314 is a new rule, included to collect in one place the special procedures followed in parentage (paternity) cases. The rule is not the source of the procedures set forth in the rule; these procedures are either dictated by statute or common law. *See, e.g.,* Minn. Stat. §§ 257.57, 257.67 (commencement of parentage action and specifying that the proper designation of parties in family court proceedings is as petitioner and respondent). Where a proceeding is commenced jointly, both parties may be designated as copetitioners or as petitioner and co-petitioner. The rule permits the parties, once properly designated in the appropriate pleadings, to be designated by less formal terms that indicate their relationship. *See* Rule 302.02(a). Parentage proceedings may be brought by a parent as well as a governmental entity, thus the provision for plural petitioners in Rule 314(b); they are commonly brought against multiple respondents.

Rule 314 provides additional rules applicable to parentage proceedings. As to a wide array of procedural matters not addressed in this rule, other rules govern their use. Rule 301.01; *see, e.g.,* Minn. R. Civ. P. 56 (summary judgment); Minn. R. Civ. P. 55 (default).

PART. B. EXPEDITED CHILD SUPPORT PROCESS RULES

1999 Order

The order of the Minnesota Supreme Court [C4-99-404] dated June 23, 1999, provides in part:

"1. The attached Expedited Child Support Process Rules are hereby prescribed and promulgated as Interim Rules to be effective beginning July 1, 1999, except that Rules 10.03 through 10.11 shall be effective on October 1, 1999. These Interim Rules shall remain in effect through June 30, 2000.

"2. The Interim Expedited Child Support Process Rules shall apply to all child support matters pending on July 1, 1999, in the administrative process authorized by Minn. Stat. §§ 518.5511 and 518.5512 and to all child support matters subject to the Interim Expedited Child Support Process Rules that are commenced on or after July 1, 1999.

"3. This court's Order Establishing Transition Rules For Child Support Matters filed on April 16, 1999, remains in full force and effect.

"4. The inclusion of Advisory Committee comments in the Interim Rules is made solely for purpose of convenience and does not reflect court approval of the comments.

2000 Order

The order of the Minnesota Supreme Court [C4–99–404] dated June 19, 2000, provides that the Interim Rules of the Expedited Child Support Process are effective from July 1, 1999, through June 30, 2001.

2001 Order

The order of the Minnesota Supreme Court [C4-99-404] dated May 30, 2001, provides in part:

"1. The attached Interim Rules of the Expedited Child Support Process are hereby repealed in its entirety effective July 1, 2001.

"2. The attached Expedited Child Support Process Rules are hereby prescribed and promulgated as Final Rules to be effective beginning July 1, 2001.

"3. These final rules shall apply to all expedited child support actions or proceedings pending on or commenced on or after the effective date.

"4. The inclusion of Advisory Committee comments in the Final Rules is made solely for the purpose of convenience and does not reflect court approval of the comments.

"IT IS FURTHER ORDERED THAT the following transition rules shall govern all support proceedings conducted in the expedited child support process:

"1. Through June 30, 2001, IV–D child support matters shall continue to be initiated and processed in conformity with the Interim Expedited Child Support Process Rules. If a proceeding is properly commenced prior to July 1, 2001, the filing of additional pleadings to maintain the action thereafter shall not be required.

"2. Any order issued in conformity with the Interim Expedited Child Support Process Rules prior to July 1, 2001 shall remain effective and fully enforceable by the district courts on and after July 1, 2001."

2003 Order

The order of the Minnesota Supreme Court [C4-99-404] dated September 23, 2003, provides in part:

"1. The attached amendments to the Rules of the Expedited Child Support Process be, and the same are, prescribed and promulgated to be effective on November 1, 2003.

"2. These amendments shall apply to all actions or proceedings pending on or commenced on or after the effective date.

"3. The inclusion of Advisory Committee comments is made for convenience and does not reflect court approval of the statements made therein."

Renumbering

The Interim Expedited Child Support Process Rules, which were adopted as a separate set of rules by court order dated June 23, 1999, were relocated to rules 351 to 375 of the General Rules of Practice for the District Courts by court order dated December 17, 1999.

I. GENERAL RULES

RULE 351. SCOPE; PURPOSE

Rule 351.01. Scope

These rules govern the procedure for all proceedings conducted in the expedited process, regardless of whether the presiding officer is a child support magistrate, family court referee, or district court judge. The Minnesota Rules of Civil Procedure, Minnesota Rules of Evidence, and other provisions of the Minnesota General Rules of Practice for the District Courts shall apply to proceedings in the expedited process unless inconsistent with these rules. These rules do not apply to matters commenced in or referred to district court.

Adopted May 30, 2001, eff. July 1, 2001.

Rule 351.02. Purposes and Goals of the Expedited Child Support Process

Subdivision 1. Purposes. The purposes of these rules are to establish an expedited process that:

(a) is streamlined;

(b) is uniform across the state;

(c) is easily accessible to the parties; and

(d) results in timely and consistent issuance of orders.

Subd. 2. Goals. These rules should be construed to:

(a) be a constitutional system;

(b) be an expedited process;

(c) be family and user friendly;

(d) be fair to the parties;

(e) be a cost-effective system;

(f) address local administration and implementation concerns;

(g) maintain simple administrative procedures and focus on problem cases;

(h) comply with federal and state laws;

(i) maximize federal financial participation;

(j) ensure consistent decisions statewide; and

(k) have adequate financial and personnel resources.

Adopted May 30, 2001, eff. July 1, 2001.

RULE 352. DEFINITIONS

Rule 352.01. Definitions

For purposes of these rules, the following terms have the following meanings:

(a) **"Answer"** means a written document responding to the allegations of a complaint or motion.

(b) **"Child support"** means basic support; child care support; and medical support. Medical support includes the obligation to carry health care coverage, costs for health care coverage, and unreimbursed / uninsured medical expenses.

(c) **"Child support magistrate"** means an individual appointed by the chief judge of the judicial district to preside over matters in the expedited process. "Child support magistrate" also means any family court referee or district court judge presiding over matters in the expedited process.

(d) **"County agency"** means the local public authority responsible for child support enforcement.

(e) **"County attorney"** means the attorney who represents the county agency, whether that person is employed by the office of the county attorney or under contract with the office of the county attorney.

(f) **"Initiating party"** means a person or county agency starting the proceeding in the expedited process by serving and filing a complaint or motion.

(g) **"IV–D case"** means any proceeding where a party has either (1) assigned to the State rights to child support because of the receipt of public assistance as defined in Minn. Stat. § 256.741, subd. 1(b) (2006), or (2) applied for child support services under Title IV–D of the Social Security Act, 42 U.S.C. § 654(4) (2006). "IV–D case" does not include proceedings where income withholding is the only service applied for or received under Minn. Stat. § 518A.53 (2006).

(h) "Noninitiating party" means a person or county agency responding to a complaint or motion, including any person who assigned to the State rights to child support because of the receipt of public assistance or applied-for child support services.

(i) "Parentage" means the establishment of the existence or non-existence of the parent-child relationship.

(j) "Parenting time" means the time a parent spends with a child regardless of the custodial designation regarding the child. "Parenting time" previously was known as "visitation."

(k) "Party" means any person or county agency with a legal right to participate in the proceedings.

(*l*) "Response" means a written answer to the complaint or motion, a "request for hearing" form, or, in a parentage matter, a "request for blood or genetic testing" form.

(m) "Support" means child support, as defined in this rule; expenses for confinement and pregnancy; arrearages; reimbursement; past support; related costs and fees; and interest and penalties. "Support" also means the enforcement of spousal maintenance when combined with basic support, child care support, or medical support

Adopted May 30, 2001, eff. July 1, 2001. Amended Nov. 12, 2008, eff. June 1, 2009.

Advisory Committee Comment—2008 Amendment

Rule 352.01 is amended to reflect the recodification, effective on January 1, 2007, of portions of the relevant statutes, that became part of Minn. Stat. ch. 518A. Rule 352.01(b) provides a new definition for "child support," replacing the definition of "support" formerly set forth in Rule 352.01(*l*).

RULE 353. TYPES OF PROCEEDINGS

Rule 353.01. Types of Proceedings

Subdivision 1. Mandatory Proceedings. Proceedings to establish, modify, and enforce support shall be conducted in the expedited process if the case is a IV–D case, except as provided in subdivision 2 and Rule 353.02. Proceedings to enforce spousal maintenance, including spousal maintenance cost-of-living adjustment proceedings, shall, if combined with a support issue, be conducted in the expedited process if the case is a IV–D case, except as provided in subdivision 2 and Rule 353.02.

Subd. 2. Permissive Proceedings.

(a) County Option. At the option of each county, the following proceedings may be initiated in the expedited process if the case is a IV–D case, except to the extent prohibited by subdivision 3:

(1) parentage actions; and

(2) civil contempt matters.

(b) Parentage Actions. Any order issued pursuant to Rule 353.01, subd. 2(b) shall address the financial issues if appropriate, whether or not agreed upon by the parties.

(1) Complete Order. Notwithstanding subdivision 3, a child support magistrate has the authority to establish the parent-child relationship, legal and physical custody, parenting time, and the legal name of the child when:

(A) the parties agree or stipulate to all of these particular issues; or

(B) the pleadings specifically address these particular issues and a party fails to serve a response or appear at the hearing.

If all of the otherwise prohibited issues above have been resolved on a permanent basis, the child support magistrate shall issue an order which shall be a final determination of all claims raised in the parentage action.

(2) Partial Order.

(A) Minimal Requirements. If the parties at least agree to the parent-child relationship and temporary or permanent physical custody, the child support magistrate shall issue an order:

(1) establishing the parent-child relationship; and

(2) establishing temporary or permanent physical custody.

(B) Further Agreed Upon Issues. The order of the child support magistrate shall also establish parenting time and the legal name of the child if the parties so agree.

The order is final as to the parent-child relationship. The order is also final as to any agreement concerning permanent legal or physical custody, parenting time, name of the child, and any financial issues decided by the child support magistrate. If there is no agreement concerning permanent legal and/or physical custody, parenting time, or the legal name of the child, those issues shall be referred to the district court. The issues referred to district court are considered pending before the district court and are not final until the district court issues an order deciding those issues. The order of the child support magistrate referring the remaining issues to district court is not appealable pursuant to Rule 378. This rule shall not limit the right to appeal the district court's order. When one or more issues are referred to district court, service of the summons and complaint in the expedited process is sufficient for the matter to proceed in district court.

(3) Order When Parent–Child Relationship Not Resolved. In an action to establish parentage, if the parties do not agree to the parent-child relationship and the temporary or permanent physical custody, the child support magistrate shall make findings and issue an order as follows.

(A) Blood or Genetic Testing Not Completed. When the issue of the parent-child relationship is not resolved and genetic testing has not been completed, the child support magistrate shall order genetic testing and shall continue the hearing in the expedited process to allow the tests to be completed and the results to be received.

(B) Blood or Genetic Testing Completed. When genetic testing has been completed, if the parties still disagree about the parent-child relationship, the child support magistrate shall refer the entire matter to district court for further proceedings. The child support magistrate may set temporary support pursuant to Rule 371.11, subd. 2.

(c) Change of Venue. Upon motion by a party for a change of venue, a child support magistrate shall issue the following order:

(1) Upon consent of all parties, a child support magistrate may issue an order changing venue. The court administrator shall forward the court file to the county that has been granted venue.

(2) If any party disputes a motion to change venue, the child support magistrate shall issue an order referring the matter to district court and the court administrator shall schedule the matter for hearing. The court administrator shall mail notice of the date, time, and location of the hearing to all parties.

Subd. 3. Prohibited Proceedings and Issues. The following proceedings and issues shall not be conducted or decided in the expedited process:

(a) non–IV–D cases;

(b) establishment, modification, or enforcement of custody or parenting time under Minn. Stat. ch. 518 (2000), unless authorized in subdivision 2;

(c) establishment or modification of spousal maintenance;

(d) issuance, modification, or enforcement of orders for protection under Minn. Stat. ch. 518B;

(e) division of marital property;

(f) determination of parentage, except as permitted by subdivision 2(b);

(g) evidentiary hearings to establish custody, parenting time, or the legal name of the child under Minn. Stat. ch. 257 (2000);

(h) evidentiary hearings in contempt matters;

(i) matters of criminal contempt;

(j) motions to change venue, except as permitted in subdivision 2;

(k) enforcement proceedings prohibited in Rule 373.01;

(*l*) matters of criminal non-support;

(m) motions to vacate a recognition of paternity or paternity adjudication; and

(n) the constitutionality of the statutes and rules.

Adopted May 30, 2001, eff. July 1, 2001. Amended Sept. 23, 2003, eff. Nov. 1, 2003.

Rule 353.02. Procedure When Prohibited Issues

Subdivision 1. Generally. These rules do not prevent a party, upon timely notice to all parties and to the county agency, from commencing a proceeding or bringing a motion in district court if the proceeding or motion involves one or more issues identified in Rule 353.01, subd. 1, and one or more issues identified in Rule 353.01, subd. 3.

Subd. 2. Multiple Issues in District Court. If a proceeding is commenced in district court, the district court judge shall decide all issues before the court. If the district court judge cannot decide the support issues without an additional hearing, the district court judge shall determine whether it is in the best interests of the parties to retain the support issues or refer them to the expedited process for decision by a magistrate. If the district court judge refers the support issues to the magistrate, the referral shall include a clear statement of the issues referred and a description of the additional information needed, and shall provide the date, time, and location of the continued hearing. If possible at the time of the referral, the district court judge shall decide temporary support. A matter referred to district court pursuant to subdivision 3 shall be decided in its entirety by the district court judge and shall not be referred back to the expedited process. After the district court judge has issued a final order in the matter, subsequent review or motions may be heard in the expedited process.

Subd. 3. Prohibited Issues in Expedited Child Support Process. If a proceeding is commenced in the expedited process and the complaint, motion, answer, responsive motion, or counter motion raises one or more issues identified in Rule 353.01, subd. 3, all parties, including the county agency, may agree in writing to refer the entire matter to district court without first appearing before the child support magistrate. Notice of the agreement must be filed with the court at least five (5) days prior to the scheduled hearing in the expedited process. The child support magistrate shall issue an order referring the entire matter to district court. Absent an agreement by all parties and upon motion of a party or upon the child support magistrate's own initiative, the child support magistrate assigned to the matter shall, either before or at the time of the hearing, decide whether to:

(a) refer the entire matter to district court; or

(b) determine the temporary support amount and refer all issues to district court. The district court judge shall issue an order addressing all issues and, with respect to support, may adopt and incorporate by reference the findings and order of the child support magistrate. If the district court judge does not adopt the findings and order of the child support magistrate, the judge shall make the necessary findings and order regarding permanent support. In the alternative, the order for temporary support shall become permanent upon the dismissal or withdrawal of the prohibited issue referred to district court. If the district court order fails to address the issue of permanent support, the order for temporary support shall become permanent and shall be deemed incorporated upon issuance of the district court order. If the district court judge fails to issue an order, on the 180th day after service of the notice of filing of the order for temporary support, the order for temporary support shall become permanent.

When a matter is referred to district court, service of the summons and complaint or notice of motion and motion in the expedited process is sufficient for the matter to proceed in district court. A child support magistrate's order that refers a matter to the district court calendar shall provide the date, time, and location of the continued hearing.

Adopted May 30, 2001, eff. July 1, 2001. Amended Sept. 23, 2003, eff. Nov. 1, 2003.

RULE 354. COMPUTATION OF TIME

Rule 354.01. Generally

All time periods shall be measured by starting to count on the first day after any event happens which by these rules starts the running of a time period. When the last day of the time period is any day other than a business day, then the last day is the next business day.

Adopted May 30, 2001, eff. July 1, 2001.

Rule 354.02. Time Periods Less Than Seven Days

When any prescribed time period is less than seven (7) days, only business days shall be counted.

Adopted May 30, 2001, eff. July 1, 2001.

Rule 354.03. "Business Day" Defined

A "business day" means any day that is not a Saturday, Sunday, or legal holiday. As used in these rules, "legal holiday" means New Year's Day, Martin Luther King's Birthday, Washington's and Lincoln's Birthday (Presidents' Day), Memorial Day, Independence Day, Labor Day, Columbus Day, Veteran's Day, Thanksgiving Day, the day after Thanksgiving Day, Christmas Day, and any other day designated as a holiday by the President or Congress of the United States, by the State, or by a county.

Adopted May 30, 2001, eff. July 1, 2001. Amended Nov. 12, 2008, eff. June 1, 2009.

Advisory Committee Comment

State-Level Judicial–Branch Holidays. The legal holidays listed in Rule 354.03 are based upon Minn. Stat. § 645.44, subd. 5 (2000), which defines state-level judicial-branch holidays. The statute further provides that when New Year's Day (January 1), Independence Day (July 4), Veteran's Day (November 11), or Christmas Day (December 25) falls on a Sunday, the following day (Monday) shall be a holiday, and that when New Year's Day, Independence Day, Veteran's Day, or Christmas Day falls on a Saturday, the preceding day (Friday) shall be a holiday. Minn. Stat. § 645.44, subd. 5, also authorizes the judicial branch to designate certain other days as holidays. The Judicial Branch Personnel Plan designates the Friday after Thanksgiving as a holiday.

County Holidays. Counties are authorized to close county offices on certain days under Minn. Stat. § 373.052 (2000). Thus, if a county closes its offices under Minn. Stat. § 373.052 on a day that is not a state-level judicial-branch holiday, such as Christopher Columbus Day (the second Monday in October), the court in that county would nevertheless include that day as a holiday for the purpose of computing time under Rule 354.03. *See Mittelstadt v. Breider*, 286 Minn. 211, 212, 175 N.W.2d 191, 192 (1970) (applying Minn. Stat. § 373.052 to filing of notice of election contest with district court). If a county does not close its offices on a day that is a state-level judicial-branch holiday, such as the Friday after Thanksgiving, the court in that county must still include that day as a holiday for the purpose of computing time under Rule 354.03.

Advisory Committee Comment—2008 Amendment

In 2006 the Minnesota Supreme Court addressed the ambiguity in the rules and the ambiguity between the rules and statutes over how Columbus Day should be treated. Columbus Day is only optionally a state holiday (by statute the different branches can elect to treat it as a holiday) but is uniformly a federal and U.S. Mail holiday. Because the rules generally allow service by mail, the Court in *Commandeur LLC v. Howard Hartry, Inc.*, 724 N.W.2d 508 (Minn. 2006), ruled that where the last day of a time period occurred on Columbus Day, service by mail permitted by the rules was timely if mailed on the following day on which mail service was available. The amendment to Rule 354.03 makes it clear that Columbus Day is a "legal holiday" for all purposes in these rules, even if that is not necessarily so by the statutory definition. Minn. Stat. § 645.44, subd. 5 (2008).

Rule 354.04. Additional Time If Service by Mail or Service Late in Day

Whenever a person has the right or is required to do an act within a prescribed period of time after service of a notice or other paper and the notice or other paper is served by U.S. mail, three (3) days shall be added to the prescribed time period. If service is made by any means other than by U.S. mail and accomplished after 5:00 p.m. Central Time, one (1) additional day shall be added to the prescribed time period.

Adopted May 30, 2001, eff. July 1, 2001.

RULE 355. METHODS OF SERVICE

Rule 355.01. Generally

Subdivision 1. Service Required. Except for ex parte motions allowed by statute or these rules, every paper or document filed with the court shall be served on all parties and the county agency.

Subd. 2. Service Upon Attorney for Party. If a party, other than the county agency, is represented by an attorney as shown by a certificate of representation in the court file, service shall be made upon the party's attorney, unless personal service upon the represented party is required under these rules. Except where personal service upon the county agency is required under these rules, service upon the county agency shall be accomplished by serving the county attorney.

Adopted May 30, 2001, eff. July 1, 2001.

Rule 355.02. Types of Service

Subdivision 1. Personal Service.

(a) *Upon Whom.*

(1) Upon an Individual. Personal service upon an individual in the state shall be accomplished by delivering a copy of the summons and complaint, notice, motion, or other document to the individual personally or by leaving a copy at the individual's house or usual place of residence with some person of suitable age and discretion who presently lives at that location. If the individual has, pursuant to statute, consented to any other method of service or appointed an agent to receive service, or if a statute designates a state official to receive service, service may be made in the manner provided by such statute. If the individual is confined to a state institution, personal service shall be accomplished by also serving a copy of the document upon the chief executive officer at the institution. Personal service upon an individual outside the state shall be accomplished according to the provisions of Minn. Stat. ch. 518C (2000) and Minn. Stat. § 543.19 (2000). Personal service may not be made on a legal holiday or election day.

(2) Upon the County Agency. Personal service upon the county agency shall be accomplished by serving the director of the county human services department or the director's designee.

(b) *By Whom Served.* Unless otherwise ordered by the child support magistrate, personal service shall be made only by the sheriff or by any other person who is at least 18 years of age who is not a party to the proceeding. Pursuant to Minn. Stat. § 518A.46, subd. 2(c)(4) (2006), an employee of the county agency may serve documents on parties.

(c) *Alternative Personal Service.*

(1) Acknowledgement by Mail. As an alternative to personal service, service may be made by U.S. mail if acknowledged in writing. Any party attempting alternative personal service shall include two copies of a notice and acknowledgment of service by mail conforming substantially to Form 22 set forth in the Minnesota Rules of Civil Procedure, along with a return envelope, postage prepaid, addressed to the sender. Any person served by U.S. mail who receives a notice and acknowledgement form shall complete the acknowledgment part of the form and return one copy of the completed form to the serving party. If the serving party does not receive the acknowledgment form within twenty (20) days, service is not valid upon that party. The serving party may then serve the summons and complaint by any means authorized under this subdivision. The child support magistrate may order the costs of personal service to be paid by the person served, if such person does not complete and return the notice and acknowledgment form within twenty (20) days.

(2) Service by Publication.

(A) Service. Service by publication means the publication of the entire summons or notice in the regular issue of a qualified newspaper, once each week for three (3) weeks. Service by publication shall be permitted only upon order of a child support magistrate. The child support magistrate may order service by publication upon the filing of an affidavit by the serving party or the serving party's attorney stating that the person to be served is not a resident of the state or cannot be found within the state, the efforts that have been made to locate the other party, and either that the serving party has mailed a copy of the summons or notice to the other party's place of residence or that such residence is not known to the serving party. When the person to be served is not a resident of the state, statutory requirements regarding long-arm jurisdiction shall be met.

(B) Defense by Noninitiating Party. If the summons or notice is served by publication and the noninitiating party receives no actual notification of the proceeding, either before judgment or within one year of entry of judgment the noninitiating party may seek relief pursuant to Minn. R. Civ. P. 4.043.

Subd. 2. Service by United States Mail. Service by United States mail means mailing a copy of the document by first-class mail, postage prepaid, addressed to the person to be served at the person's last known address. Service by mail shall be made only by the sheriff or by any other person who is at least 18 years of age who is not a party to the proceeding. Pursuant to Minn. Stat. § 518A.46, subd. 2(c)(4)

(2006), an employee of the county agency may serve documents on the parties.

Subd. 3. Service by Facsimile Transmission. Unless these rules require personal service, any document may be served by transmitting a copy by facsimile machine.

Adopted May 30, 2001, eff. July 1, 2001. Amended by Nov. 30, 2005, eff. Jan. 1, 2006; Nov. 12, 2008, eff. June 1, 2009.

Advisory Committee Comment—2008 Amendment

Rule 355.02, subds. 1 & 2, are amended to reflect the recodification, effective on January 1, 2007, of portions of the relevant statutes, that became part of Minn. Stat. ch. 518A.

Rule 355.03. Completion of Service

Personal service is complete upon delivery of the document. Service by U.S. mail is complete upon mailing. Service by publication is complete twenty-one (21) days after the first publication. Service by facsimile is complete upon completion of the facsimile transmission.

Adopted May 30, 2001, eff. July 1, 2001.

Rule 355.04. Proof of Service

Subdivision 1. Parties. All papers and documents filed with the court shall be accompanied by an affidavit of service, an acknowledgment of service by the party or party's attorney if served by alternative service, or, if served by publication, by the affidavit of the printer or the printer's designee. An affidavit of service shall describe what was served, state how the document was served, upon whom it was served, and the date, time, and place of service.

Subd. 2. Court Administrator. If the court administrator is required or permitted under these rules to serve a document, service may be proved by filing an affidavit of service, by filing a copy of the written notice, or by making a notation in the court's computerized records that service was made.

Adopted May 30, 2001, eff. July 1, 2001.

RULE 356. FEES

Rule 356.01. Collection of Fees

The court administrator shall charge and collect fees pursuant to Minnesota Statutes.

Adopted May 30, 2001, eff. July 1, 2001.

Advisory Committee Comment

Minnesota Statutes § 357.021, subdivision 2 (2000), establishes the various fees that must be charged and collected by court administrators. Specifically included is a filing fee, which is to be charged and collected from a party upon the filing of that party's first paper in the proceeding. Also included is a modification fee, which is to be paid upon the filing of a motion to modify support and upon the filing of a response to such a motion.

Rule 356.02. Waiver of Fees

If a party indicates an inability to pay any fee required under Rule 356.01, the court administrator shall explain that the party may apply for permission to proceed without payment of the fee. Upon request, the court administrator shall provide to such a party an application to proceed in forma pauperis. If a party signs and submits to the court administrator an application to proceed without payment of the fee, and such a request to waive the fee is approved by a child support magistrate, the court administrator shall not charge and collect the fee.

Adopted May 30, 2001, eff. July 1, 2001.

Advisory Committee Comment

Minnesota Statutes § 563.01, subdivision 3 (2000), provides that "the court shall allow the person to proceed in forma pauperis" if the court makes certain findings. Under this statute, only judicial officers, and not court administrators, are authorized to issue orders granting in forma pauperis status.

RULE 357. LEGAL REPRESENTATION AND APPOINTMENT OF GUARDIAN AD LITEM

Rule 357.01. Right to Representation

Each party appearing in the expedited process has a right to be represented by an attorney. A party, however, does not necessarily have the right to appointment of an attorney at public expense as provided in Rule 357.03.

Adopted May 30, 2001, eff. July 1, 2001. Amended Sept. 30, 2004, eff. Jan. 1, 2005.

Rule 357.02. Certificate of Representation

An attorney representing a party in the expedited process, other than a public defender or county attorney, shall on or before the attorney's first appearance file with the court a certificate of representation.

Adopted May 30, 2001, eff. July 1, 2001. Amended Sept. 30, 2004, eff. Jan. 1, 2005.

Rule 357.03. Appointment of Attorney at Public Expense

Unless a party voluntarily waives the right to counsel, the child support magistrate shall appoint an attorney at public expense for a party who requests an attorney and who cannot afford to retain an attorney when the case involves:

(a) establishment of parentage; or

(b) contempt proceedings in which incarceration of the party is a possible outcome of the proceeding.

Pursuant to Minn. Stat. § 257.69 (2000), a court-appointed attorney shall represent a party with respect to all issues necessary for the initial establishment of parentage, including child support, custody, parenting time, and name of the child.

Adopted May 30, 2001, eff. July 1, 2001. Amended Sept. 30, 2004, eff. Jan. 1, 2005.

Advisory Committee Comment

Parentage. The Minnesota Parentage Act, codified as Minn. Stat. §§ 257. 51—.74 (2000), provides that "the court shall appoint counsel for a party who is unable to pay timely for counsel in proceedings under sections 257.51 to 257.74." Minn. Stat. § 257.69, subd. 1 (2000). A party has a right to appointed counsel for all matters brought under the Parentage Act. See *M.T.L. v. Dempsey*, 504 N.W.2d 529, 531 (Minn. App. 1993).

Contempt. In *Cox v. Slama*, 355 N.W.2d 401, 403 (Minn. 1984), the court established the right to counsel for persons facing civil contempt for failure to pay child support when incarceration is a real possibility.

Rule 357.04. Appointment of Guardian Ad Litem

A child support magistrate may appoint a guardian ad litem for a child or minor parent who is a party in any proceeding commenced in the expedited child support process solely for purposes of having the guardian ad litem serve as a representative of that person as authorized under Rule 17.02 of the Minnesota Rules of Civil Procedure. The appointment shall be made pursuant to Rule 17.02 of the Minnesota Rules of Civil Procedure.

Adopted May 30, 2001, eff. July 1, 2001. Amended Sept. 30, 2004, eff. Jan. 1, 2005; Dec. 1, 2006, eff. Jan. 1, 2007.

RULE 358. COURT INTERPRETERS

Rule 358.01. Appointment Mandatory

The child support magistrate shall appoint a qualified interpreter in any proceeding conducted in the expedited process in which a person handicapped in communication is a party or witness. Such appointment shall be made according to the provisions of Minn. Gen. R. Prac. 8.

Adopted May 30, 2001, eff. July 1, 2001.

Rule 358.02. "Person Handicapped in Communication" Defined

For the purpose of Rule 358.01, a "person handicapped in communication" is one who, because of a hearing, speech, or other communication disorder, or because of difficulty in speaking or comprehending the English language, is unable to fully understand the proceedings in which the person is required to participate, or when named as a party to a legal proceeding is unable by reason of the handicap to obtain due process of law.

Adopted May 30, 2001, eff. July 1, 2001.

Advisory Committee Comment

Rules 358.01 and 358.02 are based upon the provisions of Minn. Stat. §§ 546.42 and 546.43 (2000) which set forth the types of proceedings in which qualified interpreters must be appointed.

RULE 359. TELEPHONE AND INTERACTIVE VIDEO

Rule 359.01. Telephone and Interactive Video Permitted

A child support magistrate may on the magistrate's own initiative conduct a hearing by telephone or, where available, interactive video. Any party may make a written or oral request to the court administrator or the court administrator's designee to appear at a scheduled hearing by telephone or, where available, interactive video. In the event the request is for interactive video, the request shall be made at least five (5) days before the date of the scheduled hearing. A child support magistrate may deny any request to appear at a hearing by telephone or interactive video.

Adopted May 30, 2001, eff. July 1, 2001.

Advisory Committee Comment

The Advisory Committee encourages the use of telephone and, where available, interactive video, to conduct proceedings in the expedited process.

Rule 359.02. Procedure

The court administrator or court administrator's designee shall arrange for any telephone or interactive video hearing approved by the child support magistrate. When conducting a proceeding by telephone or interactive video and a party or witness resides out of state, the child support magistrate shall ensure that the requirements of Minn. Stat. § 518C.316 (2000) are met. The child support magistrate shall make adequate provision for a record of any proceeding conducted by telephone or interactive video. No recording may be made of any proceeding conducted by telephone or interactive video, except the recording made as the official court record.

Adopted May 30, 2001, eff. July 1, 2001.

Rule 359.03. In–Court Appearance Not Precluded

Rule 359.01 does not preclude any party or the county attorney from being present in person before the child support magistrate at any motion or hearing.

Adopted May 30, 2001, eff. July 1, 2001.

RULE 360. INTERVENTION

Rule 360.01. County Agency

Subdivision 1. Intervention as a Matter of Right. To the extent allowed by law, the county agency may, as a matter of right, intervene as a party in any matter conducted in the expedited process. Intervention is accomplished by serving upon all parties by U.S. mail a notice of intervention. The notice of intervention and affidavit of service shall be filed with the court.

Subd. 2. Effective Date. Intervention by the county agency is effective when the last person is served with the notice of intervention.

Adopted May 30, 2001, eff. July 1, 2001.

Rule 360.02. Other Individuals

Subdivision 1. Permissive Intervention. Any person may be permitted to intervene as a party at any point in the proceeding if the child support magistrate finds that the person's legal rights, duties, or privileges will be determined or affected by the case.

Subd. 2. Procedure. A person seeking permissive intervention under subdivision 1 shall file with the court and serve upon all parties a motion to intervene. The motion shall state:

(a) how the person's legal rights, duties, or privileges will be determined or affected by the case;

(b) how the person will be directly affected by the outcome of the case;

(c) the purpose for which intervention is sought; and

(d) any statutory grounds authorizing the person to intervene.

Subd. 3. Objection to Permissive Intervention. Any existing party may file with the court and serve upon all parties and the intervenor a written objection within ten (10) days of service of the motion to intervene.

Subd. 4. Effective Date; Hearing. If a written objection is not timely served and filed and the requesting party meets the requirements of subdivisions 1 and 2, the child support magistrate may grant the motion to intervene after considering the factors set forth in subdivision 2. If written objection is timely served and filed, the child support magistrate may hold a hearing on the matter or may decide the issue without a hearing. Intervention is effective as of the date granted.

Adopted May 30, 2001, eff. July 1, 2001.

Rule 360.03. Effect of Intervention

The child support magistrate may conduct hearings, make findings, and issue orders at any time prior to intervention being accomplished or denied. Prior proceedings and decisions of the child support magistrate are not affected by intervention. Upon effective intervention the caption of the case shall be amended to include the name of the intervening party, which shall appear after the initial parties' names.

Adopted May 30, 2001, eff. July 1, 2001.

RULE 361. DISCOVERY

Rule 361.01. Witnesses

Any party may call witnesses to testify at any hearing. Any party intending to call a witness other than an employee of the county agency or any party to the proceeding shall, at least five (5) days before the hearing, provide to the other parties and the county agency written notice of the name and address of each witness.

Adopted May 30, 2001, eff. July 1, 2001.

Rule 361.02. Exchange of Documents

Subdivision 1. Documents Required to be Provided Upon Request. If a complaint or motion has been served and filed in the expedited process, a party may request any of the documents listed below. The request must be in writing and served upon the appropriate party. The request may be served along with the pleadings. A party shall provide the following documents to the requesting party no later than ten (10) days from the date of service of the written request.

(a) Verification of income, costs and availability of dependent health care coverage, child care costs, and expenses.

(b) Copies of last three months of pay stubs.

(c) A copy of last two years' State and Federal income tax returns with all schedules and attachments, including Schedule Cs, W–2s and/or 1099s.

(d) Written verification of any voluntary payments made for support of a joint child.

(e) Written verification of any other court-ordered child support obligation for a nonjoint child.

(f) Written verification of any court-ordered spousal maintenance obligation.

Subd. 2. Remedies for Non–compliance. If a party does not provide the documents, the party shall be prepared to explain the reason for the failure to the child support magistrate. If the magistrate determines that the documents should have been provided, the magistrate may impose the remedies available in Rule 361.04.

Subd. 3. Financial Statement. If a complaint or motion has been served, any party may request in writing that a financial statement be completed by a party, other than a county agency, and submitted five (5) days prior to hearing, or if no hearing is scheduled, within ten (10) days from the request being served. Failure to comply is subject to remedies under Rule 361.04. Where a financial statement requests supporting documentation, it shall be attached.

Subd. 4. Treatment of Confidential Information. To retain privacy, restricted identifiers (e.g., social security numbers, employer identification numbers, financial account numbers) must be blackened out from any documents provided under this rule and may only be submitted on a separate Confidential Information Form as required in Rule 11 of these rules. In addition, financial source documents (e.g., tax returns, wage stubs, credit card statements) must be submitted under a cover sheet entitled "Sealed Financial Source Documents" as required in Rule 11.

Adopted May 30, 2001, eff. July 1, 2001. Amended Sept. 23, 2003, eff. Nov. 1, 2003; May 6, 2005, eff. July 1, 2005; Nov. 30, 2005, eff. Jan. 1, 2006; Nov. 12, 2008, eff. June 1, 2009.

Rule 361.03. Other Discovery

Subdivision 1. Motion for Discovery. Any additional means of discovery available under the Minnesota Rules of Civil Procedure may be allowed only by order of the child support magistrate. The party seeking discovery shall bring a motion before the child support magistrate for an order permitting additional means of discovery. The motion shall include the reason for the request and shall notify the other parties of the opportunity to respond within five (5) days. The party seeking discovery has the burden of showing that the discovery is needed for the party's case, is not for purposes of delay or harassment, and that the issues or amounts in dispute justify the requested discovery. The motion shall be decided without a hearing unless the child support magistrate determines that a hearing is necessary. The child support magistrate shall issue an order granting or denying the discovery motion. If the discovery motion is granted, the requesting party must serve the approved discovery requests upon the responding party and the discovery responses are due ten (10) days following service of the discovery request, unless otherwise ordered.

Subd. 2. Objections to Discovery. If a party objects to discovery that party may serve and file a motion within five (5) days of service of discovery. The motion may be decided without a hearing unless the child support magistrate determines that a hearing is necessary.

Adopted May 30, 2001, eff. July 1, 2001. Amended Sept. 23, 2003, eff. Nov. 1, 2003.

Rule 361.04. Discovery Remedies

Subdivision 1. Motions to Compel. If a party fails to comply with an approved request for discovery or a request for documents under Rule 361.02, the party requesting the discovery may serve and file a motion for an order compelling an answer or compliance with the discovery request. The motion shall notify the other parties of the opportunity to respond within five (5) days. The motion shall be decided without a hearing unless the child support magistrate determines that a hearing is necessary.

Subd. 2. Options Available to the Child Support Magistrate. When deciding a discovery related motion or issue, or in the event a party fails to provide documents requested under Rule 361.02, the child support magistrate may:

(a) order the parties to exchange specified documents or information;

(b) deny the discovery request;

(c) affirm, modify, or quash the subpoena;

(d) issue a protective order;

(e) set or continue the hearing;

(f) conduct a hearing and keep the record open to allow for further exchange of information or response to the information provided at the hearing; or

(g) order other discovery allowable under the Minnesota Rules of Civil Procedure, if appropriate.

Subd. 3. Failure to Comply with Discovery. If a party fails to comply with an order issued pursuant to Rule 361.043, subd. 2, or Rule 361.04, the child support magistrate may:

(a) find that the subject matter of the order for discovery or any other relevant facts shall be taken as established for the purposes of the case in accordance with the claim of the party requesting the order;

(b) prohibit the non-compliant party from supporting or opposing designated claims or defenses, or prohibiting that party from introducing designated matters in evidence; or

(c) issue any other order that is appropriate in the interests of justice, including attorney fees or other sanctions.

Adopted May 30, 2001, eff. July 1, 2001. Amended Sept. 23, 2003, eff. Nov. 1, 2003.

Rule 361.05. Filing of Discovery Requests and Responses Precluded

Copies of a party's request for discovery and any responses to those requests shall not be filed with the court unless:

(a) ordered by the child support magistrate;

(b) filed in support of any motion;

(c) introduced as evidence in a hearing; or

(d) relied upon by the magistrate when approving a stipulated or default order.

To retain privacy, restricted identifiers (e.g., social security numbers, employer identification numbers, financial account numbers) must be blackened out from any documents provided under this rule and may only be submitted on a separate Confidential Information Form as required in Rule 11 of these rules. In addition, financial source documents (e.g., tax returns, wage stubs, credit card statements) must be submitted under a cover sheet entitled "Sealed Financial Source Documents" as required in Rule 11.

Adopted May 30, 2001, eff. July 1, 2001. Amended Sept. 23, 2003, eff. Nov. 1, 2003; May 6, 2005, eff. July 1, 2005.

Rule 361.06. Subpoenas

Subdivision 1. Written Request. Requests for subpoenas for the attendance of witnesses or for the production of documents shall be in writing and shall be submitted to the court administrator. The request shall specifically identify any documents requested, include the full name and home or business address of all persons to be subpoenaed, and specify the date, time, and place for responding to the subpoena. The court administrator shall issue a subpoena in accordance with Minn. R. Civ. P. 45. The party requesting the subpoena shall fill out the subpoena before having it served. An attorney as officer of the court may also issue and sign a subpoena on behalf of the court where the action is pending.

Subd. 2. Service of Subpoenas Shall be by Personal Service. All subpoenas shall be personally served by the sheriff or by any other person who is at least 18 years of age who is not a party to the action. Employees of the county agency may personally serve subpoenas. The person being served shall, at the time of service, be given the fees and mileage allowed by Minn. Stat. § 357.22 (2000). When the subpoena is requested by the county agency, fees and mileage need not be paid. The cost of service, fees, and expenses of any witnesses who have been served subpoenas shall be paid by the party at whose request the witness appears. The person serving the subpoena shall provide proof of service by filing the original subpoena with the court, along with an affidavit of personal service.

Subd. 3. Objection to Subpoena. Any person served with a subpoena who objects to the request shall serve upon the parties and file with the court an objection to subpoena. The party objecting shall state on the objection to subpoena why the request is unreasonable or oppressive. The objection to subpoena shall be filed promptly and no later than the time specified in the subpoena for compliance. A child support magistrate shall cancel or modify the subpoena if it is unreasonable or oppressive, taking into account the issues or amounts in controversy, the costs or other burdens of compliance when compared with the value of the testimony or evidence requested, and whether there are alternative methods of obtaining the desired testimony or evidence. Modification may include requiring the party requesting the subpoena to pay reasonable costs of producing documents, books, papers, or other tangible things.

Adopted May 30, 2001, eff. July 1, 2001. Amended Sept. 23, 2003, eff. Nov. 1, 2003; Nov. 30, 2005, eff. Jan. 1, 2006.

Advisory Committee Comment—2006 Amendment

Rule 361.06 is amended, effective January 1, 2006, to conform the subpoena provisions to the parallel procedures of Minn. R. Civ. P. 45, which is amended at the same time.

RULE 362. SETTLEMENT

Rule 362.01. Procedure

The parties may settle the case at any time before a hearing or, if no hearing is scheduled, before an order is issued. Alternative dispute resolution, as provided in Minn. Gen. R. Prac. 310, and settlement efforts, as provided in Minn. Gen. R. Prac. 303, do not apply to cases brought in the expedited process.

Adopted May 30, 2001, eff. July 1, 2001.

Rule 362.02. Signing of Order

Subdivision 1. Preparation and Signing. If the parties reach an agreement resolving all issues, one of the parties shall prepare an order setting forth the terms of the agreement. If the parties are not represented by counsel and the county agency is a party, the county agency shall prepare the order. All parties to the agreement, including the county agency, shall sign the original order. The order shall state that the parties have:

(a) waived the right to a hearing;

(b) waived the right to counsel where a party is not represented by counsel; and

(c) received and reviewed all documents used to prepare the order.

Subd. 2. Filing. The original order signed by all parties shall be filed with the court, who shall submit it to the child support magistrate for review and signature.

Adopted May 30, 2001, eff. July 1, 2001.

Rule 362.03. Order Accepted

The child support magistrate may sign an order filed pursuant to Rule 362. 02 if it is supported by law, and is reasonable and fair.

Adopted May 30, 2001, eff. July 1, 2001.

Rule 362.04. Order Not Accepted

The child support magistrate may reject an order filed pursuant to Rule 362.02 if the child support magistrate finds that it is contrary to law, or is unreasonable and unfair. If the child support magistrate rejects the order, the child support magistrate shall prepare a notice of deficiency, stating the reason(s) why the order cannot be signed. The notice of deficiency shall inform the parties of the following options:

(a) to file and serve any missing documents;

(b) to file and serve a revised order;

(c) to file and serve a revised order and attach any missing or additional documents;

(d) to appear at a hearing, notice of which shall be issued by the court administrator;

(e) to appear at the previously scheduled hearing; or

(f) to withdraw the matter without prejudice.

The court administrator shall mail the notice of deficiency to the parties. The parties shall either correct the deficiency or set the case on for a hearing and serve notice of the date, time, and location of the hearing pursuant to Rule 364. In matters that are pending before the court, if the parties fail to comply with the notice of deficiency within forty-five (45) days of the date the notice was mailed, the child support magistrate shall dismiss the matter without prejudice.

A stipulation or agreement shall be rejected where no underlying file exists. Neither the parties nor the child support magistrate may schedule a hearing without a party first serving and filing a summons and complaint or notice of motion and motion.

Adopted May 30, 2001, eff. July 1, 2001.

Advisory Committee Comment

After an order or a judgment and decree is issued, at a later date parties sometimes amicably agree to modify the order. These agreements are often reached without the serving and filing of any papers. Under such circumstances, the parties are required to reduce the agreement to writing in the form of a stipulation and order which a child support magistrate may accept or reject. If the stipulation and order is rejected, and there is no underlying file, the matter may not be set for hearing until such time as a complaint is filed thus giving the court jurisdiction over the parties.

RULE 363. DEFAULT

Rule 363.01. Scope

The default procedure set forth in this rule applies to actions to establish support under Minn. Stat. § 256.87 (2000) (Rule 370) and proceedings to modify support or set support (Rule 372).

Adopted May 30, 2001, eff. July 1, 2001.

Rule 363.02. Procedure

The initiating party may proceed by default if:

(a) all noninitiating parties have been properly served with the summons or notice of motion;

(b) the summons or notice of motion did not contain a hearing date; and

(c) there has been no written answer or return of the request for hearing form from any party within twenty (20) days from the date the last party was served.

The initiating party shall file an order with the court within forty-five (45) days from the date the last noninitiating party was served with the summons and complaint or notice of motion and motion. The initiating party shall also file with the court a current affidavit of default and a current affidavit of non-military status. If an order is not filed with the court within forty-five (45) days, the court administrator shall mail a notice to all parties that the matter shall be scheduled for hearing unless the initiating party files an order along with all necessary documents within ten (10) days from the date notice was mailed. If the initiating party fails to file the necessary documents within the allotted ten (10) days, the court administrator shall set the matter on for hearing and serve upon all parties and the county agency by U.S. mail at least fourteen (14) days before the scheduled hearing, notice of the date, time, and location of the hearing.

Adopted May 30, 2001, eff. July 1, 2001.

Rule 363.03. Order Accepted

The child support magistrate may sign an order filed pursuant to Rule 363. 02 if the child support magistrate finds that it is supported by law, is reasonable and fair, and that each noninitiating party:

(a) was properly served with the summons and complaint or notice of motion and motion;

(b) was notified of the requirement to either serve and file a written answer or return the request for hearing form within twenty (20) days of service of the summons and complaint or notice of motion and motion; and

(c) failed to serve and file a written answer or return the request for hearing form within twenty (20) days from the date of service.

Adopted May 30, 2001, eff. July 1, 2001.

Rule 363.04. Order Not Accepted

The child support magistrate may reject an order filed pursuant to Rule 363.02 if the child support magistrate finds the order contrary to law, or unreasonable and unfair. If the child support magistrate rejects the order, the child support magistrate shall prepare a notice of deficiency, stating the reason(s) why the order cannot be signed. The notice of deficiency shall inform the initiating party of the following options:

(a) to file and serve any missing documents;

(b) to file a revised order;

(c) to file a revised order and attach any missing or additional documents;

(d) to appear at a hearing, notice of which shall be issued by the court administrator to all parties;

(e) to appear at any previously scheduled hearing; or

(f) to withdraw the matter without prejudice.

The court administrator shall mail the notice of deficiency to the initiating party. The initiating party shall either correct the deficiency or set the case on for a hearing and serve notice of the date, time, and location of the hearing upon all parties pursuant to Rule 364. If the initiating party submits a revised order that raises new issues beyond the scope of the complaint or motion, amended pleadings shall be served on all parties and filed within 10 days from the date the notice of deficiency was mailed. If the noninitiating party chooses to respond to the amended pleadings, the response must be served and filed within 10 days from service of the amended pleadings. If the initiating party fails to schedule a hearing or comply with the notice of deficiency within forty-five (45) days of the date the notice was mailed, the child support magistrate shall dismiss the matter without prejudice.

Adopted May 30, 2001, eff. July 1, 2001. Amended Nov. 12, 2008, eff. June 1, 2009.

Advisory Committee Comment—2008 Amendment

Rule 363.04 is amended to create specific time limits for setting a case on for hearing following receipt of a notice of deficiency in an order proposed by an initiating agency or to serve amended pleadings. The amendment also establishes a specific time limit for responding to an amended pleading that may be served.

RULE 364. HEARING PROCESS

Rule 364.01. Right to Hearing

Any party has a right to a hearing unless otherwise stated in these rules.

Adopted May 30, 2001, eff. July 1, 2001.

Rule 364.02. Scheduling of Hearing

The initiating party shall schedule a hearing if a written answer or a request for hearing form is received. The initiating party shall contact the court administrator or the court administrator's designee to obtain a hearing date and shall serve upon all parties and the county agency by U.S. mail at least fourteen (14) days before the scheduled hearing, notice of the date, time, and location of the hearing.

Adopted May 30, 2001, eff. July 1, 2001.

Rule 364.03. Timing of Hearing

In the event the parties are unable to resolve the matter, a hearing shall be held no sooner than twenty (20) days after service of the summons and complaint or notice of motion and motion, unless the time period is waived by the parties. Every effort shall be made to conduct the hearing no later than sixty (60) days after service of the summons and complaint or notice of motion and motion on the last person served or, in an establishment of parentage case, no later than sixty (60) days after receipt of the genetic test results. If conducted later than sixty (60) days, the court administrator shall report that fact to the chief judge of the judicial district. Conducting a hearing later than sixty (60) days after service or receipt of blood or genetic test results does not deprive the child support magistrate of jurisdiction.

Adopted May 30, 2001, eff. July 1, 2001.

Advisory Committee Comment

Federal law requires 75% of cases commenced in the Expedited Process to be completed within 6 months from the date of service of process and 90% of the cases to be completed within 12 months from the date of service of process. 45 C.F.R. § 303.101 (2000). If the hearing is initially scheduled within 60 days under Rule 364.03 and is later continued to beyond 60 days, that fact must be reported to the chief judge of the judicial district.

Rule 364.04. Notice of Hearing

A notice of the hearing shall:

(a) state the name of the court;

(b) state the names of the parties;

(c) state the date, time, and location of the hearing;

(d) state that the parties shall appear at the hearing, unless otherwise provided in these rules;

(e) inform the parties of the requirement to bring to the hearing sufficient copies of all documents the parties intend to offer; and

(f) if possible, include the name of the child support magistrate assigned to the case.

Adopted May 30, 2001, eff. July 1, 2001.

Rule 364.05. Continuance of Hearing

Upon agreement of the parties or a showing of good cause, the child support magistrate may grant a request for continuance of a hearing. An order granting a continuance may be stated orally on the record or may be in writing. Unless time does not permit, a request for continuance shall be made in writing, and shall be filed with the court and served upon all parties at least five (5) days before the hearing. In determining whether good cause exists, due regard shall be given to the ability of the party requesting a continuance to effectively proceed without a continuance.

Adopted May 30, 2001, eff. July 1, 2001.

Advisory Committee Comment

Rule 364.05 provides that a continuance may be granted for good cause. Examples of good cause include: death or incapacitating illness of a party or attorney of a party; lack of proper notice of the hearing; a substitution of the attorney of a party; a change in the parties or pleadings requiring postponement; an agreement for a continuance by all parties provided that it is shown that more time is clearly necessary. Good cause does not include: intentional delay; unavailability of counsel due to engagement in another judicial or administrative proceeding unless all other members of the attorney's firm familiar with the case are similarly engaged, or if the notice of the other proceeding was received prior to the notice of the hearing for which the continuance is sought; unavailability of a witness if the witness' testimony can be taken by deposition; and failure of the attorney to properly utilize the statutory notice period to prepare for the hearing.

Rule 364.06. Explanation of Hearing Purpose and Procedure

At the beginning of each hearing the child support magistrate shall explain the purpose of the hearing and the process and procedures to be used during the hearing.

Adopted May 30, 2001, eff. July 1, 2001.

Rule 364.07. Hearings Open to Public

All hearings are open to the public, except as otherwise provided in these rules or by statute. For good cause shown, a child support magistrate may exclude members of the public from attending a hearing.

Adopted May 30, 2001, eff. July 1, 2001.

Advisory Committee Comment

Under Minn. Stat. § 257.70 (2000), hearings regarding the establishment of parentage are closed to the public. Other proceedings identified in Rule 353.01 are generally open to the public.

Rule 364.08. Record of Hearing

Each child support magistrate shall ensure that an accurate record is made of each hearing over which the magistrate presides.

Adopted May 30, 2001, eff. July 1, 2001.

Advisory Committee Comment

Under Minn. Stat. § 484.72, subds. 1, 6 (2000), records of hearings and other proceedings in the expedited process may be made either by competent stenographers or by use of electronic recording equipment. (1999 Minn. Laws 196, art. 1, § 3.) If electronic recording equipment is used, it must meet the minimum standards promulgated by the state court administrator and must be operated and monitored by a person who meets the minimum qualifications promulgated by the state court administrator. The minimum standards are set forth in Minnesota State Court System Administrative Policy, dated June 29, 1999.

Rule 364.09. Right to Present Evidence

Subdivision 1. Generally. Each party may present evidence, rebuttal testimony, and argument with respect to the issues.

Subd. 2. Testimony and Documents Permitted. Evidence may be presented through documents and testimony of the parties or other witnesses. Testimony may be given in narrative fashion by witnesses or by question and answer. Any party may be a witness and may present witnesses. All oral testimony shall be under oath or affirmation. The child support magistrate may exclude witnesses from the hearing room so that they cannot hear the testimony of other witnesses. In any proceeding, a sworn written affidavit of any party or witness may be offered in lieu of oral testimony.

Subd. 3. Necessary Preparation Required. The parties shall exchange copies of documents five (5) days before the hearing. If the exchange is not completed within the required time frame each party shall bring to the hearing all evidence, both oral and written, the party intends to present. Each party must have enough copies of each exhibit the party intends to offer so that a copy can be provided to all other parties and the child support magistrate at the time of the hearing. The child support magistrate shall have discretion in determining whether evidence that was not timely exchanged prior to the hearing should or should not be admitted.

Adopted May 30, 2001, eff. July 1, 2001. Amended Sept. 23, 2003, eff. Nov. 1, 2003.

Rule 364.10. Evidence

Subdivision 1. Type of Evidence Admissible. The child support magistrate may admit any evidence that possesses probative value, including hearsay, if it is the type of evidence on which reasonable, prudent persons are accustomed to rely in the conduct of their serious affairs. The child support magistrate shall give effect to the rules of privilege recognized by law. Evidence that is not related to the issue of support, is unimportant to the issue before the magistrate, or that repeats evidence that has already been provided shall not be allowed.

Subd. 2. Evidence Part of Record. All pleadings and supporting documentation previously served upon the parties and filed with the court, unless objected to, may be considered by the magistrate. Only evidence that is offered and received during the hearing or submitted following the hearing with the permission of the child support magistrate may be considered in rendering a decision, including, but not limited to, testimony, affidavits, exhibits, and financial information.

Subd. 3. Documents. Ordinarily, copies or excerpts of documents instead of originals may be received or incorporated by reference. The child support magistrate may require the original or the complete document if the copy is not legible, there is a genuine question of accuracy or authenticity, or if it would be unfair to admit the copy instead of the original. Any financial documents prepared by the employee of the county agency are admissible without requiring foundation testimony or appearance of the employee of the county agency.

Subd. 4. Notice of Facts. The child support magistrate may take judicial notice of facts not subject to reasonable dispute, but shall do so on the record and with the opportunity for any party to contest the facts so noticed.

Adopted May 30, 2001, eff. July 1, 2001.

Rule 364.11. Burden of Proof

The party proposing that certain action be taken shall prove the facts at issue by a preponderance of the evidence, unless the substantive law provides a different burden or standard. A party asserting an affirmative defense has the burden of proving the existence of the defense by a preponderance of the evidence.

Adopted May 30, 2001, eff. July 1, 2001.

Rule 364.12. Examination of Adverse Party

A party may call an adverse party or any witness for an adverse party, and may ask leading questions, cross-examine, and impeach that adverse party or witness.

Adopted May 30, 2001, eff. July 1, 2001.

Rule 364.13. Role of Child Support Magistrate

A child support magistrate may ask questions of witnesses when needed to ensure sufficient evidence to make the required findings.

Adopted May 30, 2001, eff. July 1, 2001.

Rule 364.14. Discretion to Leave Record Open

At the conclusion of a hearing, the child support magistrate may leave the record open and request or permit submission of additional documentation. Unless otherwise ordered by the child support magistrate, such additional documentation shall be submitted to the court within ten (10) days of the conclusion of the hearing. Documents submitted after the due date or without permission of the child support magistrate shall be returned to the sender and shall not be considered by the child support magistrate when deciding the case.

Adopted May 30, 2001, eff. July 1, 2001.

Rule 364.15. Close of Record

The record shall be considered closed either at the conclusion of the hearing or upon the expiration date for submission by the parties of any additional documentation authorized or requested by the child support magistrate, whichever is later. At the close of the record, the child support magistrate shall issue a decision and order pursuant to Rule 365.

Adopted May 30, 2001, eff. July 1, 2001.

RULE 365. DECISION AND ORDER OF CHILD SUPPORT MAGISTRATE

Rule 365.01. Failure to Attend Hearing

If a party fails to appear at a hearing for which notice was properly served, the child support magistrate may:

(a) decide all issues and issue an order without further notice or hearing;

(b) dismiss the matter without prejudice; or

(c) continue the hearing.

Adopted May 30, 2001, eff. July 1, 2001.

Rule 365.02. Timing

Within thirty (30) days of the close of the record the child support magistrate shall file with the court a decision and order. The child support magistrate may serve the order upon the parties at the hearing.

Adopted May 30, 2001, eff. July 1, 2001.

Rule 365.03. Effective Date; Final Order

Except as otherwise provided in these rules, the decision and order of the child support magistrate is effective and final when signed by the child support magistrate.

Adopted May 30, 2001, eff. July 1, 2001.

Rule 365.04. Notice of Filing of Order or Notice of Entry of Judgment

Subdivision 1. Service by Court Administrator. Within five (5) days of receipt of the decision and order of the child support magistrate the court administrator shall serve a notice of filing of order or notice of entry of judgment upon each party by U.S. mail, together with a copy of the order or judgment if a copy of the order was not served at the hearing. The court administrator shall use the notice of filing form prepared by the state court administrator which shall set forth the information required in subdivision 2.

Subd. 2. Content of Notice. The notice required in subdivision 1 shall include information regarding the:

(a) right to bring a motion to correct clerical mistakes pursuant to Rule 375;

(b) right to bring a motion for review of the decision and order of the child support magistrate pursuant to Rule 376;

(c) right to appeal a final order or judgment of the child support magistrate directly to the court of appeals pursuant to Rule 378;

(d) right of other parties to respond to motions to correct clerical mistakes, motions for review, and appeals pursuant to Rules 377 and 378; and

(e) authority of the child support magistrate to award costs and fees if the magistrate determines that a motion to correct clerical mistakes or a motion for review is not made in good faith or is brought for purposes of delay or harassment pursuant to Rule 377.09, subd. 6.

Subd. 3. Court Administrator Computes Dates. The court administrator shall compute, and set forth in the notice required in subdivision 1, the last day for bringing a motion for review and the last day for bringing any response to such motion.

Adopted May 30, 2001, eff. July 1, 2001.

Advisory Committee Comment

Timing and Procedure for Bringing Motions. The timing for bringing a motion for review differs from the timing for bringing an appeal to the court of appeals. Under Rule 377.02, the time within which to bring a motion for review is twenty (20) days, which begins to run on the date the court administrator serves the notice of filing of order or notice of entry of judgment.

Timing and Procedure for Bringing an Appeal to Court of Appeals. Rule 104.01 of the Minnesota Rules of Civil Appellate Procedure provides that the time within which to bring an appeal to the court of appeals is sixty (60) days which begins to run on the date of service by any party upon any other party of written notice of the filing of the order or entry of the judgment. The Advisory Committee intends that Rule 378.01 supersede Minn. R. Civ. App. P. 104.01 to provide that the sixty (60) days begins to run on the date the court administrator serves the written notice of filing of the order or notice of entry of judgment.

Options For Review and Appeal. A party may choose to bring a motion to correct clerical mistakes, a motion for review, or a combined motion, or may choose to appeal directly to the court of appeals thus bypassing the first two options. However, if a party chooses the option of appealing directly to the court of appeals without first bringing a motion for review, such an appeal will be limited to determining whether the evidence sustains the findings of fact (to which the "clearly erroneous" standard of review applies) and whether the findings support the conclusions of law and the judgment. *Kahn v. Tronnier*, 547 N.W.2d 425, 428 (Minn. App.), *rev. denied* (Minn. July 10, 1996). Thus, although a motion for review is very important to obtaining the broadcast possible appellate review, it is not an absolute prerequisite to appeal; a litigant can choose to file a direct appeal from the order of the child support magistrate, but the appeal will be limited to issues within that narrower scope of review.

RULE 366. TRANSCRIPT

Rule 366.01. Ordering of Transcript

Subdivision 1. Informational Request. Any person may request a transcript of any proceeding held before a child support magistrate, except as prohibited by statute or rule, by filing a request for transcript form with the court. The person requesting the transcript must make satisfactory arrangements for payment with the transcriber within thirty (30) days of ordering the transcript or the request for the transcript shall be deemed cancelled. The person requesting the transcript may withdraw the request any time prior to the time transcription has begun. The transcriber shall file the original with the court and serve a copy upon the requesting person. The transcriber shall also file with the court an affidavit of service verifying that service has been made upon the requesting person.

Subd. 2. Clerical or Review Requests. If a party chooses to request a transcript for purposes of bringing or responding to a motion to correct clerical mistakes, a motion for review, or a combined motion, a request for transcript form shall be filed with the court within the time required under Rule 377.02 and 377.04. The party requesting the transcript must make satisfactory arrangements for payment with the transcriber within thirty (30) days of ordering the transcript or the request for the transcript shall be deemed cancelled. The requesting party may withdraw that party's request for a transcript any time prior to the time transcription has begun. The transcriber shall file the original with the court and serve each party, including the county agency if a party, with a copy. The transcriber shall also file with the court an affidavit of service verifying that service has been made upon all parties. Ordering and filing of a transcript does not delay the due dates for the submissions described in Rule 377.02 and Rule 377.04. Filing of the transcript with the court closes the record for purposes of Rule 377.09, subd. 1.

Subd. 3. Appellate Request. If the transcript request is for appellate review, the transcriber shall comply with all appellate rules.

Adopted May 30, 2001, eff. July 1, 2001.

RULE 367. ADMINISTRATION OF EXPEDITED CHILD SUPPORT PROCESS; CHILD SUPPORT MAGISTRATES

Rule 367.01. Administration of Expedited Process

The chief judge of each judicial district shall determine whether the district will administer the expedited process within the judicial district in whole or in part, or request that the state court administrator administer the expedited process in whole or in part for the district.

Adopted May 30, 2001, eff. July 1, 2001.

Advisory Committee Comment

Rule 367.01 does not permit a judicial district to opt out of the expedited process. Rather, Rule 367.01 simply indicates that the chief judge of the district must decide who will be responsible for administering the expedited process within each judicial district.

Rule 367.02. Use and Appointment of Child Support Magistrates

The chief judge of each judicial district shall determine whether the district will use child support magistrates, family court referees, district court judges, or a combination of these individuals to preside over proceedings in the expedited process. The chief judge of each judicial district, with the advice and consent of the judges of the district, shall appoint each child support magistrate, except family court referees and district court judges, subject to confirmation by the Supreme Court. Each child support magistrate serves at the pleasure of the judges of the judicial district. Child support magistrates may be appointed on a full time, part time, or contract basis.

Adopted May 30, 2001, eff. July 1, 2001.

Advisory Committee Comment

Nothing in these rules precludes a family court referee or district court judge from serving in the capacity of a child support magistrate.

Rule 367.03. Powers and Authority

Child support magistrates shall have the powers and authority necessary to perform their duties in the expedited process pursuant to statute and rule.

Adopted May 30, 2001, eff. July 1, 2001.

Advisory Committee Comment

It is the intent of the Committee that child support magistrates have the authority to decide all issues permitted in the expedited process, including, but not limited to, awarding and modifying tax dependency exemptions, awarding costs and attorneys fees, issuing orders of direct contempt, and issuing orders to show cause.

Rule 367.04. Conflict of Interest

Subdivision 1. Generally. A child support magistrate shall not serve as:

(a) an attorney in any family law matter within any county in which the person serves as a child support magistrate; or

(b) a guardian ad litem in any family law matter, in any district in which the person serves as a child support magistrate.

Subd. 2. Disqualification. The disqualifications listed in subdivision 1 shall not be imputed to other members of a child support magistrate's law firm.

Adopted May 30, 2001, eff. July 1, 2001. Amended Sept. 30, 2004, eff. Jan. 1, 2005.

Rule 367.05. Code of Judicial Conduct

Each child support magistrate is bound by the Minnesota Code of Judicial Conduct. The exceptions set forth in the Application of the Minnesota Code of Judicial Conduct relating to part-time judges apply to child support magistrates appointed on a part-time or contract basis.

Adopted May 30, 2001, eff. July 1, 2001.

Advisory Committee Comment

A comment to the Application Section of the Minnesota Code of Judicial Conduct provides that "anyone, whether or not a lawyer, who is an officer of a judicial system and who performs judicial functions, including an officer such as a referee, special master or magistrate" is a judge within the meaning of the Minnesota Code of Judicial Conduct.

Rule 367.06. Impartiality

Each child support magistrate shall conduct each hearing in an impartial manner and shall serve only in those matters in which the magistrate can remain impartial and evenhanded. If at any time a child support magistrate is unable to conduct any proceeding in an impartial manner, the magistrate shall withdraw.

Adopted May 30, 2001, eff. July 1, 2001.

RULE 368. REMOVAL OF A PARTICULAR CHILD SUPPORT MAGISTRATE

Rule 368.01. Automatic Right to Remove Precluded

No party has an automatic right to remove a child support magistrate, family court referee, or district court judge presiding over matters in the expedited process, including motions to correct clerical mistakes under Rule 375 and motions for review under Rule 376.

Adopted May 30, 2001, eff. July 1, 2001. Amended Nov. 12, 2008, eff. June 1, 2009.

Rule 368.02. Removal for Cause

Subdivision 1. Procedure. To effect removal, a party shall serve upon the other parties and file with the court a request to remove the child support magistrate for cause within ten (10) days of service of notice of the name of the magistrate assigned to hear the matter or within ten (10) days of discovery of prejudice. If assignment of a child support magistrate is made less than ten (10) days before the hearing, the request to remove shall be made as soon as practicable after notice of assignment is given.

Subd. 2. Grounds to Remove. Removal of a child support magistrate requires an affirmative showing of prejudice. A showing that the child support magistrate might be excluded for bias from acting as a juror in the matter constitutes an affirmative showing of prejudice.

Subd. 3. Review of Denial of Removal. If the child support magistrate denies the request to remove, upon written request filed with the Court Administrator in that district, a district judge assigned to or chambered in the district shall determine whether cause exists. If that judge is the child support magistrate, the request for removal for cause shall be heard by a different judge in that district.

Adopted May 30, 2001, eff. July 1, 2001. Amended Nov. 12, 2008, eff. June 1, 2009.

Advisory Committee Comment—2008 Amendment

Rule 368.02, subd. 1, is amended to clarify the procedure for removal of an assigned child support magistrate from hearing a matter. Subdivision 3 is a new provision, designed to provide a more streamlined mechanism for review of a magistrate's decision not to order removal. The review of that decision is to be heard by a district judge who either had chambers in the county where the expedited child support case is pending or to a judge assigned to that county. This procedure obviates submission of the matter to the Chief Judge, recognizing that the Chief Judge may be far removed from the county where the case is pending.

RULE 369. ROLE OF COUNTY ATTORNEY AND EMPLOYEES OF THE COUNTY AGENCY

Rule 369.01. Role of County Attorney

Subdivision 1. Approval as to Form and Content. The county attorney shall review and approve as to form and content all legal documents prepared by employees of the county agency for use in the expedited process or in district court.

Subd. 2. Attendance at Hearings. The county agency shall appear through counsel. However, the county attorney may authorize an employee of the county agency to appear on behalf of the county attorney to present an agreement or stipulation reached by all the parties. An employee of the county agency shall not advocate a position on behalf of any party. The county attorney is not required to be present at any hearing to which the county agency is not a party.

Adopted May 30, 2001, eff. July 1, 2001.

Rule 369.02. Role of Employees of County Agency

Subdivision 1. County Attorney Direction. Under the direction of, and in consultation with, the county attorney, and consistent with Rules 5.3 and 5.5 of the Minnesota Rules of Professional Conduct, employees of the county agency may perform the following duties:

(a) meet and confer with parties by mail, telephone, electronic, or other means regarding legal issues;

(b) explain to parties the purpose, procedure, and function of the expedited child support process and the role and authority of nonattorney employees of the county agency regarding legal issues;

(c) prepare pleadings, including, but not limited to, summonses and complaints, notices, motions, subpoenas, orders to show cause, proposed orders, administrative orders, and stipulations and agreements;

(d) issue administrative subpoenas;

(e) prepare judicial notices;

(f) negotiate settlement agreements;

(g) attend and participate as witnesses in hearings and other proceedings, and if requested by the child support magistrate, present evidence, agreements and stipulations of the parties, and any other information deemed appropriate by the magistrate;

(h) participate in such other activities and perform such other duties as delegated by the county attorney; and

(i) exercise other powers and perform other duties as permitted by statute or these rules.

Employees of the county agency shall not represent the county agency at hearings conducted in the expedited process.

Subd. 2. Support Recommendations Precluded. Employees of the county agency may not offer recommendations regarding support at the hearing unless called as a witness at the hearing. Computation and presentation of support calculations are not considered recommendations as to support.

Subd. 3. County Attorney Direction Not Required. Without direction from the county attorney, employees of the county agency may perform the duties listed under Minn. Stat. § 518A.46, subd. 2(c) (2006). In addition, employees of the county agency may testify at hearings at the request of a party or the child support magistrate.

Subd. 4. Performance of Duties Not Practice of Law. Performance of the duties identified in Rule 369.02 by employees of the county agency does not constitute the unauthorized practice of law for purposes of these rules or Minn. Stat. § 481.02 (2000).

Adopted May 30, 2001, eff. July 1, 2001. Amended Nov. 12, 2008, eff. June 1, 2009.

Advisory Committee Comment—2008 Amendment

Rule 369.02, subd. 3, is amended to update the statutory references to reflect the recodification, effective on January 1, 2007, of portions of the relevant statutes, that became part of Minn. Stat. ch. 518A.

II. PROCEEDINGS

RULE 370. ESTABLISHMENT OF SUPPORT PROCEEDINGS

Rule 370.01. Commencement

An initial proceeding to establish support shall be commenced in the expedited process by service of a summons and complaint pursuant to Rule 370. 03. If the summons does not contain a hearing date, a request for hearing form and a supporting affidavit shall be attached to the summons and complaint. In addition to service of the summons and complaint, an order to show cause may be issued pursuant to Minn. Gen. R. Prac. 303.05. Service shall be made at least twenty (20) days prior to any scheduled hearing.

Adopted May 30, 2001, eff. July 1, 2001.

Rule 370.02. Content of Summons, Complaint, Supporting Affidavit, and Request for Hearing Form

Subdivision 1. Content of Summons. A summons shall:

(a) state the name of the court;

(b) state the names of the parties;

(c) state an address where the initiating party may be served;

(d) state that the purpose of the action is to establish support;

(e) either set a hearing date or attach a request for hearing form;

(f) provide information about serving and filing a written response pursuant to Rule 370.04 and Rule 370.05;

(g) state that all parties shall appear at the hearing if one is scheduled, and state that if any party fails to appear at the hearing the child support magistrate shall proceed pursuant to Rule 365.01;

(h) state that the child support magistrate may sign a default order pursuant to Rule 363.03;

(i) state that a party has the right to representation pursuant to Rule 357;

(j) state that the case may be settled informally by contacting the initiating party, and include the name, address, and telephone number of the person to contact to discuss settlement; and

(k) be signed by the initiating party or that party's attorney.

If there is reason to believe that domestic violence exists or if an order for protection has been issued, the party may provide an alternative address and telephone number. Pursuant to Minn. Stat. § 518.005, subd. 5 (2000), in all actions in which public assistance is assigned or the county agency is providing services to a party or parties to the action, information regarding the location of one party may not be released by the county agency to any other party if the county agency has knowledge that a protective order with respect to the other party has been entered or has reason to believe that the release of the information may result in physical or emotional harm to the other party.

Subd. 2. Content of Complaint. A complaint shall:

(a) state the relief the initiating party wants the child support magistrate to order;

(b) state the facts and grounds supporting the request for relief;

(c) set forth the acknowledgement required under Rule 379.04; and

(d) be signed by the initiating party or that party's attorney.

Subd. 3. Content of Supporting Affidavit. A supporting affidavit is required when the summons does not contain a hearing date. The supporting affidavit shall:

(a) state detailed facts supporting the request for relief;

(b) provide all information required by Minn. Stat. § 518A.46, subd. 3(a) (2006), if known; and

(c) be signed and sworn to under oath.

Subd. 4. Content of Request for Hearing Form. A request for hearing form shall contain the name and address of the initiating party and a short, concise statement that a noninitiating party requests a hearing.

Adopted May 30, 2001, eff. July 1, 2001. Amended Nov. 12, 2008, eff. June 1, 2009.

Advisory Committee Comment

Pursuant to Minn. Stat. § 518.5513, subd. 3(a), for all cases involving establishment or modification of support, the pleadings are to contain specific information. At times, it may be necessary to attach additional supporting documents. Each county should establish its own local policy regarding the attachment of supporting documents.

Advisory Committee Comment—2008 Amendment

Rule 370.02, subd. 3, is amended to update the statutory reference to reflect the recodification, effective on January 1, 2007, of portions of the relevant statutes, that became part of Minn. Stat. ch. 518A. Pursuant to Minn. Stat. § 518A.46, subd. 3(b), for all cases involving establishment or modification of support, the pleadings are to contain specific information. At times, it may be necessary to attach additional supporting documents. Each county should establish its own local policy regarding the attachment of supporting documents.

Rule 370.03. Service of Summons and Complaint

Subdivision 1. Who is Served. All parties, and the county agency even if not a party, shall be served pursuant to subdivision 2.

Subd. 2. How Served. The summons and complaint, and if required the supporting affidavit and request for hearing form, shall be served upon the parties by personal service, or alternative personal service, pursuant to Rule 355.02, unless personal service has been waived in writing. Where the county agency is the initiating party, a non-parent who is receiving assistance from the county or who has applied for child support services from the county may be served by any means permitted under Rule 355.02.

Adopted May 30, 2001, eff. July 1, 2001. Amended Nov. 12, 2008, eff. June 1, 2009.

Rule 370.04. Filing Requirements

Subdivision 1. Initiating Party. No later than five (5) days before any scheduled hearing or, if no hearing is scheduled, within fourteen (14) days from the date the last party was served, the initiating party shall file the following with the court:

(a) the original summons;

(b) the original complaint;

(c) the original supporting affidavit, if served;

(d) the request for hearing form, if returned to the initiating party; and

(e) proof of service upon each party pursuant to Rule 355.04.

Subd. 2. Responding Party. If a noninitiating party responds with a written answer pursuant to Rule 370.05, the following shall be filed with the court no later than five (5) days before any scheduled hearing or, if no hearing is scheduled, within twenty (20) days from the date the last party was served:

(a) the original written answer;

(b) a financial affidavit pursuant to Minn. Stat. § 518A.28 (2006); and

(c) proof of service upon each party pursuant to Rule 355.04.

Subd. 3. Facsimile Transmission. If a paper is filed by facsimile, the sender's original must not be filed but must be maintained in the files of the party transmitting it for filing and made available to the court or any party to the action upon request.

Subd. 4. Treatment of Confidential Information. To retain privacy, restricted identifiers (e.g., social security numbers, employer identification numbers, financial account numbers) must be blackened out from any documents provided under this rule and may only be submitted on a separate Confidential Information Form as required in Rule 11 of these rules. In addition, financial source documents (e.g., tax returns, wage stubs, credit card statements) must be submitted under a cover sheet entitled "Sealed Financial Source Documents" as required in Rule 11.

Adopted May 30, 2001, eff. July 1, 2001. Amended May 6, 2005, eff. July 1, 2005; Nov. 30, 2005, eff. Jan. 1, 2006; Nov. 12, 2008, eff. June 1, 2009.

Rule 370.05. Response

Subdivision 1. Hearing Date in Summons. Inclusion of a hearing date does not preclude a noninitiating party from serving and filing a written answer. Within twenty (20) days from service of the summons and complaint, a noninitiating party may serve upon all parties a written answer to the complaint. The service and filing of a written answer or the failure of a noninitiating party to appear at a hearing does not preclude the hearing from going forward, and the child support magistrate may issue an order based upon the information in the file or evidence presented at the hearing.

Subd. 2. Hearing Date Not in Summons. If the summons does not contain a hearing date, within twenty (20) days from service of the summons and complaint, a noninitiating party shall either:

(a) request a hearing by returning the request for hearing form to the initiating party; or

(b) serve upon all other parties and file with the court a written answer to the complaint.

The initiating party shall schedule a hearing upon receipt of the request for hearing form or the service of a written answer.

Adopted May 30, 2001, eff. July 1, 2001.

Rule 370.06. Amended Pleadings

Subdivision 1. Service. At any time up to ten (10) days before a scheduled hearing, the initiating party may serve and file amended pleadings. If no hearing date has been scheduled, the initiating party may serve and file amended pleadings within the time remaining for response.

Subd. 2. Response. If the noninitiating party chooses to respond to amended pleadings, the response must be made within the time remaining for response to the original pleading or within ten (10) days after service of the amended pleadings, whichever period is longer, unless the court otherwise orders.

Adopted May 30, 2001, eff. July 1, 2001.

Rule 370.07. Fees

A filing fee shall be paid pursuant to Rule 356 upon the filing of:

(a) the summons and complaint; and

(b) the written answer, if any.

Adopted May 30, 2001, eff. July 1, 2001.

Rule 370.08. Settlement Procedure

The parties may settle the case at any time pursuant to Rule 362.

Adopted May 30, 2001, eff. July 1, 2001.

Rule 370.09. Default Procedure

An action to establish support may proceed by default pursuant to Rule 363.

Adopted May 30, 2001, eff. July 1, 2001.

Rule 370.10. Hearing Procedure

Any hearing shall proceed pursuant to Rule 364. If the summons contains a hearing date, all parties shall appear at the hearing. If a party fails to appear at a hearing for which notice was properly served, the child support magistrate shall proceed pursuant to Rule 365.01.

Adopted May 30, 2001, eff. July 1, 2001.

Rule 370.11. Decision and Order

The decision and order of the court shall be issued pursuant to Rule 365.

Adopted May 30, 2001, eff. July 1, 2001.

Rule 370.12. Review and Appeal

Motions to correct clerical mistakes, if any, shall proceed pursuant to Rule 375. Review, if any, shall proceed pursuant to Rule 376. Appeal, if any, shall proceed pursuant to Rule 378.

Adopted May 30, 2001, eff. July 1, 2001.

RULE 371. PARENTAGE ACTIONS

Rule 371.01. Commencement

A proceeding to establish parentage shall be commenced in the expedited process by service of a summons and complaint pursuant to Rule 371.03. A supporting affidavit may also be served. Unless blood or genetic testing has already been completed, a request for blood or genetic testing shall be served with the summons and complaint. In addition to service of the summons and complaint, an order to show cause may be issued pursuant to Minn. Gen. R. Prac. 303.05. Service shall be completed at least twenty (20) days prior to any scheduled hearing.

Adopted May 30, 2001, eff. July 1, 2001.

Rule 371.02. Content of Summons, Complaint, and Supporting Affidavit

Subdivision 1. Content of Summons. A summons shall:

(a) state the name of the court;

(b) state the names of the parties;

(c) state an address where the initiating party may be served;

(d) state that the purpose of the action is to establish parentage;

(e) state the date, time, and location of the hearing;

(f) provide information about serving and filing a written response pursuant to Rule 371.04 and Rule 371.05;

(g) state that all parties shall appear at the hearing, and if any party fails to appear at the hearing the child support magistrate shall proceed pursuant to Rule 365.01;

(h) state that a party has the right to representation pursuant to Rule 357;

(i) state that the case may be settled informally by contacting the initiating party and include the name, address, and telephone number of the person to contact to discuss settlement; and

(j) be signed by the initiating party or that party's attorney.

If there is reason to believe that domestic violence exists or if an order for protection has been issued, a party may provide an alternative address and telephone number. Pursuant to Minn. Stat. § 257.70(b) (2000), in all actions in which public assistance is assigned or the county agency is providing services to a party or parties to the action, information regarding the location of one party may not be released by the county agency to any other party if the county agency has knowledge that a protective order with respect to the other party has been entered or has reason to believe that the release of the information may result in physical or emotional harm to the other party.

Subd. 2. Content of Complaint. A complaint shall:

(a) state the relief the initiating party wants the child support magistrate to order;

(b) state the facts and grounds supporting the request for relief;

(c) set forth the acknowledgement required under Rule 379.04; and

(d) be signed by the initiating party or that party's attorney.

Subd. 3. Content of Supporting Affidavit. A supporting affidavit shall:

(a) state detailed facts supporting the request for relief, including the facts establishing parentage;

(b) provide all information required by Minn. Stat. § 518A.46, subd. 3(a) (2006), if known; and

(c) be signed and sworn to under oath.

Adopted May 30, 2001, eff. July 1, 2001. Amended Nov. 12, 2008, eff. June 1, 2009.

Advisory Committee Comment

Pursuant to Minn. Stat. § 518.5513, subd. 3(a), for all cases involving establishment or modification of support, the pleadings are to contain specific information. At times, it may be necessary to attach additional supporting documents. Each county should establish its own local policy regarding the attachment of supporting documents.

Advisory Committee Comment—2008 Amendment

Pursuant to Minn. Stat. § 518A.46, subd. 3(a) (2006), for all cases involving establishment or modification of support, the pleadings are to contain specific information. At times, it may be necessary to attach additional supporting documents. Each county should establish its own local policy regarding the attachment of supporting documents.

Rule 371.03. Service of Summons and Complaint

Subdivision 1. Who is Served. The biological mother, each man presumed to be the father under Minn. Stat. § 257.55 (2000), each man alleged to be the biological father, and the county agency even if not a party, shall be served pursuant to subdivision 2.

Subd. 2. How Served. The summons and complaint, any supporting affidavit, and if required, a request for blood or genetic testing, shall be served upon the parties by personal service, or alternative personal service, pursuant to Rule 355.02, unless personal service has been waived in writing.

Adopted May 30, 2001, eff. July 1, 2001. Amended Sept. 23, 2003, eff. Nov. 1, 2003.

Rule 371.04. Filing Requirements

Subdivision 1. Initiating Party. No later than five (5) days before any scheduled hearing the initiating party shall file the following with the court:

(a) the original summons;

(b) the original complaint;

(c) the original supporting affidavit, if served; and

(d) proof of service upon each party pursuant to Rule 355.04.

Subd. 2. Responding Party. If a noninitiating party responds with a written response pursuant to Rule 371.05, the following, if served, shall be filed with the court no later than five (5) days before any scheduled hearing:

(a) the original written answer along with a financial affidavit pursuant to Minn. Stat. § 518A.28 (2006); or

(b) a request for blood or genetic testing; and

(c) proof of service upon each party pursuant to Rule 355.04.

Subd. 3. Facsimile Transmission. If a paper is filed by facsimile, the sender's original must not be filed but must be maintained in the files of the party transmitting it for filing and made available to the court or any party to the action upon request.

Subd. 4. Treatment of Confidential Information. To retain privacy, restricted identifiers (e.g., social security numbers, employer identification numbers, financial account numbers) must be blackened out from any documents provided under this rule and may only be submitted on a separate Confidential Information Form as required in Rule 11 of these rules. In addition, financial source documents (e.g., tax returns, wage stubs, credit card statements) must be submitted under a cover sheet entitled "Sealed Financial Source Documents" as required in Rule 11.

Adopted May 30, 2001, eff. July 1, 2001. Amended May 6, 2005, eff. July 1, 2005; Nov. 30, 2005, eff. Jan. 1, 2006; Nov. 12, 2008, eff. June 1, 2009.

Rule 371.05. Response

Subdivision 1. Response Options. In addition to appearing at the hearing as required under Rule 371.10, subd. 1, a noninitiating party may do one or more of the following:

(a) contact the initiating party to discuss settlement; or

(b) within twenty (20) days of service of the summons and complaint, serve upon all parties one or more of the written responses pursuant to subdivision 2.

Subd. 2. Types of Written Response.

(a) *Request for Blood or Genetic Test.* A noninitiating party may serve and file a request for blood or genetic testing either alleging or denying paternity. Filing of a request for blood or genetic testing shall, with the consent of the parties, extend the time for filing and serving a written answer until the blood or genetic test results have been mailed to the parties. In this event, the alleged parent shall have ten (10) days from the day the test results are mailed to the alleged parent in which to file and serve a written answer to the complaint.

(b) *Written Answer.* A noninitiating party may serve and file a written answer responding to all allegations set forth in the complaint. The matter shall proceed pursuant to Rule 353.02, subd. 3, if the written answer raises one or more of the following issues: parentage, custody, parenting time, or the legal name of the child.

Adopted May 30, 2001, eff. July 1, 2001. Amended Nov. 12, 2008, eff. June 1, 2009.

Rule 371.06. Blood or Genetic Testing Requested Before Hearing

When a request for blood or genetic testing is made prior to the hearing pursuant to Rule 371.05, the child support magistrate shall issue an order for blood or genetic testing and shall continue the hearing to allow the tests to be completed and the results to be received.

Adopted May 30, 2001, eff. July 1, 2001.

Rule 371.07. Amended Pleadings

Subdivision 1. Service. At any time up to ten (10) days before a scheduled hearing, the initiating party may serve and file amended pleadings.

Subd. 2. Response. If the noninitiating party chooses to respond to amended pleadings, the response must be made within the time remaining for response to the original pleading or within ten (10) days after service of the amended pleadings, whichever period is longer, unless the court otherwise orders.

Adopted May 30, 2001, eff. July 1, 2001.

Rule 371.08. Fees

A filing fee shall be paid pursuant to Rule 356 upon the filing of:

(a) the summons and complaint; and

(b) the written answer or the request for blood or genetic testing, if any.

Adopted May 30, 2001, eff. July 1, 2001.

Rule 371.09. Settlement Procedure

The parties may settle the case at any time pursuant to Rule 362.

Adopted May 30, 2001, eff. July 1, 2001.

Rule 371.10. Hearing Procedure

Subdivision 1. Hearing Mandatory. A hearing shall be held to determine parentage, except as provided in subdivision 2. All parties shall appear at the hearing. If a party fails to appear at a hearing for which notice was properly served, the child support magistrate shall either refer the matter to district court or proceed pursuant to Rule 365.01. The hearing shall proceed pursuant to Rule 364, except that paternity hearings from commencement through adjudication shall be closed to the public. All hearings following entry of the order determining the parent and child relationship are open to the public.

Subd. 2. Exception. If all parties, including the county agency, sign an agreement that contains all statutory requirements for a parentage adjudication, including a statement that the parties waiver their right to a hearing, the hearing may be stricken. The matter shall not be stricken from the court calendar until after the child support magistrate reviews and signs the agreement. The court administrator shall strike the hearing upon receipt of the agreement signed by the child support magistrate.

Adopted May 30, 2001, eff. July 1, 2001.

Rule 371.11. Procedure When Blood or Genetic Testing Requested

Subdivision 1. Blood or Genetic Testing Requested at Hearing. When blood or genetic testing is requested at the hearing, the child support magistrate shall issue an order for blood or genetic testing and shall continue the hearing to allow the tests to be completed and the results to be received.

Subd. 2. Blood or Genetic Testing Requested and Conducted Prior to Hearing. When blood or genetic testing is completed prior to the hearing and parentage is contested, the child support magistrate may upon motion set temporary child support pursuant to Minn. Stat. § 257.62, subd. 5 (2000), and shall refer the matter to district court pursuant to Rule 353.02, subd. 3.

Adopted May 30, 2001, eff. July 1, 2001.

Rule 371.12. Procedure When Written Answer Filed

Subdivision 1. Objections under the Parentage Act. The matter shall proceed pursuant to Rule 353.02, subd. 3, if the written answer contains an objection to one or more of the following issues: parentage, custody, parenting time, or the legal name of the child.

Subd. 2. Genetic Tests Received. When blood or genetic test results have been received and the results indicate a likelihood of paternity of ninety-two (92) percent or greater and a motion to set temporary support has been served and filed, the issue of temporary support shall be decided by the child support magistrate and the matter shall be referred to district court for further proceedings. Failure of a party to appear at the hearing shall not preclude the child support magistrate from issuing an order for temporary support.

Subd. 3. Objection to Support. A written answer objecting to any issue other than parentage, custody, parenting time, or the legal name of the child shall not prevent the hearing from proceeding. Failure of a party to appear at the hearing shall not preclude the child support magistrate from determining paternity and issuing an order for support.

Adopted May 30, 2001, eff. July 1, 2001.

Rule 371.13. Procedure When Written Answer Not Filed

If a written answer has not been served and filed by a noninitiating party and that party fails to appear at the hearing, the matter shall be heard and an order shall be issued by the child support magistrate. When the complaint, motion, or supporting affidavit contains specific requests for relief on the issue of custody, parenting time, or the legal name of the child, and proper service has been made upon all parties, the child support magistrate may grant such relief when a noninitiating party fails to appear at the hearing.

Adopted May 30, 2001, eff. July 1, 2001.

Advisory Committee Comment

Minnesota Statutes § 257.651 (2000) provides that if the alleged father fails to appear at a hearing after service duly made and proved, the court may issue an order. The Committee also intends that the court may issue an order if the mother fails to appear after service duly made and proved.

Rule 371.14. Decision and Order

The decision and order of the court shall be issued pursuant to Rule 365.

Adopted May 30, 2001, eff. July 1, 2001.

Rule 371.15. Review and Appeal

Motions to correct clerical mistakes, if any, shall proceed pursuant to Rule 375. Review, if any, shall proceed pursuant to Rule 376. Appeal, if any, shall proceed pursuant to Rule 378.

Adopted May 30, 2001, eff. July 1, 2001.

RULE 372. MOTIONS TO MODIFY, MOTIONS TO SET SUPPORT, AND OTHER MATTERS

Rule 372.01. Commencement

Subdivision 1. Motions to Modify and Motions to Set Support. A proceeding to modify an existing support order shall be commenced in the expedited process by service of a notice of motion, motion, and supporting affidavit pursuant to Rule 372.03. A proceeding to set support where a prior order reserved support may be commenced in the expedited process by service of a notice of motion and motion and supporting affidavit pursuant to Rule 372.03. If the notice of motion does not contain a hearing date, a request for hearing form shall be attached to the notice of motion. In addition to service of the notice of motion and motion, an order to show cause may be issued pursuant to Minn. Gen. R. Prac. 303.05. Service shall be made at least twenty (20) days prior to any scheduled hearing.

Subd. 2. Other Motions. Except as otherwise provided in these rules, all proceedings shall be commenced in the expedited process by service of a notice of motion, motion, and supporting affidavit. Service shall be made at least fourteen (14) days prior to the scheduled hearing.

Adopted May 30, 2001, eff. July 1, 2001. Amended Nov. 12, 2008, eff. June 1, 2009.

Rule 372.02. Content of Notice of Motion, Motion, Supporting Affidavit, and Request for Hearing Form

Subdivision 1. Content of Notice. A notice of motion shall:

(a) state the name of the court;

(b) state the names of the parties as set forth in the summons and complaint, or summons and petition, unless amended by order of the court;

(c) state an address where the initiating party may be served;

(d) state the purpose of the action;

(e) for motions brought pursuant to Rule 372.01, subd. 2, state the date, time, and location of the hearing;

(f) for motions brought pursuant to Rule 372.01, subd. 1, either state the date, time, and location of the hearing if one is scheduled or, if no hearing is scheduled, state that any party has a right to a hearing and attach a request for hearing form;

(g) provide information about serving and filing a written response pursuant to Rule 372.04 and Rule 372.05;

(h) state that all parties shall appear at the hearing if one is scheduled, and if any party fails to appear at the hearing, the child support magistrate shall proceed pursuant to Rule 365.01;

(i) state that a party has a right to representation pursuant to Rule 357;

(j) state that the case may be settled informally by contacting the initiating party and include the name, address, and telephone number of the person to contact to discuss settlement; and

(k) be signed by the initiating party or that party's attorney.

If there is reason to believe that domestic violence exists or if an order for protection has been issued, the party may provide an alternative address and telephone number. Pursuant to Minn. Stat. § 518.005, subd. 5, in all actions in which public assistance is assigned or the county agency is providing services to a party or parties to the action, information regarding the location of one party may not be released by the county agency to the other party if the county agency has knowledge that a protective order with respect to the other party has been entered or has reason to believe that the release of the information may result in physical or emotional harm to the other party.

Subd. 2. Content of Motion. A motion shall:

(a) state the relief the initiating party wants the child support magistrate to order;

(b) state the specific support that the initiating party wants the child support magistrate to order if the notice of motion does not contain a hearing date;

(c) state the facts and grounds supporting the request for relief;

(d) set forth the acknowledgement under Rule 379.04; and

(e) be signed by the initiating party or that party's attorney.

Subd. 3. Content of Supporting Affidavit. A supporting affidavit shall:

(a) state detailed facts supporting the request for relief;

(b) for motions to modify support and motions to set support, provide all information required by Minn. Stat. § 518A.46, subd. 3(a) (2006), if known; and

(c) be signed and sworn to under oath.

Subd. 4. Content of Request for Hearing Form. A request for hearing form shall contain the name and address of the initiating party, and a short and concise statement that a noninitiating party requests a hearing.

Adopted May 30, 2001, eff. July 1, 2001. Amended Nov. 12, 2008, eff. June 1, 2009.

Advisory Committee Comment

Pursuant to Minn. Stat. § 518.5513, subd. 3(a), for all cases involving establishment or modification of support, the pleadings are to contain specific information. At times, it may be necessary to attach additional supporting documents. Each county should establish its own local policy regarding the attachment of supporting documents.

Advisory Committee Comment—2008 Amendment

Pursuant to Minn. Stat. § 518A.46, subd. 3(a) (2006), for all cases involving establishment or modification of support, the pleadings are to contain specific information. At times, it may be necessary to attach additional supporting documents. Each county should establish its own local policy regarding the attachment of supporting documents.

Rule 372.03. Service of Notice of Motion and Motion

Subdivision 1. Who is Served. All parties, and the county agency even if not a party, shall be served pursuant to subdivision 2.

Subd. 2. How Served. The notice of motion, motion, supporting affidavit, and if required, the request for hearing form, may be served upon the parties either by U.S. mail, facsimile, or by personal service pursuant to Rule 355.02.

Adopted May 30, 2001, eff. July 1, 2001.

Rule 372.04. Filing Requirements

Subdivision 1. Initiating Party. No later than five (5) days before any scheduled hearing or, if no hearing is scheduled, within fourteen (14) days from the date the last party was served, the initiating party shall file the following with the court:

(a) the original notice of motion;

(b) the original motion;

(c) the original supporting affidavit;

(d) the request for hearing form, if returned to the initiating party; and

(e) proof of service upon each party pursuant to Rule 355.04.

Subd. 2. Responding Party. If a noninitiating party responds with a responsive motion or counter motion pursuant to Rule 372.05, the following shall be filed with the court no later than five (5) days before any scheduled hearing or, if no hearing is scheduled, within fourteen (14) days from the date the last party was served:

(a) the original responsive motion or counter motion; and

(b) proof of service upon each party pursuant to Rule 355.04.

Subd. 3. Facsimile Transmission. If a paper is filed by facsimile, the sender's original must not be filed but must be maintained in the files of the party transmitting it for filing and made available to the court or any party to the action upon request.

Subd. 4. Treatment of Confidential Information. To retain privacy, restricted identifiers (e.g., social security numbers, employer identification numbers, financial account numbers) must be blackened out from any documents provided under this rule and may only be submitted on a separate Confidential Information Form as required in Rule 11 of these rules. In addition, financial source documents (e.g., tax returns, wage stubs, credit card statements) must be submitted under a cover sheet entitled "Sealed Financial Source Documents" as required in Rule 11.

Adopted May 30, 2001, eff. July 1, 2001. Amended May 6, 2005, eff. July 1, 2005; Nov. 30, 2005, eff. Jan. 1, 2006.

Rule 372.05. Response

Subd. 1. Hearing Date Included in the Notice of Motions to Modify and Motions to Set Support. Inclusion of a hearing date does not preclude a noninitiating party from serving and filing a responsive motion or counter motion. A noninitiating party may serve upon all parties a responsive motion or counter motion along with a supporting affidavit at least fourteen (14) days prior to the hearing. The service and filing of a responsive motion or counter motion does not preclude the hearing from going forward and the child support magistrate may issue an order based upon the information in the file or evidence presented at the hearing if a noninitiating party fails to appear at the hearing.

Subd. 2. Hearing Date Not Included in the Notice of Motions to Modify and Motions to Set Support. If the notice of motion does not contain a hearing date, within fourteen (14) days from service of the motion, a noninitiating party shall either:

(a) request a hearing by returning the request for hearing form to the initiating party; or

(b) serve upon all other parties a responsive motion or counter motion.

The initiating party shall schedule a hearing upon receipt of a request for hearing form, a responsive motion, or counter motion. Failure of the noninitiating party to request a hearing, to serve a responsive motion, or to appear at a scheduled hearing shall not preclude the matter from going forward, and the child support magistrate may issue an order based upon the information in the file or the evidence presented at the hearing.

Subd. 3. Other Motions. Except as otherwise provided in these rules, all responsive motions shall be served upon all parties at least five (5) days prior to the hearing. A responsive motion raising new issues shall be served upon all parties at least ten (10) days prior to the hearing.

Adopted May 30, 2001, eff. July 1, 2001. Amended Sept. 23, 2003, eff. Nov. 1, 2003; Nov. 12, 2008, eff. June 1, 2009.

Advisory Committee Comment—2008 Amendment

Rule 372.05, subd. 2, is amended to apply the 14–day deadline for responding to a motion to either of the permitted responses; to request a hearing or to file a responsive motion or counter-motion. Rule 372.05, subd. 3 is added to clarify the deadlines for submitting responsive motions.

Rule 372.06. Amended Motions

Subdivision 1. Service. At any time up to ten (10) days before a scheduled hearing, the initiating party may serve and file an amended motion. If no hearing date has been scheduled, the initiating party may serve and file an amended motion within the time remaining for response.

Subd. 2. Response. If the noninitiating party chooses to respond to an amended motion, the response must be made within the time remaining for response to the original motion or within ten (10) days after service of the amended motion, whichever period is longer, unless the court otherwise orders.

Adopted May 30, 2001, eff. July 1, 2001.

Rule 372.07. Fees

Subdivision 1. Filing Fee. A filing fee shall be paid pursuant to Rule 356 upon the filing of:

(a) the notice of motion and motion; and

(b) the responsive motion or counter motion.

Subd. 2. Modification Fee. Pursuant to Minn. Stat. § 357.021, subd. 2(13), a separate fee shall also be collected upon the filing of the motion to modify and a responsive motion or counter motion.

Adopted May 30, 2001, eff. July 1, 2001. Amended Nov. 30, 2005, eff. Jan. 1, 2006.

Advisory Committee Comment—2001

The modification fee to be collected under Rule 372.07 is $20.00. (Order Setting Fee, File C9–85–1134, filed March 31, 1993).

Advisory Committee Comment—2006 Amendment

Rule 372.07, subd. 2, is amended to correct the statutory reference. In 2005, the legislature set the modification fee to be collected under Rule 372.07 at $55.00. Act of June 3, 2005, ch. 164, § 2, 2005 Minn. Laws 1878, 1879–80 (to be codified at Minn. Stat. § 357.021). Litigants are advised to review the statute or contact the court administrator for current fee amounts.

Rule 372.08. Settlement Procedure

The parties may settle the case at any time pursuant to Rule 362.

Adopted May 30, 2001, eff. July 1, 2001.

Rule 372.09. Default Procedure

An action to modify or set support may proceed by default pursuant to Rule 363.

Adopted May 30, 2001, eff. July 1, 2001.

Rule 372.10. Hearing Procedure

Any hearing shall proceed pursuant to Rule 364. If the notice of motion contains a hearing date, all parties shall appear at the hearing. If a party fails to appear at a hearing for which notice was properly served, the child support magistrate shall proceed pursuant to Rule 365.01.

Adopted May 30, 2001, eff. July 1, 2001.

Rule 372.11. Decision and Order

The decision and order of the court shall be issued pursuant to Rule 365.

Adopted May 30, 2001, eff. July 1, 2001.

Rule 372.12. Review and Appeal

Motions to correct clerical mistakes, if any, shall proceed pursuant to Rule 375. Review, if any, shall proceed pursuant to Rule 376. Appeal, if any, shall proceed pursuant to Rule 378.

Adopted May 30, 2001, eff. July 1, 2001.

RULE 373. ENFORCEMENT PROCEEDINGS

Rule 373.01. Types of Proceedings

All proceedings seeking statutory remedies shall be heard in the expedited process except as prohibited by statute or as follows:

(a) evidentiary hearings for contempt;

(b) matters of criminal non-support;

(c) motions to vacate a recognition of paternity or paternity adjudication; and

(d) matters of criminal contempt.

Civil contempt proceedings are permitted pursuant to Rule 353.01, subd. 2.

Adopted May 30, 2001, eff. July 1, 2001.

Rule 373.02. Commencement

Subdivision 1. Procedure Provided. When an enforcement proceeding is initiated pursuant to procedures set forth in statute, and a hearing is requested as permitted by statute, the matter shall be commenced in the expedited process by service of a notice of hearing. The hearing shall proceed pursuant to Rule 364.

Subd. 2. Procedure Not Provided. Any enforcement proceeding where the statute does not provide a procedure to obtain a hearing shall be commenced in the expedited process pursuant to Rule 372.

Subd. 3. Civil Contempt. Civil contempt proceedings shall be commenced pursuant to Rule 374.

Adopted May 30, 2001, eff. July 1, 2001.

RULE 374. CIVIL CONTEMPT

Rule 374.01. Initiation

Civil contempt proceedings initiated in the expedited process shall be brought according to the procedure set forth in Minn. Gen. R. Prac. 309.

Adopted May 30, 2001, eff. July 1, 2001.

Rule 374.02. Resolution of Contempt Matter

If the parties reach agreement at the initial appearance, the agreement may be stated orally on the record or the county attorney may prepare an order that shall be signed by all parties and submitted to the child support magistrate for approval. If approved, the order shall be forwarded to the court administrator for signing by a district court judge. The order is effective upon signing by a district court judge.

Adopted May 30, 2001, eff. July 1, 2001.

Rule 374.03. Evidentiary Hearing

If the parties do not reach agreement at the initial appearance, the child support magistrate shall refer the matter to the court administrator to schedule an evidentiary hearing before a district court judge or a family court referee. A child support magistrate shall not consider or decide a contempt matter, except as provided in Rule 353.01, subd. 2.

Adopted May 30, 2001, eff. July 1, 2001.

Rule 374.04. Failure to Appear

If the alleged contemnor fails to appear at the initial appearance, the child support magistrate may certify to a district court judge that the alleged contemnor failed to appear and may recommend issuance of a warrant for the person's arrest. Only a district court judge may issue arrest warrants.

Adopted May 30, 2001, eff. July 1, 2001.

III. REVIEW AND APPEAL

RULE 375. MOTION TO CORRECT CLERICAL MISTAKES

Rule 375.01. Initiation

Clerical mistakes, typographical errors, and errors in mathematical calculations in orders, including orders for temporary support, arising from oversight or omission may be corrected by the child support magistrate at any time upon the magistrate's own initiative or upon motion of any party after notice to all parties.

Adopted May 30, 2001, eff. July 1, 2001.

Rule 375.02. Procedure

A motion to correct clerical mistakes shall be brought pursuant to Rule 377 and shall be made in good faith and not for purposes of delay or harassment.

Adopted May 30, 2001, eff. July 1, 2001.

Rule 375.03. Decision

A motion to correct clerical mistakes shall be decided by the child support magistrate who issued the decision and order. If the child support magistrate who issued the order is unavailable, the motion to correct clerical mistakes may be assigned by the court administrator to another child support magistrate in the judicial district. If an appeal has been made to the court of appeals pursuant to Rule 378, a child support magistrate may correct clerical mistakes, typographical errors, and errors in mathematical calculations only upon order of the appellate court.

Adopted May 30, 2001, eff. July 1, 2001.

Rule 375.04. Combined Motions

A motion to correct clerical mistakes may be combined with a motion for review. If a party intends to bring both a motion to correct clerical mistakes under this rule and a motion for review under Rule 376.01, the combined motion shall be brought within the time prescribed by Rule 377.02. A combined motion may be decided either by the child support magistrate who issued the decision and order or, at the request of any party, by a district court judge.

Adopted May 30, 2001, eff. July 1, 2001.

RULE 376. MOTION FOR REVIEW

Rule 376.01. Initiation

Any party may bring a motion for review of the decision and order or judgment of the child support magistrate. An order for temporary support is not subject to a motion for review.

Adopted May 30, 2001, eff. July 1, 2001.

Advisory Committee Comment

A party may make a motion for review regarding an order, regardless of whether it was issued as a result of default, based upon a stipulation or agreement of the parties, or issued following a hearing.

Rule 376.02. Procedure

A motion for review or a combined motion shall be brought pursuant to Rule 377 and shall be made in good faith and not for purposes of delay or harassment.

Adopted May 30, 2001, eff. July 1, 2001.

Rule 376.03. Decision

A motion for review may be decided either by the child support magistrate who issued the decision and order or, at the request of any party, a district court judge. If the child support magistrate who issued the order is unavailable, the motion for review may be assigned by the court administrator to another child support magistrate in the judicial district. If a district court judge issued the order in question, that judge shall also decide the motion for review. If an appeal has been made to the court of appeals pursuant to Rule 378, a child support magistrate may decide a motion for review or a combined motion only upon order of the appellate court.

Adopted May 30, 2001, eff. July 1, 2001.

RULE 377. PROCEDURE ON A MOTION TO CORRECT CLERICAL MISTAKES, MOTION FOR REVIEW, OR COMBINED MOTION

Rule 377.01. Other Motions Precluded

Except for motions to correct clerical mistakes, motions for review, or motions alleging fraud, all other motions for post-decision relief are precluded, including those under Minn. R. Civ. P. 59 and 60 and Minn. Stat. § 518.145 (2000).

Adopted May 30, 2001, eff. July 1, 2001.

Rule 377.02. Timing of Motion

To bring a motion to correct clerical mistakes, the aggrieved party shall perform items (a) through (e) as soon as practicable after discovery of the error. To bring a motion for review or a combined motion, the aggrieved party shall perform items (a) through (f) within twenty (20) days of the date the court administrator served that party with the notice form as required by Rule 365.04.

(a) Complete the motion to correct clerical mistakes form, motion for review form, or combined motion form.

(b) Serve the completed motion for clerical mistakes form, motion for review form, or combined motion form upon all other parties and the county agency. Service may be made by personal service or by U.S. mail pursuant to Rule 355.02.

(c) File the original motion with the court. If the filing is accomplished by mail, the motion shall be postmarked on or before the due date set forth in the notice of filing.

(d) File the affidavit of service with the court. The affidavit of service shall be filed at the time the original motion is filed.

(e) Order a transcript of the hearing under Rule 366, if the party desires to submit a transcript.

(f) For a motion for review or combined motion, pay to the court administrator the filing fee required by Rule 356.01, if the party has not already done so. The court administrator may reject the motion papers if the appropriate fee does not accompany the papers at the time of filing.

Adopted May 30, 2001, eff. July 1, 2001.

Rule 377.03. Content of Motion

Subdivision 1. Motion to Correct Clerical Mistakes. A motion to correct clerical mistakes shall:

(a) identify by page and paragraph the clerical mistake(s) and state the correct language;

(b) include the acknowledgement as required pursuant to Rule 379.04; and

(c) be signed by the party or that party's attorney.

Subd. 2. Motion for Review or Combined Motion. A motion for review or combined motion shall:

(a) state the reason(s) the review is requested;

(b) state the specific change(s) requested;

(c) specify the evidence or law that supports the requested change(s);

(d) state whether the party is requesting that the review be by the child support magistrate that issued the order being reviewed or by a district court judge;

(e) state whether the party is requesting an order authorizing the party to submit new evidence;

(f) state whether the party requests an order granting a new hearing;

(g) include the acknowledgment as required pursuant to Rule 379.04; and

(h) be signed by the initiating party or that party's attorney.

Adopted May 30, 2001, eff. July 1, 2001.

Rule 377.04. Response to Motion

Subdivision 1. Timing of Response to Motion. A party may respond to a motion to correct clerical mistakes or a motion for review. Any response shall state why the relief requested in the motion should or should not be granted. If a responding party wishes to raise other issues, the responding party must set forth those issues as a counter motion in the response. To respond to a motion to correct clerical mistakes the party shall perform items (a) through (e) within ten (10) days of the date the party was served with the motion. To respond to a motion for review or a combined motion the party shall perform (a) through (f) within thirty (30) days of the date the party was served with the notice under Rule 365.04. To respond to a counter motion, the party shall perform items (a) through (f) within forty (40) days of the date the party was served with the notice under Rule 365.04.

(a) Complete the response to motion to correct clerical mistakes form, response to motion for review form, or response to combined motion form.

(b) Serve the completed response to motion for clerical mistakes form, response to motion for review form, or response to combined motion form upon all other parties and the county agency. Service may be made by personal service or by U.S. mail pursuant to Rule 355.02.

(c) File the original response to motion with the court. If the filing is accomplished by mail, the response to motion shall be postmarked on or before the due date set forth in the notice of filing.

(d) File the affidavit of service with the court. The affidavit of service shall be filed at the time the original response to motion is filed.

(e) Order a transcript of the hearing under Rule 366, if the party desires to submit a transcript.

(f) For a responsive motion for review or combined motion, pay to the court administrator the filing fee required by Rule 356.01, if the party has not already done so. The court administrator may reject the responsive papers if the appropriate fee does not accompany the papers at the time of filing.

Subd. 2. Content of Response to Motion

(a) Content of Response to Motion to Correct Clerical Mistakes. A response to a motion to correct clerical mistakes shall:

(1) identify by page and paragraph the clerical mistake(s) alleged by the moving party and state whether responding party agrees or opposes the corrections;

(2) include an acknowledgement as required pursuant to Rule 379.04; and

(3) be signed by the responding party or that party's attorney.

(b) Content of Response to Motion for Review, Combined Motion, or Counter Motion. A response to a motion for review, combined motion, or counter motion shall:

(1) state why the relief requested should or should not be granted;

(2) if new issues are raised, state the specific change(s) requested;

(3) if new issues are raised, specify the evidence or law that supports the requested change(s);

(4) state whether the party is requesting that the review be by the child support magistrate who issued the order being reviewed or by a district court judge;

(5) state whether the party is requesting an order authorizing the party to submit new evidence;

(6) state whether the party requests an order granting a new hearing;

(7) include an acknowledgement as required pursuant to Rule 379.04; and

(8) be signed by the responding party or that party's attorney.

Adopted May 30, 2001, eff. July 1, 2001. Amended Sept. 23, 2003, eff. Nov. 1, 2003.

Rule 377.05. Calculation of Time

Subdivision 1. Timing for Response to Motion to Correct Clerical Mistakes. To calculate the time to respond to a motion to correct clerical mistakes, three (3) days shall be added to the ten (10) days for a total of thirteen (13) days within which to respond when the motion is served by mail.

Subd. 2. Timing for Service of Motion for Review or Combined Motion. To calculate the time to serve a motion for review or combined motion, three (3) days shall be added to the twenty (20) days for a total of twenty-three (23) days within which to serve a motion when the notice form as required by Rule 365.04 is served by mail.

Subd. 3. Timing for Response to Motion for Review or Combined Motion. To calculate the time to serve a response to a motion for review or combined motion, three (3) days shall be added to the thirty (30) days for a total of thirty-three (33) days within which to respond when the notice form as required under Rule 365.04 is served by mail. If the motion for review or combined motion is served by mail, an additional three (3) days shall be added to the thirty-three (33) days for a total of thirty-six (36) days within which to respond.

Subd. 4. Timing for Response to Counter Motion. To calculate the time to serve a response to a counter motion, three (3) days shall be added to the forty (40) days for a total of forty-three (43) days within which to respond when the notice form as required under Rule 365.04 is served by mail. If the counter motion to the motion for review or combined motion is served by mail, an additional three (3) days shall be added to the forty-three (43) days for a total of forty-six (46) days within which to respond.

Adopted May 30, 2001, eff. July 1, 2001.

Rule 377.06. Review When Multiple Motions Filed—Motion for Review

If in a motion for review a party requests review by the child support magistrate and any other party requests review by a district court judge, all motions shall be assigned to a district court judge who shall either decide all issues or remand one or more issues to the child support magistrate with instructions.

Adopted May 30, 2001, eff. July 1, 2001.

Rule 377.07. Notice of Assignment of District Court Judge—Motion for Review

If a party requests that a motion for review be decided by a district court judge, upon the filing of a motion containing such a request the court administrator shall as soon as practicable notify the parties of the name of the judge to whom the motion has been assigned.

Adopted May 30, 2001, eff. July 1, 2001.

Rule 377.08. Decision and Order Not Stayed

The decision and order of the child support magistrate or district court judge remains in full force and effect and is not stayed pending a motion to correct clerical mistakes, a motion for review, or a combined motion.

Adopted May 30, 2001, eff. July 1, 2001.

Rule 377.09. Basis of Decision and Order

Subdivision 1. Timing. Within thirty (30) days of the close of the record, the child support magistrate or district court judge shall file with the court an order deciding the motion. In the event a notice to remove is granted pursuant to Rule 368, the thirty (30) days begins on the date the substitute child support magistrate or district court judge is assigned. The record shall be deemed closed upon occurrence of one of the following, whichever occurs later:

(a) filing of a response pursuant to Rule 377.04;

(b) filing of a transcript pursuant to Rule 366;

(c) withdrawal or cancellation of a request for transcript pursuant to Rule 366; or

(d) submission of new evidence under subdivision 4.

If none of the above events occur, the record on a motion for review or combined motion shall be deemed closed forty-six (46) days after service of the notice of filing as required by Rule 365.04, despite the requirements of Rule 354.04. For a motion to correct clerical mistakes and none of the above events occur, the record shall be deemed closed 15 days after service of the motion to correct clerical mistakes.

Subd. 2. Decision.

(a) Motion to Correct Clerical Mistakes. The child support magistrate or district court judge may issue an order denying the motion to correct clerical mistakes or may issue an order making such corrections as deemed appropriate. If the motion is denied, the child support magistrate or district court judge shall specifically state in the order that the findings, decision, and order are affirmed.

(b) Motion for Review. The child support magistrate or district court judge shall make an independent review of any findings or other provisions of the underlying decision and order for which specific changes are requested in the motion. The child support magistrate or district court judge may affirm the order without making additional findings. If the court determines that the findings and order are not supported by the record or the decision is contrary to law, the child support magistrate or district court judge may issue an order:

(1) denying in whole or in part the motion for review;

(2) approving, modifying, or vacating in whole or in part, the decision and order of the child support magistrate; or

(3) scheduling the matter for hearing and directing the court administrator to serve notice of the date, time, and location of the hearing upon the parties.

In addition, the district court judge may remand one or more issues back to the child support magistrate with instructions. If the child support magistrate who issued the order is unavailable, the motion may be assigned by the court administrator to another child support magistrate serving in the judicial district. If any findings or other provisions of the child support magistrate's or district court judge's decision and order are approved without change, the child support magistrate or district court judge shall specifically state in the order that those findings and other provisions are affirmed but need not make specific findings or conclusions as to each point raised in the motion. If any findings or other provisions of the child support magistrate's or district court judge's decision and order are modified, the child support magistrate or district court judge need only make specific findings or conclusions with respect to the provisions that are modified.

Subd. 3. Record on Review. The review by the child support magistrate or district court judge shall be based upon the decision of the child support magistrate or district court judge and any exhibits and affidavits filed, and, where a transcript has not been filed, may be based upon all or part of the audio or video recording of the hearing.

Subd. 4. Additional Evidence Discretionary. When bringing or responding to a motion to correct clerical mistakes, a motion for review, or a combined motion, the parties shall not submit any new evidence unless the child support magistrate or district court judge, upon written or oral notice to all parties, requests additional evidence.

Subd. 5. No Right to Hearing. A hearing shall not be held unless ordered by the child support magistrate or district court judge. The child support magistrate or district court judge may order a hearing upon motion of a party or on the court's own initiative. A party's motion shall be granted only upon a showing of good cause. In the event the child support magistrate or district court judge decides to conduct a hearing, the child support magistrate or the district court judge shall direct the court administrator to schedule a hearing date and to serve notice of the date, time, and location of the hearing upon all parties and the county agency.

Subd. 6. Costs and Fees. The child support magistrate or district court judge may award costs and fees incurred in responding to a motion to correct clerical mistakes, motion for review, or combined motion if the child support magistrate or district court judge determines that the motion is not made in good faith or is brought for purposes of delay or harassment.

Adopted May 30, 2001, eff. July 1, 2001. Amended Nov. 12, 2008, eff. June 1, 2009.

Advisory Committee Comment—2008 Amendment

Rule 377.09, subd. 2(b) is amended to correct language of the existing Rule that could be interpreted to have a mandatory meaning not intended by the Drafters. The revised rule allows the child support magistrate to affirm an order without findings, but does not require that. The rule is intended to adopt expressly a de novo standard of review. The reviewing court need not make findings if the decision is to affirm. De novo review is consistent with the reported decisions construing the former rule. *See, e.g. Kilpatrick v. Kilpatrick,* 673 N.W.2d 528, 530 n.2 (Minn. Ct. App. 2004); *Davis v. Davis,* 631 N.W.2d 822, 825 (Minn. Ct. App. 2001); *Blonigen v. Blonigen,* 621 N.W. 2d 276, 280 (Minn. Ct. App. 2001), *review denied* (Minn. Mar. 13, 2001).

Rule 377.10. Notice of Order or Judgment

Within five (5) days of receipt of an order issued as a result of a motion to correct clerical mistakes, a motion for review, or a combined motion, the court administrator shall serve a notice of filing of order or notice of entry of judgment upon each party by U.S. mail, along with a copy of the order or judgment. The notice shall state that the parties have a right to appeal to the court of appeals under Rule 378. If the order was issued by a district court judge, the court administrator shall provide a copy of the order to the child support magistrate.

Adopted May 30, 2001, eff. July 1, 2001.

Rule 377.11. Effective Date; Final Order

The order issued following a motion to correct clerical mistakes, a motion for review, or a combined motion is effective and final when signed by the child support magistrate or district court judge.

Adopted May 30, 2001, eff. July 1, 2001.

RULE 378. APPEAL TO COURT OF APPEALS

Rule 378.01. Generally

An appeal may be taken to the court of appeals from a final order or judgment of a child support magistrate or from a final order deciding a motion for review under Rule 376. Such an appeal shall be taken in accordance with the procedures set forth in the Minnesota Rules of Civil Appellate Procedure within sixty (60) days of the date the court administrator serves upon the parties the notice of filing of order or notice of entry of judgment. If any party brings a timely motion to correct clerical mistakes under Rule 375 or a timely motion for review under Rule 376, the time for appeal is extended for all parties while that motion is pending. Once the last such pending motion is decided by the child support magistrate or district court judge, the sixty (60) days to appeal from the final order or judgment of a child support magistrate or from a final order deciding a motion to correct clerical mistakes or a motion for review runs for all parties from the date the court administrator serves upon the parties the notice of filing of order or notice of entry of judgment disposing of that motion. A notice of appeal filed before the disposition of a timely motion to correct clerical mistakes or for review is premature and of no effect, and it does not divest the child support magistrate of jurisdiction to dispose of the motion. Except as otherwise provided in these rules, the Minnesota Rules of Civil Appellate Procedure shall govern the taking and processing of such appeals.

Adopted May 30, 2001, eff. July 1, 2001.

Advisory Committee Comment

Timing. Under Minn. R. Civ. App. P. 104.01, the sixty (60) days in which to bring an appeal to the court of appeals begins to run on the date of service by any party of written notice of filing of an appealable order or on the date on which an appealable judgment is entered. The Advisory Committee intends that Rule 378 supersede the appellate rule to provide that the sixty (60) days to appeal begins to run from the time the court administrator serves the written notice of filing of order or notice of entry of judgment.

Scope of Review. A party may choose to bring a motion to correct clerical mistakes, or a motion for review, or to appeal directly to the court of appeals thus bypassing the first two options. However, if a party chooses the option of appealing directly to the court of appeals without first bringing a motion for review, such an appeal will be limited to determining whether the evidence sustains the findings of fact (to which the "clearly erroneous" standard of review applies) and whether the findings support the conclusions of law and the judgment. *Kahn v. Tronnier*, 547 N. W.2d at 428, *rev. denied* (Minn. July 10, 1996). Thus, although a motion for review is very important to obtaining the broadest possible appellate review, it is not an absolute prerequisite to appeal—a litigant can choose to file a direct appeal from the order of the child support magistrate, but the appeal will be limited to issues within that narrower scope of review.

IV. FORMS

RULE 379. FORMS

Rule 379.01. Court Administrator to Provide Forms

Whenever a court administrator is required to provide forms under these rules, those forms shall be provided to the parties in the most accessible method for the parties, including fax, electronic mail, in person, by U.S. mail, or in alternate formats.

Adopted May 30, 2001, eff. July 1, 2001.

Rule 379.02. Substantial Compliance

The forms developed by the state court administrator and by the department of human services for use in the expedited process, or forms substantially in compliance with such forms, are sufficient for purposes of these rules.

Adopted May 30, 2001, eff. July 1, 2001.

Advisory Committee Comment

The Advisory Committee encourages use of the standardized forms developed by the state court administrator and department of human services. However, regardless of such standardized forms, attorneys representing the parties and the county attorney representing the interests of the county agency retain professional responsibility for the form and content of pleadings and other legal documents used in the expedited process.

Rule 379.03. Modification of Forms

Except as otherwise provided in these rules, a party has discretion to modify the standardized forms to address the factual and legal issues that cannot be adequately covered by standardized forms.

Adopted May 30, 2001, eff. July 1, 2001.

Rule 379.04. Acknowledgement

Subdivision 1. Generally. Each complaint or motion served and filed in the expedited process shall set forth an acknowledgement by the party or the party's attorney. By presenting to the court (whether by signing, filing, submitting, or later advocating) a pleading, written motion, or other paper, an attorney or pro se party is certifying that to the best of the person's knowledge, information, and belief:

(a) it is not being presented for any improper purpose, such as to harass or to cause unnecessary delay or needless increase in the cost of litigation;

(b) the claims, defenses, and other legal contentions therein are warranted by existing law or by a nonfrivolous argument for the extension, modification, or reversal of existing law or the establishment of new law;

(c) the allegations and other factual contentions have evidentiary support or, if specifically so identified, are likely to have evidentiary support after a reasonable opportunity for further investigation or discovery;

(d) the denials of factual contentions are warranted on the evidence or, if specifically so identified, are reasonably based on a lack of information or belief; and

(e) the court may impose an appropriate sanction upon the attorneys, law firms, or parties that violate the above stated representations to the court, or are responsible for the violation.

Subd. 2. Motions to Correct Clerical Mistakes and Motions for Review. In motions to correct clerical mistakes, motions for review, or combined motions, the acknowledgement shall also include the following:

(a) a statement that the existing order remains in full force and effect and the parties must continue to comply with that order until a new order is issued; and

(b) a statement that the party understands that the child support magistrate or judge will decide whether the party may submit new information or whether the party may have a hearing, and that the parties will be notified if the party's request is granted.

Adopted May 30, 2001, eff. July 1, 2001.

Rule 379.05. Deleted Nov. 12, 2008, eff. June 1, 2009

Historical Notes

Deleted Rule 379.05, adopted May 30, 2001, provided an exception for cases brought in the expedited process from the requirement that an Informational Statement and a Prehearing Statement be filed.

APPENDIX OF FORMS FOR TITLE IV. RULES OF FAMILY COURT PROCEDURE [DELETED]

All forms previously contained in Title IV have been deleted from the rules. Family Court Action forms are currently maintained on the state court website (www.mncourts.gov).

Historical Notes

The order of the Minnesota Supreme Court dated December 28, 2007, effective January 1, 2008, in amending Rule 311, included the following Advisory Committee Comment:

"The responsibility for forms development and review is being handed off to the state court administrator to permit more effective forms management and review. This process is already followed for the expedited process. Gen. R. Prac. 379.02."

TITLE V. PROBATE RULES

RULE 401. APPLICABILITY OF RULES

Rules 401 through 416 apply to all Probate proceedings.

Adopted Sept. 5, 1991, eff. Jan. 1, 1992.

Task Force Comment—1991 Adoption

Rules 401 through 416 are the Minnesota Probate Rules recodified, but not otherwise significantly changed. Rule 401 is a new rule intended to make it clear what actions are governed by these rules.

RULE 402. DEFINITIONS

(a) Formal Proceedings. A formal proceeding is a hearing conducted before the court with notice to interested persons. Formal proceedings seek a judicial determination.

(b) Informal Proceedings. An informal proceeding is conducted by the judge, the registrar, or the person or persons designated by the judge for probate of a will or appointment of a personal representative. Informal proceedings seek an administrative determination and not a judicial determination and are granted without prior notice and hearing.

(c) Supervised Administration. Supervised administration is a single, continuous, in rem proceeding commenced by a formal proceeding.

(d) Code. The code is the Uniform Probate Code as adopted by the State of Minnesota.

Adopted Sept. 5, 1991, eff. Jan. 1, 1992.

RULE 403. DOCUMENTS

(a) Preparation of Original Documents. It shall be the responsibility of lawyers and others appearing before the court or registrar to prepare for review and execution appropriate orders, decrees, statements, applications, petitions, notices and related documents, complete and properly drafted, to address the subject matter and relief requested.

(b) Official Forms. The official forms adopted by the Minnesota District Judges' Association or promulgated by the Commissioner of Commerce shall be used.

(c) Documents and Files. The court shall make its files and records available for inspection and copying.

No file, or any part thereof, shall be taken from the custody of the court, except the original court order required to be displayed to an individual or entity when the order is served. A document or exhibit which has been filed or submitted in any proceeding can thereafter be withdrawn only with the permission of the court. Any document which is written in a language other than English shall be accompanied by a verified translation into the English language.

(d) Verification of Filed Documents. Every document filed with the court must be verified as required by the code, except a written statement of claim filed with the court administrator by a creditor or a pleading signed by the lawyer for a party in accordance with the Minnesota Rules of Civil Procedure.

Adopted Sept. 5, 1991, eff. Jan. 1, 1992.

Probate Committee Comment

Original Advisory Committee Comment—Not kept current.

The court will accept photocopies of forms if the copies are made by a process that is permanent, on hard stock paper, are free of smudges and otherwise clearly legible and have been reproduced in the same length as the original form and prescribed type size. In using photocopies of forms in courts that are not utilizing a flat file system, the case heading and nomenclature must appear on the outside of the form when folded appropriately for permanent filing.

Task Force Comment—1991 Adoption

The change in this rule is made to reflect the new title of the office formerly known as Commissioner of Securities. See Minn. Stat. § 80A.14, subd. 5 (1990).

RULE 404. NOTICE IN FORMAL PROCEEDINGS

(a) General Notice Requirements. In all formal proceedings notice of a hearing on any petition shall be given as provided in the code after the court issues the order for hearing. Where mailed notice is required, proof of mailing the notice of hearing shall be filed with the court administrator before any formal order will issue. Mailed notice shall be given to any interested person as defined by the code or to the person's lawyer. Where notice by personal service or publication is required by the code, proof of personal service or publication shall be filed with the court administrator before the formal order will issue.

(b) Notice of Proceedings for Determination of Testacy and Appointment of Personal Representative. In proceedings which adjudicate testacy, notice of the hearing on the petition shall be given after the court administrator issues the order for hearing. Proof of publication of the order for hearing, in accordance with the code, shall be filed with the court administrator before the order will issue. In proceedings for the formal appointment of a personal representative, the same notice requirements shall pertain except notice by publication shall not be required if testacy has been previously determined. Where creditors claims are to be barred, the published notice shall include notice to creditors.

Mailed notice shall be given to all known heirs-at-law, all devisees under any will submitted for formal probate and all interested persons as defined by the code or ordered by the court and shall include in appropriate cases the attorney general, foreign consul and lawyers representing the interested persons.

Mailed notice shall be given to the surviving spouse of the following rights:

(1) The right to receive the decedent's wearing apparel, furniture and household goods and other personal property as provided in the code or by law.

(2) The right to receive maintenance payments during administration of the estate as provided in the code or by law.

(3) The right to take an elective share of one-third of the augmented estate as provided in the code and the homestead as provided in the code or by law.

(c) Waiver of Notice in Formal Proceedings. Except in proceedings governed by subdivision (b) of this rule, an interested person may waive notice of any formal proceeding in accordance with the code. The written waiver shall evidence the person's consent to the order sought in the proceeding.

Adopted Sept. 5, 1991, eff. Jan. 1, 1992.

Probate Committee Comment

Original Advisory Committee Comment— Not kept current.

Publication required by this notice must be completed prior to the hearing date.

RULE 405. INTERIM ORDERS

(a) Interim Orders Available From Court Only. The court has no power to intervene in any unsupervised administration unless a formal petition invoking the court's authority is filed by an interested person.

The court or registrar does not have authority to issue ex parte interim orders in unsupervised proceedings except that the registrar may issue the certificate of discharge provided for in the code.

In supervised administration, the court may issue ex parte orders only for strong and compelling reasons.

(b) [Rule 405 adopted without a paragraph (b).]

Adopted Sept. 5, 1991, eff. Jan. 1, 1992.

Probate Committee Comment

Original Advisory Committee Comment— Not kept current.

Determinations by the registrar are informal and do not bring the estate or interested persons under the supervisory authority of the court. A personal representative appointed in informal proceedings may petition the court for a formal determination as to any matter within the jurisdiction of the court. It may also be necessary to seek the formal determination of the court as to the admissibility of a will, determination of heirship, or other matters as a condition precedent to obtaining the requested relief.

RULE 406. UNCONTESTED FORMAL PROCEEDINGS

(a) Uncontested Formal Proceedings; Hearings and Proof. The court shall call the calendar in open court for all hearings set for a designated time. If a petition in a formal proceeding is unopposed, the court will enter in the record the fact that there was no appearance in opposition to the petition and that no objection has been filed with the court. Thereupon, the court shall:

(1) Make its determination after conducting a hearing in open court, requiring appearance of petitioner and testimony or other proof of the matters necessary to support the order sought; or

(2) Make its determination on the strength of the pleadings without requiring the appearance of petitioner or of petitioner's lawyer and without requiring testimony or proof other than the verified pleadings; or

(3) Make its determination based on such combination of (1) and (2) above as the court in its discretion deems proper.

In any uncontested formal proceeding, the court shall determine that (i) the time required for any notice has expired; (ii) any required notice has been given; (iii) the court has jurisdiction of the subject matter; (iv) venue is proper; and (v) the proceeding was commenced within the time limitations prescribed by the code as a prerequisite to determining other issues presented to the court for determination in the proceeding. The court shall be satisfied that the pleadings and any other proof presented support the order sought in any uncontested formal proceeding.

(b) [Rule 406 adopted without a paragraph (b).]

Adopted Sept. 5, 1991, eff. Jan. 1, 1992.

RULE 407. APPOINTMENT

(a) Nomination and Renunciation. When two or more persons have equal or higher priority to appointment as personal representative, those who do not renounce must concur in writing in nominating another to act for them, or in applying for appointment. In formal appointment proceedings, concurrence by persons who have equal or higher priority is presumed after notice has been given unless a written objection is filed.

(b) Nonresident Personal Representatives. The court or registrar may appoint a nonresident personal representative.

Adopted Sept. 5, 1991, eff. Jan. 1, 1992.

RULE 408. INFORMAL PROCEEDINGS

(a) Contents of the Application. Application for informal probate or appointment proceedings shall contain information required by the code and the approximate value of the following categories of assets:

Probate Assets	
Homestead	$________
Other Real Estate	$________
Cash	$________
Securities	$________
Other	$________
Non–Probate Assets	
Joint Tenancy	$________
Insurance	$________
Other	$________
Approximate Indebtedness	$________

In all estate proceedings, whether testate or intestate, the application must contain a statement that specifically eliminates all heirs or devisees other than those listed in the application.

Probate Committee Comment

Original Advisory Committee Comment—Not kept current.

Examples

(These are not intended to be exhaustive)

The statements will necessarily vary, depending upon who survives the decedent, and must close out any class affected:

(1) Where only the spouse survives, the application should state "That decedent left no surviving issue, natural or adopted, legitimate or illegitimate."

(2) Where only children survive, the application should state "That the decedent left surviving no spouse; no children, natural or adopted, legitimate or illegitimate, other than herein named; and no issue of any deceased children."

(3) Where the spouse and children survive, the application should state "That the decedent left surviving no children, natural or adopted, legitimate or illegitimate, other than herein named and no issue of any deceased children."

(4) Where only brothers or sisters of decedent survive, the application should state "That the decedent left surviving no spouse; issue; parents; brothers or sisters other than herein named; and no issue of deceased brothers or sisters."

(5) Where only first cousins survive, the application should state "That the decedent left surviving no spouse; issue; parents; brothers or sisters or issue thereof, grandparents; aunts or uncles; and no first cousins other than herein named."

(6) In all cases, the application should state either:

(a) That all the heirs-at-law survived the decedent for 120 hours or more; or

(b) That all the heirs-at-law survived the decedent for 120 hours or more except the following: (name or names).

(7) In all cases where a spouse and children survive, the application should state either:

(a) That all of the issue of the decedent are also issue of the surviving spouse; or

(b) That one or more of the issue of the decedent are not also issue of the surviving spouse.

(b) Will Testimony. The registrar shall not require any affidavit or testimony with respect to execution of a will prior to informal probate if it is a self-proved will or appears to have been validly executed.

Probate Committee Comment

Original Advisory Committee Comment—Not kept current.

Applicants for informal probate of a will which is not self-proved are encouraged to preserve evidence concerning the execution of the will if a formal testacy proceeding may later be required or desired.

(c) Appearances. The applicant is required to appear before the registrar unless represented by counsel. The registrar may also waive appearance by counsel.

(d) Informal Proceedings: Notice of Informal Probate of Will and Informal Appointment of Personal Representative. In informal proceedings, notice of appointment of a personal representative shall be given after the registrar issues the order appointing the personal representative. Proof of placement for publication shall be filed with the court administrator before letters will issue. Where mailed notice is required, an affidavit of mailing of the order appointing the personal representative shall be filed with the court administrator before letters will issue. If the informal proceedings include the informal probate of a will, the notice shall include notice of the issuance of the statement of informal probate of the will. Where creditors claims are to be barred, the published notice shall include notice to creditors.

Mailed notice shall be given to all known heirs-at-law, all devisees under any will submitted for informal probate and all interested persons as defined by the code and shall include in appropriate cases the attorney general, foreign consul and lawyers representing interested persons.

Mailed notice shall be given to the surviving spouse of the following rights:

(1) The right to receive the decedent's wearing apparel, furniture and household goods and other personal property as provided in the code or by law.

(2) The right to receive maintenance payments during administration of the estate as provided in the code or by law.

(3) The right to take an elective share of one-third of the augmented estate as provided in the

code and the homestead as provided in the code or by law.

Adopted Sept. 5, 1991, eff. Jan. 1, 1992.

RULE 409. FORMAL TESTACY AND APPOINTMENT PROCEEDINGS

(a) Contents of Petition. A petition in formal testacy and appointment proceedings shall contain the information required by the code and the information concerning the approximate value of assets required by Minn. Gen. R. Prac. 408(a). In all estate proceedings, whether testate or intestate, the petition must contain an allegation that specifically eliminates all heirs or devisees other than as listed in the petition.

(b) Conversion to Supervised Administration. Any estate which has been commenced as an informal proceeding or as an unsupervised formal proceeding may be converted at any time to a supervised administration upon petition. The court shall enter an order for hearing on said petition. Notice of hearing shall be given in accordance with Minn. Gen. R. Prac. 404(a). If testacy has not been adjudicated in a prior formal proceeding, notice of hearing must meet the specific notice requirements for formal testacy proceedings provided by Minn. Gen. R. Prac. 404(b) including notice by publication.

Adopted Sept. 5, 1991, eff. Jan. 1, 1992.

RULE 410. TRANSFER OF REAL ESTATE

(a) Transfers of Real Estate in Supervised and Unsupervised Administration; Transfer by Personal Representative of Real Property for Value; Documents Required. A personal representative shall provide a transferee of real property for value with the following documents:

(1) A certified copy of unrestricted letters (30 days must have elapsed since date of issuance of letters to an informally appointed personal representative);

(2) A certified copy of the will; and

(3) A personal representative's deed or other instrument transferring any interest in real property which shall contain the marital status of the decedent and the consent of spouse, if any.

(b) Distribution of Real Property; Documents Required. A personal representative shall provide a distributee of real property with the following documents:

(1) When distribution is made by decree, a certified copy of the decree of distribution assigning any interest in real property to the distributee.

(2) When distribution is made by deed from a personal representative in unsupervised administration:

(i) A certified copy of unrestricted letters (30 days must have elapsed since date of issuance of letters to an informally appointed personal representative);

(ii) A certified copy of the will; and

(iii) A personal representative's deed of distribution of any interest in real property to the distributee which shall contain the marital status of the decedent and consent of spouse, if any.

(3) When distribution is made by deed from the personal representative in supervised administration:

(i) A certified copy of unrestricted letters;

(ii) A certified copy of an order of distribution which authorizes the distribution of any interest in real property to the distributee;

(iii) A certified copy of the will; and

(iv) A personal representative's deed of distribution of any interest in real property to the distributee.

Adopted Sept. 5, 1991, eff. Jan. 1, 1992.

RULE 411. CLOSING ESTATES

(a) Notice of Formal Proceedings for Complete Settlement Under Minn. Stat. § 524.3–1001. If testacy has been adjudicated in a prior formal proceeding, notice of hearing on a petition for complete settlement under Minn. Stat. § 524.3–1001 must meet the requirements of Minn. Gen. R. Prac. 404(a), but notice by publication specifically provided for in Minn. Stat. § 524.3–403 is not required. If testacy has not been adjudicated in a prior formal proceeding, notice of hearing on a petition for complete settlement under Minn. Stat. § 524.3–1001, must meet the specific notice requirements for formal testacy proceedings provided in Minn. Stat. § 524.3–403, including notice by publication.

(b) Notice of Formal Proceedings for Settlement of Estate Under Minn. Stat. § 524.3–1002. If an estate is administered under an informally probated will and there has been no adjudication of testacy in a prior formal proceeding, the court may make a final determination of rights between the devisees under the will and against the personal representative under Minn. Stat. § 524.3–1002, if no part of the estate is intestate. The court will not adjudicate the testacy status of the decedent. Notice of hearing on a petition must meet the requirements of Minn. Stat. § 524.1–401. Notice by publication specifically provided for in Minn. Stat. § 524.3–403 is not required.

Adopted Sept. 5, 1991, eff. Jan. 1, 1992.

RULE 412. FEES, VOUCHERS, AND TAX RETURNS

(a) Fees. The court may require documentation or it may appoint counsel to determine the reasonableness of the fees charged by the lawyer and the personal representative. The court may order the fees of the appointed counsel to be paid out of the estate.

(b) Vouchers. Unless otherwise ordered by the court, vouchers for final and interim accounts need not be filed.

(c) Tax Returns. Unless ordered by the court, copies of the United States Estate Tax closing letter and the Minnesota notification of audit results need not be filed.

Adopted Sept. 5, 1991, eff. Jan. 1, 1992.

RULE 413. SUBSEQUENT PROCEEDINGS

(a) Authority of Personal Representative During One Year Period After Filing Closing Statement. For one year from the date of filing the closing statement authorized by the code, the personal representative shall have full and complete authority to execute further transfers of property; to complete transactions; to complete distributions; to correct misdescriptions or improper identification of assets; or to transfer or distribute omitted property. During this period, the personal representative shall ascertain any matters of unfinished administration which must be completed prior to the termination of the representative's authority.

(b) Authority of Personal Representative to Transfer or Distribute Omitted Property During One Year Period After Filing Closing Statement. In the case of omitted property discovered after the filing of the closing statement authorized by the code, but before termination of the personal representative's authority, the personal representative must, as required by the code, file a supplementary inventory with the court and mail a copy to any surviving spouse, other distributees, and other interested persons, including creditors whose claims are unpaid and not barred. Proof of service by mail must be filed with the court prior to any transfer of the omitted property by the personal representative.

(c) Notice of Proceedings for Subsequent Administration After Termination of Personal Representative's Authority. Appointment of a personal representative in subsequent administration may only be secured in formal proceeding. If testacy has been adjudicated in a formal proceeding, notice of hearing must meet the requirements of Minn. Gen. R. Prac. 404(a), but the notice by publication specifically provided for in Minn. Stat. § 524.3–403 is not required. If testacy has not been adjudicated previously and only appointment of a personal representative is sought, notice of hearing must meet the specific notice requirements for formal testacy proceedings provided in Minn. Stat. § 524.3–403, but notice by publication is not required. In the case of subsequent administration involving omitted property, the personal representative must comply with the inventory, mailing and filing requirements of Minn. Gen. R. Prac. 413(b).

(d) Proof Required for Formal Settlement or Distribution in Subsequent Administration. During a subsequent administration, when an order of settlement of the estate and decree or order of distribution is sought, the court must be satisfied with the pleadings and any other proof (including accounting for all assets, disbursements, and distributions made during the prior administration) before issuing its order.

Adopted Sept. 5, 1991, eff. Jan. 1, 1992.

RULE 414. FIDUCIARIES

If the lawyer for the estate, a partner, associate or employee is the personal representative of the estate, except where one of them is a family member of the decedent, the administration shall be supervised. In such a case, both the lawyer for the estate and the personal representative must keep separate time records and differentiate the charges for their duties in each capacity. The lawyer should only serve as fiduciary at the unsolicited suggestion of the client and the lawyer must realize that there are legal, ethical and practical problems that must be overcome in order to perform the duties of a fiduciary and lawyer.

Adopted Sept. 5, 1991, eff. Jan. 1, 1992.

Task Force Comment—1991 Adoption

This recommended change is made to permit family members, who happen to be lawyers, to serve as fiduciaries without automatically subjecting the estate to the burdens of supervised administration. Although supervised administration may be appropriate in individual cases, the Task Force believes that it should not be uniformly imposed on the families of lawyers.

RULE 415. REGISTRAR

(a) Authority. The functions of the registrar may be performed either by a judge of the court or by a person designated by the court in a written order filed and recorded in the office of the court, subject to the following:

(1) Each judge of the court may at any time perform the functions of registrar regardless of whether the court has designated other persons to perform those functions.

(2) The functions and powers of the registrar are limited to the acts and orders specified by the code and these rules.

(3) Any person designated registrar by the court shall be subject to the authority granted by and the continuing direction of the court.

(4) The registrar is not empowered to intervene or issue orders resolving conflicts related to the administration of the estate.

(b) Registrar Has No Continuing Authority. The registrar does not have any continuing authority over an estate after the informal probate is granted or denied and shall not require the filing of any additional documents other than are required by the code (law) and these rules.

Adopted Sept. 5, 1991, eff. Jan. 1, 1992.

RULE 416. GUARDIANSHIPS AND CONSERVATORSHIPS

(a) Responsibility of Lawyer. Upon the appointment of a conservator or guardian of the estate, the appointee shall nominate a lawyer of record for that conservatorship or guardianship, or shall advise the court that he or she shall act pro se. The named lawyer shall be the lawyer of record until terminated by the conservator or guardian, or, with the consent of the court, by withdrawal of the lawyer. If the lawyer is terminated by the conservator or guardian, written notice of substitution or pro se representation shall be given to the court (by the conservator or guardian, or by the lawyer who has received oral or written notice of termination), and until such notice, the former lawyer shall be recognized.

(b) Visitors in Guardianship and Conservatorship Proceedings. A visitor, as defined by law, may be appointed in every general guardianship or conservatorship proceeding.

Every visitor shall have training and experience in law, health care or social work, as the case may be, depending upon the circumstances of the proposed ward or conservatee.

The visitor shall be an officer of the court and shall be disinterested in the guardianship or conservatorship proceedings. If the court at any time determines that the visitor, or the firm or agency by which he or she is employed, has or had, at the time of hearing, a conflict of interest, the court shall immediately appoint a new visitor and may, if necessary, require a hearing de novo.

The visitor shall, (a) without outside interferences, meet with the proposed ward or conservatee, either once or more than once as the visitor deems necessary, (b) observe his or her appearance, lucidity and surroundings, (c) serve, read aloud, if requested, and explain the petition and notice of hearing, (d) assist, if requested, in obtaining a private or court appointed lawyer, (e) advise the proposed ward or conservatee that a report will be filed at least five (5) days before the hearing and that the report is available to the proposed ward or conservatee or the ward's or conservatee's lawyer, (f) prepare a written report to the court setting forth all matters the visitor deems relevant in determining the need for a guardian or conservator, including recommendations concerning appointment and limitation of powers, (g) file the original report with the court and, (h) serve a copy upon the petitioner or petitioner's lawyer at least five (5) days prior to the hearing, (i) appear, testify and submit to cross examination at the hearing concerning his or her observations and recommendations, unless such appearance is excused by the court.

(c) Voluntary Petition. If an adult voluntarily petitions or consents to the appointment of a guardian or conservator of the estate as set forth in the law, then it is not necessary for such adult to be an "incapacitated person" as defined by the law.

(d) Amount of Bond. The court may, at any time, require the filing of a bond in such amount as the court deems necessary and the court, either on request of an interested party, or on its own motion, may increase or decrease the amount of the bond. The court, in requiring a bond, if any, or in determining the amount thereof, shall take into account not only the nature and value of the assets, but also the qualifications of the guardian or conservator.

(e) Effect of Allowance of Accounts. The filing, examination and acceptance of an annual account, without notice of hearing, shall not constitute a determination or adjudication on the merits of the account, nor does it constitute the court's approval of the account.

(f) Required Periodic Settlement of Accounts. No order settling and allowing an annual or final account shall be issued by the court except on a hearing with notice to interested parties. A hearing for the settlement and allowance of an annual or final account may be ordered upon the request of the court or any interested party. A hearing shall be held for such purpose in each guardianship or conservatorship of the estate at least once every five years upon notice as set forth in the law, and the rules pursuant thereto. However, in estates of the value of $20,000 or less, the five year hearing requirement may be waived by the court in its discretion. Such five year hearings shall be held within 150 days after the end of the accounting period of each fifth annual unallowed account and the court administrator shall notify such guardian or conservator, the guardian's or conservator's lawyer and the court if the hearing is not held within the 150 day period.

(g) Notice of Hearing on Account. Notice of time and place for hearing on the petition for final settlement and allowance of any account shall be given to the ward or conservatee, to the guardian or conservator if such person was not the petitioner for settlement of the accounts, to the spouse, adult children and such other interested persons as the court may direct. Whenever any funds have been received by the estate from the Veterans Administration during the period of accounting, notice by mail shall be given to the regional office. The notice may be served in person or by depositing a copy in the U.S. mail to the last known address of the person or entity being served. When a ward or conservatee is restored to capacity, that person is the only interested person. When a ward or conservatee dies, the personal representative of the estate is the only interested person.

(h) Appearance on Petition for Adjudication of Accounts. When a verified annual or final account is filed in accord with the law and an adjudication is sought, and notice given as required by the law or waived as provided below, and the court determines that the account should be allowed, the account may be allowed upon the pleadings without appearance of the guardian or conservator. If the ward, conservatee or any interested person shall object to the account, or demand the appearance of the guardian or conservator for hearing on the account, at any time up to and including the date set for the hearing, the court will continue the hearing, if necessary, to a later date and require the appearance of the guardian/conservator for examination. Notice of hearing may be waived with the consent of all interested persons.

(i) Successor Guardian; Notice to Ward or Conservatee. The notice required by law shall include the right of the ward or conservatee to nominate and instruct the successor.

Adopted Sept. 5, 1991, eff. Jan. 1, 1992.

RULE 417. TRUSTEES—ACCOUNTING—PETITION FOR APPOINTMENT

Rule 417.01. Petition for Confirmation of Trustee

Except in those cases in which a trust company or national banking association having trust powers is the trustee or one of the trustees, the petition for confirmation of the appointment of the trustee or trustees shall include an inventory, including a description of the assets of the trust known to the petitioners and an estimate by them of the market value of such assets at the date of the petition. The petition shall also set forth the relationship, if any, of the trustee or trustees to the beneficiaries of the trust.

Amended Nov. 13, 1992, eff. Jan. 1, 1993.

Rule 417.02. Annual Account

Every trustee subject to the continuing supervision of the district court shall file an annual account, duly verified, of the trusteeship with the court administrator within 60 days after the end of each accounting year. Such accounts may be submitted on form 417.02 appended to these rules, and shall contain the following:

(a) Statements of the total inventory or carrying value and of the total fair market value of the assets of the trust principal as of the beginning of the accounting period. In cases where a previous account has been rendered, the totals used in these statements shall be the same as those used for the end of the last preceding accounting period.

(b) A complete itemized inventory of the assets of the trust principal as of the end of the accounting period, showing both the inventory or carrying value of each asset and also the fair market value thereof as of such end of the accounting period, unless, because such value is not readily ascertainable or for other sufficient reason, this provision cannot reasonably be complied with. Where the fair market value of any item at the end of the accounting period is not used, a notation of such fact and the reason therefor shall be indicated on the account.

(c) An itemized statement of all income transactions during the period of such account.

(d) A summary statement of all income transactions during the period of such account, including the totals of distributions of income to beneficiaries and the totals of trustees' fees and attorneys' fees charged to income.

(e) An itemized statement of all principal transactions during the period of such account.

(f) A reconciliation of all principal transactions during the period of such account, including the totals of distributions of principal to beneficiaries and the totals of trustees' fees and attorneys' fees charged to principal as well as the totals of liquidations and reinvestments of principal cash.

(g) A list of all assets that realized a net income less than one per cent of the inventory value or acquisition cost, and an explanation of the amount of net income realized and the reasons for retaining the assets.

Amended Nov. 13, 1992, eff. Jan. 1, 1993. Amended Dec. 14, 1995, eff. Jan. 1, 1996.

Advisory Committee Comments—1995 Amendments

Rule 417.02, as amended, refers to trustees subject to the continuing supervision of the district courts. The rule is intended to apply to all trusts subject to the continuing supervision of the district courts pursuant to Minn. Stat. § 501B.23 (1994), and the earlier reference to jurisdiction is deleted to avoid confusion, since all Minnesota trusts are subject to the district court's jurisdiction.

Historical Notes

The order of the Minnesota Supreme Court [CX–89–1863, C6–84–2134] dated December 14, 1995, provides in part that "(t)he attached amendments shall apply to all actions pending on the effective date and to those filed thereafter."

Rule 417.03. Taxes

Final accounts shall also disclose the state of the property of the trust estate as to unpaid or delinquent taxes and such taxes shall be paid by the trustee to the extent that the funds in the trust permit, over and beyond the cost and expenses of the trust administration, except where a special showing is made by the trustee that it is in the best interests of the trust and is lawful for the unpaid or delinquent taxes not to be paid.

Amended Nov. 13, 1992, eff. Jan. 1, 1993.

Rule 417.04. Service on Beneficiaries

There shall also be filed with the court administrator proof of mailing of such account to the last addresses known to the trustee of, or of the service of such account upon, such of the following beneficiaries or their natural or legal guardians as are known to, or reasonably ascertainable by, the trustee:

(a) Beneficiaries entitled to receive income or principal at the date of the accounting; and

(b) Beneficiaries who, were the trust terminated at the date of the accounting, would be entitled to share in distributions of income or principal.

Amended Nov. 13, 1992, eff. Jan. 1, 1993.

Rule 417.05. Court Administrator Records; Notice

The court administrator shall keep a list of trusteeships and notify each trustee and the court when any such annual account has not been filed within 120 days from the end of the accounting year.

Amended Nov. 13, 1992, eff. Jan. 1, 1993.

Rule 417.06. Hearing

Hearings upon annual accounts may be ordered upon the request of any interested party. A hearing shall be held on such annual accounts at least once every five years by mailing, at least 15 days before the date of the hearing, a copy of the order for hearing to those beneficiaries of the trust who are known to or reasonably ascertainable by the petitioner, to any other person requesting notice, or as ordered by the court. In trusts of the value of $20,000 or less, the five year hearing requirement may be waived by the court in its discretion. Any hearing on an account may be ex parte if each party in interest then in being shall execute waiver of notice in writing which shall be filed with the court administrator, but no account shall be finally allowed except upon a hearing on the record in open court. Such five year hearings shall be held within 150 days after the end of the accounting period of each fifth annual unallowed account, and the court administrator shall notify each trustee and the Court if the hearing is not held within such 150 day period.

Amended Nov. 13, 1992, eff. Jan. 1, 1993.

Advisory Committee Comment—1992 Amendments

This rule was derived from Rule 28 of the Code of Rules for the District Courts. The rule is recodified with the probate court rules because it relates to actions brought in the now-unified district court.

Rule 417.06 is amended to provide a specific method of notice rather than incorporating a specific statutory requirement. The former statute, Minn.Stat. § 501.35 was replaced by § 501B.18. The new statute, however, provides a general mechanism for order of hearing with published notice twenty days before the date of the hearing. This requirement is not necessary for hearings on accounts, as the interested parties will have been identified and known to the trustee at the time a hearing is scheduled. The rule does require notice to any party requesting notice of the hearing, and allows the court to specify another method of giving notice in a particular case. Although that might conceivably include published notice, published notice would be unusual.

RULE 418. DEPOSIT OF WILLS

(a) Deposit by Testator. Any testator may deposit his or her will with the court administrator in any county subject to the following rules. Wills shall be placed in a sealed envelope with the name, address, and birth date of the testator placed on the outside. The administrator shall give a receipt to the person depositing the will.

(b) Withdrawal by Testator or Agent. Any will may be withdrawn by the testator in person upon presentation of identification and signing an appropriate receipt. A testator's attorney or other agent may withdraw the will by presenting a written authorization signed by the testator and two witnesses with the testator's signature notarized.

(c) Examination by Guardian or Conservator. A guardian or conservator of the testator may review the will upon presentation of identification bearing the photograph of the person seeking review and a copy of valid letters of guardianship or conservatorship. If the guardianship or conservatorship proceedings are venued in a county other than that where the will is filed, the required copy of the letters shall be certified by the issuing court within 30 days of the request to review the will. The will may only be examined by the guardian or conservator in the presence of the court administrator or deputy administrator, who shall reseal it after the review is completed and shall endorse on the resealed envelope the date it was opened, by whom it was opened and that the original was placed back in the envelope.

(d) Copies. No copies of the original will shall be made during the testator's lifetime.

Adopted Oct. 10, 1996.

Advisory Committee Comment—1996 Amendment

This rule is new and is intended to provide a standard mechanism for handling wills deposited with the court for safekeeping. Minn.Stat. § 524.2–515, became effective in 1996 to permit deposit of any will by the testator. This rule is intended to provide uniform and orderly rules for deposit and withdrawal of wills that are deposited pursuant to this statute.

Historical Notes

The order of the Minnesota Supreme Court [CX-89-1863] dated October 10, 1996, provides in part that these amendments are effective July 1, 1997, except that rules 119 and 418 are effective January 1, 1997, that these amendments shall apply to all actions pending on the effective dates and to those filed thereafter, and that "(t)he inclusion of Advisory Committee comments is made for convenience and does not reflect court approval of the comments made therein".

APPENDIX OF FORMS FOR TITLE V. PROBATE RULES

FORM 417.02. TRUSTEE'S ACCOUNTING

State of Minnesota ______________ District Court
______________ COUNTY ______________ JUDICIAL DISTRICT
CASE NO. ______________

Case Type: ______________

In the Matter of the Trust Created under Article ______ of the Last Will of ______________.
ALTERNATIVE FOR INTER VIVOS TRUSTS:
In the Matter of the Trust Created under Agreement By and Between ______________, Settlor, and ________ and ________, Trustees, dated ____________.

TRUSTEE'S ANNUAL ACCOUNT

	Principal	Income
Assets on Hand as of ______ (Schedule 1)	$	$
Increases to Assets:		
Interest (Schedule 2)	$ 0.00	$
Dividends (Schedule 3)	$ 0.00	$
Capital gains distributions (Schedule 4)	$	$ 0.00
Gains on sales and other dispositions (Schedule 5)	$	$ 0.00
Return of capital (Schedule 6)	$	$ 0.00
Other increases (Schedule 7)	$	$
Decreases to Assets:		
Losses on sales and other dispositions (Schedule 8)	($)	($ .00)
Administration expenses (Schedule 9)	($)	($)
Taxes (Schedule 10)	($)	($)
Trustee fees	($)	($)
Attorney fees	($)	($)
Other decreases (Schedule 11)	($)	($)
Balance Before Distributions	$	$
Distributions to Beneficiaries (Schedule 12)	($)	($)
Principal and Income Balances	$ 0.00	$ 0.00

Total Assets on Hand as of ______________________ $______
(Income plus principal) (Schedule 13)

Assets which realized a net income of less than 1% of their inventory values or acquisition costs are listed on Schedule 14.

[NAME OF TRUST]

ASSETS ON HAND
[Beginning DATE]
Schedule 1

	Market Value as of [DATE]	Values at Cost or Basis Principal	Values at Cost or Basis Income
Cash or Cash Equivalents			
Checking account	$	$	$
Savings account	$	$	$
Money market account	$	$	$
Stocks and Bonds			
Stocks	$	$	$ 0.00
Corporate bonds	$	$	$ 0.00
Municipal bonds	$	$	$ 0.00
Real Estate	$	$	$ 0.00
Real Estate	$	$	$ 0.00
Other Assets			$
Life insurance policies (cash value)	$	$	$
Other assets	$	$	$
Total Assets on Hand as of [Date] ________.	0.00	0.00	0.00

Note: This schedule reflects assets on hand at the beginning of the period. Identify each asset thoroughly. Provide the name of the bank and account number for each account holding cash or cash equivalents. Provide the number of shares or par value of each security. Provide the address of each parcel of real estate.

[NAME OF TRUST]

INTEREST
Schedule 2

	Income
Checking account(s)	
1.	$
2.	$
Savings account(s)	
1.	$
2.	$
Corporate bonds	
1.	$
2.	$
3.	$
Municipal bonds	
1.	$
2.	$
3.	$
Other interest	

	Income
1.	$
2.	$
3.	$
Total Interest	$ 0.00

Identify each interest-producing asset. List each bank account by name and account number. Identify each bond or other asset that pays interest.

[NAME OF TRUST]

DIVIDENDS
Schedule 3

Stocks	Income
1	$
2	$
3	$
4	$
5	$
6	$
7	$
8	$
9	$
10	$
11	$
12	$
13	$
14	$
15	$
Total Dividends	0.00

Identify each security that paid dividends.

[NAME OF TRUST]

CAPITAL GAINS DISTRIBUTIONS
Schedule 4

Capital gains distributions:	Principal
1	$
2	$
3	$
4	$
5	$
6	$
7	$
8	$
9	$
10	$
11	$
12	$
13	$
14	$

	Principal
Total Capital Gains Distributions	0.00

Identify each security that paid a capital gains distribution.

[NAME OF TRUST]

GAINS ON SALES AND OTHER DISPOSITIONS
Schedule 5

			Principal
Sale of ________ shares of ____________:			
Proceeds received	$		
Less cost or basis	($)	$	0.00
Sale of ________ shares of ____________:			
Proceeds received	$		
Less cost or basis	($)	$	0.00
Sale of ________ shares of ____________:			
Proceeds received	$		
Less cost or basis	($)	$	0.00
Sale of ________ shares of ____________:			
Proceeds received	$		
Less cost or basis	($)	$	0.00
Sale of ________ shares of ____________:			
Proceeds received	$		
Less cost or basis	($)	$	0.00
Sale of ________ shares of ____________:			
Proceeds received	$		
Less cost or basis	($)	$	0.00
Sale of ________ shares of ____________:			
Proceeds received	$		
Less cost or basis	($)	$	0.00
Sale of ________ shares of ____________:			
Proceeds received	$		
Less cost or basis	($)	$	0.00
Sale of ________ shares of ____________:			
Proceeds received	$		
Less cost or basis	($)	$	0.00
Total Gains		$	0.00

[NAME OF TRUST]

RETURN OF CAPITAL
Schedule 6

	Principal
Return of capital:	
1.	$

	Principal
2.	$
3.	$
4.	$
5.	$
6.	$
7.	$
8.	$
9.	$
10.	$
11.	$
12.	$
13.	$
14.	$
Total Return of Capital	0.00

Identify each security that paid a return of capital.

[NAME OF TRUST]

OTHER INCREASES
Schedule 7

	Principal	Income
Securities added to trust by Settlor		$ 0.00
	$	$
1	$	$
2	$	$
3	$	$
4	$	$
5	$	$
6	$	$
7	$	$
8	$	$
9	$	$
Income transferred to principal	$	$ 0.00
Other increases:		
1	$	$
2	$	$
3	$	$
4	$	$
5	$	$
6	$	$
7	$	$
8	$	$
9	$	$
Total Other Increases	0.00	0.00

[NAME OF TRUST]

LOSSES ON SALES AND OTHER DISPOSITIONS
Schedule 8

	Principal
Sale of __________ shares of ________________:	

		Principal
Proceeds received	$	
Less cost or basis	($)	$ 0.00
Sale of ________ shares of ____________:		
Proceeds received	$	
Less cost or basis	($)	$ 0.00
Sale of ________ shares of ____________:		
Proceeds received	$	
Less cost or basis	($)	$ 0.00
Sale of ________ shares of ____________:		
Proceeds received	$	
Less cost or basis	($)	$ 0.00
Sale of ________ shares of ____________:		
Proceeds received	$	
Less cost or basis	($)	$ 0.00
Sale of ________ shares of ____________:		
Proceeds received	$	
Less cost or basis	($)	$ 0.00
Sale of ________ shares of ____________:		
Proceeds received	$	
Less cost or basis	($)	$ 0.00
Sale of ________ shares of ____________:		
Proceeds received	$	
Less cost or basis	($)	$ 0.00
Sale of ________ shares of ____________:		
Proceeds received	$	
Less cost or basis	($)	$ 0.00
Total Losses		$ 0.00

[NAME OF TRUST]

ADMINISTRATIVE EXPENSES
Schedule 9

	Principal	Income
Bank account fees	$	$
Check charges	$	$
Broker annual fees	$	$
Photocopies	$	$
Postage	$	$
Maintenance of real estate (schedule attached)	$	$
Other (schedule attached)	$	$

	Principal	Income
Total Administrative Expenses	$ 0.00	$ 0.00

[NAME OF TRUST]

TAXES
Schedule 10

	Principal	Income
Foreign dividend tax	$ 0.00	$
U.S. fiduciary income tax	$	$
Minnesota fiduciary income tax	$	$
Total taxes	$ 0.00	$ 0.00

Note: The portion of fiduciary income tax allocated to capital gains is charged against principal. The portion of foreign dividend tax is allocated to income.

[NAME OF TRUST]

OTHER DECREASES
Schedule 11

	Principal	Income
Income transferred to principal	$	$ 0.00
Other decreases:		
1.	$	$
2.	$	$
3.	$	$
4.	$	$
5.	$	$

	Principal	Income
6.	$	$
7.	$	$
8.	$	$
9.	$	$
10.	$	$
Total Other decreases	0.00	0.00

[NAME OF TRUST]

DISTRIBUTIONS TO BENEFICIARIES
Schedule 12

Name of each beneficiary and date and description of distribution:	Principal	Income
1.	$	$
2.	$	$
3.	$	$
4.	$	$
5.	$	$
6.	$	$
7.	$	$
8.	$	$
9.	$	$
10.	$	$
11.	$	$
12.	$	$
13.	$	$
14.	$	$
15.	$	$
Total Distributions to Beneficiaries	0.00	0.00

[NAME OF TRUST]

ASSETS ON HAND
[ending DATE]
Schedule 13

	Market Value as of [DATE]	Values at Cost or Basis Principal	Values at Cost or Basis Income
Cash or Cash Equivalents			
Checking account	$	$	$
Savings account	$	$	$
Money market account	$	$	$
Stocks and Bonds			
Stocks	$	$	$ 0.00
Corporate bonds	$	$	$ 0.00
Municipal bonds	$	$	$ 0.00
Real Estate	$	$	$ 0.00

	Market Value as of [DATE]	Values at Cost or Basis Principal	Values at Cost or Basis Income
Other Assets			$
Life insurance policies (cash value)	$	$	$
Other assets	$	$	$
Total Assets on Hand as of [Date]______.	0.00	$.	$.

Note: This schedule reflects assets on hand at the end of the accounting period. Identify each asset thoroughly. Provide the name of the bank and account number for each account holding cash or cash equivalents. Provide the number of shares or par value of each security. Provide the address of each parcel of real estate.

[NAME OF TRUST]

ASSETS WHICH REALIZED A NET INCOME OF LESS THAN 1% OF THEIR INVENTORY VALUES OR ACQUISITION COSTS
Schedule 14

	Description of Asset	Amount of Net Income Realized	Income as Percentage of Cost/Basis
1.		$	%
	Reason why this asset should be retained:		
2.		$	%
	Reason why this asset should be retained:		
3.		$	%
	Reason why this asset should be retained:		
4.		$	%
	Reason why this asset should be retained:		
5.		$	%
	Reason why this asset should be retained:		

Under penalties of perjury, we have read this Annual Account and we know or believe its contents are true and correct.

____
Trustee Date
Address:

____
Trustee Date
Address:

Notarial Stamp or Seal (or Other Title or Rank)	Signed and sworn to (or affirmed) before me on (date)__________ by__________ and__________ Trustees.
__________	Signature of Notary Public or Other Official

Amended Nov. 13, 1992, eff. Jan. 1, 1993; Dec. 14, 1995, eff. Jan. 1, 1996.

Historical Notes

Form 142.02, adopted by court order [CX–89–1863, C6–84–2134] dated September 5, 1991, effective January 1, 1992, was renumbered Form 417.02 by court order [CX–89–1863, C6–84–2134] dated November 13, 1992, effective January 1, 1993.

The order of the Minnesota Supreme Court [CX–89–1863, C6–84–2134] dated December 14, 1995, provides in part that "(t)he attaced amendments shall apply to all actions pending on the effective date and to those filed thereafter."

TITLE VI. CONCILIATION COURT RULES

Comments

The order of the Minnesota Supreme Court [C1–84–2136] dated June 22, 1993 in part amending the Conciliation Court Rules provides in part that "(t)he inclusion of Advisory Committee comments is made for convenience and does not reflect court approval of the comments made therein."

RULE 501. APPLICABILITY OF RULES

Rules 501 through 525 apply to all Conciliation Court proceedings.

Adopted Sept. 5, 1991, eff. Jan. 1, 1992. Amended June 22, 1993, eff. July 1, 1993.

RULE 502. JURISDICTION

The conciliation court shall have jurisdiction and powers as prescribed by law.

Adopted Sept. 5, 1991, eff. Jan. 1, 1992. Amended June 22, 1993, eff. July 1, 1993.

RULE 503. COMPUTATION OF TIME

(a) General. All time periods shall be measured by starting to count on the first day after any event happens which by these rules starts the running of a time period. If the last day of the time period is anything other than a working week day, then the last day is the next working week day.

(b) Time Periods Less Than Seven Days. When the time period is less than seven days, only working week days shall be counted.

(c) Working Week Day. A "working week day" means a day which is not a Saturday, Sunday or legal holiday. For purposes of this rule, a legal holiday includes all state level judicial branch holidays established pursuant to law and any other day on which county offices in the county in which the conciliation court is held are closed pursuant to law or court order. With respect to service or filing by U. S. Mail, a day that the United States Mail does not operate is not a "working week day."

Amended June 22, 1993, eff. July 1, 1993. Amended Nov. 19, 2009, eff. Jan. 1, 2010.

1993 Committee Comment

State level judicial branch holidays are defined in Minnesota Statutes, section 645.44, subd. 5 (1990), which includes: New Years Day, January 1; Martin Luther King's Birthday, the third Monday in January; Washington's and Lincoln's Birthday, the third Monday in February; Memorial Day, the last Monday in May; Independence Day, July 4; Labor Day, the first Monday in September; Veteran's Day, November 11; Thanksgiving Day, the fourth Thursday in November; and Christmas Day, December 25. Section 645.44, subdivision 5 further provides that when New Year's Day, January 1; or Independence Day, July 4; or Veteran's Day, November 11; or Christmas Day, December 25; falls on Sunday, the following day shall be a holiday and that when New Year's Day, January 1; or Independence Day, July 4; or Veteran's Day, November 11; or Christmas Day, December 25; falls on Saturday, the preceding day shall be a holiday. Section 645.44, subdivision 5, also authorizes the judicial branch to designate certain other days as holidays. The 1992 Judicial Branch Personnel Plan designates the Friday after Thanksgiving as a holiday.

Conciliation courts are housed in county buildings, and the county is authorized to close county offices on certain days pursuant to Minnesota Statutes, section 373.052 (1990). Thus, if a county closes its offices under section 373.052 on a day that is not a state level judicial branch holiday, such as Christopher Columbus Day, the second Monday in October, the conciliation court in that county would nevertheless include that day as a holiday for the purpose of computing time under Rule 503. *See Mittelstadt v. Breider,* 286 Minn. 211, 175 N.W.2d 191 (1970) (applying section 373.052 to filing of notice of election contest with district court). If a county does not close its offices on a day that is a state level judicial branch holiday, such as the Friday after Thanksgiving, the conciliation court in that county must still include that day as a holiday for the purpose of computing time under Rule 503.

Advisory Committee Comment—2009 Amendment

Rule 503(c) is amended to clarify that for service or filing by mail, if U. S. Postal Service offices are closed on a particular day, that day is not deemed a "working week day" for the purpose of the rule, effectively permitting the mailing to be made on the next day that is a "working week day." This change conforms the rule to the time calculation provision of Minn. R. Civ. P. 6.01, which in turn was amended in 2008 to conform the rule to the Minnesota Supreme Court decision in *Commandeur LLC v. Howard Hartry, Inc.*, 724 N.W.2d 508 (Minn. 2006) (holding that where the last day of a time period occurred on Columbus Day, service by mail permitted by the rules was timely if mailed on the following day on which mail service was available).

Historical Notes

The order of the Supreme Court dated November 19, 2009, provided:

"1. The attached amendments to the General Rules of Practice for the District Courts and the Special Rules of Procedure Governing Proceedings under the Minnesota Commitment and Treatment Act be, and the same are, prescribed and promulgated to be effective on January 1, 2010.

"2. The attached amendments shall apply to all actions pending on the effective date and to those filed thereafter.

"3. The inclusion of Advisory Committee comments is made for convenience and does not reflect court approval of the comments made therein."

RULE 504. JUDGE(S); ADMINISTRATOR; REPORTING

(a) Judges. The judge(s) and, where authorized by statute, full and part time judicial officers and referees of the district court shall serve as judge(s) of conciliation court for such periods and at such times as the judge(s) shall determine. A judge, judicial officer, or referee so serving shall be known as a conciliation judge.

(b) Administrator.

(1) The court administrator shall manage the conciliation court, and may delegate a deputy or deputies to assist in performing the administrator's duties. The court administrator shall keep records and accounts and perform such duties as may be prescribed by the judge(s). The court administrator shall account for, and transmit to the appropriate official, all fees received as required by statute or rule.

(2) Under supervision of the conciliation court judges, the court administrator shall explain to litigants the procedures and functions of the conciliation court and shall on request assist litigants in filling out the forms provided under rules 507(b) and 518(b) of these rules and on request shall forward properly completed statement of claim and counterclaim forms to the administrator of the appropriate conciliation court together with the applicable fees, if any. The court administrator shall also advise litigants of the availability of subpoenas to obtain witnesses and documents. The performance of these duties shall not constitute the practice of law.

(c) Reporting. Conciliation court trials and proceedings shall not be reported.

Amended June 22, 1993, eff. July 1, 1993.

1993 Committee Comment

Rule 504(b)(2) requires court administrators to advise litigants of the availability of subpoenas under Rule 512(a). The required advice may be provided orally or in writing (e.g. on the litigant's copy of a court form, an accompanying instruction sheet, or in a brochure).

RULE 505. COMMENCEMENT OF ACTION

An action is commenced against a defendant when a statement of claim as required by Rule 507 is filed with the court administrator of the conciliation court having jurisdiction and the applicable fees are paid to the administrator or the affidavit in lieu of filing fees prescribed in rule 506 is filed with the administrator.

Amended June 22, 1993, eff. July 1, 1993.

RULE 506. FEES; AFFIDAVIT IN LIEU OF FEES

The court administrator shall charge and collect a filing fee in the amount established by law and the law library fee, from every plaintiff and from every defendant when the first paper for that party is filed in any conciliation court action. If the plaintiff or defendant who is a natural person signs and files with the court administrator an affidavit claiming an inability to pay the applicable fees, no fees are required. If the affiant prevails on a claim or counterclaim, the amount of the fees which would have been payable by the affiant must be included in the order for judgment and paid to the administrator of conciliation court by the affiant out of any money recovered by the affiant on the judgment.

Amended June 22, 1993, eff. July 1, 1993.

1993 Committee Comment

Statewide conciliation court filing fees are established by the legislature (see Minnesota Statutes, section 357.022). The law library fee is established by the local law library board, and these fees typically range from $0.00 to $10.00. Minn.Stat. §§ 134A.09–.10 (1990–1991 Supp.). The fee waiver procedure under Rule 506 is essentially a clerical process, and the waiver applies to the conciliation court filing and law library fees only. The procedure for waiver of other fees [*e.g.* service fees under Rule 508(d)(3), subpoena fees under Rule 512(a), and removal/appeal fees under Rule 521(b)(4)] is set forth in Minnesota Statutes, Section 563.01 (1990), which requires a formal application to, and decision by, the court. Only a party who is a natural person may utilize the fee waiver procedures under section 563.01 and Rule 506.

RULE 507. STATEMENT OF CLAIM AND COUNTERCLAIM; CONTENTS; VERIFICATION

(a) Claim; Verification; Contents. Each statement of claim and each counterclaim shall be made in the form approved by the court and shall contain a brief statement of the amount and nature of the claim, including relevant dates, and the name and address of the plaintiff and the defendant. The court administrator shall assist with the completion of the statement of claim and counterclaim upon request. Each statement of claim and each counterclaim shall also be signed and sworn to by the party, or the lawyer representing the party, in the presence of a notary public or the court administrator.

(b) Uniform Statement of Claim or Counterclaim; Acceptance by Court. A statement of claim or counterclaim in the uniform form as published by the state court administrator shall be accepted by any conciliation court administrator when properly completed and filed with the applicable fees, if any.

Amended June 22, 1993, eff. July 1, 1993. Amended Nov. 19, 2009, eff. Jan. 1, 2010.

1993 Committee Comment

Rule 507(b) requires that all courts accept a statement of claim or counterclaim properly completed on the form set forth in the appendix. Rule 507(a) authorizes a court to tailor the forms that it makes available to litigants for use in that court or to approve forms prepared by the litigants. This rule allows both the court and the litigants to benefit from increased efficiency through the use of various preprinted forms and word processor or computer generated forms. Courts using tailored forms cannot, however, reject a statement of claim or counterclaim properly completed on the form set forth in the appendix.

Historical Notes

The order of the Supreme Court dated November 19, 2009, provided:

"1. The attached amendments to the General Rules of Practice for the District Courts and the Special Rules of Procedure Governing Proceedings under the Minnesota Commitment and Treatment Act be, and the same are, prescribed and promulgated to be effective on January 1, 2010.

"2. The attached amendments shall apply to all actions pending on the effective date and to those filed thereafter.

"3. The inclusion of Advisory Committee comments is made for convenience and does not reflect court approval of the comments made therein."

RULE 508. SUMMONS; TRIAL DATE

(a) Trial Date. When an action has been properly commenced, the court administrator shall set a trial date and prepare a summons. Unless otherwise ordered by a judge, the trial date shall not be less than 10 days from the date of mailing or service of the summons.

(b) Contents of Summons. The summons shall state the amount and nature of the claim; require the defendant to appear at the trial in person or if a corporation, by officer or agent; shall specify that if the defendant does not appear judgment by default may be entered for the amount due the plaintiff, including fees, expenses and other items provided by statute or by agreement, and where applicable, for the return of property demanded by the plaintiff; and shall summarize the requirements for filing a counterclaim.

(c) Service on Plaintiff. The court administrator shall summon the plaintiff by first class mail.

(d) Service on Defendant.

(1) If the defendant's address as shown on the statement of claim is within the county, the administrator shall summon the defendant by first class mail, except that if the claim exceeds $2,500 the summons must be served by the plaintiff by certified mail, and proof of service must be filed with the administrator. If the summons is not properly served and proof of service filed within 60 days after issuance of the summons, the action shall be dismissed without prejudice.

(2) If the defendant's address as shown on the statement of claim is outside the county but within the state, and the law provides for service of the summons anywhere within the state, the administrator shall summon the defendant by first class mail, except that if the claim exceeds $2,500 the summons must be served by the plaintiff by certified mail, and proof of service must be filed with the administrator. If the summons is not properly served and proof of service filed within 60 days after issuance of the summons, the action shall be dismissed without prejudice.

(3) If the defendant's address as shown on the statement of claim is outside the state, the administrator shall forward the summons to the plaintiff who, within 60 days after issuance of the summons, shall cause it to be served on the defendant and file proof of service with the administrator. If the summons is not properly served and proof of service filed within 60 days after issuance of the summons, the action shall be dismissed without prejudice. A party who is unable to pay the fees for service of a summons may apply for permission to proceed without payment of fees pursuant to the procedure set forth in Minnesota Statutes Section 563.01.

(4) Service by mail, whether first-class or certified, shall be effective upon mailing.

(e) Proof of Service. Service by first class mail or certified mail shall be proven by an affidavit of service in form substantially similar to that published by the state court administrator. Service may be alternatively proven, when made by the court administrator, by any appropriate notation in the court record of the date, time, method, and address used by the administrator to effect service.

Amended June 22, 1993, eff. July 1, 1993; Nov. 30, 2005, eff. Jan. 1, 2006; Nov. 19, 2009, eff. Jan. 1, 2010.

1993 Committee Comment

The territorial jurisdiction of conciliation court is limited to the county boundaries, and a summons cannot be issued outside the county except in certain situations, including: recovery of certain student loans by educational institutions located within the county; recovery of alleged dishonored checks issued within the county; certain claims arising out of rental property located within the county; actions against two or more defendants when one defendant resides in the county; actions against foreign corporations doing business in this state; and actions against non-residents other than foreign corporations when the state has jurisdiction under Minnesota Statutes, section 543.19. Minn.Stat. § 491A.01, subds. 3, 6–10 (Supp.1993). In situations in which the address of the defendant as shown on the statement of claim is outside the state, the summons is forwarded to the plaintiff who is then responsible for causing service of the summons on the defendant in the manner provided by law and filing proof of service with the court within 60 days of issuance of the summons.

Various laws govern the service of a summons on nonresident defendants. See, e.g. Minn.Stat. §§ 45.028 (foreign insurance entities doing business in this state); 303.13 (foreign corporations doing business in this state); 543.19 (other nonresident defendants subject to the jurisdiction of Minnesota's courts). The procedure under each of these laws is different, and it is the plaintiff's responsibility to ensure that the appropriate procedures are followed. For example, service on an unregistered foreign corporation pursuant to Minn.Stat. § 303.13 (1991 Supp.) can be accomplished by delivering three copies of the summons to the secretary of state and payment of a $35.00 fee. The secretary of state then mails a copy to the defendant corporation and keeps a record of the mailing. Rule 508(d) requires that the plaintiff file an affidavit of compliance which should be accompanied by the fee receipt from the secretary of state's office or a copy of the summons bearing the date and time of filing with the secretary of state. Service on an unregistered foreign insurance entity pursuant to Minn. Stat. § 45.028, subd. 2 (1990), may be accomplished by: (1) delivering a single copy of the summons to the commissioner of commerce (as of August 1, 1992, there is no filing fee); and (2) the plaintiff mailing a copy of the summons and notice of service to the foreign insurance company by certified mail; and (3) filing of an affidavit of compliance with the court. Service is not effective until all steps are completed, including the filing of the affidavit of compliance, which should be accompanied by receipts or other proof of mailing and filing with the commissioner of commerce. Finally, service on other non-residents pursuant to Minn.Stat. § 543.19 (1990) requires that the summons be "personally served" on the nonresident and proof of service filed with the court. Such "personal service" may only be made by a sheriff or any other person not less than 18 years of age who is not a party to the action. *Reichel v. Hefner,* 472 N.W.2d 346 (Minn. App.1991) (applying rule 4.02 of the rules of civil procedure for the district courts).

When service on a foreign corporation has been made under Minn.Stat. § 303.13 through the office of the secretary of state, the defendant corporation so served shall have thirty days from the date of mailing by the secretary of state in which to answer the complaint. Thus, the conciliation court trial date must be scheduled to allow the defendant the full thirty days to appear. Similarly, when certain foreign insurance entities are served under Minn. Stat. § 45.028, subd. 2, the law also provides a thirty day response period [see, e.g., Minn.Stat. § 64B.35, subd. 2 (fraternal benefit societies)] or prohibits default judgments until the expiration of thirty days from the filing of the affidavit of compliance. Minn.Stat. § 60A.21, subd. 1(4) (unauthorized foreign insurer)].

Rule 508(d) recognizes that in most situations involving resident defendants, first class mail is a sufficient method of notifying the defendant of the claim. If for some reason the summons cannot be delivered by mail, the last sentence of rule 508(a) recognizes that personal service of the summons pursuant to the rules of civil procedure for the district court is always an effective means of providing notice of the claim. The party filing the claim is responsible for obtaining personal service, including any costs involved. As indicated above, "personal service" may only be made by a sheriff or any other person not less than 18 years of age who is not a party to the action.

The provisions requiring service by certified mail were added in order to make the Rules consistent with statutes. See Minn.Stat. § 491A.01, subd. 3(b) (Supp.1993). If the claim exceeds $2,500, the plaintiff is responsible for causing service of the summons on the defendant by certified mail, and filing proof of service with the court within 60 days of issuance of the summons.

Advisory Committee Comment—2006 Amendment

Rule 508(d)(4) is a new provision, intended to remove any confusion in the rule over when service by mail is deemed complete. This question is important in determining questions of timing. Making service effective upon mailing is consistent with the provisions of Minn. R. Civ. P. 5.02 and Minn. R. Civ. App. P. 125.03

The rule has historically required proof of service, but has not specified how service is proven. Rule 508(e) specifies that an affidavit of service should be prepared in form substantially similar to new Form 508.1 to prove service by anyone other than the court administrator. Where the rule requires the administrator to effect service by mail or certified mail, it is not necessary to require an affidavit of the administrator to prove serve, and Rule 508(e) recognizes that a notation of the facts of service in the court's file will suffice to prove that service was effected.

Some courts follow the practice of using certified mail receipts as proof of service. In fact these receipts generally only prove receipt of the mailing, not the mailing itself. Although proof of receipt may be important if a question arises as to the effectiveness of service, it is not an adequate substitute for proof of the facts of service, including the date of mailing.

Advisory Committee Comment—2009 Amendment

Rules 507, 508, and 518 are amended to remove Forms UCF-8, UCF-9, UCF-10, UCF-22, and 508.1 from the rules and to correct the reference to the forms in the rule. This amendment will allow for the maintenance and publication of the forms by the state court administrator. The forms, together with other court forms, can be found at http://www.mncourts.gov/.

Forms UCF-8, UCF-9, UCF-10, UCF-22, and 508.1 should be deleted from the rules and maintained in the future on the court's website.

The order of the Supreme Court dated November 19, 2009, provided:

"1. The attached amendments to the General Rules of Practice for the District Courts and the Special Rules of Procedure Governing Proceedings under the Minnesota Commitment and Treatment Act be, and the same are, prescribed and promulgated to be effective on January 1, 2010.

"2. The attached amendments shall apply to all actions pending on the effective date and to those filed thereafter.

"3. The inclusion of Advisory Committee comments is made for convenience and does not reflect court approval of the comments made therein."

RULE 509. COUNTERCLAIM

(a) Counterclaims Allowed. The defendant may assert a counterclaim within jurisdiction of conciliation court which the defendant has against the plaintiff, whether or not arising out of the transaction or occurrence which is the subject matter of plaintiff's claim.

(b) Assertion of Counterclaim. To assert a counterclaim the defendant shall perform all the following not less than five days prior to the date set for trial of plaintiff's claim:

(1) file with the court administrator a counterclaim required by Rule 507;

(2) pay to the court administrator the applicable fees or file with the administrator the affidavit in lieu of fees prescribed in rule 506.

(c) Administrator's Duties. The court administrator shall assist with the preparation of the counterclaim on request. When the counterclaim has been properly asserted, the court administrator shall note the filing of the counterclaim on the original claim, promptly mail notice of the counterclaim to plaintiff and set the counterclaim for trial on the same date as the original claim.

(d) Late Filing. No counterclaim shall be heard if filed less than five days before the trial date of plaintiff's claim except by permission of the judge, who has discretion to allow a filing within the five day period. Should a continuance be requested by and granted to plaintiff because of the late filing, the judge may require payment of costs by defendant, absolute or conditional, not to exceed $50.00.

Amended June 22, 1993, eff. July 1, 1993.

RULE 510. COUNTERCLAIM IN EXCESS OF COURT'S JURISDICTION

(a) The court administrator shall strike plaintiff's action from the calendar if the defendant not less than five days prior to the date set for trial of plaintiff's claim, files with the court administrator an affidavit stating that:

(1) the defendant has a counterclaim against plaintiff arising out of the same transaction or occurrence as plaintiff's claim, the amount of which is beyond monetary jurisdiction of the conciliation court, and

(2) the defendant has commenced or will commence within 30 days an action against plaintiff in a court of competent jurisdiction based on such claim.

(b) The plaintiff's action shall be subject to reinstatement on the trial calendar at any time after thirty days and up to three years, upon the filing by plaintiff of an affidavit showing that the plaintiff has not been served with a summons by defendant. If the action is reinstated, the court administrator shall set the case for trial and mail notice of the trial date to the parties by first class mail.

(c) Absolute or conditional costs, not to exceed $50.00, may be imposed against the defendant if the defendant fails to commence an action as provided in paragraph (a)(2) of this rule, and the court determines that the defendant caused the plaintiff's action to be stricken from the calendar in bad faith or solely to delay the proceedings or to harass.

Amended June 22, 1993, eff. July 1, 1993.

RULE 511. NOTICE OF SETTLEMENT

If the parties agree on a settlement prior to trial, each party who has made a claim or counterclaim shall promptly advise the court in writing that the claim or counterclaim has been settled and that it may be dismissed.

Adopted June 22, 1993, eff. July 1, 1993.

RULE 512. TRIAL

(a) Subpoenas. Upon request of a party and payment of the applicable fee, the court administrator shall issue subpoenas for the attendance of witnesses and production of documentary evidence at the trial. Rule 45 of the Minnesota Rules of Civil Procedure to the extent relevant for use of subpoenas for trial applies to subpoenas issued under this rule. A party who is unable to pay the fees for issuance and service of a summons may apply for permission to proceed without payment of fees pursuant to the procedure set forth in Minnesota Statutes Section 563.01. An attorney who has appeared in an action may, as officer of the court, issue and sign a subpoena on behalf of the court where the action is pending.

(b) Testimony and Exhibits. Subject to part (d) of this rule, the judge shall hear testimony of the parties, their witnesses, and shall consider exhibits offered by the parties. The party offering an exhibit shall mark the party's name on the exhibit in a manner that will not obscure the exhibit. All exhibits will be returned to the parties at the conclusion of the trial unless otherwise ordered by the judge.

(c) Appearances. The parties shall appear in person, unless otherwise authorized by the court, and may be represented by a lawyer admitted to practice law before the courts of this state. A lawyer representing a party in conciliation court may participate in the trial to the extent and in the manner that the judge, in the judge's discretion, deems helpful.

A corporation, partnership, limited liability company, sole proprietorship, or association may be represented in conciliation court by an officer, manager, or partner, or an agent in the case of a condominium, cooperative or townhouse association, or may appoint a natural person who is an employee of the party or a commercial property manager to appear on its behalf or settle a claim in conciliation court. In the case of an officer, employee, commercial property manager, or agent of a condominium, cooperative or townhouse association, an authorized power of attorney, corporate authorization resolution, corporate by-law or other evidence of authority acceptable to the court must be filed with the claim or presented at the trial. The authority shall remain in full force and effect only as long as the case is active in conciliation court.

"Commercial property manager" means a corporation, partnership, or limited liability company or its employees who are hired by the owner of commercial real estate to perform a broad range of administrative duties at the property including tenant relations matters, leasing, repairs, maintenance, the negotiation and resolution of tenant disputes, and related matters. In order to appear in conciliation court, a property manager's employees must possess a real estate license under Minnesota Statutes, section 82.20, and be authorized by the owner of the property to settle all disputes with tenants and others within the jurisdictional limits of conciliation court.

(d) Evidence. The judge shall normally receive only evidence admissible under the rules of evidence, but in the exercise of discretion and in the interests of justice, may receive otherwise inadmissible evidence.

(e) Conciliation; Judgment. The judge may attempt to conciliate disputes and encourage fair settlements among the parties. If at the trial the parties agree on a settlement the judge shall order judgment in accordance with the settlement. If no agreement is reached, the judge shall hear, determine the cause, and order judgment. Written findings of fact or conclusions of law shall not be required.

(f) Failure of Defendant to Appear. If the defendant fails to appear at the trial, after being summoned as provided in these rules, the judge may hear the plaintiff and may:

(1) order judgment in the amount due the plaintiff, including fees, expenses and other items provided by law or by agreement, and where applicable, order return of property to the plaintiff or

(2) otherwise dispose of the matter.

(g) Failure of Plaintiff to Appear, Defendant Present. Should plaintiff fail to appear at the trial, but defendant appears, the judge may hear the defendant and may:

(1) order judgment of dismissal on the merits or order a dismissal without prejudice on the plaintiff's statement of claim, and, where applicable, order judgment on defendant's counterclaim in the amount due the defendant, including fees, expenses and other items provided by law or by agreement, and where applicable, order return of property to the defendant, or

(2) otherwise dispose of the matter.

(h) Continuances. On proper showing of good cause, a continuance may be granted by the court on request of either party. The court may require payment of costs, absolute or conditional, not to exceed $50.00, as a condition of such an order. On proper showing of good cause, requests for continuance that are made at least five days prior to the trial may be granted by the court administrator. Continuances granted by the court administrator shall be limited to one continuance per party.

Adopted Sept. 5, 1991, eff. Jan. 1, 1992. Amended June 22, 1993, eff. July 1, 1993; July 20, 1994, eff. Aug. 1, 1994; Dec. 28, 2006, eff. Jan. 1, 2007.

1993 Committee Comment

Rule 512(a) authorizes the issuance of subpoenas to secure the attendance of witnesses and production of documentary evidence. The attendance of the parties is required by Rule 512(c).

The fee for issuing a subpoena is $3.00. Minn. Stat. §§ 357.021, subd. 2(3) (1990). A subpoena may be served by the sheriff, a deputy sheriff, or any other person not less than 18 years of age who is not a party to the action. Minn.R.Civ.P. 4.02; 45.03. The sheriff's fees and mileage reimbursement rate for service of a subpoena are set by the county board. Minn.Stat. § 357.09 (1990).

Witnesses are also entitled to attendance fees and travel fees, and unless otherwise ordered by the court, a witness need not attend at the trial unless the party requesting the subpoena pays the witness one day's attendance and travel fees in advance of the trial. Minn.Stat. § 357.22 (1990) ($10.00 per day attendance fee, $.24 per mile mileage fee, to and from courthouse, measured from witness' residence, if within state, or from state boundary line, if residence is outside the state); Minn.R.Civ.P. 45.03.

A witness who is not a party or an employee of a party and who is required to provide testimony or documents relating to a profession, business, or trade, or relating to knowledge, information, or facts obtained as a result of such profession, business or trade (e.g., a banker witness subpoenaed to produce bank records), is entitled to reasonable compensation for the time and expense involved in preparing for and giving such testimony or producing such documents. The party requesting the subpoena must make arrangements for such compensation prior to the trial. Minn.R.Civ.P. 45.06; D. Herr, R. Haydock, 2 Minnesota Practice, Civil Rules Annotated, § 45.14 (1985). With respect to any subpoena requiring the production of documents, the court may also require the party requesting the subpoena to pay the reasonable costs of producing the documentary evidence. Minn. R.Civ.P. 45.02.

Rule 512(e) does not preclude a court from providing the parties with a written explanation for the court's decision. Explanations, regardless of their brevity, are strongly encouraged. Explanations provide litigants with some degree of assurance that their case received thoughtful consideration, and may help avoid unnecessary appeals. Explanations may be inserted on Form UCF–9, appended to the rules, in either the Order for Judgment section on the front of the form or in the Memorandum section on the reverse side of the court's copy of the form.

Advisory Committee Comments—2007 Amendment

Rule 512(a) is amended to include express provision for issuance of subpoenas by attorneys admitted to practice before the Court. This provision is adopted verbatim from the parallel provision in the civil rules, Minn. R. Civ. P. 45.01(c), as amended effective Jan. 1, 2006. Although subpoenas may be used for pretrial discovery from non-parties in district court proceedings, conciliation court practice does not allow pretrial discovery, so this use of subpoenas is similarly not authorized by this rule.

The rule is also amended to clarify the cross-references to Minn. R. Civ. P. 45, made necessary by the reorganization and renumbering of Rule 45 effective on Jan. 1, 2006. Rule 45 provides a comprehensive procedure for use of subpoenas that is helpful in conciliation court with one significant exception: because subpoenas are only available in conciliation court for use at trial, and not for pre-trial discovery, the portions of Rule 45 dealing with pre-trial discovery are not applicable in conciliation court.

RULE 513. ABSOLUTE OR CONDITIONAL COSTS; FILING OF ORDERS

In any case in which payment of absolute or conditional costs has been ordered as a condition of an order under any provision of these rules, the amount so ordered shall be paid to the court administrator before the order becomes effective or is filed. Conditional costs shall be held by the court administrator to be paid in accordance with the final order entered in the case; absolute costs shall be promptly transmitted by the court administrator to the other party as that party's absolute property.

Adopted Sept. 5, 1991, eff. Jan. 1, 1992. Amended June 22, 1993, eff. July 1, 1993.

RULE 514. NOTICE OF ORDER FOR JUDGMENT

The court administrator shall promptly mail to each party a notice of the order for judgment entered by the judge. The notice shall state the last day for obtaining an order to vacate (where there has been a default) or for removing the cause to the civil division of district court under these rules. The notice shall also contain a statement that if the cause is removed to district court, the court will allow the prevailing party to recover from the aggrieved party $50.00 as costs if the prevailing party on appeal is not the aggrieved party in the original action as provided in Rule 524.

Adopted Sept. 5, 1991, eff. Jan. 1, 1992. Amended June 22, 1993, eff. July 1, 1993.

1993 Committee Comment

Rules 515, 520(a), and 521(b) of these rules establish a uniform twenty day time period for obtaining an order to vacate or for removing the case to district court. The twenty days is measured from the mailing of the notice of judgment, and the law requires that an additional three days be added to the time period when notice is served by mail. *Wilkins v. City of Glencoe,* 479 N.W.2d 430 (Minn. App.1992) (construing Rule 6.05 of the Minnesota Rules of Civil Procedure). Computing the deadline can be difficult and confusing for lay persons, and Rule 514 attempts to alleviate this problem by requiring the court administrator to perform the computation and specify the resulting date in the notice of order for judgment, taking into consideration applicable rules, including Rule 503 of these rules and Rule 6.05 of the Minnesota Rules of Civil Procedure.

RULE 515. ENTRY OF JUDGMENT

The court administrator shall promptly enter judgment as ordered by the judge. The judgment shall be dated as of the date notice is sent to the parties. The judgment so entered becomes finally effective twenty days after mailing of the notice, unless:

(a) payment has been made in full, or

(b) removal to district court has been perfected, or

(c) an order vacating the prior order for judgment has been filed, or

(d) ordered by a judge.

As authorized by law, any judgment ordered may provide for satisfaction by payment in installments in amounts and at times, as the judge determines. Should any installment not be paid when due, the entire unpaid balance of the judgment ordered, becomes immediately due and payable.

Adopted Sept. 5, 1991, eff. Jan. 1, 1992. Amended June 22, 1993, eff. July 1, 1993.

1993 Committee Comment

Rule 515 provides that a judgment becomes finally effective twenty days after notice of judgment is mailed to the parties, and the law requires that an additional three days be added to the time period when notice is served by mail. *Wilkins v. City of Glencoe,* 479 N.W.2d 430 (Minn.App.1992) (construing rule 6.05 of the Minnesota Rules of Civil Procedure). Computing the effective date of the judgment can be difficult and confusing for lay persons, and Rule 514 attempts to alleviate this problem by requiring the court administrator to perform the computation and specify the resulting date in the notice of order for judgment, taking into consideration applicable rules, including rule 503 of these rules and rule 6.05 of the Minnesota Rules of Civil Procedure. The purpose of the twenty day time period specified in Rule 515 is to permit a party to obtain an order to vacate under Rule 520(a) or effect removal of the case to district court under Rule 521(b).

The legislature has determined that any judgment ordered may provide for satisfaction by payment in installments in amounts and at such times, not exceeding one year for the last installment, as the judge determines to be just and reasonable. Minn.Stat. § 491A.02, subd. 5 (Supp.1993). Rule

512(e) recognizes that the one year limit on installment payments may be waived by the parties as part of a settlement.

RULE 516. COSTS AND DISBURSEMENTS

The order for judgment shall include the fees paid or payable by the prevailing party pursuant to rules 506 and 508(d)(3) of these rules and, in the discretion of the court, may include all or part of disbursements incurred by the prevailing party which would be taxable in district court and any conditional costs previously ordered to be paid by either party.

Adopted Sept. 5, 1991, eff. Jan. 1, 1992. Amended June 22, 1993, eff. July 1, 1993.

RULE 517. PAYMENT OF JUDGMENT

A nonprevailing party must make arrangements to pay the judgment directly to the prevailing party. In the event good faith efforts to pay the judgment are not successful or the prevailing party refuses to accept tendered payment, the nonprevailing party may bring a motion to allow payment into court. Upon order of the court, the nonprevailing party may then pay all or any part of the judgment to the court administrator for benefit of the prevailing party.

The court administrator shall enter on the court's records any payment made to the administrator or to the prevailing party directly when satisfied that the direct payments have been made.

Adopted Sept. 5, 1991, eff. Jan. 1, 1992. Amended June 22, 1993, eff. July 1, 1993; Nov. 19, 2009, eff. Jan. 1, 2010.

Advisory Committee Comment—2009 Amendment

Rule 517 is amended to modify the procedure for payment of a conciliation court judgment directly to the court administrator. As amended, the rule requires that payment be made directly by the nonprevailing party to the prevailing party, and permits payment into court only if reasonable attempts to make that payment are not successful or the prevailing party will not accept payment, in which case the nonprevailing party must bring a motion to allow payment into court.

Historical Notes

The order of the Supreme Court dated November 19, 2009, provided:

"1. The attached amendments to the General Rules of Practice for the District Courts and the Special Rules of Procedure Governing Proceedings under the Minnesota Commitment and Treatment Act be, and the same are, prescribed and promulgated to be effective on January 1, 2010.

"2. The attached amendments shall apply to all actions pending on the effective date and to those filed thereafter.

"3. The inclusion of Advisory Committee comments is made for convenience and does not reflect court approval of the comments made therein."

RULE 518. DOCKETING OF JUDGMENT IN DISTRICT COURT; ENFORCEMENT

(a) Docketing. Except as otherwise provided in Rule 519 with respect to installment judgments, when a judgment has become finally effective as defined in Rule 515 of these rules the judgment creditor may obtain a transcript of the judgment from the court administrator on payment of the applicable statutory fee and file it in district court. Once filed in district court the judgment becomes and is enforceable as a judgment of district court, and the judgment will be docketed by the court administrator upon presentation of an affidavit of identification. No writ of execution or garnishment summons shall be issued out of conciliation court.

(b) Enforcement. Unless the parties have otherwise agreed, if a conciliation court judgment has been docketed in district court and the judgment is not satisfied, the district court shall upon request of the judgment creditor order the judgment debtor to mail to the judgment creditor information as to the nature, amount, identity, and location of all the debtor's assets, liabilities, and personal earnings. The information shall be provided on a form substantially similar to that published by the state court administrator, and the information shall be sufficiently detailed to enable the judgment creditor to obtain satisfaction of the judgment by way of execution on nonexempt assets and earnings of the judgment debtor. The order shall contain a notice that failure to complete the form and mail it to the judgment creditor within ten days after service of the order may result in a citation for civil contempt of court. Cash bail posted as a result of being cited for civil contempt of court order under this rule may be ordered payable to the creditor to satisfy the judgment, either partially or fully.

Adopted Sept. 5, 1991, eff. Jan. 1, 1992. Amended June 22, 1993, eff. July 1, 1993; Nov. 19, 2009, eff. Jan. 1, 2010; Dec. 1, 2009.

1993 Committee Comment

The party in whose favor the judgment was entered (the "judgment creditor") is responsible for enforcing the judgment if the other party (the "judgment debtor") does not voluntarily comply with the judgment. Obtaining a transcript of the judgment and filing it in district court under rule 518(a) is the first step in enforcing a judgment. A judgment requiring the payment of money (as opposed to a judgment requiring the return of property) will also be docketed by the court administrator upon transcription if the statutorily required affidavit of identification (Minn.Stat. § 548.09, subd. 2 (1990)) is presented. Docketing a money judgment creates a lien against all real property of the debtor in the county in which it is docketed, except for registered land, which requires an additional filing (pursuant to Minn.Stat. §§ 508.63 and 508A.63) to create a lien. Docketing must be accomplished before the judgment creditor is permitted to use the disclosure provisions of rule 518(b), which may assist in locating assets of the judgment debtor. Additional information on enforcement of judgments against non-exempt assets of the debtor is set forth in brochures and forms available from local court administration and legal aid offices.

Specific fee amounts have been deleted from these rules as the fees are subject to modification by the legislature. Minn.Stat. § 357.021 (1990) ($7.50 transcription fee). Whether a separate fee in addition to the transcription fee is required for filing and docketing is also subject to legislative modification. Under current law, no separate fee may be charged for filing and docketing a conciliation court judgment in the district court of the county in which the judgment was rendered.

Advisory Committee Comment—2009 Amendment

Rule 518 is amended to remove the automatic thirty-day stay following docketing of a judgment in district court and the commencement of discovery regarding the judgment. The thirty-day stay does not serve a useful purpose in court administration, and simply results in a thirty-day delay in resolution of these matters. Accordingly, the committee recommends that it be removed from Rule 518. This change also makes the rule consistent with statute. See MINN. STAT. § 491A.02, subd. 9.

Historical Notes

The order of the Supreme Court dated November 19, 2009, provided:

"1. The attached amendments to the General Rules of Practice for the District Courts and the Special Rules of Procedure Governing Proceedings under the Minnesota Commitment and Treatment Act be, and the same are, prescribed and promulgated to be effective on January 1, 2010.

"2. The attached amendments shall apply to all actions pending on the effective date and to those filed thereafter.

"3. The inclusion of Advisory Committee comments is made for convenience and does not reflect court approval of the comments made therein."

RULE 519. DOCKETING OF JUDGMENT PAYABLE IN INSTALLMENTS

No transcript of a judgment of conciliation court payable in installments shall be issued and filed until 20 days after default in payment of an installment due.

Adopted Sept. 5, 1991, eff. Jan. 1, 1992. Amended June 22, 1993, eff. July 1, 1993.

RULE 520. VACATION OF JUDGMENT ORDER AND JUDGMENT

(a) Vacation of Order for Judgment Within 20 Days. When a default judgment or judgment of dismissal on the merits has been ordered for failure to appear, the judge within twenty days after notice was mailed may vacate said judgment order ex parte and grant a new trial on a proper showing by the defaulting party of lack of notice, mistake, inadvertence or excusable neglect as the cause of that party's failure to appear. Absolute or conditional costs not to exceed $50.00 to the other party may be ordered as a prerequisite to that relief.

(b) Vacation of Judgment After 20 Days. A default judgment may be vacated by the judge upon a proper showing by the defendant that: (1) the defendant did not receive a summons before the trial within sufficient time to permit a defense and did not receive notice of the order for default judgment within sufficient time to permit application for relief within twenty days after notice, or (2) upon other good cause shown. Application for relief pursuant to this Rule 520(b) shall be made within a reasonable time after the applicant learns of the existence of the judgment and shall be made by motion in accordance with the procedure governing motions in the district court, except that the motion is filed with the court administrator of conciliation court. The order vacating the judgment shall grant a new trial on the merits and may be conditioned upon payment of absolute or conditional costs not to exceed $50.00.

(c) Notice. The court administrator shall promptly notify the parties by mail of a new trial date.

Adopted Sept. 5, 1991, eff. Jan. 1, 1992. Amended June 22, 1993, eff. July 1, 1993.

1993 Committee Comment

Rule 520(a) establishes a twenty day time period for obtaining an order to vacate a default judgment order or order for judgment of dismissal. The twenty days is measured from the mailing of the notice of judgment, and the law requires that an additional three days be added to the time period when notice is served by mail. *Wilkins v. City of Glencoe,* 479 N.W.2d 430 (Minn.App.1992) (construing Rule 6.05 of the Minnesota Rules of Civil Procedure). Computing the deadline can be difficult and confusing for lay persons, and Rule 514 attempts to alleviate this problem by requiring the court administrator to perform the computation and specify the resulting date in the notice of order for judgment, taking into consideration applicable rules, including Rule 503 of these rules and Rule 6.05 of the Minnesota Rules of Civil Procedure.

Rule 520(a) authorizes an informal, ex parte proceeding (involving appearance of one party only), which typically includes the presentation of an affidavit establishing lack of notice, mistake, inadvertence or excusable neglect as the cause of that party's failure to appear. In contrast, Rule 520(b) requires compliance with the formal requirements for making a motion in the district court. See Minnesota Rules of Civil Procedure 4.02, 5.02, 6.05; Minnesota General Rules of Practice for the District Courts 115.01, .02, .04–.10. Forms and instructions are available from the conciliation court.

RULE 521. REMOVAL (APPEAL) TO DISTRICT COURT

(a) Trial de novo. Any person aggrieved by an order for judgment entered in conciliation court after contested trial may remove the cause to district court for trial de novo (new trial). An "aggrieved person" may be either the judgment debtor or creditor.

(b) Removal Procedure. To effect removal, the aggrieved party must perform all the following within twenty days after the date the court administrator mailed to that party notice of the judgment order:

(1) Serve on the opposing party or the opposing party's lawyer a demand for removal of the cause to district court for trial de novo. Service shall be by first class mail. Service may also be by personal service in accordance with the provisions for personal service of a summons in district court. The demand for removal shall state whether trial demanded is to be by court or jury, and shall indicate the name, address, and telephone number of the aggrieved party's lawyer, if any. If the aggrieved party is a corporation, the demand for removal must be signed by the party's attorney.

(2) File with the court administrator the original demand for removal with proof of service. The aggrieved party may file with the court administrator within the twenty day period the original and copy of the demand together with an affidavit by the party or the party's lawyer showing that after due and diligent search the opposing party or opposing party's lawyer cannot be located. This affidavit shall serve in lieu of making service and filing proof of service. When an affidavit is filed, the court administrator shall mail the copy of the demand to the opposing party at the party's last known residence address.

(3) File with the court administrator an affidavit by the aggrieved party or that party's lawyer stating that the removal is made in good faith and not for purposes of delay.

(4) Pay to the court administrator as the fee for removal the amount prescribed by law for filing a civil action in district court, and if a jury trial is demanded under Rule 521(b)(1) of these rules, pay to the court administrator the amount prescribed by law for requesting a jury trial in a civil action in district court. A party who is unable to pay the fees may apply for permission to proceed without payment of fees pursuant to the procedure set forth in Minnesota Statutes Section 563.01.

(c) Demand for Jury Trial. Where no jury trial is demanded on removal under Rule 521(b) by the aggrieved party, if the opposing party desires a jury trial that party shall perform all the following within twenty days after the demand for removal was served on the party or lawyer:

(1) Serve a jury trial demand by first class mail upon the aggrieved party or that party's lawyer. Service may also be by personal service in accordance with the provisions for personal service of a summons in district court.

(2) File the original jury trial demand and proof of service with the court administrator.

(3) Pay to the court administrator the amount prescribed by law for requesting a jury trial in a civil action in district court and, if the demand is the first paper filed by the party in the district court proceeding, pay to the administrator the amount prescribed by law for filing a civil action in district court. A party who is unable to pay the fees may apply for permission to proceed without payment of fees pursuant to the procedure set forth in Minnesota Statutes Section 563.01.

(d) Removal Perfected; Vacating Judgment; Transmitting File. When all removal papers have been filed properly and all requisite fees paid as provided under Rule 521(b), the removal is perfected, and the court shall issue an order vacating the order for judgment in conciliation court as to the parties to the removal, and the pertinent portions of the conciliation court file of the cause shall be filed in district court.

(e) Limited Removal.

(1) When a motion for vacation of an order for judgment, or judgment under Rule 520(a) or (b) of these rules, is denied, the aggrieved party may demand limited removal to the district court for hearing de novo (new hearing) on the motion. Procedure for service and filing of the demand for limited removal and notice of hearing de novo, proof of service of the notice, and procedure in case of inability of the aggrieved party to make service on the opposing party or the opposing party's lawyer shall be in the same manner prescribed in part (b) of this Rule, except that the deadline for effecting limited removal shall be twenty days after the date that the court administrator mails notice of the denial of the motion for vacation of the order for judgment or judgment. The fee payable by the aggrieved party to the court administrator for limited removal shall be the same as the filing fee prescribed by law for filing of a civil action in district court. The court administrator shall then place the matter on the special term calendar for the date specified in the notice. At the hearing in district court, either party may be represented by a lawyer.

(2) A judge other than the conciliation court judge who denied the motion, shall hear the motion de novo (anew) and may (A) deny the motion or (B) grant the motion. In determining the motion the judge shall consider the entire file plus any affidavits submitted by either party or their lawyers.

(3) The court administrator shall send by mail a copy of the order made in district court after de novo hearing to both parties and the venue shall be transferred back to conciliation court.

Adopted Sept. 5, 1991, eff. Jan. 1, 1992. Amended June 22, 1993, eff. July 1, 1993; Dec. 8, 1997, eff. Jan. 1, 1998; Dec. 19, 2000, eff. March 1, 2001; Dec. 17, 2004, eff. Jan. 1, 2005.

1993 Committee Comment

Rule 521(b) establishes a twenty-day time period for removing the case to district court. The twenty days is measured from the mailing of the notice of judgment, and the law requires that an additional three days be added to the time period when notice is served by mail. Wilkins v. City of Glencoe, 479 N.W.2d 430 (Minn.App. 1992) (construing rule 6.05 of the Minnesota Rules of Civil Procedure). Computing the deadline can be difficult and confusing for lay persons, and Rule 514 attempts to alleviate this problem by requiring the court administrator to perform the computation and specify the resulting date in the notice of order for judgment, taking into consideration applicable rules, including rule 503 of these rules and rule 6.05 of the Minnesota Rules of Civil Procedure.

In district court, personal service may only be made by a sheriff or any other person not less than 18 years of age who is not a party to the action. Reichel v. Hefner, 472 N.W.2d 436 (Minn._App. 1991). This applies to personal service under this Rule 521. Service may not be made on Sunday, a legal holiday, or election day. Minn._Stat. §§ _624.04, 645.44, subd. 5 (1990); Minn. Const. art. VII, § 4.

Cross Reference: Minn. R. Civ. P. 4.02, 4.06, 5.02, 6.01, 6.02, and 6.05.

Advisory Committee Comment—1997 Amendment

Rule 521(e)(1), as amended in 1997, allows limited removal to district court from a denial of a motion to vacate the order for judgment or judgment made pursuant to Rule 520(a) or (b). To obtain limited removal under Rule 521(e)(1), a party must follow the same procedural steps for obtaining removal under Rule 521(b), except that the event that triggers the twenty-day time period for effecting removal is the date that the court administrator mails the notice of denial of the motion to vacate the order for judgment or judgment. The law requires that an additional three days be added to the time period when notice is served by mail. *Wilkins v. City of Glencoe*, 479 N.W.2d 430 (Minn.App.1992).

Advisory Committee Comment—2000 Amendments

Rule 521(e)(1), as amended in 1997, allows limited removal to district court from a denial of a motion to vacate the order for judgment or judgment made pursuant to Rule 520(a) or (b). To obtain limited removal under Rule 521(e)(1), a party must follow the same procedural steps for obtaining removal under Rule 521(b), except that the event that triggers the twenty-day time period for effecting removal is the date that the court administrator mails the notice of denial of the motion to vacate the order for judgment or judgment. The law requires that an additional three days be added to the time period when notice is served by mail. *Wilkins v. City of Glencoe*, 479 N.W.2d 430 (Minn. App. 1992).

Under Rule 521(b)(1) as amended in 2000, if the party seeking to remove (appeal) the case to district court is a corporation, the demand for removal must be signed by an attorney authorized to practice law in the district court. This requirement simply restates a requirement recognized by court decision. *See World Championship Fighting, Inc. v. Janos*, 609 N.W.2d 263 (Minn. App. 2000), *rev. denied* (Minn. July 25, 2000). A corporation must be represented by a licensed attorney in district court regardless of the fact that the action originated in conciliation court. *See Nicollet Restoration, Inc. v. Turnham*, 486 N.W.2d 753 (Minn. 1992).

Advisory Committee Comment—2004 Amendments

Rule 521(d) is amended in 2004 to clarify its application in a situation where one of several co-parties (either co-plaintiffs or co–defendants) removes (appeals) a conciliation court decision while another co-party does not take that action. The committee believes that the conciliation court judgment should become final against any party who does not remove the case and in favor of any party against whom removal is not sought.

Rule 521 establishes an approved and effective means of service by mail to accomplish removal of a conciliation court case to district court for trial de novo. By decision in 2004, the Minnesota Supreme Court held that a party may also rely on the different means of service by mail contained in Minn. R. Civ. P. 4.05. *See* Roehrdanz v. Brill, 682 N.W.2d 626 (Minn. 2004). Because service under that rule may require a signed receipt from the party being served, such service may not be effective.

Historical Notes

The order of the Minnesota Supreme Court [CX–89–1863] dated December 8, 1997, provides in part that "(t)he attached amendments shall apply to all actions pending on the effective date and to those filed thereafter."

The order of the Minnesota Supreme Court [CX–89–1863] dated December 8, 1997, amending the General Rules of Practice for the District Courts provides in part that "(t)he inclusion of Advisory Committee comments is made for convenience and does not reflect court approval of the comments made therein."

The order of the Minnesota Supreme Court [CX-89-1863] dated December 19, 2000, provides in part that these amendments are effective March 1, 2001, and shall apply to all actions or proceedings pending on or commenced on or after the effective date, with the exception of the amendments to Rule 114.13, which shall become effective on further order of the court following the action of the Alternative Dispute Resolution (ADR) Review Board.

The order of the Minnesota Supreme Court [CX-89-1863] dated December 19, 2000, provides in part that "(t)he inclusion of Advisory Committee comments is made for convenience and does not reflect court approval of the statements made therein".

The order of the Minnesota Supreme Court [CX–89–1863] dated December 17, 2004, provides in part that "(t)he attached amendments shall apply to all actions pending on the effective date and to those filed thereafter."

The order of the Minnesota Supreme Court [CX–89–1863] dated December 17, 2004, amending the General Rules of Practice for the District Courts provides in part that "(t)he inclusion of Advisory Committee comments is made for convenience and does not reflect court approval of the comments made therein."

RULE 522. PLEADINGS IN DISTRICT COURT

The pleadings in conciliation court shall constitute the pleadings in district court. Any party may amend its statement of claim or counterclaim if, within 30 days after removal is perfected, the party seeking the amendment serves on the opposing party and files with the court a formal complaint conforming to the Minnesota Rules of Civil Procedure. If the opposing party fails to serve and file an answer within the time permitted by the Minnesota Rules of Civil Procedure, the allegations of the formal complaint are deemed denied. Amendment of the pleadings at any other time shall be allowed in accordance with the rules of civil procedure. On the motion of any party or on its own initiative, the court may order either or both parties to prepare, serve and file formal pleadings.

Adopted Sept. 5, 1991, eff. Jan. 1, 1992. Amended June 22, 1993, eff. July 1, 1993; Dec. 17, 2002, eff. Jan. 1, 2003.

Advisory Committee Comment—2002 Amendment

Rule 522 establishes a streamlined procedure for amendment of pleadings as a matter of right during the first 30 days after an action is removed to district court. The 2002 amendment adds a sentence before the last sentence to make it clear that the parties may move for leave to amend at other times, and the court can allow amendment on its own initiative. In these situations, the standards for amendment and supplementation of pleadings contained in Rule 15 of the Minnesota Rules of Civil Procedure and the case law interpreting that rule should guide the court in deciding whether to allow amendment.

RULE 523. PROCEDURE IN DISTRICT COURT

Proceedings in the district court shall, except as otherwise expressly provided in these rules, be in accordance with the Minnesota Rules of Civil Procedure and the General Rules of Practice for the District Courts. The judge who presided in conciliation court shall not preside in district court.

Adopted Sept. 5, 1991, eff. Jan. 1, 1992. Amended June 22, 1993, eff. July 1, 1993.

1993 Committee Comment

The Minnesota Supreme Court has determined that a corporation must be represented by a licensed attorney when appearing in district court regardless of the fact that the action originated in conciliation court. *Nicollet Restoration, Inc. v. Turnham,* 486 N.W.2d 753 (Minn.1992).

RULE 524. MANDATORY COSTS IN DISTRICT COURT

(a) For the purposes of this rule, "removing party" means the first party who serves or files a demand for removal. "Opposing party" means any party as to whom the removing party seeks a reversal in whole or in part.

(b) If the removing party prevails in district court, the removing party may recover costs from the opposing party as though the action were commenced in district court. If the removing party does not prevail, the court shall award the opposing party an additional $50.00 as costs. If the removing party is eligible to proceed under Minnesota Statutes Section 563.01, the $50 costs may be waived if the court determines that a hardship exists and that the case was removed in good faith.

(c) For purposes of this rule, the removing party prevails in district court if:

(1) the removing party recovers at least $500.00 or 50 percent of the amount or value of property that the removing party requested on removal, whichever is less, when the removing party was denied any recovery in conciliation court;

(2) the opposing party does not recover any amount or any property from the removing party in district court when the opposing party recovered some amount or some property in conciliation court;

(3) the removing party recovers an amount or value of property in district court that exceeds the amount or value of property that the removing party recovered in conciliation court by at least $500.00 or 50 percent, whichever is less; or

(4) the amount or value of property that the opposing party recovers from the removing party in district court is reduced from the amount or value of property that the opposing party recovered in conciliation court by at least $500.00 or 50 percent, whichever is less.

(d) Costs or disbursements in conciliation or district court shall not be considered in determining whether there was a recovery by either party in either court or in determining the difference in recovery under this rule.

Adopted Sept. 5, 1991, eff. Jan. 1, 1992. Amended June 22, 1993, eff. July 1, 1993.

1993 Committee Comment

Rule 524 simply repeats, for the benefit of litigants, the requirements set forth by the legislature. Minn.Stat. § 491A.02, subd. 7 (Supp.1993). Statutory costs normally available in district court pursuant to Minnesota Statutes section 549.02 do not apply to conciliation court matters that have been removed to district court. Minn.Stat. § 549.02 (1992).

RULE 525. APPEAL FROM DISTRICT COURT

The judgment of the district court on removal from conciliation court in any cause may be appealed to the Court of Appeals as in other civil cases.

Adopted Sept. 5, 1991, eff. Jan. 1, 1992. Amended June 22, 1993, eff. July 1, 1993.

1993 Committee Comment

An appeal may not be taken directly from conciliation court to the court of appeals. *McConnell v. Beseres,* 358 N.W.2d 113 (1984). Removal under Rule 521(b) or limited removal under Rule 521(c), and a ruling on the removal by the district court, are jurisdictional prerequisites for an appeal to the court of appeals from an action initiated in conciliation court. *Id.*

APPENDIX OF FORMS FOR TITLE VI. CONCILIATION COURT RULES

UCF-8 STATEMENT OF CLAIM AND SUMMONS

UCF-8 (SCAO 6/93)
Statement of Claim and Summons Minn.Gen.R.Prac. 507; 508

State of Minnesota | Conciliation Court

COUNTY | JUDICIAL DISTRICT | CASE NO.

Plaintiff # 1: Name and Address ______ ZIP ______

Plaintiff # 2: Name and Address ______ ZIP ______

vs. vs.

Defendant # 1: Name and Address ______ ZIP ______

Defendant # 2: Name and Address ______ ZIP ______

Name ______ Title ______
being duly sworn says that: s/he is the above named plaintiff/plaintiff's attorney; each defendant listed above is at least 18 years old; is not now in the Military Services; defendant # 1 is a resident of ______ County, State of ______; defendant # 2 is a resident of ______ County, State of ______; and alleges that the defendant(s) is (are) indebted to the plaintiff(s) in the amount of $______ plus $______ filing fee, totaling $______ plus disbursements, by reason of the following FACTS:

STATEMENT OF CLAIM ______

NOTARY STAMP OR COURT SEAL | SUBSCRIBED AND SWORN TO BEFORE ME ON: | THE ABOVE STATEMENT OF CLAIM IS TRUE AND CORRECT TO THE BEST OF MY KNOWLEDGE

DO NOT WRITE BELOW THIS LINE

DATE ______ SIGNATURE ______

______ SIGNATURE TELEPHONE ______

THE STATE OF MINNESOTA TO THE ABOVE NAMED DEFENDANT

SUMMONS NOTICE OF HEARING

YOU ARE HEREBY SUMMONED to appear at the hearing of the above entitled case at ______m., on
time

______, at ______
Date Place

Dated: ______ Court Administrator/Deputy: ______

FAILURE TO APPEAR

Failure of defendant to appear at the hearing may result in a default judgment being entered for the plaintiff, and failure of the plaintiff to appear may result in dismissal of the action or a default judgement being entered in favor of the defendant on any counter claim that has been asserted.

UCF-8 (SCAO 6/93) Statement of Claim and Summons

Memoranda of Proceedings

Judgment becomes final and time for removal expires on ______________, 19____.

ACTION	DATE	ACTION	DATE
Claim filed		Notices Mailed	
Hearing set for		Stricken–Settled	
Notices mailed		Order of Dismissal	
Notice returned/not delivered		Judgment entered	
Notice re-mailed		Notice of Judgment mailed	
Answer/Offer filed		Judgment satisfied	
Counterclaim filed		Removal/Appeal perfected	
Notices mailed		Order Vacating Judgment	
Hearing continued/reset to		Transcript issued	
Notices mailed		Exhibit Inf. (date filed)	
Hearing continued/reset to		Exhibits returned	

Settlement Agreement

Minn. Gen. R. Prac. 512(e)

The parties hereto have agreed upon a settlement of the within controversy, which agreement is as follows:

____

____

____

____

The parties further agree that they will abide the judgment to be entered herein based upon this agreement, without removal, appeal or further litigation.

Plaintiff	Defendant
Plaintiff	Defendant
Dated: ______________	Judge

Adopted Sept. 5, 1991, eff. Jan. 1, 1992. Amended June 22, 1993, eff. July 1, 1993.

UCF-9 JUDGMENT AND NOTICE OF JUDGMENT

UCF-9 (SCAO 6/93) Judgment and Notice of Judgment Minn.Gen.R.Prac. 514

State of Minnesota Conciliation Court

COUNTY JUDICIAL DISTRICT CASE NO.

Plaintiff # 1 — NAME AND ADDRESS ______ ZIP

Plaintiff # 2 — NAME AND ADDRESS ______ ZIP

vs. vs.

Defendant # 1 — NAME AND ADDRESS ______ ZIP

Defendant # 2 — NAME AND ADDRESS ______ ZIP

Appearances: ☐ Plaintiff ☐ Defendant ☐ Neither Party ☐ Contested ☐ Default

ORDER FOR JUDGMENT ON CLAIM AND COUNTER CLAIM

Upon evidence received, IT IS HEREBY ORDERED:

☐ ______ is entitled to judgment against ______ for the sum of $______, plus fees of $______, disbursements of $______, and conditional costs of $______, for a total of $______. ☐ judgment shall be entered in favor of ______ (without damages).

☐ ______'s claim is dismissed without prejudice.

☐ ______'s claim is dismissed with prejudice.

☐ ______ shall immediately return ______ ______ to the ______, and that the Sheriff of the county in which the property is located is authorized and directed to effect repossession of such property according to M.S. § 491A.01 subd. 5, and turn the property over to ______.

☐ Other / ☐ Memo ______

Dated: ______. Judge: ______

JUDGMENT

JUDGMENT is hereby declared and entered as stated in the Court's Order for Judgment set forth above, and the judgment shall become finally effective on the date specified in the notice of judgment set forth below.

Dated: ______.Court Administrator/Deputy: ______

NOTICE OF JUDGMENT

THE PARTIES ARE HEREBY notified that Judgment has been entered as indicated above, but the Judgment is stayed by law until

______ (DATE), ______ (TIME) p.m. (to allow time for an appeal/removal if desired).

THE PARTIES ARE FURTHER NOTIFIED that if the cause is removed to district court and the removing party does not prevail as provided in Rule 524 of the Minnesota General Rules of Practice for the District Courts, the opposing party will be awarded $50 as costs.

Dated: ______.Court Administrator/Deputy: ______

TRANSCRIPT OF JUDGMENT

I certify that the above is a correct transcript of the Judgment entered by this Court.

Dated: ______.Court Administrator/Deputy: ______

UCF–9 (SCAO 6/93) Judgment and Notice of Judgment

FILE # ____________________

____________________ VS ____________________

PLAINTIFF DEFENDANT

MEMORANDUM

DATED: ____________________ ____________________

JUDGE

Order Vacating Judgment For Cause

Minn. Gen. R. Prac. 520

Upon cause shown by the ☐ Plaintiff ☐ Defendant, the written judgment is hereby vacated and costs in the amount of $____________ is hereby assessed against the ☐ Plaintiff ☐ Defendant as ☐ Absolute/ ☐ Conditional costs.

DATED: ____________________ ____________________

JUDGE

Order Vacating Judgment Upon Removal/Appeal

Minn. Gen. R. Prac. 521(e)

Removal/Appeal by the ☐ Plaintiff ☐ Defendant having been perfected, the within judgment is hereby vacated.

DATED: ____________________ ____________________

JUDGE

Adopted Sept. 5, 1991, eff. Jan. 1, 1992. Amended June 22, 1993, eff. July 1, 1993.

UCF–10 DEFENDANT'S COUNTERCLAIM

UCF–10 (SCAO 6/93) Defendant's Counterclaim — Minn.Gen.R.Prac. 519

State of Minnesota — Conciliation Court

COUNTY — JUDICIAL DISTRICTS — CASE NO.

Plaintiff #1	NAME AND ADDRESS ZIP	Plaintiff #2	NAME AND ADDRESS ZIP
	vs.		vs.
Defendant #1	NAME AND ADDRESS ZIP	Defendant #2	NAME AND ADDRESS ZIP

STATEMENT OF CLAIM

Name __________________Title __________________
being duly sworn says that: s/he is the above named defendant/defendant's attorney; each plaintiff listed above is at least 18 years old; is not now in the Military Services; and alleges that the plaintiff(s) is (are) indebted to the defendant(s) in the amount of $_______ plus $_______ filing fee, totaling $_______ plus disbursements, by reason of the following FACTS:

DO NOT WRITE BELOW THIS LINE

NOTARY STAMP OR COURT SEAL — SUBSCRIBED AND SWORN TO BEFORE ME ON: — THE ABOVE STATEMENT OF CLAIM IS TRUE AND CORRECT TO THE BEST OF MY KNOWLEDGE

DATE ________________ SIGNATURE ________________

________________ TELEPHONE ________________

SIGNATURE

SUMMONS NOTICE OF HEARINGS

THE STATE OF MINNESOTA TO THE ABOVE NAMED PLAINTIFF

YOU ARE HEREBY SUMMONED to appear at the hearing of the above entitled case at _____ m., on
time

________________, at________________________________.
DATE PLACE

Dated: ________________ Court Administrator/Deputy: ________________

FAILURE TO APPEAR

Failure of defendant to appear at the hearing may result in a default judgment being entered for the plaintiff, and failure of the plaintiff to appear may result in dismissal of the action or a default judgment being entered in favor of the defendant on any counterclaim that has been asserted.

Adopted Sept. 5, 1991, eff. Jan. 1, 1992. Amended June 22, 1993, eff. July 1, 1993.

UCF–22 FINANCIAL DISCLOSURE FORM

UCF–22 (7/94)
Financial Disclosure Form M.S. 491A.02 subd. 9, 550.011

The purpose of this Financial Disclosure Form is to tell the JUDGMENT CREDITOR what money and property you have which may be used to pay the judgment the creditor obtained against you in the lawsuit. It also allows you to tell the creditor that some or all of your property and money is "exempt," which means that it cannot be taken to pay the judgment. You must answer every question on this form. If you need additional space, continue your answer on the back of the form or attach additional sheets if necessary. If you do not understand the questions or don't know how to fill out the form, call the court administrator for assistance or consult with an attorney.

WARNING: IF YOU CLAIM AN EXEMPTION IN BAD FAITH, OR IF THE JUDGMENT CREDITOR WRONGLY OBJECTS TO AN EXEMPTION IN BAD FAITH, THE COURT MAY ORDER THE PERSON WHO ACTED IN BAD FAITH TO PAY COSTS, ACTUAL DAMAGES, ATTORNEY FEES, AND AN EXTRA $100.

1. **JUDGMENT DEBTOR Name**
2. ☐ **Individual** ☐ **Partnership** ☐ **Corporation** ☐ **Other** ______

3. **Street Address** 4. **City** 5. **State** 6. **Zip**

7. **Date of Birth** 8. **If Married, Spouse's Full Name** 9. **Home Telephone Number** ( )

10. **Employer or Business** 11. **Work Telephone Number** ( )

12. **Street Address** 13. **City** 14. **State** 15. **Zip**

16. **What are your total wages, salary, or commissions per pay period? $______**
17. **How often are you paid?** ☐ **Daily** ☐ **Weekly** ☐ **Twice a month** ☐ **Monthly** ☐ **Other** ______

18. **Do you have income from any other source?** ☐ **Yes** ☐ **No If yes, give the source and amount of the income:**

19. **By answering this question, you will be able to claim the exemptions you have for wages and income. The first exemption is already checked for you, check all others that apply:**

☑ **I claim that 75% of my disposable (after-tax) earnings or 40 times the federal minimum wage ($206 for 40–hour week) is exempt (whichever is greater), unless the judgment is for child support.**
If the judgment is for child support, I claim that the following percentage of my after tax earnings is exempt:
☐ **50% (I am supporting a spouse and/or dependent child, and the child support judgment is 12 weeks old or less).**
☐ **45% (I am supporting a spouse and/or dependent child, and the child support judgment is more than 12 weeks old).**
☐ **40% (I am not supporting a spouse and/or dependent child, and the child support judgment is 12 weeks old or less).**
☐ **35% (I am not supporting a spouse and/or dependent child, and the child support judgment is more than 12 weeks old).**

☐ **I am presently receiving or have received relief based on need in the past 6 months so all my wages are exempt. Type of relief you receive** ______

☐ **I have been an inmate in a correctional institution within the past 6 months so all my wages are exempt. Name institution and release date** ______

☐ **My income is exempt because it is:** ☐ **Unemployment Comp.** ☐ **Worker's Comp.** ☐ **V.A. Benefits** ☐ **Social Security** ☐ **Accident or Disability Benefits** ☐ **Retirement Benefits** ☐ **Other (specify)** ______

20. **Do you have a checking or savings account? (This includes any account whether you have it by yourself or with someone else, or whether it is in your name or any other name)** ☐ **Yes** ☐ **No For each, provide the following information:**

Name and Address of Bank, Credit Union or Financial Institution	Type of Account	Account Number

21. **If you claimed an exemption for your wages or income, you may claim an exemption when your money is deposited in a bank. Claim your exemptions by checking the boxes that apply to you:**
☐ **The money in my account is from exempt wages, income, or benefits.**
☐ **The money in my account is from the exempt sale of my homestead within the past year.**
☐ **The money in my account is from exempt life insurance received on the death of a spouse or parent.**
☐ **The money in my account is from other exempt property (specify)** ______

22. **Do you have any stocks, bonds, securities, certificates of deposit, mutual funds, money market account, etc.? (This includes any whether owned by you alone or with any other person, or whether it is in your name or any other name.)** ☐ **Yes** ☐ **No If yes, itemize these and the location of each:**

23. **Do you own your home?** ☐ **Yes** ☐ **No Your homestead (house owned and occupied by you) is exempt up to a value of $200,000, or if used primarily for agricultural purposes, $500,000. Do you own any other houses, land, or real estate?** ☐ **Yes** ☐ **No For each, give the following:**

Location	Estimated Value	Amount Owed (if any)	To Whom

24. **Do you own any motor vehicles, motorcycles, boats, snowmobiles, trailers, etc.?** ☐ **Yes** ☐ **No For each, provide the following:**

Make	Model	Year	Lic. Plate No.	Market Value	Amount You Owe (if any)

One motor vehicle worth up to $3,600 (or $36,000 if the vehicle has been modified at a cost of at least $2,700 to accommodate a physical disability making a disabled person eligible for a parking permit under Minnesota Statutes, section 169.345) after subtracting what you owe is exempt. Which vehicle do you want to claim as exempt?

25. Do you own any of the following property?

Cash or travelers checks	☐ Yes ☐ No	Farm supplies, implements, livestock, grain worth more than $13,000	☐ Yes ☐ No
Household goods, furnishings, and personal effects that are worth more than $8,100 total	☐ Yes ☐ No	Business equipment, tools, machinery worth more than $9,000 total	☐ Yes ☐ No
Jewelry	☐ Yes ☐ No	Inventory	☐ Yes ☐ No
Coins or stamp collections	☐ Yes ☐ No	Accounts receivable/claims	☐ Yes ☐ No
Firearms/Guns	☐ Yes ☐ No	Are you the owner or partner in any business not already listed	☐ Yes ☐ No
Life insurance policy with a cash (surrender) value more than $7,200	☐ Yes ☐ No	Any other property please specify ______	☐ Yes ☐ No
Any property that you are selling on a contract for deed	☐ Yes ☐ No		

If you answered yes to any item in question 25, provide the following information:

Description and location of property (if not at residence)	Estimated Value	Amount Owed (if any)	To Whom

If you need additional space to answer the questions, continue your answers here. Indicate the question number you are answering. Attach additional sheets if necessary.

The above information is true and correct to the best of my knowledge.

Date:______________________ Signature:______________________

NOTICE: FAILURE TO COMPLETE, SIGN, AND RETURN THIS FORM TO THE JUDGMENT CREDITOR WITHIN 10 DAYS MAY RESULT IN A CITATION FOR CIVIL CONTEMPT OF COURT.

Adopted Sept. 5, 1991, eff. Jan. 1, 1992. Amended June 22, 1993, eff. July 1, 1993; Aug. 26, 1993, eff. Aug. 26, 1993; July 20, 1994, eff. July 20, 1994; July 2, 1996, eff. July 2, 1996; Sept. 6, 1996, eff. Sept. 6, 1996; Aug. 31, 1998, eff. Aug. 31, 1998.

FORM 508.1. Conciliation Court Affidavit of Service

State of Minnesota **of Service** **District Court**

_______________ County

Judicial District: __________
Court File Number: __________
Case Type:
____

STATE OF MINNESOTA)
) ss.
COUNTY OF ________)

____
Plaintiff

vs.

Affidavit of Service

____
Defendant

_______________, being sworn/affirmed under oath, states:

Check and complete one of the following:

1. ☐ **[Service by Mail]**
☐ I am over eighteen years of age **or**
☐ I am over eighteen years of age and not a party to the action. ***[Note: A party may generally not serve process, but is allowed to serve a Conciliation Court Summons by Certified Mail and a Demand for Removal/Limited Removal by First Class Mail.]***
On the __________ day of __________, 20 ___, I served the
☐ Summons
☐ Demand For Limited Removal
☐ Other Document ____________________ (specify)
upon ____________________, (plaintiff/ defendant or attorney
for ____________________), by placing a true and correct copy of it in an envelope addressed as follows:
____
____
____
which is the last known address of said party or attorney and depositing it,
☐ first-class postage or) ***specify one or both***
☐ Certified Mail, postage prepaid), in the United States mail.

2. ☐ **[Personal Service]** I am over eighteen years of age and not a party in the above-entitled action.
I served a copy of the
☐ Summons
☐ Demand For Limited Removal
☐ Other Document ____________________ (specify)
upon ____________________, (title) ____________________,
by delivering a copy personally to him/her at ____________________
at ________ am/pm, on ____________________, 20 ____.

3. ☐ **[Service not completed; party not found.]**
I am over eighteen years of age.
After diligent search and inquiry, I was unable to locate ____________________
____________________ (name of party to be served), or any residence or business address for him/her at which service could be attempted.

Dated: ____________________ ____________________
Signature of Server

(Sign only in front of notary public or court administrator.)

Sworn/affirmed before me this

___ day of __________, 20 ___.

Telephone (___) ______________________

____

Notary Public\Deputy Court Administrator

Adopted Nov. 30, 2005, eff. Jan. 1, 2006. Amended Dec. 20, 2005, eff. Jan. 1, 2006.

TITLE VII. HOUSING COURT RULES—HENNEPIN AND RAMSEY COUNTIES

RULE 601. APPLICABILITY OF RULES

In Hennepin and Ramsey Counties, Rules 601 through 612 apply to all proceedings in Housing Court. These rules and, where not inconsistent, the Minnesota Rules of Civil Procedure, shall apply to housing court practice except where they are in conflict with applicable statutes.

Adopted Sept. 5, 1991, eff. Jan. 1, 1992.

Task Force Comment—1991 Adoption

These rules apply only in Hennepin and Ramsey Counties. Housing Courts created by the legislature exist only in those counties.

These rules were drafted as a joint effort of legal advisory committees for the Ramsey and Hennepin County Housing Courts. Those committees met on a number of occasions, and these rules are the result of significant drafting efforts and compromise. Those drafting committees included the Housing Court Referee, court administrator, judges, and practitioners of landlord and tenant law in each County. The rules are generally drawn from a current local rule, 4th Dist. R. 13 and the Housing Court Temporary Rules, Rule 17.

The Task Force is mindful that Housing Court is currently in existence in only Ramsey and Hennepin Counties, 1989 Minn. Laws ch. 328, art. 2, §§ 17, 18 & 19 (uncodified), and these rules should be reviewed and revised if Housing Courts are used in other districts.

RULE 602. HOUSING COURT REFEREE

The housing court referee may preside over all actions brought under Minnesota Statutes Chapter 504B, criminal and civil proceedings related to violations of any health, safety, housing, building, fire prevention or housing maintenance code, escrow of rent proceedings, landlord and tenant damage actions, and actions for rent and rent abatement, unless the matter has been removed for hearing before a judge.

A party may request that a judge hear a case by filing such request in writing with the court administrator at least 1 day prior to the scheduled hearing date.

Adopted Sept. 5, 1991, eff. Jan. 1, 1992. Amended Dec. 17, 1999, eff. Jan. 1, 2000.

Task Force Comment—1991 Adoption

The procedure for removal of a referee assigned in Housing Court is intended to be different, due to the exigencies of practice in that court, from the procedure created by Minn. Gen. R. Prac. 107.

Advisory Committee Comment—1999 Amendments

The former chapters 504 and 566 were consolidated into and replaced by a new chapter 504B. This change is not intended to have any substantive effect other than to correct the statutory reference.

RULE 603. PARTIES

An unlawful detainer action shall be brought in the name of the owner of the property or other person entitled to possession of the premises. No agent shall sue in the agent's own name. Any agent suing for a principal shall attach a copy of the Power of Authority to the complaint at the time of filing.

No person other than a principal or a duly licensed lawyer shall be allowed to appear in Housing Court unless the Power of Authority is attached to the complaint at the time of filing, and no person other than a duly licensed lawyer shall be allowed to appear unless the Power of Authority is so attached to the complaint. An agent or lay advocate may appear without a written Power of Authority if the party being so represented is an individual and is also present at the hearing.

Adopted Sept. 5, 1991, eff. Jan. 1, 1992.

Task Force Comment—1991 Adoption

The Task Force expresses no opinion about whether or the extent to which the role of lay advocates constitutes the unauthorized practice of law. *See* Minn. Stat. § 481.01, et seq. (1990).

RULE 604. COMPLAINT

(a) Contents of Complaint. The plaintiff in an unlawful detainer case shall file with the court administrator a complaint containing the following:

(1) A description of the premises including a street address;

(2) The legal owner of the property or other person entitled to possession of the premises;

(3) A statement of how plaintiff has complied with Minnesota Statutes § 504B.181 by written notice to the defendant, by posting or by actual knowledge of the defendant;

(4) The facts which authorize recovery; and,

(5) A request for return of possession of the property.

(b) Signature. The complaint shall be signed by the plaintiff or the plaintiff's authorized agent or a duly licensed lawyer.

(c) Termination. If the complaint contains allegations of holding over after termination of the lease, a copy of the termination notice, if any, must be attached to the complaint or provided to defendant or defendant's counsel at the initial appearance, unless the plaintiff does not possess a copy of the notice or if the defendant at the hearing acknowledges receipt of the notice.

(d) Breach. If the complaint contains allegations of breach of the lease or rental agreement, a copy of the lease or rental agreement, if any, must be attached to the complaint or provided to defendant and defendant's counsel at the initial appearance, unless the plaintiff does not possess a copy.

Adopted Sept. 5, 1991, eff. Jan. 1, 1992. Amended Dec. 17, 1999, eff. Jan. 1, 2000.

Advisory Committee Comment—1999 Amendments

The former statute § 504.22 was replaced by a new statute § 504B.181. This change is not intended to have any substantive effect other than to correct the statutory reference.

RULE 605. RETURN OF SUMMONS

All summons shall be served in the manner required by Minn. Stat. Ch. 504B and the affidavit of service shall be filed with the court by 3:00 o'clock p.m. 3 business days prior to the hearing or the matter may be stricken. The affidavit must contain the printed or typed name of the person who served the summons.

Adopted Sept. 5, 1991, eff. Jan. 1, 1992. Amended Dec. 17, 1999, eff. Dec. 1, 2000.

Advisory Committee Comment—1999 Amendments

The former chapter 560 was replaced by a new chapter 504B. This change is not intended to have any substantive effect other than to correct the statutory reference.

RULE 606. FILING OF AFFIDAVITS

Upon return of the sheriff or other process server indicating that the defendant cannot be found in the county and, in the case of a nonresidential premises, where no person actually occupies the premises described in the complaint, or, in the case the premises described in the complaint is residential, service has been attempted at least twice on different days, with at least one of the attempts having been made between the hours of 6:00 and 10:00 p.m., the plaintiff or plaintiff's lawyer shall:

(1) file an affidavit stating that the defendant cannot be found or on belief that the defendant is not in the state, and

(2) file an affidavit stating that a copy of the summons and complaint has been mailed to the defendant at the defendant's last known address or that such an address is unknown to the plaintiff.

Service of the summons may be made upon the defendant by posting the summons in a conspicuous place on the premises for not less than one week. A separate affidavit shall be filed stating that the summons has been posted and the date and location of the posting.

Adopted Sept. 5, 1991, eff. Jan. 1, 1992. Amended Dec. 8, 1997, eff. Jan. 1, 1998.

Advisory Committee Comment—1999 Amendments

This rule is amended to conform the service requirements to the service provisions of Minn. Stat. § 504B.331 (Supp. 1999). The procedure of the revised rule also streamlines the procedure for issuance, service, and filing of process, and should permit service to be accomplished at a lower cost.

Historical Notes

The order of the Minnesota Supreme Court [CX–89–1863] dated December 8, 1997, provides in part that "(t)he attached amendments shall apply to all actions pending on the effective date and to those filed thereafter."

The order of the Minnesota Supreme Court [CX–89–1863] dated December 8, 1997, amending the General Rules of Practice for the District Courts provides in part that "(t)he inclusion of Advisory Committee comments is made for convenience and does not reflect court approval of the comments made therein."

RULE 607. CALENDAR CALL

At the first call of the calendar the parties shall specify whether the case is a default or for trial, and if for trial, whether by court or jury. Proposed Order forms will be available at the hearing. It is the responsibility of the plaintiff to properly complete the proposed order prior to the case being called for hearing. When each case is called for hearing, the defendant shall be asked whether the defendant admits or denies the charges in the complaint. Matters involving unlawful ouster or lockouts, utility shutoffs and other emergency relief, and motions for temporary restraining orders shall be heard first, then default cases shall be heard in their calendar order, followed by contested cases triable to the court without a jury. If a jury trial is demanded, the jury fee must be paid before the jury is impaneled. Contested cases shall be set for trial the same day as the initial hearing, if possible, or set on the first available calendar date.

Adopted Sept. 5, 1991, eff. Jan. 1, 1992.

RULE 608. WITHHELD RENT

In any unlawful detainer case where a tenant withholds rent in reliance on a defense, the defendant shall deposit forthwith into court an amount in cash, money order or certified check payable to the District Court equal to the rent due as the same accrues or such other amount as determined by the court to be appropriate as security for the plaintiff, given the circumstances of the case.

Adopted Sept. 5, 1991, eff. Jan. 1, 1992.

RULE 609. RESTITUTION

A writ of restitution shall issue within 24 hours after the entry of judgment, excluding Saturdays, Sundays and legal holidays, unless a stay authorized by law is specifically ordered by the court.

Adopted Sept. 5, 1991, eff. Jan. 1, 1992.

RULE 610. MOTIONS

Any motion otherwise allowed by the Minnesota Rules of Civil Procedure may be made by any party orally or in writing at any time including the day of trial. Whenever possible, oral or written notice of any dispositive motions and the grounds therefore shall be provided by the moving party to all parties prior to the hearing.

All motions shall be heard by the court as soon as practicable. The court may grant a request by any party for time to prepare a response to any motion for good cause shown by the requesting party or by agreement of the parties.

The requirements of service of notice of motions and any time periods set forth in the Minnesota Rules of Civil Procedure do not apply.

Adopted Sept. 5, 1991, eff. Jan. 1, 1992.

RULE 611. REVIEW OF REFEREE'S DECISION

(a) Notice. In all cases except conciliation court actions, a party not in default may seek judge review of a decision or sentence recommended by the referee by serving and filing a notice of review on the form prescribed by the court administrator. The notice must be filed within 10 days after an oral announcement in court by the referee of the recommended order or within 13 days after service by mail of the adopted written order, whichever occurs first. Service of the written order shall be deemed complete and effective upon the mailing of a copy of the order to the last known address of the petitioner.

A judge's review of a decision recommended by the referee shall be based upon the record established before the referee. Upon the request of any party, a hearing shall be scheduled before the reviewing judge.

(b) Stays. In civil cases, filing and service of a notice of review does not stay entry of judgment nor vacate a judgment if already entered unless the petitioner requests and the referee orders a bond, payment(s) in lieu of a bond, or waiver of bond and payment(s). The decision to set or waive a bond or payment(s) in lieu of bond shall be based upon Minn. R. Civ. App. P. 108, subds. 1 & 5. A hearing on a bond or payment(s) in lieu of bond shall be scheduled before the referee, and the referee's order shall remain in effect unless a judge modifies or vacates the order.

In criminal cases, the execution of judgment or sentence shall be stayed pending review by the judge.

(c) Transcripts. The petitioner must obtain a transcript from the referee's court reporter. The petitioner must make satisfactory arrangements for payment with the court reporter or arrange for payment in forma pauperis.

Any transcript request by the petitioner must be made within 1 day of the date the notice of review is filed. The transcript must be provided within 5 business days after its purchase by the petitioner.

For good cause the reviewing judge may extend any of the time periods described in this Rule 611(c).

Adopted Sept. 5, 1991, eff. Jan. 1, 1992.

RULE 612. DISCOVERY

Because of the summary nature of proceedings in Housing Court, the parties shall cooperate with reasonable informal discovery requests by another party.

Upon the request of any party to a matter scheduled for trial, the presiding referee or judge may issue an order for an expedited discovery schedule.

Adopted Sept. 5, 1991, eff. Jan. 1, 1992.

TITLE VIII. RULES RELATING TO CRIMINAL MATTERS

RULE 701. APPLICABILITY OF RULES

These rules apply in all criminal actions, and supplement the Minnesota Rules of Criminal Procedure. In addition, Rule 707 applies in extended jurisdiction juvenile proceeding.

Adopted Sept. 5, 1991, eff. Jan. 1, 1992. Amended Dec. 17, 2004, eff. Jan. 1, 2005.

Task Force Comment—1991 Adoption

The rules set forth here are derived from existing local rules. In order to further uniformity in practice in criminal proceedings throughout the state, the Task Force reviewed the existing local rules, and combined those rules having potential usefulness in all cases into a single code. The Task Force then submitted those rules to the Minnesota Supreme Court Advisory Committee on Rules of Criminal Procedure. The recommendations of that Advisory Committee have been endorsed and ratified by this Task Force, and these rules incorporate all of the recommendations of the Advisory Committee.

Historical Notes

The order of the Minnesota Supreme Court [CX–89–1863] dated December 17, 2004, provides in part that "(t)he attached amendments shall apply to all actions pending on the effective date and to those filed thereafter."

RULE 702. BAIL

(a) Approval of Bond Procurers Required. No person shall engage in the business of procuring bail bonds, either cash or surety, for persons under detention until an application is approved by the State Court Administrator's Office. Approval shall permit the applicant to issue bail bonds throughout the State of Minnesota. Nothing in this section shall infringe upon a judge's discretion in approving a bond. The application form shall be obtained from the State Court Administrator's Office. The completed application shall then be filed with the State Court Administrator's Office stating the information requested and shall be accompanied by verification that the applicant is licensed as an insurance agent by the Minnesota Department of Commerce. The approval granted under this rule may be revoked or suspended by the State Court Administrator's Office and such revocation or suspension shall apply throughout the State of Minnesota. Approved applicants are required to apply for a renewal of approval within a time period (not less than one year) established by the State Court Administrator's Office.

(b) Corporate Sureties. Any corporate surety on a bond submitted to the judge shall be one approved by the State Court Administrator's Office and authorized to do business in the State of Minnesota.

(c) Surety Insolvency. Whenever a corporate surety becomes insolvent, the local agent shall notify the State Court Administrator's Office and the court in every county in which it has issued or applied to issue bonds, in writing immediately. Within fourteen (14) days after such notice to the court, the agent shall file with the trial court administrator a security bond to cover outstanding obligations of insolvent surety, which may be reduced automatically as the obligations are reduced. In the absence of such surety or security bond, a summons shall be sent to all principals on the bonds of the surety.

(d) Posting Bonds. Before any person is released on bond, the bond must be approved by a judge after submission to the prosecuting lawyer for approval of form and execution and filed with the court administrator during business hours or thereafter with the custodian of the jail. In cases where bail has been set by the court and the defendant has provided a bail bond with corporate surety, approval by a judge is unnecessary if the bond conforms to Form 702 as published by the state court administrator.

(e) Forfeiture of Bonds. Whenever a bail bond is forfeited by a judge, the surety and bondsman shall be notified by the court administrator in writing, and be directed to make payment in accordance with the terms of the bond within ninety (90) days from the date of the order of forfeiture. A copy of the order of forfeiture shall be forwarded with the notice.

(f) Reinstatement. Any motion for reinstatement of a forfeited bond or cash bail shall be supported by a petition and affidavit and shall be filed with the court administrator. A copy of said petition and affidavit shall be served upon the prosecuting attorney and the principal of the bond in the manner required by Minn.R.Civ.P. 4.03(e)(1). A petition for reinstatement filed within ninety (90) days of the date of the order of forfeiture shall be heard and determined by the judge who ordered forfeiture, or the chief judge. Reinstatement may be ordered on such terms and conditions as the court may require. A petition for reinstatement filed between ninety (90) days and one hundred eighty (180) days from date of forfeiture shall be heard and determined by the judge who ordered forfeiture or the judge's successor and reinstatement may be ordered on such terms and conditions as the court may require, but only with the concurrence of the chief judge and upon the condition that a minimum penalty of not less than ten percent (10%) of the forfeited bail be imposed. No reinstatement of a forfeited bail or cash bail shall be allowed unless the petition and affidavit are filed within one hundred eighty (180) days from the date of the order of forfeiture.

(g) Forfeited Bail Money. All forfeited bail money shall be deposited in the state treasury in the manner provided by law.

(h) Bonding Privilege Suspension. A failure to make payment on a forfeited bail within ninety (90) days as above provided shall automatically suspend the surety and its agent from writing further bonds. Such suspension shall apply throughout the State of Minnesota and shall continue for a period of thirty (30) days from the date the principal amount of the bond is deposited in cash with the court administrator.

Adopted Sept. 5, 1991, eff. Jan. 1, 1992. Amended Dec. 14, 1993, eff. Jan. 1, 1994; Dec. 14, 1995, eff. Jan. 1, 1996; Dec. 8, 1997, eff. Jan. 1, 1998; Dec. 17, 2004, eff. Feb. 1, 2005; Dec. 22, 2008, eff. March 1, 2009.

Task Force Comment—1991 Adoption

This Rule is derived from 4th Dist. R. 8.02. Pretrial release is governed by Minn. R. Crim. P. 6, and this rule supplements the provisions of that rule. The Task Force believes that specific, written standards relating to the issuance and forfeiture of bail bonds would be useful to practitioners, courts, and to those issuing bonds.

The Minnesota Supreme Court Advisory Committee on Rules of Criminal Procedure recommended that this local rule be incorporated in the General Rules of Practice for the District Courts for uniform statewide application and the Task Force concurs in that recommendation.

Advisory Committee Comments—1997 Amendments

This Rule is derived from 4th Dist.R. 8.02. Pretrial release is governed by Minn.R.Crim.P. 6, and this rule supplements the provisions of that rule. The Task Force believes that specific, written standards relating to the issuance and forfeiture of bail bonds would be useful to practitioners, courts, and to those issuing bonds.

The Minnesota Supreme Court Advisory Committee on Rules of Criminal Procedure recommended that this local rule be incorporated in the General Rules of Practice for the District Courts for uniform statewide application and the Task Force concurs in that recommendation. The 1997 amendment continues the practice of statewide uniformity, established an uniform bail bond application procedure and making the posting of bonds easier by using a standard form. The rule conforms the rule to the practice in use prior to 1997.

Rule 702(h) was amended in 1993, effective January 1, 1994, to establish statewide suspension of bonding privileges for a surety and a surety's agent in the event of failure to make payment on a forfeited bond. This rule is necessary to ensure that irresponsible sureties not be allowed to move from district to district.

The power to revoke bail bonding privileges must be exercised sparingly. Courts considering this action should give consideration to the appropriate procedure and the giving of notice and an opportunity to be heard if such process is due the bond person. *See, e.g., In re Cross,* 617 A.2d 97, 100–02 (R.I.1992) (show cause hearing procedure based on probable cause, with clearly defined burden of proof, not inherently unconstitutional); *American Druggists Ins. Co. v. Bogart,* 707 F.2d 1229, 1234–36 (11th Cir.1983) (corporate surety authorized by Secretary of Treasury has right under U.S. Constitution to represent bonds to court for approval.)

Advisory Committee Comment—2004 Amendments

Rule 702 is amended in 2004 to allow it to operate appropriately under the system of statewide approval of bond procurers. Under the revised rule, the State Court Administrator's Office reviews and approves bond procurers, and that approval is then applicable in all district courts. The changes in the rule are not intended to change the rule other than to effect this centralization of the agent approval process.

Advisory Committee Comment—2008 Amendment

Rule 702(d) is amended to remove Form 702 from the rules, and to permit the maintenance and publication of the form by the state court administrator. The form, together with other court forms, can be found at http://www.mncourts.gov/.

Historical Notes

The order of the Minnesota Supreme Court [CX–89–1863, C6–84–2134] dated December 14, 1995, provides in part that "(t)he attached amendments shall apply to all actions pending on the effective date and to those filed thereafter."

The order of the Minnesota Supreme Court [CX–89–1863] dated December 8, 1997, provides in part that "(t)he attached amendments shall apply to all actions pending on the effective date and to those filed thereafter."

The order of the Minnesota Supreme Court [CX–89–1863] dated December 8, 1997, amending the General Rules of Practice for the District Courts provides in part that "(t)he inclusion of Advisory Committee comments is made for convenience and does not reflect court approval of the comments made therein."

The order of the Minnesota Supreme Court [CX–89–1863] dated December 17, 2004, provides in part that "(t)he attached amendments shall apply to all actions pending on the effective date and to those filed thereafter."

The order of the Minnesota Supreme Court [CX–89–1863] dated December 17, 2004, amending the General Rules of Practice for the District Courts provides in part that "(t)he inclusion of Advisory Committee comments is made for convenience and does not reflect court approval of the comments made therein."

RULE 703. CERTIFICATES OF REPRESENTATION

In any criminal case, a lawyer representing a client, other than a public defender, shall file with the court administrator on the first appearance a "certificate of representation," in such form and substance as a majority of judges in the district specifies.

Once a lawyer has filed a certificate of representation, that lawyer cannot withdraw from the case until all proceedings have been completed, except upon written order of the court pursuant to a written motion, or upon written substitution of counsel approved by the court ex parte.

A lawyer who wishes to withdraw from a criminal case must file a written motion and serve it by mail or personal service upon the client and upon the prosecutor; and the lawyer shall have the matter heard by the court. No motion of withdrawal will be heard within 10 days of a date certain for hearing or trial.

If the court approves the withdrawal, it shall be effective when the order has been served on the client and the prosecutor by mail or personal service and due proof of such service has been filed with the court administrator.

Adopted Sept. 5, 1991, eff. Jan. 1, 1992.

Task Force Comment—1991 Adoption

This rule is derived from 4th Dist. R. 8.05.

The Minnesota Supreme Court Advisory Committee on Rules of Criminal Procedure recommended that this local rule be incorporated in the General Rules of Practice for the District Courts for uniform statewide application and the Task Force concurs in that recommendation.

RULE 704. TIMELY APPEARANCES

Once the non-felony arraignment court calendar has convened, no lawyer shall approach the courtroom clerk or the court. Any lawyer appearing late must notify the bailiff in the courtroom of his or her presence. The bailiff will then transmit the information to the court and the case will be called by instruction of the presiding judge.

Adopted Sept. 5, 1991, eff. Jan. 1, 1992.

Task Force Comment—1991 Adoption

This rule is derived from 4th Dist. R. 8.06.

The Minnesota Supreme Court Advisory Committee on Rules of Criminal Procedure recommended that this local rule be incorporated in the General Rules of Practice for the District Courts for uniform statewide application and the Task Force concurs in that recommendation.

RULE 705. COMPLAINTS AND WARRANTS—SUBMISSION TO SECOND JUDGE

A complaint or search warrant application which is found by a judge to be defective or otherwise insufficient shall not be submitted to another judge without a full and complete disclosure of such finding to the second judge.

Adopted Sept. 5, 1991, eff. Jan. 1, 1992.

Task Force Comment—1991 Adoption

This rule is derived from 4th Dist. R. 8.10.

The Minnesota Supreme Court Advisory Committee on Rules of Criminal Procedure recommended that this local rule be incorporated in the General Rules of Practice for the District Courts for uniform statewide application and the Task Force concurs in that recommendation.

RULE 706. CUSTODY OF EXHIBITS

Exhibits marked in criminal cases shall be kept by the court administrator until the time for appeal has expired or any appeal has been decided, unless surrender of the exhibits is ordered by the judged[1] before whom the case was tried or the chief judge of the district.

Adopted Sept. 5, 1991, eff. Jan. 1, 1992.

[1] So in court order as adopted September 5, 1991. Probably should read "judge".

Task Force Comment—1991 Adoption

This rule is derived from 4th Dist. R. 6.03. The Minnesota Supreme Court Advisory Committee on Rules of Criminal Procedure recommended that this local rule be incorporated in the General Rules of Practice for the District Courts for uniform statewide application and the Task Force concurs in that recommendation.

RULE 707. TRANSCRIPTION OF PLEAS, SENTENCES, AND REVOCATION HEARINGS IN FELONY, GROSS MISDEMEANOR, AND EXTENDED JURISDICTION JUVENILE PROCEEDINGS

The following provisions relate to all pleas, sentences, and revocation hearings in all felony, gross misdemeanor, and extended juvenile jurisdiction proceedings, and all grand jury proceedings. Grand jury proceedings are secret as provided in Rule 18 of the Minnesota Rules of Criminal Procedure and this rule must be construed to maintain secrecy in accordance with that rule.

(a) Court reporters and operators of electronic recording equipment shall file the stenographic notes or tape recordings of guilty plea, or sentencing and revocation hearings with the court administrator within 90 days of sentencing, and the stenographic notes or tape recordings of grand jury proceedings shall be filed with the court administrator and maintained in a non-public portion of the file at the conclusion of grand jury hearings. The reporter or operator may retrieve the notes or recordings if necessary. Minn. Stat. § 486.03 (2002) is superceded to the extent that it conflicts with this procedure.

(b) All original grand jury transcripts shall be filed within 60 days of request by the court or prosecutor or receipt of an order from the appropriate court directing transcription and shall be made available to parties other than the court or prosecutor only in accordance with that court order. The court administrator must file and maintain all grand jury transcripts in a non-public portion of the file. The court may allow extension of this 60–day deadline upon a showing of good cause.

(c) No charge may be assessed for preparation of a transcript for the district court's own use; any other person ordering a transcript as allowed under the rules shall be at the expense of that person. Transcripts ordered by the defendant or defense counsel shall be prepaid except when the defendant is represented by the public defender or assigned counsel, or when the defendant makes a sufficient affidavit of an inability to pay and the court orders that the defendant be supplied with the transcript at the expense of the appropriate governmental unit.

(d) If no district court file exists with respect to a grand jury proceeding, the administrator shall open a grand jury file upon the request of the prosecutor.

(e) The maximum rate charged for the transcription of any proceeding shall be established, until July 1, 2005, by the Conference of Chief Judges, and thereafter by the Judicial Council. Minn. Stat. § 486.06 (2002) is superceded to the extent that it conflicts with this procedure.

Adopted Dec. 17, 2004, eff. Jan. 1, 2005. Amended Nov. 19, 2009, eff. Jan. 1, 2010.

Advisory Committee Comment—2004 Amendment

Rule 707 is a new rule, designed to implement provisions of orders of the Minnesota Supreme Court in 2003 relating to the transcription of plea proceedings. *See* Order, *In re Promulgation of Amendments to the Rules of Criminal Procedure*, No. C1–84–2137 (Minn., Oct. 31, 2003); Order, *In re Promulgation of Amendments to the Rules of Juvenile Procedure*, No. CX–01–926 (Minn., Nov. 10, 2003). The rule is not intended to expand or alter the practice under these orders; it merely codifies the orders as part of the general rules.

Advisory Committee Comment—2009 Amendment

Grand jury proceedings in Minnesota are secret. See Minn. R. Crim. P. 18.08. The court and prosecutors may obtain access to grand jury records and may order a transcript; any other transcription may occur only pursuant to Minn. R. Crim. P. 18.05, subd. 1. Rule 707 is amended to provide the rules for filing and maintaining transcripts of grand jury proceedings in the limited circumstances where the transcription is permitted or ordered. The court may also enter a protective order to prohibit further disclosure of the grand jury transcript. Minn. R. Crim. P. 18.05, subd. 2.

Rule 707(d) recognizes that there are circumstances where a grand jury is not separately convened for a particular case, and there is no separate file for that grand jury. This subdivision allows the prosecutor to request that a file be opened to serve as the repository for notes, records, or transcript from that proceeding.

Historical Notes

The order of the Supreme Court dated November 19, 2009, provided:

"1. The attached amendments to the General Rules of Practice for the District Courts and the Special Rules of Procedure Governing Proceedings under the Minnesota Commitment and Treatment Act be, and the same are, prescribed and promulgated to be effective on January 1, 2010.

"2. The attached amendments shall apply to all actions pending on the effective date and to those filed thereafter.

"3. The inclusion of Advisory Committee comments is made for convenience and does not reflect court approval of the comments made therein."

The order of the Minnesota Supreme Court [CX–89–1863] dated December 17, 2004, provides in part that "(t)he attached amendments shall apply to all actions pending on the effective date and to those filed thereafter."

The order of the Minnesota Supreme Court [CX–89–1863] dated December 17, 2004, amending the General Rules of Practice for the District Courts provides in part that "(t)he inclusion of Advisory Committee comments is made for convenience and does not reflect court approval of the comments made therein."

RULE 708. ITV IN CRIMINAL CASES

Use of ITV in criminal cases is governed by the rules of criminal procedure and rule 131.07 of these rules.

Adopted Dec. 22, 2008, eff. March 1, 2009.

Advisory Committee Comments—2008 Amendment

On November 19, 2007, the Supreme Court issued an order promulgating Minn. R. Crim. P. 1.05 governing the use of interactive video teleconference (ITV) in criminal proceedings. The order referred the task of developing rules governing the administrative procedures for conducting ITV hearings in criminal matters to the Advisory Committee on General Rules of Practice for the District Courts. In the interim, the Court ordered the State Court Administrator to develop temporary administrative procedures. The administrative procedures are set forth in Rule 131.07 of the General Rules of Practice for the District Courts.

APPENDIX OF FORMS FOR TITLE VIII. RULES RELATING TO CRIMINAL MATTERS

FORM 702. BAIL BOND FOR APPEARANCE ONLY

Filed in ________________ **County District Court**

STATE OF MINNESOTA, *PLAINTIFF*

v. COURT FILE NO. ________

________________, *DEFENDANT*

Bond Amount: ________________ ($________)

Charges: ________________
(Include any amendments or lesser included charges.)

BOND OBLIGATION AND CONDITIONS

The Defendant, as Principal, and ________________ as Surety, hereby agree and acknowledge that they are indebted to pay to the District Court the Bond Amount if Defendant fails to personally appear in Court at such times and on such dates as specified by the Court to answer the charge(s) identified in this Bond, including any amendments of these charges or lesser included charges.

Provided, however, the obligation of the Surety becomes null and void upon the happening of any of the following events:

1. The dismissal of the charge(s) identified in this Bond.
2. The finding or verdict that Defendant is not guilty of the charges identified in this Bond.
3. The sentencing of Defendant (whether imposed or stayed) with respect to the charge(s) identified in this Bond.

This is an appearance bond only and does not guaranty compliance with conditional release requirements imposed upon the Defendant by the Court and shall not be used for payment of any fines, surcharges, costs, or other financial obligation imposed upon the Defendant by the Court.

By: ________________ ________________
Attorney in Fact for Surety Defendant, Principal

ACKNOWLEDGMENT OF PRINCIPAL

State of Minnesota)
) ss.
County of ________)

This instrument was acknowledged before me on ________________ (date) by ________________ (name(s) of person(s).

____
Notary Public

ACKNOWLEDGMENT OF SURETY

State of Minnesota)
) ss.
County of ________)

This instrument was acknowledged before me on ________________ (date) by ________________________________ (name(s) of person(s) as ________________________________ (type of authority or office) of ________________________________, Surety.

____
Notary Public

TO BE COMPLETED BY COURT ADMINISTRATION

Filed this ________________ day of ________________.
By: ________________________, Deputy Court Administrator

Adopted Dec. 12, 1997, eff. Jan. 1, 1998.

TITLE IX. JURY MANAGEMENT RULES

RULE 801. GENERAL POLICY

Persons shall be selected randomly for jury service, from the broadest possible cross section of people in the area served by the court. All qualified persons have an obligation to serve as jurors when summoned, and all should be considered for jury service.

Adopted Sept. 5, 1991, eff. Jan. 1, 1992.

Task Force Comment—1991 Adoption

These Jury Management Rules have already been adopted by the Minnesota Supreme Court. *See* Order Promulgating Jury Management Rules, No. C5–85–837 (Minn. Sup. Ct. June 14, 1990). The Task Force recommends that they be included as part of the General Rules of Practice for the District Courts.

RULE 802. DEFINITIONS

(a) "Court" means a district court of this state, and includes, when the context requires, any judge of the court.

(b) "Court administrator," "judicial district administrator," and "jury commissioner" include any deputy of the court designated to perform the functions listed in these rules.

(c) "Source list" means the voter registration list for the jurisdiction served by the court, which may be supplemented with names from other sources as set out in the jury administration plan.

(d) "Voter registration list" means the official record of persons registered to vote.

(e) "Drivers' license list" means the record, maintained by the department of public safety, of persons over 18 years old licensed to drive a motor vehicle or issued a state identification card.

(f) "Master list" means a list of names and addresses, or identifying numbers of prospective jurors, randomly selected from the source list.

(g) "Juror" means a person summoned for service who either is deferred to a specific future date, attends court for the purpose of serving on a jury, or is on call and available to report to court when requested.

(h) "Random selection" means the selection of names in a manner totally immune to the purposeful or inadvertent introduction of subjective bias and such that no recognizable class of the population from which names are being selected can be purposely included or excluded.

(i) "Petit jury" means a body of six persons, impaneled and sworn in any court to try and determine, by verdict, any question or issue of fact in a civil or criminal action or proceedings, according to law and the evidence as given them in court. In a criminal action where the offense charged is a felony, a petit jury is a body of 12 persons, unless a different size is established in accordance with the Minnesota Rules of Criminal Procedure.

Adopted Sept. 5, 1991, eff. Jan. 1, 1992. Amended Dec. 14, 1993, eff. Jan. 1, 1994.

Advisory Committee Comment—1994 Amendments

Rule 802(i) is amended effective January 1, 1994, to make it clear that the definition of petit jury is not intended to change in any way the mechanism for agreeing to a different sized jury in criminal cases as established in the Minnesota Rules of Criminal Procedure. This change is intended to obviate any confusion over this rule, and to eliminate the type of dispute that arose in a case brought to the Minnesota Court of Appeals. *See State v. McKenzie,* No. C7–93–1890 (Minn.Ct.App., Sept. 23, 1993) (Unpublished Order Opinion).

RULE 803. JURY COMMISSIONER

(a) A jury commissioner is established in each county to administer the jury system under the supervision and control of the chief judge of the judicial district. The jury commissioner shall be the judicial district administrator or designee. If another person is designated jury commissioner, the other person shall be responsible to the judicial district administrator in the performance of the jury commissioner's tasks.

(b) The jury commissioner shall collect and analyze information regarding the performance of the jury system on a regular basis in order to evaluate:

(1) the inclusiveness of the jury source list and the representativeness of the jury pool;

(2) the effectiveness of qualification and summoning procedures;

(3) the responsiveness of individual citizens to jury duty summonses;

(4) the efficient use of jurors; and

(5) the cost effectiveness of the jury system.

(c) The jury commissioner should seek to secure adequate and suitable facilities for juror use in each court facility in which jury trials are held.

Adopted Sept. 5, 1991, eff. Jan. 1, 1992. Amended Dec. 28, 2006, eff. Jan. 1, 2007.

Advisory Committee Comments—2007 Amendment

Rule 803(b)(1) is amended to state the jury commissioner's responsibility more precisely. Because a jury commissioner does not have control over the composition of the jury source list, the rule should not impose a duty relating to the source list. It shifts that responsibility, however, to require the jury commissioner assess the representativeness of the jury pool as a whole, not the constituent lists.

This amendment is not intended to lessen in any way the representativeness of jury pools.

RULE 804. JURY ADMINISTRATION PLAN

(a) Each jury commissioner shall develop and place into operation a written plan for the administration of the jury system. The plan shall be designed to further the policies of these rules.

(b) Each plan must

(1) describe the jury system;

(2) give a detailed description of the random selection procedures to be used in all phases of juror selection, in accordance with Rule 805;

(3) identify the lists of names, if any, which shall be used to supplement the source list, and describe the storage media by which the lists shall be maintained;

(4) indicate if a master list is to be used, and set the minimum number of names which can be used;

(5) list the conditions which will justify excusing a juror, as well as those which justify deferral;

(6) describe the juror qualification questionnaire, which will be used to gather information to determine if a prospective juror is qualified;

(7) contain policies and procedures for enforcing a summons and for monitoring failures to respond;

(8) describe juror orientation and instruction for jurors upon initial contact prior to service; upon first appearance at the courthouse; upon reporting to a courtroom for voir dire; following empanelment; during the trial; prior to deliberations; and after the verdict has been rendered or when a proceeding is terminated without a verdict.

Adopted Sept. 5, 1991, eff. Jan. 1, 1992.

RULE 805. RANDOM SELECTION PROCEDURES

(a) Random selection procedures shall be used throughout the juror selection process. Any method may be used, manual or automated, that provides each eligible and available person with an equal probability of selection.

(b) Random selection procedures shall be employed in

(1) selecting persons to be summoned for jury service;

(2) assigning prospective jurors to panels; and

(3) calling prospective jurors for voir dire.

(c) Departures from the principle of random selection are appropriate

(1) to exclude persons ineligible for service in accordance with Rule 808;

(2) to excuse or defer prospective jurors in accordance with Rule 810;

(3) to remove prospective jurors for cause or if challenged peremptorily in accordance with applicable rules of procedure;

(4) to equalize service among all prospective jurors in accordance with Rule 812.

Adopted Sept. 5, 1991, eff. Jan. 1, 1992.

RULE 806. JURY SOURCE LIST

(a) The jury commissioner for each county shall be responsible for compiling and maintaining copies of all lists to be used in the random selection of prospective jurors. These lists shall be compiled when the court finds it necessary. No names shall be placed on the source list, master list, grand jury list, or petit jury venire except as provided by the applicable jury administration plan, or these rules.

(b) The voter registration and drivers' license list for the county must serve as the source list. The source list may be supplemented with names from other lists specified in the jury administration plan. Whoever has custody, possession, or control of the lists used in compiling the source list shall provide them to the jury commissioner, upon request and for a reasonable fee, at any reasonable time. All lists shall contain the name and address of each person on the list.

(c) The source list must be used for the random selection of names or identifying numbers of prospective jurors to whom qualification questionnaires and summonses for service must be sent.

(d) When the source list is so large that its use for selecting prospective jurors and mailing out summonses and questionnaires is unreasonably cumbersome, burdensome, and noneconomical, a second list may be created. This master list shall be randomly drawn from the source list.

(e) The jury commissioner shall review the jury source list once every four years for its inclusiveness and the jury pool for its representativeness of the adult population in the county and report the results to the chief judge of the judicial district.

(f) If the chief judge, or designee, determines that improvement is needed in either the inclusiveness of the jury source list or the representativeness of the jury pool, appropriate corrective action shall be ordered.

Adopted Sept. 5, 1991, eff. Jan. 1, 1992. Amended Dec. 14, 1993, eff. Jan. 1, 1994; Dec. 28, 2007, eff. Jan. 1, 2008.

Advisory Committee Comment—1994 Amendments

Rule 802 [1] is amended to incorporate a change made in jury source list creation that predated the adoption of the Minnesota General Rules of Practice but which was not incorporated in the final draft of the rules. This change is not intended to change the existing practice in creation of jury source lists.

[1] So in original.

Advisory Committee Comment—2008 Amendment

Rules 806(e) & (f) are amended to state the jury commissioner's responsibility more precisely. Because a jury commissioner does not have control over the composition of the jury source list, the rule should not impose a duty relating to the source list. It shifts that responsibility, however, to require the jury commissioner assess the representativeness of the jury pool as a whole, not the constituent lists. This amendment is not intended to lessen in any way the representativeness of jury pools. This change is similar in purpose and form to the amendment of Minn. Gen. R. Prac. 803, effective January 1, 2007.

RULE 807. JURY QUESTIONNAIRE AND SUMMONS. ONE-STEP PROCESS

(a) The jury commissioner shall mail to every prospective juror whose name has been drawn a juror qualification questionnaire and summons for service, along with instructions to fill out and return the questionnaire by mail within ten days of receipt.

(b) The notice summoning a person to jury service and the questionnaire eliciting essential information regarding that person shall be:

(1) combined in a single mailing;

(2) phrased so as to be readily understood by an individual unfamiliar with the legal and jury systems; and

(3) delivered by first class mail.

(c) A summons shall clearly explain how and when the recipient must respond and the consequences of a failure to respond.

(d) The questionnaire shall be phrased and organized so as to facilitate quick and accurate screening, and should request only that information essential for:

(1) determining whether a person meets the criteria for eligibility;

(2) determining whether there exists a mental or physical disability which would prevent the person from rendering satisfactory jury service;

(3) providing basic background information including age, race, gender, occupation, educational level, address, marital status, prior jury service within the past four years, occupation of spouse, and the age(s) of any children; and

(4) efficiently managing the jury system.

(e) The jury commissioner shall make a list of the persons to whom the summons and questionnaire have been sent, but neither the names nor the list shall be disclosed except as provided in these rules.

Adopted Sept. 5, 1991, eff. Jan. 1, 1992.

RULE 808. QUALIFICATIONS FOR JURY SERVICE

(a) The jury commissioner shall determine on the basis of information provided on the juror qualification questionnaire, supplemented if necessary, whether the prospective juror is qualified for jury service. This determination shall be entered on the questionnaire or other record designated by the court.

(b) To be qualified to serve as a juror, the prospective juror must be:

(1) A citizen of the United States.

(2) At least 18 years old.

(3) A resident of the county.

(4) Able to communicate in the English language.

(5) Be physically and mentally capable of rendering satisfactory jury service. A person claiming disability may be required to submit a physician's certificate as to the disability, and the Judge may inquire of the certifying physician. A prospective qualified juror who is 70 years of age or older, who requests to be excused from jury service shall be automatically excused from service without having to submit evidence of an inability to serve.

(6) A person who has had their civil rights restored if they have been convicted of a felony.

(7) A person who has not served as a state or federal grand or petit juror in the past four years.

(c) A judge, serving in the judicial branch of the government, is disqualified from jury service.

Adopted Sept. 5, 1991, eff. Jan. 1, 1992. Amended Jan. 28, 2003, eff. July 1, 2003; Dec. 28, 2006, eff. May 1, 2007.

Jury Task Force Comment—2003 Amendment

The Minnesota Supreme Court Jury Task Force recommends that Rule 808(b)(7) of the General Rules of Practice for District Courts be amended to provide that "A person who has not served as a state or federal grand or petit juror in the past two years." This change will allow counties with a reduced term of service to have an appropriately large pool of eligible jurors on which to draw.

Advisory Committee Comments—2007 Amendment

Rule 808 is amended to change the exemption from repeated jury service from two to four years. This change is made on the recommendation of the Jury Managers Resource Team and reflects that fact that sufficient numbers of jurors can be obtained with a four-year exemption. This change returns the rule to the period used before 2003, when the rule was amended to shorten the period to the current two-year period. The two-year period has resulted in various disproportionate calls to jury service and to complaints from repeatedly summoned jurors.

RULE 809. DISCRIMINATION PROHIBITED

A citizen shall not be excluded from jury service in this state on account of race, color, creed, religion, sex, national origin, marital status, status with regard to public assistance disability, age, occupation, physical or sensory disability, or economic status.

Adopted Sept. 5, 1991, eff. Jan. 1, 1992. Amended Dec. 14, 1993, eff. Jan. 1, 1994.

Advisory Committee Comment—1994 Amendments

This rule is amended to add "physical or sensory disability" as types of discrimination specifically prohibited by the rule. This amendment is made to conform the rule to the legislative mandate against discrimination on these bases adopted by the legislature in 1992 and at Minn.Stat. § 593.32, subd. 1.

RULE 810. EXCUSES AND DEFERRALS

(a) All automatic excuses or disqualifications from jury service are eliminated except as provided in Rule 808.

(b) Eligible persons who are summoned may be excused from jury service only if:

(1) their ability to receive and evaluate information is so impaired that they are unable to perform their duties as jurors and they are excused for this reason by a jury commissioner or a judge;

(2) they request to be excused because their service would be a continuing hardship to them or to members of the public and they are excused for this reason by the jury commissioner.

(c) Upon request from a qualified prospective juror, the jury commissioner shall determine whether the prospective juror meets the conditions for deferral set out in the jury administration plan. The deferral shall be for a reasonable time, after which the prospective juror shall be available for jury service, in accordance with the court's direction. Deferral of jury service is encouraged as an alternative to excuse from service.

(d) The reason for the excuse or deferral of any prospective juror must be entered in the jury commissioner's records.

(e) A member, officer, or employee of the legislature is excused from jury service while the legislature is in session.

(f) A candidate who has filed an affidavit of candidacy for elected office under Minnesota Laws, chapter 103C, 122, 204B, 204D, 205, 205A, or 447 is deferred from jury service from the date of filing the affidavit until the day after the election for that office, if the person requests to be deferred for this reason.

Adopted Sept. 5, 1991, eff. Jan. 1, 1992.

RULE 811. TERM OF JURY SERVICE

The time that persons are called upon to perform jury service and be available for jury service is the shortest period consistent with the needs of justice.

(a) In counties with a population of 100,000 or more, a term of service must not exceed two weeks or the completion of one trial, whichever is longer.

(b) In counties with a population of less than 100,000 but more than 50,000, a term of service must not exceed two months. However, no person is required to continue to serve after the person has reported to the courthouse for ten days or after the completion of the trial on which the juror is sitting, whichever is longer.

(c) In counties with a population of less than 50,001 a term of service must not exceed four months. However, no person is required to continue to serve after the person has reported to the courthouse for ten days or after the completion of the trial on which the juror is sitting, whichever is longer.

(d) Chief judges and judicial district administrators shall review the frequency of juror use in each county in determining the shortest period of jury service that will enable the greatest number of citizens to have the opportunity to report to the courthouse and participate in the jury system. All courts shall adopt the shortest period of jury service that is practical.

Adopted Sept. 5, 1991, eff. Jan. 1, 1992.

RULE 812. JUROR USE

(a) Courts shall employ the services of prospective jurors so as to achieve optimum use with minimum inconvenience to jurors.

(b) Courts shall determine the minimally sufficient number of jurors needed to accommodate trial activity; this information and appropriate management techniques shall be used to adjust both the number of individuals summoned for jury duty and the number assigned to jury panels.

(c) Courts may employ procedures to ensure that each prospective juror who has reported to the courthouse is assigned to a courtroom for voir dire each day before any prospective juror is assigned a second time that day.

Adopted Sept. 5, 1991, eff. Jan. 1, 1992.

RULE 813. CHALLENGING COMPLIANCE WITH SELECTION PROCEDURE

(a) A party may move to stay the proceedings, quash the indictment or for other appropriate relief, on the ground that these rules have not been complied with. Such motion should be made within seven days after the moving party discovers or should have discovered the grounds for the motion, and in any event before the petit jury is sworn to try the case.

(b) If a motion filed under (a) contains a sworn statement of facts which, if true, constitute a substantial failure to comply with these rules, the moving party is entitled to present the testimony of the jury commissioner, any relevant records and papers even if not public or otherwise available, and any other relevant evidence in support of the motion. If the court determines that there has been a substantial failure to comply with these rules in the selection of either a grand jury or a petit jury, the court shall stay the proceedings while a jury is selected in conformity with these rules.

(c) The procedures prescribed by this Rule are the exclusive means by which a party may challenge a jury on the grounds that the jury was not selected in conformity to these rules.

Adopted Sept. 5, 1991, eff. Jan. 1, 1992.

RULE 814. RECORDS

The names of qualified prospective jurors drawn and the contents of juror qualification questionnaires shall not be disclosed except as provided by this rule or as required by Rule 813.

(a) **Public Access.** The names of the qualified prospective jurors drawn and the contents of juror qualification questionnaires, except identifying information to which access is restricted by court order and social security numbers, completed by those prospective jurors must be made available to the public upon specific requests to the court, supported by affidavit setting forth the reasons for the request, unless the court determines:

(1) in a criminal case that access to any such information should be restricted in accordance with Minn. R. Crim. P. 26.02, subd. 2(2); or

(2) in all other cases that in the interest of justice this information should be kept confidential or its use limited in whole or in part.

(b) **Limits on Access by Parties.** The contents of completed juror qualification questionnaires except juror social security numbers must be made available to lawyers upon request in advance of voir dire. The court in a criminal case may restrict access to names, telephone numbers, addresses, and other identifying information of the jurors only as permitted by Minn. R. Crim. P. 26.02, subd. 2(2). In a civil case the court may restrict access to the names, addresses, telephone numbers, and other identifying information of the jurors in the interests of justice.

(c) **Retention.** The jury commissioner shall make sure that all records and lists including any completed juror qualification questionnaires, are preserved for the length of time ordered by the court or set forth in the official retention schedule except that in criminal cases any information provided to counsel for voir dire as authorized by part (b) shall be preserved in the criminal file for at least ten years after judgment is entered.

Adopted Sept. 5, 1991, eff. Jan. 1, 1992. Amended May 6, 2005, eff. July 1, 2005; Dec. 28, 2006, eff. Jan. 1, 2007.

Advisory Committee Comment—2005 Amendment

The 2005 change to Rule 814 is intended to ensure the privacy of juror social security numbers and to reflect the constitutional limits on closure of criminal case records. Juror qualification records on a particular juror will be subject to those constitutional limits only to the extent that the juror has participated in voir dire in a criminal case. Access to completed supplemental juror questionnaires used in specific cases is governed by separate rules. *See* MINN. R. CIV. P. 47.01; MINN. R. CRIM. P. 26.02, subd. 2(3).

Advisory Committee Comments—2007 Amendment

Rule 814 is amended to delete the apparently absolute right to public access to jury questionnaires one year after the jury list is prepared, contained in Rule 814(d), The provision is replaced by the modified public access right contained in amended Rule 814(a). The procedure applies the uniform procedure of specific request to the court for access, and essentially simply removes the distinction between requests before and after the one-year anniversary.

TITLE X. RULES OF GUARDIAN AD LITEM PROCEDURE

RULE 901. SCOPE OF RULES; IMPLEMENTATION

Rule 901.01. Scope of Rules

These Rules govern the appointment, responsibilities, and removal of guardians ad litem appointed to advocate for the best interests of the child, minor parent, or incompetent adult in family and juvenile court cases. These Rules do not govern the appointment of a guardian ad litem under Minnesota Rules of Civil Procedure 17.02 in child support and paternity matters. These Rules also do not govern guardians ad litem appointed pursuant to Minnesota Statutes §§ 245.487—.4888, § 253B, § 256B.77, §§ 494.01–494.05, § 501B.19, § 501B.50, § 508.18, § 524.1–403, and § 540.08.

For purposes of Rules 902 to 907:

(a) The phrase "family court case" refers to the types of proceedings set forth in the Comment to Rule 301 of the Minnesota Rules of Family Court Procedure, including, but not limited to, marriage dissolution, legal separation, and annulment proceedings; child custody enforcement proceedings; domestic abuse and harassment proceedings; support enforcement proceedings; contempt actions in family court; parentage determination proceedings; and other proceedings that may be heard or treated as family court matters.

(b) The phrase "juvenile court case" refers to the child protection matters set forth in Rule 2.01(k) of the Minnesota Rules of Juvenile Protection Procedure, including all of the following matters: child in need of protection or services, neglected and in foster care, termination of parental rights, review of out of home placement, and other matters that may be heard or treated as child protection matters; guardianship and adoption proceedings. The phrase "juvenile court case" also refers to the juvenile delinquency proceedings set forth in Rule 1.01 of the Minnesota Rules of Juvenile Procedure.

Adopted Aug. 27, 1997, eff. Jan. 1, 1999. Amended Dec. 8, 1997, eff. Jan. 1, 1999; Sept. 30, 2004, eff. Jan. 1, 2005; Dec. 1, 2006, eff. Jan. 1, 2007.

2004 Advisory Committee Comment—2006 Amendment

The previous Rules of Guardian Ad Litem Procedure also addressed the qualifications, recruitment, screening, training, selection, supervision, and evaluation of guardians ad litem. The administration and oversight of these issues is now the responsibility of the Office of the State Court Administrator. The issues are now included in a Program Standards manual. It is the responsibility of the Office of the State Court Administrator to prepare that manual, with the advice and consent of the Judicial Council. The minimum standards set forth in the previous rules are to be maintained in the manual, together with the procedures governing complaints about the performance of a guardian ad litem. Also to be included in the manual are standards regarding knowledge and appreciation of the prevailing social and cultural standards of the Indian and other minority communities. The manual is to be published in both print and electronic forms and is available to the public on the Guardian Ad Litem page of the Judicial Branch website: www.mncourts.gov.

Historical Notes

The order of the Minnesota Supreme Court [CX–89–1863] dated December 8, 1997, provides in part that "(t)he attached amendments shall apply to all actions pending on the effective date and to those filed thereafter."

Rule 901.02. Implementation

The chief judge of the judicial district shall be responsible for insuring the implementation of the Rules of Guardian ad Litem of Procedure. The responsibilities set forth in the Rules of Guardian ad Litem of Procedure shall be carried out in each judicial district at the direction of the judicial district administrator.

Adopted Aug. 27, 1997, eff. Jan. 1, 1999. Amended Dec. 8, 1997, eff. Jan. 1, 1999; Sept. 30, 2004, eff. Jan. 1, 2005.

Historical Notes

The order of the Minnesota Supreme Court [CO–95–1475] dated August 27, 1997, adopting the Rules of Guardian Ad Litem Procedure provides in part that "(t)he inclusion of Advisory Task Force Comments is made for convenience and does not reflect court approval of the comments made therein."

The order of the Minnesota Supreme Court [CX–89–1863] dated December 8, 1997, provides in part that "(t)he attached amendments shall apply to all actions pending on the effective date and to those filed thereafter."

The order of the Minnesota Supreme Court [CX–89–1863] dated December 8, 1997, amending the General Rules of Practice for the District Courts provides in part that "(t)he inclusion of Advisory Committee comments is made for convenience and does not reflect court approval of the comments made therein."

RULE 902. MINIMUM QUALIFICATIONS

Before a person may be recommended for service as a guardian ad litem pursuant to Rule 903, the person must satisfy the minimum qualifications set forth in the Guardian Ad Litem System Program Standards as established by the Office of the State Court Administrator with the advice and consent of the Judicial Council. The Program Standards shall be published in print and electronic forms and be available to the public.

Adopted Aug. 27, 1997, eff. Jan. 1, 1999. Amended Dec. 8, 1997, eff. Jan. 1, 1999; Sept. 30, 2004, eff. Jan. 1, 2005; Dec. 1, 2006, eff. Jan. 1, 2007.

2006 Advisory Committee Comment

The Guardian Ad Litem Program Standards are available on the Guardian Ad Litem Program page located on the Supreme Court public website: www.mncourts.gov.

Historical Notes

The order of the Minnesota Supreme Court [CX–89–1863] dated December 8, 1997, provides in part that "(t)he attached amendments shall apply to all actions pending on the effective date and to those filed thereafter."

RULE 903. APPOINTMENT OF GUARDIAN AD LITEM

Rule 903.01. Order by Court; Recommendation of Guardian Ad Litem for Appointment

When the court orders the appointment of a guardian ad litem in a particular case, the district guardian ad litem manager or the manager's designee shall promptly recommend a guardian ad litem for appointment. If in the exercise of judicial discretion the court determines that the guardian ad litem recommended is not appropriate for appointment, and communicates the reasons for that determination to the district guardian ad litem manager or the manager's designee, the district guardian ad litem manager or the manager's designee shall promptly recommend another guardian ad litem for appointment. No guardian ad litem shall be appointed unless recommended by the district guardian ad litem manager or manager's designee.

Adopted Aug. 27, 1997, eff. Jan. 1, 1999. Amended Dec. 8, 1997, eff. Jan. 1, 1999; Sept. 30, 2004, eff. Jan. 1, 2005.

Historical Notes

The order of the Minnesota Supreme Court [CX–89–1863] dated December 8, 1997, provides in part that "(t)he attached amendments shall apply to all actions pending on the effective date and to those filed thereafter."

Former Rule: A former Rule 903.01, adopted Aug. 27, 1997 and amended Dec. 8, 1997, related to the recruitment of guardians ad litem.

Rule 903.02. Juvenile Court Appointment

Subd. 1. Generally. A guardian ad litem shall not be appointed or serve except upon written order of the court. The order shall set forth:

(a) the statute or rule providing for the appointment of the guardian ad litem;

(b) the provisions for parental fee collection as applicable under Minnesota Statutes §§ 260B.331, subd. 6 (a), and 260C.331, subd. 6(a), and as established by the Judicial Council, and

(c) in an adoption proceeding, authorization for the guardian to review and receive a copy of the adoption study report under Rule 37 of the Rules of Adoption Procedure and the post-placement assessment report under Rule 38 of the Rules of Adoption Procedure to the extent permitted by Minnesota Statutes § 259.53, subd. 3.

If the court has issued an order appointing a person as a guardian ad litem in a child in need of protection or services proceeding, the court may, but is not required, to issue an order reappointing the same person in the termination of parental rights or other permanent placement determination proceeding. An order is required only if a new person is being appointed as guardian ad litem.

Subd. 2. Guardian Ad Litem Shall Not Also Serve on Same Case as Petitioner. When a guardian ad litem is appointed pursuant to Minnesota Statutes § 260C.163, subd. 5(a), the court shall not appoint as guardian ad litem an individual who is the party, or an agent of the party, who has already filed the initial petition in the case pursuant to Minnesota Statutes § 260C.141.

Subd. 3. Representation of Child's Parent or Legal Custodian. The court may sua sponte or upon the written or on-the-record request of a party or participant appoint a guardian ad litem for a parent who is a party or the legal custodian if:

(a) the court determines that the parent or legal custodian is incompetent to assist counsel in the matter or understand the nature of the proceedings; or

(b) it appears at any stage of the proceedings that the parent is under eighteen (18) years of age and is without a parent or legal custodian, or that considered in the context of the matter the minor parent's parent or legal custodian is unavailable, incompetent, indifferent to, hostile to, or has interests in conflict with the interests of the minor parent.

Appointment of a guardian ad litem for a parent shall not result in discharge of counsel for the parent.

Adopted Sept. 30, 2004, eff. Jan. 1, 2005. Amended Dec. 1, 2006, eff. Jan. 1, 2007; Dec. 18, 2006, Jan. 1, 2007.

2004 Advisory Committee Comment

Rule 903.02 prohibits appointment as a guardian ad litem in a juvenile court case any individual, or the individual's agent, who has filed the initial petition in the case. The Rule is also intended to prohibit an individual serving as a guardian ad litem in both a family court matter and a juvenile court matter involving the same child, if the family court guardian ad litem has filed the initial petition in the juvenile court matter. The Rule does not prohibit a guardian ad litem already serving in a juvenile court matter from continuing to serve if, in the course of the case, the guardian ad litem files a petition or other pleadings.

2006 Advisory Committee Comment

If paragraph (c) in Rule 903.02 is not included in the initial order appointing the guardian ad litem in a juvenile protection matter, and the matter proceeds to adoption, the succeeding guardian ad litem appointment order in the adoption matter should include paragraph (c).

If the minor parent or incompetent adult is unable to admit or deny the petition, the court may choose to appoint a substitute decision maker or legal guardian to admit or deny the petition.

Historical Notes

Former Rule: A former Rule 903.02, adopted Aug. 27, 1997 and amended Dec. 8, 1997, related to the application process to become a guardian ad litem.

Rule 903.03. Family Court Appointment

A guardian ad litem shall not be appointed or serve except upon written order of the court. The order shall set forth:

(a) the statute or rule providing for the appointment of the guardian ad litem;

(b) the specific duties to be performed by the guardian ad litem in the case;

(c) to the extent appropriate, deadlines for the completion of the duties set forth;

(d) to the extent appropriate; the duration of the appointment; and

(e) the provisions for parental fee collection as applicable under Minnesota Statutes §§ 257.69, subd. 2(a),and 518.165, subd. 3 (a), and as established by the Judicial Council.

Adopted Aug. 27, 1997, eff. Jan. 1, 1999. Amended Dec. 8, 1997, eff. Jan. 1, 1999; Sept. 30, 2004, eff. Jan. 1, 2005; Dec. 1, 2006, eff. Jan. 1, 2007.

Historical Notes

The order of the Minnesota Supreme Court [CX–89–1863] dated December 8, 1997, provides in part that "(t)he attached amendments shall apply to all actions pending on the effective date and to those filed thereafter."

Former Rule: A former Rule 903.03, adopted Aug. 27, 1997 and amended Dec. 8, 1997, related to the screening process for guardians ad litem.

Rule 903.04. Other Roles Precluded

Subd. 1. Generally. A guardian ad litem under the supervision of the Office of the State Court Administrator shall not be ordered to, and shall not perform, the following roles in a case in which the person serves as a guardian ad litem:

(a) custody evaluator pursuant to Minnesota Statutes § 518.167; or

(b) parenting time evaluator; or

(c) parenting time consultant; or

(d) family group decision making facilitator; or

(e) early neutral evaluator; or

(f) mediator, as that role is prescribed in Minnesota Statutes § 518.619 and Rule 310 of the Minnesota Rules of Family Court Procedure; or

(g) arbitrator or individual authorized to decide disputes between parties; or

(h) parenting time expeditor, as that role is prescribed in Minnesota Statutes §§ 518.619 and 518.1751; or

(i) substitute decision-maker under Minnesota Statutes § 253B.092; or

(j) evaluator charged with conducting a home study under Minnesota Statutes § 245A.035 or § 259.41; or

(k) attorney for the child.

Subd. 2. Roles Distinguished. Nothing in this rule shall prevent a properly qualified person who also serves in other cases as a guardian ad litem from serving in any of the roles in subdivision 1 on a privately-paid basis. A guardian ad litem under the supervision of the Office of the State Court Administrator is not the same as a mediator, arbitrator, facilitator, custody evaluator, or neutral as those titles and roles are described in Rule 114 of the Minnesota Rules of General Practice for the District Courts.

Adopted Sept. 30, 2004, eff. Jan. 1, 2005. Amended Dec. 1, 2006, eff. Jan. 1, 2007.

Historical Notes

Former Rule: A former Rule 903.01, adopted Aug. 27, 1997 and amended Dec. 8, 1997, related to a panel of approved guardians ad litem.

RULE 904. COMPLAINT PROCEDURE; REMOVAL OR SUSPENSION OF GUARDIAN AD LITEM FROM PARTICULAR CASE

Rule 904.01. Complaint Procedure

Complaints about the performance of a guardian ad litem shall be governed by procedures and policies set forth in the Guardian Ad Litem System Program Standards established by the Office of the State Court Administrator with the advice and consent of the Judicial Council. Unless offered into evidence by the guardian ad litem or authorized by written order following an *in camera* review by the court, the complaints and complaint investigation reports shall not be received as evidence or used in any manner in any proceeding governed by these Rules.

Adopted Aug. 27, 1997, eff. Jan. 1, 1999. Amended Dec. 8, 1997, eff. Jan. 1, 1999; Sept. 30, 2004, eff. Jan. 1, 2005; Dec. 1, 2006, eff. Jan. 1, 2007.

Historical Notes

The order of the Minnesota Supreme Court [CX–89–1863] dated December 8, 1997, provides in part that "(t)he attached amendments shall apply to all actions pending on the effective date and to those filed thereafter."

Former Rule: A former Rule 904.01, adopted Aug. 27, 1997 and amended Dec. 8, 1997, related to the appointment of a guardian ad litem. See, now, MN ST Guard Ad Litem, Rule 903.01 et seq.

Rule 904.02. Removal or Suspension of Guardian Ad Litem From Particular Case

Subd. 1. A guardian ad litem appointed to serve in a particular case may be removed or suspended from the case only by order of the presiding judge. Removal or suspension may be upon initiation of the presiding judge or after hearing upon the motion of a party pursuant to subd. 2 of this Rule.

Subd. 2. A party to the case who wishes to seek the removal or suspension of a guardian ad litem for cause must proceed by written motion before the judge presiding over the case. A motion to remove or suspend a guardian ad litem for cause shall be served upon the parties and the guardian ad litem and filed and supported in compliance with the applicable rules of court. At the time the motion is served, a copy of the motion and all supporting documents shall be provided to the district guardian ad litem manager by the party making the motion.

Subd. 3. The presiding judge shall remove a guardian ad litem from a particular case:

(a) when it is shown by written communication from the district guardian ad litem manager or the manager's designee that the individual is a contract guardian ad litem who does not have a current contract with the state of Minnesota, or the guardian ad litem has been removed from the state program for cause; or

(b) upon notice of any felony, gross misdemeanor, or misdemeanor conviction of the guardian ad litem of an offense involving children or domestic assault; or

(c) upon notice of a finding by the Minnesota Department of Human Services of maltreatment of a child by the guardian ad litem.

Subd. 4. The presiding judge may remove or suspend a guardian ad litem from a particular case:

(a) for failure to comply with a directive of the court, including provisions of the order appointing the guardian ad litem; or

(b) for failure to comply with the responsibilities set forth in these Rules; or

(c) upon notice of formal sanction of the guardian ad litem by any professional or occupational licensing board; or

(d) upon formal request from the district guardian ad litem program for good cause; or

(e) for other good cause shown.

As an alternative to removal or suspension from a specific case, the presiding judge may ask the district guardian ad litem manager to provide appropriate remedial action for the guardian ad litem.

Adopted Aug. 27, 1997, eff. Jan. 1, 1999. Amended Dec. 8, 1997, eff. Jan. 1, 1999; Sept. 30, 2004, eff. Jan. 1, 2005.

Historical Notes

The order of the Minnesota Supreme Court [CO–95–1475] dated August 27, 1997, adopting the Rules of Guardian Ad Litem Procedure provides in part that "(t)he inclusion of Advisory Task Force Comments is made for convenience and does not reflect court approval of the comments made therein."

The order of the Minnesota Supreme Court [CX–89–1863] dated December 8, 1997, provides in part that "(t)he attached amendments shall apply to all actions pending on the effective date and to those filed thereafter."

The order of the Minnesota Supreme Court [CX–89–1863] dated December 8,1997, amending the General Rules of Practice for the District Courts provides in part that "(t)he inclusion of Advisory Committee comments is made for convenience and does not reflect court approval of the comments made therein."

Former Rule: A former Rule 904.02, adopted Aug. 27, 1997 and amended Dec. 8, 1997, related to the appointment of a guardian ad litem. See, now, MN ST Guard Ad Litem, Rule 903.01 et seq.

RULE 905. GENERAL RESPONSIBILITIES OF GUARDIANS AD LITEM

Rule 905.01. Generally

In every family court and juvenile court case as defined in Rule 901.01 in which a guardian ad litem is appointed, the guardian ad litem shall:

(a) conduct an independent investigation to determine the facts relevant to the situation of the child or incompetent adult and the child's parent, legal custodian, or other household or family member, which must include, unless specifically excluded by the court:

(i) reviewing relevant documents, which in the case of an adoption shall include the adoption study report and the post-placement assessment report upon order of the court to the extent permitted by Minnesota Statutes § 259.53, subd. 3(b);

(ii) meeting with and observing the child in the home setting and considering the child's or incompetent adult's wishes, as appropriate; and

(iii) interviewing parents, caregivers, and others relevant to the case;

(b) advocate for the best interests of the child or incompetent adult by participating in appropriate aspects of the case and advocating for appropriate community services when necessary;

(c) maintain the confidentiality of information related to a case, with the exception of sharing information as permitted by law to promote cooperative solutions that are in the best interests of the child or incompetent adult;

(d) monitor the best interests of the child or incompetent adult throughout the judicial proceeding; and

(e) present written reports on the best interests of the child or incompetent adult that include conclusions and recommendations, and the facts upon which they are based.

Former Rule 905, adopted Sept. 30, 2004, eff. Jan. 1, 2005. Renumbered Rule 905.01 and amended Dec. 1, 2006, eff. Jan. 1, 2007.

2006 Advisory Committee Comment

The responsibilities of a guardian ad litem are the same for all appointments made under these Rules, regardless of case type.

Historical Notes

Former Rule: A former Rule 905, adopted Aug. 27, 1997 and amended Dec. 8, 1997, related to the oath or affirmation of a guardian ad litem.

Rule 905.02. Representation of Child's Parent or Legal Custodian

In every matter where the guardian ad litem is appointed to represent a parent or legal custodian under Rule 903.02, subd. 3, the guardian ad litem shall perform the following responsibilities:

(a) conduct an investigation to determine the facts relevant to the situation of the minor parent or incompetent adult and the family, which must include, unless specifically excluded by the court:

(i) reviewing relevant documents;

(ii) meeting with and observing the minor parent or incompetent adult in the home setting and considering the minor parent's, or incompetent adult's wishes, as appropriate; and

(iii) interviewing parents, caregivers, and others relevant to the case;

(b) advocate for the minor parent's or incompetent adult's best interests by participating in appropriate aspects of the case and advocating for appropriate community services when necessary;

(c) maintain the confidentiality of information related to a case, with the exception of sharing information as permitted by law to promote cooperative solutions that are in the best interests of the minor parent or incompetent adult;

(d) monitor the minor parent's or incompetent adult's best interests throughout the judicial proceeding; and

(e) present written reports on the minor parent's or incompetent adult's best interests that include conclusions and recommendations and the facts upon which they are based.

Adopted Dec. 1, 2006, eff. Jan. 1, 2007. Amended Dec. 18, 2006, eff. Jan. 1, 2007.

RULE 906. EX PARTE CONTACT PROHIBITED

Ex parte communication with the court by a guardian ad litem is prohibited, except as to procedural matters not affecting the merits of the case.

Adopted Sept. 30, 2004, eff. Jan. 1, 2005.

Historical Notes

Former Rule: A former Rule 906, adopted Aug. 27, 1997 and amended Dec. 8, 1997, related to the supervision, evaluation, and removal of guardians ad litem.

RULE 907. RIGHTS OF GUARDIANS AD LITEM

Rule 907.01. Rights in Every Case

Subd. 1. Generally. In every case in which a guardian ad litem is appointed pursuant to Rule 903, the guardian ad litem shall have the rights set forth in clauses (a) to (d).

(a) The guardian ad litem shall have access to the child or incompetent adult including meeting with the child alone as deemed appropriate by the guardian ad litem; and shall have access to all information relevant to the child's or incompetent adult's and family's situation which is accessible under applicable state and federal laws.

(b) The guardian ad litem shall be furnished copies of all pleadings, documents, and reports by the party which served or submitted them. A party submitting, providing, or serving pleadings, documents, or reports shall simultaneously provide copies to the guardian ad litem.

(c) The guardian ad litem shall be notified of all court hearings, administrative reviews, staffings, investigations, dispositions, and other proceedings concerning the case. Timely notice of all court hearings, administrative reviews, staffings, investigations, dispositions, and other proceedings concerning the case shall be provided to the guardian ad litem by the party scheduling the proceeding.

(d) The guardian ad litem shall have the right to participate in all proceedings through submission of written and oral reports, and may initiate and respond to motions.

Subd. 2. Not Unauthorized Practice of Law. The exercise of the rights listed in subdivision 1 by a guardian ad litem shall not constitute the unauthorized practice of law.

Adopted Aug. 27, 1997, eff. Jan. 1, 1999. Amended Dec. 8, 1997, eff. Jan. 1, 1999; Sept. 30, 2004, eff. Jan. 1, 2005; Dec. 1, 2006, eff. Jan. 1, 2007.

Historical Notes

The order of the Minnesota Supreme Court [CX-89-1863] dated December 8, 1997, provides in part that "(t)he attached amendments shall apply to all actions pending on the effective date and to those filed thereafter."

Former Rule: A former Rule 907.01, adopted Aug. 27, 1997 and amended Dec. 8, 1997, related to the complaint procedure for a guardian ad litem. See, now, MN ST Guard Ad Litem, Rule 904.01.

Rule 907.02. Rights as a Party

In addition to the rights set forth in Rule 907.01 and any other rights set forth in statute, court order, or Rule, in every case in which a guardian ad litem is a party, the guardian ad litem shall have the right to:

(a) legal representation;

(b) be present at all hearings;

(c) conduct discovery;

(d) bring motions before the court;

(e) participate in settlement agreements;

(f) subpoena witnesses;

(g) make argument in support of or against the petition;

(h) present evidence;

(i) cross–examine witnesses;

(j) request review of the referee's findings and recommended order;

(k) request review of the court's disposition upon a showing of a substantial change of circumstances or that the previous disposition was inappropriate;

(*l*) bring post-trial motions; and

(m) appeal from orders of the court.

The exercise of these rights shall not constitute the unauthorized practice of law.

Adopted Aug. 27, 1997, eff. Jan. 1, 1999. Amended Dec. 8, 1997, eff. Jan. 1, 1999; Sept. 30, 2004, eff. Jan. 1, 2005.

Historical Notes

The order of the Minnesota Supreme Court [CO–95–1475] dated August 27, 1997, adopting the Rules of Guardian Ad Litem Procedure provides in part that "(t)he inclusion of Advisory Task Force Comments is made for convenience and does not reflect court approval of the comments made therein."

The order of the Minnesota Supreme Court [CX–89–1863] dated December 8, 1997, provides in part that "(t)he attached amendments shall apply to all actions pending on the effective date and to those filed thereafter."

The order of the Minnesota Supreme Court [CX–89–1863] dated December 8, 1997, amending the General Rules of Practice for the District Courts provides in part that "(t)he inclusion of Advisory Committee comments is made for convenience and does not reflect court approval of the comments made therein."

Former Rule: A former Rule 907.02, adopted Aug. 27, 1997 and amended Dec. 8, 1997, related to the removal of a guardian ad litem from a particular case. See, now, MN ST Guard Ad Litem, Rule 904.02.

RULE 908. GENERAL RESPONSIBILITIES OF GUARDIANS AD LITEM; OTHER ROLES DISTINGUISHED; CONTACT WITH COURT [Deleted Sept. 30, 2004, eff. Jan. 1, 2005]

Historical Notes

See, now, MN ST Guard Ad Litem, Rule 905.01 et seq.

RULE 909. RIGHTS AND POWERS OF GUARDIANS AD LITEM [Deleted Sept. 30, 2004, eff. Jan. 1, 2005]

Historical Notes

See, now, MN ST Guard Ad Litem, Rule 907.01 et seq.

RULE 910. PRE-SERVICE TRAINING REQUIREMENTS [Deleted Sept. 30, 2004, eff. Jan. 1, 2005]

Historical Notes

The deleted rule, which related to continuing education requirements for guardians ad litem, was derived from Aug. 27, 1997 and Dec. 8, 1997.

RULE 912. TRAINING CURRICULA; CERTIFICATION OF TRAINERS [Deleted Sept. 30, 2004, eff. Jan. 1, 2005]

RULE 913. COMMUNITY EDUCATION [Deleted Sept. 30, 2004, eff. Jan. 1, 2005]

INDEX TO GENERAL RULES OF PRACTICE FOR THE DISTRICT COURTS

SPECIAL RULES OF PRACTICE FOR THE DISTRICT COURTS

Effective January 1, 1992

Including Amendments Received Through January 1, 2014

Research Note

See Minnesota Statutes Annotated, *Volume 51, for historical notes and case annotations.*

FIRST JUDICIAL DISTRICT

SPECIAL RULES FOR THE PILOT EXPEDITED CIVIL LITIGATION TRACK

Preface

The purposes of the Expedited Litigation Track (ELT) are to promote efficiency in the processing of certain civil cases, reduce cost to the parties and the court system, maintain a system for resolution of claims that is relevant to the parties, and provide a quick and reduced-cost process for obtaining a jury trial when civil actions cannot be resolved by judicial decision (dispositive motions) or by settlement.

The core principles that support the establishment of a mandatory Expedited Litigation Track include:

1. Most civil actions can be resolved by court decision or settlement upon a sharing of basic facts regarding the claims and defenses of the parties;

2. Timely and assertive judicial attention to matters results in the resolution of actions that can be resolved through settlement and provides for customized discovery and trial procedures that will be most cost-effective for the court and the parties;

3. Attorneys and parties are hesitant to voluntarily elect expedited procedures, thus a mandatory system is required;

4. Extensive discovery through interrogatories, requests for production, and depositions is often unnecessary, unproductive, and leads to protracted litigation and unnecessary litigation costs;

5. A compact discovery schedule will reduce the time and cost of litigation for courts and litigants;

6. Mandatory disclosure of relevant information, rigorously enforced by the court, will result in disclosure of facts and information necessary to evaluate the anticipated evidence for purposes of settlement and to allow parties to prepare for trial; and

7. Expedited cases should be completed within 4-6 months.

8. Having a trial date or week certain is key to minimizing cost and delay.

9. Assignment of an expedited case to a single judge is also highly desirable, but district courts may need flexibility to ensure that trial dates are observed. This may involve assignment of a case to a pool of judges for trial or the use of adjunct judicial officers to handle case management conferences. Where possible district courts should avoid assigning judges on the day of trial to prevent the last minute striking or removal of judges that necessitates a continuance.

Adopted May 7, 2013, eff. July 1, 2013.

Rule 1. Mandatory Assignment of Certain Actions to the Expedited Litigation Track

(a) General; Effective Date. Unless excluded by an order of the court made pursuant to Rule 1(c) herein, all civil actions identified in Rule 1(b) that are filed in the First Judicial District in Dakota County and in the Sixth Judicial District in St. Louis County in Duluth on or after July 1, 2013, shall be assigned to the ELT and managed pursuant to these Special Expedited Litigation Track Rules.

(b) Actions Included. The following civil actions shall be assigned to the ELT, unless excluded pursuant to Rule 1(c) herein:

(1) in the Sixth Judicial District in St. Louis County in Duluth, all civil matters having the case type indicator Consumer Credit Contract, Other Contract, Personal Injury, or Other Civil;

(2) in the First Judicial District in Dakota County, all civil matters having the case type indicator Consumer Credit Contract, Other Contract, Personal Injury, or Other Civil, and having been randomly assigned such as by a court-assigned case file number ending in an even number or some other random selection process at filing with notice to the parties;

(3) Any action where all the parties voluntarily agree to be governed by the Special ELT Rules by including an "ELT Election" in the civil cover sheet filed under the General Rules of Practice or by jointly filing an ELT Election certificate with the court.

(c) Initial Motion for Exclusion from ELT. A party objecting to the mandatory assignment of a matter to the ELT must serve and file a motion setting forth the reasons that the matter should be removed from the ELT. Said motion papers must be served and filed within 30 days of the filing of the action. The motion shall be heard during the Case Management Conference, if any, under Rule 3 of these rules or at such other time as the court shall direct. The factors that should be considered by the court in ruling on said motion include:

(1) Multiple parties or claims;

(2) Multiple or complex theories of liability, damages, or relief;

(3) Complicated facts that require the discovery options provided by the Minnesota Rules of Civil Procedure;

(4) Substantial likelihood of dispositive motions; or

(5) Any factor that demonstrates that assignment to the ELT would substantially affect a party's right to a fair and just resolution of the matter (e.g., timing of obtaining discovery from a third party, estimated damages significantly exceeding $100,000).

(d) Subsequent Motion for Exclusion from ELT. After the time for bringing a motion under Rule 1(c) of this rule has expired and no later than the trial date, a party may by motion request that the case be removed from the ELT for good cause shown related to a new development that could not have been previously raised.

Adopted May 7, 2013, eff. July 1, 2013.

Historical and Statutory Notes

The order of the Minnesota Supreme Court [ADM04-8001, ADM09-8009, ADM-10-8051] dated May 7, 2013, provided in part the Pilot Project "be effective July 1, 2013, and shall apply to all civil actions identified therein that are filed on or after the effective date. The Pilot Project shall continue until further order of the Court."

Rule 2. Automatic Disclosures of Information

(a) Content; Timing. Each party shall prepare and serve an Automatic Disclosure of Information within 60 days after filing of the action or, where applicable, filing of the ELT Election. The Automatic Disclosure of Information shall include the following:

(1) A statement summarizing each contention in support of every claim or defense which a party will present at trial and a brief statement of the facts upon which the contentions are based.

(2) The name, address and telephone number of each individual likely to have discoverable information—along with the subjects of that information and any statement from such individual—that the disclosing party may use to support its claims or defenses. However, no party shall be required to furnish any statement (written or taped) protected by the attorney/client privilege or work-product rule.

(3) A copy—or description, by category and location—of all documents, electronically stored information, and tangible things that the disclosing party has in its possession, custody, or control and may use to support its claims or defenses.

(4) If a claim for damages is being made, a description of the precise damages being sought by the party and the method for calculation of said damages. If the party has any liability insurance coverage providing coverage for the claims being made by another party, the name of the insurance company, the limits of coverage, and the existence of any issue that could affect the availability of coverage.

(5) A brief summary of the qualifications of any expert witness the party may call at the time of trial together with a report or statement of any such expert which sets forth the subject matter of the expert witness's anticipated testimony; the substance of the facts and opinions to which the expert is expected to testify, and a brief summary of the grounds for each opinion.

(6) Any offers of stipulation of any fact that is relevant to any claim or defense in the matter.

(7) An estimate of the number of trial days that it will take to complete trial of the matter.

(b) Filing Disclosures; Privacy Considerations. Automatic disclosures under this rule need not be filed with the court unless otherwise ordered by the court. If a court directs the filing of automatic disclosures, the party filing such disclosures shall take necessary and appropriate steps to protect the privacy interests (such as, without limitation, addresses and telephone numbers) of individuals identified in the disclosures.

Adopted May 7, 2013, eff. July 1, 2013.

Historical and Statutory Notes

The order of the Minnesota Supreme Court [ADM04–8001, ADM09–8009, ADM–10-8051] dated May 7, 2013, provided in part the Pilot Project "be effective July 1, 2013, and shall apply to all civil actions identified therein that are filed on or after the effective date. The Pilot Project shall continue until further order of the Court."

Rule 3. Case Management Conference

(a) Timing; Scope. Within 45 to 60 days of the date of filing of an action, or where applicable, within 30 days of filing of the ELT Election, the court shall convene a Case Management Conference (CMC). All counsel and parties, whether represented or unrepresented, must participate in the CMC. At the CMC, the court and the parties shall address the following subjects:

(1) Any motion to exclude the matter from the ELT Rules made pursuant to ELT Rule 1(c) of these rules;

(2) The prospects for settlement via mediation, arbitration, court-conducted settlement conference, or other form of ADR;

(3) Any request for modification of the abbreviated discovery process required by the ELT Rules;

(4) The setting of a day or week certain trial date to begin no later than 120 to 180 days following filing of the action or, where applicable, the ELT Certification;

(5) The setting of a deadline for the filing of all trial documents, including witness lists, exhibit lists, jury instructions, special jury verdict forms, trial briefs and motions in limine; and

(6) The setting of the date for completion of hearing of any motions.

(b) Format; Alternative Judicial Intervention. The court may conduct the CMC by telephone or may substitute other judicial intervention (including but not limited to one or more telephone discussions or issuing a scheduling order based on information supplied by the parties in their civil cover sheet) that addresses the above subjects.

Adopted May 7, 2013, eff. July 1, 2013.

Historical and Statutory Notes

The order of the Minnesota Supreme Court [ADM04–8001, ADM09–8009, ADM–10-8051] dated May 7, 2013, provided in part the Pilot Project "be effective July 1, 2013, and shall apply to all civil actions identified therein that are filed on or after the effective date. The Pilot Project shall continue until further order of the Court."

Rule 4. Limitations on Discovery

(a) Time Period Limited. The period for conducting discovery shall continue for a period of 90 days from the Case Management Conference. Upon a request of the parties, the court, for good cause shown, may extend the period for conducting discovery for up to an additional 30 days.

(b) Written Discovery Limits; Motions to Compel. Written discovery shall be limited to 15 interrogatories, 15 requests for production of documents and things, and 25 requests for admissions. Written discovery by each party must be served within 30 days of the date of the CMC and responses thereto must be served within 30 days of the date of service. Motions to compel responses to written discovery shall be made within 15 days of the date a response was due and shall be made pursuant to the modified discovery motion procedure set forth in Rule 4(d) of these rules.

(c) Depositions. Depositions are permitted as a matter of right of the parties only but must be taken within the deadline established by the court. Except as otherwise ordered by the court, a deposition of a non-party witness shall be allowed only if the deposition is being taken in lieu of in-person trial testimony.

(d) Meet and Confer Requirement. Prior to any motion to compel discovery, the party seeking the discovery and the party from whom responses are being sought must, by and through their counsel (or a pro se litigant if unrepresented by counsel), confer in an attempt to resolve the dispute. If the dispute is not resolved, the party seeking the discovery shall contact the court and schedule a telephone conference with the court, and provide notice of the date and time of the telephone conference to all adverse parties. No later than 5 days prior to the date of the discovery dispute telephone conference, each party shall serve and file with the court a letter not exceeding 2 pages in length setting forth the party's position on the discovery dispute and providing copies of the disputed discovery. The court, in its discretion, may allow additional argument at the telephone conference. The court shall promptly rule on the discovery dispute.

Adopted May 7, 2013, eff. July 1, 2013.

Historical and Statutory Notes

The order of the Minnesota Supreme Court [ADM04–8001, ADM09–8009, ADM–10-8051] dated May 7, 2013, provided in part the Pilot Project "be effective July 1, 2013, and shall apply to all civil actions identified therein that are filed on or after the effective date. The Pilot Project shall continue until further order of the Court."

Appendix A. Sample Expedited Litigation Track Assignment Order

STATE OF MINNESOTA
COUNTY OF ________

DISTRICT COURT
______ JUDICIAL DISTRICT
CASE TYPE: ________
File Number: ________

__________, Plaintiff
v.
__________, Defendant

ELT Assignment and Case Management Conference Order

____

It is ORDERED:

1. This case is assigned to the pilot project (ELT Pilot") under the Special Rules For a Pilot Expedited Civil Litigation Track ("ELT Rules");

2. A party objecting to this assignment must make a formal motion under ELT Rule 1(c) or (d), for removal from the ELT Pilot;

3. Each party shall provide the Automatic Disclosure Of Information required under ELT Rule 2;

4. A Case Management conference shall be held on: ________, and each party shall attend the conference prepared to discuss the subjects identified in ELT Rule 3; and

5. The Limitations on Discovery set forth in ELT Rule 4 apply.

Dated: ______________ BY THE COURT:

____
Judge of District Court

Adopted May 7, 2013, eff. July 1, 2013.

Appendix B. Sample Expedited Litigation Track Case Management Order

STATE OF MINNESOTA
COUNTY OF ________

DISTRICT COURT
______ JUDICIAL DISTRICT
CASE TYPE: ________
File Number: ________

__________, Plaintiff
v.
__________, Defendant

ELT Case Management Order

____

It is ORDERED:

1. Each party shall provide the Automatic Disclosure Of Information required under Rule 2 of the Special Rules For a Pilot Expedited Civil Litigation Track ("ELT Rules")

2. ADR will/will not be used, and if used the deadline and form of ADR shall be: ______________;

3. The Limitations on Discovery set forth in ELT Rule 4 apply;

4. All motions shall be heard by: ______________;

5. The day or week certain for trial is: ______________;

6. The deadline for submitting all trial documents, including witness lists, jury instructions, special verdict forms, trial briefs, and motions in limine is: ______________.

Dated: ______________ BY THE COURT:

____
Judge of District Court

Adopted May 7, 2013, eff. July 1, 2013.

SECOND JUDICIAL DISTRICT

Rule 5. Setting Cases for Trial and Scheduling of Joint Disposition Conference

Approximately 30 days before the Pretrial Conference, a Joint Disposition Conference may be scheduled between all parties in the case at the place, date and time designated by the Court. At the scheduled conference, the parties will meet in person and complete, sign and file a Joint Disposition Conference Report in the form prescribed by the Court. If the parties meet, complete, sign and file a Joint Disposition Conference Report required by this Rule before the court scheduled conference, it shall be vacated.

The Joint Disposition Conference Report must include the following:

1. The length of time estimated for trial and trial date.

2. A statement of whether discovery has been completed as previously set by the court, or a schedule setting forth the proposed discovery to be completed and the reasons why the discovery was not completed by the time of the Joint Disposition Conference.

3. A summary of the stipulations of fact or issues that have been agreed to by the parties.

4. A general statement indicating the facts in dispute.

5. A general statement by each party indicating any known unresolved substantive issues. Any memoranda of law or citations to authority, upon which the parties will rely for their position on the unresolved issues, must be filed and served seven (7) days before the Pretrial Conference. The parties shall attempt to identify unresolved substantive issues but the failure to identify such issues shall not constitute a waiver of the right to raise such issues at a later date, except for good cause shown.

6. A list of each party's prospective witnesses, including each witness' name and address, employer and occupation, including expert witnesses and the particular area of expertise each expert will be addressing. Only witnesses so listed shall be permitted to testify at the trial, except for good cause shown.

7. A list of each party's exhibits to be offered as evidence at the trial. Only exhibits so listed shall be offered in evidence at the trial, except for good cause shown.

8. A list of the depositions each party proposes to offer in lieu of live testimony.

If a Joint Disposition Conference is not held as scheduled or a report is not filed, or an incomplete report as determined by the DCM coordinator is filed, the Court shall set the matter for hearing. If the Court finds that any party has failed to proceed with due diligence in preparing a case or has failed to cooperate, the Court may impose sanctions or take any action which it feels appropriate. (See Form DCM–2).

Form DCM–2. Joint Disposition Conference Report

STATE OF MINNESOTA COUNTY OF RAMSEY	DISTRICT COURT SECOND JUDICIAL DISTRICT CIVIL DIVISION FILE NO. _____

____

Plaintiff,

vs. JOINT DISPOSITION CONFERENCE REPORT

Defendant.

____

A time, date and place will be set for a Joint Disposition Conference. During this Conference, you are expected to discuss the issues required by Rule 5 and complete this report form. You have the option to arrange your own in-person meeting time and place so long as the report is filed by the conference date set by the Court. The failure to comply with Rule 5 may result in sanctions and a court appearance to show cause why the report was not filed timely or was incomplete.

1. All parties are prepared for trial which is scheduled to begin on __________ and will take ______ court days. A jury is _____ is not _____ requested.

2. As required by Rule 5, or as previously set by the Court, all discovery has been completed. If discovery has not been completed, attach to this form information setting forth the discovery that remains to be completed, the reason it has not been completed as required, and the estimated time needed to complete discovery. Any additional discovery must be completed by the time of the judicial pretrial conference.

3. The parties have stipulated to the following facts or issues: ____________________

____

____

____

____

____

____

____

4. The following facts are in dispute: ____________

____

____

____

____

5. (a) As to substantive issues, plaintiff contends as follows: ____________________

____

____

____

____

(b) As to substantive issues, defendant contends as follows: ____________________

____

____

____

____

Each party shall attach an addendum containing the following items:

6. A list of witnesses with their name, address, employer and occupation. Witnesses whom a party intends to qualify as expert witnesses and the area of expertise shall be indicated.

7. A list of all exhibits which a party intends to offer into evidence. All exhibits shall be made available for inspection by opposing counsel.

8. A description of depositions proposed to be offered in evidence in lieu of live testimony.

Plaintiff ____________	Defendant ____________
Attorney ____________	Attorney ____________
Attorney Reg. # ________	Attorney Reg. # ________
Firm ____________	Firm ____________
Address ____________	Address ____________
____________	____________
Telephone ____________	Telephone ____________
Date ____________	Date ____________

Plaintiff ____________	Defendant ____________
Attorney ____________	Attorney ____________
Attorney Reg. # ________	Attorney Reg. # ________
Firm ____________	Firm ____________
Address ____________	Address ____________
____________	____________
Telephone ____________	Telephone ____________
Date ____________	Date ____________

(If more space is needed to add additional information or parties, attach a separate sheet typed in the same format.)

The undersigned counsel have met and conferred this ________ day of ____________ and certify the foregoing is true and correct.

____________	____________
Signature	Signature
____________	____________
Signature	Signature

Amended Oct. 11, 1989, eff. Jan. 1, 1990; Nov. 8, 1989, eff. Jan. 1, 1990; June 13, 1990, eff. Sept. 1, 1990; Nov. 13, 1991, eff. Jan. 1, 1992.

Supersedure

Minnesota Supreme Court Order CX-89-1863, dated December 2, 1993, provides that effective July 1, 1994, this rule is superseded to the extent inconsistent with new rules 114.01 through 114.14 and amended rules 111.02(j) and 111.03(b) of the General Rules of Practice for the District Court.

Rule 24. Petty Misdemeanor Appeals from Referees

In petty misdemeanor trials heard by a referee, except Housing Court matters, the referee shall either (1) announce the recommended findings, conclusions and order orally, on the record, at the conclusion of the trial or (2) take the matter under advisement and issue written recommended findings, conclusions and order within seven days after the trial.

The referee's recommendation shall be deemed adopted when a judge reviews and countersigns the referee's sentence report calendar or written findings, conclusions and order. It shall be the duty of the criminal chambers judge to review and, if appropriate, countersign the referee's recommendation.

A defendant may appeal from the referee's order by filing with the clerk of district court a notice of appeal. The notice of appeal must be filed within ten days after the oral announcement of the referee's recommended order or within thirteen days after service by mail of the adopted written order. Service of the written order shall be deemed complete and effective upon the mailing of a copy of the order to the defendant's last known address.

Upon the timely filing of a notice of appeal, the order shall be stayed pending the determination of the appeal.

Within 15 days after filing a notice of appeal the defendant shall, at the defendant's sole expense, purchase a transcript of the trial before the referee. The transcript shall be available within 45 days after its purchase.

The appeal shall be assigned to be heard by a judge on the criminal court calendar and shall be confined to the trial record before the referee.

The parties may, but shall not be required to, present oral or written arguments or both. Written arguments shall be filed at least one day before the hearing date.

Adopted April 11, 1990, eff. April 11, 1990. Amended eff. Feb. 13, 1991.

Rule 25. Civil Alternative Dispute Resolution (ADR) Program

I. AUTHORITY

Pursuant to Minn.Stat. 484.73 and 484.74, subd. 4, the Second Judicial District has authorized the establishment of a system of Alternative Dispute Resolution (ADR) for civil cases. In this instance, ADR specifically refers to arbitration and/or mediation.

II. INITIATION

A. The Court shall review all civil cases to determine current status and possible referral to arbitration or mediation. If appropriate, the court shall mail to all parties to a civil action information concerning arbitration and mediation as alternatives to litigation.

1. Plaintiff(s) shall be responsible for reporting to the court the following:

a. The current status of the case;

b. Whether or not the parties have discussed an ADR option and which form of ADR they have chosen.

c. If the parties decide NOT to enter ADR, written reason for this decision.

2. Status conference:

a. If no response is received within 30 days from the date of the court letter, the court shall set a status conference.

b. The parties may request a status conference to discuss ADR and other case-related issues;

c. The court may set a status conference on its own motion to discuss ADR and other case-related issues.

3. Attorneys/parties shall discuss ADR options and, by filing an informational Statement, inform the court of the result of said discussions.

4. Upon motion by any party, by stipulation of the parties, at the case status conference or within the scheduling order, the court may issue an order for arbitration or mediation.

III. SELECTION OF ARBITRATORS AND/OR MEDIATORS

Once the parties or the court have selected an ADR process, the court will send all parties a list of a minimum of five court-approved arbitrators or court-approved private dispute resolution organizations or private mediators.

A. Within fifteen days thereafter, the parties:

1. Shall jointly file with the court a stipulation as to the arbitrator and/or mediator drawn from the list.

2. If no agreement as to the selection of the arbitrator and/or mediator, shall separately file with the court a list with two neutrals stricken and others ranked in order of preference. The court shall, within five days, designate the arbitrator and/or mediator from those persons not stricken.

3. May request in writing an arbitrator and/or mediator from outside the court-approved list. Prior to issuing an order for either arbitration or mediation, the court may request a written statement of the arbitrator's and/or mediator's qualifications, including educational background and relevant training and experience in the field.

B. The court shall issue and serve an order designating the arbitrator and/or mediator chosen by the parties.

IV. QUALIFICATIONS OF THE ARBITRATOR AND/OR MEDIATOR

The Second Judicial District Bench and the Ramsey County Bar Association Rules and Procedures Committee shall cooperatively determine the qualifications of arbitrators and/or mediators.

V. ADR PROCEEDINGS

A. Within fourteen days after the order designating the arbitrator and/or mediator, they/he/she shall inform the court of the initial arbitration hearing or mediation session which shall be scheduled no more than 60 days from the date of the court order.

B. ADR proceedings shall be completed no later than 90 days after the order is issued by the court.

C. Only the court may grant a continuance of the ADR proceedings beyond the time limits set forth above.

D. The arbitrator and/or mediator shall determine a suitable time and place for the ADR proceedings.

E. Pursuant to Rules 16 and 37 of the Rules of Civil Procedure, failure to appear or refusal to participate in good faith and in a meaningful manner in a court-ordered ADR proceeding may result in sanctions.

VI. EX PARTE COMMUNICATION

A. Neither parties nor their counsel shall communicate ex parte with the arbitrator.

B. Parties or their counsel may communicate with the mediator so long as such communication encourages the facilitates settlement.

VII. FEES

A. At the end of the proceeding, the parties shall divide equally and pay directly to the arbitrator and/or mediator a fee of $125 per hour. No later than at the time the final report is made to the court, other related costs, such as administrative fees and preparation costs, will be payable to the neutral as requested by the arbitrator and/or mediator.

B. If the arbitrator and/or mediator is someone outside the court-approved list, the arbitrator and/or mediator and the parties will determine an agreeable fee.

VIII. REPORT OR DECISION TO THE COURT

A. Arbitration.

1. No later than ten days from the date of the arbitration hearing or receipt of post-hearing memorandum, the arbitrator shall file with the court the decision together with proof of service by first-class mail to all parties.

2. Upon the expiration of twenty days after the award is filed, if no party has during that time period filed a request for trial as provided in these rules, the court administrator shall enter the decision as a judgment. Promptly upon entry of the decision as judgment, the court administrator shall mail notice of entry to the parties. The judgment so entered shall have the same force and effect as and is subject to all provisions of the law relating to a judgment in a civil action or proceeding, except that it is not subject to appeal and, except as provided in Sect. 4 below, may not be attacked or set aside. The judgment so entered may be enforced as if it had been rendered by the court in which it is entered.

3. No findings of fact and conclusions of law or opinions supporting an arbitrator's decision are required.

4. Within six months after its entry, a party against whom a judgment is entered pursuant to an arbitration award may move to vacate the judgment on the grounds set forth in the Uniform Arbitration Act, Chapter 572, Minnesota Statutes, and upon no other ground.

B. Mediation.

In the case of mediation, the only report to the court shall be a letter indicating whether or not the parties have settled.

1. If the case has settled, the attorneys shall cooperate in completing the appropriate court documents to bring the case to a final disposition.

2. If there has been no settlement, the parties may request that the matter be placed on the trial calendar on the first available date. If not so placed, the case shall be restored to the civil calendar in the same position as it would have had had there been no ADR.

IX. TRIAL DE NOVO (FOR ARBITRATION ONLY)

A. Within 20 days after the arbitrator files the decision with the court, any party may request a trial by filing with the court a request for trial with proof of service upon all other parties. This 20–day period shall not be extended.

B. If discovery is complete, the court will set the matter for trial on the first available date. If not so set, the case shall be restored to the civil calendar in the same position as it would have had had there been no ADR.

C. Upon request for a trial de novo, the decision of the arbitrator shall be sealed and placed in the court file.

D. If the party filing a demand for trial de novo does not improve his/her position, the prevailing party may move the court for payment of costs and disbursements, including payment of the arbitrator's fees.

E. A trial de novo shall be conducted as if there had been no arbitration. Without the consent of all parties and the approval of the court, no reference in the presence of the jury shall be made to prior arbitration proceedings.

X. CONFIDENTIALITY

A. Without the consent of all parties and an order of the court, no evidence that there has been ADR proceedings or any fact concerning them may be admitted in a trial de novo or in any subsequent proceeding involving any of the issues in or parties to the proceeding.

B. Arbitrators and attorneys for the parties cannot be called to testify as to their participation in the ADR proceeding in the trial de novo or in any subsequent trial or motion.

C. Without the agreement of the parties, there shall be no record made other than the report or decision of issues which are resolved.

D. Mediation proceedings under these rules are privileged, not subject to discovery, and without the written consent of both parties, inadmissible as evidence in any subsequent trial or motion.

XI. RULES OF EVIDENCE AT ARBITRATION PROCEEDING

A. Except where any of the parties has waived the right to be present or is absent after due notice of the hearing, the arbitrator and all parties shall be present at the taking of all evidence.

B. The Rules of Evidence apply to the conduct of the arbitration hearing and shall be construed liberally in favor of admission except:

1. Any party may offer and the arbitrator shall receive in evidence written medical and hospital reports, records and bills (including physiotherapy, nursing and prescription bills,) documentary evidence of loss of income, property damage, repair bills or estimate, and police reports concerning an accident which gave rise to the case, if copies have been delivered to all other parties at least ten days prior to the hearing. Any other party may subpoena as a witness the author of a report, bill or estimate, and examine that person as if under cross-examination. Any repair estimate offered as an exhibit as well as copies delivered to other parties shall be accompanied by a statement indicating whether or not the property was repaired and, if it was, whether the estimated repairs were made in full or in part, and by copy of the receipted bill showing the items of repair made and the amount paid. The arbitrator shall not consider any police report opinion as to ultimate fault.

2. The written statement of any other witness, including written reports of expert witnesses not enumerated above, and including statements of opinion which the witness would be qualified to express if testifying in person, may be offered and shall be received in evidence if:

a. It is made by affidavit or by declaration under penalty of perjury;

b. Copies have been delivered to all other parties at least ten days prior to the hearing; and

c. No other party has, at least five days before the hearing, delivered to the proponent of the evidence a written demand that the witness be produced in person to testify at the hearing. The arbitrator shall disregard any portion of a statement received pursuant to this rule that would be inadmissible if the witness were testifying in person, but the inclusion of inadmissible matter does not render the entire statement inadmissible.

3. Subject to objections, the deposition of any witness may be offered by any party and shall be received in evidence, notwithstanding that the deponent is not "unavailable as a witness" and no exceptional circumstances exist if:

a. The deposition was taken in the manner provided for by law or by stipulation of the parties and within the time provided for in these rules; and

b. Not less than ten days prior to the hearing, the proponent of the deposition serves on all other parties notice of his/her intention to offer the deposition in evidence. Upon receiving the notice, the other party may subpoena the deponent and the arbitrator may admit or exclude the deposition into evidence. The party who subpoenaed the deponent may further cross-examine him or her. These limitations are not applicable to a deposition admissible under the terms of Minn.R.Civ.P. 32.01.

C. As provided in Minn.R.Civ.P. 45, subpoena shall issue for the attendance of witnesses at the arbitration hearings. It shall be the duty of the party requesting the subpoena to modify the form of subpoena to show that the appearance is before the arbitrator and to give the time and place set for the arbitration hearing. At the discretion of the arbitrator, non-appearance of a properly subpoenaed witness may be grounds for an adjournment or continuance of the hearing. If any witness properly served with a subpoena fails to appear at the arbitration hearing or, having appeared, refuses to be sworn or to answer, the court may conduct proceedings to compel compliance.

D. Notwithstanding any other provisions in these rules, a party offering opinion testimony in the form of an affidavit or other statement or a deposition, shall have the right to withdraw such testimony and the attendance of the witness at the hearing shall not then be required.

XII. CONDUCT OF THE ARBITRATION HEARING

The arbitrator shall have the following powers:

A. To administer oaths or affirmations to witnesses.

B. Upon the request of a party or upon his/her own initiative, to take adjournments.

C. To permit testimony to be offered by deposition.

D. To permit evidence to be offered and introduced as provided by these rules.

E. To rule upon the admissibility and relevance of the evidence offered.

F. On reasonable notice, to invite the parties to submit pre-hearing or post-hearing briefs or pre-hearing statements of evidence.

G. To decide the law and facts of the case and make an award accordingly.

H. To award costs, within limits of statutory costs of the action.

I. To view any site or object relevant to the case; and

J. Any other powers agreed upon by the parties.

The arbitrator may make a record of the proceedings. Any record so made is deemed the arbitrator's personal notes and is not subject to discovery. The arbitrator shall not deliver the record to any party to the case or to any other person except to an employee using the record under the arbitrator's supervision or pursuant to a subpoena issued in a criminal investigation or prosecution for perjury. Except as expressly permitted by this rule, no other record shall be made. At the hearing, the arbitrator shall not permit the presence of a stenographer or court reporter or the use of any recording device.

Adopted June 13, 1990, eff. Sept. 1, 1990. Amended Dec. 11, 1991, eff. Jan. 1, 1992.

Supersedure

Minnesota Supreme Court Order CX-89-1863, dated December 2, 1993, provides that effective July 1, 1994, this rule is superseded to the extent inconsistent with new rules 114.01 through 114.14 and amended rules 111.02(j) and 111.03(b) of the General Rules of Practice for the District Court.

FOURTH JUDICIAL DISTRICT

Rule 1.01. Format/Places of Holding Court

All pleadings, motions and other documents filed in non-felony criminal and traffic matters shall bear a caption designating the venue by division as follows:

STATE OF MINNESOTA	DISTRICT COURT
COUNTY OF HENNEPIN	FOURTH JUDICIAL DISTRICT DIVISION I, MINNEAPOLIS

STATE OF MINNESOTA	DISTRICT COURT
COUNTY OF HENNEPIN	FOURTH JUDICIAL DISTRICT DIVISION II, BROOKDALE

STATE OF MINNESOTA	DISTRICT COURT
COUNTY OF HENNEPIN	FOURTH JUDICIAL DISTRICT DIVISION III, RIDGEDALE

STATE OF MINNESOTA	DISTRICT COURT
COUNTY OF HENNEPIN	FOURTH JUDICIAL DISTRICT DIVISION IV, SOUTHDALE

Arraignments, pretrial hearings, and court trials of non-felony criminal and traffic matters will be held in the following place for the municipalities specified:

Division I:
At: Government Center
Minneapolis
For: Fort Snelling
Medicine Lake
Minneapolis
St. Anthony

Arraignments, pretrial hearings, and court trials of non-felony criminal and traffic matters will be held in the following places for the municipalities specified. Suburban jury trials will be held at the Government Center in Minneapolis.

Division II (Brookdale):
At: 6125 Shingle Creek Parkway
Brooklyn Center
For: Brooklyn Center
Brooklyn Park
Champlin
Corcoran
Crystal
Dayton
Greenfield
Hassan
Hanover
New Hope
Osseo
Robbinsdale
Rockford
Rogers

Division III (Ridgedale):
At: 12601 Ridgedale Drive
Minnetonka
For: Chanhassen
Deephaven
Excelsior
Golden Valley
Greenwood
Hopkins
Independence
Lake Minnetonka Conservation District
Long Lake
Loretto
Maple Grove
Maple Plain
Medina
Minnetonka
Minnetonka Beach
Minnetrista
Mound
Orono
Plymouth
St. Bonifacius
Shorewood
Spring Park
Tonka Bay
Wayzata
Woodland

Division IV (Southdale):
At: 7009 York Avenue South
Edina
For: Bloomington
Eden Prairie
Edina
Metropolitan Airport
Richfield
St. Louis Park

Amended Nov. 1, 1991; July 30, 2002.

Historical Notes

Former Rule 1.01(d) was redesignated as Rule 1.01.

RULE 2. MEDIATION IN CONCILIATION COURT

Rule 2.1. Scope of Rule

This rule applies to all conciliation court cases in the fourth judicial district.

Adopted Dec. 17, 1999, eff. Jan. 1, 2000.

Rule 2.2. Notice and Explanation

The court may require the parties to participate in court sponsored mediation prior to their initial hearing in conciliation court. The court administrator shall notify parties that their case has been assigned to the mediation calendar and provide them with an explanation of the procedures. The notice and explanation may be in the form of a flyer or other attachment to be mailed or served with the summons and complaint.

Adopted Dec. 17, 1999, eff. Jan. 1, 2000.

Rule 2.3. Attendance; Confidentiality

Attendance at, and confidentiality of, mediation sessions is governed by Rules 114.07 and 114.08 of the General Rules of Practice for the District Court.

Adopted Dec. 17, 1999, eff. Jan. 1, 2000.

Rule 2.4. Mediator Assignment, Qualifications and Communications

Mediators shall be assigned by the court. Communications between parties and the mediator is governed by Rule 114.10 of those rules.

Adopted Dec. 17, 1999, eff. Jan. 1, 2000.

Rule 2.5. Funding

The parties shall not be required to pay for mediation services under this rule.

Adopted Dec. 17, 1999, eff. Jan. 1, 2000.

Rule 2.6. Failure to Reach Settlement

If the parties are unable to agree to a settlement of their dispute during the mediation session, the conciliation court shall promptly hear the case on the same day as the mediation session.

Adopted Dec. 17, 1999, eff. Jan. 1, 2000.

Rule 2.7. Settlement Agreement

If a settlement agreement is reached, all parties, the mediator, and the referee or judge will sign a mediated settlement agreement that includes the following terms:

(a) either party may rescind the agreement within seventy-two hours after signing it;

(b) parties must keep the court advised of their current address;

(c) if the terms of the settlement agreement are not met by the deadline agreed to, a party may request entry of judgment by filing an affidavit of non-compliance with the court;

(d) after a hearing to determine compliance issues, a judge may order that final judgment be entered in conciliation court effective immediately, and the judgment may be immediately transcribed to district court; and

(e) the parties agree to waive the thirty-day period for enforcement of a judgment set forth in Rule 518(b) of the General Rules of Practice for the District courts.

Adopted Dec. 17, 1999, eff. Jan. 1, 2000.

Rule 2.8. Non-Compliance Hearing; Judgment

Upon the filing of an affidavit of non-compliance with the court, the court administrator shall schedule a non-compliance hearing and advise the parties by mail of the date, time, and location of the hearing. If after the hearing the judge determines that a party failed to comply with the terms of the settlement agreement, the judge shall order that final judgment be entered in conciliation court effective immediately. Upon entry, the judgment may be immediately transcribed to, and enforced in, district court.

Adopted Dec. 17, 1999, eff. Jan. 1, 2000.

Advisory Committee Comment—1999 Adoption

The mandatory mediation program authorized under rule 2 began as a pilot project in 1996. *See* Order, *In re Fourth Judicial District Pilot Program for Mandatory Mediation in Conciliation Court*, No. CX–89–1863 (Minn. Sup. Ct., Oct. 29, 1996). The pilot project was successful in resolving conciliation court cases in a manner that minimized delay and financial burdens for litigants. REPORT TO THE MINNESOTA SUPREME COURT AND MINNESOTA CONFERENCE OF CHIEF JUDGES ON HENNEPIN COUNTY DISTRICT COURT MANDATORY MEDIATION PROJECT, pp. 7–11 (June 30, 1997). As a result, the program was permanently established in 1999, with directions that the program should be codified in a published court rule. *See* Order, *In re Fourth Judicial District Pilot Program for Mandatory Mediation in Conciliation Court*, No. CX–89–1863 (Minn. Sup. Ct., Mar. 23, 1999).

The references in Rules 2.3 and 2.4 to selected portions of Rule 114 of the General Rules of Practice for the District Court recognize that Rule 114 is generally not applicable to conciliation court cases. Only specific provisions of Rule 114 are made applicable to conciliation court mediation under this Rule 2.

The committee considered recommending this rule for statewide adoption, but does not believe that step would be warranted because this program is not being considered for use in other districts and because the advisory committee has not fully analyzed its operation in Hennepin County or its potential operation in other districts.

RULE 5. ARBITRATION

Supersedure

Minnesota Supreme Court Order CX-89-1863, dated December 2, 1993, provides that effective July 1, 1994, this rule is superseded to the extent inconsistent with new rules 114.01 through 114.14 and amended rules 111.02(j) and 111.03(b) of the General Rules of Practice for the District Court.

Rule 5.01. Authority

Pursuant to Minn. Stat. 484.73, the Fourth Judicial District has authorized the establishment of a system of arbitration for civil cases.

Rule 5.02. Actions Subject to Arbitration

(a) All civil actions are subject to arbitration except:

1. Actions for money damages in excess of $50,000.00;
2. Actions for money damages within the jurisdictional limit of the Hennepin County Conciliation Court;
3. Actions that include a claim for equitable relief that is neither insubstantial nor frivolous;
4. Actions removed from the Hennepin County Conciliation Court for trial de novo;
5. Class actions;
6. Actions involving family law matters;
7. Unlawful detainer actions; or
8. Actions involving the title to real estate.

(b) The Chief Judge or the judge that the case is assigned to shall have authority to order that particular actions otherwise excluded shall be submitted to arbitration.

(c) Any action otherwise excluded above may be submitted to arbitration by agreement of all parties.

Rule 5.03. Qualifications of Arbitrator

Unless otherwise ordered by the Chief Judge or his/her designee or agreed to by all parties, an arbitrator must be admitted to practice in the State of Minnesota for a minimum of five years and must sign and file an Oath of Office with the Chief Judge of the District Court.

Rule 5.04. Selection of Arbitrators

(a) Arbitrators shall be selected from members of the Bar who reside or practice in Hennepin County and who are qualified in accordance with Rule 5.03.

(b) The Court Administrator shall randomly assign arbitrators from a list of qualified arbitrators maintained by the Court.

(c) Any party or his/her attorney may file with the Court Administrator within five days of the notice of appointment and serve on the opposing party a notice to remove. Upon receipt of the notice to remove, the Court Administrator shall immediately assign another arbitrator. After a party has once disqualified an arbitrator as a matter of right, a substitute arbitrator may be disqualified by that party only by making an affirmative showing of prejudice to the Chief Judge or his/her designee.

Rule 5.05. Arbitrator's Fees

(a) The arbitrator's award or a notice of settlement signed by the parties or their counsel must be timely filed with the Court Administrator before a fee may be paid to the arbitrator.

(b) On the arbitrator's verified ex parte application, the Court may for good cause authorize payment of a fee when the award was not timely filed.

(c) The arbitrator's fee statement shall be submitted to the Court Administrator promptly upon the completion of the arbitrator's duties and shall set forth the title and number of the cause arbitrated, the date of the arbitration hearing, and the date the award or settlement was filed.

(d) The arbitrator's fee will be set by the Court with a maximum of $150.00 per day.

Rule 5.06. Communication with the Arbitrator

No ex parte disclosure of any offers of settlement shall be made to the arbitrator prior to the filing of the award.

Rule 5.07. Arbitration Hearing

(a) Within thirty (30) days after assignment, the Court Administrator shall schedule an arbitration hearing, which hearing shall be set for not more than 60 days after the deadline for completion of discovery at a specified time and place. No further extensions for discovery shall be allowed unless granted by the Chief Judge or his/her designee on motion.

(b) By agreement of all parties or by order of the court, an action may be submitted to arbitration before the deadline for completion of discovery.

(c) Failure to appear at the arbitration hearing may subject the nonappearing party or counsel, or both, to imposition by the assigned judge of appropriate sanctions.

Amended Jan. 22, 1992.

Rule 5.08. Continuances

A continuance of the arbitration hearing may be granted only by the Court Administrator.

Rule 5.09. Rules of Evidence at Hearing

(a) All evidence shall be taken in the presence of the arbitrator and all parties, except where any of the parties has waived the right to be present or is absent after due notice of the hearing.

(b) The Rules of Evidence, construed liberally in favor of admission, apply to the conduct of the arbitration hearing, except:

1. Any party may offer, and the arbitrator shall receive in evidence, written medical and hospital reports, records and bills (including physiotherapy, nursing and prescription bills), documentary evidence of loss of income, property damage, repair bills or estimates, and police reports concerning an accident which gave rise to the case, if copies have been delivered to all opposing parties at least 10 days prior to the hearing. Any other party may subpoena the author of a report, bill or estimate as a witness and examine that person as if under cross-examination. Any repair estimate offered as an exhibit, and the copies delivered to opposing parties, shall be accompanied by a statement indicating whether or not the property was repaired and if it was, whether the estimated repairs were made in full or in part, and by a copy of the receipted bill showing the items of repair made and the amount paid. The arbitrator shall not consider any opinion expressed in a police report as to ultimate fault.

2. The written statement of any other witness, including written reports of expert witnesses not enumerated above, and including statements of opinion which the witness would be qualified to express if testifying in person, may be offered and shall be received in evidence if: (i) they are made by affidavit or by declaration under penalty of perjury; (ii) copies have been delivered to all opposing parties at least 10 days prior to the hearing; and (iii) no opposing party has, at least five (5) days before the hearing, delivered to the proponent of the evidence a written demand that the witness be produced in person to testify at the hearing. The arbitrator shall disregard any portion of a statement received pursuant to this rule that would be inadmissible if the witness were testifying in person, but the inclusion of inadmissible matter does not render the entire statement inadmissible.

3. The deposition of any witness may be offered by any party and shall be received in evidence, subject to objections, notwithstanding that the deponent is not "unavailable as a witness" and no exceptional circumstances exist, if: (i) the deposition was taken in the manner provided for by law or by stipulation of the parties and within the time provided for in these rules; and (ii) not less than 10 days prior to the hearing the proponent of the deposition serves on all opposing parties notice of his/her intention to offer the deposition in evidence. The opposing party, upon receiving the notice, may subpoena the deponent and if he does so, at the discretion of the arbitrator, either the deposition may be excluded from evidence or the deposition may be admitted and the deponent may be further cross-examined by the party who subpoenaed him or her. These limitations are not applicable to a deposition admissible under the terms of Minn. R.Civ.P. 32.01.

(c) Subpoenas shall issue for the attendance of witnesses at arbitration hearings as provided in Minn. R.Civ.P. 45. It shall be the duty of the party requesting the subpoena to modify the form of subpoena to show that the appearance is before an arbitrator, and to give the time and place set for the arbitration hearing. At the discretion of the arbitrator, nonappearance of a properly subpoenaed witness may be a ground for an adjournment or continuance of the hearing. If any witness properly served with a subpoena fails to appear at the arbitration hearing or, having appeared, refuses to be sworn or to answer, proceedings to compel compliance with the subpoena on penalty of contempt may be had before the Court.

(d) Notwithstanding any other provisions in these rules, a party offering opinion testimony in the form of an affidavit or other statement, or a deposition, shall have the right to withdraw such testimony, whereupon the attendance of the witness at the hearing shall not be required.

Rule 5.10. Conduct of the Hearing

(a) The arbitrator shall have the following powers:

1. To administer oaths or affirmations to witnesses;

2. To take adjournments upon the request of party or upon his/her own initiative when deemed necessary;

3. To permit testimony to be offered by deposition;

4. To permit evidence to be offered and introduced as provided in these rules;

5. To rule upon the admissibility and relevancy of evidence offered;

6. To invite the parties, on reasonable notice, to submit pre-hearing or post-hearing briefs or pre-hearing statements of evidence;

7. To decide the law and facts of the case and make an award accordingly;

8. To award costs, not to exceed the statutory costs of the action;

9. To view any site or object relevant to the case; and

10. Any other powers agreed upon by the parties.

(b) The arbitrator may, but is not required to, make a record of the proceedings. Any records of the proceedings made by or at the direction of the arbitrator shall be deemed the arbitrator's personal notes and are not subject to discovery, and the arbitrator shall not deliver them to any party to the case or to any other person, except to an employee using the records under the arbitrator's supervision or pursuant to a subpoena issued in a criminal investigation or prosecution for perjury. No other record shall be made, and the arbitrator shall not permit the presence of a stenographer or court reporter or the use of any recording device at the hearing, except as expressly permitted by this rule.

Rule 5.11. The Award

(a) The award shall be in writing and signed by the arbitrator. It shall determine all issues properly raised by the pleadings, including a determination of any damages and an award of costs if appropriate. The arbitrator is not required to make findings of fact or conclusions of law.

(b) Within ten (10) days after the conclusion of the arbitration hearing, the arbitrator shall file his/her award with the Court Administrator, with proof of service on each party to the arbitration. On the arbitrator's application in cases of unusual length or complexity, the court may allow up to 20 additional days for the filing and service of the award. Within the time for filing the award, the arbitrator may file and serve an amended award.

(c) The Court Administrator shall enter the award as a judgment forthwith upon the expiration of twenty (20) days after the award is filed if no party has, during that period, served and filed a request for trial as provided in these rules. Promptly upon entry of the award as a judgment, the Court Administrator shall mail notice of entry of judgment to all parties who have appeared in the case and shall execute a certificate of mailing and place it in the court's file in the case. The judgment so entered shall have the same force and effect in all respects as, and is subject to all provisions of law relating to, a judgment in a civil action or proceeding, except that it is not subject to appeal and it may not be attacked or set aside except as provided in subdivision (d). The judgment so entered may be enforced as if it had been rendered by the court in which it is entered.

(d) A party against whom a judgment is entered pursuant to an arbitration award may, within six months after its entry, move to vacate the judgment on the ground that the arbitrator was subject to a disqualification not disclosed before the hearing and of which the arbitrator was then aware, or upon one of the grounds set forth in the Uniform Arbitration Act, Chapter 572, Minnesota Statutes, and upon no other grounds. The motion shall be heard by the Court upon notice to the adverse parties and to the arbitrator, and may be granted only upon clear and convincing evidence that the grounds alleged are true, and that the motion was made as soon as practicable after the moving party learned of the existence of those grounds.

Rule 5.12. Trial after Arbitration

(a) Within 20 days after the arbitration award is filed with the Court Administrator, any party may request a trial by filing with the Court Administrator a request for trial, with proof of service of a copy upon all other parties appearing in the case. The 20-day period within which to request trial may not be extended.

(b) The case shall be restored to the civil calendar in the same position on the list it would have had if there had been no arbitration in the case, unless the Court orders otherwise for good cause.

(c) The case shall be tried as though no arbitration proceedings had occurred. No reference may be made during the trial to the arbitration award, to the fact that there had been arbitration proceedings, to the evidence adduced at the arbitration hearing, or to any other aspect of the arbitration proceedings, and none of the foregoing may be used as affirmative evidence, or by way of impeachment, or for any other purpose during the trial.

SIXTH JUDICIAL DISTRICT

SPECIAL RULES FOR THE PILOT EXPEDITED CIVIL LITIGATION TRACK

Preface

The purposes of the Expedited Litigation Track (ELT) are to promote efficiency in the processing of certain civil cases, reduce cost to the parties and the court system, maintain a system for resolution of claims that is relevant to the parties, and provide a quick and reduced-cost process for obtaining a jury trial when civil actions cannot be resolved by judicial decision (dispositive motions) or by settlement.

The core principles that support the establishment of a mandatory Expedited Litigation Track include:

1. Most civil actions can be resolved by court decision or settlement upon a sharing of basic facts regarding the claims and defenses of the parties;

2. Timely and assertive judicial attention to matters results in the resolution of actions that can be resolved through settlement and provides for customized discovery and trial procedures that will be most cost-effective for the court and the parties;

3. Attorneys and parties are hesitant to voluntarily elect expedited procedures, thus a mandatory system is required;

4. Extensive discovery through interrogatories, requests for production, and depositions is often unnecessary, unproductive, and leads to protracted litigation and unnecessary litigation costs;

5. A compact discovery schedule will reduce the time and cost of litigation for courts and litigants;

6. Mandatory disclosure of relevant information, rigorously enforced by the court, will result in disclosure of facts and information necessary to evaluate the anticipated evidence for purposes of settlement and to allow parties to prepare for trial; and

7. Expedited cases should be completed within 4-6 months.

8. Having a trial date or week certain is key to minimizing cost and delay.

9. Assignment of an expedited case to a single judge is also highly desirable, but district courts may need flexibility to ensure that trial dates are observed. This may involve assignment of a case to a pool of judges for trial or the use of adjunct judicial officers to handle case management conferences. Where possible district courts should avoid assigning judges on the day of trial to prevent the last minute striking or removal of judges that necessitates a continuance.

Adopted May 7, 2013, eff. July 1, 2013.

Rule 1. Mandatory Assignment of Certain Actions to the Expedited Litigation Track

(a) General; Effective Date. Unless excluded by an order of the court made pursuant to Rule 1(c) herein, all civil actions identified in Rule 1(b) that are filed in the First Judicial District in Dakota County and in the Sixth Judicial District in St. Louis County in Duluth on or after July 1, 2013, shall be assigned to the ELT and managed pursuant to these Special Expedited Litigation Track Rules.

(b) Actions Included. The following civil actions shall be assigned to the ELT, unless excluded pursuant to Rule 1(c) herein:

(1) in the Sixth Judicial District in St. Louis County in Duluth, all civil matters having the case type indicator Consumer Credit Contract, Other Contract, Personal Injury, or Other Civil;

(2) in the First Judicial District in Dakota County, all civil matters having the case type indicator Consumer Credit Contract, Other Contract, Personal Injury, or Other Civil, and having been randomly assigned such as by a court-assigned case file number ending in an even number or some other random selection process at filing with notice to the parties;

(3) Any action where all the parties voluntarily agree to be governed by the Special ELT Rules by including an "ELT Election" in the civil cover sheet filed under the General Rules of Practice or by jointly filing an ELT Election certificate with the court.

(c) Initial Motion for Exclusion from ELT. A party objecting to the mandatory assignment of a matter to the ELT must serve and file a motion setting forth the reasons that the matter should be removed from the ELT. Said motion papers must be served and filed within 30 days of the filing of the action. The motion shall be heard during the Case

Management Conference, if any, under Rule 3 of these rules or at such other time as the court shall direct. The factors that should be considered by the court in ruling on said motion include:

(1) Multiple parties or claims;

(2) Multiple or complex theories of liability, damages, or relief;

(3) Complicated facts that require the discovery options provided by the Minnesota Rules of Civil Procedure;

(4) Substantial likelihood of dispositive motions; or

(5) Any factor that demonstrates that assignment to the ELT would substantially affect a party's right to a fair and just resolution of the matter (e.g., timing of obtaining discovery from a third party, estimated damages significantly exceeding $100,000).

(d) Subsequent Motion for Exclusion from ELT. After the time for bringing a motion under Rule 1(c) of this rule has expired and no later than the trial date, a party may by motion request that the case be removed from the ELT for good cause shown related to a new development that could not have been previously raised.

Adopted May 7, 2013, eff. July 1, 2013.

Historical and Statutory Notes

The order of the Minnesota Supreme Court [ADM04–8001, ADM09–8009, ADM–10-8051] dated May 7, 2013, provided in part the Pilot Project "be effective July 1, 2013, and shall apply to all civil actions identified therein that are filed on or after the effective date. The Pilot Project shall continue until further order of the Court."

Rule 2. Automatic Disclosures of Information

(a) Content; Timing. Each party shall prepare and serve an Automatic Disclosure of Information within 60 days after filing of the action or, where applicable, filing of the ELT Election. The Automatic Disclosure of Information shall include the following:

(1) A statement summarizing each contention in support of every claim or defense which a party will present at trial and a brief statement of the facts upon which the contentions are based.

(2) The name, address and telephone number of each individual likely to have discoverable information—along with the subjects of that information and any statement from such individual—that the disclosing party may use to support its claims or defenses. However, no party shall be required to furnish any statement (written or taped) protected by the attorney/client privilege or work-product rule.

(3) A copy—or description, by category and location—of all documents, electronically stored information, and tangible things that the disclosing party has in its possession, custody, or control and may use to support its claims or defenses.

(4) If a claim for damages is being made, a description of the precise damages being sought by the party and the method for calculation of said damages. If the party has any liability insurance coverage providing coverage for the claims being made by another party, the name of the insurance company, the limits of coverage, and the existence of any issue that could affect the availability of coverage.

(5) A brief summary of the qualifications of any expert witness the party may call at the time of trial together with a report or statement of any such expert which sets forth the subject matter of the expert witness's anticipated testimony; the substance of the facts and opinions to which the expert is expected to testify, and a brief summary of the grounds for each opinion.

(6) Any offers of stipulation of any fact that is relevant to any claim or defense in the matter.

(7) An estimate of the number of trial days that it will take to complete trial of the matter.

(b) Filing Disclosures; Privacy Considerations. Automatic disclosures under this rule need not be filed with the court unless otherwise ordered by the court. If a court directs the filing of automatic disclosures, the party filing such disclosures shall take necessary and appropriate steps to protect the privacy interests (such as, without limitation, addresses and telephone numbers) of individuals identified in the disclosures.

Adopted May 7, 2013, eff. July 1, 2013.

Historical and Statutory Notes

The order of the Minnesota Supreme Court [ADM04–8001, ADM09–8009, ADM–10-8051] dated May 7, 2013, provided in part the Pilot Project "be effective July 1, 2013, and shall apply to all civil actions identified therein that are filed on or after the effective date. The Pilot Project shall continue until further order of the Court."

Rule 3. Case Management Conference

(a) Timing; Scope. Within 45 to 60 days of the date of filing of an action, or where applicable, within 30 days of filing of the ELT Election, the court shall convene a Case Management Conference (CMC). All counsel and parties, whether represented or unrepresented, must participate in the CMC. At the CMC, the court and the parties shall address the following subjects:

(1) Any motion to exclude the matter from the ELT Rules made pursuant to ELT Rule 1(c) of these rules;

(2) The prospects for settlement via mediation, arbitration, court-conducted settlement conference, or other form of ADR;

(3) Any request for modification of the abbreviated discovery process required by the ELT Rules;

(4) The setting of a day or week certain trial date to begin no later than 120 to 180 days following

filing of the action or, where applicable, the ELT Certification;

(5) The setting of a deadline for the filing of all trial documents, including witness lists, exhibit lists, jury instructions, special jury verdict forms, trial briefs and motions in limine; and

(6) The setting of the date for completion of hearing of any motions.

(b) Format; Alternative Judicial Intervention. The court may conduct the CMC by telephone or may substitute other judicial intervention (including but not limited to one or more telephone discussions or issuing a scheduling order based on information supplied by the parties in their civil cover sheet) that addresses the above subjects.

Adopted May 7, 2013, eff. July 1, 2013.

Historical and Statutory Notes

The order of the Minnesota Supreme Court [ADM04-8001, ADM09-8009, ADM-10-8051] dated May 7, 2013, provided in part the Pilot Project "be effective July 1, 2013, and shall apply to all civil actions identified therein that are filed on or after the effective date. The Pilot Project shall continue until further order of the Court."

Rule 4. Limitations on Discovery

(a) Time Period Limited. The period for conducting discovery shall continue for a period of 90 days from the Case Management Conference. Upon a request of the parties, the court, for good cause shown, may extend the period for conducting discovery for up to an additional 30 days.

(b) Written Discovery Limits; Motions to Compel. Written discovery shall be limited to 15 interrogatories, 15 requests for production of documents and things, and 25 requests for admissions. Written discovery by each party must be served within 30 days of the date of the CMC and responses thereto must be served within 30 days of the date of service. Motions to compel responses to written discovery shall be made within 15 days of the date a response was due and shall be made pursuant to the modified discovery motion procedure set forth in Rule 4(d) of these rules.

(c) Depositions. Depositions are permitted as a matter of right of the parties only but must be taken within the deadline established by the court. Except as otherwise ordered by the court, a deposition of a non-party witness shall be allowed only if the deposition is being taken in lieu of in-person trial testimony.

(d) Meet and Confer Requirement. Prior to any motion to compel discovery, the party seeking the discovery and the party from whom responses are being sought must, by and through their counsel (or a pro se litigant if unrepresented by counsel), confer in an attempt to resolve the dispute. If the dispute is not resolved, the party seeking the discovery shall contact the court and schedule a telephone conference with the court, and provide notice of the date and time of the telephone conference to all adverse parties. No later than 5 days prior to the date of the discovery dispute telephone conference, each party shall serve and file with the court a letter not exceeding 2 pages in length setting forth the party's position on the discovery dispute and providing copies of the disputed discovery. The court, in its discretion, may allow additional argument at the telephone conference. The court shall promptly rule on the discovery dispute.

Adopted May 7, 2013, eff. July 1, 2013.

Historical and Statutory Notes

The order of the Minnesota Supreme Court [ADM04-8001, ADM09-8009, ADM-10-8051] dated May 7, 2013, provided in part the Pilot Project "be effective July 1, 2013, and shall apply to all civil actions identified therein that are filed on or after the effective date. The Pilot Project shall continue until further order of the Court."

Appendix A. Sample Expedited Litigation Track Assignment Order

STATE OF MINNESOTA
COUNTY OF ________

DISTRICT COURT
______ JUDICIAL DISTRICT
CASE TYPE: ________
File Number: ______

__________, Plaintiff
v.
__________, Defendant

ELT Assignment and Case Management Conference Order

____

It is ORDERED:

1. This case is assigned to the pilot project (ELT Pilot") under the Special Rules For a Pilot Expedited Civil Litigation Track ("ELT Rules");

2. A party objecting to this assignment must make a formal motion under ELT Rule 1(c) or (d), for removal from the ELT Pilot;

3. Each party shall provide the Automatic Disclosure Of Information required under ELT Rule 2;

4. A Case Management conference shall be held on: ________, and each party shall attend the conference prepared to discuss the subjects identified in ELT Rule 3; and

5. The Limitations on Discovery set forth in ELT Rule 4 apply.

Dated: ____________ BY THE COURT:

____
Judge of District Court

Adopted May 7, 2013, eff. July 1, 2013.

Appendix B. Sample Expedited Litigation Track Case Management Order

STATE OF MINNESOTA
COUNTY OF ________

DISTRICT COURT
______ JUDICIAL DISTRICT
CASE TYPE: ________
File Number: ______

__________, Plaintiff
v.
__________, Defendant

ELT Case Management Order

____

It is ORDERED:

1. Each party shall provide the Automatic Disclosure Of Information required under Rule 2 of the Special Rules For a Pilot Expedited Civil Litigation Track ("ELT Rules")

2. ADR will/will not be used, and if used the deadline and form of ADR shall be: __________;

3. The Limitations on Discovery set forth in ELT Rule 4 apply;

4. All motions shall be heard by: __________;

5. The day or week certain for trial is: __________;

6. The deadline for submitting all trial documents, including witness lists, jury instructions, special verdict forms, trial briefs, and motions in limine is: __________.

Dated: ____________ BY THE COURT:

____
Judge of District Court

Adopted May 7, 2013, eff. July 1, 2013.

TENTH JUDICIAL DISTRICT

Rule 14. Juvenile Court Proceedings

NOTE: References to "Rule" or "Rules" are to Rules of Procedure for Juvenile Courts.

14.01 Venue. Unless otherwise ordered by the court for good cause shown, a delinquency, petty matter or traffic trial and hearings pursuant to Rules 25 and 26 of the Rules of Procedure for Juvenile Courts, shall be held in the county where the offense is alleged to have occurred.

14.02. Discretionary Release By The Court With Conditions. Whenever the court releases a child with conditions pursuant to Rule 18.02, Subd. 2(C)(2), the conditions shall be stated on the record by the court or shall be reduced to writing and filed with the court the next court day after the conditions are imposed. [Supplementary to Rule 18.02, Subd. 2(C)(2)].

14.03. Photograph of a Line-up. Every line-up which includes a child in custody shall be photographed and the photographs shall be filed with the court with the report required pursuant to Rule 18.04, Subd. 2(D). [Supplementary to Rule 18.04, Subd. 2 (Line-up).]

14.04. Request For a Formal Review Hearing. A request for a formal review hearing pursuant to Rule 18.09, Subd. 2(B) and Rule 62.07, Subd. 2 shall be in writing and state the reasons for the request. To find a substantial basis or good cause to hold a review hearing, the court must find that the written request sets forth a showing of a significant change of circumstances so that there is good cause to believe that (a) there appears to be a change of circumstances sufficient to indicate that a change of disposition is necessary or (b) it appears that the disposition is inappropriate. [Supplementary to Rule 18.09, Subd. 2(B) and Rule 62.07, Subd. 2.]

14.05. Denial of Petition Without Personal Appearance. A denial of a petition without personal appearance pursuant to Rule 21.02, Subd. 1 (delinquency or petty matter) or Rule 36.02, Subd. 15 (traffic) may be entered by counsel with the consent of the court only after counsel has consulted with the child on the matter. In entering a denial, either on the record or in writing, counsel will assert that counsel has consulted with the child on the matter and that counsel will accept responsibility to have the child present at the next hearing at which the child's attendance is required.

A denial of a petition without personal appearance pursuant to Rule 55.02, Subd. 1 (child protection matter) may be entered by counsel with the consent of the court, only after counsel has consulted with his/her client(s) in the matter, unless counsel's client is a child under the age of 12, in which case counsel will consult with the child's guardian ad litem if there is one. In entering a denial, either on the record or in writing, counsel will assert that counsel has consulted with his/her client(s) if consultation is required by this special rule and that counsel will accept responsibility to have his/her client(s) present at the next hearing at which the attendance of the client(s) is required. [Supplementary to Rule 21.02, Subd. 1, Rule 36.02, Subd. 15 and Rule 55.02, Subd. 1.]

14.06. Counsel for Child in a Traffic Matter. For any child charged with a traffic offense which would be a misdemeanor or gross misdemeanor if committed by an adult, Rule 4.01 is adopted in lieu of Rule 36.01, Subd. 3. [Supplementary to Rule 36.01, Subd. 3 (Counsel for Child).]

14.07. Sequestration of Witnesses. Except for counsel, the child and the child's parent or guardian, the court may in its discretion sequester any witness during any hearing. In deciding whether to sequester a parent when he or she is also a witness, the court should consider whether a custodial parent will remain with the child after sequestration of a parent who is a witness. The court should also consider whether the parent is alleged to be the victim of the delinquency or is alleged to have neglected the child or to have done acts to make the child dependent. No parent shall be sequestered when he or she is a witness in an action to terminate that parent's parental rights. [Supplementary to Rule 7, Rule 36.02, Subd. 6 and Rule 42.]

14.08. Discovery of Police Reports. In addition to any court order or rule in any traffic matter, the county attorney shall make available to the child's counsel copies of any police reports concerning the alleged traffic offense, within five days after receipt of a request or as soon thereafter as the information becomes known to the county attorney. [Supplementary to Rule 36.02, Subd. 17 (Discovery).]

RULES OF JUVENILE PROCEDURE [RENUMBERED]

Rule

1.01 to 36.02. Renumbered.
37.01 to 82.06. Renumbered.

Rules 1.01 to 36.02. Renumbered as Rules of Juvenile Delinquency Procedure, Rules 1.01 to 31.02, eff. Jan. 1, 2004

Historical Notes

Rules 1.01 to 36.02 of the Rules of Juvenile Procedure were renumbered as Juvenile Delinquency Procedure Rules 1.01 to 31.02. The following table shows the disposition of each rule.

Disposition Table

Former rule	New rule
1.01	1.01
1.02	1.02
1.03	1.01
2.01	2.01
2.02	2.02
2.03	2.03
2.04	2.04
2.05	2.05
3.01	3.01
3.02	3.02
3.03	3.03
3.04	3.04
3.05	3.05
3.06	3.06
3.07	3.07
3.08	3.08
4.01	4.03
4.02	4.03
4.03	3.04
4.04	3.05
4.05	3.06
4.06	3.07
5.01	5.01
5.02	5.02
5.03	5.03
5.04	5.04
5.05	5.05
5.06	5.06
5.07	5.07
5.08	5.08
6.01	6.01
6.02	6.02
6.03	6.03
6.04	6.04
6.05	6.05
6.06	6.06
7.01	7.01
7.02	7.02
7.03	7.03
7.04	7.04
8.01	8.01
8.02	8.02
8.03	8.03
8.04	8.04
9.01	9.01
9.02	9.02
9.03	9.03
9.04	9.04
10.01	10.01
10.02	10.02
10.03	10.03
10.04	10.04
10.05	10.05
10.06	10.06
10.07	10.07
11.01	11.01
11.02	11.02
11.03	29.03
12.01	12.01
12.02	12.02
13.01	13.01
13.02	13.02
13.03	13.03
13.04	13.04
13.05	13.05
13.06	13.06
13.07	13.07
13.08	13.08
13.09	13.09
13.10	13.10
14.01	14.01
14.02	14.02
14.03	14.03
14.04	14.04
14.05	14.05
14.06	14.06
14.07	14.07
14.08	14.08
14.09	14.09
14.10	14.10
15.01	15.01
15.02	15.02
15.03	15.03
15.04	15.04
15.05	15.05
15.06	15.06
15.07	15.07
15.08	15.08
16.01	16.01
16.02	16.02
16.03	16.03
16.04	16.04
17.01	17.01
17.02	None
17.03	17.02
17.04	17.03
17.05	None
17.06	17.04
17.07	17.05
17.08	17.06
17.09	None
17.10	17.07

Former rule	New rule
17.11	17.08
17.12	None
17.13	None
17.14	17.09
17.15	None
17.16	17.10
17.17	17.11
17.18	Repealed
17.19	Repealed
18.01	18.02
18.02	18.03
18.03	18.04
18.04	18.05
18.05	18.06
18.06	18.07
18.07	18.08
18.08	None
18.09	5.08
19.01	19.01
19.02	19.02
19.03	19.03
19.04	19.04
19.05	19.05
19.06	19.07
19.07	19.09
19.08	19.10
19.09	19.11
20.01	20.01
20.02	20.02
20.03	7.04
21.01	21.01
21.02	21.02
21.03	21.03
21.04	21.04
21.05	21.05
21.06	21.06
22.01	22.01
22.02	22.02
22.03	22.03
22.04	22.04
22.05	22.05
23.01	23.01
23.02	23.02
23.03	23.03
23.04	23.04
23.05	23.05
23.06	23.06
24.01	24.01
24.02	24.02
24.03	10.06
24.04	10.07
25.01	25.01
25.02	25.02
25.03	25.03
25.04	25.04
26.01	26.01
26.02	26.02
26.03	26.03
27.01	27.01
27.02	27.02
27.03	13.03
27.04	13.04
27.05	13.06
27.06	13.09
27.07	13.10
28.01	16.01
28.02	16.03
28.03	16.04
29.01	29.01
29.02	29.02
29.03	29.03
30.01	30.01
30.02	30.02
30.03	15.03
30.04	15.04
30.05	15.05
30.06	15.06
30.07	15.08
31.01	31.01
31.02	31.02
31.03	21.03
31.04	21.04
31.05	21.05
31.06	21.06
32.01	18.02
32.02	18.03
32.03	18.04
32.04	18.05
32.05	18.06
32.06	18.07
32.07	18.08
32.08	None
32A.01	19.01
32A.02	19.02
32A.03	19.03
32A.04	19.04
32A.05	19.06
32A.06	19.07
32A.07	19.09
32A.08	19.10
32A.09	19.11
33.01	20.01
33.02	20.01
33.03	20.01
33.04	20.01
34.01	30.01
34.02	30.02
34.03	None
35.01	31.01, 31.02
36.01	17.01
36.02	17.02, 17.03, 17.04, 17.05, 17.06, 17.07, 17.08, 17.09

Rules 37.01 to 82.06. Renumbered as Rules of Juvenile Protection Procedure, Rules 1.01 to 47.06, eff. Jan. 1, 2004

Historical Notes

Rules 37.01 to 82.06 of the Rules of Juvenile Procedure were renumbered as Rules 1.01 to 47.06 of the Rules of Juvenile Protection Procedure. The following table shows the disposition of each rule.

Disposition Table

Former rule	New rule
37.01	1.01
37.02	1.02
38.01	2.01
39.01	3.01
39.02	3.02
39.03	3.03

Former rule	New rule
39.04	3.04
39.05	3.05
40.01	4.01
40.02	4.02
40.03	4.03
40.04	4.04
40.05	4.05
41.01	5.01
41.02	5.02
41.03	5.03
42.01	6.01
42.02	6.02
42.03	6.03
43.01	7.01
43.02	7.02
43.03	7.03
43.04	7.04
43.05	7.05
43.06	7.06
43.07	7.07
44.01	8.01
44.02	8.02
44.03	8.03
44.04	8.04
44.05	8.05
44.06	8.06
44.07	8.07
44.08	8.08
45.01	9.01
45.02	9.02
46.01	10.01
46.02	10.02
46.03	10.03
46.04	10.04
47.01	11.01
47.02	11.02
48.01	12.01
48.02	12.02
48.03	12.03
49.01	13.01
49.02	13.02
49.03	13.03
49.04	13.04
49.05	13.05
49.06	13.06
49.07	13.07
49.08	13.08
49.09	13.09
50.01	14.01
50.02	14.02
50.03	14.03
50.04	14.04
51.01	15.01
51.02	15.02
51.03	15.03
51.04	15.04
51.05	15.05
52.01	16.01
52.02	16.02
53.01	17.01
53.02	17.02
53.03	17.03
53.04	17.04
53.05	17.05
53.06	17.06

Former rule	New rule
54.01	18.01, 18.02
55.01	19.01
55.02	19.02
55.03	19.03
55.04	19.04
56	20
57.01	21.01
57.02	21.02
57.03	21.03
58.01	22.01
58.02	22.02
58.03	22.03
59.01	23.01
59.02	23.02
59.03	23.03
59.04	23.04
60.01	24.01
61.01	25.01
61.02	25.02
61.03	25.03
61.04	25.04
61.05	25.05
61.06	25.06
62.01	26.01
62.02	26.02
62.03	26.03
63.01	27.01
63.02	27.02
63.03	27.03
63.04	27.04
65.01	28.01
65.02	28.02
65.03	28.03
65.04	28.04
65.05	28.05
65.06	28.06
66.01	29.01
66.02	29.02
66.03	29.03
66.04	29.04
67.01	30.01
67.02	30.02
67.03	30.03
67.04	30.04
67.05	30.05
67.06	30.06
67.07	30.07
67.08	30.08
67.09	30.09
67.10	30.10
67.11	30.11
68.01	31.01
68.02	31.02
68.03	31.03
68.04	31.04
68.05	31.05
68.06	31.06
68.07	31.07
69.01	32.01
69.02	32.02
69.03	32.03
69.04	32.05
69.05	32.06
70.01	33.01
70.02	33.02
70.03	33.03
70.04	33.04

Former rule	New rule
70.05	33.05
71.01	34.01
71.02	34.02
71.03	34.03
72.01	35.01
72.02	35.02
72.03	35.03
73.01	36.01
73.02	36.02
74.01	39.01
74.02	39.02
74.03	39.03
74.04	39.04
74.05	39.05
75.01	40.01
75.02	40.02
76.01	41.01
76.02	41.02
76.03	41.03
76.04	41.04
76.05	41.05
76.06	41.06
77.01	42.01

Former rule	New rule
77.02	42.02
77.03	42.03
77.04	42.04
77.05	42.05
78.01	43.01
78.02	43.02
78.03	43.03
78.04	43.04
79.01	44.01
79.02	44.02
80.01	45.01
80.02	45.02
80.03	45.03
80.04	45.04
80.05	45.05
81.01	46.01
81.02	46.02
82.01	47.01
82.02	47.02
82.03	47.03
82.04	47.04
82.05	47.05
82.06	47.06

RULES OF JUVENILE DELINQUENCY PROCEDURE

Effective May 1, 1983

Including Amendments Received Through January 1, 2014

Research Note

See Minnesota Statutes Annotated, *Volume 52, for case annotations and cross references. The Rules of Juvenile Procedure are discussed in Scott and Sonsteng, 12 and 13* Minnesota Practice–Juvenile Law and Practice (3d Edition).

RULE 1. SCOPE, APPLICATION AND GENERAL PURPOSE

RULE 2. ATTENDANCE AT HEARINGS AND PRIVACY

RULE 3. RIGHT TO COUNSEL

RULE 4. WARRANTS

RULE 5. DETENTION

RULE 6. CHARGING DOCUMENT

RULE 7. ARRAIGNMENT

RULE 8. PLEAS

RULE 9. SETTLEMENT DISCUSSIONS AND PLEA AGREEMENTS

Rule

RULE 45. EX PARTE COMMUNICATION

45.01, 45.02. Deleted.

RULE 46. ORDERS

46.01 to 46.04. Deleted.

RULE 47. RECORDING AND TRANSCRIPTS

47.01, 47.02. Deleted.

RULE 48. USE OF TELEPHONE AND INTERACTIVE VIDEO

48.01 to 48.03. Deleted.

RULE 49. SUBPOENAS

49.01 to 49.09. Deleted.

RULE 50. CONTEMPT

50.01 to 50.04. Deleted.

RULE 51. MOTIONS

51.01 to 51.05. Deleted.

RULE 52. SIGNING OF PLEADINGS, MOTIONS, AND OTHER PAPERS; SANCTIONS

52.01, 52.02. Deleted.

RULE 53. DISCOVERY

53.01 to 53.06. Deleted.

RULE 54. DEFAULT

54.01. Deleted.

RULE 55. SETTLEMENT

55.01 to 55.04. Deleted.

RULE 56. ALTERNATIVE DISPUTE RESOLUTION

RULE 57. PARTIES

57.01 to 57.03. Deleted.

RULE 58. PARTICIPANTS

58.01 to 58.03. Deleted.

RULE 59. INTERVENTION

59.01 to 59.04. Deleted.

RULE 60. JOINDER

60.01. Deleted.

RULE 61. RIGHT TO REPRESENTATION; APPOINTMENT OF COUNSEL

61.01 to 61.06. Deleted.

RULE 62. GUARDIAN AD LITEM

62.01 to 62.03. Deleted.

Rule

RULE 63. ACCESS TO HEARINGS

63.01 to 63.04. Deleted.

RULE 64. CLOSED PROCEEDINGS

64.01. Deleted.

RULE 65. EMERGENCY PROTECTIVE CARE ORDER AND NOTICE

65.01 to 65.06. Deleted.

RULE 66. PROCEDURES DURING PERIOD OF EMERGENCY PROTECTIVE CARE

66.01 to 66.04. Deleted.

RULE 67. EMERGENCY PROTECTIVE CARE HEARING

67.01 to 67.11. Deleted.

RULE 68. METHODS OF FILING AND SERVICE

68.01 to 68.07. Deleted.

RULE 69. SUMMONS AND NOTICE

69.01 to 69.05. Deleted.

RULE 70. PETITION

70.01 to 70.05. Deleted.

RULE 71. ADMIT/DENY HEARING

71.01 to 71.03. Deleted.

RULE 72. ADMISSION OR DENIAL

72.01 to 72.03. Deleted.

RULE 73. PRETRIAL CONFERENCE

73.01, 73.02. Deleted.

RULE 74. TRIAL

74.01 to 74.05. Deleted.

RULE 75. ADJUDICATION

75.01, 75.02. Deleted.

RULE 76. DISPOSITION

76.01 to 76.06. Deleted.

RULE 77. PERMANENT PLACEMENT MATTERS

77.01 to 77.05. Deleted.

RULE 78. TERMINATION OF PARENTAL RIGHTS MATTERS

78.01 to 78.04. Deleted.

RULE 79. REVIEW OF VOLUNTARY PLACEMENT MATTERS

79.01, 79.02. Deleted.

Supersedure

The order of the Minnesota Supreme Court dated December 17, 1982 adopting the Rules of Procedure for Juvenile Court provided in part that "these Rules of Juvenile Procedure shall supersede any other rules or statutes in conflict therewith."

1996 Order

The order of the Minnesota Supreme Court [C6–84–2165] dated June 26, 1996, provides in part that Rules 1 to 36 and 37.01 (effective May 1, 1983, as amended through December 1, 1995) shall be deleted and replaced by Rules 1 to 31 and 37.01.

2012 Order

The order of the Minnesota Supreme Court [ADM10–8003] dated October 15, 2012, provides in part

"PILOT PROJECT PROVISIONS FOR E-FILING AND E-SERVICE IN JUVENILE DELINQUENCY MATTERS

"1a. Who May Electronically File and Serve. *During the Pilot Project, attorneys, government agencies, and parties designated by the State Court Administrator in consultation with the district court may, upon registering with the electronic filing service provider designated by the State Court Administrator ('Designated Provider'), electronically file documents other than charging documents with the district courts designated by the State Court Administrator ('District Courts'). Electronic filing and electronic service shall be accomplished through the Designated Provider's Internet-accessible electronic filing and service system ('E-Filing System').*

"Registered attorneys, government agencies, and parties may electronically serve documents on other registered attorneys, government agencies, and parties in juvenile cases provided that the attorney, government agency, or party to be served has designated an e-mail address for receiving electronic service in the E-Filing System.

"The District Courts may electronically file and serve any orders, notices, or other documents in juvenile cases provided that the attorney, government agency, or party to be served has designated an e-mail address for receiving electronic service in the E-Filing System.

"1b. What Documents May Be Electronically Transmitted; Alternative Method. *In addition to motions required to be served and filed under Minn. R. Juv. Del. P. 27, notices sent to counsel under Minn. R. Juv. Del. P. 25, and documents specifically authorized by court rule to be served by electronic means, other documents may be electronically filed, provided, or made available under this Order. Such documents include, but are not limited to: (a) detention reports under Minn. R. Juv. Del. P. 5.05, subd. 4; (b) predisposition reports under Minn. R. Juv. Del. P. 15.03, subd. 4; (c) certification study reports under Minn. R. Juv. Del. P. 18.04, subd. 4; and (d) extended jurisdiction juvenile study reports under Minn. R. Juv. Del. P. 19.03, subd. 4. Additionally, if authorized by the State Court Administrator in consultation with the District Court, the documents described in clauses (a)-(d) may be electronically filed with the District Court or provided or made available to government agencies via Court Integration Services. Court Integration Services facilitates application-to-application electronic exchange of data between the court and its business partners; government agencies may register for Court Integration Services under the process established by the State Court Administrator.*

"1c. Electronic Filing of Charging Documents. *If technologically feasible and if authorized by the State Court Administrator, citations, tab charges and petitions may be filed electronically via Court Integration Services. For electronically filed petitions, the signature of the prosecuting attorney under Minn. R. Juv. Del. P. 6.03, subd. 2, must comply with the electronic signature standard approved by the State Court Administrator, and the facts establishing probable cause under Minn. R. Juv. Del. P. 6.05,* *subd. 1, must be set forth in the electronically filed petition, rather than in attached police reports or affidavits.*

*"2. **Registration and Designation of E-Mail Address for Service.** An attorney, government agency, or party is registered with the Designated Provider when they have entered into a subscriber agreement with the Designated Provider and obtained an E-Filing System user identification and password generated according to the Designated Provider's protocols. Registered attorneys, government agencies, or parties electronically filing documents shall diligently monitor the E-Filing System filing queue, and designate in the E-Filing System an e-mail address for receiving electronic service, as directed by the District Court. Registered attorneys, government agencies, and parties who have used the E-Filing system for a case shall maintain a designated e-mail address for receiving electronic service until all applicable appeal periods have expired for the case.*

*"3. **Document Format.** Documents filed electronically shall be in the format required by Minn. Gen. R. Prac. 14.03.*

*"4. **Effect of Electronic Filing or Service.** A document electronically filed or served by the District Court or a registered attorney, government agency, or party under this order has the same legal effect as an original document filed or served in paper form.*

*"5. **Signatures.***

*"a. **Applicability of General Rules of Practice.** The provisions of Minn. Gen. R. Prac. 14.04, clauses (a) though (d) apply to all documents electronically filed and served using the E-Filing System.*

*"b. **Certification; Retention.** By electronically filing or submitting a document using the E-Filing System, the registered attorney, government agency, or party filing or serving is certifying compliance with the signature requirements of the applicable rules, and the signatures on the document shall have the same legal effect as the signatures on the original document. A registered attorney, government agency, or party electronically filing or serving a document using the E-Filing system shall maintain the original document bearing actual signatures, if in paper form, or electronic signatures if the original is in electronic form and shall make the original document available upon reasonable request of the District Court, the signatories, or other parties.*

*"6. **Time of Filing; Fees.** A document that is electronically filed under these provisions is deemed to have been filed with the court administrator on the date and time of its transmittal to the District Court through the E-Filing System, and the filing shall be stamped with this date and time subject to acceptance by the court administrator. If the filing is not subsequently accepted by the court administrator (e.g., for nonpayment of all applicable fees, attempted filing into the wrong case, or clearly incorrect venue as indicated in the caption), the date stamp shall be removed and the document electronically returned to the person who filed it. The District Court shall establish procedures for payment of any applicable fees electronically.*

*"7. **Effective Date of Service; Timing; Proof.***

*"a. **Service via E-Filing System.** Except when service is otherwise prohibited, service by authorized electronic means using the court's E-Filing System as defined by Minn. Gen. R. Prac. 14 is complete:*

"(1) upon completion of the electronic transmission of the document(s) to the E-Filing System if the E-Filing System service command is used; and

"(2) upon acceptance of the electronic filing by the court, as provided in Rule 14, if the E-Filing System joint service and filing command is used.

*"b. **Technical Errors; Relief.** A motion for relief because of a technical error may be made, and relief may be granted, as provided in Minn. Gen. R. Prac. 14.01(f).*

*"c. **Proof of Service; Timing.** Proof of service of documents served using the E-Filing System is governed by Minn. Gen. R. Prac. 14.05. The timing and proof of service requirements of Minn. R. Juv. Del. P. 25.03, subds. 4 and 5, that apply to service by mail also apply to electronic service.*

*"8. **Sealed and Confidential Documents.** Minn. Gen. R. Prac. 14.06 governs electronic filing of sealed and confidential documents, except that during this pilot, a document to be filed under seal or as confidential may be filed in paper form if required or permitted by the court, and a motion to file a document in paper form under seal or as confidential may, but is not required to be, filed and served electronically.*

*"9. **Records: Official; Appeal; Certified Copies.** Minn. Gen. R. Prac. 14.07 applies to documents electronically filed under this Order.*

*"10. **Access to Documents.** A document electronically filed or served under these*

provisions shall be accessible as provided in the applicable court rules and statutes, including the Rules of Public Access to Records of the Judicial Branch."

Comments

The order of the Minnesota Supreme Court [C6–84–2165] dated June 26, 1996, provides in part that "(t)he inclusion of Advisory Committee comments is made for convenience and does not reflect court approval of the comments made therein."

The order of the Minnesota Supreme Court [CX–01–926] dated July 18, 2003, provides in part that "(t)he inclusion and amendment of committee comments is made for convenience and does not reflect court approval of the comments made therein."

RULE 1. SCOPE, APPLICATION AND GENERAL PURPOSE

Rule 1.01. Scope and Application

Rules 1 through 31 govern the procedure in the juvenile courts of Minnesota for all delinquency matters as defined by Minnesota Statutes, section 260B.007, subdivision 6, juvenile petty matters as defined by Minnesota Statutes, section 260B.007, subdivision 16 and juvenile traffic matters as defined by Minnesota Statutes, section 260B.225. Procedures for juvenile traffic and petty matters are governed by Rule 17.

Where these rules require giving notice to a child, notice shall also be given to the child's counsel if the child is represented. Reference in these rules to "child's counsel" includes the child who is proceeding pro se. Reference in these rules to "counsel for the parent(s), legal guardian, or legal custodian" includes the parent, legal guardian, or legal custodian who is proceeding pro se.

Where any rule obligates the court to inform a child or other person of certain information, the information shall be provided in commonly understood, everyday language.

In cases involving an Indian child, which may be governed by the Indian Child Welfare Act, 25 U.S.C.A. Chapter 21, sections 1901–1963, these rules shall be construed to be consistent with that act. Where the Minnesota Indian Family Preservation Act, Minnesota Statutes, sections 260.751 through 260.835 applies, these rules shall be construed to be consistent with that act.

Adopted Dec. 17, 1982, eff. May 1, 1983. Amended June 26, 1996; July 18, 2003; April 23, 2004; July 11, 2005, eff. Sept. 1, 2005.

Comment—Rule 1

See comment following Rule 1.02.

Historical Notes

The order of the Minnesota Supreme Court [C6–84–2165] dated June 26, 1996, provides in part that "(t)hese amendments to the Rules of Juvenile Procedure shall govern all juvenile actions commenced or arrests made on or after 12:00 o'clock midnight August 1, 1996."

The order of the Minnesota Supreme Court [CX–01–926] dated July 18, 2003, provides in part that "(t)he attached amendments shall govern all juveniles taken into custody and all juvenile delinquency actions commenced or children taken into custody after 12 o'clock midnight September 1, 2003."

The order of the Minnesota Supreme Court [CX–01–926] dated April 23, 2004, provides in part that "(t)he attached amendments shall govern all juvenile delinquency actions commenced or children taken into custody after 12 o'clock midnight July 1, 2004."

Rule 1.02. General Purpose

The purpose of the juvenile rules is to establish uniform practice and procedures for the juvenile courts of the State of Minnesota, and to assure that the constitutional rights of the child are protected. The purpose of the laws relating to children alleged or adjudicated to be delinquent is to promote the public safety and reduce juvenile delinquency by maintaining the integrity of the substantive law prohibiting certain behavior and by developing individual responsibility for lawful behavior. This purpose should be pursued through means that are fair and just, that recognize the unique characteristics and needs of children, and that give children access to opportunities for personal and social growth. These rules shall be construed to achieve these purposes.

Adopted Dec. 17, 1982, eff. May 1, 1983. Amended June 26, 1996.

Comment—Rule 1

Minn. R. Juv. Del. P. 1.02 is based upon Minnesota Statutes, section 260B.001, subd. 2 (2002).

The Indian Child Welfare Act does not apply to placements of Indian children that are based upon an act which, if committed by an adult, would be deemed a crime. 25 U.S.C. section 1903(1) (1988). However, Minnesota Statutes, section 260.761, subd. 2 (2002) of the Minnesota Indian Family Preservation Act requires that the Indian child's tribal social service agency receive notice when the court transfers legal custody of the child under Minnesota Statutes, section 260B.198, subd. 1(c)(1), (2) and (3) (2002) following an adjudication for a misdemeanor-level delinquent act.

Historical Notes

The order of the Minnesota Supreme Court [C6–84–2165] dated June 26, 1996, provides in part that "(t)hese amendments to the Rules of Juvenile Procedure shall govern all juvenile actions commenced or arrests made on or after 12:00 o'clock midnight August 1, 1996."

Rule 1.03. Deleted June 26, 1996

Historical Notes

The order of the Minnesota Supreme Court [C6–84–2165] dated June 26, 1996, provides in part that "(t)hese amendments to the Rules

of Juvenile Procedure shall govern all juvenile actions commenced or arrests made on or after 12:00 o'clock midnight August 1, 1996."

See, now, MN ST Juv. Del., Rule 1.01.

RULE 2. ATTENDANCE AT HEARINGS AND PRIVACY

Rule 2.01. Right to Attend Hearing

Juvenile court proceedings are closed to the public except as provided by law. Only the following may attend hearings:

(A) the child, guardian ad litem appointed in the delinquency proceeding and counsel for the child;

(B) parent(s), legal guardian, or legal custodian of the child and their counsel;

(C) the spouse of the child;

(D) the prosecuting attorney;

(E) other persons requested by the parties listed in (A) through (D) and approved by the court;

(F) persons authorized by the court, including a guardian ad litem appointed for the child in another matter, under such conditions as the court may approve;

(G) persons authorized by statute, under such conditions as the court may approve; and

(H) any person who is entitled to receive a summons or notice under these rules.

Amended June 26, 1996; Sept. 30, 2004, eff. Jan. 1, 2005.

Comment—Rule 2

See comment following Rule 2.05.

Historical Notes

The order of the Minnesota Supreme Court [C6–84–2165] dated June 26, 1996, provides in part that "(t)hese amendments to the Rules of Juvenile Procedure shall govern all juvenile actions commenced or arrests made on or after 12:00 o'clock midnight August 1, 1996."

Rule 2.02. Exclusion of Persons Who Have A Right To Attend Hearings

The court may temporarily exclude any person, except counsel and the guardian ad litem appointed in the delinquency proceeding, when it is in the best interests of the child to do so. The court shall note on the record the reasons a person is excluded. Counsel for the person excluded has the right to remain and participate if the person excluded had the right to participate in the proceeding. An unrepresented child can not be excluded on the grounds that it is in the best interests of the child to do so.

Amended June 26, 1996; Sept. 30, 2004, eff. Jan. 1, 2005; Oct. 13, 2006, eff. Jan. 1, 2007.

Comment—Rule 2

See comment following Rule 2.05.

Historical Notes

The order of the Minnesota Supreme Court [C6–84–2165] dated June 26, 1996, provides in part that "(t)hese amendments to the Rules of Juvenile Procedure shall govern all juvenile actions commenced or arrests made on or after 12:00 o'clock midnight August 1, 1996."

Rule 2.03. Presence Required

Subd. 1. Child. The child shall have the right to be present at all hearings. The child is deemed to waive the right to be present if the child voluntarily and without justification is absent after the hearing has commenced or if the child disrupts the proceedings. Disruption of the proceedings occurs if the child, after warning by the court, engages in conduct which interrupts the orderly procedure and decorum of the court. The court may use all methods of restraint necessary to conduct the proceedings in an orderly manner. If the child is restrained or removed from the courtroom, the court shall state the reasons for the restraint or removal on the record. Except at trials and dispositional hearings, the child's appearance may be waived if the child is hospitalized in a psychiatric ward and the treating physician states in writing the reasons why not appearing would serve the child's best interests.

Subd. 2. Counsel.

(A) Counsel for the child shall be present at all hearings.

(B) The prosecuting attorney shall be present or available for all hearings unless excused by the court in its discretion.

Subd. 3. Parent, Legal Guardian or Legal Custodian. The parent, legal guardian or legal custodian of a child who is the subject of a delinquency or extended jurisdiction juvenile proceeding shall accompany the child to all hearings unless excused by the court for good cause shown. If such person fails to attend a hearing with the child without excuse, the court may issue an arrest warrant and/or hold the person in contempt. The court may proceed if it is in the best interests of the child to do so even if the parent, legal guardian, or legal custodian fails to appear.

Amended June 26, 1996.

Comment—Rule 2

See comment following Rule 2.05.

Historical Notes

The order of the Minnesota Supreme Court [C6–84–2165] dated June 26, 1996, provides in part that "(t)hese amendments to the Rules of Juvenile Procedure shall govern all juvenile actions commenced or arrests made on or after 12:00 o'clock midnight August 1, 1996."

Rule 2.04. Right to Participate

Subd. 1. Child and Prosecuting Attorney. The child and prosecuting attorney have the right to participate in all hearings.

Subd. 2. Guardian ad Litem. The guardian ad litem appointed in the delinquency proceeding has a right to participate and advocate for the best interests of the child at all hearings.

Subd. 3. Parent(s), Legal Guardian, or Legal Custodian. Except in their role as guardian ad litem for the child, the parent(s), legal guardian, or legal custodian may not participate separately at hearings until the dispositional stage of the proceedings and the court shall advise them of this right. A parent, legal guardian, or legal custodian for the child is not subject to the Rules of Guardian Ad Litem Procedure in Juvenile and Family Court. A parent, legal guardian, or legal custodian shall not participate as counsel for the child unless licensed to practice law.

Subd. 4. Generally. Persons represented by counsel, who have a right to participate, shall participate through their counsel. Unrepresented persons may participate on their own behalf.

Amended June 26, 1996; Sept. 30, 2004, eff. Jan. 1, 2005.

Comment—Rule 2

See comment following Rule 2.05.

Historical Notes

The order of the Minnesota Supreme Court [C6–84–2165] dated June 26, 1996, provides in part that "(t)hese amendments to the Rules of Juvenile Procedure shall govern all juvenile actions commenced or arrests made on or after 12:00 o'clock midnight August 1, 1996."

Rule 2.05. Ex–Parte Communications

The court shall not receive or consider any ex-parte communication from anyone concerning a proceeding, including conditions of release, detention, evidence, adjudication, disposition, or any other matter. The court shall fully disclose to all counsel on the record any attempted ex-parte communication.

Amended June 26, 1996.

Comment—Rule 2

Minn. R. Juv. Del. P. 2.01 allows persons authorized by statute to attend juvenile court proceedings. They include the public, in cases where a juvenile over age 16 is alleged to have committed a felony, and victims. The public is also entitled to be present during a juvenile certification hearing where a juvenile over age 16 is alleged to have committed a felony, except that the court may exclude the public from portions of a certification hearing to discuss psychological material or other evidence that would not be accessible to the public in an adult proceeding. Minnesota Statutes, section 260B.163, subd. 1(c) (2002). The statute does not currently permit exclusion when similar material is being presented in an extended jurisdiction juvenile proceeding. This may simply be an oversight. See also Minnesota Statutes, section 609.115, subd. 6 (1994).

Minn. R. Juv. Del. P. 2.02 permits exclusion of persons from hearings, even when they have a right to participate, to serve the child's best interests. For example, sometimes expert opinions are offered to the court regarding a child's psychological profile or amenability to probation supervision. Counsel are usually aware of such opinions and if it serves no useful purpose or may even be detrimental to a child's best interests to hear these opinions, it may be appropriate to temporarily exclude the child from the hearing. Obviously, this should be brought to the court's attention either before the hearing or at a bench conference. Because a child charged with a juvenile petty or juvenile traffic offense does not have a right to appointment of counsel at public expense, that child cannot be excluded unless the child is represented by counsel.

Minn. R. Juv. Del. P. 2.03, subd. 2 provides that the prosecuting attorney shall be present or available for all hearings unless excused by the court in its discretion. On occasion, because of time constraints and distance, it may be impossible for the prosecuting attorney to be present in person at a particular hearing. So long as the prosecuting attorney is available by telephone conference, the hearing could proceed without the prosecutor actually being present.

Minn. R. Juv. Del. P. 2.05 requires full disclosure by the court to all counsel on the record of any attempted ex-parte communication. Juvenile court has historically been less formal and more casual than other court proceedings. As a result, lawyers, probation and court services personnel, law enforcement, victims, and relatives of the child have sometimes attempted and succeeded in having ex-parte contact with the juvenile court judge. As the sanctions for delinquency become more severe, due process safeguards become more imperative.

Historical Notes

The order of the Minnesota Supreme Court [C6–84–2165] dated June 26, 1996, provides in part that "(t)hese amendments to the Rules of Juvenile Procedure shall govern all juvenile actions commenced or arrests made on or after 12:00 o'clock midnight August 1, 1996."

RULE 3. RIGHT TO COUNSEL

Rule 3.01. Generally

The child has the right to be represented by an attorney. This right attaches no later than when the child first appears in court. The attorney shall initially consult with the child privately, outside of the presence of the child's parent(s), legal guardian or legal custodian. The attorney shall act solely as the counsel for the child.

Amended June 26, 1996.

Comment—Rule 3

See comment following Rule 3.08.

Historical Notes

The order of the Minnesota Supreme Court [C6–84–2165] dated June 26, 1996, provides in part that "(t)hese amendments to the Rules of Juvenile Procedure shall govern all juvenile actions commenced or arrests made on or after 12:00 o'clock midnight August 1, 1996."

Rule 3.02. Appointment of Counsel

Subd. 1. Felonies and Gross Misdemeanors. In any proceeding in which the child is charged with a felony or gross misdemeanor, the court shall appoint counsel at public expense to represent the child, if the child can not afford counsel and private counsel has not been retained to represent the child. If the child waives the right to counsel, the court shall appoint stand-by counsel to be available to assist and consult with the child at all stages of the proceedings.

Subd. 2. Misdemeanors. In any proceeding in which the child is charged with a misdemeanor, the court shall appoint counsel at public expense to represent the child if the child can not afford counsel and private counsel has not been retained to represent the child, and the child has not waived the right to counsel. If the child waives the right to counsel, the court may appoint stand-by counsel to be available to assist and consult with the child at all stages of the proceedings.

Subd. 3. Out-of-Home Placement. In any proceeding in which out-of-home placement is proposed, the court shall appoint counsel at public expense to represent the child, if the child cannot afford counsel and private counsel has not been retained to represent the child. If the child waives the right to counsel, the court shall appoint stand-by counsel to be available to assist and consult with the child. No out-of-home placement may be made in disposition proceedings, in violation proceedings, or in subsequent contempt proceedings, if the child was not initially represented by counsel or stand-by counsel, except as provided herein. If out-of-home placement is based on a plea or adjudication obtained without assistance of counsel, the child has an absolute right to withdraw that plea or obtain a new trial.

Subd. 4. Probation Violation and Modification of Disposition for Delinquent Child. In any proceeding in which a delinquent child is alleged to have violated the terms of probation, or where a modification of disposition is proposed, the child has the right to appointment of counsel at public expense. If the child waives the right to counsel, the court shall appoint standby counsel.

Subd. 5. Juvenile Petty Offense or Juvenile Traffic Offense.

(A) In any proceeding in which the child is charged as a juvenile petty offender or juvenile traffic offender, the child or the child's parent may retain private counsel, but the child does not have a right to appointment of a public defender or other counsel at public expense, except:

(1) when the child may be subject to out-of-home placement as provided in Minnesota Statutes, section 260B.235, subdivision 6; or

(2) as otherwise provided pursuant to Rule 3.02, subdivisions 3, 6 and 7.

(B) Except in the discretion of the Office of the State Public Defender, a child is not entitled to appointment of an attorney at public expense in an appeal from adjudication and disposition in a juvenile petty offender or juvenile traffic offender matter.

Subd. 6. Detention. Every child has the right to be represented by an attorney at a detention hearing. An attorney shall be appointed for any child appearing at a detention hearing who cannot afford to hire an attorney. If the child waives representation, standby counsel shall be appointed.

Subd. 7. Child Incompetent to Proceed. Every child shall be represented by an attorney in any proceeding to determine whether the child is competent to proceed. An attorney shall be appointed for any child in such proceeding who cannot afford to hire an attorney.

Subd. 8. Appearance before a Grand Jury. A child appearing before a grand jury as a witness in a matter which is under the jurisdiction of the Juvenile Court shall be represented by an attorney at public expense if the child cannot afford to retain private counsel. If the child has effectively waived immunity from self-incrimination or has been granted use immunity, the attorney for the child shall be present while the witness is testifying. The attorney shall not be permitted to participate in the grand jury proceedings except to advise and consult with the child witness while the child is testifying.

Amended June 26, 1996; July 15, 1996; Dec. 12, 1997; July 18, 2003.

Comment—Rule 3

See comment following Rule 3.08.

Historical Notes

The order of the Minnesota Supreme Court [C6–84–2165] dated June 26, 1996, provides in part that "(t)hese amendments to the Rules of Juvenile Procedure shall govern all juvenile actions commenced or arrests made on or after 12:00 o'clock midnight August 1, 1996."

The order of the Minnesota Supreme Court [C6–84–2165] dated December 12, 1997, provides in part that "(t)hese amendments to the Rules of Juvenile Procedure shall govern all juvenile actions commenced or arrests made on or after 12:00 o'clock midnight January 1, 1998."

The order of the Minnesota Supreme Court [CX–01–926] dated July 18, 2003, provides in part that "(t)he attached amendments shall govern all juveniles taken into custody and all juvenile delinquency actions commenced or children taken into custody after 12 o'clock midnight September 1, 2003."

Rule 3.03. Dual Representation

A child is entitled to the effective representation of counsel. When two or more children are jointly charged or will be tried jointly pursuant to Rule 13.07, and two or more of them are represented by the same counsel, the following procedure shall be followed:

(A) The court shall address each child individually on the record. The court shall advise the child of the potential danger of dual representation and give the child the opportunity to ask the court questions about the nature and consequences of dual representation. The child shall be given the opportunity to consult with outside counsel.

(B) On the record, the court shall ask each child whether the child

(1) understands the right to be effectively represented by a lawyer;

(2) understands the details of the lawyer's possible conflict of interest;

(3) understands the possible dangers in being represented by a lawyer with these possible conflicts;

(4) discussed the issue of dual representation with a separate lawyer; and

(5) wants a separate lawyer or waives their Sixth Amendment protections.

Amended June 26, 1996; July 18, 2003.

Comment—Rule 3

See comment following Rule 3.08.

Historical Notes

The order of the Minnesota Supreme Court [C6–84–2165] dated June 26, 1996, provides in part that "(t)hese amendments to the Rules of Juvenile Procedure shall govern all juvenile actions commenced or arrests made on or after 12:00 o'clock midnight August 1, 1996."

The order of the Minnesota Supreme Court [CX–01–926] dated July 18, 2003, provides in part that "(t)he attached amendments shall govern all juveniles taken into custody and all juvenile delinquency actions commenced or children taken into custody after 12 o'clock midnight September 1, 2003."

Rule 3.04. Waiver of Right to Counsel

Subdivision 1. Conditions of Waiver. The following provision does not apply to Juvenile Petty Offenses, which are governed by Rule 17. Any waiver of counsel must be made knowingly, intelligently, and voluntarily. Any waiver shall be in writing or on the record. The child must be fully and effectively informed of the child's right to counsel and the disadvantages of self-representation by an in-person consultation with an attorney, and counsel shall appear with the child in court and inform the court that such consultation has occurred. In determining whether a child has knowingly, voluntarily, and intelligently waived the right to counsel, the court shall look to the totality of the circumstances including, but not limited to: the child's age, maturity, intelligence, education, experience, ability to comprehend, and the presence of the child's parents, legal guardian, legal custodian or guardian ad litem appointed in the delinquency proceeding. The court shall inquire to determine if the child has met privately with the attorney, and if the child understands the charges and proceedings, including the possible disposition, any collateral consequences, and any additional facts essential to a broad understanding of the case.

Subd. 2. Competency Proceedings. Any child subject to competency proceedings pursuant to Rule 20 shall not be permitted to waive counsel.

Subd. 3. Court Approval/Disapproval. If the court accepts the child's waiver, it shall state on the record the findings and conclusions that form the basis for its decision and shall appoint standby counsel as required by Rule 3.02.

Amended June 26, 1996; Dec. 12, 1997; July 18, 2003; Oct. 13, 2006, eff. Jan. 1, 2007.

Comment—Rule 3

See comment following Rule 3.08.

Historical Notes

The order of the Minnesota Supreme Court [C6–84–2165] dated June 26, 1996, provides in part that "(t)hese amendments to the Rules of Juvenile Procedure shall govern all juvenile actions commenced or arrests made on or after 12:00 o'clock midnight August 1, 1996."

The order of the Minnesota Supreme Court [C6–84–2165] dated December 12, 1997, provides in part that "(t)hese amendments to the Rules of Juvenile Procedure shall govern all juvenile actions commenced or arrests made on or after 12:00 o'clock midnight January 1, 1998."

The order of the Minnesota Supreme Court [CX–01–926] dated July 18, 2003, provides in part that "(t)he attached amendments shall govern all juveniles taken into custody and all juvenile delinquency actions commenced or children taken into custody after 12 o'clock midnight September 1, 2003."

Rule 3.05. Renewal of Advisory

After a child waives the right to counsel, the child shall be advised of the right to counsel by the court on the record at the beginning of each hearing at which the child is not represented by counsel.

Adopted June 26, 1996. Amended July 18, 2003.

Comment—Rule 3

See comment following Rule 3.08.

Historical Notes

The order of the Minnesota Supreme Court [C6–84–2165] dated June 26, 1996, provides in part that "(t)hese amendments to the Rules of Juvenile Procedure shall govern all juvenile actions commenced or arrests made on or after 12:00 o'clock midnight August 1, 1996."

The order of the Minnesota Supreme Court [CX–01–926] dated July 18, 2003, provides in part that "(t)he attached amendments shall govern all juveniles taken into custody and all juvenile delinquency actions commenced or children taken into custody after 12 o'clock midnight September 1, 2003."

Rule 3.06. Eligibility for Court Appointed Counsel at Public Expense

Subd. 1. When Parent or Child Cannot Afford to Retain Counsel. A child and his parent(s) are financially unable to obtain counsel if the child is unable to obtain adequate representation without substantial hardship for the child or the child's family. The court shall inquire to determine the financial eligibility of a child for the appointment of counsel. The ability to pay part of the cost of adequate representation shall not preclude the appointment of counsel for the child.

Subd. 2. When Parent Can Afford to Retain Counsel. If the parent(s) of a child can afford to retain counsel in whole or in part and have not retained counsel for the child, and the child cannot afford to retain counsel, the child is entitled to representation by counsel appointed by the court at public expense. After giving the parent(s) a reasonable opportunity to be heard, the court may order that service of counsel shall be at the parent(s)'s expense in whole or in part depending upon their ability to pay.

Adopted June 26, 1996.

Comment—Rule 3

See comment following Rule 3.08.

Historical Notes

The order of the Minnesota Supreme Court [C6–84–2165] dated June 26, 1996, provides in part that "(t)hese amendments to the Rules of Juvenile Procedure shall govern all juvenile actions commenced or arrests made on or after 12:00 o'clock midnight August 1, 1996."

Rule 3.07. Right of Parent(s), Legal Guardian(s), Legal Custodian(s) and Guardian ad Litem to Counsel

Subdivision 1. Right of Parent(s), Legal Guardian(s) or Legal Custodian(s). The parent(s), legal guardian(s) or legal custodian(s) of a child who is the subject of a delinquency proceeding have the right to assistance of counsel after the court has found that the allegations of the charging document have been proved. The court has discretion to appoint an attorney to represent the parent(s), legal guardian(s) or legal custodian(s) at public expense if they are financially unable to obtain counsel in any other case in which the court finds such appointment is desirable.

Subd. 2. Right of Guardian Ad Litem to Counsel. In the event of a conflict between the child and the guardian ad litem, the court may appoint separate counsel to represent the guardian ad litem appointed in the delinquency proceeding.

Adopted June 26, 1996. Amended July 18, 2003; Sept. 30, 2004, eff. Jan. 1, 2005; July 11, 2005, eff. Sept. 1, 2005.

Comment—Rule 3

See comment following Rule 3.08.

Historical Notes

The order of the Minnesota Supreme Court [C6–84–2165] dated June 26, 1996, provides in part that "(t)hese amendments to the Rules of Juvenile Procedure shall govern all juvenile actions commenced or arrests made on or after 12:00 o'clock midnight August 1, 1996."

The order of the Minnesota Supreme Court [C6-84-2165] dated December 12, 1997, amending the Rules of Juvenile Procedure provides in part that "(t)he inclusion of Advisory Committee comments is made for convenience and does not reflect court approval of the comments made therein."

The order of the Minnesota Supreme Court [CX–01–926] dated July 18, 2003, provides in part that "(t)he attached amendments shall govern all juveniles taken into custody and all juvenile delinquency actions commenced or children taken into custody after 12 o'clock midnight September 1, 2003."

Rule 3.08. Certificates of Representation

A lawyer representing a client in juvenile court, other than a public defender, shall file with the court administrator on the first appearance a certificate of representation.

Once a lawyer has filed a certificate of representation, that lawyer cannot withdraw from the case until all proceedings have been completed, except upon written order of the court pursuant to a written motion, or upon written substitution of counsel approved by the court ex parte.

A lawyer who wishes to withdraw from a case must file a written motion and serve it by mail or personal service upon the client and upon the prosecuting attorney; and the lawyer shall have the matter heard by the court. No motion of withdrawal will be heard within 10 days of a date certain for hearing or trial.

If the court approves the withdrawal, it shall be effective when the order has been served on the client and the prosecuting attorney by mail or personal service and due proof of such service has been filed with the court administrator.

Service on the prosecuting attorney under this rule may also be made by electronic means if authorized by Minnesota Supreme Court Order and if service is made in accordance with that order.

Adopted Dec. 12, 1997. Amended Oct. 15, 2012, eff. Dec. 1, 2012.

Comment—Rule 3

Minn. R. Juv. Del. P. 3 prescribes the general requirements for appointment of counsel for a juvenile. *In re Gault,* 387 U.S. 1 (1967); Minnesota Statutes, section 260B.163, subd. 4 (2002). The right to counsel at public expense does not necessarily include the right to representation by a public defender. The right to representation by a public defender is governed by Minnesota Statutes, chapter 611.

Minn. R. Juv. Del. P. 3.01 provides that the right to counsel attaches no later than the child's first appearance in juvenile court. See Minnesota Statutes, section 611.262 (2002). Whether counsel is appointed by the court or retained by the child or the child's parents, the attorney must act solely as counsel for the child. American Bar Association, Juvenile Justice Standards Relating to Counsel for Private Parties (1980). While it is certainly appropriate for an attorney representing a child to consult with the parents whose custodial interest in the child potentially may be affected by court intervention, it is essential that counsel conduct an initial interview with the child privately and outside of the presence of the parents. Following the initial private consultation, if the child affirmatively wants his or her parent(s) to be present, they may be present. The attorney may then consult with such other persons as the attorney deems necessary or appropriate. However, the child retains a right to consult privately with the attorney at any time, and either the child or the attorney may excuse the parents in order to speak privately and confidentially.

Minn. R. Juv. Del. P. 3.02 provides for the appointment of counsel for juveniles in delinquency proceedings. A parent may not represent a child unless he or she is an attorney. In *Gideon v. Wainwright,* 372 U.S. 335 (1963), the U.S. Supreme Court held that the Sixth Amendment's guarantee of counsel applied to state felony criminal proceedings. In In re Gault, the Supreme Court extended to juveniles the constitutional right to counsel in state delinquency proceedings. Minnesota Statutes, section 260B.163, subd. 4 (2002) expands the right to counsel and requires that an attorney shall be appointed in any proceeding in which a child is charged with a felony or gross misdemeanor.

If a child in a felony or gross misdemeanor case exercises the right to proceed without counsel, *Faretta v. California,* 422 U.S. 806 (1975), *State v. Richards,* 456 N.W.2d 260 (Minn. 1990), then Minn. R. Juv. Del. P. 3.02, subd. 1 requires the court to appoint standby counsel to assist and consult with the child at all stages of the proceedings. See, e.g., *McKaskle v. Wiggins,* 465 U.S. 168 (1984); *State v. Jones,* 266 N.W.2d 706 (Minn. 1978); *Burt v. State,* 256 N.W.2d 633 (Minn. 1977); *State v. Graff,* 510 N.W.2d 212 (Minn. Ct. App. 1993) pet. for rev. denied (Minn. Feb. 24, 1994); *State v. Savior,* 480 N.W.2d 693 (Minn. Ct. App. 1992); *State v. Parson,* 457 N.W.2d 261 (Minn. Ct. App. 1990) pet. for rev. denied (Minn. July 31, 1990); *State v. Lande,* 376 N.W. 2d 483 (Minn. Ct. App. 1985) pet. for rev. denied (Minn. Jan. 17, 1986).

In *McKaskle v. Wiggins,* the Supreme Court concluded that appointment of standby counsel was consistent with a defendant's Faretta right to proceed pro se, so long as standby counsel did not stifle the defendant's ability to preserve actual control over the case and to maintain the appearance of pro se representation. The child must have an opportunity to consult with standby counsel during every stage of the proceedings. *State v. Richards,* 495 N.W.2d 187 (Minn.1992). In order to vindicate this right, counsel must be physically present. "[I]t would be virtually impossible for a standby counsel to provide assistance, much less effective assistance, to a criminal client when that counsel has not been physically present during the taking of the testimony and all of the court proceedings that preceded the request ... [O]nce the trial court ... appoint[s] standby counsel, that standby counsel must be physically present in the courtroom from the time of appointment through all proceedings until the proceedings conclude." *Parson,* 457 N.W.2d at 263. Where the child proceeds pro se, it is the preferred practice for counsel to remain at the back of the courtroom and be available for consultation. *Savior,* 480 N.W.2d at 694–95; *Parson,* 457 N.W.2d at 263; *Lande,* 376 N.W.2d at 485. Moreover, standby counsel must be present at all bench and chambers conferences, even where the child is excluded. *State v. Richards,* 495 N.W.2d 187, 196 (Minn.1992).

Minn. R. Juv. Del. P. 3.02, subd. 2 requires a court to appoint counsel for a child charged with a misdemeanor unless that child affirmatively waives counsel as provided in Minn. R. Juv. Del. P. 3.04. Minn. R. Juv. Del. P. 3.02, subd. 3 requires the appointment of counsel or standby counsel in any proceeding in which out-of-home placement is proposed, and further limits those cases in which a child may waive the assistance of counsel without the appointment of standby counsel. In *Argersinger v. Hamlin,* 407 U.S. 25, 37 (1972), the Court held that "absent a knowing and intelligent waiver, no person may be imprisoned for any offense, whether classified as petty, misdemeanor or felony unless he was represented by counsel." In *Scott v. Illinois,* 440 U.S. 367 (1979), the Court clarified any ambiguity when it held that in misdemeanor proceedings, the sentence the trial judge actually imposed, i.e. whether incarceration was ordered, rather than the one authorized by the statute, determined whether counsel must be appointed for the indigent.

In *State v. Borst,* 278 Minn. 388, 154 N.W.2d 888 (1967), the Minnesota Supreme Court, using its inherent supervisory powers, anticipated the United States Supreme Court's *Argersinger* and *Scott* decisions, and shortly after *Gideon* required the appointment of counsel even in misdemeanor cases "which may lead to incarceration in a penal institution." *Id.* at 397, 154 N.W.2d at 894. *Accord City of St. Paul v. Whidby,* 295 Minn. 129, 203 N.W.2d 823 (1972); *State v. Collins,* 278 Minn. 437, 154 N.W.2d 688 (1967); *State v. Illingworth,* 278 Minn. 484, 154 N.W.2d 687 (1967) (ordinance violation). The *Borst* Court relied, in part, upon *Gault's* ruling on the need for counsel in delinquency cases to expand the scope of the right to counsel for adult defendants in any misdemeanor or ordinance prosecutions that could result in confinement. 278 Minn. at 392–93, 154 N.W.2d at 891. Like the Court in *Gault, Borst* recognized the adversarial reality of even "minor" prosecutions.

At the very least, Minn. R. Juv. Del. P. 3.02, subd. 3 places the prosecution and court on notice that out-of-home placement may not occur unless counsel or standby counsel is appointed. For example, a child appearing on a third alcohol offense faces a dispositional possibility of out-of-home placement, but cannot be placed out of the home if the child is not represented by counsel unless the child is given the opportunity to withdraw the plea or obtain a new trial. See Minn. R. Juv. Del. P. 17.02. The prosecutor should indicate, either on the petition or through a statement on the record, whether out-of-home placement will be proposed. Obviously, basing the initial decision to appoint counsel on the eventual sentence poses severe practical and administrative problems. It may be very difficult for a judge to anticipate what the eventual sentence likely would be without prejudging the child or prejudicing the right to a fair and impartial trial. Minn. R. Juv. Del. P. 3.02, subd. 3 also provides that a child retains an absolute right to withdraw any plea obtained without the assistance of counsel or to obtain a new trial if adjudicated without the assistance of counsel, if that adjudication provides the underlying predicate for an out-of-home placement.

See, e.g., *In re D.S.S.*, 506 N.W.2d 650, 655 (Minn. Ct. App. 1993) ("The cumulative history of uncounseled admissions resulting after an inadequate advisory of the right to counsel constitutes a manifest injustice"). Appointing counsel solely at disposition is inadequate to assure the validity of the underlying offenses on which such placement is based. Of course, routine appointment of counsel in all cases would readily avoid any such dilemma.

Minnesota Statutes, section 260B.007, subd. 16 defines "juvenile petty offenses," and converts most offenses that would be misdemeanors if committed by an adult into petty offenses. Minn. R. Juv. Del. P. 3.02, subd. 5 and 17.02 explain when a juvenile petty offender is entitled to court-appointed counsel. If a child is charged as a juvenile petty offender, the child or the child's parents may retain and be represented by private counsel, but the child does not have a right to the appointment of a public defender or other counsel at public expense. The denial of access to court-appointed counsel is based on the limited dispositions that the juvenile court may impose on juvenile petty offenders. Minnesota Statutes, section 260B.235, subd. 4 (2002). However, children who are charged with a third or subsequent juvenile alcohol or controlled substance offense are subject to out-of-home placement and therefore have a right to court-appointed counsel, despite their status as juvenile petty offenders. If the court is authorized to impose a disposition that includes out-of-home placement, then the provisions of Minn. R. Juv. Del. P. 3.02, subd. 5 and 17.02 are applicable and provide the child a right to counsel at public expense.

Minn. R. Juv. Del. P. 3.02, subd. 6 is an exception to the prohibition of appointment of counsel at public expense for a juvenile traffic or juvenile petty offender. If such a child is detained, at any hearing to determine if continued detention is necessary, the child is entitled to court-appointed counsel if unrepresented because substantial liberty rights are at issue.

Minn. R. Juv. Del. P. 3.02, subd. 7 is an exception to the prohibition of appointment of counsel at public expense for a juvenile traffic or juvenile petty offender. As soon as any child is alleged to be incompetent to proceed, that child has a right to be represented by an attorney at public expense for the proceeding to determine whether the child is competent to proceed. Substantial liberty rights are at issue in a competency proceeding. A finding of incompetency is a basis for a Child in Need of Protection or Services adjudication and possible out-of-home placement. Minnesota Statutes, sections 260C.007, subd. 6(15) and 260C.201 (2002). See also Minn. R. Juv. Del. P. 20.01. Because out-of-home placement is a possibility, the child is entitled to court-appointed counsel.

Minn. R. Juv. Del. P. 3.03 regarding advising children of the perils of dual representation is patterned after Minn. R. Crim. P. 17.03, subd. 5.

Minn. R. Juv. Del. P. 3.04 prescribes the circumstances under which a child charged with an offense may waive counsel. The validity of relinquishing a constitutional right is determined by assessing whether there was a "knowing, intelligent, and voluntary waiver" under the " totality of the circumstances." See, e.g., *Fare v. Michael C.*, 442 U.S. 707 (1979); *Johnson v. Zerbst*, 304 U.S. 458 (1938) (waiver of counsel); *In re M.D.S.*, 345 N.W.2d 723 (Minn. 1984); *State v. Nunn*, 297 N.W.2d 752 (Minn. 1980); *In re L.R.B.*, 373 N.W.2d 334 (Minn. Ct. App. 1985). The judicial position that a young minor can "knowingly and intelligently" waive constitutional rights is consistent with the legislature's judgment that a youth can make an informed waiver decision without parental concurrence or consultation with an attorney. Minnesota Statutes, section 260B.163, subd. 10 (2002) ("Waiver of any right ... must be an express waiver intelligently made by the child after the child has been fully and effectively informed of the right being waived").

While recognizing a right to waive counsel and proceed pro se, Minn. R. Juv. Del. P. 3.02 requires juvenile courts to appoint standby counsel to assist a child charged with a felony or gross misdemeanor, or where out-of-home placement is proposed, and to provide temporary counsel to consult with a child prior to any waiver in other types of cases. See, e.g., *State v. Rubin*, 409 N.W.2d 504, 506 (Minn. 1987) ("[A] trial court may not accept a guilty plea to a felony or gross misdemeanor charge made by an unrepresented defendant if the defendant has not consulted with counsel about waiving counsel and pleading guilty"); Jones, 266 N.W.2d 706 (standby counsel available to and did consult with defendant throughout proceedings and participated occasionally on defendant's behalf); *Burt*, 256 N.W.2d at 635 ("One way for a trial court to help ensure that a defendant's waiver of counsel is knowing and intelligent would be to provide a lawyer to consult with the defendant concerning his proposed waiver").

In *State v. Rubin*, the court described the type of "penetrating and comprehensive examination" that must precede a "knowing and intelligent" waiver and strongly recommended the appointment of counsel "to advise and consult with the defendant as to the waiver." See also ABA Standards of Criminal Justice, Providing Defense Services, sections 5–7.3 (1980); Minn. R. Crim. P. 5.04. Minn. R. Juv. Del. P. 3.04, subd. 1 prescribes the type of "penetrating and comprehensive examination" expected prior to finding a valid waiver. Prior to an initial waiver of counsel, a child must consult privately with an attorney who will describe the scope of the right to counsel and the disadvantages of self-representation. Following consultation with counsel, any waiver must be in writing and on the record, and counsel shall appear with the child to assure the court that private consultation and full discussion has occurred.

To determine whether a child "knowingly, intelligently, and voluntarily" waived the right to counsel, Minn. R. Juv. Del. P. 3.04, subd. 1 requires the court to look at the "totality of the circumstances," which includes but is not limited to the child's age, maturity, intelligence, education, experience, and ability to comprehend and the presence and competence of the child's parent(s), legal guardian or legal custodian. In addition, the court shall decide whether the child understands the nature of the charges and the proceedings, the potential disposition that may be imposed, and that admissions or findings of delinquency may be valid even without the presence of counsel and may result in more severe sentences if the child re-offends and appears again in juvenile court or in criminal court. *United States v. Nichols*, 511 U.S. 738 (1994); *United States v. Johnson*, 28 F.3d 151 (D.C. Cir. 1994) (use of prior juvenile convictions to enhance adult sentence). The court shall make findings and conclusions on the record as to why it accepts the child's waiver or appoints standby counsel to assist a juvenile who purports to waive counsel.

Even though a child initially may waive counsel, the child continues to have the right to counsel at all further stages of the proceeding. Minn. R. Juv. Del. P. 3.05 requires that at each subsequent court appearance at which a child appears without counsel, the court shall again determine on the record whether or not the child desires to exercise the right to counsel.

Minn. R. Juv. Del. P. 3.06 prescribes the standard to be applied by the court in determining whether a child or the child's family is sufficiently indigent to require appointment of counsel. The standards and methods for determining eligibility are the same as those used in the Minn. R. Crim. P. 5.04, subds. 3–5.

Minn. R. Juv. Del. P. 3.06, subd. 2 provides that if the parent(s) of a child can afford to retain counsel but have not done so and the child cannot otherwise afford to retain counsel, then the court shall appoint counsel for the child. When parents can afford to retain counsel but do not do so and counsel is appointed for the child at public expense, in the exercise of its sound discretion, the court may order reimbursement for the expenses and attorney's fees expended on behalf of the child. Minnesota Statutes, section 260B.331, subd. 5 (2002) ("[T]he court may inquire into the ability of the parents to pay for such counsel's services and, after giving the parents a reasonable opportunity to be heard, may order the parents to pay attorneys fees"). See, e.g., *In re M.S.M.*, 387 N.W.2d 194, 200 (Minn. Ct. App. 1986).

Minn. R. Juv. Del. P. 3.07 implements the rights of a child's parent(s), legal guardian or legal custodian to participate in hearings affecting the child. After a child has been found to be delinquent and state intervention potentially may intrude upon the parent's custodial interests in the child, the parent(s) have an independent right to the assistance of counsel appointed at public expense if they are eligible for such services.

Historical Notes

The order of the Minnesota Supreme Court [C6–84–2165] dated December 12, 1997, provides in part that "(t)hese amendments to the Rules of Juvenile Procedure shall govern all juvenile actions commenced or arrests made on or after 12:00 o'clock midnight January 1, 1998."

The order of the Minnesota Supreme Court [ADM10–8003] dated October 15, 2012, provides in part that the "amendments shall govern all delinquency actions pending or commenced on or after 12 o'clock midnight December 1, 2012."

RULE 4. WARRANTS

Rule 4.01. Search Warrants Upon Oral Testimony

Issuance of search warrants based on oral testimony is governed by Minnesota Rules of Criminal Procedure 33.04 and 36, except as modified by this Rule. If the focus of the warrant pertains to a juvenile, the court may designate on the face of the warrant that it shall be filed in the juvenile court. When so designated, the original warrant, the duplicate original warrant, the certified transcript of the oral application for the warrant, any longhand verbatim record, and any related documents shall be deemed to be a juvenile court record under Rule 30.

Amended June 26, 1996; Dec. 12, 1997; July 18, 2003; Nov. 19, 2010, eff. Jan. 1, 2011.

Comment—Rule 4

See comment following Rule 4.03.

Historical Notes

The order of the Minnesota Supreme Court [C6–84–2165] dated June 26, 1996, provides in part that "(t)hese amendments to the Rules of Juvenile Procedure shall govern all juvenile actions commenced or arrests made on or after 12:00 o'clock midnight August 1, 1996."

The order of the Minnesota Supreme Court [C6–84–2165] dated December 12, 1997, provides in part that "(t)hese amendments to the Rules of Juvenile Procedure shall govern all juvenile actions commenced or arrests made on or after 12:00 o'clock midnight January 1, 1998."

The order of the Minnesota Supreme Court [CX–01–926] dated July 18, 2003, provides in part that "(t)he attached amendments shall govern all juveniles taken into custody and all juvenile delinquency actions commenced or children taken into custody after 12 o'clock midnight September 1, 2003."

Rule 4.02. Search Warrants Upon Written Application

Issuance of search warrants based upon written application is governed by Minnesota Statutes, sections 626.04 through 626.18 and Minnesota Rules of Criminal Procedure 33.04, except as modified by this Rule. If the focus of the warrant pertains to a juvenile, the court may designate on the face of the warrant that it shall be filed in the juvenile court. When so designated, the search warrant, warrant application, affidavit(s) and inventories, including statements of unsuccessful execution and documents required to be served shall be deemed to be a juvenile court record under Rule 30.

Amended June 26, 1996; July 18, 2003.

Comment—Rule 4

See comment following Rule 4.03.

Historical Notes

The order of the Minnesota Supreme Court [C6–84–2165] dated June 26, 1996, provides in part that "(t)hese amendments to the Rules of Juvenile Procedure shall govern all juvenile actions commenced or arrests made on or after 12:00 o'clock midnight August 1, 1996."

The order of the Minnesota Supreme Court [CX–01–926] dated July 18, 2003, provides in part that "(t)he attached amendments shall govern all juveniles taken into custody and all juvenile delinquency actions commenced or children taken into custody after 12 o'clock midnight September 1, 2003."

Rule 4.03. Warrants for Immediate Custody

Subd. 1. Probable Cause Required. Probable cause may be established by facts set forth in writing attached to the charging document, by facts set forth in the charging document, by affidavit(s) attached to the charging document, or by sworn testimony presented to the court on the record.

Subd. 2. Warrant for Delinquent Offenders. The court may issue a warrant for immediate custody of a delinquent child or a child alleged to be delinquent if the court finds that there is probable cause to believe that the child has committed a delinquent act as defined by Minnesota Statutes, section 260B.007, subdivision 6, and:

(A) the child failed to appear after having been personally served with a summons or subpoena, or reasonable efforts to personally serve the child have failed, or there is a substantial likelihood that the child will fail to respond to a summons; or

(B) the child or others are in danger of imminent harm; or

(C) the child has left the custody of the detaining authority without permission of the court; or

(D) the child has violated a court order; or

(E) the child has violated the terms of probation.

Subd. 3. Warrant for Juvenile Petty or Traffic Offenders. The court may only issue a warrant for immediate custody of a juvenile petty or juvenile traffic offender or a child alleged to be a juvenile petty or juvenile traffic offender if the court finds that there is probable cause to believe that:

(A) the child has committed a juvenile petty offense as defined by Minnesota Statutes, section 260B.007, subdivision 16 or a juvenile traffic offense as defined by Minnesota Statutes, section 260B.225; and

(B) the child failed to appear after having been personally served with a summons or subpoena, reasonable efforts to personally serve the child have failed, or there is a substantial likelihood that the child will fail to respond to a summons.

Subd. 4. Contents of Warrant for Immediate Custody. A warrant for immediate custody shall be signed by a judge and shall:

(A) order the child to be brought immediately before the court or the child to be taken to a detention facility in accordance with Rule 5.02, subdivisions 3 and 4, to be detained pending a detention hearing or the child to be transferred to an individual or agency, including but not limited to any welfare agency or hospital as the welfare of the child might require;

(B) state the name and address of the child, or if unknown, designate the child by any name or description by which the child can be identified with reasonable certainty;

(C) state the age and sex of the child, or, if the age of the child is unknown, that the child is believed to be of an age subject to the jurisdiction of the court;

(D) state the reasons why the child is being taken into custody;

(E) where applicable, state the reasons for a limitation on the time or location of the execution of the warrant; and

(F) state the date when issued, and the county and court where issued.

Subd. 5. Who May Execute. The warrant for immediate custody may only be executed by a peace officer authorized by law to execute a warrant.

Subd. 6. How Executed. The warrant for immediate custody shall be executed by taking the child into custody.

Subd. 7. Where Executed. The warrant for immediate custody may be executed at any place in the state except where prohibited by law, unless the judge who issues the warrant limits in writing on the warrant the location where the warrant may be executed.

Subd. 8. When Executed. A warrant may be executed at any time unless the judge who issues the warrant limits in writing on the warrant the time during which the warrant may be executed. If the offense is a misdemeanor, petty offense or juvenile traffic offense, the child may not be taken into custody on Sunday or between the hours of 10:00 p.m. and 8:00 a.m. on any other day except by direction of the judge.

Subd. 9. Possession of Warrant. A warrant for immediate custody need not be in the peace officer's possession at the time the child is taken into custody.

Subd. 10. Advisory. When a warrant is executed, the child and the child's parent(s), legal guardian or legal custodian, if present, shall immediately be informed of the existence of the warrant for immediate custody and as soon as possible of the reasons why the child is being taken into custody.

Adopted July 18, 2003. Amended Oct. 11, 2007, eff. Jan. 1, 2008.

Comment—Rule 4

If the child fails to appear in response to a summons without reasonable cause, then the court may issue a warrant to take the child into immediate custody pursuant to Minn. R. Juv. Del. P. 4.03, subd. 2. See Minnesota Statutes, section 260B.154 (2002). Probable cause is required for every warrant issued. Before the court may issue a warrant, it shall make a finding of probable cause based on the contents of the charging document, any supporting affidavits or sworn supplemental testimony to believe that the child committed an act governed by Minnesota Statutes, section 260B.007, subds. 6 or 16, or Minnesota Statutes, section 260B.225. In addition, the court must also find either that the summons was personally served on the child and the child failed to appear, that service will be ineffectual, or, for a delinquent child or child alleged to be delinquent, that there is a substantial likelihood that the child will not respond to a summons, or that the child or others are in danger of imminent harm. Minnesota Statutes, section 260B.154 (2002).

Minn. R. Juv. Del. P. 4.03, subd. 4 prescribes the contents of the warrant. When a child is taken into custody, a detention hearing shall commence pursuant to Minn. R. Juv. Del. P. 5.07 within thirty-six (36) hours, excluding Saturdays, Sundays, and holidays, or within twenty-four hours, excluding Saturdays, Sundays, and holidays, if the child is detained in an adult jail or municipal lockup.

Under Minn. R. Juv. Del. P. 4.03, subd. 5, a warrant may be executed only by a peace officer. Limitations on the manner of execution are the same as those set out in Minn. R. Crim. P. 3.03, subd. 3 for adults where the offense charged is a misdemeanor or non-criminal offense. The minor nature of misdemeanors, juvenile petty and juvenile traffic offenses should not ordinarily justify taking a child into immediate custody during the proscribed period of time.

Historical Notes

The order of the Minnesota Supreme Court [CX–01–926] dated July 18, 2003, provides in part that "(t)he attached amendments shall govern all juveniles taken into custody and all juvenile delinquency actions commenced or children taken into custody after 12 o'clock midnight September 1, 2003."

Rules 4.04 to 4.06. Deleted June 26, 1996

Historical Notes

The order of the Minnesota Supreme Court [C6–84–2165] dated June 26, 1996, provides in part that "(t)hese amendments to the Rules of Juvenile Procedure shall govern all juvenile actions commenced or arrests made on or after 12:00 o'clock midnight August 1, 1996."

Deleted Rule 4.04 related to a renewal of the advisory right to counsel. See, now, Rule 3.05.

Deleted Rule 4.05 related to the eligibility for court appointed counsel at public expense. See, now, Rule 3.06.

Deleted Rule 4.06 related to the right of the parent(s), guardian(s), and guardian ad litem to counsel. See, now, Rule 3.07.

RULE 5. DETENTION

Rule 5.01. Scope and General Principles

Rule 5 governs all physical liberty restrictions placed upon a child before trial, disposition, or pending a probation violation hearing. For purposes of this Rule, the day of the act or event from which the designated period of time begins to run shall be included.

Amended June 26, 1996; July 18, 2003.

Comment—Rule 5

See comment following Rule 5.08.

Historical Notes

The order of the Minnesota Supreme Court [C6–84–2165] dated June 26, 1996, provides in part that "(t)hese amendments to the Rules of Juvenile Procedure shall govern all juvenile actions commenced or arrests made on or after 12:00 o'clock midnight August 1, 1996."

The order of the Minnesota Supreme Court [CX–01–926] dated July 18, 2003, provides in part that "(t)he attached amendments shall govern all juveniles taken into custody and all juvenile delinquency actions commenced or children taken into custody after 12 o'clock midnight September 1, 2003."

Rule 5.02. Definitions

Subd. 1. Detention. Detention includes all liberty restrictions that substantially affect a child's physical freedom or living arrangements before trial, disposition or pending a probation violation hearing. A child's physical liberty is restricted when:

(A) the child is taken into custody;

(B) the court orders detention of the child;

(C) the court orders out-of-home placement; or

(D) the court orders electronic home monitoring or house arrest with substantial liberty restrictions.

Subd. 2. Detaining Authority. The detaining officer, the detaining officer's supervisor, the person in charge of the detention facility, the prosecuting attorney or the court is a detaining authority for the purposes of this rule.

Subd. 3. Place of Detention for Juvenile Delinquent Offenders. A place of detention for a juvenile delinquent offender can be any one of the following places:

(A) the child's home subject to electronic home monitoring or house arrest with substantial liberty restrictions;

(B) a foster care or shelter care facility;

(C) a secure detention facility;

(D) a detoxification, chemical dependency, or psychiatric facility;

(E) an adult jail; or

(F) any other place of detention.

Subd. 4. Place of Detention for Juvenile Petty or Traffic Offenders. A place of detention for a juvenile petty or traffic offender can be any one of the following places:

(A) a child's relative;

(B) a designated caregiver under Minnesota Statutes, chapter 257A; or

(C) a shelter care facility.

Amended June 26, 1996; July 18, 2003; Oct. 11, 2007, eff. Jan. 1, 2008.

Comment—Rule 5

See comment following Rule 5.08.

Historical Notes

The order of the Minnesota Supreme Court [C6–84–2165] dated June 26, 1996, provides in part that "(t)hese amendments to the Rules of Juvenile Procedure shall govern all juvenile actions commenced or arrests made on or after 12:00 o'clock midnight August 1, 1996."

The order of the Minnesota Supreme Court [CX–01–926] dated July 18, 2003, provides in part that "(t)he attached amendments shall govern all juveniles taken into custody and all juvenile delinquency actions commenced or children taken into custody after 12 o'clock midnight September 1, 2003."

Rule 5.03. Detention Decision

Subd. 1. Presumption for Unconditional Release. The child shall be released unless:

(A) the child would endanger self or others; or

(B) the child would not appear for a court hearing; or

(C) the child would not remain in the care or control of the person into whose lawful custody the child is released; or

(D) the child's health or welfare would be immediately endangered.

There is a presumption that a child will not appear for a court hearing when the person to whom the child is to be released refuses to sign a written promise to bring the child to court.

Subd. 2. Detention Factors. The following non-exclusive factors may justify a decision to detain a child:

(A) the child is charged with the misdemeanor, gross misdemeanor or felony offense of arson, assault, prostitution or a criminal sexual offense;

(B) the child was taken into custody for an offense which would be a presumptive commitment to prison offense if committed by an adult, or a felony involving the use of a firearm;

(C) the child was taken into custody for additional felony charges while other delinquency charges are pending;

(D) the child was taken into custody for a felony and, as a result of prior delinquency adjudication(s), has received an out-of-home placement;

(E) the child was an escapee from an institution or other placement facility to which the court ordered the child;

(F) the child has a demonstrable recent record of willful failure to appear at juvenile proceedings;

(G) the child is a fugitive from another jurisdiction; or

(H) the above factors are not met but the detaining authority documents in writing, objective and articulable reasons why the child's welfare or public safety would be immediately endangered if the child were released.

Subd. 3. Discretion to Release Even if One or More Factors are Met. Even if a child meets one or more of the factors in Rule 5.03, subdivisions 1 and 2, the detaining authority has broad discretion to release that child before the detention hearing if other less restrictive measures would be adequate.

Subd. 4. Factors Which Can Not Support Detention Decision. In deciding whether detention is justified, the detaining authority shall not consider the child or the child's family's race, color, gender, sexual orientation, religion, national origin, economic or public assistance status, family structure or residential mobility.

Amended June 26, 1996; July 18, 2003.

Comment—Rule 5

See comment following Rule 5.08.

Historical Notes

The order of the Minnesota Supreme Court [C6–84–2165] dated June 26, 1996, provides in part that "(t)hese amendments to the Rules of Juvenile Procedure shall govern all juvenile actions commenced or arrests made on or after 12:00 o'clock midnight August 1, 1996."

The order of the Minnesota Supreme Court [CX–01–926] dated July 18, 2003, provides in part that "(t)he attached amendments shall govern all juveniles taken into custody and all juvenile delinquency actions commenced or children taken into custody after 12 o'clock midnight September 1, 2003."

Rule 5.04. Release or Continued Detention

Subd. 1. For Child Taken Into Custody Pursuant to Court Order or Warrant.

(A) *Detention Required.* Unless the court orders an earlier release, the child may be detained for thirty-six (36) hours after being taken into custody, excluding Saturdays, Sundays and holidays.

(B) *When Release is Mandatory.* Unless the time for the detention hearing is extended by twenty-four (24) hours pursuant to Rule 5.07, subdivision 7, the child shall be released no later than thirty-six (36) hours after being taken into custody, excluding Saturdays, Sundays and holidays, unless the court orders continued detention following a detention hearing commenced within that time period.

Subd. 2. For Child Taken Into Custody Without a Court Order or Warrant.

(A) *Exception Permitting Detention.* The officer taking a child into custody without a court order or warrant shall release the child unless the officer reasonably believes, after consideration of the factors set out in Rule 5.03, that:

(1) the child would endanger self or others;

(2) the child would not appear for a court hearing;

(3) the child would not remain in the care or control of the person into whose lawful custody the child is released; or

(4) the child's health or welfare would be immediately endangered.

There is a presumption that a child will not appear for a court hearing when the person to whom the child is to be released refuses to sign a written promise to bring the child to court.

(B) *Discretionary Release Any Time Before Detention Hearing.* The detaining authority has discretion to release a child any time before the detention hearing if other less restrictive measures would be adequate.

(C) *When Release is Mandatory.* Unless the time for the detention hearing is extended by twenty-four (24) hours pursuant to Rule 5.07,.subdivision 7, the child shall be released no later than thirty-six (36) hours after being taken into custody, excluding Saturdays, Sundays and holidays, unless the court orders continued detention following a detention hearing commenced within that time period.

Subd. 3. Child Taken Into Custody and Placed in an Adult Jail or Municipal Lockup.

(A) *Generally.* The child shall be released no later than twenty-four (24) hours after being taken into custody, excluding Saturdays, Sundays and legal holidays, unless within that time period, a charging document has been filed with the court and the court has determined at a detention hearing that the child shall remain detained. If the court's decision at the detention hearing is that the child shall remain detained, the child shall be detained at a juvenile facility in accordance with Rule 5.02, subdivision 3. The court may extend the time for a detention hearing for good cause pursuant to Rule 5.07, subdivision 7 only if a charging document has been filed with the court within twenty-four (24) hours of the child being taken into custody, excluding Saturdays, Sundays and legal holidays.

(B) *Adult Jail or Municipal Lockup in a Standard Metropolitan Statistical Area.* If the jail or municipal lockup is in a standard metropolitan statistical area, the child shall be held no longer than six (6) hours after the child was taken into custody including Saturdays, Sundays and holidays unless a charging document has been filed with the court within that time period and the court has determined after a detention hearing that the child shall remain detained. If the court's decision at the detention hearing is that the child shall remain detained, the child shall be detained at a juvenile facility in accordance with Rule 5.02, subdivision 3. The time for a detention hearing shall not be extended.

Subd. 4. Probable Cause Determination.

(A) *Time Limit.* The child shall be released no later than forty-eight (48) hours after being taken into custody without a court order or warrant signed by a judge, including the day the child was detained, Saturdays, Sundays and legal holidays, unless the court determines there is probable cause to believe the child committed the offense(s) alleged.

(B) *Application and Record.* The facts establishing probable cause to believe the offense(s) was committed and that the child committed the offense(s) shall be presented to the judge upon oath, either orally or in writing. Oral testimony shall be recorded and retained by the judge. Facts that are contained in a written document may be presented to the judge by telephone, facsimile, video, or other similar device. If probable cause is determined on facts contained in a written document and the judge is not personally present to sign the determination, the document shall be presented to the judge for signature within two (2) business days. The judge shall be advised if a prior request for a probable cause determination was made and turned down relative to the same incident.

(C) *Approval of Prosecuting Attorney.* No request for a probable cause determination may proceed without approval by the prosecuting attorney. The person requesting the probable cause determination shall, under oath, state that the prosecutor approves the request. If the prosecutor is unavailable, the court may make the probable cause determination if the matter should not be delayed.

(D) *Determination.* After the information is presented, the court shall determine whether there is probable cause to believe an offense(s) was committed and that the child committed the offense(s). If probable cause is found, the court may order continued detention pursuant to Rule 5, and release the child with conditions or with no conditions. A written determination of probable cause shall be filed with the court and a copy provided to the child and child's counsel.

Subd. 5. Release of Any Child at Any Time by the Court and Conditions of Release. Only the court may impose conditions of release. The court at any time may release a child and may impose one or more of the following conditions:

(A) require the parent(s), legal guardian, legal custodian or child to post bail;

(B) place restrictions on the child's travel, associations or place of abode during the period of the child's release; or

(C) electronic home monitoring or any other conditions deemed reasonably necessary and consistent with factors for detaining the child.

Unless the time for the detention hearing is extended by twenty-four (24) hours pursuant to Rule 5.07, subdivision 7, all conditions of release which restrict the physical liberty of a child terminate after thirty-six (36) hours excluding Saturdays, Sundays and legal holidays unless a detention hearing has commenced and the court has ordered continued detention.

Subd. 6. Release to Custody of Parent or Other Responsible Adult. A child released from a place of detention shall be released to the custody of the child's parent(s), legal guardian, or legal custodian if deemed appropriate by the detaining authority. If these individuals are unavailable or deemed inappropriate, the detaining authority may release the child to a member of the extended family or kinship network or other suitable adult deemed appropriate by the detaining authority and acceptable to the child.

Amended June 26, 1996; July 18, 2003; Oct. 11, 2007, eff. Jan. 1, 2008; Oct. 15, 2012, eff. Dec. 1, 2012.

Comment—Rule 5

See comment following Rule 5.08.

Historical Notes

The order of the Minnesota Supreme Court [C6–84–2165] dated June 26, 1996, provides in part that "(t)hese amendments to the Rules of Juvenile Procedure shall govern all juvenile actions commenced or arrests made on or after 12:00 o'clock midnight August 1, 1996."

The order of the Minnesota Supreme Court [CX–01–926] dated July 18, 2003, provides in part that "(t)he attached amendments shall govern all juveniles taken into custody and all juvenile delinquency actions commenced or children taken into custody after 12 o'clock midnight September 1, 2003."

The order of the Minnesota Supreme Court [ADM10–8003] dated October 15, 2012, provides in part that the "amendments shall govern all delinquency actions pending or commenced on or after 12 o'clock midnight December 1, 2012."

Rule 5.05. Detention Reports

Subd. 1. Report by Detaining Authority. When a child has been detained, the detaining officer or his agent shall file a signed report with the court and deliver a copy to the supervisor of the facility containing the following information:

(A) the time the child was taken into custody and the reasons why the child was taken into custody;

(B) the time the child was delivered to the place of detention and the reasons why the child is being held there;

(C) a statement that the child and the child's parent(s), legal guardian or legal custodian have received the notification required by Minnesota Statutes, section 260B.176, subdivisions 3 and 5, including the advisory that every child at a detention hearing has a right to counsel at public expense pursuant to Rule 3.02, subdivision 6, and the time such notification was given to each or the efforts made to notify them.

Subd. 2. Report by Supervisor of the Secure Detention Facility or Shelter Care Facility. When a child has been delivered to a secure detention facility or shelter care facility, the supervisor of the facility shall file with the court a signed report acknowledging receipt of the child and containing a statement that the child and the child's parent(s), legal guardian or legal custodian have received the notification required by Minnesota Statutes, section 260B.176, subdivisions 3 and 5 and the time such notification was given to each or the efforts made to notify them.

Subd. 3. Timing of Reports. The reports shall be filed with the court on or before the court day following detention of the child or by the time of the detention hearing, whichever is earlier.

Subd. 4. Notice to Child's Counsel; Child's Counsel Access to Child and Reports. If a child is detained pending a detention hearing in a place of detention other than home detention or at home on electronic home monitoring, the court administrator shall give the Office of the Public Defender or the child's attorney, if privately retained, notice that the child is in custody, notice of the detention hearing and provide copies of the reports filed with the court by the detaining officer and the supervisor of the place of detention. Child's counsel shall have immediate and continuing access to the child.

Amended June 26, 1996; July 18, 2003.

Comment—Rule 5

See comment following Rule 5.08.

Historical Notes

The order of the Minnesota Supreme Court [C6–84–2165] dated June 26, 1996, provides in part that "(t)hese amendments to the Rules of Juvenile Procedure shall govern all juvenile actions commenced or arrests made on or after 12:00 o'clock midnight August 1, 1996."

The order of the Minnesota Supreme Court [CX–01–926] dated July 18, 2003, provides in part that "(t)he attached amendments shall govern all juveniles taken into custody and all juvenile delinquency actions commenced or children taken into custody after 12 o'clock midnight September 1, 2003."

Rule 5.06. Identification Procedures

Subd. 1. Photographing.

(A) *Generally.* A detained child may be photographed when the child is taken into custody in accordance with the laws relating to arrests. All children in custody alleged to have committed a felony or gross misdemeanor shall be photographed without court order.

(B) *Report.* A report stating the name of the child photographed and the date the photograph was taken shall be filed with the court.

Subd. 2. Fingerprinting.

(A) *Generally.* All children in custody alleged to have committed a felony or gross misdemeanor shall be fingerprinted without court order. Otherwise, a court order is required pursuant to Rule 10.

(B) *Report.* A report stating the name of the child fingerprinted and the date of the fingerprinting shall be filed with the court.

Subd. 3. Line–Up.

(A) *Generally.* A detained child may be placed in a line-up. A child may choose not to participate in a line-up which is not related to the matter for which the child is detained unless ordered by the court to appear in a line-up pursuant to Rule 10.05, subdivision 2(A).

(B) *Right to Counsel During Line–Up for Child Alleged to be Delinquent.* A child has the right to have counsel present when placed in a line-up related to a delinquent act for which the child has been taken into custody unless exigent circumstances exist such that providing counsel would unduly interfere with a prompt investigation of the crime. When a delinquency petition has been filed, counsel for the child shall be present for any line-up. Any identification evidence obtained without the presence of counsel shall be inadmissible, unless the line-up occurred before the filing of the petition and exigent circumstances existed preventing the presence of counsel.

(C) *Report.* A report stating the name of the children who participated in the line-up and the date of the line-up shall be filed with the court.

Amended June 26, 1996; July 18, 2003.

Comment—Rule 5

See comment following Rule 5.08.

Historical Notes

The order of the Minnesota Supreme Court [C6–84–2165] dated June 26, 1996, provides in part that "(t)hese amendments to the Rules of Juvenile Procedure shall govern all juvenile actions commenced or arrests made on or after 12:00 o'clock midnight August 1, 1996."

The order of the Minnesota Supreme Court [CX–01–926] dated July 18, 2003, provides in part that "(t)he attached amendments shall govern all juveniles taken into custody and all juvenile delinquency actions commenced or children taken into custody after 12 o'clock midnight September 1, 2003."

Rule 5.07. Detention Hearing

Subd. 1. Time and Filing. For a child detained in a secure juvenile detention facility or shelter care facility, the court shall commence a detention hearing within thirty-six (36) hours of the time the child was taken into custody, excluding Saturdays, Sundays, and holidays, unless a charging document has been filed and the judge or referee determines pursuant to Minnesota Statutes, section 260B.178 that the child shall remain in detention. For a child detained in an adult jail or municipal lockup, the court shall commence a detention hearing within twenty-four (24) hours of the time the child was taken into custody, excluding Saturdays, Sundays, and holidays, or within six (6) hours of the time the child was taken into custody if the child is detained in an adult jail or municipal lockup in a standard metropolitan statistical area, including Saturdays, Sundays, and holidays, unless a charging document has been filed and the judge or referee determines pursuant to Minnesota Statutes, section 260B.178 that the child shall remain in detention.

The following documents shall be filed with the court before the detention hearing:

(A) a report or reports that the child is being held in detention filed pursuant to Rule 5.05; and

(B) a charging document with probable cause.

Subd. 2. Notice.

(A) *Child, Child's Counsel, Prosecuting Attorney, Child's Parent(s), Legal Guardian or Legal Custodian and Spouse of the Child.* The court shall inform the child, the child's counsel, the prosecuting attorney, the child's parent(s), legal guardian or legal custodian and spouse of the child of the time and place of the detention hearing pursuant to Rule 25. Failure to inform the parent(s), legal guardian or legal custodian or spouse of the child or their absence at the hearing shall not prevent the hearing from being conducted or invalidate an order of detention.

(B) *Victim.* If a detained child is charged with a crime of violence against a person or attempting a crime of violence against a person, the court administrator shall make reasonable and good faith efforts to notify the victim of the alleged crime of

(1) the time and place of the detention hearing;

(2) the name and telephone number of a person that can be contacted for additional information; and

(3) the right of the victim and victim's family to attend the detention hearing.

If the victim is incapacitated or deceased, notice must be given to the victim's family. If the victim is a minor, notice must be given to the victim's parent, legal guardian or legal custodian.

Subd. 3. Advice of Rights. At the beginning of the detention hearing, the court shall advise all persons present of:

(A) the reasons why the child was taken into custody;

(B) the allegations of the charging document;

(C) the purpose and scope of the detention hearing;

(D) the right of the child to be represented by counsel at the detention hearing and at every other stage of the proceedings, and the right of a child alleged to be delinquent to counsel at public expense; and

(E) the right of the child to remain silent.

Subd. 4. Evidence. The court may admit any evidence including reliable hearsay and opinion evidence that is relevant to the decision whether to detain the child. The court may not admit evidence of privileged communications.

Subd. 5. Findings Necessary for Continued Detention. A court may detain a child beyond the time set in subdivision 1 of this rule if, after a hearing, the court finds:

(A) probable cause to believe the child committed the offense(s) alleged pursuant to Rule 5.04, subdivision 4; and

(B) there is reason to believe that if the child were released, after consideration of the factors set forth in Rule 5.03, that:

(1) the child would endanger self or others;

(2) the child would not appear for a court hearing;

(3) the child would not remain in the care or control of the person into whose lawful custody the child is released; or

(4) the child's health or welfare would be immediately endangered.

There is a presumption that a child will not appear for a court hearing when the person to whom the child is to be released refuses to sign a written promise to bring the child to court.

Subd. 6. Order.

(A) *Release.* The child shall be released if the findings required by Rule 5.07, subdivision 5 are not made.

(B) *Detention.* If the findings required by Rule 5.07, subdivision 5 are made, the court may order continued detention or release with the posting of bail or bond and other conditions deemed appropriate by the court. An order stated on the record shall also be reduced to writing by the court within five (5) days of entry of the order.

(C) *Notice of Next Hearing.* On the record, the court shall advise all persons present of the date, time, and place of the next hearing. If persons entitled to participate at the next hearing are not present, the court shall provide those persons with notification of the next hearing by written notice of hearing. If the child is released, the child may be required to sign a promise to appear.

Subd. 7. Extension of Time for Detention Hearing. For good cause shown, the court may extend the time for a detention hearing by twenty-four (24) hours on written application of the prosecuting attorney, if the application for extension is filed with the court within the time prescribed by this rule. The court may extend the time for one additional twenty-four (24) hour period upon a second written application being filed within the extended time previously ordered by the court.

Adopted June 26, 1996; July 18, 2003. Amended Oct. 11, 2007, eff. Jan. 1, 2008.

Comment—Rule 5

See comment following Rule 5.08.

Historical Notes

The order of the Minnesota Supreme Court [C6–84–2165] dated June 26, 1996, provides in part that "(t)hese amendments to the Rules of Juvenile Procedure shall govern all juvenile actions commenced or arrests made on or after 12:00 o'clock midnight August 1, 1996."

The order of the Minnesota Supreme Court [CX–01–926] dated July 18, 2003, provides in part that "(t)he attached amendments shall govern all juveniles taken into custody and all juvenile delinquency actions commenced or children taken into custody after 12 o'clock midnight September 1, 2003."

Rule 5.08. Detention Review

Subdivision 1. Informal Review. An informal review of detention shall be made by the court every eight (8) days, excluding Saturdays, Sundays and holidays, of the child's detention. If the circumstances justifying detention have not changed, detention may be continued. If the circumstances justifying detention have changed, detention may be modified with consent of the child, child's counsel, and the prosecuting attorney. An order stated on the record shall also be reduced to writing by the court within five (5) days of entry of the order.

Subd. 2. Formal Review. The court may schedule a formal review of detention at any time.

(A) *Request by Child, Child's Counsel or Prosecuting Attorney.* If the court finds a substantial basis exists for the request to schedule a hearing to review detention, a hearing shall be scheduled as soon as possible, and at least within eight (8) days of the request.

(B) *Notice.* The person requesting a formal review shall make the request by motion as provided in Rule 27.

(C) *Relevant Evidence.* Subject to constitutional limitations and privileged communications, the court may admit any evidence, including reliable hearsay and opinion evidence that is relevant to the decision regarding continued detention of the child.

(D) *Continued Detention.* The court may continue the child in detention if the court makes findings pursuant to Rule 5.07, subdivision 5. An order stated on the record shall also be reduced to writing by the court within five (5) days of entry of the order.

Adopted June 26, 1996; July 18, 2003. Amended Oct. 11, 2007, eff. Jan. 1, 2008.

Comment—Rule 5

There is a presumption in favor of releasing an accused child unconditionally. If the child cannot be released unconditionally, the least restrictive liberty restriction is favored. The American Bar Association's *Juvenile Justice Standards Relating to Interim Status: The Release Control, and Detention of Accused Juvenile Offenders Between Arrest and Disposition* (1980) describes the general principles governing liberty restrictions. These general principles and policy considerations do not determine the outcomes of specific cases. Rather, they provide the process framework within which law enforcement and intake personnel, prosecuting attorneys and judges decide individual cases. When these decision makers decide whether or not to place a child in detention or to impose other physical liberty restrictions, the following policy considerations apply: to the greatest extent possible, any interim liberty restrictions should respect the autonomy interests of the accused child and family, ensure equality of treatment by race, class, ethnicity, and sex, ensure the child promptly receives access and continuing access to legal assistance, protect the child's access to education to the extent reasonably possible, and ensure public safety.

The primary concern of this rule is a child's physical liberty and living arrangements pending trial and disposition. For purposes of this rule, other non-physical limitations on a child's autonomy, such as a court order to avoid contact with victims or witnesses, to attend school, to remain under the control of parents or custodians, or the like, *do not constitute* liberty restrictions that invoke either the procedures of this rule or the expedited timing of procedures for youths physically detained or restricted.

Minnesota Statutes, section 260B.154 (2002) authorizes the court to issue a warrant for immediate custody for a child who fails to appear in court in response to a summons. Minnesota Statutes, section 260B.175 (2002) authorizes a child to be taken into custody: 1) when the child has failed to obey a summons or subpoena; 2) pursuant to the laws of arrest; or 3) by a peace officer or probation or parole officer when it is reasonably believed that the child has violated the terms of probation, parole, or other field supervision. Minn. R. Juv. Del. P. 5.07 defines the circumstances under which a child is subject to continuing physical restraints. Minnesota Statutes, section 260B.176 (2002) authorizes a detention hearing and provides the statutory framework that governs this rule.

Minn. R. Juv. Del. P. 5.02, subd. 3 defines the places in which a child's liberty is restricted. A child's liberty is restricted when the child is placed at home, but his or her physical mobility is limited by electronic home monitoring or house arrest with substantial liberty restrictions. In addition, the provisions of this rule apply whenever, prior to disposition, the child is placed outside of the home, whether or not the placement is in a secure facility. Thus, a child's liberty is restricted when placed in a foster care (Minnesota Statutes, section 260B.007, subd. 7 (2002)) or shelter care facility (Minnesota Statutes, section 260B.007, subd. 15 (2002)), in a detoxification or mental health treatment facility, in a secure detention facility (Minnesota Statutes, section 260B.007, subd. 14 (2002)), in an adult jail or lock-up, or other place of detention. A child who is returned to an out-of-home placement which was made voluntarily or pursuant to a CHIPS proceeding is not " detained" for the purposes of this rule.

Minn. R. Juv Del.. P. 5.03, subd. 1 establishes a general presumption in favor of unconditional release for all children taken into custody. Minn. R. Juv. Del. P. 5.03, subd. 2 provides some non-exclusive evidentiary guidelines by which detaining authorities can decide whether a child meets the criteria for detention. Under Minn. R. Juv. Del. P. 5.03, subd. 2, the detaining authority may detain a child if it believes or the court finds that the child poses a danger to other people because the child is charged with a presumptive commitment to prison offense. The presumptive commitment to prison offenses are enumerated under Section V, Offense Severity Reference Table of the Minnesota Sentencing Guidelines. In addition, an inference the child poses a danger to others applies when the child uses a firearm in the commission of a felony pursuant to Minnesota Statutes, section 260B.125, subds. 3 and 4 (2002). However, detaining authorities should exercise individualized discretion. Moreover, detaining authorities ought not detain children who meet the evidentiary criteria if other, less restrictive alternatives would assure the child's subsequent court appearance, welfare, and public safety. The non-exclusive evidentiary criteria emphasize objective indicators that the child poses a danger to self or others, or would fail to return for court appearances. The list of criteria set out in Minn. R. Juv. Del. P. 5.03, subd. 2 are examples of factors which may justify pretrial detention. If a detained child does not meet any of the enumerated criteria, the detaining authority may justify detention only if a written report is filed stating objective and articulable reasons for detention. Minn. R. Juv. Del. P. 5.03, subd. 2.

Minn. R. Juv. Del. P. 5.03 governs the initial custody decisions affecting a juvenile by the police, detention and court intake personnel, and the prosecuting attorney. Minn. R. Juv. Del. P. 5.04, subd. 1 governs the liberty restrictions on a child taken into custody pursuant to a court order or warrant. Minn. R. Juv. Del. P. 5.04, subd. 2 governs the liberty restrictions of a child taken into custody by a peace officer or other person, and then brought to a detention facility or other place of custody.

Minn. R. Juv. Del. P. 5.04, subd. 3 is based upon Minnesota Statutes, section 260B.176, subd. 2 (2002). The statute provides for an extension of the time for a detention hearing for a child detained in an adult detention facility outside of a standard metropolitan statistical area county only under two circumstances: 1) where the adult facility in which the child is detained is located where conditions of distance to be traveled or other ground transportation do not allow for court appearances within 24 hours (with the delay not to exceed 48 hours); and 2) where "conditions of safety exist" including adverse life-threatening weather conditions which do not allow for reasonably safe travel. The time for appearance may be delayed until 24 hours after the time that conditions allow for reasonably safe travel. Minnesota Statutes, section 260B.176, subd. 2 (2002). See also 42 U.S.C.A. section 5633(a)(13) and (14) (1995). Even though the statute permits an extension of the time for a detention hearing in such circumstances, the extension may be granted only if the prosecuting attorney has filed a charging document within twenty-four (24) hours of the child being taken into custody, excluding Saturdays, Sundays and legal holidays. Minn. R. Juv. Del. P. 5.04, subd. 3(A). If the court determines after the detention hearing that the child should remain detained, the child shall be detained in a juvenile facility in accordance with Minn. R. Juv. Del. P. 5.02, subd. 3. Id. See also 42 U.S.C.A. section 5633(a)(14) (1995). The placement options in Minn. R. Juv. Del. P. 5.02, subd. 4 are not referenced in Minn. R. Juv. Del. P. 5.04, subd. 3(A) and (B) because the placement limitations in Minn. Stat. § 260B.181, subds. 2 and 3 preclude the initial detention of juvenile petty offenders in an adult jail or municipal lockup.

Minn. R. Juv. Del. P. 5.04, subd. 4 is based upon Minn. R. Crim. P. 4.03. Under Minn. R. Juv. Del. P. 5.04, subd. 4, if a child arrested without a warrant is not released by law enforcement, court intake, the court, or the prosecuting attorney, then a judge or judicial officer must make a probable cause determination without unnecessary delay and in any event within forty-eight (48) hours from the time of the arrest including the day of arrest, Saturdays, Sundays, and legal holidays. If the Court determines that probable cause does not exist or if there is no determination as to probable cause within the time as provided by this rule, the person shall be released immediately. *County of Riverside v. McLaughlin,* 500 U.S. 44, 111 S.Ct. 1661, 114 L.Ed.2d 49 (1991), requires a prompt judicial determination of probable cause following a warrantless arrest. That determination must occur without unreasonable delay and in no event later than forty-eight (48) hours after the arrest. There are no exclusions in computing the forty-eight-hour time limit. Even a probable cause determination within forty-eight (48) hours will be too late if there has been unreasonable delay in obtaining the determination. "Examples of unreasonable delays are delays for the purpose of gathering additional evidence to justify the arrest, a delay motivated by ill will against the arrested individual or delay for delay's sake." *County of Riverside v. McLaughlin,* 500 U.S. 44, 64, 111 S.Ct. 1661, 1670, 114 L.Ed.2d 49 (1991). The requirements of Minn. R. Juv. Del. P. 5.04, subd. 4 are in addition to the requirement that a child arrested without a warrant must receive a detention hearing within thirty-six (36) hours after the arrest, exclusive of Saturdays, Sundays, and legal holidays. Because of the exclusion permitted in computing time under the "36–hour rule," compliance with that rule will not necessarily assure compliance with the "48–hour rule". The "48–hour rule" also applies to all misdemeanor cases.

Minn. R. Juv. Del. P. 5.05, subd. 4 requires the court administrator to notify the office of the Public Defender that a child is in custody and the time of the detention hearing and to provide facsimile copies of all reports transmitted to the court. If a specific attorney has been assigned to represent the child, that attorney should receive notice. In jurisdictions where public defenders rotate, notice to the chief public defender would be sufficient. Minnesota data privacy laws do not restrict notification of counsel of a child's detention prior to the first appearance in court and appointment of counsel. The rules of professional responsibility and attorney client privilege adequately protect the privacy of the child.

Minn. R. Juv. Del. P. 5.06, subd. 1 implements the provision of Minnesota Statutes, section 299C.10 (2002), which requires peace officers to take the fingerprints and photograph of a child taken into custody according to the laws of arrest, pursuant to Minnesota Statutes, section 260B.175, subd. 1(b) (2002). Any photograph taken of a child must be destroyed when the child reaches the age of 19 years. Minnesota Statutes, section 260B.171, subd. 5(c) (2002). Minn. R. Juv. Del. P. 5.06, subd. 2 implements the provisions of Minnesota Statutes, section 299C.10 (2002), which requires law enforcement personnel to take the fingerprints of all juveniles arrested or charged with felony- or gross misdemeanor-level offenses.

Minn. R. Juv. Del. P. 5.06, subd. 3 implements the policies of *U.S. v. Wade,* 388 U.S. 218 (1967) to provide the assistance of counsel to minimize the dangers of erroneous misidentification. See Feld, " Criminalizing Juvenile Justice: Rules of Procedure for the Juvenile Court," 62 Minn. L. Rev. 141, 209–16 (1984). Unlike the formalistic limitations imposed by *Kirby v. Illinois,* 406 U.S. 682 (1972), the rule recognizes that the dangers of unreliability, suggestibility, and error are inherent in all identification procedures. The rule attempts to balance the protection of a child from prejudicial misidentification with the State's interest in prompt investigation. A child who is in custody is entitled to have counsel present at a lineup, even prior to the filing of a delinquency petition, unless exigent circumstances exist and delay to provide counsel would unduly interfere with an expeditious investigation. *Blue v. State,* 558 P.2d 636 (Alaska 1977); *People v. Jackson,* 391 Mich. 323, 217 N.W.2d 22 (Mich. 1974); *Commonwealth v. Richman,* 238 Pa. Super. 413, 357 A.2d 585 (1976). Once an investigation proceeds beyond an immediate on-the-scene show-up, and especially once the child is in custody, there are no compelling law enforcement exigencies that offset the dangers of prejudice to the child. Since youth in custody already have a Miranda right to counsel, 384 U.S. 436 (1966), the delay involved in securing counsel will be a matter of hours at most and if conditions require immediate identification without even minimal delay or if counsel cannot be present within reasonable time, such existent circumstances will justify proceeding without counsel. *People v. Bustamante,* 30 Cal 3d 88, 634 P.2d 927 (Cal. 1981).

Minn. R. Juv. Del. P. 5.07 implements Minnesota Statutes, section 629.725 (2002) by providing that, in addition to giving notice to the child, child's counsel, prosecuting attorney, child's parent(s), legal guardian or legal custodian and spouse of the child, the court administrator must make a reasonable and good faith effort to give notice of the time and place of the detention hearing to the victim if the child is charged with a crime of violence against a person or attempting a crime of violence against a person. If the victim is deceased or incapacitated, the victim's family must receive notice. If the victim is a minor, the victim's parent or guardian must receive notice. Minnesota Statutes, section 629.725 (2002). "Crime of violence" has the meaning given it in Minnesota Statutes, section 624.712, subd. 5 (2002), and also includes Minnesota Statutes, section 609.21, gross misdemeanor violations of Minnesota Statutes, section 609.224 (2002), and nonfelony violations of Minnesota Statutes, sections 518B.01 (2002), 609.2231 (2002), 609.3451 (2002), 609.748 (2002), and 609.749 (2002). Id.

Historical Notes

The order of the Minnesota Supreme Court [C6–84–2165] dated June 26, 1996, provides in part that "(t)hese amendments to the Rules of Juvenile Procedure shall govern all juvenile actions commenced or arrests made on or after 12:00 o'clock midnight August 1, 1996."

The order of the Minnesota Supreme Court [C6-84-2165] dated December 12, 1997, amending the Rules of Juvenile Procedure provides in part that "(t)he inclusion of Advisory Committee comments is made for convenience and does not reflect court approval of the comments made therein."

The order of the Minnesota Supreme Court [CX–01–926] dated July 18, 2003, provides in part that "(t)he attached amendments shall govern all juveniles taken into custody and all juvenile delinquency actions commenced or children taken into custody after 12 o'clock midnight September 1, 2003."

RULE 6. CHARGING DOCUMENT

Rule 6.01. Generally

A charging document is a petition, tab charge or a citation, and includes charging documents filed in paper form, or by electronic means authorized by the State Court Administrator.

Amended June 26, 1996; Oct. 15, 2012, eff. Dec. 1, 2012.

Comment—Rule 6

See comment following Rule 6.08.

Historical Notes

The order of the Minnesota Supreme Court [C6–84–2165] dated June 26, 1996, provides in part that "(t)hese amendments to the Rules of Juvenile Procedure shall govern all juvenile actions commenced or arrests made on or after 12:00 o'clock midnight August 1, 1996."

The order of the Minnesota Supreme Court [ADM10–8003] dated October 15, 2012, provides in part that the "amendments shall govern all delinquency actions pending or commenced on or after 12 o'clock midnight December 1, 2012."

Rule 6.02. Tab Charge or Citation

Subdivision 1. Generally. Juvenile petty offenses as defined by Minnesota Statutes, section 260B.007, subdivision 16, misdemeanors, juvenile traffic offenses and gross misdemeanors under Minnesota Statutes, chapter 169A may be charged by tab charge or citation. Before entering a plea of guilty or not guilty to alleged misdemeanor or gross misdemeanor charge(s), the child may demand that a petition be filed with the court. If a petition is demanded, the prosecuting attorney shall have thirty (30) days to file the petition unless the child is in custody. The prosecuting attorney shall have ten (10) days to file a petition if a demand is made by a child in custody or the child shall be released.

Subd. 2. Filing. Before a tab charge or citation may be filed with the court by the peace officer or attendance officer who issued the charges, it shall be endorsed by the prosecuting attorney to permit screening for diversion programs. A tab charge or citation may be filed in paper form, or by electronic means authorized by the State Court Administrator. Filing a tab charge or citation gives the juvenile court jurisdiction over the matter.

Subd. 3. Contents of Tab Charge or Citation. Tab charges or citations shall contain:

(A) the name, address, date of birth, and race of the child;

(B) the name and address of the parent, legal guardian or legal custodian of the child;

(C) the offense charged and a reference to the statute or local ordinance which is the basis for the charge;

(D) the time and place and county of the alleged offense; and

(E) other administrative information published by the State Court Administrator.

Subd. 4. Notice of Court Appearance. When a tab charge or citation is filed with the court, the court administrator shall promptly schedule the matter for hearing and send notices as provided by Rule 25.

Adopted June 26, 1996. Amended Dec. 12, 1997; July 18, 2003; Oct. 15, 2012, eff. Dec. 1, 2012.

Comment—Rule 6

See comment following Rule 6.08.

Historical Notes

The order of the Minnesota Supreme Court [C6–84–2165] dated June 26, 1996, provides in part that "(t)hese amendments to the Rules of Juvenile Procedure shall govern all juvenile actions commenced or arrests made on or after 12:00 o'clock midnight August 1, 1996."

The order of the Minnesota Supreme Court [C6–84–2165] dated December 12, 1997, provides in part that "(t)hese amendments to the Rules of Juvenile Procedure shall govern all juvenile actions commenced or arrests made on or after 12:00 o'clock midnight January 1, 1998."

The order of the Minnesota Supreme Court [CX–01–926] dated July 18, 2003, provides in part that "(t)he attached amendments shall govern all juveniles taken into custody and all juvenile delinquency actions commenced or children taken into custody after 12 o'clock midnight September 1, 2003."

The order of the Minnesota Supreme Court [ADM10–8003] dated October 15, 2012, provides in part that the "amendments shall govern all delinquency actions pending or commenced on or after 12 o'clock midnight December 1, 2012."

Rule 6.03. Petition

Subd. 1. Generally. A child alleged to be delinquent because of a felony or gross misdemeanor offense (except gross misdemeanors under Minnesota Statutes, chapter 169A, which may be charged by tab charge or citation) shall be charged by petition. A child alleged to be delinquent because of a misdemeanor offense may be charged by petition. A child charged with a juvenile petty offense or a juvenile traffic offense may be charged by petition.

Subd. 2. Filing. Each petition shall be signed by the prosecuting attorney before it is filed with the court. The signature of the prosecuting attorney shall be an acknowledgement that the form of the petition is approved and that reasonable grounds exist to support the petition. A delinquency petition may be filed without the prosecutor's signature if the prosecutor is unavailable and a judge determines that filing and the issuance of process should not be delayed.

Subd. 3. Contents of the Delinquency Petition. Every petition alleging a child is delinquent shall contain:

(A) a concise statement alleging the child is delinquent;

(B) a description of the alleged offense and reference to the statute or ordinance which was violated;

(C) the applicable Minnesota Offense Code (MOC);

(D) the name, date of birth, address, and race of the child;

(E) the names and addresses of the child's parent(s), legal guardian, legal custodian, or nearest known relative;

(F) the name and address of the child's spouse; and

(G) other administrative information authorized by the Supreme Court Juvenile Delinquency Rules Committee and published by the State Court Administrator.

Subd. 4. Separate Counts. A petition may allege separate counts, whether the alleged delinquent acts arise out of the same or separate behavioral incidents.

Subd. 5. Contents of Petition Alleging Juvenile Petty Offender or Juvenile Traffic Offender. Every petition alleging a child is a juvenile petty offender or alleging a child is a juvenile traffic offender shall contain:

(A) a concise statement alleging that the child is a juvenile petty offender or a juvenile traffic offender;

(B) the name, address, date of birth, and for juvenile traffic offenders, the driver's license number of the child, if known;

(C) the name and address of the parent(s), legal guardian, or legal custodian of the child;

(D) a description of the offense charged and reference to the statute or ordinance which is the basis for the charge;

(E) the applicable Minnesota Offense Code (MOC);

(F) the date, county, and place of the alleged offense; and

(G) other administrative information authorized by the Supreme Court Juvenile Delinquency Rules Committee and published by the State Court Administrator.

Adopted June 26, 1996. Amended Dec. 12, 1997; July 18, 2003; Oct. 11, 2007, eff. Jan. 1, 2008.

Comment—Rule 6

See comment following Rule 6.08.

Historical Notes

The order of the Minnesota Supreme Court [C6–84–2165] dated June 26, 1996, provides in part that "(t)hese amendments to the Rules of Juvenile Procedure shall govern all juvenile actions commenced or arrests made on or after 12:00 o'clock midnight August 1, 1996."

The order of the Minnesota Supreme Court [C6–84–2165] dated December 12, 1997, provides in part that "(t)hese amendments to the Rules of Juvenile Procedure shall govern all juvenile actions commenced or arrests made on or after 12:00 o'clock midnight January 1, 1998."

The order of the Minnesota Supreme Court [CX–01–926] dated July 18, 2003, provides in part that "(t)he attached amendments shall govern all juveniles taken into custody and all juvenile delinquency actions commenced or children taken into custody after 12 o'clock midnight September 1, 2003."

Rule 6.04. Amendment

Subdivision 1. Permissive. A charging document may be amended by order of the court at any time:

(A) before the introduction of evidence at the trial by motion of the prosecuting attorney; or

(B) after the commencement of the trial with consent of the child and prosecuting attorney; or

(C) after trial but before a finding that the allegations of the charging document have been proved, upon motion of the prosecuting attorney, if no additional or different offense is alleged and if substantial rights of the child are not prejudiced.

Amendments shall be granted liberally in the interest of justice and the welfare of the child. If the court orders a charging document amended, additional time may be granted to the child or prosecuting attorney to adequately prepare for and ensure a full and fair hearing.

Subd. 2. Prohibited.

(A) A charging document alleging a child is delinquent shall not be amended to allege a child is in need of protection or services.

(B) A charging document alleging a juvenile petty or traffic offense shall not be amended to allege the child is delinquent.

(C) A petition alleging that a child is in need of protection or services shall not be amended to allege a delinquency, petty offense or juvenile traffic offense.

Adopted June 26, 1996. Amended July 11, 2005, eff. Sept. 1, 2005.

Comment—Rule 6

See comment following Rule 6.08.

Historical Notes

The order of the Minnesota Supreme Court [C6–84–2165] dated June 26, 1996, provides in part that "(t)hese amendments to the Rules of Juvenile Procedure shall govern all juvenile actions commenced or arrests made on or after 12:00 o'clock midnight August 1, 1996."

Rule 6.05. Probable Cause

Subd. 1. Establishing Probable Cause. The facts establishing probable cause may be set forth in writing in the charging document or police reports may be attached to the charging document. If police reports are attached to the charging document to establish probable cause, the child shall have the right to demand a statement establishing probable cause with specificity. Once demanded, the prosecuting attorney shall have ten (10) days to file with the court and serve on opposing counsel, the specific statement of probable cause. Probable cause may also be presented by sworn affidavits attached to a charging document or by sworn testimony presented to the court. If testimony is presented, a verbatim record of the proceedings shall be made and a transcript of the proceedings prepared and filed with the court.

Subd. 2. When Required. There must be a finding of probable cause:

(A) before the court may issue a warrant pursuant to Rule 4;

(B) before a detention hearing is held for a child taken into custody without a warrant;

(C) within ten (10) days of a court order directing the prosecuting attorney to establish probable cause on the charge(s) alleged in a charging document. The court for any reason may order the prosecutor to show probable cause and the court shall order the prosecutor to show probable cause on demand of the child; or

(D) when competency of the child has been challenged.

Subd. 3. Motion to Dismiss for Lack of Probable Cause. The child may bring a motion to dismiss the charging document for lack of probable cause. The probable cause determination is governed by the procedure set out in Minnesota Rules of Criminal Procedure 11.04.

Subd. 4. Dismissal. The court shall dismiss a charging document when a showing of probable cause has not been made. A dismissal for failure to show probable cause shall not prohibit the filing of a new charging document and further proceedings on the new charging document.

Adopted June 26, 1996. Amended July 18, 2003; July 11, 2005, eff. Sept. 1, 2005; Oct. 13, 2006, eff. Jan. 1, 2007; Nov. 19, 2010, eff. Jan. 1, 2011.

Comment—Rule 6

See comment following Rule 6.08.

Historical Notes

The order of the Minnesota Supreme Court [C6–84–2165] dated June 26, 1996, provides in part that "(t)hese amendments to the Rules of Juvenile Procedure shall govern all juvenile actions commenced or arrests made on or after 12:00 o'clock midnight August 1, 1996."

The order of the Minnesota Supreme Court [CX–01–926] dated July 18, 2003, provides in part that "(t)he attached amendments shall govern all juveniles taken into custody and all juvenile delinquency actions commenced or children taken into custody after 12 o'clock midnight September 1, 2003."

Rule 6.06. Procedure on Filing a Charging Document With the Court

Subd. 1. Dismissal. The court shall dismiss a charging document if it does not allege an act of delinquency as defined by Minnesota Statutes, section 260B.007, subdivision 6, a juvenile petty offense as defined by Minnesota Statutes, section 260B.007, subdivision 16 or a juvenile traffic offense as defined by Minnesota Statutes, section 260B.225.

Subd. 2. Arraignment. When a charging document is filed, the court administrator shall promptly schedule an arraignment on the charging document and send notices pursuant to Rule 25.

Subd. 3. Payment of Citation in Lieu of Court Appearance. When a child is charged by citation with an offense or offenses listed on the Statewide Payables List, the child may enter a plea of guilty before the scheduled arraignment date by paying the fine amount established by the Judicial Council and any applicable fees and surcharges, and by submitting a Plea and Waiver Form signed or acknowledged by the child and the child's parent.

The Plea and Waiver Form shall advise the child that payment constitutes a plea of guilty and an admission (a) that the child understands the nature of the offense alleged; (b) that the child makes no claim of innocence; (c) that the child's conduct constitutes the offense(s) to which the child is pleading guilty; (d) that the plea is made freely, under no threats or promises, and (e) that the child has the following rights which the child voluntarily waives:

(1) the right to the appointment of counsel if the child is subject to out-of-home placement as provided in Minnesota Statutes, section 260B.235, subdivision 6;

(2) the right to trial;

(3) the presumption of innocence until the prosecuting attorney proves the charges beyond a reasonable doubt;

(4) the right to remain silent;

(5) the right to testify on the child's own behalf;

(6) the right to confront witnesses against oneself;

(7) the right to subpoena witnesses;

The Plea and Waiver Form shall also advise the child that mandatory disposition requirements for a third or subsequent offense may require an appearance in court and may result in the imposition of certain dispositions including, but not limited to, those provided in Minnesota Statutes, section 260B.235, subdivision 6.

The Plea and Waiver Form shall be developed and maintained by the State Court Administrator.

Adopted June 26, 1996. Amended July 18, 2003; Nov. 19, 2010, eff. July 1, 2011.

Comment—Rule 6

See comment following Rule 6.08.

Historical Notes

The order of the Minnesota Supreme Court [C6–84–2165] dated June 26, 1996, provides in part that "(t)hese amendments to the Rules of Juvenile Procedure shall govern all juvenile actions commenced or arrests made on or after 12:00 o'clock midnight August 1, 1996."

The order of the Minnesota Supreme Court [CX–01–926] dated July 18, 2003, provides in part that "(t)he attached amendments shall govern all juveniles taken into custody and all juvenile delinquency actions commenced or children taken into custody after 12 o'clock midnight September 1, 2003."

Rule 6.07. Dismissal by Prosecuting Attorney

The prosecuting attorney may in writing or on the record, stating the reasons therefor, dismiss a petition or citation without leave of court and an indictment with leave of court.

Adopted Nov. 19, 2010, eff. Jan. 1, 2011.

Comment—Rule 6

See comment following Rule 6.08.

Rule 6.08. Dismissal by Court

If there is unnecessary delay by the prosecution in bringing a respondent to trial, the court may dismiss the petition, citation or indictment.

Adopted Nov. 19, 2010, eff. Jan. 1, 2011.

Comment—Rule 6

Previously, this rule only related to petitions in juvenile court. Due in large part to the high volume of gross misdemeanor alcohol related driving offenses, the law was amended to permit tab charges for these offenses to get cases to court more promptly.

A citation is defined as a writ issued out of a court of competent jurisdiction or an order issued by police commanding the person named to appear on a designated day and respond to a particular violation. It is most commonly used for minor offenses such as traffic violations. Some "tickets" issued by police are called "citation," some are called "complaint," and some are called "tab charge." The terms have become interchanged in everyday use.

In its revision of juvenile statutes, the legislature also expanded the list of offenses that may be charged by tab charge rather than petition in juvenile court. See Minnesota Statutes, section 260B.007, subd. 16 (2002). A tab charge is a brief statement entered upon the record by the clerk of the offense charged and citation to the statute, rule, regulation, ordinance or other provision of the law a child is alleged to have violated. The tab charge serves as a substitute for a petition. Tab charges may be used for any misdemeanor and for gross misdemeanors under Minnesota Statutes, chapter 169A. Adults have the right to demand a formal complaint in place of a tab charge. If a demand for a formal complaint is made by an adult charged with a gross misdemeanor alcohol offense, the prosecutor must file the complaint within 48 hours if the defendant is in custody, and within 10 days if not in custody. These rules have afforded juveniles the right to demand a petition where the child is charged with a misdemeanor(s) or gross misdemeanor(s).

Minn. R. Juv. Del. P. 6.06, subd. 2 provides that the court administrator shall promptly schedule the matter for hearing when a charging document is filed with the court.

Minn. R. Juv. Del. P. 6.03, subd. 2 provides that a petition shall be signed by the prosecuting attorney before it is filed with the court. Minnesota Statutes, section 260B.141, subd. 1 (2002) provides that any reputable person having knowledge of a child who is a resident of this state, who appears to be delinquent, may petition the juvenile court.

Minn. R. Juv. Del. P. 6.03, subds. 3 and 5 set forth the necessary contents of the petition. A sample petition form as well as a listing of the administrative content approved by the Juvenile Delinquency Rules Committee will be published by the State Court Administrator on the Minnesota Judicial Branch website.

The references to tab charges and citations filed by electronic means are intended to recognize that in some counties law enforcement has already begun to electronically file tab charges and citations in juvenile cases. It is understood that electronic filing of tab charges and citations is not available statewide at this time. The rule authorizes the practice in the locations where it currently exists, and authorizes the expansion of the practice as it becomes technologically feasible in other locations.

RULE 7. ARRAIGNMENT

Rule 7.01 Application

This rule is not applicable to proceedings on juvenile petty offenses or juvenile traffic offenses, which are governed by Rule 17.

Amended June 26, 1996; July 18, 2003.

Comment—Rule 7

See comment following Rule 7.04.

Historical Notes

The order of the Minnesota Supreme Court [C6–84–2165] dated June 26, 1996, provides in part that "(t)hese amendments to the Rules of Juvenile Procedure shall govern all juvenile actions commenced or arrests made on or after 12:00 o'clock midnight August 1, 1996."

The order of the Minnesota Supreme Court [CX–01–926] dated July 18, 2003, provides in part that "(t)he attached amendments shall govern all juveniles taken into custody and all juvenile delinquency actions commenced or children taken into custody after 12 o'clock midnight September 1, 2003."

Rule 7.02. Generally

Arraignment is a hearing at which the child shall enter a plea in the manner provided in Rule 8.

Amended June 26, 1996; July 18, 2003.

Comment—Rule 7

See comment following Rule 7.04.

Historical Notes

The order of the Minnesota Supreme Court [C6–84–2165] dated June 26, 1996, provides in part that "(t)hese amendments to the Rules of Juvenile Procedure shall govern all juvenile actions commenced or arrests made on or after 12:00 o'clock midnight August 1, 1996."

The order of the Minnesota Supreme Court [CX–01–926] dated July 18, 2003, provides in part that "(t)he attached amendments shall govern all juveniles taken into custody and all juvenile delinquency actions commenced or children taken into custody after 12 o'clock midnight September 1, 2003."

Rule 7.03. Timing

Upon the filing of a charging document, the court administrator shall promptly fix a time for arraignment and send notices pursuant to Rule 25.

Subd. 1. Child in Custody. The child in custody may be arraigned at a detention hearing and shall be arraigned no later than five (5) days after the detention hearing. The child has the right to have a copy of the charging document for three (3) days before being arraigned.

Subd. 2. Child Not in Custody. The child not in custody shall be arraigned no later than thirty (30) days after the filing of the charging document. The child has the right to have a copy of the charging document for three (3) days before being arraigned.

Amended June 26, 1996; July 18, 2003.

Comment—Rule 7

See comment following Rule 7.04.

Historical Notes

The order of the Minnesota Supreme Court [C6–84–2165] dated June 26, 1996, provides in part that "(t)hese amendments to the Rules of Juvenile Procedure shall govern all juvenile actions commenced or arrests made on or after 12:00 o'clock midnight August 1, 1996."

The order of the Minnesota Supreme Court [CX–01–926] dated July 18, 2003, provides in part that "(t)he attached amendments shall govern all juveniles taken into custody and all juvenile delinquency actions commenced or children taken into custody after 12 o'clock midnight September 1, 2003."

Rule 7.04. Hearing Procedure

Subd. 1. Initial Procedure. At the commencement of the hearing, the court shall on the record:

(A) verify the name, age, race, and residence of the child who is charged;

(B) determine whether all necessary persons are present and identify those present for the record;

(C) determine whether notice requirements have been met and if not, whether the affected persons waive notice;

(D) determine whether the child is either represented by counsel or waives counsel in the manner provided by Rule 3;

(E) if the child appears without counsel, and the court determines the child has properly waived the child's right to counsel, the court shall advise the child of all trial rights and other rights provided by these rules;

(F) explain to the child and the child's parent(s), legal guardian or legal custodian, if present, the child's right to remain silent in this and subsequent appearances before the court; and

(G) if two or more children are charged jointly with the same offense, advise the child of the danger of dual representation pursuant to Rule 3.03.

Subd. 2. Reading of Allegations of Charging Document. Unless waived by the child, the court shall read the allegations of the charging document to the child and determine that the child understands them, and if not, provide an explanation.

Subd. 3. Motions. The court shall hear and make findings on any motions regarding the sufficiency of the charging document, including its adequacy in stating probable cause of charges made, and the jurisdiction of the court, without requiring the child to plead guilty or not guilty to the charges stated in the charging document. A challenge on probable cause shall not delay the setting of trial proceedings in cases where the child has demanded a speedy trial.

Subd. 4. Response to Charging Document. After considering the wishes of the parties to proceed later or at once, the court may continue the arraignment without requiring that the child plead guilty or not guilty to charges stated in the charging document.

Amended June 26, 1996; Dec. 12, 1997; July 18, 2003.

Comment—Rule 7

Minn. R. Juv. Del. P. 7.04, subd. 1 (G) and Minn. R. Juv. Del. P. 3.03 regarding advising children of the perils of dual representation are patterned after Minn. R. Crim. P. 17.03, subd. 5.

Historical Notes

The order of the Minnesota Supreme Court [C6–84–2165] dated June 26, 1996, provides in part that "(t)hese amendments to the Rules of Juvenile Procedure shall govern all juvenile actions commenced or arrests made on or after 12:00 o'clock midnight August 1, 1996."

The order of the Minnesota Supreme Court [C6–84–2165] dated December 12, 1997, provides in part that "(t)hese amendments to the Rules of Juvenile Procedure shall govern all juvenile actions commenced or arrests made on or after 12:00 o'clock midnight January 1, 1998."

The order of the Minnesota Supreme Court [CX–01–926] dated July 18, 2003, provides in part that "(t)he attached amendments shall govern all juveniles taken into custody and all juvenile delinquency actions commenced or children taken into custody after 12 o'clock midnight September 1, 2003."

RULE 8. PLEAS

Rule 8.01. Application

Subd. 1. Juvenile Petty and Traffic Proceedings. Pleas in juvenile petty or juvenile traffic proceedings are governed by Rule 17.06.

Subd. 2. Extended Jurisdiction Juvenile Proceedings. Pleas in extended jurisdiction juvenile proceedings are governed by Rule 19.10, subdivision 5 and Minnesota Rules of Criminal Procedure 15.

Subd. 3. Competency Proceedings. Any child subject to competency proceedings pursuant to Rule 20 shall not be permitted to enter a plea until the court determines that the child is competent.

Amended June 26, 1996; July 18, 2003; Oct. 13, 2006, eff. Jan. 1, 2007.

Comment—Rule 8

See comment following Rule 8.04.

Historical Notes

The order of the Minnesota Supreme Court [C6–84–2165] dated June 26, 1996, provides in part that "(t)hese amendments to the Rules of Juvenile Procedure shall govern all juvenile actions commenced or arrests made on or after 12:00 o'clock midnight August 1, 1996."

The order of the Minnesota Supreme Court [CX–01–926] dated July 18, 2003, provides in part that "(t)he attached amendments shall govern all juveniles taken into custody and all juvenile delinquency actions commenced or children taken into custody after 12 o'clock midnight September 1, 2003."

Rule 8.02. Generally

If the child pleads not guilty to charges alleged in the charging document, the court shall conduct proceedings in accordance with Rules 9 through 16. If the child remains silent when confronted with charges, or if the court refuses to accept a guilty plea by the child, the court shall proceed in the same manner as if the child pled not guilty.

Adopted June 26, 1996. Amended July 18, 2003.

Comment—Rule 8

See comment following Rule 8.04.

Historical Notes

The order of the Minnesota Supreme Court [C6–84–2165] dated June 26, 1996, provides in part that "(t)hese amendments to the Rules of Juvenile Procedure shall govern all juvenile actions commenced or arrests made on or after 12:00 o'clock midnight August 1, 1996."

The order of the Minnesota Supreme Court [CX–01–926] dated July 18, 2003, provides in part that "(t)he attached amendments shall govern all juveniles taken into custody and all juvenile delinquency actions commenced or children taken into custody after 12 o'clock midnight September 1, 2003."

Rule 8.03. Plea of Not Guilty Without Appearance

Except when the child is in detention, the court may permit a written plea of not guilty or a plea of not guilty on the record to be entered by child's counsel without the personal appearance of the child, child's parent(s), legal guardian or legal custodian or their counsel. The child's counsel shall immediately furnish a copy of the written plea of not guilty to the prosecuting attorney, either personally or by mail. A copy of the written plea of not guilty may also be furnished to the prosecuting attorney by electronic means if authorized by Minnesota Supreme Court Order and if furnished in accordance with that order.

Adopted June 26, 1996. Amended July 18, 2003; Oct. 15, 2012, eff. Dec. 1, 2012.

Comment—Rule 8

See comment following Rule 8.04.

Historical Notes

The order of the Minnesota Supreme Court [C6–84–2165] dated June 26, 1996, provides in part that "(t)hese amendments to the Rules of Juvenile Procedure shall govern all juvenile actions commenced or arrests made on or after 12:00 o'clock midnight August 1, 1996."

The order of the Minnesota Supreme Court [CX–01–926] dated July 18, 2003, provides in part that "(t)he attached amendments shall govern all juveniles taken into custody and all juvenile delinquency actions commenced or children taken into custody after 12 o'clock midnight September 1, 2003."

The order of the Minnesota Supreme Court [ADM10–8003] dated October 15, 2012, provides in part that the "amendments shall govern all delinquency actions pending or commenced on or after 12 o'clock midnight December 1, 2012."

Rule 8.04. Plea of Guilty

Subd. 1. Waiver of Right to Trial. The court shall not accept a child's plea of guilty until first determining, the following, under the totality of the circumstances, and based on the child's statements, whether on the record or contained in a written document signed by the child and the child's counsel:

(A) *Charges in Charging Document; Factual Basis for Plea.* That the child understands the charges stated in the charging document, and the essential elements of each charge, and that there is a factual basis for the guilty plea;

(B) *Right to Trial.* That the child understands the child's right to have a trial, that is, to require proof of all elements of each offense stated in the charging document, and that this includes an understanding of the following related rights:

(1) the right to be presumed innocent of each charge until and unless the petitioner succeeds in proving beyond a reasonable doubt that the child is guilty;

(2) the right to remain silent during trial proceedings if the child wishes and the right of the child to testify on the child's own behalf if the child wants to;

(3) the right to call witnesses to testify on the child's behalf, including the right to use court subpoenas to require that witnesses for the child attend the trial; and

(4) the right to hear the testimony of all witnesses called by the prosecuting attorney, and to cross-examine these witnesses; and

(C) *Dispositions.* That the child understands the powers of the court to make a disposition if the court finds that the allegations in the charging document are proved, including the child's understanding that:

(1) the court's powers range up to the most severe step of placing custody of the child in an institution;

(2) the court's disposition could be for a duration ranging upward to the time the child attains age 19; and

(3) the court can modify an initial disposition, even repeatedly, for a term ranging up to the time the child attains age 19; and

(4) the child understands the potential future consequences if the court finds that the allegations in the charging document are proved, including the child's understanding of:

(a) the effect of the finding on sentencing of the child if the child, when an adult, is convicted of an adult offense; and

(b) the effect of the finding in the event the child commits any further offenses while a juvenile, including the prospects for certification of the child for an adult court prosecution or for prosecution in juvenile court as an extended jurisdiction juvenile;

(D) *Right to Counsel.* If a child charged with a misdemeanor remains without counsel or with only stand-by counsel, that the child understands the continued right to be represented by counsel, and understands that counsel:

(1) could give the child further information and advice on the child's rights and on the choice to plead guilty or not guilty to the offense(s) in the charging document; and

(2) could assist the child during a trial, to protect all rights of the child that arise in the course of a trial;

(E) *Free Choice.* That any plea of guilty is made freely, and that no one has made either threats or promises to the child to encourage a plea of guilty other than those that the parties have disclosed to the court.

(F) *No Claim of Innocence.* That the child is not making any claim of innocence.

Subd. 2. Withdrawal of Plea. The child may, on the record or by written motion filed with the court, request to withdraw a plea of guilty. The court may allow the child to withdraw a guilty plea

(A) before disposition, if it is fair and just to do so, giving due consideration to the reasons the child gives and any prejudice that withdrawal of the plea would cause because of actions taken in reliance on the child's plea; or

(B) at any time, upon showing that withdrawal is necessary to correct a manifest injustice.

Subd. 3. Plea to a Lesser Offense or a Different Offense. With the consent of the prosecuting attorney and the approval of the court, the child shall be permitted to enter:

(A) a plea of guilty to a lesser included offense or to an offense of lesser degree, or

(B) a plea of guilty to a different offense than alleged in the original charging document.

A plea of guilty to a lesser included offense or to an offense of lesser degree may be entered without an amendment of the charging document. If a plea to different offense is accepted, the charging document must be amended on the record or a new charging document must be filed with the court.

Subd. 4. Acceptance or Nonacceptance of Plea of Guilty. The court shall make a finding within fifteen (15) days of a plea of guilty:

(A) that the plea has been accepted and allegations in the charging document have been proved; or

(B) that the plea has not been accepted.

Subd. 5. Future Proceedings. If the court accepts a plea of guilty and makes a finding that the allegations in the charging document are proved, the court shall schedule further proceedings pursuant to Rules 14 and 15.

Adopted June 26, 1996. Amended July 18, 2003; April 23, 2004.

Comment—Rule 8

It is also desirable that the child be asked to acknowledge by signing the plea petition that the child has read the questions set forth in the petition or that they have been read to the child; that the child understands them; that the child gave the answers set forth in the petition; and that they are true. Suggested forms of the plea petition are appended to the rules.

Historical Notes

The order of the Minnesota Supreme Court [C6–84–2165] dated June 26, 1996, provides in part that "(t)hese amendments to the Rules of Juvenile Procedure shall govern all juvenile actions commenced or arrests made on or after 12:00 o'clock midnight August 1, 1996."

The order of the Minnesota Supreme Court [CX–01–926] dated July 18, 2003, provides in part that "(t)he attached amendments shall govern all juveniles taken into custody and all juvenile delinquency actions commenced or children taken into custody after 12 o'clock midnight September 1, 2003."

The order of the Minnesota Supreme Court [CX–01–926] dated April 23, 2004, provides in part that "(t)he attached amendments shall govern all juvenile delinquency actions commenced or children taken into custody after 12 o'clock midnight July 1, 2004."

RULE 9. SETTLEMENT DISCUSSIONS AND PLEA AGREEMENTS

Rule 9.01. Generally

In cases in which it appears that it would serve the interests of the public in the effective administration of juvenile justice under the principles set forth in this rule, the prosecuting attorney may engage in settlement discussions for the purposes of reaching a settlement agreement. If the child is represented, the prosecuting attorney shall engage in settlement discussions only through the child's counsel.

Amended June 26, 1996.

Historical Notes

The order of the Minnesota Supreme Court [C6–84–2165] dated June 26, 1996, provides in part that "(t)hese amendments to the Rules of Juvenile Procedure shall govern all juvenile actions commenced or arrests made on or after 12:00 o'clock midnight August 1, 1996."

Former Rule: A former Rule 9.01, adopted Dec. 17, 1982, defined notice, summons, and court order. The subject matter of former Rule 9.01 was incorporated into Rule 25.01 by court order dated June 26, 1996.

Rule 9.02. Relationship Between the Child and the Child's Counsel

The child's counsel shall conclude a settlement agreement only with the consent of the child and shall ensure that the decision to enter a guilty plea is ultimately made by the child.

Amended June 26, 1996.

Historical Notes

The order of the Minnesota Supreme Court [C6–84–2165] dated June 26, 1996, provides in part that "(t)hese amendments to the Rules of Juvenile Procedure shall govern all juvenile actions commenced or arrests made on or after 12:00 o'clock midnight August 1, 1996."

Rule 9.03. Disclosure of Settlement Agreement

If a settlement agreement has been reached which contemplates a guilty plea, the court shall require the disclosure of the agreement and the reasons for it before the plea. The court shall reject or accept the plea on the terms of the settlement agreement. The court may postpone its acceptance or rejection until it has received the results of a pre-disposition report. If the court rejects the settlement agreement, it shall advise the parties in open court and then ask the child to either affirm or withdraw the plea.

Amended June 26, 1996.

Historical Notes

The order of the Minnesota Supreme Court [C6–84–2165] dated June 26, 1996, provides in part that "(t)hese amendments to the Rules of Juvenile Procedure shall govern all juvenile actions commenced or arrests made on or after 12:00 o'clock midnight August 1, 1996."

Rule 9.04. Settlement Discussions and Agreements Not Admissible

If the child enters a guilty plea which is not accepted or which is withdrawn, neither the settlement discussions, nor the settlement agreement, nor the plea shall be received in evidence against or in favor of the child in any subsequent proceeding against the child.

Amended June 26, 1996.

Historical Notes

The order of the Minnesota Supreme Court [C6–84–2165] dated June 26, 1996, provides in part that "(t)hese amendments to the Rules of Juvenile Procedure shall govern all juvenile actions commenced or arrests made on or after 12:00 o'clock midnight August 1, 1996."

RULE 10. DISCOVERY

Rule 10.01. Scope and Application

Rule 10 applies to discovery for delinquency proceedings, certification hearings and extended jurisdiction juvenile proceedings and prosecutions. Pursuant to Rule 17.07, this rule may apply, in the discretion of the court, to juvenile petty and juvenile traffic proceedings. The discovery procedures provided for by this rule do not exclude other lawful methods available for obtaining evidence.

Adopted June 26, 1996. Amended July 18, 2003.

Comment—Rule 10

See comment following Rule 10.07.

Historical Notes

The order of the Minnesota Supreme Court [C6–84–2165] dated June 26, 1996, provides in part that "(t)hese amendments to the Rules of Juvenile Procedure shall govern all juvenile actions commenced or arrests made on or after 12:00 o'clock midnight August 1, 1996."

The order of the Minnesota Supreme Court [CX–01–926] dated July 18, 2003, provides in part that "(t)he attached amendments shall govern all juveniles taken into custody and all juvenile delinquency actions commenced or children taken into custody after 12 o'clock midnight September 1, 2003."

Rule 10.02. Evidence and Identification Disclosure

The prosecuting attorney shall advise the child's counsel in writing of:

(A) any evidence against the child obtained as a result of a search, seizure, wiretapping or any form of electronic or mechanical eavesdropping;

(B) any confessions, admissions, or statements in the nature of confessions made by the child;

(C) any evidence against the child discovered as a result of confessions, admissions or statements in the nature of confessions made by the child; and

(D) any identification procedures involving the child, including but not limited to line-ups or other observations of the child and the exhibition of photographs of the child.

The notice required by this rule shall be provided by the prosecutor within five (5) days of a not guilty plea by the child. If child's counsel makes a demand for disclosure pursuant to this rule, the disclosures shall be provided within five (5) days of the demand. Evidence which becomes known to the prosecutor after the deadlines for disclosure provided here, shall immediately be disclosed to child's counsel.

Adopted June 26, 1996. Amended July 18, 2003.

Comment—Rule 10

See comment following Rule 10.07.

Historical Notes

The order of the Minnesota Supreme Court [C6–84–2165] dated June 26, 1996, provides in part that "(t)hese amendments to the Rules

of Juvenile Procedure shall govern all juvenile actions commenced or arrests made on or after 12:00 o'clock midnight August 1, 1996."

The order of the Minnesota Supreme Court [CX–01–926] dated July 18, 2003, provides in part that "(t)he attached amendments shall govern all juveniles taken into custody and all juvenile delinquency actions commenced or children taken into custody after 12 o'clock midnight September 1, 2003."

Rule 10.03. Notice of Additional Offenses

The prosecuting attorney shall advise child's counsel of evidence of any additional offenses that may be offered at the trial under any exclusionary rule exceptions. Such additional acts shall be described with sufficient particularity to enable the child to prepare for the trial. The notice need not include offenses for which the child has been previously prosecuted, or that may be offered in rebuttal of character witnesses for the child or as a part of the occurrence or episode out of which the charges against the child arose. Notice of additional offenses shall be given at or before the pretrial or omnibus hearing or as soon after those hearings as the offenses become known to the prosecutor. If there is no pretrial or omnibus hearing, the notice shall be given at least seven (7) days before the trial.

Adopted June 26, 1996. Amended July 18, 2003.

Comment—Rule 10

See comment following Rule 10.07.

Historical Notes

The order of the Minnesota Supreme Court [C6–84–2165] dated June 26, 1996, provides in part that "(t)hese amendments to the Rules of Juvenile Procedure shall govern all juvenile actions commenced or arrests made on or after 12:00 o'clock midnight August 1, 1996."

The order of the Minnesota Supreme Court [CX–01–926] dated July 18, 2003, provides in part that "(t)he attached amendments shall govern all juveniles taken into custody and all juvenile delinquency actions commenced or children taken into custody after 12 o'clock midnight September 1, 2003."

Rule 10.04. Disclosure by Prosecuting Attorney

Subd. 1. Disclosure by Prosecuting Attorney Without Order of Court. After a charging document is filed, if the child's counsel makes a request, the prosecuting attorney shall make the following disclosures within five (5) days of the receipt of the request:

(A) *Trial Witnesses.* The prosecuting attorney shall disclose to the child's counsel the names and addresses of the persons the prosecuting attorney intends to call as witnesses at the trial, extended jurisdiction juvenile proceeding or prosecution or certification hearing, together with their prior record of adult convictions, any prior record of allegations of delinquency which have been proved and any prior delinquency adjudications within the actual knowledge of the prosecuting attorney. The prosecuting attorney shall permit the child's counsel to inspect and copy the witnesses' relevant written or recorded statements and any written summaries of the substance of relevant oral statements made by the witnesses to the prosecuting attorney or agents of the prosecuting attorney within the knowledge of the prosecuting attorney.

(B) *Statements of Child and Accomplices.* The prosecuting attorney shall disclose and permit the child's counsel to inspect and copy any relevant written or recorded statements made by the child and accomplices within the possession or control of the prosecuting attorney, the existence of which is known by the prosecuting attorney, and shall provide the child's counsel with the substance of any oral statements made by the child and accomplices which the prosecuting attorney intends to offer in evidence at the trial, extended jurisdiction juvenile proceeding or prosecution or certification hearing.

(C) *Documents and Tangible Objects.* The prosecuting attorney shall disclose and permit the child's counsel to inspect and copy books, papers, documents, photographs and tangible objects that the prosecutor intends to introduce in evidence at the trial, extended jurisdiction juvenile proceeding or prosecution or certification hearing, or which were obtained from or belong to the child and which the prosecuting attorney intends to offer as evidence at the trial, extended jurisdiction juvenile proceeding or prosecution or certification hearing. If the prosecuting attorney intends to offer evidence of buildings or places at the trial, extended jurisdiction juvenile proceeding or prosecution or certification hearing, the prosecuting attorney shall permit the child's counsel to inspect and photograph such buildings or places.

(D) *Reports of Examinations and Tests.* The prosecuting attorney shall disclose and permit the child's counsel to inspect and copy any results or reports of physical or mental examinations, scientific tests, experiments or comparisons made which are relevant to the case.

(E) *Record of the Child.* The prosecuting attorney shall inform the child's counsel of any prior allegations of delinquency which have been proved and of prior adjudications of delinquency of the child within the possession or control of the prosecuting attorney.

(F) *Special Education and School Disciplinary Records.* The prosecuting attorney shall disclose and permit the child's counsel to inspect and copy all special education and school disciplinary records of the child, which were transmitted by the agency reporting the crime for consideration in charging.

(G) *Exculpatory Information.* The prosecuting attorney shall disclose to the child's counsel any material or information within the possession and control of the prosecuting attorney that tends to disprove the allegation(s).

(H) *Scope of the Prosecuting Attorney's Obligations.* The prosecuting attorney's obligations under this rule extend to material and information in the possession or control of members of the prosecuting attorney's staff and of any others who have participated in the investigation or evaluation of the matter and who report to the prosecuting attorney's office.

Subd. 2. Disclosure Upon Order of Court. Upon motion of the child's counsel, the court at any time before trial may require the prosecuting attorney to disclose to the child's counsel any information requested that is relevant to guilt, innocence or culpability of the child. If the motion is denied, the court upon application of the child shall inspect and preserve any relevant information.

Subd. 3. Information Not Subject to Disclosure by Prosecuting Attorney.

(A) *Opinions, Theories or Conclusions.* Unless otherwise provided by these rules, any legal research, records, correspondence, reports or memoranda to the extent that they contain the opinions, theories or conclusions of the prosecuting attorney or members of the prosecuting attorney's staff or officials or agents of the prosecuting attorney participating in the matter are not subject to disclosure.

(B) *Reports.* Except as provided in Rule 10.04, subdivisions 1(C)–(G), reports, memoranda or internal documents made by the prosecuting attorney or members of the prosecuting attorney's staff or by agents of the prosecuting attorney in connection with the matter are not subject to disclosure.

(C) *Prosecution Witnesses Under Prosecuting Attorney's Certificate.* The information relative to the witnesses and persons described in Rule 10.04, subdivisions 1(A) and (B), shall not be subject to disclosure if approved by the court when the prosecuting attorney files a written certificate with the court that to do so may subject the witnesses or persons or others to physical harm or coercion, provided, however, that non-disclosure under this rule shall not extend beyond the time the witnesses are sworn to testify.

Adopted June 26, 1996. Amended July 18, 2003.

Comment—Rule 10

See comment following Rule 10.07.

Historical Notes

The order of the Minnesota Supreme Court [C6–84–2165] dated June 26, 1996, provides in part that "(t)hese amendments to the Rules of Juvenile Procedure shall govern all juvenile actions commenced or arrests made on or after 12:00 o'clock midnight August 1, 1996."

The order of the Minnesota Supreme Court [CX–01–926] dated July 18, 2003, provides in part that "(t)he attached amendments shall govern all juveniles taken into custody and all juvenile delinquency actions commenced or children taken into custody after 12 o'clock midnight September 1, 2003."

Rule 10.05. Disclosure by Child

Subd. 1. Information Subject to Disclosure Without Order of Court. After a charging document is filed, if the prosecuting attorney makes a request, the child's counsel shall make the following disclosures within five (5) days of the receipt of the request.

(A) *Documents and Tangible Objects.* The child's counsel shall disclose and permit the prosecuting attorney to inspect and copy books, papers, documents, photographs and tangible objects which the child intends to introduce in evidence at the trial, extended jurisdiction juvenile proceeding or prosecution or certification hearing. If the child's counsel intends to offer evidence of buildings or places at the trial, extended jurisdiction juvenile proceeding or prosecution or certification hearing, the child's counsel shall permit the prosecuting attorney to inspect and photograph such buildings or places.

(B) *Reports of Examinations and Tests.* The child's counsel shall disclose and permit the prosecuting attorney to inspect and copy any results or reports of physical or mental examinations, scientific tests, experiments and comparisons made in connection with the particular matter within the possession or control of the child which the child intends to introduce in evidence at the trial, extended jurisdiction juvenile proceeding or prosecution or certification hearing or which were prepared by a witness whom the child intends to call at the trial, extended jurisdiction juvenile proceeding or prosecution or certification hearing when the results or reports relate to the testimony of the witness.

(C) *Notice of Defense, Witnesses for the Child and Record.*

(1) Notice of Defenses. The child's counsel shall inform the prosecuting attorney in writing of any defense, other than that of a denial, on which the child intends to rely at the trial, including but not limited to the defenses of self-defense, entrapment, duress, alibi, double jeopardy, statute of limitations, collateral estoppel, a defense pursuant to Minnesota Statutes, section 609.035 or intoxication. Notice of a defense of mental illness or mental deficiency is governed by Rule 20.02, subdivision 1.

(2) Witnesses for the Child. The child's counsel shall provide the prosecuting attorney with the names and addresses of persons whom the child intends to call as witnesses at the trial, extended jurisdiction juvenile proceeding or prosecution or certification hearing together with their prior record of adult convictions, any prior record of proven allegations of delinquency and any prior delinquency adjudications within the actual knowledge of the child's counsel.

(3) Statements of Witnesses for the Child. The child's counsel shall permit the prosecuting

attorney to inspect and copy any relevant written or recorded statements of the persons whom the child intends to call as witnesses at the trial, extended jurisdiction juvenile proceeding or prosecution or certification hearing and which are within the possession or control of the child's counsel and shall permit the prosecuting attorney to inspect and copy any written summaries within the knowledge of the child or the child's counsel of the substance of any oral statements made by such witnesses to the child's counsel or obtained by the child at the direction of counsel.

(4) Alibi. If the child intends to offer evidence of an alibi, the child's counsel shall also inform the prosecuting attorney of the specific place or places where the child contends the child was when the alleged delinquent act occurred and shall inform the prosecuting attorney of the names and addresses of the witnesses the child intends to call at the trial in support of the alibi.

(5) Record. The child's counsel shall inform the prosecuting attorney of any prior allegations of a delinquency which have been proved and any prior adjudications of delinquency of the child. A child shall not be required to reveal prior offenses which might result in enhancement of pending enhanceable offenses.

Subd. 2. Disclosure Upon Order of Court.

(A) *Disclosure Procedures With Child.* Upon motion of the prosecuting attorney and a showing that one or more of the following procedures will be material in determining whether the child committed the alleged act or should be certified or is an extended jurisdiction juvenile, the court at any time before a hearing may, subject to constitutional limitations, order the child to:

(1) appear in a line-up;

(2) speak for identification by witnesses to an offense or for the purpose of taking voice prints;

(3) be fingerprinted or permit palm prints or footprints to be taken;

(4) permit measurements of the child's body to be taken;

(5) pose for photographs not involving re-enactment of a scene;

(6) permit the taking of samples of blood, hair, saliva, urine and other materials of the child's body which involve no unreasonable intrusion;

(7) provide specimens of handwriting; or

(8) submit to reasonable physical or medical inspection of the child's body.

(B) *Notice of Time and Place of Discovery Procedures With Child.* Whenever the personal appearance of the child is required for procedures ordered pursuant to Rule 10.05, subdivision 2(A), the prosecuting attorney shall inform the child's counsel of the time and place of the procedure.

(C) *Medical Supervision.* Blood tests shall be conducted under medical supervision and the court may require medical supervision for any other test ordered pursuant to this rule when the court deems such supervision necessary. Upon motion of the child's counsel, the court may order the child's appearance delayed for a reasonable time or may order that tests take place at the child's residence or some other convenient place.

(D) *Notice of Results.* The prosecuting attorney shall make available to the child's counsel the results of the procedures provided by Rule 10.05, subdivision 2(A) within five (5) days from the date the results become known to the prosecuting attorney, unless otherwise ordered by the court.

Subd. 3. Information Not Subject to Disclosure by Child.

(A) *Opinions, Theories or Conclusions.* Unless otherwise provided by these rules, any legal research, records, correspondence, reports or memoranda to the extent that they contain the opinions, theories, or conclusions of the child, the child's counsel, members of counsel's staff or counsel's agents participating in the representation of the child are not subject to disclosure.

(B) *Reports.* Except as provided by Rule 10.05, subdivisions 1(A) and (B) and (C)(2), (3), and (5), reports, memoranda or internal documents made by the child's counsel or members of counsel's staff, or counsel's agents in connection with the defense of the matter against the child are not subject to disclosure.

Adopted June 26, 1996. Amended July 18, 2003.

Comment—Rule 10

See comment following Rule 10.07.

Historical Notes

The order of the Minnesota Supreme Court [C6–84–2165] dated June 26, 1996, provides in part that "(t)hese amendments to the Rules of Juvenile Procedure shall govern all juvenile actions commenced or arrests made on or after 12:00 o'clock midnight August 1, 1996."

The order of the Minnesota Supreme Court [CX–01–926] dated July 18, 2003, provides in part that "(t)he attached amendments shall govern all juveniles taken into custody and all juvenile delinquency actions commenced or children taken into custody after 12 o'clock midnight September 1, 2003."

Rule 10.06. Regulation of Discovery

Subd. 1. Investigations Not to be Impeded.

(A) *Prosecuting Attorney.* The prosecuting attorney or agents for the prosecuting attorney shall not advise persons having relevant material or information to refrain from discussing the case with the child's counsel or from showing opposing counsel any relevant materials nor shall they otherwise impede investigation of the case by the child's counsel.

(B) *Child, Child's Counsel or Agents for Child's Counsel.* The child, child's counsel, or agents for the child or child's counsel shall not advise persons having relevant material or information to refrain from discussing the case with opposing counsel or their agents or from showing opposing counsel any relevant materials nor shall they otherwise impede opposing counsel's investigation of the case except the child's counsel may:

(1) advise the child that the child need not talk to anyone, and

(2) advise the child's parent(s), legal guardian and legal custodian that they may refrain from discussing any relevant material or information obtained as a result of privileged communication between the child and child's counsel.

Subd. 2. Continuing Duty to Disclose. If, after compliance with any discovery rule or order, the prosecuting attorney or the child's counsel discovers additional material, information or witnesses subject to disclosure, counsel shall promptly notify the opposing side of the existence of the additional material or information and the identity of the witnesses. The prosecuting attorney and the child's counsel have a continuing duty at all times before and during trial to supply the materials and information required by these rules.

Subd. 3. Time, Place and Manner of Discovery and Inspection. An order of the court permitting discovery shall specify the time, place and manner of making the discovery and inspection permitted and may prescribe such terms and conditions as are just.

Subd. 4. Custody of Materials. Any materials furnished to the prosecuting attorney or the child's counsel under discovery rules or court orders shall remain in the custody of the prosecuting attorney or the child's counsel and shall be used only for the pending case and shall be subject to such other terms and conditions as the court may prescribe.

Subd. 5. Protective Orders. Upon a showing of reasonable cause, the court may at any time order that specified disclosures be restricted or deferred or make such other order as is appropriate. However, all materials and information to which the prosecuting attorney or the child's counsel is entitled must be disclosed in time to afford the opportunity to make beneficial use of it.

Subd. 6. Excision. If only a portion of materials are discoverable under these rules, that portion shall be disclosed. If material is excised pursuant to judicial order, it shall be sealed and preserved in the records of the court to be made available to the reviewing court in the event of an appeal or habeas corpus proceeding.

Subd. 7. Sanctions.

(A) *Continuance or Order.* If at any time it is brought to the attention of the court that the prosecuting attorney, the child or child's counsel has failed to comply with an applicable discovery rule or order, the court may upon motion, order discovery or inspection, grant a continuance, or enter such order as it deems just in the circumstances.

(B) *Contempt.* Any person who willfully disobeys a court order under these discovery rules may be held in contempt.

Subd. 8. Expense. If the child or the parent(s) of the child cannot afford the costs of discovery, these costs will be at public expense in whole or in part depending on the ability of the child or the parent(s) of the child to pay.

Adopted June 26, 1996. Amended July 18, 2003.

Comment—Rule 10

See comment following Rule 10.07.

Historical Notes

The order of the Minnesota Supreme Court [C6–84–2165] dated June 26, 1996, provides in part that "(t)hese amendments to the Rules of Juvenile Procedure shall govern all juvenile actions commenced or arrests made on or after 12:00 o'clock midnight August 1, 1996."

The order of the Minnesota Supreme Court [CX–01–926] dated July 18, 2003, provides in part that "(t)he attached amendments shall govern all juveniles taken into custody and all juvenile delinquency actions commenced or children taken into custody after 12 o'clock midnight September 1, 2003."

Rule 10.07. Taking Depositions

Subd. 1. Deposition of Unavailable Witness. Upon motion, the court may order the deposition of a prospective witness when there is a reasonable probability the testimony of the witness will be used at a trial or hearing and:

(A) there is a reasonable probability the witness will be unable to be present or to testify at the trial or hearing because of the witness' physical or mental illness, infirmity, or death; or

(B) the person requesting the deposition has been unable to procure the attendance of the witness by subpoena, order of the court, or other reasonable means; or

(C) there is a stipulation by counsel; or

(D) there is another reason accepted by the court.

Subd. 2. Procedure. The court may order that the deposition be taken orally before any designated person authorized to administer oaths and that any designated book, paper, document, record, recording or other material not privileged, be produced at the same time and place. The order shall direct the child to be present when the deposition is being taken.

(A) *Oral Deposition.* Depositions shall be taken upon oral examination.

(B) *Oath and Record.* The witness shall be put under oath and a verbatim record of the testimony shall be made in the manner directed by the court.

In the event the court orders that the testimony at a deposition be recorded by other than stenographic means, the order shall designate the manner of recording, preserving and filing the deposition, and may include other provisions to assure that the recorded testimony will be accurate and trustworthy. If this order is made, the prosecuting attorney or the child's counsel may nevertheless arrange to have a stenographic transcription made at their own expense.

(C) *Scope and Manner of Examination—Objections, Motion to Terminate.*

(1) Consent Required. In no event shall the deposition of a child who is charged with an offense be taken without the child's consent.

(2) Scope and Manner of Taking. The scope and manner of examination and cross-examination in the taking of a deposition to be used at trial shall be the same as that allowed at the trial. The scope and manner of examination and cross-examination in the taking of a deposition to be used at a certification or extended jurisdiction juvenile hearing shall be the same as would be allowed at a certification or extended jurisdiction juvenile hearing.

(3) Objections. All objections made at the time of the examination to the qualifications of the person taking the deposition, or to the manner of taking it, or to the evidence presented or to the conduct of any person present at the depositions and any other objection to the proceedings shall be recorded by the person before whom the deposition is taken. Evidence objected to shall be taken subject to the objections unless the objection is based on the witness's use of the Fifth Amendment.

(4) Limitation upon Motion. At any time, on motion of the child's counsel or the prosecuting attorney, or of the deponent, the court may limit the taking of the deposition to that which is commensurate in cost and duration with the needs of the case, the resources available and the issues.

At any time during the taking of the deposition, on motion of the child's counsel or the prosecuting attorney, or of the deponent, and upon a showing that the examination is being conducted in bad faith or in such manner as to annoy, embarrass or oppress the deponent, the child, the child's counsel or prosecuting attorney or to elicit privileged testimony, the court which ordered the deposition taken may order the person conducting the examination to cease forthwith from taking the deposition or may limit the scope and manner of taking the deposition by ordering as follows:

(A) that certain matters not be inquired into or that the scope of examination be limited to certain matters, or

(B) that the examination be conducted with no one present except persons designated by the court.

Upon demand of the child's counsel, the prosecuting attorney or the deponent, the taking of the deposition shall be suspended for the time necessary to move for the order.

Subd. 3. Transcription, Certification and Filing. When the testimony is fully transcribed, the person before whom the deposition was taken shall certify on the deposition that the witness was duly sworn and that the deposition is a verbatim record of the testimony given by the witness. That person shall then securely seal the deposition in an envelope endorsed with the title of the case and marked "Deposition of (here insert name of witness)" and shall promptly file it with the court in which the case is pending or send it by registered or certified mail to the court administrator thereof for filing. Upon the request of the child's counsel or the prosecuting attorney, documents and other things produced during the examination of a witness, or copies thereof, shall be marked for identification and annexed as exhibits to the deposition, and may be inspected and copied by the child's counsel and the prosecuting attorney. The person taking the deposition shall mark the exhibits, and after giving opposing counsel an opportunity to inspect and copy them, return the exhibits to the person producing them. The exhibits may then be used in the same manner as if annexed to the deposition.

Subd. 4. Failure to Appear. Failure of the child to appear after notice is given will not prohibit the deposition from being taken.

Subd. 5. Expense of Depositions. If the child or the parent(s) of the child cannot afford the costs of depositions, these costs shall be paid at public expense in whole or in part, depending on the ability of the child or the parent(s) of the child to pay.

Adopted June 26, 1996. Amended July 18, 2003.

Comment—Rule 10

Minn. R. Juv. Del. P. 10.02 is modeled after the Minn. R. Crim. P. 7.01. A suggested form for the notice to be provided by this rule is included in the appendix of forms, following these rules.

Minn. R. Juv. Del. P. 10.03 is modeled after Minn. R. Crim. P. 7.02 and would encompass the commonly referred to *Spreigl* notice derived from *State v. Spreigl*, 139 N.W.2d 167 (1965).

Minn. R. Juv. Del. P. 10.05, subd. 1(C)(5) provides that a child is not required to reveal prior offenses which might result in enhancement of pending enhanceable offenses. An example of an "enhanceable offense" is a pending misdemeanor fifth degree assault which could be amended to a gross misdemeanor under Minnesota Statutes, section 609.224, subd. 2 (2002) if the prosecutor knew, for instance, of the child's prior adjudication for misdemeanor assault against the same victim in another county.

References in this rule to "child's counsel" include the child who is proceeding pro se. Minn. R. Juv. Del. P. 1.01.

Historical Notes

The order of the Minnesota Supreme Court [C6–84–2165] dated June 26, 1996, provides in part that "(t)hese amendments to the Rules of Juvenile Procedure shall govern all juvenile actions commenced or arrests made on or after 12:00 o'clock midnight August 1, 1996."

The order of the Minnesota Supreme Court [CX–01–926] dated July 18, 2003, provides in part that "(t)he attached amendments shall govern all juveniles taken into custody and all juvenile delinquency actions commenced or children taken into custody after 12 o'clock midnight September 1, 2003."

RULE 11. PRETRIAL CONFERENCE

Rule 11.01. Timing

The court, in its discretion or upon motion of the child's counsel or the prosecuting attorney, may order a pretrial conference. Where there has been no pretrial conference, pretrial issues and motions shall be heard immediately before trial unless the court orders otherwise for good cause.

Amended June 26, 1996.

Comment—Rule 11

See comment following Rule 11.02.

Historical Notes

The order of the Minnesota Supreme Court [C6–84–2165] dated June 26, 1996, provides in part that "(t)hese amendments to the Rules of Juvenile Procedure shall govern all juvenile actions commenced or arrests made on or after 12:00 o'clock midnight August 1, 1996."

Rule 11.02. Evidentiary and Other Issues

At the pretrial conference, the court shall determine whether there are any constitutional or evidentiary issues and, if so, schedule an omnibus hearing pursuant to Rule 12. If there is no pretrial conference, constitutional or evidentiary issues shall be raised by written motion of the child's counsel or prosecuting attorney, and the court shall schedule an omnibus hearing. The written motion must specifically set forth the issues raised.

Amended June 26, 1996; July 18, 2003.

Comment—Rule 11

References in this rule to "child's counsel" include the child who is proceeding pro se. Minn. R. Juv. Del. P. 1.01.

Historical Notes

The order of the Minnesota Supreme Court [C6–84–2165] dated June 26, 1996, provides in part that "(t)hese amendments to the Rules of Juvenile Procedure shall govern all juvenile actions commenced or arrests made on or after 12:00 o'clock midnight August 1, 1996."

The order of the Minnesota Supreme Court [CX–01–926] dated July 18, 2003, provides in part that "(t)he attached amendments shall govern all juveniles taken into custody and all juvenile delinquency actions commenced or children taken into custody after 12 o'clock midnight September 1, 2003."

Rule 11.03. Deleted June 26, 1996

Historical Notes

The order of the Minnesota Supreme Court [C6–84–2165] dated June 26, 1996, provides in part that "(t)hese amendments to the Rules of Juvenile Procedure shall govern all juvenile actions commenced or arrests made on or after 12:00 o'clock midnight August 1, 1996."

See, now, MN ST Juv. Del., Rule 29.03.

RULE 12. OMNIBUS HEARING

Rule 12.01. Scheduling of Omnibus Hearing

The court shall hold an omnibus hearing pursuant to Minnesota Rules of Criminal Procedure 11 any time before trial to determine issues raised pursuant to Rules 6, 10, or 11 upon its own motion or upon motion of the child's counsel or the prosecuting attorney.

Where new information, evidence, or issues arise during trial, the court may consider these issues at trial. Any issue not determined prior to trial shall be determined as part of the trial.

Amended June 26, 1996; July 18, 2003; Oct. 13, 2006, eff. Jan. 1, 2007.

Comment—Rule 12

See comment following Rule 12.02.

Historical Notes

The order of the Minnesota Supreme Court [C6–84–2165] dated June 26, 1996, provides in part that "(t)hese amendments to the Rules of Juvenile Procedure shall govern all juvenile actions commenced or arrests made on or after 12:00 o'clock midnight August 1, 1996."

The order of the Minnesota Supreme Court [CX–01–926] dated July 18, 2003, provides in part that "(t)he attached amendments shall govern all juveniles taken into custody and all juvenile delinquency actions commenced or children taken into custody after 12 o'clock midnight September 1, 2003."

Rule 12.02. Scheduling of Trial

If a demand for speedy trial is made, the omnibus hearing shall not extend the time for trial unless the court finds good cause for continuance of the trial date.

Amended June 26, 1996; July 18, 2003.

Comment—Rule 12

When the same judge is assigned to determine the admissibility of evidence in a suppression hearing and the guilt of the juvenile in the same proceeding, the juvenile's basic right to a fair trial by an impartial tribunal with a determination of guilt based on admissible evidence may be compromised. E.g., *In re J.P.L.*, 359 N.W.2d 622 (Minn. Ct. App. 1984). Continuances of trial beyond the time established by Minn. R. Juv. Del. P. 13.02 are not recommended. However, the child's right to a fair trial will justify a short continuance where the child seeks reassignment of the judge pursuant to Minn. R. Juv. Del. P. 22.

References in this rule to "child's counsel" include the child who is proceeding pro se. Minn. R. Juv. Del. P. 1.01.

Historical Notes

The order of the Minnesota Supreme Court [C6–84–2165] dated June 26, 1996, provides in part that "(t)hese amendments to the Rules of Juvenile Procedure shall govern all juvenile actions commenced or arrests made on or after 12:00 o'clock midnight August 1, 1996."

The order of the Minnesota Supreme Court [CX–01–926] dated July 18, 2003, provides in part that "(t)he attached amendments shall govern all juveniles taken into custody and all juvenile delinquency actions commenced or children taken into custody after 12 o'clock midnight September 1, 2003."

RULE 13. TRIALS

Rule 13.01. Purpose and Application

A trial is a hearing held to determine whether the child is guilty or not guilty of the offenses alleged in the charging document. This rule applies to all delinquency, and juvenile petty and juvenile traffic trials. Extended jurisdiction juvenile trials are governed by Rule 19.

Amended June 26, 1996; July 18, 2003.

Comment—Rule 13

See comment following Rule 13.10.

Historical Notes

The order of the Minnesota Supreme Court [C6–84–2165] dated June 26, 1996, provides in part that "(t)hese amendments to the Rules of Juvenile Procedure shall govern all juvenile actions commenced or arrests made on or after 12:00 o'clock midnight August 1, 1996."

The order of the Minnesota Supreme Court [CX–01–926] dated July 18, 2003, provides in part that "(t)he attached amendments shall govern all juveniles taken into custody and all juvenile delinquency actions commenced or children taken into custody after 12 o'clock midnight September 1, 2003."

Rule 13.02. Commencement of Trial

Subd. 1. For a Child in Detention. A trial shall be commenced within thirty (30) days from the date of a demand for a speedy trial unless good cause is shown why the trial should not be commenced within that time.

Subd. 2. For a Child Not in Detention. A trial shall be commenced within sixty (60) days from the date of a demand for a speedy trial unless good cause is shown why the trial should not be held within that time.

Subd. 3. Release. If the child is detained and the trial has not commenced within thirty (30) days of the demand and a continuance has not been granted, the child shall be released subject to such nonmonetary release conditions as may be required by the court and the trial shall commence within sixty (60) days of the original demand for a speedy trial.

Subd. 4. Dismissal. Unless there is good cause shown for the delay, the charging document shall be dismissed without prejudice if the trial has not commenced within the time set forth above and the court has not granted a continuance.

Subd. 5. Effect of Mistrial; Order For New Trial. Upon a declaration of a mistrial, or an order of the trial court or a reviewing court granting a new trial, a new trial before a new judge shall be commenced within fifteen (15) days unless good cause is shown and the court grants a continuance.

Amended June 26, 1996; July 18, 2003.

Comment—Rule 13

See comment following Rule 13.10.

Historical Notes

The order of the Minnesota Supreme Court [C6–84–2165] dated June 26, 1996, provides in part that "(t)hese amendments to the Rules of Juvenile Procedure shall govern all juvenile actions commenced or arrests made on or after 12:00 o'clock midnight August 1, 1996."

The order of the Minnesota Supreme Court [CX–01–926] dated July 18, 2003, provides in part that "(t)he attached amendments shall govern all juveniles taken into custody and all juvenile delinquency actions commenced or children taken into custody after 12 o'clock midnight September 1, 2003."

Rule 13.03. Trial

Subd. 1. Initial Procedure. At the beginning of the trial, if the court has not previously determined the following information at a prior hearing, the court shall:

(A) verify the name, age and residence of the child who is the subject of the matter;

(B) determine whether all necessary persons are present and identify those present for the record; and

(C) determine whether notice requirements have been met and if not whether the affected persons waive notice.

Subd. 2. Order of Trial. The order of the trial shall be as follows:

(A) the prosecuting attorney may make an opening statement, confining the statement to the facts that it expects to prove;

(B) the child's counsel may make an opening statement, after the prosecutor's opening statement or may reserve the opening statement until immediately before offering the defense evidence. The statement shall be confined to a statement of the defense and the facts expected to be proved;

(C) the prosecuting attorney shall offer evidence in support of the charging document;

(D) the child's counsel may offer evidence in defense of the child;

(E) the child's counsel and the prosecuting attorney shall have the right to cross-examine witnesses;

(F) the prosecuting attorney may offer evidence in rebuttal of the defense evidence, and the child's counsel may then offer evidence in rebuttal of the prosecuting attorney rebuttal evidence. In the interests of justice the court may permit either the prosecuting attorney or the child's counsel to offer evidence upon the original case;

(G) at the conclusion of the evidence, the prosecuting attorney may make a closing argument; and

(H) the child's counsel may make a closing argument.

Subd. 3. Trial on Stipulated Facts. By agreement of the child and the prosecuting attorney, a determination of the child's guilt may be submitted to and tried by the court based on stipulated facts. Before proceeding in this manner, the child shall acknowledge and waive the rights to testify at trial, to have the prosecution witnesses testify in open court in the child's presence, to question those prosecution witnesses, and to require any favorable witnesses to testify for the child in court. The agreement and the waiver shall be in writing or orally on the record. Upon submission of the case on stipulated facts, the court shall proceed as in any other trial pursuant to Rule 13.

Adopted June 26, 1996. Amended Nov. 19, 2010, eff. Jan. 1, 2011.

Comment—Rule 13

See comment following Rule 13.10.

Historical Notes

The order of the Minnesota Supreme Court [C6–84–2165] dated June 26, 1996, provides in part that "(t)hese amendments to the Rules of Juvenile Procedure shall govern all juvenile actions commenced or arrests made on or after 12:00 o'clock midnight August 1, 1996."

Rule 13.04. Evidence

The court shall admit only such evidence as would be admissible in a criminal trial.

Adopted June 26, 1996.

Comment—Rule 13

See comment following Rule 13.10.

Historical Notes

The order of the Minnesota Supreme Court [C6–84–2165] dated June 26, 1996, provides in part that "(t)hese amendments to the Rules of Juvenile Procedure shall govern all juvenile actions commenced or arrests made on or after 12:00 o'clock midnight August 1, 1996."

Rule 13.05. Use of Depositions at Trial

Subd. 1. Unavailability of Witness. At a trial or hearing, a part or all of a deposition, so far as otherwise admissible under the rules of evidence, may be used as substantive evidence if:

(A) the witness is dead or unable to be present or to testify at the trial or hearing because of the witness's existing physical or mental illness, infirmity; or

(B) the person offering the deposition has been unable to procure the attendance of the witness by subpoena, order of the court, or other reasonable means; or

(C) there is a stipulation by counsel; or

(D) for any other reason accepted by the court.

A deposition may not be used if it appears that the absence of the witness was procured or caused by the person offering the deposition, unless part of the deposition has previously been offered by another party.

Subd. 2. Inconsistent Testimony. Any deposition may be used by the child's counsel or the prosecuting attorney for the purpose of contradicting or impeaching the testimony of the deponent when they appear as a witness.

Subd. 3. Substantive Evidence. A deposition may be used as substantive evidence so far as otherwise admissible under the rules of evidence, if the witness refuses to testify despite an order of the court to do so or if the witness gives testimony at the trial or hearing which is inconsistent with the deposition.

Adopted June 26, 1996. Amended July 18, 2003.

Comment—Rule 13

See comment following Rule 13.10.

Historical Notes

The order of the Minnesota Supreme Court [C6–84–2165] dated June 26, 1996, provides in part that "(t)hese amendments to the Rules of Juvenile Procedure shall govern all juvenile actions commenced or arrests made on or after 12:00 o'clock midnight August 1, 1996."

The order of the Minnesota Supreme Court [CX–01–926] dated July 18, 2003, provides in part that "(t)he attached amendments shall govern all juveniles taken into custody and all juvenile delinquency actions commenced or children taken into custody after 12 o'clock midnight September 1, 2003."

Rule 13.06. Standard of Proof

The allegations in the charging document must be proved beyond a reasonable doubt.

Adopted June 26, 1996.

Comment—Rule 13

See comment following Rule 13.10.

Historical Notes

The order of the Minnesota Supreme Court [C6–84–2165] dated June 26, 1996, provides in part that "(t)hese amendments to the Rules of Juvenile Procedure shall govern all juvenile actions commenced or arrests made on or after 12:00 o'clock midnight August 1, 1996."

Rule 13.07. Joint Trials

Subd. 1. Generally. When two or more children are jointly charged with any offense, they may be tried separately or jointly in the discretion of the court. Where the offense is a felony, the court shall consider the nature of the offense charged, the impact on the victim, the potential prejudice to each child, and the interests of justice before ordering a joint trial. A child in a joint trial shall be found guilty or not guilty in the same manner as a child tried separately.

Subd. 2. Severance Because of Improper Joinder. Where a child was improperly joined in a proceeding, the court shall order severance upon motion of the prosecuting attorney or the child's counsel. Improper joinder is not a ground for dismissal.

Subd. 3. Severance Because of Another Child's Out-of-Court Statement. Where one child's out-of-court statement refers to, but is not admissible against another child and those children may otherwise be tried jointly, the child against whom the statement is not admissible may move for severance. If the prosecuting attorney intends to offer the statement as evidence in its case in chief, the court shall require the prosecuting attorney to elect one of the following options:

(A) a joint trial at which the statement is not received in evidence;

(B) a joint trial at which the statement is received in evidence only after all references to the child making the motion have been deleted, if admission of the statement with the deletions will not prejudice that child; or

(C) severance.

Subd. 4. Severance During Trial. If the court determines severance is necessary to achieve a fair determination of the guilt or innocence of one or more of the children in a joint trial, the court shall order severance upon a finding of manifest necessity or with the consent of the child to be tried separately.

Adopted June 26, 1996. Amended July 18, 2003.

Comment—Rule 13

See comment following Rule 13.10.

Historical Notes

The order of the Minnesota Supreme Court [C6–84–2165] dated June 26, 1996, provides in part that "(t)hese amendments to the Rules of Juvenile Procedure shall govern all juvenile actions commenced or arrests made on or after 12:00 o'clock midnight August 1, 1996."

The order of the Minnesota Supreme Court [CX–01–926] dated July 18, 2003, provides in part that "(t)he attached amendments shall govern all juveniles taken into custody and all juvenile delinquency actions commenced or children taken into custody after 12 o'clock midnight September 1, 2003."

Rule 13.08. Joinder and Severance of Offenses

Subd. 1. Joinder of Offenses. When the child's conduct constitutes more than one offense, each such offense may be charged in the same charging document in a separate count. The court, upon the prosecuting attorney's motion, may order joinder of offenses if the offenses could have been but were not joined in a single charging document. In extended jurisdiction juvenile cases, the child has the same right as an adult to sever offenses for separate trial on each offense.

Subd. 2. Severance of Offenses. On motion of the prosecuting attorney or the child's counsel, the court shall sever offenses or charges if:

(a) the offenses or charges are not related;

(b) before trial, the court determines severance is appropriate to promote a fair determination of the child's guilt or innocence of each offense or charge; or

(c) during trial, with the child's consent or upon a finding of manifest necessity, the court determines severance is necessary to achieve a fair determination of the child's guilt or innocence of each offense or charge. Misjoinder of offenses is not a ground for dismissal.

Adopted June 26, 1996. Amended July 18, 2003.

Comment—Rule 13

See comment following Rule 13.10.

Historical Notes

The order of the Minnesota Supreme Court [C6–84–2165] dated June 26, 1996, provides in part that "(t)hese amendments to the Rules of Juvenile Procedure shall govern all juvenile actions commenced or arrests made on or after 12:00 o'clock midnight August 1, 1996."

The order of the Minnesota Supreme Court [CX–01–926] dated July 18, 2003, provides in part that "(t)he attached amendments shall govern all juveniles taken into custody and all juvenile delinquency actions commenced or children taken into custody after 12 o'clock midnight September 1, 2003."

Rule 13.09. Findings

Within seven (7) days of the conclusion of the trial, the court shall make a general finding that the allegations in the charging document have or have not been proved beyond a reasonable doubt. The court shall dismiss the charging document if the allegations have not been proved. An order finding that the allegations of the charging document have been proved shall state the child's name and date of birth; and the date and county where the offense was committed. Within fifteen (15) days of the conclusion of the trial, the court shall in addition specifically find the essential facts that support a general finding that the allegations in the charging document have been proved beyond a reasonable doubt in writing. If an opinion or memorandum of decision is filed, it is sufficient if the findings of fact appear therein. If the court omits a finding on any issue of fact essential to sustain the general finding, it shall be deemed to have made a finding consistent with the general finding. Findings may be made on the record, but must be reduced to writing within the fifteen (15) days required herein.

Adopted June 26, 1996. Amended Nov. 19, 2010, eff. Jan. 1, 2011.

Comment—Rule 13

See comment following Rule 13.10.

Historical Notes

The order of the Minnesota Supreme Court [C6–84–2165] dated June 26, 1996, provides in part that "(t)hese amendments to the Rules

of Juvenile Procedure shall govern all juvenile actions commenced or arrests made on or after 12:00 o'clock midnight August 1, 1996."

Rule 13.10. Further Proceedings

If the court makes a finding that the allegations of the charging document have been proved, the court shall hold dispositional proceedings pursuant to Rule 15.

Adopted June 26, 1996. Amended July 18, 2003.

Comment—Rule 13

For children held in detention, Minn. R. Juv. Del. P. 13.02, subd. 1 requires that a trial be commenced within thirty (30) days from the date of the speedy trial demand unless good cause is shown why the trial should not be held within that time. If the trial has not commenced within the thirty (30) days and a continuance has not been granted upon a showing of good cause, the child shall be released subject to nonmonetary release conditions that the court may require. The trial must then commence within 60 days of the date of the demand for a speedy trial and not 60 days from the child's release.

For children not held in detention, Minn. R. Juv. Del. P. 13.02, subd. 2 provides that a trial shall be commenced within sixty (60) days from the date of a demand for a speedy trial unless good cause is shown why the trial should not be held within that time. The trial may be postponed for good cause beyond the time limit upon request of the prosecuting attorney or the child's counsel or upon the court's initiative. Good cause for the delay does not include court calendar congestion unless exceptional circumstances exist. See *McIntosh v. Davis,* 441 N.W.2d 115 (Minn. 1989). A delay caused by witness unavailability is permitted when the delay is "neither lengthy nor unfairly prejudicial." *In re Welfare of G.D.,* 473 N.W.2d 878 (Minn. Ct. App. 1991); see also *State v. Terry,* 295 N.W.2d 95 (Minn. 1980).

If the trial is not commenced within sixty (60) days from the date of the demand for a speedy trial and a continuance has not been granted for good cause, the charging document shall be dismissed. It is within the trial court's discretion whether it is dismissed with prejudice. See *Barker v. Wingo,* 407 U.S. 514, 92 S.Ct. 2182, 33 L.Ed.2d 101 (1972); *State v. Kasper,* 411 N.W.2d 182 (Minn. 1987); *State v. Friberg,* 435 N.W.2d 509 (Minn. 1989).

Minn. R. Juv. Del. P. 13.07 is modeled after Minn. R. Crim. P. 17.03, subds. 2 and 3. Minn. R. Juv. Del. P. 13.08 is modeled after Minn. R. Crim. P. 17.03, subds. 1, 3 and 4. Joint trials should be discouraged where one or more of the children is without counsel.

References in this rule to "child's counsel" include the child who is proceeding pro se. Minn. R. Juv. Del. P. 1.01.

Historical Notes

The order of the Minnesota Supreme Court [C6–84–2165] dated June 26, 1996, provides in part that "(t)hese amendments to the Rules of Juvenile Procedure shall govern all juvenile actions commenced or arrests made on or after 12:00 o'clock midnight August 1, 1996."

The order of the Minnesota Supreme Court [CX–01–926] dated July 18, 2003, provides in part that "(t)he attached amendments shall govern all juveniles taken into custody and all juvenile delinquency actions commenced or children taken into custody after 12 o'clock midnight September 1, 2003."

RULE 14. CONTINUANCE FOR DISMISSAL

Rule 14.01. Agreements Permitted

Subd. 1. Generally. After consideration of the victim's views and subject to the court's approval, the prosecuting attorney and the child's counsel may agree that the juvenile proceeding will be suspended for a specified period without a finding that the allegations of the charging document have been proved after which it will be dismissed as provided in Rule 14.07 on condition that the child not commit a delinquency or juvenile petty or juvenile traffic offense during the period of the continuance. The agreement shall be on the record or in writing and signed by the prosecuting attorney, the child, and the child's counsel, if any. The agreement shall contain a waiver by the child of the right to a speedy trial under Rule 13.02, subdivisions 1 and 2. The agreement may include stipulations concerning the existence of specified facts or the admissibility into evidence of specified testimony, evidence, or depositions if the suspension of prosecution is terminated and there is a trial on the allegations.

Subd. 2. Additional Conditions. Subject to the court's approval after consideration of the victim's views and upon a showing of substantial likelihood that the allegations could be proved and that the benefits to society from rehabilitation outweigh any harm to society from suspending the juvenile proceeding, the agreement may specify one or more of the following additional conditions to be observed by the child during the period of suspension:

(A) that the child not engage in specified activities, conduct, and associations bearing a relationship to the conduct upon which the allegations are based;

(B) that the child participate in a supervised rehabilitation program, which may include treatment, counseling, training, and education;

(C) that the child make restitution in a specified manner for harm or loss caused by the offense alleged;

(D) that the child perform specified community service; and

(E) that the child pay court costs.

Subd. 3. Limitations on Agreements. The agreement may not specify a period of suspension longer than the juvenile court has jurisdiction over the child nor any condition other than that which could be imposed upon probation after a finding that the offenses alleged have been proved.

Amended June 26, 1996; July 18, 2003.

Comment—Rule 14

See comment following Rule 14.10.

Historical Notes

The order of the Minnesota Supreme Court [C6–84–2165] dated June 26, 1996, provides in part that "(t)hese amendments to the Rules of Juvenile Procedure shall govern all juvenile actions commenced or arrests made on or after 12:00 o'clock midnight August 1, 1996."

The order of the Minnesota Supreme Court [CX–01–926] dated July 18, 2003, provides in part that "(t)he attached amendments shall govern all juveniles taken into custody and all juvenile delinquency actions commenced or children taken into custody after 12 o'clock midnight September 1, 2003."

Rule 14.02. Court Approval; Filing of Agreement; Release

All agreements made under Rule 14.01 of this rule must be approved by the court on the record or in writing. Promptly after any written agreement is made and approved by the court, the prosecuting attorney shall file the agreement together with a statement that pursuant to the agreement the juvenile proceeding is suspended for a period specified in the statement. Upon court approval of the agreement, the child shall be released from any custody under Rule 5.

Amended June 26, 1996; July 18, 2003.

Comment—Rule 14

See comment following Rule 14.10.

Historical Notes

The order of the Minnesota Supreme Court [C6–84–2165] dated June 26, 1996, provides in part that "(t)hese amendments to the Rules of Juvenile Procedure shall govern all juvenile actions commenced or arrests made on or after 12:00 o'clock midnight August 1, 1996."

The order of the Minnesota Supreme Court [CX–01–926] dated July 18, 2003, provides in part that "(t)he attached amendments shall govern all juveniles taken into custody and all juvenile delinquency actions commenced or children taken into custody after 12 o'clock midnight September 1, 2003."

Rule 14.03. Modification of Agreement

Subject to Rules 14.01 and 14.02 and with the court's approval on the record or in writing, the parties, by mutual consent, may modify the terms of the agreement at any time before its termination.

Adopted June 26, 1996; July 18, 2003.

Comment—Rule 14

See comment following Rule 14.10.

Historical Notes

The order of the Minnesota Supreme Court [C6–84–2165] dated June 26, 1996, provides in part that "(t)hese amendments to the Rules of Juvenile Procedure shall govern all juvenile actions commenced or arrests made on or after 12:00 o'clock midnight August 1, 1996."

The order of the Minnesota Supreme Court [CX–01–926] dated July 18, 2003, provides in part that "(t)he attached amendments shall govern all juveniles taken into custody and all juvenile delinquency actions commenced or children taken into custody after 12 o'clock midnight September 1, 2003."

Rule 14.04. Termination of Agreement; Resumption of Proceedings

Subd. 1. Upon Notice of Child or Child's Counsel. The agreement is terminated and the juvenile proceeding may resume as if there had been no agreement if the child's counsel serves upon the prosecuting attorney and files a notice with the court that the agreement is terminated.

Subd. 2. Upon Order of Court. The court may order the agreement terminated and the juvenile proceeding resumed if, upon motion of the prosecuting attorney stating facts supporting the motion and upon hearing, the court finds that:

(A) the child or child's counsel misrepresented material facts affecting the agreement, if the motion is made within six months after the date of the agreement; or

(B) the child has committed a material violation of the agreement, if the motion is made not later than one month after the expiration of the period of suspension specified in the agreement.

Adopted June 26, 1996; July 18, 2003.

Comment—Rule 14

See comment following Rule 14.10.

Historical Notes

The order of the Minnesota Supreme Court [C6–84–2165] dated June 26, 1996, provides in part that "(t)hese amendments to the Rules of Juvenile Procedure shall govern all juvenile actions commenced or arrests made on or after 12:00 o'clock midnight August 1, 1996."

The order of the Minnesota Supreme Court [CX–01–926] dated July 18, 2003, provides in part that "(t)he attached amendments shall govern all juveniles taken into custody and all juvenile delinquency actions commenced or children taken into custody after 12 o'clock midnight September 1, 2003."

Rule 14.05. Emergency Order

The court by warrant may direct any officer authorized by law to bring the child forthwith before the court for the hearing of the motion if the court finds from affidavit or testimony that:

(A) there is probable cause to believe the child committed a material violation of the agreement; and

(B) there is a substantial likelihood that the child otherwise will not attend the hearing.

In any case, the court may issue a summons instead of a warrant to secure the appearance of the child at the hearing.

Adopted June 26, 1996.

Comment—Rule 14

See comment following Rule 14.10.

Historical Notes

The order of the Minnesota Supreme Court [C6–84–2165] dated June 26, 1996, provides in part that "(t)hese amendments to the Rules

of Juvenile Procedure shall govern all juvenile actions commenced or arrests made on or after 12:00 o'clock midnight August 1, 1996."

Rule 14.06. Release Status Upon Resumption of Delinquency, Juvenile Petty or Juvenile Traffic Proceedings

If the juvenile proceeding resumes under Rule 14.04, the child shall return to the release status in effect before the juvenile proceeding was suspended unless the court imposes additional or different conditions of release under Rule 5.

Adopted June 26, 1996. Amended July 18, 2003.

Comment—Rule 14

See comment following Rule 14.10.

Historical Notes

The order of the Minnesota Supreme Court [C6–84–2165] dated June 26, 1996, provides in part that "(t)hese amendments to the Rules of Juvenile Procedure shall govern all juvenile actions commenced or arrests made on or after 12:00 o'clock midnight August 1, 1996."

The order of the Minnesota Supreme Court [CX–01–926] dated July 18, 2003, provides in part that "(t)he attached amendments shall govern all juveniles taken into custody and all juvenile delinquency actions commenced or children taken into custody after 12 o'clock midnight September 1, 2003."

Rule 14.07. Termination of Agreement; Dismissal

If no motion by the prosecuting attorney to terminate the agreement is pending, the agreement is terminated and the charging document shall be dismissed by order of the court one month after expiration of the period of suspension specified by the agreement. If such a motion is then pending, the agreement is terminated and the charging document shall be dismissed by order of the court upon entry of a final order denying the motion. Following a dismissal under this subdivision no further juvenile proceedings may be brought against the child for the offense involved.

Adopted June 26, 1996. Amended July 11, 2005, eff. Sept. 1, 2005.

Comment—Rule 14

See comment following Rule 14.10.

Historical Notes

The order of the Minnesota Supreme Court [C6–84–2165] dated June 26, 1996, provides in part that "(t)hese amendments to the Rules of Juvenile Procedure shall govern all juvenile actions commenced or arrests made on or after 12:00 o'clock midnight August 1, 1996."

Rule 14.08 Termination and Dismissal Upon Showing of Rehabilitation

The court may order the agreement terminated, dismiss the juvenile proceedings, and bar further juvenile proceedings on the offense involved if, upon motion of a party stating facts supporting the motion and opportunity to be heard, the court finds that the child has committed no later offenses as specified in the agreement and appears to be rehabilitated.

Adopted June 26, 1996.

Comment—Rule 14

See comment following Rule 14.10.

Historical Notes

The order of the Minnesota Supreme Court [C6–84–2165] dated June 26, 1996, provides in part that "(t)hese amendments to the Rules of Juvenile Procedure shall govern all juvenile actions commenced or arrests made on or after 12:00 o'clock midnight August 1, 1996."

Rule 14.09. Modification or Termination and Dismissal Upon Child's Motion

If, upon motion of the child's counsel and hearing, the court finds that the prosecuting attorney obtained the child's consent to the agreement as a result of a material misrepresentation by a person covered by the prosecuting attorney's obligation under Rule 10.04, the court may:

(A) order appropriate modification of the terms resulting from the misrepresentation; or

(B) if the court determines that the interests of justice require, order the agreement terminated, dismiss the juvenile proceeding, and bar further juvenile proceedings on the offense involved.

Adopted June 26, 1996. Amended July 18, 2003.

Comment—Rule 14

See comment following Rule 14.10.

Historical Notes

The order of the Minnesota Supreme Court [C6–84–2165] dated June 26, 1996, provides in part that "(t)hese amendments to the Rules of Juvenile Procedure shall govern all juvenile actions commenced or arrests made on or after 12:00 o'clock midnight August 1, 1996."

The order of the Minnesota Supreme Court [CX–01–926] dated July 18, 2003, provides in part that "(t)he attached amendments shall govern all juveniles taken into custody and all juvenile delinquency actions commenced or children taken into custody after 12 o'clock midnight September 1, 2003."

Rule 14.10. Court Authority to Dismiss

Nothing in this rule shall limit the inherent power of the court to continue a case for dismissal even in the absence of an agreement by the prosecutor and child's counsel. In the event the court exercises this power:

(A) The action of the court must be on the record or in writing;

(B) Unless waived by the child, the court must guarantee the child's right to a speedy trial under Rule 13.02, subdivisions 1 and 2;

(C) The continuance shall be on conditions provided in Rule 14.01 subdivisions 1 and 2, and shall be subject to limitations stated in Rule 14.01, subdivision 3;

(D) The terms of the continuance may be modified on the record or in writing, by the court, with notice to all parties; and

(E) Proceedings following the continuance shall be governed by Rules 14.04—14.08.

Adopted June 26, 1996. Amended Dec. 12, 1997; July 18, 2003.

Comment—Rule 14

Pursuant to Minn. R. Juv. Del. P. 1.01, references to "child's counsel" include the child who is proceeding pro se.

The Minnesota Supreme Court's Juvenile Rules Advisory Committee discovered that many juvenile court practitioners did not appreciate the limited benefits of withholding adjudication (now designated "continuance without adjudication") and were inadvertently misrepresenting its benefits to juveniles. See Comment to Minn. R. Juv. Del. P. 15. Many practitioners were, in effect, treating withholding of adjudication as a continuance for dismissal or pretrial diversion, similar to Minn. R. Crim. P. 27.05. In order to avoid future misuse of the continuance without adjudication and allow juvenile court practitioners the benefits of continuance for dismissal, Minn. R. Crim. P. 27.05 was incorporated into the juvenile rules. Because there is no finding that the allegations of the charging document have been proved in a continuance for dismissal, the offense should not count towards a juvenile's future criminal history score under the sentencing guidelines.

All agreements under this rule, including written agreements, must be approved by the court in writing or on the record.

A continuance for dismissal or continuance without adjudication under Minn. R. Juv. Del. P. 15.05, subd. 4 are not the only options available for dealing with an alleged juvenile offender without formal process. Every county attorney is required to have a pretrial diversion program established for certain juveniles subject to juvenile court jurisdiction, as an alternative to formal adjudication. See Minnesota Statutes, section 388. 24 (2002). With statutory pretrial diversion readily available for less serious juvenile offenders, presumably the use of continuance without adjudication and continuance for dismissal under these rules will become less common.

Minn. R. Juv. Del. P. 14 specifies the procedure to be followed when the child, child's counsel and prosecuting attorney agree to a continuance for dismissal. Rule 14.10 further provides that the court has the inherent authority to order a continuance for dismissal of its own volition without the agreement of the parties. *In re Welfare of J.B.A.*, 581 N.W.2d 37 (Minn. Ct. App. 1998).

Historical Notes

The order of the Minnesota Supreme Court [C6–84–2165] dated June 26, 1996, provides in part that "(t)hese amendments to the Rules of Juvenile Procedure shall govern all juvenile actions commenced or arrests made on or after 12:00 o'clock midnight August 1, 1996."

The order of the Minnesota Supreme Court [C6–84–2165] dated December 12, 1997, provides in part that "(t)hese amendments to the Rules of Juvenile Procedure shall govern all juvenile actions commenced or arrests made on or after 12:00 o'clock midnight January 1, 1998."

The order of the Minnesota Supreme Court [CX–01–926] dated July 18, 2003, provides in part that "(t)he attached amendments shall govern all juveniles taken into custody and all juvenile delinquency actions commenced or children taken into custody after 12 o'clock midnight September 1, 2003."

RULE 15. DELINQUENCY DISPOSITION

Rule 15.01. Generally

Subd. 1. Findings on Charges. All references in this rule to findings that allegations in the charging document have been proved include findings pursuant to a plea of guilty by the child under Rule 8.04 and findings after trial pursuant to Rule 13.09.

Subd. 2. Application. This rule applies to delinquency dispositions. Rule 17 governs dispositions for juvenile petty offenses and juvenile traffic offenses. Rule 19 provides for sentence and disposition in extended jurisdiction juvenile cases.

Adopted June 26, 1996. Amended July 18, 2003.

Comment—Rule 15

See comment following Rule 15.08.

Historical Notes

The order of the Minnesota Supreme Court [C6–84–2165] dated June 26, 1996, provides in part that "(t)hese amendments to the Rules of Juvenile Procedure shall govern all juvenile actions commenced or arrests made on or after 12:00 o'clock midnight August 1, 1996."

The order of the Minnesota Supreme Court [CX–01–926] dated July 18, 2003, provides in part that "(t)he attached amendments shall govern all juveniles taken into custody and all juvenile delinquency actions commenced or children taken into custody after 12 o'clock midnight September 1, 2003."

Rule 15.02. Timing

Subdivision 1. Hearing. After the court makes a general finding that the allegations in the charging document have been proved beyond a reasonable doubt, the court may conduct a disposition hearing immediately or continue the matter for a disposition hearing at a later time as follows:

(A) for a child not held in detention, within forty-five (45) days from the finding that the allegations in the charging document have been proved beyond a reasonable doubt; or

(B) for a child held in detention, within fifteen (15) days from the finding that the allegations in the charging document have been proved beyond a reasonable doubt; or

(C) in cases involving a transfer of the file under subdivision 4, for a child not held in detention, as early as practicable but within ninety (90) days from the finding that the allegations in the charging document have been proved beyond a reasonable doubt.

Subd. 2. Order. The court shall enter a dispositional order pursuant to Rule 15.05 within three (3) days of the disposition hearing. For good cause, the court may extend the time to enter a dispositional order to fifteen (15) days from the disposition hearing.

Subd. 3. Delay. For good cause, the court may extend the time period to conduct a disposition hearing for one additional period of thirty (30) days for a child not held in detention or fifteen (15) days for a child held in detention. Except in extraordinary circumstances, if the court fails to conduct a disposition hearing or enter a dispositional order for a child held in detention within the time limits prescribed by this rule, the child shall be released from detention. If a disposition hearing is not conducted or a dispositional order is not entered within the time limits prescribed by this rule, the court may dismiss the case.

Subd. 4. Transfer of File. If the matter is to be transferred to the child's county of residence for disposition, the court shall direct the court administrator to transfer the file to the child's home county within five (5) days of the finding that the offense(s) charged have been proved. Venue transfers in juvenile court are governed by Minnesota Statutes, section 260B.105. For convenience of the participants, the court which accepts a plea may determine the disposition for the court which will supervise the child's probation, if the transferring court has conferred with the receiving court and there is agreement regarding the disposition.

Adopted June 26, 1996. Amended July 18, 2003; Nov. 19, 2010, eff. Jan. 1, 2011.

Comment—Rule 15

See comment following Rule 15.08.

Historical Notes

The order of the Minnesota Supreme Court [C6–84–2165] dated June 26, 1996, provides in part that "(t)hese amendments to the Rules of Juvenile Procedure shall govern all juvenile actions commenced or arrests made on or after 12:00 o'clock midnight August 1, 1996."

The order of the Minnesota Supreme Court [CX–01–926] dated July 18, 2003, provides in part that "(t)he attached amendments shall govern all juveniles taken into custody and all juvenile delinquency actions commenced or children taken into custody after 12 o'clock midnight September 1, 2003."

Rule 15.03. Predisposition Reports

Subd. 1. Investigations and Evaluations. The court may order an investigation of the personal and family history and environment of the child, and medical, psychological or chemical dependency evaluations of the child:

(A) at any time after the charges in the charging document have been proved; or

(B) with the consent of the child, child's counsel, if any, and the parent(s), legal guardian or legal custodian of the child, before the charges in the charging document have been proved.

Subd. 2. Placement. With the consent of the child at any time or without consent of the child after the delinquency charges of a charging document pursuant to Minnesota Statutes, section 260B.007, subdivisions 6(a)(1) or (2) have been proved, the court may place the child with the consent of the Commissioner of Corrections in an institution maintained by the Commissioner of Corrections for the detention, diagnosis, custody and treatment of persons adjudicated to be delinquent in order that the investigation and evaluations may be conducted pursuant to Rule 15.03, subdivision 1.

Subd. 3. Advisory. The court shall advise the child, the child's counsel, the prosecuting attorney and the child's parent(s), legal guardian or legal custodian and their counsel present in court that a predisposition investigation is being ordered, the nature of the evaluations to be included and the date when the reports resulting from the investigation are to be filed with the court.

Subd. 4. Filing and Inspection of Reports. The person making the report shall file the report three (3) days prior to the time scheduled for the disposition hearing and the reports shall be available for inspection and copying by the child, the child's counsel, the prosecuting attorney and counsel for the parent(s), legal guardian or legal custodian of the child. The court administrator shall not otherwise disclose the report except by court order.

Amended June 26, 1996; Dec. 12, 1997; July 18, 2003; July 11, 2005, eff. Sept. 1, 2005.

Comment—Rule 15

See comment following Rule 15.08.

Historical Notes

The order of the Minnesota Supreme Court [C6–84–2165] dated June 26, 1996, provides in part that "(t)hese amendments to the Rules of Juvenile Procedure shall govern all juvenile actions commenced or arrests made on or after 12:00 o'clock midnight August 1, 1996."

The order of the Minnesota Supreme Court [C6–84–2165] dated December 12, 1997, provides in part that "(t)hese amendments to the Rules of Juvenile Procedure shall govern all juvenile actions commenced or arrests made on or after 12:00 o'clock midnight January 1, 1998."

The order of the Minnesota Supreme Court [CX–01–926] dated July 18, 2003, provides in part that "(t)he attached amendments shall govern all juveniles taken into custody and all juvenile delinquency actions commenced or children taken into custody after 12 o'clock midnight September 1, 2003."

Rule 15.04. Hearing

Subd. 1. Procedure. Disposition hearings shall be separate from the hearing at which the charges are proved and may be held immediately following that hearing. Disposition hearings shall be conducted in a manner designed to facilitate opportunity for all participants to be heard. The child and the child's counsel, if any, shall appear at all disposition hearings. The child's parents and their counsel, if any, may also participate in the hearing. The child has the right of allocution at the disposition hearing, prior to any disposition being imposed.

Subd. 2. Evidence. The court may receive any information, except privileged communication, that is relevant to the disposition of the case including reliable hearsay and opinions. Anyone with the right to participate in the disposition hearing pursuant to Rule 2 may call witnesses, subject to cross-examination, regarding an appropriate disposition and may cross-examine any persons who have prepared a written report relating to the disposition.

Amended June 26, 1996; July 18, 2003.

Comment—Rule 15

See comment following Rule 15.08.

Historical Notes

The order of the Minnesota Supreme Court [C6–84–2165] dated June 26, 1996, provides in part that "(t)hese amendments to the Rules of Juvenile Procedure shall govern all juvenile actions commenced or arrests made on or after 12:00 o'clock midnight August 1, 1996."

The order of the Minnesota Supreme Court [CX–01–926] dated July 18, 2003, provides in part that "(t)he attached amendments shall govern all juveniles taken into custody and all juvenile delinquency actions commenced or children taken into custody after 12 o'clock midnight September 1, 2003."

Rule 15.05. Dispositional Order

Subdivision 1. Adjudication and Disposition. On each of the charges found by the court to be proved, the court shall either:

(A) adjudicate the child delinquent pursuant to Minnesota Statutes, section 260B.198, subdivision 1; or

(B) continue the case without adjudicating the child delinquent and order a disposition pursuant to Minnesota Statutes, section 260B.198, subdivisions 1(1) or (2).

The adjudication or continuance without adjudication shall occur at the same time and in the same court order as the disposition.

Subd. 2. Considerations; Findings.

(A) The dispositional order made by the court shall contain written findings of fact to support the disposition ordered and shall set forth in writing the following information:

(1) why public safety and the best interests of the child are served by the disposition ordered;

(2) what alternative dispositions were recommended to the court and why such recommendations were not ordered; and

(3) if the disposition changes the place of custody of the child:

(a) the reasons why public safety and the best interest of the child are not served by preserving the child's present custody; and

(b) suitability of the placement, taking into account the program of the placement facility and assessment of the child's actual needs.

(B) When making a disposition, the court shall consider whether a particular disposition will serve established principles of dispositions, including but not limited to:

(1) Necessity. It is arbitrary and unjust to impose a disposition that is not necessary to restore law abiding conduct. Considerations bearing on need are:

(a) Public Safety. The risk to public safety, taking into account:

(i) the seriousness of the alleged offense in terms of community protection, including the existence of any aggravating factors recognized by the Minnesota Sentencing Guidelines, the use of a firearm, and the impact on any victim;

(ii) the culpability of the child in committing the alleged offense, including the level of the child's participation in planning and carrying out the offense and the existence of any mitigating factors recognized by the Minnesota Sentencing Guidelines;

(iii) the child's prior record of delinquency;

(iv) the child's programming history, including the child's past willingness to participate meaningfully in available programming; and

(b) Proportionality. The principle that the disposition be proportional, that is, the least restrictive action consistent with the child's circumstances.

(2) Best Interests. A disposition must serve the best interests of the child, but this does not supersede the requirement that the disposition be necessary. The promise of benefits in a disposition, or even the suggestion that a particular disposition is best for the child, does not permit a disposition that is not necessary.

(3) Out-of-Home Placement. Public policy mandates that the best interests of the child are normally served by parental custody. Where an out-of-home placement is being considered, the placement should be suitable to the child's needs. A placement that is not suited to the actual needs of the child cannot serve the child's best interests.

(4) Sanctions. Sanctions, such as post-adjudication placement in a secure facility, are appropriate where such measures are necessary to promote public safety and reduce juvenile delinquency, provided that the sanctions are fair and just, recognize the unique characteristics and needs of the child and give the child access to opportunities for personal and social growth. In determining whether to order secure placement, the court shall consider the necessity of protecting the public, protecting program residents and staff, and preventing juveniles with histories of absconding from leaving treatment programs. Other factors that may impact on what sanctions

are necessary include: any prior adjudication for a felony offense against a person, prior failures to appear in court, or prior incidents of running away from home.

(5) Local Dispositional Criteria. The disposition should reflect the criteria used for determining delinquency dispositions in the local judicial district.

Subd. 3. Duration. A dispositional order transferring legal custody of the child pursuant to Minnesota Statutes, section 260B.198, subdivision 1(c) shall be for a specified length of time. The court may extend the duration of a placement but only by instituting a modification proceeding pursuant to Rule 15.08. Orders for probation shall be for an indeterminate length of time unless otherwise specified by the court and shall be reviewed by the court at least annually.

Subd. 4. Continuance without Adjudication.

(A) *Generally.* When it is in the best interests of the child and the protection of the public to do so, the court may continue the case without adjudicating the child. The court may not grant a continuance without adjudication where the child has been designated an extended jurisdiction juvenile.

(B) *Child Not in Detention.* If the child is not held in detention, the court may continue the case without adjudication for a period not to exceed ninety (90) days from the date of disposition. The court may extend the continuance for an additional successive period not to exceed ninety (90) days.

(C) *Child in Detention.* If the child is held or is to be held in detention, the court may continue the case without adjudication and enter an order to hold the child in detention for a period not to exceed fifteen (15) days from the date of disposition. If the child is in detention, this continuance must be for the purpose of completing any consideration, or any investigation or examination ordered pursuant to Rule 15.03, subdivision 1. The court may extend this continuance and enter an order to hold the child in detention for an additional successive period not to exceed fifteen (15) days.

(D) *Dispositions During Continuance.* During any continuance without adjudication of delinquency, the court may enter a disposition order pursuant to Minnesota Statutes, section 260B.198, subdivisions 1(a) or (b).

(E) *Adjudication after Continuance.* Adjudicating a child for an offense after initially granting a continuance without adjudication is a probation revocation and must be accomplished pursuant to Rule 15.07.

(F) *Termination of Jurisdiction.* A probation revocation proceeding to adjudicate the child on any allegation initially continued without adjudication must be commenced within the period prescribed by Rule 15.05, subdivisions 4 (B) or (C), or juvenile court jurisdiction over the charges terminates.

Adopted June 26, 1996. Amended July 18, 2003; Oct. 15, 2012, eff. Dec. 1, 2012.

Comment—Rule 15

See comment following Rule 15.08.

Historical Notes

The order of the Minnesota Supreme Court [C6–84–2165] dated June 26, 1996, provides in part that "(t)hese amendments to the Rules of Juvenile Procedure shall govern all juvenile actions commenced or arrests made on or after 12:00 o'clock midnight August 1, 1996."

The order of the Minnesota Supreme Court [CX–01–926] dated July 18, 2003, provides in part that "(t)he attached amendments shall govern all juveniles taken into custody and all juvenile delinquency actions commenced or children taken into custody after 12 o'clock midnight September 1, 2003."

The order of the Minnesota Supreme Court [ADM10–8003] dated October 15, 2012, provides in part that the "amendments shall govern all delinquency actions pending or commenced on or after 12 o'clock midnight December 1, 2012."

Rule 15.06. Informal Review

The court shall review all disposition orders, except commitments to the Commissioner of Corrections, at least every six (6) months.

If, upon review, the court finds there is good cause to believe a modification of the disposition is warranted under Rule 15.08, subdivision 8, the court may commence a modification proceeding pursuant to Rule 15.08.

Adopted June 26, 1996. Amended July 18, 2003.

Comment—Rule 15

See comment following Rule 15.08.

Historical Notes

The order of the Minnesota Supreme Court [C6–84–2165] dated June 26, 1996, provides in part that "(t)hese amendments to the Rules of Juvenile Procedure shall govern all juvenile actions commenced or arrests made on or after 12:00 o'clock midnight August 1, 1996."

The order of the Minnesota Supreme Court [CX–01–926] dated July 18, 2003, provides in part that "(t)he attached amendments shall govern all juveniles taken into custody and all juvenile delinquency actions commenced or children taken into custody after 12 o'clock midnight September 1, 2003."

Rule 15.07. Probation Violation

Subd. 1. Commencement of Proceedings. Proceedings for revocation of probation may be commenced based upon a written report showing probable cause to believe the juvenile has violated any conditions of probation. Based upon the report, the court may issue a warrant as provided by Rule 4.03, or the court may schedule a review hearing and provide notice of the hearing as provided in Rule 25. If the juvenile fails to appear in response to a summons, the court may issue a warrant.

(A) *Contents of Probation Violation Report.* The probation violation report and supporting affidavits, if any, shall include:

(1) the name, date of birth and address of the child;

(2) the name and address of the child's parent(s), legal guardian, or legal custodian;

(3) the underlying offense or offenses and date(s) of offense for which violation of probation is alleged; and

(4) a description of the surrounding facts and circumstances upon which the request for revocation is based.

(B) *Notice.* The court shall give notice of the admit/deny hearing on the probation violation to all persons entitled to notice pursuant to Rule 25.

Subd. 2. Detention Hearing. Detention pending a probation violation hearing is governed by Rule 5.

Subd. 3. Admit/Deny Hearing. The child shall either admit or deny the allegations of the of the probation violation report at the admit/deny hearing.

(A) *Timing.* The admit/deny hearing shall be held:

(1) for a child in custody, at or before the detention hearing; or

(2) for a child not in custody, within a reasonable time of the filing of the motion.

(B) *Advisory.* Prior to the child admitting or denying the violation, the court shall advise the child of the following:

(1) that the child is entitled to counsel appointed at public expense at all stages of the proceedings;

(2) that, unless waived, a revocation hearing will be commenced to determine whether there is clear and convincing evidence that the child violated a dispositional order of the court and whether the court should change the existing dispositional order because of the violation;

(3) that before the revocation hearing, all evidence to be used against the child shall be disclosed to the child and the child shall be provided access to all official records pertinent to the proceedings;

(4) that at the hearing, both the prosecuting attorney and the child shall have the right to offer evidence, present arguments, subpoena witnesses, and call and cross-examine witnesses. Additionally, the child shall have the right at the hearing to present mitigating circumstances or other reasons why the violation, if proved, should not result in revocation; and

(5) that the child has the right of appeal from the determination of the court following the revocation hearing.

(C) *Denial.* If the child denies the allegations, the matter shall be set for a revocation hearing which shall be held in accordance with the provisions of Rule 15.07, subdivision 4.

Subd. 4. Revocation Hearing.

(A) *Generally.* At the hearing, both the prosecuting attorney and the child shall have the right to offer evidence, present arguments, subpoena witnesses, and call and cross-examine witnesses, provided, however, that the child may be denied confrontation by the court when good cause is shown that a substantial risk of serious harm to others would exist if it were allowed. Additionally, the child shall have the right at the hearing to present mitigating circumstances or other reasons why the violation, if proved, should not result in revocation.

(B) *Timing.* The revocation hearing shall be held within seven (7) days after the child is taken into custody or, if the child is not in custody, within a reasonable time after the filing of the denial. If the child has allegedly committed a new offense, the court may postpone the revocation hearing pending disposition of the new offense whether or not the child is in custody.

(C) *Violation Not Proved.* If the court finds that a violation of the dispositional order has not been established by clear and convincing evidence, the revocation proceedings shall be dismissed, and the child shall continue under the dispositional order previously ordered by the court.

(D) *Violation Proved.* If the court finds by clear and convincing evidence, or the child admits violating the terms of the dispositional order, the court may proceed as follows:

(1) order a disposition pursuant to Minnesota Statutes, section 260B.198; or

(2) for a child who was previously granted a continuance without adjudication pursuant to Rule 15.05, subdivision 4, adjudicate the child and order a disposition pursuant to Minnesota Statutes, section 260B.198.

The dispositional order shall comply with Rule 15.05, subdivisions 2 and 3.

Rule 15.02 governs the timing of dispositional orders in probation violation matters.

Adopted June 26, 1996. Amended Dec. 12, 1997; July 18, 2003; Oct. 13, 2006, eff. Jan. 1, 2007; Oct. 11, 2007, eff. Jan. 1, 2008.

Comment—Rule 15

See comment following Rule 15.08.

Historical Notes

The order of the Minnesota Supreme Court [C6–84–2165] dated June 26, 1996, provides in part that "(t)hese amendments to the Rules of Juvenile Procedure shall govern all juvenile actions commenced or arrests made on or after 12:00 o'clock midnight August 1, 1996."

The order of the Minnesota Supreme Court [C6–84–2165] dated December 12, 1997, provides in part that "(t)hese amendments to the Rules of Juvenile Procedure shall govern all juvenile actions commenced or arrests made on or after 12:00 o'clock midnight January 1, 1998."

The order of the Minnesota Supreme Court [CX–01–926] dated July 18, 2003, provides in part that "(t)he attached amendments shall govern all juveniles taken into custody and all juvenile delinquency actions commenced or children taken into custody after 12 o'clock midnight September 1, 2003."

Rule 15.08. Other Modifications

Subd. 1. Generally. Rule 15.08 governs the procedure to be followed when any party, including the court, seeks modification of a disposition.

Subd. 2. Modification by Agreement. A disposition may be modified by agreement of all the parties, either in writing or on the record. All agreements to modify a disposition must be approved by the court, and the court may order the parties to appear at a hearing to examine the merits of the modification and verify the voluntariness of the agreement on the record.

Subd. 3. Motion for Modification. All modification proceedings, shall be commenced by the filing of a motion or petition to modify the disposition. The motion for modification shall be in writing and shall be served and filed along with accompanying affidavits, if any, in accordance with Rule 27. The motion or its attachments shall state the proposed modification and the facts and circumstances supporting such a modification.

Subd. 4. Written Request for Modification. If a child is not represented by counsel, the child or the child's parent may submit to the court a written request for modification and send a copy of the written request to the prosecuting attorney.

Subd. 5. Good Cause. Within ten (10) days of filing a motion or written request, the court shall determine from the written request or motion and accompanying affidavits, if any, whether there is good cause to believe that a modification of the disposition is warranted under Rule 15.08, subdivision 8. If the court finds that good cause exists the court shall schedule a modification hearing within ten (10) days of such finding and issue a notice in lieu of summons or a summons in accordance with Rule 15.08, subdivision 6(A). If the court finds that good cause does not exist, the court shall issue an order denying the motion or written request for modification.

Subd. 6. Summons and Warrant.

(A) *Summons.* Notice in lieu of summons or a summons to the modification hearing shall be served upon the child, the child's counsel, the prosecuting attorney, the parent(s), legal guardian or legal custodian of the child, and any agency or department with legal custody of or supervisory responsibility over the child, pursuant to Rule 25. The summons shall be personally served upon the child.

(B) *Warrant.* The court may issue a warrant for immediate custody of a delinquent child or a child alleged to be delinquent if the court finds that there is probable cause to believe that the child has violated the terms of probation or a court order and:

(1) the child failed to appear after having been personally served with a summons or subpoena, or reasonable efforts to personally serve the child have failed, or there is a substantial likelihood that the child will fail to respond to a summons; or

(2) the child or others are in danger of imminent harm; or

(3) the child has left the custody of the detaining authority without permission of the court.

Subd. 7. Hearing.

(A) *Timing.* Except in extraordinary circumstances, the hearing shall be held within twenty (20) days of the date of filing of the modification request.

(B) *Hearing.* The modification hearing shall be conducted in accordance with Rule 15.04. The moving party bears the burden of proving that modification is warranted under Rule 15.08, subdivision 8 by clear and convincing evidence.

Subd. 8. Grounds for Modification. The court may order modification of the disposition after a hearing upon a showing that there has been a substantial change of circumstances such that the original disposition is:

(A) insufficient to restore the child to lawful conduct; or

(B) inconsistent with the child's actual rehabilitative needs.

The modification order shall comply with Rule 15.05, subdivisions 2 and 3.

Adopted June 26, 1996. Amended Dec. 12, 1997; July 18, 2003.

Comments—Rule 15

The disposition for a child who has been designated an extended jurisdiction juvenile is also governed by Minn. R. Juv. Del. P. 19.10.

Dispositional choices are enumerated in Minnesota Statutes, section 260B.198, subds. 1 and 2 (2002). Probation revocation proceedings for a child who has been designated an extended jurisdiction juvenile are governed by Minn. R. Juv. Del. P. 19.11.

Minn. R. Juv. Del. P. 15.02, subd. 3 is intended to address the deficiency noted by various appellate decisions that the juvenile rules do not specify a sanction for violation of the time limits in this rule. See *In re Welfare of C.T.T.,* 464 N.W.2d 751, 753 (Minn. Ct. App. 1991) pet. for rev. denied (Minn. Mar. 15, 1991); *In re Welfare of J.D.K.,* 449 N.W.2d 194, 196 (Minn. Ct. App. 1989).

The juvenile court and court personnel should make every effort to utilize culturally-specific evaluation and assessment programs whenever predisposition reports for juveniles are ordered under Minn.

R. Juv. Del. P. 15.03. The juvenile court should also keep in mind possible cultural issues and biases when evaluating predisposition reports, particularly when a culture-specific evaluation program is not available. See Minnesota Supreme Court Task Force on Racial Bias in the Judicial System, Final Report p. 46–47, 104, 108 (1994).

Before placing a child in a secure treatment facility the court may conduct a subjective assessment to determine whether the child is a danger to self or others or would abscond from a nonsecure facility or if the child's health or welfare would be endangered if not placed in a secure facility; conduct a culturally appropriate psychological evaluation which includes a functional assessment of anger and abuse issues; and conduct an educational and physical assessment of the juvenile. *See* Minn.Stat. § 260B.198, subd. 4 (2002).

When the child has counsel, counsel has the right and the duty to appear at and participate in the disposition hearing.

As a matter of due process, the child has the absolute right to call and cross-examine the authors of any reports, object to the competency of the evidence contained in the reports, and otherwise respond to any adverse facts contained therein. *See In re Welfare of N.W.*, 405 N.W.2d 512, 516–17 (Minn. Ct. App. 1987) (citing *Scheibe v. Scheibe*, 241 N.W.2d 100 (Minn. 1976); *VanZee v. VanZee*, 226 N.W.2d 865 (Minn. 1974); *Stanford v. Stanford*, 123 N.W. 2d 187 (Minn. 1963)).

The child and other participants in the disposition hearing have the right to cross-examine the authors of any written report. However, Rules 15.03 and 15.04 do not mandate that the authors appear at the disposition hearing. Counsel may subpoena the authors of written reports for purposes of cross–examination.

Under Minn. R. Juv. Del. P. 15.05, subd. 1, the decision to either adjudicate the child or grant a continuance without adjudication and the choice of disposition shall be made at the same time and in a single dispositional order. Accord Minn. R. Juv. Del. P. 21.03, subd. 1. The purpose of this rule is to eliminate multiple appeals. Because both an adjudicatory order and a dispositional order are final, appealable orders, if the court adjudicates the child or grants a continuance without adjudication and then enters a dispositional order at a later date, the child is forced to appeal twice: once from the adjudicatory order and once from the dispositional order. By requiring the court to defer the adjudicatory decision until the time of disposition, the child can appeal both orders at the same time in one appeal.

Requiring that the adjudicatory decision be deferred until the time of disposition should also eliminate the problem that arose in *In re Welfare of M.D.S.*, 514 N.W.2d 308 (Minn. Ct. App. 1994). There, the juvenile court entered an order finding that the allegations of the petition had been proved. The order also stated that adjudication was withheld but only for the purpose of transferring the case to the child's home county for disposition and further proceedings. The child attempted to appeal the order finding that the allegations of the petition had been proved. The appellate court held that the order was not appealable because it neither adjudicated the child delinquent nor finally determined that adjudication was withheld. Because the juvenile court is prohibited from adjudicating the child or granting a continuance without adjudication until the time of disposition under Minn. R. Juv. Del. P. 15.05, subd. 1, it should be clear that there can be no appeal of the finding that the allegations of the charging document have been proved until after the court enters a dispositional order.

An order adjudicating a child delinquent prior to disposition is ineffective and not appealable. But the order becomes appealable as part of the disposition once a dispositional order is made. *See In re Welfare of G.M.*, 533 N.W.2d 883, C9–95–812 (Minn. Ct.App. July 3, 1995).

A copy of the order adjudicating a child delinquent for committing felony-level criminal sexual conduct should be forwarded to the Bureau of Criminal Apprehension by the court in accordance with Minnesota Statutes, section 260B.171, subd. 2(a) (2002).

Minnesota Statutes, section 260B.198, subd. 1 (2002) requires written findings on disposition in every case. Although this statute seemingly invades the province of the judiciary to govern its own procedures. Minn. R. Juv. Del. P. 15.05, subd. 2(A) reiterates the statutory principle.

Minn. R. Juv. Del. P. 15.05, subd. 2(B) recites some of the general principles relating to dispositions that have developed under Minnesota law.

a. The content of Minn. R. Juv. Del. P. 15.05, subd. 2(B) is largely derived from Minnesota Statutes, section 260B.001, subd. 2 (2002); Minnesota Statutes, section 260B.198, subd. 1 (2002); *In re Welfare of A.R.W. & Y.C.W.*, 268 N.W.2d 414, 417 (Minn. 1978) cert. denied 439 U.S. 989 (1978); *In re Welfare of D.S.F.*, 416 N.W.2d 772 (Minn. Ct. App. 1987) pet. for rev. denied (Minn. Feb. 17, 1988); and *In re Welfare of L.K.W.*, 372 N.W.2d 392 (Minn. Ct. App. 1985). See also Institute of Judicial Administration–American Bar Association, Juvenile Justice Standards: Standards Relating to Dispositions (1980). This rule does not create any substantive standards or limit the development of the law but is intended to assist the court when choosing a disposition by focusing on those standards that are already part of established Minnesota law. The court is not required to make findings on each of these factors in every case, although such findings may be helpful in contentious cases.

b. The overriding purpose in every juvenile delinquency disposition, declared by statute, is to "promote the public safety and reduce juvenile delinquency by maintaining the integrity of the substantive law prohibiting certain behavior and by developing individual responsibility for lawful behavior." Minn.Stat. § 260B.001, subd. 2 (2002). This statute and another declare the means to be employed by the juvenile court to serve its public safety purpose. First, the purpose of the court "should be pursued through means that are fair and just, that recognize the unique characteristics and needs of children, and that give children access to opportunities for personal and social growth." *Id.* Second, the court is to employ dispositions that are "deemed necessary to the rehabilitation of the child." Minn.Stat. § 260B.198, subd. 1 (2002). Each judicial district, after consultation with local county attorneys, public defenders, corrections personnel, victim advocates, and the public, is required to have written criteria for determining delinquency dispositions develop by September 1, 1995. *See* 1994 Minn.Laws ch. 576, § 59.

Where appropriate, the court should make every effort to use any available culturally-specific programs when making a disposition for a juvenile. The court should also be aware of racial disparities in dispositions among similarly situated juveniles, particularly for those offenses which have historically resulted in more severe sanctions for minorities. *See* Minnesota Supreme Court Task Force on Racial Bias in the Judicial System, Final Report p. 103–04, 108–09.

Minn. R. Juv. Del. P. 15.05, subd. 3 provides that a dispositional order that transfers legal custody of the child under Minnesota Statutes, section 260B.198, subd. 1(c) (2002) shall be for a specified length of time. See Minnesota Statutes, section 260B.198, subd. 9 (2002).

The duration of a disposition that transfers custody of the child to the Commissioner of Corrections pursuant to Minnesota Statutes, section 260B.198, subd. 1(d)(2002) is determined by the Commissioner. *See In re Welfare of M.D.A,* 237 N.W.2d 827 (Minn. 1975).

"Withholding of adjudication" was redesignated as "continuance without adjudication" to conform with the statutory language of Minnesota Statutes, section 260.185, subd. 3 (1994). Continuance without adjudication is now authorized by Minnesota Statutes, section 260B.198, subd. 7 (2002). The court must find that the allegations of the charging document have been proved before it can continue a case without adjudication. *Id.* The court may not grant a continuance without adjudication in an extended juvenile jurisdiction proceeding. *Id.*

Continuance without adjudication (or withholding of adjudication) has a material effect on a child's juvenile record. Prior to 1983, the Minnesota Sentencing Guidelines assigned one criminal history point for every two felony-level "juvenile adjudications." See Minnesota Sentencing Guidelines II.B.4 (1982). In *State v. Peterson,* 331 N.W.2d 483 (Minn. 1983), the defendant claimed that it was error to use juvenile offenses for which there had been findings but no adjudication when calculating his criminal history score under the sentencing guidelines. The supreme court did not reach the defendant's argument but suggested that the Sentencing Guidelines Commission amend the guidelines to avoid the issue raised by defendant. *Id.* at 486. The guidelines were subsequently amended in 1983 to assign one criminal history point for every two felony-level offenses "committed and prosecuted as a juvenile", provided the juvenile court made findings pursuant to an admission or trial. Minnesota Sentencing Guidelines II.B.4 (2002). Because Minnesota Statutes, section 260B.198, subd. 7 requires a finding that the juvenile committed the offense alleged in the charging document before the court may continue the case without an adjudication, which finding satisfies the requirements of the sentencing guidelines for counting a juvenile offense in the criminal history score, a continuance without adjudication (or withholding of adjudication) will not exclude the juvenile offense from a subsequent criminal history score. See John O. Sonsteng, et. al. 12 Minnesota Practice at 215 (1997). Continuance without adjudication may prevent the operation of some statutes which still require that the child be adjudicated delinquent. See, e.g., Minnesota Statutes, section 609.117, subd. 1(3) (2002) (provision of biological specimens for DNA analysis).

A continuance without adjudication or continuance for dismissal under Minn. R. Juv. Del. P. 14 are not the only options available for dealing with an alleged juvenile offender without formal process. Every county attorney should have a pretrial diversion program established for certain juveniles subject to juvenile court jurisdiction, as an alternative to formal adjudication. See Minnesota Statutes, section 388.24 (2002). With statutory pretrial diversion readily available for less serious juvenile offenders, presumably the use of continuance without adjudication and continuance for dismissal under these rules will become less common.

Much of Minn. R. Juv. Del. P. 15.07 was taken from Minn. R. Crim. P. 27.04. There was question as to whether probation officers could detain juveniles pending a probation violation hearing for 72 hours pursuant to Minn. Stat. §§ 244.195, subd. 2 (2004) and 401.025, subd. 1 (2004). Minn. R. Juv. Del. P. 15.07, subd. 2 was clarified to indicate that the maximum period for the detention of juveniles pending a probation violation hearing is 36 hours pursuant to Minn. R. Juv. Del. P. 5 and Minn. Stat. § 260B.176, subd. 2 (2004).

The three-step *Austin* analysis (*see State v. Austin,* 295 N.W.2d 246 (Minn. 1980)) is not required when revoking a juvenile's probation under Minn. R. Juv. Del. P. 15.07, subd. 4(D) "because the juvenile rules afford non–EJJ juvenile probationers better protection against the reflexive execution of a stayed disposition requiring confinement in a secure facility than *Austin* would afford." *In re Welfare of R.V.,* 702 N.W.2d 294 (Minn. Ct. App. 2005).

Unless all the parties agree to a proposed modification, the court may not order modification of the disposition after an informal review without commencing a modification proceeding pursuant to Minn. R. Juv. Del. P. 15.08 in order to give the parties an opportunity to contest the proposed modification before it is imposed.

Under Minn. R. Juv. Del. P. 15.08, subd. 2, the court is not required to hold a hearing to examine a modification agreement on the record in every case. But agreements to make upward modifications to a disposition will normally require a court appearance and approval on the record in order to ensure that the proposed modification complies with the law, and that the child appreciates the significance of the modification and voluntarily consents to the modification. The discretion to approve a modification without an appearance is intended to be reserved for relatively minor, usually downward, modifications.

Rule 15.08 does not apply to probation revocations, the procedure for which is governed by Rule 15.07.

Minnesota Statutes, section 260B.154 (2002) addresses the court's authority to issue a warrant for immediate custody for the child. Minnesota Statutes, section 260B. 175, subd. 1(c) addresses the authority of a peace officer or probation officer to take a child into custody for allegedly violating the terms of probationary supervision.

Counsel for the child has the right and duty to appear at and participate in all probation revocation and modification proceedings and hearings. See Minn. R. Juv. Del. P. 3.02, subd. 4.

Reference in this rule to "counsel for the parent(s), legal guardian, or legal custodian" includes the parent, legal guardian, or legal custodian who is proceeding pro se. Minn. R. Juv. Del. P. 1.01.

Historical Notes

The order of the Minnesota Supreme Court [C6–84–2165] dated June 26, 1996, provides in part that "(t)hese amendments to the Rules of Juvenile Procedure shall govern all juvenile actions commenced or arrests made on or after 12:00 o'clock midnight August 1, 1996."

The order of the Minnesota Supreme Court [C6–84–2165] dated December 12, 1997, provides in part that "(t)hese amendments to the Rules of Juvenile Procedure shall govern all juvenile actions commenced or arrests made on or after 12:00 o'clock midnight January 1, 1998."

The order of the Minnesota Supreme Court [CX–01–926] dated July 18, 2003, provides in part that "(t)he attached amendments shall govern all juveniles taken into custody and all juvenile delinquency actions commenced or children taken into custody after 12 o'clock midnight September 1, 2003."

RULE 16. POST-TRIAL MOTIONS

Rule 16.01. Post-trial Motions

Subd. 1. Grounds. The court, on written motion of the child's counsel, may grant a new trial on any of the following grounds:

(A) if required in the interests of justice;

(B) irregularity in the proceedings of the court or in any court order or abuse of discretion by the court, if the child was deprived of a fair trial;

(C) misconduct of the prosecuting attorney;

(D) accident or surprise which could not have been prevented by ordinary prudence;

(E) material evidence, newly discovered, which with reasonable diligence could not have been found and produced at the trial;

(F) errors of law occurring at the trial and objected to at the time or, if no objection is required, assigned in the motion;

(G) the finding that the allegations of the charging document are proved is not justified by the evidence or is contrary to law; or

(H) ineffective assistance of child's counsel.

Subd. 2. Basis of Motion. A motion for a new trial shall be made and heard on the files, exhibits and minutes of the court. Pertinent facts that would not be a part of the minutes may be shown by affidavit except as otherwise provided by these rules. A full or partial transcript of the court reporter's notes of the testimony taken at the trial or other verbatim recording thereof may be used on the hearing of the motion.

Subd. 3. Time for Motion.

(A) *Generally.* Notice of a motion for a new trial shall be served within fifteen (15) days after the court's specific findings are made pursuant to Rule 13.09. The motion shall be heard within thirty (30) days after the court's specific findings are made pursuant to Rule 13.09 unless the time for the hearing is extended by the court for good cause shown within the thirty (30) day period.

(B) *New Evidence.* Notice of a motion for a new trial based on new evidence shall be served and filed within fifteen (15) days of the filing of the court's order for adjudication and disposition. The motion shall be heard within fifteen (15) days of the filing of the notice of motion for new trial. Upon a showing that new evidence exists, the court shall order that a new trial be held within thirty (30) days, unless the court extends this time period for good cause shown within the thirty (30) days.

Subd. 4. Time for Serving Affidavits. When a motion for new trial is based on affidavits, they shall be served with the notice of motion. The prosecuting attorney shall have ten (10) days after such service in which to serve responsive affidavits. The period may be extended by the court upon an order extending the time for hearing under this rule. The court may permit reply affidavits.

Amended June 26, 1996; Nov. 19, 2010, eff. Jan. 1, 2011.

Comment—Rule 16

See comment following Rule 16.05.

Historical Notes

The order of the Minnesota Supreme Court [C6–84–2165] dated June 26, 1996, provides in part that "(t)hese amendments to the Rules of Juvenile Procedure shall govern all juvenile actions commenced or arrests made on or after 12:00 o'clock midnight August 1, 1996."

Rule 16.02. Motion to Vacate the Finding that the Allegations of the Charging Document are Proved

The court, on motion of the child's counsel, shall vacate the finding that the allegations of the charging document are proved and dismiss the charging document if it fails to charge an offense or if the court was without jurisdiction of the offense charged. The motion shall be made within fifteen (15) days of the finding that the allegations of the charging document are proved or within such time as the court may fix during the fifteen (15) day period. If the motion is granted, the court shall make written findings specifying its reasons for vacating the finding that the allegations of the charging document are proved and dismissing the charging document.

Amended June 26, 1996; July 11, 2005, eff. Sept. 1, 2005.

Comment—Rule 16

See comment following Rule 16.05.

Historical Notes

The order of the Minnesota Supreme Court [C6–84–2165] dated June 26, 1996, provides in part that "(t)hese amendments to the Rules of Juvenile Procedure shall govern all juvenile actions commenced or arrests made on or after 12:00 o'clock midnight August 1, 1996."

Rule 16.03. Joinder of Motions

Any motion to vacate the finding that the allegations of the charging document are proved shall be joined with a motion for a new trial.

Amended June 26, 1996.

Comment—Rule 16

See comment following Rule 16.05.

Historical Notes

The order of the Minnesota Supreme Court [C6–84–2165] dated June 26, 1996, provides in part that "(t)hese amendments to the Rules of Juvenile Procedure shall govern all juvenile actions commenced or arrests made on or after 12:00 o'clock midnight August 1, 1996."

Rule 16.04. New Trial on Court's Own Motion

The court, on its own motion, may order a new trial upon any of the grounds specified in Rule 16.01, subdivision 1 within fifteen (15) days after the finding that the allegations of the charging document are proved and with the consent of the child.

Adopted June 26, 1996. Amended July 18, 2003.

Comment—Rule 16

See comment following Rule 16.05.

Historical Notes

The order of the Minnesota Supreme Court [C6–84–2165] dated June 26, 1996, provides in part that "(t)hese amendments to the Rules of Juvenile Procedure shall govern all juvenile actions commenced or arrests made on or after 12:00 o'clock midnight August 1, 1996."

The order of the Minnesota Supreme Court [CX–01–926] dated July 18, 2003, provides in part that "(t)he attached amendments shall govern all juveniles taken into custody and all juvenile delinquency actions commenced or children taken into custody after 12 o'clock midnight September 1, 2003."

Rule 16.05. Order

Orders issued pursuant to this rule shall be in writing.

Adopted Oct. 11, 2007, eff. Jan. 1, 2008.

Comment—Rule 16

References to "child's counsel" includes the child who is proceeding pro se. Minn. R. Juv. Del. P. 1.01.

Minn. R. Juv. Del. P. 16.01, subd. 3 provides that notice of a motion for a new trial shall be served within fifteen (15) days after the finding that the allegations of the charging document are proved, except for a motion for new trial based on the grounds of new evidence. Minnesota Statutes, section 260B.411 (2002) provides for a different time for filing a motion for new trial which is premised on the discovery of new evidence. There, a child must bring a motion for new trial based on new evidence within fifteen (15) days of the filing of the court's order for adjudication and disposition. *Id.* Motions for new trial brought on other grounds must be brought within fifteen (15) days after the finding that the allegations of the charging document are proved as provided by this rule. Minn. R. Juv. Del. P. 16.01, subd. 3.

In re Welfare of D.N. held that a juvenile must move for a new trial to raise an appealable issue on evidentiary rulings. *In re Welfare of D.N.*, 523 N.W.2d 11, 13 (Minn. Ct. App. 1994), *review denied* (Minn. Nov. 29, 1994). It should be noted that D.N. was a child in need of protection or services and not a delinquent. The procedures for delinquent children are more closely aligned with the rules of adult criminal court.

RULE 17. JUVENILE PETTY OFFENDER AND JUVENILE TRAFFIC OFFENDER

Rule 17.01. Scope, Application and General Purpose

Rule 17 applies to children alleged to be juvenile petty offenders as defined by Minnesota Statutes, section 260B.007, subdivision 16 or juvenile traffic offenders as defined by Minnesota Statutes, section 260B.225. The purpose of Rule 17 is to provide a uniform and streamlined procedure for juvenile petty and juvenile traffic offenders which is sensitive to the fact that neither has the right to counsel at public expense, except as provided in Rule 3.02, subd. 5. Except as otherwise provided in this rule, the general rules of juvenile delinquency procedure apply to juvenile petty and juvenile traffic matters.

Subd. 1. Juvenile Petty Offender. A juvenile petty offender is a child who has committed a juvenile petty offense as defined by Minnesota Statutes, section 260B.007, subdivision 16. The prosecuting attorney may designate a child a juvenile petty offender despite the child's history of misdemeanor-level offenses.

Subd. 2. Juvenile Traffic Offender. A juvenile traffic offender is any child alleged to have committed a traffic offense except those children under the jurisdiction of adult court as provided in Minnesota Statutes, section 260B.225. A traffic offense is any violation of a state or local traffic law, ordinance, or regulation, or a federal, state or local water traffic law.

Adopted June 26, 1996. Amended July 18, 2003.

Comment—Rule 17

See comment following Rule 17.11.

Historical Notes

The order of the Minnesota Supreme Court [C6–84–2165] dated June 26, 1996, provides in part that "(t)hese amendments to the Rules of Juvenile Procedure shall govern all juvenile actions commenced or arrests made on or after 12:00 o'clock midnight August 1, 1996."

The order of the Minnesota Supreme Court [CX–01–926] dated July 18, 2003, provides in part that "(t)he attached amendments shall govern all juveniles taken into custody and all juvenile delinquency actions commenced or children taken into custody after 12 o'clock midnight September 1, 2003."

Rule 17.02. Right to Counsel

Subd. 1. Generally. In any proceeding in which a child is charged as a juvenile petty offender or a juvenile traffic offender, the child or the child's parent may retain private counsel, but the child does not have a right to counsel at public expense, except:

(A) when the child may be subject to out-of-home placement as provided in Minnesota Statutes, section 260B.235, subdivision 6; or

(B) as otherwise provided pursuant to Rule 3.02, subdivisions 3, 6 and 7.

Subd. 2. Waiver. Any waiver of counsel must be knowing, intelligent, and voluntary. A waiver of counsel shall be in writing or made orally on the record.

Subd. 3. For Appeal. A child adjudicated a juvenile petty offender or juvenile traffic offender does not have the right to counsel at public expense for the purposes of appeal except at the discretion of the Office of the State Public Defender as set out in Rule 21.02, subdivision 2.

Subd. 4. Parent, Legal Guardian or Legal Custodian as Counsel. A parent, legal guardian or legal custodian may not represent the child unless licensed as an attorney.

Adopted June 26, 1996. Amended Dec. 12, 1997; July 18, 2003.

Comment—Rule 17

See comment following Rule 17.11.

Historical Notes

The order of the Minnesota Supreme Court [C6–84–2165] dated June 26, 1996, provides in part that "(t)hese amendments to the Rules of Juvenile Procedure shall govern all juvenile actions commenced or arrests made on or after 12:00 o'clock midnight August 1, 1996."

The order of the Minnesota Supreme Court [C6–84–2165] dated December 12, 1997, provides in part that "(t)hese amendments to the Rules of Juvenile Procedure shall govern all juvenile actions commenced or arrests made on or after 12:00 o'clock midnight January 1, 1998."

The order of the Minnesota Supreme Court [CX–01–926] dated July 18, 2003, provides in part that "(t)he attached amendments shall govern all juveniles taken into custody and all juvenile delinquency actions commenced or children taken into custody after 12 o'clock midnight September 1, 2003."

Rule 17.03. Warrants

The issuance of warrants under this Rule is governed by Rule 4.

Adopted June 26, 1996. Amended July 18, 2003.

Comment—Rule 17

See comment following Rule 17.11.

Historical Notes

The order of the Minnesota Supreme Court [C6–84–2165] dated June 26, 1996, provides in part that "(t)hese amendments to the Rules of Juvenile Procedure shall govern all juvenile actions commenced or arrests made on or after 12:00 o'clock midnight August 1, 1996."

The order of the Minnesota Supreme Court [CX–01–926] dated July 18, 2003, provides in part that "(t)he attached amendments shall govern all juveniles taken into custody and all juvenile delinquency actions commenced or children taken into custody after 12 o'clock midnight September 1, 2003."

Rule 17.04. The Charging Document and Notice of Arraignment

A child shall be charged as a juvenile petty offender or juvenile traffic offender pursuant to Rule 6 with proper notice given pursuant to Rule 25. The time for an arraignment shall be the same as that for a delinquency proceeding, and the child may resolve the case by paying a citation in lieu of appearing at arraignment as provided in Rule 6.

Adopted June 26, 1996. Amended July 18, 2003; Nov. 19, 2010, eff. Jan. 1, 2011.

Comment—Rule 17

See comment following Rule 17.11.

Historical Notes

The order of the Minnesota Supreme Court [C6–84–2165] dated June 26, 1996, provides in part that "(t)hese amendments to the Rules of Juvenile Procedure shall govern all juvenile actions commenced or arrests made on or after 12:00 o'clock midnight August 1, 1996."

The order of the Minnesota Supreme Court [CX–01–926] dated July 18, 2003, provides in part that "(t)he attached amendments shall govern all juveniles taken into custody and all juvenile delinquency actions commenced or children taken into custody after 12 o'clock midnight September 1, 2003."

Rule 17.05. Arraignment

Subd. 1. Generally. An arraignment is a hearing in which a child shall enter a plea of guilty or not guilty in the manner provided in Rule 17.06.

Subd. 2. Timing. Upon the filing of a charging document, the court administrator shall promptly fix a time for arraignment and send notices pursuant to Rule 25. The time for an arraignment shall be the same as that for a delinquency proceeding, that is:

(A) *Child in Custody.* The child in custody may be arraigned at a detention hearing and shall be arraigned no later than five (5) days after the detention hearing. The child has the right to have a copy of the charging document for three (3) days before being arraigned.

(B) *Child Not in Custody.* The child not in custody shall be arraigned no later than thirty (30) days after the filing of the charging document. The child has the right to have a copy of the charging document for three (3) days before being arraigned.

Subd. 3. Hearing Procedure. Children alleged to be juvenile petty offenders or juvenile traffic offenders may be arraigned as a group and shall be arraigned individually and confidentially upon request. At the start of the arraignment, the court shall inform the child(ren) of the following rights and possible dispositions:

(A) the right to remain silent;

(B) the right to counsel at any point throughout the proceedings, including the limited right to appointment of counsel at public expense;

(C) the right to plead not guilty and have a trial in which the child is presumed innocent unless and until the prosecuting attorney proves the allegations beyond a reasonable doubt;

(D) the right of the child to testify on the child's own behalf;

(E) the right to call witnesses using the court's subpoena powers;

(F) *For a Juvenile Petty Offender.*

(1) the dispositions that may be imposed pursuant to Minnesota Statutes, section 260B.235, subdivisions 4, 5 and 6 if the child pleads guilty or, after a trial, the court finds that the allegations of the charging document have been proven beyond a reasonable doubt; and

(2) if the offense is a second misdemeanor-level petty offense, the possibility that any same or similar offense will be charged as a misdemeanor in a delinquency petition;

(G) *For a Juvenile Traffic Offender.* The dispositions that may be imposed pursuant to Minnesota Statutes, section 260B.225, subdivision 9 if the child pleads guilty or, after a trial, the court finds that the allegations of the charging document have been proven beyond a reasonable doubt.

Subd. 4. Reading of Allegations of Charging Document. The court shall read the allegations of the charging document to the child and determine that the child understands them, and, if not, provide an explanation.

Subd. 5. Motions. The court shall hear and make findings on any motions regarding the sufficiency of the charging document, including its adequacy in stating probable cause of the charges made and the jurisdiction of the court, without requiring the child to plead guilty or not guilty to the charges in the charging document. A challenge of probable cause shall not delay the setting of trial proceedings in cases where the child has demanded a speedy trial.

Subd. 6. Response to Charging Document. After considering the wishes of the parties to proceed later or at once, the court may continue the arraignment without requiring the child to plead guilty or not guilty to the charges stated in the charging document.

Adopted June 26, 1996. Amended July 18, 2003.

Comment—Rule 17

See comment following Rule 17.11.

Historical Notes

The order of the Minnesota Supreme Court [C6–84–2165] dated June 26, 1996, provides in part that "(t)hese amendments to the Rules of Juvenile Procedure shall govern all juvenile actions commenced or arrests made on or after 12:00 o'clock midnight August 1, 1996."

The order of the Minnesota Supreme Court [CX–01–926] dated July 18, 2003, provides in part that "(t)he attached amendments shall govern all juveniles taken into custody and all juvenile delinquency actions commenced or children taken into custody after 12 o'clock midnight September 1, 2003."

Rule 17.06. Pleas

Subd. 1. Plea of Guilty. Before the court accepts a plea of guilty, the court shall determine under the totality of the circumstances whether the child understands all applicable rights. The court shall on the record, or by written plea petition if the child is represented by counsel, determine:

(A) whether the child understands:

(1) the nature of the offense alleged:

(2) the right to the appointment of counsel if the child is subject to out-of-home placement as provided in Minnesota Statutes, section 260B.235, subdivision 6;

(3) the right to trial;

(4) the presumption of innocence until the prosecuting attorney proves the charges beyond a reasonable doubt;

(5) the right to remain silent;

(6) the right to testify on the child's own behalf;

(7) the right to confront witnesses against oneself;

(8) the right to subpoena witnesses;

(9) that the child's conduct constitutes the offense to which the child pled guilty;

(B) whether the child makes any claim of innocence; and

(C) whether the plea is made freely, under no threats or promises other than those the parties have disclosed to the court.

Subd. 2. Plea of Not Guilty. Upon a plea of not guilty, the matter shall be set for trial and the court shall advise the child of the discovery procedures as set forth in Rule 17.07.

Subd. 3. Withdrawal of Plea. The child may, on the record or by written motion filed with the court, request to withdraw a plea of guilty. The court may allow the child to withdraw a guilty plea:

(A) before disposition, for any just reason;

(B) at any time, if out-of-home placement is proposed based upon a plea or adjudication obtained without the assistance of counsel; or

(C) after disposition, upon showing that withdrawal is necessary to correct a manifest injustice.

Subd. 4. Plea to a Lesser Offense or a Different Offense. With the consent of the prosecuting attorney and approval of the court, the child shall be permitted to enter:

(A) a plea of guilty to a lesser included offense or to an offense of a lesser degree; or

(B) a plea of guilty to a different offense than that alleged in the charging document.

A plea of guilty to a lesser included offense or to an offense of a lesser degree may be entered without an amendment of the charging document. If a plea to different offense is accepted, the charging document must be amended on the record or a new charging document must be filed with the court.

Subd. 5. Acceptance or Nonacceptance of Plea of Guilty and Future Proceedings. The court shall make a finding within fifteen (15) days of the plea of guilty:

(A) that the plea has been accepted and the allegations in the charging document have been proved; or

(B) that the plea has not been accepted.

If the court accepts a plea of guilty and makes a finding that the allegations in the charging document have been proved, the court shall schedule further proceedings pursuant to Rule 17.09.

Adopted June 26, 1996. Amended July 18, 2003.

Comment—Rule 17

See comment following Rule 17.11.

Historical Notes

The order of the Minnesota Supreme Court [C6-84-2165] dated June 26, 1996, provides in part that "(t)hese amendments to the Rules of Juvenile Procedure shall govern all juvenile actions commenced or arrests made on or after 12:00 o'clock midnight August 1, 1996."

The order of the Minnesota Supreme Court [CX-01-926] dated July 18, 2003, provides in part that "(t)he attached amendments shall govern all juveniles taken into custody and all juvenile delinquency actions commenced or children taken into custody after 12 o'clock midnight September 1, 2003."

Rule 17.07. Discovery

At the court's discretion, discovery may be conducted in the manner provided for delinquency proceedings pursuant to Rule 10. Otherwise discovery shall proceed as follows: The prosecuting attorney shall, as soon as possible, provide the child with copies of statements and police reports. At least ten (10) days before trial, the parties shall exchange the names of witnesses they intend to have testify at trial as well as exhibit lists.

Adopted June 26, 1996. Amended July 18, 2003.

Comment—Rule 17

See comment following Rule 17.11.

Historical Notes

The order of the Minnesota Supreme Court [C6-84-2165] dated June 26, 1996, provides in part that "(t)hese amendments to the Rules of Juvenile Procedure shall govern all juvenile actions commenced or arrests made on or after 12:00 o'clock midnight August 1, 1996."

The order of the Minnesota Supreme Court [CX-01-926] dated July 18, 2003, provides in part that "(t)he attached amendments shall govern all juveniles taken into custody and all juvenile delinquency actions commenced or children taken into custody after 12 o'clock midnight September 1, 2003."

Rule 17.08. Pretrial and Omnibus Hearing

Upon request of either party, the court shall hold a pretrial and/or an omnibus hearing in the manner provided for delinquency proceedings pursuant to Rules 11 and 12.

Adopted June 26, 1996. Amended July 18, 2003.

Comment—Rule 17

See comment following Rule 17.11.

Historical Notes

The order of the Minnesota Supreme Court [C6-84-2165] dated June 26, 1996, provides in part that "(t)hese amendments to the Rules of Juvenile Procedure shall govern all juvenile actions commenced or arrests made on or after 12:00 o'clock midnight August 1, 1996."

The order of the Minnesota Supreme Court [CX-01-926] dated July 18, 2003, provides in part that "(t)he attached amendments shall govern all juveniles taken into custody and all juvenile delinquency actions commenced or children taken into custody after 12 o'clock midnight September 1, 2003."

Rule 17.09. Adjudication and Disposition

Subd. 1. Predisposition Reports. Before finding that the allegations of the charging document have been proved, the court may order an investigation of the personal and family history and environment of the child and outpatient psychological or chemical dependency evaluations of the child. The information and recommendations contained in the predisposition report(s) shall be made known to the child, child's parent(s), legal guardian or legal custodian before the disposition hearing.

Subd. 2. Adjudication and Disposition. Within forty-five (45) days from the finding that the allegations of the charging document are proved, the court shall:

(A) *For a Juvenile Petty Offender.* Adjudicate the child a juvenile petty offender and order a disposition pursuant to Minnesota Statutes, section 260B.235, subdivisions 4, 5, and 6.

(B) *For a Juvenile Traffic Offender.* Adjudicate the child a juvenile traffic offender and order a disposition pursuant to Minnesota Statutes, section 260B.225, subdivision 9.

The order may be in writing or on the record. If the order is on the record, the child may request written findings, and the court shall make and file written findings within seven (7) days of the request. The court administrator shall serve the written findings as provided in Rule 28.

Subd. 3. Probation Revocation. Probation revocation proceedings shall be conducted in the same manner as delinquency probation violation proceedings pursuant to Rule 15.07 except for the following:

(A) *Warrant.* The court may only issue a warrant for immediate custody of a juvenile petty or juvenile traffic offender if the court finds that there is probable cause to believe that: the child failed to appear after having been personally served with a summons or subpoena, reasonable efforts to personally serve the child have failed, or there is a substantial likelihood that the child will fail to respond to a summons.

(B) *Advisory.* Prior to the child admitting or denying the allegations in the probation violation report, the court shall advise the child of the following:

(1) that, at all stages of the proceedings, the child has the right to be represented by counsel but does not have the right to counsel at public expense, unless the child is subject to out-of-home placement;

(2) that, unless waived, a revocation hearing will be commenced to determine whether there is clear and convincing evidence that the child violated a dispositional order of the court and whether the court should change the existing dispositional order because of the violation;

(3) that before the revocation hearing, all evidence to be used against the child shall be disclosed to the child and the child shall be provided access to all official records pertinent to the proceedings;

(4) that at the hearing, both the prosecuting attorney and the child shall have the right to offer evidence, present arguments, subpoena witnesses, and call and cross-examine witnesses, provided, however, that the child may be denied confrontation by the court when good cause is shown that a substantial risk of serious harm to others would exist if it were allowed. Additionally, the child shall have the right at the hearing to present mitigating circumstances or other reasons why the violation, if proved, should not result in revocation;

(5) that the child has the right of appeal from the determination of the court following the revocation hearing.

(C) *Violation Proved.* If the court finds by clear and convincing evidence, or the child admits violating the terms of the dispositional order, the court may order a disposition pursuant to Minnesota Statutes, section 260B.235, subdivisions 4, 5, and 6 for a juvenile petty offender or a disposition pursuant to Minnesota Statutes, section 260B.225, subdivision 9 for a juvenile traffic offender.

Subd. 4. Other Modifications. Other modification proceedings shall be conducted in the same manner as delinquency modification proceedings pursuant to Rule 15.08 except that the court may not order a delinquency disposition. For a juvenile petty offender, the court may order a disposition pursuant to Minnesota Statutes, section 260B.235, subdivisions 4, 5, and 6 and for a juvenile traffic offender, the court may order a disposition pursuant to Minnesota Statutes, section 260B.225, subdivision 9. The modification order may be in writing or on the record. If the order is on the record, the child may request written findings, and the court shall make and file written findings within seven (7) days of the request.

Adopted June 26, 1996. Amended July 18, 2003; Oct. 11, 2007, eff. Jan. 1, 2008.

Comment—Rule 17

See comment following Rule 17.11.

Historical Notes

The order of the Minnesota Supreme Court [C6–84–2165] dated June 26, 1996, provides in part that "(t)hese amendments to the Rules of Juvenile Procedure shall govern all juvenile actions commenced or arrests made on or after 12:00 o'clock midnight August 1, 1996."

The order of the Minnesota Supreme Court [CX–01–926] dated July 18, 2003, provides in part that "(t)he attached amendments shall govern all juveniles taken into custody and all juvenile delinquency actions commenced or children taken into custody after 12 o'clock midnight September 1, 2003."

Rule 17.10. Transfer to Adult Court of Juvenile Traffic Matter

Subd. 1. On Motion of Court or Prosecuting Attorney. The court, after a hearing and on its own motion or on motion of the prosecuting attorney, may transfer a juvenile traffic offender case to adult court if it makes a written order to transfer which finds that the welfare of the child or public safety would be better served under the laws relating to adult traffic matters.

Subd. 2. Method of Transfer. The court shall transfer the case by forwarding all documents in the court file to adult court together with the order to transfer.

Subd. 3. Effect of Transfer. Upon transfer, jurisdiction of the juvenile court is deemed not to have attached and the adult shall proceed with the case as if it had never been in juvenile court.

Adopted June 26, 1996. Amended July 18, 2003.

Comment—Rule 17

See comment following Rule 17.11.

Historical Notes

The order of the Minnesota Supreme Court [C6–84–2165] dated June 26, 1996, provides in part that "(t)hese amendments to the Rules of Juvenile Procedure shall govern all juvenile actions commenced or arrests made on or after 12:00 o'clock midnight August 1, 1996."

The order of the Minnesota Supreme Court [CX–01–926] dated July 18, 2003, provides in part that "(t)he attached amendments shall govern all juveniles taken into custody and all juvenile delinquency actions commenced or children taken into custody after 12 o'clock midnight September 1, 2003."

Rule 17.11. Child Incompetent to Proceed

If a child is believed to be incompetent to proceed, the court may proceed according to Rule 20, direct that civil commitment proceedings be initiated, direct that Child in Need of Protection or Services (CHIPS) proceedings be initiated or dismiss the case.

Adopted June 26, 1996. Amended July 18, 2003.

Comment—Rule 17

In 1995, the legislature expanded the definition of "juvenile petty offense." Pursuant to Minnesota Statutes, section 260.015, subd. 21 (Supp. 1995), a juvenile petty offense included the following:

(a) a juvenile alcohol offense;

(b) a juvenile controlled substance offense;

(c) a violation of section 609.685;

(d) a violation of a local ordinance, which by its terms prohibits conduct by a child under the age of 18 years which would be lawful conduct if committed by an adult;

(e) an offense, other than a violation of section 609.224, 609.324, 609.563, 609.576, or 617.23, that would be a misdemeanor if committed by an adult if:

(1) the child has not been found to be a juvenile petty offender on more than two prior occasions for a misdemeanor-level offense;

(2) the child has not previously been found to be delinquent for a misdemeanor, gross misdemeanor, or felony offense; or

(3) the county attorney designates the child on the petition as a juvenile petty offender, notwithstanding the child's prior record of misdemeanor-level juvenile petty offenses. Minnesota Statutes, section 260.015, subd. 21 (Supp. 1995).

This definition of juvenile petty offense applied to crimes committed on or after July 1, 1995. 1995 Minn. Laws Ch. 226, Art. 3, Sec. 65.

In 1996, the legislature again revised the definition of "juvenile petty offense." Pursuant to 1996 Minn. Laws Ch. 408, Art. 6, Sec. 1, a juvenile petty offense included:

(a) a juvenile alcohol offense;

(b) a juvenile controlled substance offense;

(c) a violation of section 609.685;

(d) a violation of local ordinance, which by its terms prohibits conduct by a child under the age of 18 years which would be lawful conduct if committed by an adult; and

(e) an offense that would be a misdemeanor if committed by an adult, except:

(1) a misdemeanor-level violation of section 588.20, 609.224, 609.2242, 609.324, 609.563, 609.576, 609.66, or 617.23;

(2) a major traffic offense or an adult court traffic offense, as described in section 260.193;

(3) a misdemeanor-level offense committed by a child whom the juvenile court previously has found to have committed a misdemeanor, gross misdemeanor, or felony offense; or

(4) a misdemeanor-level offense committed by a child whom the juvenile court has found to have committed a misdemeanor-level juvenile petty offense on two or more prior occasions, unless the county attorney designates the child on the petition as a juvenile petty offender notwithstanding this prior record. As used in this clause, "misdemeanor-level juvenile petty offense" included a misdemeanor-level offense that would have been a juvenile petty offense if it had been committed on or after July 1, 1995. 1996 Minn. Laws Ch. 408, Art. 6, Sec. 1.

This definition of juvenile petty offense applied to crimes committed on or after August 1, 1996. 1996 Minn. Laws Ch. 408, Art. 6, Sec. 13. Minn. R. Juv. Del. P. 17.01, subd. 1 reflected the definition of "juvenile petty offense" set forth pursuant to 1996 Minn. Laws Ch. 408, Art. 6, Sec. 1. However, because this definition often changed, Rule 17.01, subd. 1 now refers to the applicable statute. See Minnesota Statutes, section 260B.007, subd. 16 (2002).

The legislature reorganized the law relating to juvenile delinquency and child protection in 1999. 1999 Minn. Laws Ch. 139. This recodification is found in Minnesota Statutes, sections 260B.001–260B.446 for juvenile delinquency.

Minnesota Statutes, section 260B.225, subd. 2 (2002) provides that the prosecutor may allege the child is delinquent based upon a traffic offense but the court must find as a further fact that the child is delinquent within the meaning and purpose of the laws relating to juvenile court. Such matter shall be initiated and shall proceed in the same manner as any other delinquency.

At the arraignment, the court may inform each child of his or her rights and the possible consequences by reading and having each child sign a sheet outlining those rights. A suggested form for this rights sheet is included in the appendix of forms, following these rules.

Minn. R. Juv. Del. P. 17.10 is based on Minnesota Statutes, section 260B.225, subd. 7 (2002), which provides that the juvenile court may transfer a juvenile traffic offender case to adult court after a hearing if the juvenile court finds that the welfare of the child or public safety would be better served under the laws relating to adult traffic matters.

The right to appeal is set forth in Minnesota Statutes, section 260B.415, subd. 1 (2002).

Historical Notes

The order of the Minnesota Supreme Court [C6–84–2165] dated June 26, 1996, provides in part that "(t)hese amendments to the Rules of Juvenile Procedure shall govern all juvenile actions commenced or arrests made on or after 12:00 o'clock midnight August 1, 1996."

The order of the Minnesota Supreme Court [CX–01–926] dated July 18, 2003, provides in part that "(t)he attached amendments shall govern all juveniles taken into custody and all juvenile delinquency actions commenced or children taken into custody after 12 o'clock midnight September 1, 2003."

Rule 17.12 to 17.19. Repealed and Renumbered July 18, 2003

Historical Notes

See, now, generally, Minn. R. Juv. Del. P. Rules 17.01 to 17.11.

RULE 18. CERTIFICATION OF DELINQUENCY MATTERS

Rule 18.01. Application

Subd. 1. Generally. This rule is applicable when the prosecutor moves for certification and a child is alleged to have committed, after becoming fourteen (14) years of age, an offense that would be a felony if committed by an adult.

Subd. 2. First Degree Murder Accusation. The district court has original and exclusive jurisdiction in criminal proceedings concerning a child alleged to have committed murder in the first degree after becoming sixteen (16) years of age. Upon the filing of a complaint or indictment charging a sixteen (16) or seventeen (17) year old child in adult proceedings with the offense of first degree murder, juvenile court jurisdiction terminates for all proceedings arising out of the same behavioral incident.

Adopted July 18, 2003.

Comment—Rule 18

See comment following Rule 18.09.

Historical Notes

The order of the Minnesota Supreme Court [CX–01–926] dated July 18, 2003, provides in part that "(t)he attached amendments shall govern all juveniles taken into custody and all juvenile delinquency actions commenced or children taken into custody after 12 o'clock midnight September 1, 2003."

Rule 18.02. Initiation of Certification Proceedings of Delinquency Matters

Subd. 1. Generally. Proceedings to certify delinquency matters pursuant to Minnesota Statutes, section 260B.125 may be initiated upon motion of the prosecuting attorney after a delinquency petition has been filed. The motion may be made at the first appearance of the child pursuant to Rules 5 or 7, or within ten (10) days of the first appearance or before jeopardy attaches, whichever of the latter two occurs first. The motion shall be in writing and comply with the provisions of Rule 27, and shall include a statement of the grounds supporting the certification.

Subd. 2. First Degree Murder Accusation. When the delinquency petition that is the basis for the motion for certification alleges that a child under age sixteen (16) committed the offense of murder in the first degree, the prosecuting attorney shall present the case to the grand jury for consideration of an indictment under Minnesota Statutes, chapter 628 within fourteen (14) days after the petition is filed.

Amended June 26, 1996; July 18, 2003.

Comment—Rule 18

See comment following Rule 18.09.

Historical Notes

The order of the Minnesota Supreme Court [C6-84-2165] dated June 26, 1996, provides in part that "(t)hese amendments to the Rules of Juvenile Procedure shall govern all juvenile actions commenced or arrests made on or after 12:00 o'clock midnight August 1, 1996."

The order of the Minnesota Supreme Court [CX–01–926] dated July 18, 2003, provides in part that "(t)he attached amendments shall govern all juveniles taken into custody and all juvenile delinquency actions commenced or children taken into custody after 12 o'clock midnight September 1, 2003."

Rule 18.03. Notice of Certification

Notice of the initial appearance under Rule 18.05, subdivision 2 together with a copy of the motion for certification and a copy of the delinquency petition shall be served pursuant to Rule 25.

Amended June 26, 1996; July 18, 2003.

Comment—Rule 18

See comment following Rule 18.09.

Historical Notes

The order of the Minnesota Supreme Court [C6-84-2165] dated June 26, 1996, provides in part that "(t)hese amendments to the Rules of Juvenile Procedure shall govern all juvenile actions commenced or arrests made on or after 12:00 o'clock midnight August 1, 1996."

The order of the Minnesota Supreme Court [CX–01–926] dated July 18, 2003, provides in part that "(t)he attached amendments shall govern all juveniles taken into custody and all juvenile delinquency actions commenced or children taken into custody after 12 o'clock midnight September 1, 2003."

Rule 18.04. Certification Study

Subd. 1. Order. The court on its own motion or on the motion of the child's counsel or the prosecuting attorney, may order social, psychiatric, or psychological studies concerning the child who is the subject of the certification proceeding.

Subd. 2. Content of Reports. If the person preparing the report includes a recommendation on the court's actions: (a) the report shall address each of the public safety considerations of Rule 18.06, subdivision 3; and (b) the report shall address all options of the trial court under Rule 18.07, namely: (i) certification; (ii) retention of jurisdiction for extended jurisdiction juvenile proceedings; and (iii) retention of juvenile court jurisdiction in non-presumptive certification cases.

Subd. 3. Costs. Preparation costs and court appearance expenses for person(s) appointed by the court to conduct studies shall be paid at public expense.

Subd. 4. Filing and Access to Reports. The person(s) making a study shall file a written report with the court and provide copies to the prosecuting attorney and the child's counsel four (4) days, excluding Saturdays, Sundays, and legal holidays, prior to the time scheduled for the hearing. The court administrator shall not otherwise disclose the report except by court order.

Subd. 5. Admissibility. Any matters disclosed by the child to the examiner during the course of the study may not be used as evidence or the source of evidence against the child in any subsequent trial.

Amended June 26, 1996; July 18, 2003; July 11, 2005, eff. Sept. 1, 2005.

Comment—Rule 18

See comment following Rule 18.09.

Historical Notes

The order of the Minnesota Supreme Court [C6-84-2165] dated June 26, 1996, provides in part that "(t)hese amendments to the Rules of Juvenile Procedure shall govern all juvenile actions commenced or arrests made on or after 12:00 o'clock midnight August 1, 1996."

The order of the Minnesota Supreme Court [CX-01-926] dated July 18, 2003, provides in part that "(t)he attached amendments shall govern all juveniles taken into custody and all juvenile delinquency actions commenced or children taken into custody after 12 o'clock midnight September 1, 2003."

Rule 18.05. Hearing

Subd. 1. In General.

(A) *Limited Public Access.* The court shall exclude the general public from certification hearings and shall admit only those persons who, in the discretion of the court, have a direct interest in the case or the work of the court, including victims. The court shall open the hearings to the public in certification proceedings where the child is alleged to have committed an offense or has been proven to have committed an offense that would be a felony if committed by an adult and the child was at least sixteen (16) years of age at the time of the offense, except that the court may exclude the public from portions of a certification hearing to consider psychological material or other evidence that would not be accessible to the public in an adult proceeding.

(B) *Timing.* The certification hearing shall be held within thirty (30) days of the filing of the certification motion. Only if good cause is shown by the prosecuting attorney or the child may the court extend the time for a hearing for another sixty (60) days. Unless the child waives the right to the scheduling of the hearing within specified time limits, if the hearing is not commenced within thirty (30) days, or within the extended period ordered pursuant to this subdivision, the child, except in extraordinary circumstances, shall be released from custody subject to such nonmonetary release conditions as may be required by the court under Rule 5.

(C) *Waiver.* The child may waive the right to a certification hearing provided that the child does so knowingly, voluntarily, and intelligently on the record after being fully and effectively informed of the right to a certification hearing by counsel. In determining whether the child has knowingly, voluntarily, and intelligently waived this right the court shall look at the totality of the circumstances. These circumstances include but are not limited to: the presence of the child's parent(s), legal guardian, legal custodian or guardian ad litem appointed in the delinquency proceeding; and the child's age, maturity, intelligence, education, experience, and ability to comprehend the proceedings and consequences.

(D) *Discovery.* The child and prosecuting attorney are entitled to discovery pursuant to Rule 10.

Subd. 2. Initial Appearance in Certification Proceeding. At the initial appearance following the motion for certification the court shall:

(A) verify the name, age and residence of the child who is the subject of the matter;

(B) determine whether all necessary persons are present and identify those present for the record;

(C) appoint counsel, if not previously appointed;

(D) determine whether notice requirements have been met and if not whether the affected persons waive notice;

(E) schedule further hearings including: a probable cause hearing, unless waived; the certification hearing under Rule 18.05 subdivision 4; and a prehearing conference if requested; and

(F) order studies pursuant to Rule 18.04, if appropriate.

Subd. 3. Probable Cause Determination.

(A) *Timing.* Unless waived by the child or based upon an indictment, a hearing and court determination on the issue of probable cause shall be completed within fourteen (14) days of filing the certification motion. The court may, on the record, extend this time for good cause.

(B) *Standard.* A showing of probable cause to believe the child committed the offense alleged by the delinquency petition shall be made pursuant to Minnesota Rules of Criminal Procedure 11.

(C) *Presumption.* Upon a finding of probable cause, the court shall determine whether the presumption for certification under Rule 18.06, subdivision 1 applies.

(D) *Waiver.* The child may waive a probable cause hearing and permit a finding of probable cause without a hearing, provided that the child does so knowingly, voluntarily, and intelligently on the record after being fully and effectively informed of the right to a probable cause hearing by counsel.

Subd. 4. Conduct and Procedure for Certification Hearing.

(A) *Hearing Rights.* The child's counsel and the prosecuting attorney shall have the right to:

(1) present evidence;

(2) present witnesses;

(3) cross-examine witnesses; and

(4) present arguments for or against certification.

(B) *Evidence.* All evidence considered by the court on the certification question shall be made a part of the court record. The court may receive any information, except privileged communication, that is relevant to the certification issue, including reliable hearsay and opinions.

(C) *Order of Hearing; Presumptive Certification.*

(1) The child's counsel may make an opening statement, confining the statement to the facts that the child expects to prove.

(2) The prosecuting attorney may make an opening statement, or may make it immediately before offering evidence. The statement shall be confined to the facts expected to be proved.

(3) The child's counsel shall offer evidence against certification.

(4) The prosecuting attorney may offer evidence in support of the motion for certification.

(5) The child's counsel may offer evidence in rebuttal of the evidence for certification, and the prosecuting attorney may then offer evidence in rebuttal of the child's rebuttal evidence. In the interests of justice, the court may permit either party to offer additional evidence.

(6) At the conclusion of the evidence, the prosecuting attorney may make a closing argument.

(7) The child's counsel may make a closing argument.

(D) *Order of Hearing; Non-presumptive Certification.*

(1) The prosecuting attorney may make an opening statement, confining the statement to the facts that the prosecutor expects to prove.

(2) The child's counsel may make an opening statement, or may make it immediately before offering evidence. The statement shall be confined to a statement of the defense and the facts expected to be proved.

(3) The prosecuting attorney shall offer evidence in support of certification, or alternatively, designation as an extended jurisdiction juvenile proceeding.

(4) The child's counsel may offer evidence in defense of the child.

(5) The prosecuting attorney may offer evidence in rebuttal of the defense evidence, and the child's counsel may then offer evidence in rebuttal of the prosecuting attorney's rebuttal evidence. In the interests of justice the court may permit either party to offer additional evidence.

(6) At the conclusion of the evidence, the prosecuting attorney may make a closing argument.

(7) The child's counsel may make a closing argument.

(E) *Burdens of Proof.* In a presumptive certification hearing under Rule 18.06, subdivision 1, the child shall have the burden to prove by clear and convincing evidence that retaining the proceeding in juvenile court serves public safety. In non-presumptive certification hearings under Rule 18.06, subdivision 2, the prosecuting attorney shall have the burden to prove by clear and convincing evidence that retaining the proceeding in juvenile court does not serve public safety.

Amended June 26, 1996; July 18, 2003; Oct. 13, 2006, eff. Jan. 1, 2007.

Comment—Rule 18

See comment following Rule 18.09.

Historical Notes

The order of the Minnesota Supreme Court [C6-84-2165] dated June 26, 1996, provides in part that "(t)hese amendments to the Rules of Juvenile Procedure shall govern all juvenile actions commenced or arrests made on or after 12:00 o'clock midnight August 1, 1996."

The order of the Minnesota Supreme Court [CX-01-926] dated July 18, 2003, provides in part that "(t)he attached amendments shall govern all juveniles taken into custody and all juvenile delinquency actions commenced or children taken into custody after 12 o'clock midnight September 1, 2003."

Rule 18.06. Certification Determination

Subd. 1. Presumption of Certification. Pursuant to Minnesota Statutes, section 260B.125, subdivision 3, it is presumed that a child will be certified for action under the laws and court procedures controlling adult criminal violations if:

(A) the child was sixteen (16) or seventeen (17) years old at the time of the offense;

(B) the delinquency petition alleges that the child committed an offense that would result in a presumptive commitment to prison under the sentencing guidelines and applicable statutes, or a felony offense in which the child allegedly used a firearm; and

(C) probable cause has been determined pursuant to Rule 18.05, subdivision 3.

The presumption of certification is overcome if the child demonstrates by clear and convincing evidence that retaining the proceedings in juvenile court serves public safety.

Subd. 2. Non-presumptive Certification. If there is no presumption of certification as defined by subdivision 1, the court may order certification only if the prosecuting attorney has demonstrated by clear and convincing evidence that retaining the proceeding in juvenile court does not serve public safety.

Subd. 3. Public Safety. In determining whether the public safety is served by certifying the matter, or in designating the proceeding an extended jurisdiction juvenile proceeding, the court shall consider the following factors:

(A) the seriousness of the alleged offense in terms of community protection, including the existence of any aggravating factors recognized by the Minnesota Sentencing Guidelines, the use of a firearm, and the impact on any victim;

(B) the culpability of the child in committing the alleged offense, including the level of the child's participation in planning and carrying out the offense and the existence of any mitigating factors recognized by the Minnesota Sentencing Guidelines;

(C) the child's prior record of delinquency;

(D) the child's programming history, including the child's past willingness to participate meaningfully in available programming;

(E) the adequacy of the punishment or programming available in the juvenile justice system; and

(F) the dispositional options available for the child.

In considering these factors, the court shall give greater weight to the seriousness of the alleged offense and the child's prior record of delinquency than to the other factors listed in this subdivision.

Subd. 4. Prior Certification. The court shall order certification in any felony case if the prosecutor shows that the child was previously prosecuted and convicted in adult proceedings that were certified pursuant to Minnesota Statutes, section 260B.125, subdivision 5.

Subd. 5. Extended Juvenile Court Jurisdiction.

(A) *Presumptive Certification.* If the juvenile court does not order certification in a presumptive certification case, the court shall designate the proceeding an extended jurisdiction juvenile prosecution.

(B) *Non-presumptive Certification.* If the court does not order certification in a non-presumptive certification case, the court may consider designating the proceeding an extended jurisdiction juvenile prosecution. Designation as an extended jurisdiction juvenile prosecution may only occur if the prosecuting attorney has shown by clear and convincing evidence that the designation would serve public safety, taking into account the factors specified in Rule 18.06, subdivision 3. Absent this showing the case shall proceed as a delinquency proceeding in juvenile court.

Amended June 26, 1996; July 18, 2003; July 11, 2005, eff. Sept. 1, 2005.

Comment—Rule 18

See comment following Rule 18.09.

Historical Notes

The order of the Minnesota Supreme Court [C6-84-2165] dated June 26, 1996, provides in part that "(t)hese amendments to the Rules of Juvenile Procedure shall govern all juvenile actions commenced or arrests made on or after 12:00 o'clock midnight August 1, 1996."

The order of the Minnesota Supreme Court [CX-01-926] dated July 18, 2003, provides in part that "(t)he attached amendments shall govern all juveniles taken into custody and all juvenile delinquency actions commenced or children taken into custody after 12 o'clock midnight September 1, 2003."

Rule 18.07. Order

Subdivision 1. Decision, Timing, and Content of Order Following Waiver of Certification Hearing and Stipulation to Certification Order. When a child waives the right to a certification hearing and stipulates to certification, the court shall, within five (5) days of that hearing, file an order with written findings of fact and conclusions of law that states:

(A) that adult court prosecution is to occur on the alleged offense(s) specified in the certification order;

(B) a finding of probable cause in accordance with Rule 18.05, subdivision 3, unless the accused was presented by means of an indictment;

(C) findings of fact as to:

(1) the child's date of birth; and

(2) the date of the alleged offense; and

(D) if the child is currently being detained, that:

(1) the child be detained in an adult detention facility; and

(2) the child be brought before the appropriate court (as determined pursuant to Rule 18.08) without unnecessary delay, and in any event, not more than thirty-six (36) hours after filing of the certification order, exclusive of the day of filing, Sundays, or legal holidays, or as soon thereafter as a judge is available.

Subd. 2. Decision, Timing, and Content of Order Following Contested Hearing. Within fifteen (15) days of the certification hearing the court shall file an order with written findings of fact and conclusions of law as set forth in this subdivision.

(A) *Certification of the Alleged Offense for Prosecution under the Criminal Laws.* If the court orders a certification for adult prosecution, the order shall state:

(1) that adult court prosecution is to occur on the alleged offense(s) specified in the certification order;

(2) a finding of probable cause in accordance with Rule 18.05, subdivision 3 unless the accusation was presented by means of an indictment;

(3) findings of fact as to:

(a) the child's date of birth;

(b) the date of the alleged offense;

(c) why the court upheld the presumption of certification under Rule 18.06, subdivision 1 or, if the presumption of certification does not apply but the court orders certification, why public safety, as defined in Rule 18. 06, subdivision 3, is not served by retaining the proceeding in juvenile court; and

(4) if the child is currently being detained, that (a) the child be detained in an adult detention facility, and (b) the child be brought before the appropriate court (as determined pursuant to Rule 18.08) without unnecessary delay, and in any event, not more than thirty-six (36) hours after filing of the certification order, exclusive of the day of filing, Sundays or legal holidays or as soon thereafter as a judge is available.

(B) *Retention of Jurisdiction by Juvenile Court as an Extended Jurisdiction Juvenile.*

(1) If the court does not order certification in a presumptive certification case, the court shall designate the proceeding an extended jurisdiction juvenile prosecution. The order shall state why certification is not ordered with specific reference as to why designation as an extended jurisdiction juvenile prosecution serves public safety under the factors listed in Rule 18.06, subdivision 3.

(2) If the court does not order certification in a non-presumptive certification case, the court may designate the proceeding an extended jurisdiction juvenile prosecution pursuant to Rule 18.06, subdivision 5(B). The order shall state why certification was not ordered and why the proceeding was designated as an extended jurisdiction juvenile prosecution.

If the court designates the case as an extended jurisdiction juvenile prosecution, the case shall proceed pursuant to Rule 19.09.

(C) *Retention of Jurisdiction by Juvenile Court.* If the court does not order certification or extended jurisdiction juvenile prosecution in a non-presumptive certification case, the order shall state why certification or extended jurisdiction juvenile prosecution was not ordered with specific reference to why retention of the matter in juvenile court serves public safety, considering the factors listed in Rule 18.06, subdivision 3. Further proceedings shall be held pursuant to Rule 7.

Subd. 3. Delay. For good cause, the court may extend the time period to file its order for an additional fifteen (15) days. If the order is not filed within fifteen (15) days, or within the extended period ordered by the court pursuant to this subdivision, the child, except in extraordinary circumstances, shall be released from custody subject to such nonmonetary release conditions as may be required by the court under Rule 5.

Subd. 4. Final Order. Any order issued pursuant to this rule is a final order.

Subd. 5. Appeal. An appeal of the final order pursuant to this rule shall follow the procedure set forth in Rule 21.

Amended June 26, 1996; July 18, 2003; July 11, 2005, eff. Sept. 1, 2005; Oct. 13, 2006, eff. Jan. 1, 2007.

Comment—Rule 18

See comment following Rule 18.09.

Historical Notes

The order of the Minnesota Supreme Court [C6-84-2165] dated June 26, 1996, provides in part that "(t)hese amendments to the Rules of Juvenile Procedure shall govern all juvenile actions commenced or arrests made on or after 12:00 o'clock midnight August 1, 1996."

The order of the Minnesota Supreme Court [CX–01–926] dated July 18, 2003, provides in part that "(t)he attached amendments shall govern all juveniles taken into custody and all juvenile delinquency actions commenced or children taken into custody after 12 o'clock midnight September 1, 2003."

Rule 18.08. Termination of Jurisdiction Upon Certification

Subd. 1. Child Not in Detention. Once the court enters an order certifying a proceeding, the jurisdiction of the juvenile court terminates immediately over a child who is not then detained in custody. All subsequent steps in the case are governed by the Minnesota Rules of Criminal Procedure.

Subd. 2. Child in Detention. If the child is detained at the time certification is ordered:

(A) If the alleged offense was committed in the same county where certification is ordered, juvenile court jurisdiction terminates immediately and the prosecuting attorney shall file an appropriate adult criminal complaint at or before the time of the next appearance of the child that is stated in the certification order pursuant to Rule 18.07, subdivision 2(A)(4).

(B) If the alleged offense was committed in a county other than where certification is ordered, juvenile court jurisdiction terminates in five (5) days or before if the prosecuting attorney files a complaint as provided under Minnesota Rules of Criminal Procedure 2. If juvenile court jurisdiction has terminated under this subsection before an appearance of a detained child following issuance of an order certifying the case, the appearance shall constitute a first appearance in criminal proceedings as provided in the Minnesota Rules of Criminal Procedure. If juvenile court jurisdiction has not terminated by the time a detained juvenile first appears following issuance of an order certifying, the juvenile court shall determine conditions of release in accordance with the provisions of Minnesota Rules of Criminal Procedure 5.01(d) and 6.02; for these purposes, the juvenile court petition shall serve in lieu of a criminal complaint as the charging instrument.

Subd. 3. Stay. Notwithstanding the preceding provisions of subdivision 1 and 2, certification and the termination of juvenile court jurisdiction may be stayed as provided in Rule 21.03, subdivision 3. A motion for stay of the certification order pending appeal shall first be heard by the juvenile court.

Amended June 26, 1996; July 18, 2003; Oct. 13, 2006, eff. Jan. 1, 2007; Nov. 19, 2010, eff. Jan. 1, 2011.

Comment—Rule 18

See comment following Rule 18.09.

Historical Notes

The order of the Minnesota Supreme Court [C6-84-2165] dated June 26, 1996, provides in part that "(t)hese amendments to the Rules of Juvenile Procedure shall govern all juvenile actions commenced or arrests made on or after 12:00 o'clock midnight August 1, 1996."

The order of the Minnesota Supreme Court [CX-01-926] dated July 18, 2003, provides in part that "(t)he attached amendments shall govern all juveniles taken into custody and all juvenile delinquency actions commenced or children taken into custody after 12 o'clock midnight September 1, 2003."

Rule 18.09. Withdrawal of Waiver of Certification Hearing

Subd. 1. General Procedure. A child may bring a motion to withdraw the waiver of certification hearing and stipulation to certification order:

(A) within fifteen (15) days of the filing of the order for certification, upon showing that it is fair and just to do so; or

(B) at any time prior to trial, upon showing that withdrawal is necessary to correct a manifest injustice.

The motion shall be made in the juvenile court that entered the certification order. A motion shall also be filed for a stay of proceedings in the adult court to which the case was certified.

Subd. 2. Basis for Motion. The motion shall state with particularity one of the following bases for granting withdrawal of waiver:

(A) the waiver was not knowingly, voluntarily, and intelligently made;

(B) the child alleges ineffective assistance of counsel; or

(C) withdrawal of waiver is appropriate in the interests of justice.

Subd. 3. Timing and Effect of Hearing. A hearing shall be held within fifteen (15) days of the filing of the motion. Following the hearing, if the court grants the motion to withdraw the waiver of certification hearing: 1) the court shall vacate the order for certification, and proceedings will resume in juvenile court pursuant to Rule 18; and 2) the court shall review the order for custody or conditions of release. If the court denies the motion to withdraw the waiver for certification hearing, the certification order shall remain in effect, and proceedings will resume in adult court.

Adopted July 18, 2003.

Comment—Rule 18

Pursuant to Minnesota Statutes, section 260B.125, subd. 6 (2002), on a proper motion, the court may hold a certification hearing for an adult charged with a juvenile offense if:

(1) the adult was alleged to have committed an offense before his or her 18th birthday; and

(2) a petition was timely filed under Minnesota Statutes, sections 260B.141 (2002) and 628.26 (2002). The court may not certify the matter if the adult demonstrates that the delay was purposefully caused by the state in order to gain an unfair advantage. Minn. Stat. § 260B.125, subd. 6 (2002); *see also In re Welfare of A.N.J.*, 521 N.W.2d 889, 891 (Minn. Ct. App. 1994). Juvenile court retains jurisdiction to hear a certification motion filed after the child's 19th birthday provided a delinquency petition has been timely filed and the delay was not the result of an improper state purpose.

Much of the text of Minn. R. Juv. Del. P. 18.05, subd. 1(A) is taken from Minnesota Statutes, section 260B.163 (2002).

The sanction for delay in Minn. R. Juv. Del. P. 18.05, subd. 1(B) and 18.07, subd. 3 is modeled after Minn. R. Crim. P. 11.10, which as of January 1, 2010 is now Minn. R. Crim. P. 11.09. See *In re Welfare of J.J.H.*, 446 N.W.2d 680, 681–82 (Minn. Ct. App. 1989) (order issued 66 days after hearing, 38 days after submission of written argument; because rule contains no sanction, reversal denied). See also *McIntosh v. Davis*, 441 N.W.2d 115 (Minn. 1989) (where alternative remedies available, mandamus not appropriate to enforce time limit of Minn. R. Crim. P. 11.10 speedy trial rule).

On continuation questions under Minn. R. Juv. Del. P. 18.05, subd. 1(B), the victim should have input but does not have the right of a party to appear and object.

Most of the waiver language in Minn. R. Juv. Del. P. 18.05, subd. 1(C) is taken from the 1983 version of Minn. R. Juv. P. 15.03.

Minn. R. Juv. Del. P. 18.05, subd. 2(B) requires a determination on appearances of necessary persons. Under Minnesota Statutes, section 260B.163, subd. 7 (2002) the custodial parent or guardian of the child who is the subject of the certification proceedings must accompany the child at each hearing, unless the court excuses the parent or guardian from attendance for good cause shown. The failure of a parent or guardian to comply with this duty may be punished as provided in Minnesota Statutes, section 260B.154 (2002).

Much of the content of Minn. R. Juv. Del. P. 18.05, subd. 3 is modeled after Minn. R. Crim. P. 11.04 and 18.05, subd. 1. The court may employ police statements for probable cause determinations in the same manner as permitted in adult proceedings under Minn. R. Crim. P. 11.04. Also note *In re Welfare of E.Y.W.*, 496 N.W.2d 847, 850 (Minn. Ct. App. 1993) (juvenile not entitled to exclusionary hearing before decision on probable cause).

Minn. R. Juv. Del. P. 18.05, subd. 3 and 18.07, subd. 2(A)(2) eliminate the need for a probable cause finding when a delinquency accusation is presented by an indictment. Accusation by indictment is uncommon, but might occur more often as the result of grand jury proceedings conducted after 1994 statutory amendments on the question of whether a juvenile is to be accused of first degree murder in adult proceedings. See Minnesota Statutes, section 260B.007, subd. 6 (2002). Minn. R. Juv. Del. P. 18.05, subd. 4(B) is consistent with case law. Because the certification question is dispositional in nature, strict application of the rules of evidence is thought to be inappropriate. Minn. R. Juv. Del. P. 18.05 does not address the consequences of the child's testimony at a hearing. See *Simmons v. United States*, 390 U.S. 377 (1968) and *State v. Christenson*, 371 N.W.2d 228 (Minn. Ct. App. 1985). Cf. *Harris v. New York*, 401 U.S. 222 (1971).

When a child waives probable cause solely for the purpose of certification, that waiver does not preclude the child from litigating probable cause in a subsequent prosecution on the underlying offense.

Following presentation of evidence by the party with the burden of proof under Minn. R. Juv. Del. P. 18.05, subd. 4(C) or (D), the adverse party may move the court for directed relief on the grounds that the burden of proof has not been met by the evidence presented.

The determination under Minn. R. Juv. Del. P. 18.06, subd. 1 whether an offense would result in a presumptive commitment to prison under the Minnesota Sentencing Guidelines should be analyzed pursuant to those guidelines. The public safety factors listed in Rule 18.06, subd. 3 mirror those set forth in Minnesota Statutes, section 260B.125, subd. 4 and eliminate the need for non-offense related evidence of dangerousness. See *In re Welfare of D.M.D.*, 607 N.W.2d 432 (Minn. 2000).

Under Minnesota Statutes, sections 260B.101, subd. 2, 260B.007, subd. 6(b), and 260B.125, subd. 10 (2002), the accusation of first degree murder by a 16 or 17 year old child takes the case out of the delinquency jurisdiction of the juvenile court. If this accusation is first made by complaint, and is followed by an indictment that does not accuse the child of first degree murder but of some other crime, the proceedings come within the exclusive jurisdiction of the juvenile court, but subject to action of the juvenile court on any motion for certification of the proceedings to adult court. In these circumstances, the juvenile court would deal with an accusation by indictment in the same fashion as proceedings might otherwise occur on a juvenile court petition. Once adult court proceedings begin on an indictment for first degree murder, regardless of the ultimate conviction, the proceedings remain within adult court jurisdiction. Indictments may be received by any district court judge including one sitting in juvenile court.

Under Minn. R. Crim. P. 17.01, first degree murder cases are prosecuted by an indictment, but the proceedings can begin by complaint. *State v. Behl*, 564 N.W.2d 560 (Minn. 1997). As a result, the prosecuting attorney can initiate a first degree murder accusation in adult court proceedings.

Minn. R. Juv. Del. P. 18.02, subd. 2 repeats the procedural requirement stated in Minnesota Statutes, section 260B.125, subd. 9 (2002).

Rule 18 previously contained a provision that allowed jail credit for time spent in custody in connection with the offense or behavioral incident on which further proceedings are to occur. See Minn. R. Juv. Del. P. 18.06, subd. 1(D) (repealed 2003). That provision was deleted because jail credit is awarded at the time of sentencing in adult court, and is thus governed by the Minnesota Rules of Criminal Procedure, not the Minnesota Rules of Juvenile Procedure. See Minn. R. Crim. P. 27.03, subd. 4(B).

References in this rule to "child's counsel" include the child who is proceeding pro se. Minn. R. Juv. Del. P. 1.01.

Historical Notes

The order of the Minnesota Supreme Court [CX–01–926] dated July 18, 2003, provides in part that "(t)he attached amendments shall govern all juveniles taken into custody and all juvenile delinquency actions commenced or children taken into custody after 12 o'clock midnight September 1, 2003."

RULE 19. EXTENDED JURISDICTION JUVENILE PROCEEDINGS AND PROSECUTION

Rule 19.01. Initiation of Extended Jurisdiction Juvenile Proceedings and Prosecution

Subd. 1. Authority. Extended jurisdiction juvenile prosecutions are initiated pursuant to Minnesota Statutes, sections 260B.125 and 260B.130, Rule 18.06, subdivisions 5(A) and (B), and Rule 19.

Subd. 2. Definitions.

(A) "Extended jurisdiction juvenile" is a child who has been given a stayed adult criminal sentence, a disposition under Minnesota Statutes, section 260B.198, and for whom jurisdiction of the juvenile court may continue until the child's twenty-first (21st) birthday.

(B) "Extended jurisdiction juvenile proceeding" includes the process to determine whether a child should be prosecuted as an extended jurisdiction juvenile. Extended jurisdiction juvenile proceedings may be initiated pursuant to Rule 19.01, subdivisions 3 and 4.

(C) "Extended jurisdiction juvenile prosecution" includes the trial, disposition, and subsequent proceedings after the determination that a child should be prosecuted as an extended jurisdiction juvenile. Extended jurisdiction juvenile prosecutions may be initiated pursuant to Rule 19.06.

Subd. 3. Designation by Prosecuting Attorney. The court shall commence an extended jurisdiction juvenile proceeding when a delinquency petition filed pursuant to Rule 6:

(A) alleges a felony offense committed after the child's sixteenth (16th) birthday and the offense would, if committed by an adult, result in a presumptive commitment to prison under the sentencing guidelines and applicable statutes, or a felony offense in which the child allegedly used a firearm; and

(B) the prosecuting attorney designates on the petition that the case should be an extended jurisdiction juvenile prosecution.

This designation may be made at the time the petition is filed, and may be withdrawn by the prosecuting attorney any time before jeopardy attaches.

Subd. 4. Motion by Prosecuting Attorney. The prosecuting attorney may make a written motion pursuant to this Rule to have the court commence an extended jurisdiction juvenile proceeding when a delinquency petition has been filed pursuant to Rule 6 alleging a felony offense committed after the child's fourteenth (14th) birthday. The motion may be made at the first appearance on the delinquency petition, or within ten (10) days after the first appearance pursuant to Rules 5 and 7 or before jeopardy attaches, whichever of the later two occurs first.

Amended June 26, 1996; July 18, 2003; Oct. 13, 2006, eff. Jan. 1, 2007.

Comment—Rule 19

See comment following Rule 19.11.

Historical Notes

The order of the Minnesota Supreme Court [C6-84-2165] dated June 26, 1996, provides in part that "(t)hese amendments to the Rules of Juvenile Procedure shall govern all juvenile actions commenced or arrests made on or after 12:00 o'clock midnight August 1, 1996."

The order of the Minnesota Supreme Court [CX-01-926] dated July 18, 2003, provides in part that "(t)he attached amendments shall govern all juveniles taken into custody and all juvenile delinquency actions commenced or children taken into custody after 12 o'clock midnight September 1, 2003."

Rule 19.02. Notice of the Extended Jurisdiction Juvenile Proceeding

A notice of the initial appearance under Rule 19.04, subdivision 2, together with a copy of the petition and designation, or a copy of the motion and petition, shall be served pursuant to Rule 25.

Amended June 26, 1996; July 18, 2003.

Comment—Rule 19

See comment following Rule 19.11.

Historical Notes

The order of the Minnesota Supreme Court [C6-84-2165] dated June 26, 1996, provides in part that "(t)hese amendments to the Rules of Juvenile Procedure shall govern all juvenile actions commenced or arrests made on or after 12:00 o'clock midnight August 1, 1996."

The order of the Minnesota Supreme Court [CX-01-926] dated July 18, 2003, provides in part that "(t)he attached amendments shall govern all juveniles taken into custody and all juvenile delinquency actions commenced or children taken into custody after 12 o'clock midnight September 1, 2003."

Rule 19.03. Extended Jurisdiction Juvenile Study

Subdivision 1. Order. The court on its own motion or on the motion of the child's counsel or the prosecuting attorney, may order social, psychiatric, or psychological studies concerning the child who is the subject of the extended jurisdiction juvenile proceeding.

Subd. 2. Content of Reports. If study reports include a recommendation on the court's actions, the report shall address each of the public safety considerations of Rule 19.05.

Subd. 3. Costs. Preparation costs and court appearance expenses for the person(s) appointed by the court to conduct studies shall be paid at public expense.

Subd. 4. Filing and Access to Reports. The person(s) making a study shall file a written report with the court and provide copies to the prosecuting attorney and the child's counsel four (4) days, excluding Saturdays, Sundays, and legal holidays, prior to the time scheduled for the hearing. The court administrator shall not otherwise disclose the report except by court order.

Subd. 5. Admissibility of Study. Any matters disclosed by the child to the examiner during the course of the study may not be used as evidence or the source of evidence against the child in any subsequent trial.

Amended June 26, 1996; July 18, 2003; July 11, 2005, eff. Sept. 1, 2005.

Comment—Rule 19

See comment following Rule 19.11.

Historical Notes

The order of the Minnesota Supreme Court [C6-84-2165] dated June 26, 1996, provides in part that "(t)hese amendments to the Rules of Juvenile Procedure shall govern all juvenile actions commenced or arrests made on or after 12:00 o'clock midnight August 1, 1996."

The order of the Minnesota Supreme Court [CX-01-926] dated July 18, 2003, provides in part that "(t)he attached amendments shall govern all juveniles taken into custody and all juvenile delinquency actions commenced or children taken into custody after 12 o'clock midnight September 1, 2003."

Rule 19.04. Hearings on Extended Jurisdiction Juvenile Proceedings

Subd. 1. In General.

(A) *Limited Public Access.* The court shall exclude the general public from extended jurisdiction juvenile proceedings and shall admit only those persons who, in the discretion of the court, have a direct interest in the case or the work of the court including victims. The court shall open the hearings to the public in extended jurisdiction juvenile proceedings where the child is alleged to have committed an offense or has been proven to have committed an offense that would be a felony if committed by an adult and the child was at least sixteen (16) years of age at the time of the offense, except that the court may exclude the public from portions of a extended jurisdiction juvenile proceedings hearing to consider psychological material or other evidence that would not be accessible to the public in an adult proceeding.

(B) *Timing.* The contested hearing to determine whether the matter will be an extended jurisdiction juvenile prosecution shall be held within thirty (30) days of the filing of the extended jurisdiction juvenile proceeding motion. Only if good cause is shown by the prosecuting attorney or the child may the court extend the time for the contested hearing for up to an additional sixty (60) days.

(C) *Waiver.* The child may waive the right to an extended jurisdiction juvenile proceeding hearing provided that the child does so knowingly, voluntarily, and intelligently on the record after being fully and effectively informed of all rights by counsel. In determining whether the child has knowingly, voluntarily, and intelligently waived this right the court shall look at the totality of the circumstances. These circumstances include but are not limited to: the presence of the child's parent(s), legal guardian, legal custodian or guardian ad litem appointed in the delinquency proceeding, the child's age, maturity, intelligence, education, experience, and ability to comprehend the proceedings and consequences.

(D) *Discovery.* The child and prosecuting attorney are entitled to discovery pursuant to Rule 10.

Subd. 2. Initial Appearance and Probable Cause Determination.

(A) *Timing.* Unless waived by the child, or based upon an indictment, an initial appearance and court determination on the issue of probable cause shall be completed within fourteen (14) days of the filing of the petition designating an extended jurisdictional juvenile proceeding or the filing of the extended jurisdictional juvenile proceedings motion. The court may, on the record, extend this time for good cause.

(B) At the initial appearance hearing, the court shall:

(1) verify the name, age, race, and residence of the child who is the subject of the matter;

(2) determine whether all necessary persons are present, and identify those persons for the record;

(3) appoint counsel if not previously appointed;

(4) determine whether notice requirements have been met and if not whether the affected persons waive notice;

(5) schedule further hearings including: a probable cause hearing, unless waived; the contested hearing required by Rule 19.04, 4 subdivision 3; and a pre-hearing conference if requested; and

(6) order studies pursuant to Rule 19.03, if appropriate.

(C) *Offense Probable Cause.* A showing of probable cause to believe that the child committed the offense alleged by the delinquency petition shall be made pursuant to Minnesota Rules of Criminal Procedure 11.

(D) *Designation Probable Cause.* If the prosecuting attorney has designated the proceeding an extended jurisdiction juvenile proceeding pursuant to Rule 19.01, subdivision 3 and the court finds that:

(1) probable cause exists for an offense that, if committed by an adult, would be a presumptive commitment to prison under the Sentencing Guidelines and applicable statutes or alleges a felony offense in which the child allegedly used a firearm; and

(2) the child was at least sixteen (16) years old at the time of the offense, the court shall order that the matter proceed as an extended jurisdiction juvenile prosecution pursuant to Rule 19.09.

(E) *Waiver.* The child may waive a probable cause hearing and permit a finding of probable cause without a hearing, provided that the child does so knowingly, voluntarily, and intelligently on the record after being fully and effectively informed of the right to a probable cause hearing by counsel.

Subd. 3. Conduct and Procedure for Extended Jurisdiction Juvenile Proceeding Contested Hearing.

(A) *Hearing Rights.* The child's counsel and the prosecuting attorney shall have the right to:

(1) present evidence;

(2) present witnesses;

(3) cross-examine witnesses; and

(4) present arguments for or against extended jurisdiction juvenile prosecution.

(B) *Evidence.* All evidence considered by the court on the extended juvenile jurisdiction question shall be made a part of the court record. The court may receive any information, except privileged communication, that is relevant to the issue of extended jurisdiction juvenile prosecution, including reliable hearsay and opinions.

(C) *Order of Hearing.*

(1) The prosecuting attorney may make an opening statement, confining the statement to the facts expected to be proved.

(2) The child's counsel may make an opening statement, or may make it immediately before offering evidence. The statement shall be confined to a statement of the defense and the facts expected to be proved.

(3) The prosecuting attorney shall offer evidence in support of extended jurisdiction juvenile prosecution.

(4) The child's counsel may offer evidence on behalf of the child.

(5) The prosecuting attorney may offer evidence in rebuttal of the defense evidence, and the child's counsel may then offer evidence in response to the prosecuting attorney's rebuttal evidence. In the interests of justice the court may permit either party to offer additional evidence.

(6) At the conclusion of the evidence, the prosecuting attorney may make a closing argument.

(7) The child's counsel may make a closing argument.

(D) *Burdens of Proof.* The prosecuting attorney shall prove by clear and convincing evidence that the case meets the criteria for extended jurisdiction juvenile prosecution, pursuant to Rule 19.05.

Amended June 26, 1996; Dec. 12, 1997; July 18, 2003; Oct. 13, 2006, eff. Jan. 1, 2007.

Comment—Rule 19

See comment following Rule 19.11.

Historical Notes

The order of the Minnesota Supreme Court [C6-84-2165] dated June 26, 1996, provides in part that "(t)hese amendments to the Rules of Juvenile Procedure shall govern all juvenile actions commenced or arrests made on or after 12:00 o'clock midnight August 1, 1996."

The order of the Minnesota Supreme Court [C6–84–2165] dated December 12, 1997, provides in part that "(t)hese amendments to the Rules of Juvenile Procedure shall govern all juvenile actions commenced or arrests made on or after 12:00 o'clock midnight January 1, 1998."

The order of the Minnesota Supreme Court [CX–01–926] dated July 18, 2003, provides in part that "(t)he attached amendments shall govern all juveniles taken into custody and all juvenile delinquency actions commenced or children taken into custody after 12 o'clock midnight September 1, 2003."

Rule 19.05. Public Safety Determination

In determining whether public safety would be served, the court shall take into account the following factors:

(A) the seriousness of the alleged offense in terms of community protection, including the existence of any aggravating factors recognized by the Minnesota Sentencing Guidelines, the use of a firearm, and the impact on the victim;

(B) the culpability of the child in committing the alleged offense, including the level of the child's participation in planning and carrying out the offense and the existence of any mitigating factors recognized by the Minnesota Sentencing Guidelines;

(C) the child's prior record of delinquency;

(D) the child's programming history, including the child's past willingness to participate meaningfully in available programming;

(E) the adequacy of the punishment or programming available in the juvenile justice system; and

(F) the dispositional options available for the child.

In considering these factors, the court shall give greater weight to the seriousness of the alleged offense and the child's prior record of delinquency than to the other factors listed in this subdivision.

Amended June 26, 1996; July 18, 2003.

Comment—Rule 19

See comment following Rule 19.11.

Historical Notes

The order of the Minnesota Supreme Court [C6-84-2165] dated June 26, 1996, provides in part that "(t)hese amendments to the Rules of Juvenile Procedure shall govern all juvenile actions commenced or arrests made on or after 12:00 o'clock midnight August 1, 1996."

The order of the Minnesota Supreme Court [CX–01–926] dated July 18, 2003, provides in part that "(t)he attached amendments shall govern all juveniles taken into custody and all juvenile delinquency actions commenced or children taken into custody after 12 o'clock midnight September 1, 2003."

Rule 19.06. Extended Jurisdiction Juvenile Prosecution Determination

Subd. 1. Extended Jurisdiction Juvenile Prosecution Required. The court shall designate the proceeding an extended jurisdiction juvenile prosecution:

(A) following a motion for certification in a presumptive certification case pursuant to Minnesota Statutes, section 260B.125, subdivision 3:

(1) when the court finds, after a contested hearing pursuant to Rule 18.05, that the child has shown by clear and convincing evidence that retaining the proceeding in juvenile court serves public safety pursuant to Rule 18.06, subdivision 3; or

(2) when the parties agree that extended jurisdiction juvenile prosecution is appropriate; or

(B) following designation by the prosecuting attorney and findings by the court pursuant to Rule 19.04, subdivision 2(D).

Subd. 2. Extended Jurisdiction Juvenile Prosecution Discretionary. The court may designate the proceeding an extended jurisdiction juvenile prosecution:

(A) following a motion for certification in a non-presumptive certification case:

(1) when the court finds, after a contested certification hearing, that the prosecutor has not demonstrated by clear and convincing evidence that retaining the proceeding in juvenile court does not serve public safety pursuant to Rule 18.06, subdivision 3, and the court determines that extended jurisdiction juvenile prosecution is appropriate; or

(2) when the parties agree that extended jurisdiction juvenile prosecution is appropriate and the child waives the right to a contested hearing; or

(B) following a motion for extended jurisdiction juvenile proceeding:

(1) when the court finds, after a contested extended jurisdiction juvenile hearing conducted pursuant to Rule 19.04, that designating the proceeding an extended jurisdiction juvenile prosecution serves public safety pursuant to Rule 19.05; or

(2) when the parties agree that extended jurisdiction juvenile prosecution is appropriate and the child waives the right to a contested hearing.

Adopted July 18, 2003.

Comment—Rule 19

See comment following Rule 19.11.

Historical Notes

The order of the Minnesota Supreme Court [CX–01–926] dated July 18, 2003, provides in part that "(t)he attached amendments shall govern all juveniles taken into custody and all juvenile delinquency actions commenced or children taken into custody after 12 o'clock midnight September 1, 2003."

Rule 19.07. Order

Subd. 1. Decision, Timing, and Content of Order Following Waiver of Extended Jurisdiction Juvenile Hearing and Stipulation to Extended Jurisdiction Juvenile Order. When a child waives the right to a contested hearing and stipulates to entry of an order that the child is subject to an extended jurisdiction juvenile prosecution, the court shall, within five (5) days of that hearing, enter a written order stating:

(A) that extended jurisdiction juvenile prosecution shall occur for the offense(s) alleged in the delinquency petition filed pursuant to Rule 6.03;

(B) a finding of probable cause in accordance with Rule 19.04, subdivision 2(C), unless the accusation was presented by means of an indictment; and

(C) findings of fact as to:

(1) the child's date of birth; and

(2) the date of the alleged offense(s).

Subd. 2. Decision, Timing, and Content of Order Following Contested Hearing. Within fifteen (15) days of the contested hearing, the court shall file an order with written findings of fact and conclusions of law as provided in this subdivision.

(A) If the court orders that the proceeding be an extended jurisdiction juvenile prosecution, the order shall state:

(1) that extended jurisdiction juvenile prosecution shall occur for the offense(s) alleged in the delinquency petition filed pursuant to Rule 6.03;

(2) a finding of probable cause in accordance with Rule 19.04, subdivision 2(C), unless the accusation was presented by means of an indictment; and

(3) findings of fact as to:

(a) the child's date of birth;

(b) the date of the alleged offense(s); and

(c) why the court found that designating the proceeding as an extended jurisdiction juvenile prosecution serves public safety pursuant to Rule 19.05.

(B) If the court does not order that the proceeding be an extended jurisdiction juvenile prosecution, the court order shall state:

(1) that the case shall proceed as a delinquency proceeding in juvenile court;

(2) a finding of probable cause in accordance with Rule 19.04, subdivision 2(C), unless the accusation was presented by means of an indictment; and

(3) findings of fact as to:

(a) the child's date of birth;

(b) the date of the alleged offense(s);

(c) why the court found that retaining the proceeding in juvenile court serves public safety pursuant to Rule 19.05.

Subd. 3. Delay. For good cause, the court may extend the time period to file its order for an additional fifteen (15) days. If the order is not filed within fifteen (15) days, or within the extended period ordered by the court pursuant to this subdivision, the child, except in extraordinary circumstances, shall be released from custody subject to such nonmonetary release conditions as may be required by the court under Rule 5.

Subd. 4. Venue Transfer. When the court deems it appropriate, taking into account the best interest of the child or of society, or the convenient administration of the proceedings, the court may transfer venue of the case to the juvenile court of the county of the child's residence. With the consent of the receiving court, the court may also transfer the case to the juvenile court of the county where the child is found or the county where the alleged offense occurred. The transfer shall be processed in the manner provided by Minnesota Statutes, section 260B.105. The receiving court thereafter has venue for purposes of all proceedings under Rules 19.10 (disposition and sentencing upon conviction in extended jurisdiction juvenile proceedings) and 19.11 (revocation of stay of adult criminal sentence).

Subd. 5. Final Order. Any order issued pursuant to this rule is a final order.

Subd. 6. Appeal. An appeal of the final order pursuant to this rule shall follow the procedure set forth in Rule 21.

Amended June 26, 1996; July 18, 2003; July 11, 2005, eff. Sept. 1, 2005; Aug. 17, 2006, eff. Oct. 1, 2006; Oct. 13, 2006, eff. Jan. 1, 2007.

Comment—Rule 19

See comment following Rule 19.11.

Historical Notes

The order of the Minnesota Supreme Court [C6-84-2165] dated June 26, 1996, provides in part that "(t)hese amendments to the Rules of Juvenile Procedure shall govern all juvenile actions commenced or arrests made on or after 12:00 o'clock midnight August 1, 1996."

The order of the Minnesota Supreme Court [CX-01-926] dated July 18, 2003, provides in part that "(t)he attached amendments shall govern all juveniles taken into custody and all juvenile delinquency actions commenced or children taken into custody after 12 o'clock midnight September 1, 2003."

Rule 19.08. Withdrawal of Waiver of Extended Jurisdiction Juvenile Hearing

Subd. 1. General Procedure. A child may bring a motion to withdraw the waiver of extended jurisdiction juvenile hearing and stipulation to extended jurisdiction juvenile prosecution order:

(A) within fifteen (15) days of the filing of the order, upon showing that it is fair and just to do so; or

(B) at any time prior to trial, upon showing that withdrawal is necessary to correct a manifest injustice.

The motion shall be made in the juvenile court that entered the extended jurisdiction juvenile prosecution order.

Subd. 2. Basis for Motion. The motion shall state with particularity one of the following bases for granting withdrawal of the waiver:

(A) the waiver was not knowingly, voluntarily, or intelligently made;

(B) the child alleges ineffective assistance of counsel; or

(C) withdrawal is appropriate in the interests of justice.

Subd. 3. Timing and Effect of Hearing. A hearing shall be held within fifteen (15) days of the filing of the motion. Following the hearing, if the court grants the motion to withdraw the waiver of extended jurisdiction juvenile hearing, the court shall vacate the order for extended jurisdiction juvenile prosecution, and proceedings will resume pursuant to Rule 19.04. If the court denies the motion to withdraw the waiver for extended jurisdiction juvenile hearing, the order for extended jurisdiction juvenile prosecution shall remain in effect, and proceedings will resume pursuant to Rule 19.09.

Adopted July 18, 2003.

Comment—Rule 19

See comment following Rule 19.11.

Historical Notes

The order of the Minnesota Supreme Court [CX-01-926] dated July 18, 2003, provides in part that "(t)he attached amendments shall govern all juveniles taken into custody and all juvenile delinquency actions commenced or children taken into custody after 12 o'clock midnight September 1, 2003."

Rule 19.09. Extended Jurisdiction Juvenile Prosecution and Procedure for Seeking an Aggravated Adult Criminal Sentence

Subdivision 1. General Procedure and Timing. Minnesota Statutes, chapters 260 and 260B and these Rules apply to extended jurisdiction juvenile prosecutions. However, every child who is the subject of an extended jurisdiction juvenile prosecution is entitled to trial by jury on the underlying offense pursuant to Minnesota Rules of Criminal Procedure 26. The court shall schedule a hearing for the child to enter a plea to the charges. If the child pleads not guilty, the court shall schedule an omnibus hearing prior to the trial and shall also schedule the trial. The trial shall be scheduled pursuant to Rule 13.02, except:

(A) The time shall run from the date of the filing of the extended jurisdiction juvenile order.

(B) In cases where the child is in detention, if the extended jurisdiction juvenile hearing is commenced within thirty (30) days of the prosecution motion for designation as an extended jurisdiction juvenile prosecution, the trial shall be scheduled within sixty (60) days of the court's order designating the child an extended jurisdiction juvenile, unless good cause is shown why the trial should not be held within that time. If the hearing on the motion to designate the child as an extended jurisdiction juvenile is commenced more than thirty (30) days from the filing of the motion, the trial shall be commenced within thirty (30) days of entry of the court's order designating the child an extended jurisdiction juvenile.

Subd. 2. Notice and Procedure for Seeking an Aggravated Adult Criminal Sentence.

(A) *Notice.* Within seven (7) days after filing of a designation of the proceeding as an extended jurisdiction juvenile prosecution by the court or prosecutor, or at such later time if permitted by the court upon good cause shown and upon such conditions as will not unfairly prejudice the child, the prosecutor shall serve and file on the child's attorney written notice of intent to seek an aggravated adult criminal sentence as defined in Minnesota

Rules of Criminal Procedure 1.04(d). The notice shall include the grounds or statutes relied upon and a summary statement of the factual basis supporting the aggravated adult criminal sentence.

(B) *Procedure.* If the prosecutor has filed and served notice under this rule of intent to seek an aggravated adult criminal sentence, a hearing shall be held to determine whether the law and proffered evidence support an aggravated adult criminal sentence and, if so, whether the issues will be presented to the jury in a unitary or bifurcated trial. The hearing shall be held prior to trial.

In deciding whether to bifurcate the trial, the court shall consider whether the evidence in support of an aggravated adult criminal sentence is otherwise admissible in the guilt phase of the trial and whether unfair prejudice would result to the child in a unitary trial. A bifurcated trial shall be ordered where evidence in support of an aggravated adult criminal sentence includes evidence that is inadmissible during the guilt phase of the trial or would result in unfair prejudice to the child. If the court orders a unitary trial the court may still order separate final arguments on the issues of guilt and the aggravated adult criminal sentence.

Except as modified by these rules, procedures relating to an aggravated adult criminal sentence are governed by the Minnesota Rules of Criminal Procedure.

Adopted June 26, 1996. Amended July 18, 2003; Aug. 17, 2006, eff. Oct. 1, 2006; Oct. 13, 2006, eff. Jan. 1, 2007.

Comment—Rule 19

See comment following Rule 19.11.

Historical Notes

The order of the Minnesota Supreme Court [C6-84-2165] dated June 26, 1996, provides in part that "(t)hese amendments to the Rules of Juvenile Procedure shall govern all juvenile actions commenced or arrests made on or after 12:00 o'clock midnight August 1, 1996."

The order of the Minnesota Supreme Court [CX-01-926] dated July 18, 2003, provides in part that "(t)he attached amendments shall govern all juveniles taken into custody and all juvenile delinquency actions commenced or children taken into custody after 12 o'clock midnight September 1, 2003."

Rule 19.10. Disposition

Subdivision 1. Procedure. Upon a guilty plea or conviction, the court shall:

(A) order one or more dispositions under Minnesota Statutes, section 260B.198; and

(B) impose an adult criminal sentence under Minnesota Law, except that the court shall stay execution of that sentence on the conditions that the child not violate the provisions of the disposition ordered in subdivision 1(A) above or commit a new offense.

Subd. 2. Length of Stayed Sentence. Unless the stayed sentence is executed after a revocation hearing pursuant to Rule 19.11, jurisdiction of the juvenile court shall terminate on the child's twenty-first (21st) birthday or at the end of the maximum probationary term, whichever occurs first. The court may terminate jurisdiction earlier pursuant to Rule 15.08.

Subd. 3. Limitation on Certain Extended Jurisdiction Juvenile Dispositions. If an extended jurisdiction juvenile prosecution, initiated by designation by the prosecuting attorney, results in a guilty plea or a conviction for an offense other than a presumptive commitment to prison under the Minnesota Sentencing Guidelines or a felony committed using a firearm, the court shall only impose one or more dispositions under Minnesota Statutes, section 260B.198. But if the child has plead guilty and consents, even if the plea or the conviction is for an offense other than a presumptive commitment under the guidelines, the court may also impose a stayed adult criminal sentence under Rule 19.10, subdivision 1.

Subd. 4. Venue. If the child's county of residence is not the same county where the offense occurred, venue of the case may be transferred as provided by Minnesota Statutes, section 260B.105. The conditions under which the execution of any adult sentence are stayed shall be determined by the juvenile court having jurisdiction to impose and supervise any juvenile court disposition. The stayed adult sentence may be pronounced by the judge who presided over the trial or who accepted a plea of guilty. If venue for the juvenile disposition is being transferred to the child's county of residence, prior to making the transfer, the transferring court shall prepare and file with the receiving court, a copy of the juvenile's file, including the plea and sentencing transcript, if any, and the adult stayed sentence form or order.

Subd. 5. Record of Proceedings. (A) A verbatim record shall be made of all plea and sentencing proceedings.

(B) A record of the adult stayed sentence shall also be recorded in a sentencing order that, at a minimum, contains:

(1) the child's name;

(2) case number;

(3) for each count:

(a) if the child pled guilty to or was found guilty of the offense:

(i) the offense date;

(ii) a citation to the offense statute;

(iii) the precise terms of the adult criminal sentence, and that execution has been stayed;

(iv) the level of sentence; and

(v) the amount of time spent in custody, if any; or

(b) if the child did not plead guilty to or was not found guilty of the offense, that the child was acquitted or the count was dismissed; and

(4) the signature of the sentencing judge.

Where venue is transferred as provided in subdivision 4, a copy of the sentencing order shall be filed with the transferring court.

Adopted June 26, 1996. Amended Dec. 12, 1997; July 18, 2003; Nov. 10, 2003, eff. Nov. 14, 2003; June 9, 2005, eff. Aug. 1, 2005; Oct. 13, 2006, eff. Jan. 1, 2007.

Comment—Rule 19

See comment following Rule 19.11.

Historical Notes

The order of the Minnesota Supreme Court [C6-84-2165] dated June 26, 1996, provides in part that "(t)hese amendments to the Rules of Juvenile Procedure shall govern all juvenile actions commenced or arrests made on or after 12:00 o'clock midnight August 1, 1996."

The order of the Minnesota Supreme Court [C6–84–2165] dated December 12, 1997, provides in part that "(t)hese amendments to the Rules of Juvenile Procedure shall govern all juvenile actions commenced or arrests made on or after 12:00 o'clock midnight January 1, 1998."

The order of the Minnesota Supreme Court [CX–01–926] dated July 18, 2003, provides in part that "(t)he attached amendments shall govern all juveniles taken into custody and all juvenile delinquency actions commenced or children taken into custody after 12 o'clock midnight September 1, 2003."

The order of the Minnesota Supreme Court [CX–01–926] dated November 10, 2003, provides in part:

"1. The attached amendments to the Minnesota Rules of Juvenile Procedure are prescribed and promulgated for the regulation of practice and procedure in juvenile delinquency matters in the courts of the State of Minnesota to be effective November 14, 2003.

"2. Transcripts for extended jurisdiction juvenile guilty plea, sentencing, or probation revocation hearings held prior to November 14, 2003, shall be paid in accordance with Minn. R. Juv. P. 19.10, subd. 5 and 19.11, subd. 3(F) as they existed prior to the amendments provided for in this order if the transcripts for those hearings are filed within thirty days of the extended jurisdiction juvenile guilty plea, sentencing, or probation revocation hearing.

"3. Form 17 is a model of the adult stayed sentence form provided for in Minn. R. Juv. P. 19.10, subd. 5, as amended by this order. The form will be made available in electronic format in the Court Rules section of the Supreme Court public website: http://www.courts.state.mn.us. The Supreme Court Technology Planning Committee is directed to develop, through the MNCIS project and in consultation with appropriate criminal justice partners, a standardized, uniform state-wide adult stayed sentence form or order that captures for immediate transmission essential sentencing information consistent with Minn. R. Juv. P. 19.10, subd. 5, as amended herein. The form shall be completed and implemented in conjunction with the MNCIS rollout.

"4. Court reporters and operators of electronic recording equipment shall file the stenographic notes or tape recordings of extended jurisdiction juvenile guilty plea, sentencing, or probation revocation hearings with the court administrator within 90 days of the sentencing or probation revocation hearing. The reporter or operator may retrieve the notes or recordings if necessary. Minnesota Statutes § 486.03 (2002) is superceded to the extent that it conflicts with this procedure.

"5. No charge may be assessed for preparation of a transcript for the district court's own use. Any person authorized to obtain a transcript pursuant to Minn. R. Juv. P. 29.02 may order a transcript at his or her own expense. Any other person may order a transcript at his or her own expense if the proceedings are open to the public pursuant to Minn. Stat. § 260B.163, subd. 1(c)(2) (2002).

"6. The maximum rate charged for the transcription of any proceeding shall be established by the Conference of Chief Judges. Minnesota Statutes § 486.06 (2002) is superceded to the extent that it conflicts with this procedure.

"7. The Supreme Court Advisory Committee on General Rules of Practice shall draft rules in accordance with paragraphs 4, 5, and 6 of this order, and may recommend additional procedures for ensuring the availability and transcribability of the record, such as requiring that the court reporter file or make available his or her personal stenographic dictionary."

Rule 19.11. Revocation

Subd. 1. Commencement of Proceedings.

(A) *Issuance of Revocation Warrant or Summons.* Proceedings for the revocation of a stayed sentence shall be commenced by the issuance of a warrant or a summons by the court. The warrant or summons shall be based upon a written report showing probable cause to believe that the probationer has violated any of the provisions of the disposition order or committed a new offense. The written report shall include a description of the surrounding facts and circumstances upon which the request for revocation is based. The court may issue a summons instead of a warrant whenever it is satisfied that a warrant is unnecessary to secure the appearance of the probationer. The court may issue a warrant for immediate custody of the probationer if the court finds that there is probable cause to believe that the probationer has violated the terms of probation or a court order, and:

(1) the probationer failed to appear after having been personally served with a summons or subpoena, or reasonable efforts to personally serve the probationer have failed, or there is a substantial likelihood that the probationer will fail to respond to a summons; or

(2) the probationer or others are in danger of imminent harm; or

(3) the probationer has left the custody of the detaining authority without permission of the court.

(B) *Contents of Warrant and Summons.* Both the warrant and summons shall contain the name of the probationer, a description of the stayed sentence sought to be revoked, the signature of the issuing judge or judicial officer of the district court, and shall be accompanied by the written report upon which it was based. The amount of any bail or other conditions of release may be set by the issuing judge or judicial officer and endorsed on the warrant. The warrant shall direct that the probationer be brought promptly before the court. The warrant shall direct that the probationer be brought before a judge or judicial officer without unnecessary delay, and in any event not later than thirty-six (36) hours after the arrest exclusive of the day of arrest. The summons shall summon the probationer to appear at a stated time and place to respond to the revocation charges.

(C) *Place of Detention.* If the probationer is under eighteen (18) years of age and is to be detained prior to the revocation hearing, the probationer may only be detained in a juvenile facility. If the probationer is eighteen (18) years of age or older and is to be detained, the probationer may be detained in an adult facility.

(D) *Execution or Service of Warrant or Summons; Certification.* Execution, service, and certification of the warrant or summons shall be as provided in Minnesota Rules of Criminal Procedure 3.03.

Subd. 2. First Appearance.

(A) *Advice to Probationer.* A probationer who initially appears before the court pursuant to a warrant or summons concerning an alleged probation violation, shall be advised of the nature of the violation charged. The probationer shall also be given a copy of the written report upon which the warrant or summons was based if the probationer has not previously received such report. The judge, judicial officer, or other duly authorized personnel shall further advise the probationer substantially as follows:

(1) the probationer is entitled to counsel at all stages of the proceedings, and if financially unable to afford counsel, one will be appointed for the probationer and, if counsel is waived, standby counsel will be appointed;

(2) unless waived, a revocation hearing will be held to determine whether there is clear and convincing evidence that the probationer violated any provisions of the disposition order or committed a new offense and that the stayed sentence should therefore be revoked;

(3) before the revocation hearing, all evidence to be used against the probationer shall be disclosed to the probationer and the probationer shall be provided access to all official records pertinent to the proceedings;

(4) at the hearing, both the prosecuting attorney and the probationer shall have the right to offer evidence, present arguments, subpoena witnesses, and call and cross-examine witnesses, provided, however, the probationer may be denied confrontation by the court when good cause is shown that a substantial risk of serious harm to others would exist if it were allowed. Additionally, the probationer shall have the right at the revocation hearing to present mitigating circumstances or other reasons why the violation, if proved, should not result in revocation; and

(5) the probationer has the right of appeal from the determination of the court following the revocation hearing.

(B) *Appointment of Counsel.* If the probationer is financially unable to afford counsel, one will be appointed for the probationer and, if counsel is waived, standby counsel shall be appointed.

(C) *Conditions of Release.* The probationer may be released pending appearance at the revocation hearing. In deciding whether and upon what conditions to release the probationer, the court shall take into account the conditions of release and the factors determining the conditions of release as provided by Rule 5 and Minnesota Rules of Criminal Procedure 6.02, subdivisions 1 and 2. The probationer has the burden of establishing that he or she will not flee or will not be a danger to any other person or the community.

(D) *Time of Revocation Hearing.* The court shall set a date for the revocation hearing to be held within a reasonable time. If the probationer is in custody as a result of the revocation proceedings, the revocation hearing shall be held within seven (7) days. If the probationer has allegedly committed a new offense the court may postpone the revocation hearing pending disposition of the new offense whether or not the probationer is in custody.

(E) *Record.* A verbatim record shall be made of the proceedings at the probationer's initial appearance.

Subd. 3. Revocation Hearing.

(A) *Hearing Procedures.* The hearing shall be held in accordance with the provisions of Rule 19.11, subdivisions 2(A)(1), (2), (3), and (4).

(B) *Finding of No Violation of Terms and Conditions of Disposition.* If the court finds that a violation of the terms and conditions of the disposition order was not established by clear and convincing evidence, the revocation proceedings shall be dismissed, and the probationer's stayed sentence shall be continued under conditions ordered by the court.

(C) *Finding of Violation of Terms and Conditions of Disposition.*

(1) If the court finds upon clear and convincing evidence that any provisions of the disposition order were violated, or if the probationer admits the violation, the court may revoke the probationer's extended jurisdiction juvenile status. Upon revocation of extended jurisdiction juvenile status, the court shall treat the offender as an adult and may order any of the adult sanctions authorized by Minnesota Statutes, section 609.14, subdivision 3.

(2) To execute the stayed prison sentence after revocation of extended jurisdiction juvenile status, the court must make written findings that:

(a) one or more conditions of probation were violated;

(b) the violation was intentional or inexcusable; and

(c) the need for confinement outweighs the policies favoring probation.

(3) If the extended jurisdiction juvenile conviction was for an offense with a presumptive prison sentence or the probationer used a firearm, and the court has made findings pursuant to clause (2), the court shall order execution of the sen-

tence unless the court makes written findings indicating the mitigating factors that justify continuing the stay.

(D) *Jail Credit for Juvenile Facility Custody.* If the court revokes the probationer's extended jurisdiction juvenile status, the court shall ensure that the record accurately reflects all time spent in custody in connection with the underlying offense at juvenile facilities where the level of confinement and limitations are the functional equivalent of a jail, workhouse, or regional correctional facility. Such time shall be deducted from any adult sentence imposed pursuant to Minnesota Statutes, section 609.14, subdivision 3.

(E) *Record of Findings.* A verbatim record shall be made of the proceedings at the revocation hearing and in any contested hearing the court shall make written findings of fact on all disputed issues including a summary of the evidence relied upon and a statement of the court's reasons for its determination.

(F) *Appeal.* The probationer or the prosecuting attorney may appeal from the court's decision according to the procedure provided for appeal in Rule 21.

Adopted June 26, 1996. Amended Dec. 12, 1997; July 18, 2003; Nov. 10, 2003, eff. Nov. 14, 2003; April 23, 2004; July 11, 2005, eff. Sept. 1, 2005; Oct. 13, 2006, eff. Jan. 1, 2007.

Comment—Rule 19

The determination of "presumptive prison" under the Minnesota Sentencing Guidelines should be analyzed pursuant to those guidelines.

The sanction for delay in Minn. R. Juv. Del. P. 19.04, subd. 1(B) and 19.06, subd. 3 is modeled after Minn. R. Crim. P. 11.10, which as of January 1, 2010 is now Minn. R. Crim. P. 11.09. See *In re Welfare of J.J.H.,* 446 N.W.2d 680, 681–82 (Minn. Ct. App. 1989) (order issued 66 days after hearing, 38 days after submission of written argument; because rule contains no sanction, reversal denied). See also *McIntosh v. Davis,* 441 N.W.2d 115 (Minn. 1989) (where alternative remedies available mandamus not appropriate to enforce time limit of Minn. R. Crim. P. 11.10 speedy trial rule).

Most of the waiver language in Minn. R. Juv. Del. P. 19.04 subd. 1(C) is taken from the 1983 version of Minn. R. Juv. P. 15.03.

Minn. R. Juv. Del. P. 19.04 does not address the consequences of the child's testimony at a hearing or whether it can be subsequently used against the child. See *Simmons v. United States,* 390 U.S. 377 (1968); *State v. Christenson,* 371 N.W.2d 228 (Minn. Ct. App. 1985) (impeachment); cf. *Harris v. New York,* 401 U.S. 222 (1971).

On continuation questions under Minn. R. Juv. Del. P. 19.04, subd. 1(B), the victim should have input but does not have the right of a party to appear and object.

Previously, the last sentence to Rule 19.04, subd. 2(A) stated. "If witnesses are to be called, the court may continue the hearing." This statement was deleted because the committee felt it was redundant in light of the previous sentence, which allows the court to extend the time of the hearing for good cause.

Much of the content of Minn. R. Juv. Del. P. 19.04, subd. 3 is modeled after Minn. R. Crim. P 11.04 and 18.05, subd. 1. The court may employ police statements for probable cause determinations in the same manner as permitted in adult proceedings under Minn. R. Crim. P. 11.04. Also note, *In re Welfare of E.Y.W.,* 496 N.W.2d 847, 850 (Minn. Ct. App. 1993) (juvenile not entitled to exclusionary hearing before decision on probable cause).

Minn. R. Juv. Del. P. 19.04, subd. 3 eliminates the need for a probable cause finding when a delinquency accusation is presented by an indictment. Accusation by indictment is uncommon, but might occur more often as a result of grand jury proceedings conducted after 1994 statutory amendments on the question of whether a child is to be accused of first degree murder in adult proceedings. See Minnesota Statutes, section 260B.007, subd. 6 (2002).

When a juvenile waives probable cause solely for the purpose of an extended jurisdiction juvenile proceeding, that waiver does not preclude the child from litigating probable cause in a subsequent prosecution on the underlying offense.

Minn. R. Juv. Del. P. 19.04, subd. 3(B) is consistent with case law. Because the extended jurisdiction juvenile prosecution question is dispositional in nature, strict application of the rules of evidence is thought to be inappropriate.

The public safety factors listed in Minn. R. Juv. Del. P. 19.05 mirror those set forth in Minnesota Statutes, section 260B.125, subd. 4 (2002), and eliminate the need for non-offense related evidence of dangerousness. See In re Welfare of D.M.D., 607 N.W.2d 432 (Minn. 2000).

Rule 19.09(B) was amended to clarify that a continuance beyond the timelines prescribed by the Rule may be necessary in limited circumstances. For example, a reasonable delay may be appropriate to facilitate necessary scientific testing. The Committee adopted a "good cause" standard for use in determining whether to grant a continuance. "Good cause" is defined in case law; however, the Committee intends a strict application of the standard. Time is of the essence in an extended jurisdiction juvenile prosecution. Juvenile dispositional options and treatment opportunities may be lost if the trial is unnecessarily delayed. The court should consider the unique nature of extended jurisdiction juvenile when deciding whether to grant a continuance for good cause.

Following the presentation of evidence by the prosecuting attorney the child may move the court for directed relief on the grounds that the burden of proof has not been met.

Under Minnesota Statutes, section 260B.163, subd. 7 (2002) the custodial parent or guardian of the child alleged or found to be delinquent or prosecuted as an extended jurisdiction juvenile, must accompany the child at each hearing held during the delinquency or extended juvenile jurisdiction proceedings, unless the court excuses the parent or guardian from attendance for good cause shown. The failure of a parent or guardian to comply with this duty may be punished as provided in Minnesota Statutes, section 260B.154 (2002).

Pursuant to Minnesota Statutes, section 260B.245 (2002), if a child is convicted as an extended jurisdiction juvenile, the child will be assigned points for the purpose of computing a criminal history score pursuant to the Minnesota Sentencing Guidelines, as if the child were an adult.

A disposition form developed by the Minnesota Sentencing Guidelines Commission shall be completed by the court in addition to the findings of facts, conclusions of law and order.

A sentencing worksheet developed by the Minnesota Sentencing Guidelines Commission shall be completed by the probation department pursuant to Minn. R. Crim. P. 27, and Minnesota Statutes, sections 609.115 and 631.20 (2002). The court shall send a copy of this worksheet to the Minnesota Sentencing Guidelines Commission pursuant to Minn. R. Crim. P. 27.03, subd. 4(C).

In accordance with the procedure and law set forth in State v. B.Y., 659 N.W.2d 763 (Minn. 2003), Minn. R. Juv. Del. P. 19.11, subd. 3 incorporates consideration of the Austin factors (see State v. Austin, 295 N.W.2d 246 (Minn. 1980) into the court's determination of whether to revoke the stayed prison sentence of an EJJ probationer. This is in contrast to the decision to revoke probation in delinquency cases, for which consideration of the *Austin* factors is not required. *In re Welfare of R.V.*, 702 N.W.2d 294 (Minn. Ct. App. 2005).

The court's holdings in *State v. Garcia*, 683 N.W.2d 294 (Minn. 2004) and *Asfaha v. State*, 665 N.W.2d 523 (Minn. 2003) found Minn. Stat. § 260B.130, subd. 5 (2002) unconstitutional to the extent it denied credit for time spent in custody in juvenile facilities. Minn. R. Juv. Del. P. 19.11, subd. 3 has been amended to require the court to calculate and record the amount of time the probationer spent in custody at juvenile facilities where the level of confinement and limitations were the functional equivalent of a jail, workhouse, or correctional facility. Such time must be deducted from any adult sentence imposed after revocation of extended jurisdiction juvenile status.

The decision in *In Re Welfare of T.C.J.*, 689 N.W.2d 787 (Minn. Ct. App. 2004), that Minnesota Statutes, section 260B.130, subd. 4(b) violates the Equal Protection Clause, raises an issue regarding the application of Minn. R. Juv. Del. P. 19.10, subd. 3, which was modeled after the statute.

References in this rule to "child's counsel" include the child who is proceeding pro se. Minn. R. Juv. Del. P. 1.01.

Historical Notes

The order of the Minnesota Supreme Court [C6-84-2165] dated June 26, 1996, provides in part that "(t)hese amendments to the Rules of Juvenile Procedure shall govern all juvenile actions commenced or arrests made on or after 12:00 o'clock midnight August 1, 1996."

The order of the Minnesota Supreme Court [C6–84–2165] dated December 12, 1997, provides in part that "(t)hese amendments to the Rules of Juvenile Procedure shall govern all juvenile actions commenced or arrests made on or after 12:00 o'clock midnight January 1, 1998."

The order of the Minnesota Supreme Court [CX–01–926] dated July 18, 2003, provides in part that "(t)he attached amendments shall govern all juveniles taken into custody and all juvenile delinquency actions commenced or children taken into custody after 12 o'clock midnight September 1, 2003."

The order of the Minnesota Supreme Court [CX–01–926] dated November 10, 2003, provides in part:

"1. The attached amendments to the Minnesota Rules of Juvenile Procedure are prescribed and promulgated for the regulation of practice and procedure in juvenile delinquency matters in the courts of the State of Minnesota to be effective November 14, 2003.

"2. Transcripts for extended jurisdiction juvenile guilty plea, sentencing, or probation revocation hearings held prior to November 14, 2003, shall be paid in accordance with Minn. R. Juv. P. 19.10, subd. 5 and 19.11, subd. 3(F) as they existed prior to the amendments provided for in this order if the transcripts for those hearings are filed within thirty days of the extended jurisdiction juvenile guilty plea, sentencing, or probation revocation hearing.

"3. Form 17 is a model of the adult stayed sentence form provided for in Minn. R. Juv. P. 19.10, subd. 5, as amended by this order. The form will be made available in electronic format in the Court Rules section of the Supreme Court public website: http://www.courts.state.mn.us. The Supreme Court Technology Planning Committee is directed to develop, through the MNCIS project and in consultation with appropriate criminal justice partners, a standardized, uniform state-wide adult stayed sentence form or order that captures for immediate transmission essential sentencing information consistent with Minn. R. Juv. P. 19.10, subd. 5, as amended herein. The form shall be completed and implemented in conjunction with the MNCIS rollout.

"4. Court reporters and operators of electronic recording equipment shall file the stenographic notes or tape recordings of extended jurisdiction juvenile guilty plea, sentencing, or probation revocation hearings with the court administrator within 90 days of the sentencing or probation revocation hearing. The reporter or operator may retrieve the notes or recordings if necessary. Minnesota Statutes § 486.03 (2002) is superceded to the extent that it conflicts with this procedure.

"5. No charge may be assessed for preparation of a transcript for the district court's own use. Any person authorized to obtain a transcript pursuant to Minn. R. Juv. P. 29.02 may order a transcript at his or her own expense. Any other person may order a transcript at his or her own expense if the proceedings are open to the public pursuant to Minn. Stat. § 260B.163, subd. 1(c)(2) (2002).

"6. The maximum rate charged for the transcription of any proceeding shall be established by the Conference of Chief Judges. Minnesota Statutes § 486.06 (2002) is superceded to the extent that it conflicts with this procedure.

"7. The Supreme Court Advisory Committee on General Rules of Practice shall draft rules in accordance with paragraphs 4, 5, and 6 of this order, and may recommend additional procedures for ensuring the availability and transcribability of the record, such as requiring that the court reporter file or make available his or her personal stenographic dictionary."

The order of the Minnesota Supreme Court [CX–01–926] dated April 23, 2004, provides in part that "(t)he attached amendments shall govern all juvenile delinquency actions commenced or children taken into custody after 12 o'clock midnight July 1, 2004."

RULE 20. CHILD INCOMPETENT TO PROCEED AND DEFENSE OF MENTAL ILLNESS OR MENTAL DEFICIENCY

Rule 20.01. Proceeding When Child is Believed to be Incompetent

Subd. 1. Incompetency to Proceed Defined. A child is incompetent and shall not be permitted to enter a plea, be tried, or receive a disposition for any offense when the child lacks sufficient ability to:

(A) consult with a reasonable degree of rational understanding with the child's counsel; or

(B) understand the proceedings or participate in the defense due to mental illness or mental deficiency.

Subd. 2. Counsel. Any child subject to competency proceedings shall be represented by counsel.

Subd. 3. Proceedings. The prosecuting attorney, the child's counsel or the court shall bring a motion to determine the competency of the child if there is reason to doubt the competency of the child during the pending proceedings.

The motion shall set forth the facts constituting the basis for the motion but the child's counsel shall not divulge communications in violation of the attorney-client privilege. The bringing of the motion by the child's counsel does not waive the attorney-client privilege. Any such motion may be brought over the objection of the child. Upon such motion, the court shall suspend the proceedings and shall proceed as follows:

(A) *Felony or Gross Misdemeanor.* If the offense is a felony or gross misdemeanor, the court shall determine whether there is sufficient probable cause to believe the child committed the offense charged before proceeding pursuant to this rule. If there is sufficient showing of probable cause, the court shall proceed according to this rule. If the court finds insufficient probable cause to believe the child committed the offense charged, the charging document against the child shall be dismissed.

(B) *Other Matters.* If the offense is a misdemeanor, juvenile petty matter or juvenile traffic offense, the court having trial jurisdiction shall proceed according to this rule, or dismiss the case in the interests of justice.

(C) *Examination.* If there is probable cause, the court shall proceed as follows. The Court shall suspend the proceedings and appoint at least one examiner as defined in the Minnesota Commitment Act, Minnesota Statutes, Chapter 253B to examine the child and report to the court on the child's mental condition.

The court may not order confinement for the examination if the child is otherwise entitled to release and if the examination can be done adequately on an outpatient basis. The court may require the completion of an outpatient examination as a condition of release.

The court may order confinement for an inpatient examination for a specified period not to exceed sixty (60) days if the examination cannot be adequately done on an outpatient basis or if the child is not entitled to be released.

The court shall permit examination of the child or observation of such examination by a qualified psychiatrist, clinical psychologist or qualified physician retained and requested by the child's counsel or prosecuting attorney.

The court shall further direct the mental-health professionals to notify promptly the prosecuting attorney, the child's counsel, and the court if such mental-health professionals conclude, upon examination, that the child presents an imminent risk of serious danger to another person, is imminently suicidal, or otherwise needs emergency intervention.

(D) *Report of Examination.* Within sixty (60) days, the examiner shall send a written report to the judge who ordered such examination, the prosecuting attorney and the child's counsel. The report contents shall not be otherwise disclosed until the hearing on the child's competency. The report shall include:

(1) A diagnosis of the mental condition of the child;

(2) If the child is mentally ill or mentally deficient, an opinion as to:

(a) whether the child can understand the proceedings and participate in the defense;

(b) whether the child presents an imminent risk of serious danger to another person, is imminently suicidal, or otherwise needs emergency intervention;

(c) whether the child requires any treatment to attain competency and if so, the appropriate treatment alternatives by order of choice, the extent to which the child can be treated as an outpatient and the reasons for rejecting such treatment if institutionalization is recommended; and

(d) whether, with treatment, there is a substantial probability that the child will attain competency and if so, when the child is expected to attain competency and the availability of inpatient and outpatient treatment agencies or facilities in the local geographical area;

(3) A statement of the factual basis upon which the diagnosis and opinion are based; and

(4) If the examination could not be conducted because the child is unwilling to participate, a statement to that effect with an opinion, if possible, as to whether the child's unwillingness was the result of mental illness or deficiency.

Subd. 4. Hearing and Determination of Competency.

(A) *Hearing and Notice.* Upon receipt of the report and notice to the parties, the court shall hold a hearing within ten (10) days to review the report with the parties. If either party objects to the report's conclusion regarding the child's competency to proceed, the court shall hold a hearing within ten

(10) days on the issue of the child's competency to proceed.

(B) *Going Forward with Evidence.* If the child's counsel moved for the examination, the child's counsel shall go forward first with evidence at the hearing. If the prosecuting attorney or the court on its own initiative, moved for the examination, the prosecuting attorney shall go forward with evidence unless the court otherwise directs.

(C) *Report and Evidence.* The examination report and other evidence as to the child's mental condition may be admitted at the hearing. The person who prepared the report or any individual designated by that person as a source of information for preparation of the report, other than the child or the child's counsel, is considered the court's witness and may be called and cross-examined as such by either party.

(D) *Child's Counsel as Witness.* The child's counsel may testify as to personal observations of and conversations with the child to the extent that attorney-client privilege is not violated, and continue to represent the child. The prosecuting attorney may examine the child's counsel testifying to such matter.

The court may inquire of the child's counsel concerning the attorney-client relationship and the child's ability to communicate effectively with the child's counsel. However, the court may not require the child's counsel to divulge communications in violation of the attorney-client privilege. The prosecuting attorney may not cross-examine the child's counsel responding to the court's inquiry.

(E) *Decision and Sufficiency of Evidence.* If the court determines that the child is competent by the greater weight of evidence, the court shall enter a written order finding competency. Otherwise, the court shall enter a written order finding incompetency. The court shall enter its written order within fifteen (15) days of the hearing.

Subd. 5. Effect of Finding on Issue of Competency to Proceed.

(A) *Finding of Competency.* If the court determines that the child is competent to proceed, the proceedings against the child shall resume.

(B) *Finding of Incompetency.* If the offense is a misdemeanor, petty matter, or juvenile traffic offense, and the court determines that the child is incompetent to proceed, the matter shall be dismissed. If the offense is a gross misdemeanor, and the court determines that the child is incompetent to proceed, the court has the discretion to dismiss or suspend the proceedings against the child except as provided by Rule 20.01, subdivision 7. If the offense is a felony, and the court determines that the child is incompetent to proceed, the proceedings against the child shall be further suspended except as provided by Rule 20.01, subdivision 7.

(1) If the court determines that the child is mentally ill or deficient so as to be incapable of understanding the proceedings or participation in the defense, the court shall order any existing civil commitment continued. If the child is not under commitment, the court may direct civil commitment proceedings be initiated, and the child confined in accordance with the provisions of the Minnesota Commitment Act, Chapter 253B.

(2) If it is determined that commitment proceedings are inappropriate and a petition has been filed alleging the child is in need of protection or services (CHIPS), the court shall order such jurisdiction be continued. If the child is not under CHIPS jurisdiction, the court may order the child held for up to seventy-two (72) hours and direct CHIPS proceedings to be initiated.

(3) If it is determined that neither commitment proceedings nor CHIPS proceedings are appropriate, the child shall be released to the child's parent(s), legal guardian or legal custodian under conditions deemed appropriate to the court.

Subd. 6. Continuing Supervision by the Court. In felony and gross misdemeanor cases in which proceedings have been suspended, the person charged with the child's supervision, such as the head of the institution to which the child is committed, shall report to the trial court on the child's mental condition and competency to proceed at least every six (6) months unless otherwise ordered. Copies of the reports shall also be sent to the prosecuting attorney and to the child's counsel.

Unless the charging document against the child has been dismissed as provided by Rule 20.01, subdivision 7, the trial court, child's counsel and the prosecuting attorney shall be notified of any proposed institutional transfer, partial institutionalization status, and any proposed termination, discharge, or provisional discharge of the juvenile protection case. The prosecuting attorney shall have the right to participate as a party in any proceedings concerning such proposed changes in the child's commitment or status.

Subd. 7. Dismissal of Proceedings.

(A) Delinquency and extended jurisdiction juvenile proceedings shall be dismissed upon the earlier of the following:

(1) the child's nineteenth (19th) birthday in the case of a delinquency, or twenty-first (21st) birthday if a designation or motion for extended jurisdiction juvenile proceedings is pending;

(2) for all cases except murder, the expiration of one (1) year from the date of the finding of the child's incompetency to proceed unless the prosecuting attorney, before the expiration of the one (1) year period, files a written notice of intention to prosecute the child when the child has been restored to competency. Such a notice shall ex-

tend the suspension of proceeding for one (1) year from the date of filing subject to Rule 20.01, subdivision 7(A).

(B) For all cases pending certification except murder, proceedings shall be dismissed upon the expiration of three (3) years from the date of the finding of the child's incompetency unless the prosecuting attorney, before the expiration of the three (3) year period, files a written notice of intention to prosecute the child when the child has been restored to competency. Murder charges shall not be dismissed based upon a finding of incompetency.

Subd. 8. Determination of Legal Issues Not Requiring Child's Participation. The fact that the child is incompetent to proceed shall not preclude the child's counsel from making any legal objection or defense that can be fairly determined without the personal participation of such child.

Subd. 9. Admissibility of Child's Statements. When a child is examined under this rule, any statement made by the child for the purpose of the examination and any evidence derived from the examination shall be admissible in evidence only at the proceedings to determine whether the child is competent to proceed.

Adopted June 26, 1996. Amended Dec. 12, 1997; July 18, 2003; July 11, 2005, eff. Sept. 1, 2005; Oct. 11, 2007, eff. Jan. 1, 2008; Nov. 19, 2010, eff. Jan. 1, 2011.

Comment—Rule 20

See comment following Rule 20.02.

Historical Notes

The order of the Minnesota Supreme Court [C6-84-2165] dated June 26, 1996, provides in part that "(t)hese amendments to the Rules of Juvenile Procedure shall govern all juvenile actions commenced or arrests made on or after 12:00 o'clock midnight August 1, 1996."

The order of the Minnesota Supreme Court [C6–84–2165] dated December 12, 1997, provides in part that "(t)hese amendments to the Rules of Juvenile Procedure shall govern all juvenile actions commenced or arrests made on or after 12:00 o'clock midnight January 1, 1998."

The order of the Minnesota Supreme Court [CX–01–926] dated July 18, 2003, provides in part that "(t)he attached amendments shall govern all juveniles taken into custody and all juvenile delinquency actions commenced or children taken into custody after 12 o'clock midnight September 1, 2003."

Rule 20.02. Defense of Mental Illness or Mental Deficiency at the Time of the Offense

Subd. 1. When Raised.

(A) If the child intends to raise mental illness or mental deficiency as a defense, the child's counsel shall advise the court and prosecuting attorney in writing at the omnibus hearing or no less than ten (10) days before the trial, whichever is earlier. The notice shall provide the court and prosecuting attorney with a statement of particulars showing the nature of the mental illness or mental deficiency expected to be proved and the names and addresses of witnesses expected to prove it.

(B) The court, upon good cause shown and in its discretion, may waive these requirements and permit the introduction of the defense, or may continue the hearing for the purpose of an examination in accordance with the procedures in this rule.

(C) A continuance granted for an examination will toll the speedy trial rule and the limitation on detention pending adjudication and disposition.

Subd. 2. Examination of the Child. If the defense of mental illness or mental deficiency is raised, the court shall order an examination as described in Rule 20.01, subdivision 3(C). The court may order that the examination for competency under Rules 20.01 and 20.02 be conducted simultaneously.

Subd. 3. Refusal of the Child to be Examined. If the child does not participate in the examination so that the examiner is unable to make an adequate report to the court, the court may:

(A) prohibit the child from introducing evidence of the child's mental illness or mental deficiency;

(B) strike any such evidence previously introduced;

(C) permit any other party to comment on and to introduce evidence of the child's refusal to cooperate to the trier of the facts; and

(D) make any such other ruling as it deems just.

Subd. 4. Disclosure of Reports and Records of Child's Mental Illness or Mental Deficiency Examinations.

(A) *Order for Disclosure.* If a child raises the defense of mental illness or mental deficiency, the trial court, on motion of the prosecuting attorney and notice to the child's counsel may order the child to furnish either to the court or to the prosecuting attorney copies of all medical reports and hospital and medical records previously or thereafter made concerning the mental illness or mental deficiency of the child and relevant to the issue of the defense of mental illness or mental deficiency. If the copies of the reports and records are furnished to the court, the court shall inspect them to determine their relevancy. If the court determines they are relevant, they shall be delivered to the prosecuting attorney. Otherwise, they shall be returned to the child. If the child is unable to comply with the court order, a subpoena duces tecum may be issued.

(B) *Use of Reports and Records.* If an order for disclosure of reports and records under this subdivision is entered and copies are furnished to the prosecuting attorney, the reports and records and any evidence obtained from them may be admitted in evidence only upon the issue of the defense of mental illness or mental deficiency.

Subd. 5. Report of Examination. At the conclusion of the examination, a written report of the examination shall be forwarded to the judge who ordered the examination, the prosecuting attorney and to the child's counsel. The court administrator shall not otherwise disclose the report except by court order. The report of the examination shall contain:

(A) A diagnosis of the child's mental illness or mental deficiency as requested by the court;

(B) If so directed by the court, an opinion as to whether, because of mental illness or deficiency, the child at the time of the commission of the offense charged was laboring under such a defect of reason as not to know the nature of the act constituting the offense with which child is charged or that it was wrong;

(C) Any opinion requested by the court that is based on the examiner's diagnosis;

(D) A statement of the factual basis upon which the diagnosis and any opinion are based; and

(E) If the examination cannot be conducted by reason of the child's unwillingness to participate, the report shall so state and shall include, if possible, an opinion as to whether the unwillingness of the child was the result of mental illness or deficiency.

Subd. 6. Admissibility of Evidence at Trial. No evidence derived from the examination shall be received against the child unless the child has previously made his or her mental illness or mental deficiency an issue in the case. If the child's mental illness or mental deficiency is an issue, any party may call the person who examined the child at the direction of the court to testify as a witness at the trial. The report or portions thereof may be received in evidence to impeach the testimony of the person making it.

Subd. 7. Trial. When a child is examined under Rules 20.01 or 20.02, the admissibility at trial of any statements made by the child for the purposes of the examination and any evidence obtained as a result of such statements shall be determined by the following rules:

(A) *Notice by Child of Sole Defense of Mental Illness or Mental Deficiency.* If a child notifies the court and prosecuting attorney under Rule 20.02, subdivision 1 of an intention to rely solely on the defense of mental illness or deficiency, any statements made by the child for the purpose of the mental examination and evidence obtained as a result of the statements shall be admissible at the trial upon that issue.

(B) *Separate Trial of Defenses.* If a child notifies the court and prosecuting attorney under Rule 20.02, subdivision 1 of an intention to rely on the defense of mental illness or deficiency together with a defense of not guilty, there shall be a separation of the two defenses with a sequential order of proof before the court in a continuous trial in which the defense of not guilty shall be heard and determined first, and then the defense of the child's mental illness or deficiency.

(C) *Effect of Separate Trial.* If the child relies on the two defenses, the statements made by the child for the purpose of the mental examination and any evidence obtained as a result of such statements shall be admissible against the child only at that stage of the trial relating to the defense of mental illness or mental deficiency.

(D) *Procedure Upon Separated Trial of Defenses.*

(1) Court Trial for Child Alleged to be Delinquent or Charged with a Juvenile Petty or Juvenile Traffic Offense. Upon the trial of the defense of not guilty the court shall determine whether the elements of the offense charged have been proved beyond a reasonable doubt. If the court determines that the elements of the offense have not been proved beyond a reasonable doubt, the court shall enter findings and order a dismissal pursuant to Rule 13.09. If the court determines that the elements of the offense have been proved beyond a reasonable doubt and the child is relying on the sole defense of mental illness or mental deficiency, the defense of mental illness or mental deficiency shall then be tried and determined by the court. The child shall have the burden of proving the defense of mental illness or mental deficiency by a preponderance of the evidence. Based upon that determination the court shall make a finding of:

(a) not guilty by reason of mental illness; or

(b) not guilty by reason of mental deficiency; or

(c) guilty.

The court shall enter findings pursuant to Rule 13.09.

(2) Extended Jurisdiction Juvenile Proceedings. A court trial in an extended jurisdiction juvenile proceeding shall be conducted pursuant to Rule 20.02, subdivision 7(D)(1). A jury trial in an extended jurisdiction juvenile proceeding shall be conducted pursuant to Minnesota Rules of Criminal Procedure 20.02, subdivision 7.

Subd. 8. Procedure After Hearing.

(A) *Mental Illness or Mental Deficiency Not Proven.* After a finding of guilty and the defense of mental illness or deficiency not proven, the court shall schedule and conduct a disposition hearing. The issues of the child's mental illness or deficiency shall be considered by the court at disposition.

(B) *Mental Illness or Mental Deficiency Proven.* When a child is found not guilty by reason of mental illness or mental deficiency.

(1) the court shall order any existing civil commitment continued. If the child is not under commitment, the court may order the child held at a shelter or treatment facility for up to seven-

ty-two (72) hours and shall direct civil commitment proceedings be initiated;

(2) if it is determined that the child does not meet the criteria for civil commitment jurisdiction and the child is under CHIPS jurisdiction, the court shall order such jurisdiction be continued. If the child is not under CHIPS jurisdiction, the court may order the child held for up to seventy-two (72) hours in an appropriate facility and shall direct CHIPS proceedings be initiated.

Adopted June 26, 1996. Amended July 18, 2003; July 11, 2005, eff. Sept. 1, 2005; Nov. 19, 2010, eff. Jan. 1, 2011.

Comment—Rule 20

Minn. R. Juv. Del. P. 20 is based upon Minn. R. Crim. P. 20.

Under Minn. R. Juv. Del. P. 20.01, subd. 3(C), the court shall permit examination of the child or observation of such examination by a qualified medical personnel retained and requested by the child's counsel or prosecuting attorney. The court has the authority to order payment of reasonable and necessary costs of evaluation of the child at public expense pursuant to Minnesota Statutes, section 260B.331, subd. 1 (2002). Furthermore, under Minnesota Statutes, section 260.042 (2002), the court shall make an orientation and educational program available for juveniles and their families in accordance with the program established, if any, by the Minnesota Supreme Court.

"A determination of competency, even in the context of juvenile adjudicatory proceedings, is a fundamental right. Because of this and because dispositions in juvenile proceedings, including rehabilitative dispositions, may involve both punishment and a substantial loss of liberty, the level of competence required to permit a child's participation in juvenile court proceedings can be no less than the competence demanded for trial or sentencing of an adult." In re Welfare of D.D.N., 582 N.W.2d 278, 281 (Minn. Ct. App. 1998) (citation omitted). The court has a continuing obligation to inquire into a juvenile's competency to stand trial when substantial information exists, or the child's observed demeanor raises doubts as to competency. In re Welfare of S.W.T., 277 N.W.2d 507, 512 (Minn. 1979). C.f. Drope v. Missouri, 420 U.S. 162, 179 (1975); Pate v. Robinson, 383 U.S. 375, 385 (1966); State v. Jensen, 278 Minn. 212, 215, 153 N.W.2d 339 (Minn. 1967).

A juvenile delinquency proceeding is not a criminal proceeding. See Minnesota Statutes, section 260B.225 (2002) (stating a violation of a state or local law or ordinance by a child before becoming 18 is not a crime). Although the right to counsel has been recognized for juveniles in In re Gault, 387 U.S. 1, 41 (1967), the corollary right to self-representation has not been established in the juvenile context. The committee recognized that children subject to competency proceedings may be vulnerable; therefore, it would not be appropriate to allow a child to waive counsel prior to a court determining that the child is competent.

Historical Notes

The order of the Minnesota Supreme Court [C6-84-2165] dated June 26, 1996, provides in part that "(t)hese amendments to the Rules of Juvenile Procedure shall govern all juvenile actions commenced or arrests made on or after 12:00 o'clock midnight August 1, 1996."

The order of the Minnesota Supreme Court [CX-01-926] dated July 18, 2003, provides in part that "(t)he attached amendments shall govern all juveniles taken into custody and all juvenile delinquency actions commenced or children taken into custody after 12 o'clock midnight September 1, 2003."

Rule 20.03. Deleted June 26, 1996

Historical Notes

The order of the Minnesota Supreme Court [C6-84-2165] dated June 26, 1996, provides in part that "(t)hese amendments to the Rules of Juvenile Procedure shall govern all juvenile actions commenced or arrests made on or after 12:00 o'clock midnight August 1, 1996."

See, now, MN ST Juv. Del., Rule 7.04.

RULE 21. APPEALS

Rule 21.01. Generally

This rule governs the procedure for appeals from juvenile traffic and juvenile petty, delinquency, extended jurisdiction juvenile, and certification proceedings in district court. Except as provided by these rules, Minnesota Rules of Civil Appellate Procedure shall govern appeals from juvenile court proceedings. These rules do not limit a child's right to seek extraordinary writs. In order to expedite its decision or for other good cause shown, the court of appeals may suspend any of these rules, except the time for filing a notice of appeal. The court of appeals shall expedite all appeals from juvenile court proceedings pursuant to Rule 21.07.

A party may petition to the Supreme Court of Minnesota for review pursuant to Minnesota Rules of Civil Appellate Procedure 117 or 118.

Amended June 26, 1996; July 18, 2003; July 11, 2005, eff. Sept. 1, 2005.

Comment—Rule 21

See comment following Rule 21.07.

Historical Notes

The order of the Minnesota Supreme Court [C6-84-2165] dated June 26, 1996, provides in part that "(t)hese amendments to the Rules of Juvenile Procedure shall govern all juvenile actions commenced or arrests made on or after 12:00 o'clock midnight August 1, 1996."

The order of the Minnesota Supreme Court [CX-01-926] dated July 18, 2003, provides in part that "(t)he attached amendments shall govern all juveniles taken into custody and all juvenile delinquency actions commenced or children taken into custody after 12 o'clock midnight September 1, 2003."

Rule 21.02. Proceedings in Forma Pauperis

Subdivision 1. Generally. An indigent child wanting to appeal, cross-appeal, or defend an appeal taken by the prosecuting attorney shall make application to the office of the state public defender.

Upon the administrative determination by the state public defender's office that the applicant is financially and otherwise eligible for representation, the state public defender is automatically appointed for that purpose without order of the trial court. Any applicant who contests a decision of the state public defender's office regarding eligibility may apply to the Minnesota Supreme Court for relief.

If the parents of a child are financially able to contribute to some or all of the costs of representation, they may be ordered to pay the State of Minnesota all or a portion of those costs.

Subd. 2. Exception for Juvenile Petty Offenders and Juvenile Traffic Offenders. The state public defender may, in its discretion, agree to represent a juvenile traffic offender or a juvenile petty offender who wants to appeal, cross-appeal, or defend an appeal taken by the prosecuting attorney if, after an administrative determination by the state public defender's office, the child is found financially eligible for representation.

Amended June 26, 1996; Oct. 11, 2007, eff. Jan. 1, 2008.

Comment—Rule 21

See comment following Rule 21.07.

Historical Notes

The order of the Minnesota Supreme Court [C6-84-2165] dated June 26, 1996, provides in part that "(t)hese amendments to the Rules of Juvenile Procedure shall govern all juvenile actions commenced or arrests made on or after 12:00 o'clock midnight August 1, 1996."

Rule 21.03. Appeal by Child

Subdivision 1. Right of Appeal. A child may appeal as of right from an adverse final order and certain non final orders, as enumerated in Rule 21.03, subdivisions 1(A) and (B). In addition, a child shall be permitted to seek a discretionary appeal as provided for in Minnesota Rules of Criminal Procedure 28.02, subdivision 3. A motion for a new trial is not necessary in order to appeal.

(A) *Final Orders.* Final orders include orders for:

(1) certification to adult court, whether the order is entered or stayed pursuant to Rule 21.03, subdivision 3;

(2) continuance without adjudication and disposition in delinquency proceedings;

(3) adjudication and disposition in delinquency proceedings;

(4) adjudication and disposition in juvenile petty or juvenile traffic offender proceedings;

(5) denial of motion for new trial;

(6) extended jurisdiction juvenile prosecution designation, whether the order is entered or stayed pursuant to Rule 21.03, subdivision 3;

(7) conviction, disposition, and sentencing of an extended jurisdiction juvenile;

(8) an order, on the prosecuting attorney's motion, finding the child incompetent, if the underlying offense would be a felony or a gross misdemeanor if the offense were committed by an adult;

(9) an order modifying a disposition;

(10) an order revoking probation including an order adjudicating a child delinquent after the child was granted a continuance without adjudication;

(11) an order revoking extended jurisdiction juvenile status; and

(12) an order revoking the stay of the adult sentence of an extended jurisdiction juvenile.

(B) *Non Final Orders.* A child may appeal from the following non final orders:

(1) an order refusing or imposing conditions of release; and

(2) an order granting a new trial when a child's motion for acquittal is denied, if the underlying offense would be a felony or a gross misdemeanor if the offense were committed by an adult.

Subd. 2. Procedure for Appeals.

(A) *Orders Revoking Extended Jurisdiction Juvenile Status and Orders Revoking the Stayed Adult Sentence of an Extended Jurisdiction Juvenile.* Probationer appeals under Rule 21.03, subdivision 1(A)(11) and (12) shall be governed by the procedure provided for appeal from a sentence by Minnesota Rules of Criminal Procedure 27.04, subdivision 3(4) and 28.05.

(B) *All Other Appealable Orders.* All other juvenile appeals shall proceed as follows:

(1) Time for Taking an Appeal. An appeal shall be taken within thirty (30) days after service of the notice of filing of the appealable order upon the child's counsel by the court administrator as provided in Rule 28.

(2) Notice of Appeal and Filing. The appellant shall file the following documents with the clerk of the appellate courts:

(a) a notice of appeal naming the party taking the appeal, identifying the order being appealed, and listing the names, addresses, and telephone numbers of all counsel;

(b) proof of service of notice of appeal on the adverse party, the district court administrator, and the court reporter;

(c) a certified copy of the judgment or order appealed from; and

(d) two copies of the statement of the case as provided for by Minnesota Rules of Civil Appellate Procedure 133.03.

When the disposition is ordered in a county other than the one in which the child pled guilty or was found to have committed the offense(s), the appellant shall serve notice of appeal on the prosecuting attorney, district court administrator and court reporter in the county where the child pled guilty or was found to have committed the offense(s) as well as the prosecuting attorney, district court administrator and court reporter where the disposition was ordered. Proof of service of notice of appeal on all of these persons shall be filed with the clerk of the appellate courts.

Whether a filing fee is required shall be determined pursuant to Minnesota Rules of Civil Appellate Procedure 103.01, subdivision 3. A cost bond is not required.

Except for the timely filing of the notice of appeal, if a party fails to comply with these rules, the validity of the appeal may not be affected except as deemed appropriate by the court of appeals.

(3) *Transcript of Proceedings and Transmission of the Transcript and Record.* The Minnesota Rules of Civil Appellate Procedure shall govern the transcription of the proceedings and the transmission of the transcript and record to the court of appeals except as modified here:

(a) Within ten (10) days of filing the notice of appeal, appellant shall order the necessary transcript and notify the court reporter that the transcript is due within thirty (30) days of the court reporter's receipt of the appellant's request for transcript.

(b) For parties represented by the state public defender, payment for transcripts will be made after receipt of the transcripts.

(c) If the parties have stipulated to the accuracy of a transcript of videotape or audiotape exhibits and made the transcript part of the district court record, it becomes part of the record on appeal, and it is not necessary for the court reporter to transcribe the exhibits. If no such transcript exists, a transcript need not be prepared unless expressly requested by the appellant or the respondent. If the exhibit must be transcribed, the court reporter need not certify the correctness of this transcript.

(4) *Briefs.* The Minnesota Rules of Civil Appellate Procedure shall govern the form and filing of briefs except as modified here:

(a) Extended Jurisdiction Juvenile and Certification Determinations.

(i) The appellant shall serve and file the appellant's brief and appendix within thirty (30) days after delivery of the transcript by the reporter. If the transcript is obtained prior to appeal or if the record on appeal does not include a transcript, then the appellant shall serve and file the appellant's brief and appendix within thirty (30) days after the filing of the notice of appeal.

(ii) The appellant's brief shall contain a statement of the procedural history.

(iii) The respondent shall serve and file the respondent's brief and appendix, if any, within thirty (30) days after service of the brief of appellant.

(iv) The appellant may serve and file a reply brief within fifteen (15) days after service of the respondent's brief.

(b) Briefs For Cases Other Than Extended Jurisdiction Juvenile and Certification Determinations.

(i) The appellant shall serve and file the appellant's brief and appendix within forty-five (45) days after delivery of the transcript by the reporter. If the transcript is obtained prior to appeal or if the record on appeal does not include a transcript, then the appellant shall serve and file the appellant's brief and appendix within forty-five (45) days after the filing of the notice of appeal.

(ii) The appellant's brief shall contain a statement of the procedural history.

(iii) The respondent shall serve and file the respondent's brief and appendix, if any, within thirty (30) days after service of the brief of appellant.

(iv) The appellant may serve and file a reply brief within fifteen (15) days after service of the respondent's brief.

Subd. 3. Stay Pending Appeal. (A) *Generally.* Pending an appeal, a stay may be granted by the juvenile court or the court of appeals. A motion for stay initially shall be presented to the juvenile court.

In cases certified to adult court, if a stay was granted by the juvenile court, the district court shall stay further adult criminal proceedings pending the filing of a final decision on appeal. By agreement of the parties, the adult case may proceed through the omnibus hearing.

If a stay is granted, conditions of release must be set pursuant to Rule 21.03, subdivision 4(B).

(B) *Placement Pending Appeal.*

(1) Upon Certification. If the district court determines that a certified child should be detained, placement pending appeal shall be governed by Minnesota Rules of Criminal Procedure 6.02, and detention in an adult facility shall be presumed.

(2) Other Cases. If the child is detained, the reasons for the place of detention must be stated on the record, and the detention must comply with Minnesota Statute, section 260B.176.

Subd. 4. Release of Child.

(A) *Motion for Release Pending Appeal.* When release is not addressed in the motion for a stay, application for release pending appeal shall be made to the trial court. If the trial court refuses to release a child pending appeal, or imposes conditions of release, the trial court shall state the reasons on the record. Thereafter, if an appeal is pending, a motion for release or for modification of the conditions of release pending review may be made to the court of appeals. The motion shall be determined upon such papers, affidavits, and portions of the record as the parties shall present. The court of appeals may order the release of a child with or without conditions, pending disposition of the motion. The motion shall be determined on an expedited basis.

(B) *Conditions of Release.* Minnesota Rules of Criminal Procedure 6.02 shall govern conditions of release upon certification. If a stay is granted under Rule 21.03, subdivision 3 of this rule, Minnesota Statutes, section 260B.176 shall govern conditions of release. The child has the burden of proving that the appeal is not frivolous or taken for delay and that the child does not pose a risk for flight, is not likely to commit a serious crime, and is not likely to tamper with witnesses. The trial court shall make written findings on each of the above factors. The trial court shall take into consideration that:

(1) the child may be compelled to serve the sentence or disposition imposed before the appellate court has an opportunity to decide the case; and

(2) the child may be confined for a longer time pending the appeal than would be possible under the potential sentence or disposition for the offense charged.

(C) *Credit for Time Spent in Custody.* The time a child is in custody pending an appeal may be considered by the trial court in determining the disposition imposed in juvenile proceedings.

Amended June 26, 1996; July 18, 2003; July 11, 2005, eff. Sept. 1, 2005; Oct. 13, 2006, eff. Jan. 1, 2007; Oct. 11, 2007, eff. Jan. 1, 2008; Nov. 19, 2010, eff. Jan. 1, 2011.

Comment—Rule 21

See comment following Rule 21.07.

Historical Notes

The order of the Minnesota Supreme Court [C6-84-2165] dated June 26, 1996, provides in part that "(t)hese amendments to the Rules of Juvenile Procedure shall govern all juvenile actions commenced or arrests made on or after 12:00 o'clock midnight August 1, 1996."

The order of the Minnesota Supreme Court [CX-01-926] dated July 18, 2003, provides in part that "(t)he attached amendments shall govern all juveniles taken into custody and all juvenile delinquency actions commenced or children taken into custody after 12 o'clock midnight September 1, 2003."

Rule 21.04. Appeal by Prosecuting Attorney

Subdivision 1. Scope of Appeal. The prosecuting attorney may appeal as of right from:

(A) sentences or dispositions imposed or stayed in extended jurisdiction juvenile cases;

(B) denial of a motion for certification or denial of a motion for designation as an extended jurisdiction juvenile prosecution;

(C) denial of a motion to revoke extended jurisdiction juvenile status following an admission of a violation of probation or a determination that a violation of probation has been proven;

(D) denial of a motion to revoke the stay of the adult sentence of an extended jurisdiction juvenile following an admission of a violation of probation or a determination that a violation of probation has been proven;

(E) pretrial orders, including suppression orders; and

(F) orders dismissing the charging document for lack of probable cause when the dismissal was based solely on a question of law.

Appeals from disposition or sentence shall only include matters that arose after adjudication or conviction. In addition to all powers of review presently existing, the appellate court may review the sentence or disposition to determine whether it is consistent with the standards set forth in Rule 15.05, subdivisions 2 and 3.

Subd. 2. Attorney Fees. The child shall be allowed reasonable attorney fees and costs incurred for appeal. The child's attorney fees and costs shall be paid by the governmental unit responsible for prosecution of the case.

Subd. 3. Procedure for Appeals.

(A) Prosecutorial appeals under Rule 21.04, subdivision 1(A), (B), and (F) shall be governed by Rule 21.03, subdivision 2.

(B) Prosecutorial appeals under Rule 21.04, subdivision 1(C) and (D) shall be governed by the procedure provided for appeal from a sentence by Minnesota Rules of Criminal Procedure 27.04, subdivision 3(4) and 28.05.

(C) Prosecutorial appeals under Rule 21.04, subdivision 1(E) shall proceed as follows:

(1) Time for Appeal. The prosecuting attorney may not appeal until all issues raised during the evidentiary hearing and pretrial conference have been determined by the trial court. The appeal shall be taken within twenty (20) days after notice of entry of the appealable order is served upon the prosecuting attorney by the district court administrator. An appeal by the prosecuting attorney under this rule bars any further appeal by the prosecuting attorney from any existing orders not included in the appeal. No appeal of a pretrial order by the prosecuting attorney shall be taken after jeopardy has attached. An appeal under this rule does not deprive the trial court of jurisdiction over pending matters not included in the appeal.

(2) Notice of Appeal and Filing. Rule 21.03, subdivision 2(B) shall govern notice of appeal and filing of an appeal by the prosecuting attorney except that the prosecuting attorney must file a statement of the case as provided for by Minnesota Rules of Civil Appellate Procedure 133.03. In addition, if a transcript of the proceedings is necessary, the prosecuting attorney must file a copy of the request for transcript with the clerk of the appellate court.

(3) *Briefs.* The Minnesota Rules of Civil Appellate Procedure shall govern the form and filing of briefs except as modified here:

(a) Within fifteen (15) days of delivery of the transcripts, appellant shall file the appellant's brief with the clerk of the appellate courts together with proof of service upon the respondent.

(b) The appellant's brief shall contain a statement of the procedural history.

(c) Within eight (8) days of service of appellant's brief upon respondent, the respondent shall file the respondent's brief with the appellate court clerk together with proof of service upon the appellant.

Subd. 4. Stay. Upon oral notice that the prosecuting attorney intends to appeal a pretrial order, the trial court shall order a stay of the proceedings for twenty (20) days to allow time to perfect the appeal.

Subd. 5. Conditions of Release. Upon appeal by the prosecuting attorney of a pretrial order, the conditions for the child's release pending the appeal shall be governed by Rule 5 or, for children certified to adult court, Minnesota Rules of Criminal Procedure 6.02, subdivisions 1 and 2. The trial court shall consider whether the child may be confined for a longer time pending the appeal than would be possible under the potential sentence or disposition for the offense charged.

Subd. 6. Cross–Appeal by Child. Upon appeal by the prosecuting attorney, the child may obtain review of any pretrial order which will adversely affect the child by filing a notice of cross-appeal with the clerk of the appellate courts and the trial court administrator together with proof of service on the prosecuting attorney. The notice of cross-appeal shall be filed within ten (10) days after service of notice of the appeal by the prosecuting attorney. Failure to serve the notice does not deprive the court of appeals of jurisdiction over a child's cross-appeal but is ground for such action as the court of appeals deems appropriate, including dismissal of the cross-appeal.

Adopted June 26, 1996. Amended July 18, 2003; July 11, 2005, eff. Sept. 1, 2005; Oct. 13, 2006, eff. Jan. 1, 2007; Oct. 11, 2007, eff. Jan. 1, 2008; Nov. 19, 2010, eff. Jan. 1, 2011.

Comment—Rule 21

See comment following Rule 21.07.

Historical Notes

The order of the Minnesota Supreme Court [C6-84-2165] dated June 26, 1996, provides in part that "(t)hese amendments to the Rules of Juvenile Procedure shall govern all juvenile actions commenced or arrests made on or after 12:00 o'clock midnight August 1, 1996."

The order of the Minnesota Supreme Court [CX–01–926] dated July 18, 2003, provides in part that "(t)he attached amendments shall govern all juveniles taken into custody and all juvenile delinquency actions commenced or children taken into custody after 12 o'clock midnight September 1, 2003."

Rule 21.05. Appeal by Parent(s), Legal Guardian or Legal Custodian of the Child

A parent, legal guardian, or legal custodian who participated separately pursuant to Rule 2.04, subdivision 3 may appeal from a disposition.

A parent, legal guardian, or legal custodian who is indigent may apply to the office of the state public defender for legal representation.

Parents' right to appeal is limited to cases where they have a liberty or property interest involved and their interest is adverse to that of the child.

The procedure for appeals by a parent, legal guardian, or legal custodian shall be governed by Rule 21.03, subdivision 2.

Adopted June 26, 1996. Amended July 18, 2003.

Comment—Rule 21

See comment following Rule 21.07.

Historical Notes

The order of the Minnesota Supreme Court [C6-84-2165] dated June 26, 1996, provides in part that "(t)hese amendments to the Rules of Juvenile Procedure shall govern all juvenile actions commenced or arrests made on or after 12:00 o'clock midnight August 1, 1996."

The order of the Minnesota Supreme Court [CX–01–926] dated July 18, 2003, provides in part that "(t)he attached amendments shall govern all juveniles taken into custody and all juvenile delinquency actions commenced or children taken into custody after 12 o'clock midnight September 1, 2003."

Rule 21.06. Certified Questions to the Court of Appeals

After adjudication or sentencing, or before hearing on a motion to dismiss, the trial court may report any question of law which is important and doubtful to the court of appeals, if the child requests or consents. Upon report of the question all further district court proceedings shall be stayed. Other cases pending in the trial court which involve or depend on the same question shall also be stayed if a stay is requested or consented to by the juvenile involved.

The aggrieved party shall file a brief with the court of appeals and serve it on all parties within fifteen (15) days of the trial court's report of the question. Other parties shall have eight (8) days to file responsive briefs. The court of appeals shall expedite its decision on certified questions.

Adopted June 26, 1996.

Historical Notes

The order of the Minnesota Supreme Court [C6-84-2165] dated June 26, 1996, provides in part that "(t)hese amendments to the Rules of Juvenile Procedure shall govern all juvenile actions commenced or arrests made on or after 12:00 o'clock midnight August 1, 1996."

Rule 21.07. Time for Issuance of Decision

All decisions regarding appeals of certification determinations pursuant to Rule 18.07 or extended jurisdiction juvenile determinations pursuant to Rule 19.07 shall be issued within sixty (60) days of the date the case is deemed submitted pursuant to the Rules of Civil Appellate Procedure. The court of appeals shall issue its decision in all other appeals within ninety (90) days of the date the case is deemed submitted pursuant to the Rules of Civil Appellate Procedure.

Adopted July 11, 2005, eff. Sept. 1, 2005.

Comment—Rule 21

An appeal may be taken by petitioning the Supreme Court of Minnesota for review pursuant to Minn R. Civ. App. P. 117 or by petitioning for accelerated review pursuant to Minn. R. Civ. App. P. 118.

The scope of review shall be pursuant to Minn. R. Civ. App. P. 103.04.

Minn. R. Juv. Del. P. 21.03, subd. 1(A) (7) and (10) includes the right to appeal a stayed sentence and the execution of a stayed sentence. See Minn. R. Crim. P. 27.04, subd. 3(4) and 28.05, subd. 2. An order continuing the matter without adjudication and imposing a disposition pursuant to Minnesota Statutes, section 260B.198, subds. 1(a) or (b)(2002) is an appealable final order as is a subsequent order adjudicating the child and imposing a disposition pursuant to Minnesota Statutes, section 260B.198, subd. 1 (2002).

A child's representation by the public defender is governed by Minnesota Statutes, chapter 611. The public defender is not required to appeal from misdemeanor dispositions or adjudications, but may do so at its discretion.

The parents or the child may be required to contribute to some or all of the costs of representation. See Minn. R. Juv. Del. P. 3.06, subd. 2. See also Minnesota Statutes, section 260B.331, subd. 5 (2002).

Minn. R. Juv. Del. P. 21.03, subd. 2(C)(1) refers to "necessary transcripts" because in some cases only a partial transcript will be required. Minn. R. Civ. App. P. 110.02 shall govern partial transcripts.

Whether or not the order for certification should be stayed is discretionary with the court. Certification orders are governed by Minn. R. Juv. Del. P. 18.07. If a stay is granted, the child will be detained in a juvenile facility if detention is necessary. If the stay of the certification order is not granted and detention is necessary, the child will more likely be detained in an adult facility pending the appeal.

Minn. R. Juv. Del. P. 21.04, subd. 1(D), which allows prosecutors to appeal orders dismissing a charging document for lack of probable cause when dismissed solely on a question of law, is based on *In re Welfare of C.P.W.*, 601 N.W.2d 204, 207 (Minn. Ct. App. 1999).

RULE 22. SUBSTITUTION OF JUDGE

Rule 22.01. Before or During Trial

If by reason of death, sickness or other disability, the judge before whom pretrial proceedings or a jury trial has commenced is unable to proceed, any other judge sitting in or assigned to the court, upon certification of familiarity with the record of the proceedings or trial, may proceed with and finish the proceedings or trial.

Amended June 26, 1996.

Comment—Rule 22

See comment following Rule 22.04.

Historical Notes

The order of the Minnesota Supreme Court [C6-84-2165] dated June 26, 1996, provides in part that "(t)hese amendments to the Rules of Juvenile Procedure shall govern all juvenile actions commenced or arrests made on or after 12:00 o'clock midnight August 1, 1996."

Rule 22.02. After Verdict or Finding of Guilt

If by reason of absence, death, sickness, or other disability, the judge before whom the child has been tried is unable to perform the duties to be performed by the court after a verdict or finding of guilt, any other judge sitting in or assigned to the court may perform those duties; but if such other judge is satisfied that those duties cannot be performed because of not presiding at the trial, such judge may grant a new trial.

Amended June 26, 1996.

Comment—Rule 22

See comment following Rule 22.04.

Historical Notes

The order of the Minnesota Supreme Court [C6-84-2165] dated June 26, 1996, provides in part that "(t)hese amendments to the Rules of Juvenile Procedure shall govern all juvenile actions commenced or arrests made on or after 12:00 o'clock midnight August 1, 1996."

Rule 22.03. Notice to Remove

Subdivision 1. Service and Filing. The child's counsel or the prosecuting attorney may serve on the other parties and file with the court administrator a notice to remove the judge assigned to a trial or hearing. The notice shall be served and filed within seven (7) days after the child's counsel or the prosecuting attorney receives written notice, or oral notice in court on the record, of which judge is to preside at the trial or hearing but, in any event, not later than the commencement of the trial or the hearing.

Subd. 2. Removal of Presiding Judge. No notice shall be effective against a judge who has already presided at the trial, probable cause hearing, or other evidentiary hearing of which the party had notice, except where a party shows cause why a judge should be removed. After a party has once disqualified a presiding judge as a matter of right, that party may disqualify the substitute judge only upon an affirmative showing of cause.

Amended June 26, 1996; July 18, 2003; April 23, 2004.

Comment—Rule 22

See comment following Rule 22.04.

Historical Notes

The order of the Minnesota Supreme Court [C6-84-2165] dated June 26, 1996, provides in part that "(t)hese amendments to the Rules of Juvenile Procedure shall govern all juvenile actions commenced or arrests made on or after 12:00 o'clock midnight August 1, 1996."

The order of the Minnesota Supreme Court [CX-01-926] dated July 18, 2003, provides in part that "(t)he attached amendments shall govern all juveniles taken into custody and all juvenile delinquency actions commenced or children taken into custody after 12 o'clock midnight September 1, 2003."

The order of the Minnesota Supreme Court [CX-01-926] dated April 23, 2004, provides in part that "(t)he attached amendments shall govern all juvenile delinquency actions commenced or children taken into custody after 12 o'clock midnight July 1, 2004."

Rule 22.04. Assignment of New Judge

Upon the removal, disqualification, disability, recusal or unavailability of a judge under this rule, the chief judge of the judicial district shall assign any other judge within the district to hear the matter. If there is no other judge of the district who is qualified to hear the matter, the chief judge of the district shall notify the chief justice. The chief justice shall then assign a judge of another district to preside over the matter.

Amended June 26, 1996.

Comment—Rule 22

This rule is modeled after Minn. R. Crim. P. 26.03, subd. 14. The rule permits the child's counsel or prosecuting attorney to serve and file a notice to remove a judge as a matter of right without cause. Only one such removal as a matter of right is permitted to a party. Other removals must be for cause.

The right to a fair trial before an impartial tribunal is a fundamental due process requirement. *See, e.g., Estes v. Texas,* 381 U.S. 532, 85 S.Ct. 1628, 14 L.Ed.2d 543 (1965). The Supreme Court in *In re Murchison,* 349 U.S. 133, 75 S.Ct. 623 (1955), explained the importance of an impartial tribunal: "Fairness of course requires an absence of actual bias in the trial of cases. But our system of law has always endeavored to prevent even the probability of unfairness ... [T]o perform its high function in the best way, 'justice must satisfy the appearance of justice.'" 349 U.S. at 136 *citing Offutt v. United States,* 348 U.S. 11, 14, 75 S.Ct. 11, 13 (1954). Moreover, the fact finder must make a determination based only on the evidence in the record in order to ensure effective appellate review. *See, e.g., Patterson v. Colorado,* 205 U.S. 454 (1907).

The appearance, if not the actuality, of neutral and unbiased fact-finding may be compromised if the judge has actual knowledge of the social history or prior court history of the child. *See, e.g., In re Gladys R.,* 1 Cal.3d 855, 464 P.2d 127, 83 Cal.Rptr. 671 (1970) (reversible error for juvenile court to review social study report before jurisdictional hearing). The problem is especially acute in delinquency proceedings because juveniles, with the exception of extended jurisdiction juveniles, do not have the right to a jury trial. *McKeiver v. Pennsylvania,* 403 U.S. 528, 91 S.Ct. 1976, 29 L.Ed. 647 (1970). Whenever a judge knows information that is not admissible at trial but is prejudicial to a child, the impartiality of the tribunal is open to question. *A.B.A. Juvenile Justice Standards Relating to Adjudication, Standard 4.1* at 54. The problem of impartiality is particularly troublesome in juvenile court proceedings because the same judge typically handles the same case at different stages. For example, at a detention hearing, a judge may be exposed to a youth's social history file and prior record of police contacts and delinquency adjudications, all of which bear on the issue of appropriate pretrial placement. When the same judge is subsequently called upon to determine the admissibility of evidence in a suppression hearing and the guilt of the juvenile in the same proceeding, the juvenile's basic right to a fair trial by an impartial tribunal with a determination of guilt based on admissible evidence may be compromised. *E.g., In re Welfare of J.P.L.,* 359 N.W.2d 622 (Minn.Ct.App.1984).

References in this rule to "child's counsel" includes the child who is proceeding pro se. Minn. R. Juv. Del. P. 1.01.

Historical Notes

The order of the Minnesota Supreme Court [C6-84-2165] dated June 26, 1996, provides in part that "(t)hese amendments to the Rules of Juvenile Procedure shall govern all juvenile actions commenced or arrests made on or after 12:00 o'clock midnight August 1, 1996."

Rule 22.05. Deleted June 26, 1996

Historical Notes

The order of the Minnesota Supreme Court [C6-84-2165] dated June 26, 1996, provides in part that "(t)hese amendments to the Rules of Juvenile Procedure shall govern all juvenile actions commenced or arrests made on or after 12:00 o'clock midnight August 1, 1996."

RULE 23. REFEREE

Rule 23.01. Authorization to Hear Cases

A referee may hear matters as authorized by statute.

Amended June 26, 1996.

Comment—Rule 23

See comment following Rule 23.06.

Historical Notes

The order of the Minnesota Supreme Court [C6-84-2165] dated June 26, 1996, provides in part that "(t)hese amendments to the Rules of Juvenile Procedure shall govern all juvenile actions commenced or arrests made on or after 12:00 o'clock midnight August 1, 1996."

Rule 23.02. Objection to Assignment of Referee

The child's counsel or the prosecuting attorney may object to a referee presiding at a hearing. This objection shall be in writing and filed with the court within three (3) days after being informed that the matter is to be heard by a referee or the right to object is waived. The court may permit the filing of a written objection at any time. After the filing of an objection, a judge shall hear any motion and preside at any hearing.

Amended June 26, 1996; April 23, 2004.

Comment—Rule 23

See comment following Rule 23.06.

Historical Notes

The order of the Minnesota Supreme Court [C6-84-2165] dated June 26, 1996, provides in part that "(t)hese amendments to the Rules of Juvenile Procedure shall govern all juvenile actions commenced or arrests made on or after 12:00 o'clock midnight August 1, 1996."

The order of the Minnesota Supreme Court [CX-01-926] dated April 23, 2004, provides in part that "(t)he attached amendments shall govern all juvenile delinquency actions commenced or children taken into custody after 12 o'clock midnight July 1, 2004."

Rule 23.03. Notice to Remove a Particular Referee

The child's counsel or the prosecuting attorney may serve on the other party and file with the court administrator a notice to remove a particular referee assigned to a trial or hearing in the same manner as a judge may be removed under Rule 22. After a party has once disqualified a referee as a matter of right, that party may disqualify the substitute judge or referee only upon an affirmative showing of cause.

Amended June 26, 1996; July 18, 2003.

Comment—Rule 23

See comment following Rule 23.06.

Historical Notes

The order of the Minnesota Supreme Court [C6-84-2165] dated June 26, 1996, provides in part that "(t)hese amendments to the Rules of Juvenile Procedure shall govern all juvenile actions commenced or arrests made on or after 12:00 o'clock midnight August 1, 1996."

The order of the Minnesota Supreme Court [CX-01-926] dated July 18, 2003, provides in part that "(t)he attached amendments shall govern all juveniles taken into custody and all juvenile delinquency actions commenced or children taken into custody after 12 o'clock midnight September 1, 2003."

Rule 23.04. Transmittal of Findings

Upon the conclusion of a hearing, the referee shall transmit to the judge findings and recommendations in writing. Notice of the findings of the referee together with a statement relative to the right to a review before a judge shall be given either orally on the record, or in writing to the child, the child's counsel, the child's parent(s), legal guardian or legal custodian and their counsel, the prosecuting attorney and to any other person that the court may direct.

Amended June 26, 1996.

Comment—Rule 23

See comment following Rule 23.06.

Historical Notes

The order of the Minnesota Supreme Court [C6-84-2165] dated June 26, 1996, provides in part that "(t)hese amendments to the Rules of Juvenile Procedure shall govern all juvenile actions commenced or arrests made on or after 12:00 o'clock midnight August 1, 1996."

Rule 23.05. Review

Subdivision 1. Generally. A matter which has been decided by a referee may be reviewed in whole or in part by a judge.

Subd. 2. Filing. A motion for a review by a judge must be filed with the court within ten (10) days after the referee's findings and recommendations have been provided to the child, child's counsel, prosecuting attorney, child's parents, legal guardian or legal custodian and their counsel pursuant to Rule 28.

Subd. 3. Right of Review Upon Filing of Timely Motion.

(A) *Right of Child.* The child is entitled to a review by a judge in any matter upon which a referee has made findings or recommendations.

(B) *Right of Prosecuting Attorney.* The prosecuting attorney is entitled to a review by a judge from any pre-trial findings or recommendations of a referee. The prosecuting attorney is not entitled to a review on any pretrial findings by a judge after jeopardy has attached.

(C) *Right of Parent(s), Legal Guardian or Legal Custodian.* The child's parent(s), legal guardian or legal custodian are entitled to a review by a judge of a referee's findings or recommendations made after the allegations of a charging document have been proved.

Subd. 4. The Court. The judge may grant a review at any time before confirming the findings and recommendation of the referee.

Subd. 5. Procedure. A review by a judge may be of the verbatim record or de novo in whole or in part.

Adopted June 26, 1996. Amended July 18, 2003.

Comment—Rule 23

See comment following Rule 23.06.

Historical Notes

The order of the Minnesota Supreme Court [C6-84-2165] dated June 26, 1996, provides in part that "(t)hese amendments to the Rules of Juvenile Procedure shall govern all juvenile actions commenced or arrests made on or after 12:00 o'clock midnight August 1, 1996."

The order of the Minnesota Supreme Court [CX-01-926] dated July 18, 2003, provides in part that "(t)he attached amendments shall govern all juveniles taken into custody and all juvenile delinquency actions commenced or children taken into custody after 12 o'clock midnight September 1, 2003."

Rule 23.06. Order of the Court

The findings and recommendations of the referee become the order of the court when confirmed by the judge subject to review pursuant to Rule 23.05.

Adopted June 26, 1996. Amended July 18, 2003.

Comment—Rule 23

References in this rule to "child's counsel" include the child who is proceeding pro se. Minn. R. Juv. Del. P. 1.01.

Historical Notes

The order of the Minnesota Supreme Court [C6-84-2165] dated June 26, 1996, provides in part that "(t)hese amendments to the Rules of Juvenile Procedure shall govern all juvenile actions commenced or arrests made on or after 12:00 o'clock midnight August 1, 1996."

The order of the Minnesota Supreme Court [CX-01-926] dated July 18, 2003, provides in part that "(t)he attached amendments shall govern all juveniles taken into custody and all juvenile delinquency actions commenced or children taken into custody after 12 o'clock midnight September 1, 2003."

RULE 24. GUARDIAN AD LITEM

Rule 24.01. Appointment

(A) Except as provided in Rule 24.01 (B), the court shall appoint a guardian ad litem, to act in place of a parent, legal guardian or legal custodian to protect the best interest of the child when it appears, at any stage of the proceedings, that the child is without a parent, legal guardian or legal custodian. If the parent, legal guardian or legal custodian is unavailable, incompetent, indifferent to, hostile to, or has interests in conflict with the child's best interests, a guardian ad litem shall be appointed.

(B) The court may determine not to appoint a guardian ad litem when:

(1) counsel has been appointed or is otherwise retained for the child, and

(2) the court finds that the best interests of the child are otherwise protected.

(C) The court may appoint a guardian ad litem on its own motion or on the motion of the child's counsel or the prosecuting attorney when the court determines that an appointment is in the best interests of the child.

Amended June 26, 1996; July 18, 2003; Sept. 30, 2004, eff. Jan. 1, 2005.

Historical Notes

The order of the Minnesota Supreme Court [C6-84-2165] dated June 26, 1996, provides in part that "(t)hese amendments to the Rules of Juvenile Procedure shall govern all juvenile actions commenced or arrests made on or after 12:00 o'clock midnight August 1, 1996."

The order of the Minnesota Supreme Court [CX-01-926] dated July 18, 2003, provides in part that "(t)he attached amendments shall govern all juveniles taken into custody and all juvenile delinquency actions commenced or children taken into custody after 12 o'clock midnight September 1, 2003."

Rule 24.02. General Responsibilities of Guardians Ad Litem

In every juvenile delinquency court case in which a guardian ad litem is appointed, the guardian ad litem shall:

(1) conduct an independent investigation to determine the facts relevant to the situation of the child and the family, which must include, unless specifically excluded by the court: reviewing relevant documents; meeting with and observing the child in the home setting and considering the child's wishes, as appropriate; and interviewing parents, caregivers, and others relevant to the case;

(2) advocate for the child's best interests by participating in appropriate aspects of the case and advocating for appropriate community services when necessary;

(3) maintain the confidentiality of information related to a case, with the exception of sharing information as permitted by law to promote cooperative solutions that are in the best interests of the child;

(4) monitor the child's best interests throughout the judicial proceeding; and

(5) present written reports on the child's best interests that include conclusions and recommendations and the facts upon which they are based.

Adopted Sept. 30, 2004, eff. Jan. 1, 2005.

Rule 24.03. Guardian ad Litem not Counsel for Child

When the court appoints a guardian ad litem, the guardian ad litem shall not be the child's counsel.

Amended June 26, 1996; Sept. 30, 2004, eff. Jan. 1, 2005.

Historical Notes

The order of the Minnesota Supreme Court [C6-84-2165] dated June 26, 1996, provides in part that "(t)hese amendments to the Rules of Juvenile Procedure shall govern all juvenile actions commenced or arrests made on or after 12:00 o'clock midnight August 1, 1996."

Rule 24.04. Deleted June 26, 1996

Historical Notes

The order of the Minnesota Supreme Court [C6-84-2165] dated June 26, 1996, provides in part that "(t)hese amendments to the Rules

of Juvenile Procedure shall govern all juvenile actions commenced or arrests made on or after 12:00 o'clock midnight August 1, 1996."

RULE 25. NOTICE

Rule 25.01. Summons, Notice in Lieu of Summons, Oral Notice on the Record, Service by Facsimile or Other Electronic Transmission and Notice by Telephone

Subd. 1. Summons. A summons is a document personally served on a person directing that person to appear before the court at a specified time and place. If the person summoned fails to appear, the court may issue an arrest warrant or, for the child, a warrant for immediate custody.

Subd. 2. Notice in Lieu of Summons. A notice in lieu of summons is a document mailed by the court administrator to a person who is directed to appear in court at a specified time and place. If a person appears pursuant to the mailed notice, the person waives the right to personal service of the summons. If the person fails to appear, the court shall not issue a warrant until personal service is made or attempted unless grounds exist under Rule 4.03.

Subd. 3. Oral Notice on the Record. The court may schedule further proceedings by oral notice to all persons present. Oral notice on the record shall be sufficient notice to all persons present. Any person not present who is entitled to notice, shall receive written notice.

Subd. 4. Detention Hearings: Service by Facsimile or Other Electronic Transmission or Notice by Telephone Permitted.

(A) *Service By Facsimile or Other Electronic Transmission.*

(1) Notice to Defense Counsel; Defense Counsel Access to Child and Reports. If a child is detained pending a detention hearing in a place of detention other than home detention or at home on electronic home monitoring, the court administrator shall give the Office of the Public Defender or the child's attorney, if privately retained, notice that the child is in custody, and notice of the detention hearing. The court administrator shall also provide to the Office of the Public Defender or the child's attorney copies of the reports filed with the court by the detaining officer and the supervisor of the place of detention. Defense counsel shall have immediate and continuing access to the child. The notice in lieu of summons and copies of the reports may be provided by facsimile transmission or hand delivery if mailed notice would not be effective given the time remaining before the detention hearing.

(2) Notice to Prosecuting Attorney. If mailed notice in lieu of summons would not be effective given the time remaining before the detention hearing, notice in lieu of summons may be provided by facsimile transmission or hand delivery.

(3) Notice to Defense Counsel and the Prosecuting Attorney may also be provided by electronic means if authorized by Minnesota Supreme Court Order and if notice is provided in accordance with that order.

(B) *Notice By Telephone.* If the child, child's attorney, prosecuting attorney, child's parent(s), legal guardian(s) or legal custodian(s) or spouse of the child has not received notice of the time and place of the detention hearing and effective service by mail or facsimile transmission or hand delivery of the notice in lieu of summons is not possible, the court administrator may provide notice of the time and place of the detention hearing by telephone call.

Amended June 26, 1996; July 18, 2003; Oct. 15, 2012, eff. Dec. 1, 2012.

Comment—Rule 25

See comment following Rule 25.04.

Historical Notes

The order of the Minnesota Supreme Court [C6-84-2165] dated June 26, 1996, provides in part that "(t)hese amendments to the Rules of Juvenile Procedure shall govern all juvenile actions commenced or arrests made on or after 12:00 o'clock midnight August 1, 1996."

The order of the Minnesota Supreme Court [CX-01-926] dated July 18, 2003, provides in part that "(t)he attached amendments shall govern all juveniles taken into custody and all juvenile delinquency actions commenced or children taken into custody after 12 o'clock midnight September 1, 2003."

The order of the Minnesota Supreme Court [ADM10-8003] dated October 15, 2012, provides in part that the "amendments shall govern all delinquency actions pending or commenced on or after 12 o'clock midnight December 1, 2012."

Rule 25.02. Content

Any summons or notice in lieu of summons shall include:

(A) a copy of the charging document, court order, motion, affidavit or other legal documents, filed with the court which require a court appearance;

(B) a statement of the time and place of the hearing;

(C) a brief statement describing the purpose of the hearing;

(D) a brief statement of rights of the child and parents;

(E) notice to the child and parent that a failure to appear in court could result in a warrant; and

(F) such other matters as the court may direct.

Amended June 26, 1996; July 11, 2005, eff. Sept. 1, 2005.

Comment—Rule 25

See comment following Rule 25.04.

Historical Notes

The order of the Minnesota Supreme Court [C6-84-2165] dated June 26, 1996, provides in part that "(t)hese amendments to the Rules

of Juvenile Procedure shall govern all juvenile actions commenced or arrests made on or after 12:00 o'clock midnight August 1, 1996."

Rule 25.03. Procedure for Notification

Subdivision 1. First Notice by Mail. After a charging document has been filed, the court administrator shall schedule a hearing as required by these rules. A notice in lieu of summons shall be served by first class mail on the following:

(A) child and parent(s) or person(s) with custody of the child; and

(B) child's counsel, prosecuting attorney, spouse of child and their counsel.

The court may waive notice to the parent(s), legal guardian, legal custodian, or spouse of the child if it would be in the child's best interest to proceed without their presence. Notice may also be served by electronic means if authorized by Minnesota Supreme Court Order and if notice is served in accordance with that order.

Subd. 2. Personal Service. If the child and/or parent(s) fail to appear in response to one or more notices in lieu of summons served by mail, a summons may be served personally in the manner provided by Minnesota law. The summons shall advise the person served that a failure to appear may result in the court issuing a warrant for arrest.

Subd. 3. Warrant for Arrest or Immediate Custody. A warrant for arrest or immediate custody may be issued by the court for a child or parent(s) who fail to appear in response to a summons which has been personally served or where reasonable efforts at personal service have been made.

Subd. 4. Timing. A summons shall be personally served at least five (5) days before the hearing. A notice in lieu of summons shall be mailed at least eight (8) days before the hearing. These times may be waived by a person or by the court for good cause shown.

Subd. 5. Proof of Service.

(A) *Personal Service.* On or before the date set for appearance, the person who served a summons by personal service shall file a written statement with the court showing:

(1) that the summons was served;

(2) the person on whom the summons was served; and

(3) the date, time, and place of service.

(B) *Service by Mail.* On or before the date set for appearance, the person who served notice in lieu of summons by mail shall file a written statement with the court showing:

(1) the name of the person to whom the summons or notice was mailed;

(2) the date the summons or notice was mailed; and

(3) whether the summons or notice was sent by certified mail.

(C) *Notice of Detention Hearing: Service by Facsimile Transmission.* The person providing notice of a detention hearing by facsimile transmission shall file a written statement with the court showing:

(1) the name, address and facsimile number of the person to whom the notice was sent by facsimile transmission;

(2) the time and date the facsimile transmission was sent or the efforts to do so; and

(3) the reason why notice was not sent by First Class Mail.

(D) *Notice of Detention Hearing: Telephone Call.* The person providing notice of a detention hearing by telephone call shall file a written statement with the court showing:

(1) the name, address and telephone number of the person who was contacted with notice of the detention hearing;

(2) the date and time of the telephone call or the efforts to do so; and

(3) the reason why notice in lieu of summons was not sent by First Class Mail and, in the case of the child's attorney or the prosecuting attorney, why the notice in lieu of summons was not sent by facsimile transmission.

Adopted June 26, 1996. Amended July 18, 2003; Oct. 15, 2012, eff. Dec. 1, 2012.

Comment—Rule 25

See comment following Rule 25.04.

Historical Notes

The order of the Minnesota Supreme Court [C6-84-2165] dated June 26, 1996, provides in part that "(t)hese amendments to the Rules of Juvenile Procedure shall govern all juvenile actions commenced or arrests made on or after 12:00 o'clock midnight August 1, 1996."

The order of the Minnesota Supreme Court [CX-01-926] dated July 18, 2003, provides in part that "(t)he attached amendments shall govern all juveniles taken into custody and all juvenile delinquency actions commenced or children taken into custody after 12 o'clock midnight September 1, 2003."

The order of the Minnesota Supreme Court [ADM10-8003] dated October 15, 2012, provides in part that the "amendments shall govern all delinquency actions pending or commenced on or after 12 o'clock midnight December 1, 2012."

Rule 25.04. Waiver

Service is waived by voluntary appearance in court or by a written waiver of service filed with the court.

Adopted June 26, 1996.

Comment—Rule 25

Pursuant to Minnesota Statutes, section 260.141, subd. 1 (1994), notices of juvenile court proceedings were to be made by personal service or if made pursuant to Minn. R. Civ. P. 4.02, by mail with an acknowledgement returned to the court. That was not the practice throughout the state. This rule is written to reflect the common practice of simply mailing the notice (called a notice in lieu of summons) and charging document by first class mail. If those served do not appear in response to the notice, the court can proceed with personal service of a summons and follow up with a warrant if there is still a failure to appear. Appearance rates are generally high with just a mailed notice and the costs of process are significantly increased by mailed service with acknowledgement or by personal service. The legislature has since amended Minnesota Statutes, section 260.141, subd. 1 to comport with this rule. 1996 Minn. Laws Ch. 408, Art, 6, Secs. 3 and 12; see Minn. Stat. sec. 260B.152, subd. 1 (2002).

This rule allows for notice of a detention hearing to be provided by facsimile transmission or telephone call when, given the time remaining before the detention hearing, mailed notice in lieu of summons would not be effective. Notice by facsimile transmission or telephone is not permitted for any other type of hearing.

Historically, there have been some informal service methods for service of the prosecuting attorney and the public defender by each other and by the court, which were instituted for efficiency and cost-effectiveness. However, where the rules require a specific method of service, these informal methods of service may not be used. See City of Albert Lea v. Harrer, 381 N.W.2d 499 (Minn. Ct. App. 1986) (stating "[t]he clerk and the city attorney cannot agree to ignore the rules").

In the appendix of these rules are samples of a notice in lieu of summons and a summons.

The amendments to Rule 25 that allow for service on counsel by electronic means if authorized by an order of the Minnesota Supreme Court are intended to facilitate a pilot project on electronic service and filing in certain pilot districts, and are designed to be a model for the implementation of electronic filing and service if the pilot project is made permanent and statewide. The rule makes service by electronic means effective in accordance with the rule for the pilot project. Personal service or service by mail on the child and others of documents such as summonses, subpoenas and warrants is still required under the rules that govern those documents, and electronic service is not an authorized means of service.

Historical Notes

The order of the Minnesota Supreme Court [C6-84-2165] dated June 26, 1996, provides in part that "(t)hese amendments to the Rules of Juvenile Procedure shall govern all juvenile actions commenced or arrests made on or after 12:00 o'clock midnight August 1, 1996."

RULE 26. SUBPOENAS

Rule 26.01. Motion or Request for Subpoenas

On the court's own motion or at the request of the child's counsel or the prosecuting attorney, the clerk shall issue subpoenas requiring the attendance and testimony of witnesses and the production of records, documents or other tangible objects at any hearing.

Counsel for the parent(s), legal guardian and legal custodian of the child have the right to request the issuance of subpoenas requiring the attendance and testimony of witnesses and the production of records, documents or other tangible objects at any hearing after the allegations of the charging document have been proved.

Amended June 26, 1996.

Comment—Rule 26

See comment following Rule 26.02.

Historical Notes

The order of the Minnesota Supreme Court [C6-84-2165] dated June 26, 1996, provides in part that "(t)hese amendments to the Rules of Juvenile Procedure shall govern all juvenile actions commenced or arrests made on or after 12:00 o'clock midnight August 1, 1996."

Rule 26.02. Expense

The fees and mileage of witnesses shall be paid at public expense if the subpoena is issued by the court on its own motion or at the request of the prosecuting attorney.

If a subpoena is issued at the request of the child's counsel or counsel for the parent(s), legal guardian, or legal custodian, and the child or parent(s) of the child are unable to pay the fees and mileage of witnesses, these costs shall be paid at public expense, upon approval by the court, in whole or in part, depending on the ability of the child and the parent(s) of the child to pay. All other fees shall be paid by the requesting person unless otherwise ordered by the court.

Amended June 26, 1996.

Comment—Rule 26

References in this rule to "child's counsel" includes the child who is proceeding pro se. Minn. R. Juv. Del. P. 1.01.

Reference in this rule to "counsel for the parent(s), legal guardian, or legal custodian" includes the parent, legal guardian, or legal custodian who is proceeding pro se. Minn. R. Juv. Del. P. 1.01.

Historical Notes

The order of the Minnesota Supreme Court [C6-84-2165] dated June 26, 1996, provides in part that "(t)hese amendments to the Rules of Juvenile Procedure shall govern all juvenile actions commenced or arrests made on or after 12:00 o'clock midnight August 1, 1996."

Rule 26.03. Deleted June 26, 1996

Historical Notes

The order of the Minnesota Supreme Court [C6-84-2165] dated June 26, 1996, provides in part that "(t)hese amendments to the Rules of Juvenile Procedure shall govern all juvenile actions commenced or arrests made on or after 12:00 o'clock midnight August 1, 1996."

RULE 27. MOTIONS

Rule 27.01. Motions to be Signed

Every motion shall be in writing, state with particularity the grounds, be signed by the person making the motion and filed with the court unless it is made in court and on the record.

Amended June 26, 1996.

Comment—Rule 27

See comment following Rule 27.02.

Historical Notes

The order of the Minnesota Supreme Court [C6-84-2165] dated June 26, 1996, provides in part that "(t)hese amendments to the Rules of Juvenile Procedure shall govern all juvenile actions commenced or arrests made on or after 12:00 o'clock midnight August 1, 1996."

Former Rule: A former Rule 27.01, adopted Dec. 17, 1982, related generally to trials. The subject matter of former Rule 27.01 was incorporated into Rule 13.01 by court order dated June 26, 1996.

Rule 27.02. Service of Motions

Subdivision 1. When Required. Every written motion along with any supporting affidavits shall be served on the child, the child's counsel, the prosecuting attorney and the parent(s), legal guardian or legal custodian of the child.

Subd. 2. How Made. The moving party shall serve the other parties. If the other parties are represented by counsel, the moving party shall serve the other parties' counsel unless the court orders otherwise. Service of motions may be made by personal service or by mail. Service by mail shall be complete upon mailing to the last known address of the person to be served. Service may be made by electronic means if authorized by an order of the Minnesota Supreme Court and if service is made in accordance with that order; service by electronic means is complete as provided in that order.

Subd. 3. Time. Any motion required by this rule to be served, along with any supporting affidavits, shall be served at least three (3) days before it is to be heard unless the court for good cause shown permits a motion to be made and served less than three (3) days before it is to be heard.

Amended June 26, 1996; Oct. 15, 2012, eff. Dec. 1, 2012.

Comment—Rule 27

The amendment to Rule 27 that allows for service on counsel by electronic means if authorized by an order of the Minnesota Supreme Court is intended to facilitate a pilot project on electronic service and filing in certain pilot districts, and is designed to be a model for the implementation of electronic filing and service if the pilot project is made permanent and statewide. The rule makes service by electronic means effective in accordance with the rule for the pilot project.

Historical Notes

The order of the Minnesota Supreme Court [C6-84-2165] dated June 26, 1996, provides in part that "(t)hese amendments to the Rules of Juvenile Procedure shall govern all juvenile actions commenced or arrests made on or after 12:00 o'clock midnight August 1, 1996."

The order of the Minnesota Supreme Court [ADM10–8003] dated October 15, 2012, provides in part that the "amendments shall govern all delinquency actions pending or commenced on or after 12 o'clock midnight December 1, 2012."

Former Rule: A former Rule 27.02, adopted Dec. 17, 1982, related to the timing of trials. The subject matter of former Rule 27.02 was incorporated into Rule 13.02 by court order dated June 26, 1996.

Rules 27.03 to 27.07. Deleted June 26, 1996

Historical Notes

The order of the Minnesota Supreme Court [C6-84-2165] dated June 26, 1996, provides in part that "(t)hese amendments to the Rules of Juvenile Procedure shall govern all juvenile actions commenced or arrests made on or after 12:00 o'clock midnight August 1, 1996."

For subject matter of former Rule 27.03, see, now, Rule 13.03.

For subject matter of former Rule 27.04, see, now, Rule 13.04.

For subject matter of former Rule 27.05, see, now, Rule 13.06.

For subject matter of former Rule 27.06, see, now, Rule 13.09.

For subject matter of former Rule 27.07, see, now, Rule 13.10.

RULE 28. NOTICE OF ORDERS OR JUDGMENTS

Within five (5) days of filing of a written order or decision or entry of a judgment, the court administrator shall serve a copy of the written order on the child, the child's counsel, prosecuting attorney, probation officer, the parent(s), the legal guardian or legal custodian of the child and their counsel. The order shall be accompanied by a notice of filing, which shall include notice of the right to appeal a final order pursuant to Rule 21. The State Court Administrator shall develop a "notice of filing" form, which shall be used by court administrators.

Adopted June 26, 1996. Amended July 18, 2003; Oct. 11, 2007, eff. Jan. 1, 2008.

Historical Notes

The order of the Minnesota Supreme Court [C6-84-2165] dated June 26, 1996, provides in part that "(t)hese amendments to the Rules of Juvenile Procedure shall govern all juvenile actions commenced or arrests made on or after 12:00 o'clock midnight August 1, 1996."

The order of the Minnesota Supreme Court [CX–01–926] dated July 18, 2003, provides in part that "(t)he attached amendments shall govern all juveniles taken into custody and all juvenile delinquency actions commenced or children taken into custody after 12 o'clock midnight September 1, 2003."

Rules 28.01 to 28.03. Deleted June 26, 1996

Historical Notes

The order of the Minnesota Supreme Court [C6-84-2165] dated June 26, 1996, provides in part that "(t)hese amendments to the Rules of Juvenile Procedure shall govern all juvenile actions commenced or arrests made on or after 12:00 o'clock midnight August 1, 1996."

For subject matter of former Rule 28.01, see, now, Rule 16.01.

For subject matter of former Rule 28.02, see, now, Rule 16.03.

For subject matter of former Rule 28.03, see, now, Rule 16.04.

RULE 29. RECORDING

Rule 29.01. Procedure

A verbatim recording of all hearings shall be made by a stenographic reporter or by an electronic reporter. If the recording is made by an electronic reporter, any requested transcripts shall be prepared by personnel assigned by the court.

Amended June 26, 1996; Nov. 10, 2003, eff. Nov. 14, 2003.

Comment—Rule 29

See comment following Rule 29.03.

Historical Notes

The order of the Minnesota Supreme Court [C6-84-2165] dated June 26, 1996, provides in part that "(t)hese amendments to the Rules of Juvenile Procedure shall govern all juvenile actions commenced or arrests made on or after 12:00 o'clock midnight August 1, 1996."

Rule 29.02. Availability of Transcripts

Subdivision 1. Child's Counsel and Prosecuting Attorney. Transcripts of hearings for further use in the hearing or subsequent hearings, appeal, habeas corpus action or for other use as the court may approve, shall be made available to the child's counsel or the prosecuting attorney upon written request to the court reporter.

Subd. 2. Counsel for Parent(s), Legal Guardian or Legal Custodian. Transcripts of hearings for use at dispositional hearings, for appeal from disposition hearings, or for other use as the court approves, shall be made available to counsel for the parent(s), legal guardian or legal custodian of the child when they participate pursuant to Rule 2.04, subdivision 3. Applications for transcripts shall be made to the court in writing or on the record.

Amended June 26, 1996; July 18, 2003.

Comment—Rule 29

See comment following Rule 29.03.

Historical Notes

The order of the Minnesota Supreme Court [C6-84-2165] dated June 26, 1996, provides in part that "(t)hese amendments to the Rules of Juvenile Procedure shall govern all juvenile actions commenced or arrests made on or after 12:00 o'clock midnight August 1, 1996."

The order of the Minnesota Supreme Court [CX–01–926] dated July 18, 2003, provides in part that "(t)he attached amendments shall govern all juveniles taken into custody and all juvenile delinquency actions commenced or children taken into custody after 12 o'clock midnight September 1, 2003."

Rule 29.03. Expense

If the person requesting a transcript is unable to pay the preparation cost, the person may apply to the court for an order directing the preparation and delivery of the transcript to the person requesting it, at public expense. Depending on the ability of the person to pay, the court may order partial reimbursement for the cost of transcript.

Amended June 26, 1996.

Comment—Rule 29

References in this rule to "child's counsel" include the child who is proceeding pro se. Minn. R. Juv. Del. P. 1.01.

Reference in this rule to "counsel for the parent(s), legal guardian, or legal custodian" includes the parent, legal guardian, or legal custodian who is proceeding pro se. Minn. R. Juv. Del. P. 1.01.

Historical Notes

The order of the Minnesota Supreme Court [C6-84-2165] dated June 26, 1996, provides in part that "(t)hese amendments to the Rules of Juvenile Procedure shall govern all juvenile actions commenced or arrests made on or after 12:00 o'clock midnight August 1, 1996."

RULE 30. RECORDS

Rule 30.01. Generally

Subdivision 1. Records Defined. Juvenile court records include:

(A) all documents filed with the court;

(B) all documents maintained by the court;

(C) all reporter's notes and tapes, electronic recordings and transcripts of hearings and trials; and

(D) as relates to delinquency matters, all documents maintained by juvenile probation officers, county home schools and county detention agencies.

Subd. 2. Duration of Maintaining Records. The juvenile court shall maintain records as required by Minnesota Statute.

Amended June 26, 1996.

Comment—Rule 30

See comment following Rule 30.02.

Historical Notes

The order of the Minnesota Supreme Court [C6-84-2165] dated June 26, 1996, provides in part that "(t)hese amendments to the Rules of Juvenile Procedure shall govern all juvenile actions commenced or arrests made on or after 12:00 o'clock midnight August 1, 1996."

Rule 30.02. Availability of Juvenile Court Records

Subdivision 1. By Statute or Rule. Juvenile Court records shall be available for inspection, copying and release as required by statute or these rules. Access to all reporter's tapes and electronic recordings shall be governed by the Rules of Public Access to Records of the Judicial Branch.

Subd. 2. No Order Required.

(A) *Court and Court Personnel.* Juvenile court records shall be available to the court and court personnel without a court order.

(B) *Child's Counsel, Guardian Ad Litem, and Counsel for the Child's Parent(s), Legal Guardian, or*

Legal Custodian. Juvenile court records of the child shall be available for inspection, copying and release to the following without court order:

(1) the child's counsel and guardian ad litem appointed in the delinquency proceeding;

(2) counsel for the child's parent(s), legal guardian or legal custodian subject to restrictions on copying and release imposed by the court.

(C) *Prosecuting Attorney.* Juvenile court records shall be available for inspection, copying or release to the prosecuting attorney.

(D) *Other.* The juvenile court shall forward data to agencies and others as required by Minnesota Statute.

Subd. 3. Court Order Required.

(A) *Person(s) with Custody or Supervision of the Child, and Others.* The court may order juvenile court records to be made available for inspection, copying, disclosure or release, subject to such conditions as the court may direct, to:

(1) a representative of a state or private agency providing supervision or having custody of the child under order of the court; or

(2) any individual for whom such record is needed to assist or to supervise the child in fulfilling a court order; or

(3) any other person having a legitimate interest in the child or in the operation of the court.

(B) *Public.* A court order is required before any inspection, copying, disclosure or release to the public of the record of a child. Before any court order is made the court must find that inspection, copying, disclosure or release is:

(1) in the best interests of the child; or

(2) in the interests of public safety; or

(3) necessary for the functioning of the juvenile court system.

(C) *Disclosure Prohibited.* The record of the child shall not be inspected, copied, disclosed or released to any present or prospective employer of the child or the military services.

(D) *Disclosure Limited.* The inspection, copying, disclosure, or release of the juvenile records listed below is limited pursuant to the identified Rules of Juvenile Delinquency Procedure:

(1) Predisposition report (Rule 15.03, subd. 4);

(2) Juvenile certification study (Rule 18.04, subd. 4);

(3) Extended jurisdiction juvenile study (Rule 19.03, subd. 4); and

(4) Competency examination (Rule 20.02, subd. 5).

Amended June 26, 1996; April 23, 2004; Sept. 30, 2004, eff. Jan. 1, 2005; July 11, 2005, eff. Sept. 1, 2005; Oct. 13, 2006, eff. Jan. 1, 2007; Nov. 19, 2010, eff. Jan. 1, 2011.

Comment—Rule 30

Legal records as defined in Minnesota Statutes, section 260B.171, subd. 1 (2002), are the petition, summons, notice, findings, orders, decrees, judgments and motions and such other matters as the court deems necessary and proper. Minnesota Statutes, section 260B.171, subd. 4 (2002), provides exceptions to public access of "legal records," arising under Minnesota Statutes, section 260B.163, subd. 1 (2002), delinquency proceedings alleging or proving a felony level violation by a juvenile at least 16 years old at the time of violation, along with the following exclusions: (1) Minnesota Statutes, section 245A.04, subd. 3(d) (2002), which directs the court to provide juvenile court records to the Commissioner of Human Services; and (2) Minnesota Statutes, sections 611A.03, 611A.04, 611A.06 and 629.73 (2002), which provide for the rights of victims in delinquency proceedings, juvenile traffic proceedings involving driving under the influence of alcohol or drugs and proceedings involving any other act committed by a juvenile that would be a crime as defined in Minnesota Statutes, section 609. 02 (2002), if committed by an adult.

The juvenile court shall maintain records pertaining to juvenile delinquency adjudications until the juvenile reaches 28 years of age. Records pertaining to convictions of extended jurisdiction juveniles shall be maintained for as long as they would be maintained if the offender had been an adult.

References in this rule to "child's counsel" includes the child who is proceeding pro se. Minn. R. Juv. Del. P. 1.01.

"Prosecuting attorney" as used in this rule also includes adult court prosecuting attorneys.

Pursuant to Minnesota Statutes, section 260B.171, subd. 2 (2002), the juvenile court shall forward data for juvenile delinquents adjudicated delinquent for felony- or gross misdemeanor-level offenses. The court shall also forward data to the BCA on persons convicted as extended jurisdiction juveniles.

Reference in this rule to "counsel for the parent(s), legal guardian, or legal custodian" includes the parent, legal guardian, or legal custodian who is proceeding pro se. Minn. R. Juv. Del. P. 1.01.

If a juvenile is enrolled in school, the juvenile's probation officer shall transmit a copy of the court's disposition order if the juvenile is adjudicated delinquent for committing an act on school property or if the juvenile is adjudicated delinquent for one of the offenses enumerated in Minnesota Statutes, section 260B.171, subd. 3(a) (2002). When the probation officer transmits a disposition order to a school, the probation officer shall notify the parent, legal guardian or legal custodian that this information has been sent to the juvenile's school.

Historical Notes

The order of the Minnesota Supreme Court [C6-84-2165] dated June 26, 1996, provides in part that "(t)hese amendments to the Rules of Juvenile Procedure shall govern all juvenile actions commenced or arrests made on or after 12:00 o'clock midnight August 1, 1996."

The order of the Minnesota Supreme Court [CX-01-926] dated April 23, 2004, provides in part that "(t)he attached amendments shall govern all juvenile delinquency actions commenced or children taken into custody after 12 o'clock midnight July 1, 2004."

Rules 30.03 to 30.07. Deleted June 26, 1996

Historical Notes

The order of the Minnesota Supreme Court [C6-84-2165] dated June 26, 1996, provides in part that "(t)hese amendments to the Rules of Juvenile Procedure shall govern all juvenile actions commenced or arrests made on or after 12:00 o'clock midnight August 1, 1996."

For subject matter of former Rule 30.03, see, now, Rule 15.03.

For subject matter of former Rule 30.04, see, now, Rule 15.04.

For subject matter of former Rule 30.05, see, now, Rule 15.05.

For subject matter of former Rule 30.06, see, now, Rule 15.06.

For subject matter of former Rule 30.07, see, now, Rule 15.08.

RULE 31. TIMING

Rule 31.01. Computation

Unless otherwise provided by statute or specific Minnesota Rules of Juvenile Procedure, the day of the act or event from which the designated period of time begins to run shall not be included. The last day of the period shall be included, unless it is a Saturday, a Sunday, or a legal holiday, in which event the period runs until the end of the next day which is not a Saturday, a Sunday or legal holiday. When a period of time prescribed or allowed is three days or less, intermediate Saturdays, Sundays and legal holidays shall be excluded in the computation. As used in these rules, "legal holiday" includes New Year's Day, Martin Luther King's Birthday, Washington's Birthday (Presidents' Day), Memorial Day, Independence Day, Labor Day, Columbus Day, Veterans Day, Thanksgiving Day, the day after Thanksgiving Day, Christmas Day, and any other day appointed as a holiday by the President or Congress of the United States or by the State.

Amended June 26, 1996; July 18, 2003.

Historical Notes

The order of the Minnesota Supreme Court [C6-84-2165] dated June 26, 1996, provides in part that "(t)hese amendments to the Rules of Juvenile Procedure shall govern all juvenile actions commenced or arrests made on or after 12:00 o'clock midnight August 1, 1996."

The order of the Minnesota Supreme Court [CX–01–926] dated July 18, 2003, provides in part that "(t)he attached amendments shall govern all juveniles taken into custody and all juvenile delinquency actions commenced or children taken into custody after 12 o'clock midnight September 1, 2003."

Rule 31.02. Additional Time After Service by Mail

Whenever a person has the right or is required to do an act within a prescribed period after the service of a notice or other paper and the notice or other paper is served by mail, three (3) days shall be added to the prescribed period.

Amended June 26, 1996.

Historical Notes

The order of the Minnesota Supreme Court [C6-84-2165] dated June 26, 1996, provides in part that "(t)hese amendments to the Rules of Juvenile Procedure shall govern all juvenile actions commenced or arrests made on or after 12:00 o'clock midnight August 1, 1996."

Rules 31.03 to 31.06. Deleted June 26, 1996

Historical Notes

The order of the Minnesota Supreme Court [C6-84-2165] dated June 26, 1996, provides in part that "(t)hese amendments to the Rules of Juvenile Procedure shall govern all juvenile actions commenced or arrests made on or after 12:00 o'clock midnight August 1, 1996."

Deleted Rule 31.03 related to appeals by a child. See, now, Rule 21.03.

Deleted Rule 31.04 related to appeals by a prosecuting authority. See, now, Rule 21.04.

Deleted Rule 31.05 related to appeals by parent(s) or guardian of the child. See, now, Rule 21.05.

Deleted Rule 31.06 related to certified questions to the court of appeals. See, now, Rule 21.06.

RULE 32. CERTIFICATION OF DELINQUENCY MATTERS

Rules 32.01 to 32.08. Deleted June 26, 1996

Historical Notes

The order of the Minnesota Supreme Court [C6-84-2165] dated June 26, 1996, provides in part that "(t)hese amendments to the Rules of Juvenile Procedure shall govern all juvenile actions commenced or arrests made on or after 12:00 o'clock midnight August 1, 1996."

The deleted rules related to the reference of delinquency matters. See, now, Rules 18.01 to 18.08.

RULE 32A. EXTENDED JURISDICTION JUVENILE PROCEEDINGS AND PROSECUTION

Rules 32A.01 to 32A.09. Deleted June 26, 1996

Historical Notes

The order of the Minnesota Supreme Court [C6-84-2165] dated June 26, 1996, provides in part that "(t)hese amendments to the Rules of Juvenile Procedure shall govern all juvenile actions commenced or arrests made on or after 12:00 o'clock midnight August 1, 1996."

The deleted rules related to extended jurisdiction juvenile proceedings and prosecution.

See, now, Rules 19.01 to 19.09.

RULE 33. PROCEEDINGS WHEN CHILD IS BELIEVED TO BE MENTALLY ILL OR MENTALLY DEFICIENT

Rules 33.01 to 33.04. Deleted June 26, 1996

Historical Notes

The order of the Minnesota Supreme Court [C6-84-2165] dated June 26, 1996, provides in part that "(t)hese amendments to the Rules of Juvenile Procedure shall govern all juvenile actions commenced or arrests made on or after 12:00 o'clock midnight August 1, 1996."

The deleted rules related to proceedings when a child is believed to be mentally ill or mentally deficient.

See, now, Rule 20.01.

RULE 34. RECORDS

Rules 34.01 to 34.03. Deleted June 26, 1996

Historical Notes

The order of the Minnesota Supreme Court [C6-84-2165] dated June 26, 1996, provides in part that "(t)hese amendments to the Rules of Juvenile Procedure shall govern all juvenile actions commenced or arrests made on or after 12:00 o'clock midnight August 1, 1996."

The deleted rules related to the availability of juvenile court records.

See, now, Rules 30.01 and 30.02.

RULE 35. TIME

Rule 35.01. Deleted June 26, 1996

Historical Notes

The order of the Minnesota Supreme Court [C6-84-2165] dated June 26, 1996, provides in part that "(t)hese amendments to the Rules of Juvenile Procedure shall govern all juvenile actions commenced or arrests made on or after 12:00 o'clock midnight August 1, 1996."

The deleted rule related to the computation of time.

See, now, MN ST Juv. Del., Rules 31.01 and 31.02.

JUVENILE TRAFFIC OFFENDER

RULE 36. JUVENILE TRAFFIC OFFENDER

Rules 36.01, 36.02. Deleted June 26, 1996

Historical Notes

The order of the Minnesota Supreme Court [C6-84-2165] dated June 26, 1996, provides in part that "(t)hese amendments to the Rules of Juvenile Procedure shall govern all juvenile actions commenced or arrests made on or after 12:00 o'clock midnight August 1, 1996."

The deleted rules related to juvenile traffic offenders.

See, now, Rules 17.01 to 17.19.

JUVENILE PROTECTION RULES

1999 Order

The order of the Minnesota Supreme Court [C4–97–1693] dated December 20, 1999, as amended by the order [C4–97–1693] dated December 29, 1999, revised the Juvenile Protection Rules, substituting present rules 37 to 82.06 for former rules 37 to 65.02 (adopted by order dated December 17, 1982).

2003 Order

The order of the Minnesota Supreme Court [C1-01-927] dated November 12, 2003, amending Rules 37 to 82 of the Rules of Juvenile Procedure and renumbering them as Rules 1 to 47 of the Rules of Juvenile Protection Procedure, provides in part that the amendments are effective January 1, 2004, and shall apply to all juvenile protection matters filed on or after that date.

RULE 37. SCOPE AND PURPOSE

Rules 37.01, 37.02. Deleted Nov. 12, 2003

Historical Notes

The order of the Minnesota Supreme Court [C1-01-927] dated November 12, 2003, amending Rules 37 to 82 of the Rules of Juvenile Procedure and renumbering them as Rules 1 to 47 of the Rules of Juvenile Protection Procedure, provides in part that the amendments are effective January 1, 2004, and shall apply to all juvenile protection matters filed on or after that date.

See, now, Rules 1.01 and 1.02 of the Rules of Juvenile Protection Procedure.

RULE 38. DEFINITIONS

Rule 38.01. Deleted Nov. 12, 2003

Historical Notes

The order of the Minnesota Supreme Court [C1-01-927] dated November 12, 2003, amending Rules 37 to 82 of the Rules of Juvenile Procedure and renumbering them as Rules 1 to 47 of the Rules of Juvenile Protection Procedure, provides in part that the amendments are effective January 1, 2004, and shall apply to all juvenile protection matters filed on or after that date.

See, now, MN ST Juv. Del., Rule 2.01.

RULE 39. APPLICABILITY OF OTHER RULES AND STATUTES

Rules 39.01 to 39.05. Deleted Nov. 12, 2003

Historical Notes

The order of the Minnesota Supreme Court [C1-01-927] dated November 12, 2003, amending Rules 37 to 82 of the Rules of Juvenile Procedure and renumbering them as Rules 1 to 47 of the Rules of Juvenile Protection Procedure, provides in part that the amendments are effective January 1, 2004, and shall apply to all juvenile protection matters filed on or after that date.

See, now, Rules 3.01 to 3.05 of the Rules of Juvenile Protection Procedure.

RULE 40. TIME; TIMELINE

Rules 40.01 to 40.05. Deleted Nov. 12, 2003

Historical Notes

The order of the Minnesota Supreme Court [C1-01-927] dated November 12, 2003, amending Rules 37 to 82 of the Rules of Juvenile Procedure and renumbering them as Rules 1 to 47 of the Rules of Juvenile Protection Procedure, provides in part that the amendments are effective January 1, 2004, and shall apply to all juvenile protection matters filed on or after that date.

See, now, Rules 4.01 to 4.05 of the Rules of Juvenile Protection Procedure.

RULE 41. CONTINUANCES

Rules 41.01 to 41.03. Deleted Nov. 12, 2003

Historical Notes

The order of the Minnesota Supreme Court [C1-01-927] dated November 12, 2003, amending Rules 37 to 82 of the Rules of Juvenile Procedure and renumbering them as Rules 1 to 47 of the Rules of Juvenile Protection Procedure, provides in part that the amendments are effective January 1, 2004, and shall apply to all juvenile protection matters filed on or after that date.

See, now, Rules 5.01 to 5.03 of the Rules of Juvenile Protection Procedure.

RULE 42. SCHEDULING ORDER

Rules 42.01 to 42.03. Deleted Nov. 12, 2003

Historical Notes

The order of the Minnesota Supreme Court [C1-01-927] dated November 12, 2003, amending Rules 37 to 82 of the Rules of Juvenile

Procedure and renumbering them as Rules 1 to 47 of the Rules of Juvenile Protection Procedure, provides in part that the amendments are effective January 1, 2004, and shall apply to all juvenile protection matters filed on or after that date.

See, now, Rules 6.01 to 6.03 of the Rules of Juvenile Protection Procedure.

RULE 43. REFEREES AND JUDGES

Rules 43.01 to 43.07. Deleted Nov. 12, 2003

Historical Notes

The order of the Minnesota Supreme Court [C1-01-927] dated November 12, 2003, amending Rules 37 to 82 of the Rules of Juvenile Procedure and renumbering them as Rules 1 to 47 of the Rules of Juvenile Protection Procedure, provides in part that the amendments are effective January 1, 2004, and shall apply to all juvenile protection matters filed on or after that date.

See, now, Rules 7.01 to 7.07 of the Rules of Juvenile Protection Procedure.

RULE 44. ACCESS TO JUVENILE PROTECTION CASE RECORDS

Rules 44.01 to 44.08. Deleted Nov. 12, 2003

Historical Notes

The order of the Minnesota Supreme Court [C1-01-927] dated November 12, 2003, amending Rules 37 to 82 of the Rules of Juvenile Procedure and renumbering them as Rules 1 to 47 of the Rules of Juvenile Protection Procedure, provides in part that the amendments are effective January 1, 2004, and shall apply to all juvenile protection matters filed on or after that date.

See, now, Rules 8.01 to 8.08 of the Rules of Juvenile Protection Procedure.

RULE 45. EX PARTE COMMUNICATION

Rules 45.01, 45.02. Deleted Nov. 12, 2003

Historical Notes

The order of the Minnesota Supreme Court [C1-01-927] dated November 12, 2003, amending Rules 37 to 82 of the Rules of Juvenile Procedure and renumbering them as Rules 1 to 47 of the Rules of Juvenile Protection Procedure, provides in part that the amendments are effective January 1, 2004, and shall apply to all juvenile protection matters filed on or after that date.

See, now, Rules 9.01 and 9.02 of the Rules of Juvenile Protection Procedure.

RULE 46. ORDERS

Rules 46.01 to 46.04. Deleted Nov. 12, 2003

Historical Notes

The order of the Minnesota Supreme Court [C1-01-927] dated November 12, 2003, amending Rules 37 to 82 of the Rules of Juvenile Procedure and renumbering them as Rules 1 to 47 of the Rules of Juvenile Protection Procedure, provides in part that the amendments are effective January 1, 2004, and shall apply to all juvenile protection matters filed on or after that date.

See, now, Rules 10.01 to 10.04 of the Rules of Juvenile Protection Procedure.

RULE 47. RECORDING AND TRANSCRIPTS

Rules 47.01, 47.02. Deleted Nov. 12, 2003

Historical Notes

The order of the Minnesota Supreme Court [C1-01-927] dated November 12, 2003, amending Rules 37 to 82 of the Rules of Juvenile Procedure and renumbering them as Rules 1 to 47 of the Rules of Juvenile Protection Procedure, provides in part that the amendments are effective January 1, 2004, and shall apply to all juvenile protection matters filed on or after that date.

See, now, Rules 11.01 and 11.02 of the Rules of Juvenile Protection Procedure.

RULE 48. USE OF TELEPHONE AND INTERACTIVE VIDEO

Rules 48.01 to 48.03. Deleted Nov. 17, 2003

Historical Notes

The order of the Minnesota Supreme Court [C1-01-927] dated November 12, 2003, amending Rules 37 to 82 of the Rules of Juvenile Procedure and renumbering them as Rules 1 to 47 of the Rules of Juvenile Protection Procedure, provides in part that the amendments are effective January 1, 2004, and shall apply to all juvenile protection matters filed on or after that date.

See, now, Rules 12.01 to 12.03 of the Rules of Juvenile Protection Procedure.

RULE 49. SUBPOENAS

Rules 49.01 to 49.09. Deleted Nov. 12, 2003

Historical Notes

The order of the Minnesota Supreme Court [C1-01-927] dated November 12, 2003, amending Rules 37 to 82 of the Rules of Juvenile Procedure and renumbering them as Rules 1 to 47 of the Rules of Juvenile Protection Procedure, provides in part that the amendments are effective January 1, 2004, and shall apply to all juvenile protection matters filed on or after that date.

See, now, Rules 13.01 to 13.09 of the Rules of Juvenile Protection Procedure.

RULE 50. CONTEMPT

Rules 50.01 to 50.04. Deleted Nov. 12, 2003

Historical Notes

The order of the Minnesota Supreme Court [C1-01-927] dated November 12, 2003, amending Rules 37 to 82 of the Rules of Juvenile Procedure and renumbering them as Rules 1 to 47 of the Rules of Juvenile Protection Procedure, provides in part that the amendments are effective January 1, 2004, and shall apply to all juvenile protection matters filed on or after that date.

See, now, Rules 14.01 to 14.04 of the Rules of Juvenile Protection Procedure.

RULE 51. MOTIONS

Rules 51.01 to 51.05. Deleted Nov. 12, 2003

Historical Notes

The order of the Minnesota Supreme Court [C1-01-927] dated November 12, 2003, amending Rules 37 to 82 of the Rules of Juvenile Procedure and renumbering them as Rules 1 to 47 of the Rules of Juvenile Protection Procedure, provides in part that the amendments are effective January 1, 2004, and shall apply to all juvenile protection matters filed on or after that date.

See, now, Rules 15.01 to 15.05 of the Rules of Juvenile Protection Procedure.

RULE 52. SIGNING OF PLEADINGS, MOTIONS, AND OTHER PAPERS; SANCTIONS

Rules 52.01, 52.02. Deleted Nov. 12, 2003

Historical Notes

The order of the Minnesota Supreme Court [C1-01-927] dated November 12, 2003, amending Rules 37 to 82 of the Rules of Juvenile Procedure and renumbering them as Rules 1 to 47 of the Rules of Juvenile Protection Procedure, provides in part that the amendments are effective January 1, 2004, and shall apply to all juvenile protection matters filed on or after that date.

See, now, Rules 16.01 and 16.03 of the Rules of Juvenile Protection Procedure.

RULE 53. DISCOVERY

Rules 53.01 to 53.06. Deleted Nov. 12, 2003

Historical Notes

The order of the Minnesota Supreme Court [C1-01-927] dated November 12, 2003, amending Rules 37 to 82 of the Rules of Juvenile Procedure and renumbering them as Rules 1 to 47 of the Rules of Juvenile Protection Procedure, provides in part that the amendments are effective January 1, 2004, and shall apply to all juvenile protection matters filed on or after that date.

See, now, Rules 17.01 to 17.06 of the Rules of Juvenile Protection Procedure.

RULE 54. DEFAULT

Rule 54.01. Deleted Nov. 12, 2003

Historical Notes

The order of the Minnesota Supreme Court [C1-01-927] dated November 12, 2003, amending Rules 37 to 82 of the Rules of Juvenile Procedure and renumbering them as Rules 1 to 47 of the Rules of Juvenile Protection Procedure, provides in part that the amendments are effective January 1, 2004, and shall apply to all juvenile protection matters filed on or after that date.

See, now, MN ST Juv. Prot., Rule 18.01.

RULE 55. SETTLEMENT

Rules 55.01 to 55.04. Deleted Nov. 12, 2003

Historical Notes

The order of the Minnesota Supreme Court [C1-01-927] dated November 12, 2003, amending Rules 37 to 82 of the Rules of Juvenile Procedure and renumbering them as Rules 1 to 47 of the Rules of Juvenile Protection Procedure, provides in part that the amendments are effective January 1, 2004, and shall apply to all juvenile protection matters filed on or after that date.

See, now, Rules 19.01 to 19.04 of the Rules of Juvenile Protection Procedure.

RULE 56. ALTERNATIVE DISPUTE RESOLUTION

[Reserved for future use.]

Historical Notes

The order of the Minnesota Supreme Court [C4-97-1693] dated December 20, 1999, as amended by the order [C4-97-1693] dated December 29, 1999, provides in part that the Juvenile Protection Rules are effective March 1, 2000, and apply to all juvenile protection matters filed on or after that date.

RULE 57. PARTIES

Rules 57.01 to 57.03. Deleted Nov. 12, 2003

Historical Notes

The order of the Minnesota Supreme Court [C1-01-927] dated November 12, 2003, amending Rules 37 to 82 of the Rules of Juvenile Procedure and renumbering them as Rules 1 to 47 of the Rules of Juvenile Protection Procedure, provides in part that the amendments are effective January 1, 2004, and shall apply to all juvenile protection matters filed on or after that date.

See, now, Rules 21.01 to 21.03 of the Rules of Juvenile Protection Procedure.

RULE 58. PARTICIPANTS

Rules 58.01 to 58.03. Deleted Nov. 12, 2003

Historical Notes

The order of the Minnesota Supreme Court [C4-97-1693] dated December 20, 1999, as amended by the order [C4-97-1693] dated December 29, 1999, provides in part that the Juvenile Protection Rules are effective March 1, 2000, and apply to all juvenile protection matters filed on or after that date.

The order of the Minnesota Supreme Court [C1-01-927] dated November 12, 2003, amending Rules 37 to 82 of the Rules of Juvenile Procedure and renumbering them as Rules 1 to 47 of the Rules of Juvenile Protection Procedure, provides in part that the amendments are effective January 1, 2004, and shall apply to all juvenile protection matters filed on or after that date.

See, now, Rules 22.01 to 22.03 of the Rules of Juvenile Protection Procedure.

RULE 59. INTERVENTION

Rules 59.01 to 59.04. Deleted Nov. 12, 2003

Historical Notes

The order of the Minnesota Supreme Court [C1-01-927] dated November 12, 2003, amending Rules 37 to 82 of the Rules of Juvenile Procedure and renumbering them as Rules 1 to 47 of the Rules of Juvenile Protection Procedure, provides in part that the amendments are effective January 1, 2004, and shall apply to all juvenile protection matters filed on or after that date.

See, now, Rules 23.01 to 23.04 of the Rules of Juvenile Protection Procedure.

RULE 60. JOINDER

Rule 60.01. Deleted Nov. 12, 2003

Historical Notes

The order of the Minnesota Supreme Court [C1-01-927] dated November 12, 2003, amending Rules 37 to 82 of the Rules of Juvenile Procedure and renumbering them as Rules 1 to 47 of the Rules of Juvenile Protection Procedure, provides in part that the amendments are effective January 1, 2004, and shall apply to all juvenile protection matters filed on or after that date.

See, now, MN ST Juv. Prot., Rule 24.01.

RULE 61. RIGHT TO REPRESENTATION; APPOINTMENT OF COUNSEL

Rules 61.01 to 61.06. Deleted Nov. 12, 2003

Historical Notes

The order of the Minnesota Supreme Court [C1-01-927] dated November 12, 2003, amending Rules 37 to 82 of the Rules of Juvenile

Procedure and renumbering them as Rules 1 to 47 of the Rules of Juvenile Protection Procedure, provides in part that the amendments are effective January 1, 2004, and shall apply to all juvenile protection matters filed on or after that date.

See, now, Rules 25.01 to 25.06 of the Rules of Juvenile Protection Procedure.

RULE 62. GUARDIAN AD LITEM

Rules 62.01 to 62.03. Deleted Nov. 12, 2003

Historical Notes

The order of the Minnesota Supreme Court [C1-01-927] dated November 12, 2003, amending Rules 37 to 82 of the Rules of Juvenile Procedure and renumbering them as Rules 1 to 47 of the Rules of Juvenile Protection Procedure, provides in part that the amendments are effective January 1, 2004, and shall apply to all juvenile protection matters filed on or after that date.

See, now, Rules 26.01 to 26.03 of the Rules of Juvenile Protection Procedure.

RULE 63. ACCESS TO HEARINGS

Rules 63.01 to 63.04. Deleted Nov. 12, 2003

Historical Notes

The order of the Minnesota Supreme Court [C1-01-927] dated November 12, 2003, amending Rules 37 to 82 of the Rules of Juvenile Procedure and renumbering them as Rules 1 to 47 of the Rules of Juvenile Protection Procedure, provides in part that the amendments are effective January 1, 2004, and shall apply to all juvenile protection matters filed on or after that date.

See, now, Rules 27.01 to 27.04 of the Rules of Juvenile Protection Procedure.

RULE 64. CLOSED PROCEEDINGS

Rule 64.01. Deleted eff. July 1, 2002

RULE 65. EMERGENCY PROTECTIVE CARE ORDER AND NOTICE

Rules 65.01 to 65.06. Deleted Nov. 12, 2003

Historical Notes

The order of the Minnesota Supreme Court [C1-01-927] dated November 12, 2003, amending Rules 37 to 82 of the Rules of Juvenile Procedure and renumbering them as Rules 1 to 47 of the Rules of Juvenile Protection Procedure, provides in part that the amendments are effective January 1, 2004, and shall apply to all juvenile protection matters filed on or after that date.

See, now, Rules 28.01 to 28.06 of the Rules of Juvenile Protection Procedure.

RULE 66. PROCEDURES DURING PERIOD OF EMERGENCY PROTECTIVE CARE

Rules 66.01 to 66.04. Deleted Nov. 12, 2003

Historical Notes

The order of the Minnesota Supreme Court [C1-01-927] dated November 12, 2003, amending Rules 37 to 82 of the Rules of Juvenile Procedure and renumbering them as Rules 1 to 47 of the Rules of Juvenile Protection Procedure, provides in part that the amendments are effective January 1, 2004, and shall apply to all juvenile protection matters filed on or after that date.

See, now, Rules 29.01 to 29.04 of the Rules of Juvenile Protection Procedure.

RULE 67. EMERGENCY PROTECTIVE CARE HEARING

Rules 67.01 to 67.11. Deleted Nov. 12, 2003

Historical Notes

The order of the Minnesota Supreme Court [C1-01-927] dated November 12, 2003, amending Rules 37 to 82 of the Rules of Juvenile Procedure and renumbering them as Rules 1 to 47 of the Rules of Juvenile Protection Procedure, provides in part that the amendments are effective January 1, 2004, and shall apply to all juvenile protection matters filed on or after that date.

See, now, Rules 30.01 to 30.11 of the Rules of Juvenile Protection Procedure.

RULE 68. METHODS OF FILING AND SERVICE

Rules 68.01 to 68.07. Deleted Nov. 12, 2003

Historical Notes

The order of the Minnesota Supreme Court [C1-01-927] dated November 12, 2003, amending Rules 37 to 82 of the Rules of Juvenile Procedure and renumbering them as Rules 1 to 47 of the Rules of Juvenile Protection Procedure, provides in part that the amendments are effective January 1, 2004, and shall apply to all juvenile protection matters filed on or after that date.

See, now, Rules 31.01 to 31.07 of the Rules of Juvenile Protection Procedure.

RULE 69. SUMMONS AND NOTICE

Rules 69.01 to 69.05. Deleted Nov. 12, 2003

Historical Notes

The order of the Minnesota Supreme Court [C1-01-927] dated November 12, 2003, amending Rules 37 to 82 of the Rules of Juvenile Procedure and renumbering them as Rules 1 to 47 of the Rules of Juvenile Protection Procedure, provides in part that the amendments are effective January 1, 2004, and shall apply to all juvenile protection matters filed on or after that date.

See, now, Rules 32.01 to 32.03, 32.05, and 32.06 of the Rules of Juvenile Protection Procedure.

RULE 70. PETITION

Rules 70.01 to 70.05. Deleted Nov. 12, 2003

Historical Notes

The order of the Minnesota Supreme Court [C1-01-927] dated November 12, 2003, amending Rules 37 to 82 of the Rules of Juvenile Procedure and renumbering them as Rules 1 to 47 of the Rules of Juvenile Protection Procedure, provides in part that the amendments are effective January 1, 2004, and shall apply to all juvenile protection matters filed on or after that date.

See, now, Rules 33.01 to 33.05 of the Rules of Juvenile Protection Procedure.

RULE 71. ADMIT/DENY HEARING

Rules 71.01 to 71.03. Deleted Nov. 12, 2003

Historical Notes

The order of the Minnesota Supreme Court [C1-01-927] dated November 12, 2003, amending Rules 37 to 82 of the Rules of Juvenile Procedure and renumbering them as Rules 1 to 47 of the Rules of Juvenile Protection Procedure, provides in part that the amendments

are effective January 1, 2004, and shall apply to all juvenile protection matters filed on or after that date.

See, now, Rules 34.01 to 34.03 of the Rules of Juvenile Protection Procedure.

RULE 72. ADMISSION OR DENIAL

Rules 72.01 to 72.03. Deleted Nov. 12, 2003

Historical Notes

The order of the Minnesota Supreme Court [C1-01-927] dated November 12, 2003, amending Rules 37 to 82 of the Rules of Juvenile Procedure and renumbering them as Rules 1 to 47 of the Rules of Juvenile Protection Procedure, provides in part that the amendments are effective January 1, 2004, and shall apply to all juvenile protection matters filed on or after that date.

See, now, Rules 35.01 to 35.03 of the Rules of Juvenile Protection Procedure.

RULE 73. PRETRIAL CONFERENCE

Rules 73.01, 73.02. Deleted Nov. 12, 2003

Historical Notes

The order of the Minnesota Supreme Court [C1-01-927] dated November 12, 2003, amending Rules 37 to 82 of the Rules of Juvenile Procedure and renumbering them as Rules 1 to 47 of the Rules of Juvenile Protection Procedure, provides in part that the amendments are effective January 1, 2004, and shall apply to all juvenile protection matters filed on or after that date.

See, now, Rules 36.01 and 36.02 of the Rules of Juvenile Protection Procedure.

RULE 74. TRIAL

Rules 74.01 to 74.05. Deleted Nov. 12, 2003

Historical Notes

The order of the Minnesota Supreme Court [C1-01-927] dated November 12, 2003, amending Rules 37 to 82 of the Rules of Juvenile Procedure and renumbering them as Rules 1 to 47 of the Rules of Juvenile Protection Procedure, provides in part that the amendments are effective January 1, 2004, and shall apply to all juvenile protection matters filed on or after that date.

See, now, Rules 39.01 to 39.05 of the Rules of Juvenile Protection Procedure.

RULE 75. ADJUDICATION

Rules 75.01, 75.02. Deleted Nov. 12, 2003

Historical Notes

The order of the Minnesota Supreme Court [C1-01-927] dated November 12, 2003, amending Rules 37 to 82 of the Rules of Juvenile Procedure and renumbering them as Rules 1 to 47 of the Rules of Juvenile Protection Procedure, provides in part that the amendments are effective January 1, 2004, and shall apply to all juvenile protection matters filed on or after that date.

See, now, Rules 40.01 and 40.02 of the Rules of Juvenile Protection Procedure.

RULE 76. DISPOSITION

Rules 76.01 to 76.06. Deleted Nov. 12, 2003

Historical Notes

The order of the Minnesota Supreme Court [C1-01-927] dated November 12, 2003, amending Rules 37 to 82 of the Rules of Juvenile Procedure and renumbering them as Rules 1 to 47 of the Rules of Juvenile Protection Procedure, provides in part that the amendments are effective January 1, 2004, and shall apply to all juvenile protection matters filed on or after that date.

See, now, Rules 41.01 to 41.06 of the Rules of Juvenile Protection Procedure.

RULE 77. PERMANENT PLACEMENT MATTERS

Rules 77.01 to 77.05. Deleted Nov. 12, 2003

Historical Notes

The order of the Minnesota Supreme Court [C1-01-927] dated November 12, 2003, amending Rules 37 to 82 of the Rules of Juvenile Procedure and renumbering them as Rules 1 to 47 of the Rules of Juvenile Protection Procedure, provides in part that the amendments are effective January 1, 2004, and shall apply to all juvenile protection matters filed on or after that date.

See, now, Rules 42.01 to 42.05 of the Rules of Juvenile Protection Procedure.

RULE 78. TERMINATION OF PARENTAL RIGHTS MATTERS

Rules 78.01 to 78.04. Deleted Nov. 12, 2003

Historical Notes

The order of the Minnesota Supreme Court [C1-01-927] dated November 12, 2003, amending Rules 37 to 82 of the Rules of Juvenile Procedure and renumbering them as Rules 1 to 47 of the Rules of Juvenile Protection Procedure, provides in part that the amendments are effective January 1, 2004, and shall apply to all juvenile protection matters filed on or after that date.

See, now, Rules 43.01 to 43.04 of the Rules of Juvenile Protection Procedure.

RULE 79. REVIEW OF VOLUNTARY PLACEMENT MATTERS

Rules 79.01, 79.02. Deleted Nov. 12, 2003

Historical Notes

The order of the Minnesota Supreme Court [C1-01-927] dated November 12, 2003, amending Rules 37 to 82 of the Rules of Juvenile Procedure and renumbering them as Rules 1 to 47 of the Rules of Juvenile Protection Procedure, provides in part that the amendments are effective January 1, 2004, and shall apply to all juvenile protection matters filed on or after that date.

See, now, Rules 44.01 and 44.02 of the Rules of Juvenile Protection Procedure.

RULE 80. POST–TRIAL MOTIONS

Rules 80.01 to 80.05. Deleted Nov. 12, 2003

Historical Notes

The order of the Minnesota Supreme Court [C1-01-927] dated November 12, 2003, amending Rules 37 to 82 of the Rules of Juvenile Procedure and renumbering them as Rules 1 to 47 of the Rules of Juvenile Protection Procedure, provides in part that the amendments are effective January 1, 2004, and shall apply to all juvenile protection matters filed on or after that date.

See, now, Rules 45.01 to 45.05 of the Rules of Juvenile Protection Procedure.

RULE 81. RELIEF FROM ORDER

Rules 81.01, 81.02. Repealed Nov. 12, 2003

Historical Notes

The order of the Minnesota Supreme Court [C1-01-927] dated November 12, 2003, amending Rules 37 to 82 of the Rules of Juvenile Procedure and renumbering them as Rules 1 to 47 of the Rules of Juvenile Protection Procedure, provides in part that the amendments are effective January 1, 2004, and shall apply to all juvenile protection matters filed on or after that date.

See, now, Rules 46.01 and 46.02 of the Rules of Juvenile Protection Procedure.

RULE 82. APPEAL

Rules 82.01 to 82.06. Deleted Nov. 12, 2003

Historical Notes

The order of the Minnesota Supreme Court [C1-01-927] dated November 12, 2003, amending Rules 37 to 82 of the Rules of Juvenile Procedure and renumbering them as Rules 1 to 47 of the Rules of Juvenile Protection Procedure, provides in part that the amendments are effective January 1, 2004, and shall apply to all juvenile protection matters filed on or after that date.

See, now, Rules 47.01 to 47.06 of the Rules of Juvenile Protection Procedure.

JUVENILE DELINQUENCY FORMS

INTRODUCTORY STATEMENT

The following forms are provided as an aid to practitioners and the court in the juvenile justice system. The forms are not mandatory, but shall be accepted by the court if offered by any party or counsel for their designated purpose. The Advisory Committee on Juvenile Delinquency Rules strongly recommends that Forms 12 through 16 be used in all felony level or enhanceable cases. A sample petition may be found on the Minnesota Judicial Branch website.

Amended Oct. 11, 2007, eff. Jan. 1, 2008.

Form 1. Petition [Deleted Oct. 11, 2007, eff. Jan. 1, 2008]

Form 2. Notice of the Rights of Victims in Juvenile Court

NOTICE OF THE RIGHTS OF VICTIMS IN JUVENILE COURT

1. Right to Participation

Minnesota law (Minn. Stat. § 260B.163, subd.1 (2002) and § 611A.01, et seq. (2002)) prohibits the public from attending juvenile hearings in most cases. However, a person who has a direct interest in the case, such as a crime victim, has the following rights to participate:

a. The right to have input in a pretrial diversion program decision;
b. The right to object to the proposed disposition and a plea agreement;
c. The right to request the prosecutor make a demand for a speedy trial;
d. The right to be present in court at the time of the disposition hearing (sentencing); and
e. The right to submit an impact statement to the judge orally or in writing, at the time of disposition (sentencing) hearing.

2. Right to Notification

You have a right to be notified of certain information such as the following:

a. The contents of any plea agreement;
b. The schedule changes in court proceedings if you have been subpoenaed or requested to testify;
c. The information regarding the detention hearing of an arrested or detained juvenile;
d. The final disposition of the case;
e. The transfer of the juvenile to a less secure correctional facility;
f. The release of the juvenile from a custodial institution; and
g. The escape and apprehension of the juvenile from a custodial institution.

3. Right to Protection

As a victim and/or witness, you have certain rights to protection such as the following:

a. The right to a safe and secure waiting area during the court process, if available;
b. The right to ask a law enforcement agency to withhold public access to data revealing your identity;
c. The right not to give your home or business address in open court; and
d. The right not to be retaliated against by employers if you are called to testify as a victim or witness.

4. Right to Financial Assistance

You may be eligible for financial assistance from the state through the Crime Victims' Reparations Board if you have suffered economic loss as a result of a violent crime. Also, you may ask the court to order the juvenile to pay restitution under Minn. Stat. §611A.04. If the juvenile fails to pay restitution as ordered, you have the right to ask the juvenile's probation officer to request a probation review hearing.

5. Additional Rights

In cases involving sex offenses, you have the right to be notified whether the offender has any sexually transmitted diseases, and may also have the right to ask that the offender submit to HIV-testing.

Page 1 of 2 (10/02)

TERMS USED IN JUVENILE COURT PROCEEDINGS

DETENTION

A juvenile can be detained in foster care, at a shelter care facility, at a secure detention facility, at a detoxification, chemical dependency or psychiatric facility, at an adult jail, or in the juvenile's home subject to electronic home monitoring. Most juveniles must appear before the court within 36 hours of being taken into custody for a detention hearing.

ARRAIGNMENT

At the arraignment hearing, the juvenile will appear in court and be asked to plead guilty or not guilty to the charges. Juveniles are entitled to representation by an attorney. A plea of guilty leads to a disposition (sentencing) hearing. If a juvenile pleads not guilty, there will be a trial.

PRETRIAL HEARING

In some cases, the judge orders a pretrial hearing to decide issues of law and allow the parties the opportunity to settle the case before trial.

TRIAL

A juvenile has the same legal protections during trial as an adult charged with a crime. Most juvenile trials are held before a judge who will decide whether the juvenile is guilty or not guilty. If the petition has been proved, there will be a disposition hearing.

DISPOSITION

The disposition may include restitution, fines, community service, probation, out-of-home placement, counseling or treatment, and/or victim/offender mediation. The court will take into consideration the seriousness of the offense, the child's prior history of offenses, and available programs and services.

Page 2 of 2 (10/02)

Adopted July 18, 2003, eff. Sept. 1, 2003.

Form 3. Notice in Lieu of Summons

STATE OF MINNESOTA	DISTRICT COURT - JUVENILE DIVISION
COUNTY OF ______________	_______ JUDICIAL DISTRICT

In the Matter of the Welfare of:	NOTICE IN LIEU OF SUMMONS
______________________________ Child	Court File No. __________

TO: The above-named child and to the child's parent(s), legal guardian(s), legal custodian(s) or person having custody and control of child:

ADDRESS: [ ]

PLEASE take notice that a petition has been filed with this Court alleging that the child is a:

- ☐ juvenile traffic offender
- ☐ juvenile petty offender
- ☐ juvenile delinquent

and the Court has directed that a hearing be held in this matter at the _____ Courthouse, Courtroom _____,

in _____, Minnesota on ______at ______before a District Court Judge or Referee.

YOU ARE entitled to have a summons requiring your appearance served upon you. The Court has directed that this notice be mailed to you instead of issuing a summons. However, if you do not appear at the hearing, a summons will be issued.

Attached is a copy of the:

- ☐ charging document
- ☐ court order
- ☐ motion
- ☐ affidavit
- ☐ other: ______________________

ALSO attached is a statement describing the purpose of the hearing, the possible consequences of the hearing and an explanation of the child's basic rights, including the right of the child's parent(s), legal guardian(s), or legal custodian(s) to participate. PLEASE READ ATTACHED ITEMS CAREFULLY.

DATE:	BY THE COURT:
BY: ______________________ Deputy	______________________ Court Administrator

Served by Regular Mail:	
DATE:	BY: ______________________

(11/02)

Adopted July 18, 2003, eff. Sept. 1, 2003.

Form 4. Summons

STATE OF MINNESOTA **DISTRICT COURT - JUVENILE DIVISION**

COUNTY OF ______________ ______ **JUDICIAL DISTRICT**

In the Matter of the Welfare of: **SUMMONS**

______________________________ Child

Court File No. ____________

TO: The above-named child and to the child's parent(s), legal guardian(s), legal custodian(s) or person having custody and control of child:

ADDRESS:

PLEASE take notice that a petition has been filed with this Court alleging that the child is a:

☐ juvenile traffic offender
☐ juvenile petty offender
☐ juvenile delinquent

and the Court has directed that a hearing be held in this matter at the _____ Courthouse, Courtroom _____, in _____, Minnesota on _____ at _____ before a District Court Judge or Referee.

Attached is a copy of the:

☐ charging document
☐ court order
☐ motion
☐ affidavit
☐ other: ____________________

ALSO attached is a statement describing the purpose of the hearing, the possible consequences of the hearing and an explanation of the child's basic rights, including the right of the child's parent(s), legal guardian(s), or legal custodian(s) to participate. PLEASE READ ATTACHED ITEMS CAREFULLY.

TAKE NOTICE THAT if you fail to appear in response to this Summons, the Court may: (1) issue a warrant for your arrest; and (2) conduct a hearing without your presence and grant appropriate relief. Further information concerning the date and consequences of later hearings, if any, may be obtained from the Court by a request in writing.

DATE: BY THE COURT:

BY: ____________________ ____________________
Deputy Court Administrator

☐ Served by Certified Mail ☐ Served Personally

DATE: ____________ BY: ____________________

(11/02)

Adopted July 18, 2003, eff. Sept. 1, 2003.

Form 5. Prosecutor's Request for Disclosure

STATE OF MINNESOTA **DISTRICT COURT - JUVENILE DIVISION**

COUNTY OF ______________ ______ **JUDICIAL DISTRICT**

In the Matter of the Welfare of:

PROSECUTOR'S REQUEST FOR DISCLOSURE

______________________________ Child

Court File No. __________

Pursuant to Rule 10.05 of the Minnesota Rules of Juvenile Procedure, the County Attorney requests the child to make disclosure of the following items, which the child intends to introduce into evidence at the trial, certification, or extended jurisdiction juvenile hearing:

(1) documents and tangible objects;
(2) reports of examinations and tests;
(3) notice of defenses;
(4) names, addresses, and record of criminal convictions or delinquency adjudications of child's witnesses;
(5) statements of child's witnesses;
(6) details of and witnesses to the defense of alibi; and
(7) record of child's prior proven or admitted delinquency offenses.

This request for disclosure incorporates by reference the language of Rule 10.05 and shall be deemed to be a request for disclosure of all information to which the County Attorney is entitled under the provisions of that Rule.

Date: ______________

____
__________ County Attorney

(11/02)

Adopted July 18, 2003, eff. Sept. 1, 2003.

Form 6. Prosecutor Notice of Evidence and Identification Procedures

STATE OF MINNESOTA **DISTRICT COURT - JUVENILE DIVISION**

COUNTY OF ______________ ______ **JUDICIAL DISTRICT**

In the Matter of the Welfare of:

______________________ Child

PROSECUTOR NOTICE OF EVIDENCE AND IDENTIFICATION PROCEDURES

Court File No. ____________

TO: THE ABOVE-NAMED CHILD AND COUNSEL FOR CHILD:

Pursuant to Rule 10.02 of the Minnesota Rules of Juvenile Procedure, you are advised that in the above-captioned case, the Prosecutor has:

☐ Evidence obtained as a result of a search, search and seizure, wiretapping, or other forms of electronic or mechanical eavesdropping;

☐ Confessions, admissions or statements in the nature of confessions made by the child;

☐ Evidence discovered as a result of confessions, admissions or statements in the nature of confessions made by the child;

☐ Identification procedures used during the investigation were:

- ☐ Line-ups
- ☐ Observations of the respondent
- ☐ Exhibition of photographs
- ☐ Other ______________________________
- ☐ None of above is known to the prosecution at this time; you will be notified if any is discovered.

Date: ______________

____

__________ County Attorney

(11/02)

Adopted July 18, 2003, eff. Sept. 1, 2003.

Form 7. Petition to Proceed as Pro Se in Juvenile Delinquency Proceeding

STATE OF MINNESOTA **DISTRICT COURT - JUVENILE DIVISION**

COUNTY OF ________________ ________ **JUDICIAL DISTRICT**

In the Matter of the Welfare of:

______________________________ Child

PETITION TO PROCEED PRO SE IN JUVENILE DELINQUENCY PROCEEDING

Court File No. ____________

My full name is ______________________________, and I am the child in the above-entitled action.
I request the Court allow me to represent myself and state as follows:

1. I am ______ years old. My date of birth is ________. The last grade I attended in school is ________.
2. I have received and read the charging document in this matter.
3. I understand the charge(s) made against me in this case.
4. I understand that I have been charged with the offense(s) of:

   ____

   committed on or about __________ in ______________ County, Minnesota.
5. I have discussed my desire to represent myself with an attorney whose name is ____________.
6. I (have) (have not) been a patient in a mental hospital.
7. I (have) (have not) talked with or been treated by a psychiatrist or other person for a nervous or mental condition.
8. I (have) (have not) been ill recently.
9. I (have) (have not) recently taken pills or medicine.
10. I understand that I have the right to have an attorney represent me in these proceedings. I understand that if the Court grants my petition to represent myself, I will be responsible for preparing my case for trial and trying my case. I understand that I will be bound by the same rules as an attorney. I understand that if I fail to do something in a timely manner or make a mistake because of my unfamiliarity with the law, I will be bound by those decisions and must deal with them myself.
11. In making my decisions regarding the conduct of this case, I have the right to consult with standby counsel if one is assigned to this case.
12. I understand the Court will schedule a probable cause hearing if one has not already been held. At the probable cause hearing, I can request that the petition or indictment filed against me be dismissed for lack of probable cause. The preparation for, conduct of, and decisions made relating to that hearing will be my sole responsibility.
13. I understand that I am entitled to a court trial. I further understand that I will conduct all phases of the trial, including but not limited to writing and filing motions, making arguments to the Court, cross-examination of the witnesses for the prosecution, direct examination of my witnesses, making objections, opening statement and closing argument.
14. I understand I am entitled to require any witnesses I think are favorable to me to appear and testify at my trial by use of a subpoena.

Page 1 of 2 (11/02)

15. I understand that a person who has a prior delinquency record can be given a longer out-of-home placement. The maximum statutory penalty the Court could impose if I am adjudicated delinquent is commitment to the Commissioner of Corrections until my 19th birthday. The maximum statutory penalty the court could impose if I am certified to adult court or prosecuted as an extended jurisdiction juvenile is commitment to the Commissioner of Corrections for a term as determined by the Minnesota Sentencing Guidelines.

16. I understand the Court may appoint a public defender to act as standby counsel in this case. However, I am under no obligation to seek advice from standby counsel. I understand that the role of standby counsel is as follows:

   a. Standby counsel will be physically present in the courtroom during all proceedings in my case.
   b. Standby counsel will respond to requests for advice from me. Standby counsel will not initiate such discussion.
   c. Support staff of the public defender, such as investigators, secretaries, law clerks, and legal service advisors will not be available to me.
   d. If I need investigative services, expert services, waivers of fees, research, secretarial services, or any other assistance, I must ask the Court for the relief or assistance I need. Such request is made pursuant to Minnesota Statutes, section 611.21.
   e. If I desire to conduct legal research, I will be expected to do it myself.
   f. Standby counsel will not be prepared to try my case on the trial date unless ordered to prepare to do so by the Court.
   g. Standby counsel will be present for all court appearances to consult with me if I request. Standby counsel will be seated either at the back of the courtroom or at counsel table, based on my wishes and the Court's order. In an effort to support my constitutional right to self-representation, standby counsel will not initiate motions, objections, arguments to the Court, or any other aspect of representation unless I have given approval to that specific aspect of representation.
   h. If I wish to give up my right to represent myself, I know the Court will not automatically grant my request. The Court will consider the following in granting or denying that request: the stage of the proceedings, whether standby counsel is prepared to take over, the length of the continuance necessary for standby counsel to assume representation, the prejudice to either party, and any other relevant considerations.
   i. If the Court grants my request to represent myself and orders standby counsel, the trial date may be continued if requested by the standby counsel.
   j. If the Court orders standby counsel to represent me after the trial has started and jeopardy has attached, the Court may grant a mistrial if requested by my new attorney and reset the trial date. It is solely up to the Court whether to grant a mistrial.

17. I have read the above two pages, discussed them with counsel, and I understand the rights and responsibilities I have in representing myself. In consideration of those rights and responsibilities, I want to give up my right to be represented by an attorney and will represent myself.

Date: ____________________ ______________________________
Child

Page 2 of 2 (11/02)

Adopted July 18, 2003, eff. Sept. 1, 2003.

Form 8. Statement of Rights: Juvenile Delinquency Proceedings

STATEMENT OF RIGHTS
JUVENILE DELINQUENCY PROCEEDINGS

You have been charged with a delinquent act by a document filed in Juvenile Court. You are presumed innocent of the charge(s) unless and until the state is able to prove guilt beyond a reasonable doubt. You have the following rights:

1. The right to understand the charge(s) against you.

2. The right to be represented by an attorney. If you cannot afford an attorney, the judge will appoint an attorney for you at public expense. The judge may order you or your parent(s), legal guardian(s), or legal custodian(s) to pay some or all of the attorney expense depending on the ability to pay. You may not be represented in court by anyone who is not an attorney, even if that person is your parent.

3. The right to plead guilty, plead not guilty, or remain silent. If you remain silent, the judge will enter a not guilty plea for you and the case will go to trial.

4. If you plead not guilty, you have additional rights including:

   a. The right to a trial before a judge;
   b. The right to require the state to prove beyond a reasonable doubt that you committed the offense(s);
   c. The right to cross-examine witnesses called by the state;
   d. The right to subpoena witnesses and present evidence on your own behalf; and
   e. The right not to testify or to give an explanation of your actions.

5. If you plead guilty, you give up the rights listed in paragraph 4. The judge will ask you what you did. The judge cannot accept your guilty plea unless you admit doing something that is against the law.

6. Your guilty plea must be made freely and voluntarily, without threats or promises by anyone, with the exception of any plea agreement.

7. If you plead guilty or the judge finds you guilty, the judge may:

   a. Counsel you and your parent(s), legal guardian(s) or legal custodian(s).
   b. Place you on probation in your own home under conditions established by the court;
   c. Transfer your legal custody under court supervision and place you out of your home;
   d. Transfer your legal custody by commitment to the Commissioner of Corrections;
   e. Order restitution for any damage done to person(s) and/or property;
   f. Order special treatment or care for your physical or mental health;
   g. Recommend to the Commissioner of Public Safety that your driver's license be canceled;

Page 1 of 2 (11/02)

h. Order community work service and/or a fine up to $700.00;
i. Require you to attend school until age 18 or completion of graduation requirements;
j. Consider imposition of additional consequences if you committed a "crime of violence" and/or if a gun or dangerous weapon was involved;
k. Require you to submit a DNA sample if you have been charged with a felony; and/or
l. Require you to have a psychosexual evaluation, register as a predatory offender, and submit a DNA sample if you have been charged with a sexual offense or predatory offense.

8. If you plead guilty or the judge finds you guilty of a felony after your 14th birthday, this case may be used as a basis for additional jail or prison time if you are sentenced for another felony as an adult before your 25th birthday.

9. If you plead guilty or the judge finds you guilty of an offense, this case may be used as a basis to transfer any future felony-level case to adult court or treat it as an extended jurisdiction juvenile prosecution.

10. Your parent(s), legal guardian(s), or legal custodian(s) may not participate in the hearing until you either plead guilty or the judge finds you guilty of the offense. At that time your parent(s), legal guardian(s), or legal custodian(s) has the right to present information to the judge and may be represented by an attorney.

IF YOU HAVE ANY QUESTIONS ABOUT YOUR RIGHTS, ASK YOUR ATTORNEY BEFORE THE HEARING OR ASK THE JUDGE DURING YOUR HEARING.

DATE: ____________________ ____________________
(Signature of Child)

DATE: ____________________ ____________________
(Signature of Parent, Legal Guardian, or Legal Custodian)

Page 2 of 2 (11/02)

Adopted July 18, 2003, eff. Sept. 1, 2003.

Form 9. Statement of Rights: Juvenile Petty Offender Proceedings

STATEMENT OF RIGHTS
JUVENILE PETTY OFFENDER PROCEEDINGS

You have been charged with a petty offense by a document filed in Juvenile Court. You are presumed innocent of the charge(s) unless and until the state is able to prove guilt beyond a reasonable doubt. You have the following rights:

1. The right to understand the charge(s) against you.

2. The right to be represented by an attorney that you hire. You do not have a right to appointment of a public defender or other counsel at public expense. If you wish to be represented by an attorney, you or your parent(s), legal guardian(s), or legal custodian(s) must hire one and pay the cost. You may not be represented in court by anyone who is not an attorney, even if that person is your parent.

3. The right to plead guilty, plead not guilty, or remain silent. If you remain silent, the judge will enter a not guilty plea for you and the case will go to trial.

4. If you plead not guilty, you have additional rights including:

   a. The right to a trial before a judge;
   b. The right to require the state to prove beyond a reasonable doubt that you committed the offense(s);
   c. The right to cross-examine witnesses called by the state;
   d. The right to subpoena witnesses and present evidence on your own behalf; and
   e. The right not to testify or to give an explanation of your actions.

5. If you plead guilty, you give up the rights listed in paragraph 4. The judge will ask you what you did. The judge cannot accept your plea unless you admit doing something that is an offense.

6. Your guilty plea must be made freely and voluntarily, without threats or promises by anyone, with the exception of any plea agreement.

7. If you plead guilty or the judge finds you guilty of an offense, the judge may:

   a. Require you to pay a fine of up to $100;
   b. Require you to take part in a community service project;
   c. Require you to participate in a drug awareness program;
   d. Place you on probation for up to six months;
   e. Order you to undergo a chemical dependency evaluation and participate in an outpatient treatment program;
   f. Order restitution for any damage to person(s) and/or property; and/or
   g. Order you to perform other activities or participate in other outpatient treatment programs deemed appropriate by the judge.

Page 1 of 2 (11/02)

8. If you plead guilty or the judge finds you guilty of a second or subsequent juvenile alcohol or controlled substance offense, in addition to the above penalties, the judge may:

a. Send your driver's license or driving permit to the Commissioner of Public Safety who shall revoke it for one year or until your 18th birthday, whichever is longer.
b. Suspend your driver's license or driving permit for up to 90 days, but allow you to travel to work.
c. If you do not have a driver's license or driving permit, the judge may order denial of your driving privileges for one year or until your 18th birthday, whichever is longer.

9. If you plead guilty to, or the judge finds you committed a third juvenile alcohol or controlled substance offense, and a chemical dependency evaluation recommends inpatient treatment, you have a right to appointment of a public defender or other counsel at public expense.

10. Your parent(s), legal guardian(s), or legal custodians(s) may not participate in the hearing until you have either pled guilty or the judge finds you guilty of the offense. At that time, your parent(s), legal guardian(s), or legal custodian(s) has the right to present information to the judge and may be represented by an attorney.

IF YOU HAVE ANY QUESTIONS ABOUT YOUR RIGHTS, ASK YOUR ATTORNEY BEFORE THE HEARING. IF YOU DO NOT HAVE AN ATTORNEY, ASK THE JUDGE DURING YOUR HEARING.

DATE: ________________ ________________________________
(Signature of Child)

DATE: ________________ ________________________________
(Signature of Parent, Legal Guardian, or Legal Custodian)

Page 2 of 2 (11/02)

Adopted July 18, 2003, eff. Sept. 1, 2003.

Form 10. Statement of Rights: Juvenile Traffic Offender Proceedings

STATEMENT OF RIGHTS
JUVENILE TRAFFIC OFFENDER PROCEEDINGS

You have been charged as a juvenile traffic offender by a document filed in Juvenile Court. You are presumed innocent of the charge(s) unless and until the state is able to prove guilt beyond a reasonable doubt. You have the following rights:

1. The right to understand the charge(s) against you.

2. The right to be represented by an attorney that you hire. You do not have a right to appointment of a public defender or other counsel at public expense. If you wish to be represented by an attorney, you or your parent(s), legal guardian(s), or legal custodian(s) must hire one and pay the cost. You may not be represented in court by anyone who is not an attorney, even if that person is your parent.

3. The right to plead guilty, plead not guilty, or remain silent. If you remain silent, the judge will enter a not guilty plea for you and the case will go to trial.

4. If you plead not guilty, you have additional rights including:

   a. The right to a trial before a judge;
   b. The right to require the state to prove beyond a reasonable doubt that you committed the offense(s);
   c. The right to cross-examine witnesses called by the state;
   d. The right to subpoena witnesses and present evidence on your own behalf; and
   e. The right not to testify or to give an explanation of your actions.

5. If you plead guilty, you give up the rights listed in paragraph 4. The judge will ask you what you did. The judge cannot accept your plea unless you admit doing something that is an offense.

6. Your guilty plea must be made freely and voluntarily, without threats or promises by anyone, with the exception of any plea agreement.

7. If you plead guilty or the judge finds you guilty of an offense, the judge may:

   a. Reprimand you and counsel you and your parent(s), legal guardian(s) or legal custodian(s);
   b. Continue the case for a reasonable period under such conditions governing your use and operation of motor vehicles or watercraft as the court may set;
   c. Require you to attend a driver improvement course;
   d. Recommend that the Commissioner of Public Safety suspend your driver's license;

Page 1 of 2 (11/02)

e. If you are found to have committed two moving highway traffic violations or to have contributed to a highway accident involving death, injury, or physical damage in excess of $100, the judge may recommend that the Commissioner of Public Safety cancel your driver's license until you are 18;

f. Place you on probation in your own home under conditions set by the judge including reasonable rules relating to the operation and use of motor vehicles or watercraft;

g. Order restitution for any damage to person(s) and/or property;

h. Order community work service or a fine up to $700; and/or

i. Order a chemical assessment for alcohol-related driving offenses and charge $75.00 for the assessment.

8. Your parent(s), legal guardian(s), or legal custodian(s) may not participate in the hearing until you have either pled guilty or the judge finds you guilty of the offense. At that time, your parent(s), legal guardian(s), or legal custodian(s) has the right to present information to the judge and may be represented by an attorney.

IF YOU HAVE ANY QUESTIONS ABOUT YOUR RIGHTS, ASK YOUR ATTORNEY BEFORE THE HEARING. IF YOU DO NOT HAVE AN ATTORNEY, ASK THE JUDGE DURING YOUR HEARING.

DATE: ______________________ ______________________________

(Signature of Child)

DATE: ______________________ ______________________________

(Signature of Parent, Legal Guardian, or Legal Custodian)

Page 2 of 2 (11/02)

Adopted July 18, 2003, eff. Sept. 1, 2003.

Form 11. Statement of Rights: Juvenile Probation Revocation

STATEMENT OF RIGHTS
JUVENILE PROBATION REVOCATION

A probation revocation is a hearing before a judge to decide if a juvenile violated a term or condition of probation, and if so, whether the judge should change the disposition.

You will be asked to admit or deny the allegations of the probation violation. You have the following rights:

1. You have the right to have an attorney represent you. You may have the right to an attorney appointed at public expense.

2. If you deny the allegations of the probation violation, you have a right to a hearing before a judge. The hearing must be held within seven days if you are removed from your home. If you are allowed to remain in your home pending the probation revocation hearing, the hearing must be held within a reasonable time. If you admit the probation violation, you give up your right to a probation revocation hearing.

3. Before the hearing, you are entitled to receive all the evidence of the probation violation that will be used against you, including probation revocation reports and all records relating to the proceedings.

4. At the probation revocation hearing, both you and the prosecuting attorney have the right to offer evidence, make arguments, subpoena witnesses, and call and cross-examine witnesses. You may testify in your own defense or remain silent throughout the hearing. You may present mitigating circumstances or other reasons why the probation violation, if proved, should not result in a change in the disposition order.

5. The probation violation must be proved by clear and convincing evidence. You have the right to appeal the decision of the court after a revocation hearing.

DATE: ____________________ ______________________________
(Signature of Child)

DATE: ____________________ ______________________________
(Signature of Parent, Legal Guardian, or Legal Custodian)

(11/02)

Adopted July 18, 2003, eff. Sept. 1, 2003.

Form 12. Waiver of Right to Contested Hearing in an Extended Jurisdiction Juvenile Case

STATE OF MINNESOTA | DISTRICT COURT - JUVENILE DIVISION

COUNTY OF ______________ ______ JUDICIAL DISTRICT

In the Matter of the Welfare of:

____
Child

WAIVER OF RIGHT TO CONTESTED HEARING IN AN EXTENDED JURISDICTION JUVENILE CASE

Court File No. ________

I have been advised by my attorney and I understand the following rights:

1. My full name is ______________ and I have been charged by Delinquency Petition in juvenile court with the offense(s) of: ______________ which would be a felony if committed by an adult. This felony carries a presumptive sentence of ______ months in prison under the Minnesota Sentencing Guidelines and applicable statutes. [range]
2. The offense(s) is alleged to have occurred on ______________ and I was at least 14 years old at the time, having a date of birth of ______________
3. For the purpose of this waiver only, I submit there is probable cause to believe I committed the offense(s).
4. I understand that I have a right to an attorney.
5. The prosecutor has brought a motion for extended jurisdiction juvenile prosecution, and I understand I have a right to a hearing before a judge.
6. At that hearing, the prosecutor must show by clear and convincing evidence that designating the proceeding as an extended jurisdiction juvenile prosecution serves public safety. I have discussed the public safety factors with my attorney.
7. I understand I could present witnesses and evidence at that hearing.
8. I understand I could cross-examine all witnesses who testify for the state.
9. I understand I could present arguments against the extended jurisdiction juvenile prosecution.
10. I understand that by waiving my right to a hearing I agree that my case can proceed to a jury trial on the above-named offense(s). If I am found guilty, I will be subject to the penalties of both juvenile and adult court, including a stayed sentence under Minnesota Sentencing Guidelines and criminal statutes.
11. I have discussed with my attorney and understand the potential maximum penalties under the Minnesota Sentencing Guidelines and criminal statutes. I have discussed and understand that if I violate the terms of the stayed adult sentence, I have a right to a hearing, but if the court finds the violation proven, I will be in the adult court system where a prison sentence could be imposed. We have discussed and I understand that there may be sentencing departures, either upward if the court finds aggravating circumstances, or downward if the court finds mitigating factors in the case.

☐ No promise of any agreement has been made to me.

☐ The following agreement has been reached in exchange for my waiver:

Page 1 of 2 (11/02)

12. I understand I have a right to discuss my case with my parent(s), legal guardian(s), or legal custodian(s), and I have either done so or waive my right to do so.

13. I understand the court will find I represent a danger to the public safety if kept solely within the juvenile system and will order an extended jurisdiction juvenile prosecution.

14. If a psychological evaluation has been completed, I understand I may request additional psychological evaluations and explore alternative treatment programs to find a suitable juvenile disposition option and demonstrate to the court that I do not represent a danger to the public safety if I remain in the juvenile system.

15. Based upon all of this information and investigation, I am choosing to waive or give up my right to have an extended jurisdiction juvenile hearing.

16. No threats have been made to coerce me into waiving these rights. No promises have been made to me except as set forth in paragraph 11.

17. I am waiving or giving up my rights freely and voluntarily. I have had sufficient time to discuss my rights and options with my attorney.

DATE: ____________ ______________________________
Child

DATE: ____________ ______________________________
Child's Attorney

Page 2 of 2 (11/02)

Adopted July 18, 2003, eff. Sept. 1, 2003.

Form 13. Waiver of Right to Contested Hearing in a Non–Presumptive Certification Case

STATE OF MINNESOTA DISTRICT COURT - JUVENILE DIVISION

COUNTY OF ______________ ______ JUDICIAL DISTRICT

In the Matter of the Welfare of:

____
Child

WAIVER OF RIGHT TO CONTESTED HEARING IN A NON-PRESUMPTIVE CERTIFICATION CASE

Court File No. ____________

I have been advised by my attorney and I understand the following rights:

1. My full name is ______________________________ and I have been charged by Delinquency Petition in juvenile court with the offense(s) of: ______________________________ which would be a felony if committed by an adult. This felony carries a presumptive sentence of ________ months in prison under the Minnesota Sentencing Guidelines and applicable statutes. [range]
2. The offense(s) is alleged to have occurred on ______________________________ and I was at least 14 years old at the time, having a date of birth of __________.
3. For the purpose of this waiver only, I submit there is probable cause to believe I committed the offense(s).
4. I understand that I have a right to an attorney.
5. The prosecutor has brought a motion for certification, and I understand I have a right to a hearing before a judge.
6. At that hearing, it is the prosecutor's burden to demonstrate to the judge by clear and convincing evidence that retaining my case in juvenile court does not serve public safety. I have discussed the public safety factors with my attorney.
7. I understand I could present witnesses and evidence at that hearing.
8. I understand I could cross-examine all witnesses who testify for the state.
9. I understand I could present arguments against certification.
10. I understand that by waiving my right to a hearing I agree that my case can proceed to adult court for a jury trial on the above-named offense(s) and be subject to the penalties under Minnesota Sentencing Guidelines and criminal statutes.
11. I have discussed with my attorney and understand the potential maximum penalties under the Minnesota Sentencing Guidelines and criminal statutes. We have discussed and I understand that there may be sentencing departures, either upward if the court finds aggravating circumstances, or downward if the court finds mitigating factors in the case.

☐ No promise of any agreement has been made to me.

☐ The following agreement has been reached in exchange for my waiver:

12. I understand I have a right to discuss my case with my parent(s), legal guardian(s), or legal custodian(s), and I have either done so or waive my right to do so.
13. I understand the court will find that I represent a danger to the public safety if kept within the juvenile system and will order certification for trial as an adult.
14. If a psychological evaluation has been completed, I understand I may request additional psychological evaluations and explore alternative treatment programs to find a suitable juvenile disposition option and demonstrate to the court that I do not represent a danger to the public safety if my case is kept in the juvenile system.
15. Based upon all of this information and investigation, I am choosing to waive or give up my right to have a contested certification hearing.
16. No threats have been made to coerce me into waiving these rights. No promises have been made to me except as set forth in paragraph 11.
17. I am waiving or giving up my rights freely and voluntarily. I have had sufficient time to discuss my rights and options with my attorney.

DATE: ________	________________ Child
DATE: ________	________________ Child's Attorney

Page 2 of 2 (11/02)

Adopted July 18, 2003, eff. Sept. 1, 2003.

Form 14. Waiver of Right to Contested Hearing in a Presumptive Certification Case

STATE OF MINNESOTA **DISTRICT COURT - JUVENILE DIVISION**

COUNTY OF ______________ ________ **JUDICIAL DISTRICT**

In the Matter of the Welfare of:

______________________________ Child

WAIVER OF RIGHT TO CONTESTED HEARING IN A PRESUMPTIVE CERTIFICATION CASE

Court File No. ____________

I have been advised by my attorney and I understand the following rights:

1. My full name is ______________________ and I have been charged by Delinquency Petition in juvenile court with the offense(s) of: ______________________ which would be a felony if committed by an adult. This felony carries a presumptive sentence of ________ months in prison under the Minnesota Sentencing Guidelines and applicable statutes. [range]
2. The offense(s) is alleged to have occurred on ______________________ and I was 16 or 17 years old at the time, having a date of birth of __________ .
3. For the purpose of this waiver only, I submit there is probable cause to believe I committed the offense(s).
4. I understand that I have a right to an attorney.
5. The prosecutor has brought a motion for certification, and I understand I have a right to a hearing before a judge.
6. At that hearing, it is my burden to show the judge by clear and convincing evidence that retaining my case in juvenile court serves public safety. I have discussed the public safety factors with my attorney.
7. I understand I could present witnesses and evidence at that hearing.
8. I understand I could cross-examine all witnesses who testify for the state.
9. I understand I could present arguments against certification. I further understand that if I prevailed at the certification hearing, the court must order that my case proceed as an extended jurisdiction juvenile prosecution.
10. I understand that by waiving my right to a hearing I agree that my case can proceed to adult court for a jury trial on the above-named offense(s) and be subject to the penalties under Minnesota Sentencing Guidelines and criminal statutes.
11. I have discussed with my attorney and understand the potential maximum penalties under the Minnesota Sentencing Guidelines and criminal statutes. I have discussed and understand that the charged offenses presume an executed prison sentence. We have discussed and I understand that there may be sentencing departures, either upward if the court finds aggravating circumstances, or downward if the court finds mitigating factors in the case.

☐ No promise of any agreement has been made to me.

☐ The following agreement has been reached in exchange for my waiver:

Page 1 of 2 (11/02)

12. I understand I have a right to discuss my case with my parent(s), legal guardian(s), or legal custodian(s), and I have either done so or waive my right to do so.
13. I understand the court will find that I represent a danger to the public safety if kept within the juvenile system and will order certification for trial as an adult.
14. If a psychological evaluation has been completed, I understand I may request additional psychological evaluations and explore alternative treatment programs to find a suitable juvenile disposition option and demonstrate to the court that I do not represent a danger to the public safety if returned to the extended jurisdiction juvenile system.
15. Based upon all of this information and investigation, I am choosing to waive or give up my right to have a contested certification hearing.
16. No threats have been made to coerce me into waiving these rights. No promises have been made to me except as set forth in paragraph 11.
17. I am waiving or giving up my rights freely and voluntarily. I have had sufficient time to discuss my rights and options with my attorney.

DATE:	______________	______________________________ Child
DATE:	______________	______________________________ Child's Attorney

Page 2 of 2 (11/02)

Adopted July 18, 2003, eff. Sept. 1, 2003.

Form 15. Petition to Enter Plea of Guilty in an Extended Jurisdiction Juvenile Case

STATE OF MINNESOTA **DISTRICT COURT - JUVENILE DIVISION**

COUNTY OF ______________ ______ **JUDICIAL DISTRICT**

In the Matter of the Welfare of:

____
Child

PETITION TO ENTER PLEA OF GUILTY IN EXTENDED JURISDICTION JUVENILE CASE

Court File No. ____________

---

1. My full name is ______________________________ and I have been charged by Delinquency Petition in juvenile court with the offense(s) of: ______________________________ which would be a felony if committed by an adult. This felony carries a presumptive sentence of ________ [range] months in prison under the Minnesota Sentencing Guidelines and applicable statutes.
2. The offense(s) is alleged to have occurred on ______________________________ and I was ________ years old at the time, having a date of birth of ____________ .
3. In understand the charge(s) against me in this case.
4. I understand that I have a right to an attorney.
5. I am represented by an attorney, and:
   a. I feel that I have had sufficient time to discuss my case with my attorney.
   b. I am satisfied that my attorney is fully informed as to the facts of this case.
   c. My attorney has discussed possible defenses that I may have.
   d. I am satisfied that my attorney has represented my interests and has fully advised me.
6. I understand I have the right to a jury trial, and at that trial I have the following rights:
   a. The right to be presumed innocent unless and until proven guilty beyond a reasonable doubt.
   b. The right to be present and cross-examine all witnesses brought by the prosecutor.
   c. The right to subpoena and bring in my own witnesses.
   d. The right to remain silent or testify in my own defense. I understand that if I choose to remain silent, my silence could not be used against me.
   e. The right to a unanimous verdict by the jury.
7. I understand that if I enter a plea of guilty to an offense, I give up the rights listed above in #6.
8. I understand that the judge will not accept a plea from someone who says they are innocent. I am not saying that I am innocent of the charge(s) to which I am pleading guilty.
9. I am entering my plea of guilty freely and voluntarily.

☐ No promise of any agreement has been made to me.

☐ The following agreement has been reached in exchange for my plea:

Page 1 of 2 (11/02)

10. If the court does not accept my guilty plea, I have a right to withdraw my plea and anything said in court cannot be used against me. However, if the court accepts my guilty plea, there will be a disposition in juvenile court and an adult prison sentence will be stayed.

11. I have discussed with my attorney and understand the potential maximum penalties under the Minnesota Sentencing Guidelines and criminal statutes. We have discussed and I understand that there may be sentencing departures, either upward if the court finds aggravating circumstances, or downward if the court finds mitigating factors in the case. I understand that if the court finds I have violated the terms of the stayed prison sentence, the court can send me to prison.

12. I understand I have a right to discuss my case with my parent(s), legal guardian(s), or legal custodian(s), and I have either done so or waive my right to do so.

13. I understand I could be on probation until my 21st birthday.

14. I understand that my plea may increase the penalties for future offenses, and this plea will be used to compute my adult criminal history score.

15. If I plead guilty and I am adjudicated for a "crime of violence," it may be illegal for me to possess any firearm.

16. If I plead guilty to a felony, I may be required to submit a DNA sample. For felony driving while impaired offenses and most sex offenses, a mandatory period of conditional release will follow the adult prison sentence if it is executed. Violating the terms of this conditional release may increase the time I serve in prison. In this case, the period of conditional release is _____ years.

17. If I plead guilty to a sexual offense or predatory offense, I may be required to have a psychosexual evaluation, register as a predatory offender, and submit a DNA sample.

18. I understand that if I am not a citizen of the United States, my guilty plea may result in deportation, exclusion from admission to the United States, or denial of naturalization as a United States citizen.

19. I understand that my probation or parole could be revoked because of the guilty plea to this offense.

20. I (have) (have not) been a patient in a mental hospital.

21. I (have) (have not) talked with or been treated by a psychiatrist or other person for a nervous or mental condition.

22. I (have) (have not) been ill recently.

23. I (have) (have not) recently taken pills or medicine.

24. Based upon all of this information, I am choosing to waive or give up my right to have a jury trial.

25. No threats have been made to coerce me into waiving these rights. No promises have been made to me except as set forth in paragraph 9.

26. I am waiving or giving up my rights freely and voluntarily. I have had sufficient time to discuss my rights and options with my attorney.

DATE: ______________	______________________________ Child
DATE: ______________	______________________________ Child's Attorney

Page 2 of 2 (11/02)

Adopted July 18, 2003, eff. Sept. 1, 2003.

Form 16. Petition to Enter Plea of Guilty in a Juvenile Delinquency Matter

STATE OF MINNESOTA DISTRICT COURT - JUVENILE DIVISION

COUNTY OF ________ ________ JUDICIAL DISTRICT

In the Matter of the Welfare of:

____

Child

PETITION TO ENTER PLEA OF GUILTY IN JUVENILE DELINQUENCY MATTER

Court File No. ________

1. My full name is ________________________. I am ______ years old, and my date of birth is ______. The last grade that I went through in school is ______ or I am currently attending the ______ grade in school.
2. I have received and read a copy of the charging document, and discussed it with my attorney.
3. I understand the charge(s) made against me in this case.
4. I understand that I have been charged with the offense(s) of:

   ____

   committed on or about ________ in ________________ County, Minnesota.
5. I am represented by an attorney, whose name is ________________ and:
   a. I feel that I have had sufficient time to discuss my case with my attorney.
   b. I am satisfied that my attorney is fully informed as to the facts of this case.
   c. My attorney has discussed possible defenses that I may have.
   d. I am satisfied that my attorney has represented my interests and has fully advised me.
6. I understand I have the right to a trial before a judge, and at that trial I have the following rights:
   a. The right to be presumed innocent unless and until the prosecutor proves me guilty beyond a reasonable doubt.
   b. The right to be present and ask questions of all witnesses brought by the prosecutor.
   c. The right to subpoena and bring in my own witnesses.
   d. The right to testify on my behalf or remain silent. I understand if I choose to remain silent the court cannot use my silence against me.
7. I understand that if I plead guilty to an offense, I give up my right to a trial in this case, including the rights stated in #6.
8. I understand that the judge will not accept a plea from someone who says they are innocent. I am not saying that I am innocent of the charge(s) to which I am pleading guilty.
9. I am entering my plea of guilty freely and voluntarily.

   ☐ No promise of any agreement has been made to me.

   ☐ The following agreement has been reached in exchange for my plea:

Page 1 of 2 (11/02)

10. If the court does not accept my guilty plea:
    a. I have the right to withdraw my guilty plea and have a trial.
    b. Anything I said in court about my plea cannot be used against me.
11. I understand that if the court accepts my guilty plea, there will be a disposition or sentencing.
12. I understand that the court could place me on probation until my 19th birthday. During that time, the court may change the disposition.
13. I understand that the court can:
    a. Place me out of home;
    b. Require me to participate in education and/or treatment programs;
    c. Require me to do community work service and/or pay a fine;
    d. Require me to pay restitution;
    e. Order cancellation, revocation, or suspension of my driver's license; and/or
    f. Require me to meet school graduation requirements.
14. If I violate the conditions of probation or commit a new offense, I could be arrested and placed in detention.
15. If the court adjudicates me for the offense I am admitting, I will have a juvenile court record.
16. I understand this offense could be used against me if I commit a future felony-level offense and the prosecutor in that case wishes to move for extended jurisdiction juvenile or certify me to adult court.
17. If I am admitting a felony offense today, and the offense was committed after my 14th birthday, I understand it will be used to compute my adult criminal history score.
18. If I plead guilty and I am adjudicated for a "crime of violence," it may be illegal for me to possess any firearm.
19. If I plead guilty to a felony, I may be required to submit a DNA sample.
20. If I plead guilty to a sexual offense or predatory offense, I may be required to have a psychosexual evaluation, register as a predatory offender, and submit a DNA sample.
21. I understand that if I am not a citizen of the United States, my guilty plea may result in deportation, exclusion from admission to the United States, or denial of naturalization as a United States citizen.
22. I understand that my probation or parole could be revoked because of the guilty plea to this offense.
23. I understand that my plea may result in increasing the level of a future offense to a gross misdemeanor or felony.
24. I (have) (have not) been a patient in a mental hospital.
25. I (have) (have not) talked with or been treated by a psychiatrist or other person for a nervous or mental condition.
26. I (have) (have not) been ill recently.
28. I (have) (have not) recently taken pills or medicine.
29. I have read this petition to plead guilty and I understand it. I am waiving or giving up my rights freely and voluntarily. I have had sufficient time to discuss my rights and options with my attorney.

DATE: ____________	____________________ Child
DATE: ____________	____________________ Child's Attorney

Page 2 of 2 (11/02)

Adopted July 18, 2003, eff. Sept. 1, 2003.

Form 17. EJJ Adult Stayed Sentence

State of Minnesota District Court

County | Judicial District | Case Number

State of Minnesota
vs.
____________________, Defendant.

CRIMINAL JUDGMENT / WARRANT OF COMMITMENT

TERMS AND CONDITIONS OF SENTENCE Date Pronounced: ____

Charge Resulting in Plea or Finding of Guilt	Minn. Stat. §	Count	Level of Offense

Offense Date: | Non-Conviction Dispositions: Count Number(s): ____ ☐ Dismissed ☐ Acquitted

☐ **FELONY LEVEL SENTENCE**

☐ Imposition of sentence is stayed for ____ years, ____ months, and ____ days; **OR**

☐ Commitment to the custody of the Commissioner of Corrections for ____ years, ____ months, and ____ days. The sentence consists of two parts: a minimum term of imprisonment equal to two-thirds (2/3) of the total executed sentence, and a maximum supervised release term equal to one-third (1/3) of the total executed sentence.

☐ Execution of this sentence is stayed for ____ years, ____ months.

☐ Execution of this sentence is stayed until the EJJ offender's 21st birthday on the condition that the EJJ offender not violate the terms of the juvenile disposition and not commit a new offense.

☐ Defendant shall pay a fine of $____, of which $____ is stayed for ____ years, ____ months.

☐ Other ____________________

☐ **MISDEMEANOR** ☐ **GROSS MISDEMEANOR LEVEL SENTENCE**

☐ Stay of imposition for ____ years, ____ months; **OR**

☐ Sentenced to jail for ____ days at this location: ____. In lieu of jail, may serve: ____. ☐ Execution of this sentence is stayed for ____ years, ____ months.

☐ Defendant shall pay a fine of $____, of which $____ is stayed for ____ years, ____ months.

☐ **JAIL CREDIT:** Credit for time spent in custody: ____ days.

☐ **SENTENCE DEPARTURE:** Sentence departs from the presumptive sentence under the Minnesota Sentencing Guidelines. **Attach a departure report.** Send a copy of this form and the attached departure report to the Minnesota Sentencing Guidelines Commission.

☐ **PROBATION:** The Defendant is placed on probation.

FINANCIAL CONDITIONS

The following financial conditions also apply to Case# ____ Count(s) ____
Fine Imposed $____ Fine Stayed $____
Restitution jointly and severally with: ____.

☐ Restitution $____
☐ Surcharge $____
☐ Law Library $____
☐ Court Costs $____
☐ Chem Fee $____
☐ Other: ____ $____
☐ Other: ____ $____
TOTAL $____

ADDITIONAL CONDITIONS

☐ ____ days in jail as a condition of a stayed sentence. In lieu of jail, defendant may: ____.
☐ Commit no felonies, gross misdemeanors or misdemeanors.
☐ No alcohol/illegal drug use. ☐ Enforce with random drug testing.
☐ Complete these evaluations/programs and follow recommendations:
☐ Domestic Abuse ☐ Chemical Dependency
☐ Sex Offender ☐ Psychological Evaluation/ Counseling
☐ Other: ____
☐ Other: ____
☐ ____ hours community service by ____.
☐ Other: ____
☐ Other: ____
☐ Other: ____

COMMENTS:

Sentencing Judge: Date:
I understand the terms and conditions of my sentence:
Defendant: Date:

Adopted Nov. 10, 2003, eff. Nov. 14, 2003.

INDEX TO RULES OF JUVENILE DELINQUENCY PROCEDURE

RULES OF JUVENILE PROTECTION PROCEDURE

Effective January 1, 2004

Including Amendments Received Through January 1, 2014

Research Note

See Minnesota Statutes Annotated, *Volume 52, for case annotations and cross references. The Rules of Juvenile Procedure are discussed in Scott and Sonsteng, 12 and 13* Minnesota Practice–Juvenile Law and Practice (3d Edition).

2003 Order

The order of the Minnesota Supreme Court [C1-01-927] dated November 12, 2003, amending Rules 37 to 82 of the Rules of Juvenile Procedure and renumbering them as Rules 1 to 47 of the Rules of Juvenile Protection Procedure, provides in part that the amendments are effective January 1, 2004, and shall apply to all juvenile protection matters filed on or after that date.

A. SCOPE AND PURPOSE

RULE 1. SCOPE AND PURPOSE

Rule 1.01. Scope

These rules govern the procedure for juvenile protection matters in the juvenile courts in Minnesota. Juvenile protection matters include all matters defined in Rule 2.01(14).

Amended Nov. 12, 2003; June 10, 2009, eff. Aug. 1, 2009.

Historical Notes

The order of the Minnesota Supreme Court [C1-01-927] dated June 10, 2009, amending the Rules of Juvenile Protection Procedure and the Rules of Adoption Procedure, provides in part that the amendments are effective August 1, 2009, and shall apply to all actions or proceedings pending on or commenced on or after the effective date.

The order of the Minnesota Supreme Court [C1-01-927] dated November 12, 2003, amending Rules 37 to 82 of the Rules of Juvenile Procedure and renumbering them as Rules 1 to 47 of the Rules of Juvenile Protection Procedure, provides in part that the amendments are effective January 1, 2004, and shall apply to all juvenile protection matters filed on or after that date.

Rule 1.02. Purpose

These rules establish uniform practice and procedure for juvenile protection matters in the juvenile courts of Minnesota. The purpose of these rules is to:

(a) secure for each child under the jurisdiction of the court a home that is safe and permanent;

(b) secure for each child under the jurisdiction of the court the care and guidance, preferably in the child's own home, that will best serve the physical, emotional, spiritual, and mental welfare of the child;

(c) provide judicial procedures which protect and promote the safety and welfare of the child;

(d) whenever possible and in the best interests of the child, preserve and strengthen the child's family ties, removing the child from the custody of the child's parent or legal custodian only when the child's safety and welfare cannot otherwise be adequately safeguarded;

(e) secure for the child such custody, care, and discipline, as nearly as possible equivalent to that which should have been given by the child's parent or legal custodian, when removal from the child's parent or legal custodian is necessary and in the child's best interests;

(f) provide a just, thorough, speedy, and efficient determination of each juvenile protection matter before the court and ensure due process for all persons involved in the proceedings;

(g) establish a uniform system for judicial oversight of case planning and reasonable efforts, or active efforts in the case of an Indian child, aimed at preventing or eliminating the need for removal of the child from the care of the child's parent or legal custodian;

(h) ensure a coordinated decision-making process;

(i) reduce unnecessary delays in court proceedings; and

(j) encourage the involvement of parents and children in the proceedings.

Amended Nov. 12, 2003.

1999 Advisory Committee Comment—2003 Amendments

The purpose statement is not intended to be a rule of construction. Rather, it is intended as a guide for judges, attorneys, social services personnel, families, and other judicial system stakeholders to articulate that the overall objective of juvenile court is to move expeditiously toward a resolution of the matter in such a way as to secure that which is in the best interests of the child while ensuring due process for all of the parties.

The purpose statement reflects the policy set forth in the federal Adoption and Safe Families Act of 1997, 42 U.S.C. §§ 601, 603, 622, 629, 653, 675, 670–679, and 1320,, which emphasizes that the overriding objective in any juvenile protection matter is to timely provide a safe, permanent home for the child. The purpose statement also reflects the policy set forth in Minnesota Statutes § 260C.001, subd. 2, which provides, in pertinent part, as follows:

> The paramount consideration in all proceedings concerning a child alleged or found to be in need of protection or services is the health, safety, and best interests of the child ... The purpose of the laws relating to juvenile courts is to secure for each child alleged or adjudicated in need of protection or services and under the jurisdiction of the court, the care and guidance, preferably in the child's own home, as will best serve the spiritual, emotional, mental, and physical welfare of the child; to provide judicial procedures which protect the welfare of the child; to preserve and strengthen the child's family ties whenever possible and in the child's best interests, removing the child from the custody of parents only when the child's welfare or safety cannot be adequately safeguarded without removal; and, when removal from the child's own family is necessary and in the child's best interests, to secure for the child custody, care and discipline as nearly as possible equivalent to that which should have been given by the parents.

Rule 1.02(h) calls for coordinated decision-making in those cases where one family is involved in simultaneous juvenile, criminal, and family court matters. The parties and the court should coordinate the separate proceedings to assure a consistent outcome that is in the best interests of the child.

Historical Notes

The order of the Minnesota Supreme Court [C1-01-927] dated November 12, 2003, amending Rules 37 to 82 of the Rules of Juvenile Procedure and renumbering them as Rules 1 to 47 of the Rules of Juvenile Protection Procedure, provides in part that the amendments are effective January 1, 2004, and shall apply to all juvenile protection matters filed on or after that date.

RULE 2. DEFINITIONS

Rule 2.01. Definitions

The terms used in these rules shall have the following meanings:

(1) *"Adjudicated father"* means an individual determined by a court, or pursuant to a recognition of parentage under Minnesota Statutes § 257.75 to be the biological father of the child.

(2) *"Alleged father"* means an individual claimed by a party or participant to be the biological father of a child.

(3) *"Child placing agency"* means any agency licensed pursuant to Minnesota Statutes § 245A.02 to § 245A.16 or § 252.28, subd. 2.

(4) *"Child custody proceeding,"* as defined in the Indian Child Welfare Act, 25 U.S.C. § 1903(1), and Minnesota Statutes § 260.755, subd. 3, means and includes:

(a) "foster care placement" which means any action removing an Indian child from the child's parent or Indian custodian for temporary placement in a foster home, institution, or the home of a guardian or conservator where the parent or Indian custodian cannot have the child returned upon demand, but where parental rights have not been terminated;

(b) "termination of parental rights" which means any action resulting in the termination of the parent-child relationship;

(c) "preadoptive placement" which means the temporary placement of an Indian child in a foster home or institution after the termination of parental rights, but prior to or in lieu of adoptive placement; and

(d) "adoptive placement" which means the permanent placement of an Indian child for adoption, including any action resulting in a final decree of adoption.

Such term or terms shall not include a placement based upon an act which, if committed by an adult, would be deemed a crime, or an award of custody to one of the parents in a divorce proceeding.

(5) *"Emergency protective care"* means the placement status of a child when:

(a) taken into custody by a peace officer pursuant to Minnesota Statutes § 260C.151, subd. 6; § 260C.154; or § 260C.175; or

(b) returned home before an emergency protective care hearing pursuant to Rule 30 with court ordered conditions of release.

(6) *"Extended family member,"* as defined in the Indian Child Welfare Act, 25 U.S.C. § 1903(2), shall be as defined by the law or custom of the Indian child's tribe or, in the absence of such law or custom, shall be a person who has reached the age of eighteen (18) and who is the Indian child's grandparent, aunt or uncle, brother or sister, brother-in-law or sister-in-law, niece or nephew, first or second cousin, or stepparent.

(7) *"Foster care"* means the 24-hour-a-day substitute care for a child placed away from the child's parents or guardian and for whom a responsible social services agency has placement and care responsibilities under Minnesota Statutes § 260C.007, subd. 18. "Foster care" includes, but is not limited to, placement in foster family homes, foster homes of relatives, group homes, emergency shelters, residential facilities not excluded in this subdivision, child care institutions, and preadoptive homes. A child is in foster care under this definition regardless of whether the facility is licensed and payments are made for the cost of care. Nothing in this definition creates any authority to place a child in a home or facility that is required to be licensed which is not licensed. "Foster care" does not include placement in any of the following facilities: hospitals, inpatient chemical dependency treatment facilities, facilities that are primarily for delinquent children, any corrections facility or program within a particular correction's facility not meeting requirements for Title IV–E facilities as determined by the commissioner, facilities to which a child is committed under the provision of chapter 253B, forestry camps, or jails.

(8) *"Independent living plan"* is a plan for a child age sixteen (16) or older who is in placement as a result of a permanency disposition which includes the objectives set forth in Minnesota Statutes § 260C.212, subd. 1(c)(8).

(9) *"Indian child,"* as defined in the Indian Child Welfare Act, 25 U.S.C. § 1903(4), and modified by Minnesota Statutes § 260.755, subd. 8, means any unmarried person who is under age eighteen (18) and is either (a) a member of an Indian tribe or (b) eligible for membership in an Indian tribe.

(10) *"Indian custodian,"* as defined in the Indian Child Welfare Act, 25 U.S.C. § 1903(6), and Minnesota Statutes § 260.755, subd. 10, means an Indian person who has legal custody of an Indian child under tribal law or custom or under state law, or to whom temporary physical care, custody, and control has been transferred by the parent of such child.

(11) *"Indian child's tribe,"* as defined in the Indian Child Welfare Act, 25 U.S.C. § 1903(5), and Minnesota Statutes § 260.755, subd. 9, means:

(a) the Indian tribe in which an Indian child is a member or eligible for membership; or

(b) in the case of an Indian child who is a member of or eligible for membership in more than one tribe, the Indian tribe with which the Indian child has the most significant contacts.

(12) *"Indian tribe,"* as defined in the Indian Child Welfare Act, 25 U.S.C. § 1903(8), and Minnesota Statutes § 260.755, subd. 12, means an Indian tribe, band, nation, or other organized group or community of Indians recognized as eligible for the services provided to Indians by the Secretary of the Interior because of their status as Indians, including any Alaska Native village as defined in 43 U.S.C. § 1602(c), and exercising tribal governmental powers.

(13) *"Juvenile protection case records"* means all records of the juvenile court regarding a particular case or controversy, including all records filed with the court and the official transcript. Juvenile protection case records do not include reporter's notes and tapes, electronic recordings, and unofficial transcripts of hearings and trials. See also "records" defined in subdivision (24).

(14) *"Juvenile protection matter"* means any of the following types of matters:

(a) child in need of protection or services matters as defined in Minnesota Statutes § 260C.007, subd. 6, including habitual truant and runaway matters;

(b) neglected and in foster care matters as defined in Minnesota Statutes § 260C.007, subd. 24;

(c) review of voluntary foster care matters as defined in Minnesota Statutes § 260C.141, subd. 2;

(d) review of out-of-home placement matters as defined in Minnesota Statutes § 260C.212;

(e) termination of parental rights matters as defined in Minnesota Statutes § 260C.301 to § 260C.328; and

(f) permanent placement matters as defined in Minnesota Statutes § 260C.201, subd. 11, including transfer of permanent legal and physical custody to a relative matters; termination of parental rights matters; long-term foster care matters; foster care for a specified period of time matters; and guardianship and legal custody to human services matters.

(15) *"Legal custodian"* means a person, including a legal guardian, who by court order or statute has sole or joint legal or physical custody of the child.

(16) *"Parent"* as adapted from Minnesota Statutes § 260C.007, subd. 25, means the birth, legally adjudicated, or adoptive parent of a minor child. For an Indian child, pursuant to Minnesota Statutes § 260.755, subd. 14, parent also includes any Indian person who has legally adopted an Indian child including a person who has adopted a child by tribal law or custom, but "parent" does not include an unmarried father whose paternity has not been acknowledged or established.

(17) *"Person,"* as defined in Minnesota Statutes § 260C.007, subd. 26, includes any individual, association, corporation, partnership, and the state or any of its political subdivisions, departments, or agencies.

(18) *"Presumed father"* means an individual who is presumed to be the biological father of a child under Minnesota Statutes § 257.55, subd. 1.

(19) *"Protective care"* means the right of the responsible social services agency or child-placing agency to temporary physical custody and control of a child for purposes of foster care placement, and the right and duty of the responsible social services agency or child-placing agency to provide the care, food, lodging, training, education, supervision, and treatment the child needs.

(20) *"Protective supervision,"* as referenced in Minnesota Statutes § 260C.201, subd. 1(a)(1), means the right and duty of the responsible social services agency or child-placing agency to monitor the conditions imposed by the court directed to the correction of the child's need for protection or services while in the care of the child's parent or legal custodian.

(21) *"Qualified expert witness,"* as defined in Minnesota Administrative Rule 9560.0221, subp. 3G, means:

(a) a member of an Indian child's tribe who is recognized by the tribal community as knowledgeable in tribal customs of family organization and child rearing;

(b) a lay expert witness having substantial experience in the delivery of child and family services to Indians, and extensive knowledge of prevailing social and cultural standards and child rearing practices within the Indian child's tribe; or

(c) a professional person having substantial education and experience in the area of the professional person's specialty, along with substantial knowledge of prevailing social and cultural standards and child-rearing practices within the Indian community.

(22) *"Reasonable efforts to prevent placement,"* as defined in Minnesota Statutes § 260.012(d) means:

(a) the agency has made reasonable efforts to prevent the placement of the child in foster care; or

(b) given the particular circumstances of the child and family at the time of the child's removal, there are no service or efforts available which could allow the child to safely remain in the home.

"Reasonable efforts" are made upon the exercise of due diligence by the responsible social services agency to use culturally appropriate and available services to meet the needs of the child and the child's family.

(23) *"Reasonable efforts to finalize a permanent plan for the child,"* as defined in Minnesota Statutes § 260.012(e) means due diligence by the responsible social services agency:

(a) to reunify the child with the parent or guardian from whom the child was removed;

(b) to assess a noncustodial parent's ability to provide day-to-day care for the child and, where appropriate, provide services necessary to enable the noncustodial parent to safely provide the care, as required by Minnesota Statutes § 260C.212, subd. 4;

(c) to conduct a relative search as required under Minnesota Statutes § 260C.212, subd. 5; and

(d) when the child cannot return to the parent or guardian from whom the child was removed, to plan for and finalize a safe and legally permanent alternative home for the child, and consider permanent alternative homes for the child inside or outside of the state, preferably through adoption or transfer of permanent legal and physical custody of the child.

"Reasonable efforts" are made upon the exercise of due diligence by the responsible social services agency to use culturally appropriate and available services to meet the needs of the child and the child's family.

(24) *"Records"* means any recorded information that is collected, created, received, maintained, or disseminated by a court or court administrator, regardless of its physical form or method of storage, and specifically excludes judicial work product and drafts as defined in the Rules of Public Access to Records of the Judicial Branch. See also "juvenile protection case records" defined in subdivision (13).

(25) *"Relative"* as defined in Minnesota Statutes § 260C.007, subd. 27, means a person related to the child by blood, marriage, or adoption, or an individual who is an important friend with whom the child has resided or had significant contact. For an Indian child, relative includes members of the extended family as defined by the law or custom of the Indian child's tribe or, in the absence of laws or custom, nieces, nephews, or first or second cousins, as provided in the Indian Child Welfare Act of 1978, 25 U.S.C. § 1903(2).

(26) *"Removed from home"* means the child has been taken out of the care of the parent or legal

custodian, including a substitute caregiver, and placed in foster care or in a shelter care facility.

(27) *"Reservation,"* as defined in the Indian Child Welfare Act, 25 U.S.C. § 1903(10), means Indian country as defined in 18 U.S.C. § 1151 and any lands, not covered under such section, title to which is either held by the United States in trust for the benefit of any Indian tribe or individual or held by any Indian tribe or individual subject to a restriction by the United States against alienation.

(28) *"Shelter care facility,"* as adapted from Minnesota Statutes § 260C.007, subd. 30, means a physically unrestricting facility, including but not limited to, a hospital, a group home, or a facility licensed for foster care pursuant to Minnesota Statutes Chapter 245A, used for the temporary care of a child during the pendency of a juvenile protection matter.

(29) *"Trial home visit,"* as defined in Minnesota Statutes § 260C.201, subd. 1(a)(3), means the child is returned to the care of the parent or legal custodian from whom the child was removed for a period not to exceed six months, with agency authority and responsibilities set forth in the statute.

(30) *"Tribal court,"* as defined in the Indian Child Welfare Act, 25 U.S.C. § 1903(12), means a court with jurisdiction over child custody proceedings and which is either a Court of Indian Offenses, a court established and operated under the code or custom of an Indian tribe, or any other administrative body of a tribe which is vested with authority over child custody proceedings.

(31) *"Voluntary foster care"* means placement of a child in foster care based on a written agreement between the responsible social services agency or child placing agency and the child's parent, guardian, or legal custodian. The voluntary foster care agreement gives the agency legal responsibility for the placement of the child. The voluntary foster care agreement is based on both the agency's and the parent's, guardian's, or legal custodian's assessment that placement is necessary and in the child's best interests. See Minnesota Statutes § 260C.212, subd. 8, and § 260D.02, subd. 5.

(32) *"Voluntary foster care of an Indian child,"* as defined in Minnesota Statutes § 260.755, subd. 22, means a decision in which there has been participation by a local social services agency or private child-placing agency resulting in the temporary placement of an Indian child away from the home of the child's parent or Indian custodian in a foster home, institution, or the home of a guardian, and the parent or Indian custodian may have the child returned upon demand.

Amended Nov. 12, 2003; Dec. 1, 2006, eff. Jan. 1, 2007; June 10, 2009, eff. Aug. 1, 2009.

Historical Notes

The order of the Minnesota Supreme Court [C1–01–927] dated June 10, 2009, amending the Rules of Juvenile Protection Procedure and the Rules of Adoption Procedure, provides in part that the amendments are effective August 1, 2009, and shall apply to all actions or proceedings pending on or commenced on or after the effective date.

The order of the Minnesota Supreme Court [C1-01-927] dated November 12, 2003, amending Rules 37 to 82 of the Rules of Juvenile Procedure and renumbering them as Rules 1 to 47 of the Rules of Juvenile Protection Procedure, provides in part that the amendments are effective January 1, 2004, and shall apply to all juvenile protection matters filed on or after that date.

RULE 3. APPLICABILITY OF OTHER RULES AND STATUTES

Rule 3.01 Rules of Civil Procedure

Except as otherwise provided by statute or these rules, the Minnesota Rules of Civil Procedure do not apply to juvenile protection matters.

Amended Nov. 12, 2003.

Historical Notes

The order of the Minnesota Supreme Court [C1-01-927] dated November 12, 2003, amending Rules 37 to 82 of the Rules of Juvenile Procedure and renumbering them as Rules 1 to 47 of the Rules of Juvenile Protection Procedure, provides in part that the amendments are effective January 1, 2004, and shall apply to all juvenile protection matters filed on or after that date.

Rule 3.02. Rules of Evidence

Subd. 1. Generally. Except as otherwise provided by statute or these rules, in a juvenile protection matter the court shall only admit evidence that would be admissible in a civil trial pursuant to the Minnesota Rules of Evidence.

Subd. 2. Certain Out–of–Court Statements Admissible. An out-of-court statement not otherwise admissible by statute or rule of evidence is admissible as evidence in a juvenile protection matter if:

(a) the statement was made by a child under ten (10) years of age or by a child ten (10) years of age or older who is mentally impaired as defined in Minnesota Statutes § 609.341, subd. 6;

(b) the statement alleges, explains, denies, or describes:

(1) any act of sexual penetration or contact performed with or on the child;

(2) any act of sexual penetration or contact with or on another child observed by the child making the statement;

(3) any act of physical abuse or neglect of the child by another; or

(4) any act of physical abuse or neglect of another child observed by the child making the statement;

(c) the court finds that the time, content, and circumstances of the statement and the reliability of the person to whom the statement is made provide sufficient indicia of reliability; and

(d) the proponent of the statement notifies all other parties of the particulars of the statement and the intent to offer the statement sufficiently in advance of the proceeding at which the proponent intends to offer the statement into evidence to provide the parties with a fair opportunity to respond to the statement.

For purposes of this subdivision, an out-of-court statement includes a video, audio, or other recorded statement.

Subd. 3. Judicial Notice. In addition to the judicial notice permitted under the Rules of Evidence, the court, upon its own motion or the motion of any party or the county attorney, may take judicial notice only of findings of fact and court orders in the juvenile protection court file and in any other proceeding in any other court file involving the child or the child's parent or legal custodian.

Amended Nov. 12, 2003.

Historical Notes

The order of the Minnesota Supreme Court [C1-01-927] dated November 12, 2003, amending Rules 37 to 82 of the Rules of Juvenile Procedure and renumbering them as Rules 1 to 47 of the Rules of Juvenile Protection Procedure, provides in part that the amendments are effective January 1, 2004, and shall apply to all juvenile protection matters filed on or after that date.

Rule 3.03. Indian Child Welfare Act

Juvenile protection matters concerning an Indian child shall be governed by the Indian Child Welfare Act, 25 U.S.C. § 1901 to § 1963; the Minnesota Indian Family Preservation Act, Minnesota Statutes § 260.751 to § 260.835; and by these rules when these rules are not inconsistent with the Indian Child Welfare Act or the Minnesota Indian Family Preservation Act.

Amended Nov. 12, 2003.

Historical Notes

The order of the Minnesota Supreme Court [C1-01-927] dated November 12, 2003, amending Rules 37 to 82 of the Rules of Juvenile Procedure and renumbering them as Rules 1 to 47 of the Rules of Juvenile Protection Procedure, provides in part that the amendments are effective January 1, 2004, and shall apply to all juvenile protection matters filed on or after that date.

Rule 3.04. Rules of Guardian Ad Litem Procedure

The Rules of Guardian Ad Litem Procedure apply to juvenile protection matters.

Amended Nov. 12, 2003.

Historical Notes

The order of the Minnesota Supreme Court [C1-01-927] dated November 12, 2003, amending Rules 37 to 82 of the Rules of Juvenile Procedure and renumbering them as Rules 1 to 47 of the Rules of Juvenile Protection Procedure, provides in part that the amendments are effective January 1, 2004, and shall apply to all juvenile protection matters filed on or after that date.

Rule 3.05. Court Interpreter Statutes, Rules, and Court Policies

The statutes, court rules, and court policies regarding appointment of court interpreters apply to juvenile protection matters. The court may appoint an interpreter of its own selection and may fix reasonable compensation pursuant to such statutes, court rules and court policies.

Amended Nov. 12, 2003.

Historical Notes

The order of the Minnesota Supreme Court [C1-01-927] dated November 12, 2003, amending Rules 37 to 82 of the Rules of Juvenile Procedure and renumbering them as Rules 1 to 47 of the Rules of Juvenile Protection Procedure, provides in part that the amendments are effective January 1, 2004, and shall apply to all juvenile protection matters filed on or after that date.

Rule 3.06. General Rules Practice for the District Courts

Rule 10 of the General Rules of Practice for the District Courts applies to juvenile protection matters.

Amended June 10, 2009, eff. Aug. 1, 2009.

2008 Advisory Committee Comment

Consistent with the Indian Child Welfare Act, 25 U.S.C. § 1911(d), Rule 10 of the General Rules of Practice for the District Courts addresses recognition of tribal court orders, judgments, and other judicial acts.

Historical Notes

The order of the Minnesota Supreme Court [C1–01–927] dated June 10, 2009, amending the Rules of Juvenile Protection Procedure and the Rules of Adoption Procedure, provides in part that the amendments are effective August 1, 2009, and shall apply to all actions or proceedings pending on or commenced on or after the effective date.

B. GENERAL OPERATING RULES

RULE 4. TIME; TIMELINE

Rule 4.01. Computation of Time

Unless otherwise provided by statute, the day of the act or event from which the designated period of time begins to run shall not be included in the computation of time. The last day of the period shall be included, unless it is a Saturday, Sunday, or legal holiday, in which event the period runs until the end of the next day that is not a Saturday, Sunday, or legal holiday. When a period of time prescribed or allowed is three (3) days or less, intermediate Saturdays, Sundays, and legal holidays shall be excluded in the computation. As used in these rules, "legal holiday" includes New Year's Day, Martin Luther King's Birthday, Washington's Birthday (Presidents' Day), Memorial Day, Independence Day, Labor Day, Veteran's Day, Thanksgiving Day, the day after Thanksgiving Day, Christmas Day, and any other day designated as a holiday by the President, Congress of the United States, or by the State.

Amended Nov. 12, 2003.

Historical Notes

The order of the Minnesota Supreme Court [C1-01-927] dated November 12, 2003, amending Rules 37 to 82 of the Rules of Juvenile Procedure and renumbering them as Rules 1 to 47 of the Rules of Juvenile Protection Procedure, provides in part that the amendments are effective January 1, 2004, and shall apply to all juvenile protection matters filed on or after that date.

Rule 4.02. Additional Time After Service by Mail or Other Means

Whenever a person has the right or is required to do an act within a prescribed period after the service of a notice or other paper and the notice or other paper is served by mail, three (3) days shall be added to the prescribed period. If service is made by any means other than mail and accomplished after 5:00 p.m. local time on the day of service, one (1) additional day shall be added to the prescribed period.

Amended Nov. 12, 2003.

Historical Notes

The order of the Minnesota Supreme Court [C1-01-927] dated November 12, 2003, amending Rules 37 to 82 of the Rules of Juvenile Procedure and renumbering them as Rules 1 to 47 of the Rules of Juvenile Protection Procedure, provides in part that the amendments are effective January 1, 2004, and shall apply to all juvenile protection matters filed on or after that date.

Rule 4.03. Timeline

Subd. 1. Child in Need of Protection or Services Matters.

(a) *Emergency Protective Care Hearing.* If a child has been removed from the home of the parent or legal custodian pursuant to Rule 28.01, the court shall hold an emergency protective care hearing within seventy-two (72) hours of the child's removal pursuant to Rule 30.01.

(b) *Admit/Deny Hearing.* Pursuant to Rule 34.02, subd. 1(a), when the child is removed from home by court order, an admit/deny hearing shall be held within ten (10) days of the date of the emergency protective care hearing. Pursuant to Rule 34.02, subd. 2(a), when the child is not removed from home by court order, an admit/deny hearing shall be held no sooner than three (3), and no later than twenty (20) days after the parties have been served with the summons and petition.

(1) **Parent's, Indian Custodian's or Tribe's Identity Known.** In matters governed by the Indian Child Welfare Act, 25 U.S.C. § 1901 et seq., the admit/deny hearing on a petition requesting the foster care placement of an Indian child, the permanent placement of an Indian child, or the termination of parental rights to an Indian child shall not be held until at least ten (10) days after receipt of the notice required under Rule 32.06, 25 U.S.C. § 1912(a), and Minnesota Statutes § 260.761, subd. 3. The parent, Indian custodian, or child's tribe shall, upon request, be granted up to twenty (20) additional days from receipt of the notice to prepare for the admit/deny hearing.

(2) **Parent's, Indian Custodian's, or Child's Tribe's Identity Unknown.** If the identity or location of the parent, Indian custodian, or child's tribe cannot be determined, the notice required under Rule 32.06, 25 U.S.C. § 1912(a), and Minnesota Statutes § 260.761, subd. 3, shall be sent to the Secretary of the Interior who shall have fifteen (15) days to provide the requisite notice to the parent or Indian custodian and the tribe. The admit/deny hearing shall be held at least twenty-five (25) days after receipt of the notice by the Secretary. The parent, Indian custodian, or child's tribe shall, upon request, be granted up to twenty (20) additional days from receipt of the notice to prepare for the admit/deny hearing.

(c) *Scheduling Order.* Pursuant to Rule 6.02, the court shall issue a scheduling order at the admit/deny hearing held pursuant to Rule 34 or within fifteen (15) days of the admit/deny hearing.

(d) *Pretrial Hearing.* Pursuant to Rule 36.01, the court shall convene a pretrial hearing at least ten (10) days prior to trial.

(e) *Trial.* Pursuant to Rule 39.02, subd. 1(a), when the statutory grounds set forth in the petition are denied, a trial regarding a child in need of protection or services matter shall commence within sixty (60) days from the date of the emergency protective care hearing or the admit/deny hearing, whichever is earlier, and testimony shall be concluded within thirty (30) days from the date of commencement of the trial and whenever possible should be over consecutive days.

(f) *Findings/Adjudication.* Pursuant to Rule 39.05, subd. 1, within fifteen (15) days of the conclusion of the testimony, during which time the court may require simultaneous written arguments to be filed and served, the court shall issue its findings and order regarding whether one or more statutory grounds set forth in the petition have been proved. The court may extend the period for issuing an order for an additional fifteen (15) days if the court finds that an extension of time is required in the interests of justice and the best interests of the child.

(g) *Disposition.* Pursuant to Rule 41.02, to the extent practicable, the court shall conduct a disposition hearing and enter a disposition order the same day it makes a finding that the statutory grounds set forth in the petition have been proved. In the event disposition is not ordered at the same time as the adjudication, the disposition order shall be issued within ten (10) days of the date the court finds the statutory grounds set forth in the petition have been proved.

(h) *Review of Legal Custody.* When the disposition is transfer of legal custody to the responsible social services agency pursuant to Rule 41.06, the court shall conduct a review hearing at least every ninety (90) days to review whether foster care is necessary and continues to be appropriate or whether the child should be returned to the home of the parent or legal custodian from whom the child was removed. Any party or the county attorney may request a review hearing before ninety (90) days.

(i) *Review of Protective Supervision.* When the disposition is protective supervision pursuant to Rule 41.06, subd. 1, the court shall review the disposition in court at least every six (6) months from the date of the disposition.

Subd. 2. Permanent Placement Matters—Notice of Timeline for Permanency Proceedings. In the case of a child who is alleged or found to be in need of protection or services and ordered into foster care or the home of a noncustodial parent, and where reasonable efforts for reunification are required, pursuant to Rule 42. 01, subd. 1, the court in its first order placing the child in foster care or the home of a noncustodial parent shall set the date or deadline for the admit/deny hearing commencing permanent placement determination proceedings and the permanency progress review hearing required for a child who is under age eight (8) at the time the petition is filed alleging the child to be in need of protection or services. Pursuant to Rule 42.01, subd. 5, not later than when the court sets the date or deadline for the admit/deny hearing commencing the permanent placement determination proceedings and the permanency progress review hearing, the court shall notify the parties and participants of the following requirements:

(a) *Requirement of Six (6) Month Hearing for Child Under Eight (8) Years of Age.* For a child who is under eight (8) years of age at the time a petition is filed alleging the child to be in need of protection or services, pursuant to Rule 42.01, subd. 5(a), the court shall conduct a permanency progress review hearing not later than six (6) months after the child is placed in foster care or in the home of a noncustodial parent to review the progress of the case, the parent's progress on the out-of-home placement plan, and the provision of services. At the hearing required under this paragraph, the court may conduct a permanency progress review hearing for any sibling of the child, regardless of age, when the sibling is also in foster care or in the home of a noncustodial parent.

(b) *Requirement of Twelve (12) Month Hearing.* Pursuant to Rule 42.01, subd. 5(b), the court shall commence permanent placement determination proceedings to determine the permanent status of the child, regardless of age, not later than twelve (12) months after the child is placed in foster care or in the home of a noncustodial parent.

Subd. 3. Permanent Placement Petition and Trial for Child Under Eight (8) Years of Age. In the case of a child under eight (8) years of age at the time the child in need of protection or services petition is filed, if the court determines at the permanency progress review hearing required under Rule 42.01, subd. 1(b), that the parent or legal custodian has not maintained regular contact with the child as outlined in the visitation plan or is not complying with the case plan or out-of-home placement pursuant to Rule 42.04(a) a petition supporting the permanency plan shall be filed and served within thirty (30) days of the hearing under this paragraph. Pursuant to Rule 39.02, subd. 1(b), a trial on the petition shall be commenced within thirty (30) days of the filing of a petition in the case of a transfer of legal custody or within ninety (90) days of the filing of the petition in the case of a petition for termination of parental rights, and testimony shall be concluded within thirty (30) days from the date of commencement of the trial and whenever possible should be over consecutive days. Pursuant to Rule 39.05, subd. 1, within fifteen (15) days of the conclusion of the testimony, during which time the court may require simultaneous written arguments to be filed and served, the court shall issue its findings and order regarding whether the statutory grounds set forth in the petition have or have not been proved. The court may extend the period for issuing an order for an additional fifteen (15) days if the court finds that an extension of time is required in the interests of justice and the best interests of the child.

Subd. 4. Termination of Parental Rights and Other Permanent Placement Matters at Twelve (12) Months.

(a) *Admit/Deny Hearing.* Pursuant to Rule 34.02 subd. 1(b), an admit/deny hearing shall be held not less than ten (10) days after service of the summons and petition upon the parties.

(1) **Parent's, Indian Custodian's, or Child's Tribe's Identity Known.** In matters governed by the Indian Child Welfare Act, 25 U.S.C. § 1901 et seq., the admit/deny hearing on a petition requesting the foster care placement of an Indian child, the permanent placement of an Indian child, or the termination of parental rights to an Indian child shall not be held until at least ten (10) days after receipt of the notice required under Rule 32.06, 25 U.S.C. § 1912(a), and Minnesota Statutes § 260.761, subd. 3. The parent, Indian custodian, or child's tribe shall, upon request, be granted up to twenty (20) additional days from receipt of the notice to prepare for the admit/deny hearing.

(2) **Parent's, Indian Custodian's, or Child's Tribe's Identity Unknown.** If the identity or location of the parent, Indian custodian, or child's tribe cannot be determined, the notice required under Rule 32.06, 25 U.S.C. § 1912(a), and Minnesota Statutes § 260.761, subd. 3, shall be sent to the Secretary of the Interior who shall have fifteen (15) days to provide the requisite notice to the parent or Indian custodian and the tribe. The admit/deny hearing shall be held at least twenty-five (25) days after receipt of the notice by the Secretary. The

parent, Indian custodian, or child's tribe shall, upon request, be granted up to twenty (20) additional days from receipt of the notice to prepare for the admit/deny hearing.

(b) *Pretrial Hearing.* Pursuant to Rule 36.01, the court shall convene a pretrial hearing at least ten (10) days prior to trial.

(c) *Trial.* Pursuant to Rule 39.02, subd. 1(c), a trial regarding a termination of parental rights matter or other permanent placement matter shall commence within sixty (60) days of the first scheduled admit/deny hearing and testimony shall be concluded within thirty (30) days from the date of commencement of the trial and whenever possible should be over consecutive days.

(d) *Findings/Adjudication.* Pursuant to Rule 39.05 subd. 1, within fifteen (15) days of the conclusion of the testimony, during which time the court may require simultaneous written arguments to be filed and served, the court shall issue its findings and order regarding whether the statutory grounds set forth in the petition have or have not been proved. The court may extend the period for issuing an order for an additional fifteen (15) days if the court finds that an extension of time is required in the interests of justice and the best interests of the child.

(e) *Post–Permanency Review Hearings.*

(1) If the court orders termination of parental rights and adoption as the permanency plan, pursuant to Rule 42.08, subd. 5, the court shall conduct a review hearing ninety (90) days from the date of the termination of parental rights order is filed, and at least every ninety (90) days thereafter, for the purpose of reviewing the progress towards finalization of the adoption.

(2) If the court orders transfer of permanent legal and physical custody to a relative, pursuant to Rule 42.07, subds. 3 and 7, the court may order further in-court review hearings at such intervals as it determines to be in the best interests of the child to ensure that the appropriate services are being delivered to the child and permanent legal physical custodian or that conditions ordered by the court relating to the care and custody of the child are met.

(3) If the court orders long-term foster care, pursuant to Rule 42.11, subd. 4, the court shall review the matter in court at least every twelve (12) months to consider whether long term foster care continues to be the best permanent plan for the child.

(4) If the court orders foster care for a specified period of time, pursuant to Rule 42.12, subd. 3, not later than twelve (12) months after the child was ordered into foster care for a specified period of time the matter shall be returned to court for a review of the appropriateness of continuing the child in foster care and of the responsible social service agency's reasonable efforts to finalize a permanent plan for the child.

(f) *Review When Child Removed from Permanent Placement Within One (1) Year.* Pursuant to Rule 42.15, subd. 1, if a child is removed from a permanent placement disposition within one year after the placement was made:

(a) the child shall be returned to the foster home where the child was placed immediately preceding the permanent placement; or

(b) the court shall conduct a hearing within ten (10) days after the child is removed from the permanent placement to determine where the child is to be placed.

Subd. 5. Hearing for Child on a Trial Home Visit. Pursuant to Rule 42.01, subd. 2, when the child has been ordered on a trial home visit which continues at the time the court is required to commence permanent placement determination proceedings under Rule 42.01, within twelve (12) months of the date a child is placed in foster care the court shall hold a hearing pursuant to Rule 42.13 to determine the continued status of the child.

Subd. 6. Cases Where Reasonable Efforts For Reunification Are Not Required. Pursuant to Rule 42.01, subd. 6, when the court finds that the petition states a prima facie case that one or more of the five (5) circumstances under Minnesota Statutes § 260.012(a) and Rule 30.09, subd. 3, exist where reasonable efforts for reunification are not required, the court shall order that an admit/deny hearing under Rule 34 be conducted within thirty (30) days and a trial be conducted within ninety (90) days of its prima facie finding. Unless a permanency or termination of parental rights petition under Rule 33 has already been filed, the county attorney requesting the prima facie determination shall file a permanency or termination of parental rights petition that permits the completion of service by the court at least ten (10) days prior to the admit/deny hearing.

Amended Nov. 12, 2003; Dec. 1, 2006, eff. Jan. 1, 2007; June 10, 2009, eff. Aug. 1, 2009.

1999 Advisory Committee Comment (amended 2003 and 2009)

The timeline set forth in Rule 4.03 is intended as an overall guide for juvenile protection matters and is based upon the requirements of Minnesota Statutes § 260C.176; § 260C.201, subds. 10 and 11; § 260C.178, subd. 6; the Indian Child Welfare Act, 25 U.S.C. § 1901 to § 1963; and the Adoption and Safe Families Act of 1997, 42 U.S.C. §§ 601, 603, 622, 629, 653, 675, 670–679, and 1320. Specific time requirements are set forth in each individual rule.

Rule 4.03, subd. 1, sets forth the timeline for child in need of protection or services matters. The following timeline is an example of how a case would proceed if it related to a non-Indian child who has been removed from the child's home:

Day	Event
1	Child removed from home
3	Emergency Protective Care Hearing
3–13	Admit/Deny Hearing
14–53	Pretrial Hearing
63	Trial
79	Findings/Adjudication
79–88	Disposition Hearing
168–178	Disposition Review Hearing
180	Permanency Progress Review Hearing
258–268	Disposition Review Hearing
335	Permanency Petition Filed
348–358	Disposition Review Hearing
365	Admit/Deny Hearing on Permanency Petition
455+	Post–Permanency Review Hearings (if appropriate)

Historical Notes

The order of the Minnesota Supreme Court [C1–01–927] dated June 10, 2009, amending the Rules of Juvenile Protection Procedure and the Rules of Adoption Procedure, provides in part that the amendments are effective August 1, 2009, and shall apply to all actions or proceedings pending on or commenced on or after the effective date.

Rule 4.04. Sanctions for Violation

The court may impose sanctions upon any county attorney, party, or counsel for a party who willfully fails to follow the timelines set forth in these rules.

Amended Nov. 12, 2003.

Historical Notes

The order of the Minnesota Supreme Court [C1-01-927] dated November 12, 2003, amending Rules 37 to 82 of the Rules of Juvenile Procedure and renumbering them as Rules 1 to 47 of the Rules of Juvenile Protection Procedure, provides in part that the amendments are effective January 1, 2004, and shall apply to all juvenile protection matters filed on or after that date.

Rule 4.05. Application of Timing Provisions

The timing provisions set forth in this rule are subject to the continuance provisions of Rule 5 and any other timing provisions set forth in each specific rule.

Amended Nov. 12, 2003; June 10, 2009, eff. Aug. 1, 2009.

Historical Notes

The order of the Minnesota Supreme Court [C1–01–927] dated June 10, 2009, amending the Rules of Juvenile Protection Procedure and the Rules of Adoption Procedure, provides in part that the amendments are effective August 1, 2009, and shall apply to all actions or proceedings pending on or commenced on or after the effective date.

The order of the Minnesota Supreme Court [C1-01-927] dated November 12, 2003, amending Rules 37 to 82 of the Rules of Juvenile Procedure and renumbering them as Rules 1 to 47 of the Rules of Juvenile Protection Procedure, provides in part that the amendments are effective January 1, 2004, and shall apply to all juvenile protection matters filed on or after that date.

RULE 5. CONTINUANCES

Rule 5.01. Findings

Subd. 1. Generally. Upon its own motion or motion of a party or the county attorney the court may continue a scheduled hearing or trial to a later date so long as the timelines for achieving permanency as set forth in these rules are not delayed. To grant a continuance, the court must make written findings or oral findings on the record that the continuance is necessary for the protection of the child, for accumulation or presentation of evidence or witnesses, to protect the rights of a party, or for other good cause shown.

Subd. 2. Trials. Trials may not be continued or adjourned for more than one (1) week unless the court makes specific findings that the continuance or adjournment is in the best interests of the child.

Amended Nov. 12, 2003.

1999 Advisory Committee Comment

Although the court may grant a continuance in appropriate circumstances, the court should not grant a continuance that would defeat the federal and state statutory time requirements for permanency determinations.

Historical Notes

The order of the Minnesota Supreme Court [C1-01-927] dated November 12, 2003, amending Rules 37 to 82 of the Rules of Juvenile Procedure and renumbering them as Rules 1 to 47 of the Rules of Juvenile Protection Procedure, provides in part that the amendments are effective January 1, 2004, and shall apply to all juvenile protection matters filed on or after that date.

Rule 5.02. Notice of Continuance

The court shall, either in writing or orally on the record, provide notice to the parties and the county attorney of the date and time of the continued hearing or trial.

Amended Nov. 12, 2003.

Historical Notes

The order of the Minnesota Supreme Court [C1-01-927] dated November 12, 2003, amending Rules 37 to 82 of the Rules of Juvenile Procedure and renumbering them as Rules 1 to 47 of the Rules of Juvenile Protection Procedure, provides in part that the amendments are effective January 1, 2004, and shall apply to all juvenile protection matters filed on or after that date.

Rule 5.03. Existing Orders; Interim Orders

Unless otherwise ordered, existing orders shall remain in full force and effect during a continuance. When a continuance is ordered, the court may make any interim orders it deems to be in the best interests of the child in accordance with the provisions of Minnesota Statutes § 260C.001 to § 260C.451.

Amended Nov. 12, 2003.

Historical Notes

The order of the Minnesota Supreme Court [C1-01-927] dated November 12, 2003, amending Rules 37 to 82 of the Rules of Juvenile Procedure and renumbering them as Rules 1 to 47 of the Rules of Juvenile Protection Procedure, provides in part that the amendments are effective January 1, 2004, and shall apply to all juvenile protection matters filed on or after that date.

RULE 6. SCHEDULING ORDER

Rule 6.01. Purpose

The purpose of this rule is to provide a uniform system for scheduling matters for trial and disposition and for achieving permanency within the timelines set forth in these rules.

Amended Nov. 12, 2003.

Historical Notes

The order of the Minnesota Supreme Court [C1-01-927] dated November 12, 2003, amending Rules 37 to 82 of the Rules of Juvenile Procedure and renumbering them as Rules 1 to 47 of the Rules of Juvenile Protection Procedure, provides in part that the amendments are effective January 1, 2004, and shall apply to all juvenile protection matters filed on or after that date.

Rule 6.02. Order

Subd. 1. When Issued. The court shall issue a scheduling order at the admit/deny hearing held pursuant to Rule 34 or within fifteen (15) days of the admit/deny hearing.

Subd. 2. Contents of Order. The scheduling order shall establish a deadline or specific date for:

(a) completion of discovery and other pretrial preparation;

(b) serving, filing, or hearing motions;

(c) submission of the proposed case plan;

(d) the pretrial conference;

(e) the trial;

(f) the disposition hearing;

(g) the permanency placement determination hearing; and

(h) any other events deemed necessary or appropriate.

Amended Nov. 12, 2003; June 10, 2009, eff. Aug. 1, 2009.

1999 Advisory Committee Comment—2003 Amendments

Rule 6.02 does not require the court to actually calendar time for any of the events described in the order. Rather, the court may simply set deadlines without establishing a date certain. For example, without setting a specific date the court may order that discovery must be completed at least ten days prior to trial.

Historical Notes

The order of the Minnesota Supreme Court [C1–01–927] dated June 10, 2009, amending the Rules of Juvenile Protection Procedure and the Rules of Adoption Procedure, provides in part that the amendments are effective August 1, 2009, and shall apply to all actions or proceedings pending on or commenced on or after the effective date.

The order of the Minnesota Supreme Court [C1-01-927] dated November 12, 2003, amending Rules 37 to 82 of the Rules of Juvenile Procedure and renumbering them as Rules 1 to 47 of the Rules of Juvenile Protection Procedure, provides in part that the amendments are effective January 1, 2004, and shall apply to all juvenile protection matters filed on or after that date.

Rule 6.03. Amendment

The court may amend a scheduling order as necessary, so long as the permanency timelines set forth in these rules are not delayed.

Amended Nov. 12, 2003.

Historical Notes

The order of the Minnesota Supreme Court [C1-01-927] dated November 12, 2003, amending Rules 37 to 82 of the Rules of Juvenile Procedure and renumbering them as Rules 1 to 47 of the Rules of Juvenile Protection Procedure, provides in part that the amendments are effective January 1, 2004, and shall apply to all juvenile protection matters filed on or after that date.

RULE 7. REFEREES AND JUDGES

Rule 7.01. Referee Authorization to Hear Matter

A referee may, as authorized by the chief judge of the judicial district, hear any juvenile protection matter under the jurisdiction of the juvenile court.

Amended Nov. 12, 2003.

Historical Notes

The order of the Minnesota Supreme Court [C1-01-927] dated November 12, 2003, amending Rules 37 to 82 of the Rules of Juvenile Procedure and renumbering them as Rules 1 to 47 of the Rules of Juvenile Protection Procedure, provides in part that the amendments are effective January 1, 2004, and shall apply to all juvenile protection matters filed on or after that date.

Rule 7.02. Objection to Referee Presiding Over Matter

A party or the county attorney may object to having a referee preside over a matter. The right to object shall be deemed waived unless the objection is in writing, filed with the court, and served upon all other parties and the county attorney within three (3) days after being informed that the matter is to be heard by a referee. Upon the filing of an objection, a judge shall hear any motion and shall preside at all further motions and proceedings involving the matter.

Amended Nov. 12, 2003.

Historical Notes

The order of the Minnesota Supreme Court [C1-01-927] dated November 12, 2003, amending Rules 37 to 82 of the Rules of Juvenile Procedure and renumbering them as Rules 1 to 47 of the Rules of Juvenile Protection Procedure, provides in part that the amendments are effective January 1, 2004, and shall apply to all juvenile protection matters filed on or after that date.

Rule 7.03. Removal of Particular Referee

Subd. 1. Notice to Remove. A party or the county attorney may file with the court and serve upon all other parties a notice to remove a particular referee. The notice shall be served and filed within ten (10) days of the date the party or county attorney receives notice of the name of the referee who will preside at the hearing or trial, but not later than the commencement of the hearing or trial. A notice to remove may not be filed by a party or the county attorney against a referee who has presided at a motion or at any other proceeding in the matter of which the party or the county attorney had notice. A referee who has presided at a motion or other proceeding may not be removed except upon an affirmative showing of prejudice on the part of the referee. A judge shall rule on a motion to remove a referee who has already presided over the proceeding.

Subd. 2. Prejudice. If a party or the county attorney has once disqualified a referee as a matter of right, that party or the county attorney may disqualify the substitute referee, but only upon an affirmative showing of prejudice. A showing that the referee might be excluded for bias from acting as a juror in the matter constitutes an affirmative showing of prejudice. A judge shall rule on a motion to remove a substitute referee.

Subd. 3. Assignment of Another Referee. Upon the filing of a notice to remove a particular referee, or if a party or the county attorney makes an affirmative showing of prejudice against a substitute referee, the chief judge of the judicial district shall assign another juvenile court referee or a judge to hear the matter.

Subd. 4. Termination of Parental Rights Matters and Permanent Placement Matters. When a termination of parental rights matter or a permanent placement matter is filed in connection with a child who is the subject of a pending child in need of protection or services matter, the termination or permanency matter shall be considered a continuation of the protection matter. If the referee assigned to the protection matter is assigned to hear the termination or permanency matter, the parties and the county attorney shall not have the right to disqualify the assigned referee as a matter of right.

Amended Dec. 12, 2003.

1999 Advisory Committee Comment

A party may not remove a particular referee and then object to having the case heard by any referee. If a judge is assigned to hear a matter after a party has objected to a particular referee hearing the matter, the party may not seek removal of the judge as a matter of right but may only seek removal of a subsequent judge for cause.

Historical Notes

The order of the Minnesota Supreme Court [C1-01-927] dated November 12, 2003, amending Rules 37 to 82 of the Rules of Juvenile Procedure and renumbering them as Rules 1 to 47 of the Rules of Juvenile Protection Procedure, provides in part that the amendments are effective January 1, 2004, and shall apply to all juvenile protection matters filed on or after that date.

Rule 7.04. Transmittal of Referee's Findings and Recommended Order

Subd. 1. Transmittal. Upon the conclusion of a hearing, the referee shall transmit to a judge the written findings and recommended order. Notice of the findings and recommended order, along with notice of the right to review by a judge, shall be given either orally on the record or in writing to all parties, the county attorney, and to any other person as directed by the court.

Subd. 2. Effective Date. The recommended order is effective upon signing by the referee, unless stayed, reversed, or modified by a judge upon review.

Amended Nov. 12, 2003.

Historical Notes

The order of the Minnesota Supreme Court [C1-01-927] dated November 12, 2003, amending Rules 37 to 82 of the Rules of Juvenile Procedure and renumbering them as Rules 1 to 47 of the Rules of Juvenile Protection Procedure, provides in part that the amendments are effective January 1, 2004, and shall apply to all juvenile protection matters filed on or after that date.

Rule 7.05. Review of Referee's Findings and Recommended Order

Subd. 1. Right to Review. A matter that has been decided by a referee may be reviewed in whole or in part by a judge. Review, if any is requested, shall be from the referee's written findings and recommended order. Upon request for review, the recommended order shall remain in effect unless stayed by a judge.

Subd. 2. Motion for Review. Any motion for review of the referee's findings and recommended order, together with a memorandum of law, shall be filed with the court and served on all parties and the county attorney within five (5) days of the filing of the referee's findings and recommended order. Upon the filing of a motion for review, the court administrator shall notify each party and the county attorney of the name of the judge to whom the review has been assigned.

Subd. 3. Response to Motion for Review. The parties and the county attorney shall file and serve any responsive motion and memorandum within three (3) days from the date of service of the motion for review.

Subd. 4. Timing. Failure to timely file and serve a submission may result in dismissal of the motion for review or disallowance of the submissions.

Subd. 5. Basis of Review. The review shall be based on the record before the referee and no additional evidence may be filed or considered. No personal appearances will be permitted, except upon order of the court for good cause shown.

Subd. 6. Transcripts. Any party or county attorney desiring to submit a transcript of the hearing held before the referee shall make arrangements with the court reporter at the earliest possible time. The court reporter shall advise the parties and the court of the day by which the transcript will be filed.

Amended Nov. 12, 2003.

1999 Advisory Committee Comment

If a party or the county attorney cannot obtain the transcript in time to file it with the motion for review, the motion should set forth the date the transcript will be submitted. The motion, recommended order, and memorandum of law must still be filed within the five day time period prescribed by the rule, but the decision of the court may be delayed until the court has the opportunity to review the transcript.

Historical Notes

The order of the Minnesota Supreme Court [C1-01-927] dated November 12, 2003, amending Rules 37 to 82 of the Rules of Juvenile Procedure and renumbering them as Rules 1 to 47 of the Rules of Juvenile Protection Procedure, provides in part that the amendments are effective January 1, 2004, and shall apply to all juvenile protection matters filed on or after that date.

Rule 7.06. Order of the Court

When no review is requested, or when the right to review is waived, the findings and recommended order of the referee become the order of the court when confirmed by the judge as written or when modified by the judge sua sponte. The order shall be confirmed or modified by the court within fifteen (15) days of the transmittal of the findings and proposed order.

Amended Nov. 12, 2003; June 10, 2009, eff. Aug. 1, 2009.

Historical Notes

The order of the Minnesota Supreme Court [C1–01–927] dated June 10, 2009, amending the Rules of Juvenile Protection Procedure and the Rules of Adoption Procedure, provides in part that the amendments are effective August 1, 2009, and shall apply to all actions or proceedings pending on or commenced on or after the effective date.

The order of the Minnesota Supreme Court [C1-01-927] dated November 12, 2003, amending Rules 37 to 82 of the Rules of Juvenile Procedure and renumbering them as Rules 1 to 47 of the Rules of Juvenile Protection Procedure, provides in part that the amendments are effective January 1, 2004, and shall apply to all juvenile protection matters filed on or after that date.

Rule 7.07. Removal of Judge

Subd. 1. Disability of Judge. If by reason of death, sickness, or other disability a judge before whom a proceeding in the matter has been tried is unable to perform judicial duties after a decision is made or findings of fact and conclusions of law are filed, any other judge regularly sitting in or assigned to the court in which the action was tried may perform those duties; but if such other judge is satisfied that the duties cannot be performed because that judge did not preside at the trial, or for any other reason, that judge may exercise discretion to grant a new trial. If there is no other judge of the district who is qualified, the chief judge shall immediately notify the Chief Justice of the Minnesota Supreme Court.

Subd. 2. Interest or Bias. No judge shall preside over any case if that judge is interested in its determination or if that judge might be excluded for bias from acting as a juror in the matter.. If there is no other judge of the district who is qualified, the chief judge shall immediately notify the Chief Justice of the Minnesota Supreme Court.

Subd. 3. Notice to Remove.

(a) *Procedure.* A party or the county attorney may file with the court and serve upon all other parties a notice to remove. The notice shall be served and filed within ten (10) days of the date the party receives notice of the name of the judge who is to preside over the proceeding, but not later than the commencement of the proceeding.

(b) *Presiding Judge.* A notice to remove shall not be filed against a judge who has presided at a motion or any other proceeding in the matter of which the party or the county attorney had notice. A judge who has presided at a motion or other proceeding may not be removed except upon an affirmative showing of prejudice on the part of the judge.

(c) *Showing of Prejudice.* After a party or the county attorney has once disqualified a presiding judge as a matter of right, that party may disqualify the substitute judge, but only by making an affirmative showing of prejudice. A showing that the judge might be excluded for bias from acting as a juror in the matter constitutes an affirmative showing of prejudice.

(d) *Assignment of Another Judge.* Upon the filing of a notice to remove, or if a party or the county attorney makes an affirmative showing of prejudice against a substitute judge, the chief judge of the judicial district shall assign any other judge of any court within the district to hear the matter. If there is no other judge of the district who is qualified, the chief judge shall immediately notify the Chief Justice of the Minnesota Supreme Court.

Subd. 4. Termination of Parental Rights Matters and Permanent Placement Matters. When a termination of parental rights matter or a permanent placement matter is filed in connection with a child who is the subject of a pending child in need of protection or services matter, the termination or permanency matter shall be considered a continuation of the protection matter. If the judge assigned to the protection matter is assigned to hear the termination or permanency matter, the parties and the county attorney shall not have the right to disqualify the assigned judge as a matter of right.

Amended Nov. 12, 2003; Dec. 1, 2006, eff. Jan. 1, 2007.

2003 Advisory Committee Comment

While there was consensus that the one-judge one-family concept should be an aspirational goal of all juvenile courts, there was also consensus that a rule mandating implementation of the one-judge one-family concept may not be practical or enforceable in all situations. Instead, the Committee recommends that courts implement the one-judge one-family concept to the greatest extent possible.

Historical Notes

The order of the Minnesota Supreme Court [C1-01-927] dated November 12, 2003, amending Rules 37 to 82 of the Rules of Juvenile Procedure and renumbering them as Rules 1 to 47 of the Rules of Juvenile Protection Procedure, provides in part that the amendments are effective January 1, 2004, and shall apply to all juvenile protection matters filed on or after that date.

RULE 8. ACCESSIBILITY OF JUVENILE PROTECTION CASE RECORDS

Rule 8.01. Presumption of Access to Records

Except as otherwise provided in this Rule, all juvenile protection case records relating to juvenile protection matters, as those terms are defined in Rule 2.01, are presumed to be accessible to any party and any member of the public for inspection, copying, or release. Records or information to which access is restricted under Rule 8.04 shall not be redacted prior to transmission to the clerk of appellate courts. If a party or a member of the public requests access to the juvenile protection case record during the appeal, the portion of the case record requested shall be returned to the trial court to be redacted pursuant to Rule 8.04 before access shall be allowed. The Minnesota Court of Appeals or the Minnesota Supreme Court shall deny access to the case records during the appeal if providing access would unduly delay the conclusion of the appeal. An order prohibiting access to the court file, or any record in such file, shall be accessible to the public.

Amended Nov. 12, 2003; June 10, 2009, eff. Aug. 1, 2009.

2001 Advisory Committee Comment—2003 Amendments

Rule 8.01 establishes a presumption of public access to juvenile protection case records, and exceptions to this presumption are set forth in the remaining provisions of Rule 8. Rule 8.01 does not apply to any case records relating to adoption proceedings, which remain inaccessible to the public.

Historical Notes

The order of the Minnesota Supreme Court [C1–01–927] dated June 10, 2009, amending the Rules of Juvenile Protection Procedure and the Rules of Adoption Procedure, provides in part that the amendments are effective August 1, 2009, and shall apply to all actions or proceedings pending on or commenced on or after the effective date.

The order of the Minnesota Supreme Court [C1-01-927] dated November 12, 2003, amending Rules 37 to 82 of the Rules of Juvenile Procedure and renumbering them as Rules 1 to 47 of the Rules of Juvenile Protection Procedure, provides in part that the amendments are effective January 1, 2004, and shall apply to all juvenile protection matters filed on or after that date.

Rule 8.02. Effective Date

Subd. 1. Open Hearings Pilot Project Counties. All juvenile protection case records deemed to be accessible to the public pursuant to this rule and filed in any of the twelve open hearings pilot project counties on or after June 28, 1998, shall be accessible to the public for inspection, copying, or release. All juvenile protection case records deemed to be accessible to the public pursuant to this rule and filed in any of the twelve open hearings pilot project counties before June 28, 1998, shall not be accessible to the public for inspection, copying, or release.

Subd. 2. Non-Open Hearings Pilot Project Counties. All juvenile protection case records deemed to be accessible to the public pursuant to this rule and filed in any non-open hearings pilot project county on or after July 1, 2002, shall be accessible to the public for inspection, copying, or release. All juvenile protection case records deemed to be accessible to the public pursuant to this rule and filed in any non-open hearings pilot project county before to July 1, 2002, shall not be accessible to the public for inspection, copying, or release.

Amended Nov. 12, 2003.

2001 Advisory Committee Comment—2003 Amendments

Rule 8.02 identifies different effective dates for the pilot project counties (June 1998) and non-pilot project counties (July 2002) because the twelve pilot counties already permit public access to hearings and records under the open hearings pilot project. Twelve counties participated in the open hearings pilot project from June 28, 1998, through June 30, 2002: Goodhue and LeSueur (First Judicial District); Houston (Third Judicial District); Hennepin (Fourth Judicial District); Watonwan (Fifth Judicial District); St. Louis—Virginia (Sixth Judicial District); Clay (Seventh Judicial District); Stevens (Eighth Judicial District); Marshall, Pennington, and Red Lake (Ninth Judicial District); and Chisago (Tenth Judicial District).

Historical Notes

The order of the Minnesota Supreme Court [C1-01-927] dated November 12, 2003, amending Rules 37 to 82 of the Rules of Juvenile Procedure and renumbering them as Rules 1 to 47 of the Rules of Juvenile Protection Procedure, provides in part that the amendments are effective January 1, 2004, and shall apply to all juvenile protection matters filed on or after that date.

Rule 8.03. Applicability of Rules of Public Access to Records of the Judicial Branch

Except where inconsistent with this rule, the Rules of Public Access to Records of the Judicial Branch promulgated by the Minnesota Supreme Court shall apply to juvenile protection case records relating to juvenile protection matters. Subdivisions 1(a) and 1(c) of Rule 4 of the Rules of Public Access to Records of the Judicial Branch, which prohibit public access to domestic abuse restraining orders and judicial work products and drafts, are not inconsistent with this rule.

Amended Nov. 12, 2003.

2001 Advisory Committee Comment—2003 Amendments

Rule 8.03 incorporates the provisions of the Rules of Public Access to Records of the Judicial Branch promulgated by the Minnesota Supreme Court ("Access Rules"), except to the extent that the Access Rules are inconsistent with this rule. The Access Rules establish the procedure for requesting access, the timing and format of the response, and an administrative appeal process. The Access Rules also define "case records" as a subcategory of records maintained by a court. Thus, "case records" would not include items that are not made a part of the court file, such notes of a social worker or guardian ad litem. Aggregate statistics on juvenile protection cases that do not identify parties or participants or a particular case are included in the "administrative records" category and are accessible to the public under the Access Rules. Such statistics are routinely published by the courts in numerous reports and studies. These procedures and definitions are consistent with this rule.

One significant aspect of both this rule and the Access Rules is that they govern public access only. Parties and participants in a juvenile protection matter may have greater access rights than the general public. See, e.g., Minn. R. Juv. P. 17 (2001).

Rule 8.03 preserves the confidentiality of domestic abuse restraining orders issued pursuant to Minn. Stat. § 518B.01 (Supp. 2001). The address of a petitioner for a restraining order under section 518B.01 must not be disclosed to the public if nondisclosure is requested by the petitioner. Minn. Stat. § 518B.01, subd. 3b (Supp. 2001). All other case records regarding the restraining order must not be disclosed until the temporary order made pursuant to subdivision 5 or 7 of section 518B.01 is served on the respondent. Access Rule 4, subd. 1(a) (Supp. 2001).

Rule 8.03 prohibits public access to judicial work products and drafts. These include notes, memoranda, and drafts prepared by a judge or court employed attorney, law clerk, legal assistant, or secretary and used in the process of preparing a decision or order, except the official court minutes prepared pursuant to Minn. Stat. § 546.24—.25 (Supp. 2001). Access Rule 4, subd. 1(c) (2001).

The "Court Services Records" provision of Access Rule 4, subd. 1(b), is inconsistent with this rule. The Advisory Committee is of the opinion that public access to reports and recommendations of social workers and guardians ad litem, which become case records, is an integral component of the increased accountability that underlies the concept of public access to juvenile protection matters. Court rulings will necessarily incorporate significant portions of what is set forth in those reports, and similar information is routinely disclosed in family law cases.

Historical Notes

The order of the Minnesota Supreme Court [C1-01-927] dated November 12, 2003, amending Rules 37 to 82 of the Rules of Juvenile Procedure and renumbering them as Rules 1 to 47 of the Rules of Juvenile Protection Procedure, provides in part that the amendments are effective January 1, 2004, and shall apply to all juvenile protection matters filed on or after that date.

Rule 8.04. Records Not Accessible to the Public or Parties

The following records (a)—(m) in the court file are not accessible to the public. Unless otherwise ordered by the court, parties shall have access for inspection and copying to all records in the court file, except records (b), (d), and (e) listed below.

(a) official transcript of testimony taken during portions of proceedings that are closed by the presiding judge;

(b) audio tapes or video tapes of a child alleging or describing physical abuse, sexual abuse, or neglect of any child;

(c) victims' statements;

(d) portions of juvenile protection case records that identify reporters of abuse or neglect;

(e) HIV test results;

(f) medical records, chemical dependency evaluations and records, psychological evaluations and records, and psychiatric evaluations and records;

(g) sexual offender treatment program reports;

(h) portions of photographs that identify a child;

(i) applications for ex parte emergency protective custody orders, and any resulting orders, until the hearing where all parties have an opportunity to be heard on the custody issue, provided that, if the order is requested in a child in need of protection or services (CHIPS) petition, only that portion of the petition that requests the order shall be deemed to be the application for purposes of this section (i);

(j) records or portions of records that specifically identify a minor victim of an alleged or adjudicated sexual assault;

(k) notice of pending court proceedings provided to an Indian tribe by the responsible social services agency pursuant to the Indian Child Welfare Act, 25 U.S.C. § 1912;

(*l*) records or portions of records which the court in exceptional circumstances has deemed to be inaccessible to the public; and

(m) records or portions of records that identify the name, address, home, or location of any shelter care or foster care facility in which a child is placed pursuant to an emergency protective care placement, foster care placement, pre-adoptive placement, adoptive placement, or any other type of court ordered placement.

Amended Nov. 12, 2003; June 10, 2009, eff. Aug. 1, 2009.

2001 Advisory Committee Comment—2003 Amendments

Rule 8.04(a) prohibits public access to testimony of anyone taken during portions of a proceeding that are closed to the public by the presiding judge. Hearings or portions of hearings may be closed by the presiding judge only in exceptional circumstances.

Rule 8.04(b) prohibits public access to audio tapes and video tapes of a child alleging or describing physical abuse, sexual abuse, or neglect of any child. This includes all tapes made pursuant to Minn. Stat. § 626.561, subd. 3 (Supp. 2001), during the course of a child abuse assessment, criminal investigation, or prosecution. This is consistent with Minn. Stat. § 13.391 (Supp. 2001), which prohibits an individual who is a subject of the tape from obtaining a copy of the tape without a court order. See also *In re Application of KSTP Television v. Ming Sen Shiue*, 504 F. Supp. 360 (D. Minn. 1980) (television station not entitled to view and copy three hours of video tapes received in evidence in criminal trial). Similarly, Rule 8.04(c)prohibits public access to victims' statements, and this includes written records of interviews of victims made pursuant to Minn. Stat. § 626.561, subd. 3 (Supp. 2001). This is consistent with Minn. Stat. § 609.115, subds. 1, 5; § 609.2244; and § 611A.037 (Supp. 2001) (pre–sentence investigations to include victim impact statements; no public access; domestic abuse victim impact statement confidential).

Although victims' statements and audio tapes and video tapes of a child alleging or describing abuse or neglect of any child are inaccessible to the public under Rule 8.04(b) and (c), this does not prohibit the attorneys for the parties or the court from including information from the statements or tapes in the petition, court orders, and other documents that are otherwise accessible to the public. In contrast, Rule 8.04(d) prohibits public access to "portions of juvenile protection case records that identify reporters of abuse or neglect. " By precluding public access to "portions of records that identify reporters of abuse or neglect," the Advisory Committee did not intend to preclude public access to any other information included in the same document. Thus, courts and court administrators must redact identifying information from otherwise publicly accessible documents and then make the edited documents available to the public for inspection and copying. Similarly, Rule 8.04(e) requires that courts and court administrators redact from any publicly accessible juvenile court record any reference to HIV test results, and Rule 8.04(h) requires administrators to redact the face or other identifying features in a photograph of a child.

The prohibition of public access to the identity of reporters of abuse or neglect under Rule 8.04(d) is consistent with state law governing access to this information in the hands of social services, law enforcement, court services, schools, and other agencies. Minn. Stat. § 626.556 (Supp. 2001). Rule 8.04(d) is also intended to help preserve federal funds for child abuse prevention and treatment programs. See 42 U.S.C. § 5106a(b)(2)(A) and § 5106a(b)(3) (1998); 45 C.F.R. § 1340.1 to § 1340.20 (1997). Rule 8.04(d) does not, however, apply to testimony of a witness taken during a proceeding that is open to the public.

Rule 8.04(e) prohibits public access to HIV test results. This is consistent with state and federal laws regarding court ordered testing for HIV. Minn. Stat. § 611A.19 (Supp. 2001) (defendant convicted for criminal sexual conduct; no reference to the test, the motion requesting the test, the test order, or the test results may appear in the criminal record or be maintained in any record of the court or court services); 42 U.S.C. § 14011 (1998) (defendant charged with crime; test result may be disclosed to victim only). The Committee is also aware that federal funding for early intervention services requires confidential treatment of this information. 42 U.S.C. § 300ff–61(a); § 300ff–63 (1998).

Rule 8.04(f) and (g) prohibit public access to medical records, chemical dependency evaluations and records, psychological evaluations and records, psychiatric evaluations and records, and sexual offender treatment program reports, unless admitted into evidence under Rule 8.05. This is consistent with public access limitations in criminal and juvenile delinquency proceedings that are open to the public. See, e.g., Minn. Stat. § 609.115, subd. 6 (Supp. 2001) (pre–sentence investigation reports). Practitioners and the courts must be careful not to violate applicable federal laws. Under 42 U.S.C. § 290dd–2 (1998), records of all federally assisted or regulated substance abuse treatment programs, including diagnosis and evaluation records, and all confidential communications made therein, except information required to be reported under a state mandatory child abuse reporting law, are confidential and may not be disclosed by the program unless disclosure is authorized by consent or court order. Thus, practitioners will have to obtain the relevant written consents from the parties or court orders, including protective orders, before disclosing certain medical records in their reports and submissions to the court. See 42 C.F.R. § 2.1 to 2.67 (1997) (comprehensive regulations providing procedures that must be followed for consent and court-ordered disclosure of records and confidential communications).

Although similar requirements apply to educational records under the Federal Educational Rights and Privacy Act (FERPA), 20 U.S.C. § 1232g, 1417, and § 11432 (1998); 34 C.F.R. § 99.1 to § 99.67 (1997), FERPA allows schools to disclose education records without consent or court order in certain circumstances, including disclosures to state and local officials under laws in effect before November 19, 1974. 20 U.S.C. § 1232g(b)(1)(E) (i) (1998); 34 C.F.R. § 99.31(a)(5)(i)(A) (1997). Authorization to disclose truancy to the county attorney, for example, was in effect before that date and continues under current law. See Minn. Stat. § 120.12 (1974) (superintendent to notify county attorney if truancy continues after notice to parent); 1987 Minn. Laws ch. 178 § 10 (repealing section 120.12 and replacing with current section 120.103, which adds mediation process before notice to county attorney); see also Minn. Stat. § 260A.06–.07 (Supp. 2001) (referral to county attorney from school attendance review boards; county attorney truancy mediation program notice includes warning that court action may be taken). Practitioners will have to review the procedures under which they receive education records from schools and, where necessary, obtain relevant written consents or protective orders before disclosing certain education records in their reports and submissions to the court. Additional information regarding FERPA may be found in Sharing Information: A Guide to the Family Educational Rights and Privacy Act and Participation in Juvenile justice Programs (U.S. Dept. of Justice, Office of Juvenile Justice and Delinquency Prevention, Washington, D.C. 20531, June 1997) (includes hypothetical disclosure situations and complete set of federal regulations).

Rule 8.04(h) prohibits public access to portions of photographs that identify a child, and requires administrators to redact the face or other identifying features in a photograph of a child before permitting public access. Any appropriate concern regarding public access to the remaining portions of such a photograph can be addressed through a protective order (see Rule 8.07).

Rule 8.04(i) precludes public access to an ex parte emergency protective custody order, until the hearing where all parties have an opportunity to be heard on the custody issue. This provision is designed to reduce the risk that a parent or legal custodian would try to hide a child before the child can be placed in protective custody or to take the child from custody before the court can hear the matter. See, e. g., Minn. R. Juv. P. 65 (Supp. 2001) (order must either direct that child be brought immediately before the court or taken to a placement facility designated by the court; parent or legal custodian, if present when child is taken into custody, shall immediately be informed of existence of order and reasons why child is being taken into custody). Rule 8.04(i) also precludes public access to the application or request for the protective custody order, except that if the request is made in a Child In Need of Protection or Services (CHIPS) petition, only that portion of the petition that requests the order is inaccessible to the public.

Rule 8.04(j) precludes public access to portions of records that specifically identify a minor victim of sexual assault. This will require court administrators to redact information from case records that specifically identifies the minor victim, including the victim's name and address. Rule 8.04(j) does not preclude public access to other information in the particular record. This is intended to parallel the treatment of victim identities in criminal and juvenile delinquency proceedings involving sexual assault charges under Minn. Stat. § 609.3471 (Supp. 2001). Thus, the term "sexual assault" includes any act described in Minnesota Statutes § 609.342, § 609.343, § 609.344, and § 609.345. The Committee considered using the term "sexual abuse" but felt that it was a limited subcategory of "sexual assault." See Minn. Stat. § 626.556, subd. 2(a) (Supp. 2001) ("sexual abuse" includes violations of § 609.342—.345 committed by person in a position of authority, responsible for child's care, or having a significant relationship with the child). Rule 8.04(j) does not require a finding that sexual assault occurred. An allegation of sexual assault is sufficient.

Rule 8.04(k) precludes public access to the notice of pending proceedings given by the responsible social services agency to an Indian child's tribe or to the Secretary of the Interior pursuant to 25 U.S.C. § 1912(a) (1998). The notice includes extensive personal information about the child, including all known information on direct lineal ancestors, and requires parties who receive the notice to keep it confidential. 25 C.F.R. § 23.11(d), (e) (1997). Notices are routinely given in doubtful cases because lack of notice can be fatal to a state court proceeding. See 25 U.S.C. § 1911 (1998) (exclusive jurisdiction of tribes; right to intervene; transfer of jurisdiction). The Committee believed that public access to information regarding the child's tribal heritage is appropriately given whenever a tribe intervenes or petitions for transfer of jurisdiction. Rule 8.04(k) does not preclude public access to intervention motions or transfer petitions.

Rule 8.04(*l*) recognizes that courts may, in exceptional circumstances, issue protective orders precluding public access to certain records or portions of records. Records of closed proceedings are inaccessible to the public under Rule 8.04(a). Procedures for issuing protective orders are set forth in Rule 8.07.

Rule 8.04(m) prohibits public access to the names, addresses, home, location, or other identifying information about the foster parents, foster care institutions, adoptive parents, and other persons and institutions providing care or pre-adoptive care of the child. This is consistent with the confidentiality accorded adoption proceedings. It is also designed to reduce the risk of continuing contact by someone whose parental rights have been terminated or who is a potentially dangerous family member. If deemed appropriate, the name, address, home, location, or other identifying information about a child's foster placement may be protected from a party through issuance of a protective order pursuant to Rule 8.07

Notwithstanding the list of inaccessible case records in Rule 8.04(a) through (m), many juvenile protection case records will typically be accessible to the public. Examples include: petitions, other than petitions for paternity; summons; affidavits of publication or service; certificates of representation; orders; hearing and trial notices; subpoenas; names of witnesses; motions and supporting affidavits and legal memoranda; transcripts; and reports of social workers and guardians ad litem. With the exception of information that must be redacted under Rule 8.04(d), (e), and (h), these records will be accessible to the public notwithstanding that they contain a summary of information derived from another record that is not accessible to the public. For example, a social services or guardian ad litem report might discuss the results of a chemical dependency evaluation. Although the chemical dependency evaluation itself is not accessible to the public under Rule 8.04(f), discussion of the details of that evaluation in the social services or guardian ad litem report need not be redacted before public disclosure of the report. Finally, it must be remembered that public access under this rule would not apply to records filed with the court before the effective date of this rule (see Rule 8.02) or to reports of a social worker or guardian ad litem that have not been made a part of the court file (see Rule 8.03).

2006 Advisory Committee Comment

The child's name and other identifying information are not to be redacted from records that are accessible to the public, except under Rule 8.04(j) when the child is the victim of an alleged or adjudicated sexual assault and under Rule 8.04(d) where the child is specifically identified as the reporter of the abuse or neglect. In the latter instance, the child's name and other identifying information should be redacted only in those instances where it is used as the reporter of abuse or neglect but should not be redacted when referenced elsewhere in the record.

Historical Notes

The order of the Minnesota Supreme Court [C1–01–927] dated June 10, 2009, amending the Rules of Juvenile Protection Procedure and the Rules of Adoption Procedure, provides in part that the amendments are effective August 1, 2009, and shall apply to all actions or proceedings pending on or commenced on or after the effective date.

The order of the Minnesota Supreme Court [C1-01-927] dated November 12, 2003, amending Rules 37 to 82 of the Rules of Juvenile Procedure and renumbering them as Rules 1 to 47 of the Rules of Juvenile Protection Procedure, provides in part that the amendments are effective January 1, 2004, and shall apply to all juvenile protection matters filed on or after that date.

Rule 8.05. Access to Exhibits

Case records received into evidence as exhibits shall be accessible to the public unless subject to a protective order issued pursuant to Rule 8.07.

Amended Nov. 12, 2003.

2001 Advisory Committee Comment

Rule 8.05 permits public access to records that have been received in evidence as an exhibit, unless the records are subject to a protective order (see Rule 8.07). Thus, any of the records identified in Rule 8.04(b) through (k) that have been admitted into evidence as an exhibit are accessible to the public, unless there is a protective order indicating otherwise. An exhibit that has been offered, but not expressly admitted by the court, does not become accessible to the public under Rule 8.05. Exhibits admitted during a trial or hearing must be distinguished from items attached as exhibits to a petition or a report of a social worker or guardian ad litem. Merely attaching something as an "exhibit" to another filed document does not render the "exhibit" to be accessible to the public under Rule 8.05.

Historical Notes

The order of the Minnesota Supreme Court [C1-01-927] dated November 12, 2003, amending Rules 37 to 82 of the Rules of Juvenile Procedure and renumbering them as Rules 1 to 47 of the Rules of Juvenile Protection Procedure, provides in part that the amendments are effective January 1, 2004, and shall apply to all juvenile protection matters filed on or after that date.

Rule 8.06. Access to Court Information Systems

Except where authorized by the district court, there shall be no direct public access to juvenile protection case records maintained in electronic format in court information systems.

Amended Nov. 12, 2003.

2001 Advisory Committee Comment—2003 Amendments

Rule 8.06 prohibits direct public access to case records maintained in electronic format in court information systems unless authorized by the court. Rule 44.06 intentionally limits access to electronic formats as a means of precluding widespread distribution of case records about children into larger, private databases that could be used to discriminate against children for insurance, employment, and other purposes. This concern also led the Advisory Committee to recommend that case titles in the petition and other documents include only the names of the parent or legal custodian, and exclude the names or initials of the children (see Rule 8.08). Rule 8.06 allows the courts to prepare calendars that identify cases by the appropriate caption. To the extent that court information systems can provide appropriate electronic formats for public access, Rule 8.06 allows the district court to make those accessible to the public.

Historical Notes

The order of the Minnesota Supreme Court [C1-01-927] dated November 12, 2003, amending Rules 37 to 82 of the Rules of Juvenile Procedure and renumbering them as Rules 1 to 47 of the Rules of Juvenile Protection Procedure, provides in part that the amendments are effective January 1, 2004, and shall apply to all juvenile protection matters filed on or after that date.

Rule 8.07. Protective Order

Subd. 1. Orders Regarding the Public. The court may sua sponte, or upon motion and hearing, issue an order prohibiting public access to juvenile protection case records that are otherwise accessible to the public only if the court finds that an exceptional circumstance exists. The protective order shall state the reason for issuance of the order. If the court issues a protective order on its own motion and without a hearing, the court shall schedule a hearing on the order as soon as possible at the request of any person. A protective order issued pursuant to this subdivision is accessible to the public.

Subd. 2. Orders Regarding Parties. The court may sua sponte, or upon motion and hearing, issue a protective order prohibiting a party's access to juvenile protection case records that are otherwise accessible to the party. The protective order shall state the reason for issuance of the order. If the court issues a protective order on its own motion and without a hearing the court shall schedule a hearing on the order as soon as possible at the request of any person. A protective order issued pursuant to this subdivision is accessible to the public.

Amended Nov. 12, 2003.

2001 Advisory Committee Comment—2003 Amendments

Rule 8.07 establishes two categories of protective orders. One is made on motion of a party after a hearing, and the other is made on the court's own motion without a hearing, subject to a later hearing if requested by any person, including representatives of the media. In any case, a protective order may issue only in exceptional circumstances. The Advisory Committee felt that these procedures would provide adequate protection and flexibility.

Historical Notes

The order of the Minnesota Supreme Court [C1-01-927] dated November 12, 2003, amending Rules 37 to 82 of the Rules of Juvenile Procedure and renumbering them as Rules 1 to 47 of the Rules of Juvenile Protection Procedure, provides in part that the amendments are effective January 1, 2004, and shall apply to all juvenile protection matters filed on or after that date.

Rule 8.08. Case Captions and Text of Decisions and Other Records

Subd. 1. District Court.

All juvenile protection court files opened and any petitions, pleadings, reports, orders, or other documents or records filed in any

(i) of the twelve open hearings pilot project counties on or after June 22, 1998, or

(ii) non–open hearings pilot project county on or after July 1, 2002, shall be captioned in the name of the child's parent(s) or legal custodian(s), as follows: "In the Matter of the Welfare of the Child(ren) of __________, Parent(s)/ Legal Custodian(s)." The caption shall not include the child's name or initials. The body of any petitions, pleadings, reports, orders, or other documents or records filed with the court shall include the child's and parent's or legal custodian's full name, not their initials. The case caption shall not be modified upon the issuance of an order terminating parental rights.

Subd. 2. Appellate Court. All juvenile protection court files opened in any Minnesota appellate court shall be captioned in the initials of the parent(s) or legal custodian(s) as follows: "In the Matter of the Welfare of the Child(ren) of __________, Parent(s)/Legal Custodian(s)." The caption shall not include the child's name or initials. The body of any decision filed in any Minnesota appellate court shall use the parent's and child's initials, not their names. Upon the filing of an appeal pursuant to Rule 47.02, the appellant shall provide to the court administrator, the appellate court, and the parties and participants notice of the correct appellate case caption required under this Rule. This Rule supercedes Rule 143.01 of the Rules of Civil Appellate Procedure regarding the provisions relating to case captions upon appeal.

Amended Nov. 12, 2003.

2001 Advisory Committee Comment—2003 Amendments

Twelve counties participated in the pilot project from June 28, 1998, through June 30, 2002: Goodhue and LeSueur (First Judicial District); Houston (Third Judicial District); Hennepin (Fourth Judicial District); Watonwan (Fifth Judicial District); St. Louis—Virginia (Sixth Judicial District); Clay (Seventh Judicial District); Stevens (Eighth Judicial District); Marshall, Pennington, and Red Lake (Ninth Judicial District); and Chisago (Tenth Judicial District).

The change in case captions under Rule 8.08 is designed to minimize the stigma to children involved in juvenile protection matters that are accessible to the public. It is more appropriate to label these cases in the name of the adults involved, who are often the perpetrators of abuse or neglect.

Historical Notes

The order of the Minnesota Supreme Court [C1-01-927] dated November 12, 2003, amending Rules 37 to 82 of the Rules of Juvenile Procedure and renumbering them as Rules 1 to 47 of the Rules of Juvenile Protection Procedure, provides in part that the amendments are effective January 1, 2004, and shall apply to all juvenile protection matters filed on or after that date.

RULE 9. EX PARTE COMMUNICATION

Rule 9.01. Ex Parte Communication Prohibited

Ex parte communication is prohibited, except as to procedural matters not affecting the merits of the case. All communications between the court and a party or participant shall be in the presence of all other parties or in writing with copies to the parties or, if represented, the party's attorney, except as otherwise permitted by statute or these rules. The court shall not consider any ex parte communication from anyone concerning a proceeding, including conditions of release, evidence, adjudication, disposition, or any other matter.

Amended Nov. 12, 2003.

1999 Advisory Committee Comment—2003 Amendments

Rule 9.01 reflects the prohibition against ex parte communication set forth in Rule 3.5(g) of the Rules of Professional Conduct and Cannon 3A(7) of the Code of Judicial Conduct.

Historical Notes

The order of the Minnesota Supreme Court [C1-01-927] dated November 12, 2003, amending Rules 37 to 82 of the Rules of Juvenile Procedure and renumbering them as Rules 1 to 47 of the Rules of Juvenile Protection Procedure, provides in part that the amendments are effective January 1, 2004, and shall apply to all juvenile protection matters filed on or after that date.

Rule 9.02. Disclosure

The court shall fully disclose to all parties any attempted prohibited ex parte communication.

Amended Nov. 12, 2003.

Historical Notes

The order of the Minnesota Supreme Court [C1-01-927] dated November 12, 2003, amending Rules 37 to 82 of the Rules of Juvenile Procedure and renumbering them as Rules 1 to 47 of the Rules of Juvenile Protection Procedure, provides in part that the amendments are effective January 1, 2004, and shall apply to all juvenile protection matters filed on or after that date.

RULE 10. ORDERS

Rule 10.01. Written or Oral Orders; Timing

Court orders may be written or stated on the record. An order stated on the record shall also be reduced to writing by the court. Except for orders issued following a trial pursuant to Rule 39.05, all orders shall be filed with the court administrator within fifteen (15) days of the conclusion of the testimony, unless the court finds that a fifteen (15)–day extension is required in the interests of justice or the best interests of the child. Each order issued following a hearing shall include the name and contact information of the court reporter. Failure to include the court reporter contact information does not extend the timeline for appeal. An order shall remain in full force and effect until the first occurrence of one of the following:

(a) issuance of an inconsistent order;

(b) the order ends pursuant to the terms of the order; or

(c) jurisdiction of the juvenile court is terminated.

Amended Nov. 12, 2003; June 10, 2009, eff. Aug. 1, 2009.

2008 Advisory Committee Comment

To easily identify court reporters for the purpose of timely requesting a transcript for purposes of appeal, Rule 10.01 requires each order issued follow a hearing to include the name and contact information of the court reporter.

Historical Notes

The order of the Minnesota Supreme Court [C1–01–927] dated June 10, 2009, amending the Rules of Juvenile Protection Procedure and the Rules of Adoption Procedure, provides in part that the amendments are effective August 1, 2009, and shall apply to all actions or proceedings pending on or commenced on or after the effective date.

The order of the Minnesota Supreme Court [C1-01-927] dated November 12, 2003, amending Rules 37 to 82 of the Rules of Juvenile Procedure and renumbering them as Rules 1 to 47 of the Rules of Juvenile Protection Procedure, provides in part that the amendments are effective January 1, 2004, and shall apply to all juvenile protection matters filed on or after that date.

Rule 10.02. Immediate Effect of Oral Order

Unless otherwise ordered by the court, an order stated on the record shall be effective immediately.

Amended Nov. 12, 2003.

Historical Notes

The order of the Minnesota Supreme Court [C1-01-927] dated November 12, 2003, amending Rules 37 to 82 of the Rules of Juvenile Procedure and renumbering them as Rules 1 to 47 of the Rules of Juvenile Protection Procedure, provides in part that the amendments are effective January 1, 2004, and shall apply to all juvenile protection matters filed on or after that date.

Rule 10.03. Method and Timing of Service; Persons to be Served

Service of court orders shall be made by the court administrator upon each party, county attorney, and such other persons as the court may direct, and may be made by delivery at the hearing, by U.S. mail, or as otherwise directed by the court. If a party is represented by counsel, delivery or service shall be upon counsel. If service of the summons was by publication and the person has not appeared either personally or through counsel, service of court orders upon the person is not required. Service of the order by the court administrator shall be accomplished within five (5) days of the date the judicial officer delivers the order to the court administrator. In a termination of parental rights matter or other permanency matter, service by the court administrator of the findings and order terminating parental rights or establishing other permanency for the child shall be accomplished within three (3) days of the date the judicial officer delivers the order to the court administrator.

Amended Nov. 12, 2003; Dec. 1, 2006, eff. Jan. 1, 2007; June 26, 2007, eff. July 1, 2007; June 10, 2009, eff. Aug. 1, 2009.

Historical Notes

The order of the Minnesota Supreme Court [C1–01–927] dated June 10, 2009, amending the Rules of Juvenile Protection Procedure and the Rules of Adoption Procedure, provides in part that the amendments are effective August 1, 2009, and shall apply to all actions or proceedings pending on or commenced on or after the effective date.

The order of the Minnesota Supreme Court [C1-01-927] dated November 12, 2003, amending Rules 37 to 82 of the Rules of Juvenile Procedure and renumbering them as Rules 1 to 47 of the Rules of Juvenile Protection Procedure, provides in part that the amendments are effective January 1, 2004, and shall apply to all juvenile protection matters filed on or after that date.

Rule 10.04. Notice of Filing of Order

Each order delivered or mailed to the parties and the county attorney shall be accompanied by a notice of filing of order, which shall include notice of the right to appeal a final order pursuant to Rule 47.02. The State Court Administrator shall develop a "notice of filing" form which shall be used by court administrators.

Amended Nov. 12, 2003; June 10, 2009, eff. Aug. 1, 2009.

Historical Notes

The order of the Minnesota Supreme Court [C1–01–927] dated June 10, 2009, amending the Rules of Juvenile Protection Procedure and the Rules of Adoption Procedure, provides in part that the amendments are effective August 1, 2009, and shall apply to all actions or proceedings pending on or commenced on or after the effective date.

The order of the Minnesota Supreme Court [C1-01-927] dated November 12, 2003, amending Rules 37 to 82 of the Rules of Juvenile Procedure and renumbering them as Rules 1 to 47 of the Rules of Juvenile Protection Procedure, provides in part that the amendments

are effective January 1, 2004, and shall apply to all juvenile protection matters filed on or after that date.

RULE 11. RECORDING AND TRANSCRIPTS

Rule 11.01. Procedure

A verbatim recording of all hearings shall be made by a stenographic reporter or by an electronic sound recording device. If the recording is made by an electronic sound recording device, qualified personnel shall be assigned by the court to operate the device. Any required transcripts shall be prepared by personnel assigned by the court.

Amended Nov. 12, 2003.

Historical Notes

The order of the Minnesota Supreme Court [C1-01-927] dated November 12, 2003, amending Rules 37 to 82 of the Rules of Juvenile Procedure and renumbering them as Rules 1 to 47 of the Rules of Juvenile Protection Procedure, provides in part that the amendments are effective January 1, 2004, and shall apply to all juvenile protection matters filed on or after that date.

Rule 11.02. Availability of Transcripts

Transcripts may be requested by the county attorney, parties, and participants. The court upon a showing of good cause may grant any other person's written or on the record request for a transcript.

Amended Nov. 12, 2003.

Historical Notes

The order of the Minnesota Supreme Court [C1-01-927] dated November 12, 2003, amending Rules 37 to 82 of the Rules of Juvenile Procedure and renumbering them as Rules 1 to 47 of the Rules of Juvenile Protection Procedure, provides in part that the amendments are effective January 1, 2004, and shall apply to all juvenile protection matters filed on or after that date.

Rule 11.03. Expense

If a party requesting a transcript is unable to pay the preparation cost, the party may apply to the court for an order directing the preparation and delivery of the transcript to the party requesting it, at public expense. A party's request for a transcript shall be accompanied by an In Forma Pauperis (IFP) application. Upon a finding of the party's ability to do so, the court may order partial reimbursement for the cost of the transcript.

Adopted Nov. 12, 2003.

Historical Notes

The order of the Minnesota Supreme Court [C1-01-927] dated November 12, 2003, amending Rules 37 to 82 of the Rules of Juvenile Procedure and renumbering them as Rules 1 to 47 of the Rules of Juvenile Protection Procedure, provides in part that the amendments are effective January 1, 2004, and shall apply to all juvenile protection matters filed on or after that date.

RULE 12. USE OF TELEPHONE AND INTERACTIVE VIDEO

Rule 12.01. Motions and Conferences

The court may hear motions and conduct conferences with counsel by telephone or interactive video.

Amended Nov. 12, 2003.

1999 Advisory Committee Comment—2003 Amendments

Rule 12.01 authorizes the court to use telephone and interactive video to hear motions where testimony is not required and to resolve procedural matters with counsel for the parties.

Historical Notes

The order of the Minnesota Supreme Court [C1-01-927] dated November 12, 2003, amending Rules 37 to 82 of the Rules of Juvenile Procedure and renumbering them as Rules 1 to 47 of the Rules of Juvenile Protection Procedure, provides in part that the amendments are effective January 1, 2004, and shall apply to all juvenile protection matters filed on or after that date.

Rule 12.02. Hearings and Taking Testimony

By agreement of the parties, or in exceptional circumstances upon motion of a party or the county attorney, the court may hold hearings and take testimony by telephone or interactive video.

Amended Nov. 12, 2003.

1999 Advisory Committee Comment

Rule 12.02 authorizes the court to hold hearings and take testimony by telephone or interactive video only upon agreement of the parties or in exceptional circumstances upon motion. The intent of this rule is to ensure that parties are permitted to fully participate in hearings and to be present when testimony is offered. The rule provides that the court has the opportunity, in all but the most exceptional cases, to personally observe witnesses in order to effectively weigh credibility. However, it also gives the court some flexibility in those exceptional cases.

Historical Notes

The order of the Minnesota Supreme Court [C1-01-927] dated November 12, 2003, amending Rules 37 to 82 of the Rules of Juvenile Procedure and renumbering them as Rules 1 to 47 of the Rules of Juvenile Protection Procedure, provides in part that the amendments are effective January 1, 2004, and shall apply to all juvenile protection matters filed on or after that date.

Rule 12.03. In Court Appearance Not Precluded

This rule shall not preclude a party or the county attorney from being present in person before the court at a hearing.

Amended Nov. 12, 2003.

Historical Notes

The order of the Minnesota Supreme Court [C1-01-927] dated November 12, 2003, amending Rules 37 to 82 of the Rules of Juvenile Procedure and renumbering them as Rules 1 to 47 of the Rules of Juvenile Protection Procedure, provides in part that the amendments are effective January 1, 2004, and shall apply to all juvenile protection matters filed on or after that date.

RULE 13. SUBPOENAS

Rule 13.01. Subpoena for a Hearing or Trial

At the request of any party or the county attorney, the court administrator shall issue a subpoena for a witness in a matter pending before the court.

Amended Nov. 12, 2003.

Historical Notes

The order of the Minnesota Supreme Court [C1-01-927] dated November 12, 2003, amending Rules 37 to 82 of the Rules of Juvenile Procedure and renumbering them as Rules 1 to 47 of the Rules of Juvenile Protection Procedure, provides in part that the amendments are effective January 1, 2004, and shall apply to all juvenile protection matters filed on or after that date.

Rule 13.02. Form; Issuance; Notice

Subd. 1. Form. Every subpoena shall be issued by the court administrator under the seal of the court, shall state the name of the court and the title of the action, and shall command each person to whom it is directed to attend and give testimony at a specified time and place or to produce books, papers, documents, or other tangible things designated in the subpoena. The court administrator shall issue a subpoena, or a subpoena for the production of documentary evidence or tangible things, signed and sealed, but otherwise in blank, to a party or county attorney requesting it, who shall fill it in before service.

Subd. 2. Issuance. A subpoena shall be issued only for appearance at a hearing, a deposition pursuant to Rule 17, a trial pursuant to Rule 39, or to produce books, papers, documents, or other tangible things designated in the subpoena.

Subd. 3. Notice. Every subpoena shall contain a notice to the person to whom it is directed advising the person of the right to reimbursement for certain expenses pursuant to Rule 13.08.

Amended Nov. 12, 2003.

Historical Notes

The order of the Minnesota Supreme Court [C1-01-927] dated November 12, 2003, amending Rules 37 to 82 of the Rules of Juvenile Procedure and renumbering them as Rules 1 to 47 of the Rules of Juvenile Protection Procedure, provides in part that the amendments are effective January 1, 2004, and shall apply to all juvenile protection matters filed on or after that date.

Rule 13.03. Service

A subpoena may be served by the sheriff, a deputy sheriff, or any other person over the age of 18 who is not a party to the proceeding. Service of a subpoena upon a person named in the subpoena shall be made by delivering a copy of the subpoena to the named person or by leaving a copy at the person's usual place of abode with some person of suitable age and discretion residing at such abode.

Amended Nov. 12, 2003.

Historical Notes

The order of the Minnesota Supreme Court [C1-01-927] dated November 12, 2003, amending Rules 37 to 82 of the Rules of Juvenile Procedure and renumbering them as Rules 1 to 47 of the Rules of Juvenile Protection Procedure, provides in part that the amendments are effective January 1, 2004, and shall apply to all juvenile protection matters filed on or after that date.

Rule 13.04. Motion to Quash a Subpoena

Upon motion pursuant to Rule 15, a person served with a subpoena may move to quash or modify the subpoena. Upon hearing a motion to quash a subpoena, the court may:

(a) direct compliance with the subpoena;

(b) modify the subpoena if it is unreasonable or oppressive;

(c) deny the motion to quash the subpoena on the condition that the person requesting the subpoena prepay the reasonable cost of producing the books, papers, documents, or tangible things; or

(d) quash the subpoena.

Amended Nov. 12, 2003.

Historical Notes

The order of the Minnesota Supreme Court [C1-01-927] dated November 12, 2003, amending Rules 37 to 82 of the Rules of Juvenile Procedure and renumbering them as Rules 1 to 47 of the Rules of Juvenile Protection Procedure, provides in part that the amendments are effective January 1, 2004, and shall apply to all juvenile protection matters filed on or after that date.

Rule 13.05. Objection

The person to whom the subpoena is directed may, within five (5) days after service of the subpoena or on or before the time specified in the subpoena for compliance if such time is less than five (5) days after service, serve upon the party serving the subpoena a written objection to the taking of the deposition or the production, inspection, or copying of any or all of the designated materials. If objection is made, the party serving the subpoena shall not be entitled to inspect or copy the materials, except pursuant to an order of the court from which the subpoena was issued. If objection is made, the party serving the subpoena may, at any time before or during the taking of the deposition, and upon notice and motion to the deponent, request an order requiring compliance with the subpoena.

Amended Nov. 12, 2003.

Historical Notes

The order of the Minnesota Supreme Court [C1-01-927] dated November 12, 2003, amending Rules 37 to 82 of the Rules of Juvenile Procedure and renumbering them as Rules 1 to 47 of the Rules of Juvenile Protection Procedure, provides in part that the amendments are effective January 1, 2004, and shall apply to all juvenile protection matters filed on or after that date.

Rule 13.06. Production of Documentary Evidence

A subpoena may also command the person to whom it is directed to produce books, papers, documents, or tangible things designated in the subpoena.

Amended Nov. 12, 2003.

Historical Notes

The order of the Minnesota Supreme Court [C1-01-927] dated November 12, 2003, amending Rules 37 to 82 of the Rules of Juvenile Procedure and renumbering them as Rules 1 to 47 of the Rules of

Juvenile Protection Procedure, provides in part that the amendments are effective January 1, 2004, and shall apply to all juvenile protection matters filed on or after that date.

Rule 13.07. Subpoena for Taking Depositions; Place of Examination

Subd. 1. Proof of Service. Proof of service of notice to take a deposition, as provided in Rule 17, constitutes a sufficient authorization for the issuance of a subpoena for the person named or described in the subpoena.

Subd. 2. Location. A resident of the state may be required to attend an examination only in the county in which the resident resides or is employed or transacts business in person, or at such other convenient place as is fixed by order of the court. A nonresident of the state may be required to attend in any county of the state.

Amended Nov. 12, 2003.

Historical Notes

The order of the Minnesota Supreme Court [C1-01-927] dated November 12, 2003, amending Rules 37 to 82 of the Rules of Juvenile Procedure and renumbering them as Rules 1 to 47 of the Rules of Juvenile Protection Procedure, provides in part that the amendments are effective January 1, 2004, and shall apply to all juvenile protection matters filed on or after that date.

Rule 13.08. Expenses

Subdivision 1. Witnesses. If the subpoena is issued at the request of the State of Minnesota, a political subdivision of the State, or an officer or agency of the State, witness fees and mileage shall be paid by public funds. If the subpoena is issued at the request of a party who is unable to pay witness fees and mileage, these costs shall upon order of the court be paid in whole or in part at public expense, depending upon the ability of the party to pay. All other fees and mileage shall be paid by the requesting party, unless otherwise ordered by the court upon motion.

Subd. 2. Expenses of Experts. Subject to the provisions of Rule 17, a witness who is not a party to the action or an employee of a party and who is required to give testimony or produce documents relating to a profession, business, or trade, or relating to knowledge, information, or facts obtained as a result of activities in such profession, business, or trade, is entitled to reasonable compensation for the time and expense involved in preparing for and giving such testimony or producing such documents. The party serving the subpoena shall make arrangements for such reasonable compensation prior to the time of the taking of the testimony. If such arrangements are not made, the person subpoenaed may proceed pursuant to Rule 13.04 or Rule 13.05. If the deponent has moved to quash or otherwise objected to the subpoena, the party serving the subpoena may, upon notice and motion to the deponent and all parties and the county attorney, move for an order directing the amount of such compensation at any time before the taking of the deposition.

Amended Nov. 12, 2003.

Historical Notes

The order of the Minnesota Supreme Court [C1-01-927] dated November 12, 2003, amending Rules 37 to 82 of the Rules of Juvenile Procedure and renumbering them as Rules 1 to 47 of the Rules of Juvenile Protection Procedure, provides in part that the amendments are effective January 1, 2004, and shall apply to all juvenile protection matters filed on or after that date.

Rule 13.09. Failure to Appear

If any person personally served with a subpoena fails, without reasonable cause, to appear or bring the child if ordered to do so, or if the court has reason to believe the person is avoiding personal service, the court may sua sponte or upon the motion of a party or the county attorney pursuant to Rule 15 proceed against the person for civil contempt of court pursuant to Rule 14 or the court may issue a warrant for the person's arrest, or both. When it appears to the court that service will be ineffectual, or that the welfare of the child requires that the child be immediately brought into the custody of the court, the court may issue a warrant for immediate custody of the child.

Amended Nov. 12, 2003.

Historical Notes

The order of the Minnesota Supreme Court [C1-01-927] dated November 12, 2003, amending Rules 37 to 82 of the Rules of Juvenile Procedure and renumbering them as Rules 1 to 47 of the Rules of Juvenile Protection Procedure, provides in part that the amendments are effective January 1, 2004, and shall apply to all juvenile protection matters filed on or after that date.

RULE 14. CONTEMPT

Rule 14.01. Initiation

Contempt proceedings shall be initiated by personal service upon the alleged contemnor of an order to show cause together with a motion for contempt and an affidavit supporting the motion. The order to show cause shall direct the alleged contemnor to appear and show cause why he or she should not be held in contempt of court and why the moving party should not be granted the relief requested in the motion. The order to show cause shall contain at least the following:

(a) a reference to the specific order of the court alleged to have been violated and date of filing of the order;

(b) a quotation of the specific applicable provisions ordered;

(c) a statement identifying the alleged contemnor's ability to comply with the order; and

(d) a statement identifying the alleged contemnor's failure to comply with the order.

Amended Nov. 12, 2003.

Historical Notes

The order of the Minnesota Supreme Court [C1-01-927] dated November 12, 2003, amending Rules 37 to 82 of the Rules of Juvenile Procedure and renumbering them as Rules 1 to 47 of the Rules of Juvenile Protection Procedure, provides in part that the amendments are effective January 1, 2004, and shall apply to all juvenile protection matters filed on or after that date.

Rule 14.02. Supporting and Responsive Affidavits

The supporting affidavit of the moving party shall set forth with particularity the facts constituting each alleged violation of the order. Any responsive affidavit shall set forth with particularity any defenses the alleged contemnor will present to the court. The supporting affidavit and the responsive affidavit shall contain paragraphs which shall be numbered to correspond to the paragraphs of the motion where possible.

Amended Nov. 12, 2003.

Historical Notes

The order of the Minnesota Supreme Court [C1-01-927] dated November 12, 2003, amending Rules 37 to 82 of the Rules of Juvenile Procedure and renumbering them as Rules 1 to 47 of the Rules of Juvenile Protection Procedure, provides in part that the amendments are effective January 1, 2004, and shall apply to all juvenile protection matters filed on or after that date.

Rule 14.03. Hearing

The alleged contemnor must appear in person before the court to be afforded the opportunity to oppose the motion for contempt by sworn testimony. The court shall not act upon affidavit alone, absent express waiver by the alleged contemnor of the right to offer sworn testimony.

Amended Nov. 12, 2003.

Historical Notes

The order of the Minnesota Supreme Court [C1-01-927] dated November 12, 2003, amending Rules 37 to 82 of the Rules of Juvenile Procedure and renumbering them as Rules 1 to 47 of the Rules of Juvenile Protection Procedure, provides in part that the amendments are effective January 1, 2004, and shall apply to all juvenile protection matters filed on or after that date.

Rule 14.04. Sentencing

Subd. 1. Default of Conditions for Stay. Where the court has entered an order for contempt with a stay of sentence and there has been a default in the performance of the condition(s) for the stay, before a writ of attachment or bench warrant may be issued, an affidavit of non-compliance and request for writ of attachment must be served upon the defaulting party, unless the person is shown to be avoiding service.

Subd. 2. Writ of Attachment. The writ of attachment shall direct law enforcement officers to bring the defaulting party before the court for a hearing to show cause why the stay of sentence should not be revoked. The moving party shall submit a proposed order for writ of attachment to the court.

Subd. 3. Sanctions. Upon evidence taken, the court shall determine the guilt or innocence of the alleged contemnor. If the court determines that the alleged contemnor is guilty, the court shall order punishment by fine or imprisonment for not more than six (6) months, or both.

Subd. 4. Authority of Court. Nothing in these rules shall be interpreted to limit the inherent authority of the court to enforce its own orders.

Amended Nov. 12, 2003.

Historical Notes

The order of the Minnesota Supreme Court [C1-01-927] dated November 12, 2003, amending Rules 37 to 82 of the Rules of Juvenile Procedure and renumbering them as Rules 1 to 47 of the Rules of Juvenile Protection Procedure, provides in part that the amendments are effective January 1, 2004, and shall apply to all juvenile protection matters filed on or after that date.

RULE 15. MOTIONS

Rule 15.01. Form

Subd. 1. Generally. An application to the court for an order shall be by motion.

Subd. 2. Motions to Be in Writing. Except as permitted by subdivision 3, a motion shall be in writing and shall:

(a) set forth the relief or order sought;

(b) state with particularity the grounds for the relief or order sought;

(c) be signed by the person making the motion;

(d) be filed with the court, unless it is made orally in court on the record; and

(e) be accompanied by a supporting affidavit or other supporting documentation or a memorandum of law, unless it is made orally in court on the record.

The requirement of writing is fulfilled if the motion is stated in a written notice of motion. The parties may agree to written submission to the court for decision without oral argument unless the court directs otherwise.

Subd. 3. Exception. Unless another party or the county attorney objects, a party or the county attorney may make an oral motion during a hearing. All oral motions and objections to oral motions shall be made on the record. When an objection is made, the court shall determine whether there is good cause to permit the oral motion and, before issuing an order, shall allow the objecting party reasonable time to respond.

Amended Nov. 12, 2003.

Historical Notes

The order of the Minnesota Supreme Court [C1-01-927] dated November 12, 2003, amending Rules 37 to 82 of the Rules of Juvenile Procedure and renumbering them as Rules 1 to 47 of the Rules of Juvenile Protection Procedure, provides in part that the amendments are effective January 1, 2004, and shall apply to all juvenile protection matters filed on or after that date.

Rule 15.02. Service and Notice of Motions

Subd. 1. Upon Whom.

(a) *Generally.* The moving party shall serve the notice of motion and motion, along with any supporting affidavit or other supporting documentation or a memorandum of law, upon all parties, the county attorney, and any other persons designated by the court. If service of the petition was by publication and the address of the person remains unknown, service of a motion shall be deemed sufficient if it is mailed to the person's last known address. The moving party shall serve only the notice of the hearing and not the motion upon all participants.

(b) *Motion to Transfer Juvenile Protection Matter to Jurisdiction of Tribal Court.* In addition to providing service as required in subdivision 1(a), a motion to transfer a juvenile protection matter to jurisdiction of the Indian child's tribal court under Rule 48.01, or a response to such motion, shall also be served upon the child's parents and any Indian child age twelve (12) or older regardless of party status.

Subd. 2. How Made. Service of a motion may be made by personal service, by mail, or by transmitting a copy by facsimile transmission pursuant to Rule 31.

Subd. 3. Time. Any written motion, along with any supporting affidavit or other supporting documentation or memorandum of law, shall be served at least five (5) days before it is to be heard, unless the court for good cause shown permits a motion to be made and served less than five (5) days before it is to be heard. The filing and service of a motion shall not extend the permanency timelines set forth in these rules.

Amended Nov. 12, 2003; June 10, 2009, eff. Aug. 1, 2009.

2008 Advisory Committee Comment

Service of Motion to Transfer Juvenile Protection Matter to Jurisdiction of Tribal Court on Child Age 12 or Older. The Indian Child Welfare Act (ICWA) permits the district court to deny a request to transfer to tribal court when there is "good cause" to deny the transfer. 25 U.S.C. § 1911(b). While "good cause" to deny the transfer is not defined in the ICWA, it is addressed in the *Bureau of Indian Affairs Guidelines for State Courts: Indian Child Custody Proceedings* (*BIA Guidelines*), which provides that "Good cause not to transfer the proceeding may exist if any of the following circumstances exists ... [t]he Indian child is over twelve years of age and objects to the transfer." *BIA Guidelines* C.3 and C.3 Commentary, 44 Fed. Reg. 67584, 67591 at C.3 (Nov. 26, 1979). Requiring service of the motion to transfer jurisdiction to tribal court upon a child age twelve (12) or older permits the child to be aware of the request to transfer and to raise an objection.

Historical Notes

The order of the Minnesota Supreme Court [C1–01–927] dated June 10, 2009, amending the Rules of Juvenile Protection Procedure and the Rules of Adoption Procedure, provides in part that the amendments are effective August 1, 2009, and shall apply to all actions or proceedings pending on or commenced on or after the effective date.

The order of the Minnesota Supreme Court [C1-01-927] dated November 12, 2003, amending Rules 37 to 82 of the Rules of Juvenile Procedure and renumbering them as Rules 1 to 47 of the Rules of Juvenile Protection Procedure, provides in part that the amendments are effective January 1, 2004, and shall apply to all juvenile protection matters filed on or after that date.

Rule 15.03. Ex Parte Motion and Hearing

Subd. 1. Motion. A motion may be made ex parte when permitted by statute or these rules. Every ex parte motion shall be accompanied by an explanation of the efforts made to notify all parties and the county attorney of the motion or an explanation of why such notice would place the child in danger of imminent harm or could result in the child being hidden or removed from the court's jurisdiction.

Subd. 2. Hearing. When the court issues an ex parte order removing a child from the care of a parent or legal custodian, the court shall schedule a hearing to review the order within seventy-two (72) hours of the child's removal. Upon issuance of an ex parte order in cases of domestic child abuse, the court shall schedule a hearing pursuant to the requirements of Minnesota Statutes § 260C.148. Upon issuance of any other ex parte order, a hearing shall be scheduled on the request of a party or the county attorney at the earliest possible date.

Amended Nov. 12, 2003; Dec. 1, 2006, eff. Jan. 1, 2007.

Historical Notes

The order of the Minnesota Supreme Court [C1-01-927] dated November 12, 2003, amending Rules 37 to 82 of the Rules of Juvenile Procedure and renumbering them as Rules 1 to 47 of the Rules of Juvenile Protection Procedure, provides in part that the amendments are effective January 1, 2004, and shall apply to all juvenile protection matters filed on or after that date.

Rule 15.04. Motion to Dismiss Petition

Any party or the county attorney may bring a motion to dismiss the petition upon any of the following grounds:

(a) lack of jurisdiction over the subject matter;

(b) lack of jurisdiction over the child; or

(c) at or prior to the admit/deny hearing, failure of the petition to state facts which, if proven, establish a prima facie case to support the statutory grounds set forth in the petition.

Amended Nov. 12, 2003.

Historical Notes

The order of the Minnesota Supreme Court [C1-01-927] dated November 12, 2003, amending Rules 37 to 82 of the Rules of Juvenile Procedure and renumbering them as Rules 1 to 47 of the Rules of Juvenile Protection Procedure, provides in part that the amendments are effective January 1, 2004, and shall apply to all juvenile protection matters filed on or after that date.

Rule 15.05. Motion to Strike Document

If a motion to strike a document or any portion of a document is granted, the document or portion of document shall be marked by the judge as stricken, but the document shall remain in the court file.

Amended Nov. 12, 2003; Dec. 1, 2006, eff. Jan. 1, 2007.

Historical Notes

The order of the Minnesota Supreme Court [C1-01-927] dated November 12, 2003, amending Rules 37 to 82 of the Rules of Juvenile Procedure and renumbering them as Rules 1 to 47 of the Rules of Juvenile Protection Procedure, provides in part that the amendments are effective January 1, 2004, and shall apply to all juvenile protection matters filed on or after that date.

Rule 15.06. Obtaining Hearing Date; Notice to Parties

Upon request of a party who intends to file a notice of motion and motion, the court administrator shall schedule a hearing which shall take place within fifteen (15) days of the request. A party obtaining a date and time for a hearing on a motion shall file and serve the notice of motion and motion pursuant to Rule 15.02, subd. 3.

Adopted June 10, 2009, eff. Aug. 1, 2009.

Historical Notes

The order of the Minnesota Supreme Court [C1–01–927] dated June 10, 2009, amending the Rules of Juvenile Protection Procedure and the Rules of Adoption Procedure, provides in part that the amendments are effective August 1, 2009, and shall apply to all actions or proceedings pending on or commenced on or after the effective date.

Former rule: Former Rule 15.06, which related to the timing of a decision, was renumbered and amended as Rule 15.07 by court order dated June 10, 2009.

Rule 15.07. Timing of Decision

Orders regarding motions shall be filed with the court administrator within fifteen (15) days of the conclusion of the hearing. Orders shall be served by the court administrator pursuant to Rule 10.03.

Former Rule 15.06, adopted Dec. 1, 2006, eff. Jan. 1. 2006. Renumbered Rule 15.07 and amended June 10, 2009, eff. Aug. 1, 2009.

Historical Notes

The order of the Minnesota Supreme Court [C1–01–927] dated June 10, 2009, amending the Rules of Juvenile Protection Procedure and the Rules of Adoption Procedure, provides in part that the amendments are effective August 1, 2009, and shall apply to all actions or proceedings pending on or commenced on or after the effective date.

RULE 16. SIGNING OF PLEADINGS, MOTIONS, AND OTHER DOCUMENTS; SERVICE AND FILING OF MOTIONS AND OTHER DOCUMENTS; SANCTIONS

Rule 16.01. Signature

Subd. 1. Generally. Except as otherwise provided in these rules, every pleading, written motion, and other paper shall be signed by at least one attorney of record in the attorney's individual name, or, if the party is not represented by an attorney, shall be signed by the party. Each paper shall state the signer's name, address, telephone number, and attorney registration number if signed by an attorney. If providing a party's address and telephone number would endanger the party, the address and telephone number may be provided to the court in a separate information statement and shall not be accessible to the public or to the parties. Upon notice and motion, the court may disclose the address and telephone number as it deems appropriate. Except when otherwise specifically provided by rule or statute, pleadings need not be verified or accompanied by affidavit. An unsigned paper shall be stricken unless omission of the signature is corrected promptly after being called to the attention of the attorney or party.

Subd. 2. Exception—Social Worker and Guardian Ad Litem Reports. Reports filed by social workers and guardians ad litem under Rule 38 need not be signed.

Amended Nov. 12, 2003; Dec. 1, 2006, eff. Jan. 1, 2007.

Historical Notes

The order of the Minnesota Supreme Court [C1-01-927] dated November 12, 2003, amending Rules 37 to 82 of the Rules of Juvenile Procedure and renumbering them as Rules 1 to 47 of the Rules of Juvenile Protection Procedure, provides in part that the amendments are effective January 1, 2004, and shall apply to all juvenile protection matters filed on or after that date.

Rule 16.02. Representations to Court

By presenting to the court, whether by signing, filing, submitting, or later advocating, a pleading, motion, report, or other paper, an attorney or unrepresented party is certifying to the best of the person's knowledge, information, and belief, formed after an inquiry reasonable under the circumstances, that:

(a) it is not being presented for any improper purpose, such as to harass or to cause unnecessary delay or needless increase in the cost of litigation;

(b) the claims, defenses, and other legal contentions therein are warranted by existing law or by a nonfrivolous argument for the extension, modification, or reversal of existing law or the establishment of new law;

(c) the allegations and other factual contentions have evidentiary support or, if specifically so identified, are likely to have evidentiary support after a reasonable opportunity for further investigation or discovery; and

(d) the denials of factual contentions are warranted on the evidence or, if specifically so identified, are reasonably based on a lack of information or belief.

Adopted Dec. 1, 2006, eff. Jan. 1, 2007.

Rule 16.03. Service and Filing of Motions and Other Documents

Except as otherwise provided in this Rule, the party filing a motion or other document, except a pleading, shall be responsible for serving the motion or other document upon the parties or, if represented, upon the attorneys for such individuals. The court administrator shall serve the motion or other document if the address of the person being served is confidential.

Former Rule 16.02, adopted Nov. 12, 2003. Renumbered Rule 16.03, Dec. 1, 2006, eff. Jan. 1, 2007.

Historical Notes

The order of the Minnesota Supreme Court [C1-01-927] dated November 12, 2003, amending Rules 37 to 82 of the Rules of Juvenile Procedure and renumbering them as Rules 1 to 47 of the Rules of Juvenile Protection Procedure, provides in part that the amendments are effective January 1, 2004, and shall apply to all juvenile protection matters filed on or after that date.

Rule 16.04. Sanctions

If a pleading, motion, or other paper is not signed, it shall be stricken unless it is signed promptly after the omission is called to the attention of the pleader or movant. If a pleading, motion, or other paper is signed in violation of this rule, the court, upon motion or upon its own initiative, shall impose upon the person who signed it, a represented party, or both, an appropriate sanction, which may include an order to pay to the other party or parties the amount of the reasonable expenses incurred because of the filing of the pleading, motion, or other paper, including reasonable attorney fees.

Former Rule 16.03, adopted Nov. 12, 2003. Renumbered Rule 16.04, Dec. 1, 2006, eff. Jan. 1, 2007

Historical Notes

The order of the Minnesota Supreme Court [C1-01-927] dated November 12, 2003, amending Rules 37 to 82 of the Rules of Juvenile Procedure and renumbering them as Rules 1 to 47 of the Rules of Juvenile Protection Procedure, provides in part that the amendments are effective January 1, 2004, and shall apply to all juvenile protection matters filed on or after that date.

RULE 17. DISCOVERY

Rule 17.01. Disclosure by Petitioner Without Court Order

Upon the request of any party, the petitioner shall without court order make the following disclosures:

(a) Documents and Tangible Items. The petitioner shall allow access at any reasonable time to all information, material, and items within the petitioner's possession or control which relate to the case. The petitioner shall permit inspection and copying of any relevant documents, recorded statements, or other tangible items which relate to the case within the possession or control of the petitioner and shall provide any party with the substance of any oral statements which relate to the case. The copying of a videotaped statement of a child abuse victim or alleged victim shall be governed by Minnesota Statutes § 611A.90. The petitioner shall not disclose the name of or any identifying information regarding a reporter of maltreatment except as provided in Minnesota Statutes § 626.556, subd. 11.

(b) Witnesses. The petitioner shall disclose to all other parties and the county attorney the names and addresses of the persons intended to be called as witnesses at trial. The county attorney or petitioner shall permit all other parties to inspect and copy such witnesses' written or recorded statements that relate to the case within the petitioner's knowledge.

(c) Expert Witnesses. Petitioner shall disclose to all other parties and the county attorney:

(1) the names and addresses of all persons intended to be called as expert witnesses at trial;

(2) the subject matter about which each expert witness is expected to testify; and

(3) a summary of the grounds for each opinion to be offered.

Amended Nov. 12, 2003.

Historical Notes

The order of the Minnesota Supreme Court [C1-01-927] dated November 12, 2003, amending Rules 37 to 82 of the Rules of Juvenile Procedure and renumbering them as Rules 1 to 47 of the Rules of Juvenile Protection Procedure, provides in part that the amendments are effective January 1, 2004, and shall apply to all juvenile protection matters filed on or after that date.

Rule 17.02. Disclosure by Other Parties Without Court Order

Upon the request of a party or the county attorney, any party who is not the petitioner shall without court order make the following disclosures:

(a) Documents and Tangible Objects. The party shall disclose and permit the county attorney, attorney for petitioner, or any other party to inspect and copy any book, paper, report, exam, scientific test, comparison, document, photograph, or tangible object which the party intends to introduce in evidence at the trial or concerning which the party intends to offer evidence at the trial.

(b) Witnesses. Each party shall disclose to every other party and the county attorney the names and addresses of the persons the party intends to call as witnesses at trial. Each party shall permit every other party and the county attorney to inspect and copy such witnesses' written or recorded statements within the party's knowledge as relates to the case.

(c) Expert Witnesses. Each party shall disclose to all other parties and the county attorney:

(1) the names and addresses of all persons intended to be called as expert witnesses at trial;

(2) the subject matter about which each expert witness is expected to testify; and

(3) a summary of the grounds for each opinion to be offered.

Amended Nov. 12, 2003.

Historical Notes

The order of the Minnesota Supreme Court [C1-01-927] dated November 12, 2003, amending Rules 37 to 82 of the Rules of Juvenile Procedure and renumbering them as Rules 1 to 47 of the Rules of Juvenile Protection Procedure, provides in part that the amendments are effective January 1, 2004, and shall apply to all juvenile protection matters filed on or after that date.

Rule 17.03. Information Not Discoverable

The following information shall not be discoverable by any party or the county attorney with or without a court order:

(a) documents containing privileged information between an attorney and client, legal research, records, correspondence, reports, or memoranda to the extent they contain the opinions, theories, or conclusions of the attorney for a party or other staff of an attorney for a party; and

(b) except as otherwise required by this rule, reports, memoranda, or internal documents made by an attorney for a party or staff of an attorney for a party.

Amended Nov. 12, 2003.

Historical Notes

The order of the Minnesota Supreme Court [C1-01-927] dated November 12, 2003, amending Rules 37 to 82 of the Rules of Juvenile Procedure and renumbering them as Rules 1 to 47 of the Rules of Juvenile Protection Procedure, provides in part that the amendments are effective January 1, 2004, and shall apply to all juvenile protection matters filed on or after that date.

Rule 17.04. Discovery Upon Court Order

Upon written motion of any party or the county attorney, the court may authorize other discovery methods, including, but not limited to, the following:

(a) Physical and Mental Examinations.

(1) *Examination by Licensed Professional.* If the physical or mental condition of a party is in controversy, the court may order the party to submit to a physical or mental examination by a licensed professional of the moving party's choice. The examination shall be at the moving party's expense. The order shall specify the time, place, manner, conditions, and the scope of the examination.

(2) *Copy of Report.* The examiner shall prepare a detailed report of the findings and conclusions of the examination and shall provide the report to the moving party who shall forward it to all other parties and the county attorney unless otherwise ordered by the court.

(b) Depositions.

(1) *Agreement of Parties.* A deposition may be taken upon agreement of the parties.

(2) *Order of Court.* Following the initial appearance, any party or the county attorney may move the court to order the testimony of any other person or party be taken by deposition upon oral examination, if:

(i) there is a reasonable probability that the witness will be unable to be present or to testify at the hearing or trial because of the witness' existing physical or mental illness, infirmity, or death;

(ii) the party taking the deposition cannot procure the attendance of the witness at a hearing or trial by a subpoena, order of the court, or other reasonable means: or

(iii) upon a showing that the information sought cannot be obtained by other means.

(3) *Subpoena.* Attendance of witnesses at oral deposition may be compelled by subpoena as provided by Rule 13. Attendance of parties at oral deposition shall be ordered by the court when the court grants a motion pursuant to subdivision 2(b) and shall be procured through service of the order and a notice of the time and place of the taking of the deposition on the party.

(4) *Notice.* A party or the county attorney taking a deposition shall give reasonable notice of the deposition. The deposition shall be taken before an officer authorized to administer oaths by the laws of the United States, or before a person appointed by the court in which the matter is pending. The parties shall agree on or the court shall order the manner of recording of the deposition. A stenographic transcription may be made at a party's request. Examination and cross-examination of witnesses shall be as permitted at trial. However, the deponent shall answer any otherwise objectionable question, except that which would reveal privileged material unless the privilege does not apply pursuant to Minnesota Statutes § 626.556, subd. 8, so long as it leads to or is reasonably calculated to lead to the discovery of any relevant data.

(c) Reports or Examinations and Tests. Upon motion and order of the court, any party shall disclose and permit the county attorney, attorney for petitioner, and other parties to inspect and copy any results or reports of physical or mental examinations, chemical dependency assessments and treatment records, scientific tests, experiments, and comparisons relating to the particular case. It is not grounds for objection that the information sought will be inadmissible at trial if the information sought appears reasonably calculated to lead to the discovery of admissible evidence. Privileged communications are discoverable in accordance with Minnesota Statutes § 626.556, subd. 8.

(d) Experts. Discovery of facts known and opinions held by experts, otherwise discoverable pursuant to these rules and acquired or developed in anticipation of litigation or for trial, may be obtained only as follows:

(1) Upon motion, the court may order further discovery by means other than as provided in Rules 17.01 and 17.02, subject to such restrictions as to scope and such provisions concerning fees and expenses as the court may deem appropriate.

(2) A party may discover facts known or opinions held by an expert who has been retained or specially employed by another party in anticipation of litigation or preparation for trial and who is not expected to be called as a witness at trial, only upon a showing of exceptional circumstances under which it is impracticable for the party seeking discovery to obtain facts or opinions on the same subject by other means.

(3) Unless manifest injustice would result,

(i) the court shall require the party seeking discovery to pay the expert a reasonable fee for time spent in responding to discovery pursuant to this rule, and

(ii) with respect to discovery obtained pursuant to this rule, the court shall require the party seeking discovery to pay the other party a fair portion of the fees and expenses reasonably incurred by the latter party in obtaining facts and opinions from the expert.

Amended Nov. 12, 2003.

Historical Notes

The order of the Minnesota Supreme Court [C1-01-927] dated November 12, 2003, amending Rules 37 to 82 of the Rules of Juvenile Procedure and renumbering them as Rules 1 to 47 of the Rules of Juvenile Protection Procedure, provides in part that the amendments are effective January 1, 2004, and shall apply to all juvenile protection matters filed on or after that date.

Rule 17.05. Time, Place, and Manner of Discovery

An order of the court granting discovery shall specify the time, place, and manner of discovery and inspection permitted and may prescribe such terms and conditions as are just.

Amended Nov. 12, 2003.

Historical Notes

The order of the Minnesota Supreme Court [C1-01-927] dated November 12, 2003, amending Rules 37 to 82 of the Rules of Juvenile Procedure and renumbering them as Rules 1 to 47 of the Rules of Juvenile Protection Procedure, provides in part that the amendments are effective January 1, 2004, and shall apply to all juvenile protection matters filed on or after that date.

Rule 17.06. Regulation of Discovery

Subd. 1. Continuing Duty to Disclose. Whenever a party or the county attorney discovers additional material, information, or witnesses subject to disclosure, that party or the county attorney shall promptly notify the other parties and the county attorney of the existence of the additional material or information and the identity of the witnesses.

Subd. 2. Protective Orders. The trial court may order that specified disclosures be restricted or deferred, or make such other order as is appropriate to protect the child.

Subd. 3. Timely Discovery. Unless a court order otherwise provides, all material and information to which a party or the county attorney is entitled must be disclosed within fourteen (14) days of a request for disclosure.

Subd. 4. Sanctions. If, at any time, it is brought to the attention of the court that a party or the county attorney has failed to comply with an applicable discovery rule or order, or has failed to appear pursuant to a notice of taking of deposition, be sworn, or answer questions, the court may, upon motion, order such party or the county attorney to permit the discovery or inspection, grant a continuance, or enter such order as it deems just under the circumstances including:

(a) an order that the matters regarding which the order was made, or the other designated facts, shall be taken to be established for purposes of the proceedings, in accordance with the claim of the party who obtained the order;

(b) an order refusing to allow the disobedient party to support or oppose designated claims, or prohibiting the disobedient party from introducing designated matters in evidence;

(c) an order striking the petition or parts of the petition, answer, or parts of an answer, dismissing the proceeding, or entering a finding that the petition is proved or that certain facts alleged in the petition are proved;

(d) in lieu of any of the foregoing, an order treating as a contempt of court the failure to obey any order; or

(e) the court shall require the party or county attorney failing to act or the party's counsel, or both, to pay the reasonable expenses, including attorney's fees, caused by the failure, unless the court finds the failure was substantially justified or that other circumstances make an award of expenses unjust.

Subd. 5. Failure to Act. Failure to act as described in this rule may not be excused on the ground that the discovery sought is objectionable unless the party or county attorney failing to act has applied for a protective order as provided in subdivision 2.

Amended Nov. 12, 2003; Dec. 1, 2006, eff. Jan. 1, 2007.

Historical Notes

The order of the Minnesota Supreme Court [C1-01-927] dated November 12, 2003, amending Rules 37 to 82 of the Rules of Juvenile Procedure and renumbering them as Rules 1 to 47 of the Rules of Juvenile Protection Procedure, provides in part that the amendments are effective January 1, 2004, and shall apply to all juvenile protection matters filed on or after that date.

RULE 18. DEFAULT

Rule 18.01. Failure to Appear

Except as otherwise provided in Rule 35.02, subd. 1, if a parent, legal custodian, or Indian custodian fails to appear for an admit-deny hearing, a pretrial hearing, or a trial after being properly served with a summons pursuant to Rule 32.02 or a notice pursuant to Rule 32.03 or 32.04, the court may receive evidence in support of the petition or reschedule the hearing.

Amended Nov. 12, 2003.

Historical Notes

The order of the Minnesota Supreme Court [C1-01-927] dated November 12, 2003, amending Rules 37 to 82 of the Rules of Juvenile Procedure and renumbering them as Rules 1 to 47 of the Rules of Juvenile Protection Procedure, provides in part that the amendments are effective January 1, 2004, and shall apply to all juvenile protection matters filed on or after that date.

Rule 18.02. Default Order

If the petition is proved by the applicable standard of proof, the court may enter an order granting the relief sought in the petition as to that parent, legal custodian, or Indian custodian.

Adopted Nov. 12, 2003. Amended Dec. 1, 2006, eff. Jan. 1, 2007.

Historical Notes

The order of the Minnesota Supreme Court [C1-01-927] dated November 12, 2003, amending Rules 37 to 82 of the Rules of Juvenile Procedure and renumbering them as Rules 1 to 47 of the Rules of Juvenile Protection Procedure, provides in part that the amendments are effective January 1, 2004, and shall apply to all juvenile protection matters filed on or after that date.

RULE 19. SETTLEMENT

Rule 19.01. Generally

Settlement discussions may be utilized to achieve one or more of the purposes set forth in Rule 1.02.

Amended Nov. 12, 2003.

Historical Notes

The order of the Minnesota Supreme Court [C1-01-927] dated November 12, 2003, amending Rules 37 to 82 of the Rules of Juvenile Procedure and renumbering them as Rules 1 to 47 of the Rules of Juvenile Protection Procedure, provides in part that the amendments are effective January 1, 2004, and shall apply to all juvenile protection matters filed on or after that date.

Rule 19.02. Content of Settlement Agreement

Any settlement agreement shall include a statement of:

(a) the statutory grounds to be admitted;

(b) the statutory grounds to be dismissed, if any;

(c) the factual allegations to be admitted;

(d) the factual allegations asserted by the petitioner but not admitted;

(e) whether the court will enter or withhold adjudication; and

(f) the issues to be addressed at the disposition hearing or the agreed upon disposition and case plan.

Amended Nov. 12, 2003.

Historical Notes

The order of the Minnesota Supreme Court [C1-01-927] dated November 12, 2003, amending Rules 37 to 82 of the Rules of Juvenile Procedure and renumbering them as Rules 1 to 47 of the Rules of Juvenile Protection Procedure, provides in part that the amendments are effective January 1, 2004, and shall apply to all juvenile protection matters filed on or after that date.

Rule 19.03. Procedure

Every settlement agreement shall be filed with the court or stated and agreed to on the record by the settling parties. Before approving a settlement agreement, the court shall determine that the agreement is in the best interests of the child and that each party to the agreement understands the content and consequences of the admission or settlement agreement and voluntarily consents to the agreement. When a party makes an admission, the court may accept or reject the admission based upon the terms of the settlement agreement or may conditionally accept or reject the admission pending receipt of a predisposition report prepared for the disposition hearing. The court may accept a settlement agreement that resolves the issues with respect to the petitioner and one or more but not all parties, and proceed with the matter with respect to the non-settling parties. If the court approves the settlement agreement, it shall proceed pursuant to Rule 40. If the court rejects the settlement agreement, it shall advise the parties and the county attorney of this decision in writing or on the record and shall call upon the parties to either affirm or withdraw the admission. If the admission is withdrawn, the court shall make a finding that the admission is not accepted and proceed pursuant to Rule 39.

Amended Nov. 12, 2003.

Historical Notes

The order of the Minnesota Supreme Court [C1-01-927] dated November 12, 2003, amending Rules 37 to 82 of the Rules of Juvenile Procedure and renumbering them as Rules 1 to 47 of the Rules of Juvenile Protection Procedure, provides in part that the amendments are effective January 1, 2004, and shall apply to all juvenile protection matters filed on or after that date.

Rule 19.04. Objection to Settlement Agreement—Termination of Parental Rights Matters and Permanent Placement Matters

If a party objects to a settlement agreement in a termination of parental rights matter or a permanent placement matter, that party shall, within five (5) days of service of notice of the proposed settlement agreement, adopt the existing pleadings and assume the burden of proof or file pleadings in support of an alternative. The matter shall be set for trial within the timelines set forth in Rule 39.

Amended Nov. 12, 2003.

Historical Notes

The order of the Minnesota Supreme Court [C1-01-927] dated November 12, 2003, amending Rules 37 to 82 of the Rules of Juvenile Procedure and renumbering them as Rules 1 to 47 of the Rules of Juvenile Protection Procedure, provides in part that the amendments are effective January 1, 2004, and shall apply to all juvenile protection matters filed on or after that date.

RULE 20. ALTERNATIVE DISPUTE RESOLUTION

[Reserved for future use.]

1999 Advisory Committee Comment

The Committee recommends the appointment of a separate advisory committee to research, draft, and recommend rules for alternative dispute resolution in juvenile protection matters. In the meantime, the absence of a rule is not intended to imply that parties may not use mediation or other alternative dispute resolution to achieve results in the best interests of the child.

Historical Notes

The order of the Minnesota Supreme Court [C1-01-927] dated November 12, 2003, amending Rules 37 to 82 of the Rules of Juvenile Procedure and renumbering them as Rules 1 to 47 of the Rules of Juvenile Protection Procedure, provides in part that the amendments are effective January 1, 2004, and shall apply to all juvenile protection matters filed on or after that date.

C. PARTIES AND PARTICIPANTS

RULE 21. PARTIES

Rule 21.01. Party Status

Subd. 1. Parties Generally. Parties to a juvenile protection matter shall include:

(a) the child's guardian ad litem;

(b) the child's legal custodian;

(c) in the case of an Indian child, the child's parents as defined in Rule 2.01(16), the child's Indian custodian, and the Indian child's tribe through the tribal representative;

(d) the petitioner;

(e) any person who intervenes as a party pursuant to Rule 23;

(f) any person who is joined as a party pursuant to Rule 24; and

(g) any other person who is deemed by the court to be important to a resolution that is in the best interests of the child.

Subd. 2. Habitual Truant, Runaway, and Child Prostitution Matters. In addition to the parties identified in subdivision 1, in any matter alleging a child to be a habitual truant, a runaway, or engaged in prostitution, the child, regardless of age, shall also be a party. In any matter alleging a child to be a habitual truant, the child's school district may be joined as a party pursuant to Rule 24.

Subd. 3. Termination of Parental Rights Matters and Permanent Placement Matters. In addition to the parties identified in subdivision 1, in any termination of parental rights matter or permanent placement matter the parties shall also include:

(a) the child's parents, including any noncustodial parent and any adjudicated or presumed father;

(b) any person entitled to notice of any adoption proceeding involving the child;

(c) the responsible social services agency when the agency is not the petitioner; and

(d) any other person who is deemed by the court to be important to a resolution that is in the best interests of the child.

Subd. 4. Relatives Recommended as Permanent Custodians. If, in a proceeding involving a child in need of protection or services, the responsible social services agency recommends transfer of permanent legal and physical custody to a relative, the relative has a right to participate as a party and shall receive notice of all hearings and copies of all orders.

Amended Nov. 12, 2003; Dec. 1, 2006, eff. Jan. 1, 2007; June 10, 2009, eff. Aug. 1, 2009.

Historical Notes

The order of the Minnesota Supreme Court [C1–01–927] dated June 10, 2009, amending the Rules of Juvenile Protection Procedure and the Rules of Adoption Procedure, provides in part that the amendments are effective August 1, 2009, and shall apply to all actions or proceedings pending on or commenced on or after the effective date.

The order of the Minnesota Supreme Court [C1-01-927] dated November 12, 2003, amending Rules 37 to 82 of the Rules of Juvenile Procedure and renumbering them as Rules 1 to 47 of the Rules of Juvenile Protection Procedure, provides in part that the amendments are effective January 1, 2004, and shall apply to all juvenile protection matters filed on or after that date.

Rule 21.02. Rights of Parties

A party shall have the right to:

(a) notice pursuant to Rule 32;

(b) legal representation pursuant to Rule 25;

(c) be present at all hearings unless excluded pursuant to Rule 27;

(d) conduct discovery pursuant to Rule 17;

(e) bring motions before the court pursuant to Rule 15;

(f) participate in settlement agreements pursuant to Rule 19;

(g) subpoena witnesses pursuant to Rule 13;

(h) make argument in support of or against the petition;

(i) present evidence;

(j) cross-examine witnesses;

(k) request review of the referee's findings and recommended order pursuant to Rule 7;

(*l*) request review of the court's disposition upon a showing of a substantial change of circumstances or that the previous disposition was inappropriate;

(m) bring post-trial motions pursuant to Rule 45;

(n) appeal from orders of the court pursuant to Rule 47; and

(*o*) any other rights as set forth in statute or these rules.

Amended Nov. 12, 2003.

1999 Advisory Committee Comment—2003 Amendments

The former rules did not distinguish between parties and participants. Rule 21 delineates the status and rights of parties, and Rule 22 delineates the status and rights of participants. There may be many individuals concerned about the best interests of a child who do not have the immediate connection to the child that justifies treating them as parties. The intent of this rule is to ensure that such individuals are aware of the proceedings and are available to provide information useful to the court in making decisions concerning that child. A person with participant status may intervene as a party pursuant to Rule 23 or may be joined as a party pursuant to Rule 24.

Historical Notes

The order of the Minnesota Supreme Court [C1-01-927] dated November 12, 2003, amending Rules 37 to 82 of the Rules of Juvenile Procedure and renumbering them as Rules 1 to 47 of the Rules of Juvenile Protection Procedure, provides in part that the amendments are effective January 1, 2004, and shall apply to all juvenile protection matters filed on or after that date.

Rule 21.03. Parties' Addresses

It shall be the responsibility of the petitioner to set forth in the petition the names and addresses of all parties if known to the petitioner after reasonable inquiry, and to specify that each such person has party status. It shall be the responsibility of each party to inform the court administrator of any change of address. If a party is endangered, the party may ask the court to keep the party's address confidential.

Amended Nov. 12, 2003.

Historical Notes

The order of the Minnesota Supreme Court [C1-01-927] dated November 12, 2003, amending Rules 37 to 82 of the Rules of Juvenile Procedure and renumbering them as Rules 1 to 47 of the Rules of Juvenile Protection Procedure, provides in part that the amendments are effective January 1, 2004, and shall apply to all juvenile protection matters filed on or after that date.

RULE 22. PARTICIPANTS

Rule 22.01. Participant Status

Unless already a party pursuant to Rule 21, or unless otherwise specified, participants to a juvenile protection matter shall include:

(a) the child;

(b) any parent who is not a legal custodian and any alleged, adjudicated, or presumed father;

(c) the responsible social services agency, when the responsible social services agency is not the petitioner;

(d) any guardian ad litem for the child's legal custodian;

(e) grandparents with whom the child has lived within the two (2) years preceding the filing of the petition;

(f) relatives or other persons providing care for the child and other relatives who request notice;

(g) current foster parents, persons proposed as long-term foster care parents, and persons proposed as pre-adoptive parents;

(h) the spouse of the child, if any; and

(i) any other person who is deemed by the court to be important to a resolution that is in the best interests of the child.

Amended Nov. 12, 2003; June 26, 2007, eff. July 1, 2007.

1999 Advisory Committee Comment—2003 Amendments

The former rules did not distinguish between parties and participants. Rule 21 delineates the status and rights of parties, and Rule 22 delineates the status and rights of participants. There may be many individuals concerned about the best interests of a child who do not have the immediate connection to the child that justifies treating them as parties. The intent of this rule is to ensure that such individuals are aware of the proceedings and are available to provide information useful to the court in making decisions concerning that child. A person with participant status may intervene as a party pursuant to Rule 23 or may be joined as a party pursuant to Rule 24.

Historical Notes

The order of the Minnesota Supreme Court [C1-01-927] dated November 12, 2003, amending Rules 37 to 82 of the Rules of Juvenile Procedure and renumbering them as Rules 1 to 47 of the Rules of Juvenile Protection Procedure, provides in part that the amendments are effective January 1, 2004, and shall apply to all juvenile protection matters filed on or after that date.

Rule 22.02. Rights of Participants

Subd. 1. Generally. Unless a participant intervenes as a party pursuant to Rule 23, or is joined as a party pursuant to Rule 24, the rights of a participant shall be limited to:

(a) notice and a copy of the petition pursuant to Rule 32;

(b) attending hearings pursuant to Rule 27; and

(c) offering information at the discretion of the court, except as provided in subdivision 2.

Subd. 2. Foster Parents, Pre–Adoptive Parents, and Relatives Providing Care. Notwithstanding subdivision 1, any foster parent, pre-adoptive parent, relative providing care for the child, or relative to whom the responsible social services agency recommends transfer of permanent legal and physical custody of the child shall have a right to be heard in any hearing regarding the child. Any other relative may request an opportunity to be heard. This subdivision does not require that a foster parent, pre-adoptive parent, or relative providing care for the child be made a party to the matter. Each party and the county attorney shall be provided an opportunity to respond to any presentation by a foster parent, pre-adoptive parent, or relative.

Amended Nov. 12, 2003; June 26, 2007, eff. July 1, 2007.

Historical Notes

The order of the Minnesota Supreme Court [C1-01-927] dated November 12, 2003, amending Rules 37 to 82 of the Rules of Juvenile Procedure and renumbering them as Rules 1 to 47 of the Rules of Juvenile Protection Procedure, provides in part that the amendments are effective January 1, 2004, and shall apply to all juvenile protection matters filed on or after that date.

Rule 22.03. Participants' Addresses

It shall be the responsibility of the petitioner to set forth in the petition the names and addresses of all participants if known to the petitioner after reasonable inquiry, and to specify that each such person has participant status. It shall be the responsibility of each participant to inform the court administrator of any change of address. If a participant is endangered, the participant may ask the court to keep the participant's address confidential.

Amended Nov. 12, 2003.

Historical Notes

The order of the Minnesota Supreme Court [C1-01-927] dated November 12, 2003, amending Rules 37 to 82 of the Rules of Juvenile Procedure and renumbering them as Rules 1 to 47 of the Rules of Juvenile Protection Procedure, provides in part that the amendments are effective January 1, 2004, and shall apply to all juvenile protection matters filed on or after that date.

RULE 23. INTERVENTION

Rule 23.01. Intervention of Right

Subd. 1. Child. A child who is the subject of the juvenile protection matter shall have the right to intervene as a party.

Subd. 2. Grandparents. Any grandparent of the child shall have the right to intervene as a party if the child has lived with the grandparent within the two (2) years preceding the filing of the petition.

Subd. 3 Parent. Any parent who is not a legal custodian of the child shall have the right to intervene as a party.

Subd. 4. Social Services Agency. The responsible social services agency shall have the right to intervene as a party in a case where the responsible social services agency is not the petitioner.

Amended Nov. 12, 2003.

Historical Notes

The order of the Minnesota Supreme Court [C1-01-927] dated November 12, 2003, amending Rules 37 to 82 of the Rules of Juvenile Procedure and renumbering them as Rules 1 to 47 of the Rules of Juvenile Protection Procedure, provides in part that the amendments are effective January 1, 2004, and shall apply to all juvenile protection matters filed on or after that date.

Rule 23.02. Permissive Intervention

Any person may be permitted to intervene as a party if the court finds that such intervention is in the best interests of the child.

Amended Nov. 12, 2003.

Historical Notes

The order of the Minnesota Supreme Court [C1-01-927] dated November 12, 2003, amending Rules 37 to 82 of the Rules of Juvenile Procedure and renumbering them as Rules 1 to 47 of the Rules of Juvenile Protection Procedure, provides in part that the amendments are effective January 1, 2004, and shall apply to all juvenile protection matters filed on or after that date.

Rule 23.03. Procedure

Subd. 1. Intervention of Right. A person with a right to intervene pursuant to Rule 23.01 shall file with the court and serve upon all parties and the county attorney a notice of intervention, which shall include the basis for a claim to intervene. The notice of intervention as a matter of right form shall be available from the court administrator. The intervention shall be deemed accomplished upon service of the notice of intervention, unless a party or the county attorney files and serves a written objection within ten (10) days of the date of service. If a written objection is timely filed and served, the court shall schedule a hearing for the next available date.

Subd. 2. Permissive Intervention. A person, including the county attorney in a case where the responsible social services agency is not the petitioner, seeking permissive intervention pursuant to Rule 23.02 shall file with the court and serve upon all parties and the county attorney a notice of motion and motion to intervene pursuant to Rule 15. The notice shall state the nature and extent of the person's interest in the child and the reason(s) that the person's intervention would be in the best interests of the child. A hearing on a motion to intervene shall be held within ten (10) days of the filing of the motion to intervene.

Amended Nov. 12, 2003.

Historical Notes

The order of the Minnesota Supreme Court [C1-01-927] dated November 12, 2003, amending Rules 37 to 82 of the Rules of Juvenile Procedure and renumbering them as Rules 1 to 47 of the Rules of Juvenile Protection Procedure, provides in part that the amendments are effective January 1, 2004, and shall apply to all juvenile protection matters filed on or after that date.

Rule 23.04. Effect of Intervention

The court may conduct hearings, make findings, and issue orders at any time prior to intervention being accomplished or denied. The intervention shall be effective as of the date granted and prior proceedings and decisions of the court shall not be affected.

Amended Nov. 12, 2003.

Historical Notes

The order of the Minnesota Supreme Court [C1-01-927] dated November 12, 2003, amending Rules 37 to 82 of the Rules of Juvenile Procedure and renumbering them as Rules 1 to 47 of the Rules of Juvenile Protection Procedure, provides in part that the amendments are effective January 1, 2004, and shall apply to all juvenile protection matters filed on or after that date.

RULE 24. JOINDER

Rule 24.01. Procedure

The court, upon its own motion or motion of a party or the county attorney pursuant to Rule 15, may join a person or entity as a party if the court finds that joinder is:

(a) necessary for a just and complete resolution of the matter; and

(b) in the best interests of the child.

The moving party shall serve the motion upon all parties, the county attorney, and the person proposed to be joined.

Amended Nov. 12, 2003.

2003 Advisory Committee Comment

In *In Re the Welfare of Q.T.B.*, Nos. C7–97–2093 and C9–97–2094, (Minn. Ct. App. May 26, 1998), *rev. denied* (Minn. July 16, 1998), an unpublished decision of the Court of Appeals, the court considered the appellant's claim that she should have been joined as a party to a child in need of protection or services proceeding because she was at risk of losing her visitation rights with the infant who was the subject of the petition. The court cited Minn. R. Civ. P. 19.01 and determined that the rights of the appellant did not rise to the level of requiring joinder under Rule 19.01. While *In Re the Welfare of Q.T.B.* denies joinder under the specific facts of that case, it implies that joinder is permissible thus authorizing joinder in juvenile protection matters.

Historical Notes

The order of the Minnesota Supreme Court [C1-01-927] dated November 12, 2003, amending Rules 37 to 82 of the Rules of Juvenile Procedure and renumbering them as Rules 1 to 47 of the Rules of Juvenile Protection Procedure, provides in part that the amendments are effective January 1, 2004, and shall apply to all juvenile protection matters filed on or after that date.

RULE 25. RIGHT TO REPRESENTATION; APPOINTMENT OF COUNSEL

Rule 25.01. Right to Representation

Every party and participant has the right to be represented by counsel in every juvenile protection matter, including through appeal, if any. This right attaches no later than when the party or participant first appears in court.

Amended Nov. 12, 2003.

1999 Advisory Committee Comment—2003 Amendments

Rule 25.01 sets forth the basic principle that each person appearing in court has the right to be represented by counsel. Each person, however, does not necessarily have the right to court appointed counsel as provided in Rule 25.02.

Historical Notes

The order of the Minnesota Supreme Court [C1-01-927] dated November 12, 2003, amending Rules 37 to 82 of the Rules of Juvenile Procedure and renumbering them as Rules 1 to 47 of the Rules of Juvenile Protection Procedure, provides in part that the amendments are effective January 1, 2004, and shall apply to all juvenile protection matters filed on or after that date.

Rule 25.02. Appointment of Counsel

Subd. 1. Child. Each child has the right to effective assistance of counsel in connection with a juvenile protection matter. Counsel for the child shall not also act as the child's guardian ad litem.

(a) *Juvenile Protection Matters.* Except in proceedings where the sole basis for the petition is habitual truancy, if the child desires counsel but is financially unable to employ it, the court shall appoint counsel to represent the child who is ten (10) years of age or older and may appoint counsel to represent a child under age ten (10) in any case in which the court determines that such appointment is appropriate.

(b) *Truancy Matters.* In any proceeding where the sole basis for the petition is habitual truancy, the child does not have the right to appointment of a public defender or other counsel at public expense. However, before any out-of-home placement, including foster care or inpatient treatment, can be ordered, the court shall appoint a public defender or other counsel at public expense to represent the child.

(c) *Indian Child.* In any juvenile protection matter involving an Indian child, the court may, in its discretion, appoint counsel for an Indian child upon a finding that such appointment is in the best interests of the child.

(d) *Request; Timing.* The court may sua sponte appoint counsel for the child, or may do so upon the request of any party or participant. Any such appointment of counsel for the child shall occur as soon as practicable after the request is made. For purposes of appeal, appointment of counsel in a juvenile protection matter shall be made within three (3) days of the request for counsel. When possible, the trial court attorney should be appointed as appellate counsel.

Subd. 2. Parent, Legal Custodian, or Indian Custodian. Each parent, legal custodian, or Indian custodian has the right to effective assistance of counsel in connection with a juvenile court proceeding.

(a) *Juvenile Protection Matters.* Except in proceedings where the sole basis for the petition is habitual truancy, if the child's parent or legal custodian desires counsel but is financially unable to employ it, the court shall appoint counsel to represent the parent or legal custodian in any juvenile protection matter in which the court determines that such appointment is appropriate.

(b) *Truancy Matters.* In any proceeding where the sole basis for the petition is habitual truancy, the parent or legal custodian does not have the right to appointment of a public defender or other counsel at public expense. However, before any out-of-home placement, including foster care or inpatient treatment, can be ordered, the court shall appoint a public defender or other counsel at public expense to represent the parent in accordance with subdivision 2(a).

(c) *Indian Parent or Custodian.* In any juvenile protection matter involving an Indian child, if the child's parent or Indian custodian is unable to afford it, the court shall appoint counsel to represent the parent or Indian custodian.

(d) *Timing.* The appointment of counsel for the parent, legal custodian, or Indian custodian shall occur as soon as practicable after the request is made. For purposes of appeal, appointment of counsel in a juvenile protection matter shall be made within three (3) days of the request for counsel. When possible, the trial court attorney should be appointed as appellate counsel.

Subd. 3. Guardian Ad Litem. The court may appoint separate counsel for the guardian ad litem if necessary. A public defender may not be appointed as counsel for a guardian ad litem. For purposes of appeal, appointment of counsel in a juvenile protection matter shall be made within three (3) days of the request for counsel. When possible, the trial court attorney should be appointed as appellate counsel.

Subd. 4. Child's Preference. In any juvenile protection matter where the child is not represented by counsel, the court shall determine the child's preferences regarding the proceedings, if the child is of suitable age to express a preference.

Amended Nov. 12, 2003; Dec. 1, 2006, eff. Jan. 1, 2007; June 10, 2009, eff. Aug. 1, 2009.

Historical Notes

The order of the Minnesota Supreme Court [C1–01–927] dated June 10, 2009, amending the Rules of Juvenile Protection Procedure and the Rules of Adoption Procedure, provides in part that the amendments are effective August 1, 2009, and shall apply to all actions or proceedings pending on or commenced on or after the effective date.

The order of the Minnesota Supreme Court [C1-01-927] dated November 12, 2003, amending Rules 37 to 82 of the Rules of Juvenile Procedure and renumbering them as Rules 1 to 47 of the Rules of Juvenile Protection Procedure, provides in part that the amendments are effective January 1, 2004, and shall apply to all juvenile protection matters filed on or after that date.

Rule 25.03. Reimbursement

When counsel is appointed for a child, the court may inquire into the ability of the parent or legal custodian to pay for the attorney's services and, after giving the parent or legal custodian a reasonable opportunity to be heard, may order the parent or legal custodian to pay the attorney's fees. The parent or legal custodian shall have an ongoing duty to disclose any change in the person's financial circumstances.

Amended Nov. 12, 2003; Dec. 1, 2006, eff. Jan. 1, 2007.

Historical Notes

The order of the Minnesota Supreme Court [C1-01-927] dated November 12, 2003, amending Rules 37 to 82 of the Rules of Juvenile Procedure and renumbering them as Rules 1 to 47 of the Rules of Juvenile Protection Procedure, provides in part that the amendments are effective January 1, 2004, and shall apply to all juvenile protection matters filed on or after that date.

Rule 25.04. Notice of Right to Representation

Any child, parent, or legal custodian who appears in court and is not represented by counsel shall be advised by the court on the record of the right to representation pursuant to Rule 25.

Amended Nov. 12, 2003.

Historical Notes

The order of the Minnesota Supreme Court [C1-01-927] dated November 12, 2003, amending Rules 37 to 82 of the Rules of Juvenile Procedure and renumbering them as Rules 1 to 47 of the Rules of Juvenile Protection Procedure, provides in part that the amendments are effective January 1, 2004, and shall apply to all juvenile protection matters filed on or after that date.

Rule 25.05. Certificate of Representation

An attorney representing a client in a juvenile protection matter, other than a public defender or county attorney, shall on or before the attorney's first appearance file with the court a certificate of representation.

Amended Nov. 12, 2003.

Historical Notes

The order of the Minnesota Supreme Court [C1-01-927] dated November 12, 2003, amending Rules 37 to 82 of the Rules of Juvenile Procedure and renumbering them as Rules 1 to 47 of the Rules of Juvenile Protection Procedure, provides in part that the amendments are effective January 1, 2004, and shall apply to all juvenile protection matters filed on or after that date.

Rule 25.06. Withdrawal or Discharge of Counsel

An attorney representing a party in a juvenile protection matter, including a public defender, shall continue representation until such time as:

(a) all district court proceedings in the matter have been completed, including filing and resolution of all post-trial motions under Rules 45 and 46;

(b) the attorney has been discharged by the client in writing or on the record;

(c) the court grants the attorney's ex parte motion for withdrawal upon good cause shown; or

(d) the court approves the attorney's ex parte written substitution of counsel.

If the court grants an attorney's ex parte motion for withdrawal, the withdrawing attorney shall serve upon all parties and the county attorney a copy of the order permitting withdrawal.

Amended Nov. 12, 2003; Dec. 1, 2006, eff. Jan. 1, 2007.

Historical Notes

The order of the Minnesota Supreme Court [C1-01-927] dated November 12, 2003, amending Rules 37 to 82 of the Rules of Juvenile Procedure and renumbering them as Rules 1 to 47 of the Rules of Juvenile Protection Procedure, provides in part that the amendments are effective January 1, 2004, and shall apply to all juvenile protection matters filed on or after that date.

RULE 26. GUARDIAN AD LITEM

Rule 26.01. Appointment for Child

Subd. 1. Mandatory Appointment Generally Required. Pursuant to the procedures set forth in the Rules of Guardian Ad Litem Procedure in Juvenile and Family Court, the court shall issue an order appointing a guardian ad litem to advocate for the best interests of the child in each child in need of protection or services matter, termination of parental rights matter, and other permanent placement matter where such appointment is mandated by Minnesota Statutes § 260C.163, subd. 5. If the court has issued an order appointing a person as a guardian ad litem in a child in need of protection or services matter, the court may, but is not required to, issue an order reappointing the same person in the termination of parental rights or other permanent placement matter. An appointment order is required only if a new person is being appointed as guardian ad litem.

Subd. 2. Discretionary Appointment. Pursuant to the procedures set forth in the Rules of Guardian Ad Litem Procedure in Juvenile and Family Court, in all other cases, except as provided in subdivision 1, the court may appoint a guardian ad litem to advocate for the best interests of the child as permitted by Minnesota Statutes § 260C.163, subd. 5.

Subd. 3. Timing; Method of Appointment. Appointment of a guardian ad litem shall occur prior to the Emergency Protective Care Hearing or the Admit–Deny Hearing, whichever occurs first. The court may appoint a person to serve as guardian ad litem for more than one child in a proceeding. The appointment of a guardian ad litem shall be made pursuant to the Rules of Guardian ad Litem Procedure in Juvenile and Family Court.

Subd. 4. Responsibilities; Rights. The guardian ad litem shall carry out the responsibilities set forth in the Rules of Guardian ad Litem Procedure in Juvenile and Family Court. The guardian ad litem shall have the rights set forth in the Rules of Guardian Ad Litem Procedure in Juvenile and Family Court.

Subd. 5. Guardian Ad Litem Not Also Attorney for Child. Counsel for the child shall not also serve as the child's guardian ad litem or as legal counsel for the guardian ad litem.

Amended Nov. 12, 2003; Sept. 30, 2004, eff. Jan. 1, 2005; Dec. 1, 2006, eff. Jan. 1, 2007; June 26, 2007, eff. July 1, 2007.

1999 Advisory Committee Comment—2004 Amendments

Rule 26.01 is consistent with Minnesota Statutes § 260C.163, subd. 5, which provides in part:

(a) The court shall appoint a guardian ad litem to protect the interests of the minor when it appears, at any stage of the proceedings, that the minor is without a parent or guardian, or that the minor's parent is a minor or incompetent, or that the parent or guardian is indifferent or hostile to the minor's interests, and in every proceeding alleging a child's need for protection or services under Minnesota Statutes § 260C.007, subd. 4.

With respect to the appointment of guardians ad litem, Minnesota Statutes § 260C.163, subd. 5, complies with the federal Child Abuse Prevention and Treatment Act (CAPTA), 42 U.S.C. § 5106a(b)(2)(A). CAPTA mandates that for a state to qualify to receive federal grants for child protection prevention and treatment services, the state must have in place:

[P]rovisions and procedures requiring that in every case involving an abused or neglected child which results in a judicial proceeding, a guardian ad litem, who has received training appropriate to the role, and who may be an attorney or a court appointed special advocate (or both), shall be appointed to represent the child in such proceedings—

(I) to obtain first-hand, a clear understanding of the situation and needs of the child; and

(II) to make recommendations to the court concerning the best interests of the child . . .

42 U.S.C. § 5106a(b)(2)(A)(xiii) (2002).

The types of cases to which guardians ad litem must be appointed are much more expansive under Minnesota's statutes than under federal statutes. Minnesota requires the appointment of a guardian ad litem not only in cases where the act of an adult places the child in need of protection or services, but also in cases where the child's act or status places the child in need of protection or services. Minn. Stat. § 260C.163, subd. 5.

Historical Notes

The order of the Minnesota Supreme Court [C1-01-927] dated November 12, 2003, amending Rules 37 to 82 of the Rules of Juvenile Procedure and renumbering them as Rules 1 to 47 of the Rules of Juvenile Protection Procedure, provides in part that the amendments are effective January 1, 2004, and shall apply to all juvenile protection matters filed on or after that date.

Rule 26.02. Discretionary Appointment for Child's Parent or Legal Custodian

Subd. 1. Appointment. Pursuant to the procedures set forth in the Rules of Guardian Ad Litem Procedure in Juvenile and Family Court, the court may sua sponte or upon the written or on-the-record request of a party or participant appoint a guardian ad litem for a parent who is a party or the legal custodian if the court determines that the parent or legal custodian:

(a) is incompetent to assist counsel in the matter or understand the nature of the proceedings; or

(b) it appears at any stage of the proceedings that the parent is under eighteen (18) years of age and is without a parent or legal custodian, or that considered in the context of the matter the minor parent's parent or legal custodian is unavailable, incompetent, indifferent to, hostile to, or has interests in conflict with the interests of the minor parent.

Subd. 2. Attorney Not Discharged. Appointment of a guardian ad litem for a parent or legal custodian shall not result in discharge of counsel for the parent or legal custodian.

Subd. 3. Responsibilities; Rights. The guardian ad litem shall carry out the responsibilities set forth in the Rules of Guardian Ad Litem Procedure in Juvenile and Family Court. The guardian ad litem shall have the rights set forth in the Rules of Guardian Ad Litem Procedure in Juvenile and Family Court.

Amended Nov. 12, 2003; Sept. 30, 2004, eff. Jan. 1, 2005; Dec. 1, 2006, eff. Jan. 1, 2007.

2004 Advisory Committee Comment

If the minor parent or incompetent adult is unable to admit or deny the petition, the court may choose to appoint a substitute decisionmaker or legal guardian to admit or deny the petition.

Historical Notes

The order of the Minnesota Supreme Court [C1-01-927] dated November 12, 2003, amending Rules 37 to 82 of the Rules of Juvenile Procedure and renumbering them as Rules 1 to 47 of the Rules of Juvenile Protection Procedure, provides in part that the amendments are effective January 1, 2004, and shall apply to all juvenile protection matters filed on or after that date.

Rule 26.03. Term of Service of Guardian Ad Litem

Unless otherwise ordered by the court, upon appointment to a juvenile protection matter the guardian ad litem shall serve as follows:

(a) when the permanency plan for the child is to return the child home, the court shall issue an order dismissing the guardian ad litem from the case upon issuance of an order returning the child to the child's home and terminating the juvenile protection matter;

(b) when the permanency plan for the child is transfer of permanent legal and physical custody to a relative, the court shall issue an order dismissing the guardian ad litem from the case upon issuance of the order transferring custody and terminating the juvenile protection matter;

(c) when the permanency plan for the child is termination of parental rights leading to adoption, the guardian ad litem shall continue to serve as a party until the adoption decree is entered;

(d) when the permanency plan for the child is long-term foster care, the guardian ad litem shall continue to serve as a party for the purpose of monitoring the child's welfare, and shall provide the foster parent and child, if of suitable age, with the address and phone number of the guardian ad litem so that they may contact the guardian ad litem if necessary. The guardian ad litem shall be provided notice of all social services administrative reviews and shall be consulted regarding development of any case plan, out-of-home placement plan, or independent living plan required pursuant to Rule 37.

Amended Nov. 12, 2003; June 10, 2009, eff. Aug. 1, 2009.

Historical Notes

The order of the Minnesota Supreme Court [C1–01–927] dated June 10, 2009, amending the Rules of Juvenile Protection Procedure and the Rules of Adoption Procedure, provides in part that the amendments are effective August 1, 2009, and shall apply to all actions or proceedings pending on or commenced on or after the effective date.

The order of the Minnesota Supreme Court [C1-01-927] dated November 12, 2003, amending Rules 37 to 82 of the Rules of Juvenile Procedure and renumbering them as Rules 1 to 47 of the Rules of Juvenile Protection Procedure, provides in part that the amendments are effective January 1, 2004, and shall apply to all juvenile protection matters filed on or after that date.

Rule 26.04. Request for Appointment of Counsel for Child

The guardian ad litem shall request appointment of counsel for a child if the guardian ad litem determines that the appointment is necessary to protect the legal rights or legal interests of the child.

Adopted Nov. 12, 2003.

2003 Advisory Committee Comment

In deciding whether to request appointment of counsel for the child, the guardian ad litem should assess the following, among other factors: the child's ability to work with counsel, whether the guardian ad litem's recommendation is contrary to the child's expressed preference, whether the child's siblings are represented, and the complexity of the issues involved.

Historical Notes

The order of the Minnesota Supreme Court [C1-01-927] dated November 12, 2003, amending Rules 37 to 82 of the Rules of Juvenile

Procedure and renumbering them as Rules 1 to 47 of the Rules of Juvenile Protection Procedure, provides in part that the amendments are effective January 1, 2004, and shall apply to all juvenile protection matters filed on or after that date.

Rule 26.05. Reimbursement

The court may inquire into the ability of the parent or legal custodian to pay for the guardian ad litem's services and, after giving the parent or legal custodian a reasonable opportunity to be heard, may order the parent or legal custodian to pay the guardian ad litem's fees. The parent or legal custodian shall have an ongoing duty to disclose any change in the person's financial circumstances.

Adopted Nov. 12, 2003. Amended Dec. 1, 2006, eff. Jan. 1, 2007.

Historical Notes

The order of the Minnesota Supreme Court [C1-01-927] dated November 12, 2003, amending Rules 37 to 82 of the Rules of Juvenile Procedure and renumbering them as Rules 1 to 47 of the Rules of Juvenile Protection Procedure, provides in part that the amendments are effective January 1, 2004, and shall apply to all juvenile protection matters filed on or after that date.

RULE 27. ACCESS TO HEARINGS

Rule 27.01. Presumption of Public Access to Hearings

Absent exceptional circumstances, hearings in juvenile protection matters are presumed to be accessible to the public. Hearings, or portions of hearings, may be closed to the public by the court only in exceptional circumstances. The closure of any hearing shall be noted on the record and the reasons for the closure given. Closure of all or part of a hearing shall not prevent the court from proceeding with the hearing or issuing a decision. Minnesota Statutes § 260C.163, subd. 1(c), is superseded insofar as it applies to public access to hearings in juvenile protection matters. An order closing a hearing or portion of a hearing to the public shall be accessible to the public.

Amended Nov. 12, 2003.

Historical Notes

The order of the Minnesota Supreme Court [C1-01-927] dated November 12, 2003, amending Rules 37 to 82 of the Rules of Juvenile Procedure and renumbering them as Rules 1 to 47 of the Rules of Juvenile Protection Procedure, provides in part that the amendments are effective January 1, 2004, and shall apply to all juvenile protection matters filed on or after that date.

Rule 27.02. Party and Participant Attendance at Hearings

Notwithstanding the closure of a hearing to the public pursuant to Rule 27.01, any party who is entitled to summons pursuant to Rule 32.02 or any participant who is entitled to notice pursuant to Rule 32.03, or any person who is summoned or given notice, shall have the right to attend the hearing to which the summons or notice relates unless excluded pursuant to Rule 27.04.

Amended Nov. 12, 2003.

1999 Advisory Committee Comment—2003 Amendment

Pursuant to Rule 21, a party has the right to be present in person at any hearing. For a child, the person with physical custody of the child should generally be responsible for ensuring the child's presence in court. When a child is in emergency protective care or protective care, the responsible social services agency is responsible for ensuring the child's presence in court. If the child is in the custody of the responsible social services agency in out-of-home placement, the agency should transport the child to the hearing. If the agency fails to make arrangements for the child to attend the hearing, the child's attorney or guardian ad litem may need to ask for a continuance and for an order requiring the child to be brought to the next hearing.

Historical Notes

The order of the Minnesota Supreme Court [C1-01-927] dated November 12, 2003, amending Rules 37 to 82 of the Rules of Juvenile Procedure and renumbering them as Rules 1 to 47 of the Rules of Juvenile Protection Procedure, provides in part that the amendments are effective January 1, 2004, and shall apply to all juvenile protection matters filed on or after that date.

Rule 27.03. Absence Does Not Bar Hearing

The absence from a hearing of any party or participant shall not prevent the hearing from proceeding provided appropriate notice has been served.

Amended Nov. 12, 2003.

Historical Notes

The order of the Minnesota Supreme Court [C1-01-927] dated November 12, 2003, amending Rules 37 to 82 of the Rules of Juvenile Procedure and renumbering them as Rules 1 to 47 of the Rules of Juvenile Protection Procedure, provides in part that the amendments are effective January 1, 2004, and shall apply to all juvenile protection matters filed on or after that date.

Rule 27.04. Exclusion of Parties or Participants from Hearings

The court may exclude from any hearing any party or participant, other than a guardian ad litem or counsel for any party or participant, only if it is in the best interests of the child to do so or the person engages in conduct that disrupts the court. The exclusion of any party or participant from a hearing shall be noted on the record and the reason for the exclusion given. The exclusion of any party or participant shall not prevent the court from proceeding with the hearing or issuing a decision. An order excluding a party or participant from a hearing shall be accessible to the public.

Amended Nov. 12, 2003.

Historical Notes

The order of the Minnesota Supreme Court [C1-01-927] dated November 12, 2003, amending Rules 37 to 82 of the Rules of Juvenile

Procedure and renumbering them as Rules 1 to 47 of the Rules of Juvenile Protection Procedure, provides in part that the amendments are effective January 1, 2004, and shall apply to all juvenile protection matters filed on or after that date.

D. COURSE OF CASE

RULE 28. EMERGENCY PROTECTIVE CARE ORDER AND NOTICE

Rule 28.01. Emergency Protective Care Defined

A child is in "emergency protective care" when:

(1) taken into custody by a peace officer pursuant to Minnesota Statutes § 260C.151, subd. 6; § 260C.154; or § 260C.175; or

(2) returned home before an Emergency Protective Care Hearing pursuant to Rule 30 with court ordered conditions of release.

Amended Nov. 12, 2003.

1999 Advisory Committee Comment

A child taken into emergency protective care should never be held in secure detention.

Historical Notes

The order of the Minnesota Supreme Court [C1-01-927] dated November 12, 2003, amending Rules 37 to 82 of the Rules of Juvenile Procedure and renumbering them as Rules 1 to 47 of the Rules of Juvenile Protection Procedure, provides in part that the amendments are effective January 1, 2004, and shall apply to all juvenile protection matters filed on or after that date.

Rule 28.02. Ex Parte Order for Emergency Protective Care

Subd. 1. Generally. When the court makes individualized, explicit findings, the court may issue an ex parte order for emergency protective care if it finds from the facts set forth in the petition or any supporting affidavits or sworn testimony that:

(a) the child has left or been removed from a court-ordered placement; or

(b) there is a prima facie showing that the child is in surroundings or conditions that endanger the child's health, safety, or welfare and that require that responsibility for the child's care and custody be immediately assumed by the responsible social services agency; and

(c) continuation of the child in the custody of the parent or legal custodian is contrary to the child's welfare.

Subd. 2. Habitual Truant, Runaway, Prostitution, Delinquent Under Age 10, Incompetent to Proceed, and Domestic Abuse Matters. In addition to the provisions of subdivision 1, the court may issue an ex parte order for emergency protective care if it finds from the facts set forth in the petition or any supporting affidavits or sworn testimony that:

(a) there is a prima facie showing that pursuant to Minnesota Statutes § 260C.007, subd. 6, the child has engaged in prostitution, is a habitual truant, is a runaway, has committed a delinquent act before becoming ten (10) years of age, has been found incompetent to proceed or not guilty by reason of mental illness or mental deficiency, or has been found by the court to have committed domestic abuse; and

(b) the child failed to appear after having been personally served with a summons or subpoena, reasonable efforts to personally serve the child have failed, or there is a substantial likelihood that the child will fail to respond to a summons; and

(c) continuation of the child in the custody of the parent or legal custodian is contrary to the child's welfare.

Amended Nov. 12, 2003; Dec. 1, 2006, eff. Jan. 1, 2007.

Historical Notes

The order of the Minnesota Supreme Court [C1-01-927] dated November 12, 2003, amending Rules 37 to 82 of the Rules of Juvenile Procedure and renumbering them as Rules 1 to 47 of the Rules of Juvenile Protection Procedure, provides in part that the amendments are effective January 1, 2004, and shall apply to all juvenile protection matters filed on or after that date.

Rule 28.03. Contents of Order

An order for emergency protective care shall be signed by a judge, shall include the findings required under Rule 28.02, subds. 1 and 2, and shall:

(a) order the child to be taken to an appropriate relative, a designated caregiver pursuant to Minnesota Statutes § 260C.181, or a shelter care facility designated by the court pending an emergency protective care hearing;

(b) state the name and address of the child, unless such information would endanger the child, or, if unknown, designate the child by any name or description by which the child can be identified with reasonable certainty;

(c) state the age and gender of the child or, if the age of the child is unknown, that the child is believed to be of an age subject to the jurisdiction of the court;

(d) state the reasons why the child is being taken into emergency protective care;

(e) state the reasons for any limitation on the time or location of the execution of the emergency protective care order;

(f) state the date when issued and the county and court where issued; and

(g) state the date, time, and location of the emergency protective care hearing.

Amended Nov. 12, 2003.

Historical Notes

The order of the Minnesota Supreme Court [C1-01-927] dated November 12, 2003, amending Rules 37 to 82 of the Rules of Juvenile Procedure and renumbering them as Rules 1 to 47 of the Rules of Juvenile Protection Procedure, provides in part that the amendments are effective January 1, 2004, and shall apply to all juvenile protection matters filed on or after that date.

Rule 28.04. Execution of Order

An order for emergency protective care:

(a) may only be executed by a peace officer authorized by law to execute a warrant;

(b) shall be executed by taking the child into custody;

(c) may be executed at any place in the state except where prohibited by law or unless otherwise ordered by the court;

(d) may be executed at any time unless otherwise ordered by the court; and

(e) need not be in the peace officer's possession at the time the child is taken into emergency protective care.

Amended Nov. 12, 2003.

Historical Notes

The order of the Minnesota Supreme Court [C1-01-927] dated November 12, 2003, amending Rules 37 to 82 of the Rules of Juvenile Procedure and renumbering them as Rules 1 to 47 of the Rules of Juvenile Protection Procedure, provides in part that the amendments are effective January 1, 2004, and shall apply to all juvenile protection matters filed on or after that date.

Rule 28.05. Notice

When an order for emergency protective care is executed, the peace officer shall notify the child and the child's parent or legal custodian:

(a) of the existence of the order for emergency protective care;

(b) of the reasons why the child is being taken into emergency protective care;

(c) of the time and place of the emergency protective care hearing;

(d) of the name, address, and telephone number of the responsible social services agency; and

(e) that the parent or legal custodian or child may request that the court place the child with a relative or a designated caregiver rather than in a shelter care facility.

The notice shall be delivered in written form and, when possible, the content of the notice shall also be orally summarized and explained. If the parent or legal custodian is not present when the child is removed from the premises, the notice shall be left with an adult on the premises. If no adult is present at the time the child is removed, the notice shall be left in a conspicuous place on the premises.

Amended Nov. 12, 2003.

Historical Notes

The order of the Minnesota Supreme Court [C1-01-927] dated November 12, 2003, amending Rules 37 to 82 of the Rules of Juvenile Procedure and renumbering them as Rules 1 to 47 of the Rules of Juvenile Protection Procedure, provides in part that the amendments are effective January 1, 2004, and shall apply to all juvenile protection matters filed on or after that date.

Rule 28.06. Enforcement of Order

An emergency protective care order shall be enforceable by any peace officer in any jurisdiction.

Amended Nov. 12, 2003.

Historical Notes

The order of the Minnesota Supreme Court [C1-01-927] dated November 12, 2003, amending Rules 37 to 82 of the Rules of Juvenile Procedure and renumbering them as Rules 1 to 47 of the Rules of Juvenile Protection Procedure, provides in part that the amendments are effective January 1, 2004, and shall apply to all juvenile protection matters filed on or after that date.

RULE 29. PROCEDURES DURING PERIOD OF EMERGENCY PROTECTIVE CARE

Rule 29.01. Release from Emergency Protective Care

Subd. 1. Child Taken Into Emergency Protective Care Pursuant to Court Order.

(a) *Release Prohibited.* A child taken into emergency protective care pursuant to a court order shall be held for seventy-two (72) hours unless the court issues an order authorizing release.

(b) *Release Required.* A child taken into emergency protective care pursuant to a court order shall not be held in emergency protective care for more than seventy-two (72) hours unless an emergency protective care hearing has commenced pursuant to Rule 30 and the court has ordered continued protective care.

Subd. 2. Child Taken Into Emergency Protective Care Without Court Order.

(a) *Release Required.* A child taken into emergency protective care without a court order shall be released unless an emergency protective care hearing pursuant to Rule 30 has commenced within seventy-two (72) hours of the time the child was removed from home and the court has ordered continued protective care.

(b) *Discretionary Release by Peace Officer or County Attorney.* When a peace officer has taken a child into emergency protective care without a court order, the peace officer, peace officer's supervisor, or the county attorney may release the child any time prior to an emergency protective care hearing. The peace officer, the peace officer's supervisor, or the county attorney who releases the child may not place any conditions of release on the child.

Amended Nov. 12, 2003.

2003 Advisory Committee Comment

When calculating the seventy-two (72) hour period referenced in Rule 29.01, pursuant to Rule 4.01 the day the child was removed from home and any Saturday, Sunday, or legal holiday is not counted. The last day of the period shall be included, unless it is a Saturday, Sunday, or legal holiday in which event the period runs to the end of the next day that is not a Saturday, Sunday, or legal holiday.

Historical Notes

The order of the Minnesota Supreme Court [C1-01-927] dated November 12, 2003, amending Rules 37 to 82 of the Rules of Juvenile Procedure and renumbering them as Rules 1 to 47 of the Rules of Juvenile Protection Procedure, provides in part that the amendments are effective January 1, 2004, and shall apply to all juvenile protection matters filed on or after that date.

Rule 29.02. Discretionary Release by Court; Custodial Conditions

The court at any time before an emergency protective care hearing may release a child and may:

(a) place restrictions on the child's travel, associations, or place of abode during the period of the child's release; and

(b) impose any other conditions upon the child or the child's parent or legal custodian deemed reasonably necessary and consistent with criteria for protecting the child.

Any conditions terminate after seventy-two (72) hours unless a hearing has commenced pursuant to Rule 30 and the court has ordered continuation of the condition.

Amended Nov. 12, 2003.

Historical Notes

The order of the Minnesota Supreme Court [C1-01-927] dated November 12, 2003, amending Rules 37 to 82 of the Rules of Juvenile Procedure and renumbering them as Rules 1 to 47 of the Rules of Juvenile Protection Procedure, provides in part that the amendments are effective January 1, 2004, and shall apply to all juvenile protection matters filed on or after that date.

Rule 29.03. Release to Custody of Parent or Other Suitable Person

A child released from emergency protective care shall be released to the custody of the child's parent, legal custodian, or other suitable person.

Amended Nov. 12, 2003.

Historical Notes

The order of the Minnesota Supreme Court [C1-01-927] dated November 12, 2003, amending Rules 37 to 82 of the Rules of Juvenile Procedure and renumbering them as Rules 1 to 47 of the Rules of Juvenile Protection Procedure, provides in part that the amendments are effective January 1, 2004, and shall apply to all juvenile protection matters filed on or after that date.

Rule 29.04. Reports

Subd. 1. Report by Peace Officer. Any report required by Minnesota Statutes § 260C.176, subd. 6, shall be filed with the court on or before the first court day following placement of the child and the report shall include at least:

(a) the time the child was taken into emergency protective care;

(b) the time the child was delivered for transportation to the shelter care facility;

(c) the reasons why the child was taken into emergency protective care;

(d) the reasons why the child has been placed;

(e) a statement that the child and the child's parent or legal custodian have received the advisory required by Minnesota Statutes § 260C.176, subd. 3, or the reasons why the advisory has not been made; and

(f) reasons to support the non-disclosure, if disclosure of the location of the placement has not been made because there is reason to believe that the child's health and welfare would be immediately endangered.

Subd. 2. Report by Supervisor of Shelter Care Facility. Any report required by Minnesota Statutes § 260C.176, subd. 6, shall be filed with the court on or before the first court day following placement. The report shall include, at least, acknowledgement of receipt of the child and state the time the child arrived at the shelter care facility.

Amended Nov. 12, 2003.

Historical Notes

The order of the Minnesota Supreme Court [C1-01-927] dated November 12, 2003, amending Rules 37 to 82 of the Rules of Juvenile Procedure and renumbering them as Rules 1 to 47 of the Rules of Juvenile Protection Procedure, provides in part that the amendments are effective January 1, 2004, and shall apply to all juvenile protection matters filed on or after that date.

RULE 30. EMERGENCY PROTECTIVE CARE HEARING

Rule 30.01. Timing

Subd. 1. Generally. The court shall hold an emergency protective care hearing within seventy-two (72) hours of the child being taken into emergency protective care unless the child is released pursuant to Rule 29. The purpose of the hearing shall be to determine whether the child shall be returned home or placed in protective care.

Subd. 2. Continuance. The court may, upon its own motion or upon the written or oral motion of a party made at the emergency protective care hearing, continue the emergency protective care hearing for a period not to exceed eight (8) days. A continuance may be granted:

(a) upon a determination by the court that there is a prima facie showing that the child should be held in emergency protective care pursuant to Rule 28; and

(b) if the court finds that a continuance is necessary for the protection of the child, for the accumulation or presentation of necessary evidence or witnesses, to protect the rights of a party, or for other good cause shown.

Amended Nov. 12, 2003.

1999 Advisory Committee Comment

Subdivision 2 requires that the court make certain findings before permitting a continuance. This provision recognizes that parties may need time to prepare for the hearing, but assures that a child will not be held unnecessarily during the continuance.

Historical Notes

The order of the Minnesota Supreme Court [C1-01-927] dated November 12, 2003, amending Rules 37 to 82 of the Rules of Juvenile Procedure and renumbering them as Rules 1 to 47 of the Rules of Juvenile Protection Procedure, provides in part that the amendments are effective January 1, 2004, and shall apply to all juvenile protection matters filed on or after that date.

Rule 30.02. Notice of Hearing

The court administrator, or designee, shall inform the county attorney; the responsible social services agency; the child; and the child's counsel, guardian ad litem, parent, legal custodian, spouse, Indian custodian, Indian tribe, and school district of residence as required by Minnesota Statutes § 127A.47, subd. 6, of the time and place of the emergency protective care hearing.

Amended Nov. 12, 2003.

Historical Notes

The order of the Minnesota Supreme Court [C1-01-927] dated November 12, 2003, amending Rules 37 to 82 of the Rules of Juvenile Procedure and renumbering them as Rules 1 to 47 of the Rules of Juvenile Protection Procedure, provides in part that the amendments are effective January 1, 2004, and shall apply to all juvenile protection matters filed on or after that date.

Rule 30.03. Inspection of Reports

Prior to the emergency protective care hearing, the parties shall be permitted to inspect reports or other written information or records that any party intends to present at the hearing.

Amended Nov. 12, 2003.

1999 Advisory Committee Comment—2003 Amendment

Rule 30.03 places upon each party the burden of providing to opposing parties all documentation the party intends to introduce at the hearing. The rule is intended to ensure that the parties have the relevant information before the hearing so they are prepared to respond. This rule is not intended to limit discovery allowed by Rule 17.

Historical Notes

The order of the Minnesota Supreme Court [C1-01-927] dated November 12, 2003, amending Rules 37 to 82 of the Rules of Juvenile Procedure and renumbering them as Rules 1 to 47 of the Rules of Juvenile Protection Procedure, provides in part that the amendments are effective January 1, 2004, and shall apply to all juvenile protection matters filed on or after that date.

Rule 30.04. Determination Regarding Notice

During the hearing, the court shall determine whether all persons identified in Rule 30.02 have been informed of the time and place of the emergency protective care hearing and what further efforts, if any, must be taken to notify all parties and participants as rapidly as possible of the pendency of the matter and the date and time of the next hearing. Before the emergency protective care hearing, the court administrator, or designee, shall file with the court a written statement describing the efforts to inform the persons identified in Rule 30.02 of the emergency protective care hearing, including the date, time, and method of each effort to inform each such person and whether contact was actually made.

Amended Nov. 12, 2003.

Historical Notes

The order of the Minnesota Supreme Court [C1-01-927] dated November 12, 2003, amending Rules 37 to 82 of the Rules of Juvenile Procedure and renumbering them as Rules 1 to 47 of the Rules of Juvenile Protection Procedure, provides in part that the amendments are effective January 1, 2004, and shall apply to all juvenile protection matters filed on or after that date.

Rule 30.05. Advisory

At the beginning of the emergency protective care hearing the court shall on the record advise all parties and participants present of:

(a) the reasons why the child was taken into emergency protective care;

(b) the substance of the statutory grounds and supporting factual allegations set forth in the petition;

(c) the purpose and scope of the hearing;

(d) the possible consequences of the proceedings;

(e) the right of the parties and participants to legal representation, including the right of the child, the child's parent or legal custodian, and the child's Indian custodian to court appointed counsel pursuant to Rule 25;

(f) the right of the parties to present evidence and to cross-examine witnesses regarding whether the child should return home with or without conditions or whether the child should be placed in protective care; and

(g) that failure to appear at future hearings could result in a finding that the petition has been proved, issuance of an order adjudicating the child in need of protection or services, and an order transferring permanent legal and physical custody of the child to another.

Amended Nov. 12, 2003.

Historical Notes

The order of the Minnesota Supreme Court [C1-01-927] dated November 12, 2003, amending Rules 37 to 82 of the Rules of Juvenile Procedure and renumbering them as Rules 1 to 47 of the Rules of Juvenile Protection Procedure, provides in part that the amendments

are effective January 1, 2004, and shall apply to all juvenile protection matters filed on or after that date.

Rule 30.06. Evidence

The court may admit any evidence, including reliable hearsay and opinion evidence, that is relevant to the decision of whether to continue protective care of the child or return the child home. Privileged communications may be admitted in accordance with Minnesota Statutes § 626.556, subd. 8.

Amended Nov. 12, 2003.

Historical Notes

The order of the Minnesota Supreme Court [C1-01-927] dated November 12, 2003, amending Rules 37 to 82 of the Rules of Juvenile Procedure and renumbering them as Rules 1 to 47 of the Rules of Juvenile Protection Procedure, provides in part that the amendments are effective January 1, 2004, and shall apply to all juvenile protection matters filed on or after that date.

Rule 30.07. Filing and Service of Petition

A petition shall be filed with the court and may be served at or before the emergency protective care hearing.

Amended Nov. 12, 2003.

Historical Notes

The order of the Minnesota Supreme Court [C1-01-927] dated November 12, 2003, amending Rules 37 to 82 of the Rules of Juvenile Procedure and renumbering them as Rules 1 to 47 of the Rules of Juvenile Protection Procedure, provides in part that the amendments are effective January 1, 2004, and shall apply to all juvenile protection matters filed on or after that date.

Rule 30.08. Protective Care Determinations

Subd. 1. Initial Findings.

(a) *Prima Facie Showing.* The court shall dismiss the petition if it finds that the petition fails to establish a prima facie showing that a juvenile protection matter exists and that the child is the subject of that matter.

(b) *Endangerment.*

(1) *Findings.* If the court finds that the petition establishes a prima facie showing that a juvenile protection matter exists and that the child is the subject of that matter, the court shall then determine whether the petition also makes a prima facie showing that:

(i) the child or others would be immediately endangered by the child's actions if the child were released to the care of the parent or legal custodian; or

(ii) the child's health, safety, or welfare would be immediately endangered if the child were released to the care of the parent or legal custodian.

(2) *Determination.* If the court finds that endangerment exists pursuant to this subdivision, the court shall continue protective care or release the child to the child's parent or legal custodian and impose conditions to ensure the safety of the child or others. If the court finds that endangerment does not exist, the court shall release the child to the child's parent or legal custodian subject to reasonable conditions of release.

(3) *Continued Custody by Parent Contrary to Welfare of Child.* The court may not order or continue the foster care placement of the child unless the court makes explicit, individualized findings that continued custody of the child by the parent or legal custodian is contrary to the welfare of the child.

Subd. 2. Indian Child Determination. The court shall determine whether the child is an Indian child through review of the petition and other documents and an on-the-record inquiry. If the court is unable to determine whether the child is an Indian child, the court shall direct the petitioner to make further inquiry and provide to the court and parties additional information regarding whether the child is an Indian child.

Subd. 3. Emergency Removal and Placement Authority For Indian Child Ward, Resident, or Domiciliary.

(a) *Finding.* If the district court finds from review of the petition or other information that an Indian child resides or is domiciled on an Indian reservation or that an Indian child is a ward of tribal court but is temporarily located off the reservation, the district court may order emergency removal of the child from the child's parent or Indian custodian and emergency placement in foster care.

(b) *Required Actions for Wards of Tribal Court.* If the district court finds from review of the petition or other information that an Indian child is a ward of tribal court, the court shall order that the child be expeditiously returned to the jurisdiction of the Indian child's tribe and shall consult with the tribal court regarding the child's safe transition pursuant to Rule 48.02, subd. 1.

Amended Nov. 12, 2003; June 10, 2009, eff. Aug. 1, 2009.

1999 Advisory Committee Comment—2003 Amendment

Rule 30.08 is consistent with Minnesota Statutes § 260C.178, subd. 1(b), which provides:

> Unless there is reason to believe that the child would endanger self or others, not return for a court hearing, run away from the child's parent, guardian, or custodian or otherwise not remain in the care or control of the person to whose lawful custody the child is released, or that the child's health or welfare would be immediately endangered, the child shall be released to the custody of a parent, guardian, custodian, or other suitable person, subject to reasonable conditions of release including, but not limited to, a requirement that the child undergo a chemical use assessment as provided in [Minnesota Statutes §] 260C.157, subd. 1.

2008 Advisory Committee Comment

Child's Status as Indian Child Unknown. In cases where the application of the Indian Child Welfare Act (ICWA) is unclear, such as when it is not yet known whether the child is or is not an Indian child, it is advisable to proceed pursuant to the requirements of the ICWA unless or until a determination is otherwise made in order to fulfill the Congressional purposes of the ICWA, to ensure that the child's Indian tribe is involved, and to avoid invalidation of the action pursuant to 25 U.S.C. § 1914 and Rule 46.03.

Exclusive Jurisdiction. With respect to exclusive jurisdiction, the Indian Child Welfare Act (ICWA) provides:

"An Indian tribe shall have jurisdiction exclusive as to any State over any child custody proceeding involving an Indian child who resides or is domiciled within the reservation of such tribe, except where such jurisdiction is otherwise vested in the State by existing Federal law. Where an Indian child is a ward of a tribal court, the Indian tribe shall retain exclusive jurisdiction, notwithstanding the residence or domicile of the child."

25 U.S.C. § 1911(a). The language in the Minnesota Indian Family Preservation Act (MIFPA), Minn. Stat. § 260.771, subd. 1., is nearly identical. For a full discussion of "domicile" under the ICWA, see Mississippi Band of Choctaw Indians v. Holyfield, 490 U.S. 30 (1989).

There are differences of opinion regarding application of Public Law 83–280, codified at 25 U.S.C. § 1322, as it may intersect with exclusive jurisdiction requirements in child welfare proceedings governed by the ICWA. *See California v. Cabazon Band of Mission Indians*, 480 U.S. 202, 207–14 (1987); *Doe v. Mann (Mann II)*, 415 F.3d 1038, 1047–68 (9th Cir. 2005); *Native Village of Venetie I.R.A. Council v. Alaska (Venetie II)*, 944 F.2d 548, 559–62 (9th Cir. 1991); *Teague v. Bad River Band of the Lake Superior Tribe of Chippewa Indians*, 612 N.W.2d 709, 717–18 (Wis. 2000); *In re M.A.*, 40 Cal. Rptr. 3d 439, 441–43 (Cal. Ct. App. 2006); *State ex rel Dep't of Human Servs. V. Whitebreast*, 409 N.W.2d 460, 461–64 (Iowa 1987); 78 Wis. Op. Att'y Gen. 122 (1989).

Historical Notes

The order of the Minnesota Supreme Court [C1–01–927] dated June 10, 2009, amending the Rules of Juvenile Protection Procedure and the Rules of Adoption Procedure, provides in part that the amendments are effective August 1, 2009, and shall apply to all actions or proceedings pending on or commenced on or after the effective date.

The order of the Minnesota Supreme Court [C1-01-927] dated November 12, 2003, amending Rules 37 to 82 of the Rules of Juvenile Procedure and renumbering them as Rules 1 to 47 of the Rules of Juvenile Protection Procedure, provides in part that the amendments are effective January 1, 2004, and shall apply to all juvenile protection matters filed on or after that date.

Rule 30.09. Factors

Subd. 1. Generally. Except in cases described in subdivision 3, or when the parental rights of the parent to a sibling of the child have been terminated involuntarily, or the child is presumed to be an abandoned infant under Minnesota Statutes § 260C.301, subd. 2, at the emergency protective care hearing the court shall require petitioner to present information regarding the following issues:

(a) whether the responsible social services agency made reasonable efforts, or active efforts in the case of an Indian child, to prevent placement or eliminate the need for removal of the child from the home;

(b) whether there are services the court could order that would allow the child to safely return home;

(c) whether responsible relatives or other responsible adults are available to provide services or to serve as placement options if licensed;

(d) whether the placement proposed by the agency is the least restrictive and most home-like setting that meets the needs of the child;

(e) whether restraining orders, or orders expelling an allegedly abusive parent or legal custodian from the home, are appropriate;

(f) whether orders are needed for examinations, evaluations, or immediate services;

(g) the terms and conditions for parental visitation; and

(h) what consideration has been given for financial support of the child.

Subd. 2. Determination Regarding Reasonable or Active Efforts. Based upon the information provided to the court in the petition, sworn affidavit, certified report, or on the record, the court shall make a determination whether reasonable efforts, or active efforts in the case of an Indian child, were made to prevent the child's out-of-home placement. The court shall also determine whether there are available services that would prevent the need for further placement. In the alternative, the court shall determine that reasonable efforts are not required if the court makes a prima facie determination that one of the circumstances under subdivision 3 exists.

Subd. 3. Cases Permitting By–Pass of Child in Need of Protection or Services Proceedings.

(a) *Permanency Determination.* At the emergency protective care hearing, or at any time prior to adjudication, and upon notice and request of the county attorney, the court shall determine whether a petition has been filed stating a prima facie case that:

(1) the parent has subjected a child to egregious harm as defined in Minnesota Statutes § 260C.007, subd. 14;

(2) the parental rights of the parent to another child have been terminated involuntarily;

(3) the child is presumed to be an abandoned infant under Minnesota Statutes § 260C.301, subd. 2(a);

(4) the parent's custodial rights to another child have been involuntarily transferred to a relative

under Minnesota Statutes § 260C.201, subd. 11(d)(1) or a similar law of another jurisdiction; or

(5) the provision of services or the provision of further services for the purpose of rehabilitation and reunification is futile and therefore unreasonable under the circumstances.

(b) *Permanency Hearing Required.* Once the court makes the determination required in subdivision 3(a), the court shall schedule a permanent placement determination hearing pursuant to Rule 42 within thirty (30) days.

Amended Nov. 12, 2003; Dec. 1, 2006, eff. Jan. 1, 2007; June 10, 2009, eff. Aug. 1, 2009.

2003 Advisory Committee Comment

Consistent with Minnesota Statutes § 260C.178, Rule 30.09 requires the court to make a determination about whether the responsible social services agency made reasonable, or active efforts in the case of an Indian child, to prevent the removal of the child. Unless the child's removal is due to circumstances which do not require efforts to reunify the child with the parent or legal custodian, the responsible social services agency should provide services to prevent the child's removal. The circumstances where reunification efforts are not required are set out in subdivision 3. When the removal occurs due to an emergency, the agency should consider what services it might put into the child's home to allow the child to return home or whether the child's safety could be met by excluding from the child's home the individual responsible for abuse or neglect of the child. When the agency documents the services provided or attempted, or other measures it considered but rejected, to provide for the child's safety, and the court finds such actions reasonable, the court may properly find the agency has made reasonable efforts to prevent the removal of the child.

Historical Notes

The order of the Minnesota Supreme Court [C1–01–927] dated June 10, 2009, amending the Rules of Juvenile Protection Procedure and the Rules of Adoption Procedure, provides in part that the amendments are effective August 1, 2009, and shall apply to all actions or proceedings pending on or commenced on or after the effective date.

The order of the Minnesota Supreme Court [C1-01-927] dated November 12, 2003, amending Rules 37 to 82 of the Rules of Juvenile Procedure and renumbering them as Rules 1 to 47 of the Rules of Juvenile Protection Procedure, provides in part that the amendments are effective January 1, 2004, and shall apply to all juvenile protection matters filed on or after that date.

Rule 30.10. Protective Care Findings and Order

Within three (3) days of the conclusion of the emergency protective care hearing the court shall issue a written order which shall include findings pursuant to Rules 30.08 and 30.09 and which shall order:

(a) that the child:

(1) continue in protective care;

(2) return home with conditions to ensure the safety of the child or others;

(3) return home with reasonable conditions of release; or

(4) return home with no conditions;

(b) conditions pursuant to subdivision (a), if any, to be imposed upon the parent, legal custodian, or a party;

(c) services, if any, to be provided to the child and the child's family;

(d) terms of parental and sibling visitation pending further proceedings;

(e) the parent's responsibility for costs of care pursuant to Minnesota Statutes § 260C.331, subd. 1;

(f) if the court knows or has reason to know that the child is an Indian child, notice of the proceedings shall be sent to the Indian child's parents or Indian custodian and Indian child's tribe consistent with 25 U.S.C. § 1912(a); Minnesota Statutes § 260.761, subd. 3; and Rule 32.06; and

(g) if the child is determined to be an Indian child and is proposed to be placed in foster care, testimony, pursuant to Rule 49, of a qualified expert witness.

Amended Nov. 12, 2003; Dec. 1, 2006, eff. Jan. 1, 2007; June 10, 2009, eff. Aug. 1, 2009.

1999 Advisory Committee Comment—2003 Amendments

Minnesota Statutes § 260C.178, subd. 1(c), provides as follows:

[In a proceeding regarding a child in need of protection or services,] the court, before determining whether a child should continue in custody, shall also make a determination, consistent with [Minnesota Statutes §] 260.012 as to whether reasonable efforts, or in the case of an Indian child, active efforts, according to the Indian Child Welfare Act of 1978, United States Code, title 25, section 1912(d), were made to prevent placement. The court shall also determine whether there are available services that would prevent the need for further detention.

In compliance with the statutory mandate of Minnesota Statutes § 260C.178, Rules 30.08 and 30.09 require the court to elicit relevant evidence from the petitioner and make findings as to whether the child is in imminent danger, whether the county made reasonable efforts to prevent removal or eliminate the need for removal, and whether there are services the court could order to allow the child to safely return home. Rule 30.10 requires that the court issue a written order that includes specific findings in support of the order.

2006 Advisory Committee Comment—2009 Amendments

When the court orders a child into "protective care," the court is ordering the child placed in foster care. That means the responsible social services agency has the right to temporary physical custody and control of the child. *See Rule 2.01(19); Minn. Stat. §§ 260C.178, subd. 1; and 260C.007, subd. 18.*

The responsible social services agency must make an individualized determination that the placement selected is in the best interests of the child using the eight factors set out in the statute. *Minn. Stat. § 260C.201, subd. 1(a)(2)(ii),* and *§ 260C.212, subd. 2.* The agency documents its use of the eight best interest factors in the Out-of-Home Placement Plan required under *Minn. Stat. § 260C.212, subd. 1,* and *Rule 37.02.* The court reviews the agency's use of the eight statutory best interest factors during the hearing required under *Rule 41* and *Minn. Stat. § 260C.193, subd. 3.*

When a child is in foster care, the agency is responsible for the cost of placement, and may seek reimbursement from the child and parent under *Minn. Stat. § 260C.331, subd. 1,* and, in the case of eligible children, from the federal government under Title IV–E of the Social Security Act, *42 U.S.C. § 670 et al.* Federal reimbursement to counties for the cost of foster care in Minnesota is about 50% of the cost and offers the opportunity for significant savings to counties. One of the requirements for federal reimbursement is that the agency be the entity responsible for selecting the placement. The federal regulation that accompanies Title IV–E states "FFP [Federal Financial Participation—that is, Title IV–E reimbursement] is not available when a court orders a placement with a specific foster care provider." *See 45 CFR § 1356.21(g).* The Minnesota Department of Human Services recommends that orders for specific placements be limited to help ensure that Title IV–E reimbursements are not jeopardized. *See Minn. Dept. of Human Servs., Bull. No. 01–68–04, Title IV–E Updates (Apr. 11, 2001).* The only specific authority under Minnesota's statutes for the court to order a particular placement is *Minn. Stat. § 260C.193, subd. 3,* which permits the court to order a child placed with a relative who qualifies to be licensed if the agency has not made efforts to locate a relative as required under *Minn. Stat. § 260C.212, subd. 5.* For these reasons, Rule 30.10 omits any requirement that the court order the child placed in a particular facility or with a particular relative.

2008 Advisory Committee Comment

Notice to Indian Child's Parent, Indian Custodian, and Indian Tribe Required under ICWA. See the 2008 Advisory Committee Comment following Rule 34.03 for information about the notice required under the Indian Child Welfare Act (ICWA) to be provided to the Indian child's parent, Indian custodian, and Indian tribe, including timing of the notice and time to respond.

Emergency Protective Care Placement Pending ICWA Notice. While both the ICWA and Minnesota law require notice to the Indian child's parent or Indian custodian and Indian child's tribe regarding the juvenile protection proceeding, 25 U.S.C. § 1922 provides that a state may take emergency action to protect an Indian child who is domiciled or resides on a reservation but is temporarily located off the reservation. While there is no such explicit provision in the ICWA regarding an Indian child who is not domiciled on or a resident of a reservation, by analogy there is general recognition that the state may take emergency action to protect an Indian child who is not domiciled on or resident of a reservation. It is not possible to send the ICWA notice referred to in Rule 32.06 and meet the timing requirements of 25 U.S.C. § 1912(a) before the emergency removal hearing. The ICWA notice that the court will direct be provided under Rule 30.10(f) is required under Rule 32.06 before the Admit/Deny Hearing may be held. The timing of the Admit/Deny Hearing in matters governed by the ICWA may be different due to the notice requirement of Rule 32.06.

Historical Notes

The order of the Minnesota Supreme Court [C1–01–927] dated June 10, 2009, amending the Rules of Juvenile Protection Procedure and the Rules of Adoption Procedure, provides in part that the amendments are effective August 1, 2009, and shall apply to all actions or proceedings pending on or commenced on or after the effective date.

The order of the Minnesota Supreme Court [C1–01–927] dated November 12, 2003, amending Rules 37 to 82 of the Rules of Juvenile Procedure and renumbering them as Rules 1 to 47 of the Rules of Juvenile Protection Procedure, provides in part that the amendments are effective January 1, 2004, and shall apply to all juvenile protection matters filed on or after that date.

Rule 30.11. Protective Care Review

Subd. 1. Consent for Continued Protective Care. The court may, with the consent of the parties and the county attorney, order that the child continue in protective care even if the circumstances of the parent, legal custodian, or child have changed.

Subd. 2. Release from Protective Care on Consent of Parties and the County Attorney. The court may, with the consent of the parties and the county attorney, order that a child be released from protective care. If the child has no guardian ad litem, the court may not release the child from protective care without a court hearing.

Subd. 3. Formal Review.

(a) *On Motion of Court.* The court may on its own motion schedule a formal review hearing at any time.

(b) *On Request of a Party or the County Attorney.* A party or the county attorney may request a formal hearing concerning continued protective care by filing a motion with the court. The court shall schedule a hearing and provide notice pursuant to Rule 32 if the motion states:

(1) that the moving party has new evidence concerning whether the child should be continued in protective care; or

(2) that the party has an alternate arrangement to provide for the safety and protection of the child.

(c) *Evidence.* The court may admit any evidence, including reliable hearsay and opinion evidence, which is relevant to the decision whether to continue protective care of the child or return the child home. Privileged communications may be admitted in accordance with Minnesota Statutes § 626.556, subd. 8.

(d) *Findings and Order.* At the conclusion of the formal review hearing the court shall:

(1) return the child to the care of the parent or legal custodian with or without reasonable conditions of release if the court does not make findings pursuant to subdivision 3(d)(2);

(2) continue the child in protective care or release the child with conditions to assure the safety of the child or others if the court finds that the petition states a prima facie case to believe that a child protection matter exists and that the child is the subject of that matter, and (a) the child or others would be immediately endangered by the child's actions if the child were released to the care of the parent or legal custodian or (b) the child's health, safety or welfare would be immediately endangered if the child were released to the care of the parent or legal custodian; or

(3) modify the conditions of release.

Amended Nov. 12, 2003.

Historical Notes

The order of the Minnesota Supreme Court [C1-01-927] dated November 12, 2003, amending Rules 37 to 82 of the Rules of Juvenile Procedure and renumbering them as Rules 1 to 47 of the Rules of Juvenile Protection Procedure, provides in part that the amendments are effective January 1, 2004, and shall apply to all juvenile protection matters filed on or after that date.

Rule 30.12. Notification When Child Returned Home

If the parents comply with the conditions of the court order and the child is returned home, including under protective supervision, the county attorney shall immediately file with the court and serve upon all parties a notice stating the date the child was returned home.

Adopted Nov. 12, 2003.

Historical Notes

The order of the Minnesota Supreme Court [C1-01-927] dated November 12, 2003, amending Rules 37 to 82 of the Rules of Juvenile Procedure and renumbering them as Rules 1 to 47 of the Rules of Juvenile Protection Procedure, provides in part that the amendments are effective January 1, 2004, and shall apply to all juvenile protection matters filed on or after that date.

RULE 31. METHODS OF FILING AND SERVICE

Rule 31.01. Types of Filing

Subd. 1. Generally. Any paper may be filed with the court either personally, by U.S. mail, or by facsimile transmission.

Subd. 2. Filing by Facsimile Transmission.

(a) Any paper may be filed with the court by facsimile transmission. Filing shall be deemed complete at the time that the facsimile transmission is received by the court. The facsimile shall have the same force and effect as the original. Only facsimile transmission equipment that satisfies the published criteria of the supreme court shall be used for filing in accordance with this rule.

(b) Within five (5) days after the court has received the transmission, the party filing the document shall forward the following to the court:

(1) a $25 transmission fee for each 50 pages, or part thereof, of the filing, unless otherwise provided by statute or rule or otherwise ordered by the court;

(2) any bulky exhibits or attachments; and

(3) the applicable filing fee or fees, if any.

(c) If a paper is filed by facsimile, the sender's original must not be filed but must be maintained in the files of the party transmitting it for filing and made available to the court or any party to the action upon request.

(d) Upon failure to comply with the requirements of this rule, the court in which the action is pending may make such orders as are just including, but not limited to, an order striking pleadings or parts thereof, staying further proceedings until compliance is complete, or dismissing the action, proceeding, or any part thereof.

Amended Nov. 12, 2003; Dec. 1, 2006, eff. Jan. 1, 2007.

2006 Advisory Committee Comment

Rule 31.01, subd. 2, regarding facsimile filing is amended in format and substance consistent with the amendments made to the Rules of Civil Procedure. Specifically, it is amended to delete the requirement that an "original" document follow the filing by facsimile. The requirement of a double filing causes confusion and unnecessary burdens for court administrators, and with the dramatic improvement in quality of received faxes since initial implementation of the Civil Rule in 1988, it no longer serves a useful purpose. Under the amended rule, the document filed by facsimile is the original for all purposes unless an issue arises as to its authenticity, in which case the version transmitted electronically and retained by the sender can be reviewed.

The filing fee for fax filings is changed from $5.00 to $25.00 because fax filings, even under the streamlined procedures of the amended rule, still impose significant administrative burdens on court staff, and it is therefore appropriate that this fee, unchanged since its adoption in the Rules of Civil Procedure in 1988, be increased. A number of committee members expressed the view that facsimile filing was, and still is, intended to be a process used on a limited basis in exigent or at least unusual circumstances. It is not intended to be a routine filing method.

The rule does not provide a specific mechanism for collecting the transmission fee required under the rule. Because prejudice may occur to a party if a filing is deemed ineffective, the court should determine the appropriate consequences of failure to pay the necessary fee.

Historical Notes

The order of the Minnesota Supreme Court [C1-01-927] dated November 12, 2003, amending Rules 37 to 82 of the Rules of Juvenile Procedure and renumbering them as Rules 1 to 47 of the Rules of Juvenile Protection Procedure, provides in part that the amendments are effective January 1, 2004, and shall apply to all juvenile protection matters filed on or after that date.

Rule 31.02. Types of Service

Subd. 1. Personal Service. Personal service means personally delivering the original document to the person to be served or leaving it at the person's home or usual place of abode with a person of suitable age and discretion residing therein, unless the court authorizes service by publication. Unless otherwise provided by these rules or ordered by the court, the sheriff or other person not less than 18 years of age and not a party to the action may make personal service of a summons or other process. The social services reports and guardian ad litem reports required under Rule 38 may be served directly by the social worker and guardian ad litem.

(a) *Personal Service Outside State.* Personal service of a summons outside the state, proved by the affidavit of the person making the same sworn to before a person authorized to administer an oath, shall have the same effect as the published notice.

(b) *Service Outside United States.* Unless otherwise provided by law, service upon an individual, other than an infant or an incompetent person, may be effected in a place not within the state:

(1) by any internationally agreed means reasonably calculated to give notice, such as those means authorized by the Hague Convention on the Service Abroad of Judicial and Extrajudicial Documents; or

(2) if there is no internationally agreed means of service or the applicable international agreement allows other means of service, provided that service is reasonably calculated to give notice:

(a) in the manner prescribed by the law of the foreign country for service in that country in an action in any of its courts of general jurisdiction; or

(b) as directed by the foreign authority in response to a letter rogatory or letter of request; or

(c) unless prohibited by the law of the foreign country, by:

(i) delivery to the individual personally of a copy of the summons and the complaint; or

(ii) any form of mail requiring a signed receipt, to be addressed and dispatched by the court administrator to the party to be served; or

(3) by other means not prohibited by international agreement as may be directed by the court.

Subd. 2. U.S. Mail. Service by U.S. Mail means placing a copy of the document in the U.S. mail, first class, postage prepaid, addressed to the person to be served.

Subd. 3. Publication. Service by publication means the publication in full of the summons, notice, or other papers in the regular issue of a qualified newspaper, once each week for the number of weeks specified pursuant to Rule 32.02. Service by publication substitutes for personal service where authorized by the court. The court shall authorize service by publication only if the petitioner has filed a written statement or affidavit describing unsuccessful efforts to locate the party to be served.

Subd. 4. Facsimile Service. Service by facsimile means transmission by facsimile equipment that satisfies the published criteria of the supreme court, addressed to the person to be served.

Amended Nov. 12, 2003; Dec. 1, 2006, eff. Jan. 1, 2007.

Historical Notes

The order of the Minnesota Supreme Court [C1-01-927] dated November 12, 2003, amending Rules 37 to 82 of the Rules of Juvenile Procedure and renumbering them as Rules 1 to 47 of the Rules of Juvenile Protection Procedure, provides in part that the amendments are effective January 1, 2004, and shall apply to all juvenile protection matters filed on or after that date.

Rule 31.03. Service by Facsimile Transmission

Unless these rules require personal service, by agreement of the parties any document may be served by facsimile transmission. The facsimile shall have the same force and effect as the original.

Amended Nov. 12, 2003.

Historical Notes

The order of the Minnesota Supreme Court [C1-01-927] dated November 12, 2003, amending Rules 37 to 82 of the Rules of Juvenile Procedure and renumbering them as Rules 1 to 47 of the Rules of Juvenile Protection Procedure, provides in part that the amendments are effective January 1, 2004, and shall apply to all juvenile protection matters filed on or after that date.

Rule 31.04. Service Upon Counsel; Social Services Agency

Unless personal service upon a party is required, service upon counsel for a party or counsel for a participant shall be deemed service upon the party or participant. Service upon the county attorney shall be deemed to be service upon the responsible social services agency. Reports and other documents that are not court orders shall not be served directly upon a represented party.

Amended Nov. 12, 2003; Dec. 1, 2006, eff. Jan. 1, 2007.

Historical Notes

The order of the Minnesota Supreme Court [C1-01-927] dated November 12, 2003, amending Rules 37 to 82 of the Rules of Juvenile Procedure and renumbering them as Rules 1 to 47 of the Rules of Juvenile Protection Procedure, provides in part that the amendments are effective January 1, 2004, and shall apply to all juvenile protection matters filed on or after that date.

Rule 31.05. Service of Subpoena

A subpoena requiring the attendance of a witness at a hearing or trial may be served at any place within the state

Amended Nov. 12, 2003.

Historical Notes

The order of the Minnesota Supreme Court [C1-01-927] dated November 12, 2003, amending Rules 37 to 82 of the Rules of Juvenile Procedure and renumbering them as Rules 1 to 47 of the Rules of Juvenile Protection Procedure, provides in part that the amendments are effective January 1, 2004, and shall apply to all juvenile protection matters filed on or after that date.

Rule 31.06. Completion of Service

Service by mail is complete upon mailing to the last known address of the person to be served. Service by facsimile is complete upon completion of the facsimile transmission.

Amended Nov. 12, 2003.

Historical Notes

The order of the Minnesota Supreme Court [C1-01-927] dated November 12, 2003, amending Rules 37 to 82 of the Rules of Juvenile Procedure and renumbering them as Rules 1 to 47 of the Rules of Juvenile Protection Procedure, provides in part that the amendments are effective January 1, 2004, and shall apply to all juvenile protection matters filed on or after that date.

Rule 31.07. Proof of Service

Subd. 1. Generally. On or before the date set for appearance, the person serving the document shall file with the court a notarized affidavit of service stating:

(a) whether the document was served;

(b) the method of service;

(c) the name of the person served; and

(d) the date and place of service.

Subd. 2. Exceptions.

(a) *Social Worker and Guardian Ad Litem Court Reports.* Social workers and guardians ad litem are not required to file proof of service when serving the court reports required under Rule 38 and, instead, shall include with their report a non-notarized certificate of distribution stating:

(1) the name of the person served,

(2) the method of service,

(3) the date and place of service, and

(4) the name of the person submitting the certificate of distribution.

(b) *Court Administrators.* If the court administrator served the document, the court administrator may file a written statement in lieu of an affidavit.

Amended Nov. 12, 2003; Dec. 1, 2006, eff. Jan. 1, 2007.

Historical Notes

The order of the Minnesota Supreme Court [C1-01-927] dated November 12, 2003, amending Rules 37 to 82 of the Rules of Juvenile Procedure and renumbering them as Rules 1 to 47 of the Rules of Juvenile Protection Procedure, provides in part that the amendments are effective January 1, 2004, and shall apply to all juvenile protection matters filed on or after that date.

RULE 32. SUMMONS AND NOTICE

Rule 32.01. Commencement

A juvenile protection matter is commenced by filing a petition with the court.

Amended Nov. 12, 2003.

Historical Notes

The order of the Minnesota Supreme Court [C1-01-927] dated November 12, 2003, amending Rules 37 to 82 of the Rules of Juvenile Procedure and renumbering them as Rules 1 to 47 of the Rules of Juvenile Protection Procedure, provides in part that the amendments are effective January 1, 2004, and shall apply to all juvenile protection matters filed on or after that date.

Rule 32.02. Summons

Subd. 1. Definition. A summons is a document issued by the court that orders the initial appearance in court of the person to whom it is directed.

Subd. 2. Upon Whom; Cost.

(a) *Generally.* The court shall serve a summons and petition upon each party identified in Rule 21, except as provided in subdivision 3(b), and upon any other person whose presence the court deems necessary to a determination concerning the best interests of the child. The cost of service of a summons and petition filed by someone other than a non-profit or public agency shall be paid by the petitioner.

(b) *Termination of Parental Rights Matters.* In addition to the requirements of subdivision 2(a), in any termination of parental rights matter the court administrator shall serve the summons and petition upon the county attorney, any guardian ad litem for the child's legal custodian, and any attorney representing a party in an ongoing child in need of protection or services proceeding involving the subject child.

Subd. 3. Service.

(a) *Generally.* Unless the court orders service by publication pursuant to Rule 31.02, subd. 3, the summons and petition shall be personally served upon the child's parent or legal custodian, and the summons shall be served personally or by U.S. mail upon all other parties and attorneys.

(b) *Habitual Truant, Runaway, and Prostitution Matters.*

(1) **Initial Service.** Notwithstanding the requirements of subdivisions 2(a) and 3(a), when the sole allegation is that the child is a habitual truant, a runaway, or engaged in prostitution, initial service may be made as follows:

(i) in lieu of a summons, the court may send a notice of hearing and a copy of the petition by U.S. mail to the legal custodian, the person with custody or control of the child, and each party and participant; or

(ii) a peace officer may issue a notice to appear or a citation.

(2) **Failure to Appear.** If the child or the child's parent or legal custodian or the person with custody or control of the child fails to appear in response to the initial service, the court shall order such person to be personally served with a summons.

(c) *Voluntary Placement—Service by Mail.* In all cases involving a voluntary placement of a child pursuant to Rule 44, the summons shall be served by U.S. mail upon the parent or legal custodian.

Subd. 4. Content.

(a) *Generally.* A summons shall contain or have attached:

(1) a copy of the petition, court order, motion, affidavit or other legal documents not previously provided; however, these documents shall not be contained in or attached to the summons and complaint if the court has authorized service of the summons by publication pursuant to Rule 32.02, subd. 3(a);

(2) a statement of the time and place of the hearing;

(3) a statement describing the purpose of the hearing;

(4) a statement explaining the right to representation pursuant to Rule 25; and

(5) a statement that failure to appear may result in:

(i) the child being removed from home pursuant to a child in need of protection or services petition;

(ii) the parent's parental rights being permanently severed pursuant to a termination of parental rights petition;

(iii) permanent transfer of the child's legal and physical custody to a relative;

(iv) a finding that the statutory grounds set forth in the petition have been proved; and

(v) an order granting the relief requested.

(b) *Child in Need of Protection or Services Matters.* In addition to the content requirements set forth in subdivision 4(a), in any child in need of protection or services matter the summons shall also contain or have attached a statement pursuant to Rule 18.01 that:

(1) if the person summoned fails to appear, the court may conduct the hearing in the person's absence; and

(2) a possible consequence of the hearing is that the child may be removed from the home of the parent or legal custodian and placed in foster care, and such removal may lead to other proceedings for permanent out-of-home placement of the child or termination of parental rights.

(c) *Termination of Parental Rights Matters.* In addition to the content requirements set forth in subdivision 4(a), in any termination of parental rights matter the summons shall also contain or have attached a statement pursuant to Rule 18.01 that if the person summoned fails to appear the court may conduct the hearing in the person's absence and the hearing may result in termination of the person's parental rights.

(d) *Permanent Placement Matters.* In addition to the content requirements set forth in subdivision 4(a), in any permanent placement matter the summons shall also contain or have attached a statement pursuant to Rule 18.01 that if the person summoned fails to appear the court may conduct the hearing in the person's absence and the hearing may result in an order granting the relief requested in the petition.

Subd. 5. Timing of Service of Summons and Petition.

(a) *Generally.* The summons and petition shall be served either at or before the emergency protective care hearing held pursuant to Rule 30, or at least three (3) days prior to the admit/deny hearing, whichever is earlier. At the request of a party, the hearing shall not be held at the scheduled time if the summons and petition have been served less than three (3) days before the hearing. If service is made outside the state or by publication, the summons shall be personally served, mailed, or last published at least ten (10) days before the hearing. In cases where publication of a child in need of protection or services petition is ordered, published notice shall be made one time with the last publication at least ten (10) days before the date of the hearing. Service by publication shall be made pursuant to Rule 31.02, subd. 3.

(b) *Termination of Parental Rights Matters and Permanent Placement Matters.* In any termination of parental rights matter or permanent placement matter the summons and petition shall be served upon all parties in a manner that will allow for completion of service at least ten (10) days prior to the date set for the admit/deny hearing. In cases where publication of a termination of parental rights or other permanency summons is ordered, published notice shall be made once per week for three (3) weeks with the last publication at least ten (10) days before the date of the hearing. Pursuant to Minnesota Statutes § 260C.307, subd. 3, notice sent by certified mail to the last known address shall be mailed at least twenty (20) days before the date of the hearing. Service by publication shall be made pursuant to Rule 31.02, subd. 3.

Subd. 6. Waiver. Service is waived by voluntary appearance in court or by a written waiver of service filed with the court.

Subd. 7. Failure to Appear. If any person personally served with a summons or subpoena fails, without reasonable cause, to appear or bring the child if ordered to do so, or if the court has reason to believe the person is avoiding personal service, the court may sua sponte or upon the motion of a party or the county attorney pursuant to Rule 15proceed against the person for contempt of court or the court may issue a warrant for the person's arrest, or both. When it appears to the court that service will be ineffectual, or that the welfare of the child requires that the child be immediately brought into the custody of the court, the court may issue a warrant for immediate custody of the child.

Amended Nov. 12, 2003; Dec. 1, 2006, eff. Jan. 1, 2007.

1999 Advisory Committee Comment—2003 Amendments

Rule 32.02 specifies the procedure for summoning a party to his or her first appearance in a case. Rule 32.03 specifies the procedure for providing initial notice to a participant. While failure to notify a non-legal custodial parent does not create a jurisdictional defect, the best practice is to invite that parent to participate in the proceedings, as failure to do so may create substantial barriers to permanency.

Historical Notes

The order of the Minnesota Supreme Court [C1-01-927] dated November 12, 2003, amending Rules 37 to 82 of the Rules of Juvenile Procedure and renumbering them as Rules 1 to 47 of the Rules of Juvenile Protection Procedure, provides in part that the amendments are effective January 1, 2004, and shall apply to all juvenile protection matters filed on or after that date.

Rule 32.03. Notice of Emergency Protective Care or Admit/Deny Hearing

Subd. 1. Definition. A notice is a document issued by the court notifying the person to whom it is addressed of the specific time and place of a hearing.

Subd. 2. Upon Whom.

(a) *Emergency Protective Care Hearing.* If the initial hearing is an emergency protective care hearing, written notice is not required to be served. Instead, the court administrator, or designee, shall use whatever method is available to inform all parties and participants identified by the petitioner in the petition, and their attorneys, of the date, time, and location of the hearing.

(b) *Admit/Deny Hearing.* If the initial hearing is an admit/deny hearing, the court administrator shall serve a summons and petition upon all parties identified in Rule 21, and a notice of hearing and petition upon all participants identified in Rule 22, the county attorney, any attorney representing a party in the matter, and the child through the child's attorney, if represented, or the child's physical custodian.

Subd. 3. Content. A notice shall contain or have attached:

(a) a copy of the petition, but only if it is the initial hearing or the person has intervened or been joined as a party and previously has not been served with a copy of the petition;

(b) a statement of the time and place of the hearing;

(c) a statement describing the purpose of the hearing;

(d) a statement explaining the right to representation pursuant to Rule 25;

(e) a statement explaining intervention as of right and permissive intervention pursuant to Rule 23;

(f) a statement pursuant to Rule 18.01 that failure to appear may result in:

(1) the child being removed from home pursuant to a child in need of protection or services petition;

(2) the parent's parental rights being permanently severed pursuant to a termination of parental rights petition;

(3) permanent transfer of the child's legal and physical custody to a relative;

(4) a finding that the statutory grounds set forth in the petition have been proved; and

(5) an order granting the relief requested; and

(g) a statement that it is the responsibility of the individual to notify the court administrator of any change of address.

Subd. 4. Service by Mail or Delivery at Hearing. Notice shall be served by U.S. Mail or may be delivered at a hearing. The court may order service of notice to be by personal service.

Amended Nov. 12, 2003; Dec. 1, 2006, eff. Jan. 1, 2007; June 10, 2009, eff. Aug. 1, 2009.

1999 Advisory Committee Comment—2003 Amendments

Rule 32.02 specifies the procedure for summoning a party to his or her first appearance in a case. Rule 32.03 specifies the procedure for providing initial notice to a participant. While failure to notify a non-legal custodial parent does not create a jurisdictional defect, the best practice is to invite that parent to participate in the proceedings as failure to do so may create substantial barriers to permanency.

Historical Notes

The order of the Minnesota Supreme Court [C1–01–927] dated June 10, 2009, amending the Rules of Juvenile Protection Procedure and the Rules of Adoption Procedure, provides in part that the amendments are effective August 1, 2009, and shall apply to all actions or proceedings pending on or commenced on or after the effective date.

The order of the Minnesota Supreme Court [C1-01-927] dated November 12, 2003, amending Rules 37 to 82 of the Rules of Juvenile Procedure and renumbering them as Rules 1 to 47 of the Rules of Juvenile Protection Procedure, provides in part that the amendments are effective January 1, 2004, and shall apply to all juvenile protection matters filed on or after that date.

Rule 32.04. Notice of Subsequent Hearings

For each hearing following the emergency protective care or admit/deny hearing, the court administrator shall serve upon each party, participant, and attorney a written notice of the date, time, and location of the next hearing. Such notice shall be delivered at the close of each hearing or mailed at least five (5) days before the date of the hearing or ten (10) days before the date of the hearing if mailed to an address outside the state. If written notice is delivered at the end of the hearing, later written notice is not required.

Adopted Nov. 12, 2003. Amended Dec. 1, 2006, eff. Jan. 1, 2007.

Historical Notes

The order of the Minnesota Supreme Court [C1-01-927] dated November 12, 2003, amending Rules 37 to 82 of the Rules of Juvenile Procedure and renumbering them as Rules 1 to 47 of the Rules of Juvenile Protection Procedure, provides in part that the amendments are effective January 1, 2004, and shall apply to all juvenile protection matters filed on or after that date.

Rule 32.05. Orders on the Record

An oral order stated on the record directed to the parties which either separately or with written supplementation contains the information required by this rule is sufficient to provide notice and compel the presence of the parties at a stated time and place. Such an order shall be reduced to writing pursuant to Rule 10.

Amended Nov. 12, 2003.

Historical Notes

The order of the Minnesota Supreme Court [C1-01-927] dated November 12, 2003, amending Rules 37 to 82 of the Rules of Juvenile Procedure and renumbering them as Rules 1 to 47 of the Rules of Juvenile Protection Procedure, provides in part that the amendments are effective January 1, 2004, and shall apply to all juvenile protection matters filed on or after that date.

Rule 32.06. Petitioner's Notice Responsibility Under Indian Child Welfare Act

Pursuant to 25 U.S.C. § 1912(a), in any juvenile protection proceeding where the court knows or has reason to know that an Indian child is involved, the party seeking the foster care placement of, or termination of parental rights to, an Indian child shall notify the parent or Indian custodian and the Indian child's tribe of the pending proceedings and of the right of intervention pursuant to Rule 23. Such notice shall be by registered mail with return receipt requested, unless personal service has been accomplished. If the identity or location of the parent or Indian custodian and the tribe cannot be determined, such notice shall be given to the Secretary of the Interior in like manner, who shall have fifteen (15) days after receipt to provide the requisite notice to the parent or Indian custodian and the tribe. No foster care placement or termination of parental rights proceeding shall be held until at least ten (10) days after receipt of notice by the parent or Indian custodian and the tribe or the Secretary of the Interior, provided that the parent or Indian custodian or the tribe shall, upon request, be granted up to twenty (20) additional days to prepare for such proceeding. The original or a copy of each notice shall be filed with the court together with any return receipts or other proof of service.

Amended Nov. 12, 2003; Dec. 1, 2006, eff. Jan. 1, 2007; June 10, 2009, eff. Aug. 1, 2009.

2008 Advisory Committee Comments

Notice to Indian Child's Parent, Indian Custodian, and Indian Tribe Required under ICWA. See the 2008 Advisory Committee Comment following Rule 34.03 for information about the notice required under the Indian Child Welfare Act (ICWA) to be provided to the Indian child's parent, Indian custodian, and Indian tribe, including timing of the notice and time to respond.

Content of ICWA Notice. The *Bureau of Indian Affairs Guidelines for State Courts: Indian Child Custody Proceedings* (*BIA Guidelines*) provides as follows regarding the content of the notice required to be provided under Rule 32.06 to the Indian child's parent or Indian custodian and the Indian child's tribe:

"Notice Requirements

"a. In any involuntary child custody proceeding, the state court shall make inquiries to determine if the child involved is a member of an Indian tribe or if a parent of the child is a member of an Indian tribe and the child is eligible for membership in an Indian tribe.

"b. In any involuntary Indian child custody proceeding, notice of the proceeding shall be sent to the parents and Indian custodians, if any, and to any tribes that may be the Indian child's tribe by registered mail with return receipt requested. The notice shall be written in clear and understandable language and include the following information:

"i. The name of the Indian child.

"ii. His or her tribal affiliation.

"iii. A copy of the petition, complaint or other document by which the proceeding was initiated.

"iv. The name of the petitioner and the name and address of the petitioner's attorney.

"v. A statement of the right of the biological parents or Indian custodians and the Indian child's tribe to intervene in the proceeding.

"vi. A statement that if the parents or Indian custodians are unable to afford counsel, counsel will be appointed to represent them.

"vii. A statement of the right of the natural parents or Indian custodians and the Indian child's tribe to have, on request, twenty days (or such additional time as may be permitted under state law) to prepare for the proceedings.

"viii. The location, mailing address and telephone number of the court.

"ix. A statement of the right of the parents or Indian custodians or the Indian child's tribe to petition the court to transfer the proceeding to the Indian child's tribal court.

"x. The potential legal consequences of an adjudication on future custodial rights of the parents or Indian custodians.

"xi. A statement in the notice to the tribe that since child custody proceedings are usually conducted on a confidential basis, tribal officials should keep confidential the information contained in the notice concerning the particular proceeding and not reveal it to anyone who does not need the information in order to exercise the tribe's right under the Act."

BIA Guidelines, 44 Fed. Reg. 67584, 67588, 67591 at B.5 (Nov. 26, 1979).

Historical Notes

The order of the Minnesota Supreme Court [C1–01–927] dated June 10, 2009, amending the Rules of Juvenile Protection Procedure and the Rules of Adoption Procedure, provides in part that the amendments are effective August 1, 2009, and shall apply to all actions or proceedings pending on or commenced on or after the effective date.

The order of the Minnesota Supreme Court [C1-01-927] dated November 12, 2003, amending Rules 37 to 82 of the Rules of Juvenile Procedure and renumbering them as Rules 1 to 47 of the Rules of Juvenile Protection Procedure, provides in part that the amendments are effective January 1, 2004, and shall apply to all juvenile protection matters filed on or after that date.

RULE 33. PETITION

Rule 33.01. Drafting; Filing; Service

Subd. 1. Generally. A petition may be drafted and filed by the county attorney or any responsible person. A petition shall be served pursuant to Rule 32.02. If the petition contains any information under Rule 8.04 that is inaccessible to the public, the petitioner shall file with the court the original petition and a copy of the petition from which the inaccessible information has been redacted.

Subd. 2. Habitual Truant and Runaway Matters. A matter based solely on grounds that a child is a habitual truant or a runaway may be initiated by citation issued by a peace officer or school attendance officer. A citation shall contain:

(a) the name, address, date of birth, and race of the child;

(b) the name and address of the parent or legal custodian of the child;

(c) the offense alleged and a reference to the statute which is the basis for the charge; and

(d) the time and place the alleged offense was committed. In the event the child is alleged to be a runaway, the place where the offense was committed may be stated in the notice as either the child's parent's residence or lawful placement or where the child was found by the officer. In the event the child is alleged to be a habitual truant, the place where the offense was committed may be stated as the school or the place where the child was found by the officer.

Subd. 3. Termination of Parental Rights Matters.

(a) *Drafting.* A termination of parental rights petition may be drafted and filed by the county attorney or any responsible person.

(b) *Filing and Service.* Any termination of parental rights petition shall be filed in the child in need of protection or services file, if one exists. A petition shall be served pursuant to Rule 32.02.

(c) *Egregious Harm, Abandonment of an Infant, Previous Involuntary Termination of Parental Rights, or Previous Involuntary Transfer of Permanent Legal and Physical Custody Matters.* The county attorney shall file a termination of parental rights petition within thirty (30) days of the responsible social services agency determining that a child:

(1) has been subjected to egregious harm as defined in Minnesota Statutes § 260C.007, subd. 14;

(2) is the sibling of another child who was subjected to egregious harm by the parent;

(3) is an abandoned infant as defined in Minnesota Statutes § 260C.301, subd. 2;

(4) is a child of a parent whose parental rights to another child have been involuntarily terminated; or

(5) is the child of a parent whose custodial rights to another child have been involuntarily transferred to a relative under Minnesota Statutes § 260C.201, subd. 11, or similar law of another jurisdiction.

(d) *Joinder of Social Services Agency.* If the termination of parental rights petition has been filed by a party other than the responsible social services agency, that party shall join the responsible social services agency as a party pursuant to Rule 24.

(e) *Termination of Parental Rights or Other Permanency Petition.* The county attorney need not file a termination of parental rights petition if the county attorney files with the court:

(1) a petition for transfer of permanent legal and physical custody to a relative, including a determination that such transfer is in the best interests of the child; or

(2) a petition alleging the child and, where appropriate, the child's siblings to be in need of protection or services and such petition is accompanied by a case plan or out-of-home placement plan prepared by the responsible social services agency documenting a compelling reason why filing a termination of parental rights petition is not in the best interests of the child.

Subd. 4. Permanent Placement Matters.

(a) *Generally.* Any permanent placement petition required under Rule 42 shall be filed in the child in need of protection or services file, if one exists.

(b) *Filing by Whom; Service.* The county attorney shall file a permanent placement petition in juvenile court to determine the permanent placement of a child. The county attorney may seek any alternative permanent placement relief, and any other party may seek only termination of parental rights or transfer of permanent legal and physical custody to a relative. A party, including a guardian ad litem for the child, shall file a permanent placement petition if the party disagrees with the permanent placement determination set forth in the petitions filed by other parties. A petition shall be served pursuant to Rule 32.02.

Amended Nov. 12, 2003; Dec. 1, 2006, eff. Jan. 1, 2007.

1999 Advisory Committee Comment

If a child in need of protection or services matter is pending at the time a termination of parental rights matter is filed regarding the same child, the termination petition should be filed in the same file as the child in need of protection or services matter.

Historical Notes

The order of the Minnesota Supreme Court [C1-01-927] dated November 12, 2003, amending Rules 37 to 82 of the Rules of Juvenile Procedure and renumbering them as Rules 1 to 47 of the Rules of Juvenile Protection Procedure, provides in part that the amendments are effective January 1, 2004, and shall apply to all juvenile protection matters filed on or after that date.

Rule 33.02. Content

Subd. 1. Generally. Every petition filed with the court in a juvenile protection matter, or a sworn affidavit accompanying such petition, shall contain:

(a) a statement of facts that, if proven, would support the relief requested in the petition;

(b) the child's name, date of birth, race, gender, current address unless stating the address would endanger the child or seriously risk disruption of the current placement, and, if the child is believed to be an Indian child, the name of the child's tribe;

(c) the names, race, dates of birth, residences, and post office addresses of the child's parents when known, and, if the child is believed to be an Indian child, the name of the child's tribe;

(d) the name, residence, and post office address of the child's legal custodian, the person having custody or control of the child, the nearest known relative if no parent or legal custodian can be found, and, if the child is believed to be an Indian child, the name and post office address of the child's Indian custodian, if any, and the Indian custodian's tribal affiliation;

(e) the name, residence, and post office address of the spouse of the child;

(f) the statutory grounds on which the petition is based, together with a recitation of the relevant portion of the subdivision(s);

(g) a statement regarding the applicability of the Indian Child Welfare Act;

(h) the names and addresses of the parties identified in Rule 21, as well as a statement designating them as parties;

(i) the names and addresses of the participants identified in Rule 22, as well as a statement designating them as participants;

(j) if the child is believed to be an Indian child, a statement regarding:

(1) the specific actions that have been taken to prevent the child's removal from, and to safely return the child to, the custody of the parents or Indian custodian;

(2) whether the residence of the child is believed to be on an Indian reservation and, if so, the name of the reservation;

(3) whether the child is a ward of a tribal court and, if so, the name of the tribe; and

(4) whether the child's tribe has exclusive jurisdiction pursuant to 25 U.S.C. § 1911(a).

If any information required by subdivision 1 is unknown at the time of the filing of the petition, as soon as such information becomes known to the petitioner it shall be provided to the court and parties either orally on the record, by sworn affidavit, or by amended petition. If presented orally on the record, the court shall annotate the petition to reflect the updated information.

Subd. 2. Child in Need of Protection or Services Matters.

(a) *Petitions Drafted and Filed by County Attorney.* A child in need of protection or services matter is defined in Minnesota Statutes § 260C.007, subd. 6. All child in need of protection or services petitions shall be drafted and filed under the supervision of the county attorney, except as provided in Minnesota Statutes § 260C.141, subd. 1, and subdivision 2(b) of this rule.

(b) *Petitions Drafted and Filed By Others.*

(1) **Petition Form.** A child in need of protection or services petition filed by an individual who is not a county attorney or an agent of the Commissioner of Human Services shall be filed on a form developed by the state court administrator. Copies of the form shall be available from the court administrator in each county.

(2) **Additional Content Requirements for Petitions Not Filed by County Attorney.** In addition to the content requirements set forth in subdivision 1, a petition filed by an individual who is not a county attorney or an agent of the Commissioner of Human Services shall contain:

(i) a statement that the petitioner has reported the circumstances underlying the petition to the responsible social services agency and that protection or services were not provided to the child;

(ii) a statement, including court file numbers where possible, of pending juvenile or family court proceedings and prior or present juvenile or family court orders relating to the child;

(iii) a statement regarding the relationship of the petitioner to the child and to any other parties; and

(3) **Review by Court Administrator.** Any petition filed by an individual who is not a county attorney or an agent of the Commissioner of Human Services shall be reviewed by the court administrator before it is filed to determine whether it is complete. The court administrator may reject the petition as incomplete if it does not indicate that the petitioner has contacted the responsible social services agency.

(4) **Court Review.** Within three (3) days of the date a petition is filed by a person who is not a county attorney or an agent of the Commissioner of Human Services, the court shall review the petition. If the court determines that the petition and attachments establish a prima facie case that a child in need of protection or services matter exists and that the child is the subject of that matter, the court shall set the matter for an admit/deny hearing pursuant to Rule 34 and shall direct notice pursuant to Rule 32. The court shall not allow a petition to proceed if it appears that the sole purpose of the petition is to modify custody between the parents or if it fails to set forth the information required in subdivisions 1 and 2(b) of this rule.

(c) *Petition Based Upon Prima Facie Case.*

(1) **When Required.** In addition to the content requirements of subdivisions 1 and 2(b), a petition establishing a prima facie case that a child in need of protection or services matter exists and that the child is the subject of that matter shall be filed with the court:

(i) before the court may issue an ex parte order for emergency protective care pursuant to Rule 28; or

(ii) before an emergency protective care hearing is held pursuant to Rule 30 for a child taken into emergency protective care without a court order.

(2) **Manner.** The facts establishing a prima facie case that a child in need of protection or services matter exists and that the child is the subject of that matter may be set forth in writing in or with the petition, or in supporting affidavits, and may be supplemented by sworn testimony of witnesses taken before the court. If such testimony is taken, a note stating this fact shall be made by the court on the petition. The testimony shall be recorded pursuant to Rule 11.

Subd. 3. Termination of Parental Rights Matters.

(a) *Generally.* A termination of parental rights matter shall be entitled "Petition to Terminate Parental Rights" and shall conform to the requirements of Minnesota Statutes § 260C.141.

(b) *Petitions Drafted and Filed By Others.*

(1) **Petition Form.** A termination of parental rights petition filed by an individual who is not a county attorney or responsible social services agency shall be filed on a form developed by the state court administrator. Copies of the form shall be available from the court administrator in each county.

(2) **Additional Content Requirements for Petitions Not Filed by County Attorney.** In addition to the content requirements set forth in subdivision 1, a petition filed by an individual who is not a county attorney or an agent of the Commissioner of Human Services shall contain:

(i) a statement, including court file numbers where possible, of pending juvenile or family court proceedings and prior or present juvenile or family court orders relating to the child;

(ii) a statement regarding the relationship of the petitioner to the child and to any other parties; and

(iii) a statement identifying any past or pending cases involving the child or family that is the subject of the petition.

(3) **Review by Court Administrator.** Any petition filed by an individual who is not a county attorney or an agent of the Commissioner of Human Services shall be reviewed by the court administrator before it is filed to determine whether it is complete. The court administrator may reject the petition if incomplete.

(c) *Petitions Seeking Alternative Permanent Placement Relief.* In addition to the content requirements set forth in subdivision 1, any termination of parental rights petition filed by the county attorney or agent of the Commissioner of Human Services may seek alternative permanent placement relief, and any other party may seek only transfer of permanent legal and physical custody to a relative as the alternative to termination of parental rights. A petition seeking alternative permanent placement relief shall identify which proposed permanent placement option the petitioner believes is in the best interests of the child. A petition may seek separate permanent placement relief for each child named as a subject of the petition as long as the petition identifies which option(s) is sought for each child and why that option(s) is in the best interests of the child. At the admit/deny hearing on a petition that seeks alternative relief, each party shall identify on the record the permanent placement option that is in the best interests of the child.

Subd. 4. Permanent Placement Matters.

(a) *Captions and Title.* Each petition in a permanent placement matter, or a sworn affidavit accompanying each petition, shall contain a title denoting the permanent relief sought:

(1) A transfer of permanent legal and physical custody matter shall be entitled "Juvenile Protection Petition to Transfer Permanent Legal and Physical Custody" and shall name a fit and willing relative as a proposed permanent legal and physical custodian.

(2) A request for long-term foster care shall be entitled "Juvenile Protection Petition for Long–Term Foster Care."

(3) A request for foster care for a specified period of time for a child adjudicated to be in need of protection or services solely on the basis of the child's behavior shall be entitled "Juvenile Protection Petition for Foster Care for a Specific Period of Time."

(b) *Petitions Seeking Alternative Placement Relief.* Any permanent placement petition filed by the county attorney or agent of the Commissioner of Human Services may seek alternative permanent placement relief, including termination of parental rights, transfer of permanent legal and physical custody to a relative, or placement of the child in long-term foster care. Any permanent placement petition filed by a party who is not the county attorney or agent of the Commissioner of Human Services may seek only transfer of permanent legal and physical custody to a relative as the alternative to termination of parental rights. A petition seeking alternative permanent placement relief shall identify which permanent placement option the petitioner believes is in the best interests of the child. A petition may seek separate permanent placement relief for each child named as a subject of the petition as long as the petition identifies which option(s) is sought for each child and why that option is in the best interests of the child. At the admit/deny hearing on a petition that seeks alternative relief, each party shall identify on the record the permanent placement option that is in the best interests of the child. If another party files a permanent placement petition in response to the county's petition, it must be filed and served at least fifteen (15) days prior to the date of trial.

Subd. 5. Out of State Party. If a party resides out of state, or if there is likelihood of interstate litigation, the petition or an attached affidavit shall include a statement regarding the whereabouts of the party and any other information required by the Uniform Child Custody Jurisdiction and Enforcement Act, Minnesota Statutes § 518D.101 to § 518D.317.

Subd. 6. Disclosure of Name and Address—Endangerment. If there is reason to believe that an individual may be endangered by disclosure of a name or address required to be provided pursuant to this rule, that name or address may be provided to the court in a separate informational statement and shall not be accessible to the public or to the parties. Upon notice and motion, the court may disclose the name or address as it deems appropriate.

Amended Nov. 12, 2003; Dec. 1, 2006, eff. Jan. 1, 2007; Dec. 18, 2006, eff. Jan. 1, 2007; Jan. 4, 2007, eff. retroactive Jan. 1, 2007; June 10, 2009, eff. Aug. 1, 2009.

2008 Advisory Committee Comment

For a quote from the Indian Child Welfare Act (ICWA) that addresses "exclusive jurisdiction," see the 2008 Advisory Committee Comment following Rule 30.08.

Historical Notes

The order of the Minnesota Supreme Court [C1–01–927] dated June 10, 2009, amending the Rules of Juvenile Protection Procedure and the Rules of Adoption Procedure, provides in part that the amendments are effective August 1, 2009, and shall apply to all actions or proceedings pending on or commenced on or after the effective date.

The order of the Minnesota Supreme Court [C1-01-927] dated November 12, 2003, amending Rules 37 to 82 of the Rules of Juvenile Procedure and renumbering them as Rules 1 to 47 of the Rules of Juvenile Protection Procedure, provides in part that the amendments are effective January 1, 2004, and shall apply to all juvenile protection matters filed on or after that date.

Rule 33.03. Verification

A petition shall be verified by a person having knowledge of the facts and may be verified on information and belief.

Amended Nov. 12, 2003.

Historical Notes

The order of the Minnesota Supreme Court [C1-01-927] dated November 12, 2003, amending Rules 37 to 82 of the Rules of Juvenile Procedure and renumbering them as Rules 1 to 47 of the Rules of Juvenile Protection Procedure, provides in part that the amendments are effective January 1, 2004, and shall apply to all juvenile protection matters filed on or after that date.

Rule 33.04. Amendment

Subd. 1. Prior to Trial. The petition may be amended at any time prior to the commencement of the trial, including, in a child in need of protection or services matter, adding a child as the subject matter of the petition. The petitioner shall provide written or on-the-record notice of the amendment to all parties and participants. When the petition is amended, the court shall grant all other parties sufficient time to respond to the amendment.

Subd. 2. After Trial Begins. The petition may be amended after the trial has commenced if the court finds that the amendment does not prejudice a party and all parties are given sufficient time to respond to the proposed amendment. Upon receipt of approval from the court, the petitioner shall provide written or on-the-record notice of the proposed amendment to all parties and participants.

Amended Nov. 12, 2003; Dec. 1, 2006, eff. Jan. 1, 2007.

Historical Notes

The order of the Minnesota Supreme Court [C1-01-927] dated November 12, 2003, amending Rules 37 to 82 of the Rules of Juvenile

Procedure and renumbering them as Rules 1 to 47 of the Rules of Juvenile Protection Procedure, provides in part that the amendments are effective January 1, 2004, and shall apply to all juvenile protection matters filed on or after that date.

Rule 33.05. Timing

If a child is in emergency protective care pursuant to Rule 28, the petition shall be filed at or prior to the time of the emergency protective care hearing held pursuant to Rule 30.

Amended Nov. 12, 2003.

1999 Advisory Committee Comment

Minnesota Statutes § 260C.143 provides that a peace officer or school attendance officer may issue a notice to a child to appear in court and file the notice with the juvenile court.

Historical Notes

The order of the Minnesota Supreme Court [C1-01-927] dated November 12, 2003, amending Rules 37 to 82 of the Rules of Juvenile Procedure and renumbering them as Rules 1 to 47 of the Rules of Juvenile Protection Procedure, provides in part that the amendments are effective January 1, 2004, and shall apply to all juvenile protection matters filed on or after that date.

RULE 34. ADMIT/DENY HEARING

Rule 34.01. Generally

An admit/deny hearing is a hearing at which the statutory grounds set forth in the petition are admitted or denied pursuant to Rule 35.

Amended Nov. 12, 2003.

Historical Notes

The order of the Minnesota Supreme Court [C1-01-927] dated November 12, 2003, amending Rules 37 to 82 of the Rules of Juvenile Procedure and renumbering them as Rules 1 to 47 of the Rules of Juvenile Protection Procedure, provides in part that the amendments are effective January 1, 2004, and shall apply to all juvenile protection matters filed on or after that date.

Rule 34.02. Timing

Subd. 1. Child in Placement.

(a) *Generally.* When the child is placed out of the child's home by court order, an admit/deny hearing shall be held within ten (10) days of the date of the emergency protective care hearing. Upon agreement of the parties, an admit/deny hearing may be combined with an emergency protective care hearing held pursuant to Rule 30.

(b) *Termination of Parental Rights Matters.* In a termination of parental rights matter the admit/deny hearing shall be held not less than ten (10) days after service of the summons and petition is complete upon the party.

(c) *Permanent Placement Matters.* In a permanent placement matter the admit/deny hearing shall be held not less than ten (10) days after service of the summons and petition is complete upon the party.

(d) *Indian Child Welfare Act Matters.*

(1) **Parent's, Indian Custodian's or Tribe's Identity Known.** In matters governed by the Indian Child Welfare Act, 25 U.S.C. § 1901 et seq., the admit/deny hearing on a petition requesting the foster care placement of an Indian child, the permanent placement of an Indian child, or the termination of parental rights to an Indian child shall not be held until at least ten (10) days after receipt of the notice required under Rule 32.06, 25 U.S.C. § 1912(a), and Minnesota Statutes § 260.761, subd. 3. The parent, Indian custodian, or tribe shall, upon request, be granted up to twenty (20) additional days from receipt of the notice to prepare for the admit/deny hearing.

(2) **Parent's, Indian Custodian's, or Tribe's Identity Unknown.** If the identity or location of the parent or Indian custodian and the tribe cannot be determined, the notice required under Rule 32.06, 25 U.S.C. § 1912(a), and Minnesota Statutes § 260.761, subd. 3, shall be sent to the Secretary of the Interior who shall have fifteen (15) days to provide the requisite notice to the parent or Indian custodian and the tribe. The admit/deny hearing shall be held at least twenty-five (25) days after receipt of the notice by the Secretary. The parent, Indian custodian, or tribe shall, upon request, be granted up to twenty (20) additional days from receipt of the notice to prepare for the admit/deny hearing.

Subd. 2. Child Not in Placement.

(a) *Generally.* When the child is not placed outside the child's home by court order, an admit/deny hearing shall be held no sooner than five (5) days and no later than twenty (20) days after the parties have been served with the summons and petition.

(b) *Child's Behavior.* In matters where the sole allegation is that the child's behavior is the basis for the petition and the child is not in placement, an admit/deny hearing shall be commenced within a reasonable time after service of the summons and petition upon the child.

Subd. 3. Possession of Petition. The parties have the right to have a copy of the petition at least three (3) days before the admit/deny hearing.

Amended Nov. 12, 2003; Dec. 1, 2006, eff. Jan. 1, 2007; June 10, 2009, eff. Aug. 1, 2009.

Historical Notes

The order of the Minnesota Supreme Court [C1-01-927] dated June 10, 2009, amending the Rules of Juvenile Protection Procedure and the Rules of Adoption Procedure, provides in part that the amendments are effective August 1, 2009, and shall apply to all actions or proceedings pending on or commenced on or after the effective date.

The order of the Minnesota Supreme Court [C1-01-927] dated November 12, 2003, amending Rules 37 to 82 of the Rules of Juvenile Procedure and renumbering them as Rules 1 to 47 of the Rules of Juvenile Protection Procedure, provides in part that the amendments are effective January 1, 2004, and shall apply to all juvenile protection matters filed on or after that date.

Rule 34.03. Hearing Procedure

Subd. 1. Initial Procedure. At the commencement of the hearing the court shall on the record:

(a) verify the child's name, date of birth, race, gender, current address unless stating the address would endanger the child or seriously risk disruption of the current placement, and, if the child is believed to be an Indian child, the name of the child's tribe;

(b) inquire whether the child is an Indian child and, if so, determine whether the Indian child's tribe, parent, and Indian custodian have been notified;

(c) determine whether all parties are present and identify those present for the record;

(d) advise any child and the child's parent or legal custodian who appears in court and is not represented by counsel of the right to representation pursuant to Rule 25;

(e) determine whether notice requirements have been met and, if not, whether the affected person waives notice;

(f) if the child who is a party or the child's parent or legal custodian appears without counsel, explain basic trial rights;

(g) determine whether the child and the child's parent or legal custodian understand the statutory grounds and the factual allegations set forth in the petition and, if not, provide an explanation;

(h) explain the purpose of the hearing and the possible transfer of custody of the child from the parent or legal custodian to another, when such transfer is permitted by law and the permanency requirements of Minnesota Statutes § 260C.201, subd. 11;

(i) if the Admit/Deny Hearing is the first hearing in the juvenile protection matter, and if the court knows or has reason to know that the child is an Indian child, determine whether notice has been sent pursuant to Rule 32.06; 25 U.S.C. § 1912(a); and Minnesota Statutes § 260.761, subd. 3; and

(j) if the district court finds from review of the petition or other information that an Indian child is a ward of tribal court, pursuant to Rule 48.02, subd. 1, adjourn the hearing to consult with the tribal court regarding the safe and expeditious return of the child to the jurisdiction of the tribe and dismiss the juvenile protection matter.

Subd. 2. Child in Need of Protection or Services Matters.

(a) In each child in need of protection or services matter, after completing the initial inquiries set forth in subdivision 1, the court shall determine whether the petition establishes a prima facie showing that a juvenile protection matter exists and that the child is the subject of the matter, unless the prima facie determination was made at the emergency protective care hearing pursuant to Rule 30.08. The court shall dismiss the petition if it finds that the petition fails to establish a prima facie showing that a juvenile protection matter exists and that the child is the subject of that matter.

(b) In addition to the initial procedures set forth in subdivision 1, in each child in need of protection or services matter the court shall also advise all persons present that if the petition is proven and the child is not returned home:

(1) a permanency progress review hearing shall be held within six (6) months of the date of the child's placement in foster care or in the home of a noncustodial parent if the child was under eight (8) years of age at the time of the filing of the petition; and

(2) a permanent placement determination hearing shall be held within twelve (12) months of the date of the child's placement in foster care or in the home of a noncustodial parent.

Subd. 3. Termination of Parental Rights Matters.

(a) In each termination of parental rights matter, after completing the initial inquiries set forth in subdivision 1, the court shall determine whether the petition states a prima facie case in support of one or more statutory grounds set forth in the petition to terminate parental rights and a prima facie showing that a juvenile protection matter exists and that the child is the subject of the matter. The court shall dismiss the petition if it finds that the petition fails to establish a prima facie showing that a juvenile protection matter exists and that the child is the subject of that matter.

(b) When the petition alleges that reasonable efforts, or active efforts in the case of an Indian child, have been made to reunify the child with the parent or legal custodian, the court shall enter a separate finding regarding whether the factual allegations contained in the petition state a prima facie case that the agency has provided reasonable efforts, or active efforts in the-case of an Indian child, to reunify the child and the parent or legal custodian. In the alternative, the court may enter a finding that reasonable efforts, to reunify the child and the parent or legal custodian were not required under Minnesota Statutes § 260.012.

(c) If the court determines that the petition states a prima facie case in support of termination of parental rights, the court shall proceed pursuant to Rule 35. If the court determines that the petition fails to state a prima facie case in support of termination of parental rights, the court shall:

(i) return the child to the care of the parent or legal custodian;

(ii) give the petitioner ten (10) days to file an amended petition or supplementary information if the petitioner represents there are additional facts which, if presented to the court, would establish a prima facie case in support of termination of parental rights;

(iii) give the petitioner ten (10) days to file a child in need of protection or services petition; or

(iv) dismiss the petition.

Subd. 4. Permanent Placement Matters.

(a) In each permanent placement matter, after completing the initial inquiries set forth in subdivision 1, the court shall review the facts set forth in the petition, consider such argument as the parties may make, and determine whether the petition states a prima facie case in support of one or more of the permanent placement options.

(b) When the petition seeking permanent placement of the child away from the parent or legal custodian requires a determination by the court that reasonable efforts, or active efforts in the case of an Indian child, have been made to reunify the child with the parent or legal custodian, the court shall enter a separate finding regarding whether the factual allegations in the petition state a prima face case that the agency has provided reasonable efforts, or active efforts in the case of an Indian child, to reunify the child and the parent or legal custodian. In the alternative, the court may enter a finding that reasonable efforts were not required under Minnesota Statutes § 260.012.

(c) If the court determines that the petition states a prima facie case, the court shall proceed pursuant to Rule 35. If the court determines that the petition fails to state a prima facie case, the court may:

(i) return the child to the care of the parent;

(ii) give the petitioner ten (10) days to file an amended petition or supplementary information if the petitioner represents there are additional facts which, if presented to the court, would establish a prima facie case; or

(iii) dismiss the petition.

Subd. 5 Motions. The court shall hear any motions, made pursuant to Rule 15, addressed to the sufficiency of the petition or jurisdiction of the court without requiring any person to admit or deny the statutory grounds set forth in the petition prior to making a finding on the motion.

Amended Nov. 12, 2003; Dec. 1, 2006, eff. Jan. 1, 2007; June 26, 2007, eff. July 1, 2007; June 10, 2009, eff. Aug. 1, 2009.

1999 Advisory Committee Comment (amended 2003 and 2008)

Rule 34.03, subd. 2, is consistent with Minnesota Statutes § 260C.201, subd. 11, which provides that a permanency progress review hearing must be held within six (6) months of a child's removal from the home if the child is under eight (8) years of age at the time the petition is filed. The requirements of Rule 34.03, subds. 3 and 4, are consistent with federal requirements regarding the timing of reasonable efforts determinations and permanency hearings.

2008 Advisory Committee Comment

Notice to Indian Child's Parent, Indian Custodian, and Indian Tribe Required Under ICWA. For a juvenile protection matter involving an Indian child, the Indian Child Welfare Act (ICWA), 25 U.S.C. § 1912(a); Minnesota Statutes § 260.761, subd. 3; and Rule 32.06 require that notice of the proceeding and of the right to intervene in the proceeding shall be given by registered mail with return receipt requested to the Indian child's parent or Indian custodian and the Indian child's tribe by the person seeking foster care placement or termination of parental rights. Minnesota Statutes § 260.761, subd. 2, also requires notice to the Indian child's tribe whenever the agency's involvement with the Indian child could lead to out-of-home placement and requires agency involvement longer than thirty (30) days. This requirement supports the practice of early involvement of the child's Indian tribe in planning for the child's safety and services for the family.

Timing of ICWA Notice. The ICWA, 25 U.S.C. § 1912(a), provides that no foster care placement or termination of parental rights proceeding shall be held until at least ten (10) days after receipt of notice by the Indian child's parent or Indian custodian and the Indian child's tribe, provided that the parent or Indian custodian or the tribe shall, upon request, be granted up to twenty (20) additional days from receipt of the notice to prepare for such proceeding.

Emergency Protective Care Placement Pending ICWA Notice. See 2008 Advisory Committee Comment to Rule 30.10.

Historical Notes

The order of the Minnesota Supreme Court [C1–01–927] dated June 10, 2009, amending the Rules of Juvenile Protection Procedure and the Rules of Adoption Procedure, provides in part that the amendments are effective August 1, 2009, and shall apply to all actions or proceedings pending on or commenced on or after the effective date.

The order of the Minnesota Supreme Court [C1-01-927] dated November 12, 2003, amending Rules 37 to 82 of the Rules of Juvenile Procedure and renumbering them as Rules 1 to 47 of the Rules of Juvenile Protection Procedure, provides in part that the amendments are effective January 1, 2004, and shall apply to all juvenile protection matters filed on or after that date.

RULE 35. ADMISSION OR DENIAL

Rule 35.01. Generally

Subd. 1. Parent or Legal Custodian.

(a) *Generally.* Unless the child's parent or legal custodian is the petitioner, a parent who is a party or a legal custodian shall admit or deny the statutory grounds set forth in the petition or remain silent. If the parent or legal custodian denies the statutory grounds set forth in the petition or remains silent, or if the court refuses to accept an admission, the court shall enter a denial of the petition on the record.

(b) *Termination of Parental Rights Matters.* In a termination of parental rights matter, only the parents of the child are required to admit or deny the petition. A party who is not required to admit or deny the petition may object to the admission if that party has filed a petition pursuant to Rule 33.

(c) *Permanent Placement Matters.* In a permanent placement matter:

(1) Only the legal custodian of the child who is not the petitioner is required to admit or deny the petition. A party who is not required to admit or deny the petition may object to the entry of the proposed permanent placement order if that party has filed a petition pursuant to Rule 33.

(2) When there is a petition for transfer of permanent legal and physical custody to a relative who is not represented by counsel, the court may not enter an order granting the transfer of custody unless there is testimony from the proposed custodian establishing that the proposed custodian understands:

(i) the legal consequences of a transfer of permanent legal and physical custody;

(ii) the nature and amount of financial support and services that will be available to help care for the child;

(iii) how the custody order can be modified; and

(iv) any other permanent placement options available for the subject child.

Subd. 2. Child.

(a) *Generally.* Except as otherwise provided in this rule, the child shall not admit or deny the petition.

(b) *Child's Behavior.* In matters where the sole allegation is that the child's behavior is the basis for the petition, only the child shall admit or deny the statutory grounds set forth in the petition or remain silent.

Subd. 3. Contested Petition. Any party has the right to contest the basis of a petition. The county attorney has the right to contest the basis of a petition filed by an individual who is not a county attorney or an agent of the Commissioner of Human Services.

Amended Nov. 12, 2003; Dec. 1, 2006, eff. Jan. 1, 2007.

Historical Notes

The order of the Minnesota Supreme Court [C1-01-927] dated November 12, 2003, amending Rules 37 to 82 of the Rules of Juvenile Procedure and renumbering them as Rules 1 to 47 of the Rules of Juvenile Protection Procedure, provides in part that the amendments are effective January 1, 2004, and shall apply to all juvenile protection matters filed on or after that date.

Rule 35.02. Denial

Subd. 1. Denial Without Appearance. A written denial or a denial on the record of the statutory grounds set forth in a petition may be entered by counsel without the personal appearance of the person represented by counsel.

Subd. 2. Further Proceedings After Denial. When a denial by any party is entered, the court shall schedule further proceedings pursuant to Rule 36 or Rule 39.

Amended Nov. 12, 2003.

Historical Notes

The order of the Minnesota Supreme Court [C1-01-927] dated November 12, 2003, amending Rules 37 to 82 of the Rules of Juvenile Procedure and renumbering them as Rules 1 to 47 of the Rules of Juvenile Protection Procedure, provides in part that the amendments are effective January 1, 2004, and shall apply to all juvenile protection matters filed on or after that date.

Rule 35.03. Admission

Subd. 1. Admission Under Oath. Any admission must be made under oath.

Subd. 2. Admission Without Appearance. Upon approval of the court, a written admission of the statutory grounds set forth in the petition, made under oath, may be entered by counsel without personal appearance of the person represented by counsel.

Subd. 3. Questioning of Person Making Admission.

(a) *Generally.* Before accepting an admission the court shall determine on the record or by written document signed by the person admitting and the person's counsel, if represented, whether:

(1) the person admitting acknowledges an understanding of:

(i) the nature of the statutory grounds set forth in the petition;

(ii) if unrepresented, the right to representation pursuant to Rule 25;

(iii) the right to a trial;

(iv) the right to testify; and

(v) the right to subpoena witnesses; and

(2) the person admitting acknowledges an understanding that the facts being admitted establish the statutory grounds set forth in the petition.

(b) *Child in Need of Protection or Services Matters, and Habitual Truant, Runaway, and Prostitution Matters.* In addition to the questions set forth in subdivision 3(a), before accepting an admission in a child in need of protection or services matter or a matter alleging a child to be a habitual truant, a runaway, or engaged in prostitution, the court shall also determine on the record or by written document signed by the person admitting and the person's counsel, if represented, whether the person admitting acknowledged an understanding that:

(1) a possible effect of a finding that the statutory grounds are proved may be the transfer of legal custody of the child to another or other permanent placement option including termination of parental rights to the child; and

(2) if the child is in out-of-home placement, a permanency progress review hearing will be held within six (6) months of the date the child is ordered placed in foster care or in the home of a noncustodial parent if the child was under eight (8) years of age at the time of the filing of the petition, and a permanent placement determination hearing will be held within twelve (12) months of the date the child is ordered placed in foster care or in the home of a noncustodial parent.

Subd. 4. Basis for Admission. The court shall refuse to accept an admission unless there is a factual basis for the admission.

(a) *Full Admission.* A party may admit all of the statutory grounds set forth in the petition.

(b) *Partial Admission.* Pursuant to a Rule 19 settlement agreement, a person may admit some, but not all, of the statutory grounds set forth in the petition.

Subd. 5. Withdrawal of Admission. After filing a motion with the court:

(a) an admission may be withdrawn at any time upon a showing that withdrawal is necessary to correct a manifest injustice; or

(b) the court may allow a withdrawal of an admission before a finding on the petition for any fair and just reason.

Subd. 6. Acceptance or Non–Acceptance of Admission. At the time of the admission, the court shall make a finding that:

(a) the admission has been accepted and the statutory grounds admitted have been proved;

(b) the admission has been conditionally accepted pending the court's approval of a settlement agreement pursuant to Rule 19; or

(c) the admission has not been accepted.

Subd. 7. Further Proceedings. If the court makes a finding that the admission is accepted and the statutory grounds admitted are proved, or that the admission is conditionally accepted pending the court's approval of a settlement agreement pursuant to Rule 19, the court shall enter an order with respect to adjudication pursuant to Rule 40 and proceed to disposition. If the court makes a finding that the admission has not been accepted, the court shall schedule further proceedings pursuant to Rule 36 or Rule 39.

Amended Nov. 12, 2003; Dec. 1, 2006, eff. Jan. 1, 2007.

Historical Notes

The order of the Minnesota Supreme Court [C1-01-927] dated November 12, 2003, amending Rules 37 to 82 of the Rules of Juvenile Procedure and renumbering them as Rules 1 to 47 of the Rules of Juvenile Protection Procedure, provides in part that the amendments are effective January 1, 2004, and shall apply to all juvenile protection matters filed on or after that date.

RULE 36. PRETRIAL HEARING

Rule 36.01. Timing

The court shall convene a pretrial hearing at least ten (10) days prior to trial.

Amended Nov. 12, 2003; Dec. 1, 2006, eff. Jan. 1, 2007; June 10, 2009, eff. Aug. 1, 2009.

Historical Notes

The order of the Minnesota Supreme Court [C1–01–927] dated June 10, 2009, amending the Rules of Juvenile Protection Procedure and the Rules of Adoption Procedure, provides in part that the amendments are effective August 1, 2009, and shall apply to all actions or proceedings pending on or commenced on or after the effective date.

The order of the Minnesota Supreme Court [C1-01-927] dated November 12, 2003, amending Rules 37 to 82 of the Rules of Juvenile Procedure and renumbering them as Rules 1 to 47 of the Rules of Juvenile Protection Procedure, provides in part that the amendments are effective January 1, 2004, and shall apply to all juvenile protection matters filed on or after that date.

Rule 36.02. Purpose

The purposes of a pretrial hearing shall be to:

(a) determine whether a settlement of any or all of the issues has occurred or is possible;

(b) determine whether all parties have been served and, if not, review the efforts that have taken place to date to serve all parties;

(c) advise any child or the child's parent or legal custodian who appears in court and is unrepresented of the right to representation pursuant to Rule 25. If counsel is appointed at the pretrial hearing, the hearing shall be reconvened at a later date;

(d) determine whether the child shall be present and testify at trial and, if so, under what circumstances;

(e) identify any unresolved discovery matters;

(f) resolve any pending pretrial motions;

(g) identify and narrow issues of law and fact for trial, including identification of:

(1) the factual allegations admitted or denied;

(2) the statutory grounds admitted or denied;

(3) any stipulations to foundation and relevance of documents; and

(4) any other stipulations, admissions, or denials;

(h) exchange witness lists and a brief summary of each witness' testimony;

(i) exchange exhibit lists;

(j) confirm the trial date and estimate the length of trial;

(k) determine the need for, and date for submission of, proposed findings; and

(*l*) determine any other relevant issues.

Amended Nov. 12, 2003; Dec. 1, 2006, eff. Jan. 1, 2007; June 10, 2009, eff. Aug. 1, 2009.

1999 Advisory Committee Comment—2003 Amendments

Rule 36.02(d) addresses the need to determine whether the child will testify. The intent of the rule is to provide that an order protecting the child from testifying or placing conditions on the child's testimony can only be made after notice of motion and a hearing. The Committee intends that any such motion be heard and resolved at the pretrial conference.

Historical Notes

The order of the Minnesota Supreme Court [C1-01-927] dated June 10, 2009, amending the Rules of Juvenile Protection Procedure and the Rules of Adoption Procedure, provides in part that the amendments are effective August 1, 2009, and shall apply to all actions or proceedings pending on or commenced on or after the effective date.

The order of the Minnesota Supreme Court [C1-01-927] dated November 12, 2003, amending Rules 37 to 82 of the Rules of Juvenile Procedure and renumbering them as Rules 1 to 47 of the Rules of Juvenile Protection Procedure, provides in part that the amendments are effective January 1, 2004, and shall apply to all juvenile protection matters filed on or after that date.

Rule 36.03. Pretrial Order

The pretrial order shall be filed within ten (10) days of the hearing and shall include the information specified in Rule 36.02 and shall specify all factual allegations and statutory grounds admitted and denied.

Former Rule 36.02. Renumbered Rule 36.03 and amended Dec. 1, 2006, eff. Jan. 1, 2007; June 10, 2009, eff. Aug. 1, 2009.

Historical Notes

The order of the Minnesota Supreme Court [C1-01-927] dated June 10, 2009, amending the Rules of Juvenile Protection Procedure and the Rules of Adoption Procedure, provides in part that the amendments are effective August 1, 2009, and shall apply to all actions or proceedings pending on or commenced on or after the effective date.

Rule 36.04. Continuing Obligation to Update Information

From the date of the pretrial hearing through the date of trial, the parties shall have a continuing obligation to update information provided during the pretrial hearing.

Former Rule 36.02. Renumbered Rule 36.04 and amended Dec. 1, 2006, eff. Jan. 1, 2007

RULE 37. CASE AND OUT-OF-HOME PLACEMENT PLANS

Rule 37.01. Case and Out-of-Home Placement Plans and Reports Generally

When the responsible social services agency is the petitioner, the agency shall file with the court and provide to the parties and foster parent a case plan or out-of-home placement plan for the child and the parents or legal custodians, as appropriate. A case plan shall be prepared according to the requirements of Minnesota Statutes § 245.4871, subds. 19 or 21; § 245.492, subd. 16; § 256B.092; § 260C.212, subd. 1; or § 626.556, subd. 10, whichever is applicable.

Adopted Nov. 12, 2003. Amended Dec. 1, 2006, eff. Jan. 1, 2007.

Historical Notes

The order of the Minnesota Supreme Court [C1-01-927] dated November 12, 2003, amending Rules 37 to 82 of the Rules of Juvenile Procedure and renumbering them as Rules 1 to 47 of the Rules of Juvenile Protection Procedure, provides in part that the amendments are effective January 1, 2004, and shall apply to all juvenile protection matters filed on or after that date.

Rule 37.02. Child in Court-Ordered Foster Care: Out-of-Home Placement Plan

Subd. 1. Plan Required. When a child is placed in foster care by court order, the responsible social services agency shall file with the court and provide to the parties and foster parents the out-of-home placement plan required under Minnesota Statutes § 260C.212, subd. 1.

Subd. 2. Timing. The out-of-home placement plan shall be filed with the court and provided to the parties and foster parents by the responsible social services agency within thirty (30) days of the court order placing the child in foster care, an order for protective care, or order transferring legal custody to the responsible social services agency, whichever is earliest.

Subd. 3. Content. The out-of-home placement plan shall include a statement about whether the child and parent, legal custodian, or Indian custodian, participated in the preparation of the plan. If a parent or legal custodian refuses to participate in the preparation of the plan or disagrees with the services recommended in the plan by the responsible social services agency, the agency shall state in the plan the attempts made to engage the parent, legal custodian, and child in case planning and note such refusal or disagreement. The plan shall also include a statement about whether the child's guardian ad litem; the child's tribe, if the child is an Indian child; and the child's foster parent or representative of the residential facility have been consulted in the plan's preparation. The agency shall document whether the parent, legal custodian, or Indian custodian; child, if appropriate; the child's tribe, if the child is an Indian child; and foster parents have received a copy of the plan. When the child is in foster care due solely or in part to the child's emotional disturbance, the child's mental health treatment provider shall also be consulted in preparation of the plan and the agency shall document such consultation in the plan filed with the court.

Subd. 4. Procedure for Approving or Ordering Out-of-Home Placement Plan Prior to Disposition.

(a) *Court's Approval of Plan.* Upon the filing of the out-of-home placement plan, together with the information about whether the parent or legal custodian; the child, if appropriate; the child's tribe, if the child is an Indian child; and the foster parents have received a copy of the plan, the court may, based upon the allegations in the petition, approve the responsible social services agency's implementation of the plan if it was developed jointly with the parent and in consultation with others required under this Rule and Minnesota Statutes § 260C.212, subd. 1. The court shall send written notice of the approval of the plan to all parties and the county attorney, or may state such approval on the record at a hearing after the plan has been filed with the court and provided to the parties, foster parents, and the child, as appropriate.

(b) *Refusal to Participate in Development of Plan or Disagreement With Services.* When a parent or legal custodian refuses to participate in the preparation of the out-of-home placement plan or disagrees with the services recommended by the responsible social services agency, the agency shall notify the court of the services it will provide or efforts it will attempt under the plan notwithstanding the parent's refusal to cooperate or disagreement with the services. Any party may ask the court to modify the plan to require different or additional services. The court may approve the plan as presented by the agency or may modify the plan to require services requested. The court's approval of the plan shall be based upon the content of the petition or amended petition.

(c) *Voluntary or Court–Ordered Compliance with Plan.* A parent may voluntarily agree to comply with the terms of an out-of-home placement plan filed with the court. Unless the parent voluntarily agrees to the plan, the court may not order a parent to comply with the plan until there is a disposition ordered under Minnesota Statutes § 260C.201, subd. 1, and Rule 41. However, the court may find that the responsible social services agency has made reasonable efforts to finalize a permanent placement plan for the child if the agency makes efforts to implement the terms of an out-of-home placement plan approved under this rule and Minnesota Statutes § 260C.178, subd. 7.

(d) *Copy of Plan.* When the out-of-home placement plan is either ordered or approved, a copy of the plan shall be incorporated into the order by reference. The plan need not be served with the order, unless the plan has been modified.

Subd. 5. Procedure for Ordering Out–of–Home Placement Plan at Disposition. Rule 41 governs the ordering of an Out–of–Home Placement Plan at the time of Disposition.

Adopted Nov. 12, 2003. Amended Dec. 1, 2006, eff. Jan. 1, 2007; June 10, 2009, eff. Aug. 1, 2009.

Historical Notes

The order of the Minnesota Supreme Court [C1–01–927] dated June 10, 2009, amending the Rules of Juvenile Protection Procedure and the Rules of Adoption Procedure, provides in part that the amendments are effective August 1, 2009, and shall apply to all actions or proceedings pending on or commenced on or after the effective date.

The order of the Minnesota Supreme Court [C1-01-927] dated November 12, 2003, amending Rules 37 to 82 of the Rules of Juvenile Procedure and renumbering them as Rules 1 to 47 of the Rules of Juvenile Protection Procedure, provides in part that the amendments are effective January 1, 2004, and shall apply to all juvenile protection matters filed on or after that date.

Rule 37.03. Child in Voluntary Foster Care: Out-of-Home Placement Plan

Subd. 1. Child in Voluntary Foster For Reasons Other than for Treatment.

(a) *Timing.* The out-of-home placement plan required under Minnesota Statutes § 260C.212, subd. 1, shall be filed and served with the petition asking the court to review a voluntary placement of a child in placement when the placement is not due solely to the child's disability under Minnesota Statutes § 260C.141, subd. 2, and Rule 44.

(b) *Content.* The plan shall include a statement about whether the child and parent, legal custodian, or Indian custodian participated in the preparation of the plan. The plan shall also include a statement about whether the child's guardian ad litem; the child's tribe, if the child is an Indian child; and the child's foster parent or representative of the residential facility have been consulted in the plan's preparation. The agency shall document whether the parent, legal custodian, or Indian custodian; the child, if appropriate; the child's tribe, if the child is an Indian child; and foster parents have received a copy of the plan. When a child is in foster care due solely or in part to the child's emotional disturbance, the child's mental health treatment provider shall also be consulted in preparation of the plan and the agency shall document such consultation in the plan filed with the court.

Subd. 2. Procedure for Approving Out-of-Home Placement Plan for Child in Voluntary Foster Care. The court shall consider the appropriateness of the case plan or out-of-home placement plan in determining whether the voluntary placement is in the best interests of the child as required under Rule 44.02.

Adopted Nov. 12, 2003. Amended Dec. 1, 2006, eff. Jan. 1, 2007; June 10, 2009, eff. Aug. 1, 2009.

Historical Notes

The order of the Minnesota Supreme Court [C1–01–927] dated June 10, 2009, amending the Rules of Juvenile Protection Procedure and the Rules of Adoption Procedure, provides in part that the amendments are effective August 1, 2009, and shall apply to all actions or proceedings pending on or commenced on or after the effective date.

The order of the Minnesota Supreme Court [C1-01-927] dated November 12, 2003, amending Rules 37 to 82 of the Rules of Juvenile Procedure and renumbering them as Rules 1 to 47 of the Rules of Juvenile Protection Procedure, provides in part that the amendments are effective January 1, 2004, and shall apply to all juvenile protection matters filed on or after that date.

Rule 37.04. Child Not in Foster Care: Child Protective Services Case Plan

A responsible social services agency may file a petition alleging that the child is in need of protection or services seeking to ensure the provision of adequate child protective services as required under Minnesota Statutes § 626.556, subd. 10, and Minnesota Rule 9560.0228.

(a) *Timing.* When the child is not in foster care, the child protective services plan required under Minnesota Statutes § 626.556, subd. 10, and Minnesota Rule 9560.0228 shall be filed with the petition alleging the child to be in need of protection or services unless the responsible social services agency includes a statement in the petition explaining why it has not been possible to develop the plan, which may include exigent circumstances or the non-cooperation of the child's parents or guardian. The child protective services plan shall be provided to the parties by the responsible social services agency at the time it is filed with the court.

(b) *Procedure for Ordering Child Protective Services Plan.* When the child is not in foster care or is not recommended to continue in foster care, but the court finds endangerment under Rule 30, the court may order the parties to comply with the provisions of the child protective services plan as a condition of the child remaining in the care of the parent, guardian, or custodian. The court may also order the parties to comply with the provisions of the plan as part of a disposition under Rule 41. When the court orders a child protection services plan, a copy of the plan shall be attached to the court's order and incorporated into it by reference.

Adopted Nov. 12, 2003. Amended Dec. 1, 2006, eff. Jan. 1, 2007.

Historical Notes

The order of the Minnesota Supreme Court [C1-01-927] dated November 12, 2003, amending Rules 37 to 82 of the Rules of Juvenile Procedure and renumbering them as Rules 1 to 47 of the Rules of Juvenile Protection Procedure, provides in part that the amendments are effective January 1, 2004, and shall apply to all juvenile protection matters filed on or after that date.

Rule 37.05. Child with Disability: Case Plan

Subd. 1. Procedure. If a child found to be in need of protection or services has a physical or mental disability and a case plan is required under Minnesota Statutes § 245.4871, subd. 19 or 21; § 245.492, subd. 16; or § 256B.092, the plan shall be filed with the court. Services may be ordered provided to the child according to the provisions of Minnesota Statutes § 260C.201, subd. 1(a)(3). When an out-of-home placement plan is required under Rule 37.02 or a child protective services plan is required under Rule 37.04, the requirements of a plan under this paragraph may be included in such plans and need not be a separate document.

Subd. 2. Timing. The case plan shall be provided to the parties by the responsible social services agency at the time it is filed with the court.

Adopted Nov. 12, 2003. Amended Dec. 1, 2006, eff. Jan. 1, 2007.

Historical Notes

The order of the Minnesota Supreme Court [C1-01-927] dated November 12, 2003, amending Rules 37 to 82 of the Rules of Juvenile Procedure and renumbering them as Rules 1 to 47 of the Rules of Juvenile Protection Procedure, provides in part that the amendments are effective January 1, 2004, and shall apply to all juvenile protection matters filed on or after that date.

Rule 37.06. Non–Child Protection Cases; Child Not in Out–of–Home Care

Subd. 1. Timing of Filing of Case Plan for Child Under Protective Supervision, in Need of Special Care or Services, Allowed to Live Independently, or Who is a Runaway or Habitual Truant. When a petition is filed alleging a child to be in need of protection or services and no plan is required under Rule 37.02, 37.04, or 37.05, the responsible social services agency or other agency shall file a case plan designed to correct the conditions underlying the allegations that make the child in need of protection or services and may be based on the investigation and report required under subdivision 2. The case plan must be filed and served not later than five (5) days prior to the date of the disposition hearing.

Subd. 2. Predisposition Investigation and Report. Upon request of the court, the responsible social services agency or probation officer shall investigate the personal and family history and environment of any minor coming within the jurisdiction of the court under Minnesota Statutes § 260C.101 and shall report its findings to the court. The court may order any minor coming within its jurisdiction to be examined by a duly qualified physician, psychiatrist, or psychologist appointed by the court, the cost of which shall be paid pursuant to Minnesota Statutes § 260C.331, subd. 1. The predisposition report shall be governed by Rule 41.

Adopted Nov. 12, 2003.

Historical Notes

The order of the Minnesota Supreme Court [C1-01-927] dated November 12, 2003, amending Rules 37 to 82 of the Rules of Juvenile Procedure and renumbering them as Rules 1 to 47 of the Rules of Juvenile Protection Procedure, provides in part that the amendments are effective January 1, 2004, and shall apply to all juvenile protection matters filed on or after that date.

RULE 38. REPORTS TO THE COURT

Rule 38.01. Social Services Court Reports—Generally

Subd. 1. Periodic Reports Required. After an out-of-home placement plan or case plan is approved or ordered by the court pursuant to Rule 37 or Rule 41, the responsible social services agency shall make periodic certified reports to the court regarding progress made on the plan. When the report relates to plans for siblings who are in foster care, the agency may combine information related to each child's plan into one report as long as the report addresses each child's individual needs and circumstances. The agency may also submit written information from collateral sources regarding assessments or the delivery of services or any other relevant information regarding the child's safety, health, or welfare in support of the report or as a supplement to the report. Such reports may be supplemented at or before the hearing either orally or in writing.

Subd. 2. Content. Although pursuant to Rule 16 a report is not required to be signed, each report shall include the name of the person submitting the report; a statement certifying the content as true based upon personal observation, first-hand knowledge, or information and belief; and shall include the case caption, the date of the report, and the date of the hearing at which the report is to be considered. Each report shall contain or have attached the certificate of distribution required under Rule 31.07, subd. 2.

Subd. 3. Timing of Reports. Periodic reports required under this Rule shall be filed with the court and served upon the parties by the responsible social services agency not later than five (5) business days prior to each review hearing required under Rule 41.06, permanent placement determination hearing required under Rule 42.04, and as otherwise directed by the court.

Adopted Nov. 12, 2003. Amended Dec. 1, 2006, eff. Jan. 1, 2007.

Historical Notes

The order of the Minnesota Supreme Court [C1-01-927] dated November 12, 2003, amending Rules 37 to 82 of the Rules of Juvenile Procedure and renumbering them as Rules 1 to 47 of the Rules of Juvenile Protection Procedure, provides in part that the amendments are effective January 1, 2004, and shall apply to all juvenile protection matters filed on or after that date.

Rule 38.02. Social Services Court Reports—Child Ordered into Foster Care

Subd. 1. Content. In addition to the requirements of Rule 38.01, subd. 2, each certified report regarding an out-of-home placement plan shall include the name of the person submitting the report and the following:

(a) *Identifying Information.* Identifying and baseline placement information regarding the child shall be included as follows:

(1) the child's name and date of birth and, in the case of an Indian child, the Tribe in which the child is enrolled or eligible for membership;

(2) the names of the child's parents or legal custodians;

(3) the dates of birth of the child's parents who are minors;

(4) the date the child was first placed in foster care;

(5) the date the child was ordered placed in foster care;

(6) the total length of time the child has been in foster care, including all cumulative time the child may have experienced within the previous five (5) years;

(7) the number of moves the child has experienced while in foster care, including all moves during the previous five (5) years;

(8) if the child's placement has changed since the out-of-home placement plan was approved or ordered, a description of how the child's placement meets the child's best interests as set out in the modified out–of–home placement plan, or in the case of an Indian child, whether the placement complies with placement preferences established in 25 U.S.C. § 1915; and

(9) when the child has siblings, the names and ages of the child's siblings, the residence or placement status of each sibling and, where appropriate, the efforts the agency has made to place the children together; and

(b) *Review of Out–of–Home Placement Plan.* As applicable, a description of:

(1) the agency's efforts to implement the out-of-home placement plan requirements;

(2) the parent's or legal custodian's compliance with the plan requirements;

(3) services provided to the child;

(4) the child's adjustment in placement;

(5) visitation between the parents or legal custodian and the child and between the child and any siblings; and

(6) the agency's efforts to finalize adoption; and

(c) *Placement with Relatives.* At least once during the first six (6) months the child is in placement or until placement is made with a relative or the court finds the agency's efforts adequate under Minnesota Statutes § 260C.212, subd. 5, the report shall describe the efforts the agency has made to identify and notify relatives, or in the case of an Indian child the report shall describe how the placement complies with requirements of 25 U.S.C. § 1915; and

(d) *Independent Living Plan.* When the child is age sixteen (16 or older, the report shall include a description of the elements of the child's independent living plan and how the child is progressing on that plan; and

(e) *Child with Emotional Disturbance.* For a child in placement due solely or in part to the child's emotional disturbance, the report shall include diagnostic and assessment information, specific services relating to meeting the mental health care needs of the child, and treatment outcomes; and

(f) *Recommendations.* The report shall include recommendations to the court for modification of the plan or for actions the parents or legal custodian must take to provide protection or services for the child.

Subd. 2. Reports Between Disposition Review Hearings. Once disposition has been ordered pursuant to Rule 41, the responsible social services agency, through the county attorney, may ask the court for orders related to meeting the safety, protection, and best interests of the child based upon a certified report that meets the requirements of Rule 38.01, subd. 2, and states the child's identifying and baseline placement information and the factual basis for the request including, where appropriate, other relevant reports or data. Such reports shall be filed with the court together with proof of service upon all parties by the responsible social services agency. Any party may request a hearing regarding the agency's report. Pending hearing, if any, upon two (2) day's actual notice and based upon the report the court may issue an order that is in the best interests of the child. Upon a finding that an emergency exists, the court may issue a temporary order that is in the best interests of the child.

Adopted Nov. 12, 2003. Amended Dec. 1, 2006, eff. Jan. 1, 2007.

Historical Notes

The order of the Minnesota Supreme Court [C1-01-927] dated November 12, 2003, amending Rules 37 to 82 of the Rules of Juvenile Procedure and renumbering them as Rules 1 to 47 of the Rules of Juvenile Protection Procedure, provides in part that the amendments are effective January 1, 2004, and shall apply to all juvenile protection matters filed on or after that date.

Rule 38.03. Social Services Court Reports—Child Not in Foster Care

In addition to the requirements of Rule 38.01, subd. 2, each certified report regarding the case plan shall include the name of the person submitting the report and the following:

(a) ***Identifying Information.*** Identifying information regarding the child shall be included as follows:

(1) the child's name and date of birth and, in the case of an Indian child, the Tribe in which the child is enrolled or eligible for membership;

(2) a statement about whether the child is an Indian child, whether or not the Indian Child Welfare Act applies, and in the case of an Indian child the Tribe in which the child is enrolled or is eligible for membership;

(3) the names of the child's parents or legal custodians;

(4) the dates of birth of the child's parents who are minors;

(5) the child's residence and, if the child's residence has changed since the case plan was ordered, the date of the change;

(6) the date the case was most recently opened for services in the responsible social services agency;

(7) the date of all other case openings for this child and the child's siblings with the responsible social services agency and, if known, case openings for this child or the child's siblings with any other social services agency responsible for providing child welfare or child protection services to this child; in addition to the date of other case openings, the report should contain a brief description of the nature of the contact with the responsible or other social services agency; and

(b) ***Review of Plan.*** As applicable, a description of:

(1) the agency's efforts to implement the case plan;

(2) the parents' or legal custodian's and child's compliance with plan requirements; and

(3) the services provided to the child; and

(c) ***Recommendations.*** The report shall include recommendations to the court for modification of the plan or for actions the parent or legal custodian must take to provide adequate protection or services for the child.

Adopted Nov. 12, 2003. Amended Dec. 1, 2006, eff. Jan. 1, 2007.

Historical Notes

The order of the Minnesota Supreme Court [C1-01-927] dated November 12, 2003, amending Rules 37 to 82 of the Rules of Juvenile Procedure and renumbering them as Rules 1 to 47 of the Rules of Juvenile Protection Procedure, provides in part that the amendments are effective January 1, 2004, and shall apply to all juvenile protection matters filed on or after that date.

Rule 38.04. Objections to Agency's Report or Recommendations

Any party objecting to the content or recommendations of the responsible agency's report may submit a written objection to the report either before or at the hearing at which the report is to be considered. The objection shall include a statement certifying the content as true based upon personal observation, firsthand knowledge, or information and belief. The certified objection shall be supported by a sworn statement of the party's factual basis for the objection and may state other or additional facts on information and belief and argument that the court should consider in making its determinations or orders. An objection may also be supported by reports from collateral service providers or assessors. Objections to the agency's report and recommendations may also be stated on the record as long as the court gives the agency a reasonable opportunity to respond to the party's objection.

Adopted Nov. 12, 2003.

Historical Notes

The order of the Minnesota Supreme Court [C1-01-927] dated November 12, 2003, amending Rules 37 to 82 of the Rules of Juvenile Procedure and renumbering them as Rules 1 to 47 of the Rules of Juvenile Protection Procedure, provides in part that the amendments

are effective January 1, 2004, and shall apply to all juvenile protection matters filed on or after that date.

Rule 38.05. Reports to the Court by Child's Guardian ad Litem

Subd. 1. Periodic Reports Required. The guardian ad litem for the child shall submit periodic certified written reports to the court which may be supplemented at or before the hearing either orally or in writing.

Subd. 2. Content. Although pursuant to Rule 16 a report is not required to be signed, each report shall include the name of the person submitting the report, a statement certifying the content as true based upon personal observation, first-hand knowledge, or information and belief, and shall include the following:

(a) the child's name, date of birth, and age at the time the report is filed;

(b) the names of the child's parents or legal custodians;

(c) the case caption;

(d) the date of the report;

(e) the date of the hearing at which the report is to be considered;

(f) the date the guardian ad litem was appointed by the court;

(g) a brief summary of the issues that brought the child and family into the court system;

(h) a list of the resources or persons contacted who provided information to the guardian ad litem since the date of the last court hearing;

(i) a list of the dates and types of contacts the guardian ad litem had with the child(ren) since the date of the last court hearing;

(j) a list of all documents relied upon when generating the court report;

(k) a summary of information gathered regarding the child and family since the date of the last hearing relevant to the pending hearing;

(*l*) a list of any issues of concern to the guardian ad litem about the child's or family's situation; and

(m) a list of recommendations designed to address the concerns and advocate for the best interests of the child.

Each report shall contain or have attached the certificate of distribution required under Rule 31.07, subd. 2.

Subd. 3. Timing of Reports. Except for an emergency protective care hearing for which no written report is required, reports required under this rule shall be filed with the court and served upon the parties by the guardian ad litem not later than five (5) business days prior to each review hearing required under Rule 41.06, permanent placement determination hearing required under Rule 42, and as otherwise directed by the court.

Subd. 4. Objections to Guardian Ad Litem's Report or Recommendations. Any party objecting to the content or recommendations of the guardian ad litem's /may submit a written objection to the report either before or at the hearing at which the report is to be considered. The objection shall include a statement certifying the content as true based upon personal observation, first-hand knowledge, or information and belief. The certified objection shall be supported by a sworn statement of the party's factual basis for the objection and may state other or additional facts on information and belief and argument that the court should consider in making its determinations or orders. An objection may also be supported by reports from collateral service providers or assessors. Objections to the guardian ad litem's report and recommendations may also be stated on the record as long as the court gives the guardian ad litem a reasonable opportunity to respond to the party's objection.

Adopted Nov. 12, 2003. Amended Dec. 1, 2006, eff. Jan. 1, 2007.

Historical Notes

The order of the Minnesota Supreme Court [C1-01-927] dated November 12, 2003, amending Rules 37 to 82 of the Rules of Juvenile Procedure and renumbering them as Rules 1 to 47 of the Rules of Juvenile Protection Procedure, provides in part that the amendments are effective January 1, 2004, and shall apply to all juvenile protection matters filed on or after that date.

RULE 39. TRIAL

Rule 39.01. Generally

A trial is a hearing to determine whether the statutory grounds set forth in the petition are or are not proved.

Amended Nov. 12, 2003.

Historical Notes

The order of the Minnesota Supreme Court [C1-01-927] dated November 12, 2003, amending Rules 37 to 82 of the Rules of Juvenile Procedure and renumbering them as Rules 1 to 47 of the Rules of Juvenile Protection Procedure, provides in part that the amendments are effective January 1, 2004, and shall apply to all juvenile protection matters filed on or after that date.

Rule 39.02. Timing

Subd. 1. Trial.

(a) *Child in Need of Protection or Services Matters.* A trial regarding a child in need of protection or services matter shall commence within sixty (60) days from the date of the emergency protective care hearing or the admit/deny hearing, whichever is earlier, and testimony shall be concluded within thirty (30) days from the date of commencement of the trial and whenever possible should be over consecutive days.

(b) *Trial Following Permanency Progress Review Hearing for Child Under Age 8.* A trial required by

Rule 42.04(c) following a Permanency Progress Review Hearing shall be commenced within thirty (30) days of the filing of a petition in the case of a transfer of legal custody or within ninety (90) days of the filing of the petition in the case of a petition for termination of parental rights, and testimony shall be concluded within thirty (30) days from the date of commencement of the trial and whenever possible should be over consecutive days.

(c) *Termination of Parental Rights and Other Permanent Placement Matters.* Unless otherwise provided by these rules, a trial regarding a termination of parental rights matter or other permanent placement matter shall commence within sixty (60) days of the first scheduled admit/deny hearing, and testimony shall be concluded within thirty (30) days from the date of commencement of the trial and whenever possible should be over consecutive days.

(d) *Simultaneous Criminal Proceedings.* If criminal charges have been filed against a parent arising out of conduct alleged to constitute egregious harm, the county attorney shall determine whether the criminal matter or the juvenile court matter should proceed to trial first, consistent with the best interests of the child and subject to the defendant's right to a speedy trial.

Subd. 2. Continuance. The court may, either on its own motion or upon motion of a party or the county attorney, continue or adjourn a trial to a later date upon written findings or oral findings made on the record that a continuance is necessary for the protection of the child, for accumulation or presentation of evidence or witnesses, to protect the rights of a party, or for other good cause shown, so long as the permanency time requirements set forth in these rules are not delayed. Failure to conduct a pretrial hearing shall not constitute good cause.

Subd. 3. Effect of Mistrial; Order for New Trial. Upon a declaration of a mistrial, or an order of the trial court or a reviewing court granting a new trial, a new trial shall be commenced within thirty (30) days of the order.

Amended Nov. 12, 2003; Dec. 1, 2006, eff. Jan. 1, 2007; June 10, 2009, eff. Aug. 1, 2009.

Historical Notes

The order of the Minnesota Supreme Court [C1–01–927] dated June 10, 2009, amending the Rules of Juvenile Protection Procedure and the Rules of Adoption Procedure, provides in part that the amendments are effective August 1, 2009, and shall apply to all actions or proceedings pending on or commenced on or after the effective date.

The order of the Minnesota Supreme Court [C1-01-927] dated November 12, 2003, amending Rules 37 to 82 of the Rules of Juvenile Procedure and renumbering them as Rules 1 to 47 of the Rules of Juvenile Protection Procedure, provides in part that the amendments are effective January 1, 2004, and shall apply to all juvenile protection matters filed on or after that date.

Rule 39.03. Procedure

Subd. 1. Initial Procedure. At the beginning of the trial the court shall on the record:

(a) verify the name, age, race, and current address of the child who is the subject of the matter, unless stating the address would endanger the child or seriously risk disruption of the current placement;

(b) inquire whether the child is an Indian child and, if so, determine whether the Indian child's tribe has been notified;

(c) determine whether all parties are present and identify those present for the record;

(d) determine whether any child or the child's parent or legal custodian is present without counsel and, if so, explain the right to representation pursuant to Rule 25;

(e) determine whether notice requirements have been met and, if not, whether the affected person waives notice;

(f) if the child who is a party or the child's parent or legal custodian appears without counsel, explain basic trial rights;

(g) determine whether the child and the child's parent or legal custodian understand the statutory grounds and the factual allegations set forth in the petition and, if not, provide an explanation; and

(h) explain the purpose of the hearing and the possible transfer of custody of the child from the parent or legal custodian to another when such transfer is permitted by law and the permanency requirements of Minnesota Statutes § 260C.201, subd. 11.

Subd. 2. Conduct and Procedure.

(a) *Trial Rights.* The parties and the county attorney shall have the right to:

(1) present evidence;

(2) present witnesses;

(3) cross–examine witnesses;

(4) present arguments in support of or against the statutory grounds set forth in the petition; and

(5) ask the court to order that witnesses be sequestered.

(b) *Trial Procedure.* The trial shall proceed as follows:

(1) the party that drafted and filed the petition pursuant to Rule 33 may make an opening statement confining the statement to the facts expected to be proved;

(2) the other parties, in order determined by the court, may make an opening statement or may make a statement immediately before offering evidence, and the statement shall be confined to the facts expected to be proved;

(3) the party that drafted and filed the petition pursuant to Rule 33 shall offer evidence in support of the petition;

(4) the other parties, in order determined by the court, may offer evidence;

(5) the party that drafted and filed the petition pursuant to Rule 33 may offer evidence in rebuttal;

(6) the other parties, in order determined by the court, may offer evidence in rebuttal;

(7) when evidence is presented, other parties may, in order determined by the court, cross-examine witnesses;

(8) at the conclusion of the evidence the parties, other than the party that drafted and filed the petition pursuant to Rule 33, in order determined by the court, may make a closing statement;

(9) the party that drafted and filed the petition pursuant to Rule 33 may make a closing statement; and

(10) if written argument is to be submitted, it shall be submitted within fifteen (15) days of the conclusion of testimony, and the trial is not considered completed until the time for written arguments to be submitted has expired.

Amended Nov. 12, 2003.

Historical Notes

The order of the Minnesota Supreme Court [C1-01-927] dated November 12, 2003, amending Rules 37 to 82 of the Rules of Juvenile Procedure and renumbering them as Rules 1 to 47 of the Rules of Juvenile Protection Procedure, provides in part that the amendments are effective January 1, 2004, and shall apply to all juvenile protection matters filed on or after that date.

Rule 39.04. Standard of Proof

Subd. 1. Generally. Pursuant to Minnesota Statutes § 260C.163, subd. 1(a), and the Indian Child Welfare Act, 25 U.S.C. § 1912(e), in a child in need of protection or services matter, the standard of proof is clear and convincing evidence.

Subd. 2. Termination of Parental Rights and Other Permanent Placement Matters.

(a) *Non–Indian Child.* Pursuant to Minnesota Statutes § 260C.317, subd. 1, in a termination of parental rights or other permanency matter involving a non-Indian child, the standard of proof is clear and convincing evidence.

(b) *Indian Child.* Pursuant to the Indian Child Welfare Act, 25 U.S. C. § 1912(f), in a termination of parental rights matter involving an Indian child, the standard of proof is beyond a reasonable doubt.

Amended Nov. 12, 2003; June 10, 2009, eff. Aug. 1, 2009.

1999 Advisory Committee Comment

In *In Re the Matter of M.S.S.,* 465 N.W.2d 412 (Minn. Ct. App. 1991), the court held that the parental rights to an Indian child may not be terminated unless the county proves beyond a reasonable doubt that it has complied with section 1912(f) of the Indian Child Welfare Act, 25 U.S.C. § 1901 *et. seq.*, requiring the county to make active efforts to prevent or avoid placement.

Historical Notes

The order of the Minnesota Supreme Court [C1–01–927] dated June 10, 2009, amending the Rules of Juvenile Protection Procedure and the Rules of Adoption Procedure, provides in part that the amendments are effective August 1, 2009, and shall apply to all actions or proceedings pending on or commenced on or after the effective date.

The order of the Minnesota Supreme Court [C1-01-927] dated November 12, 2003, amending Rules 37 to 82 of the Rules of Juvenile Procedure and renumbering them as Rules 1 to 47 of the Rules of Juvenile Protection Procedure, provides in part that the amendments are effective January 1, 2004, and shall apply to all juvenile protection matters filed on or after that date.

Rule 39.05. Decision

Subd. 1. Timing. Within fifteen (15) days of the conclusion of the testimony, during which time the court may require simultaneous written arguments to be filed and served, the court shall issue its findings and order regarding whether one or more statutory grounds set forth in the petition have been proved. The court may extend the period for issuing an order for an additional fifteen (15) days if the court finds that an extension of time is required in the interests of justice and the best interests of the child.

Subd. 2. Child in Need of Protection or Services Matters and Habitual Truant, Runaway, and Prostitution Matters. The court shall dismiss the petition if the statutory grounds have not been proved. If the court finds that one or more statutory grounds set forth in the petition have been proved, the court shall either enter or withhold adjudication pursuant to Rule 40 and schedule the matter for further proceedings pursuant to Rule 41. The findings and order shall be filed with the court administrator who shall proceed pursuant to Rule 10.

Subd. 3. Termination of Parental Rights and Other Permanency Matters.

(a) *Generally.* If the court finds that the statutory grounds set forth in the petition are not proved, the court shall either dismiss the petition or determine that the child is in need of protection or services. If the court determines that the child is in need of protection or services, the court shall either enter or withhold adjudication pursuant to Rule 40 and schedule further proceedings pursuant to Rule 41. If the court finds that one or more statutory grounds set forth in the termination of parental rights petition are proved, the court may terminate parental rights. If the court finds that any other permanency petition is proved, the court may order relief consistent with that petition. The findings and order shall be filed with the court administrator who shall proceed pursuant to Rule 10.

(b) *Particularized Findings.* In addition to making the findings in subdivision (a), the court shall also make findings regarding the following as appropriate:

(1) **Non–Indian Child.** In any termination of parental rights matter, the court shall make specific findings regarding the nature and extent of efforts made by the responsible social services agency to rehabilitate the parent and reunite the family, including, where applicable, a statement that reasonable efforts to prevent placement and for rehabilitation and reunification are not required as provided under Minnesota Statutes § 260.012(a).

(2) **Indian Child.** In any termination of parental rights proceeding involving an Indian child, the court shall make specific findings regarding the following:

(i) *Active Efforts.* The petitioner has proven beyond a reasonable doubt that active efforts have been made to provide remedial services and rehabilitative programs designed to prevent the breakup of the Indian family and that these efforts have proved unsuccessful.

(ii) *Serious Emotional or Physical Damage.* Based upon the testimony, pursuant to Rule 49, of at least one qualified expert witness, that the continued custody of the child by the parent or Indian custodian is likely to result in serious emotional or physical damage to the child.

(3) **Best Interests of the Child.** Before ordering termination of parental rights, the court shall make a specific finding that termination is in the best interests of the child and shall analyze:

(i) the child's interests in preserving the parent-child relationship;

(ii) the parent's interests in preserving the parent-child relationship; and

(iii) any competing interests of the child.

(4) **Best interests of an Indian Child.** In proceedings involving an Indian child, the best interests of the child shall be determined consistent with the Indian Child Welfare Act, 25 U.S.C. § 1901 et seq.

(5) **Child's Interests Paramount.** Where the interests of parent and child conflict, the interests of the child are paramount.

Amended Nov. 12, 2003; Dec. 1, 2006, eff. Jan. 1, 2007; June 26, 2007, eff. July 1, 2007; June 10, 2009, eff. Aug. 1, 2009.

Historical Notes

The order of the Minnesota Supreme Court [C1–01–927] dated June 10, 2009, amending the Rules of Juvenile Protection Procedure and the Rules of Adoption Procedure, provides in part that the amendments are effective August 1, 2009, and shall apply to all actions or proceedings pending on or commenced on or after the effective date.

The order of the Minnesota Supreme Court [C1-01-927] dated November 12, 2003, amending Rules 37 to 82 of the Rules of Juvenile Procedure and renumbering them as Rules 1 to 47 of the Rules of Juvenile Protection Procedure, provides in part that the amendments are effective January 1, 2004, and shall apply to all juvenile protection matters filed on or after that date.

RULE 40. ADJUDICATION

Rule 40.01. Adjudication

If the court makes a finding that the statutory grounds set forth in a petition alleging a child to be in need of protection or services are proved, the court shall:

(a) adjudicate the child as in need of protection or services and proceed to disposition pursuant to Rule 41; or

(b) withhold adjudication of the child pursuant to Rule 40.02.

Amended Nov. 12, 2003.

Historical Notes

The order of the Minnesota Supreme Court [C1-01-927] dated November 12, 2003, amending Rules 37 to 82 of the Rules of Juvenile Procedure and renumbering them as Rules 1 to 47 of the Rules of Juvenile Protection Procedure, provides in part that the amendments are effective January 1, 2004, and shall apply to all juvenile protection matters filed on or after that date.

Rule 40.02. Withholding Adjudication

Subd. 1. Generally. When it is in the best interests of the child to do so, the court may withhold an adjudication that the child is in need of protection or services. The court may withhold adjudication for a period not to exceed ninety (90) days from the finding that the statutory grounds set forth in the petition have been proved. During the withholding of an adjudication, the court may enter a disposition order pursuant to Rule 41.

Subd. 2. Further Proceedings. At a hearing, which shall be held within ninety (90) days following the court's withholding of adjudication, the court shall either:

(a) dismiss the matter without an adjudication if both the child and the child's legal custodian have complied with the terms of the continuance; or

(b) adjudicate the child in need of protection or services if either the child or the child's legal custodian has not complied with the terms of the continuance. If the court enters an adjudication, the court shall proceed to disposition pursuant to Rule 41.

Amended Nov. 12, 2003.

Historical Notes

The order of the Minnesota Supreme Court [C1-01-927] dated November 12, 2003, amending Rules 37 to 82 of the Rules of Juvenile Procedure and renumbering them as Rules 1 to 47 of the Rules of Juvenile Protection Procedure, provides in part that the amendments are effective January 1, 2004, and shall apply to all juvenile protection matters filed on or after that date.

RULE 41. DISPOSITION

Rule 41.01. Disposition

After an adjudication that a child is in need of protection or services pursuant to Rule 40.01, the court shall conduct a hearing to determine disposition. Dispositions in regard to review of voluntary foster care matters shall be pursuant to Minnesota Statutes § 260C.205 and § 127A.47.

Amended Nov. 12, 2003; Dec. 1, 2006, eff. Jan. 1, 2007.

Historical Notes

The order of the Minnesota Supreme Court [C1-01-927] dated November 12, 2003, amending Rules 37 to 82 of the Rules of Juvenile Procedure and renumbering them as Rules 1 to 47 of the Rules of Juvenile Protection Procedure, provides in part that the amendments are effective January 1, 2004, and shall apply to all juvenile protection matters filed on or after that date.

Rule 41.02. Timing

To the extent practicable, the court shall conduct a disposition hearing and enter a disposition order the same day it makes a finding that the statutory grounds set forth in the petition have been proved. In the event disposition is not ordered at the same time as the adjudication, the disposition order shall be issued within ten (10) days of the date the court finds that the statutory grounds set forth in the petition have been proved.

Amended Nov. 12, 2003; June 10, 2009, eff. Aug. 1, 2009.

Historical Notes

The order of the Minnesota Supreme Court [C1–01–927] dated June 10, 2009, amending the Rules of Juvenile Protection Procedure and the Rules of Adoption Procedure, provides in part that the amendments are effective August 1, 2009, and shall apply to all actions or proceedings pending on or commenced on or after the effective date.

The order of the Minnesota Supreme Court [C1-01-927] dated November 12, 2003, amending Rules 37 to 82 of the Rules of Juvenile Procedure and renumbering them as Rules 1 to 47 of the Rules of Juvenile Protection Procedure, provides in part that the amendments are effective January 1, 2004, and shall apply to all juvenile protection matters filed on or after that date.

Rule 41.03. Pre–Disposition Reports

Subd. 1. Investigations and Evaluations. At any time after the court accepts or conditionally accepts an admission pursuant to Rule 35 or finds that the statutory grounds set forth in the petition have been proved, the court may, upon its own motion or the motion of a party or the county attorney, order a pre-disposition report which may include:

(a) an investigation of the personal and family history and environment of the child;

(b) medical, psychological, psychiatric, or chemical dependency evaluations of the child and any parent who is a party; and

(c) information regarding the factors set forth in Rule 41.05.

Subd. 2. Advisory. The court shall advise the persons present in court that a pre-disposition investigation is being ordered, the nature of the evaluations to be included, the date when the reports resulting from the investigation are to be filed with the court, and the right of each party to present opposing evidence and reports.

Subd. 3. Pre–Disposition Reports.

(a) *Filing and Service.* The person who intends to offer the pre-disposition report shall file the report with the court and serve the report on all parties at least forty-eight (48) hours prior to the time scheduled for the hearing. When the child or the child's parent or legal custodian is not represented by counsel, the court may limit the inspection of reports by the child or the child's parent and legal custodian if the court determines it is in the best interests of the child. Any party or the person making the pre-disposition report may by motion request a protective order limiting the release of confidential or sensitive information contained in the report.

(b) *Consideration of Reports.* Before making a disposition in a case, terminating parental rights, or appointing a legal guardian for a child, the court may consider any report or recommendation made by the responsible social services agency, probation officer, licensed child-placing agency, foster parent, guardian ad litem, tribal representative, the child's health or mental health care provider, or other authorized advocate for the child or child's family, a school district concerning the effect on student transportation of placing a child in a school district in which the child is not a resident, or any other information deemed material by the court.

Subd. 4. Discussion of Contents of Reports. The person making the pre-disposition report may discuss the contents of the report with all parties and the county attorney.

Subd. 5. Discussion of Content of Report—Limitation by Court. The court may upon a showing of good cause limit the extent of the discussion of the contents of the pre-disposition report with the parties if the court finds the limitation to be in the best interests of the child. The limitation may be made:

(a) on the court's own motion; or

(b) upon the written or on-the-record motion of a party, the county attorney, or the person making the pre-disposition report.

Amended Nov. 12, 2003; Dec. 1, 2006, eff. Jan. 1, 2007.

Historical Notes

The order of the Minnesota Supreme Court [C1-01-927] dated November 12, 2003, amending Rules 37 to 82 of the Rules of Juvenile Procedure and renumbering them as Rules 1 to 47 of the Rules of Juvenile Protection Procedure, provides in part that the amendments are effective January 1, 2004, and shall apply to all juvenile protection matters filed on or after that date.

Rule 41.04. Procedure; Evidence

Disposition hearings shall be conducted in an informal manner designed to facilitate the opportunity for all parties to be heard.

The court may admit any evidence, including reliable hearsay and opinion evidence, which is relevant to the disposition of the matter. Privileged communications may be admitted in accordance with Minnesota Statutes § 626.556, subd. 8.

Amended Nov. 12, 2003.

Historical Notes

The order of the Minnesota Supreme Court [C1-01-927] dated November 12, 2003, amending Rules 37 to 82 of the Rules of Juvenile Procedure and renumbering them as Rules 1 to 47 of the Rules of Juvenile Protection Procedure, provides in part that the amendments are effective January 1, 2004, and shall apply to all juvenile protection matters filed on or after that date.

Rule 41.05. Disposition Order

Subd. 1. Findings. The disposition order shall contain written findings of fact to support the disposition ordered and shall also set forth in writing the following information:

(a) a statement explaining how the disposition serves the best interests and safety of the child;

(b) a statement of all alternative dispositions or services under the case plan or out-of-home placement plan considered by the court and why such dispositions or services are not appropriate in the instant case;

(c) if the disposition is transfer of legal custody to a responsible social services agency, a statement about whether the proposed placement meets the child's needs and is in the child's best interests and reviewing the agency's use of the factors set out below in making the child's foster care placement:

(1) the child's current functioning and behaviors;

(2) the medical, educational, and developmental needs of the child;

(3) the child's history and past experience;

(4) the child's religious and cultural needs;

(5) the child's connection with a community, school, and faith community;

(6) the child's interests and talents;

(7) the child's relationship to current caretakers, parents, siblings, and relatives; and

(8) reasonable preference of the child, if the court deems the child to be of sufficient age to express a preference; and

(d) a brief description of the efforts made to prevent or eliminate the need for removal of the child from home and to reunify the family after removal, and why further efforts could not have prevented or eliminated the necessity of removal or that reasonable efforts were not required under Minnesota Statutes §§ 260.012 or 260C.178, subd. 1.

The court may authorize or continue an award of legal custody to the responsible social services agency despite a finding that the agency's preventive or reunification efforts have not been reasonable if the court finds that further preventive or reunification efforts could not permit the child to safely remain at home.

If the child has been identified by the responsible social services agency as the subject of concurrent permanency planning, the court shall review and make findings regarding the reasonable efforts of the agency to recruit, identify, and make a placement with a foster parent or relative who has committed to providing the legally permanent home for the child in the event reunification efforts are not successful.

(e) In the case of an Indian child, the foster care placement of the child shall be ordered only upon the testimony, pursuant to Rule 49, of at least one qualified expert witness that the continued custody of the child by the parent or legal custodian or Indian custodian is likely to result in serious emotional or physical damage to the child.

Subd. 2. Content.

(a) *Mandatory Provisions.* The court shall enter an order making one of the following dispositions for the child:

(1) **Protective Supervision.** Place the child under the protective supervision of the responsible services agency or child-placing agency in the home of a parent or legal custodian under conditions directed to correction of the child's need for protection or services:

(i) the court may order the child into the home of a parent who does not otherwise have legal custody of the child, however, an order under this section does not confer legal custody on that parent;

(ii) if the court orders the child into the home of a father who has not been adjudicated as such, the order shall require the alleged or presumed father to cooperate with paternity establishment proceedings regarding the child in the appropriate jurisdiction as one of the conditions prescribed by the court for the child to continue in his home; and

(iii) the court may order the child into the home of a noncustodial parent with conditions and may also order both the noncustodial and the custodial parent to comply with the requirements of a case plan under subdivision 2; or

(2) **Transfer Legal and Physical Custody to Agency.** Transfer legal custody to a child-placing agency or the responsible social services agency, which shall have legal responsibility for the child's placement in foster care, including making an individualized determination of how the particular placement is in the child's best interests using the consideration for relatives and the best interest

factors in Minnesota Statutes § 260C.212, subdivision 2(b); or

(3) **Trial Home Visit.** Order a trial home visit, as defined in Rule 2.01(x), without modifying the transfer of legal custody to the responsible social services agency under subdivision 2(a)(2) of this Rule; or

(4) **Special Services.** If the child has been adjudicated as a child in need of protection or services because the child is in need of special services or care to treat or ameliorate a physical or mental disability or emotional disturbance as defined in Minnesota Statutes § 245.4871, subd. 15, the court may order the child's parent, guardian or custodian to provide it. The court may order the child's health plan company to provide mental health services to the child. Minnesota Statutes § 62Q.535 applies to an order for mental health services directed to the child's health plan company. If the health plan, the child's parent or legal custodian fails or is unable to provide the treatment or care, the court may order it provided. Absent specific written findings by the court that the child's disability is the result of abuse or neglect by the child's parent or guardian, the court shall not transfer legal custody of the child for the purpose of obtaining special treatment or care solely because the parent is unable to provide the treatment or care. If the court's order for mental health treatment is based on a diagnosis made by a treatment professional, the court may order that the diagnosing professional not provide the treatment to the child if it finds that such an order is in the child's best interests; or

(5) **Independent Living.** Allow a child sixteen (16) years old or older to live independently under appropriate supervision, if the court determines that the child has sufficient maturity and judgment, and the responsible social services agency after consultation with the court has specifically authorized this alternative.

(6) **Monitoring.** When a parent has complied with a case plan and the child is in the care of the parent, the court may order the responsible social services agency to monitor the parent's continued ability to maintain the child safely in the home under such terms and conditions as the court determines appropriate under the circumstances.

(b) *Additional Provisions.* As part of the disposition order the court shall also:

(1) approve or modify the plan for supervised or unsupervised visitation for the child's parent or legal custodian, relatives, and siblings of the child, if siblings are not in out-of-home placement together, as set out in the out-of-home placement plan; the court may set reasonable rules for visitation that contribute to the objectives of the court order and the maintenance of the familial relationship; the court may deny visitation when visitation would act to prevent the achievement of the court's disposition order or would endanger the child's physical or emotional well-being;

(1) review the case plan, make modifications supported by the evidence appropriate, and approve the plan;

(2) order all parties to comply with the approved case plan;

(3) incorporate into the order by reference the approved case plan and attach a copy of the plan only if it has been modified;

(4) give notice to the parent on the record and in writing of the requirements of Minnesota Statutes § 260C.201, subds. 11 and 11a; and

(5) set the date and time for the admit/deny hearing pursuant to Rule 42.

(c) *Habitual Truant and Runaway Matters.* If the child is adjudicated in need of protection or services because the child is a habitual truant or a runaway, the court may order any of the following dispositions in addition to or as alternatives to the dispositions ordered under subdivisions (a) and (b):

(1) counseling for the child or the child's parent or legal custodian;

(2) place the child under the supervision of a probation officer or other suitable person in the child's own home under conditions prescribed by the court, including reasonable rules for the child's conduct and the conduct of the parent or legal custodian designed for the physical, mental, and moral well-being and behavior of the child;

(3) with the consent of the commissioner of corrections, place the child in a group foster care facility that is under the commissioner's management and supervision;

(4) subject to the court's supervision, transfer legal custody of the child to one of the following:

(i) a reputable person of good moral character; or

(ii) a county probation officer for placement in a group foster home established under the direction of the juvenile court and licensed pursuant to Minnesota Statutes § 241.021;

(5) require the child to pay a fine of up to $100, to be paid in a manner that will not impose undue financial hardship upon the child;

(6) require the child to participate in a community service project;

(7) order the child to undergo a chemical dependency evaluation and, if warranted by the evaluation, order participation by the child in a drug awareness program or an inpatient or outpatient chemical dependency treatment program;

(8) order the commissioner of public safety to cancel the child's driver's license or permit or, for a

child who does not have a driver's license or permit, order a denial of driving privileges for any period up to the child's 18th birthday; or

(9) order the child's parent or legal custodian to deliver the child to school at the beginning of each school day for a period of time specified by the court.

Amended Nov. 12, 2003; Dec. 1, 2006, eff. Jan. 1, 2007; Dec. 18, 2006, eff. Jan. 1, 2007; June 10, 2009, eff. Aug. 1, 2009.

2006 Advisory Committee Comment

Minnesota Statutes § 260C.331, subd. 1(a)(3), provides that "whenever a child is given physical or mental examinations or treatment under order of the court, and no provision is otherwise made by law for payment for the care, examination, or treatment of the child, those costs are a charge upon the welfare funds of the county in which proceedings are held upon certification of the judge of juvenile court."

Historical Notes

The order of the Minnesota Supreme Court [C1–01–927] dated June 10, 2009, amending the Rules of Juvenile Protection Procedure and the Rules of Adoption Procedure, provides in part that the amendments are effective August 1, 2009, and shall apply to all actions or proceedings pending on or commenced on or after the effective date.

The order of the Minnesota Supreme Court [C1-01-927] dated November 12, 2003, amending Rules 37 to 82 of the Rules of Juvenile Procedure and renumbering them as Rules 1 to 47 of the Rules of Juvenile Protection Procedure, provides in part that the amendments are effective January 1, 2004, and shall apply to all juvenile protection matters filed on or after that date.

Rule 41.06. Hearings to Review Disposition

Subd. 1. Timing. When disposition is an award of legal custody to the responsible social services agency, the court shall review the disposition in court at least every ninety (90) days. Any party or the county attorney may request a review hearing before ninety (90) days. When the disposition is protective supervision, the court shall review the disposition in court at least every six (6) months from the date of disposition.

Subd. 2. Procedure in Reviewing Disposition.

(a) *Legal Custody to Agency With Foster Care.* When the disposition is transfer of legal custody to the responsible social services agency, the court shall conduct a hearing at least every ninety (90) days to review whether foster care is necessary and continues to be appropriate or whether the child should be returned to the home of the parent or legal custodian from whom the child was removed. The review shall include the following:

(1) whether the out-of-home placement plan is relevant to the safety and best interests of the child;

(2) whether the agency is making reasonable or, in the case of an Indian child, active efforts to implement the requirements of the out-of-home placement plan;

(3) the extent of progress which has been made toward alleviating or mitigating the causes necessitating placement;

(4) whether the parents or legal custodian of the child are visiting the child and, if not, what barriers exist to visitation;

(5) whether the agency has made diligent efforts to identify both parents of the child as required under Minnesota Statutes § 260C.212, subd. 4, and whether the case plan or out-of-home placement plan addresses the need for services of both parents;

(6) whether the child is receiving appropriate services under the out-of-home placement plan;

(7) when a child has siblings in foster care:

(i) whether the child resides with the siblings;

(ii) when the child and siblings are not placed together, whether further efforts are appropriate to place the siblings together; and

(iii) when the child and siblings are not placed together, whether there is visitation amongst siblings;

(8) when a child is not placed with a relative, whether the agency's efforts under Minnesota Statutes § 260C.212, subd. 5, are adequate; in the case of an Indian child, whether the placement preferences of 25 U.S.C. § 1915 are met;

(9) when the agency is utilizing concurrent permanency planning, the agency's efforts to place the child with a relative or a foster parent who has committed to providing the child's legally permanent home in the event reunification efforts are not successful; and

(10) whether the parent or legal custodian understands the requirements of Minnesota Statutes § 260C.201, subd. 11, related to the required permanency placement determination hearing, including the projected date by which the child will be returned home or the hearing will be held.

(b) *Legal Custody to Agency with Trial Home Visit.* When the disposition is a trial home visit:

(1) the responsible social services agency shall advise the court and parties within three (3) days of the date a trial home visit is terminated by the responsible social services agency without a court order;

(2) the responsible social services agency shall prepare a report for the court when the trial home visit is terminated, whether by the agency or court order, which describes the child's circumstances during the trial home visit and recommends appropriate orders, if any, for the court to enter to provide for the child's safety and stability. In the event a trial home visit is terminated by the agency by removing the child to foster care without prior court order or authorization, the court shall conduct a hearing within ten (10) days of receiving notice of

the termination of the trial home visit by the agency and shall order disposition under this subdivision or conduct a permanency hearing under Rule 42. The time period for the hearing may be extended by the court for good cause shown and if it is in the best interests of the child as long as the total time the child spends in foster care without a permanent placement determination hearing does not exceed twelve (12) months;

(3) while the child is in trial home placement the matter shall be reviewed in court at least every ninety (90) days to determine whether the trial home visit continues to be necessary. At least five (5) business days prior to the hearing, the responsible social services agency shall file with the court and serve upon the parties a report describing the services provided to the child and parent and the parent's progress on the case plan; and

(c) *Protective Supervision in Home of Parent.* When the disposition is protective supervision of the child in the home of a custodial parent, the court shall conduct a review hearing at least every six (6) months. When the disposition is protective supervision of the child in the home of a noncustodial parent, the court shall conduct a review hearing at least every ninety (90) days. At the hearing, the court shall review:

(1) whether the agency has submitted a case plan for the parents or legal custodian and child as required under Rule 37;

(2) after the agency has submitted a plan to the court as required under Rule 37, whether the plan continues to be relevant to the safety and best interests of the child;

(3) whether the agency is making appropriate efforts to implement the plan;

(4) whether the agency, child's attorney and the guardian ad litem have reasonable access to the child to determine the child's safety, health, and well-being;

(5) whether the parents or legal custodian are able to utilize the services set out in the plan to correct the conditions which led to the court's determination that the child is in need of protection or services, and if not, what other services might be appropriate; and

(6) whether the child is receiving necessary services identified in the plan and whether those services are meeting the best interests of the child.

Subd. 3. Procedure. Any party or the county attorney may seek modification of a disposition order by motion made pursuant to Rule 15. The motion may be heard at the scheduled review hearing or at an earlier date or may be considered by the court without hearing if no party objects.

Subd. 4. Modification of Disposition; Modification of Case or Out–of–Home Placement Plan.

(a) *Agreement.* The court, on its own motion or that of any party, may modify the disposition or order the case plan or out-of-home placement plan modified when all parties agree the modification is in the best interests of the child and:

(1) a change of circumstances requires a change in the disposition or modification of the case plan or out-of-home placement plan; or

(2) the original disposition or case plan or out-of-home placement plan is inappropriate.

(b) *Objection.* If a party objects to a proposed modification, or if the child does not have a guardian ad litem at the time the motion is made, the court shall schedule a hearing for the next available date. A party has a right to request a court review of the reasonableness of the case plan or out-of-home placement plan upon a showing of a substantial change in circumstances. The court may also:

(1) order the agency to make further efforts to identify and place a child with a relative if the court finds the agency has failed to perform duties required under Minnesota Statutes § 260C.212, subds. 2 and 5; or

(2) find that the agency has performed required duties under Minnesota Statutes § 260C.212, subd. 5, and no further efforts to locate relatives are required; or

(3) in the case of an Indian child, unless good cause is found under 25 U.S.C. § 1915, order the agency to make additional efforts to comply with the placement preferences of 25 U.S.C. § 1915.

Subd. 5. Notice. Notice of the review hearing shall be given to all parties and participants.

Subd. 6. Procedure. Review hearings shall be conducted pursuant to Rule 41.04.

Subd. 7. Findings and Order. In the event the disposition is modified, the court shall issue a disposition order in accordance with Rule 41.05.

Amended Nov. 12, 2003; Dec. 1, 2006, eff. Jan. 1, 2007; June 10, 2009, eff. Aug. 1, 2009.

2008 Advisory Committee Comment

To ensure that each child's developmental needs are timely met, federal and state statutes have established a 12–month permanent placement determination timeline. A trial home visit is a tool designed to support reunification efforts, while simultaneously ensuring the child's safety. Consistent with Rule 41.06, which requires 90–day review hearings for other types of dispositions, Rule 41.06, subd. 2(b), provides that in cases where a trial home visit has been ordered the disposition review hearing must occur at least every 90 days. However, to better support reunification efforts, the best practice is to hold such disposition review hearings more often than every 90 days and to establish the hearing frequency and date in court.

Historical Notes

The order of the Minnesota Supreme Court [C1–01–927] dated June 10, 2009, amending the Rules of Juvenile Protection Procedure and the Rules of Adoption Procedure, provides in part that the amendments are effective August 1, 2009, and shall apply to all actions or proceedings pending on or commenced on or after the effective date.

The order of the Minnesota Supreme Court [C1-01-927] dated November 12, 2003, amending Rules 37 to 82 of the Rules of Juvenile Procedure and renumbering them as Rules 1 to 47 of the Rules of Juvenile Protection Procedure, provides in part that the amendments are effective January 1, 2004, and shall apply to all juvenile protection matters filed on or after that date.

RULE 42. PERMANENT PLACEMENT AND TERMINATION OF PARENTAL RIGHTS MATTERS; POST–PERMANENCY REVIEW REQUIREMENTS

Rule 42.01. Timing

Subd. 1. Timing of Required Permanency Proceedings for Child in Need of Protection or Services Matters. In the case of a child who is alleged or found to be in need of protection or services, ordered into foster care or the home of a noncustodial parent, and where reasonable efforts for reunification are required, the first order placing the child in foster care or the home of a noncustodial parent shall set the date or deadline for:

(a) the admit/deny hearing commencing permanent placement determination proceedings; and

(b) the permanency progress review hearing required for a child who is under age eight (8) at the time the petition alleging the child to be in need of protection or services is filed.

Subd. 2. Timing of Hearing for Child on a Trial Home Visit. When the child has been ordered on a trial home visit which continues at the time the court is required to commence permanent placement determination proceedings under Rule 42.01, within twelve (12) months of the date a child is placed in foster care the court shall hold a hearing pursuant to Rule 42.13 to determine the continued status of the child.

Subd. 3. Calculating Time Period

The child shall be considered placed in foster care or the home of a noncustodial parent at the earlier of:

(a) the date of the child's placement in foster care or in the care of a noncustodial parent by court order; or

(b) sixty (60) days after the date on which the child has been voluntarily placed in foster care as a result of a voluntary placement agreement between the parents and the responsible social services agency.

Subd. 4. Accumulation of Out-of-Home Placement Time

The time period requiring the court to commence permanent placement determination proceedings shall be calculated as follows:

(a) during the pendency of a petition alleging a child to be in need of protection or services, all time periods during which a child is placed in foster care or in the home of a noncustodial parent are accumulated;

(b) if a child has been placed in foster care within the previous five years under one or more previous petitions, the lengths of all prior time periods during which the child was placed in foster care within the previous five years are accumulated. If a child under this clause has been in foster care for twelve (12) months or more, the court, if it is in the best interests of the child and for compelling reasons, may extend the total time the child may continue out of the home under the current petition up to an additional six (6) months before making a permanency determination; and

(c) time spent on a trial home visit under Minnesota Statutes § 260C.201, subd. 1(a)(3), counts toward the requirement that the court commence permanency proceedings under this rule. However, if the child is on a trial home visit at the time the court is required to commence permanency proceedings, the court may conduct the hearing under Rule 42.13. If a trial home visit is ordered or continued at the time set for the court to commence permanency proceedings or if the child is ordered returned to the parent's home as a trial home visit at the conclusion of permanency proceedings under this rule, and the child is subsequently returned to foster care, the court shall re-commence proceedings to determine an appropriate permanent order for the child not later than thirty (30) days after the child returns to foster care.

Subd. 5. Notification of Timing. Not later than when the court sets the date or deadline for the admit/deny hearing commencing the permanent placement determination proceedings and the permanency progress review hearing, the court shall notify the parties and participants of the following requirements:

(a) *Requirement of Six (6) Month Hearing for Child Under Eight (8) Years of Age.* For a child who is under eight (8) years of age at the time a petition is filed alleging the child to be in need of protection or services, the court shall conduct a permanency progress review hearing to review the progress of the case, the parent's progress on the case plan or out-of-home placement plan, and the provision of services not later than six (6) months after the child is placed in foster care or in the home of a noncustodial parent. At the hearing required under this paragraph, the court may conduct a permanency progress review hearing for any sibling of the child, regardless of age, when the sibling is also in foster care or in the home of a noncustodial parent.

(b) *Requirement of Twelve (12) Month Hearing.* The court shall commence permanent placement determination proceedings to determine the permanent status of the child, regardless of age, not later than twelve (12) months after the child is placed in foster care or in the home of a noncustodial parent.

Subd. 6. Timing for Cases Where Reasonable Efforts For Reunification Are Not Required. When the court finds that the petition states a prima facie case that one or more of the five circumstances under Minnesota Statutes § 260.012 and Rule 30.09, subd. 3, exist where reasonable efforts for reunification are not required, the court shall order that an admit/deny hearing under Rule 34 be conducted within thirty (30) days and a trial be conducted within ninety (90) days of its prima facie finding. Unless a permanency or termination of parental rights petition under Rule 33 has already been filed, the county attorney requesting the prima facie determination shall file a permanency or termination of parental rights petition that permits the completion of service by the court at least ten (10) days prior to the admit/deny hearing.

Amended Nov. 12, 2003; Dec. 1, 2006, eff. Jan. 1, 2007. Former Rules 42.02 and 42.03 renumbered as Rule 42.01, subds. 3 and 4, and amended June 10, 2009, eff. Aug. 1, 2009.

Historical Notes

The order of the Minnesota Supreme Court [C1–01–927] dated June 10, 2009, amending the Rules of Juvenile Protection Procedure and the Rules of Adoption Procedure, provides in part that the amendments are effective August 1, 2009, and shall apply to all actions or proceedings pending on or commenced on or after the effective date.

The order of the Minnesota Supreme Court [C1-01-927] dated November 12, 2003, amending Rules 37 to 82 of the Rules of Juvenile Procedure and renumbering them as Rules 1 to 47 of the Rules of Juvenile Protection Procedure, provides in part that the amendments are effective January 1, 2004, and shall apply to all juvenile protection matters filed on or after that date.

Former rule: A former Rule 42.01, subd. 2, amended by court orders dated November 12, 2003, and December 1, 2006, related to the purpose of permanent placement determination and progress review hearings. The subject matter of former Rule 42.01, subd. 2, was incorporated into Rule 42.02 by court order dated June 10, 2009, effective August 1, 2009.

Rule 42.02. Purpose of Permanent Placement Determination Proceeding and Permanency Progress Review Hearing

Subd. 1. Any Child in Foster Care or in Home of a Noncustodial Parent. The purpose of permanent placement determination proceedings is to determine the permanent status of a child, including a review of the progress of the case and the parent's progress on the case plan or out-of-home placement plan, the services provided by the responsible social services agency, and whether or not the conditions that led to the child's placement in foster care or in the home of a noncustodial parent have been corrected so that the child can return to the care of the parent or custodian from whom the child was removed. The court shall determine whether the child shall be returned home or, if not, order permanent placement of the child consistent with the child's best interests and the pleadings and proof presented to the court.

Subd. 2. Permanency Progress Review: Child Under Eight (8) Years of Age. The purpose of the permanency progress review hearing is to review the progress of the case, the parent's progress on the case plan or out-of-home placement plan, and the provision of services by the responsible social services agency. The court shall determine whether the parents or legal custodian have maintained regular contact with the child, the parents are complying with the court-ordered case plan or out-of-home placement plan, and the child would benefit from continuing this relationship.

Subd. 3. Matters Where Reasonable Efforts for Reunification Are Not Required. The purpose of holding the trial on the petition within ninety (90) days of the prima facie determination permitted under Rule 30.09, subd. 3, and Minnesota Statutes § 260.012 in cases where reasonable efforts for reunification are not required is to ensure timely decision by the court that either:

(a) there is a sufficient evidentiary basis for an order for termination of parental rights or permanent placement of the child away from the parent and for finding the order for termination of parental rights or permanent placement away from the parent is in the child's best interests; or

(b) there is an insufficient evidentiary basis for the order or that the order is not in the best interests of the child.

Amended Nov. 12, 2003; Dec. 1, 2006, eff. Jan. 1, 2007. Former Rule 42.01, subd. 2, renumbered as Rule 42.02 and amended June 10, 2009, eff. Aug. 1, 2009.

Historical Notes

The order of the Minnesota Supreme Court [C1–01–927] dated June 10, 2009, amending the Rules of Juvenile Protection Procedure and the Rules of Adoption Procedure, provides in part that the amendments are effective August 1, 2009, and shall apply to all actions or proceedings pending on or commenced on or after the effective date.

The order of the Minnesota Supreme Court [C1-01-927] dated November 12, 2003, amending Rules 37 to 82 of the Rules of Juvenile Procedure and renumbering them as Rules 1 to 47 of the Rules of Juvenile Protection Procedure, provides in part that the amendments are effective January 1, 2004, and shall apply to all juvenile protection matters filed on or after that date.

Former rule: A former Rule 42.02, amended by court orders dated November 12, 2003, and December 1, 2006, related to the calculation of the time period after which a child is considered placed out of the care of the parent. The subject matter of former Rule 42.02 was incorporated into Rule 42.01 as subd. 3 by court order dated June 10, 2009, effective August 1, 2009.

Rule 42.03. Procedures for Permanency Progress Review Hearing

The following procedures govern a permanency progress review hearing required within six (6) months of placement for a child under the age of eight (8) at the time the petition was filed alleging the child to be in need of protection or services and may also apply to any sibling of the child, regardless of age, when the sibling also is in foster care or the home of a noncustodial parent.

(a) *Written Report.* Not later than ten (10) days prior to the hearing, the county attorney shall file with the court and serve upon the parties a written report prepared by the responsible social services agency describing the progress of the case and the case plan or out-of-home placement plan including the services provided to the parents.

(b) *Court Determination.*

(1) **Regular Contact Maintained and Parent Complying.** If the court determines that parent or legal custodian has maintained regular contact with the child, the parent is complying with the court-ordered case plan or out-of-home placement plan, and the child would benefit from continuing this relationship, the court may either:

(i) return the child home, if the conditions which led to the out-of-home placement have been sufficiently mitigated and it is safe and in the child's best interests to return home; or

(ii) continue the matter up to a total of six (6) additional months.

(2) **Regular Contact Not Maintained or Parent Not Complying.** If the court determines that the parent or legal custodian has not maintained regular contact with the child as outlined in the visitation plan required under the case plan or out-of-home placement plan or the parent is not complying with the case plan or out-of-home placement plan, the court may order the responsible social services agency to develop a plan for permanent placement of the child away from the parent and to file a petition to support an order for the permanent placement plan within thirty (30) days of the hearing. A trial on the petition shall be held as provided in subdivision (c).

(c) *Responsible Agency's or County Attorney's Duties.* Following the review under this subdivision:

(1) if the court either returns the child home or continues the matter up to a total of six (6) additional months, the agency shall continue to provide services to support the child's return home or continue to make reasonable efforts to achieve reunification of the child and the parent as ordered by the court under an approved case plan;

(2) if the court orders the agency to develop a plan for the transfer of permanent legal and physical custody of the child to a relative, a petition supporting the plan shall be filed with the court within thirty (30) days of the hearing required under this subdivision and a trial on the petition shall be held within thirty (30) days of the filing of the petition; or

(3) if the court orders the agency to file a termination of parental rights petition, unless the county attorney can show cause why a termination of parental rights petition should not be filed, a petition for termination of parental rights shall be filed with the court within thirty (30) days of the hearing required under this subdivision and a trial on the petition shall be held within ninety (90) days of the filing of the petition.

Amended Nov. 12, 2003; Dec. 1, 2006, eff. Jan. 1, 2007. Former Rule 42.04, subd. 1, renumbered as Rule 42.03 and amended June 10, 2009, eff. Aug. 1, 2009.

Historical Notes

The order of the Minnesota Supreme Court [C1–01–927] dated June 10, 2009, amending the Rules of Juvenile Protection Procedure and the Rules of Adoption Procedure, provides in part that the amendments are effective August 1, 2009, and shall apply to all actions or proceedings pending on or commenced on or after the effective date.

The order of the Minnesota Supreme Court [C1-01-927] dated November 12, 2003, amending Rules 37 to 82 of the Rules of Juvenile Procedure and renumbering them as Rules 1 to 47 of the Rules of Juvenile Protection Procedure, provides in part that the amendments are effective January 1, 2004, and shall apply to all juvenile protection matters filed on or after that date.

Former rule: A former Rule 42.03, amended by court orders dated November 12, 2003, and December 1, 2006, related to the accumulation of out-of-home placement time. The subject matter of former Rule 42.03 was incorporated into Rule 42.01 as subd. 4 by court order dated June 10, 2009, effective August 1, 2009.

Rule 42.04. Procedures for Permanent Placement Determination Proceedings for a Child Eight (8) Years of Age or Older or a Child Under Age Eight (8) for Whom Permanency Has Not Been Ordered; Admit/Deny Hearing Required at Month 12

The following procedures govern permanent placement determination proceedings for a child eight (8) years of age or older, or a child under age eight (8) for whom permanency has not been ordered, who has not been returned home within twelve (12) months of an order placing the child in foster care or in the home of a noncustodial parent:

(a) *Petition.* Unless the responsible social services agency recommends return of the child to the custodial parent or files a petition and motion pursuant to Rule 42.14, not later than thirty (30) days prior to the admit/deny hearing required in paragraph (b) the responsible social services agency shall file with the court a petition required under Rule 33.01 to establish the basis for the juvenile court to order permanent placement of the child according to Rules 42.06 to 42.12.

(b) *Admit/Deny Hearing on Permanency Petition.* The court shall commence and complete an admit/deny hearing pursuant to Rule 34 on the permanency petition, termination of parental rights petition, or petition for alternative permanent placement relief under Rule 33.01 not later than twelve (12) months after the child is placed in foster care or in the care of a noncustodial parent.

(c) *Trial.* The court shall commence and complete any trial on the permanency petition within the time specified in Rule 39.

Amended Nov. 12, 2003; Dec. 1, 2006, eff. Jan. 1, 2007; June 10, 2009, eff. Aug. 1, 2009.

Historical Notes

The order of the Minnesota Supreme Court [C1–01–927] dated June 10, 2009, amending the Rules of Juvenile Protection Procedure and the Rules of Adoption Procedure, provides in part that the amendments are effective August 1, 2009, and shall apply to all actions or proceedings pending on or commenced on or after the effective date.

The order of the Minnesota Supreme Court [C1-01-927] dated November 12, 2003, amending Rules 37 to 82 of the Rules of Juvenile Procedure and renumbering them as Rules 1 to 47 of the Rules of Juvenile Protection Procedure, provides in part that the amendments are effective January 1, 2004, and shall apply to all juvenile protection matters filed on or after that date.

Former rule: A former Rule 42.04, subd. 1, amended by court orders dated November 12, 2003, and December 1, 2006, related to the procedures for permanency progress review hearings. The subject matter of former Rule 42.04, subd. 1, was incorporated into Rule 42.03 by court order dated June 10, 2009, effective August 1, 2009.

Rule 42.05. Permanent Placement Findings and Order

Subd. 1. Findings. Except in the case of an order terminating parental rights governed by Rule 42.08, an order permanently placing the child out of the home of the parent or guardian shall include the following findings:

(a) how the child's best interests are served by the order;

(b) the nature and extent of the responsible social services agency's reasonable efforts, or in the case of an Indian child active efforts, to reunify the child with the parent or guardian where reasonable efforts are required;

(c) the parent's efforts and ability to use services to correct the conditions which led to the out-of-home placement; and

(d) that the conditions which led to the out-of-home placement have not been corrected so that the child can safely return home.

Subd. 2. Order. At the conclusion of the permanent placement determination proceedings the court shall order one of the following permanency dispositions:

(a) Return the child home pursuant to Rule 42.06;

(b) Transfer permanent legal and physical custody to a relative pursuant to Rule 42.07;

(c) Terminate parental rights pursuant to Rule 42.08;

(d) Guardianship and legal custody to the Commissioner of Human Services upon consent by the child's parent to adopt pursuant to Rule 42.09;

(e) Long term foster care pursuant to Rule 42.11; or

(f) Foster care for a specified period of time pursuant to Rule 42.12.

Amended Nov. 12, 2003; Dec. 1, 2006, eff. Jan. 1, 2007; June 10, 2009, eff. Aug. 1, 2009.

Historical Notes

The order of the Minnesota Supreme Court [C1–01–927] dated June 10, 2009, amending the Rules of Juvenile Protection Procedure and the Rules of Adoption Procedure, provides in part that the amendments are effective August 1, 2009, and shall apply to all actions or proceedings pending on or commenced on or after the effective date.

The order of the Minnesota Supreme Court [C1-01-927] dated November 12, 2003, amending Rules 37 to 82 of the Rules of Juvenile Procedure and renumbering them as Rules 1 to 47 of the Rules of Juvenile Protection Procedure, provides in part that the amendments are effective January 1, 2004, and shall apply to all juvenile protection matters filed on or after that date.

Former rule: A former Rule 42.05, amended by court orders dated November 12, 2003, and December 1, 2006, related to permanent placement orders. The subject matter of former Rule 42.05 was incorporated into Rules 42.06, 42.07, 42.09, 42.11, and 42.12, all by court order dated June 10, 2009, effective August 1, 2009.

Rule 42.06. Return Child Home

If the court orders the child to be returned to the care of a parent, the court may enter or continue a prior finding that the child is in need of protection or services and may order conditions directed to correction of the child's need for protection or services. The court may order:

(a) the child returned on a trial home visit pursuant to Rule 41.05, subd. 2(a)(3);

(b) the child placed under the protective supervision of the responsible social services agency under Rule 41.05, subd. 2(a)(1); or

(c) monitoring of the parent's continued ability to maintain the child safely in the home under Rule 41.05, subd. 2(a)(6).

Former Rule 42.05, subd. 2, par. (a), amended Nov. 12, 2003; Dec. 1, 2006. Renumbered Rule 42.06 and amended June 10, 2009, eff. Aug. 1, 2009.

Historical Notes

The order of the Minnesota Supreme Court [C1–01–927] dated June 10, 2009, amending the Rules of Juvenile Protection Procedure and the Rules of Adoption Procedure, provides in part that the amendments are effective August 1, 2009, and shall apply to all actions or proceedings pending on or commenced on or after the effective date.

Former rule: A former Rule 42.06, adopted by court order dated December 1, 2006, and relating to a motion by the responsible social services agency to modify adjudication and transfer of a custody order for a child who continues in placement due solely to the child's emotional disturbance or developmental disability, was deleted by court order dated June 10, 2009, effective August 1, 2009.

Rule 42.07. Transfer of Permanent Legal and Physical Custody to a Relative

Subd. 1. Order. The court may order transfer of permanent legal and physical custody to a fit and willing relative pursuant to Minnesota Statutes § 260C.201, subd. 11(d)(1).

Subd. 2. Jurisdiction Terminated Unless Retained. If the court transfers permanent legal and physical custody to a relative, juvenile court jurisdiction is terminated unless specifically retained by the court in its order.

Subd. 3. Further Hearings If Jurisdiction Retained. If the court retains jurisdiction, the court may order further in-court hearings at such intervals as it determines to be in the best interests of the child pursuant to subdivision 7.

Subd. 4. Order and Further Proceedings in Family Court. When juvenile court jurisdiction is terminated, the court shall include an order directing the juvenile court administrator to file the order with the family court. Any further proceedings for modification of the order transferring permanent legal and physical custody to a relative shall be brought in the family court of the county where the original order was filed. The review shall be pursuant to Minnesota Statutes § 518.18 and § 518.185. Notice of any family court proceedings shall be provided by the court administrator to the responsible social services agency which shall be a party to the family court proceeding pursuant to Minnesota Statutes § 260C.201, subd. 11(j).

Subd. 5. Voluntary Transfer of Custody. A parent or legal custodian may voluntarily agree to transfer permanent legal and physical custody of the child to a fit and willing relative by either filing a petition to transfer permanent legal and physical custody pursuant to Rule 33.01 and establishing that such transfer is in the child's best interests under Minnesota Statutes § 260C.201, subd. 11, or by entering an admission to such a petition filed by another party and stating, under oath, that the parent or legal custodian believes such a transfer is in the child's best interests and establishes good cause for the transfer on the record before the court.

Subd. 6. Order Requirements. In addition to the findings required under Rule 42.05, the order transferring permanent legal and physical custody shall address parental and sibling visitation and ongoing services to be delivered to the child while the juvenile court has jurisdiction, and shall state whether the transfer was voluntary or involuntary. The order shall state whether a child support order exists or if the issue is reserved for future determination.

Subd. 7. Review for a Child Who is with a Relative Who Has Permanent Legal and Physical Custody

When the court orders transfer of permanent legal and physical custody to a relative under this Rule, the court may retain jurisdiction over the responsible social services agency, the parents or guardian of the child, the child, and the permanent legal and physical custodian. The court may conduct reviews at such frequency as the court determines will serve the child's best interests for the purpose of ensuring:

(a) appropriate services are delivered to the child and the permanent legal and physical custodian; or

(b) conditions ordered by the court relating to the care and custody of the child are met.

Former Rule 42.05, subd. 2, par. (b), amended Nov. 12, 2003; Dec. 1, 2006. Renumbered Rule 42.07 and amended June 10, 2009, eff. Aug. 1, 2009.

Historical Notes

The order of the Minnesota Supreme Court [C1–01–927] dated June 10, 2009, amending the Rules of Juvenile Protection Procedure and the Rules of Adoption Procedure, provides in part that the amendments are effective August 1, 2009, and shall apply to all actions or proceedings pending on or commenced on or after the effective date.

Rule 42.08. Involuntary and Voluntary Termination of Parental Rights Proceedings

Subd. 1. Involuntary Termination of Parental Rights Proceedings. Upon petition pursuant to Minnesota Statutes § 260C.301, subd. 1(b), and after an admit/deny hearing under Rule 34 or a trial under Rule 39, as appropriate, the court may issue an order granting or denying a petition to involuntarily terminate parental rights which shall include the following:

(a) a statement of the facts upon which the court bases its order;

(b) findings regarding how the order is in the best interests of the child;

(c) findings regarding the responsible social services agency's reasonable efforts, or, in the case of an Indian child active efforts, to reunify the child and the parent or that reasonable efforts for reunification are not required under Minnesota Statutes § 260.012;

(d) if the child is an Indian child, findings regarding the testimony, pursuant to Rule 49, of at least one qualified expert witness;

(e) if termination of parental rights is ordered, the specific statutory grounds under Minnesota Statutes § 260C.301, subd. 1(b), upon which the court issued its order and the facts supporting those grounds; and

(f) the effective date of the order.

Subd. 2. Voluntary Termination of Parental Rights Proceedings.

(a) *Petition and Consent.* Upon petition pursuant to Minnesota Statutes § 260C.301, subd. 1(a), and voluntary consent of the parent, the court shall conduct a hearing regarding the voluntary termination of the person's parental rights.

(b) *Oath.* At the hearing, the parent shall be placed under oath for the purpose of:

(1) asking that the petition be granted; and

(2) establishing that there is good cause for termination of parental rights and that it is in the best interests of the child to terminate parental rights.

(c) *Hearing.* During the hearing, the court shall:

(1) advise the parent of the right to representation by counsel pursuant to Rule 25;

(2) determine whether the parent fully understands the consequences of termination of parental rights and the alternatives to termination;

(3) inquire as to the true voluntary nature of the parent's consent; and

(4) obtain a waiver of the right to trial on the involuntary petition when the parent is voluntarily consenting to termination of parental rights after an involuntary termination of parental rights petition has been filed.

(d) if the parent is not present in court but has signed a voluntary consent to termination of parental rights, the court shall determine whether there has been compliance with all statutory requirements regarding a written consent to termination of parental rights and whether the parent was thoroughly advised of and understood the right to trial, the right to representation by counsel, the consequences of termination of parental rights, and the alternatives to termination.

Subd. 3. Voluntary Termination of Parental Rights in Matters Governed by the Indian Child Welfare Act

When the child is an Indian child and the matter is governed by the Indian Child Welfare Act, 25 U.S.C. § 1913, the following procedures apply to a voluntary termination of parental rights by an Indian parent.

(a) *Procedures for Consent.* The consent to terminate parental rights by the parent shall not be valid unless:

(1) executed in writing;

(2) recorded before the judge; and

(3) accompanied by the presiding judge's certificate that the terms and consequences of the consent were explained in detail and were fully understood by the parent or Indian custodian. The court shall also certify that the parent or Indian custodian fully understood the explanation in English or that it was translated into a language that the parent or Indian custodian understood.

(b) *Timing of Consent.* Any consent to termination of parental rights given prior to, or within ten days after, the birth of the Indian child shall not be valid.

(c) *Parent's Right to Withdraw Consent.* Any consent to termination of parental rights by a parent of an Indian child may be withdrawn by the parent at any time prior to the time the final order terminating the parent's rights.

Subd. 4. Notice to Parents Whose Rights Have Been Terminated Upon entry of an order terminating the parental rights of any person who is identified as a parent on the original birth record of the child, the court shall serve upon that person at the person's last known address written notice setting forth a statement regarding:

(a) the right of the person at any time to file with the state registrar of vital statistics a consent to disclosure, as defined in Minnesota Statutes § 144.212, subd. 11;

(b) the right of the person at any time to file with the state registrar of vital statistics an affidavit stating that the information on the original birth record shall not be disclosed as provided in Minnesota Statutes § 144.2252;

(c) the effect of failure to file either a consent to disclosure or an affidavit stating that the information on the original birth record shall not be disclosed; and

(d) the right of the parent to file an appeal pursuant to Rule 47.

Subd. 5. Review When Child is Under the Guardianship of the Commissioner of Human Services.

If the court terminates parental rights, the court shall schedule a review hearing ninety (90) days from the date the termination order is filed with the court, and at least every ninety (90) days thereafter, for the purpose of reviewing the progress towards finalization of adoption. Review under this rule is required unless the court has ordered the child into long-term foster care. The court shall notify the county attorney, responsible social services agency, the child's guardian ad litem, the child, the child's attorney, and the child's foster parent, pre-adoptive parent, and relative caregiver of the date and time of the hearing. In lieu of the court report required under Rule 38, not later than five (5) business days before the hearing the responsible social services agency shall file with the court and serve upon the parties a report which addresses the following:

(a) where the child currently resides, the length of time the child has resided in the current placement, the number of other placements the child has experienced, and whether the current foster care provider is willing to adopt the child;

(b) whether the responsible social services agency has made adequate efforts to identify, locate, and place the child with a relative willing to adopt the child; if the child is an Indian child, the agency's plan to meet the adoptive placement preferences of 25 U.S.C. § 1915;

(c) if the child has siblings in out-of-home placement or previously placed for adoption, whether the child is placed with the siblings; if the child is not placed with siblings, whether the agency:

(1) must make further efforts to place the child with siblings; or

(2) obtain the consent of the Commissioner of Human Services to separate the child from siblings for adoption under Minnesota Statutes § 259.24,

subd. 1(e), and Minnesota Rules 9560.0450, subp. 2; and

(3) has developed a visitation plan for the siblings; if no visitation plan exists, the reason why;

(d) the efforts the agency has made to identify nonrelative adoptive resources for the child including utilizing the State of Minnesota Adoption Registry and other strategies for identifying potential adoptive homes for the child; and

(e) if an adoptive home has been identified whether:

(1) placement has been made in the home;

(2) a preadoptive placement agreement has been signed;

(3) the child qualifies for adoption assistance payments, and if so, what the status of the adoption assistance agreement is;

(4) an adoption petition has been filed;

(5) a finalization hearing has been scheduled; and

(6) there are barriers to adoption and how those barriers might be removed.

(f) At least every twelve (12) months, the court shall enter a finding regarding whether or not the responsible social services agency has made reasonable efforts to finalize the permanent plan for the child as long as the permanent plan remains adoption.

(g) When an adoptive placement was made more than twelve (12) months prior to the review hearing and no hearing to finalize the adoption has been scheduled, a hearing under Minnesota Statutes § 259.22, subd. 4, shall be scheduled.

Former Rules 43.01, 43.03, subd. 1, and 43.04, amended Nov. 12, 2003; Dec. 1, 2006; Dec. 12, 2006. Renumbered Rule 42.08 and amended June 10, 2009, eff. Aug. 1, 2009.

2008 Advisory Committee Comment

See the 2008 Advisory Committee Comment to Rule 49.03 regarding qualified expert witness.

Historical Notes

The order of the Minnesota Supreme Court [C1–01–927] dated June 10, 2009, amending the Rules of Juvenile Protection Procedure and the Rules of Adoption Procedure, provides in part that the amendments are effective August 1, 2009, and shall apply to all actions or proceedings pending on or commenced on or after the effective date.

Rule 42.09. Guardianship and Legal Custody to the Commissioner of Human Services Upon Consent by the Child's Parent to Adopt Under Minn. Stat. § 260C.201, subd. 11(d)

Subd. 1. Procedures. Without terminating parental rights, the court may award guardianship and legal custody to the Commissioner of Human Services under the following procedures:

(a) *Voluntary Consent and Identified Prospective Adoptive Home.* When there is an identified prospective adoptive home agreed to by the responsible social services agency that has agreed to adopt the child and the court accepts the parent's voluntary consent to adopt under Minnesota Statutes § 259.24.

(b) *Copies of Consent and Order to Commissioner.* The court shall forward to the Commissioner of Human Services one copy of the consent to adopt, together with a certified copy of the order transferring guardianship and legal custody to the Commissioner.

Subd. 2. When Consent is Irrevocable. Consent to adoption executed by a parent under Minnesota Statute § 260C.201, subd. 11(d)(5), is irrevocable upon acceptance by the court unless fraud is established and an order issues permitting revocation. In a matter governed by the Indian Child Welfare Act, 25 U.S.C. § 1913, a consent to adopt given by the parent of an Indian child is revocable at any time prior to finalization of the adoption.

Subd. 3. Ninety (90) Day Review. The matter shall be reviewed in court at least every ninety (90) days under the requirements of Rule 42.08, subd. 5, as if a termination of parental rights had occurred.

Former Rule 42.05, subd. 2, par. (d), amended Nov. 12, 2003; Dec. 1, 2006. Renumbered Rule 42.09 and amended June 10, 2009, eff. Aug. 1, 2009.

Historical Notes

The order of the Minnesota Supreme Court [C1–01–927] dated June 10, 2009, amending the Rules of Juvenile Protection Procedure and the Rules of Adoption Procedure, provides in part that the amendments are effective August 1, 2009, and shall apply to all actions or proceedings pending on or commenced on or after the effective date.

Rule 42.10. Order for Guardianship and Legal Custody When Parental Rights Are Terminated or When Parent Consents to Adoption

Subd. 1. Procedures. In addition to the findings and order for termination of parental rights requirements of Rule 42.08, or when the parent consents to adoption of the child under Rule 42.09, the court shall order guardianship and legal custody according to the following requirements:

(a) *Order When Parental Rights of Both Parents Terminated.* When an order terminates the rights of the only known living parent of the child, the rights of both parents of the child, or where the rights of the other parent of the child were previously terminated, the court shall issue an order transferring guardianship and legal custody to:

(1) the Commissioner of Human Services;

(2) a licensed child placing agency; or

(3) an individual who is willing and capable of assuming the appropriate duties and responsibilities to the child.

(b) *Order When Parental Rights of Both Parents Not Terminated.* When the rights of both known, living parents are not terminated at the same time, the order terminating the rights of one parent, but not both parents, shall not award guardianship and legal custody to a person or entity until and unless the rights of both parents are terminated or the child is free for adoption due to consent of a parent to adoption under Minnesota Statutes § 260C.201, subd. 11, or § 259.24. The order may continue legal custody of the child with the responsible social services agency.

(c) *Order When Parents Rights are Terminated in Separate Orders.* When the court issues separate orders terminating parental rights to a child or an order freeing a child for adoption due to consent by a parent to adoption under Minnesota Statutes § 260C.201, subd. 11(d), or § 259.24, the second order terminating parental rights or freeing the child for adoption shall reference by filing date and jurisdiction the previous order and shall award guardianship and legal custody to:

(1) the Commissioner of Human Services;

(2) a licensed child placing agency; or

(3) an individual who is willing and capable of assuming the appropriate duties and responsibilities to the child.

Subd. 2. Conditions—Limits on When Commissioner of Human Services May Become Guardian or Legal Custodian.

(a) *Limits on Appointment of Commissioner of Human Services When no Appointment under Probate Code.* The court may transfer guardianship and legal custody to the Commissioner of Human Services if, upon petition to the juvenile court by a reputable person, including but not limited to an agency of the Commissioner of Human Services, and upon trial the court finds:

(1) that both parents or the only known legal parent are or is deceased;

(2) no appointment has been made or petition for appointment filed under Minnesota Statutes § 524.5–102 to 524.5–317; and

(3) there is no individual who is willing and capable of assuming the appropriate duties and responsibilities to the child.

(b) *Responsible Social Services Agency Has Permanency Planning Responsibility.* The court shall order transfer of guardianship and legal custody of a child to the Commissioner of Human Services only when the responsible county social services agency had legal responsibility for planning for the permanent placement of the child and the child was in foster care under the legal responsibility of the responsible county social services agency at the time the court orders guardianship and legal custody transferred to the commissioner.

Subd. 3. Certified Copy of Orders. The court administrator shall forward one certified copy of the findings and order terminating parental rights and awarding guardianship and legal custody to the Commissioner of Human Services, the agency to which guardianship is transferred, or the individual to whom guardianship is transferred. The court also shall issue a separate order for guardianship and legal custody and provide a certified copy to the guardian.

Subd. 4. Copy of Order Terminating Guardianship. If the court issues an order terminating guardianship with the Commissioner of Human Services, an agency, or an individual by other than an order for adoption, the court administrator shall send a copy of the order terminating the guardianship to the former guardian.

Former Rule 43.02, amended Nov. 12, 2003. Renumbered Rule 42.10, subd. 1, and amended June 10, 2009, eff. Aug. 1, 2009.

2008 Advisory Committee Comment

Rule 42.10, subd. 2, reflects requirements of Minnesota Statutes § 260C.325, subds. 1(b) and 3. Rule 42.10, subd. 3, requires the court to issue a separate order regarding the award of guardianship to enable the guardian to demonstrate legal decision-making authority for the child without disclosing all of the findings contained in the order terminating parental rights.

Historical Notes

The order of the Minnesota Supreme Court [C1–01–927] dated June 10, 2009, amending the Rules of Juvenile Protection Procedure and the Rules of Adoption Procedure, provides in part that the amendments are effective August 1, 2009, and shall apply to all actions or proceedings pending on or commenced on or after the effective date.

Rule 42.11. Long-term Foster Care

Subd. 1. Requirements for Compelling Reasons Why Permanent Legal and Physical Custody and Adoption is Not in the Child's Best Interests. The court may order long term foster care only if it approves the responsible social services agency's compelling reasons that neither an award of permanent legal and physical custody to a relative, nor termination of parental rights, is in the child's best interests and all of the requirements of Minnesota Statutes § 260C.201, subd. 11(d)(3), are met.

Subd. 2. Disruption. Pursuant to Rule 42.15, if the long-term foster care placement disrupts, the responsible social services agency shall return the matter to court within ten (10) days of the disruption for review of the matter.

Subd. 3. Long–Term Foster Care For State Wards.

(a) *Limits on Circumstances When Long-term Foster Care Ordered.* The responsible social services agency may make a determination of compelling reasons for a child who is a ward of the Commissioner of Human Services to be in long-term foster care when the agency has made exhaustive efforts to recruit, identify, and place the child in an adoptive home, and the child continues in foster care for at least twenty-four (24) months after the court has issued the order terminating parental rights. If the court approves the agency's determination of compelling reasons, the court may order the child placed in long-term foster care.

(b) *Jurisdiction through Child's Minority.* In a case where long-term foster care is the permanent disposition, the court shall retain jurisdiction through the child's minority, unless the court extends jurisdiction to age nineteen (19).

Subd. 4. Annual Review When Child is Ordered into Long–Term Foster Care.

(a) *Review of Appropriateness of Order for Long-term Foster Care.* When a child has been ordered into long-term foster care, the court shall review the matter in court at least every twelve (12) months to consider whether long-term foster care continues to be the best permanent plan for the child.

(b) *Reasonable Efforts.* The court shall also review the reasonable efforts of the agency to:

(1) identify a specific long-term foster home or other legally permanent home for the child, if one has not already been identified;

(2) support continued placement of the child in the identified home, if one has been identified;

(3) ensure appropriate services are provided to the child during the period of long-term foster care; and

(4) plan for the child's independence upon the child's leaving long-term foster care living as required under Minnesota Statutes § 260C.212, subd. 1(c)(8).

(c) *Additional Requirements for Youth Age 16 or Older.* When the child is age sixteen (16) or older, the court shall review the agency's reasonable efforts to implement the independent living plan required under Minnesota Statutes § 260C.212, subd. 1(c)(8), and the provision of services to the child related to the well-being of the child as the child prepares to leave foster care. The court's review shall include the actual plans related to each item in the plan necessary to the child's future safety and well-being when the child is no longer in foster care. The court shall make findings regarding progress toward or accomplishment of the following goals:

(1) the child has obtained a high school diploma or its equivalent;

(2) the child has completed a driver's education course or has demonstrated the ability to use public transportation in the child's community;

(3) the child is employed or enrolled in postsecondary education;

(4) the child has applied for and obtained postsecondary education financial aid for which the child is eligible;

(5) the child has health care coverage and health care providers to meet the child's physical and mental health needs;

(6) the child has applied for and obtained disability income assistance for which the child is eligible;

(7) the child has obtained affordable housing with necessary supports, which does not include a homeless shelter;

(8) the child has saved sufficient funds to pay for the first month's rent and a damage deposit;

(9) the child has an alternative affordable housing plan, which does not include a homeless shelter, if the original housing plan is unworkable;

(10) the child, if male, has registered for the Selective Service; and

(11) the child has a permanent connection to a caring adult.

(d) *Agency Responsibility for Notice When Child is Seventeen (17).* When the child is age seventeen (17), the responsible social services agency shall establish for the court that it has given the notice required under Minnesota Administrative Rules, part 9560.0660, regarding the right to continued access to services for children in foster care past age eighteen (18), including the right to appeal a denial of social services under Minnesota Statutes § 256.045. If the agency is unable to establish that the notice, including the right to appeal a denial of social services, has been given, the court shall order the agency to give it.

Subd. 5. Modifying an Order for Long-term Foster Care for a Child Who is Not a State Ward.

(a) *Modification by Parent.* A parent may seek modification of an order for long-term foster care only upon motion and a showing by the parent of a substantial change in the parent's circumstances such that the parent could provide appropriate care for the child and that removal of the child from the child's permanent placement and the return to the parent's care would be in the best interest of the child.

(b) *Modification by Agency.* The responsible social services agency may ask the court to vacate an order for long-term foster care upon a prima facie showing that there is a factual basis for the court to order another permanent placement under this rule and that the placement is in the child's best interests. If the agency's request is to terminate parental rights, the county attorney shall file a petition under Rule 33 and the court shall proceed under Rule 34. If the agency's request is transfer of permanent legal and physical custody to a relative, the county attorney may file a motion under Rule 15 to modify the permanency order establishing long-term foster care for the child. If a party entitled to notice of the motion opposes the transfer of permanent legal and physical custody to a fit and willing relative, the responsible social services agency and county attorney shall establish:

(1) that the relative is fit and willing; and

(2) that the transfer is in the best interest of the child.

Subd. 6. Order. Upon a hearing or trial where the court determines that there is a factual basis for vacating the order for long-term foster care and that another permanent order regarding the placement of the child is in the child's best interests, the court may vacate the order for long-term foster care and enter a different order for permanent placement that is in the child's best interests.

Subd. 7. Further Reasonable Efforts Not Required. The court shall not require further reasonable efforts to reunify the child with the parent or guardian as a basis for vacating the order for long-term foster care and ordering a different permanent placement in the child's best interests.

Subd. 8. Jurisdiction. The court shall retain jurisdiction through the child's minority in a case where long-term foster care is the permanent disposition, unless the court extends jurisdiction to age nineteen (19).

Former Rule 42.05, subd. 2, pars. (e), (h), amended Nov. 12, 2003; Dec. 1, 2006; former Rule 43.03, subds. 2, 3, amended Nov. 12, 2003; Dec. 1, 2006. Renumbered Rule 42.11 and amended June 10, 2009, eff. Aug. 1, 2009.

Historical Notes

The order of the Minnesota Supreme Court [C1–01–927] dated June 10, 2009, amending the Rules of Juvenile Protection Procedure and the Rules of Adoption Procedure, provides in part that the amendments are effective August 1, 2009, and shall apply to all actions or proceedings pending on or commenced on or after the effective date.

Rule 42.12. Foster Care for a Specified Period of Time

Subd. 1. Requirements for Compelling Reasons Why Permanent Legal and Physical Custody and Adoption is Not in the Child's Best Interests. The court may order foster care for a specified period of time only if it approves the responsible social services agency's compelling reasons that neither an award of permanent legal and physical custody to a relative, nor termination of parental rights, is in the child's best interests and all of the requirements of Minnesota Statutes § 260C.201, subd. 11(d)(4), are met.

Subd. 2. Periodic Review. If the court orders foster care for a specified period of time, the court shall order in-court review hearings at intervals as will serve the child's best interests not to exceed a total of twelve (12) months after the date the order is entered for foster care for a specified period of time pursuant to subdivision 3.

Subd. 3. Continued Reviews of Foster Care for a Specified Period of Time.

If it is necessary for a child who has been ordered into foster care for a specified period of time to be in foster care longer than one year, then not later than twelve (12) months after the time the child was ordered into foster care for a specified period of time the matter shall be returned to court for a review of the appropriateness of continuing the child in foster care and of the responsible social services agency's reasonable efforts to finalize a permanent plan for the child. If it is the child's best interests to continue the order for foster care for a specified period of time past a total of twelve (12) months, the court shall set objectives for the child's continuation in foster care, specify any further amount of time the child may be in foster care, and review the plan for the safe return of the child to the parent.

Former Rule 42.05, subd. 2, pars. (f), (g), amended Nov. 12, 2003; Dec. 1, 2006. Renumbered Rule 42.12 and amended June 10, 2009, eff. Aug. 1, 2009.

Historical Notes

The order of the Minnesota Supreme Court [C1–01–927] dated June 10, 2009, amending the Rules of Juvenile Protection Procedure and the Rules of Adoption Procedure, provides in part that the amendments are effective August 1, 2009, and shall apply to all actions or proceedings pending on or commenced on or after the effective date.

Rule 42.13. Hearing for Child on Trial Home Visit at Time for Commencement of Permanency Proceedings

Subd. 1. Hearing. When the child has been ordered on a trial home visit which continues at the time the court is required to commence permanent placement determination proceedings under Rule 42.01, the court shall hold a hearing to determine the continued status of the child on the trial home visit and shall review:

(a) the child's progress during the trial home visit;

(b) the parent's progress during the trial home visit;

(c) the agency's reasonable efforts to finalize the child's safety and permanent return to the care of the parent.

Subd. 2. Required Findings. The court shall make findings regarding the reasonableness of the agency's efforts to finalize the child's return home as the permanent order in the best interests of the child and may continue the trial home visit for a period not to exceed a total of six (6) months. If the court finds that the responsible social services agency has not made reasonable efforts to finalize the child's return home as the permanent order in the best interests of the child, the court may order other or additional efforts to support the child remaining in the care of the parent.

Subd. 3. Procedure When Child Returns to Foster Care. If an order for a trial home visit is continued at or after a hearing under subdivision 1 and the child is subsequently returned to foster care, the court shall commence proceedings to determine an appropriate permanent order for the child not later than thirty (30) days after the child returns to foster care.

Adopted June 10, 2009, eff. Aug. 1, 2009.

Historical Notes

The order of the Minnesota Supreme Court [C1–01–927] dated June 10, 2009, amending the Rules of Juvenile Protection Procedure and the Rules of Adoption Procedure, provides in part that the amendments are effective August 1, 2009, and shall apply to all actions or proceedings pending on or commenced on or after the effective date.

Rule 42.14. Terminating Jurisdiction When Child is Continued in Voluntary Foster Care for Treatment Under Minnesota Statutes Chapter 260D

Subd. 1. Voluntary Placement as Prerequisite to Review. If a child has been ordered into foster care under Rules 30 or 41 and Minnesota Statutes § 260C.178 or § 260C.201, subd. 1, and the conditions that led to the court's order have been corrected so that the child could safely return home except for the child's need to continue in foster care for treatment due to the child's disability, the child's parent and the agency may enter into a voluntary foster care agreement under Minnesota Statutes § 260D.

Subd. 2. Motion and Petition to Terminate Jurisdiction. When the agency and the parent agree to voluntary placement of the child for treatment, the agency shall file a motion to terminate jurisdiction under Minnesota Statutes § 260C.193, subd. 6, which also terminates the order for foster care under Rules 30 or 41 and Minnesota Statutes § 260C.178 or § 260C. 201, subd. 1, together with the petition required under Rule 43.04. subd. 2, and Minnesota Statutes § 260D.07(b), for permanency review and the court's approval of the voluntary arrangement.

Subd. 3. Timing of Motion and Petition. The motion and petition shall be filed no later than the time the agency is required to file a petition for permanent placement under Minnesota Statutes § 260C.201, subd. 11, but may be filed as soon as the agency and the parent agree that the child should remain in foster care under a voluntary foster care agreement, because the child needs treatment and voluntary foster care is in the child's best interest.

Subd. 4. Service. The court shall serve the motion and the petition filed under subdivision 2 together with a notice of hearing by U.S. mail.

Subd. 5. Continuous Agency Authority for Foster Care. The parent and agency may execute the voluntary foster care agreement at or before the permanency review hearing required under Rule 43.04, subd. 3, and Minnesota Statutes Chapter 260D.

Subd. 6. Permanency Review Hearing Required Under Rule 43.04. When the court grants the agency's motion to terminate jurisdiction under this rule, the court shall proceed on the Petition for Permanency Review regarding a Child in Voluntary Placement for Treatment and conduct the Permanency Review hearing required under Rule 43.04. subd. 3.

Adopted June 10, 2009, eff. Aug. 1, 2009.

2008 Advisory Committee Comment

Rule 42.14, subd. 5, reflects the requirement under Minnesota Statutes § 260D.09(e) that, in order for the agency to have continuous legal authority to place the child, the parent and the agency shall execute a voluntary foster care agreement for the child's continuation in foster care for treatment prior to the termination of the order for foster care under Rules 30 or 41 and Minnesota Statutes § 260C.178 or § 260C.201, subd. 1.

Historical Notes

The order of the Minnesota Supreme Court [C1–01–927] dated June 10, 2009, amending the Rules of Juvenile Protection Procedure and the Rules of Adoption Procedure, provides in part that the amendments are effective August 1, 2009, and shall apply to all actions or proceedings pending on or commenced on or after the effective date.

Rule 42.15. Review of Child Who Experiences Disruption of a Permanent Placement

Subd. 1. Review Required When Child Removed from Permanent Placement Within One (1) Year. If a child is removed from a permanent placement disposition ordered under Rule 42 and Minnesota Statutes § 260C.201, subd. 1, within one year after the placement was made:

(a) the child shall be returned to the foster home where the child was placed immediately preceding the permanent placement; or

(b) the court shall conduct a hearing within ten (10) days after the child is removed from the permanent placement to determine where the child is to be placed.

Subd. 2. Further Planning for Child. The court shall also review what further planning is appropriate to meet the child's need for safety and stability and to address the well-being of the child, including the child's physical and mental health and educational needs.

Adopted June 10, 2009, eff. Aug. 1, 2009.

2008 Advisory Committee Comment

Rule 42.15, subd. 2, delineates what orders are to be reviewed under Minnesota Statute § 260C.212, subd. 6.

Historical Notes

The order of the Minnesota Supreme Court [C1–01–927] dated June 10, 2009, amending the Rules of Juvenile Protection Procedure and the Rules of Adoption Procedure, provides in part that the amendments are effective August 1, 2009, and shall apply to all actions or proceedings pending on or commenced on or after the effective date.

RULE 43. REVIEW OF CHILDREN IN VOLUNTARY FOSTER CARE FOR TREATMENT

Rule 43.01. Generally

Subd. 1. Scope of Rule. This rule governs review of all voluntary foster care for treatment placements made pursuant to Minnesota Statutes § 260D.01.

Subd. 2. Jurisdiction. The court assumes jurisdiction to review the voluntary foster care placement of a child pursuant to Minnesota Statutes § 260D.01 upon the filing of a report by the responsible social services agency pursuant to Minnesota Statutes § 260D.06.

Subd. 3. Court File Required. Upon the filing of a report under this rule, the court administrator shall open a voluntary foster care for treatment file.

Adopted June 10, 2009, eff. Aug. 1, 2009.

Historical Notes

The order of the Minnesota Supreme Court [C1–01–927] dated June 10, 2009, amending the Rules of Juvenile Protection Procedure and the Rules of Adoption Procedure, provides in part that the amendments are effective August 1, 2009, and shall apply to all actions or proceedings pending on or commenced on or after the effective date.

Former rule: Former Rule 43.01, amended November 12, 2003, related to the disclosure of birth certificate information in the event of a termination of parental rights. The subject matter of former Rule 43.01 was incorporated into Rule 42.08 as subd. 4 by court order dated June 10, 2009, effective August 1, 2009.

Rule 43.02. Report by Agency

Subd. 1. Content and Timing of Report. Within 165 days of the date of the voluntary foster care agreement the responsible social services agency shall file with the court and serve upon the county attorney; the responsible social services agency; the parent; the parent's attorney; the foster parent or foster care facility; the child, if age twelve (12) or older; the child's attorney, if one is appointed; the child's guardian ad litem, if one is appointed; and the child's Indian tribe, if the child is an Indian child, a written report which shall contain or have attached:

(a) a statement of facts that necessitate the child's foster care placement;

(b) the child's name, date of birth, race, gender, and current address;

(c) the name, race, date of birth, residence, and post office address of the child's parents or legal custodian;

(d) a statement regarding the child's eligibility for membership or enrollment in an Indian tribe and the agency's compliance with applicable provisions of Minnesota Statutes §§ 260.751—835;

(e) the name and address of the child's foster parents or chief administrator of the facility in which the child is placed;

(f) a copy of the out-of-home placement plan required under subdivision 5 and Minnesota Statutes § 260C.212, subd. 1;

(g) a written summary of the proceedings of the administrative review required under Minnesota Statutes § 260C.212, subd. 7, and § 260D.03;

(h) a statement that the parent, representative of the foster care facility, and the child have been notified of their right to request a hearing; and

(i) any other information the agency, parent or legal custodian, child, or foster parent or other residential facility wants the court to consider.

Subd. 2. Additional Report Requirements for Child Who Is Emotionally Disturbed. In the case of a child in placement due to emotional disturbance, the written report shall include, as an attachment, the child's individual treatment plan developed by the child's treatment professional, as provided in Minnesota Statutes § 245.4871, subd. 21, or the child's individual interagency intervention plan, as provided in Minnesota Statutes § 125A.023, subd. 3(c).

Subd. 3. Additional Report Requirements for Child Who Has a Developmental Disability. In the case of a child in placement due to developmental disability or a related condition, the written report shall include, as an attachment, the child's individual service plan as provided in Minnesota Statutes § 256B.092, subd. 1b; the child's individual program plan as provided in Minnesota Rules 9525.0004, subpart 11; the child's waiver care plan; or the child's individual interagency intervention plan as provided in Minnesota Statutes § 125A.023, subd. 3(c).

Subd. 4. Report Requirement to Include Information About Child's Disagreement. If, at the time required for the report under this rule, a child age twelve (12) or older disagrees about the foster care facility or services provided under the out-of-home placement plan required under Minnesota Statutes § 260C.212, subd. 1, the agency shall include in the report information regarding the child's disagreement and, to the extent possible, the basis for the child's disagreement.

Subd. 5. Content of Case Plan. The out-of-home placement plan required under Minnesota Statutes § 260C.212, subd. 1, shall include a statement about whether the child and parent, legal custodian or Indian custodian participated in the preparation of the plan. The plan shall also include a statement about whether the child's guardian ad litem; the child's tribe, if the child is an Indian child; and the child's foster parent or representative of the residential facility have been consulted in the plan's preparation. The agency shall document whether the the child, if appropriate; the child's parent, legal custodian, or Indian custodian; the child's tribe, if the child is an Indian child; and the foster parents have received a copy of the plan. When a child is in foster care due solely to the child's emotional disturbance, the child's mental health treatment provider shall also be consulted in preparation of the plan and the agency shall document such consultation with the plan filed with the court.

Adopted June 10, 2009, eff. Aug. 1, 2009.

Historical Notes

The order of the Minnesota Supreme Court [C1–01–927] dated June 10, 2009, amending the Rules of Juvenile Protection Procedure and the Rules of Adoption Procedure, provides in part that the amendments are effective August 1, 2009, and shall apply to all actions or proceedings pending on or commenced on or after the effective date.

Former rule: Former Rule 43.02, amended November 12, 2003, related to orders for guardianship. The subject matter of former Rule 43.02 was incorporated into Rule 42.10 as subd. 1 by court order dated June 10, 2009, effective August 1, 2009.

Rule 43.03. Court Review and Determinations Based on Court Report

Subd. 1. Determinations Based on Report. After receiving the report required under Rule 43.02 and Minnesota Statutes § 260D.06, subd. 2, the court has jurisdiction to make the following determinations and shall do so within ten (10) days of the filing of the report, regardless of whether a hearing is requested under subdivision 2:

(a) whether the voluntary foster care arrangement is in the child's best interests;

(b) whether the parent and agency are appropriately planning for the child; and

(c) in the case of a child age twelve (12) or older who disagrees with the foster care facility or services provided under the out-of-home placement plan, whether it is appropriate to appoint counsel and a guardian ad litem for the child using standards and procedures under Minnesota Statutes § 260C.163.

Subd. 2. Hearing.

(a) *Hearing Not Required.* Unless requested by a parent, representative of the foster care facility, or child age twelve (12) or older, no in-court hearing is required in order for the court to make findings and issue an order under subdivision 3.

(b) *Hearing Requested.* If a hearing is requested by a parent, representative of the foster care facility, or child age twelve (12) or older, the hearing shall be promptly scheduled so that the judge may make the findings required in Rule 43.03 within ten (10) days of the date the report is filed.

Subd. 3. Order

(a) *Procedure When Voluntary Foster Care is in Child's Best Interests.* If the court finds that the voluntary foster care arrangement is in the child's best interests and that the agency and parent are appropriately planning for the child, the court shall issue an order containing explicit, individualized findings to support its determination. The individualized findings shall be based on the responsible social services agency's written report and other materials and information submitted to the court. The court may make this determination notwithstanding the child's disagreement, if any, reported under Rule 43.02, subd. 4.

(b) *Service.* The court shall serve a copy of the order upon the county attorney; the responsible social services agency; the parent; the parent's attorney; the foster parent or foster care facility; the child, if age twelve (12) or older; the child's attorney, if one is appointed; the child's guardian ad litem, if one is appointed; and the child's Indian tribe, if the child is an Indian child.

(c) *Required Notice of Permanency Review.* The court shall also serve the parent, the child if age twelve (12) or older, and the foster parent or representative of the foster care facility notice of the permanency review hearing required under Rule 43.04 and Minnesota Statutes § 260D.07(f).

(d) *Procedure When Voluntary Foster Care Not in Child's Best Interests.* If the court finds that continuing the voluntary foster care for treatment arrangement is not in the child's best interests or that the agency or the parent are not appropriately planning for the child, the court shall:

(1) notify the county attorney; the responsible social services agency; the parent; the parent's attorney; the foster parent or foster care facility; the child, if age twelve (12) or older; the child's attorney, if one is appointed; the child's guardian ad litem, if one is appointed; and the child's Indian tribe, if the child is an Indian child, of the court's determinations and the basis for the court's determinations; and

(2) set the matter for hearing within ten (10) days and, if a guardian ad litem has not already been appointed, appoint a guardian ad litem for the child under Minnesota Statutes § 260C.163, subd. 5.

Adopted June 10, 2009, eff. Aug. 1, 2009.

Historical Notes

The order of the Minnesota Supreme Court [C1–01–927] dated June 10, 2009, amending the Rules of Juvenile Protection Procedure and the Rules of Adoption Procedure, provides in part that the amendments are effective August 1, 2009, and shall apply to all actions or proceedings pending on or commenced on or after the effective date.

Former rule: Former Rule 43.03, amended November 12, 2003, and December 1, 2006, related to court review of adoption and foster care orders. The subject matter of former Rule 43.03 was incorporated into Rules 42.08 and 42.11 by court order dated June 10, 2009, effective August 1, 2009.

Rule 43.04. Required Permanency Review Hearing

Subd. 1. Required Agency Action. When the court finds that the voluntary arrangement is in the child's best interests and that the agency and parent are appropriately planning for the child pursuant to the report submitted under Rule 43.02 and Minnesota Statutes § 260D.06, and the child continues in voluntary foster care for treatment as defined in Minnesota Statutes § 260D.02, subd. 5, for thirteen (13) months from the date of the voluntary foster care agreement, or has been in placement for fifteen (15) of the last twenty-two (22) months, and the agency determines there are compelling reasons to continue the voluntary foster care arrangement, the agency shall request judicial approval of its determination.

Subd. 2. Petition. When the agency requests the court's approval of its determination that there are compelling reasons to continue the voluntary foster care arrangement, the agency shall file a "Petition for Permanency Review Regarding a Child in Voluntary Foster Care for Treatment."

(a) *Drafted or Approved by County Attorney.* The "Petition for Permanency Review Regarding a Child in Voluntary Foster Care for Treatment" shall be drafted or approved by the county attorney.

(b) *Oath and Content.* The petition shall be under oath and include:

(1) the date of the voluntary foster care agreement;

(2) whether the voluntary foster care placement is due to the child's developmental disability or emotional disturbance;

(3) the plan for the ongoing care of the child and the parent's participation in the plan;

(4) a description of the parent's visitation and contact with the child;

(5) either:

(i) the date of the court finding that the voluntary foster care placement was in the best interests of the child, if required under Minnesota Statutes § 260D.06, or

(ii) the date the agency filed the motion under Rule 42.14 and Minnesota Statutes § 260D.09(b);

(6) the agency's reasonable efforts to finalize the permanency plan for the child, including returning the child to the care of the child's family;

(7) the length of time, including cumulated time, the child has been in foster care;

(8) a citation to Minnesota Statutes Chapter 260D as the basis for the petition; and

(9) a statement of what findings are requested from the court.

(c) *Out-of-Home Placement Plan.* An updated copy of the out-of-home placement plan required under Minnesota Statutes § 260C.212, subd. 1, shall be filed with the petition.

(d) *Manner of Service.* The court shall serve the petition together with a notice of hearing by U.S. mail upon the county attorney; the responsible social services agency; the parent; the parent's attorney; the foster parent or foster care facility; the child, if age twelve (12) or older; the child's attorney, if one is appointed; the child's guardian ad litem, if one is appointed; and the child's Indian tribe, if the child is an Indian child.

Subd. 3. Hearing Regarding Petition for Child in Voluntary Foster Care for Treatment.

(a) *Timing.* The court shall conduct a permanency review hearing on the petition:

(1) no later than fourteen (14) months after the date of the voluntary foster care agreement; or

(2) within thirty (30) days of the filing of the petition when the child has been in placement fifteen (15) of the last twenty-two (22) months; or

(3) within fifteen (15) days of a motion to terminate jurisdiction and to dismiss an order for foster care under Minnesota Statutes § 260C.201, subd. 1, as provided in Minnesota Statutes § 260D.09(b) and Rule 42.14.

(b) *Conduct of Hearing; Inquiries of Parents and Others.* At the permanency review hearing, the court shall:

(1) inquire of the parent whether the parent has reviewed the "Petition for Permanency Review Regarding a Child in Voluntary Foster Care for Treatment," whether the petition is accurate, and whether the parent agrees to the continued voluntary foster care arrangement as being in the child's best interests;

(2) inquire of the parent whether the parent is satisfied with the agency's reasonable efforts to finalize the permanent plan for the child, including whether there are services available and accessible to the parent that might allow the child to safely be with the child's family;

(3) inquire of the parent whether the parent consents to the court entering an order that:

(i) approves the agency's reasonable efforts to finalize the permanent plan for the child, which includes ongoing future planning for the safety, health, and best interests of the child; and

(ii) approves the agency's determination that there are compelling reasons why the continued voluntary foster care arrangement is in the child's best interests; and

(4) inquire of the child's guardian ad litem and any other party whether the guardian ad litem or the party agrees that:

(i) the court should approve the responsible agency's reasonable efforts to finalize the permanent plan for the child, which includes ongoing and future planning for the safety, health, and best interests of the child; and

(ii) the court should approve of the responsible agency's determination that there are compelling reasons why the continued voluntary foster care arrangement is in the child's best interests.

(c) *Court Actions Based on Consent of Parent.* At the permanency review hearing, the court may take the following actions based on the contents of the sworn petition and the consent of the parent:

(1) approve the agency's compelling reasons that the voluntary foster care arrangement is in the best interests of the child; and

(2) find that the agency has made reasonable efforts to finalize a plan for the permanent plan for the child.

(d) *Objection by Child.* A child age twelve (12) or older may object to the agency's request that the court approve its compelling reasons for the continued voluntary arrangement and may be heard on the reasons for the objection. After hearing from the child, and notwithstanding the child's objection, the court may approve the agency's compelling reasons and the voluntary arrangement.

(e) *Findings and Order Approving Continued Voluntary Arrangement.* When the court approves the responsible social services agency's compelling reasons for the child to continue in voluntary foster care for treatment, and finds that the agency has made reasonable efforts to finalize a permanent plan for the child, the court shall issue an order approving the continued voluntary foster care for treatment arrangement, and continuing the matter under the court's jurisdiction for the purpose of reviewing the child's placement every twelve (12) months while the child is in foster care.

(f) *Continued Voluntary Arrangement Not in Child's Best Interests.* If the court does not approve the voluntary arrangement after hearing from the child or the child's guardian ad litem, the court shall dismiss the petition. The agency shall either:

(1) return the child to the care of the parent; or

(2) when there is a legal basis, file a petition under Minnesota Statutes § 260C.141 requesting appropriate relief under Minnesota Statutes § 260C.201, subd. 11, or § 260C.301.

(g) *Notice of Required Annual Review.* At the Permanency Review Hearing and in the Notice of Filing of the Order from the hearing, the court shall give notice to the parent, child if age twelve (12) or older, and the foster parent or foster care facility of the continued review requirements under Rule 43.05 and Minnesota Statutes § 260D.09.

Adopted June 10, 2009, eff. Aug. 1, 2009.

2008 Advisory Committee Comment

When the timing requirements in Rule 43.04, subd. 1, are met or when otherwise appropriate and the agency determines there are not compelling reasons to continue the voluntary arrangement, Minnesota Statutes § 260D.10 permits the agency to terminate the voluntary foster care agreement and return the child home or to file a petition for the termination of parental rights when there are grounds to do so.

Under Minnesota Statutes § 260D.07(1), a finding that the court approves the continued voluntary placement means that the responsible social services agency has continued legal authority to place the child while the voluntary foster care agreement remains in effect. The parent or the agency may terminate a voluntary agreement as provided in Minnesota Statutes § 260D. 10. Termination of a voluntary foster care placement of an Indian child by a parent is governed by Minnesota Statutes § 260.765, subd. 4.

Historical Notes

The order of the Minnesota Supreme Court [C1–01–927] dated June 10, 2009, amending the Rules of Juvenile Protection Procedure and the Rules of Adoption Procedure, provides in part that the amendments are effective August 1, 2009, and shall apply to all actions or proceedings pending on or commenced on or after the effective date.

Former rule: Former Rule 43.04, amended November 12, 2003, and December 18, 2006, related to voluntary termination of parental rights matters. The subject matter of former Rule 43.04 was incorporated into Rule 42.08 by court order dated June 10, 2009, effective August 1, 2009.

Rule 43.05. Annual Review

Subd. 1. Required Annual Review.

(a) *Timing.* After the court conducts a permanency review hearing under Rule 43.04 and Minnesota Statutes § 260D.07, the matter shall be returned to the court for further review of the child's foster care placement at least every twelve (12) months while the child is in foster care.

(b) *Annual Report to the Court.* When the child continues in foster care, the responsible social services agency shall annually file a report that sets forth facts that address the required determinations the court shall make under subdivision 2. The agency's report shall be accompanied by proof of the agency's service of the report by U.S. Mail upon the parent, the child if age twelve (12) or older, the child's guardian ad litem, if one has been appointed, and counsel for any party and the child. The report shall be filed with the court at least thirty (30) days prior to the time required for annual review under this rule.

(c) *Timing of Hearing.* The court shall set a date for the annual review hearing not later than twelve (12) months after the Permanency Review Hearing and at least every twelve (12) months thereafter as requested in the report from the agency.

(d) *Service.* At least ten (10) days prior to the date set for the annual review hearing, the court shall give notice by U.S. Mail of the date and time of the hearing to the county attorney; the responsible social services agency; the parent; the parent's attorney; the foster parent or foster care facility; the child, if age twelve (12) or older; the child's attorney, if one is appointed; the child's guardian ad litem, if one is appointed; and the child's Indian tribe, if the child is an Indian child.

Subd. 2. Conduct of Hearing.

(a) *Required Reasonable Efforts Determination.* At the annual review the court shall determine whether the agency made reasonable efforts to finalize the permanency plan for the child, which means the exercise of due diligence by the agency to:

(1) ensure that the agreement for voluntary foster care is the most appropriate legal arrangement to meet the child's safety, health, and best interests;

(2) engage and support the parent in continued involvement in planning and decision making for the needs of the child;

(3) strengthen the child's ties to the parent, relatives, and community;

(4) implement the out-of-home placement plan required under Minnesota Statutes § 260C.212, subd. 1; and

(5) ensure that the plan requires the provision of appropriate services to address the physical health, mental health, and educational needs of the child.

(b) Review for Youth Age 16 or Older. When a child is age sixteen (16) or older, the court shall also review the agency's reasonable efforts to implement the independent living plan required under Minnesota Statutes § 260C.212, subd. 1(c)(8), and the provision of services to the child related to the well-being of the child as the child prepares to leave foster care. The court's review shall include the findings and review required under Rule 42.11, subd. 4(c).

Subd. 3. Order. At the conclusion of the hearing or within five (5) days of the hearing, the court shall issue an order making the findings required under subdivision 2(a) and (b), as appropriate.

Subd. 4. Service of Order. The court administrator shall serve the order upon the county attorney; the responsible social services agency; the parent; the parent's attorney; the foster parent or foster care facility; the child, if age twelve (12) or older; the child's attorney, if one is appointed; the child's guardian ad litem, if one is appointed; and the child's Indian tribe, if the child is an Indian child.

Adopted June 10, 2009, eff. Aug. 1, 2009.

Historical Notes

The order of the Minnesota Supreme Court [C1–01–927] dated June 10, 2009, amending the Rules of Juvenile Protection Procedure and the Rules of Adoption Procedure, provides in part that the amendments are effective August 1, 2009, and shall apply to all actions or proceedings pending on or commenced on or after the effective date.

RULE 44. REVIEW OF VOLUNTARY PLACEMENT MATTERS

Rule 44.01. Generally

Subd. 1. Scope of Review. This rule governs review of all voluntary foster care placements made pursuant to Minnesota Statutes § 260C.212, subd. 8.

Subd. 2. Jurisdiction. The court assumes jurisdiction to review a voluntary foster care placement of a child pursuant to Minnesota Statutes § 260C.212, subd. 8, upon the filing of a petition pursuant to Minnesota Statutes § 260C.141, subd. 2..

Subd. 3. Court File Required. Upon the filing of a petition under this Rule, the court administrator shall open a juvenile protection file which is part of the juvenile protection case record related to the matter. If a child in need of protection or services file regarding this child already exists, the petition shall be filed in that file.

Amended Nov. 12, 2003; Dec. 1, 2006, eff. Jan. 1, 2007; June 10, 2009, eff. Aug. 1, 2009.

Historical Notes

The order of the Minnesota Supreme Court [C1–01–927] dated June 10, 2009, amending the Rules of Juvenile Protection Procedure and the Rules of Adoption Procedure, provides in part that the amendments are effective August 1, 2009, and shall apply to all actions or proceedings pending on or commenced on or after the effective date.

The order of the Minnesota Supreme Court [C1-01-927] dated November 12, 2003, amending Rules 37 to 82 of the Rules of Juvenile Procedure and renumbering them as Rules 1 to 47 of the Rules of Juvenile Protection Procedure, provides in part that the amendments are effective January 1, 2004, and shall apply to all juvenile protection matters filed on or after that date.

Rule 44.02. Petition and Hearing

Subd. 1. Timing of Petition When the responsible social services agency expects the child's need for voluntary foster care placement will not exceed a total of 180 days and the child's safety, health, and best interests do not require the court to order the child in foster care, a petition shall be filed within ninety (90) days of the date of the voluntary placement agreement and shall state the reasons why the child is in placement, the progress on the out-of-home placement plan required pursuant to Minnesota Statutes § 260C.212, subd. 1, and the statutory basis for the petition pursuant to Minnesota Statutes § 260C.007, subd. 6. A copy of the out-of-home placement plan shall be filed with the petition.

Subd. 2. Service of Petition. Upon the filing of the petition, the court administrator shall serve the petition, together with out-of-home placement plan, upon the parties by U.S. Mail and shall schedule a hearing pursuant to subdivision 3.

Subd. 3. Timing of Hearing. When a petition is filed under subdivision 1, the matter shall be set for hearing within twenty (20) days of service of the petition.

Subd. 4. Initial Hearing.

(a) *Agreement to Continue.* At the initial hearing following the filing of a petition under subdivision 1, if all parties agree to the findings under paragraph (b) of this subdivision, the matter may be continued without the requirement of the parent or legal custodian entering an admission or denial to the petition. The matter may be continued for up to a total of ninety (90) more days during which time the child may continue in foster care on a voluntary basis.

(b) *Findings.* When all parties agree and the court finds that it is in the best interests of the child, the court may find the petition states a prima facie case that:

(1) the child's needs are being met;

(2) the placement of the child in foster care is in the best interests of the child;

(3) reasonable efforts to reunify the child and the parent or legal custodian are being made; and

(4) the child will be returned home in the next ninety (90) days.

(c) *Approval of Placement.* If the court makes the findings required pursuant paragraph (b), the court shall approve the voluntary arrangement and continue the matter for up to ninety (90) days to ensure the child returns to the parent's home or that the matter is returned to court as required under subdivision 5(b).

Subd. 5. Further Proceedings.

(a) *Agency Report to Court Upon Child's Return Home.* The responsible social services agency shall report to the court when the child returns home and the progress made by the parent on the case plan required pursuant to Minnesota Statutes § 260C.212, subd. 1. Upon receiving the report that the child has returned home, the court shall dismiss the petition.

(b) *Return to Court When Child Not Home.* If the child does not return home within the ninety (90) days approved by the court:

(1) the matter shall be returned to court for:

(i) an emergency protective care hearing pursuant to Rule 30 if the petition filed under item (2) of this paragraph asks the court to order protective care, or

(ii) for an admit/deny hearing pursuant to Rule 34 if the petition does not ask the court to order protective care; and

(2) the responsible social services agency shall file a new petition alleging the child's need for protection or services and explaining why the child's foster care placement shall exceed the 180–day statutory maximum permitted for voluntary placements under Minnesota Statutes § 260C.212, subd. 8. The petition shall:

(i) state a prima facie basis for the court to order the child to continue in foster care under Rule 30 and Minnesota Statute § 260C.178; or

(ii) have sufficient facts to support a disposition of legal custody to the agency for continued foster care under Rule 41.

(c) *Trial.* If the petition is not admitted at the hearing scheduled under subdivision 4(a), the matter shall be set for trial.

Subd. 6. Disagreement with Voluntary Placement. If any party or the child disagrees with the voluntary placement or the sufficiency of the services offered by the responsible social services agency at the time of the initial hearing, or if the court finds that the placement or case plan is not in the best interests of the child, the court shall schedule a trial to determine what is in the best interests of the child..

Subd. 7. Calculating Time Period. When a child is placed in foster care pursuant to a voluntary placement agreement pursuant to Minnesota Statutes § 260C.212, subd. 8, the time period the child is considered to be in foster care for purposes of determining whether to proceed pursuant to Minnesota Statutes § 260C.201, subd. 11, is sixty (60) days after the voluntary placement agreement is signed, or the date the court orders the child in protective care, whichever is earlier.

Amended Nov. 12, 2003; Dec. 1, 2006, eff. Jan. 1, 2007; June 10, 2009, eff. Aug. 1, 2009.

2008 Advisory Committee Comment

Rule 44.02, subds. 5(a) and (b), deal with the child's return home. A child may not continue in foster care on a voluntary basis longer than 180 days unless the child is in foster care treatment under Minnesota Statutes Chapter 260D. *See* Minnesota Statutes § 260C.212, subd. 8. The parent may agree that the child needs to continue in foster care longer than 180 days, in which case the parent may admit a petition alleging the child in need of protection or services which states the basis for the child's need to continue in foster care. Under these circumstances the court has a legal basis to order the child to continue in foster care. If the parent does not agree, the agency shall return the child to the care of the parent unless there is a basis for an order for emergency protective care under Rule 30 and Minnesota Statutes § 260C.178.

Historical Notes

The order of the Minnesota Supreme Court [C1–01–927] dated June 10, 2009, amending the Rules of Juvenile Protection Procedure and the Rules of Adoption Procedure, provides in part that the amendments are effective August 1, 2009, and shall apply to all actions or proceedings pending on or commenced on or after the effective date.

The order of the Minnesota Supreme Court [C1-01-927] dated November 12, 2003, amending Rules 37 to 82 of the Rules of Juvenile Procedure and renumbering them as Rules 1 to 47 of the Rules of Juvenile Protection Procedure, provides in part that the amendments are effective January 1, 2004, and shall apply to all juvenile protection matters filed on or after that date.

Rule 44.03. Procedures When Court–Ordered Foster Care, Permanent Placement, or Termination of Parental Rights Sought

Subd. 1. Applicable Rules When Other than Voluntary Review is Sought. When a child enters foster care pursuant to a voluntary placement agreement under Minnesota Statutes § 260C.212, subd. 8, and there is a sufficient evidentiary basis, the responsible social services agency may file a petition for termination of parental rights, a petition for permanent placement of the child away from the parent, or a petition alleging the child to be in need of protection or services stating sufficient facts to meet any definition of Minnesota Statutes § 260C.007(6). The matter shall proceed under:

(a) Rule 30 if the petition requests an order for protective care under Rule 30.10 and Minnesota Statutes § 260C.178; or

(b) Rule 34 if an order for protective care is not requested.

Subd. 2. Timing of Hearing. When a petition is filed under subdivision 1, timing of the required hearing shall be pursuant to:

(a) Rule 30.01 if the petition requests an order for protective care under Rule 30.10 and Minnesota Statutes § 260C.178; or

(b) Rule 34.02 if an order for protective care is not requested.

Adopted June 10, 2009, eff. Aug. 1, 2009.

Historical Notes

The order of the Minnesota Supreme Court [C1–01–927] dated June 10, 2009, amending the Rules of Juvenile Protection Procedure and the Rules of Adoption Procedure, provides in part that the amendments are effective August 1, 2009, and shall apply to all actions or proceedings pending on or commenced on or after the effective date.

RULE 45. POST-TRIAL MOTIONS

Rule 45.01. Procedure and Timing

Subd. 1. Timing. All post-trial motions shall comply with Rule 15 and shall be filed with the court and served upon the parties within ten (10) days of the service of notice by the court administrator of the filing of the court's order finding that the statutory grounds set forth in the petition are or are not proved. Any response to a post-trial motion shall comply with Rule 15 and shall be filed with the court and served upon the parties within five (5) days of service of the post-trial motion.

Subd. 2. Basis of Motion. A post-trial motion shall be made and decided on the files, exhibits, and minutes of the court. Pertinent facts that would not be a part of the minutes may be shown by affidavit except as otherwise provided by these rules. A full or partial transcript of the court reporter's notes of the testimony taken at the trial or other verbatim recording thereof may be used in deciding the motion.

Subd. 3. Time for Serving Affidavits. When a post-trial motion is based upon affidavits, such affidavits shall be served with the notice of motion. The parties and the county attorney shall have five (5) days after such service in which to serve opposing affidavits pursuant to Rule 15. The court may permit reply affidavits so long as the time for issuing a decision is not extended beyond the time permitted in Rule 45.05.

Subd. 4. Hearing. If the trial court grants a hearing on a post-trial motion, the hearing shall take place within ten (10) days of the date the post-trial motion is filed.

Amended Nov. 12, 2003; Dec. 1, 2006, eff. Jan. 1, 2007; June 10, 2009, eff. Aug. 1, 2009.

Historical Notes

The order of the Minnesota Supreme Court [C1–01–927] dated June 10, 2009, amending the Rules of Juvenile Protection Procedure and the Rules of Adoption Procedure, provides in part that the amendments are effective August 1, 2009, and shall apply to all actions or proceedings pending on or commenced on or after the effective date.

The order of the Minnesota Supreme Court [C1-01-927] dated November 12, 2003, amending Rules 37 to 82 of the Rules of Juvenile Procedure and renumbering them as Rules 1 to 47 of the Rules of Juvenile Protection Procedure, provides in part that the amendments are effective January 1, 2004, and shall apply to all juvenile protection matters filed on or after that date.

Rule 45.02. New Trial on Court's Own Motion

Not later than fifteen (15) days after finding that the statutory grounds set forth in the petition are or are not proved, the court may upon its own initiative order a new trial for any reason for which it might have granted a new trial on a motion. After giving appropriate notice and an opportunity to be heard, the court may grant a motion for a new trial, timely served, for reasons not stated in the motion. In either case, the court shall specify in the order the basis for ordering a new trial.

Amended Nov. 12, 2003.

Historical Notes

The order of the Minnesota Supreme Court [C1-01-927] dated November 12, 2003, amending Rules 37 to 82 of the Rules of Juvenile Procedure and renumbering them as Rules 1 to 47 of the Rules of Juvenile Protection Procedure, provides in part that the amendments are effective January 1, 2004, and shall apply to all juvenile protection matters filed on or after that date.

Rule 45.03. Amendment of Findings

Upon motion, the court may amend its findings or make additional findings, and may amend the order accordingly. The motion may be made with a motion for a new trial and may be made on the files, exhibits, and minutes of the court. The question of sufficiency of the evidence to support the findings may be raised whether or not the party raising the question has made in the district court an objection to such findings or has made a motion to amend the order.

Adopted Dec. 1, 2006, eff. Jan. 1, 2007.

Rule 45.04. Grounds for New Trial

A new trial may be granted on all or some of the issues for any of the following reasons:

(a) irregularity in the proceedings of the court, referee, or prevailing party, or any order or abuse of discretion whereby the moving party was deprived of a fair trial;

(b) misconduct of counsel;

(c) fraud, misrepresentation, or other misconduct of the county attorney, any party, their counsel, or their guardian ad litem;

(d) accident or surprise that could not have been prevented by ordinary prudence;

(e) material evidence, newly discovered, which with reasonable diligence could not have been found and produced at the trial;

(f) errors of law occurring at the trial and objected to at the time, or if no objection need have been made, then plainly assigned in the motion;

(g) a finding that the statutory grounds set forth in the petition are proved is not justified by the evidence or is contrary to law; or

(h) if required in the interests of justice.

Former Rule 45.03, amended Nov. 12, 2003. Renumbered Rule 45.04, Dec. 1, 2006, eff. Jan. 1, 2007.

Historical Notes

The order of the Minnesota Supreme Court [C1-01-927] dated November 12, 2003, amending Rules 37 to 82 of the Rules of Juvenile Procedure and renumbering them as Rules 1 to 47 of the Rules of Juvenile Protection Procedure, provides in part that the amendments are effective January 1, 2004, and shall apply to all juvenile protection matters filed on or after that date.

Rule 45.05. Decision

The court shall rule on all post-trial motions within ten (10) days of the conclusion of the hearing, which shall include the time for filing written arguments, if any. The findings and order shall be filed with the court administrator, who shall proceed pursuant to Rule 10.

Former Rule 45.04, amended Nov. 12, 2003. Renumbered Rule 45.05, Dec. 1, 2006, eff. Jan. 1, 2007. Amended June 10, 2009, eff. Aug. 1, 2009.

Historical Notes

The order of the Minnesota Supreme Court [C1–01–927] dated June 10, 2009, amending the Rules of Juvenile Protection Procedure and the Rules of Adoption Procedure, provides in part that the amendments are effective August 1, 2009, and shall apply to all actions or proceedings pending on or commenced on or after the effective date.

The order of the Minnesota Supreme Court [C1-01-927] dated November 12, 2003, amending Rules 37 to 82 of the Rules of Juvenile Procedure and renumbering them as Rules 1 to 47 of the Rules of Juvenile Protection Procedure, provides in part that the amendments are effective January 1, 2004, and shall apply to all juvenile protection matters filed on or after that date.

Rule 45.06. Relief

In response to any post-trial motion, including a motion for a new trial, the court may:

(a) conduct a new trial;

(b) reopen the proceedings and take additional testimony;

(c) amend the findings of fact and conclusions of law; or

(d) make new findings and conclusions as required.

Former Rule 45.05, amended Nov. 12, 2003. Renumbered Rule 45.06, Dec. 1, 2006, eff. Jan. 1, 2007

Historical Notes

The order of the Minnesota Supreme Court [C1-01-927] dated November 12, 2003, amending Rules 37 to 82 of the Rules of Juvenile Procedure and renumbering them as Rules 1 to 47 of the Rules of Juvenile Protection Procedure, provides in part that the amendments are effective January 1, 2004, and shall apply to all juvenile protection matters filed on or after that date.

RULE 46. RELIEF FROM ORDER

Rule 46.01. Clerical Mistakes

Clerical mistakes in judgments, orders, or other parts of the record and errors arising from oversight or omission may be corrected by the court at any time upon its own initiative or upon motion of any party and after such notice, if any, as the court orders. During the pendency of an appeal, such mistakes may be so corrected with leave of the appellate court.

Amended Nov. 12, 2003.

Historical Notes

The order of the Minnesota Supreme Court [C1-01-927] dated November 12, 2003, amending Rules 37 to 82 of the Rules of Juvenile Procedure and renumbering them as Rules 1 to 47 of the Rules of Juvenile Protection Procedure, provides in part that the amendments are effective January 1, 2004, and shall apply to all juvenile protection matters filed on or after that date.

Rule 46.02. Mistakes; Inadvertence; Excusable Neglect; Newly Discovered Evidence; Fraud

Upon motion and upon such terms as are just, the court may relieve a party or the party's legal representatives from a final order or proceeding, including a default order, and may order a new trial or grant such other relief as may be just for any of the following reasons:

(a) mistake, inadvertence, surprise, or excusable neglect;

(b) newly discovered evidence which by due diligence could not have been discovered in time to move for a new trial;

(c) fraud (whether denominated intrinsic or extrinsic), misrepresentation, or other misconduct of an adverse party;

(d) the judgment is void; or

(e) any other reason justifying relief from the operation of the order.

The motion shall be made within a reasonable time, but in no event shall it be more than ninety (90) days following the service of notice by the court administrator of the filing of the court's order.

Amended Nov. 12, 2003; Dec. 1, 2006, eff. Jan. 1, 2007.

Historical Notes

The order of the Minnesota Supreme Court [C1-01-927] dated November 12, 2003, amending Rules 37 to 82 of the Rules of Juvenile

Procedure and renumbering them as Rules 1 to 47 of the Rules of Juvenile Protection Procedure, provides in part that the amendments are effective January 1, 2004, and shall apply to all juvenile protection matters filed on or after that date.

Rule 46.03. Invalidation of Action Under ICWA

Subd. 1. Petition or Motion. Pursuant to 25 U.S.C. § 1914, any Indian child who is the subject of any action for foster care placement or termination of parental rights, any parent or Indian custodian from whose custody an Indian child was removed, or the Indian child's tribe may seek to invalidate the action upon a showing that such action violates the Indian Child Welfare Act, 25 U.S.C. §§ 1911—1913.

(a) *Motion.* A motion to invalidate may be brought regarding a pending juvenile protection matter.

(b) *Petition.* A petition to invalidate may be brought regarding a juvenile protection matter in which juvenile court jurisdiction has been terminated.

Subd. 2. Form and Service. A motion or petition to invalidate shall be in writing pursuant to Rule 15.01 and shall be filed and served pursuant to Rule 15.02. Both a motion and a petition to invalidate shall be processed by the court as a motion. Upon receipt of a petition to invalidate a proceeding in which juvenile court jurisdiction has been terminated, the court administrator shall re-open the original juvenile protection file related to the petition.

Subd. 3. Hearing. Within thirty (30) days of the filing of a motion or petition to invalidate, the court shall hold an evidentiary hearing of sufficient length to address the issue raised in the motion or petition. A motion filed thirty (30) or more days prior to trial shall be heard prior to trial and the decision shall be issued prior to trial. A motion filed less than thirty (30) days prior to trial shall not delay commencement of the trial and the decision shall be issued as part of the trial decision.

Subd. 4. Findings and Order. Within fifteen (15) days of the conclusion of the evidentiary hearing on the motion or petition to invalidate, the court shall issue findings of fact, conclusions of law, and an order regarding the petition or motion to invalidate.

Adopted Nov. 12, 2003. Amended June 10, 2009, eff. Aug. 1, 2009.

2008 Advisory Committee Comment

Grounds for Petition to Invalidate. Rule 46.03 establishes a procedure for filing a petition or motion to invalidate an action under the Indian Child Welfare Act (ICWA). 25 U.S.C. § 1914. Section 1914 of the ICWA permits an Indian child, the Indian child's parent or Indian custodian, or the Indian child's tribe to petition the court to invalidate any action for foster care placement or termination of parental rights upon a showing that the action violated the ICWA § 1911 (dealing with exclusive jurisdiction and transfer to tribal court), § 1912 (dealing with notice to the Indian child's tribe regarding the district court proceedings, appointment of counsel, examination of reports, and testimony of a qualified expert witness), or § 1913 (dealing with voluntary consent to foster care placement and termination of parental rights). Section 14 of the ICWA is silent about the time for bringing a petition to invalidate, the relief available, and whether relief is available even if there was no objection below.

Time Limit for Filing Petition to Invalidate. Although there is no time limit for bringing a petition to invalidate contained in section 1914 of the ICWA, the Alaska Supreme Court has held that a challenge to an adoption under section 1914 shall be brought within a year. *In re Adoption of Erin G.*, 140 P.3d 886, 891 (Alaska 2006). In a slightly later case, the Alaska Supreme Court suggested that the time limit in an ICWA challenge brought under 42 U.S.C. § 1983 would be two years. *Dept. of Health & Soc. Servs. v. Native Village of Curyung*, 151 P.3d 388, 411 (Alaska 2006). The authors of *A Practical Guide to the Indian Child Welfare Act* do not cite any other cases, but they disagree that there should be time limits which vary from state to state. Native American Rights Fund, *A Practical Guide to the Indian Child Welfare Act* 161 (2007). The authors of *The Indian Child Welfare Act Handbook* recommend using the two-year time limit contained in § 1913(d). B.J. Jones, M. Tilden & K. Gaines–Stoner, *The Indian Child Welfare Act Handbook: A Legal Guide to the Custody and Adoption of Native American Children 156* (2d ed. 2008).

Reach of Relief Available. There are a number of cases which hold that section 1914 of the ICWA is not available to attack an ICWA violation occurring during the foster care placement proceeding (i.e., child in need of protection or services (CHIPS)) as part of the termination of parental rights proceeding. *In Re Welfare of the Children of S.W., et.al., Parents*, 727 N.W.2d 144 (Minn. Ct. App. 2007); *Interest of J.D.B.*, 584 N.W.2d 577 (Iowa Ct. App. 1998); *Interest of J.W.*, 528 N.W.2d 657, 661 (Iowa Ct. App. 1995); *D.E.D. v. State*, 704 P.2d 774, 782 (Alaska 1985); *In Re M.E.M.*, 679 P.2d 1241, 1243–44 (Mont. 1984). Although these courts have rejected this sort of collateral attack, there is some suggestion in all four of these cases that a different decision might have resulted if the termination of parental rights judge had made extensive use of the evidence introduced in the foster care placement proceeding in which the violations occurred. The North Dakota Supreme Court appears to agree. *See B.R.T. v. Social Serv. Bd.*, 391 N.W.2d 594, 600 n. 10 (N.D. 1986).

The Native American Rights Fund cites three cases that, it says, compel vacation of the adjudication for specific ICWA violations: *Interest of H.D.*, 729 P.2d 1234, 1240–41 (Kansas Ct. App. 1986); *In Re L.A.M.*, 727 P.2d 1057, 1060 (Alaska 1986); and *Morgan v. Morgan et al.*, 364 N.W.2d 754, 758 (Mich. Ct. App. 1985). Native American Rights Fund, *A Practical Guide to the Indian Child Welfare Act* 162 (2007). But none of these three cases invalidates a subsequent termination of parental rights because of ICWA violations occurring during the foster care placement proceeding.

In an American Bar Association treatise on the subject, the authors argue a broader role for section 1914, including collateral attack in federal court. *See* B.J. Jones, M. Tilden & K. Gaines–Stoner, *The Indian Child Welfare Act Handbook: A Legal Guide to the Custody and Adoption of Native American Children*, pp. 153–56 (2d ed. 2008).

Necessity of Objection During Trial Court Proceeding. Although it is not a section 1914 case, *Matter of L.A.M.*, 727 P.2d 1057, 1059 (Alaska 1986), specifically holds that objection during the trial court proceeding is not required to preserve an objection on appeal to a section 1912 violation. The Native American Rights Fund lists two cases which hold that an objection below is not necessary to seek relief under section 1914: *In re S.R.M.*, 153 P.3d 438 (Colo. Ct. App. 2006); and *In re S.M.H.*, 103 P.3d 976, 982 (Kan. Ct. App. 2005). Native American Rights Fund, *A Practical Guide to the Indian Child Welfare Act* 161 (2007).

Historical Notes

The order of the Minnesota Supreme Court [C1-01-927] dated November 12, 2003, amending Rules 37 to 82 of the Rules of Juvenile Procedure and renumbering them as Rules 1 to 47 of the Rules of Juvenile Protection Procedure, provides in part that the amendments are effective January 1, 2004, and shall apply to all juvenile protection matters filed on or after that date.

RULE 47. APPEAL

Rule 47.01. Applicability of Rules of Civil Appellate Procedure

Except as provided in Rule 47.02, appeals of juvenile protection matters shall be in accordance with the Rules of Civil Appellate Procedure.

Amended Nov. 12, 2003.

Historical Notes

The order of the Minnesota Supreme Court [C1-01-927] dated November 12, 2003, amending Rules 37 to 82 of the Rules of Juvenile Procedure and renumbering them as Rules 1 to 47 of the Rules of Juvenile Protection Procedure, provides in part that the amendments are effective January 1, 2004, and shall apply to all juvenile protection matters filed on or after that date.

Rule 47.02. Procedure

Subd. 1. Appealable Order. An appeal may be taken by the aggrieved person from a final order of the juvenile court affecting a substantial right of the aggrieved person, including but not limited to an order adjudicating a child to be in need of protection or services, neglected and in foster care.

Subd. 2. Timing of Filing Notice of Appeal. Any appeal shall be taken within twenty (20) days of the service of notice by the court administrator of the filing of the court's order. In the event of the filing and service of a timely and proper post-trial motion under Rule 45, or motion for relief under Rule 46 if the motion is filed within the time specified in Rule 45.01, subd. 1, the provisions of Minnesota Rules of Civil Appellate Procedure Rule 104.01, subd. 2 and 3, apply, except that the time for appeal runs for all parties from the service of notice by the court administrator of the filing of the order disposing of the last post-trial motion.

Subd. 3. Service and Filing of Notice of Appeal. Within the time allowed for an appeal, as provided in subdivision 2, the party appealing shall:

(a) serve a notice of appeal upon the county attorney and all parties or their counsel if represented, including notice of the correct case caption pursuant to Rule 8.08; and

(b) file with the clerk of appellate courts a notice of appeal, together with proof of service upon all parties, including notice of the correct case caption pursuant to Rule 8.08.

A notice of appeal shall be accompanied by a copy of the request for transcript required by subdivision 5.

Subd. 4. Notice to Court Administrator. At the same time as the appeal is filed, the appellant shall provide notice of the appeal to the court administrator. Failure to notify the court administrator does not deprive the court of appeals of jurisdiction.

Subd. 5. Request for Transcript. At or before the time for serving the notice of appeal, the appellant shall serve on the court reporter a written request for a transcript. At the same time, the appellant shall also provide the court reporter with a signed Certificate as to Transcript, which the court reporter shall sign and file with the clerk of appellate courts, with a copy to the trial court, unrepresented parties, and counsel of record, within ten (10) days of the date the transcript was ordered.

Subd. 6. Failure to File Proof of Service. Failure to file proof of service does not deprive the court of appeals of jurisdiction over the appeal, but is grounds only for such action as the court of appeals deems appropriate, including a dismissal of the appeal.

Subd. 7. Notice to Legal Custodian. The court administrator shall notify the child's legal custodian of the appeal. Failure to notify the legal custodian does not affect the jurisdiction of the court of appeals.

Subd. 8. Timing of Briefs. Rule 131.01 of the Rules of Civil Appellate Procedure applies to the timing of briefs in juvenile protection matters, except that the respondent shall serve and file a brief and any appendix within twenty (20) days after service of the brief of the appellant; within twenty (20) days after service of the last appellant's brief, if there are multiple appellants; or within twenty (20) days after delivery of a transcript ordered by respondent pursuant to Civil Appellate Procedure Rule 110.02, subd. 1, whichever is later.

Amended Nov. 12, 2003; Dec. 1, 2006, eff. Jan. 1, 2007; June 10, 2009, eff. Aug. 1, 2009.

2003 Advisory Committee Comment

The committee recognizes that the timing provision of Rule 47.02 is a departure from the Rules of

Civil Appellate Procedure. This departure is intended to expedite the appellate process, which the committee deems to be in the best interests of the child.

2004 Advisory Committee Comment—2006 Amendment

Minnesota Statutes § 260C.415 provides that an appeal shall be taken within 30 days of the filing of the appealable order and "as in other civil cases" under the Rules of Civil Appellate Procedure. The Committee recognizes that the timing provision of Rule 47.02, subd. 2, which provides that the appeal time begins to run from the court administrator's service of notice of the filing of the order, is a departure from the statute and the Minnesota Rules of Civil Appellate Procedure. This departure is intended to expedite the appellate process, which the Committee deems to be in the best interests of the child. The appeal time and procedures are governed by these rules, specifically established for juvenile protection proceedings, and not by the more general provisions of the appellate rules. *See In Re Welfare of J.R., Jr.*, 655 N.W.2d 1 (Minn. 2003).

2004 Advisory Committee Comment—2006 Amendment, 2009 Amendment

Minnesota Statutes § 260C.415 provides that an appeal shall be taken within 30 days of the filing of the appealable order and "as in other civil cases" under the Rules of Civil Appellate Procedure. The Committee recognizes that the timing provision of Rule 47.02, subd. 2, which provides that the appeal time begins to run from the court administrator's service of notice of the filing of the order, is a departure from the Rules of Civil Appellate Procedure. This departure is intended to expedite the appellate process, which the Committee deems to be in the best interests of the child. The appeal time and procedures are governed by these rules, specifically established for juvenile protection proceedings, and not by the more general provisions of the appellate rules. *See In re Welfare of J.R., Jr.*, 655 N.W.2d 1 (Minn. 2003).

Historical Notes

The order of the Minnesota Supreme Court [C1–01–927] dated June 10, 2009, amending the Rules of Juvenile Protection Procedure and the Rules of Adoption Procedure, provides in part that the amendments are effective August 1, 2009, and shall apply to all actions or proceedings pending on or commenced on or after the effective date.

The order of the Minnesota Supreme Court [C1-01-927] dated November 12, 2003, amending Rules 37 to 82 of the Rules of Juvenile Procedure and renumbering them as Rules 1 to 47 of the Rules of Juvenile Protection Procedure, provides in part that the amendments are effective January 1, 2004, and shall apply to all juvenile protection matters filed on or after that date.

Rule 47.03. Application for Stay of Trial Court Order

The service and filing of a notice of appeal does not stay the order of the juvenile court. The order of the juvenile court shall stand pending the determination of the appeal, but the juvenile court may in its discretion and upon application stay the order. If the juvenile court denies an application for stay pending appeal, upon motion, a stay may be granted by the court of appeals.

Amended Nov. 12, 2003; June 26, 2007, eff. July 1, 2007.

Historical Notes

The order of the Minnesota Supreme Court [C1-01-927] dated November 12, 2003, amending Rules 37 to 82 of the Rules of Juvenile Procedure and renumbering them as Rules 1 to 47 of the Rules of Juvenile Protection Procedure, provides in part that the amendments are effective January 1, 2004, and shall apply to all juvenile protection matters filed on or after that date.

Rule 47.04. Right to Additional Review

Upon an appeal, any party or the county attorney may obtain review of an order entered in the same case which may adversely affect that person by filing a notice of review with the clerk of appellate courts. The notice of review shall specify the order to be reviewed, shall be served and filed within fifteen (15) days after service of the notice of appeal, and shall contain proof of service.

Amended Nov. 12, 2003.

Historical Notes

The order of the Minnesota Supreme Court [C1-01-927] dated November 12, 2003, amending Rules 37 to 82 of the Rules of Juvenile Procedure and renumbering them as Rules 1 to 47 of the Rules of Juvenile Protection Procedure, provides in part that the amendments are effective January 1, 2004, and shall apply to all juvenile protection matters filed on or after that date.

Rule 47.05. Transcript of Proceedings

The requirements regarding preparation of a transcript shall be governed by Rule 110.02 of the Rules of Civil Appellate Procedure, except that the estimated completion date contained in the certificate of transcript shall not exceed thirty (30) days from the date the request for transcript is received.

Amended Nov. 12, 2003; June 10, 2009, eff. Aug. 1, 2009.

Historical Notes

The order of the Minnesota Supreme Court [C1–01–927] dated June 10, 2009, amending the Rules of Juvenile Protection Procedure and the Rules of Adoption Procedure, provides in part that the amendments are effective August 1, 2009, and shall apply to all actions or proceedings pending on or commenced on or after the effective date.

The order of the Minnesota Supreme Court [C1-01-927] dated November 12, 2003, amending Rules 37 to 82 of the Rules of Juvenile Procedure and renumbering them as Rules 1 to 47 of the Rules of Juvenile Protection Procedure, provides in part that the amendments are effective January 1, 2004, and shall apply to all juvenile protection matters filed on or after that date.

Rule 47.06. Time for Rendering Decision by Minnesota Court of Appeals

All decisions regarding juvenile protection matters shall be issued by the appellate court within forty-five

(45) days of the date the case is deemed submitted pursuant to the Rules of Civil Appellate Procedure.

Amended Nov. 12, 2003; June 10, 2009, eff. Aug. 1, 2009.

Historical Notes

The order of the Minnesota Supreme Court [C1-01-927] dated June 10, 2009, amending the Rules of Juvenile Protection Procedure and the Rules of Adoption Procedure, provides in part that the amendments are effective August 1, 2009, and shall apply to all actions or proceedings pending on or commenced on or after the effective date.

The order of the Minnesota Supreme Court [C1-01-927] dated November 12, 2003, amending Rules 37 to 82 of the Rules of Juvenile Procedure and renumbering them as Rules 1 to 47 of the Rules of Juvenile Protection Procedure, provides in part that the amendments are effective January 1, 2004, and shall apply to all juvenile protection matters filed on or after that date.

Rule 47.07. Petition in Supreme Court for Review of Decisions of the Court of Appeals

Rule 117 of the Rules of Civil Appellate Procedure applies to petitions for review of decisions of the court of appeals in juvenile protection matters, except that any petition for further review shall be filed with the clerk of the appellate courts and served upon the parties within fifteen (15) days of the filing of the court of appeals' decision, and any response to such petition shall be filed with the clerk of appellate courts and served upon the parties within ten (10) days of service of the petition.

Adopted June 10, 2009, eff. Aug. 1, 2009.

Historical Notes

The order of the Minnesota Supreme Court [C1-01-927] dated June 10, 2009, amending the Rules of Juvenile Protection Procedure and the Rules of Adoption Procedure, provides in part that the amendments are effective August 1, 2009, and shall apply to all actions or proceedings pending on or commenced on or after the effective date.

RULE 48. TRANSFER TO CHILD'S TRIBE

Rule 48.01. Transfer of Juvenile Protection Matter to the Tribe

Subd. 1. Motion or Request to Transfer. An Indian child's parent, Indian custodian, or tribe may request transfer of the juvenile protection matter to the Indian child's tribe by:

(a) filing with the court and serving a motion or any other written document pursuant to Rule 15; or

(b) making an on-the-record request which shall be reflected in the court's findings.

Subd. 2. Service and Filing Requirements for Motion, Request, or Objection to Transfer Matter to Tribe.

(a) When a motion or other written document is filed pursuant to subdivision 1(a), the service and notice provisions of Rule 15.02, subd. 1, apply.

(b) When an on-the-record request is made pursuant to subdivision 1(b), the objection and continuance provisions of Rule 15.01, subd. 3, apply.

Subd. 3. Transfer Required Absent Objection by Parent or Good Cause Finding. Upon motion or request of an Indian child's parent, Indian custodian, or tribe pursuant to subdivision 1, the court shall issue an order transferring the juvenile protection matter to the Indian child's tribe absent objection by either parent pursuant to subdivision 4 or a finding of good cause to deny transfer pursuant to subdivision 6(b), and shall proceed pursuant to Rule 48.02. The order transferring the juvenile protection matter to the Indian child's tribe shall order jurisdiction of the matter retained pursuant to subdivision 7 until the Indian child's tribe exercises jurisdiction over the matter.

Subd. 4. Objection to Transfer by Parent. A parent of an Indian child may object to transfer of a juvenile protection matter to the Indian child's tribe.

(a) *Form of Objection.* The parent's objection shall be in writing or stated on the record. The writing may be in any form sufficient for the court to determine that the parent objects to the request to transfer the matter to the Indian child's tribe.

(b) *Timing of Filing and Service.* Any written objection shall be filed with the court and served upon those who are served with the motion pursuant to Rule 15.02, subd. 1, either:

(1) within fifteen (15) days of service of the motion, written request, or on-the-record request to transfer the juvenile protection matter to the Indian child's tribe under subdivision 1; or

(2) at or before the time scheduled for hearing on a motion to deny transfer for good cause, if any, under subdivision 6.

(c) *Method of Filing and Service.* Service of any notice of objection shall be by U.S. Mail, facsimile, or personal service and shall be accomplished by the parent's attorney or by the court administrator when the parent is not represented by counsel. The court shall include a parent's on-the-record objection to the transfer as a finding in its order denying the motion to transfer.

(d) *No Hearing Required.* A hearing on an objection to transfer by parent is not required.

(e) *Decision and Order.* Upon objection by a parent, the court shall deny the request to transfer the juvenile protection matter to the Indian child's tribe and issue its findings and order pursuant to Rule 10.01.

Subd. 5. Request to Deny Transfer by Child or Party Who is Not a Parent.

(a) *Child.* A child age twelve (12) or older, regardless of party status, may request that the juvenile protection matter not be transferred to the Indian child's tribe by filing with the court, within fifteen (15) days of receiving the request to transfer the matter to the tribe, a written document stating the child's request to deny transfer. The writing may be in any form. If the child is represented by an attorney, the attorney shall serve the written document and the notice of hearing. If the child is not represented by an attorney, the court administrator shall serve the written request and notice of hearing. Service of the written document and the notice of hearing by either the child's attorney or the court administrator shall be pursuant to Rule 15.02, subd. 1.

(b) *Party Who is Not a Parent.* A party who is not a parent may request that the juvenile protection matter not be transferred to the Indian child's tribe by filing with the court and serving a notice of motion and motion pursuant to subdivision 1(a) and Rule 15 within fifteen (15) days of receiving the request to transfer the matter to the tribe. The party opposing transfer shall provide a written explanation of the reason for the opposition.

(c) *Establishment of Good Cause.* The child or party opposing transfer of the juvenile protection matter has the burden of establishing good cause not to transfer. The request to deny transfer shall be scheduled for hearing pursuant to subdivision 6.

Subd. 6. Hearing on Request to Deny Transfer to Tribal Court.

(a) *Hearing.* Within fifteen (15) days of the filing of a written request to deny transfer of the juvenile protection matter to the Indian child's tribe, the court shall conduct a hearing to determine whether good cause exists to deny the transfer to the tribe pursuant to 25 U.S.C. § 1911(b).

(b) *Decision.* The court shall make findings regarding the existence of good cause to deny transfer. If good cause to deny transfer is not found, the court shall order the matter transferred to tribal court and shall proceed pursuant to Rule 48.02. If good cause to deny transfer is found, the court may either deny the request to transfer or order the matter transferred to tribal court.

(c) *Order.* The court shall issue its findings and order pursuant to Rule 10.01.

Subd. 7. Retention of District Court Jurisdiction until Notice from the Indian Child's Tribe.

(a) *District Court Jurisdiction.* The district court shall retain jurisdiction over the juvenile protection matter by written order until the district court judge receives information from the tribal court that the tribe has exercised jurisdiction over the matter. Pending exercise of jurisdiction by the Indian child's tribe, the district court has continued authority to:

(1) approve or modify services to be provided to the child and the child's family pursuant to Rule 30.10; or

(2) approve or modify the case plan pursuant to Rules 41.05 and 41.06; and

(3) make other orders that ensure a smooth transition of the matter to the tribe.

(b) *Hearings in District Court Pending Dismissal.* The district court may conduct hearings as required by Minnesota Statutes Chapter 260C and these Rules and shall conduct a review hearing at least every ninety (90) days until the Indian child's tribe exercises jurisdiction over the juvenile protection matter or the tribal court declines the transfer in response to the district court's order to transfer the matter to the tribe. Such hearings shall be for the purpose of reviewing the provision of services under the case plan or the provision of services to the child and family and to update the court regarding exercise of jurisdiction over the matter by the Indian child's tribe.

(c) *Exercise of Jurisdiction by Indian Child's Tribe.* The district court may accept and rely on any reasonable form of communication indicating the tribe has exercised jurisdiction over the juvenile protection matter. The district court shall acknowledge receipt of the communication and the exercise of jurisdiction over the matter by the tribe by forwarding to the tribal court of, or designated by, the Indian child's tribe an order terminating the district court's jurisdiction over the matter under paragraph (e).

(d) *Declination of Transfer by Tribal Court.* Upon declination of the exercise of jurisdiction over the juvenile protection matter by a tribal court, the district court shall proceed as if the matter was not transferred to tribal court.

(e) *Order Terminating District Court Jurisdiction.* After issuing the order transferring the juvenile protection matter to the Indian child's tribe pursuant to subdivision 6(b), and once the district court judge receives information that the tribe has exercised jurisdiction over the matter pursuant to paragraph (a), the district court judge shall issue an order terminating jurisdiction over the matter which shall include provisions:

(1) stating the factual basis for the judge's determination that the Indian child's tribe has exercised jurisdiction;

(2) terminating jurisdiction over all parties, the Indian child's parent or Indian custodian, and the Indian child;

(3) terminating the responsible social services agency's legal responsibility for the Indian child's placement when the district court has ordered the child into protective care under Rule 30.10 and Minnesota Statute § 260C.178;

(4) terminating the responsible social services agency's legal custody of the child when the court has transferred legal custody to the responsible social services agency under Rule 41.05 and Minnesota Statute § 260C.201, subdivision 1;

(5) discharging the Commissioner of Human Services as guardian and terminating the order for legal custody to the commissioner when the court has ordered guardianship and legal custody to the commissioner; and

(6) discharging court appointed attorneys and the guardian ad litem for the child and for the parent, if any.

Adopted June 10, 2009, eff. Aug. 1, 2009.

2008 Advisory Committee Comment

"Tribe," "Tribal Court," and "Tribal Social Services." Throughout the Indian Child Welfare Act (ICWA), 25 U.S.C. §§ 1901–1963, the phrases "tribe," "tribal court," and "tribal social services" are used. In an effort to remain consistent with the ICWA, Rule 48 mirrors the use of those phrases.

Tribe's Method of Communicating Exercise of Jurisdiction. Rule 48.01, subd. 7(c), provides "The district court may accept and rely on any reasonable form of communication indicating the tribe has exercised jurisdiction over the juvenile protection matter." The information received may be in a written order or letter, a telephone call, a faxed or emailed message, a copy of a hearing notice setting the matter for hearing in tribal court, or any other form of communication between the tribe and the district court judge regarding the tribe's action in regard to the district court order transferring the matter to the Indian child's tribe.

Transfer of Juvenile Protection Matter After Termination of Parental Rights. The Indian Child Welfare Act (ICWA) does not preclude the transfer of matters to tribal court following termination of parental rights. Rule 48.04, subd. 7(e)(5), recognizes the practice of transferring cases to the tribe after termination of parental rights and requires certain orders when such a transfer is made, *inter alia,* discharging the Commissioner of Human Services as the guardian for the child.

Transfer to Tribe Other Than Indian Child's Tribe. The Indian Child Welfare Act (ICWA) provides for the transfer of jurisdiction from State court to the "the Indian child's tribe." 25 U.S.C. § 1911. Rule 48.01, subd. 7(c), recognizes that some Indian tribes are exercising jurisdiction over child custody proceedings by designating other tribes to act on their behalf to receive the transferred case.

"Good Cause" to Deny Transfer. Consistent with the Indian Child Welfare Act (ICWA), 25 U.S.C. § 1911(b), Rule 48.01, subd. 3, mandates that transfer to the Indian child's tribe must occur upon motion absent objection by a parent or a finding of "good cause to deny transfer." "Good cause" is not defined in the ICWA. Good cause not to transfer a proceeding may exist if a child age twelve (12) or older objects to the transfer. *Bureau of Indian Affairs Guidelines for State Courts: Indian Child Custody Proceedings,* 44 Fed Reg. 67584, 67590 at C3(b)(i) (Nov. 26, 1979) [hereinafter *"BIA Guidelines"*]. "Good cause" is discussed in the *BIA Guidelines.* 44 Fed Reg. at 67583, 67590 at C.3 Commentary (Nov. 26, 1979). See also *In Re the Welfare of the Child of: T.T.B. & G.W.,* 724 NW2d 300 (Minn. 2006), and *In Re the Welfare of the Children of R.M.B. & R.E.R.,* 735 NW2d 348 (Minn. Ct. App. 2007) *rev. denied* (Minn. Sept. 26, 2007). *See BIA Guidelines,* 44 Fed. Reg. 67,584, 67,591 at C.3(b)(i)–(iv), (c), (d) (Nov. 26, 1979) (as modified).

Historical Notes

The order of the Minnesota Supreme Court [C1–01–927] dated June 10, 2009, amending the Rules of Juvenile Protection Procedure and the Rules of Adoption Procedure, provides in part that the amendments are effective August 1, 2009, and shall apply to all actions or proceedings pending on or commenced on or after the effective date.

Rule 48.02. Communication Between District Court and Tribal Court Judges

Subd. 1. Child Ward of Tribal Court.

(a) When the child is a ward of tribal court, prior to directing the return of the child to tribal court the district court judge shall communicate with a tribal court judge pursuant to subdivision 4 to:

(1) inform the tribal court judge that the district court has ordered the emergency removal of the ward; and

(2) inquire of the tribal court judge about any orders regarding the safe transition of the ward so that such orders can be enforced by the district court pursuant to the full faith and credit provisions of 25 U.S.C. § 1911(d) and Minnesota General Rules of Practice for the District Courts Rule 10.

(b) The district court judge may order the responsible social services agency and attorney for the parties to communicate with their respective tribal counterparts or to take any other reasonable steps to ensure that the ward's tribe is timely aware of the district court's order for emergency removal of the ward.

(c) Communication permitted under this rule shall facilitate expeditious return of the ward to the jurisdiction of the Indian child's tribe and consultation regarding the safe transition of the child.

Subd. 2. Child Domiciled or Residing on a Reservation.

(a) When the child resides or is domiciled on a reservation, prior to ordering transfer of the juvenile protection matter to tribal court, the district court judge shall communicate with a tribal court judge pursuant to subdivision 4 to:

(1) inform the tribal court judge that the district court has ordered the emergency removal of an Indian child; and

(2) inquire of the tribal court judge about any requirements or conditions that should be put in place regarding the safe transition of the child to the jurisdiction of the child's tribe.

(b) The district court judge may order the responsible social services agency and attorneys for the parties to communicate with their respective tribal counterparts or to take any other reasonable steps to ensure that the Indian child's tribe is timely aware of the request to transfer the matter to the tribe.

(c) Communication permitted under this rule shall facilitate timely transfer of the matter to tribal court or return of the Indian child to the child's parent or Indian custodian.

Subd. 3. Child Not a Ward of Tribal Court, Not a Resident or Domiciliary of the Reservation.

(a) When a child is not a ward of tribal court, or does not reside on or is not domiciled on the reservation, prior to ordering transfer of the juvenile protection matter to tribal court the district court judge shall communicate with a tribal court judge pursuant to subdivision 4 to:

(1) inquire whether the tribal court will accept the transfer and, if so, order the transfer absent objection by either parent pursuant to Rule 48. 01, subd. 4, or a finding of good cause to deny the transfer pursuant to Rule 48.01, subd. 6(b), and proceed pursuant to Rule 48.01, subd. 7; and

(2) inquire of the child's tribe what district court orders should be made regarding the child's safe transition to the jurisdiction of the Indian child's tribe when 25 U.S.C. § 1911(b) applies.

(b) The district court judge may order the responsible social services agency and counsel for the parties to communicate with their respective tribal counterparts or to take any other reasonable steps to ensure that the Indian child's tribe is timely aware of the request to transfer the matter to the tribe.

(c) Communication permitted under this rule shall facilitate timely transfer of the matter to tribal court.

Subd. 4. Method of Communication; Inclusion of Parties; Recording

(a) *Method of Communication.* Communication between the district court judge and the tribal court judge may be in writing, by telephone, or by electronic means.

(b) *Inclusion of Parties.* The district court judge may allow the parties to participate in the communication with the tribal court judge. Participation may be in any form, including a hearing on-the-record or a telephonic communication.

(c) *Record of Communication.* Except as otherwise provided in paragraph (d), a record shall be made of a communication under this rule. If the parties or any party did not participate in the communication, the court shall promptly inform the parties of the communication and grant access to the record. The record may be a written or on-the-record summary of any telephone or verbal communication or a copy of any electronic communication.

(d) *Administrative Communication.* Communication between courts on administrative matters may occur without informing the parties and a record need not be made.

Adopted June 10, 2009, eff. Aug. 1, 2009.

2008 Advisory Committee Comment

Rule 48.02, subd. 4, regarding communication between courts includes language similar to certain provisions in the Uniform Child Custody Jurisdiction and Enforcement Act (UCCJEA), Minn. Stat. § 518D.110. Not all provisions in the "communication between courts" provisions of the UCCJEA are included in this Rule because the UCCJEA is not applicable when the case is governed by the ICWA. *See* Minn. Stat. § 518D.104(a). The purpose of requiring court-to-court communication is to facilitate expeditious return or transfer by timely and direct contact between judges. Nothing in this rule shall be construed to delay return or transfer of the matter to tribal court. Administrative matters may include schedules, calendars, court records, and similar matters. Communication may include receipt of a tribal court order.

Historical Notes

The order of the Minnesota Supreme Court [C1–01–927] dated June 10, 2009, amending the Rules of Juvenile Protection Procedure and the Rules of Adoption Procedure, provides in part that the amendments are effective August 1, 2009, and shall apply to all actions or proceedings pending on or commenced on or after the effective date.

Rule 48.03. Court Administrator's Duties

Upon receiving an order transferring a juvenile protection matter to tribal court, the court administrator shall file the order and serve it on all parties, participants, the Indian child's parents, and the Indian child as directed by the court according to the requirements of Rule 10. The court administrator shall forward a certified copy of the complete court file by U.S. Mail, courier, hand-delivery, or any other means calculated to ensure timely receipt of the file by the tribal court.

Adopted June 10, 2009, eff. Aug. 1, 2009.

Historical Notes

The order of the Minnesota Supreme Court [C1–01–927] dated June 10, 2009, amending the Rules of Juvenile Protection Procedure and the Rules of Adoption Procedure, provides in part that the amendments are effective August 1, 2009, and shall apply to all actions or proceedings pending on or commenced on or after the effective date.

RULE 49. QUALIFIED EXPERT WITNESS REQUIREMENT UNDER THE INDIAN CHILD WELFARE ACT

Rule 49.01. Timing—Temporary Emergency Custody

Absent extraordinary circumstances, temporary emergency custody of an Indian child shall not be continued for more than ninety (90) days without a determination by the court, supported by the testimony of at least one qualified expert witness that the continued custody of the child by the parent or Indian custodian is likely to result in serious emotional or physical damage to the child.

Adopted June 10, 2009, eff. Aug. 1, 2009.

Historical Notes

The order of the Minnesota Supreme Court [C1–01–927] dated June 10, 2009, amending the Rules of Juvenile Protection Procedure and the Rules of Adoption Procedure, provides in part that the amendments are effective August 1, 2009, and shall apply to all actions or proceedings pending on or commenced on or after the effective date.

Rule 49.02. Foster Care Placement

In the case of an Indian child, foster care placement shall not be ordered in the absence of testimony of at least one qualified expert witness, as defined in Rule 2.01(21), that the continued custody of the child by the parent or Indian custodian is likely to result in serious emotional or physical damage to the child.

Adopted June 10, 2009, eff. Aug. 1, 2009.

Historical Notes

The order of the Minnesota Supreme Court [C1–01–927] dated June 10, 2009, amending the Rules of Juvenile Protection Procedure and the Rules of Adoption Procedure, provides in part that the amendments are effective August 1, 2009, and shall apply to all actions or proceedings pending on or commenced on or after the effective date.

Rule 49.03. Termination of Parental Rights

In the case of an Indian child, termination of parental rights shall not be ordered in the absence of testimony of at least one qualified expert witness that the continued custody of the child by the parent or Indian custodian is likely to result in serious emotional or physical damage to the child.

Adopted June 10, 2009, eff. Aug. 1, 2009.

2008 Advisory Committee Comment

Voluntary Versus Involuntary Termination of Parental Rights. Minnesota law distinguishes between voluntary and involuntary termination of parental rights. The Indian Child Welfare Act (ICWA) does not distinguish between voluntary and involuntary termination of parental rights and, for that reason, Rule 49 simply restates the ICWA.

Qualified Expert Witness. Rule 49 recognizes the unique requirements for and qualifications of the qualified expert witness whose testimony must be presented to the court before the court may order foster care placement or termination of parental rights under the ICWA. Rule 49.03 is a restatement of the *Bureau of Indian Affairs Guidelines for State Courts; Indian Child Custody Proceedings* (hereinafter *BIA Guidelines)* regarding the timing of qualified expert testimony when there is an emergency removal of an Indian child. *See* BIA Guidelines, 44 Fed. Reg. 67,584, 67,589–90 at B.7(d) (Nov. 26, 1979). Compliance with the requirement for a qualified expert witness is best achieved by timely notice to the child's tribe, ensuring that the county agency works with the child's tribe to discuss the need for placement, identifying extended family who can serve as placement resources and support for the family, ensuring that culturally appropriate services are delivered to the family, and requesting qualified expert witness testimony from the tribe or elsewhere. When the court has determined that the ICWA applies, but the child's tribe has not participated in planning for the child, or when the child's tribe does not support placement of the child in foster care or termination or parental rights, the requirements of this rule may be met by a person who meets the criteria of Rule 2.01(21)(b) or (c).

Historical Notes

The order of the Minnesota Supreme Court [C1–01–927] dated June 10, 2009, amending the Rules of Juvenile Protection Procedure and the Rules of Adoption Procedure, provides in part that the amendments are effective August 1, 2009, and shall apply to all actions or proceedings pending on or commenced on or after the effective date.

INDEX TO RULES OF JUVENILE PROTECTION PROCEDURE

RULES OF ADOPTION PROCEDURE

Effective January 1, 2005

Including Amendments Received Through January 1, 2014

RULE 1. SCOPE AND PURPOSE

Rule 1.01. Scope

These rules govern the procedure in the juvenile courts of Minnesota for all adoptions pursuant to Minn. Stat. § 259.20 to § 259.89. These rules do not apply to a change of name under Minn. Stat. § 259.10 to § 259.13.

Adopted Sept. 30, 2004, eff. Jan. 1, 2005.

Rule 1.02. Purpose

These rules establish uniform practice and procedure for adoption matters in the juvenile courts of Minnesota. The purpose of these rules is to ensure that:

(a) the best interests of the child are met in the planning and granting of an adoption, including an individualized determination of the child's needs and how the adoptive placement will serve the child's needs;

(b) there is recognition of the diversity of Minnesota's population and the diverse needs of persons affected by adoption; and

(c) the processes are culturally responsive.

Adopted Sept. 30, 2004, eff. Jan. 1, 2005.

2004 Advisory Committee Comment

Rule 1.02 reflects the policy set forth in Minn. Stat. § 259.20 and § 259.29. The purpose statement also reflects the policy set forth in the federal Adoption and Safe Families Act of 1997, 42 U.S.C. §§ 601, 603, 622, 629, 653, 675, 670–679, and 1320, which emphasizes that the overriding objective in any juvenile protection matter is to timely provide a safe, stable, permanent home for the child.

RULE 2. DEFINITIONS

Rule 2.01. Definitions

The terms used in these rules shall have the following meanings:

(a) **"Adjudicated father"** means an individual determined by a court, or pursuant to a Recognition of Parentage under Minn. Stat. § 257.75, subd. 3, to be the biological father of the child.

(b) **"Adoption case records"** means all records of the court regarding a particular adoption matter, including all records filed with the court, all records maintained by the court, and all reporter's notes and tapes, electronic recordings, and transcripts of hearings and trials relating to the adoption matter.

(c) **"Adoption matter"** means any proceeding for adoption of a child or an adult in the juvenile courts of Minnesota, including a step-parent adoption, relative adoption, intercountry adoption, adoption resulting from a juvenile protection matter, and any other type of adoption proceeding.

(d) **"Agency,"** as defined in Minn. Stat. § 259.21, subd. 6, and as referenced in Minn. Stat. § 245A.02 to § 245A.16 and § 252.28, subd. 2, means an organization or department of government designated or authorized by law to place children for adoption or any person, group of persons, organization, association, or society licensed or certified by the Commissioner of Human Services to place children for adoption, including a Minnesota federally recognized tribe.

(e) **"Birth relative,"** for purposes of entering into a communication or contact agreement pursuant to Rule 34, means a parent, stepparent, grandparent, brother, sister, uncle, or aunt of a child. This relationship may be by blood, adoption, or marriage. "Birth relative" of an Indian child includes members of the extended family as defined by the law or custom of the Indian child's tribe or, in the absence of laws or custom, also includes any person age eighteen (18) or older who is the Indian child's niece, nephew, first or second cousin, brother-in-law, or sister-in-law as provided in the Indian Child Welfare Act, 25 U.S.C. § 1903(2).

(f) **"Child"** means a person under the age of 18 years.

(g) **"Child placing agency"** means a private agency making or supervising an adoptive placement.

(h) **"Commissioner"** means the Commissioner of Human Services of the State of Minnesota.

(i) **"Contested adoption"** means an adoption matter where:

(1) there are two or more adoption petitions regarding the same child;

(2) a party has filed a written challenge to the adoption; or

(3) the Commissioner of Human Services or a legal custodian or legal guardian who is not a parent has withheld consent.

(j) **"Direct placement adoption"** means the placement of a child by a biological parent or legal guardian, other than an agency, under the procedure for adoption authorized by Minnesota Statutes § 259.47.

(k) **"Father."** See "adjudicated father" and "putative father" as defined in this rule.

(*l*) **"Indian child"** as defined in the Indian Child Welfare Act, 25 U.S.C. § 1903(4), and modified by Minnesota Statutes § 260.755, subd. 8, means any unmarried person who is under age eighteen (18) and is either (1) a member of an Indian tribe or (2) is eligible for membership in an Indian tribe.

(m) **"Indian custodian,"** as defined in the Indian Child Welfare Act, 25 U.S.C. § 1903(1)(6), and Minn. Stat. § 260.755, subd. 10, means an Indian person who has legal custody of an Indian child pursuant to tribal law or custom or under State law, or to whom temporary physical care, custody, and control has been transferred by the parent of such child.

(n) **"Indian tribe,"** as defined in the Indian Child Welfare Act, 25 U.S.C. § 1903(1)(8), and Minn. Stat. § 260.755, subd. 12, means an Indian tribe, band, nation, or other organized group or community of Indians recognized as eligible for the services provided to Indians by the Secretary of the Interior because of their status as Indians, including any band under the Alaska Native Claims Settlement Act, 43 U.S.C. § 1602(c).

(*o*) **"Individual related to child,"** as defined under Minn. Stat. § 245A.02, subd. 13, means a spouse, a parent, a biological or adopted child or stepchild, a stepparent, a stepbrother, a stepsister, a niece, a nephew, an adoptive parent, a grandparent, a sibling, an aunt, an uncle, or a legal guardian. Distinguish "relative" under Rule 2.01(x).

(p) **"Legal custodian"** means a person, including a legal guardian, who by court order or statute has sole or joint legal custody of the child.

(q) **"Legal guardian"** means a person who is the court-appointed legal guardian of the child pursuant to Minn. Stat. § 260C.325, subds. 1 and 3, or Minn. Stat. Chapter 525 or an equivalent law in another jurisdiction.

(r) **"Local social services agency"** means the agency in the county of the petitioner's residence.

(s) **"Parent"** means the biological or adoptive parent of a child, including an adjudicated father. Pursuant to Minn. Stat. § 260.755, subd. 14, "parent" also means the biological parent of an Indian child, or any Indian person who has lawfully adopted an Indian child, including a person who has adopted a child by tribal law or custom. "Parent" does not mean an unmarried father whose paternity has not been acknowledged or established.

(t) **"Petitioner"** means a person, with a spouse, if any, petitioning for the adoption of any person pursuant to Minn. Stat. § 259.21 to § 259.63.

(u) **"Placement"** means the transfer of physical custody of a child from a biological parent, legal guardian, or agency with placement authority to a prospective adoptive home.

(v) **"Placement activities"** means any of the following:

(1) placement of a child;

(2) arranging or providing short-term foster care pending an adoptive placement;

(3) facilitating placement by maintaining a list in any form of biological parents or prospective adoptive parents;

(4) collecting health and social histories of a birth family;

(5) conducting an adoption study;

(6) witnessing consents to an adoption; or

(7) engaging in any activity listed in clauses (1) to (6) for purposes of fulfilling any requirements of the Interstate Compact on the Placement of Children, Minn. Stat. § 260.851 to § 260.91.

(w) **"Putative father"** means a man, including a male who is less than 18 years of age, who may be a child's father, but who:

(1) is not married to the child's mother on or before the date that the child was or is to be born; and

(2) has not established paternity of the child according to Minn. Stat. § 257.57 in a court proceeding before the filing of an adoption petition regarding the child; or

(3) has not signed a recognition of parentage under Minn. Stat. § 257.75, which has not been revoked or vacated.

(x) **"Relative"** means a person related to the child by blood, marriage, or adoption, or an individual who is an important friend with whom the child has resided or had significant contact. For an Indian child, relative includes members of the extended family as defined by the law or custom of the Indian child's tribe or, in the absence of laws or custom, any person age 18 or older who is the Indian child's grandparent, aunt, uncle, brother, sister, niece, nephew, first or second cousin, brother-in-law, sister-in-law, or stepparent as provided in the Indian Child Welfare Act of 1978, 25 U.S.C. § 1903(2). Distinguish "Individual Related to Child" under Rule 2.01(*o*).

(y) **"Responsible social services agency"** means the county agency acting on behalf of the Commissioner of Human Services as legal guardian or legal custodian of the child.

(z) **"Working day"** refers solely to revocation of consents and means Monday through Friday, excluding any holiday as defined under Minn. Stat. § 645.44, subd. 5.

(aa) **"Intercountry adoption"** means adoption of a child by a Minnesota resident under the laws of a foreign country or the adoption under the laws of Minnesota of a child born in another country.

Adopted Sept. 30, 2004, eff. Jan. 1, 2005. Amended Dec. 1, 2006, eff. Jan. 1, 2007.

RULE 3. APPLICABILITY OF OTHER RULES AND STATUTES

Rule 3.01. Rules of Civil Procedure

Except as otherwise provided by statute or these rules, the Minnesota Rules of Civil Procedure do not apply to adoption matters.

Adopted Sept. 30, 2004, eff. Jan. 1, 2005.

Rule 3.02. Rules of Evidence

The Minnesota Rules of Evidence apply to adoption matters.

Adopted Sept. 30, 2004, eff. Jan. 1, 2005.

Rule 3.03. Rules of Guardian Ad Litem Procedure

The Minnesota Rules of Guardian Ad Litem Procedure apply to adoption matters.

Adopted Sept. 1, 2004, eff. Jan. 1, 2005.

Rule 3.04. Indian Child Welfare Act and Other Minnesota Statutes

Adoption matters concerning an Indian child shall be governed by the Indian Child Welfare Act, 25 U.S.C. § 1901 to § 1963; the Minnesota Indian Family Preservation Act, Minn. Stat. § 260.751 to § 260.835; and by these rules when these rules are not inconsistent with the Indian Child Welfare Act or the Minnesota Indian Family Preservation Act.

Adopted Sept. 1, 2004, eff. Jan. 1, 2005.

Rule 3.05. Court Interpreter Statutes, Rules, and Court Policies

The statutes, court rules, and court policies regarding appointment of court interpreters apply to adoption matters. The court may appoint an interpreter of its own selection and may fix reasonable compensation pursuant to such statutes, court rules, and court policies.

Adopted Sept. 1, 2004. eff. Jan. 1, 2005.

Rule 3.06. Interstate Compact on the Placement of Children

Adoption matters concerning children crossing state lines for the purpose of adoption are subject to the provisions of the Interstate Compact on the Placement of Children, Minn. Stat. § 260.851 to § 260.91.

Adopted Sept. 30, 2004, eff. Jan. 1, 2005.

Rule 3.07. Human Services Licensing Act

The Human Services Licensing Act, Minn. Stat. § 245A.03, applies to adoption matters.

Adopted Sept. 30, 2004, eff. Jan. 1, 2005.

2004 Advisory Committee Comment

The Human Services Licensing Act establishes that only Minnesota licensed adoption agencies or county social services agencies are authorized to complete adoption "placement activities" defined under Rule 2.01(v). Minn. Stat. § 245A.03, subds. 1 and 2.

RULE 4. TIME; TIMELINES

Rule 4.01. Computation of Time

Unless otherwise provided by statute or these rules, the day of the act or event from which the designated period of time begins shall not be included in the computation of time. The last day of the period shall be included, unless it is a Saturday, Sunday or legal holiday, in which event the period runs until the end of the next day that is not a Saturday, Sunday or legal holiday. When a period prescribed or allowed is three (3) days or less, intermediate Saturdays, Sundays, and legal holidays shall be excluded in the computation. As used in these rules, "legal holiday" includes New Year's Day, Martin Luther King's Birthday, Washington's Birthday (Presidents' Day), Memorial Day, Independence Day, Labor Day, Veteran's Day, Thanksgiving Day, the day after Thanksgiving Day, Christmas Day, and any other day designated as a holiday by the President, Congress of the United States, or by the State. For purposes of calculating time for the revocation of consent under Rule 33, the definition of "working day" under Rule 2.01(z) applies.

Adopted Sept. 30, 2004, eff. Jan. 1, 2005. Amended Dec. 1, 2006, eff. Jan. 1, 2007.

Rule 4.02. Additional Time After Service by Means Other Than Mail

Whenever a person has the right or is required to do an act within a prescribed period after the service of a notice or other paper served by mail, three (3) days shall be added to the prescribed period. If service is made by any means other than mail and accomplished after 5:00 p.m. local time on the day of service, one (1) additional days shall be added to the prescribed period.

Adopted Sept. 30, 2004, eff. Jan. 2005.

RULE 5. CONTINUANCES

Rule 5.01. Findings

Upon its own motion or motion of a party, the court may continue a scheduled hearing or trial to a later date. To grant a continuance, the court shall make written findings or oral findings on the record that the continuance is necessary for the accumulation or presentation of evidence or witnesses, to protect the rights of a party, or for other good cause shown. A final hearing pursuant to Rule 41 and a trial pursuant to Rule 44 shall be commenced and completed not sooner than ninety (90) days after the child is placed, unless there is a waiver of the residency requirement pursuant to Rule 35, but not later than ninety (90) days after the petition is filed.

Adopted Sept. 30, 2004, eff. Jan. 1, 2005. Amended Dec. 1, 2006, eff. Jan. 1, 2007.

Rule 5.02. Notice of Continuance

The court shall provide written notice to the parties of the date and time of the continued hearing or trial.

Adopted Sept. 30, 2004, eff. Jan. 1, 2005.

Rule 5.03. Existing Orders; Interim Orders

Unless otherwise ordered, existing orders shall remain in full force and effect during a continuance. When a continuance is ordered, the court may make any interim orders it deems to be in the best interests of the child in accordance with Minn. Stat. § 259.20 to § 259.89.

Adopted Sept. 30, 2004, eff. Jan. 1, 2005.

RULE 6. REFEREES AND JUDGES

Rule 6.01. Referee Authorization to Hear Matter

A referee may, as authorized by the chief judge of the judicial district, hear any adoption matter under the jurisdiction of the juvenile court.

Adopted Sept. 30, 2004, eff. Jan. 1, 2005.

Rule 6.02. Objection to Referee Presiding Over Matter

A party may object to having a referee preside over an adoption matter. A party's right to object shall be deemed waived unless the objection is in writing, filed with the court, and served upon all other parties within three (3) days after being informed that the matter is to be heard by a referee. Upon the filing of an objection, a judge shall hear any motion and shall preside at all further motions and proceedings involving the adoption matter.

Adopted Sept. 30, 2004, eff. Jan. 1, 2005.

Rule 6.03. Removal of Particular Referee

Subd. 1. Notice to Remove. A party may file with the court and serve upon all other parties a notice to remove a particular referee. The notice shall be served and filed within ten (10) days of the date the party receives notice of the name of the referee who will preside at the hearing or trial, but not later than the commencement of the hearing or trial. A notice to remove may not be filed by a party against a referee who has presided at a motion or at any other proceeding in the matter of which the party had notice. A referee who has presided at a motion or other proceeding may not be removed except upon an affirmative showing of prejudice on the part of the referee. A judge shall rule on a motion to remove a referee who has already presided over the proceeding.

Subd. 2. Prejudice. If a party has once disqualified a referee as a matter of right, that party may disqualify the substitute referee, but only upon an affirmative showing of prejudice. A showing that the referee might be excluded for bias from acting as a juror in the matter constitutes an affirmative showing of prejudice. A judge shall rule on a motion to remove a substitute referee.

Subd. 3. Assignment of Another Referee. Upon the filing of a notice to remove a particular referee, or if a party makes an affirmative showing of prejudice against a substitute referee, the chief judge of the judicial district shall assign another juvenile court referee or a judge to hear the matter.

Adopted Sept. 30, 2004, eff. Jan. 1, 2005.

2004 Advisory Committee Comment

A party may not remove a particular referee and then object to having the case heard by any referee.

Rule 6.04. Transmittal of Referee's Findings and Recommended Order

Subd. 1. Transmittal. Upon the conclusion of a hearing, the referee shall provide to a judge the written findings and recommended order, including the findings of fact, conclusions of law, order for judgment, and adoption decree required pursuant to Rule 45. Notice of the findings and recommended order, along with notice of the right to review by a judge, shall be given either orally on the record or in writing to all parties, and to any other person as directed by the court.

Subd. 2. Effective Date. The recommended order is effective upon signing by the referee unless stayed, reversed, or modified by a judge upon review.

Adopted Sept. 30, 2004, eff. Jan. 1, 2005. Amended Dec. 1, 2006, eff. Jan. 1, 2007.

Rule 6.05. Review of Referee's Findings and Recommended Order

Subd. 1. Right to Review. A matter that has been decided by a referee may be reviewed in whole or in part by a judge. Review, if any is requested, shall be from the referee's written findings and recommended order. Upon request for review, the recommended order shall remain in effect unless stayed by a judge.

Subd. 2. Motion for Review. Any motion for review of the referee's findings and recommended order, together with a memorandum of law, shall be filed with the court and served on all parties within five (5) days of the filing of the referee's findings and recommended order. Upon the filing of a motion for review, the court administrator shall notify each party of the name of the judge to whom the review has been assigned.

Subd. 3. Response to Motion for Review. The parties shall file and serve any responsive motion and memorandum within three (3) days from the date of service of the motion for review.

Subd. 4. Timing. Failure to timely file and serve a submission may result in dismissal of the motion for review or disallowance of the submissions.

Subd. 5. Basis of Review. The review shall be based on the record before the referee and no additional evidence may be filed or considered. No personal appearances will be permitted, except upon order of the court for good cause shown.

Subd. 6. Transcripts. Any party desiring to submit a transcript of the hearing held before the referee shall make arrangements with the court reporter at the earliest possible time. The court reporter shall advise the parties and the court of the day by which the transcript will be filed.

Adopted Sept. 30, 2004, eff. Jan. 1, 2005.

2004 Advisory Committee Comment

If a party cannot obtain the transcript in time to file it with the motion for review, the motion should set forth the date the transcript will be submitted. The motion, recommended order, and memorandum of law must still be filed within the five-day time period prescribed by the rule, but the decision of the court may be delayed until the court has the opportunity to review the transcript.

Rule 6.06. Order of the Court

When no review is requested, or when the right to review is waived, the findings and recommended order of the referee become the order of the court when confirmed by the judge as written or when modified by the judge sua sponte. The order shall be confirmed or modified by the court within three (3) days of the transmittal of the findings and proposed order.

Adopted Sept. 30, 2004, eff. Jan. 1, 2005. Amended June 10, 2009, eff. Aug. 1, 2009.

Historical Notes

The order of the Minnesota Supreme Court [C1–01–927] dated June 10, 2009, amending the Rules of Juvenile Protection Procedure and the Rules of Adoption Procedure, provides in part that the amendments are effective August 1, 2009, and shall apply to all actions or proceedings pending on or commenced on or after the effective date.

Rule 6.07. Removal of Judge

Subd. 1. Disability of Judge. If by reason of death, sickness, or other disability a judge before whom a proceeding in the matter has been tried is unable to perform judicial duties after a decision is made or findings of fact and conclusions of law are filed, any other judge regularly sitting in or assigned to the court in which the action was tried may perform those duties; but if such other judge is satisfied that the duties cannot be performed because that judge did not preside at the trial, or for any other reason, that judge may exercise discretion to grant a new trial. If there is no other judge of the district who is qualified, the chief judge shall immediately notify the Chief Justice of the Minnesota Supreme Court.

Subd. 2. Interest or Bias. No judge shall preside over any adoption matter if that judge is interested in its determination or if that judge might be excluded for bias from acting as a juror in the matter. If there is no other judge of the district who is qualified, the chief judge shall immediately notify the Chief Justice of the Minnesota Supreme Court.

Subd. 3. Notice to Remove.

(a) *Procedure.* A party or the county attorney may file with the court and serve upon all other parties a notice to remove. The notice shall be served and filed within ten (10) days of the date the party receives notice of the name of the judge who is to preside over the proceeding, but not later than the commencement of the proceeding.

(b) *Presiding Judge.* A notice to remove shall not be filed against a judge who has presided at a motion or at any other proceeding in the matter of which the party had notice. A judge who has presided at a motion or other proceeding may not be removed except upon an affirmative showing of prejudice on the part of the judge.

(c) *Showing of Prejudice.* After a party or the county attorney has once disqualified a presiding judge as a matter of right, that party may disqualify the substitute judge, but only by making an affirmative showing of prejudice. A showing that the judge might be excluded for bias from acting as a juror in the matter constitutes an affirmative showing of prejudice.

(d) *Assignment of Another Judge.* Upon the filing of a motion to remove, or if a party or the county attorney makes an affirmative showing of prejudice against a substitute judge, the chief judge of the judicial district shall assign any other judge of any court within the district to hear the matter. If there is no other judge of the district who is qualified, the chief judge shall immediately notify the Chief Justice of the Minnesota Supreme Court.

Adopted Sept. 30, 2004, eff. Jan. 1, 2005. Amended Dec. 1, 2006, eff. Jan. 1, 2007; Dec. 18, 2006, eff. Jan. 1, 2007.

RULE 7. ACCESS TO ADOPTION CASE RECORDS AND BIRTH RECORD INFORMATION

Rule 7.01. Access to Adoption Case Records Limited

Adoption case records and files maintained by the court relating to adoption matters shall not be available for inspection or copying by any person except:

(a) the court and court personnel;

(b) the Commissioner of Human Services or the Commissioner's representatives, including the responsible social services agency, local social services agency, or child placing agency;

(c) an agency acting under Minn. Stat. § 259.47, subd. 10; or

(d) upon an order of the court expressly permitting inspection and copying pursuant to a petition filed as provided in Rule 7.02.

Adopted Sept. 30, 2004, eff. Jan. 1, 2005.

2004 Advisory Committee Comment

Rule 7.01 mirrors Minn. Stat. § 259.61, which does not permit party access to adoption case records or court files relating to adoption matters.

Rule 7.02. Petition to Access Adoption Case Records and Birth Record Information

Subd. 1. Content of Petition. A person not listed in Rule 7.01 may only access adoption case records or birth record information relating to an adoption matter by filing with the court in the county which issued the final adoption decree a petition which sets forth the reasons why the person is requesting access to the case records or birth record information and shall include the following, if known:

(a) the procedural history of the adoption proceeding, including the date of adoption or of adoptive placement;

(b) the names and addresses of all persons who may be affected by the request;

(c) a factual statement about how granting the petitioner access to the adoption case records would be of greater benefit than not granting access;

(d) the particular information sought, including whether the request for disclosure includes the name of the biological parent;

(e) the date the petitioner contacted the Department of Health requesting identifying information on a birth record, if the petitioner is requesting identifying information in a birth record; and

(f) the legal basis, if any, given to the petitioner by the Department of Health, the Department of Human Services, or agency responsible for supervising the adoptive placement for the Department's or agency's refusal to disclose the requested information.

Subd. 2. Service of Petition.

(a) *Request for Access to Identifying Information in Birth Record—Commissioner of Health.* Where access to identifying information in the birth record is sought, the court administrator shall serve the petition on the Commissioner of Health by U.S. mail. Upon service of the petition on the Commissioner of Health, the Commissioner shall supply to the court any affidavit of notification it has from the Department of Human Services pursuant to Minn. Stat. § 259.89 and any other information the Commissioner of Health has regarding the legal basis for its refusal to disclose the requested information, including whether:

(1) the biological parent has consented to disclosure of identifying information in the adoption record or birth record;

(2) the biological parent has filed an affidavit objecting to the release of identifying information which remains unrevoked; and

(3) the biological parent is living or deceased.

(b) *Request for Access to Agency Records—Agency Supervising Adoptive Placement.* When access to records of the agency responsible for supervising the adoptive placement is requested, the court administrator shall serve the petition on the director of the agency by U.S. mail.

(c) *Other Persons.* The court may order the petition to be served on such other persons as are necessary to its determination regarding whether nondisclosure of the requested information is of greater benefit than disclosure. If the court orders service upon the biological parent when the biological parent's address is known to the Department or the agency, the court may order the Department or the agency to disclose the biological parent's name and address to the court administrator who shall maintain the information in a confidential manner and cause the petition to be served on the biological parent in a confidential manner by certified U.S. Mail designated "deliver to addressee only."

Subd. 3. Access to Information—Other Agencies. The court shall forward data and information to agencies and others as required by statute or these rules.

Subd. 4. Tribal Affiliation Information. Upon application by an Indian person who has reached the age of eighteen (18) and who was the subject of an adoptive placement, the court which entered the final adoption decree shall inform such individual of the tribal affiliation, if any, of the individual's biological parents and provide such other information as may be necessary to protect any rights flowing from the individual's tribal relationship.

Subd. 5. Counsel Sharing Record with Client. Unless otherwise expressly ordered by the court, counsel for a party may only share adoption case records with that party consistent with state and federal access rules.

Adopted Sept. 30, 2004, eff. Jan. 1, 2005.

2004 Advisory Committee Comment

Rule 7.01, subd. 4, sets forth the substantive law of the Indian Child Welfare Act.

Rule 7.03. Stepparent Adoption

In a stepparent adoption, upon written request from a parent whose parental rights would be or have been severed by the adoption under Minn. Stat. § 259.59, the court may confirm in writing whether or not the adoption decree has been granted, and if so, the date of the adoption decree.

Adopted Sept. 2004, eff. Jan. 1, 2005.

Rule 7.04. Disclosure to Employer and Military Prohibited

Adoption case records and court files relating to adoption matters shall not be inspected, copied, disclosed, or released to the military services or to any present or prospective employer of the adopted person.

Adopted Sept. 30, 2004, eff. Jan. 1, 2005.

Rule 7.05. Protective Order

Upon motion pursuant to Rule 15, and for good cause shown, the court may at any time issue a protective order regarding any adoption case record or portion of such a record.

Adopted Sept. 30, 2004, eff. Jan. 1, 2005.

Rule 7.06. Suitability of Proposed Adoptive Parents

Pursuant to Minn. Stat. § 259.53, subd. 3(b), a judge of the court having jurisdiction of the adoption matter shall upon request disclose to a party to the proceedings or the party's counsel any portion of a report or record that relates only to the suitability of the proposed adoptive parents. In this disclosure, the judge may withhold the identity of individuals providing information in the report or record. When the judge is considering whether to disclose the identity of individuals providing information, the agency with custody of the report or record shall be permitted to present reasons for or against disclosure.

Adopted Sept. 30, 2004, eff. Jan. 1, 2005.

Rule 7.07. Release of Identifying Information

Subd. 1. Request for Identifying Information. After first accessing or attempting to access the requested information pursuant to Minn. Stat. § 259.83 and 259.89, an adopted person who is age nineteen (19) or older may petition the court for release of identifying information about a biological parent.

Subd. 2. Notice to Biological Parent. Upon petition for release of identifying information under Rule 7.02, including service of the petition on the agency that supervised the adoptive placement, the court may order such agency to locate and identify the biological parent's current address, including contacting the biological parent in a confidential manner as required under Minn. Stat. § 259.83. Pursuant to Minn. Stat. § 259.83, the agency may charge the petitioner a reasonable fee for its efforts to locate the biological parent. Not later than ninety (90) days after the order, or sooner if exigent circumstances exist, the agency shall inform the court of the results of the search.

Subd. 3. Biological Parent's Response to Notice.

(a) *Biological Parent's Consent.* If the biological parent has been located and consents to release of the identifying information, the petitioner shall advise the court when the requested identifying information is received at which time the court shall dismiss the petition.

(b) *Biological Parent's Refusal.* If the biological parent refuses release of identifying information, including through an affidavit objecting to the release of identifying information under Minn. Stat. § 259.83, the agency shall inform the court of the parent's refusal. If the parent's address is known, it shall be provided to the court administrator who shall maintain it in a confidential manner. Upon receipt of the parent's address, the court shall serve a copy of the petition requesting release of information and any supporting documentation on the biological parent by Certified U.S. Mail designated "deliver to addressee only".

(c) *Biological Parent Cannot be Located.* If the agency is unable to locate the biological parent's address, the agency shall inform the court about the efforts made to locate the parent's address. The court may then either direct the agency to conduct further search or grant the request for release of identifying information.

Subd. 4. Objection to Release of Identifying Information. A biological parent objecting to the release of identifying information shall have the opportunity to present evidence to the court that nondisclosure of identifying information is of greater benefit to the biological parent than disclosure to the adopted person. Such an objection shall be filed with the court within thirty (30) days of the contact and such objection shall be maintained by the court in a confidential manner.

Adopted Sept. 30, 2004, eff. Jan. 1, 2005.

Rule 7.08. Access to Original Birth Record Information; Decision

Subd. 1. Adoptions Prior to August 1, 1977. A person adopted prior to August 1, 1977, may petition the court for disclosure of the original birth record. The petition shall include information necessary for the court to make the decision required in subdivision 2. Pursuant to Minn. Stat. § 259.89, for adoptions occurring prior to August 1, 1977, and after consideration of the interests of all known persons involved, if the biological parent is deceased and the court determines that disclosure of the birth record information would be of greater benefit than nondisclosure, the court shall grant the petition and order the Commissioner of Health to disclose identifying information including the name of the biological parent on the original birth record.

Subd. 2. Adoptive Placements After August 1, 1982. Pursuant to Minn. Stat. § 259.83 for adoptive placements made on or after August 1, 1982, and after consideration of the interests of all known persons involved, if a living biological parent has filed an unrevoked affidavit objecting to the release of identifying information and the court determines that disclosure of the birth record information would be of greater benefit than nondisclosure, the court shall grant the petition and order the agency responsible for supervising the adoptive placement to disclose identifying information retained by the agency including the name of the biological parent, the biological parent's last known address, the birth date, and birth place of the biological parent named on the adopted person's original birth record.

Adopted Sept. 30, 2004, eff. Jan. 1, 2005.

2004 Advisory Committee Comment

In many situations where adult adopted persons seek information about their adoptions including the names of biological parents, the Department of Health or the agency responsible for supervising the adoptive placement have legal authority to release the requested information. The instances where the Department of Health and responsible agencies do not have such legal authority are covered by Rule 7.08.

Rule 7.09. Information to Adopted Persons and Others About Access to Birth and Adoption Records

Upon inquiry from an adopted person, a biological or adopted parent, or an adult genetic sibling, the court administrator shall give information about access to information about original birth records or adoption records as provided in Minn. Stat. § 259.83 and § 259.89 on an information sheet prepared by the State Court Administrator's Office.

Adopted Sept. 30, 2004, eff. Jan. 1, 2005.

RULE 8. PRESENCE AT HEARINGS

Rule 8.01. Attendance at Hearings

Only the parties, their legal counsel, their witnesses, persons entitled to notice pursuant to Rule 31, and any other persons authorized by the court may attend hearings relating to adoption matters.

Adopted Sept. 30, 2004, eff. Jan. 1, 2005. Amended Dec. 1, 2006, eff. Jan. 1, 2007.

Rule 8.02. Absence Does Not Bar Hearing

The absence from a hearing of any person who is entitled to notice of the hearing, except the petitioners, shall not prevent the hearing from proceeding, provided appropriate notice has been served.

Adopted Sept. 30, 2004, eff. Jan. 1, 2005.

Rule 8.03. Exclusion of Persons Who Have Right to Attend Hearings

In any hearing the court may temporarily exclude the presence of any person other than counsel or the guardian ad litem when it is in the best interests of the child to do so. If a person other than counsel or the guardian ad litem engages in conduct that disrupts the court, the person may be excluded from the courtroom. The exclusion of the person shall not prevent the court from proceeding with the hearing.

Adopted Sept. 30, 2004, eff. Jan. 1, 2005.

Rule 8.04. Record of Exclusion and Right to Continued Participation

Any exclusion of a person who has the right to attend a hearing shall be noted on the record and the reasons for the exclusion given. The counsel and guardian ad litem of the excluded person have the right to remain and participate in the hearing.

Adopted Sept. 30, 2004, eff. Jan. 1, 2005.

RULE 9. EX PARTE COMMUNICATION

Rule 9.01. Ex Parte Communication Prohibited

Ex parte communication is prohibited, except as to procedural matters not affecting the merits of the case. All communications between the court and a party shall be in the presence of all other parties or in writing with copies to the parties or, if represented, the party's attorney, except as otherwise permitted by statute or these rules.

Adopted Sept. 30, 2004, eff. Jan. 1, 2005.

2004 Advisory Committee Comment

Rule 9.01 reflects the prohibition against ex parte communication set forth in Rule 3.5(g) of the Minnesota Rules of Professional Conduct and Cannon 3A(7) of the Code of Judicial Conduct.

Rule 9.02. Disclosure

The court shall fully disclose to all parties any prohibited ex parte communication.

Adopted Sept. 30, 2004, eff. Jan. 1, 2005.

RULE 10. ORDERS

Rule 10.01. Written or Oral Orders

Court orders may be written or stated on the record. An order stated on the record shall also be reduced to writing by the court. Except for orders issued following a trial pursuant to Rule 44.06, all orders shall be filed with the court administrator within fifteen (15) days of the conclusion of the hearing. An order shall remain in full force and effect until the occurrence of any of the following:

(a) issuance of an inconsistent order;

(b) the order ends pursuant to the terms of the order; or

(c) jurisdiction of the juvenile court is terminated.

Adopted Sept. 30, 2004, eff. Jan. 1, 2005. Amended June 10, 2009, eff. Aug. 1, 2009.

Historical Notes

The order of the Minnesota Supreme Court [C1–01–927] dated June 10, 2009, amending the Rules of Juvenile Protection Procedure and the Rules of Adoption Procedure, provides in part that the amendments are effective August 1, 2009, and shall apply to all actions or proceedings pending on or commenced on or after the effective date.

Rule 10.02. Immediate Effect of Oral Order

Unless otherwise ordered by the court, an order stated on the record shall be effective immediately.

Adopted Sept. 30, 2004, eff. Jan. 1, 2005.

Rule 10.03. Delivery; Mailing

Subd. 1. Court Orders. Court orders shall be delivered at the hearing or mailed by the court administrator to each party and such other persons as the court may direct. If a party is represented by counsel, delivery or service shall be upon such counsel. Filing and mailing of an order by the court administrator shall be accomplished within ten (10) days of the date the judicial officer delivers the order to the court administrator.

Subd. 2. Adoption Decree. The findings of fact, conclusions of law, order for judgment, and adoption decree issued pursuant to Rule 45 shall be delivered at the hearing or mailed by the court administrator to:

(a) each party;

(b) the Commissioner of Human Services for children who are:

(i) under guardianship of the Commissioner or a licensed child-placing agency according to Minnesota Statutes § 260C.201, subd. 11, or § 260C.317;

(ii) placed by the commissioner, commissioner's agent, or licensed child-placing agency after a consent to adopt according to Minnesota Statutes § 259.24 or under an agreement conferring authority to place for adoption according to Minnesota Statutes § 259.25; or

(iii) adopted after a direct adoptive placement approved by the district court under Minnesota Statutes § 259.47;

(c) the Secretary of the Interior and the child's tribal social services agency, if the child is an Indian child; and

(d) such other persons as the court may direct.

If a party is represented by counsel, delivery or service shall be upon such counsel. Filing and mailing of the adoption decree by the court administrator shall be accomplished within five (5) days of the date the judicial officer delivers the adoption decree to the court administrator. Upon request and payment of the applicable fee, the court administrator shall provide a certified copy of the adoption decree to persons entitled to receive a copy as permitted by statute or these rules.

Subd. 3. Replacement Birth Record. Upon the court administrator's receipt of the fee for the replacement birth record made payable to the Department of Health or equivalent agency in another state, the court administrator shall complete the certificate of adoption and send it to the Commissioner of Health in Minnesota or to the equivalent agency in any other state so that a replacement birth record may be generated. Any fee required by the Department of Health or equivalent agency in another state for a replacement birth record shall be paid by the petitioner. Any such fee shall be submitted by the petitioner to the court administrator at the time the request for a replacement birth record is made and shall be forwarded by the court administrator to the Department of Health.

Adopted Sept. 30, 2004, eff. Jan. 1, 2005. Amended Dec. 1, 2006, eff. Jan. 1, 2007; June 10, 2009, eff. Aug. 1, 2009.

Historical Notes

The order of the Minnesota Supreme Court [C1–01–927] dated June 10, 2009, amending the Rules of Juvenile Protection Procedure and the Rules of Adoption Procedure, provides in part that the amendments are effective August 1, 2009, and shall apply to all actions or proceedings pending on or commenced on or after the effective date.

Rule 10.04. Notice of Filing of Order and Adoption Decree

Each order or adoption decree delivered or mailed pursuant to Rule 10.03 shall be accompanied by a notice of filing of order. The State Court Administrator shall develop a "notice of filing" form, which shall be used by court administrators.

Adopted Sept. 30, 2004, eff. Jan. 1, 2005.

RULE 11. RECORDING AND TRANSCRIPTS

Rule 11.01. Procedure

A verbatim recording of all hearings shall be made by a stenographic reporter or by an electronic sound recording device. If the recording is made by an electronic sound recording device, qualified personnel shall be assigned by the court to operate the device. Any required transcripts shall be prepared by personnel assigned by the court.

Adopted Sept. 30, 2004, eff. Jan. 1, 2005.

Rule 11.02. Availability of Transcripts

Transcripts shall be available only to the parties or their counsel if represented.

Adopted Sept. 30, 2004, eff. Jan. 1, 2005.

Rule 11.03. Expense

If a party requesting a transcript is unable to pay the preparation cost, the party may apply to the court for an order directing the preparation and delivery of the transcript to the party requesting it, at public expense. A party's request for a transcript shall be accompanied by an In Forma Pauperis application.

Upon a finding of the party's ability to do so, the court may order partial reimbursement for the cost of the transcript.

Adopted Sept. 30, 2004, eff. Jan. 1, 2005.

RULE 12. USE OF TELEPHONE AND INTERACTIVE VIDEO

Rule 12.01. Motions and Conferences

The court may hear motions and conduct conferences by telephone or interactive video where testimony is not required and to resolve procedural matters.

Adopted Sept. 30, 2004, eff. Jan. 1, 2005.

Rule 12.02. Hearings and Taking Testimony

By agreement of the parties, or in exceptional circumstances upon motion of a party, the court may hold hearings and take testimony by telephone or interactive video.

Adopted Sept. 30, 2004, eff. Jan. 1, 2005.

Rule 12.03. In Court Appearance Not Precluded

This rule shall not preclude a party from being present in person before the court at a hearing.

Adopted Sept. 30, 2004, eff. Jan. 1, 2005.

RULE 13. SUBPOENAS

Rule 13.01. Subpoena for a Hearing or Trial

At the request of any party, the court administrator shall issue a subpoena for a witness in an adoption matter pending before the court.

Adopted Sept. 30, 2004, eff. Jan. 1, 2005.

Rule 13.02. Form; Purpose; Notice

Subd. 1. Form. Every subpoena shall be issued by the court administrator under seal of the court and shall state the name of the court and the title of the action. The court administrator shall issue a subpoena signed and sealed but otherwise in blank to a party requesting it, who shall fill it in before service.

Subd. 2. Purpose. A subpoena shall command each person to whom it is directed to, at a specified time and place:

(a) attend and give testimony at a final hearing pursuant to Rule 41, a deposition pursuant to Rule 17, or trial pursuant to Rule 44;

(b) bring the child to court; or

(c) produce books, papers, documents, or other tangible things designated in the subpoena.

Subd. 3. Notice. Every subpoena shall contain a notice to the person to whom it is directed advising the person of the right to reimbursement for certain expenses pursuant to Rule 13.07.

Adopted Sept. 1, 2004, eff. Jan. 1, 2005. Amended Dec. 1, 2006, eff. Jan. 1, 2007.

Rule 13.03. Service

A subpoena may be served by the sheriff, a deputy sheriff, or any other person over the age of eighteen (18) who is not a party to the proceeding. Service of a subpoena upon a person named in the subpoena shall be made by delivering a copy of the subpoena to the named person or by leaving a copy at the person's usual place of abode with a person of suitable age and discretion residing at such abode. A subpoena may be served by mail upon agreement of the witness.

Adopted Sept. 30, 2004, eff. Jan. 1, 2005.

Rule 13.04. Motion to Quash a Subpoena

Upon motion pursuant to Rule 15, a person served with a subpoena may move to quash or modify the subpoena. Upon hearing a motion to quash a subpoena, the court may:

(a) direct compliance with the subpoena;

(b) modify the subpoena if it is unreasonable or oppressive;

(c) deny the motion to quash the subpoena on the condition that the person requesting the subpoena prepay the reasonable cost of producing the books, papers, documents, or tangible things; or

(d) quash the subpoena.

Adopted Sept. 30, 2004, eff. Jan. 1, 2005.

Rule 13.05. Objection

The person to whom the subpoena is directed may, within five (5) days after service of the subpoena or on or before the time specified in the subpoena for compliance if such time is less than five (5) days after service, serve upon the party serving the subpoena a written objection to the taking of the deposition or the production, inspection, or copying of any or all of the designated materials. If objection is made, the party serving the subpoena shall not be entitled to inspect or copy the materials, except pursuant to an order of the court from which the subpoena was issued. If objection is made, the party serving the subpoena may, at any time before or during the taking of the deposition, and upon notice of motion and motion to the deponent, request an order requiring compliance with the subpoena.

Adopted Sept. 30, 2004, eff. Jan. 1, 2005.

Rule 13.06. Subpoena for Taking Deposition; Place of Deposition

Subd. 1. Proof of Service. Proof of service of notice to take a deposition, as provided in Rule 17, constitutes a sufficient authorization for the issuance of a subpoena for the person named or described in the subpoena.

Subd. 2. Location. A resident of the state may be required to attend a deposition only in the county in which the resident resides or is employed or transacts business in person, or at such other convenient place as is designated by order of the court. A nonresident of the state may be required to attend in any county of the state.

Adopted Sept. 30, 2004, eff. Jan. 1, 2005.

Rule 13.07. Expenses

Subd. 1. Witnesses. If the subpoena is issued at the request of the State of Minnesota, a political subdivision of the State, or an officer or agency of the State, witness fees and mileage shall be paid by public funds. If the subpoena is issued at the request of a party who is unable to pay witness fees and mileage, these costs shall upon order of the court be paid in whole or in part at public expense, depending upon the ability of the party to pay. All other fees and mileage shall be paid by the requesting party, unless otherwise ordered by the court upon motion.

Subd. 2. Expenses of Experts. Subject to the provisions of Rule 17, a witness who is not a party to the action or an employee of a party and who is required to give testimony or produce documents relating to a profession, business, or trade, or relating to knowledge, information, or facts obtained as a result of activities in such profession, business, or trade, is entitled to reasonable compensation for the time and expense involved in preparing for and giving such testimony or producing such documents. The party serving the subpoena shall make arrangements for such reasonable compensation prior to the time of the taking of the testimony. If such arrangements are not made, the person subpoenaed may proceed pursuant to Rule 13.04 or Rule 13.05. If the deponent has moved to quash or otherwise objected to the subpoena, the party serving the subpoena may, upon notice and motion to the deponent and all parties, move for an order directing the amount of such compensation at any time before the taking of the deposition.

Adopted Sept. 30, 2004, eff. Jan. 1, 2005.

Rule 13.08. Failure to Appear

If any person personally served with a subpoena fails, without reasonable cause, to appear or bring the child if ordered to do so, or if the court has reason to believe the person is avoiding personal service, the court may sua sponte or upon the motion of a party pursuant to Rule 15 proceed against the person for civil contempt of court pursuant to Rule 14, or the court may issue a warrant for the person's arrest, or both.

Adopted Sept. 30, 2004, eff. Jan. 1, 2005.

RULE 14. CONTEMPT

Rule 14.01. Initiation

Contempt proceedings shall be initiated upon the alleged contemnor by personal service of an order to show cause, a motion for contempt, and an affidavit supporting the motion. The order to show cause shall direct the alleged contemnor to appear and show cause why he or she should not be held in contempt of court and why the moving party should not be granted the relief requested in the motion. The order to show cause shall contain at least the following:

(a) a reference to the specific order of the court alleged to have been violated and date of filing of the order;

(b) a quotation of the specific applicable provisions ordered;

(c) a statement identifying the alleged contemnor's ability to comply with the order; and

(d) a statement identifying the alleged contemnor's failure to comply with the order.

Adopted Sept. 30, 2004, eff. Jan. 1, 2005.

Rule 14.02. Supporting and Responsive Affidavits

The supporting affidavit of the moving party shall set forth with particularity the facts constituting each alleged violation of the order. Any responsive affidavit shall set forth with particularity any defenses the alleged contemnor will present to the court. When possible, the supporting affidavit and the responsive affidavit shall contain paragraphs numbered to correspond to the paragraphs of the motion.

Adopted Sept. 30, 2004, eff. Jan. 1, 2005.

Rule 14.03. Hearing

The alleged contemnor shall appear in person before the court to be afforded an opportunity to oppose the motion for contempt by sworn testimony. The court shall not act upon affidavit alone, absent express waiver by the alleged contemnor of the right to offer sworn testimony.

Adopted Sept. 30, 2004, eff.Jan. 1, 2005.

Rule 14.04. Sentencing

Subd. 1. Default of Conditions for Stay. Where the court has entered an order for contempt with a stay of sentence and there has been a default in the performance of the condition(s) for the stay, before a writ of attachment or bench warrant may be issued, an affidavit of non-compliance and request for writ of attachment shall be served upon the defaulting party, unless the person is shown to be avoiding service.

Subd. 2. Writ of Attachment or Bench Warrant. The writ of attachment or bench warrant shall direct law enforcement officers to bring the defaulting party before the court for a hearing to show cause why the stay of sentence should not be revoked. The moving party shall submit a proposed order for writ of attachment or bench warrant to the court.

Subd. 3. Sanctions. Upon evidence taken, the court shall determine the guilt or innocence of the alleged contemnor. If the court determines that the alleged contemnor is guilty, the court shall order punishment by fine or imprisonment for not more than six (6) months, or both.

Subd. 4. Authority of Court. Nothing in these rules shall be interpreted to limit the inherent authority of the court to enforce its own orders.

Adopted Sept. 30, 2004, eff. Jan. 1, 2005.

RULE 15. MOTIONS

Rule 15.01. Form

Subd. 1. Generally. An application to the court for an order shall be by motion. Motions may be made for any purpose authorized by statute or these rules.

Subd. 2. Motions to Be in Writing. Except as permitted by subdivision 3, a motion shall be in writing and shall:

(a) set forth the relief or order sought;

(b) state with particularity the grounds for the relief or order sought;

(c) be signed by the person making the motion;

(d) be filed with the court;

(e) be accompanied by a supporting affidavit; and

(f) be accompanied by a memorandum of law, if appropriate.

The requirement of writing is fulfilled if the motion is stated in a written notice of motion. The parties may agree to written submission to the court for decision without oral argument unless the court directs otherwise.

Subd. 3. Exception to Requirement of Written Motion. Unless another party objects, a party may make an oral motion during a hearing. All oral motions and objections to oral motions shall be made on the record. When an objection is made, the court shall determine whether there is good cause to permit the oral motion and, before issuing an order, shall allow the objecting party reasonable time to respond.

Adopted Sept. 30, 2004, eff. Jan. 1, 2005.

Rule 15.02. Service and Notice of Motion

Subd. 1. Upon Whom. The moving party shall serve the notice of motion and motion, along with any supporting affidavit or other supporting documentation or a memorandum of law, on all parties and any other persons designated by the court.

Subd. 2. How Made. Service of a motion may be made by personal service, by mail, or by transmitting a copy by facsimile transmission.

Subd. 3. Time.

(a) *Motion.* Except for motions pursuant to Rule 29, no motion shall be heard until the moving party serves a copy of the following documents on the other parties and files the original with the court administrator at least fourteen (14) days prior to the hearing:

(1) notice of motion and motion;

(2) proposed order;

(3) any affidavits and exhibits to be submitted in conjunction with the motion; and

(4) any memorandum of law the party intends to submit.

(b) *Response.* Any party responding to the motion shall serve a copy of the following documents on the moving party and other interested parties and shall file the original with the court administrator at least seven (7) days prior to the hearing:

(1) any memorandum of law the party intends to submit; and

(2) any relevant affidavits and exhibits.

(c) *Reply Memorandum.* The moving party may submit a reply memorandum, limited to new legal or factual matters raised by an opposing party's response to a motion, by serving a copy of such memorandum upon the party or parties and filing the original with the court administrator at least three (3) days before the hearing.

Adopted Sept. 30, 2004, eff. Jan. 1, 2005. Amended Dec. 1, 2006, eff. Jan. 1, 2007.

Rule 15.03. Ex Parte Motion

A motion may be made ex parte without a hearing when permitted by statute or these rules. Upon issuance of an ex parte order, a hearing shall be scheduled at the earliest possible date upon the request of a party.

Adopted Sept. 30, 2004, eff. Jan. 1, 2005.

RULE 16. SIGNING OF PLEADINGS, MOTIONS, AND OTHER DOCUMENTS; SANCTIONS

Rule 16.01. Signing of Pleadings, Motions and Other Documents

Subd. 1. Party Represented by an Attorney. When a party is represented by an attorney, every pleading, motion, and other paper filed with the court shall be personally signed by at least one attorney of record in the attorney's individual name and shall state the attorney's address, telephone number, and attorney registration number.

Subd. 2. Party Not Represented by an Attorney. A party who is not represented by an attorney shall personally sign the pleading, motion, or other paper filed with the court and shall state the party's address and telephone number. If a party asserts that providing the address and telephone number is not in the best interests of the child, the address and telephone number may be provided to the court in a separate informational statement and shall not be accessible to the public or to the parties. Upon notice of motion and motion, the court may disclose the address and telephone number as it deems appropriate.

Subd. 3. Signing Constitutes Certification. Except when otherwise specifically provided by rule or statute, pleadings need not be verified by affidavit or accompanied by affidavit. The signature of an attorney or party constitutes a certification that:

(a) the pleading, motion, or other paper has been read;

(b) to the best of the signer's knowledge, information, and belief, formed after reasonable inquiry, the pleading, motion, or other paper is well-grounded in fact and is warranted by existing law or a good-faith argument for the extension, modification, or reversal of existing law; and

(c) it is not interposed for any improper purpose, such as to harass or cause unnecessary delay or needless increase in the cost of litigation.

Adopted Sept. 30, 2004, eff. Jan. 1, 2005.

Rule 16.02. Sanctions

If a pleading, motion, affidavit, or other paper is not signed, it shall be stricken unless it is signed promptly after the omission is called to the attention of the pleader or movant. If a pleading, motion, affidavit, or other paper is signed in violation of this rule, the court, upon motion or upon its own initiative, may impose upon the person who signed it, a represented party, or both, an appropriate sanction, including sanctions permitted pursuant to Rule 11 of the Minnesota Rules of Civil Procedure, which may include an order to pay to the other party or parties the amount of the reasonable expenses incurred because of the filing of the pleading, motion, affidavit, or other paper, including reasonable attorney fees.

Adopted Sept. 30, 2004, eff. Jan. 1, 2005.

RULE 17. DISCOVERY

Rule 17.01. Applicability

These discovery rules apply only to contested adoption matters and only to the extent permitted and upon the conditions ordered by the court. To the extent that there are any discovery issues that arise out of an uncontested adoption matter, any requests for information shall be addressed to the court which shall determine whether such discovery will be allowed and, if so, in what form and whether any protective order shall be issued.

Adopted Sept. 30, 2004, eff. Jan. 1, 2005.

Rule 17.02. Regulation of Discovery

Discovery in adoption matters shall be governed by Rules 26 through 37 of the Minnesota Rules of Civil Procedure.

Adopted Sept. 30, 2004, eff. Jan. 1, 2005.

RULE 18. DEFAULT

Rule 18.01. Procedure

If a party fails to appear, as that term is defined in Rule 5.01 of the Minnesota Rules of Civil Procedure, after being properly served with a notice pursuant to Rule 31, the court may take testimony in support of the petition. If the court determines that the petition is proven in accordance with the applicable standard of proof and the adoption is in the best interests of the child, the court shall enter an order granting the relief sought. The court shall not grant a default if a party was not served with notice within the time period set forth in Rule 31. The court shall not grant a default regarding the issue of consent to adopt.

Adopted Sept. 30, eff. Jan. 1, 2005. Amended Dec. 1, 2006, eff. Jan. 1, 2007.

2004 Advisory Committee Comment

If consent is required and has not been given, the procedure that must be followed is to initiate a termination of parental rights proceeding pursuant to the Minnesota Rules of Juvenile Protection Procedure.

RULE 19. SETTLEMENT

Rule 19.01. Generally

Settlement discussions may be utilized to achieve one or more of the purposes set forth in these rules.

Adopted Sept. 30, 2004, eff. Jan. 1, 2005.

Rule 19.02. Partial Settlement

The parties may enter into a settlement of one or more issues and shall proceed to final hearing pursuant to Rule 41. Any remaining contested issues shall proceed to trial pursuant to Rule 44.

Adopted Sept. 30, 2004, eff. Jan. 1, 2005. Amended Dec. 1, 2006, eff. Jan. 1, 2007.

Rule 19.03. Content of Settlement Agreement

Any settlement agreement shall include information that identifies:

(a) the parties to the agreement;

(b) the attorneys for the parties, if any;

(c) the judicial officer receiving the settlement;

(d) the date, time, and place the settlement was reached;

(e) any and all necessary statutory grounds and factual allegations to support the settlement agreement; and

(f) signatures and notarizations of all parties to the settlement.

Adopted Sept. 30, 2004, eff. Jan. 1, 2005.

Rule 19.04. Procedure

Every settlement agreement shall be filed with the court or stated and agreed to on the record by the settling parties. Before approving a settlement agreement, the court shall determine that the agreement is in the best interests of the child and that each party to the agreement understands the content and consequences of the settlement agreement and voluntarily consents to the agreement. If the court approves the settlement agreement, it shall issue an order, judgment, or decree as appropriate. If the court rejects the settlement agreement, it shall advise the parties of this decision in writing or on the record and the matter shall proceed as any other contested adoption matter.

Adopted Sept. 30, 2004, eff. Jan. 1, 2005.

RULE 20. PARTIES

Rule 20.01. Party Status

Parties to an adoption matter shall include:

(a) the child's guardian ad litem;

(b) the adoptee, if age ten (10) or older;

(c) the child's legal custodian;

(d) the child's legal guardian;

(e) the petitioner;

(f) the child's biological parent, if the consent of the biological parent is required and has not been executed pursuant to Rule 33;

(g) the child's Indian tribe, if the child is an Indian child and the tribe is or was a party in an underlying juvenile protection matter as defined in Rule 2.01(k) of the Minnesota Rules of Juvenile Protection Procedure;

(h) the responsible social services agency, if the child is under the guardianship of the Commissioner of Human Services;

(i) the child placing agency, if the child has been placed;

(j) any person who intervenes as a party pursuant to Rule 21; and

(k) any person who is joined as a party pursuant to Rule 22.

Adopted Sept. 30, 2004, eff. Jan. 1, 2005. Amended Dec. 1, 2006, eff. Jan. 1, 2007.

Rule 20.02. Rights of Parties

A party shall have the right to:

(a) notice pursuant to Rule 31;

(b) legal representation pursuant to Rule 23;

(c) be present at all hearings unless excluded pursuant to Rule 8;

(d) conduct discovery pursuant to Rule 17;

(e) bring motions before the court pursuant to Rule 15;

(f) participate in settlement agreements pursuant to Rule 19;

(g) subpoena witnesses pursuant to Rule 13;

(h) make argument in support of or against the petition;

(i) present evidence;

(j) cross–examine witnesses;

(k) ask the court to order that witnesses be sequestered;

(*l*) request review of the referee's findings and recommended order pursuant to Rule 6, if a referee presides over the matter;

(m) bring post-trial motions pursuant to Rules 46 and 47;

(n) appeal from orders of the court pursuant to Rule 48; and

(*o*) any other rights as set forth in statute or these rules.

Adopted Sept. 30, 2004, eff. Jan. 1, 2005. Amended Dec. 1, 2006, eff. Jan. 1, 2007.

Rule 20.03. Parties' Addresses

It shall be the responsibility of the petitioner to set forth in the petition the names and addresses of all parties if known to the petitioner after reasonable inquiry. It shall be the responsibility of each party to inform the court administrator of any change of address. For good cause shown, the court may grant a party's request to keep the party's address confidential.

Adopted Sept. 30, 2004, eff. Jan. 1, 2005.

RULE 21. INTERVENTION

Rule 21.01. Intervention of Right

Subd. 1. Child. A child younger than age ten (10) who is the subject of the adoption matter has the right to intervene as a party at any point in the proceeding.

Subd. 2. Indian Tribe. In any adoption matter relating to an Indian child, if the child's Indian tribe is not already a party pursuant to Rule 20.01(g), the child's tribe has the right to intervene as a party at any point in the proceeding.

Subd. 3. Local Social Services Agency. The local social services agency has the right to intervene as a party at any point in the proceeding.

Subd. 4. Procedure. A child younger than age ten (10), the child's Indian tribe, or the local social services agency may intervene as a party by filing with the court and serving upon the parties a notice of intervention as a matter of right. The notice of intervention form shall be available from the court administrator. The intervention shall be deemed accomplished upon service of the notice of intervention, unless a party files and serves a written objection within ten (10) days of the date of service.

Adopted Sept. 30, 2004, eff. Jan. 1, 2005.

Rule 21.02. Parent Intervention Prohibited

No parent who has executed a valid consent to the adoption or whose parental rights to the child who is the subject of the adoption petition have been terminated may intervene in an adoption matter.

Adopted Sept. 30, 2004, eff. Jan. 1, 2005.

Rule 21.03. Permissive Intervention

Subd. 1. Generally. Any person or agency may be permitted to intervene as a party if the court finds that such intervention is in the best interests of the child.

Subd. 2. Procedure. A person or agency seeking permissive intervention shall file with the court and serve upon all parties a notice of motion and motion to intervene pursuant to Rule 15. The motion form shall be available from the court administrator and shall state the nature and extent of the person's interest in the child and the reason(s) that the person's intervention would be in the best interests of the child. A hearing on a motion to intervene shall be held within ten (10) days of the filing of the motion to intervene.

Adopted Sept. 30, 2004, eff. Jan. 1, 2005.

Rule 21.04. Effect of Intervention

The court may conduct hearings, make findings, and issue orders at any time before intervention is accomplished or denied. The intervention shall be effective as of the date accomplished or granted and shall not affect prior proceedings and decisions of the court, unless otherwise ordered by the court or required by the Indian Child Welfare Act, 25 U.S.C. § 19.01, et seq.

Adopted Sept. 1, 2004, eff. Jan. 1, 2005.

RULE 22. JOINDER

Rule 22.01. Procedure

The court sua sponte, or upon notice of motion and motion of a party pursuant to Rule 15, may join a person or entity as a party if the court finds that joinder is:

(a) necessary for a just and complete resolution of the matter; and

(b) in the best interests of the child.

The moving party shall serve the motion upon all parties and the person proposed to be joined.

Adopted Sept. 30, 2004, eff. Jan. 1, 2005.

RULE 23. RIGHT TO REPRESENTATION; APPOINTMENT OF COUNSEL

Rule 23.01. Right to Representation

Every party has the right to be represented by counsel in an adoption matter, including through appeal if any. This right attaches no later than when the party first appears in court.

Adopted Sept. 30, 2004, eff. Jan. 1, 2005.

Rule 23.02. Appointment of Counsel

Subd. 1. Adoptee. Pursuant to Minn. Stat. § 259.65, in any adoption matter the court may appoint an attorney for the person being adopted. The court may inquire into the ability of the adopting parent to pay for the attorney's services and, after giving the adopting parent a reasonable opportunity to be heard, may order the adopting parent to pay the attorney's fees.

Subd. 2. Putative Father. Pursuant to Minn. Stat. § 259.52, subd. 12, upon proof of indigency, a putative father who has registered with the Minnesota Fathers' Adoption Registry, has received a notice to registered putative father, and has timely filed an intent to claim paternal rights form with the court administrator, shall be appointed counsel at public expense.

Adopted Sept. 30, 2004, eff. Jan. 1, 2005.

2004 Advisory Committee Comment

Rule 23.01 sets forth the basic principle that each party appearing in court has the right to be represented by counsel. Each party, however, does not necessarily have the right to court appointed counsel as provided in Rule 23.02. The phrase "at public expense" is not defined in the statute.

Rule 23.01, subd. 1, is consistent with Minn. Stat. § 259.65, which provides: "In any adoption proceeding, the court may appoint an attorney or guardian ad litem, or both, for the person being adopted. The court may order the adopting parents to pay the costs of services rendered by guardians or attorneys appointed, . . . provided that such parents be given a reasonable opportunity to be heard."

Rule 23.02, subd. 2, is consistent with Minn. Stat. § 259.52, subd. 12, which provides: "Upon proof of indigency, a putative father who has registered with the Minnesota Fathers' Adoption Registry, has received a notice to registered putative father, and has timely filed an intent to claim paternal rights form with the court administrator must have counsel appointed at public expense."

Rule 23.03. Representation of Responsible Social Services Agency

In any adoption matter in which the Commissioner of Human Services is the legal guardian for the child, the responsible social services agency shall be represented by its county attorney.

Adopted Sept. 30, 2004, eff. Jan. 1, 2005.

Rule 23.04. Biological Parent Counsel in Direct Placement Adoption

Subd. 1. Right to Counsel. Pursuant to Minnesota Statutes § 259.47, subd. 5, in a direct placement adoption, upon the request of a biological parent, separate legal counsel shall be made available to the biological parent at the expense of the prospective adoptive parents for legal services provided in a direct placement adoption. The prospective adoptive parent shall be required to provide legal counsel for only one parent unless the biological parents elect joint legal representation.

Subd. 2. Waiver of Right to Counsel. A biological parent may waive the right to counsel only by written waiver signed and filed with the court at the time the biological parent's consent to the adoption is executed pursuant to Minn. Stat. § 259.47, subd. 7.

Subd. 3. Expiration of Right to Counsel. The right to legal counsel shall continue until consents become irrevocable, but not longer than seventy (70) days after placement. If the parent's consent to adoption has not been executed within sixty (60) days of placement, the right to counsel under Rule 23 and Minn. Stat. § 259.47, subd. 5, shall end at that time.

Subd. 4. Dual Representation Prohibited. Representation of a biological parent and a prospective adoptive parent by the same attorney is prohibited.

Adopted Sept. 30, 2004, eff. Jan. 1, 2005. Amended Dec. 1, 2006, eff. Jan. 1, 2007.

Rule 23.05. Certificate of Representation

An attorney representing a client in an adoption matter, other than a public defender or county attorney, shall on or before the attorney's first appearance file with the court a certificate of representation.

Adopted Sept. 30, 2004, eff. Jan. 1, 2005.

Rule 23.06. Withdrawal of Counsel

An attorney representing a party in an adoption matter, including a public defender, shall continue representation until such time as:

(a) all proceedings in the matter have been completed;

(b) the attorney has been discharged by the client in writing or on the record;

(c) the court grants the attorney's ex parte motion for withdrawal; or

(d) the court approves the attorney's ex parte written substitution of counsel.

If the court grants an attorney's ex parte motion for withdrawal, the withdrawing attorney shall serve upon all parties and the county attorney a copy of the order permitting withdrawal.

Adopted Sept. 30, 2004, eff. Jan. 1, 2005.

Rule 23.07. Appointment of Counsel in Adoption Involving an Indian Child

Subd. 1. Parent or Indian Custodian. In any case in which the court determines indigency, the parent or Indian custodian shall have the right to court appointed counsel in any removal, placement, or termination proceeding.

Subd. 2. Indian Child. The court may, in its discretion, appoint counsel for an Indian child upon a finding that such appointment is in the best interests of the child.

Adopted Dec. 1, 2006, eff. Jan. 1, 2007.

RULE 24. GUARDIAN AD LITEM

Rule 24.01. Appointment

Subd. 1. Generally. A guardian ad litem appointed to serve in a juvenile protection matter, as defined in Rule 2.01(k) of the Minnesota Rules of Juvenile Protection Procedure, shall continue to serve in the adoption matter following a termination of parental rights or transfer of guardianship to the Commissioner of Human Services. In any other adoption matter, the court may appoint a guardian ad litem. The guardian ad litem shall advocate for the best interests of the child and shall continue to serve until the adoption decree is entered pursuant to Rule 45.

Subd. 2. Guardian Ad Litem Not Also Attorney for Child. Counsel for the child shall not also serve as the child's guardian ad litem or as legal counsel for the guardian ad litem.

Adopted Sept. 30, 2004, eff. Jan. 1, 2005. Amended Dec. 1, 2006, eff. Jan. 1, 2007.

2004 Advisory Committee Comment

Rule 24.01, subd. 1, is consistent with Minn. Stat. § 259.65, which provides: "In any adoption proceeding, the court may appoint an attorney or a guardian ad litem, or both, for the person being adopted."

Rule 24.01 is intended to reflect the clear legislative mandate that the guardian ad litem in a juvenile protection matter shall continue to serve until the adoption decree is entered. See Minn. Stat. § 260C.317, subd. 3(b), and Rule 26.03 of the Minnesota Rules of Juvenile Protection Procedure. It is preferable that the same individual serve continuously as the child's guardian ad litem for both the juvenile protection matter and the adoption matter. However, if that is not practicable, the guardian ad litem program shall assign another individual to serve as the child's guardian ad litem in the adoption matter following the termination of parental rights in the juvenile protection matter. Upon the assignment of a new individual to serve as guardian ad litem, the court shall issue a new appointment order.

Rule 24.02. Responsibilities

The guardian ad litem shall carry out the responsibilities set forth in the Minnesota Rules of Guardian Ad Litem Procedure. The guardian ad litem shall have the rights and powers set forth in the Minnesota Rules of Guardian Ad Litem Procedure.

Adopted Sept. 30, 2004, eff. Jan. 1, 2005.

Rule 24.03. Reimbursement

The court may inquire into the ability of the adopting parent to pay for the guardian ad litem's services and, after giving the adopting parent a reasonable opportunity to be heard, may order the adopting parent to pay the guardian ad litem's fees.

Adopted Sept. 30, 2004, eff. Jan. 1, 2005.

2004 Advisory Committee Comment

Rule 24.03 is consistent with Minn. Stat. § 259.65, which provides: "The court may order the adopting parents to pay the costs of services rendered by guardians or attorneys appointed, ... provided that such parents shall be given a reasonable opportunity to be heard."

RULE 25. METHODS OF FILING AND SERVICE

Rule 25.01. Types of Filing

Subd. 1. Generally. Any paper may be filed with the court either personally, by U.S. mail, or by facsimile transmission.

Subd. 2. Filing by Facsimile Transmission. Any paper may be filed with the court by facsimile transmission. Filing shall be deemed complete at the time the facsimile transmission is received by the court. The facsimile shall have the same force and effect as the original. Only facsimile transmission equipment that satisfies the published criteria of the supreme court shall be used for filing in accordance with this rule.

Subd. 3. Fees; Original Document. Within five (5) days after the court has received the facsimile transmission, the party filing the document shall forward the following to the court:

(a) a $25 transmission fee for each 50 pages, or part thereof, of the filing, unless otherwise provided by statute or rule or otherwise ordered by the court;

(b) any bulky exhibits or attachments; and

(c) the applicable filing fee or fees, if any.

If a paper is filed by facsimile, the sender's original must not be filed but must be maintained in the files of the party transmitting it for filing and made available to the court or any party to the action upon request.

Subd. 4. Noncompliance. Upon failure to comply with the requirements of this rule, the court may make such orders as are just including, but not limited to, an order striking pleadings or parts thereof, staying further proceedings until compliance is complete, or dismissing the adoption matter, proceeding, or any part thereof.

Adopted Sept. 30, 2004, eff. Jan. 1, 2005. Amended Dec. 18, 2006, eff. Jan. 1, 2007.

Rule 25.02. Types of Service

Subd. 1. Personal Service. Personal service means personally delivering the original document to the person to be served or leaving it at the person's home or usual place of abode with a person of suitable age and discretion residing therein, unless the court authorizes service by publication.

Subd. 2. U.S. Mail. Service by U.S. Mail means placing a copy of the document in the U.S. mail, first class, postage prepaid, addressed to the person to be served.

Subd. 3. Publication. Service by publication means the publication in full of the summons, notice of hearing, or other papers in the regular issue of a qualified newspaper, once each week for the number of weeks specified pursuant to Rule 31.04, subd. 2. Service by publication substitutes for personal service where authorized by the court. The court shall authorize service by publication only if the petitioner has filed a written statement or affidavit describing unsuccessful efforts to locate the party to be served. Service by publication shall be completed by the petitioner in a location approved by the court. If the summons is required to be published, the case caption shall identify the child by the child's initials rather than by full name. In cases involving an Indian child, if the identity or location of the parent or Indian custodian and the child's Indian tribe cannot be determined, the summons and petition shall be served upon the Secretary of the Interior pursuant to 25 U.S.C. § 1912.

Subd. 4. Facsimile Service. Service by facsimile means transmission by facsimile equipment that satisfies the published criteria of the supreme court, addressed to the person to be served.

Adopted Sept. 30, 2004, eff. Jan. 1, 2005. Amended Dec. 1, 2006, eff. Jan. 1, 2007.

Rule 25.03. Service by Facsimile Transmission

Unless these rules require personal service, any document may be served by facsimile transmission upon agreement of the parties. The facsimile shall have the same force and effect as the original.

Adopted Sept. 30, 2004, eff. Jan. 1, 2005.

Rule 25.04. Service Upon Counsel; Social Services Agency

Unless personal service upon a party is required, service upon counsel for a party shall be deemed service upon the party. Service upon the county attorney shall be deemed to be service upon the responsible social services agency.

Adopted Sept. 30, 2004, eff. Jan. 1, 2005.

Rule 25.05. Service of Subpoena

A subpoena requiring the attendance of a witness at a hearing or trial may be served upon the witness at any place within the state.

Adopted Sept. 30, 2004, eff. Jan. 1, 2004.

Rule 25.06. Completion of Service

Service by mail is complete upon mailing to the last known address of the person to be served. Service by facsimile is complete upon completion of the facsimile transmission.

Adopted Sept. 30, 2004, eff. Jan. 1, 2005.

Rule 25.07. Proof of Service

On or before the date set for appearance, the person serving the document shall file with the court an affidavit of service stating:

(a) whether the document was served;

(b) how the document was served;

(c) the person on whom the document was served; and

(d) the date, time, and place of service.

If the court administrator served the document, the court administrator may file a written statement in lieu of an affidavit.

Adopted Sept. 30, 2004, eff. Jan. 1, 2005.

RULE 26. COMMENCEMENT OF ADOPTION MATTER

Rule 26.01. Commencement of an Adoption Matter

An adoption matter is commenced by filing:

(a) a motion for a direct placement preadoptive custody order pursuant to Rule 29;

(b) an adoption petition; or

(c) a motion for waiver of agency placement pursuant to Minnesota Statutes § 259.22, subd. 2(d).

Adopted Sept. 30, 2004, eff. Jan. 1, 2005. Amended Dec. 1, 2006, eff. Jan. 1, 2007.

Rule 26.02. Post–Permanency Review Hearings Continue

The filing of an adoption petition does not terminate the in-court review hearings required at least every ninety (90) days under Rule 41.06 of the Minnesota Rules of Juvenile Protection Procedure.

Former Rule 26.01, adopted Sept. 30, 2004, eff. Jan. 1, 2005. Renumbered Rule 26.02, Dec. 1, 2006, eff. Jan. 1, 2007.

RULE 27. STEPPARENT ADOPTION

A stepparent adoption shall be commenced by the filing of a petition pursuant to Rule 35. All other Rules apply to stepparent adoptions, except for Rule 28 dealing with agency adoptions, Rule 29 dealing with direct placement adoptions, and Rule 30 dealing with intercountry adoptions.

Adopted Dec. 1, 2006, eff. Jan. 1, 2007.

RULE 28. AGENCY ADOPTION

An agency adoption shall be commenced by the filing of a petition pursuant to Rule 35. All other Rules apply to agency adoptions, except for Rule 27 dealing with stepparent adoptions, Rule 29 dealing with direct placement adoptions, and Rule 30 dealing with intercountry adoptions.

Adopted Dec. 1, 2006, eff. Jan. 1, 2007.

RULE 29. DIRECT PLACEMENT ADOPTION

Rule 29.01. Notice of Motion and Motion for Preadoptive Custody Order

In a direct placement adoption, whether involving an emergency or non-emergency situation, the petitioner shall file with the court and serve a notice of motion and motion for a preadoptive custody order upon:

(a) the biological mother;

(b) the biological father if his consent is required;

(c) any parent whose consent is required; and

(d) the Indian tribe, if the child is an Indian child.

Former Rule 27.01, adopted Sept. 30, 2004, eff. Jan. 1, 2005. Renumbered Rule 29.01 and amended Dec. 1, 2006, eff. Jan. 1, 2007.

Rule 29.02. Timing

A notice of motion and motion for a preadoptive custody order may be filed up to sixty (60) days before the adoptive placement is to be made and may be filed prior to the birth of the baby.

Former Rule 27.02, adopted Sept. 30, 2004, eff. Jan. 1, 2005. Renumbered Rule 29.02 and amended Dec. 1, 2006, eff. Jan. 1, 2007.

Rule 29.03. Content

Subd. 1. Non–Emergency Direct Placement. In a non-emergency situation, a notice of motion and motion for a preadoptive custody order in a direct placement adoption shall be in writing and shall contain or have attached:

(a) a statement that the biological parents have:

(1) provided the social and medical history to the prospective adoptive parent using the form prescribed by the Commissioner of Human Services;

(2) received a written statement of their legal rights and responsibilities prepared by the Department of Human Services; and

(3) been notified of their right to receive counseling;

(b) the name of the agency chosen by the adoptive parent to supervise the adoptive placement and complete the post-placement assessment;

(c) affidavits from the biological parents stating their support of the motion or, if there is no affidavit from the biological father, an affidavit from the biological mother that describes her good faith efforts, or efforts made on her behalf, to identify and locate the biological father for purposes of securing his consent. In the following circumstances the biological mother may instead submit an affidavit stating on which of the following grounds she is exempt from making efforts to identify and locate the father:

(1) the child was conceived as the result of incest or rape;

(2) efforts to locate the biological father by the affiant or anyone acting on the affiant's behalf could reasonably result in physical harm to the biological mother or the child; or

(3) efforts to locate the biological father by the affiant or anyone acting on the affiant's behalf could reasonably result in severe emotional distress of the biological mother or child;

(d) a statement that the prospective adoptive parent meets the residence requirements;

(e) an affidavit of intent to remain a resident of the state for at least three (3) months after the child is placed in the prospective adoptive home;

(f) a notice of intent to file an adoption petition;

(g) the adoption study report required pursuant to Rule 37;

(h) an itemized statement of expenses that have been paid and an estimate of expenses that will be paid by the prospective adoptive parents to the biological parents, any agency, attorney, or other party in connection with the prospective adoption; and

(i) the name of counsel for each party, if any.

Subd. 2. Emergency Direct Placement. In an emergency situation, a notice of motion and motion for a preadoptive custody order in a direct placement adoption shall be in writing and shall contain or have attached:

(a) affidavits from the prospective adoptive parents and biological parents stating that an emergency order is needed because of the unexpected premature birth of the child or other extraordinary circumstances which prevented the completion of the requirements under subdivision 1;

(b) affidavits from the biological parents stating their support of the motion or, if there is no affidavit from the biological father, an affidavit from the biological mother that describes her good faith efforts, or efforts made on her behalf, to identify and locate the biological father for purposes of securing his consent. In the following circumstances the biological mother may instead submit an affidavit stating on which of the following grounds she is exempt from making efforts to identify and locate the father:

(1) the child was conceived as the result of incest or rape;

(2) efforts to locate the father by the affiant or anyone acting on the affiant's behalf could reasonably result in physical harm to the biological mother or child; or

(3) efforts to locate the father by the affiant or anyone acting on the affiant's behalf could reasonably result in severe emotional distress of the biological mother or child;

(c) a statement that the biological parents:

(1) have received the written statement of their legal rights and responsibilities prepared by the Department of Human Services; and

(2) have been notified of their right to receive counseling; and

(d) either:

(1) the adoption study report pursuant to Rule 37; or

(2) sworn affidavits stating whether the prospective adoptive parents or any person residing in the household have been convicted of a crime.

Former Rule 27.03, adopted Sept. 30, 2004, eff. Jan. 1, 2005. Renumbered Rule 29.03 and amended Dec. 1, 2006, eff. Jan. 1, 2007.

Rule 29.04. Decision and Order

Subd. 1. Non–Emergency Direct Placement. In a non-emergency situation, the court shall decide a motion for a preadoptive custody order within fifteen (15) days of the filing of the motion or by the anticipated placement date stated in the motion, whichever is earlier.

Subd. 2. Emergency Direct Placement.

(a) *Expedited Emergency Order.* An order granting or denying a motion for an emergency preadoptive custody order shall be issued within twenty-four (24) hours of the time it is filed. Any district court judge may decide a motion for emergency preadoptive custody. An order granting the motion shall direct that an adoption study be commenced immediately, if that has not already occurred, and that the agency conducting the study shall supervise the emergency placement.

(b) *Expiration of Emergency Order.* A court may issue an emergency order granting preadoptive custody of a child to a prospective adoptive parent for up to fourteen (14) days. An emergency order under this rule expires fourteen (14) days after it is issued. If the requirements for non-emergency direct placement under this Rule are completed and a preadoptive custody motion is filed on or before the expiration of the emergency order, placement may continue until the court decides the motion. The court shall decide the preadoptive custody motion within seven (7) days of filing.

Former Rule 27.04, adopted Sept. 30, 2004, eff. Jan. 1, 2005. Renumbered Rule 29.04 and amended Dec. 1, 2006, eff. Jan. 1, 2007; June 10, 2009, eff. Aug. 1, 2009.

Historical Notes

The order of the Minnesota Supreme Court [C1–01–927] dated June 10, 2009, amending the Rules of Juvenile Protection Procedure and the Rules of Adoption Procedure, provides in part that the amendments are effective August 1, 2009, and shall apply to all actions or proceedings pending on or commenced on or after the effective date.

RULE 30. INTERCOUNTRY ADOPTIONS

Rule 30.01. Adoption of a Child by a Resident of Minnesota Under the Laws of a Foreign Country

Subd. 1. Validity of a Foreign Adoption. The adoption of a child by a resident of Minnesota under the laws of a foreign country is valid and binding under the laws of Minnesota if the validity of the foreign adoption has been verified by the granting of an IR–3 visa for the child by the United States Citizenship and Immigration Services.

Subd. 2. New Birth Record.

(a) *Petition.* The adoption of a child under the laws of a foreign country is valid in Minnesota pursuant to Rule 30.01 and the petitioner may petition the court in petitioner's county of residence for a decree:

(1) confirming and recognizing the adoption;

(2) changing the child's legal name, if requested; and

(3) authorizing the Commissioner of Health to create a new birth record for the child pursuant to Minnesota Statutes § 144.218, subd. 2.

(b) *Documents to be Submitted.* The court shall issue the decree described in subdivision 2(a) upon receipt of the following documents:

(1) a signed, sworn, and notarized petition by the adoptive parent:

(i) stating that the adoptive parent completed the adoption of the child under the laws of a foreign county;

(ii) stating that the adoption is valid in this state under Rule 30.01; and

(iii) requesting that the court issue a decree confirming and recognizing the adoption and authorizing the Commissioner of Health to issue a new birth record for the child;

(2) a copy of the child's original birth record, if available;

(3) a copy of the final adoption certificate or equivalent as issued by the foreign jurisdiction;

(4) a copy of the child's passport, including the United States visa indicating IR–3 immigration status; and

(5) a certified English translation of any of the documents listed in (2) through (4) above.

Subd. 3. Action Upon Issuance of Adoption Decree. Upon issuing an adoption decree under this Rule, the court shall forward a copy of the adoption decree to the Commissioner of Human Services. The court shall also complete and forward to the Commissioner of Health the certificate of adoption, unless another form has been specified by the Commissioner of Health.

Former Rules 47.01 and 47.02, adopted Sept. 30, 2004, eff. Jan. 1, 2005. Renumbered Rule 30.01 and amended Dec. 1, 2006, eff. Jan. 1, 2007.

Rule 30.02. Adoption Under the Laws of Minnesota of a Child Born in Another Country

Subd. 1. Agency Adoption. An adoption of a child placed by an agency shall be commenced by the filing of a petition or other document pursuant to Rule 35 and thereafter shall proceed pursuant to Rule 28 dealing with agency adoptions.

Subd. 2. Direct Placement Adoption. A direct placement adoption of a child born in another country shall be commenced by the filing of a petition or other document pursuant to Rule 35 and thereafter shall proceed pursuant to Rule 29 dealing with direct placement adoptions.

Adopted Dec. 1, 2006, eff. Jan. 1, 2007.

Rule 30.03. Post–Adoption Report

If a child is adopted by a resident of Minnesota under the laws of a foreign country or if a resident of Minnesota brings a child into the state under an IR–3 or IR–4 visa issued for the child by the United States Citizenship and Immigration Services, the post-adoption reporting requirements of the country in which the child was adopted, applicable at the time of the child's adoption, shall be given full faith and credit by the courts of Minnesota and apply to the adoptive placement of the child.

Former Rule 47.03, adopted Sept. 30, 2004, eff. Jan. 1, 2005. Renumbered Rule 30.03 and amended Dec. 1, 2006, eff. Jan. 1, 2007.

RULE 31. NOTICE OF FINAL HEARING OR TRIAL

Rule 31.01. Notice

Subd. 1. Definition. A notice of hearing is a document providing notice of the specific date, time and place of a hearing or trial upon an adoption petition.

Subd. 2. Upon Whom. A notice of hearing shall be served by the petitioner upon:

(a) all parties under Rule 20;

(b) the parent of a child if:

(1) the person's name appears on the child's birth record as a parent;

(2) the person has substantially supported the child;

(3) the person either was married to the person designated on the birth record as the biological mother within the 325 days before the child's birth or married that person within the ten (10) days after the child's birth;

(4) the person is openly living with the child or the person designated on the birth record as the biological mother of the child, or both;

(5) the person has been adjudicated the child's parent;

(6) the person has filed a paternity action within thirty (30) days after the child's birth and the action is still pending; or

(7) the person and the mother of the child signed a declaration of parentage before August 1, 1995, which has not been revoked or a recognition of parentage which has not been revoked or vacated;

(c) a person who has timely registered pursuant to Minnesota Statutes § 259.52;

(d) the responsible social services agency;

(e) any parent who has abandoned the child or who has lost custody of the child through a divorce decree or dissolution of marriage; and

(f) the child's Indian tribe, if the child is an Indian child.

Former Rule 29.01, adopted Sept. 30, 2004, eff. Jan. 1, 2005. Renumbered Rule 31.01 and amended Dec. 1, 2006, eff. Jan. 1, 2007.

Rule 31.02. Notice Not Required

Without express order of the court, a notice of the hearing shall not be served upon:

(a) persons whose parental rights have been terminated;

(b) persons who have not timely registered pursuant to Minnesota Statutes § 259.52;

(c) persons who have waived notice of hearing pursuant to Minnesota Statutes § 259.49, subd. 1;

(d) a putative father who has timely registered with the Minnesota Fathers' Adoption Registry pursuant to Minnesota Statutes § 259.52, but who fails to timely file an intent to claim parental rights form with the court; and

(e) a putative father who has registered with the Minnesota Fathers' Adoption Registry pursuant to Minnesota Statutes § 259.52 and who has filed a completed denial of paternity form and a consent to adoption form.

Former Rule 29.02, adopted Sept. 30, 2004, eff. Jan. 1, 2005. Renumbered Rule 31.02 and amended Dec. 1, 2006, eff. Jan. 1, 2007.

Rule 31.03. Content of Notice of Hearing

A notice of hearing shall contain or have attached:

(a) an adoption petition;

(b) a statement setting forth the time and place of the hearing;

(c) a statement describing the purpose of the hearing as either:

(1) a final hearing pursuant to Rule 41 if it is an uncontested adoption matter; or

(2) a pretrial conference pursuant to Rule 43 if it is a contested adoption matter;

(d) a statement explaining the right to representation pursuant to Rule 23;

(e) a statement explaining intervention pursuant to Rule 21;

(f) a statement explaining that if the person fails to appear at the hearing, the court may still conduct the hearing and grant the adoption pursuant to Rule 18; and

(g) a statement explaining that it is the responsibility of the individual to notify the court administrator of any change of address.

Former Rule 29.03, adopted Sept. 30, 2004, eff. Jan. 1, 2005. Renumbered Rule 31.03 and amended Dec. 1, 2006, eff. Jan. 1, 2007.

Rule 31.04. Service of Notice of Hearing

Subd. 1. Timing. A notice of hearing shall be served, within or without the state, at least ten (10) days before the date of a final hearing in an uncontested matter and at least thirty (30) days before the date of the commencement of the trial in a contested matter.

Subd. 2. Method of Service—Parent.

(a) *Personal Service.* The petitioner shall serve the notice of hearing upon the child's parents by personal service.

(b) *Service by Publication.* If personal service cannot be made upon the parent, the petitioner or petitioner's attorney shall file an affidavit setting forth the effort that was made to locate the parent, and the names and addresses of the known kin of the child. If satisfied that the parent cannot be served personally, the court shall order three (3) weeks of published notice to be given, the last publication to be at least ten (10) days before the date set for the hearing. Service by publication shall be completed by the petitioner in a location approved by the court. Where service is made by publication, the court may cause such further notice to be given as it deems just. If, in the course of the proceedings, the court determines that the interests of justice will be promoted, it may continue the proceeding and require that such notice as it deems proper shall be served on any person. In the course of the proceedings the court may enter reasonable orders for the protection of the child if the court determines that the best interests of the child require such an order.

Subd. 3. U.S. Mail. The petitioner shall serve the notice of hearing by U.S. Mail upon the child's guardian ad litem; the child, if age ten (10) or older; the child's Indian custodian, if the child is an Indian child; the child's legal custodian or legal guardian, if other than the Commissioner of Human Services; any person who has intervened as a party; any person who has been joined as a party; the responsible social services agency; and any person who has timely complied with the requirements of Minn. Stat. § 259.52.

Subd. 4. Registered Mail. The petitioner shall serve the notice of hearing by registered mail with return receipt requested upon the Indian tribe if the child is an Indian child.

Former Rule 29.04, adopted Sept. 30, 2004, eff. Jan. 1, 2005. Renumbered Rule 31.04 and amended Dec. 1, 2006, eff. Jan. 1, 2007.

RULE 32. MINNESOTA FATHERS' ADOPTION REGISTRY

Rule 32.01. Requirement to Search Minnesota Fathers' Adoption Registry Before Adoption Petition Granted; Proof of Search

Subd. 1. Requirement to Search Registry. Except for intercountry adoptions, an adoption petition for a child born on or after January 1, 1998, shall not be granted unless the Minnesota Fathers' Adoption Registry has been searched to determine whether a putative father is registered in relation to the child who is the subject of the adoption petition. The search shall be conducted no sooner than thirty-one (31) days following the birth of the child.

Subd. 2. Proof of Search. A search of the registry may be proven by the production of a certified copy of the registration form or by a certified statement of the Commissioner of Health that after a search no registration of a putative father in relation to a child who is or may be the subject of an adoption petition could be located. Certification that the Minnesota Fathers' Adoption Registry has been searched shall be filed with the court prior to entry of any final adoption decree. The filing of a certified copy of the order from a juvenile protection matter containing a finding that certification of the requisite search of the Minnesota Fathers' Adoption Registry was filed with the court in that matter shall constitute proof of search.

Former Rule 30.01, adopted Sept. 30, 2004, eff. Jan. 1, 2005. Renumbered Rule 32.01, Dec. 1, 2006, eff. Jan. 1, 2007.

2004 Advisory Committee Comment

For children born before January 1, 1998, the Advisory Committee recommends that the best practice is for the petitioner to include with the petition a confirmation from the Department of Health that no one has filed a notice of intent to retain parental rights.

Rule 32.02. Fees for Minnesota Fathers' Adoption Registry

Pursuant to Minnesota Statutes § 259.52, subd. 14, in addition to any other filing fees, the court administrator shall assess an adoption filing fee surcharge on each adoption petition filed in the district court for the purpose of implementing and maintaining the Minnesota Fathers' Adoption Registry. The court administrator shall forward fees collected under this rule to the Commissioner of Finance for deposit into the state government special revenue fund to be appropriated to the Commissioner of Health to administer the Minnesota Fathers' Adoption Registry. The fee shall not be assessed in adoptions or re-adoptions of children adopted in intercountry adoptions.

Former Rule 30.02, adopted Sept. 30, 2004, eff. Jan. 1, 2005. Renumbered Rule 32.02 and amended Dec. 1, 2006, eff. Jan. 1, 2007.

RULE 33. CONSENT TO ADOPTION

Rule 33.01. Persons and Agencies Required to Consent

Written consent to an adoption is required by the following:

(a) the child to be adopted, if the child is fourteen (14) years of age or older, and the child's consent must be consent to adoption by a particular person;

(b) the adult to be adopted, whose consent shall be the only consent required;

(c) a registered putative father, if pursuant to Rule 32 he has:

(1) been notified under the Minnesota Fathers' Adoption Registry;

(2) timely filed an intent to claim parental rights form; and

(3) timely filed a paternity action;

(d) the child's parents or legal guardian, except:

(1) a parent not entitled to notice of the proceedings;

(2) a parent who has abandoned the child or a parent who has lost custody of the child through a divorce decree or a decree of dissolution and upon whom notice has been served as required under Rule 31; and

(3) a parent whose parental rights to the child have been terminated by a juvenile court order or through a decree in a prior adoption matter;

(e) if there is no parent or legal guardian qualified to consent to the adoption, the consent shall be given by the Commissioner of Human Services;

(f) the agency having authority to place the child for adoption, which shall have the exclusive right to consent to the adoption of such child; and

(g) the Commissioner of Human Services when the Commissioner is the legal guardian or legal custodian of the child, who shall have the exclusive right to consent to the adoption of such child.

Former Rule 31.01, adopted Sept. 30, 2004, eff. Jan. 1, 2005. Renumbered Rule 33.01 and amended Dec. 1, 2006, eff. Jan. 1, 2007; June 10, 2009, eff. Aug. 1, 2009.

2004 Advisory Committee Comment

The Advisory Committee recommends that, with respect to a parent who has abandoned the child or a parent who has lost custody of the child through a divorce decree or a decree of dissolution, it is best practice to either obtain a parent's consent as provided under Rule 31 or to commence a termination of parental rights proceeding pursuant to the Minnesota Rules of Juvenile Protection Procedure.

Historical Notes

The order of the Minnesota Supreme Court [C1-01-927] dated June 10, 2009, amending the Rules of Juvenile Protection Procedure and the Rules of Adoption Procedure, provides in part that the amendments are effective August 1, 2009, and shall apply to all actions or proceedings pending on or commenced on or after the effective date.

Rule 33.02. Notice of Intent to Consent to Adoption

Subd. 1. Consent of Biological Parents. Unless all biological parents from whom consent is required under Rule 33.01 are involved in making the adoptive placement and intend to consent to the adoption, a biological parent who intends to execute a consent to an adoption shall give notice to the child's other biological parent of the intent to consent to the adoption prior to or within seventy-two (72) hours following the placement of the child if the other biological parent's consent to the adoption is required under Rule 33.01. Notice of intent to consent to adoption shall be provided to the other biological parent according to the Minnesota Rules of Civil Procedure for service of a summons and complaint. The biological parent who receives notice shall have sixty (60) days after the placement of the child to serve upon the other biological parent either a consent pursuant to Rule 33.01 or a written objection to the adoption. If the biological parent who receives notice fails to consent or to respond with a written objection to the adoption within sixty (60) days after the adoptive placement, that parent shall be deemed to have irrevocably consented to the child's adoption.

Subd. 2. Consent of Minors. If an unmarried parent who consents to the adoption of a child is under eighteen (18) years of age, the consent of the minor parent's parents or legal custodian or legal guardian, if any, also shall be required. If either or both parents are not required to consent pursuant to Rule 33.01(d), the consent of such parent shall be waived and the consent of the legal custodian or legal guardian only shall be sufficient. If there be neither parent nor legal custodian or legal guardian qualified to give such consent, the consent may be given by the Commissioner of Human Services. The responsible social services agency overseeing the adoption matter shall ensure that the minor parent is offered the opportunity to consult with an attorney, a member of the clergy, or a physician before consenting to adoption of the child. The advice or opinion of the attorney, clergy member, or physician shall not be binding on the minor parent. If the minor parent cannot afford the cost of consulting with an attorney, a member of the clergy, or a physician, the county shall bear that cost. A parent or legal custodian or legal guardian of a minor or incapacitated person may not delegate the power to consent to adoption of a minor ward under Minnesota Statutes §§ 524.5-101 to 524.5-502.

Former Rule 31.02, adopted Sept. 30, 2004, eff. Jan. 1, 2005. Renumbered Rule 33.02 and amended Dec. 1, 2006, eff. Jan. 1, 2007.

Rule 33.03. Execution of Consent to Adoption

Subd. 1. Requirements of Consent. Except as provided in subdivision 3, all consents to an adoption shall:

(a) be in writing;

(b) be executed before two competent witnesses;

(c) be acknowledged by the consenting party;

(d) be executed before a representative of the Commissioner of Human Services, the Commissioner's agent, or a licensed child-placing agency;

(e) include a notice to the parent of the substance of Minnesota Statutes § 259.24, subd. 6a, providing for the right to withdraw consent; and

(f) include the following written notice in all capital letters at least one-eighth inch high: "This agency will submit your consent to adoption to the court. The consent itself does not terminate your parental rights. Parental rights to a child may be terminated only by an adoption decree or by a court order terminating parental rights. Unless the child is adopted or your parental rights are terminated, you may be asked to support the child."

Subd. 2. Consents Taken Outside of Minnesota. A consent executed and acknowledged outside of Minnesota, either in accordance with the law of this state or in accordance with the law of the place where executed, is valid.

Subd. 3. Exceptions to Consent Requirements. The requirements of subdivision 1 do not apply to:

(a) consents to adoption by:

(1) the Commissioner of Human Services or the Commissioner's agent;

(2) a licensed child-placing agency;

(3) an adult adoptee;

(4) the child's parent in a petition for adoption by a stepparent; or

(5) a parent or legal guardian when executed, together with a waiver of notice of hearing, before a judicial officer;

(b) a Minnesota Fathers' Adoption Registry consent to adoption; or

(c) consent to the adoption of an Indian child.

Former Rule 31.03, adopted Sept. 30, 2004, eff. Jan. 1, 2005. Renumbered Rule 33.03 and amended Dec. 1, 2006, eff. Jan. 1, 2007.

Rule 33.04. Timing of Consent

A consent to adoption form shall not be signed sooner than seventy-two (72) hours after the birth of a child. The seventy-two (72) hours is computed excluding the date of the birth and including Saturdays, Sundays, and legal holidays. A consent to adoption shall be executed by any person whose consent is required under Rule 33 within sixty (60) days after the child's placement in a prospective adoptive home.

Former Rule 31.04, adopted Sept. 30, 2004, eff. Jan. 1, 2005. Renumbered Rule 33.04 and amended Dec. 1, 2006, eff. Jan. 1, 2007.

Rule 33.05. Failure to Execute Consent

With the exception of cases where a person receives notice under Minnesota Statutes § 259.24, subd. 2a, if a biological parent whose consent is required under Rule 33 does not execute a consent by the end of the period specified in Rule 33.04, the child placing agency shall notify the court and the court shall issue an order regarding continued placement of the child. The court shall order the local social services agency to determine whether to commence proceedings for termination of parental rights on grounds of abandonment as defined in Minnesota Statutes § 260C.301, subd. 2. The court may disregard the six-month and twelve-month requirements of Minnesota Statutes § 260C. 201, subd. 11, in finding abandonment if the biological parent has failed to execute a consent within the time required under Rule 33.04 and has made no effort to obtain custody of the child.

Former Rule 31.05, adopted Sept. 30, 2004, eff. Jan. 1, 2005. Renumbered Rule 33.05 and amended Dec. 1, 2006, eff. Jan. 1, 2007.

Rule 33.06. Agreement Conferring Authority to Place for Adoption

Subd. 1. Parties to Agreement. The parents and legal custodian or legal guardian, if there be one, of a child may enter into a written agreement with the Commissioner of Human Services or an agency giving the Commissioner or such agency authority to place the child for adoption. If an unmarried parent is under eighteen (18) years of age, the written consent of the parents and legal custodian or legal guardian, if any, of the minor parent also shall be required. If either or both of the parents are disqualified from giving such consent for any of the reasons enumerated in Minnesota Statutes § 259.24, subd. 1, the written consent of the legal custodian or legal guardian shall be required.

Subd. 2. Format of Agreement. The agreement and consent shall be in the form prescribed by the Commissioner of Human Services and shall contain notice to the parent of the substance of Minn. Stat. § 259.59, subd. 2a, providing for the right to revoke the agreement.

Subd. 3. Content of Agreement. The agreement and consent shall contain the following written notice in all capital letters at least one-eighth inch high: "This agency will submit your consent to adoption to the court. The consent itself does not terminate your parental rights. Parental rights to a child may be terminated only by an adoption decree or by a court order terminating parental rights. Unless the child is adopted or your parental rights are terminated, you may be asked to support the child."

Subd. 4. Execution of Agreement. The agreement shall be executed by the Commissioner of Human Services or agency, or one of their authorized agents, and all other necessary parties, and shall be filed, together with the consent, in the proceedings for the adoption of the child. If, after the execution of an agreement and consent under this rule, the child is diagnosed with a medical or psychological condition that may present a substantial barrier to adoption, the child-placing agency shall make reasonable efforts to give notice of this fact to a party to the agreement and consent. If a child is not adopted within two (2) years after an agreement and consent are executed under this rule, the agency that executed the agreement shall so notify a parent who was a party to the agreement and request the parent to take custody of the child or to file a petition for termination of parental rights. This notice shall be provided to the parent in a personal and confidential manner. A parent who has executed an agreement under this rule shall, upon request to the agency, be informed of whether the child has been adopted.

Former Rule 31.06, adopted Sept. 30, 2004, eff. Jan. 1, 2005. Renumbered Rule 33.06 and amended Dec. 1, 2006, eff. Jan. 1, 2007.

Rule 33.07. Consent to a Direct Placement Adoption Under Minnesota Statutes § 259.47

Subd. 1. Presence of Legal Counsel for Biological Parent. If a biological parent has chosen to have legal counsel pursuant to Rule 23.04, the attorney shall be present at the execution of any consent. If a biological parent waives counsel, the parent's written waiver shall be filed with the consent to the adoption.

Subd. 2. Execution of Consent Before Judicial Officer—When Required. A biological parent whose consent to a direct placement adoption is required under Minn. Stat. § 259.24 and who has chosen not to receive counseling through a licensed agency or a licensed social services professional trained in adoption issues, shall appear before a judicial officer at a consent hearing as described in subdivision 4 to execute consent to the adoption.

Subd. 3. Execution of Consent Before Judicial Officer—When Optional. A biological parent whose consent to a direct placement adoption is required under Minnesota Statutes 259.24 and who has received counseling through a licensed agency or a licensed social services professional trained in adoption issues, or any other parent or legal guardian whose consent to a direct placement adoption is required under Minnesota Statutes 259.24, subd. 2, may choose to execute consent to the adoption under the procedures set forth in Minnesota Statutes 259.24, subd. 5, and Rule 33.03, subd. 1, or at a consent hearing as described in subdivision 4.

Subd. 4. Consent Hearing. Notwithstanding where the prospective adoptive parent resides, a consent hearing may be held in any county in this state where the biological parent is found. If the consent hearing is held in a county other than where the prospective adoptive parent resides, the court shall forward the executed consent to the district court in the county where the prospective adoptive parent resides.

Subd. 5. Consent Format. The written consent form to be used in a direct placement adoption under this rule shall be on a form prepared by the Commissioner of Human Services and made available to agencies and court administrators for public distribution. The form shall state:

(a) the biological parent has had the opportunity to consult with independent legal counsel at the expense of the prospective adoptive parent, unless the biological parent knowingly waived the opportunity;

(b) the biological parent has been notified of the right to receive counseling at the expense of the prospective adoptive parent and has chosen to exercise or waive that right; and

(c) the biological parent has been informed that if the biological parent withdraws consent, the prospective adoptive parent cannot require the biological parent to reimburse any costs the prospective adoptive parent has incurred in connection with the adoption, including payments made to or on behalf of the biological parent.

Former Rule 31.07, adopted Sept. 30, 2004, eff. Jan. 1, 2005. Renumbered Rule 33.07, Dec. 1, 2006, eff. Jan. 1, 2007. Amended Dec. 18, 2006, eff. Jan. 1, 2007.

Rule 33.08. Revocation of Consent to Adoption of a Non–Indian Child Under Minnesota Statutes § 259.24

A parent's consent to adoption may be withdrawn for any reason within ten (10) working days after the consent is executed and acknowledged or pursuant to the law of the state where the consent is executed. Written notification of withdrawal of consent shall be received by the agency to which the child was surrendered no later than the tenth working day after the consent is executed and acknowledged. On the day following the tenth working day after execution and acknowledgment, the consent shall become irrevocable, except upon order of a court of competent jurisdiction after written findings that the consent was obtained by fraud. In proceedings to determine the existence of fraud, the adoptive parents and the child shall be made parties. The proceedings shall be conducted to preserve the confidentiality of the adoption process. There shall be no presumption in the proceedings favoring the biological parents over the adoptive parents. Failure to comply with the terms of a communication or contact agreement order entered by the court under Rule 34 is not grounds for revocation of a written consent to an adoption after that consent has become irrevocable.

Former Rule 31.08, adopted Sept. 30, 2004, eff. Jan. 1, 2005. Renumbered Rule 33.08 and amended Dec. 1, 2006, eff. Jan. 1, 2007.

Rule 33.09. Consent to Adoption of an Indian Child

Subd. 1. Requirements of Consent. If the child to be adopted is an Indian child, the consent of the parent or Indian custodian shall not be valid unless:

(a) executed in writing;

(b) recorded before the judge; and

(c) accompanied by the presiding judge's certificate that the terms and consequences of the consent were explained in detail and were fully understood by the parent or Indian custodian. The court shall also certify that the parent or Indian custodian fully understood the explanation in English or that it was translated into a language that the parent or Indian custodian understood. Any consent given prior to, or within ten (10) days after, the birth of the Indian child shall not be valid.

Subd. 2. Revocation of Consent to Adoption of an Indian Child. In any voluntary proceeding for adoptive placement of an Indian child, the consent of the parent may be withdrawn for any reason at any time prior to the entry of an adoption decree and the child shall be returned to the parent.

Subd. 3. Vacation of an Adoption Decree of an Indian Child. After the entry of an adoption decree of an Indian child in any State court, the parent may withdraw consent thereto upon the grounds that consent was obtained through fraud or duress and may petition the court to vacate such decree. Upon a finding that such consent was obtained through fraud or duress, the court shall vacate such decree and return the child to the parent. No adoption of an Indian child which has been effective for at least two (2) years may be invalidated under the Indian Child Welfare Act, 25 U.S.C. § 1913, unless otherwise permitted under state law.

Former Rule 31.09, adopted Sept. 30, 2004, eff. Jan. 1, 2005. Renumbered Rule 33.09 and amended Dec. 1, 2006, eff. Jan. 1, 2007.

2004 Advisory Committee Comment

Rule 33.09 mirrors the provisions of the Indian Child Welfare Act, 25 U.S.C. § 1913. The Guidelines of the Bureau of Indian Affairs provide additional guidance as follows:

"A consent to termination of parental rights or adoption may be withdrawn by the parent at any time prior to entry of a *final decree of voluntary termination or adoption* by filing an instrument executed under oath by the parent stipulating his or her intention to withdraw such consent. The clerk of court where the withdrawal of consent is filed shall promptly notify the party or agency by or through whom the adoptive placement has been arranged of such filing and that party or agency shall insure the return of the child to the parent as soon as practicable." The *Commentary* to the guideline further provides that "This provision recommends that the clerk of court be responsible for notifying the family with whom the child has been placed that consent has been withdrawn. The court's involvement frequently may be necessary [because] the biological parents are often not told who the adoptive parents are."

Bureau of Indian Affairs Guidelines for State Courts—Indian Child Custody Proceedings, Section E.4 and *Commentary (emphasis included in original).*

RULE 34. COMMUNICATION OR CONTACT AGREEMENT

Rule 34.01. Persons Who May Enter Into a Communication or Contact Agreement

Subd. 1. Parties. A communication or contact agreement shall be in writing and may be entered into between the following persons:

(a) the adopting parent and a biological parent;

(b) the adopting parent and any other birth relative, including a sibling, or foster parent with whom the child resided before being adopted; or

(c) the adopting parent and any other birth relative, including a sibling, if the child is adopted by a birth relative upon the death of both biological parents.

Subd. 2. Approval. A communication or contact agreement shall be approved as follows:

(a) The responsible social services agency shall approve, in writing, any agreement involving a child in the legal custody or guardianship of the Commissioner of Human Services.

(b) A child placing agency shall approve, in writing, any agreement involving a child under its legal custody or guardianship.

(c) A biological parent shall approve in writing an agreement between an adopting parent and any other birth relative or foster parent, unless an action has been filed against the biological parent by a county under Minn. Stat. Chapter 260C.

Former Rule 32.01, adopted Sept. 30, 2004, eff. Jan. 1, 2005. Renumbered Rule 34.01, Dec. 1, 2006, eff. Jan. 1, 2007.

2004 Advisory Committee Comment

For siblings who grow up in foster care under the guardianship of the Commissioner of Human Services, a communication or contact agreement may be one way to ensure the children are able to maintain their sibling relationship.

Rule 34.02. Filing of Agreement

The signed communication or contact agreement shall be filed with the court after the petition has been filed and prior to finalization of the adoption.

Former Rule 32.02, adopted Sept. 30, 2004, eff. Jan. 1, 2005. Renumbered Rule 34.02, Dec. 1, 2006, eff. Jan. 1, 2007.

Rule 34.03. Written Order Required

A communication or contact agreement is not legally enforceable unless the terms of the agreement are contained in a written court order entered pursuant to these rules, which shall be separate from the findings of fact, conclusions of law, order for judgment, and adoption decree issued pursuant to Rule 45.

Former Rule 32.03, adopted Sept. 30, 2004, eff. Jan. 1, 2005. Renumbered Rule 34.03 and amended Dec. 1, 2006, eff. Jan. 1, 2007.

Rule 34.04. Timing

A communication or contact agreement order shall be issued by the court within fifteen (15) days of being submitted to the court or by the date the adoption decree is issued, whichever is earlier.

Former Rule 32.04, adopted Sept. 30, 2004, eff. Jan. 1, 2005. Renumbered Rule 34.04, Dec. 1, 2006, eff. Jan. 1, 2007; June 10, 2009, eff. Aug. 1, 2009.

Historical Notes

The order of the Minnesota Supreme Court [C1–01–927] dated June 10, 2009, amending the Rules of Juvenile Protection Procedure and the Rules of Adoption Procedure, provides in part that the amendments are effective August 1, 2009, and shall apply to all actions or proceedings pending on or commenced on or after the effective date.

Rule 34.05. Requirements for Entry of Order

A communication or contact agreement order under this rule need not disclose the identity of the parties. The court shall not enter an order unless the court finds that the communication or contact between the child, the adoptive parent, and a birth relative as agreed upon and contained in the proposed order is in the child's best interests.

Former Rule 32.05, adopted Sept. 30, 2004, eff. Jan. 1, 2005. Renumbered Rule 34.05, Dec. 1, 2006, eff. Jan. 1, 2007.

Rule 34.06. Service of Order

The court administrator shall mail a certified copy of the communication or contact agreement order to the parties to the agreement or their legal representatives at the addresses provided by the petitioners.

Former Rule 32.06, adopted Sept. 30, 2004, eff. Jan. 1, 2005. Renumbered Rule 34.06, Dec. 1, 2006, eff. Jan. 1, 2007.

Rule 34.07. Enforcement—Family Court

Subd. 1. Filing Requirement. A communication or contact agreement order entered under this rule may be enforced by filing with the family court:

(a) a petition or motion;

(b) a certified copy of the communication or contact agreement order; and

(c) an affidavit that the parties have mediated or attempted to mediate any dispute under the agreement or that the parties agree to a proposed modification.

Subd. 2. Attorneys Fees. The prevailing party upon a motion to enforce a communication or contact agreement order may be awarded reasonable attorney's fees and costs.

Former Rule 32.07, adopted Sept. 30, 2004, eff. Jan. 1, 2005. Renumbered Rule 34.07, Dec. 1, 2006, eff. Jan. 1, 2007.

Rule 34.08. Failure to Comply with Order

Failure to comply with the terms of a communication or contact agreement order is not grounds for:

(a) setting aside an adoption decree; or

(b) revocation of a written consent to an adoption after that consent has become irrevocable.

Former Rule 32.08, adopted Sept. 30, 2004, eff. Jan. 1, 2005. Renumbered Rule 34.08, Dec. 1, 2006, eff. Jan. 1, 2007.

Rule 34.09. Modification

The court shall not modify a communication or contact agreement order unless it finds that the modification is necessary to serve the best interests of the child, and:

(a) the modification is agreed to by the parties to the agreement; or

(b) exceptional circumstances have arisen since the agreed order was entered that justify modification of the order.

Former Rule 32.09, adopted Sept. 30, 2004, eff. Jan. 1, 2005. Renumbered Rule 34.09, Dec. 1, 2006, eff. Jan. 1, 2007.

RULE 35. PETITION

Rule 35.01. Residency of Petitioner

Subd. 1. Residency Requirement. Any person who has resided in the state for one (1) year or more may petition to adopt.

Subd. 2. Exception to Residency Requirement. The one (1) year residency requirement may be reduced to thirty (30) days by the court in the best interests of the child. The court may waive any residency requirement of this rule if the petitioner is an individual related to the child, as defined in Rule 2.01(*o*), or as a member of a child's extended family or important friend with whom the child has resided or had significant contact or, upon a showing of good cause, the court is satisfied that the proposed adoptive home and the child are suited to each other.

Former Rule 33.01, adopted Sept. 30, 2004, eff. Jan. 1, 2005. Renumbered Rule 35.01, Dec. 1, 2006, eff. Jan. 1, 2007.

Rule 35.02. Residency of Child to be Adopted

Unless waived by the court, no petition shall be granted until the child has lived three (3) months in the proposed home, subject to a right of visitation by the Commissioner of Human Services or an agency or their authorized representatives. If the three-month residency requirement is waived by the court, at least ten (10) days notice of the hearing shall be provided by certified mail to the local social services agency.

Former Rule 33.02, adopted Sept. 30, 2004, eff. Jan. 1, 2005. Renumbered Rule 35.02 and amended Dec. 1, 2006, eff. Jan. 1, 2007.

Rule 35.03. Timing

Subd. 1. Generally. An adoption petition shall be filed not later than twelve (12) months after a child is placed in a prospective adoptive home. If a petition is not filed by that time, the agency that placed the child or, in a direct placement adoption, the agency that is supervising the placement, shall file with the court in the county where the prospective adoptive parent resides, or in the county where the court is reviewing progress towards adoption of a child under the guardianship or legal custody of the Commissioner of Human Services, a motion for an order and a report recommending one of the following:

(a) that the time for filing a petition be extended because of the child's special needs as specified under Minnesota Statutes § 259.22, subd. 4,

(b) that, based on a written plan for completing filing of the petition, including a specific timeline, to which the prospective adoptive parents have agreed, the time for filing a petition be extended long enough to complete the plan because such an extension is in the best interests of the child and additional time is needed for the child to adjust to the adoptive home; or

(c) that the child be removed from the prospective adoptive home.

Subd. 2. Exceptions—Stepparent and Relative Adoptions. The timing specified in subdivision 1 does not apply to stepparent adoptions or adoptions by an individual related to the child not involving a placement as defined in Rule 2.01(*o*).

Former Rule 33.03, adopted Sept. 30, 2004, eff. Jan. 1, 2005. Renumbered Rule 35.03 and amended Dec. 1, 2006, eff. Jan. 1, 2007.

Rule 35.04. Conditions for Filing Petition for Adoption of a Child; Exceptions

Subd. 1. Generally. No petition for adoption of a child may be filed unless the adoptive placement of the child was made by:

(a) the Commissioner of Human Services;

(b) an agent of the Commissioner of Human Services; or

(c) a child-placing agency as defined in Rule 2.01(g).

Subd. 2. Exceptions. The requirements of subdivision 1 shall not apply if:

(a) the child is over fourteen (14) years of age;

(b) the petitioner is an individual who is related to the child as defined in Rule 2.01(*o*);

(c) the child has been lawfully placed under the laws of another state while the child and the petitioner resided in that state;

(d) the court waives the requirement of subdivision 1 in the best interests of the child and the placement is not made by transfer of physical custody of the child from a biological parent or legal guardian to the prospective adoptive home; or

(e) the child has been lawfully placed pursuant to an order for direct placement pursuant to Rule 29.

Former Rule 33.04, adopted Sept. 30, 2004, eff. Jan. 1, 2005. Renumbered Rule 35.04 and amended Dec. 1, 2006, eff. Jan. 1, 2007.

Rule 35.05. Content

Subd. 1. Case Caption. In all adoption proceedings, except as otherwise stated in this subdivision, the case caption shall be "In Re the Petition of _________ and _________ (petitioners) to adopt _________ (child's birth name)." In proceedings commenced before the birth of the child being adopted, the case caption shall be "In Re the Petition of _________ and _________ (petitioners) to adopt _________ (unborn child of _________)."

Subd. 2. Allegations. An adoption petition may be filed regarding one or more children, shall be verified by the petitioner upon information and belief, and shall allege:

(a) the full name, age, and place of residence of the petitioner, except as provided in Rule 7;

(b) if married, the date and place of marriage, and the name of any parent who will retain legal rights;

(c) the date the petitioner acquired physical custody of the child and from what person or agency or, in the case of a stepparent adoption or adoption by an individual related to the child as defined in Rule 2.01(*o*), the date the petitioner began residing with the child;

(d) the date of birth of the child, if known, and the county, state, and country where born;

(e) the name of the child's parents, if known, and the legal custodian or legal guardian if there be one;

(f) the actual name of the child, if known, and any known aliases;

(g) the name to be given the child, if a change of name is desired;

(h) the description and value of any real or personal property owned by the child;

(i) the relationship of the petitioner to the child, if any;

(j) whether the Indian Child Welfare Act does or does not apply;

(k) the name and address of the parties identified in Rule 20;

(*l*) whether the child has been placed with petitioner for adoption by an agency and, if so, the date of the adoptive placement; and

(m) that the petitioner desires that the relationship of parent and child be established between petitioner and the child, and that it is in the best interests of the child to be adopted by the petitioner.

Subd. 3. Exception to Content. In agency placements, the information required in subdivision 2(e) and (f) shall not be required to be alleged in the petition but shall be provided to the court by the Commissioner of Human Services. In the case of an adoption by a stepparent, the parent who is the stepparent's spouse shall not be required to join the petition.

Subd. 4. Attachments. The following shall be filed with the petition:

(a) the adoption study report required under Rule 37;

(b) any biological parent history required under Minnesota Statutes § 259.43, except if the petitioner is the child's stepparent;

(c) the request, if any, under Rule 38.04 to waive the post-placement assessment report and background check; and

(d) proof of service.

Subd. 5. Other Documents to be Filed. The following shall be filed with the court prior to finalization of the adoption:

(a) a certified copy of the child's birth record;

(b) a certified copy of the findings and order for termination of parental rights, if any;

(c) a copy of the communication or contact agreement, if any;

(d) certification that the Minnesota Fathers' Adoption Registry has been searched as required under Rule 32;

(e) the original of each consent to adoption required under Rule 33; and

(f) the post-placement assessment report required under Rule 38.

Subd. 6. Missing Information. If any information required by subdivision 2 or 3 is unknown at the time of the filing of the petition, as soon as such information becomes known to the petitioner it shall be provided to the court and parties either orally on the record, by sworn affidavit, or by amended petition. If presented orally on the record, the court shall annotate the petition to reflect the updated information.

Subd. 7. Acceptance Despite Missing Information. The court administrator shall accept a petition for filing even if, on its face, the petition appears to be incomplete or does not include all information specified in subdivision 2 and 3. The presiding judge shall determine whether the petition complies with the requirements of these rules.

Former Rule 33.05, adopted Sept. 30, 2004, eff. Jan. 1, 2005. Renumbered Rule 35.05 and amended Dec. 1, 2006, eff. Jan. 1, 2007. Amended June 26, 2007, eff. July 1, 2007.

Rule 35.06. Verification

The petition shall be signed and dated by the petitioner and verified upon information and belief.

Former Rule 33.06, adopted Sept. 30, 2004, eff. Jan. 1, 2005. Renumbered Rule 35.06, Dec. 1, 2006, eff. Jan. 1, 2007.

Rule 35.07. Amendment

Subd. 1. Uncontested Petitions. An adoption petition may be amended at any time prior to the conclusion of the final hearing pursuant to Rule 41.

Subd. 2. Contested Petitions.

(a) *Prior to Trial.* An adoption petition may be amended at any time prior to the commencement of a trial pursuant to Rule 44. The petitioner shall provide notice of the amendment to all parties at least seven (7) days prior to the commencement of the trial. When the petition is amended, the court shall grant all other parties sufficient time to respond to the amendment.

(b) *After Trial Begins.* The petition may be amended after the trial has commenced if the court finds that the amendment does not prejudice a party and all parties are given sufficient time to respond to the proposed amendment.

Former Rule 33.07, adopted Sept. 30, 2004, eff. Jan. 1, 2005. Renumbered Rule 35.07 and amended Dec. 1, 2006, eff. Jan. 1, 2007.

Rule 35.08. Statement of Expenses

Upon the filing of an adoption petition, the agency shall file with the court a statement of expenses that have been paid or are to be paid by the prospective adoptive parent in connection with the adoption. In a direct placement adoption, the statement of expenses shall be filed by the prospective adoptive parent.

Former Rule 33.08, adopted Sept. 30, 2004, eff. Jan. 1, 2005. Renumbered Rule 35.08 and amended Dec. 1, 2006, eff. Jan. 1, 2007.

RULE 36. ACTIONS UPON FILING OF PETITION

Upon the filing of an adoption petition, the court administrator shall immediately provide a copy of the petition to:

(a) the Commissioner of Human Services; and

(b) if the petition relates to a child, the agency identified below:

(1) in an agency or a direct placement adoption, the court shall provide the petition to the agency supervising the placement; and

(2) in all other instances not described in clause (1), the court shall provide the petition to the local social services agency of the county in which the prospective adoptive parent lives if the child is to be adopted by an individual who is related to the child as defined in Rule 2.01(*o*).

Former Rule 34.01, adopted Sept. 30, 2004, eff. Jan. 1, 2005. Renumbered Rule 36 and amended Dec. 1, 2006, eff. Jan. 1, 2007.

RULE 37. ADOPTION AND BACKGROUND STUDY

Rule 37.01. Adoption Study and Background Study Required; Exception

An approved adoption study, completed background study as required under Minnesota Statutes § 245C.33, and written adoption study report must be completed before the child is placed in a prospective adoptive home, except as allowed by Minnesota Statutes § 259.47, subd. 6. An approved adoption study, which includes the background study, shall be completed by a licensed child-placing agency and must be thorough and comprehensive. The study shall be paid for by the prospective adoptive parent, except as otherwise required under Minnesota Statutes § 259.67 or 259.73. A placement for adoption with an individual who is related to the child, as defined by Minnesota Statutes § 245A.02, subd. 13, is not subject to this rule except as required by Minnesota Statutes § 245C.33 and § 259.53, subd. 2(c). In the case of a licensed foster parent seeking to adopt a child who is in the foster parent's care, any portions of the foster care licensing process that duplicate requirements of the adoption study may be submitted in satisfaction of the relevant requirements of this rule.

Former Rule 35.01, adopted Sept. 30, 2004, eff. Jan. 1, 2005. Renumbered Rule 37.01 and amended Dec. 1, 2006, eff. Jan. 1, 2007; June 10, 2009, eff. Aug. 1, 2009.

Historical Notes

The order of the Minnesota Supreme Court [C1–01–927] dated June 10, 2009, amending the Rules of Juvenile Protection Procedure and the Rules of Adoption Procedure, provides in part that the amendments are effective August 1, 2009, and shall apply to all actions or proceedings pending on or commenced on or after the effective date.

Rule 37.02. Adoption Study Report

The adoption study is the basis for completion of a written report which must be in a format specified by the Commissioner of Human Services. An adoption study report must include at least one in-home visit with each prospective adoptive parent. At a minimum, the report must document the following information about each prospective adoptive parent:

(a) a background study pursuant to Minnesota Statutes § 259.41, subd. 3, and § 245C.33, including:

(i) an assessment of the data and information required in Minnesota Statutes § 245C.33, subd. 4, to determine if the prospective adoptive parent and any other person over the age of 13 living in the home has a felony conviction consistent with subdivision 3 and section 471(a)(2) of the Social Security Act; and

(ii) an assessment of the effect of any conviction or finding of substantiated maltreatment on the capacity of the prospective adoptive parent to safely care for and parent a child;

(b) an assessment of medical and social history;

(c) an assessment of current health;

(d) an assessment of potential parenting skills;

(e) an assessment of ability to provide adequate financial support for a child;

(f) an assessment of the level of knowledge and awareness of adoption issues, including, where appropriate, matters relating to interracial, cross-cultural, and special needs adoptions; and

(g) recommendations regarding the suitability of the subject of the study to be an adoptive parent..

Former Rule 35.02, adopted Sept. 30, 2004, eff. Jan. 1, 2005. Renumbered Rule 37.02 and amended Dec. 1, 2006, eff. Jan. 1, 2007; June 10, 2009, eff. Aug. 1, 2009.

Historical Notes

The order of the Minnesota Supreme Court [C1–01–927] dated June 10, 2009, amending the Rules of Juvenile Protection Procedure and the Rules of Adoption Procedure, provides in part that the amendments are effective August 1, 2009, and shall apply to all actions or proceedings pending on or commenced on or after the effective date.

Rule 37.03. Direct Placement Adoption; Background Study Incomplete

Unless otherwise ordered by the court, in a direct placement adoption the child may be placed in the preadoptive home prior to completion of the background study if each prospective adopting parent has completed and filed with the court a sworn affidavit stating whether the affiant or any person residing in the household has been convicted of a crime. The affidavit shall also:

(a) state whether the adoptive parent or any other person residing in the household is the subject of an open investigation of, or has been the subject of a substantiated allegation of, child or vulnerable adult maltreatment within the past ten (10) years;

(b) include a complete description of the crime, open investigation, or substantiated allegation of child abuse or vulnerable adult maltreatment, and a complete description of any sentence, treatment, or disposition; and

(c) include the following statement: "Petitioner acknowledges that if, at any time before the adoption is final, a court receives evidence leading to a conclusion that a prospective adoptive parent knowingly gave false information in the affidavit, it shall be determined that the adoption of the child by the prospective adoptive parent is not in the best interests of the child."

Former Rule 35.03, adopted Sept. 30, 2004, eff. Jan. 1, 2005. Renumbered Rule 37.03 and amended Dec. 1, 2006, eff. Jan. 1, 2007; June 10, 2009, eff. Aug. 1, 2009.

Historical Notes

The order of the Minnesota Supreme Court [C1–01–927] dated June 10, 2009, amending the Rules of Juvenile Protection Procedure and the Rules of Adoption Procedure, provides in part that the amendments are effective August 1, 2009, and shall apply to all actions or proceedings pending on or commenced on or after the effective date.

Rule 37.04. Background Study; Timing

Subd. 1. Timing of Background Study. The background study required in Rule 37.03 shall be completed before an adoption petition is filed.

Subd. 2. Direct Placement Adoption. In a direct placement adoption, if an adoption study report has been submitted to the court before the background study is complete, an updated adoption study report which includes the results of the background study shall be filed with the adoption petition.

Subd. 3. Agency Unable to Complete Background Study. In the event that an agency is unable to complete the background study, the agency shall submit with the adoption petition an affidavit documenting the agency's efforts to complete the background study.

Former Rule 35.04, adopted Sept. 30, 2004, eff. Jan. 1, 2005. Renumbered Rule 37.04 and amended Dec. 1, 2006, eff. Jan. 1, 2007; June 10, 2009, eff. Aug. 1, 2009.

Historical Notes

The order of the Minnesota Supreme Court [C1–01–927] dated June 10, 2009, amending the Rules of Juvenile Protection Procedure and the Rules of Adoption Procedure, provides in part that the amendments are effective August 1, 2009, and shall apply to all actions or proceedings pending on or commenced on or after the effective date.

Rule 37.05. Updates to Adoption Study Report; Period of Validity

An adoption study report is valid if the report has been completed or updated within twelve (12) months of the adoptive placement.

Former Rule 35.05, adopted Sept. 30, 2004, eff. Jan. 1, 2005. Renumbered Rule 37.05, Dec. 1, 2006, eff. Jan. 1, 2007.

Rule 37.06. Filing of Adoption Study Report

Subd. 1. Agency Placement. The adoption study report shall be filed with the court at the time the adoption petition is filed.

Subd. 2. Direct Placement Adoption. The adoption study report shall be filed with the court pursuant to Rule 29 in support of a motion for a non-emergency preadoptive custody order or, if the study and report are complete, in support of an emergency preadoptive custody order .

Former Rule 35.06, adopted Sept. 30, 2004, eff. Jan. 1, 2005. Renumbered Rule 37.06 and amended Dec. 1, 2006, eff. Jan. 1, 2007.

Rule 37.07. Foster Parent Assessment May be Used for Adoption Study

A licensed foster parent seeking to adopt a child in the foster parent's care may submit any portion of the foster care licensing assessment that duplicates requirements of the adoption study report in satisfaction of the adoption study report requirements.

Former Rule 35.07, adopted Sept. 30, 2004, eff. Jan. 1, 2005. Renumbered Rule 37.07, Dec. 1, 2006, eff. Jan. 1, 2007.

RULE 38. POST–PLACEMENT ASSESSMENT REPORT

Rule 38.01. Timing

Subd. 1. Generally. Unless waived by the court pursuant to Rule 38.04 and Minnesota Statutes § 259.53, the supervising agency, or if there is no such agency the local social services agency, shall conduct a post-placement assessment and file a report with the court within ninety (90) days of receipt of a copy of the adoption petition. A post-placement assessment report is valid for twelve (12) months following its date of completion.

Subd. 2. Failure to Comply. If, through no fault of the petitioner, the agency fails to complete the assessment and file the report within ninety (90) days of the date it received a copy of the adoption petition, the court may hear the petition upon giving the agency five (5) days notice by mail of the time and place of the hearing.

Former Rule 36.01, adopted Sept. 30, 2004, eff. Jan. 1, 2005. Renumbered Rule 38.01 and amended Dec. 1, 2006, eff. Jan. 1, 2007.

Rule 38.02. Content

The post-placement assessment report shall provide an individualized determination of the needs of the child and how the adoptive placement will serve the needs of the child. The report shall include a recommendation to the court as to whether the adoption petition should or should not be granted. In making evaluations and recommendations, the post-placement assessment report shall, at a minimum, address the following:

(1) the level of adaptation by the prospective adoptive parents to parenting the child;

(2) the health and well-being of the child in the prospective adoptive parent's home;

(3) the level of incorporation by the child into the prospective adoptive parent's home, extended family, and community; and

(4) the level of inclusion of the child's previous history into the prospective adoptive home, such as cultural or ethnic practices, or contact with former foster parents or biological relatives.

Former Rule 36.02, adopted Sept. 30, 2004, eff. Jan. 1, 2005. Renumbered Rule 38.02, Dec. 1, 2006, eff. Jan. 1, 2007.

Rule 38.03. Background Study

If an adoption study is not required because the petitioner is an individual who is related to the child as defined in Rule 2.01(*o*), the agency, as part of its post-placement assessment report, shall conduct a background study meeting the requirements of Minnesota Statutes § 259.41, subd. 3(b).

Former Rule 36.03, adopted Sept. 30, 2004, eff. Jan. 1, 2005. Renumbered Rule 38.03 and amended Dec. 1, 2006, eff. Jan. 1, 2007; June 10, 2009, eff. Aug. 1, 2009.

Historical Notes

The order of the Minnesota Supreme Court [C1–01–927] dated June 10, 2009, amending the Rules of Juvenile Protection Procedure and the Rules of Adoption Procedure, provides in part that the amendments are effective August 1, 2009, and shall apply to all actions or proceedings pending on or commenced on or after the effective date.

Rule 38.04. Waiver by Court

Subdivision 1. Post–Placement Assessment Waiver Permitted. The post-placement assessment report may be waived by the court pursuant to Minnesota Statutes § 259.53. A request to waive a post-placement assessment report shall be in writing and shall be filed and served with the petition pursuant to Rule 35.05. A request to waive a post-placement assessment report shall be decided by the court within fifteen (15) days of filing, unless a written objection to the waiver is filed, in which case a hearing must be conducted as soon as practicable.

Subd. 2. Background Study Waiver Prohibited. The court shall not waive the background study.

Former Rule 36.04, adopted Sept. 30, 2004, eff. Jan. 1, 2005. Renumbered Rule 38.04 and amended Dec. 1, 2006, eff. Jan. 1, 2007; June 10, 2009, eff. Aug. 1, 2009.

Historical Notes

The order of the Minnesota Supreme Court [C1–01–927] dated June 10, 2009, amending the Rules of Juvenile Protection Procedure and the Rules of Adoption Procedure, provides in part that the amendments are effective August 1, 2009, and shall apply to all actions or proceedings pending on or commenced on or after the effective date.

RULE 39. ANSWER WHEN CONTESTED ADOPTION MATTER

Rule 39.01. Answer When Contested

Within twenty (20) days after service of the adoption petition, or as soon thereafter as the party or agency becomes aware that the matter is contested, a Notice of Contested Adoption and, if appropriate, a competing adoption petition, shall be filed by:

(a) any party or agency opposing the adoption;

(b) any party or agency with knowledge of two or more adoption petitions regarding the same child; or

(c) the Commissioner of Human Services or responsible social services agency if consent to adopt is being withheld from the petitioner.

Former Rule 37.01, adopted Sept. 30, 2004, eff. Jan. 1, 2005. Renumbered Rule 39.01 and amended Dec. 1, 2006, eff. Jan. 1, 2007.

Rule 39.02. Notice of Contested Adoption

Subd. 1. Content. A Notice of Contested Adoption shall:

(a) set forth the allegations upon which the adoption is being contested; and

(b) be signed by the party or by an agent of the agency opposing the adoption.

Subd. 2. Service. The Notice of Contested Adoption shall be served upon all parties in the same fashion as other motions are served under these Rules.

Former Rule 37.02, adopted Sept. 30, 2004, eff. Jan. 1, 2005. Renumbered Rule 39.02 and amended Dec. 1, 2006, eff. Jan. 1, 2007.

Rule 39.03. Pretrial Conference

The court shall schedule a pretrial conference within fifteen (15) days of the filing of a Notice of Contested Adoption and provide notice of hearing to the parties.

Former Rule 37.03, adopted Sept. 30, 2004, eff. Jan. 1, 2005. Renumbered Rule 39.03, Dec. 1, 2006, eff. Jan. 1, 2007.

RULE 40. VOLUNTARY WITHDRAWAL; INVOLUNTARY DISMISSAL; SUMMARY JUDGMENT

Rule 40.01. Voluntary Withdrawal of Petition

A petition may be withdrawn or dismissed by a petitioner without order of the court by filing:

(a) at any time a notice of withdrawal along with proof of service upon all parties; or

(b) a stipulation of dismissal signed by all parties who have appeared in the matter.

Former Rule 38.01, adopted Sept. 30, 2004, eff. Jan. 1, 2005. Renumbered Rule 40.01 and amended Dec. 1, 2006, eff. Jan. 1, 2007.

Rule 40.02. Involuntary Dismissal of Petition

Pursuant to the timing, notice, and format requirements of Rule 7 of the Minnesota Rules of Civil Procedure, the court, upon its own initiative or upon motion of a party, may dismiss a petition or grant judgment on the pleadings. Grounds for such dismissal or judgment on the pleadings shall include, but not be limited to:

(a) failure to comply with these rules;

(b) failure to move forward on the petition;

(c) failure to state a claim upon which relief may be granted;

(d) lack of jurisdiction over the subject matter;

(e) lack of jurisdiction over the person;

(f) insufficiency of service of process; and

(g) failure to join a necessary party.

Furthermore, after a petitioner has completed the presentation of evidence, any other party to the proceeding, without waiving the right to offer evidence in the event the motion is not granted, may move for dismissal on the ground that based upon the facts and the law, the petitioner has shown no right to relief.

Former Rule 38.02, adopted Sept. 30, 2004, eff. Jan. 1, 2005. Renumbered Rule 40.02 and amended Dec. 1, 2006, eff. Jan. 1, 2007.

Rule 40.03. Summary Judgment

Pursuant to the timing, notice, and format requirements of Rule 7 of the Minnesota Rules of Civil Procedure, a party may move with or without supporting affidavits for summary judgment. Judgment shall be rendered forthwith if the pleadings, depositions, answers to interrogatories, and admissions on file, together with the affidavits, if any, show that there is no genuine issue as to any material fact, and that a moving party is entitled to judgment as a matter of law.

Former Rule 38.03, adopted Sept. 30, 2004, eff. Jan. 1, 2005. Renumbered Rule 40.03, Dec. 1, 2006, eff. Jan. 1, 2007.

RULE 41. FINAL HEARING IN UNCONTESTED MATTERS

Rule 41.01. Generally

A final hearing is a hearing to determine whether an uncontested adoption petition should be granted.

Former Rule 39.01, adopted Sept. 30, 2004, eff. Jan. 1, 2005. Renumbered Rule 41.01, Dec. 1, 2006, eff. Jan. 1, 2007.

Rule 41.02. Commencement

A final hearing relating to an uncontested adoption petition shall be held not sooner than ninety (90) days after the child is placed, unless there is a waiver of the residency requirement pursuant to Rule 35, but not later than ninety (90) days after the adoption petition is filed. If the petitioner has not requested a hearing date within sixty (60) days of the filing of the petition, the court administrator may schedule a hearing and serve notice of such hearing pursuant to Rule 31.04.

Former Rule 39.02, adopted Sept. 30, 2004, eff. Jan. 1, 2005. Renumbered Rule 41.02 and amended Dec. 1, 2006, eff. Jan. 1, 2007.

Rule 41.03. Hearing Procedure

At the beginning of the final hearing, the court shall on the record:

(a) verify the name, age, and current address of the child who is the subject of the proceeding, except as provided in Rule 20.03;

(b) determine whether the Indian child's tribe has been notified, if the child has been determined to be an Indian child;

(c) determine whether all parties are present and identify those present for the record;

(d) determine whether any necessary biological parent, guardian, or other person from whom consent to the adoption is required or whose parental rights will need to be terminated is present;

(e) determine whether notice requirements have been met, and, if not, whether the affected person waives notice; and

(f) determine whether the Interstate Compact on the Placement of Children, Minnesota Statutes §§ 260.851–.91, applies.

Former Rule 39.03, adopted Sept. 30, 2004, eff. Jan. 1, 2005. Renumbered Rule 41.03 and amended Dec. 1, 2006, eff. Jan. 1, 2007.

Rule 41.04. Standard of Proof

The petitioner shall prove by a preponderance of evidence the facts alleged in the adoption petition and that the adoption is in the best interests of the child.

Former Rule 39.04, adopted Sept. 30, 2004, eff. Jan. 1, 2005. Renumbered Rule 41.04, Dec. 1, 2006, eff. Jan. 1, 2007.

2004 Advisory Committee Comment

The Indian Child Welfare Act, 25 U.S.C. § 1901, et. seq., does not state a standard of proof for adoption matters as it does for foster care and termination of parental rights matters.

Rule 41.05. Timing of Decision

Within fifteen (15) days of the conclusion of the final hearing in an uncontested adoption, the court shall issue findings of fact, conclusions of law, order for judgment, and adoption decree pursuant to Rule 45. For good cause, the court may extend this period for an additional fifteen (15) days.

Former Rule 39.05, adopted Sept. 30, 2004, eff. Jan. 1, 2005. Renumbered Rule 41.05 and amended Dec. 1, 2006, eff. Jan. 1, 2007.

RULE 42. CONSOLIDATION; BIFURCATION

Rule 42.01. Consolidation Generally

When matters involving the adoption of the same child or children are pending before the court, the court may:

(a) order a joint hearing or trial of any or all the adoption matters;

(b) order consolidation of all such adoption matters;

(c) order that the matters be heard sequentially; and

(d) make any orders appropriate to avoid unnecessary delay or costs.

Former Rule 40.01, adopted Sept. 30, 2004, eff. Jan. 1, 2005. Renumbered Rule 42.01, Dec. 1, 2006, eff. Jan. 1, 2007.

Rule 42.02. Consolidation with Other Proceedings; Competing Petitions

Subd. 1. Consolidation with Other Proceedings. Upon notice of motion and motion and for good cause shown, the court may order the consolidation of the adoption matter with any related proceeding, including a custody proceeding, paternity proceeding, termination of parental rights proceeding, or other proceeding regarding the same child.

Subd. 2. Competing Petition. When multiple adoption petitions have been filed with respect to the same child who is under the guardianship of the Commissioner of Human Services, the court shall consolidate the matters for trial. In all other cases, when two or more parties have petitioned for the adoption of the same child, the court may, after consideration of the factors specified in subdivision 4, order the petitions to be tried together.

Subd. 3. Cross–County Matters. Upon motion for a change of venue and for good cause shown, the court may order the consolidation of the adoption matter with any related proceeding in another county regarding the same child.

Subd. 4. Factors to Consider. In making the determinations required under subdivisions 1 to 3, the court shall consider the best interests of the child, any potential breaches of confidentiality of the adoption matter, the additional complexity or judicial economies of a joint proceeding, and any other relevant factors.

Former Rule 40.02, adopted Sept. 30, 2004, eff. Jan. 1, 2005. Renumbered Rule 42.02, Dec. 1, 2006, eff. Jan. 1, 2007.

2004 Advisory Committee Comment

In determining whether to consolidate an adoption matter and termination of parental rights proceeding, the court shall consider the impact of the consolidation on the eligibility of the child for financial adoption assistance or other financial benefits available under Minn. Stat. § 259.67.

Rule 42.03. Bifurcation

Subd. 1. Permissive Bifurcation. The court may order a trial pursuant to Rule 44 to be bifurcated as to one or more claims or issues.

Subd. 2. Mandatory Bifurcation. In cases where the child is under the guardianship of the Commissioner of Human Services, the court shall bifurcate the trial on the contested adoption petitions as follows:

(a) A trial shall first be held to determine whether the consent to the adoption by the Commissioner of Human Services was unreasonably withheld from the petitioner. The responsible social services agency shall proceed first with evidence about the reason for the withholding of consent. The petitioner who has not obtained consent shall then have the burden of showing by a preponderance of the evidence that the consent was unreasonably withheld.

(b) If the court determines that the consent of the Commissioner of Human Services was not unreasonably withheld, the court shall dismiss the adoption petition of the petitioner who did not obtain consent, and proceed to trial on the remaining adoption petitions, if any.

(c) If the court determines that the consent of the Commissioner of Human Services was unreasonably withheld from any petitioner, the court shall not dismiss that petition for lack of consent. The court shall proceed to trial on all the contested adoption petitions, and shall determine whether adoption is in the best interests of the child, and, if so, adoption by whom.

Former Rule 40.03, adopted Sept. 30, 2004, eff. Jan. 1, 2005. Renumbered Rule 42.03 and amended Dec. 1, 2006, eff. Jan. 1, 2007.

RULE 43. PRETRIAL CONFERENCE IN CONTESTED MATTERS

Rule 43.01. Timing

The court may convene a pretrial conference sua sponte or upon the motion of any party. Any pretrial conference shall take place at least ten (10) days prior to trial.

Former Rule 41.01, adopted Sept. 30, 2004, eff. Jan. 1, 2005. Renumbered Rule 43.01, Dec. 1, 2006, eff. Jan. 1, 2007.

Rule 43.02. Purpose

The purposes of a pretrial conference shall be to:

(a) determine whether a settlement of any or all of the issues has occurred or is possible;

(b) determine whether all parties have been served and, if not, review the efforts that have taken place to date to serve all parties;

(c) determine whether all parties who seek legal representation have obtained legal representation and determine that attorneys of record have filed certificates of representation with the court;

(d) identify any unresolved discovery matters;

(e) resolve any pending pretrial motions;

(f) determine the order in which evidence will be presented pursuant to Rule 45;

(g) identify and narrow issues of law and fact for trial, including identification of:

(1) the factual allegations admitted or denied;

(2) any stipulations to foundation and relevance of documents; and

(3) any other stipulations, admissions, or denials;

(h) exchange witness lists and a brief summary of each witness' testimony;

(i) set a deadline for the exchange of exhibits prior to trial and determine how exhibits shall be marked prior to the start of trial;

(j) confirm the trial date and estimate the length of trial; and

(k) determine any other relevant issues.

Former Rule 41.02, adopted Sept. 30, 2004, eff. Jan. 1, 2005. Renumbered Rule 43.02 and amended Dec. 1, 2006, eff. Jan. 1, 2007.

Rule 43.03. Pretrial Order

Within fifteen (15) days of the pretrial conference, the court shall issue a pretrial order which shall specify all determinations required by this rule. From the date of the pretrial conference to the commencement of the trial, the parties shall have a continuing obligation to update information provided during the pretrial conference.

Former Rule 41.03, adopted Sept. 30, 2004, eff. Jan. 1, 2005. Renumbered Rule 43.03, Dec. 1, 2006, eff. Jan. 1, 2007; June 10, 2009, eff. Aug. 1, 2009.

Historical Notes

The order of the Minnesota Supreme Court [C1–01–927] dated June 10, 2009, amending the Rules of Juvenile Protection Procedure and the Rules of Adoption Procedure, provides in part that the amendments are effective August 1, 2009, and shall apply to all actions or proceedings pending on or commenced on or after the effective date.

RULE 44. TRIAL IN CONTESTED MATTERS

Rule 44.01. Generally

A trial is a hearing to determine whether an adoption petition should be granted.

Former Rule 42.01, adopted Sept. 30, 2004, eff. Jan. 1, 2005. Renumbered Rule 44.01, Dec. 1, 2006, eff. Jan. 1, 2007.

Rule 44.02. Commencement

A trial on a contested adoption petition shall commence within ninety (90) days of the filing of the petition or notice of a contested hearing, whichever is later. The trial shall be completed within thirty (30) days of commencement. Either or both deadlines may be extended for up to an additional thirty (30) days upon a showing of good cause and a finding by the court that the extension is in the best interests of the child.

Former Rule 42.02, adopted Sept. 30, 2004, eff. Jan. 1, 2005. Renumbered Rule 44.02 and amended Dec. 1, 2006, eff. Jan. 1, 2007.

Rule 44.03. Trial Procedure

Subd. 1. Initial Procedure. At the beginning of the trial, the court shall on the record:

(a) verify the name, age, and current address of the child who is the subject of the proceeding, except as provided in Rule 20.03;

(b) determine whether the Indian child's tribe has been notified, if the child has been determined to be an Indian child;

(c) determine whether all parties are present and identify those present for the record;

(d) determine whether any necessary biological parent, guardian, or other person from whom consent to the adoption or whose parental rights will need to be terminated is present; and

(e) determine whether notice requirements have been met, and, if not, whether the affected person waives notice.

Subd. 2. Order of Evidence. That trial shall proceed as follows:

(a) The parties, in the order determined by the court at the pretrial conference, may make an opening statement or may make a statement immediately before offering evidence on their own petition and the statement shall be confined to the facts expected to be proved.

(b) The parties, in the order determined by the court at the pretrial conference, may offer evidence.

(c) The parties, in the order determined by the court at the pretrial conference, may offer evidence in rebuttal.

(d) When evidence is presented, the parties may, in the order determined by the court at the pretrial conference, cross-examine the witnesses.

(e) At the conclusion of the evidence, the parties may make closing statements in the reverse order in which they presented their evidence.

(f) If a written argument is to be submitted, it shall be submitted within fifteen (15) days of the conclusion of testimony, and the trial is not considered completed until the time for written arguments to be submitted has expired.

Former Rule 42.03, adopted Sept. 30, 2004, eff. Jan. 1, 2005. Renumbered Rule 44.03, Dec. 1, 2006, eff. Jan. 1, 2007.

Rule 44.04. Standard of Proof

The petitioner shall prove by a preponderance of evidence the facts alleged in the adoption petition and that the adoption is in the best interests of the child.

Former Rule 42.04, adopted Sept. 30, 2004, eff. Jan. 1, 2005. Renumbered Rule 44.04, Dec. 1, 2006, eff. Jan. 1, 2007.

2004 Advisory Committee Comment

The Indian Child Welfare Act, 25 U.S.C. § 1901, et. seq., does not state a standard of proof for adoption matters as it does for foster care and termination of parental rights matters.

Rule 44.05. Motion for Judgment at Conclusion of Trial

A motion for a judgment may be made at the close of the evidence offered by an opponent or at the close of all evidence. A party who moves for a judgment at the close of the evidence offered by an opponent shall, after denial of the motion, have the right to offer evidence as if the motion had not been made. A motion for a judgment shall state the specific grounds therefore.

Former Rule 42.05, adopted Sept. 30, 2004, eff. Jan. 1, 2005. Renumbered Rule 44.05, Dec. 1, 2006, eff. Jan. 1, 2007.

Rule 44.06. Timing of Decision; Delay of Issuance of Order if Adoption Assistance Not Yet Acted Upon

Subd. 1. Generally. Within fifteen (15) days of the conclusion of the trial in a contested matter, the court shall issue findings of fact, conclusions of law, an order for judgment, and an adoption decree pursuant to Rule 45. If written argument is to be submitted, such argument must be submitted within fifteen (15) days of the conclusion of testimony. For good cause, the court may extend this period for an additional fifteen (15) days. The trial is not considered completed until written arguments, if any, are submitted or the time for submission of written arguments has expired.

Subd. 2. Delay of Issuance of Order if Adoption Assistance Not Yet Acted Upon. For adoption matters involving a child who is a ward of the Commissioner of Human Services, if there has been no opportunity for the adopting parent to apply for adoption assistance, the court shall delay issuing its findings of fact, conclusions of law, order for judgment, and adoption decree pursuant to Rule 45 until such time as the responsible social services agency documents for the court that either the Commissioner has acted upon an adoption assistance application made on behalf of the adopting parent and child or the adopting parent has declined in writing to apply for adoption assistance. "Acted upon" means the commissioner or commissioner's delegate has signed an adoption assistance agreement or denied adoption assistance eligibility pursuant to a completed application submitted to the Department of Human Services. Nothing in this rule grants jurisdiction over the commissioner in regard to procedures or substantive decisions regarding the award or denial of adoption assistance.

Former Rule 42.06, adopted Sept. 30, 2004, eff. Jan. 1, 2005. Renumbered Rule 44.06 and amended Dec. 1, 2006, eff. Jan. 1, 2007; June 10, 2009, eff. Aug. 1, 2009.

2008 Advisory Committee Comment

Rule 44.06, subd. 2, requires the court to delay issuing its order after a final hearing or trial on an adoption matter relating to a child who is a state ward if the adopting parent has not had the opportunity to apply for adoption assistance or if the responsible agency has not documented in writing signed by the adopting parent that the adopting parent was advised of the opportunity to apply for adoption assistance and has declined adoption assistance. The reason for requiring the delay is because there may not have been an adoption assistance application by, or agency discussion of the opportunity to apply for adoption assistance with, the adopting parent when two or more competing adoption petitions regarding the same child are heard and the Commissioner of Human Services has given consent to the adoption, as required under Minn. Stat. § 259.24, subd. 1(d), by a different prospective adoptive petitioner than the adopting parent whose petition the court is granting. There may be an adoption assistance agreement for the parent to whom the Commissioner gave consent, but no application may have been made in regard to the competing petitioner. The court is required to delay issuing the adoption decree to give the responsible social services agency time to discuss the opportunity to apply for adoption assistance on behalf of the child with family whose petition the court is granting and for the commissioner to act on any application that is made. This will mean more certain eligibility for adoption assistance and timely start of adoption assistance payments after the decree is issued, if the child and adoptive parent are determined eligible.

Historical Notes

The order of the Minnesota Supreme Court [C1–01–927] dated June 10, 2009, amending the Rules of Juvenile Protection Procedure and the Rules of Adoption Procedure, provides in part that the amendments are effective August 1, 2009, and shall apply to all actions or proceedings pending on or commenced on or after the effective date.

RULE 45. FINDINGS OF FACT, CONCLUSIONS OF LAW, ORDER FOR JUDGMENT, AND ADOPTION DECREE

Rule 45.01. Denial of Adoption Petition

If the court finds that the consent of the adult person to be adopted is not valid, the court shall deny the petition. The court may dismiss an adoption petition if appropriate legal grounds have not been proved. If the court is not satisfied that the proposed adoption is in the best interests of the child, the court shall deny the petition and:

(a) order that the child be returned to the custody of the person or agency legally vested with permanent custody; or

(b) order the case transferred for appropriate action and disposition by the court having jurisdiction to determine the custody and guardianship of the child.

Former Rule 43.01, adopted Sept. 30, 2004, eff. Jan. 1, 2005. Renumbered Rule 45.01, Dec. 1, 2006, eff. Jan. 1, 2007.

Rule 45.02. Granting Adoption Petition

If the court finds that it is in the best interests of the child that the petition be granted, the court shall issue findings of fact, conclusions of law, an order for judgment, and an adoption decree that the person shall be the child of the petitioner. If the person being adopted is an adult, the court shall grant an adoption decree if the court finds that the person's consent is valid. Once the court issues an adoption decree, the court shall also direct the court administrator to complete the appropriate forms so that a new birth record may be issued and notify the prevailing petitioner and his or her attorney of the determination, and provide them with an opportunity to obtain a certified copy of the adoption decree and new birth record prior to the closing of the file.

Former Rule 43.02, adopted Sept. 30, 2004, eff. Jan. 1, 2005. Renumbered Rule 45.02, Dec. 1, 2006, eff. Jan. 1, 2007.

Rule 45.03. Findings of Fact, Conclusions of Law, Order for Judgment, and Adoption Decree

Subd. 1. Separate Orders For Each Child. Although multiple children may be listed in an adoption petition, for each such child the court shall issue a separate findings of fact, conclusions of law, order for judgment, and adoption decree.

Subd. 2. Findings of Fact in a Contested Adoption Matter. In its decision in a contested adoption matter, the court shall make findings about:

(a) the petitioner's full name and date of birth;

(b) the petitioner's marital status;

(c) whether petitioner has resided in Minnesota for at least one (1) year prior to filing the adoption petition or whether the residency requirement has been waived pursuant to Rule 35.01;

(d) the date petitioner acquired physical custody of the child and from whom;

(e) the type of placement, including whether it is an agency placement, a direct preadoptive placement, a relative placement, or some other type of placement;

(f) whether three (3) months have passed since the date petitioner acquired physical custody of the child or whether the residency requirement has been waived pursuant to Rule 35.02;

(g) the child's date of birth and the child's city, county, state, and country of birth;

(h) whether a certified copy of the birth record of the child or of the adult to be adopted has been filed with the court;

(i) whether the post-placement assessment report required under Rule 38 and the adoption study report required under Rule 37 have been filed with the court;

(j) whether the child owns property and, if so, a list of such property;

(k) whether all consents required under Rule 33 have been properly executed and filed with the court or whether orders for termination of parental rights have been entered;

(*l*) whether all notices required under Rule 31 have been properly served and proof of service has been filed with the court;

(m) whether, if applicable, a communication or contact agreement pursuant to Rule 34 has been properly executed and filed with the court and whether the court finds that the communication or contact agreement is in the best interests of the child;

(n) whether a statement of expenses paid by the petitioner has been filed with the court pursuant to Rule 35.08 and whether the expenses are approved;

(*o*) whether a search of the Minnesota Fathers' Adoption Registry has been conducted and the results have been filed with the court pursuant to Rule 32; and

(p) whether the social and medical history form has been completed by the biological mother and biological father and has been filed with the court.

Subd. 3. Findings of Fact in an Uncontested Adoption Matter. In its decision in an uncontested adoption matter, the court:

(a) shall include findings about the issues identified in subdivision 2 (a), (b), (c), (d), (g), (j), and (m); and

(b) may include findings about the issues identified in subdivision 2 (e), (f), (h), (i), (k), (*l*), (n), (*o*), and (p).

Subd. 4. Conclusions of Law. In its decision, the court shall make conclusions of law about whether all of the allegations contained in the adoption petition have been proved in accordance with the applicable standard of proof and whether the adoption is in the child's best interests.

Subd. 5. Order for Judgment. If the court decides to grant the adoption petition, in its decision the court shall include an order stating:

(a) the child's new name;

(b) that the child is the child of the petitioner; and

(c) that an adoption decree shall be issued.

Subd. 6. Adoption Decree. If the court decides to grant the adoption petition, in its decision the court shall order that the child is the child of the petitioner and of any parent retaining parental rights.

Former Rule 43.03, adopted Sept. 30, 2004, eff. Jan. 1, 2005. Renumbered Rule 45.03 and amended Dec. 1, 2006, eff. Jan. 1, 2007.

Rule 45.04. Filing and Service

The findings of fact, conclusions of law, order for judgment, and adoption decree shall be filed and served pursuant to Rule 10.03, subd. 2. If the adoptee is an Indian child, the court administrator shall provide the Secretary of the Interior with a copy of the adoption decree, along with such other information as may be necessary to show the following:

(a) the child's name and tribal affiliation;

(b) the names and addresses of the child's biological parents;

(c) the names and addresses of the child's adoptive parents; and

(d) the identity of any agency having files or information relating to such adoptive placement.

Former Rule 43.04, adopted Sept. 30, 2004, eff. Jan. 1, 2005. Renumbered Rule 45.04, Dec. 1, 2006, eff. Jan. 1, 2007.

RULE 46. POST-TRIAL MOTIONS

Rule 46.01. Motion for Amended Findings

Upon motion of a party served and heard not later than the time allowed for a motion for a new trial pursuant to Rule 46.02, the court may amend its findings or make additional findings, and may amend the judgment accordingly if judgment has been entered. The motion may be made with a motion for a new trial and may be made on the files, exhibits, and minutes of the court. The question of the sufficiency of the evidence to support the findings may be raised on appeal regardless of whether the party raising the question has made in the district court an objection to such findings or has made a motion to amend them or a motion for judgment.

Former Rule 44.01, adopted Sept. 30, 2004, eff. Jan. 1, 2005. Renumbered Rule 46.01 and amended Dec. 1, 2006, eff. Jan. 1, 2007.

Rule 46.02. Motion for New Trial

Subd. 1. Grounds. A motion for a new trial may be granted to any or all of the parties on all or part of the issues for any of the following causes:

(a) irregularity in the proceedings of the court, referee, or prevailing party, or any order or abuse of discretion whereby the moving party was deprived of a fair trial;

(b) misconduct of the prevailing party;

(c) accident or surprise which could not have been prevented by ordinary prudence;

(d) material evidence newly discovered, which with reasonable diligence could not have been found and produced at the trial;

(e) errors of law occurring at the trial, and objected to at the time, or, if no objection need have been made pursuant to these rules, plainly assigned in the notice of motion;

(f) the decision is not justified by the evidence or is contrary to law; but, unless it be so expressly stated in the order granting a new trial, it shall not be presumed on appeal to have been made on the ground that the decision was not justified by the evidence; or

(g) in the interest of justice.

Upon a motion for a new trial, the court may open the judgment if one has been entered, take additional testimony, amend findings of fact and conclusions of law, or make new findings and conclusions, and direct entry of a new judgment.

Subd. 2. Basis Of Motion. A motion for a new trial shall be made pursuant to Rule 15 and shall be made based upon on the files, exhibits, and minutes of the court. Pertinent facts that would not be a part of the minutes may be shown by affidavit. A full or partial transcript of the court reporter's notes may be used on the hearing of the motion.

Subd. 3. Time For Serving and Filing Motion. A notice of motion and motion for a new trial shall be served and filed within fifteen (15) days after service of notice by the court administrator of the filing of the decision or order pursuant to Rule 10. The motion shall be heard within thirty (30) days after such notice of filing.

Subd. 4. Time For Serving and Filing Affidavits. When a motion for a new trial is based upon affidavits, they shall be served and filed with the notice of motion. The opposing party shall have ten (10) days after such service in which to serve and file opposing affidavits, which period may be extended by the court for good cause. The court may permit reply affidavits.

Subd. 5. Order for New Trial On Court's Initiative. Not later than fifteen (15) days after a general verdict or the filing of the decision or order, the court upon its own initiative may order a new trial for any reason for which it might have granted a new trial on a motion of a party. After giving the parties notice and an opportunity to be heard on the matter, the court may grant a motion for a new trial, timely served, for a reason not stated in the motion. The court shall specify in the order the grounds therefore.

Former Rule 44.02, adopted Sept. 30, 2004, eff. Jan. 1, 2005. Renumbered Rule 46.02, Dec. 1, 2006, eff. Jan. 1, 2007.

Rule 46.03. Timing of Decision

Within fifteen (15) days of the conclusion of the hearing on the motion the court shall issue its decision and order. For good cause shown, the court may extend this period for an additional fifteen (15) days.

Former Rule 44.03, adopted Sept. 30, 2004, eff. Jan. 1, 2005. Renumbered Rule 46.03, Dec. 1, 2006, eff. Jan. 1, 2007.

RULE 47. RELIEF FROM ORDER

Rule 47.01. Clerical Mistakes

Clerical mistakes in judgments, orders, or other parts of the record and errors arising from oversight or omission may be corrected by the court at any time upon its own initiative or upon motion of any party and after such notice, if any, as the court orders. During the pendency of an appeal, such mistakes may be so corrected with leave of the appellate court.

Former Rule 45.01, adopted Sept. 30, 2004, eff. Jan. 1, 2005. Renumbered Rule 47.01, Dec. 1, 2006, eff. Jan. 1, 2007.

Rule 47.02. Mistakes; Inadvertence; Excusable Neglect; Newly Discovered Evidence; Fraud

Upon motion and upon such terms as are just, the court may relieve a party or the party's legal representatives from a final order or proceeding and may order a new trial or grant such other relief as may be just for any of the following reasons:

(a) mistake, inadvertence, surprise, or excusable neglect;

(b) newly discovered evidence which by due diligence could not have been discovered in time to move for a new trial;

(c) fraud (whether denominated intrinsic or extrinsic), misrepresentation, or other misconduct of an adverse party;

(d) the judgment is void; or

(e) any other reason justifying relief from the operation of the order.

The motion shall be made within a reasonable time, but in no event shall it be more than ninety (90) days following the filing of the court's order.

Former Rule 45.02, adopted Sept. 30, 2004, eff. Jan. 1, 2005. Renumbered Rule 47.02, Dec. 1, 2006, eff. Jan. 1, 2007.

Rule 47.03. Invalidation of District Court Action—Indian Child Cases

Subd. 1. Petition. Any Indian child who is the subject of an adoption proceeding under State law, parent or Indian custodian from whose custody such child was removed, and the Indian child's tribe may file with any court of competent jurisdiction a petition to invalidate such action upon a showing that such action violates any provisions of the Indian Child Welfare Act, 25 U.S.C. §§ 1911, 1912, or 1913.

Subd. 2. Evidentiary Hearing. Upon the filing of a petition to invalidate, the court shall schedule an evidentiary hearing. The form and content of the petition to invalidate shall be governed by Rule 15.

Subd. 3. Findings and Order. Within fifteen (15) days of the conclusion of the evidentiary hearing, the court shall issue a written order which shall include findings of fact and conclusions of law.

Former Rule 45.03, adopted Sept. 30, 2004, eff. Jan. 1, 2005. Renumbered Rule 47.03 and amended Dec. 1, 2006, eff. Jan. 1, 2007; June 10, 2009, eff. Aug. 1, 2009.

Historical Notes

The order of the Minnesota Supreme Court [C1-01-927] dated June 10, 2009, amending the Rules of Juvenile Protection Procedure and the Rules of Adoption Procedure, provides in part that the amendments are effective August 1, 2009, and shall apply to all actions or proceedings pending on or commenced on or after the effective date.

Rule 47.04. Vacation of Adoption Decree—Indian Child Cases

Subd. 1. Petition to Vacate. After the entry of an adoption decree of an Indian child in any State court, the parent may withdraw consent upon the grounds that the consent was obtained through fraud or duress and may petition the court to vacate such decree. Upon a finding that such consent was obtained through fraud or duress, the court shall vacate such decree and return the child to the parent. No adoption which has been effective for at least two (2) years may be invalidated under the provisions of this rule unless otherwise permitted under State law.

Subd. 2. Evidentiary Hearing. Upon the filing of a petition to vacate, the court shall schedule an evidentiary hearing. The form and content of the petition to vacate shall be governed by Rule 15.

Subd. 3. Findings and Order. At the conclusion of the evidentiary hearing the court shall issue a written order which shall include findings of fact and conclusions of law.

Former Rule 45.04, adopted Sept. 30, 2004, eff. Jan. 1, 2005. Renumbered Rule 47.04, Dec. 1, 2006, eff. Jan. 1, 2007.

RULE 48. APPEAL

Rule 48.01. Applicability of Rules of Civil Appellate Procedure

Except as provided in this rule, appeals of adoption matters shall be in accordance with the Minnesota Rules of Civil Appellate Procedure.

Former Rule 46.01, adopted Sept. 30, 2004, eff. Jan. 1, 2005. Renumbered Rule 48.01, Dec. 1, 2006, eff. Jan. 1, 2007.

Rule 48.02. Procedure

Subd. 1. Appealable Order. An appeal may be taken by an aggrieved person from a final order of the juvenile court affecting a substantial right of the aggrieved person.

Subd. 2. Timing. Any appeal shall be taken within thirty (30) days of the service of notice by the court administrator of the filing of the court's order. In the event of the filing and service of a timely and proper post-trial motion under Rule 46, or for relief under Rule 47 if the motion is filed within the time specified in Rule 46.02, subd. 3, the provisions of Minnesota Rules of Civil Appellate Procedure Rule 104.01, subds. 2 and 3, apply, except that the time for appeal runs for all parties from the service of notice by the court administrator of the filing of the order disposing of the last post-trial motion.

Subd. 3. Service and Filing of Notice of Appeal. Within the time allowed for an appeal from an appealable order, the person appealing shall:

(a) serve a notice of appeal upon all parties or their counsel if represented, including notice of the correct case caption pursuant to Rule 8. 08 of the Minnesota Rules of Juvenile Protection Procedure; and

(b) file with the clerk of appellate courts a notice of appeal, together with proof of service upon all parties, including notice of the correct case caption as required under Rule 8.08 of the Minnesota Rules of Juvenile Protection Procedure.

Subd. 4. Notice to Court Administrator. At the same time as the appeal is filed the appellant shall provide notice of the appeal to the court administrator. Failure to notify the court administrator does not deprive the court of appeals of jurisdiction.

Subd. 5. Failure to File Proof of Service. Failure to file proof of service does not deprive the court of appeals of jurisdiction over the appeal, but is grounds only for such action as the court of appeals deems appropriate, including a dismissal of the appeal.

Subd. 6. Notice to Legal Custodian. The court administrator shall notify the child's legal custodian of the appeal. Failure to notify the legal custodian does not affect the jurisdiction of the court of appeals.

Former Rule 46.02, adopted Sept. 30, 2004, eff. Jan. 1, 2005. Renumbered Rule 48.02 and amended Dec. 1, 2006, eff. Jan. 1, 2007.

2004 Advisory Committee Comment—2006 Amendment

Minnesota Statutes § 259.63 provides that adoption appeals are taken "as in other civil cases" under the Rules of Civil Appellate Procedure. The Committee recognizes that the timing provision of Rule 48.02, subd. 2, is a departure from the Minnesota Rules of Civil Appellate Procedure in that under these Rules the appeal period now starts to run for all parties from the service of the Notice of Filing of Order by the court administrator rather than from the service of notice of filing by a party. In addition, the time for appeal is decreased to 30 days, consistent with the child's need for timely permanency. This departure is intended to expedite the appellate process, which the Committee deems to be in the best interests of the child. The appeal time and procedures are governed by these rules, specifically established for adoption proceedings, and not by the more general provisions of the appellate rules. *See In Re Welfare of J.R., Jr.*, 655 N.W.2d 1 (Minn. 2003).

Rule 48.03. Application for Stay of Trial Court Order

The service and filing of a notice of appeal does not stay the order of the trial court. The order of the juvenile court shall stand pending the determination of the appeal, but the reviewing court may in its discretion and upon application stay the order.

Former Rule 46.03, adopted Sept. 30, 2004, eff. Jan. 1, 2005. Renumbered Rule 48.03, Dec. 1, 2006, eff. Jan. 1, 2007.

Rule 48.04. Right to Additional Review

Upon an appeal, any party or the county attorney may obtain review of an order entered in the same case which may adversely affect that person by filing a notice of review with the clerk of appellate courts. The notice of review shall specify the order to be reviewed, shall be served and filed within fifteen (15) days after service of the notice of appeal, and shall contain proof of service.

Former Rule 46.04, adopted Sept. 30, 2004, eff. Jan. 1, 2005. Renumbered Rule 48.04, Dec. 1, 2006, eff. Jan. 1, 2007.

Rule 48.05. Transcript of Proceedings

The requirements regarding preparation of a transcript shall be governed by Rule 110.02 of the Minnesota Rules of Civil Appellate Procedure, except that the estimated completion date contained in the certificate of transcript shall not exceed thirty (30) days.

Former Rule 46.05, adopted Sept. 30, 2004, eff. Jan. 1, 2005. Renumbered Rule 48.05, Dec. 1, 2006, eff. Jan. 1, 2007.

Rule 48.06. Time for Rendering Decisions

All decisions regarding adoption matters shall be issued by the appellate court within sixty (60) days of the date the case is deemed submitted pursuant to the Minnesota Rules of Civil Appellate Procedure.

Former Rule 46.06, adopted Sept. 30, 2004, eff. Jan. 1, 2005. Renumbered Rule 48.06, Dec. 1, 2006, eff. Jan. 1, 2007.

RULE 49. VENUE

Rule 49.01. Venue

Subd. 1. Generally. Except as provided in subdivision 2, venue for an adoption proceeding shall be the county of the petitioner's residence.

Subd. 2. Child Under Guardianship of Commissioner. Venue for the adoption of a child committed to the guardianship of the Commissioner of Human Services shall be the county with jurisdiction in the matter according to Minnesota Statutes § 260C.317, subd. 3.

Adopted Dec. 1, 2006, eff. Jan. 1, 2007.

Rule 49.02. Request to Transfer Venue

Upon the petitioner's motion served and filed pursuant to Rule 15, the court having jurisdiction over the matter under Minnesota Statutes § 260C.317, subd. 3, may transfer venue of an adoption proceeding involving a child under the guardianship of the Commissioner of Human Services to the county of the petitioner's residence upon determining that:

(a) the Commissioner of Human Services has given consent to the petitioner's adoption of the child or that consent is unreasonably withheld;

(b) there is no other adoption petition for the child that has been filed or is reasonably anticipated by the Commissioner of Human Services or the Commissioner's delegate to be filed; and

(c) transfer of venue is in the best interests of the child.

Adopted Dec. 1, 2006, eff. Jan. 1, 2007.

Rule 49.03. Transfer of Venue Procedures

If the court grants a motion to transfer venue, the court shall do so by ordering a continuance and by forwarding to the court administrator of the appropriate court a certified copy of all papers filed, together with an order of transfer. The transferring court also shall provide copies of the order of transfer to the Commissioner of Human Services and any agency participating in the proceedings. The judge of the receiving court shall accept the order of the transfer and any other documents transmitted and hear the case.

Adopted Dec. 1, 2006, eff. Jan. 1, 2007.

RULE 50. ADOPTIVE PLACEMENTS—INDIAN CHILD

Rule 50.01. Placement Preferences

Subd. 1. Generally. In any adoptive placement of an Indian child, a preference shall be given, in the absence of good cause to the contrary, to a placement with:

(a) a member of the Indian child's extended family;

(b) other members of the Indian child's tribe; or

(c) other Indian families.

Subd. 2. Preadoptive Placements.

An Indian child accepted for preadoptive placement shall be placed in the least restrictive setting which most approximates a family and in which the child's special needs, if any, may be met. The child shall also be placed within reasonable proximity to his or her home, taking into account any special needs of the child. In any preadoptive placement, a preference shall be given, in the absence of good cause to the contrary, to a placement with:

(a) a member of the Indian child's extended family;

(b) a foster home licensed, approved, or specified by the Indian child's tribe;

(c) an Indian foster home licensed or approved by an authorized non–Indian licensing authority; or

(d) an institution for children approved by an Indian tribe or operated by an Indian organization which has a program suitable to meet the Indian child's needs.

Adopted Dec. 1, 2006, eff. Jan. 1, 2007.

Rule 50.02. Tribal Resolution for Different Order of Preference; Personal Preference Considered; Anonymity in Application of Preferences

In the case of a placement under Rule 50.01, if the Indian child's tribe establishes a different order of preference by resolution, the agency or court effecting the placement shall follow such order so long as the placement is the least restrictive setting appropriate to the particular needs of the child, as provided in Rule 50.01, subd. 2. Where appropriate, the preference of the Indian child or parent shall be considered, provided that where a consenting parent evidences a desire for anonymity, the court or agency shall give weight to such desire in applying the preferences.

Adopted Dec. 1, 2006, eff. Jan. 1, 2007.

Rule 50.03. Social and Cultural Standards Applicable

The standards to be applied in meeting the preference requirements of Rule 50 shall be the prevailing social and cultural standards of the Indian community in which the parent or extended family resides or with which the parent or extended family members maintain social and cultural ties.

Adopted Dec. 1, 2006, eff. Jan. 1, 2007.

Rule 50.04. Record of Placement

A record of each placement, under State law, of an Indian child shall be maintained by the State in which the placement was made, evidencing the efforts to comply with the order of preference specified in this section. Such record shall be made available at any time upon the request of the Secretary of the Interior or the Indian child's tribe.

Adopted Dec. 1, 2006, eff. Jan. 1, 2007.

INDEX TO RULES OF ADOPTION PROCEDURE

RULE ON PUBLIC ACCESS TO RECORDS RELATING TO OPEN JUVENILE PROTECTION PROCEEDINGS [REPEALED]

Historical Notes

The order of the Minnesota Supreme Court [C2-95-1476] dated December 26, 2001, provides in part that effective July 1, 2002, the Rule on Public Access to Records Relating to Open Juvenile Protection Proceedings is repealed and its provisions as amended by this order are incorporated into Rule 44 of the Rules of Juvenile Procedure.

TAX COURT RULES OF PROCEDURE

Effective December 9, 1996

Including Amendments Received Through January 1, 2014

Rules 8600.0200 to 8600.9960. Repealed Dec. 2, 1996, eff. Dec. 9, 1996

Historical Notes

The repealed rules related to various aspects of tax court procedures.

See, now, Rules 8610.0010 to 8610.0150.

Rule 8610.0010. Representation

The following persons may practice before the tax court in a regular division matter:

A. a lawyer licensed to practice law in Minnesota;

B. a lawyer licensed to practice law in a jurisdiction other than Minnesota who complies with part 8610.0020;

C. an individual, when representing the individual or a partnership in which the individual is a general partner; and

D. the sole shareholder of a corporation or sole member of a limited liability company, when representing the corporation or limited liability company. Except as provided in this item, a lawyer must represent a corporation or limited liability company.

Adopted Dec. 2, 1996, eff. Dec. 9, 1996.

Rule 8610.0020. Practice before tax court by nonresident lawyers

Subpart 1. Affidavit required. A lawyer licensed to practice in the trial courts of a jurisdiction other than Minnesota may, in the discretion of the tax court, appear before the tax court if:

A. the nonresident lawyer files an affidavit with the tax court and serves the affidavit on opposing counsel at the time an appeal is filed under Minnesota Statutes, chapter 271, or at the time a petition is filed under Minnesota Statutes, chapter 278;

B. the affidavit establishes that the nonresident lawyer is familiar with and prepared and willing to follow Minnesota's:

(1) Rules of Civil Procedure;

(2) Rules of Evidence;

(3) Rules of Professional Conduct;

(4) Rules on Lawyers Professional Responsibility; and

(5) Tax Court Rules of Procedure; and

C. the nonresident lawyer includes with the affidavit a certificate of good standing from the jurisdiction issuing the nonresident lawyer's license to practice law.

Subp. 2. Motion to oppose; denial of privilege. No later than 30 days before the first scheduled hearing on the matter, opposing counsel may move the tax court for a hearing to oppose the practice of the nonresident lawyer before the tax court. The opposing counsel has the burden of establishing cause to deny the nonresident lawyer the privilege of practicing before the tax court. This hearing may be conducted by telephone. Failure of opposing counsel to respond within the specified time period waives opposing counsel's right to contest the nonresident lawyer's practice before the tax court. The tax court may, for cause, deny the nonresident lawyer the privilege of practicing before the tax court.

Subp. 3. Subject to discipline; jurisdiction of courts. A lawyer appearing pursuant to this part is subject to the disciplinary rules and regulations governing Minnesota lawyers and is subject to the jurisdiction of the Minnesota courts.

Adopted Dec. 2, 1996, eff. Dec. 9, 1996.

Rule 8610.0030. Extension of time to appeal from an order of commissioner of revenue

A request for an extension of time to appeal from an order of the commissioner of revenue should be made to the tax court either by telephone or by mail to the main office of the tax court in St. Paul, Minnesota.

If the request for an extension of time is received within 60 days of the making and filing of the order, the tax court will extend the time to appeal for an additional 30 days. If the request for an extension is made more than 60 days after the making and filing of the order, the tax court may, for cause shown, extend the time for appeal to a date not more than 90 days from the date of the making and filing of the order of the commissioner. A request for an extension made more than 60 days after the making and filing of the order must explain why the extension was not requested within the original 60–day period.

Adopted Dec. 2, 1996, eff. Dec. 9, 1996.

Rule 8610.0040. Form for appeal from order of commissioner

Subpart 1. Caption. A notice of appeal from an order of the commissioner of revenue and all other papers filed with the tax court in its St. Paul office or in district court must contain a caption in the following form:

STATE OF MINNESOTA
TAX COURT

________________ Appellant,	In The Matter of the Appeal from the Commissioner's Order dated ________________ relating to
vs.	________________ (type of) tax of ________________ for the
Commissioner of Revenue, Appellee.	year ending ________________

Subp. 2. Notice of appeal. A notice of appeal must refer to the order appealed from, state specifically the points of law and fact questioned by the appellant, and provide an address where service of notice and other papers in the matter may be made upon the appellant.

Subp. 3. Parties. In all appeals under this part the appellee is the commissioner of revenue, who shall be designated by the official title without naming the individual holding the office. If a change occurs in the individual holding the office while an appeal is pending, the appeal does not abate and no substitution of parties is necessary.

The appellant is the taxpayer or the person or agency authorized by Minnesota Statutes, chapter 271, to appeal from an order of the commissioner.

Subp. 4. Small claims. If the appellant elects to file the appeal in the small claims division, the appeal must contain the following statement:

THE APPELLANT(S) IS (ARE) AWARE OF THE FACT THAT NO APPEAL MAY BE HAD FROM A SMALL CLAIMS DECISION AND AGREE(S) THAT THE DECISION OF THE TAX COURT SHALL BE CONCLUSIVE.

Adopted Dec. 2, 1996, eff. Dec. 9, 1996.

Rule 8610.0050. Form for petition relating to property taxes

Subpart 1. Caption. A petition and all other papers in matters arising under Minnesota property tax laws must contain a caption in the following form:

STATE OF MINNESOTA	COURT (DISTRICT OR TAX)
	JUDICIAL DISTRICT
COUNTY OF ______	______ DIVISION (REGULAR or SMALL CLAIMS)

________________,

Petitioner(s),

vs.

County of ________,

Respondent. Court File No. ____________

Subp. 2. Petition relating to real property tax. A petition under this part must be in substantially the following form:

1. Petitioner(s) has/have an interest pursuant to Minnesota Statutes, section 278.01, in that tract of land situated in the city/township of ...., county of ...., State of Minnesota, described as follows:

[insert here official description of land]

2. The assessment date at issue is January 2, ..., for taxes payable in year ....

3. Petitioner(s) claim(s) that

[insert here claim and relief requested]

[Examples of claims include the estimated market value is greater than the property's actual market value as of the assessment date at issue; the subject property is unequally assessed when compared with other property; the classification of the property is incorrect; the subject property is exempt from taxation; and other claims over which the court has jurisdiction.]

WHEREFORE, petitioner(s) pray(s) for a determination of the claim before the tax court.

Subp. 3. Small claims. If the petitioner elects to file the petition in the small claims division, it must contain the following statement:

THE PETITIONER(S) IS (ARE) AWARE OF THE FACT THAT NO APPEAL MAY BE HAD FROM A SMALL CLAIMS DECISION AND

AGREE(S) THAT THE DECISION OF THE TAX COURT SHALL BE CONCLUSIVE.

Adopted Dec. 2, 1996, eff. Dec. 9, 1996.

Rule 8610.0060. Continuances

The tax court reserves the right to order continuances or postponements on its own motion.

Adopted Dec. 2, 1996, eff. Dec. 9, 1996.

Rule 8610.0070. Motion practice

Subpart 1. Scope and application. Except as otherwise provided in Minnesota Statutes, chapters 271 and 278, this part governs pretrial motion practice before the tax court, other than motions to continue or motions to consolidate.

Subp. 2. Definitions. Motions are either dispositive or nondispositive, as defined in items A and B.

A. "Dispositive motions" are motions that seek to dispose of all or part of the claims or parties, except motions for default judgment. They include motions to dismiss a party or claim, motions for summary judgment, and motions under Minnesota Rules of Civil Procedure 12.02(a)–(f).

B. "Nondispositive motions" are all other motions, including, but not limited to, discovery, third party practice, temporary relief, intervention, and amendment of pleadings.

Subp. 3. Time. The time limits in this part are to provide the tax court adequate opportunity to prepare for and promptly rule on matters, and the tax court may modify the time limits. The time allowed for summary judgment motions, however, may not be less than the time established by Minnesota Rules of Civil Procedure 56.03. If this part requires documents to be filed with the tax court administrator within a prescribed period of time before a specific event, filing may be accomplished by mail, subject to the following:

A. three days must be added to the prescribed period; and

B. filing may not be considered timely unless the documents are deposited in the mail within the prescribed period.

Minnesota Rules of Civil Procedure, 5.02 and 6.05, apply regarding service of documents by mail.

Subp. 4. Obtaining hearing date; notice to parties. A hearing date and time must be obtained from the tax court administrator. A party obtaining a date and time for a hearing on a motion or for any other calendar setting, shall promptly give notice advising all other parties who have appeared in the action so that cross motions may, insofar as possible, be heard on a single hearing date. The notice to the other parties must contain a statement describing the nature of the motion and the relief sought.

Subp. 5. Dispositive motions.

A. No dispositive motion may be heard until the moving party serves a copy of the following documents on opposing counsel or party if that party is pro se and files the original with the tax court administrator at least 28 days prior to the hearing:

(1) notice of motion and motion;

(2) proposed order;

(3) any affidavits and exhibits to be submitted in conjunction with the motion; and

(4) memorandum of law.

B. The party responding to the motion shall serve a copy of the following documents on opposing counsel or party if that party is pro se and shall file the originals with the tax court administrator at least nine days prior to the hearing:

(1) memorandum of law; and

(2) any supplementary affidavits and exhibits to be submitted in conjunction with the response.

C. The moving party may submit a reply memorandum, limited to new legal or factual matters raised by an opposing party's response to a motion, by serving a copy on opposing counsel or party if that party is pro se and filing the original with the tax court administrator at least three days before the hearing.

D. For summary judgment motions, the memorandum of law must include:

(1) A statement by the moving party of the issues involved that are the grounds for the motion for summary judgment.

(2) A statement identifying all documents, such as depositions or excerpts of depositions, pleadings, exhibits, admissions, interrogatory answers, and affidavits, which comprise the record on which the motion is made. Opposing parties shall identify in their responding memorandum of law any additional documents on which they rely.

(3) A recital by the moving party of the material facts that are not in genuine dispute, with a specific citation to that part of the record supporting each fact, such as deposition page and line or page and paragraph of an exhibit. A party opposing the motion shall make a similar recital of any material facts claimed to be in dispute.

(4) The party's argument and authorities. Subitem (3) is excluded from the page limitations of subpart 7.

Subp. 6. Nondispositive motions.

A. No nondispositive motion may be heard until the moving party serves a copy of the following documents on opposing counsel or party if that party is pro se and files the original with the tax court administrator at least 14 days prior to the hearing:

(1) notice of motion and motion;

(2) proposed order;

(3) any affidavits and exhibits to be submitted in conjunction with the motion; and

(4) any memorandum of law.

B. The party responding to the nondispositive motion shall serve a copy of the following documents on opposing counsel or party if that party is pro se and shall file the original with the tax court administrator at least seven days prior to the hearing:

(1) a memorandum of law; and

(2) any relevant affidavits and exhibits to be submitted in conjunction with the response.

C. The moving party may submit a reply memorandum, limited to new legal or factual matters raised by an opposing party's response to a motion, by serving a copy on opposing counsel or party if that party is pro se and filing the original with the tax court administrator at least three days before the hearing.

Subp. 7. Page limits. No memorandum of law submitted in connection with either a dispositive or nondispositive motion may exceed 35 pages, exclusive of the recital of facts required for each motion, except with permission of the tax court. For motions involving discovery requests, the moving party's memorandum must set forth only the particular discovery requests and the response or objection to them which are the subject of the motion, and a concise recitation of why the response or objection is improper. If a reply memorandum of law is filed, the cumulative total of the original memorandum and the reply memorandum must not exceed 35 pages, except with permission of the tax court.

Subp. 8. Failure to comply. If the moving papers are not properly served and filed, the hearing may be canceled by the tax court. If responsive papers are not properly served and filed in a nondispositive motion, the tax court may consider the motion unopposed and may grant the relief requested without a hearing. For a dispositive motion, the tax court, in its discretion, may refuse to permit oral argument by the party not filing the required documents, may allow reasonable attorney's fees, or may take other appropriate action.

Subp. 9. Relaxation of time limits. If irreparable harm will result without immediate action by the court, or if the interests of justice otherwise require, the tax court may waive or modify the time limits established by this part.

Subp. 10. Witnesses. No testimony will be taken at motion hearings except under unusual circumstances. A party seeking to present witnesses at a motion hearing must obtain prior consent of the tax court and must notify the adverse party in the motion papers of the names and addresses of the witnesses that party intends to call at the hearing.

Subp. 11. Telephone hearings. If a motion is authorized by the tax court to be heard by telephone conference call, the moving party shall either initiate the conference call or comply with the court's instructions on initiation of the conference call. Dispositive motions must be recorded. Nondispositive motions may be recorded at the request of either party or on motion of the tax court. "Recorded" for this purpose means by tape recording or by a court reporter, as determined by the tax court.

Adopted Dec. 2, 1996, eff. Dec. 9, 1996.

Rule 8610.0100. Stipulation of facts

The parties may stipulate in writing to any or all questions of fact involved in the appeal or petition. An original and one copy of the stipulation must be filed with the tax court.

Adopted Dec. 2, 1996, eff. Dec. 9, 1996.

Rule 8610.0110. Submission without hearing

If all parties to an appeal or petition by written stipulation waive their right to a public hearing, the parties may submit the matter to the tax court on written stipulation of facts and briefs. After the submission the court may, in its discretion, require appearance for the taking of further testimony or for oral argument. If an appearance is required, notice must be given by mail to all parties at least ten days before the hearing.

Adopted Dec. 2, 1996, eff. Dec. 9, 1996.

Rule 8610.0120. Hearings

Subpart 1. Open to public. Hearings before the tax court are open to the public. All findings and decisions of the tax court, after they have been filed with the court administrator, are a matter of public record.

Subp. 2. Additional hearings. If, after the holding of any hearings in any matter, the tax court finds the rights of the parties will be better served by the holding of a further hearing in the matter, the court may order a further hearing and provide notice to all parties to the proceeding.

Adopted Dec. 2, 1996, eff. Dec. 9, 1996.

Rule 8610.0130. Documentary evidence

If originals of books, documents, records, or other papers have been received in evidence, a copy of them, or of so many of them as may be material or relevant, may in the discretion of the court be substituted. Copies of documents will be admitted as evidence under the Rules of Evidence.

Originals of books, documents, records, diagrams, or other exhibits introduced in evidence before the court may be withdrawn from the custody of the court in the manner and upon the terms the court in its discretion prescribes.

An original and one copy of all exhibits must be furnished to the court, and a copy must be furnished to opposing counsel or the opposing party if the party is pro se.

Adopted Dec. 2, 1996, eff. Dec. 9, 1996.

Rule 8610.0140. Amicus curiae briefs

A person interested in or affected by a matter pending before the tax court may petition the court for leave to file a brief amicus curiae. The tax court in its discretion may grant or deny the petition.

Adopted Dec. 2, 1996, eff. Dec. 9, 1996.

Rule 8610.0150. Request for costs and disbursements

No later than 90 days after the date of a final order of the tax court, a party may file a motion that costs and disbursements be granted to the prevailing party in the case of a commissioner of revenue matter under Minnesota Statutes, chapter 271, or be included in the judgment in the case of a real estate tax appeal under Minnesota Statutes, chapter 278. The moving party must file an affidavit with the tax court outlining the basis for granting costs and itemizing the items and amounts to be granted. The moving party shall serve a copy of the affidavit on the other party to the action and file proof of service with the tax court. Within ten days of being served, the other party must notify the moving party and the tax court of any objection to the request for costs and disbursements and the basis of the objection. The objection to an award must clearly state the basis of the objection and copies of the objection must be served on the moving party and proof of service filed with the tax court. The tax court may order a hearing within 20 days of receiving an objection to determine whether costs and disbursements will be awarded. The hearing may be conducted by telephone. Failure to respond within the ten-day period waives the other party's right to contest awarding costs.

Adopted Dec. 2, 1996, eff. Dec. 9, 1996.

to orders issued or the opposing party or the party's proposed [illegible].

Adopted Dec. 2, 1986, eff. Dec. 8, 1986.

Rule 8610.0140. Amicus curiae briefs

A person interested in or affected by a matter pending before the tax court may petition the court for leave to file a brief amicus curiae. The tax court may [illegible] an amicus curiae brief [illegible].

Adopted Dec. 2, 1986, eff. Dec. 8, 1986.

Rule 8610.0150. Request for costs and disbursements

No later than 30 days after the date of the final order of the tax court, a party may file a motion that costs and disbursements be granted to the prevailing party in the case of a commissioner of revenue matter under Minnesota Statutes, chapter 271, or be included in the judgment in the case of a real estate tax appeal under Minnesota Statutes, chapter 278. The moving party must file an affidavit with the tax court itemizing the basis for granting costs and itemizing the costs and amounts to be granted. The moving party must serve a copy of the affidavit on the other party to the action and file proof of service with the tax court. Within [illegible] days of being served, the other party may notify the moving party and the tax court of any objections to the requested costs and disbursements and the basis of the objection. The objection to an award must state the basis of the objection and copies of the objection must be served on the moving party and proof of service filed with the tax court. The tax court may order a hearing within 20 days of receiving an objection to determine whether costs and disbursements will be awarded. The hearing may be conducted by telephone conference. Failure to respond within the time [illegible] waives the objecting party's right to contest the costs [illegible].

Adopted Dec. 2, 1986, eff. Dec. 8, 1986.

SPECIAL RULES OF PROCEDURE GOVERNING PROCEEDINGS UNDER THE MINNESOTA COMMITMENT ACT OF 1982 [Repealed November 10, 1999 effective January 1, 2000]

SPECIAL RULES OF PROCEDURE GOVERNING PROCEEDINGS UNDER THE MINNESOTA COMMITMENT AND TREATMENT ACT

Effective November 10, 1999

Including Amendments Received Through January 1, 2014

Research Note

See Minnesota Statutes Annotated, *Volume 16B, for case annotations and historical notes.*

RULE 1. GENERAL

(a) Scope. The Special Rules shall apply in proceedings under the 1997 Minnesota Commitment and Treatment Act, Minn. Stat. ch. 253B, including its amendments, and Minn. Stat. ch. 253D, the Minnesota Commitment and Treatment Act: Sexually Dangerous Persons and Sexual Psychopathic Personalities.

(b) Rules Superseded. The Special Rules shall supersede any other body of rules otherwise applicable (e.g., the Rules of Civil Procedure for the District Courts, Probate Court Rules, etc.) in conflict with these Special Rules.

(c) Citation. These Special Rules may be cited as Commitment and Treatment Act Rules.

Adopted Nov. 10, 1999, eff. Jan. 1, 2000. Amended eff. Sept. 18, 2013.

Advisory Comment—1999

The Act, as codified under Minn. Stat. ch. 253B, is detailed and the practitioner must be familiar with both the Act and these rules.

Historical Notes

The order of the Minnesota Supreme Court [C4-94-1646] dated November 10, 1999, adopting the Special Rules of Procedure Governing Proceedings Under the Minnesota Commitment and Treatment Act, provides in part that "(t)he inclusion of Advisory Committee comments is made for convenience and does not reflect court approval of the comments made therein."

The order of the Minnesota Supreme Court [ADM10–8046] dated September 18, 2013, provided in part that "the amendments shall apply to all proceedings pending or commenced on or after the effective date."

RULE 2. COMPUTATION OF TIME

Except as provided by these Special Rules, the Minnesota Rules of Civil Procedure govern the computation of any time periods prescribed by Minn. Stat. ch. 253B or Minn. Stat. ch. 253D. If a respondent is represented by an attorney, whenever an act is required within a certain time after a written demand or service of a document upon a party or entity other than the court, time shall begin to run once both the party and the parties' attorneys have received notice of the document, regardless of the method of service, and shall not include weekends and holidays. The 72–hour absence that triggers the missing respondent procedures under Minn. Stat. § 253B.141, subd. 1, commences when the respondent was due to return to the facility and includes weekends and holidays.

Adopted Nov. 10, 1999, eff. Jan. 1, 2000. Amended eff. Sept. 18, 2013.

Advisory Committee Comment—1999

These rules contemplate that service may be effected personally, by mail, or by fax. There are instances in the statute when a notice or a report does not need to be "given" to an attorney. The rule ensures that the attorneys know the basis of any hearing scheduled by the court upon receipt of a filed document. When a party requests a hearing after notice that the treatment center or designated agency intends to take some action (as in the case of revocation of provisional discharge), this rule expands the period of time if the notice was mailed to the attorneys. If the notice was faxed, the time to request the hearing is not expanded.

Historical Notes

The order of the Minnesota Supreme Court [C4-94-1646] dated November 10, 1999, adopting the Special Rules of Procedure Governing Proceedings Under the Minnesota Commitment and Treatment Act, provides in part that "(t)he inclusion of Advisory Committee comments is made for convenience and does not reflect court approval of the comments made therein."

The order of the Minnesota Supreme Court [ADM10–8046] dated September 18, 2013, provided in part that "the amendments shall apply to all proceedings pending or commenced on or after the effective date."

RULE 3. SERVICE

Whenever a person is required to give or serve any document under this chapter to any party, attorney, or entity other than the court, service may be made in any manner allowed under the Minnesota Rules of Civil Procedure. Attorneys for both parties must also be served whether or not service upon counsel is specifically required by statute.

Adopted Nov. 10, 1999, eff. Jan. 1, 2000.

Advisory Committee Comment—1999

See comment to Rule 2.

RULE 4. CONSECUTIVE HOLD ORDERS PROHIBITED

A person held under a 72–hour emergency hold must be released by the facility within 72 hours unless a court order to hold the person is obtained. A consecutive hold order not issued by the district court is expressly prohibited, whether or not issued by the same physician or other authority.

Adopted Nov. 10, 1999, eff. Jan. 1, 2000.

RULE 5. CASE CAPTIONS

Civil commitment proceedings shall be captioned in the name of the person subject to the petition as follows: *In the Matter of the Civil Commitment of: (Full Name of Respondent), Respondent.*

Adopted Nov. 10, 1999, eff. Jan. 1, 2000.

Advisory Committee Comment—1999

A person subject to commitment proceedings is referred to as the respondent throughout these rules. The court and counsel shall be sensitive to the correct pronunciation of a respondent's name.

Historical Notes

The order of the Minnesota Supreme Court [C4-94-1646] dated November 10, 1999, adopting the Special Rules of Procedure Governing Proceedings Under the Minnesota Commitment and Treatment Act, provides in part that "(t)he inclusion of Advisory Committee comments is made for convenience and does not reflect court approval of the comments made therein."

RULE 6. COMMENCEMENT

A proceeding for commitment or early intervention is commenced upon filing a petition with the District Court pursuant to Minn. Stat. ch. 253B or Minn. Stat. ch. 253D.

The petition should be filed in the county of financial responsibility as defined in Minn. Stat. § 253B.045, subd. 2. If the county of financial responsibility refuses to file a petition, the county where the respondent is present must file the petition if statutory conditions for commitment are present. Financial responsibility for the costs of the proceedings and treatment will be resolved by subsequent administrative process.

Adopted Nov. 10, 1999, eff. Jan. 1, 2000. Amended eff. Sept. 18, 2013.

Advisory Committee Comment—1999

The committee has attempted to address concerns where conflicts occur between the county of financial responsibility (respondent's residence) and the county where respondent is present, regarding who shall file the petitions, and to provide guidance in light of short statutory time constraints. The committee did not intend to remove discretion from the county attorney in the county where the respondent is present. If statutory conditions are present for commitment and the county attorney in the county where the respondent is present determines that a commitment is necessary and reasonable for the protection of the respondent or others, then the petition must be filed. Ultimate financial responsibility will be resolved in accordance with Minn. Stat. § 256G.01–.12.

See also Minn. Stat. § 253B.07, subd. 2a, when dealing with a person subject to Minn. R. Crim. P. 20.01 or 20.02. It is not the intent of the committee to affect venue when the person is subject to a proceeding governed by Minn. R. Crim. P. 20.01 or 20.02 or Minn. R. Juv. Del. P. 20.01 or 20.02.

A petition for commitment as a sexual psychopathic personality or a sexually dangerous person may also be filed in a county where a related criminal conviction was entered. *See* Minn. Stat. § 253B.185, subd. 1.

Historical Notes

The order of the Minnesota Supreme Court [C4-94-1646] dated November 10, 1999, adopting the Special Rules of Procedure Governing Proceedings Under the Minnesota Commitment and Treatment Act, provides in part that "(t)he inclusion of Advisory Committee comments is made for convenience and does not reflect court approval of the comments made therein."

The order of the Minnesota Supreme Court [ADM10–8046] dated September 18, 2013, provided in part that "the amendments shall apply to all proceedings pending or commenced on or after the effective date."

RULE 7. PETITIONS

A petition filed pursuant to Minn. R. Crim. P. 20.01 or Minn. R. Juv. Del. P. 20.01 is sufficient if it contains a judicial determination that the defendant is incompetent to stand trial or be sentenced for the offense. A petition filed pursuant to Minn. R. Crim. P. 20.02 or Minn. R. Juv. Del. P. 20.02 is sufficient if it contains a judicial determination that the defendant was found not guilty, by reason of mental illness or mental deficiency, of the crime with which the defendant was charged.

Adopted Nov. 10, 1999, eff. Jan. 1, 2000.

Advisory Committee Comment—1999

This rule clarifies that petitions pursuant to Minn. R. Crim. P. 20 or Minn. R. Juv. Del. P. 20 need not include all of the specific requirements of the law relating to petitions for judicial commitment, which arise from referrals to the pre-petition screening team. For example, an examiner's statement in support of commitment is not required, since the basis of the petition is a judicial determination.

Historical Notes

The order of the Minnesota Supreme Court [C4-94-1646] dated November 10, 1999, adopting the Special Rules of Procedure Governing Proceedings Under the Minnesota Commitment and Treatment Act, provides in part that "(t)he inclusion of Advisory Committee comments is made for convenience and does not reflect court approval of the comments made therein."

RULE 8. SUMMONS

Once a petition has been filed, the court shall issue a summons to be personally served upon the respondent. The summons shall direct the respondent to appear at the times and places stated in the summons for psychiatric, psychological, and medical examination and court hearing. The summons shall state in bold print that an order to apprehend and hold the respondent may be issued if the respondent does not appear as directed. The court need not issue a summons if the respondent is already under a medical or judicial hold.

The court shall direct that a copy of the pre-petition screening report, the petition, and the examiner's supporting statement be personally served upon the respondent with the summons if issued, and that a copy be distributed to the petitioner, the proposed patient, the patient's counsel, the county attorney, and any person authorized by the patient, and any other person as the court directs.

Adopted Nov. 10, 1999, eff. Jan. 1, 2000.

RULE 9. APPOINTMENT AND ROLE OF COUNSEL

Immediately upon the filing of a petition for commitment or early intervention the court shall appoint a qualified attorney to represent the respondent at public expense at any subsequent proceeding under Minn. Stat. ch. 253B or Minn. Stat. ch. 253D. The attorneys shall represent the respondent until the court dismisses the petition or the commitment and discharges the attorney.

The respondent may employ private counsel at the respondent's expense. If private counsel is employed, the court shall discharge the appointed counsel.

In order to withdraw, counsel must file a motion and obtain the court's approval.

Counsel for the respondent is not required to file an appeal or commence any proceeding under Minn. Stat. ch. 253B or Minn. Stat. ch. 253D if, in the opinion of counsel, there is an insufficient basis for proceeding.

Adopted Nov. 10, 1999, eff. Jan. 1, 2000. Amended eff. Sept. 18, 2013.

Historical and Statutory Notes

The order of the Minnesota Supreme Court [ADM10–8046] dated September 18, 2013, provided in part that "the amendments shall apply to all proceedings pending or commenced on or after the effective date."

RULE 10. ATTORNEY–CLIENT PRIVILEGE

The content of attorney-client communications by telephone, mail, or conference at the facility, shall not be monitored, censored, or made part of a respondent's medical record. The facility may open and inspect, but not read, a letter or package, and must do so in the respondent's presence.

Adopted Nov. 10, 1999, eff. Jan. 1, 2000.

RULE 11. EXAMINER'S LIST

The court administrator shall prepare and maintain a list of examiners. A statement of the manner and rate of compensation of examiners shall be attached to the list. Examiners shall be paid at a rate of compensation fixed by the court. If a party seeks appointment of an examiner not on the list, or at a rate of compensation exceeding that fixed by the court, the party shall seek approval of the court prior to appointment.

Adopted Nov. 10, 1999, eff. Jan. 1, 2000.

RULE 12. EXAMINER REPORTS

Each court-appointed examiner shall examine the respondent and prepare a separate report stating the examiner's opinion and the facts upon which the opinion is based. The report shall address:

(a) Whether the respondent is mentally ill, mentally retarded, chemically dependent, mentally ill and dangerous to the public, a sexually dangerous person, or a sexual psychopathic personality;

(b) Whether the examiner recommends commitment;

(c) The appropriate form, location, and conditions of treatment, including likelihood of the need for treatment with neuroleptic medication;

(d) The respondent's capacity to make decisions about neuroleptic medication, if needed; and

(e) If the petition alleges that the respondent is mentally ill and dangerous to the public, whether there is a substantial likelihood that respondent will engage in acts capable of inflicting serious physical harm on another.

(f) If the petition alleges that the respondent is a sexual psychopathic personality and/or a sexually dangerous person, the report shall address each element set out in Minn. Stat. § 253D.02, subds. 11 and 12 respectively, including an opinion as to the likelihood that the respondent will engage in future dangerous behavior.

The court shall send a copy of the examiner's report to the petitioner's attorney, the respondent and respondent's attorney immediately upon receiving the report.

Adopted Nov. 10, 1999, eff. Jan. 1, 2000. Amended eff. Sept. 18, 2013.

Historical and Statutory Notes

The order of the Minnesota Supreme Court [ADM10–8046] dated September 18, 2013, provided in part that "the amendments shall apply to all proceedings pending or commenced on or after the effective date."

RULE 13. MEDICAL RECORDS

The county attorney, respondent, respondent's attorney, court-appointed examiner, guardian ad litem, substitute decision-maker, and their agents and experts retained by them shall have access to all of the respondent's medical records and the reports of the court-appointed examiners. The records and reports may not be disclosed to any other person without court authorization or the respondent's signed consent. Except for a preliminary hearing, each party shall disclose to the other party or parties at least 24 hours in advance of the hearing which of the respondent's medical records the party intends to introduce at the hearing.

Adopted Nov. 10, 1999, eff. Jan. 1, 2000. Amended eff. Sept. 18, 2013.

Historical and Statutory Notes

The order of the Minnesota Supreme Court [ADM10–8046] dated September 18, 2013, provided in part that "the amendments shall apply to all proceedings pending or commenced on or after the effective date."

RULE 14. LOCATION OF HEARING, RULES OF DECORUM, ALTERNATIVE METHODS OF PRESENTING EVIDENCE

The judge or judicial officer shall assure the decorum and orderliness of any hearing held pursuant to Minn. Stat. ch. 253B or Minn. Stat. ch. 253D. The judge or judicial officer shall afford to respondent an opportunity to be dressed in conformity with the dignity of court appearances.

A hearing may be conducted or an attorney for a party, a party, or a witness may appear by telephone, audiovisual, or other electronic means if the party intending to use electronic means notifies the other party or parties at least 24 hours in advance of the hearing and the court approves. If a witness will be testifying electronically, the notice must include the name, address, and telephone number where the witness may be reached in advance of the hearing. This rule does not supersede Minn. Stat. §§ 595.02–595.08 (competency and privilege). Respondent's counsel will be physically present with the patient. The court shall insure that the respondent has adequate opportunity to speak privately with counsel, including, where appropriate, suspension of the audio recording or allowing counsel to leave the conference table to communicate with the client in private.

Adopted Nov. 10, 1999, eff. Jan. 1, 2000. Amended Dec. 22, 2008, eff. March 1, 2009; Nov. 19, 2009, eff. Jan. 1, 2010; eff. Sept. 18, 2013.

General Rules of Practice Advisory Committee Comment—2008 Amendment

Rule 14 is amended to lengthen the amount of notice required to be given by a litigant desiring to have a matter heard by electronic means, typically either telephone or interactive television. The seven days required by the rule can be adjusted by the court if necessary.

Advisory Committee Comment—2009 Amendment

Rule 14 is amended to change the amount of notice required to be given by a litigant desiring to have a matter heard by electronic means, typically either telephone or interactive television. The 24 hours required by the rule represents the bare minimum of what may be necessary to allow for necessary electronic equipment to be made available. This deadline can be adjusted by the court if necessary.

Historical Notes

The order of the Supreme Court dated November 19, 2009, provided:

"1. The attached amendments to the General Rules of Practice for the District Courts and the Special Rules of Procedure Governing Proceedings under the Minnesota Commitment and Treatment Act be, and the same are, prescribed and promulgated to be effective on January 1, 2010.

"2. The attached amendments shall apply to all actions pending on the effective date and to those filed thereafter.

"3. The inclusion of Advisory Committee comments is made for convenience and does not reflect court approval of the comments made therein."

The order of the Minnesota Supreme Court [ADM10–8046] dated September 18, 2013, provided in part that "the amendments shall apply to all proceedings pending or commenced on or after the effective date."

RULE 15. EVIDENCE

The court may admit all relevant, reliable evidence, including but not limited to the respondent's medical records, without requiring foundation witnesses.

Adopted Nov. 10, 1999, eff. Jan. 1, 2000. Amended eff. Sept. 18, 2013.

Historical and Statutory Notes

The order of the Minnesota Supreme Court [ADM10–8046] dated September 18, 2013, provided in part that "the amendments shall apply to all proceedings pending or commenced on or after the effective date."

RULE 16. RIGHTS OF PATIENTS

In every order for commitment, the committing court shall order that the Rights of Patients, provided at Minn. Stat. § 253B.03, Minn. Stat. § 253D.17, and Minn. Stat. § 253D.18, be incorporated in the order by reference.

Adopted Nov. 10, 1999, eff. Jan. 1, 2000. Amended eff. Sept. 18, 2013.

Historical and Statutory Notes

The order of the Minnesota Supreme Court [ADM10–8046] dated September 18, 2013, provided in part that "the amendments shall apply to all proceedings pending or commenced on or after the effective date."

RULE 17. PETITION TO DETERMINE NEED FOR CONTINUED CARE

Upon the filing of a petition to determine the need for continued care pursuant to Minn. Stat. § 253B.17, the court shall cause the hearing to be held within 14 days of filing. The hearing may be continued for up to 30 days upon a showing of good cause. The court shall give the respondent, respondent's attorney, county attorney, guardian ad litem, and substitute decision maker, as well as such other interested persons as the court may direct, at least 10 days' notice of the date and time of the hearing.

Adopted Nov. 10, 1999, eff. Jan. 1, 2000. Amended eff. Sept. 18, 2013.

Historical and Statutory Notes

The order of the Minnesota Supreme Court [ADM10–8046] dated September 18, 2013, provided in part that "the amendments shall apply to all proceedings pending or commenced on or after the effective date."

RULE 18. RECOMMITMENT

For recommitments pursuant to Minn. Stat. § 253B.13, the court shall append the immediately preceding commitment file to the file on the new petition.

Adopted Nov. 10, 1999, eff. Jan. 1, 2000.

RULE 19. TERMINATION OF EARLY INTERVENTION

Any petition for involuntary commitment filed at the termination of court-ordered early intervention under Minn. Stat. § 253B.065 shall be treated as an initial commitment petition and not a recommitment.

Adopted Nov. 10, 1999, eff. Jan. 1, 2000.

RULE 20. TERMINATION OF COMMITMENT

The court shall order termination of the commitment when the commitment expires, or upon a direct discharge by the treatment facility, or upon a discharge by the Commissioner of Human Services.

The order shall also discharge the court-appointed attorney.

Adopted Nov. 10, 1999, eff. Jan. 1, 2000.

Advisory Committee Comment—1999

Minn. Stat. § 253B.12, subd. 1(e), provides for an order terminating the commitment if a 60–90 day report is not timely filed or if the report describes the respondent as not in need of further institutional care and treatment. There is no similar provision for terminating the commitment if the report required by Minn. Stat. § 253B.16 is not filed or if there is a final discharge under Minn. Stat. § 253B.16 or if a provisional discharge expires under Minn. Stat. § 253B.15, subd. 9. This rule insures a formal termination of the proceeding and discharge of the respondent's court-appointed attorney.

Historical Notes

The order of the Minnesota Supreme Court [C4-94-1646] dated November 10, 1999, adopting the Special Rules of Procedure Governing Proceedings Under the Minnesota Commitment and Treatment Act, provides in part that "(t)he inclusion of Advisory Committee comments is made for convenience and does not reflect court approval of the comments made therein."

RULE 21. PUBLIC ACCESS TO RECORDS

(a) Except as provided in these Special Rules, and as limited by court order, all court files relating to civil commitment shall be available to the public for inspection, copying, or release.

(b) The court administrator shall create a separate section or file in which the prepetition screening report, court appointed examiner's report, and all medical records shall be filed. Records in that section or file shall not be disclosed to the public except by express order of the district court. This provision shall not limit the parties' ability to mention the contents of the pre-petition screening report, court appointed examiner's report and medical records in the course of proceedings under Minn. Stat. ch. 253B or Minn. Stat. ch. 253D.

Adopted Nov. 10, 1999, eff. Jan. 1, 2000. Amended eff. Sept. 18, 2013.

Historical and Statutory Notes

The order of the Minnesota Supreme Court [ADM10–8046] dated September 18, 2013, provided in part that "the amendments shall apply to all proceedings pending or commenced on or after the effective date."

RULE 22. STAYED ORDERS (MENTALLY ILL AND DANGEROUS TO THE PUBLIC, SEXUALLY DANGEROUS PERSONS, AND SEXUAL PSYCHOPATHIC PERSONALITIES)

Stayed orders for commitment as mentally ill and dangerous to the public, sexually dangerous person, or a sexual psychopathic personality may be issued only by agreement of the parties and approval by the court.

Adopted Nov. 10, 1999, eff. Jan. 1, 2000.

RULE 23. EVALUATION AND FINAL HEARINGS IN CASES GOVERNED BY MINN. STAT. §§ 253B.18, 253B.185, AND MINN. STAT. CH. 253D

(a) For persons who have been committed as mentally ill and dangerous to the public, sexually dangerous persons, or as sexual psychopathic personalities, the head of treatment facility shall file the report required by Minn. Stat. § 253B.18. The evaluation may be conducted at a secure treatment facility or at a correctional facility. If transport is needed, the court shall designate the agency responsible to do it.

(b) Prior to making the final determination with regard to a person initially committed as mentally ill and dangerous to the public, as a sexually dangerous person, or as a sexual psychopathic personality, the court shall hold a hearing. The head of the treatment facility shall file the report required by Minn. Stat. § 253B.18, subd. 2. The hearing for final determination shall be held within 14 days of the court's receipt of the report from the head of the treatment facility or within 90 days of the date of initial commitment, whichever is earlier, unless continued by agreement of the parties, or by the court for good cause shown. As its final determination, the court may, subject to Minn. R. Crim. P. 20.01, subd. 4:

(1) Discharge the respondent's commitment;

(2) Commit the respondent as mentally ill only, in which case the respondent's commitment shall be deemed to have commenced upon the date of initial commitment, for purposes of determining the maximum length of the determinate commitment; or

(3) Commit the respondent for an indeterminate period as mentally ill and dangerous to the public, as a sexually dangerous person, or as a sexual psychopathic personality.

(c) At the request of the respondent, the court shall appoint an examiner of the respondent's choice for purposes of the hearing required by this rule.

(d) The written report of the head of the treatment facility pursuant to Minn. Stat. § 253B.18, subd. 2, shall address the criteria for commitment and whether there has been any change in the respondent's condition since the commitment hearing. The report shall provide the following information:

(1) the respondent's diagnosis;

(2) the respondent's present condition and behavior;

(3) the facts, if any, that establish that the respondent continues to satisfy the statutory requirements for commitment;

(4) a description of treatment efforts and response to treatment by the respondent during hospitalization;

(5) the respondent's prognosis;

(6) the respondent's individual treatment plan;

(7) an opinion as to whether the respondent is in need of further care and treatment;

(8) an opinion as to the program or facility best able to provide further care and treatment, if needed;

(9) an opinion as to whether respondent is dangerous to the public or himself. All supportive data and documentation shall be attached to the report.

(e) At the hearing, the court shall consider all competent evidence relevant to the respondent's present need for continued commitment. The burden of proof at the hearing is upon the proponent of indeterminate commitment to establish by clear and convincing evidence that the statutory requirements for commitment under Minn. Stat. ch. 253B or Minn. Stat. ch. 253D continue to be met.

Adopted Nov. 10, 1999, eff. Jan. 1, 2000. Amended eff. Sept. 18, 2013.

Advisory Committee Comment—1999

This rule is intended to require final resolution, with due diligence, of the commitment process of a respondent who is mentally ill and dangerous to the public, a sexually dangerous person, or a sexual psychopathic personality. An initial hearing should not be "reviewed" years later. The rule is not intended to dictate where a committed person should be confined. If a commitment is sustained upon review and the individual is still subject to commitment to the Commissioner of Corrections the balance of the sentence is to be served in a correctional institution.

Historical Notes

The order of the Minnesota Supreme Court [C4-94-1646] dated November 10, 1999, adopting the Special Rules of Procedure Governing Proceedings Under the Minnesota Commitment and Treatment Act, provides in part that "(t)he inclusion of Advisory Committee comments is made for convenience and does not reflect court approval of the comments made therein."

The order of the Minnesota Supreme Court [ADM10–8046] dated September 18, 2013, provided in part that "the amendments shall apply to all proceedings pending or commenced on or after the effective date."

RULE 24. EXPEDITING TRANSCRIPTS FOR CHAPTER 253B OR CHAPTER 253D APPEALS

In addition to satisfying the requirements of the Rules of Civil Appellate Procedure, any party initiating an appeal of an order entered under Minn. Stat. ch. 253B or Minn. Stat. ch. 253D shall, at or before the date of filing the notice of appeal, (a) serve on each court reporter who recorded the proceedings a copy of the notice of appeal and a request for transcripts the appellant deems necessary for the appeal and (b) file with the notice of appeal a copy of the request(s) for transcripts, along with an affidavit of service of the request(s) on opposing counsel, the court administrator of the court that issued the order appealed, and the court reporter or reporters, unless at the time of filing the notice of appeal all transcripts necessary for the appeal have already been transcribed. The transcript request(s) shall require completion of the transcripts no more than 25 days after the filing of the notice of appeal, unless the 25th day falls on a Saturday, Sunday or a holiday, in which case the transcripts shall be completed on the next business day. The Court of Appeals may modify the deadline for completion of the transcripts if necessary. Failure of an appellant who intends to order a transcript to serve on the court reporter(s) a request for transcripts the appellant deems necessary for the appeal at the date of filing the notice of appeal does not deprive the Court of Appeals of jurisdiction over the appeal, but extends the time for the Court of Appeals to hear the appeal by the period of delay between the filing of the appeal and service of the transcript request(s).

Adopted Dec. 12, 2008, eff. July 1, 2009. Amended eff. Sept. 18, 2013.

Historical and Statutory Notes

The order of the Minnesota Supreme Court [ADM10–8046] dated September 18, 2013, provided in part that "the amendments shall apply to all proceedings pending or commenced on or after the effective date."

RULE 25. SUBPOENA FOR PRODUCTION OF RECORDS

Where a party in a proceeding under Minn. Stat. ch. 253B or Minn. Stat. ch. 253D uses a subpoena to obtain production of records, the advance-service and advance-notice requirements under Minn. R. Civ. P. 45.02(a) and 45.04(a)(5) shall be 24 hours, rather than seven days.

Adopted May 3, 2010, eff. July 1, 2010. Amended eff. Sept. 18, 2013.

Historical and Statutory Notes

The order of the Minnesota Supreme Court [ADM10–8046] dated September 18, 2013, provided in part that "the amendments shall apply to all proceedings pending or commenced on or after the effective date."

RULES OF PUBLIC ACCESS TO RECORDS OF THE JUDICIAL BRANCH

Effective July 1, 1988

Including Amendments Received Through January 1, 2014

RULE 1. SCOPE OF RULES

These rules govern access to the records of all courts and court administrators of the judicial branch of the state of Minnesota. They do not govern access to records of the Tax Court or the Workers' Compensation Court of Appeals, which are part of the executive branch of the state. In addition, these rules do not govern access to records of the various Boards or Commissions of the Supreme Court as they are governed by independent rules promulgated or approved by the Supreme Court. A partial list of Boards and Commissions is set forth in Appendix A.

Finally, except as provided in Rule 4, subdivision 1(b) with respect to case records, these rules do not govern access to records of judicial branch court services departments or probation authorities. Access to these records is governed by MINN. STAT. § 13.84 and any successor, and other applicable court rules and statutes.

Nothing in these rules shall affect the disposition of records as authorized by MINN. STAT. § 138.17 or any successor or prevent the return of documents or physical objects to any person or party in accordance with a court rule or order.

Adopted Feb. 1, 1988, eff. July 1, 1988. Amended May 6, 2005, eff. July 1, 2005.

RULE 2. GENERAL POLICY

Records of all courts and court administrators in the state of Minnesota are presumed to be open to any member of the public for inspection or copying at all times during the regular office hours of the custodian of the records. Some records, however, are not accessible to the public, at least in the absence of a court order, and these exceptions to the general policy are set out in Rules 4, 5, 6, and 8.

Adopted Feb. 1, 1988, eff. July 1, 1988. Amended May 6, 2005, eff. July 1, 2005.

RULE 3. DEFINITIONS

Subdivision 1. Custodian. The custodian is the person responsible for the safekeeping of any records held by any court, court administrator, or clerk of court. In the absence of the person usually responsible, the person who is temporarily responsible for the records is the custodian. For purposes of remote and bulk electronic access under Rule 8, the state court administrator shall be the custodian for case records that are maintained in computer systems administered by the state court administrator.

Subd. 2. Judge. "Judge" means any justice, judge, judicial officer, referee, magistrate, court-appointed arbitrator or other person exercising adjudicatory powers.

Subd. 3. Court. "Court" means the Supreme Court, the Court of Appeals, District Court, and any other court established as part of the judicial branch of the state.

Subd. 4. Court Administrator. "Court administrator" means a person employed or appointed for the purpose of administering the operations of any court or court system, including the clerk of the appellate courts, state court administrator, judicial district administrator, and court administrator of district court.

Subd. 5. Records. "Records" means any recorded information that is collected, created, received, maintained, or disseminated by a court or court administrator, regardless of physical form or method of storage. A "record" does not necessarily constitute an entire file, as a file may contain several "records." Court reporters' notes shall be available to the court for the preparation of a transcript.

(a) *Case Records.* "Case records" means all records of a particular case or controversy.

(b) *Administrative Records.* "Administrative records" means all records pertaining to the administration of the courts or court systems.

(c) *Vital Statistics Records.* "Vital statistics records" means all certificates or reports of birth, death, fetal death, induced abortion, marriage, dissolution and annulment, and related records.

Adopted Feb. 1, 1988, eff. July 1, 1988. Amended May 6, 2005, eff. July 1, 2005.

RULE 4. ACCESSIBILITY TO CASE RECORDS

Subd. 1. Accessibility. All case records are accessible to the public except the following:

(a) *Domestic Abuse Records.* Records maintained by a court administrator in accordance with the domestic abuse act, MINN. STAT. § 518B.01, until a court order as authorized by subdivision 5 or 7 of section 518B.01 is executed or served upon the record subject who is the respondent to the action;

(b) *Court Services Records.* Records on individuals maintained by a court, other than records that have been admitted into evidence, that are gathered at the request of a court to:

(1) determine an individual's need for counseling, rehabilitation, treatment or assistance with personal conflicts,

(2) assist in assigning an appropriate sentence or other disposition in a case,

(3) provide the court with a recommendation regarding the custody of minor children, or

(4) provide the court with a psychological evaluation of an individual.

Provided, however, that the following information on adult individuals is accessible to the public: name, age, sex, occupation, and the fact that an individual is a parolee, probationer, or participant in a diversion program, and if so, at what location; the offense for which the individual was placed under supervision; the dates supervision began and ended and the duration of supervision; information which was public in a court or other agency which originated the data; arrest and detention orders; orders for parole, probation or participation in a diversion program and the extent to which those conditions have been or are being met; identities of agencies, units within agencies and individuals providing supervision; and the legal basis for any change in supervision and the date, time and locations associated with the change.

(c) *Judicial Work Product and Drafts.* All notes and memoranda or drafts thereof prepared by a judge or by a court employed attorney, law clerk, legal assistant or secretary and used in the process of preparing a final decision or order, except the official minutes prepared in accordance with MINN. STAT. §§ 546.24–.25.

(d) *Juvenile Appeal Cases.* Case records arising from an appeal from juvenile court proceedings that are not open to the public, except the appellate court's written opinion or unless otherwise provided by rule or order of the appellate court.

(e) *Race Records.* The contents of completed race census forms obtained from participants in criminal, traffic, juvenile and other matters, and the contents of race data fields in any judicial branch computerized information system, except that:

(1) the records may be disclosed in bulk format if the recipient of the records:

(A) executes a nondisclosure agreement in a form approved by the state court administrator in which the recipient of the records agrees not to disclose to any third party any information in the records from which either the identity of any participant or other characteristic that could uniquely identify any participant is ascertainable; and

(B) obtains an order from the supreme court authorizing the disclosure;

(2) A juror's race may be disclosed to the parties or their attorneys as part of the juror profile information unless otherwise provided by law or court rule.

Nothing in this section (e) shall prevent public access to source documents such as complaints or petitions that are otherwise accessible to the public.

(f) *Genetic Information.* Records on genetic information, other than records that have been admitted into evidence in a hearing or trial, that are from medical or scientific professionals, including but not limited to reports and affidavits. For purposes of this rule, "genetic information" means information about a specific human being that is derived from the presence, absence, alteration, or mutation of a gene or genes, or the presence or absence of a specific deoxyribonucleic acid or ribonucleic acid marker or markers, and which has been obtained from an analysis of an individual's biological information or specimen or the biological information or specimen of a person to whom an individual is genetically related.

(g) *Other.* Case records that are made inaccessible to the public under:

(1) state statutes, other than Minnesota Statutes, chapter 13;

(2) court rules or orders; or

(3) other applicable law.

The state court administrator shall maintain, publish and periodically update a partial list of case records that are not accessible to the public.

Subd. 2. Restricting Access; Procedure. Procedures for restricting access to case records shall be as provided in the applicable court rules.

Subd. 3. Access to Recordings. This subdivision governs access to recordings of proceedings in the district court:

(a) **General.** Recordings of proceedings in the district court, including without limitation those used as a back-up to a stenographically recorded proceeding or as the electronic recording, are intended to assist in the preparation of a transcript. The transcript, and not the recording, is the official record of the proceedings. Recordings of proceedings in the district court may only be used as authorized in this or other applicable rules or orders promulgated by the Supreme Court.

(b) **Off the Record Remarks.** Any spoken words in the courtroom that are not a part of a proceeding, hearing or trial of a specific case are not intended to be recorded. Recordings of such words may not be listened to or used in any way other than by authorized operators of the recording equipment to orient themselves on recording content.

(c) **Playback.** Playback of any part of the recording of a proceeding, hearing, or trial of a specific case is authorized in only the following situations:

(1) during the proceeding, hearing or trial at the direction of the court;

(2) by authorized operators of the recording equipment or an official court reporter or other authorized reporting service employee for the purpose of creating a transcript as the official record; and

(3) at the direction of the court for the use of the court.

(d) **Disseminate by Transcript Only.** Except as provided in part (c) of this rule, the contents of the recording shall be disseminated by transcript only, which transcript, and not the recording, shall be the official record.

(e) **No Transcripts in Conciliation Court.** Nothing in this rule shall permit the transcription of conciliation court proceedings, hearings or trials. Playback of any part of the recordings of conciliation court proceeding, hearing or trial is authorized only at the direction of the court for the use of the court.

Adopted Feb. 1, 1988, eff. July 1, 1988. Amended May 6, 2005, eff. July 1, 2005; June 17, 2005, eff. July 1, 2005; April 27, 2007, eff. July 1, 2007; Dec. 28, 2007, eff. March 1, 2008.

Advisory Committee Comment–2005

The 2005 deletion of the word "temporary" in Rule 4, subd. 1(a), reflects statutory changes that allow the initial, ex parte order to be the permanent order of the court if no hearing is requested. See 1995 MINN. LAWS ch. 142, §§ 4, 5 (amending MINN. STAT. § 518B.01, subds. 5, 7).

The 2005 reorganization of Rule 4, subd. 1, parts (d) and (f) is not substantive in nature. Trial level juvenile court proceedings that are not accessible to the public include adoption (MINN. STAT. § 259.61 (2004); MINN. R. ADOPT. PROC. 8.01 (effective 1–1–2005), delinquency and extended jurisdiction juveniles (except where there are felony level charges and the juvenile was at least 16 years old at the time of the offense) (MINN. STAT. § 260B.163, subd. 1(c)(2004); MINN. R. JUV. DEL. PROC. 2.01), and other proceedings closed to the public by order of the court on a case-by-case basis (*see, e.g.*, MINN. R. JUV. PROT. PROC. 27.01 (permitting closure of child protection proceeding only in exceptional circumstances, and requiring public access to closure order)). If a trial level juvenile court proceeding is not accessible to the public, then Rule 4, subd. 1(d) precludes public access to the appellate records related to that proceeding except the written opinion of the appellate court or unless otherwise ordered by the court.

The 2005 addition of race records in Rule 4, subd. 1(e) is based on the understanding that race and ethnicity information is not solicited from participants for the purpose of reselling race status of individuals to commercial enterprises. The goal is to ensure fair resolution of cases, and the rule attempts to provide a limited right of public access consistent with that goal. Access to race records, e.g., for research purposes, can be obtained under a nondisclosure agreement that limits ultimate public disclosure to aggregate statistics that do not identify individual participants. The Supreme Court has a longstanding tradition of authorizing disclosure of juvenile court records for scholarly research using nondisclosure agreements. *See, e.g., Order Authorizing Disclosure of Juvenile Court Database for Research Purposes*, No. C4–85–1848 (Minn. S. Ct. filed May 14, 2001).

The substitution of a periodically updated list of inaccessible case records for the former Appendix B in Rule 4, subd. 1(f) recognizes that the state court administrator maintains an updated list of statutes (and court rules and other legal authority) that identify case records that are not accessible to the public. The list is updated as necessary, whereas the former Appendix B quickly became obsolete soon after it was first published. It is contemplated that the list will be posted on the main state court website (www.courts.state.mn.us) for access by the general public.

The 2005 changes to Rule 4, subd. 2, recognize that a number of rules address restrictive orders. The factors to consider in seeking a protective order in regard to criminal case records are discussed in Rule 25, Rules of Criminal Procedure, *Minneapolis Star & Tribune v. Kammeyer*, 341 N.W.2d 550 (Minn. 1983), and *Northwest Publications, Inc. v.*

Anderson, 259 N.W.2d 254 (Minn. 1977). For civil cases, see Rule 26.03, Rules of Civil Procedure and *Minneapolis Star & Tribune Co. v. Schumacher*, 392 N.W.2d 197 (Minn. 1986). For child in need of protective services cases, see Rule 8.07, Rules of Juvenile Protection Procedure. For juvenile delinquency cases, see Rule 10.06, subd. 5, Rules of Juvenile Delinquency Procedure.

Advisory Committee Comment–2007

The 2007 addition of Rule 4, subd. 1(f), is designed to provide some privacy protection for genetic information about individuals. The definition of "genetic information" is based in part on the privacy law governing executive branch genetic information. Act of June 1, 2006, ch. 253 § 4, 2006 MINN. LAWS 424, 426 (codified at MINN. STAT. § 13.386 (2006)). Genetic information can affect not only a party, witness or victim, but also his or her genetic relatives. Courts and parties need to consider the scope of this information when admitting and offering to admit such information into evidence. Rule 4, subd. 2, recognizes that, when necessary, protective orders can be issued under applicable procedural rules. The factors to consider in seeking a protective order in regard to criminal case records are discussed in Rule 25, Rules of Criminal Procedure, *Minneapolis Star & Tribune v. Kammeyer*, 341 N.W.2d 550 (Minn. 1983), and *Northwest Publications, Inc. v. Anderson*, 259 N.W.2d 254 (Minn. 1977). For civil cases, see Rule 26.03, Rules of Civil Procedure, and *Minneapolis Star & Tribune v. Schumacher*, 392 N.W.2d 197 (Minn. 1986).

Advisory Committee Comment–2008

The 2008 addition of Rule 4, subd. 1(e)(2), is designed to recognize that race data is routinely disclosed to parties as part of juror profile information for purposes of voir dire.

The 2008 addition of Rule 4, subd. 3, is based in part on IL. 18TH CIR. R. 1.03. Rule 4, subd. 3, attempts to clarify the application of the Rules to recordings of testimony in light of Supreme Court policy limiting audio and video coverage of trial court proceedings, and to clarify the proper scope and role of recordings in preparing and preserving the official record.

The broad definition of "records" in Rule 3, subd. 1, appears to include recordings of court proceedings, but arguably may not include court reporter's notes. Assuming that recordings are included, it is not clear whether recordings would then be subject to the work product exception to public access (Rule 4, subd. 1(c)) or the presumption of public access (Rule 2). Assuming the presumption applies, public access creates significant administrative burdens, unresolved issues regarding what constitutes the official record, and conflicts with the Supreme Court's policy limiting audio and video coverage of trial court proceedings. MINN. GEN. R. PRAC. 4; MN. CODE JUD. CONDUCT CANON 3A(11); MINN. S. CT. ORDER, IN RE MODIFICATION OF SECTION 3A(10) OF THE MINNESOTA CODE OF JUDICIAL CONDUCT, # C7–81–300 (filed Jan. 11, 1996) (reinstating experimental program for audio and video coverage of trial court proceedings). Although the conflict might be partially reduced by permitting public access but no public dissemination of copies of the recordings, this conflicts with the policy in Rule 2 permitting both inspection and copying. Rule 4, subd. 3, provides a straightforward resolution of all conflicts and it includes controlled playback access in appropriate circumstances.

Rule 4, subd. 3(a), recognizes that the transcript is the official record and that recordings are intended to support the creation of that record. Use of recordings is limited as provided in the rule or in other rules or orders promulgated by the Supreme Court.

Rule 4, subd. 3 (b), recognizes that courtroom microphones may inadvertently pick up conversation that is intended to be protected by the attorney client privilege or is simply intended to be private conversation. The rule does not permit public access to portions of recordings that contain this material.

The controlled playback access in Rule 4, subd. 3(c), reflects what typically occurs in practice. To the extent that any abuses occur, actions of the court in controlling playback are subject to appellate review. *See, e.g., Blanchard v. Golden*, No. C8–95–2390 (Minn. App. filed Feb. 29, 1996) (unpublished interim order) (denying appellant's motion for correction of transcript where trial court provided opportunity to listen to backup tape).

Rule 4, subd. 3(e), reflects the requirement of MINN. GEN. R. PRAC. 504(c) which provides that conciliation court proceedings and trials shall not be reported. Judges presiding in conciliation court often use recordings to supplement their notes. Access to the recordings of conciliation court proceedings, hearings or trials is treated in the same manner as judge's notes under Rule 4, subd. 1(c), and their playback is subject to the control of the court.

Rule 4, subd. 3, does not address the procedures for requesting and obtaining transcripts, or for correcting or modifying the same. These matters are addressed in other appropriate rules and statutes. *See, e.g.*, MINN. R. CIV. APP. P. 110; MINN. R. CRIM. P. 28.02, subds. 8, 9; MINN. STAT. §§ 486.02–.03 (2006).

RULE 5. ACCESSIBILITY TO ADMINISTRATIVE RECORDS

All administrative records are accessible to the public except the following:

Subdivision 1. Personnel Records. Records on individuals collected because the individual is or was an employee of, performs services on a voluntary basis for, or acts as an independent contractor with the judicial branch, provided, however, that the following information is accessible to the public: name; actual gross salary; salary range; contract fees; actual gross pension; the value and nature of employer-paid fringe benefits; the basis for and the amount of any added remuneration, including expense reimbursement, in addition to salary; job title and bargaining unit; job description; education and training background; previous work experience; date of first and last employment; the status of any complaints or charges against the employee, whether or not the complaint or charge resulted in a disciplinary action; the final disposition of any disciplinary action and supporting documentation, excluding information that would identify confidential sources who are employees of the judicial branch; the terms of any agreement settling any dispute arising out of an employment relationship; work location; a work telephone number; honors and awards received; payroll time sheets or other comparable data, that are only used to account for employee's work time for payroll purposes, to the extent that they do not reveal the employee's reasons for the use of sick or other medical leave or other information that is not public; and county of residence.

(a) For purposes of this subdivision, a final disposition occurs when the person or group that is authorized to take the disciplinary action makes its final decision about the disciplinary action, regardless of the possibility of any later court proceedings or other proceedings. In the case of arbitration proceedings arising under collective bargaining agreements, a final disposition occurs at the conclusion of the arbitration proceedings, or upon the failure of the employee to elect arbitration within the time provided by the collective bargaining agreement. Final disposition includes a resignation by an individual when the resignation occurs after the final decision of the person, group, or arbitrator that is authorized to take disciplinary action.

(b) Notwithstanding contrary provisions in these rules, a photograph of a current or former employee may be displayed to a prospective witness as part of an investigation of any complaint or charge against the employee.

(c) Notwithstanding contrary provisions in these rules, if an appointed officer resigns or is terminated from employment while the complaint or charge is pending, all information relating to the complaint or charge is public, unless access to the information would jeopardize an active investigation or reveal confidential sources. For purposes of this paragraph, "appointed officer" means the clerk of the appellate courts, the state court administrator, a judicial district administrator, and a court administrator of district court.

(d) Records under subdivision 1 may be disseminated to a law enforcement agency for the purpose of reporting a crime or alleged crime committed by an employee, volunteer or independent contractor, or for the purpose of assisting law enforcement in the investigation of a crime committed or allegedly committed by an employee, volunteer, or independent contractor.

(e) Records under subdivision 1 must be disclosed to the Department of Employment and Economic Development for the purpose of administration of an unemployment benefits program under state law including without limitation the investigation, prosecution, settlement or defense of a claim related thereto.

(f) Records under subdivision 1 must be disclosed to the Department of Employee Relations and the Department of Labor and Industry for the purpose of administering workers compensation programs including without limitation the investigation, prosecution, settlement or defense of a claim related thereto.

(g) Records under subdivision 1 may be disseminated to labor organizations to the extent that the custodian determines that the dissemination is necessary to conduct elections, notify employees of fair share fee assessments, and implement the provisions of MINN. STAT. §§ 179 and 179A. Records under subdivision 1 shall be disseminated to labor organizations and to the Bureau of Mediation Services to the extent the dissemination is ordered or authorized by the Commissioner of the Bureau of Mediation Services.

(h) If the custodian determines that the release of records under subdivision 1 is necessary to protect an employee, volunteer or independent contractor from harm to self or to protect another person who may be harmed by the employee, volunteer, or independent contractor, records that are relevant to the concerns for safety may be released to: the person who may be harmed and to that person's attorney when the records are relevant to obtaining a restraining order; to a prepetition screening team conducting an investigation under section 253B.07, subdivision 1; or to a court, law enforcement agency, or prosecuting authority. If the person who may be harmed or that person's attorney receives records under this subdivision, the records may be used or released further only to the extent necessary to protect that person from harm.

Subd. 2. Personnel Related Records

(a) *Collective Bargaining Planning Records.* Management positions on economic and noneconomic labor relations items that have not been presented during the collective bargaining process or interest arbitration, including information specifically collected or created to prepare the management position.

(b) *Applicant Records.* Records on individuals collected because the individual is or was an applicant for employment with the judicial branch, provided, however, that the following information is accessible to the public: veteran status; relevant test scores; rank on eligible lists; job history; education and training; work availability; and, after the applicant has been certified by the appointing authority to be a finalist for a position in public employment, the name of the applicant.

Subd. 3. Correspondence. Correspondence between individuals and judges; but such correspondence may be made accessible to the public by the sender or the recipient.

Subd. 4. Schedules and Assignments. The identity of appellate judges or justices assigned to or participating in the preparation of a written decision or opinion, until the decision or opinion is released.

Subd. 5. Security Records. Records that would be likely to substantially jeopardize the security of information, possessions, individuals, or property in the possession or custody of the courts against theft, tampering, improper use, illegal disclosure, trespass, or physical injury, such as security plans or codes.

Subd. 6. State Owned or Licensed Trade Secrets. Records revealing a common law trade secret or a trade secret as defined in MINN.STAT.. § 325C.01 that is owned or licensed by the state and is maintained by a court or court administrator; provided, that the following are accessible to the public: the existence of any contract, the parties to the contract, and the material terms of the contract, including price, projected term, and scope of work.

Subd. 7. Copyrighted Material. Computer programs and related records, including but not limited to technical and user manuals, for which the judicial branch has acquired or is in the process of acquiring, a patent or copyright, or a license to use the same; provided, that the following are accessible to the public: the existence of any contract, the parties to the contract, and the material terms of the contract, including price, projected term, and scope of work.

Subd. 8. Competitive Bidding Records.

(a) *Sealed Bids.* Sealed bids and responses to judicial branch bid or procurement requests or solicitations, including the number of bids or responses received, before the opening of the bids or responses at the time specified in the judicial branch request or solicitation.

(b) *Submission of Trade Secret.* Except as provided in subparagraph (c) of this subdivision, a common law trade secret or a trade secret as defined in MINN. STAT. § 325C.01 that is required to be submitted a judicial branch bid or procurement request provided that:

(1) the submitting party marks the document(s) containing the trade secret "CONFIDENTIAL;"

(2) the submitting party submits as part of the bid or response a written request to maintain confidentiality; and

(3) the trade secret information is not publicly available, already in the possession of the judicial branch, or known to or ascertainable by the judicial branch from third parties.

(c) Contract. The existence of any resulting contract, the parties to the contract, and the material terms of the contract, including price, projected term, and scope of work, shall be accessible to the public.

Subd. 9. Compliance Records. Records and reports and drafts thereof maintained by the judicial branch information systems for purposes of compliance with MINN. STAT. § 546.27.

Subd. 10. Library Records. Records maintained by the State Law Library which: (a) link a patron's name with materials requested or borrowed by the patron or which links a patron's name with a specific subject about which the patron has requested information or materials; or (b) are submitted by a person applying for a borrower's card, other than the name of the person to whom a borrower's card has been issued.

Subd. 11. Passport Records. Passport applications and accompanying documents received by court administrators, and lists of applications that have been transmitted to the United States Passport Services Office.

Subd. 12. Attorney Work Product. The work product of any attorney or law clerk employed by or representing the judicial branch that is produced in the regular course of business or representation of the judicial branch.

Subd. 13. Judicial Branch Internal Audit Records. Information, notes, and preliminary drafts of reports relating to an audit or investigation, created, collected, and maintained by the internal auditor or audit committee of the judicial branch, or persons performing audits for the judicial branch; provided that upon the release of a final audit report by the judicial branch auditor or if the audit or investigation is no longer being pursued actively, such audit records shall be accessible to the public except as otherwise provided by applicable law or rule.

(a) *Auditor access; personnel records.* This subdivision does not limit in any way disclosures required under MINN. STAT. §§ 609.456 or 3.978, or public access to records classified as accessible to the public by Rule 5, subd. 1.

(b) *Confidential sources.* Records on an individual who supplies information for an audit or investigation, that could reasonably be used to determine the individual's identity, are not accessible to the public if the information supplied was needed for an audit or investigation and would not have been provided to the internal auditor or person performing audits without an assurance to the individual that the individual's identity would remain not accessible to the public.

(c) *Access to records by audit committee members.* Members of an audit committee have access to records that are collected or used by the judicial branch auditor and that have been classified as not accessible to the public only as authorized by resolution of the committee.

(d) *Unreleased records.* Records related to an audit but not released in a final audit report and that the judicial branch auditor reasonably believes will be used in litigation are not accessible to the public until the litigation has been completed or is no longer being actively pursued.

(e) *Review of Records.* If, before releasing a final audit report, the judicial branch auditor provides a person with records relating to the audit for the purpose of review and verification of the records, that person shall not disclose the records to anyone else unless and until the information becomes accessible to the public under these rules.

(f) *Duties Concerning Misuse of Public Money or Other Resources.* If the judicial branch auditor's examination discloses misuse of public money or other public resources, the judicial branch auditor may disclose records relating to the examination to the attorney general to assist in the recovery of money and other resources and to the appropriate prosecuting authority to assist in the prosecution of criminal proceedings as the evidence may warrant.

Subd. 14. Other. Matters that are made inaccessible to the public under:

(a) state statute, other than MINN. STAT. ch. 13, or

(b) federal law; or

(c) rule or order of the Supreme Court.

The state court administrator shall maintain, publish and periodically update a partial list of administrative records that are not accessible to the public.

Adopted Feb. 1, 1988, eff. July 1, 1988. Amended May 6, 2005, eff. July 1, 2005; April 27, 2007, eff. July 1, 2007; Dec. 28, 2007, eff. March 1, 2008.

Advisory Committee Comment–2005

The 2005 changes to Rule 5, subds. 6, 7 and 8, reflect the existing practice. Trade secrets and copyrights are subject to state and federal law, and the specifics are generally clarified in procurement documents, from requests for bids to contracts, in the manner set forth in the rule. Once a vendor enters into a contract, the basic parameters of the contract relationship become accessible under Rule 5, subd. 1. These revisions provide notice to potential vendors of what to expect and are intended to ensure consistent results.

The 2005 changes to Rule 5, subd. 10, regarding State Law Library records provides consistent protection to information held by the library.

The 2005 addition of Rule 5, subd. 13, is based on policy applicable to executive branch audit records. *See* MINN. STAT. §§ 3.979, 13.392 (2004). An internal audit function is being implemented by the judicial branch as part of the transition to state funding of district court administrative costs. The scope of the audit function is currently limited to financial audits but program audits could be added later. Subdivision 13 encompasses both types of audits.

Subdivision 13 is not intended to provide a safe harbor to deny public access to records that would otherwise be accessible to the public. If an audit involves personnel records, for example, to the extent that those personnel records are accessible to the public in the hands of a supervisor or human resources office, they will continue to be accessible only from that source and would not be accessible from the auditor until a final audit report is released. Conversely, to the extent that any personnel records are not accessible to the public from the supervisor or human resources office, the records would remain off limits to the public even after the auditor releases a final report. Subdivision 13, clause (a) includes an express reference to personnel records under Rule 5, subd. 1, as audits often involve personnel records.

Implementation of the audit function includes establishment of an audit committee to provide oversight and advice to the auditor. Although the structure of that committee has not yet been finalized, subdivision 13(c) assumes that such a committee would exist and would have some access to the auditor's records via formal resolutions adopted by the committee. The requirement of a resolution prevents individual audit committee members from independently obtaining access to the auditor's records and places consistent limitations on re-disclosure to the extent that audit committee members obtain such records.

A confidential source clause is included under subd. 13(b) to protect individuals who want to cooperate with an audit or investigation. Subdivision 13(d) addresses unreleased records when litigation is a concern. Subdivision 13(e) allows the auditor to control the distribution of draft reports or record summaries to a specified "person." This process allows for verification of facts before the release of the final audit report.

The 2005 substitution of a periodically updated list for the former Appendix C in Rule 5, subd. 14 recognizes that the state court administrator maintains an updated list of statutes (and court rules and other legal authority) that identify administrative records that are not accessible to the public. The list is updated as necessary, whereas the former Appendix C became obsolete soon after it was first published. It is contemplated that the list will be posted on the main state court website (www.courts.state.mn. us) for access by the general public.

Advisory Committee Comment–2007

The 2005 changes to Rule 5, subd. 1, are based on policy applicable to employee records held by the executive branch. MINN. STAT. § 13.43 (2004). There are, however, some subtle differences from executive branch policy, including the fact that judicial employee discipline is governed by a separate set of procedures and access provisions. *See* RULES OF THE BOARD ON JUDICIAL STANDARDS. In addition, judicial branch e-mail addresses are not accessible to the public unless individual employees authorize disclosure. Limiting access helps minimize the potential for ex parte contact prohibited by law. *See* MINN. CODE JUD. CONDUCT, CANON § 3A(7).

The 2007 addition of Rule 5, subd. 2(a), is based on policy applicable to collective bargaining records held by the executive branch. MINN. STAT. § 13.37, subd. 1(e) (2006).

Advisory Committee Comment–2008

The 2008 addition of subd. 13(f) is based on policy applicable to records of the legislative auditor. *See* MINN. STAT. § 3.975 (2006) (legislative auditor). To the extent that misuse is uncovered as part of a personnel investigation, Rule 5, subd. 1(d), authorizes disclosure of the pertinent personnel records to law enforcement. Subd. 13(f) extends the same authority to the judicial branch auditor, who may be in a better position to report and assist law enforcement, particularly when misuse occurs in a court office that does not have the staff or technical ability to thoroughly investigate and report on the matter.

RULE 6. VITAL STATISTICS RECORDS

Vital statistics records held by any court or court administrator shall be accessible to the public except as provided by statute. The state court administrator shall maintain, publish and periodically update a partial list of vital statistics records that are not accessible to the public.

Adopted Feb. 1, 1988, eff. July 1, 1988. Amended May 6, 2005, eff. July 1, 2005.

Advisory Committee Comment–2005

The 2005 substitution of a periodically updated list for the former Appendix D in Rule 6 recognizes that the state court administrator maintains an updated list of statutes (and court rules and other legal authority) that identify vital statistics records that are not accessible to the public. The list is updated as necessary, whereas the former Appendix D became obsolete soon after it was first published. It is contemplated that the list will be posted on the main state court website (www.courts.state.mn.us) for access by the general public.

RULE 7. PROCEDURE FOR REQUESTING RECORD ACCESS OR CASE RECORD CORRECTION

Subdivision 1. To Whom Request is Made. A request to inspect or obtain copies of records that are accessible to the public shall be made to the custodian and may be made orally or in writing. The custodian may insist on a written request only if the complexity of the request or the volume of records requested would jeopardize the efficiency and accuracy of the response to an oral request. All requests must include sufficient information to reasonably identify the data being sought, but the requesting person shall not be required to have detailed knowledge of the agency's filing system or procedures, nor shall the requesting person be required to disclose the purpose of the request.

Subd. 2. Response. The custodian shall respond to the request as promptly as practical.

Subd. 3. Delay or Denial; Explanation. If a request cannot be granted promptly, or at all, an explanation shall be given to the requesting person as soon as possible. The requesting person has the right to at least the following information: the nature of any problem preventing access, and the specific statute, federal law, or court or administrative rule that is the basis of the denial. The explanation shall be in writing if desired by the requesting person. Appeals are governed by Rule 9 of these rules.

Subd. 4. Referral in Certain Cases. If the custodian is uncertain of the status of a record, the custodian may ask for a status determination from the state court administrator. The state court administrator shall promptly make a determination and forward it either orally or in writing to the custodian.

Subd. 5. Correction of Case Records. An individual who believes that a case record contains clerical errors may submit a written request for correction to the court administrator of the court that maintains the record, with a copy served on all parties to the case. Such request shall be no longer than two pages in length. The court administrator shall promptly do one of the following: (a) correct a clerical error for which no court order is required; (b) forward the request to the court to be considered informally; or (c) forward the request to the party or participant who submitted the record containing the alleged clerical error who in turn may seek appropriate relief from the court. Upon forwarding under clause (b), the court may either correct the error on its own initiative or direct that the request will only be considered pursuant to a motion requesting correction. The court's directive may also establish appropriate notice requirements for a motion. The request for correction authorized in this subdivision need not be exhausted before other relief is requested.

Adopted Feb. 1, 1988, eff. July 1, 1988. Amended May 6, 2005, eff. July 1, 2005.

Advisory Committee Comment–2005

The 2005 addition in Rule 7, subd. 3, of a cross reference to appeals under Rule 9 is added as a convenience to counterbalance the growing complexity of these rules. The 2005 deletion of the phrase "by phone or by mail" in Rule 7, subd. 4, recognizes that a determination is often issued in electronic format, such as e-mail or facsimile transmission.

The 2005 addition of subdivision 5 regarding correction of case records is based in part on MINN. GEN. R. PRAC. 115.11 (motions to reconsider). In the context of Internet publication of court records, a streamlined process is particularly appropriate for clerical-type errors, and should allow for prompt resolution of oversights and omissions. For example, to the extent that the register of actions, court calendar, or index in a court's case management system incorrectly incorporates provisions of a court order, judgment, or pleading, such data entry inaccuracies are typically corrected without a court order by court administration staff promptly upon learning of the inaccuracy.

A party is not required to utilize the procedure set forth in subdivision 5 before making a formal motion for correction of a case record in the first instance. Alleged inaccuracies in orders and judgments themselves must be brought to the attention of the court in accordance with procedures established for that purpose. Clerical errors in judgments and orders typically can be addressed by motion. *See, e.g.*, MINN. GEN. R. PRAC. 375 (expedited child support process: clerical mistakes, typographical errors, and errors in mathematical calculations in orders ... arising from oversight or omission may be corrected by the child support magistrate at any time upon the magistrate's own initiative or upon motion of any party after notice to all parties); MINN. R. CIV. P. 60.01 (civil cases: clerical mistakes in judgments, orders, or other parts of the record and errors therein arising from oversight or omission may be corrected by the court at any time on its own initiative or on the motion of any party after such notice, if any, the court orders); MINN. R. CRIM. P. 27.03, subds. 8, 9 (criminal cases: clerical mistakes in judgments, orders, or other parts of the record or errors in the record arising from oversight or omission may be corrected by the court at any time and after such notice, if any, as the court orders; the court may at any time correct a sentence not authorized by law); MINN. R. JUV. PROT. P. 46.01 (juvenile protection cases: clerical mistakes in judgments, orders, or other parts of the record and errors arising from oversight or omission may be corrected by the court at any time upon its own initiative or upon motion of any party and after such notice, if any, as the court orders; during the pendency of an appeal, such mistakes can be corrected with leave of the appellate court); MINN. R. CIV. APP. P. 110.05 (differences as to whether the transcript or other parts of the record on appeal truly disclose what occurred in the trial court are to be submitted to and determined by the trial court; material omissions or misstatements may be resolved by the trial court, stipulation of the parties, or by the appellate court on motion by a party or on its own initiative).

Alleged inaccuracies in the records submitted by the parties and other participants in the litigation must also be brought to the attention of the court through existing procedures for introducing and challenging evidence. These procedures typically have deadlines associated with the progress of the case and failure to act in a timely fashion may preclude relief.

RULE 8. INSPECTION, COPYING, BULK DISTRIBUTION AND REMOTE ACCESS

Subdivision 1. Access to Original Records. Upon request to a custodian, a person shall be allowed to inspect or to obtain copies of original versions of records that are accessible to the public in the place where such records are normally kept, during regular working hours. However, copies, edited copies, reasonable facsimiles or other appropriate formats may be produced for inspection if access to the original records would: result in disclosure of information to which access is not permitted; provide remote or bulk access that is not permitted under this rule; jeopardize the security of the records; or prove otherwise impractical. Unless expressly allowed by the custodian, records shall not be removed from the area where they are normally kept.

Subd. 2. Remote Access to Electronic Records.

(a) **Remotely Accessible Electronic Records.** Except as otherwise provided in Rule 4 and parts (b) and (c) of this subdivision 2, a custodian that maintains the following electronic case records must provide remote electronic access to those records to the extent that the custodian has the resources and technical capacity to do so.

(1) register of actions (a register or list of the title, origination, activities, proceedings and filings in each case [MINN. STAT. § 485.07(1)]);

(2) calendars (lists or searchable compilations of the cases to be heard or tried at a particular court house or court division [MINN. STAT. § 485.11]);

(3) indexes (alphabetical lists or searchable compilations for plaintiffs and for defendants for all cases including the names of the parties, date commenced, case file number, and such other data as the court directs [MINN. STAT. § 485.08]);

(4) judgment docket (alphabetical list or searchable compilation including name of each judgment debtor, amount of the judgment, and precise time of its entry [MINN. STAT. § 485.07(3)]);

(5) judgments, orders, appellate opinions, and notices prepared by the court.

All other electronic case records that are accessible to the public under Rule 4, and that have been in existence for not more than ninety (90) years, shall not be made remotely accessible but shall be made accessible in either electronic or in paper form at the court facility.

(b) **Certain Data Not To Be Disclosed.** Notwithstanding Rule 8, subd. 2 (a), the public shall not have remote access to the following data fields in the register of actions, calendars, index, and judgment docket, with regard to parties or their family members, jurors, witnesses (other than expert witnesses), or victims of a criminal or delinquent act:

(1) social security numbers and employer identification numbers;

(2) street addresses except that street addresses of parties may be made available by access agreement in a form prepared by the state court administrator and approved by the Judicial Council;

(3) telephone numbers;

(4) financial account numbers; and

(5) in the case of a juror, witness, or victim of a criminal or delinquent act, information that either specifically identifies the individual or from which the identity of the individual could be ascertained.

Without limiting any other applicable laws or court rules, and in order to address privacy concerns created by remote access, it is recommended that court personnel preparing judgments, orders, appellate opinions and notices limit the disclosure of items (2), (3) and (5) above to what is necessary and relevant for the purposes of the document. Under GEN. R. PRAC. 11, inclusion of items (1) and (4) in judgments, orders, appellate opinions and notices is to be made using the confidential information form 11.1. Disclosure of juror information is also subject to GEN. R. PRAC. 814, R. CRIM. P. 26.02, subd. 2, and Minn. R. CIV. P. 47.01.

(c) **Preconviction Criminal Records.** The Information Technology Division of the Supreme Court shall make reasonable efforts and expend reasonable and proportionate resources to prevent preconviction criminal records and preconviction or preadjudication juvenile records from being electronically searched by defendant name by the majority of known, mainstream automated tools, including but not limited to the court's own tools. A "preconviction criminal record" is a record, other than an appellate court record, for which there is no conviction as defined in MINN. STAT. § 609.02, subd. 5 (2006), on any of the charges. A "preconviction or preadjudication juvenile record" is a record, other than an appellate court record, for which there is no adjudication of delinquency, adjudication of traffic offender, or extended jurisdiction juvenile conviction as provided in the applicable RULES OF JUVENILE DELINQUENCY PROCEDURE and related MINNESOTA STATUTES, on any of the charges. For purposes of this rule, an "appellate court record" means the appellate court's opinions, orders, judgments, notices and case management system records, but not the trial court record related to an appeal.

(d) **"Remotely Accessible" Defined.** "Remotely accessible" means that information in a court record can be electronically searched, inspected, or copied without the need to physically visit a court facility. The state court administrator may designate publicly-accessible facilities other than court facilities as official locations for public access to court records where records can be electronically searched, inspected or copied without the need to physically visit a court. This shall not be remote access for purposes of these rules.

(e) **Exceptions**

(1) *Particular Case.* After notice to the parties and an opportunity to be heard, the presiding judge may by order direct the court administrator to provide remote electronic access to records of a particular case that would not otherwise be remotely accessible under parts (a), (b), or (c) of this rule.

(2) *Appellate Briefs.* The State Law Library may, to the extent that it has the resources and technical capacity to do so, provide remote access to appellate court briefs provided that the following are redacted: appendices to briefs, data listed in Rule 8, subd. 2(b) of these rules, and other records that are not accessible to the public.

(3) *E-mail and Facsimile Transmission.* Any record custodian may, in the custodian's discretion and subject to applicable fees, provide public access by e-mail or facsimile transmission to publicly accessible records that would not otherwise be remotely accessible under parts (a), (b) or (c) of this rule.

(4) *E-filed Records.* Documents electronically filed or served using the E–Filing System designated by the state court administrator shall be remotely accessible to the person filing or serving them and the recipient of them, on the E–Filing System for the period designated by the court, and on the court's case management system to the extent technically feasible.

(f) **Delayed Application.** To reduce the burden and costs of modifying existing case management systems scheduled to be replaced by MNCIS, the remote access provisions of Rule 8, subd. 2, shall only apply to the individual district courts to the extent that they have transferred case management to MNCIS, provided that: (1) such courts shall not modify the remote access to case records that they are providing as of the issuance of this order other than to comply with any other rules or laws limiting access to records or in preparation of compliance with Rule 8, subd. 2; and (2) such courts shall comply with Rule 8, subd. 3, as if Rule 8, subd. 2, were in effect.

Subd. 3. Bulk Distribution of Court Records. A custodian shall, to the extent that the custodian has the resources and technical capacity to do so, provide bulk distribution of its electronic case records as follows:

(a) Preconviction criminal records and preconviction or preadjudication juvenile records shall be provided only to an individual or entity which enters into an agreement in the form approved by the state court administrator providing that the individual or entity will not disclose or disseminate the data in a manner that identifies specific individuals who are the subject of such data. If the state court administrator determines that a bulk data recipient has utilized data in a manner inconsistent with such agreement, the state court administrator shall not allow further release of bulk data to that individual or entity except upon order of a court.

(b) All other electronic case records that are remotely accessible to the public under Rule 8, subd. 2, shall be provided to any individual or entity.

Subd. 4. Criminal Justice and Other Government Agencies.

(a) *Authorized by Law.* Criminal justice agencies, including public defense agencies, and other state or local government agencies may obtain remote and bulk case record access where access to the records in any format by such agency is authorized by law.

(b) *Discretionary Authorization for Statewide Access to Certain Case Records.* Except with respect to race data under Rule 4, subd. 1(e), Minnesota County attorneys, Minnesota state public defenders, Minnesota state and local corrections agencies, and Minnesota state and local social services agencies may obtain remote and bulk access to statewide case records in MNCIS that are not accessible to the public and are classified as Civil Domestic Violence, Juvenile, and Parent/Child Relationship case records, if the recipient of the records:

(1) executes a nondisclosure agreement in form and content approved by the state court administrator; and

(2) the custodian of the records reasonably determines that the recipient has a legitimate business need for the records and disclosure to the recipient will not compromise the confidentiality of any of the records.

Subd. 5. Access to Certain Evidence. Except where access is restricted by court order or the evidence is no longer retained by the court under a court rule, order or retention schedule, documents and physical objects admitted into evidence in a proceeding that is open to the public shall be available for public inspection under such conditions as the court administrator may deem appropriate to protect the security of the evidence.

Subd. 6. Fees. When copies are requested, the custodian may charge the copy fee established by statute but, unless permitted by statute, the custodian shall not require a person to pay a fee to inspect a record. When a request involves any person's receipt of copies of publicly accessible information that has commercial value and is an entire formula, pattern, compilation, program, device, method, technique, process, data base, or system developed with a significant expenditure of public funds by the judicial branch, the custodian may charge a reasonable fee for the information in addition to costs of making, certifying, and compiling the copies. The custodian may grant a person's request to permit the person to make copies, and may specify the condition under which this copying will be permitted.

Adopted Feb. 1, 1988, eff. July 1, 1988. Amended May 6, 2005, eff. July 1, 2005; April 27, 2007, eff. July 1, 2007; Dec. 28, 2007, eff. March 1, 2008; May 24, 2012, eff. Sept. 1, 2012.

Advisory Committee Comment–2005

The 2005 addition of a new Rule 8, subd. 2, on remote access establishes a distinction between public access at a court facility and remote access over the Internet. Subdivision 2 attempts to take a measured step into Internet access that provides the best chance of successful implementation given current technology and competing interests at stake. The rule limits Internet access to records that are created by the courts as this is the only practical method of ensuring that necessary redaction will occur. Redaction is necessary to prevent Internet access to clear identity theft risks such as social security numbers and financial account numbers. The rule recognizes a privacy concern with respect to remote access to telephone and street addresses, or the identities of witnesses or jurors or crime victims. The identity of victims of a criminal or delinquent act are already accorded confidentiality in certain contexts [Minn. Stat. § 609.3471 (2004) (victims of criminal sexual conduct)], and the difficulty of distinguishing such contexts from all others even in a data warehouse environment may establish practical barriers to Internet access.

Internet access to preconviction criminal records may have significant social and racial implications, and the requirements of Rule 8, subd. 2(c) are intended to minimize the potential impact on persons of color who may be disproportionately represented in criminal cases, including dismissals. The rule contemplates the use of log-ins and other technology that require human interaction to prevent automated information harvesting by software programs. One such technology is referred to as a "Turing test" named after British mathematician Alan Turing. The "test" consists of a small distorted picture of a word and if the viewer can correctly type in the word, access or log in to the system is granted. Presently, software programs do not read clearly enough to identify such pictures. The rule contemplates that the courts will commit resources to staying ahead of technology developments and implementing necessary new barriers to data harvesting off the courts' web site, where feasible.

Some district courts currently allow public access to records of other courts within their district through any public access terminal located at a court facility in that district. The definition of "remote access" has been drafted to accommodate this practice. The scope of the definition allows statewide access to the records in Rule 8, subd. 2, from any single courthouse terminal in the state, which is the current design of the new district court computer system referred to as MNCIS.

The exception in Rule 8, subd. 2(e), for allowing remote access to additional documents, is intended for individual cases when Internet access to documents will significantly reduce the administrative burdens associated with responding to multiple or voluminous access requests. Examples include high-volume or high-profile cases. The exception is intended to apply to a specific case and does not authorize a standing order that would otherwise swallow the rule.

The 2005 addition of a new Rule 8, subd. 3, on bulk distribution, complements the remote access established under the preceding subdivision. Courts have been providing this type of bulk data to the public for the past ten years, although distribution has mainly been limited to noncommercial entities and the media. The bulk data would not include the data set forth in Rule 8, subd. 2(b), or any case records that are not accessible to the public. The bulk data accessible to the public would, however, include preconviction criminal records as long as the individual or entity requesting the data enters into an agreement in the form approved by the state court administrator that provides that the individual or entity will not disclose or disseminate the data in a manner that identifies specific individuals who are the subject of such data.

The 2005 addition of new Rule 8, subd. 4(a), regarding criminal justice and other governmental agencies, recognizes that the courts are required to report certain information to other agencies and that the courts are participating in integration efforts (e.g., CriMNet) with other agencies. The access is provided remotely or via regular (e.g., nightly or even annually) bulk data exchanges. The provisions on remote and bulk record access are not intended to affect these interagency disclosures. Additional discretionary disclosures are authorized under subd. 4(b).

The 2005 changes to Rule 8, subd. 5, regarding access to certain evidence, are intended to address the situation in which the provisions appear to completely cut off public access to a particular document or parts of it even when the item is formally admitted into evidence (*i.e.*, marked as an exhibit and the record indicates that its admission was approved by the court) in a publicly accessible court proceeding. *See, e.g.*, MINN. STAT. § 518.146 (2004) (prohibiting public access to, among other things, tax returns submitted in dissolution cases). The process for formally admitting evidence provides an opportunity to address privacy interests affected by an evidentiary item. Formal admission into evidence has been the standard for determining when most court services records become accessible to the public under Rule 4, subd. 1(b), and this should apply across the board to documents that are admitted into evidence.

The changes also recognize that evidentiary items may be subject to protective orders or retention schedules or other orders. As indicated in Rule 4, subd. 2, and its accompanying advisory committee comment, the procedures for obtaining a protective order are addressed in other rules. Similarly, as indicated in Rule 1, the disposition, retention and return of records and objects is addressed elsewhere.

Advisory Committee Comment–2007

The 2007 modifications to Rule 8, subd. 2(b), recognize the feasibility of controlling remote access to identifiers in data fields and the impracticability of controlling them in text fields such as documents. Data fields in court computer systems are designed to isolate specific data elements such as social security numbers, addresses, and names of victims. Access to these isolated elements can be systematically controlled by proper computer programming. Identifiers that appear in text fields in documents are more difficult to isolate. In addition, certain documents completed by court personnel occasionally require the insertion of names, addresses and/or telephone numbers of parties, victims, witnesses or jurors. Examples include but are not limited to appellate opinions where victim or witness names may be necessary for purposes of clarity or comprehensibility, "no-contact" orders that require identification of victims or locations for purposes of enforceability, orders directing seizure of property, and various notices issued by the court.

The use of the term "recommends" intentionally makes the last sentence of the rule hortatory in nature, and is designed to avoid creating a basis for appeals. The reference to other applicable laws and rules recognizes that there are particular provisions that may control the disclosure of certain information in certain documents. For example, the disclosure of restricted identifiers (which includes social security numbers, employer identification numbers, and financial account numbers) on judgments, orders, decisions and notices is governed by MINN. GEN. R. PRAC. 11. Rules governing juror-related records include MINN. GEN. R. PRAC. 814, MINN. R. CRIM. P. 26.02, subd. 2, and MINN. R. CIV. P. 47.01.

The 2007 modifications to Rule 8, subd. 2(c), recognize that criminal cases often involve a conviction on less than all counts charged, and that appellate records that have long been remotely accessible have included pretrial and preconviction appeals. The clarification regarding automated tools recognizes that the participant index on the court's case management system is included in the scope of the limits on remote searching of preconviction records.

The 2007 modification to Rule 8, subd. 2(d), authorizes the state court administrator to designate additional locations as court facilities for purposes of remote access. For example, a government service center, registrar of titles office or similar location that is not in the same building as the court's offices could be designated as a location where the public could have access to court records without the limitations on remote access. In some counties, these types of offices are located in the courthouse and in other counties they are in a separate building. This change allows such offices to provide the same level of access to court records regardless of where they are located.

The 2007 addition of Rule 8, subd. 2(e)(3), is intended to reinstate the routine disclosure, by facsimile transmission or e-mail, of criminal complaints, pleadings, orders, disposition bulletins, and other documents to the general public. These disclosures were unintentionally cut off by the definition of remote access under Rule 8, subd. 2(d), which technically includes facsimile and e-mail transmissions. Limiting disclosures to the discretion of the court administrator relies on the common sense of court staff to ensure that this exception does not swallow the limits on remote and bulk data access. The rule also recognizes that copy fees may apply. Some but not all courts are able to process electronic (i.e., credit card) fee payments.

ACCESS RULE 8, subd. 4(b), authorizes disclosure of certain records to executive branch entities pursuant to a nondisclosure agreement. Minnesota Statutes § 13.03, subd. 4(a) (2006), provides a basis for an executive branch entity to comply with the nondisclosure requirements.. It is recommended that this basis be expressly recognized in the nondisclosure agreement and that the agreement limit the executive branch agency's use of the nonpublicly-accessible court records to that necessary to carry out its duties as required by law in connection with any civil, criminal, administrative, or arbitral proceeding in any federal or state court, or local court or agency or before any self-regulated body.

Advisory Committee Comment–2008

The 2008 modifications to Rule 8, subd. 2(a), recognize that privacy concerns in regard to remote access, such as identity theft, subside over time while the historical value of certain records may increase. The rule permits remote access to otherwise publicly accessible records as long as the records have been in existence for 90 years or more. This provision is based in part on the executive branch data practices policy of allowing broader access to records that are approximately a lifetime in age. *See* Minn. Stat. § 13.10, subd. 2 (2006) (private and confidential data on decedents becomes public when ten years have elapsed from the actual or presumed death of the individual and 30 years have elapsed from the creation of the data; "an individual is presumed to be dead if either 90 years elapsed since the creation of the data or 90 years have elapsed since the individual's birth, whichever is earlier, except that an individual is not presumed to be dead if readily available data indicate that the individual is still living").

The 2008 modifications to Rule 8, subds. 2(c) and 3, recognize that certain juvenile court records are accessible to the public and that the remote access policy for preconviction criminal records needs to be consistently applied in the juvenile context. There are both adjudications and convictions in the juvenile process. Delinquency adjudications are governed by MINN. R. JUV. DEL. P. 15.05, subd. 1(A), and MINN. STAT. § 260B.198, subd. 1 (Supp. 2007); traffic offender adjudications are governed by MINN. R. JUV. DEL. P. 17.09, subd. 2(B) and MINN. STAT. § 260B.225, subd. 9 (2006); and extended jurisdiction juvenile convictions are governed by MINN. R. JUV. DEL. P. 19.10, subd. 1(A) and MINN. STAT. § 260B.130, subd. 4 (2006). Juvenile records that are otherwise publicly accessible but have not reached the appropriate adjudication or conviction are not remotely accessible under Rule 8, subds. 2(c) and 3.

Advisory Committee Comment—2012 Amendment

The 2012 addition of Rule 8, subd. 2(e)(4), is intended to recognize that documents electronically filed with the courts or electronically served using the court's internet-accessible electronic filing and electronic service system can be made remotely accessible to the parties filing or serving the same and to the recipients of such service. This continues remote access that was established through the Judicial District E–Filing Pilot Project Provisions, adopted by the court on October 21, 2010, and amended on March 10, 2011. Those provisions are being replaced by permanent rules.

Historical Notes

The order of the Minnesota Supreme Court [ADM 10–8011] dated May 24, 2012, provided in part that "These amendments shall apply to all actions or proceedings commenced on or after the effective date."

RULE 9. APPEAL FROM DENIAL OF ACCESS

If the custodian, other than a judge, denies a request to inspect records, the denial may be appealed in writing to the state court administrator. The state court administrator shall promptly make a determination and forward it in writing to the interested parties as soon as possible. This remedy need not be exhausted before other relief is sought.

Adopted Feb. 1, 1988, eff. July 1, 1988. Amended May 6, 2005, eff. July 1, 2005.

Advisory Committee Comment–2005

The 2005 deletion of the phrase "by mail" in Rule 9 recognizes that a determination is often issued in electronic format, such as e-mail or facsimile transmission.

RULE 10. CONTRACTING WITH VENDORS FOR INFORMATION TECHNOLOGY SERVICES

If a court or court administrator contracts with a vendor to perform information technology related services for the judicial branch: (a) "court records" shall include all recorded information collected, created, received, maintained or disseminated by the vendor in the performance of such services, regardless of physical form or method of storage, excluding any vendor-owned or third-party-licensed intellectual property (trade secrets or copyrighted or patented materials) expressly identified as such in the contract; (b) the vendor shall not, unless expressly authorized in the contract, disclose to any third party court records that are inaccessible to the public under these rules; (c) unless assigned in the contract to the vendor in whole or in part, the court shall remain the custodian of all court records for the purpose of providing public access to publicly accessible court records in accordance with these rules, and the vendor shall provide the court with access to such records for the purpose of complying with the public access requirements of these rules.

Adopted May 6, 2005, eff. July 1, 2005.

Advisory Committee Comment–2005

The 2005 addition of Rule 10 is necessary to ensure the proper protection and use of court records when independent contractors are used to perform information technology related services for the courts. Where the service involves coding, designing, or developing software or managing a software development project for a court or court administrator, the court or court administrator would typically retain all record custodian responsibilities under these rules and the contract would, among other things: (a) require the vendor to immediately notify the court or court administrator if the vendor receives a request for release of, or access to, court records; (b) prohibit the disclosure of court records that are inaccessible to the public under these rules; (c) specify the uses the vendor may make of the court records; (d) require the vendor to take all reasonable steps to ensure the confidentiality of the court records that are not accessible to the public, including advising all vendor employees who are permitted access to the records of the limitations on use and disclosure; (e) require the vendor, other than a state agency, to indemnify and hold the court or court administrator and its agents harmless from all violations of the contract; (f) provide the court or court administrator with an explicit right to injunctive relief without the necessity of showing actual harm for any violation or threatened violation of the contract; (g) be governed by Minnesota law, without giving effect to Minnesota's choice of law provisions; (h) include the consent of the vendor to the personal jurisdiction of the state and federal courts within Minnesota; and (i) require all disputes to be venued in a state or federal court situated within the state of Minnesota.

RULE 11. IMMUNITY

Absent willful or malicious conduct, the custodian of a record shall be immune from civil liability for conduct relating to the custodian's duties of providing access under these rules.

Adopted May 6, 2005, eff. July 1, 2005.

Advisory Committee Comment–2005

The 2005 addition of Rule 11 is intended to allow record custodians to promptly and effectively discharge their obligations under these rules without undue concern over liability for inadvertent errors. The burden of redacting each and every reference to specific pieces of information from voluminous records is a daunting task, and the threat of liability could turn even the more routine, daily access requests into lengthy processes involving nondisclosure/indemnity agreements. The court has established immunity for records custodians in other contexts. *See, e.g.*, R. Bd. Jud. Stds. 3 (members of the Board on Judicial Standards are absolutely immune from suit for all conduct in the course of their official duties); R. Lawyers Prof. Resp. 21(b) (Lawyers Professional Responsibility Board members, other panel members, District Committee members, the Director, and the Director's staff, and those entering agreements with the Director's office to supervise probation are immune from suit for any conduct in the course of their official duties); Minn R. Admission to the Bar 12.A. (the Board of Law Examiners and its members, employees and agents are immune from civil liability for conduct and communications relating to their duties under the Rules of Admission to the Bar or the Board's policies and procedures); Minn. R. Bd. Legal Cert. 120 (the Board of Legal Certification and its members, employees, and agents are immune from civil liability for any acts conducted in the course of their official duties); Minn. R. Client Sec. Bd. 1.05 (the Client Security Board and its staff are absolutely immune from civil liability for all acts in the course of their official capacity). Rule 11 does not, however, avoid an administrative appeal of a denial of access under Rule 9, declaratory judgment, writ of mandamus, or other similar relief that may otherwise be available for a violation of these rules.

APPENDICES

APPENDIX A

Boards and Commissions that are governed by independent rules promulgated by the Supreme Court include, but are not limited to, the following:

Lawyers Professional Responsibility Board

Lawyer Trust Account Board

Client Security Fund Board

State Board of Legal Certification

Board of Continuing Education

State Board of Law Examiners

State Bar Advisory Council

Board on Judicial Standards

Standing Committee on No Fault Arbitration

Legal Services Advisory Committee

Adopted Feb. 1, 1988, eff. July 1, 1988.

APPENDIX B. [Deleted May 6, 2005, eff. July 1, 2005]

APPENDIX C. [Deleted May 6, 2005, eff. July 1, 2005]

APPENDIX D. [Deleted May 6, 2005, eff. July 1, 2005]

PAPER SIZE FOR COURT FILINGS

ORDER MANDATING 8½ × 11 INCH SIZE PAPER FOR ALL FILINGS IN ALL COURTS IN THE STATE

WHEREAS, the District Administrators presented a Resolution to the Conference of Chief and Assistant Chief Judges at their December 2, 1981, meeting recommending the adoption of 8½ × 11 inch paper in all courts, and

WHEREAS, the Conference of Chief and Assistant Chief Judges considered and unanimously adopted said Resolution, and

WHEREAS, the Supreme Court was requested to promulgate a rule mandating the exclusive use of 8½ × 11 inch size paper in all courts in the State effective July 1, 1983, and

WHEREAS, the Supreme Court held a public hearing on this petition on Friday, April 9, 1982.

NOW, THEREFORE, IT IS HEREBY ORDERED that effective July 1, 1983, only the standard size of 8½ × 11 inch paper will be used for all filings, pleadings, motions, and petitions in all courts in the State of Minnesota.

Dated April 16, 1982

FACSIMILE TRANSMISSION

Research Note

These rules may be searched electronically on Westlaw in the MN–RULES database; updates to these rules may be found on Westlaw in MN–RULESUPDATES. For search tips and a summary of database content, consult the Westlaw Scope Screens for each database.

Orders

USE OF FACSIMILE TRANSMISSION AND CONSIDERATION BY RULES COMMITTEES

WHEREAS, by Order # C2–87–1853 dated October 3, 1988, this Court extended the authorization for filing of papers and issuance of orders and warrants by use of facsimile transmission equipment until January 1, 1989; and

WHEREAS, filing papers by the use of facsimile transmission has been incorporated into the Rules of Civil Procedure by an amendment effective January 1, 1989; and

WHEREAS, incorporation of the use of facsimile transmission, where appropriate, into other rules promulgated by this Court will provide clear notice of such use to all members of the practicing bar and the public;

NOW, THEREFORE, IT IS ORDERED that, effective January 1, 1989, facsimile transmission is allowed subject to the following conditions:

A. Equipment. Only facsimile transmission equipment that satisfies the published criteria of the Supreme Court shall be used for filing and issuance of orders and warrants under this Order.

B. Permitted Use.

(1) *Issuance of Orders or Warrants.*

(a) Facsimile transmission may be used for the issuance of all orders and warrants including, but not limited to, the following circumstances:

(i) Criminal matters for the issuance of arrest and search warrants;

(ii) Juvenile matters for the issuance of orders or warrants for taking a juvenile into custody and for the release or detention of the juvenile;

(iii) Family matters for the issuance of ex parte temporary orders for protection; and

(iv) Civil cases for the issuance of temporary restraining orders.

(b) All procedural and statutory requirements for the issuance of a warrant or order, including the making of a record of the proceedings, shall be met.

(c) For all procedural and statutory purposes, the facsimile shall have the same force and effect as the original.

(d) The original order or warrant, along with any other documents, including affidavits, shall be delivered to the court administrator of the county where the request or application for the order or warrant was made.

(2) *Filing.* Filing of all papers in the district court shall be permitted by use of facsimile transmission pursuant to the terms and conditions of Rule 5.05 of the Minnesota Rules of Civil Procedure for the District Court.

IT IS FURTHER ORDERED that all advisory committees established by this Court in regard to rules governing procedure in appeals and criminal, juvenile, probate, commitment, and family law matters shall consider the adoption of appropriate amendments that will incorporate the use of facsimile transmission into the rules of procedure and report their recommendations to this Court at the next available opportunity.

Dated November 21, 1988.

ORDER ADOPTING CRITERIA FOR COURT OPERATED FACSIMILE EQUIPMENT

WHEREAS, by Order # C2–87–1853 dated November 21, 1988, this Court authorized the filing of papers and issuance of warrants and orders by use of facsimile transmission equipment that satisfies the published criteria of this Court; and

WHEREAS, the fair and efficient administration of justice requires the establishment of a uniform standard for facsimile transmission equipment operated by the courts of this state; and

WHEREAS, the International Telegraph and Telephone Consultative Committee (CCITT) of the International Telecommunications Union has established standards for facsimile transmission equipment, and

WHEREAS, facsimile transmission equipment that meets the standards established for the CCITT category "Group 3" provides the highest operating speed and image resolution available for use over the public telephone network;

NOW, THEREFORE, IT IS HEREBY ORDERED that, until further order of this Court, facsimile transmission equipment operated by the courts of this state for the purposes of filing of papers and issuance of warrants and orders shall comply with the standards for Group 3 apparatus established by the CCITT [currently set forth in Recommendations T.4 and T.30, Vol. VII—Fascicle VII.3, *CCITT Red Book; Malaga–Torremolinos 1984* (U.N. Bookstore Code ITU 6731)]. At the discretion of the court or judicial district operating such equipment, such equipment may also be compatible with machines in CCITT Groups 1 and 2.

IT IS FURTHER ORDERED that it is the responsibility of persons desiring to file documents with the courts of this state by the use of facsimile transmission equipment to utilize facsimile transmission equipment that is compatible with facsimile transmission equipment operated by the courts of this state.

Dated January 31, 1989

MINNESOTA NO–FAULT, COMPREHENSIVE OR COLLISION DAMAGE AUTOMOBILE INSURANCE ARBITRATION RULES

Generally Effective January 1, 1991

Including Amendments Received Through January 1, 2014

Rule

RULE 1. PURPOSE AND ADMINISTRATION

(a) The purpose of the Minnesota no-fault arbitration system is to promote the orderly and efficient administration of justice in this State. To this end, the Court, pursuant to Minn. Stat. § 65B.525 and in the exercise of its rule making responsibilities, does hereby adopt these rules. These rules are intended to implement the Minnesota No–Fault Act.

(b) Arbitration under Minn.Stat. 65B.525 shall be administered by a standing committee of twelve members to be appointed by the Minnesota Supreme Court. Initially, the twelve members shall be appointed for terms to commence January 1, 1975, and the Supreme Court shall designate three such members for a one-year term, three for a two-year term, three for a three-year term, and three for a four-year term commencing on January 1 of each succeeding year. After July 1, 1988, no member shall serve more than two full terms and any partial term.

(c) The day-to-day administration of arbitration under Minn. Stat. 65B.525 shall be by an arbitration organization designated by the Standing Committee with the concurrence of the Supreme Court. The administration shall be subject to the continuing supervision of the Standing Committee.

RULE 2. APPOINTMENT OF ARBITRATOR

The Standing Committee may conditionally approve and submit to the arbitration organization nominees to the panel of arbitrators quarterly in March, June, September and December of each year, commencing March 1988. These nominees then may be included in the panel of arbitrators that the Standing Committee shall nominate annually for approval by the Supreme Court. The panel appointed by the Supreme Court shall be certified by the Standing Committee to the arbitration organization.

RULE 3. NAME OF TRIBUNAL

Any tribunal constituted by the parties for the settlement of their dispute under these rules shall be called the Minnesota No-Fault Arbitration Tribunal.

RULE 4. ADMINISTRATOR

When parties agree to arbitrate under these rules, or when they provide for arbitration by the arbitration organization and an arbitration is initiated thereunder, they thereby constitute the arbitration organization the administrator of the arbitration.

RULE 5. INITIATION OF ARBITRATION

(a) Mandatory Arbitration (for claims of $10,000 or less at the commencement of arbitration). At such time as the respondent denies a claim, the respondent shall advise the claimant of claimant's right to demand arbitration.

(b) Nonmandatory Arbitration (for claims over $10,000). At such time as the respondent denies a claim, the respondent shall advise the claimant whether or not it is willing to submit the claim to arbitration.

(c) All Cases. In all cases the respondent shall also advise the claimant that information on arbitration procedures may be obtained from the arbitration organization, giving the arbitration organization's current address. On request, the arbitration organization will provide a claimant with a petition form for initiating arbitration together with a copy of these rules. Arbitration is commenced by the filing of the signed, executed form, together with the required filing fee, with the arbitration organization. If the claimant asserts a claim against more than one insurer, claimant shall so designate upon the arbitration petition. In the event that a respondent claims or asserts that another insurer bears some or all of the responsibility for the claim, respondent shall file a petition identifying the insurer and setting forth the amount of the claim that it claims is the responsibility of another insurer. Regardless of the number of respondents identified on the claim petition, the claim is subject to the jurisdictional limits set forth in Rule 6.

(d) Denial of Claim. If a respondent fails to respond in writing within 30 days after reasonable proof of the fact and the amount of loss is duly presented to the respondent, the claim shall be deemed denied for the purpose of activating these rules.

(e) Itemization of claim. At the time of filing the arbitration from or within 30 days after, the claimant shall file an itemization of benefits claimed and supporting documentation. Medical and replacement services claims must detail the name of providers, dates of services claimed, and total amounts owing. Income loss claims must detail employers, rates of pay, dates of loss, method of calculation, and total amounts owing.

(f) Within 30 days after receipt of the itemization of benefits claimed and supporting documentation from claimant, respondent shall serve a response to the petition setting forth all grounds upon which the claim is denied and accompanied by all documents supporting denial of the benefits claimed.

RULE 6. JURISDICTION IN MANDATORY CASES

By statute, mandatory arbitration applies to all claims for no-fault benefits or comprehensive or collision damage coverage where the total amount of the claim, at the commencement of arbitration, is in an amount of $10,000 or less. In cases where the amount of the claim continues to accrue after the petition is filed, the arbitrator shall have jurisdiction to determine all amounts claimed including those in excess of $10,000.

If the claimant waives a portion of the claim in order to come within the $10,000.00 jurisdictional limit, the claimant must specify within thirty (30) days of filing the claims in excess of the $10,000.00 being waived.

RULE 7. NOTICE

Upon the filing of the petition form by either party, the arbitration organization shall send a copy of the petition to the other party together with a request for payment of the filing fee. The responding party will then have 20 days to notify the arbitration organization of the name of counsel, if any.

RULE 8. SELECTION OF ARBITRATOR AND CHALLENGE PROCEDURE

The arbitration organization shall send simultaneously to each party to the dispute an identical list of four names of persons chosen from the panel. Each party to the dispute shall have seven business days from the mailing date in which to cross out a maximum of one name objected to, number the remaining names in order of preference and return the list to the arbitration organization. In the event of multiparty arbitration, the arbitration organization may increase the number of potential arbitrators and divide the strikes so as to afford an equal number of strikes to each adverse interest. If a party does not return the list within the time specified, all persons named therein shall be deemed acceptable.

One of the persons who has been approved on both lists shall be invited by the arbitration organization to serve in accordance with the designated order of the mutual preference. Any objection to an arbitrator based on the arbitrator's post-appointment disclosure must be made within seven business days from the mailing date of the arbitrator disclosure form. Failure to object to the appointed arbitrator based upon the post-appointment disclosure within seven business days constitutes waiver of any objections based on the post-appointment disclosure. An objection to a potential arbitrator shall be determined initially by the arbitration organization, subject to appeal to the Standing Committee. If an acceptable arbitrator is unable to act, or for any other reason the appointment cannot be made from the submitted list, the arbitration organization shall have the power to make the appointment from among other members of the panel without the submission of additional lists. If any arbitrator should resign, be disqualified or unable to perform the duties of the office, the arbitration organization shall appoint another arbitrator from the no-fault panel to the case.

RULE 9. NOTICE TO ARBITRATOR OF APPOINTMENT

Notice of the appointment of the neutral arbitrator, whether appointed mutually by the parties or by the arbitration organization, shall be mailed to the arbitrator by the arbitration organization, together with a copy of these rules, and the signed acceptance of the arbitrator shall be filed with the arbitration organization prior to the opening of the first hearing.

RULE 10. QUALIFICATION OF ARBITRATOR AND DISCLOSURE PROCEDURE

a. Every member of the panel shall be a licensed attorney at law of this state or a retired attorney or judge in good standing. Effective January 1, 2004, requirements for qualification as an arbitrator shall be: (1) at least 5 years in practice in this state; (2) at least one-third of the attorney's practice is with auto insurance claims or, for an attorney not actively representing clients, at least one-third of an ADR practice is with motor vehicle claims or not-fault matters; (3) completion of an arbitrator training program approved by the No–Fault Standing Committee prior to appointment to the panel; (4) at least three CLE hours on no-fault issues within their reporting period; and (5) arbitrators will be required to recertify each year, confirming at the time of recertification that they continue to meet the above requirements.

b. No person shall serve as an arbitrator in any arbitration in which he or she has a financial or personal conflict of interest. Under procedures established by the Standing Committee and immediately following appointment to a case, every arbitrator shall be required to disclose any circumstances likely to create a presumption or possibility of bias or conflict that may disqualify the person as a potential arbitrator. Every arbitrator shall supplement the disclosures as circumstances require. The fact that an arbitrator or the arbitrator's firm represents automobile accident claimants against insurance companies or self-insureds, including the respondent, does not create a presumption of bias. It is a financial conflict of interest if, within the last year, the appointed arbitrator or the arbitrator's firm has been hired by the respondent to represent the respondent or respondent's insureds in a dispute for which respondent provides insurance coverage. It is a financial conflict of interest if the appointed arbitrator is aware of having received referrals within the last year from officers, employees or agents of any entity whose bills are in dispute in the arbitration or the arbitrator's firm has received such referrals and the arbitrator is aware of them.

c. If an arbitrator has been certified and has met the requirements of subdivision (a) for the past five years but becomes ineligible for certification under Rule 10(a) due to retirement or change in practice, the arbitrator may continue to seek annual certification for up to five years from the date of retirement or practice change if the following requirements are satisfied:

The arbitrator completes and files an annual No–Fault Arbitrator Recertification form which certifies that

1. He or she is an attorney licensed to practice law in Minnesota and is in good standing;

2. He or she has retained current knowledge of the Minnesota No–Fault Act (Minn. Stat. §§ 65B.41–65B.71), Minnesota appellate court decisions interpreting the Act, the Minnesota No–Fault Arbitration Rules and the Arbitrators' Standards of Conduct; and

3. He or she has attended CLE course(s) in the last year containing at least three credits relating to no-fault matters.

The rules regarding bias and conflict of interest as set forth in subdivision (b) remain applicable to arbitrators who are recertified under this subdivision (c).

Amended Nov. 19, 2007, eff. Jan. 1, 2008; May 3, 2010, eff. June 1, 2010.

Comment to Rule 10

In recent years, there have been inconsistencies in district court rulings and in determinations by the Standing Committee as to what constitutes a conflict of interest for no-fault arbitrators. In response, the Standing Committee wishes to clarify what constitutes a conflict of interest for both respondents' and claimants' attorneys. The Committee recognizes that the Amendments will limit the number of arbitrators, especially in certain out state areas. But the Amendments are necessary to clarify the law and stem the tide of parties seeking removal of arbitrators in the district court. The Amendments also establish, for the first time, that a conflict exists if an arbitrator who is to rule on a disputed bill for a medical provider is aware that the provider has made referrals to the arbitrator within the last year.

RULE 11. VACANCIES

If for any reason an arbitrator should be unable to perform the duties of the office, the arbitration organization may, on proof satisfactory to it, declare the office vacant. Vacancies shall be filed in accordance with the applicable provisions of these rules.

RULE 12. DISCOVERY

The voluntary exchange of information is encouraged. Formal discovery is discouraged except that a party is entitled to:

1) exchange of medical reports;

2) medical authorizations directed to all medical providers consulted by the claimant in the 7 years prior to the accident;

3) employment records and authorizations for 2 years prior to the accident, when wage loss is in dispute;

4) supporting documentation required under No-Fault Arbitration Rule 5; and

5) other exhibits to be offered at the hearing.

However, upon application and good cause shown by any party, the arbitrator may permit any discovery allowable under the Minnesota Rules of Civil Procedure for the District Courts. Any medical examination for which the respondent can establish good cause shall be completed within 90 days following the commencement of the case unless extended by the arbitrator for good cause.

RULE 13. WITHDRAWAL

A claimant may withdraw a petition up until ten (10) days prior to the hearing. The claimant will be responsible for the arbitrator's fee, if any, upon withdrawal. If the petition is withdrawn after a panel of arbitrators is submitted and if the claimant shall file another petition arising from the same accident against the same insurer, the same panel of arbitrators shall be resubmitted to the claimant and the respondent. If the petition is withdrawn after the arbitrator is selected and if the claimant shall file another petition arising from the same accident against the same insurer, the same arbitrator who was earlier assigned shall be reassigned. The claimant who withdraws a petition shall be responsible for all parties' filing fees incurred upon the refiling of the petition.

RULE 14. TIME AND PLACE OF ARBITRATION

An informal arbitration hearing will be held in the arbitrator's office or some other appropriate place in the general locale within a 50–mile radius of the claimant's residence, or other place agreed upon by the parties. If the claimant resides outside of the state of Minnesota, arbitration organization shall designate the appropriate place for the hearing. The arbitrator shall fix the time and place for the hearing. At least 14 days prior to the hearing, the arbitration organization shall mail notice thereof to each party or to a party's designated representative. Notice of hearing may be waived by any party. When an arbitration hearing has been scheduled for a day certain, the courts of the state shall recognize the date as the equivalent of a day certain court trial date in the scheduling of their calendars.

RULE 15. POSTPONEMENTS

The arbitrator, for good cause shown, may postpone any hearing upon the request of a party or upon the arbitrator's own initiative, and shall also grant such postponement when all of the parties agree thereto. The party requesting a postponement will be billed for the cost of the rescheduling; if, however, the arbitrator determines that a postponement was necessitated by a party's failure to cooperate in providing information required under Rule 5 or Rule 12, the arbitrator may assess the rescheduling fee to that party.

Amended Dec. 19, 2005, eff. Jan. 1, 2006.

RULE 16. REPRESENTATION

Any party may be represented by counsel or other representative named by that party. A party intending to be so represented shall notify the other party and the arbitration organization of the name and address of the representative at least three days prior to the date set for the hearing at which that person is first to appear. When such a representative initiates an arbitration or responds for a party, notice is deemed to have been given.

RULE 17. STENOGRAPHIC RECORD

Any party desiring a stenographic record shall make arrangements directly with a stenographer and shall notify the other party of these arrangements at least 24 hours in advance of the hearing. The requesting party or parties shall pay the cost of the record. If the transcript is agreed by the parties to be, or determined by the arbitrator to be, the official record of the proceeding, it must be made available to the arbitrator and to the other parties for inspection, at a date, time and place determined by the arbitrator.

RULE 18. INTERPRETERS

Any party desiring an interpreter shall make all arrangements directly with the interpreter and shall assume the costs of the service. The arbitrator may assess the cost of an interpreter pursuant to Rule 42.

RULE 19. ATTENDANCE AT HEARINGS

The arbitrator shall maintain the privacy of the hearings. Any person having a direct interest in the arbitration is entitled to attend hearings. The arbitrator shall otherwise have the power to require the exclusion of any witness, other than a party or other essential person, during the testimony of any other witness.

RULE 20. OATHS

Arbitrators, upon accepting appointment to the panel, shall take an oath or affirmation of office. The arbitrator may require witnesses to testify under oath or affirmation.

RULE 21. ORDER OF PROCEEDINGS AND COMMUNICATION WITH ARBITRATOR

The hearing shall be opened by the recording of the date, time and place of the hearing, and the presence of the arbitrator, the parties, and their representatives, if any. Either party may make an opening statement regarding the claim. The claimant shall then present evidence to support the claim. The respondent shall then present evidence supporting the defense. Witnesses for each party shall submit to questions or other examination. The arbitrator has the discretion to vary this procedure, but shall afford a full and equal opportunity to all parties for the presentation of any material and relevant evidence. Exhibits, when offered by either party, may be received in evidence by the arbitrator.

The names and addresses of all witnesses and description of the exhibits in the order received shall be made part of the record. There shall be no direct communication between the arbitrator and the parties other than at the hearing, unless the parties and the arbitrator agree otherwise. However, pre-hearing exhibits can be sent directly to the arbitrator, delivered in the same manner and at the same time to the opposing party. Parties are encouraged to submit any pre-hearing exhibits at least 24 hours in advance of the scheduled hearing. If the exhibits are not provided to opposing counsel and the arbitrator at least 24 hours before the hearing or if the exhibits contain new information and opposing counsel has not had a reasonable amount of time to review and respond to the information, the arbitrator may hold the record open until the parties have had time to review and respond to the material or reconvene the arbitration at a later date. Any other oral or written communication from the parties to the arbitrator shall be directed to the arbitration organization for transmittal to the arbitrator.

Amended Nov. 19, 2007, eff. Jan. 1, 2008.

Comment to Rule 21

The change in Rule 21 merely formalizes a practice common to the No–Fault arena. More often parties are delaying the submission of their pre-hearing exhibits until the day of the hearing, which does not allow the arbitrator ample time to prepare before the hearing. This rule not only discourages that practice, it allows time for the other party to refute new claims presented by opposing counsel.

RULE 22. ARBITRATION IN THE ABSENCE OF A PARTY OR REPRESENTATIVE

Unless the law provides to the contrary, the arbitration may proceed in the absence of any party or representative who, after due notice, fails to be present or fails to obtain a postponement. An award shall not be made solely on the default of a party. The arbitrator shall require the party who is present to submit such evidence as the arbitrator may require for the making of an award.

RULE 23. WITNESSES, SUBPOENAS AND DEPOSITIONS

(a) Through the arbitration organization, the arbitrator may, on the arbitrator's initiative or at the request of any party, issue subpoenas for the attendance of witnesses at the arbitration hearing or at such deposition as ordered under Rule 12, and the production of books, records, documents and other evidence. The subpoenas so issued shall be served, and upon application to the district court by either party or the arbitrator, enforced in the manner provided by law for the service and enforcement of subpoenas for a civil action.

(b) All provisions of law compelling a person under subpoena to testify are applicable.

(c) Fees for attendance as a witness shall be the same as for a witness in the district courts.

RULE 24. EVIDENCE

The parties may offer such evidence as they desire and shall produce such additional evidence as the arbitrator may deem necessary to an understanding and determination of the issues. The arbitrator shall be the judge of the relevancy and materiality of any evidence offered, and conformity to legal rules of evidence shall not be necessary. The parties shall be encouraged to offer, and the arbitrator shall be encouraged to receive and consider, evidence by affidavit or other document, including medical reports, statements of witnesses, officers, accident reports, medical texts, and other similar written documents which would not ordinarily be admissible as evidence in the courts of this state. In receiving this evidence, the arbitrator shall consider any objections to its admission in determining the weight to which he or she deems it is entitled.

RULE 25. CLOSE OF HEARING

The arbitrator shall specifically inquire of all parties as to whether they have any further evidence. If they do not, the arbitrator shall declare the hearing closed. If briefs or documents are to be filed, the hearing shall be declared closed as of the final date set by the arbitrator for the receipt of said briefs or documents. The time limit within which the arbitrator is required to make his award shall commence to run upon the close of the hearing.

RULE 26. REOPENING THE HEARING

At any time before the award is made, a hearing may be reopened by the arbitrator on the arbitrator's own motion, or upon application of a party for good cause shown.

RULE 27. WAIVER OF ORAL HEARING

The parties may provide, by written agreement, for the waiver of oral hearings in any case. If the parties are unable to agree as to the procedure, the arbitration organization shall specify a fair and equitable procedure.

RULE 28. EXTENSIONS OF TIME

The parties may modify any period of time by mutual agreement. The arbitration organization or the arbitrator may for good cause extend any period of time established by these rules, except the time for making the award. The arbitration organization shall notify the parties of any extension.

RULE 29. SERVING OF NOTICE

Each party waives the requirements of Minn. Stat. § 572.23 and shall be deemed to have agreed that any papers, notices or process necessary or proper for the initiation or continuation of an arbitration under these rules; for any court action in connection herewith including application for the confirmation, vacation, modification or correction of an award issued hereunder as provided in Rule 38; or for the entry of judgment on any award made under these rules may be served on a party by mail or facsimile addressed to the party or its representative at the last known address or by personal service, in or outside the state where the arbitration is to be held, provided that reasonable opportunity to be heard with regard thereto has been granted to the party. The arbitration organization and the parties may also use facsimile transmission, telex, telegram or other written forms of electronic communication to give the notices required by these rules and to serve process for an application for the confirmation, vacation, modification or correction of an award issued hereunder.

RULE 30. TIME OF AWARD

The award shall be made promptly by the arbitrator, unless otherwise agreed by the parties or specified by law, no later than 30 days from the date of closing the hearing, or if oral hearings have been waived, from the date of the arbitration organization's transmittal of the final statements and proofs to the arbitrator.

RULE 31. FORM OF AWARD

The award shall be in writing and shall be signed by the arbitrator. It shall be executed in the manner required by law.

RULE 32. SCOPE OF AWARD

The arbitrator may grant any remedy or relief that the arbitrator deems just and equitable consistent with the Minnesota No–Fault Act. The arbitrator may, in the award, include arbitration fees, expenses, rescheduling fees and compensation as provided in sections 39, 40, 41 and 42 in favor of any party and, in the event that any administrative fees or expenses are due the arbitration organization, in favor of the arbitration organization, except that the arbitrator must award interest when required by Minn. Stat. 65B.54. The arbitrator may not, in the award, include attorneys fees for either party.

Given the informal nature of no-fault arbitration proceedings, the no-fault award shall not be the basis for a claim of estoppel or waiver in any other proceeding.

RULE 33. DELIVERY OF AWARD TO PARTIES

Parties shall accept as legal delivery of the award the placing of the award or a true copy thereof in the mail addressed to a party or its representative at the last known address, personal service of the award, or the filing of the award in any other manner that is permitted by law.

RULE 34. WAIVER OF RULES

Any party who proceeds with the arbitration after knowledge than any provision or requirement of these rules has not been complied with and who fails to state an objection thereto in writing shall be deemed to have waived the right to object.

RULE 35. INTERPRETATION AND APPLICATION OF RULES

The arbitrator shall interpret and apply these rules insofar as they relate to the arbitrator's powers and duties. All other rules shall be interpreted by the arbitration organization.

RULE 36. RELEASE OF DOCUMENTS FOR JUDICIAL PROCEEDINGS

The arbitration organization shall, upon the written request of a party, furnish to the party, at its expense, certified copies of any papers in the arbitration organization's possession that may be required in judicial proceedings relating to the arbitration.

RULE 37. APPLICATIONS TO COURT AND EXCLUSION OF LIABILITY

(a) No judicial proceedings by a party relating to the subject matter of the arbitration shall be deemed a waiver of the party's right to arbitrate.

(b) Neither the arbitration organization nor any arbitrator in a proceeding under these rules can be made a witness or is a necessary party in judicial proceedings relating to the arbitration.

(c) Parties to these rules shall be deemed to have consented that judgment upon the arbitration award may be entered in any federal or state court having jurisdiction thereof.

(d) Neither the arbitration organization nor any arbitrator shall be liable to any party for any act or omission in connection with any arbitration conducted under these rules.

RULE 38. CONFIRMATION, VACATION, MODIFICATION OR CORRECTION OF AWARD

The provisions of Minn. Stat. § 572.10 through § 572.26 shall apply to the confirmation, vacation, modification or correction of award issued hereunder, except that service of process pursuant to Minn. Stat. § 572.23 shall be made as provided in Rule 29 of these rules.

RULE 39. ADMINISTRATIVE FEES

The initial fee is due and payable at the time of filing and shall be paid as follows: by the claimant, $45.00; by the respondent, $155.00. In the event that there is more than one respondent in an action, each respondent shall pay the $155.00 fee.

The American Arbitration Association may, in the event of extreme hardship on the part of any party, defer or reduce the administrative fee.

Amended May 14, 2004, eff. July 1, 2004; July 1, 2008, eff. July 1, 2008.

RULE 40. ARBITRATOR'S FEES

(a) An arbitrator shall be compensated for services and for any use of office facilities in the amount of $300 per case.

(b) If the arbitration organization is notified of a settlement or a withdrawal of a claim at any time up to 24 hours prior to the scheduled hearing, but after the appointment of the arbitrator, the arbitrator's fee shall be $50. If the arbitration organization is notified of a postponement, settlement or a withdrawal of a claim 24 hours or less prior to the scheduled hearing, the arbitrator's fee shall be $300. Unless the parties agree otherwise, the fee in a settlement shall be assessed equally to the parties, the fee in a withdrawal shall be borne by claimant, and the fee in a postponement shall be borne by the requesting party. Regardless of the resolution of the case, the arbitrator's fee shall not exceed $300 and is subject to the provisions of Rule 15.

(c) Once a hearing is commenced, the arbitrator shall direct assessment of the fee.

Amended Nov. 19, 2007, eff. Jan. 1, 2008.

Comment to Rule 40

It is becoming increasingly common for parties to request a last-minute postponement of a hearing, sometimes on multiple occasions. This change encourages the parties to consider the time the arbitrator has set aside to hear the matter and places postponed hearings more in line with the fee structure for settled cases. This rule also formalizes the practice of assessing the postponement fee to the requesting party. Finally, this rule specifies that the arbitrator's fee shall not exceed $300. This has become necessary as an increasing number of arbitrators have requested a larger fee because of time devoted to a particular case.

RULE 41. POSTPONEMENT FEES

A postponement fee of $100.00, $150.00, and $200.00 shall be charged against each party requesting a rescheduling for their first, second and additional postponements respectively.

Amended May 14, 2004, eff. July 1, 2004; Dec. 19, 2005, eff. Jan. 1, 2006; July 1, 2008, eff. July 1, 2008.

RULE 42. EXPENSES

Generally each side should pay its own expenses. An arbitrator does, however, have the discretion to direct a party or parties to pay expenses as part of an award.

RULE 43. AMENDMENT OR MODIFICATION

The standing committee may propose amendments to these rules as circumstances may require. All changes in these rules, and all other determinations of the standing committee shall be subject to review and approval by the Minnesota Supreme Court.

FORMS

TO BE PRINTED ON BACK OF OATH OF ARBITRATOR FORM: ARBITRATOR'S CONTINUING REPRESENTATION

THE ARBITRATOR ON OATH CERTIFIES THAT:

1. I will act in good faith and with integrity and fairness.
2. I have disclosed to the parties (and co-arbitrators) prior to this hearing any interest or relationship likely to affect impartiality or which might create an appearance of partiality or bias. (Canon II, Code of Ethics for Arbitrators in Commercial Disputes).

CANON II.

An Arbitrator should disclose any interests or relationship likely to affect impartiality or which might create an appearance of partiality or bias.

Safeco Insurance Co. v. *Stariha*, 346 N.W.2d 663 (Minn.Ct.App.1984).

3. I have had no ex parte contacts with regard to this arbitration proceeding, either orally or in writing, with any of the parties to this arbitration or their counsel except:

   a. Communications concerning scheduling and anticipated duration of arbitration hearing. (Rule 11).

   b. Pre-arbitration proceedings as described in Rule 10 of Minnesota No-Fault Automobile Insurance Arbitration Rules.

Crosby-Ironton Federation of Teachers v. *Independent School District No. 182*, 285 N.W.2d 667 (Minn.1979).

Beebout v. *St. Paul Fire & Marine Ins. Co.*, 365 N.W.2d 271 (Minn.Ct.App.1985).

CODE OF JUDICIAL CONDUCT

Effective January 1, 1996

Including Amendments Received Through January 1, 2014

Research Note

See Minnesota Statutes Annotated, *Volume 52, for case annotations, cross references, and historical notes.*

CODE OF JUDICIAL CONDUCT

CODE OF JUDICIAL CONDUCT

Effective July 1, 2009

PREAMBLE

An independent, fair, and impartial judiciary is indispensable to our system of justice. The United States legal system is based upon the principle that an independent, impartial, and competent judiciary, composed of men and women of integrity, will interpret and apply the law that governs our society. Thus, the judiciary plays a central role in preserving the principles of justice and the rule of law. Inherent in all the Rules contained in this Code are the precepts that judges, individually and collectively, must respect and honor the judicial office as a public trust and strive to maintain and enhance confidence in the legal system.

Judges should maintain the dignity of judicial office at all times, and avoid both impropriety and the appearance of impropriety in their professional and personal lives. They should aspire at all times to conduct that ensures the greatest possible public confidence in their independence, impartiality, integrity, and competence.

The Code of Judicial Conduct establishes standards for the ethical conduct of judges and judicial candidates. It is not intended as an exhaustive guide for the conduct of judges and judicial candidates, who are governed in their judicial and personal conduct by general ethical standards as well as by the Code. The Code is intended, however, to provide guidance and assist judges in maintaining the highest standards of judicial and personal conduct, and to provide a basis for regulating their conduct through disciplinary agencies.

SCOPE

The Code of Judicial Conduct consists of four Canons, numbered Rules under each Canon, and Comments that generally follow and explain each Rule. Scope and Terminology sections provide additional guidance in interpreting and applying the Code. An Application section establishes when the various Rules apply to a judge or judicial candidate.

The Canons state overarching principles of judicial ethics that all judges must observe. Although a judge may be disciplined only for violating a Rule, the Canons provide important guidance in interpreting the Rules. Where a Rule contains a permissive term, such as "may" or "should," the conduct being addressed is committed to the personal and professional discretion of the judge or candidate in question, and no disciplinary action should be taken for action or inaction within the bounds of such discretion.

The Comments that accompany the Rules serve two functions. First, they provide guidance regarding the purpose, meaning, and proper application of the Rules. They contain explanatory material and, in some instances, provide examples of permitted or prohibited conduct. Comments neither add to nor subtract from the binding obligations set forth in the Rules. Therefore, when a Comment contains the term "must," it does not mean that the Comment itself is binding or enforceable; it signifies that the Rule in question, properly understood, is obligatory as to the conduct at issue.

Second, the Comments identify aspirational goals for judges. To implement fully the principles of this Code as articulated in the Canons, judges should strive to exceed the standards of conduct established by the Rules, holding themselves to the highest ethical standards and seeking to achieve those aspirational goals, thereby enhancing the dignity of the judicial office.

The Rules of the Code of Judicial Conduct are rules of reason that should be applied consistent with constitutional requirements, statutes, other court rules, and decisional law, and with due regard for all relevant circumstances. The Rules should not be interpreted to impinge upon the essential independence of judges in making judicial decisions.

Although the black letter of the Rules is binding and enforceable, it is not contemplated that every transgression will result in imposition of discipline. Whether discipline should be imposed should be determined through a reasonable and reasoned application of the Rule(s), and should depend upon factors such as the seriousness of the transgression, the facts and circumstances that existed at the time of the transgression, the extent of any pattern of improper activity, whether there have been previous violations, and the effect of the improper activity upon the judicial system or others.

The Code is not designed or intended as a basis for civil or criminal liability. Neither is it intended to be the basis for litigants to seek collateral remedies against each other or to obtain tactical advantages in proceedings before a court.

TERMINOLOGY

"Aggregate," in relation to contributions for a candidate, means not only contributions in cash or in kind made directly to a candidate's campaign committee, but also all contributions made indirectly with the understanding that they will be used to support the election of a candidate or to oppose the election of the candidate's opponent. See Rule 4.4.

"Appropriate authority" means the authority having responsibility for initiation of disciplinary process in connection with the violation to be reported. See Rules 2.14 and 2.15.

"Contribution" means money, a negotiable instrument, or a donation in kind that is given to a political committee, political fund, principal campaign committee, or party unit as defined in Minn. Stat. 10A.01. "Contribution" includes a loan or advance of credit to a political committee, political fund, principal campaign committee, or party unit, if the loan or advance of credit is: (1) forgiven; or (2) repaid by an individual or an association other than the political committee, political fund, principal campaign committee, or party unit to which the loan or advance of credit was made. If an advance of credit or a loan is forgiven or repaid as provided in this paragraph, it is a contribution in the year in which the loan or advance of credit was made. "Contribution" does not include services provided without compensation by an individual volunteering personal time on behalf of a candidate, ballot question, political committee, political fund, principal campaign committee, or party unit, or the publishing or broadcasting of news items or editorial comments by the news media. See Rules 4.1 and 4.4.

"De minimis," in the context of interests pertaining to disqualification of a judge, means an insignificant interest that could not raise a reasonable question regarding the judge's impartiality. See Rule 2.11.

"Economic interest" means ownership of more than a de minimis legal or equitable interest. Except for situations in which the judge participates in the management of such a legal or equitable interest, or the interest could be substantially affected by the outcome of a proceeding before a judge, it does not include:

(1) an interest in the individual holdings within a mutual or common investment fund;

(2) an interest in securities held by an educational, religious, charitable, fraternal, or civic organization in which the judge or the judge's spouse, parent, child, a person with whom the judge has an intimate relationship, or a member of the judge's household serves as a director, an officer, an advisor, or other participant;

(3) a deposit in a financial institution, or deposits or proprietary interests the judge may maintain as a member of a mutual savings association or credit union, or similar proprietary interests; or

(4) an interest in the issuer of government securities held by the judge.

See Rules 1.3 and 2.11.

"Fiduciary" includes relationships such as executor, administrator, trustee, or guardian. See Rules 2.11, 3.2, and 3.8.

"Impartial," "impartiality," and **"impartially"** mean absence of bias or prejudice in favor of, or against, particular parties or classes of parties, as well as maintenance of an open mind in considering issues that may come before a judge. See Canons 1, 2, and 4, and Rules 1.2, 2.2, 2. 10, 2.11, 2.13, 3.1, 3.12, 3.13, 4.1, and 4.2.

"Impending matter" is a matter that is imminent or expected to occur in the near future. See Rules 2.9, 2.10, 3.13, and 4.1.

"Impropriety" includes conduct that violates the law, court rules, or provisions of this Code, and conduct that undermines a judge's independence, integrity, or impartiality. See Canon 1 and Rule 1.2.

"Independence" means a judge's freedom from influence or controls other than those established by law. See Canons 1 and 4, and Rules 1.2, 3.1, 3.12, 3.13, and 4.2.

"Integrity" means probity, fairness, honesty, uprightness, and soundness of character. See Canon 1 and Rule 1.2.

"Intimate relationship" means a continuing relationship involving sexual relations as defined in Rule 1.8(j)(1) of the Rules of Professional Conduct.

"Judicial candidate" means any person, including a sitting judge, who is seeking selection for judicial office by election or appointment. A person becomes a candidate for judicial office as soon as he or she makes a public announcement of candidacy, declares or files as a candidate with the election or appointment authority, authorizes or, where permitted, engages in solicitation or acceptance of contributions or support, or is nominated for election or appointment to office. See Rules 2.11, 4.1, 4.2, and 4.4.

"Knowingly," "knowledge," "known," and **"knows"** mean actual knowledge of the fact in question. A person's knowledge may be inferred from circumstances. See Rules 2.11, 2.15, 2.16, 3.6, and 4.1.

"Law" encompasses court rules as well as statutes, constitutional provisions, and decisional law. See Rules 1.1, 2.1, 2.2, 2.6, 2.7, 2.9, 3.1, 3.4, 3.9, 3.12, 3.13, 3.14, 4.1, 4.2, 4.4, and 4.5.

"Leader in a political organization" is one who holds an elective, representative, or appointed position in a political organization. See Rule 4.1.

"Member of the candidate's family" means a spouse, child, grandchild, parent, grandparent, or other relative or person with whom the candidate maintains a close familial relationship. See Rules 4.1 and 4.2.

"Member of the judge's family" means a spouse, child, grandchild, parent, grandparent, or other relative or person with whom the judge maintains a close familial relationship. See Rules 3.7, 3.8, 3.10, 3.11, 4.1, and 4.2.

"Member of a judge's family residing in the judge's household" means any relative of a judge by blood or marriage, or a person treated by a judge as a member of the judge's family, who resides in the judge's household. See Rules 2.11.

"Nonpublic information" means information that is not available to the public. Nonpublic information may include, but is not limited to, information that is sealed by statute or court order or impounded or communicated in camera, and information offered in grand jury proceedings, presentencing reports, dependency cases, or psychiatric reports. See Rule 3. 5.

"Pending matter" is a matter that has commenced. A matter continues to be pending through any appellate process until final disposition. See Rules 2.9, 2.10, 3.13, and 4.1.

"Personally solicit" means a direct request made by a judge or a judicial candidate for financial support or in-kind services, whether made by letter, telephone, or any other means of communication. See Rules 4.1, 4. 2 and 4.4.

"Political organization" means a political party or other group sponsored by or affiliated with a political party or candidate, the principal purpose of which is to further the election or appointment of candidates for political office. For purposes of this Code, the term does not include a judicial candidate's campaign committee created as authorized by Rule 4.4. See Rules 4.1 and 4.2.

"Public election" includes primary and general elections. See Rules 4.2 and 4.4.

"Third degree of relationship" includes the following persons: great-grandparent, grandparent, parent, uncle, aunt, brother, sister, child, grandchild, great-grandchild, nephew, and niece. See Rule 2.11.

APPLICATION

The Application section establishes when the various Rules apply to a judge or judicial candidate.

I. Applicability of This Code

(A) The provisions of the Code apply to all full-time judges. Parts II through V of this section identify those provisions that apply to four distinct categories of part-time judges. The four categories of judicial service in other than a full-time capacity are necessarily defined in general terms because of the widely varying forms of judicial service. Canon 4 applies to judicial candidates.

(B) A judge, within the meaning of this Code, is anyone who is employed by the judicial branch of state government to perform judicial functions, including an officer such as a magistrate under Minn. Stat. § 484. 702, court commissioner under Minn. Stat. § 489.01, referee, or judicial officer under Minn. Stat. § 487.08.

Comment

[1] The Rules in this Code have been formulated to address the ethical obligations of any person who serves a judicial function, and are premised upon the supposition that a uniform system of ethical principles should apply to all those authorized to perform judicial functions. By statute the legislature has applied the Code of Judicial Conduct to judges of the Tax Court (Minn. Stat. § 271.01, subd. 1), the Worker's Compensation Court of Appeals (Minn. Stat. § 175A.01, subd. 4), and the Office of Administrative Hearings (Minn. Stat. § 14.48, subds. 2 and 3(d)).

[2] The determination of which category and, accordingly, which specific Rules apply to an individual judicial officer, depends upon the facts of the particular judicial service.

[3] In recent years many jurisdictions have created what are often called "problem-solving" courts, in which judges are authorized by court rules to act in nontraditional ways. For example, judges presiding in drug courts and monitoring the progress of participants in those courts' programs may be authorized and even encouraged to communicate directly with social workers, probation officers, and others outside the context of their usual judicial role as independent decision makers on issues of fact and law. When court rules specifically authorize conduct not otherwise permitted under these Rules, they take precedence over the provisions set forth in the Code. Nevertheless, judges serving on "problem-solving" courts shall comply with this Code except to the extent court rules provide and permit otherwise.

II. Retired Judge Subject to Recall

A retired judge subject to recall for service, who by law is not permitted to practice law, is not required to comply:

(A) with Rule 3.9 (Service as Arbitrator or Mediator), except while serving as a judge; or

(B) at any time with Rule 3.8 (Appointments to Fiduciary Positions).

Comment

[1] For the purposes of this section, as long as a retired judge is subject to being recalled for service, the judge is considered to "perform judicial functions."

III. Continuing Part–Time Judge

A judge who serves repeatedly on a part-time basis under a continuing appointment,

(A) is not required to comply:

(1) with Rules 2.10(A) and 2.10(B) (Judicial Statements on Pending and Impending Cases), except while serving as a judge; or

(2) at any time with Rules 3.4 (Appointments to Governmental Positions), 3.8 (Appointments to Fiduciary Positions), 3.9 (Service as Arbitrator or Mediator), 3.10 (Practice of Law), 3.11 (Financial, Business, or Remunerative Activities), 3.14 (Re-

imbursement of Expenses and Waivers of Fees or Charges), 3.15 (Reporting Requirements), 4.1 (Political and Campaign Activities of Judges and Judicial Candidates in General), 4.2 (Political and Campaign Activities of Judicial Candidates in Public Elections), 4.3 (Activities of Candidates for Appointive Judicial Office), 4.4 (Campaign Committees), and 4.5 (Activities of Judges Who Become Candidates for Nonjudicial Office); and

(B) shall not practice law in the district court of the county in which the judge serves, or, if the court is divided into divisions, in the division of the court on which the judge serves, or in any court subject to the appellate jurisdiction of the court on which the judge serves. This paragraph shall not apply to lawyers who are appointed pursuant to Minn. Stat. § 484.013, Minn. Stat. § 491A.03, subd. 1, or such other appointments as ordered by the Supreme Court. However, in no event shall the judge act as a lawyer in a proceeding in which the judge has served as a judge or in any other proceeding related thereto.

Comment

[1] When a person who has been a continuing part-time judge is no longer a continuing part-time judge, including a retired judge no longer subject to recall, that person may act as a lawyer in a proceeding in which he or she has served as a judge or in any other proceeding related thereto only with the informed consent of all parties, and pursuant to Rule 1.12 of the Rules of Professional Conduct.

IV. Periodic Part–Time Judge

A periodic part-time judge who serves or expects to serve repeatedly on a part-time basis, but under a separate appointment for each limited period of service or for each matter,

(A) is not required to comply:

(1) with Rule 2.10 (Judicial Statements on Pending and Impending Cases), except while serving as a judge; or

(2) at any time with Rules 3.4 (Appointments to Governmental Positions), 3.7 (Participation in Educational, Religious, Charitable, Fraternal, or Civic Organizations and Activities), 3.8 (Appointments to Fiduciary Positions), 3.9 (Service as Arbitrator or Mediator), 3.10 (Practice of Law), 3.11 (Financial, Business, or Remunerative Activities), 3. 13 (Acceptance and Reporting of Gifts, Loans, Bequests, Benefits, or Other Things of Value), 3.15 (Reporting Requirements), 4.1 (Political and Campaign Activities of Judges and Judicial Candidates in General), and 4.5 (Activities of Judges Who Become Candidates for Nonjudicial Office); and

(B) shall not practice law in the district court of the county in which the judge serves, or, if the court is divided into divisions, in the division of the court on which the judge serves, or in any court subject to the appellate jurisdiction of the court on which the judge serves. This paragraph shall not apply to lawyers who are appointed pursuant to Minn. Stat. § 484.013, Minn. Stat. § 491A.03, subd. 1, or such other appointments as ordered by the Supreme Court. However, in no event shall the judge act as a lawyer in a proceeding in which the judge has served as a judge or in any other proceeding related thereto.

V. Pro Tempore Part–Time Judge

A pro tempore part-time judge who serves or expects to serve once or only sporadically on a part-time basis under a separate appointment for each period of service or for each case heard is not required to comply:

(A) except while serving as a judge, with Rules 1.2 (Promoting Confidence in the Judiciary), 2.4 (External Influences on Judicial Conduct), 2.10 (Judicial Statements on Pending and Impending Cases), or 3.2 (Appearances before Governmental Bodies and Consultation with Government Officials); or

(B) at any time with Rules 3.4 (Appointments to Governmental Positions), 3.6 (Affiliation with Discriminatory Organizations), 3.7 (Participation in Educational, Religious, Charitable, Fraternal, or Civic Organizations and Activities), 3.8 (Appointments to Fiduciary Positions), 3.9 (Service as Arbitrator or Mediator), 3.10 (Practice of Law), 3.11 (Financial, Business, or Remunerative Activities), 3.13 (Acceptance and Reporting of Gifts, Loans, Bequests, Benefits, or Other Things of Value), 3.15 (Reporting Requirements), 4.1 (Political and Campaign Activities of Judges and Judicial Candidates in General), and 4.5 (Activities of Judges Who Become Candidates for Nonjudicial Office).

VI. Time for Compliance

A person to whom this Code becomes applicable shall comply immediately with its provisions, except that those judges to whom Rules 3.8 (Appointments to Fiduciary Positions) and 3.11 (Financial, Business, or Remunerative Activities) apply shall comply with those Rules as soon as reasonably possible, but in no event later than one year after the Code becomes applicable to the judge.

Amended eff. Jan. 1, 2011.

Comment

[1] If serving as a fiduciary when selected as judge, a new judge may, notwithstanding the prohibitions in Rule 3.8, continue to serve as fiduciary, but only for that period of time necessary to avoid serious adverse consequences to the beneficiaries of the fiduciary relationship and in no event longer than one year. Similarly, if engaged at the time of judicial selection in a business activity, a new judge may, notwithstanding the prohibitions in Rule 3.11, continue in that activity for a reasonable period but in no event longer than one year.

Canon 1

A Judge Shall Uphold and Promote the Independence, Integrity, and Impartiality of the Judiciary, and Shall Avoid Impropriety and the Appearance of Impropriety.

Rule 1.1. Compliance With the Law

A judge shall comply with the law, including the Code of Judicial Conduct.

Adopted Dec. 18, 2008, eff. July 1, 2009.

Historical Notes

The order of the Minnesota Supreme Court [C4–85–697] dated December 18, 2008, substantially revising the Code of Judicial Conduct by adopting in large measure the 2007 American Bar Association Model Code of Judicial Conduct, provided in part that the revised Code of Judicial Conduct was promulgated, and the existing Code of Judicial Conduct abrogated, effective July 1, 2009, and that the revised Code shall apply to all conduct on or after July 1, 2009.

Rule 1.2. Promoting Confidence in the Judiciary

A judge shall act at all times in a manner that promotes public confidence in the independence, integrity, and impartiality of the judiciary, and shall avoid impropriety and the appearance of impropriety.

Adopted Dec. 18, 2008, eff. July 1, 2009.

Comment

[1] Public confidence in the judiciary is eroded by improper conduct and conduct that creates the appearance of impropriety. This principle applies to both the professional and personal conduct of a judge.

[2] A judge should expect to be the subject of public scrutiny that might be viewed as burdensome if applied to other citizens, and must accept the restrictions imposed by the Code.

[3] Conduct that compromises or appears to compromise the independence, integrity, and impartiality of a judge undermines public confidence in the judiciary. Because it is not practicable to list all such conduct, the Rule is necessarily cast in general terms.

[4] Judges should participate in activities that promote ethical conduct among judges and lawyers, support professionalism within the judiciary and the legal profession, and promote access to justice for all.

[5] Actual improprieties include violations of law, court rules, or provisions of this Code. The test for appearance of impropriety is whether the conduct would create in reasonable minds a perception that the judge violated this Code or engaged in other conduct that reflects adversely on the judge's honesty, impartiality, temperament, or fitness to serve as a judge.

[6] A judge should initiate and participate in community outreach activities for the purpose of promoting public understanding of and confidence in the administration of justice. In conducting such activities, the judge must act in a manner consistent with this Code.

Historical Notes

The order of the Minnesota Supreme Court [C4–85–697] dated December 18, 2008, substantially revising the Code of Judicial Conduct by adopting in large measure the 2007 American Bar Association Model Code of Judicial Conduct, provided in part that the revised Code of Judicial Conduct was promulgated, and the existing Code of Judicial Conduct abrogated, effective July 1, 2009, and that the revised Code shall apply to all conduct on or after July 1, 2009.

Rule 1.3. Avoiding Abuse of the Prestige of Judicial Office

A judge shall not abuse the prestige of judicial office to advance the personal or economic interests of the judge or others, or allow others to do so.

Adopted Dec. 18, 2008, eff. July 1, 2009.

Comment

[1] It is improper for a judge to use or attempt to use his or her position to gain personal advantage or deferential treatment of any kind. For example, it would be improper for a judge to allude to his or her judicial status to gain favorable treatment in encounters with traffic officials. Similarly, a judge must not use judicial letterhead to gain an advantage in conducting his or her personal business.

[2] A judge may provide a reference or recommendation for an individual based upon the judge's personal knowledge. The judge may use official letterhead if the judge indicates that the reference is personal and if there is no likelihood that the use of the letterhead would reasonably be perceived as an attempt to exert pressure by reason of the judicial office.

[3] Judges may participate in the process of judicial selection by cooperating with appointing authorities and screening committees, and by responding to inquiries from such entities concerning the professional qualifications of a person being considered for judicial office.

[4] Special considerations arise when judges write or contribute to publications of for-profit entities, whether related or unrelated to the law. A judge should not permit anyone associated with the publication of such materials to exploit the judge's office in a manner that violates this Rule or other applicable law. In contracts for publication of a judge's writing, the judge should retain sufficient control over the advertising to avoid such exploitation.

Historical Notes

The order of the Minnesota Supreme Court [C4–85–697] dated December 18, 2008, substantially revising the Code of Judicial Conduct by adopting in large measure the 2007 American Bar Association Model Code of Judicial Conduct, provided in part that the revised Code of Judicial Conduct was promulgated, and the existing Code of Judicial Conduct abrogated, effective July 1, 2009, and that the revised Code shall apply to all conduct on or after July 1, 2009.

Canon 2

A Judge Shall Perform the Duties of Judicial Office Impartially, Competently, and Diligently.

Rule 2.1. Giving Precedence to the Duties of Judicial Office

The duties of judicial office, as prescribed by law, shall take precedence over all of a judge's personal and extrajudicial activities.

Adopted Dec. 18, 2008, eff. July 1, 2009.

Comment

[1] To ensure that judges are available to fulfill their judicial duties, judges must conduct their personal and extrajudicial activities to minimize the risk of conflicts that would result in frequent disqualification. See Canon 3.

[2] Although it is not a duty of judicial office unless prescribed by law, judges are encouraged to participate in activities that promote public understanding of and confidence in the justice system.

Historical Notes

The order of the Minnesota Supreme Court [C4–85–697] dated December 18, 2008, substantially revising the Code of Judicial Conduct by adopting in large measure the 2007 American Bar Association Model Code of Judicial Conduct, provided in part that the revised Code of Judicial Conduct was promulgated, and the existing Code of Judicial Conduct abrogated, effective July 1, 2009, and that the revised Code shall apply to all conduct on or after July 1, 2009.

Rule 2.2. Impartiality and Fairness

A judge shall uphold and apply the law, and shall perform all duties of judicial office fairly and impartially.

Adopted Dec. 18, 2008, eff. July 1, 2009.

Comment

[1] To ensure impartiality and fairness to all parties, a judge must be objective and open-minded.

[2] Although each judge comes to the bench with a unique background and personal philosophy, a judge must interpret and apply the law without regard to whether the judge approves or disapproves of the law in question.

[3] When applying and interpreting the law, a judge sometimes may make good-faith errors of fact or law. Errors of this kind do not violate this Rule.

[4] It is not a violation of this Rule for a judge to make reasonable accommodations to ensure pro se litigants the opportunity to have their matters fairly heard.

Historical Notes

The order of the Minnesota Supreme Court [C4–85–697] dated December 18, 2008, substantially revising the Code of Judicial Conduct by adopting in large measure the 2007 American Bar Association Model Code of Judicial Conduct, provided in part that the revised Code of Judicial Conduct was promulgated, and the existing Code of Judicial Conduct abrogated, effective July 1, 2009, and that the revised Code shall apply to all conduct on or after July 1, 2009.

Rule 2.3. Bias, Prejudice, and Harassment

(A) A judge shall perform the duties of judicial office, including administrative duties, without bias or prejudice.

(B) A judge shall not, in the performance of judicial duties, by words or conduct manifest bias or prejudice, or engage in harassment, including but not limited to bias, prejudice, or harassment based upon race, sex, gender, religion, national origin, ethnicity, disability, age, sexual orientation, marital status, socioeconomic status, or political affiliation, and shall not permit court staff, court officials, or others subject to the judge's direction and control to do so.

(C) A judge shall require lawyers in proceedings before the court to refrain from manifesting bias or prejudice, or engaging in harassment, against parties, witnesses, lawyers, or others based upon attributes including but not limited to race, sex, gender, religion, national origin, ethnicity, disability, age, sexual orientation, marital status, socioeconomic status, or political affiliation.

(D) The restrictions of paragraphs (B) and (C) do not preclude judges or lawyers from making legitimate reference to the listed factors, or similar factors, when they are relevant to an issue in a proceeding.

Adopted Dec. 18, 2008, eff. July 1, 2009.

Comment

[1] A judge who manifests bias or prejudice in a proceeding impairs the fairness of the proceeding and brings the judiciary into disrepute.

[2] Examples of manifestations of bias or prejudice include but are not limited to epithets; slurs; demeaning nicknames; negative stereotyping; attempted humor based upon stereotypes; threatening, intimidating, or hostile acts; suggestions of connections between race, ethnicity, or nationality and crime; and irrelevant references to personal characteristics. Even facial expressions and body language can convey to parties and lawyers in the proceeding, jurors, the media, and others an appearance of bias or prejudice. A judge must avoid conduct that may reasonably be perceived as prejudiced or biased.

[3] Harassment, as referred to in paragraphs (B) and (C), is verbal or physical conduct that denigrates or shows hostility or aversion toward a person on bases such as race, sex, gender, religion, national origin, ethnicity, disability, age, sexual orientation, marital status, socioeconomic status, or political affiliation.

[4] Sexual harassment includes but is not limited to sexual advances, requests for sexual favors, and other verbal or physical conduct of a sexual nature that is unwelcome.

Historical Notes

The order of the Minnesota Supreme Court [C4–85–697] dated December 18, 2008, substantially revising the Code of Judicial Conduct by adopting in large measure the 2007 American Bar Association Model Code of Judicial Conduct, provided in part that the revised Code of Judicial Conduct was promulgated, and the existing Code of Judicial Conduct abrogated, effective July 1, 2009, and that the revised Code shall apply to all conduct on or after July 1, 2009.

Rule 2.4. External Influences on Judicial Conduct

(A) A judge shall not be swayed by public clamor or fear of criticism.

(B) A judge shall not permit family, social, political, financial, or other interests or relationships to influence the judge's judicial conduct or judgment.

(C) A judge shall not convey or permit others to convey the impression that any person or organization is in a position to influence the judge.

Adopted Dec. 18, 2008, eff. July 1, 2009.

Comment

[1] An independent judiciary requires that judges decide cases according to the law and facts, without regard to whether particular laws or litigants are popular or unpopular with the public, the media, government officials, or the judge's friends or family. Confidence in the judiciary is eroded if judicial decision making is perceived to be subject to inappropriate outside influences.

Historical Notes

The order of the Minnesota Supreme Court [C4–85–697] dated December 18, 2008, substantially revising the Code of Judicial Conduct by adopting in large measure the 2007 American Bar Association Model Code of Judicial Conduct, provided in part that the revised Code of Judicial Conduct was promulgated, and the existing Code of Judicial Conduct abrogated, effective July 1, 2009, and that the revised Code shall apply to all conduct on or after July 1, 2009.

Rule 2.5. Competence, Diligence, and Cooperation

(A) A judge shall perform judicial and administrative duties competently and diligently.

(B) A judge shall cooperate with other judges and court officials in the administration of court business.

Adopted Dec. 18, 2008, eff. July 1, 2009.

Comment

[1] Competence in the performance of judicial duties requires the legal knowledge, skill, thoroughness, and preparation reasonably necessary to perform a judge's responsibilities of judicial office.

[2] A judge should seek the necessary docket time, court staff, expertise, and resources to discharge all adjudicative and administrative responsibilities.

[3] Prompt disposition of the court's business requires a judge to devote adequate time to judicial duties, to be punctual in attending court and expeditious in determining matters under submission, and to take reasonable measures to ensure that court officials, litigants, and their lawyers cooperate with the judge to that end.

[4] In disposing of matters promptly and efficiently, a judge must demonstrate due regard for the rights of parties to be heard and to have issues resolved without unnecessary cost or delay. A judge should monitor and supervise cases in ways that reduce or eliminate dilatory practices, avoidable delays, and unnecessary costs.

Historical Notes

The order of the Minnesota Supreme Court [C4–85–697] dated December 18, 2008, substantially revising the Code of Judicial Conduct by adopting in large measure the 2007 American Bar Association Model Code of Judicial Conduct, provided in part that the revised Code of Judicial Conduct was promulgated, and the existing Code of Judicial Conduct abrogated, effective July 1, 2009, and that the revised Code shall apply to all conduct on or after July 1, 2009.

Rule 2.6. Ensuring the Right to Be Heard

(A) A judge shall accord to every person who has a legal interest in a proceeding, or that person's lawyer, the right to be heard according to law.

(B) A judge may encourage parties to a proceeding and their lawyers to settle matters in dispute but shall not act in a manner that coerces any party into settlement.

Adopted Dec. 18, 2008, eff. July 1, 2009.

Comment

[1] The right to be heard is an essential component of a fair and impartial system of justice. Substantive rights of litigants can be protected only if procedures protecting the right to be heard are observed.

[2] The judge plays an important role in overseeing the settlement of disputes, but should be careful that efforts to further settlement do not undermine any party's right to be heard according to law. The judge should keep in mind the effect that the judge's participation in settlement discussions may have, not only on the judge's own views of the case, but also on the perceptions of the lawyers and the parties if the case remains with the judge after settlement efforts are unsuccessful. Among the factors that a judge should consider when deciding upon an appropriate settlement practice for a case are (1) whether the parties have requested or voluntarily consented to a certain level of participation by the judge in settlement discussions, (2) whether the parties and their counsel are relatively sophisticated in legal matters, (3) whether the case will be tried by the judge or a jury, (4) whether the parties participate with their counsel in settlement discussions, (5) whether any parties are unrepresented by counsel, and (6) whether the matter is civil or criminal.

[3] Judges must be mindful of the effect settlement discussions can have, not only on their objectivity and impartiality, but also on the appearance of their objectivity and impartiality. Despite a judge's best efforts, there may be instances when information obtained during settlement discussions could influence a judge's decision making during trial, and, in such instances, the judge should consider whether disqualification may be appropriate. See Rule 2.11(A)(1).

Historical Notes

The order of the Minnesota Supreme Court [C4–85–697] dated December 18, 2008, substantially revising the Code of Judicial Conduct by adopting in large measure the 2007 American Bar Association Model Code of Judicial Conduct, provided in part that the revised Code of Judicial Conduct was promulgated, and the existing Code of

Judicial Conduct abrogated, effective July 1, 2009, and that the revised Code shall apply to all conduct on or after July 1, 2009.

Rule 2.7. Responsibility to Decide

A judge shall hear and decide matters assigned to the judge, except when disqualification is required by Rule 2.11 or other law.

Adopted Dec. 18, 2008, eff. July 1, 2009.

Comment

[1] Judges must be available to decide the matters that come before the court. Although there are times when disqualification is necessary to protect the rights of litigants and preserve public confidence in the independence, integrity, and impartiality of the judiciary, judges must be available to decide matters that come before the courts. Unwarranted disqualification may bring public disfavor to the court and to the judge personally. The dignity of the court, the judge's respect for fulfillment of judicial duties, and a proper concern for the burdens that may be imposed upon the judge's colleagues require that a judge not use disqualification to avoid cases that present difficult, controversial, or unpopular issues.

Historical Notes

The order of the Minnesota Supreme Court [C4–85–697] dated December 18, 2008, substantially revising the Code of Judicial Conduct by adopting in large measure the 2007 American Bar Association Model Code of Judicial Conduct, provided in part that the revised Code of Judicial Conduct was promulgated, and the existing Code of Judicial Conduct abrogated, effective July 1, 2009, and that the revised Code shall apply to all conduct on or after July 1, 2009.

Rule 2.8. Decorum, Demeanor, and Communication with Jurors

(A) A judge shall require order and decorum in proceedings before the court.

(B) A judge shall be patient, dignified, and courteous to litigants, jurors, witnesses, lawyers, court staff, court officials, and others with whom the judge deals in an official capacity, and shall require similar conduct of lawyers, court staff, court officials, and others subject to the judge's direction and control.

(C) A judge shall not commend or criticize jurors for their verdict other than in a court order or opinion in a proceeding.

Adopted Dec. 18, 2008, eff. July 1, 2009.

Comment

[1] The duty to hear all proceedings with patience and courtesy is not inconsistent with the duty imposed in Rule 2.5 to dispose promptly of the business of the court. Judges can be efficient and businesslike while being patient and deliberate.

[2] Commending or criticizing jurors for their verdict may imply a judicial expectation in future cases and may impair a juror's ability to be fair and impartial in a subsequent case.

[3] A judge who is not otherwise prohibited by law from doing so may meet with jurors who choose to remain after trial but should be careful not to discuss the merits of the case.

Historical Notes

The order of the Minnesota Supreme Court [C4–85–697] dated December 18, 2008, substantially revising the Code of Judicial Conduct by adopting in large measure the 2007 American Bar Association Model Code of Judicial Conduct, provided in part that the revised Code of Judicial Conduct was promulgated, and the existing Code of Judicial Conduct abrogated, effective July 1, 2009, and that the revised Code shall apply to all conduct on or after July 1, 2009.

Rule 2.9. Ex Parte Communications

(A) A judge shall not initiate, permit, or consider ex parte communications, or consider other communications made to the judge outside the presence of the parties or their lawyers, concerning a pending or impending matter, except as follows:

(1) When circumstances require it, ex parte communication for scheduling, administrative, or emergency purposes, which does not address substantive matters, is permitted, provided:

(a) the judge reasonably believes that no party will gain a procedural, substantive, or tactical advantage as a result of the ex parte communication; and

(b) the judge makes provision promptly to notify all other parties of the substance of the ex parte communication, and gives the parties an opportunity to respond.

(2) A judge may obtain the written advice of a disinterested expert on the law applicable to a proceeding before the judge if the judge gives advance notice to the parties of the person to be consulted and the subject matter of the advice to be solicited, and affords the parties a reasonable opportunity to object and respond to the notice and to the advice received.

(3) A judge may consult with court staff and court officials whose functions are to aid the judge in carrying out the judge's adjudicative responsibilities, or with other judges, provided the judge makes reasonable efforts to avoid receiving factual information that is not part of the record, and does not abrogate the responsibility personally to decide the matter.

(4) A judge may, with the consent of the parties, confer separately with the parties and their lawyers in an effort to settle matters pending before the judge.

(5) A judge may initiate, permit, or consider any ex parte communication when expressly authorized by law to do so.

(B) If a judge inadvertently receives an unauthorized ex parte communication bearing upon the substance of a matter, the communication should be noted as received and returned to the sender without review by the judge. If a judge inadvertently reviews an unauthorized ex parte communication bearing upon the substance of a matter, the judge shall make provision to notify the parties promptly of the substance of the communication and provide the parties with an opportunity to respond.

(C) A judge shall not investigate facts in a matter independently, and shall consider only the evidence presented and any facts that may properly be judicially noticed.

(D) A judge shall make reasonable efforts, including providing appropriate supervision, to ensure that this Rule is not violated by court staff, court officials, and others subject to the judge's direction and control.

Adopted Dec. 18, 2008, eff. July 1, 2009.

Comment

[1] To the extent reasonably possible, all parties or their lawyers shall be included in communications with a judge.

[2] Whenever the presence of a party or notice to a party is required by this Rule, it is the party's lawyer, or if the party is unrepresented, the party, who is to be present or to whom notice is to be given.

[3] The proscription against communications concerning a proceeding includes communications with lawyers, law teachers, and other persons who are not participants in the proceeding, except to the limited extent permitted by this Rule.

[4] A judge may initiate, permit, or consider ex parte communications expressly authorized by law, such as when serving on therapeutic or problem-solving courts, mental health courts, or drug courts. In this capacity, judges may assume a more interactive role with parties, treatment providers, probation officers, social workers, and others.

[5] A judge may consult with other judges on pending matters, but must avoid ex parte discussions of a case with judges who have previously been disqualified from hearing the matter, and with judges who have appellate jurisdiction over the matter.

[6] The prohibition against a judge investigating the facts in a matter extends to information available in all mediums, including electronic.

[7] A judge may consult ethics advisory committees, outside counsel, or legal experts concerning the judge's compliance with this Code. Such consultations are not subject to the restrictions of paragraph (A)(2).

Historical Notes

The order of the Minnesota Supreme Court [C4–85–697] dated December 18, 2008, substantially revising the Code of Judicial Conduct by adopting in large measure the 2007 American Bar Association Model Code of Judicial Conduct, provided in part that the revised Code of Judicial Conduct was promulgated, and the existing Code of Judicial Conduct abrogated, effective July 1, 2009, and that the revised Code shall apply to all conduct on or after July 1, 2009.

Rule 2.10. Judicial Statements on Pending and Impending Cases

(A) A judge shall not make any public statement that might reasonably be expected to affect the outcome or impair the fairness of a matter pending or impending in any court, or make any nonpublic statement that might substantially interfere with a fair trial or hearing.

(B) A judge shall not, in connection with cases, controversies, or issues that are likely to come before the court, make pledges, promises, or commitments that are inconsistent with the impartial performance of the adjudicative duties of judicial office.

(C) A judge shall require court staff, court officials, and others subject to the judge's direction and control to refrain from making statements that the judge would be prohibited from making by paragraphs (A) and (B).

(D) Notwithstanding the restrictions in paragraph (A), a judge may make public statements in the course of official duties, may explain court procedures, and may comment on any proceeding in which the judge is a litigant in a personal capacity.

(E) Subject to the requirements of paragraph (A), a judge may respond directly or through a third party to allegations in the media or elsewhere concerning the judge's conduct in a matter.

Adopted Dec. 18, 2008, eff. July 1, 2009.

Comment

[1] This Rule's restrictions on judicial speech are essential to the maintenance of the independence, integrity, and impartiality of the judiciary.

[2] This Rule does not prohibit a judge from commenting on proceedings in which the judge is a litigant in a personal capacity. In cases in which the judge is a litigant in an official capacity, such as a writ of mandamus, the judge must not comment publicly.

[3] Depending upon the circumstances, the judge should consider whether it may be preferable for a third party, rather than the judge, to respond or issue statements in connection with allegations concerning the judge's conduct in a matter.

Historical Notes

The order of the Minnesota Supreme Court [C4–85–697] dated December 18, 2008, substantially revising the Code of Judicial Conduct by adopting in large measure the 2007 American Bar Association Model Code of Judicial Conduct, provided in part that the revised Code of Judicial Conduct was promulgated, and the existing Code of Judicial Conduct abrogated, effective July 1, 2009, and that the revised Code shall apply to all conduct on or after July 1, 2009.

Rule 2.11. Disqualification

(A) A judge shall disqualify himself or herself in any proceeding in which the judge's impartiality might reasonably be questioned, including but not limited to the following circumstances:

(1) The judge has a personal bias or prejudice concerning a party or a party's lawyer, or personal knowledge of facts that are in dispute in the proceeding.

(2) The judge knows that the judge, the judge's spouse, a person with whom the judge has an intimate relationship, a member of the judge's household, or a person within the third degree of relationship to any of them, or the spouse or person in an intimate relationship with such a person is:

(a) a party to the proceeding, or an officer, director, general partner, managing member, or trustee of a party;

(b) acting as a lawyer in the proceeding;

(c) a person who has more than a de minimis interest that could be substantially affected by the proceeding; or

(d) likely to be a material witness in the proceeding.

(3) The judge knows that he or she, individually or as a fiduciary, or the judge's spouse, parent, child, or any other member of the judge's family residing in the judge's household, a person with whom the judge has an intimate relationship, or any other member of the judge's household, has an economic interest in the subject matter in controversy or in a party to the proceeding.

(4) The judge, while a judge or a judicial candidate, has made a public statement, other than in a court proceeding, judicial decision, or opinion, that commits or appears to commit the judge to reach a particular result or rule in a particular way in the proceeding or controversy.

(5) The judge:

(a) served as a lawyer in the matter in controversy, or was associated with a lawyer who participated substantially as a lawyer in the matter during such association;

(b) served in governmental employment, and in such capacity participated personally and substantially as a lawyer or public official concerning the proceeding, or has publicly expressed in such capacity an opinion concerning the merits of the particular matter in controversy;

(c) was a material witness concerning the matter; or

(d) previously presided as a judge over the matter in another court.

(B) A judge shall keep informed about the judge's personal and fiduciary economic interests, and make a reasonable effort to keep informed about the personal economic interests of the judge's spouse, a person with whom the judge has an intimate relationship, and any member of the judge's household.

(C) A judge subject to disqualification under this Rule, other than for bias or prejudice under paragraph (A)(1), may disclose on the record the basis of the judge's disqualification and may ask the parties and their lawyers to consider, outside the presence of the judge and court personnel, whether to waive disqualification. If, following the disclosure, the parties and lawyers agree, without participation by the judge or court personnel, that the judge should not be disqualified, the judge may participate in the proceeding. The agreement shall be incorporated into the record of the proceeding.

Adopted Dec. 18, 2008, eff. July 1, 2009.

Comment

[1] Under this Rule, a judge is disqualified whenever the judge's impartiality might reasonably be questioned, regardless of whether any of the specific provisions of paragraphs (A)(1) through (5) apply. In many jurisdictions, the term "recusal" is used interchangeably with the term "disqualification."

[2] A judge's obligation not to hear or decide matters in which disqualification is required applies regardless of whether a motion to disqualify is filed.

[3] The rule of necessity may override the rule of disqualification. For example, a judge might be required to participate in judicial review of a judicial salary statute, or might be the only judge available in a matter requiring immediate judicial action, such as a hearing on probable cause or a temporary restraining order. In matters that require immediate action, the judge must disclose on the record the basis for possible disqualification and make reasonable efforts to transfer the matter to another judge as soon as practicable.

[4] The fact that a lawyer in a proceeding is affiliated with a law firm with which a relative of the judge is affiliated does not itself disqualify the judge. If, however, the judge's impartiality might reasonably be questioned under paragraph (A), or the relative is known by the judge to have an interest in the law firm that could be substantially affected by the proceeding under paragraph (A)(2)(c), the judge's disqualification is required.

[5] A judge should disclose on the record information that the judge believes the parties or their lawyers might reasonably consider relevant to a possible motion for disqualification, even if the judge believes there is no basis for disqualification.

[6] "Economic interest," as set forth in the Terminology section, means ownership of more than a de minimis legal or equitable interest. Except for situations in which a judge participates in the management of such a legal or equitable interest, or the interest could be substantially affected by the outcome of a proceeding before a judge, it does not include:

(1) an interest in the individual holdings within a mutual or common investment fund;

(2) an interest in securities held by an educational, religious, charitable, fraternal, or civic organization in which the judge or the judge's spouse, parent, child, a member of the judge's household, or a person with whom the judge has an intimate relationship serves as a director, officer, advisor, or other participant;

(3) a deposit in a financial institution or deposits or proprietary interests the judge may maintain as a member of a mutual savings association or credit union, or similar proprietary interests; or

(4) an interest in the issuer of government securities held by the judge.

Historical Notes

The order of the Minnesota Supreme Court [C4–85–697] dated December 18, 2008, substantially revising the Code of Judicial Conduct by adopting in large measure the 2007 American Bar Association Model Code of Judicial Conduct, provided in part that the revised Code of Judicial Conduct was promulgated, and the existing Code of Judicial Conduct abrogated, effective July 1, 2009, and that the revised Code shall apply to all conduct on or after July 1, 2009.

Rule 2.12. Supervisory Duties

(A) A judge shall require court staff, court officials, and others subject to the judge's direction and control to act in a manner consistent with the judge's obligations under this Code.

(B) A judge with supervisory authority for the performance of other judges shall take reasonable measures to ensure that those judges properly discharge their judicial responsibilities, including the prompt disposition of matters before them.

Adopted Dec. 18, 2008, eff. July 1, 2009.

Comment

[1] A judge is responsible for his or her own conduct and for the conduct of others, such as staff, when those persons are acting at the judge's direction or control. A judge may not direct court personnel to engage in conduct on the judge's behalf or as the judge's representative when such conduct would violate the Code if undertaken by the judge.

[2] Public confidence in the judicial system depends upon timely justice. To promote the efficient administration of justice, a judge with supervisory authority must take the steps needed to ensure that judges under his or her supervision administer their workloads promptly.

Historical Notes

The order of the Minnesota Supreme Court [C4–85–697] dated December 18, 2008, substantially revising the Code of Judicial Conduct by adopting in large measure the 2007 American Bar Association Model Code of Judicial Conduct, provided in part that the revised Code of Judicial Conduct was promulgated, and the existing Code of Judicial Conduct abrogated, effective July 1, 2009, and that the revised Code shall apply to all conduct on or after July 1, 2009.

Rule 2.13. Administrative Appointments

(A) In making administrative appointments, a judge:

(1) shall exercise the power of appointment impartially and on the basis of merit; and

(2) shall avoid nepotism, favoritism, and unnecessary appointments.

(B) A judge shall not approve compensation of appointees beyond the fair value of services rendered.

Adopted Dec. 18, 2008, eff. July 1, 2009.

Comment

[1] Appointees of a judge include assigned counsel, officials such as referees, commissioners, special masters, receivers, and guardians, and personnel such as clerks, secretaries, and bailiffs. Consent by the parties to an appointment or an award of compensation does not relieve the judge of the obligation prescribed by paragraph (A).

[2] Unless otherwise defined by law, nepotism is the appointment or hiring of any relative within the third degree of relationship of the judge, the judge's spouse, a person in an intimate relationship with the judge, a member of the judge's household, or the spouse or person in an intimate relationship with such person.

Historical Notes

The order of the Minnesota Supreme Court [C4–85–697] dated December 18, 2008, substantially revising the Code of Judicial Conduct by adopting in large measure the 2007 American Bar Association Model Code of Judicial Conduct, provided in part that the revised Code of Judicial Conduct was promulgated, and the existing Code of Judicial Conduct abrogated, effective July 1, 2009, and that the revised Code shall apply to all conduct on or after July 1, 2009.

Rule 2.14. Disability and Impairment

A judge having a reasonable belief that the performance of a lawyer or another judge is impaired by drugs or alcohol, or by a mental, emotional, or physical condition, shall take appropriate action, which may include a confidential referral to a lawyer or judicial assistance program.

Adopted Dec. 18, 2008, eff. July 1, 2009.

Comment

[1] "Appropriate action" means action intended and reasonably likely to help the judge or lawyer in question address the problem and prevent harm to the justice system. Depending upon the circumstances, appropriate action may include but is not limited to speaking directly to the impaired person, notifying an individual with supervisory responsibility over the impaired person, or making a referral to an assistance program.

[2] Taking or initiating corrective action by way of referral to an assistance program may satisfy a judge's responsibility under this Rule. Assistance programs have many approaches for offering help to impaired judges and lawyers, such as intervention, counseling, or referral to appropriate health care professionals. Depending upon the gravity of the conduct that has come to the judge's attention, however, the judge may be required to take other action, such as reporting the impaired judge or lawyer to the appropriate authority, agency, or body. See Rule 2.15.

Historical Notes

The order of the Minnesota Supreme Court [C4–85–697] dated December 18, 2008, substantially revising the Code of Judicial Conduct by adopting in large measure the 2007 American Bar Association Model Code of Judicial Conduct, provided in part that the revised Code of Judicial Conduct was promulgated, and the existing Code of Judicial Conduct abrogated, effective July 1, 2009, and that the revised Code shall apply to all conduct on or after July 1, 2009.

Rule 2.15. Responding to Judicial and Lawyer Misconduct

(A) A judge having knowledge that another judge has committed a violation of this Code that raises a substantial question regarding the judge's honesty, trustworthiness, or fitness as a judge in other respects shall inform the appropriate authority.

(B) A judge having knowledge that a lawyer has committed a violation of the Rules of Professional Conduct that raises a substantial question regarding the lawyer's honesty, trustworthiness, or fitness as a lawyer in other respects shall inform the appropriate authority.

(C) A judge who receives credible information indicating a substantial likelihood that another judge has committed a violation of this Code shall take appropriate action.

(D) A judge who receives credible information indicating a substantial likelihood that a lawyer has committed a violation of the Rules of Professional Conduct shall take appropriate action.

Adopted Dec. 18, 2008, eff. July 1, 2009.

Comment

[1] Taking action to address known misconduct is a judge's obligation. Paragraphs (A) and (B) impose an obligation on the judge to report to the appropriate disciplinary authority the known misconduct of another judge or a lawyer that raises a substantial question regarding the honesty, trustworthiness, or fitness of that judge or lawyer. Ignoring or denying known misconduct among one's judicial colleagues or members of the legal profession undermines a judge's responsibility to participate in efforts to ensure public respect for the justice system. This Rule limits the reporting obligation to those offenses that an independent judiciary must vigorously endeavor to prevent.

[2] A judge who does not have actual knowledge that another judge or a lawyer may have committed misconduct, but receives credible information indicating a substantial likelihood of such misconduct, is required to take appropriate action under paragraphs (C) and (D). Appropriate action may include, but is not limited to, communicating directly with the judge who may have violated this Code, communicating with a supervising judge, or reporting the suspected violation to the appropriate authority or other agency or body. Similarly, actions to be taken in response to credible information indicating that a lawyer has committed a violation of the Rules of Professional Conduct may include, but are not limited to, communicating directly with the lawyer who may have committed the violation, or reporting the suspected violation to the appropriate authority or other agency or body.

Historical Notes

The order of the Minnesota Supreme Court [C4–85–697] dated December 18, 2008, substantially revising the Code of Judicial Conduct by adopting in large measure the 2007 American Bar Association Model Code of Judicial Conduct, provided in part that the revised Code of Judicial Conduct was promulgated, and the existing Code of Judicial Conduct abrogated, effective July 1, 2009, and that the revised Code shall apply to all conduct on or after July 1, 2009.

Rule 2.16. Cooperation with Disciplinary Authorities

(A) A judge shall cooperate and be candid and honest with judicial and lawyer disciplinary agencies.

(B) A judge shall not retaliate, directly or indirectly, against a person known or suspected to have assisted or cooperated with an investigation of a judge or a lawyer.

Adopted Dec. 18, 2008, eff. July 1, 2009.

Comment

[1] Cooperation with investigations and proceedings of judicial and lawyer discipline agencies, as required in paragraph (A), instills confidence in judges' commitment to the integrity of the judicial system and the protection of the public.

Historical Notes

The order of the Minnesota Supreme Court [C4–85–697] dated December 18, 2008, substantially revising the Code of Judicial Conduct by adopting in large measure the 2007 American Bar Association Model Code of Judicial Conduct, provided in part that the revised Code of Judicial Conduct was promulgated, and the existing Code of Judicial Conduct abrogated, effective July 1, 2009, and that the revised Code shall apply to all conduct on or after July 1, 2009.

Canon 3

A Judge Shall Conduct the Judge's Personal and Extrajudicial Activities to Minimize the Risk of Conflict with the Obligations of Judicial Office.

Rule 3.1. Extrajudicial Activities in General

A judge may engage in extrajudicial activities, except as prohibited by law or this Code. However, when engaging in extrajudicial activities, a judge shall not:

(A) participate in activities that will interfere with the proper performance of the judge's judicial duties;

(B) participate in activities that will lead to frequent disqualification of the judge;

(C) participate in activities that would appear to a reasonable person to undermine the judge's independence, integrity, or impartiality;

(D) engage in conduct that would appear to a reasonable person to be coercive; or

(E) make use of court premises, staff, stationery, equipment, or other resources, except for incidental use for activities that concern the law, the legal system, or the administration of justice, or unless such additional use is permitted by law or Judicial Branch policy.

Adopted Dec. 18, 2008, eff. July 1, 2009.

Comment

[1] To the extent that time permits, and judicial independence and impartiality are not compromised, judges are encouraged to engage in appropriate extrajudicial activities. Judges are uniquely qualified to engage in extrajudicial activities that concern the law, the legal system, and the administration of justice, such as by speaking, writing, teaching, or participating in scholarly research projects. In addition, judges are permitted and encouraged to engage in educational, religious, charitable, fraternal, or civic extrajudicial activities not conducted for profit, even when the activities do not involve the law. See Rule 3.7.

[2] Participation in both law-related and other extrajudicial activities helps integrate judges into their communities, and furthers public understanding of and respect for courts and the judicial system.

[3] Discriminatory actions and expressions of bias or prejudice by a judge, even outside the judge's official or judicial actions, are likely to appear to a reasonable person to call into question the judge's integrity and impartiality. Examples include jokes or other remarks that demean individuals based upon their race, sex, gender, religion, national origin, ethnicity, disability, age, sexual orientation, or socioeconomic status. For the same reason, a judge's extrajudicial activities must not be conducted in connection or affiliation with an organization that practices unlawful discrimination. See Rule 3.6.

[4] While engaged in permitted extrajudicial activities, judges must not coerce others or take action that would reasonably be perceived as coercive. For example, depending upon the circumstances, a judge's solicitation of contributions or memberships for an organization, even as permitted by Rule 3.7(A), might create the risk that the person solicited would feel obligated to respond favorably, or would do so to curry favor with the judge.

Historical Notes

The order of the Minnesota Supreme Court [C4–85–697] dated December 18, 2008, substantially revising the Code of Judicial Conduct by adopting in large measure the 2007 American Bar Association Model Code of Judicial Conduct, provided in part that the revised Code of Judicial Conduct was promulgated, and the existing Code of Judicial Conduct abrogated, effective July 1, 2009, and that the revised Code shall apply to all conduct on or after July 1, 2009.

Rule 3.2. Appearances before Governmental Bodies and Consultation with Government Officials

A judge shall not appear voluntarily at a public hearing before, or otherwise consult with, an executive or a legislative body or official, except:

(A) in connection with matters concerning the law, the legal system, or the administration of justice;

(B) in connection with matters about which the judge acquired knowledge or expertise in the course of the judge's judicial duties; or

(C) when the judge is acting pro se in a matter involving the judge's legal or economic interests, or when the judge is acting in a fiduciary capacity.

Adopted Dec. 18, 2008, eff. July 1, 2009.

Comment

[1] Judges possess special expertise in matters of law, the legal system, and the administration of justice, and may properly share that expertise with governmental bodies and executive or legislative branch officials.

[2] In appearing before governmental bodies or consulting with government officials, judges must be mindful that they remain subject to other provisions of this Code, such as Rule 1.3, prohibiting judges from using the prestige of office to advance their own or others' interests, Rule 2.10, governing public comment on pending and impending matters, and Rule 3.1(C), prohibiting judges from engaging in extrajudicial activities that would appear to a reasonable person to undermine the judge's independence, integrity, or impartiality.

[3] In general, it would be an unnecessary and unfair burden to prohibit judges from appearing before governmental bodies or consulting with government officials on matters that are likely to affect them as private citizens, such as zoning proposals affecting their real property. In engaging in such activities, however, judges must not refer to their judicial positions, and must otherwise exercise caution to avoid using the prestige of judicial office.

Historical Notes

The order of the Minnesota Supreme Court [C4–85–697] dated December 18, 2008, substantially revising the Code of Judicial Conduct by adopting in large measure the 2007 American Bar Association Model Code of Judicial Conduct, provided in part that the revised Code of Judicial Conduct was promulgated, and the existing Code of Judicial Conduct abrogated, effective July 1, 2009, and that the revised Code shall apply to all conduct on or after July 1, 2009.

Rule 3.3. Testifying as a Character Witness

A judge shall not testify as a character witness in a judicial, administrative, or other adjudicatory proceeding or otherwise vouch for the character of a person in a legal proceeding, except when duly summoned.

Adopted Dec. 18, 2008, eff. July 1, 2009.

Comment

[1] A judge who, without being subpoenaed, testifies as a character witness abuses the prestige of judicial office to advance the interests of another. See Rule 1.3. Except in unusual circumstances where the demands of justice require, a judge should discourage a party from requiring the judge to testify as a character witness.

Historical Notes

The order of the Minnesota Supreme Court [C4–85–697] dated December 18, 2008, substantially revising the Code of Judicial Conduct by adopting in large measure the 2007 American Bar Association Model Code of Judicial Conduct, provided in part that the revised Code of Judicial Conduct was promulgated, and the existing Code of Judicial Conduct abrogated, effective July 1, 2009, and that the revised Code shall apply to all conduct on or after July 1, 2009.

Rule 3.4. Appointments to Governmental Positions

A judge shall not accept appointment to a governmental committee, board, commission, or other governmental position, unless it is one that concerns the law, the legal system, or the administration of justice.

Adopted Dec. 18, 2008, eff. July 1, 2009.

Comment

[1] Rule 3.4 implicitly acknowledges the value of judges accepting appointments to entities that concern the law, the legal system, or the administration of justice. Even in such instances, however, a judge should assess the appropriateness of accepting an appointment, paying particular attention to the subject matter of the appointment and the availability and allocation of judicial resources, including the judge's time commitments, and giving due regard to the requirements of the independence and impartiality of the judiciary.

[2] A judge may represent his or her country, state, or locality on ceremonial occasions or in connection with historical, educational, or cultural activities. Such representation does not constitute acceptance of a government position.

Historical Notes

The order of the Minnesota Supreme Court [C4–85–697] dated December 18, 2008, substantially revising the Code of Judicial Conduct by adopting in large measure the 2007 American Bar Association Model Code of Judicial Conduct, provided in part that the revised Code of Judicial Conduct was promulgated, and the existing Code of Judicial Conduct abrogated, effective July 1, 2009, and that the revised Code shall apply to all conduct on or after July 1, 2009.

Rule 3.5. Use of Nonpublic Information

A judge shall not intentionally disclose or use nonpublic information acquired in a judicial capacity for any purpose unrelated to the judge's judicial duties.

Adopted Dec. 18, 2008, eff. July 1, 2009.

Comment

[1] In the course of performing judicial duties, a judge may acquire information of commercial or other value that is unavailable to the public. The judge must not reveal or use such information for personal gain or for any purpose unrelated to his or her judicial duties.

[2] This rule is not intended, however, to affect a judge's ability to act on information as necessary to protect the health or safety of the judge or a member of a judge's family, court personnel, or other judicial officers if consistent with other provisions of this Code.

Historical Notes

The order of the Minnesota Supreme Court [C4–85–697] dated December 18, 2008, substantially revising the Code of Judicial Conduct by adopting in large measure the 2007 American Bar Association Model Code of Judicial Conduct, provided in part that the revised Code of Judicial Conduct was promulgated, and the existing Code of Judicial Conduct abrogated, effective July 1, 2009, and that the revised Code shall apply to all conduct on or after July 1, 2009.

Rule 3.6. Affiliation with Discriminatory Organizations

(A) A judge shall not knowingly hold membership in any organization that practices unlawful discrimination.

(B) A judge shall not use the benefits or facilities of an organization if the judge knows or should know that the organization practices unlawful discrimination. A judge's attendance at an event in a facility of an organization that the judge is not permitted to join is not a violation of this Rule when the judge's attendance is an isolated event that could not reasonably be perceived as an endorsement of the organization's practices.

Adopted Dec. 18, 2008, eff. July 1, 2009.

Comment

[1] A judge's public manifestation of approval of unlawful discrimination on any basis gives rise to the appearance of impropriety and diminishes public confidence in the integrity and impartiality of the judiciary. A judge's membership in an organization that practices unlawful discrimination creates the perception that the judge's impartiality is impaired.

[2] An organization is generally said to discriminate unlawfully if it arbitrarily excludes from membership on the basis of race, sex, gender, religion, national origin, ethnicity, sexual orientation, or other classification protected by law, persons who would otherwise be eligible for admission. Whether an organization practices unlawful discrimination is a complex question to which judges should be attentive. The answer cannot be determined from a mere examination of an organization's current membership rolls, but rather, depends upon how the organization selects members, as well as other relevant factors, such as whether the organization is dedicated to the preservation of religious, ethnic, or cultural values of legitimate common interest to its members, or whether it is an intimate, purely private organization whose membership limitations could not constitutionally be prohibited.

[3] When a judge learns that an organization to which the judge belongs engages in unlawful discrimination, the judge must resign immediately from the organization.

[4] A judge's membership in a religious organization as a lawful exercise of the freedom of religion is not a violation of this Rule.

[5] This Rule does not apply to national or state military service.

Historical Notes

The order of the Minnesota Supreme Court [C4–85–697] dated December 18, 2008, substantially revising the Code of Judicial Conduct by adopting in large measure the 2007 American Bar Association Model Code of Judicial Conduct, provided in part that the revised Code of Judicial Conduct was promulgated, and the existing Code of Judicial Conduct abrogated, effective July 1, 2009, and that the revised Code shall apply to all conduct on or after July 1, 2009.

Rule 3.7. Participation in Educational, Religious, Charitable, Fraternal, or Civic Organizations and Activities

(A) Subject to the requirements of Rule 3.1, a judge may participate in activities sponsored by organizations or governmental entities concerned with the law, the legal system, or the administration of justice, and those sponsored by or on behalf of educational, religious, charitable, fraternal, or civic organizations not conducted for profit, including but not limited to the following activities:

(1) assisting such an organization or entity in planning related to fund-raising, and participating in the management and investment of the organization's or entity's funds;

(2) soliciting funds and services for such an organization or entity, but only from members of the judge's family, from a person with whom the judge has an intimate relationship, or from judges over whom the judge does not exercise supervisory or appellate authority;

(3) soliciting membership for such an organization or entity, if there are no dues or fees required for membership;

(4) appearing or speaking at, receiving an award or other recognition at, being featured on the program of, and permitting his or her title to be used in connection with an event of such an organization or entity, unless the event serves a fund-raising purpose;

(5) making recommendations to an organization or entity of which the judge is a member or director concerning its fund-granting programs and activities; and

(6) serving as an officer, director, trustee, or nonlegal advisor of such an organization or entity, unless it is likely that the organization or entity:

(a) will be engaged in proceedings that would ordinarily come before the judge; or

(b) will frequently be engaged in adversary proceedings in the court of which the judge is a member, or in any court subject to the appellate jurisdiction of the court of which the judge is a member.

(B) A judge may encourage lawyers to provide pro bono publico legal services.

Adopted Dec. 18, 2008, eff. July 1, 2009.

Comment

[1] The activities permitted by paragraph (A) generally include those sponsored by or undertaken on behalf of public or private not-for-profit educational institutions, and other not-for-profit organizations, including law-related, charitable, and other organizations.

[2] Even for law-related organizations, a judge should consider whether the membership and purposes of the organization, or the nature of the judge's participation in or association with the organization, would conflict with the judge's obligation to refrain from activities that reflect adversely upon a judge's independence, integrity, and impartiality.

[3] Mere attendance at an event, whether or not the event serves a fund-raising purpose, does not constitute a violation of paragraph (A)(4). It is also generally permissible for a judge to serve as an usher or a food server or preparer, or to perform similar functions, at fund-raising events sponsored by educational, religious, charitable, fraternal, or civic organizations. Such activities are not solicitation and do not present an element of coercion or abuse the prestige of judicial office.

[4] In addition to appointing lawyers to serve as counsel for indigent parties in individual cases, a judge may promote broader access to justice by encouraging lawyers to participate in pro bono publico legal services, if in doing so the judge does not employ coercion, or abuse the prestige of judicial office. Such encouragement may take many forms, including providing lists of available programs, training lawyers to do pro bono publico legal work, and participating in events recognizing lawyers who have done pro bono publico work.

Historical Notes

The order of the Minnesota Supreme Court [C4–85–697] dated December 18, 2008, substantially revising the Code of Judicial Conduct by adopting in large measure the 2007 American Bar Association Model Code of Judicial Conduct, provided in part that the revised Code of Judicial Conduct was promulgated, and the existing Code of Judicial Conduct abrogated, effective July 1, 2009, and that the revised Code shall apply to all conduct on or after July 1, 2009.

Rule 3.8. Appointments to Fiduciary Positions

(A) A judge shall not accept appointment to serve in a fiduciary position, such as executor, administrator, trustee, guardian, attorney in fact, or other personal representative, except for the estate, trust, or person of a member of the judge's family, a person with whom the judge has an intimate relationship, or a member of the judge's household and then only if such service will not interfere with the proper performance of judicial duties.

(B) A judge shall not serve in a fiduciary position if the judge as fiduciary will likely be engaged in proceedings that would ordinarily come before the judge, or if the estate, trust, or ward becomes involved in adversary proceedings in the court on which the judge serves, or one under its appellate jurisdiction.

(C) A judge acting in a fiduciary capacity shall be subject to the same restrictions on engaging in financial activities that apply to a judge personally.

(D) If a person who is serving in a fiduciary position becomes a judge, he or she must comply with this Rule as soon as reasonably practicable, but in no event later than one year after becoming a judge.

Adopted Dec. 18, 2008, eff. July 1, 2009.

Comment

[1] A judge should recognize that other restrictions imposed by this Code may conflict with a judge's obligations as a fiduciary; in such circumstances, a judge should resign as fiduciary. For example, serving as a fiduciary might require frequent disqualification of a judge under Rule 2.11 because a judge is deemed to have an economic interest in shares of stock held by a trust if the amount of stock held is more than de minimis.

Historical Notes

The order of the Minnesota Supreme Court [C4–85–697] dated December 18, 2008, substantially revising the Code of Judicial Conduct by adopting in large measure the 2007 American Bar Association Model Code of Judicial Conduct, provided in part that the revised Code of Judicial Conduct was promulgated, and the existing Code of Judicial Conduct abrogated, effective July 1, 2009, and that the revised Code shall apply to all conduct on or after July 1, 2009.

Rule 3.9. Service as Arbitrator or Mediator

A judge shall not act as an arbitrator or a mediator or otherwise perform judicial functions in a private capacity unless expressly authorized by law. A retired judge may act as mediator or arbitrator if:

(A) The judge does not act as an arbitrator or mediator during the period of any judicial assignment;

(B) The judge is disqualified from mediation and arbitration in matters in which the judge served as judge, and is disqualified as judge from matters in which the judge acted as mediator or arbitrator, unless all parties to the proceeding consent after consultation with their attorneys; and

(C) Acting as arbitrator or mediator does not reflect adversely on the judge's impartiality.

Adopted Dec. 18, 2008, eff. July 1, 2009.

Comment

[1] This Rule does not prohibit a judge from participating in arbitration, mediation, or settlement conferences performed as part of assigned judicial duties. Rendering dispute resolution services apart from those duties, whether or not for economic gain, is prohibited unless it is expressly authorized by law.

[2] A retired judge may act as a mediator or arbitrator under the conditions set forth in the rule.

Historical Notes

The order of the Minnesota Supreme Court [C4–85–697] dated December 18, 2008, substantially revising the Code of Judicial Conduct by adopting in large measure the 2007 American Bar Association Model Code of Judicial Conduct, provided in part that the revised Code of Judicial Conduct was promulgated, and the existing Code of Judicial Conduct abrogated, effective July 1, 2009, and that the revised Code shall apply to all conduct on or after July 1, 2009.

Rule 3.10. Practice of Law

A judge shall not practice law. A judge may act pro se and may, without compensation, give legal advice to and draft or review documents for a member of the judge's family, a person with whom the judge has an intimate relationship, or a member of the judge's household, but is prohibited from serving as the lawyer for any such person in any forum.

Adopted Dec. 18, 2008, eff. July 1, 2009.

Comment

[1] A judge may act pro se in all legal matters, including matters involving litigation and matters involving appearances before or other dealings with governmental bodies. A judge must not use the prestige of office to advance the judge's personal or family interests. See Rule 1.3.

Historical Notes

The order of the Minnesota Supreme Court [C4–85–697] dated December 18, 2008, substantially revising the Code of Judicial Conduct by adopting in large measure the 2007 American Bar Association Model Code of Judicial Conduct, provided in part that the revised Code of Judicial Conduct was promulgated, and the existing Code of Judicial Conduct abrogated, effective July 1, 2009, and that the revised Code shall apply to all conduct on or after July 1, 2009.

Rule 3.11. Financial, Business, or Remunerative Activities

(A) A judge may hold and manage investments of the judge and members of the judge's family and of persons with whom the judge has an intimate relationship or who are members of the judge's household.

(B) A judge shall not serve as an officer, director, manager, general partner, advisor, or employee of any business entity except that a judge may manage or participate in:

(1) a business closely held by the judge or members of the judge's family or by a person with whom the judge has an intimate relationship or who is a member of the judge's household; or

(2) a business entity primarily engaged in investment of the financial resources of the judge, members of the judge's family, or a person with whom the judge has an intimate relationship or who is a member of the judge's household.

(C) A judge shall not engage in financial activities permitted under paragraphs (A) and (B) if they will:

(1) interfere with the proper performance of judicial duties;

(2) lead to frequent disqualification of the judge;

(3) involve the judge in frequent transactions or continuing business relationships with lawyers or other persons likely to come before the court on which the judge serves; or

(4) result in violation of other provisions of this Code.

Adopted Dec. 18, 2008, eff. July 1, 2009.

Comment

[1] Judges are generally permitted to engage in financial activities, including managing real estate and other investments for themselves, for members of their families, and for those with whom they have

intimate relationships or who are members of their households. Participation in these activities, like participation in other extrajudicial activities, is subject to the requirements of this Code. For example, it would be improper for a judge to spend so much time on business activities that it interferes with the performance of judicial duties. See Rule 2.1. Similarly, it would be improper for a judge to use his or her official title or appear in judicial robes in business advertising, or to conduct his or her business or financial affairs in such a way that disqualification is frequently required. See Rules 1.3 and 2.11.

[2] As soon as practicable without serious financial detriment, the judge must divest himself or herself of investments and other financial interests that might require frequent disqualification or otherwise violate this Rule.

Historical Notes

The order of the Minnesota Supreme Court [C4–85–697] dated December 18, 2008, substantially revising the Code of Judicial Conduct by adopting in large measure the 2007 American Bar Association Model Code of Judicial Conduct, provided in part that the revised Code of Judicial Conduct was promulgated, and the existing Code of Judicial Conduct abrogated, effective July 1, 2009, and that the revised Code shall apply to all conduct on or after July 1, 2009.

Rule 3.12. Compensation for Extrajudicial Activities

A judge may accept reasonable compensation for extrajudicial activities permitted by this Code or other law unless such acceptance would appear to a reasonable person to undermine the judge's independence, integrity, or impartiality.

Adopted Dec. 18, 2008, eff. July 1, 2009.

Comment

[1] A judge is permitted to accept honoraria, stipends, fees, wages, salaries, royalties, or other compensation for speaking, teaching, writing, and other extrajudicial activities, provided the compensation is reasonable and commensurate with the task performed. The judge should be mindful, however, that judicial duties must take precedence over other activities. See Rule 2.1.

[2] Compensation derived from extrajudicial activities may be subject to public reporting. See Rule 3.15.

Historical Notes

The order of the Minnesota Supreme Court [C4–85–697] dated December 18, 2008, substantially revising the Code of Judicial Conduct by adopting in large measure the 2007 American Bar Association Model Code of Judicial Conduct, provided in part that the revised Code of Judicial Conduct was promulgated, and the existing Code of Judicial Conduct abrogated, effective July 1, 2009, and that the revised Code shall apply to all conduct on or after July 1, 2009.

Rule 3.13. Acceptance and Reporting of Gifts, Loans, Bequests, Benefits, or Other Things of Value

(A) A judge shall not accept any gifts, loans, bequests, benefits, or other things of value, if acceptance is prohibited by law or would appear to a reasonable person to undermine the judge's independence, integrity, or impartiality.

(B) Unless otherwise prohibited by law, or by paragraph (A), a judge may accept the following without publicly reporting such acceptance:

(1) items with little intrinsic value, such as plaques, certificates, trophies, and greeting cards;

(2) gifts, loans, bequests, benefits, or other things of value from friends, relatives, or other persons, including lawyers, whose appearance or interest in a proceeding pending or impending before the judge would in any event require disqualification of the judge under Rule 2.11;

(3) ordinary social hospitality;

(4) commercial or financial opportunities and benefits, including special pricing and discounts, and loans from lending institutions in their regular course of business, if the same opportunities and benefits or loans are made available on the same terms to similarly situated persons who are not judges;

(5) rewards and prizes given to competitors or participants in random drawings, contests, or other events that are open to persons who are not judges;

(6) scholarships, fellowships, and similar benefits or awards, if they are available to similarly situated persons who are not judges, based upon the same terms and criteria;

(7) books, magazines, journals, audiovisual materials, and other resource materials supplied by publishers on a complimentary basis for official use;

(8) gifts, awards, or benefits associated with the business, profession, or other separate activity of a spouse, a person with whom the judge has an intimate relationship, or a member of the judge's household, but that incidentally benefit the judge;

(9) gifts incident to a public testimonial;

(10) an invitation to the judge and the judge's spouse, a person in an intimate relationship with the judge, a member of the judge's household, or a guest to attend without charge:

(a) an event associated with a bar-related function or other activity relating to the law, the legal system, or the administration of justice; or

(b) an event associated with any of the judge's educational, religious, charitable, fraternal, or civic activities permitted by this Code, if the same invitation is offered to non-judges who are engaged in similar ways in the activity as is the judge; or

(11) any other gift, loan, bequest, benefit, or other thing of value with a value not exceeding $150, if the source is not a party or other person who, directly or indirectly, has come or is likely to come

before the judge, or whose interests have come or are likely to come before the judge.

(C) Unless otherwise prohibited by law or by paragraph (A), a judge may accept the following items, and must report such acceptance in the same manner as the judge reports compensation under Rule 3.15:

(1) any other gift, loan, bequest, benefit, or other thing of value not described in paragraphs (B)(1)–(10) above with a value exceeding $150; and

(2) any other gift, loan, bequest, benefit, or other thing of value not described in paragraphs (B)(1)–(10) above, if the source is a party or other person who, directly or indirectly, has come before the judge or is likely to come before the judge, or whose interests have come or are likely to come before the judge.

Adopted Dec. 18, 2008, eff. July 1, 2009.

Comment

[1] Whenever a judge accepts a gift or other thing of value without paying fair market value, there is a risk that the benefit might be viewed as intended to influence the judge's decision in a case. Rule 3.13 imposes restrictions upon the acceptance of such benefits, according to the magnitude of the risk. Paragraph (A) prohibits acceptance where expressly prohibited by law or where the judge's independence, integrity, or impartiality would be compromised by acceptance. Paragraph (B) identifies circumstances in which the risk that the acceptance would appear to undermine the judge's independence, integrity, or impartiality is low, and explicitly provides that such items need not be publicly reported. As the value of the benefit or the likelihood that the source of the benefit will appear before the judge increases, the judge is either prohibited under paragraph (A) from accepting the gift, or required under paragraph (C) to publicly report it.

[2] Gift-giving between friends and relatives is a common occurrence, and ordinarily does not create an appearance of impropriety or cause reasonable persons to believe that the judge's independence, integrity, or impartiality has been compromised. In addition, when the appearance of friends or relatives in a case would require the judge's disqualification under Rule 2.11, there would be no opportunity for a gift to influence the judge's decision making. Paragraph (B)(2) places no restrictions upon the ability of a judge to accept gifts or other things of value from friends or relatives under these circumstances, and does not require public reporting.

[3] Businesses and financial institutions frequently make available special pricing, discounts, and other benefits, either in connection with a temporary promotion or for preferred customers, based upon longevity of the relationship, volume of business transacted, and other factors. A judge may freely accept such benefits if they are available to the general public, or if the judge qualifies for the special price or discount according to the same criteria as are applied to persons who are not judges. As an example, loans provided at generally prevailing interest rates are not gifts, but a judge could not accept a loan from a financial institution at below-market interest rates unless the same rate was being made available to the general public for a certain period of time or only to borrowers with specified qualifications that the judge also possesses.

[4] Rule 3.13 applies only to acceptance of gifts or other things of value by a judge. Nonetheless, if a gift or other benefit is given to the judge's spouse, a person in an intimate relationship with the judge, or a member of the judge's household, it may be viewed as an attempt to evade Rule 3.13 and influence the judge indirectly. Where the gift or benefit is being made primarily to such other persons, and the judge is merely an incidental beneficiary, this concern is reduced. A judge should, however, remind family, intimates, and household members of the restrictions imposed upon judges, and urge them to take these restrictions into account when making decisions about accepting such gifts or benefits.

[5] Rule 3.13 does not apply to contributions to a judge's campaign for judicial office. Such contributions are governed by other Rules of this Code, including Rules 4.1, 4.2, and 4.4.

Historical Notes

The order of the Minnesota Supreme Court [C4–85–697] dated December 18, 2008, substantially revising the Code of Judicial Conduct by adopting in large measure the 2007 American Bar Association Model Code of Judicial Conduct, provided in part that the revised Code of Judicial Conduct was promulgated, and the existing Code of Judicial Conduct abrogated, effective July 1, 2009, and that the revised Code shall apply to all conduct on or after July 1, 2009.

Rule 3.14. Reimbursement of Expenses and Waivers of Fees or Charges

(A) Unless otherwise prohibited by Rules 3.1 and 3.13(A) or other law, a judge may accept reimbursement of necessary and reasonable expenses for travel, food, lodging, or other incidental expenses, or a waiver or partial waiver of fees or charges for registration, tuition, and similar items, from sources other than the judge's employing entity, if the expenses or charges are associated with the judge's participation in extrajudicial activities permitted by this Code.

(B) Reimbursement of expenses for necessary travel, food, lodging, or other incidental expenses shall be limited to the actual costs reasonably incurred by the judge and, when appropriate to the occasion, by the judge's spouse, person with whom the judge has an intimate relationship, or guest.

Adopted Dec. 18, 2008, eff. July 1, 2009.

Comment

[1] Educational, civic, religious, fraternal, and charitable organizations often sponsor meetings, seminars, symposia, dinners, awards ceremonies, and similar events. Judges are encouraged to attend educational programs, as both teachers and participants, in law-related and academic disciplines,

in furtherance of their duty to remain competent in the law. Participation in a variety of other extrajudicial activity is also permitted and encouraged by this Code.

[2] Not infrequently, sponsoring organizations invite certain judges to attend seminars or other events on a fee-waived or partial-fee-waived basis, and sometimes include reimbursement for necessary travel, food, lodging, or other incidental expenses. A judge's decision whether to accept reimbursement of expenses or a waiver or partial waiver of fees or charges in connection with these or other extrajudicial activities must be based upon an assessment of all the circumstances. The judge must undertake a reasonable inquiry to obtain the information necessary to make an informed judgment about whether acceptance would be consistent with the requirements of this Code.

[3] A judge must assure himself or herself that acceptance of reimbursement or fee waivers would not appear to a reasonable person to undermine the judge's independence, integrity, or impartiality. The factors that a judge should consider when deciding whether to accept reimbursement or a fee waiver for attendance at a particular activity include:

(a) whether the sponsor is an accredited educational institution or bar association rather than a trade association or a for-profit entity;

(b) whether the funding comes largely from numerous contributors rather than from a single entity and is earmarked for programs with specific content;

(c) whether the content is related or unrelated to the subject matter of litigation pending or impending before the judge, or to matters that are likely to come before the judge;

(d) whether the activity is primarily educational rather than recreational, and whether the costs of the event are reasonable and comparable to those associated with similar events sponsored by the judiciary, bar associations, or similar groups;

(e) whether information concerning the activity and its funding sources is available upon inquiry;

(f) whether the sponsor or source of funding is generally associated with particular parties or interests currently appearing or likely to appear in the judge's court, thus possibly requiring disqualification of the judge under Rule 2.11;

(g) whether differing viewpoints are presented; and

(h) whether a broad range of judicial and nonjudicial participants are invited, whether a large number of participants are invited, and whether the program is designed specifically for judges.

Historical Notes

The order of the Minnesota Supreme Court [C4–85–697] dated December 18, 2008, substantially revising the Code of Judicial Conduct by adopting in large measure the 2007 American Bar Association Model Code of Judicial Conduct, provided in part that the revised Code of Judicial Conduct was promulgated, and the existing Code of Judicial Conduct abrogated, effective July 1, 2009, and that the revised Code shall apply to all conduct on or after July 1, 2009.

Rule 3.15. Reporting Requirements

(A) In addition to any other reporting required by law, a judge shall publicly report, in the manner and time directed by this Rule, the source and amount or value of:

(1) compensation received for extrajudicial activities as permitted by Rule 3.12; and

(2) gifts and other things of value for which reporting is required by Rule 3.13(C).

(B) When public reporting is required by paragraph (A), a judge shall report the date, place, and nature of the activity for which the judge received any compensation; and the description of any gift, loan, bequest, benefit, or other thing of value accepted.

(C) The public report required by paragraph (A) and filed as required by paragraph (D) shall be made annually.

(D) Reports made in compliance with this Rule shall be filed annually on or before the first day of May as public documents in the office of the State Court Administrator.

(E) Income from investments, including real or personal property, pension plans, deferred compensation plans, and other lawful sources where the judge does not render current or future service in exchange for the income is not extra-judicial compensation to the judge for purposes of the reporting required by this Rule.

Adopted Dec. 18, 2008, eff. July 1, 2009. Amended Dec. 31, 2013, eff. Dec. 31, 2013.

Historical Notes

The order of the Minnesota Supreme Court [C4–85–697] dated December 18, 2008, substantially revising the Code of Judicial Conduct by adopting in large measure the 2007 American Bar Association Model Code of Judicial Conduct, provided in part that the revised Code of Judicial Conduct was promulgated, and the existing Code of Judicial Conduct abrogated, effective July 1, 2009, and that the revised Code shall apply to all conduct on or after July 1, 2009.

The order of the Minnesota Supreme Court [ADM08–8004] dated December 31, 2013, provided in part that the amendments were effective December 31, 2013, and "shall apply to all conduct on or after the effective date."

Canon 4

A Judge or Candidate for Judicial Office Shall Not Engage in Political or Campaign Activity that is Inconsistent with the Independence, Integrity, or Impartiality of the Judiciary.

Rule 4.1. Political and Campaign Activities of Judges and Judicial Candidates in General

(A) Except as permitted by law, or by Rules 4.2, 4.3, and 4.4, a judge or a judicial candidate shall not:

(1) act as a leader in a political organization;

(2) make speeches on behalf of a political organization;

(3) publicly endorse or, except for the judge or candidate's opponent, publicly oppose another candidate for public office;

(4) (a) solicit funds for a political organization or a candidate for public office, or

(b) make a contribution to a candidate for public office;

(5) attend or purchase tickets for dinners or other events sponsored by a candidate for public office;

(6) personally solicit or accept campaign contributions other than as authorized by Rules 4.2 and 4.4;

(7) use or permit the use of campaign contributions for the private benefit of the judge, the candidate, or others;

(8) use court staff, facilities, or other court resources in a campaign for judicial office in a manner prohibited by state law or Judicial Branch personnel policies;

(9) knowingly, or with reckless disregard for the truth, make any false or misleading statement;

(10) make any statement that would reasonably be expected to affect the outcome or impair the fairness of a matter pending or impending in any court; or

(11) in connection with cases, controversies, or issues that are likely to come before the court, make pledges, promises, or commitments that are inconsistent with the impartial performance of the adjudicative duties of judicial office.

(B) A judge or judicial candidate shall take reasonable measures to ensure that other persons do not undertake, on behalf of the judge or judicial candidate, any activities prohibited under paragraph (A), except as permitted by Rule 4.4.

Adopted Dec. 18, 2008, eff. July 1, 2009.

Comment

General Considerations

[1] Even when subject to public election, a judge plays a role different from that of a legislator or executive branch official. Rather than making decisions based upon the expressed views or preferences of the electorate, a judge makes decisions based upon the law and the facts of every case. Therefore, in furtherance of this interest, judges and judicial candidates must, to the greatest extent possible, be free and appear to be free from political influence and political pressure. This Canon imposes narrowly tailored restrictions upon the political and campaign activities of all judges and judicial candidates, taking into account the various methods of selecting judges.

[2] When a person becomes a judicial candidate, this Canon becomes applicable to his or her conduct.

Participation in Political Activities

[3] Public confidence in the independence and impartiality of the judiciary is eroded if judges or judicial candidates are perceived to be subject to political influence. Although judges and judicial candidates may register to vote as members of a political party, they are prohibited by paragraph (A)(1) from assuming leadership roles in political organizations. Examples of such leadership roles include precinct or block captains and delegates or alternates to political conventions. Such positions would be inconsistent with an independent and impartial judiciary.

[4] Paragraphs (A)(2) and (A)(3) prohibit judges and judicial candidates from making speeches on behalf of political organizations or publicly endorsing or opposing candidates for public office, respectively, to prevent them from abusing the prestige of judicial office to advance the interests of others. See Rule 1.3.

[5] Although members of the families of judges and judicial candidates are free to engage in their own political activity, including running for public office, there is no "family exception" to the prohibition in paragraph (A)(3) against a judge or candidate publicly endorsing candidates for public office. A judge or judicial candidate must not become involved in, or publicly associated with, a family member's political activity or campaign for public office. To avoid public misunderstanding, judges and judicial candidates should take, and should urge members of their families to take, reasonable steps to avoid any implication that they endorse any family member's candidacy or other political activity.

[6] Judges and judicial candidates retain the right to participate in the political process as voters in both primary and general elections. For purposes of this Canon, participation in a caucus-type election procedure does not constitute public support for or endorsement of a political organization or candidate, and is not prohibited by paragraphs (A)(2) or (A)(3).

Statements and Comments Made during a Campaign for Judicial Office

[7] Judicial candidates must be scrupulously fair and accurate in all statements made by them and by their campaign committees. Paragraph (A)(9) obligates candidates and their committees to refrain from knowingly making statements that are false or misleading, or that omit facts necessary to make the communication considered as a whole not materially misleading.

[8] Judicial candidates are sometimes the subject of false, misleading, or unfair allegations made by opposing candidates, third parties, or the media. For example, false or misleading statements might be made regarding the identity, present position, experience, qualifications, or judicial rulings of a candidate. In other situations, false or misleading allegations may be made that bear upon a candidate's integrity or fitness for judicial office. As long as the candidate does not violate paragraphs (A)(9), (A)(10), or (A)(11), the candidate may make a factually accurate public response. In addition, when an independent third party has made unwarranted attacks on a candidate's opponent, the candidate may disavow the attacks, and request the third party to cease and desist.

[9] Subject to paragraph (A)(10), a judicial candidate is permitted to respond directly to false, misleading, or unfair allegations made against him or her during a campaign, although it is preferable for someone else to respond if the allegations relate to a pending case.

[10] Paragraph (A)(10) prohibits judicial candidates from making comments that might impair the fairness of pending or impending judicial proceedings. This provision does not restrict arguments or statements to the court or jury by a lawyer who is a judicial candidate, or rulings, statements, or instructions by a judge that may appropriately affect the outcome of a matter.

Pledges, Promises, or Commitments Inconsistent with Impartial Performance of the Adjudicative Duties of Judicial Office

[11] The role of a judge is different from that of a legislator or executive branch official, even when the judge is subject to public election. Campaigns for judicial office must be conducted differently from campaigns for other offices. The narrowly drafted restrictions upon political and campaign activities of judicial candidates provided in Canon 4 allow candidates to conduct campaigns that provide voters with sufficient information to permit them to distinguish between candidates and make informed electoral choices.

[12] Paragraph (A)(11) makes applicable to both judges and judicial candidates the prohibition that applies to judges in Rule 2.10(B), relating to pledges, promises, or commitments that are inconsistent with the impartial performance of the adjudicative duties of judicial office.

[13] The making of a pledge, promise, or commitment is not dependent upon, or limited to, the use of any specific words or phrases; instead, the totality of the statement must be examined to determine if a reasonable person would believe that the candidate for judicial office has specifically undertaken to reach a particular result. Pledges, promises, or commitments must be contrasted with statements or announcements of personal views on legal, political, or other issues, which are not prohibited. When making such statements, a judge should acknowledge the overarching judicial obligation to apply and uphold the law, without regard to his or her personal views.

[14] A judicial candidate may make campaign promises related to judicial organization, administration, and court management, such as a promise to dispose of a backlog of cases, start court sessions on time, or avoid favoritism in appointments and hiring. A candidate may also pledge to take action outside the courtroom, such as working toward an improved jury selection system, or advocating for more funds to improve the physical plant and amenities of the courthouse.

[15] Judicial candidates may receive questionnaires or requests for interviews from the media and from issue advocacy or other community organizations that seek to learn their views on disputed or controversial legal or political issues. Paragraph (A)(11) does not specifically address judicial responses to such inquiries. Depending upon the wording and format of such questionnaires, candidates' responses might be viewed as pledges, promises, or commitments to perform the adjudicative duties of office other than in an impartial way. To avoid violating paragraph (A)(11), therefore, candidates who respond to media and other inquiries should also give assurances that they will keep an open mind and will carry out their adjudicative duties faithfully and impartially if elected. Candidates who do not respond may state their reasons for not responding, such as the danger that answering might be perceived by a reasonable person as undermining a successful candidate's independence or impartiality, or that it might lead to frequent disqualification. See Rule 2.11.

Historical Notes

The order of the Minnesota Supreme Court [C4–85–697] dated December 18, 2008, substantially revising the Code of Judicial Conduct by adopting in large measure the 2007 American Bar Association Model Code of Judicial Conduct, provided in part that the revised Code of Judicial Conduct was promulgated, and the existing Code of Judicial Conduct abrogated, effective July 1, 2009, and that the revised Code shall apply to all conduct on or after July 1, 2009.

Rule 4.2. Political and Campaign Activities of Judicial Candidates in Public Elections

(A) A judicial candidate in a public election shall:

(1) act at all times in a manner consistent with the independence, integrity, and impartiality of the judiciary;

(2) comply with all applicable election, election campaign, and election campaign fund-raising laws and regulations of this jurisdiction;

(3) review and approve the content of all campaign statements and materials produced by the candidate or his or her campaign committee, as authorized by Rule 4.4, before their dissemination;

(4) take reasonable measures to ensure that other persons do not undertake on behalf of the candidate activities, other than those described in Rule 4.4, that the candidate is prohibited from doing by Rule 4.1; and

(5) take reasonable measures to ensure that the candidate will not obtain any information identifying those who contribute or refuse to contribute to the candidate's campaign.

(B) A candidate for elective judicial office may, unless prohibited by law:

(1) establish a campaign committee pursuant to the provisions of Rule 4.4;

(2) speak on behalf of his or her candidacy through any medium, including but not limited to advertisements, websites, or other campaign literature; and

(3) (a) make a general request for campaign contributions when speaking to an audience of 20 or more people;

(b) sign letters, for distribution by the candidate's campaign committee, soliciting campaign contributions, if the letters direct contributions to be sent to the address of the candidate's campaign committee and not that of the candidate; and

(c) personally solicit campaign contributions from members of the judge's family, from a person with whom the judge has an intimate relationship, or from judges over whom the judge does not exercise supervisory or appellate authority.

Adopted Dec. 18, 2008, eff. July 1, 2009.

Comment

[1] Paragraph (B) permits judicial candidates in public elections to engage in some political and campaign activities otherwise prohibited by Rule 4.1.

[2] Despite paragraph (B), judicial candidates for public election remain subject to many of the provisions of Rule 4.1. For example, a candidate continues to be prohibited from soliciting funds for a political organization, knowingly making false or misleading statements during a campaign, or making certain promises, pledges, or commitments related to future adjudicative duties. See Rule 4.1, paragraphs (A)(4), (A)(9), and (A)(11).

[3] Judicial candidates are permitted to attend or purchase tickets for dinners and other events sponsored by political organizations.

Historical Notes

The order of the Minnesota Supreme Court [C4–85–697] dated December 18, 2008, substantially revising the Code of Judicial Conduct by adopting in large measure the 2007 American Bar Association Model Code of Judicial Conduct, provided in part that the revised Code of Judicial Conduct was promulgated, and the existing Code of Judicial Conduct abrogated, effective July 1, 2009, and that the revised Code shall apply to all conduct on or after July 1, 2009.

Rule 4.3. Activities of Candidates for Appointive Judicial Office

A candidate for appointment to judicial office may:

(A) communicate with the appointing or confirming authority, including any selection, screening, or nominating commission or similar agency; and

(B) seek support for the appointment from organizations and from individuals to the extent requested, required, or permitted by the appointing authority or the nominating commission.

Adopted Dec. 18, 2008, eff. July 1, 2009.

Comment

[1] When seeking support or endorsement, or when communicating directly with an appointing or confirming authority, a candidate for appointive judicial office must not make any pledges, promises, or commitments that are inconsistent with the impartial performance of the adjudicative duties of the office. See Rule 4.1(A)(11).

Historical Notes

The order of the Minnesota Supreme Court [C4–85–697] dated December 18, 2008, substantially revising the Code of Judicial Conduct by adopting in large measure the 2007 American Bar Association Model Code of Judicial Conduct, provided in part that the revised Code of Judicial Conduct was promulgated, and the existing Code of Judicial Conduct abrogated, effective July 1, 2009, and that the revised Code shall apply to all conduct on or after July 1, 2009.

Rule 4.4. Campaign Committees

(A) A judicial candidate subject to public election may establish a campaign committee to manage and conduct a campaign for the candidate, subject to the provisions of this Code. The candidate is responsible for ensuring that his or her campaign committee complies with applicable provisions of this Code and other applicable law.

(B) A judicial candidate subject to public election shall direct his or her campaign committee:

(1) to solicit and accept only campaign contributions in an amount allowed by law;

(2) to comply with all applicable statutory requirements for reporting, disclosure, and divestiture of campaign contributions; and

(3) not to disclose to the candidate the identity of campaign contributors nor to disclose to the candidate the identity of those who were solicited for contribution and refused such solicitation. The candidate may be advised of aggregate contribution information in a manner that does not reveal the source(s) of the contributions.

Adopted Dec. 18, 2008, eff. July 1, 2009. Amended Dec. 31, 2013, eff. Dec. 31, 2013.

Comment

[1] Judicial candidates are prohibited from personally soliciting campaign contributions or personally accepting campaign contributions except as provided by Rule 4.2(B)(3). See Rule 4.1(A)(6). This Rule recognizes that judicial candidates must raise campaign funds to support their candidacies, and permits candidates, other than candidates for appointive judicial office, to establish campaign committees to solicit and accept contributions.

[2] Campaign committees may solicit and accept campaign contributions, manage the expenditure of campaign funds, and generally conduct campaigns. Candidates are responsible for compliance with the requirements of election law and other applicable law, and for the activities of their campaign committees.

[3] At the start of a campaign, the candidate must instruct the campaign committee to solicit or accept only such contributions as are appropriate and in conformity with applicable law. Although lawyers and others who might appear before a successful candidate for judicial office are permitted to make campaign contributions, the candidate should instruct his or her campaign committee to be especially cautious in connection with such contributions, so they do not create grounds for disqualifica-

tion if the candidate is elected to judicial office. See Rule 2.11.

Historical Notes

The order of the Minnesota Supreme Court [C4–85–697] dated December 18, 2008, substantially revising the Code of Judicial Conduct by adopting in large measure the 2007 American Bar Association Model Code of Judicial Conduct, provided in part that the revised Code of Judicial Conduct was promulgated, and the existing Code of Judicial Conduct abrogated, effective July 1, 2009, and that the revised Code shall apply to all conduct on or after July 1, 2009.

The order of the Minnesota Supreme Court [ADM08–8004] dated December 31, 2013, provided in part that the amendments were effective December 31, 2013, and "shall apply to all conduct on or after the effective date."

Rule 4.5. Activities of Judges Who Become Candidates for Nonjudicial Office

(A) Upon becoming a candidate for a nonjudicial elective office, a judge shall resign from judicial office, unless permitted by law to continue to hold judicial office.

(B) Upon becoming a candidate for a nonjudicial appointive office, a judge is not required to resign from judicial office, provided that the judge complies with the other provisions of this Code.

Adopted Dec. 18, 2008, eff. July 1, 2009.

Comment

[1] In campaigns for nonjudicial elective public office, candidates may make pledges, promises, or commitments related to positions they would take and ways they would act if elected to office. Although appropriate in nonjudicial campaigns, this manner of campaigning is inconsistent with the role of a judge, who must remain fair and impartial to all who come before him or her. The potential for misuse of the judicial office, and the political promises that the judge would be compelled to make in the course of campaigning for nonjudicial elective office, together dictate that a judge who wishes to run for such an office must resign upon becoming a candidate.

[2] The "resign to run" rule set forth in paragraph (A) ensures that a judge cannot use the judicial office to promote his or her candidacy, and prevents post-campaign retaliation from the judge in the event the judge is defeated in the election. When a judge is seeking appointive nonjudicial office, however, the dangers are not sufficient to warrant imposing the "resign to run" rule.

[3] Minnesota Constitution, Article VI, Section 6 prohibits a judge from holding any office under the United States, except a commission in a reserve component of the military forces of the United States, or any other office of the State of Minnesota and provides that the judge's term of office shall terminate at the time the judge files as a candidate for an elective office of the United States or for a nonjudicial office of the State of Minnesota.

Historical Notes

The order of the Minnesota Supreme Court [C4–85–697] dated December 18, 2008, substantially revising the Code of Judicial Conduct by adopting in large measure the 2007 American Bar Association Model Code of Judicial Conduct, provided in part that the revised Code of Judicial Conduct was promulgated, and the existing Code of Judicial Conduct abrogated, effective July 1, 2009, and that the revised Code shall apply to all conduct on or after July 1, 2009.

RULES OF BOARD ON JUDICIAL STANDARDS

Effective January 1, 1996

Including Amendments Received Through January 1, 2014

Research Note

See Minnesota Statutes Annotated, *Volume 52, for case annotations and cross references.*

DEFINITIONS

"Censure" is a formal public sanction by the Supreme Court based on a finding that the judge has committed serious misconduct.

"Complaint" is any communication, oral or written, made by judges, lawyers, court personnel or any member of the general public regarding the conduct of a judge.

"Deferred Disposition Agreement" is an agreement between the judge and the board or hearing panel for the judge to undergo treatment, participate in education programs, or take other corrective action, based upon misconduct or disability that can be addressed through treatment or a rehabilitation program.

"Disability" is a physical or mental condition of a judge that seriously interferes with the capacity of the judge to perform judicial duties, including, but not limited to, impairment due in whole or in part from habitual or excessive use of intoxicants, drugs, or controlled substances. A disability may be permanent or temporary.

"Evaluation" is a prompt and discreet inquiry by the executive secretary into the facts and circumstances of any complaint or information that alleges conduct listed in Rule 4(a).

"Formal Complaint" is a complaint upon which the board has determined to conduct a public hearing.

"Formal Statement of Disability Proceeding" is a statement that the board has determined to conduct a public hearing to determine the appropriate action with regard to a judge alleged to have a disability.

"Investigation" is a full inquiry by the executive secretary, with the authorization of the board, into the facts and circumstances of any complaint or information that alleges conduct listed in Rule 4(a).

"Judge" is any judge, including full-time, part-time, and retired judges, judicial officer, referee, magistrate, or other hearing officer employed in the judicial branch of the state of Minnesota, any judge of the Minnesota Tax Court, or any judge of the Workers' Compensation Court of Appeals.

"Letter of Caution" is a nondisciplinary letter that advises the judge regarding future conduct.

"Private Admonition" is a nonpublic sanction imposed by the board for misconduct of an isolated and non-serious nature.

"Public Reprimand" is a public sanction imposed by the board or hearing panel based on a finding that the judge has committed serious misconduct.

"Reasonable Cause" is a reasonable belief in the existence of facts warranting discipline or a finding of disability.

Adopted May 20, 1986, eff. July 1, 1986. Amended Dec. 27, 1989, eff. Jan. 1, 1990; Nov. 1, 1995; March 31, 2009, eff. July 1, 2009.

Historical Notes

The order of the Minnesota Supreme Court [C4–85–697] dated November 1, 1995, provides in part that the Code of Judicial Conduct and the Rules of the Board on Judicial Standards, as amended, "shall govern all matters which come before the Board on Judicial Standards on or after the 1st day of January 1996."

RULE 1. ORGANIZATION OF BOARD

(a) Appointment of Members. The Board on Judicial Standards shall consist of one judge of the Court of Appeals, three judges of district court, two lawyers who have practiced law in the state for at least ten years and four resident citizens of Minnesota who are not judges, retired judges or lawyers. The executive secretary, who shall be an attorney licensed to practice law in Minnesota, with a minimum of fifteen years' experience in the practice of law, including any service as a judge, shall be appointed by the board. All members shall be appointed by the governor with the advice and consent of the senate except that senate confirmation shall not be required for judicial members.

(b) Term of Office.

(1) The term of each member shall be four years.

(2) No member shall serve more than two full four-year terms or their equivalent, not to exceed eight years.

(c) Vacancy.

(1) A vacancy on the board shall be deemed to occur:

(i) When a member retires from the board; or

(ii) When a judge who is a member of the board ceases to hold the judicial office held at the time of selection; or

(iii) When a lawyer who is a member of the board ceases to be in good standing to practice law in the courts of this state or is appointed or elected to a judicial office; or

(iv) When a lay member becomes a lawyer; or

(v) When a member is no longer a resident citizen.

(2) Vacancies shall be filled by selection of a successor in the same manner as required for the selection of the predecessor in office. A member selected to fill a vacancy shall hold office for the unexpired term of the predecessor. All vacancies on the board shall be filled within 90 days after the vacancy occurs.

(3) Members of the board may retire therefrom by submitting their resignation to the board, which shall certify the vacancy to the governor.

(d) Duties and Responsibilities of Executive Secretary. The executive secretary shall have duties and responsibilities prescribed by the board, including the authority to:

(1) Receive complaints and allegations as to misconduct or disability;

(2) Make preliminary evaluations;

(3) Conduct investigations of complaints as directed by the board;

(4) Recommend dispositions;

(5) Maintain the board's records;

(6) Maintain statistics concerning the operation of the board and make them available to the board and to the Supreme Court;

(7) Prepare the board's budget for approval by the board and administer its funds;

(8) Employ and supervise other members of the board's staff;

(9) Prepare an annual report of the board's activities for presentation to the board, to the Supreme Court, and to the public;

(10) Employ, with the approval of the board, special counsel, private investigators or other experts as necessary to investigate and process matters before the board and before the Supreme Court. The use of the attorney general's staff prosecutors or law enforcement officers for this purpose is not allowed. The use of the director and staff of the Office of Lawyers Professional Responsibility for this purpose is allowed if the matter involves conduct of a judge, other than a Supreme Court Justice, that occurred prior to the judge assuming judicial office. Individuals employed or providing assistance under this section shall be deemed to be counsel to the Board on Judicial Standards for the purposes of these rules.

(e) Performance Review of Executive Secretary. The board shall annually conduct a performance review of the executive secretary.

(f) Quorum and Chairperson.

(1) A quorum for the transaction of business by the board shall be six members of the board.

(2) The board shall elect from its members a chairperson and vice-chairperson, each of whom shall serve a term of two years. The vice-chairper-

son shall act as chairperson in the absence of the chairperson.

(g) Meetings of the Board. Meetings of the board shall be held at the call of the chairperson, the vice-chairperson, the executive secretary or the written request of three members of the board.

(h) Annual Report. At least once a year the board shall prepare a report summarizing its activities during the preceding year. One copy of this report shall be filed with the Supreme Court.

(i) Expenses of the Board and Staff.

(1) The expenses of the board shall be paid from appropriations of funds to the Board on Judicial Standards.

(2) Members of the board shall be compensated for their services as provided by law.

(3) In addition to the executive secretary, the board may appoint other employees to perform such duties as it shall direct, subject to the availability of funds under its budget.

(j) Code of Ethics. The board shall maintain a Code of Ethics setting forth the ethical standards expected of board members in the performance of the board's responsibilities.

Adopted July 5, 1978. Amended May 20, 1986, eff. July 1, 1986; Dec. 27, 1989, eff. Jan. 1, 1990; Nov. 1, 1995; March 30, 1999, eff. March 30, 1999; March 31, 2009, eff. July 1, 2009.

Advisory Committee Comment—1999 Amendment

Rule 1(d)(10) has been modified to allow the use of the director and staff of the Office of Lawyers Professional Responsibility to provide investigative and support services in situations involving conduct that occurred prior to a judge assuming judicial office. Related changes grant the Lawyers Professional Responsibility Board jurisdiction to consider whether such conduct warrants lawyer discipline. R.Bd.Jud.Std. 2; R.L.Prof. Resp. 6Z(a). It is contemplated that complaints about the conduct of a judge occurring prior to the judge assuming judicial office will be investigated in the first instance by the Office of Lawyers Professional Responsibility [R.Bd.Jud.Std. 6Z(b); R.L.Prof.Resp. 6Z(b)(2)], and the results would be disclosed to the Board on Judicial Standards. R.Bd.Jud.Std. 5(a)(4); R.L.Prof.Resp. 20(a)(10). This allows for efficient and effective use of investigative resources by both disciplinary boards. Related changes also authorize the use of the hearing record, findings, and recommendations of the lawyer disciplinary process in the judicial disciplinary process. R.Bd.Jud.Std. 6Z(d); R.L.Prof.Resp. 6Z(b)(4).

Rule 1(d)(10) prohibits the use of the staff of the Office of Lawyers Professional Responsibility when the pre-bench conduct at issue involves a Supreme Court Justice because the office's director and staff are appointed and compensated by the Court. If such a case were to arise, it is contemplated that the Office of Lawyers Professional Responsibility would follow existing conflict procedures, which include assigning a former attorney or former board member to review and follow up on patently frivolous complaints and hiring outside counsel and investigators to handle other complaints. The prohibition against the use of office staff does not prohibit communication of confidential information between the two boards regarding matters involving the conduct of a justice occurring prior to assumption of judicial office.

Modifications to Rule 1(d)(10) also clarify that individuals employed or providing assistance to the executive secretary and the board are considered counsel to the board for purposes of these rules. This ensures, for example, that the immunity and privilege provisions under Rule 3 and the confidentiality and work product provisions under Rule 5 apply to these individuals when they are assisting the executive secretary and the board.

Historical Notes

The order of the Minnesota Supreme Court [C4–85–697] dated November 1, 1995, provides in part that the Code of Judicial Conduct and the Rules of the Board on Judicial Standards, as amended, "shall govern all matters which come before the Board on Judicial Standards on or after the 1st day of January 1996."

The order of the Minnesota Supreme Court [C4–85–697] dated March 30, 1999, amending the Rules of the Board on Judicial Standards provides in part that the "(t)he inclusion of Advisory Committee comments is made for convenience and does not reflect court approval of the comments made therein."

RULE 2. JURISDICTION AND POWERS OF BOARD

(a) Powers of the Board.

(1) *Disposition of Complaints.* The board shall have the power to receive complaints, investigate, conduct hearings, make certain summary dispositions, and make recommendations to the Supreme Court concerning:

(i) Allegations of judicial misconduct;

(ii) Allegations of physical or mental disability of judges;

(iii) Matters of voluntary retirement for disability; and

(iv) Review of a judge's compliance with Minn. Stat. § 546.27.

(2) *Advisory Opinions.* The board may issue advisory opinions on proper judicial conduct with respect to the provisions of the Code of Judicial Conduct. An advisory opinion may be requested by a judge or a candidate for judicial office. A request for an advisory opinion shall relate to prospective conduct only, and shall be submitted in writing and contain a complete statement of all facts pertaining to the intended conduct and a clear, concise question of judicial ethics. The board shall issue a written opinion within 30 days after receipt of the written request, unless the time period is extended by the board. The fact that the judge or judicial candidate requested and relied on an advisory opinion shall be taken into account in any subsequent disciplinary proceedings. The advisory opinion

shall not be binding on the hearing panel or the Supreme Court in the exercise of their judicial-discipline responsibilities.

(b) Jurisdiction Over Judges. The board shall have jurisdiction over allegations of misconduct and disability for all judges.

(c) Conduct Prior to Assuming Judicial Office. The board's jurisdiction shall include conduct that occurred prior to a judge assuming judicial office. The Office of Lawyers Professional Responsibility shall have jurisdiction to consider whether discipline as a lawyer is warranted in matters involving conduct of any judge occurring prior to the assumption of judicial office.

(d) Jurisdiction Over Former Judge. The board shall have jurisdiction over an inquiry, investigation, Formal Complaint, or Formal Statement of Disability Proceeding commenced before a judge left judicial office provided the conduct at issue occurred while the judge was in judicial office and the conduct at issue occurred in the judge's judicial capacity. The board may at any time dismiss a matter involving a former judge if the board determines that pursuing the matter further is not a prudent use of the board's resources. The Office of Lawyers Professional Responsibility shall have jurisdiction over a lawyer who is no longer a judge to consider whether discipline is warranted with reference to allegedly unethical conduct that occurred during the time when the lawyer held judicial office. The board shall notify the Office of Lawyers Professional Responsibility if a judge leaves judicial office while an inquiry, investigation, Formal Complaint, or Formal Statement of Disability Proceeding is pending.

(e) Subpoena and Depositions.

(1) *Depositions Limited.* Depositions shall not be allowed, provided that, for good cause shown, a deposition may be taken of a witness living outside the state or physically unable to attend the hearing.

(2) *Subpoenas for Investigation.* During the investigative stage of a proceeding, prior to a finding of reasonable cause to proceed, and subject to the limitations of Rule 2(e)(1):

(i) Upon resolution of the board, the executive secretary may make application for the issuance of a subpoena compelling any person, including a judge, to attend and give testimony, and to produce documents, books, accounts and other records. Such subpoena shall issue upon a showing that the information sought appears reasonably calculated to lead to the discovery of admissible evidence.

(ii) Failure or refusal of a judge who is the subject of information to cooperate or the intentional misrepresentation of a material fact by the judge shall constitute conduct prejudicial to the administration of justice and may provide reasonable cause for the board to proceed under Rule 2(e)(3).

(3) *Subpoenas for Hearing.* At all other stages of the proceeding following a finding of reasonable cause to proceed, and subject to the limitations of Rule 2(e)(1), both the board and the judge being investigated shall be entitled to compel, by subpoena, attendance and testimony of witnesses, including the judge as a witness, and the inspection of documents, books, accounts, and other records.

(4) *Issuing Subpoenas.* The District Court of Ramsey County shall issue subpoenas.

(5) *Motions.* Prior to the appointment of a hearing panel pursuant to Rule 8(b), the District Court of Ramsey County shall have jurisdiction over motions arising from Rule 2(e) requests. Following the appointment of a panel, the presider of the panel before whom the matter is pending shall have jurisdiction over motions arising from Rule 2(e) requests and shall have all the powers of a district court judge. Any resulting decision or order of the presider of the panel or the District Court of Ramsey County may not be appealed before entry of the final order in the disciplinary proceeding. The judge shall be denominated by number or randomly selected initials in any District Court proceedings.

(f) Impeachment. Nothing in these rules shall affect the impeachment of judges under the Minnesota Constitution, Art. 8.

Adopted July 5, 1978. Amended March 26, 1981; May 20, 1986, eff. July 1, 1986; Dec. 27, 1989, eff. Jan. 1, 1990; Nov. 1, 1995; March 30, 1999, eff. March 30, 1999; March 31, 2009, eff. July 1, 2009.

Advisory Committee Comment—1999 Amendment

Rule 2(a) has been amended to recognize that the board may make certain summary dispositions. These dispositions include proposed public reprimands under Rule 6(d)(1)(ii), which are subject to a judge's right to demand a formal hearing before the reprimand is made public, and nonpublic warnings, conditions, counseling, treatment, and assistance directed by the board under Rule 6(f).

Rule 2(b) has been modified to permit the Lawyers Professional Responsibility Board to also exercise jurisdiction to consider whether discipline as a lawyer is warranted in matters involving conduct of any judge occurring prior to the assumption of judicial office. As set forth in the definition section of these rules, the term "judge" includes any judge, judicial officer, referee or other hearing officer employed in the judicial branch, and any judge of the Minnesota Tax Court or Worker's Compensation Court of Appeals. See Minn. Stat. §§ 490.15–.18; 175A.01, subd. 4; 271.01 (1998). The procedure to be followed in situations involving pre-bench conduct is set forth in rule 6Z of these rules.

Historical Notes

The order of the Minnesota Supreme Court [C4–85–697] dated November 1, 1995, provides in part that the Code of Judicial Conduct and the Rules of the Board on Judicial Standards, as amended, "shall govern all matters which come before the Board on Judicial Standards on or after the 1st day of January 1996."

The order of the Minnesota Supreme Court [C4–85–697] dated March 30, 1999, amending the Rules of the Board on Judicial Standards provides in part that the "(t)he inclusion of Advisory Committee comments is made for convenience and does not reflect court approval of the comments made therein."

RULE 3. IMMUNITY; PRIVILEGE

Information submitted to the board or its staff and testimony given in the proceedings under these rules shall be absolutely privileged, and no civil action predicated thereon may be instituted against the complainant or witness, or their counsel. Members of the board, referees, board counsel and staff shall be absolutely immune from suit for all conduct in the course of their official duties.

Adopted July 5, 1978. Amended May 20, 1986, eff. July 1, 1986; Dec. 27, 1989, eff. Jan. 1, 1990; Nov. 1, 1995.

Historical Notes

The order of the Minnesota Supreme Court [C4–85–697] dated November 1, 1995, provides in part that the Code of Judicial Conduct and the Rules of the Board on Judicial Standards, as amended, "shall govern all matters which come before the Board on Judicial Standards on or after the 1st day of January 1996."

RULE 4. GROUNDS FOR DISCIPLINE OR OTHER ACTION

(a) Grounds for Discipline or Other Action Shall Include:

(1) Conviction of a crime punishable as a felony under state or federal law or any crime involving moral turpitude;

(2) A persistent failure to perform judicial duties;

(3) Pattern of incompetence in the performance of judicial duties;

(4) Habitual intemperance;

(5) Conduct prejudicial to the administration of justice that brings the judicial office into disrepute, including, but not limited to, discrimination against or harassment of persons on the basis of race, color, creed, religion, national origin, sex, marital status, sexual preference, disability, or age;

(6) Conduct that constitutes a violation of the Code of Judicial Conduct or Professional Responsibility;

(7) *Disability.*

(b) Disposition of Criminal Charges. A conviction, acquittal, or other disposition of any criminal charge filed against a judge shall not preclude action by the board with respect to the conduct upon which the charge was based.

(c) Proceedings Not Substitute for Appeal. In the absence of fraud, corrupt motive, or bad faith, the board shall not take action against a judge for making findings of fact, reaching a legal conclusion, or applying the law as understood by the judge. Claims of error shall be left to the appellate process.

Adopted July 5, 1978. Amended May 20, 1986, eff. July 1, 1986; Dec. 27, 1989, eff. Jan. 1, 1990; Nov. 1, 1995; March 31, 2009, eff. July 1, 2009.

Advisory Committee Comment—2009 Amendment

Retaliatory behavior by the judge related to a complaint may be grounds for discipline under the Code of Judicial Conduct or Professional Responsibility. See, e.g., Inquiry into the Conduct of Murphy, 737 N.W.2d 355, 360 (Minn. 2007).

Historical Notes

The order of the Minnesota Supreme Court [C4–85–697] dated March 31, 2009, amending the Rules of the Board on Judicial Standards provides in part that the "The Advisory Committee comments are included for convenience and do not reflect court approval of the comments made therein."

The order of the Minnesota Supreme Court [C4–85–697] dated November 1, 1995, provides in part that the Code of Judicial Conduct and the Rules of the Board on Judicial Standards, as amended, "shall govern all matters which come before the Board on Judicial Standards on or after the 1st day of January 1996."

RULE 5. CONFIDENTIALITY

(a) Before Formal Complaint and Response. Except as otherwise provided in this rule or Rule 16(f), all proceedings shall be confidential until the Formal Complaint or Formal Statement of Disability Proceeding and response, if any, have been filed with the Supreme Court pursuant to Rule 8. The board shall establish procedures for enforcing the confidentiality provided by this rule.

(1) If at any time the board issues a public reprimand, such action shall be a matter of public record.

(2) If the board issues a dismissal with a letter of caution or enters into a deferred disposition agreement, this action may be disclosed to the chief justice, chief judge, and/or district administrator of the judicial district in which the judge sits. Such disclosure is at the discretion of the board and shall be for the purpose of monitoring future conduct of the judge and for assistance to the judge in modifying the judge's conduct. To the extent that any information is disclosed by the board pursuant to this provision, the chief justice, chief judge and/or district administrator shall maintain the confidentiality of the information in accordance with Rule 5.

(3) Information may be disclosed between the Board on Judicial Standards or executive secretary and the Lawyers Professional Responsibility Board or the director in furtherance of their duties to investigate and consider conduct that occurred prior to a judge assuming judicial office.

(b) After Formal Complaint or Formal Statement of Disability Proceeding and Response. Upon the filing of the Formal Complaint or Formal Statement of Disability Proceeding and written response, if any, with the Supreme Court, except as providing in Rule 16(f) the proceedings become public, but the files of the board, other than the Formal Complaint or Formal Statement of Disability Proceeding and the written response thereto, shall remain confidential unless and until any documents, statements, depositions or other evidence in the files of the board are introduced or used in a public hearing as provided in Rule 10.

(c) Notice to Complainant. The board shall promptly notify the complainant, if any, of the board's action and give a brief explanation of the action. The notice shall disclose the names of the board members who did not participate in the action. If the board's action is issuance of a Formal Complaint or Formal Statement of Disability Proceeding, the board shall notify the complainant of the issuance of the Formal Complaint or Formal Statement of Disability Proceeding, the hearing panel's action, and the action, if any, of the Supreme Court.

(d) Work Product. The work product of the executive secretary and board counsel, and the records of the board's deliberations, shall not be disclosed.

(e) Public Statements by Board.

(1) In any case in which the subject matter becomes public through independent sources or through a waiver of confidentiality by the judge, the board may issue statements as it deems appropriate in order to confirm the pendency of the investigation, to clarify the procedural aspects of the disciplinary proceedings, to explain the right of the judge to a fair hearing without prejudgment and to state that the judge denies the allegations. The statement shall be first submitted to the judge involved for comments and criticisms prior to its release, but the board in its discretion may release the statement as originally prepared.

(2) If the inquiry was initiated as a result of notoriety or because of conduct that is a matter of public record, information concerning the lack of cause to proceed may be released by the board. If the inquiry was initiated after the statutory filing period for judicial office has opened, the board may issue a public statement as deemed appropriate pursuant to Rule 6(e).

(3) The board may make such disclosures as it deems appropriate whenever the board has determined that there is a need to notify another person or agency in order to protect the public or the administration of justice.

(f) Disclosure in Event of Application to the Governor for Retirement. The board may disclose to the governor information about the existence, status, and nature of pending complaints regarding judges who have applied to the governor for disability retirement as provided in Rule 20.

(g) Disclosure for Judicial Selection, Appointment, Election, or Assignment. When any state or federal agency seeks material in connection with the selection or appointment of judges or the assignment of a retired judge to judicial duties, the board may release information from its files only: (1) if the judge in question agrees to such dissemination; and (2) if the file reflects some action of the board pursuant to Rule 6(f). If the board action was taken on or after January 1, 1996, such information may also be released if a judge is involved in a contested election, subject to the same restrictions.

(h) Disclosure to Judge. The judge who is the subject of a complaint shall, upon request, have access to the file relative to the complaint at any stage of the proceedings, including witness statements and notes of witness interviews. Except as provided in the first sentence, the work product of the executive secretary and board counsel, including their notes, and the records of the board's and hearing panel's deliberations shall not be required to be disclosed.

(i) Waiver of Confidentiality. A respondent judge may waive confidentiality at any time during the proceedings.

Adopted July 5, 1978. Amended May 20, 1986, eff. July 1, 1986; Dec. 27, 1989, eff. Jan. 1, 1990; Nov. 1, 1995; March 30, 1999, eff. March 30, 1999; March 31, 2009, eff. July 1, 2009.

Advisory Committee Comment—1999 Amendment

Rule 5(a) has been modified by the addition of clause (4) to permit the exchange of information between the two disciplinary boards and their staff in situations involving conduct of a judge that occurred prior to the judge assuming judicial office. See also R.L.Prof.Resp. 20(a)(10). Both the Board on Judicial Standards and the Lawyers Professional Responsibility Board have jurisdiction in such cases. R.Bd.Jud.Std. 2(b); R.L.Prof.Resp. 6Z.

Historical Notes

The order of the Minnesota Supreme Court [C4–85–697] dated November 1, 1995, provides in part that the Code of Judicial Conduct and the Rules of the Board on Judicial Standards, as amended, "shall govern all matters which come before the Board on Judicial Standards on or after the 1st day of January 1996."

The order of the Minnesota Supreme Court [C4–85–697] dated March 30, 1999, amending the Rules of the Board on Judicial Standards provides in part that the "(t)he inclusion of Advisory Committee comments is made for convenience and does not reflect court approval of the comments made therein."

RULE 6. SCREENING AND INVESTIGATION

(a) Initiation of Inquiry. An inquiry may be initiated as follows:

(1) An inquiry relating to conduct of a judge may be initiated upon a complaint.

(2) The board may on its own motion make an inquiry into the conduct or physical or mental condition of a judge.

(3) Upon request of the Chief Justice of the Supreme Court, the board shall make an inquiry into the conduct or physical or mental condition of a judge.

(b) Screening. The executive secretary shall review the complaint or information resulting in the initiation of an inquiry. If the matters alleged in the complaint or information would not constitute misconduct or disability if true, the executive secretary shall dismiss the complaint or end the inquiry, subject to review and approval by a board member as assigned by the chair, or, if appropriate, refer the matter to another agency or court. If the matters alleged in the complaint or information would constitute judicial misconduct or disability if true, the executive secretary shall conduct a preliminary evaluation.

(c) Evaluation. If after screening, the executive secretary determines the complaint raises allegations as to conduct that might constitute grounds for discipline or other action, the executive secretary shall conduct a prompt, discreet and confidential evaluation. The results of all evaluations shall be routinely submitted to the board.

(d) Investigation; Notice.

(1) Upon review of the preliminary evaluation, or on its own motion, the board may, by resolution:

(i) stay proceedings pending action by another agency or court;

(ii) dismiss the complaint or end the inquiry; or

(iii) authorize an investigation.

(2) Within ten (10) business days after an investigation has been authorized by the board, the executive secretary shall give the following notice to the judge whose conduct is being investigated:

(i) a specific statement of the allegations and possible violations of the Code of Judicial Conduct being investigated, including notice that the investigation can be expanded if appropriate;

(ii) the judge's duty to respond under to Rule 6(d)(5);

(iii) the judge's opportunity to appear before the board or panel of the board under to Rule 6(d)(6); and

(iv) the name of the complainant, unless the board determines there is good cause to withhold that information.

Except as provided in clause (3), the executive secretary shall not commence a formal investigation until such notice is sent to the judge.

(3) The board may defer notice for specific reasons, but when notice is deferred, the executive secretary shall give notice to the judge before making a recommendation as to discipline.

(4) Notice shall be sent immediately upon request of the judge whose conduct or physical or mental condition is the subject of the inquiry if the inquiry has been made public.

(5) Upon request of the executive secretary, the judge shall file a written response within thirty (30) days after service of the notice under Rule 6(d)(2).

(6) Before the board determines its disposition of the inquiry, either the board or the judge may request that the judge appear before the board or a panel of the board to respond to questions. The appearance shall be granted. If the board requests the judge's appearance, the executive secretary shall give the judge 20 days notice and the testimony shall be sworn.

(e) Investigation of Complaints Filed During an Election. The board may expedite its investigation into a complaint against a judge who is a candidate for judicial office if the complaint was filed after the statutory filing period for judicial office has opened. If after investigation the board determines the complaint has no merit, the board may dismiss the complaint and issue an appropriate public statement under Rule 5(e)(2).

(f) Disposition After Investigation.

(1) Upon conclusion of an investigation or determination by another agency or court, the executive secretary may recommend disposition to the board.

(2) The board shall review the results of the investigation or determination by another agency or court and the recommendations of the executive secretary and determine whether there is reasonable cause to believe the judge committed misconduct.

(3) A finding of reasonable cause shall require the concurrence of a majority of the full board.

(4) Upon determination that there is not reasonable cause to believe the judge committed misconduct, the board shall dismiss the complaint or end the inquiry. Upon dismissal or termination of the inquiry, the board may issue a letter of caution that addresses the judge's conduct.

(5) If the board finds there is reasonable cause to believe the judge committed misconduct, it may:

(i) enter into a deferred disposition agreement for a period of time, and the agreement may specify the disposition upon completion;

(ii) if the misconduct appears to be of an isolated and non-serious nature, issue a private admonition, which may include conditions;

(iii) issue a public reprimand, which may include conditions; or

(iv) issue a Formal Complaint;

(6) Prior to issuance of a private admonition, the board shall serve the judge with a copy of the proposed private admonition and a notice stating that within 20 days after service of the proposed private admonition, the judge may serve the board with either a written demand for a private hearing before the board, or the written comments and criticisms of the judge regarding the proposed admonition. If the judge makes a timely demand for a private hearing, the board shall comply. If no

timely demand for a hearing is made, the board may consider the comments and criticisms, if any, but may in its discretion release the private admonition as originally prepared.

(7) Prior to issuance of a public reprimand, the board shall serve the judge with a copy of the proposed reprimand and a notice stating that within 20 days of service of the proposed reprimand, the judge may serve the board with either a written demand for a formal hearing as provided in Rule 8, or the written comments and criticisms of the judge regarding the proposed reprimand. If the judge makes a timely demand for a formal hearing, the board shall comply with Rule 8. If no timely demand for a hearing is made, the board may consider the comments and criticisms, if any, but may in its discretion release the reprimand as originally prepared.

(8) The board shall notify the judge of its action and shall disclose the names of the board members who did not participate in the action.

(g) Representation by Counsel. A judge may be represented by counsel, at the judge's expense, at any stage of the proceedings under these rules.

Adopted July 5, 1978. Amended May 20, 1986, eff. July 1, 1986; Dec. 27, 1989, eff. Jan. 1, 1990; Nov. 1, 1995; March 30, 1999, eff. March 30, 1999; March 31, 2009, eff. July 1, 2009.

ADVISORY COMMITTEE COMMENT—1999 AMENDMENT

The change in Rule 6(d)(1)(i) recognizes that the Board on Judicial Standards may proceed directly to issuance of a formal complaint under Rule 8 when there has been a related public proceeding before the Lawyers Professional Responsibility Board involving conduct of a judge that occurred prior to the judge assuming judicial office. In these circumstances the procedure under Rule 7 may only serve to delay the disciplinary process.

Modifications to Rule 6(d)(1)(ii) allow the board to submit a proposed public reprimand to the judge for conduct that is unacceptable but not so serious as to warrant further discipline, e.g., a censure, by the Supreme Court. Disciplinary bodies in other jurisdictions have similar authority. See, e.g., Rule 6(g)(1), Rules of Procedure for the Arizona Commission on Judicial Conduct; Rules of the Georgia Judicial Qualifications Commission, Definition (c). The change is intended to provide the board with guidance regarding when it is appropriate to proceed directly to a proposed reprimand (which is subject to a judge's right to demand a formal hearing before the reprimand is made public) in lieu of formal charges under Rules 7 and 8.

Advisory Committee Comment—2009 Amendment

Rule 6(d)(1)(i) allows the board to stay proceedings pending action by another agency or court. Such proceedings include criminal prosecution, civil litigation, and administrative action by regulatory agencies.

Historical Notes

The order of the Minnesota Supreme Court [C4–85–697] dated March 31, 2009, amending the Rules of the Board on Judicial Standards provides in part that the "The Advisory Committee comments are included for convenience and do not reflect court approval of the comments made therein."

The order of the Minnesota Supreme Court [C4–85–697] dated November 1, 1995, provides in part that the Code of Judicial Conduct and the Rules of the Board on Judicial Standards, as amended, "shall govern all matters which come before the Board on Judicial Standards on or after the 1st day of January 1996."

The order of the Minnesota Supreme Court [C4–85–697] dated March 30, 1999, amending the Rules of the Board on Judicial Standards provides in part that the "(t)he inclusion of Advisory Committee comments is made for convenience and does not reflect court approval of the comments made therein."

RULE 6Z. PROCEDURE FOR CONDUCT OCCURRING PRIOR TO ASSUMPTION OF JUDICIAL OFFICE

(a) Complaint; Notice. If either the executive secretary or the Office of Lawyers Professional Responsibility initiates an inquiry or investigation, or receives a complaint, concerning the conduct of a judge occurring prior to assumption of judicial office, it shall so notify the other. Notice is not required if all proceedings relating to the inquiry, investigation, or complaint have been resolved before the judge assumes judicial office.

(b) Investigation. Complaints of a judge's unprofessional conduct occurring prior to the judge assuming judicial office shall be investigated by the Office of Lawyers Professional Responsibility and processed pursuant to the Rules on Lawyers Professional Responsibility. The Board on Judicial Standards may suspend a related inquiry pending the outcome of the investigation and/or proceedings.

(c) Authority of Board on Judicial Standards to Proceed Directly to Public Charges. If probable cause has been determined under Rule 9(i)(ii) of the Rules on Lawyers Professional Responsibility or proceedings before a referee or the Supreme Court have been commenced under those rules, the Board on Judicial Standards may, after finding reasonable cause under Rule 6 of the Rules of the Board on Judicial Standards, proceed directly to the issuance of a Formal Complaint under Rule 8 of those rules.

(d) Record of Lawyer Discipline Admissible in Judicial Disciplinary Proceeding. If there is a hearing under Rule 9 or Rule 14 of the Rules on Lawyers Professional Responsibility, the record of the hearing, including the transcript, and the findings and conclusions of the panel, referee, and/or the Supreme Court shall be admissible in any hearing convened under Rule 10 of the Rules of the Board on Judicial Standards. Counsel for the judge and the board may be permitted to introduce additional evidence, relevant to alleged violations of the Code of Judicial Conduct, at the hearing under rule 10.

Adopted March 30, 1999, eff. March 30, 1999. Amended March 31, 2009, eff. July 1, 2009.

Advisory Committee Comment—1999 Amendment

Rule 6Z outlines the process for handling complaints concerning conduct by a judge before assuming judicial office. Related changes grant the Lawyers Professional Responsibility Board jurisdiction to consider whether such conduct warrants lawyer discipline, while the Board on Judicial Standards retains jurisdiction to consider whether the same conduct warrants judicial discipline. R.Bd.Jud.Std. 2; R.L.Prof.Resp. 6Z(a).

The provisions of Rule 6Z(a)–(d) are repeated in R.L.Prof.Resp. 6Z(b)(1)–(4). The committee felt that repetition of the significant procedural provisions was more convenient and appropriate than a cross-reference.

Rule 6Z(a) requires the staff of the Lawyers Professional Responsibility Board and the Judicial Standards Board to notify each other about complaints concerning conduct by a judge occurring before the judge assumed judicial office. Notice is not required if all proceedings relating to the inquiry, investigation, or complaint have been resolved before the judge assumed judicial office.

Rule 6Z(a) neither increases nor decreases the authority of the executive secretary or Office of Lawyers Professional Responsibility to investigate or act on any matter. That authority is governed by other rules. Rule 6Z(a) merely establishes a mutual duty to provide notice about complaints or inquiries concerning conduct of a judge occurring before the judge assumed judicial office.

Although a fair number of complaints received by the executive secretary and the Office of Professional Responsibility are frivolous, there have been relatively few complaints concerning conduct occurring prior to a judge assuming judicial office. Thus, the committee believes that this procedure will not result in a needless duplication of efforts.

Under rule 6Z(b) it is contemplated that complaints about the conduct of a judge occurring prior to the judge assuming judicial office will be investigated in the first instance by the Office of Lawyers Professional Responsibility, and the results would be disclosed to the Board on Judicial Standards. R.Bd.Jud.Std. 5(a)(4); R.L.Prof.Resp. 20(a)(10). This allows for efficient and effective use of investigative resources by both disciplinary boards.

Rule 6Z(c) authorizes the Board on Judicial Standards to proceed directly to issuance of a formal complaint under Rule 8 when there has been a related public proceeding under the Rules on Lawyers Professional Responsibility involving conduct of a judge that occurred prior to the judge assuming judicial office. In these circumstances the procedure under Rule 7 may only serve to delay the disciplinary process.

Rule 6Z(c) does not prohibit the Board on Judicial Standards from proceeding to public disciplinary proceedings in cases in which only private discipline (e.g., an admonition) has been imposed under the Rules on Lawyers Professional Responsibility for conduct of a judge occurring prior to the judge assuming judicial office. In these cases, the Board on Judicial Standards would be required to follow Rule 7 (unless, of course, the matter is resolved earlier, for example, by dismissal or public reprimand).

Rule 6Z(d) authorizes the use of the hearing record and the findings and recommendations of the lawyer disciplinary process in the judicial disciplinary process. This is intended to streamline the judicial disciplinary hearing when there has already been a formal fact finding hearing in the lawyer disciplinary process, and permits the Supreme Court to rule on both disciplinary matters as quickly as possible.

Under Rule 6Z(d) it is contemplated that the hearing record and the findings and conclusions of the lawyer disciplinary process will be the first evidence introduced in the rule 10 judicial disciplinary hearing. Counsel for the board and the judge may be permitted to introduce additional evidence relevant to alleged Code of Judicial Conduct violations at the hearing. Counsel must be aware that there may be situations in which the introduction of additional evidence will not be permitted. See, e.g., In re Gillard, 260 N.W.2d 562, 564 (Minn. 1977) (after review of hearing record and findings and conclusions from lawyer disciplinary process, Supreme Court ruled that findings would not be subject to collateral attack in the related judicial disciplinary proceeding and that additional evidence may be introduced only as a result of a stipulation or order of the fact finder); In re Gillard, 271 N.W.2d 785, 809–11 (Minn. 1978) (upholding removal and disbarment where Board on Judicial Standards as factfinder refused to consider additional testimony but allowed filing of deposition and exhibits and made alternative findings based on those filings). Although the rules do not expressly provide for a pre-hearing conference, it is contemplated that admissibility issues will be resolved by the presider of the fact finding panel sufficiently in advance of the hearing to allow the parties adequate time to prepare for the hearing.

Historical Notes

The order of the Minnesota Supreme Court [C4–85–697] dated March 31, 2009, amending the Rules of the Board on Judicial Standards provides in part that the "The Advisory Committee comments are included for convenience and do not reflect court approval of the comments made therein."

The order of the Minnesota Supreme Court [C4–85–697] dated March 30, 1999, amending the Rules of the Board on Judicial Standards provides in part that the "(t)he inclusion of Advisory Committee comments is made for convenience and does not reflect court approval of the comments made therein."

RULE 7. [Deleted March 31, 2009, eff. July 1, 2009]

Historical Notes

Deleted Rule 7, adopted by court order dated July 5, 1978, and amended by orders dated May 20, 1986, Dec. 27, 1989, Nov. 1, 1995, and March 30, 1999, related to the procedure to follow upon a finding of sufficient cause to proceed.

RULE 8. FORMAL COMPLAINT OR FORMAL STATEMENT OF DISABILITY PROCEEDING AND NOTICE

(a) Formal Complaint or Formal Statement of Disability Proceeding.

(1) The Formal Complaint or Formal Statement of Disability Proceeding shall set forth the charges against the judge, the factual allegations and the time within which these rules require the judge to serve a written response. Where more than one act of misconduct is alleged, each shall be clearly set forth.

(2) The judge shall be served promptly with a copy of the Formal Complaint or Formal Statement of Disability Proceeding. Service shall be accomplished in accordance with the Rules of Civil Procedure.

(3) The judge shall serve a written response on the board within 20 days after service of the Formal Complaint or Formal Statement of Disability Proceeding.

(4) The executive secretary shall file the Formal Complaint or Formal Statement of Disability Proceeding and the written response, if any, with the Supreme Court, within 30 days of service of the Formal Complaint or Formal Statement of Disability Proceeding unless the matter is resolved. The filing time may be extended by agreement of the board and the judge.

(b) Hearing Panel. The public hearing on the Formal Complaint or Formal Statement of Disability Proceeding shall be conducted before a three-member hearing panel. Members of the panel shall be appointed by the Chief Justice of the Supreme Court within 14 days of the filing of the Formal Complaint or Formal Statement of Disability Proceeding with the Supreme Court. The panel shall consist of one judge or retired judge in good standing, one lawyer, and one member of the public. Whenever possible, the public member shall be a former member of the board. The judge or retired judge member shall be the presider, and shall have the powers of a judge of the district court for these proceedings.

(c) Notice of Hearing.

(1) The hearing panel shall schedule a public hearing. The date shall be selected to afford the judge ample time to prepare for the hearing, but shall not be later than 90 days after the filing of the Formal Complaint or Formal Statement Of Disability Proceeding with the Supreme Court. The judge and all counsel shall be notified of the time and place of the hearing.

(2) In extraordinary circumstances, the hearing panel shall have the authority to extend the hearing date as it deems proper.

Adopted July 5, 1978. Amended May 20, 1986, eff. July 1, 1986; Dec. 27, 1989, eff. Jan. 1, 1990; Nov. 1, 1995; March 31, 2009, eff. July 1, 2009.

Historical Notes

The order of the Minnesota Supreme Court [C4–85–697] dated November 1, 1995, provides in part that the Code of Judicial Conduct and the Rules of the Board on Judicial Standards, as amended, "shall govern all matters which come before the Board on Judicial Standards on or after the 1st day of January 1996."

RULE 9. DISCOVERY

(a) Witnesses; Depositions. Within 20 days after the service of a response, or after the expiration of the time for service of a response, whichever occurs first, counsel for the board and the judge shall exchange the names and addresses of all persons known to have knowledge of the relevant facts. The presider of the hearing panel shall set a date for the exchange of the names and addresses of all witnesses the parties intend to call at the hearing. Subpoenas and depositions shall be governed by Rule 2(e).

(b) Other Evidence. Counsel for the board and the judge shall exchange:

(1) non-privileged evidence relevant to the Formal Complaint, documents to be presented at the hearing, witness statements, and summaries of interviews with witnesses who will be called at the hearing; and

(2) other material only upon good cause shown to the presider of the panel.

The presider may authorize service of interrogatories upon request by the board or the judge.

(c) Exculpatory Evidence. Counsel for the board and the executive secretary shall provide the judge with exculpatory evidence relevant to the Formal Complaint.

(d) Duty of Supplementation. Both the board and the judge have a continuing duty to supplement information required to be exchanged under this rule.

(e) Completion of Discovery. All discovery shall be completed within 60 days of the service of the response or the expiration of the time for service of the response, whichever occurs first.

(f) Failure to Disclose. The presider of the hearing panel may preclude either party from calling a witness at the hearing if the party has not provided the opposing party with the witness' name and address, any statements taken from the witness, or summaries of any interviews with the witness.

(g) Resolution of Disputes. Disputes concerning discovery shall be determined by the presider of the hearing panel before whom the matter is pending. The decisions of the presider may not be appealed before entry of the panel's disposition in the disciplinary proceeding.

(h) Civil Rules Not Applicable. Proceedings under these rules are not subject to the Rules of Civil Procedure regarding discovery except Rules 26.03, 30.02–.07, 32.04–.05, and 37.04.

Adopted July 5, 1978. Amended May 20, 1986, eff. July 1, 1986; Dec. 27, 1989, eff. Jan. 1, 1990; Nov. 1, 1995; March 31, 2009, eff. July 1, 2009.

Historical Notes

The order of the Minnesota Supreme Court [C4–85–697] dated November 1, 1995, provides in part that the Code of Judicial Conduct and the Rules of the Board on Judicial Standards, as amended, "shall govern all matters which come before the Board on Judicial Standards on or after the 1st day of January 1996."

RULE 10. PUBLIC HEARING

(a) Rules of Evidence. All testimony shall be under oath, and the Rules of Evidence shall apply except that affidavits and depositions are admissible in lieu of testimony.

(b) Presentation: Burden of Proof; Cross–Examination; Recording.

(1) An attorney or attorneys of the board's staff, or special counsel retained for the purpose, shall present the matter to the panel.

(2) The board has the burden of proving by clear and convincing evidence the facts justifying action.

(3) The judge shall be permitted to adduce evidence and produce and cross-examine witnesses, subject to the Rules of Evidence.

(4) Every formal hearing conducted under these rules shall be recorded verbatim.

(c) Amendments. By leave of the presider of the panel for good cause shown or by consent of the judge, the Formal Complaint or Formal Statement of Disability Proceeding may be amended after commencement of the hearing if the judge and the judge's counsel are given adequate time to prepare a response.

Adopted July 5, 1978. Amended May 20, 1986, eff. July 1, 1986; Dec. 27, 1989, eff. Jan. 1, 1990; Nov. 1, 1995; March 31, 2009, eff. July 1, 2009.

Historical Notes

The order of the Minnesota Supreme Court [C4–85–697] dated November 1, 1995, provides in part that the Code of Judicial Conduct and the Rules of the Board on Judicial Standards, as amended, "shall govern all matters which come before the Board on Judicial Standards on or after the 1st day of January 1996."

RULE 11. FINDINGS, DISPOSITION, AND APPEAL

(a) Findings. The hearing panel shall make findings of fact and conclusions of law as to whether there is clear and convincing evidence that the judge committed misconduct under the grounds for discipline in Rule 4. If the panel finds there is not clear and convincing evidence, the panel shall dismiss the case. If the panel finds there is clear and convincing evidence, the panel shall impose or recommend sanctions under Rule 11(b).

(b) Disposition. If the hearing panel finds clear and convincing evidence of misconduct, the panel may:

(1) enter into a deferred disposition agreement for a specified period of time upon reasonable conditions, and the agreement may specify the disposition upon completion;

(2) issue a public reprimand; or

(3) recommend any of the following sanctions to the Supreme Court:

(i) Removal;

(ii) Retirement;

(iii) Imposing discipline as an attorney;

(iv) Imposing limitations or conditions on the performance of judicial duties;

(v) Censure;

(vi) Imposing a civil penalty;

(vii) Suspension with or without pay; or

(viii) Any combination of the above sanctions.

(c) Filing and Service. The hearing panel must file its findings of fact, conclusions of law, and disposition with the Supreme Court within 7 days after issuance of the disposition. The panel shall serve copies on the board and respondent judge. Proof of service shall also be filed with the Supreme Court.

(d) Appeal. The board or judge may appeal the disposition of the hearing panel. The appeal shall proceed under Rule 14. The disposition of the panel becomes final if no appeal is taken within 60 days after issuance of the disposition. If the panel determines it is appropriate to issue a public reprimand, the reprimand shall be stayed until the time for appeal has run or any appeal is completed.

Adopted July 5, 1978. Amended May 20, 1986, eff. July 1, 1986; Dec. 27, 1989, eff. Jan. 1, 1990; Nov. 1, 1995; March 30, 1999, eff. March 30, 1999; March 31, 2009, eff. July 1, 2009.

Advisory Committee Comment—1999 Amendment

Rule 11(d)(5) has been modified by deleting reprimand from the list of sanctions that may be issued after a formal hearing. Under Rule 6(d)(1)(ii), a reprimand may be issued by the board without resort to formal proceedings in situations involving conduct that is unacceptable under one of the grounds for judicial discipline but not so serious as to warrant further discipline, such as a censure, by the Supreme Court.

Historical Notes

The order of the Minnesota Supreme Court [C4–85–697] dated November 1, 1995, provides in part that the Code of Judicial Conduct and the Rules of the Board on Judicial Standards, as amended, "shall govern all matters which come before the Board on Judicial Standards on or after the 1st day of January 1996."

The order of the Minnesota Supreme Court [C4–85–697] dated March 30, 1999, amending the Rules of the Board on Judicial Standards provides in part that the "(t)he inclusion of Advisory Committee comments is made for convenience and does not reflect court approval of the comments made therein."

RULE 12. COSTS

(a) Witness Fees.

(1) All witnesses shall receive fees and expenses to the same extent allowable in an ordinary civil action.

(2) Expenses of witnesses shall be borne by the party calling them, unless:

(i) Physical or mental disability of the judge is in issue, in which case the board shall reimburse the judge for the reasonable expenses of the witnesses whose testimony is related to the disability; or

(ii) The judge is exonerated of the charges, in which case the Supreme Court may determine that the imposition of costs and expert witness fees would work a financial hardship or injustice and shall then order that those fees be reimbursed.

(b) Transcript Cost. A transcript of all proceedings shall be provided to the judge without cost.

(c) Other Costs. All other costs of these proceedings shall be at public expense.

Adopted July 5, 1978. Amended May 20, 1986, eff. July 1, 1986; Dec. 27, 1989, eff. Jan. 1, 1990; Nov. 1, 1995.

Historical Notes

The order of the Minnesota Supreme Court [C4–85–697] dated November 1, 1995, provides in part that the Code of Judicial Conduct and the Rules of the Board on Judicial Standards, as amended, "shall govern all matters which come before the Board on Judicial Standards on or after the 1st day of January 1996."

RULE 13. DISPOSITION BY CONSENT

(a) Agreement. At any time after issuance of the Formal Complaint or Formal Statement of Disability Proceeding and before conclusion of any hearing panel proceedings under Rules 10, 11, and 16, the judge and the board may enter into an agreement in which the judge admits to any or all of the charges or allegations of disability in exchange for a stated disposition. Entry into the agreement shall stay the proceedings of the panel. The agreement shall set forth:

(1) a statement of the facts;

(2) the allegations to which the judge is admitting; and

(3) the agreed-upon disposition.

(b) Disposition. If the agreed-upon disposition is one the board is authorized to impose under Rule 6(f)(4), proceedings before the hearing panel shall terminate, and the board shall impose the disposition. If the agreed-upon disposition is one the Board is not authorized to impose under Rule 6(f)(4), the agreement shall be submitted to the Supreme Court. The Court shall either enter an order implementing or rejecting the agreement. If the stated disposition is rejected by the Supreme Court, the agreement may be withdrawn but the facts admitted to in the agreement can be used against the judge in such further proceedings as the Court may direct.

Adopted March 31, 2009, eff. July 1, 2009.

RULE 14. SUPREME COURT REVIEW

(a) Prompt Consideration. Upon the filing of a recommendation for discipline or disability retirement, the Court shall promptly docket the matter for expedited consideration, but not sooner than the end of the time allowed for appeal of the panel's disposition by the board or judge. If the board or judge appeals the disposition of the hearing panel, the Court shall consider the recommended disposition under Rule 11(b)(3) or Rule 16(f)(1)(ii) at the same time as any appeal regarding those recommendations.

(b) Briefs. The board shall, and the judge may, file briefs with the Court in accordance with the requirements of Rule 128, Rules of Civil Appellate Procedure. Any party seeking to challenge a finding of fact by the panel shall order a transcript.

(c) Additional Findings and Filings; Supplemental Record.

(1) If the Court desires an expansion of the record or additional findings with respect either to the recommendation for discipline or to the sanction to be imposed, it shall remand the matter to the hearing panel with appropriate directions, retaining jurisdiction, and shall stay proceedings pending receipt of the panel's filing of the additional record.

(2) The Court may order additional filings or oral argument as to specified issues or the entire matter.

(3) The Court without remand and prior to the imposition of discipline may accept or solicit supplementary filings with respect to medical or other information, provided that the parties have notice and an opportunity to be heard.

(d) Delay for Further Proceedings. The Court, on receipt of notice of an additional proceeding before the board involving the same judge, may stay proceedings pending the board's termination of this additional proceeding. In the event that additional recommendations for discipline of the judge are filed, the Court may impose a single sanction covering all recommendations.

(e) Decision. When the hearing panel recommends the Supreme Court impose sanctions under Rule 11(b)(3), the Court shall review the record of the proceedings, giving deference to the facts, and shall file a written opinion and judgment directing such discipline or other action as it concludes is just and proper. If the judge or board has filed an appeal under Rule 11(d), the Court may accept the recommendation of the panel, or reject or modify it in whole or in part.

(f) Consideration of Lawyer Discipline. When the hearing panel recommends the removal of a judge, the Court shall promptly notify the judge and the Lawyers Professional Responsibility Board and give them an opportunity to be heard in the Court on the issue of lawyer discipline.

(g) Charge Against Supreme Court Justice. When any Formal Complaint or Formal Statement of Disability Proceeding has been filed against a member of the Supreme Court, the review under Rule 14 shall be submitted to and heard by a panel consisting of the Chief Judge of the Court of Appeals or designee and six others chosen at random from among the judges of the Court of Appeals by the Chief Judge or designee.

(h) Petition for Rehearing. In its decision, the Court may direct that no petition for rehearing will be entertained, in which event its decision shall be final upon filing. If the Court does not so direct, the respondent may file a petition for rehearing in accordance with the requirements of Rule 140, Rules of Civil Appellate Procedure.

Adopted July 5, 1978. Amended May 20, 1986, eff. July 1, 1986; Dec. 27, 1989, eff. Jan. 1, 1990; Nov. 1, 1995; March 31, 2009, eff. July 1, 2009.

Historical Notes

The order of the Minnesota Supreme Court [C4–85–697] dated November 1, 1995, provides in part that the Code of Judicial Conduct and the Rules of the Board on Judicial Standards, as amended, "shall govern all matters which come before the Board on Judicial Standards on or after the 1st day of January 1996."

RULE 15. INTERIM SUSPENSION

(a) Pending Criminal Prosecution. The Supreme Court may, without the necessity of board action, suspend a judge with pay upon the filing of an indictment or complaint charging the judge with a crime punishable as a felony under state or federal law. The Supreme Court may suspend the pay of such judge upon a conviction of a crime punishable as a felony under state or federal law or any other crime involving moral turpitude. If the conviction is reversed, suspension terminates and the judge shall be paid the salary for the period of suspension.

(b) Pending Final Decision. Interim suspension, with pay, pending final decision as to ultimate discipline, may be ordered by the Supreme Court in any proceeding under these rules.

(c) Review of Permissive Suspension. Any judge suspended under section (b) of this rule shall be given a prompt hearing and determination by the Supreme Court upon application for review of the interim suspension order.

Adopted July 5, 1978. Amended May 20, 1986, eff. July 1, 1986; Dec. 27, 1989, eff. Jan. 1, 1990; Nov. 1, 1995; March 31, 2009, eff. July 1, 2009.

Historical Notes

The order of the Minnesota Supreme Court [C4–85–697] dated November 1, 1995, provides in part that the Code of Judicial Conduct and the Rules of the Board on Judicial Standards, as amended, "shall govern all matters which come before the Board on Judicial Standards on or after the 1st day of January 1996."

RULE 16. SPECIAL PROVISIONS FOR CASES INVOLVING DISABILITY

(a) Proceedings In General. When an inquiry alleges facts that could constitute disability, the board shall follow the same procedures used with respect to misconduct, except as modified by this rule.

(b) Initiation of Proceedings. The board may initiate an inquiry into a case involving disability:

(1) upon receiving a complaint alleging a disability;

(2) when an investigation indicates the alleged conduct may be due to disability; or

(3) when the judge asserts inability to defend in a disciplinary proceeding due to a disability.

(c) Evaluation. Upon initiation of an inquiry into a case involving disability, the executive secretary shall conduct an evaluation pursuant to Rule 6(c).

(d) Investigation; Notice; Medical Privilege.

(1) If upon review of the preliminary evaluation, or on its own motion, the board authorizes an investigation under Rule 6(d), the board shall give notice pursuant to Rule 6(d)(2) to the judge alleged to have a disability. The notice shall instruct the judge that when providing a written response under Rule 6(d)(5), the judge shall admit or deny the disability.

(2) The purpose of an investigation conducted under this rule is to determine whether there is reasonable cause to believe the judge has a disability.

(3) If the judge admits to a disability or provides affirmative evidence of a disability as a defense in a disciplinary proceeding, the admission or provision of evidence shall constitute reasonable cause to believe the judge has a disability and waiver of medical privilege as to records relevant to the alleged disability.

If the judge denies the disability, the board shall determine whether there is credible evidence of a disability. The board may consult with a qualified professional in the area of the alleged disability to determine whether the evidence before the board constitutes credible evidence. If there is credible evidence of a disability, the denial constitutes a waiver of medical privilege as to records relevant to the alleged disability. If there is not credible evidence of a disability, the judge does not waive medical privilege, and the board shall continue the investigation under Rule 6 as a disciplinary proceeding.

(4) If medical privilege is waived, the board may require the judge to provide medical records relevant to the alleged disability. Disputes concerning the relevancy of medical records shall be determined by the Supreme Court or its designee.

(5) If medical privilege is waived, the board may request that the judge consent to a physical or mental examination by a qualified medical practitioner designated by the board. The purpose of the examination is to assist the board in determining whether there is reasonable cause to believe the judge has a disability. The report of the medical practitioner shall be furnished to the board and the judge. If the judge fails or refuses to submit to a medical examination, the judge may not present as evidence the results of any medical examinations done on the judge's behalf, and the board may consider the judge's refusal or failure as evidence that the judge has a disability.

The judge has the right to an additional independent medical examination provided by experts other than those designated by the board, but the examination shall be at the sole expense of the judge, and written reports of any examination shall be provided to the board as soon as medically feasible.

(e) Disposition After Investigation.

(1) If the board determines there is not reasonable cause to believe the judge has a disability, the board shall determine whether a disciplinary disposition under Rule 6(f) is appropriate.

(2) If the board determines there is reasonable cause to believe the judge has a disability, the board may:

(i) enter into a deferred disposition agreement as provided in Rule 6(f)(5)(i); or

(ii) issue a Formal Statement of Disability Proceeding.

(f) Hearing. Upon issuance of a Formal Statement of Disability Proceeding, a hearing shall be held under Rules 10 and 11 to determine whether there is clear and convincing evidence the judge has a disability. If the board has also filed a Formal Complaint, the hearing panel shall determine whether there is clear and convincing evidence that the judge committed misconduct and whether the misconduct was related to a disability. The panel may exclude the public from portions of the proceedings to hear evidence on psychological or medical materials or other evidence that would not be accessible to the public.

(1) If the hearing panel finds clear and convincing evidence of a disability, the panel may:

(i) enter into a deferred disposition agreement as provided in Rule 11(b)(1); or

(ii) recommend any of the following actions to the Supreme Court:

(A) Removal;

(B) Disability retirement if the disability is or is likely to become permanent;

(C) Imposition of limitations or conditions on the performance of judicial duties;

(D) Suspension with or without pay; or

(E) Any combination of the above actions.

(2) The hearing panel may also impose or recommend a disciplinary disposition with regard to misconduct, if applicable, pursuant to Rule 11(b).

(3) Any disposition of the hearing panel is public.

(4) The board or judge may appeal the decision of the hearing panel as provided in Rule 11(d).

(g) Petition for Reinstatement After Disability Suspension.

(1) A judge suspended by the Supreme Court due to disability may petition the board for reinstatement. Reinstatement may only be effected by order of the Supreme Court.

(2) The judge shall provide to the board the name of each qualified medical, psychological, or other expert, or qualified program or referral by whom or in which the judge has been examined or treated relevant to the disability since suspension. The judge shall furnish to the board written consent to the release of information and records from these sources.

(3) Upon the filing of a petition for reinstatement, the board may take or direct whatever action it deems necessary to determine whether the disability has been removed, including requesting the judge to consent to a physical or mental examination by a qualified professional in the area of the disability designated by the board.

(4) If the board determines, after conducting a review under paragraph (3), the judge has been restored to capacity to perform judicial duties, the board shall recommend to the Supreme Court that the judge be reinstated. If the board determines that the judge continues to have a disability, it shall notify the judge of its determination. The judge shall have 20 days after service of the notice to either accept the determination of the board or request a formal hearing on the petition. If the judge accepts the determination of the board, there will be no further proceedings on the petition. If the judge requests a formal hearing, proceedings will continue under Rule 16(f), but the petition shall replace the Formal Statement of Disability Proceeding.

(h) Representation by Counsel. If the judge in any proceeding under this rule is not represented by counsel, the board or, if a hearing panel has been appointed, the presider of the panel, shall appoint an attorney to represent the judge at public expense.

Adopted July 5, 1978. Amended May 20, 1986, eff. July 1, 1986; Dec. 27, 1989, eff. Jan. 1, 1990; Nov. 1, 1995; March 31, 2009, eff. July 1, 2009.

Historical Notes

The order of the Minnesota Supreme Court [C4–85–697] dated November 1, 1995, provides in part that the Code of Judicial Conduct and the Rules of the Board on Judicial Standards, as amended, "shall govern all matters which come before the Board on Judicial Standards on or after the 1st day of January 1996."

RULE 17. INVOLUNTARY RETIREMENT

(a) Procedure. A judge who refuses to retire voluntarily may be involuntarily retired by the Supreme Court. If attempts to convince a judge to retire voluntarily fail, then the board shall proceed as provided in Rules 8, 9, 10, and 11. The Supreme Court shall then proceed as provided in Rule 13.

(b) Effect of Involuntary Retirement. A judge who is involuntarily retired shall be ineligible to perform judicial duties pending further order of the Supreme Court and may, upon order of the Supreme Court, be transferred to inactive status or indefinitely suspended from practicing law in the jurisdiction.

Adopted July 5, 1978. Amended May 20, 1986, eff. July 1, 1986; Dec. 27, 1989, eff. Jan. 1, 1990; Nov. 1, 1995; March 31, 2009, eff. July 1, 2009.

Historical Notes

The order of the Minnesota Supreme Court [C4–85–697] dated November 1, 1995, provides in part that the Code of Judicial Conduct and the Rules of the Board on Judicial Standards, as amended, "shall govern all matters which come before the Board on Judicial Standards on or after the 1st day of January 1996."

RULE 18. APPLICATION TO THE GOVERNOR FOR DISABILITY RETIREMENT

If a judge applies to the Governor for disability retirement, the Governor may make a written request that the board provide the Governor with information about the existence, status, and nature of any pending complaints or investigations relating to the judge. The board must promptly provide the information to the Governor. Upon receipt of a written waiver by the judge, the board may also provide the Governor with any of the board's documents related to the complaint, investigation, or the judge. The Governor may further disclose the information for the purpose of consulting with a qualified professional in the area of the alleged disability.

Adopted March 31, 2009, eff. July 1, 2009.

RULE 19. EXPUNGEMENT

The executive secretary shall expunge records as follows:

(a) Dismissals. All records or evidence of a complaint where the board did not find reasonable cause to believe the judge committed misconduct or where the board did not find reasonable cause to believe the judge has a disability shall be destroyed three years after the board receives the complaint or authorizes an investigation, whichever occurs first. If the board receives a new complaint involving the same judge within the three years, the new complaint shall renew the three-year period.

(b) Case Files on Deceased Judges. All case files on deceased judges shall be destroyed.

(c) Exceptions. Upon application by the executive secretary to the chair for good cause shown and with notice and opportunity to be heard to the judge, records which would otherwise be expunged under this rule may be retained for such additional time as the chair may deem appropriate.

Adopted Nov. 5, 1995. Amended March 31, 2009, eff. July 1, 2009.

Historical Notes

The order of the Minnesota Supreme Court [C4–85–697] dated November 1, 1995, provides in part that the Code of Judicial Conduct and the Rules of the Board on Judicial Standards, as amended, "shall govern all matters which come before the Board on Judicial Standards on or after the 1st day of January 1996."

RULE 20. USE OF ALLEGATIONS FROM DISMISSED INQUIRIES.

(a) Use of Allegations in General. Allegations from an inquiry that was dismissed shall not be referred to by the board in any subsequent proceedings or used for any purpose in any judicial or lawyer disciplinary proceeding against the judge, except as provided in this rule.

Allegations from a dismissed inquiry may be reinvestigated with permission of the board if, within three years after dismissal, additional information becomes known to the board regarding the inquiry.

(b) Use of Allegations From Dismissal with Letter of Caution. Allegations from an inquiry dismissed with a letter of caution may be used within three years after dismissal in subsequent proceedings only as follows:

(i) The fact that the inquiry was dismissed with a letter of caution may not be used to establish the misconduct alleged in a subsequent proceeding. However, the underlying conduct described in the letter of caution may be charged in a subsequent Formal Complaint, and evidence in support thereof may be presented to the hearing panel at the public hearing under Rule 10.

(ii) If the underlying conduct described in the letter of caution is charged in a subsequent Formal Complaint, and the hearing panel finds the judge committed misconduct with respect to the facts underlying the dismissal with letter of caution, the letter of caution may be considered by the panel in determining an appropriate sanction.

Adopted March 31, 2009, eff. July 1, 2009.

RULE 21. PERIODIC REVIEW

The Supreme Court may periodically appoint a committee to review the records and proceedings of the board for the purpose of evaluating the effectiveness of the disciplinary process. The records and proceedings reviewed by the committee shall be maintained as confidential except for records and proceedings that have already been made public. The final written and oral report of the committee may present information about the board as long as it contains no specific information that would easily identify a judge, witness, or complainant.

Adopted March 31, 2009, eff. July 1, 2009.

RULE 22. AMENDMENT OF RULES

As procedural and other experience may require or suggest, the board may petition the Supreme Court for further rules of implementation or for necessary amendments to these rules.

Adopted July 5, 1978. Amended May 20, 1986, eff. July 1, 1986; Dec. 27, 1989, eff. Jan. 1, 1990; Nov. 1, 1995; March 31, 2009, eff. July 1, 2009.

Historical Notes

The order of the Minnesota Supreme Court [C4–85–697] dated November 1, 1995, provides in part that the Code of Judicial Conduct and the Rules of the Board on Judicial Standards, as amended, "shall govern all matters which come before the Board on Judicial Standards on or after the 1st day of January 1996."

MINNESOTA RULES OF PROFESSIONAL CONDUCT

Effective September 1, 1985

Including Amendments Received Through January 1, 2014

Comments

The Comments were included in the order of the Minnesota Supreme Court dated June 13, 1985 enacting the Minnesota Rules of Professional Conduct and repealing the former Minnesota Code of Professional Responsibility.

The order of the Minnesota Supreme Court dated December 27, 1989 amending Rules 1.6, 1.15, 7.2, and 8.4 provided in part that "(t)he comments are included for convenience and the Supreme Court does not necessarily approve the content of the comments." The order of the Minnesota Supreme Court dated April 14, 1992 amending Rules 1.6, 8.3, and 8.4 provided in part that "(t)he comments are included for convenience and the Supreme Court does not approve the content of the comments."

The order of the Minnesota Supreme Court dated December 11, 1995, adopting Rule 1.17 and amending Rules 5.4, 6.1, 7.2, and 7.4, provided in part that "(t)he inclusion of comments is made for convenience and does not reflect court approval of the comments made therein."

PREAMBLE: A LAWYER'S RESPONSIBILITIES

[1] A lawyer, as a member of the legal profession, is a representative of clients, an officer of the legal system and a public citizen having special responsibility for the quality of justice.

[2] As a representative of clients, a lawyer performs various functions. As advisor, a lawyer provides a client with an informed understanding of the client's legal rights and obligations and explains their practical implications. As advocate, a lawyer zealously asserts the client's position under the rules of the adversary system. As negotiator, a lawyer seeks a result advantageous to the client but consistent with requirements of honest dealings with others. As evaluator, a lawyer examines a client's legal affairs and reports about them to the client or to others.

[3] In addition to these representational functions, a lawyer may serve as a third-party neutral, a nonrepresentational role helping the parties to resolve a dispute or other matter. Some of these rules apply directly to lawyers who are or have served as third-party neutrals. See, e.g., Rules 1.12 and 2.4. In addition, there are rules that apply to lawyers who are not active in the practice of law or to practicing lawyers even when they are acting in a nonprofessional capacity. For example, a lawyer who commits fraud in the conduct of a business is subject to discipline for engaging in conduct involving dishonesty, fraud, deceit, or misrepresentation. See Rule 8.4.

[4] In all professional functions a lawyer should be competent, prompt, and diligent. A lawyer should maintain communication with a client concerning the representation. A lawyer should keep in confidence information relating to the representation of a client except so far as disclosure is required or permitted by the Rules of Professional Conduct or other law.

[5] A lawyer's conduct should conform to the requirements of the law, both in professional service to clients and in the lawyer's business and personal affairs. A lawyer should use the law's procedures only for legitimate purposes and not to harass or intimidate others. A lawyer should demonstrate respect for the legal system and for those who serve it, including judges, other lawyers, and public officials. While it is a lawyer's duty, when necessary, to challenge the rectitude of official action, it is also a lawyer's duty to uphold legal process.

[6] As a public citizen, a lawyer should seek improvement of the law, access to the legal system, the administration of justice and the quality of service rendered by the legal profession. As a member of a learned profession, a lawyer should cultivate knowledge of the law beyond its use for clients, employ that knowledge in reform of the law and work to strengthen legal education. In addition, a lawyer should further the public's understanding of and confidence in the rule of law and the justice system because legal institutions in a constitutional democracy depend on popular participation and support to maintain their authority. A lawyer should be mindful of deficiencies in the administration of justice and of the fact that the poor, and sometimes persons who are not poor, cannot afford adequate legal assistance. Therefore, all lawyers should devote professional time and resources and use civic influence to ensure equal access to our system of justice for all those who because of economic or social barriers cannot afford or secure adequate legal counsel. A lawyer should aid the legal profession in pursuing these objectives and should help the bar regulate itself in the public interest.

[7] Many of a lawyer's professional responsibilities are prescribed in the Rules of Professional Conduct, as well as substantive and procedural law. However, a lawyer is also guided by personal conscience and the approbation of professional peers. A lawyer should strive to attain the highest level of skill, to improve the law and the legal profession, and to exemplify the legal profession's ideals of public service.

[8] A lawyer's responsibilities as a representative of clients, an officer of the legal system and a public citizen are usually harmonious. Thus, when an opposing party is well represented, a lawyer can be a zealous advocate on behalf of a client and at the same time assume that justice is being done. So also, a lawyer can be sure that preserving client confidences ordinarily serves the public interest because people are more likely to seek legal advice, and thereby heed their legal obligations, when they know their communications will be private.

[9] In the nature of law practice, however, conflicting responsibilities are encountered. Virtually all difficult ethical problems arise from the conflict between a lawyer's responsibilities to clients, the legal system and the lawyer's own interest in remaining an ethical person while earning a satisfactory living. The Rules of Professional Conduct often prescribe terms for resolving such conflicts. Within the framework of these rules, however, many difficult issues of professional discretion can arise. Such issues must be re-

solved through the exercise of sensitive professional and moral judgment guided by the basic principles underlying the rules. These principles include the lawyer's obligation to zealously protect and pursue a client's legitimate interests, within the bounds of the law, while maintaining a professional, courteous, and civil attitude toward all persons involved in the legal system.

[10] The legal profession is largely self-governing. Although other professions also have been granted powers of self-government, the legal profession is unique in this respect because of the close relationship between the profession and the processes of government and law enforcement. This connection is manifested in the fact that ultimate authority over the legal profession is vested largely in the courts.

[11] To the extent that lawyers meet the obligations of their professional calling, the occasion for government regulation is obviated. Self-regulation also helps maintain the legal profession's independence from government domination. An independent legal profession is an important force in preserving government under law, for abuse of legal authority is more readily challenged by a profession whose members are not dependent on government for the right to practice.

[12] The legal profession's relative autonomy carries with it special responsibilities of self-government. The profession has a responsibility to assure that its regulations are conceived in the public interest and not in furtherance of parochial or self-interested concerns of the bar. Every lawyer is responsible for observance of the Rules of Professional Conduct. A lawyer should also aid in securing observance of these rules by other lawyers. Neglect of these responsibilities compromises the independence of the profession and the public interest which it serves.

[13] Lawyers play a vital role in the preservation of society. The fulfillment of this role requires an understanding by lawyers of their relationship to our legal system. The Rules of Professional Conduct, when properly applied, serve to define that relationship.

Adopted June 13, 1985, eff. Sept. 1, 1985. Amended June 17, 2005, eff. Oct. 1, 2005.

SCOPE

[14] The Rules of Professional Conduct are rules of reason. They should be interpreted with reference to the purposes of legal representation and of the law itself. Some of the rules are imperatives, cast in the terms "shall" or "shall not." These define proper conduct for purposes of professional discipline. Others, generally cast in the term "may," are permissive and define areas under the rules in which the lawyer has discretion to exercise professional judgment. No disciplinary action should be taken when the lawyer chooses either not to act or to act within the bounds of such discretion. Other rules define the nature of relationships between the lawyer and others. The rules are thus partly obligatory and disciplinary and partly constitutive and descriptive in that they define a lawyer's professional role. Many of the comments use the term "should." Comments do not add obligations to the rules but provide guidance for practicing in compliance with the rules.

[15] The rules presuppose a larger legal context shaping the lawyer's role. That context includes court rules and statutes relating to matters of licensure, laws defining specific obligations of lawyers and substantive and procedural law in general. The comments are sometimes used to alert lawyers to their responsibilities under such other law.

[16] Compliance with the rules, as with all law in an open society, depends primarily upon understanding and voluntary compliance, secondarily upon reinforcement by peer and public opinion and finally, when necessary, upon enforcement through disciplinary proceedings. The rules do not, however, exhaust the moral and ethical considerations that should inform a lawyer, for no worthwhile human activity can be completely defined by legal rules. For example, Minnesota's Professionalism Aspirations provide guidance on best practices in situations typical in the practice of law. The rules simply provide a framework for the ethical practice of law.

[17] Furthermore, for purposes of determining the lawyer's authority and responsibility, principles of substantive law external to these rules determine whether a client-lawyer relationship exists. Most of the duties flowing from the client-lawyer relationship attach only after the client has requested the lawyer to render legal services and the lawyer has agreed to do so. But there are some duties, such as that of confidentiality under Rule 1.6, that attach when the lawyer agrees to consider whether a client-lawyer relationship shall be established. See Rule 1.18. Whether a client-lawyer relationship exists for any specific purpose can depend on the circumstances and may be a question of fact.

[18] Under various legal provisions, including constitutional, statutory and common law, the responsibilities of government lawyers may include authority concerning legal matters that ordinarily reposes in the client in private client-lawyer relationships. For example, a lawyer for a government agency may have authority on behalf of the government to decide upon settlement or whether to appeal from an adverse judgment. Such authority in various respects is generally vested in the attorney general and the state's attorney in state government, and their federal counterparts, and the same may be true of other government law officers. Also, lawyers under the supervision of these officers may be authorized to represent several government agencies in intragovernmental legal controversies in circumstances where a private lawyer could not represent multiple private clients. These rules do not abrogate any such authority.

[19] Failure to comply with an obligation or prohibition imposed by a rule is a basis for invoking the disciplinary process. The rules presuppose that disciplinary assessment of a lawyer's conduct will be made on the basis of the facts and circumstances as they existed at the time of the conduct in question and in recognition of the fact that a lawyer often has to act upon uncertain or incomplete evidence of the situation. Moreover, the rules presuppose that whether discipline should be imposed for a violation, and the severity of a sanction, depend on all the circumstances, such as the willfulness and seriousness of the violation, extenuating factors and whether there have been previous violations.

[20] Violation of a rule should not itself give rise to a cause of action against a lawyer nor should it create any presumption in such a case that a legal duty has been breached. In addition, violation of a rule does not necessarily warrant any other nondisciplinary remedy, such as disqualification of a lawyer in pending litigation. The rules are designed to provide guidance to lawyers and to provide a structure for regulating conduct through disciplinary agencies. They are not designed to be a basis for civil liability. Furthermore, the purpose of the rules can be subverted when they are invoked by opposing parties as procedural weapons. The fact that a rule is a just basis for a lawyer's self-assessment, or for sanctioning a lawyer under the administration of a disciplinary authority, does not imply that an antagonist in a

collateral proceeding or transaction has standing to seek enforcement of the rule. Nevertheless, because the rules do establish standards of conduct for lawyers, a lawyer's violation of a rule may be evidence of breach of the applicable standard of conduct.

[21] The comment accompanying each rule explains and illustrates the meaning and purpose of the rule. The Preamble and this note on Scope provide general orientation. The comments are intended as guides to interpretation, but the text of each rule is authoritative.

Adopted June 13, 1985, eff. Sept. 1, 1985. Amended June 17, eff. Oct. 1, 2005.

Rule 1.0. Terminology

(a) "Belief" or "believes" denotes that the person involved actually supposed the fact in question to be true. A person' s belief may be inferred from circumstances.

(b) "Confirmed in writing," when used in reference to the informed consent of a person, denotes informed consent that is given in writing by the person or a writing that a lawyer promptly transmits to the person confirming an oral informed consent. See paragraph (f) for the definition of "informed consent." If it is not feasible to obtain or transmit the writing at the time the person gives informed consent, then the lawyer must obtain or transmit it within a reasonable time thereafter.

(c) "Consult" or "consultation" denotes communication of information reasonably sufficient to permit the client to appreciate the significance of the matter in question.

(d) "Firm" or "law firm" denotes a lawyer or lawyers in a law partnership, professional corporation, sole proprietorship, or other association authorized to practice law; or lawyers employed in a legal services organization or the legal department of a corporation or other organization.

(e) "Fraud" or "fraudulent" denotes conduct that is fraudulent under the substantive or procedural law of the applicable jurisdiction and has a purpose to deceive.

(f) "Informed consent" denotes the agreement by a person to a proposed course of conduct after the lawyer has communicated adequate information and explanation about the material risks of and reasonably available alternatives to the proposed course of conduct.

(g) "Knowingly," "known," or " knows" denotes actual knowledge of the fact in question. A person's knowledge may be inferred from circumstances.

(h) "Partner" denotes a member of a partnership, a shareholder in a law firm organized as a professional corporation, or a member of an association authorized to practice law.

(i) "Reasonable" or "reasonably" when used in relation to conduct by a lawyer denotes the conduct of a reasonably prudent and competent lawyer.

(j) "Reasonable belief" or "reasonably believes" when used in reference to a lawyer denotes that the lawyer believes the matter in question and that the circumstances are such that the belief is reasonable.

(k) "Reasonably should know" when used in reference to a lawyer denotes that a lawyer of reasonable prudence and competence would ascertain the matter in question.

(*l*) "Screened" denotes the isolation of a lawyer from any participation in a matter through the timely imposition of procedures within a firm that are reasonably adequate under the circumstances to protect information that the isolated lawyer is obligated to protect under these rules or other law.

(m) "Substantial" when used in reference to degree or extent denotes a material matter of clear and weighty importance.

(n) "Tribunal" denotes a court, an arbitrator in a binding arbitration proceeding, or a legislative body, administrative agency, or other body acting in an adjudicative capacity. A legislative body, administrative agency, or other body acts in an adjudicative capacity when a neutral official, after the presentation of evidence or legal argument by a party or parties, will render a binding legal judgment directly affecting a party's interests in a particular matter.

(*o*) "Writing" or "written" denotes a tangible or electronic record of a communication or representation, including handwriting, typewriting, printing, photostating, photography, audio or videorecording, and e-mail. A "signed" writing includes an electronic sound, symbol or process attached to or logically associated with a writing and executed or adopted by a person with the intent to sign the writing.

Adopted June 13, 1985, eff. Sept. 1, 1985. Amended June 17, 2005, eff. Oct. 1, 2005.

Comment—2005

Confirmed in Writing

[1] If it is not feasible to obtain or transmit a written confirmation at the time the client gives informed consent, then the lawyer must obtain or transmit it within a reasonable time thereafter. If a lawyer has obtained a client's informed consent, the lawyer may act in reliance on that consent so long as it is confirmed in writing within a reasonable time thereafter.

Firm

[2] Whether two or more lawyers constitute a firm within paragraph (d) can depend on the specific facts. For example, two practitioners who share office space and occasionally consult or assist each other ordinarily would not be regarded as constituting a firm. However, if they present themselves to the public in a way that suggests that they are a firm or conduct themselves as a firm, they should be regarded as a firm for purposes of the rules. The terms of any formal agreement between associated lawyers are relevant in determining whether they are a firm, as is the fact that they have mutual

access to information concerning the clients they serve. Furthermore, it is relevant in doubtful cases to consider the underlying purpose of the rule that is involved. A group of lawyers could be regarded as a firm for purposes of the rule that the same lawyer should not represent opposing parties in litigation, while it might not be so regarded for purposes of the rule that information acquired by one lawyer is attributed to another.

[3] With respect to the law department of an organization there is ordinarily no question that the members of the department constitute a firm within the meaning of the Rules of Professional Conduct. There can be uncertainty, however, as to the identity of the client. For example, it may not be clear whether the law department of a corporation represents a subsidiary or an affiliated corporation, as well as the corporation by which the members of the department are directly employed. A similar question can arise concerning an unincorporated association and its local affiliates.

[4] Similar questions can also arise with respect to lawyers in legal aid and legal services organizations. Depending upon the structure of the organization, the entire organization or different components of it may constitute a firm or firms for purposes of these rules.

Fraud

[5] When used in these rules, the terms "fraud" or "fraudulent" refer to conduct that is characterized as such under the substantive or procedural law of the applicable jurisdiction and has a purpose to deceive. This does not include merely negligent misrepresentation or negligent failure to apprise another of relevant information. For purposes of these rules, it is not necessary that anyone has suffered damages or relied on the misrepresentation or failure to inform.

Informed Consent

[6] Many of the Rules of Professional Conduct require the lawyer to obtain the informed consent of a client or other person (e.g., a former client or, under certain circumstances, a prospective client) before accepting or continuing representation or pursuing a course of conduct. See, e.g., Rules 1.2(c), 1.6(b) and 1.7(b). The communication necessary to obtain such consent will vary according to the rule involved and the circumstances giving rise to the need to obtain informed consent. The lawyer must make reasonable efforts to ensure that the client or other person possesses information reasonably adequate to make an informed decision. Ordinarily, this will require communication that includes a disclosure of the facts and circumstances giving rise to the situation, any explanation reasonably necessary to inform the client or other person of the material advantages and disadvantages of the proposed course of conduct and a discussion of the client's or other person's options and alternatives. In some circumstances it may be appropriate for a lawyer to advise a client or other person to seek the advice of other counsel. A lawyer need not inform a client or other person of facts or implications already known to the client or other person; nevertheless, a lawyer who does not personally inform the client or other person assumes the risk that the client or other person is inadequately informed and the consent is invalid. In determining whether the information and explanation provided are reasonably adequate, relevant factors include whether the client or other person is experienced in legal matters generally and in making decisions of the type involved, and whether the client or other person is independently represented by other counsel in giving the consent. Normally, such persons need less information and explanation than others, and generally a client or other person who is independently represented by other counsel in giving the consent should be assumed to have given informed consent.

[7] Obtaining informed consent will usually require an affirmative response by the client or other person. In general, a lawyer may not assume consent from a client's or other person's silence. Consent may be inferred, however, from the conduct of a client or other person who has reasonably adequate information about the matter. A number of rules require that a person's consent be confirmed in writing. See Rules 1.7(b) and 1.9(a). For a definition of "writing" and "confirmed in writing," see paragraphs (*o*) and (b). Other rules require that a client's consent be obtained in a writing signed by the client. See, e.g., Rules 1.8(a) and (g). For a definition of "signed," see paragraph (*o*).

Screened

[8] This definition applies to situations where screening of a personally disqualified lawyer is permitted to remove imputation of a conflict of interest under Rule 1.10, 1.11, 1.12 or 1.18.

[9] The purpose of screening is to assure the affected parties that confidential information known by the personally disqualified lawyer remains protected. The personally disqualified lawyer should acknowledge the obligation not to communicate with any of the other lawyers in the firm with respect to the matter. Similarly, other lawyers in the firm who are working on the matter should be informed that the screening is in place and that they may not communicate with the personally disqualified lawyer with respect to the matter. Additional screening measures that are appropriate for the particular matter will depend on the circumstances. To implement, reinforce and remind all affected lawyers of the presence of the screening, it may be appropriate for the firm to undertake such procedures as a written undertaking by the screened lawyer to avoid any communication with other firm personnel and any contact with any firm files or other materials relating to the matter, written notice and instructions to all other firm personnel forbidding any communication with the screened lawyer relating to the matter, denial of access by the screened lawyer to firm files or other materials relating to the matter, and periodic reminders of the screen to the screened lawyer and all other firm personnel.

[10] In order to be effective, screening measures must be implemented as soon as practical after a lawyer or law firm knows or reasonably should know that there is a need for screening.

CLIENT–LAWYER RELATIONSHIP

Rule 1.1. Competence

A lawyer shall provide competent representation to a client. Competent representation requires the legal knowledge, skill, thoroughness, and preparation reasonably necessary for the representation.

Adopted June 13, 1985, eff. Sept. 1, 1985. Amended June 17, 2005, eff. Oct. 1, 2005.

Comment—2005

Legal Knowledge and Skill

[1] In determining whether a lawyer employs the requisite knowledge and skill in a particular matter, relevant factors include the relative complexity and specialized nature of the matter, the lawyer's general experience, the lawyer's training and experience in the field in question, the preparation and study the lawyer is able to give the matter, and whether it is feasible to refer the matter to, or associate or consult with, a lawyer of established competence in the field in question. In many instances, the required proficiency is that of a general practitioner. Expertise in a particular field of law may be required in some circumstances.

[2] A lawyer need not necessarily have special training or prior experience to handle legal problems of a type with which the lawyer is unfamiliar. A newly admitted lawyer can be as competent as a practitioner with long experience. Some important legal skills, such as the analysis of precedent, the evaluation of evidence and legal drafting, are required in all legal problems. Perhaps the most fundamental legal skill consists of determining what kind of legal problems a situation may involve, a skill that necessarily transcends any particular specialized knowledge. A lawyer can provide adequate representation in a wholly novel field through necessary study. Competent representation can also be provided through the association of a lawyer of established competence in the field in question.

[3] In an emergency, a lawyer may give advice or assistance in a matter in which the lawyer does not have the skill ordinarily required where referral to or consultation or association with another lawyer would be impractical. Even in an emergency, however, assistance should be limited to that reasonably necessary in the circumstances, for ill-considered action under emergency conditions can jeopardize the client's interest.

[4] A lawyer may accept representation where the requisite level of competence can be achieved by reasonable preparation. This applies as well to a lawyer who is appointed as counsel for an unrepresented person. See also Rule 6.2.

Thoroughness and Preparation

[5] Competent handling of a particular matter includes inquiry into and analysis of the factual and legal elements of the problem, and use of methods and procedures meeting the standards of competent practitioners. It also includes adequate preparation. The required attention and preparation are determined in part by what is at stake; major litigation and complex transactions ordinarily require more extensive treatment than matters of lesser complexity and consequence. An agreement between the lawyer and the client regarding the scope of the representation may limit the matters for which the lawyer is responsible. See Rule 1.2(c).

Maintaining Competence

[6] To maintain the requisite knowledge and skill, a lawyer should keep abreast of changes in the law and its practice, engage in continuing study and education and comply with all continuing legal education requirements to which the lawyer is subject.

Historical Notes

This rule is similar to provisions of former DR 6–101 of Minn. Code of Prof. Responsibility.

Rule 1.2. Scope of Representation and Allocation of Authority Between Client and Lawyer

(a) Subject to paragraphs (c) and (d), a lawyer shall abide by a client's decisions concerning the objectives of representation and, as required by Rule 1.4, shall consult with the client as to the means by which they are to be pursued. A lawyer may take such action on behalf of the client as is impliedly authorized to carry out the representation. A lawyer shall abide by a client's decision whether to settle a matter. In a criminal case, the lawyer shall abide by the client's decision, after consultation with the lawyer, as to a plea to be entered, whether to waive a jury trial and whether the client will testify.

(b) A lawyer's representation of a client, including representation by appointment, does not constitute an endorsement of the client's political, economic, social, or moral views or activities.

(c) A lawyer may limit the scope of the representation if the limitation is reasonable under the circumstances and the client gives informed consent.

(d) A lawyer shall not counsel a client to engage, or assist a client, in conduct that the lawyer knows is criminal or fraudulent, but a lawyer may discuss the legal consequences of any proposed course of conduct with a client and may counsel or assist a client to make a good faith effort to determine the validity, scope, meaning, or application of the law.

Adopted June 13, 1985, eff. Sept. 1, 1985. Amended June 17, 2005, eff. Oct. 1, 2005.

Comment—2005

Allocation of Authority between Client and Lawyer

[1] Paragraph (a) confers upon the client the ultimate authority to determine the purposes to be served by legal representation, within the limits

imposed by law and the lawyer's professional obligations. The decisions specified in paragraph (a), such as whether to settle a civil matter, must also be made by the client. See Rule 1.4(a)(1) for the lawyer's duty to communicate with the client about such decisions. With respect to the means by which the client's objectives are to be pursued, the lawyer shall consult with the client as required by Rule 1.4(a)(2) and may take such action as is impliedly authorized to carry out the representation.

[2] On occasion, however, a lawyer and a client may disagree about the means to be used to accomplish the client's objectives. Clients normally defer to the special knowledge and skill of their lawyer with respect to the means to be used to accomplish their objectives, particularly with respect to technical, legal, and tactical matters. Conversely, lawyers usually defer to the client regarding such questions as the expense to be incurred and concern for third persons who might be adversely affected. Because of the varied nature of the matters about which a lawyer and client might disagree and because the actions in question may implicate the interests of a tribunal or other persons, this rule does not prescribe how such disagreements are to be resolved. Other law, however, may be applicable and should be consulted by the lawyer. The lawyer should also consult with the client and seek a mutually acceptable resolution of the disagreement. If such efforts are unavailing and the lawyer has a fundamental disagreement with the client, the lawyer may withdraw from the representation. See Rule 1.16(b)(4). Conversely, the client may resolve the disagreement by discharging the lawyer. See Rule 1.16(a)(3).

[3] At the outset of a representation, the client may authorize the lawyer to take specific action on the client's behalf without further consultation. Absent a material change in circumstances and subject to Rule 1.4, a lawyer may rely on such an advance authorization. The client may, however, revoke such authority at any time.

[4] In a case in which the client appears to be suffering from diminished capacity, the lawyer's duty to abide by the client's decisions is to be guided by reference to Rule 1.14.

Independence from Client's Views or Activities

[5] Legal representation should not be denied to people who are unable to afford legal services, or whose cause is controversial or the subject of popular disapproval. By the same token, representing a client does not constitute approval of the client's views or activities.

Agreements Limiting Scope of Representation

[6] The objectives or scope of services to be provided by a lawyer may be limited by agreement with the client or by the terms under which the lawyer's services are made available to the client. When a lawyer has been retained by an insurer to represent an insured, for example, the representation may be limited to matters related to the insurance coverage. A limited representation may be appropriate because the client has limited objectives for the representation. In addition, the terms upon which representation is undertaken may exclude specific means that might otherwise be used to accomplish the client's objectives. Such limitations may exclude actions that the client thinks are too costly or that the lawyer regards as repugnant or imprudent.

[7] Although this rule affords the lawyer and client substantial latitude to limit the representation, the limitation must be reasonable under the circumstances. If, for example, a client's objective is limited to securing general information about the law the client needs in order to handle a common and typically uncomplicated legal problem, the lawyer and client may agree that the lawyer's services will be limited to a brief telephone consultation. Such a limitation, however, would not be reasonable if the time allotted was not sufficient to yield advice upon which the client could rely. Although an agreement for a limited representation does not exempt a lawyer from the duty to provide competent representation, the limitation is a factor to be considered when determining the legal knowledge, skill, thoroughness, and preparation reasonably necessary for the representation. See Rule 1.1.

[8] All agreements concerning a lawyer's representation of a client must accord with the Rules of Professional Conduct and other law. See, e.g., Rules 1.1, 1.8 and 5.6.

Criminal, Fraudulent and Prohibited Transactions

[9] Paragraph (d) prohibits a lawyer from knowingly counseling or assisting a client to commit a crime or fraud. This prohibition, however, does not preclude the lawyer from giving an honest opinion about the actual consequences that appear likely to result from a client's conduct. Nor does the fact that a client uses advice in a course of action that is criminal or fraudulent of itself make a lawyer a party to the course of action. There is a critical distinction between presenting an analysis of legal aspects of questionable conduct and recommending the means by which a crime or fraud might be committed with impunity.

[10] When the client's course of action has already begun and is continuing, the lawyer's responsibility is especially delicate. The lawyer is required to avoid assisting the client, for example, by drafting or delivering documents that the lawyer knows are fraudulent or by suggesting how the wrongdoing might be concealed. A lawyer may not continue assisting a client in conduct that the lawyer originally supposed was legally proper but then discovers is criminal or fraudulent. The lawyer must, therefore, withdraw from the representation of the client in the matter. See Rule 1.16(a). In some cases, withdrawal alone might be insufficient. It may be necessary for the lawyer to give notice of the fact of withdrawal and to disaffirm any opinion, document, affirmation, or the like. See Rule 4.1.

[11] Where the client is a fiduciary, the lawyer may be charged with special obligations in dealings with a beneficiary.

[12] Paragraph (d) applies regardless of whether the defrauded party is a party to the transaction. Hence, a lawyer must not participate in a transaction to effectuate criminal or fraudulent avoidance of tax liability. Paragraph (d) does not preclude undertaking a criminal defense incident to a general

retainer for legal services to a lawful enterprise. The last clause of paragraph (d) recognizes that determining the validity or interpretation of a statute or regulation may require a course of action involving disobedience of the statute or regulation or of the interpretation placed upon it by governmental authorities.

[13] If a lawyer comes to know or reasonably should know that a client expects assistance not permitted by the Rules of Professional Conduct or other law or if the lawyer intends to act contrary to the client's instructions, the lawyer must consult with the client regarding the limitations on the lawyer's conduct. See Rule 1.4(a)(5).

Historical Notes

This rule is similar, in part, to provisions of former EC 7–7, EC 7–8 and former DR 7–102(A)(7) of the Minn. Code of Prof. Responsibility.

Rule 1.3. Diligence

A lawyer shall act with reasonable diligence and promptness in representing a client.

Adopted June 13, 1985, eff. Sept. 1, 1985.

Comment—2005

[1] A lawyer should pursue a matter on behalf of a client despite opposition, obstruction, or personal inconvenience to the lawyer, and take whatever lawful and ethical measures are required to vindicate a client's cause or endeavor. A lawyer must also act with commitment and dedication to the interests of the client and with zeal in advocacy upon the client's behalf. A lawyer is not bound, however, to press for every advantage that might be realized for a client. For example, a lawyer may have authority to exercise professional discretion in determining the means by which a matter should be pursued. See Rule 1.2. The lawyer's duty to act with reasonable diligence does not require the use of offensive tactics or preclude the treating of all persons involved in the legal process with courtesy and respect.

[2] A lawyer's work load must be controlled so that each matter can be handled competently.

[3] Perhaps no professional shortcoming is more widely resented than procrastination. A client's interests often can be adversely affected by the passage of time or the change of conditions; in extreme instances, as when a lawyer overlooks a statute of limitations, the client's legal position may be destroyed. Even when the client's interests are not affected in substance, however, unreasonable delay can cause a client needless anxiety and undermine confidence in the lawyer's trustworthiness. A lawyer's duty to act with reasonable promptness, however, does not preclude the lawyer from agreeing to a reasonable request for a postponement that will not prejudice the lawyer's client.

[4] Unless the relationship is terminated as provided in Rule 1.16, a lawyer should carry through to conclusion all matters undertaken for a client. If a lawyer's employment is limited to a specific matter, the relationship terminates when the matter has been resolved. If a lawyer has served a client over a substantial period in a variety of matters, the client sometimes may assume that the lawyer will continue to serve on a continuing basis unless the lawyer gives notice of withdrawal. Doubt about whether a client-lawyer relationship still exists should be clarified by the lawyer, preferably in writing, so that the client will not mistakenly suppose the lawyer is looking after the client's affairs when the lawyer has ceased to do so. For example, if a lawyer has handled a judicial or administrative proceeding that produced a result adverse to the client and the lawyer and the client have not agreed that the lawyer will handle the matter on appeal, the lawyer must consult with the client about the possibility of appeal before relinquishing responsibility for the matter. See Rule 1.4(a)(2). Whether the lawyer is obligated to prosecute the appeal for the client depends on the scope of the representation the lawyer has agreed to provide to the client. See Rule 1.2.

[5] To prevent neglect of client matters in the event of a sole practitioner's death or disability, the duty of diligence may require that each sole practitioner prepare a plan, in conformity with applicable rules, that designates another competent lawyer to review client files, notify each client of the lawyer's death or disability, and determine whether there is a need for immediate protective action. Cf. Rule 28 of the American Bar Association Model Rules for Lawyer Disciplinary Enforcement (providing for court appointment of a lawyer to inventory files and take other protective action in absence of a plan providing for another lawyer to protect the interests of the clients of a deceased or disabled lawyer).

Historical Notes

This rule is similar to provisions of former DR 6–101(A)(3) and DR 7–101(A)(1) of the Minn. Code of Prof. Responsibility.

Rule 1.4. Communication

(a) A lawyer shall

(1) promptly inform the client of any decision or circumstance with respect to which the client's informed consent, as defined in Rule 1.0(f), is required by these rules;

(2) reasonably consult with the client about the means by which the client's objectives are to be accomplished;

(3) keep the client reasonably informed about the status of the matter;

(4) promptly comply with reasonable requests for information; and

(5) consult with the client about any relevant limitation on the lawyer's conduct when the lawyer knows that the client expects assistance not permitted by the Rules of Professional Conduct or other law.

(b) A lawyer shall explain a matter to the extent reasonably necessary to permit the client to make informed decisions regarding the representation.

Adopted June 13, 1985, eff. Sept. 1, 1985. Amended June 17, 2005, eff. Oct. 1, 2005.

Comment—2005

[1] Reasonable communication between the lawyer and the client is necessary for the client effectively to participate in the representation.

Communicating with Client

[2] If these rules require that a particular decision about the representation be made by the client, paragraph (a)(1) requires that the lawyer promptly consult with and secure the client's consent prior to taking action unless prior discussions with the client have resolved what action the client wants the lawyer to take. For example, a lawyer who receives from opposing counsel an offer of settlement in a civil controversy or a proffered plea bargain in a criminal case must promptly inform the client of its substance unless the client has previously indicated that the proposal will be acceptable or unacceptable or has authorized the lawyer to accept or to reject the offer. See Rule 1.2(a).

[3] Paragraph (a)(2) requires the lawyer to reasonably consult with the client about the means to be used to accomplish the client's objectives. In some situations—depending on both the importance of the action under consideration and the feasibility of consulting with the client—this duty will require consultation prior to taking action. In other circumstances, such as during a trial when an immediate decision must be made, the exigency of the situation may require the lawyer to act without prior consultation. In such cases the lawyer must nonetheless act reasonably to inform the client of actions the lawyer has taken on the client's behalf. Additionally, paragraph (a)(3) requires that the lawyer keep the client reasonably informed about the status of the matter, such as significant developments affecting the timing or the substance of the representation.

[4] A lawyer's regular communication with clients will minimize the occasions on which a client will need to request information concerning the representation. When a client makes a reasonable request for information, however, paragraph (a)(4) requires prompt compliance with the request, or if a prompt response is not feasible, that the lawyer, or a member of the lawyer's staff, acknowledge receipt of the request and advise the client when a response may be expected. Client telephone calls should be promptly returned or acknowledged.

Explaining Matters

[5] The client should have sufficient information to participate intelligently in decisions concerning the objectives of the representation and the means by which they are to be pursued, to the extent the client is willing and able to do so. Adequacy of communication depends in part on the kind of advice or assistance that is involved. For example, when there is time to explain a proposal made in a negotiation, the lawyer should review all important provisions with the client before proceeding to an agreement. In litigation a lawyer should explain the general strategy and prospects of success and ordinarily should consult the client on tactics that might or are likely to result in significant expense or to injure or coerce others. On the other hand, a lawyer ordinarily will not be expected to describe trial or negotiation strategy in detail. The guiding principle is that the lawyer should fulfill reasonable client expectations for information consistent with the duty to act in the client's best interests, and the client's overall requirements as to the character of representation. In certain circumstances, such as when a lawyer asks a client to consent to a representation affected by a conflict of interest, the client must give informed consent, as defined in Rule 1.0(f).

[6] Ordinarily, the information to be provided is that appropriate for a client who is a comprehending and responsible adult. However, fully informing the client according to this standard may be impracticable, for example, where the client is a child or suffers from diminished capacity. See Rule 1.14. When the client is an organization or group, it is often impossible or inappropriate to inform every one of its members about its legal affairs; ordinarily, the lawyer should address communications to the appropriate officials of the organization. See Rule 1.13. Where many routine matters are involved, a system of limited or occasional reporting may be arranged with the client.

Withholding Information

[7] In some circumstances, a lawyer may be justified in delaying transmission of information when the client would be likely to react imprudently to an immediate communication. Thus, a lawyer might withhold a psychiatric diagnosis of a client when the examining psychiatrist indicates that disclosure would harm the client. A lawyer may not withhold information to serve the lawyer's own interest or convenience or the interests or convenience of another person. Rules or court orders governing litigation may provide that information supplied to a lawyer may not be disclosed to the client. Rule 3.4(c) directs compliance with such rules or orders.

Historical Notes

This rule is similar to provisions of former EC 7–8 and EC 9–2 of the Minn. Code of Prof. Responsibility.

Rule 1.5. Fees

(a) A lawyer shall not make an agreement for, charge, or collect an unreasonable fee or an unreasonable amount for expenses. The factors to be considered in determining the reasonableness of a fee include the following:

(1) the time and labor required, the novelty and difficulty of the questions involved, and the skill requisite to perform the legal service properly;

(2) the likelihood, if apparent to the client, that the acceptance of the particular employment will preclude other employment by the lawyer;

(3) the fee customarily charged in the locality for similar legal services;

(4) the amount involved and the results obtained;

(5) the time limitations imposed by the client or by the circumstances;

(6) the nature and length of the professional relationship with the client;

(7) the experience, reputation, and ability of the lawyer or lawyers performing the services; and

(8) whether the fee is fixed or contingent.

(b) The scope of the representation and the basis or rate of the fee and expenses for which the client will be responsible shall be communicated to the client, preferably in writing, before or within a reasonable time after commencing the representation, except when the lawyer will charge a regularly represented client on the same basis or rate. Any changes in the basis or rate of the fee or expenses shall also be communicated to the client. Except as provided below, fee payments received by a lawyer before legal services have been rendered are presumed to be unearned and shall be held in a trust account pursuant to Rule 1.15.

(1) A lawyer may charge a flat fee for specified legal services, which constitutes complete payment for those services and may be paid in whole or in part in advance of the lawyer providing the services. If agreed to in advance in a written fee agreement signed by the client, a flat fee shall be considered to be the lawyer's property upon payment of the fee, subject to refund as described in Rule 1.5(b)(3). Such a written fee agreement shall notify the client:

(i) of the nature and scope of the services to be provided;

(ii) of the total amount of the fee and the terms of payment;

(iii) that the fee will not be held in a trust account until earned;

(iv) that the client has the right to terminate the client-lawyer relationship; and

(v) that the client will be entitled to a refund of all or a portion of the fee if the agreed-upon legal services are not provided.

(2) A lawyer may charge a fee to ensure the lawyer's availability to the client during a specified period or on a specified matter in addition to and apart from any compensation for legal services performed. Such an availability fee shall be reasonable in amount and communicated in a writing signed by the client. The writing shall clearly state that the fee is for availability only and that fees for legal services will be charged separately. An availability fee may be considered to be the lawyer's property upon payment of the fee, subject to refund in whole or in part should the lawyer not be available as promised.

(3) Fee agreements may not describe any fee as nonrefundable or earned upon receipt but may describe the advance fee payment as the lawyer's property subject to refund. Whenever a client has paid a flat fee or an availability fee pursuant to Rule 1.5(b)(1) or (2) and the lawyer-client relationship is terminated before the fee is fully earned, the lawyer shall refund to the client the unearned portion of the fee. If a client disputes the amount of the fee that has been earned, the lawyer shall take reasonable and prompt action to resolve the dispute.

(c) A fee may be contingent on the outcome of the matter for which the service is rendered, except in a matter in which a contingent fee is prohibited by paragraph (d) or other law. A contingent fee agreement shall be in a writing signed by the client and shall state the method by which the fee is to be determined, including the percentage or percentages that shall accrue to the lawyer in the event of settlement, trial or appeal; litigation and other expenses to be deducted from the recovery; and whether such expenses are to be deducted before or after the contingent fee is calculated. The agreement must clearly notify the client of any expenses for which the client will be liable whether or not the client is the prevailing party. Upon conclusion of a contingent fee matter, the lawyer shall provide the client with a written statement stating the outcome of the matter and, if there is a recovery, showing the remittance to the client and the method of its determination.

(d) A lawyer shall not enter into an arrangement for, charge, or collect:

(1) any fee in a domestic relations matter, the payment or amount of which is contingent upon the securing of a divorce or upon the amount of alimony or support, or property settlement in lieu thereof; or

(2) a contingent fee for representing a defendant in a criminal case.

(e) A division of a fee between lawyers who are not in the same firm may be made only if

(1) the division is in proportion to the services performed by each lawyer or each lawyer assumes joint responsibility for the representation;

(2) the client agrees to the arrangement, including the share each lawyer will receive, and the agreement is confirmed in writing; and

(3) the total fee is reasonable.

Adopted June 13, 1985, eff. Sept. 1, 1985. Amended June 17, 2005, eff. Oct. 1, 2005; Dec. 17, 2010, eff. July 1, 2011; April 7, 2011, eff. July 1, 2011.

Comment—2005

Reasonableness of Fee and Expenses

[1] Paragraph (a) requires that lawyers charge fees that are reasonable under the circumstances. The factors specified in (1) through (8) are not exclusive. Nor will each factor be relevant in each instance. Paragraph (a) also requires that expenses for which the client will be charged must be reasonable. A lawyer may seek reimbursement for the cost of services performed in-house, such as copying, or for other expenses incurred in-house, such as telephone charges, either by charging a reasonable amount to which the client has agreed in advance or

by charging an amount that reasonably reflects the cost incurred by the lawyer.

Basis or Rate of Fee

[2] When the lawyer has regularly represented a client, they ordinarily will have evolved an understanding concerning the basis or rate of the fee and the expenses for which the client will be responsible. In a new client-lawyer relationship, however, an understanding as to fees and expenses must be promptly established. Generally, it is desirable to furnish the client with at least a simple memorandum or copy of the lawyer's customary fee arrangements that states the general nature of the legal services to be provided, the basis, rate or total amount of the fee and whether and to what extent the client will be responsible for any costs, expenses or disbursements in the course of the representation. A written statement concerning the terms of the engagement reduces the possibility of misunderstanding.

[3] Contingent fees, like any other fees, are subject to the reasonableness standard of paragraph (a) of this rule. In determining whether a particular contingent fee is reasonable, or whether it is reasonable to charge any form of contingent fee, a lawyer must consider the factors that are relevant under the circumstances. Applicable law may impose limitations on contingent fees, such as a ceiling on the percentage allowable, or may require a lawyer to offer clients an alternative basis for the fee. Applicable law also may apply to situations other than a contingent fee, for example, government regulations regarding fees in certain tax matters.

Terms of Payment

[4] A lawyer may require advance payment of a fee, but is obliged to return any unearned portion. See Rule 1.16(d). A lawyer may accept property in payment for services, such as an ownership interest in an enterprise, providing this does not involve acquisition of a proprietary interest in the cause of action or subject matter of the litigation contrary to Rule 1.8 (i). However, a fee paid in property instead of money may be subject to the requirements of Rule 1.8(a) because such fees often have the essential qualities of a business transaction with the client.

[5] An agreement may not be made whose terms might induce the lawyer improperly to curtail services for the client or perform them in a way contrary to the client's interest. For example, a lawyer should not enter into an agreement whereby services are to be provided only up to a stated amount when it is foreseeable that more extensive services probably will be required, unless the situation is adequately explained to the client. Otherwise, the client might have to bargain for further assistance in the midst of a proceeding or transaction. However, it is proper to define the extent of services in light of the client's ability to pay. A lawyer should not exploit a fee arrangement based primarily on hourly charges by using wasteful procedures.

Prohibited Contingent Fees

[6] Paragraph (d) prohibits a lawyer from charging a contingent fee in a domestic relations matter when payment is contingent upon the securing of a divorce or upon the amount of alimony or support or property settlement to be obtained. This provision does not preclude a contract for a contingent fee for legal representation in connection with the recovery of post-judgment balances due under support, alimony, or other financial orders because such contracts do not implicate the same policy concerns.

Division of Fee

[7] A division of fee is a single billing to a client covering the fee of two or more lawyers who are not in the same firm. A division of fee facilitates association of more than one lawyer in a matter in which neither alone could serve the client as well, and most often is used when the fee is contingent and the division is between a referring lawyer and a trial specialist. Paragraph (e) permits the lawyers to divide a fee either on the basis of the proportion of services they render or if each lawyer assumes responsibility for the representation as a whole. In addition, the client must agree to the arrangement, including the share that each lawyer is to receive, and the agreement must be confirmed in writing. Contingent fee agreements must be in a writing signed by the client and must otherwise comply with paragraph (c) of this rule. Joint responsibility for the representation entails financial and ethical responsibility for the representation as if the lawyers were associated in a partnership. A lawyer should only refer a matter to a lawyer whom the referring lawyer reasonably believes is competent to handle the matter. See Rule 1.1.

[8] Paragraph (e) does not prohibit or regulate division of fees to be received in the future for work done when lawyers were previously associated in a law firm.

Disputes over Fees

[9] If a procedure has been established for resolution of fee disputes, such as an arbitration or mediation procedure established by the bar, the lawyer must comply with the procedure when it is mandatory, and, even when it is voluntary, the lawyer should conscientiously consider submitting to it. The law may prescribe a procedure for determining a lawyer's fee, for example, in representation of an executor or administrator, a class or a person entitled to a reasonable fee as part of the measure of damages. The lawyer entitled to such a fee and a lawyer representing another party concerned with the fee should comply with the prescribed procedure.

Historical Notes

This rule is similar, in part, to provisions of former EC 2–19, EC 2–20, DR 2–106 and DR 2–107 of the Minn. Code of Prof. Responsibility.

Rule 1.6. Confidentiality of Information

(a) Except when permitted under paragraph (b), a lawyer shall not knowingly reveal information relating to the representation of a client.

(b) A lawyer may reveal information relating to the representation of a client if:

(1) the client gives informed consent;

(2) the information is not protected by the attorney-client privilege under applicable law, the client has not requested that the information be held inviolate, and the lawyer reasonably believes the disclosure would not be embarrassing or likely detrimental to the client;

(3) the lawyer reasonably believes the disclosure is impliedly authorized in order to carry out the representation;

(4) the lawyer reasonably believes the disclosure is necessary to prevent the commission of a fraud that is reasonably certain to result in substantial injury to the financial interests or property of another and in furtherance of which the client has used or is using the lawyer's services or to prevent the commission of a crime;

(5) the lawyer reasonably believes the disclosure is necessary to rectify the consequences of a client's criminal or fraudulent act in the furtherance of which the lawyer's services were used;

(6) the lawyer reasonably believes the disclosure is necessary to prevent reasonably certain death or substantial bodily harm;

(7) the lawyer reasonably believes the disclosure is necessary to secure legal advice about the lawyer's compliance with these rules;

(8) the lawyer reasonably believes the disclosure is necessary to establish a claim or defense on behalf of the lawyer in an actual or potential controversy between the lawyer and the client, to establish a defense in a civil, criminal, or disciplinary proceeding against the lawyer based upon conduct in which the client was involved, or to respond in any proceeding to allegations by the client concerning the lawyer's representation of the client;

(9) the lawyer reasonably believes the disclosure is necessary to comply with other law or a court order; or

(10) the lawyer reasonably believes the disclosure is necessary to inform the Office of Lawyers Professional Responsibility of knowledge of another lawyer's violation of the Rules of Professional Conduct that raises a substantial question as to that lawyer's honesty, trustworthiness, or fitness as a lawyer in other respects. See Rule 8.3.

Adopted June 13, 1985, eff. Sept. 1, 1985. Amended Dec. 27, 1989, eff. Jan. 1, 1990; April 14, 1992; June 17, 2005, eff. Oct. 1, 2005.

Comment—2005

[1] This rule governs the disclosure by a lawyer of information relating to the representation of a client during the lawyer's representation of the client. See Rule 1.18 for the lawyer's duties with respect to information provided to the lawyer by a prospective client, Rule 1.9(c)(2) for the lawyer's duty not to reveal information relating to the lawyer's prior representation of a former client and Rules 1.8(b) and 1.9(c)(1) for the lawyer's duties with respect to the use of such information to the disadvantage of clients and former clients.

[2] A fundamental principle in the client-lawyer relationship is that, in the absence of the client's informed consent, the lawyer must not reveal information relating to the representation. See Rule 1.0(f) for the definition of informed consent. This contributes to the trust that is the hallmark of the client-lawyer relationship. The client is thereby encouraged to seek legal assistance and to communicate fully and frankly with the lawyer even as to embarrassing or legally damaging subject matter. The lawyer needs this information to represent the client effectively and, if necessary, to advise the client to refrain from wrongful conduct. Almost without exception, clients come to lawyers in order to determine their rights and what is, in the complex of laws and regulations, deemed to be legal and correct. Based upon experience, lawyers know that almost all clients follow the advice given, and the law is upheld.

[3] The principle of client-lawyer confidentiality is given effect by related bodies of law; the attorney-client privilege, the work-product doctrine and the rule of confidentiality established in professional ethics. The attorney-client privilege and work-product doctrine apply in judicial and other proceedings in which a lawyer may be called as a witness or otherwise required to produce evidence concerning a client. The rule of client-lawyer confidentiality applies in situations other than those where evidence is sought from the lawyer through compulsion of law. The confidentiality rule, for example, applies not only to matters communicated in confidence by the client but also to all information relating to the representation, whatever its source. A lawyer may not disclose such information except as authorized or required by the Rules of Professional Conduct or other law. See also Scope.

[4] Paragraph (a) prohibits a lawyer from revealing information relating to the representation of a client. This prohibition also applies to disclosures by a lawyer that do not in themselves reveal protected information but could reasonably lead to the discovery of such information by a third person. A lawyer's use of a hypothetical to discuss issues relating to the representation is permissible so long as there is no reasonable likelihood that the listener will be able to ascertain the identity of the client or the situation involved.

Authorized Disclosure

[5] Except to the extent that the client's instructions or special circumstances limit that authority, a lawyer is impliedly authorized to make disclosures about a client when appropriate in carrying out the representation. In some situations, for example, a lawyer may be impliedly authorized to admit a fact that cannot properly be disputed or to make a disclosure that facilitates a satisfactory conclusion to a matter. Lawyers in a firm may, in the course of the firm's practice, disclose to each other information relating to a client of the firm, unless the client has instructed that particular information be confined to specified lawyers.

Disclosure Adverse to Client

[6] Although the public interest is usually best served by a strict rule requiring lawyers to preserve the confidentiality of information relating to the representation of their clients, the confidentiality rule is subject to limited exceptions. Paragraph (b)(6) recognizes the overriding value of life and physical integrity and permits disclosure reasonably necessary to prevent reasonably certain death or substantial bodily harm. Such harm is reasonably certain to occur if it will be suffered imminently or if there is a present and substantial threat that a person will suffer such harm at a later date if the lawyer fails to take action necessary to eliminate the threat. Thus, a lawyer who knows that a client has accidentally discharged toxic waste into a town's water supply may reveal this information to the authorities if there is a present and substantial risk that a person who drinks the water will contract a life-threatening or debilitating disease and the lawyer's disclosure is necessary to eliminate the threat or reduce the number of victims.

[7] A lawyer's confidentiality obligations do not preclude a lawyer from securing confidential legal advice about the lawyer's personal responsibility to comply with these rules. In most situations, disclosing information to secure such advice will be impliedly authorized for the lawyer to carry out the representation. Even when the disclosure is not impliedly authorized, paragraph (b)(7) permits such disclosure because of the importance of a lawyer's compliance with the Rules of Professional Conduct.

[8] Where a legal claim or disciplinary charge alleges complicity of the lawyer in a client's conduct or other misconduct of the lawyer involving representation of the client, the lawyer may respond to the extent the lawyer reasonably believes necessary to establish a defense. The same is true with respect to a claim involving the conduct or representation of a former client. Such a charge can arise in a civil, criminal, disciplinary or other proceeding and can be based on a wrong allegedly committed by the lawyer against the client or on a wrong alleged by a third person, for example, a person claiming to have been defrauded by the lawyer and client acting together. The lawyer's right to respond arises when an assertion of such complicity has been made. Paragraph (b)(8) does not require the lawyer to await the commencement of an action or proceeding that charges such complicity, so that the defense may be established by responding directly to a third party who has made such an assertion. The right to defend also applies, of course, where a proceeding has been commenced.

[9] A lawyer entitled to a fee is permitted by paragraph (b)(8) to prove the services rendered in an action to collect it. This aspect of the rule expresses the principle that the beneficiary of a fiduciary relationship may not exploit it to the detriment of the fiduciary.

[10] Other law may require that a lawyer disclose information about a client, Whether such a law supersedes Rule 1.6 is a question of law beyond the scope of these rules. When disclosure of information relating to the representation appears to be required by other law, the lawyer must discuss the matter with the client to the extent required by Rule 1.4. If, however, the other law supersedes this rule and requires disclosure, paragraph (b)(9) permits the lawyer to make such disclosures as are necessary to comply with the law.

[11] A lawyer may be ordered to reveal information relating to the representation of a client by a court or by another tribunal or governmental entity claiming authority pursuant to other law to compel the disclosure. Absent informed consent of the client to do otherwise, the lawyer should assert on behalf of the client all nonfrivolous claims that the order is not authorized by other law or that the information sought is protected against disclosure by the attorney-client privilege or other applicable law. In the event of an adverse ruling, the lawyer must consult with the client about the possibility of appeal to the extent required by Rule 1.4, Unless review is sought, however, paragraph (b)(9) permits the lawyer to comply with the court' s order.

[12] Paragraph (b) permits disclosure only to the extent the lawyer reasonably believes the disclosure is necessary to accomplish one of the purposes specified. Where practicable, the lawyer should first seek to persuade the client to take suitable action to obviate the need for disclosure. In any case, a disclosure adverse to the client's interest should be no greater than the lawyer reasonably believes necessary to accomplish the purpose. If the disclosure will be made in connection with a judicial proceeding, the disclosure should be made in a manner that limits access to the information to the tribunal or other persons having a need to know it and appropriate protective orders or other arrangements should be sought by the lawyer to the fullest extent practicable.

[13] Paragraph (b) permits but does not require the disclosure of information relating to a client's representation to accomplish the purposes specified in paragraphs (b)(1) through (b)(10). In exercising the discretion conferred by this rule, the lawyer may consider such factors as the nature of the lawyer's relationship with the client and with those who might be injured by the client, the lawyer's own involvement in the transaction and factors that may extenuate the conduct in question. A lawyer's decision not to disclose as permitted by paragraph (b) does not violate this rule. Disclosure may be required, however, by other rules. Some rules require disclosure only if such disclosure would be permitted by paragraph (b). See Rules 8.1 and 8.3. Rule 3.3, on the other hand, requires disclosure in some circumstances regardless of whether such disclosure is permitted by this rule. See Rule 3.3(c).

Withdrawal

[14] If the lawyer's services will be used by the client in materially furthering a course of criminal or fraudulent conduct, the lawyer must withdraw, as stated in Rule 1.16(a)(1). After withdrawal the lawyer is required to refrain from making disclosure of the client's confidences, except as otherwise permitted in Rule 1.6. Neither this rule nor Rule 1.8(b) nor Rule 1.16(d) prevents the lawyer from giving notice of the fact of withdrawal, and the lawyer may also withdraw or disaffirm any opinion, document, affirmation, or the like. Where the client

is an organization, the lawyer may be in doubt whether contemplated conduct will actually be carried out by the organization. Where necessary to guide conduct in connection with this rule, the lawyer may make inquiry within the organization as indicated in Rule 1.13(b).

Acting Competently to Preserve Confidentiality

[15] A lawyer must act competently to safeguard information relating to the representation of a client against inadvertent or unauthorized disclosure by the lawyer or other persons who are participating in the representation of the client or who are subject to the lawyer's supervision. See Rules 1.1, 5.1 and 5.3.

[16] When transmitting a communication that includes information relating to the representation of a client, the lawyer must take reasonable precautions to prevent the information from coming into the hands of unintended recipients. This duty, however, does not require that the lawyer use special security measures if the method of communication affords a reasonable expectation of privacy. Special circumstances, however, may warrant special precautions. Factors to be considered in determining the reasonableness of the lawyer's expectation of confidentiality include the sensitivity of the information and the extent to which the privacy of the communication is protected by law or by a confidentiality agreement. A client may require the lawyer to implement special security measures not required by this rule or may give informed consent to the use of a means of communication that would otherwise be prohibited by this rule.

Former Client

[17] The duty of confidentiality continues after the client-lawyer relationship has terminated. See Rule 1.9(c)(2). See Rule 1.9(c)(1) for the prohibition against using such information to the disadvantage of the former client.

Historical Notes

This rule is similar to provisions of former DR 4–101 of the Minn. Code of Prof. Responsibility.

Rule 1.7. Conflict of Interest: Current Clients

(a) Except as provided in paragraph (b), a lawyer shall not represent a client if the representation involves a concurrent conflict of interest. A concurrent conflict of interest exists if:

(1) the representation of one client will be directly adverse to another client; or

(2) there is a significant risk that the representation of one or more clients will be materially limited by the lawyer's responsibilities to another client, a former client or a third person, or by a personal interest of the lawyer.

(b) Notwithstanding the existence of a concurrent conflict of interest under paragraph (a), a lawyer may represent a client if:

(1) the lawyer reasonably believes that the lawyer will be able to provide competent and diligent representation to each affected client;

(2) the representation is not prohibited by law;

(3) the representation does not involve the assertion of a claim by one client against another client represented by the lawyer in the same litigation or other proceeding before a tribunal; and

(4) each affected client gives informed consent, confirmed in writing.

Adopted June 13, 1985, eff. Sept. 1, 1985. Amended June 17, 2005, eff. Oct. 1, 2005.

Comment—2005

General Principles

[1] Loyalty and independent judgment are essential elements in the lawyer's relationship to a client. Concurrent conflicts of interest can arise from the lawyer's responsibilities to another client a former client or a third person or from the lawyer's own interests. For specific rules regarding certain concurrent conflicts of interest, see Rule 1.8. For former client conflicts of interest, see Rule 1.9. For conflicts of interest involving prospective clients, see Rule 1.18. For definitions of "informed consent" and "confirmed in writing," see Rule 1.0(f) and (b).

[2] Resolution of a conflict of interest problem under this rule requires the lawyer to; 1) clearly identify the client or clients; 2) determine whether a conflict of interest exists; 3) decide whether the representation may be undertaken despite the existence of a conflict, i.e., whether the conflict is consentable; and 4) if so, consult with the clients affected under paragraph (a) and obtain their informed consent, confirmed in writing. The clients affected under paragraph (a) include both of the clients referred to in paragraph (a)(1) and the one or more clients whose representation might be materially limited under paragraph (a)(2).

[3] A conflict of interest may exist before representation is undertaken, in which event the representation must be declined, unless the lawyer obtains the informed consent of each client under the conditions of paragraph (b). To determine whether a conflict of interest exists, a lawyer should adopt reasonable procedures, appropriate for the size and type of firm and practice, to determine in both litigation and non-litigation matters the persons and issues involved. See also Comment to Rule 5.1. Ignorance caused by a failure to institute such procedures will not excuse a lawyer's violation of this rule. As to whether a client- lawyer relationship exists or, having once been established, is continuing, see Comment to Rule 1.3 and Scope.

[4] If a conflict arises after representation has been undertaken, the lawyer ordinarily must withdraw from the representation, unless the lawyer has obtained the informed consent of the client under the conditions of paragraph (b). See Rule 1.16. Where more than one client is involved, whether the lawyer may continue to represent any of the clients is determined both by the lawyer's ability to comply with duties owed to the former client and by the lawyer's ability to represent adequately the remaining client or clients, given the lawyer's duties to the

former client. See Rule 1.9. See also Comments [5] and [29].

[5] Unforeseeable developments, such as changes in corporate and other organizational affiliations or the addition or realignment of parties in litigation, might create conflicts in the midst of a representation, as when a company sued by the lawyer on behalf of one client is bought by another client represented by the lawyer in an unrelated matter. Depending on the circumstances, the lawyer may have the option to withdraw from one of the representations in order to avoid the conflict. The lawyer must seek court approval where necessary and take steps to minimize harm to the clients. See Rule 1.16. The lawyer must continue to protect the confidences of the client from whose representation the lawyer has withdrawn. See Rule 1.9(c).

Identifying Conflicts of Interest; Directly Adverse

[6] Loyalty to a current client prohibits undertaking representation directly adverse to that client without that client's informed consent. Thus, absent consent, a lawyer may not act as an advocate in one matter against a person the lawyer represents in some other matter, even when the matters are wholly unrelated. The client as to whom the representation is directly adverse is likely to feel betrayed, and the resulting damage to the client-lawyer relationship is likely to impair the lawyer's ability to represent the client effectively. In addition, the client on whose behalf the adverse representation is undertaken reasonably may fear that the lawyer will pursue that client's case less effectively out of deference to the other client, i.e., that the representation may be materially limited by the lawyer's interest in retaining the current client. Similarly, a directly adverse conflict may arise when a lawyer is required to cross-examine a client who appears as a witness in a lawsuit involving another client, as when the testimony will be damaging to the client who is represented in the lawsuit. On the other hand, simultaneous representation in unrelated matters of clients whose interests are only economically adverse, such as representation of competing economic enterprises in unrelated litigation, does not ordinarily constitute a conflict of interest and thus may not require consent of the respective clients.

[7] Directly adverse conflicts can also arise in transactional matters. For example, if a lawyer is asked to represent the seller of a business in negotiations with a buyer represented by the lawyer, not in the same transaction but in another, unrelated matter, the lawyer could not undertake the representation without the informed consent of each client.

Identifying Conflicts of Interest: Material Limitation

[8] Even where there is no direct adverseness, a conflict of interest exists if there is a significant risk that a lawyer 's ability to consider, recommend or carry out an appropriate course of action for the client will be materially limited as a result of the lawyer's other responsibilities or interests. For example, a lawyer asked to represent several individuals seeking to form a joint venture is likely to be materially limited in the lawyer's ability to recommend or advocate all possible positions that each might take because of the lawyer's duty of loyalty to the others. The conflict in effect forecloses alternatives that would otherwise be available to the client. The mere possibility of subsequent harm does not itself require disclosure and consent. The critical questions are the likelihood that a difference in interests will eventuate and, if it does, whether it will materially interfere with the lawyer's independent professional judgment in considering alternatives or foreclose courses of action that reasonably should be pursued on behalf of the client.

Lawyer's Responsibilities to Former Clients and Other Third Persons

[9] In addition to conflicts with other current clients, a lawyer's duties of loyalty and independence may be materially limited by responsibilities to former clients under Rule 1.9 or by the lawyer's responsibilities to other persons, such as fiduciary duties arising from a lawyer's service as a trustee, executor or corporate director.

Personal Interest Conflicts

[10] The lawyer's own interests should not be permitted to have an adverse effect on representation of a client. For example, if the probity of a lawyer's own conduct in a transaction is in serious question, it may be difficult or impossible for the lawyer to give a client detached advice. Similarly, when a lawyer has discussions concerning possible employment with an opponent of the lawyer's client, or with a law firm representing the opponent, such discussions could materially limit the lawyer's representation of the client. In addition, a lawyer may not allow related business interests to affect representation, for example, by referring clients to an enterprise in which the lawyer has an undisclosed financial interest. See Rule 1.8 for specific rules pertaining to a number of personal interest conflicts, including business transactions with clients. See also Rule 1.10 (personal interest conflicts under Rule 1.7 ordinarily are not imputed to other lawyers in a law firm).

[11] When lawyers representing different clients in the same matter or in substantially related matters are closely related by blood or marriage, there may be a significant risk that client confidences will be revealed and that the lawyer's family relationship will interfere with both loyalty and independent professional judgment. As a result, each client is entitled to know of the existence and implications of the relationship between the lawyers before the lawyer agrees to undertake the representation. Thus, a lawyer related to another lawyer, e.g., as parent, child, sibling or spouse, ordinarily may not represent a client in a matter where that lawyer is representing another party, unless each client gives informed consent. The disqualification arising from a close family relationship is personal and ordinarily is not imputed to members of firms with whom the lawyers are associated. See Rule 1.10.

[12] A lawyer is prohibited from engaging in sexual relationships with a client unless the sexual relationship predates the formation of the client-lawyer relationship. See Rule 1.8(j).

Interest of Person Paying for a lawyer's Service

[13] A lawyer may be paid from a source other than the client, including a co-client, if the client is informed of that fact and consents and the arrangement does not compromise the lawyer's duty of loyalty or independent judgment to the client. See Rule 1.8(f). If acceptance of the payment from any other source presents a significant risk that the lawyer's representation of the client will be materially limited by the lawyer's own interest in accommodating the person paying the lawyer's fee or by the lawyer's responsibilities to a payer who is also a co-client, then the lawyer must comply with the requirements of paragraph (b) before accepting the representation, including determining whether the conflict is consentable and, if so, that the client has adequate information about the material risks of the representation.

Prohibited Representations

[14] Ordinarily, clients may consent to representation notwithstanding a conflict. However, as indicated in paragraph (b), some conflicts are nonconsentable, meaning that the lawyer involved cannot properly ask for such agreement or provide representation on the basis of the client's consent. When the lawyer is representing more than one client, the question of consentability must be resolved as to each client.

[15] Consentability is typically determined by considering whether the interests of the clients will be adequately protected if the clients are permitted to give their informed consent to representation burdened by a conflict of interest. Thus, under paragraph (b)(1), representation is prohibited if under the circumstances the lawyer cannot reasonably conclude that the lawyer will be able to provide competent and diligent representation. See Rule 1.1 (competence) and Rule 1.3 (diligence).

[16] Paragraph (b)(2) describes conflicts that are nonconsentable because the representation is prohibited by applicable law.

[17] Paragraph (b)(3) describes conflicts that are nonconsentable because of the institutional interest in vigorous development of each client's position when the clients are aligned directly against each other in the same litigation or other proceeding before a tribunal. Whether clients are aligned directly against each other within the meaning of this paragraph requires examination of the context of the proceeding. Although this paragraph does not preclude a lawyer's multiple representation of adverse parties to a mediation (because mediation is not a proceeding before a "tribunal" under Rule 1.0(n)), such representation may be precluded by paragraph (b)(1).

Informed Consent

[18] Informed consent requires that each affected client be aware of the relevant circumstances and of the material and reasonably foreseeable ways that the conflict could have adverse effects on the interests of that client. See Rule 1.0(f) (informed consent). The information required depends on the nature of the conflict and the nature of the risks involved. When representation of multiple clients in a single matter is undertaken, the information must include the implications of the common representation, including possible effects on loyalty, confidentiality and the attorney-client privilege and the advantages and risks involved. See Comments [30] and [31] (effect of common representation on confidentiality).

[19] Under some circumstances it may be impossible to make the disclosure necessary to obtain consent. For example, when the lawyer represents different clients in related matters and one of the clients refuses to consent to the disclosure necessary to permit the other client to make an informed decision, the lawyer cannot properly ask the latter to consent. In some cases the alternative to common representation can be that each party may have to obtain separate representation with the possibility of incurring additional costs. These costs, along with the benefits of securing separate representation, are factors that may be considered by the affected client in determining whether common representation is in the client's interests.

Consent Confirmed in Writing

[20] Paragraph (b) requires the lawyer to obtain the informed consent of the client, confirmed in writing. Such a writing may consist of a document executed by the client or one that the lawyer promptly records and transmits to the client following an oral consent. See Rule 1.0(b). See also Rule 1.0(*o*) (writing includes electronic transmission). If it is not feasible to obtain or transmit the writing at the time the client gives informed consent, then the lawyer must obtain or transmit it within a reasonable time thereafter. See Rule 1.0(b). The requirement of a writing does not supplant the need in most cases for the lawyer to talk with the client, to explain the risks and advantages, if any, of representation burdened with a conflict of interest, as well as reasonably available alternatives, and to afford the client a reasonable opportunity to consider the risks and alternatives and to raise questions and concerns. Rather, the writing is required in order to impress upon clients the seriousness of the decision the client is being asked to make and to avoid disputes or ambiguities that might later occur in the absence of a writing.

Revoking Consent

[21] A client who has given consent to a conflict may revoke the consent to the client's own representation and, like any other client, may terminate the lawyer's representation at any time. Whether revoking consent to the client's own representation precludes the lawyer from continuing to represent other clients depends on the circumstances, including the nature of the conflict, whether the client revoked consent because of a material change in circumstances, the reasonable expectations of the other client and whether material detriment to the other clients or the lawyer would result.

Consent to Future Conflict

[22] Whether a lawyer may properly request a client to waive conflicts that might arise in the future is subject to the test of paragraph (b). The effectiveness of such waivers is generally determined by the extent to which the client reasonably understands the material risks that the waiver en-

tails. The more comprehensive the explanation of the types of future representations that might arise and the actual and reasonably foreseeable adverse consequences of those representations, the greater the likelihood that the client will have the requisite understanding. Thus, if the client agrees to consent to a particular type of conflict with which the client is already familiar, then the consent ordinarily will be effective with regard to that type of conflict. If the consent is general and open- ended, then the consent ordinarily will be ineffective, because it is not reasonably likely that the client will have understood the material risks involved. On the other hand, if the client is an experienced user of the legal services involved and is reasonably informed regarding the risk that a conflict may arise, such consent is more likely to be effective, particularly if, e.g., the client is independently represented by other counsel in giving consent and the consent is limited to future conflicts unrelated to the subject of the representation. In any case, advance consent cannot be effective if the circumstances that materialize in the future are such as would make the conflict nonconsentable under paragraph (b).

Conflicts in Litigation

[23] Paragraph (b)(3) prohibits representation of opposing parties in the same litigation, regardless of the clients' consent. On the other hand, simultaneous representation of parties whose interests in litigation may conflict, such as coplaintiffs or codefendants, is governed by paragraph (a)(2). A conflict may exist by reason of substantial discrepancy in the parties' testimony, incompatibility in positions in relation to an opposing party or the fact that there are substantially different possibilities of settlement of the claims or liabilities in question. Such conflicts can arise in both criminal and civil cases. The potential for conflict of interest in representing multiple defendants in a criminal case is so grave that ordinarily a lawyer should decline to represent more than one codefendant. On the other hand, common representation of persons having similar interest is proper if the risk of adverse effect is minimal and the requirements of paragraph (b) are met.

[24] Ordinarily a lawyer may take inconsistent legal positions in different tribunals at different times on behalf of different clients. The mere fact that advocating a legal position on behalf of one client might create precedent adverse to the interests of a client represented by the lawyer in an unrelated matter does not create a conflict of interest. A conflict of interest exists, however, if there is a significant risk that a lawyer's action on behalf of one client will materially limit under Rule 1.7 (a)(2) the lawyer's effectiveness in representing another client in a different case.

[25] When a lawyer represents or seeks to represent a class of plaintiffs or defendants in a class-action lawsuit, unnamed members of the class are ordinarily not considered to be clients of the lawyer for purposes of applying paragraph (a)(1) of this rule. Thus, the lawyer does not typically need to get the consent of such a person before representing a client suing the person in an unrelated matter. Similarly, a lawyer seeking to represent an opponent in a class action does not typically need the consent of an unnamed member of the class whom the lawyer represents in an unrelated matter.

Nonlitigation Conflicts

[26] Conflicts of interest under paragraphs (a)(1) and (a)(2) arise in contexts other than litigation. For a discussion of directly adverse conflicts in transactional matters, see Comment [7]. Relevant factors in determining whether there is significant potential for material limitation include the duration and intimacy of the lawyer's relationship with the client or clients involved, the functions being performed by the lawyer, the likelihood that disagreements will arise and the likely prejudice to the client from the conflict. The question is often one of proximity and degree. See Comment [8].

[27] For example, conflict questions may arise in estate planning and estate administration. A lawyer may be called upon to prepare wills for several family members, such as husband and wife, and, depending upon the circumstances, a conflict of interest may be present. In estate administration the identity of the client may be unclear to the parties involved. In order to comply with conflict of interest rules, the lawyer should make clear the lawyer's relationship to the parties involved.

[28] Whether a conflict is consentable depends on the circumstances. For example, a lawyer may not represent multiple parties to a negotiation whose interests are fundamentally antagonistic to each other, but common representation is permissible where the clients are generally aligned in interest even though there is some difference in interest among them. Thus, a lawyer may seek to establish or adjust a relationship between clients on an amicable and mutually advantageous basis; for example, the lawyer may help to organize a business in which two or more clients are entrepreneurs, working out the financial reorganization of an enterprise in which two or more clients have an interest or arranging a property distribution in settlement of an estate. The lawyer seeks to resolve potentially adverse interests by developing the parties' mutual interests. Otherwise, each party might have to obtain separate representation, with the possibility of incurring additional cost, complication or even litigation. Given these and other relevant factors, the clients may prefer that the lawyer act for all of them.

Special Considerations in Common Representation

[29] In considering whether to represent multiple clients in the same matter, a lawyer should be mindful that if the common representation fails because the potentially adverse interests cannot be reconciled, the result can be additional cost, embarrassment and recrimination. Ordinarily, the lawyer will be forced to withdraw from representing all of the clients if the common representation fails. In some situations, the risk of failure is so great that multiple representation is plainly impossible. For example, a lawyer cannot undertake common representation of clients where contentious litigation or negotiations between them are imminent or contemplated. Moreover, because the lawyer is required to be impartial between commonly repre-

sented clients, representation of multiple clients is improper when it is unlikely that impartiality can be maintained. Generally, if the relationship between the parties has already assumed antagonism, the possibility that the clients' interests can be adequately served by common representation is not very good. Other relevant factors are whether the lawyer subsequently will represent both parties on a continuing basis and whether the situation involves creating or terminating a relationship between the parties.

[30] A particularly important factor in determining the appropriateness of common representation is the effect on client-lawyer confidentiality and the attorney-client privilege. With regard to the attorney-client privilege, the prevailing rule is that, as between commonly represented clients, the privilege does not attach. Hence, it must be assumed that if litigation eventuates between the clients, the privilege will not protect any such communications, and the clients should be so advised.

[31] As to the duty of confidentiality, continued common representation will almost certainly be inadequate if one client asks the lawyer not to disclose to the other client information relevant to the common representation. This is so because the lawyer has an equal duty of loyalty to each client, and each client has the right to be informed of anything bearing on the representation that might affect that client's interests and the right to expect that the lawyer will use that information to that client's benefit. See Rule 1.4. The lawyer should, at the outset of the common representation and as part of the process of obtaining each client's informed consent, advise each client that information will be shared and that the lawyer will have to withdraw if one client decides that some matter material to the representation should be kept from the other. In limited circumstances, it may be appropriate for the lawyer to proceed with the representation when the clients have agreed, after being properly informed, that the lawyer will keep certain information confidential. For example, the lawyer may reasonably conclude that failure to disclose one client's trade secrets to another client will not adversely affect representation involving a joint venture between the clients and agree to keep that information confidential with the informed consent of both clients.

[32] When seeking to establish or adjust a relationship between clients, the lawyer should make clear that the lawyer's role is not that of partisanship normally expected in other circumstances and, thus, that the clients may be required to assume greater responsibility for decisions than when each client is separately represented. Any limitations on the scope of the representation made necessary as a result of the common representation should be fully explained to the clients at the outset of the representation. See Rule 1.2(c).

[33] Subject to the above limitations, each client in the common representation has the right to loyal and diligent representation and the protection of Rule 1.9 concerning the obligations to a former client. The client also has the right to discharge the lawyer as stated in Rule 1.16.

Organizational Clients

[34] A lawyer who represents a corporation or other organization does not, by virtue of that representation, necessarily represent any constituent or affiliated organization, such as a parent or subsidiary. See Rule 1.13(a). Thus, the lawyer for an organization is not barred from accepting representation adverse to an affiliate in an unrelated matter, unless the circumstances are such that the affiliate should also be considered a client of the lawyer, there is an understanding between the lawyer and the organizational client that the lawyer will avoid representation adverse to the client's affiliates, or the lawyer's obligations to either the organizational client or the new client are likely to limit materially the lawyer's representation of the other client.

[35] A lawyer for a corporation or other organization who is also a member of its board of directors should determine whether the responsibilities of the two roles may conflict. The lawyer may be called on to advise the corporation in matters involving actions of the directors. Consideration should be given to the frequency with which such situations may arise, the potential intensity of the conflict, the effect of the lawyer's resignation from the board and the possibility of the corporation's obtaining legal advice from another lawyer in such situations. If there is material risk that the dual role will compromise the lawyer's independence of professional judgment, the lawyer should not serve as a director or should cease to act as the corporation's lawyer when conflicts of interest arise. The lawyer should advise the other members of the board that in some circumstances matters discussed at board meetings while the lawyer is present in the capacity of director might not be protected by the attorney-client privilege and that conflict of interest considerations might require the lawyer's recusal as a director or might require the lawyer and the lawyer' s firm to decline representation of the corporation in a matter.

Historical Notes

This rule is similar to provisions of former DR 5–101(A) and DR 5–105(A) to (C) of the Minn. Code of Prof. Responsibility.

Rule 1.8. Conflict of Interest: Current Clients: Specific Rules

(a) A lawyer shall not enter into a business transaction with a client or knowingly acquire an ownership, possessory, security, or other pecuniary interest adverse to a client unless:

(1) the transaction and terms on which the lawyer acquires the interest are fair and reasonable to the client and are fully disclosed and transmitted in writing in a manner that can be reasonably understood by the client;

(2) the client is advised in writing of the desirability of seeking and is given a reasonable opportunity to seek the advice of independent legal counsel on the transaction; and

(3) the client gives informed consent, in a document signed by the client separate from the transaction documents, to the essential terms of the transaction and the lawyer's role in the transaction, including whether the lawyer is representing the client in the transaction.

(b) A lawyer shall not use information relating to representation of a client to the disadvantage of the client unless the client gives informed consent, except as permitted or required by these rules.

(c) A lawyer shall not prepare an instrument giving the lawyer or a person related to the lawyer as parent, child, sibling, or spouse any substantial gift from a client, including a testamentary gift, except where the client is related to the donee.

(d) Prior to the conclusion of representation of a client, a lawyer shall not make or negotiate an agreement giving the lawyer literary or media rights to a portrayal or account based in substantial part on information relating to the representation.

(e) A lawyer shall not provide financial assistance to a client in connection with pending or contemplated litigation, except that:

(1) a lawyer may advance court costs and expenses of litigation, the repayment of which may be contingent on the outcome of the matter;

(2) a lawyer representing an indigent client may pay court costs and expenses of litigation on behalf of the client; and

(3) a lawyer may guarantee a loan reasonably needed to enable the client to withstand delay in litigation that would otherwise put substantial pressure on the client to settle a case because of financial hardship rather than on the merits, provided the client remains ultimately liable for repayment of the loan without regard to the outcome of the litigation and, further provided, that no promise of such financial assistance was made to the client by the lawyer, or by another in the lawyer's behalf, prior to the employment of that lawyer by that client.

(f) A lawyer shall not accept compensation for representing a client from one other than the client unless:

(1) the client gives informed consent or the acceptance of compensation from another is impliedly authorized by the nature of the representation;

(2) there is no interference with the lawyer's independence of professional judgment or with the client-lawyer relationship; and

(3) information relating to representation of a client is protected as required by Rule 1.6.

(g) A lawyer who represents two or more clients shall not participate in making an aggregate settlement of the claims of or against the clients unless each client gives informed consent in a writing signed by the client. The lawyer's disclosure shall include the existence and nature of all the claims involved and of the participation of each person in the settlement.

(h) A lawyer shall not:

(1) make an agreement prospectively limiting the lawyer's liability to a client for malpractice unless the client is independently represented in making the agreement; or

(2) settle a claim or potential claim for such liability with an unrepresented client or former client unless that person is advised in writing of the desirability of seeking and is given a reasonable opportunity to seek the advice of independent legal counsel in connection therewith.

(i) A lawyer shall not acquire a proprietary interest in the cause of action or subject matter of litigation the lawyer is conducting for a client, except that the lawyer may:

(1) acquire a lien authorized by law to secure the lawyer's fee or expenses; and

(2) contract with a client for a reasonable contingent fee in a civil case.

(j) A lawyer shall not have sexual relations with a client unless a consensual sexual relationship existed between them when the client-lawyer relationship commenced. For purposes of this paragraph:

(1) "sexual relations" means sexual intercourse or any other intentional touching of the intimate parts of a person or causing the person to touch the intimate parts of the lawyer;

(2) if the client is an organization, any individual who oversees the representation and gives instructions to the lawyer on behalf of the organization shall be deemed to be the client; in–house attorneys while representing governmental or corporate entities are governed by Rule 1.7 rather than by this rule with respect to sexual relations with other employees of the entity they represent;

(3) this paragraph does not prohibit a lawyer from engaging in sexual relations with a client of the lawyer's firm provided that the lawyer has no involvement in the performance of the legal work for the client;

(4) if a party other than the client alleges violation of this paragraph, and the complaint is not summarily dismissed, the Director of the Office of Lawyers Professional Responsibility, in determining whether to investigate the allegation and whether to charge any violation based on the allegations, shall consider the client's statement regarding whether the client would be unduly burdened by the investigation or charge.

(k) While lawyers are associated in a firm, a prohibition in the foregoing paragraphs (a) through (i) that applies to any one of them shall apply to all of them.

Adopted June 13, 1985, eff. Sept. 1, 1985. Amended June 20, 1994, eff. July 1, 1994; July 28, 1999, eff. Aug. 1, 1999; June 17, 2005, eff. Oct. 1, 2005.

Comment—2005

[1] A lawyer's legal skill and training, together with the relationship of trust and confidence between lawyer and client, create the possibility of overreaching when the lawyer participates in a business, property or financial transaction with a client, for example, a loan or sales transaction or a lawyer investment on behalf of a client. The requirements of paragraph (a) must be met even when the transaction is not closely related to the subject matter of the representation, as when a lawyer drafting a will for a client learns that the client needs money for unrelated expenses and offers to make a loan to the client, The rule applies to lawyers engaged in the sale of goods or services related to the practice of law, for example, the sale of title insurance or investment services to existing clients of the lawyer's legal practice. See Rule 5.7. It also applies to lawyers purchasing property from estates they represent. It does not apply to ordinary fee arrangements between client and lawyer, which are governed by Rule 1.5, although its requirements must be met when the lawyer accepts an interest in the client's business or other nonmonetary property as payment of all or part of a fee. In addition, the rule does not apply to standard commercial transactions between the lawyer and the client for products or services that the client generally markets to others, for example, banking or brokerage services, medical services, products manufactured or distributed by the client, and utilities services. In such transactions, the lawyer has no advantage in dealing with the client, and the restrictions in paragraph (a) are unnecessary and impracticable.

[2] Paragraph (a)(1) requires that the transaction itself be fair to the client and that its essential terms be communicated to the client, in writing, in a manner that can be reasonably understood. Paragraph (a)(2) requires that the client also be advised, in writing, of the desirability of seeking the advice of independent legal counsel. It also requires that the client be given a reasonable opportunity to obtain such advice. Paragraph (a)(3) requires that the lawyer obtain the client's informed consent, in a document signed by the client separate from the transaction documents, both to the essential terms of the transaction and to the lawyer's role. When necessary, the lawyer should discuss both the material risks of the proposed transaction, including any risk presented by the lawyer's involvement, and the existence of reasonably available alternatives and should explain why the advice of independent legal counsel is desirable. See Rule 1.0(f) (definition of informed consent).

[3] The risk to a client is greatest when the client expects the lawyer to represent the client in the transaction itself or when the lawyer's financial interest otherwise poses a significant risk that the lawyer's representation of the client will be materially limited by the lawyer's financial interest in the transaction. Here the lawyer's role requires that the lawyer must comply, not only with the requirements of paragraph (a), but also with the requirements of Rule 1.7. Under that rule, the lawyer must disclose the risks associated with the lawyer's dual role as both legal adviser and participant in the transaction, such as the risk that the lawyer will structure the transaction or give legal advice in a way that favors the lawyer's interests at the expense of the client. Moreover, the lawyer must obtain the client's informed consent. In some cases, the lawyer's interest may be such that Rule 1.7 will preclude the lawyer from seeking the client's consent to the transaction.

[4] If the client is independently represented in the transaction, paragraph (a)(2) of this rule is inapplicable, and the paragraph (a)(1) requirement for full disclosure is satisfied either by a written disclosure by the lawyer involved in the transaction or by the client's independent counsel. The fact that the client was independently represented in the transaction is relevant in determining whether the agreement was fair and reasonable to the client as paragraph (a)(1) further requires.

Use of Information Related to Representation

[5] Use of information relating to the representation to the disadvantage of the client violates the lawyer's duty of loyalty. Paragraph (b) applies when the information is used to benefit either the lawyer or a third person, such as another client or business associate of the lawyer. For example, if a lawyer learns that a client intends to purchase and develop several parcels of land, the lawyer may not use that information to purchase one of the parcels in competition with the client or to recommend that another client make such a purchase. The rule does not prohibit uses that do not disadvantage the client. For example, a lawyer who learns a government agency's interpretation of trade legislation during the representation of one client may properly use that information to benefit other clients. Paragraph (b) prohibits disadvantageous use of client information unless the client gives informed consent, except as permitted or required by these rules. See Rules 1.2(d), 1.6, 1.9(c), 3.3, 4.1(b), 8.1 and 8.3.

Gifts to Lawyers

[6] A lawyer may accept a gift from a client, if the transaction meets general standards of fairness. For example, a simple gift such as a present given at a holiday or as a token of appreciation is permitted. If a client offers the lawyer a more substantial gift, paragraph (c) does not prohibit the lawyer from accepting it, although such a gift may be voidable by the client under the doctrine of undue influence. In any event, due to concerns about overreaching and imposition on clients, a lawyer may not suggest that a substantial gift be made to the lawyer or for the lawyer's benefit, except where the lawyer is related to the client as set forth in paragraph (c).

[7] If effectuation of a substantial gift requires preparing a legal instrument such as a will or conveyance the client should have the detached advice that another lawyer can provide. The sole exception to this rule is where the client is a relative of the donee.

[8] This rule does not prohibit a lawyer from seeking to have the lawyer or a partner or associate of the lawyer named as executor of the client's estate or to another potentially lucrative fiduciary

position. Nevertheless, such appointments will be subject to the general conflict of interest provision in Rule 1.7 when there is a significant risk that the lawyer's interest in obtaining the appointment will materially limit the lawyer's independent professional judgment in advising the client concerning the choice of an executor or other fiduciary. In obtaining the client's informed consent to the conflict, the lawyer should advise the client concerning the nature and extent of the lawyer's financial interest in the appointment, as well as the availability of alternative candidates for the position.

Literary Rights

[9] An agreement by which a lawyer acquires literary or media rights concerning the conduct of the representation creates a conflict between the interests of the client and the personal interests of the lawyer. Measures suitable in the representation of the client may detract from the publication value of an account of the representation. Paragraph (d) does not prohibit a lawyer representing a client in a transaction concerning literary property from agreeing that the lawyer's fee shall consist of a share in ownership in the property, if the arrangement conforms to Rule 1.5 and paragraphs (a) and (i).

Financial Assistance

[10] Lawyers may not subsidize lawsuits brought on behalf of their clients, such as by making loans to their clients for living expenses, because to do so would encourage clients to pursue lawsuits that might not otherwise be brought and because such assistance gives lawyers too great a financial stake in the litigation. These dangers do not warrant a prohibition on a lawyer lending a client court costs and litigation expenses, including the expenses of medical examination and the costs of obtaining and presenting evidence, because these advances are virtually indistinguishable from contingent fees and help ensure access to the courts. Similarly, an exception allowing lawyers representing indigent clients to pay court costs and litigation expenses regardless of whether these funds will be repaid is warranted. A lawyer may guarantee a loan to enable the client to withstand delay in litigation under the circumstances stated in Rule 1.8 (e)(3).

Person Paying for a Lawyer's Services

[11] Lawyers are frequently asked to represent a client under circumstances in which a third person will compensate the lawyer, in whole or in part. The third person might be a relative or friend, an indemnitor (such as a liability insurance company) or a co-client (such as a corporation sued along with one or more of its employees). Because third-party payers frequently have interests that differ from those of the client, including interests in minimizing the amount spent on the representation and in learning how the representation is progressing, lawyers are prohibited from accepting or continuing such representations unless the lawyer determines that there will be no interference with the lawyer's independent professional judgment and there is informed consent from the client, or acceptance of compensation from another is impliedly authorized by the nature of the representation. See also Rule 5.4(c) (prohibiting interference with a lawyer's professional judgment by one who recommends, employs or pays the lawyer to render legal services for another).

[12] Sometimes, it will be sufficient for the lawyer to obtain the client's informed consent regarding the fact of the payment and the identity of the third-party payer. If, however, the fee arrangement creates a conflict of interest for the lawyer, then the lawyer must comply with Rule. 1.7. The lawyer must also conform to the requirements of Rule 1.6 concerning confidentiality. Under Rule 1.7(a), a conflict of interest exists if there is significant risk that the lawyer's representation of the client will be materially limited by the lawyer's own interest in the fee arrangement or by the lawyer's responsibilities to the third-party payer (for example, when the third-party payer is a co–client). Under Rule 1.7(b), the lawyer may accept or continue the representation with the informed consent of each affected client, unless the conflict is nonconsentable under that paragraph. Under Rule 1.7(b), the informed consent must be confirmed in writing.

Aggregate Settlements

[13] Differences in willingness to make or accept an offer of settlement are among the risks of common representation of multiple clients by a single lawyer. Under Rule 1.7, this is one of the risks that should be discussed before undertaking the representation, as part of the process of obtaining the clients' informed consent. In addition, Rule 1.2(a) protects each client's right to have the final say in deciding whether to accept or reject an offer of settlement. The rule stated in this paragraph is a corollary of both these rules and provides that, before any settlement offer is made or accepted on behalf of multiple clients, the lawyer must inform each of them about all the material terms of the settlement, including what the other clients will receive or pay if the settlement is accepted. See also Rule 1.0(f) (definition of informed consent). Lawyers representing a class of plaintiffs or defendants, or those proceeding derivatively, may not have a full client-lawyer relationship with each member of the class; nevertheless, such lawyers must comply with applicable rules regulating notification of class members and other procedural requirements designed to ensure adequate protection of the entire class.

Limiting Liability and Settling Malpractice Claims

[14] Agreements prospectively limiting a lawyer's liability for malpractice are prohibited unless the client is independently represented in making the agreement because such agreements are likely to undermine competent and diligent representation. Also, many clients are unable to evaluate the desirability of making such an agreement before a dispute has arisen, particularly if they are then represented by the lawyer seeking the agreement. This paragraph does not, however, prohibit a lawyer from entering into an agreement with the client to arbitrate legal malpractice claims, provided such agreements are enforceable and the client is fully informed of the scope and effect of the agreement. Nor does this paragraph limit the ability of lawyers to practice in the form of a limited-liability entity,

where permitted by law, provided that each lawyer remains personally liable to the client for his or her own conduct and the firm complies with any conditions required by law, such as provisions requiring client notification or maintenance of adequate liability insurance. Nor does it prohibit an agreement in accordance with Rule 1.2 that defines the scope of the representation, although a definition of scope that makes the obligations of representation illusory will amount to an attempt to limit liability.

[15] Agreements settling a claim or a potential claim for malpractice are not prohibited by this rule. Nevertheless, in view of the danger that a lawyer will take unfair advantage of an unrepresented client or former client, the lawyer must first advise such a person in writing of the appropriateness of independent representation in connection with such a settlement. In addition, the lawyer must give the client or former client a reasonable opportunity to find and consult independent counsel.

Acquiring Proprietary Interest in Litigation

[16] Paragraph (i) states the traditional general rule that lawyers are prohibited from acquiring a proprietary interest in litigation. Like paragraph (e), the general rule has its basis in common law champerty and maintenance and is designed to avoid giving the lawyer too great an interest in the representation. In addition, when the lawyer acquires an ownership interest in the subject of the representation, it will be more difficult for a client to discharge the lawyer if the client so desires. The rule is subject to specific exceptions developed in decisional law and continued in these rules. The exception for certain advances of the costs of litigation is set forth in paragraph (e). In addition, paragraph (i) sets forth exceptions for liens authorized by law to secure the lawyer's fees or expenses and contracts for reasonable contingent fees. The law of each jurisdiction determines which liens are authorized by law. These may include liens granted by statute, liens originating in common law and liens acquired by contract with the client. When a lawyer acquires by contract a security interest in property other than that recovered through the lawyer's efforts in the litigation, such an acquisition is a business or financial transaction with a client and is governed by the requirements of paragraph (a), Contracts for contingent fees in civil cases are governed by Rule 1.5.

Client–Lawyer Sexual Relationships

[17] The relationship between lawyer and client is a fiduciary one in which the lawyer occupies the highest position of trust and confidence. The relationship is almost always unequal; thus, a sexual relationship between lawyer and client can involve unfair exploitation of the lawyer's fiduciary role, in violation of the lawyer's basic ethical obligation not to use the trust of the client to the client's disadvantage. In addition, such a relationship presents a significant danger that, because of the lawyer's emotional involvement, the lawyer will be unable to represent the client without impairment of the exercise of independent professional judgment. Moreover, a blurred line between the professional and personal relationships may make it difficult to predict to what extent client confidences will be protected by the attorney-client evidentiary privilege, since client confidences are protected by privilege only when they are imparted in the context of the client-lawyer relationship. Because of the significant danger of harm to client interests and because the client's own emotional involvement renders it unlikely that the client could give adequate informed consent, this rule prohibits the lawyer from having sexual relations with a client regardless of whether the relationship is consensual and regardless of the absence of prejudice to the client.

[18] Sexual relationships that predate the client-lawyer relationship are not prohibited. Issues relating to the exploitation of the fiduciary relationship and client dependency are diminished when the sexual relationship existed prior to the commencement of the client-lawyer relationship. However, before proceeding with the representation in these circumstances, the lawyer should consider whether the lawyer's ability to represent the client will be materially limited by the relationship. See Rule 1.7(a)(2).

[19] When the client is an organization, paragraph (j) of this rule prohibits a lawyer for the organization from having a sexual relationship with a person who oversees the representation and gives instructions to the lawyer on behalf of the organization.

Imputation of Prohibitions

[20] Under paragraph (k), a prohibition on conduct by an individual lawyer in paragraphs (a) through (i) also applies to all lawyers associated in a firm with the personally prohibited lawyer. For example, one lawyer in a firm may not enter into a business transaction with a client of another member of the firm without complying with paragraph (a), even if the first lawyer is not personally involved in the representation of the client. The prohibition set forth in paragraph (j) is personal and is not applied to associated lawyers.

Historical Notes

This rule is similar, in part, to provisions of former DR 4–101B, EC 5–5, DR 5–103, DR 5–104, DR 5–106, DR 5–107(A), (B) and DR 6–102 of the Minn. Code of Prof. Responsibility.

Rule 1.9. Duties to Former Clients

(a) A lawyer who has formerly represented a client in a matter shall not thereafter represent another person in the same or a substantially related matter in which that person's interests are materially adverse to the interests of the former client unless the former client gives informed consent, confirmed in writing.

(b) A lawyer shall not knowingly represent a person in the same or a substantially related matter in which a firm with which the lawyer formerly was associated had previously represented a client whose interests are materially adverse to that person and about whom the lawyer had acquired information protected by Rules 1.6 and 1.9(c) unless the former client gives informed consent, confirmed in writing.

(c) A lawyer who has formerly represented a client in a matter or whose present or former firm has formerly represented a client in a matter shall not thereafter:

(1) use information relating to the representation to the disadvantage of the former client except as these rules would permit or require with respect to a client, or when the information has become generally known; or

(2) reveal information relating to the representation except as these rules would permit or require with respect to a client.

Adopted June 13, 1985, eff. Sept. 1, 1985. Amended June 17, 2005, eff. Oct. 1, 2005.

Comment—2005

[1] After termination of a client-lawyer relationship, a lawyer has certain continuing duties with respect to confidentiality and conflicts of interest and thus may not represent another client except in conformity with this rule. Under this rule, for example, a lawyer could not properly seek to rescind on behalf of a new client a contract drafted on behalf of the former client. So also a lawyer who has prosecuted an accused person could not properly represent the accused in a subsequent civil action against the government concerning the same transaction. Nor could a lawyer who has represented multiple clients in a matter represent one of the clients against the others in the same or a substantially related matter after a dispute arose among the clients in that matter, unless all affected clients give informed consent. See Comment [9]. Current and former government lawyers must comply with this rule to the extent required by Rule 1.11.

[2] The scope of a "matter" for purposes of this rule depends on the facts of a particular situation or transaction. The lawyer's involvement in a matter can also be a question of degree. When a lawyer has been directly involved in a specific transaction, subsequent representation of other clients with materially adverse interests in that transaction clearly is prohibited. On the other hand, a lawyer who recurrently handled a type of problem for a former client is not precluded from later representing another client in a factually distinct problem of that type even though the subsequent representation involves a position adverse to the prior client. Similar considerations can apply to the reassignment of military lawyers between defense and prosecution functions within the same military jurisdictions. The underlying question is whether the lawyer was so involved in the matter that the subsequent representation can be justly regarded as a changing of sides in the matter in question.

[3] Matters are "substantially related" for purposes of this rule if they involve the same transaction or legal dispute or if there otherwise is a substantial risk that confidential factual information as would normally have been obtained in the prior representation would materially advance the client's position in the subsequent matter. For example, a lawyer who has represented a businessperson and learned extensive private financial information about that person may not then represent that person's spouse in seeking a divorce. Similarly, a lawyer who has previously represented a client in securing environmental permits to build a shopping center would be precluded from representing neighbors seeking to oppose rezoning of the property on the basis of environmental considerations; however, the lawyer would not be precluded, on the grounds of substantial relationship, from defending a tenant of the completed shopping center in resisting eviction for nonpayment of rent. Information that has been disclosed to the public or to other parties adverse to the former client ordinarily will not be disqualifying. Information acquired in a prior representation may have been rendered obsolete by the passage of time, a circumstance that may be relevant in determining whether two representations are substantially related. In the case of an organizational client, general knowledge of the client's policies and practices ordinarily will not preclude a subsequent representation; on the other hand, knowledge of specific facts gained in a prior representation that are relevant to the matter in question ordinarily will preclude such a representation. A former client is not required to reveal the confidential information learned by the lawyer in order to establish a substantial risk that the lawyer has confidential information to use in the subsequent matter. A conclusion about the possession of such information may be based on the nature of the services the lawyer provided the former client and information that would in ordinary practice be learned by a lawyer providing such services.

Lawyers Moving Between Firms

[4] When lawyers have been associated within a firm but then end their association, the question of whether a lawyer should undertake representation is more complicated. There are several competing considerations. First, the client previously represented by the former firm must be reasonably assured that the principle of loyalty to the client is not compromised. Second, the rule should not be so broadly cast as to preclude other persons from having reasonable choice of legal counsel. Third, the rule should not unreasonably hamper lawyers from forming new associations and taking on new clients after having left a previous association. In this connection, it should be recognized that today many lawyers practice in firms, that many lawyers to some degree limit their practice to one field or another, and that many move from one association to another several times in their careers. If the concept of imputation were applied with unqualified rigor, the result would be radical curtailment of the opportunity of lawyers to move from one practice setting to another and of the opportunity of clients to change counsel.

[5] Paragraph (b) operates to disqualify the lawyer only when the lawyer involved has actual knowledge of information protected by Rules 1.6 and 1.9(c). Thus, if a lawyer while with one firm acquired no knowledge or information relating to a particular client of the firm, and that lawyer later joined another firm, neither the lawyer individually

nor the second firm is disqualified from representing another client in the same or a related matter even though the interests of the two clients conflict. See Rule 1.10(b) for the restrictions on a firm once a lawyer has terminated association with the firm.

[6] Application of paragraph (b) depends on a situation's particular facts, aided by inferences, deductions or working presumptions that reasonably may be made about the way in which lawyers work together. A lawyer may have general access to files of all clients of a law firm and may regularly participate in discussions of their affairs; it should be inferred that such a lawyer in fact is privy to all information about all the firm's clients. In contrast, another lawyer may have access to the files of only a limited number of clients and participate in discussions of the affairs of no other clients; in the absence of information to the contrary, it should be inferred that such a lawyer in fact is privy to information about the clients actually served but not those of other clients. In such an inquiry, the burden of proof should rest upon the firm whose disqualification is sought.

[7] Independent of the question of disqualification of a firm, a lawyer changing professional association has a continuing duty to preserve confidentiality of information about a client formerly represented. See Rule 1.6 and 1.9(c).

[8] Paragraph (c) provides that information acquired by the lawyer in the course of representing a client may not subsequently be used or revealed by the lawyer to the disadvantage of the client. However, the fact that a lawyer has once served a client does not preclude the lawyer from using generally known information about that client when later representing another client.

[9] The provisions of this rule are for the protection of former clients and can be waived if the client gives informed consent, which consent must be confirmed in writing under paragraphs (a) and (b). See Rule 1.0(f). With regard to the effectiveness of an advance waiver, see Comment [22] to Rule 1.7. With regard to disqualification of a firm with which a lawyer is or was formerly associated, see Rule 1.10.

Historical Notes

This rule is similar, in part, to provisions of former DR 4-101(B) of the Minn. Code of Prof. Responsibility.

Rule 1.10. Imputation of Conflicts of Interest: General Rule

(a) While lawyers are associated in a firm, none of them shall knowingly represent a client when any one of them practicing alone would be prohibited from doing so by Rule 1.7 or 1.9, unless the prohibition is based on a personal interest of the prohibited lawyer and does not present a significant risk of materially limiting the representation of the client by the remaining lawyers in the firm.

(b) When a lawyer becomes associated with a firm, and the lawyer is prohibited from representing a client pursuant to Rule 1.9(b), other lawyers in the firm may represent that client if there is no reasonably apparent risk that confidential information of the previously represented client will be used with material adverse effect on that client because:

(1) any confidential information communicated to the lawyer is unlikely to be significant in the subsequent matter;

(2) the lawyer is subject to screening measures adequate to prevent disclosure of the confidential information and to prevent involvement by that lawyer in the representation; and

(3) timely and adequate notice of the screening has been provided to all affected clients.

(c) When a lawyer has terminated an association with a firm, the firm is not prohibited from thereafter representing a person with interests materially adverse to those of a client represented by the formerly associated lawyer and not currently represented by the firm, unless:

(1) the matter is the same or substantially related to that in which the formerly associated lawyer represented the client; and

(2) any lawyer remaining in the firm has information protected by Rules 1.6 and 1.9(c) that is material to the matter.

(d) A disqualification prescribed by this rule may be waived by the affected client under the conditions stated in Rule 1.7.

(e) The disqualification of lawyers associated in a firm with former or current government lawyers is governed by Rule 1.11.

Adopted June 13, 1985, eff. Sept. 1, 1985. Amended July 28, 1999, eff. Aug. 1, 1999; June 17, 2005, eff. Oct. 1, 2005.

Comment—2005

Definition of "Firm"

[1] For purposes of the Rules of Professional Conduct, the term " firm" denotes lawyers in a law partnership, professional corporation, sole proprietorship or other association authorized to practice law; or lawyers employed in a legal services organization or the legal department of a corporation or other organization. See Rule 1.0(d). Whether two or more lawyers constitute a firm within this definition can depend on the specific facts. See Rule 1.0, Comments [2]–[4].

Principles of Imputed Disqualification

[2] The rule of imputed disqualification stated in paragraph (a) gives effect to the principle of loyalty to the client as it applies to lawyers who practice in a law firm. Such situations can be considered from the premise that a firm of lawyers is essentially one lawyer for purposes of the rules governing loyalty to the client, or from the premise that each lawyer is vicariously bound by the obligation of loyalty owed by each lawyer with whom the lawyer is associated. Paragraph (a) operates only among the lawyers currently associated in a firm. When a

lawyer moves from one firm to another, the situation is governed by Rules 1.9(b) and 1.10(b) and (c).

[3] The rule in paragraph (a) does not prohibit representation where neither questions of client loyalty nor protection of confidential information are presented. Where one lawyer in a firm could not effectively represent a given client because of strong political beliefs, for example, but that lawyer will do no work on the case and the personal beliefs of that lawyer will not materially limit the representation by others in the firm, the firm should not be disqualified. On the other hand, if an opposing party in a case were owned by a lawyer in the law firm, and others in the firm would be materially limited in pursuing the matter because of loyalty to that lawyer, the personal disqualification of the lawyer would be imputed to all others in the firm.

[4] The rule in paragraph (a) also does not prohibit representation by others in the law firm where the person prohibited from involvement in a matter is a nonlawyer, such as a paralegal or legal secretary. Nor does paragraph (a) prohibit representation if the lawyer is prohibited from acting because of events before the person became a lawyer, for example, work that the person did while a law student. Such persons, however, ordinarily must be screened from any personal participation in the matter to avoid communication to others in the firm of confidential information that both the nonlawyers and the firm have a legal duty to protect. See Rules 1.0(*l*) and 5.3.

[5] Rule 1.10(c) operates to permit a law firm, under certain circumstances, to represent a person with interests directly adverse to those of a client represented by a lawyer who formerly was associated with the firm. The rule applies regardless of when the formerly associated lawyer represented the client. However, the law firm may not represent a person with interests adverse to those of a present client of the firm, which would violate Rule 1.7. Moreover, the firm may not represent the person where the matter is the same or substantially related to that in which the formerly associated lawyer represented the client and any other lawyer currently in the firm has material information protected by Rules 1.6 and 1.9(c).

[6] Rule 1.10(d) removes imputation with the informed consent of the affected client or former client under the conditions stated in Rule 1.7. The conditions stated in Rule 1.7 require the lawyer to determine that the representation is not prohibited by Rule 1.7(b) and that each affected client or former client has given informed consent to the representation, confirmed in writing. In some cases, the risk may be so severe that the conflict may not be cured by client consent. For a discussion of the effectiveness of client waivers of conflicts that might arise in the future, see Rule 1.7, Comment [22]. For a definition of informed consent, see Rule 1.0(f).

[7] Where a lawyer has joined a private firm after having represented the government, imputation is governed by Rule 1.11(b) and (c), not this rule. Under Rule 1.11(d), where a lawyer represents the government after having served clients in private practice, nongovernmental employment or in another government agency, former-client conflicts are not imputed to government lawyers associated with the individually disqualified lawyer.

[8] Where a lawyer is prohibited from engaging in certain transactions under Rule 1.8, paragraph (k) of that rule, and not this rule, determines whether that prohibition also applies to other lawyers associated in a firm with the personally prohibited lawyer.

Historical Notes

This rule is similar, in part, to provisions of former DR 5–105(D) of the Minn. Code of Prof. Responsibility.

Rule 1.11. Special Conflicts of Interest for Former and Current Government Officers and Employees

(a) Except as the law may otherwise expressly permit, a lawyer who has formerly served as a public officer or employee of the government:

(1) is subject to Rule 1.9(c); and

(2) shall not otherwise represent a client in connection with a matter in which the lawyer participated personally and substantially as a public officer or employee, unless the appropriate government agency gives its informed consent, confirmed in writing, to the representation.

(b) When a lawyer is disqualified from representation under paragraph (a), no lawyer in a firm with which that lawyer is associated may knowingly undertake or continue representation in such a matter unless:

(1) the disqualified lawyer is timely screened from any participation in the matter and is apportioned no part of the fee therefrom; and

(2) written notice is promptly given to the appropriate government agency to enable it to ascertain compliance with the provisions of this rule.

(c) Except as the law may otherwise expressly permit, a lawyer having information that the lawyer knows is confidential government information about a person acquired when the lawyer was a public officer or employee, may not represent a private client whose interests are adverse to that person in a matter in which the information could be used to the material disadvantage of that person. As used in this rule, the term " confidential government information" means information that has been obtained under governmental authority and which, at the time this rule is applied, the government is prohibited by law from disclosing to the public or has a legal privilege not to disclose and which is not otherwise available to the public. A firm with which that lawyer is associated may undertake or continue representation in the matter only if the disqualified lawyer is timely screened from any participation in the matter and is apportioned no part of the fee therefrom.

(d) Except as law may otherwise expressly permit, a lawyer currently serving as a public officer or employee:

(1) is subject to Rules 1.7 and 1.9; and

(2) shall not:

(i) participate in a matter in which the lawyer participated personally and substantially while in private practice or nongovernmental employment, unless the appropriate government agency gives its informed consent, confirmed in writing; or

(ii) negotiate for private employment with any person who is involved as a party or as lawyer for a party in a matter in which the lawyer is participating personally and substantially, except that a lawyer serving as a law clerk to a judge, other adjudicative officer, or arbitrator may negotiate for private employment as permitted by Rule 1.12(b) and subject to the conditions stated in Rule 1.12(b).

(e) As used in this rule, the term "matter" includes:

(1) any judicial or other proceeding, application, request for a ruling or other determination, contract, claim, controversy, investigation, charge, accusation, arrest or other particular matter involving a specific party or parties, and

(2) any other matter covered by the conflict of interest rules of the appropriate government agency.

Adopted June 13, 1985, eff. Sept. 1, 1985. Amended June 17, 2005, eff. Oct. 1, 2005.

Comment—2005

[1] A lawyer who has served or is currently serving as a public officer or employee is personally subject to the Rules of Professional Conduct, including the prohibition against concurrent conflicts of interest stated in Rule 1.7. In addition, such a lawyer may be subject to statutes and government regulations regarding conflicts of interest. Such statutes and regulations may circumscribe the extent to which the government agency may give consent under this rule. See Rule 1.0(f) for the definition of informed consent. It is generally improper for a county attorney to accept the defense of a criminal case in another county, and for a city attorney to accept a criminal case that arises within the boundaries of the city or municipality that he or she represents. In extraordinary circumstances, where the accused would otherwise be deprived of competent counsel, a county attorney may seek to represent a client accused of a crime in another county by obtaining permission from the court before which the matter will be tried. The disqualification of county and city attorneys is only imputed to those lawyers in the county or city attorney's law firm who actually participate in representing the county or the city.

[2] Paragraphs (a)(1), (a)(2) and (d)(1) restate the obligations of an individual lawyer who has served or is currently serving as an officer or employee of the government toward a former government or private client. Rule 1.10 is not applicable to the conflicts of interest addressed by this rule. Rather, paragraph (b) sets forth a special imputation rule for former government lawyers that provides for screening and notice. Because of the special problems raised by imputation within a government agency, paragraph (d) does not impute the conflicts of a lawyer currently serving as an officer or employee of the government to other associated government officers or employees, although ordinarily it will be prudent to screen such lawyers.

[3] Paragraphs (a)(2) and (d)(2) apply regardless of whether a lawyer is adverse to a former client and are thus designed not only to protect the former client, but also to prevent a lawyer from exploiting public office for the advantage of another client. For example, a lawyer who has pursued a claim on behalf of the government may not pursue the same claim on behalf of a later private client after the lawyer has left government service, except when authorized to do so by the government agency under paragraph (a). Similarly, a lawyer who has pursued a claim on behalf of a private client may not pursue the claim on behalf of the government, except when authorized to do so by paragraph (d). As with paragraphs (a)(1) and (d)(1). Rule 1.10 is not applicable to the conflicts of interest addressed by these paragraphs.

[4] This rule represents a balancing of interests. On the one hand, where the successive clients are a government agency and another client, public or private, the risk exists that power or discretion vested in that agency might be used for the special benefit of the other client. A lawyer should not be in a position where benefit to the other client might affect performance of the lawyer's professional functions on behalf of the government. Also, unfair advantage could accrue to the other client by reason of access to confidential government information about the client's adversary obtainable only through the lawyer's government service. On the other hand, the rules governing lawyers presently or formerly employed by a government agency should not be so restrictive as to inhibit transfer of employment to and from the government. The government has a legitimate need to attract qualified lawyers as well as to maintain high ethical standards. Thus a former government lawyer is disqualified only from particular matters in which the lawyer participated personally and substantially. The provisions for screening and waiver in paragraph (b) are necessary to prevent the disqualification rule from imposing too severe a deterrent against entering public service. The limitation of disqualification in paragraphs (a)(2) and (d)(2) to matters involving a specific party or parties, rather than extending disqualification to all substantive issues on which the lawyer worked, serves a similar function.

[5] When a lawyer has been employed by one government agency and then moves to a second government agency, it may be appropriate to treat that second agency as another client for purposes of this rule, as when a lawyer is employed by a city and subsequently is employed by a federal agency.

However, because the conflict of interest is governed by paragraph (d), the latter agency is not required to screen the lawyer as paragraph (b) requires a law firm to do. The question of whether two government agencies should be regarded as the same or different clients for conflict of interest purposes is beyond the scope of these rules. See Rule 1.13, Comment [6].

[6] Paragraphs (b) and (c) contemplate a screening arrangement. See Rule 1.0(*l*) (requirements for screening procedures). These paragraphs do not prohibit a lawyer from receiving a salary or partnership share established by prior independent agreement, but that lawyer may not receive compensation directly relating the lawyer's compensation to the fee in the matter in which the lawyer is disqualified.

[7] Notice, including a description of the screened lawyer's prior representation and of the screening procedures employed, generally should be given as soon as practicable after the need for screening becomes apparent.

[8] Paragraph (c) operates only when the lawyer in question has knowledge of the information, which means actual knowledge; it does not operate with respect to information that merely could be imputed to the lawyer.

[9] Paragraphs (a) and (d) do not prohibit a lawyer from jointly representing a private party and a government agency when doing so is permitted by Rule 1.7 and is not otherwise prohibited by law.

[10] For purposes of paragraph (e) of this rule, a "matter" may continue in another form. In determining whether two particular matters are the same, the lawyer should consider the extent to which the matters involve the same basic facts, the same or related parties, and the time elapsed.

Historical Notes

This rule is similar, in part, to provisions of former EC 9–3 and DR 9–101(B) of the Minn. Code of Prof. Responsibility.

Rule 1.12. Former Judge, Arbitrator, Mediator, or Other Third–Party Neutral

(a) Except as stated in paragraph (d), a lawyer shall not represent anyone in connection with a matter in which the lawyer participated personally and substantially as a judge or other adjudicative officer or law clerk to such a person, or as an arbitrator, mediator, or other third-party neutral, unless all parties to the proceeding give informed consent, confirmed in writing.

(b) A lawyer shall not negotiate for employment with any person who is involved as a party or as lawyer for a party in a matter in which the lawyer is participating personally and substantially as a judge or other adjudicative officer or as an arbitrator, mediator, or other third-party neutral. A lawyer serving as a law clerk to a judge or other adjudicative officer may negotiate for employment with a party or lawyer involved in a matter in which the clerk is participating personally and substantially, but only after the lawyer has notified the judge or other adjudicative officer.

(c) If a lawyer is disqualified by paragraph (a), no lawyer in a firm with which that lawyer is associated may knowingly undertake or continue representation in the matter unless:

(1) the disqualified lawyer is timely screened from any participation in the matter and is apportioned no part of the fee therefrom; and

(2) written notice is promptly given to the parties and any appropriate tribunal to enable them to ascertain compliance with the provisions of this rule.

(d) An arbitrator selected as a partisan of a party in a multimember arbitration panel is not prohibited from subsequently representing that party.

Adopted June 13, 1985, eff. Sept. 1, 1985. Amended June 17, 2005, eff. Oct. 1, 2005.

Comment—2005

[1] This rule generally parallels Rule 1.11. The term "personally and substantially" signifies that a judge who was a member of a multimember court, and thereafter left judicial office to practice law, is not prohibited from representing a client in a matter pending in the court, but in which the former judge did not participate. So also, the fact that a former judge exercised administrative responsibility in a court does not prevent the former judge from acting as a lawyer in a matter where the judge had previously exercised remote or incidental administrative responsibility that did not affect the merits. Compare Comment to Rule 1.11. The term "adjudicative officer" includes such officials as judges pro tempore, referees, special masters, hearing officers and other parajudicial officers, and also lawyers who serve as part-time judges. Paragraphs C(2), D(2), and E(2) of the Application section of the Model Code of Judicial Conduct provide that a part-time judge, judge pro tempore, or retired judge recalled to active service, may not "act as a lawyer in a proceeding in which the judge served as a judge or in any other proceeding related thereto." Although phrased differently from this rule, those rules correspond in meaning.

[2] Like former judges, lawyers who have served as arbitrators, mediators or other third-party neutrals may be asked to represent a client in a matter in which the lawyer participated personally and substantially. This rule forbids such representation unless all of the parties to the proceedings give their informed consent, confirmed in writing. See Rule 1.0(f) and (b). Other law or codes of ethics governing third-party neutrals may impose more stringent standards of personal or imputed disqualification. See Rule 2.4.

[3] Although lawyers who serve as third-party neutrals do not have information concerning the parties that is protected under Rule 1.6, they typically owe the parties an obligation of confidentiality under law or codes of ethics governing third-party neutrals. Thus, paragraph (c) provides that conflicts of the personally disqualified lawyer will be imputed to other lawyers in a law firm unless the conditions of this paragraph are met.

[4] Requirements for screening procedures are stated in Rule 1.0(l). Paragraph (c)(1) does not prohibit the screened lawyer from receiving a salary or partnership share established by prior independent agreement, but that lawyer may not receive compensation directly related to the matter in which the lawyer is disqualified.

[5] Notice, including a description of the screened lawyer's prior representation and of the screening procedures employed, generally should be given as soon as practicable after the need for screening becomes apparent.

Historical Notes

This rule is similar, in part, to provisions of former DR 9–101(A) of the Minn. Code of Prof. Responsibility.

Rule 1.13. Organization as Client

(a) A lawyer employed or retained by an organization represents the organization acting through its duly authorized constituents.

(b) If a lawyer for an organization knows that an officer, employee or other person associated with the organization is engaged in action, intends to act, or refuses to act in a matter related to the representation that is a violation of a legal obligation to the organization, or a violation of law that reasonably might be imputed to the organization, and that is likely to result in substantial injury to the organization, then the lawyer shall proceed as is reasonably necessary in the best interest of the organization.

Unless the lawyer reasonably believes that it is not necessary in the best interests of the organization to do so, the lawyer shall refer the matter to higher authority in the organization, including, if warranted by the circumstances, to the highest authority that can act on behalf of the organization as determined by applicable law.

(c) If, despite the lawyer's efforts in accordance with paragraph (b), the highest authority that can act on behalf of the organization insists upon or fails to address in a timely and appropriate manner an action, or a refusal to act, that is clearly a violation of the law, the lawyer may resign in accordance with Rule 1.16 and may disclose information in conformance with Rule 1.6.

(d) A lawyer who reasonably believes that he or she has been discharged because of the lawyer's actions taken pursuant to paragraph (b) or (c), or who withdraws under circumstances that require or permit the lawyer to take action under either of those paragraphs, shall proceed as the lawyer reasonably believes necessary to assure that the organization's highest authority is informed of the lawyer's discharge or withdrawal.

(e) In dealing with an organization's directors, officers, employees, members, shareholders, or other constituents, a lawyer shall explain the identity of the client when the lawyer knows or reasonably should know that the organization's interests are adverse to those of the constituents with whom the lawyer is dealing.

(f) A lawyer representing an organization may also represent any of its directors, officers, employees, members, shareholders, or other constituents, subject to the provisions of Rule 1.7. If the organization's consent to the dual representation is required by Rule 1.7, the consent shall be given by an appropriate official of the organization other than the individual who is to be represented, or by the shareholders.

Adopted June 13, 1985, eff. Sept. 1, 1985. Amended June 17, 2005, eff. Oct. 1, 2005.

Comment—2005

The Entity as the Client

[1] An organizational client is a legal entity, but it cannot act except through its officers, directors, employees, shareholders, and other constituents. Officers, directors, employees, and shareholders are the constituents of the corporate organizational client. The duties defined in this comment apply equally to unincorporated associations. " Other constituents" as used in this comment means the positions equivalent to officers, directors, employees, and shareholders held by persons acting for organizational clients that are not corporations.

[2] When one of the constituents of an organizational client communicates with the organization's lawyer in that person's organizational capacity, the communication is protected by Rule 1.6. Thus, by way of example, if an organizational client requests its lawyer to investigate allegations of wrongdoing, interviews made in the course of that investigation between the lawyer and the client's employees or other constituents are covered by Rule 1.6. This does not mean, however, that constituents of an organizational client are the clients of the lawyer. The lawyer may not disclose to such constituents information relating to the representation except for disclosures explicitly or impliedly authorized by the organizational client in order to carry out the representation or as otherwise permitted by Rule 1.6.

[3] When constituents of the organization make decisions for it, the decisions ordinarily must be accepted by the lawyer even if their utility or prudence is doubtful. Decisions concerning policy and operations, including ones entailing serious risk, are not as such in the lawyer's province. Paragraph (b) makes clear, however, that when the lawyer knows that the organization is likely to be substantially injured by action of an officer or other constituent that violates a legal obligation to the organization or is in violation of law that might be imputed to the organization the lawyer must proceed as is reasonably necessary in the best interest of the organization. As defined in Rule 1.0(f), knowledge can be inferred from circumstances, and a lawyer cannot ignore the obvious.

[4] In determining how to proceed under paragraph (b), the lawyer should give due consideration to the seriousness of the violation and its consequences, the responsibility in the organization and the apparent motivation of the person involved, the

policies of the organization concerning such matters, and any other relevant considerations. Ordinarily, referral to a higher authority would be necessary. In some circumstances, however, it may be appropriate for the lawyer to ask the constituent to reconsider the matter; for example, if the circumstances involve a constituent's innocent misunderstanding of law and subsequent acceptance of the lawyer's advice, the lawyer may reasonably conclude that the best interest of the organization does not require that the matter be referred to higher authority. If a constituent persists in conduct contrary to the lawyer's advice, it will be necessary for the lawyer to take steps to have the matter reviewed by a higher authority in the organization. If the matter is of sufficient seriousness and importance or urgency to the organization, referral to a higher authority in the organization may be necessary even if the lawyer has not communicated with the constituent. Any measures taken should, to the extent practicable, minimize the risk of revealing information relating to the representation to persons outside the organization. Even in circumstances where a lawyer is not obligated by Rule 1.13 to proceed, a lawyer may bring to the attention of an organization client, including its highest authority, matters that the lawyer reasonably believes to be of sufficient importance to warrant doing so in the best interest of the organization.

[5] Paragraph (b) also makes clear that when it is reasonably necessary to enable the organization to address the matter in a timely and appropriate manner, the lawyer must refer the matter to higher authority, including, if warranted by the circumstances, the highest authority that can act on behalf of the organization under applicable law. The organization's highest authority to whom a matter may be referred ordinarily will be the board of directors or similar governing body. However, applicable law may prescribe that under certain conditions the highest authority reposes elsewhere, for example, in the independent directors of a corporation.

Relation to Other Rules

[6] The authority and responsibility provided in this rule are concurrent with the authority and responsibility provided in other rules. In particular, this rule does not limit or expand the lawyer's responsibility under Rule 1.6, 1.8, 1.16, 3.3, or 4.1. Paragraph (c) of this rule does not modify, restrict, or limit the provisions of Rule 1.6(b). Under paragraph (c), the lawyer may reveal confidential information only when the organization's highest authority insists upon or fails to address threatened or ongoing action that is clearly a violation of law. If the lawyer's services are being used by an organization to further a crime or fraud by the organization, Rule 1.6(b) may permit the lawyer to disclose confidential information. In such circumstances Rule 1.2(d) may also be applicable, in which event withdrawal from the representation under Rule 1.16(a)(1) may be required.

[7] A lawyer who reasonably believes that he or she has been discharged because of the lawyer's actions taken pursuant to paragraph (b) or (c), or who withdraws in circumstances that require or permit the lawyer to take action under either of these paragraphs, must proceed as the lawyer reasonably believes necessary to assure that the organization's highest authority is informed of the lawyer's discharge or withdrawal.

Government Agency

[8] The duty defined in this rule applies to governmental organizations. Defining precisely the identity of the client and prescribing the resulting obligations of such lawyers may be more difficult in the government context and is a matter beyond the scope of these rules. See Scope [18]. Although in some circumstances the client may be a specific agency, it may also be a branch of government, such as the executive branch, or the government as a whole. For example, if the action or failure to act involves the head of a bureau, either the department of which the bureau is a part or the relevant branch of government may be the client for purposes of this rule. Moreover, in a matter involving the conduct of government officials, a government lawyer may have authority under applicable law to question such conduct more extensively than that of a lawyer for a private organization in similar circumstances. Thus, when the client is a governmental organization, a different balance may be appropriate between maintaining confidentiality and assuring that the wrongful act is prevented or rectified, for public business is involved. In addition, duties of lawyers employed by the government or lawyers in military service may be defined by statutes and regulation. This rule does not limit that authority. See Scope.

Clarifying the Lawyer's Role

[9] There are times when the organization's interest may be or become adverse to those of one or more of its constituents. In such circumstances the lawyer should advise any constituent, whose interest the lawyer finds adverse to that of the organization of the conflict or potential conflict of interest, that the lawyer cannot represent such constituent, and that such person may wish to obtain independent representation. Care must be taken to assure that the individual understands that, when there is such adversity of interest, the lawyer for the organization cannot provide legal representation for that constituent individual, and that discussions between the lawyer for the organization and the individual may not be privileged.

[10] Whether such a warning should be given by the lawyer for the organization to any constituent individual may turn on the facts of each case.

Dual Representation

[11] Paragraph (f) recognizes that a lawyer for an organization may also represent a principal officer or major shareholder.

Derivative Actions

[12] Under generally prevailing law, the shareholders or members of a corporation may bring suit to compel the directors to perform their legal obligations in the supervision of the organization. Members of unincorporated associations have essentially the same right. Such an action may be brought nominally by the organization, but usually

is, in fact, a legal controversy over management of the organization.

[13] The question can arise whether counsel for the organization may defend such an action. The proposition that the organization is the lawyer's client does not alone resolve the issue. Most derivative actions are a normal incident of an organization's affairs, to be defended by the organization's lawyer like any other suit. However, if the claim involves serious charges of wrongdoing by those in control of the organization, a conflict may arise between the lawyer's duty to the organization and the lawyer's relationship with the board. In those circumstances, Rule 1.7 governs who should represent the directors and the organization.

Historical Notes

This rule is similar, in part, to provisions of former EC 5–18 of the Minn. Code of Prof. Responsibility.

Rule 1.14. Client with Diminished Capacity

(a) When a client's capacity to make adequately considered decisions in connection with a representation is diminished, whether because of minority, mental impairment, or some other reason, the lawyer shall, as far as reasonably possible, maintain a normal client-lawyer relationship with the client.

(b) When the lawyer reasonably believes that the client has diminished capacity, is at risk of substantial physical, financial, or other harm unless action is taken and cannot adequately act in the client's own interest, the lawyer may take reasonably protective action, including consulting individuals or entities that have the ability to take action to protect the client and, in appropriate cases, seeking the appointment of a guardian ad litem, conservator, or guardian.

(c) Information relating to the representation of a client with diminished capacity is protected by Rule 1.6. When taking protective action pursuant to paragraph (b), the lawyer is impliedly authorized under Rule 1.6(b)(3) to reveal information about the client, but only to the extent reasonably necessary to protect the client's interests.

Adopted June 13, 1985, eff. Sept. 1, 1985. Amended June 17, 2005, eff. Oct. 1, 2005.

Comment—2005

[1] The normal client-lawyer relationship is based on the assumption that the client, when properly advised and assisted, is capable of making decisions about important matters. When the client is a minor or suffers from a diminished mental capacity, however, maintaining the ordinary client-lawyer relationship may not be possible in all respects. In particular, a severely incapacitated person may have no power to make legally binding decisions. Nevertheless, a client with diminished capacity often has the ability to understand, deliberate upon, and reach conclusions about matters affecting the client's own well-being. For example, children as young as five or six years of age, and certainly those of ten or twelve, are regarded as having opinions that are entitled to weight in legal proceedings concerning their custody. So also, it is recognized that some persons of advanced age can be quite capable of handling routine financial matters while needing special legal protection concerning major transactions.

[2] The fact that a client suffers an impairment does not diminish the lawyer's obligation to treat the client with attention and respect. Even if the person has a legal representative, the lawyer should as far as possible accord the represented person the status of client, particularly in maintaining communication.

[3] The client may wish to have family members or other persons participate in discussions with the lawyer. When necessary to assist in the representation, the presence of such persons generally does not affect the applicability of the attorney-client evidentiary privilege. Nevertheless, the lawyer must keep the client's interests foremost and, except for protective action authorized under paragraph (b), must look to the client, and not family members, to make decisions on the client's behalf.

[4] If a legal representative has already been appointed for the client, the lawyer should ordinarily look to the representative for decisions on behalf of the client. In matters involving a minor, whether the lawyer should look to the parents as natural guardians may depend on the type of proceeding or matter in which the lawyer is representing the minor. If the lawyer represents the guardian as distinct from the ward, and is aware that the guardian is acting adversely to the ward' s interest, the lawyer may have an obligation to prevent or rectify the guardian's misconduct. See Rule 1.2(d).

Taking Protective Action

[5] If a lawyer reasonably believes that a client is at risk of substantial physical, financial or other harm unless action is taken, and that a normal client-lawyer relationship cannot be maintained as provided in paragraph (a) because the client lacks sufficient capacity to communicate or to make adequately considered decisions in connection with the representation, then paragraph (b) permits the lawyer to take protective measures deemed necessary. Such measures could include: consulting with family members, using a reconsideration period to permit clarification or improvement of circumstances, using voluntary surrogate decisionmaking tools, such as durable powers of attorney or consulting with support groups, professional services, adult-protective agencies, or other individuals or entities that have the ability to protect the client. In taking any protective action, the lawyer should be guided by such factors as the wishes and values of the client to the extent known, the client's best interests and the goals of intruding into the client's decisionmaking autonomy to the least extent feasible, maximizing client capacities, and respecting the client's family and social connections.

[6] In determining the extent of the client's diminished capacity, the lawyer should consider and balance such factors as: the client's ability to articulate reasoning leading to a decision, variability of state of mind and ability to appreciate consequences

of a decision, the substantive fairness of a decision, and the consistency of a decision with the known long-term commitments and values of the client. In appropriate circumstances, the lawyer may seek guidance from an appropriate diagnostician.

[7] If a legal representative has not been appointed, the lawyer should consider whether appointment of a guardian ad litem, conservator, or guardian is necessary to protect the client's interests. Thus, if a client with diminished capacity has substantial property that should be sold for the client's benefit, effective completion of the transaction may require appointment of a legal representative. In addition, rules of procedure in litigation sometimes provide that minors or persons with diminished capacity must be represented by a guardian or next friend if they do not have a general guardian. In many circumstances, however, appointment of a legal representative may be more expensive or traumatic for the client than circumstances in fact require. Evaluation of such circumstances is a matter entrusted to the professional judgment of the lawyer. In considering alternatives, however, the lawyer should be aware of any law that requires the lawyer to advocate the least restrictive action on behalf of the client.

Disclosure of the Client's Condition

[8] Disclosure of the client's diminished capacity could adversely affect the client's interests. For example, raising the question could, in some circumstances, lead to proceedings for involuntary commitment. Information relating to the representation is protected by Rule 1.6. Therefore, unless authorized to do so, the lawyer may not disclose such information. When taking protective action pursuant to paragraph (b), the lawyer is impliedly authorized to make the necessary disclosures, even when the client directs the lawyer to the contrary. Nevertheless, given the risks of disclosure, paragraph (c) limits what the lawyer may disclose in consulting other individuals or entities or seeking the appointment of a legal representative. At the very least, the lawyer should determine whether it is likely that the person or entity consulted will act adversely to the client's interests before discussing matters related to the client. The lawyer's position in such cases is an unavoidably difficult one.

Emergency Legal Assistance

[9] In an emergency where the health, safety, or financial interest of a person with seriously diminished capacity is threatened with imminent and irreparable harm, a lawyer may take legal action on behalf of such a person even though the person is unable to establish a client-lawyer relationship or to make or express considered judgments about the matter, when the person or another acting, in good faith on that person's behalf has consulted the lawyer. Even in such an emergency, however, the lawyer should not act unless the lawyer reasonably believes that the person has no other lawyer, agent, or other representative available. The lawyer should take legal action on behalf of the person only to the extent reasonably necessary to maintain the status quo or otherwise avoid imminent and irreparable harm. A lawyer who undertakes to represent a person in such an exigent situation has the same duties under these rules as the lawyer would with respect to a client.

[10] A lawyer who acts on behalf of a person with seriously diminished capacity in an emergency should keep the confidences of the person as if dealing with a client, disclosing them only to the extent necessary to accomplish the intended protective action. The lawyer should disclose to any tribunal involved and to any other counsel involved the nature of his or her relationship with the person. The lawyer should take steps to regularize the relationship or implement other protective solutions as soon as possible. Normally, a lawyer would not seek compensation for such emergency actions taken.

Historical Notes

This rule is similar, in part, to provisions of former EC 7–11 of the Minn. Code of Prof. Responsibility.

Rule 1.15. Safekeeping Property

(a) All funds of clients or third persons held by a lawyer or law firm in connection with a representation shall be deposited in one or more identifiable trust accounts as set forth in paragraphs (d) through (g) and as defined in paragraph (*o*). No funds belonging to the lawyer or law firm shall be deposited therein except as follows:

(1) funds of the lawyer or law firm reasonably sufficient to pay service charges may be deposited therein;

(2) funds belonging in part to a client or third person and in part presently or potentially to the lawyer or law firm must be deposited therein.

(b) A lawyer must withdraw earned fees and any other funds belonging to the lawyer or the law firm from the trust account within a reasonable time after the fees have been earned or entitlement to the funds has been established, and the lawyer must provide the client or third person with: (i) written notice of the time, amount, and purpose of the withdrawal; and (ii) an accounting of the client's or third person's funds in the trust account. If the right of the lawyer or law firm to receive funds from the account is disputed by the client or third person claiming entitlement to the funds, the disputed portion shall not be withdrawn until the dispute is finally resolved. If the right of the lawyer or law firm to receive funds from the account is disputed within a reasonable time after the funds have been withdrawn, the disputed portion must be restored to the account until the dispute is resolved.

(c) A lawyer shall:

(1) promptly notify a client or third person of the receipt of the client's or third person's funds, securities, or other properties;

(2) identify and label securities and properties of a client or third person promptly upon receipt and place them in a safe deposit box or other place of safekeeping as soon as practicable;

(3) maintain complete records of all funds, securities, and other properties of a client or third person coming into the possession of the lawyer and render appropriate accounts to the client or third person regarding them;

(4) promptly pay or deliver to the client or third person as requested the funds, securities, or other properties in the possession of the lawyer which the client or third person is entitled to receive; and

(5) except as specified in Rule 1.5(b)(1) and (2), deposit all fees received in advance of the legal services being performed into a trust account and withdraw the fees as earned.

(d) Each trust account referred to in paragraph (a) shall be an account in an eligible financial institution selected by a lawyer in the exercise of ordinary prudence.

(e) A lawyer who receives client or third person funds shall maintain a pooled trust account ("IOLTA account") for deposit of funds that are nominal in amount or expected to be held for a short period of time.

(f) All client or third person funds shall be deposited in the account specified in paragraph (e) unless they are deposited in a:

(1) separate trust account for the particular third person, client, or client's matter on which the earnings, net of any transaction costs, will be paid to the client or third person; or

(2) pooled trust account with subaccounting which will provide for computation of earnings accrued on each client's or third person's funds and the payment thereof, net of any transaction costs, to the client.

(g) In determining whether to use the account specified in paragraph (e) or an account specified in paragraph (f), a lawyer shall take into consideration the following factors:

(1) the amount of earnings which the funds would accrue during the period they are expected to be deposited;

(2) the cost of establishing and administering the account, including the cost of the lawyer's services;

(3) the capability of financial institutions described in paragraph (d) to calculate and pay earnings to individual clients.

Only funds that could not accrue earnings for the client, net of the costs described in subparagraph (2) above, may be placed or retained in the account specified in paragraph (e).

(h) Every lawyer engaged in private practice of law shall maintain or cause to be maintained on a current basis books and records sufficient to demonstrate income derived from, and expenses related to, the lawyer's private practice of law, and to establish compliance with paragraphs (a) through (f). Equivalent books and records demonstrating the same information in an easily accessible manner and in substantially the same detail are acceptable. The books and records shall be preserved for at least six years following the end of the taxable year to which they relate or, as to books and records relating to funds or property of clients or third persons, for at least six years after completion of the employment to which they relate.

(i) Every lawyer subject to paragraph (h) shall certify, in connection with the annual renewal of the lawyer's registration and in such form as the Clerk of the Appellate Court may prescribe, that the lawyer or the lawyer's law firm maintains books and records as required by paragraph (h). The Lawyers Professional Responsibility Board shall publish annually the books and records required by paragraph (h).

(j) Lawyer trust accounts, including IOLTA accounts, shall be maintained only in eligible financial institutions approved by the Office of Lawyers Professional Responsibility. Every check, draft, electronic transfer, or other withdrawal instrument or authorization shall be personally signed or, in the case of electronic, telephone, or wire transfer, directed by one or more lawyers authorized by the law firm.

(k) A financial institution, to be approved as a depository for lawyer trust accounts, must files with the Office of Lawyers Professional Responsibility an agreement, in a form provided by the Office, to report to the Office in the event any properly payable instrument is presented against a lawyer trust account containing insufficient funds, irrespective of whether the instrument is honored. The Lawyers Professional Responsibility Board shall establish rules governing approval and termination of approved status for financial institutions, and shall annually publish a list of approved financial institutions. No trust account shall be maintained in any financial institution that does not agree to make such reports. Any such agreement shall apply to all branches of the financial institution and shall not be canceled except upon three days notice in writing to the Office.

(*l*) The overdraft notification agreement shall provide that all reports made by the financial institution shall be in the following format:

(1) in the case of a dishonored instrument, the report shall be identical to the overdraft notice customarily forwarded to the depositor, and should include a copy of the dishonored instrument, if such a copy is normally provided to depositors;

(2) in the case of an instrument that is presented against insufficient funds but which instrument is honored, the report shall identify the financial institution, the lawyer or law firm, the account number, the date of presentation for payment, and the date paid, as well as the amount of overdraft created thereby.

Such reports shall be made simultaneously with, and within the time provided by law for notice of dishonor, if any. If an instrument presented against insufficient funds is honored, then the report shall be made within five banking days of the date of presentation for payment against insufficient funds.

(m) Every lawyer practicing or admitted to practice in this jurisdiction shall, as a condition thereof, be conclusively deemed to have consented to the reporting and production requirements mandated by this Rule.

(n) Nothing herein shall preclude a financial institution from charging a particular lawyer or law firm for the reasonable cost of producing the reports and records required by this rule.

(*o*) Definitions.

"Trust account" is an account denominated as such in which a lawyer or law firm holds funds on behalf of a client or third person(s) and is: 1) an interest-bearing checking account; 2) a money market account with or tied to check-writing; 3) a sweep account which is a money market fund or daily overnight financial institution repurchase agreement invested solely in or fully collateralized by U.S. Government Securities; or 4) an open-end money market fund solely invested in or fully collateralized by U.S. Government Securities. An open-end money market fund must hold itself out as a money market fund as defined by applicable federal statutes and regulations under the Investment Act of 1940, and, at the time of the investment, have total assets of at least $250,000,000. "U.S. Government Securities" refers to U.S. Treasury obligations and obligations issued or guaranteed as to principal and interest by the United States or any agency or instrumentality thereof. A daily overnight financial institution repurchase agreement may be established only with an institution that is deemed to be "well capitalized" or "adequately capitalized" as defined by applicable federal statutes and regulations.

"IOLTA account" is a pooled trust account in an eligible financial institution that has agreed to:

(1) remit the earnings accruing on this account, net of any allowable reasonable fees, monthly to the IOLTA program as established by the Minnesota Supreme Court;

(2) transmit with each remittance a report that shall identify each lawyer or law firm for whom the remittance is sent, the amount of remittance attributable to each IOLTA account, the rate and type of earnings applied, the amount of earnings accrued, the amount and type of fees deducted, if any, and the average account balance for the period in which the report is made; and

(3) transmit to the depositing lawyer or law firm a report in accordance with normal procedures for reporting to its depositors.

An approved eligible financial institution must pay no less on IOLTA accounts than (i) the highest earnings rate generally available from the institution to its non–IOLTA customers on each IOLTA account that meets the same minimum balance or other eligibility qualifications, or, (ii) 80% of the Federal Funds Target Rate on all its IOLTA accounts. The rate to be paid shall be fixed on the first day of each month, subject to rate changes during the month reflected in normal month-end calculations. Accrued earnings and fees shall be calculated in accordance with the eligible financial institution's standard practice, but institutions may elect to pay a higher earnings rate and may elect to waive any fees on IOLTA accounts. A financial institution may choose to pay the higher sweep or money market account rates on a qualifying IOLTA checking account.

"Allowable reasonable fees" for IOLTA accounts are per check charges, per deposit charges, sweep fees and similar charges assessed against comparable accounts by the eligible financial institution. All other fees are the responsibility of, and may be charged to, the lawyer maintaining the IOLTA account. Fees or charges in excess of the earnings accrued on the account for any month or quarter shall not be taken from earnings accrued on other IOLTA accounts or from the principal of the account. Eligible financial institutions may elect to waive any or all fees on IOLTA accounts.

"Eligible financial institution" for trust accounts is a bank or savings and loan association authorized by federal or state law to do business in Minnesota, the deposits of which are insured by an agency of the federal government, or is an open-end investment company registered with the Securities and Exchange Commission authorized by federal or state law to do business in Minnesota.

"Properly payable" refers to an instrument which, if presented in the normal course of business, is in a form requiring payment under the laws of this jurisdiction.

"Notice of dishonor" refers to the notice which an eligible financial institution is required to give, under the laws of this jurisdiction, upon presentation of an instrument that the institution dishonor.

Adopted June 13, 1985, eff. Sept. 1, 1985. Amended Dec. 27, 1989, eff. Jan. 1, 1990; July 28, 1999, eff. Aug. 1, 1999; June 17, 2005, eff. Oct. 1, 2005; Dec. 21, 2006, eff. July 1, 2007; April 1, 2010, eff. July 1, 2010; Dec. 17, 2010, eff. July 1, 2011.

Comment—2005

[1] A lawyer should hold property of others with the care required of a professional fiduciary. Securities should be kept in a safe deposit box, except when some other form of safekeeping is warranted by special circumstances. All property that is the property of clients or third persons, including prospective clients, must be kept separate from the lawyer's business and personal property and, if

monies, in one or more trust accounts. Separate trust accounts may be warranted when administering estate monies or acting in similar fiduciary capacities.

[2] While normally it is impermissible to commingle the lawyer's own funds with client funds, paragraph (a) (1) provides that it is permissible when necessary to pay bank service charges on that account. Accurate records must be kept regarding which part of the funds is the lawyer's.

[3] Lawyers often receive funds from which the lawyer's fee will be paid. The lawyer is not required to remit to the client funds that the lawyer reasonably believes represent fees owed. However, a lawyer may not hold funds to coerce a client into accepting the lawyer's contention. The disputed portion of the funds must be kept in a trust account and the lawyer should suggest means for prompt resolution of the dispute, such as arbitration. The undisputed portion of the funds shall be promptly distributed.

[4] Paragraph (b) also recognizes that third parties may have lawful claims against specific funds or other property in a lawyer's custody, such as a client's creditor who has a lien on funds recovered in a personal injury action. A lawyer may have a duty under applicable law to protect such third-party claims against wrongful interference by the client. In such cases, when the third-party claim is not frivolous under applicable law, the lawyer must refuse to surrender the property to the client until the claims are resolved. A lawyer should not unilaterally assume to arbitrate a dispute between the client and the third party, but, when there are substantial grounds for dispute as to the person entitled to the funds, the lawyer may file an action to have a court resolve the dispute.

[5] The obligations of a lawyer under this rule are independent of those arising from activity other than rendering legal services. For example, a lawyer who serves only as an escrow agent is governed by the applicable law relating to fiduciaries even though the lawyer does not render legal services in the transaction and is not governed by this rule.

Historical Notes

This rule is similar to provisions of former DR 9–102 to DR 9–104 of Minn. Code of Prof. Responsibility.

Rule 1.16. Declining or Terminating Representation

(a) Except as stated in paragraph (c), a lawyer shall not represent a client or, where representation has commenced, shall withdraw from the representation of a client if:

(1) the representation will result in violation of the Rules of Professional Conduct or other law;

(2) the lawyer's physical or mental condition materially impairs the lawyer's ability to represent the client; or

(3) the lawyer is discharged.

(b) Except as stated in paragraph (c), a lawyer may withdraw from representing a client if:

(1) withdrawal can be accomplished without material adverse effect on the interests of the client;

(2) the client persists in a course of action involving the lawyer's services that the lawyer reasonably believes is criminal or fraudulent;

(3) the client has used the lawyer's services to perpetrate a crime or fraud;

(4) the client insists upon taking action that the lawyer considers repugnant or with which the lawyer has a fundamental disagreement;

(5) the client fails substantially to fulfill an obligation to the lawyer regarding the lawyer's services and has been given reasonable warning that the lawyer will withdraw unless the obligation is fulfilled;

(6) the representation will result in an unreasonable financial burden on the lawyer or has been rendered unreasonably difficult by the client; or

(7) other good cause for withdrawal exists.

(c) A lawyer must comply with applicable law requiring notice to or permission of a tribunal when terminating a representation. When ordered to do so by a tribunal, a lawyer shall continue representation notwithstanding good cause for terminating the representation.

(d) Upon termination of representation, a lawyer shall take steps to the extent reasonably practicable to protect a client's interests, such as giving reasonable notice to the client, allowing time for employment of other counsel, surrendering papers and property to which the client is entitled, and refunding any advance payment of fees or expenses that has not been earned or incurred.

(e) Papers and property to which the client is entitled include the following, whether stored electronically or otherwise;

(1) in all representations, the papers and property delivered to the lawyer by or on behalf of the client and the papers and property for which the client has paid the lawyer's fees and reimbursed the lawyer's costs;

(2) in pending claims or litigation representations:

(i) all pleadings, motions, discovery, memoranda, correspondence and other litigation materials which have been drafted and served or filed, regardless of whether the client has paid the lawyer for drafting and serving the document(s), but shall not include pleadings, discovery, motion papers, memoranda and correspondence which have been drafted, but not served or filed if the client has not paid the lawyer's fee for drafting or creating the documents; and

(ii) all items for which the lawyer has agreed to advance costs and expenses regardless of whether the client has reimbursed the lawyer for the costs and expenses including depositions, expert opinions and statements, business records, witness statements, and other materials that may have evidentiary value;

(3) in non-litigation or transactional representations, client files, papers, and property shall not include drafted but unexecuted estate plans, title opinions, articles of incorporation, contracts, partnership agreements, or any other unexecuted document which does not otherwise have legal effect, where the client has not paid the lawyer's fee for drafting the document(s).

(f) A lawyer may charge a client for the reasonable costs of duplicating or retrieving the client's papers and property after termination of the representation only if the client has, prior to termination of the lawyer's services, agreed in writing to such a charge.

(g) A lawyer shall not condition the return of client papers and property on payment of the lawyer's fee or the cost of copying the files or papers.

Adopted June 13, 1985, eff. Sept. 1, 1985. Amended June 17, 2005, eff. Oct. 1, 2005.

Comment—2005

[1] A lawyer should not accept representation in a matter unless it can be performed competently, promptly, without improper conflict of interest and to completion. Ordinarily, a representation in a matter is completed when the agreed-upon assistance has been concluded. See Rules 1.2(c) and 6.5. See also Rule 1.3, Comment [4].

Mandatory Withdrawal

[2] A lawyer ordinarily must decline or withdraw from representation if the client demands that the lawyer engage in conduct that is illegal or violates the Rules of Professional Conduct or other law. The lawyer is not obliged to decline or withdraw simply because the client suggests such a course of conduct; a client may make such a suggestion in the hope that a lawyer will not be constrained by a professional obligation.

[3] When a lawyer has been appointed to represent a client, withdrawal ordinarily requires approval of the appointing authority. See also Rule 6.2. Similarly, court approval or notice to the court is often required by applicable law before a lawyer withdraws from pending litigation. Difficulty may be encountered if withdrawal is based on the client's demand that the lawyer engage in unprofessional conduct. The court may request an explanation for the withdrawal, while the lawyer may be bound to keep confidential the facts that would constitute such an explanation. The lawyer's statement that professional considerations require termination of the representation ordinarily should be accepted as sufficient. Lawyers should be mindful of their obligations to both clients and the court under Rules 1.6 and 3.3.

Discharge

[4] A client has a right to discharge a lawyer at any time, with or without cause, subject to liability for payment for the lawyer's services. Where future dispute about the withdrawal may be anticipated, it may be advisable to prepare a written statement reciting the circumstances.

[5] Whether a client can discharge appointed counsel may depend on applicable law. A client seeking to do so should be given a full explanation of the consequences. These consequences may include a decision by the appointing authority that appointment of successor counsel is unjustified, thus requiring self-representation by the client.

[6] If the client has severely diminished capacity, the client may lack the legal capacity to discharge the lawyer, and in any event the discharge may be seriously adverse to the client's interests. The lawyer should make special effort to help the client consider the consequences and may take reasonably necessary protective action as provided in Rule 1.14.

Optional Withdrawal

[7] A lawyer may withdraw from representation in some circumstances. The lawyer has the option to withdraw if it can be accomplished without material adverse effect on the client's interests. Withdrawal is also justified if the client persists in a course of action that the lawyer reasonably believes is criminal or fraudulent, for a lawyer is not required to be associated with such conduct even if the lawyer does not further it. Withdrawal is also permitted if the lawyer's services were misused in the past even if that would materially prejudice the client. The lawyer may also withdraw where the client insists on taking action that the lawyer considers repugnant or with which the lawyer has a fundamental disagreement.

[8] A lawyer may withdraw if the client refuses to abide by the terms of an agreement relating to the representation, such as an agreement concerning fees or court costs or an agreement limiting the objectives of the representation.

Historical Notes

This rule is similar to provisions of former DR 2–110 of the Minn. Code of Prof. Responsibility.

Rule 1.17. Sale of Law Practice

(a) A lawyer shall not sell or buy a law practice unless:

(1) the seller sells the practice as an entirety, as defined in paragraph (c) of this rule, to a lawyer or firm of lawyers licensed to practice law in Minnesota; and

(2) the seller sends a written notification that complies with paragraph (d) of this rule to all clients whose files are currently active and all clients whose inactive files will be taken over by the buying lawyer or firm of lawyers.

(b) The buying lawyer or firm of lawyers shall not increase the fees charged to clients by reason of the sale for a period of at least one year from the date of the sale. The buying lawyer or firm of lawyers shall honor all existing fee agreements for at least one year from the date of the sale and shall continue to completion, on the same terms agreed to by the selling lawyer and the client, any matters that the selling lawyer has agreed to do on a pro bono publico basis or for a reduced fee.

(c) For purposes of this rule, a practice is sold as an entirety if the buying lawyer or firm of lawyers assumes responsibility for at least all of the currently active files except those that deal with matters that the buying lawyer or firm of lawyers would not be competent to handle, those that the buying lawyer or firm of lawyers would be barred from handling because of a conflict of interest, or those from which the selling lawyer is denied permission to withdraw by a tribunal in a matter subject to Rule 1.16(c).

(d) The written notification that the selling lawyer must send pursuant to paragraph (a)(2) of this rule must include at a minimum:

(1) A statement that the law practice of the selling lawyer has been sold to the buying lawyer or law firm;

(2) A summary of the buying lawyer's or law firm's professional background, including education and experience and the length of time that the buying lawyer or members of the buying law firm have been in practice;

(3) A statement that the client has the right to continue to retain the buying lawyer under the same fee arrangement as the client had with the selling lawyer or to have the client's complete file sent to the client or to another lawyer of the client's choice.

(e) If the written notification described in paragraph (d) has actually reached the client through personal service or by certified mail, the notification may include a provision stating that if the client does not respond to the buying lawyer by ninety days from the date that the client receives the notification, the client's silence shall be deemed to be the client's waiver of confidentiality and the client's consent to the buying lawyer representing the client in the matter that was the subject of the selling lawyer's representation. The client's failure to respond within that time shall be such a waiver and consent.

(f) The transaction may include a promise by the selling lawyer that the selling lawyer will not engage in the practice of law for a reasonable period of time within a reasonable geographic area and will not advertise for or solicit clients within that area for that time.

(g) The selling lawyer shall retain responsibility for the proper management and disposition of all inactive files that are not transferred as part of the sale of the law practice.

(h) For purposes of this rule, the term "lawyer" means an individual lawyer or a law firm that buys or sells a law practice.

Adopted Dec. 11, 1995, eff. Jan. 1, 1996. Amended June 17, 2005, eff. Oct. 1, 2005.

Comment—2005

[1] A representative of a deceased, disabled or disappeared lawyer may sell the lawyer's law practice under the same restrictions as imposed by this rule. See Rule 5.4 (a)(2).

[2] Rule 1.6 on Confidentiality of Information limits the amount and type of information that the selling lawyer may give to the potential buying lawyer during negotiations. Before the prospective buyer could see the client's files, the selling lawyer would be required to obtain from the affected client a waiver of confidentiality.

[3] The selling lawyer should consider extending malpractice insurance for some reasonable period of time following the sale to insure against losses arising from errors that might come to light after the sale.

Rule 1.18. Duties to Prospective Client

(a) A person who discusses with a lawyer the possibility of forming a client-lawyer relationship with respect to a matter is a prospective client.

(b) Even when no client-lawyer relationship ensues, a lawyer who has had discussions with a prospective client shall not use or reveal information learned in the consultation, except as Rule 1.9 would permit with respect to information of a former client.

(c) A lawyer subject to paragraph (b) shall not represent a client with interests materially adverse to those of a prospective client in the same or a substantially related matter if the lawyer received information from the prospective client that could be significantly harmful to that person in the matter, except as provided in paragraph (d). If a lawyer is disqualified from representation under this paragraph, no lawyer in a firm with which that lawyer is associated may knowingly undertake or continue representation in such a matter, except as provided in paragraph (d).

(d) When the lawyer has received disqualifying information as defined in paragraph (c), representation is permissible if:

(1) both the affected client and the prospective client have given informed consent, confirmed in writing; or

(2) the lawyer who received the information took reasonable measures to avoid exposure to more disqualifying information than was reasonably necessary to determine whether to represent the prospective client, and

(i) the disqualified lawyer is timely screened from any participation in the matter and is apportioned no part of the fee therefrom; and

(ii) written notice is promptly given to the prospective client.

Adopted June 17, 2005, eff. Oct. 1, 20005.

Comment—2005

[1] Prospective clients, like clients, may disclose information to a lawyer, place documents or other property in the lawyer's custody, or rely on the lawyer's advice. A lawyer's discussions with a prospective client usually are limited in time and depth and leave both the prospective client and the lawyer free (and sometimes required) to proceed no further. Hence, prospective clients should receive some but not all of the protection afforded clients.

[2] Not all persons who communicate information to a lawyer are entitled to protection under this rule. A person who communicates information unilaterally to a lawyer, without any reasonable expectation that the lawyer is willing to discuss the possibility of forming a client-lawyer relationship, is not a "prospective client" within the meaning of paragraph (a).

[3] It is often necessary for a prospective client to reveal information to the lawyer during an initial consultation prior to the decision about formation of a client-lawyer relationship. The lawyer often must learn such information to determine whether there is a conflict of interest with an existing client and whether the matter is one that the lawyer is willing to undertake. Paragraph (b) prohibits the lawyer from using or revealing that information, except as permitted by Rule 1.9, even if the client or lawyer decides not to proceed with the representation. The duty exists regardless of how brief the initial conference may be.

[4] In order to avoid acquiring disqualifying information from a prospective client, a lawyer considering whether or not to undertake a new matter should limit the initial interview to only such information as reasonably appears necessary for that purpose. Where the information indicates that a conflict of interest or other reason for non-representation exists, the lawyer should so inform the prospective client or decline the representation. If the prospective client wishes to retain the lawyer, and if consent is possible under Rule 1.7, then consent from all affected present or former clients must be obtained before accepting the representation.

[5] A lawyer may condition conversations with a prospective client on the person's informed consent that no information disclosed during the consultation will prohibit the lawyer from representing a different client in the matter. See Rule 1.0(f) for the definition of informed consent. If the agreement expressly so provides, the prospective client may also consent to the lawyer's subsequent use of information received from the prospective client.

[6] Even in the absence of an agreement, under paragraph (c), the lawyer is not prohibited from representing a client with interests adverse to those of the prospective client in the same or a substantially related matter unless the lawyer has received from the prospective client information that could be significantly harmful if used against the prospective client in the matter.

[7] Under paragraph (c), the prohibition in this rule is imputed to other lawyers as provided in Rule 1.10, but, under paragraph (d), imputation may be avoided if the lawyer obtains the informed consent, confirmed in writing, of both the prospective and affected clients. In the alternative, imputation may be avoided if all disqualified lawyers are timely screened and written notice is promptly given to the prospective client. See Rule 1.0(*l*) (requirements for screening procedures). Paragraph (d)(1) does not prohibit the screened lawyer from receiving a salary or partnership share established by prior independent agreement, but that lawyer may not receive compensation directly related to the matter in which the lawyer is disqualified.

[8] Notice, including a description of the screened lawyer's prior representation and of the screening procedures employed, generally should be given as soon as practicable after the need for screening becomes apparent. When disclosure is likely to significantly injure the client, a reasonable delay may be justified.

[9] For the duty of competence of a lawyer who gives assistance on the merits of a matter to a prospective client, see Rule 1.1. For a lawyer's duties when a prospective client entrusts valuables or papers to the lawyer's care, see Rule 1.15.

COUNSELOR

Rule 2.1. Advisor

In representing a client, a lawyer shall exercise independent professional judgment and render candid advice. In rendering advice, a lawyer may refer not only to the law but to other considerations such as moral, economic, social, and political factors, that may be relevant to the client's situation.

Adopted June 13, 1985, eff. Sept. 1, 1985. Amended June 17, 2005, eff. Oct. 1, 2005.

Comment—2005

Scope of Advice

[1] A client is entitled to straightforward advice expressing the lawyer's honest assessment. Legal advice often involves unpleasant facts and alternatives that a client may be disinclined to confront. In presenting advice, a lawyer endeavors to sustain the client's morale and may put advice in as acceptable a form as honesty permits. However, a lawyer should not be deterred from giving candid advice by the prospect that the advice will be unpalatable to the client.

[2] Advice couched in narrow legal terms may be of little value to a client, especially where practical considerations, such as cost or effects on other people, are predominant. Purely technical legal advice, therefore, can sometimes be inadequate. It is proper for a lawyer to refer to relevant moral and ethical considerations in giving advice. Although a lawyer is not a moral advisor as such, moral and ethical considerations impinge upon most legal

questions and may decisively influence how the law will be applied.

[3] A client may expressly or impliedly ask the lawyer for purely technical advice. When such a request is made by a client experienced in legal matters, the lawyer may accept it at face value. When such a request is made by a client inexperienced in legal matters, however, the lawyer's responsibility as advisor may include indicating that more may be involved than strictly legal considerations.

[4] Matters that go beyond strictly legal questions may also be in the domain of another profession. Family matters can involve problems within the professional competence of psychiatry, clinical psychology or social work; business matters can involve problems within the competence of the accounting profession or of financial specialists. Where consultation with a professional in another field is itself something a competent lawyer would recommend, the lawyer should make such a recommendation. At the same time, a lawyer's advice at its best often consists of recommending a course of action in the face of conflicting recommendations of experts.

Offering Advice

[5] In general, a lawyer is not expected to give advice until asked by the client. However, when a lawyer knows that a client proposes a course of action that is likely to result in substantial adverse legal consequences to the client, the lawyer's duty to the client under Rule 1.4 may require that the lawyer offer advice if the client's course of action is related to the representation. Similarly, when a matter is likely to involve litigation, it may be necessary under Rule 1.4 to inform the client of forms of dispute resolution that might constitute reasonable alternatives to litigation. A lawyer ordinarily has no duty to initiate investigation of a client's affairs or to give advice that the client has indicated is unwanted, but a lawyer may initiate advice to a client when doing so appears to be in the client's interest.

Historical Notes

This rule is similar to provisions of EC 7–8 of the Minn. Code of Prof. Responsibility.

Rule 2.2. Intermediary [Deleted June 17, 2005, eff. Oct. 1, 2005]

Rule 2.3. Evaluation for Use by Third Persons

(a) A lawyer may provide an evaluation of a matter affecting a client for the use of someone other than the client if the lawyer reasonably believes that making the evaluation is compatible with other aspects of the lawyer's relationship with the client.

(b) When the lawyer knows or reasonably should know that the evaluation is likely to affect the client's interests materially and adversely, the lawyer shall not provide the evaluation unless the client gives informed consent.

(c) Except as disclosure is authorized in connection with a report of an evaluation, information relating to the evaluation is otherwise protected by Rule 1.6.

Adopted June 13, 1985, eff. Sept. 1, 1985. Amended June 17, 2005, eff. Oct. 1, 2005.

Comment—2005

Definition

[1] An evaluation may be performed at the client's direction or when impliedly authorized in order to carry out the representation. See Rule 1.2. Such an evaluation may be for the primary purpose of establishing information for the benefit of third parties; for example, an opinion concerning the title of property rendered at the behest of a vendor for the information of a prospective purchaser, or at the behest of a borrower for the information of a prospective lender. In some situations, the evaluation may be required by a government agency; for example, an opinion concerning the legality of the securities registered for sale under the securities laws. In other instances, the evaluation may be required by a third person, such as a purchaser of a business.

[2] A legal evaluation should be distinguished from an investigation of a person with whom the lawyer does not have a client-lawyer relationship. For example, a lawyer retained by a purchaser to analyze a vendor's title to property does not have a client-lawyer relationship with the vendor. So also, an investigation into a person's affairs by a government lawyer, or by special counsel employed by the government, is not an evaluation as that term is used in this rule. The question is whether the lawyer is retained by the person whose affairs are being examined. When the lawyer is retained by that person, the general rules concerning loyalty to client and preservation of confidences apply, which is not the case if the lawyer is retained by someone else. For this reason, it is essential to identify the person by whom the lawyer is retained. This should be made clear not only to the person under examination, but also to others to whom the results are to be made available.

Duties Owed to Third Person and Client

[3] When the evaluation is intended for the information or use of a third person, a legal duty to that person may or may not arise. That legal question is beyond the scope of this rule. However, since such an evaluation involves a departure from the normal client-lawyer relationship, careful analysis of the situation is required. The lawyer must be satisfied as a matter of professional judgment that making the evaluation is compatible with other functions undertaken on behalf of the client. For example, if the lawyer is acting as advocate in defending the client against charges of fraud, it would normally be incompatible with that responsibility for the lawyer to perform an evaluation for others concerning the same or a related transaction. Assuming no such impediment is apparent, however, the lawyer should advise the client of the implications of the evaluation, particularly the lawyer's responsibilities to third persons and the duty to disseminate the findings.

Access to and Disclosure of Information

[4] The quality of an evaluation depends on the freedom and extent of the investigation upon which it is based. Ordinarily a lawyer should have whatever latitude of investigation seems necessary as a matter of professional judgment. Under some circumstances, however, the terms of the evaluation may be limited. For example, certain issues or sources may be categorically excluded, or the scope of search may be limited by time constraints or the noncooperation of persons having relevant information. Any such limitations that are material to the evaluation should be described in the report. If after a lawyer has commenced an evaluation, the client refuses to comply with the terms upon which it was understood the evaluation was to have been made, the lawyer's obligations are determined by law, having reference to the terms of the client's agreement and the surrounding circumstances. In no circumstance is the lawyer permitted to knowingly make a false statement of material fact or law in providing an evaluation under this rule. See Rule 4.1.

Obtaining Client's Informed Consent

[5] Information relating to an evaluation is protected by Rule 1.6. In many situations, providing an evaluation to a third party poses no significant risk to the client; thus, the lawyer may be impliedly authorized to disclose information to carry out the representation. See Rule 1.6(b)(3). Where, however, it is reasonably likely that providing the evaluation will affect the client's interests materially and adversely, the lawyer must first obtain the client's consent after the client has been adequately informed concerning the important possible effects on the client's interests. See Rules 1.6(a) and 1.0(f).

Financial Auditors' Requests for Information

[6] When a question concerning the legal situation of a client arises at the instance of the client's financial auditor and the question is referred to the lawyer, the lawyer's response may be made in accordance with procedures recognized in the legal profession. Such a procedure is set forth in the American Bar Association Statement of Policy Regarding Lawyers' Responses to Auditors' Requests for Information, adopted in 1975.

Rule 2.4. Lawyer Serving as Third-Party Neutral

(a) A lawyer serves as a third-party neutral when the lawyer assists two or more persons who are not clients of the lawyer to reach a resolution of a dispute or other matter that has arisen between them. Service as a third-party neutral may include service as an arbitrator, a mediator or in such other capacity as will enable the lawyer to assist the parties to resolve the matter.

(b) A lawyer serving as a third-party neutral shall inform unrepresented parties that the lawyer is not representing them. When the lawyer knows or reasonably should know that a party does not understand the lawyer's role in the matter, the lawyer shall explain the difference between the lawyer's role as a third-party neutral and a lawyer's role as one who represents a client.

Adopted June 17, 2005, eff. Oct. 1, 2005.

Comment—2005

[1] Alternative dispute resolution has become a substantial part of the civil justice system. Aside from representing clients in dispute-resolution processes, lawyers often serve as third-party neutrals. A third-party neutral is a person, such as a mediator, arbitrator, conciliator or evaluator, who assists the parties, represented or unrepresented, in the resolution of a dispute or in the arrangement of a transaction. Whether a third-party neutral serves primarily as a facilitator, evaluator or decisionmaker depends on the particular process that is either selected by the parties or mandated by a court.

[2] The role of a third-party neutral is not unique to lawyers, although, in some court-connected contexts, only lawyers are allowed to serve in this role or to handle certain types of cases. In performing this role, the lawyer may be subject to court rules or other law that apply either to third-party neutrals generally or to lawyers serving as third-party neutrals. Lawyer–neutrals may also be subject to various codes of ethics, such as the Code of Ethics for Arbitration in Commercial Disputes prepared by a joint committee of the American Bar Association and the American Arbitration Association or the Model Standards of Conduct for Mediators jointly prepared by the American Bar Association, the American Arbitration Association and the Society of Professionals in Dispute Resolution.

[3] Unlike nonlawyers who serve as third-party neutrals, lawyers serving in this role may experience unique problems as a result of differences between the role of a third-party neutral and a lawyer's service as a client representative. The potential for confusion is significant when the parties are unrepresented in the process. Thus, paragraph (b) requires a lawyer-neutral to inform unrepresented parties that the lawyer is not representing them. For some parties, particularly parties who frequently use dispute-resolution processes, this information will be sufficient. For others, particularly those who are using the process for the first time, more information will be required. Where appropriate, the lawyer should inform unrepresented parties of the important differences between the lawyer's role as third-party neutral and a lawyer's role as a client representative, including the inapplicability of the attorney-client evidentiary privilege. The extent of disclosure required under this paragraph will depend on the particular parties involved and the subject matter of the proceeding, as well as the particular features of the dispute- resolution process selected.

[4] A lawyer who serves as a third-party neutral subsequently may be asked to serve as a lawyer representing a client in the same matter. The conflicts of interest that arise for both the individual lawyer and the lawyer's law firm are addressed in Rule 1.12.

[5] Lawyers who represent clients in alternative dispute-resolution processes are governed by the Rules of Professional Conduct. When the dispute-resolution process takes place before a tribunal, as in binding arbitration (see Rule 1.0(n)), the lawyer's duty of candor is governed by Rule 3.3. Otherwise, the lawyer's duty of candor toward both the third-party neutral and other parties is governed by Rule 4.1.

ADVOCATE

Rule 3.1. Meritorious Claims and Contentions

A lawyer shall not bring or defend a proceeding, or assert or controvert an issue therein, unless there is a basis in law and fact for doing so that is not frivolous, which includes a good faith argument for an extension, modification, or reversal of existing law. A lawyer for a defendant in a criminal proceeding, or a respondent in a proceeding that could result in incarceration, may nevertheless so defend the proceeding as to require that every element of the case be established.

Adopted June 13, 1985, eff. Sept. 1, 1985. Amended June 17, 2005, eff. Oct. 1, 2005.

Comment—2005

[1] The advocate has a duty to use legal procedure for the fullest benefit of the client's cause, but also a duty not to abuse legal procedure. The law, both procedural and substantive, establishes the limits within which an advocate may proceed. However, the law is not always clear and never is static. Accordingly, in determining the proper scope of advocacy, account must be taken of the law's ambiguities and potential for change.

[2] The filing of an action or defense or similar action taken for a client is not frivolous merely because the facts have not first been fully substantiated or because the lawyer expects to develop vital evidence only by discovery. What is required of lawyers, however, is that they inform themselves about the facts of their clients' cases and the applicable law and determine that they can make good faith arguments in support of their clients' positions. Such action is not frivolous even though the lawyer believes that the client's position ultimately will not prevail. The action is frivolous, however, if the lawyer is unable either to make a good faith argument on the merits of the action taken or to support the action taken by a good faith argument for an extension, modification or reversal of existing law.

[3] The lawyer's obligations under this rule are subordinate to federal or state constitutional law that entitles a defendant in a criminal matter to the assistance of counsel in presenting a claim or contention that otherwise would be prohibited by this rule.

Historical Notes

This rule is similar to provisions of former DR 2–109 and DR 7–102(A)(2) of the Minn. Code of Prof. Responsibility.

Rule 3.2. Expediting Litigation

A lawyer shall make reasonable efforts to expedite litigation consistent with the interests of the client.

Adopted June 13, 1985, eff. Sept. 1, 1985.

Comment—2005

[1] Dilatory practices bring the administration of justice into disrepute. Although there will be occasions when a lawyer may properly seek a postponement for personal reasons, it is not proper for a lawyer to routinely fail to expedite litigation solely for the convenience of the advocates. Nor will a failure to expedite be reasonable if done for the purpose of frustrating an opposing party's attempt to obtain rightful redress or repose. It is not a justification that similar conduct is often tolerated by the bench and bar. The question is whether a competent lawyer acting in good faith would regard the course of action as having some substantial purpose other than delay. Realizing financial or other benefit from otherwise improper delay in litigation is not a legitimate interest of the client.

Historical Notes

This rule is similar to provisions of former DR 7–102(A)(1) of the Minn. Code of Prof. Responsibility.

Rule 3.3. Candor Toward the Tribunal

(a) A lawyer shall not knowingly:

(1) make a false statement of fact or law to a tribunal, or fail to correct a false statement of material fact or law previously made to the tribunal by the lawyer;

(2) fail to disclose to the tribunal legal authority in the controlling jurisdiction known to the lawyer to be directly adverse to the position of the client and not disclosed by opposing counsel; or

(3) offer evidence that the lawyer knows to be false. If a lawyer, the lawyer's client, or a witness called by the lawyer has offered material evidence and the lawyer comes to know of its falsity, the lawyer shall take reasonable remedial measures, including, if necessary, disclosure to the tribunal. A lawyer may refuse to offer evidence, other than the testimony of a defendant in a criminal matter, that the lawyer reasonably believes is false.

(b) A lawyer who represents a client in an adjudicative proceeding and who knows that a person intends to engage, is engaging or has engaged in criminal or fraudulent conduct related to the proceeding shall take reasonable remedial measures, including, if necessary, disclosure to the tribunal.

(c) The duties stated in paragraphs (a) and (b) continue to the conclusion of the proceeding and apply even if compliance requires disclosure of information otherwise protected by Rule 1.6.

(d) In an ex parte proceeding, a lawyer shall inform the tribunal of all material facts known to the lawyer that will enable the tribunal to make an informed decision, whether or not the facts are adverse.

Adopted June 13, 1985, eff. Sept. 1, 1985. Amended June 17, 2005, eff. Oct. 1, 2005.

Comment—2005

[1] This Rule governs the conduct of a lawyer who is representing a client in the proceedings of a tribunal. See Rule 1.0(n) for the definition of "tribunal." It also applies when the lawyer is representing a client in an ancillary proceeding conducted pursuant to the tribunal's adjudicative authority, such as a deposition. Thus, for example, paragraph (a)(3) requires a lawyer to take reasonable remedial measures if the lawyer comes to know that a client who is testifying in a deposition has offered evidence that is false.

[2] This Rule sets forth the special duties of lawyers as officers of the court to avoid conduct that undermines the integrity of the adjudicative process. A lawyer acting as an advocate in an adjudicative proceeding has an obligation to present the client's case with persuasive force. Performance of that duty while maintaining confidences of the client, however, is qualified by the advocate's duty of candor to the tribunal. Consequently, although a lawyer in an adversary proceeding is not required to present an impartial exposition of the law or to vouch for the evidence submitted in a cause, the lawyer must not allow the tribunal to be misled by false statements of law or fact or evidence that the lawyer knows to be false.

Representations by a Lawyer

[3] An advocate is responsible for pleadings and other documents prepared for litigation, but is usually not required to have personal knowledge of matters asserted therein, for litigation documents ordinarily present assertions by the client, or by someone on the client's behalf, and not assertions by the lawyer. Compare Rule 3.1. However, an assertion purporting to be on the lawyer's own knowledge, as in an affidavit by the lawyer or in a statement in open court, may properly be made only when the lawyer knows the assertion is true or believes it to be true on the basis of a reasonably diligent inquiry. There are circumstances where failure to make a disclosure is the equivalent of an affirmative misrepresentation. The obligation prescribed in Rule 1.2(d) not to counsel a client to commit or assist the client in committing a fraud applies in litigation. Regarding compliance with Rule 1.2(d), see the comment to that rule. See also Comment to Rule 8.4(b).

Legal Argument

[4] Legal argument based on a knowingly false representation of law constitutes dishonesty toward the tribunal. A lawyer is not required to make a disinterested exposition of the law, but must recognize the existence of pertinent legal authorities. Furthermore, as stated in paragraph (a) (2), an advocate has a duty to disclose directly adverse authority in the controlling jurisdiction that has not been disclosed by the opposing party. The underlying concept is that legal argument is a discussion seeking to determine the legal premises properly applicable to the case.

Offering Evidence

[5] Paragraph (a)(3) requires that the lawyer refuse to offer evidence that the lawyer knows to be false, regardless of the client's wishes. This duty is premised on the lawyer's obligation as an officer of the court to prevent the trier of fact from being misled by false evidence. A lawyer does not violate this rule if the lawyer offers the evidence for the purpose of establishing its falsity.

[6] If a lawyer knows that the client intends to testify falsely or wants the lawyer to introduce false evidence, the lawyer should seek to persuade the client that the evidence should not be offered. If the persuasion is ineffective and the lawyer continues to represent the client, the lawyer must refuse to offer the false evidence. If only a portion of a witness's testimony will be false, the lawyer may call the witness to testify but may not elicit or otherwise permit the witness to present the testimony that the lawyer knows is false.

[7] The duties stated in paragraphs (a) and (b) apply to all lawyers, including defense counsel in criminal cases. See also Comment [9].

[8] The prohibition against offering false evidence only applies if the lawyer knows that the evidence is false. A lawyer's reasonable belief that evidence is false does not preclude its presentation to the trier of fact. A lawyer's knowledge that evidence is false, however, can be inferred from the circumstances. See Rule 1.0(g). Thus, although a lawyer should resolve doubts about the veracity of testimony or other evidence in favor of the client, the lawyer cannot ignore an obvious falsehood.

[9] Although paragraph (a)(3) only prohibits a lawyer from offering evidence the lawyer knows to be false, it permits the lawyer to refuse to offer testimony or other proof that the lawyer reasonably believes is false. Offering such proof may reflect adversely on the lawyer's ability to discriminate in the quality of evidence and thus impair the lawyer's effectiveness as an advocate. Because of the special protections historically provided criminal defendants, however, this rule does not permit a lawyer to refuse to offer the testimony of such a client where the lawyer reasonably believes but does not know that the testimony will be false. Unless the lawyer knows the testimony will be false, the lawyer must honor the client's decision to testify. See also Comment [7].

Remedial Measures

[10] Having offered material evidence in the belief that it was true, a lawyer may subsequently come to know that the evidence is false. Or, a lawyer may be surprised when the lawyer's client, or another witness called by the lawyer, offers testimony the lawyer knows to be false, either during the lawyer's direct examination or in response to cross-examination by the opposing lawyer. In such situations or if the lawyer knows of the falsity of testimony elicited from the client during a deposition, the lawyer must take reasonable remedial

measures. In such situations, the advocate's proper course is to remonstrate with the client confidentially, advise the client of the lawyer's duty of candor to the tribunal and seek the client's cooperation with respect to the withdrawal or correction of the false statements or evidence. If that fails, the advocate must take further remedial action. If withdrawal from the representation is not permitted or will not undo the effect of the false evidence, the advocate must make such disclosure to the tribunal as is reasonably necessary to remedy the situation, even if doing so requires the lawyer to reveal information that otherwise would be protected by Rule 1.6. It is for the tribunal then to determine what should be done — making a statement about the matter to the trier of fact, ordering a mistrial or perhaps nothing.

[11] The disclosure of a client's false testimony can result in grave consequences to the client, including not only a sense of betrayal but also loss of the case and perhaps a prosecution for perjury. But the alternative is that the lawyer cooperate in deceiving the court, thereby subverting the truth-finding process which the adversary system is designed to implement. See Rule 1.2(d). Furthermore, unless it is clearly understood that the lawyer will act upon the duty to disclose the existence of false evidence, the client can simply reject the lawyer's advice to reveal the false evidence and insist that the lawyer keep silent. Thus the client could in effect coerce the lawyer into being a party to fraud on the court.

Preserving Integrity of Adjudicative Process

[12] Lawyers have a special obligation to protect a tribunal against criminal or fraudulent conduct that undermines the integrity of the adjudicative process, such as bribing, intimidating or otherwise unlawfully communicating with a witness, juror, court official or other participant in the proceeding, unlawfully destroying or concealing documents or other evidence or failing to disclose information to the tribunal when required by law to do so. Thus, paragraph (b) requires a lawyer to take reasonable remedial measures, including disclosure if necessary, whenever the lawyer knows that a person, including the lawyer's client, intends to engage, is engaging or has engaged in criminal or fraudulent conduct related to the proceeding.

Duration of Obligation

[13] A practical time limit on the obligation to rectify false evidence or false statements of law and fact has to be established. The conclusion of the proceeding is a reasonably definite point for the termination of the obligation. A proceeding has concluded within the meaning of this Rule when a final judgment in the proceeding has been affirmed on appeal or the time for review has passed.

Ex Parte Proceedings

[14] Ordinarily, an advocate has the limited responsibility of presenting one side of the matters that a tribunal should consider in reaching a decision; the conflicting position is expected to be presented by the opposing party. However, in any ex parte proceeding, such as an application for a temporary restraining order, there is no balance of presentation by opposing advocates. The object of an ex parte proceeding is nevertheless to yield a substantially just result. The judge has an affirmative responsibility to accord the absent party just consideration. The lawyer for the represented party has the correlative duty to make disclosures of material facts known to the lawyer and that the lawyer reasonably believes are necessary to an informed decision.

Withdrawal

[15] Normally, a lawyer's compliance with the duty of candor imposed by this rule does not require that the lawyer withdraw from the representation of a client whose interests will be or have been adversely affected by the lawyer's disclosure. The lawyer may, however, be required by Rule 1.16(a) to seek permission of the tribunal to withdraw if the lawyer's compliance with this rule's duty of candor results in such an extreme deterioration of the client-lawyer relationship that the lawyer can no longer competently represent the client. Also see Rule 1.16(b) for the circumstances in which a lawyer will be permitted to seek a tribunal's permission to withdraw. In connection with a request for permission to withdraw that is premised on a client's misconduct, a lawyer may reveal information relating to the representation only to the extent reasonably necessary to comply with this rule or as otherwise permitted by Rule 1.6.

Historical Notes

This rule is similar, in part, to provisions of former DR 7–102(A)(3) to (5), (B) and DR 7–106(B)(1) of the Minn. Code of Prof. Responsibility.

Rule 3.4. Fairness to Opposing Party and Counsel

A lawyer shall not:

(a) unlawfully obstruct another party's access to evidence or unlawfully alter, destroy, or conceal a document or other material having potential evidentiary value. A lawyer shall not counsel or assist another person to do any such act;

(b) falsify evidence, counsel or assist a witness to testify falsely, or offer an inducement to a witness that is prohibited by law;

(c) knowingly disobey an obligation under the rules of a tribunal except for an open refusal based on an assertion that no valid obligation exists;

(d) in pretrial procedure, make a frivolous discovery request or fail to make a reasonably diligent effort to comply with a legally proper discovery request by an opposing party;

(e) in trial, allude to any matter that the lawyer does not reasonably believe is relevant or that will not be supported by admissible evidence, assert personal knowledge of facts in issue except when testifying as a witness, or state a personal opinion as to the justness of a cause, the credibility of a witness, the culpability of a civil litigant or the guilt or innocence of an accused; or

(f) request a person other than a client to refrain from voluntarily giving relevant information to another party unless:

(1) the person is a relative or an employee or other agent of a client; and

(2) the lawyer reasonably believes that the person's interests will not be adversely affected by refraining from giving such information.

Adopted June 13, 1985, eff. Sept. 1, 1985. Amended June 17, 2005, eff. Oct. 1, 2005.

Comment—2005

[1] The procedure of the adversary system contemplates that the evidence in a case is to be marshalled competitively by the contending parties. Fair competition in the adversary system is secured by prohibitions against destruction or concealment of evidence, improperly influencing witnesses, obstructive tactics in discovery procedure, and the like.

[2] Documents and other items of evidence are often essential to establish a claim or defense. Subject to evidentiary privileges, the right of an opposing party, including the government, to obtain evidence through discovery or subpoena is an important procedural right. The exercise of that right can be frustrated if relevant material is altered, concealed or destroyed.

[3] With regard to paragraph (b), it is not improper to pay a witness's expenses or to compensate an expert witness on terms permitted by law.

[4] Paragraph (f) permits a lawyer to advise employees of a client to refrain from giving information to another party, for the employees may identify their interests with those of the client. See also Rule 4.2.

Historical Notes

This rule is similar, in part, to provisions of former DR 7–102(A)(6), DR 7–104(A)(2), DR 7–106(A), (C)(1) to (C)(4) and DR 7–109 of the Minn. Code of Prof. Responsibility.

Rule 3.5. Impartiality and Decorum of the Tribunal

(a) Before the trial of a case, a lawyer connected therewith shall not, except in the course of official proceedings, communicate with or cause another to communicate with anyone the lawyer knows to be a member of the venire from which the jury will be selected for the trial of the case.

(b) During the trial of the case:

(1) a lawyer connected therewith shall not, except in the course of official proceedings, communicate with or cause another to communicate with any member of the jury.

(2) a lawyer who is not connected therewith shall not, except in the course of official proceedings, communicate with or cause another to communicate with a juror concerning the case.

(c) After discharge of the jury from further consideration of a case with which the lawyer was connected, the lawyer shall not ask questions of or make comments to a member of that jury that are calculated merely to harass or embarrass the juror or to influence the juror's actions in future jury service.

(d) A lawyer shall not conduct or cause another, by financial support or otherwise, to conduct a vexatious or harassing investigation of a juror or prospective juror.

(e) All restrictions imposed by this Rule apply also to communications with or investigations of members of a family of a juror or prospective juror.

(f) A lawyer shall reveal promptly to the court improper conduct by, or by another toward, a juror or prospective juror or a member of the family thereof, of which the lawyer has knowledge.

(g) In an adversary proceeding a lawyer shall not communicate or cause another to communicate as to the merits of the case with the judge or an official before whom a proceeding is pending except:

(1) in the course of official proceedings;

(2) in writing, if the lawyer promptly delivers a copy of the writing to opposing counsel or to the adverse party if the party is not represented by a lawyer;

(3) orally upon adequate notice to opposing counsel or to the adverse party if the adverse party is not represented by a lawyer; or

(4) as otherwise authorized by law.

(h) A lawyer shall not engage in conduct intended to disrupt a tribunal.

Adopted June 13, 1985, eff. Sept. 1, 1985. Amended June 17, 2005, eff. Oct. 1, 2005.

Comment—2005

[1] Many forms of improper influence upon a tribunal are proscribed by criminal law. Others are specified in the ABA Model Code of Judicial Conduct, with which an advocate should be familiar. A lawyer is required to avoid contributing to a violation of such provisions.

[2] The advocate's function is to present evidence and argument so that the cause may be decided according to law. Refraining from abusive or obstreperous conduct is a corollary of the advocate's right to speak on behalf of litigants. A lawyer may stand firm against abuse by a judge but should avoid reciprocation; the judge's default is no justification for similar dereliction by an advocate. An advocate can prevent the cause, protect the record for subsequent review and preserve professional integrity by patient firmness no less effectively than by belligerence or theatrics.

Historical Notes

This rule is similar to provisions of former DR 7–106(C)(6), DR 7–108, and DR 7–110(B) of the Minn. Code of Prof. Responsibility.

Rule 3.6. Trial Publicity

(a) A lawyer who is participating or has participated in the investigation or litigation of a criminal matter shall not make an extrajudicial statement about the matter that the lawyer knows or reasonably should know will be disseminated by means of public communication and will have a substantial likelihood of materially prejudicing a jury trial in a pending criminal matter.

(b) Notwithstanding paragraph (a), a lawyer may make a statement that a reasonable lawyer would believe is required to protect a client from the substantial undue prejudicial effect of recent publicity not initiated by the lawyer or the lawyer's client. A statement made pursuant to this paragraph shall be limited to such information as is necessary to mitigate the recent adverse publicity.

(c) No lawyer associated in a firm or government agency with a lawyer subject to paragraph (a) shall make a statement prohibited by paragraph (a).

Adopted June 13, 1985, eff. Sept. 1, 1985. Amended June 17, 2005, eff. Oct. 1, 2005.

Comment—2005

[1] It is difficult to strike a balance between protecting the right to a fair trial and safeguarding the right of free expression. Preserving the right to a fair trial necessarily entails some curtailment of the information that may be disseminated about a party prior to trial, particularly where trial by jury is involved. If there were no such limits, the result would be the practical nullification of the protective effect of the rules of forensic decorum and the exclusionary rules of evidence. On the other hand, there are vital social interests served by the free dissemination of information about events having legal consequences and about legal proceedings themselves. The public has a right to know about threats to its safety and measures aimed at assuring its security. It also has a legitimate interest in the conduct of judicial proceedings, particularly in matters of general public concern. Furthermore, the subject matter of legal proceedings is often of direct significance in debate and deliberation over questions of public policy.

[2] The rule sets forth a basic general prohibition against a lawyer's making statements that the lawyer knows or should know will have a substantial likelihood of materially prejudicing a pending criminal jury trial. Recognizing that the public value of informed commentary is great and the likelihood of prejudice to a proceeding by the commentary of a lawyer who is not involved in the proceeding is small, the rule applies only to lawyers who are or who have been involved in the investigation or litigation of a case, and their associates.

[3] Extrajudicial statements that might otherwise raise a question under this rule may be permissible when they are made in response to statements made publicly by another party, another party's lawyer, or third persons, where a reasonable lawyer would believe a public response is required in order to avoid prejudice to the lawyer's client. When prejudicial statements have been publicly made by others, responsive statements may have the salutary effect of lessening any resulting adverse impact on the adjudicative proceeding. Such responsive statements should be limited to contain only such information as is necessary to mitigate undue prejudice created by the statements made by others.

[4] See Rule 3.8(f) for additional duties of prosecutors in connection with extrajudicial statements about criminal proceedings.

Historical Notes

This rule is similar to provisions of former DR 7–107 of the Minn. Code of Prof. Responsibility.

Rule 3.7. Lawyer as Witness

(a) A lawyer shall not act as advocate at a trial in which the lawyer is likely to be a necessary witness unless:

(1) the testimony relates to an uncontested issue;

(2) the testimony relates to the nature and value of legal services rendered in the case; or

(3) disqualification of the lawyer would work substantial hardship on the client.

(b) A lawyer may act as an advocate in a trial in which another lawyer in the lawyer's firm is likely to be called as a witness unless precluded from doing so by Rule 1.7 or Rule 1.9.

Adopted June 13, 1985, eff. Sept. 1, 1985. Amended July 16, 1987; June 17, 2005, eff. Oct. 1, 2005.

Comment—2005

[1] Combining the roles of advocate and witness can prejudice the tribunal and the opposing party and can also involve a conflict of interest between the lawyer and client.

Advocate–Witness Rule

[2] The tribunal has proper objection when the trier of fact may be confused or misled by a lawyer serving as both advocate and witness. The opposing party has proper objection where the combination of roles may prejudice that party's rights in the litigation. A witness is required to testify on the basis of personal knowledge, while an advocate is expected to explain and comment on evidence given by others. It may not be clear whether a statement by an advocate-witness should be taken as proof or as an analysis of the proof.

[3] To protect the tribunal, paragraph (a) prohibits a lawyer from simultaneously serving as advocate and necessary witness except in those circumstances specified in paragraphs (a)(1) through (a)(3). Paragraph (a) (1) recognizes that if the testimony will be uncontested, the ambiguities in the dual role are purely theoretical. Paragraph (a)(2) recognizes that where the testimony concerns the extent and value of legal services rendered in the action in which the testimony is offered, permitting the lawyers to testify avoids the need for a second trial with new counsel to resolve that issue. Moreover, in such a situation the judge has firsthand knowl-

edge of the matter in issue; hence, there is less dependence on the adversary process to test the credibility of the testimony.

[4] Apart from these two exceptions, paragraph (a)(3) recognizes that a balancing is required between the interests of the client and those of the tribunal and the opposing party. Whether the tribunal is likely to be misled or the opposing party is likely to suffer prejudice depends on the nature of the case, the importance and probable tenor of the lawyer's testimony, and the probability that the lawyer's testimony will conflict with that of other witnesses. Even if there is risk of such prejudice, in determining whether the lawyer should be disqualified, due regard must be given to the effect of disqualification on the lawyer's client. It is relevant that one or both parties could reasonably foresee that the lawyer would probably be a witness. The conflict of interest principles stated in Rules 1.7, 1.9 and 1.10 have no application to this aspect of the problem.

[5] Because the tribunal is not likely to be misled when a lawyer acts as advocate in a trial in which another lawyer in the lawyer's firm will testify as a necessary witness, paragraph (b) permits the lawyer to do so except in situations involving a conflict of interest.

Conflict of Interest

[6] In determining if it is permissible to act as advocate in a trial in which the lawyer will be a necessary witness, the lawyer must also consider that the dual role may give rise to a conflict of interest that will require compliance with Rule 1.7 or 1. 9. For example, if there is likely to be substantial conflict between the testimony of the client and that of the lawyer, the representation involves a conflict of interest that requires compliance with Rule 1.7. This would be true even though the lawyer might not be prohibited by paragraph (a) from simultaneously serving as advocate and witness because the lawyer's disqualification would work a substantial hardship on the client. Similarly, a lawyer who might be permitted to simultaneously serve as an advocate and a witness by paragraph (a)(3) might be precluded from doing so by Rule 1.9. The problem can arise whether the lawyer is called as a witness on behalf of the client or is called by the opposing party. Determining whether or not such a conflict exists is primarily the responsibility of the lawyer involved. If there is a conflict of interest, the lawyer must secure the client's informed consent, confirmed in writing. In some cases, the lawyer will be precluded from seeking the client's consent. See Rule 1.7. See Rule 1.0(b) for the definition of "confirmed in writing" and Rule 1.0(f) for the definition of "informed consent."

[7] Paragraph (b) provides that a lawyer is not disqualified from serving as an advocate because a lawyer with whom the lawyer is associated in a firm is precluded from doing so by paragraph (a). If, however, the testifying lawyer would also be disqualified by Rule 1.7 or Rule 1.9 from representing the client in the matter, other lawyers in the firm will be precluded from representing the client by Rule 1.10 unless the client gives informed consent under the conditions stated in Rule 1.7.

Rule 3.8. Special Responsibilities of a Prosecutor

The prosecutor in a criminal case shall:

(a) refrain from prosecuting a charge that the prosecutor knows is not supported by probable cause;

(b) make reasonable efforts to assure that the accused has been advised of the right to, and the procedure for obtaining, counsel and has been given reasonable opportunity to obtain counsel;

(c) not seek to obtain from an unrepresented accused a waiver of important pretrial rights, such as the right to a preliminary hearing;

(d) make timely disclosure to the defense of all evidence or information known to the prosecutor that tends to negate the guilt of the accused or mitigates the offense, and, in connection with sentencing, disclose to the defense and to the tribunal all unprivileged mitigating information known to the prosecutor, except when the prosecutor is relieved of this responsibility by a protective order of the tribunal;

(e) not subpoena a lawyer in a grand jury or other criminal proceeding to present evidence about a past or present client unless the prosecutor reasonably believes:

(1) the information sought is not protected from disclosure by any applicable privilege;

(2) the evidence sought is essential to the successful completion of an ongoing investigation or prosecution;

(f) exercise reasonable care to prevent employees or other persons assisting or associated with the prosecutor in a criminal case and over whom the prosecutor has direct control from making an extrajudicial statement that the prosecutor would be prohibited from making under Rule 3.6.

Adopted June 13, 1985, eff. Sept. 1, 1985. Amended June 17, 2005, eff. Oct. 1, 2005.

Comment—2005

[1] A prosecutor has the responsibility of a minister of justice and not simply that of an advocate. This responsibility carries with it specific obligations to see that the defendant is accorded procedural justice and that guilt is decided upon the basis of sufficient evidence. Precisely how far the prosecutor is required to go in this direction is a matter of debate and varies in different jurisdictions. Many jurisdictions have adopted the ABA Standards of Criminal Justice Relating to the Prosecution Function, which in turn are the product of prolonged and careful deliberation by lawyers experienced in both criminal prosecution and defense. Applicable law may require other measures by the prosecutor and knowing disregard of those obligations or a systematic abuse of prosecutorial discretion could constitute a violation of Rule 8.4.

[2] In some jurisdictions, a defendant may waive a preliminary hearing and thereby lose a valuable opportunity to challenge probable cause. Accordingly, prosecutors should not seek to obtain waivers of preliminary hearings or other important pretrial rights from unrepresented accused persons. Paragraph (c) does not apply, however, to an accused appearing *pro se* with the approval of the tribunal. Nor does it forbid the lawful questioning of an uncharged suspect who has knowingly waived the rights to counsel and silence.

[3] The exception in paragraph (d) recognizes that a prosecutor may seek an appropriate protective order from the tribunal if disclosure of information to the defense could result in substantial harm to an individual or to the public interest.

[4] Paragraph (e) is intended to limit the issuance of lawyer subpoenas in grand jury and other criminal proceedings to those situations in which there is a genuine need to intrude into the client-lawyer relationship.

[5] Paragraph (f) supplements Rule 3.6, which prohibits extrajudicial statements that have a substantial likelihood of prejudicing an adjudicatory proceeding. In the context of a criminal prosecution, a prosecutor's extrajudicial statement can create the additional problem of increasing public condemnation of the accused. Although the announcement of an indictment for example, will necessarily have severe consequences for the accused, a prosecutor can, and should, avoid comments which have no legitimate law enforcement purpose and have a substantial likelihood of increasing public opprobrium of the accused. Nothing in this comment is intended to restrict the statements which a prosecutor may make which comply with Rule 3.6(b) or 3.6(c).

[6] Like other lawyers, prosecutors are subject to Rules 5.1 and 5.3, which relate to responsibilities regarding lawyers and nonlawyers who work for or are associated with the lawyer's office. Paragraph (f) reminds the prosecutor of the importance of these obligations in connection with the unique dangers of improper extrajudicial statements in a criminal case.

Historical Notes

This rule is similar, in part, to provisions of former DR 7–103 and DR 7–107(J) of the Minn. Code of Prof. Responsibility.

Rule 3.9. Advocate in Nonadjudicative Proceedings

A lawyer representing a client before a legislative body or administrative agency in a nonadjudicative proceeding shall disclose that the appearance is in a representative capacity and shall conform to the provisions of Rules 3.3(a) through (c), 3.4(a) through (c), and 3.5.

Adopted June 13, 1985, eff. Sept. 1, 1985. Amended June 17, 2005, eff. Oct. 1, 2005.

Comment—2005

[1] In representation before bodies such as legislatures, municipal councils, and executive and administrative agencies acting in a rule-making or policy-making capacity, lawyers present facts, formulate issues and advance argument in the matters under consideration. The decision-making body, like a court, should be able to rely on the integrity of the submissions made to it. A lawyer appearing before such a body must deal with it honestly and in conformity with applicable rules of procedure. See Rules 3.3(a) through (c), 3.4(a) through (c) and 3.5.

[2] Lawyers have no exclusive right to appear before nonadjudicative bodies, as they do before a court. The requirements of this rule therefore may subject lawyers to regulations inapplicable to advocates who are not lawyers. However, legislatures and administrative agencies have a right to expect lawyers to deal with them as they deal with courts.

[3] This rule only applies when a lawyer represents a client in connection with an official hearing or meeting of a governmental agency or a legislative body to which the lawyer or the lawyer's client is presenting evidence or argument. It does not apply to representation of a client in a negotiation or other bilateral transaction with a governmental agency or in connection with an application for a license or other privilege or the client's compliance with generally applicable reporting requirements, such as the filing of income-tax returns. Nor does it apply to the representation of a client in connection with an investigation or examination of the client's affairs conducted by government investigators or examiners. Representation in such matters is governed by Rules 4.1 through 4.4.

Historical Notes

This rule is similar to provisions of former EC 7–15 and EC 7–16 of the Minn. Code of Prof. Responsibility.

TRANSACTIONS WITH PERSONS OTHER THAN CLIENTS

Rule 4.1. Truthfulness in Statements to Others

In the course of representing a client a lawyer shall not knowingly make a false statement of fact or law.

Adopted June 13, 1985, eff. Sept. 1, 1985.

Comment—2005

Misrepresentation

[1] A lawyer is required to be truthful when dealing with others on a client's behalf, but generally has no affirmative duty to inform an opposing party of relevant facts. A misrepresentation can occur if the lawyer incorporates or affirms a statement of another person that the lawyer knows is false. Misrepresentations can also occur by partially true but misleading statements or omissions that are the equivalent of affirmative false statements. For dishonest conduct that does not amount to a false statement or for misrepresentations by a law-

yer other than in the course of representing a client, see Rule 8.4.

Statements of Fact

[2] This rule refers to statements of fact. Whether a particular statement should be regarded as one of fact can depend on the circumstances. Under generally accepted conventions in negotiation, certain types of statements ordinarily are not taken as statements of material fact. Estimates of price or value placed on the subject of a transaction and a party's intentions as to an acceptable settlement of a claim are ordinarily in this category, and so is the existence of an undisclosed principal except where nondisclosure of the principal would constitute fraud. Lawyers should be mindful of their obligations under applicable law to avoid criminal and tortious misrepresentation.

Historical Notes

This rule is similar to provisions of former DR 7–102(A)(5) of the Minn. Code of Prof. Responsibility.

Rule 4.2. Communication with Person Represented by Counsel

In representing a client, a lawyer shall not communicate about the subject of the representation with a person the lawyer knows to be represented by another lawyer in the matter, unless the lawyer has the consent of the other lawyer or is authorized to do so by law or a court order.

Adopted June 13, 1985, eff. Sept. 1, 1985. Amended Dec. 12, 1994; June 17, 2005, eff. Oct. 1, 2005.

Comment—2005

[1] This rule contributes to the proper functioning of the legal system by protecting a person who has chosen to be represented by a lawyer in a matter against possible overreaching by other lawyers who are participating in the matter, interference by those lawyers with the client-lawyer relationship and the uncounselled disclosure of information relating to the representation.

[2] This rule applies to communications with any person who is represented by counsel concerning the matter to which the communication relates.

[3] The rule applies even though the represented person initiates or consents to the communication. A lawyer must immediately terminate communication with a person if, after commencing communication, the lawyer learns that the person is one with whom communication is not permitted by this rule.

[4] This rule does not prohibit communication with a represented person, or an employee or agent of such a person, concerning matters outside the representation. For example, the existence of a controversy between a government agency and a private party, or between two organizations, does not prohibit a lawyer for either from communicating with nonlawyer representatives of the other regarding a separate matter. Nor does this rule preclude communication with a represented person who is seeking advice from a lawyer who is not otherwise representing a client in the matter. A lawyer may not make a communication prohibited by this rule through the acts of another. See Rule 8.4(a). Parties to a matter may communicate directly with each other, and a lawyer is not prohibited from advising a client concerning a communication that the client is legally entitled to make. Also, a lawyer having independent justification or legal authorization for communicating with a represented person is permitted to do so.

[5] Communications authorized by law may include communications by a lawyer on behalf of a client who is exercising a constitutional or other legal right to communicate with the government. Communications authorized by law may also include investigative activities of lawyers representing governmental entities, directly or through investigative agents, prior to the commencement of criminal or civil enforcement proceedings. When communicating with the accused in a criminal matter, a government lawyer must comply with this rule in addition to honoring the constitutional rights of the accused. The fact that a communication does not violate a state or federal constitutional right is insufficient to establish that the communication is permissible under this rule.

[6] A lawyer who is uncertain whether a communication with a represented person is permissible may seek a court order. A lawyer may also seek a court order in exceptional circumstances to authorize a communication that would otherwise be prohibited by this rule, for example, where communication with a person represented by counsel is necessary to avoid reasonably certain injury.

[7] In the case of a represented organization, this rule prohibits communications with a constituent of the organization who supervises, directs or regularly consults with the organization's lawyer concerning the matter or has authority to obligate the organization with respect to the matter or whose act or omission in connection with the matter may be imputed to the organization for purposes of civil or criminal liability. The term "constituent" is defined in Comment [1] to Rule 1.13. Consent of the organization's lawyer is not required for communication with a former constituent. If a constituent of the organization is represented in the matter by his or her own counsel, the consent by that counsel to a communication will be sufficient for purposes of this rule. Compare Rule 3.4(f). In communicating with a current or former constituent of an organization, a lawyer must not use methods of obtaining evidence that violate the legal rights of the organization. See Rule 4.4.

[8] The prohibition on communications with a represented person only applies in circumstances where the lawyer knows that the person is in fact represented in the matter to be discussed. This means that the lawyer has actual knowledge of the fact of the representation; but such actual knowledge may be inferred from the circumstances. See Rule 1.0(g). Thus, the lawyer cannot evade the requirement of obtaining the consent of counsel by closing eyes to the obvious.

[9] In the event the person with whom the lawyer communicates is not known to be represented by

counsel in the matter, the lawyer's communications are subject to Rule 4.3.

Historical Notes

The order of the Minnesota Supreme Court dated December 12, 1994, provides in part that the amendments to the Rules on Lawyers Professional Responsibility and the Rules of Professional Conduct shall govern all lawyer disciplinary actions commenced on or after January 1, 1995.

This rule is similar to provisions of former DR 7–104(A)(1) of the Minn. Code of Prof. Responsibility.

Rule 4.3. Dealing with Unrepresented Person

In dealing on behalf of a client with a person who is not represented by counsel;

(a) a lawyer shall not state or imply that the lawyer is disinterested;

(b) a lawyer shall clearly disclose that the client's interests are adverse to the interests of the unrepresented person, if the lawyer knows or reasonably should know that the interests are adverse;

(c) when a lawyer knows or reasonably should know that the unrepresented person misunderstands the lawyer's role in the matter, the lawyer shall make reasonable efforts to correct the misunderstanding; and

(d) a lawyer shall not give legal advice to the unrepresented person, other than the advice to secure counsel, if the lawyer knows or reasonably should know that the interests of the unrepresented person are or have a reasonable possibility of being in conflict with the interests of the client.

Adopted June 13, 1985, eff. Sept. 1, 1985. Amended June 17, 2005, eff. Oct. 1, 2005.

Comment—2005

[1] An unrepresented person, particularly one not experienced in dealing with legal matters, might assume that a lawyer is disinterested in loyalties or is a disinterested authority on the law even when the lawyer represents a client. In order to avoid a misunderstanding, a lawyer will typically need to identify the lawyer's client and, where the lawyer knows or reasonably should know that the interests are adverse, disclose that the client has interests opposed to those of the unrepresented person. For misunderstandings that sometimes arise when a lawyer for an organization deals with an unrepresented constituent, see Rule 1.13(d).

[2] The rule distinguishes between situations involving unrepresented persons whose interests may be adverse to those of the lawyer's client and those in which the person's interests are not in conflict with the client's. In the former situation, the possibility that the lawyer will compromise the unrepresented person's interests is so great that the rule prohibits the giving of any advice, apart from the advice to obtain counsel. Whether a lawyer is giving impermissible advice may depend on the experience and sophistication of the unrepresented person, as well as the setting in which the behavior and comments occur. This rule does not prohibit a lawyer from negotiating the terms of a transaction or settling a dispute with an unrepresented person. So long as the lawyer has explained that the lawyer represents a party whose interests are adverse and is not representing the person, the lawyer may inform the person of the terms on which the lawyer's client will enter into an agreement or settle a matter, prepare documents that require the person's signature and explain the lawyer's own view of the meaning of the document or the lawyer's view of the underlying legal obligations.

Historical Notes

This rule is similar, in part, to provisions of former DR 7–104(A)(2) of the Minn. Code of Prof. Responsibility.

Rule 4.4. Respect for Rights of Third Persons

(a) In representing a client, a lawyer shall not use means that have no substantial purpose other than to embarrass, delay, or burden a third person, or use methods of obtaining evidence that violate the legal rights of such a person.

(b) A lawyer who receives a document relating to the representation of the lawyer's client and knows or reasonably should know that the document was inadvertently sent shall promptly notify the sender.

Adopted June 13, 1985, eff. Sept. 1, 1985. Amended June 17, 2005, eff. Oct. 1, 2005.

Comment—2005

[1] Responsibility to a client requires a lawyer to subordinate the interests of others to those of the client, but that responsibility does not imply that a lawyer may disregard the rights of third persons. It is impractical to catalogue all such rights, but they include legal restrictions on methods of obtaining evidence from third persons and unwarranted intrusions into privileged relationships, such as the client-lawyer relationship.

[2] Paragraph (b) recognizes that lawyers sometimes receive documents that were mistakenly sent or produced by opposing parties or their lawyers. If a lawyer knows or reasonably should know that such a document was sent inadvertently, then this rule requires the lawyer to promptly notify the sender in order to permit that person to take protective measures. Whether the lawyer is required to take additional steps, such as returning the original document, is a matter of law beyond the scope of these rules, as is the question of whether the privileged status of a document has been waived. Similarly, this rule does not address the legal duties of a lawyer who receives a document that the lawyer knows or reasonably should know may have been wrongfully obtained by the sending person. For purposes of this rule, "document" includes e-mail or other electronic modes of transmission subject to being read or put into readable form.

[3] Some lawyers may choose to return a document unread, for example, when the lawyer learns before receiving the document that it was inadvertently sent to the wrong address. Where a lawyer is not required by applicable law to do so, the

decision to voluntarily return such a document is a matter of professional judgment ordinarily reserved to the lawyer. See Rules 1.2 and 1.4.

Historical Notes

This rule is similar to provisions of former DR 7-102(A)(1) of the Minn. Code of Prof. Responsibility.

LAW FIRMS AND ASSOCIATIONS

Rule 5.1. Responsibilities of a Partner or Supervisory Lawyer

(a) A partner in a law firm, and a lawyer who individually or together with other lawyers possesses comparable managerial authority in a law firm, shall make reasonable efforts to ensure that the firm has in effect measures giving reasonable assurance that all lawyers in the firm conform to the Rules of Professional Conduct.

(b) A lawyer having direct supervisory authority over another lawyer shall make reasonable efforts to ensure that the other lawyer's conduct conforms to the Rules of Professional Conduct.

(c) A lawyer shall be responsible for another lawyer's violation of the Rules of Professional Conduct if:

(1) the lawyer orders or, with knowledge of the specific conduct, ratifies the conduct involved; or

(2) the lawyer is a partner or has comparable managerial authority in the law firm in which the other lawyer practices, or has direct supervisory authority over the other lawyer, and knows of the conduct at a time when it consequences can be avoided or mitigated but fails to take reasonable remedial action.

Adopted June 13, 1985, eff. Sept. 1, 1985. Amended June 17, 2005, eff. Oct. 1, 2005.

Comment—2005

[1] Paragraph (a) applies to lawyers who have managerial authority over the professional work of a firm. See Rule 1.0(d). This includes members of a partnership, the shareholders in a law firm organized as a professional corporation, and members of other associations authorized to practice law; lawyers having comparable managerial authority in a legal services organization or a law department of an enterprise or government agency; and lawyers who have intermediate managerial responsibilities in a firm. Paragraph (b) applies to lawyers who have supervisory authority over the work of other lawyers in a firm.

[2] Paragraph (a) requires lawyers with managerial authority within a firm to make reasonable efforts to establish internal policies and procedures designed to provide reasonable assurance that all lawyers in the firm will conform to the Rules of Professional Conduct. Such policies and procedures include those designed to detect and resolve conflicts of interest, identify dates by which actions must be taken in pending matters, account for client funds and property, and ensure that inexperienced lawyers are properly supervised.

[3] Other measures that may be required to fulfill the responsibility prescribed in paragraph (a) can depend on the firm's structure and the nature of its practice. In a small firm of experienced lawyers, informal supervision and periodic review of compliance with the required systems ordinarily will suffice. In a large firm, or in practice situations in which difficult ethical problems frequently arise, more elaborate measures may be necessary. Some firms, for example, have a procedure whereby junior lawyers can make confidential referral of ethical problems directly to a designated senior partner or special committee. See Rule 5.2. Firms, whether large or small, may also rely on continuing legal education in professional ethics. In any event, the ethical atmosphere of a firm can influence the conduct of all its members and the partners may not assume that all lawyers associated with the firm will inevitably conform to the rules.

[4] Paragraph (c) expresses a general principle of personal responsibility for acts of another. See also Rule 8.4(a).

[5] Paragraph (c)(2) defines the duty of a partner or other lawyer having comparable managerial authority in a law firm, as well as a lawyer who has direct supervisory authority over performance of specific legal work by another lawyer. Whether a lawyer has supervisory authority in particular circumstances is a question of fact. Partners and lawyers with comparable authority have at least indirect responsibility for all work being done by the firm, while a partner or manager in charge of a particular matter ordinarily also has supervisory responsibility for the work of other firm lawyers engaged in the matter. Appropriate remedial action by a partner or managing lawyer would depend on the immediacy of that lawyer's involvement and the seriousness of the misconduct. A supervisor is required to intervene to prevent avoidable consequences of misconduct if the supervisor knows that the misconduct occurred. Thus, if a supervising lawyer knows that a subordinate misrepresented a matter to an opposing party in negotiation, the supervisor as well as the subordinate has a duty to correct the resulting misapprehension.

[6] Professional misconduct by a lawyer under supervision could reveal a violation of paragraph (b) on the part of the supervisory lawyer even though it does not entail a violation of paragraph (c) because there was no direction, ratification, or knowledge of the violation.

[7] Apart from this rule and Rule 8.4(a), a lawyer does not have disciplinary liability for the conduct of a partner, associate, or subordinate. Whether a lawyer may be liable civilly or criminally for another lawyer's conduct is a question of law beyond the scope of these rules.

[8] The duties imposed by this rule on managing and supervising lawyers do not alter the personal

duty of each lawyer in a firm to abide by the Rules of Professional Conduct. See Rule 5.2(a).

Historical Notes

This rule is similar to provisions of former DR 3–101 of the Minn. Code of Prof. Responsibility.

Rule 5.2. Responsibilities of a Subordinate Lawyer

(a) A lawyer is bound by the Rules of Professional Conduct notwithstanding that the lawyer acted at the direction of another person.

(b) A subordinate lawyer does not violate the Rules of Professional Conduct if that lawyer acts in accordance with a supervisory lawyer's reasonable resolution of an arguable question of professional duty.

Adopted June 13, 1985, eff. Sept. 1, 1985.

Comment—2005

[1] Although a lawyer is not relieved of responsibility for a violation by the fact that the lawyer acted at the direction of a supervisor, that fact may be relevant in determining whether a lawyer had the knowledge required to render his conduct a violation of the rules. For example, if a subordinate filed a frivolous pleading at the direction of a supervisor, the subordinate would not be guilty of a professional violation unless the subordinate knew of the document's frivolous character.

[2] When lawyers in a supervisor-subordinate relationship encounter a matter involving professional judgment as to ethical duty, the supervisor may assume responsibility for making the judgment. Otherwise a consistent course of action or position could not be taken. If the question can reasonably be answered only one way, the duty of both lawyers is clear and they are equally responsible for fulfilling it. However, if the question is reasonably arguable, someone has to decide upon the course of action. That authority ordinarily reposes in the supervisor, and a subordinate may be guided accordingly. For example, if a question arises whether the interests of two clients conflict under Rule 1.7, the supervisor's reasonable resolution of the question should protect the subordinate professionally if the resolution is subsequently challenged.

Rule 5.3. Responsibilities Regarding Nonlawyer Assistants

With respect to a nonlawyer employed or retained by or associated with a lawyer:

(a) a partner and a lawyer, who individually or together with other lawyers possess comparable managerial authority in a law firm, shall make reasonable efforts to ensure that the firm has in effect measures giving reasonable assurance that nonlawyer's conduct is compatible with the professional obligations of the lawyer;

(b) a lawyer having direct supervisory authority over the nonlawyer shall make reasonable efforts to ensure that the person's conduct is compatible with the professional obligations of the lawyer; and

(c) a lawyer shall be responsible for the conduct of a nonlawyer that would be a violation of the Rules of Professional Conduct if engaged in by a lawyer if:

(1) the lawyer orders or, with the knowledge of the specific conduct, ratifies the conduct involved; or

(2) the lawyer is a partner or has comparable managerial authority in the law firm in which the person is employed, or has direct supervisory authority over the person, and knows of the conduct at a time when its consequences can be avoided or mitigated but fails to take reasonable remedial action.

Adopted June 13, 1985, eff. Sept. 1, 1985. Amended June 17, 2005, eff. Oct. 1, 2005.

Comment—2005

[1] Lawyers generally employ assistants in their practice, including secretaries, investigators, law student interns, and paraprofessionals. Such assistants, whether employees or independent contractors, act for the lawyer in rendition of the lawyer's professional services. A lawyer must give such assistants appropriate instruction and supervision concerning the ethical aspects of their employment, particularly regarding the obligation not to disclose information relating to representation of the client, and should be responsible for their work product. The measures employed in supervising nonlawyers should take account of the fact that they do not have legal training and are not subject to professional discipline.

[2] Paragraph (a) requires lawyers with managerial authority within a law firm to make reasonable efforts to establish internal policies and procedures designed to provide reasonable assurance that nonlawyers in the firm will act in a way compatible with the Rules of Professional Conduct. See Comment [1] to Rule 5.1. Paragraph (b) applies to lawyers who have supervisory authority over the work of a nonlawyer. Paragraph (c) specifies the circumstances in which a lawyer is responsible for conduct of a nonlawyer that would be a violation of the Rules of Professional Conduct if engaged in by a lawyer.

Rule 5.4. Professional Independence of a Lawyer

(a) A lawyer or law firm shall not share legal fees with a nonlawyer, except that:

(1) an agreement by a lawyer with the lawyer's firm, partner, or associate may provide for the payment of money, over a reasonable period of time after the lawyer's death, to the lawyer's estate or to one or more specified persons;

(2) a lawyer who purchases the practice of a deceased, disabled, or disappeared lawyer may, pursuant to the provisions of Rule 1.17, pay to the estate or other representative of that lawyer the agreed-upon purchase price;

(3) a lawyer or law firm may include nonlawyer employees in a compensation or retirement plan, even though the plan is based in whole or in part on a profit-sharing arrangement;

(4) subject to full disclosure and court approval, a lawyer may share court-awarded legal fees with a nonprofit organization that employed, retained, or recommended employment of the lawyer in the matter; and

(5) a lawyer who undertakes to complete unfinished legal business of a deceased lawyer may pay to the estate of the deceased lawyer the proportion of the total compensation that fairly represents the services rendered by the deceased lawyer.

(b) A lawyer shall not form a partnership with a nonlawyer if any of the activities of the partnership consist of the practice of law.

(c) A lawyer shall not permit a person who recommends, employs, or pays the lawyer to render legal services for another to direct or regulate the lawyer's professional judgment in rendering such legal services.

(d) A lawyer shall not practice with or in the form of a professional corporation or association authorized to practice law for a profit, if

(1) a nonlawyer owns any interest therein, except that a fiduciary representative of the estate of a lawyer may hold the stock or interest of the lawyer for a reasonable time during administration;

(2) a nonlawyer possesses governance authority, unless permitted by the Minnesota Professional Firms Act; or

(3) a nonlawyer has the right to direct or control the professional judgment of a lawyer.

Adopted June 13, 1985, eff. Sept. 1, 1985. Amended Dec. 11, 1995, eff. Jan. 1, 1996; July 28, 1999, eff. Aug. 1, 1999; June 17, 2005, eff. Oct. 1, 2005.

Comment—2005

[1] The provisions of this rule express traditional limitations on sharing fees. These limitations are to protect the lawyer's professional independence of judgment. Where someone other than the client pays the lawyer's fee or salary, or recommends employment of the lawyer, that arrangement does not modify the lawyer's obligation to the client. As stated in paragraph (c), such arrangements should not interfere with the lawyer's professional judgment.

[2] This rule also expresses traditional limitations on permitting a third party to direct or regulate the lawyer's professional judgment in rendering legal services to another. See also Rule 1.8 (f).

Historical Notes

This rule is similar to provisions of former DR 3-102, DR 3-103, and DR 5-107(B), (C) of the Minn. Code of Prof. Responsibility.

Rule 5.5. Unauthorized Practice of Law; Multijurisdictional Practice of Law

(a) A lawyer shall not practice law in a jurisdiction in violation of the regulation of the legal profession in that jurisdiction, or assist another in doing so, except that a lawyer admitted to practice in Minnesota does not violate this rule by conduct in another jurisdiction that is permitted in Minnesota under Rule 5.5 (c) and (d) for lawyers not admitted to practice in Minnesota.

(b) A lawyer who is not admitted to practice in this jurisdiction shall not:

(1) except as authorized by these rules or other law, establish an office or other systematic and continuous presence in this jurisdiction for the practice of law; or

(2) hold out to the public or otherwise represent that the lawyer is admitted to practice law in this jurisdiction.

(c) A lawyer admitted in another United States jurisdiction, and not disbarred or suspended from practice in any jurisdiction, may provide legal services on a temporary basis in this jurisdiction which:

(1) are undertaken in association with a lawyer who is admitted to practice in this jurisdiction and who actively participates in the matter;

(2) are in or reasonably related to a pending or potential proceeding before a tribunal in this or another jurisdiction, if the lawyer, or a person the lawyer is assisting, is authorized by law or order to appear in the proceeding or reasonably expects to be so authorized;

(3) are in or reasonably related to a pending or potential arbitration, mediation, or other alternative dispute resolution proceeding in this or another jurisdiction, if the services arise out of or are reasonably related to the lawyer's practice in a jurisdiction in which the lawyer is admitted to practice and are not services for which the forum requires pro hac vice admission; or

(4) are not within paragraphs (c)(2) or (c)(3) and arise out of or are reasonably related to the lawyer's practice in a jurisdiction in which the lawyer is admitted to practice.

(d) A lawyer admitted in another United States jurisdiction, and not disbarred or suspended from practice in any jurisdiction, may provide legal services in this jurisdiction that are services that the lawyer is authorized to provide by federal law or other law of this jurisdiction.

Adopted June 13, 1985, eff. Sept. 1, 1985. Amended June 17, 2005, eff. Oct. 1, 2005.

Comment—2005

[1] A lawyer may practice law only in a jurisdiction in which the lawyer is authorized to practice. A lawyer may be admitted to practice law in a jurisdiction on a regular basis or may be authorized

by court rule or order or by law to practice for a limited purpose or on a restricted basis. Paragraph (a) applies to unauthorized practice of law by a lawyer, whether through the lawyer's direct action or by the lawyer assisting another person. The exception is intended to permit a Minnesota lawyer, without violating this rule, to engage in practice in another jurisdiction as Rule 5.5 (c) and (d) permit a lawyer admitted to practice in another jurisdiction to engage in practice in Minnesota. A lawyer who does so in another jurisdiction in violation of its law or rules may be subject to discipline or other sanctions in that jurisdiction.

[2] The definition of the practice of law is established by law and varies from one jurisdiction to another. Whatever the definition, limiting the practice of law to members of the bar protects the public against rendition of legal services by unqualified persons. This rule does not prohibit a lawyer from employing the services of paraprofessionals and delegating functions to them, so long as the lawyer supervises the delegated work and retains responsibility for their work. See Rule 5.3.

[3] A lawyer may provide professional advice and instruction to nonlawyers whose employment requires knowledge of the law; for example, claims adjusters, employees of financial or commercial institutions, social workers, accountants, and persons employed in government agencies. Lawyers also may assist independent nonlawyers, such as paraprofessionals, who are authorized by the law of a jurisdiction to provide particular law- related services. In addition, a lawyer may counsel nonlawyers who wish to proceed pro se.

[4] Other than as authorized by law or this rule, a lawyer who is not admitted to practice generally in this jurisdiction violates paragraph (b) if the lawyer establishes an office or other systematic and continuous presence in this jurisdiction for the practice of law. Presence may be systematic and continuous even if the lawyer is not physically present here. Such a lawyer must not hold out to the public or otherwise represent that the lawyer is admitted to practice law in this jurisdiction. See also Rules 7.1 and 7.5(b).

[5] There are occasions in which a lawyer admitted to practice in another United States jurisdiction, and not disbarred or suspended from practice in any jurisdiction, may provide legal services on a temporary basis in this jurisdiction under circumstances that do not create an unreasonable risk to the interests of their clients, the public, or the courts. Paragraph (c) identifies four such circumstances. The fact that conduct is not so identified does not imply that the conduct is or is not authorized. With the exception of paragraph (d), this rule does not authorize a lawyer to establish an office or other systematic and continuous presence in this jurisdiction without being admitted to practice generally here.

[6] There is no single test to determine whether a lawyer's services are provided on a "temporary basis" in this jurisdiction, and may therefore be permissible under paragraph (c). Services may be "temporary" even though the lawyer provides services in this jurisdiction on a recurring basis or for an extended period of time, as when the lawyer is representing a client in a single lengthy negotiation or litigation.

[7] Paragraphs (c) and (d) apply to lawyers who are admitted to practice law in any United States jurisdiction, which includes the District of Columbia, and any state, territory, or commonwealth of the United States. The word "admitted" in paragraph (c) contemplates that the lawyer is authorized to practice in the jurisdiction in which the lawyer is admitted and excludes a lawyer who while technically admitted is not authorized to practice because, for example, the lawyer is on inactive status.

[8] Paragraph (c)(1) recognizes that the interests of clients and the public are protected if a lawyer admitted only in another jurisdiction associates with a lawyer licensed to practice in this jurisdiction. For this paragraph to apply, however, the lawyer admitted to practice in this jurisdiction must actively participate in and share responsibility for the representation of the client.

[9] Lawyers not admitted to practice generally in a jurisdiction may be authorized by law or order of a tribunal or an administrative agency to appear before the tribunal or agency. This authority may be granted pursuant to formal rules governing admission pro hac vice or pursuant to informal practice of the tribunal or agency. Under paragraph (c)(2), a lawyer does not violate this rule when the lawyer appears before a tribunal or agency pursuant to such authority. To the extent that a court rule or other law of this jurisdiction requires a lawyer who is not admitted to practice in this jurisdiction to obtain admission pro hac vice before appearing before a tribunal or administrative agency, this rule requires the lawyer to obtain that authority.

[10] Paragraph (c)(2) also provides that a lawyer rendering services in this jurisdiction on a temporary basis does not violate this rule when the lawyer engages in conduct in anticipation of a proceeding or hearing in a jurisdiction in which the lawyer is authorized to practice law or in which the lawyer reasonably expects to be admitted pro hac vice. Examples of such conduct include meetings with the client, interviews of potential witnesses, and the review of documents. Similarly, a lawyer admitted only in another jurisdiction may engage in conduct temporarily in this jurisdiction in connection with pending litigation in another jurisdiction in which the lawyer is or reasonably expects to be authorized to appear, including taking depositions in this jurisdiction.

[11] When a lawyer has been or reasonably expects to be admitted to appear before a court or administrative agency, paragraph (c)(2) also permits conduct by lawyers who are associated with that lawyer in the matter, but who do not expect to appear before the court or administrative agency. For example, subordinate lawyers may conduct research, review documents, and attend meetings with witnesses in support of the lawyer responsible for the litigation.

[12] Paragraph (c)(3) permits a lawyer admitted to practice law in another jurisdiction to perform

services on a temporary basis in this jurisdiction if those services are in or reasonably related to a pending or potential arbitration, mediation, or other alternative dispute resolution proceeding in this or another jurisdiction, if the services arise out of or are reasonably related to the lawyer's practice in a jurisdiction in which the lawyer is admitted to practice. The lawyer, however, must obtain admission pro hac vice in the case of a court-annexed arbitration or mediation or otherwise if court rules or law so require.

[13] Paragraph (c)(4) permits a lawyer admitted in another jurisdiction to provide certain legal services on a temporary basis in this jurisdiction that arise out of or are reasonably related to the lawyer's practice in a jurisdiction in which the lawyer is admitted but are not within paragraphs (c)(2) or (c)(3). These services include both legal services and services that nonlawyers may perform but that are considered the practice of law when performed by lawyers.

[14] Paragraphs (c)(3) and (c)(4) require that the services arise out of or be reasonably related to the lawyer's practice in a jurisdiction in which the lawyer is admitted. A variety of factors evidence such a relationship. The lawyer's client may have been previously represented by the lawyer, or may be resident in or have substantial contacts with the jurisdiction in which the lawyer is admitted. The matter, although involving other jurisdictions, may have a significant connection with that jurisdiction. In other cases, significant aspects of the lawyer's work might be conducted in that jurisdiction or a significant aspect of the matter may involve the law of that jurisdiction. The necessary relationship might arise when the client's activities or the legal issues involve multiple jurisdictions, such as when the officers of a multinational corporation survey potential business sites and seek the services of their lawyer in assessing the relative merits of each. In addition, the services may draw on the lawyer's recognized expertise developed through the regular practice of law on behalf of clients in matters involving a particular body of federal, nationally-uniform, foreign, or international law.

[15] Paragraph (d) identifies a circumstance in which a lawyer who is admitted to practice in another United States jurisdiction, and is not disbarred or suspended from practice in any jurisdiction, may establish an office or other systematic and continuous presence in this jurisdiction for the practice of law as well as provide legal services on a temporary basis. Except as provided in paragraph (d), a lawyer who is admitted to practice law in another jurisdiction and who establishes an office or other systematic or continuous presence in this jurisdiction must become admitted to practice law generally in this jurisdiction.

[16] Paragraph (d) recognizes that a lawyer may provide legal services in a jurisdiction in which the lawyer is not licensed when authorized to do so by federal or other law, which includes statute, court rule, executive regulation, or judicial precedent.

[17] A lawyer who practices law in this jurisdiction pursuant to paragraphs (c) or (d) or otherwise is subject to the disciplinary authority of this jurisdiction. See Rule 8.5(a).

[18] In some circumstances, a lawyer who practices law in this jurisdiction pursuant to paragraphs (c) or (d) may have to inform the client that the lawyer is not licensed to practice law in this jurisdiction. For example, such notice may be required when the representation occurs primarily in this jurisdiction and requires knowledge of the law of this jurisdiction. See Rule 1.4(b).

[19] Paragraphs (c) and (d) do not authorize communications advertising legal services to prospective clients in this jurisdiction by lawyers who are admitted to practice in other jurisdictions. Whether and how lawyers may communicate the availability of their services to prospective clients in this jurisdiction is governed by Rules 7.1 to 7.5.

Rule 5.6. Restrictions on Right to Practice

A lawyer shall not participate in offering or making:

(a) a partnership, shareholder, operating, employment, or other similar type of agreement that restricts the right of a lawyer to practice after termination of the relationship, except an agreement concerning benefits upon retirement; or

(b) an agreement in which a restriction on the lawyer's right to practice is part of the settlement of a client controversy.

Adopted June 13, 1985, eff. Sept. 1, 1985. Amended June 17, 2005, eff. Oct. 1, 2005.

Comment—1985

An agreement restricting the right of partners or associates to practice after leaving a firm not only limits their professional autonomy but also limits the freedom of clients to choose a lawyer. Paragraph (a) prohibits such agreements except for restrictions incident to provisions concerning retirement benefits from service with the firm.

Paragraph (b) prohibits a lawyer from agreeing not to represent other persons in connection with settling a claim on behalf of a client.

Comment—2005

[1] An agreement restricting the right of lawyers to practice after leaving a firm not only limits their professional autonomy but also limits the freedom of clients to choose a lawyer. Paragraph (a) prohibits such agreements except for restrictions incident to provisions concerning retirement benefits for service with the firm.

[2] Paragraph (b) prohibits a lawyer from entering into an agreement not to represent other persons in connection with settling a claim on behalf of a client.

[3] This rule does not apply to prohibit restrictions that may be included in the terms of the sale of a law practice pursuant to Rule 1.17.

Historical Notes

This rule is similar to provisions of former DR 2–108 of the Minn. Code of Prof. Responsibility.

Rule 5.7. Responsibilities Regarding Law–Related Services

(a) A lawyer shall be subject to the Rules of Professional Conduct with respect to the provision of law-related services, as defined in paragraph (b), if the law-related services are provided:

(1) by the lawyer in circumstances that are not distinct from the lawyer's provision of legal services to clients; or

(2) in other circumstance by an entity controlled by the lawyer individually or with others if the lawyer fails to take reasonable measures to assure that a person obtaining the law-related services knows that the services are not legal services and that the protections of the client-lawyer relationship do not exist.

(b) The term "law-related services" denotes services which might reasonably be performed in conjunction with and in substance are related to the provision of legal services and which are not prohibited as the unauthorized practice of law when provided by a nonlawyer.

Adopted July 28, 1999, eff. Aug. 1, 1999. Amended June 17, 2005, eff. Oct. 1, 2005.

Comment—2005

[1] When a lawyer performs law-related services or controls an organization that does so, there exists the potential for ethical problems. Principal among these is the possibility that the person for whom the law-related services are performed fails to understand that the services may not carry with them the protections normally afforded as part of the client-lawyer relationship. The recipient of the law-related services may expect, for example, that the protection of client confidences, prohibitions against representation of persons with conflicting interests, and obligations of a lawyer to maintain professional independence apply to the provision of law-related services when that may not be the case.

[2] Rule 5.7 applies to the provision of law-related services by a lawyer even when the lawyer does not provide any legal services to the person for whom the law-related services are performed and whether the law- related services are performed through a law firm or a separate entity. The rule identifies the circumstances in which all of the Rules of Professional Conduct apply to the provision of law-related services. Even when those circumstances do not exist, however, the conduct of a lawyer involved in the provision of law-related services is subject to those rules that apply generally to lawyer conduct, regardless of whether the conduct involves the provision of legal services. See, e.g., Rule 8.4.

[3] When law-related services are provided by a lawyer under circumstances that are not distinct from the lawyer's provision of legal services to clients, the lawyer in providing the law-related services must adhere to the requirements of the Rules of Professional Conduct as provided in paragraph (a)(1). Even when the law-related and legal services are provided in circumstances that are distinct from each other, for example through separate entities or different support staff within the law firm, the Rules of Professional Conduct apply to the lawyer as provided in paragraph (a)(2) unless the lawyer takes reasonable measures to assure that the recipient of the law-related services knows that the services are not legal services and that the protections of the client-lawyer relationship do not apply.

[4] Law–related services also may be provided through an entity that is distinct from that through which the lawyer provides legal services. If the lawyer individually or with others has control of such an entity's operations, the rule requires the lawyer to take reasonable measures to assure that each person using the services of the entity knows that the services provided by the entity are not legal services and that the Rules of Professional Conduct that relate to the client-lawyer relationship do not apply. A lawyer's control of an entity extends to the ability to direct its operation. Whether a lawyer has such control will depend upon the circumstances of the particular case.

[5] When a client-lawyer relationship exists with a person who is referred by a lawyer to a separate law-related service entity controlled by the lawyer, individually or with others, the lawyer must comply with Rule 1.8(a).

[6] In taking the reasonable measures referred to in paragraph (a)(2) to assure that a person using law-related services understands the practical effect or significance of the inapplicability of the Rules of Professional Conduct, the lawyer should communicate to the person receiving the law- related services, in a manner sufficient to assure that the person understands the significance of the fact, that the relationship of the person to the business entity will not be a client-lawyer relationship. The communication should be made before entering into an agreement for provision of or providing law-related services, and preferably should be in writing.

[7] The burden is upon the lawyer to show that the lawyer has taken reasonable measures under the circumstances to communicate the desired understanding. For instance, a sophisticated user of law-related services, such as a publicly held corporation, may require a lesser explanation than someone unaccustomed to making distinctions between legal services and law- related services, such as an individual seeking tax advice from a lawyer- accountant or investigative services in connection with a lawsuit.

[8] Regardless of the sophistication of potential recipients of law- related services, a lawyer should take special care to keep separate the provision of law-related and legal services in order to minimize the risk that the recipient will assume that the law-related services are legal services. The risk of such confusion is especially acute when the lawyer renders both types of services with respect to the same matter. Under some circumstances the legal and law-related services may be so closely entwined that they cannot be distinguished from each other, and the requirement of disclosure and consultation imposed by paragraph (a)(2) of the rule cannot be met.

In such a case a lawyer will be responsible for assuring that both the lawyer's conduct and, to the extent required by Rule 5.3, the conduct of nonlawyer employees in the distinct entity that the lawyer controls complies in all respects with the Rules of Professional Conduct.

[9] A broad range of economic and other interests of clients may be served by lawyers engaging in the delivery of law-related services. Examples of law-related services include providing title insurance, financial planning, accounting, trust services, real estate counseling, legislative lobbying, economic analysis, social work, psychological counseling, tax preparation, and patent, medical or environmental consulting.

[10] When a lawyer is obliged to accord the recipients of such services the protections of those rules that apply to the client-lawyer relationship, the lawyer must take special care to heed the proscriptions of the rules addressing conflict of interest (Rules 1.7 through 1.11, especially Rules 1.7(a)(2) and 1.8(a), (b) and (f)), and to scrupulously adhere to the requirements of Rule 1.6 relating to disclosure of confidential information. The promotion of the law-related services must also in all respects comply with Rules 7.1 through 7.3, dealing with advertising and solicitation. In that regard, lawyers should take special care to identify the obligations that may be imposed as a result of a jurisdiction's decisional law.

[11] When the full protections of all of the Rules of Professional Conduct do not apply to the provision of law-related services, principles of law external to the rules, for example, the law of principal and agent, govern the legal duties owed to those receiving the services. Those other legal principles may establish a different degree of protection for the recipient with respect to confidentiality of information, conflicts of interest, and permissible business relationships with clients. See also Rule 8.4 (Misconduct).

Rule 5.8 Employment of Disbarred, Suspended, or Involuntarily Inactive Lawyers

(a) For purposes of this rule "employ" means to engage the services of another, including employees, agents, independent contractors, and consultants, regardless of whether any compensation is paid.

(b) A lawyer shall not employ, associate professionally with, or aid a person the lawyer knows or reasonably should know has been disbarred, suspended, or placed on disability inactive status by order of the court to do any of the following on behalf of the lawyer's client:

(1) render legal consultation or advice to the client;

(2) appear on behalf of the client in any hearing or proceeding or before any judicial officer, arbitrator, mediator, court, public agency, referee, magistrate, commissioner, or hearing officer, unless the rules of the tribunal involved permit representation by nonlawyers and the client has been informed of the lawyer's suspension, disbarment, or disability inactive status;

(3) appear as a representative of the client at a deposition or other discovery matter;

(4) negotiate or transact any matter for or on behalf of the client with third parties;

(5) receive, disburse, or otherwise handle the client's funds; or

(6) engage in activities that constitute the practice of law.

(c) A lawyer may employ, associate professionally with, or aid a disbarred, suspended, or disability inactive lawyer to perform research, drafting, clerical, or similar activities, including but not limited to:

(1) performing legal work of a preparatory nature for the active lawyer's review, such as legal research, gathering information, and drafting pleadings, briefs, and other similar documents;

(2) directly communicating with the client or third parties regarding matters such as scheduling, billing, updates, information gathering, and confirmation of receipt or sending of correspondence and messages; or

(3) accompanying an active lawyer to a deposition or other discovery matter for the limited purpose of providing clerical assistance to the active lawyer who will appear as the representative of the client.

(d) Prior to or at the time of employing a person the lawyer knows or reasonably should know is a disbarred, suspended, or disability inactive lawyer, the lawyer shall serve upon the Office of Lawyers Professional Responsibility written notice of the employment, including a full description of such person's current license status. The notice shall state that the suspended, disbarred, or disability inactive lawyer shall not be employed to perform any of the activities prohibited by paragraph (b).

(e) Upon terminating the employment of the disbarred, suspended, or disability inactive lawyer, the employing lawyer shall promptly serve upon the Office of Lawyers Professional Responsibility written notice of the termination.

Amended June 17, 2005, eff. Oct. 1, 2005.

PUBLIC SERVICE

Rule 6.1. Voluntary Pro Bono Publico Service

Every lawyer has a professional responsibility to provide legal services to those unable to pay. A lawyer should aspire to render at least 50 hours of pro bono publico legal services per year. In fulfilling this responsibility, the lawyer should:

(a) provide a substantial majority of the 50 hours of legal services without fee or expectation of fee to:

(1) persons of limited means; or

(2) charitable, religious, civic, community, governmental, and educational organizations in matters that are designed primarily to address the needs of persons of limited means; and

(b) provide any additional services through:

(1) delivery of legal services at no fee or substantially reduced fee to individuals, groups, or organizations seeking to secure or protect civil rights, civil liberties, or public rights, or charitable, religious, civic, community, governmental, and educational organizations in matters in furtherance of their organizational purposes, where the payment of standard legal fees would significantly deplete the organization's economic resources or would be otherwise inappropriate;

(2) delivery of legal services at a substantially reduced fee to persons of limited means; or

(3) participation in activities for improving the law, the legal system, or the legal profession.

In addition, a lawyer should voluntarily contribute financial support to organizations that provide legal services to persons of limited means.

Adopted June 13, 1985, eff. Sept. 1, 1985. Amended Dec. 11, 1995, eff. Jan. 1, 1996; June 17, 2005, eff. Oct. 1, 2005.

Comment—2005

[1] Every lawyer, regardless of professional prominence or professional work load, has a responsibility to provide legal services to those unable to pay, and personal involvement in the problems of the disadvantaged can be one of the most rewarding experiences in the life of a lawyer. The Minnesota State Bar Association urges all lawyers to provide a minimum of 50 hours of pro bono services annually. It is recognized that in some years a lawyer may render greater or fewer hours than the annual standard specified but, during the course of his or her legal career, each lawyer should render on average per year the number of hours set forth in this rule. Services can be performed in civil matters or in criminal or quasi-criminal matters for which there is no government obligation to provide funds for legal representation, such as postconviction death penalty appeal cases.

[2] Paragraphs (a)(1) and (2) recognize the critical need for legal services that exists among persons of limited means by providing that a substantial majority of the legal services rendered annually to the disadvantaged be furnished without fee or expectation of fee. Legal services under these paragraphs consist of a full range of activities, including individual and class representation, the provision of legal advice, legislative lobbying, administrative rule- making, and the provision of free training or mentoring to those who represent persons of limited means. The variety of these activities should facilitate participation by government lawyers, even when restrictions exist on their engaging in the outside practice of law.

[3] Persons eligible for legal services under paragraphs (a)(1) and (2) are those who qualify for participation in programs funded by the Legal Services Corporation and those whose incomes and financial resources are slightly above the guidelines utilized by such programs but nevertheless, cannot afford counsel. Legal services can be rendered to individuals or to organizations such as homeless shelters, battered women's centers, and food pantries that serve those of limited means. The term "governmental organizations" includes, but is not limited to, public protection programs and sections of governmental or public sector agencies.

[4] Because service must be provided without fee or expectation of fee, the intent of the lawyer to render free legal services is essential for the work performed to fall within the meaning of paragraphs (a)(1) and (2). Accordingly, services rendered cannot be considered pro bono if an anticipated fee is uncollected, but the award of statutory attorneys' fees in a case originally accepted as pro bono would not disqualify such services from inclusion under this section. Lawyers who do receive fees in such cases are encouraged to contribute an appropriate portion of such fees to organizations or projects that benefit persons of limited means.

[5] While it is possible for a lawyer to fulfill the annual responsibility to perform pro bono services exclusively through activities described in paragraphs (a)(1) and (2), to the extent that any hours of service remained unfulfilled, the remaining commitment can be met in a variety of ways as set forth in paragraph (b). Constitutional, statutory, or regulatory restrictions may prohibit or impede government and public sector lawyers and judges from performing the pro bono services outlined in paragraphs (a)(1) and (2). Accordingly, where those restrictions apply, government and public sector lawyers and judges may fulfill their pro bono responsibility by performing services outlined in paragraph (b).

[6] Paragraph (b)(1) includes the provision of certain types of legal services to those whose incomes and financial resources place them above limited means. It also permits the pro bono lawyer to accept a substantially reduced fee for services. Examples of the types of issues that may be addressed under this paragraph include First Amendment claims, Title VII claims, and environmental protection claims. Additionally, a wide range of organizations may be represented, including social service, medical research, cultural, and religious groups.

[7] Paragraph (b)(2) covers instances in which lawyers agree to and receive a modest fee for furnishing legal services to persons of limited means. Participation in judicare programs and acceptance of court appointments in which the fee is substantially below a lawyer's usual rate are encouraged under this section.

[8] Paragraph (b)(3) recognizes the value of lawyers engaging in activities that improve the law, the

legal system, or the legal profession. Serving on bar association committees, serving on boards of pro bono or legal services programs, taking part in Law Day activities, acting as a continuing legal education instructor, a mediator, or an arbitrator and engaging in legislative lobbying to improve the law, the legal system, or the legal profession are a few examples of the many activities that fall within this paragraph.

[9] Because the provision of pro bono services is a professional responsibility, it is the individual ethical commitment of each lawyer. Nevertheless, there may be times when it is not feasible for a lawyer to engage in pro bono services. At such times, a lawyer may discharge the pro bono responsibility by providing financial support to organizations providing free legal services to persons of limited means. Such financial support should be reasonably equivalent to the value of the hours of service that would have otherwise been provided. In addition, at times it may be more feasible to satisfy the pro bono responsibility collectively, as by a firm's aggregate pro bono activities.

[10] Because the efforts of individual lawyers are not enough to meet the need for free legal services that exists among persons of limited means, the government and the profession have instituted additional programs to provide those services. Every lawyer should financially support such programs, in addition to either providing direct pro bono services or making financial contributions when pro bono service is not feasible.

[11] Law firms should act reasonably to enable and encourage all lawyers in the firm to provide the pro bono legal services called for by this rule.

[12] The responsibility set forth in this rule is not intended to be enforced through disciplinary process.

Historical Notes

This rule is similar to provisions of former EC 2–25 of the Minn. Code of Prof. Responsibility.

Rule 6.2. Accepting Appointments

A lawyer shall not seek to avoid appointment by a tribunal to represent a person except for good cause, such as:

(a) representing the client is likely to result in violation of the Rules of Professional Conduct or other law;

(b) representing the client is likely to result in an unreasonable financial burden on the lawyer; or

(c) the client or the cause is so repugnant to the lawyer as to be likely to impair the client-lawyer relationship or the lawyer's ability to represent the client.

Adopted June 13, 1985, eff. Sept. 1, 1985. Amended June 17, 2005, eff. Oct. 1, 2005.

Comment—2005

[1] A lawyer ordinarily is not obliged to accept a client whose character or cause the lawyer regards as repugnant. The lawyer's freedom to select clients is, however, qualified. All lawyers have a responsibility to assist in providing pro bono publico service. See Rule 6.1. An individual lawyer fulfills this responsibility by accepting a fair share of unpopular matters or indigent or unpopular clients. A lawyer may also be subject to appointment by a court to serve unpopular clients or persons unable to afford legal services.

Appointed Counsel

[2] For good cause a lawyer may seek to decline an appointment to represent a person who cannot afford to retain counsel or whose cause is unpopular. Good cause exists if the lawyer could not handle the matter competently, see Rule 1.1, or if undertaking the representation would result in an improper conflict of interest, for example, when the client or the cause is so repugnant to the lawyer as to be likely to impair the client-lawyer relationship or the lawyer's ability to represent the client. A lawyer may also seek to decline an appointment if acceptance would be unreasonably burdensome, for example, when it would impose a financial sacrifice so great as to be unjust.

[3] An appointed lawyer has the same obligations to the client as retained counsel, including the obligations of loyalty and confidentiality, and is subject to the same limitations on the client-lawyer relationship, such as the obligation to refrain from assisting the client in violation of the rules.

Historical Notes

This rule is similar, in part, to provisions of former EC 2–29 and EC 2–30 of the Minn. Code of Prof. Responsibility.

Rule 6.3. Membership in Legal Services Organization

A lawyer may serve as a director, officer, or member of a legal services organization, apart from the law firm in which the lawyer practices, notwithstanding that the organization serves persons having interests adverse to a client of the lawyer. The lawyer shall not knowingly participate in a decision or action of the organization:

(a) if participating in the decision or action would be incompatible with the lawyer's obligations to a client under Rule 1.7; or

(b) where the decision or action could have a material adverse effect on the representation of a client of the organization whose interests are adverse to a client of the lawyer.

Adopted June 13, 1985, eff. Sept. 1, 1985. Amended June 17, 2005, eff. Oct. 1, 2005.

Comment—2005

[1] Lawyers should be encouraged to support and participate in legal service organizations. A lawyer who is an officer or a member of such an organization does not thereby have a client-lawyer relationship with persons served by the organization. However, there is potential conflict between the interests of such persons and the interests of the law-

yer's clients. If the possibility of such conflict disqualified a lawyer from serving on the board of a legal services organization, the profession's involvement in such organizations would be severely curtailed.

[2] It may be necessary in appropriate cases to reassure a client of the organization that the representation will not be affected by conflicting loyalties of a member of the board. Established, written policies in this respect can enhance the credibility of such assurances.

Rule 6.4. Law Reform Activities Affecting Client Interests

A lawyer may serve as a director, officer, or member of an organization involved in reform of the law or its administration notwithstanding that the reform may affect the interests of a client of the lawyer. When the lawyer knows that the interests of a client may be materially benefited by a decision in which the lawyer participates, the lawyer shall disclose that fact but need not identify the client.

Adopted June 13, 1985, eff. Sept. 1, 1985. Amended June 17, 2005, eff. Oct. 1, 2005.

Comment—2005

Lawyers involved in organizations seeking law reform generally do not have a client-lawyer relationship with the organization. Otherwise, it might follow that a lawyer could not be involved in a bar association law reform program that might indirectly affect a client. See also Rule 1.2(b). For example, a lawyer specializing in antitrust litigation might be regarded as disqualified from participating in drafting revisions of rules governing that subject. In determining the nature and scope of participation in such activities, a lawyer should be mindful of obligations to clients under other rules, particularly Rule 1.7. A lawyer is professionally obligated to protect the integrity of the program by making an appropriate disclosure within the organization when the lawyer knows a private client might be materially benefited.

Rule 6.5. Pro Bono Limited Legal Services Programs

(a) A lawyer who, under the auspices of a program offering pro bono legal services, provides short-term limited legal services to a client without expectation by either the lawyer or the client that the lawyer will provide continuing representation in the matter:

(1) is subject to Rules 1.7 and 1.9(a) only if the lawyer knows that the representation of the client involves a conflict of interest; and

(2) is subject to Rule 1.10 only if the lawyer knows that another lawyer associated with the lawyer in a law firm is disqualified by Rule 1.7 or 1.9(a) with respect to the matter.

(b) Except as provided in paragraph (a)(2), Rule 1.10 is inapplicable to a representation governed by this rule.

Adopted June 17, 2005, eff. Oct. 1, 2005.

Comment—2005

[1] Legal services organizations, courts and various organizations have established programs through which lawyers provide short-term limited legal services—such as advice or the completion of legal forms-that will assist persons to address their legal problems without further representation by a lawyer. In these programs, such as legal-advice hotlines, advice-only clinics or pro se counseling programs, a client-lawyer relationship is established, but there is no expectation that the lawyer's representation of the client will continue beyond the limited consultation. Such programs are normally operated under circumstances in which it is not feasible for a lawyer to systematically screen for conflicts of interest as is generally required before undertaking a representation. See, e.g., Rules 1.7, 1.9 and 1.10.

[2] A lawyer who provides short-term limited legal services pursuant to this rule must secure the client's informed consent to the limited scope of the representation. See Rule 1.2(c). If a short-term limited representation would not be reasonable under the circumstances, the lawyer may offer advice to the client but must also advise the client of the need for further assistance of counsel. Except as provided in this rule, the Rules of Professional Conduct, including Rules 1.6 and 1.9(c), are applicable to the limited representation.

[3] Because a lawyer who is representing a client in the circumstances addressed by this rule ordinarily is not able to check systematically for conflicts of interest, paragraph (a) requires compliance with Rule 1.7 or 1.9(a) only if the lawyer knows that the representation presents a conflict of interest for the lawyer, and with Rule 1.10 only if the lawyer knows that another lawyer in the lawyer's firm is disqualified by Rule 1.7 or 1.9(a) in the matter.

[4] Because the limited nature of the services significantly reduces the risk of conflicts of interest with other matters being handled by the lawyer's firm, paragraph (b) provides that Rule 1.10 is inapplicable to a representation governed by this rule except as provided by paragraph (a)(2). Paragraph (a)(2) requires the participating lawyer to comply with Rule 1.10 when the lawyer knows that the lawyer's firm is disqualified by Rule 1.7 or 1.9(a). By virtue of paragraph (b), however, a lawyer's participation in a short-term limited legal services program will not preclude the lawyer's firm from undertaking or continuing the representation of a client with interests adverse to a client being represented under the program's auspices. Nor will the personal disqualification of a lawyer participating in the program be imputed to other lawyers participating in the program.

[5] If, after commencing a short-term limited representation in accordance with this rule, a lawyer undertakes to represent the client in the matter on

an ongoing basis, Rules 1.7, 1.9(a) and 1.10 become applicable.

INFORMATION ABOUT LEGAL SERVICES

Rule 7.1. Communications Concerning a Lawyer's Services

A lawyer shall not make a false or misleading communication about the lawyer or the lawyer's services. A communication is false or misleading if it contains a material misrepresentation of fact or law, or omits a fact necessary to make the statement considered as a whole not materially misleading.

Adopted June 13, 1985, eff. Sept. 1, 1985. Amended June 17, 2005, eff. Oct. 1, 2005.

Comment—2005

[1] This rule governs all communications about a lawyer's services, including advertising permitted by Rule 7.2. Whatever means are used to make known a lawyer's services, statements about them must be truthful.

[2] Truthful statements that are misleading are also prohibited by this rule. A truthful statement is misleading if it omits a fact necessary to make the lawyer's communication considered as a whole not materially misleading. A truthful statement is also misleading if there is a substantial likelihood that it will lead a reasonable person to formulate a specific conclusion about the lawyer or the lawyer's services for which there is no reasonable factual foundation.

[3] An advertisement that truthfully reports a lawyer's achievements on behalf of clients or former clients may be misleading if presented so as to lead a reasonable person to form an unjustified expectation that the same results could be obtained for other clients in similar matters without reference to the specific factual and legal circumstances of each client's case. Similarly, an unsubstantiated comparison of the lawyer's services or fees with the services or fees of other lawyers may be misleading if presented with such specificity as would lead a reasonable person to conclude that the comparison can be substantiated. The inclusion of an appropriate disclaimer or qualifying language may preclude a finding that a statement is likely to create unjustified expectations or otherwise mislead a prospective client.

[4] See also Rule 8.4(e) for the prohibition against stating or implying an ability to influence improperly a government agency or official or to achieve results by means that violate the Rules of Professional Conduct or other law.

Historical Notes

This rule is similar to provisions of former DR 2–101(A), B(1) to (4) of the Minn. Code of Prof. Responsibility.

Rule 7.2. Advertising

(a) Subject to the requirements of Rules 7.1 and 7.3, a lawyer may advertise services through written, recorded, or electronic communications, including public media.

(b) A lawyer shall not give anything of value to a person for recommending the lawyer's services except that a lawyer may

(1) pay the reasonable costs of advertisements or communications permitted by this rule;

(2) pay the usual charges of a legal service plan or a not-for- profit lawyer referral service;

(3) pay for a law practice in accordance with Rule 1.17; and

(4) refer clients to another lawyer or a nonlawyer professional pursuant to an agreement not otherwise prohibited under these rules that provides for the other person to refer clients or customers to the lawyer, if

(i) the reciprocal referral agreement is not exclusive, and

(ii) the client is informed of the existence and nature of the agreement.

(c) Any communication made pursuant to this rule shall include the name of at least one lawyer or law firm responsible for its content.

Adopted June 13, 1985, eff. Sept. 1, 1985. Amended Dec. 27, 1989, eff. Jan. 1, 1990; August 31, 1993, eff. August 31, 1993; Dec. 11, 1995, eff. Jan. 1, 1996; June 17, 2005, eff. Oct. 1, 2005.

Comment—2005

[1] To assist the public in obtaining legal services, lawyers should be allowed to make known their services not only through reputation but also through organized information campaigns in the form of advertising. Advertising involves an active quest for clients, contrary to the tradition that a lawyer should not seek clientele. However, the public's need to know about legal services can be fulfilled in part through advertising. This need is particularly acute in the case of persons of moderate means who have not made extensive use of legal services. The interest in expanding public information about legal services ought to prevail over considerations of tradition. Nevertheless, advertising by lawyers entails the risk of practices that are misleading or overreaching.

[2] This rule permits public dissemination of information concerning a lawyer's name or firm name, address and telephone number; the kinds of services the lawyer will undertake; the basis on which the lawyer's fees are determined, including prices for specific services and payment and credit arrangements; a lawyer's foreign language ability; names of references and, with their consent, names of clients regularly represented; and other informa-

tion that might invite the attention of those seeking legal assistance.

[3] Questions of effectiveness and taste in advertising are matters of speculation and subjective judgment. Some jurisdictions have had extensive prohibitions against television advertising, against advertising going beyond specified facts about a lawyer, or against "undignified" advertising. Television is now one of the most powerful media for getting information to the public, particularly persons of low and moderate income; prohibiting television advertising, therefore, would impede the flow of information about legal services to many sectors of the public. Limiting the information that may be advertised has a similar effect and assumes that the bar can accurately forecast the kind of information that the public would regard as relevant.

[4] Neither this rule nor Rule 7.3 prohibits communications authorized by law, such as notice to members of a class in class action litigation.

Paying Others to Recommend a Lawyer

[5] Lawyers are not permitted to pay others for channeling professional work. Paragraph (b)(1), however, allows a lawyer to pay for advertising and communications permitted by this rule, including the costs of print directory listings, on- line directory listings, newspaper ads, television and radio airtime, domain- name registrations, sponsorship fees, banner ads, and group advertising. A lawyer may compensate employees, agents and vendors who are engaged to provide marketing or client-development services, such as publicists, public- relations personnel, business-development staff and website designers. See Rule 5.3 for the duties of lawyers and law firms with respect to the conduct of nonlawyers who prepare marketing materials for them.

[6] A lawyer may pay the usual charges of a legal service plan or a not-for-profit lawyer referral service. A legal service plan is a prepaid or group legal service plan or a similar delivery system that assists prospective clients to secure legal representation. A lawyer referral service, on the other hand, is any organization that holds itself out to the public as a lawyer referral service. Such referral services are understood by laypersons to be consumer-oriented organizations that provide unbiased referrals to lawyers with appropriate experience in the subject matter of the representation and afford other client protections, such as complaint procedures or malpractice insurance requirements. Consequently, this rule only permits a lawyer to pay the usual charges of a not-for-profit lawyer referral service.

[7] A lawyer who accepts assignments or referrals from a legal service plan or referrals from a not-for-profit lawyer referral service must act reasonably to assure that the activities of the plan or service are compatible with the lawyer's professional obligations. See Rule 5.3. Legal service plans and lawyer referral services may communicate with prospective clients, but such communication must be in conformity with these rules. Thus, advertising must not be false or misleading, as would be the case if the communications of a group advertising program or a group legal services plan would mislead prospective clients to think that it was a lawyer referral service sponsored by a state agency or bar association. Nor could the lawyer allow in-person or telephonic contacts that would violate Rule 7.3.

[8] A lawyer also may agree to refer clients to another lawyer or a nonlawyer professional, in return for the undertaking of that person to refer clients or customers to the lawyer. Such reciprocal referral arrangements must not interfere with the lawyer's professional judgment as to making referrals or as to providing substantive legal services. See Rules 2.1 and 5.4(c). Except as provided in Rule 1.5(e), a lawyer who receives referrals from a lawyer or nonlawyer professional must not pay anything solely for the referral, but the lawyer does not violate paragraph (b) of this rule by agreeing to refer clients to the other lawyer or nonlawyer professional, so long as the reciprocal referral agreement is not exclusive and the client is informed of the referral agreement. Conflicts of interest created by such arrangements are governed by Rule 1.7. Reciprocal referral agreements should not be of indefinite duration and should be reviewed periodically to determine whether they comply with these rules. This rule does not restrict referrals or divisions of revenues or net income among lawyers within a firm.

Historical Notes

This rule is similar, in part, to provisions of former DR 2–102(A), DR 2–103(A) and DR 2–104(D) of the Minn. Code of Prof. Responsibility.

Rule 7.3. Direct Contact with Prospective Clients

(a) A lawyer shall not by in-person or live telephone contact solicit professional employment from a prospective client when a significant motive for the lawyer's doing so is the lawyer's pecuniary gain, unless the person contacted:

(1) is a lawyer; or

(2) has a family, close personal, or prior professional relationship with the lawyer.

(b) A lawyer shall not solicit professional employment from a prospective client by written, recorded, or electronic communication or by in-person or telephone contact even when not otherwise prohibited by paragraph (a) if:

(1) the prospective client has made known to the lawyer a desire not to be solicited by the lawyer; or

(2) the solicitation involves coercion, duress, or harassment.

(c) Every written, recorded, or electronic communication from a lawyer soliciting professional employment from a prospective client known to be in need of legal services in a particular matter shall clearly and conspicuously include the words "Advertising Material" on the outside envelope, if any, and within any written, recorded, or electronic communication, unless the recipient of the communication is a person specified in paragraphs (a)(1) or (a)(2).

(d) Notwithstanding the prohibitions in paragraph (a), a lawyer may participate with a prepaid or group legal service plan operated by an organization not owned or directed by the lawyer that uses in-person or telephone contact to solicit memberships or subscriptions for the plan from persons who are not known to need legal services in a particular matter covered by the plan.

Adopted June 13, 1985, eff. Sept. 1, 1985. Amended August 31, 1993, eff. August 31, 1993; June 17, 2005, eff. Oct. 1, 2005.

Comment—2005

[1] There is a potential for abuse inherent in direct in-person or live telephone contact by a lawyer with a prospective clients known to need legal services. These forms of contact between a lawyer and a prospective client subject the layperson to the private importuning of the trained advocate in a direct interpersonal encounter. The prospective client, who may already feel overwhelmed by the circumstances giving rise to the need for legal services, may find it difficult fully to evaluate all available alternatives with reasoned judgment and appropriate self-interest in the face of the lawyer's presence and insistence upon being retained immediately. The situation is fraught with the possibility of undue influence, intimidation, and over-reaching.

[2] This potential for abuse inherent in direct in-person or live telephone solicitation of prospective clients justifies its prohibition, particularly since lawyer advertising and written and recorded communication permitted under Rule 7.2 offer alternative means of conveying necessary information to those who may be in need of legal services. Advertising and written and recorded communications which may be mailed or autodialed make it possible for a prospective client to be informed about the need for legal services, and about the qualifications of available lawyers and law firms, without subjecting the prospective client to direct in- person or telephone persuasion that may overwhelm the client's judgment.

[3] The use of general advertising and written, recorded or electronic communications to transmit information from lawyer to prospective client, rather than direct in-person or live telephone contact will help to assure that the information flows cleanly as well as freely. The contents of advertisements and communications permitted under Rule 7.2 can be permanently recorded so that they cannot be disputed and may be shared with others who know the lawyer. This potential for informal review is itself likely to help guard against statements and claims that might constitute false and misleading communications, in violation of Rule 7.1. The contents of direct in-person or live telephone conversations between a lawyer and a prospective client can be disputed and may not be subject to third-party scrutiny. Consequently, they are much more likely to approach (and occasionally cross) the dividing line between accurate representations and those that are false and misleading.

[4] There is far less likelihood that a lawyer would engage in abusive practices against an individual who is a former client, or with whom the lawyer has a close personal or family relationship, or in situations in which the lawyer is motivated by considerations other than the lawyer's pecuniary gain. Nor is there a serious potential for abuse when the person contacted is a lawyer. Consequently, the general prohibition in Rule 7.3(a) and the requirements of Rule 7.3(c) are not applicable in those situations. Also, paragraph (a) is not intended to prohibit a lawyer from participating in constitutionally protected activities of public or charitable legal- service organizations or bona fide political, social, civic, fraternal, employee or trade organizations whose purposes include providing or recommending legal services to its members or beneficiaries.

[5] But even permitted forms of solicitation can be abused. Thus, any solicitation which contains information which is false or misleading within the meaning of Rule 7.1, which involves coercion, duress or harassment within the meaning of Rule 7.3(b)(2), or which involves contact with a prospective client who has made known to the lawyer a desire not to be solicited by the lawyer within the meaning of Rule 7.3(b)(1) is prohibited. Moreover, if after sending a letter or other communication to a client as permitted by Rule 7.2 the lawyer receives no response, any further effort to communicate with the prospective client may violate the provisions of Rule 7.3(b).

[6] This rule is not intended to prohibit a lawyer from contacting representatives of organizations or groups that may be interested in establishing a group or prepaid legal plan for their members, insureds, beneficiaries or other third parties for the purpose of informing such entities of the availability of and details concerning the plan or arrangement which the lawyer or lawyer's firm is willing to offer. This form of communication is not directed to a prospective client. Rather, it is usually addressed to an individual acting in a fiduciary capacity seeking a supplier of legal services for others who may, if they choose, become prospective clients of the lawyer. Under these circumstances, the activity which the lawyer undertakes in communicating with such representatives and the type of information transmitted to the individual are functionally similar to and serve the same purpose as advertising permitted under Rule 7.2.

[7] The requirement in Rule 7.3(c) that certain communications be marked "Advertising Material" does not apply to communications sent in response to requests of potential clients or their spokespersons or sponsors. General announcements by lawyers, including changes in personnel or office location, do not constitute communications soliciting professional employment from a client known to be in need of legal services within the meaning of this rule.

[8] Paragraph (d) of this rule permits a lawyer to participate with an organization which uses personal contact to solicit members for its group or prepaid legal service plan, provided that the personal contact is not undertaken by any lawyer who would be a provider of legal services through the plan. The organization must not be owned by or directed

(whether as manager or otherwise) by any lawyer or law firm that participates in the plan. For example, paragraph (d) would not permit a lawyer to create an organization controlled directly or indirectly by the lawyer and use the organization for the in-person or telephone solicitation of legal employment of the lawyer through memberships in the plan or otherwise. The communication permitted by these organizations also must not be directed to a person known to need legal services in a particular matter, but is to be designed to inform potential plan members generally of another means of affordable legal services. Lawyers who participate in a legal service plan must reasonably assure that the plan sponsors are in compliance with Rules 7. 1, 7.2 and 7.3(b). See 8.4(a).

Historical Notes

This rule is similar to provisions of former DR 2–103 of the Minn. Code of Prof. Responsibility.

Rule 7.4. Communication of Fields of Practice and Certification

(a) A lawyer may communicate the fact that the lawyer does or does not practice in particular fields of law.

(b) A lawyer admitted to engage in patent practice before the United States Patent and Trademark Office may use the designation " Patent Attorney" or a substantially similar designation.

(c) A lawyer engaged in admiralty practice may use the designation "Admiralty," "Proctor in Admiralty," or a substantially similar designation.

(d) In any communication subject to Rules 7.2, 7.3, or 7.5, a lawyer shall not state or imply that a lawyer is a specialist or certified as a specialist in a particular field of law except as follows;

(1) the communication shall clearly identify the name of the certifying organization, if any, in the communication; and

(2) if the attorney is not certified as a specialist or if the certifying organization is not accredited by the Minnesota Board of Legal Certification, the communication shall clearly state that the attorney is not certified by any organization accredited by that Board, and in any advertising subject to Rule 7.2, this statement shall appear in the same sentence that communicates the certification.

Adopted June 13, 1985, eff. Sept. 1, 1985. Amended Dec. 11, 1995, eff. Jan. 1, 1996; June 17, 2005, eff. Oct. 1, 2005.

Comment—2005

[1] Paragraph (a) of this rule permits a lawyer to indicate areas of practice in communications about the lawyer's services. If a lawyer practices only in certain fields, or will not accept matters except in a specified field or fields, the lawyer is permitted to so indicate. A lawyer is generally permitted to state that the lawyer is a "specialist," practices a "specialty," or "specializes in" particular fields, but such communications are subject to the "false and misleading" standard applied in Rule 7.1 to communications concerning a lawyer's services.

[2] Paragraph (b) recognizes the long-established policy of the Patent and Trademark Office for the designation of lawyers practicing before the Office. Paragraph (c) recognizes that designation of Admiralty practice has a long historical tradition associated with maritime commerce and the federal courts.

[3] Paragraph (d) permits a lawyer to state that the lawyer is certified as a specialist in a field of law if such certification is granted by an organization that has been accredited by the Board on Legal Certification. Certification signifies that an objective entity has recognized an advanced degree of knowledge and experience in the specialty area greater than is suggested by general licensure to practice law. Certifying organizations may be expected to apply standards of experience, knowledge and proficiency to insure that a lawyer's recognition as a specialist is meaningful and reliable. In order to insure that consumers can obtain access to useful information about an organization granting certification, the name of the certifying organization must be included in any communication regarding the certification.

[4] Lawyers may also be certified as specialists by organizations that either have not yet been accredited to grant such certification or have been disapproved. In such instances, the consumer may be misled as to the significance of the lawyer's status as a certified specialist. The rule therefore requires that a lawyer who chooses to communicate recognition by such an organization also clearly state the absence or denial of the organization's authority to grant such certification. Because lawyer advertising through public media and written or recorded communications invites the greatest danger of misleading consumers, the absence or denial of the organization's authority to grant certification must be clearly stated in such advertising in the same sentence that communicates the certification.

Historical Notes

This rule is similar, in part, to provisions of former DR 2–105 of Minn. Code of Prof. Responsibility.

Rule 7.5. Firm Names and Letterheads

(a) A lawyer shall not use a firm name, letterhead, or other professional designation that violates Rule 7.1. A trade name may be used by a lawyer in private practice if it does not imply a connection with a government agency or with a public or charitable legal services organization and is not otherwise in violation of Rule 7.1.

(b) A law firm with offices in more than one jurisdiction may use the same name or other professional designation in each jurisdiction, but identification of the lawyers in an office of the firm shall indicate the jurisdictional limitations on those not licensed to practice in the jurisdiction where the office is located.

(c) The name of a lawyer holding a public office shall not be used in the name of a law firm, or in communications on its behalf, during any substantial period in which the lawyer is not actively and regularly practicing with the firm.

(d) Lawyers may state or imply that they practice in a partnership or other organization only when that is the fact.

Adopted June 13, 1985, eff. Sept. 1, 1985. Amended June 17, 2005, eff. Oct. 1, 2005.

Comment—2005

[1] A firm may be designated by the names of all or some of its members, by the names of deceased members where there has been a continuing succession in the firm's identity or by a trade name such as the "ABC Legal Clinic." A lawyer or law firm may also be designated by a distinctive website address or comparable professional designation. Although the United States Supreme Court has held that legislation may prohibit the use of trade names in professional practice, use of such names in law practice is acceptable so long as it is not misleading. If a private firm uses a trade name that includes a geographical name such as "Springfield Legal Clinic," an express disclaimer that it is a public legal aid agency may be required to avoid a misleading implication. It may be observed that any firm name including the name of a deceased partner is, strictly speaking, a trade name. The use of such names to designate law firms has proven a useful means of identification. However, it is misleading to use the name of a lawyer not associated with the firm or a predecessor of the firm.

[2] With regard to paragraph (d), lawyers sharing office facilities, but who are not in fact associated with each other in a law firm, may not denominate themselves as, for example, "Smith and Jones," for that title suggests that they are practicing law together in a firm.

Historical Notes

This rule is similar to provisions of former DR 2–102 of the Minn. Code of Prof. Responsibility.

MAINTAINING THE INTEGRITY OF THE PROFESSION

Rule 8.1. Bar Admission and Disciplinary Matters

An applicant for admission to the bar, or a lawyer in connection with a bar admission application or in connection with a disciplinary matter, shall not:

(a) knowingly make a false statement of material fact; or

(b) fail to disclose a fact necessary to correct a misapprehension known by the person to have arisen in the matter, or knowingly fail to respond to a lawful demand for information from an admissions or disciplinary authority, except that this rule does not require disclosure of information otherwise protected by Rule 1.6.

Adopted June 13, 1985, eff. Sept. 1, 1985. Amended June 17, 2005, eff. Oct. 1, 2005.

Comment—2005

[1] The duty imposed by this rule extends to persons seeking admission to the bar as well as to lawyers. Hence, if a person makes a material false statement in connection with an application for admission, it may be the basis for subsequent disciplinary action if the person is admitted, and in any event may be relevant in a subsequent admission application. The duty imposed by this rule applies to a lawyer's own admission or discipline as well as that of others. Thus, it is a separate professional offense for a lawyer to knowingly make a misrepresentation or omission in connection with a disciplinary investigation of the lawyer's own conduct. Paragraph (b) of this rule also requires correction of any prior misstatement in the matter that the applicant or lawyer may have made and affirmative clarification of any misunderstanding on the part of the admissions or disciplinary authority of which the person involved becomes aware.

[2] This rule is subject to the provisions of the Fifth Amendment of the United States Constitution and corresponding provisions of state constitutions. A person relying on such a provision in response to a question, however, should do so openly and not use the right of nondisclosure as a justification for failure to comply with this rule.

[3] A lawyer representing an applicant for admission to the bar, or representing a lawyer who is the subject of a disciplinary inquiry or proceeding, is governed by the rules applicable to the client-lawyer relationship, including Rule 1.6 and, in some cases, Rule 3.3.

Historical Notes

This rule is similar to provisions of former DR 1–101 and DR 1–103(B) of the Minn. Code of Prof. Responsibility.

Rule 8.2. Judicial and Legal Officials

(a) A lawyer shall not make a statement that the lawyer knows to be false or with reckless disregard as to its truth or falsity concerning the qualifications or integrity of a judge, adjudicatory officer, or public legal officer, or of a candidate for election or appointment to judicial or legal office.

(b) A lawyer who is a candidate for judicial office shall comply with the applicable provisions of the Code of Judicial Conduct.

Adopted June 13, 1985, eff. Sept. 1, 1985. Amended June 17, 2005, eff. Oct. 1, 2005.

Comment—2005

[1] Assessments by lawyers are relied on in evaluating the professional or personal fitness of per-

sons being considered for election or appointment to judicial office and to public legal offices, such as attorney general, prosecuting attorney and public defender. Expressing honest and candid opinions on such matters contributes to improving the administration of justice. Conversely, false statements by a lawyer can unfairly undermine public confidence in the administration of justice.

[2] When a lawyer seeks judicial office, the lawyer should be bound by applicable limitations on political activity.

[3] To maintain the fair and independent administration of justice, lawyers are encouraged to continue traditional efforts to defend judges and courts unjustly criticized.

Historical Notes

This rule is similar to provisions of former DR 8–102 and DR 8–103 of the Minn. Code of Prof. Responsibility.

Rule 8.3. Reporting Professional Misconduct

(a) A lawyer who knows that another lawyer has committed a violation of the Rules of Professional Conduct that raises a substantial question as to that lawyer's honesty, trustworthiness, or fitness as a lawyer in other respects, shall inform the appropriate professional authority.

(b) A lawyer who knows that a judge has committed a violation of the applicable Code of Judicial Conduct that raises a substantial question as to the judge's fitness for office shall inform the appropriate authority.

(c) This rule does not require disclosure of information that Rule 1.6 requires or allows a lawyer to keep confidential or information gained by a lawyer or judge while participating in a lawyers assistance program or other program providing assistance, support, or counseling to lawyers who are chemically dependent or have mental disorders.

Adopted June 13, 1985, eff. Sept. 1, 1985. Amended April 14, 1992; April 17, 2000, eff. July 1, 2000; June 17, 2005, eff. Oct. 1, 2005.

Comment—2005

[1] Self–regulation of the legal profession requires that members of the profession initiate disciplinary investigation when they know of a violation of the Rules of Professional Conduct. Lawyers have a similar obligation with respect to judicial misconduct. An apparently isolated violation may indicate a pattern of misconduct that only a disciplinary investigation can uncover. Reporting a violation is especially important where the victim is unlikely to discover the offense.

[2] A report about misconduct is not required where it would involve violation of Rule 1.6. However, a lawyer should encourage a client to consent to disclosure where prosecution would not substantially prejudice the client's interests.

[3] If a lawyer were obliged to report every violation of the rules, the failure to report any violation would itself be a professional offense. Such a requirement existed in many jurisdictions but proved to be unenforceable. This rule limits the reporting obligation to those offenses that a self-regulating profession must vigorously endeavor to prevent. A measure of judgment is, therefore, required in complying with the provisions of this rule. The term "substantial" refers to the seriousness of the possible offense and not the quantum of evidence of which the lawyer is aware. A report should be made to the bar disciplinary agency unless some other agency, such as a peer review agency, is more appropriate in the circumstances. Similar considerations apply to the reporting of judicial misconduct.

[4] The duty to report professional misconduct does not apply to a lawyer retained to represent a lawyer whose professional conduct is in question. Such a situation is governed by the rules applicable to the client- lawyer relationship.

[5] Information about a lawyer's or judge's misconduct or fitness may be received by a lawyer in the course of that lawyer's participation in a bona fide lawyers assistance program or other program that provides assistance, support or counseling to lawyers, including lawyers and judges who may be impaired due to chemical abuse or dependency, behavioral addictions, depression or other mental disorders. In that circumstance, providing for the confidentiality of information obtained by a lawyer-participant encourages lawyers and judges to participate and seek treatment through such programs. Conversely, without such confidentiality, lawyers and judges may hesitate to seek assistance, which may then result in additional harm to themselves, their clients, and the public. The rule therefore exempts lawyers participating in such programs from the reporting obligation of paragraphs (a) and (b) with respect to information they acquire while participating. A lawyer exempted from mandatory reporting under part (c) of the rule may nevertheless report misconduct in the lawyer's discretion, particularly if the impaired lawyer or judge indicates an intent to engage in future illegal activity, for example, the conversion of client funds. See the comments to Rule 1.6.

Historical Notes

This rule is similar, in part, to provisions of former DR 1–103(A) of the Minn. Code of Prof. Responsibility.

Rule 8.4. Misconduct

It is professional misconduct for a lawyer to:

(a) violate or attempt to violate the Rules of Professional Conduct, knowingly assist or induce another to do so, or do so through the acts of another;

(b) commit a criminal act that reflects adversely on the lawyer's honesty, trustworthiness, or fitness as a lawyer in other respects;

(c) engage in conduct involving dishonesty, fraud, deceit, or misrepresentation;

(d) engage in conduct that is prejudicial to the administration of justice;

(e) state or imply an ability to influence improperly a government agency or official or to achieve results by means that violate the Rules of Professional Conduct or other law;

(f) knowingly assist a judge or judicial officer in conduct that is a violation of applicable rules of judicial conduct or other law;

(g) harass a person on the basis of sex, race, age, creed, religion, color, national origin, disability, sexual orientation, or marital status in connection with a lawyer's professional activities;

(h) commit a discriminatory act prohibited by federal, state, or local statute or ordinance that reflects adversely on the lawyer's fitness as a lawyer. Whether a discriminatory act reflects adversely on a lawyer's fitness as a lawyer shall be determined after consideration of all the circumstances, including:

(1) the seriousness of the act,

(2) whether the lawyer knew that the act was prohibited by statute or ordinance,

(3) whether the act was part of a pattern of prohibited conduct, and

(4) whether the act was committed in connection with the lawyer's professional activities; or

(i) refuse to honor a final and binding fee arbitration award after agreeing to arbitrate a fee dispute.

Adopted June 13, 1985, eff. Sept. 1, 1985. Amended Dec. 27, 1989, eff. Jan. 1, 1990; April 14, 1992; June 17, 2005, eff. Oct. 1, 2005.

Comment—2005

[1] Lawyers are subject to discipline when they violate or attempt to violate the Rules of Professional Conduct, knowingly assist or induce another to do so or do so through the acts of another, as when they request or instruct an agent to do so on the lawyer's behalf. Paragraph (a), however, does not prohibit a lawyer from advising a client concerning action the client is legally entitled to take.

[2] Many kinds of illegal conduct reflect adversely on fitness to practice law, such as offenses involving fraud and the offense of willful failure to file an income tax return. Although a lawyer is personally answerable to the entire criminal law, a lawyer should be professionally answerable only for offenses that indicate lack of those characteristics relevant to the practice of law. Offenses involving violence, dishonesty, or breach of trust, or serious interference with the administration of justice are in that category. A pattern of repeated offenses, even ones of minor significance when considered separately, can indicate indifference to legal obligation.

[3] Lawyers holding public office assume legal responsibilities going beyond those of other citizens. A lawyer's abuse of public office can suggest an inability to fulfill the professional role of attorney. The same is true of abuse of positions of private trust such as trustee, executor, administrator, guardian, agent and officer, director or manager of a corporation or other organization.

[4] Paragraph (g) specifies a particularly egregious type of discriminatory act-harassment on the basis of sex, race, age, creed, religion, color, national origin, disability, sexual orientation, or marital status. What constitutes harassment in this context may be determined with reference to antidiscrimination legislation and case law thereunder. This harassment ordinarily involves the active burdening of another, rather than mere passive failure to act properly.

[5] Harassment on the basis of sex, race, age, creed, religion, color, national origin, disability, sexual orientation, or marital status may violate either paragraph (g) or paragraph (h). The harassment violates paragraph (g) if the lawyer committed it in connection with the lawyer's professional activities. Harassment, even if not committed in connection with the lawyer's professional activities, violates paragraph (h) if the harassment (1) is prohibited by antidiscrimination legislation and (2) reflects adversely on the lawyer's fitness as a lawyer, determined as specified in paragraph (h).

[6] Paragraph (h) reflects the premise that the concept of human equality lies at the very heart of our legal system. A lawyer whose behavior demonstrates hostility toward or indifference to the policy of equal justice under the law may thereby manifest a lack of character required of members of the legal profession. Therefore, a lawyer's discriminatory act prohibited by statute or ordinance may reflect adversely on his or her fitness as a lawyer even if the unlawful discriminatory act was not committed in connection with the lawyer's professional activities.

[7] Whether an unlawful discriminatory act reflects adversely on fitness as a lawyer is determined after consideration of all relevant circumstances, including the four factors listed in paragraph (h). It is not required that the listed factors be considered equally, nor is the list intended to be exclusive. For example, it would also be relevant that the lawyer reasonably believed that his or her conduct was protected under the state or federal constitution or that the lawyer was acting in a capacity for which the law provides an exemption from civil liability. *See, e.g.,* Minn. Stat. Section 317A.257 (unpaid director or officer of nonprofit organization acting in good faith and not willfully or recklessly).

[8] A lawyer may refuse to comply with an obligation imposed by law upon a good faith belief that no valid obligation exists. The provisions of Rule 1.2(d) concerning a good faith challenge to the validity, scope, meaning or application of the law apply to challenges of legal regulation of the practice of law.

Historical Notes

This rule is similar, in part, to provisions of former DR 1–102 and DR 9–101(C) of the Minn. Code of Prof. Responsibility.

Rule 8.5. Disciplinary Authority; Choice of Law

(a) Disciplinary Authority. A lawyer admitted to practice in this jurisdiction is subject to the disciplinary authority of this jurisdiction, regardless of where the lawyer's conduct occurs. A lawyer not admitted in this jurisdiction is also subject to the disciplinary authority of this jurisdiction if the lawyer provides or offers to provide any legal services in this jurisdiction. A lawyer may be subject to the disciplinary authority of both this jurisdiction and another jurisdiction for the same conduct.

(b) Choice of Law. In any exercise of the disciplinary authority of this jurisdiction, the rules of professional conduct to be applied shall be as follows:

(1) for conduct in connection with a matter pending before a tribunal, the rules of the jurisdiction in which the tribunal sits, unless the rules of the tribunal provide otherwise; and

(2) for any other conduct, the rules of the jurisdiction in which the lawyer's conduct occurred, or, if the predominant effect of the conduct is in a different jurisdiction, the rules of that jurisdiction shall be applied to the conduct. A lawyer shall not be subject to discipline if the lawyer's conduct conforms to the rules of a jurisdiction in which the lawyer reasonably believes the predominant effect of the lawyer's conduct will occur.

Adopted June 13, 1985, eff. Sept. 1, 1985. Amended June 17, 2005, eff. Oct. 1, 2005.

Comment—2005

Disciplinary Authority

[1] It is longstanding law that the conduct of a lawyer admitted to practice in this jurisdiction is subject to the disciplinary authority of this jurisdiction. Extension of the disciplinary authority of this jurisdiction to other lawyers who provide or offer to provide legal services in this jurisdiction is for the protection of the citizens of this jurisdiction. Reciprocal enforcement of a jurisdiction's disciplinary findings and sanctions will further advance the purposes of this rule.

See Rules 6 and 22, ABA *Model Rules for Lawyer Disciplinary Enforcement.* A lawyer who is subject to the disciplinary authority of this jurisdiction under Rule 8.5(a) is subject to service of process in accordance with Rule 12, Rules on Lawyers Professional Responsibility. The fact that the lawyer is subject to the disciplinary authority of this jurisdiction may be a factor in determining whether personal jurisdiction may be asserted over the lawyer for civil matters.

Choice of Law

[2] A lawyer potentially may be subject to more than one set of rules of professional conduct that impose different obligations. The lawyer may be licensed to practice in more than one jurisdiction with differing rules, or may be admitted to practice before a particular court with rules that differ from those of the jurisdiction or jurisdictions in which the lawyer is licensed to practice. Additionally, the lawyer's conduct may involve significant contacts with more than one jurisdiction.

[3] Paragraph (b) seeks to resolve such potential conflicts. Its premise is that minimizing conflicts between rules, as well as uncertainty about which rules are applicable, is in the best interests of both clients and the profession (as well as the bodies having authority to regulate the profession). Accordingly, it takes the approach of (i) providing that any particular conduct of a lawyer shall be subject to only one set of rules of professional conduct; (ii) making the determination of which set of rules applies to particular conduct as straightforward as possible, consistent with recognition of appropriate regulatory interests of relevant jurisdictions and (iii) providing protection from discipline for lawyers who act reasonably in the face of uncertainty.

[4] Paragraph (b)(1) provides that as to a lawyer's conduct relating to a proceeding pending before a tribunal, the lawyer shall be subject only to the rules of the jurisdiction in which the tribunal sits unless the rules of the tribunal, including its choice of law rule, provide otherwise. As to all other conduct, including conduct in anticipation of a proceeding not yet pending before a tribunal, paragraph (b) (2) provides that a lawyer shall be subject to the rules of the jurisdiction in which the lawyer's conduct occurred, or, if the predominant effect of the conduct is in another jurisdiction, the rules of that jurisdiction shall be applied to the conduct. In the case of conduct in anticipation of a proceeding that is likely to be before a tribunal, the predominant effect of such conduct could be where the conduct occurred, where the tribunal sits, or in another jurisdiction.

[5] When a lawyer's conduct involves significant contacts with more than one jurisdiction, it may not be clear whether the predominant effect of the lawyer's conduct will occur in a jurisdiction other than the one in which the conduct occurred. So long as the lawyer's conduct conforms to the rules of a jurisdiction in which the lawyer reasonably believes the predominant effect will occur, the lawyer shall not be subject to discipline under this rule.

[6] If two admitting jurisdictions were to proceed against a lawyer for the same conduct, they should, applying this rule, identify the same governing ethics rules. They should take all appropriate steps to see that they do apply the same rule to the same conduct, and in all events should avoid proceeding against a lawyer on the basis of two inconsistent rules.

[7] The choice of law provision applies to lawyers engaged in transnational practice, unless international law, treaties or other agreements between competent regulatory authorities in the affected jurisdictions provide otherwise.

APPENDIX 1. MAINTENANCE OF BOOKS AND RECORDS

Pursuant to Rule 1.15(i), Minnesota Rules of Professional Conduct (MRPC), and adoption of Appendix 1 to the Minnesota Rules of Professional Conduct by the Lawyers Professional Responsibility Board, the following books and records are required pursuant to Rule 1.15(h), MRPC:

Every attorney engaged in the private practice of law must maintain the books and records described in this

Appendix to comply with the applicable provisions of the MRPC relating to funds and property received and disbursed on behalf of clients or otherwise held in a fiduciary capacity. Equivalent books and records demonstrating the same information in an easily accessible manner and in substantially the same detail are acceptable. Books and records may be prepared manually or by computer.

I. **Trust Account Records.** The following books and records must be maintained for funds and property received and disbursed in a fiduciary capacity, whether for clients or for others:

1. An identification of all trust accounts maintained, including the name of the bank or other depository, account number, account name, date account opened, and an agreement with the bank establishing each account and its interest bearing nature. A record should also be maintained showing clearly the type of each such account whether pooled, with net interest paid to the IOLTA program, pooled with allocation of interest, or individual, including the client name. See Rules 1.15(e), (f)(1), and (f)(2), MRPC.
2. A check register for each trust account that chronologically shows all deposits and checks.
   a. Each deposit entry must include the date of the deposit, the amount, the identity of the client(s) for whom the funds were deposited, and the purpose of the deposit.
   b. Each check entry must include the date the check was issued, the payee, the amount, the identity of the client for whom the check was issued (if not the payee), and the purpose of the check.
3. Subsidiary ledgers for each client matter for whom the attorney receives trust funds.
   a. For every trust account transaction, attorneys must record on the appropriate client subsidiary ledger the date of receipt or disbursement, the amount, the payee and check number (for disbursements), the purpose of the transaction, and the balance of funds remaining in the account on behalf of that client matter. An attorney shall not disburse funds from the trust account that would create a negative balance on behalf of an individual client matter.
   b. A separate subsidiary ledger for nominal funds of the attorney held in the trust account pursuant to > Rule 1.15(a)(1), MRPC, to accommodate reasonably expected bank fees and charges. This ledger should also record any monthly service charges not offset or waived by the bank in the same month. A separate ledger should be maintained to record interest accrued but not transferred by the bank to the IOLTA program in the same month it is credited.
   c. An attorney maintaining non-IOLTA accounts pursuant to Rule 1.15(f), MRPC, shall record on each client subsidiary ledger the monthly accrual of interest, and the date and amount of each interest disbursement, including disbursements from accrued interest for costs of establishing and administering the account.
4. A monthly trial balance of the subsidiary ledgers identifying each client matter, the balance of funds held on behalf of the client matter at the end of each month, and the total of all the client balances. No balance for a client matter may be negative at any time.
5. A monthly reconciliation of the checkbook balance, the subsidiary ledger trial balance total, and the adjusted bank statement balance. The adjusted bank statement balance is determined from the month-end bank statement balance by adding outstanding deposits and subtracting outstanding checks.

   [Sample trial balances and reconciliations are available from the Office of Lawyers Professional Responsibility].
6. Bank statements, canceled checks or copies of canceled checks if they are provided with the bank statements, bank wire or electronic fund transfer confirmations and duplicate deposit slips. Cash fee payments must be documented by copies of receipts countersigned by the payor. Attorneys making deposits using substitute checks pursuant to the Check Clearing for the 21st Century Act must request and retain image statements from the bank for each such deposit. For withdrawal by bank wire or electronic fund transfer, an attorney or law firm must create a written memorandum authorizing the transaction, signed by the attorney responsible for the transaction. The bank wire or electronic fund transfer must be entered in the check register and include all the identifying information listed in paragraphs I(2)(b) and I(3)(a) of this Appendix.
7. **Electronic Record Retention.** An attorney who maintains trust account records by computer must print and retain, on a monthly basis, the checkbook register, the trial balance of the subsidiary ledgers, and the reconciliation report. The checkbook register must contain all of the information identified in paragraph 2. Electronic records should be regularly backed up by an appropriate storage device. The frequency of the back-up

procedure should be directly related to the volume of activity in the trust account.

8. A record showing all property, specifically identified, other than cash, held in trust from time-to-time for clients or others, provided that routine files, documents and items, such as real estate abstracts, which are not expected to be held indefinitely, need not be so recorded but should be documented in the files of the lawyer as to receipt and delivery.

II. **Business Account Records.** An attorney or law firm must maintain at least one bank account, other than the trust account, for funds and property received and disbursed outside the attorney's fiduciary capacity. The following books and records should be maintained for such accounts:

1. A record in the form of a fees book or file of copies of billing invoices reflecting all fees charged and other billings to clients.
2. Copies of receipts, countersigned by the payor, for all cash fee payments.
3. Check registers, bank statements, canceled checks, and duplicate deposit slips sufficient to establish the receipt of earned fee payments from clients, costs advanced on behalf of clients, and similar receipts and disbursements.
4. A periodic reconciliation of the checkbook balance and the bank statement balance.

PROFESSIONALISM ASPIRATIONS [1]

[1] A summary form of these Professionalism Aspirations is included at the end of the document. This summary version is intended to permit the standards to be posted, included in literature, or otherwise made available where the entire text would be cumbersome.

Adopted January 11, 2001

I. Our Legal System

A lawyer owes personal dignity, integrity, and independence to the administration of justice. A lawyer's conduct should be characterized at all times by personal courtesy and professional integrity in the fullest sense of those terms.

A. Respect And Dignity. We will uphold the respect and dignity of judges, each member of the Bar, the law and the legal system.

B. Honesty. We will conduct our affairs with candor and honesty. Our word is our bond.

C. Equal Access. We will dedicate and commit ourselves to equal access to the legal system.

D. Education. We will educate our clients, the public, and other lawyers regarding the spirit and letter of these Professional Aspirations.

E. Appearance of Impropriety. We will always endeavor to conduct ourselves in such a manner as to avoid even the appearance of impropriety.

II. Lawyer to Client

A lawyer owes allegiance, learning, skill, and industry to a client. As lawyers, we shall employ appropriate legal procedures to protect and advance our clients' legitimate rights, claims, and objectives. In fulfilling our duties to each client, we will be mindful of our obligation to the administration of justice, which is a truth-seeking process designed to resolve human and societal problems in a rational, peaceful, and efficient manner.

A. Independent Judgment.

1. We will be loyal and committed to our clients' lawful objectives, but will not permit that loyalty and commitment to interfere with our duty to provide objective and independent advice.

2. We will always be conscious of our duty to the system of justice.

3. We reserve the right to determine whether to grant accommodations to opposing counsel in all matters that do not adversely affect our clients' lawful objectives.

4. We will advise our clients, if necessary, that they do not have a right to demand that we engage in abusive or offensive conduct and we will not engage in such conduct.

5. We will neither encourage nor cause clients to do anything that would be unethical or inappropriate if done by us.

B. Proper Conduct on Behalf of Clients.

1. We will affirm among parties and other lawyers that civility and courtesy are expected and are not a sign of weakness.

2. We will endeavor to achieve our clients' legitimate objectives in our office practice work and in litigation as expeditiously and economically as possible.

3. We will not employ tactics that are designed primarily to delay resolution of a matter or to harass or drain the financial resources of the parties.

III. Lawyer to Lawyer

A lawyer owes courtesy, candor, cooperation, and compliance with all agreements and mutual understandings to opposing counsel, in the conduct of an office practice and in pursuit of the resolution of legal issues. As professionals, ill feelings between clients should not influence our conduct, attitude, or demeanor toward opposing counsel. Conduct that may be characterized as uncivil, abrasive, abusive, hostile, or obstructive impedes the fundamental goal of resolving disputes rationally, peacefully, and efficiently. A lawyer owes the same duty to an opposing party who is pro se.

A. Courtesy and Punctuality.

1. We will practice our profession with a continuing awareness that our role is to advance the legitimate interests of our clients. In our dealings with others we will not reflect the ill feelings of our clients. We will treat all other counsel, parties, and witnesses in a civil and courteous manner, not only in court, but also in all other written and oral communications.

2. We will not, even when called upon by a client to do so, abuse others or indulge in offensive conduct

directed to other counsel, parties, or witnesses. We will abstain from disparaging personal remarks or acrimony toward other counsel, parties, or witnesses. We will treat adverse witnesses and parties with fair consideration.

3. We will be courteous, civil and prompt in oral and written communications and punctual in honoring scheduled appearances, meetings, depositions, appointments, etc. with opposing counsel.

4. We will disagree without being disagreeable. We recognize that effective representation does not require antagonistic or obnoxious behavior.

5. We will not, without good cause, attribute bad motives or unethical conduct to opposing counsel nor bring the profession into disrepute by unfounded accusations or acrimony toward opposing counsel, parties, and witnesses.

6. We will not ask a witness or an opposing party a question solely for the purpose of harassing or embarrassing that individual.

7. We will adhere to all express promises and to agreements with other counsel, whether oral or in writing, and will adhere in good faith to all agreements implied by the circumstances or local customs.

B. Drafting.

1. We will not quarrel over matters of form or style, but concentrate on matters of substance.

2. We will try to achieve the common goal in the preparation of agreements.

3. When we purport to identify for other counsel or parties changes we make in documents submitted for their review, we will identify all such changes accurately.

4. We will carefully craft document production requests so they are limited to those documents we reasonably believe are necessary for the prosecution or defense of an action. We will not design production requests to place an undue burden or expense on a party.

5. We will respond to document requests reasonably and not strain to interpret the request in an artificially restrictive manner to avoid disclosure of relevant and non-privileged documents. We will not produce documents in a manner designed to hide or obscure the existence of particular documents.

6. When a draft order is to be prepared by counsel to reflect a court ruling, we will draft an order that accurately and completely reflects the court's ruling. We will promptly prepare and submit a proposed order to other counsel and attempt to reconcile any differences before the draft order is presented to the court.

C. Scheduling, Extensions, Cancellations.

1. We will not arbitrarily schedule a meeting, deposition, court appearance, hearing, or other proceeding until a good faith effort has been made to schedule it by agreement. If we are unable to contact the other lawyer, we will send written correspondence suggesting a time or times that will become operative unless an informal objection is directed to us within a set reasonable time.

2. We will endeavor in good faith to honor previously scheduled trial or hearing settings, vacations, seminars, meetings or other functions that produce good faith calendar conflicts on the part of opposing counsel. We will not seek accommodation from another member of the Bar for the rescheduling of any court setting, discovery, hearing, meeting, etc. unless a legitimate need exists.

3. We will agree to reasonable requests for extensions of time and for waiver of procedural formalities, provided legitimate objectives of our clients will not be adversely affected.

4. We will not request an extension of time solely for the purpose of unjustified delay or to obtain a tactical advantage.

5. We will notify other counsel and, if appropriate, the court or other persons, at the earliest possible time when hearings, depositions, meetings, or conferences are to be canceled or postponed.

D. Discovery.

1. We will make reasonable efforts to conduct discovery by agreement.

2. We will refrain from excessive and/or abusive discovery.

3. We will comply with all reasonable discovery requests. We will not resist discovery requests that are not objectionable.

4. We will not seek court intervention to obtain discovery that is clearly improper and not desirable.

5. We will take depositions only when actually needed to ascertain facts or information or to perpetuate testimony. We will not take depositions for the purposes of harassment or to increase litigation expenses.

6. During depositions we will ask only those questions we reasonably believe are necessary for the prosecution or defense of an action.

7. We will carefully craft interrogatories so they are limited to those matters we reasonably believe are necessary for the prosecution or defense of an action, and we will not design them to place an undue burden or expense on a party.

8. We will respond to interrogatories reasonably and will not strain to interpret them in an artificially restrictive manner to avoid disclosure of relevant and non-privileged information.

9. We will not engage in any conduct during a deposition that would not be appropriate in the presence of a judge. We will not make objections nor give instructions to a witness for the purpose of delaying or

obstructing the discovery process. We will encourage witnesses to respond to all deposition questions that are reasonably understandable.

10. We will not use any form of discovery or discovery scheduling as a means of harassment.

11. We will make good faith efforts to resolve by agreement our objections to matters contained in pleadings and discovery requests and objections.

E. Sanctions. We will not seek or threaten sanctions or disqualifications without first conducting a reasonable investigation and unless it is necessary for protection of our client's lawful objectives or fully justified by the circumstances.

F. Opportunity to Respond.

1. We will not serve motions, pleadings or briefs in any manner that unfairly limits another party's opportunity to respond. We will not seek ex parte relief without first attempting to notify the opposing party or attorney. We will not file memoranda or affidavits that are not permitted by court rules. We will furnish opposing counsel copies of all submissions to the court either contemporaneously or as soon as practical.

2. We will not cause a default or dismissal to be entered, when we know the identity of an opposing counsel, without first making a good faith attempt to inquire about the counsel's intention to proceed.

G. Settlement.

1. We will readily stipulate to undisputed facts in order to avoid needless costs or inconvenience for any party.

2. We will endeavor to confer early with other counsel to assess settlement possibilities. We will not falsely hold out the possibility of settlement as a means to adjourn discovery or to delay trial.

H. Request During Trial or Hearing. During trial or hearing we will honor reasonable requests of opposing counsel that do not prejudice the rights of our clients or sacrifice tactical advantage.

I. Conduct of Others. We will not encourage or knowingly authorize any person under our control to engage in conduct that would be improper if we were to engage in such conduct.

IV. Lawyer and Judge

Lawyers and judges owe each other respect, diligence, punctuality, and protection against unjust and improper criticism and attack. Lawyers and judges are equally responsible to protect the dignity and independence of the court and the profession.

A. Lawyers' Duties to Court and Administrative Tribunal.

1. We will speak and write civilly and respectfully in all communications with the court or administrative tribunal.

2. We will be punctual and prepared for all appearances so that all hearings, conferences, and trials may commence on time to the greatest extent possible.

3. We will be considerate of the time constraints and pressures on the court and court staff inherent in their efforts to administer justice.

4. We will not engage in any conduct that brings disorder or disruption to the courtroom or administrative hearing area. We will advise our clients and witnesses appearing in these settings of the proper conduct expected and required there and, to the best of our ability, prevent our clients and witnesses from creating disorder or disruption.

5. We will not knowingly misrepresent, mischaracterize, misquote, or miscite facts or authorities in any oral or written communication to the court or administrative hearing officer.

6. We will avoid argument or posturing through sending copies of correspondence between counsel to the court, unless specifically permitted or invited by the court.

7. Before dates for hearings or trials are set, or if that is not feasible, immediately after such dates have been set, we will attempt to verify the availability of necessary participants and witnesses so we can promptly notify the court of any problems.

8. We will act and speak civilly to all other court staff with an awareness that they, too, are an integral part of the judicial system.

B. The Duties of Judges, Referees, and Administrative Law Judges to Lawyers and Parties.

1. We will be courteous, respectful, and civil to lawyers, parties, and witnesses. We will maintain control of the proceedings, recognizing that we have both the obligation and the authority to insure that all proceedings are conducted in a civil manner.

2. If we observe a lawyer being uncivil to another lawyer or others, we will call it to the attention of the offending lawyer on our own initiative.

3. We will not employ hostile, demeaning, or humiliating words in opinions or in written or oral communications with lawyers, parties, or witnesses.

4. We will be punctual in convening all hearings, meetings, and conferences; if delayed, we will notify counsel, if possible.

5. In scheduling all hearings, meetings and conferences, we will be considerate of time schedules of lawyers, parties, and witnesses.

6. We will make all reasonable efforts to decide promptly all matters presented to us for decision.

7. We will give the issues in controversy deliberate, impartial, and studied analysis and consideration.

8. While endeavoring to resolve disputes efficiently, we will be considerate of the time constraints and

pressures imposed on lawyers by exigencies of litigation practice.

9. We recognize that a lawyer has a right and a duty to present a cause fully and properly, and that a party has a right to a fair and impartial hearing. Within the practical limits of time, we will allow lawyers to present proper arguments and to make a complete and accurate record.

10. We will not impugn the integrity or professionalism of any lawyer on the basis of the clients whom, or the causes which, a lawyer represents.

11. We will do our best to insure that court personnel act civilly toward lawyers, parties, and witnesses.

12. We will not adopt procedures that needlessly increase litigation expense.

C. The Duties of Judges, Referees, and Administrative Law Judges to Each Other.

1. We will be courteous, respectful, and civil in opinions, ever mindful that a position articulated by another judge is the result of that judge's earnest effort to interpret the law and the facts correctly.

2. In all written and oral communications, we will abstain from disparaging personal remarks, criticisms, or sarcastic or demeaning comments about another colleague.

3. We will endeavor to work with other judges in an effort to foster a spirit of cooperation in our mutual goal of enhancing the administration of justice.

Summary Standards

I. Our Legal System

A lawyer owes personal dignity, integrity, and independence to the administration of justice. A lawyer's conduct should be characterized at all times by personal courtesy and professional integrity in the fullest sense of those terms.

II. Lawyer to Client

A lawyer owes allegiance, learning, skill, and diligence to a client. As lawyers, we shall employ appropriate legal procedures to protect and advance our client's legitimate rights, claims, and objectives. In fulfilling our duties to each client, we will be mindful of our obligation to the administration of justice, which is a truth-seeking process designed to resolve human and societal problems in a rational, peaceful, and efficient manner.

III. Lawyer to Lawyer

A lawyer owes courtesy, candor, cooperation, and compliance with all agreements and mutual understandings to opposing counsel whether in the conduct of an office practice or in the pursuit of litigation. As professionals, ill feelings between clients should not influence our conduct, attitude, or demeanor toward opposing counsel. Conduct that may be characterized as uncivil, abrasive, abusive, hostile, or obstructive impedes the fundamental goal of resolving disputes rationally, peacefully, and efficiently. A lawyer owes the same duty to an opposing party who is pro se.

IV. Lawyer And Judge

Lawyers and judges owe each other respect, diligence, punctuality, and protection against unjust and improper criticism and attack. Lawyers and judges are equally responsible to protect the dignity and independence of the court and the profession.

LAWYERS PROFESSIONAL RESPONSIBILITY BOARD OPINIONS

Including Amendments Received Through January 1, 2014

Opinion

OPINION 1. THE LEGAL FORCE AND EFFECT OF OPINIONS ISSUED BY THE STATE BOARD OF PROFESSIONAL RESPONSIBILITY

It is the policy of the State Board of Professional Responsibility to issue, from time to time, advisory opinions as to the professional conduct of lawyers, whether as a result of a specific request or its own initiative, on matters deemed important by the Board.

The Board and the Supreme Court consider these opinions as rule interpretations that guide attorneys' professional conduct even though they are not binding on the Court. *See, In re Admonition Issued in Panel File No. 99-42,* 621 N.W.2d 240 (Minn. 2001).

Opinions issued by the Board will be subject to change from time to time as deemed necessary by the Board, or as required by decisions of the Minnesota Supreme Court.

Adopted October 27, 1972. Amended December 4, 1987; January 26, 2006.

OPINION 2. DEFENSE OF CRIMINAL CASES BY A COUNTY ATTORNEY [Repealed January 26, 2006]

OPINION 3. PRACTICE OF LAW BY PART-TIME JUDGES [Repealed October 25, 2002]

OPINION 4. WITHDRAWAL FOR NON-PAYMENT OF FEES [Repealed October 25, 2002]

OPINION 5. FAILURE TO COMPLY WITH FEE ARBITRATION DECISION [Repealed January 26, 2006]

OPINION 6. DEFENSE OF CRIMINAL CASES BY MUNICIPAL ATTORNEYS [Repealed January 26, 2006]

OPINION 7. INDEBTEDNESS INCURRED FOR PROFESSIONAL SERVICES ON BEHALF OF CLIENTS [Repealed January 7, 1983]

OPINION 8. ATTORNEYS' GUIDELINES FOR LAW OFFICE SERVICES BY NON-LAWYERS

Except to the extent permitted by the Supreme Court of the State of Minnesota, (e.g., Student Practice Rules) neither law students nor any other person not duly admitted to the practice of law shall be named on pleadings under any identification.

Legal assistants, or other paralegal employees, may be listed on professional cards, professional announcement cards, office signs, letterheads, telephone directory listings, law lists, legal directory listings, or similar professional notices or devices, so long as the paralegals are clearly identified as such, and so long as no false, fraudulent, misleading, or deceptive statements or claims are made concerning said paralegals, their legal status and authority, or their relationships to the firms by which they are employed. Paralegals may use business cards so identifying themselves, which cards carry the law firm's name and address.

Such a paralegal, so identified, may sign correspondence on behalf of the law firm, provided he or she does so by direction of an attorney-employer.

Non-lawyers must be supervised by an attorney who is responsible for their work. See, Rules 5.3 and 5.5 and Comments, Minnesota Rules of Professional Conduct.

Adopted June 26, 1974. Amended June 18, 1980; December 4, 1987; January 26, 2006.

OPINION 9. MAINTENANCE OF BOOKS AND RECORDS [Repealed January 26, 2006]

OPINION 10. DEBT COLLECTION PROCEDURES [Repealed October 25, 2002]

OPINION 11. ATTORNEYS' LIENS [Repealed January 26, 2006]

OPINION 12. TRUST ACCOUNT SIGNATORIES [Repealed January 26, 2006]

OPINION 13. COPYING COSTS OF CLIENT FILES, PAPERS AND PROPERTY

Client files, papers and property, whether printed or electronically stored, shall include:

1. All papers and property provided by the client to the lawyer.

2. All pleadings, motions, discovery, memorandums, and other litigation materials which have been executed and served or filed regardless of whether the client has paid the lawyer for drafting and serving and/or filing the document(s).

3. All correspondence regardless of whether the client has paid the lawyer for drafting or sending the correspondence.

4. All items for which the lawyer has advanced costs and expenses regardless of whether the client has reimbursed the lawyer for the costs and expenses including depositions, expert opinions and statements, business records, witness statements, and other materials which may have evidentiary value.

Client files, papers and property, whether printed or electronically stored, shall not include:

1. Pleadings, discovery, motion papers, memoranda and correspondence which have been drafted, but not sent or served if the client has not paid for legal services in drafting or creating the documents.

2. In non-litigation settings, client files, papers and property shall not include drafted but unexecuted estate plans, title opinions, articles of incorporation, contracts, partnership agreements, or any other unexecuted document which does not otherwise have legal effect, where the client has not paid the lawyer for the services in drafting the document(s).

A lawyer who has withdrawn from representation or has been discharged from representation, may charge a former client for the costs of copying or electronically retrieving the client's files, papers and property only if the client has, prior to termination of the lawyer's services, agreed in writing to such a charge. Such copying charges must be reasonable. Copying charges which substantially exceed the charges of a commercial copy service are normally unreasonable.

A lawyer may not condition the return of client files, papers and property on payment of copying costs. Nor may the lawyer condition return of client files, papers or property upon payment of the lawyer's fee. *See* Rule 1.16(g), Minnesota Rules of Professional Conduct.

A lawyer may withhold documents not constituting client files, papers and property until the outstanding fee is paid unless the client's interests will be substantially prejudiced without the documents. Such circumstances shall include, but not necessarily be limited to, expiration of a statute of limitations or some other litigation imposed deadline. A lawyer who withholds documents not constituting client files, papers or property for nonpayment of fees may not assert a claim against the client for the fees incurred in preparing or creating the withheld document(s).

Adopted June 15, 1989. Amended January 22, 2010.

OPINION 14. ATTORNEY LIENS ON CLIENT HOMESTEADS [Repealed April 4, 2003]

OPINION 15. ADVANCE FEE PAYMENTS AND AVAILABILITY OR NON-REFUNDABLE RETAINERS [Repealed January 26, 2006]

OPINION 16. INTEREST AND LATE CHARGES ON ATTORNEYS FEES [Repealed October 25, 2002]

OPINION 17. ACCEPTING GRATUITIES FROM COURT REPORTING SERVICES AND OTHER SIMILAR SERVICES

A lawyer ought not to accept, or to permit any nonlawyer employee to accept, a gratuity offered by a court reporting service or other similar service for which a client is expected to pay unless the client consents after consultation. However, a lawyer may accept nominal gifts, such as pens, coffee mugs, and other similar advertising-type gifts without consent of the client. *See* Rules 1.4, 1.5(a), 1.8(f)(1) and 5.3, Minnesota Rules of Professional Conduct (MRPC). *See also* Rule 1.0(c), MRPC.

Adopted June 18, 1993. Amended January 26, 2006.

OPINION 18. SECRET RECORDINGS OF CONVERSATIONS [Repealed April 18, 2002]

OPINION 19. USING TECHNOLOGY TO COMMUNICATE CONFIDENTIAL INFORMATION TO CLIENTS

A lawyer may use technological means such as electronic mail (e-mail) and cordless and cellular telephones to communicate confidential client information without violating Rule 1.6, Minnesota Rules of Professional Conduct (MRPC). Such use is subject to the following conditions:

1. E-mail without encryption may be used to transmit and receive confidential client information;

2. Digital cordless and cellular telephones may be used by a lawyer to transmit and receive confidential client information when used within a digital service area;

3. When the lawyer knows, or reasonably should know, that a client or other person is using an insecure means, to communicate with the lawyer about confidential client information, the lawyer shall consult with the client about the confidentiality risks associated with inadvertent interception and obtain the client's consent.

Adopted January 22, 1999. Amended January 22, 2010.

Comment

A lawyer may not knowingly reveal a confidence or secret of a client. Rule 1.6(a)(1). A lawyer should exercise care to prevent unintended disclosure. See Comment to Rule 1.6. For example, the lawyer should avoid professional discussions in the company of persons to whom the attorney-client privilege does not extend. Id. Similarly, a lawyer should take reasonable steps to prevent interception or unintended disclosure of confidential communications. All communication carries with it some such risk, for example by eavesdropping, wiretapping, or theft of mail. The precautions to be taken by a lawyer depend on the circumstances, including the sensitivity of the information, the manner of communication, the apparent risks of interception or unintended disclosure, and the client's wishes.

The purpose of this opinion is to address concerns that certain devices or methods may not be used by lawyers to communicate client confidences or secrets because they do not guarantee security. The committee believes absolute security is not required, and that the use of new technology is subject to the same analysis as the use of more traditional methods of communication.

This opinion reflects the prevalent view of other states and technology experts, that communications by facsimile, e-mail, and digital cordless or cellular phones, like those by mail and conventional corded telephone, generally are considered secure; their interception involves intent, expertise, and violation of federal law. Some states have required client consent or encryption for the use of e-mail, but the majority of recent state ethics opinions sanction the use of e-mail without such requirements. The committee finds the reasoning of the latter opinions persuasive.

The opinion intentionally omits facsimile machines, which typically transmit data over conventional telephone lines. With facsimile machines, the concerns are less with interception than with unintended dissemination of the communication at its destination, where the communication may be received in a common area of the workplace or home and may be read by persons other than the intended recipient. The Director has received client complaints involving such situations and cautions lawyers to take reasonable precautions to prevent unintended dissemination. Similar concerns may be raised by voice-mail and answering machine messages.

OPINION 20. USE OF THE WORD "ASSOCIATES" IN A LAW FIRM NAME

The use of the word "Associates" or the phrase "& Associates" in a law firm name, letterhead or other professional designation is false and misleading if the use conveys the impression the law firm has more attorneys practicing law in the firm than is actually the case.

Adopted June 18, 2009.

Comment

Subject to qualifications below, the use of the word "Associates" in a law firm name, letterhead or other professional designation—such as "Doe Associates"—is false and misleading if there are not at least two licensed attorneys practicing law with the firm. Similarly, the use of the phrase "& Associates" in a firm name, letterhead or other professional designation—such as "Doe & Associates"—is false and misleading if there are not at least three licensed attorneys practicing law with the firm.

Rule 7.5(a), Minnesota Rules of Professional Conduct ("MRPC"), states:

> A lawyer shall not use a firm name, letterhead, or other professional designation that violates Rule 7.1. A trade name may be used by a lawyer in private practice if it . . . is not otherwise in violation of Rule 7.1.

Comment 1 to Rule 7.5, MRPC, states, in pertinent part, that "the use of trade names . . . is acceptable so long as it is not misleading."

Rule 7.1, MRPC, states:

A lawyer shall not make a false or misleading communication about the lawyer or the lawyer's services. A communication is false or misleading if it contains a material misrepresentation of fact or law, or omits a fact necessary to make the statement considered as a whole not materially misleading.

Comment 2 to Rule 7.1, MRPC, provides:

Truthful statements that are misleading are also prohibited by this rule. A truthful statement is misleading if it omits a fact necessary to make the lawyer's communication considered as a whole not materially misleading. A truthful statement is also misleading if there is a substantial likelihood that it will lead a reasonable person to formulate a specific conclusion about the lawyer or the lawyer's services for which there is no reasonable factual foundation.

While the word "Associates" and the phrase "& Associates" undoubtedly have other meanings and connotations in other contexts, in the practice of law the word and the phrase have been used and are perceived as referring to an attorney practicing law in a law firm. *See In re Sussman*, 405 P.2d 355, 356 (Or. 1965) ("Principally through custom the word ["associates"] when used on the letterheads of law firms has come to be regarded as describing those who are employees of the firm. Because the word has acquired this special significance in connection with the practice of law the use of the word to describe lawyer relationships other than that of employer-employee is likely to be misleading."); St. B. of N.M. Ethics Advisory Comm., Formal Op. 2006–1 (2006) ("It is well accepted in the legal community that an 'associate' is an attorney that works for a firm. 'Associates,' at least in the legal context, do not include support staff such as legal assistants or investigators."); Ass'n of the B. of the City of N.Y. Comm. on Prof'l & Jud. Ethics, Formal Op. 1996–8 (1996), 1996 WL 416301 ("[T]he term ['associate'] has been interpreted by courts and other ethics committees to mean a salaried lawyer-employee who is not a partner of a firm."); Utah St. B. Ethics Advisory Op. Comm., Op. 04–03 (2004), 2004 WL 1304775 ("We believe that, if a member of the public examined a firm name such as 'John Doe & Associates,' he would conclude that John Doe works regularly with at least two other lawyers.").

While some members of the public may care little about the number of attorneys practicing law at a law firm, clearly some members of the public seeking legal counsel do care whether there is more than one attorney at a firm available to provide legal services. "A client may wish to be represented by a law firm comprised of several or many lawyers, and the implications of the law firm name may affect the client's decision. Any communication that suggests multiple lawyers creates the appearance that the totality of the lawyers of the law firm could and would be available to render legal counsel to any prospective client ..." Cal. St. B. Standing Comm. on Prof'l Responsibility & Conduct, Formal Op. 1986–90 (1986), 1986 WL 69070 (opining that solo practitioners may not ethically advertise using a group trade name such as "XYZ Associates" unless the advertisement affirmatively discloses they are solo practitioners). A law firm name which suggests there are multiple attorneys to service a client's needs when there is only one attorney is inherently misleading.

The Board's opinion is consistent with decisions and ethics opinions from other jurisdictions which have held that the use of "associates" in the name of a law firm with one practicing lawyer is false and misleading. *See, e.g., In re Mitchell*, 614 S.E.2d 634 (S.C. 2005) (holding a solo practitioner made false and misleading communications by using the word "associates" in his firm name); *In re Brandt*, 670 N.W.2d 552, 554–55 (Wis. 2003) (solo practitioner holding himself out as "Brandt & Associates" was in violation of ethics rule prohibiting false and misleading communications); *Portage County B. Ass'n v. Mitchell*, 800 N.E.2d 1106 (Ohio 2003) (solo practitioner engaged in misleading conduct by holding himself out as "Mitchell and Associates"); *Office of Disciplinary Counsel v. Furth*, 754 N.E.2d 219, 224, 231 (Ohio 2001) (a solo practitioner's use of letterhead referring to his firm as "Tom Furth and Associates, Attorneys & Counselors at Law" was misleading); S.C. B. Ethics Advisory Comm., Op. 05–19 (2005), 2005 WL 3873354 (opining that a solo practitioner's use of a firm name such as "John Doe and Associates, P.A." is misleading); Utah St. B. Ethics Advisory Op. Comm., Op. 138 (1994), 1994 WL 579848 ("[A] sole practitioner may not use a firm name of the type 'Doe & Associates' if he has no associated attorneys, even if the firm formerly had such associates or employs one or more associated nonlawyers such as paralegals or investigators.").

The use of "Associates" or "& Associates" in a firm name, letterhead or other professional designation by lawyers who share office space or who associate with other lawyers on a particular legal matter but who do not otherwise practice together as a law firm is false and misleading.

Whether or not a law firm name using the word "Associates" or the phrase "& Associates" is false and misleading will depend on the particular facts and circumstances of each case. For example, there may be circumstances where three attorneys with a law firm name such as "Doe & Associates" may lose one of the firm's attorneys. In that event, if another attorney joins the firm within a reasonable period of time thereafter, or if the firm reasonably and objectively anticipates another attorney joining the firm within a reasonable period of time, it is not false or misleading for the firm to continue using "& Associates" in its name during the interim period. If neither circumstance exists, the continued use of "& Associates" would be considered false and misleading. In addition, there may be circumstances where one or more of the attorneys practicing with a firm may be working part-time. As long as the requisite minimum number of attorneys, part-time or otherwise, regularly and actively practice with the firm, the use of "Associates" or "& Associates" would not be considered false or misleading.

The proper use of "Associates" or "& Associates" in a firm name, letterhead or other professional designation previously has not been the subject of guidance from the Board. Therefore, the Office of Lawyers Professional Responsibility will defer invoking this opinion in disciplinary proceedings under Rules 7.1 and 7.5, MRPC, until January 1, 2010. For the same reason, to the extent a lawyer has already contracted for an advertisement or other promotional material using a name contrary to Opinion No. 20, the continued availability of the advertisement or other material for the duration of the contract term should not be the basis for discipline.

OPINION 21. A LAWYER'S DUTY TO CONSULT WITH A CLIENT ABOUT THE LAWYER'S OWN MALPRACTICE

A lawyer who knows that the lawyer's conduct could reasonably be the basis for a non-frivolous malpractice claim by a current client that materially affects the client's interests has one or more duties to act under the Minnesota Rules of Professional Conduct. The requirements of Rules 1.4 and 1.7 are implicated in such a circumstance and the lawyer must determine what actions may be required under the Rules, with particular attention to Rules 1.4 and 1.7.

Since the possibility of a malpractice claim that arises during representation may cause a lawyer to be concerned with the prospect of legal liability for the malpractice, the provisions of Rule 1.7 dealing with a "concurrent conflict of interest" must be considered to determine whether the personal interest of the lawyer poses a significant risk that the continued representation of the client will be materially limited. [1] Under Rule 1.7 the lawyer must withdraw from continued representation unless circumstances giving rise to an exception are present. [2] Assuming continued representation is not otherwise prohibited, to continue the representation the lawyer must reasonably believe he or she may continue to provide competent and diligent representation. [3] If so, the lawyer must obtain the client's "informed consent," confirmed in writing, to the continued representation. [4] Whenever the rules require a client to provide "informed consent," the lawyer is under a duty to promptly disclose to the client the circumstances giving rise to the need for informed consent. [5] In this circumstance, "informed consent" requires that the lawyer communicate adequate information and explanation about the material risks of and reasonably available alternatives to the continued representation. [6]

Regardless of whether the possibility of a malpractice claim creates a conflict of interest under Rule 1.7, the lawyer also has duties of communication with the client under Rule 1.4 that may apply. When the lawyer knows the lawyer's conduct may reasonably be the basis for a non-frivolous malpractice claim by a current client that materially affects the client's interests, the lawyer shall inform the client about that conduct to the extent necessary to achieve each of the following objectives:

1) keeping the client reasonably informed about the status of the representation, [7]

2) permitting the client to make informed decisions regarding the representation, [8]

3) assuring reasonable consultation with the client about the means by which the client's objectives are to be accomplished. [9]

Adopted October 2, 2009.

1 Rule 1.7(a)(2).

2 Rule 1.7(a).

3 Rule 1.7(b)(1) and (2).

4 Rule 1.7(b)(4).

5 Rule 1.4(a)(1).

6 Rule 1.0(f).

7 Rule 1.4 (a)(3).

8 Rule 1.4 (b).

9 Rule 1.4 (a)(2).

Comment

The issue of when and what to say to a client when a lawyer knows that the lawyer's conduct described in Opinion 21 could reasonably be expected to be the basis for a malpractice claim is difficult and may create inherent conflicts. The Board is issuing Opinion No. 21 to apprise the Bar of the Board's position on the matter and to provide guidance to lawyers who may confront the issue.

In consulting with the current client about the possible malpractice claim, the lawyer should bear in mind Comment 5 to Rule 1.4, which provides that "[t]he guiding principle is that the lawyer should fulfill reasonable client expectations for information consistent with the duty to act in the client's best interests, and the client's overall requirements as to the character of representation."

Other jurisdictions have recognized a lawyer's ethical duty to disclose to the client conduct which may constitute malpractice. *See, e.g., Tallon v. Comm. on Prof'l Standards*, 447 N.Y.S.2d 50, 51 (App. Div. 1982) ("An attorney has a professional duty to promptly notify his client of his failure to act and of the possible claim his client may thus have against him."); Colo. B. Ass'n Ethics Comm., Formal Op. 113 (2005) ("When, by act or omission, a lawyer has made an error, and that error is likely to result in prejudice to a client's right or claim, the lawyer must promptly disclose the error to the client."); Wis. St. B. Prof'l Ethics Comm., Formal Op. E–82–12 ("[A]n attorney is obligated to inform his or her client that an omission has occurred which may constitute malpractice and that the client may have a claim against him or her for such an omission."); N.Y. St. B. Ass'n Comm. on Prof'l Ethics, Op. 734 (2000), 2000 WL 33347720 (Generally, an attorney "has an obligation to report to the client that [he or she] has made a significant error or omission that may give rise to a possible malpractice claim."); N.J. Sup. Ct. Advisory Comm. on Prof'l Ethics, Op. 684 ("The Rules of Professional Conduct still require an attorney to notify the client that he or she may have a legal malpractice claim even if notification is against the attorney's own interest.").

In re SRC Holding Corp., 352 B.R. 103 (Bankr. D. Minn. 2006), aff'd in part and rev'd in part *In re SRC Holding Corp.*, 364 B.R. 1 (D. Minn. 2007), reversed *Leonard v. Dorsey & Whitney LLP*, 553 F.3d 609 (8th Cir. 2009) discuss certain matters addressed in Opinion 21. In *Leonard*, the Eighth Circuit held that the bankruptcy court had relied too heavily on ethics rules in determining whether the law firm had violated a legal duty to consult with its client about the law firm's possible malpractice. The Eighth Circuit said "[d]emonstrating that an ethics rule has been violated, by itself, does not give rise to a cause of action against the lawyer and does not give rise to a presumption that a legal duty has been breached." 553 F.3d 628. In predicting how the Minnesota Supreme Court would rule on an attorney's legal duty to consult with a client about the law firm's possible malpractice, the Eighth Circuit did not opine on a law firm's ethical duties to consult about such a claim. Recognizing the distinction, this Opinion does not opine on a law firm's legal duties to consult about such a claim.

A lawyer's obligation to report a possible malpractice claim to the lawyer's client also is discussed in a local article written by Charles E. Lundberg, entitled *Self-Reporting Malpractice or Ethics Problems*, 60 Bench & B. of Minn. 8, Sept. 2003, and more recently and extensively in Benjamin P. Cooper's article, *The Lawyer's Duty to Inform His Client of His Own Malpractice*, 61 Baylor L. Rev. 174 (2009) and Brian Pollock's article, *Surviving a Screwup*, 34 ABA Litig. Mag. 2, Winter 2008.

OPINION 22. A LAWYER'S ETHICAL OBLIGATIONS REGARDING METADATA

A lawyer has a duty under the Minnesota Rules of Professional Conduct (MRPC), not to knowingly reveal information relating to the representation of a client, except as otherwise provided by the Rules, and a duty to act competently to safeguard information relating to the representation of a client against inadvertent or unauthorized disclosure. *See* Rules 1.1, 1.6, MRPC. The lawyer's duties with respect to such information extends to and includes metadata in electronic documents. Accordingly, a lawyer is ethically required to act competently to avoid improper disclosure of confidential and privileged information in metadata in electronic documents.

If a lawyer receives a document which the lawyer knows or reasonably should know inadvertently contains confidential or privileged metadata, the lawyer shall promptly notify the document's sender as required by Rule 4.4(b), MRPC.

Adopted March 26, 2010.

Comment

Metadata Generally

Metadata, sometimes defined as data within data, is used in this Opinion to refer to information generated and embedded in electronically created documents. Metadata is generated automatically by software when an electronic document is created, accessed and modified and typically may include such information as the date the document was created, the author, and the date changes were made to the document. Other times metadata may be purposely created, such as when the author adds comments or other information visible in the document's electronic format but which may not be visible in its printed version. When electronic documents are transmitted electronically—for example, as a Word document attached to an e-mail —the metadata is transmitted with the document.

Metadata can be "scrubbed" or removed from an electronic document by various means, including the use of special software programs or by scanning a printed copy of the document and sending it in a PDF format. Transmission of metadata can also be avoided by transmitting hard copies of the document rather than electronic copies or by faxing the document.

Metadata embedded in an electronic document can be "mined" or viewed by a recipient of the document. Some metadata can be accessed simply by right-clicking a mouse or selecting "properties" or "show markup" on a Word document. Other metadata can be accessed by the use of special software programs.

There are many types of metadata, many ways of creating metadata, and many means for removing and accessing metadata, all of which will undoubtedly continue to expand and evolve with technological innovation.

Most metadata is not confidential, and the disclosure of metadata may often be intentional and for the mutual benefit of clients with adverse interests. Other metadata may contain confidential information the disclosure of which can have serious adverse consequences to a client. For example, a lawyer may use a template for pleadings, discovery and affidavits which contain metadata within the document with names and other important information about a particular matter which should not be disclosed to another party in another action. Also as an example, a lawyer may circulate within the lawyer's firm a draft pleading or legal memorandum on which other lawyers may add comments about the strengths and weaknesses of a client's position which are embedded in the document but not apparent in the document's printed form. Similarly, documents used in negotiating a price to pay in a transaction or in the settlement of a lawsuit may contain metadata about how much or how little one side or the other may be willing to pay or to accept.

Due to the hidden, or not readily visible, nature of metadata and the ease with which electronic documents can be transmitted, a potential exists for the inadvertent disclosure of confidential or privileged information in the form of metadata in both a litigation and non-litigation setting, which in turn could give rise to violations of a lawyer's ethical duties.

Applicable Rules

Rule 1.1, Minnesota Rules of Professional Conduct (MRPC), states that "[a] lawyer shall provide competent representation to a client." Comment 5 to Rule 1.1 provides that "[c]ompetent handling of a particular matter includes . . . use of methods and procedures meeting the standards of competent practitioners."

As noted in American Bar Association Formal Opinion 06–442 (2006) at 1:

In modern legal practice, lawyers regularly receive email, sometimes with attachments such as proposed contracts, from opposing counsel and other parties. Lawyers also routinely receive electronic documents that have been made available by opponents, such as archived e-mail and other documents relevant to potential transactions or to past events. Receipt may occur in the course of negotiations, due diligence review, litigation, investigation, and other circumstances.

Competence requires that lawyers who use electronic documents understand that metadata is created in the generation of electronic documents, that transmission of electronic documents will include transmission of metadata, that recipients of the documents can access metadata, and that actions can be taken to prevent or minimize the transmission of metadata.

Rule 1.6(a), MRPC, states that, "[e]xcept when permitted under paragraph (b), a lawyer shall not knowingly reveal information relating to the representation of a client." Comment 2 to the rule explains that "[a] fundamental principle in the client-lawyer relationship is that, in the absence of the client's informed consent, the lawyer must not reveal information relating to the representation." Comment 15 provides that "[a] lawyer must act competently to safeguard information relating to the representation of a client against inadvertent or unauthorized disclosure by the lawyer or other persons who are participating in the representation of the client or who are subject to the lawyer's supervision"; and Comment 16 further provides that "when transmitting a communication that includes information relating to the representation of a client, the lawyer must take reasonable precautions to prevent the information from coming into the hands of unintended recipients."

Opinion No. 22 makes clear that the duty imposed by Rule 1.6(a), MRPC, regarding client information extends to and includes metadata in electronic documents. Thus, a lawyer must take reasonable steps to prevent the disclosure of confidential metadata. *See* ABA/BNA Lawyers' Manual on Professional Conduct 55:401 (2008) ("When a lawyer sends, receives, or stores client information in electronic form, the lawyer's duty to protect that information from disclosure to unauthorized individuals is the same as it is for information communicated or kept in any other form.").

Rule 4.4(b), MRPC, states that "[a] lawyer who receives a document relating to the representation of the lawyer's client and knows or reasonably should know that the document was inadvertently sent shall promptly notify the sender." Comment 2 to the Rule explains that lawyers sometimes receive documents that were mistakenly sent and that "[i]f a lawyer knows or reasonably should know that such a document was sent inadvertently, then this rule requires the lawyer to promptly notify the sender in order to permit that person to take protective measures." Comment 2 states that "[f]or purposes of this rule, 'document' includes email or other electronic modes of transmission subject to being read or put into readable form. Opinion No. 22 makes clear that the duty imposed by Rule 4.4(b) regarding documents extends to metadata in electronic documents.

"Whether the lawyer is required to take additional steps, such as returning the original document, is a matter of law beyond the scope of these Rules, as is the question of whether the privileged status of a document has been waived." Comment 2 to Rule 4.4, MRPC.

The generation, transmittal and receipt of documents containing metadata also implicates ethical obligations under Rules 5.1 and 5.3, MRPC.

Opinion 22 is not meant to suggest there is an ethical obligation on a receiving lawyer to look or not to look for metadata in an electronic document. Whether and when a lawyer may be advised to look or not to look for such metadata is a fact specific question beyond the scope of this Opinion.

A lawyer may be subject to a number of obligations other than those provided by the MRPC in connection with the transmission and receipt of metadata, including obligations under the Federal Rules of Civil Procedure and the Minnesota Rules of Civil Procedure. Removing metadata from evidentiary documents in the context of litigation or in certain other circumstances may be impermissible or illegal. Opinion No. 22 addresses only a lawyer's ethical obligations regarding metadata under the Minnesota Rules of Professional Conduct.

Adopted: March 26, 2010.

RULES ON LAWYERS PROFESSIONAL RESPONSIBILITY

Effective January 1, 1989

Including Amendments Received Through January 1, 2014

Research Note

See Minnesota Statutes Annotated, *Volume 52, for case annotations and cross references.*

These rules may be searched electronically on Westlaw in the MN–RULES database; updates to these rules may be found on Westlaw in MN–RULESUPDATES. For search tips and a summary of database content, consult the Westlaw Scope Screens for each database.

RULE 1. DEFINITIONS

As used in these Rules:

(1) "Board" means the Lawyers Professional Responsibility Board.

(2) "Chair" means the Chair of the Board.

(3) "Executive Committee" means the committee appointed by the Chair under Rule 4(d).

(4) "Director" means the Director of the Office of Lawyers Professional Responsibility.

(5) "District Bar Association" includes the Range Bar Association.

(6) "District Chair" means the Chair of a District Bar Association's Ethics Committee.

(7) "District Committee" means a District Bar Association's Ethics Committee.

(8) "Notify" means to give personal notice or to mail to the person at the person's last known address or the address maintained on this Court's attorney registration records, or to the person's attorney if the person is represented by counsel.

(9) "Panel" means a panel of the Board.

Adopted Nov. 1, 1976, eff. Jan. 1, 1977. Amended June 18, 1986, eff. July 1, 1986; April 27, 1987, eff. July 1, 1987; Sept. 14, 1988, eff. Jan. 1, 1989; Feb. 11, 1991, eff. March 1, 1991.

RULE 2. PURPOSE

It is of primary importance to the public and to the members of the Bar that cases of lawyers' alleged disability or unprofessional conduct be promptly investigated and disposed of with fairness and justice, having in mind the public, the lawyer complained of and the profession as a whole, and that disability or disciplinary proceedings be commenced in those cases where investigation discloses they are warranted. Such investigations and proceedings shall be conducted in accordance with these Rules.

Adopted Nov. 1, 1976, eff. Jan. 1, 1977. Amended July 22, 1982; June 18, 1986, eff. July 1, 1986; April 27, 1987, eff. July 1, 1987; Sept. 14, 1988, eff. Jan. 1, 1989.

RULE 3. DISTRICT ETHICS COMMITTEE

(a) Composition. Each District Committee shall consist of:

(1) A Chair appointed by this Court for such time as it designates and serving at the pleasure of this Court but not more than six years as Chair; and

(2) Four or more persons whom the District Bar Association (or, upon failure thereof, this Court) may appoint to three-year terms except that shorter terms shall be used where necessary to assure that approximately one-third of all terms expire annually. No person may serve more than two consecutive three-year terms, nor more than a total of four three-year terms, in addition to any additional shorter term for which the person was originally appointed and any period served as District Chair. At least 20 percent of each District Committee's members shall be nonlawyers. Every effort shall be made to appoint lawyer members from the various areas of practice. The Board shall monitor District Committee compliance with this objective and the District Committee shall include information on compliance in its annual report to the Court.

(b) Duties. The District Committee shall investigate complaints of lawyers' alleged unprofessional conduct and make reports and recommendations thereon as provided in these Rules in a format prescribed by the Executive Committee. It shall meet at least annually and from time to time as required. The District Chair shall prepare and submit an annual report to the Board and this Court in a format specified by the Executive Committee and make such other reports as the Executive Committee may require.

Adopted Nov. 1, 1976, eff. Jan. 1, 1977. Amended June 18, 1986, eff. July 1, 1986; April 27, 1987, eff. July 1, 1987; Sept. 14, 1988, eff. Jan. 1, 1989; Feb. 11, 1991, eff. March 1, 1991.

RULE 4. LAWYERS PROFESSIONAL RESPONSIBILITY BOARD

(a) Composition. The Board shall consist of:

(1) A Chair appointed by this Court for such time as it designates and serving at the pleasure of this Court but not more than six years as Chair; and

(2) Thirteen lawyers having their principal office in this state, six of whom the Minnesota State Bar Association may nominate, and nine nonlawyers resident in this State, all appointed by this Court to three-year terms except that shorter terms shall be used where necessary to assure that as nearly as may be one-third of all terms expire each February 1. No person may serve more than two three-year terms, in addition to any additional shorter term for which the person was originally appointed and any period served as Chair. To the extent possible, members shall be geographically representative of the state and lawyer members shall reflect a broad cross section of areas of practice.

(b) Compensation. The Chair, other Board members, and other panel members shall serve without compensation, but shall be paid their reasonable and necessary expenses incurred in the performance of their duties.

(c) Duties. The Board shall have general supervisory authority over the administration of the Office of Lawyers Professional Responsibility and these Rules, and may, from time to time, issue opinions on questions of professional conduct. The Board shall prepare and submit to this Court an annual report covering the operation of the lawyer discipline and disability system. The Board may elect a Vice–Chair and specify the Vice–Chair's duties. Board meetings are open to the public, except the Board may go into closed session not open to the public to discuss matters protected by Rule 20 or for other good cause.

(d) Executive Committee. The Executive Committee, consisting of the Chair, and two lawyers and two nonlawyers designated annually by the Chair, shall be responsible for carrying out the duties set forth in these Rules and for the general supervision of the Office of Lawyers Professional Responsibility. The Executive Committee shall act on behalf of the Board between Board meetings. If requested by the Executive Committee, it shall have the assistance of the State Court Administrator's office in carrying out its responsibilities. Members shall have served at least one year as a member of the Board prior to appointment to the Executive Committee. Members shall not be assigned to Panels during their terms on the Executive Committee.

(e) Panels. The Chair shall divide the Board into Panels, each consisting of not less than three Board members and at least one of whom is a nonlawyer, and shall designate a Chair and a Vice–Chair for each Panel. Three Panel members, at least one of whom is a nonlawyer and at least one of whom is a lawyer, shall constitute a quorum. No Board member shall be assigned to a matter in which disqualification would be required of a judge under Canon 3 of the Code of Judicial Conduct. The Board's Chair or the Vice-Chair may designate substitute Panel members from current or former Board members or current or former District Committee members for the particular matter, provided, that any panel with other than current Board members must include at least one current lawyer Board member. A Panel may refer any matters before it to the full Board, excluding members of the Executive Committee.

(f) Assignment to Panels. The Director shall assign matters to Panels in rotation. The Executive Committee may, however, redistribute case assignments to balance workloads among the Panels, appoint substitute panel members to utilize Board member or District Committee member expertise, and assign appeals of multiple admonitions issued to the same lawyer to the same Panel for hearing.

(g) Approval of petitions. Except as provided in these Rules or ordered by this Court, no petition for disciplinary action shall be filed with this Court without the approval of a Panel or the Board.

Adopted Nov. 1, 1976, eff. Jan. 1, 1977. Amended May 11, 1978, eff. May 11, 1978; July 22, 1982; June 18, 1986, eff. July 1, 1986; April 27, 1987, eff. July 1, 1987; Sept. 14, 1988, eff. Jan. 1, 1989; Feb. 11, 1991, eff. March 1, 1991; Dec. 12, 1994.

Historical Notes

The order of the Minnesota Supreme Court dated December 12, 1994, provides in part that the amendments to the Rules on Lawyers Professional Responsibility and the Rules of Professional Conduct shall govern all lawyer disciplinary actions commenced on or after January 1, 1995.

RULE 5. DIRECTOR

(a) Appointment. The Director shall be appointed by and serve at the pleasure of this Court, and shall be paid such salary as this Court shall fix. The Board shall review the performance of the Director every 2 years or at such times as this Court directs and the Board shall make recommendations to this Court concerning the continuing service of the Director.

(b) Duties. The Director shall be responsible and accountable directly to the Board and through the Board to this Court for the proper administration of the Office of Lawyers Professional Responsibility and these Rules. The Director shall prepare and submit to the Board an annual report covering the operation of the Office of Lawyers Professional Responsibility and shall make such other reports to the Board as the Board or this Court through the Board may order.

(c) Employees. The Director when authorized by the Board may employ, on behalf of this Court persons at such compensation as the Board shall recommend and as this Court may approve.

(d) Client Security Board Services. Subject to the approval of this court, the Client Security Board and the Lawyers Board, the Director may provide staff investigative and other services to the Client Security Board. Compensation for such services may be paid by the Client Security Board to the Director's office upon such terms as are approved by the Lawyers Board and the Client Security Board. The Lawyers Board and the Client Security Board may also establish further terms for the provision by the Director of such services.

Adopted Nov. 1, 1976, eff. Jan. 1, 1977. Amended July 22, 1982; June 18, 1986, eff. July 1, 1986; April 27, 1987, eff. July 1, 1987; May 21, 1987, eff. July 1, 1987; Sept. 14, 1988, eff. Jan. 1, 1989.

RULE 6. COMPLAINTS

(a) Investigation. All complaints of lawyers' alleged unprofessional conduct or allegations of disability shall be investigated pursuant to these Rules. No District Committee investigator shall investigate a matter in which disqualification would be required of a judge under Canon 3 of the Code of Judicial Conduct. No employee of the office of Lawyers Professional Responsibility shall be assigned to a matter if the employee's activities outside the Office are such that a judge with similar activities would be disqualified under Canon 3 of the Code of Judicial Conduct.

(b) Notification: referral. If a complaint of a lawyer's alleged unprofessional conduct is submitted to a District Committee, the District Chair promptly shall notify the Director of its pendency. If a complaint is submitted to the Director, it shall be referred for investigation to the District Committee of the district where the lawyer's principal office is located or in exceptional circumstances to such other District Committee as the Director reasonably selects, unless the Director determines to investigate it without referral or that discipline is not warranted.

(c) Copies of Investigator's Report. Upon the request of the lawyer being investigated, the Director shall provide a copy of the investigator's report, whether that investigation was undertaken by the District Committee or the Director's Office.

(d) Opportunity to respond to statements. The District Committee or the Director's Office shall afford the complainant an opportunity to reply to the lawyer's response to the complaint.

Adopted Nov. 1, 1976, eff. Jan. 1, 1977. Amended July 22, 1982; June 18, 1986, eff. July 1, 1986; April 27, 1987, eff. July 1, 1987; June 30, 1981, eff. July 1, 1981; Sept. 14, 1988, eff. Jan. 1, 1989; Feb. 11, 1991, eff. March 1, 1991; Dec. 12, 1994.

Historical Notes

The order of the Minnesota Supreme Court dated December 12, 1994, provides in part that the amendments to the Rules on Lawyers Professional Responsibility and the Rules of Professional Conduct shall govern all lawyer disciplinary actions commenced on or after January 1, 1995.

RULE 6X. PILOT MEDIATION PROGRAM FOR COMPLAINTS AGAINST LAWYERS IN THE THIRD, FOURTH, AND TWELFTH BAR ASSOCIATION DISTRICTS [Deleted July 28, 1999, eff. Aug. 1, 1999]

RULE 6Y. PILOT MANDATORY ARBITRATION PROGRAM FOR ATTORNEY-CLIENT FEE DISPUTES INVOLVING LAWYERS IN THE SECOND, SIXTH AND FOURTEENTH BAR ASSOCIATION DISTRICTS [Deleted July 28, 1999, eff. Aug. 1, 1999]

RULE 6Z. COMPLAINTS INVOLVING JUDGES

(a) Jurisdiction. The Lawyers Professional Responsibility Board has jurisdiction to consider whether discipline as a lawyer is warranted in matters involving conduct of any judge occurring prior to the assumption of judicial office and conduct of a part-time judge, including referees of conciliation court, not occurring in a judicial capacity. The Board on Judicial Standards may also exercise jurisdiction to consider whether judicial discipline is warranted in such matters.

(b) Procedure for Conduct Occurring Prior to Assumption of Judicial Office.

(1) *Complaint; Notice.* If either the executive secretary or the Office of Lawyers Professional Responsibility makes an inquiry or investigation, or receives a complaint, concerning the conduct of a judge occurring prior to assumption of judicial office, it shall so notify the other. Notice is not required if all proceedings relating to the inquiry, investigation or complaint have been resolved before the judge assumes judicial office.

(2) *Investigation.* Complaints of a judge's unprofessional conduct occurring prior to the judge assuming judicial office shall be investigated by the Office of Lawyers Professional Responsibility and processed pursuant to the Rules on Lawyers Professional Responsibility. The Board on Judicial Standards may suspend a related inquiry pending the outcome of the investigation and/or proceedings.

(3) *Authority of Board on Judicial Standards to Proceed Directly to Public Charges.* If probable cause has been determined under Rule 9(i)(ii) of the Rules on Lawyers Professional Responsibility or proceedings before a referee or the Supreme Court have been commenced under those rules, the Board on Judicial Standards may, after finding sufficient cause under Rule 6 of the Rules of the Board on Judicial Standards, proceed directly to the issuance of a formal complaint under Rule 8 of those rules.

(4) *Record of Lawyer Discipline Admissible in Judicial Disciplinary Proceeding.* If there is a hearing under rule 9 or rule 14 of the Rules on Lawyers Professional Responsibility, the record of the hearing, including the transcript, and the findings and conclusions of the panel, referee, and/or the Court shall be admissible in any hearing convened pursuant to rule 10 of the Rules of the Board on Judicial Standards. Counsel for the judge and the Board on Judicial Standards may be permitted to introduce additional evidence, relevant to violations of the Code of Judicial Conduct, at the hearing under rule 10.

Adopted March 30, 1999, eff. March 30, 1999.

Advisory Committee Comment—1999 Amendment

Rule 6Z outlines the process for handling complaints concerning conduct by a judge before assuming judicial office. Rule 6Z(a) grants the Lawyers Professional Responsibility Board jurisdiction to consider whether such conduct warrants lawyer discipline, while the Board on Judicial Standards retains jurisdiction to consider whether the same conduct warrants judicial discipline. R.Bd.Jud.Std.2.

The procedural provisions of Rule 6Z(b)(1)-(4) are identical to those in R.Bd.Jud.Stds 6Z(a)-(d). The committee felt that repetition of the significant procedural provisions was more convenient and appropriate than a cross-reference.

Rule 6Z(b)(1) is identical to R.Bd.Jud.Std. 6Z(a) and requires the staff of the Lawyers Professional Responsibility Board and the Judicial Standards Board to notify each other about complaints concerning conduct by a judge occurring before the judge assumed judicial office. Notice is not required if all proceedings relating to the inquiry, investigation or complaint have been resolved before the judge assumed judicial office.

Rule 6Z(b)(1) neither increases nor decreases the authority of the executive secretary or Office of Lawyers Professional Responsibility to investigate or act on any matter. That authority is governed by other rules. Rule 6Z(b)(1) merely establishes a mutual duty to provide notice about complaints or inquiries concerning conduct of a judge occurring before the judge assumed judicial office.

Although a fair number of complaints received by the executive secretary and the Office of Professional Responsibility are frivolous, there have been relatively few complaints concerning conduct occurring prior to a judge assuming judicial office. Thus, the committee believes that this procedure will not result in a needless duplication of efforts.

Under rule 6Z(b)(2) and its counterpart R.Bd. Jud.Std. 6Z(b), it is contemplated that complaints about the conduct of a judge occurring prior to the judge assuming judicial office will be investigated in the first instance by the Office of Lawyers Professional Responsibility, and the results would be disclosed to the Board on Judicial Standards. R.Bd. Jud.Std. 5(a)(4); R.L.Prof.Resp. 20(a)(10). This allows for efficient and effective use of investigative resources by both disciplinary boards.

Rule 6Z(b)(3) is identical to R.Bd.Jud.Std. 6Z(C) and authorizes the Board on Judicial Standards to proceed directly to issuance of a formal complaint under R.Bd.Jud.Std. 8 when there has been a related public proceeding under the Rules on Lawyers Professional Responsibility involving conduct of a judge that occurred prior to the judge assuming judicial office. In these circumstances the procedure under R.Bd.Jud.Std. 7 may only serve to delay the judicial disciplinary process.

Rule 6Z(b)(3) does not prohibit the Board on Judicial Standards from proceeding to public disciplinary proceedings in cases in which only private discipline (e.g., an admonition) has been imposed under the Rules on Lawyers Professional Responsibility for conduct of a judge occurring prior to the judge assuming judicial office. In these cases, the Board on Judicial Standards would be required to follow R.Bd.Jud.Std. 7 (unless, of course, the matter is resolved earlier, for example, by dismissal or public reprimand).

Rule 6Z(b)(4) is identical to R.Bd.Jud.Std. 6Z(d) and authorizes the use of the hearing record and the findings and recommendations of the lawyer disciplinary process in the judicial disciplinary process. This is intended to streamline the judicial disciplinary hearing when there has already been a formal fact finding hearing in the lawyer disciplinary process, and permits the Supreme Court to rule on both disciplinary matters as quickly as possible.

Under rule 6Z(b)(4) it is contemplated that the hearing record and the findings and conclusions of the lawyer disciplinary process will be the first evidence introduced in the judicial disciplinary hearing. Counsel for the Board on Judicial Standards and the judge may be permitted to introduce additional evidence relevant to alleged Code of Judicial Conduct violations at the judicial disciplinary hearing. Counsel must be aware that there may be situations in which the introduction of additional evidence will not be permitted. See, e.g., In re Gillard, 260 N.W.2d 562, 564 (Minn. 1977) (after review of hearing record and findings and conclusions from lawyer disciplinary process, Supreme Court ruled that findings would not be subject to collateral attack in the related judicial disciplinary proceeding and that additional evidence may be introduced only as a result of a stipulation or order of the fact finder); In re Gillard, 271 N.W.2d 785, 809 (Minn. 1978) (upholding removal and disbarment where Board on Judicial Standards as factfinder refused to consider additional testimony but allowed filing of deposition and exhibits and made alternative findings based on those filings). Although the Rules of the Board on Judicial Standards do not expressly provide for a pre-hearing conference, it is contemplated that admissibility issues will be resolved by the presider of the fact finding panel sufficiently in advance of the hearing to allow the parties adequate time to prepare for the hearing.

Historical Notes

The order of the Minnesota Supreme Court [C4–85–697] dated March 30, 1999, amending the Rules on Lawyers Professional Responsibility provides in part that the "(t)he inclusion of Advisory Committee comments is made for convenience and does not reflect court approval of the comments made therein."

RULE 7. DISTRICT COMMITTEE INVESTIGATION

(a) Assignment; Assistance. The District Chair may investigate or assign investigation of the complaint to one or more of the Committee's members, and may request the Director's assistance in making the investigation. The investigation may be conducted by means of written and telephonic communication and personal interviews.

(b) Report. The investigator's report and recommendations shall be submitted for review and approval to the District Chair, the Chair's designee or to a committee designated for this purpose by the District Chair, prior to its submission to the Director. The report shall include a recommendation that the Director:

(1) Determine that discipline is not warranted;

(2) Issue an admonition;

(3) Refer the matter to a Panel; or

(4) Investigate the matter further.

If the report recommends discipline not warranted or admonition, the investigator shall include in the report a draft letter of disposition in a format prescribed by the Director.

(c) Time. The investigation shall be completed and the report made promptly and, in any event within 90 days after the District Committee received the complaint, unless good cause exists. If the report is not made within 90 days, the District Chair or the Chair's designee within that time shall notify the Director of the reasons for the delay. If a District Committee has a pattern of responding substantially beyond the 90 day limitation, the Director shall advise the Board and the Chair shall seek to remedy the matter through the President of the appropriate District Bar Association.

(d) Removal. The Director may at any time and for any reason remove a complaint from a District Committee's consideration by notifying the District Chair of the removal.

(e) Notice to Complainant. The Director shall keep the complainant advised of the progress of the proceedings.

Adopted Nov. 1, 1976, eff. Jan. 1, 1977. Amended July 22, 1982; June 18, 1986, eff. July 1, 1986; April 27, 1987, eff. July 1, 1987; Sept. 14, 1988, eff. Jan. 1, 1989; Feb. 11, 1991, eff. March 1, 1991; July 28, 1999, eff. Aug. 1, 1999.

RULE 8. DIRECTOR'S INVESTIGATION

(a) Initiating investigation. At any time, with or without a complaint or a District Committee's report, and upon a reasonable belief that professional misconduct may have occurred, the Director may make such investigation as the Director deems appropriate as to the conduct of any lawyer or lawyers; provided, however, that investigations to be commenced upon the sole initiative of the Director shall not be commenced without the prior approval of the Executive Committee.

(b) Complaints by criminal defendants. No investigation shall commence on a complaint by or on behalf of a party represented by court appointed counsel, insofar as the complaint against the court appointed attorney alleges incompetent representation by the attorney in the pending matter. Any such complaint shall be summarily dismissed without prejudice. The Director's dismissal shall inform the complainant that the complaint may be sent to the chief district judge or trial court judge involved in the pending matter. The judge may, at any time, refer the matter to the Director for investigation. The Director may communicate with the appropriate court regarding the complaint and its disposition.

(c) Investigatory subpoena. With the Board Chair or Vice–Chair's approval upon the Director's application showing that it is necessary to do this before issuance of charges under Rule 9(a), the Director may subpoena and take the testimony of any person believed to possess information concerning possible unprofessional conduct of a lawyer. The examination shall be recorded by such means as the Director designates. The District Court of Ramsey County shall have jurisdiction over issuance of subpoenas and over motions arising from the examination.

(d) Disposition.

(1) *Determination discipline not warranted.* If, in a matter where there has been a complaint, the Director concludes that discipline is not warranted, the Director shall so notify the lawyer involved, the complainant, and the Chair of the District Committee, if any, that has considered the complaint. The notification shall:

(i) Set forth a brief explanation of the Director's conclusion;

(ii) Set forth the complainant's identity and the complaint's substance; and

(iii) Inform the complainant of the right to appeal under subdivision (e).

(2) *Admonition.* In any matter, with or without a complaint, if the Director concludes that a lawyer's conduct was unprofessional but of an isolated and non-serious nature, the Director may issue an admonition. The Director shall issue an admonition if so directed by a Board member reviewing a complainant appeal, under the circumstances identified in Rule 8(e). The Director shall notify the lawyer in writing:

(i) Of the admonition;

(ii) That the admonition is in lieu of the Director's presenting charges of unprofessional conduct to a Panel;

(iii) That the lawyer may, by notifying the Director in writing within fourteen days, demand that the Director so present the charges to a Panel which shall consider the matter de novo or instruct the Director to file a Petition for Disciplinary Action in this Court; and

(iv) That unless the lawyer so demands, the Director after that time will notify the complainant, if any, and the Chair of the District Committee, if any, that has considered the complaint, that the Director has issued the admonition.

If the lawyer makes no demand under clause (iii), the Director shall notify as provided in clause (iv). The notification to the complainant, if any, shall inform the complainant of the right to appeal under subdivision (e).

(3) *Stipulated probation.*

(i) In any matter, with or without a complaint, if the Director concludes that a lawyer's conduct was unprofessional and that a private probation is appropriate, and the Board Chair or Vice–Chair approves, the Director and the lawyer may agree that the lawyer will be subject to private probation for a specified period up to two years, provided the lawyer throughout the period complies with specified reasonable conditions. At any time during the period, with the Board Chair or Vice–Chair's approval, the Director and the lawyer may agree to modify the agreement or to one extension of it for a specified period up to two additional years. The Director shall maintain a permanent disciplinary record of all stipulated probations.

(ii) The Director shall notify the complainant, if any, and the Chair of the District Committee, if any, that has considered the complaint, of the agreement and any modification. The notification to the complainant, if any, shall inform the complainant of the right to appeal under subdivision (e).

(iii) If it appears that the lawyer has violated the conditions of the probation, or engaged in further misconduct, the Director may either submit the matter to a Panel or upon a motion made with notice to the attorney and approved by a Panel Chair chosen in rotation, file a petition for disciplinary action under Rule 12. A lawyer may, in the stipulation for probation, waive the right to such consideration by the Panel or Panel Chair.

(4) *Submission to Panel.* The Director shall submit the matter to a Panel under Rule 9 if:

(i) In any matter, with or without a complaint, the Director concludes that public discipline is warranted;

(ii) The lawyer makes a demand under subdivision (d)(2)(iii);

(iii) A reviewing Board member so directs upon an appeal under subdivision (e); or

(iv) The Director determines that a violation of the terms of a conditional admission agreement warrants revocation of the conditional admission.

(5) *Extension or Modification of a Conditional Admission Agreement.* If, in a matter involving a complaint against a conditionally admitted lawyer the Director determines that the conditional admission agreement was violated, the Director may en-

ter into an agreement with the lawyer and the Board of Law Examiners to modify or extend the terms of the agreement for a period not to exceed two years.

(e) Review by Lawyers Board. If the complainant is not satisfied with the Director's disposition under Rule 8(d)(1), (2) or (3), the complainant may appeal the matter by notifying the Director in writing within fourteen days. The Director shall notify the lawyer of the appeal and assign the matter by rotation to a board member, other than an Executive Committee member, appointed by the Chair. The reviewing Board member may:

(1) approve the Director's disposition; or

(2) direct that further investigation be undertaken; or

(3) if a district ethics committee recommended discipline, but the Director determined that discipline is not warranted, the Board member may instruct the Director to issue an admonition; or

(4) in any case that has been investigated, if the Board member concludes that public discipline is warranted, the Board member may instruct the Director to issue charges of unprofessional conduct for submission to a Panel other than the Board member's own.

The reviewing Board member shall set forth an explanation of the Board member's action. A summary dismissal by the Director under Rule 8(b) shall be final and may not be appealed to a Board member for review under this section.

Adopted Nov. 1, 1976, eff. Jan. 1, 1977. Amended July 22, 1982; June 18, 1986, eff. July 1, 1986; April 27, 1987, eff. July 1, 1987; Sept. 14, 1988, eff. Jan. 1, 1989; Feb. 11, 1991, eff. March 1, 1991; Dec. 12, 1994; Aug. 10, 2005, eff. Sept. 1, 2005.

Historical Notes

The order of the Minnesota Supreme Court dated December 12, 1994, provides in part that the amendments to the Rules on Lawyers Professional Responsibility and the Rules of Professional Conduct shall govern all lawyer disciplinary actions commenced on or after January 1, 1995.

RULE 9. PANEL PROCEEDINGS

(a) Charges. If the matter is to be submitted to a Panel, the matter shall proceed as follows:

(1) The Director shall prepare charges of unprofessional conduct, assign them to a Panel by rotation, and notify the lawyer of the Charges, the name, address, and telephone number of the Panel Chair and Vice Chair, and the provisions of this Rule. Within 14 days after the lawyer is notified of the Charges, the lawyer shall submit an answer to the Charges to the Panel Chair and the Director and may submit a request that the Panel conduct a hearing. Within ten days after the lawyer submits an answer, the Director and the lawyer may submit affidavits and other documents in support of their positions.

(2) The Panel shall make a determination in accordance with paragraph (j) within 40 days after the lawyer is notified of the Charges based on the documents submitted by the Director and the lawyer, except in its discretion, the Panel may hear oral argument or conduct a hearing. If the Panel orders a hearing, the matter shall proceed in accordance with subdivisions (b) through (i). If the Panel does not order a hearing, subdivisions (b) through (i) do not apply.

(3) The Panel Chair may extend the time periods provided in this subdivision for good cause.

(b) Setting Pre-Hearing Meeting. If the Panel orders a hearing, the Director shall notify the lawyer of:

(1) The time and place of the pre-hearing meeting; and

(2) The lawyer's obligation to appear at the time set unless the meeting is rescheduled by agreement of the parties or by order of the Panel Chair or Vice-Chair.

(c) Request for Admission. Either party may serve upon the other a request for admission. The request shall be made before the prehearing meeting or within ten days thereafter. The Rules of Civil Procedure for the District Courts applicable to requests for admissions govern, except that the time for answers or objections is ten days and the Panel Chair or Vice-Chair shall rule upon any objections. If a party fails to admit, the Panel may award expenses as permitted by the Rules of Civil Procedure for District Courts.

(d) Deposition. Either party may take a deposition as provided by the Rules of Civil Procedure for the District Courts. A deposition under this Rule may be taken before the pre-hearing meeting or within ten days thereafter. The District Court of Ramsey County shall have jurisdiction over issuance of subpoenas and over motions arising from the deposition. The lawyer shall be denominated by number or randomly selected initials in any District Court proceedings.

(e) Pre-Hearing Meeting. The Director and the lawyer shall attend a pre-hearing meeting. At the meeting:

(1) The parties shall endeavor to formulate stipulations of fact and to narrow and simplify the issues in order to expedite the Panel hearing; and

(2) Each party shall mark and provide the other party with a copy of each affidavit or other exhibit to be introduced at the Panel hearing. The genuineness of each exhibit is admitted unless objection is served within ten days after the pre-hearing meeting. If a party objects, the Panel may award expenses of proof as permitted by the Rules of Civil Procedure for the District Courts. No additional

exhibit shall be received at the Panel hearing without the opposing party's consent or the Panel's permission.

(f) Setting Panel Hearing. Promptly after the prehearing meeting, the Director shall schedule a hearing by the Panel on the charges and notify the lawyer of:

(1) The time and place of the hearing;

(2) The lawyer's right to be heard at the hearing; and

(3) The lawyer's obligation to appear at the time set unless the hearing is rescheduled by agreement of the parties or by order of the Panel Chair or Vice–Chair. The Director shall also notify the complainant, if any, of the hearing's time and place. The Director shall send each Panel member a copy of the charges, of any stipulations, and of the prehearing statement. Each party shall provide to each Panel member in advance of the Panel hearing, copies of all documentary exhibits marked by that party at the pre-hearing meeting, unless the parties agree otherwise or the Panel Chair or Vice–Chair orders to the contrary.

(g) Referee Probable Cause Hearing. Upon the certification of the Panel Chair and the Board Chair to the Court that extraordinary circumstances indicate that a matter is not suitable for submission to a Panel under this Rule, because of exceptional complexity or other reasons, the Court may appoint a referee with directions to conduct a probable cause hearing acting as a Panel would under this Rule, or the Court may remand the matter to a Panel under this Rule with instructions, or the Court may direct the Director to file with this Court a petition for disciplinary action under Rule 12(a). If a referee is appointed to substitute for a Panel, the referee shall have the powers of a district court judge and Ramsey County District Court shall not exercise such powers in such case. If the referee so appointed determines there is probable cause as to any charge and a petition for disciplinary action is filed in this Court, the Court may appoint the same referee to conduct a hearing on the petition for disciplinary action under Rule 14. If a referee appointed under Rule 14 considers all of the evidence presented at the probable cause hearing, a transcript of that hearing shall be made part of the public record.

(h) Form of Evidence at Panel Hearing. The Panel shall receive evidence only in the form of affidavits, depositions or other documents except for testimony by:

(1) The lawyer;

(2) A complainant who affirmatively desires to attend; and

(3) A witness whose testimony the Panel Chair or Vice–Chair authorized for good cause. If testimony is authorized, it shall be subject to cross-examination and the Rules of Evidence and a party may compel attendance of a witness or production of documentary or tangible evidence as provided in the Rules of Civil Procedure for the District Courts. The District Court of Ramsey County shall have jurisdiction over issuance of subpoenas, motions respecting subpoenas, motions to compel witnesses to testify or give evidence, and determinations of claims of privilege. The lawyer shall be denominated by number or randomly selected initials in any district court proceedings.

(i) Procedure at Panel Hearing. Unless the Panel for cause otherwise permits, the Panel hearing shall proceed as follows:

(1) The Chair shall explain the purpose of the hearing, which is:

(i) to determine whether there is probable cause to believe that public discipline is warranted, and the Panel will terminate the hearing on any charge whenever it is satisfied that there is or is not such probable cause;

(ii) if an admonition has been issued under Rule 8(d)(2) or 8(e), to determine whether the Panel should affirm the admonition on the ground that it is supported by clear and convincing evidence, should reverse the admonition, or, if there is probable cause to believe that public discipline is warranted, should instruct the Director to file a petition for disciplinary action in this Court; or

(iii) to determine whether there is probable cause to believe that a conditional admission agreement has been violated, thereby warranting revocation of the conditional admission to practice law, and that the Panel will terminate the hearing whenever it is satisfied there is or is not such probable cause.

(2) The Director shall briefly summarize the matters admitted by the parties, the matters remaining for resolution, and the proof which the Director proposes to offer thereon;

(3) The lawyer may respond to the Director's remarks;

(4) The parties shall introduce their evidence in conformity with the Rules of Evidence except that affidavits and depositions are admissible in lieu of testimony;

(5) The parties may present oral arguments;

(6) The complainant may be present for all parts of the hearing related to the complainant's complaint except when excluded for good cause; and

(7) The Panel shall either recess to deliberate or take the matter under advisement.

(j) Disposition. The Panel shall make one of the following determinations:

(1) In the case of charges of unprofessional conduct, the Panel shall:

(i) determine that there is not probable cause to believe that public discipline is warranted, or that there is not probable cause to believe that revocation of a conditional admission is warranted;

(ii) if it finds probable cause to believe that public discipline is warranted, instruct the Director to file in this Court a petition for disciplinary action. The Panel shall not make a recommendation as to the matter's ultimate disposition;

(iii) if it concludes that the attorney engaged in conduct that was unprofessional but of an isolated and nonserious nature, the Panel shall state the facts and conclusions constituting unprofessional conduct and issue an admonition. If the Panel issues an admonition based on the parties' submissions without a hearing, the lawyer shall have the right to a hearing de novo before a different Panel. If the Panel issues an admonition following a hearing, the lawyer shall have the right to appeal in accordance with Rule 9(m); or

(iv) if it finds probable cause to revoke a conditional admission agreement, instruct the Director to file in this Court a petition for revocation of conditional admission.

(2) If the Panel held a hearing on a lawyer's appeal of an admonition that was issued under Rule 8(d)(2), or issued by another panel without a hearing, the Panel shall affirm or reverse the admonition, or, if there is probable cause to believe that public discipline is warranted, instruct the Director to file a petition for disciplinary action in this Court.

(k) Notification. The Director shall notify the lawyer, the complainant, if any, and the District Committee, if any, that has the complaint, of the Panel's disposition. The notification to the complainant, if any, shall inform the complainant of the right to petition for review under subdivision (*l*). If the Panel affirmed the Director's admonition, the notification to the lawyer shall inform the lawyer of the right to appeal to the Supreme Court under subdivision (m).

(*l*) Complainant's Petition for Review. If not satisfied with the Panel's disposition, the complainant may within 14 days file with the Clerk of the Appellate Courts a petition for review. The complainant shall, prior to or at the time of filing, serve a copy of the petition for review upon the respondent and the Director and shall file an affidavit of service with the Clerk of the Appellate Courts. The respondent shall be denominated by number or randomly selected initials in the proceeding. This Court will grant review only if the petition shows that the Panel acted arbitrarily, capriciously, or unreasonably. If the Court grants review, it may order such proceedings as it deems appropriate. Upon conclusion of such proceedings, the Court may dismiss the petition or, if it finds that the Panel acted arbitrarily, capriciously, or unreasonably, remand the matter to the same or a different Panel, direct the filing of a petition for disciplinary action or a petition for revocation of conditional admission, or take any other action as the interest of justice may require.

(m) Respondent's Appeal to Supreme Court. The lawyer may appeal a Panel's affirmance of the Director's admonition or an admonition issued by a Panel by filing a notice of appeal and seven copies thereof with the Clerk of Appellate Courts and by serving a copy on the Director within 30 days after being notified of the Panel's action. The respondent shall be denominated by number or randomly selected initials in the proceeding. The Director shall notify the complainant, if any, of the respondent's appeal. This Court may review the matter on the record or order such further proceedings as it deems appropriate. Upon conclusion of such proceedings, the Court may either affirm the decision or make such other disposition as it deems appropriate.

(n) Manner of Recording. The Director shall arrange for a court reporter to make a record of the proceedings as in civil cases.

(*o*) Panel Chair Authority. Requests or disputes arising under this Rule before the Panel hearing commences may be determined by the Panel Chair or Vice–Chair. For good cause shown, the Panel Chair or Vice–Chair may shorten or enlarge time periods for discovery under this Rule.

Adopted Nov. 1, 1976, eff. Jan. 1, 1977. Amended July 22, 1982; Oct. 22, 1984; June 18, 1986, eff. July 1, 1986; April 27, 1987, eff. July 1, 1987; Jan. 14, 1988; Sept. 14, 1988, eff. Jan. 1, 1989; Feb. 11, 1991, eff. March 1, 1991; Dec. 12, 1994; June 13, 1996, eff. June 13, 1996; June 24, 1996, eff. June 24, 1996; July 28, 1999, eff. Aug. 1, 1999; Aug. 10, 2005, eff. Sept. 1, 2005; March 24, 2009, eff. July 1, 2009.

Historical Notes

The order of the Minnesota Supreme Court dated December 12, 1994, provides in part that the amendments to the Rules on Lawyers Professional Responsibility and the Rules of Professional Conduct shall govern all lawyer disciplinary actions commenced on or after January 1, 1995.

RULE 10. DISPENSING WITH PANEL PROCEEDINGS

(a) Agreement of parties. The parties by written agreement may dispense with some or all procedures under Rule 9 before the Director files a petition under Rule 12.

(b) Admission. If the lawyer admits some or all charges, the Director may dispense with some or all procedures under Rule 9 and file a petition for disciplinary action together with the lawyer's admission. This Court may act thereon with or without any of the procedures under Rules 12, 13, or 14.

(c) Criminal conviction or guilty plea. If a lawyer pleads guilty to or is convicted of a felony under Minnesota statutes, a crime punishable by incarceration for more than one year under the laws of any other jurisdiction, or any lesser crime a necessary element of which involves interference with the administration of justice, false swearing, misrepresentation, fraud, willful extortion, misappropriation, theft, or an attempt, conspiracy, or solicitation of another to commit such a crime, the Director may either submit the matter to a Panel or, with the approval of the Chair of the Board, file a petition under Rule 12.

(d) Other Serious Matters. In matters in which there are an attorney's admissions, civil findings, or apparently clear and convincing documentary evidence of an offense of a type for which the Court has suspended or disbarred lawyers in the past, such as misappropriation of funds, repeated non-filing of personal income tax returns, flagrant non-cooperation including failure to submit an answer or failure to attend a pre-hearing meeting as required by Rule 9, fraud and the like, the Director may either submit the matter to a Panel or upon a motion made with notice to the attorney and approved by the Panel Chair, file the petition under Rule 12.

(e) Additional Charges. If a petition under Rule 12 is pending before this Court, the Director must present the matter to the Panel Chair, or if the matter was not heard by a Panel or the Panel Chair is unavailable, to the Board Chair or Vice–Chair, for approval before amending the petition to include additional charges based upon conduct committed before or after the petition was filed.

(f) Discontinuing Panel proceedings. The Director may discontinue Panel proceedings for the matter to be disposed of under Rule 8(d)(1), (2) or (3).

Adopted Nov. 1, 1976, eff. Jan. 1, 1977. Amended July 22, 1982; June 18, 1986, eff. July 1, 1986; April 27, 1987, eff. July 1, 1987; Sept. 14, 1988, eff. Jan. 1, 1989; Feb. 11, 1991, eff. March 1, 1991; March 24, 2009, eff. July 1, 2009.

RULE 11. RESIGNATION

This Court may at any time, with or without a hearing and with any conditions it may deem appropriate, grant or deny a lawyer's petition to resign from the bar. A lawyer's petition to resign from the bar shall be served upon the Director. The original petition with proof of service and one copy shall be filed with this Court. If the Director does not object to the petition, the Director shall promptly advise the Court. If the Director objects, the Director shall also advise the Court, but then submit the matter to a Panel, which shall conduct a hearing and make a recommendation to the Court. The recommendation shall be served upon the petitioner and filed with the Court.

Adopted Nov. 1, 1976, eff. Jan. 1, 1977. Amended Oct. 16, 1981; June 18, 1986, eff. July 1, 1986; April 27, 1987, eff. July 1, 1987; Sept. 14, 1988, eff. Jan. 1, 1989.

RULE 12. PETITION FOR DISCIPLINARY ACTION

(a) Petition. When so directed by a Panel or by this Court or when authorized under Rule 10 or this Rule, the Director shall file with this Court a petition for disciplinary action or a petition for revocation of conditional admission. An original and nine copies shall be filed. The petition shall set forth the unprofessional conduct charges. When a lawyer is subject to a probation ordered by this Court and the Director concludes that the lawyer has breached the conditions of the probation or committed additional serious misconduct, the Director may file with this Court a petition for revocation of probation and further disciplinary action.

(b) Service. The Director shall cause the petition to be served upon the respondent in the same manner as a summons in a civil action. If the respondent has a duly appointed resident guardian or conservator service shall be made thereupon in like manner.

(c) Respondent not found.

(1) *Suspension.* If the respondent cannot be found in the state, the Director shall mail a copy of the petition to the respondent's last known address and file an affidavit of mailing with this Court. Thereafter the Director may apply to this Court for an order suspending the respondent from the practice of law. A copy of the order, when made and filed, shall be mailed to each district court judge of this state. Within one year after the order is filed, the respondent may move this Court for a vacation of the order of suspension and for leave to answer the petition for disciplinary action.

(2) *Order to show cause.* If the respondent does not so move, the Director shall petition this Court for an order directing the respondent to show cause to this Court why appropriate disciplinary action should not be taken. The order to show cause shall be returnable not sooner than 20 days after service. The order may be served on the respondent by publishing it once each week for three weeks in the regular issue of a qualified newspaper published in the county in this state in which the respondent was last known to practice or reside. The service shall be deemed complete 21 days after the first publication. Personal service of the order without the state, proved by the affidavit of the person making the service, sworn to before a person authorized to administer an oath, shall have the same effect as service by publication. Proof of service shall be filed with this Court. If the respondent fails to respond to the order to show cause, this Court may proceed under Rule 15.

(d) Reciprocal discipline. Upon learning from any source that a lawyer licensed to practice in Minnesota has been publicly disciplined or is subject to public disciplinary charges in another jurisdiction, the Director may commence an investigation and, without further proceedings, may file a petition for disciplinary action this Court.[1] A lawyer subject to such charges or discipline shall notify the Director. If the lawyer has been publicly disciplined in another jurisdiction, this Court may issue an order directing that the lawyer and the Director inform the Court within thirty (30) days whether either or both believe the imposition of the identical discipline by this Court would be unwarranted and the reasons for that claim. Without further proceedings this Court may thereafter impose the identical discipline unless it appears that discipline procedures in the other jurisdiction were unfair, or the imposition of the same discipline would be unjust or substantially different from discipline warranted in Minnesota. If this Court determines that imposition of the identical discipline is not appropriate, it may order such other discipline or such other proceedings as it deems appropriate. Unless the Court determines otherwise, a final adjudication in another jurisdiction that a lawyer had committed certain misconduct shall establish conclusively the misconduct for purposes of disciplinary proceedings in Minnesota.

Adopted Nov. 1, 1976, eff. Jan. 1, 1977. Amended July 22, 1982; Feb. 21, 1984, eff. Feb. 21, 1984; June 18, 1986, eff. July 1, 1986; April 27, 1987, eff. July 1, 1987; Sept. 14, 1988, eff. Jan. 1, 1989; Feb. 11, 1991, eff. March 1, 1991; Aug. 10, 2005, eff. Sept. 1, 2005.

1 So in original.

RULE 13. ANSWER TO PETITION FOR DISCIPLINARY ACTION

(a) Filing. Within 20 days after service of the petition, the respondent shall file an original and seven copies of an answer in this Court. The answer may deny or admit any accusations or state any defense, privilege, or matter in mitigation.

(b) Failure to file. If the respondent fails to file an answer within the time provided or any extension of time this Court may grant, the allegations shall be deemed admitted and this Court may proceed under Rule 15.

Adopted Nov. 1, 1976, eff. Jan. 1, 1977. Amended Feb. 21, 1984, eff. Feb. 21, 1984; June 18, 1986, eff. July 1, 1986; April 27, 1987, eff. July 1, 1987; Sept. 14, 1988, eff. Jan. 1, 1989.

RULE 14. HEARING ON PETITION FOR DISCIPLINARY ACTION

(a) Referee. This Court may appoint a referee with directions to hear and report the evidence submitted for or against the petition for disciplinary action or petition for revocation of conditional admission.

(b) Conduct of Hearing Before Referee. Unless this Court otherwise directs, the hearing shall be conducted in accordance with the Rules of Civil Procedure applicable to district courts and the referee shall have all the powers of a district court judge.

(c) Subpoenas. The District Court of Ramsey County shall issue subpoenas. The referee shall have jurisdiction to determine all motions arising from the issuance and enforcement of subpoenas.

(d) Record. The referee shall appoint a court reporter to make a record of the proceedings as in civil cases.

(e) Referee's Findings, Conclusions, and Recommendations. The referee shall make findings of fact, conclusions, and recommendations, file them with this Court, and notify the respondent and the Director of them. In revocation of conditional admission matters, the referee shall also notify the Director of the Board of Law Examiners. Unless the respondent or Director, within ten days, orders a transcript and so notifies this Court, the findings of fact and conclusions shall be conclusive. If either the respondent or the Director so orders a transcript, then none of the findings of fact or conclusions shall be conclusive, and either party may challenge any findings of fact or conclusions. A party ordering a transcript shall, within ten days of the date the transcript is ordered, file with the clerk of appellate courts a certificate as to transcript signed by the court reporter. The certificate shall contain the date on which the transcript was ordered, the estimated completion date (which shall not exceed 30 days from the date the transcript was ordered), and a statement that satisfactory financial arrangements have been made for the transcription. A party ordering a transcript shall order and pay for an original transcript for the Court plus two copies, one copy for the respondent and one for the Director. A party ordering a transcript shall specify in the initial brief to the Court the referee's findings of fact, conclusions and recommendations that are disputed.

(f) Panel as Referee. Upon written agreement of an attorney, the Panel Chair and the Director, at any time, this Court may appoint the Panel which is to conduct or has already conducted the probable cause hearing as its referee to hear and report the evidence submitted for or against the petition for disciplinary action. Upon such appointment, the Panel shall proceed under Rule 14 as the Court's referee, except that if the Panel considers evidence already presented at the Panel hearing, a transcript of the hearing shall be made part of the public record. The District Court of Ramsey County shall continue to have the jurisdiction over discovery and subpoenas in Rule 9(d) and (h).

(g) Hearing Before Court. This Court within thirty days of the referee's findings, conclusions and recommendations, shall set a time for hearing before this Court. The order shall specify times for briefs and oral arguments. In all matters in which the Director seeks discipline, the cover of the main brief of the Director shall be blue; the main brief of the respondent, red; and any reply brief shall be gray. In a matter in which reinstatement is sought pursuant to Rule 18 of these Rules, the cover of the respondent's main brief shall be blue; that of the main brief of the Director, red; and that of any reply brief, gray.

The matter shall be heard upon the record, briefs, and arguments.

Adopted Nov. 1, 1976, eff. Jan. 1, 1977. Amended Oct. 22, 1984; June 18, 1986, eff. July 1, 1986; April 27, 1987, eff. July 1, 1987; Sept. 14, 1988, eff. Jan. 1, 1989; Feb. 11, 1991, eff. March 1, 1991; July 28, 1999, eff. Aug. 1, 1999; Aug. 10, 2005, eff. Sept. 1, 2005; March 24, 2009, eff. July 1, 2009.

RULE 15. DISPOSITION; PROTECTION OF CLIENTS

(a) Disposition. Upon conclusion of the proceedings, this Court may:

(1) Disbar the lawyer;

(2) Suspend the lawyer indefinitely or for a stated period of time;

(3) Order the lawyer to pay costs:

(4) Place the lawyer on a probationary status for a stated period, or until further order of this Court, with such conditions as this Court may specify and to be supervised by the Director;

(5) Reprimand the lawyer;

(6) Order the lawyer to successfully complete within a specified period such written examination as may be required of applicants for admission to the practice of law by the State Board of Law Examiners on the subject of professional responsibility;

(7) Make such other disposition as this Court deems appropriate;

(8) Require the lawyer to pay costs and disbursements; in addition, in those contested cases where the lawyer has acted in the proceedings in bad faith, vexatiously, or for oppressive reasons, order the lawyer to pay reasonable attorney fees;

(9) Dismiss the petition for disciplinary action or petition for revocation of conditional admission, in which case the Court's order may denominate the lawyer by number or randomly selected initials and may direct that the remainder of the record be sealed; or

(10) Revoke, modify or extend a conditional admission agreement.

(b) Protection of clients. When a lawyer is disciplined or permitted to resign, this Court may issue orders as may be appropriate for the protection of clients or other persons.

(c) Petition for rehearing. A petition for rehearing may be filed regarding an order of the Court under this rule, by following the procedures of Rule 140, Rules of Civil Appellate Procedure. The filing of a petition for rehearing shall not stay this Court's order.

Adopted Nov. 1, 1976, eff. Jan. 1, 1977. Amended Oct. 16, 1981; July 22, 1982; April 26, 1983; June 18, 1986, eff. July 1, 1986; April 27, 1987, eff. July 1, 1987; Sept. 14, 1988, eff. Jan. 1, 1989; Feb. 11, 1991, eff. March 1, 1991; Aug. 10, 2005, eff. Sept. 1, 2005; March 24, 2009, eff. July 1, 2009.

RULE 16. TEMPORARY SUSPENSION PENDING DISCIPLINARY PROCEEDINGS

(a) Petition for temporary suspension. In any case where the Director files or has filed a petition under Rule 12, if it appears that a continuation of the lawyer's authority to practice law pending final determination of the disciplinary proceeding poses a substantial threat of serious harm to the public, the Director may file with this Court an original and seven copies of a petition for suspension of the lawyer pending final determination of the disciplinary proceeding. The petition shall set forth facts as may constitute grounds for the suspension and may be supported by a transcript of evidence taken by a Panel, court records, documents or affidavits.

(b) Service. The Director shall cause the petition to be served upon the lawyer in the same manner as a petition for disciplinary action.

(c) Answer. Within 20 days after service of the petition or such shorter time as this Court may order, the lawyer shall file in this Court an original and seven copies of an answer to the petition for temporary suspension. If the lawyer fails to do so within that time or any extension of time this Court may grant, the petition's allegations shall be deemed admitted and this Court may enter an order suspending the lawyer pending final determination of disciplinary proceedings. The answer may be supported by a transcript of any evidence taken by the Panel, court records, documents, or affidavits.

(d) Hearing; disposition. If this Court after hearing finds a continuation of the lawyer's authority to practice law poses a substantial threat of serious harm to the public, it may enter an order suspending the lawyer pending final determination of disciplinary proceedings.

(e) Interim suspension. Upon a referee disbarment recommendation, the lawyer's authority to practice law shall be suspended pending final determination of the disciplinary proceeding, unless the referee directs otherwise or the Court orders otherwise.

Adopted Nov. 1, 1976, eff. Jan. 1, 1977. Amended July 22, 1982; Feb. 21, 1984, eff. Feb. 21, 1984; June 18, 1986, eff. July 1, 1986; April 27, 1987, eff. July 1, 1987; Sept. 14, 1988, eff. Jan. 1, 1989; Feb. 11, 1991, eff. March 1, 1991; Dec. 12, 1994.

Historical Notes

The order of the Minnesota Supreme Court dated December 12, 1994, provides in part that the amendments to the Rules on Lawyers Professional Responsibility and the Rules of Professional Conduct shall govern all lawyer disciplinary actions commenced on or after January 1, 1995.

RULE 17. FELONY CONVICTION

(a) Duty of the court administrator. Whenever a lawyer is convicted of a felony, the court administrator shall send the Director a certified copy of the judgment of conviction.

(b) Other cases. Nothing in these Rules precludes disciplinary proceedings, where appropriate, in case of conviction of an offense not punishable by incarceration for more than one year or in case of unprofessional conduct for which there has been no criminal conviction or for which a criminal conviction is subject to appellate review.

Adopted Nov. 1, 1976, eff. Jan. 1, 1977. Amended July 22, 1982; June 18, 1986, eff. July 1, 1986; April 27, 1987, eff. July 1, 1987; Sept. 14, 1988, eff. Jan. 1, 1989.

RULE 18. REINSTATEMENT

(a) Petition for Reinstatement. A petition for reinstatement to practice law shall be served upon the Director. The original petition, with proof of service, and seven copies, shall then be filed with this Court. Together with the petition served upon the Director's Office, a petitioner seeking reinstatement shall pay to the Director a fee in the same amount as that required by Rule 12(B), Rules for Admission to the Bar, for timely filings. Applications for admission to the bar following a revocation of conditional admission shall be filed with the Board of Law Examiners pursuant to Rule 16, Rules for Admission to the Bar.

(b) Investigation; Report.

(1) The Director shall publish an announcement of the petition for reinstatement in a publication of general statewide circulation to attorneys soliciting comments regarding the appropriateness of the petitioner's reinstatement. Any comments made in response to such a solicitation shall be absolutely privileged and may not serve as a basis for liability in any civil lawsuit brought against the person making the statement.

(2) The Director shall investigate and report the Director's conclusions to a Panel.

(c) Recommendation. The Panel may conduct a hearing and shall make its recommendation. The recommendation shall be served upon the petitioner and filed with this Court.

(d) Hearing Before Court. There shall be a hearing before this Court on the petition unless otherwise ordered by this Court. This Court may appoint a referee. If a referee is appointed, the same procedure shall be followed as under Rule 14.

(e) General Requirements for Reinstatement.

(1) Unless such examination is specifically waived by this Court, no lawyer, after having been disbarred by this Court, may petition for reinstatement until the lawyer shall have successfully completed such written examinations as may be required of applicants for admission to the practice of law by the State Board of Law Examiners.

(2) No lawyer ordered reinstated to the practice of law after having been suspended or transferred to disability inactive status by this Court, and after petitioning for reinstatement under subdivision (a), shall be effectively reinstated until the lawyer shall have successfully completed such written examination as may be required for admission to the practice of law by the State Board of Law Examiners on the subject of professional responsibility.

(3) Unless specifically waived by this Court, any lawyer suspended for a fixed period of ninety (90) days or less, and any suspended lawyer for whom the Court waives the requirements of subdivisions (a) through (d), must, within one year from the date of the suspension order, successfully complete such written examination as may be required for admission to the practice of law by the State Board of Law Examiners on the subject of professional responsibility. Except upon motion and for good cause shown, failure to successfully complete this examination shall result in automatic suspension of the lawyer effective one year after the date of the original suspension order.

(4) Unless specifically waived by this Court, no lawyer shall be reinstated to the practice of law following the lawyer's resignation, suspension, disbarment, or transfer to disability inactive status by this Court until the lawyer shall have satisfied (1) the requirements imposed under the rules for Continuing Legal Education on members of the bar as a condition to a change from a restricted to an active status and (2) any subrogation claim against the lawyer by the Client Security Board.

(f) Reinstatement by Affidavit. Unless otherwise ordered by this Court, subdivisions (a) through (d) shall not apply to lawyers who have been suspended for a fixed period of ninety (90) days or less. Such a suspended lawyer, and any suspended lawyer for whom the Court waives the requirements of subdivisions (a) through (d), may apply for reinstatement by filing an affidavit with the Clerk of Appellate Courts and the Director, stating that the suspended lawyer has complied with Rules 24 and 26 of these rules, is current in Continuing Legal Education requirements, and has complied with all other conditions for reinstatement imposed by the Court. After receiving the lawyer's affidavit, the Director shall promptly file a proposed order and an affidavit regarding the lawyer's compliance or lack thereof with the requirements for reinstatement. The lawyer shall not resume the practice of law unless and until this Court issues a reinstatement order.

Adopted Nov. 1, 1976, eff. Jan. 1, 1977. Amended Oct. 16, 1981; Feb. 21, 1984, eff. Feb. 21, 1984; June 18, 1986, eff. July 1, 1986; April 27, 1987, eff. July 1, 1987; Sept. 14, 1988, eff. Jan. 1, 1989; Feb. 11, 1991, eff. March 1, 1991; July 28, 1999, eff. Aug. 1, 1999; Aug. 10, 2005, eff. Sept. 1, 2005; March 24, 2009, eff. July 1, 2009.

RULE 19. EFFECT OF PREVIOUS PROCEEDINGS

(a) Criminal Conviction. A lawyer's criminal conviction in any American jurisdiction, even if upon a plea of nolo contendere or subject to appellate review, is, in proceedings under these Rules, conclusive evidence that the lawyer committed the conduct for which the lawyer was convicted. The same is true of a conviction in a foreign country if the facts and circumstances surrounding the conviction indicate that the lawyer was accorded fundamental fairness and due process.

(b) Disciplinary Proceedings.

(1) *Conduct Previously Considered And Investigated Where Discipline Was Not Warranted.* Conduct considered in previous lawyer disciplinary proceedings of any jurisdiction, including revocation of conditional admission proceedings, is inadmissible if it was determined in the proceedings that discipline was not warranted, except to show a pattern of related conduct, the cumulative effect of which constitutes an ethical violation, except as provided in subsection (b)(2).

(2) *Conduct Previously Considered Where No Investigation Was Taken And Discipline Was Not Warranted.* Conduct in previous lawyer disciplinary proceedings of any jurisdiction, including revocation of conditional admission proceedings which was not investigated, is admissible, even if it was determined in the proceedings without investigation that discipline was not warranted.

(3) *Previous Finding.* A finding in previous disciplinary proceedings that a lawyer committed conduct warranting discipline or revocation, modification or extension of conditional admission is, in proceedings under these Rules, conclusive evidence that the lawyer committed the conduct.

(4) *Previous Discipline.* The fact that the lawyer received discipline in previous disciplinary proceedings, including revocation, modification or extension of conditional admission, is admissible to determine the nature of the discipline to be imposed, but is not admissible to prove that a violation occurred and is not admissible to prove the character of the lawyer in order to show that the lawyer acted in conformity therewith; provided, however, that evidence of such prior discipline may be used to prove:

(i) A pattern of related conduct, the cumulative effect of which constitutes a violation;

(ii) The current charge (e.g., the lawyer has continued to practice despite suspension);

(iii) For purposes of impeachment (e.g., the lawyer denies having been disciplined before); or

(iv) Motive, opportunity, intent, preparation, plan, knowledge, identity, or absence of mistake or accident.

(c) Stipulation. Unless the referee or this Court otherwise directs or the stipulation otherwise provides, a stipulation before a Panel remains in effect at subsequent proceedings regarding the same matter before the referee or this Court.

(d) Panel Proceedings. Subject to the Rules of Civil Procedure for District Courts and the Rules of Evidence, evidence obtained through a request for admission, deposition, or hearing under Rule 9 is admissible in proceedings before the referee or this Court.

(e) Admission. Subject to the Rules of Evidence, a lawyer's admission of unprofessional conduct or of violating a conditional admission agreement is admissible in proceedings under these Rules.

Adopted Nov. 1, 1976, eff. Jan. 1, 1977. Amended May 29, 1980; June 26, 1980; Jan. 12, 1981; July 22, 1982; June 18, 1986, eff. July 1, 1986; April 27, 1987, eff. July 1, 1987; Sept. 14, 1988, eff. Jan. 1, 1989; July 28, 1999, eff. Aug. 1, 1999; Aug. 10, 2005, eff. Sept. 1, 2005.

RULE 20. CONFIDENTIALITY; EXPUNCTION

(a) General Rule. The files, records, and proceedings of the District Committees, the Board, and the Director, as they may relate to or arise out of any complaint or charge of unprofessional conduct against or investigation of a lawyer, shall be deemed confidential and shall not be disclosed, except:

(1) As between the Committees, Board and Director in furtherance of their duties;

(2) After probable cause has been determined under Rule 9(j)(1)(ii) or (iv) or proceedings before a referee or this Court have been commenced under these Rules;

(3) As between the Director and a lawyer admission or disciplinary authority of another jurisdiction in which the lawyer affected is admitted to practice or seeks to practice;

(4) Upon request of the lawyer affected, the file maintained by the Director shall be produced including any district committee report; however, the Director's work product shall not be required to be produced, nor shall a member of the District Ethics Committee or the Board, the Director, or the Director's staff be subject to deposition or compelled testimony, except upon a showing to the court issuing the subpoena of extraordinary circumstance and compelling need. In any event, the mental impressions, conclusions, opinions and legal theories of the Director and Director's staff shall remain protected.

(5) If the complainant is, or at the time of the actions complained of was, the lawyer's client, the lawyer shall furnish to the complainant copies of the lawyer's written responses to investigation requests by the Director and District Ethics Committee, except that, insofar as a response does not relate to the client's complaint or involves information as to

which another client has a privilege, portions may be deleted;

(6) Where permitted by this Court; or

(7) Where required or permitted by these Rules.

(8) Nothing in this rule shall be construed to require the disclosure of the mental processes or communications of the Committee or Board members made in furtherance of their duties.

(9) As between the Director and the Client Security Board in furtherance of their duties to investigate and consider claims of client loss allegedly caused by the intentional dishonesty of a lawyer.

(10) As between the Director and the Board on Judicial Standards or its executive secretary in furtherance of their duties to investigate and consider conduct of a judge that occurred prior to the judge assuming judicial office.

(11) As between the Director and the Board of Law Examiners in furtherance of their duties under these rules.

(b) Special Matters. The following may be disclosed by the Director:

(1) The fact that a matter is or is not being investigated or considered by the Committee, Director, or Panel;

(2) With the affected lawyer's consent, the fact that the Director has determined that discipline is not warranted;

(3) The fact that the Director has issued an admonition;

(4) The Panel's disposition under these Rules;

(5) The fact that stipulated probation has been approved under Rule 8(d)(3) or 8(e);

(6) The fact that the terms of a conditional admission agreement have been modified or extended under Rule 8(d)(5);

(7) Information to other members of the lawyer's firm necessary for protection of the firm's clients or appropriate for exercise of responsibilities under Rules 5.1 and 5.2, Rules of Professional Conduct.

Notwithstanding any other provision of this Rule, the records of matters in which it has been determined that discipline is not warranted shall not be disclosed to any person, office or agency except to the lawyer and as between Committees, Board, Director, Referee or this Court in furtherance of their duties under these Rules.

(c) Records after Determination of Probable Cause or Commencement of Referee or Court Proceedings. Except as ordered by the referee or this Court and except for work product, after probable cause has been determined under Rule 9(j)(1)(ii) or (iv) or proceedings before a referee or this Court have been commenced under these Rules, the files, records, and proceedings of the District Committee, the Board, and the Director relating to the matter are not confidential.

(d) Referee or Court proceedings. Except as ordered by the referee or this Court, the files, records, and proceedings before a referee or this Court under these Rules are not confidential.

(e) Expunction of records. The Director shall expunge records relating to dismissed complaints as follows:

(1) *Destruction schedule.* All records or other evidence of a dismissed complaint shall be destroyed three years after the dismissal;

(2) *Retention of records.* Upon application by the Director to a Panel Chair chosen in rotation, for good cause shown and with notice to the respondent and opportunity to be heard, records which should otherwise be expunged under this Rule may be retained for such additional time not exceeding three years as the Panel Chair deems appropriate.

(f) Advisory Opinions, Overdraft Notification Program Files, and Probation Files. The files, notes, and records maintained by the Director relating to advisory opinions, trust account overdraft notification, and monitoring of lawyers on probation shall be deemed confidential and shall not be disclosed except:

(1) in the course of disciplinary proceedings arising out of the facts or circumstances of the advisory opinion, overdraft notification, or probation; or

(2) upon consent of the lawyer who requested the advisory opinion or was the subject of the overdraft notification or probation.

Adopted Nov. 1, 1976, eff. Jan. 1, 1977. Amended April 26, 1983; June 18, 1986, eff. July 1, 1986; April 27, 1987, eff. July 1, 1987; May 21, 1987, eff. July 1, 1987; Sept. 14, 1988, eff. Jan. 1, 1989; Feb. 11, 1991, eff. March 1, 1991; Dec. 12, 1994; March 30, 1999, eff. March 30, 1999; Aug. 10, 2005, eff. Sept. 1, 2005; March 24, 2009, eff. July 1, 2009.

Advisory Committee Comment—1999 Amendment

Rule 20 has been modified to permit the exchange of information between the two disciplinary boards and their staff in situations involving conduct of a judge that occurred prior to the judge assuming judicial office. See also R.L.Prof.Resp. 20(a)(10). Both the Board on Judicial Standards and the Lawyers Professional Responsibility Board have jurisdiction in such cases. R.Bd.Jud.Std. 2(b); R.L.Prof. Resp. 62.

Historical Notes

The order of the Minnesota Supreme Court dated December 12, 1994, provides in part that the amendments to the Rules on Lawyers Professional Responsibility and the Rules of Professional Conduct shall govern all lawyer disciplinary actions commenced on or after January 1, 1995.

The order of the Minnesota Supreme Court [C4–85–697] dated March 30, 1999, amending the Rules on Lawyers Professional Responsibility provides in part that the "(t)he inclusion of Advisory Committee comments is made for convenience and does not reflect court approval of the comments made therein."

RULE 21. PRIVILEGE: IMMUNITY

(a) Privilege. A complaint or charge, or statement relating to a complaint or charge, of a lawyer's alleged unprofessional conduct, to the extent that it is made in proceedings under these Rules, or to the Director or a person employed thereby or to a District Committee, the Board or this Court, or any member thereof, is absolutely privileged and may not serve as a basis for liability in any civil lawsuit brought against the person who made the complaint, charge, or statement.

(b) Immunity. Board members, other Panel members, District Committee members, the Director, and the Director's staff, and those entering into agreements with the Director's Office to supervise probations, shall be immune from suit for any conduct in the course of their official duties.

Adopted Nov. 1, 1976, eff. Jan. 1, 1977. Amended May 29, 1980; July 22, 1982; June 18, 1986, eff. July 1, 1986; April 27, 1987, eff. July 1, 1987; Sept. 14, 1988, eff. Jan. 1, 1989; Feb. 11, 1991, eff. March 1, 1991.

RULE 22. PAYMENT OF EXPENSES

Payment of necessary expenses of the Director and the Board and its members incurred from time to time and certified to this Court as having been incurred in the performance of their duties under these Rules and the compensation of the Director and persons employed by the Director under these Rules shall be made upon vouchers approved by this Court from its funds now or hereafter to be deposited to its credit with the State of Minnesota or elsewhere.

Adopted Nov. 1, 1976, eff. Jan. 1, 1977. Amended June 18, 1986, eff. July 1, 1986; April 27, 1987, eff. July 1, 1987; Sept. 14, 1988, eff. Jan. 1, 1989.

RULE 23. SUPPLEMENTAL RULES

The Board and each District Committee may adopt rules and regulations, not inconsistent with these Rules, governing the conduct of business and performance of their duties.

Adopted Nov. 1, 1976, eff. Jan. 1, 1977. Amended June 18, 1986, eff. July 1, 1986; April 27, 1987, eff. July 1, 1987; Sept. 14, 1988, eff. Jan. 1, 1989.

RULE 24. COSTS AND DISBURSEMENTS

(a) Costs. Unless this Court orders otherwise or specifies a higher amount, the prevailing party in any disciplinary proceeding or revocation of conditional admission proceeding decided by this Court shall recover costs in the amount of $900.

(b) Disbursements. Unless otherwise ordered by this Court, the prevailing party in any disciplinary proceedings or revocation of conditional admission proceedings decided by this Court shall recover, in addition to the costs specified in subdivision (a), all disbursements necessarily incurred after the filing of a petition for disciplinary action or a petition for revocation of conditional admission under Rule 12. Recoverable disbursements in proceedings before a referee or this Court shall include those normally assessed in appellate proceedings in this Court, together with those which are normally recoverable by the prevailing party in civil actions in the district court.

(c) Time and Manner for Taxation of Costs and Disbursements. The procedures and times governing the taxation of costs and disbursements and for making objection to same and for appealing from the clerk's taxation shall be as set forth in the Rules of Civil Appellate Procedure.

(d) Judgment for Costs and Disbursements. Costs and disbursements taxed under this Rule shall be inserted in the judgment of this Court in any disciplinary proceeding wherein suspension, disbarment, or revocation of conditional admission is ordered. No suspended attorney shall be permitted to resume practice and no disbarred attorney may file a petition for reinstatement if the amount of the costs and disbursements taxed under this Rule has not been fully paid. A lawyer whose conditional admission has been revoked may not file an application for admission to the bar until the amount of the costs and disbursements taxed under this Rule has been fully paid.

Adopted May 29, 1980, eff. May 29, 1980. Amended June 18, 1986, eff. July 1, 1986; April 27, 1987, eff. July 1, 1987; Sept. 14, 1988, eff. Jan. 1, 1989; June 13, 1996, eff. June 13, 1996; Aug. 10, 2005, eff. Sept. 1, 2005.

RULE 25. REQUIRED COOPERATION

(a) Lawyer's duty. It shall be the duty of any lawyer who is the subject of an investigation or proceeding under these Rules to cooperate with the District Committee, the Director, or the Director's staff, the Board, or a Panel, by complying with reasonable requests, including requests to:

(1) Furnish designated papers, documents or tangible objects;

(2) Furnish in writing a full and complete explanation covering the matter under consideration;

(3) Appear for conferences and hearings at the times and places designated;

(4) Execute authorizations and releases necessary to investigate alleged violations of a conditional admission agreement.

Such requests shall not be disproportionate to the gravity and complexity of the alleged ethical violations. The District Court of Ramsey County shall have jurisdiction over motions arising from Rule 25 requests. The lawyer shall be denominated by number or randomly selected initials in any District Court proceeding. Copies of documents shall be permitted in lieu of the original in all proceedings under these Rules. The Director shall promptly return the originals to the respondent after they have been copied.

(b) Grounds of discipline. Violation of this Rule is unprofessional conduct and shall constitute a ground for discipline; provided, however, that a lawyer's challenge to the Director's requests shall not constitute lack of cooperation if the challenge is promptly made, is in good faith and is asserted for a substantial purpose other than delay.

Adopted Oct. 16, 1981. Amended June 18, 1986, eff. July 1, 1986; April 27, 1987, eff. July 1, 1987; Sept. 14, 1988, eff. Jan. 1, 1989; Aug. 10, 2005, eff. Sept. 1, 2005.

RULE 26. DUTIES OF DISCIPLINED, DISABLED, CONDITIONALLY ADMITTED, OR RESIGNED LAWYER

(a) Notice to Clients in Nonlitigation Matters. Unless this Court orders otherwise, a disbarred, suspended or resigned lawyer, a lawyer whose conditional admission has been revoked, or a lawyer transferred to disability inactive status, shall notify each client being represented as of the date of the resignation or the order imposing discipline or transferring the lawyer to disability inactive status in a pending matter other than litigation or administrative proceedings of the lawyer's disbarment, suspension, resignation, revocation of conditional admission, or disability. The notification shall urge the client to seek legal advice of the client's own choice elsewhere, and shall include a copy of the Court's order.

(b) Notice to Parties and Tribunal in Litigation. Unless this Court orders otherwise, a disbarred, suspended or resigned lawyer, a lawyer whose conditional admission has been revoked, or a lawyer transferred to disability inactive status, shall notify each client, opposing counsel (or opposing party acting pro se) and the tribunal involved in pending litigation or administrative proceedings as of the date of the resignation or the order imposing discipline or transferring the lawyer to disability inactive status of the lawyer's disbarment, suspension, resignation, revocation of conditional admission, or disability. The notification to the client shall urge the prompt substitution of other counsel in place of the disbarred, suspended, or resigned, disabled lawyer, or a lawyer whose conditional admission has been revoked, and shall include a copy of the Court's order.

(c) Manner of notice. Notices required by this Rule shall be sent by certified mail, return receipt requested, within ten (10) days of the Court's order.

(d) Client papers and property. A disbarred, suspended, resigned or disabled lawyer, or a lawyer whose conditional admission has been revoked, shall make arrangements to deliver to each client being represented in a pending matter, litigation or administrative proceeding any papers or other property to which the client is entitled.

(e) Proof of Compliance. Within fifteen (15) days after the effective date of the Court's order, the disbarred, suspended, resigned or disabled lawyer, or a lawyer whose conditional admission has been revoked, shall file with the Director an affidavit showing:

(1) That the affiant has fully complied with the provisions of the order and with this Rule;

(2) All other State, Federal and administrative jurisdictions to which the affiant is admitted to practice; and

(3) The residence or other address where communications may thereafter be directed to the affiant.

Copies of all notices sent by the disbarred, suspended, resigned or disabled lawyer, or lawyer whose conditional admission has been revoked, shall be attached to the affidavit, along with proof of mailing by certified mail. The returned receipts from the certified mailing shall be provided to the Director within two months of the mailing of notices.

(f) Maintenance of Records. A disbarred, suspended, resigned or disabled lawyer, or a lawyer whose conditional admission has been revoked, shall keep and maintain records of the actions taken to comply with this Rule so that upon any subsequent proceeding being instituted by or against the lawyer, proof of compliance with this Rule and with the disbarment, suspension, resignation, disability, or revocation of conditional admission order will be available.

(g) Condition of Reinstatement. Proof of compliance with this Rule shall be a condition precedent to any petition or affidavit for reinstatement made by a disbarred, suspended, resigned or disabled lawyer, or to an application for admission submitted to the Board of Law Examiners after revocation of a lawyer's conditional admission.

Adopted Oct. 16, 1981. Amended June 18, 1986, eff. July 1, 1986; April 27, 1987, eff. July 1, 1987; Sept. 14, 1988, eff. Jan. 1, 1989; Feb. 11, 1991, eff. March 1, 1991; Aug. 10, 2005, eff. Sept. 1, 2005; March 24, 2009, eff. July 1, 2009.

RULE 27. TRUSTEE PROCEEDING

(a) Appointment of trustee. Upon a showing that a lawyer is unable to properly discharge responsibilities to clients due to disability, disappearance or death, or that a suspended, disbarred, resigned, or disabled lawyer, or a lawyer whose conditional admission has been revoked, has not complied with Rule 26, and that no arrangement has been made for another lawyer to discharge such responsibilities, this Court may appoint a lawyer to serve as the trustee to inventory the files of the disabled, disappeared, deceased, suspended, disbarred or resigned lawyer, or a lawyer whose conditional admission has been revoked, and to take whatever other action seems indicated to protect the interests of the clients and other affected parties.

(b) Protection of records. The trustee shall not disclose any information contained in any inventoried file without the client's consent, except as necessary to execute this Court's order appointing the trustee.

Adopted Oct. 16, 1981. Amended June 18, 1986, eff. July 1, 1986; April 27, 1987, eff. July 1, 1987; Jan. 14, 1988; Sept. 14, 1988, eff. Jan. 1, 1989; Feb. 11, 1991, eff. March 1, 1991; Aug. 10, 2005, eff. Sept. 1, 2005.

RULE 28. DISABILITY STATUS

(a) Transfer to disability inactive status. A lawyer whose physical condition, mental illness, mental deficiency, senility, or habitual and excessive use of intoxicating liquors, narcotics, or other drugs prevents the lawyer from competently representing clients shall be transferred to disability inactive status.

(b) Immediate transfer. This Court may immediately transfer a lawyer to disability inactive status upon proof that the lawyer has been found in a judicial proceeding to be a mentally ill, mentally deficient, incapacitated, or inebriate person.

(c) Asserting Disability in Disciplinary Proceeding. A lawyer's assertion of disability in defense or mitigation in a disciplinary proceeding or a revocation of conditional admission proceeding shall be deemed a waiver of the doctor-patient privilege. The referee may order an examination or evaluation by such person or institution as the referee designates. If a lawyer alleges disability during a disciplinary investigation or proceeding or a revocation of conditional admission proceeding, and therefore is unable to assist in the defense, the Director shall inform the Court of the allegation and of the Director's position regarding the allegation. The Court may:

(1) Transfer the lawyer to disability inactive status;

(2) Order the lawyer to submit to a medical examination by a designated professional;

(3) Appoint counsel if the lawyer has not retained counsel and the lawyer is financially eligible for appointed counsel. Financial eligibility shall be determined by the referee appointed by the Court to hear the disciplinary or disability petition in the same manner as eligibility for appointment of a public defender in a criminal case;

(4) Stay disciplinary proceedings or revocation of conditional admission proceedings until it appears the lawyer can assist in the defense;

(5) Direct the Director to file a petition under Rule 12;

(6) Appoint a referee with directions to make findings and recommendations to the Court regarding the disability allegation or to proceed under Rule 14;

(7) Make such or further orders as the Court deems appropriate.

(d) Reinstatement. This Court may reinstate a lawyer to active status upon a showing that the lawyer is fit to resume the practice of law. The parties shall proceed as provided in Rule 18. The lawyer's petition for reinstatement:

(1) Shall be deemed a waiver of the doctor-patient privilege regarding the incapacity; and

(2) Shall set forth the name and address of each physician, psychologist, psychiatrist, hospital or other institution that examined or treated the lawyer since the transfer to disability inactive status.

(e) Transfer following hearing. In cases other than immediate transfer to disability inactive status, and other than cases in which the lawyer asserts personal disability, this Court may transfer a lawyer to or from disability inactive status following a proceeding initiated by the Director and conducted in the same manner as a disciplinary proceeding under these Rules. In such proceeding:

(1) If the lawyer does not retain counsel, counsel may be appointed to represent the lawyer; and

(2) Upon petition of the Director and for good cause shown, the referee may order the lawyer to submit to a medical examination by an expert appointed by the referee.

Adopted July 22, 1982. Amended June 18, 1986, eff. July 1, 1986; April 27, 1987, eff. July 1, 1987; Sept. 14, 1988, eff. Jan. 1, 1989; Aug. 10, 2005, eff. Sept. 1, 2005; March 24, 2009, eff. July 1, 2009.

RULE 29. EX PARTE COMMUNICATIONS

Ex parte communications to any adjudicatory body including panels, referees and this Court are strongly disfavored. Such communications should not occur except after first attempting to contact the adversary and then only if the adversary is unavailable and an emergency exists. Such communications should be strictly limited to the matter relating to the emergency and the adversary notified at the earliest practicable time of the prior attempted contact and of the ex parte communication.

Adopted June 18, 1986, eff. July 1, 1986. Amended April 27, 1987, eff. July 1, 1987; Sept. 14, 1988, eff. Jan. 1, 1989.

RULE 30. ADMINISTRATIVE SUSPENSION

(a) Upon receipt of a district court order or a report from an Administrative Law Judge or public authority pursuant to Minn. Stat. § 518A.66 finding that a licensed Minnesota attorney is in arrears in payment of maintenance or child support and has not entered into or is not in compliance with an approved payment agreement for such support, the Director's Office shall serve and file with the Supreme Court a motion requesting the administrative suspension of the attorney until such time as the attorney has paid the arrearages or entered into or is in compliance with an approved payment plan. The Court shall suspend the lawyer or take such action as it deems appropriate.

(b) Any attorney administratively suspended under this rule shall not practice law or hold himself or herself out as authorized to practice law until reinstated pursuant to paragraph (c). The attorney shall, within 10 days of receipt of an order of administrative suspension, send written notice of the suspension to all clients, adverse counsel and courts before whom matters are pending and shall file an affidavit of compliance with this provision with the Director's Office.

(c) An attorney administratively suspended under this rule may be reinstated by filing an affidavit with supporting documentation averring that he or she is no longer in arrears in payment of maintenance or child support or that he or she has entered into and is in compliance with an approved payment agreement for payment of such support. Within 15 days of the filing of such an affidavit the Director's Office shall verify the accuracy of the attorney's affidavit and file a proposed order for reinstatement of the attorney requesting an expedited disposition.

(d) Nothing in this rule precludes disciplinary proceedings, if the attorney's conduct also violates the Minnesota Rules of Professional Conduct.

Adopted June 13, 1996, eff. June 13, 1996. Amended June 24, 1996, eff. June 24, 1996; May 14, 2010, eff. May 14, 2010.

RULES OF LAWYER TRUST ACCOUNT BOARD [REPEALED]

Historical Notes

The order of the Minnesota Supreme Court [C1-84-2140] dated April 1, 2010, repealed the Rules for the Lawyer Trust Account Board, effective July 1, 2010, and ordered that the administration of the Interest on Lawyer Trust Account (IOLTA) funds be transferred to the Legal Services Advisory Committee.

Rule 1. Repealed July 1, 2010.

Historical Notes

The order of Minnesota Supreme Court [C1-84-2140] dated April 1, 2010, repealed Rules 1 through 7 of the Lawyer Trust Account Board.

Rule 2. Repealed July 1, 2010.

Historical Notes

The order of Minnesota Supreme Court [C1-84-2140] dated April 1, 2010, repealed Rules 1 through 7 of the Lawyer Trust Account Board.

Rule 3. Repealed July 1, 2010.

Historical Notes

The order of Minnesota Supreme Court [C1-84-2140] dated April 1, 2010, repealed Rules 1 through 7 of the Lawyer Trust Account Board.

Rule 4. Repealed July 1, 2010.

Historical Notes

The order of Minnesota Supreme Court [C1-84-2140] dated April 1, 2010, repealed Rules 1 through 7 of the Lawyer Trust Account Board.

Rule 5. Repealed July 1, 2010.

Historical Notes

The order of Minnesota Supreme Court [C1-84-2140] dated April 1, 2010, repealed Rules 1 through 7 of the Lawyer Trust Account Board.

Rule 6. Repealed July 1, 2010.

Historical Notes

The order of Minnesota Supreme Court [C1-84-2140] dated April 1, 2010, repealed Rules 1 through 7 of the Lawyer Trust Account Board.

Rule 7. Repealed July 1, 2010.

Historical Notes

The order of Minnesota Supreme Court [C1-84-2140] dated April 1, 2010, repealed Rules 1 through 7 of the Lawyer Trust Account Board.

RULES OF LAWYER TRUST ACCOUNT BOARD [REPEALED]

RULES OF THE SUPREME COURT AND OF THE STATE BOARD OF LAW EXAMINERS FOR ADMISSION TO THE BAR [REPEALED]

Historical Notes

The order of the Minnesota Supreme Court [C5–84–2139] dated August 18, 1998, which promulgated the Rules for Admission to the Bar, provides in part that the Rules of the Minnesota Supreme Court and State Board of Law Examiners for Admission to the Bar are repealed retroactive to August 18, 1998.

CHARACTER AND FITNESS STANDARDS OF THE SUPREME COURT AND OF THE STATE BOARD OF LAW EXAMINERS FOR ADMISSION TO THE BAR OF MINNESOTA [Repealed August 26, 1998]

RULES FOR ADMISSION TO THE BAR

Effective July 1, 1998

Including Amendments Received Through January 1, 2014

Research Note

See Minnesota Statutes Annotated, *Volume 52, for case annotations and cross references.*

Rule 1. Purpose

The Board of Law Examiners is established to ensure that those who are admitted to the bar have the necessary competence and character to justify the trust and confidence that clients, the public, the legal system, and the legal profession place in lawyers.

Adopted Aug. 26, 1998. Amended Aug. 25, 2004, eff. Sept. 1, 2004; June 12, 2007, eff. July 1, 2007.

Historical Notes

The order of the Minnesota Supreme Court [C5–84–2139] dated August 26, 1998, provides in part that except as otherwise provided in Rule 6(E)(2), relating to the Performance Test which commences with the February 2001 bar examination, the Rules for Admission to the Bar are adopted retroactive to August 18, 1998.

Rule 2. Definitions and Due Date Provisions

A. Definitions. As used in these Rules:

(1) "Application file" means all information relative to an individual applicant to the bar collected by or submitted to the Board while the application is pending and during any conditional admission period.

(2) "Approved law school" means a law school provisionally or fully approved by the American Bar Association.

(3) "Board" means the Minnesota State Board of Law Examiners.

(4) "Court" means the Minnesota Supreme Court.

(5) "Director" means the staff director for the Board.

(6) "Full-time faculty member" means a person whose professional responsibilities are consistent with the definition of "full-time faculty member" set forth in the *Standards for Approval of Law Schools*, published by the American Bar Association's Section of Legal Education and Admissions to the Bar.

(7) "Good character and fitness" means traits, including honesty, trustworthiness, diligence and reliability, that are relevant to and have a rational connection with the applicant's present fitness to practice law.

(8) "Jurisdiction" means the District of Columbia or any state or territory of the United States.

(9) "Legal services program" means a program existing primarily for the purpose of providing legal assistance to indigent persons in civil or criminal matters.

(10) "Notify" or "give notice" means to mail or deliver a document to the last known address of the applicant or the applicant's lawyer. Notice is com-

plete upon mailing, but extends the applicant's period to respond by three days.

(11) "Principal occupation" means an applicant's primary professional work or business.

(12) "Uniform Bar Examination" or "UBE" is an examination prepared by the National Conference of Bar Examiners (NCBE), comprised of six Multistate Essay Examination questions, two Multistate Performance Test questions, and the Multistate Bar Examination.

B. Due Dates Provisions. Due dates specified under these Rules shall be strictly enforced and shall mean no later than 4:30 p.m. on the date stated; if the date falls on Saturday, Sunday, or a legal holiday, the deadline shall be the first working day thereafter. Postmarks dated on the due date will be accepted.

Adopted Aug. 26, 1998. Amended March 14, 2000, eff. March 14, 2000; Aug. 25, 2004, eff. Sept. 1, 2004; June 12, 2007, eff. July 1, 2007; June 27, 2011, eff. Sept. 1, 2011; Jan. 17, 2013, eff. Feb. 1, 2013.

Historical Notes

The order of the Minnesota Supreme Court [C5–84–2139] dated August 26, 1998, provides in part that except as otherwise provided in Rule 6(E)(2), relating to the Performance Test which commences with the February 2001 bar examination, the Rules for Admission to the Bar are adopted retroactive to August 18, 1998.

The order of the Minnesota Supreme Court [ADM10–8008] dated June 27, 2011, provides in part that "These amendments shall apply to all applications for bar examinations to be administered in February 2012 and thereafter. These amendments shall also apply to all applications for admission without examination under Rule 7 and for house counsel licenses under Rules 9 and 10 filed on or after September 1, 2011."

The order of the Minnesota Supreme Court [ADM10–8008] dated January 17, 2013, provides in part that the amendments are effective February 1, 2013, and "shall apply to bar examinations administered in February 2014 and thereafter."

Rule 3. State Board of Law Examiners

A. Composition. The Board shall consist of nine members, including a president. Seven of the members shall be lawyers having their principal office in this state and two shall be non-lawyer public members, each appointed by the Court for a term of three years or until a successor is appointed and qualifies. With the exception of the president, Board members may serve no more than three successive three-year terms. The president shall be appointed by the Court and shall serve as president, at the pleasure of the Court, for no more than six years. The terms of office may be staggered by the Court by any method it deems appropriate. The Board shall select a secretary from among its members.

B. Authority. The Board is authorized:

(1) Subject to the approval of the Court, to employ a director on a full-time or part-time basis, to prescribe duties, and to fix compensation;

(2) To secure examination questions and other testing instruments that the Board finds valid and reliable in measuring the competence of applicants to practice law, and to pay reasonable compensation for them;

(3) To employ examination graders;

(4) To establish a minimum passing score for the examinations;

(5) To conduct investigations of applicants' backgrounds as may be reasonably related to fitness to practice or eligibility under the Rules, and to require applicants to pay the costs of the investigations;

(6) To recommend to the Court the admission and licensure of applicants to practice law in Minnesota;

(7) To administer these Rules and adopt policies and procedures consistent with these Rules;

(8) To delegate to its president and director authority to make necessary determinations to implement the Board's policies and procedures and these Rules;

(9) To prepare and disseminate information to prospective applicants and the public about procedures and standards for admission to practice law in this state.

C. Board Meetings and Quorum.

(1) *Meetings.* Board meetings are open to the public except when the Board is considering the following:

(a) Examination materials;

(b) Any information concerning an applicant, potential applicant, or conditionally admitted lawyer;

(c) Personnel matters;

(d) Any information that is confidential or private under Rule 14;

(e) Legal advice from its counsel.

(2) *Minutes.* Minutes of the public portions of Board meetings are available upon request from the Board office.

(3) *Meeting Attendance.* Board members may attend meetings in person or, in extraordinary circumstances, by conference call.

(4) *Quorum.* A quorum of the Board shall be a majority of its sitting members.

Adopted Aug. 26, 1998. Amended Aug. 25, 2004, eff. Sept. 1, 2004; June 12, 2007, eff. July 1, 2007; June 27, 2011, eff. Sept. 1, 2011.

Historical Notes

The order of the Minnesota Supreme Court [C5–84–2139] dated August 26, 1998, provides in part that except as otherwise provided in Rule 6(E)(2), relating to the Performance Test which commences with the February 2001 bar examination, the Rules for Admission to the Bar are adopted retroactive to August 18, 1998.

The order of the Minnesota Supreme Court [ADM10–8008] dated June 27, 2011, provides in part that "These amendments shall apply to all applications for bar examinations to be administered in February 2012 and thereafter. These amendments shall also apply to all applications for admission without examination under Rule 7 and for house counsel licenses under Rules 9 and 10 filed on or after September 1, 2011."

Rule 4. General Requirements for Admission

A. Eligibility for Admission. The applicant has the burden to prove eligibility for admission by providing satisfactory evidence of the following:

(1) Age of at least 18 years;

(2) Good character and fitness as defined by these Rules;

(3) Either of the following:

(a) Graduation with a J.D. or LL.B. degree from a law school that is provisionally or fully approved by the American Bar Association; or

(b)(i) A bachelor's degree from an institution that is accredited by an agency recognized by the United States Department of Education;

(ii) a J.D. degree from a law school located within any state or territory of the United States or the District of Columbia;

(iii) and that the applicant has been licensed to practice law in any state or territory of the United States or the District of Columbia in 60 of the previous 84 months; and

(iv) the applicant has been engaged, as principal occupation, in the practice of law for 60 of the previous 84 months in one or more of the activities listed in Rule 7A(1)(c).

(4) Passing score on the written examination under Rule 6 or qualification under Rules 7A, 7B, 7C, 8, 9, or 10. An applicant eligible under Rule 4A(3)(b) but not under Rule 4A(3)(a) must provide satisfactory evidence of a passing score on the written examination under Rule 6 and is not eligible for admission under Rules 7A, 7B, 7C, 8, 9, or 10;

(5) A scaled score of 85 or higher on the Multistate Professional Responsibility Examination (MPRE); and

(6) Not currently suspended or disbarred from the practice of law in another jurisdiction.

B. Deleted effective February 1, 2013.

C. Application for Admission. To be accepted as complete, an application must be submitted on a form prescribed by the Board together with the following:

(1) A fee in an amount prescribed by Rule 12;

(2) A notarized authorization for release of information form;

(3) For applicants seeking admission by examination, a passport-style photo;

(4) Two notarized affidavits of good character from persons who have known the applicant for at least one year. To be acceptable, each affidavit shall:

(a) Be executed by a person who is unrelated to the applicant by blood or marriage and not living in the same household;

(b) Be executed by a person who was not a fellow law students during the applicant's enrollment;

(c) Describe the duration of time and circumstances under which the affiant has known the applicant;

(d) Describe what the affiant knows about the applicant's character and general reputation; and

(e) Provide other information bearing on the applicant's character and fitness to practice law.

D. Evidence of Graduation (Conferral of Degree). At least 30 days prior to the examination, each applicant shall file, or cause to be filed, an original document from the applicant's law school, signed by the dean or other authorized person stating:

(1) That the law school has conferred a J.D. or LL.B. degree upon the applicant; or

That the applicant has completed all coursework 30 days prior to the examination for which the applicant has applied, fulfilled all requirements for conferral of degree, and will be awarded a J.D. or LL.B. degree within 120 days following that examination. An applicant filing evidence of conferral of degree pursuant to Rule 4D(2) shall cause to be filed a certified transcript verifying the award of the degree within 120 days following the examination.

E. Additional Filing When Admitted Elsewhere. An applicant who has been admitted to practice in another jurisdiction shall also file or cause to be filed at the time of the application:

(1) A copy of the application for admission to the bar from the bar admissions authority in each jurisdiction in which the applicant has applied for admission to the practice of law;

(2) A document from the proper authority in each other jurisdiction where admitted showing the date of admission to the bar;

(3) A document from the proper authority in each other jurisdiction where admitted stating that the applicant is in good standing; and

(4) A document from the proper authority in each other jurisdiction where admitted indicating whether the applicant is the subject of any pending complaint or charge of misconduct.

F. Applicant Without MPRE Score. An applicant may file an application without having taken the MPRE. However, the applicant shall not be admitted until he or she has submitted evidence of an MPRE scaled score of 85 or higher. Such applicants must be admitted within 12 months of the date of a written notice from the Board or the application will be considered to have been withdrawn.

G. Additional Information Required. At the request of the Board, an applicant will be required to obtain and submit additional information.

H. Continuing Obligation to Update Application. An applicant has a continuing obligation to provide written updates to the application. This obligation continues until such time as the applicant is admitted, the application is withdrawn, or there is a final determination by the Board or Supreme Court. Applicants conditionally admitted under Rule 16 must continue to update their application for the term of the consent agreement.

I. Required Cooperation.

(1) An applicant has the duty to cooperate with the Board and the director by timely complying with requests, including requests to:

(a) Provide complete information, documents, and signed authorizations for release of information;

(b) Obtain reports or other information necessary for the Board to properly evaluate the applicant's fitness to practice;

(c) Appear for interviews to determine eligibility for admission or facilitate the background investigation.

(2) An applicant shall not discourage a person from providing information to the Board or retaliate against a person for providing information to the Board.

(3) If the Board determines that an applicant has breached the duty to cooperate, the Board may deem the application withdrawn, may deny the applicant an opportunity to test, or may deny admission.

J. Repeat Examinee. An applicant who has been unsuccessful on a prior Minnesota Bar Examination may reapply by submitting:

(1) A new application for admission pursuant to Rule 4C;

(2) The proper fee under Rule 12;

(3) A notarized authorization for release of information on a form prescribed by the Board;

(4) A passport-style photo; and

(5) If the original application is more than two years old, new affidavits as described in Rule 4C(4) of these Rules.

K. Incomplete Application. An application determined to be incomplete shall be returned to the applicant.

L. Withdrawal of Application. An applicant may withdraw the application by notifying the Board in writing at any time prior to the issuance of an adverse determination.

Adopted Aug. 26, 1998. Amended March 14, 2000, eff. March 14, 2000; Aug. 25, 2004, eff. Sept. 1, 2004; June 12, 2007, eff. July 1, 2007; June 27, 2011, eff. Sept. 1, 2011; Aug. 15, 2011, eff. Sept. 1, 2011; Aug. 30, 2011, eff. Sept. 1, 2011; Jan. 17, 2013, eff. Feb. 1, 2013.

Historical Notes

The order of the Minnesota Supreme Court [C5–84–2139] dated August 26, 1998, provides in part that except as otherwise provided in Rule 6(E)(2), relating to the Performance Test which commences with the February 2001 bar examination, the Rules for Admission to the Bar are adopted retroactive to August 18, 1998.

The orders of the Minnesota Supreme Court [ADM10–8008] dated June 27, 2011, August 15, 2011, and August 30, 2011, provide in part that "These amendments shall apply to all applications for bar examinations to be administered in February 2012 and thereafter. These amendments shall also apply to all applications for admission without examination under Rule 7 and for house counsel licenses under Rules 9 and 10 filed on or after September 1, 2011."

The order of the Minnesota Supreme Court [ADM10–8008] dated January 17, 2013, provides in part that the amendments are effective February 1, 2013, and "shall apply to bar examinations administered in February 2014 and thereafter."

Rule 5. Standards for Admission

A. Essential Eligibility Requirements. Applicants must be able to demonstrate the following essential eligibility requirements for the practice of law:

(1) The ability to be honest and candid with clients, lawyers, courts, the Board, and others;

(2) The ability to reason, recall complex factual information, and integrate that information with complex legal theories;

(3) The ability to communicate with clients, lawyers, courts, and others with a high degree of organization and clarity;

(4) The ability to use good judgment on behalf of clients and in conducting one's professional business;

(5) The ability to conduct oneself with respect for and in accordance with the law;

(6) The ability to avoid acts which exhibit disregard for the rights or welfare of others;

(7) The ability to comply with the requirements of the Rules of Professional Conduct, applicable state, local, and federal laws, regulations, statutes, and any applicable order of a court or tribunal;

(8) The ability to act diligently and reliably in fulfilling one's obligations to clients, lawyers, courts, and others;

(9) The ability to use honesty and good judgment in financial dealings on behalf of oneself, clients, and others; and

(10) The ability to comply with deadlines and time constraints.

B. Character and Fitness Standards and Investigation.

(1) *Purpose.* The purpose of the character and fitness investigation before admission to the bar is to protect the public and to safeguard the justice system.

(2) *Burden of Proof.* The applicant bears the burden of proving good character and fitness to practice law.

(3) *Relevant Conduct.* The revelation or discovery of any of the following shall be treated as cause for further inquiry before the Board determines whether the applicant possesses the character and fitness to practice law:

(a) Unlawful conduct;

(b) Academic misconduct;

(c) Misconduct in employment;

(d) Acts involving dishonesty, fraud, deceit, or misrepresentation;

(e) Acts which demonstrate disregard for the rights or welfare of others;

(f) Abuse of legal process, including the filing of vexatious or frivolous lawsuits;

(g) Neglect of financial responsibilities;

(h) Neglect of professional obligations;

(i) Violation of an order of a court, including child support orders;

(j) Conduct that evidences current mental or emotional instability that may impair the ability to practice law;

(k) Conduct that evidences current drug or alcohol dependence or abuse that may impair the ability to practice law;

(*l*) Denial of admission to the bar in another jurisdiction on character and fitness grounds;

(m) Disciplinary action by a lawyer disciplinary agency or other professional disciplinary agency of any jurisdiction;

(n) The making of false statements, including omissions, on bar applications in this state or any other jurisdiction.

(4) *Considerations.* The Board shall determine whether the present character and fitness of an applicant qualifies the applicant for admission. In making this determination, the following factors shall be considered in assigning weight and significance to prior conduct:

(a) The applicant's age at the time of the conduct;

(b) The recency of the conduct;

(c) The reliability of the information concerning the conduct;

(d) The seriousness of the conduct;

(e) The factors underlying the conduct;

(f) The cumulative effect of the conduct or information;

(g) The evidence of rehabilitation as defined in Rule 5B(5);

(h) The applicant's candor in the admissions process; and

(i) The materiality of any omissions or misrepresentations.

(5) *Rehabilitation.* An applicant who affirmatively asserts rehabilitation from past conduct may provide evidence of rehabilitation by submitting one or more of the following:

(a) Evidence that the applicant has acknowledged the conduct was wrong and has accepted responsibility for the conduct;

(b) Evidence of strict compliance with the conditions of any disciplinary, judicial, administrative, or other order, where applicable;

(c) Evidence of lack of malice toward those whose duty compelled bringing disciplinary, judicial, administrative, or other proceedings against applicant;

(d) Evidence of cooperation with the Board's investigation;

(e) Evidence that the applicant intends to conform future conduct to standards of good character and fitness for legal practice;

(f) Evidence of restitution of funds or property, where applicable;

(g) Evidence of positive social contributions through employment, community service, or civic service;

(h) Evidence that the applicant is not currently engaged in misconduct;

(i) Evidence of a record of recent conduct that demonstrates that the applicant meets the essential eligibility requirements for the practice of law and justifies the trust of clients, adversaries, courts, and the public;

(j) Evidence that the applicant has changed in ways that will reduce the likelihood of recurrence of misconduct; or

(k) Other evidence that supports an assertion of rehabilitation.

(6) *Continuing Obligation.* The applicant has a continuing obligation to update the application with respect to all matters inquired of on the application. This obligation continues during the pendency of the application, including the period when the matter is on appeal to the Board or the Court and during any period of conditional admission.

(7) *Determination.* A character and fitness determination shall be made with respect to each applicant who is a successful examinee or who is qualified by practice for admission under these Rules. An adverse determination on character and fitness grounds may be appealed under Rule 15.

(8) *Advisory Opinions.*

(a) A law student may request a written advisory opinion from the Board with respect to his or her character and fitness for admission by filing a completed application for admission, a fee in the amount required under Rule 12L, two notarized affidavits as required by Rule 4C(4), and an authorization for release of information as required by Rule 4C(2).

(b) Advisory opinions will not be binding on the Board.

Adopted Aug. 26, 1998. Amended Aug. 25, 2004, eff. Sept. 1, 2004; June 12, 2007, eff. July 1, 2007; June 27, 2011, eff. Sept. 1, 2011.

Historical Notes

The order of the Minnesota Supreme Court [C5-84-2139] dated August 26, 1998, provides in part that except as otherwise provided in Rule 6(E)(2), relating to the Performance Test which commences with the February 2001 bar examination, the Rules for Admission to the Bar are adopted retroactive to August 18, 1998.

The order of the Minnesota Supreme Court [ADM10-8008] dated June 27, 2011, provides in part that "These amendments shall apply to all applications for bar examinations to be administered in February 2012 and thereafter. These amendments shall also apply to all applications for admission without examination under Rule 7 and for house counsel licenses under Rules 9 and 10 filed on or after September 1, 2011."

Rule 6. Admission by Examination

A. Dates of Examinations. Examinations shall be held the last Tuesday and Wednesday of the months of February and July each year, at a place to be determined by the Board.

B. Timely Filing Deadlines. An application for admission by examination shall be filed in the office of the Board by October 15 for the February examination, or by March 15 for the July examination. Due dates shall be strictly enforced as specified in Rule 2B.

C. Late Filing Deadlines. Late applications will be accepted on or before December 1 for the February examination, or on or before May 1 for the July examination, but must be accompanied by the late filing fee pursuant to Rule 12. No applications shall be accepted after the late filing deadline. Due dates shall be strictly enforced as specified in Rule 2B.

D. Denial of Opportunity to Test. An applicant may be denied permission to take an examination:

(1) When the applicant has failed to comply with the requirements of Rule 4C, 4D, or 4I; or

(2) When the Board has determined the applicant has not satisfied the good character and fitness requirement of Rule 4A(2).

E. Scope of Examination. The Minnesota Bar Examination shall be the Uniform Bar Examination prepared by the National Conference of Bar Examiners, comprised of six Multistate Essay Examination (MEE) questions, two Multistate Performance Test (MPT) questions, and the Multistate Bar Examination (MBE).

(1) *Essay Questions.* The essay examination is comprised of six 30-minute MEE questions, covering any one or more of the following subjects:

Business Associations (Agency and Partnership; Corporations; and Limited Liability Companies)
Conflict of Laws
Constitutional Law
Contracts (including contracts under the Uniform Commercial Code (UCC))
Criminal Law and Procedure
Evidence
Family Law
Federal Civil Procedure
Negotiable Instruments (Commercial Paper) under the UCC
Real Property
Secured Transactions under the UCC
Torts
Trusts and Estates (Decedents' Estates; Trusts and Future Interests)

(2) *Multistate Performance Test.* The performance test shall include two 90-minute questions testing the applicant's ability to perform a lawyering task using legal and factual materials provided.

F. Testing Accommodations. An applicant whose disability requires testing accommodations shall submit with the application a written request pursuant to the Board's testing accommodations policy and shall describe:

(1) The type of accommodation requested;

(2) The reasons for the requested accommodation, including medical documentation in a format set forth in the policy referenced above.

The Board shall notify the applicant of its decision. A denial or modification of a request for testing accommodations constitutes an adverse determination of the Board and may be appealed pursuant to Rule 15.

G. Computer Use. Any applicant requesting to use a laptop computer to write the essay and performance test portion of the bar examination shall submit a computer registration form with the application and pay the required fee.

H. Examination Results. The results of the examination shall be released to examinees by regular mail to the address listed in the files of the Board, and successful examination numbers will be posted at the Court, on the Board's website, and at each Minnesota law school. The date of the release shall be announced at the examination.

I. Failing Examination Scores. A failing score on the bar examination is a final decision of the Board and does not afford the applicant the appeal and hearing rights set forth in Rule 15.

J. Stale Examination Scores. A passing score on the Minnesota Bar Examination is valid for 36 months from the date of the examination. Applicants must be admitted within 36 months of the examination.

Adopted Aug. 26, 1998. Amended Aug. 25, 2004, eff. Sept. 1, 2004; June 12, 2007, eff. July 1, 2007; June 27, 2011, eff. Sept. 1, 2011; Jan. 17, 2013, eff. Feb. 1, 2013.

Historical Notes

The order of the Minnesota Supreme Court [C5–84–2139] dated August 26, 1998, provides in part that except as otherwise provided in Rule 6(E)(2), relating to the Performance Test which commences with the February 2001 bar examination, the Rules for Admission to the Bar are adopted retroactive to August 18, 1998.

The order of the Minnesota Supreme Court [ADM10–8008] dated June 27, 2011, provides in part that "These amendments shall apply to all applications for bar examinations to be administered in February 2012 and thereafter. These amendments shall also apply to all applications for admission without examination under Rule 7 and for house counsel licenses under Rules 9 and 10 filed on or after September 1, 2011."

The order of the Minnesota Supreme Court [ADM10–8008] dated January 17, 2013, provides in part that the amendments are effective February 1, 2013, and "shall apply to bar examinations administered in February 2014 and thereafter."

Rule 7. Admission Without Examination

A. Eligibility by Practice.

(1) *Requirements.* An applicant may be eligible for admission without examination if the applicant otherwise qualifies for admission under Rule 4 (excluding applicants who qualify only under Rule 4A(3)(b)) and provides documentary evidence showing that for at least 60 of the 84 months immediately preceding the application, the applicant was:

(a) Licensed to practice law;

(b) In good standing before the highest court of all jurisdictions where admitted; and

(c) Engaged, as principal occupation, in the lawful practice of law as a:

i. Lawyer representing one or more clients;

ii. Lawyer in a law firm, professional corporation, or association;

iii. Judge in a court of law;

iv. Lawyer for any local or state governmental entity;

v. House counsel for a corporation, agency, association, or trust department;

vi. Lawyer with the federal government or a federal governmental agency including service as a member of the Judge Advocate General's Department of one of the military branches of the United States;

vii. Full-time faculty member in any approved law school; and/or

viii. Judicial law clerk whose primary responsibility is legal research and writing.

(2) *Jurisdiction.* The lawful practice of law described in Rule 7A(1)(c)(i) through (v) must have been performed in a jurisdiction in which the applicant is admitted, or performed in a jurisdiction that permits the practice of law by a lawyer not admitted in that jurisdiction. Practice described in Rule 7A(1)(c)(vi) through (viii) may have been performed outside the jurisdiction where the applicant is licensed.

B. Eligibility for Admission by MBE Score. An applicant may be eligible for admission without examination under Rule 4A(4) if the applicant has received a scaled score of 145 or higher on the MBE taken as a part of and at the same time as the essay or other part of a written bar examination given by another jurisdiction, was successful on that bar examination, and was subsequently admitted in that jurisdiction. The applicant shall submit evidence of the score and a completed application to the Board within 24 months of the date of the qualifying examination being used as the basis for the admission.

C. Eligibility for Admission by UBE Score. An applicant may be eligible for admission without examination under Rule 4A(4) if the applicant has received a scaled score of 260 or higher earned in another jurisdiction on the UBE and the score is certified as a UBE score by the National Conference of Bar Examiners. The applicant shall submit evidence of the score and a complete application for admission to the Board within 36 months of the date of the qualifying examination being used as the basis for the admission.

D. Transfer of MBE or UBE Score. An applicant seeking to transfer a MBE or UBE score achieved in another jurisdiction to Minnesota shall submit a written request for transfer to the National Conference of Bar Examiners.

E. MBE Score Advisory. Upon written request, the director will advise an applicant or potential applicant who took and passed a bar examination in another jurisdiction whether or not his or her MBE score satisfies the requirements of Rule 7B. Requests for score advisory shall include the following:

(1) Complete name and social security number of the examinee; and

(2) Month, year, and jurisdiction of test administration.

F. No Waiver of Time Requirements. The minimum time requirements and the timely filing requirements of this Rule shall be strictly enforced.

G. Eligibility After Unsuccessful Examination. An applicant may be eligible for admission without examination under this Rule notwithstanding a prior failure on the Minnesota Bar Examination.

Adopted Aug. 26, 1998. Amended March 14, 2000, eff. March 14, 2000; Aug. 25, 2004, Sept. 1, 2004; June 12, 2007, eff. July 1, 2007; June 27, 2011, eff. Sept. 1, 2011; Aug. 30, 2011, eff. Sept. 1, 2011; Jan. 17, 2013, eff. Feb 1, 2013.

Historical Notes

The order of the Minnesota Supreme Court [C5–84–2139] dated August 26, 1998, provides in part that except as otherwise provided in Rule 6(E)(2), relating to the Performance Test which commences with the February 2001 bar examination, the Rules for Admission to the Bar are adopted retroactive to August 18, 1998.

The orders of the Minnesota Supreme Court [ADM10–8008] dated June 27, 2011, and August 30, 2011, provide in part that "These amendments shall apply to all applications for bar examinations to be administered in February 2012 and thereafter. These amendments shall also apply to all applications for admission without examination under Rule 7 and for house counsel licenses under Rules 9 and 10 filed on or after September 1, 2011."

The order of the Minnesota Supreme Court [ADM10–8008] dated January 17, 2013, provides in part that the amendments are effective February 1, 2013, and "shall apply to bar examinations administered in February 2014 and thereafter."

Rule 8. Admission by Temporary License for Legal Services Programs

A. Eligibility. A lawyer licensed in another jurisdiction may apply for and be admitted under a temporary license to practice law in Minnesota when the applicant has accepted employment in Minnesota as a lawyer for a legal services program.

B. Filing. In order to qualify for the license, the lawyer must comply with the requirements of Rule 4A(1), (2), (3)(a), and (6) and must file with the Board, the following:

(1) A completed application for temporary license to practice law in Minnesota for a legal services program;

(2) A certificate or certificates from the proper authority in each jurisdiction certifying that the lawyer is in good standing and that no charges of professional misconduct are pending;

(3) An affidavit from the applicant's employer attesting to his or her knowledge of the applicant's competence and good character, and the fact that the applicant has accepted employment as a lawyer for a legal services program in Minnesota and will be supervised by a licensed Minnesota lawyer;

(4) Two additional affidavits of character as prescribed by Rule 4C(4), and a fee consistent with Rule 12G of these Rules.

C. Certification of Applicant's Good Character and Fitness. The office of the Board shall conduct an expedited character and fitness investigation and certify the applicant's good character and fitness prior to issuance of a license under this Rule.

D. Limitation. A license granted pursuant to this Rule shall authorize the lawyer to practice solely on behalf of the indigent clients of the designated legal services program.

E. Duration and Revocation. This temporary license shall be valid for a period of no more than 15 months from the date of issuance. Upon notice to the Clerk of the Appellate Courts, the Board shall have authority to revoke a temporary license issued pursuant to this Rule upon the occurrence of any of the following:

(1) The holder's admission to practice law in Minnesota pursuant to Rule 6 (Admission by Examination), Rule 7A (Eligibility by Practice) or 7B (Eligibility by Test Score);

(2) Termination of the holder's employment with the employer referred to in Rule 8B(3);

(3) The lapse of 15 months from the date of issuance;

(4) The holder's failure of the Minnesota Bar Examination; or

(5) Issuance by the Board of an adverse determination relative to the applicant's character and fitness.

F. Credit for Admission Without Examination. Time in the practice of law in the State of Minnesota under this temporary license may be counted toward the applicant's eligibility for admission without examination under Rule 7A.

Adopted Aug. 26, 1998. Amended Aug. 25, 2004, eff. Sept. 1, 2004; June 12, 2007, eff. July 1, 2007; Aug. 30, 2011, eff. Sept. 1, 2011.

Historical Notes

The order of the Minnesota Supreme Court [C5–84–2139] dated August 26, 1998, provides in part that except as otherwise provided in Rule 6(E)(2), relating to the Performance Test which commences with the February 2001 bar examination, the Rules for Admission to the Bar are adopted retroactive to August 18, 1998.

The order of the Minnesota Supreme Court [ADM10–8008] dated August 30, 2011, provides in part that these amendments "shall apply to all applications for bar examinations to be administered in February 2012 and thereafter."

Rule 9. Admission by Temporary House Counsel License

A. Practice by House Counsel. A lawyer licensed in another jurisdiction shall not practice law in Minnesota as house counsel unless he or she is admitted to practice in Minnesota under this Rule, Rule 6 (Admission by Examination), Rule 7 (Admission Without Examination), or Rule 10 (Admission by House Counsel License).

B. Eligibility. A lawyer licensed in another jurisdiction may apply for and be admitted under a temporary house counsel license when the lawyer:

(1) Is employed in Minnesota as house counsel solely for a single corporation (or its subsidiaries), association, business, or governmental entity whose lawful business consists of activities other than the practice of law or the provision of legal services; and

(2) Has practiced law by engaging in one or more of the activities listed in Rule 7A for at least 36 of the previous 60 months; and

(3) Complies with the eligibility provisions of Rule 4A(1), (2), (3)(a), (4), and (6).

The practice of law during the qualifying period must have been performed in a jurisdiction where the applicant is licensed or performed in a jurisdiction that permits the practice of law by a lawyer not licensed in that jurisdiction, unless the applicant, during the qualifying period, was practicing as house counsel for a corporation, agency, association, or trust department.

C. Requirements. In order to qualify for the temporary house counsel license, the applicant shall comply with the requirements of these Rules and file the following with the Board:

(1) An application for license to practice law in Minnesota as described in Rule 4C;

(2) The documents listed in Rules 4D and 4E;

(3) An affidavit from an officer, director, or general counsel of applicant's employer or parent company employer stating the date of employment and attesting to the fact that applicant is employed as house counsel solely for said employer, that applicant is an individual of good character, and that the nature of the employment meets the requirements of Rule 9B(1);

(4) A fee consistent with Rule 12F; and

(5) Other information, if requested by the Board.

D. Limitation. A license issued pursuant to this Rule authorizes the holder to practice solely for the employer designated in the affidavit required by Rule 9C(3), except that the lawyer is authorized to provide "pro bono legal representation" to a "pro bono client" referred to the lawyer through an "approved legal services provider" as these phrases are defined in Rule 2S, Rule 2R, and Rule 2B, respectively, of the Rules of the Supreme Court for Continuing Legal Education of the Bar.

E. Issuance of Temporary House Counsel License. An expedited character and fitness investigation will be conducted, and if the Board finds that the applicant's present character and fitness qualifies the applicant for admission, a temporary license will be issued.

F. Duration and Expiration of Temporary License. The temporary license shall expire 12 months from the date of issuance, or sooner, upon the occurrence of any of the following:

(1) Termination of the holder's employment with the employer referenced in Rule 9C(3); or

(2) Admission to practice law in Minnesota pursuant to Rule 6 (Admission by Examination), Rule 7 (Admission Without Examination), or Rule 10 (Admission by House Counsel License); or

(3) Issuance of an adverse determination pursuant to Rule 15A.

After expiration of a temporary house counsel license, the former license holder, unless already admitted to practice law in Minnesota under another of these Rules, shall not practice law in Minnesota or otherwise represent that he or she is admitted to practice law in Minnesota.

G. House Counsel License Without Time Limitation. An applicant for or holder of a temporary house counsel license who anticipates practicing in Minnesota for more than 12 months should also apply for a house counsel license under Rule 10 or another license under these Rules.

H. Notice of Termination of Employment. A holder of a temporary house counsel license shall notify both the Board and the Lawyer Registration Office in writing within 10 business days of termination of employment with the employer referenced in Rule 9C(3).

I. Credit for Admission Without Examination. Time in the practice of law under the temporary house counsel license may be counted toward eligibility for admission without examination under Rule 7A.

J. Professional Conduct and Responsibility. A lawyer licensed under this Rule shall abide by and be subject to all laws and rules governing lawyers admitted to the practice of law in this state.

Adopted Aug. 26, 1998. Amended Aug. 25, 2004, eff. Sept. 1, 2004; June 12, 2007, eff. July 1, 2007; July 23, 2007, eff. July 23, 2007; June 27, 2011, eff. Sept. 1, 2011; Aug. 30, 2011, eff. Sept. 1, 2011; Jan. 17, 2013, eff. Feb. 1, 2013.

Historical Notes

The order of the Minnesota Supreme Court [C5–84–2139] dated August 26, 1998, provides in part that except as otherwise provided in Rule 6(E)(2), relating to the Performance Test which commences with the February 2001 bar examination, the Rules for Admission to the Bar are adopted retroactive to August 18, 1998.

The orders of the Minnesota Supreme Court [ADM10–8008]dated June 27, 2011, and August 30, 2011, provide in part that "These amendments shall apply to all applications for bar examinations to be administered in February 2012 and thereafter. These amendments shall also apply to all applications for admission without examination under Rule 7 and for house counsel licenses under Rules 9 and 10 filed on or after September 1, 2011."

The order of the Minnesota Supreme Court [ADM10–8008] dated January 17, 2013, provides in part that the amendments are effective February 1, 2013, and "shall apply to bar examinations administered in February 2014 and thereafter."

Rule 10. Admission by House Counsel License

A. Practice by House Counsel. A lawyer licensed in another jurisdiction shall not practice law in Minnesota as house counsel unless he or she is admitted to practice in Minnesota under this Rule, Rule 6 (Admission by Examination), Rule 7 (Admission Without Examination), or Rule 9 (Admission by Temporary House Counsel License).

B. Eligibility. A lawyer licensed in another jurisdiction or the holder of a temporary house counsel license issued pursuant to Rule 9B and 9C, who intends to practice in Minnesota for more than 12 months, may apply for a house counsel license when the lawyer:

(1) Is employed in Minnesota as house counsel solely for a single corporation (or its subsidiaries), association, business, or governmental entity whose lawful business consists of activities other than the practice of law or the provision of legal services; and

(2) Has practiced law by engaging in one or more of the activities listed in Rule 7A for at least 36 of the previous 60 months; and

(3) Complies with the eligibility provisions of Rule 4A(1), (2), (3)(a), (4), and (6).

C. **Requirements.** In order to qualify for the house counsel license, the applicant shall comply with the requirements of these Rules and file the following with the Board:

(1) An application for a license to practice law in Minnesota as described in Rule 4C;

(2) The documents listed in Rules 4D and 4E;

(3) An affidavit from an officer, director, or general counsel of applicant's employer or parent company stating the date of employment and attesting to the fact that applicant is employed as house counsel solely for that employer, that applicant is an individual of good character, and that the nature of the employment meets the requirements of Rule 10B(1);

(4) A fee consistent with Rule 12F; and

(5) Other information, as requested by the Board.

D. **Limitation.** A license issued pursuant to this Rule authorizes the holder to practice solely for the employer designated in the Rule 10C(3) affidavit, except that the lawyer is authorized to provide "pro bono legal representation" to a "pro bono client" referred to the lawyer through an "approved legal services provider" as these phrases are defined in Rule 2S, Rule 2R, and Rule 2B, respectively of the Rules of the Supreme Court for Continuing Legal Education of the Bar.

E. **Expiration of House Counsel License.** The house counsel license shall expire upon termination of the holder's employment with the employer referenced in Rule 10C(3). After a house counsel license expires, the former license holder, unless already admitted to practice law in Minnesota under another of these Rules, shall not practice law in Minnesota or otherwise represent that he or she is admitted to practice law in Minnesota.

F. **Notice of Termination of Employment.** A house counsel license holder shall notify both the Board and the Lawyer Registration Office in writing within 10 business days of termination of employment with the employer referenced in Rule 10C(3).

G. **Re-issuance of House Counsel License.** At the director's discretion, a house counsel license that has expired due to termination of holder's employment may be reissued if re-issuance is requested within 90 days of the expiration of the license, provided that the other requirements of this Rule are met at the time of the request for re-issuance. The fee for re-issuance shall be consistent with Rule 12M.

H. **Credit for Admission Without Examination.** Time in the practice of law under the house counsel license may be counted toward eligibility for admission without examination under Rule 7A.

I. **Professional Conduct and Responsibility.** A lawyer licensed under this Rule shall abide by and be subject to all laws and rules governing lawyers admitted to the practice of law in this state.

Adopted Aug. 25, 2004, eff. Sept. 1, 2004. Amended June 12, 2007, eff. July 1, 2007; July 23, 2007, eff. July 23, 2007; June 27, 2011, eff. Sept. 1, 2011; June 27, 2011, eff. Sept. 1, 2011; Aug. 30, 2011, eff. Sept. 1, 2011; Jan. 17, 2013, eff. Feb. 1, 2013.

Historical Notes

The orders of the Minnesota Supreme Court [ADM10–8008] dated June 27, 2011 and August 30, 2011, provide in part that "These amendments shall apply to all applications for bar examinations to be administered in February 2012 and thereafter. These amendments shall also apply to all applications for admission without examination under Rule 7 and for house counsel licenses under Rules 9 and 10 filed on or after September 1, 2011."

The order of the Minnesota Supreme Court [ADM10–8008] dated January 17, 2013, provides in part that the amendments are effective February 1, 2013, and "shall apply to bar examinations administered in February 2014 and thereafter."

Rule 11. License for Foreign Legal Consultants

A. **Eligibility.** A person who is admitted to practice in a foreign country as a lawyer or counselor at law may apply for, and, at the discretion of the Board, may obtain a license to render services as a foreign legal consultant in this state, without examination, subject to the limitations set forth in this Rule.

B. **Requirements.** In order to qualify for the license the applicant must:

(1) Have been admitted to practice in a foreign country as a lawyer or counselor at law or the equivalent;

(2) As principal occupation, have been engaged in the practice of law of that country for at least five of the seven years immediately preceding the application;

(3) Be in current good standing as a lawyer or counselor at law or the equivalent in that country, and have remained in good standing throughout the period of his or her practice;

(4) Possess the good character and fitness required for admission to practice in this state;

(5) Have been awarded a post-secondary degree in law;

(6) Intend to practice as a foreign legal consultant in this state; and

(7) Maintain an office in this state for the purpose of practicing as a foreign legal consultant.

C. **Applications.** In order to qualify for the foreign legal consultant license, an applicant must file with the Board the following documents, together with duly authenticated English translations, if the documents are not in English:

(1) A sworn and notarized typewritten Application for Foreign Legal Consultant License;

(2) An authentic certificate from the authority having final jurisdiction over professional discipline

in the foreign country in which the applicant is admitted to practice, which shall be accompanied by the official seal, if any, of such authority, and which shall certify:

(a) The authority's jurisdiction in such matters;

(b) The applicant's admission to practice in the foreign country, the date of admission, and the applicant's good standing as a lawyer or counselor at law or the equivalent in that jurisdiction;

(3) An authentic document from the authority having final jurisdiction over professional discipline in any foreign country or jurisdiction in which the applicant has been licensed as a lawyer or as a foreign legal consultant indicating whether any charge or complaint has ever been filed against the applicant with the authority, and, if so, the substance of each charge or complaint, and the adjudication or resolution of each charge or complaint;

(4) A letter of recommendation signed by, and accompanied with the official seal, if any, of one of the members of the executive body of the authority having final jurisdiction over professional discipline or from one of the judges of the highest court of law of the foreign country, certifying to the applicant's professional qualifications;

(5) Letters of recommendation from at least three lawyers or counselors at law or the equivalent admitted in and practicing in the foreign country where the applicant is admitted, setting forth the length of time, and under what circumstances they have known the applicant and stating their appraisal of the applicant's good character and fitness for admission;

(6) Notarized letters of recommendation from at least two members in good standing of the Minnesota Bar, setting forth the length of time, and under what circumstances they have known the applicant and their appraisal of the applicant's good character and fitness for admission;

(7) Any other evidence as to the applicant's educational and professional qualifications, good character and fitness and compliance with the requirements of this rule as the Board may require;

(8) A statement that the foreign legal consultant has read, understood, and made a commitment to observe the Minnesota Rules of Professional Conduct;

(9) A score report showing that the applicant received a scaled score of 85 or higher on the Multistate Professional Responsibility Examination, or a sworn statement attesting to the applicant's attendance, within the previous 12 months, of no fewer than six hours of coursework in legal ethics accredited by the Minnesota Board of Continuing Legal Education;

(10) Evidence of professional liability insurance in an amount deemed sufficient by the director;

(11) A written and notarized statement setting forth the foreign legal consultant's address within the State of Minnesota and designating the Clerk of Appellate Courts as agent for the service of process for all purposes;

(12) An affidavit stating that the foreign legal consultant shall notify the Board of any resignation or revocation of such foreign legal consultant's admission to practice in the foreign country of admission, or in any other state or jurisdiction in which the foreign legal consultant has been licensed as a lawyer or counselor at law or equivalent or as a foreign legal consultant, or of any censure, suspension, or expulsion in respect of such admission;

(13) If employed as house counsel, an affidavit from an officer, director, or general counsel of applicant's employer attesting to the fact that applicant is employed as house counsel solely for that employer and agreeing to notify the Board if the applicant's employment is terminated; and

(14) A fee in the amount of $1,200.

D. Investigation. The Board shall conduct an investigation into the applicant's background and verify the applicant's supporting documents as the Board deems appropriate or necessary in the circumstances.

E. Scope of Practice. A person licensed as a foreign legal consultant under this Rule may render legal services in this state respecting the laws of the country in which the foreign legal consultant is admitted to practice as a lawyer, counselor at law or equivalent.

(1) The foreign legal consultant shall not conduct any activity or render any services constituting the practice of the law of the United States, of this state, or of any other state, commonwealth or territory of the United States or the District of Columbia including, but not limited to, the restrictions that the foreign legal consultant shall not:

(a) Appear for another person as a lawyer in any court or before any magistrate or other judicial officer or before any federal, state, county or municipal governmental agency, quasi-judicial or quasi-governmental authority in this state, or prepare pleadings or any other papers in any action or proceedings brought in any such court or before any judicial officer, except as authorized in any rule or procedure relating to admission pro hac vice, or pursuant to administrative rule;

(b) Provide legal advice in connection with the preparation of any deed, mortgage, assignment, discharge, lease, agreement of sale, or any other instrument affecting title to real property located in the United States;.

(c) Prepare any will or trust instrument affecting the disposition of any property located in the United States and owned by a resident thereof any instrument relating to the administration of a decedent's estate in the United States;

(d) Prepare any instrument in respect of the marital relations, rights or duties of a resident of the United States or the custody or care of the children of a resident;

(e) Render professional legal advice on the law of this state or the United States or any other state, subdivision, commonwealth or territory of the United States or the District of Columbia (whether rendered incident to the preparation of a legal instrument or otherwise);

(f) In any way represent that the foreign legal consultant is admitted to the Minnesota Bar or is licensed as a lawyer or foreign legal consultant in another state, territory or the District of Columbia, or as a lawyer or counselor at law or the equivalent in a foreign country, unless so licensed;

(g) Use any title other than "Foreign Legal Consultant, Admitted to the Practice of Law in [name of country]". The foreign legal consultant's authorized title and firm name in the foreign country in which the foreign legal consultant is admitted to practice as a lawyer or counselor at law or the equivalent may be used if the title, firm name, and the name of the foreign country are stated together with the above-mentioned designation;

(h) Render any legal services for a client without utilizing a written retainer agreement which shall specify in bold type that the foreign legal consultant is not admitted to practice law in this state, nor licensed to advise on the laws of the United States or the District of Columbia, and that the practice of the foreign legal consultant is limited to the laws of the foreign country where such person is admitted to practice as a lawyer or counselor at law or the equivalent; or

(i) Hold any client funds or valuables without entering into a written retainer agreement which shall specify in bold type the name of a Minnesota lawyer licensed in good standing who is also representing the particular client in the particular matter at hand.

(2) A foreign legal consultant who is employed in Minnesota as house counsel solely for a single corporation (or its subsidiaries), association, business, or governmental entity is not subject to the restrictions as to scope of practice set forth in Rule 11E(1) (e), (f), (g) (h), and (i) provided that the practice is performed exclusively for the employer referenced above. A foreign legal consultant employed as house counsel may use the title "counsel."

F. Disciplinary Provisions.

(1) A foreign legal consultant is expressly subject to:

(a) the Minnesota Rules of Professional Conduct and all laws and rules governing lawyers admitted to the practice of law in this state;

(b) continuing review by the Board of qualifications to retain the license granted hereunder;and

(c) the disciplinary jurisdiction of the Minnesota Office of Lawyers Professional Responsibility and the Minnesota Supreme Court.

(2) Rule 11F(1) above shall not be construed to limit in any way concurrent disciplinary procedures to which the foreign legal consultant may be subject in the country of admission.

G. Rights and Obligations. A foreign legal consultant shall be entitled to the rights and obligations of a member of the Minnesota Bar with respect to:

(1) Affiliation in the same law firm with one or more members of the Minnesota Bar, including by employing one or more members of the bar; being employed by one or more members of the bar or by any partnership or professional corporation that includes members of the Minnesota Bar or that maintains an office in Minnesota; and being a partner in any partnership or shareholder in any professional corporation that includes members of the Minnesota Bar or that maintains an office in Minnesota; and

(2) Attorney–client privilege, work product protection, and similar professional privileges.

H. Re–Certification and Renewal Fees.

(1) Every three years a foreign legal consultant shall submit to the Board:

(a) A sworn statement attesting to the foreign legal consultant's continued good standing as a lawyer or counselor at law or equivalent in the foreign country in which the foreign legal consultant is admitted to practice;

(b) A sworn and notarized typewritten Application for Foreign Legal Consultant License; and

(c) A fee in the amount of $300.

(2) On an annual basis, a foreign legal consultant shall submit to the Minnesota Lawyer Registration Office a lawyer registration fee equivalent to the renewal fees paid by Minnesota licensed lawyers pursuant to the Rules of the Supreme Court for Registration of Lawyers.

I. Admission to Bar. If the Board determines that a foreign legal consultant under this Rule is subsequently admitted as a member of the Minnesota Bar, the foreign legal consultant's license shall be deemed superceded by the license to practice law in Minnesota.

J. Revocation and Expiration. If the Board determines that a foreign legal consultant no longer meets the requirements for licensure set forth in this Rule, the license shall expire. If the foreign legal consultant is employed as house counsel, the foreign legal consultant license shall expire on the date of the termination of the foreign legal consultant's employment by the employer referenced in Rule 11C(13).

Adopted Aug. 26, 1998. Amended Aug. 25, eff. Sept. 1, 2004; June 12, 2007, eff. July 1, 2007; July 23, 2007, eff. July 23, 2007.

Historical Notes

The order of the Minnesota Supreme Court [C5–84–2139] dated August 26, 1998, provides in part that except as otherwise provided in Rule 6(E)(2), relating to the Performance Test which commences with the February 2001 bar examination, the Rules for Admission to the Bar are adopted retroactive to August 18, 1998.

Rule 12. Fees

A. General. Applicants shall pay application fees or other fees required under these Rules by personal check or money order made payable to the Board. At the Board's discretion, fees may be accepted by credit card or electronic funds transfer. The applicable fee is determined as of the date of filing of a complete application under Rule 4.

B. Fee for Examination, Not Previously Admitted. An applicant who meets the following criteria shall submit a fee of $500:

(1) Applying to take the Minnesota examination for the first time; and

(2) Not admitted to practice in another jurisdiction; and

(3) Filing on or before the timely filing deadline (October 15 for the February examination, or March 15 for the July examination).

An applicant meeting the criteria in (1) and (2) above, who files after the timely filing deadline but before the late filing deadline (December 1 for the February examination, or May 1 for the July examination) shall submit a fee of $650. Applications will not be accepted after the late filing deadline.

C. Fee for Examination, Prior Admission. An applicant who meets the following criteria shall submit a fee of $950:

(1) Licensed to practice in another jurisdiction more than six months prior to the date of the applicant's Minnesota application; and

(2) Filing on or before the timely filing deadline (October 15 for the February examination, or March 15 for the July examination).

An applicant meeting the criteria in (1) above, who files after the timely filing deadline but before the late filing deadline (December 1 for the February examination, or May 1 for the July examination) shall submit a fee of $1100. Applications will not be accepted after the late filing deadline.

D. Fee for Examination for Recently Admitted Applicants. An applicant applying to take the Minnesota examination who has been licensed to practice in another jurisdiction fewer than six months prior to the date of the applicant's Minnesota application shall submit the fee for examination required by paragraph B of this Rule.

E. Repeat Examinations. An applicant who was unsuccessful on the Minnesota examination and is filing on or before December 1 for the February examination, or on or before May 1 for the July examination, shall submit a fee of $500 and comply with Rule 4J.

F. Fee for Admission Without Examination. An applicant for admission without examination pursuant to Rule 7 (Admission Without Examination) or Rule 10 (Admission by House Counsel License) shall submit a fee of $950. An applicant for admission pursuant to Rule 9 (Admission by Temporary House Counsel License) shall submit a fee of $700.

G. Fee for Temporary License for Legal Services Program Practice. A fee in the amount of $75 must accompany an application for Temporary License pursuant to Rule 8. Payment of an additional fee, as required by Rule 12B, will qualify applicants under Rule 6. Payment of an additional fee, as required by Rule 12C, will qualify applicants under Rule 7A or 7B.

H. Transfer of Rule 8 Application to Rule 6 or Rule 7 Application. Documents submitted in support of a Rule 8 (Temporary License for Legal Services Programs) application for license may, upon the written request of applicant, constitute application pursuant to Rule 6 (Admission by Examination) or Rule 7 (Admission Without Examination) of these Rules, provided additional fees required by Rule 12 are submitted.

I. Refunds of Fees. An applicant who submits a written request to withdraw a bar examination application 15 or more days before the examination for which the applicant applied shall receive a refund in the amount of:

(1) $150, if the fee paid was in an amount specified by either Rule 12B or Rule 12E;

(2) $300, if the fee paid was in an amount specified by Rule 12C.

No other requests for refund will be granted.

J. Carry-over of Fees.

(1) *Applicants Ineligible Under Rule 7 (Admission Without Examination).* The fee of an applicant declared ineligible under Rule 7 (Admission Without Examination) shall, upon the applicant's written request, be applied to

(a) An examination held within the succeeding 15 months; or

(b) An application made under Rules 8, 9, or 10.

The written request must be received by the Board within 30 days of notice of the denial. No other carry-over of fees, other than those provided for in the following paragraph, shall be granted.

(2) *Medical Emergencies.* An applicant who is unable to take the examination due to a medical emergency and who notifies the Board in writing or by telephone prior to the start of the examination, may request carry-over of the application fee to the next examination. Such requests must be made in writing, received in the Board office no later than 14 days following the examination, and be accompanied by written documentation of the medical emergency. The applicant shall submit a fee of $50 when reapplying for the next examination.

K. Copies of Examination Answers. An unsuccessful applicant may request copies of the applicant's essay answers. The request shall be in writing, submitted within 60 days of the release of the examination results, and accompanied by a fee of $20.

L. Fees for Advisory Opinions. An application filed for the purpose of receiving an advisory opinion from the Board must be accompanied by a fee in the amount of $100.

M. Fee for Reissuance of House Counsel License. An applicant for re-issuance of a house counsel license under Rule 10G shall submit a fee of $275.

N. Other Fees. The Board may require an applicant to bear the expense of obtaining reports or other information necessary for the Board's investigation. The Board may require applicants to pay a reasonable application processing fee. The Board may charge reasonable fees for collection and publication of any information permitted to be released. For matters not covered in these Rules, the director may set reasonable fees which reflect the administrative costs associated with the service.

Adopted Aug. 26, 1998. Amended Dec. 17, 2002, eff. Jan. 1, 2003; Aug. 25, 2004, eff. Sept. 1, 2004; June 12, 2007, eff. July 1, 2007; Sept. 24, 2007, eff. Jan. 1, 2008; June 27, 2011, eff. Sept. 1, 2011.

Historical Notes

The order of the Minnesota Supreme Court [C5–84–2139] dated August 26, 1998, provides in part that except as otherwise provided in Rule 6(E)(2), relating to the Performance Test which commences with the February 2001 bar examination, the Rules for Admission to the Bar are adopted retroactive to August 18, 1998.

The order of the Minnesota Supreme Court [ADM10-8008] dated June 27, 2011, provides in part that "These amendments shall apply to all applications for bar examinations to be administered in February 2012 and thereafter. These amendments shall also apply to all applications for admission without examination under Rule 7 and for house counsel licenses under Rules 9 and 10 filed on or after September 1, 2011."

Rule 13. Immunity

A. Immunity of the Board. The Board and its members, employees, agents, and monitors of conditionally admitted lawyers are immune from civil liability for conduct and communications relating to their duties under these Rules or the Board's policies and procedures.

B. Immunity of Persons or Entities Providing Information to the Board. Any person or entity providing to the Board or its members, employees, agents, or monitors, any information, statements of opinion, or documents regarding an applicant, potential applicant, or conditionally admitted lawyer, is immune from civil liability for such communications.

Adopted Aug. 26, 1998. Amended Aug. 25, 2004, eff. Sept. 1, 2004; June 12, 2007, eff. July 1, 2007.

Historical Notes

The order of the Minnesota Supreme Court [C5–84–2139] dated August 26, 1998, provides in part that except as otherwise provided in Rule 6(E)(2), relating to the Performance Test which commences with the February 2001 bar examination, the Rules for Admission to the Bar are adopted retroactive to August 18, 1998.

Rule 14. Confidentiality and Release of Information

A. Application File. An applicant may review the contents of his or her application file with the exception of the work product of the Board and its staff. Such review must take place within two years after the filing of the last application for admission in Minnesota, at such times and under such conditions as the Board may provide.

B. Work Product. The Board's work product shall not be produced or otherwise discoverable, nor shall any member of the Board or its staff be subject to deposition or compelled testimony except upon a showing of extraordinary circumstances and compelling need and upon order of the Court. In any event, the mental impressions, conclusions, and opinions of the Board or its staff shall be protected and not subject to compelled disclosure.

C. Examination Data.

(1) *Statistics.* Statistical information relating to examinations and admissions may be released at the discretion of the Board.

(2) *MBE Score Advisory.* The director may release individual MBE scores as provided in Rule 7E.

(3) *Transfer of MBE Score.* The score of an examinee may be disclosed to the bar admission authority of another jurisdiction, upon the examinee's written request to the National Conference of Bar Examiners (NCBE).

(4) *Transfer of UBE Score.* The score of an examinee may be disclosed to the examinee or to the bar admission authority of another jurisdiction, upon the examinee's written request to the National Conference of Bar Examiners (NCBE).

(5) *Release of Examination Scores and Essays to Unsuccessful Examinees.* The director may release to an unsuccessful examinee the scores assigned to each of the various portions of the examination; and, upon payment of the fee specified by Rule 12K, the director may release copies of an unsuccessful examinee's answers to the MEE and MPT questions.

(6) *Release of Examination Scores to Law Schools.* At the discretion of the Board, the examination scores of an examinee may be released to the law school from which the examinee graduated.

D. Release of Information to Other Agencies. Information may be released to the following:

(1) Any authorized lawyer disciplinary agency;

(2) Any bar admissions authority; or

(3) Persons or other entities in furtherance of the character and fitness investigation.

E. Referrals. Information relating to the misconduct of an applicant may be referred to the appropriate authority.

F. Confidentiality. Subject to the exceptions in this Rule, all other information contained in the files of the office of the Board is confidential and shall not be released to anyone other than the Court except upon order of the Court.

Adopted Aug. 26, 1998. Amended Aug. 25, 2004, eff. Sept. 1, 2004; June 12, 2007, eff. July 1, 2007; Jan. 17, 2013, eff. Feb 1, 2013.

Historical Notes

The order of the Minnesota Supreme Court [C5–84–2139] dated August 26, 1998, provides in part that except as otherwise provided in Rule 6(E)(2), relating to the Performance Test which commences with the February 2001 bar examination, the Rules for Admission to the Bar are adopted retroactive to August 18, 1998.

The order of the Minnesota Supreme Court [ADM10–8008] dated January 17, 2013, provides in part that the amendments are effective February 1, 2013, and "shall apply to bar examinations administered in February 2014 and thereafter."

Rule 15. Adverse Determinations and Hearings

A. Adverse Determination. When an adverse determination relating to an applicant's character, fitness, or eligibility is made by the Board, the director shall notify the applicant of the determination, the reasons for the determination, the right to request a hearing, the right to be represented by counsel, and the right to present witnesses and evidence.

B. Request for Hearing. Within 20 days of notice of an adverse determination, the applicant may make a written request for a hearing. If the applicant does not timely request a hearing, the adverse determination becomes the final decision of the Board.

C. Scheduling of Hearing. The Board shall schedule a hearing upon receipt of the applicant's request for a hearing. At least 45 days prior to the hearing, the Board shall notify the applicant of the time and place.

D. Proceedings. At the discretion of the Board president, the hearing may be held before the full Board, before a sub-committee of the Board appointed by the president, or before a hearing examiner appointed by the president. The Board may employ special counsel. The hearing shall be recorded and a transcript shall be provided to the applicant on request at a reasonable cost. The applicant has the burden of proving by clear and convincing evidence that the applicant possesses good character and fitness to practice law and is eligible for admission.

E. Pre-hearing Conference. The Board president or designee shall conduct a pre-hearing conference at least 30 days prior to the hearing for the purpose of addressing procedural issues. Unless the president or designee orders otherwise, Board counsel and the applicant shall exchange exhibit lists; the names and addresses of witnesses; proposed findings of fact, conclusions of law, and final decisions; or stipulations at least 15 days before the hearing.

F. Subpoenas. Upon written authorization of the Board president or designee, the applicant and Board counsel may subpoena evidence and witnesses for the hearing. The District Court of Ramsey County shall have jurisdiction over issuance of subpoenas.

G. Continuances. A written request for a continuance of a scheduled hearing shall be considered and decided by the Board president or designee, who shall grant such request only upon a showing of good cause.

H. Final Decision. Following the hearing, the Board shall notify the applicant in writing of its findings of fact, conclusions of law and final decision.

Adopted Aug. 26, 1998. Amended Aug. 25, 2004, eff. Sept. 1, 2004; June 12, 2007, eff. July 1, 2007; June 27, 2011, eff. Sept. 1, 2011.

Historical Notes

The order of the Minnesota Supreme Court [C5–84–2139] dated August 26, 1998, provides in part that except as otherwise provided in Rule 6(E)(2), relating to the Performance Test which commences with the February 2001 bar examination, the Rules for Admission to the Bar are adopted retroactive to August 18, 1998.

The order of the Minnesota Supreme Court [ADM10-8008] dated June 27, 2011, provides in part that "These amendments shall apply to all applications for bar examinations to be administered in February 2012 and thereafter. These amendments shall also apply to all applications for admission without examination under Rule 7 and for house counsel licenses under Rules 9 and 10 filed on or after September 1, 2011."

Rule 16. Conditional Admission

A. Conditional Admission. The Board, upon its own initiative or the initiative of the applicant, may recommend to the Court that the applicant be admitted on a conditional basis.

B. Circumstances Warranting Conditional Admission. The Board may consider for conditional admission an applicant whose past conduct raises concerns under Rule 5, but whose current record of conduct evidences a commitment to rehabilitation and an ability to meet the essential eligibility requirements of the practice of law. The Board shall prescribe the terms and conditions of conditional admission in a consent agreement entered into by the Board and the applicant.

C. Consent Agreement. The consent agreement shall set forth the terms and conditions of conditional admission, shall be signed by the president or designee and by the applicant, and shall be made a part of the conditionally admitted lawyer's application file. The consent agreement shall remain confidential subject to the provisions of these Rules and of the Rules on Lawyers Professional Responsibility.

D. Transmittal to the Office of Lawyers Professional Responsibility. A list of conditionally admitted lawyers shall be transmitted each month to the Office of Lawyers Professional Responsibility (OLPR). In the event a complaint of unprofessional conduct or violation of the consent agreement is filed against the conditionally admitted lawyer, the application file shall be transmitted to the OLPR upon the request of that office.

E. Length of Conditional Period. The initial conditional admission period shall not exceed 24 months, unless a complaint for a violation of the consent agreement or a complaint of unprofessional conduct has been filed with the OLPR. The filing of any complaint with the OLPR shall extend the conditional admission until disposition of the complaint by the OLPR.

F. Consequences of Failure to Fulfill the Conditional Terms. Failure to fulfill the terms of the consent agreement may result in the suspension or revocation of the conditional admission license or such other action as is appropriate under the Rules on Lawyers Professional Responsibility.

G. Monitoring of Consent Agreement by Conditional Admission Committee. During the conditional admission period, the conditionally admitted lawyer's compliance with the terms of the consent agreement shall be monitored by a Conditional Admission Committee (CAC), a committee of no fewer than three Board members appointed by the president. The CAC shall conduct such investigation and take such action as is necessary to monitor compliance with the terms of the consent agreement, including, but not limited to, requiring the conditionally admitted lawyer to:

(1) submit written verification of compliance with conditions;

(2) appear before the CAC; and

(3) respond to any requests for evidence concerning compliance.

H. Procedure After Finding of Violation of Consent Agreement. If the CAC finds that a term or terms of the consent agreement have been violated, the CAC may request that the President convene the Board for the purpose of determining whether to file a complaint with OLPR or take other action to address the violation. The Board shall notify the conditionally admitted lawyer of the Board's decision if a complaint is filed.

I. Complaint for Violation of Consent Agreement; Disposition of Complaint. Any complaint for violation of the consent agreement filed with the OLPR shall set forth the basis for finding that a term or terms of the consent agreement have been violated.

J. Appeal. Appeal rights are limited to those set forth in Rule 15 and Rule 17.

Adopted Aug. 25, 2004, eff. Sept. 1, 2004. Amended June 12, 2007, eff. July 1, 2007; June 27, 2011, eff. Sept. 1, 2011.

Historical Notes

The order of the Minnesota Supreme Court [ADM10-8008] dated June 27, 2011, provides in part that "These amendments shall apply to all applications for bar examinations to be administered in February 2012 and thereafter. These amendments shall also apply to all applications for admission without examination under Rule 7 and for house counsel licenses under Rules 9 and 10 filed on or after September 1, 2011."

Rule 17. Appeal to the Supreme Court

A. Petition for Review. Any applicant who is adversely affected by a final decision of the Board may appeal to the Court by filing a petition for review with the Clerk of Appellate Courts within 20 days of receipt by the applicant of a final decision of the Board together with proof of service of the petition on the director of the Board. The petition shall briefly state the facts that form the basis for the complaint, and the applicant's reasons for believing the Court should review the decision.

B. Board Response. Within 20 days of service of the petition, the Board shall serve and file a response to the petition and a copy of the final decision of the Board. Thereupon the Court shall give such directions, hold such hearings, and make such order as it may in its discretion deem appropriate.

Adopted Aug. 26, 1998. Amended Aug. 25, 2004, eff. Sept. 1, 2004; June 12, 2007, eff. July 1, 2007.

Historical Notes

The order of the Minnesota Supreme Court [C5–84–2139] dated August 26, 1998, provides in part that except as otherwise provided in Rule 6(E)(2), relating to the Performance Test which commences with the February 2001 bar examination, the Rules for Admission to the Bar are adopted retroactive to August 18, 1998.

Rule 18. Reapplication

Unless the Board designates a shorter time period in its final decision, an applicant who has not satisfied the character and fitness requirement is prohibited from applying for admission to practice in Minnesota for three years from the date of the Board's final decision. An applicant whose conditional admission license has been revoked is prohibited from applying for admission for three years from the date of the revocation.

Adopted Aug. 26, 1998. Amended Aug. 25, 2004, eff. Sept. 1, 2004; June 12, 2007, eff. July 1, 2007.

Historical Notes

The order of the Minnesota Supreme Court [C5–84–2139] dated August 26, 1998, provides in part that except as otherwise provided in Rule 6(E)(2), relating to the Performance Test which commences with the February 2001 bar examination, the Rules for Admission to the Bar are adopted retroactive to August 18, 1998.

Rule 19. Bar Admissions Advisory Council

A. Creation. There shall be an Advisory Council consisting of representatives of the Minnesota State Bar Association and of each of the Minnesota law schools to consult with the Board on matters of general policy concerning admissions to the bar, amendments to the Rules, and other matters related to the work of the Board.

B. Meetings. The secretary of the Board shall call a joint meeting of the Advisory Council and the Board at least once each year. The Advisory Council shall meet at such other time as it may determine or when called by the Court or the Board.

C. Expenses. The members of the Advisory Council shall receive no compensation or reimbursement of expenses and shall serve for terms of three years.

Adopted Aug. 26, 1998. Amended Aug. 25, 2004, eff. Sept. 1, 2004; June 12, 2007, eff. July 1, 2007.

Historical Notes

The order of the Minnesota Supreme Court [C5–84–2139] dated August 26, 1998, provides in part that except as otherwise provided in Rule 6(E)(2), relating to the Performance Test which commences with the February 2001 bar examination, the Rules for Admission to the Bar are adopted retroactive to August 18, 1998.

INDEX TO RULES FOR ADMISSION TO THE BAR

RULES OF THE SUPREME COURT ON LAWYER REGISTRATION

Revised February 10, 1983

Including Amendments Received Through January 1, 2014

Research Note

See Minnesota Statutes Annotated, *Volume 52, for historical notes.*

These rules may be searched electronically on Westlaw in the MN–RULES database; updates to these rules may be found on Westlaw in MN–RULESUP-DATES. For search tips and a summary of database content, consult the Westlaw Scope Screens for each database.

PREAMBLE

Admission to the bar of the State of Minnesota, disciplinary proceedings, and continuing legal education for members of the legal profession shall be conducted in accordance with rules promulgated by this court.

Adopted Aug. 4, 1970. Amended Feb. 10, 1983; July 12, 2006, eff. Oct. 1, 2006.

RULE 1. DEFINITIONS

A. "Active Status" means a lawyer or judge who (i) has paid the applicable required lawyer registration fee for the current year, (ii) is in compliance with the requirements of the Minnesota State Board of Continuing Legal Education or of continuing judicial education, (iii) is not disbarred, suspended, or on permanent disability status pursuant to Rule 28 of the Rules on Lawyers Professional Responsibility, (iv) is in compliance with Rule 1.15(i), Minnesota Rules of Professional Conduct (MRPC), and (v) is in compliance with Rule 6 of these rules. A lawyer or judge on active status is in good standing and is authorized to practice law in this state.

B. "Inactive Status" means a lawyer or judge who has elected to be on inactive status pursuant to Rule 2C1, 2C2, 2C3, 2C4, 2C5 or 2C6 of these rules and who meets the criteria set forth in subparts (i) through (v) in the definition of Active Status, above. A lawyer or judge on inactive status is in good standing but is not authorized to practice law in this state.

C. "Judge" means any judicial officer, referee, or other hearing officer employed in the judicial branch of the State of Minnesota.

D. "Lawyer" means a person admitted to practice law in this state pursuant to the Rules for Admission to the Bar.

E. "Lawyer Registration Statement" means a document prepared by the Lawyer Registration Office that informs a lawyer or judge of the lawyer registration fee due and on which the lawyer or judge can certify the lawyer's or judge's status and compliance with Rule 1.15(i), MRPC, and Rule 6 of these rules.

F. "Non–Compliant Status" means a lawyer or judge who has not met all the criteria to be on active status or inactive status. A lawyer or judge who is on non-compliant status is not in good standing and is not authorized to practice law in this state.

G. "Online Registration System" means the Internet lawyer registration system maintained by the Lawyer Registration Office. Lawyers and judges who elect to use this system manage the information required by these rules in their lawyer profile, complete their annual registration statement and pay their annual fee electronically.

H. "Private Client." For the purpose of reporting professional liability insurance coverage, the term "private client" excludes the clients of government lawyers and house counsel.

Adopted July 12, 2006, eff. Oct. 1, 2006. Amended Aug. 16, 2006, eff. Oct. 1, 2006; June 22, 2010, eff. July 1, 2010.

RULE 2. REGISTRATION FEE

A. Required Fee.

In order to defray the expenses of examinations and investigation for admission to the bar and disciplinary proceedings, to defray the expenses of administering continuing legal education, to provide an adequate client security fund, to help fund legal services programs, and to help fund a lawyers assistance program, each lawyer and each judge must pay to the Lawyer Registration Office an annual registration fee.

B. Active Statuses.

Each lawyer and judge must pay an annual registration fee of $254 or such lesser sum as is set forth in the following sections.

1. Active Status—Income Less Than $25,000.

A lawyer or judge on active status who certifies that the lawyer's or judge's gross income from all sources, excluding the income of a spouse, is less than $25,000 per year must pay an annual registration fee of 226.

2. Active Status—Lawyers on Full–Time Military Duty.

A lawyer or judge on full-time duty in the armed forces of the United States must pay an annual registration fee of $131.

3. Active Status—Lawyers on Full–Time Military Duty—Income Less Than $25,000.

A lawyer or judge on full-time duty in the armed forces of the United States who certifies that the lawyer's or judge's gross income from all sources, excluding the income of a spouse, is less than $25,000 per year must pay an annual registration fee of $103.

4. Active Status—Lawyers Admitted Fewer Than Three Years.

A lawyer or judge who has been admitted to practice law fewer than three years in each and every licensing jurisdiction, including Minnesota, must pay an annual registration fee of $120.

5. Active Status—Lawyers Admitted Fewer Than Three Years—Income Less Than $25,000.

A lawyer or judge who has been admitted to practice law fewer than three years in each and every licensing jurisdiction, including Minnesota, and certifies that the lawyer's or judge's gross income from all sources, excluding the income of a spouse, is less than $25,000 per year must pay an annual registration fee of $106.

C. Inactive Statuses.

1. Inactive Status—Out-of-State.

A lawyer or judge who files with the Lawyer Registration Office on or before the date the lawyer's registration fee is due an affidavit stating that the lawyer or judge (i) is a permanent resident of a state other than Minnesota, (ii) is currently in good standing, (iii) does not hold judicial office in Minnesota, and (iv) is not engaged in the practice of law in Minnesota must pay an annual registration fee of $211.

2. Inactive Status—Out-of-State—Income Less Than $25,000.

A lawyer or judge who files with the Lawyer Registration Office on or before the date the lawyer's registration fee is due an affidavit stating that the lawyer or judge (i) is a permanent resident of a state other than Minnesota, (ii) is currently in good standing, (iii) does not hold judicial office in Minnesota, (iv) is not engaged in the practice of law in Minnesota, and (v) certifies that the lawyer's or judge's gross income from all sources, excluding the income of a spouse, is less than $25,000 per year must pay an annual registration fee of $183.

3. Inactive Status—Minnesota.

A lawyer who files with the Lawyer Registration Office on or before the date the lawyer's registration fee is due an affidavit stating that the lawyer (i) is a resident of the State of Minnesota, (ii) is currently in good standing, (iii) does not hold judicial office in this state, and (iv) is not engaged in the practice of law in this state must pay an annual registration fee of $211.

4. Inactive Status—Minnesota—Income Less Than $25,000.

A lawyer who files with the Lawyer Registration Office on or before the date the lawyer's registration fee is due an affidavit stating that the lawyer (i) is a resident of the State of Minnesota, (ii) is currently in good standing, (iii) does not hold judicial office in this state, (iv) is not engaged in the practice of law in this state, and (v) certifies that the lawyer's or judge's gross income from all sources, excluding the income of a spouse, is less than $25,000 per year must pay an annual registration fee of $183.

5. Inactive Status—Retired.

A lawyer or judge who files with the Lawyer Registration Office a Retirement Affidavit stating that the lawyer or judge (i) is currently on active or inactive status, (ii) does not hold judicial office in this state, (iii) is not engaged in the practice of law in this state, (iv) is at least 62 years of age, and (v) is retired from any gainful employment is exempt from payment of any registration fee during the period of the lawyer's or judge's retirement. A Retirement Affidavit, once filed, is effective for each succeeding year unless the lawyer or judge transfers to active status pursuant to section C7 of this rule. Notwithstanding the above, a lawyer or judge who has filed an affidavit in accordance with this rule may engage in the pro bono legal representation of pro bono clients pursuant to Rule 14 of the Rules of the Minnesota State Board of Continuing Legal Education.

6. Inactive Status—Permanent Disability.

A lawyer or judge who files with the Lawyer Registration Office a Disability Affidavit stating that the lawyer or judge (i) is currently on active or inactive status, (ii) does not hold judicial office in this state, (iii) is not engaged in the practice of law in this state, and (iv) is totally disabled is exempt from payment of any registration fee during the period of the lawyer's or judge's disability. A Disability Affidavit, once filed, is effective for each succeeding year unless the lawyer or judge transfers to active status pursuant to section C7 of this rule.

7. Transfer from Inactive Status to Active Status.

A lawyer or judge who is on inactive status must, prior to practicing law or assuming judicial responsibilities, (i) promptly notify the Lawyer Registration Office, (ii) complete a lawyer registration statement, (iii) pay the applicable registration fee, (iv) complete all continuing legal education (CLE) requirements and be transferred to CLE active status, (v) comply with Rule 1.15(i), MRPC, and (vi) comply with Rule 6 of these rules.

D. Allocation of Fees.

Fees paid pursuant to this rule are allocated according to the following schedule:

(1) Payments of $254 are allocated as follows:

a. $23 to the State Board of Law Examiners;

b. $6 to the State Board of Continuing Legal Education;

c. $122 to the Lawyers Professional Responsibility Board;

d. $12 to the Client Security Fund;

e. $75 to the Legal Services Advisory Committee; and

f. $16 to the Lawyer Trust Account Board for a lawyers assistance program.

(2) Payments of $226 are allocated as follows:

a. $23 to the State Board of Law Examiners;

b. $6 to the State Board of Continuing Legal Education;

c. $122 to the Lawyers Professional Responsibility Board;

d. $12 to the Client Security Fund;

e. $47 to the Legal Services Advisory Committee; and

f. $16 to the Lawyer Trust Account Board for a lawyers assistance program.

(3) Payments of $211 are allocated as follows:

a. $23 to the State Board of Law Examiners;

b. $6 to the State Board of Continuing Legal Education;

c. $83 to the Lawyers Professional Responsibility Board;

d. $12 to the Client Security Fund;

e. $71 to the Legal Services Advisory Committee; and

f. $16 to the Lawyer Trust Account Board for a lawyers assistance program.

(4) Payments of $183 are allocated as follows:

a. $23 to the State Board of Law Examiners;

b. $6 to the State Board of Continuing Legal Education;

c. $83 to the Lawyers Professional Responsibility Board;

d. $12 to the Client Security Fund;

e. $43 to the Legal Services Advisory Committee; and

f. $16 to the Lawyer Trust Account Board for a lawyers assistance program.

(5) Payments of $131 are allocated as follows:

a. $23 to the State Board of Law Examiners;

b. $5 to the State Board of Continuing Legal Education;

c. $24 to the Lawyers Professional Responsibility Board;

d. $63 to the Legal Services Advisory Committee; and

e. $16 to the Lawyer Trust Account Board for a lawyers assistance program.

(6) Payments of $103 are allocated as follows:

a. $23 to the State Board of Law Examiners;

b. $5 to the State Board of Continuing Legal Education;

c. $24 to the Lawyers Professional Responsibility Board;

d. $35 to the Legal Services Advisory Committee; and

e. $16 to the Lawyer Trust Account Board for a lawyers assistance program.

(7) Payments of $120 are allocated as follows:

a. $23 to the State Board of Law Examiners;

b. $6 to the State Board of Continuing Legal Education;

c. $26 to the Lawyers Professional Responsibility Board;

d. $12 to the Client Security Fund;

e. $37 to the Legal Services Advisory Committee; and

f. $16 to the Lawyer Trust Account Board for a lawyers assistance program.

(8) Payments of $106 are allocated as follows:

a. $23 to the State Board of Law Examiners;

b. $6 to the State Board of Continuing Legal Education;

c. $26 to the Lawyers Professional Responsibility Board;

d. $12 to the Client Security Fund;

e. $23 to the Legal Services Advisory Committee; and

f. $16 to the Lawyer Trust Account Board for a lawyers assistance program.

E. Due Date.

Fees under this rule are due and payable on or before the first day of January, April, July, or October of each year as requested by the Lawyer Registration Office.

F. Notification of Fee Due.

The Lawyer Registration Office must annually one month prior to the date due, either mail a lawyer registration statement or email a notice of registration to each lawyer and judge then in good standing except those who have elected inactive retired status pursuant to section C5, above, or permanent disability status pursuant to section C6 above. A lawyer registration statement must be mailed to the lawyer's or judge's postal address on file with the Lawyer Registration Office. For those electing to use the online registration system, a notice of registration must be sent to the lawyer's or judge's email address on file with the Lawyer Registration Office. Failure to receive a lawyer registration statement or a notice of registration shall not excuse payment of the fee.

G. Obligation to Notify of Address Change.

Every lawyer or judge must immediately notify the Lawyer Registration Office of any change of postal address. Every lawyer or judge who elects to use the online registration system must immediately update their online registration profile to reflect any change of their postal address and email address.

H. Penalty for Failure to Comply—Non-Compliant Status—Administrative Suspension.

A lawyer or judge who fails to meet all of the criteria to be on either active or inactive status is placed on non-compliant status, and the right to practice law in this state is automatically suspended. A lawyer or judge on non-compliant status is not in good standing. A lawyer or judge on non-compliant status must not practice law in this state, must not hold out himself or herself as authorized to practice law, or in any manner represent that he or she is qualified or authorized to practice law while on non-compliant status. Any lawyer or judge who violates this rule is subject to all the penalties and remedies provided by law for the unauthorized practice of law in the State of Minnesota. It is the duty of each judge to enjoin persons who are not on active status from appearing and practicing law in that judge's court.

I. Reinstatement.

A lawyer or judge who is on non-compliant status, who seeks to be reinstated to active status or inactive status, must (i) notify the Lawyer Registration Office, (ii) complete a lawyer registration statement, (iii) pay all delinquent registration fees, (iv) pay the applicable registration fee for the current year, (v) pay a late penalty of $75, (vi) complete all CLE requirements and be transferred to CLE active status, (vii) comply with Rule 1.15(i), MRPC, and (viii) comply with Rule 6 of these rules. The Lawyer Registration Office may, in hardship cases, waive payment of delinquent lawyer registration fees and late penalties. All late penalty payments are allocated to the Lawyer Registration Office to defray registration costs.

Adopted Aug. 4, 1970. Amended Aug. 1, 1977; July 28, 1978; July 17, 1979; Aug. 12, 1980; May 18, 1982, eff. July 1, 1982; Feb. 10, 1983; July 25, 1984, eff. Oct. 1, 1984; April 7, 1987, eff. July 1, 1988; April 19, 1990; May 22, 1990; Nov. 14, 1990; April 15, 1992; Dec. 3, 1993; June 13, 1996; Feb. 5, 1997; Aug. 6, 1997; May 22, 1998; April 18, 2000, eff. July 1, 2000; May 8, 2000, eff. July 1, 2000; May 28, 2002, eff. July 1, 2003; Dec. 18, 2002, eff. July 1, 2003; June 17, 2003, eff. July 1, 2003; July 12, 2006, eff. Oct. 1, 2006. Aug. 16, 2006, eff. Oct. 1, 2006; Sept. 24, 2007, eff. Jan. 1, 2008; March 19, 2008, eff. July 1, 2008; July 22, 2008, eff. Oct. 1, 2008; July 28, 2008, eff. Oct. 1, 2008; April 1, 2010, eff. July 1, 2010; June 22, 2010, eff. July 1, 2010; March 2, 2011, eff. Oct. 1, 2011; March 15, 2013, eff. July 1, 2013.

Historical Notes

The order of the Minnesota Supreme Court dated November 14, 1990 amending Rule 2 provides in part that these amendments shall become effective with payments due on or after July 1, 1991 and shall remain in effect until July 1, 1995.

The April 15, 1992 order amending Rule 2 contained 2 amendments. The order provided in part that the first amendment is effective with attorney registration payments due between July 1, 1992 and June 30, 1993, and that the second amendment is effective with attorney registration payments due on and after July 1, 1993.

The order of the Minnesota Supreme Court dated June 13, 1996, provides in part that the increase in attorney registration fees shall be effective for licenses due for renewal on October 1, 1996, and for new licenses issued on or after October 1, 1996.

The order of the Minnesota Supreme Court [C9-81-1206] dated February 5, 1997, provides in part that "(t)he increase in attorney registration fees shall be effective for licenses due for renewal on July 1, 1997, and for new licenses issued on or after July 1, 1997."

The order of the Minnesota Supreme Court [C9-81-1206] dated August 6, 1997, provides in part that "(t)he increase in attorney registration fees shall be effective for licenses being renewed on or after August 6, 1997, and for new licenses issued on or after August 6, 1997. This allocation shall continue in effect until June 30, 1998."

The order of the Minnesota Supreme Court dated May 22, 1998, provides in part that the temporary reallocation of attorney registration fees for the Board of Continuing Legal Education contained in the August 6, 1997 order is revoked July 1, 1998, and the changes in the allocation of attorney registration fees based on the May 22, 1998 order shall be effective July 1, 1998, and for new licenses issued on or after July 1, 1998 and will remain in effect until July 1, 1999.

The order of the Minnesota Supreme Court dated May 20, 1999, provides in part that the attorney registration fee allocation set forth in the May 22, 1998 order of the court be continued until further order of the court.

The order of the Minnesota Supreme Court [C9-81-1206] dated May 28, 2002, provides in part that the amendment of Rule 2 is effective for registration fees due on and after July 1, 2003.

The order of the Minnesota Supreme Court [C1-81-1206] dated December 18, 2002, provides in part that the amendment of Rule 2 is effective for registration fees due July 1, 2003.

The order of the Minnesota Supreme Court [C9–81–1206] dated July 28, 2008, correcting inadvertent errors made by the order of the Minnesota Supreme Court dated July 22, 2008, provided in part that the amendments were effective with the October 1, 2008, registration cycle deadline and expire with the July 1, 2009, registration cycle deadline.

An order of the Minnesota Supreme Court [C9–81–1206] dated July 15, 2009, provided:

"By an order filed July 28, 2008, this court promulgated amendments to the Rules of the Supreme Court on Lawyer Registration that changed registration fees to reflect a one-year reduction in the amount collected for the Client Security Board. The board has informed the Court that the reduction should be extended for an additional year.

"NOW, THEREFORE, IT IS HEREBY ORDERED that the reduction of the fee for the Client Security Board shall be extended for one year, expiring with the July 1, 2010 registration cycle deadline."

The order of the Minnesota Supreme Court dated November 4, 2009, provides:

"The Board of Public Defense and the Legal Services Planning Committee have filed petitions with this court seeking an increase in the annual lawyer registration fee. The Board of Public Defense requests the court to increase the annual lawyer registration fee by $75.00 per year and allocate this money to the Board to provide additional funding for legal representation of its clients. The Legal Services Planning Committee requests the court to increase the amount of the annual lawyer registration fee allocated to the Legal Services Advisory Committee by $25.00 per year, the additional funds to be distributed by the Legal Services Advisory Committee for civil legal services for low-income and disadvantaged Minnesotans. In an order filed on June 11, 2009, the court invited written comments on the proposed amendments. The comment period has now expired.

"The court has reviewed the petitions and the comments received and is advised in the premises.

"Pursuant to the inherent authority of the court,

"IT IS HEREBY ORDERED THAT:

"1. The petitions are granted effective for annual registration fees due and payable by October 1, 2009 and expiring with annual registration fees due and payable by July 1, 2011. Effective commencing with fees due and payable by October 1, 2009 and expiring with fees due and payable by July 1, 2011, the annual lawyer registration fee shall be $317 or such lesser sum as is set forth below:

"Active Status—Income Less than $25,000	$280.50
"Active Status—Lawyers on Full-Time Military Duty	$172.00
"Active Status—Lawyers on Full-Time Military Duty—Income Less than $25, 000	$136.00
"Active Status—Lawyers Admitted Fewer Than Three Years	$140.00
"Active Status—Lawyers Admitted Fewer Than Three Years—Income Less Than $25,000	$122.00
"Inactive Status—Out-of-State	$260.00
"Inactive Status—Out-of-State—Income Less Than $25,000	$223.50
"Inactive Status—Minnesota	$260.00
"Inactive Status—Minnesota—Income Less Than $25,000	$223.50
"Inactive Status—Retired	Exempt
"Inactive Status—Permanent Disability	Exempt

"While this order is in effect, these annual registration fees are in lieu of the fees set forth in Rule 2 of the Rules of the Supreme Court on Lawyer Registration. The fee increase is temporary only, and upon the expiration of this fee increase, the annual registration fee shall revert to the amounts set forth in Rule 2.

"2. For registration fees due and payable by October 1, 2009, payment of the temporary fee increase imposed by this order is deferred and the increase shall be payable along with the registration fees due and payable by October 1, 2010.

"3. Seventy-five percent of the additional funds generated by this temporary fee increase shall be allocated to the Board of Public Defense; the remaining twenty-five percent of the additional funds generated by this temporary fee increase shall be allocated to the Legal Services Advisory Committee."

The order of the Minnesota Supreme Court dated March 2, 2011, provides:

"By order filed November 4, 2009, we granted requests from the Board of Public Defense and the Legal Services Planning Committee to increase temporarily the annual lawyer registration fee to provide additional funding for representation of indigent criminal defendants and civil litigants. We increased the annual lawyer registration fee by $100 per year, allocating $75 of the increase to the Board of Public Defense to provide additional funding for legal representation of its clients and $25 to the Legal Services Advisory Committee to be distributed by the Committee for civil legal services for low-income and disadvantaged Minnesotans. We approved the increase reluctantly, to meet exceptional financial circumstances, and its duration was limited, expiring with the fees due and payable by July 1, 2011.

"The Board of Public Defense has filed a petition with this court requesting that the $75 temporary increase in the annual lawyer registration fee allocated to the Board be extended indefinitely, and the Legal Services Planning Committee has filed a petition requesting that the $25 temporary fee increase allocated for civil legal services be made permanent. In orders filed September 23 and November 24, 2010, we invited comments and scheduled a hearing on the petitions for December 14, 2010.

"The exceptional financial circumstances facing the courts and the State in general that we acknowledged and responded to in our November 4, 2009, order have not abated. Indeed, the economic challenges facing the courts and the State for the upcoming biennium have, if anything, worsened. For the reasons stated, and based on the authority recognized, in our November 4, 2009, order we extend the fee increases.

"In doing so, we caution the Legislature and the Governor, our coordinate branches of government that are responsible together for creation of the State's biennial budgets, that we will not continue, beyond this second temporary fee increase, to rely on lawyer registration fees to fund the constitutional obligation of the State to provide defense counsel for indigent criminal defendants. We call on the Legislature and the Governor to fulfill their constitutional responsibilities to provide adequate funding for the public defense system, with the knowledge that the additional temporary funding provided by this fee increase will note be extended beyond the July 2013 fees provided for in this order.

"Pursuant to the inherent authority of the court,

"IT IS HEREBY ORDERED THAT:

"1. The petition of the Legal Services Planning Committee to incorporate into Rule 2 of the Rules of the Supreme Court on Lawyer Registration the previous temporary increase of $25 in the annual lawyer registration fee allocated to the Legal Services Advisory Committee be, and the same is, granted, and the attached amendments to Rule 2 are prescribed and promulgated to be effective with the lawyer registration fees due and payable by October 1, 2011.

"2. The petition of the Board of Public Defense to extend indefinitely the previous temporary increase of $75 in the annual lawyer registration fee allocated to the Board be, and the same is denied, but the increase is extended for one additional temporary period, effective with the lawyer registration fees due and payable by October 1, 2011, and expiring with fees due and payable by July 1, 2013.

"3. With the amendment to Rule 2 promulgated by this order, the 2-year extension of the temporary fee increase for the Board of Public Defense, and the expiration of the 2-year hiatus in collection of the portion of the lawyer registration fees allocated to the Client Security Board, commencing with fees due and payable by October 1, 2011, the annual lawyer registration fee shall be $329 or such lesser sum as is set forth below:

Active Status - Income Less than $25,000	$292.50
Active Status - Lawyers on Full-Time Military Duty	$172.00
Active Status - Lawyers on Full-Time Military Duty - Income Less than $25,000	$136.00
Active Status - Lawyers Admitted Fewer Than Three Years	$152.00
Active Status - Lawyers Admitted Fewer Than Three Years - Income Less Than $25,000	$134.00
Inactive Status - Out-of-State	$272.00
Inactive Status - Out-of-State - Income Less Than $25,000	$235.50
Inactive Status - Minnesota	$272.00
Inactive Status - Minnesota - Income Less Than $25,000	$235.50
Inactive Status - Retired	Exempt
Inactive Status - Permanent Disability	Exempt

"While this order is in effect, these annual registration fees are in lieu of the fees set forth in Rule 2 of the Rules of the Supreme Court on Lawyer Registration. The $75 fee increase allocated to the Board of Public Defense remains temporary only, and upon the expiration of this temporary fee increase, the annual registration fees shall revert to the amounts set forth in Rule 2, as amended by this order.

"4. The additional funds generated by the temporary $75 fee increase shall be allocated to the Board of Public Defense; the remaining funds generated by the attorney registration fees shall be allocated as provided in Rule 2, as amended by this order."

RULE 3. LICENSE

A. Upon payment of the lawyer registration fee and completion of a lawyer registration statement, the Lawyer Registration Office must issue and mail to the lawyer or judge a license in such form as may be provided by this court, showing the license status of the lawyer or judge.

B. Upon request and the payment of a fee of $25, the Lawyer Registration Office must provide to any lawyer or judge a certificate of active status and good standing, provided the lawyer or judge is entitled to the same.

Adopted Aug. 4, 1970. Amended Feb. 10, 1983; July 12, 2006, eff. Oct. 1, 2006.

RULE 4. SPECIAL FUND

All money collected from applicants for admission to the bar or as an annual registration fee or as payment for a certificate of active status and good standing as provided herein shall be deposited in a special fund, as desired by this court, and shall be disbursed therefrom only upon vouchers signed by a member of this court.

Adopted Aug. 4, 1970. Amended Feb. 10, 1983; July 12, 2006, eff. Oct. 1, 2006.

RULE 5. NONRESIDENT COUNSEL

Nothing herein shall prevent any court in this state from granting special permission to nonresident counsel to appear and participate in a particular action or proceeding in association with an authorized lawyer of this state.

Adopted Aug. 4, 1970. Amended Feb. 10, 1983; July 12, 2006, eff. Oct. 1, 2006.

RULE 6. ANNUAL REPORTING OF PROFESSIONAL LIABILITY INSURANCE COVERAGE

Each lawyer on active status must certify on the lawyer registration statement

(1) whether the lawyer represents private clients;

(2) if the lawyer represents private clients, whether the lawyer is currently covered by professional liability insurance;

(3) if the lawyer is covered by professional liability insurance, the name of the primary carrier;

Each lawyer on active status must notify the Lawyer Registration Office either by letter or by updating the lawyer's online registration profile within 30 days if the insurance policy providing coverage lapses, is no longer in effect, or terminates for any reason, unless the policy is renewed or replaced without substantial interruption.

Adopted July 12, 2006, eff. Oct. 1, 2006. Amended June 22, 2010, eff. July 1, 2010.

RULE 7. ACCESS TO LAWYER REGISTRATION RECORDS

Lawyer registration records are accessible only as provided in this rule.

A. **Public Inquiry Concerning Specific Lawyer.** Upon inquiry, the Lawyer Registration Office may disclose to the public the name, postal address, admission date, continuing legal education category, current status, professional liability insurance coverage information submitted under Rule 6 of these rules, and license number of a registered lawyer or judge, provided that each inquiry and disclosure is limited to a single registered lawyer or judge.

B. Publicly Available List. The Lawyer Registration Office may also disclose to the public a complete list of the name, city, and zip code of all registered lawyers and judges.

C. Lists Available to Continuing Legal Education Providers and the Courts. Upon written request and payment of the required fee, the Lawyer Registration Office may disclose to a bona fide continuing legal education business a complete list of the name, postal address, admission date, continuing legal education category, current status, and license number of all registered lawyers and judges. The Lawyer Registration Office may also disclose the same information to a court or judicial district solely for use in updating mailing addresses of lawyers and judges to be included in a judicial evaluation program.

D. Trust Account Information. Trust account information submitted by lawyers and judges as part of the lawyer registration process is not accessible to the public.

E. Use in Case Management Systems. Lawyer registration records may be imported into case management systems for the purpose of linking lawyers to cases and storing accurate identification information. When imported into a case management system, lawyer registration records may thereafter be disclosed in connection with corresponding case information provided that bulk distribution of such records must comply with Rule 7.B of these rules.

Adopted Feb. 13, 1986. Amended Sept. 26, 2000, eff. July 1, 2001; Aug. 4, 2003, eff. Aug. 4, 2003; May 6, 2005, eff. July 1, 2005; July 12, 2006, eff. Oct. 1, 2006; June 22, 2010, eff. July 1, 2010.

RULES OF THE SUPREME COURT FOR CONTINUING LEGAL EDUCATION OF MEMBERS OF THE BAR [REPEALED]

Historical Notes

The order of the Minnesota Supreme Court [C2–84–2163] dated April 17, 2000, which promulgated the Rules of the Minnesota Board of Continuing Legal Education, provides in part that the Rules of the Minnesota Supreme Court and the State Board for Continuing Legal Education of Members of the Bar are repealed effective July 1, 2000.

RULES OF THE BOARD OF CONTINUING LEGAL EDUCATION [REPEALED]

Historical Notes

The order of the Minnesota Supreme Court [C2–84–2163] dated April 17, 2000, which promulgated the Rules of the Minnesota Board of Continuing Legal Education, provides in part that the Rules of the Minnesota Supreme Court and the State Board for Continuing Legal Education of Members of the Bar are repealed effective July 1, 2000.

RULES OF THE MINNESOTA STATE BOARD OF CONTINUING LEGAL EDUCATION

Rule 1. Purpose

The purpose of these Rules is to require that lawyers continue their legal education and professional development throughout the period of their active practice of law; to establish the minimum requirements for continuing legal education; to improve lawyers' knowledge of the law; and through continuing legal education courses, to address the special responsibilities that lawyers as officers of the court have to improve the quality of justice administered by the legal system and the quality of service rendered by the legal profession.

Adopted April 17, 2000, eff. July 1, 2000. Amended Dec. 10, 2003, eff. Feb. 1, 2004.

Rule 2. Definitions

Rule effective until July 1, 2014. See, also, rule effective July 1, 2014.

In these Rules,

A. "Approved course" means a course approved by the Board.

B. "Approved legal services provider" means a legal services organization that meets at least one of the following criteria:

(1) Funded by the Legal Services Corporation or the Minnesota Legal Services Advisory Committee; or

(2) Designated by the Minnesota Legal Services Advisory Committee as an approved legal service provider. Eligibility for designation is limited to:

(a) Programs providing pro bono legal representation within 501(c)(3) nonprofit organizations that have as their primary purpose the furnishing of legal services to individuals with limited means.

(b) Law firms, law libraries, or bar associations that conduct programs that have as their primary purpose the furnishing of legal services to individuals with limited means and are under the supervision of a pro bono coordinator or designated lawyer.

(c) Law firms that provide pro bono legal services on behalf of a Minnesota Judicial Branch program, including but not limited to, the Guardian ad Litem Program.

C. "Board" means the State Board of Continuing Legal Education.

D. "Chairperson" means the Chairperson of the Board.

E. "Classroom setting" means a room, including an office, suitably appointed with chairs, writing surfaces, lecterns and other normal accouterments of a teaching room, which is exclusively devoted to the educational activity being presented.

F. "Course in ethics or professional responsibility" means a course or session within a course that deals with the Minnesota Rules of Professional Conduct, the ABA Model Rules of Professional Conduct, the rules of professional conduct or professional responsibility of other jurisdictions, or the opinions and case law arising from the application of any of the above-specified rules, including a course or session within a course that addresses in a specific way concepts such as professionalism, civility and ethical conduct in the practice of law and in the legal profession.

G. "Course in the elimination of bias in the legal profession and in the practice of law" means a course directly related to the practice of law that is designed to educate attorneys to identify and eliminate from the legal profession and from the practice of law biases against persons because of race, gender, economic status, creed, color, religion, national origin, disability, age or sexual orientation.

H. "Court" means the Supreme Court of the State of Minnesota.

I. "Director" means the Director of the Board.

J. "Emeritus status" is the status of a lawyer who has filed a Retirement Affidavit pursuant to Rule 2(C)(5) of the Rules of the Supreme Court on Lawyer Registration, is not on involuntary restricted status, has submitted an Affidavit of Emeritus Status Appendix IV showing compliance with the requirements of CLE Rule 14, and is authorized by Rule 14 to provide pro bono legal representation to a pro bono client when referred by an approved legal services provider. Emeritus status lawyers remain on restricted status.

K. "Established continuing legal education course sponsor," for the purposes of Rule 5B, is a person or entity regularly retained by firms or organizations for the purpose of presenting continuing legal education programs, which is completely independent of the firm or organization for whose members the continuing legal education course is presented.

L. "Fee" means funds made payable to the Minnesota State Board of Continuing Legal Education.

M. "In–house course" means a course sponsored by a single private law firm, a single corporation or financial institution, or by a single federal, state or local governmental agency for lawyers who are members or employees of any of the above organizations.

N. "Involuntary restricted status" means the status of a lawyer licensed in Minnesota who is not in compliance with the educational and reporting requirements of these Rules and who has been involuntarily placed in that status by order of the Court. See Rule 12 for additional provisions.

O. "Laboratory setting" means a mock courtroom, law office, negotiation table, or other simulated setting in which demonstrations are given, role-playing is carried out or lawyers' activities are taught by example or participation.

P. "Law and literature course" means a course otherwise meeting the requirements of Rules 4D and 5A, based upon a literary text and designed to generate discussion, insight, and learning about topics such as the practice of law, the history and philosophy of law, rhetoric, lawyers' professional or ethical responsibilities, professional development, and the elimination of bias in the legal profession and in the practice of law.

Q. "Moderator" means an individual, knowledgeable in the topic or topics addressed by the course, who guides the discussion and answers questions related to the material presented.

R. "Participant" means a lawyer licensed in Minnesota attending an approved course and actively engaged in the subject matter being presented.

S. "Pro bono client" means an individual, who is not a corporation or other organizational entity, and who has been referred to the lawyer by an approved legal services provider or by a state or federal court program.

T. "Pro bono legal representation" means providing legal representation to a pro bono client without compensation, expectation of compensation, or other direct or indirect pecuniary gain.

U. "Professional development course" means a course or session within a course designed to enhance the development and performance of lawyers by addressing issues such as career satisfaction and renewal, stress management, mental or emotional health, substance abuse, and gambling addiction. Professional development courses do not include individual or group therapy sessions.

V. "Restricted status" means the status of a lawyer licensed in Minnesota who has voluntarily chosen not to comply with the educational and reporting requirements of these Rules. See Rule 12 for additional provisions.

W. "Submit" means to communicate information to the Board office in writing or electronic submission:

(1) through the Board's Online Attorney and Sponsor Integrated System (OASIS);

(2) by regular U.S. Mail; or

(3) by delivery.

Adopted April 17, 2000, eff. July 1, 2000. Amended Dec. 10, 2003, eff. Feb. 1, 2004; Jan. 31, 2008, eff. July 1, 2008; June 30, 2008, eff. July 1, 2008; Jan. 6, 2010, eff. Feb. 1, 2010; April 1, 2010, eff. July 1, 2010; March 15, 2013, eff. July 1, 2013.

Rule 2. Definitions

Rule effective July 1, 2014. See, also, rule effective until July 1, 2014.

In these Rules,

A. "Approved course" means a course approved by the Board.

B. "Approved legal services provider" means a legal services organization that meets at least one of the following criteria:

(1) Funded by the Legal Services Corporation or the Minnesota Legal Services Advisory Committee; or

(2) Designated by the Minnesota Legal Services Advisory Committee as an approved legal service provider. Eligibility for designation is limited to:

(a) Programs providing pro bono legal representation within 501(c)(3) nonprofit organizations that have as their primary purpose the furnishing of legal services to individuals with limited means.

(b) Law firms, law libraries, or bar associations that conduct programs that have as their primary purpose the furnishing of legal services to individuals with limited means and are under the supervision of a pro bono coordinator or designated lawyer.

(c) Law firms that provide pro bono legal services on behalf of a Minnesota Judicial Branch program, including but not limited to, the Guardian ad Litem Program.

C. "Board" means the State Board of Continuing Legal Education.

D. "Chairperson" means the Chairperson of the Board.

E. "Classroom setting" means a room, including an office, suitably appointed with chairs, writing surfaces, lecterns and other normal accouterments of a teaching room, which is exclusively devoted to the educational activity being presented.

F. "Course in ethics or professional responsibility" means a course or session within a course that deals with the Minnesota Rules of Professional Conduct, the ABA Model Rules of Professional Conduct, the rules of professional conduct or professional responsibility of other jurisdictions, or the opinions and case law arising from the application of any of the above-specified rules, including a course or session within a course that addresses in a specific way concepts such as professionalism, civility and ethical conduct in the practice of law and in the legal profession.

G. "Course in the elimination of bias in the legal profession and in the practice of law" means a course directly related to the practice of law that is designed to educate attorneys to identify and eliminate from the legal profession and from the practice of law biases against persons because of race, gender, economic status, creed, color, religion, national origin, disability, age or sexual orientation.

H. "Court" means the Supreme Court of the State of Minnesota.

I. "Director" means the Director of the Board.

J. "Emeritus status" is the status of a lawyer who has filed a Retirement Affidavit pursuant to Rule 2(C)(5) of the Rules of the Supreme Court on Lawyer Registration, is not on involuntary restricted status, has submitted an Affidavit of Emeritus Status Appendix IV showing compliance with the requirements of CLE Rule 14, and is authorized by Rule 14 to provide pro bono legal representation to a pro bono client when referred by an approved legal services provider. Emeritus status lawyers remain on restricted status.

K. "Established continuing legal education course sponsor," for the purposes of Rule 5B, is a person or entity regularly retained by firms or organizations for the purpose of presenting continuing legal education programs, which is completely independent of the firm or organization for whose members the continuing legal education course is presented.

L. "Fee" means funds made payable to the Minnesota State Board of Continuing Legal Education.

M. "In–house course" means a course sponsored by a single private law firm, a single corporation or financial institution, or by a single federal, state or local governmental agency for lawyers who are members or employees of any of the above organizations.

N. "Involuntary restricted status" means the status of a lawyer licensed in Minnesota who is not in compliance with the educational and reporting requirements of these Rules and who has been involuntarily placed in that status by order of the Court. See Rule 12 for additional provisions.

O. "Laboratory setting" means a mock courtroom, law office, negotiation table, or other simulated setting in which demonstrations are given, role-playing is carried out or lawyers' activities are taught by example or participation.

P. "Law and literature course" means a course that meets the requirements of Rules 4D and 5A, based upon a literary text and designed to generate discussion, insight, and learning about topics such as the practice of law, the history and philosophy of law, rhetoric, lawyers' professional or ethical responsibilities, professional development, and the elimination of bias in the legal profession and in the practice of law.

Q. "Moderator" means an individual, knowledgeable in the topic or topics addressed by the course, who guides the discussion and answers questions related to the material presented.

R. "On–Demand course" means archived CLE programming that meets all the requirements of Rule 5A and is available to participants at any time.

S. "Participant" means a lawyer licensed in Minnesota attending an approved course and actively engaged in the subject matter being presented.

T. "Pro bono client" means an individual, who is not a corporation or other organizational entity, and who has been referred to the lawyer by an approved legal services provider or by a state or federal court program.

U. "Pro bono legal representation" means providing legal representation to a pro bono client without compensation, expectation of compensation, or other direct or indirect pecuniary gain.

V. "Professional development course" means a course or session within a course designed to enhance the development and performance of lawyers by addressing issues such as career satisfaction and renewal, stress management, mental or emotional health, substance abuse, and gambling addiction. Professional development courses do not include individual or group therapy sessions.

W. "Restricted status" means the status of a lawyer licensed in Minnesota who has voluntarily chosen not to comply with the educational and reporting requirements of these Rules. See Rule 12 for additional provisions.

X. "Submit" means to communicate information to the Board office in writing or electronic submission:

(1) through the Board's Online Attorney and Sponsor Integrated System (OASIS);

(2) by regular U.S. Mail; or

(3) by delivery.

Adopted April 17, 2000, eff. July 1, 2000. Amended Dec. 10, 2003, eff. Feb. 1, 2004; Jan. 31, 2008, eff. July 1, 2008; June 30, 2008, eff. July 1, 2008; Jan. 6, 2010, eff. Feb. 1, 2010; April 1, 2010, eff. July 1, 2010; March 15, 2013, eff. July 1, 2013; Dec. 6, 2012, eff. July 1, 2014.

Rule 3. State Board of Continuing Legal Education

A. Membership of the Board. The Court shall appoint twelve members and a Chairperson. The membership of the Board shall consist of:

(1) 3 members of the public;

(2) 1 member who is a district court judge;

(3) 6 lawyer members who are nominated by the Minnesota State Bar Association; and

(4) 3 lawyer members who are nominated by the Court.

B. Terms of Members. Appointments shall be for staggered 3–year terms, with no member serving more than two 3–year terms, and each member serving until a successor is appointed and qualifies.

C. Officers of the Board.

(1) *Chairperson.* The Chairperson of the Board shall be appointed by the Court for such time as it shall designate and shall serve at the pleasure of the Court.

(2) *Vice Chairperson.* A Vice Chairperson shall be designated by the Chairperson and shall maintain the minutes of meetings of the Board.

D. Authority of the Board. Subject to the general direction of the Court in all matters, the Board shall have supervisory authority over the administration of these Rules, shall approve courses and programs which satisfy the educational requirements of these Rules, and shall have authority with respect to the following:

(1) *Waivers and Extensions.* Waivers of strict compliance with these Rules or extensions of time deadlines provided in these Rules may be made in cases of hardship or other compelling reasons.

(2) **Supplemental Policies.** The Board may adopt policies and forms not inconsistent with these Rules governing the conduct of business and performance of its duties.

E. Board Procedures. Robert's Rules of Order shall govern the conduct of Board meetings where practicable.

F. Confidentiality. Unless otherwise directed by the Court, the files, records, and proceedings of the Board, as they may relate to or arise out of any failure of an active lawyer to satisfy the continuing legal education requirements, shall be deemed confidential and shall not be disclosed except in furtherance of the Board's duties, or upon request of the lawyer affected, or as they may be introduced in evidence or otherwise produced in proceedings in accordance with these Rules.

G. Persons with Disabilities. It is the policy of the Board to administer these Rules in a manner consistent with state and federal laws prohibiting discrimination against persons with disabilities and to make reasonable modifications in any policies, practices, and procedures that might otherwise deny equal access to individuals with disabilities.

H. Payment of Expenses. The Chairperson, the Vice Chairperson and other members of the Board shall serve without compensation, but shall be paid reasonable and necessary expenses certified to have been incurred in the performance of their duties.

Adopted April 17, 2000, eff. July 1, 2000. Amended Dec. 10, 2003, eff. Feb. 1, 2004; Jan. 6, 2010, eff. Feb. 1, 2010.

Rule 4. Applying for Credit

Rule effective until July 1, 2014. See, also, rule effective July 1, 2014.

A. Course Approval and Fee Information. No segment of any course shall be approved in more than one credit category. In applying for course approval, a sponsoring agency or lawyer shall submit to the Board an application for course approval (see Appendix I) and include the following:

(1) Name and contact information for the sponsor;

(2) Title of the program under consideration;

(3) City and state where the program is held;

(4) Names and credentials of the speakers, including those of persons designated to act as moderators for video or satellite programs;

(5) Type of presentation;

(6) Agenda or course schedule showing beginning and ending times of each session and the date(s) on which the program is presented;

(7) For each segment of the course, credit may be requested in one of the following categories:

(a) standard

(b) ethics and/or professional responsibility

(c) elimination of bias

(d) law office management

(e) professional development.

(8) Fee in the amount of $35. This fee may be subject to waiver under the provisions of Rule 3D(1). A fee is not required when submitting an application for either of the following types of courses meeting Rule 4 and Rule 5 requirements:

(a) a previously approved course that has been recorded and is replayed at a later date in its entirety; or

(b) a course 60 minutes or less in duration.

(9) Expected audience or target audience to which the program is marketed; and

(10) Such other information as the Board may require.

B. Professional Responsibility or Ethics: General Treatment. Every application for course approval must include:

(1) A description of the general treatment of professional responsibility or ethical considerations; or

(2) An explanation of why professional responsibility or ethical considerations are not included.

C. Sanctions for Failure to Include Ethics. If in the opinion of the Board, the general treatment of professional responsibility or legal ethics topics within courses approved as standard continuing legal education is inadequate without satisfactory explanation, the Board may refuse to grant full credit for all hours in attendance, impose a deduction from credit hours which would otherwise be granted, and in the case of persistent refusal to cover these topics, refuse to grant further credit for courses offered by the sponsor.

D. Law and Literature. A "law and literature course" that otherwise meets the course approval requirements set forth in Rule 5(A) will be approved for credit if the application for course approval includes the following:

(1) A narrative describing the course learning goals and discussion topics.

(2) Evidence that program registrants are instructed to read the designated literary text prior to attending the course.

No credit will be granted for the time that participants spend reading the designated literary text prior to attending the course.

E. Notice of Credit. The Board shall inform the sponsor or applicant of the number and type of credit hours granted or denied. This information will also be posted on the Board's website.

Adopted April 17, 2000, eff. July 1, 2000. Amended Dec. 10, 2003, eff. Feb. 1, 2004; Jan. 6, 2010, eff. Feb. 1, 2010.

Rule 4. Applying for Credit

Rule effective July 1, 2014. See, also, rule effective until July 1, 2014.

A. Course Approval and Fee Information. No segment of any course shall be approved in more than one credit category. In applying for course approval, a sponsoring agency or lawyer shall submit to the Board an application for course approval (see Appendix I) and include the following:

(1) Name and contact information for the sponsor;

(2) Title of the program under consideration;

(3) City and state where the program is held;

(4) Names and credentials of the speakers, including those of persons designated to act as moderators for video or satellite programs;

(5) Type of presentation;

(6) Agenda or course schedule showing beginning and ending times of each session and the date(s) on which the program is presented;

(7) For each segment of the course, credit may be requested in one of the following categories:

(a) standard

(b) ethics and/or professional responsibility

(c) elimination of bias

(d) law office management

(e) professional development.

(8) Fee in the amount of $35. This fee may be subject to waiver under the provisions of Rule 3D(1). A fee is not required when submitting an application for either of the following types of courses meeting Rule 4 and Rule 5 requirements:

(a) A previously approved course that has been recorded and is replayed in its entirety with a live moderator present during the scheduled question and answer period of the program; or

(b) A live course 60 minutes or less in duration.

(9) Expected audience or target audience to which the program is marketed; and

(10) Such other information as the Board may require.

B. Professional Responsibility or Ethics: General Treatment. Every application for course approval must include:

(1) A description of the general treatment of professional responsibility or ethical considerations; or

(2) An explanation of why professional responsibility or ethical considerations are not included.

C. Sanctions for Failure to Include Ethics. If in the opinion of the Board, the general treatment of professional responsibility or legal ethics topics within courses approved as standard continuing legal education is inadequate without satisfactory explanation, the Board may refuse to grant full credit for all hours in attendance, impose a deduction from credit hours which would otherwise be granted, and in the case of persistent refusal to cover these topics, refuse to grant further credit for courses offered by the sponsor.

D. Law and Literature. A "law and literature course" that otherwise meets the course approval requirements set forth in Rule 5(A) will be approved for credit if the application for course approval includes the following:

(1) A narrative describing the course learning goals and discussion topics.

(2) Evidence that program registrants are instructed to read the designated literary text prior to attending the course.

No credit will be granted for the time that participants spend reading the designated literary text prior to attending the course.

E. Notice of Credit. The Board shall inform the sponsor or applicant of the number and type of credit hours granted or denied. This information will also be posted on the Board's website.

Adopted April 17, 2000, eff. July 1, 2000. Amended Dec. 10, 2003, eff. Feb. 1, 2004; Jan. 6, 2010, eff. Feb. 1, 2010; Dec. 6, 2013, eff. July 1, 2014.

Rule 5. Standards for Course Approval

Rule effective until July 1, 2014. See, also, rule effective July 1, 2014.

A. General Standards. A course must meet the following standards before approval is granted.

(1) The course shall have significant intellectual or practical content.

(2) The course shall deal primarily with matter directly related to the practice of law, the professional responsibility or ethical obligations of lawyers, the elimination of bias in the legal profession and in the practice of law, law office management, or the professional development of lawyers.

(3) The course shall be taught by faculty members qualified by practical or academic experience to teach the specified subject matter. Legal subjects shall be taught by lawyers.

(4) Any written materials should be thorough, high quality, readable, carefully prepared, and distributed to all participants at or before the time the course is offered.

(5) The course shall be presented and attended in a suitable classroom or laboratory setting. Courses presented via video recording, simultaneous broadcast, teleconference, or audiotape may be approved provided that a faculty member or moderator is in attendance at all presentations, either in person or through live transmission, allowing all participants to hear and participate in the question and answer session. Subject to the exception of paragraph (11) below, no course will be approved which involves solely television or video viewing in the home or office, or correspondence work or self-study, including online self-study.

(6) Credit will not normally be given for speeches at luncheons or banquets.

(7) A list of all participants shall be maintained by the course sponsor and transmitted to the Board upon request, following the presentation of the course.

(8) Credit shall be awarded on the basis of one credit hour for each 60 minutes of instruction at an approved course.

(9) A lawyer shall not receive credit for any course attended before being admitted to practice law in Minnesota, but one so admitted may receive credit of one hour for each 60 minutes actually spent in attendance, for attending for credit or as an auditor, a regular course offered by a law school approved by the American Bar Association.

(10) Notwithstanding the provisions of paragraph (9) above, a person who takes approved courses or teaches in an approved course after sitting for the Minnesota Bar Examination, but before admission to practice, may claim credit for the courses taken or the teaching done, if he or she passes that bar examination.

(11) Lawyers residing or working outside of the State of Minnesota during the CLE reporting period who, because of nonresidence are unable in good faith to attend courses approved as "elimination of bias" as defined in these Rules, may receive up to 2 hours of credit in fulfillment of the elimination of bias requirement by viewing a video or webcast of a course or courses that otherwise meet the requirements of these Rules. If a lawyer is a participant in an elimination of bias course not previously approved for credit under these Rules, the lawyer may seek approval by completing and submitting an application for course approval as described in Rule 4A.

B. Standards for Course Approval for In-House Courses.

(1) An in-house course as defined in Rule 2M will be approved if:

(a) The requirements of Rule 5A and other applicable Rules are met;

(b) 25% of the hours of approved instruction are taught by instructors having no continuing relationship or employment with the sponsoring firm, department, financial institution or agency; and

(c) Notice of the course is given to enough outside lawyers so that the audience can potentially be composed of at least 25% participants who are not lawyers working in or for the sponsoring firm, department, institution or agency.

(2) An in-house course as defined in Rule 2M that is presented and controlled by an established continuing legal education course sponsor as defined in Rule 2K, may be approved for credit, notwith-

standing the fact that the course does not comply with requirements of Rule 5B(1) (b) and (c) above.

(3) An in-house course as defined in Rule 2M shall not be approved for credit if it is presented primarily for clients or clients' counsel.

Adopted April 17, 2000, eff. July 1, 2000. Amended Dec. 10, 2003, eff. Feb. 1, 2004; Jan. 6, 2010, eff. Feb. 1, 2010; March 15, 2013, eff. July 1, 2013.

Rule 5. Standards for Course Approval

Rule effective July 1, 2014. See, also, rule effective until July 1, 2014.

A. General Standards. A course must meet the following standards before approval is granted.

(1) The course shall have current, significant intellectual or practical content, and shall be presented in a high-quality manner permitting participants to hear all of the audio and see all of the video portions of the program, including presentations, audience questions, responses to questions, embedded videos, and other program materials.

(2) The course shall deal primarily with matter directly related to the practice of law, the professional responsibility or ethical obligations of lawyers, the elimination of bias in the legal profession and in the practice of law, law office management, or the professional development of lawyers.

(3) The course shall be taught by faculty members qualified by practical or academic experience to teach the specified subject matter. Legal subjects shall be taught by lawyers.

(4) Any written materials should be thorough, high quality, readable, carefully prepared, and distributed to all participants at or before the time the course is offered.

(5) The course shall be presented and attended in a suitable classroom or laboratory setting. A course presented via video recording, simultaneous broadcast, teleconference, or audiotape, or available on-demand or by podcast, may be approved provided that it complies with Rule 6E and a faculty member or moderator is accessible to all participants, either in person or via electronic means, allowing all participants to have access to and participate in the question and answer session. No course will be approved which involves solely correspondence work or self-study.

(6) Credit will not normally be given for speeches at luncheons or banquets.

(7) A list of all participants shall be maintained by the course sponsor and transmitted to the Board upon request, following the presentation of the course.

(8) Credit shall be awarded on the basis of one credit hour for each 60 minutes of instruction at an approved course.

(9) A lawyer shall not receive credit for any course attended before being admitted to practice law in Minnesota, but one so admitted may receive credit of one hour for each 60 minutes actually spent in attendance, for attending for credit or as an auditor, a regular course offered by a law school approved by the American Bar Association.

(10) Notwithstanding the provisions of paragraph (9) above, a person who takes approved courses or teaches in an approved course after sitting for the Minnesota Bar Examination, but before admission to practice, may claim credit for the courses taken or the teaching done, if he or she passes that bar examination.

B. Standards for Course Approval for In–House Courses.

(1) An in-house course as defined in Rule 2M will be approved if:

(a) The requirements of Rule 5A and other applicable Rules are met;

(b) 25% of the hours of approved instruction are taught by instructors having no continuing relationship or employment with the sponsoring firm, department, financial institution or agency; and

(c) Notice of the course is given to enough outside lawyers so that the audience can potentially be composed of at least 25% participants who are not lawyers working in or for the sponsoring firm, department, institution or agency.

(2) An in-house course as defined in Rule 2M that is presented and controlled by an established continuing legal education course sponsor as defined in Rule 2K, may be approved for credit, notwithstanding the fact that the course does not comply with requirements of Rule 5B(1) (b) and (c) above.

(3) An in-house course as defined in Rule 2M shall not be approved for credit if it is presented primarily for clients or clients' counsel.

Adopted April 17, 2000, eff. July 1, 2000. Amended Dec. 10, 2003, eff. Feb. 1, 2004; Jan. 6, 2010, eff. Feb. 1, 2010; March 15, 2013, eff. July 1, 2013; Dec. 6, 2013, eff. July 1, 2014.

Rule 6. Special Categories of Credit

Rule effective until July 1, 2014. See, also, rule effective July 1, 2014.

A. Ethics and Professional Responsibility. Courses or sessions within courses approved as courses in ethics or professional responsibility:

(1) Must be at least 30 minutes in length; and

(2) Must be separately identified as ethics or professional responsibility on the course agenda and on the Course Approval Form at Appendix I.

B. Elimination of Bias in the Legal Profession and in the Practice of Law. Courses or sessions within courses approved as courses in the elimination of bias in the legal profession and in the practice of law:

(1) Must be at least 60 minutes in length;

(2) Must be identified on the application as fulfilling the elimination of bias requirement and be accompanied by a narrative describing how the course or segments of the course meet one or more of the learning goals as described in the Course Approval Form at Appendix I;

(3) Must focus on issues in the legal profession and in the practice of law and not issues of bias in society in general; and

(4) Must not include courses on the substantive law of illegal discrimination unless such courses meet one or more of the learning goals for elimination of bias courses set forth in the Course Approval Form at Appendix I.

C. Law Office Management. A lawyer may receive credit for attendance at a course on law office management, which includes the topics of mentoring, staff development, and technology related to law office management, up to a maximum of 6 credit hours per reporting period. The course must be submitted for approval pursuant to Rule 4. Law office management courses that specifically address elimination of bias in the law office or in the practice of law may be approved instead as courses in the elimination of bias and when so designated are not subject to the 6–hour maximum on law office management courses.

D. Pro bono Legal Representation. A lawyer may claim 1 hour of standard CLE credit for every 6 hours of pro bono legal representation as defined by Rule 2T that the lawyer provides to a pro bono client as defined by Rule 2S in a legal matter that has been referred to the lawyer by an approved legal services provider as defined by Rule 2B or by a state court or federal court program. No more than 6 hours of credit may be claimed per reporting period by a lawyer for pro bono legal representation. In order to receive CLE credit the lawyer must submit an Affidavit of Pro Bono Representation to the Board (see Appendix II).

Adopted April 17, 2000, eff. July 1, 2000. Amended Dec. 10, 2003, eff. Feb. 1, 2004; Jan. 31, 2008, eff. July 1, 2008; June 30, 2008, eff. July 1, 2008; Jan. 6, 2010, eff. Feb. 1, 2010; March 15, 2013, eff. July 1, 2013.

Rule 6. Special Categories of Credit

Rule effective July 1, 2014. See, also, rule effective until July 1, 2014.

A. Ethics and Professional Responsibility. To be approved for ethics credit, the courses or sessions within the courses approved must meet the following requirements:

(1) Be at least 30 minutes in length; and

(2) Be separately identified as ethics or professional responsibility on the course agenda and on the Course Approval Form at Appendix I.

B. Elimination of Bias in the Legal Profession and in the Practice of Law. To be approved for elimination of bias credit, the courses or sessions within such courses must meet the following requirements:

(1) Be at least 60 minutes in length;

(2) Be identified on the application as fulfilling the elimination of bias requirement and be accompanied by a narrative describing how the course or sessions of the course meet one or more of the learning goals as described in the Course Approval Form at Appendix I;

(3) Focus on issues in the legal profession and in the practice of law and not issues of bias in society in general; and

(4) Not include courses on the substantive law of illegal discrimination unless such courses meet one or more of the learning goals for elimination of bias courses set forth in the Course Approval Form at Appendix I.

C. Law Office Management. A lawyer may receive credit for attendance at a course on law office management, which includes the topics of mentoring, staff development, and technology related to law office management, up to a maximum of 6 credit hours per reporting period. The course must be submitted for approval pursuant to Rule 4. Law office management courses that specifically address elimination of bias in the law office or in the practice of law may be approved instead as courses in the elimination of bias and when so designated are not subject to the 6–hour maximum on law office management courses.

D. Pro Bono Legal Representation. A lawyer may claim 1 hour of standard CLE credit for every 6 hours of pro bono legal representation as defined by Rule 2U that the lawyer provides to a pro bono client as defined by Rule 2T in a legal matter that has been referred to the lawyer by an approved legal services provider as defined by Rule 2B or by a state court or federal court program. No more than 6 hours of credit may be claimed per reporting period by a lawyer for pro bono legal representation. In order to receive CLE credit the lawyer must submit an Affidavit of Pro Bono Representation to the Board (see Appendix II).

E. On–Demand Courses. A lawyer may claim up to 15 hours of credit within the 45 hour CLE period for on-demand courses as defined in Rule 2R, subject to the following provisions:

(1) The course meets all other requirements of Rules 2, 5, & 6;

(2) The course sponsor agrees to have one or more faculty members accessible to all participants via electronic or other means through the 24 month

period during which the program is approved for Minnesota CLE credit;

(3) The course sponsor or course applicant completes and submits to the Board an Application for Course Approval; and

(4) The approval for an on-demand course is valid for 24 months after the date of approval by the Board office.

Adopted April 17, 2000, eff. July 1, 2000. Amended Dec. 10, 2003, eff. Feb. 1, 2004; Jan. 31, 2008, eff. July 1, 2008; June 30, 2008, eff. July 1, 2008; Jan. 6, 2010, eff. Feb. 1, 2010; March 15, 2013, eff. July 1, 2013; Dec. 6, 2013, eff. July 1, 2014.

Rule 7. Other Credit

Text of subd. A. effective until July 1, 2014.

A. Teaching Credit. Credit for teaching in an approved course shall be awarded to presenting faculty on the basis of one credit for each 60 minutes spent by the faculty preparing the presentation and materials for the course and teaching the course. No credit shall be awarded for teaching directed primarily to persons preparing for admission to practice law. A lawyer seeking credit for teaching and preparation for teaching shall submit to the Board all information called for on the Affidavit of CLE Compliance at Appendix III.

Text of subd. A. effective July 1, 2014.

A. Teaching Credit. Credit for teaching in an approved, live (not previously recorded) course shall be awarded to presenting faculty on the basis of one credit for each 60 minutes spent by the faculty preparing the presentation and materials for the course and teaching the course. No credit shall be awarded for teaching directed primarily to persons preparing for admission to practice law. A lawyer seeking credit for teaching and preparation for teaching shall submit to the Board all information called for on the Affidavit of CLE Compliance at Appendix III.

B. Courses at Universities. Courses that are part of a regular curriculum at a college or university, other than a law school, may be approved for a maximum of 15 hours per course when the lawyer requesting approval submits evidence supporting the conclusion that the course meets the Rule 5A(1) through (5) criteria and that it is directly related to the requesting lawyer's practice of law. Teaching credit shall not be awarded for courses approved under this paragraph.

C. Retroactive Credit. A lawyer, or a course sponsor, may seek retroactive approval of courses by submitting the necessary information and fees required in Rule 4A. (See Course Approval Form at Appendix I.)

Adopted April 17, 2000, eff. July 1, 2000. Amended Dec. 10, 2003, eff. Feb. 1, 2004; Jan. 6, 2010, eff. Feb. 1, 2010; Dec. 6, 2013, eff. July 1, 2014.

Rule 8. Announcement of Approval

Any person may announce, as to an approved course: This course has been approved by the Minnesota State Board of Continuing Legal Education for ___ hours in the following category or categories of credit:

(a) standard continuing legal education;

(b) ethics or professional responsibility continuing legal education;

(c) elimination of bias continuing legal education; or

(d) law office management continuing legal education.

Adopted April 17, 2000, eff. July 1, 2000. Amended Dec. 10, 2003, eff. Feb. 1, 2004; Jan. 6, 2010, eff. Feb. 1, 2010.

Rule 9. Affidavit of CLE Compliance

Rule effective until July 1, 2014. See, also, rule effective July 1, 2014.

A. Contents of Affidavit. To maintain active status, a lawyer shall report attendance or participation in no fewer than 45 credit hours of approved continuing legal education courses. A lawyer may report the credits through the Board's Online Attorney and Sponsor Integrated System (OASIS) or by Affidavit of CLE Compliance (Appendix III). Effective July 1, 2010, the Affidavit of CLE Compliance (Appendix III) must be accompanied by a $10 processing fee. There is no processing fee for submission through OASIS.

B. Special Categories of Credit. Lawyers must report:

(1) no fewer than 3 hours of approved courses in ethics or professional responsibility;

(2) no fewer than 2 hours of approved courses in the elimination of bias in the legal profession and in the practice of law;

(3) no more than 6 hours of approved courses in law office management; and

(4) no more than 6 hours of credit for pro bono legal representation provided pursuant to Rule 6D and reported by Appendix II.

C. Timely Affidavit. The affidavit must be received by the Board office or postmarked no later than August 31 following the close of the final year of the 3-year period specified by the Lawyer Registration Office as a lawyer's continuing legal education category. Electronic affidavits must be submitted on or before August 31.

D. Late Affidavit Fee. A lawyer who submits an Affidavit of CLE Compliance after the deadline specified in paragraph C above, but before issuance of a notice of noncompliance, shall submit along with the late affidavit a late filing fee in the amount of $75.00. This fee is payable notwithstanding the Board's grant of an extension of time. Additional late fees will not be charged for late affidavits filed within a single reporting period.

E. Notice of Noncompliance Fee. A lawyer who submits an Affidavit of CLE Compliance after the Board has issued a notice of noncompliance, but before the Court has issued an order placing the lawyer on involuntary restricted status, shall submit along with the affidavit a notice of noncompliance fee in the amount of $200.

F. Active Duty Military Service. A lawyer called to active duty military service who requests an extension of time to complete CLE requirements because of active duty military service shall be granted an extension of at least six months from the date of return from active duty status. Upon request, the Board shall grant a waiver of a late filing fee or a notice of non-compliance fee assessed as a result of the lawyer's active duty military status.

Adopted April 17, 2000, eff. July 1, 2000. Amended Dec. 10, 2003, eff. Feb. 1, 2004; Jan. 6, 2010, eff. Feb. 1, 2010.

Rule 9. Affidavit of CLE Compliance

Rule effective July 1, 2014. See, also, rule effective until July 1, 2014.

A. Contents of Affidavit. To maintain active status, a lawyer shall report participation in no fewer than 45 credit hours of approved continuing legal education courses within a single reporting period that are in compliance with the provisions of Rule 9B. A lawyer may report the credits through the Board's Online Attorney and Sponsor Integrated System (OASIS) or by Affidavit of CLE Compliance (Appendix III). Effective July 1, 2010, the Affidavit of CLE Compliance (Appendix III) must be accompanied by a $10 processing fee. There is no processing fee for submission through OASIS.

B. Special Categories of Credit. Lawyers must report:

(1) no fewer than 3 hours of approved courses in ethics or professional responsibility;

(2) no fewer than 2 hours of approved courses in the elimination of bias in the legal profession and in the practice of law;

(3) no more than 6 hours of approved courses in law office management;

(4) no more than 6 hours of credit for pro bono legal representation provided pursuant to Rule 6D and reported by Appendix II; and

(5) no more than 15 hours of credit for on-demand courses.

C. Timely Affidavit. The affidavit must be received by the Board office or postmarked no later than August 31 following the close of the final year of the 3–year period specified by the Lawyer Registration Office as a lawyer's continuing legal education category. Electronic affidavits must be submitted on or before August 31.

D. Late Affidavit Fee. A lawyer who submits an Affidavit of CLE Compliance after the deadline specified in paragraph C above, but before issuance of a notice of noncompliance, shall submit along with the late affidavit a late filing fee in the amount of $75.00. This fee is payable notwithstanding the Board's grant of an extension of time. Additional late fees will not be charged for late affidavits filed within a single reporting period.

E. Notice of Noncompliance Fee. A lawyer who submits an Affidavit of CLE Compliance after the Board has issued a notice of noncompliance, but before the Court has issued an order placing the lawyer on involuntary restricted status, shall submit along with the affidavit a notice of noncompliance fee in the amount of $200.

F. Active Duty Military Service. A lawyer called to active duty military service who requests an extension of time to complete CLE requirements because of active duty military service shall be granted an extension of at least six months from the date of return from active duty status. Upon request, the Board shall grant a waiver of a late filing fee or a notice of non-compliance fee assessed as a result of the lawyer's active duty military status.

Adopted April 17, 2000, eff. July 1, 2000. Amended Dec. 10, 2003, eff. Feb. 1, 2004; Jan. 6, 2010, eff. Feb. 1, 2010; Dec. 6, 2013, eff. July 1, 2014.

Rule 10. Director's Determinations and Board Review

Text of subd. A. effective until July 1, 2014.

A. Director's Determinations. The Director has the following authority and responsibility:

(1) To respond in writing to written requests for course approval, giving reasons for the determination;

(2) To grant credit to lawyers for attending or teaching approved courses;

(3) To grant or deny requests for transfer, waiver, extension of time deadlines or interpretation of these Rules; and

(4) To inform the Board about determinations made since the Board's last meeting, together with observations and comments relating to matters under the Board's jurisdiction.

Text of subd. A. effective July 1, 2014.

A. Director's Determinations. The Director has the following authority and responsibility:

(1) To respond in writing to written requests for course approval, giving reasons for the determination;

(2) To grant credit to lawyers for participating in or teaching approved courses;

(3) To grant or deny requests for transfer, waiver, extension of time deadlines or interpretation of these Rules; and

(4) To inform the Board about determinations made since the Board's last meeting, together with observations and comments relating to matters under the Board's jurisdiction.

B. Board Review. A lawyer or sponsoring agency affected by an adverse determination of the Director may request Board review of the determination and may present information to the Board in writing and in person. The Board may take such action as it deems appropriate and shall advise the lawyer or sponsoring agency of its determination.

Adopted April 17, 2000, eff. July 1, 2000. Amended Dec. 10, 2003, eff. Feb. 1, 2004; Jan. 6, 2010, eff. Feb. 1, 2010; Dec. 6, 2013, eff. July 1, 2014.

Rule 11. Notice of Noncompliance

A. Notice Required. The Director shall send a notice of noncompliance to any lawyer who:

(1) Fails to meet the requirements of these Rules; and

(2) Fails to request and obtain an extension of time in which to file an Affidavit of CLE Compliance as required by these Rules.

B. Service of Notice. The notice shall be sent by regular mail to the lawyer's address of record with the Lawyer Registration Office.

C. Contents of Notice. The notice shall state the nature of the noncompliance and shall inform the lawyer of the right to request a hearing within 30 days of the mailing of the notice, the right to be represented by counsel, and the right to present witnesses and evidence.

D. Effect of Notice. If no hearing is requested, the Director's determination of noncompliance shall become final and shall be reported to the Court with the recommendation that the lawyer be placed on involuntary restricted status.

E. Board Hearing. If a hearing is requested, the following apply:

(1) The Board may employ special counsel;

(2) The Chairperson shall preside at the hearing, which may be held before the entire Board or a committee appointed by the Chairperson, and shall make necessary rulings; and

(3) The hearing shall be recorded and a transcript shall be provided to the lawyer at a reasonable cost.

F. Decision. Following the hearing, the Board shall issue a written decision. If the lawyer is determined to be in noncompliance with these Rules, the Board may recommend to the Court that the lawyer be placed on involuntary restricted status or take other appropriate action.

G. Petition for Review. A lawyer who is adversely affected by the decision of the Board may appeal to the Court by filing a petition for review with the Clerk of Appellate Courts within 20 days of receipt by the lawyer of the decision together with proof of service of the petition on the Director. The petition shall state briefly the facts that form the basis for the petition and the lawyer's reasons for believing the Court should review the decision. Within 20 days of service of the petition, the Board shall serve and file a response to the petition and a copy of the final decision of the Board. Thereupon, the Court shall give such direction, hold such hearings and issue such orders as it may in its discretion deem appropriate.

Adopted April 17, 2000, eff. July 1, 2000. Amended Dec. 10, 2003, eff. Feb. 1, 2004.

Rule 12. Restricted and Involuntary Restricted Status

Text of subd. A. effective until July 1, 2014.

A. Election of Restricted Status. A lawyer duly admitted to practice in this state may elect restricted status as defined in Rule 2V by sending written notice of such election to the Director, except that a referee or judicial officer of any court of record of the State of Minnesota or lawyer employed and serving as attorney or legal counsel for any employer, including any governmental unit of the State of Minnesota, is not eligible to apply for restricted status. A lawyer on restricted status shall not be required to satisfy the educational and reporting requirements of these Rules.

Text of subd. A. effective July 1, 2014.

A. Election of Restricted Status. A lawyer duly admitted to practice in this state may elect restricted status as defined in Rule 2W by sending written notice of such election to the Director, except that a referee or judicial officer of any court of record of the State of Minnesota or lawyer employed and serving as attorney or legal counsel for any employer, including any governmental unit of the State of Minnesota, is not eligible to apply for restricted status. A lawyer on restricted status shall not be required to satisfy the educational and reporting requirements of these Rules.

B. Restrictions imposed. A lawyer on restricted or involuntary restricted status shall be subject to the following provisions and restrictions:

(1) The lawyer may not engage in the practice of law or represent any person or entity in any legal matter or proceedings within the State of Minnesota other than himself or herself, except as provided in Rule 14.

(2) The name of the lawyer may not appear on law firm letterhead without a qualification that the lawyer's Minnesota license is restricted. A law firm name may continue to include the lawyer's name if the name was included prior to the lawyer's place-

ment on restricted or involuntary restricted status. The lawyer may not be listed "of counsel" or otherwise be represented to clients or others as being able to undertake legal business.

(3) The lawyer may not have a financial interest in a law firm that is a professional corporation.

C. Transfer from Restricted Status to Active Status.

(1) Notice to Director and Fee. Unless otherwise ordered by the Court, a lawyer on restricted status who desires to resume active status shall notify the Director in writing of the lawyer's intention to resume active status and submit a transfer fee of $125.

(2) Transfer Requirements. ***A lawyer on restricted status shall be transferred to active status upon the Director's determination that the lawyer has fulfilled the requirements of (a) or (b) below:***

(a) Automatic transfer requirements. The lawyer has completed the number of CLE hours that the lawyer would have had to complete to meet reporting requirements and to be current on a proportional basis had the lawyer not been on restricted status, or

(b) Discretionary transfer requirements. The lawyer has completed such lesser requirements as the Director determines are adequate provided that the number of hours completed total no fewer than 45 hours during the 3 years immediately preceding transfer. The Director will specify no more than 90 hours. Determinations will be made subject to the criteria set forth in paragraph (c) below. The Director shall report to the Board at its next meeting the terms and conditions upon which each transfer to active status was made.

(c) Discretionary transfer criteria. The Director may transfer a lawyer to active status when the lawyer has fulfilled appropriate CLE conditions precedent or agreed to fulfill appropriate CLE conditions subsequent as determined by the Director. In making discretionary transfer decisions, the Director will take the following into consideration:

i. The number of CLE hours the lawyer has taken in the past;

ii. The lawyer's other educational activity;

iii. The lawyer's practice of law in another jurisdiction;

iv. The lawyer's law-related work other than the practice of law;

v. Whether the lawyer acted reasonably in not anticipating the need to take the appropriate number of CLE hours before being transferred from active status; and

vi. Whether the lawyer has demonstrated circumstances of hardship or other compelling reasons that show that the lawyer should be transferred to active status before completing the appropriate number of CLE hours.

(3) Failure to Abide by Transfer Conditions. A lawyer who fails to comply with the conditions of transfer shall be restored to restricted status upon notice from the Director sent by regular mail to the lawyer's last known address.

(4) Appeal to the Board. Upon written request from a lawyer, the Board shall review the Director's determination of transfer requirements and notify the lawyer in writing regarding the outcome of that review.

D. Transfer from Involuntary Restricted Status to Active Status.

(1) Notice to Director and Fee. Unless otherwise ordered by the Court, a lawyer on involuntary restricted status who desires to resume active status shall notify the Director in writing of the lawyer's intention to resume active status and submit a transfer fee of $250.

(2) Transfer Requirements. Unless otherwise ordered by the Court, the Director shall recommend to the Court that a lawyer on involuntary restricted status be transferred to active status upon the Director's determination that the lawyer has completed the number of CLE hours that the lawyer would have had to complete to meet reporting requirements and to be current on a proportional basis had the lawyer not been placed on involuntary restricted status, or that the lawyer has completed such lesser requirements as the Director determines are adequate provided that the number of hours completed total no fewer than 45 hours during the 3 years immediately preceding transfer. The Director will specify no more than 90 hours. The Director may recommend to the Court that a lawyer on involuntary restricted status be transferred to active status when the lawyer has fulfilled appropriate CLE conditions precedent or agreed to fulfill appropriate CLE conditions subsequent as determined by the Director. In making such a recommendation, the Director will take into consideration the discretionary transfer criteria in section (C)(2)(c) of this Rule.

(3) Appeal to the Board. Upon written request from a lawyer, the Board shall review the Director's determination of transfer requirements and notify the lawyer in writing regarding the outcome of that review.

E. Transfer from Involuntary Restricted Status to Voluntary Restricted Status. Unless otherwise ordered by the Court, a lawyer on involuntary restricted status who desires to transfer to restricted status shall notify the Director in writing and submit a transfer fee in the amount of $250.

Adopted April 17, 2000, eff. July 1, 2000. Amended Dec. 10, 2003, eff. Feb. 1, 2004; Jan. 6, 2010, eff. Feb. 1, 2010; March 15, 2013, eff. July 1, 2013; Dec. 6, 2013, eff. July 1, 2014.

Rule 13. Retired Status

A. Transfer from Active Status to Retired Status. A lawyer who files a Retirement Affidavit with the Lawyer Registration Office and who is placed on inactive status by the Lawyer Registration Office shall be transferred to voluntary restricted status by the CLE Board,

B. Transfer from Retired Status to Active Status. In addition to notifying the Lawyer Registration Office of the lawyer's intention to transfer to active status, a lawyer must satisfy the provision of Rule 12C before the Board returns the lawyer to active CLE status.

Adopted April 17, 2000, eff. July 1, 2000. Amended Dec. 10, 2003, eff. Feb. 1, 2004; Jan. 6, 2010, eff. Feb. 1, 2010.

Rule 14. Emeritus Status

A. Qualification. A lawyer who has filed a Retirement Affidavit pursuant to Rule 2(C)(5) of the Rules of the Supreme Court on Lawyer Registration and who has elected restricted status under the CLE Rules may elect emeritus status by complying with the requirements for emeritus status listed below.

B. Limitation of Practice. A lawyer on emeritus status is authorized solely to provide pro bono legal representation to a pro bono client in a matter referred to the lawyer by an approved legal services provider.

C. Contents of Emeritus Affidavit Appendix IV. Prior to representation as described by Rule 14B, the lawyer shall complete and submit to the Board an affidavit of emeritus status (Appendix IV) which shall include the following:

(1) The list of approved CLE courses that the lawyer has attended or participated in during the 90–day period immediately preceding the submission of the emeritus affidavit, totaling no fewer than 5 credit hours of approved continuing legal education courses, and including:

a. 3 credit hours in approved courses in the substantive area of law in which the lawyer intends to be performing pro bono services;

b. 1 credit hour approved as ethics or professional responsibility; and

c. 1 credit hour approved as elimination of bias in the legal profession and in the practice of law;

(2) A certification signed by the emeritus lawyer, affirming that if the lawyer provides pro bono representation in multiple areas such as in a brief advice clinic, the lawyer shall obtain the necessary training and resources to provide those services in a competent and ethical manner.

D. Transfer to Emeritus Status. When a lawyer submits an affidavit of emeritus status, the Board office shall verify the information and shall, for a period of three years, maintain a public posting on the Board's website listing the lawyer's name as being on emeritus status.

E. Expiration of Emeritus Status. Emeritus status shall expire three years from the date that the lawyer's name is posted. A lawyer shall not represent clients after expiration of the lawyer's emeritus status.

F. Renewal of Emeritus Status. Prior to the expiration of a lawyer's emeritus status, the lawyer may renew emeritus status by submitting to the Board an affidavit of emeritus status (Appendix IV) which shall include the following:

(1) The list of approved CLE courses attended or participated in by the lawyer during the three-year period immediately preceding the submission of the emeritus affidavit, totaling no fewer than 5 credit hours of approved continuing legal education courses, and including:

a. 3 credit hours in approved courses in the substantive area of law in which the lawyer intends to perform pro bono services;

b. 1 credit hour approved as ethics or professional responsibility; and

c. 1 credit hour approved as elimination of bias in the legal profession and in the practice of law.

(2) A certification signed by the emeritus lawyer, affirming that when the lawyer provides pro bono representation in multiple areas such as in a brief advice clinic, the lawyer shall obtain the necessary training and resources to provide those services in a competent and ethical manner.

Adopted March 15, 2013, eff. July 1, 2013.

APPENDICES

APPENDIX I. COURSE APPROVAL FORM

MINNESOTA STATE BOARD OF CONTINUING LEGAL EDUCATION

180 E. 5th Street, Suite 950, St. Paul, Minnesota 55101

651–297–7100 www.mbcle.state.mn.us

The Rules of the Board of Continuing Legal Education are on the Board's website, and published in the Court Rules volume of the Minnesota Statutes.

Fee: Check one of the following:
$35 fee is enclosed. Rule 4A(8)
No fee is required because the program is a video replay of a previously approved course. Rule 4A(8)(a)
No fee is required because the program is 1 hour or less in length. Rule 4A(8)(b)

Sponsor Name

Street Address City State Zip Code

Contact Person Email Address Telephone (area code)

Submitted by: Name: ______ Check one: ___ course sponsor or ___ course participant

Describe the expected audience or target audience to which the program is being marketed (if known): ______

The course sponsor must maintain a list of Minnesota participants and make this list available to the Board upon request. See Rule 5A(7). If you are the course sponsor, do you agree to maintain a list of Minnesota participants and make it available to the Board upon request? Yes ___ No ___

Course Title

Date(s) of course City and State course held

Check those which apply:

___ live lecture
___ in-house course (see Rule 5B)
___ demonstration, role play, mock trial
___ study tour
___ videotape/film (must have live faculty member)
___ live teleconference
___ live satellite broadcast or webcast (question and answer participation)

You must attach the program agenda or course schedule. You must include the following information:

(1) Start and stop times for each course segment. Rule 4A(6)

(2) Names and brief description of the credentials of the speakers and faculty members, including those

persons designated to act as moderators for video or satellite programs. Rule 4A(4).

(3) The type of CLE credit for which approval is sought for each segment of the course. Types of CLE Credit, include:

- Standard CLE (Rule 5A)
- Ethics CLE (Rule 2H, Rule 5A and Rule 6A)
- Elimination of Bias CLE (Rule 2G, Rule 5A, and Rule 6B)
- Law Office Management CLE (Rule 5A and Rule 6C)
- Professional Development CLE (Rule 2T and Rule 5A)

(4) **Optional**: Course materials distributed to participants may, but are not required to be, submitted along with the application. Do not send voluminous materials.

Credit is awarded on the basis of one hour for each 60 minutes of actual classroom training.

When a course has been submitted for approval and not yet approved, sponsors must advertise credit as "applied for".

ETHICS OR PROFESSIONAL RESPONSIBILITY CONTENT: Check one of the following to describe the treatment of **ethics or professional responsibility** content in the program:

___ A portion of the program 30 minutes or more in length addresses **ethics or professional responsibility** and is marked as "ethics" on the attached program agenda. Rule 6A.

___ Ethics or professional responsibility concerns are addressed throughout the program but no distinct segment is 30 minutes or more in length. Rule 4B(1).

___ No portion of the program addresses ethics or professional responsibility. Attached is an explanation of why ethics or professional responsibility content is not present in this program. Rule 4B(2).

ELIMINATION OF BIAS EDUCATION CONTENT: Check one of the following to indicate whether Elimination of Bias credit is requested for this program:

___ No credit for Elimination of Bias is sought.

___ Elimination of Bias credit is sought and a narrative is attached.

CLE Rule 6B describes course requirements for CLE on the "elimination of bias in the legal profession and in the practice of law." In order to be afforded **"elimination of bias" credit, such courses or segments of courses must be at least 60 minutes in length.** The course must focus on issues in the legal profession and in the practice of law and not on issues of bias in society in general. If elimination of bias credit is sought for some portion of this course, please do the following:

1. Review the "elimination of bias" goals listed below and the definition of elimination of bias course under Rule 2G and the requirements of Rule 6B;

2. Mark the segment or segments on the agenda that the sponsor believes fulfill these requirements; and

3. Attach a brief written narrative describing how the course segment or segments meet one or more of the "Learning Goals for Minnesota Elimination of Bias Courses" listed below.

Please note that courses or segments of courses may address ethics and elimination of bias topics. A sponsor may seek credit in one category or the other, but a course or segment will not be accredited in both categories simultaneously. The Board will determine in which category credit will be granted, based upon the course description and the sponsor's narrative.

LEARNING GOALS FOR MINNESOTA ELIMINATION OF BIAS COURSES

Courses accredited as "elimination of bias" must be at least **60 continuous minutes in duration**, must be directly related to the practice of law, must meet all other requirements of Rule 5 of the CLE rules and must be designed to meet one or more of the following goals:

1. To educate lawyers about the elimination of bias or prejudice in the legal profession, in the practice of law, and/or in the administration of justice;

2. To educate lawyers regarding barriers to hiring, retention, promotion, professional development and full participation of lawyers of color, women, and those persons referenced in the "course in the elimination of bias in the legal profession and in the practice of law" definition (Rule 2G) of the CLE rules, both in the public and private sector of the legal profession and in the practice of law; or

3. To educate lawyers about the problems identified in the Supreme Court's Race Bias and Gender Fairness Task Force Reports, as well as in other studies, reports or treatises which describe bias and prejudice in the legal profession, in the practice of law, and/or in the administration of justice.

Yes ___ No ___ If the application is seeking elimination of bias credit, I have attached a narrative explanation describing how the elimination of bias learning goals are met and how the program focuses on elimination of bias in the legal profession and not merely elimination of bias in society in general.

LAW AND LITERATURE

Yes ___ No ___ This law and literature course is accompanied by documentation on Rule 4D.

Yes ___ No ___ This law and literature course was designed to meet the standard CLE requirements set forth in Rule 5A.

APPENDIX II. AFFIDAVIT OF PRO BONO REPRESENTATION

MINNESOTA STATE BOARD OF CONTINUING LEGAL EDUCATION

180 E. 5th Street, Suite 950, St. Paul, Minnesota 55101

651–297–7100 www.mbcle.state.mn.us

An Affidavit of Pro Bono Representation must be submitted for each legal services provider for whom you provided pro bono service.

License Number: ________ Name: ________________

CLE Category:[1] Firm Name: ________________

☐ 1 Street Address:[2] ________________

☐ 2 Street Address: ________________

☐ 3 City State, and Zip: ________________

☐ Other ____ Email:[3] ________________

Telephone: ________________

Name and address of referring legal services provider: ________________

____

Name and phone number of contact person at legal services provider: ________

____

Type(s) of Representation Provided:

☐ Consumer ☐ Economic Assistance ☐ Education ☐ Employment

☐ Family Law ☐ Health ☐ Housing ☐ Immigration/Refugee ☐ Individual Rights

☐ Juvenile ☐ Seniors ☐ Wills or Probate ☐ Other: ________________

Date range of representation:[4] ________________

# of hours of pro bono legal representation: ____ # of CLE credit hours claimed:[5] ________

____

By signing this affidavit I swear (affirm) that:

- I give permission to the Minnesota Board of Continuing Legal Education to contact the referring legal services provider to verify that the information I have provided is true and accurate; and
- I understand that the Board may use this information that I have provided six (6) hours of pro bono legal representation for each one (1) hour of CLE credit claimed and that the pro bono legal representation provided qualifies in all respects under Rules 2R, 2S, 2T, and 6D.

Lawyer Signature: ________________ Date: ________________

1 Your CLE reporting category is found on your lawyer license card issued by the Lawyer Registration Office and online at http://www.mncourts.gov/mars/.

2 Address changes must be made by sending a written notice to the Lawyer Registration Office, 25 Rev. Dr. Martin Luther King Jr. Blvd., Room 305, St. Paul, Minnesota 55155.

3 An email confirmation will be sent after credits are approved or denied.

4 If representation covers more than one reporting period, submit a separate Affidavit of Pro Bono Representation for each reporting period. If representation is ongoing, write "ongoing" as the date representation ended.

5 You may claim 1 hour of CLE credit for every 6 hours of pro bono legal representation up to a maximum of 6 hours. Record credits in increments no smaller than.25 hours.

APPENDIX III. AFFIDAVIT OF CLE COMPLIANCE

MINNESOTA STATE BOARD OF CONTINUING LEGAL EDUCATION

180 E. 5th Street, Suite 950 St. Paul, Minnesota 55101

651–297–7100 www.mbcle.state.mn.us

As of July 1, 2010, a $10 processing fee must be submitted with this form.

The processing fee is not assessed when you file courses online through OASIS (www.mbcle.state.mn.us)

License Number: ________ Name: ________________
CLE Category: ________ Address: ________________
Period Covered: ________ Address: ________________
Telephone Number: ________ Email Address: ________________

I swear that the information below is an accurate and complete record of my attendance.

Lawyer Signature ________________ Date: ________

ATTENDANCE INFORMATION

SPONSORING AGENCY	COURSE TITLE AND EVENT CODE (if known)	COURSE DATE(S)	# OF HOURS				
			STANRD CLE	LAW OFFICE MNGT	PROF DVLPMT	* ETHICS	ELIMN OF BIAS
1.							
2.							
3.							
4.							

Please retain a copy of this form for your records.

(USE ADDITIONAL SHEETS IF NECESSARY)

a. HOURS OF PREPARATION AND TEACHING INFORMATION

SPONSORING AGENCY	COURSE TITLE AND EVENT CODE (if known)	COURSE DATE(S)	# OF HOURS				
			STANRD CLE	LAW OFFICE MNGT	PROF DVLPMT	ETHICS	ELIMN OF BIAS
1.							
2.							
3.							
4.							

Please note:

• Lawyers must report at least 45 credit hours, including 3 hours of Ethics CLE and at least 2 hours of Elimination of Bias CLE. You may report more than the minimum required number of ethics and bias credits. All ethics and bias credits count towards your 45 hour requirement.

• The event code assigned to the program and the number and type of credits awarded to the program are found at the Board's website at http://www.mbcle.state.mn.us. A course segment will be accredited as one credit type, and will not be accredited as both Ethics and Elimination of Bias.

• Law Office Management credits are capped at 6 hours per 3–year period.

• There is no limit on the number of hours of professional development CLE you may claim.

COMPLIANCE INSTRUCTIONS

REQUIREMENTS: The CLE Rules require that each lawyer holding an active license complete a minimum of 45 credit hours including at least 3 ethics credits and 2 elimination of bias credits, every three years. A reporting category number is assigned to each lawyer and is printed on the face of the lawyer's license card.

CLE 1 reports attendance from (July 1, 2009 to June 30, 20012);

CLE 2 reports attendance from (July 1, 2007 to June 30, 2010);

CLE 3 reports attendance from (July 1, 2008 to June 30, 2011).

The credits must be taken during the reporting period. There is no carry-over of credits from one reporting period to the next.

DEADLINES: Courses should be completed prior to June 30 of the reporting year. A lawyer due to report must file an affidavit of attendance with the Board (or enter the information through OASIS) on or before August 31 of the lawyer's reporting year. Postmarks dated on or before the due date are accepted as timely. A $75.00 late filing fee must be included with your Affidavit if you are filing after the deadline, even if an extension has been granted.

SANCTIONS: The Board will issue a Notice of Noncompliance pursuant to Rule 9E to a lawyer who fails to comply with the Rule requirements. A lawyer who submits an affidavits after the issuance of a Notice of Noncompliance must submit a $200.00 Notice of Noncompliance fee. Failure to comply with the CLE requirements after receiving the Notice of Noncompliance will result in the lawyer's license being placed on involuntary restricted status by Court order.

RECORDKEEPING: It is the responsibility of the lawyer to maintain records of courses taken and to submit reports to file promptly with the Board. The lawyer may submit the affidavit of CLE compliance (1) by mail; (2) by bringing the affidavit to the Board office; (3) by reporting attendance electronically through the Board's online reporting system (OASIS); or (4) by submitting a signed copy of a certificate of completion from the course sponsor in lieu of an affidavit.

Affidavit processing may be delayed if the affidavit does not correctly and completely identify the course sponsor, the course title, and the dates of each program. To expedite processing, include the course event codes on the affidavit form. Event codes for approved or pending courses can be found on the Board's website www.mbcle.state.mn.us.

ELIGIBLE COURSES: A lawyer will not receive credit for a course unless the course has been accredited under Minnesota CLE rules. Courses accredited by other states may not be accredited in Minnesota. In addition to the course accreditation criteria in CLE Rule 5, courses should comply with the Rule 4 ethical content requirement. The Course Accreditation Forms may be submitted either by the sponsor or by a lawyer who attended the course.

RESTRICTED STATUS: A lawyer who no longer practices law in Minnesota may elect voluntary restricted status pursuant to Rule 12A by sending a written request to the Board. A lawyer on restricted status is not required to comply with the CLE attendance requirements.

INFORMATION: The course event code and the number and type of course credits may be found on the Board's website (www.mbcle.state.mn.us) under the "Search Courses" tab. A lawyer may also request this information from the course sponsor. Forms and other information , including frequently asked questions, can also be found on the Board's website,

CLAIMING TEACHING CREDIT

CLE Rule 7(A) states as follows regarding teaching credit: Credit for teaching in an approved course shall be awarded to presenting faculty on the basis of one credit for each 60 minutes spent by the faculty preparing the presentation and materials for the course and teaching the course. No credit shall be awarded for teaching directed primarily to persons preparing for admission to practice law. A lawyer seeking credit for teaching and preparation for teaching shall submit to the Board all information called for on the Affidavit of CLE Compliance at Appendix III.

Under the provisions of Rule 7A, a lawyer presenting a course may claim the time spent in presenting the course and time in attendance at the course, as well as the hours spent in preparation for the presentation. There is no limit to the number of hours that may be claimed for preparation.

Credit for teaching and/or preparation can be claimed only when the lawyer actually **teaches** in an accredited course. A lawyer who prepares materials that are distributed at the course but who does not present during the program cannot claim credit for the lawyer's scholarly efforts in preparing the program or in preparing materials for the program. Lawyers may not claim credit for writing a law review article or other scholarly articles.

A lawyer who organizes the program **cannot** claim time for administrative tasks, including identifying and persuading speakers to participate, arranging for the written materials or conferring with speakers about the allocation of responsibility for subject areas.

APPENDIX IV. AFFIDAVIT OF EMERITUS STATUS

MINNESOTA STATE BOARD OF CONTINUING LEGAL EDUCATION

180 E. 5th Street, Suite 950, St. Paul, Minnesota 55101

651–297–7100 www.mbcle.state.mn.us

For details regarding Emeritus Status, see Rule 2J and Rule 14 of the Rules of the Minnesota State Board of Continuing Legal Education at www.mbcle.state.mn.us/MBCLE/pages/rules.asp.

Name: ____________________ License Number: _______________
Email [1]: ____________________ Phone: _______________
Address [2]: ____
City: ____________________ State: ________ Zip: ______

☐ First Affidavit for Emeritus Status ☐ Renewal Affidavit for Emeritus Status

ATTENDANCE INFORMATION

SPONSORING AGENCY	COURSE TITLE & EVENT CODE (if known)	COURSE DATE(S)	STANRD CLE	ETHICS	ELIMN OF BIAS
1.					
2.					
3.					
4.					
5.					
		Hours Total:			

Name & address of referring approved legal services provider:

____

____

Name & phone # of contact at legal services provider:

____

____

Area of law in which pro bono service will be provided:

____

____

Please initial the following statements and sign this affidavit swearing (affirming) to the following:

___ I have filed a Retirement Affidavit with the Lawyer Registration Office pursuant to Rule 2(C)(5) of the Rules on Lawyer Registration and am on Inactive–Retired Status with Lawyer Registration. Record can be verified at: www.mncourts.gov/mars/default.aspx

___ I am on voluntary (not involuntary) restricted status. See CLE Rules 2N and 2V.

___ At least 3 of the substantive law CLE credit hours listed above are in the substantive area of law in which I intend to provide pro bono legal representation, and I affirm that prior to providing legal advice or representation in another substantive law area I will obtain 3 substantive credit hours in that area of law.

___ If providing pro bono service in a brief advice clinic, I will have received or will obtain the necessary training to provide that service.

___ I give permission to the Minnesota Board of Continuing Legal Education to verify this information by contacting the approved legal services provider.

___ I understand that the Emeritus Status will expire 3 years from the day the CLE Board posts my Emeritus status on the CLE website, unless prior to the expiration I file an Emeritus Status renewal Affidavit in compliance with Rule 14.

___ I shall limit my practice to providing pro bono legal representation to one or more pro bono clients in matters referred to me by an approved legal services provider.

Lawyer Signature: ________________ Date: ____________

A lawyer on Emeritus Status who seeks to transfer to Active Status must follow the requirements of Rule 12 (and return to an active fee status with the Lawyer Registration Office) See Rule 12 of the CLE Rules.

Adopted March 15, 2013, eff. July 1, 2013.

[1] An email confirmation will be sent after the lawyer is placed on Emeritus Status.

[2] Address changes must be made in writing by sending notice to the Lawyer Registration Office, 25 Rev. Dr. Martin Luther King Jr. Blvd., Room 205, St. Paul, Minnesota 55155.

RULE ON THE PROVISION OF LEGAL SERVICES FOLLOWING DETERMINATION OF A MAJOR DISASTER

Adopted December 10, 2009

Rule on the Provision of Legal Services Following the Determination of a Major Disaster

Subd. 1. Determination of Existence of Major Disaster. Solely for purposes of this rule, the Supreme Court shall determine when an emergency affecting the justice system, as a result of a natural or other major disaster has occurred in:

(1) This jurisdiction and whether the emergency caused by the major disaster affects the entirety or only apart of this jurisdiction, or

(2) Another jurisdiction but only after such a determination and its geographical scope have been made by the highest court of that jurisdiction. The authority to engage in the temporary practice of law in this jurisdiction pursuant to subdivision 3 shall extend only to lawyers who principally practice in the area of such other jurisdiction determined to have suffered a major disaster causing an emergency affecting the justice system and the provision of legal services.

Subd. 2. Temporary Practice in this Jurisdiction Following Major Disaster. Following the determination of an emergency affecting the justice system in this jurisdiction pursuant to subdivision 1 of this rule, or a determination that persons displaced by a major disaster in another jurisdiction and residing in this jurisdiction are in need of pro bono services and the assistance of lawyers from outside this jurisdiction is required to help provide such assistance, a lawyer authorized to practice law in another United States jurisdiction, and not disbarred, suspended from practice or otherwise restricted from practice in any jurisdiction, may provide legal services in this jurisdiction on a temporary basis. Such legal services must be provided on a pro bono basis without compensation, expectation of compensation or other direct or indirect pecuniary gain to the lawyer. Such legal services shall be assigned and supervised through an established not-for-profit bar association, pro bono program or legal services program or through such organizations specifically designated by the Supreme Court.

Subd. 3. Temporary Practice in this Jurisdiction Following Major Disaster in Another Jurisdiction. Following the determination of a major disaster in another United States jurisdiction, a lawyer who is authorized to practice law and who principally practices in that affected jurisdiction, and who is not disbarred, suspended from practice or otherwise restricted from practice in any jurisdiction, may provide legal services in this jurisdiction on a temporary basis. Those legal services must arise out of and be reasonably related to that lawyer's practice of law in the jurisdiction, or area of such other jurisdiction, where the major disaster occurred.

Subd. 4. Duration of Authority for Temporary Practice. The authority to practice law in this jurisdiction granted by subdivision 1 of this rule shall end when the Supreme Court determines that the conditions caused by the major disaster in this jurisdiction have ended except that a lawyer then representing clients in this jurisdiction pursuant to subdivision 2 is authorized to continue the provision of legal services for such time as is reasonably necessary to complete the representation, but the lawyer shall not thereafter accept new clients. The authority to practice law in this jurisdiction granted by subdivision 3 of this rule shall end 60 days after the Supreme Court declares that the conditions caused by the major disaster in the affected jurisdiction have ended.

Subd. 5. Court Appearances. The authority granted by this rule does not include appearances in court except:

(1) Pursuant to the court's pro hac vice admission rule and, if such authority is granted, any fees for such admission shall be waived; or

(2) If the Supreme Court, in any determination made under subdivision 1, grants blanket permission to appear in all or designated courts of this jurisdiction to lawyers providing legal services pursuant to subdivision 2. If such an authorization is included, any pro hac vice admission fees shall be waived.

Subd. 6. Disciplinary Authority and Registration Requirement. Lawyers providing legal services in this jurisdiction pursuant to subdivisions 1 or 2 are subject to the Supreme Court's disciplinary authority and the Rules of Professional Conduct of this jurisdiction as provided in Rule 8.5 of the Rules of Professional Conduct. Lawyers providing legal services in this jurisdiction under subdivisions 1 or 2 shall, within 30 days from the commencement of the provision of legal services, file a registration statement with the Lawyer Registration Office. The registration statement shall be in a form prescribed by the Supreme Court. Any lawyer who provides legal services pursuant to this rule shall not be considered to be engaged in the unlawful practice of law in this jurisdiction.

Subd. 7. Notification to Clients. Lawyers authorized to practice law in another United States jurisdiction who provide legal services pursuant to this rule shall inform clients in this jurisdiction of the jurisdiction in which they are authorized to practice law, any Limits of that authorization, and that they are not authorized to practice law in this jurisdiction except as permitted by this rule. They shall not state or imply to any person that they are otherwise authorized to practice law in this jurisdiction.

Adopted Dec. 10, 2009, eff. Jan. 1, 2010.

STUDENT PRACTICE RULES

Adopted May 24, 1982

Including Amendments Received Through January 1, 2014

RULE 1. GENERAL STUDENT PRACTICE

RULE 2. CLINICAL STUDENT PRACTICE

RULE 3. STUDENT OBSERVATION OF PROFESSIONAL ACTIVITIES

RULE 1. GENERAL STUDENT PRACTICE

Rule 1.01. Representation

An eligible law student not enrolled in a law school clinical program may, under the supervision of a member of the bar, perform all functions that an attorney may perform in representing and appearing on behalf of any state, local, or other government unit or agency, or any indigent person who is a party to a civil action or who is accused of a crime, or a petty misdemeanor.

Adopted May 24, 1982.

Rule 1.02. Eligible Law Students

An eligible law student is one who:

(1) is duly enrolled at the time of original certification in a school of law approved by the American Bar Association;

(2) has completed at the time of original certification legal studies equivalent to at least two semesters of full-time study;

(3) has been certified by the state, local, or other government unit or agency, or organization or persons representing indigents as being a paid or unpaid intern working for said unit, agency, organization, or persons;

(4) has been certified by the dean or designee of the law school as being of good academic standing; and

(5) has been identified as a student and accepted by the client.

Adopted May 24, 1982. Amended eff. Aug. 6, 2013.

Historical Notes

The order of the Minnesota Supreme Court [C6-02-1906] dated November 20, 2002, provides in part:

"IT IS HEREBY ORDERED that the petition for an exemption from Minn. Student Prac. R. 1.02(1) is granted, and students enrolled at the University of St. Thomas School of Law who otherwise satisfy all conditions of eligibility may practice under the supervision of a member of the bar as provided in Minn. Student Prac. R. 1.01. This exemption expires October 1, 2003, or upon a decision from the American Bar Association on the University of St. Thomas School of Law's application for provisional accreditation whichever occurs sooner."

Rule 1.03. Certification

The state, local, or other government unit or agency or organization or persons representing indigent clients shall submit in writing to the student's law school the student's name and a statement that the student will be properly supervised under the provisions of this practice rule. The student's law school shall then certify the student's academic standing and file this certification with the Board of Law Examiners for approval. Written notification of approval shall be provided to the law school. The certification shall remain in effect for twelve (12) months after the date filed. Law students may be recertified for additional twelve-month periods. Certification shall terminate sooner than twelve (12) months upon the occurrence of the following events:

(1) Certification is withdrawn by the unit, agency, organization, or person by mailing notice to that effect to the law student, the law school, and the Board of

Law Examiners along with the reason(s) for such withdrawal;

(2) Certification is terminated by the Board of Law Examiners by mailing notice to that effect to the law student, the law school, and the unit, agency, organization or person along with the reason(s) for such termination;

(3) Certification shall terminate upon the student being placed on academic probation;

(4) The student does not take the first bar examination following his or her graduation, upon which the certification will terminate on the first day of the exam;

(5) The student takes but fails the bar examination, upon which the certification will terminate upon notice to the dean and the law student of such failure; or

(6) The student takes and passes the bar examination and is admitted to the bar of the court.

Adopted May 24, 1982. Amended eff. May 1, 2013.

Rule 1.04. Supervisory Attorney

The attorney who supervises a student shall:

(1) be a member of the bar of this court;

(2) assume personal professional responsibility for and supervision of the student's work;

(3) assist the student to the extent necessary;

(4) sign all pleadings;

(5) appear with the student in all trials;

(6) appear with the student at all other proceedings unless the attorney deems his or her personal appearance unnecessary to assure proper supervision. This authorization shall be made in writing and shall be available to the judge or other official conducting the proceedings upon request.

Adopted May 24, 1982.

Rule 1.05. Miscellaneous

Nothing contained in this rule shall affect the existing rules of this court or the right of any person who is not admitted to practice law to do anything that he or she might lawfully do prior to the adoption of this rule.

Adopted May 24, 1982. Amended eff. May 1, 2013; Aug. 6, 2013.

RULE 2. CLINICAL STUDENT PRACTICE

Rule 2.01. Representation

An eligible law student may, under the supervision of a member of the bar, perform all functions that an attorney may perform in representing and appearing on behalf of a client.

Adopted May 24, 1982.

Rule 2.02. Eligible Law Students

An eligible law student is one who:

(1) is duly enrolled at the time of original certification in a school of law approved by the American Bar Association;

(2) has completed at the time of original certification legal studies equivalent to at least two semesters of full-time study;

(3) is enrolled at the time of original certification in a law school clinical program;

(4) has been certified by the dean or designee of the law school as being of good academic standing; and

(5) has been identified as a student and accepted by the client.

Adopted May 24, 1982. Amended eff. Aug. 6, 2013.

Rule 2.03. Certification

Certification of a student by the law school shall be filed with the Board of Law Examiners for approval. Written notification of approval shall be provided to the law school. The certification shall remain in effect for twelve (12) months after the date filed. Law students may be recertified for additional 12–month periods. Certification shall terminate sooner than twelve (12) months upon the occurrence of the following events:

(1) Certification is withdrawn by the dean by mailing notice to that effect to the law student and the Board of Law Examiners along with the reason(s) for such withdrawal;

(2) Certification is terminated by the Board of Law Examiners by mailing a notice to that effect to the law student and to the dean along with the reason(s) for such termination;

(3) The student does not take the first bar examination following his or her graduation, upon which the certification will terminate on the first day of the exam;

(4) The student takes but fails in the bar examination, upon which the certification will terminate upon notice to the dean and the law student of such failure; or

(5) The student takes and passes the bar examination and is admitted to the bar of this court.

Adopted May 24, 1982. Amended eff. May 1, 2013.

Rule 2.04. Supervisory Attorney

The attorney who supervises a student shall:

(1) be a member of the bar of this court;

(2) assume personal professional responsibility for and supervision of the student's work;

(3) assist the student to the extent necessary;

(4) sign all pleadings;

(5) appear with the student in all trials;

(6) appear with the student at all other proceedings unless the attorney deems his or her personal appearance unnecessary to assure proper supervision. This authorization shall be made in writing and shall be available to the judge or other official conducting the proceedings upon request.

Adopted May 24, 1982.

Rule 2.05. Miscellaneous

Nothing contained in this rule shall affect the existing rules of this court or the right of any person who is not admitted to practice law to do anything that he or she might lawfully do prior to the adoption of this rule.

Adopted May 24, 1982. Amended eff. May 1, 2013; Aug. 6, 2013.

RULE 3. STUDENT OBSERVATION OF PROFESSIONAL ACTIVITIES

Rule 3.01. Observation of Professional Activities

An eligible law student may, under the supervision of a member of the bar, observe any and all professional activities of a member of the bar, including client communications. Communications between the client and the student shall be privileged under the same rules that govern the attorney-client privilege and work product doctrine, and the presence of the student during communications between the lawyer and client shall not, standing alone, waive these evidentiary privileges.

The law student's observation must be part of an academic program or a course for academic credit.

Adopted April 23, 2009, eff. April 23, 2009.

Rule 3.02. Eligible Law Students

An eligible law student is one who:

(1) is duly enrolled at the time of original certification in a school of law approved by the American Bar Association;

(2) has been certified by the dean or designee of the law school as being of good academic standing;

(3) has signed a statement certifying that the student will maintain the confidentiality that a lawyer is required to maintain under Rule 1.6 of the Minnesota Rules of Professional Conduct; and

(4) has been identified as a student and accepted by the client.

Adopted April 23, 2009, eff. April 23, 2009. Amended eff. Aug. 6, 2013.

Rule 3.03. Certification

Certification of a student by the law school shall be filed with the Board of Law Examiners for approval. Written notification of approval shall be provided to the law school. The certification shall remain in effect for twelve (12) months after the date filed. Law students may be recertified for additional twelve-month periods. Certification shall terminate sooner than twelve (12) months upon the occurrence of the following events:

(1) Certification is withdrawn by the dean by mailing notice to that effect to the law student and the Board of Law Examiners along with the reason(s) for such withdrawal;

(2) Certification is terminated by the Board of Law Examiners by mailing a notice to that effect to the law student and to the dean along with the reason(s) for such termination;

(3) The student does not take the first bar examination following his or her graduation, upon which the certification will terminate on the first day of the exam;

(4) The student takes but fails the bar examination, upon which the certification will terminate upon notice to the dean and the law student of such failure; or

(5) The student takes and passes the bar examination and is admitted to the bar of this court.

Adopted April 23, 2009, eff. April 23, 2009. Amended eff. May 1, 2013.

Rule 3.04. Supervisory Attorney

The attorney who supervises a student under Rule 3 shall:

(1) be a member of the bar of this court;

(2) assume personal professional responsibility for and supervision of the student's conduct;

(3) be present with the student during all interactions with the client; and

(4) report to the law school supervisor for the academic program or course as required by the law school supervisor.

Adopted April 23, 2009, eff. April 23, 2009.

Rule 3.05. Miscellaneous

Nothing contained in this rule shall affect the existing rules of this court or the right of any person who is not admitted to practice law to do anything that he or she might lawfully do prior to the adoption of this rule.

Adopted April 23, 2009, eff. April 23, 2009. Amended eff. May 1, 2013; Aug. 6, 2013.

PLAN FOR THE MINNESOTA STATE BOARD OF LEGAL CERTIFICATION [REPEALED]

Historical Notes

The order of the Minnesota Supreme Court [CX–84–1651] dated March 14, 2002, which adopted the Rules of the Minnesota State Board of Legal Certification, provides in part that the Plan of the Minnesota Supreme Court and the Rules of the Board of Legal Certification are repealed effective March 14, 2002.

INTERNAL RULES FOR THE STATE BOARD OF LEGAL CERTIFICATION [REPEALED]

Historical Notes

The order of the Minnesota Supreme Court [CX–84–1651] dated March 14, 2002, which adopted the Rules of the Minnesota State Board of Legal Certification, provides in part that the Plan of the Minnesota Supreme Court and the Rules of the Board of Legal Certification are repealed effective March 14, 2002.

RULES OF THE MINNESOTA STATE BOARD OF LEGAL CERTIFICATION

Effective March 14, 2002

Including Amendments Received Through January 1, 2014

PREAMBLE

The following rules establish procedures for continued operation of the Minnesota State Board of Legal Certification. As of the effective date of their adoption by the Minnesota Supreme Court, these rules will supersede and replace the original Plan of the Supreme Court (adopted October 10, 1985) and the Rules of the Board of Legal Certification (adopted December 15, 1986).

Adopted March 14, 2002, eff. March 14, 2002.

RULE 100. PURPOSE OF THE BOARD OF LEGAL CERTIFICATION

The purpose of the Minnesota State Board of Legal Certification (Board) is to accredit agencies that certify lawyers as specialists, so that public access to appropriate legal services may be enhanced. In carrying out its purpose, the Board shall provide information about certification of lawyers as specialists for the benefit of the profession and the public.

Adopted March 14, 2002, eff. March 14, 2002.

RULE 101. DEFINITIONS

a. "Applicant agency" means an entity that submits a proposal to become an accredited agency in a field of law.

b. "Applicant lawyer" means a lawyer who seeks certification from an accredited agency.

c. "Board" means the Minnesota State Board of Legal Certification.

d. "Certified lawyer" means a lawyer who has received certification from an accredited agency.

e. "Accredited agency" means an entity that has applied for and has been accredited by the Board to certify lawyers in a field of law.

f. "Rules" means rules promulgated by the Supreme Court governing the Minnesota State Board of Legal Certification.

g. "Field of law" means a field of legal practice that is identified, defined and approved by the Board as appropriate for specialist designation.

Adopted March 14, 2002, eff. March 14, 2002.

RULE 102. COMPOSITION OF THE BOARD

a. The Supreme Court shall appoint twelve (12) members of the Board, of whom nine (9) shall have active licenses to practice law in the state and represent various fields of legal practice. Three (3) attorney members shall be nominated by the Minnesota State Bar Association and three (3) shall be non-attorney public members. The Supreme Court shall designate a lawyer member as chairperson and the Board may elect other officers, including a vice-chair who will serve in the absence of the chairperson.

b. Members shall be appointed for three-year terms. The terms of one (1) public member and one (1) member nominated by the State Bar shall expire each year. Any vacancy on the Board shall be filled by the Supreme Court by appointment for the unexpired term. No member may serve more than two (2) three-year terms with the exception of the sitting chairperson, who may be appointed for a third three-year term or such additional period as the court may order.

c. Members shall serve without compensation, but shall be paid their regular and necessary expenses.

Adopted March 14, 2002, eff. March 14, 2002.

RULE 103. MEETINGS

a. Meetings of the Board shall be held at regular intervals and at times and places set by the chairperson.

b. Meetings are open to the public except when the Board is considering:

(1) personnel matters;

(2) examination materials;

(3) legal advice from its counsel;

(4) any information which is confidential or private under Rule 106b(5).

c. The Board may make determinations by a majority vote of those present at a meeting, with the exception of the following which must be made by a majority of the members of the Board:

(1) recommendations for changes in rules of the Board;

(2) determinations to approve or rescind an agency's accreditation.

d. The Board may meet by conference call or make determinations through mail vote.

Adopted March 14, 2002, eff. March 14, 2002.

RULE 104. CONFLICT OF INTEREST

A Board member who in the past twelve (12) months has served in a decision-making capacity for an agency that is, or seeks to become, a Minnesota accredited agency shall disclose such service to the Board and shall recuse him/herself from any vote relating to the agency's accreditation.

Adopted March 14, 2002, eff. March 14, 2002.

RULE 105. POWERS OF THE BOARD

The Board is authorized:

a. To identify, define and approve a definition or definitions of a field of law, on its own motion, or in response to an application or applications from an applicant agency.

b. To develop standards, application verification procedures, testing procedures, and other criteria for reviewing and evaluating applicant and accredited agencies.

c. To take one of the following actions with regard to an applicant agency or accredited agency:

(1) grant accreditation or conditional accreditation;

(2) deny accreditation;

(3) rescind accreditation.

d. To review and evaluate the programs and examinations of an applicant agency or accredited agency to assure compliance with these rules.

e. To investigate an applicant agency or accredited agency concerning matters contained in the application and, if necessary, to conduct an on-site inspection.

f. To require reports and other information from the applicant agency or accredited agency regarding the certification program.

g. To monitor lawyer representations concerning certification status.

h. To adopt policies and charge fees reasonably related to the certification program and not inconsistent with these rules.

Adopted March 14, 2002, eff. March 14, 2002.

RULE 106. DUTIES OF THE BOARD

a. The chairperson shall convene the Board as necessary, and between meetings shall act on behalf of the Board. The chairperson may appoint subcommittees of the Board.

b. The Board shall:

(1) Hire a Director to administer the Board's programs and to perform duties as assigned by the Board.

(2) Provide information about lawyer certification programs for the benefit of the profession and the public.

(3) Disseminate accurate information regarding lawyers' certification status.

(4) File with the Supreme Court an annual report detailing the work of the Board.

(5) Report to the Lawyers Professional Responsibility Board any lawyers who may violate the provisions of these rules or other rules concerning certification matters.

(6) Maintain appropriate records of accredited agencies and certified lawyers.

(7) Communicate with groups, agencies, and other boards and organizations regarding matters of common interest.

(8) Make rulings on applications, conduct hearings, and take other actions as are necessary to carry out the Board's purpose.

Adopted March 14, 2002, eff. March 14, 2002.

RULE 107. BOARD DISPOSITION OF AGENCY APPLICATIONS

The Board shall take the following action with respect to the agency application:

a. Grant the agency's application for accreditation.

b. Grant conditional accreditation to an applicant agency subject to receipt of evidence showing satisfaction of specific conditions imposed by the Board.

c. Deny the agency's application and issue a written decision stating the reasons for the denial. An application may be denied for any of the following reasons:

(1) The agency fails to meet criteria set forth in these rules.

(2) The application is incomplete, investigation has revealed inaccuracies, or the applicant agency has been uncooperative in the initial review.

(3) The proposed definition of the field of law is rejected by the Board.

(4) The agency's goals and methods of measuring attainment of those goals are not appropriate or not well defined.

(5) The agency's tests and other performance criteria are inadequate.

d. Rescind the agency's previously granted accreditation if the agency is found to have violated these rules.

Adopted March 14, 2002, eff. March 14, 2002.

RULE 108. APPLICATION AFTER DENIAL

An applicant agency denied accreditation may not reapply for twelve (12) months following the Board's disposition.

Adopted March 14, 2002, eff. March 14, 2002.

RULE 109. BOARD HEARINGS

An agency whose application has been denied pursuant to Rule 107c or rescinded pursuant to Rule 107d has the right to a hearing if the agency makes a written request for hearing within twenty (20) days of its receipt of notice of denial. The hearing shall be promptly scheduled before the full Board or a subcommittee thereof appointed by the chairperson. Representatives of the agency may appear personally or through counsel and may present evidence and testimony. The hearing shall be recorded. Following the hearing, the Board shall provide written notice of its decision setting forth reasons for the decision.

Adopted March 14, 2002, eff. March 14, 2002.

RULE 110. BOARD INFORMATION DISCLOSURE

The Board has the following public disclosure obligations:

a. To provide public notice when an accreditation application has been received for a particular field of law.

b. To make available for inspection, at reasonable times, applications for accreditation submitted by applicant agencies.

c. To publish the definitions of each field of law and the address and telephone number of each applicant agency or accredited agency, along with the name of the agency's contact person.

Adopted March 14, 2002, eff. March 14, 2002.

RULE 111. BOARD SPECIFIED FEES

The Board shall periodically set and publish a schedule of reasonable fees for the costs incidental to administering these rules.

Adopted March 14, 2002, eff. March 14, 2002.

RULE 112. THRESHOLD CRITERIA FOR AGENCY AUTHORITY TO CERTIFY

An agency applying to the Board for accreditation in a field of law must complete an agency application form and submit it along with necessary documentation and fees to the Board office. An applicant agency must meet the following criteria:

a. Have among its permanent staff, operating officers, or Board of Directors at least three (3) legal practitioners not from the same law firm or business whose daily work fulfills the substantial involvement requirement in the field of law as defined in Rule 114b, and whose role in the agency includes evaluating the qualifications of specialist lawyers.

b. Provide evidence that the certification program is available to lawyers without discrimination because of a lawyer's geographic location or non-membership in an organization.

c. Provide evidence that the applicant agency is an ongoing entity capable of operating an acceptable certification program for an indefinite period of time.

d. Agree to publicize the certification program in a manner designed to reach lawyers licensed to practice in Minnesota who may be interested in the field of law.

e. Agree to be subject to Minnesota law and rules regulating lawyers.

f. Agree to keep statistical records concerning certified lawyers and to report such numbers to the Board on an annual basis.

g. Agree to provide written notice to each certified specialist stating that if he/she communicates the specialty status, he/she shall do so in a manner consistent with the requirements of Rule 119 of these rules, as well as with the requirements of Rule 7.4 of the Minnesota Rules of Professional Conduct.

h. Provide evidence that the following have been adopted and are in use in the agency:

(1) Procedures that will assure the periodic review and recertification of certified lawyers.

(2) Due process procedures for lawyers denied certification.

(3) Procedures that will assure the periodic evaluation of the certification program.

(4) Procedures that will assure accurate ongoing reporting to the Board concerning the certification program.

Adopted March 14, 2002, eff. March 14, 2002.

RULE 113. AGENCY OBLIGATIONS

An accredited agency must provide the Board with the following:

a. At least 60 days prior to the effective date, a written summary of proposed changes in an accredited agency's standards for certification.

b. An updated lawyer application and such other information as the Board may require.

c. Within 30 days of certifying lawyers, a roster listing the certified lawyers' names, Minnesota license numbers, home and work addresses, and other states where licensed; this document must be verified by the director of the accredited agency, and accompanied by the initial fee.

d. Within 30 days of denying or revoking a lawyer's certification, the name, Minnesota license number, work address, and reason for denial or revocation.

e. By January 20 of each year, an annual statistical and summary report showing the progress of its certification program.

f. By January 20 of each year, or at such time as is mutually agreed, submit payment of annual attorneys' fees as defined in Rule 111.

Adopted March 14, 2002, eff. March 14, 2002.

RULE 114. AGENCY STANDARDS FOR CERTIFYING LAWYERS

Accredited agencies shall certify lawyers for a period not exceeding six (6) years. The following are minimum standards for lawyers certified by an accredited agency:

a. The lawyer is licensed and on active status in Minnesota.

b. The lawyer shows by independent evidence "substantial involvement" in the field of law during the three-year period immediately preceding certification. "Substantial involvement" means at least 25% of the lawyer's practice is spent in the field of law of the certification.

c. The accredited agency verifies at least three (3) written peer recommendations, in addition to references from lawyers or judges unrelated to and not in legal practice with the lawyer.

d. The lawyer successfully completes a written examination of the lawyer's knowledge of the substantive, procedural and related ethical law in the field of law; grading standards for the examination must be made available prior to test administration; model answers must be made available for inspection after test results are determined.

e. The lawyer provides evidence of having completed at least 20 hours every three (3) years of approved CLE activity that is directly related to the certified specialist's field of law, sufficiently rigorous and otherwise appropriate for a certified specialist.

f. The lawyer provides evidence of being current with CLE credit requirements for every state of active licensure and having been current throughout the period of application or recertification.

g. The lawyer signs a release to share information with the Board from the files of the accredited agency.

Adopted March 14, 2002, eff. March 14, 2002.

RULE 115. AGENCY STANDARDS FOR AUTOMATIC/DISCRETIONARY DENIAL OR REVOCATION OF LAWYER CERTIFICATION.

a. **Automatic denial or revocation.** An agency will automatically deny or revoke a lawyer's certification upon the occurrence of any of the following:

(1) A finding by the agency that the lawyer failed to complete 20 CLE credits in the field of law within his/her three-year reporting period or the equivalent CLE reporting period.

(2) Suspension or disbarment of the lawyer from the practice of law in any jurisdiction in which the lawyer is licensed.

(3) Suspension of the lawyer for nonpayment of license fees or for failing to maintain mandatory CLE credits in any jurisdiction in which the lawyer is licensed.

(4) Failure of the lawyer to complete satisfactorily the recertification process or failure to pay the required certification fees.

(5) Written notice from the lawyer that he/she seeks decertification.

b. **Discretionary denial or revocation of certification.** An agency may deny or revoke a lawyer's certification if:

(1) The lawyer fails to cooperate with the certifying agency, or submits false or misleading information during the certification or recertification process.

(2) The lawyer's record contains evidence of personal or professional misconduct which is inconsistent with the standards of conduct adopted by the accredited agency.

(3) The lawyer falsely or improperly announces the field of law or certification.

Adopted March 14, 2002, eff. March 14, 2002.

RULE 116. RENEWAL OF AGENCY ACCREDITATION

Agencies are required to apply to the Board for accreditation renewal at least once every three (3) years.

a. The following must be submitted to the Board for renewal of accreditation:

(1) A completed application form seeking renewal of accreditation and a fee in an amount specified by Rule 111.

(2) A written critique of the agency's own certification program, which includes written evaluations from certified lawyers and a written analysis of achievement of program goals.

(3) Copies of examinations and model answers for the most recent examinations administered since accreditation or last renewal of accreditation.

(4) Statistical information concerning the progress of the program since the original accreditation or last renewal of accreditation.

b. The Board may require the agency to provide the following as part of the accreditation renewal process:

(1) Opportunity for Board representatives to conduct an on-site inspection of the agency.

(2) An audit of agency records by Board representatives, including a review of certified lawyers' references.

(3) Opportunity for a personal meeting with representatives of the accredited agency.

(4) Such other information as is needed to evaluate the certification program.

Adopted March 14, 2002, eff. March 14, 2002.

RULE 117. AGENCY ANNOUNCEMENT OF ACCREDITATION

An accredited agency may publish the following statement with respect to its certification status: "This agency is accredited by the Minnesota State Board of Legal Certification to certify lawyers as specialists in the field of [name of field of law]." If conditional accreditation has been granted publication of that fact must be made.

Adopted March 14, 2002, eff. March 14, 2002.

RULE 118. AGENCY ANNOUNCEMENT OF REVOCATION OF ACCREDITATION

In the event that the Board revokes the accreditation of an agency, the agency shall contact each certified lawyer and shall advise him/her to cease all advertising, announcements and publications referencing Board authorization.

Adopted March 14, 2002, eff. March 14, 2002.

RULE 119. LAWYER ANNOUNCEMENT OF CERTIFICATION

The certified lawyer may announce that he/she is a certified specialist in a field of law and that the agency granting the certification is an agency accredited by the Minnesota State Board of Legal Certification to certify lawyers as specialists in a designated field of law. The lawyer shall not represent, either expressly or implicitly, that the specialist status is conferred by the Minnesota Supreme Court.

Adopted March 14, 2002, eff. March 14, 2002.

RULE 120. IMMUNITY

The Board and its members, employees, and agents are immune from civil liability for any acts conducted in the course of their official duties.

Adopted March 14, 2002, eff. March 14, 2002.

RULES OF THE MINNESOTA CLIENT SECURITY BOARD

Effective July 1, 1987

Including Amendments Received Through January 1, 2014

I. RULES GOVERNING THE CLIENT SECURITY BOARD

Rule 1.01. Membership of the Board

The Supreme Court shall appoint seven members to the Client Security Board. Five shall be lawyers actively practicing in the state, three of whom shall be nominees of the Minnesota State Bar Association, and two shall be public members. The Board shall elect Chair from its members.

Adopted April 7, 1987, eff. July 1, 1987. Amended June 27, 1995, eff. July 1, 1995.

Rule 1.02. Terms of Office

Two members of the Board shall be appointed for one year, two members for two years and three members for three years, and thereafter appointments shall be for three-year terms. The terms of public members shall be staggered. Any vacancy on the Board shall be filled by appointment of the Supreme Court for the unexpired term. No member may serve more than two consecutive three-year terms, in addition to any additional shorter term for which the person was originally appointed.

Adopted April 7, 1987, eff. July 1, 1987. Amended June 27, 1995, eff. July 1, 1995.

Rule 1.03. Reimbursement

Members shall serve without compensation, but shall be paid their regular and necessary expenses.

Adopted April 7, 1987, eff. July 1, 1987. Amended June 27, 1995, eff. July 1, 1995.

Rule 1.04. Meetings

The Board shall meet at least annually, and at other times as scheduled by the Chair. A quorum shall consist of four members.

Adopted April 7, 1987, eff. July 1, 1987. Amended June 27, 1995, eff. July 1, 1995.

Rule 1.05. Immunity

The Board and its staff are absolutely immune from civil liability for all acts in the course of their official duties.

Adopted April 7, 1987, eff. July 1, 1987. Amended June 27, 1995, eff. July 1, 1995.

Rule 1.06. Duties of the Board

The Board is authorized:

a. To administer and operate the Minnesota Client Security Fund, pursuant to statutes, court rules and internal procedures;

b. To make final determinations on disbursement from the Fund;

c. To recommend to the Supreme Court limits for the amount payable per claim against the Fund, and for total reimbursement for claims arising from one lawyer's misconduct;

d. To undertake investigation of claims, coordinating with the Office of Lawyers Professional Responsibility;

e. To recommend to the Supreme Court means available to cover extraordinary losses in excess of the assets of the Fund;

f. To annually establish an administrative budget which may be paid from the Fund;

g. To enforce subrogation and lien rights of the Fund;

h. To sue in the name of the Fund for restitution of payments made pursuant to claims;

i. To cooperate in educational activities for theft prevention and risk management, and for remedial services for problem lawyers;

j. To certify the financial condition of the Fund;

k. To employ and compensate consultants, legal counsel and employees;

l. To adopt internal rules of procedure not inconsistent with these rules, and make recommendations to the Supreme Court on rule changes.

Adopted April 7, 1987, eff. July 1, 1987. Amended June 27, 1995, eff. July 1, 1995.

Rule 1.07. Conflict of Interest

a. A member of the Board who has or had a lawyer-client relationship or financial relationship with a claimant or the lawyer subject to the claim shall not participate in the investigation or adjudication of the matter.

b. A member of the Board who is a member or of counsel in the same law firm or company as the lawyer subject to the claim shall not participate in the matter.

Adopted April 7, 1987, eff. July 1, 1987. Amended June 27, 1995, eff. July 1, 1995.

Rule 1.08. Duties of the Director

The Board may recommend to the Supreme Court a Director, who shall serve at the pleasure of the Court, to perform duties assigned to the Board, including but not limited to:

a. Screening claims, coordinating investigations with the Lawyers Professional Responsibility Board, and presenting claims at Board hearings;

b. Coordinating enforcement of liens, restitution and subrogation rights of the Fund;

c. Maintaining records of the Board suitable for audit of the Fund;

d. Keeping current on legal and procedural developments of the client security funds in other states;

e. Performing other duties as assigned by the Board.

Adopted April 7, 1987, eff. July 1, 1987. Amended June 27, 1995, eff. July 1, 1995.

Rule 1.09. Confidentiality

Claims, proceedings and reports involving claims for reimbursement are confidential until the Board authorizes reimbursement to the claimant, except as provided below.

a. After payment of the reimbursement, the Board shall publicize the nature of the claim, the amount of reimbursement and the name of the lawyer. The name and the address of the claimant shall not be publicized by the Board unless specific permission has been granted by the claimant.

b. This Rule shall not be construed to deny access to relevant information by professional disciplinary agencies or other law enforcement authorities as the Board shall authorize the release of statistical information which does not disclose the identity of the lawyer or the parties.

Adopted April 7, 1987, eff. July 1, 1987. Amended June 27, eff. July 1, 1995.

Rule 1.10. Annual Report

At least once a year and at such other times as the Supreme Court may order, the Board shall file with the Court a written report reviewing in detail the administration of the Fund, its operation, its assets and liabilities.

Adopted April 7, 1987, eff. July 1, 1987. Amended June 27, 1995, eff. July 1, 1995.

II. RULES GOVERNING THE FUND

Rule 2.01. Establishment of the Fund

There is created a Minnesota Client Security Fund to aid those persons directly injured by the dishonest conduct of any lawyer during an attorney-client or fiduciary relationship.

Adopted April 7, 1987, eff. July 1, 1987. Amended June 27, 1995, eff. July 1, 1995.

Rule 2.02. Financing

The Fund shall be financed from:

a. Lawyer restitution and subrogation for claims paid;

b. Gifts and contributions;

c. Upon order of the Supreme Court, assessments of licensed lawyers.

Adopted April 7, 1987, eff. July 1, 1987. Amended June 27, 1995, eff. July 1, 1995.

Historical Notes

The order of the Minnesota Supreme Court dated April 7, 1987, which adopted the Rules of the Minnesota Client Security Board and amended Rule 2 of the Rules of the Supreme Court for Registration of Attorneys, also provided:

"IT IS FURTHER ORDERED that a Client Security Fund shall be established and financed in part by an assessment of licensed lawyers pursuant to Rule 2.02(c) of the Rules of the Minnesota Client Security Board in the following manner:

a. A lawyer admitted to practice law in this state for more than three years and a member of the judiciary who is required to be admitted to practice as a prerequisite to holding office shall pay $100 for the fiscal year of July 1, 1987–June 30, 1988;

b. A lawyer or judge whose permanent residence is outside the State of Minnesota and who does not practice law within this state, a lawyer who has been admitted to practice for three years or less and a lawyer on duty in the armed forces of the United States shall pay $50 for the fiscal year of July 1, 1987–June 30, 1988, and $50 for the fiscal year the lawyer becomes subject to the first paragraph of Rule 2, Rules of the Supreme Court for Registration of Attorneys;

c. A lawyer or judge who is retired from any gainful employment or permanently disabled, and who files annually with the clerk of the appellate courts an affidavit that he or she is so retired or disabled and not engaged in the practice of law shall be exempt from the assessment.

d. A lawyer or judge who is currently retired or disabled and who is not otherwise engaged in the active practice of law or who is currently suspended from the practice of law shall pay $100 in the fiscal year in which he or she resumes active status.

Nothing in this order shall preclude this Court from imposing further assessments as may become necessary;".

Rule 2.03. Ordering, Reinstatement and Cancellation of Assessments

The Supreme Court may order, reinstate or cancel the collection of assessments after review of the financial condition of the Fund certified by the Client Security Board in its annual report.

Adopted April 7, 1987, eff. July 1, 1987. Amended June 27, 1995, eff. July 1, 1995.

Rule 2.04. Failure to Pay Assessment

Upon failure to pay the assessment when due, the lawyer's right to practice law in the state shall be automatically suspended.

Adopted April 7, 1987, eff. July 1, 1987. Amended June 27, 1995, eff. July 1, 1995.

Rule 2.05. Disbursements from the Fund

a. Upon written authorization of the Board, claims may be paid from the Fund.

b. The Board shall annually prepare an administrative budget to be approved by the Supreme Court, from which the Board may pay necessary expenses.

c. The Fund shall be invested as provided by law.

Adopted April 7, 1987, eff. July 1, 1987. Amended June 27, 1995, eff. July 1, 1995.

III. RULES GOVERNING THE CLAIM PROCESS

Rule 3.01. Claims Payment Discretionary

Reimbursements of losses by the Board are discretionary, and not a matter of right. No person shall have a right in the Fund as a third party beneficiary or otherwise either before or after allowance of a claim.

Adopted April 7, 1987, eff. July 1, 1987. Amended June 27, 1995, eff. July 1, 1995.

Rule 3.02. Filing Claims

The Board shall consider a claim filed on forms provided by the Board if:

a. The claimant experienced a loss of money or property, excluding loss of profit, consequential damages, interest, and costs of recovery; and

b. The loss of the claimant arose out of and during the course of a lawyer-client relationship of a matter in this state, or a fiduciary relationship between the lawyer and the claimant which arose out of a lawyer-client relationship in this state; and

c. The loss was caused by the dishonest conduct of the lawyer and the claim was not based on negligence; and

d. There is no reasonably available collateral source for reimbursement to the claimant, such as insurance, surety, bond, or some other fund; and

e. Reasonable efforts have been made by the claimant to exhaust administrative and civil remedies; and

f. The lawyer was licensed to practice law in this state at the time of the misconduct or was licensed within three years prior to the misconduct; and

g. Less than three years have elapsed between the filing of the claim and the date the claimant knew or should have known of the dishonest conduct; and

h. The dishonest conduct occurred on or after January 1, 1964.

i. As used in these Rules, "dishonest conduct" means wrongful acts committed by a lawyer in the nature of theft or embezzlement of money or the wrongful taking or conversion of money, property or other things of value, including but not limited to:

(1) Refusal or failure to refund an advance fee when the lawyer performed no work whatever, or an insignificant portion of the services that he or she agreed to perform. All other instances of a lawyer failing to return an unearned fee or the disputed portion of a fee are outside the scope of the Fund.

(2) Obtaining money or property from a client representing that it was to be used for investment purposes when no such investment was made. The failure of an investment to perform as represented to, or anticipated by, the applicant is outside the scope of the Fund.

j. For purposes of these Rules, including but not limited to those acts set out in Rule 3.02(i), all payments made by the lawyer to the client following the dishonest conduct, however denominated by the lawyer, shall be treated as restitution of principal.

Adopted April 7, 1987, eff. July 1, 1987. Amended June 27, 1995, eff. July 1, 1995.

Rule 3.03. Privileged Complaints

A claim filed pursuant to these Rules is absolutely privileged and may not serve as a basis for liability in any civil lawsuit brought against the claimant.

Adopted April 7, 1987, eff. July 1, 1987. Amended June 27, 1995, eff. July 1, 1995.

Rule 3.04. Screening Claims

The Chair shall designate a Board member or the Director to screen a claim and to advise the lawyer named in the claim that the lawyer has 20 days to respond to the Board in writing. The lawyer shall receive a copy of the claim, by first class mail sent to the lawyer's last known address.

Adopted April 7, 1987, eff. July 1, 1987. Amended June 27, 1995, eff. July 1, 1995.

Rule 3.05. Claim Investigation

If a claim is sufficient, the Director shall promptly request the Office of Lawyers Professional Responsibility to furnish a report on any investigation matter.

Adopted April 7, 1987, eff. July 1, 1987. Amended June 27, 1995, eff. July 1, 1995.

Rule 3.06. Rights of Lawyer Subject to Claim

A lawyer subject to a claim shall be entitled to receive a copy of the claim, to respond to the claim in writing to the Board, and to request an evidentiary hearing as provided by Rules 3.12.

Adopted April 7, 1987, eff. July 1, 1987. Amended June 27, 1995, eff. July 1, 1995.

Rule 3.07. Lawyer Cooperation

It shall be the duty of a lawyer subject to a claim to cooperate and comply with the reasonable requests of the Board and the Board's investigator by furnishing papers, documents or objects, providing a full written explanation, and appearing at conferences and hearings. The lawyer's failure to respond or cooperate may be reported to the Office of Lawyers Professional Responsibility for possible discipline under this rule.

Adopted April 7, 1987, eff. July 1, 1987. Amended June 27, 1995, eff. July 1, 1995.

Rule 3.08. Subpoena

With the approval of the Board Chair, the Director may subpoena and take testimony of any person believed to possess information concerning a claim.

Adopted April 7, 1987, eff. July 1, 1987. Amended June 27, 1995, eff. July 1, 1995.

Rule 3.09. Jurisdiction

The district court of Ramsey County shall have jurisdiction over issuance of subpoenas and over motions arising from the investigation of a claim.

Adopted April 7, 1987, eff. July 1, 1987. Amended June 27, 1995, eff. July 1, 1995.

Rule 3.10. Action After Investigation

No later than 120 days from the date of the notification to the Office of Lawyers Professional Responsibility, whether or not the Director has received a report from the Lawyers Professional Responsibility Board, the Chair shall determine whether additional investigation should be conducted, a hearing should be held, or a determination may be immediately rendered.

Adopted April 7, 1987, eff. July 1, 1987. Amended June 27, 1995, eff. July 1, 1995.

Rule 3.11. Panels

The Chair may divide the Board into panels, each consisting of not less than three Board members and at least one of whom is a nonlawyer, and shall designate a Chair for each panel. A panel may be assigned to consider a matter and make a recommendation to the entire Board, or may conduct a hearing under Rule 3.12 in lieu of a hearing before the entire Board.

Adopted April 7, 1987, eff. July 1, 1987. Amended June 27, 1995, eff. July 1, 1995.

Rule 3.12. Request for Hearing

If the claimant or the lawyer subject to the claim requests an evidentiary hearing, the Chair may order such a hearing, defer the matter for further investigation or until any proceedings of the Lawyers Professional Responsibility Board have been completed, or deny the request.

Adopted April 7, 1987, eff. July 1, 1987. Amended June 27, 1995, eff. July 1, 1995.

Rule 3.13. Hearing

If an evidentiary hearing under Rule 3.12 is ordered, both the claimant and the lawyer and their representatives may appear. The hearing shall be recorded and preserved for five years.

Adopted April 7, 1987, eff. July 1, 1987. Amended June 27, 1995, eff. July 1, 1995.

Rule 3.14. Determination

a. Payment of a claim from the Fund shall be made only on affirmative vote of four members.

b. In determining the amount of any payment, the Board may consider:

(1) Monies available and likely to become available to the Fund for payment of claims;

(2) Size and number of claims presented and likely to be presented in the future;

(3) The amount of a claimant's loss compared with losses sustained by others;

(4) The comparative hardship suffered by a claimant because of a loss;

(5) The total amount of losses caused by the dishonest conduct of any one lawyer;

(6) The culpability or negligence of the claimant contributing to the loss;

(7) The extent to which there is a collateral source for reimbursement to the claimant;

(8) The effort made by the claimant to exhaust administrative and civil remedies;

(9) Other factors as appear to be just and proper.

c. The maximum amount that may be paid to any claimant for a single claim is $150,000. In exceptional circumstances, the Board may allow a greater or lesser amount based on the factors set forth in subdivision (b) of this rule.

d. The Board may, in its discretion, award interest on any award at the rate of interest payable under Minnesota § 549.049 from the date of filing the claim. In determining the amount of interest, if any, the Board may consider:

(1) The length of time between filing the claim and its disposition;

(2) The existence of third-party litigation; and

(3) Other factors outside the control of the Board.

Adopted April 7, 1987, eff. July 1, 1987. Amended Dec. 3, 1993; June 27, 1995, eff. July 1, 1995; Sept. 14, 2001.

Historical Notes

The order of the Minnesota Supreme Court dated December 3, 1993, amending Rule 3.14, provides in part that this amendment is retroactively effective for all claims filed on or after February 1, 1993.

The order of the Minnesota Supreme Court dated September 14, 2001, amending Rule 3.14, provides in part that this amendment shall be applicable prospectively and to all unresolved claims filed with the Client Security Board as of September 14, 2001.

Rule 3.15. Denial

If the Board determines that the criteria of Rule 3.02 have not been met, the Board may deny the claim. The Board may authorize payment of that portion of a claim proved, although the entire amount of a claim is undetermined. The Board may defer payment of a claim in order to await completion of investigations of related claims, or for payment in subsequent fiscal years. The claimant and the lawyer shall be notified in writing of the Board's determination.

Adopted April 7, 1987, eff. July 1, 1987. Amended June 27, 1995, eff. July 1, 1995.

Rule 3.16. Reconsideration

If a claim has been reduced or denied by the Board, a claimant may request reconsideration of the determination within 30 days by submitting a written request to the Board. A claimant may not seek reconsideration if the full claim is allowed but a lesser amount has been authorized for payment under Rule 3.14(b) or (c), or on the basis that the Board did not award interest under Rule 3.14(d).

Adopted April 7, 1987, eff. July 1, 1987. Amended June 27, 1995, eff. July 1, 1995.

Rule 3.17. Subrogation

A claim paid pursuant to these Rules shall be repaid to the Fund by the lawyer. The Board shall obtain a subrogation agreement from the claimant. The Board may bring an action against the lawyer, the lawyer's assets, the lawyer's estate, the lawyer's law firm or partner(s) or any other person(s) or entities against which subrogation rights may be enforced, or may file liens against the property of the lawyer in the name of the Fund, in an amount equal to the sum paid the claimant plus the Board's attorney fees and costs. The claimant shall be notified of any action and may join in the action to press a claim for the loss in excess of the amount paid by the Fund, but the Fund shall have first priority to any recovery in the suit.

Adopted April 7, 1987, eff. July 1, 1987. Amended June 27, 1995, eff. July 1, 1995.

Rule 3.18. Notification of Claim Paid

a. The Board shall advise the Office of Lawyers Professional Responsibility of any claim paid, the amount paid, and the name of the lawyer.

b. Upon request of the lawyer, the Board may advise a lawyer admission or discipline authority of another jurisdiction the status of any file on the lawyer.

Adopted April 7, 1987, eff. July 1, 1987. Amended June 27, 1995, eff. July 1, 1995.

Rule 3.19. [Deleted June 27, 1995, eff. July 1, 1995]

IV. RULE GOVERNING EDUCATION

Rule 4.01. Education

The Board or the Director shall conduct research, analyze statistics, and categorize claims to determine whether there are methods and programs that would minimize lawyer misconduct resulting in claims against the Fund. The Board shall make recommendations to the Court of any such programs.

Adopted April 7, 1987, eff. July 1, 1987. Amended June 27, 1995, eff. July 1, 1995.

CODE OF PROFESSIONAL RESPONSIBILITY FOR INTERPRETERS IN THE MINNESOTA STATE COURT SYSTEM

Adopted Effective January 1, 1996

Including Amendments Received Through January 1, 2014

PREAMBLE

Many persons who come before the courts are partially or completely excluded from full participation in the proceedings due to limited English proficiency, or a speech or hearing impairment. It is essential that the resulting communication barrier be removed, as far as possible, so that these persons are placed in the same position as similarly situated persons for whom there is no such barrier. As officers of the court, interpreters help assure that such persons may enjoy equal access to justice and that court proceedings and court support services function efficiently and effectively. Interpreters are highly skilled professionals who fulfill an essential role in the administration of justice.

Adopted Sept. 18, 1995, eff. Jan. 1, 1996.

APPLICABILITY

This code shall guide and be binding upon all persons, agencies and organizations who administer, supervise, use, or deliver interpreting services within the Minnesota state court system.

Adopted Sept. 18, 1995, eff. Jan. 1, 1996.

Commentary

The use of the term "shall", is reserved for the black letter principles. Statements in the commentary use the term "should" to describe behavior that illustrates or elaborates upon the principles. The commentaries are intended to convey what the drafters of this code believe to be probable and expected behaviors. Wherever a court policy or routine practice appears to conflict with the commentary in this code, it is recommended that the reasons for the policy or practice as it applies to court interpreters be reviewed for possible modification.

Canon 1
Accuracy and Completeness

Interpreters shall render a complete and accurate interpretation or sight translation, without altering, omitting, or adding anything to the meaning of what is stated or written, and without explanation.

Adopted Sept. 18, 1995, eff. Jan. 1, 1996.

Commentary

The interpreter has a twofold duty:

1) to ensure that the proceedings reflect in English precisely what was said by a non-English speaking person, and

2) to place the non-English speaking person on an equal footing with those who understand English.

This creates an obligation to conserve every element of information contained in a source language communication when it is rendered in the target language.

Therefore interpreters are obligated to apply their best skills and judgment to faithfully preserve the meaning of what is said in court, including the style or register of speech. Verbatim, "word for word" or literal oral interpretations are not appropriate when they distort the meaning of what was said in the source language, but every spoken statement, even if it appears non-responsive, obscene, rambling, or incoherent should be interpreted. This includes apparent misstatements.

Interpreters should never interject any statement or elaboration of their own. If the need arises to explain an interpreting problem (e.g. a term or phrase with no direct equivalent in the target language or a misunderstanding that only the interpreter can clarify), the interpreter should ask the court's permission to provide an explanation. Spoken language interpreters should convey the emotional emphasis of the speaker without reenacting or mimicking the speaker's emotions, or dramatic gestures. Sign language interpreters, however, must employ all of the visual cues that the language they are interpreting for requires—including facial expressions and body language, in addition to hand gestures. Judges, therefore, should ensure that court participants do not confuse these essential elements of the interpreted language with inappropriate interpreter conduct. Any challenge to the interpreter's conduct should be directed to the judge.

The obligation to preserve accuracy includes the interpreter's duty to correct any errors of interpretation discovered by the interpreter during the proceeding. Interpreters should demonstrate their professionalism by objectively analyzing any challenge to their performance.

The ethical responsibility to accurately and completely interpret includes the responsibility of being properly prepared for interpreting assignments. Interpreters are encouraged to obtain documents and other information necessary to familiarize themselves with the nature and purpose of a proceeding. Prior preparation is especially required when testimony or documents include highly specialized terminology and subject matter.

Canon 2
Representation of Qualifications

Interpreters shall accurately and completely represent their certifications, training, and pertinent experience.

Adopted Sept. 18, 1995, eff. Jan. 1, 1996.

Commentary

Acceptance of a case by an interpreter conveys linguistic competency in legal settings. Withdrawing or being asked to withdraw from a case after it begins causes a disruption of court proceedings and is wasteful of scarce public resources. It is therefore essential that interpreters present a complete and truthful account of their training, certification and experience prior to appointment so the officers of the court can fairly evaluate their qualifications for delivering interpreting services.

Canon 3
Impartiality and Avoidance of Conflict of Interest

Interpreters shall be impartial and unbiased and shall refrain from conduct that may give an appearance of bias. Interpreters shall disclose any real or perceived conflict of interest.

Adopted Sept. 18, 1995, eff. Jan. 1, 1996.

Commentary

The interpreter serves as an officer of the court and the interpreter's duty in a court proceeding is to serve the court and the public to which the court is a servant. This is true regardless of whether the interpreter is publicly retained at government expense or retained privately at the expense of one of the parties.

The interpreter of record should avoid any conduct or behavior that presents the appearance of favoritism toward any of the parties. Interpreters should maintain professional relationships with their clients, and should not take an active part in any of the proceedings. The interpreter should discourage a non-English speaking party's personal dependence.

During the course of the proceedings, interpreters of record should not converse with parties, witnesses, jurors, attorneys, or with friends or relatives of any party, except in the discharge of their official functions. Official functions may include an informal preappearance assessment to include the following:

1. culturally appropriate introductions;

2. a determination of variety, mode, or level of communication;

3. a determination of potential conflicts of interest; and

4. a description of the interpreter's role and function.

The interpreter should strive for professional detachment. Verbal and nonverbal displays of personal attitudes, prejudices, emotions, or opinions should be avoided at all times.

Any condition that interferes with the objectivity of an interpreter constitutes a conflict of interest and must be disclosed to the judge. The interpreter should only divulge necessary information when disclosing the conflict of interest. The following are circumstances that create potential conflicts of interest that must be disclosed:

1. the interpreter is a friend, associate, or relative of a party or counsel for a party involved in the proceedings;

2. the interpreter or the interpreter's friend, associate, or relative has a financial interest in the subject matter in controversy, a financial interest in a party to the proceeding, or any other interest that would be affected by the outcome of the case;

3. the interpreter has served in an investigative capacity for any party involved in the case at issue;

4. the interpreter has previously been retained by a law enforcement agency to assist in the preparation of the criminal case at issue;

5. the interpreter has been involved in the choice of counsel or law firm for that case at issue;

6. the interpreter is an attorney in the case at issue;

7. the interpreter has previously been retained for private employment by one of the parties to interpret in the case at issue; or

8. for any other reason, the interpreter's independence of judgment would be compromised in the course of providing services.

The existence of any one of the above-mentioned circumstances does not alone disqualify an interpreter from providing services as long as the interpreter is able to render services objectively. An interpreter may serve if the judge and all parties consent. If an actual or apparent conflict of interest exists the interpreter may, without explanation to any of the parties or the judge, decline to provide services.

Should an interpreter become aware that a non-English speaking participant views the interpreter as having a bias or being biased, the interpreter should disclose that knowledge to the judge.

Canon 4
Professional Demeanor

Interpreters shall conduct themselves in a manner consistent with the dignity of the court.

Adopted Sept. 18, 1995, eff. Jan. 1, 1996.

Commentary

Interpreters should know and observe the established protocol, rules, and procedures for delivering interpreting services. When speaking in English, interpreters should speak at a rate and volume that enables them to be heard and understood throughout the courtroom. If an interpreter is not actively interpreting, the interpreter should not engage in any distracting activity in the courtroom such as reading newspapers or magazines or engaging in conduct that may call inappropriate attention to the interpreter. Interpreters should dress in a manner that is consistent with the dignity of the proceedings of the court.

Interpreters should avoid obstructing the view of any of the individuals involved in the proceedings, but should be appropriately positioned to facilitate communication. Interpreters who use sign language or other visual modes of communication must, however, be positioned so that signs, facial expressions, and whole body movements, are visible to the person for whom they are interpreting.

Interpreters are encouraged to avoid personal or professional conduct which could discredit the court.

Canon 5
Confidentiality

Interpreters shall protect the confidentiality of all privileged and other confidential information.

Adopted Sept. 18, 1995, eff. Jan. 1, 1996.

Commentary

Interpreters must protect and uphold the confidentiality of all privileged information obtained during the course of their duties. It is especially important that the interpreter understand and uphold the attorney-client privilege that requires confidentiality with respect to any communication between attorney and client. This rule also applies to other types of privileged communications.

Interpreters must also refrain from repeating or disclosing information obtained by them in the course of their employment that may be relevant to the legal proceeding.

In the event that an interpreter becomes aware of information that indicates probable imminent harm to someone or relates to a crime being committed during the course of the proceedings, the interpreter should immediately disclose the information to the presiding judge. If the judge is not available, the interpreter should disclose the information to an appropriate authority in the judiciary.

Canon 6
Restriction of Public Comment

Interpreters shall not publicly discuss, report, or offer an opinion concerning a matter in which they are or have been engaged, even when that information is not privileged or required by law to be confidential, except to facilitate training and education.

Adopted Sept. 18, 1995, eff. Jan. 1, 1996.

Commentary

Generally, interpreters should not discuss outside of the interpreter's official duties, interpreter assignments, persons involved or the facts of the case. However, interpreters may share information for training and educational purposes. Interpreters should only share as much information as is required to accomplish their purpose. An interpreter must not reveal privileged or confidential information.

Canon 7
Scope of Practice

Interpreters shall limit themselves to interpreting or translating and shall not give legal advice, express personal opinions to individuals for whom they are interpreting, or engage in any other activities which may be construed to constitute a service other than interpreting or translating while serving as an interpreter.

Adopted Sept. 18, 1995, eff. Jan. 1, 1996.

Commentary

Since interpreters are responsible only for enabling others to communicate, they should limit themselves to the activity of interpreting or translating only, including official functions as described in the commentary to Canon 3. Interpreters, however, may be required to initiate communications during a proceeding when they find it necessary to seek direction from the court in performing their duties. Examples of such circumstances include seeking direction from the court when unable to understand or express a word or thought, requesting speakers to moderate their rate of communication or repeat or rephrase something, correcting their own interpreting errors, or notifying the court of reservations about their ability to satisfy an assignment competently. In such instances they should make it clear that they are speaking for themselves.

An interpreter may convey legal advice from an attorney to a person only while that attorney is giving it. An interpreter should not explain the purpose or contents of forms, services, or otherwise act as counselors or advisors unless they are interpreting for someone who is acting in that official capacity. The interpreter may translate language on a form for a person who is filling out the form, but should not explain the form or its purpose for such a person.

While engaged in the function of interpreting, interpreters should not personally perform official acts that are the official responsibility of other court officials including, but not limited to, court clerks, pretrial release investigators or interviewers, or probation counselors.

Canon 8
Assessing and Reporting Impediments to Performance

Interpreters shall assess at all times their ability to deliver their services. When interpreters have any reservation about their ability to satisfy an assignment competently, they shall immediately convey that reservation to the appropriate judicial authority.

Adopted Sept. 18, 1995, eff. Jan. 1, 1996.

Commentary

If the communication mode or language variety of the non-English-speaking person cannot be readily interpreted, the interpreter should notify the appropriate judicial authority, which includes a supervisory interpreter, a judge, or another official with jurisdiction over interpreter matters.

Interpreters should notify the appropriate judicial authority of any environmental or physical limitation that impedes or hinders their ability to deliver interpreting services adequately e.g., the court room is not quiet enough for the interpreter to hear or be heard by the non-English speaker, more than one person at a time is speaking, or principals or witnesses of the court are speaking at a rate of speed that is too rapid for the interpreter to adequately interpret. Sign language interpreters must ensure that they can both see and convey the full range of visual language elements that are necessary for communication, including facial expressions and body movement, as well as hand gestures.

Interpreters should notify the judge of the need to take periodic breaks in order to maintain mental and physical alertness and prevent interpreter fatigue. Interpreters should recommend and encourage the use of team interpreting whenever necessary.

Interpreters are encouraged to make inquiries as to the nature of a case whenever possible before accepting an assignment. This enables interpreters to match more closely their professional qualifications, skills, and experience to potential assignments and more accurately assess their ability to satisfy competently those assignments.

Even competent and experienced interpreters may encounter situations where routine proceedings suddenly involve technical or specialized terminology unfamiliar to the interpreter, e.g., the unscheduled testimony of an expert witness. When such situations occur, interpreters should request a brief recess in order to familiarize themselves with the subject matter. If familiarity with the terminology requires extensive time or more intensive research, interpreters should inform the judge.

Interpreters should refrain from accepting a case if they feel the language and subject matter of that case is likely to exceed their skills or capacities. Interpreters should notify the judge if they feel unable to perform competently, due to lack of familiarity with terminology, preparation, or difficulty in understanding a witness or defendant.

Canon 9
Duty to Report Ethical Violations

Interpreters shall report to the proper judicial authority any effort to impede their compliance with any law, any provision of this code, or any other official policy governing court interpreting and translating.

Adopted Sept. 18, 1995, eff. Jan. 1, 1996.

Commentary

Because the users of interpreting services frequently misunderstand the proper role of the interpreter, they may ask or expect the interpreter to perform duties or engage in activities that run counter to the provisions of this code or other laws, rules, regulations, or policies governing court interpreters. It is incumbent upon the interpreter to explain their professional obligations to the user. If, having been apprised of these obligations, the person persists in demanding that the interpreter violate them, the interpreter should turn to a supervisory interpreter, a judge, or another official with jurisdiction over interpreter matters to resolve the situation.

Canon 10
Professional Development

Interpreters shall continually strive to improve their skills and knowledge and advance the profession through activities such as professional training and education, and interaction with colleagues, and specialists in related fields.

Adopted Sept. 18, 1995, eff. Jan. 1, 1996.

Commentary

Interpreters must continually strive to improve their interpreting skills and increase their knowledge of the languages they work in professionally, including past and current trends in technical terminology and social and regional dialects as well as their application within court proceedings.

Interpreters should keep informed of all statutes, rules of court and policies of the judiciary that govern the performance of their professional duties.

An interpreter should seek to elevate the standards of the profession through participation in workshops, professional meetings, interaction with colleagues, and reading current literature in the field.

RULES ON CERTIFICATION OF COURT INTERPRETERS

Historical Notes

The order of the Minnesota Supreme Court dated October 13, 2005, provided in part:

"1. The Rules on Certification of Court Interpreters shall no longer exist as stand-alone rules. All rules pertaining to the certification and regulation of interpreters shall be contained within the General Rules of Practice for the District Courts.

"2. The attached amendments to the General Rules of Practice for the District Courts are prescribed and promulgated for the regulation of the Minnesota Court Interpreter Program and the use of interpreters in the courts of the State of Minnesota to be effective January 1, 2006."

See, now, Rule 8 of the General Rules Of Practice for the District Courts.